ENGLISH
DICTIONARY
FOR
STUDENTS

This dictionary is also available on CD-ROM:
English Dictionary for Students (CD-ROM)   1-901659-36-4

This dictionary has a companion workbook and thesaurus:
Check Your Vocabulary for English   1-901659-11-9
English Thesaurus for Students   1-901659-31-3

Dictionary Titles in the Series:
Dictionary of Accounting   0-948549-27-0
Dictionary of Agrigulture, 2nd ed   0-948549-78-5
Dictionary of American Business   0-948549-11-4
Dictionary of Automobile Engineering   0-948549-66-1
Dictionary of Banking & Finance   0-948549-12-2
Dictionary of Business, 2nd ed   0-948549-51-3
Dictionary of Computing, 3rd ed   1-901659-04-6
Dictionary of Ecology & Environment, 3rd ed   0-948549-74-2
Dictionary of Government & Politics, 2nd ed   0-948549-89-0
Dictionary of Hotels, Tourism, Catering Management   0-948549-40-8
Dictionary of Human Resources & Personnel, 2nd ed   0-948549-79-3
Dictionary of Information Technology, 2nd ed   0-948549-88-2
Dictionary of Law, 3rd ed   1-901659-43-7
Dictionary of Library & Information Management   0-948549-68-8
Dictionary of Marketing   0-948549-73-4
Dictionary of Medicine, 3rd ed   1-901659-45-3
Dictionary of Printing & Publishing, 2nd ed   0-948549-99-8
Dictionary of Science & Technology   0-948549-67-X
English Dictionary for Students   1-901659-06-2

Professional Dictionary Series:
Dictionary of Astronomy   0-948549-43-2
Dictionary of Multimedia, 2nd ed   1-901659-01-1
Dictionary of PC & the Internet, 2nd ed   1-901659-12-7

Check your Vocabulary Workbooks:
Vocabulary for Banking & Finance   0-948549-96-3
Vocabulary for Business, 2nd ed   1-901659-27-5
Vocabulary for Colloquial English   0-948549-97-1
Vocabulary for Computing, 2nd ed   0-948549-72-6
Vocabulary for English   1-901659-11-9
Vocabulary for Hotels, Tourism   0-948549-75-0
Vocabulary for Law, 2nd ed   1-901659-21-6
Vocabulary for Marketing   1-901659-48-8
Vocabulary for Medicine, 2nd ed   1-901659-47-X

Visit our web site for full details of all our books
http://www.pcp.co.uk

ENGLISH
DICTIONARY
FOR
STUDENTS

PETER COLLIN PUBLISHING

First published in Great Britain 1999
reprinted 2000

Published by Peter Collin Publishing Ltd
1 Cambridge Road, Teddington, Middlesex, TW11 8DT

British Library Cataloguing-in-Publication Data

A catalogue record for this book is available from the British Library

ISBN 1-901659-06-2

Text processing and computer typesetting by PCP
Printed and bound in Finland by WSOY

General editor
PH Collin

Editorial contributors
Hazel Curties, Stephen Curtis, Liz Greasby,
Rupert Livesey, Martin Mellor

Readers
Gill Francis, Françoise Laurendeau,
Elizabeth Manning, Christina Rammell,
John Williams

Preface to the first edition

This dictionary aims to provide a modern vocabulary of British, American and International English for the student.

The vocabulary of over 25,000 words and phrases has been selected firstly according to various word frequency counts available both in Europe and in the USA, then by looking at the various syllabuses for national examinations. The words and phrases have then been supplemented with a wider selection of more specialized words and phrases (such as *greenhouse gases, peace process, search and replace*) which are very common in current English usage.

Each word, even derived words such as adverbs, is clearly defined, and we have also given examples of each word and phrase in simple illustrative contexts, so as to show how the words can be used in practice.

Because the dictionary is aimed at a wide spectrum of students, especially older students, we have included over 300 encyclopaedic comments on cultural and historical matters (*Pancake Day, weddings, Estuary English, Guy Fawkes, Magna Carta, Stonehenge,* and so on) and on more technical subjects (*search engines, the periodic table, the Internet, the metric system,* etc.) which may be of interest.

Some words in the dictionary are trademarks, and these have been indicated as such.

Layout of the dictionary

We have tried to lay the dictionary out as clearly as possible, in order to make it as easy as possible for the student to use.

Each entry begins with a main word, followed by the pronunciation in international phonetic symbols; this is followed by the part of speech. Entries where the same word occurs as two or more different parts of speech are split by numbers. Within each entry, major differences of meaning are highlighted by letter divisions.

The meanings of the words are written as simply as possible, using only a small defining vocabulary, supplemented as necessary by other words which appear in the dictionary. For most words we give examples of usage, and for the commonest words we give very many examples, all set in contexts which are easy to understand. Common idiomatic expressions and collocations are highlighted, explained, and examples are given for them also.

Throughout the book, usage notes (beginning with the word NOTE:) give irregular forms, British vs American usage, constructions, registers, derived words, words which can be confused, etc. These notes are also used to give information about the countries of the world which appear as entries.

Some words have fuller encyclopaedic comments in boxes, and these give more information than can be given within a simple definition.

Phonetics

The following symbols have been used to show the pronunciation of the main words in the dictionary.

Stress has been indicated by a main stress mark ('), but these are only guides as the stress of the word may change according to its position in the sentence.

Vowels		*Consonants*	
æ	back	b	buck
ɑː	harm	d	dead
ɒ	stop	ð	other
aɪ	type	dʒ	jump
aʊ	how	f	fare
aɪə	hire	g	gold
aʊə	hour	h	head
ɔː	course	j	yellow
ɔɪ	loyalty	k	cab
e	head	l	leave
eə	fair	m	mix
eɪ	make	n	nil
ə	abroad	ŋ	bring
əʊ	float	p	post
əʊə	lower	r	rule
ɜː	word	s	save
iː	keep	ʃ	shop
ɪ	fit	t	take
ɪə	near	tʃ	change
u	supreme	χ	loch
uː	pool	θ	theft
ʊ	book	v	value
ʌ	shut	w	work
		z	zone
		ʒ	measure

Aa

A, a [eɪ] first letter of the alphabet, followed by B; *do you mean 'dependant' spelt with an 'a' or with an 'e'?*; **from A to Z** = completely, all the way through; **the A to Z** = street guide for a town, especially one for London; *you can find us in the A to Z*

a, an [ə or æn] *article* **(a)** one; *I want a cup of tea*; *she's bought a new car*; *an enormous hole*; *we had to wait an hour for the bus*; *a useful guidebook* **(b)** for each or to each; *apples cost 50p a kilo*; *the car was travelling at 50 kilometres an hour*; *he earns £100 a day* (NOTE: **an** is used in front of words beginning with **a, e, i, o, u** and with **h** if the **h** is not pronounced (**an apple; an hour**); **a** is used in front of all other letters and also in front of **u** where **u** is pronounced [juː] (**a useful guidebook**))

AA ['eɪ 'eɪ] AUTOMOBILE ASSOCIATION

aback [ə'bæk] *adverb* **taken aback** = surprised and shocked by something unpleasant; *she was somewhat taken aback when he asked her to pay for the meal*

abaft [ə'bɑːft] *adverb* (*nautical*) **(a)** towards the stern of a ship **(b)** behind another ship

abandon [ə'bændən] *verb* **(a)** to leave; *he abandoned his wife and children*; *the crew abandoned the sinking fishing boat* **(b)** to give up, to stop doing something; *the company has decided to abandon the project*; *we abandoned the idea of setting up a London office*

abandoned [ə'bændənd] *adjective* no longer used or lived in; *squatters moved into the abandoned farmhouse*

abandonment [ə'bændənmənt] *noun* giving up; *the abandonment of a project*

abate [ə'beɪt] *verb* (*formal*) to become less strong; *the winds will abate during the next twenty-four hours*; *they waited for the rain to abate before starting their walk*

abatement [ə'beɪtmənt] *noun* **(a)** reduction; **Noise Abatement Society** = society which aims to reduce noise **(b) tax abatement** = decrease in tax

abbess ['æbes] *noun* woman in charge of a convent; *a new abbess was elected as head of the convent* (NOTE: plural is **abbesses**)

abbey ['æbi] *noun* religious establishment for monks or nuns; *when you go to Yorkshire, don't miss a visit to Fountains Abbey*; *Westminster Abbey is near the Houses of Parliament*

abbot ['æbət] *noun* man in charge of a monastery; *the abbot is quite elderly*

abbreviate [ə'briːvieɪt] *verb* **(a)** to shorten a word by leaving out some of the letters; *'Limited Company' is usually abbreviated to 'Ltd'* **(b)** to shorten a piece of writing by leaving out part of it; *this is the abbreviated version of the text*

abbreviation [əbriːvi'eɪʃn] *noun* shortened form of a word; *'Mr' is the abbreviation for 'Mister'*; *NATO is not an abbreviation but an acronym; compare* ACRONYM

ABC [eɪbiː'siː] *noun* the alphabet (from the first letters of the Roman alphabet); *my little sister is learning her ABC*; **it's as easy as ABC** = it's very easy

abdomen ['æbdəmen] *noun* (*formal*) part of body, the space in the front part of the body, below the diaphragm, containing the stomach, intestines, liver and other organs; *the child is complaining of severe pain in the right lower part of the abdomen*

abdominal [æb'dɒmɪnl] *adjective* referring to the abdomen; *these exercises are meant to strengthen the abdominal muscles*; **abdominal cavity** = space in the body below the chest; **abdominal pain** = pain in the abdomen caused by indigestion or something more serious; *he's feverish and is complaining of abdominal pain*

abduct [æb'dʌkt] *verb* to take a person away, usually by force; *kidnappers abducted the president's daughter at gunpoint*; *a woman abducted a two-day old baby from the Maternity Hospital*

abduction [æb'dʌkʃn] *noun* taking someone away, usually by force; *every single newspaper mentions the abduction of the president's daughter*

abductor [æb'dʌktə] *noun* **(a)** person who abducts someone, usually by force; *the child abductors collected the ransom and were never caught*; *she was able to give a fairly good description of her abductor* **(b) abductor muscle** = muscle which pulls a part of the body

aberrant [ə'berənt] *adjective* not normal

aberration [æbə'reɪʃn] *noun* action or thing which is not normal; *chromosome aberration is an abnormality in the number or arrangement of chromosomes*; **mental aberration** = mistake made by doing something without thinking; *in a moment of mental aberration, she answered her home phone as if she were still at the office*

abhor [əb'hɔː] *verb* (*formal*) to hate something, to feel horror for something; *don't ever offer him cucumber sandwiches, he absolutely abhors them*

abhorrence [əb'hɒrəns] *noun* hatred, horror; *everyone is aware of his abhorrence of racial discrimination*

abhorrent [əb'hɒrənt] *adjective* horrible, disgusting; *is there a crime more abhorrent than child abuse?*

abide [ə'baɪd] *verb* **(a) to abide by** = to follow rules, orders, etc.; *you must abide by the rules of the game*; *we have to abide by the decision of the referee*; **to abide by a promise** = to keep a promise **(b)** (*with negative*) **can't abide something** = to dislike something or someone, not to be able to put up with something; *I can't abide the smell of cigars*; *if you can't abide me, why do you accept his invitation?*

abiding [ə'baɪdɪŋ] *adjective* which stays for a long time; *an abiding feeling of shame*; *his abiding interest in gardening will always be remembered by his friends*

ability [ə'bɪlɪti] *noun* **(a)** having the force to do something; *he has many abilities but singing isn't one of them* (NOTE: plural in this meaning is **abilities**) **(b)**

being clever; *he's a man of great or outstanding ability*; **I'll do it to the best of my ability** = I'll do it as well as I can

abject ['æbdʒekt] *adjective* **(a) abject poverty** = being poor and very miserable; *the refugees were living in abject poverty* **(b)** cowardly, which makes you ashamed; *he made an abject apology*

ablaze [ə'bleɪz] *adverb* **(a)** on fire; *thirty hectares of woodland were ablaze* **(b)** shining brightly; *Oxford Street was ablaze with lights*

able ['eɪbl] *adjective* **to be able to do something** = to have the capability or chance to do something; *she wasn't able to breathe* = she could not breathe; **will you be able to come to the meeting?** = can you come to the meeting?; *they weren't able to find the house* (NOTE: **able** is only used with **to** and a verb)

ablutions [ə'blu:ʃənz] *noun (formal, usually humorous)* **to perform one's ablutions** = to wash yourself

abnormal [æb'nɔ:ml] *adjective* not normal; *is this abnormal or is it something that happens often?*; *the animal's behaviour seemed slightly abnormal to me*

abnormality [æbnɔ:'mælɪti] *noun* **(a)** state of being abnormal; *everyone recognizes the abnormality of the situation* **(b)** something which is abnormal; *the slightest abnormality will show up on the scan* (NOTE: plural is **abnormalities**)

abnormally [æb'nɔ:məli] *adverb* in a way which is different from normal; *the number of absentees is abnormally high*

aboard [ə'bɔ:d] *adverb & preposition* on a ship or other vehicle; *the train ran into a bus with twenty passengers aboard*; *the passengers went aboard the 'Queen Elizabeth' at 10 p.m.*; *when the ship docked, customs officers came aboard to inspect the cargo*; **all aboard!** = everyone get on, please!

abolish [ə'bɒlɪʃ] *verb* to get rid of (a law, a right); *Parliament voted to abolish capital punishment*

abolition [æbə'lɪʃn] *noun* act of abolishing; *to campaign for the abolition of the death penalty*

aboriginal [æbə'rɪdʒɪnəl] **1** *adjective* referring to aborigines; *a museum of aboriginal art and artefacts* **2** *noun* aborigine, original inhabitant

aborigine [æbə'rɪdʒɪni] *noun* original inhabitant of a place, usually referring to the original inhabitants of Australia; *the early settlers drove the aborigines from their tribal lands*

abort [ə'bɔ:t] *verb* **(a)** to stop something taking place; *the space mission was aborted* **(b)** to perform an abortion; *the doctors decided to abort the fetus* **(c)** *(of a woman)* to have an abortion; *she was pregnant, but she was aborted at ten weeks* **(d)** *(of woman)* to have a miscarriage; *she was pregnant, but she aborted at ten weeks*

abortion [ə'bɔ:ʃn] *noun* ending of a woman's pregnancy; *she did not want the baby, so asked to have an abortion*

abortive [ə'bɔ:tɪv] *adjective* unsuccessful; *the leaders of the abortive coup were arrested*

abound [ə'baʊnd] *verb* **to abound in** *or* **with** = to be full of; *the forests abound in game*

about [ə'baʊt] **1** *preposition* **(a)** referring to; *he told me all about his operation*; *what do you want to speak to the doctor about?*; *she's worried about her heart problems* **(b) to be about to do something** = to be just going to do something; *we were about to go home when you arrived* **2** *adverb* **(a)** approximately; *the table is about two metres long*; *I've been waiting for about four hours*; *she's only about fifteen years old* **(b)** in various places; *there were papers lying about on the floor*; *there is a lot of flu about during the winter months*

about-turn *or* **about-face**   [əbaʊt'tɜ:n *or* əbaʊt'feɪs] *noun* **(a)** *(in the army)* order to turn to face the opposite direction **(b)** changing your plans or policy to the opposite of what you did before; *the government has done a complete about-turn on pensioners' rights* (NOTE: you can also say **U-turn** in this meaning)

above [ə'bʌv] **1** *preposition* higher than; *the plane was flying above the clouds*; *the temperature in the street was above 30 degrees*; *at prices above £2.00, nobody will buy it*; *if you are above 18, you have to pay the full fare* **2** *noun* **the above** = people mentioned earlier; *all the above have passed the test*

above board [ə'bʌv 'bɔ:d] *adjective* open and legal as everyone can see; *everything's completely above board regarding the contract*

abrasive [ə'breɪzɪv] **1** *adjective* **(a)** which rubs away a surface; *they rubbed the surface of the metal with abrasive paper*; *use abrasive cleaning powder to get rid of these stains* **(b)** sharp way of speaking; *his manner sounded very abrasive on the phone* **2** *noun* substance which rubs away a surface; *avoid using abrasives to clean this surface*

abreast [ə'brest] *adverb* **(a)** side by side; *they were cycling three abreast* **(b) to keep abreast of something** = to keep up to date with something; *she wants to keep abreast of the latest developments in cancer therapy*

abridge [ə'brɪdʒ] *verb* to shorten a book, play, etc.; *the text is too long - it really needs to be abridged*

abridged [ə'brɪdʒd] *adjective* shortened; *I'm reading an abridged version of 'War and Peace'*

abridgement [ə'brɪdʒmənt] *noun* shortened version of a book, play, etc.; *I didn't read the whole book, just an abridgement*

abroad [ə'brɔ:d] *adverb* in another country; to another country; *he travels abroad a lot on business*; *they've gone abroad on holiday*; *holidays abroad are more and more popular*; *she lives abroad and only comes back here for her holidays*

abrupt [ə'brʌpt] *adjective* **(a)** sudden; *the committee made an abrupt change of plan*; *the bus made an abrupt turn* **(b)** short and not very polite; *his reply was abrupt and to the point*

abscess ['æbses] *noun* collection of pus in the body; *the dentist said he had an abscess under his tooth*; *the doctor decided to lance the abscess* (NOTE: plural is **abscesses**)

abscond [əb'skɒnd] *verb* to run away; *two of the prisoners have absconded*

absence ['æbsəns] *noun* **(a)** being away from a place; *she did not explain her absence from the meeting*; *the former president was sentenced in his absence*; **in the absence of** = without someone being there; *in the absence of the chairman, his deputy took the chair*; **leave of absence** = permission to be away from work; *he asked for leave of absence to visit his* *wife in hospital* (b) lack of something; *in the absence of any town plans we had to ask our way*

absent *adjective* ['æbsənt] not there; *the chairman was absent from the meeting*; *ten of the staff are absent with flu*; *let's drink a toast to absent friends*

absentee [æbsən'ti:] *noun* person who is not there; *there were three absentees at the meeting*; *the number of absentees is abnormally high for the time of year*; **absentee landlord** = owner of a property who lives a long way away and uses agents to deal with his tenants; *with an absentee landlord, it always takes months to get permission for repairs to be undertaken*

absent-minded ['æbsənt'maɪndɪd] *adjective* forgetful; *grandfather's getting very absent-minded - he went off to the library in his slippers*

absolute ['æbsəlu:t] *adjective* complete, total; *the general assumed absolute power*; *he's an absolute idiot - he should have accepted the offer immediately*; **absolute majority** = majority over all the others; *the government has an absolute majority of fifteen*; **absolute zero** = the lowest possible temperature

absolutely ['æbsəlu:tli] *adverb* completely, totally; *I am absolutely sure I left the keys in my coat pocket*

absorb [əb'zɔ:b] *verb* (a) to take in (a liquid, etc.); *the liquid should be absorbed by the paper*; *salt absorbs moisture from the air* (b) to reduce a shock; *the car's springs are supposed to absorb any shock from the road surface* (c) **absorbed in** = totally interested in; *he was so absorbed in his newspaper that he didn't notice that the toast had burnt*

absorbent [əb'zɔ:bənt] *adjective* which can absorb; *a wad of absorbent cotton*; *wipe the liquid with this soft cloth, it's more absorbent*

absorbing [əb'zɔ:bɪŋ] *adjective* very interesting; *it's an absorbing story*; *I find my new job so absorbing that time simply flies*

absorption [əb'zɔ:pʃən] *noun* (a) being absorbed; *the absorption of the drug into the bloodstream* (b) being very interested in something; *her total absorption in her family* (NOTE: the spellings: **absorb** but **absorption**)

abstain [əb'steɪn] *verb* (a) deliberately not to do something; *please abstain from smoking during the flight*; *he was recommended to abstain from drinking coffee for the next six months* (NOTE: you abstain **from** doing something) (b) not to vote; *Mr Smith abstained*; *sixty MPs abstained in the vote on capital punishment*

abstention [əb'stenʃn] *noun* deliberately not voting; *there were several abstentions during the vote on capital punishment*; *the motion was carried by 200 votes to 150, with 60 abstentions*

abstinence ['æbstɪnəns] *noun* not doing something, especially not drinking alcohol; *many people have a period of abstinence during Lent*; **total abstinence** = not drinking any alcohol; not having sexual relations; *total abstinence from sex is essential during the course of treatment*

abstract ['æbstrækt] 1 *adjective* (a) not concrete, which exists only in the mind; *she has lots of abstract theories about how to reorganize society* (b) *(art)* which does not reproduce something exactly, as opposed to figurative art; *an abstract painting*; *an abstract painter* 2 *noun* (a) something which exists in the mind only; **in the abstract** = in a general way (b) an abstract painting; *he started by painting abstracts and then turned to portraits* (c) short form of a report or document; *to make an abstract of a report*

abstraction [əb'strækʃən] *noun* (a) removing; *the abstraction of water from a river* (b) vague general idea, as opposed to a concrete example; *he talks in abstractions, and never cites real cases*

abstruse [əb'stru:s] *adjective* difficult to understand; *the professor has written some very abstruse books on atomic physics*

absurd [əb'sɜ:d] *adjective* ridiculous; *it's absurd to expect you will win the lottery*; *she was wearing a really absurd hat*

absurdity [əb'sɜ:dɪti] *noun* being absurd; *do you realize the absurdity of what you're proposing?*

abundance [ə'bʌndəns] *noun* large quantity; *there is an abundance of wild life in the national park*; **abundance** = in large quantities; *the fridge was full, so we had food and drink in abundance*

abundant [ə'bʌndənt] *adjective* in large quantities; *the cottage has abundant stocks of wood for the stove*

abuse 1 *noun* [ə'bju:s] (a) bad use; *the minister's action is an abuse of power* (b) rude words; *the strikers shouted abuse at the police*; **a term of abuse** = a rude word (c) very bad treatment; *she suffered physical abuse in prison*; *sexual abuse of children* (NOTE: no plural for meanings (b) and (c)) 2 *verb* [ə'bju:z] (a) to make the wrong use of; *he abused his position as finance director*; *he abused my confidence* = he took advantage of my trust in him (b) to treat very badly, usually sexually; *as a child, she was abused by her uncle* (c) to say rude things about someone; *the crowd sang songs abusing the president's wife*

abusive [ə'bju:sɪv] *adjective* rude and insulting; *we received an abusive letter from our neighbours*; *he had too much to drink and became abusive*

abysmal [ə'bɪzml] *adjective* extremely bad; *the weather was abysmal during our holiday*; *an abysmal election result*

abysmally [ə'bɪzməli] *adverb* extremely badly; *our team did abysmally in the championship*; *the level of the candidates who applied for the job was abysmally low*

abyss [ə'bɪs] *noun* (a) deep hole; *she went to the edge of the cliff and peered down into the abyss* (b) horrifying situation; *after the election, the party found itself on the brink of the abyss* (NOTE: only singular in meaning (b); the plural is **abysses**)

AC = ALTERNATING CURRENT

academic [ækə'demɪk] 1 *adjective* (a) theoretical; *it is only of academic interest* (b) referring to study at a university; *members of the academic staff received a letter from the principal*; **academic year** *or* **school year** = period which starts in September and finishes in August; *the academic year starts in September* 2 *noun* a university teacher; *she teaches at a university and all her friends are academics*

academy [ə'kædəmi] *noun* (a) college where specialized subjects are taught; *a military academy*; *an academy of music* (b) *(in Scotland)* selective secondary school; *he went to Stirling Academy* (c) private society for the study of art or science; *the Russian Academy of Sciences*; **the Royal Academy of Arts** = private London society for teaching art and putting on art exhibitions

ACAS ['eɪkæs] = ADVISORY, CONCILIATION AND ARBITRATION SERVICE

accelerate [æk'seləreɪt] *verb* **(a)** to go faster; *he pressed down on the pedal and the car accelerated*; *don't accelerate when you get to traffic lights* **(b)** to make something go faster; *the drug accelerates the heart rate* (NOTE: the opposite is **decelerate**)

acceleration [æksələ'reɪʃn] *noun* **(a)** *(of a car, etc.)* the action of going faster; *acceleration in this year's model is superior to that of last year's* **(b)** the action of going at a faster speed; *the nurse noted an acceleration of the patient's pulse rate*

accelerator [æk'seləreɪtə] *noun* pedal which makes a car go faster; *he put his foot down on the accelerator and the car shot forward*

accent *noun* ['æksənt] **(a)** particular way of pronouncing; *she has an Irish accent*; *he speaks with an American accent* **(b)** sign over a printed letter; **an acute accent** = sign sloping forwards over a vowel, such as é; *'résumé' has two acute accents*; **a grave accent** = sign sloping backwards over a vowel, such as è; *'crèche' can be written with a grave accent* **(c)** stress in speaking; *in the word 'haberdashery' the accent is on the first syllable* **(d)** emphasis; *the accent is on youth unemployment*

accentuate [ək'sentjueɪt] *verb* to emphasize; *he accentuated the importance of remaining calm when faced with an angry mob*; *the treatment only seems to accentuate the pain*; *painting the walls in a light colour will accentuate the brightness of the room*

accentuation [əksentju'eɪʃn] *noun* emphasizing something; *the accentuation of the difference between the two plans*

accept [ək'sept] *verb* **(a)** to take a present; *we hope you will accept this little gift* **(b)** to say 'yes' or to agree to something; *she accepted the offer of a job in Australia*; *I invited her to come with us and she accepted* **(c)** to agree to handle something; *several currencies accepted on the ferry*; *'all major credit cards accepted'*; *do you accept traveller's cheques?* (NOTE: do not confuse with **except**)

acceptable [ək'septəbl] *adjective* easily accepted; *a small gift of flowers would be very acceptable*; *the offer is not acceptable to the vendor*

acceptance [ək'septəns] *noun* **(a)** taking something which is offered; *he indicated his acceptance of the offer* **(b)** agreement; *we received her letter of acceptance this morning*

accepted [ək'septɪd] *adjective* which is taken as correct by most people; *this is not a painkiller in the accepted sense of the word*

access ['ækses] **1** *noun* **(a)** way of getting to a place; *an access road*; *the concert hall has access for wheelchairs*; *at present there is no access to the site* **(b) to have (easy) access to** = to be able to get easily; *the company has access to substantial funds* **2** *verb* to get information from a computer; *she tried to access the address list*

accessible [ək'sesɪbl] *adjective* **(a)** easily reached; *the island is only accessible by boat in fine weather*; *they live in a farm which is not accessible by car* **(b)** easy to read or understand; *his style of writing is quite accessible*

accession [æk'seʃn] *noun* **accession to the throne** = action of becoming king or queen; *on his accession to the throne, he took the title Alexander III*

accessory [ək'sesəri] *noun* **(a)** useful piece of equipment, added to others; *a shop which sells cameras and photographic accessories*; **accessory bag** = bag for carrying extra equipment **(b)** small items of clothing; *she had a brown silk dress with yellow accessories* = a dress with yellow belt, handbag, gloves, shoes, etc. **(c)** person who helps someone commit a crime; *he was charged with being an accessory to the crime* (NOTE: plural is **accessories**)

accident ['æksɪdənt] *noun* **(a)** something which happens by chance; *he discovered the missing papers by accident* **(b)** unpleasant thing which happens and causes damage; *the accident happened or took place at a dangerous corner*; *she was involved in a car accident and had to go to hospital*; *thirty people were killed in the air accident*; *he missed his flight, because his bus had an accident on the way to the airport*; **industrial accident** = accident which takes place at work

accidental [æksɪ'dentl] *adjective* which happens by accident; *his death was not accidental*; **an accidental injury** = an injury due to an accident

accidentally [æksɪ'dentəli] *adverb* by chance; *he discovered the missing papers accidentally*

accident-prone ['æksɪdəntprəun] *adjective* likely to have accidents often; *the new sales manager seems to be accident-prone*

acclaim [ə'kleɪm] **1** *noun* great praise; *his film was greeted with great acclaim* **2** *verb* to greet with praise; *she was acclaimed as the best novelist of the decade*

acclimatization *US* **acclimation** [əklaɪmətaɪ'zeɪʃn *or* əklaɪ'meɪʃn] *noun* the process of becoming acclimatized to something; *the acclimatization of animals to a colder climate*; *the period of acclimatization needed will be of up to 6 months*

acclimatize *US* **acclimate** [ə'klaɪmətaɪz *or* ə'klaɪmət] *verb* **to become acclimatized to something** = to become used to something; *gradually, the animals became acclimatized to their new habitat*; *did you ever become acclimatized to living in Hong Kong?*

accolade ['ækɒleɪd] *noun* award given to someone as a sign of praise; *he received the highest accolade the society could give - its gold medal*

accommodate [ə'kɒmədeɪt] *verb* to provide a place to live; *the hotel can accommodate up to two hundred visitors*

accommodating [ə'kɒmədeɪtɪŋ] *adjective* helpful; *the staff in the hotel were very accommodating*

accommodation [əkɒmə'deɪʃən] *noun* **(a)** place to live; *all the available accommodation in the town has been taken by journalists*; *visitors have difficulty in finding hotel accommodation during the summer*; *they are living in furnished accommodation* **(b)** compromise, agreement; *he reached an accommodation with his creditors* **(c) accommodation address** = address used for receiving messages but which is not the real address of a company (NOTE: no plural in British English but American English uses **accommodations** in the first meaning)

accompaniment [ə'kʌmpnɪmənt] *noun* **(a)** thing which accompanies; *as an accompaniment to the* cheese, we had a glass of red wine; *they served cranberry sauce as an accompaniment to the turkey* **(b)** music played to accompany a singer or instrumentalist; *a piece for violin with piano accompaniment*; **to the accompaniment of** = accompanied by; *he sang a rude song to the accompaniment of loud whistles from the audience*

accompanist [ə'kʌmpənɪst] *noun* person who plays an instrument to accompany a soloist; *he's a very experienced piano accompanist*

accompany [ə'kʌmpni] *verb* **(a)** to go with; *he accompanied his wife to the hospital*; *the pain was accompanied by high temperature*; *pork is served accompanied by apple sauce* **(b)** to play a musical instrument, when someone else plays or sings; *she sang and was accompanied on the piano by her father* (NOTE: accompanied **by** someone *or* something)

accomplice [ə'kʌmplɪs] *noun* person who helps another person to commit a crime; *one of the thieves was caught, but his accomplice escaped*; *it was discovered that his brother had acted as his accomplice*

accomplish [ə'kʌmplɪʃ] *verb* to achieve something successfully; *what do you hope to accomplish at the meeting?*; *I don't think he accomplished very much in his first year as head of the museum*

accomplished [ə'kʌmplɪʃt] *adjective* talented, skilled; *he's an accomplished musician*; *she is an accomplished cook*

accomplishment [ə'kʌmplɪʃmənt] *noun* **(a)** the successful finishing of something after a lot of work; *winning three gold medals was a remarkable accomplishment for someone who is still not 21* **(b)** **accomplishments** = skills; *he's a man of many accomplishments*; *among her many accomplishments she is a fine skier*

accord [ə'kɔːd] **1** *noun* **(a)** agreement; *they are still discussing the terms of the Dayton Accord*; **with one accord** = with the agreement of everyone **(b)** **of your own accord** = voluntarily, without being ordered by anyone; *of his own accord he decided to sell the business and retire to a Greek island* **2** *verb* **(a)** *(formal)* to give as an honour; *he was accorded a civic reception* **(b)** **to accord with** = to agree with; *his way of behaving does not accord with his principles*

accordance [ə'kɔːdəns] *noun* **in accordance with** = in agreement with *or* following; *I am submitting the claim for damages in accordance with the advice of our lawyers*; *in accordance with your instructions we have sold the house*

accordingly [ə'kɔːdɪŋli] *adverb* as a result of something just mentioned; *we have received your letter and have altered the booking accordingly*; *he's an experienced gardener and should be paid accordingly*

according to [ə'kɔːdɪŋ tu] *adverb* **(a)** as someone says *or* writes; *the washing machine was installed according to the manufacturer's instructions*; *according to the witness, the car was going too fast* **(b)** in relation to; *the teachers have separated the children into classes according to their ages*

accordion [ə'kɔːdiən] *noun* **(piano) accordion** = musical instrument, played with a keyboard on the side, which makes a sound by air pumped by hand; *he played the accordion in a Paris bar*

account [ə'kaʊnt] **1** *noun* **(a)** **bank account** = arrangement which you make with a bank to keep your money safely; *I put all my savings into my bank account*; *this type of bank account pays 10% interest*; **to open a bank account** = to start keeping money in a bank; **to close a bank account** = to stop keeping money in a bank; **current account** *or* **cheque account** *US* **checking account** = account which pays little or no interest but from which the customer can withdraw money when he wants by writing cheques; **deposit account** = account which pays interest but on which notice usually has to be given to withdraw money; **savings account** = account where you put money in regularly and which pays interest, often at a higher rate than a deposit account **(b)** *(in a shop)* arrangement which a customer has to buy goods and pay for them later; *put it on my account or charge it to my account*; *(of a customer)* **to open an account** = to ask a shop to supply goods which you will pay for later; *(of a shop)* **to open an account** *or* **to close an account** = to start *or* to stop supplying a customer on credit; **to settle an account** = to pay all the money owed on an account **(c)** **on account of** = because of, due to; *the trains are late on account of the fog*; *we don't use the car much on account of the price of petrol* **(d)** **on account** = as part of a total bill; **to pay money on account** = to pay to settle part of a bill **(e)** **to take something into account** *or* **to take account of something** = to consider something; *we have to take the weather into account* **(f)** story; *they listened to his account of the journey*; **by all accounts** = as everyone says; *by all accounts, she is a very attractive woman* **(g)** **the accounts of a business** *or* **a company's accounts** = detailed records of a company's financial affairs; **to keep the accounts** = to write each sum of money in the account book; **profit and loss account (P&L account)** = statement of company expenditure and income over a period of time, showing whether the company has made a profit or loss; **accounts department** = department in a company which deals with money paid, received, borrowed or owed **2** *verb* **to account for** = to explain; *he was asked to account for all his expenditure*

accountable [ə'kaʊntəbl] *adjective* having to explain money transactions; *we try to make councillors more accountable to the finance department* (NOTE: you are accountable **to** someone **for** something)

accountancy [ə'kaʊntənsi] *noun* study of the work of being an accountant; *he is studying accountancy or he is an accountancy student* (NOTE: American English uses **accounting** in this meaning)

accountant [ə'kaʊntənt] *noun* person who deals with accounts; *I send all my tax queries to my accountant*; *she has an appointment with her accountant to go over her tax form*; **chartered accountant** = qualified accountant

accounting [ə'kaʊntɪŋ] *noun* work of recording money paid, received, borrowed or owed; **false accounting** = offence of changing financial records (NOTE: the word **accounting** is used in the USA to mean the subject as a course of study, where British English uses **accountancy**)

accredit [ə'kredɪt] *verb* to make someone an official representative; *our ambassador was accredited to the government of Brazil*; *he is accredited to the United Nations*

accrue [ə'kru:] *verb* to increase and accumulate; *the accrued interest is added to your account each month*; *interest accrues from the beginning of the month*

accumulate [ə'kju:mjʊleɪt] *verb* to grow larger; *she allowed the interest in her account to accumulate*; *fat had accumulated in the arteries*

accumulation [əkju:mjʊ'leɪʃn] *noun* **(a)** action of accumulating; *he devoted his life to the accumulation of information about climate change* **(b)** heap; *an accumulation of dirty papers was blocking the gutter*; *the drug aims at clearing the accumulation of fatty deposits in the arteries*

accuracy ['ækjʊrəsi] *noun* being correct in every detail; *accuracy is very important when drawing maps*; *he works quickly but with great accuracy*; *the police doubt the accuracy of the witnesses' statements*

accurate ['ækjʊrət] *adjective* correct in all details; *are the figures accurate?*; *we asked them to make an accurate copy of the plan*

accurately ['ækjʊrətli] *adverb* correctly; *the TV weathermen accurately forecast the storm*

accusation [ækjʊ'zeɪʃn] *noun* statement that someone has done wrong; *the secretary made an accusation against her boss*; *he denied the accusations against him*

accuse [ə'kju:z] *verb* to say that someone has done something wrong; *the police accused her of stealing the money*; *she was accused of stealing from the petty cash box* (NOTE: you accuse someone **of** a crime or **of** doing something)

accused [ə'kju:zd] *noun* **the accused** = person or persons charged with a crime; *all the accused pleaded not guilty*; *the police brought the accused into the court* (NOTE: can be singular or plural: **the six accused all plead guilty**)

accustom [ə'kʌstəm] *verb* **to accustom someone to something** = to make someone used to something; *they had to accustom themselves to working in Swedish*; *it took him some time to become accustomed to driving on the right-hand side of the road*

accustomed [ə'kʌstəmd] *adjective* normal, usual; *that day he wasn't sitting in his accustomed chair*; **accustomed to** = used to; *she was accustomed to walking her dog in the park every morning*; *he is accustomed to having a car and chauffeur provided by the firm*

ace [eɪs] *noun* **(a)** playing card with one spot; *the ace of spades* **(b)** someone who is brilliant at doing something; *he's our ace batsman* **(c)** *(in tennis)* service which the opponent cannot return; *Henman has served four aces so far*

ache [eɪk] **1** *noun* pain; *he felt a dull ache in his shoulder*; *she complained of various aches and pains in her legs*; *see also* TOOTHACHE, HEADACHE **2** *verb* to hurt; *my head really aches*

achieve [ə'tʃi:v] *verb* to succeed in doing something; *what do you hope the achieve by writing to your MP?*; *the theatre company has achieved great success in the USA*; *he achieved all his objectives*

achievement [ə'tʃi:vmənt] *noun* thing which has been done successfully; *coming sixth was a great achievement, since he had never raced before*; *she is excessively modest about her achievements*

achiever [ə'tʃi:və] *noun* person who achieves something by hard work; *he's not an achiever - he'll always be at the bottom of his class*

aching ['eɪkɪŋ] *adjective* which hurts; *put your aching feet in a bath of warm water*; *that aching tooth needs to be looked at by a dentist*

acid ['æsɪd] **1** *noun* chemical substance containing hydrogen that forms a salt when combined with an alkali, and turns litmus paper red; *the muggers threw acid in her face* (NOTE: the opposite is **alkali**) **2** *adjective* sour; *the acid taste of lemons*

acidic [ə'sɪdɪk] *adjective* which has a sour taste; *if you have problems with your digestion, avoid orange juice as it's very acidic*

acidity [ə'sɪdɪti] *noun* **(a)** percentage of acid in something; *pH is the measurement of acidity*; *an alkaline solution may help to reduce acidity* **(b)** bitter taste; *the acidity of a green apple*

> COMMENT: acidity and alkalinity are measured according to the pH scale. pH7 is neutral; numbers above pH7 show alkalinity, while pH6 and below is acid

acid rain ['æsɪd 'reɪn] *noun* polluted rain which kills trees; *acid rain falls a long distance away from the source of the pollution*

acknowledge [ək'nɒlɪdʒ] *verb* **(a)** to say that something has been received; *I am writing to acknowledge receipt of your letter of the 15th*; *he has still not acknowledged my letter of the 24th* **(b)** to admit that something is true; *in the end, they acknowledged defeat* *or* *they acknowledged that they were beaten*; *he acknowledged that what she said was true*

acknowledgement [ək'nɒlɪdʒmənt] *noun* **(a)** reply to say that something has been received; *she sent a letter of acknowledgement*; *I sent a cheque as a deposit two weeks ago but have not received any acknowledgement* **(b)** admission that something is true; *his acknowledgement that he had made a mistake*; *the party's acknowledgement of defeat in the general election* **(c)** *(in a book)* **acknowledgements** = list of people an author thanks for help

acne ['ækni] *noun* spots on the skin, usually on the face, neck and shoulders; *he has acne*; *she is using a cream to clear up her acne*

acorn ['eɪkɔ:n] *noun* fruit of an oak tree; *if you plant an acorn in front of your house, don't expect an oak tree to grow overnight*

acoustic [ə'ku:stɪk] *adjective* referring to sound; **acoustic guitar** = ordinary guitar, as opposed to an electric guitar

acquaint [ə'kweɪnt] *verb* **(a)** **to be acquainted with something** *or* **someone** = to know something *or* someone; *is he acquainted with the details of the case?*; *she is acquainted with my father* **(b)** *(formal)* to inform; *we had to acquaint him with the correct procedure*

acquaintance [ə'kweɪntəns] *noun* **(a)** knowledge of someone; *my first acquaintance with him was in Hong Kong in 1997*; **to make the acquaintance of** = to get to know someone for the first time; *I made her acquaintance when we were at college together* **(b)** person you know; *she has many acquaintances in the publishing industry but no real friends*

acquiesce [ækwɪˈes] *verb (formal)* to acquiesce in *or* to something = to agree to something without protesting about it; *in the end the old man acquiesced in the sale of the house*; *the students asked to have the exam postponed and the teacher acquiesced*

acquiescence [ækwɪˈesəns] *noun (formal)* agreement without protest; *all we needed was the acquiescence of the local chief of police*

acquiescent [ækwˈɪesənt] *adjective (formal)* agreeing with some action without protesting; *he's too acquiescent to be a good manager*

acquire [əˈkwaɪə] *verb* to obtain or to get; *she has acquired a large collection of shoes*; **acquired immunodeficiency syndrome** see AIDS; **acquired taste** = something which you come to like after a time; *oysters are something of an acquired taste*

acquisition [ækwɪˈzɪʃn] *noun* (a) act of acquiring; *his acquisition of half the shares in the company shocked the staff* (b) thing which has been acquired; *you simply must see his latest acquisition - a pink Rolls Royce!*

acquit [əˈkwɪt] *verb* (a) to declare formally that a person is not guilty; *he was acquitted of the crime*; *the court acquitted two of the accused* (b) **to acquit yourself well** = to do well when trying something difficult or for the first time; *she said she had never played tennis before, but in the event she acquitted herself very well*; *how well did she acquit herself in her first public recital?* (NOTE: **acquitting - acquitted**)

acquittal [əˈkwɪtəl] *noun* decision by a court that someone is not guilty; *after his acquittal he left the court with a smile on his face*; *his acquittal was quite unexpected*

acre [ˈeɪkə] *noun* measure of land, 4840 square yards or 0.4047 hectares (NOTE: the plural is used with figures, except before a noun: **he has bought a farm of 250 acres** *or* **he has bought a 250-acre farm**)

acrid [ˈækrɪd] *adjective* with a bitter smell; *acrid black smoke poured out the building*

acrimonious [ækrɪˈməʊniəs] *adjective* angry and bitter; *the conversation started pleasantly but soon turned acrimonious*; *there was an acrimonious argument between the lawyers*; *she arrived in the middle of an acrimonious dispute*

acrobat [ˈækrəbæt] *noun* person who performs spectacular physical movements for the public; *anyone who climbs up a pylon to repair electric cables must have the agility of an acrobat*; **circus acrobats** = people who perform exercises as part of a circus show; *even experienced acrobats have asked for safety nets to be installed*

acrobatic [ækrəˈbætɪk] *adjective* moving in an artistic way, like an acrobat; *she performed breathtaking acrobatic exercises*

acrobatics [ækrəˈbætɪks] *noun* acrobatic exercises; *all these acrobatics with the new plane are meant to impress potential customers*

acronym [ˈækrənɪm] *noun* word made from the first letters of the name of something; *NATO and AIDS are both acronyms*; *compare* ABBREVIATION

across [əˈkrɒs] **1** *preposition* (a) from one side to the other; *he helped the old lady across the street*; *don't run across the road without looking to see if there is any traffic coming* (b) on the other side; *he called to her from across the street*; *their house is across the street from ours* = it is just opposite our house **2** *adverb* from one side to the other; *the river is only twenty feet across*; *the stream is very narrow - you can easily jump across*

acrylic [əˈkrɪlɪk] **1** *adjective* **acrylic paints** = paints made from a plastic **2** *noun* plastic paint; *the picture is painted in acrylics*

act [ækt] **1** *noun* (a) thing which is done; *he didn't forget the many acts of kindness she had shown him over the years* (b) part of a play, of a show; *Act II of the play takes place in the garden*; *the circus has acts by clowns and wild animals*; *(informal)* **to get your act together** = to organize yourself properly; *if they don't get their act together, they'll miss the last date for entries to the competition*; *let's try and get our act together* (c) law passed by Parliament; *an act to ban the sale of weapons* **2** *verb* (a) to take part in a film, play, etc.; *she's acted on TV many times*; *he acted the part of Hamlet in the film* (b) to do something; *you will have to act quickly if you want to stop the fire*; *she acted in a very responsible way* (c) to behave; *he's started acting very strangely*

acting [ˈæktɪŋ] **1** *adjective* taking the place of someone who is absent; *Mr Smith is the acting chairman while Sir James is in hospital* **2** *noun* profession of an actor; *he has decided to take up a career in acting*

action [ˈækʃən] *noun* (a) doing something; *what action are you going to take to prevent accidents?*; **out of action** = not working; *the car has been out of action for a week*; *the goalkeeper broke his leg and will be out of action for some time*; **to take industrial action** = to do something (usually to go on strike) to show that you are not happy with conditions at work (b) what happens in a play, film, etc.; *the action of the play takes place in a flat in London* (c) instruction to start filming; *camera, lights, action!* (d) case in a law court where someone sues someone else; *an action for libel or a libel action*; **to bring an action for damages against someone**; **to take legal action against someone** = to sue someone

activate [ˈæktɪveɪt] *verb* (a) to make something start to work; *he touched the door handle and that activated an alarm signal*; *pressing F10 activates the printer* (b) to start a chemical reaction

active [ˈæktɪv] *adjective* (a) energetic or positive; *my grandmother is still very active at the age of 88*; *he didn't play an active part in the attack on the police station* (b) *(volcano)* which is erupting; *scientists think the volcano is no longer active* (c) **on active service** US **on active duty** = serving in the armed services in time of war; *he was killed on active service*

actively [ˈæktɪvli] *adverb* in an active way; *the store is actively recruiting new staff*

activist [ˈæktɪvɪst] *noun* person who vigorously supports a political party; *the meeting was disrupted by an argument between the chairman and left-wing activists*

activity [ækˈtɪvɪti] *noun* (a) being active; *there is a possibility of volcanic activity*; *there was a lot of activity on the stock market* (b) occupation, pastime; *children are offered various holiday activities - sailing, windsurfing, water-skiing, etc.*; **activity holiday** = planned holiday where you do certain things (such as painting, rock-climbing, etc.) (NOTE: plural in this meaning is **activities**)

act on ['ækt 'ɒn] *verb* to do something after something has been said; *the police acted on his suggestion*

actor *or* **actress** ['æktə *or* 'æktrəs] *noun* person who acts in the theatre, in films, on television; *a famous TV actor* (NOTE: the plural of actress is **actresses**; note also that the feminine form **actress** is less used nowadays)

actual ['æktjʊəl] *adjective* real; *it looks quite small but the actual height is 5 metres*; *her actual words were much stronger*; **in actual fact** = really; *in spite of what the newspapers said, in actual fact he did sell his shares*

actuality [æktjʊ'ælɪti] *noun* (*formal*) reality; **in actuality** = really; *in actuality, he is totally incompetent*

actually ['æktjʊəli] *adverb* really; *it looks quite small, but actually it is over 5 metres high*; *he said he was ill, but actually he wanted to go to the football match*

acupuncture ['ækjʊpʌŋktʃə] *noun* (*Chinese medicine*) treatment originating in China, where needles are inserted through the skin into nerve centres in order to relieve pain or to treat a disorder, etc.; *one of the doctors at the clinic practices acupuncture*; *she goes to an acupuncture clinic for her bad back*

acupuncturist [ækjʊ'pʌŋktʃərɪst] *noun* person who practises acupuncture; *there is an acupuncturist attached to the clinic*

acute [ə'kjuːt] *adjective* (**a**) serious illness or pain which starts suddenly and lasts for a short time; *he felt acute chest pains*; *the pain was very acute*; *a child with acute bronchitis compare* CHRONIC (**b**) **acute angle** = angle which is less than 90° (**c**) keen; *dogs have an acute sense of smell*

acute accent [ə'kjuːt 'æksənt] *noun* mark sloping forwards over a vowel, indicating a change of sound; *'café has an acute accent on the 'e'*

acutely [ə'kjuːtli] *adverb* strongly; *she is acutely aware of the problem*; *his behaviour was acutely embarrassing to his family*

ad [æd] *noun* (*informal*) = ADVERTISEMENT; *if you want to sell your car quickly, put an ad in the paper*; **classified ads** = newspaper advertisements which are listed under special headings, such as 'jobs wanted' or 'household items for sale'; **small ads** = small advertisements for jobs, for things for sale; *I was just looking through the small ads when I saw that they wanted a gardener*

AD ['eɪ'diː] *abbreviation for* Anno Domini (Latin for 'in the year of our Lord'), used in dates; *Claudius invaded Britain in 43 AD* (NOTE: for dates before the birth of Christ, use BC: *Julius Caesar died in 44 BC*)

adage ['ædɪdʒ] *noun* old saying; *according to the old adage, time is the great healer*

adamant ['ædəmənt] *adjective* with firm opinions; *he was adamant that the police should not be told*; *we must leave no later than 6 o'clock - father is quite adamant about it*

Adam's apple ['ædəmz 'æpl] *noun* piece of cartilage in the front of the larynx, which can sometimes easily be seen; *with his double chin, you can't see his Adam's apple*

COMMENT: men have deeper voices than women because their larynxes are bigger; hence the Adam's apple is more usually seen in men than women, and also why it is called Adam's apple and not Eve's

adapt [ə'dæpt] *verb* (**a**) to change something so that it fits; *the play has been adapted for the cinema*; *she adapted the story for TV*; *the car has been adapted for the disabled* (**b**) to change to become more suitable; *the country will have to adapt to the new political system*

adaptable [ə'dæptəbl] *adjective* who is able to change to deal with a new situation; *she's very adaptable, I'm sure that she will accept to alter her timetable*

adaptation [ædæp'teɪʃn] *noun* (**a**) change which fits new conditions; *like everyone else, he'll have to go through a period of adaptation when he starts his new job*; *the adaptation of the eye to different levels of brightness* (**b**) film, play, etc., which has been adapted from another; *it is an adaptation of a play by Shakespeare*; *a new adaptation of 'Pickwick Papers' for television*

adaptor *or* **adapter** [ə'dæptə] *noun* (**a**) person who adapts (a play, etc.) (**b**) device which allows two or more pieces of equipment to be connected together; **adaptor plug** = plug which allows a piece of equipment to be plugged into a different sized socket; *my hair-drier won't work here in France, because I haven't brought my adaptor*

add [æd] *verb* (**a**) to make a total of numbers; *if you add all these numbers together it should make fifty* (NOTE: **add** is usually shown by the sign + : **10 + 4 = 14**: say 'ten add four equals fourteen') (**b**) to join to something else; *interest is added to the account monthly*; *add two cupfuls of sugar*; *put some tea into the pot and add boiling water*; *by building the annexe, they have added thirty rooms to the hotel*; *this paint is too thick - add some water to it*

added ['ædɪd] *adjective* which has been added; *not only did we have a puncture on the motorway, but we had the added problem of not being able to speak German*; *this marmalade has no added sugar*

adder ['ædə] *noun* type of poisonous European snake (NOTE: also called a **viper**)

addict ['ædɪkt] *noun* person who cannot stop doing something; **drug addict** = person who takes drugs as a habit; *a centre for drug addicts*

addicted [ə'dɪktɪd] *adjective* (person) who cannot stop doing something; *people addicted to alcohol can be treated at the centre*

addiction [ə'dɪkʃn] *noun* being unable to stop doing something; *alcohol addiction*; *drug addiction*; *addiction to heroin*

addictive [ə'dɪktɪv] *adjective* (**a**) which is habit-forming, which people can become addicted to; *certain narcotic drugs are addictive* (**b**) which you can get used to doing; *watching the Olympics on TV can become addictive*

addition [ə'dɪʃn] *noun* (**a**) action of adding figures to make a total; *you don't need a calculator to do a simple addition* (**b**) thing or person added; *the latest addition to the family*; *he showed us the additions to his collection of paintings* (**c**) **in addition** = also; *in*

addition to = as well as; *there are twelve registered letters to be sent in addition to this parcel*

additional [ə'dɪʃənəl] *adjective* more; *additional duty will have to be paid*

additionally [æ'dɪʃənəli] *adverb* in addition; *the price includes the camera, the case and additionally six free films*

additive ['ædɪtɪv] *noun* substance which is added; *the orange juice contains a number of additives*; *be sure to buy a brand of ice cream which is additive-free*

> COMMENT: colour additives are added to food to improve its appearance. Some are natural organic substances like saffron, carrot juice or caramel, but other colour additives are synthetic. Other substances are added to food to prevent decay or to keep the food in the right form: these can be emulsifiers, which bind different foods together as mixtures in sauces, for example, and stabilizers, which can keep a sauce semi-liquid and prevent it from separating into solids and liquids. The European Community allows certain additives to be added to food and these are given E numbers

address [ə'dres] 1 *noun* (a) details of the number of a house, the name of a street and the town where someone lives or works; *what is the doctor's address?*; *he wrote his address on a piece of paper*; *our address is: 1 Cambridge Road, Teddington, Middlesex*; **accommodation address** = address used for receiving messages but which is not the real address of a company; **business address** = address of a business (as opposed to private address); *my business address and phone number are printed on the card*; **home address** *or* **private address** = address of a house or flat where someone lives; *please send the plane tickets to my home address*; **address book** = special notebook, with columns printed in such a way that names, addresses and phone numbers can be entered; **address list** = list of addresses (b) formal speech; *he made an address to the Parliament* (NOTE: plural is **addresses**) 2 *verb* (a) to write the details of name, street, town, etc., on a letter or parcel; *that letter is addressed to me - don't open it!* (b) to speak to, to write to; *please address your inquiries to the information office*; *teachers are not normally addressed as 'Sir' in the USA* (c) to make a formal speech; *the chairman addressed the meeting* (d) to examine a problem; *this is an important issue which must be addressed at the next meeting*; *the committee failed to address the question of sexual harassment*

add up ['æd 'ʌp] *verb* (a) to put several figures together to make a total; *just add up this column of figures*; *the waiter added up the bill wrongly*; **the figures do not add up** = the total given is not correct (b) **it doesn't add up** = it doesn't make sense, it is confusing; *the story she told the police simply did not add up*

add up to ['æd 'ʌp tu] *verb* to make a total of; *the total cost adds up to more than £1,000*

adept ['ædept] 1 *adjective* skilful at doing something; *she's adept at avoiding paying her bills* 2 *noun* person who is skilful at doing something; *he's an adept at car maintenance*

adequacy ['ædɪkwəsi] *noun* being adequate; *no one even thought of questioning the adequacy of the alarm system*

adequate ['ædɪkwət] *adjective* enough; *his salary is barely adequate to support his family*; *we don't have adequate supplies for the whole journey*

adhere to [əd'hiːə 'tu] *verb* (a) to stick to; *this type of glue won't adhere to china*; *the suction pads allow the machine to adhere firmly to the bench* (b) to follow rules; *she refused to adhere to the conditions attached to the competition*

adherence [əd'hiːrəns] *noun* closely following; *our adherence to the principle of non-interference*

adherent [əd'hiːrənt] *noun* person who supports a policy or a religion; *the government persecuted the adherents of the old religion*

adhesive [əd'hiːzɪv] 1 *adjective* which sticks; *adhesive tape*; *adhesive plaster*; **self-adhesive** = which sticks to itself; *self-adhesive envelopes* 2 *noun* glue; *a tube of adhesive*

ad hoc ['æd 'hɒk] *Latin phrase* (meaning 'for this particular purpose') (a) arranged for a particular case; *an ad hoc decision*; **an ad hoc committee** = a temporary committee set up to study a particular problem (b) **on an ad hoc basis** = done without planning; *the decision was taken on an ad hoc basis*

adjacent [ə'dʒeɪsənt] *adjective* very close to, almost touching; *we went to the museum and parked in the adjacent car park*; **adjacent to** = very near to; *the house is adjacent to the garden centre*

adjectival [ædʒek'taɪvl] *adjective* used like an adjective; *the adjectival use of nouns and verbs is common in English*; *an adjectival phrase is usually made up of an adverb and an adjective, such as 'completely silent'*

adjective ['ædʒektɪv] *noun* word which describes a noun; *in the phrase 'a big black cloud', 'big' and 'black' are both adjectives*

adjoin [ə'dʒɔɪn] *verb* to be next to; *here is your bedroom, and there is an adjoining bathroom*; *the back of the office adjoins the garden of the French restaurant*; **adjoining rooms** = rooms which are next to each other; *they asked to be put in adjoining rooms*

adjourn [ə'dʒɜːn] *verb* to postpone to a later date; *the meeting was adjourned until the 25th*; *the court adjourned for lunch*; *the appeal was adjourned while further evidence was being produced*; **let's adjourn to the bar** = let's go on talking in the bar

adjudicate [ə'dʒuːdɪkeɪt] *verb* (a) to give an official decision (in a dispute); *he was asked to adjudicate in the argument between the management and unions*; *he was adjudicated bankrupt* (b) to act as the judge in a competition; *she adjudicated the poetry competition*

adjudication [ədʒuːdɪ'keɪʃn] *noun* (a) official decision in a dispute; *we have to wait until next month for the adjudication* (b) judging of a competition; *the adjudication of the poetry competition is taking place in the town hall*

adjudicator [ə'dʒuːdɪkeɪtə] *noun* (a) person who gives an official decision in a dispute; *the case was referred to an adjudicator*; *he has been appointed an adjudicator in the industrial dispute* (b) person who judges a competition; *one of the adjudicators is ill so the result of the competition has had to be postponed*

adjunct ['ædʒʌŋkt] *noun* **an adjunct to something** = something which is joined to something else; *a report and its adjuncts*

adjust [ə'dʒʌst] *verb* **(a)** to make a slight change to; *if the trousers are too tight, we can easily adjust the fitting* **(b) to adjust to** = to change and adapt to; *it's difficult adjusting to living in a tropical climate*

adjustable [ə'dʒʌstəbl] *adjective* which can be adjusted; *the height of these office chairs is adjustable*; **adjustable spanner** = spanner which can be screwed to fit different nuts (NOTE: also called **monkey wrench**)

adjustment [ə'dʒʌsmənt] *noun* slight change to make something work well; *he made a slight adjustment to the central heating pump*

admin ['ædmɪn] *noun* (*informal*) **(a)** work of administration, paperwork; *all this admin takes up a lot of time*; *the admin people have asked for more figures* **(b)** staff dealing with administration; *admin say they want the report by four o'clock*

administer [əd'mɪnɪstə] *verb* **(a)** (*a country, an office, a company*) to manage, to organize; *the province was administered by Portugal for many years* **(b)** to give; *to administer a drug to a patient* **(c)** to **administer an oath** = to make someone swear an oath

administration [ədmɪnɪ'streɪʃn] *noun* **(a)** action of organizing; *hospital administration must be improved*; *who's in charge of administration here?* **(b)** the administration = the government; *the Reagan Administration* **(c)** the **administration of justice** = providing justice

administrative [əd'mɪnɪstrətɪv] *adjective* referring to administration; *his duties are almost entirely administrative*; *administrative expenses are rising all the time*; *there are more administrative staff than workers*

administrator [əd'mɪnɪstreɪtə] *noun* **(a)** ruler, governor; *the country's administrators are to blame for what has happened* **(b)** person who runs an organization; *we are advertising for a new chief administrator for the society*

admirable ['ædmərəbl] *adjective* which must be admired; *her work is entirely admirable*; *an admirable display of courage*

admiral ['ædmərəl] *noun* **(a)** high naval officer; *her father was an admiral in the French Navy* **(b) red admiral** = common summer butterfly with black and red wings

admiration [ædmə'reɪʃn] *noun* respect for; *I have great admiration for her*; *everyone looked on in admiration as she showed how to toss pancakes*

admire [əd'maɪə] *verb* to look at someone *or* something with respect; *we admired his garden*; *everyone admires her paintings*; *he was admired for his skill as a violinist*; *a much-admired chief minister*

admirer [əd'maɪərə] *noun* person who loves someone or is attracted by someone; *he's had a Valentine card from a secret admirer*

admission [əd'mɪʃn] *noun* **(a)** being allowed to enter; *there is a £1 admission charge*; *admission to the exhibition is free on Sundays*; *my friend was refused admission to the restaurant because he was not wearing a tie* **(b)** statement saying that something is true; *his admission of fraud*; *her admission that she had taken the watch*

admit [əd'mɪt] *verb* **(a)** to allow someone to go in; *children are admitted free, but adults have to pay*; *this ticket admits three persons* **(b)** to say that something is

true; *he admitted stealing the car*; *she admitted she had taken the watch* (NOTE: **admitting - admitted**)

admittance [əd'mɪtəns] *noun* (*formal*) allowing someone to go into a place; *'No admittance except on business'*; *he gained admittance to the building by a side door which had been left unlocked*

admittedly [əd'mɪtədli] *adverb* admitting that this is true; *admittedly, the restaurant didn't charge us for the glasses that the children broke*; *he is admittedly one of the leading experts in the field*

admonish [əd'mɒnɪʃ] *verb* (*formal*) to criticize or warn; *no one admonished her for her rudeness to the president's wife*

admonishment [əd'mɒnɪʃmənt] *noun* (*formal*) warning given to someone; *he received no admonishment*

admonition [ædmə'nɪʃn] *noun* (*formal*) warning given to someone; *the admonition came in the form of a letter signed by the dean of the faculty*

adolescence [ædə'lesns] *noun* period between childhood and adulthood, between the ages of 12 and 18; *adolescence is a period of strong emotional changes*; *wait until she reaches adolescence, that's when real problems will start*; *skin troubles in adolescence must be taken seriously*

adolescent [ædə'lesnt] **1** *adjective* referring to the period between childhood and adulthood; *she teaches a class of adolescent boys* **2** *noun* young person between 12 and 18; *all adolescents rebel against authority*

adopt [ə'dɒpt] *verb* **(a)** to take legally as a son or daughter; *they have adopted a little boy* **(b)** to take; *the opposition parties have adopted a different line of argument*; *he adopted an air of superiority* **(c)** to tell all students to use; *the book has been adopted for use in all English classes* **(d)** (*of a political party*) to choose a candidate; *James Black was adopted as the candidate for our constituency*

adopted [ə'dɒptɪd] *adjective* **adopted child** = child who has been taken legally as someone's son or daughter; *their adopted son has won a scholarship*

adoption [ə'dɒpʃn] *noun* **(a)** legally taking as son or daughter; *the adoption papers were signed yesterday*; **to put up for adoption** = to offer a child to be adopted **(b)** choosing as an official candidate; *there were 250 local party members at the adoption meeting*

adoptive [ə'dɒptɪv] *adjective* **adoptive parents** = parents who have adopted a child as a son or daughter

adorable [ə'dɔːrəbl] *adjective* lovely and attractive; *what an adorable little cottage!*; *our little granddaughter is adorable*

adoration [ædə'reɪʃn] *noun* **(a)** admiration, love; *his adoration for his young wife* **(b)** (*art*) **the Adoration of the Magi** = painting showing the Three Wise Men coming to present gifts to the infant Jesus

adore [ə'dɔː] *verb* to like very much; *he adored his father*; *she adores Italian food*; *we adore going shopping in Bond Street*

adoring [ə'dɔːrɪŋ] *adjective* who or which adores; *he was surrounded by his adoring family*; *the adoring glances of his sisters*; *the pop group was greeted by shrieks from their adoring fans*

adorn [ə'dɔːn] *verb* to decorate with ornaments; *the walls of the cave were adorned with paintings of deer* *and elephants; there was a period when ladies wore huge hats adorned with feathers*

adornment [əˈdɔːnmənt] *noun* decorating with ornaments; *she wore no adornment except a large brooch*

adrenalin [əˈdrenəlɪn] *noun* hormone secreted by glands in the body; *an injection of adrenalin may be needed if the body doesn't produce enough naturally;* **to get the adrenalin going** *or* **flowing = ** to make someone excited and energetic; *the preparation for the great race got the adrenalin going*

> COMMENT: adrenalin is produced when a person or animal is experiencing surprise, shock, fear, excitement: it speeds up the heartbeat and raises the blood pressure

Adriatic [ˈeɪdriˈætɪk] *noun* sea to the east of Italy; *we spent the summer cruising in the Adriatic; Dubrovnik is one of the most beautiful towns on the Adriatic*

adrift [əˈdrɪft] *adverb* **(a)** drifting, not being steered by anyone; *the mutineers took over the ship and set the officers adrift in a small boat* **(b)** not connected; *it won't work because the wire has come adrift from the plug* **(c)** *(informal)* not correct; *I think we are about £250 adrift in our calculations*

adroit [əˈdrɔɪt] *adjective* clever, especially in negotiating; *he showed himself to be particularly adroit at dealing with the unions*

adroitly [əˈdrɔɪtli] *adverb* skilfully; *he adroitly avoided answering the reporters' questions*

adulation [ædjuˈleɪʃn] *noun* excessive praise; *she enjoys the adulation of the teenage audiences*

adult [ˈædʌlt] **1** *adjective* **(a)** fully grown; *an adult tiger* **(b)** referring to grown-up people; *adult education; adult fiction* **2** *noun* grown-up person; *children are admitted free, but adults have to pay*

adulterate [əˈdʌltəreɪt] *verb* **(a)** to add water to milk, wine; *wine can be adulterated by simply adding water* **(b)** to make something less pure by adding an inferior substance to it; *pure alcohol is adulterated by an addition of methyl alcohol to make it unpleasant to drink*

adulteration [ədʌltəˈreɪʃn] *noun* making something less pure; *adulteration of wine by adding water happens in some restaurants*

adulterer *or* **adulteress** [əˈdʌltərə or əˈdʌltərəs] *noun* person who commits adultery

adulterous [əˈdʌltərəs] *adjective* referring to adultery; *her adulterous relationship with the owner of the local garage; he was accused of having an adulterous liaison with one of his staff*

adultery [əˈdʌltri] *noun* *(of married person)* sexual intercourse with someone who is not your husband or wife; *she committed adultery with the ski instructor; he was found guilty of adultery*

adulthood [ˈædʌlthʊd] *noun* period when someone is adult; *in theory, young people reach adulthood at the age of 18*

advance [ədˈvɑːns] **1** *noun* **(a)** movement forwards; *the police have made some advances in their fight against crime* **(b)** **in advance** = early; *if you want to get good seats for the play, you need to book three weeks in advance; you must phone well in advance to make an appointment; they asked us to pay £200 in advance* **(c)** money paid as a loan or as a part of a payment to be made later; *she received an advance from the purchaser; can I have an advance of £50 against next month's salary?* **2** *verb* **(a)** to go forward; *the police slowly advanced across the square* **(b)** to pay as a loan; *he advanced me £100* **(c)** to bring a date forward; *the date of the meeting has been advanced by a week* **(d)** to move a clock to a later time; *when crossing from England to France, watches should be advanced by one hour; see also* PUT FORWARD

advanced [ədˈvɑːnst] *adjective* **(a)** which is studied after studying for several years'; *he is taking advanced mathematics; she is studying for an advanced degree;* **advanced level examination (A level)** = examination taken at about 18, at the end of secondary school, which is used as a basis for entry to university or college **(b)** which has moved forward; *in an advanced state of decay*

advancement [ədˈvɑːnsmənt] *noun* **(a)** moving something forwards; *it contributes to the advancement of human knowledge* **(b)** promotion; *his advancement has been blocked by his boss*

advantage [ədˈvɑːntɪdʒ] *noun* thing which will help you to be successful; *being able to drive a car is an advantage; knowledge of two foreign languages is an advantage in this job; she has several advantages over the other candidates for the job;* **to take advantage of** = to profit from; *they took advantage of the cheap fares on offer;* **to take advantage of someone** = to cheat someone; *he took advantage of the old lady;* **to advantage** = to make someone look perfect; *her dress shows off her figure to advantage;* **to use to great advantage** = to use in a way which helps you win

advantageous [ædvənˈteɪdʒəs] *adjective* profitable, likely to help; *the contract would certainly be advantageous to us*

advent [ˈædvent] *noun* arrival; *the advent of spring; the advent of the industrial revolution changed the world*

adventure [ədˈventʃə] *noun* new, exciting and dangerous experience; *I must tell you about our adventures in the Gobi desert*

adventurer [ədˈventʃərə] *noun* person who travels in dangerous parts of the world; *crossing the Sahara desert is the dream of any young adventurer*

adventurous [ədˈventʃərəs] *adjective* **(a)** *(person)* bold, happy to do something risky; *my sister is not very adventurous, she's never been any further than the south coast; investing in the Far East can be an adventurous undertaking; she's quite adventurous, she's decided to learn to fly* **(b)** exciting, full of adventure; *he leads an adventurous life studying polar bears in the North Pole*

adverb [ˈædvɜːb] *noun* word which modifies a verb, an adjective, another adverb or a whole sentence; *in the phrase 'he walked slowly, because the snow was very thick', 'slowly' and 'very' are both adverbs*

adversary [ˈædvəsri] *noun* opponent, the person you are fighting; *his first adversary in the ring was known as 'Man Mountain'* (NOTE: plural is **adversaries**)

adverse [ˈædvɜːs] *adjective* **(a)** *(wind)* which blows against you; *adverse winds prevented the ships leaving the harbour* **(b)** *(conditions)* which go against you; *will the plan have any adverse effects?; his condition is an adverse reaction to the drug which he has been* *prescribed*; **adverse balance of trade** = situation where a country imports more than it exports

adversity [əd'vɜːsɪti] *noun* difficult times, when you have to face all sorts of problems; *in his adversity he had the support of his wife*

advert ['ædvɜːt] *noun GB (informal)* = ADVERTISEMENT

advertise ['ædvətaɪz] *verb* to make sure that people know that something is for sale, that something is going to happen, that a show is on; *there are posters all over the town advertising the circus*; *I sent away for a watch which I saw advertised in the paper*; *did you see that the restaurant is advertising cheap meals on Sundays?*; *the company is advertising for secretaries*

advertisement [əd'vɜːtɪzmənt] *noun* announcement which tries to make sure that people know that something is for sale, that something is going to happen, that a show is on; *he put an advertisement in the paper*; *she answered an advertisement in the paper*; **classified advertisements** = advertisements listed in a newspaper under special headings, such as 'property for sale' or 'jobs wanted'

advertiser ['ædvətaɪzə] *noun* person who advertises; *the advertiser will pay for postage on orders placed before the end of the month*

advertising ['ædvətaɪzɪŋ] *noun* the action of making sure that people know that something is for sale, that something is going to happen, that a show is on; *they spent millions on the advertising campaign*; *the company has increased the amount of money it spends on advertising*; **advertising agency** = agency which organizes advertisements for other companies

advice [əd'vaɪs] *noun* saying what should be done; *he went to the bank manager for advice on how to pay his debts*; *they would not listen to the doctor's advice*; *my grandfather gave me a very useful piece of advice*; *his mother's advice was to stay in bed*; *she took or followed the doctor's advice and stopped smoking* (NOTE: no plural: **some advice**; for one item say **a piece of advice**)

advisable [əd'vaɪzəbl] *adjective* which is recommended; *it is advisable to take warm clothing*; *I didn't think it advisable to tell her the bad news just before her interview*

advise [əd'vaɪz] *verb* to suggest what should be done; *he advised her to put all her money into a deposit account*

advise against [əd'vaɪz ə'genst] *verb* to suggest that something should not be done; *he advised against buying the house*

advisedly [əd'vaɪzədli] *adverb* deliberately, after a lot of thought; *the police advisedly refused to publish the photograph of the suspect*

adviser *or* **advisor** [əd'vaɪzə] *noun* person who gives advice; *he is consulting his financial adviser*

advisory [əd'vaɪzəri] *adjective* giving advice; *she acts in an advisory capacity*; *the council runs an advisory service for immigrants*; **Advisory, Conciliation and Arbitration Service (ACAS)** = British government service which arbitrates in disputes between management and employees

advocacy ['ædvəkəsi] *noun* support for a cause; *her advocacy of the cause of homeless families*

advocate 1 *noun* ['ædvəkət] person who pleads for a cause; *the advocates of capital punishment* **2** ['ædvəkeɪt] *verb* to recommend; *she advocates the introduction of capital punishment*

aerial ['eəriəl] **1** *adjective* referring to the air; **aerial spraying** = spraying from the air **2** *noun* device for receiving radio or TV signals; *we have fixed a TV aerial on the roof* (NOTE: American English is **antenna**)

aerie ['ɪəri] *US* = EYRIE

aerobic [eə'rəʊbɪk] *adjective* using or needing oxygen; *aerobic exercises help keep you fit*; *the bacillus which causes tetanus is an aerobic bacillus* (NOTE: opposite is **anaerobic**)

aerobics [eə'rəʊbɪks] *noun* active exercises which aim to increase the amount of oxygen taken into the body; *I don't like doing aerobics, I'd rather cycle or run*; *we both missed our aerobics class last Friday*

aerodrome ['eərədrəʊm] *noun* small airfield; *the local aerodrome is used by small executive aircraft*

aerodynamic [eərədaɪ'næmɪk] *adjective* referring to the movement of objects through the air; *the aerodynamic design of a car*

aerodynamics [eərədaɪ'næmɪks] *noun* **(a)** science of the movement of objects through the air; *knowledge of aerodynamics is necessary for the design of aircraft* **(b)** way in which a machine moves through the air; *the aerodynamics of the car are superb*

aeroplane ['eərəpleɪn] *noun* plane or aircraft, a machine which flies in the air, carrying passengers or cargo; *we all got into the little aeroplane and it took off*

aerosol ['eərəsɒl] *noun* **(a)** can which sprays a liquid such as an insecticide, medicine, etc., in the form of tiny drops; *don't throw the empty aerosol into the fire*; *it's much easier to use an aerosol to spray the insecticide on the plants*; *paint is spread more evenly with an aerosol* **(b)** tiny particles of a chemical in the air; *an insecticide in aerosol form*

aerospace ['eərəʊspeɪs] *noun* the space around the earth; **the aerospace industry** = the industry involved in making and flying planes

aesthetic *US* **esthetic** [iːs'θetɪk] *adjective* pleasant, from an artistic point of view; *they criticized the plane from a practical point of view but didn't mention its aesthetic merits*; *the colour scheme shocks my aesthetic sense*

aesthetically *US* **esthetically** [iːs'θetɪkli] *adverb* from an artistic point of view; *the whole town is aesthetically very pleasing*

aesthetics *US* **esthetics** [iː'sθetɪks] *noun* science of and study of beauty, especially in art; *this design goes against all the rules of aesthetics*; *the colour scheme shocks my sense of aesthetics*

afar [ə'fɑː] *adverb (formal)* **from afar** = from a long way away; *travellers came from afar to the great market at Samarkand*

affability [æfə'bɪlɪti] *noun* being pleasant and easy to talk to; *he is well-known for his affability*

affable ['æfəbl] *adjective* pleasant and easy to talk to; *the old boss always had an affable word for each member of staff*

affair [ə'feə] *noun* **(a)** thing which concerns someone; *that's his affair - it's nothing to do with me*; *it's an affair for the police*; *she's always sticking her nose into other people's affairs*; *his business affairs were* *very complicated* **(b)** **(love)** **affair** = sexual relationship; *he's having an affair with his boss's wife* **(c)** state of affairs = general situation; *the present state of affairs* **(d)** affairs of state = government business

affect [ə'fekt] *verb* to have an influence on, to change; *the new regulations have affected our business*; *train services have been seriously affected by the strike*

affecting [ə'fektɪŋ] *adjective* which touches your emotions; *she made an affecting appeal to the judge*

affection [ə'fekʃn] *noun* liking or love; *she felt great affection for her youngest grandson*

affectionate [ə'fekʃənət] *adjective* showing love; *our dog is wonderfully affectionate with the children*; *he gave her an affectionate kiss*

affidavit [æfi'deɪvɪt] *noun* written statement which is signed and sworn before a solicitor and which can then be used as evidence in court; *the solicitor came in with the affidavit which had to be signed*

affiliate [ə'fɪliet] **1** *noun* company linked to another one; *we have affiliates in several European countries* **2** *verb* to link to a larger group; *a union which is affiliated to the Labour Party*; *the college is affiliated to an American university*

affiliated [ə'fɪlietɪd] *adjective* **affiliated to** *or* **with** = linked to *or* with; *he runs one of our affiliated companies*; *one of their affiliated companies has had to close down*

affiliation [əfɪlɪ'eɪʃn] *noun* being affiliated; **political affiliation** = link to a particular political party; *because of his strong political affiliations, he cannot be considered as an independent advisor*

affinity [ə'fɪnɪti] *noun* being similar in character; *a certain degree of affinity exists between the two organizations*; **to feel an affinity for** = to feel a special link with; *she feels an affinity for homeless people*; **affinity card** = credit card which pays a percentage of turnover to a charity (NOTE: plural is **affinities**)

affirm [ə'fɜːm] *verb (formal)* **(a)** to state publicly that something is true; *he continued to affirm his innocence* **(b)** to make a statement in court that you will tell the truth, though this is not sworn on oath

affirmation [æfə'meɪʃn] *noun* **(a)** statement that something is true; *despite her affirmation that she was away when I called, I am fairly sure she was at home all the time*; *in spite of all his affirmations to the contrary, the evidence seems to show that he knew the money had been stolen* **(b)** statement in court that you will tell the truth, though this is not sworn on oath

affirmative [ə'fɜːmətɪv] **1** *adjective* meaning 'yes'; *we are waiting for an affirmative response from our German partners*; **US affirmative action program** = program to avoid racial or sexual discrimination (NOTE: the British equivalent is **equal opportunities**) **2** *noun* meaning 'yes'; **the answer is in the affirmative** = the answer is 'yes'

affix [ə'fɪks] *verb (formal)* to fix something; *he affixed the seal to the contract*; *there is no need to affix a stamp on a prepaid envelope*

afflict [ə'flɪkt] *verb* **(a)** to make someone very sad; *she was much afflicted by the news of her father's death* **(b)** to make someone suffer; *the country has been afflicted by civil wars and natural disasters*

affliction [ə'flɪkʃn] *noun* suffering or pain, or something that causes suffering or pain; *in moments of*

affliction it is good to know that your friends will stand by you; *no affliction can be more depressing than Alzheimer's disease*; *I hope I'll never have to face the afflictions of old age*

affluence ['æfluəns] *noun* wealth; *the country is poor but the capital shows signs of great affluence*

affluent ['æfluənt] *adjective* very rich; *affluent people are not always those who give most generously to good causes*; **affluent society** = society where most people are rich; *who doesn't want to live in an affluent society?*

afford [ə'fɔːd] *verb* to have enough money to pay for; *we can't afford to run a large car these days*; *he couldn't afford the time to take a holiday* (NOTE: only used after **can, cannot, could, could not, able to**)

affordable [ə'fɔːdəbl] *adjective* which can be afforded; *the price of the meal was quite affordable*; *we are looking for more affordable air fares to Spain*; *living in London is not affordable any more*

affront [ə'frʌnt] **1** *noun (formal)* action which insults; *he considered it an affront to be made to stand in a queue* **2** *verb* to insult; *I did not expect him to feel so affronted by my remarks*

afield [ə'fiːld] *adverb* **far afield** = a long way away; *people come from far afield to visit the grave*

afloat [ə'fləʊt] *adverb* **(a)** floating, not sinking; *she kept afloat by holding on to a piece of wood*; *our boat was driven onto the beach by the storm, but we managed to get it afloat again* **(b)** *(of company)* not in difficulties; *I wonder how they manage to stay afloat when the market is so difficult*

afoot [ə'fʊt] *adverb* in the process of being planned; *there's a plan afoot*

aforementioned [ə'fɔːmenʃnd] *(formal)* **1** *adjective* mentioned earlier; *the aforementioned company was awarded the contract* **2** *noun* someone *or* something mentioned earlier; *none of the aforementioned must be allowed to leave the country*

afraid [ə'freɪd] *adjective* **(a) to be afraid of something** = to be frightened of something; *I am afraid of snakes*; *she is afraid of going out alone*; *he's afraid to climb the ladder* **(b) to be afraid (that)** = to be sorry to say; *I'm afraid that all the cakes have been sold*; *you can't see the boss - I'm afraid he's ill*; *have you got a pocket calculator? - no, I'm afraid not* (NOTE: **afraid** cannot be used in front of a noun: **the girl's afraid** but **a frightened girl**)

Africa ['æfrɪkə] *proper noun* large continent, to the south of the Mediterranean, between the Atlantic Ocean and the Indian Ocean; *they want to go to Africa on holiday*; *after ten days at sea, they saw the coast of North Africa in the distance*

African ['æfrɪkən] **1** *adjective* referring to Africa; *the African jungle*; **African elephant** = type of elephant with large ears (the other type is the Indian elephant) **2** *noun* person from Africa; *the guitarist is an African*

aft [ɑːft] *adverb* in the back of a ship or plane; *they went aft*; *you will find the toilets aft* (NOTE: the opposite is **forward**)

after ['ɑːftə] **1** *preposition* **(a)** following or next in order; *what's the letter after Q in the alphabet?*; *if today is Tuesday, the day after tomorrow is Thursday*; *they spoke one after the other*; **after you** = you go first; **after you with the milk** = pass me the milk when you have finished with it **(b)** later than; *we arrived after six* *o'clock*; *he should be in bed - it's after ten o'clock*; *we don't let the children go out alone after dark* **(c)** to be **after someone** = (i) to be looking for someone; (ii) to be angry with someone; *the police are after him*; *if you leave mud all over the kitchen floor, your mother will be after you*; **what's she after?** = what does she want? **2** *conjunction* later than a time; *after the snow fell, the motorways were blocked*; *after the driver had got in, the coach started*; *phone me after you get home* (NOTE: **after** is used with many verbs: **look after**, **take after**, etc.)

after all ['ɑːftə 'ɔːl] *adverb* **(a)** in spite of everything; *she changed her mind and decided to come with us after all* **(b)** the fact is; *I think I'll go out in the car - after all, it's a fine day and I've finished my work*

aftercare ['ɑːftəkeə] *noun* care of a patient after an operation, etc.; *aftercare treatment also involves helping a patient to look after himself again*

after-effects [ɑːftər'fekts] *noun* effects which follow after something; *the after-effects of the bomb lasted for years*; *the operation can have some unpleasant after-effects*

after-hours ['ɑːftə'auəz] *adjective* **after-hours trading** = trading after a stock exchange has closed

aftermath ['ɑːtəmɑːθ] *noun* time after a catastrophe; *they had to clear up in the aftermath of the typhoon*; *the scene after the office party resembled the aftermath of the Battle of Waterloo*

afternoon [ɑːftə'nuːn] *noun* time between lunchtime and the evening; *he always has a little sleep in the afternoon*; *the shop is closed on Wednesday afternoons*; *can we meet this afternoon?*; *there is an afternoon flight to Paris*; *I'm playing tennis tomorrow afternoon*; **afternoon tea** = meal taken in the afternoon, usually with small sandwiches, cakes, and tea

afters ['ɑːftəz] *noun* GB *(informal)* dessert course; *what do you want for afters?*; *what's on the menu for afters?* (NOTE: very informal, used often by children, but also sometimes by adults as a joke)

after-school ['ɑːftə'skuːl] *adjective* taking place when school has finished; *he takes part in lots of after-school activities, such as the astronomy club*

afterthought ['ɑːftəθɔːt] *noun* thing which you only think of or do later; **as an afterthought** = showing that you have just thought of something new; *he signed the letter and as an afterthought added a row of kisses*; *the last chapter of the book was an afterthought and it changes the emphasis totally*

afterwards ['ɑːftəwədz] *adverb* later; *we'll have lunch first and go shopping afterwards*; *she felt fine before dinner but was ill afterwards*

again [ə'gen] *adverb* **(a)** another time, once more; *he wrote again to say he was ill*; *we'd love to come to see you again*; *he had to take his driving test again* **(b)** back as you were before; *although I like going on holiday, I'm always glad to be home again*; *she brought the jeans back again to the shop because they didn't fit*

◊ **once again** ['wʌns ə'gen] another time; *once again, the train was late*

◊ **yet again** ['jet ə'gen] once more after many times; *she's taking her driving test yet again*

against [ə'genst] *preposition* **(a)** touching; *he was leaning against the wall*; *she hit her head against the*

low doorway **(b)** not as someone proposes; **it's against the rules** *or* **against the law** = it's not as the rules say *or* as the law says; *it's against the law to drive in the dark without lights*; *you mustn't hold the football in your hands - it's against the rules*; **what do you have against the plan?** = why don't you agree with the plan?; *she was against the idea of going to the cinema* **(c)** opposite; *England is playing against South Africa tomorrow*; *it's hard cycling uphill against the wind* **(d)** as part of; *can I have an advance against next month's salary?*

age [eidʒ] *noun* **(a)** the number of years which you have lived; *what age will he be on his next birthday?*; *she is thirty years of age*; *he looks younger than his age*; **old age** = period when you are old; **under age** = younger than the legal age to do something; *under-age drinkers* **(b)** a very long time; *I've been waiting here for ages*; *it took us ages to get served*

aged *adjective* **(a)** [eidʒd] with the age of; *a girl aged nine*; *she died last year, aged 83* **(b)** ['eidʒid] very old; *an aged man*

age group ['eidʒ 'gruːp] *noun* all people of a certain age; *the book is aimed at the 13-16 age group*

ageing *US* **aging** ['eidʒiŋ] *adjective* which is becoming older; *the ageing population*

agency ['eidʒənsi] *noun* office which represents another firm; *we have the agency for Ford cars*; *an advertising agency*; **estate agency** = office which arranges for the sale of houses, flats, etc.; **travel agency** = office which sells air tickets, organizes tours, etc. (NOTE: plural is **agencies**)

agenda [ə'dʒendə] *noun* list of points for discussion; *we will now take item five on the agenda*; *after two hours we were still discussing the first item on the agenda*; **what's on the agenda?** = what are we going to discuss?

agent ['eidʒənt] *noun* person who works for or represents someone else; *our head office is in London but we have an agent in Paris*; **travel agent** = person who sells tickets, organizes tours, etc.; *I bought my plane tickets at the travel agent's*

aggravate ['ægrəveit] *verb* to make something worse; *playing football aggravates his knee injury*; *the treatment seems to aggravate the disease*; **aggravated damages** = extra damages awarded by a court against a defendant who has behaved particularly badly

aggregate ['ægrɪgət] *noun* **(a)** grand total; *the aggregate of the team's scores*; **on aggregate** *or* **in the aggregate** = as a final total; *Liverpool won 7 -2 on aggregate* **(b)** mixture of sand and gravel used to make roads; *lorries transporting aggregate to the building site*

aggression [ə'greʃn] *noun* feeling of anger against someone; *she had never experienced aggression from her husband before*; **an act of aggression** = an attack on someone

aggressive [ə'gresiv] *adjective* ready to attack; *he's very aggressive towards his family*; *why are you getting so aggressive?*

aggressively [ə'gresivli] *adverb* as if wanting to attack; *she glared at him aggressively*

aggressor [ə'gresə] *noun* person or country that attacks another; *they were the aggressors in the civil war*; *the girl said that the boy next door was the aggressor*

aggrieved [ə'griːvd] *adjective* annoyed because you have been badly treated; *she was aggrieved because she had not been invited to the wedding; (legal)* **aggrieved party** = party who has been harmed; *the aggrieved party was not represented in court*

agile ['ædʒaɪl] *adjective* that can move easily; *he's very agile - he can climb up a rope easily*

agitate ['ædʒɪteɪt] *verb* **to agitate for** *or* **against something** = to stir up public opinion for *or* against something; *they are agitating for a change in the law*

agitated ['ædʒɪteɪtɪd] *adjective* very nervous, worried or upset, not able to keep still; *the police tried to calm the agitated relatives of the miners trapped in the mine*

agitation [ædʒɪ'teɪʃn] *noun* **(a)** nervous worry; *she came to see me in a state of considerable agitation* **(b)** political agitation = struggle for political change; *the election campaign has begun against a background of widespread political agitation*

agitator ['ædʒɪteɪtə] *noun* person who stirs up political unrest; *the current political unrest is the work of a handful of agitators*

AGM ['eɪ dʒiː 'em] = ANNUAL GENERAL MEETING

agnostic [æg'nɒstɪk] **1** *adjective* believing that no one can know if God exists; *no agnostic writer could defend that theory* **2** *noun* person who believes that no one can know if God exists; *agnostics see no point in going to church; compare* ATHEIST

ago [ə'gəʊ] *adverb* in the past; *he phoned a few minutes ago; she came to England two years ago; this all happened a long time ago* (NOTE: **ago** always follows a word meaning time)

agonizing ['ægənaɪzɪŋ] *adjective* **(a)** very sharp; *an agonizing pain* **(b)** very painful and difficult; *the family went through an agonizing time while the police were searching for the missing girl;* **an agonizing decision** = a decision which is difficult to take; *it was an agonizing decision whether to have the operation or not*

agony ['ægəni] *noun* **(a)** extreme pain; *after the accident, she was in agony for weeks; she went through agonies of worry, waiting to see if had got the job* **(b) agony aunt** = person who writes an agony column; **agony column** = newspaper column giving advice on personal problems

agrarian [ə'greəriən] *adjective* referring to farming; **agrarian reform** = land reform

agree [ə'griː] *verb* **(a)** to say yes; *we asked her to come with us and she agreed; he nodded to show that he agreed; most of the group agreed with his suggestion; after some discussion he agreed to our plan* (NOTE: you agree **to** *or* **on** a plan) **(b) to agree with someone** = to think the same way as someone; *I agree with you that most people drive too fast* **(c)** not **to agree with someone** = to make someone ill; *all this rich food does not agree with me* **(d) to agree to do something** = to say that you will do something; *she agreed to babysit for us; the bank will never agree to lend the company £250,000*

agreeable [ə'griːəbl] *adjective* **(a)** pleasant; *we spent a very agreeable weekend by the sea* **(b)** *(formal)* **to be agreeable to** = to be in agreement with; *are they all agreeable to the plan?*

agreed [ə'griːd] *adjective* which has been accepted; *the deal was struck on agreed terms; the agreed amount we will pay for your old car is £1500*

agreement [ə'griːmənt] *noun* **(a)** thinking the same; *to reach an agreement or to come to an agreement on salaries; agreement between the two sides is still a long way off;* **they are in agreement with our plan** = they agree with our plan; *we discussed the plan with them and they are in agreement* **(b)** contract; *we signed an agreement with the Italian company; to draw up or to draft an agreement*

agricultural [ægrɪ'kʌltʃərəl] *adjective* referring to agriculture; **agricultural machinery**

agriculture ['ægrɪkʌltʃə] *noun* growing crops or raising animals on farms; *not many people work in agriculture compared with fifty years ago; the country's agriculture is based on wheat*

agronomist [ə'grɒnəmɪst] *noun* person who studies agronomy; *agronomists were sent to the region to ensure that the new methods of cultivation were correctly implemented*

agronomy [ə'grɒnəmi] *noun* scientific study of soil management and the cultivation of crops; *this is the only university in the country which has a faculty of agronomy*

aground [ə'graʊnd] *adverb* stuck on sand or rocks, not afloat; **the ship ran aground** *or* **went aground** = the ship hit sand or rocks; *the emergency services received a message saying that the ship had run aground during the storm*

ah [ɑː] **1** *interjection* showing surprise; *Ah! Wilkins, how nice to see you!; the audience let out 'oohs' and 'ahs' as they watched the lion tamers* **2** *verb see* UM

ahead [ə'hed] *adverb* in front; *our team was losing, but now we are ahead again; run on ahead and find some seats for us; you need to go straight ahead, and then turn left;* **full steam ahead!** = go forwards as fast as possible; **to draw ahead** = to become the leader in a race, etc.

ahead of [ə'hed 'ɒv] *preposition* **(a)** in front of; *ahead of us was a steep hill; you have a mass of work ahead of you; they ran on ahead of the others* **(b)** *(informal)* before; *they drafted in extra police ahead of the international match*

aid [eɪd] *noun* **(a)** help; *aid to Third World countries;* **aid agency; aid worker** **(b) first aid** = help for injured people; *we keep a first-aid kit in the office* **(c) in aid of** = to help; *we give money in aid of the Red Cross; they are collecting money in aid of refugees* *(informal)* **what's all this in aid of?** = what's all the fuss about? **(d)** device which helps; *he wears a hearing aid; food processors are useful aids in the kitchen*

aide [eɪd] *noun* assistant to an important person; *the minister came with two of his aides*

AIDS [eɪdz] = ACQUIRED IMMUNODEFICIENCY SYNDROME viral infection which breaks down the body's immune system; *he died from AIDS; a clinic for people with AIDS*

aileron ['eɪlərɒn] *noun* flap on the wing of an aircraft; *the pilot noticed that one of the ailerons wasn't functioning properly*

ailing ['eɪlɪŋ] *adjective* **(a)** sick; *she spends all her time looking after her ailing parents* **(b)** in financial difficulties; *the government is planning to help the ailing bank*

ailment ['eɪlmənt] *noun* illness, though not generally a very serious one; *measles is one of the common childhood ailments; it's only a minor ailment, nothing to be worried about*

aim [eɪm] **1** *noun* what you are trying to do; *his aim is to do well at school and then go to university; one of our aims is to increase the speed of service* **2** *verb* **(a)** to plan to do something; *we aim to go on holiday in June* **(b)** to point a weapon at something; *he was not aiming at the target*

aimless ['eɪmləs] *adjective* without any particular plan; *the chairman tried to put an end to the aimless discussion; his aimless wanderings round the streets brought him to the British Museum*

aimlessly ['eɪmləsli] *adverb* without any particular plan; *she wandered aimlessly round the museum*

ain't ['eɪnt] *verb (slang)* = IS NOT; *it ain't fair*

air [eə] *noun* **(a)** mixture of gases (mainly oxygen and nitrogen) which cannot be seen, but which is all around us and which every animal breathes; *his breath was like steam in the cold air; the mountain air feels cold; he threw the ball up into the air* **(b)** method of travelling (or sending goods) using aircraft; **air fares** = different types of fares charged for travel on aircraft; **air letter** = a special sheet of thin blue paper which when folded can be sent by air mail without an envelope

◊ **by air** ['baɪ 'eə] in an aircraft; *we are going to France by ferry, not by air; send the letter by air if you want it to arrive before Christmas*

air bag ['eə 'bæg] *noun* bag in a car which inflates when there is an accident and protects the driver or passenger; *some people say that air bags can be dangerous for babies*

airborne ['eəbɔːn] *adjective* **(a)** carried in the air; *airborne infection* **(b)** carried by an aircraft; *an airborne invasion*

air-conditioned ['eə kən'dɪʃənd] *adjective* having the temperature controlled by an air-conditioner; *the office is air-conditioned*

air-conditioner ['eə kən'dɪʃənə] *noun* device which filters and cools the air in a room; *how can we turn the air-conditioner off?*

air-conditioning ['eə kən'dɪʃənɪŋ] *noun* system of controlling the temperature in a room or office or train, etc.; *if you hire a car in Texas, make sure it has air-conditioning;* **to turn the air-conditioning on** = to start the cooling; **to turn the air-conditioning off** = to stop the cooling; **to turn the air-conditioning down** = to make a room warmer; **to turn the air-conditioning up** = to make a room cooler

aircraft ['eəkrɑːft] *noun* machine which flies in the air; *the passengers got into the aircraft; the airline has a fleet of ten aircraft; the president came down the aircraft steps* (NOTE: plural is **aircraft: one aircraft, six aircraft**)

aircraft carrier ['eəkrɑːft 'kæriə] *noun* warship which carries aircraft; *an American aircraft carrier could be seen in the distance*

aircrew ['eəkruː] *noun* crew of an aircraft; *none of the aircrew survived the crash*

airfield ['eəfiːld] *noun* small, usually military, airport; *the military airfield is no longer operational*

airflow ['eəfləʊ] *noun* movement of air in a certain direction; *the prevailing westerly airflow across the country*

air force ['eə 'fɔːs] *noun* a country's military air organization; *he's joined the Belgian Air Force; American Air Force fighters*

air hostess ['eə 'həʊstəs] *noun* woman who serves food and drinks to passengers on an aircraft; *a friend of mine became an air hostess because she wanted an opportunity to work and travel* (NOTE: also called a **stewardess;** the term for a man who does this job is a **steward**)

airless ['eələs] *adjective* without any air; *a hot airless day, when all you want to do is sit by the swimming pool*

airlift ['eəlɪft] **1** *noun* emergency transport by air; *an airlift of emergency supplies* **2** *verb* to transport emergency supplies, etc., by air; *the climbers were airlifted to safety*

airline ['eəlaɪn] *noun* company which runs air services; *which airline are you flying with?; he's an airline pilot; the airline has been voted the most popular with business travellers*

airliner ['eəlaɪnə] *noun* large aircraft that carries passengers; *the airliner crashed in thick jungle*

airmail ['eəmeɪl] **1** *noun* way of sending letters or parcels by air; *we sent the package by airmail;* **airmail envelope** = very light envelope for sending airmail letters; **airmail sticker** = blue sticker with the words 'by air mail' which can be stuck to an envelope or packet to show it is being sent by air **2** *verb* to send letters or parcels by air; *we airmailed the documents to New York*

airman ['eəmən] *noun* man who serves in an Air Force; *he was an airman during the war* (NOTE: plural is **airmen**)

airplane ['eəpleɪn] *noun US* aeroplane, aircraft; *a four-engined airplane; the president came down the airplane steps*

airport ['eəpɔːt] *noun* place where aircraft land and take off; *you can take the underground to the airport; we are due to arrive at London Airport at midday; we leave from London Airport at 10.00;* **airport bus** = bus which takes passengers to and from an airport; *there is an airport bus which takes passengers to the centre of town*

air power ['eə 'paʊə] *noun* strength of an Air Force; *the enemy air power was stronger than we expected*

air raid ['eə 'reɪd] *noun* attack by military aircraft; *people had to hide in underground stations during the air raids on London; his father built an air raid shelter in the garden*

airship ['eəʃɪp] *noun* large balloon driven by an engine; *the R-100 was a famous airship*

airsick ['eəsɪk] *adjective* sick when travelling by air; *take one of these tablets if you're feeling airsick*

airsickness ['eəsɪknəs] *noun* feeling of being airsick; *take some airsickness tablets before the plane takes off*

airstream ['eəstriːm] *noun* flow of air in a certain direction; *a westerly airstream is flowing across the country*

air strike ['eə 'straɪk] *noun* sudden attack by military aircraft; *bombers carried out a series of air strikes on the capital*

airstrip ['eəstrɪp] *noun* small runway; *they landed on an airstrip in the jungle*

airtight ['eətaɪt] *adjective* which does not allow air to get in or out; *the films must be kept in airtight boxes*

air traffic controller [eə 'træfɪk kən'trəʊlə] *noun* person at an airport who controls the movements of aircraft as they land or take off; *we can't fly to Paris because of a strike by the French air traffic controllers*

airwaves ['eəweɪvz] *noun (old)* **on the airwaves** = on the radio; *his was a familiar voice on the airwaves in the 1950s*

airway ['eəweɪ] *noun* **(a)** name given to an airline; *British Airways*; *Virgin Atlantic Airways* **(b)** passage for air; *the glottis is an opening in the larynx between the vocal cords, the entry to the main airway*

airy ['eəri] *adjective* **(a)** full of fresh air; *light airy rooms* **(b)** vague; *he made a lot of airy promises* (NOTE: **airier - airiest**)

aisle [aɪl] *noun* **(a)** gangway between seats (in a plane, theatre, church, etc.); *please do not put luggage in the aisles*; **aisle seat** = seat which is next to an aisle; *I always ask for an aisle seat on long-distance flights* (NOTE: the opposite is a **window seat**) **(b)** side part of a church; *the church was ruined in the earthquake - only one aisle and part of the nave are left* (NOTE: do not confuse with **isle**)

akin [ə'kɪn] *adjective* **akin to** = similar to; *she experienced a sensation akin to burning on her skin*; *this situation is not akin to anything I've experienced before*

à la mode [ælæ'mɒd] *adverb US* served with ice cream; *do you want apple pie à la mode?*

alarm [ə'lɑːm] **1** *noun* **(a)** loud warning; *an alarm will sound if someone touches the wire*; **to raise the alarm** = to warn everyone of danger; *it was only a false alarm* = it was only a wrong warning **(b)** burglar alarm = device which rings if someone enters a building; **fire alarm** = bell which sounds if there is a fire; **alarm (clock)** = clock which can ring at a certain time; *I set my alarm for 5.30 because I had to catch the 7 o'clock plane; see also* BELL **(c)** being afraid; *the expression on his face increased her alarm*; *there's no cause for alarm, the injection won't hurt at all* **2** *verb* to warn or frighten; *I don't want to alarm you, but the police say a dangerous criminal has been seen in the village*

alarmed [ə'lɑːmd] *adjective* worried and frightened; *they were alarmed to see that their car was missing with the baby in it*; *don't leave without telling your parents, they'll just get alarmed*

alarming [ə'lɑːmɪŋ] *adjective* frightening; *what was most alarming was to see soldiers on the village green*; *going up in a hot-air balloon was not such an alarming experience after all*; *we are using up the earth's diminishing sources of energy at an alarming rate*

alas [ə'læs] *interjection showing sadness*; *he died in the war, alas*; *alas, there is no time left to continue the discussion*

albatross ['æbətrɒs] *noun* very large white sea bird, which flies for long distances but is awkward when

walking on the ground; *it's part of sea lore that it is unlucky to kill an albatross*

albeit [ɔːl'biːɪt] *conjunction (formal)* although; *he's still an excellent tennis player, albeit a rather elderly one*

album ['ælbəm] *noun* **(a)** large book; *an album of photos or a photo album*; *he showed me his stamp album* **(b)** collections of songs on a CD, cassette, etc.; *this is her latest album*

alcohol ['ælkəhɒl] *noun* intoxicating liquid, beer, wine, etc.; *they will not serve alcohol to anyone under the age of 18*

alcoholic [ælkə'hɒlɪk] **1** *adjective* referring to alcohol; *an alcoholic drink* **2** *noun* person who is addicted to alcohol; *she went to a clinic for alcoholics*

alcoholism ['ælkəhɒlɪzm] *noun* drinking so much alcohol that it becomes addictive; *alcoholism is a very serious social problem*

alcove ['ælkəʊv] *noun* recess, part of the wall of a room which is set back; *the large stone urn stands in the alcove by the doorway*; *the statues were removed from the alcoves on either side of the altar*

ale [eɪl] *noun* British-type beer, especially bitter beer, but not lager; *ale is stronger, darker and more bitter than lager*

alert [ə'lɜːt] **1** *adjective* watchful, on your guard; *after a short sleep he was bright and alert*; *the guard must remain alert at all times* **2** *noun* warning signal; *he gave the alert*; **to be on the alert** = to watch out for something **3** *verb* to alert someone to = to warn someone of something; *she was alerted to the dangers of smoking*

A Level ['eɪ 'levəl] = ADVANCED LEVEL examination taken at about 18, at the end of secondary school; *if you pass your A Levels, you can go on to higher education*

alfresco [æl'freskəʊ] *adjective* in the open air; *we had an alfresco meal on the terrace overlooking the sea* (NOTE: do not confuse with **fresco**)

algae ['ældʒiː] *noun* tiny plants living in water or in moist conditions, which contain chlorophyll and have no stems or roots or leaves; *the old posts are green with algae*; *be careful, the rocks are covered with algae and can be very slippery*

algebra ['ældʒɪbrə] *noun* type of mathematics where letters are used to represent quantities; *algebra was the branch of mathematics I always enjoyed at school*

algebraic [ældʒɪ'breɪɪk] *adjective* referring to algebra; *try and memorize these algebraic symbols*

Algeria [æl'dʒɪəriə] *noun* country in North Africa on the Mediterranean, east of Morocco and west of Tunisia; *she travelled a lot in Algeria when she was young*; *he has to go to Algeria on a business trip* (NOTE: capital: **Algiers**; people: **Algerians**; language: **Arabic**; currency: **Algerian dinar**)

Algerian [æl'dʒɪəriən] **1** *adjective* referring to Algeria; *have you ever tasted typically Algerian food?*; *the Algerian ambassador was interviewed on the radio this morning* **2** *noun* person from Algeria; *three Algerians were killed in the accident*

alias ['eɪliəs] **1** *adverb* otherwise known as; *John Smith, alias 'The Bulldog'* **2** *noun* assumed name; *he travelled under the alias of Dupont*; *the confidence trickster used several aliases* (NOTE: plural is **aliases**)

alibi ['ælɪbaɪ] *noun* plea that a person charged with a crime was somewhere else when the crime was committed; *does he have an alibi for the time the crime was committed?*; *the task of the prosecution is to try to break his alibi*

alien ['eɪliən] **1** *adjective* foreign, from another country; *the soldiers wandered away from the camp into alien territory*; *speaking foreign languages is alien to the British way of life* **2** *noun* foreigner, a person who is not a citizen of the country; *aliens are not permitted to travel outside the capital*; *when you arrive at the airport, you must go through the door marked 'aliens'*; **undesirable alien** = foreigner who is not welcome in a country, and who can be expelled

alienate ['eɪliəneɪt] *verb* **(a)** to make someone no longer friendly; *their father's will alienated the sisters from their brother* **(b)** to make someone not want to support you; *his speech alienated many party members*

alienation [eɪliə'neɪʃn] *noun* feeling that you are not wanted, that you have no place in society; *he suddenly felt a sense of total alienation from his family*

alight [ə'laɪt] **1** *verb* (*formal*) to get off a vehicle; *she alighted from the bus*; *alight here for the Post Office* **2** *adjective* on fire; *soon the whole house was alight*; *after pouring petrol on the car he set it alight*

align [ə'laɪn] *verb* **(a)** to arrange in line with; *she took her car to the garage to have the wheels aligned* **(b)** to **align yourself with** = to adopt a similar policy as another country; *the three neighbouring states aligned themselves with the USA*; **non-aligned state** = country which is not allied to a superpower; *after independence, India joined the group of non-aligned states*

alignment [ə'laɪnmənt] *noun* **(a)** row; *a prehistoric alignment of stones*; **out of alignment** = not parallel; *I think the front wheels are out of alignment* **(b)** grouping together on the same side in politics; *a new political alignment*; *see also* REALIGNMENT

alike [ə'laɪk] *adjective* very similar; *the two sisters are very alike*

alive [ə'laɪv] *adjective* not dead; *he was still alive when he was rescued, even though he had been in the sea for hours*; *when my grandfather was alive, there was no television* (NOTE: **alive** cannot be used in front of a noun: **the fish is alive** but **a live fish**)

alkali ['ælkəlaɪ] *noun* substance that neutralizes acids and forms salts; *an alkali plus an acid gives a salt* (NOTE: British English plural is **alkalis**, but American English is **alkalies**)

alkaline ['ælkəlaɪn] *adjective* containing more alkali than acid; *an alkaline solution*; *the soil is very alkaline and is good for growing root vegetables*

alkalinity [ælkə'lɪnɪti] *noun* amount of alkali in something such as soil or water; *the alkalinity of a substance is measured in pH*

> COMMENT: alkalinity and acidity are measured according to the pH scale. pH7 is neutral, and pH8 and upwards are alkaline. One of the commonest alkalis is caustic soda, used to clear blocked drains

all [ɔːl] **1** *adjective & pronoun* everything *or* everyone; *did you pick all (of) the tomatoes?*; *where are all the children?*; *they all like coffee or all of them like coffee*; *all trains stop at Clapham Junction*; *let's sing the* song **all together** = everyone at the same time **2** *adverb* **(a)** completely; *the ground was all white after the snow fell*; *I forgot all about her birthday* **(b) all by yourself** = all alone; *you can't do it all by yourself*; *I'm all by myself this evening - my girlfriend's gone out*; *he drove the lorry all by himself*

◊ **not at all** ['nɒt ət 'ɔːl] certainly not; *do you mind waiting for a few minutes? - not at all!*; *she wasn't at all annoyed*

all along ['ɔːl ə'lɒŋ] *adverb* right from the beginning; *I knew all along that he was cheating me*

all at once ['ɔːl ət 'wʌns] suddenly; *all at once the telephone rang*

allay [ə'leɪ] *verb* (*formal*) to calm; *he tried to allay her fears*

All Blacks ['ɔːl 'blæks] *noun* (*informal*) the New Zealand international rugby team; *compare* SPRINGBOKS, WALLABIES

all but ['ɔːl 'bʌt] *adverb* almost; *it's all but impossible to find anything to eat after 11 o'clock at night*

allegation [ælɪ'geɪʃn] *noun* suggestion that someone has possibly done something wrong; *she made several allegations about her boss*; *he denied the allegations made against him*

allege [ə'ledʒ] *verb* to suggest that someone may have done something wrong; *the police alleged that the accused was inside the building when the theft took place*

alleged [ə'ledʒd] *adjective* suggested; *the alleged victim refused to make a statement to the police*

allegedly [ə'ledʒɪdli] *adverb* as has been suggested, but not proved; *the student allegedly offered her drugs*; *this painting is allegedly by Picasso*

allegiance [ə'liːdʒəns] *noun* being loyal; **an oath of allegiance** = oath which is sworn to put the person under the orders or rules of a country, an army, etc.; *he swore (an oath of) allegiance to the new president*

allegorical [ælɪ'gɒrɪkl] *adjective* referring to allegory; *his allegorical depictions of hell are frightening*

allegory ['ælɪgəri] *noun* painting or story where the characters represent abstract ideas or are symbols of something else; *the story is an allegory of life in a police state*

allergic [ə'lɜːdʒɪk] *adjective* **(a)** suffering from an allergy; **to be allergic to** = to react badly to; *many people are allergic to grass pollen*; *she is allergic to cats*; *he showed an allergic reaction to peanuts* **(b) to be allergic to** = to dislike; *he is allergic to jazz*; *she is allergic to men with beards*

allergy ['ælədʒi] *noun* reaction to a substance; *she has an allergy to household dust*; *the baby has a wheat allergy*

alleviate [ə'liːvieɪt] *verb* to make less painful; *she tried to alleviate the suffering of the refugees*; *he was given injections to alleviate the pain*

alleviation [əliːvi'eɪʃn] *noun* making less painful; *alleviation of the pain was their first priority*

alley ['æli] *noun* **(a)** narrow little street; *the shop is down an alley near the High Street* **(b) skittle alley** *or* **bowling alley** = place for playing bowls, skittles; *we can't go and play bowls, since there's no bowling alley near here*

alleyway ['æliweɪ] *noun* little alley for pedestrians; *go along past the chemist's, and you'll see an alleyway leading to the car park*

alliance [ə'laɪəns] *noun* formal link between two groups or countries; *the alliance between England and France*

allied ['ælaɪd] *adjective* (a) linked in an alliance; *the allied powers* (b) **allied to** = linked with; *his poor health allied to his age means that he will not be able to run the marathon*

alligator ['ælɪgeɪtə] *noun* large reptile like a crocodile, found in the southern parts of the USA; *if you go to Florida you will see alligators*

all in ['ɔːl 'ɪn] *adjective* (a) including everything; **all-in rate** *or* **all-in price** = price which covers all items (goods, delivery, tax, insurance, etc.); *they quoted us an all-in price of £250.00* (b) *(informal)* tired out; *after moving all my stuff to my new flat I was all in*

all-inclusive ['ɔːl ɪn'kluːsɪv] *adjective* that includes everything; *an all-inclusive price; is the rate quoted all-inclusive?*

alliteration [əlɪtə'reɪʃn] *noun* using words which begin with the same sound to make special effects in poetry; *'the forest's ferny floor' is an example of an alliteration*

allocate ['æləkeɪt] *verb* to give out to various people; *we have allocated £2,500 to buying furniture for the office; our group were allocated rooms in the hotel annexe*

allocation [ælə'keɪʃn] *noun* giving as a share; *they set up a committee to supervise the allocation of the money; room allocation is on a first come, first served basis*

all of a sudden ['ɔːl ɒv ə 'sʌdn] *phrase* suddenly, all at once; *all of a sudden she had a brilliant idea*

allot [ə'lɒt] *verb* to give something to someone as a share of something; *you have been allotted ten minutes at the beginning of the meeting; when I arrived for work I was allotted a desk and a bookshelf* (NOTE: **allotting - allotted**)

allotment [ə'lɒtmənt] *noun* (a) giving out money; *the allotment of funds to a project* (b) plot of land which belongs to a local council and which can be rented for growing vegetables; *he grows vegetables on his allotment*

all-out ['ɔːl'aʊt] *adjective* total, involving a lot of work; *we must make an all-out effort to solve the problem*

all over ['ɔːl 'əʊvə] (a) everywhere; *she poured cream all over the strawberries; water was pouring all over the floor* (b) finished; *when the game was all over we went home*

allow [ə'laʊ] *verb* (a) to let someone do something; *she allowed me to borrow her book; smoking is not allowed in the restaurant; you are allowed to take two pieces of hand luggage onto the plane* (b) to give; *we will allow you a discount* (c) to agree to or to accept legally; *to allow a claim for damages*

allowance [ə'laʊəns] *noun* (a) money paid regularly; *she gets a weekly allowance from her father* (b) something which is allowed; **baggage allowance** = weight of baggage which an air passenger is allowed to take free when he travels; *see also* DUTY-FREE (c) amount of money which you are allowed to earn without paying tax; *allowances for married couples have been increased in the budget* (d) **to make allowances for** = to take someone's failings into account; *you must make allowances for his age*

allow for [ə'laʊ 'fɔː] *verb* to allocate a certain amount of time or money; *to allow 10% extra for postage and packing; allow 28 days for delivery*

alloy ['ælɔɪ] **1** *noun* mixture of metals; *brass is a well-known alloy of copper and zinc* **2** *verb* to mix metals; *you alloy copper and zinc to get brass*

all-purpose ['ɔːl'pɜːpəs] *adjective* that can be used in many different situations; *an all-purpose knife for campers; she only uses all-purpose flour*

all right ['ɔːl 'raɪt] **1** *adjective* well; *she was ill yesterday but is all right now* **2** *interjection* (meaning 'yes') all right, here's your money; will you answer the telephone for me? - all right! (NOTE: OK is often used in the this meaning)

all-rounder [ɔːl'raʊndə] *noun* person who is good at anything; *he's not a specialist, just a good all-rounder, which is what we need*

all-star ['ɔːlstɑː] *adjective* with many stars; *an all-star show*

all the same ['ɔːl ðə 'seɪm] *adverb* in spite of this; *she smokes too much, but she's a nice girl all the same*

all-time ['ɔːltaɪm] *adjective* biggest, best, worst, etc., ever; *the stock market is at an all-time high; our sales have reached an all-time low*

allude [ə'luːd] *verb* **to allude to something** = to refer briefly to something in an indirect way; *he alluded to it in his speech, without giving any details*

allure [ə'ljʊə] **1** *noun* mysterious attraction; *the allure of India* **2** *verb* to attract someone; *allured by the high salary offered, he answered the advertisement*

alluring [ə'ljʊrɪŋ] *adjective* very attractive; *the alluring promise of a high salary; what an alluring offer!; she should have been suspicious of his alluring smile*

allusion [ə'luːʒn] *noun* referring indirectly to something; *I didn't understand his allusion to peppermints; let's hope that nobody will make any allusion(s) to his driving test*

alluvial [ə'luːviəl] *adjective* deposited by rivers; *river deltas are created by alluvial deposits;* **the alluvial plain** = flat area along a river where silt is deposited when the river floods; *alluvial plains are subject to flooding*

alluvium [ə'luːviəm] *noun* silt deposited by rivers; *alluvium is responsible for some of the most fertile soils*

ally 1 *noun* ['ælaɪ] person who is on the same side; *he's a close ally of the leader of the opposition; when one of our allies is attacked, we have to come to their defence* (NOTE: plural is **allies**) **2** *verb* [ə'laɪ]; **to ally oneself with** *or* **to someone** = to join forces with someone; *the nationalists have allied themselves with the socialists*

almighty [ɔːl'maɪti] **1** *adjective* (informal) very powerful, very loud; *there was an almighty crash from the kitchen; they had an almighty row* **2** *noun* **the Almighty** = God; *we pray to the Almighty every day that they find our daughter alive*

almond ['ɑːmənd] *noun* (a) type of nut; *a bag of almonds; add the almond essence to the cake mixture;*

almond oil is used in the preparation of skin creams; *almond-shaped eyes are very attractive* **(b)** **almond (tree)** = tree which produces these nuts; *do almonds or almond trees grow in cold climates?*

almost ['ɒlməʊst] *adverb* nearly; *London is almost as far from here as Paris*; *she's almost as tall as I am*; *she'll eat almost anything*; *hurry up, it's almost time for the train to leave*

aloft [ə'lɒft] *adverb (formal)* high in the air; *he was photographed holding the flag aloft above his head*

alone [ə'ləʊn] **1** *adjective* with no one else; *she lives alone with her cats*; *he was all alone in the shop*; *we don't let the children go out alone after dark*; *I want to talk to you alone* = just the two of us together **2** *adverb* **(a)** **to leave someone alone** = not to bother someone; *leave that cat alone and come and have your tea* **(b)** **let alone** = and certainly not; *he can't ride a bike let alone drive a car*

along [ə'lɒŋ] **1** *preposition* **(a)** by the side of; *he has planted fruit trees along both sides of the garden path*; *the river runs along one side of the castle* **(b)** from one end to the other; *she ran along the pavement*; *walk along the street until you come to the post office* **2** *adverb* **(a)** **to get along with someone** = to agree with or to work well with someone; *she doesn't get along very well with her new boss*; *they don't get along very well together* **(b)** **to go along** *or* **to come along** = to go with *or* to come with; *come along to the party*; *after the accident, she was taken along to the police station*

alongside [əlɒŋ'saɪd] **1** *preposition* beside; *the ship was tied up alongside the quay* **2** *adverb* beside; *we had stopped at a red light when a police car pulled up alongside*

aloof [ə'luːf] **1** *adjective* reserved, unfriendly to other people; *he's a cold aloof person* **2** *adverb* **to keep yourself aloof** *or* **to stand aloof from** = to keep separate from, not to get involved with other people; *they kept themselves aloof from the rest of the crowd*

aloud [ə'laʊd] *adverb* in a voice which can be heard; *she read the poem aloud*; *he insists on reading the football scores out aloud*

alpha ['ælfə] *noun* the first letter of the Greek alphabet (α) mark showing top-class results; *he got an alpha plus for his essay*

alphabet ['ælfəbet] *noun* series of letters in order, A, B, C, etc.; *A is the first letter of the alphabet, and B is the second*; *G comes before L in the alphabet*; *if you're going to Greece on holiday, you ought to learn the Greek alphabet*

alphabetical [ælfə'betɪkl] *adjective* referring to the alphabet; *an alphabetical list of names*; **in alphabetical order** = in order of the first letter of each word; *the words in the dictionary are in alphabetical order*; *sort out the address cards into alphabetical order of their names*

alphabetize [ælfəbe'taɪz] *verb* to put into alphabetical order automatically; *it will be much quicker if you can use a computer program to alphabetize the list of names*

alpine ['ælpaɪn] **1** *adjective* referring to high mountains, especially the Alps; *herdsmen take their flocks to alpine pastures in the summer*; *alpine vegetation grows high above the forests* **2** *noun* plant which grows on or originally comes from high mountains; *she grows alpines in her garden*

Alps [ælps] *noun* high mountains, especially the mountains running from France, through Switzerland and Italy to Austria and Slovenia; *we spend our Easter holidays in the Swiss Alps*; *he was killed climbing in the French Alps*

already [ɔːl'redi] *adverb* **(a)** before now, before a certain time; *I've already done my shopping*; *it was already past ten o'clock when he arrived*; **I have seen that film already** = I've seen that film before **(b)** sooner than expected; *have you finished your work already?*

Alsatian [æl'seɪʃn] *noun* breed of large dog, often used as guard dogs; *Alsatians are excellent guard dogs which look a bit like wolves* (NOTE: American English is **German shepherd**)

also ['ɔːlsəʊ] *adverb* too, as well as; *she sings well and can also play the violin*; *they came to visit us, and their children also came*

altar ['ɒltə] *noun* table in church on which the priest celebrates communion or mass; *the main altar is at the east end of the church*; **to lead someone to the altar** = to marry someone; *grandfather led his wife to the altar when he was only 22 years old* (NOTE: do not confuse with **alter**)

alter ['ɒltə] *verb* to change; *they wanted to alter the terms of the contract after they had signed it*; *he has altered so much I didn't recognize him* (NOTE: do not confuse with **altar**)

alteration [ɒltə'reɪʃn] *noun* change; *she made some alterations to the design*; *he made some slight alterations to his will*

alternate 1 *adjective* [ɔːl'tɜːnət] every other one; *we see each other on alternate Sundays* **2** *verb* ['ɔːltəneɪt] to put in place of something, then switch them round; *fill the pot with alternating slices of potato and onion*; *she alternated between excitement and gloom*

alternating current (AC) ['ɔːltəneɪtɪŋ 'kʌrənt] *noun* electric current which changes direction all the time, as opposed to 'direct current' (DC) which flows in one direction

alternative [ɔːl'tɜːnətɪv] **1** *adjective* **(a)** in place of something else; *if the plane is full, we will put you on an alternative flight* **(b)** following a different way from usual; *alternative energy*; *alternative medicine* **2** *noun* something which takes the place of something else; *now that she's got measles, do we have any alternative to calling the holiday off?*; **there is no alternative** = there is nothing else we can do

alternatively [ɔːl'tɜːnətɪvli] *adverb* on the other hand; *we can give you tickets for next week or alternatively you can have a refund*

although [ɔːl'ðəʊ] *conjunction* in spite of the fact that; *although it was freezing, she didn't put a coat on*; *I've never been into that shop although I've often walked past it*

altitude ['æltɪtjuːd] *noun* height above sea level; *the plane was cruising at an altitude of 10,000m*; *at what altitude does the pine forest start?*; **altitude sickness** = sickness, where a person suffers from a lack of oxygen because of being at a high altitude, as when you are on a mountain; *if you're staying high up in the mountains, wait at least a day before you start skiing, because altitude sickness may affect you*

alto ['æltəʊ] *noun* **(a)** high singing voice of a man or boy; *he's the only boy in the group to sing alto* **(b)** man or boy with a high-pitched voice; *we need more altos in our choir* (NOTE: plural is **altos**)

altogether [ɔːltəˈgeðə] *adverb* **(a)** taking everything together; *the food was £10 and the drinks £5, so that makes £15 altogether; the staff of the three shops come to 200 altogether* **(b)** completely; *he's altogether a happier man since he got married; their situation is altogether different from ours*

altruistic [æltruˈɪstɪk] *adjective* not selfish; *his motives in offering to help his mother clean the house were not entirely altruistic - he wants to borrow her car at the weekend*

aluminium *US* **aluminum** [æljuˈmɪnjəm or əˈluːmɪnəm] *noun* silver-coloured metal which is extremely light; *we were given a set of aluminium saucepans for our wedding; cover the meat in a sheet of aluminium foil* (NOTE: Chemical element: chemical symbol: **Al**; atomic number: **13**)

alumnus [əˈlʌmnəs] *noun US* a former student at a university or college or high school; *letters of invitation to the concert were sent to all the university alumni* (NOTE: plural is **alumni** [əˈlʌmnaɪ])

always [ɔːlweɪz] *adverb* **(a)** every time; *she is always late for work; why does it always rain when we want to go for a walk?* **(b)** continually; *it's always hot in tropical countries* **(c)** again and again; *she's always asking me to lend her money*

Alzheimer's disease [æltseɪməz dɪˈziːz] *noun* disease of the brain where loss of brain tissue leads to memory loss and eventually complete disablement; *his wife has just died - she had had Alzheimer's disease for some time; it has been discovered that plaques form on the brains of Alzheimer's patients*

am [æm] *see* BE

a.m. *US* **A.M.** [ˈeɪ ˈem] *adverb* before midday, in the morning; *I have to catch the 7 a.m. train to work every day; telephone calls made before 6 a.m. are charged at the cheap rate* (NOTE: **a.m.** is usually used to show the exact hour and the word **o'clock** is left out)

amalgam [əˈmælgəm] *noun (formal)* mixture, especially the mixture of mercury and silver used by dentists to fill holes in teeth; *ask the dentist to use gold instead of amalgam for your filling*

amalgamate [əˈmælgəmeɪt] *verb* to combine together; *our college amalgamated with Kings College a few years ago; the two paragraphs are so short that they can be amalgamated into one*

amalgamation [əmælgəˈmeɪʃn] *noun* act of combining together; *the shareholders voted against the amalgamation of the two companies, so they will remain independent*

amass [əˈmæs] *verb* to collect a lot of money, information, things; *before you start writing a historical novel, you have to spend months amassing dates and facts; he amassed his fortune in the 1980s; the police are amassing evidence against him*

amateur [ˈæmətə] **1** *noun* **(a)** unpaid sportsman; *the golf tournament is open to amateurs* **(b)** someone who does something because he likes doing it; *for an amateur he's a very good painter* **2** *adjective* **(a)** not paid; *he plays for the local amateur football team; our amateur theatre club is putting on 'Henry V'* **(b)** doing something as a hobby rather than to earn money; *he's an amateur painter*

amateurish [ˈæmətərɪʃ] *adjective* not well done, not done in a professional way; *their performance was quite amateurish*

amaze [əˈmeɪz] *verb* to surprise very much; *your attitude amazes me*

amazed [əˈmeɪzd] *adjective* very surprised; *she was amazed at or by the result; he was amazed to learn that she was over thirty; I'm amazed that you're still working there - I thought you hated it; he won the race, watched by his amazed and delighted parents*

amazement [əˈmeɪzmənt] *noun* great surprise; *the tourists watched the changing of the guard in amazement; to our amazement we won a prize*

amazing [əˈmeɪzɪŋ] *adjective* **(a)** very surprising; *it was amazing that she never suspected anything* **(b)** extremely interesting and unusual; *it was an amazing experience, sailing down the Nile*

ambassador [æmˈbæsədə] *noun* the representative of a country in another country; *His Excellency, the French Ambassador; see also* CONSUL, EMBASSY

amber [ˈæmbə] **1** *adjective* orange coloured; *you are not supposed to go through an amber (traffic) light* **2** *noun* **(a)** yellow stone, which is fossilized resin; *her father bought an amber necklace for her in one of the Baltic countries; amber sometimes contains fossilized insects* **(b)** orange traffic light; *the traffic light was at amber*

COMMENT: in America, traffic lights change from green to amber to red and then back to green, while in the UK they change from green to amber to red, before changing back to red and amber together and then green again

ambience [ˈæmbiəns] *noun* character and atmosphere surrounding a place; *the new landlord has given the pub a friendly ambience*

ambiguity [æmbɪˈgjuːti] *noun* having two meanings; *there is a certain ambiguity about his statement; we want to clear up some ambiguities in the contract* (NOTE: plural is **ambiguities**)

ambiguous [æmˈbɪgjuəs] *adjective* which has two meanings, which is not clear; *as it stands, the phrase is very ambiguous*

ambition [æmˈbɪʃn] *noun* desire to become great, rich or famous; *his great ambition is to ride on an elephant*

ambitious [æmˈbɪʃəs] *adjective* with high aims; *I'm not very ambitious; she's a very ambitious young woman - she wants to be a judge*

ambivalence [æmˈbɪvələns] *noun* not being sure about something; *her ambivalence towards him*

ambivalent [æmˈbɪvələnt] *adjective* not sure, undecided; *he is ambivalent about the proposal*

amble [ˈæmbl] *verb* to walk in a relaxed way without hurrying; *he was ambling along in the sunshine when someone suddenly called out to him from the other side of the street*

ambulance [ˈæmbjuləns] *noun* van which carries sick or injured people; *when she fell down the stairs, her husband called an ambulance; he pulled into the side of the road when he saw the ambulance coming*

ambulanceman [ˈæmbjulənsmən] *noun* person who drives or assists in an ambulance; *ambulancemen* *raced to take the accident victims to hospital* (NOTE: plural is **ambulancemen**)

ambush ['æmbʊʃ] **1** *noun* surprise attack by people who have been hiding; *the guerrillas lay in ambush beside the path* (NOTE: plural is **ambushes**) **2** *verb* to wait hidden and attack someone by surprise; *the soldiers were ambushed as they went along the mountain path*

ameba [ə'miːbə] *US* = AMOEBA

ameliorate [ə'miːljəreɪt] *verb* (*formal*) to make something better, to improve something; *he wants to ameliorate the conditions of the workers in the plantations*

amelioration [əmiːljə'reɪʃn] *noun* (*formal*) becoming better; *the doctors reported no amelioration in her condition*

amen [ɑː'men *or* eɪ'men] *interjection* meaning 'let this be so' used at the end of Christian prayers; *I didn't understand a word of the prayer, except for 'amen' at the end*; *I say amen to that* = I agree with that

amend [ə'mend] *verb* to change for the better; *the Prime Minister amended the text of the speech in several places*

amendment [ə'mendmənt] *noun* (a) change; *he has made several amendments to the text* (b) proposed change to a law, to a proposal; *to propose an amendment to the constitution*; *US* the Fifth Amendment = amendment to the American constitution which allows someone not to give evidence which might be used against themselves

amenity [ə'miːnɪti] *noun* ease of doing something; *the town has many amenities, that's why it is so popular*; **amenity bed** = bed, usually in a separate room, in an NHS hospital, for which the patient pays extra; *you will have to stay in the ward a little longer - there are no amenity beds free*; **amenity centre** = sports and entertainment centre; *the mayor opened the new amenity centre* (NOTE: plural is **amenities**)

America [ə'merɪkə] *proper noun* (a) one of two large continents between the Atlantic and Pacific Oceans; *in the year 1492 Columbus discovered America*; *they went to America by boat across the Atlantic* (b) the United States; *she spent all her savings on a holiday in America*; *send your furniture to America by sea - it would be much too expensive by air*

◊ **Central America** ['sentrəl ə'merɪkə] *noun* part of the American continent between North and South America, containing Mexico, Costa Rica, etc.; *our cruise took us to several ports in Central America*

◊ **North America** ['nɔːθ ə'merɪkə] *noun* northern part of the American continent containing the USA and Canada; *they travelled extensively in North America*

◊ **South America** ['saʊθ ə'merɪkə] *noun* southern part of the American continent containing Brazil, Argentina, Chile and several other countries; *he is hiding from the police somewhere in South America*

American [ə'merɪkən] **1** *adjective* referring to America or to the United States of America; *an American dollar*; *the American president*; *I'm letting my house to an American family for the summer*; *I'm reading about the American presidential election*; *his wife is American* **2** *noun* person from the United States of America; *I met a group of Americans on the train*; *the Americans won several gold medals*

American football [ə'merɪkən 'fʊtbɔːl] *noun* type of football played in the USA, similar to rugby (NOTE: American usage is simply **football**; **soccer is used in American English** to refer to what is simply **football** in British English)

COMMENT: the game is played between two teams of eleven players who score points by moving the oval ball (slightly bigger than a rugby ball) across the opponents' goal line by passing or running with it, or by kicking it over the crossbar. Play is not continuous but stops whenever the ball-carrier is tackled, when a pass is incomplete or after a score is made. A touchdown worth 6 points is scored when the ball is carried or passed over the opposing team's goal line and a further point is scored if it is successfully converted by kicking the ball between the posts. A game has four 15-minute quarters but as the clock only runs when the ball is actually in play, and most games last for nearly three hours. Each player wears a helmet with a face mask or guard and mouthpiece, and pads (especially large shoulder pads) to protect vulnerable parts of the body

amiable ['eɪmiəbl] *adjective* friendly and pleasant; *I met her aunt and found her a very amiable person*; *we had an amiable discussion about the project*

amicable ['æmɪkəbl] *adjective* done in a friendly way; *following an amicable discussion he accepted the cancellation of the agreement*

amid [ə'mɪd] *preposition* (*formal*) in the middle of; *the family stood amid the ruins of their shop*

amidships [ə'mɪdʃɪps] *adverb & preposition* in the middle of a ship; *the torpedo struck the cruiser amidships*

amidst [ə'mɪdst] *preposition* (*formal*) in the middle of; *amidst the panic caused by the assassination of the president*

amino acid [ə'miːnəʊ 'æsɪd] *noun* chemical compound which is broken down from proteins in the digestive system and then used by the body to form its own protein; *proteins are first broken down into amino acids*; **essential amino acids** = eight amino acids which are essential for growth, but which cannot be synthesized and so must be obtained from food or medicinal substances

COMMENT: amino acids all contain carbon, hydrogen, nitrogen and oxygen, as well as other elements. Some amino acids are produced in the body itself, but others have to be absorbed from food. The eight essential amino acids are: isoleucine, leucine, lysine, methionine, phenylalanine, threonine, tryptophan and valine

ammonia (NH_3) [ə'məʊnɪə] *noun* gas with a strong smell, a compound of nitrogen and hydrogen; *ammonia is used to make artificial fertilizers*; *she tried to clean the drains with ammonia*

ammunition [æmjʊ'nɪʃn] *noun* bullets, shells, etc.; *they fought all day until their ammunition started to run low*; *the rioters used beer bottles as ammunition against the police* (NOTE: no plural)

amnesty ['æmnəsti] *noun* pardon given to criminals; *the government has offered an amnesty to everyone holding an illegal weapon*

amoeba [əˈmiːbə] *noun* single cell organism, which constantly changes its shape (NOTE: plural is **amoebae**; American spelling is **ameba**)

among *or* **amongst** [əˈmʌŋ or əˈmʌŋst] *preposition* **(a)** surrounded by, in the middle of; *in the campsite, the tents were put up among the trees*; *among the people at the party was a woman who does the TV weather forecasts*; *he was standing amongst a crowd of tourists* **(b)** between various people in a group; *the Christmas cake was divided among the class of children*; *we had to share one towel amongst the three of us*

amorphous [əˈmɔːfəs] *adjective* with no particular shape; *an amorphous mass of broken branches*; *can you give me a few more days to make these amorphous ideas into a proper plan?*

amount [əˈmaunt] *noun* quantity of something, such as money; *the amount in my bank account has reached £1,000*; *this make of car uses by far the least amount of petrol*; **a certain amount** = some; *the storm did a certain amount of damage*; *painting the house will take a certain amount of time*

amount to [əˈmaunt tʊ] *verb* **(a)** to make a total of; *the total bill amounts to over £100* **(b) to amount to the same thing** = to mean the same, to be the same; *whether he took cash or free holidays, it all amounts to the same thing*

amp *or* **ampere** [æmp or ˈæmpeə] *noun* SI measurement of electric current; *you need a 13-amp fuse for that mixer*

amphetamine [æmˈfetəmiːn] *noun* stimulating drug; *amphetamines are commonly abused*

amphibian [æmˈfibiən] *noun* animal that lives both in water and on land; *frogs, toads and other amphibians*

amphibious [æmˈfibiəs] *adjective* that lives both in water and on land; *frogs and toads and other amphibious animals*; **amphibious vehicle** = vehicle which can travel on land and in the water; *the army brought amphibious vehicles to cross the river*

amphitheatre *US* **amphitheater** [ˈæmfɪθɪətə] *noun* **(a)** circular Greek or Roman theatre; *the tour includes the ancient Roman amphitheatre* **(b)** semi-circular lecture hall; *since he's a very popular speaker, we easily filled the amphitheatre*

ample [ˈæmpl] *adjective* sufficient; *we have ample funds to pay for the development programme*; *four hours should be ample time to get to Glasgow*

amplification [æmplɪfɪˈkeɪʃn] *noun* **(a)** making a sound louder; *increase the amplification of the input signal*; *the amplification is so high, the signal is distorted* **(b)** more detailed explanation; *we sent the proposal back for further amplification*

amplifier [ˈæmplɪfaɪə] *noun* device which makes sound louder; *the sound goes from the receiver through an amplifier to the loudspeakers*

amplify [ˈæmplɪfaɪ] *verb* **(a)** to make a sound louder; *the received signal needs to be amplified before it can be processed* **(b)** to explain something in more detail; *there is no need to amplify your story with details which are not relevant*

amputate [ˈæmpjuteɪt] *verb* to cut off an arm, leg, finger or toe; *he developed gangrene and they had to amputate his leg*

amuse [əˈmjuːz] *verb* **(a)** to make someone laugh; *the story about the Prime Minister's cat will amuse you*; *I was amused to hear that you and Jim are sharing an office*; *the boss was not at all amused to get a Valentine's card* **(b)** to make the time pass pleasantly; **to amuse yourself** = to play, to get pleasure from what you are doing; *the children amused themselves quietly while their parents talked*

amused [əˈmjuːzd] *adjective* thinking that something is funny; *we were all amused to hear her story*; *he was very amused by the film*; **to keep someone amused** = to keep someone interested and happy; *this jigsaw will keep the children amused for hours*

amusement [əˈmjuːzmənt] *noun* **(a)** pleasure; *when the rain stopped the tennis match, the group sang for the crowd's amusement*; **amusement arcade** = hall with slot machines for playing games, etc.; **amusement park** = open-air park with various types of entertainment, such as roundabouts, shooting galleries, etc. **(b) to someone's amusement** = making someone laugh; *much to her amusement, the band played 'Happy Birthday to you!'* **(c) amusements** = things which amuse people; *there are all sorts of amusements on the pier*

amusing [əˈmjuːzɪŋ] *adjective* which makes you laugh; *it was amusing to hear about your journey*; *he stayed late, telling us amusing stories about his life in the army*

an [æn or ən] *see* A

anachronism [əˈnækrənɪzm] *noun* thing which is out of date and does not belong to the present time; *judges with wigs will certainly be considered an anachronism in 21st century England*

anachronistic [ənækrəˈnɪstɪk] *adjective* which does not fit the period when a play, film, etc., is supposed to take place; *making Julius Caesar look at his watch is a bit anachronistic*

anaconda [ænəˈkɒndə] *noun* large snake from South America, which winds itself round its victims before eating them; *I took this picture of an anaconda on my trip to South America*

anaemia *US* **anemia** [əˈniːmiə] *noun* condition where the level of red blood cells is less than normal; *the child who is always tired and pale may have anaemia*

anaemic *US* **anemic** [əˈniːmɪk] *adjective* **(a)** having anaemia; *anaemic children always look very pale* **(b)** looking weak and pale; *these plants look very anaemic - you'd better give them some fertilizer*

anaerobic [æneəˈrəubɪk] *adjective* not needing oxygen to exist (NOTE: opposite is **aerobic**)

anaesthetic *US* **anesthetic** [ænəsˈθetɪk] *noun* substance given to a patient to remove feeling, so that he or she can undergo an operation without feeling pain; **general anaesthetic** = substance given to make a patient lose consciousness so that a major surgical operation can be carried out; *you will have to be given a general anaesthetic for this operation*; **local anaesthetic** = substance which removes the feeling in a certain part of the body only; *this operation can be carried out under local rather than general anaesthetic*

anaesthetist *US* **anesthetist** [əˈniːsθətɪst] *noun* specialist who gives anaesthetics; *the anaesthetist gave her an injection*

anaesthetize *US* **anesthetize** [ə'niːsθətaɪz] *verb* to give a patient an anaesthetic; *the patient was anaesthetized before the operation*

anal ['eɪnl] *adjective* referring to the anus; *the anal region*

analgesic [ænəl'dʒiːzɪk] **1** *adjective* which kills pain, without making you lose consciousness; *don't take any other analgesic drug than the one which is prescribed* **2** *noun* painkilling drug which does not make you lose consciousness; *the doctor prescribed a strong analgesic to relieve the pain*

analogous [ə'næləgəs] *adjective (formal)* similar; *it seems we are in a situation analogous to or with that of the Christians facing lions in a Roman arena*

analogy [ə'nælədʒi] *noun* similarity between two things; *historians can see analogies between the two events*; **to draw an analogy between** = to show how two things are similar; *he drew an analogy between raising children and growing plants*

analyse *or* **analyze** ['ænəlaɪz] *verb* to examine closely and scientifically; *to analyse the market potential for golfing holidays*; *when the food was analysed it was found to contain bacteria*

analysis [ə'næləsɪs] *noun* close examination; *job analysis*; *systems analysis*; to make an analysis of the sales *or* a sales analysis; *to carry out an analysis of the market potential* (NOTE: plural is **analyses** [ə'næləsiːz])

analyst ['ænəlɪst] *noun* **(a)** person who carries out analyses; *political analysts are examining the results of the election*; **systems analyst** = person who examines computer systems **(b)** psychoanalyst, doctor who is trained in psychoanalysis; *my analyst says I haven't got an Oedipus complex*

analytical [ænə'lɪtɪkl] *adjective* examining in detail; *his analytical mind should be able to find a solution to our little problem*; *taking an analytical approach from the start would have been better*

anarchic *or* **anarchical** [ə'nɑːkɪk(l)] *adjective* without any law or order; *the anarchical state of the country after the coup*; *his anarchic views don't go down well with his colleagues on the committee*

anarchist ['ænəkɪst] *noun* person who believes in anarchy, who tries to destroy a government by violent means, without planning to replace it in any way; *an attack by anarchists on the Prime Minister*

anarchy ['ænəki] *noun* absence of law and order, because the government has lost control or because there is no government; *when the president was assassinated, the country fell into anarchy*; *the situation is so bad, it's verging on anarchy* (NOTE: no plural)

anathema [ə'næθəmə] *noun* thing which you dislike very much; **it's anathema to her** = she dislikes it intensely; *his way of teaching is anathema to the older teachers*

anatomical [ænə'tɒmɪkl] *adjective* referring to the structure of the body; *anatomical drawings*; *the anatomical features of a fetus*

anatomy [ə'nætəmi] *noun* **(a)** structure of the body or of part of the body; *you'll find a detailed illustration of the anatomy of a bone on page 9*; **human anatomy** = structure and shape of the human body **(b)** detailed examination; *an anatomy of the state of the economy* (NOTE: plural in meanings (a) and (b) is **anatomies**) **(c)** study of the structure of the body; *he is studying*

anatomy; *she failed her anatomy examination*; *he's the professor of human anatomy* **(d)** *(informal)* your own body; *I went riding yesterday and parts of my anatomy are still sore*

ancestor ['ænsestə] *noun* former member of a family; *his ancestors built a castle here in the 13th century*

ancestral [æn'sestrəl] *adjective* referring to a family over many generations; *our ancestral home*

ancestry ['ænsestri] *noun* your family going back over a long period; *we're trying to trace our ancestry*; **she is of French ancestry** = originally her family came from France

anchor ['æŋkə] **1** *noun* large metal hook which holds a ship in place; *the ship was (riding) at anchor*; **to drop anchor** = to let an anchor fall to the bottom of the sea to hold a ship steady; *the ship dropped anchor in the bay* **2** *verb* **(a)** *(of ship)* to drop an anchor to stay in the same place; *the ship anchored in the mouth of the river* **(b)** to hold firm; *the electricity pylon was anchored to the ground with wire cables*

anchorage ['æŋkərɪdʒ] *noun* water where ships can anchor safely; *the harbour provided a safe anchorage*

anchovy ['æntʃəvi *or* æn'tʃəuvi] *noun* small very salty fish; *although I love anchovies, I don't like anchovy paste* (NOTE: plural is **anchovies**)

ancient ['eɪnʃənt] *adjective* very old; *she's studying ancient history*; *he was riding an ancient bicycle*; **ancient monument** = old building which is protected and looked after by the government

and [ænd *or* nd] *conjunction used to join two words or phrases*; *all my uncles and aunts live in the country*; *use a knife and fork to eat your meat*; *the children were running about and singing*; *come and sit down next to me* (NOTE: **and** is used to say numbers after 100: **seven hundred and two (702)**

and so on [nd 'səʊ ɒn] *adverb* with other things; *he talked about plants: flowers, vegetables, and so on*

anecdotal [ænɪk'dəʊtl] *adjective* which comes from stories of individual people; *this report is purely anecdotal and has very little value*; **anecdotal evidence** = evidence which comes in the form of stories told by individual people; *all the police have against him is based on anecdotal evidence*

anecdote ['ænɪkdəʊt] *noun* usually humorous story based on something which has taken place; *she kept us amused with anecdotes about her first months in the UK*

anemia, anemic *US see* ANAEMIA, ANAEMIC

anesthesia, anesthetic, anesthetist *US see* ANAESTHESIA, ANAESTHETIC, ANAESTHETIST

anew [ə'njuː] *adverb (formal)* again; *deer antlers are shed and grown anew each year*

angel ['eɪndʒl] *noun* **(a)** heavenly being; *this grave has a statue of an angel* **(b)** *(informal)* sweet, kind person; *be an angel and get me my slippers* **(c)** *(informal)* person who backs a theatre production financially; *when the play flopped, the angels lost all their money*

angelic [æn'dʒelɪk] *adjective* like an angel, looking innocent; *she looks angelic singing in the school choir, but at home she's a real little devil*

anger ['æŋgə] **1** *noun* annoyance; *I felt no anger, only great disappointment* **2** *verb* to make someone annoyed; *her lateness angered him*

angina [æn'dʒaɪnə] *noun* severe pains in the centre of the chest caused by inadequate supply of blood to the heart muscles, following exercise or eating, because of narrowing of the arteries; *the pain of angina may radiate down the arms and also up into the jaw*

angle ['æŋgl] *noun* **(a)** corner between two lines; *she planted the tree in the angle of the two walls*; **right angle** = 90° angle; **acute angle** = angle less than 90°; **obtuse angle** = angle more than 90°; **angle bracket** = L-shaped metal bracket **(b)** point of view; *what's the government's angle on the story?*

angle for ['æŋgl 'fɔ:] *verb* to try to get; *he was just angling for compliments* = he was trying to get someone to compliment him

angler ['æŋglə] *noun* fisherman who fishes for pleasure; *anglers sitting on the river bank*

Anglican ['æŋglɪkən] **1** *adjective* **the Anglican Church** = the Protestant church which is the official religion of England, with the Queen as its head, and other similar churches in other countries (NOTE: also called the **Church of England**) **2** *noun* member of the Anglican Church

angling ['æŋglɪŋ] *noun* catching fish with a rod; *they go angling every weekend*; *do you belong to an angling club?*

angrily ['æŋgrɪli] *adverb* in an angry way; *he shouted angrily when the children climbed over the fence*

angry ['æŋgri] *adjective* upset and annoyed, and sometimes wanting to harm someone; *the shopkeeper is angry with the schoolchildren because they broke his window*; *he gets angry if the post is late*; *I am angry that the government is doing nothing to prevent crime*; *when the cashier still hadn't arrived at midday the boss got angrier and angrier* (NOTE: **angrier - angriest**)

angst [æŋst] *noun* great worry about life; *all her angst showed in her letters and poems*

anguish ['æŋgwɪʃ] **1** *noun* great mental suffering; *she caused her parents great anguish* (NOTE: no plural) **2** *verb* to worry very much; *she anguished over what decision to take*

anguished ['æŋgwɪʃd] *adjective* showing or feeling great suffering; *his anguished shouts brought people out into the street*

angular ['æŋgjulə] *adjective* **(a)** with sharp corners; *the new car design is very angular* **(b)** with sharp visible bones; *he has a thin angular face*

animal ['ænɪməl] *noun* living and moving thing (but usually not people); *I like to have animals about the house: we have two dogs and three cats*; *the football crowd behaved like animals*

animated ['ænɪmeɪtɪd] *adjective* full of life and energy; *an animated discussion*; *an animated street market*

animation [ænɪ'meɪʃn] *noun* **(a)** being lively; *there was a lot of animation in the market* **(b)** making cartoons; *he worked for a while in an animation studio*; *the film was made using computer animation*

animosity *or* **animus** [ænɪ'mɒsɪti *or* 'ænɪməs] *noun* very unfriendly attitude; *his animosity against or towards people in authority*; *she was accused of trying to stir up racial animosity*

aniseed ['ænɪsi:d] *noun* plant with a sharp taste, used for flavouring drinks, sweets, etc.

ankle ['æŋkəl] *noun* part of the body, where your leg joins your foot; *I couldn't swim, the water only came up to my ankles*; *she twisted her ankle when she slipped on the stairs*; **ankle socks** = short socks

annex [ə'neks] *verb* to take possession of a territory which belongs to another state; *the island was annexed by the neighbouring republic*

annexation [ænek'seɪʃn] *noun* attaching one country to another; *they proceeded to carry out the annexation of the neighbouring state*

annexe ['æneks] *noun* less important building attached to another building; *we have a single room available in the hotel annexe*

annihilate [ə'naɪəleɪt] *verb* to destroy something completely; *there is enough ammunition to annihilate the entire population of the UK*

annihilation [ənaɪə'leɪʃn] *noun* total destruction; *he thinks that a meteorite hit the earth and caused the annihilation of the dinosaurs*

anniversary [ænɪ'vɜ:səri] *noun* same date as an important historical event; *the fiftieth anniversary of the end of the Second World War*; *1966 was the nine-hundredth anniversary of the Battle of Hastings*; **wedding anniversary** = date which is the date of a wedding; *see also* GOLDEN, SILVER (NOTE: plural is **anniversaries**)

annotate ['ænəteɪt] *verb* to add notes to a text; *he annotated the draft of her speech*

annotated ['ænəteɪtɪd] *adjective* with added notes; *don't forget to buy the annotated edition of the text*; *this is the original copy, annotated by the author*

annotation [ænə'teɪʃn] *noun* **(a)** action of adding notes to a text; *the annotation of the whole text took nearly three months* **(b)** note added to a text; *the director's annotations to the play are most useful to the actors*

announce [ə'naʊns] *verb* to say officially or in public; *he announced his resignation*; *she announced that she would be standing for parliament*; *she announced the results of the competition*

announcement [ə'naʊnsmənt] *noun* statement made in public; *the managing director made an announcement to the staff*; *there were several loudspeaker announcements concerning flight changes*

announcer [ə'naʊnsə] *noun* person who reads the news or announces programmes on radio or TV; *a well-known radio announcer*; *he's an announcer with Channel 4*

annoy [ə'nɔɪ] *verb* to make someone irritated; *you can tell he's annoyed by the way his ears go red*; *he gets very annoyed if you keep him waiting*; *try not to annoy your father*

annoyance [ə'nɔɪəns] *noun* feeling annoyed; *she showed her annoyance by throwing the book down on the table*; **to someone's annoyance** = which makes someone annoyed; *I took both sets of keys home with me, much to his annoyance*

annoyed [əˈnɔɪd] *adjective* angry; *he was annoyed with his neighbours for cutting down one of his trees; I was annoyed to find someone had stolen my car; we came back from holiday to find some very annoyed letters from the gas company*

annoying [əˈnɔɪɪŋ] *adjective* which makes you angry; *it is highly annoying to have to try and get my car back from the police station; I find it very annoying that the post doesn't come before 10 o'clock; how annoying! - I've got to go back to the shop because I forgot to buy some milk; the baby has an annoying cough which won't go away*

annual [ˈænjuəl] **1** *adjective* happening once a year; *the village fête is an annual event* **2** *noun* flower which grows from a seed and flowers and dies, all in the same year; *we will put tall plants at the back of the flowerbed and annuals in front; compare* BIENNIAL, PERENNIAL

annual general meeting (AGM) [ˈænjuəl ˈdʒenərəl ˈmiːtɪŋ] *noun* yearly meeting of shareholders of a company; *the chairman announced his retirement at the AGM*

annuity [əˈnjuːɪtɪ] *noun* amount of money paid annually to someone; *her annuity is not enough to live on comfortably, so she has to go out to work; he receives an annuity from the government or a government annuity* (NOTE: plural is **annuities**)

annul [əˈnʌl] *verb* **(a)** to cancel or stop something having a legal effect; *they have written to say that they want to annul the contract* **(b)** to cancel a marriage by stating that it no longer exists; *soon after his first marriage was annulled, he married his secretary* (NOTE: **annulling - annulled**)

annulment [əˈnʌlmənt] *noun* ending of a marriage, a contract, etc., by stating that it no longer exists; *the annulment of the contract was the only way out of a very awkward situation*

anode [ˈænəʊd] *noun* positive terminal on an electric battery; *the positive terminal of a battery, or anode, is indicated by a plus sign* (NOTE: the opposite is a **cathode**)

anomalous [əˈnɒmələs] *adjective* unusual, unexpected; *she's in an anomalous position, being the owner's only daughter*

anomaly [əˈnɒməlɪ] *noun* unusual thing; *the anomaly remained undetected for several years; being left-handed used to be considered an anomaly* (NOTE: plural is **anomalies**)

anonymous [əˈnɒnɪməs] *adjective* without stating a name; *the police have received several anonymous phone calls; the club has had a donation from a businessman who wants to remain anonymous;* **anonymous letter** = letter with no name or signature

anorak [ˈænəræk] *noun* waterproof jacket; *you need a warm anorak when climbing mountains in winter* (NOTE: American English is **windbreaker** or **parka**)

anorexia nervosa [ænəˈreksɪə nɜːˈvəʊsə] *noun* condition usually found in girls where the patient refuses to eat because of a fear of becoming fat; *the girls' school reported two cases of anorexia nervosa*

anorexic [ænəˈreksɪk] *adjective* referring to anorexia; *the school has developed a programme of counselling for anorexic students*

another [əˈnʌðə] *adjective and pronoun* **(a)** one more (like others); *would you like another drink?; I'd*

like another one of those cakes, please; there is only another week before we go on holiday **(b)** a different (one); *he's bought another car; can I have another plate, please, this one's dirty?; she tried on one dress after another, but couldn't find anything she liked; see also* EACH OTHER, ONE ANOTHER

answer [ˈɑːnsə] **1** *noun* reply, letter or conversation after someone has written or spoken to you, asking you a question; *I phoned his office but there was no answer; have you had an answer to your letter yet?;* **in answer to** = as a reply to; *I am writing in answer to your letter of October 6th* **2** *verb* **(a)** to reply, to speak or write words as a response to someone who has spoken to you or asked you a question; *he never answers my letters; when he asked us if we had enjoyed the meal we all answered 'yes'* **(b)** **to answer the phone** = to lift the receiver when the phone rings and listen to what the caller is saying; *when I called, it was his secretary who answered the phone;* **to answer the door** = to open the door when someone knocks or rings; *he leapt out of the shower and answered the door dripping wet with a towel round his waist*

answerable [ˈɑːnsərəbl] *adjective* **to be answerable to someone for something** = to be responsible to someone for your actions; *the manager is answerable to the directors for the smooth running of the office; Simon's my boss - I'm answerable to him*

answer back [ˈɑːnsə ˈbæk] *verb* to speak to someone in a rude way; *don't answer back if the teacher tells you to be quiet*

answering [ˈɑːnsrɪŋ] *adjective* in reply; *'what do we want?' - 'action now' came the answering cry;* **answering machine** = machine which answers the telephone automatically when someone is not in the office or at home, and allows messages to be recorded; **answering service** = office which answers the telephone and takes messages for someone

answerphone [ˈɑːnsəfəʊn] *noun* machine which answers the telephone automatically when someone is not in the office or at home, and allows messages to be recorded; *I left a message for him on his answerphone*

ant [ænt] *noun* small insect; *I found some ants in our kitchen*

antagonism [ænˈtægənɪzm] *noun* hatred; *his antagonism towards anyone in authority; his speech stirred up old antagonisms in the party*

antagonist [ænˈtægənɪst] *noun* bitter opponent; *I know Jones - he's an old antagonist of mine*

antagonistic [æntægəˈnɪstɪk] *adjective* very hostile; **antagonistic to** *or* **towards something** = very hostile to, very much against something; *the demonstrations against fox-hunting just show how antagonistic these people are to the idea; you would never believe how antagonistic she was towards my plan*

antagonize [ænˈtægənaɪz] *verb* to make someone very hostile; *don't antagonize him by telling him what he ought to do*

the Antarctic *or* **Antarctica** [ænˈtɑːktɪk(ə)] *noun* large continent, forming the region around the South Pole; *Antarctica is home to Emperor penguins; two scientists have left for the Antarctic to study the weather; the Antarctic Treaty was signed to prevent the exploitation of the Antarctic region;* **the Antarctic Circle** = parallel running round the earth at latitude 66°32S

antecedent [æntɪ'siːdənt] *noun* **(a)** *(formal)* something that existed earlier but is similar to what exists now; *the common law of the Middle Ages was an antecedent of the modern English legal system* **(b)** family background; *do you know anything of his antecedents?*

antelope ['æntɪləup] *noun* African deer which can run very fast; *vultures were circling above the dead antelope; gazelles are a type of small antelope which run and leap in the air* (NOTE: usually no plural: **a herd of antelope**)

antenna [æn'tenə] *noun* **(a)** feeler of an insect; *the butterfly has two antennae with which it senses* **(b)** senses of a person; *his political antennae told him that the members of the party were not satisfied* (NOTE: plural is **antennae** [æn'teniː]) **(c)** *US* device for receiving radio or TV signals; *a bigger TV antenna should give better reception; signal reception is bad with that type of antenna* (NOTE: plural is **antennas**. Note also that British English is **aerial**)

anthem ['ænθəm] *noun* solemn song for a choir; *the choir sang an anthem at the end of the funeral service; his poem is an anthem to the beauties of nature*; **national anthem** = piece of music which is used to represent the nation officially, and is played at official ceremonies; *everyone stood up when the National Anthem was played; the British National Anthem is 'God Save the Queen'*

anther ['ænθə] *noun* the part of a flower that carries pollen; *each stamen is like a fine stalk bearing an anther*

anthology [æn'θɒlədʒi] *noun* collection of stories, poems, etc; *he has compiled an anthology of political speeches; this poem by Victor Hugo is in every anthology of French poetry* (NOTE: plural is **anthologies**)

anthropological [ænθrəpə'lɒdʒɪkl] *adjective* referring to anthropology; *he specializes in anthropological research*

anthropologist [ænθrə'pɒlədʒɪst] *noun* scientist who studies people and culture; *as an anthropologist, he's very interested in the Inuit culture*

anthropology [ænθrə'pɒlədʒi] *noun* the study of people and culture; *don't miss the next anthropology lecture - it promises to be very interesting; she studied anthropology at university, then she lived with the Inuits for a year to study their culture* (NOTE: no plural)

anti- ['ænti] *prefix* meaning 'against'; *an anti-nuclear protest*

antibiotic [æntɪbaɪ'ɒtɪk] **1** *adjective* which kills bacteria; *she's taking a new antibiotic drug* **2** *noun* substance which kills bacteria; *the doctor prescribed some antibiotics; he was given a course of antibiotics*

antibody ['æntɪbɒdi] *noun* natural substance produced by the body to fight disease; *antibodies fight bacteria* (NOTE: plural is **antibodies**)

anticipate [æn'tɪsɪpeɪt] *verb* to expect something to happen; *we are anticipating bad weather; I don't anticipate taking a later flight*

anticipation [æntɪsɪ'peɪʃn] *noun* **(a)** excitement because you expect that something will happen; *she was full of anticipation at the thought of seeing her again* **(b)** **in anticipation of** = because you expect something to happen; *we closed our shop in anticipation of riots after the football match*

anticlimax [æntɪ'klaɪmæks] *noun* feeling of disappointment when something does not turn out as expected; *after weeks of preparation, it was something of an anticlimax when we discovered that we couldn't leave because of the weather* (NOTE: plural is **anticlimaxes**)

anticlockwise [æntɪ'klɒkwaɪz] *adverb & adjective* in the opposite direction to the hands of a clock; *an anticlockwise movement; turn the hands of the clock anticlockwise; he was driving anticlockwise round the ring road when the accident took place* (NOTE: American English is **counterclockwise**; the opposite is **clockwise**)

antics ['æntɪks] *noun* funny or silly behaviour; *the antics of the clowns in the circus; the students' antics cost them their places at university*

anticyclone ['æntisaɪkləun] *noun* area of high pressure usually associated with fine dry weather in summer and fog in winter; *compare* CYCLONE

antidote ['æntɪdəut] *noun* **(a)** substance which counteracts the effect of a poison; *there is no satisfactory antidote to cyanide* **(b)** something which counteracts a bad influence; *a holiday is a good antidote to feelings of depression*

antihistamine [ænti'hɪstəmiːn] *noun* drug which controls the effects of an allergy; *she takes antihistamines for her hayfever*

antipathy [æn'tɪpəθi] *noun* dislike; *she couldn't hide her feeling of antipathy towards her new boss* (NOTE: no plural)

antiquated ['æntɪkweɪtɪd] *adjective* very old and out-of-date; *he arrived driving an antiquated Morris; she was wearing an antiquated hat with a feather in it*

antique [æn'tiːk] **1** *adjective* old and valuable; *an antique Chinese vase* **2** *noun* valuable old object; *their house if full of antiques*; **antique shop** = shop which sells antiques

antiquity [æn'tɪkwɪti] *noun* **(a)** ancient times; **lost in the mists of antiquity** = very, very old; *the source of the drama is lost in the mists of antiquity* **(b)** **antiquities** = old items from ancient times; *do you know of a good book on the Roman antiquities of Sussex?*

antiseptic [ænti'septɪk] **1** *adjective* which prevents germs spreading or a wound becoming septic; *an antiseptic dressing; she gargled with an antiseptic mouthwash* **2** *noun* substance which prevents germs growing or spreading; *the nurse painted the wound with antiseptic*

antisocial [ænti'səuʃl] *adjective* unfriendly, not wanting to meet other people; *he's very antisocial, he never goes to parties*; **antisocial behaviour** = rowdiness or bad behaviour in public; *the antisocial behaviour of a few football fans can ruin everybody's enjoyment*; **antisocial hours** = work outside the normal hours of work; *in this job, you may have to work antisocial hours*

antithesis [æn'tɪθəsɪs] *noun* the exact opposite of something; *physically he is the antithesis of his sister: she is tall and fair, with blue eyes, while he is short and dark; her taste in food is the complete antithesis of mine* (NOTE: plural is **antitheses** [æn'tɪθəsiːz])

antitrust [ænti'trʌst] *adjective* **antitrust laws** *or* **antitrust legislation** = laws which attack monopolies and encourage competition; *price-fixing amongst rival* *companies is forbidden according to USA anti-trust legislation*

antlers ['æntləz] *noun* horns of a deer; *deer grow new antlers each summer and then shed them in the winter*

antonym ['æntənɪm] *noun* word which means the opposite; *can you find more than one antonym of the word 'different'?* (NOTE: the opposite, a word which means the same as another, is a **synonym**)

anus ['eɪnəs] *noun* opening at the end of the rectum between the buttocks, leading outside the body and through which faeces are passed; *solid food goes into the body by the mouth, and that which is not absorbed is excreted through the anus* (NOTE: plural is **anuses**)

anvil ['ænvɪl] *noun* **(a)** block on which a blacksmith hits pieces of hot metal to shape them; *you could hear the blacksmith hammering away at his anvil* **(b)** one of the three little bones in the middle ear

anxiety [æŋ'zaɪəti] *noun* nervous worry about something; *her anxiety about her job prospects*; *in his anxiety to get away quickly, he forgot to lock the door*

anxious ['æŋkʃəs] *adjective* nervous and very worried about something; *she's anxious about the baby*; **anxious to do something** = nervous and eager for something, wanting something very much; *she's always anxious to please*

anxiously ['æŋkʃəsli] *adverb* in a nervous worried way; *she peered anxiously through the window*; *they are waiting anxiously for the results of the tests*

any ['eni] **1** *adjective and pronoun* **(a)** it doesn't matter which; *take any book you like*; *I'm free any day next week except Tuesday*; *I don't like any of the paintings in the exhibition* **(b)** a quantity; *have you any money left?*; *is there any food for me?*; *would you like any more to eat?*; *will any of your friends be there?* **(c)** not...any = none; *there isn't any food left - they've eaten it all*; *can you lend me some money - I haven't got any?* **2** *adverb* used to emphasize comparatives; **not...any** = not even a little (more); *can't you sing any louder?*; *he can't cycle any faster*; *she's been in hospital for two weeks and isn't any better*

◊ **any more** [eni'mɔː] *adverb* **(a)** a certain number more; *do you have any more books on gardening?* **(b)** **not ... any more** = no longer; *we don't go there any more*

anybody ['enibɒdi] *see* ANYONE

anyhow ['enɪhaʊ] *adverb* **1** in a careless way; *he piled up the books anyhow* **2** = ANYWAY

anyone *or* **anybody** ['eniwʌn *or* 'enibɒdi] *pronoun* **(a)** it doesn't matter who; *anyone can learn to ride a bike*; *anybody could tell you that* **(b)** *(after questions, negatives)* any person; *can anybody lend me some money?*; *did anyone telephone while I was out?*; **we didn't meet anybody** = we met no one

anyplace ['enipleɪs] *adverb US* = ANYWHERE; *anyplace you want to go, she'll want to go too*

anything ['eniθɪŋ] *pronoun* **(a)** it doesn't matter what; *you can eat anything you want*; *our dog will bite anything that moves* **(b)** *(in questions, negatives)* something; *did you do anything interesting during the weekend?*; *did you hear anything make a noise during the night?*; *has anything happened to the plans for the party?*; *do you want anything more to drink?*; **he didn't eat anything** = he ate nothing

anything else ['eniθɪŋ 'els] *pronoun* any other thing; *do you want anything else to drink?*; *is there*

anything else you would like to know about?; *she must have a doll which closes its eyes - anything else won't do*

any time ['eni 'taɪm] *adverb* at any time; *come any time you like*

anyway ['eniweɪ] *adverb* in any case; *I'm not supposed to drink during the daytime, but I'll have a beer anyway*; *I think it's time to leave, anyway, the last bus is at 11.40*

anywhere ['eniweə] *adverb* **(a)** it doesn't matter where; *put the chair anywhere* **(b)** *(in questions, negatives)* somewhere; *did you go anywhere at the weekend?*; *is there anywhere where I can sit down?*; *I can't see your wallet anywhere* (NOTE: American English is also **anyplace**)

aorta [eɪ'ɔːtə] *noun* large artery which takes blood away from the left side of the heart and carries it to other arteries; *red blood is pumped by the heart into the aorta*

apart [ə'pɑːt] *adverb* **(a)** separated; *the two churches are about six miles apart* **(b)** not living together; *they were married but now they're living apart* **(c)** in separate pieces; **the watch came apart** = the watch came to pieces; *he took the watch apart* **(d)** to tell **something** *or* **someone apart** = to identify two things or people that are similar; *the twins are very alike - how can you tell them apart?*

apart from [ə'pɑːt frɒm] *phrase* except, other than; *do you have any special interests apart from your work?*; *I'm feeling fine, apart from a slight cold*

apartment [ə'pɑːtmənt] *noun* separate set of rooms for living in; *she has an apartment in downtown New York*; **an apartment block** *or* **a block of apartments** = large building divided into many apartments; **apartment house** = large house which has been divided up into apartments; **a studio apartment** = apartment with one main room, plus kitchen and bathroom (NOTE: British English is usually **flat**)

apathetic [æpə'θetɪk] *adjective* not bothering about anything, not interested in anything; *since he was made redundant he's become so apathetic, he just sits all day in front of the TV*; *she's quite apathetic about the campaign to prevent the building of the bypass*

apathy ['æpəθi] *noun* not having any interest in anything; *he showed total apathy towards her new project* (NOTE: no plural)

ape [eɪp] *noun* a large monkey; *is man really descended from the apes?*

aperitif *or* **apéritif** [ə'peritiːf] *noun* alcoholic drink taken before a meal to give you an appetite; *we had aperitifs before the meal*; *would you like an aperitif?*

aperture ['æpətʃə] *noun* **(a)** little hole; *some light came through a small aperture in the door*; **aperture envelope** = envelope with a hole in it so that the address on the letter inside can be seen **(b)** the opening in the front of a camera lens, which can be made larger or smaller; *to take a photograph when it is so grey outside, you need to use a large aperture*

apex ['eɪpeks] *noun* the top of a triangle or a pyramid; *the rock is shaped like a triangle with its apex 150 metres above the sea* (NOTE: plural is **apexes**)

Apex fare ['eɪpeks 'feə] *noun* specially cheap air fare which must be booked a certain time before the flight, usually three weeks, and which can only be changed or cancelled once it has been booked on payment of an extra charge; *the Apex fare to Montreal has been discontinued* (NOTE: it stands for **Advance Purchase Excursion**)

aphid *or* **aphis** ['eɪfɪd *or* 'eɪfɪs] *noun* small insect, such as a blackfly or greenfly, which sucks sap from plants and can multiply very rapidly; *I must spray the aphids in our apple trees*

apiece [ə'piːs] *adverb* each; *she gave the children £1 apiece*; *the oranges cost 50p apiece*

Apocalypse [ə'pɒkəlɪps] *noun* **(a)** last book of the New Testament; **the Four Horsemen of the Apocalypse** = symbols of death, famine, war and disease **(b)** the catastrophe at the end of the world; *the ice storm was so destructive, it looked like a scene from the Apocalypse*

apocalyptic [əpɒkə'lɪptɪk] *adjective* which warns about the catastrophe at the end of the world; *the apocalyptic scenes of destruction caused by the volcano*

Apocrypha [ə'pɒkrɪfə] *noun* parts of the Old Testament which are of doubtful origin (NOTE: the word is plural)

apocryphal [ə'pɒkrɪfl] *adjective* famous, but probably untrue; *the very funny, but probably apocryphal, story of Queen Victoria and the bottle of gin*

apologetic [əpɒlə'dʒetɪk] *adjective* showing that you are sorry for something; *he was very apologetic when we complained about the slow service*; *she wrote us an apologetic letter*

apologize [ə'pɒlədʒaɪz] *verb* to say you are sorry; *did you apologize to your mother for what you said?*; *he shouted at her and then apologized*; *she apologized for being late*

apology [ə'pɒlədʒi] *noun* saying sorry; *he wrote a letter of apology*; *I enclose a cheque for £10 with apologies for the delay in answering your letter*; *my apologies for being so late*; *I expect we will receive an apology in due course* (NOTE: plural is **apologies**)

apostle [ə'pɒsl] *noun* **(a) the Apostles** = twelve people who were sent by Jesus Christ to preach the gospel **(b)** person who tries to persuade other people that an idea is good; *she was the apostle of free enterprise*

apostrophe [ə'pɒstrəfi] *noun* printing sign:'; *'it's' written with an apostrophe means 'it is'*

> COMMENT: an apostrophe either shows that a letter has been left out (weren't) or is used with 's' to show possession: before an 's' with singular words, after the 's' with plural words (a boy's coat, the girls' team)

appal *US* **appall** [ə'pɔːl] *verb* to horrify, to shock; *her rude behaviour appalled us*; *the tourists were appalled by the dirt in the streets*

appalled [ə'pɔːld] *adjective* very shocked; *he was appalled that no one had told him about the accident*; *the appalled hotel manager called the police*

appalling [ə'pɔːlɪŋ] *adjective* horrible, shocking; *the appalling injuries caused by the bomb*; *her table manners are appalling*; *it's an appalling waste of money*

apparatus [æpə'reɪtəs] *noun* scientific or medical equipment; *he dropped an expensive piece of apparatus in the lab this morning*; *the oxygen apparatus a diver carries on his back is called an 'aqualung'*; *the firemen had to wear breathing apparatus to enter the burning building* (NOTE: no plural: for one item say **a piece of apparatus**)

apparel [ə'pærəl] *noun* *(formal)* clothes; *gentlemen's apparel*

apparent [ə'pærənt] *adjective* obvious, which seems to be; *it was apparent to everyone that there had been an accident*; *there is an apparent mistake in the accounts*

apparently [ə'pærəntli] *adverb* as it seems; *apparently she took the last train home and then disappeared*; *he didn't come to work today - he's got a cold apparently*

apparition [æpə'rɪʃn] *noun* ghost, something which you think you see; *according to the legend, the apparition was seen walking down the stairs*

appeal [ə'piːl] **1** *noun* **(a)** asking for help; *the police have made an appeal for witnesses*; *the hospital is launching an appeal to raise £50,000* **(b)** legal request to reconsider a verdict; *his appeal was rejected*; *the verdict was overturned on appeal*; **Court of Appeal** *or* **Appeal Court** = law court which decides on appeals **(c)** attraction; *the appeal of Greece as a holiday destination*; **sex appeal** = being attractive to the opposite sex **2** *verb* **(a) to appeal for** = to ask for; *they appealed for money to continue their work* **(b) to appeal against a verdict** = to make a legal request to reconsider a verdict; *he has appealed against the sentence* **(c) to appeal to** = to attract; *these CDs appeal to the teenage market*; *the idea of working in Australia for six months appealed to her*

appealing [ə'piːlɪŋ] *adjective* attractive; *an appealing offer*; *the thought of a week on a Greek island is very appealing*

appear [ə'pɪə] *verb* **(a)** to start to be seen; *a ship appeared through the fog* **(b)** to seem; *there appears to be a mistake*; *he appears to have forgotten the time*; *she appeared rather cross*

appearance [ə'pɪərəns] *noun* **(a)** look; *you could tell from his appearance that he had been sleeping rough* **(b)** being present, being there; *this is her second appearance in a film*; **to put in an appearance** = to arrive at, to come to a meeting, etc.

appearances [ə'pɪərənsɪz] *noun* looks; *appearances can be deceptive; by all appearances, the house is empty*; **to keep up appearances** = to try to show that you are still as rich or important as you were before

appease [ə'piːz] *verb* **(a)** to try to satisfy; *I hope the letter will appease her anger*; *he ate an apple to appease his hunger* **(b)** to make concessions to another country in the hope that they will not start a war; *to avoid the use of arms, they tried to appease their enemy by making various promises which they found difficult to keep*

appeasement [ə'piːzmənt] *noun* policy of avoiding war by making concessions; *the government is convinced that the new policy of appeasement will prevent a disastrous war*

appellation [æpə'leɪʃn] *noun (formal)* name; *did the former Prime Minister deserve the appellation of 'Iron Lady'?*

appellation contrôlée [æpə'læsiən kɒn'trəuleɪ] *French noun* official name of a certain type of wine

appendicitis [əpendɪ'saɪtɪs] *noun* inflammation of the appendix; *they diagnosed acute appendicitis*

> COMMENT: appendicitis takes several forms, the main ones being: acute appendicitis, which is a sudden attack of violent pain in the right lower part of the abdomen, accompanied by a fever. Acute appendicitis normally requires urgent surgery. A second form is chronic appendicitis, where the appendix is continually slightly inflamed, giving a permanent dull pain or a feeling of indigestion

appendix [ə'pendɪks] *noun* **(a)** little sac attached to the intestine, which serves no function but can become infected, causing appendicitis; *she had her appendix removed* (NOTE: plural is **appendixes**) **(b)** section at the back of a book, containing additional information; *there is an appendix giving the names of all the presidents of the USA; see appendices B and C for further details* (NOTE: plural is **appendices** [ə'pendɪsi:z])

appetite ['æpɪtaɪt] *noun* **(a)** wanting to eat; *going for a long walk has given me an appetite*; *he's not feeling well and has lost his appetite*; **good appetite** = interest in eating food; *the baby has a good appetite*; **poor appetite** = lack of interest in eating food **(b)** strong desire for something; *she has an appetite for hard work*

appetizer ['æpɪtaɪzə] *noun* little snack before a main meal; *raw carrots, celery sticks and black olives were served as appetizers*

appetizing ['æpɪtaɪzɪŋ] *adjective* which looks or smells good and makes you want to eat it; *a very appetizing smell of fresh bread came from the bakery; that dish doesn't look very appetizing* (NOTE: the opposite is **unappetizing**)

applaud [ə'plɔ:d] *verb* to clap to show that you like something; *the audience applauded the singers at the end of the concert*

applause [ə'plɔ:z] *noun* clapping; *at the end of the concert there was a storm of applause*

apple ['æpl] *noun* **(a)** common hard round sweet fruit, growing on a tree; *don't eat unripe apples - they'll make you ill*; **cooking apple** = sour apple which is good for cooking, not for eating raw; **eating apple** = apple which is good to eat raw, rather than to be cooked **(b)** **apple (tree)** = tree which apples grow on; *there's an old apple tree behind our house*

apple pie ['æpl 'paɪ] *noun* pie made with apples and sugar; *do you want any more apple pie?; she gave him a huge helping of apple pie and cream*

appliance [ə'plaɪəns] *noun* machine, especially an electrical machine used in the home, such as a washing machine; *household appliances should be properly earthed*

applicable [ə'plɪkəbl] *adjective* which can be applied in certain cases; *the rule is only applicable on Sundays; the duty is applicable to imports from outside the EU*

applicant ['æplɪkənt] *noun* person who applies for something; *applicants for visas will have to wait at least two weeks*

application [æplɪ'keɪʃn] *noun* **(a)** putting on (of medicine); *several applications of the cream will be necessary*; **for external application only** = to be used on the skin only **(b)** applying for a job, etc.; *he wrote a letter of application*; *we've received dozens of applications for the job of barman*; **application form** = form to be filled in when applying; *she filled in an application form*

apply [ə'plaɪ] *verb* **(a)** **to apply for a job** = to ask for a job; *she applied for a job in the supermarket*; *he's applying for a job as a teacher* **(b)** to put on; *wait until the first coat of paint is dry before you apply the second* **(c)** **to apply to** = to affect or to relate to; *this rule only applies to people coming from outside the EU*

appoint [ə'pɔɪnt] *verb* to give (a job) to someone; *he was appointed (as) manager* or *to the post of manager*; *we want to appoint someone to manage our sales department* (NOTE: you appoint a person **to** a job)

appointee [əpɔɪn'ti:] *noun* person who is appointed to a post; *new appointees have to go through a period of training*

appointment [ə'pɔɪntmənt] *noun* **(a)** being given a job; **on her appointment as manager** = when she was made manager; *she had a rise on her appointment as manager* **(b)** agreed time for a meeting; *I want to make an appointment to see the doctor; she was late for her appointment; I have an appointment with Dr Jones;* **a dentist's appointment** = arrangement to see a dentist; **appointments book** = book in which you write down the time and place of meetings

appraisal [ə'preɪzəl] *noun* report on the value of someone or something; *did you read her appraisal of the current situation?;* **staff appraisals** = annual reports on how well each member of staff is working; *annual staff appraisals are company policy*

appraise [ə'preɪz] *verb* to judge how successful someone or something is working; *in our company, managers have to appraise their staff every year; give me some more time to appraise the situation fully*

appreciate [ə'pri:ʃieɪt] *verb* **(a)** to recognize the value of; *shoppers always appreciate good value; customers don't appreciate having to wait to be served* **(b)** to increase in value; *the pound appreciated against the peseta*

appreciation [əpri:ʃi'eɪʃn] *noun* **(a)** showing that you recognize the value of something; *she is taking an art appreciation course; the company presented him with a watch in appreciation of his years of service* **(b)** increase in value; *the appreciation of the pound against the dollar*

appreciative [ə'pri:ʃjətɪv] *adjective* **(a)** full of gratitude; *she was very appreciative of our efforts to help* **(b)** showing enjoyment; *the audience burst into appreciative laughter when he finished telling the joke*

apprehend [æprɪ'hend] *verb* (formal) to arrest a criminal; *he was apprehended as he was getting on the plane; the accused was apprehended at the scene of the crime*

apprehension [æprɪ'henʃn] *noun* **(a)** worry about what is going to happen; *she showed understandable apprehension on going into the interview; his apprehension showed on his face; compare* MISAPPREHENSION **(b)** (formal) act of arresting someone; *this led to the apprehension of the killer*

apprehensive [æprɪ'hensɪv] *adjective* worried about the future; *we are apprehensive about our daughter's safety*

apprentice [ə'prentɪs] **1** *noun* young person who works under contract with a skilled workman to learn from him; *the new apprentice is working very well - he will go far* **2** *verb* **to be apprenticed to someone** = to work with a skilled workman to learn from him; *he has been apprenticed to one of the best printers in the country*

apprenticeship [ə'prentɪsʃɪp] *noun* **(a)** contract of an apprentice; *he signed an apprenticeship with a builder* **(b)** time spent as an apprentice; *he served a six-year apprenticeship in the furniture factory*

approach [ə'prəʊtʃ] **1** *noun* **(a)** coming closer; *with the approach of winter we need to get the central heating serviced* **(b)** way which leads to; *the approaches to the city were crowded with coaches*; **approach road** = road leading to a main road **(c)** way of dealing with a situation; *his approach to the question was different from hers* **(d)** proposal; *he made approaches to her to leave her job and come to work for him* (NOTE: plural is **approaches**) **2** *verb* **(a)** to come near; *the plane was approaching London airport when the lights went out* **(b)** to deal with a problem; *he approached the question in an entirely new way* **(c)** to make a proposal; *our company was approached with a takeover bid; he approached his bank with a request for a loan*

approaching [ə'prəʊtʃɪŋ] *adjective* coming closer; *the approaching winter; she was dreading the approaching new term*

appropriate 1 *adjective* [ə'prəʊpriət] suitable; *that short skirt is not really appropriate for gardening; we leave it to you to take appropriate action* **2** *verb* [ə'prəʊprieɪt] **(a)** to seize property; *the authorities appropriated the land to build a new hospital* **(b)** to put a sum of money aside for a special purpose; *they appropriated £100,000 to the reserve fund*

appropriation [əprəʊprɪ'eɪʃn] *noun* **(a)** seizure of property; *the council have voted the appropriation of derelict land in the centre of town to build a new town hall* **(b)** act of putting money aside for a particular purpose; *the appropriation of £600,000 to the reserves was agreed*

approval [ə'pruːvəl] *noun* **(a)** agreeing with; *does the choice of colour have your approval or meet with your approval?; the committee gave their approval to the scheme*; **approval rating** = points system showing how many people approve of something, usually of a politician's work; *the Prime Minister's approval rating has fallen to an all-time low* **(b)** **on approval** = (merchandise) taken by a customer to use and see if he or she likes it; *the shop let us have the photocopier for two weeks on approval*

approve [ə'pruːv] *verb* **(a)** **to approve of** = to think something is good; *he doesn't approve of loud music* **(b)** to agree to something officially; *the committee approved the scheme*

approximate 1 *adjective* [ə'prɒksɪmət] more or less correct; *the approximate cost will be £600; these figures are only approximate* **2** *verb* [ə'prɒksɪmeɪt] to be nearly correct; *the cost of the sports stadium will approximate to two million pounds*

approximately [ə'prɒksɪmətli] *adverb* roughly; *it takes approximately 35 minutes to get to central London from here*

approximation [əprɒksɪ'meɪʃn] *noun* approximate amount; *the figure is just a rough approximation*

apricot ['eɪprɪkɒt] *noun* **(a)** stone fruit with yellow flesh, like a small peach, but not as juicy; *she bought a bag of apricots; you have a choice of marmalade or apricot jam for breakfast* **(b)** **apricot (tree)** = tree which bears this fruit; *we planted two apricots against a south-facing wall*

April ['eɪprɪl] *noun* the fourth month of the year, the month after March and before May; *her birthday is in April; we went on holiday last April; today is April 5th* US *April 5*; **April 1st** = *see* APRIL FOOL'S DAY (NOTE: **April 5th** *or* **April 5**: say 'the fifth of April' or 'April the fifth'; American English: 'April fifth')

April fool ['eɪprəl 'fuːl] *noun* person who is tricked on April 1st; *she told me I had jam on my chin, and then called me an April fool*

April Fools' Day ['eɪprəl 'fuːlz deɪ] *noun* April 1st, the day when you play tricks on people

apron ['eɪprən] *noun* **(a)** cloth worn over your clothes when cooking or doing housework; *the chef came out in his white hat and apron to talk to the customers* **(b)** *(at an airport)* piece of tarmac on which planes can be parked for unloading, waiting, cleaning, etc.

apt [æpt] *adjective* **(a)** which fits well; *she made some very apt comments* **(b)** **apt to** = tending to; *our old car was apt to break down on motorways*

aptitude ['æptɪtjʊd] *noun* skill or ability in doing something; *she shows great aptitude for French*; **aptitude test** = test of someone's ability; *twenty young people will take the aptitude test this month*

aqualung ['ækwəlʌŋ] *noun* oxygen apparatus which a diver carries on his back; *it is easy to learn to swim under water, but you also have to learn to breathe with an aqualung*

aquarium [ə'kweəriəm] *noun* **(a)** tank for keeping tropical fish; *he keeps an aquarium with little blue fish in the kitchen* **(b)** building with an exhibition of fish; *we went to the aquarium on Saturday afternoon*

Aquarius [ə'kweəriəs] *noun* one of the signs of the Zodiac, shaped like a person carrying water; *my grandson is (an) Aquarius - his birthday is the 31st of January*

aquatic [ə'kwætɪk] *adjective* **(a)** *(animal or plant)* which lives in water, not on land; *aquatic animals, such as otters* (NOTE: animals and plants that live on land are **terrestrial**) **(b)** which takes place in water; *it's the ideal place for aquatic sports*

aqueduct ['ækwɪdʌkt] *noun* construction like a high bridge, carrying water over a valley, etc.; *we visited a Roman aqueduct in the south of France*

Arab ['ærəb] **1** *adjective* referring to the countries of the Middle East where Arabic is the language; *Foreign Ministers of the Arab countries have met in Jordan* **2** *noun* person who speaks Arabic and who comes from one of the countries in the Middle East

Arabian [ə'reɪbiən] *adjective* referring to Arabia; **Arabian camel** = the dromedary, a camel with one hump

Arabic ['ærəbɪk] **1** *noun* language spoken by Arabs; *he studied Arabic at university* **2** *adjective* **Arabic**

numerals = numbers written 1, 2, 3, 4, etc. *compare* ROMAN NUMERALS

arable ['ærəbl] *adjective* referring to the growing of crops; **arable farming** = growing crops, as opposed to dairy farming, sheep farming, etc.; **arable land** = land which has been ploughed and is used for growing crops

arbiter ['ɑːbɪtə] *noun (formal)* person who decides on what is fashionable; *she is trying to play the role of arbiter of fashion*

arbitrary ['ɑːbɪtrəri] *adjective* done at random, without any reason; *an arbitrary decision to sell the company; the referee's decision seemed quite arbitrary to me*

arbitrate ['ɑːbɪtreɪt] *verb* **to arbitrate in a dispute** = to act as an official judge in a dispute; *he has been asked to arbitrate in the dispute between the company and the union* (NOTE: American English is to **arbitrate a dispute**)

arbitration [ɑːbɪ'treɪʃn] *noun* settling of a dispute by an official judge, accepted by both sides; *to submit a dispute to arbitration; to go to arbitration;* **arbitration board** *or* **arbitration tribunal** = committee which arbitrates in industrial disputes; *to accept the ruling of the arbitration board*

arbitrator ['ɑːbɪtreɪtə] *noun* person who acts as the official judge in a dispute; *the dispute has gone before an industrial arbitrator*

arboreal [ɑː'bɔːriəl] *adjective* referring to trees; living in trees; *the koala bear is a well-known Australian arboreal animal*

arc [ɑːk] *noun* **(a)** curve, like part of a circle; *the moon slowly moves in an arc across the sky* **(b)** bright electric spark between two points; *see also* ARC-LAMP (NOTE: do not confuse with **ark**)

arcade [ɑː'keɪd] *noun* covered walkway round a square, with pillars and shops; **shopping arcade** = covered shopping street with an arched glass roof; **amusement arcade** = place with slot machines for playing games

arcane [ɑː'keɪn] *adjective (formal)* mysterious and secret; *an arcane religious sect*

arch [ɑːtʃ] *noun* **(a)** round structure forming a roof or doorway; *the church roof is formed of tall stone arches;* **Norman arch** = arch in the shape of a half-circle; **Gothic arch** = arch which is pointed **(b)** **triumphal arch** = large building over a roadway, to celebrate a victory; *there are the ruins of a Roman triumphal arch in the centre of the square* (NOTE: plural is **arches**)

archaeological [ɑːkiə'lɒdʒɪkl] *adjective* referring to archaeology; *an archaeological excavation*

archaeologist [ɑːkɪ'ɒlədʒɪst] *noun* person who studies or is a specialist in archaeology; *an archaeologist came to look at the site*

archaeology [ɑːkɪ'ɒlədʒi] *noun* digging up of buried remains of buildings to study ancient civilizations; *she's a specialist in Roman archaeology;* **industrial archaeology** = study of old factories, old machines, etc.; **marine archaeology** = study of old ships

archaic [ɑː'keɪɪk] *adjective* **(a)** dating from ancient times; *an archaic language* **(b)** old-fashioned; *her methods for bringing up children are very archaic*

archaism ['ɑːkeɪɪzm] *noun* word or term which was used in ancient times; *two archaisms, 'thou' and 'thee', were old forms of 'you'*

archbishop [ɑːtʃ'bɪʃəp] *noun* bishop holding the highest rank; *the Archbishop of Canterbury is the religious head of the Church of England*

arched ['ɑːtʃd] *adjective* made with an arch; *an arched doorway*

archer ['ɑːtʃə] *noun* person who shoots with a bow and arrows; *the archers stood in line with their bows and arrows ready*

archery ['ɑːtʃəri] *noun* sport of shooting arrows at targets; *both my children took part in the archery competition*

archetypal [ɑːkɪ'taɪpəl] *adjective* very typical; *he's the archetypal Englishman*

archetype ['ɑːkɪtaɪp] *noun* typical example of something; *she's the archetype of the young successful career woman*

archipelago [ɑːkɪ'peləgəʊ] *noun* group of islands; *the Galapagos Archipelago* (NOTE: plural is **archipelagos**)

architect ['ɑːkɪtekt] *noun* person who designs buildings; *which architect designed the new town hall?; we've asked a local architect to submit plans for a new house*

architectural [ɑːkɪ'tektʃərel] *adjective* referring to architecture; *the town hall won an architectural design award*

architecture ['ɑːkɪtektʃə] *noun* design of buildings; *she is studying architecture* or *she's an architecture student; he doesn't like modern architecture*

archives ['ɑːkaɪvz] *noun* collection of documents; *the town's archives go back to its foundation in 1140*

archway ['ɑːtʃweɪ] *noun* passage which goes under an arch; *go through the archway and turn left*

arc-lamp *or* **arc-light** ['ɑːklæmp *or* 'ɑːklaɪt] *noun* very bright light caused by an electric spark between two points; *the accident site was lit by arc-lights*

arctic ['ɑːktɪk] **1** *adjective* **(a)** referring to the area round the North Pole; *polar bears hibernate during the long arctic winters; two arctic explorers have reached the North Pole;* **the Arctic Circle** = parallel running round the earth at latitude 66°32N **(b)** extremely cold; *we've had some really arctic weather this winter* **2** *noun* **the Arctic** = the area round the North Pole; *the Arctic is home to polar bears*

ardent ['ɑːdənt] *adjective* very keen; *an ardent lover; he's an ardent cricket fan*

ardour *US* **ardor** ['ɑːdə] *noun (formal)* violent feelings of love or enthusiasm; *he showed no ardour for the battle; by the time he had reached the third year, all his youthful ardour for study had vanished*

arduous ['ɑːdjʊəs] *adjective* needing a lot of effort or work; *an arduous climb; the work is very arduous, so it's hardly surprising not many people want to do it*

are [ɑː] *see* BE

area ['eəriə] *noun* **(a)** space; *the whole area round the town hall is going to be rebuilt; we always sit in the 'no smoking' area* **(b)** measurement of the space taken up by something (calculated by multiplying the length by the width); *the area of the room is four square metres; we are looking for a shop with a sales area of about*

100 square metres (c) subject; *it's a problem area for the government*; *he's an expert in the area of crowd control* (d) district, part of a town or country; *our house is near the commercial area of the town*; *the factory is in a very good area for getting to the motorways and airports*; **the London area** = the part of England round London; *houses in the London area are more expensive than elsewhere in the country*

area code ['eəriə'kəud] *noun* special telephone number which is given to a particular area; *the area code for central London is 0171*

> COMMENT: area codes always start with 0, and may have three further digits for large towns (Central London is 0171, Liverpool is 0151) or several digits for smaller towns (Oxford is 01865). These are spoken as 'oh one eight one, oh one eight six five,' etc.

arena [ə'ri:nə] *noun* (a) building with seats for spectators, where sports and fights are held; *the boys went skating at the school arena* (b) field of activity where something happens; *she decided to enter the political arena*

aren't [ɑ:nt] *see* BE

Argentina [ɑ:dʒən'ti:nə] *noun* large country in South America; *our rep is leaving for Argentina soon*; *we spent three weeks in Argentina, visiting relatives* (NOTE: capital: **Buenos Aires** people: **Argentinians**; language: **Spanish**; currency: **Argentinian peso**)

Argentinian [ɑ:dʒən'tınjən] **1** *adjective* referring to Argentina; *we do a lot of business with an Argentinian importer* **2** *noun* person from Argentina; *these Argentinians speak very good English*

argon ['ɑ:gɒn] *noun* inert gas which is found in small quantities in air, and which is used in electric light bulbs (NOTE: Chemical element: chemical symbol: **Ar**; atomic number: **18**)

arguable ['ɑ:gjuəbl] *adjective* which is possibly not true; *it's arguable whether travel is faster now than it was fifty years ago*; *his claim to be a descendant of Charles II is arguable*

arguably ['ɑ:gjuəbli] *adverb* quite possibly true; *it is arguably the best restaurant in London*

argue ['ɑ:gju:] *verb* to discuss without agreeing; *they argued over the prices*; *she argued with the waiter about the bill*; *I could hear them arguing in the next room* (NOTE: you argue **with** someone **about** or **over** something)

argument ['ɑ:gju:mənt] *noun* quarrel; *nobody would back her up in her argument with the boss*; *the argument took place in the restaurant*; **to get into an argument with someone** = to start to argue with someone; *he got into an argument with the customs officials*

argumentative [ɑ:gju'mentətɪv] *adjective* who likes to argue; *the boss was very argumentative this morning*

aria ['ɑ:riə] *noun* solo song in an opera; *she sang an aria from the 'Marriage of Figaro'*

arid ['ærɪd] *adjective* extremely dry; where there is very little rain; *deserts are arid regions with less than 400mm of rain per year*

Aries ['eəri:z] *noun* one of the signs of the Zodiac, shaped like a ram; *she's (an) Aries - her birthday is 22nd March*

arise [ə'raɪz] *verb* (a) to start, to appear; *a problem has arisen in connection with the tickets* (b) **to arise from** = to result from, to happen because of; *the misunderstanding arose from a mistake in her instructions* (NOTE: arising - arose [ə'rəuz] - arisen [ə'rɪzn])

aristocracy [ærɪ'stɒkrəsi] *noun* the nobility, the people of the highest class in society, usually with titles such as Lord, Duke, etc.; *the aristocracy supported the military dictatorship*; *his family is part of the old aristocracy*

aristocrat ['ærɪstəkræt *US* ə'rɪstəkræt] *noun* member of the aristocracy; *many aristocrats were killed during the French Revolution*

aristocratic [ærɪstə'krætɪk] *adjective* referring to the aristocracy; *he comes from an old aristocratic family*; *his aristocratic attitude to his staff* = the very superior attitude which he adopts towards his staff

arithmetic [ə'rɪθmətɪk] *noun* calculations with figures; *children must concentrate on reading, writing and arithmetic*; *I got the arithmetic slightly wrong*

arithmetical [ærɪθ'metɪkl] *adjective* referring to arithmetic; *the arithmetical problems were more difficult to solve than I expected*

ark [ɑ:k] *noun* (a) *(literary)* large ship; *the Bible says that two of each animal went into the Ark*; *the Flood is the story in the Bible of the time when the earth was covered with water and only Noah and his family and animals were saved in the Ark*; **Noah's Ark** = model of the ship in which Noah escaped from the Flood with two of each animal (NOTE: the name **Ark Royal** is still used for a ship in the Royal Navy: it was first used in the time of Henry VIII) (b) hut for pigs (NOTE: do not confuse with **arc**)

arm [ɑ:m] **1** *noun* (a) part of your body which goes from your shoulder to your hand; *he held the parcel under his arm*; *she tripped over the pavement and broke her arm*; *lift your arms up above your head*; **arm in arm** = with their arms linked; *they walked down the street arm in arm*; **to welcome someone with open arms** = to welcome someone eagerly; *the villagers welcomed the UN soldiers with open arms*; *see also* COST (b) sleeve, the part of a coat, shirt, etc., which you put your arm into; *there was a hole under the arm of her favourite T-shirt* (c) part of a chair which you can rest your arms on; *he put his coffee cup on the arm of his chair* **2** *verb* to equip with weapons; *the farm workers have all been armed because of possible attacks*; *the soldiers were armed with guns*

armada [ɑ:'mɑ:də] *noun* (a) fleet of warships; *the Spanish Armada* (b) fleet of any ships; *an armada of little yachts followed the liner into port*

armaments ['ɑ:məmənts] *noun* heavy weapons; *an important armaments manufacturer*; *Britain has been supplying armaments to the Middle Eastern countries*

armband ['ɑ:mbænd] *noun* band of cloth which goes round your arm; *the mourners all wore black armbands*; *cyclists should wear reflective armbands when cycling in the dark*

armchair ['ɑ:mtʃeə] *noun* chair with arms; *each room in the hotel is furnished with two armchairs and a TV*; *she settled down in a comfortable armchair to read*

armed [ɑ:md] *adjective* *(person)* carrying weapons; *most British policemen are not armed*; *armed police* *guarded the house*; **the armed forces** = the army, navy and air force of a country *(informal)* **armed to the teeth** = carrying lots of weapons; *the robbers were armed to the teeth*

armistice ['ɑːmɪstɪs] *noun* agreement to stop fighting; *the two generals signed an armistice*; *we visited the train carriage where the armistice was signed in 1918*

Armistice Day ['ɑːmɪstɪs 'deɪ] *noun* November 11th, or the nearest Sunday, celebrating the end of the First World War and remembering the dead of both World Wars; *we all bought poppies for Armistice Day*; *see comments at* POPPY, REMEMBRANCE (NOTE: also called **Remembrance Day** *or* **Poppy Day**)

armour *US* **armor** ['ɑːmə] *noun* **(a)** protective metal clothing for medieval soldiers; *a suit of armour* **(b)** protective covering for ships or tanks; *the gun is capable of piercing a tank's steel armour*

armoured *US* **armored** ['ɑːməd] *adjective* protected by armour; **armoured car** = military vehicle which is protected by thick metal; **armoured column** = series of armoured cars or tanks in a line; *the armoured column moved off down the road*

armour-plated ['ɑːməˈpleɪtɪd] *adjective* protected by thick sheets of metal; *the President drove past in his armour-plated limousine*

armour-plating ['ɑːməˈpleɪtɪŋ] *noun* protective metal covering for ships or tanks; *the gun is capable of piercing a tank's steel armour-plating*

armoury *US* **armory** ['ɑːməri] *noun* **(a)** store for weapons; *their main target was the enemy's armoury* **(b)** a country's arms; *Russia's nuclear armoury*

armpit ['ɑːmpɪt] *noun* part of your body, the place under your arm where it joins your body; *there are lymph glands under the armpits*

arms [ɑːmz] *noun* **(a)** weapons, such as guns or bombs; *he's a well-known arms dealer*; *they were selling arms to Arab countries* **(b) up in arms about** = very annoyed about; *they are up in arms about the new bus timetable*

army ['ɑːmi] *noun* all the soldiers of a country, trained for fighting on land; *he left school at 16 and joined the army*; *an army spokesman held a news conference* (NOTE: plural is **armies**)

aroma [əˈrəʊmə] *noun* pleasant smell of something you can eat or drink; *the aroma of fresh coffee*

aromatherapy [ərəʊməˈθerəpi] *noun* treatment with pleasant-smelling oils; *have you considered aromatherapy to help you to relax?*

aromatic [ærəˈmætɪk] *adjective* with a strong pleasant smell; *the aromatic smell of Indian spices*; **aromatic herbs** = plants used to make perfume, or which form condiments and spices; *the unforgettable smell of aromatic herbs in the market*

arose [əˈrəʊz] *verb see* ARISE

around [əˈraʊnd] **1** *preposition* **(a)** going all round something; *she had a gold chain around her neck*; *the flood water was all around the village*; *the police car drove around the town* **(b)** close to, nearby; *a few boys hung around the bus stop* **(c)** in various places; *we have lots of computers scattered around the office*; *it's hard to find your way around Rome without a map* **(d)** more or less; *it will cost around £200*; *around sixty people came to the meeting* **2** *adverb* **(a)** in various

places; *papers were lying around all over the floor*; *the restaurants were all full, so we walked around for some time* **(b)** all round; *a castle with water all around* **(c)** close to, nearby; *the children stood around waiting for the bus* **(d)** in existence; *she's one of the best eye surgeons around*; *the new coins have been around for some weeks now*

arousal [əˈraʊzəl] *noun* making someone interested, especially sexually excited; *sexual arousal*

arouse [əˈraʊz] *verb* **(a)** to excite emotion; *she only wanted to arouse our sympathy*; **he is easily aroused** = it is easy to make him angry **(b)** to make someone interested. excited, etc.; *the proposal has aroused a lot of opposition among the people of the village*; *the painting has aroused the interest of several collectors* **(c)** to make someone sexually excited; *compare* ROUSE

arrange [əˈreɪndʒ] *verb* **(a)** to put in order; *the chairs are arranged in rows*; *the books are arranged in alphabetical order*; *the ground floor is arranged as an open-plan area with a little kitchen at the side* **(b)** to organize; *let's arrange to meet somewhere before we go to the theatre*; *the tour has been arranged by the travel agent*; *she arranged for a taxi to meet him at the airport*; *I've arranged with my mother that she will feed the cat while we're away* (NOTE: you arrange **for** someone to do something; you arrange **for** something to be done; or you arrange **to** do something)

arrangement [əˈreɪndʒmənt] *noun* **(a)** putting into an order; *the arrangement of the pictures in a book* **(b)** organizing; *all the arrangements for the wedding were left to the bride's mother* **(c)** general agreement; *we have an arrangement by which we meet for lunch every Tuesday*

array [əˈreɪ] *noun* display; *an array of flowers in front of the house*

arrears [əˈrɪəz] *noun* **(a)** money which should have been paid earlier; *she arranged to pay the arrears of rent in monthly instalments*; *he let the payments fall into arrears* **(b) to be in arrears** = to owe money which should have been paid earlier; *the payments are six months in arrears*; *he is six weeks in arrears with his rent*

arrest [əˈrest] **1** *noun* holding someone for breaking the law; *the police made several arrests at the demonstration*; **under arrest** = held by the police; *after the demonstration, three people were under arrest* **2** *verb* to hold someone for breaking the law; *the police arrested two men and took them to the police station*; *he ended up getting arrested by the police*; *he was arrested for stealing, but the judge let him off with a fine*

arrival [əˈraɪvl] *noun* **(a)** action of reaching a place; *we announce the arrival of flight AB 987 from Tangiers*; *the time of arrival is 5 p.m.*; *we apologize for the late arrival of the 14.25 Intercity express from Edinburgh*; **on arrival** = when you arrive; *on arrival at the hotel, members of the party will be allocated rooms* **(b)** person who has arrived; *he's a new arrival on our staff* **(c) arrivals** = part of an airport that deals with passengers who are arriving; *I'll wait for you in arrivals*; *compare* DEPARTURES **(d)** birth of a baby; *the arrival of their son was announced in the newspapers*

arrive [ə'raɪv] *verb* to reach a place; *the train from Paris arrives in London at 5 p.m.*; *when we arrived at the cinema we found it was full*; *they arrived home tired out* (NOTE: that you arrive **in a town** or **in a country** but **at a place**)

arrogance ['ærəgəns] *noun* being very proud of yourself, feeling that you are much better than others; *I can't stand his arrogance and pomposity*

arrogant ['ærəgənt] *adjective* very proud in an unpleasant way; *I've never known such an arrogant young man*; *because he was so arrogant, the people in his department refused to have anything to do with him*; *what an arrogant way to treat customers!*

arrow ['ærəʊ] *noun* (a) piece of wood with a sharp point, shot by a bow; *King Harold was killed by an arrow at the Battle of Hastings* (b) printed sign which points to something; *follow the arrows to the exhibition*

arrowhead ['ærəʊhed] *noun* sharp metal head attached to the end of an arrow; *the Battle of Hastings ended when an arrowhead entered King Harold's eye*

arse [ɑːs] *noun (vulgar)* buttocks, the part of the body you sit on; *he just sits on his arse all day while I have to do all the work*

arsenal ['ɑːsənl] *noun* (a) store of weapons; *all the weapons were removed from the arsenal before it was rebuilt*; *they agreed to destroy their nuclear arsenal* (b) collection of things which can be used; *the central bank has an arsenal of measures to control the economy*

arsenic ['ɑːsnɪk] *noun* very poisonous substance used for killing; *several pesticides contain arsenic* (NOTE: Chemical element: chemical symbol: **As**; atomic number: **33**)

arson ['ɑːsn] *noun* crime of setting fire to a building; *he was charged with arson*; *the police are treating it as a case of arson*; **an arson attack on a house** = setting fire to a house; *the arson attack on the house was racially motivated* (NOTE: no plural)

arsonist ['ɑːsənɪst] *noun* person who sets fire to buildings on purpose; *the arsonists who set fire to the church have still not been arrested*

art [ɑːt] *noun* (a) painting, drawing, etc.; *she is taking art lessons*; *he went to an exhibition at the local art college*; *when in Washington, do not miss the Museum of Modern Art*; **art gallery** = museum of paintings, sculptures, etc. (b) playing music, singing, etc.; *a musician who lives for her art*; *see also* ARTS

artefact ['ɑːtɪfækt] *noun* object made by man, such as a tool, dish, etc.; *the archaeological team found several artefacts dating from the Roman period*

arterial [ɑː'tɪəriəl] *adjective* (a) referring to arteries; *arterial blood is red blood which has received oxygen in the lungs and is being taken to the tissues* (b) **an arterial road** = a main road linking two towns

artery ['ɑːtəri] *noun* tube carrying blood from the heart round the body; *a main artery runs down the side of the neck*; *compare* VEIN (NOTE: plural is **arteries**)

artful ['ɑːtfʊl] *adjective* clever, good at tricking people; *he's an artful little chap!*

artfully ['ɑːtfʊli] *adverb* cleverly, in a way which deceives; *she artfully put the bright red apples on top of the rotten ones*

arthritic [ɑː'θrɪtɪk] **1** *adjective* affected by arthritis; *he has an arthritic hip* **2** *noun* person with arthritis; *her old mother is an arthritic and has great difficulty in walking*

arthritis [ɑː'θraɪtɪs] *noun* painful inflammation of a joint; *a joint which is badly damaged by arthritis may need to be replaced*; *her hands were swollen with arthritis*; **rheumatoid arthritis** = general painful disabling disease affecting any joint, but especially the hands, feet, and hips, making them swollen and inflamed; *more women than men are affected by rheumatoid arthritis*

artichoke ['ɑːtɪtʃəʊk] *noun* sort of vegetable; *the first time I was served an artichoke, I didn't know how to eat it*; *cook, drain and mash the Jerusalem artichokes, and then add butter, salt and pepper*

> COMMENT: there are two types of artichoke: the globe artichoke, a tall thistle-like plant (you boil the head and then eat the base of the leaves) and the Jerusalem artichoke, a tall plant which develops tubers like lumpy potatoes

article ['ɑːtɪkl] *noun* (a) report in a newspaper; *there's an interesting article on fishing in the newspaper*; *did you read the article on skiing in yesterday's paper?* (b) section of a legal agreement; *see article 8 of the treaty* (c) object, thing; *several articles of clothing were found near the road* (d) one of the parts of speech; *'the' is the definite article; 'a' is the indefinite article*

articulate 1 *verb* [ɑː'tɪkjʊleɪt] to speak words; *she articulated clearly so as to be understood* **2** *adjective* [ɑː'tɪkjʊlət] who expresses thoughts clearly; *she's very articulate for a seven-year-old*

articulated lorry [ɑː'tɪkjʊleɪtɪd 'lɒri] *noun* lorry with a trailer; *an articulated lorry overturned on the motorway*

articulation [ɑːtɪkjʊ'leɪʃn] *noun* (a) movement in a joint or series of joints; *inflammation is limiting his shoulder articulation* (b) speaking each sound clearly; *you need clear articulation for the post of telephonist*; *following his stroke he had to see the speech therapist to improve his articulation*

artifact ['ɑːtɪfækt] = ARTEFACT

artificial [ɑːtɪ'fɪʃl] *adjective* not real; *she was wearing artificial pearls*; **to give someone artificial respiration** = to revive someone who is almost dead by blowing air into their lungs

artillery [ɑː'tɪləri] *noun* guns in the army; **heavy artillery** = big guns

artisan [ɑːtɪ'zæn] *noun* craftsman, skilled person who works with his hands; *a colony of artisans and artists live in the Cornish village*

artist ['ɑːtɪst] *noun* person who paints, draws, etc.; *he collects paintings by 19th-century artists*; **pavement artist** = artist who draws pictures on the pavement with coloured chalks

artiste [ɑː'tiːst] *noun* professional singer, dancer, acrobat, etc.; *she belongs to a family of artistes, most of whom are dancers or tightrope walkers*

artistic [ɑː'tɪstɪk] *adjective* with feeling for art; *she is very artistic*; *he has an artistic temperament*

artistry ['ɑːtɪstri] *noun* skill in a particular art; *the samples of peasant embroidery show a high degree of artistry*

arts [ɑːts] **(a)** all work connected with art; *the Arts Minister or the Minister for the Arts* **(b)** subject taught which is not a science; *she has an arts degree*

artwork ['ɑːtwɜːk] *noun* drawings, designs, etc., which are to be used for printing in a book or as a poster, etc.; *the artwork has to be delivered by August 17th*; *the book is ready for printing and the artwork for the cover hasn't arrived*

arty (crafty) ['ɑːti 'krɑːfti] *adjective (informal)* pretending to be artistic; making artistic things; *his mother always looks very arty while his father, the judge, wears pinstripe suits*

as [æz] **1** *conjunction* **(a)** because; *as you can't drive, you'll have to go by bus*; *as it's cold, you should wear an overcoat* **(b)** at the same time as; *as he was getting into the bath, the telephone rang*; *the little girl ran into the road as the fire engine was turning the corner* **(c)** in this way; *leave everything as it is*; *you should take a holiday as the doctor told you* **2** *preposition* **(a)** in a certain job; *he had a job as a bus driver* **(b)** because you are; *as a doctor, he has to know the symptoms of all the common diseases* **(c)** like; *she was dressed as a nurse*; *they treated him as a friend of the family*

◊ **as...as** [æz] *(making comparative)* like; *she is as tall as I am*; *as black as coal*; *I can't run as fast as you*

◊ **as for** ['æz 'fɔː] *preposition* referring to; *as for him - he will have to take the bus*; *you play cards if you want to - as for me, I'm going to watch TV*

◊ **as from** ['æz 'frɒm] *preposition* from a time; *as from next Friday* = starting from next Friday

◊ **as if** *or* **as though** [əz 'ɪf *or* əz 'ðəʊ] in the same way as; *it looks as if it is going to be fine for the cricket match*; *she looked as if she was going to cry*; *he spoke very slowly, as though he was talking to a little child*

◊ **as well** ['æz 'wel] *phrase* in addition, also; *she came to have tea and brought her sister as well*; *we visited the castle and swam in the pool as well*

◊ **as well as** [əz 'wel æz] *phrase* in addition to, together with; *he has a cottage in the country as well as a flat in town*; *as well as being a maths teacher, he is a part-time policeman*

asap *or* **ASAP** [eɪeɪeɪ'piː] *(informal)* = AS SOON AS POSSIBLE; *I want it done asap*

asbestos [æs'bestəs] *noun* mineral which does not burn, used to protect against fire; *asbestos is now recognized as carcinogenic*

> COMMENT: asbestos was formerly widely used in cement and fireproof construction materials; it is now recognized that asbestos dust can cause many lung diseases, leading in some cases to forms of cancer

ascend [ə'send] *verb (formal)* **(a)** to go up; *the balloon rapidly ascended to 3000m* **(b)** to ascend the throne = to become king or queen; *the year 1509, in which Henry VIII ascended the throne*

ascendancy [ə'senəndsi] *noun* strong influence; *the Prime Minister is struggling to maintain his ascendancy over the party*; *she gained ascendancy over the rest of the staff*

ascendant [ə'sendənt] *noun* to be in the ascendant = to be becoming powerful or important; *the once powerless ecology committee has been in the ascendant since last year*

ascension [ə'senʃn] *noun (formal)* **(a)** moving upwards; *the rapid ascension of the balloon to 3000m* **(b)** ascension to the throne = becoming king or queen; *the Prince's ascension to the throne is automatic on the death of his father*

ascent [ə'sent] *noun* climbing up; *the first ascent of Everest was in 1952*; *tourists make the ascent to the monastery on donkeys* (NOTE: do not confuse with **assent**)

ascertain [æsə'teɪn] *verb (formal)* to check facts to see if they are true; *when will you be able to ascertain if any criminals are involved?*

ascetic [ə'setɪk] **1** *adjective* austere, without personal comforts or pleasures; *he lives an ascetic existence* **2** *noun* religious person who refuses comforts or pleasures; *he leads the life of an ascetic, praying most of the time and eating very little*

ascot ['æskət] *noun US* type of coloured scarf worn by men knotted round the neck inside the shirt; *ascots are not fashionable any more* (NOTE: British English is **cravat**)

ascribe [ə'skraɪb] *verb (formal)* to ascribe something to something *or* someone = to say that something is caused by something *or* someone; *he ascribed his business failures to bad luck*

asexual [eɪ'seksjʊəl] *adjective* without having sex; *a clone is derived from a cell by asexual reproduction*

ash [æʃ] *noun* **(a)** grey dust left after a fire, volcanic eruption, etc.; *there was a pile of ash left after the bonfire*; *a thick layer of ash from the volcano* (NOTE: no plural in this meaning, but see also **ashes**) **(b)** tree growing in the northern part of Europe; *ash trees have black buds and are the last trees to have leaves in springtime*

ashamed [ə'ʃeɪmd] *adjective* embarrassed and sorry (for what you have done or not done); *I am ashamed to say that I have never been to the Tate Gallery*; *she was ashamed of herself*; *it's nothing to be ashamed of*

ashen ['æʃən] *adjective* of a very pale grey colour; *she looked ashen as she came out of hospital*

ashes ['æʃɪz] *noun* **(a)** remains of someone who has been cremated; *he asked for his ashes to be scattered in the sea*; *her ashes were buried in the garden of remembrance* **(b)** the Ashes = cricket trophy given to the winner of test matches between England and Australia; *who won the Ashes two years ago?*

ashore [ə'ʃɔː] *adverb* onto land; *we went ashore at 3 p.m. and were back on board ship at four o'clock*; *the ship put its passengers ashore for a three-hour tour of the market*; *see also* SHORE

ashtray ['æʃtreɪ] *noun* little dish for cigarette ash; *there was no ashtray, so he asked the waiter for one*

Ash Wednesday ['æʃ 'wenzdi] *noun* the first day of Lent, the day after Shrove Tuesday

Asia ['eɪʒə] *noun* large continent running from the east of Europe to China and Japan; *the Trans-Siberian Railway crosses the deserts of central Asia*

Asian ['eɪʒən] **1** *adjective* referring to Asia **2** *noun* person coming from one of the countries of Asia

aside [ə'saɪd] *adverb* **(a)** to one side; *he took me aside and whispered in my ear*; *to put aside or to set aside* = to save money; *he is putting £50 aside each* *week to pay for his car* (b) *usually US* aside from = apart from; *aside from a minor infection, his health has been remarkably good*

ask [ɑːsk] *verb* (a) to put a question to get information; *she asked a policeman the way to the hospital*; *she went to the railway station to ask about cheap tickets*; *ask her how much her shoes cost* (b) to put a question to get someone to do something; *ask your father to teach you how to drive*; *can I ask you not to make so much noise?* (c) to invite; *we asked them round for dinner*; **to ask someone out** = to ask someone to go out to a restaurant, to a film, etc., with you; *don't ask her out - she always orders the most expensive things on the menu*

ask for ['ɑːsk 'fɔː] *verb* to say that you want something; *he asked Father Christmas for a new bike*; *she asked her boss for more money*; *someone came into the shop and asked for the manager*; **he asked for his book back** = he said that he wanted to have the book that he had lent

asking price ['ɑːskɪŋ 'praɪs] *noun* price at which the seller wants to sell something; *the asking price is £24,000*; *the buyer offered £5000 more than the asking price*

asleep [ə'sliːp] *adjective* sleeping; *he was asleep and didn't hear the fire alarm*; *they were lying asleep on the ground*; **she fell asleep** = she began to sleep; *see also* FAST ASLEEP (NOTE: **asleep** cannot be used in front of a noun: **the cat is asleep** but **a sleeping cat**)

asparagus [ə'spærəgəs] *noun* vegetable, a plant of which the young shoots are cut when they are about 25cm long and are eaten cooked; *asparagus is an expensive delicacy in winter*; *we used to grow asparagus in the garden*

aspect ['æspekt] *noun* (a) way of considering a situation, a problem; *I will examine several aspects of the problem* (b) direction which a house faces; *the living room has a southerly aspect*

aspen ['æspən] *noun* small tree of the poplar family, with pale leaves which flutter in the wind

asphalt ['æsfælt] 1 *noun* mixture of tar, small stones and sand used for making roads; *asphalt is normally used to make road surfaces* 2 *verb* to cover a road with asphalt; *the path will be asphalted during the summer*

asphyxia [əs'fɪksiə] *noun* suffocation, condition where someone is prevented from breathing and therefore cannot take oxygen into the bloodstream; *artificial respiration is often given in cases of asphyxia*

> COMMENT: asphyxia can be caused by strangling, or by breathing poisonous gases or by having your head in a plastic bag, etc.

asphyxiate [əs'fɪksɪeɪt] *verb* to stop someone breathing; *he was asphyxiated by the smoke*

asphyxiation [əsfɪksɪ'eɪʃn] *noun* death by being unable to breathe; *the verdict was: asphyxiation by smoke inhalation*

aspiration [æspɪ'reɪʃn] *noun* (*formal*) ambition; *he has aspirations to become a concert pianist*

aspire [ə'spaɪə] *verb* **to aspire to something** = to have the ambition to get something; *he aspires to great success as an actor*

aspirin ['æsprɪn] *noun* (a) common drug, used to stop the symptoms of flu, colds, headaches, etc.; *she always keeps a bottle of aspirin in her bag*; *aspirin inhibits the clotting of blood* (b) one tablet of aspirin; *take a couple of aspirins and lie down*

aspiring [ə'spaɪrɪŋ] *adjective* hoping to get something; *a crowd of aspiring actors*

ass [æs] *noun* (a) (*old*) donkey; *the men were riding asses* (b) (*informal*) stupid person; *don't be such an ass!*; *he's an ass - he should have accepted straight away* (NOTE: plural is **asses**)

assail [ə'seɪl] *verb* (*formal*) to attack; *the bus was assailed with a shower of stones*; *he was assailed with doubts*

assailant [ə'seɪlənt] *noun* (*formal*) person who attacks; *she did not see her assailant very clearly in the dark*

assassin [ə'sæsɪn] *noun* person who kills someone famous for political reasons; *the assassins were waiting for the President's car to turn the corner*; *the hired assassin took the money and then vanished*

assassinate [ə'sæsɪneɪt] *verb* to kill a famous person for political reasons; *do you remember the day when the President was assassinated?*

assassination [əsæsɪ'neɪʃn] *noun* political killing; *an assassination attempt against the President*

assault [ə'sɔːlt] 1 *noun* attack; *troops are getting ready for the assault*; *he was accused of assault on a police officer* 2 *verb* to attack; *he was arrested for assaulting a police officer*

assault force [ə'sɔːlt 'fɔːs] *noun* group of soldiers who attack something; *the assault force was led by a young inexperienced officer*

assemble [ə'sembl] *verb* (a) to come together; *the fans assembled at the gates of the football ground* (b) to put together; *the cars are assembled in Scotland*

assembly [ə'sembli] *noun* (a) meeting; *the General Assembly of the United Nations*; **school assembly** = meeting of all the children in a school, normally at the beginning of the morning, when prayers are said, and notices read out (NOTE: plural in this meaning is **assemblies**) (b) putting together; *the parts are shipped to Hong Kong for assembly*; **assembly line** = moving line in a factory, where the product moves slowly past workers who add pieces to it as it goes past; *he works on an assembly line* or *he is an assembly line worker*

assent [ə'sent] 1 *noun* (*formal*) agreement; *she gave her assent to the plan*; **Royal Assent** = formal passing of a Bill into law to become an Act of Parliament (NOTE: do not confuse with **ascent**) 2 *verb* **to assent to something** = to agree to something; *the committee assented to the suggestion*

assert [ə'sɜːt] *verb* to state firmly; *he asserted that he had never seen her before*; *she continues to assert her innocence*; **to assert yourself** = to make your opinions felt

assertion [ə'sɜːʃn] *noun* statement of something which you believe to be true; *counsel made a series of assertions which were disputed by the witness*

assertive [ə'sɜːtɪv] *adjective* confident and forceful; *her assertive tone of voice silenced her critics*; *you should try to be a little more assertive*

assess [ə'ses] *verb* (a) to calculate an amount to be paid; *damages were assessed at £1m* (b) to calculate the value of; *how do you assess United's performance today?; teachers have to assess each student once a term*

assessment [ə'sesmənt] *noun* (a) calculation of amount to be paid; *assessment of the damages will take about a week; see also* SELF-ASSESSMENT (b) calculation of value; *what's your assessment of United's performance today?; student assessments showed that some were failing behind*

assessor [ə'sesə] *noun* (a) person who calculates how much insurance should be paid; *the insurance assessor must see your car to judge the extent of the damage* (b) person who calculates the value of something; *he's a very experienced assessor, and I am sure that the value he gave is correct* (c) person who calculates the results of candidates in an examination; *the assessor found that a mistake had been made in calculating the marks*

asset ['æsɪt] *noun* (a) valuable quality; *knowing several languages is an asset* (b) assets = valuable things which are owned; *they will have to sell some of their assets to repay the debt*

assiduity [æsɪ'djuːɪti] *noun (formal)* working in a careful and regular way; *her lack of assiduity lost her her job*

assiduous [ə'sɪdjuəs] *adjective* careful and regular; *these students are very assiduous workers - I wouldn't want to see them fail the course*

assign [ə'saɪn] *verb* (a) to assign someone to = to appoint someone to do something; *she was assigned to the ear, nose and throat section of the hospital; we are assigning you to work in the accounts department* (b) to assign something to someone = to give or allocate something to someone; *he was assigned the job of cleaning the kitchen; she was assigned a bedroom on the ground floor*

assignment [ə'saɪnmənt] *noun* (a) appointment of someone to a job; *Inspector Murray's assignment to the investigation did not please everyone* (b) job of work; *he was given the assignment of reporting on the war* (c) written work given to a student; *I have two assignments which must be in by the end of the week*

assimilate [ə'sɪmɪleɪt] *verb* (a) to learn and understand; *he quickly assimilated the instructions he had been given* (b) to digest food; *she has difficulty in assimilating greasy food* (c) to assimilate *or* to be assimilated into a group = to become part of a group; *she assimilated into the teaching community very easily*

assimilation [əsɪmɪ'leɪʃn] *noun* action of assimilating; *the soldiers' rapid assimilation of difficult instructions was surprising; this medicine will help the assimilation of calcium; his assimilation into the group was not without problems*

assist [ə'sɪst] *verb (formal)* to help; *he assists me with my income tax forms; I will be assisted in my work by Miss Smith* (NOTE: you assist someone **in** doing something or **with** something)

assistance [ə'sɪstəns] *noun* help; *he was trying to change the wheel, when a truck drew up and the driver offered his assistance; he asked if he could be of any assistance; she will need assistance with her luggage;* financial assistance = help in the form of money

assistant [ə'sɪstənt] *noun* person who helps; *his assistant works in the office next door;* shop assistant = person who serves the customers in a shop; assistant manager = person who is second-in-command to a manager

associate 1 [ə'səʊsieɪt] *verb* to associate with = to be linked with, to have dealings with; *I don't want you to associate with that family - they've all been in trouble with the police; the government is closely associated with the project* **2** [ə'səʊsiət] *noun* person who works in the same business as someone; *she is a business associate of mine*

associated [ə'səʊsieɪtɪd] *adjective* linked with; *the sales division and all associated departments*

association [əsəʊsi'eɪʃn] *noun* (a) official group, group of companies in the same trade; *an association offering support to victims of street violence; the Association of British Travel Agents* (b) connection between things; *for some people, a black cat has an association with luck; Manchester has strong family associations for him* (c) in association with = together with, sponsored by; *the guidebook is published in association with the local tourist board; this programme is brought to you in association with British Airways*

assorted [ə'sɔːtɪd] *adjective* various, mixed; *the sweets come in assorted colours*

assortment [ə'sɔːtmənt] *noun* mixture of different shapes, colours, styles, etc.; *the shop has a wide assortment of women's clothes*

assuage [ə'sweɪdʒ] *verb (formal)* to calm or soothe something unpleasant; *she tried to assuage his grief after the death of his son*

assume [ə'sjuːm] *verb* (a) to suppose; *let's assume that he is innocent; I assume you have enough money to pay for the meal?* (b) to take on; *when she was twenty-one, she assumed complete control of the family business; he has assumed responsibility for fire safety*

assumed name [ə'sjuːmd 'neɪm] *noun* false name; *he travelled to Russia under an assumed name*

assuming [ə'sjuːmɪŋ] *conjunction* supposing; *your luggage, assuming you have any, will be sent on ahead; assuming that the car really has been stolen, then we need to inform the police*

assumption [ə'sʌmpʃn] *noun* (a) supposing something is true; *we must go on the assumption that she was murdered* (b) *(formal)* assumption of office = starting your duties

assurance [ə'ʃʊərəns] *noun* (a) promise; *she gave her assurance that she would not do it again* (b) guarantee; *there is no assurance that he will ever pay the damages* (c) life assurance = insurance which pays if someone dies; *she took out a life assurance policy* (NOTE: **assurance** is used in Britain for insurance policies relating to something which will certainly happen, such as death; otherwise, **insurance** is used)

assure [ə'ʃʊə] *verb* (a) to state definitely; *I can assure you we will do everything to try to find your missing daughter* (b) to make sure; *you are assured of a warm welcome in that hotel* (c) to insure; *to assure someone's life*

assured [ə'ʃʊəd] *adjective* very certain and confident; *she looks so assured up there on the stage*

asterisk ['æstərɪsk] *noun* printing sign (*) like a star, used to refer to something such as a footnote; *put an asterisk next to the word which is explained in the footnote*

astern [ə'stɜːn] *adverb* **(a)** behind a ship; *we left the Statue of Liberty astern* **(b)** *(of a ship)* **to go astern** = to go backwards; *the ferry had to go full speed astern so as not to hit the barge*

asteroid ['æstərɔɪd] *noun* little planet; *asteroids vary in sizes, the smallest ones can be only 100m across*

COMMENT: asteroids belong to the solar system: most are in orbit between Mars and Jupiter

asthma ['æsmə] *noun* breathing difficulty, often caused by an allergy; *she has chronic asthma*

asthmatic [æs'mætɪk] **1** *adjective* referring to asthma; *he has an asthmatic attack every spring*; *their little girl is asthmatic* **2** *noun* person who has asthma; *being an asthmatic he always carries an inhaler with him*

astonish [ə'stɒnɪʃ] *verb* to surprise very much; *his confidence astonished everyone who met him*; *it astonishes me that he ever manages to get to work on time*

astonished [ə'stɒnɪʃt] *adjective* very surprised; *we were astonished to learn that he had died*; *she stood on a table and started to dance, watched by an astonished crowd*

astonishing [ə'stɒnɪʃɪŋ] *adjective* very surprising; *they spent an astonishing amount of money buying Christmas presents*; *for an eight-year-old her violin technique is astonishing*

astonishingly [ə'stɒnɪʃɪŋli] *adverb* very surprisingly; *the teacher was astonishingly calm considering she was surrounded by screaming children*

astonishment [ə'stɒnɪʃmənt] *noun* great surprise; *he turned pale in astonishment at the sight*; *she could not hide her astonishment at the news*; *to my great astonishment they paid the bill in full*

astound [ə'staund] *verb* to surprise someone completely; *the club's win astounded their fans*; *the results of the test astounded the doctors*

astounded [ə'staundɪd] *adjective* very surprised; *he waved his hands above his head to the cheers of his astounded fans*; *we were all astounded to hear that he had got married*; *I'm astounded that he hasn't phoned*

astounding [ə'staundɪŋ] *adjective* very surprising; *it was an astounding circus performance*; *it was astounding that no one was killed in the accident*

astral ['æstrəl] *adjective* referring to stars

astray [ə'streɪ] *adverb* **to go astray** = to get lost; *yet another spoon seems to have gone astray, we can't find it anywhere*; **to lead someone astray** = to encourage someone to bad habits; *it appears that the boy was led astray by some of the older boys at school*

astringent [ə'strɪndʒənt] **1** *adjective* **(a)** harsh or severe; *some astringent remarks by the chairman* **(b)** which helps stop the skin being oily and also stops bleeding; *an astringent cream* **2** *noun* ointment for making the skin less oily or for stopping bleeding; *use an astringent to stop the bleeding on your cheek*

astrologer [ə'strɒlədʒə] *noun* person who forecasts what will happen from the positions of the planets and stars; *to give you an accurate horoscope, an astrologer must know not only your date of birth, but also the place and time*

astrological [æstrə'lɒdʒɪkl] *adjective* referring to astrology; *astrological horoscopes are based on the position of the stars and planets in the sky*

astrology [ə'strɒlədʒi] *noun* foretelling the future from the stars; *he is a great believer in astrology - he reads his horoscope in the paper every day* (NOTE: no plural)

astronaut ['æstrənɔːt] *noun* person who travels into space in a spacecraft; *one of the astronauts had to get out of the spacecraft to do some repair work*

astronomer [ə'strɒnəmə] *noun* person who studies astronomy; *a group of astronomers met to observe the comet*

astronomical [æstrə'nɒmɪkl] *adjective* **(a)** referring to astronomy; *using a radio telescope gives much more accurate astronomical measurements* **(b)** *(informal)* very large; *he was paid an astronomical sum*; *she earns an astronomical salary*

astronomy [ə'strɒnəmi] *noun* study of the stars, sun, planets; *more people are interested in astronomy since the papers wrote about the comet*

astute [ə'stjuːt] *adjective* clever at understanding things quickly; *she's a very astute businesswoman*; *he's astute at getting the best deal possible*; *the board was impressed by his astute answers to their questions during the interview*

asylum [ə'saɪləm] *noun* safe refuge from enemies; *people seeking asylum in Britain*; **to ask for political asylum** = to ask permission to stay in another country, because the political situation in your own country makes it unsafe for you to stay there (NOTE: no plural)

asylum seeker [ə'saɪləm 'siːkə] *noun* person who asks for political asylum; *the government insists that all asylum seekers should follow the correct procedure*

at [æt] *preposition* **(a)** *(showing time)* *we'll meet at eleven o'clock*; *you must put your lights on when you drive at night*; *at the weekend, we went to see my mother*; *we went to Paris at Easter* **(b)** *(showing place)* *meet us at the post office*; *she's got a job at the supermarket*; *he's not at home, he's at work* **(c)** *(showing speed)* *the train was travelling at 200 kilometres an hour* **(d)** *(showing direction)* *they threw rotten eggs at the speaker* (NOTE: **at** is often used after verbs: **look at, point at**, etc.)

ate [eɪt] *see* eat

atheism ['eɪθiɪzm] *noun* belief that there is no god; *he ended his book on religions with a chapter on atheism*

atheist ['eɪθiɪst] *noun* person who believes there is no god; *by the age of 17 he had become an atheist and remained so until his death*; *compare* AGNOSTIC

athlete ['æθliːt] *noun* sportsman who competes in races, etc.; *the Olympic athletes marched round the stadium*

athletic [æθ'letɪk] *adjective* referring to sport; *the athletic events start at 2.30*

athletics [æθ'letɪks] *noun* organized sports; *at school I hated athletics*; *we spent the afternoon watching athletics on TV*

Atlantic (Ocean) [ət'læntɪk 'əuʃən] *noun* ocean between the Americas and Europe and Africa; *she sailed across the Atlantic on her own*

atlas ['ætləs] *noun* book of maps; *can you find Montserrat in the Atlas?* (NOTE: plural is **atlases**)

ATM ['eɪtiː'em] = AUTOMATED TELLER MACHINE

atmosphere ['ætməsfɪə] *noun* **(a)** air around the earth; *the atmosphere surrounds the earth to a height of several hundred kilometres* **(b)** general feeling; *the atmosphere in the office was tense*; *I like the friendly atmosphere in our college*

atmospheric [ætməs'ferɪk] *adjective* **(a)** referring to the atmosphere; *signal reception is bad due to unsettled atmospheric conditions*; **atmospheric pressure** = normal pressure of the air on the surface of the earth; *atmospheric pressure decreases with altitude - it is lower at 5000m than at 500m* **(b)** mysterious, beautiful; *the lighting under the trees created an atmospheric effect in the gardens*

atoll ['ætɒl] *noun* coral island shaped like a ring; *the atolls of the Pacific Ocean*

atom ['ætəm] *noun* **(a)** basic particle of matter; *all substances are composed of atoms*; *splitting an atom releases energy* **(b)** very small thing; *not an atom of dust must get into the watch*; *there's not an atom of evidence against him*

atomic [ə'tɒmɪk] *adjective* referring to atoms; **atomic bomb** = bomb using nuclear energy; **atomic energy** = energy created during a nuclear reaction, as in a nuclear reactor

atomizer ['ætəmaɪzə] *noun* device which sprays liquid, such as perfume, in a mist; *perfume in an atomizer is more expensive*

atrium ['eɪtriəm] *noun* **(a)** very large open space in a building, usually with a glass roof, fountains and plants, which acts as a central meeting point; *we'll meet in the atrium of the conference hotel* **(b)** one of the two chambers in the heart (NOTE: plural is **atria**)

atrocity [ə'trɒsɪti] *noun* very wicked deed; *atrocities were committed by both armies* (NOTE: plural is **atrocities**)

atrocious [ə'trəuʃəs] *adjective* **(a)** very bad; *the weather on holiday was absolutely atrocious*; *the fog caused atrocious driving conditions on the motorway*; *she has an atrocious singing voice* **(b)** very wicked; *the army committed atrocious acts of brutality against the refugees*

atrophy ['ætrəfi] **1** *noun* wasting away of an organ or other part of the body **2** *verb* to waste away, to become smaller; *his muscles had atrophied from lying in bed so long*

attach [ə'tætʃ] *verb* **(a)** to fasten; *the gate is attached to the post*; *I am attaching a copy of my previous letter* **(b)** to consider that something has a particular quality; *she attaches great importance to hygiene*

attaché [ə'tæʃeɪ] *noun* diplomat who deals with a special type of work; *a commercial attaché*; *a military attaché*

attaché case [ə'tæʃeɪ 'keɪs] *noun* briefcase for papers; *an elegant leather attaché case could cost around £100*

attachment [ə'tætʃmənt] *noun* **(a)** thing which can be attached to something; *the camera has several attachments*; *I don't use half the attachments which come with the food processor* **(b)** affection; *everyone knew of his attachment to her*; *he formed an attachment to the girl next door* **(c)** *(formal)* **attachment of earnings** = legal power to take money from a person's salary to pay money which is owed to the courts; *he will be subject to an attachment of earnings if he doesn't pay the fine on time*

attack [ə'tæk] **1** *noun* **(a)** trying to hurt someone or something; *they made an attack on the town*; **under attack** = being attacked; *the town is under attack from rebel guerrillas* **(b)** criticism; *he launched an attack on the government* **(c)** sudden illness; *she had an attack of malaria* **2** *verb* to try to hurt someone or something; *three men attacked her and stole her watch*; *the old lady was attacked by muggers*; *they attacked the enemy camp*

attacker [ə'tækə] *noun* person who attacks; *can you describe your attacker?*

attain [ə'teɪn] *verb (formal)* to reach; *he attained the position of manager*

attainment [ə'teɪnmənt] *noun* **(a)** reaching; *his attainment of his sales target* **(b) attainments** = successes; *his attainments on the sports field*

attempt [ə'tempt] **1** *noun* try; *he failed in his attempt to climb Mount Everest*; *all his attempts to get a job have failed*; *we closed down one shop in an attempt to cut costs*; *she passed her driving test at her second attempt* **2** *verb* to try; *she attempted to commit suicide*

attempted [ə'temptɪd] *adjective* which has been tried; *he was accused of attempted murder*

attend [ə'tend] *verb* to be present at; *she attended the wedding*; *they organized a protest meeting but only one or two people attended*

attendance [ə'tendəns] *noun* **(a)** being present; *your attendance at the opening ceremony is required*; **in attendance** = being present as helper; *the Queen unveiled the memorial, with Major Jones in attendance* **(b)** the number of people present; *there was huge attendance on the first day of the show* (NOTE: no plural)

attendant [ə'tendənt] *noun* **(a)** person on duty; *ask the lavatory attendant if he found your wallet*; **flight attendant** = air hostess or steward, person who looks after passengers on a plane; *press the button to call the flight attendant* **(b)** person on duty in a museum; *the attendant asked her to open her bag* **(c)** person who helps someone during a ceremony; *one of the bride's attendants fainted*

attend to [ə'tend 'tuː] *verb* **(a)** to give careful thought to something and deal with it; *the manager will attend to your complaint himself* **(b)** to attend to someone *or* to someone's needs = to look after a customer, patient, etc.; *wait here, please, someone will attend to you in a moment*

attention [ə'tenʃən] *noun* **(a)** careful thinking; *don't distract the driver's attention*; **for the attention of (FAO)** = words written on a letter to show that a certain person must see it and deal with it; *mark your letter 'for the attention of the Managing Director'*; **to pay attention to** = to note and think about something carefully; *pay attention to the instructions in the leaflet*; *don't pay any attention to what she says!* **(b)** position of a soldier, standing straight, with heels together and looking straight ahead; *the guards stood to attention at the entrance of the palace*

attentive [ə'tentɪv] *adjective* **(a)** being careful when dealing with someone; *the manager was very attentive to her needs* **(b)** listening carefully; *the students were very attentive as the teacher explained the problem*

attest [ə'test] *verb (formal)* **to attest to something** = to swear that something is true; *many people attested to his honesty*; **attested herd of cows** = cows which have been tested and found to be free of tuberculosis

attestation [ætes'teɪʃn] *noun (formal)* legal statement that something is true; *his attestation was sworn before a solicitor*

attic ['ætɪk] *noun* room at the top of a house under a roof; *he slowly climbed up the stairs to the attic*; *the house has two attic bedrooms* (NOTE: also called a **loft**)

attire [ə'taɪə] *noun (formal)* clothing; *the men were all dressed in evening attire* (NOTE: no plural)

attired [ə'taɪəd] *adjective (formal)* dressed; *they were attired more for the beach than for the office*; **attired in** = wearing; *she was attired in purple silk*

attitude ['ætɪtjuːd] *noun* **(a)** way of standing, sitting, etc.; *his portrait shows him in a thoughtful attitude* **(b)** way of thinking; *what is the government's attitude to the problem?*

attorney [ə'tɜːni] *noun* **(a)** *(especially US)* lawyer; *after his arrest he tried to call his attorney* **(b)** **power of attorney** = written document, which gives someone power to act on behalf of someone else; *she's going to the solicitor's today to sign the power of attorney*

Attorney-General [ə'tɜːni 'dʒenrəl] *noun* **(a)** *GB* one of the Law Officers in the government; *this legal matter falls within the competence of the Attorney-General* **(b)** *US* head of legal affairs in the federal government; *the new Attorney-General is well known in the legal world*

COMMENT: in the US federal government, the Attorney-General is in charge of the Department of Justice

attract [ə'trækt] *verb* to make someone come near; *the shops are lowering their prices to attract more customers*; *the exhibition attracted hundreds of visitors*; *we must see if we can attract more candidates for the job*; **to be attracted to someone** = to feel a sexual interest in someone; *I can't understand why she's attracted to him*

attraction [ə'trækʃn] *noun* **(a)** the ability to attract; *the attraction of a large salary*; *what is the attraction of cricket?* **(b)** something which attracts people; *the Tower of London is a great tourist attraction* **(c)** *(in physics)* act of attracting something; *the attraction of magnets* (NOTE: the opposite in this meaning is **repulsion**)

attractive [ə'træktɪv] *adjective* **(a)** pleasant-looking; *they found the Lake District very attractive*; *she's an attractive young girl* **(b)** which attracts; *there are some attractive bargains on offer*; *the rival firm made him a very attractive offer*; **attractive salary** = good salary to make sure many people will apply for the job

attributable [ə'trɪbjutəbl] *adjective* which probably was caused by; *the disaster is attributable to a simple error*

attribute 1 *noun* ['ætrɪbjuːt] quality; *loyalty and a good sense of humour are the most important attributes of a secretary* **2** *verb* [ə'trɪbjuːt]; **to attribute something to** = (i) to say that something was caused by

something; (ii) to say that something was said or written by someone; *the accident was attributed to faulty brakes*; *the remark was attributed to his father*

attribution [ætrɪ'bjuːʃn] *noun* **attribution to** = (i) saying that something was caused by something; (ii) saying that something was said or written by someone; *the inspectors' attribution of the accident to faulty brakes*; *his attribution of the poem to Shakespeare*

attributive [ə'trɪbjuːtɪv] *adjective* **attributive adjective** = adjective which comes before a noun and describes it

COMMENT: in 'the cold weather' the word 'cold' is attributive (as opposed to 'the weather is cold' where it is predicative)

attrition [ə'trɪʃn] *noun* wearing down of an enemy, etc., until they become weak; *they won their case by a process of attrition*; **war of attrition** = war where you try to wear down the enemy; *to wage a war of attrition*

atypical [eɪ'tɪpɪkl] *adjective* not typical; *this behaviour is quite atypical of monkeys*

aubergine ['əubəʒiːn] *noun* dark purple shiny fruit of a small plant, used as a vegetable; *she had stuffed aubergines as a starter* (NOTE: American English is **eggplant**)

auburn ['ɔːbən] *adjective* reddish-brown, like chestnuts; *she has long auburn hair*

auction ['ɔːkʃn] **1** *noun* sale to the person who makes the highest bid in public; *the house was sold by auction*; *I bought the painting at an auction*; **to put something up for auction** = to offer something for sale at an auction **2** *verb* to sell to the person who makes the highest bid in public; *they are auctioning all grandmother's possessions*; *the princess's dresses will be auctioned for charity*

auctioneer [ɔːkʃə'nɪə] *noun* person who runs an auction; *the auctioneer started the bidding at £500*

auction off ['ɔːkʃən 'ɒf] *verb* to get rid of by auction; *the company was put into liquidation and its stock was auctioned off*

auction rooms ['ɔːkʃən 'ruːmz] *noun* place where auctions are held; *the auction rooms were filled with antique dealers*

audacious [ɔː'deɪʃəs] *adjective* very brave or risky; *it was audacious of him to try to dance with the mafia boss's daughter*; *they rejected his audacious request for a salary increase after only four weeks in the job*

audacity [ɔː'dæsɪti] *noun* great daring; *he had the audacity to come in here and ask me for money, when he already owes me thousands of pounds!*

audible ['ɔːdɪbl] *adjective* which can be heard; *there was an audible sigh of relief from the audience when the heroine was rescued*

audience ['ɔːdɪəns] *noun* **(a)** people at a theatre, cinema, concert hall, or watching TV or listening to the radio; *members of the audience cheered*; *there was a huge audience on the first night of the play* **(b)** allowing you to speak to someone; *the ambassador had an audience with the President*

audio- ['ɔːdɪəu] *prefix* referring to sound; **audiocassette** = cassette with sound; **audio tape** = special magnetic tape on which sounds can be recorded

audit ['ɔːdɪt] **1** *noun* official check of accounts; *the auditors are carrying out the annual audit* **2** *verb* to check accounts officially; *the accounts have not yet been audited*

audition [ɔː'dɪʃn] **1** *noun* test for actors, singers, dancers, etc., to see if they will be given a part in a play or film; *we are holding an audition tomorrow morning*; *I'm going for an audition for a part in 'Hamlet'* **2** *verb* **(a)** to test actors, singers, dancers, etc.; *they auditioned fifty-five little girls before they found the right one* **(b)** *(of actor)* **to audition for a part** = to do a test; *two hundred children auditioned for the part of the Artful Dodger*

auditor ['ɔːdɪtə] *noun* accountant who checks accounts officially; *the company's auditors are appointed at the AGM*

auditorium [ɔːdɪ'tɔːriəm] *noun* large hall for concerts, ceremonies, etc.; *the prize-giving will be held in the school auditorium* (NOTE: plural is **auditoriums** or **auditoria**)

augment [ɔːg'ment] *verb* (*formal*) to increase; *you can augment your resistance to illness by adopting a more healthy diet*; *pensioners' allowances will be augmented by £5 a week from January*

augmentation [ɔːgmen'teɪʃn] *noun* (*formal*) increase; *there will be no augmentation in the allowances paid to pensioners*

August ['ɔːgəst] *noun* eighth month of the year, the month after July and before September; *my birthday is in August*; *I left my job last August*; *today is August 15th US August 15* (NOTE: **August 15th** or **August 15:** say 'August the fifteenth' or 'the fifteenth of August'; American English: 'August fifteenth')

aunt [ɑːnt] *noun* sister of mother or father; wife of an uncle; *say goodbye to Aunt Anne*; *she lives next door to my aunt*

au pair [əʊ 'peə] *noun* person, usually a girl, who lives with a family in another country to learn the language while looking after children and doing light housework; *she is going to Germany to work as an au pair in a doctor's family* (NOTE: plural is **au pairs**)

aura ['ɔːrə] *noun* general feeling or quality; *the aura of victory which hung over him has begun to slip*

aural ['ɔːrəl] *adjective* referring to hearing; *people with a good aural memory can play music by ear* (NOTE: do not confuse with **oral**)

auspices ['ɔːspɪsɪz] *noun* **under the auspices of** = subsidized by or organized by; *the concert is being held under the auspices of the local Chamber of Commerce*

auspicious [ɔː'spɪʃəs] *adjective* which is going to be successful; *today is a very auspicious occasion for our school*

Aussie ['ɒzi] *noun & adjective* (*informal*) Australian; *there was a group of Aussies in the restaurant* (NOTE: plural is **Aussies**)

austere [ɔː'stɪə] *adjective* **(a)** plain, with no ornaments; *an austere mountain chapel*; *an austere looking priest* **(b)** without luxury; *the austere life of the monks*

austerity [ɔː'sterɪti] *noun* **(a)** lack of luxury; being austere; *the austerity of the inside of the great cathedral* **(b)** poor living conditions because people do not have much money; *in times of austerity, people ate very little*; **austerity programme** = planned way of cutting down on expenditure; *the government has*

introduced an austerity programme to try to rescue the economy

Australia [ɒs'treɪliə] *proper noun* large country, covering a whole continent in the south west of the Pacific Ocean; *they went to Australia by boat*; *she spent all her savings on a holiday in Australia* (NOTE: capital: **Canberra**; people: **Australians**; language: **English**; currency: **Australian dollar**)

Australian [ɒs'treɪliən] **1** *adjective* referring to Australia; *an Australian dollar*; *the Australian Prime Minister*; *I'm letting my house to an Australian family for the summer*; *his wife is Australian* **2** *noun* person who lives in or comes from Australia; *we beat the Australians at cricket last year*; *I met an Australian in the train*

Australian Rules football [ɒs'treɪliən 'ruːlz 'fʊtbɒl] *noun* sport played by two teams of eighteen players on an oval field with an oval ball - the object being to score points by kicking the ball over the opponents' goal line (NOTE: in Australia the game is often called **Footie**)

COMMENT: the pitches are often cricket pitches out of season and at each end have two tall goal posts without a crossbar. A goal worth 6 points is scored by a player kicking the ball cleanly through the two goal posts. The game is divided into four 25-minute quarters and each side is allowed two interchangeable substitutes. Despite being definitely a contact sport, the players do not wear any protective clothing. Players may run with the ball - as long as they bounce it or touch it to the ground every 15m - or they may kick it and punch it but are not allowed to throw it.

Austria ['ɒstriə] *noun* country in central Europe, south of Germany and east of Switzerland; *we often go skiing in Austria*; *they are moving to Austria as her father has a business in Vienna* (NOTE: capital: **Vienna**; people: **Austrians**; language: **German**; currency: **schilling, euro**)

Austrian ['ɒstriən] **1** *adjective* referring to Austria; *you can get Austrian wine in some supermarkets*; *an Austrian family has bought the house next door to us* **2** *noun* person from Austria; *the group was made up mainly of Germans and Austrians*

authentic [ɔː'θentɪk] *adjective* genuine; *is it an authentic Picasso or a copy?*; *he believed the diaries to be authentic*

authenticate [ɔː'θentɪkeɪt] *verb* to prove that something is genuine; *the old map which was found recently has been authenticated as a genuine and important document*

authentication [ɔːθentɪ'keɪʃn] *noun* proving that something is genuine; *the painting was sent to experts for authentication*

authenticity [ɔːθen'tɪsɪti] *noun* being genuine; *the police are checking the authenticity of the letter*

author ['ɔːθə] *noun* writer; *the books are written under a pseudonym and no one knows who the author is*; *she is the author of a popular series of children's books*

authoritarian [ɔːθɒrɪ'teəriən] *adjective* controlling people strictly; *Victorian fathers are often pictured as authoritarian*

authoritative [ɔː'θɒrɪtətɪv] *adjective* **(a)** in a commanding way; *he spoke in an authoritative voice* **(b)** which is an authority; *this is the authoritative work on the meaning of Shakespeare's 'Macbeth'*

authority [ɔː'θɒrɪti] *noun* **(a)** power to do something; *he has no authority to act on our behalf* **(b)** permission to do something; *he signed without having my authority to do so* **(c)** source of information; *what is his authority for the story?* **(d)** ruling organization; *the education authority pays teachers' salaries*; **local authority** = council which runs a town or country area; **the authorities** = the government; *the authorities have cancelled his visa* **(e)** expert; *he's an authority on Greek literature* (NOTE: plural is **authorities**)

authorization [ɔːθəraɪ'zeɪʃn] *noun* official permission; *she wrote the letter without our authorization*; *do you have authorization for this expenditure?*; *he has no authorization to act on our behalf*

authorize ['ɔːθəraɪz] *verb* to give permission for something to be done; *to authorize payment of £10,000*; *to authorize someone to act on the company's behalf*

authorship ['ɔːθəʃɪp] *noun* being an author; the identity of an author; *the authorship of the letters is in doubt*

autism ['ɔːtɪzm] *noun* condition of children and adolescents where patients are completely absorbed in themselves and pay no attention to anyone else

autistic [ɔː'tɪstɪk] *adjective* having autism; *the school caters for children with special needs, such as autistic children*

auto ['ɔːtəʊ] *noun* car; *he runs a small auto spares store*; **auto insurance** = insurance covering a car, its driver and others

autobiographical [ɔːtəbaɪə'græfɪkl] *adjective* referring to the writer's life; *her latest novel is supposed to be autobiographical*

autobiography [ɔːtəbaɪ'ɒgrəfi] *noun* story of the life of a person written by himself or herself; *he's writing his autobiography*; *I'm reading the autobiography of a cabinet minister*

autocracy [ɔː'tɒkrəsi] *noun* government by an autocrat; *what can be said in favour of autocracy?*

autocrat ['ɔːtəkræt] *noun* (*often as criticism*) dictator, a ruler with total power over the people he rules; *like any other autocrat, he does exactly as he wants*

autocratic [ɔːtə'krætɪk] *adjective* ruling like an autocrat; *his autocratic style annoyed some of the staff*; **autocratic regime** = government by autocrats; *under the autocratic regime of the generals, all free newspapers were suppressed*

autograph ['ɔːtəgrɑːf] *noun* signature of a famous person; *he asked the footballer for his autograph*; **autograph hunter** = person who tries to meet famous people to get their autographs

automaker ['ɔːtəʊmeɪkə] *noun US* company which makes cars (NOTE: British English is **car manufacturer**)

automate ['ɔːtəmeɪt] *verb* to put in machines to do work which formerly was done by people; *we are in the process of automating our invoice system*

automated ['ɔːtəmeɪtɪd] *adjective* using machines in place of people; *the car factory is almost completely*

automated; *a fully automated assembly plant has opened recently*; *US* **automated teller machine (ATM)** = machine outside a bank from which you can get money when you insert a card and follow certain instructions (NOTE: British English is a **cashpoint machine**)

automatic [ɔːtə'mætɪk] **1** *adjective* which works by itself; *there is an automatic device which cuts off the electric current*; **automatic pilot** = device which flies a plane, allowing the pilot to rest **2** *noun* **(a)** gun which goes on firing as long as the trigger is being pulled; *he was shot with an automatic* **(b)** car which has automatic gear change; *I prefer driving automatics to manual models*

automatically [ɔːtə'mætɪkli] *adverb* working by itself; *the doors open automatically when someone comes near them*

automation [ɔːtə'meɪʃn] *noun* installing machinery in place of workers; *automation can be a mixed blessing - machines usually tend to be out of order when you need them most*

automobile ['ɔːtəməbiːl] *noun* (*especially US*) car; *the automobile industry*

Automobile Association (AA) [ɔːtə'məʊbaɪl əsəʊsi'eɪʃn] *noun* British organization which offers services to its members, such as insurance, emergency repairs to vehicles, maps and guide books, etc.

automotive [ɔːtə'məʊtɪv] *adjective* referring to cars, lorries, etc.; *the automotive industry*; *the college's department of automotive studies has closed down*

autonomous [ɔː'tɒnəməs] *adjective* self-governing; *these former provinces have now become autonomous regions*

autonomy [ɔː'tɒnəmi] *noun* **(a)** self-government; *the island was a colony but now enjoys its autonomy* **(b)** being able to decide what to do yourself; *we aim for complete autonomy of each department in the organization*

autopilot ['ɔːtəʊpaɪlət] *noun* automatic pilot, a device which can fly a plane, allowing the pilot to rest; *the plane was on autopilot when it hit the tropical storm*

autopsy ['ɔːtɒpsi] *noun* examination of a corpse to find the cause of death; *the autopsy revealed nothing about the cause of death*; *the police pathologist performed the autopsy* (NOTE: plural is **autopsies**)

autumn ['ɔːtəm] *noun* season of the year between summer and winter; *in autumn, the leaves turn brown*; *we went on a walking holiday last autumn*; *they say the building will be finished next autumn*; *I'll be starting my new job in the autumn* (NOTE: in American English this is **the fall**)

autumnal [ɔː'tʌmnl] *adjective* referring to autumn; *the autumnal colours of the trees*; *it's raining and the leaves are falling - it looks very autumnal*

auxiliary [ɔːg'zɪliəri] **1** *adjective* which gives help; *when the power failed, the hospital switched on its auxiliary generator* **2** *noun* **(a)** person who helps other workers; **a nursing auxiliary** = helper who does general work in a hospital or clinic; *the nurse is busy at the moment, so an auxiliary will take you to the right department* **(b)** verb which forms part of a verb phrase, such as 'have'; *write one example with the verb 'to eat' and the auxiliary 'have', and one with the same verb* and the auxiliary 'be'; see also MODAL (NOTE: plural is **auxiliaries**)

> COMMENT: the auxiliary verbs in English are **be, do, have**

availability [əveɪlə'bɪlɪti] *noun* being available; **subject to availability** = if available; *the goods will be supplied subject to availability; the availability of hard drugs to primary school children is shocking*

available [ə'veɪləbl] *adjective* **(a)** which can be obtained; *the tablets are available from most chemists* **(b) to make oneself available** = to arrange to be free to do something; *I can make myself available to meet you next week; the manager is never available when customers want to complain*

avalanche ['ævəlɑːnʃ] *noun* fall of masses of snow down the side of a mountain; *two climbers were lost in an avalanche in the Alps*; **the avalanche season** = late spring, when increasing temperatures make the snow melt on high mountains, and cause avalanches

avant-garde [ævɒŋ'gɑːd] *adjective* new, experimental and not traditional music, painting, etc.; *during his lifetime he was regarded as an avant-garde author, but now seems quite traditional; his ideas are rather avant-garde - I hope your parents won't be shocked*

avarice ['ævərɪs] *noun (formal)* desire to have and keep a lot of money; *all he thinks about is to amass money without spending it - I call that avarice*

Ave = AVENUE

avenge [ə'vendʒ] *verb (formal)* to hurt someone because they have hurt you; *he set out to avenge his father's murder*; **to avenge yourself on** = to get your own back on someone; *she wanted to avenge herself on her rival*; compare REVENGE

avenue ['ævənjuː] *noun* wide street in a town, often with trees along the side; *a leafy suburban avenue*; **Fifth Avenue** = famous shopping street in New York; *we went into the stores on Fifth Avenue* (NOTE: in names of streets, usually shortened to **Ave: 15 Laurel Ave**)

average ['ævərɪdʒ] **1** *noun* **(a)** number calculated by adding several figures and dividing by the number of figures added; *the temperature has been above the average for the time of year; the average for the last three months or the last three months' average* **(b) on average** = as a rule; *on average, £15 worth of goods are stolen every day* **2** *adjective* **(a)** ordinary; *it was an average working day at the office; their daughter is of above average intelligence* **(b)** calculated by dividing the total by the number of quantities; *his average speed was 30 miles per hour* **3** *verb* to work out as an average; *price increases have averaged 10% per annum*

averse [ə'vɜːs] *adjective (formal)* **to be averse to** = to dislike; *I'm averse to people smoking in pubs*; **not to be averse to** = to like; *she is not averse to hard work; he is not averse to the odd glass of wine with his meals* (NOTE: usually used in the negative form: **not averse to**)

aversion [ə'vɜːʃn] *noun* **(a) aversion to** *or* **towards** = dislike of; *she has a great aversion to men with beards; you can't ask them together because of their mutual aversion towards each other* **(b) pet aversion** = main thing which is disliked; *burnt toast is one of her pet aversions*

avert [ə'vɜːt] *verb* to prevent; *the negotiators are aiming to avert a strike*

aviary ['eɪviəri] *noun* large cage or building for keeping birds; *he filled the aviary with parrots*

aviation [eɪvɪ'eɪʃn] *noun* action of flying aircraft; *he's planning a career in aviation*; **aviation fuel** = special fuel used by aircraft; **civil aviation** = flying commercial or passenger planes, not war planes

avid ['ævɪd] *adjective* eager; *they are always avid for news of their families back home; she's an avid filmgoer - she goes to the cinema almost every day; he's an avid reader of gardening magazines*

avocado (pear) [ævə'kɑːdəʊ ('peə)] *noun* tropical fruit with yellow flesh and a very large stone, eaten as a vegetable; *add slices of avocado pear to your salad*; **avocado (green)** = greyish green; *the bathroom suite is avocado green* (NOTE: plural is **avocados**)

avocet ['ævəset] *noun* black and white wading bird with a bill which is curved upwards; *I've seen pictures of avocets in books but never the bird itself*

avoid [ə'vɔɪd] *verb* **(a)** to keep away from; *travel early to avoid the traffic jams; aircraft fly high to avoid storms; you must avoid travelling on Friday evenings* **(b)** to try not to do something; *he's always trying to avoid taking a decision* (NOTE: you avoid something or avoid **doing** something)

avoidance [ə'vɔɪdəns] *noun* act of avoiding; *in some cases, the avoidance of danger amounts to cowardice*; **tax avoidance** = trying legally to minimize the amount of tax you pay; *tax avoidance, as opposed to tax evasion, is not illegal*

avoirdupois [ævədə'pɔɪz] *noun* non-metric system of weights used in the UK, the USA and some other countries

> COMMENT: avoirdupois weight is divided into ounces (16 ounces = one pound); pounds (112 pounds = 1 hundredweight); hundredweight (20 hundredweight = 1 ton). Avoirdupois weights are slightly heavier than troy weights with the same names: the avoirdupois pound equals 0.45kg, whereas the troy pound equals 0.37kg

avowed [ə'vaʊd] *adjective* who admits; *he's an avowed communist*

await [ə'weɪt] *verb (formal)* to wait for; *we are awaiting the decision of the court*

awake [ə'weɪk] **1** *verb* **(a)** to stop somebody sleeping; *he was awoken by the sound of the telephone* **(b)** to wake up; *he awoke when he heard them knocking on the door; they awoke to find a fox in their tent* (NOTE: awaking - awoke [ə'wəʊk] - has awoken) **2** *adjective* not asleep; *I can't get to sleep - it's 2 o'clock and I'm still awake*; **wide awake** = completely awake (NOTE: awake cannot be used in front of a noun)

awaken [ə'weɪkn] *verb* **(a)** to wake up; *we awakened early to find it had snowed during the night* **(b)** to wake someone up; *everyone was awakened by her screams*; **to awaken someone to a danger** = to warn someone of a danger; *the president was finally awakened to the possibility of war*

award [ə'wɔːd] **1** *noun* **(a)** prize; *the coffee maker has won a design award; the school has been nominated for an award; we all went to London for the award-giving ceremony* **(b)** decision which settles a dispute; *the latest pay award has been announced* **2**

verb to give compensation, a prize, etc., to someone; *he was awarded first prize*; *she was awarded damages*

award-winning [ə'wɔːd'wɪnɪŋ] *adjective* which has won awards; *an award-winning film*

aware [ə'weə] *adjective* knowing; *is he aware that we have to decide quickly?*; *I am not aware of any problem*; **not that I am aware of** = not as far as I know; *has there ever been an accident here before? - not that I am aware of*

awareness [ə'weənəs] *noun* being aware; *the police are trying to increase public awareness of car crime*

awash [ə'wɒʃ] *adjective* **awash with** = covered with something, especially a liquid; *the deck of the boat was awash*; *just at the moment the company is awash with cash* (NOTE: **awash** cannot be used in front of a noun)

away [ə'weɪ] **1** *adverb* **(a)** at a distance; *they've gone away on holiday*; *the nearest shop is three kilometres away*; *go away! - I don't want to see you*; *we all waved as the bus moved away* **(b)** *(as emphasis, after verbs)* without stopping; *the birds were singing away in the garden* **(c)** not here, somewhere else; *the managing director is away on business*; *my secretary is away sick* **(d)** *(in sports)* at your opponents' sports ground; *our team is playing away next Saturday* (NOTE: the opposite is **at home**) **2** *adjective* **away game** = game played at your opponents' sports ground (NOTE: the opposite is **home game**)

awe [ɔː] *noun* great fear; *he inspires considerable awe in the younger members of staff*; **to be in awe of someone** = to be frightened of; *she is in awe of her father*

awe-inspiring *or* **awesome** [ɔː'ɪnspaɪrɪŋ or 'ɔːsəm] *adjective* frightening and impressive; *an awe-inspiring cathedral*; *his awesome memory for dates*

awful ['ɔːfəl] *adjective* very bad, very unpleasant; *turn off the television - that programme's awful!*; *she felt awful about missing the party*; *he's got an awful cold*

awfully ['ɔːflɪ] *adverb* (*informal*) very; *I'm awfully sorry to have to disturb you*; *she was awfully upset by the news*; *it was awfully cold in Moscow*

awhile [ə'waɪl] *adverb* (*literary*) for a short time; *let's rest here awhile before going on with our journey*

awkward ['ɔːkwəd] *adjective* **(a)** difficult to do; *I couldn't reach the handle - it's in a very awkward position*; *the lock is awkward and stiff* **(b)** embarrassing; *it's awkward for us to invite him and his second wife, when his first wife is a friend of my sister*; *when he asked for the loan the bank started to ask some very awkward questions* **(c)** not convenient; *next Thursday is awkward for me - what about Friday?*

awkwardly ['ɔːkwədlɪ] *adverb* **(a)** in an awkward way; *she walked awkwardly across the stage* **(b)** inconveniently; *the meeting is very awkwardly timed - it's in the middle of my summer holiday*

awning ['ɔːnɪŋ] *noun* roof made of canvas or other cloth, used to keep the sun or rain off; *coloured awnings in front of the shops*

awoke, awoken [ə'wəʊk or ə'wəʊkn] *see* AWAKE

axe *US* **ax** [æks] **1** *noun* **(a)** instrument for chopping; *he chopped the tree down with an axe* **(b)** **to get the axe** = to be stopped; *the project got the axe*; **to have an axe to grind** = to have a personal reason for doing something, a personal point of view which you keep repeating; *you can ask him what he thinks as he doesn't have any particular axe to grind on this issue* **2** *verb* to get rid of; *the government has promised to axe spending on defence*; **to axe staff** = to sack staff; *two hundred jobs are going to be axed*

axiom ['æksɪəm] *noun* rule or statement that most people think is true; *here is a good axiom for you: time is money*

axiomatic [æksɪə'mætɪk] *adjective* which everyone knows is true; *it is axiomatic that the more people work on a project the sooner it will be finished*

axis ['æksɪs] *noun* imaginary line through the centre of a round object, such as a ball; *the Earth turns on its axis once every 24 hours* (NOTE: plural is **axes** ['æksiːz])

axle ['æksl] *noun* rod which bears the wheels in a vehicle; *the front axle was damaged in the accident and needs replacing*

aye [aɪ] **1** *noun* yes vote; **the ayes have it** = the yes votes have won **2** *interjection (in the navy)* **aye aye sir!** = yes, sir!

azalea [ə'zeɪlɪə] *noun* shrub with bright white, orange, purple or pink flowers, similar to a rhododendron, but smaller; *you should visit Kew Gardens in March, when the azaleas are in flower*

Bb

B, b [biː] second letter of the alphabet, between A and C; *he initialled the document with a large 'BB' for Ben Brown*

B & B *or* **b. & b.** ['biː ənd 'biː] *noun* = BED AND BREAKFAST; *we want to find a B & B away from the main road* (NOTE: plural is **B & Bs**)

BA [biː'eɪ] = BACHELOR OF ARTS; *she has a BA in Italian and music* (NOTE: written after the name: **Jane Bushell BA**)

babble ['bæbl] **1** *noun* **(a)** little trickling sound made by water; *or the babble of the stream* **(b)** sound of people chattering; *a babble of voices in the next room* **2** *verb* **(a)** to make a trickling sound; *we sat on the grass by a babbling brook* **(b)** to speak in a confused way; *she babbled a few words and collapsed*; *what's he babbling on about?*

babe [beɪb] *noun* **(a)** *(formal)* baby; **a babe in arms** = a very small baby; *he inherited his grandfather's castle when he was still a babe in arms* **(b)** *(informal)* girl; *come on, babe, let's hit the town*

baboon [bə'buːn] *noun* type of large African monkey

baby ['beɪbi] *noun* **(a)** very young child; *most babies start to walk when they are about a year old*; *I've known him since he was a baby*; **to have a baby** = to give birth to a baby; *she's going into hospital to have her baby*; *see also* BATH WATER **(b)** very young animal; *baby rabbit* (NOTE: plural is **babies**; note also that if you do not know if a baby is a boy or a girl, you can always call it **it: the baby was sucking its thumb**)

baby carriage ['beɪbi 'kærɪdʒ] *noun usually US* small carriage in which you can push a baby; *she pushed the baby carriage round the park* (NOTE: British English is **pram, pushchair**)

babyish ['beɪbiɪʃ] *adjective* like a baby; *that book's too babyish for him - he's five, you know*; *it's very babyish to cry because you got a smaller piece of cake*

baby-sit ['beɪbɪsɪt] *verb* to look after children in a house, while their parents are out; *she baby-sits for me while I go to my evening classes*; *I'm baby-sitting my little brother tonight* (NOTE: **baby-sitting - baby-sat**)

baby-sitter ['beɪbɪsɪtə] *noun* person who baby-sits; *we have to find a reliable baby-sitter for next Thursday evening*

baby talk ['beɪbi 'tɔːk] *noun* way of speaking like a baby; *if you speak normally to your little daughter she'll learn to speak properly from the start - we don't encourage baby talk*

bachelor ['bætʃələ] *noun* **(a)** man who is not married; *he's still a bachelor and I'm beginning to wonder if he'll ever get married*; **bachelor pad** = small flat for a single person; *see also* ELIGIBLE **(b)** person with a first degree from a university; *she has a bachelor's degree from Edinburgh University*; **Bachelor of Arts (BA)** = first degree in an arts subject from a university; **Bachelor of Science (BSc)** = first degree in a science subject from a university; *he left university in 1988 with a Bachelor of Science degree*

bacillus [bə'sɪləs] *noun* type of bacteria shaped like a rod; *bacteria, especially bacilli, can move and reproduce very rapidly* (NOTE: plural is **bacilli** [bə'sɪlaɪ])

back [bæk] **1** *noun* **(a)** part of your body which is not in front; *she went to sleep lying on her back*; *he carried his son on his back*; *don't lift that heavy box, you may hurt your back*; *she stood with her back to the wall*; **he did it behind my back** = he did it without telling me; **we were glad to see the back of him** = we were glad to see him leave; **to put someone's back up** = to annoy someone; **we've broken the back of the work** = we've done most of the work **(b)** the opposite part to the front; *he wrote his address on the back of the envelope*; *she sat in the back of the bus and went to sleep*; *the dining room is at the back of the house*; **he knows London like the back of his hand** = he knows London very well; **he put his trousers on back to front** = he put them on the wrong way round **(c)** *(in many sports)* person who defends the goal area; *(in rugby)* one of the attacking players immediately behind the forwards; *the backs stayed back to defend the goal* **2** *adjective* **(a)** on the opposite side to the front; *he knocked at the back door of the house*; *the back tyre of my bicycle is flat* **(b)** referring to the past; **back pay** = salary which has not been paid; *I am owed £500 in back pay* **3** *adverb* **(a)** towards the back; *he stepped back from the edge of the platform*; *she leant back in her armchair*; *please sit back, I can't see the screen* **(b)** in the state where things were before; *put the telephone back on the table*; *she watched him drive away and then went back into the house*; *she gave me back the money she had borrowed*; *I'll phone you as soon as I get back to the office* **(c)** in the past; *back in the 1950s, life was much less complicated than it is today* **4** *verb* **(a)** to go backwards; to make something go backwards; *he backed (his car) down the drive*; **to back away from** = to go backwards from something frightening; *she backed away from the dog* **(b)** to support with money; *she is backing her son's restaurant* **(c)** to bet on something happening; *we're backing the Prime Minister to win the election* (NOTE: **back** is often used after verbs: **to give back, to go back, to pay back**, etc.)

backache ['bækeɪk] *noun* pain in the back; *I've had backache for several days*

backbencher *or* **backbench MP** [bæk'benʃə or 'bækbenʃ em'piː] *noun* ordinary Member of Parliament who does not sit on the front benches (and is not a government minister or a member of the Opposition shadow cabinet); *some backbenchers voted against the bill*; *compare* FRONT BENCH

backbone ['bækbəun] *noun* **(a)** the spine, the series of bones which link together down a person's or an animal's back; *if you're careful, you ought to be able to lift the backbone off the fish before eating it* **(b)**

strength of character; *it takes someone with backbone to stand up to the government*

backcloth *or* **backdrop** ['bækklɒθ or 'bækdrɒp] *noun* **(a)** *(in a theatre)* the painted sheet at the back of the stage; *the backdrop is meant to represent a forest* **(b)** background; *against a backcloth of* = with this going on in the background; *the wedding took place against a backdrop of family arguments*; *talks started against a backcloth of continuing conflict in the Middle East*

backdate [bæk'deɪt] *verb* to put an earlier date on something; *backdate your invoice to April 1st*

back door ['bæk'dɔ:] *noun* door at the back of a house; *I locked the front door but I'm not sure whether the back door is locked or not*; **backdoor negotiations** = negotiations which are hidden from the public; *I suspect some sort of backdoor deal has been reached*

backdrop ['bækdrɒp] *see* BACKCLOTH

backer ['bækə] *noun* **(a)** person who supports a project with money; *one of the company's backers has withdrawn* **(b)** person who gambles on a horse, a team, etc., to win; *several backers lost thousands when the favourite fell at the last fence*

backfire ['bækfaɪə] *verb* **(a)** *(of a car)* to make a loud bang, when unburnt petrol explodes in the cylinder; *the motorbike backfired several times when I started it this morning* **(b)** *(of a plan)* to go wrong, to turn out exactly the opposite to what was expected; *he was sure that everything would go according to plan and had never even thought it could backfire*; *all their holiday plans backfired when their children got chickenpox*

background ['bækgraʊnd] *noun* **(a)** part of a picture which seems farther away; *the photograph is of a house with mountains in the background*; *his white shirt stands out against the dark background*; *compare* FOREGROUND **(b)** **background music** = music played quietly in a film, restaurant, etc.; *the background music was too loud, so we asked for it to be turned down* **(c)** past life or experience; *he comes from a working class background*; *do you know anything about her background?*; *his background is in the restaurant business* **(d)** past details; *he explained the background of the claim for damages*

backing ['bækɪŋ] *noun* **(a)** financial support; *he has the backing of a French bank* **(b)** action of going backwards; *backing your car round corners is always difficult* **(c)** music played to accompany a singer; *she sings with an Irish backing group*

backlash ['bæklæʃ] *noun* reaction against something; *we can expect some sort of backlash from the public against the rise in prices*

backlog ['bæklɒg] *noun* a lot of work, such as orders or letters, which has not been dealt with yet; *my secretary can't cope with the backlog of paperwork*

back out ['bæk 'aʊt] *verb* **(a)** to make a car go backwards out of a place; *he backed (the car) out of the garage into the main road* **(b)** to decide not to support a project; *we had to cancel the project when the bank backed out*

backpack ['bækpæk] *noun* rucksack, a large bag carried on the back when walking; *I'll have to lighten my backpack - it's much too heavy*

backpacker ['bækpækə] *noun* person who goes walking, carrying a backpack; *we picked up two backpackers who were hitching a lift into the Rockies*

backpacking ['bækpækɪŋ] *noun* going on a long distance walk, carrying a backpack; *we went backpacking round Greece*

backpedal [bæk'pedəl] *verb* to change your point of view and do the opposite of what you had promised; *the government is starting to backpedal over its pledge to cut taxes*; *the minister had to backpedal rapidly when the papers found out about his speech* (NOTE: **backpedalling - backpedalled** but American spelling is **backpedaling - backpedaled**)

back room ['bæk 'rʊm] *noun* room at the back of an office, where secret work is done; *they were working away in a back room and the managers didn't know anything about what they were doing*; **back-room boys** = people, especially scientists, who do important work without publicity; *he was one of the back-room boys, so his name was never mentioned in the papers*

backside ['bæksaɪd] *noun* *(informal)* buttocks, the part of the body you sit on; *get off your backside and come and do some work*

backstage ['bæksteɪdʒ] **1** *adverb* **(a)** off the stage in a theatre; *the actors gathered backstage to wait for the audience to settle down* **(b)** hidden from view; *she did a lot of work backstage to help the party win the election* **2** *adjective* hidden from view; *the football club has several backstage supporters who keep it afloat*; *he did a lot of backstage work to help the poor people of the town*

back street ['bæk 'stri:t] **1** *noun* street away from the main streets; *he grew up in the back streets of the city* **2** *adjective* hidden, in the back streets; *she went to see a disreputable backstreet doctor*

backstroke ['bækstrəʊk] *noun* swimming style where the swimmer lies on his back and moves his arms backwards; *let's practise the backstroke*; *he won the 100m backstroke*

back up ['bæk 'ʌp] *verb* **(a)** to help someone; *nobody would back her up when she complained about the service*; *will you back me up in the vote?* **(b)** to make a copy of a computer file; *don't forget to back up your work before you go home in the evening* **(c)** *US* to make a car go backwards; *can you back up, please? I want to get out of the parking lot* (NOTE: British English for this is simply to **back**)

backup ['bækʌp] *adjective* supporting, helping; *we offer a free backup service to customers*; **backup copy** = copy of a computer disk to be kept in case the original disk is damaged or lost

backward ['bækwəd] **1** *adjective* **(a)** not as advanced as normal; *he is backward for his age* **(b)** not industrially advanced; *poor and backward countries* **2** *adverb* *US* = BACKWARDS

backward-looking ['bækwəd'lʊkɪŋ] *adjective* not looking to the future; *it was a backward-looking move to keep the old currency*

backwards *US* **backward** ['bækwədz] *adverb* from the front towards the back; *don't step backwards*; *'tab' is 'bat' spelt backwards*; *she looked backwards at the next person in the queue*; **backwards and forwards** = in one direction, then in the opposite direction; *the policeman was walking backwards and forwards in front of the bank*; *(informal)* **to bend over**

backwards *or* **to lean over backwards to do something** = to do everything you can to be helpful; *we bent over backwards to get her a mortgage, and then she decided not to buy the house; the social services leant over backwards to help the family*

backwater ['bækwɔːtə] *noun* quiet country place, away from the capital city; *they used to live in the centre of London, but they retired to a peaceful rural backwater*

backyard [bæk'jɑːd] *noun* **(a)** *GB* paved area behind a house; *we keep our bikes in the backyard* **(b)** neighbourhood; *they have no idea of what's going on in their own backyard* **(c)** *US* yard, piece of land behind a house where you can grow flowers and vegetables; *they moved to the USA where they bought a nice house with a big backyard where the children can play* (NOTE: British English is **garden**)

bacon ['beɪkən] *noun* salted or smoked meat from a pig, usually cut in thin slices; **bacon and eggs** = fried bacon and fried eggs (served at breakfast) (NOTE: no plural: **some bacon; a pound of bacon**; for a single piece say **a rasher**)

COMMENT: bacon is cured in brine for several days; some bacon is also smoked by hanging in smoke, which improves its taste; unsmoked bacon is also known as 'green' bacon

bacteria [bæk'tɪərɪə] *noun* tiny organisms, which can cause disease; *the cleaning liquid will kill harmful bacteria* (NOTE: the word is plural; the singular is **bacterium** [bæk'tɪərɪəm])

COMMENT: bacteria can be shaped like rods (bacilli), balls (cocci) or have a spiral form (spirochaetes). Bacteria, especially bacilli and spirochaetes, can move and reproduce very rapidly

bacterial [bæk'tɪərɪəl] *adjective* referring to bacteria; *these children are very susceptible to bacterial infection*; **bacterial warfare** = war where bacteria are used to kill the enemy; *they are rumoured to be planning to develop bacterial weapons*

Bactrian camel ['bæktrɪən 'kæməl] *noun* Asian camel which has two humps

COMMENT: the Arabian camel or dromedary has only one hump

bad [bæd] *adjective* **(a)** not good; *eating too much fat is bad for you*; *I think it would be a bad idea* **(b)** of poor quality; *he's a bad driver*; *she's good at singing but bad at playing the piano* **(c)** unpleasant; *he's got a bad cold*; *she's in a bad temper*; *I've got some bad news for you*; *the weather was bad when we were on holiday in August* **(d)** *(food)* which is not fresh, which has started to rot; *the meat we bought yesterday has started to go bad* (NOTE: **bad - worse** [wɜːs] **- worst** [wɜːst])

◊ **not bad** ['nɒt 'bæd] quite good; *the food in this restaurant isn't bad*; *what did you think of the film? - not bad!*

bad debt ['bæd 'det] *noun* debt which will never be paid (usually because the debtor has gone out of business) and which has to be written off in the accounts; *the company has written off £30,000 in bad debts*

baddy ['bædi] *noun (informal)* villain (in a film, etc.); *in the end, the baddies all got killed* (NOTE: the opposite is **goodies**)

badge [bædʒ] *noun* small sign pinned to someone's clothes (to show who he or she is, what company he or she belongs to, etc.); *all the staff at the exhibition must wear badges*

badger ['bædʒə] **1** *noun* wild animal, with short legs and a black and white striped head, which lives in holes in the ground; *farmers say that cows can catch TB from badgers* **2** *verb* **to badger someone into doing something** = to keep on asking someone so often that in the end they do what you want; *she badgered me into giving her the key*

badlands ['bædlændz] *noun US* eroded land which is unsuitable for cultivation; *the badlands of Dakota*

badly ['bædli] *adverb* **(a)** not well; *she did badly in her driving test* **(b)** seriously; *he was badly injured in the motorway accident* **(c)** very much; *his hair badly needs cutting* (NOTE: **badly - worse - worst**)

badly-off ['bædli 'ɒf] *adjective* not having very much money, quite poor; *when her husband died she was left quite badly-off* (NOTE: **badly-off - worse-off - worst-off**)

badminton ['bædmɪntən] *noun* game for two or four people, similar to tennis, played with a different type of racket and a shuttlecock; *do you want a game of badminton?*; *the badminton tournament starts on Saturday*

COMMENT: named after Badminton House, in Gloucestershire, where the sport was developed

bad-tempered [bæd'tempəd] *adjective* in a bad temper; *she's always bad-tempered in the morning*

baffle ['bæfl] **1** *noun* shield to reduce noise or air; *they built baffles between the airport runway and the road* **2** *verb* to puzzle; *I'm baffled as to why the car won't start*; *it baffles us that she sold her house so cheaply*

bag [bæg] **1** *noun* **(a)** container made of paper, plastic, etc., in which you can carry things; *he put the apples in a paper bag*; **to let the cat out of the bag** = to tell a secret by accident; *her husband let the cat out of the bag and it was all over the newspapers the following morning*; **carrier bag** = large paper or plastic bag with handles, for carrying shopping, often given by a shop, with the shop's name on it; *have you got a carrier bag for all this shopping?*; **doggy bag** = bag in which you can put food which you didn't eat in a restaurant to take home; **shopping bag** = bag for carrying your shopping in; **shoulder bag** = bag which you carry on a strap over your shoulder; **sleeping bag** = comfortable warm bag for sleeping in, often used by campers; **string bag** = bag made like a net **(b)** what is contained in a bag; *a bag of potatoes*; *a small bag of flour*; *(informal)* **bags of** = a large amount of; *let him pay the bill if he wants to - he's got bags of money* **(c)** = HANDBAG; *my keys are in my bag* **(d)** suitcase, piece of luggage; *I always pack my bags at the last minute*; *(informal)* **to tell someone to pack their bags** = to tell someone to leave, to sack someone; *when he got home, she told him to pack his bags* **2** *verb (informal)* **(a)** to catch, kill or destroy; *we bagged a brace of pheasants*; *he bagged three enemy planes* **(b)** **bags I go first** = let me go first, I claim the right to go first (NOTE: **bagging - bagged**)

bagel ['beɪgl] *noun* small hard loaf of bread, shaped like a ring; *he bought bagels and cream cheese for breakfast*

bagful ['bægful] *noun* amount contained in a bag; *she cooked a whole bagful of potatoes*

baggage ['bægɪdʒ] *noun* luggage, cases and bags which you take with you when travelling; *she brought a huge amount of baggage with her*; **excess baggage** = cases which weigh more than you are allowed when travelling by air, and for which you must pay extra; **unaccompanied baggage** = cases which are sent by air, with no passenger travelling with them; *I'm sending three cases as unaccompanied baggage*; **baggage allowance** = weight of baggage which an air passenger is allowed to take free when he travels; **baggage handler** = person who deals with passengers' luggage at an airport; *US (at airport)* **baggage cart** = little cart with wheels which you use to carry your luggage at an airport; *there's a row of baggage carts near where you reclaim your baggage* (NOTE: British English for this is **luggage trolley**); **baggage rack** = device above the seats in a train for holding baggage; *US* **baggage room** = room at a railway station, coach station, ferry terminal or airport where suitcases, bags and parcels can be left (NOTE: British English for this is **left luggage office**. Note also **baggage** has no plural; to show one suitcase, etc., you can say **a piece of baggage**. Note also that British English uses **luggage** more often than **baggage**)

baggy ['bægi] *adjective (of clothes)* too big, hanging in folds; *he wore a pair of baggy trousers* (NOTE: **baggier - baggiest**)

bagpipes ['bægpaɪps] *noun* musical instrument used especially in Scotland, Ireland and Brittany, which is played by blowing air into a bag and then pumping it through pipes; *she was woken up by someone playing the bagpipes near the castle*

bail [beɪl] 1 *noun* **(a)** money paid to a court as surety for the release of a prisoner; *she was released on bail of £5000*; **to jump bail** = not to appear in court after being released on bail; *the police are afraid he will jump bail* **(b) bails** = two pieces of wood on top of the stumps in cricket 2 *verb* to scoop water out of a boat; *we're filling up with water - start bailing!* (NOTE: do not confuse with **bale**)

bailer ['beɪlə] *noun* instrument for scooping water out of a boat; *before you set off, make sure you have the bailer on board*

bailiff ['beɪlɪf] *noun* **(a)** court official whose responsibility is to see that court orders are obeyed; *the court ordered the bailiff to seize his property because he had not paid his debt*; *we were having breakfast when the bailiffs arrived and seized our car* **(b)** person employed to manage a farm for a landowner; *we are looking for a bailiff for one of our farms*

bail out ['beɪl 'aut] *verb* **(a)** to help someone in difficulty; *when he couldn't pay his rent, he asked his father to bail him out* **(b)** to pay money to a court to have a prisoner released; *he phoned his lawyer to see if someone could bail him out* **(c)** to scoop water out of a boat; *I'll try to plug the hole, if you start to bail out* **(d)** = BALE OUT

bairn [beən] *noun (in Scotland)* child; *he's only a wee bairn*

bait [beɪt] 1 *noun* something used to attract fish or animals so that you can catch them; *we must put down some more bait to try to get rid of the mice*; **to rise to**

the bait *or* **to take the bait** = to allow yourself to get caught by a tempting offer 2 *verb* to attach bait (to a hook); *he baited his line with a worm*

bake [beɪk] *verb* to cook in an oven; *Mum's baking a cake for my birthday*; *do you like baked potatoes?*; *bake the pizza for 35 minutes*

baked beans ['beɪkt 'biːnz] *noun* dried white beans cooked in tomato sauce; *we had baked beans on toast for supper*; *can you go to the grocer's and get me a tin of baked beans?*

baker ['beɪkə] *noun* person who makes bread and cakes; *bakers start work very early in the morning*; **the baker's** = shop where you can buy bread and cakes; *can you go to the baker's and get a loaf of brown bread?*; *see also* DOZEN

bakery ['beɪkəri] *noun* place where bread and cakes are made; *there's no bakery near us, so we have to go to the next village to buy our bread* (NOTE: plural is **bakeries**)

baking ['beɪkɪŋ] 1 *noun* cooking in an oven, especially bread and cakes; *there was a wonderful smell of baking coming from the kitchen*; **baking dish** = dish which goes into the oven 2 *adjective (informal)* very hot; *it's baking (hot) in here*

balance ['bæləns] 1 *noun* **(a)** staying steady; *you need a good sense of balance to walk along the top of a fence*; **to keep your balance** = not to fall over; **to lose your balance** = to fall down; *as he was crossing the river on the tightrope he lost his balance and fell* **(b)** money left in an account; *I have a balance of £25 in my bank account*; **balance of payments** = the difference in value between a country's imports and exports; *the government is trying to reduce the balance of payments deficit* **(c)** money left to be paid; *you can pay £100 down and the balance in three instalments*; *the balance outstanding is now £5000* 2 *verb* **(a)** to stand without falling; *the cat balanced on the top of the fence* **(b)** to make something stand without falling; *the waiter balanced a pile of dirty plates on his arm* **(c)** to make accounts balance *or* **to balance the accounts** = to make income and expenditure equal in accounts

balanced ['bælənst] *adjective* **(a)** which is not excessive, which has equal quantities; *a balanced diet* **(b)** not in profit or loss; *a balanced budget* **(c)** sensible; *to express a balanced opinion*

balance of power ['bæləns əv 'pauə] *noun* **(a)** situation where two powerful states are roughly equal in power; *the rise of the military government has threatened the balance of power in the region* **(b)** *(of a small group)* **to hold the balance of power** = to be in a situation where no large group has a majority and so hold power by being able to decide which group to ally with; *although the Liberals only have two seats on the council, they hold the balance of power because the other two parties have twenty seats each*

balance sheet ['bæləns 'ʃiːt] *noun* statement of a company's financial position at the end of a period of time; *the accountants have prepared a balance sheet to present to the committee meeting*

> COMMENT: the balance sheet shows the state of a company's finances at a certain date; the profit and loss account shows the movements which have taken place since the end of the previous accounting period

balcony ['bælkəni] *noun* **(a)** small terrace jutting out from the upper level of a building; *the flat has a balcony overlooking the harbour*; *breakfast is served on the balcony* **(b)** upper rows of seats in a theatre or cinema; *we booked seats at the front of the balcony* (NOTE: plural is **balconies**)

bald [bɔːld] *adjective* **(a)** who has no hair; *his grandfather is quite bald*; *he is beginning to go bald* **(b)** straightforward, without any explanation; *after the fire, the police issued a bald statement* **(c)** a bald tyre = a tyre with a worn tread

balding ['bɔːldɪŋ] *adjective* going bald; *the attacker was a man of about thirty, balding, with a small beard*

bale [beɪl] **1** *noun* large pack of wool, paper, cotton, etc.; *a bale of cotton*; *they used bales of straw to make walls alongside the racetrack* **2** *verb* to bale out = to jump out of a plane with a parachute; *as the plane exploded, the pilot managed to bale out* (NOTE: do not confuse with **bail**)

baler ['beɪlə] *noun* machine which makes bales of straw, etc.; *he was feeding straw into the baler when the accident happened*

balk [bɔːlk] *verb* = BAULK

ball [bɔːl] *noun* **(a)** round thing for throwing, kicking, playing games, etc.; *they played in the garden with an old tennis ball*; *he kicked the ball into the goal*; *he threw the ball and I caught it*; to keep the ball rolling = to keep everything moving, especially a conversation; *John kept the ball rolling by telling a long story about his trip to Egypt*; I'll start the ball rolling = I'll start things going; he's on the ball = he knows his job, he's clever in business; *I'll ask Mary to do it - she's been here a long time and is really on the ball*; they won't play ball = they won't cooperate **(b)** any round thing; *a ball of wool*; *he crumpled the paper up into a ball* **(c)** formal dance; *Cinderella lost her shoe at the ball* (*informal*) to have a ball = to enjoy yourself; *the children don't want to leave - they're having a ball*

ballad ['bæləd] *noun* simple romantic song; *a concert of folk ballads*

ballast ['bæləst] *noun* **(a)** material carried in a ship to give it extra weight, so that it will keep steady even if it is not carrying any cargo; *the ship was in ballast* **(b)** small stones placed under railway sleepers to give a base for the track; *there will be some disruption to services while new ballast is being laid*

ball-bearing ['bɔːl 'beərɪŋ] *noun* **(a)** small steel ball; *I tried to mend my bicycle wheel and lost one of the ball-bearings* **(b)** ring of small steel balls which allows a metal rod to turn easily; *the ball-bearings in the bicycle wheel had to be replaced*

ballerina [bælə'riːnə] *noun* woman ballet dancer; *if she wants to become a ballerina she'll have to go to a ballet school*; prima ballerina = leading female dancer in a ballet company; *the prima ballerina was magnificent in last night's performance*

ballet ['bæleɪ *US* bæ'leɪ] *noun* **(a)** type of dance, given as a public entertainment, where dancers perform a story to music; *she's taking ballet lessons* or *she's going to ballet school* **(b)** a performance of this type of dance; *Tchaikovsky's ballet 'Swan Lake'*; *we went to the ballet last night*

ball game ['bɔːl 'geɪm] *noun* **(a)** any game played with a ball; *football, tennis and other ball games* **(b)** *US* a game of baseball **(c)** general way in which things are managed; a whole new ball game = an entirely new state of affairs; *it's opened up a whole new ball game*

ballistics [bə'lɪstɪks] *noun* science of projectiles that are shot through the air, such as bullets; *the revolver was examined by a police ballistics expert*

balloon [bə'luːn] *noun* large ball which is blown up with air or gas; *he was blowing up balloons for the party*; hot-air balloon = very large balloon which rises into the air as the air inside it is heated, with people travelling in a basket attached underneath; *we went for a ride in a hot-air balloon*

ballot ['bælət] **1** *noun* way of voting where voters mark papers with a cross; postal ballot = ballot where the votes are sent by post; ballot box = box for putting voting papers into; ballot paper = paper on which the voter marks a vote; ballot-rigging = arranging a dishonest result in an election **2** *verb* **(a)** to get people to vote on something; *the union is balloting its members on the strike* **(b)** to vote by marking papers with a cross; *they balloted for the place on the committee*

ballpark ['bɔːlpɑːk] *US* place for playing baseball; *the team's gone to the ballpark*

ballpark figure ['bɔːlpɑːk 'fɪgə] *noun* general figure which can be used as the basis for discussion; *I estimate the cost at £900, but this is just a ballpark figure*

ball point (pen) ['bɔːl pɔɪnt 'pen] *noun* pen which writes using a small ball covered with ink; *don't write in ball point, use a pencil*

ballroom ['bɔːlrʊm] *noun* large room for formal dances; *the reception will take place in the hotel ballroom*; ballroom dancing = formal dancing; *the hotel is booked tonight for a ballroom dancing competition*

ballyhoo [bælɪ'huː] *noun* excited and energetic publicity; *all this ballyhoo about the new digital camera is all over the top*

balm [bɑːm] *noun* soothing ointment; *apply some lip balm if your lips are dry*

Baltic ['bɒltɪk] *noun* sea south of Sweden and Finland, and north of Poland; *we spent the summer cruising along the Baltic coast*; the Baltic States = Latvia, Lithuania and Estonia

balustrade [bælə'streɪd] *noun* series of small pillars with a bar across the top, forming a wall round a balcony or formal garden; *the balcony is dangerous, the balustrade is not high enough*

bamboo [bæm'buː] *noun* tropical plant, which grows very tall and of which the stems are used as supports or in making furniture; *we bought some bamboo chairs for the living room*; *train the beans to climb up bamboo poles*; bamboo shoots = young shoots of bamboo, eaten especially in Chinese cooking; *she made a stir-fry of vegetables and bamboo shoots*

ban [bæn] **1** *noun* order which forbids something; *the government has introduced a ban on smoking in cinemas*; *they imposed a ban on cycling in the park* **2** *verb* to forbid; *smoking has been banned in cinemas*; *she was banned from driving for three years* (NOTE: banning - banned)

banal [bə'nɑːl] *adjective* quite ordinary and uninteresting; *the story is terribly banal, but the music is excellent*

banality [bə'nælɪti] *noun* **(a)** being ordinary; *the banality of the sitcom drives me mad* **(b)** banalities =

ordinary, uninteresting things; *his speech was full of banalities*

banana [bə'nɑːnə] *noun* **(a)** long yellow, slightly curved fruit which grows in hot countries; *she was peeling a banana*; *can I have a banana milk shake?*; **banana split** = dessert made of a banana with ice cream, cream and chocolate sauce; usually served in a long dish **(b)** *(informal)* **to go bananas** = to go mad, to get very annoyed; *when he saw what they had done to his car, he went bananas*

band [bænd] **1** *noun* **(a) elastic band** *or* **rubber band** = thin circle of rubber for holding things together; *the roll of papers was held together with a rubber band*; *put a band round the cards to stop them getting mixed* **(b)** group of people who play music together; *the soldiers were marching after the band*; *the dance band played all night* **(c)** range of things taken together; *he's in the £50 - 60,000 salary band*; *we're looking for something in the £10 - £15 price band* **2** *verb* **to band together** = to form a group; *they banded together to form a pressure group*

bandage ['bændɪdʒ] **1** *noun* cloth for putting round a wound, an injured limb, etc.; *the nurse put a bandage round his knee*; *his head was covered in bandages* **2** *verb* to put a cloth round a wound, an injured limb, etc.; *she took him to the hospital and the nurse bandaged his knee*

BandAid ['bændeɪd] *noun* US *(trademark)* small strip of cloth with gauze in the middle, which can be stuck to the skin to cover a wound; *let me put a BandAid on your finger* (NOTE: British English is **sticking plaster)**

bandit ['bændɪt] *noun* robber; *their car was stopped by bandits on a quiet mountain road*

bandwagon ['bændwægən] *noun* **to jump on the bandwagon** = to do what everyone else is doing; *once the prince had praised the ecological movement, everyone wanted to jump on the bandwagon*

bane [beɪn] *noun* **it's the bane of my life** = it's very annoying; *the neighbour's dog is the bane of our lives*; *being up during the night with young children is the bane of the life of most parents*

bang [bæŋ] **1** *noun* sudden noise like that made by a gun; *the car started with a series of loud bangs*; *there was a bang and the tyre went flat* **2** *verb* to hit hard, so as to make a loud noise; *can't you stop the door banging?*; *he banged (on) the table with his hand* **3** *interjection* (showing the something makes a sudden noise) *a firework suddenly went bang*; **bang in the middle** = right in the middle; *bang in the middle of his speech, someone's mobile phone started to ring*

banger ['bæŋə] *noun* **(a)** type of firework which makes a bang; *keep the dog indoors on November 5th - she doesn't like bangers* **(b)** *(slang)* old car; *I'm surprised his old banger is still on the road* **(c)** *(informal)* sausage; **bangers and mash** = fried sausages and mashed potatoes

Bangladesh [bæŋlə'deʃ] *noun* country in the Indian subcontinent, to the east of India; *the family who have bought the corner shop come from Bangladesh* (NOTE: capital: **Dacca**; people: **Bangladeshis**; language: **Bengali**; currency: **taka)**

Bangladeshi [bæŋlə'deʃi] **1** *adjective* referring to Bangladesh; *a Bangladeshi family has moved in next door* **2** *noun* person from Bangladesh; *the new teacher is a Bangladeshi*

bangle ['bæŋgl] *noun* metal bracelet worn round the wrist or ankle; *a girl with a thin silver bangle round her ankle*

banish ['bænɪʃ] *verb* **(a)** to exile, to send someone to live a long distance away (usually out of the country, or in a distant part of the country) as a punishment; *she was banished to a small island for ten years*; *he was banished to Siberia* **(b)** to send away from a particular place; *she was banished from the front desk to a little office on the fifth floor* **(c)** to get rid of; *the aim is to banish poverty by the year 2010*

banishment ['bænɪʃmənt] *noun* act of banishing or state of being banished; *the banishment of political opponents to distant parts of the empire* (NOTE: no plural)

banisters ['bænɪstəz] *noun* handrail on top of a series of poles along the side of stairs; *the children loved to slide down the banisters when they were little*

banjo ['bændʒəʊ] *noun* stringed instrument with a round body and a long neck; *the singer was accompanied by three musicians playing banjos or playing the banjo* (NOTE: plural is **banjos)**

bank [bæŋk] **1** *noun* **(a)** business which holds money for its clients, which lends money at interest and trades generally in money; *I must go to the bank to get some money*; *how much money do you have in the bank?*; *she took all her money out of the bank to buy a car* **(b)** land along the side of a river; *he sat on the river bank all day, trying to catch fish*; *there is a path along the bank of the canal* **2** *verb* to put money away into a bank; *have you banked the money yet?*; *I banked the cheque as soon as it arrived*

bank account ['bæŋk ə'kaʊnt] *noun* arrangement which you make with a bank to keep your money safely, where you can deposit and withdraw money as you want; *I put all my savings into my bank account*; **to open a bank account** = to start keeping money in a bank; *he opened a bank account when he started his first job*; **to close a bank account** = to stop having an account with a bank

bankbook ['bæŋkbʊk] *noun* book which records how much money you put in or take out of your savings account in a bank or with a building society; *next time, bring your bankbook so we can bring it up to date* (NOTE: also called **passbook)**

banker ['bæŋkə] *noun* person who has a senior post in a bank; *he works as a banker in the City*

bank holiday ['bæŋk 'hɒlɪdeɪ] *noun* special day when most people do not go to work and the banks are closed; *Christmas Day is a bank holiday*

COMMENT: bank holidays in England and Wales are: New Year's Day, Good Friday, Easter Monday, the first Monday in May (May Day), the last Monday in May (Spring Bank Holiday), the last Monday in August (Summer Bank Holiday), Christmas Day and Boxing Day (December 26th). In Scotland, the first Monday in August and January 2nd are also Bank Holidays, but Easter Monday and the last Monday in August are not. In the USA, New Year's Day, 21st January (Martin Luther King Day), February 12th (Lincoln's Birthday), the third Monday in February (Washington's birthday), the last Monday in May (Memorial Day), July 4th (Independence Day), the first Monday in September (Labor Day), the second Monday in October (Columbus Day), 11th November (Veterans' Day), the fourth Thursday in November (Thanksgiving) and Christmas Day are public holidays nationally, although there are other local holidays

banking ['bæŋkɪŋ] *noun* (a) the profession of working in a bank; *he is planning a career in banking* (b) the business of working in a bank; *some supermarkets now offer banking services*; **banking hours** = time when a bank is open for its customers; *you cannot get money out of the bank after banking hours*

bank manager ['bæŋk 'mænədʒə] *noun* person in charge of a branch of a bank; *he asked his bank manager for a loan*

banknote ['bæŋknəʊt] *noun* piece of paper money; *he pulled out a pile of new banknotes* (NOTE: American English is **bill**)

bank on ['bæŋk 'ɒn] *verb* to be sure that something will happen; *don't bank on getting any more money from your father; can we bank on fine weather for the school sports day ?*

bankrupt ['bæŋkrʌpt] **1** *adjective* not able to pay your debts; *he has been declared bankrupt* **2** *noun* person who cannot pay his debts; *a bankrupt cannot be a member of parliament*

bankruptcy ['bæŋkrʌptsi] *noun* being bankrupt; *when his business failed he faced bankruptcy; bankruptcies increased during the recession* (NOTE: plural is **bankruptcies**)

COMMENT: 'bankruptcy' and 'bankrupt' are applied to people, and 'insolvency' and 'insolvent' are usually applied to companies

banner ['bænə] *noun* (a) long flag; *they hung banners from the tops of buildings for the festival* (b) large piece of cloth with a slogan on it; *the demonstrators carried banners with the words 'Power to the People'* (c) **banner headline** = newspaper headline printed in very large letters

banquet ['bæŋkwɪt] *noun* formal dinner for important guests; *the president gave a banquet for the visiting prime minister; the Queen made a speech at a state banquet given in her honour*

banquette ['bɒŋket] *noun* seat along a wall in a restaurant; *shall we sit on the banquette?*

bantam ['bæntəm] *noun* small breed of chicken, most kinds being about half the size and weight of an ordinary chicken; *he raises bantams on his farm*

bantamweight ['bæntəmweɪt] *noun* weight of boxer between flyweight and featherweight; *this young boxer is a bantamweight; a bantamweight title fight; the bantamweight champion*

banter ['bæntə] *noun* talking with joking comments; *the two leaders exchanged banter at the press conference after the summit; the guests engaged in idle banter while waiting for the bride to arrive*

bantering ['bæntərɪŋ] *adjective* joking and teasing; *they made some bantering remarks about the waitresses*

baptism ['bæptɪzm] *noun* (a) religious ceremony where someone, usually a baby, is welcomed into the Christian church and given a Christian name after being sprinkled with holy water; *all the family came together*

for the baptism (b) **baptism of fire** = the first time someone has faced the enemy or a difficult situation; *giving a speech to the sales conference was her baptism of fire as sales manager*

baptize [bæp'taɪz] *verb* to receive someone, usually a baby, into a Christian church in a ceremony during which he or she is sprinkled with holy water and given a Christian name; *our granddaughter was baptized last Sunday; her father was baptized a Roman Catholic; none of her children has been baptized*

bar [bɑː] **1** *noun* (a) long piece of something hard; *the yard was full of planks and metal bars* (b) solid rectangular piece of material; *put a new bar of soap by the bath; she was munching a bar of chocolate* (c) long piece of wood or metal which closes a door or window; **bars** = pieces of metal in front of a prison window; *he was put behind bars for several years; the prisoners escaped by sawing through the bars* (d) long metal or plastic key on a typewriter or computer keyboard; **space bar** = long bar at the bottom of the keyboard on a typewriter or computer which inserts a single space into text (e) place in a hotel or pub where you can buy and drink alcohol; *let's meet in the bar before dinner; the reps met in the bar of the hotel* (f) small shop where you can buy food; **coffee bar** = small restaurant which sells coffee, cakes and sandwiches; **sandwich bar** = small shop which mainly sells sandwiches; **snack bar** = small restaurant where you can eat simple meals; *she bought a pie and salad in the snack bar at Waterloo Station* (g) obstacle, thing which prevents something happening; *I don't think it should be a bar to your promotion*; **colour bar** = using the colour of someone's skin as an obstacle to something (h) the profession of a barrister; **to be called to the bar** = to become a barrister (i) division within a piece of music; *let's play the first few bars again* **2** *preposition* except; *all of the suppliers replied bar one; all bar two of the players in the team are British* **3** *verb* (a) to block; *the road was barred by the police; the path is barred to cyclists* (b) **to bar someone from doing something** = to prevent someone doing something; *she was barred from entering the USA* (NOTE: **barring - barred**)

barbarian [bɑː'beərɪən] *noun* wild and uncivilized person; *the barbarians invaded the Roman Empire in the fifth century*

barbaric [bɑː'bærɪk] *adjective* cruel and uncivilized; *such barbaric treatment of prisoners of war is not allowed under the Geneva Convention*

barbarous ['bɑːbərəs] *adjective* very cruel; *what a barbarous way of slaughtering animals!*

barbecue ['bɑːbɪkjuː] **1** *noun* (a) metal grill for cooking out of doors; *light the barbecue at least half an hour before you start cooking* (b) food cooked on a barbecue; *here is a recipe for chicken barbecue* (c) meal or party where food is cooked out of doors; *we had a barbecue for twenty guests; they were invited to a barbecue* **2** *verb* to cook on a barbecue; *barbecued spare ribs are on the menu; she was barbecuing sausages for lunch when it started to rain*

barbed ['bɑːbd] *adjective* (a) with sharp hooks; *it was impossible to remove the barbed hook from her hand without cutting into the flesh* (b) sharply critical remark; *she made some barbed comments about her former husband*

barbed wire ['bɑːbd 'waɪə] *noun* wire with sharp spikes, used to make fences; *the Ministry of Defence buildings are surrounded by barbed wire fences; see also* ENTANGLEMENT

barber ['bɑːbə] *noun* person who cuts men's hair; **barber's** *US* **barber shop** = shop where men have their hair cut; *I'm just going to the barber's*

> COMMENT: traditionally, a barber's shop has a red and white striped pole outside, as an advertisement

bar code ['bɑː 'kəʊd] *noun* printed lines which can be read by a computer; *there doesn't seem to be a price on the packet - just a bar code* (NOTE: also called **universal product code**)

> COMMENT: bar codes are found on most goods and their packages; the width and position of the stripes can be recognized by the computer's reader and give the shop information about the goods sold, such as price, stock quantities, etc.

bard [bɑːd] *noun (formal)* poet; **the Bard (of Avon)** = Shakespeare

bare ['beə] **1** *adjective* **(a)** naked, with no clothes on; *he walked on the beach in his bare feet* **(b)** with no leaves on, no furnishings on, etc.; *in winter, the branches are all bare; they slept on the bare floorboards; they saw the bare bones of dead animals in the desert* **(c)** **bare living** = just enough to live on; *he makes a bare living selling T-shirts to tourists;* **bare minimum** = the smallest amount needed; *the flat is furnished with the bare minimum of furniture* **2** *verb* to make part of the body bare by removing clothes; *men should bare their heads on entering the church* (NOTE: do not confuse with **bear**)

barefoot ['beəfʊt] *adjective & adverb* without shoes; *she walked barefoot in the grass; the children were barefoot*

bareheaded [beə'hedɪd] *adjective & adverb* not wearing a hat; *bareheaded mourners followed the coffin to the cemetery; it was silly to go out bareheaded in a snowstorm; the mourners stood bareheaded by the graveside*

barelegged ['beəlegd] *adjective & adverb* not wearing clothes on your legs; *barelegged children were fishing for shrimps; the children played barelegged in the puddles*

barely ['beəli] *adverb* scarcely, almost not enough; *she barely had enough money to pay the bill; he barely had time to get dressed before the police arrived; the noise in the iron foundry is barely tolerable*

bargain ['bɑːgɪn] **1** *noun* **(a)** an agreed deal; **to strike a bargain** = to agree terms; *we shook hands and the bargain was struck;* **he drives a hard bargain** = he is a tough negotiator **(b)** **into the bargain** = as well as other things; *the plane was late and they lost my suitcase into the bargain* **(c)** something bought more cheaply than usual; *the car was a real bargain at £500;* **bargain basement** = cheap department in the basement of a shop; *you'll find cheaper items in the bargain basement;* **bargain offer** *or* **bargain sale** = sale at a specially low price **2** *verb* **(a)** to negotiate terms; *after bargaining with the doorman, we managed to get into the club* **(b)** to haggle, to discuss a price; *if you bargain with the man in the antique shop, you'll probably get something knocked off the price* **(c)** to bargain for

something = to expect something to happen; *I hadn't bargained for him being away and leaving me to do all the work;* **I got more than I bargained for** = the deal had unpleasant results which I did not expect (NOTE: you bargain **with** someone **over** *or* **about** *or* **for** something)

bargaining ['bɑːgənɪŋ] *noun* discussing prices or terms; *the bargaining for the carpet took two hours or more;* **collective bargaining** = wage negotiations between management and unions

barge [bɑːdʒ] **1** *noun* cargo boat (often long and narrow) on a river or canal; *we watched the barges go past along the Rhine* **2** *verb* **to barge in** = to interrupt; *we were having a quiet chat when he came barging in*

> COMMENT: barges on English canals are also called 'narrow boats' because they are long and narrow

barge pole ['bɑːdʒ 'pəʊl] *noun (informal)* **I wouldn't touch it with a barge pole** = I would advise you not to get involved in that

baritone ['bærɪtəʊn] **1** *noun* singer with a voice which is higher than a bass and lower than a tenor; *the baritone sang a duet with the soprano* **2** *adjective* higher than a bass and lower than a tenor; *he has a rich baritone voice*

barium ['beərɪəm] *noun* white metal; **barium meal** = solution containing barium which a patient drinks to give a better contrast when taking X-rays of the stomach, etc. (NOTE: Chemical element: chemical symbol: **Ba**; atomic number: **56**)

bark [bɑːk] **1** *noun* **(a)** hard outer layer of a tree; *the rough bark of a pine tree; the bark of silver birch trees comes off in strips* **(b)** call of a dog; *the dog gave a bark of greeting as we came into the house;* **his bark is worse than his bite** = he is not as frightening as he seems; *don't be afraid of Aunt Bessie - her bark is much worse than her bite* **2** *verb* **(a)** to scrape your skin; *he barked his shin climbing over the wall* **(b)** to make a call like a dog; *the dogs barks every time he hears the postman;* **to bark up the wrong tree** = to be mistaken; *they don't know what the problem is - they're barking up the wrong tree*

barley ['bɑːli] *noun* common cereal crop grown in temperate areas; *barley is rarely used for making flour but it is used to make beer;* **pearl barley** = barley used in soup and puddings; *Scotch broth is a hearty soup made of mutton, vegetables and pearl barley;* **barley sugar** = sweet of boiled sugar; *I bought a bag of barley sugar; there are only three barley sugars left in the tin;* **barley wine** = very strong beer

barmaid ['bɑːmeɪd] *noun* woman who serves drinks in a bar; *she works as a barmaid in the local pub*

barman ['bɑːmən] *noun* man who serves drinks in a bar; *the barman didn't know how to make cocktails* (NOTE: plural is **barmen**)

bar mitzvah ['bɑː 'mɪtsvə] *noun* ceremony where a Jewish boy is made a full member of his community at the age of 13

barn [bɑːn] *noun* large farm building for storing produce; *the barn is full of hay*

barnstorming ['bɑːnstɔːmɪŋ] *adjective* full of wild political oratory; *he gave a barnstorming performance at the party conference and had all the delegates shouting and cheering*

barnyard ['bɑːnjɑːd] *noun* part of a farm, the space round barns and other farm buildings; *he parked the tractor in the barnyard*

barometer [bə'rɒmɪtə] *noun* instrument which measures changes in atmospheric pressure and can be used to forecast the weather; *take an umbrella - the barometer's falling*

barometric [bærə'metrɪk] *adjective* referring to a barometer; **barometric pressure** = atmospheric pressure shown by a barometer

baron ['bærən] *noun* **(a)** lowest rank of peer in the House of Lords **(b)** title given to a life peer **(c)** important person; **a drugs baron** = an important drugs dealer; *they aim to put the country's drugs barons behind bars*; **a press baron** = an important newspaper owner; **a robber baron** = a medieval lord who spent his time robbing people (NOTE: do not confuse with **barren**)

COMMENT: life peers and peeresses are barons and baronesses; barons are addressed as 'Lord' followed by their family name and baronesses as 'Lady'. In some European countries, the word is used as a form of address: so, Baron Smith is addressed as 'Lord Smith', but Baron Schmidt is addressed as 'Baron'

baroness [bærə'nes] *noun* **(a)** wife of a baron **(b)** title given to a female life peer *see note at* BARON

baronet ['bærənet] *noun* hereditary knight, a member of one of the lowest ranks of the aristocracy

COMMENT: baronets are addressed as 'Sir', followed by their Christian name and family name; their wives are addressed as 'Lady' followed by the family name (hence Sir John Smith's wife is addressed as 'Lady Smith'). The title passes to the heir but does not qualify the holder for a seat in the House of Lords; baronets can be Members of Parliament

baroque [bə'rɒk] *adjective* highly decorated European artistic, architectural and musical style of the late 17th and 18th centuries; *the baroque churches of south Germany*; *I don't really enjoy baroque music*

barrack ['bærək] *verb* to shout at someone who is speaking; *the speaker was constantly barracked by hecklers*

barracks ['bærəks] *noun* **(a)** building where soldiers are housed; *the soldiers marched into their barracks* **(b)** cold building; *the school was housed in a barracks of a building* (NOTE: **barracks** is both singular and plural)

barrage ['bærɑːʒ] *noun* **(a)** heavy gunfire, mass of things thrown; *the enemy started an artillery barrage*; *the police were met by a barrage of stones and bottles*; *he faced a barrage of questions from reporters when he arrived at the airport* **(b)** dam made of a wall of soil or stones which blocks a river; *they built a barrage to help control the water level in the river*

barrel ['bærəl] *noun* **(a)** round wooden container for liquid; *a barrel of beer*; *we sell wine by the barrel*; **he's got me over a barrel** = I'm placed in very awkward situation **(b)** amount contained in a barrel; *the price of oil has reached $30 a barrel*; *the oil well produces thousands of barrels of oil per day* **(c)** firing tube of a gun; *you need to clean the barrel of a rifle very carefully*

barren ['bærən] *adjective* **(a)** barren land = land which is not fertile and cannot grow crops; *barren land stretches for miles around the reactor site* **(b)** *(old)* (animals) which cannot bear young; *a barren cow* **(c)** *(plants)* which do not produce fruit; *one pear tree on its own will be barren - you need two trees to produce fruit* (NOTE: do not confuse with **baron**)

barricade [bærɪ'keɪd] **1** *noun* pile of stones, burnt cars, etc., built to block a street; *protesters built barricades across several of the main streets* **2** *verb* to build a barricade; *protesters barricaded the streets*; **to barricade yourself inside** = to block a door with furniture, etc., so that no one else can get inside; *he barricaded himself inside the flat*

barrier ['bæriə] *noun* bar which blocks a passage; thing which prevents the spread of a disease, the import of goods, etc.; *he lifted the barrier and we drove across the border*; **barrier reef** = coral reef enclosing a lagoon; **crush barriers** = metal fences which are put up to control crowds; *the fans simply climbed over the crush barriers to get at the pop group's car*; **customs barriers** *or* **trade barriers** = special taxes to prevent imports; *to impose trade barriers on certain goods*

barring ['bɑːrɪŋ] *preposition* unless there are; *barring any unforeseen hitches the new shop should be open to the public next Monday*

barrister ['bærɪstə] *noun GB* lawyer who can present cases in court; *they hired one of the top barristers to defend them*; *see also* BAR (NOTE: the term is not used in the USA; also called **counsel**)

COMMENT: barristers are members of one of the Inns of Court. They are instructed by solicitors, and never by the client whom they are representing. Important barristers are nominated to become QCs

barrow ['bærəʊ] *noun* **(a)** wheeled handcart for selling fruit and vegetables; *an old man used to sell apples from a barrow on the corner of the street* **(b)** mound of earth over the tomb of a prehistoric leader; *archaeologists are excavating an old barrow*

barter ['bɑːtə] **1** *noun* system where goods are exchanged for other goods and not sold for money; *the company has agreed a barter deal with Bulgaria* **2** *verb* to barter something for something = to exchange goods for other goods, and not buy them for money; *they agreed a deal to barter tractors for barrels of wine*

basal ['beɪsəl] *adjective* referring to a base; **basal joint** = joint at the base of a leaf

basalt ['bæsɔːlt] *noun* black rock produced by volcanoes; *they visited the basalt cliffs by boat*

base [beɪs] **1** *noun* **(a)** bottom part; *the table lamp has a flat base* **(b)** place where you work from; *he lives in London but uses Paris as his base when travelling in France*; **a military base** = a camp for soldiers; *he was posted to an air base in East Anglia* **(c)** one of the marked spots in baseball where a player is safe; *players have to run from base to base*; **to touch base with someone** = to get in touch with someone again; *I'm calling because I wanted to touch base with you* **2** *verb* to use as a base; *the company is based in Paris, it is not London-based as you might expect*; *the theory is based on research done in Russia*; *he based his article on work done at Harvard University*

baseball ['beɪsbɔːl] *noun* **(a)** American game for two teams of nine players, in which a player hits a ball with a bat and players from the other team try to catch it; he scores points by running round the field from base to base (there are four bases in all); *we went to the baseball game last Saturday*; **baseball cap** = soft cotton cap with a large peak; *she was also wearing a baseball cap back to front* **(b)** the hard ball used in playing baseball; *we lost yet another baseball in the river*

COMMENT: the field is diamond-shaped; the batter stands over home plate (the base of the diamond) and attempts to hit a ball thrown by the pitcher standing on a slightly raised mound in the centre of the diamond. The other three points of the diamond constitute first, second and third bases and it is round these a batter must run in an anti-clockwise direction before returning to home plate, in order to score a run. He may pause at any of the bases before going on when a team-mate makes another hit from home plate. A home run is scored if a batter manages to touch all three bases and return to home plate without stopping

baseboard ['beɪsbɔːd] *noun US* board along the bottom of the wall in a room; *the wall was painted yellow and the baseboard white* (NOTE: British English is **skirting board**)

baseline ['beɪslaɪn] *noun* line at the back of a tennis court, etc.; *players have to stand behind the baseline when serving*; *his lob fell just over the baseline*

basement ['beɪsmənt] *noun* floor in a building below the ground level; *we keep the washing machine in the basement*; *she lives in a basement flat in Kensington see also* BARGAIN (NOTE: also called **lower ground floor**)

base metal ['beɪs 'metəl] *noun* metal, like iron, which is not particularly valuable; *gold and silver are precious metals while lead and iron are base metals*

base rate ['beɪs 'reɪt] *noun* basic rate of interest set by a central bank on which other banks calculate the actual rate of interest on loans; *bank base rates are likely to rise before Christmas* (NOTE: the American equivalent is the **prime rate**)

bash [bæʃ] **1** *noun* **(a)** knock; *I see your car has had a bash* **(b)** *(informal)* **have a bash** = go on, try to do it; *waterskiing looks fun - do you think I could have a bash at it?* **(c)** *(informal)* party; *are you going to Jane's bash tomorrow?* (NOTE: plural is **bashes**) **2** *verb* to hit hard; *he bashed her over the head with a stick*; *she was bashing stakes into the ground with a mallet*

basic ['beɪsɪk] *adjective* elementary; *being able to swim is a basic requirement if you are going canoeing*; *knowledge of basic Spanish will be enough for the job*; **basic vocabulary** = most common words in a language

basically ['beɪsɪkli] *adverb* (*used when stating the simplest fact*) at the simplest level; *basically, he's fed up with his job*

basics ['beɪsɪks] *noun* basic facts; *the course teaches you the basics of photography*; **to get back to basics** = to concentrate on the main points again; *all these new theories are very interesting, but we need to get back to basics again*

basil ['bæzl] *noun* herb used in cooking, especially with Italian dishes; *add fresh basil to your tomato salad*

basilica [bə'zɪlɪkə] *noun* **(a)** early form of Christian churches, built as a long rectangle **(b)** important Catholic church; *St Peter's Basilica is the most important church in Rome*

basin ['beɪsən] *noun* large bowl; *follow the recipe and mix the flour and butter in a basin*; **wash basin** = large bowl in the bathroom, used for washing your hands and face

basis ['beɪsɪs] *noun* **(a)** general facts on which something is based; *what is the basis for these proposals?*; **on the basis of** = based on; *the calculations are done on the basis of an exchange rate of 2.5 marks to the pound* **(b)** general terms of an agreement; *she is working for us on a freelance basis*; *many of the helpers at the hospice work on a voluntary basis* (NOTE: plural is **bases** ['beɪsiːz])

basis point ['beɪsɪs 'pɔɪnt] *noun* one hundredth of a percentage point (0.01%), the measurement used in showing movements of interest rates; *interest rates moved up by two basis points*

bask [bɑːsk] *verb* to lie happily in warm sunshine or in a pleasant atmosphere; *seals lay basking on rocks*; *he basked in the glory of his prize*

basket ['bɑːskɪt] *noun* container made of thin pieces of wood, wire, grass, etc., woven together; **shopping basket** = basket used for carrying shopping; *if you're going shopping, don't forget your shopping basket*; **wastepaper basket** = container into which paper or pieces of rubbish can be put; *he threw the letter into the wastepaper basket*

basketball ['bɑːskɪtbɔːl] *noun* **(a)** game played by two teams of five players; *he plays in the college basketball team* **(b)** the ball used when playing basketball

COMMENT: the game is played between two teams of five players, the aim being to throw the ball through a metal hoop over an open net hung high up at each end of the playing area (this is called the 'basket'). Players may pass or dribble the ball by bouncing it with one hand each time a step is taken but may not walk or run with the ball in their hands; as soon as a player uses two hands he must either shoot or pass the ball

basketful ['bɑːskɪtfʊl] *noun* amount you can put into a basket; *they brought basketfuls of apples to the farmhouse*

bass [beɪs] **1** *adjective* referring to a low-pitched voice or music; *he has a pleasant bass voice*; **bass guitar** *or* **bass trombone** = guitar or trombone which plays a lower range of notes; *he plays bass guitar in a pop group*; *see also* CLEF **2** *noun* **(a)** singer with deep voice; *the famous Russian bass* **(b)** (**double**) **bass** = musical instrument like a very large violin; *she plays the double bass in the city orchestra* (NOTE: plural is **basses**; do not confuse with **base**)

bassist ['beɪsɪst] *noun* person who plays a bass instrument, such as a double bass; *he's a bassist in a pop group*

bassoon [bə'suːn] *noun* long wooden wind instrument, with a low tone; *a bassoon has a range of over four octaves*

bassoonist [bə'suːnɪst] *noun* person who plays a bassoon; *he's not only an excellent pianist but a well-known bassoonist*

bastard ['bɑːstəd] **1** *adjective* with parents who are not married; *the bastard son of the last duke* **2** *noun* **(a)** person whose parents are not married; *technically speaking, many children are born bastards nowadays* **(b)** *(informal) (generally offensive)* nasty person, nasty thing; *the bastard walked out without paying; the written driving test is a real bastard*

baste [beɪst] *verb* **(a)** to sew a piece of clothing loosely, so that the stitches can be taken apart if it doesn't fit properly; *baste the sleeves and try on the dress: if it fits, then you can sew the sleeves on properly* **(b)** to pour melted fat and juices over meat as it is cooking; *don't forget to baste the chicken two or three times while it is roasting*

bastion ['bæstiən] *noun* **(a)** stronghold, part of a castle wall which sticks out from the face of the wall; *the gate was protected by bastions at each corner* **(b)** place which protects some particular good way of living; **a bastion of democracy =** a country which is firmly democratic; *Rome is famous as the bastion of Catholicism*

bat [bæt] **1** *noun* **(a)** piece of wood used for hitting a ball; *a baseball bat; a cricket bat;* **he did it off his own bat =** he decided to do it himself without asking anyone **(b)** little animal, similar to a mouse, which can fly; *bats were flying all round the trees in the garden; bats hang upside down* **2** *verb* **(a)** *(in cricket)* to be one of the two batsmen or to be the team which is batting; *Atherton is batting; England batted all day* **(b)** *(in baseball)* to be the batter; *I watched him batting on TV his afternoon* **(c)** **he never batted an eyelid =** he showed no surprise at all (NOTE: **batting - batted**)

batch [bætʃ] *noun* number of things made at one time; *she baked a batch of cakes; the department processed a batch of orders;* **batch number =** number printed on a batch of units made at one time; *when making a complaint, please quote the batch number on the packet* (NOTE: plural is **batches**)

bath [bɑːθ] **1** *noun* **(a)** large container in which you can sit and wash your whole body; *there's a wash basin and a bath in the bathroom; the bath has not been cleaned properly* (NOTE: American English is **bathtub** or **tub**) **(b)** washing your whole body; *he had a bath when he came home from work; my father has a cold bath every morning; (informal)* **to throw the baby out with the bath water =** to get rid of something good and useful at the same time as you are getting rid of something useless **(c)** **public baths =** large building belonging to a local council, with saunas and swimming pools; **swimming baths =** large building with a swimming pool; *he goes to the municipal swimming baths every day before breakfast* (NOTE: you say **one bath** [bɑːθ] but **two baths** [bɑːðz]) **2** *verb* to wash all over; *she's bathing the baby* (NOTE: do not confuse with **bathe**; note also **baths** [bɑːθs] - **bathing** ['bɑːθɪŋ] - **bathed** [bɑːθt])

bath chair ['bɑːθ 'tʃeə] *noun (old)* chair with wheels, in which a patient sat and could be moved by pulling or pushing

bathe [beɪð] **1** *noun* act of swimming in a pool, a river, the sea, etc.; *we all went for an early-morning bathe before breakfast* **2** *verb* **(a)** to go into water; *thousands of pilgrims come to bathe in the Ganges* **(b)** to wash a wound carefully; *the nurse bathed his wound before applying a dressing* **(c)** *US* to have a bath; *I just have enough time to bathe before my dinner guests*

arrive (NOTE the pronunciation (and compare to **bath**): **bathes** [beɪðz] - **bathing** ['beɪðɪŋ] - **bathed** [beɪðd])

bathing ['beɪðɪŋ] *noun* swimming, or just going into the sea, a lake, etc.; *the bathing is very safe here because the water is shallow*

bathing costume ['beɪðɪŋ 'kɒstjuːm] *noun (old)* piece of clothing worn when swimming; *she didn't go swimming, because she had forgotten her bathing costume* (NOTE: also called a **swimsuit**)

bath mat ['bɑːθmæt] *noun* little carpet in a bathroom; *he got out of the bath and stood dripping on the bath mat*

bathrobe ['bɑːθrəʊb] *noun* **(a)** loose coat of towelling, worn when you get out of a bath; *she came out of the bathroom dressed in a pink bathrobe* **(b)** *US* also dressing gown, a long robe worn over pyjamas or nightdress before getting dressed

bathroom ['bɑːθruːm] *noun* **(a)** room in a house with a bath, a wash basin and usually a lavatory; *the house has two bathrooms* **(b)** *(said instead of)* toilet; *where's the bathroom?; can I use your bathroom, please?*

bathtowel ['bɑːθtaʊəl] *noun* very large towel; *remind me to give you a clean bathtowel*

bathtub ['bɑːθtʌb] *noun especially US* bath, the container in which you sit and wash your body; *I'd rather have a shower than a bathtub in the bathroom* (NOTE: British English prefers simply **bath**)

batman ['bætmən] *noun* officer's servant in the army; *when he commanded a regiment he had a batman who did everything for him* (NOTE: do not confuse with **batsman**; plural is **batmen**)

baton ['bætn] *noun* **(a)** large stick used to hit with; *the crowd was stopped by a row of policemen carrying batons;* **baton charge =** charge by police using batons against a mob **(b)** **a conductor's baton =** thin white stick used to conduct an orchestra **(c)** stick which is passed from runner to runner in a relay race; **to pass the baton =** (i) to hand the stick on to the next runner; (ii) to pass control of something to your successor; *as he passed the baton the other runner dropped it*

batsman ['bætsmən] *noun (in cricket)* the player who is batting; *the last batsman batted on for two hours* (NOTE: plural is **batsmen**; compare also **batter**)

battalion [bə'tæliən] *noun* a section of the army, usually commanded by a lieutenant-colonel; *the battalion marched out of the barracks*

batter ['bætə] **1** *noun* **(a)** liquid mixture of flour and milk; *fish coated in batter and fried* **(b)** *(in baseball)* the player who has the bat and hits the ball (NOTE: compare **batsman**) **2** *verb* to hit often; *he was accused of battering the baby to death*

battered ['bætəd] *adjective* **(a)** ill-treated by being often hit; *battered babies; battered wives* **(b)** covered with batter and cooked; *battered prawns*

battery ['bætəri] *noun* **(a)** little device for storing electric energy; *my calculator needs a new battery; the battery has given out so I can't use my radio; my mobile phone has a rechargeable battery* **(b)** series of small cages in which thousands of chickens are kept; **battery chicken =** chicken which spends its life confined in a small cage; *we never eat battery chicken, only free-range* (NOTE: plural is **batteries**)

COMMENT: battery farming is a very efficient method of egg production; it is criticized, however, because of the quality of the eggs, the possibility of disease and also on the grounds of cruelty because of the stress caused to the birds

battery-operated or **battery-powered** ['bætərɪ'ɒpəreɪtɪd or 'bætərɪ'pauwəd] *adjective* driven by a battery; *a battery-powered calculator*

battle ['bætl] **1** *noun* **(a)** important fight between armed forces; *many of the soldiers died in battle; Napoleon was beaten at the Battle of Waterloo; Nelson was killed at the Battle of Trafalgar;* **pitched battle** = battle where the opposing sides stand and face each other; **running battle** = battle which moves around; *the police were engaged in running battles with the protesters* **(b)** fight against something; *the government's constant battle against inflation; he lost his battle against cancer* **2** *verb* **to battle against** = to fight against; *she had to battle against the other members of the board; his last years were spent battling against cancer*

battleaxe ['bætəlæks] *noun (old)* large difficult woman; *the receptionist at the surgery is a real old battleaxe*

battledress ['bætəldres] *noun* uniform worn by soldiers going into battle; *the soldiers marched down the street in khaki battledress*

battlefield ['bætəlfiːld] *noun* site of a battle; *we went to visit the battlefields of northern France*

battleground ['bætəlɡraund] *noun* battlefield, place where a battle was fought; *as we were crossing northern France, we drove through the First World War battleground*

battlements ['bætəlmənts] *noun* top part of a castle wall, with places where soldiers could shoot at attackers; *soldiers were firing from the battlements*

battleship ['bætəlʃɪp] *noun* largest type of warship with big guns; *after the Second World War most battleships were scrapped*

baulk [bɔːlk] *verb* **to baulk at something** = to refuse to do something which is dangerous or unpleasant; *he does all sorts of work in the office but baulked at having to clean the toilets; she didn't go to the concert because she baulked at the cost of the tickets* (NOTE: also spelled **balk**)

bawl [bɔːl] *verb* to shout loudly; *the baby was bawling in its pram*

bawl out ['bɔːl 'aut] *verb US* **to bawl someone out** = to criticize someone sharply; *she bawled him out for having left the house in a mess*

bay [beɪ] *noun* **(a)** large inwards curve in a coast; *the Bay of Biscay* **(b) bay window** = window which sticks out from a flat wall; *can we sit at that table in the bay window?* **(c) loading bay** = place for loading lorries in a warehouse; **parking bay** = place for one car in a car park; *you can park in the visitors' parking bay* **(d) to keep someone at bay** = to stop someone attacking; *he tried to keep the bank manager at bay by promising to repay the loan in ten days' time; some farmers use llamas to protect their lambs by keeping foxes at bay* **(e)** shrub with leaves used in cooking; *add a bay leaf to the soup*

bayonet ['beɪənət] *noun* **(a)** sharp blade fitted at the end of a rifle; *the soldiers were ordered to fix bayonets*

(b) bayonet fitting = light bulb fitting with two pins, which you push into a socket and turn, as opposed to a screw fitting; *bayonet light bulbs are the norm in Britain*

bazaar [bə'zɑː] *noun* **(a)** Indian or Middle Eastern market; *we visited the busy bazaar to try to buy spices* **(b) charity bazaar** = sale of goods donated by people to be sold for charity; *we're holding a bazaar at the hospital on Saturday*

BBC [biːbiː'siː] = BRITISH BROADCASTING CORPORATION; *we were listening to the BBC news or to the news on the BBC; the BBC broadcasts to many countries in the world; a BBC reporter wanted to interview her*

BC ['biː'siː] *abbreviation for 'before Christ', used in dates; Julius Caesar died in 44 BC* (NOTE: for dates after the birth of Christ, use **AD: Claudius invaded Britain in 43 AD**)

be [biː] **1** *verb* **(a)** *(describing a person or thing)* our *house is older than yours; she is bigger than her brother; lemons are yellow; the soup is hot; are you tired after your long walk?; put on your coat - it is cold outside; I'm cold after standing waiting for the bus* **(b)** *(showing age or time)* he's twenty years old; she will be two next month; it is nearly ten o'clock; it is time to get up; September is the beginning of autumn **(c)** *(showing price)* onions are 80p a kilo; the cakes are 50p each; my car was worth £10,000 when it was new **(d)** *(showing a job)* his father is a bus driver; he wants to be a teacher **(e)** *(showing size, weight, height, etc.)* he's 1.70m tall; the room is three metres square; our house is ten miles from the nearest station **(f)** *(meaning to add up to)* two and two are four **(g)** *(showing that something exists)* where are we?; there's your hat!; there was a crowd of people waiting for the shop to open; there were only two people left on the bus **(h)** *(meaning to go or visit)* the police have been into every room; have you ever been to Spain?; we have been to see the film three times **2** *(making part of a verb)* **(a)** *(making a present tense)* don't make a noise when he's watching the football on TV; I'm waiting for the bank to open; we are hoping to go on holiday in June **(b)** *(making a past tense)* he was singing in the bath; we were walking towards the post office when we met her **(c)** *(making a future tense)* we will be going to Germany next week **(d)** *(showing a passive)* he was killed by a train; the children were sent home by the teacher*

beach [biːtʃ] **1** *noun* area of sand or pebbles by the edge of the sea; *let's go to the beach this afternoon; many of the beaches were covered with oil from the tanker; we walked along the beach and looked for shells;* **beach towel** = large towel normally used on the beach; *she was wrapped in a bright blue and yellow beach towel;* **beach umbrella** = large coloured umbrella to use on a beach (NOTE: plural is **beaches**) **2** *verb* to bring onto a beach; *they beached the boat near the harbour; at high tide we will try to return the beached whale to the sea* (NOTE: do not confuse with **beech**)

beacon ['biːkən] *noun* light which warns; *there is a beacon on the cliff, warning ships that there are dangerous rocks nearby; beacons on the ground show pilots the route into the runway;* **radio beacon** = transmitter which aircraft can follow to bring them to an airport; *see also* BELISHA

bead [biːd] *noun* little decorative piece of wood, plastic, glass, etc., with a hole in it, used to make a necklace; *she was wearing a string of red beads*; *beads are back in fashion again*

beak [biːk] *noun* hard part of a bird's mouth; *the bird was carrying the worm in its beak*

beaker ['biːkə] *noun* **(a)** drinking cup with or without a handle; drinking cup for very small children, with or without a handle, and sometimes with a spout; *we'll use these glasses and the children can have the plastic beakers*; *she's just started to drink from a beaker* **(b)** glass jar used in chemical experiments; *you need a beaker and a Bunsen burner for this experiment*

beam [biːm] **1 (a)** long block of wood or metal which supports a structure, especially a roof; *you can see the old beams in the ceiling* **(b)** ray of light; *beams of sunlight came through the stained glass windows*; *the beam from the car's headlights shone into the barn*; **dipped beam** = lowered headlights of a car **2** *verb* to give a wide smile; *the little girl beamed at him*

beaming ['biːmɪŋ] *adjective* with a wide smile; *she gave him a beaming smile*; *the beaming faces of children in the playground*

bean [biːn] *noun* **(a)** long thin green vegetable, of which you eat the pod or seeds; *we had veal with French beans or green beans* (informal) **full of beans** = full of energy; *she's full of beans today*; (informal) **I haven't got a bean** = I have no money at all; *see also* BAKED BEANS, SPILL **(b) coffee beans** = seeds of the coffee bush, which are roasted and ground to make coffee; **soya beans** = beans of the soya plant, which have a high protein and fat content and very little starch; *soya sauce is made from soya beans*; **bean curd** = soft white paste made from soya beans (NOTE: **bean curd** is also called **tofu**)

bean bag ['biːn 'bæg] *noun* **(a)** large bag full of polystyrene granules, used as a chair **(b)** little bag with beans inside, used to throw, or to form the body of a little doll; *she was playing with her bean bag frog*

beanie ['biːni] *noun US* sort of small cap, worn by sports fans

bear [beə] **1** *noun* **(a)** large wild animal covered with fur; *they say that bears like honey*; *there are bears near the campsite in the mountains*; **polar bear** = big white bear which lives in the snow near the North Pole; *the explorers were attacked by polar bears*; **teddy bear** = toy bear; *she came carrying her favourite teddy bear*; (informal) **like a bear with a sore head** = very bad-tempered; *what's the matter with him, he's like a bear with a sore head this morning* (NOTE: usually simply called a **teddy**) **(b)** person who believes that share prices will fall; **bear market** = period when prices on the stock market fall as shareholders sell shares because they think share prices will fall further (NOTE: the opposite is **bull**) **2** *verb* **(a)** to carry, to produce; *this apple tree has borne fruit every year for the last twenty years*; *the letter bore a London postmark*; *a bond which bears interest at 5%* **(b) not to bear** = not to like; *I can't bear the smell of cooking fish* **(c)** to turn slightly; *bear right at the crossroads* (NOTE: **bearing - bore** [bɔː] **- has borne** [bɔːn])

beard ['biːəd] *noun* hair growing on a man's chin; *Father Christmas has a long white beard*

bearded ['biːədɪd] *adjective* with a beard; *the driver was a big bearded man*

bearer ['beərə] *noun* **(a)** (formal) person who carries something; *he said he was the bearer of bad news*; *flag bearers walked in front of the groups of soldiers* **(b)** person who owns a legal document, such as a cheque; *this card entitles the bearer to a discount*; **the cheque is payable to bearer** = the cheque can be paid only to the person who holds it, not to any named person

bearing ['beərɪŋ] *noun* **(a) (ball) bearings** = set of little balls inside which an axle turns; *the bearings in the bicycle wheel had to be replaced* **(b)** calculation to show where you are; *you need a compass to take a bearing*; **to get your bearings** = to find out where you are; *give me a few moments to get my bearings*; **to lose your bearings** = to get lost; *I'm sorry I'm late, but I didn't have a map and lost my bearings* **(c) bearing on something** = connection to something; *the letter had no bearing on the result of the trial*

bearish ['beərɪʃ] *adjective* feeling that the stock market is likely to fall; *sell now before the market turns bearish again* (NOTE: the opposite is **bullish**)

bear out ['beə 'aʊt] *verb* to confirm; *the statistics bear out our conclusions*

bear up ['beə 'ʌp] *verb* to survive cheerfully; *they're bearing up under the strain*

bear with ['beə 'wɪθ] *verb* to wait patiently; *please bear with me while I fill in the form*

beast [biːst] *noun* **(a)** wild animal; **beast of burden** = animal which carries loads (such as a donkey) **(b)** nasty person; *the beast! he left the restaurant without paying his share*

beat [biːt] **1** *noun* **(a)** regular sound; *the patient's heart has an irregular beat*; *see also* HEARTBEAT **(b)** (in music) regular sound of a piece of music; *they danced to the beat of the steel band* **(c)** area patrolled by a police officer on foot; *here policemen on the beat have to go round in pairs* **2** *verb* **(a)** to make a regular sound; *his heart was still beating when the ambulance arrived*; *her heart beat faster as she went into the interview* **(b)** to hit hard; *the schoolboy was taken and beaten by a gang of youths*; *she hung the carpet on the line and beat it with a stick to remove the dust* **(c)** to do better than someone else, than another team in a game; *they beat their rivals into second place*; *our football team beat France 2 - 0*; *they beat us by 10 goals to 2*; *we beat the Australians at cricket last year* **(d)** (informal) **beat it!** = go away! (NOTE: **beating - beat - has beaten**)

beat down ['biːt 'daʊn] *verb* **(a)** to make someone reduce a price; *I beat down his price or I beat him down* **(b)** to fall hard on; *the sun was beating down so we looked for some shade*; *the rain beat down on the marchers*

beaten ['biːtən] *adjective* **(a)** defeated; *the beaten team was very disappointed* **(b) off the beaten track** = away from main roads; *luckily, our village is off the beaten track*

beater ['biːtə] *noun* **(a)** device for beating things, such as eggs; *I always whisk egg whites with a hand beater* **(b)** person who drives birds towards hunters; *the hunters waited for the beaters to drive the birds towards them*

beating ['biːtɪŋ] *noun* act of hitting or defeating; *they gave our team a beating*

beat up ['biːt 'ʌp] *verb* to attack someone; *three muggers beat him up and stole his wallet*

beat-up [ˈbiːtʌp] *adjective (informal)* wrecked and useless; *he drives a beat-up old Ford*

Beaujolais [ˈbəʊʒəleɪ] *noun* light French red wine from Burgundy; *a bottle of Beaujolais would go well with this meal*; **Beaujolais nouveau** = Beaujolais wine which has just been made, sold from November onwards, i.e. only a few weeks after the grapes have been picked

beautiful [ˈbjuːtɪfʊl] *adjective* very nice, especially to look at; *the beautiful colours of the autumn leaves*; *Mr Smith and his three beautiful daughters*; *what beautiful weather!*; *they have a beautiful house in the country*

beautifully [ˈbjuːtɪfʊli] *adverb* in a very pleasing way; *she sang the song beautifully*

beautify [ˈbjuːtɪfaɪ] *verb* to make someone *or* something beautiful; *they cleaned, they painted, they planted flowers, in fact they did everything they could to beautify the place*

beauty [ˈbjuːti] *noun* **(a)** quality of being beautiful; *her beauty was legendary*; *the beauty of the maples against the background of the blue lake* **(b)** beautiful woman; beautiful thing; *at 18 she was a real beauty*; *his motorbike is a beauty - I must buy one like it*; *look at these apples, they're real beauties*

beauty salon *or* **beauty shop** [ˈbjuːti ˈsælɒn *or* ˈbjuːti ˈʃɒp] *noun* place which offers treatments for hair, nails, skin, etc., to help women look more beautiful

beaver [ˈbiːvə] **1** *noun* American animal with sharp teeth and a broad flat tail, which lives in water; *beavers cut down young trees to build their homes* **2** *verb* to **beaver away at something** = to work hard at something; *they were beavering away at building the wall*

became [bɪˈkeɪm] *see* BECOME

because [bɪˈkɒz] *conjunction* for this reason; *I was late because I missed the train*; *the dog's wet because he's been in the river*; *just because I'm lending you my car this time, it doesn't mean you can borrow it when you like*

because of [bɪˈkɒz ɒv] *preposition* on account of, due to; *the trains are late because of the fog*; *we don't often use the car because of the price of petrol*

beckon [ˈbekən] *verb* to **beckon to someone** = to make a sign with your hand telling someone to come; *the nurse beckoned to her to come into the room*

become [bɪˈkʌm] *verb* **(a)** to change to something different; *the sky became dark and the wind became stronger*; *they became good friends*; *as she got older she became rather deaf*; *it soon became obvious that he didn't understand a word of what I was saying* **(b)** to start to work as; *he wants to become a doctor* **(c)** to **become of** = to happen to; *I never saw her brother again, I wonder what became of him* **(d)** *(formal)* to suit; *such behaviour hardly becomes a young lady* (NOTE: **becoming - became** [bɪˈkeɪm] **- has become**)

becoming [bɪˈkʌmɪŋ] *adjective (old)* which is suitable; **her dress is very becoming** = her dress suits her

bed [bed] **1** *noun* **(a)** piece of furniture for sleeping on; *lie down on my bed if you're tired*; **double bed** = bed for two people; **single bed** = bed for one person; **to go to bed** = to get into your bed for the night; *she always goes to bed at 9 o'clock*; **to be in bed** = to be sitting or lying in bed; *she's in bed with a cold*; *he was*

sitting up in bed drinking a cup of coffee; **to make a bed** = to make it tidy or change the bedclothes after someone has slept in it; *have you made your bed?*; *you can't go into your hotel room because the beds haven't been made*; *see also* WRONG **(b)** piece of ground specially for plants; *a strawberry bed*; *a bed of roses*; **her life isn't a bed of roses** = she leads a life full of difficulties **(c)** ground at the bottom of water; *the sandy bed of a river*; **oyster bed** = place where oysters are cultivated in the sea **2** *verb* **to bed out plants** = to put plants into a flowerbed; *it's still too cold to start bedding out the geraniums*

bed and breakfast (b. & b.) *or* **B & B)** [ˈbed n ˈbrekfəst] *noun* **(a)** staying for a night in a hotel, etc., and having breakfast but no other meals; *I only want to have bed and breakfast* **(b)** guesthouse offering accommodation and breakfast; *we got a list of bed and breakfasts from the tourist office*

bedclothes [ˈbedkləʊðz] *noun* sheets and blankets which cover a bed; *she woke up when all her bedclothes fell off*

bedcover [ˈbedkʌvə] *noun* decorated cloth put over a bed, a bedspread; *she bought a yellow bedcover for her daughter's room*

bedding [ˈbedɪŋ] *noun* **(a)** bedclothes, sheets, blankets, etc.; *when you rent a cottage the bedding is usually provided* **(b)** straw for horses' stables **(c) bedding (out)** = putting plants in flower beds; *bedding out must be done this weekend or it'll be too late*; **bedding plants** = small plants that are planted in flower beds in early summer; *the garden centre has sold out of bedding plants* (NOTE: no plural)

bed linen [ˈbed ˈlɪnɪn] *noun* sheets and pillowcases used on a bed; *I have no bed linen for the single bed I've just bought*

bedraggled [bɪˈdrægəld] *adjective* dirty, untidy and wet; *they came back from their walk in the rain looking very bedraggled*; *the dogs were all bedraggled after swimming in the lake*

bedrock [ˈbedrɒk] *noun* **(a)** bottom layer of rock under the earth **(b)** basic principles; *socialism is the bedrock of the party's manifesto*

bedroom [ˈbedruːm] *noun* room where you sleep; *my bedroom is on the first floor*; *the hotel has twenty-five bedrooms*; *shut your bedroom door if you want to be quiet*

bedside [ˈbedsaɪd] *noun* the side of a bed; *his wife was sitting at his bedside*; *there's a small lamp on the bedside table*; **bedside manner** = way in which a doctor behaves towards a patient, especially a patient who is in bed; *he has a good bedside manner* = he comforts and reassures his patients

bedsit *or* **bed-sitter** [bedˈsɪt *or* bedˈsɪtə] *noun* combined bedroom and living room which is rented; *she lives in a bedsit in Earl's Court*

bedsore [ˈbedsɔː] *noun* sore which you get from lying in bed; *bedsores can be prevented by the use of special mattresses*

bedspread [ˈbedspred] *noun* a bedcover, a decorated cloth put over a bed; *she decided on a pink and white bedspread to match her bedroom curtains*

bedstead [ˈbedsted] *noun* wooden or metal frame of a bed; *metal bedsteads have become fashionable again*

bedtime [ˈbedtaɪm] *noun* time when you go to bed; *10 o'clock is my bedtime*; *she read the children a* *bedtime story*; **go to bed - it's past your bedtime** = it's later than the time when you normally go to bed

bee [biː] *noun* insect which makes honey, and can sting you if it is annoyed; *the bee moved from flower to flower collecting pollen*

> COMMENT: in a bee colony, the main female bee is the **queen**; the other females are the **workers**, and the males are the **drones**

Beeb [biːb]; **the Beeb** = BRITISH BROADCASTING CORPORATION

beech [biːtʃ] *noun* **(a) beech (tree)** = common hardwood tree; *beeches are common on the chalk hills in the south of England* (NOTE: plural in this meaning is **beeches**) **(b)** wood from this tree; *a beech table*; *the floor is made of beech* (NOTE: do not confuse with **beach**)

beef [biːf] **1** *noun* meat from a cow or bull; *a plate of roast beef and Yorkshire pudding* **2** *verb* (*informal*) **to beef about** = to grumble about; *what's he beefing on about, tell him to shut up!*; **to beef up** = to make bigger or stronger; *we will have to beef up our advertising budget*

beefburger ['biːfbɜːgə] *noun* cake of grilled minced beef, usually served in a roll; *she ordered a beefburger and fries*

beehive ['biːhaɪv] *noun* box for bees to make a nest in which makes it easier for the beekeeper to gather the honey; *take the honeycomb carefully out of the beehive*

beekeeper ['biːkiːpə] *noun* person who keeps bees for their honey; *the beekeeper opened one of the hives and took out a honeycomb*

beeline ['biːlaɪn] *noun* straight line; **to make a beeline for** = to go straight towards; *he made a beeline for the prettiest girl in the room*; *she made a beeline for the chocolate cakes*

been [biːn] *see* BE

beep ['biːp] **1** *noun* audible warning sound; *the printer will make a beep when it runs out of paper* **2** *verb* to make a beep; *the computer beeped when I hit the wrong key*; *see also* BLEEP

beeper ['biːpə] *see* BLEEPER

beer [bɪə] *noun* **(a)** alcoholic drink made from grain (barley, rice, etc.) and water; *can I have a glass of beer?*; *British beer is flavoured with hops* **(b)** a glass of beer; *three beers, please* (NOTE: the plural **beers** is used to mean **glasses of beer**)

beer garden ['bɪə 'gɑːdən] *noun* garden behind a pub, with tables where you can sit and drink beer; *as it was fine and hot, we took our drinks out into the beer garden*

beet [biːt] *noun* **(a) sugar beet** = root vegetable used for making sugar **(b)** *US* beetroot, vegetable with a dark red root; *boil young fresh beets, and serve them with butter*; **as red as a beet** = very red in the face; *you've stayed in the sun too long - you're as red as a beet* (NOTE: do not confuse with **beat**)

beetle ['biːtl] *noun* insect with hard covers on its wings; *there were black beetles in the kitchen*; *some beetles, such as ladybirds, are useful in the garden*

beetroot ['biːtruːt] *noun* vegetable with a dark red root, eaten cooked and pickled with vinegar to make a salad; **as red as a beetroot** = very red in the face; *he*

went as red as a beetroot when we asked him about his girlfriend (NOTE: American English is simply **beet**)

befall [bɪ'fɔːl] *verb* (*formal*) to happen to; *he is worried that some accident might befall her*; *what calamity has befallen her this time?* (NOTE: **befalling - befell - has befallen**)

befit [bɪ'fɪt] *verb* (*formal*) to suit; *he wore a grey suit, as befitted his position as manager* (NOTE: **befitting - befitted**)

before [bɪ'fɔː] **1** *adverb* earlier; *why didn't you tell me before?*; *I didn't see him last week, I saw him the week before* **2** *preposition* earlier than; *they should have arrived before now*; *you must be home before 9 o'clock*; *G comes before H in the alphabet* **3** *conjunction* earlier than; *before you sit down, can you switch on the light?*; *the police got there before I did*; *think carefully before you start to answer the exam questions*; *wash your hands before you have your dinner*

beforehand [bɪ'fɔːhænd] *adverb* in advance; *you must tell me beforehand if you want to borrow any more money*

befriend [bɪ'frend] *verb* (*formal*) to become friendly with someone and help them; *he befriended a lonely student whom he met at Waterloo Station*

beg [beg] *verb* **(a)** to ask for money; *she sat begging on the steps of the station* **(b)** to ask someone in an emotional way to do something, to give something; *his mother begged him not to go*; *children were begging for food*; *he begged for more time to find the money* **(c) to beg a favour of someone** = to ask someone to do something for you **(d) I beg your pardon!** = excuse me, forgive me; *I beg your pardon, I didn't hear what you said*; *I do beg your pardon - I didn't know you were busy* (NOTE: **begging - begged**)

began [bɪ'gæn] *see* BEGIN

beggar ['begə] *noun* **(a)** person who lives by asking for money; *I'm always sad to see so many beggars outside the railway stations* **(b)** (*informal*) **lucky beggar!** = lucky person; *he just won the lottery - lucky beggar!*

begin [bɪ'gɪn] *verb* to start; *the children began to cry*; *she has begun to knit the pullover*; *the house is beginning to warm up*; *his surname begins with an S*; *the meeting is due to begin at ten o'clock sharp*; **to begin again** = to start a second time; *he forgot to save his file and had to begin keyboarding all over again* (NOTE: **beginning - began** [bɪ'gæn] **- has begun** [bɪ'gʌn])

beginner [bɪ'gɪnə] *noun* person who is starting; *he can't paint well, he's only a beginner*

beginning [bɪ'gɪnɪŋ] *noun* first part; *the beginning of the film is rather boring*; *hurry up if you want to see the beginning of the news*

begun [bɪ'gʌn] *see* BEGIN

behalf [bɪ'hɑːf] *noun* **(a) on behalf of** = acting for someone; *she is speaking on behalf of the trade association*; *he was chosen to speak on behalf of the other workers on the shopfloor* **(b) acting on my behalf** = acting as my representative; *the solicitor acting on my behalf* **(c) don't worry on my behalf** = don't worry about me

behave [bɪ'heɪv] *verb* to act in a certain way with someone; *he behaved very pleasantly towards his staff*; *she was behaving in a funny way (of children)* to

behave (yourself) = to be good; *if you don't behave (yourselves) you won't have any ice cream*

-behaved [bɪ'heɪvd] *suffix* referring to behaviour; *he's a very well-behaved little boy*; *the girls are badly-behaved*

behaviour *US* **behavior** [bɪ'heɪvjə] *noun* way of doing things; *his behaviour was quite natural*; *visitors complained about the behaviour of football fans*

behavioural *US* **behavioral** [bɪ'heɪvjərəl] *adjective* referring to human behaviour; *people with behavioural problems*

behead [bɪ'hed] *verb* to cut off someone's head; *Queen Anne Boleyn was beheaded in the Tower of London*

behind [bɪ'haɪnd] **1** *preposition* **(a)** at the back of; *they hid behind the door*; *I dropped my pen behind the bed*; *he was second, only three metres behind the winner*; *she's behind the rest of class* = not as advanced as the others; *see also* TIME **(b)** responsible for; *the police believe they know who is behind the bombing campaign* **(c)** supporting; *all his colleagues were behind his decision*; *we're behind you!* **2** *adverb* **(a)** at the back; *he was first, the rest of the runners were a long way behind*; *he left his wallet behind* = he forgot to take his wallet with him; *when the others went out, he stayed behind to watch TV* = he stayed at home when the others went out **(b)** later than you should be; *I am behind with my correspondence*; *the company has fallen behind with its deliveries* **3** *noun* (*informal*) part of the body which you sit on; *I'll kick your behind if you don't get a move on*; *there was some water on the chair and my behind's all wet*; *he's so lazy! - he needs a good kick up the behind*

behind-the-scenes [bɪ'haɪnd ðə 'siːnz] *adjective* hidden, not in public; *there was a lot of behind-the-scenes activity getting the room ready for the wedding reception*

behold [bɪ'həʊld] *verb* **(a)** (*old*) to see; *the happiness on the little children's faces was marvellous to behold* **(b)** lo and behold! = all of a sudden (something happened); *we had been waiting for hours for a bus when, lo and behold, three came together*

beholden [bɪ'həʊldən] *adjective* (*formal*) to be beholden to someone for something = to be grateful to someone; *the family is particularly beholden to the neighbours for their help*

beige [beɪʒ] *adjective & noun* very pale brown colour; *he was wearing a beige pullover*

being ['biːɪŋ] *see* HUMAN, TIME

Belarus *or* **Bielorussia** [belə'rʊs *or* bjeləʊ'rʌʃə] *noun* country in eastern Europe, between Poland and Russia (NOTE: capital: **Minsk**; people: **Belarusians**; language: **Belarusian**: currency: **rouble**)

Belarusian [belə'rʌʃən] **1** *adjective* referring to Belarus **2** *noun* **(a)** person from Belarus **(b)** language spoken in Belarus

belated [bɪ'leɪtɪd] *adjective* later than should be; *he sent a rather belated thank you letter*

belch [beltʃ] **1** *noun* allowing air in the stomach to come up through the mouth; *he finished his meal and let out a loud belch* (NOTE: plural is **belches**) **2** *verb* **(a)** to make air in the stomach come up through the mouth; *he wiped his mouth and belched* **(b)** to pour out of; *dark smoke belched from the power station* **(c)** to

belch out = to send out large amounts of smoke, fumes, flames; *the power station was belching out dark smoke*

beleaguered [bɪ'liːgəd] *adjective* (*formal*) surrounded by difficulties or by enemies; *can the government do anything to help the beleaguered coal industry?*

belfry ['belfri] *noun* church tower where bells are; *the belfry was hit by lightning* (NOTE: plural is **belfries**)

Belgian ['beldʒən] **1** *adjective* referring to Belgium; *Belgian chocolates are very popular in England*; *all Belgian motorways are lit up at night* **2** *noun* person from Belgium; *there were ten people at the meeting, and two of them were Belgians*

Belgium ['beldʒəm] *noun* country on the North Sea, between France and Holland; *if you're driving to Denmark, it is quicker to drive through Belgium into Germany* (NOTE: capital: **Brussels**; people: **Belgians**; languages: **Flemish, French**; currency: **Belgian franc, euro**)

belie [bɪ'laɪ] *verb* (*formal*) **(a)** to hide; *his brusque manner belies his gentle nature* **(b)** to show that something is false; *his exam results belied his teachers' reports*

belief [bɪ'liːf] *noun* feeling sure that something is true; *his firm belief in the power of law*; *her strong belief in God*; *it is my belief* = I believe; *it's my belief that the problems have been grossly exaggerated*; *to the best of my belief* = as far as I know; *to the best of my belief, no one else has seen this document*; *beyond belief* = quite incredible; *that she did not know that there were drugs in the parcel is quite beyond belief*

believable [bɪ'liːvəbl] *adjective* which can be believed; *her story was hardly believable*

believe [bɪ'liːv] *verb* **(a)** to be sure that something is true, although you can't prove it; *people used to believe that the earth was flat*; *don't believe anything he tells you* **(b)** not to be absolutely sure; *I don't believe I have ever met your father*; *I believe I have been here before* **(c)** to believe in = to be sure that something exists; *do you believe in flying saucers?*; *some people believe in miracles* **(d)** can't *or* couldn't believe your eyes *or* ears = be very surprised to see *or* hear something; *she couldn't believe her eyes when she saw the car he had bought her*

believer [bɪ'liːvə] *noun* person who believes in a particular religion or idea; *the prophet was followed by a crowd of believers*; *he's a great believer in cold showers*

Belisha beacon [bɪ'liːʃə 'biːkən] *noun* flashing light at a zebra crossing

belittle [bɪ'lɪtl] *verb* (*formal*) to make something seem unimportant; *he tried to belittle her achievements*; *don't belittle her first attempts at drawing, she's only two years old, after all*

bell [bel] *noun* **(a)** metal object, like a cup, which makes a ringing noise when hit; electric device which makes a ringing noise if you push a button; *the church bells were damaged during the war*; *the alarm bell rings if you touch the door*; *the postman rang the door bell*; *you ought to have a bell on your bicycle*; *they rang the church bells at the wedding*; *that rings a bell* = that reminds me of something; *does the name Forsyth ring a bell?* **(b)** (*informal*) to give someone a bell = to phone someone; *I'll give you a bell when we've sorted out the details*

bellboy ['belbɔɪ] *noun* messenger who carries messages, takes luggage, etc., in a hotel; *the bellboy will carry your cases up to your room* (NOTE: American English is **bellhop**)

bellhop ['belhɒp] *noun US* messenger who carries messages, takes luggage, etc., in a hotel; *the bellhop will carry your cases up to your room* (NOTE: British English is **bellboy**)

bellicose ['belɪkəʊs] *adjective (formal)* wanting to fight; *when the chef is in a bellicose mood, we know that he has slept badly*

belligerent [bə'lɪdʒərənt] **1** *adjective* **(a)** wanting to go to war; *the country has turned increasingly belligerent towards its neighbours* **(b)** *(person)* aggressive, wanting to argue with other people; *ask the manager about it tomorrow, he's in a belligerent mood at the moment* **2** *noun* country that is at war; *the belligerents refused to accept the ruling of the international mediators*

bellow ['beləʊ] **1** *noun* loud deep cry; *the deer raised its head and gave a loud bellow* **2** *verb* **(a)** to make a loud cry; *he bellowed with pain*; *the bull was bellowing in the farmyard* **(b)** to shout; *he bellowed to the swimmers to come back to the beach*

bellows ['beləʊz] *noun* device used to blow air onto a fire; *we have an old pair of bellows at home which we never use* (NOTE: no singular: to show one item, say **a pair of bellows**)

belly ['beli] *noun (informal)* stomach and intestines, the front part of the body below the chest; *the little boy lifted his T-shirt to show his round belly* (NOTE: plural is **bellies**)

bellyache ['belieɪk] **1** *noun* pain in the abdomen or stomach; *she had a bellyache after eating green apples* **2** *verb (informal)* to bellyache about something = to complain about something; *nothing seems to make her happy - she's always bellyaching about something*

belly button ['beli 'bʌtən] *noun (children's language)* navel, the depression in the middle of the abdomen where the umbilical cord was detached after birth; *my doll has a belly button just like a real baby*

belong [bɪ'lɒŋ] *verb* **(a)** to belong to someone = to be the property of someone; *does the car really belong to you?* **(b)** to belong to a group or club = to be a member of a group or club; *which tennis club do you belong to?* **(c)** to belong with = to be part of, to be stored with; *these plates belong with the big dinner service*

belongings [bɪ'lɒŋɪŋz] *noun* personal property; *her belongings were scattered all over the room*; *please be sure to take all personal belongings with you when you leave the aircraft*

beloved [bɪ'lʌvɪd] **1** *adjective* which is loved; *she doesn't want to leave her beloved childhood home*; *he was very upset at the death of his beloved grandfather* **2** *noun (old)* person you love most; *he was reunited with his beloved*

below [bɪ'ləʊ] **1** *adverb* lower down; *standing on the bridge we looked at the river below*; *these toys are for children of two years and below* **2** *preposition* lower down than; *the temperature was below freezing*; *in Singapore, the temperature never goes below 25°C*; *can you see below the surface of the water?*; *do not write anything below this line*; *these tablets should not be given to children below the age of twelve*

belt [belt] **1** *noun* **(a)** strap which goes round your waist (to hold up a skirt or trousers); *she wore a bright red belt*; *this silver belt comes from Thailand* **(b)** seat belt *or* safety belt = belt which you wear in a car or a plane to stop you being hurt if there is an accident; *please fasten your seat belts as we are preparing to land*; *the police caught him driving without a seat belt* **(c)** person who wears a particular coloured belt worn when playing judo; *he's a black belt* **(d)** zone around something; **commuter belt** = area round a large town, where commuters live; *they live in the Surrey commuter belt*; **Green Belt** = area of farming land or woods and parks, which surrounds a town, and on which building is restricted or completely banned; *they can't put houses in Old Oak Wood, it's Green Belt land* **2** *verb (informal)* **(a)** to travel fast; *the car was belting along the motorway at over 100 miles an hour* **(b)** to belt out = to sing very loudly; *the fans were belting out football songs*

belt up ['belt 'ʌp] *verb (informal)* **(a)** to stop talking; **belt up!** = be quiet! **(b)** to attach your seat belt; *make sure everyone in the car belts up*

bemoan [bɪ'məʊn] *verb (formal)* to complain about something; *she bemoaned the lack of a good bus service*

bemused [bɪ'mju:zd] *adjective* puzzled and confused; *she looked bemused by her success*; *three rather bemused English girls came to collect their prizes*

bench [bentʃ] *noun* **(a)** long wooden seat; *we sat down on one of the park benches* **(b)** (work) bench = table in a workshop at which someone works; *the carpenter was standing at his bench* **(c)** the bench = magistrates sitting in court; *he was up before the bench for speeding* **(d)** *(in Parliament)* long seats in the House of Commons; **front bench** = seat where ministers sit; *he's hoping for a seat on the front bench*; **back benches** = seats where ordinary MPs sit (NOTE: plural is **benches**)

benchmark ['bentʃmɑ:k] *noun* standard for testing; *we are using the results of the first tests as a benchmark*

bend [bend] **1** *noun* **(a)** curve (in a road, line, etc.); *don't drive too fast, there's a sudden bend in the road*; *the pipe under the sink has an awkward S-bend* **(b)** *(informal)* round the bend = mad; *he's completely round the bend*; *she'll go round the bend when she hears that*; *that music is driving me round the bend* **2** *verb* **(a)** to make something curved; *you will have to bend the pipe to fit round the corner* **(b)** to curve; *the road bends sharply after the bridge* (NOTE: **bending - bent** [bent])

bend down *or* **bend over** ['bend 'daʊn *or* 'əʊvə] *verb* to stoop, so that your head is lower than your waist; *he dropped his pen and bent down to pick it up*; *she was bending over the sink*; *see also* BACKWARDS

bends [bendz] *noun* the bends = illness of divers, with pains in the joints and dizziness, caused when a diver moves up from a deep part of the sea too quickly

beneath [bɪ'ni:θ] **1** *adverb* underneath; *from the bridge we watched the river flowing beneath* **2** *preposition* **(a)** under; *there are dangerous rocks beneath the surface of the lake*; *the river flows very fast beneath the bridge* **(b)** not suitable, not important enough; *he thinks it is beneath him to make the coffee himself*

benefactor *or* **benefactress** ['benɪfæktə *or* 'benɪfæktrəs] *noun* person who gives money to an organization such as a charity; *some benefactors did not approve of the party's decision and cancelled their contributions*; *the college refused to accept any financial help from overseas benefactors*

beneficent [bɪ'nefɪsənt] *adjective (formal)* who does good to others; *a beneficent god*

beneficial [benɪ'fɪʃl] *adjective* which helps; *a regular walk every morning is beneficial to your general health*

beneficiary [benɪ'fɪʃəri] *noun* **(a)** person who inherits something in a will; *the main beneficiaries were his three children* **(b)** someone, or a group, who is helped by something; *who will be the main beneficiaries of this new law? - surely not small firms* (NOTE: plural is **beneficiaries**)

benefit ['benɪfɪt] **1** *noun* **(a)** advantage; *what benefit would I get from joining the club?*; *see also* FRINGE BENEFITS **(b)** payment by the state; *unemployment benefit*; *maternity benefit* **2** *verb* **(a)** to be useful to someone; *the book will benefit anyone who is planning to do some house repairs* **(b)** to benefit from *or* by something = to get an advantage from; *British tourists will benefit from the strong pound*; *pensioners can benefit from free bus passes*

benevolence [bɪ'nevələns] *noun* being good and kind; *the old doctor's benevolence was well-known in the village*

benevolent [bɪ'nevələnt] *adjective* good and kind; *he's in a particularly benevolent mood this morning, so you can ask him for time off*; *the government has never been benevolent towards single parents in the past*

benign [bɪ'naɪn] *adjective* **(a)** kind and pleasant; *the police officer looked at the little boy with a benign smile and took him to find his mother* **(b)** benign growth = a harmless or non-cancerous growth; *at first they thought the growth was benign, but in fact it was malignant* (NOTE: a tumour which is cancerous is **malignant**) **(c)** mild, not very cold; *I don't like cold winters - I think we should move to a country with a more benign climate*

bent [bent] **1** *adjective* **(a)** curved; *these nails are bent so we can't use them* **(b)** to be bent on = to be very keen on doing something; *he is bent on buying the car even if he can't afford it* **2** *noun* instinct; *she has a natural bent to be a nurse*; *he followed his bent and joined the navy* **3** *verb see also* BEND

benzene ['benziːn] *noun* simple liquid hydrocarbon used in making plastic and petrol (it is very carcinogenic); *benzene is found in car exhaust fumes*

bequeath [bɪ'kwiːð] *verb* **to bequeath something to someone** = to leave property (but not freehold land) to someone in a will; *he bequeathed his shares to his son*

bequest [bɪ'kwest] *noun* giving of property, money, etc. (but not freehold land) to someone in a will; *in his will, he made several bequests to his staff*

berate [bɪ'reɪt] *verb (formal)* to criticize in an angry tone; *he berated the restaurant staff for being badly dressed*; *the newspapers berated the minister for her eccentric decision*

bereaved [bɪ'riːvd] **1** *adjective* who has a close relative or friend who has died; *we sent our condolences to the bereaved families* **2** *noun* **the bereaved** = the family or friends of a person who has died; *the priest was trying to console the bereaved after the funeral*

bereavement [bɪ'riːvmənt] *noun (formal)* loss of a friend or relative through death; *it seems that we have had one bereavement after another this winter*

bereft [bɪ'reft] *adjective (formal)* **bereft of** = without; *he was left bereft of all income when his business collapsed*; *the children were bereft of medical care*; **bereft of hope** = without any hope or plans for the future

beret ['bereɪ] *noun* round cap without a peak; *he thinks he looks very French with his beret*

berry ['beri] *noun* small fruit; *they spent the afternoon picking berries in the woods* (NOTE: plural is **berries**; also used frequently after other words: **blackberry, blueberry, gooseberry**, etc.; do not confuse with **bury**)

berserk [bə'zɜːk] *adjective* **to go berserk** = to get angry and wild; *when he heard that she had sold his collection of stamps he went berserk*

berth [bɜːθ] **1** *noun* **(a)** place where a ship ties up in a harbour; *there are no berths free - the ferry will have to wait at anchor outside the harbour for a while* **(b)** **to give someone *or* something a wide berth** = to avoid someone *or* something; *dad is in a bad mood - I'd give him a wide berth if I were you* **(c)** bunk bed on a ship or train; *do you want the upper or lower berth?* **2** *verb (of ship)* to tie up in a harbour; *the ship won't berth until late this evening*

beseech [bɪ'siːtʃ] *verb (formal)* **to beseech someone to do something** = to ask someone earnestly to do something; *she beseeched them to think again*; *do not do this, I beseech you* (NOTE: **beseeched** *or* **besought** [bɪ'sɔːt])

beset [bɪ'set] *adjective* **beset with** = surrounded with difficulties, problems, etc.; *the move to new offices was beset with problems*

beside [bɪ'saɪd] *preposition* **(a)** at the side of someone or something; *come and sit down beside me*; *the office is just beside the railway station*; **it's beside the point** = it's got nothing to do with the main subject; *whether or not the coat matches your hat is beside the point - it's simply too big for you* **(b)** **to be beside yourself with** = to be mad with; *the parents were beside themselves with worry when the little daughter did not come home from school*; *she was beside herself with grief*

besides [bɪ'saɪdz] **1** *preposition* as well as; *they have two other cars besides the big Ford*; *besides the football team, our town also has a hockey team*; *besides managing the shop, he also teaches in the evening* **2** *adverb* **(a)** as well; *he paints, plays chess and has lots of other interests besides* **(b)** in any case; *I don't want to go for a picnic - besides, it's starting to rain*

besiege [bɪ'siːdʒ] *verb (of soldiers, newspaper reporters)* to surround (a castle, a house, etc.); *the cameramen besieged the house*; *the army besieging the town directed their artillery against the weakest part of the city walls*

besmirch [bɪˈsmɜːtʃ] *verb (formal)* to make dirty; *the news story was trying to besmirch the Prime Minister's reputation*

besotted [bɪˈsɒtɪd] *adjective* **besotted with someone** = madly in love with someone; *I don't see what he sees in her, but he's completely besotted; she's besotted with her new baby*

best [best] **1** *adjective* **(a)** very good, better than anything else; *she's my best friend; what is the best way of getting to London from here?; he put on his best suit to go to the interview* **(b)** *for the best part of* = for most of; *she's been in bed for the best part of a week* **2** *noun* **(a)** thing which is better than anything else; *the picture shows her at her best;* **to do your best** = to do as well as you can; *she did her best, but didn't win* **(b) to make the best of something** = to take what advantage you can from something; *they say it will rain this afternoon, so we'd better make the best of the sunshine while it's here;* **to make the best of a bad job** = to do something in spite of terrible conditions; *it was raining when we stopped for a picnic, so we made the best of a bad job and had our sandwiches in the car* **(c)** *(informal)* best clothes; *the children were all in their Sunday best* **(d)** *(informal)* best bitter beer; *two pints of best, please!* **3** *adverb* in the best way; *which of you knows London best?; the engine works best when it's warm; oranges grow best in hot countries;* **as best you can** = in the best way you can, even though this may not be perfect; *he repaired the dent in the car door as best he could* (NOTE: **best** is the superlative of both **good** and **well**)

bestial [ˈbestjəl] *adjective* savage, horrible; *he carried out a series of bestial attacks on old people*

best man [ˈbest ˈmæn] *noun* man who helps the bridegroom at a wedding; *the best man had put the wedding rings in his pocket; the best man gave a speech and told some funny stories about the groom when he was a student*

bestow [bɪˈstəʊ] *verb (formal)* to give; *the government bestowed many honours on him*

best regards *or* **best wishes** [ˈbest rɪˈɡɑːdz *or* ˈwɪʃɪz] *noun* greeting sent to someone; *give my best wishes to your father*

bestseller [bestˈselə] *noun* item, especially a book, which sells very well; *he has written three bestsellers; her book has been in the bestseller list for several weeks*

bestselling [bestˈselɪŋ] *adjective* which sells in very large numbers; *these computer disks are our bestselling line; this is the bestselling car in the range;* **bestselling author** *or* **writer** = writer whose books sell very well; *our bestselling author left us for another publishing house*

bet [bet] **1** *noun* money which is risked by trying to say which horse will come first in a race, which side will win a competition, etc.; *he placed a bet on his friend's horse but lost his bet when the horse came last; I've got a bet on England to win the next World Cup;* **safe bet** = bet which you are not likely to lose; *it's a safe bet that if we decide to go camping it will rain* **2** *verb* to risk money by saying which horse you think will come first in a race, which team will win, etc.; *he bet me £10 the Prime Minister would lose the election; I bet you she's going to be late* = I am quite sure she's going to be late *(informal)* **you bet!** = of course; *do you want to go to the pub? - you bet!* (NOTE: **betting - bet**)

beta [ˈbiːtə] *noun* the second letter of the Greek alphabet (β) mark showing a second level; *he only got a beta minus for his essay*

beta blockers [ˈbiːtə ˈblɒkəz] *noun* drugs which reduce the heart's activity; *hypertension can be treated with drugs such as beta blockers*

betray [bɪˈtreɪ] *verb* **(a)** to harm someone by telling their secrets; *he was betrayed to the enemy by his best friend; the scientist was accused of betraying secrets to the enemy* **(b)** to show a feeling which you want to keep hidden; *the tears in her eyes betrayed her emotion*

betrayal [bɪˈtreɪəl] *noun* giving someone's secrets to an enemy; not doing what you had promised to do; *selling the farm to a property developer is a betrayal of all our principles; he felt a sense of betrayal when he heard the news*

betrothal [bɪˈtrəʊðəl] *noun (formal)* engagement, promise to marry; *special robes are worn at the betrothal ceremony*

betrothed [bɪˈtrəʊðd] *noun (old, formal)* person you are engaged to marry; *his betrothed decided in the end that she would not marry him*

better [ˈbetə] **1** *adjective* **(a)** good when compared to something else; *the weather is better today than it was yesterday; his latest book is better than the first one he wrote; she's better at maths than English; brown bread is better for you than white; we will shop around to see if we can get a better price* **(b)** healthy again; *I had a cold last week but I'm better now; I hope your sister will be better soon* **2** *adverb* well as compared to something else; *she sings better than her sister; my old knife cuts better than the new one;* **to think better of something** = to decide that something is not a good idea; *he was going to drive to London, but thought better of it when he saw the traffic* (NOTE: **better** is the comparative of both **good** and **well**) **3** *noun* **the better of someone** = to beat someone; *no one can get the better of him at poker;* **for the better** = which makes the situation better; *he's earning more money now, and his financial situation has changed for the better; he took a turn for the better* = his health began to improve

◊ **had better** [ˈhæd ˈbetə] it would be a good thing if; *you had better wear a coat - I think it's starting to snow; she'd better go to bed if she's got flu; hadn't you better answer the phone?*

betting shop [ˈbetɪŋ ˈʃɒp] *noun* shop where you can place bets on races; *young people are not allowed in betting shops*

bettor [ˈbetə] *noun* person who bets (on a horse, etc.) (NOTE: do not confuse with **better**)

between [bɪˈtwiːn] *preposition* **(a)** placed with things on both sides; *there's only a thin wall between his office and mine, so I hear everything he says; don't sit between him and his girlfriend* **(b)** connecting two places; *the bus goes between Oxford and London* **(c)** in the interval separating two times; *I'm have a meeting between 10 o'clock and 12; can you come to see me between now and next Monday?* **(d)** in the space separating two amounts; *the parcel weighs between four and five kilos; cherries cost between £2 and £3 per kilo* **(e)** showing a difference; *she's colour-blind - she can't tell the difference between red and green* **(f)** sharing; *we only had £10 between the three of us* **(g)** among; *she could choose between courses in German, Chinese or Russian* **(h)** between

you and me = speaking privately; *between you and me, I don't think he's very good at his job*

◊ **in between** [ɪn bɪ'twiːn] in the middle, with things on both sides; *the hotel looks over the river, with a railway line in between*; *he had two meetings in the morning but managed to fit in a game of tennis in between*

beverage ['bevərɪdʒ] *noun (formal)* drink; *Coca Cola is a popular non-alcoholic beverage*

beware [bɪ'weə] *verb* to watch out for; *beware of the dog!*; *beware of pickpockets!*

bewilder [bɪ'wɪldə] *verb* to make someone puzzled; *all these road signs just bewilder drivers*

bewildered [bɪ'wɪldəd] *adjective* confused or puzzled; *he was bewildered to find himself alone in the castle*; *a bewildered young girl was standing all by herself in the middle of the room*

bewildering [bɪ'wɪldərɪŋ] *adjective* confusing or puzzling; *she tried to follow the bewildering instructions in the manufacturer's handbook*; *all these different prices and discounts are quite bewildering*

bewilderment [bɪ'wɪldəmənt] *noun* confusion, being puzzled; *in some bewilderment she tried to discover who had sent her the bunch of flowers*

beyond [bɪ'jɒnd] **1** *preposition* **(a)** further away than; *the post office is beyond the bank*; *it is beyond my means* = it is too expensive for me to buy it; *I'd love to buy a sports car, but I think it would be beyond my means* **(b)** later than; *the party went on till beyond midnight* **2** *adverb* further away, on the other side; *she stared through the window at the fields beyond*

biannual [baɪ'ænjʊəl] *adjective* which happens twice a year; *there is a biannual review of progress on the construction* (NOTE: do not confuse with **biennial**)

bias ['baɪəs] *noun* fixed opinion in one direction only; *the judges in the beauty competition were accused of bias*

biased ['baɪəst] *adjective* prejudiced; *we felt the decision was biased*; *the court was biased in favour of the president's daughter*

biathlon [baɪ'æθlɒn] *noun* Winter Olympic sport in which skiers with rifles shoot at targets along a cross-country course; *compare* TRIATHLON

COMMENT: originally for men, but included as a discipline for women in the 1992 Winter Olympics at Albertville, France

bib [bɪb] *noun* **(a)** little piece of cloth which is tied round a baby's neck, under its chin; *don't forget to put his bib on when he's eating spinach* **(b)** top part of an apron or dungarees, covering your chest

Bible ['baɪbl] *noun* Christian and Jewish book of scriptures; *he reads from the Bible every evening*

COMMENT: the Bible is formed of the Old Testament (the Jewish scriptures) and New Testament, the writings concerned with the life and works of Christ and the early Christian church

biblical ['bɪblɪkl] *adjective* referring to the Bible; *I'm trying to remember that biblical passage about the Flood*

bibliographical [bɪblɪə'græfɪkl] *adjective* referring to a list of publications on a particular subject; *for further bibliographical information, please refer to the supplement*

bibliography [bɪblɪ'ɒgrəfi] *noun* list of publications about a special subject; *he compiled a bibliography of works on Shakespeare's poems*; *there is a full bibliography at the back of the book* (NOTE: plural is **bibliographies**)

biceps ['baɪseps] *noun* any muscle formed of two parts, especially the muscle in the front of the upper arm; *he's doing gym exercises to develop his biceps* (NOTE: plural is **biceps**)

bicker ['bɪkə] *verb* to quarrel about something; *they're constantly bickering about money*

bicycle ['baɪsɪkl] *noun* vehicle with two wheels which is ridden by one person who makes it go by pushing on the pedals and steers with the handlebars; *he goes to school by bicycle every day*; *she's going to do the shopping on her bicycle*; *he's learning to ride a bicycle*; **bicycle pump** = small hand pump for blowing up bicycle tyres; *we blew up the mattress with a bicycle pump*; *see also* BIKE, TANDEM (NOTE: also called a **bike**. The person who rides a bicycle is a **cyclist**. Note also that to show the difference with a motorcycle, a bicycle is sometimes called a **push bike**)

bicyclist ['baɪsɪklɪst] *noun* person who rides a bicycle (NOTE: usually **cyclist**)

bid [bɪd] **1** *noun* **(a)** offer to buy at an auction; *his bid for the painting was too low* **(b)** attempt to do something; *he made a bid for power* = he tried to seize power; **takeover bid** = attempt to take over a company by offering to buy most of its shares **2** *verb* to make an offer to buy something at an auction; *he bid £500 for the car* (NOTE: **bidding - bid**)

bidder ['bɪdə] *noun* person who makes an offer to buy something, especially at an auction; *several bidders made offers for the house*; **the highest bidder** = the person who makes the best offer; *the lot was sold to the highest bidder*

bidet ['biːdeɪ] *noun* small low bath for washing your buttocks, etc.; *each bathroom has a shower and a bidet*

biennial [baɪ'enjəl] **1** *adjective* **(a)** **biennial plant** = plant which flowers in its second year of growth and then dies **(b)** *(event)* which happens every two years; *the athletics competition is a biennial event* (NOTE: do not confuse with **biannual**) **2** *noun* plant which flowers in its second year of growth and then dies; *we plant biennials at the back of the flowerbed and annuals in front*; *compare with* ANNUAL, PERENNIAL

big [bɪg] *adjective* of a large size; *I don't want a small car - I want a big one*; *his father has the biggest restaurant in town*; *I'm not afraid of him - I'm bigger than he is*; *we had a big order from Germany*; **big toe** = the largest of the five toes (NOTE: **bigger - biggest**)

bigamist ['bɪgəmɪst] *noun* person who is illegally married to two people at the same time; *it turned out that he was a bigamist, with one wife in Hong Kong and another in England*

bigamous ['bɪgəməs] *adjective* **bigamous marriage** = marriage to someone when you are already married; *he went through a bigamous wedding ceremony in Malta*

bigamy ['bɪgəmi] *noun* crime of going through a ceremony of marriage to someone when you are already married to someone else; *he was charged with bigamy*; *compare* MONOGAMY, POLYGAMY

Big Ben ['bɪg 'ben] *noun* clock and bell at the top of the tower of the Houses of Parliament in London; *Big Ben strikes the hours for the TV news*

big business ['bɪg 'bɪznɪs] *noun* very large commercial companies, seen as a group; *big business exerts a lot of pressure on the government*

big-city ['bɪg 'sɪti] *adjective* referring to a very large town; *the big-city bustle of New York scares me*

big deal ['bɪg 'diːl] *noun* **(a)** important business transaction; *it's one of the biggest deals we have ever signed* **(b)** *(used sarcastically)* **big deal!** = that's not a very good deal; *he offered me £20 for the car - big deal!*

bigheaded ['bɪghedɪd] *adjective (informal)* too proud of yourself; *he's got so bigheaded since he won the prize*

big money ['bɪg 'mʌni] *noun (informal)* a lot of money; *there's big money involved in the deal*; *he works as a computer programmer and makes really big money*

big name ['bɪg 'neɪm] *noun* important person; *he's a big name in the music business*

bigoted ['bɪgətɪd] *adjective* with very strong and unreasonable ideas about something; *the president made a bigoted reference to women directors*

bigotry ['bɪgətri] *noun* attitude where you dislike something strongly for no particular reason; *his speech played on the bigotry of the crowd*; *a new wave of bigotry and racism is sweeping the country*

big time ['bɪg 'taɪm] *noun* being at the top level in show business; *he toured the country doing conjuring tricks, and then suddenly hit the big time with a TV show*

big top ['bɪg 'tɒp] *noun* very large circus tent; *they're putting up the big top on the sports field*

bike [baɪk] *noun (informal)* = BICYCLE; *he goes to school by bike*; *she was knocked off her bike by a car*; *although he is over eighty he still rides a bike* or *goes for a bike ride every day*; **exercise bike** = bicycle fixed to the floor, which you can pedal on as exercise; *he does ten minutes on his exercise bike before breakfast*; **mountain bike** = strong bicycle with wider tyres, used for country cycling; *she rode her mountain bike along the hill paths*; **push bike**; *see note at* BICYCLE

biker ['baɪkə] *noun* motorcyclist, a person who rides a motorcycle; *a gang of bikers arrived in the village*

bikini [bɪ'kiːni] *noun* woman's small two-piece bathing costume; *women in bikinis strolled around the pool*

bilateral [baɪ'lætərəl] *adjective* involving two sides; *the two countries have signed a bilateral trade agreement*

bilberry ['bɪlbəri] *noun* wild berry, which is blue when ripe, eaten raw with sugar and cream, or cooked in pies and jams; *she made a bilberry pie*; **bilberry bush** = little bush which has these berries (NOTE: plural is **bilberries**; also called **blueberry**)

bile [baɪl] *noun* thick bitter brownish-yellow fluid produced by the liver, which helps to digest fatty substances; **bile duct** = tube carrying bile to the intestines

COMMENT: in attacks of jaundice, excess bile pigments flow into the blood and make the skin turn yellow

bilingual [baɪ'lɪŋgwəl] *adjective* using two languages; *unfortunately he's not bilingual and everything has to be translated for him*; **a bilingual dictionary** = dictionary which gives translations from one language into another; *he carries a bilingual German-Spanish glossary with him*; **she is bilingual in French and Spanish** = she can speak French and Spanish equally well

bilious ['bɪliəs] *adjective* feeling sick, especially when bile comes up into your mouth; *she had a bilious attack after the dinner*

bill [bɪl] *noun* **(a)** piece of paper showing the amount of money you have to pay (in a restaurant, for repairs, etc.); *the total bill came to more than £200*; *does the bill include VAT ?*; *ask the waiter for the bill*; *don't forget to pay the gas bill* (NOTE: in American English in a restaurant or hotel, this is **check**) **(b)** hard part of a bird's mouth; *the bird was picking up food with its bill* **(c)** *US* piece of paper money; *a 10-dollar bill* (NOTE: British English for this is **note**: **a 5-pound note**) **(d)** proposed act of parliament which, if passed by parliament, becomes law; *Parliament will consider two bills this week*; *he has drafted a bill to ban the sale of guns*

billboard ['bɪlbɔːd] *noun especially US* large outdoor panel for posters; *billboards were advertising the new fares to the Far East* (NOTE: British English is **hoarding**)

billfold ['bɪlfəʊld] *noun US* small flat leather case for credit cards and banknotes, carried in your pocket; *his billfold was stolen from his back pocket*; *never leave your billfold on the car seat* (NOTE: British English is **wallet**)

billiards ['bɪljədz] *noun* game where two players with long cues hit their own white ball against a red ball or the opponent's ball, scoring points; *they played a game of billiards*; *the club has bought a new billiard table* *compare* SNOOKER (NOTE: the word **billiards** loses the 's' when it is in front of another noun)

COMMENT: The game is played on a rectangular table covered with smooth green baize and with raised cushioned edges (or 'cushions') and six small net bags (or 'pockets') situated at each corner and in the middle of the two long sides

billion ['bɪljən] *noun* **(a)** one thousand million *(sometimes)* one million million; *the government raises billions in taxes each years* **(b)** a great many; *billions of Christmas cards are sent every year* (NOTE: in American English it has always meant one thousand million, but in British English it formerly meant one million million, and it is still sometimes used with this meaning. With figures it is usually written **bn**: **$5bn** say 'five billion dollars')

billionaire [bɪljə'neə] *noun* person who is worth one billion pounds or dollars; *the billionaire head of a computer company*

bill of exchange ['bɪl əv ɪks'tʃeɪnʒ] *noun* document signed by the person authorizing it, which tells someone else to pay money to a named person on a certain date (usually used in payments in foreign currency)

Bill of Rights [ˈbɪl əv ˈraɪts] *noun* the first ten amendments to the constitution of the United States, which refer to the rights and privileges of individual citizens

billow [ˈbɪləʊ] **1** *noun* **(a)** *(formal)* very large wave **(b)** mass of moving smoke; *we could see billows of smoke rising from the volcano* **2** *verb* **(a)** to become full of air; *the sails of the yachts billowed in the breeze* **(b)** to move in large waves; *smoke billowed out of the building*

billy goat [ˈbɪlɪ ˈɡəʊt] *noun (children's word)* male goat (NOTE: a female goat is a **nanny goat**)

bimbo [ˈbɪmbəʊ] *noun (slang)* attractive (but usually rather stupid) girl; *he came to the wedding with some bimbo from the office*

bin [bɪn] **1** *noun* **(a)** metal box for keeping things; **bread bin** = metal box for keeping bread in **(b)** container for putting rubbish; *don't throw your litter on the floor - pick it up and put it in the bin*; **pedal bin** = container for rubbish which opens with a pedal **2** *verb (informal)* to throw away into a rubbish bin; *he just binned the demand for payment* (NOTE: **binning - binned**)

binary system [ˈbaɪnəri ˈsɪstəm] *noun* numerical system which only uses the digits 1 and 0; *the binary system is used in computer programs*; **binary digit** = *see* BIT

bind [baɪnd] *verb* **(a)** to tie; *they bound her to the tree with ropes* **(b)** to force someone to do something; *the contract binds him to make regular payments* **(c)** to put a cover on a book; *the book is bound in blue leather*; *see also* BOUND (NOTE: **binding - bound** [baʊnd])

binder [ˈbaɪndə] *noun* **(a)** person or company that binds books; *the book has been printed and is now at the binder's* **(b)** stiff cardboard cover for papers; *write to the publisher to get a free binder for your magazines*; **ring binder** = cover with rings in it which fit into special holes made in sheets of paper; *he keeps his letters in a ring binder* **(c)** *US* letter giving agreement for insurance sent before the policy is issued; *this binder is valid for thirty days* (NOTE: the British English for this is **cover note**) **(d)** *US* money paid as part of an agreement to buy something, especially a property; *a binder of $5000 will secure the purchase of the property* (NOTE: the British English for this is **deposit**)

binding [ˈbaɪndɪŋ] **1** *adjective* legally enforceable; *this contract is binding on both parties* **2** *noun* cover of a book; *the book has a leather binding*

binge [bɪndʒ] *noun (informal)* time when you drink alcohol, eat or do something else to excess; *after last night's binge he had to stay in bed*; *she went on a chocolate binge that lasted the whole summer*; *shopping binges are not uncommon during sales time*

bingo [ˈbɪŋgəʊ] **1** *noun* game of chance, where each player has a card with numbers on it, numbers are called out and when you have marked off a whole row of numbers, you win; *she goes to play bingo every Friday night*; *he won quite a lot at bingo* **2** *interjection* showing surprise; *he opened the envelope and bingo! a key fell out*

binoculars [bɪˈnɒkjʊləz] *noun* powerful glasses looking at things which are too far away to see clearly, such a when birdwatching, etc.; *he watched the yachts through his binoculars*; *don't forget to bring your binoculars* (NOTE: plural; if you want to indicate one item, say **a pair of binoculars**)

biochemical [baɪəʊˈkemɪkl] *adjective* referring to biochemistry; *she's involved in very advanced biochemical research*

biochemist [baɪəʊˈkemɪst] *noun* scientist who specializes in biochemistry; *she's not an ordinary chemist, but a biochemist*

biochemistry [baɪəʊˈkemɪstri] *noun* science and study of the chemistry of living things (animals, plants, etc.); *biochemistry is a fascinating subject*

biodegradable [baɪəʊdiˈgreɪdəbl] *adjective* which can easily be decomposed by organisms such as bacteria, or by sunlight, sea water, etc.; *many companies are developing biodegradable packaging*

biodiversity [baɪəʊdaɪˈvɜːsɪti] *noun* richness of the number of species in a certain area; *the biodiversity of the area will be destroyed by cutting down too many trees*

bioengineering [baɪəʊendʒɪˈnɪəɪŋ] *noun* use of biochemical processes in industry to produce drugs, foodstuffs, etc.

biographer [baɪˈɒgrəfə] *noun* person who writes a biography; *he is the biographer of Charles Dickens*

biographical [baɪəˈgræfɪkl] *adjective* referring to a biography; *the novel is partly biographical*

biography [baɪˈɒgrəfi] *noun* the story of someone's life; *have you read the new biography of Churchill?*; *she's the author of a biography of Henry VIII*

biological [baɪəˈlɒdʒɪkl] *adjective* **(a)** referring to living things; *the biological balance in the North Sea* **(b)** using germs; *biological warfare* **(c)** **biological mother** = mother who gave birth to a child (as opposed to an adoptive mother, foster mother, etc.)

biologist [baɪˈɒlədʒɪst] *noun* scientist who specializes in biology; *Darwin was a famous biologist*

biology [baɪˈɒlədʒi] *noun* study of living organisms; *she took biology and chemistry as exam subjects*; *biology students spend some of their time in the research lab*

biosphere [ˈbaɪəsfɪə] *noun* part of the earth and its atmosphere where living organisms exist; *there is a great variety of ecosystems within the biosphere*

biotechnology [baɪəʊtekˈnɒlədʒi] *noun* technology which manipulates and combines different living materials, such as cells, to produce organisms with particular characteristics; *a biotechnology company is developing a range of new pesticides*; *artificial insemination of cattle was one of the first examples of biotechnology*

> COMMENT: biotechnology offers great potential to increase farm production and food processing efficiency, to lower food costs, to enhance food quality and to increase commercial competitiveness; there is however a danger that it may permanently affect natural organisms in ways which cannot be predicted and could be harmful

bipartisan [baɪpɑːtɪˈzæn] *adjective* accepted by the Opposition as well as by the Government; *when will there be a bipartisan approach to European monetary policy?*; **a bipartisan foreign policy** = a foreign policy agreed between the Government and the Opposition

birch [bɜːtʃ] *noun* **silver birch** = northern tree, with small leaves and white bark which peels off in strips; *the birch forests of Russia* (NOTE: plural is **birches**)

bird [bɜːd] *noun* **(a)** animal with wings and feathers; *most birds can fly, but penguins can't*; *she keeps a little bird in a cage*; **a little bird told me** = someone told me the secret, but I can't tell you who it was; **a bird in the hand is worth two in the bush** = be satisfied with what you have, rather than hope for something better which may never come *see also* EARLY **(b)** *(informal)* person; *she's a funny old bird* **(c)** *(informal)* girl; *who's that new bird in the accounts department?*; *did you see the bird he was with last night?*

birdie ['bɜːdi] *noun* **(a)** *(child's name for bird)* *look at the little birdies on the lawn!* **(b)** *(in golf)* using one stroke less than the normal number of strokes to get the ball into a hole; *he had a birdie at the fifth hole*

bird of prey ['bɜːd ʌv 'preɪ] *noun* bird which kills animals and other birds for food; *birds of prey like owls and buzzards help keep down the numbers of small rodents*

bird's nest soup ['bɜːdz nest 'suːp] *noun* delicate Chinese soup made from the nests of a species of swallow; *we ended the meal with a bowl of bird's nest soup*

bird-table ['bɜːd'teɪbl] *noun* small flat surface on which food can be put for wild birds during the winter; *in the winter lots of finches come to our bird-table looking for nuts*

birdwatcher ['bɜːdwɒtʃə] *noun* person who looks at birds for pleasure, or for scientific purposes; *birdwatchers set up hides all round the lake* (NOTE: a fanatical birdwatcher is called a **twitcher**)

birdwatching ['bɜːdwɒtʃɪŋ] *noun* looking at birds for pleasure, or for scientific purposes; *he goes birdwatching every weekend*; *she belongs to a birdwatching club*; *we often go to a nature reserve in Suffolk to do some birdwatching and walk by the sea*

biro ['baɪrəʊ] *noun* *(trademark)* ballpoint pen; *use a biro to fill in the form, so that it will go through all four copies* (NOTE: plural is **biros**)

birth [bɜːθ] *noun* being born; *he was a big baby at birth*; **to give birth to** = to have a baby; *she gave birth to a boy last week*; **birth certificate** = official document which says when and where someone was born; **date of birth** = day, month and year when a person was born; *he put his date of birth as 15th June 1935*

birth control ['bɜːθ kən'trəʊl] *noun* restricting the number of children born by using contraception; *couples are encouraged to practise birth control*; *in some countries, birth control is the only way to deal with potential food shortages*

birthday ['bɜːθdeɪ] *noun* date on which you were born; *April 23rd is Shakespeare's birthday*; *my birthday is on 25th June*; *what do you want for your birthday?*; *he'll be 10 years old next birthday* = on his next birthday he will be 10 years old; **birthday cake** = cake made specially for a birthday and decorated with icing, candles, etc.; **birthday card** = card sent to someone to wish him or her good luck on their birthday; *remind me to send her a birthday card, it's her birthday next Tuesday*; **birthday party** = party held for a birthday; **birthday presents** = presents given to someone for his or her birthday; *the watch was a birthday present from my father*

◊ **Happy Birthday** ['hæpi 'bɜːθdeɪ] greeting said to someone on their birthday; *'Happy Birthday to you!'* = song sung at a birthday party; *we all sang 'Happy Birthday to you' and then she blew out the candles on her cake*

birthmark ['bɜːθmɑːk] *noun* mark on skin which a baby has from birth and which usually cannot be removed; *he has a birthmark on his stomach*

birthplace ['bɜːθpleɪs] *noun* **(a)** place where someone was born; *they visited Shakespeare's birthplace in Stratford* **(b)** place where something was invented; *China was the birthplace of gunpowder*

birth rate ['bɜːθ 'reɪt] *noun* number of children born per thousand of the population; *the birth rate is declining in parts of Western Europe*

biscuit ['bɪskɪt] *noun* small flat hard cake, usually sweet; *a packet of chocolate biscuits*; **cheese and biscuits** = cheese served with biscuits (which are not sweet); *they had cheese and biscuits after the meal* (NOTE: American English for sweet biscuits is **cookies**; biscuits which are not sweet are also called **crackers**)

bisexual [baɪ'seksjuəl] *adjective* sexually attracted to both men and women; *only after he died did his wife discover that he was bisexual* *compare* HETEROSEXUAL, HOMOSEXUAL

bishop ['bɪʃəp] *noun* **(a)** Christian church leader; *the Bishop of London* **(b)** piece in chess, which looks like a bishop's hat or mitre; *she took both his bishops in three moves*

bishopric ['bɪʃəprɪk] *noun* position of a bishop; *he was offered the bishopric of Durham*

bismuth ['bɪzməθ] *noun* white metal used in medicines, especially to treat indigestion (NOTE: Chemical element: chemical symbol: **Bi**; atomic number: 83)

bison ['baɪsn] *noun* large wild animal with long hair, like a large ox, which used to be common in Europe and North America; *European bison are still found in some countries of eastern Europe* (NOTE: plural is **bison**; note also that the **American bison** is also called a **buffalo**)

bit [bɪt] **1** *noun* **(a)** little piece; *he tied the bundle of sticks together with a bit of string*; *would you like another bit of cake?*; **to come to bits** = to fall apart; *the chair has come to bits*; **to take something to bits** = to put it in pieces to mend it; *he's taking my old clock to bits* **(b)** **a bit** = a little; *the painting is a bit too dark*; *let him sleep a little bit longer*; *have you got a piece of wood a bit bigger than this one?*; *can you wait a bit, I'm not ready yet*; **a bit much** = not fair; *being told it was my fault when I wasn't even there is a bit much*; **not the slightest bit** = not at all; *she didn't sound the slightest bit worried* **(c)** binary digit (i) the smallest unit in binary notation, which has the value of 0 or 1; (ii) the smallest unit of data that a system can handle *compare* BYTE **(d)** tool which fits into a brace, used for making holes; *have you seen the bit for the drill anywhere?* **(e)** metal rod which is in a horse's mouth, and which is used to control the horse through the reins *see also* CHAMP **2** *verb see* BITE

◊ **bit by bit** ['bɪt baɪ 'bɪt] *phrase* not all at the same time, little by little; *he paid back the money he owed, bit by bit*; *he inched himself forward, bit by bit, towards the edge of the cliff*

bitch [bɪtʃ] **1** *noun* **(a)** female animal, especially a female dog; *they have two dogs - a male and a bitch*; *the bitch has given birth to five puppies* **(b)** *(informal)* nasty woman; *that bitch is going round spreading rumours about me* (NOTE: plural is **bitches**) **2** *verb* *(informal)* to complain; *what's she bitching about now?*

bitchy [ˈbɪtʃi] *adjective (informal)* making unpleasant remarks about someone; *don't be so bitchy about her*; *she made some really bitchy remarks about the secretary*

bite [baɪt] **1** *noun* **(a)** mouthful; *all I had for lunch was a bite of bread and cheese*; *she took a big bite out of the sandwich* **(b)** place where someone has been bitten; **insect bite** = sting caused by an insect which goes through the skin and irritates; *some insect bites can be very painful*; *her arms were covered with mosquito bites* (NOTE: do not confuse with **byte**) **2** *verb* **(a)** to cut with your teeth; *the dog tried to bite the postman*; *she bit a piece out of the pie* **(b)** *(of an insect)* to sting; *she's been bitten by a mosquito* (NOTE: **biting - bit** [bɪt] **- has bitten** [ˈbɪtn])

bitten [ˈbɪtn] *verb see* BITE

bitter [ˈbɪtə] **1** *adjective* **(a)** not sweet; *this black coffee is too bitter* **(b)** angry and resentful; *she was very bitter about the way the company treated her*; **to the bitter end** = to the very end; *they resisted the changes to the bitter end* **(c)** very cold; *a bitter December night*; *bitter weather coming from the Arctic* **2** *noun* ordinary pale British beer which is not sweet; *a pint of bitter, please* (NOTE: usually no plural: **bitters** means glasses of bitter: two bitters and a packet of crisps, please. However, see also BITTERS below)

bitterly [ˈbɪtəli] *adverb* **(a)** deeply; *he bitterly regrets what he said* **(b) bitterly cold** = very cold; *it was bitterly cold in the tent*

bitters [ˈbɪtəz] *noun* sharp-tasting liquid made from tropical plants, used to give drinks a sharp flavour; *he added a drop of bitters to his gin and tonic*

bitumen [ˈbɪtjumən] *noun* black substance similar to tar, which comes from petroleum; *bitumen is used to make road surfaces*

bituminous [bɪˈtjuːmɪnəs] *adjective* referring to bitumen; **bituminous coal** = coal which contains bitumen

bizarre [bɪˈzɑː] *adjective* very strange; *I find it bizarre that no one told her that the house had been sold*; *she's started to wear the most bizarre clothes*

bizarrely [bɪˈzɑːli] *adverb* in a very strange way; *he's been behaving very bizarrely lately*; *during the night thieves stole the clock from the town hall and, bizarrely, no one noticed*

blab [blæb] *verb (informal)* to tell someone a secret; *we thought we wouldn't be caught, and then she went blabbing to her mother* (NOTE: **blabbing - blabbed**)

black [blæk] **1** *adjective* **(a)** very dark colour, the opposite to white; *he was wearing a black suit*; *a black and white photograph*; **black coffee** = coffee with no milk in it; *do you want your coffee black or white?* **(b) black economy** = goods and services which are paid for in cash, and not declared to the income tax authorities (NOTE: **blacker - blackest**) **2** *noun* **(a)** the colour of black; **in the black** = in credit, in profit; *the company went into the black last year*; *my bank account is still in the black* **(b)** person whose skin is dark coloured **3** *verb* to forbid trading in certain goods or with certain suppliers; *three firms were blacked by the government*

blackberry [ˈblækbəri] *noun* **(a)** small black fruit that grows on a thorny bush; *for dessert we're having blackberry and apple pie* **(b)** the bush this fruit grows on; *we had to struggle through blackberry bushes which had grown over the path* (NOTE: the wild form is also called **bramble**)

blackbird [ˈblækbɜːd] *noun* common garden bird with black feathers and a yellow beak; *listen to the blackbird singing*

blackboard [ˈblækbɔːd] *noun* dark board on the wall of a classroom, etc., which you can write on with chalk; *he wrote the instructions for the exam on the blackboard*; *some dishes are not on the menu, but are written on a blackboard*

black box [ˈblæk ˈbɒks] *noun* flight recorder, a device carried in an aircraft which records what happens during a flight, including conversations between pilots and the control tower; *the first priority after a crash is to find the plane's black box*

blackcurrant [blækˈkʌrənt] *noun* **(a)** garden fruit with little black berries which are usually eaten cooked; *a jar of blackcurrant jam*; *the blackcurrants need more sugar - they're very sour* **(b)** the small bush this fruit grows on; *I planted six blackcurrants in the garden*

Black Death [ˈblæk ˈdeθ] *noun* the name given to bubonic plague in the Middle Ages; *the Black Death killed millions of people in the fourteenth century*

blacken [ˈblækən] *verb* to make black; *the walls of the cave were blackened with smoke*; **to blacken someone's reputation** = to say things which harm someone's reputation; *in order to blacken his reputation, the newspapers said that he was having an affair with his secretary*

blackfly [ˈblækflaɪ] *noun* small black aphid which sucks sap from garden plants; *the roses are covered with blackfly*; *use a spray to try to get rid of the blackfly*; *there is or are a lot of blackfly on the roses* (NOTE: plural is **blackfly**)

Black Forest gâteau [ˈblæk fɒrɪst ˈgætəʊ] *noun* chocolate cake with cream and cherry filling covered with whipped cream and chocolate shavings; *they had some Black Forest gâteau and coffee*

black hole [ˈblæk ˈhəʊl] *noun* zone in space from which no radiation can escape; *the speed of stars near the centre of a galaxy may indicate the presence of black holes*; *nothing can escape from black holes, not even light*

blackleg [ˈblækleg] *noun* worker who goes on working when there is a strike; *the pickets shouted 'blackleg' as he arrived for work*

blacklist [ˈblæklɪst] **1** *noun* list of unacceptable things or people; *his name is on the blacklist* **2** *verb* to put on a list of unacceptable things or people; *the company has been blacklisted by the government*

blackmail [ˈblækmeɪl] **1** *verb* to threaten to do something harmful unless a demand is met, to threaten to reveal a scandal unless paid; *her former cook tried to blackmail her*; *they tried to blackmail the government into releasing prisoners of war* **2** *noun* act of blackmailing; *the government will not give in to terrorist blackmail*

blackmailer ['blækmeɪlə] *noun* person who blackmails someone; *the blackmailer contacted the store, asking for £2m by the following day*

black mark ['blæk 'mɑːk] *noun* bad report; *it's a black mark on the council's environmental record*

black market ['blæk 'mɑːkɪt] *noun* buying and selling goods in a way which is not allowed by law (as in a time of rationing); *there is a flourishing black market in gold coins*

black marketeer ['blæk mɑːkə'tiːə] *noun* person who sells things on the black market; *black marketeers make a lot of money selling illegal CDs*

blackness ['blæknəs] *noun* being completely black or dark; *you couldn't see anything in the pitch blackness of the cave*

blackout ['blækaʊt] *noun* (a) fainting fit, sudden loss of consciousness; *he must have had a blackout while driving* (b) period when there is no electricity, or when there are no lights; *the snowstorm caused a blackout* (c) **news blackout** = stoppage of all news; *the government imposed a total news blackout until the treaty had been signed*

black out ['blæk 'aʊt] *verb* (a) to have a fainting fit; *I suddenly blacked out and I can't remember anything more* (b) to make all the lights switch off over a large area; *the storm blacked out half the town*

black pepper ['blæk 'pepə] *noun* pepper from whole dried pepper berries; *do you want some black pepper on top of the pizza?* (NOTE: pepper from berries which have had the outer layer removed is **white pepper**)

black sheep ['blæk 'ʃiːp] *noun* **the black sheep of the family** = the member of the family who behaves badly; *everyone turned up for the funeral except Eugene, the black sheep of the family*

blacksmith ['blæksmɪθ] *noun* person who works with red-hot iron, hammering it into different shapes; person who will repair and fit horseshoes; *she asked the blacksmith to make her a new garden gate; the blacksmith was shoeing a horse*

black spot ['blæk 'spɒt] *noun* place on a road where accidents often happen; *this corner used to be an accident black spot until they installed better lighting*

bladder ['blædə] *noun* (a) any organ in the shape of a sac inside the body; **gall bladder** = sac underneath the liver, in which bile produced by the liver is stored; *she had her gall bladder removed* (b) especially, the sac where urine collects before being passed out of the body; *she is taking antibiotics for a bladder infection* (c) light balloon full of air inside a football; *the nail went right through the football and pierced the bladder*

blade [bleɪd] *noun* sharp cutting part; *the blades of a pair of scissors; be careful - that knife has a very sharp blade*

blame [bleɪm] **1** *noun* criticism for having done something (even if you did not do it); *I'm not going to take the blame for something I didn't do*; **to get the blame for** = to be accused of; *who got the blame for breaking the window? - me, of course!* **2** *verb* **to blame someone for something** *or* **to blame something on someone** = to say that someone is responsible for something; *blame my sister for the awful food, not me; he blamed the accident on the bad weather*; **I don't blame you** = I think you're right to do that; *I don't blame you for being annoyed, when everyone else got*

a present and you didn't; **he has only himself to blame** = no one else is responsible for what happened; *he has only himself to blame if he missed the chance of a free ticket to Thailand*; **to be to blame for** = to be responsible for; *the manager is to blame for the bad service*

blameworthy ['bleɪmwɜːði] *adjective* who or which can be blamed for something; *his actions were considered blameworthy*

blanch [blɑːntʃ] *verb* (a) to cook for a short time in boiling water; *blanch the asparagus for two minutes* (b) to put vegetables, etc., in boiling water to remove the skin; *blanch the tomatoes first to remove the skin; almonds should be blanched before being roasted and salted* (c) to cover growing plants so that they become white; *celery needs to be blanched by covering it with earth to get really white stems* (d) to turn white with fright or worry; *she blanched at the news*

bland [blænd] *adjective* (a) dull and uninteresting, not giving any information; *he gave a bland reply* (b) without much flavour; *some people don't like avocados because they find them too bland; the sauce needs more herbs - it's far too bland*; **bland diet** = diet where the patient eats mainly milk-based food, boiled vegetables and white meat

blank [blæŋk] **1** *adjective* (a) (paper) with no writing on it; *she took a blank piece of paper and drew a map* (b) **he looked blank** = he didn't seem to know anything about it; *when she mentioned the money he owed, he just looked blank* **2** *noun* (a) empty space on a piece of paper; *just fill in the blanks on the form*; **my mind is a blank** = I can't remember anything about it; **to draw a blank** = to get no result; *when she tried to trace her father, she drew a blank* (b) cartridge without a bullet in it; *the police fired blanks into the crowd of protesters* **3** *verb* **to blank out** = to cover up something (which has been written); *he showed her the letter with the signature blanked out*

blank cheque ['blæŋk 'tʃek] *noun* (a) cheque which has not been filled in; *a book of blank cheques* (b) a cheque which has been signed, but without any details; *her father gave her a blank cheque for her birthday and told her to fill in any amount she liked* (c) total freedom to do anything; *the planners have been given a blank cheque to do what they like with the town centre*

blanket ['blæŋkɪt] **1** *noun* (a) thick cover which you put over you to keep warm; *he woke up when the blankets fell off the bed; she wrapped the children up in blankets to keep them warm*; **wet blanket** = miserable person who spoils an activity; *don't ask her to the party - she's such a wet blanket* (b) **blanket refusal** = general refusal to accept various things; *we put forward various suggestions and got a blanket refusal* (c) thick layer; *a blanket of snow covered the fields; the motorway was covered in a blanket of fog* **2** *verb* to cover with something; *the whole area was blanketed with snow*

blare ['bleə] **1** *noun* loud unpleasant noise; *the blare of car horns in the street outside our hotel* **2** *verb* to make a loud unpleasant noise; *the night club has music blaring away in the middle of the night; he drives around with his radio blaring*

blaspheme [blæs'fiːm] *verb* to speak in a rude way about god or religion; *the way she blasphemes, she'll shock even the most broad-minded person*

blasphemous ['blæsfəməs] *adjective* rude towards god or religion; *his blasphemous book was burnt in public*

blasphemy ['blæsfəmi] *noun* being rude about god, religion or established principles; *he uttered blasphemies against the church; he was accused of blasphemy; for him, any criticism of the royal family amounts to blasphemy*

blast [blɑːst] **1** *noun* **(a)** explosion; *windows were shattered by the blast* **(b)** strong gust of wind; *an icy blast from the north* **(c)** sharp blow on a signal or whistle; *three blasts of the alarm means that passengers should go on deck* **(d)** going full blast = going at full power; *they kept the heating going full blast even in summer* **2** *verb* **(a)** to destroy with an explosive or bullets; *the burglars blasted their way into the safe; they blasted their way out of the police trap* **(b)** to ruin; *the accident blasted his hopes of a sporting career*

blasted ['blɑːstɪd] *adjective (informal)* awful, terrible; *can't someone stop that blasted noise?*

blast furnace ['blɑːst 'fɜːnɪs] *noun* furnace where air is blown onto iron ore which is heated until it produces iron; *blast furnaces were developed in the 18th century*

blast off ['blɑːst 'ɒf] *verb (of rocket)* to take off; *the rocket blasted off from Cape Canaveral yesterday morning*

blast-off ['blɑːstɒf] *noun* time when a rocket leaves the earth; *the scientists were still checking their instruments in the last moments before blast-off*

blatant ['bleɪtənt] *adjective* obviously bad; *an act of blatant aggression; that is a blatant lie*

blatantly ['bleɪtəntli] *adverb* in an obviously bad way; *he blatantly disregarded the instructions on the package*

blaze [bleɪz] **1** *noun* **(a)** large bright fire; *five fire engines were called to the blaze* **(b)** to work like blazes = to work very hard; *they worked like blazes to get the house ready* **2** *verb* **(a)** to burn fiercely; *the camp fire was blazing and everyone sang songs* **(b)** to blaze away = to shoot fiercely; *they blazed away at the enemy for several minutes*

blazer ['bleɪzə] *noun* jacket, often with a club badge; *she was wearing a blue blazer with brass buttons*; **school blazer** = blazer of a special colour with the badge of the school on it; *a crowd of boys and girls in school blazers got onto the bus*

blazing ['bleɪzɪŋ] *adjective* **(a)** burning strongly; *they sat around the blazing bonfire* **(b)** a blazing row = a big quarrel; *I walked into the middle of a blazing row between the MD and his secretary*

bleach [bliːtʃ] **1** *noun* chemical substance which cleans things or kills harmful bacteria; *she poured bleach into the lavatory; even a small drop of bleach will remove colour; do not use bleach on this material* **2** *verb* to remove colour; *he's bleached his hair; her hair was bleached by the sun*

bleachers ['bliːtʃəz] *noun US* open-air seats in a sports stadium; *the crowd in the bleachers soon started shouting and throwing cans*

bleak [bliːk] *adjective* cold and miserable; *the path led across bleak mountains; she gave him a bleak stare* (NOTE: **bleaker - bleakest**)

bleary-eyed ['blɪriˈaɪd] *adjective* with eyes half closed from lack of sleep; *he staggered into work at ten o'clock, bleary-eyed*

bleat [bliːt] **1** *noun* sound made by a sheep or goat; *we heard a faint bleat from the corner of the field and found an injured lamb; see also* GRUNT, LOW, NEIGH **2** *verb* **(a)** *(of sheep or goats)* to make a sound; *the lambs were bleating in the snow* **(b)** *(informal)* to complain in a whining voice; *what's he bleating on about?*

bleed [bliːd] **1** *noun see* NOSEBLEED **2** *verb* to lose blood; *his chin bled after he cut himself while shaving; he was bleeding heavily from his wound* (NOTE: **bleeding - bled** ['bled])

bleeding ['bliːdɪŋ] *adjective (informal)* awful; *stop that bleeding noise!*

bleep [bliːp] **1** *noun* little noise from a computer, radio, etc., to attract attention; *the computer made a bleep and the screen went blank; the printer will make a bleep when it runs out of paper* **2** *verb* **(a)** *(of a computer, radio, etc)* to make a bleep; *excuse me a moment, my mobile has just bleeped* **(b)** to call someone on a mobile phone or pager; *I've been bleeped, so I've got to go to the hospital; see also* BEEP

bleeper ['bliːpə] *noun* device which makes a bleep to warn you; *he's in the factory somewhere - we'll try to find him on his bleeper*

blemish ['blemɪʃ] **1** *noun* mark which makes something look less perfect; *our fruit have no blemishes; the fine for speeding is a blemish on his otherwise clean driving licence* **2** *verb* to spoil something; *being arrested for theft blemished his reputation*

blend [blend] **1** *noun* mixture; *different blends of coffee* **2** *verb* **(a)** to mix; *blend the eggs, milk and flour together* **(b)** *(of colour)* to go well together, not to contrast with each other; *the grey curtains blend with the pale wallpaper*

blender ['blendə] *noun* kitchen device for mixing different food items together thoroughly; *don't forget to put the top on the blender before you switch it on*

bless [bles] *verb* **(a)** to make sacred by prayers, etc.; *the church was blessed by the bishop* **(b)** to bring happiness or good fortune; *their marriage was blessed with two fine sons* **(c)** *(old) (showing surprise)* well I'm blessed! - *we've had a postcard from Jane* **(d)** *(informal) (said when someone sneezes)* bless you! (NOTE: **blessing - blessed** [blest])

blessed ['blesɪd] *adjective* **(a)** protected by God; *the church of the Blessed Virgin Mary* **(b)** *(informal)* cursed; *the blessed engine won't start!*

blessing ['blesɪŋ] *noun* **(a)** prayer which blesses; *the priest gave his blessing to the congregation* **(b)** to give your blessing to something = to approve something officially; *the chairman gave his blessing to the new design* **(c)** something which brings happiness; *she enjoyed the blessings of good health and a happy family;* **it was a blessing in disguise** = it was good thing, even if at first it seemed bad; *breaking his leg was a blessing in disguise - it meant he could spend more time studying;* **it's a mixed blessing** = in has both advantages and disadvantages; *automation can be a mixed blessing - machines usually tend to be out of order when you need them most*

blew [blu:] *see* BLOW

blind [blaɪnd] **1** *adjective* **(a)** not able to see; *he's not only blind, he's also very deaf*; **to turn a blind eye to something** = not to bother about something, even if you know it exists; *we turn a blind eye to minor cases of theft in the office* **(b)** *(informal)* none at all; *he didn't pay a blind bit of notice to the regulations; it didn't make a blind bit of difference* **2** *noun* **(a)** covering over a window that can be pulled up and down; *they must still be asleep - their blinds are closed; he pulled down the blind to keep out the sun* **(b)** **the blind** = people who cannot see; *the town hall has excellent facilities for the blind* **3** *verb* to make someone unable to see; *she was blinded by the bright lights of the oncoming cars*

blind date ['blaɪnd 'deɪt] *noun* social meeting arranged in advance, but with someone you do not know; *they met on a blind date*

blinders ['blaɪndəz] *noun US* = BLINKERS

blindfold ['blaɪndfəʊld] **1** *noun* cloth put over someone's eyes to prevent him or her seeing; *her kidnappers did not let her take off the blindfold* **2** *verb* to put a piece of cloth over someone's eyes to prevent him or her seeing; *he was blindfolded and bundled into the back of a car* **3** *adverb* wearing a blindfold; *I could find my way here blindfold*

blinding ['blaɪndɪŋ] *adjective* so bright or intense as to stop you seeing properly; *there was a blinding flash; they couldn't see anything in the blinding snowstorm; she had a blinding headache*

blindly ['blaɪndli] *adverb* without being able to see; *he groped blindly around the room, feeling for a light switch*

blind man's buff ['blaɪnd mænz 'blʌf] *noun* children's game, where one person is blindfolded and tries to catch the others

blindspot ['blaɪndspɒt] *noun* area at the side of a car which the driver cannot see in his rear view mirrors; *he didn't see the bicycle in his blind spot*

blink [blɪŋk] **1** *noun* **(a)** action of quickly opening and shutting your eyes; *he heard the news without a blink* **(b)** *(informal)* **on the blink** = not working, out of action; *the telephone's on the blink* **2** *verb* **(a)** to close your eyelids very quickly; *he blinked when the light was switched on; she watched the bull come towards her without blinking* **(b)** *(of lights)* to go on and off; *the alarm light is blinking*

blinkers ['blɪŋkəz] *noun* shades which cover the sides of a horse's eyes, to prevent it looking sideways; *our horse seems less nervous if it has blinkers* (NOTE: American English is **blinders**)

blip [blɪp] *noun* **(a)** little dot on a computer screen; *a blip appeared on the radar screen* **(b)** temporary bad result; *we hope that this month's bad export figures are only a blip*

bliss [blɪs] *noun* great happiness; *that chocolate pudding was pure bliss; it was sheer bliss to be walking in the country, away from the office* (NOTE: no plural)

blissful ['blɪsfʊl] *adjective* very pleasant or happy; *it's blissful, sitting on the beach when everyone else is working in the office!; we spent a blissful three weeks on a Greek island*

blister ['blɪstə] **1** *noun* **(a)** swelling on the skin with liquid beneath; *I can't run - I've got a blister on my heel* **(b)** **blister pack** = plastic bubble packaging; *each toy comes in a separate blister pack* **2** *verb* to make a

blister on a surface; *the heat had blistered the paint; his hands were blistered in the fire*

COMMENT: blisters can be caused by rubbing, burning or by a disease such as chickenpox

blistering ['blɪstərɪŋ] *adjective* **(a)** very hot; *walking in the blistering desert is impossible* **(b)** very fast; *the defence could not keep up with blistering pace of the winger* **(c)** strong (criticism); *his blistering attack on his host bewildered everyone present*

blithe [blaɪð] *adjective* not worrying about anything; *he showed a blithe disregard for the regulations*

blitz [blɪts] **1** *noun* **(a)** bombing by planes; *she was born during the London Blitz* **(b)** *(informal)* **to have a blitz on something** = to make a sudden effort to do something; *we'll have to have a blitz on this pile of orders* (NOTE: plural is **blitzes**) **2** *verb* to bomb; *the factories were blitzed by the enemy bombers*

blizzard ['blɪzəd] *noun* snowstorm with strong wind; *there were blizzards in the highlands during the weekend*

bloated ['bloʊtɪd] *adjective* fatter or fuller than usual; swollen with air; *after the Indian meal she felt bloated; bloated corpses lay in the streets*

blob [blɒb] *noun* small spot of sticky stuff; *put a blob of glue on the back of the poster*

bloc [blɒk] *noun* political group of states; *the Eastern European bloc has now split up*

block [blɒk] **1** *noun* **(a)** large building; *they live in a block of flats* **(b)** *US* section of buildings surrounded by streets; *he lives two blocks away* **(c)** large piece; *blocks of ice were floating in the river* **(d)** group of things together; *they booked a block of seats in the middle of the plane*; **block vote** = casting of a large number of votes at the same time by one person who represents a large number of people at a meeting **2** *verb* to prevent something passing along something; *the pipe is blocked with dead leaves; the crash blocked the road for hours; what can I take for my blocked nose?*

blockade [blɒ'keɪd] **1** *noun* preventing supplies arriving; *the fishermen decided that a blockade of their harbour would help them in their fight with the EU* **2** *verb* to prevent supplies coming in; *the fleet blockaded the port for several months*

blockage ['blɒkɪdʒ] *noun* something which blocks; being blocked; *there was a blockage in the tube; the blockage in the artery was caused by a blood clot*

blockbuster ['blɒkbʌstə] *noun* very successful big book or film; *have you read her latest blockbuster?; the blockbuster movie took $25m in box office sales*

block capitals ['blɒk 'kæpɪtəlz] *noun* letters written as A, B, C, D, etc., and not a, b, c, d; *write your name in block capitals at the top of the form*

block up ['blɒk 'ʌp] *verb* to stop up a hole; *we need to block up the hole to stop the water leaking*

bloke [bloʊk] *noun* *(informal)* man; *I bought the car from a bloke I know at work*

blond [blɒnd] *adjective* fair, or with fair hair; *is her blond hair natural?; two little blond children*

blonde [blɒnd] **1** *adjective* fair, or with fair hair; *she has lovely long blonde hair* **2** *noun* woman with fair hair; *he came to the party with a gorgeous blonde*

blood [blʌd] *noun* red liquid in the body; *blood was pouring out of the wound on his head*

COMMENT: blood is formed of red and white cells or corpuscles, platelets and plasma. Blood circulates round the body, going from the heart and lungs along arteries and returning to the heart through the veins. As it moves round the body, blood takes oxygen to the tissues and removes waste matter which is cleaned through the kidneys. An adult has about six litres of blood in his or her body

blood cell ['blʌd 'sel] *noun* cell in the blood (NOTE: also called **corpuscle**)

COMMENT: there are two types of blood cell: white blood cells which fight disease and form antibodies, and red blood cells which contain haemoglobin and carry oxygen to the tissues. It is the red blood cells which give blood its colour

blood clot ['blʌd 'klɒt] *noun* soft mass of coagulated blood in a vein or an artery; *the doctor diagnosed a blood clot in the brain*; *the blockage in the artery was caused by a blood clot*

bloodcurdling ['blʌdkɜːdlɪŋ] *adjective* very frightening; *suddenly they heard a bloodcurdling cry*; *we watched a bloodcurdling film on television*

blood donor ['blʌd 'dəunə] *noun* person who gives blood; *after the rail crash the hospital called for blood donors*

blood group ['blʌd 'gruːp] *noun* (people with the same) type of blood; *do you know your blood group?*

COMMENT: blood is classified in various ways. The most common classifications are by factors in the red blood corpuscles (factors A and B) and by the Rhesus factor. Blood can therefore have either factor (Group A and Group B), or both factors (Group AB) or neither factor (Group O), and each of these groups can be Rhesus negative or positive

bloodhound ['blʌdhaund] *noun* large dog which can follow a trail by scent

blood poisoning [blʌd 'pɔɪznɪŋ] *noun* condition caused by the presence of bacteria in the blood; *blood poisoning during pregnancy can be very dangerous* (NOTE: also called **septicaemia** *or* **toxaemia**)

blood pressure ['blʌd 'preʃə] *noun* pressure at which the heart pumps blood; *he has to take pills for his high blood pressure*

bloodshed ['blʌdʃed] *noun* killing people; *the United Nations is trying to prevent further bloodshed in the civil war* (NOTE: no plural)

bloodstain ['blʌdsteɪn] *noun* red mark of blood on a surface; *the police found bloodstains on the carpet*

bloodstained ['blʌdsteɪnd] *adjective* covered with bloodstains; *they found a bloodstained shirt in his suitcase*

bloodstream ['blʌdstriːm] *noun* flow of blood round the body; *the antibiotics are injected into the bloodstream*; *hormones are carried by the bloodstream to various parts of the body*

blood test ['blʌd 'test] *noun* laboratory test of a sample of blood to analyze its chemical composition; *they did a blood test which proved negative*; *the doctor's going to do a blood test*

blood transfusion ['blʌd trænz'fjuːʒn] *noun* giving blood to someone; *after the operation she had a blood transfusion*

blood vessel ['blʌd 'vesl] *noun* **(a)** any tube, artery or vein, which carries blood round the body; *the wound is bleeding profusely because a blood vessel has been cut* **(b) to burst a blood vessel** = to get violently angry; *the boss will burst a blood vessel when he hears the news*

bloody ['blʌdi] *adjective* **(a)** with much blood; *a bloody battle* **(b)** (*slang*) awful, terrible; *stop that bloody noise!* (NOTE: **bloodier - bloodiest**)

bloom [bluːm] **1** *noun* flower; **the apple trees are in full bloom** = the apple trees are in flower **2** *verb* **(a)** to flower; *the flowers are blooming in the greenhouses* **(b)** to flourish; *the country's economy is blooming*

blooming ['bluːmɪŋ] *adjective* **(a)** full of brightness and life; *she's positively blooming* **(b)** (*slang*) awful; *it's a blooming shame that his mother won't let him come out to play football!*

blossom ['blɒsəm] **1** *noun* mass of flowers on trees; *the hedges are covered with hawthorn blossom*; *the trees are in full blossom* **2** *verb* **(a)** to flower; *the roses were blossoming round the cottage door* **(b)** to flourish; *she's blossomed since she got married*

blot [blɒt] **1** *noun* drop of ink; *the boy with blots of ink on his shirt is our son*; *the painting he sent to the art show was just a series of coloured blots* **2** *verb* **(a) to blot something out** = to hide something completely; *the thick fog blotted out the details of the landscape* **(b) he blotted his copybook** = he ruined his reputation; *he blotted his copybook when he was found kissing the chairman's wife* (NOTE: **blotting - blotted**)

blouse [blauz] *noun* woman's shirt; *she wore a pink blouse and white jeans*

blow [bləu] *verb* to make air move; *the wind had been blowing hard all day*; *blow on your soup if it's too hot*; **to blow your nose** = to clear a blocked nose by blowing down into a handkerchief; *she has a cold and keeps having to blow her nose* (NOTE: **blowing - blew** [bluː] - **has blown** [bləun])

blow away ['bləu ə'weɪ] *verb* **(a)** to go away by blowing; *his hat blew away* **(b)** to make something go away by blowing; *the wind will blow the fog away*

blow down ['bləu 'daun] *verb* **(a)** to make something fall down by blowing; *six trees were blown down in the storm* **(b)** to fall down by blowing; *the school fence has blown down*

blow off ['bləu 'ɒf] *verb* to make something go away by blowing; *the wind blew his hat off*; *the wind has blown all the leaves off the trees*

blow out ['bləu 'aut] *verb* to make something go out by blowing; *she blew out the candles on her birthday cake*

blow up ['bləu 'ʌp] *verb* **(a)** to make something get bigger by blowing into it; *he blew up balloons for the party*; *your front tyre needs blowing up* **(b)** to destroy something with explosives; *the soldiers blew up the railway bridge* **(c)** to make a photograph bigger; *the article was illustrated with a blown-up picture of the little girl and her stepfather* **(d)** to make something seem more important than it really is; *the story has been blown up by the papers*

bludgeon ['blʌdʒən] **1** *noun* heavy stick for hitting; *bands of rioters carrying bludgeons and axes roamed* the streets **2** verb **(a)** to beat with a heavy stick; *the young student was bludgeoned and left for dead*; *the rioters bludgeoned him to the ground* **(b)** to bludgeon someone into doing something = to force someone to do something; *he was bludgeoned into agreeing with the proposal*

blue [blu:] **1** adjective **(a)** coloured like the colour of the sky; *he wore a pale blue shirt*; *they live in the house with the dark blue door*; *all their children have got blue eyes* **(b)** sad or miserable; *when you're feeling blue just sing a song and you'll feel better* (NOTE: **bluer - bluest**) **2** noun **(a)** the colour of the sky; *have you a cloth of a darker blue than this?*; *she was dressed all in blue*; *(informal)* the boys in blue = the police **(b)** out of the blue = suddenly; *out of the blue came an offer of a job in Australia*; *see also* BOLT

bluebell ['blu:bel] noun wild plant with blue flowers like a series of little bells; *we went into the woods to see if there were any bluebells*

blueberry ['blu:bəri] noun wild berry, which is dark blue when ripe, eaten raw with sugar and cream, or cooked in pies and jams; *blueberry pie and whipped cream*; *blueberries are expensive this year*

blue chip shares or **blue chips** ['blu: tʃip 'ʃeəz] noun safe investments, low risk shares in good companies; *I wouldn't dare buy anything other than blue chips*

blue collar worker ['blu: kɒlə 'wɜːkə] noun manual worker in a factory; *this factory is going to close but all the blue collar workers have been offered other jobs* (NOTE: office staff are called **whitecollar workers**)

blue-eyed [blu:'eɪd] adjective **(a)** with blue eyes; *they have two little blue-eyed children* **(b)** blue-eyed boy = favourite; *James is the manager's blue-eyed boy*

blue jeans ['blu: 'dʒiːnz] noun popular blue trousers made of denim, a type of strong cotton; *she came into the restaurant in her blue jeans*; *I bought a pair of blue jeans* (NOTE: usually called simply **jeans**)

blue moon ['blu: 'muːn] noun once in a blue moon = very rarely; *I only see them once in a blue moon*

blueprint ['blu:prɪnt] noun **(a)** photographic print of a plan which consists of blue lines on a white background or white lines on a blue background; *here's the blueprint of the new engine* **(b)** plan for doing something; *the deal will act as a blueprint for future cooperation*

blues [blu:z] noun sad songs from the southern USA; *Bessie Smith, the great blues singer*

blue whale ['blu: 'weɪl] noun very large whale, the largest mammal that exists; *children love looking at the blue whale in the Natural History Museum*

bluff [blʌf] **1** noun **(a)** threat to do something which cannot be carried out; *don't believe what he says, it's all just bluff*; to call someone's bluff = to show that someone is lying; *he said he would blow up the building but the police called his bluff* **(b)** steep rocky hill; *the soldiers climbed the bluff and found the enemy waiting for them on top* **2** adjective straightforward, not very sensitive; *he's a bluff individual, but you can trust what he says* **3** verb to do something by trickery; *he said he was a naval officer, but he was just bluffing*; to bluff your way = to get somewhere by pretending to be someone; *he bluffed his way into the first-class cabin*

blunder ['blʌndə] **1** noun mistake; *a dreadful blunder by the goalkeeper allowed their opponents to equalize*; *what a blunder, to ask her to dinner at the same time as her ex-husband!* **2** verb to make a careless mistake; *he blundered badly when he made the deal with the Chinese company*

blunder into ['blʌndə 'ɪntu] verb **(a)** to bump into; *she was running in the dark and blundered into a glass door* **(b)** to interrupt by mistake; *quite by chance the two cops blundered into a meeting of gangsters*

blunt [blʌnt] **1** adjective **(a)** not sharp; *he tried to cut the meat with a blunt knife*; blunt instrument = something used as a weapon such as a piece of wood or hammer, which is not sharp; *the pathologist says the wounds were caused by a blunt instrument* **(b)** almost rude (way of speaking); *his blunt manner made people say he was rude* (NOTE: **blunter - bluntest**) **2** verb to make blunt; *using the knife to open tins has blunted it*

bluntly ['blʌntli] adverb quite rudely; *he told her bluntly that she had failed her exam*; to put it bluntly, *you're just no good as a shop assistant*

blur [blɜː] **1** noun indistinct image; *he was hit on the head, and everything became a blur*; *you must have moved - the photograph is just a blur* **2** verb to become indistinct, to make indistinct; *his vision became blurred*; *the paper printed a rather blurred photograph of the house* (NOTE: **blurring - blurred**)

blurb [blɜːb] noun short publicity piece which describes a book; *the blurb says that it is a gripping story of love in the Middle Ages*

blurt [blɜːt] verb to blurt out = to give away a secret suddenly, without intending to; *he blurted out that she had been sacked*

blush [blʌʃ] **1** noun **(a)** red colour of the skin; *the blush of a peach*; *a blush tinged her cheeks pink* **(b)** at first blush = at first sight; *at first blush, the deal looks a good one* (NOTE: plural is **blushes**) **2** verb to go red in the face because you are ashamed or embarrassed; *she blushed when he spoke to her*

bluster ['blʌstə] **1** noun loud violent talk; *his threat of legal action is just bluster* **2** verb to speak loudly and angrily; *he went blustering on about taking us to court*

BO = BODY ODOUR

boa constrictor ['bəuə kən'strɪktə] noun large snake found in South America, which kills animals by wrapping itself round them and squeezing them

boar [bɔː] noun **(a)** wild boar = wild pig; *wild boar is common in Germany, but there are very few in England*; *have you ever eaten wild boar?* **(b)** male pig; *we have a boar and two sows* (NOTE: do not confuse with **bore**)

board [bɔːd] **1** noun **(a)** long flat piece of wood, etc.; *the floor of the bedroom was just bare boards*; ironing board = long narrow table for ironing; board games = games (like chess) which are played on a flat piece of wood **(b)** blackboard; *the teacher wrote on the board* **(c)** food; board and lodging = meals and accommodation; full board = rate for bedroom and all meals in a hotel; half board = rate for breakfast and dinner at a hotel, but not lunch **(d)** group of directors; *she was asked to join the board*; *the board meets every month* **(e)** to go on board = to go on to a ship, train, plane, etc.; *we went on board at 9.30 and the ship sailed at 12.00* **2** verb to go on to a ship, train, plane, etc.; *six passengers boarded at Belgrade*; *customs* *officials boarded the ship in the harbour; the 16.50 train to Paris is now ready for boarding at platform 5*

boarder ['bɔːdə] *noun* pupil who lives in a boarding school; *both day pupils and boarders will have the afternoon off* (NOTE: do not confuse with **border**)

boarding card US **boarding pass** ['bɔːdɪŋ 'kaːd] *noun* card which allows you to go on board a plane; *here's your ticket and your boarding card*

boarding house ['bɔːdɪŋ 'haʊs] *noun* house where you pay to live; *we get a lot of tourists here and there are not enough hotels and boarding houses*

boarding school ['bɔːdɪŋ 'skuːl] *noun* school where the children live at the school during term time; *at eleven, he was sent away to boarding school*

boardroom ['bɔːdruːm] *noun* room where directors meet; *the directors hurried into the boardroom and shut the door*

board up ['bɔːd 'ʌp] *verb* to cover windows, doors, etc., with boards; *the shops were boarded up to prevent looting*

boardwalk ['bɔːdwɔːk] *noun* usually US path made of planks, usually alongside the seashore; *in Atlantic City we walked along the famous boardwalk*

boast [bəʊst] **1** *noun* act of boasting; *their proudest boast is that they never surrendered* **2** *verb* **(a)** to boast of *or* about something = to say how good, etc., you are; *he was boasting of how he had climbed the three mountains in a day* **(b)** to have something good; *the house boasts a conservatory and patio; the town boasts an 18-hole golf course*

boastful ['bəʊstfʊl] *adjective* saying how good, etc., you are; *he annoyed everyone with his boastful talk of his salary and new car*

boat [bəʊt] *noun* small ship; *they sailed their boat across the lake; they went to Spain by boat; when is the next boat to Calais?;* a rowing boat; *US* a rowboat = small boat which is rowed with oars; *we hired a rowing boat and went down the river;* a sailing boat *US* a sailboat = boat which has sails; *two sailing boats capsized during the race;* a fishing boat = boat used for catching fish at sea; *the fishing boats are back, let's buy some fish on the pier;* (informal) we're all in the same boat = we're all in the same situation; *it's a shame about the redundancies, but if the firm goes bust we'll all be in the same boat*

boating ['bəʊtɪŋ] *noun* going in small boats for pleasure, rowing or sailing; *a boating holiday on the lakes*

boatman ['bəʊtmən] *noun* person who sails boats, or is in charge of boats; *a boatman rowed us across the lake* (NOTE: plural is **boatmen**)

the Boat Race [ðə 'bəʊt 'reɪs] *noun* the annual race on the Thames between rowing eights from Oxford and Cambridge universities; *we watched the Boat Race on TV*

COMMENT: the race is rowed each year over a course of 4 miles, 374 yards, on the Thames between Putney and Mortlake in the west of London. The race has been rowed each year since 1864, and to date Cambridge have won 75 times and Oxford 68 times, with one dead heat. The fastest time for the race is 16 minutes, 45 seconds

bob [bɒb] **1** *noun* woman's or girl's hair style, where the hair is cut fairly short so that it is the same length all round the head; *she had her hair in a bob* **2** *verb* to move up and down; *pieces of wood were bobbing about on the water* (NOTE: **bobbing - bobbed**)

bobbin ['bɒbɪn] *noun* little device with thread wound round it; *the bobbin on the sewing machine has blue thread on it*

bobble [bɒbl] *noun* fluffy ball made of wool; **bobble hat** = woollen hat with a fluffy ball on top

bobby ['bɒbi] *noun (informal)* policeman; *the local bobby does his rounds on a bicycle* (NOTE: plural is **bobbies**)

bobby-pin ['bɒbɪpɪn] *noun* US piece of bent wire used to keep your hair in place; *use these bobby-pins to keep your hair off your face* (NOTE: British English is **hairpin** *or* **grip**)

bobsleigh US **bobsled** ['bɒbsleɪ *or* 'bɒbsled] *noun* sleigh which can be steered, for racing down a special track; *the bobsleigh raced down the track at frightening speed*

bode [bəʊd] *verb (formal)* to bode ill = to be a bad sign; *it bodes ill for their project if the local council has refused them a grant*

bodily ['bɒdɪli] **1** *adjective* referring to the body; *the main bodily functions are those of important organs such as the heart, the lungs, etc.;* to cause someone grievous bodily harm = to attack someone causing serious injury **2** *adverb* moving the whole of someone's body at the same time; *they carried him out bodily* = they lifted him up and carried him out

body ['bɒdi] *noun* **(a)** the whole of a person or of an animal; *he had pains all over his body; the dead man's body was found in the river* **(b)** the main part of an animal or person, but not the head and arms and legs; *she was beaten on the arms and the upper part of her body* **(c)** the main part of a car, plane, text, etc.; *the car has an all aluminium body; the body of the text is printed in black* (NOTE: plural is **bodies** for meanings (a), (b) and (c)) **(d)** strength, solidity; *the conditioner will give your hair body; the wine has a good body*

bodyguard ['bɒdɪgaːd] *noun* **(a)** person who guards someone; *the attacker was overpowered by the president's bodyguards* **(b)** group of people who guard someone; *he has a bodyguard of six people or a six-man bodyguard*

body language ['bɒdi 'læŋgwɪdʒ] *noun* movements of the body which show what someone is thinking; *he seemed reluctant to talk to her, but his body language was quite the opposite; the interviewer observed the body language of the candidates very carefully*

body odour (BO) ['bɒdi 'əʊdə] *noun* unpleasant smell caused by perspiration; *use the spray to prevent unpleasant body odour*

bodywork ['bɒdɪwɜːk] *noun* metal outer covering of a car; *the car is in quite good condition, except for some scratches on the bodywork*

bog [bɒg] *noun* marshland; *watch out when you're walking near the bog - the ground is very soft*

bog down ['bɒg 'daʊn] *verb* to get bogged down = to get stuck; *the negotiations are getting bogged down over the question of salaries; the discussion got bogged down in arguments over the number of staff to be made redundant*

bogey ['bəʊgi] *noun* **(a)** weird creature that frightens children; *the bogey or bogeyman will come to get you if you're naughty* (NOTE: also called **bogeyman** in this meaning) **(b)** (*in golf*) using one more stroke than the normal number of strokes to get the ball into a hole; *he had a bogey at the fifth hole*

boggle ['bɒgl] *verb* **to boggle at something** = to be doubtful about being able to do something; *he boggled at the idea of crossing the Atlantic in such a small boat*; **the mind simply boggles** = I can't imagine how this can be done; *when I think how much work we have left to do by next Friday, my mind simply boggles or it makes the mind boggle*; *see also* MIND-BOGGLING

bogus ['bəʊgəs] *adjective* false, pretending to be real; *he got the job with bogus references*; *the old lady was robbed of all her savings by a bogus gasman*

bohemian [bəʊ'hi:miən] **1** *adjective* referring to a very relaxed or artistic way of life; *he led a very bohemian existence in Paris as a young man*; *she brought along some of her bohemian friends* **2** *noun* person who lives a very relaxed or artistic way of life; *he's a bohemian at heart, but he has to do a proper office job to feed his family*

boil [bɔɪl] **1** *noun* **(a)** infected swelling; *he has a boil on the back of his neck* **(b)** when water is boiling; **the kettle is on the boil** = the water in the kettle is boiling; **bring the water to the boil** = to heat the water until it boils **2** *verb* **(a)** (*of water or other liquid*) to bubble and change into steam or gas because of being very hot; *put the egg in when you see that the water's boiling*; *don't let the milk boil*; **the kettle's boiling** = the water in the kettle is boiling **(b)** to heat water (or another liquid) until it changes into steam; *can you boil some water so we can make tea?*; *boil the water before you drink it* **(c)** to cook (vegetables, eggs, etc.) in boiling water; *small potatoes do not take long to boil*; *would you like a boiled egg for breakfast?*; **soft-boiled egg** = egg cooked by boiling in water until it is hot, but with the yolk still more or less liquid; **hard-boiled egg** = egg that has been boiled until it is hard; *I need two hard-boiled eggs for the salad*

boil down ['bɔɪl 'daʊn] *verb* to be reduced to; *it all boils down to whether he will accept the deal now or not*

boiler ['bɔɪlə] *noun* apparatus for boiling water; heater for central heating; *naturally the boiler broke down just before Christmas*

boiler room ['bɔɪlə 'ruːm] *noun* room where a central heating boiler is in a factory

boiler suit ['bɔɪlə 'suːt] *noun* one-piece item of clothing, often worn over other clothes; *he was in his boiler suit repairing the car exhaust* (NOTE: also called **overalls**)

boiling ['bɔɪlɪŋ] **1** *noun* action of heating a liquid to the point where it becomes vapour or gas; *boiling water for five minutes will kill germs in it* **2** *adjective* **(a)** which has started to boil (i.e., for water, at 100°); *put the potatoes in a pan of boiling water* **(b)** very hot; *it is boiling in this room* **3** *adverb* **boiling hot** = very hot; *it's boiling hot in our office*; *a pan of boiling hot oil fell on her foot*

boiling point ['bɔɪlɪŋ 'pɔɪnt] *noun* **(a)** temperature at which a liquid boils, i.e. when it turns into steam or gas; *100°C is the boiling point of water* **(b)** very critical point; *the UN must do something quickly because the situation has reached boiling point*

boil over ['bɔɪl 'əʊvə] *verb* (*of liquid*) to rise up when boiling and run over the side of the pan; *the milk boiled over and made a mess*

boisterous ['bɔɪstrəs] *adjective* energetic and noisy; *a boisterous crowd of children*

bold [bəʊld] **1** *adjective* **(a)** strong in colour or design; *she likes bold colours*; *the wallpaper is a bold design of dark green leaves* **(b)** brave; *she was bold enough to say 'no' to the Prime Minister*; *may I be so bold as to ask if you are free for dinner this evening?* (NOTE: **bolder - boldest**) **2** *noun* printing type with thick black letters; *the main words in this dictionary are set in bold* (NOTE: the other two styles of print are **italic** and **roman**)

boldly ['bəʊldli] *adverb* in a brave way; *she boldly went up to the boss and asked him for an increase in pay*

Bolivia [bə'lɪviə] *noun* country in the Andes in South America (NOTE: capital: **La Paz**; people: **Bolivians**; language: **Spanish**; currency: **boliviano**)

Bolivian [bə'lɪviən] **1** *adjective* referring to Bolivia **2** *noun* person from Bolivia

bolster ['bəʊlstə] **1** *noun* long round pillow; *you often find bolsters in French hotels* **2** *verb* to support; *the money from the village fête has bolstered the church funds*; *learning that he will be out of hospital next week has bolstered his spirits*

bolt [bəʊlt] **1** *noun* **(a)** long metal rod with a screw thread, fastened with a nut; *the legs of the table are secured to the top with bolts* **(b)** long metal rod which is pushed into a hole to bar a door; *she peered through the window and after a long pause pulled back the bolts* **(c)** flash of lightning; *he had taken shelter under a tree that was hit by a bolt of lightning*; **it came as a bolt from the blue** = it came as a complete surprise **(d)** **to make a bolt for** = to rush towards; *at the end of the show everyone made a bolt for the door*; **to make a bolt for it** = to run away; *when the guards weren't looking two prisoners tried to make a bolt for it* **2** *verb* **(a)** to run fast, to escape; *the horse bolted* **(b)** to fasten with a bolt; *he bolted the door when he went to bed*; *the tables are bolted to the floor* **(c)** to eat quickly; *don't bolt your food* **3** *adverb* **sitting bolt upright** = sitting with your back very straight

bomb [bɒm] **1** *noun* explosive weapon, dropped from an aircraft or placed by hand; *the bomb was left in a suitcase in the middle of the station*; *they phoned to say that a bomb had been planted in the main street*; *enemy aircraft dropped bombs on the army base* **2** *verb* **(a)** to drop bombs on something; *enemy aircraft bombed the power station* **(b)** (*informal*) to go very fast; *we bombed down the motorway to Bristol*

bombard [bɒm'bɑːd] *verb* **(a)** to attack again and again with heavy guns or bombs; *the town was bombarded for ten days before surrendering* **(b)** to send again and again; *he was bombarded with offers of jobs*; *she was bombarded with letters from the solicitors*

bombardment [bɒm'bɑːdmənt] *noun* attack by heavy guns or bombs; *there was a heavy air bombardment of the town before the troops attacked*

bomber ['bɒmə] *noun* **(a)** person who plants bombs; *the bombers managed to escape after planting the*

bomb (b) aircraft for dropping bombs; *the bombers were out during the night, attacking enemy targets*

bombshell ['bɒmʃel] *noun* very unpleasant surprise; *the letter from the bank came as a bombshell*

bona fide ['bəʊnə 'faɪdi] *adjective* acting in good faith; *a bona fide offer*; *he's a bona fide purchaser*

bona fides ['bəʊnə 'faɪdiːz] *noun* real identity; *the police are checking on his bona fides*

bonanza [bə'nænzə] *noun* situation where you can make a lot of money; *1990 was a bonanza year for the computer industry*; *he won £5000 on the lottery - a real bonanza for the family*

bond [bɒnd] **1** *noun* **(a)** document showing a loan to the government; *government bonds are a very safe form of investment*; **premium bond** = government bond which gives a prize in a draw, instead of paying interest **(b)** link between two people; *there is a close bond between her and her sister* **(c)** contract; *his word is his bond* **(d)** goods in bond = goods which are held by the customs until duty has been paid **2** *verb* to link tightly; *cover the two surfaces with glue and hold them tightly until they bond*

bondage ['bɒndɪdʒ] *noun* being a slave; *the missionaries rescued her from a life of bondage*

bonded warehouse ['bɒndɪd 'weəhaʊs] *noun* warehouse where goods are stored in bond until duty is paid; *the goods are being kept in a bonded warehouse by the customs*

bondholder ['bɒndhəʊldə] *noun* person who holds government bonds; *bondholders with mature bonds should redeem them within 3 months*

bone [bəʊn] **1** *noun* **(a)** one of the solid pieces in the body, which make up the skeleton; *the bone in the thigh is called the femur*; *be careful when you're eating fish - they have lots of little bones*; *the two dogs were fighting over a bone*; **I've got a bone to pick with you** = I want to complain about something you have done **(b)** bone dry = extremely dry; *don't put your shirt on until it is bone dry* **2** *verb* to remove bones from meat; *a boned leg of lamb* (NOTE: when taking the bones out of fish, it is more usual to say **fillet**)

bone marrow ['bəʊn 'mærəʊ] *noun* soft tissue inside a bone; **red bone marrow** = the bone marrow in flat bones where blood cells are formed; **bone marrow transplant** = transplant of marrow from a donor to a recipient; *they think that a bone marrow transplant could offer a possible cure*

bonfire ['bɒnfaɪə] *noun* outdoor fire; *he put the dead leaves on the bonfire*; *they sat around the bonfire singing songs*; **Bonfire Night** = 5th November, when the attempt by Guy Fawkes to blow up the Houses of Parliament in 1605 is remembered; *see note at* GUY FAWKES

bonkers ['bɒŋkəz] *adjective (informal)* **to go bonkers** = to go mad; *they sold their big house and bought a little caravan - has the family gone bonkers?*

bonnet ['bɒnɪt] *noun* **(a)** metal cover for the front part of a car, covering the engine; *he lifted up the bonnet and looked at the steam pouring out of the engine* (NOTE: American English for this is **hood**) **(b)** close-fitting warm hat for a baby; *tie her bonnet under her chin* **(c)** *(old-fashioned)* close-fitting hat for a woman; *old women in black bonnets and shawls sat knitting outside their houses*

bonus ['bəʊnəs] *noun* **(a)** extra money; *salesmen earn a bonus if they sell more than their quota*; **no claims bonus** = reduced insurance premium because no claims have been made against the policy; *the insurance premium is £300 but I have a 50% no claims bonus*; *because of the accident, he lost his no claims bonus* **(b)** advantage; *it was an added bonus that the plane arrived early, as we were able to catch an earlier bus home* (NOTE: plural is **bonuses**)

bony ['bəʊni] *adjective* **(a)** thin, with bones which you can see easily; *she was riding a bony horse*; *he grabbed her arm with his bony hand* **(b)** with many bones; *I don't like kippers, they're usually too bony* (NOTE: **bonier - boniest**)

boo [buː] **1** *interjection* showing that you do not like an actor, singer, politician, etc.; *everyone shouted 'boo' when he announced that taxes would have to go up*; *the wicked pirate's appearance was greeted with boos and hisses* **2** *verb* to make a 'boo' sound to show that you do not like an actor, singer, politician, etc.; *the crowd booed the referee*; *the dancers' performance was terrible and the audience booed them at the end of the ballet*; **she was booed off the stage** = the audience shouted 'boo' so loudly that she had to leave the stage

boob [buːb] **1** *noun* **(a)** *(informal)* silly mistake; *what a boob!*; *he's made yet another boob!* (NOTE: American English for this is **boo-boo**) **(b)** *(slang)* woman's breast; *she doesn't like having big boobs* **2** *verb* to make a silly mistake; *we boobed badly when we said we didn't want to do business with them*

boo-boo ['buːbuː] *noun* mainly US *(informal)* silly mistake; *I made a boo-boo - I gave her the wrong phone number*

boobytrap ['buːbɪtræp] *noun* hidden bomb; *they soldiers went forward slowly, in case there was a boobytrap*

boobytrapped ['buːbɪtræpt] *adjective* full of boobytraps; *the police think the house has been boobytrapped*

book [bʊk] **1** *noun* **(a)** sheets of printed paper attached together, usually with a stiff cover; *I'm reading a book on the history of London*; *he wrote a book about butterflies*; **coffee table book** = heavy expensive book with many illustrations, which can be left on a table for people to look at; **phone book** *or* **telephone book** = book which lists names of people and businesses in alphabetical order with their addresses and telephone numbers; *he looked up the number of the company in the phone book*; **picture book** = book with mainly pictures and not much text; *the book shop has a few picture books for the under twos*; **reference book** = book (such as a dictionary or an encyclopedia) where you can look up information; **school book** = book used when learning a subject in school; *I've lost one of my school books, my French vocabulary* **(b)** sheets of paper attached together; **account book** = book which records sales and purchases; **chequebook** *US* **checkbook** = set of blank cheques attached together in a cover; *don't leave your chequebook on the counter*; **exercise book** = note book which you can write school exercises in; *this exercise book is for my English homework*; **a book of stamps** = several stamps attached inside a little paper cover; **a book of matches** = set of cardboard matches attached together in a paper cover; *he collect books of matches* **(c)** **books** = business records; *her job its to keep the firm's books up to date*; *we have no one on our books* with that name; *we have ten houses for sale on our books* **2** *verb* **(a)** to reserve a place, a seat, a table in a restaurant or a room in a hotel; *we have booked a table for tomorrow evening; I want to book two seats for Friday evening; I'm afraid the dentist is fully booked until the end of next week; I'm sorry, the concert is sold out - all the seats have been booked* **(b)** to charge someone with an offence; *the police officer booked him for speeding*

bookcase ['bʊkkeɪs] *noun* cupboard with shelves for keeping books; *he keeps his best books in the bookcase*

booked up ['bʊkd 'ʌp] *adjective* with all rooms or seats reserved; *the restaurant is booked up for Christmas*; **the hotel is booked up** = all the rooms have been taken in advance

bookie ['bʊki] *noun (informal)* bookmaker, person who takes bets on the result of races; *the favourite horse won, and the bookies had to pay out a lot of money*

book into ['bʊk 'ɪn tu:] *verb* to reserve a room (in a hotel); *I've booked into the Castle Hotel; after we've booked into our hotel I want to do some sightseeing*; **to book someone into a hotel** = to reserve a hotel room for someone else

booking ['bʊkɪŋ] *noun* reservation of seats, places, etc.; *we had to cancel our booking and travel the next day*; **to make a booking** = to reserve a room, a seat, a table, etc.; *we tried to make a booking for the week beginning May 1st, but the hotel was full*

booking office ['bʊkɪŋ 'ɒfɪs] *noun* office in a cinema, theatre, etc., where you can buy tickets in advance; *phone the booking office to see if there are any seats left for tonight*

bookkeeper ['bʊkki:pə] *noun* person who keeps the accounts of a company; *she works as a bookkeeper in a law firm*

bookkeeping ['bʊkki:pɪŋ] *noun* keeping of a company's accounts; *she studied bookkeeping and now works in the accounts department of the local authority*

booklet ['bʊklət] *noun* book of information with only a few pages; *you'll find booklets about the town at the Tourist Information Office*

bookmaker ['bʊkmeɪkə] *noun* person who takes bets on the result of races; *the bookmakers stood around the course, taking bets* (NOTE: also often called a **bookie**; the official term is **turf accountant**)

book on ['bʊk 'ɒn tu:] *verb* **to book someone on(to) a flight** = to order a plane ticket for someone else; *I've booked you on the 10 o'clock flight to New York*

bookseller ['bʊkselə] *noun* person who sells books, who runs a bookshop; *our local bookseller has retired and his bookshop has been sold; the book should be available at your local bookseller's*

bookshelf ['bʊkʃelf] *noun* shelf for keeping books; *his study was lined with bookshelves* (NOTE: plural is **bookshelves**)

bookshop ['bʊkʃɒp] *noun* shop which sells books; *the local bookshop has books on local history* (NOTE: American English is usually **bookstore**)

bookstall *or* **bookstand** ['bʊkstɔ:l *or* 'bʊkstænd] *noun* small shop or kiosk selling books, newspapers and magazines; *she bought a magazine at the station bookstall* (NOTE: American English is also **newsstand**)

bookstore ['bʊkstɔ:] *noun US* store which sells books; *there's a good bookstore just across the street from our apartment* (NOTE: British English is **bookshop**)

boom [bu:m] **1** *noun* **(a)** increase in prosperity; *the economy is improving and everyone is forecasting a boom for next year* **(b)** loud noise, like a muffled bang; *there was such a loud boom that everyone jumped* **2** *verb* to become more prosperous, to increase; *sales to Europe are booming*

boomerang ['bu:məræŋ] **1** *noun* curved piece of wood, invented in Australia, which twists as it flies and returns to you when you throw it in a special way **2** *verb (of a plan)* to go wrong, to turn out exactly the opposite to what was expected; *the plan boomeranged, and he ended up being sued for damages*

boon [bu:n] **1** *noun* very useful thing; *the car has been a real boon to her since the bus company stopped the service to their village* **2** *adjective* **boon companion** = great friend; *they are boon companions and always go on holiday together*

boor ['bʊə] *noun (old)* rude and badly-behaved man

boorish ['bʊərɪʃ] *adjective* rude and badly-behaved; *people have complained about the boorish behaviour of some of the rugby fans*

boost [bu:st] **1** *noun* help or increase; *it gave a boost to our sales* **2** *verb* to help to increase; *the TV commercial should boost our sales*

booster ['bu:stə] *noun* thing which gives extra help or support; *winning the competition was a much needed morale booster for her*; **booster rocket** = rocket which gives more power to a main rocket; **booster (injection, shot)** = a second (or third, etc.) injection of vaccine given some time after the first injection so as to keep the immunizing effect; *come back in June for your polio booster; she should have a booster injection next year*

boot [bu:t] **1** *noun* **(a)** strong shoe which covers your foot and goes above your ankle; *the policemen were wearing long black boots; put on your boots if you're going to dig the garden; bring walking boots with you as we will be climbing in the hills*; **football boots** = boots to wear when playing football; **ski boots** = boots to wear when skiing; *see also* **WELLINGTONS** **(b)** **give someone the boot** = to sack someone; *if he carries on like that he'll be given the boot* **(c)** the space at the back of a car where luggage is put; *put the cases in the boot; this packing case won't fit into the boot* (NOTE: American English for this is the **trunk**) **2** *verb (informal)* **to boot someone out** = to throw someone out; *he was booted out of the police force for taking bribes*

booth [bu:ð] *noun* **(a)** small place for one person to stand or sit; **polling booth** = small enclosed space in a polling station, where the voter goes to mark his ballot paper in private; **telephone booth** = public box with a telephone; *there's a telephone booth near the supermarket - we can phone from there*; **ticket booth** = place outdoors where a person sells tickets **(b)** *US* separate section of a commercial fair where a company exhibits its products or services; *the American publisher wants us to meet him at his booth* (NOTE: British English for this is a **stand**) **(c)** *US* separate section of a restaurant with one table; *we sat in a booth by the bar and listened to the jazz*

bootleg ['buːtleg] *adjective* illegal; *a shipment of bootleg whisky*

booty ['buːti] *noun* treasure taken by soldiers, sailors, etc., during fighting; *the pirates hid their booty in a chest on the island* (NOTE: no plural)

booze [buːz] **1** *noun (informal)* alcoholic drink; *he's too fond of (the) booze to work well* (NOTE: no plural) **2** *verb (informal)* to drink alcohol; *he was out all night boozing with his friends*

bop [bɒp] *verb (informal)* **(a)** to hit with your hand or with something held in your hand; *she bopped him over the head with a rolled-up newspaper* **(b)** to dance to pop music; *some of the partygoers were still bopping at three o'clock in the morning* (NOTE: **bopping - bopped**)

Bordeaux [bɔː'dəʊ] *noun* wine from the Bordeaux region in the west of France; *some Bordeaux would be excellent with the venison*; *I've ordered a bottle of Bordeaux* (NOTE: there are both red and white Bordeaux wines; red Bordeaux wine is also called **claret**)

border ['bɔːdə] **1** *noun* **(a)** frontier between countries; *they managed to cross the border into Switzerland*; *there was nothing to show that we had crossed the border*; *the enemy shelled several border towns*; *he was killed by the border guards* **(b)** edge; **flower border** = flower bed by the side of a path or lawn (NOTE: do not confuse with **boarder**) **2** *verb* to be along the edge of something; *the path is bordered with rose bushes*

bordering ['bɔːdərɪŋ] *adjective* which in on a border; *bordering countries are worried by the renewed fighting*

borderline ['bɔːdəlaɪn] *noun* line between two things; **borderline candidate** = someone who may have either passed or failed an exam; *candidates on the borderline or borderline candidates will be given an oral test*; **borderline case** = case on the dividing line between two things; *the surgeons are not sure whether to operate - it's a borderline case*

border on ['bɔːdə 'ɒn] *verb* to be almost; *the book borders on the obscene*; **bordering on** = close to; *he was exhausted, bordering on total collapse*

bore [bɔː] **1** *noun* **(a)** thing which makes you bored; *he went on talking non-stop and in the end it became a bit of a bore*; **what a bore!** = what a nuisance **(b)** dull, uninteresting person; *I don't want to sit next to him, he's such a bore* **(c)** measurement of the inside of a pipe or gun barrel; *a small-bore shotgun* (NOTE: do not confuse with **boar**) **2** *verb* **(a)** to make a round hole in something; *bore three holes two centimetres apart* **(b)** to make someone fed up with what you are saying or doing; *I won't bore you with the details of my operation*

bored [bɔːd] *adjective* fed up, not interested in what is happening; *you get very bored having to do the same work every day*; *I'm bored - let's go out to the club*; **bored with** = fed up with; *I'm bored with this programme, can't we change to another channel* (informal) **bored stiff** = very bored; *can't we switch on the TV? - I'm bored stiff waiting for the rain to stop* (NOTE: do not confuse with **board**)

boredom ['bɔːdəm] *noun* state of being bored; *the boredom of sitting keyboarding all day would drive me mad*; *he started flicking bits of paper round the office out of sheer boredom*; *they were looking for something to do to relieve the boredom*

boring ['bɔːrɪŋ] *adjective* dull, not interesting; *I don't want to watch that boring TV programme*

born [bɔːn] *verb* **to be born** = to begin to live; *he was born in Scotland*; *she was born in 1956*; *he's American-born but was brought up in the UK*; *the baby was born last week* (informal) **I wasn't born yesterday** = I'm not as stupid as you think (NOTE: **born** is usually only used with **was** or **were**)

born-again ['bɔːn ə'gen] *adjective* **born-again Christian** = someone who has been converted again to Christianity, after not having been very religious before

borough ['bʌrə] *noun* large town run by a town council; *the borough council is responsible for roads*

> COMMENT: a borough is an officially incorporated town, which has a charter granted by Parliament. A borough is run by an elected council, with a mayor as its official head. Most boroughs are represented in Parliament by at least one MP

borrow ['bɒrəʊ] *verb* **(a)** to take something for a short time, usually with the permission of the owner; *can I borrow your car to go to the shops?*; *she borrowed three books from the school library*; *he wants to borrow one of my CDs* **(b)** to take money for a time, usually paying interest; *he borrowed £10 from me and never paid it back*; *companies borrow from banks to finance their business*; *she borrowed £100,000 from the bank to buy a flat*; compare LEND

borrower ['bɒrəʊə] *noun* person who borrows; *the interest rate for borrowers is 18.5%*

borrowing ['bɒrəʊwɪŋ] *noun* action of taking money for a time; **borrowing power** = amount of money which a company or person can borrow; *he has enormous debts, so his borrowing power is very limited*

borrowings ['bɒrəʊwɪŋz] *noun* money which is borrowed; *the company has borrowings of over £200,000*

bosom ['bʊzəm] *noun* **(a)** *(formal)* woman's breast **(b)** **bosom companion** or **bosom friend** = great friend; *they've been bosom pals since they were at college together* **(c)** **in the bosom of** = among; *he retired to live in the bosom of his family*

boss [bɒs] **1** *noun (informal)* person in charge, owner (of a business); *if you want a day off, ask the boss*; *I left because I didn't get on with my boss* (NOTE: plural is **bosses**) **2** *verb* **to boss someone about** or **around** = to tell someone what to do all the time; *she's always bossing her little brother about*; *stop bossing me around!*

bossy ['bɒsi] *adjective* always telling people what to do; *he's so bossy that it annoys everyone and no one wants to work with him*; *don't be so bossy - I'll do what I like!* (NOTE: **bossier - bossiest**)

botanical [bə'tænɪkl] *adjective* referring to plants or to botany; **botanical gardens** = scientific gardens; *when in Oxford, don't forget to visit the botanical gardens*; **botanical name** = scientific Latin name of a plant; *in this book, plants are listed according to both their botanical names and their common names*

botanist ['bɒtənɪst] *noun* scientist who studies plants; *botanists are setting up a seed bank at Kew Gardens*

botany ['botəni] *noun* science and study of plants; *I enjoy botany but I can never remember the long Latin names of plants*

botch [botʃ] *verb* to do or make something badly; *they made a botched job of paving the patio*; *he took the free kick and botched it*

both [bəʊθ] *adjective & pronoun* **(a)** two people together, two things together; *hold onto the handle with both hands*; *both my shoes have holes in them*; *both her brothers are very tall*; *she has two brothers, both of them in Canada*; *she and her brother both go to the same school*; *I'm talking to both of you* **(b)** *(for emphasis) she is both clever and modest*

bother ['boðə] **1** *noun* trouble or worry; *we found the shop without any bother*; *it was such a bother getting packed that we nearly didn't go on holiday* **2** *verb* **(a)** to annoy, to cause trouble; *stop bothering me, I'm trying to read*; **to be hot and bothered** = to be annoyed and nervous about something **(b)** **to bother to do something** = to take the time or trouble to do something; *don't bother to come with me to the station - I can find my way easily* **(c)** **can't be bothered to** = don't have the time to, don't have the energy to; *I can't be bothered to iron the sheets*; *he couldn't be bothered to answer my letters* **3** *interjection (informal)* used to show annoyance; *bother! I've left my umbrella on the train*

bottle ['botl] **1** *noun* **(a)** tall plastic or glass container for liquids; *he bought two bottles of red wine*; *she drank the water straight out of the bottle*; *he bought his wife a bottle of perfume in the duty-free shop* **(b) hot water bottle** = rubber bottle filled with hot water, for warming the bed **(c)** *(informal)* courage; *he hasn't got the bottle to do it* **2** *verb* **(a)** to put in bottles; *the wine is bottled in Germany*; *only bottled water is safe to drink*; *she perfected a process for speeding up the bottling system* **(b)** *(informal)* **to bottle out** = to decide not to do something because you are scared; *he was ready to jump but bottled out at the last minute*

bottle bank ['botl 'bæŋk] *noun* place where you can throw away empty bottles for recycling; *there's a box of bottles ready to be taken to the bottle bank*

bottleful ['botlful] *noun* amount contained in a bottle; *you need to put a bottleful of brown beer into the Christmas pudding*

bottle opener ['botl 'əʊpnə] *noun* little tool for taking the caps off bottles; *the top of this bottle unscrews so you don't need a bottle opener*

bottom ['botəm] **1** *noun* **(a)** lowest point; *is there any honey left in the bottom of the jar?*; *the ship sank to the bottom of the sea*; *turn left at the bottom of the hill*; *he's bottom of his class* = he gets the worst marks; **to get to the bottom of a problem** = to find the real cause of a problem **(b)** far end; *go down to the bottom of the street and you will see the post office on your left*; *the greenhouse is at the bottom of the garden* **(c)** part of the body on which you sit; *if you are naughty again, you will get a smack on your bottom*; *see also* BEHIND **(d)** lower part of two-piece clothing; *he was wearing just his track suit bottom*; *I can't find my bikini bottom* **(e)** **from the bottom of my heart** = deeply and sincerely; *I want to thank you all from the bottom of my heart* **2** *adjective* lowest; *the jam is on the bottom shelf*; *he was standing on the bottom rung of the ladder*

bottom line ['botəm 'laın] *noun* **(a)** last line on a profit-and-loss account indicating the total profit or loss; *the boss is interested only in the bottom line* **(b)** fact which must be accepted; *the bottom line is that we will have to sell our flat*

bough [baʊ] *noun (formal)* branch of a tree (NOTE: do not confuse with **bow**)

bought [bɔːt] *adjective* **bought ledger** = account book in which purchases are recorded (NOTE: also called **purchase ledger**); *see also* BUY

boulder ['bəʊldə] *noun* large rock; *the landslide brought huge boulders down the side of the mountain*

boulevard ['buːləvɑːd] *noun* wide road in a town, usually with trees along it; *in the evening, they strolled along the boulevard*

bounce [baʊns] **1** *noun* **(a)** movement up and down; *he hit the ball on the second bounce* **(b)** energy; *she's always full of bounce* **2** *verb* to spring up and down or off a surface; *the ball bounced down the stairs*; *he kicked the ball but it bounced off the post*

bouncer ['baʊnsə] *noun* **(a)** *(in cricket)* fast ball which bounces very high; *he was hit on the head by a bouncer* **(b)** doorman at a night club, whose job is to stop people getting in or to throw people out; *the bouncers wouldn't let her in because she'd caused trouble before*

bouncing ['baʊnsıŋ] *adjective* which bounces; **bouncing baby** = very healthy baby

bouncy ['baʊnsı] *adjective* **(a)** which bounces; *a big bouncy red ball*; **bouncy castle** = big inflated plastic castle for children to bounce inside **(b)** full of energy; *it's quite tiring working with her because she's so bouncy*

bound [baʊnd] **1** *noun* great jump; **in leaps and bounds** = very rapidly; *the project is going forward in leaps and bounds* **2** *adjective* **(a) bound for** = on the way to; *a ship bound for the Gulf*; **homeward bound** = on the way home **(b)** tied up; *the boy was left bound to a tree*; *the burglars left him bound hand and foot*; *a bundle of old letters bound in pink ribbon* **(c)** obliged; *he felt bound to help her*; *he is bound by the contract he signed last year* **(d)** very likely; *they are bound to be late* **(e)** *see also* BIND **3** *verb* to leap; to run fast; *she bounded into the room*; *he bounded out of his chair*; *the dog bounded into the bushes* **4** *suffix* meaning unable to move; *see* FOGBOUND, STRIKEBOUND

boundary ['baʊndrı] *noun* limit of property, knowledge, etc.; *the white fence marks the boundary between our land and his*; **the boundaries of knowledge** *or* **of science** = the furthest point in human knowledge; *scientists are trying to push back the boundaries of human knowledge*; *(in cricket)* **to hit a boundary** = to hit the ball beyond the edge of the playing field (and score four runs) (NOTE: plural is **boundaries**)

bounds [baʊndz] *noun* limits; *you must keep your expenditure within bounds*; **out of bounds** = where people are forbidden to go; *the bar is out of bounds to soldiers on duty*

bountiful ['baʊntıful] *adjective* very large (amount of); *the campsite has a bountiful supply of fresh water*

bounty ['baʊntı] *noun* money given as a reward; *he gets a bounty for every escaped prisoner he catches* (NOTE: plural is **bounties**)

bouquet [bu'keı] *noun* **(a)** beautifully arranged bunch of flowers; *he bought a bouquet of white roses*; *a little girl presented the princess with a bouquet* **(b)** the aroma of a wine; *a wine with a delicate bouquet*

bourbon ['bɜːbən] *noun US* whiskey, an alcoholic drink distilled from rye; a glass of this drink; *he drank a couple of bourbons or a couple of glasses of bourbon*

bourgeois ['buəʒwɑː] **1** *adjective* referring to the middle-class; *they want to go on living their bourgeois existence*; *he accuses his parents of being terribly bourgeois and swears he won't be like them* **2** *noun* middle-class person; *the bourgeois refused to see their living standards fall* (NOTE: plural is **bourgeois**)

bourgeoisie [buəʒwɑ'ziː] *noun* the middle classes; *the bourgeoisie stands to lose most by the change of government*

bout [baut] *noun* **(a)** sporting fight or contest; *Lewis won that bout* **(b)** attack of illness; *she had a bout of flu*

boutique [buːˈtiːk] *noun* **(a)** small specialized shop, especially for up-to-date fashionable clothes; *a jeans boutique*; *a ski boutique* **(b)** section of a department store selling up-to-date clothes; *you may find what you're looking for in our dress boutique on the next floor*

bovine ['bəuvaın] *adjective* referring to cattle *(of a person)* **she has a bovine look** = she looks stupid, rather like a cow; **bovine spongiform encephalopathy (BSE)** = fatal disease of cows, also called 'mad cow disease'

bow 1 ['bəu] *noun* **(a)** weapon used for shooting arrows; *the archers drew their bows and shot arrows into the air* **(b)** piece of wood with strings, used for playing a string instrument; *he slowly drew the bow across the strings of his violin* **(c)** ribbon knotted in a shape like a butterfly; *the parcel was tied up with red bows*; **bow tie** = tie which is tied in the shape of a butterfly; *I've only ever seen him with a bow tie* **2** [bau] *noun* **(a)** bending the body forward as a mark of respect; *he made a deep bow to the queen*; **to take a bow** = to step forward on a stage and bow to the audience to thank them for their applause; *the actors took their bows one after the other* **(b)** *(also* **bows)** front part of a ship; *the captain posted a lookout in the bow(s)* **bow wave** = big wave which forms at the front of a boat **(c)** rower who sits nearest to the bow of a boat; *he rowed bow for Cambridge; compare* STROKE (NOTE: do not confuse with **bough**) **3** [bau] *verb* to bend forward in salute; *he bowed to the queen*; *the congregation bowed to the altar*

bowels *or* **bowel** ['bauəlz] *noun* **(a)** intestines, the tract from the stomach to the anus in which food is digested as it passes through; **bowel movement** = action of passing faeces from the bowel through the anus; *the patient had a bowel movement this morning* **(b) in the bowels of the earth** = deep underground

bower ['bauə] *noun (formal)* shelter made of shrubs and trees; *they sat in a bower at the end of the lake*

bowl [bəul] **1** *noun* **(a)** wide container for food, water, etc.; *put the egg whites in a bowl and whisk them*; **salad bowl** = special bowl for salad; **soup bowl** = special bowl for soup **(b)** the food or liquid contained in a bowl; *he was eating a bowl of rice; give the dog a bowl of water; a bowl of hot thick soup is just what you need in this cold weather* **(c)** large heavy ball, used for

playing the game of bowls or the game of bowling; *she picked up the bowl and stepped up to take her turn* **2** *verb* **(a)** *(especially in cricket)* to throw a ball (to a batsman); *just as the bowler ran up to bowl, a pigeon landed on the pitch*; *it's your turn to bowl*; **to bowl someone (out)** = to beat someone with a ball and hit his wicket; *he was bowled for three* **(b)** *(in a game of bowls)* to roll a bowl (to try to get close to the target)

bowler ['bəulə] *noun* **(a)** person who plays bowls **(b)** *(in cricket)* person who throws the ball to the batsman; *a fast bowler* **(c)** **bowler (hat)** = round-topped hat; *forty years ago, many London office workers wore bowler hats*

bowling ['bəulıŋ] *noun* game of knocking down skittles; *we're going bowling tomorrow night*; **bowling alley** = large room for bowling; *see also* TEN-PIN BOWLING

bowling green ['bəulıŋ 'griːn] *noun* level area of closely cut grass on which games of bowls are played; *they were playing bowls on the bowling green down by the river*

bowls [bəulz] *noun* game where teams of players roll large balls towards a small ball (the 'jack') thrown as a target; *their team are the bowls champions*

COMMENT: points are scored according to the number of bowls lying closer to the jack than the opponent's closest bowl. The winner rolls the jack back down the green in the opposite direction as far as he or she likes and follows it with his or her first bowl. Strategy often involves knocking the jack away from your opponent's bowls or their bowls away from the jack. The wooden balls (called 'bowls' or 'woods') have unequal flattened sides to make them curve when rolled

bow window ['bəu 'wındəu] *noun* curved window which sticks out from a wall; *there were roses climbing round the bow window of the cottage*

box [bɒks] **1** *noun* **(a)** container made of wood, plastic, metal, etc., with a lid; *the baker put the cakes into a box*; **cash box** = metal box for keeping cash in **(b)** a container and its contents; *he took a box of matches from his pocket*; *he gave her a box of chocolates for her birthday* **(c)** **letter box** *or* **pillar box** = container for posting letters; *she posted her cards in the letter box on the corner*; **P.O. box number** = address with a number at a post office **(d)** **callbox** = public telephone kiosk; *not a single callbox at the station was free* **(e)** line running round a section of text or an illustration; *in this dictionary, the comments are in boxes* **(f)** small separate section in a theatre; *they took a box for the performance of the 'Magic Flute'*; **royal box** = special section in a theatre where a king or queen sits (NOTE: plural is **boxes**) **2** *verb* to fight with your fists; *he learnt to box at a gym in the East End*

boxed ['bɒkst] *adjective* **(a)** packed in a box, sold in a box; *a boxed set of knives, forks and spoons for four people* **(b) boxed in** = tightly enclosed, not able to move; *we feel boxed in, with all the office blocks round our little shop*

boxer ['bɒksə] *noun* fighter who fights with his fists; *the two boxers came together in the ring*; **boxer shorts** = men's underwear shaped like sports shorts

boxing ['bɒksıŋ] *noun* sport in which two opponents fight each other in a ring with gloved fists; **boxing gloves** = thickly padded mittens, laced at the wrist, worn for boxing; **boxing ring** = square area with a stiff canvas floor, surrounded with a rope fence, in which boxing matches take place; *the two boxers climbed into the boxing ring; see also* BANTAMWEIGHT, FEATHERWEIGHT, FLYWEIGHT, HEAVYWEIGHT, LIGHTWEIGHT, MIDDLEWEIGHT, WELTERWEIGHT

COMMENT: a fight lasts a specified number (usually 10 or 15 in professional boxing) of 3-minute rounds with a 1-minute rest between rounds, the object being to knock out or score more points than your opponent. Blows must land above the waist on the front and sides of the body and on the head. A referee in the ring supervises the fight. If one boxer is knocked down he is allowed ten seconds, counted out loud by the referee, to get up; if at the end of ten seconds he is still down, he is counted out and the result declared a knockout (KO)

Boxing Day ['bɒksɪŋ 'deɪ] 26th December, the day after Christmas Day; *we're going to see my grandparents on Boxing Day*

COMMENT: traditionally, Boxing Day was the occasion when gifts in the form of Christmas boxes were given to tradesmen and staff. The Boxing Day holiday is moved to the Monday if the 26th December falls on a Saturday or Sunday

box office ['bɒks 'ɒfɪs] *noun* office where you buy tickets in a theatre; *call the box office and see if there are any seats left*; *the blockbuster movie took $25m in box office sales*

boy [bɔɪ] *noun* **(a)** male child; *a boy from our school won the tennis match*; *when I was a boy, hardly anyone in the village had a television set*; *I knew him when he was a boy*; **paper boy** = boy who delivers newspapers to your house; *the paper boy comes every morning at seven o'clock*; **a boys' school** = a school for boys only; *see also* OLD BOY, SCHOOLBOY, SCOUT, TOY BOY **(b)** a son; *her three boys are all at university*

boycott ['bɔɪkɒt] **1** *noun* action of refusing to deal with someone; *the boycott of the company lasted three months* **2** *verb* to refuse to deal with someone; *we are boycotting all food imports from that country*

boyfriend ['bɔɪfrend] *noun* man, usually young, that a girl is having a relationship with; *she's got a new boyfriend*; *she brought her boyfriend to the party*

boyhood ['bɔɪhʊd] *noun* time of life when someone is or was a boy; *his boyhood was spent in India*

boyish ['bɔɪʃ] *adjective* looking like a boy; acting like a little boy; *with her short hair and tight jeans, she looked very boyish*; *his enthusiasm was very boyish*

bra [brɑː] *noun (informal)* brassiere, a woman's undergarment covering the breasts; *don't wear a black bra under that white shirt*

brace [breɪs] **1** *noun* **(a)** support which makes a bone straight; *she wears braces on her teeth* **(b) braces** = straps over your shoulders to hold up your trousers; *he wore bright red braces with his jeans* (NOTE: American English is **suspenders**) **(c) a brace of** = two, a pair of; *a brace of grouse*; *we bought a brace of pheasants* (NOTE: only used with birds which have been killed) **(d) a brace and bit** = tool holding a bit **2** *verb* **to brace yourself for** = to prepare yourself for something nasty

to happen; *when the phone rang, she braced herself for the shock of hearing his voice again*; *the pilot told us to brace ourselves for a crash landing*

bracelet ['breɪslət] *noun* chain or other ornament worn round your wrist or arm; *he gave her a bracelet for her birthday*

bracing ['breɪsɪŋ] *adjective* cool and healthy; *the bracing climate of East Anglia*

bracken ['brækən] *noun* wild fern; *a section of the park is covered with bracken* (NOTE: no plural)

bracket ['brækɪt] **1** *noun* **(a)** piece of metal or wood, which is attached to a wall to support a shelf; *the shelf is held up by two solid brackets*; **angle bracket** = L-shaped metal bracket **(b)** printing sign [ ] or ( ) to show that a piece of text is separated from the rest; *the words in brackets can be deleted*; *the four words underlined should be put in brackets*; **round brackets** = parentheses, printing symbol ( ) which encloses words or characters and separates them from the rest of the text; **square brackets** = printing symbol [ ] used to enclose certain types of text; *in this dictionary, the phonetics are in square brackets* **(c)** group of items or people taken together for administrative purposes; **people in the middle-income bracket** = people with average incomes, not high or low; **he is in the top tax bracket** = he pays the highest level of tax **2** *verb* **(a)** to put brackets round something; *bracket the whole sentence* **(b)** to link together; to treat several items together in the same way; *his name has been bracketed with that of one of the local gang leaders*; *in the sales report, all European countries are bracketed together*

brag [bræg] *verb* to boast about something; *he's always bragging about his business deals* (NOTE: **bragging - bragged**)

braggart ['brægət] *noun* person who boasts all the time; *don't believe all he says - he's such a braggart!*

Brahmin ['brɑːmɪn] *noun* **(a)** highest-ranking Hindu according to the caste system **(b)** *US* important person from an old family; *the board of the trust is made up of Boston Brahmins* (NOTE: compare the British use of **mandarin: Whitehall mandarins**)

braid [breɪd] **1** *noun* **(a)** decoration made of plaited ribbon or thread; *admirals have gold braid on their caps* **(b)** plaited hair; *this is a picture of her when she was ten and still had her hair in braids* **2** *verb* to plait (hair, ribbon, etc.); *she braided her hair before going swimming*

Braille ['breɪl] *noun* system of writing using raised dots on paper to indicate letters, which allows a blind person to read by passing his or her fingers over the page; *the book has been published in Braille*

brain [breɪn] *noun* **(a)** nerve centre in the head, which controls all the body; *the brain is the most important part of the body* **(b)** intelligence; **use your brain** = think hard; **she's got brains** *or* **she's got a good brain** = she's intelligent

brainchild ['breɪntʃaɪld] *noun* original plan that someone has thought of; *the one-way system was the brainchild of a group of architects*

brain drain ['breɪn 'dreɪn] *noun* movement of clever people from one country to another to find better paid jobs; *the brain drain has meant that some of our best scientists are now working in the US*

brainless ['breɪnləs] *adjective* absolutely stupid; *you brainless fool - that plug goes into the computer not the wall socket!*

brainwash ['breɪnwɒʃ] *verb* to make someone believe something is true by repeating it and forcing them to believe it; *she was brainwashed into leaving her family and joining a religious group*

brainwashing [breɪnwɒʃɪŋ] *noun* action of making people believe something; *the brainwashing of the entire population into believing that the end of the world is near*

brainwave ['breɪnweɪv] *noun* sudden brilliant idea; *I've had a brainwave: let's postpone the meeting until the New Year, so that we can assess the Christmas sales; I don't know how the problem can be solved - if any of you has a brainwave let me know!*

brainy ['breɪni] *adjective (informal)* very intelligent; *she was always the brainiest of the family* (NOTE: **brainier - brainiest**)

braise [breɪz] *verb* to cook food in a pot with very little liquid; *why don't you braise the vegetables?*; *braised ham and mashed potatoes*

brake [breɪk] **1** *noun* device for stopping a vehicle or making it go slower; *put the brake on when you go down a hill*; *the brakes aren't working!*; **hand brake** = brake which is worked by hand, using a lever; *he managed to stop the car safely using the hand brake*; *release the hand brake before you start*; **foot brake** = brake which is worked by foot, using a pedal; **brake lights** = red lights at the back of a car which light up when you put the brakes on; *do you know that one of your brake lights isn't working?*; **brake pedal** = pedal in a car which you press with your foot to make the brakes work; *see also* **JAM 2** *verb* to slow down by pressing the brakes; *the driver of the little white van braked but too late to avoid the dog* (NOTE: do not confuse with **break**)

bramble ['bræmbl] *noun* wild blackberry bush; *the rabbit disappeared back into the brambles*; **bramble jelly** = jam made with wild blackberries

bran [bræn] *noun* the outside part of wheat seeds; *bran is an important source of roughage* (NOTE: no plural)

branch [brɑːnʃ] **1** *noun* **(a)** thick part of a tree, growing out of the trunk; *he hit his head against a low branch* **(b)** local office of an organization; *he's the manager of our local branch of Lloyds Bank*; *the store has branches in most towns in the south of the country* (NOTE: plural is **branches**) **2** *verb* **to branch off** = to come off a main road; *drive along for about a mile and you will see a small road branching off on the left*; **to branch out** = to start to do something different, as well as what you normally do; *the greengrocer has branched out and now sells flowers*

brand [brænd] **1** *noun* **(a)** product with a name; *a well-known brand of soap* **(b)** mark burnt with a hot iron on an animal's hide, to show who owns the animal **2** *verb* **(a)** to name publicly; *he was branded as a thief*; *the minister was publicly branded a liar in the newspaper* **(b)** to mark an animal's hide with a hot iron; *the cattle were corralled before being branded*

brandish ['brændɪʃ] *verb* to wave something about; *the cook ran out of the kitchen brandishing a knife*; *she burst into the room brandishing a letter*

brand name ['brænd 'neɪm] *noun* name of a product; *popular brand names are easily recognised by the public*

brand-new [brænd'njuː] *adjective* completely new; *these shoes are brand-new - I bought them for the wedding*

brandy ['brændi] *noun* **(a)** alcohol distilled from wine; glass of this alcohol; *I was given a bottle of excellent brandy*; *he ordered three brandies* **(b)** **brandy snap** = thin rolled ginger biscuit; *they served brandy snaps with vanilla ice cream*

> COMMENT: brandy is made in most wine-producing countries, such as Spain and Greece. Brandy from the Bordeaux region of France is called 'cognac'; that from south-west France is called 'armagnac'. In Germany, brandy is called 'Brandwein'

brash [bræʃ] *adjective* confident, loud and vulgar; *he's too brash, he should try to be less forceful*; *when you paint the room use a soft colour, not a brash yellow or pink*

brass [brɑːs] *noun* **(a)** mixture of copper and zinc; *the doctor has a brass name plate on his door* **(b)** musical instruments made of brass (such as the trumpet or trombone); *a brass band led the parade*; **the brass section** *or* **the brass** = section of an orchestra with brass instruments **(c)** medieval metal plate set in the floor of a church, showing where someone is buried; **brass rubbing** = copy of a brass made by placing a sheet of paper over it and rubbing it with coloured pencils

brasserie ['bræsəri] *French noun (meaning 'brewery')* a name for a continental-style restaurant or bar; *let's have lunch at the brasserie next door*

> COMMENT: in France, brasseries belong to breweries and serve mainly beer, and also food. In England, they serve mainly wine

brassiere ['bræziə] *noun (formal)* woman's undergarment covering the breasts (NOTE: usually simply called a **bra**)

brat [bræt] *noun* badly-behaved child; *her children are just spoilt brats*

bravado [brə'vɑːdəʊ] *noun* actions to show how recklessly brave you are; *stealing the bus was just an act of bravado* (NOTE: no plural)

brave [breɪv] **1** *adjective* full of courage; *it was very brave of him to dive into the river to try to rescue the little girl* (NOTE: **braver - bravest**) **2** *verb* to be brave enough to do something dangerous; *the ambulance braved the snowstorm to answer the 999 call*

bravery ['breɪvəri] *noun* being brave when in a dangerous situation; *he showed considerable bravery in tackling the bull*; *he won a medal for bravery* (NOTE: no plural)

bravura [brə'vjʊərə] *noun* showing great brilliance in painting, dancing, singing, etc.; *she gave a bravura performance as Madame Butterfly*

brawl [brɔːl] **1** *noun* wild fight; *coming out of the pub, he got into a brawl with some soldiers* **2** *verb* to fight wildly; *after the match ended spectators were brawling on the terraces*

brawn [brɔːn] *noun* **(a)** muscle power; *he has more brawn than brains* **(b)** cooked meat from the head of a pig, pressed and then sliced (NOTE: no plural)

brawny ['brɔːni] *adjective* strong and muscular; *he brought along two brawny helpers when he came to collect the money we owed him*

bray [breɪ] *verb* to make a loud noise like a donkey; *there's a donkey in the farm next door, and you can hear it braying from time to time*

brazen ['breɪzn] **1** *adjective* with no shame; *what you say is a brazen lie* **2** *verb* **to brazened it out** = to get through a difficult situation by seeming to be sure of yourself; *in spite of what the papers said, he managed to brazen it out*

brazier ['breɪzɪə] *noun* metal basket for burning fuel; *the men on the picket line took turns to sit round the brazier to warm up*

Brazil [brə'zɪl] *noun* large country on the Atlantic coast of South America; *don't just go to Rio de Janeiro, you must visit the rest of Brazil* (NOTE: capital: **Brasilia**; people: **Brazilians**; language: **Portuguese**; currency: **rial**)

Brazilian [brə'zɪlɪən] **1** *adjective* referring to Brazil **2** *noun* person from Brazil

brazil nut [brə'zɪl 'nʌt] *noun* large sweet nut from a tropical tree; *there were only a couple of brazil nuts in this bag of mixed nuts*

breach [briːtʃ] **1** *noun* breaking the law, a promise; *this is a breach of the undertaking they made last year*; **breach of the peace** = rowdy behaviour; *they were arrested for a breach of the peace*; **breach of faith** = going back on a promise; **in breach of** = breaking; *in breach of their agreement, they started negotiating with our rivals behind our backs* (NOTE: plural is **breaches**) **2** *verb* **(a)** to make a hole; *the enemy guns breached the town's defences* **(b)** to go against rules, etc.; *the pay settlement has breached the government's guidelines*; *he was arrested for breaching the peace*

bread [bred] *noun* food made from flour and water baked in an oven; *can you get a loaf of bread from the baker's?*; *she cut thin slices of bread for sandwiches*; **bread and butter** = slices of bread covered with butter; **brown bread** = bread made from brown flour; **white bread** = bread made from white flour; **French bread** = bread in the form of a long thin stick (NOTE: do not confuse with **bred**; not also there is no plural: **some bread**; for one piece say **a loaf of bread, a slice of bread**, etc.)

breadcrumbs ['bredkrʌmz] *noun* little pieces of dried bread; *the fish is covered in breadcrumbs and then fried*

breaded ['bredɪd] *adjective* covered with breadcrumbs; *breaded fish fillets*

breadth [bredθ] *noun* **(a)** *(formal)* measurement of how broad something is; *the breadth of the vacant plot of land is over 300m*; *we walked the length and breadth of the field and found no wild strawberries* **(b)** wideness of knowledge; *his answers show the breadth of his knowledge of the subject*

break [breɪk] **1** *noun* **(a)** space; *you can see blue sky through a break in the clouds* **(b)** short rest; *there will be a 15-minute break in the middle of the meeting*; *they worked for three hours without a break* = they worked without stopping; **to take a break** = to have a short rest; *we'll take a break now, and start again in*

fifteen minutes; **coffee break** *or* **tea break** = short rest in the middle of work when you drink coffee or tea; *we'll have a coffee break now* **(c)** *(in schools)* **morning break** *or* **afternoon break** = short period for rest and play in the middle of the morning and afternoon; *we couldn't go out during the morning break because it was raining* **(d)** short holiday; **weekend break** = short holiday over a weekend; *we went away for a weekend break in Brighton*; **city break** = short holiday in a large and famous town; *we took a city break in Prague* **(e)** move away from someone or something; *I thought they were in love, so the break came as a surprise*; *it's not always easy to make a break with the past* **(f)** **(commercial) break** = short period between TV programmes or parts of programmes when advertisements are shown; *we will continue with the news after this break* **(g)** crack in a broken bone, piece of china, etc.; *the break is clean so it should heal quite quickly* **(h)** stop in something regular; *there's a break in the pattern which shouldn't be there* **2** *verb* **(a)** to make something come apart in pieces; *he dropped the plate on the floor and broke it*; *she broke her leg when she was skiing* **(b)** to come apart in pieces; *the clock fell on the floor and broke* **(c)** **to break a record** = to do better than a previous record; *he broke the record for the 2000 metres* **(d)** **to break your journey** = to stop for a while before going on; *we'll break our journey in Edinburgh* **(e)** **to break a silence** = to make a noise; *the silence was broken by the sound of a dripping tap*; **to break your silence** = to talk about something which has been kept secret for a long time; *at long last he broke his silence about the affair* **(f)** **to break with the past** = to cut your links with people you used to know, places you used to visit; *they decided to break with the past and emigrate to New Zealand* **(g)** to fail to carry out the duties of a contract; *the company has broken its agreement*; **to break a promise** = not to do what you had promised to do; *he broke his promise and wrote to her again*; **to break a contract** = to cancel a contract **(h)** to start; *we woke up as day was breaking* **(i)** **to break it to someone** *or* **to break the news to someone** = to tell someone bad news; *we will have to break it to her as gently as possible* (NOTE: do not confuse with **brake**; note also **breaking** - **broke** [brəʊk] - **has broken** ['brəʊkn])

breakable ['breɪkəbl] *adjective* that can break easily; *don't put anything breakable in your suitcase*

breakages ['breɪkɪdʒɪz] *noun* things which have been broken; *all breakages have to be paid for*

breakaway ['breɪkəweɪ] *adjective* which has become detached; *the breakaway nationalist party*

break down ['breɪk 'daʊn] *verb* **(a)** *(of machine)* to stop working; *the lift has broken down again*; *the car broke down and we had to push it* **(b)** to show all the items in a total list; *can you break down this invoice into travel costs and extras?*

breakdown ['breɪkdaʊn] *noun* **(a)** failure of a system to work properly; *there has been a breakdown in communications between them* **(b)** physical collapse; **nervous breakdown** = severe depression; *he had a breakdown after he was made redundant* **(c)** *(of machine)* stopping working; *we had a breakdown on the motorway*; *a breakdown truck came to tow us to the garage* **(d)** showing details item by item; *give me a breakdown of the travel costs*

breaker ['breɪkə] *noun* **(a)** **breakers** = big waves; *the breakers were so big that it would have been* *dangerous to try to swim* **(b)** person who buys old cars for scrap; *the car was badly damaged and had to be sold to a breaker*; we went to a breaker's yard to try to *find some cheap spare parts*

break even ['breɪk 'iːvən] *phrase* not to make a loss or a profit; *we are just about breaking even*; *the business broke even in the first year*

breakeven point ['breɪkiːvn 'pɔɪnt] *noun* point where sales cover costs, but do not show a profit; *we have just about reached breakeven point*

breakfast ['brekfəst] *noun* first meal of the day; *I had a boiled egg for breakfast*; *she didn't have any breakfast because she was in a hurry*; *the hotel serves breakfast from 7.30 to 9.30 every day*; **breakfast TV** = TV show at breakfast time; **working breakfast** = breakfast where you discuss business; **continental breakfast** = light breakfast of rolls, croissants, and coffee (as opposed to a 'full English breakfast'); **full English breakfast** *or* **cooked breakfast** = cereals, bacon, eggs, sausages, etc.

COMMENT: a traditional 'full English breakfast' may include cereals, porridge, or stewed fruit (such as prunes), and a choice of grilled fish (such as kippers), bacon and eggs, sausages, kidneys, fried or grilled tomatoes or mushrooms and fried bread, followed by toast and marmalade and tea or coffee

break in ['breɪk 'ɪn] *verb* **(a)** to break someone *or* an animal in = to train someone *or* an animal; *he rode a mustang which he'd broken in himself* **(b)** to break in *or* to break into a building = to use force to get into a building; *burglars broke into the office during the night*

break-in ['breɪkɪn] *noun* burglary; *they had a break-in when they were on holiday*

break off ['breɪk 'ɒf] *verb* **(a)** to make something come off by breaking; to come off; *he broke a piece off his pie and gave it to his dog*; *the handle broke off the cup in the dishwasher*; *several branches broke off in the wind* **(b)** to stop something suddenly; *he broke off in the middle of his story*; *they broke off the discussions*; *they were going to get married, but she broke it off*

break out ['breɪk 'aʊt] *verb* **(a)** to start; *war broke out between the countries in the area*; to break out into a rash = to have a rash which starts suddenly **(b)** to escape; *three prisoners broke out of jail*

breakout ['breɪkaʊt] *noun* escape from a prison; *during the breakout one of the prisoners was shot in the leg by a guard*

breakthrough ['breɪkθruː] *noun* sudden success; *we have had or have made a breakthrough in our search for a cure for cancer*

break up ['breɪk 'ʌp] *verb* **(a)** to come to pieces; *the oil tanker was breaking up on the rocks* **(b)** to stop being together; *we broke up last year*; *their marriage broke up after 25 years* **(c)** to stop being in a group; *the meeting broke up at 3 p.m.*; *the group broke up when the lead singer started singing solo* **(d)** school breaks up next week = the school holidays start next week **(e)** come on, break it up! = stop fighting!

breakup ['breɪkʌp] *noun* coming to pieces, stopping being together; *the board has recommended the breakup of the company into smaller independent*

divisions; *the breakup of their marriage was a surprise to everyone*

breakwater ['breɪkwɔːtə] *noun* wall that is built into the sea as a protection against the action of strong waves; *big boulders will be used to build new breakwaters*

breast [brest] *noun* **(a)** one of two parts on a woman's chest which produce milk; **breast cancer** = malignant tumour in the breast **(b)** meat from the chest part of a bird; *do you want a wing or a slice of breast?*; *we bought some chicken breasts to make a stir-fry*

breastbone ['brestbəʊn] *noun* the bone which is in the centre of the front of the chest and to which most of the ribs are attached; *the false ribs are not directly attached to the breastbone* (NOTE: also called the **sternum**)

breastfeed ['brestfiːd] *verb* to give a baby milk from the breast; *she was too weak to breastfeed her first baby*; *all her children were breastfed* (NOTE: **breastfeeding - breastfed**)

breastfeeding ['brestfiːdɪŋ] *noun* giving milk from the breast to a baby (as opposed to giving milk from a bottle)

breast stroke ['brest 'strəʊk] *noun* swimming stroke where the swimmer is face downwards, pushing the arms out in front and bringing them back to the sides while the feet are kicking

breath [breθ] *noun* **(a)** air which goes into and out of the body through the nose or mouth; *you should smell his breath - he must have eaten garlic last night*; out of breath *or* gasping for breath = having difficulty in breathing; *he ran all the way to the station, got there out of breath, and then saw the train leaving*; to get your breath back = to breathe normally again, after exercise; *first get your breath back, then tell me all about it*; to hold your breath = to keep air in your lungs to go under water, as a test or because you are afraid that something will happen; *she held her breath under water for a minute*; we're all holding our breath to see if he wins = we're all waiting anxiously to see if he wins; to take a deep breath = to breathe in as much air as you can; *take a deep breath for the X-ray*; to take someone's breath away = to astonish; *the huge size of ruins took my breath away*; under your breath = quietly; *he cursed under his breath*; **breath test** = test for a driver to see if he has been drinking; *the police stopped him and made him take a random breath test*; *the breath test showed he was way over the limit* **(b)** a breath of wind = slight movement of air; *there wasn't a breath of wind all day*

breathe [briːð] *verb* to take air into the lungs or let it out; *take your hand off my mouth, I can't breathe*; *I want to listen to your chest, so breathe in and then out when I tell you to*; *do you know how fish breathe?*; *she breathed a sigh of relief*; breathe deeply = take in a lot of air; **he's breathing down my neck all the time** = he's always watching how I'm working

breather ['briːðə] *noun (informal)* time when you can rest; *you all can take a breather now*

breathing ['briːðɪŋ] *noun* taking air in and out of the lungs; *his breathing became more difficult*; **breathing apparatus** = mask and oxygen cylinder; **breathing space** = period when you can rest between activities; *the chairman called for five minutes' adjournment to allow everyone a little breathing space*

breathless ['breθləs] *adjective* out of breath; finding it difficult to breathe; *she was breathless after running upstairs*

breathtaking ['breθteɪkɪŋ] *adjective* very striking; *the view across the lake to the snow-capped mountains is breathtaking; a breathtaking display of acrobatics*

bred [bred] *verb; see* BREED (NOTE: do not confuse with **bread**)

breech [briːtʃ] *noun* (a) rear part of a gun, where bullets or shells are put in; *the shell stuck in the breech and exploded* (b) **breech birth** *or* **breech delivery** = birth where the baby's buttocks appear first; *they are expecting a breech delivery and she may need a caesarean section* (NOTE: plural is **breeches**)

breeches ['briːtʃɪz] *noun* (a) knee-length trousers which fasten just below the knee; *have you got a pair of riding breeches to lend me?* (b) **breeches buoy** = rescue device where a person's legs fit into a harness which is pulled on a rope from a wreck, etc.; *the crew were winched to safety by breeches buoy*

breed [briːd] **1** *noun* race of animal or plant; *Alsatians and other large breeds of dog* **2** *verb* (a) to produce young (animals); *rabbits breed very rapidly* (b) **I was born and bred in the country** = I was born and grew up in the country; **well-bred** = polite, well-educated (c) to raise new plants; *they are breeding new strains of wheat* (NOTE: **breeding - bred** [bred])

breeder ['briːdə] *noun* person who breeds animals or plants; *a pigeon breeder*

breeding ['briːdɪŋ] *noun* (a) raising animals or plants; *because of the smell, pig breeding is strictly controlled*; *you can't shoot pheasants during the breeding season* (b) good education, background and behaviour; *it was obvious that his secretary was a girl of good breeding*

breeding ground ['briːdɪŋ 'graʊnd] *noun* (a) place where an animal breeds; *the area is the breeding ground of several rare birds*; *stagnant water is a breeding ground for mosquitoes* (b) place where something unpleasant develops; *that amusement arcade is a breeding ground for drugs*

breeze [briːz] *noun* slight wind; *a cool breeze is welcome on a hot day like this*; **a stiff breeze** = a strong wind; *there was a stiff breeze blowing from the south*

breeze block ['briːz 'blɒk] *noun* concrete building block, much larger than a brick; *they built the inside walls with breeze blocks*

breezy ['briːzi] *adjective* (a) windy; *it is very hot, but slightly breezy which makes it more comfortable; it's a little breezy in here, let's shut the French windows* (b) happy-go-lucky; *a breezy youth looking as if he didn't have a care in the world*

brethren ['breðrən] *noun* brothers; *let us now pray for our brethren who died in the explosion* (NOTE: a plural noun only referring to members of religious groups)

brevity ['brevɪti] *noun* (*of time*) being very short; *the visit to the palace was disappointing in its brevity; she thought deeply on the brevity of life*

brew [bruː] **1** *verb* (a) to make beer; *they've been brewing beer in this town for over two hundred years* (b) to make tea or coffee; *let's brew some tea before we sit down and talk* (c) **there's trouble brewing** = there will soon be trouble; *the police moved in when they sensed trouble brewing in the crowd* **2** *noun* (*informal*)

a brew = a cup of tea; *he makes a good strong brew; do you fancy a brew?*

brewer ['bruːə] *noun* person or company that makes beer; *they are one of the biggest brewers in the south of England*; **brewer's yeast** = yeast used in brewing and for making bread; *either fresh or dried brewer's yeast can be used for making bread*

brewery ['bruːəri] *noun* factory where beer is made; *they have been making beer in that brewery for many, many years* (NOTE: plural is **breweries**)

bribe [braɪb] **1** *noun* illegal payment to someone to get something done; *he offered the witness a bribe to say nothing* **2** *verb* to give an illegal payment to someone; *she planned to bribe customs officials to get her case through customs*

bribery ['braɪbəri] *noun* act of bribing; *bribery is common in some parts of the world*

bric-a-brac ['brɪkəbræk] *noun* attractive little ornaments which are not very valuable; *we bought some souvenirs from a bric-a-brac shop by the church*

brick [brɪk] *noun* (a) hard block of baked clay used for building; *you'll need more than eighty bricks to build a wall* (b) **to drop a brick** = to make an unfortunate remark (c) (*old*) good dependable person; *he's been a real brick over the whole business*

brickie ['brɪki] *noun* (*informal*) = BRICKLAYER; *a group of brickies whistled as she walked past*

bricklayer ['brɪkleɪə] *noun* person who builds walls with bricks; *he works as a bricklayer to earn some money during the vacations*

brick up ['brɪk 'ʌp] *verb* to fill a hole with bricks; *they bricked up one of the windows*

brickwork ['brɪkwɜːk] *noun* building work with bricks; *I wonder when the conservatory will be ready - the brickwork isn't finished yet*

brickworks *or* **brickyard** ['brɪkwɜːks or 'brɪkjɑːd] *noun* factory for making bricks; *his father used to say that there was an old brickyard near here*

bridal ['braɪdəl] *adjective* referring to a wedding; *a bridal bouquet of yellow roses; the hotel bridal suite is not available next Saturday* (NOTE: do not confuse with **bridle**)

bride [braɪd] *noun* woman who is getting married; *the bride wore white; the bride was given away by her father; it is usual for the bride to arrive a few minutes late*

bridegroom ['braɪdgruːm] *noun* man who is getting married; *the bridegroom and best man waited nervously in front of the altar; the parents of the bridegroom came all the way from New Zealand* (NOTE: often just called the **groom**)

bridesmaid ['braɪdzmeɪd] *noun* girl who is one of the bride's attendants at a wedding; *three bridesmaids followed the bride into the church* (NOTE: a boy who does the same is a **page**)

bridge [brɪdʒ] *noun* (a) construction built over a road, river, etc., so that you can walk or drive from one side to the other; *there are a dozen bridges across the Thames in London*; **railway bridge** = bridge which carries a railway (b) part of a ship where the captain and crew can keep watch and steer; *the captain was on the bridge when the accident occurred* (c) card game for four people; *they played bridge until midnight*

bridging loan *US* **bridge loan**

['brɪdʒɪŋləʊn] or ['brɪdʒ ləʊn] *noun* short-term loan to help someone buy a new house when his old house has not yet been sold; *you pay a high rate of interest on a bridging loan*

bridle ['braɪdl] **1** *noun* straps put round a horse's head; *she had some difficulty in putting the bridle on the horse* **2** *verb* **to bridle at** = to take offence at; *she bridled at his suggestion* (NOTE: do not confuse with **bridal**)

brief [briːf] **1** *adjective* short; *he wrote a brief note of thanks; the meeting was very brief; tell me what happened, but be brief as we don't have much time* **2** *noun* instructions given to a professional; *his brief was to overhaul the accounts system* **3** *verb* **(a)** to give information or instructions to someone; *he briefed the staff on the latest stage in the negotiations; she was briefed to look for new office premises* **(b)** to give a case to a lawyer and explain the details; *my solicitor will brief the barrister tomorrow morning*

briefcase ['briːfkeɪs] *noun* thin case for carrying papers, documents, etc.; *he put all the files into his briefcase*

briefing ['briːfɪŋ] *noun* meeting where information is given; *the salesmen seemed confident after the briefing on the new product*

briefly ['briːfli] *adverb* for a short time; *she spoke briefly about the work of the hospital*

briefs [briːfs] *noun* short underwear for men or women; *before the medical, the doctor asked him to strip down to his briefs* (NOTE: plural; for one item say **a pair of briefs**)

brigade [brɪ'geɪd] *noun* **(a)** section of the army; *the general sent an infantry brigade to the region* **(b) fire brigade** = group of fire fighters; *she called the fire brigade when she saw smoke coming out of the windows*

brigadier [brɪgə'dɪə] *noun* high-ranking army officer in charge of a brigade; *the brigadier gave a press conference after the attack*

bright [braɪt] *adjective* **(a)** shining strongly; *bright sunshine* **(b)** with a very strong colour; *they have painted their front door bright orange* **(c)** intelligent; *he's a bright little boy; both their children are very bright; she's the brightest of the class;* **bright idea** = clever thought; *I've had a bright idea - let's all go to the beach!* **(d)** clear and sunny; *there will be bright periods during the afternoon* **(e)** cheerful; *she gave me a bright smile* (NOTE: **brighter - brightest**)

brighten ['braɪtən] *verb* to make bright; *light-coloured paint on the walls would brighten the room*

brighten up ['braɪtən 'ʌp] *verb* **(a)** *(of person)* to become more cheerful; *she brightened up when she saw him* **(b)** *(of weather)* to become sunnier; *the weather is brightening up*

brightly ['braɪtli] *adverb* **(a)** in a bright way; *a children's book with brightly painted pictures; the streets were brightly lit for Christmas* **(b)** cheerfully; *she smiled brightly as she went into the hospital*

brill [brɪl] *adjective* (*informal*) = BRILLIANT; *it was an absolutely brill evening; listen to this brill idea!*

brilliance ['brɪljəns] *noun* being very intelligent; *because of his brilliance at A level maths, several universities offered him places*

brilliant ['brɪljənt] *adjective* **(a)** extremely clever; *he's the most brilliant student of his year; she had a brilliant idea* **(b)** (*informal*) very good; *the graphics on this website are brilliant* **(c)** shining brightly; *she stepped out into the brilliant sunshine*

brilliantly ['brɪljəntli] *adverb* in a brilliant way; *the gold roofs of the temples shone brilliantly in the sun; he did brilliantly at university*

brim [brɪm] **1** *noun* **(a)** edge; *the glass was filled to the brim* **(b)** flat part around a hat; *a hat with a wide brim* **2** *verb* **to brim over** = to overflow; *the glass was brimming over with wine* (NOTE: **brimming - brimmed**)

bring [brɪŋ] *verb* to come with someone or something to this place; *she brought the books to school with her; he brought his girlfriend home for tea; are you bringing any friends to the party?* (NOTE: **bringing - brought** [brɔːt])

bring about ['brɪŋ ə'baʊt] *verb* to make something happen; *the burglary brought about a change in security arrangements*

bring along ['brɪŋ ə'lɒŋ] *verb* to bring with you; *he brought his girlfriend along*

bring back ['brɪŋ 'bæk] *verb* to carry something back; *you must bring the book back to the library by Monday; he brought back presents for all his family from Germany*

bring down ['brɪŋ 'daʊn] *verb* **(a)** to carry something down to here; *can you bring down the television from the bedroom?* **(b)** to make something less; *we've brought down all our prices*

bring forward ['brɪŋ 'fɔːwəd] *verb* to arrange something to be done at an earlier date than had been planned; *to bring forward the date of the meeting*

bring in(to) ['brɪŋ 'ɪntʊ] *verb* to come with something or somebody in here; *the dog's all wet - don't bring him into the kitchen; the police brought the accused into the courtroom*

bring on ['brɪŋ 'ɒn] *verb* to produce; *standing in the rain brought on an attack of rheumatism;* **he brought it on himself** = he has himself to blame for what happened to him

bring out ['brɪŋ 'aʊt] *verb* to make something come out; *the publishers have brought out a new book on Spain; our Sunday paper is bringing out a special supplement for the royal wedding;* **to bring out the colour** = to make the colour more striking; *the white background brought out the main colours in the painting*

bring out in ['brɪŋ 'aʊt 'ɪn] *verb* **to bring someone out in** = to make someone have (a rash, etc.); *eating crab brings her out in spots*

bring round *US* **bring around** ['brɪŋ 'raʊnd or 'brɪŋ ə'raʊnd] *verb* **(a)** to bring to someone's house; *they brought round their holiday photographs* **(b)** to revive someone who is unconscious; *the nurse brought her round by putting cold water on her face*

bring up ['brɪŋ 'ʌp] *verb* **(a)** to look after and educate a child; *he was born in the USA but brought up in England; he was brought up by his uncle in Scotland* **(b)** to mention a problem; *he brought up the question of the noise* **(c)** to vomit; *she's got a stomach upset and brought up all her breakfast*

brink [brɪŋk] *noun* edge; **on the brink of** = very close to; *the company is on the brink of collapse*; *she was on the brink of a nervous breakdown*

brisk [brɪsk] *adjective* rapid; *we went for a brisk walk along the beach* (NOTE: **brisker - briskest**)

brisket ['brɪskɪt] *noun* piece of beef which comes from the breast of the animal; *she bought a piece of brisket*

briskly ['brɪskli] *adverb* rapidly; *she walked briskly into the room and sat down at the head of the table*

bristle ['brɪsl] **1** *noun* **(a)** bristles = short stiff hairs on plants, or animals such as pigs; *you could see the bristles on the back of the sow's neck* **(b)** bristles = short stiff hairs on a brush; *the bristles of my toothbrush are coming off - I must get a new one* **2** *verb* **(a)** to bristle at = to take offence at; *she bristled at the suggestion* **(b)** to be bristling with = to be covered with; *the hijackers were bristling with weapons*

bristly ['brɪstli] *adjective* covered with short stiff hairs; *the bristly back of the pig*; *he hadn't shaved for three days, so he gave her a rather bristly kiss*

Brit [brɪt] *noun (informal)* a Briton; *the cross-channel ferry was full of Brits going on holiday*

Britain ['brɪtən] *noun* **(Great) Britain** = country formed of England, Scotland and Wales (which with Northern Ireland makes up the United Kingdom); *we sometimes go abroad for our holidays, but we mostly stay in Britain*; *in 1814 Britain was at war with France or Britain and France were at war*; *in Britain, cars drive on the left hand side of the road see also* GREAT BRITAIN, UNITED KINGDOM (NOTE: the word **England** is often used instead of Britain, and this is a mistake, as England is only one part of Britain; note also the capital: **London**; people: **British**; language: **English**; currency: **pound sterling (£)**)

British ['brɪtɪʃ] **1** *adjective* referring to Great Britain; *a British citizen*; *the British army*; *the British press reported a plane crash in Africa*; *the ship was flying a British flag*; **the British government** = the government of the United Kingdom; **the British Isles** = the islands which make up Great Britain and Ireland (NOTE: the word **English** is often used instead of British, and this is a mistake, as England is only one part of Great Britain; you say **the British Prime Minister** and not **the English Prime Minister**) **2** *noun* **the British** = the people of Great Britain

British Broadcasting Corporation (BBC) ['brɪtɪʃ 'brɔːdkɑːstɪŋ kɔːpə'reɪʃn] *noun* British national radio and TV company (NOTE: often called **the Beeb**)

Briton ['brɪtn] *noun* person from Great Britain; *three Britons were injured in the plane crash*

brittle ['brɪtl] *adjective* which breaks easily; *old peoples' bones can be very brittle*

broad [brɔːd] *adjective* **(a)** very wide; *a broad river* **(b)** *(as an emphasis)* **in broad daylight** = in the daytime; *the gang attacked the bank in broad daylight*; **a broad Irish accent** = a strong Irish accent **(c)** **broad beans** = large flat pale green beans (NOTE: **broader - broadest**)

broadcast ['brɔːdkɑːst] **1** *noun* radio or TV programme; *the broadcast came live from outside Buckingham Palace*; **outside broadcast** = programme not done in the studio **2** *verb* **(a)** to send out on radio or TV; *the programme will be broadcast on Monday at 8 p.m.*; *the police broadcast an appeal for information*

(b) to tell everyone; **don't broadcast the fact** = keep it a secret (NOTE: **broadcasting - broadcast**)

broadcaster ['brɔːdkɑːstə] *noun* person who works on radio or TV but is not an actor; *a veteran BBC broadcaster*

broadcasting ['brɔːdkɑːstɪŋ] *noun* sending out on radio or TV; *many companies now have broadcasting licences*

broaden ['brɔːdən] *verb* **(a)** to make something wider; to become wider; *part of their plan is to broaden the road*; *the river broadens to form a small lake* **(b)** **to broaden the mind** = to increase knowledge; *travel broadens the mind*

broadly ['brɔːdli] *adverb* widely; *he smiled broadly as he handed her the parcel*; **broadly speaking** = roughly, speaking in a general way; *broadly speaking, you can calculate that 10 francs equals one pound*

broad-minded ['brɔːd'maɪndɪd] *adjective* not shocked by other people's behaviour or words; *you can tell him the story - he's very broad-minded*; *the way she swears, she would shock even the most broad-minded person*

broadsheet ['brɔːdʃiːt] *noun* large format newspaper; *the broadsheets all have pictures of the crash on their front pages* (NOTE: small format newspapers are called **tabloids**)

Broadway ['brɔːdweɪ] *noun* street in New York, where the major theatres are located; *the play was a big hit on Broadway but flopped in London*; **off Broadway** = smaller New York theatres, putting on more experimental plays (NOTE: the British equivalents are the **West End theatres** and the **fringe theatre**)

broccoli ['brɒkəli] *noun* vegetable of which the green (or sometimes purple) flower buds are eaten; *would you like some more broccoli?*; *do-you think broccoli would grow in my garden?* (NOTE: no plural)

brochure ['brəʊʃə] *noun* small pamphlet; *I picked up a brochure about ferry services*; *can you get some holiday brochures from the travel agent's?*

broke [brəʊk] *adjective (informal)* with no money; *it's the end of the month and, as usual, I'm broke*; **to be flat broke** = to have no money at all; *see also* BREAK

broken ['brəʊkən] *adjective* **(a)** in pieces; *she tried to mend the broken vase*; **a broken home** = a family where the parents have separated; *the girl comes from a broken home* **(b)** not working; *they came to mend the broken TV*; *we can't use the lift because it's broken* **(c)** not complete; *after so many broken nights, she's looking forward to the day when the baby will sleep all night without waking* **(d)** not fluent; **broken English** = English spoken with a foreign accent and mistakes; *he only spoke broken English when he arrived, but was soon speaking fluently* **(e)** discouraged; *he was pardoned, but came out of prison a broken man*; *see also* BREAK

broken-down [brəʊkən'daʊn] *adjective* not working; *a breakdown van came to tow away the broken-down lorry*

brokenhearted [brəʊkən'hɑːtɪd] *adjective* very sad; *she was brokenhearted when her cat died*

broker ['brəʊkə] *noun* dealer in shares or insurance; *he works as an insurance broker*; **to play the honest broker** = to be a mediator

brokerage *or* **broker's commission**
['brəʊkərɪdʒ *or* 'brəʊkəz kə'mɪʃən] *noun* payment to a broker for a deal carried out; *when a broker buys and sells shares for a customer, he charges a broker's commission*

brolly ['brɒli] *noun (informal)* umbrella; *thank goodness I brought my brolly - just look at the rain!* (NOTE: plural is **brollies**)

bronchi ['brɒŋkiː] *noun* air passages leading from the trachea into the lungs; *inflammation of the bronchi* (NOTE: plural noun; the singular is **bronchus**)

bronchial ['brɒŋkiəl] *adjective* referring to the bronchi; *inflammation of the bronchial tubes*

bronchitis [brɒŋ'kaɪtɪs] *noun* inflammation of membranes in the bronchi; *a child with bronchitis should stay indoors if it is cold outside*

bronze [brɒnz] *noun* (a) mixture of copper and tin; *they have repainted the ornamental bronze gates to the palace* (b) bronze (**medal**) = medal given to someone who finishes third in a race or competition; *Britain won a gold and three bronzes at the athletics meeting; see also* GOLD, SILVER

brooch [brəʊtʃ] *noun* piece of women's jewellery fastened to clothes with a pin; *she wore her favourite brooch to the wedding* (NOTE: plural is **brooches**)

brood [bruːd] **1** *noun* family of chicks or small children; *some birds raise only one brood of chicks a year*; *Simon and his brood came for lunch yesterday* **2** *verb* to think gloomy thoughts; *he's in the garden, brooding as usual*; *she's brooding over the possibility that she might lose her job*

brooding ['bruːdɪŋ] *adjective* gloomy and threatening; *the scenery was dismal, with dark brooding mountains in the distance*

brook [brʊk] **1** *noun* small stream; *they jumped over the brook and walked on up the hill* **2** *verb (formal)* to **brook no interference** = not to allow anyone to interfere

broom [bruːm] *noun* (a) long-handled brush used to sweep floors; *she swept the kitchen with a broom*; **new broom** = person who takes up a managerial job and makes a lot of changes; *he came in as a new broom and sacked half the staff* (b) bush with yellow flowers, found in sandy places and cultivated in gardens; *broom flowers early in the summer*

broth [brɒθ] *noun* light meat soup; *use freshly made chicken broth for this dish*; **Scotch broth** = thick soup with barley, vegetables and lamb; *a hot bowl of Scotch broth will be very welcome*

brothel ['brɒθl] *noun* house for prostitutes; *a street of brothels*

brother ['brʌðə] *noun* boy or man who has the same mother and father as someone else; *my brother John is three years older than me*; *she came with her three brothers*

brotherhood ['brʌðəhʊd] *noun* links between people; *the brotherhood of man*

brother-in-law ['brʌðərɪnlɔː] *noun* brother of husband or wife; husband of your sister; husband of a husband's or wife's sister; *they went to his sister and brother-in-law's for Christmas* (NOTE: plural is **brothers-in-law**)

brotherly ['brʌðəli] *adjective* (a) kind or protective like a brother; *she was expecting some brotherly advice, instead of which her brother told her she was a fool* (b) **brotherly love** = love for your fellow human beings

brought [brɔːt] *see* BRING

brow [braʊ] *noun* (a) forehead; *she wrinkled or knit her brow as she tried to understand the guidebook*; **by the sweat of your brow** = with a lot of hard work; *he became a millionaire by the sweat of his brow* (b) eyebrow, line of hair above the eye; *he's instantly recognizable with those dark bushy brows* (c) top of a hill; *having reached the brow of the hill they stopped to look at the view*

brown [braʊn] **1** *adjective* with a colour like the earth or wood; *she has brown hair and blue eyes*; *it's autumn and the leaves are turning brown*; *he's very brown - he must have been sitting in the sun*; *I like brown bread better than white* (NOTE: **browner - brownest**) **2** *noun* the colour brown; *I'd prefer a darker brown than this* **3** *verb* to cook until brown; *brown the onions in a little butter*

brown bear ['braʊn 'beə] *noun* large fierce mammal, found in mountain areas; *as the weather get warmer, brown bears are coming out of hibernation*

browned off ['braʊnd 'ɒf] *adjective (informal)* fed up, annoyed and rather depressed; *the staff are browned off because there are no Christmas bonuses this year*

brownie ['braʊni] *noun* (a) **Brownie** = little girl in the Girl Guides; *at what age can little girls join the Brownies?* (b) US small chocolate cake usually with nuts; *an American friend gave me a good recipe for brownies*

brownie points ['braʊni 'pɔɪnts] *noun (informal)* good marks for something you have done; *the government won't earn any brownie points for its policy on single-parent families*

brownstone ['braʊnstəʊn] *noun* US (a) reddish-brown building stone mainly used in New York (b) a house with a front built of this stone; *they live in a New York brownstone*

browse [braʊz] *verb* (a) *(of animal)* to eat grass; *the snow has gone, and the cows are browsing in the fields again* (b) *(of person)* to wander around looking at things for sale; *do you need any help? - no, I'm just browsing* (c) to look through a book, newspaper or magazine, without reading it properly; *I browsed through several magazines at the doctor's surgery*

bruise [bruːz] **1** *noun* dark, painful area on the skin, following a blow; *she had bruises all over her arms* **2** *verb* (a) to make a bruise; *she bruised her knee on the corner of the table* (b) **to bruise easily** = to get bruises easily because your skin is delicate; *she bruises easily, even a little blow gives her a bruise*; *peaches are delicate fruit - they bruise easily*

bruising ['bruːzɪŋ] **1** *noun* area of bruises; *the baby has bruising on the back and legs* **2** *adjective* painful or unpleasant; *a bruising encounter with the police*

brunch [brʌntʃ] *noun* a meal taken from about 10 o'clock in the morning onwards, a combination of breakfast and lunch; *the hotel serves Sunday brunch in the main dining room*

brunette [bruː'net] *noun* person, usually a woman, with dark brown hair; *I saw him with a very pretty brunette yesterday*

brunt [brʌnt] *noun* **to bear the brunt of** = to suffer most effects of; *the west coast bore the brunt of the storm*; *she bore the brunt of the criticism*

brush [brʌʃ] **1** *noun* **(a)** tool made of a handle and hairs or wire, used for cleaning, painting, etc.; *you need a stiff brush to get the mud off your shoes*; *she used a very fine brush to paint the details*; *he was painting the front of the house with a large brush* (NOTE: plural is **brushes**) **(b)** act of cleaning with a brush; *she gave the coat a good brush* **(c)** land covered with bushes or low trees; *they walked through the brush for several miles* **(d)** near miss, when something nearly happens to harm you; *they had a brush with death on the motorway*; *he's had several brushes with the law recently* **2** *verb* to clean with a brush; *he brushed his shoes before going to the office*; *remember always to brush your teeth before you go to bed*

brush off ['brʌʃ 'ɒf] *verb* to clean something off with a brush; *he brushed the mud off his boots*

brush up ['brʌʃ 'ʌp] *verb* to make your knowledge better; *he's brushing up his French before going on holiday*; *you'll have to brush up your German if you are going to work in Berlin*

brusque [bruːsk] *adjective* abrupt and rude, using very few words; *the salesman was so brusque that I just walked out of the shop*; *she gave a brusque reply to the reporter's questions*

brusquely ['bruːskli] *adverb* rudely, using few words; *he brusquely ended the conversation*

Brussels sprouts ['brʌsəl 'sprauts] *noun* small round green edible shoots from a type of cabbage; *don't overcook the Brussels sprouts or they'll go soggy* (NOTE: also sometimes called simply **sprouts**)

COMMENT: Brussels sprouts are traditionally served with the turkey at Christmas

brutal ['bruːtəl] *adjective* cruel and violent; *the police said it had been a particularly brutal murder*

brutality [bruːˈtæliti] *noun* violent actions; *the brutality shown in the video shocked the viewers*; *he accused them of brutality towards the demonstrators* (NOTE: usually no plural: to indicate a plural you can say **acts of brutality**)

brutally ['bruːtəli] *adverb* in a cruel and violent way; *she had been brutally beaten and then stabbed*

brute [bruːt] **1** *noun* **(a)** violent person; *her husband's such a brute, sometimes I fear for her safety*; *(joking)* the brute didn't even ring me up to let me know he was getting married; *you brute!* you could have given me a lift **(b)** large animal; *three bears came near our camp and one big brute tried to get into my tent* **2** *adjective* **to use brute force** = to use rough methods; *he managed to get the door open using brute force*

BSc [biːesˈsiː] = BACHELOR OF SCIENCE; *she has a BSc in Chemistry* (NOTE: written after the name: **Jane Bushell BSc**)

BSE [biːesˈiː] = BOVINE SPONGIFORM ENCEPHALOPATHY; *the public has lost confidence in beef as a result of BSE*

bubble ['bʌbl] **1** *noun* **(a)** air or gas trapped in liquid; *bubbles of gas rose to the surface of the lake*; *he blew bubbles in his drink*; **bubble bath** = bath with special soapy liquid which makes foam; *she relaxed in a hot bubble bath* **(b)** *(informal)* **bubble and squeak** = fried potatoes and cabbage **2** *verb* to make bubbles, to have bubbles inside; *the porridge was bubbling in the pan*; **to bubble up** = to come to the surface as bubbles; *gas was bubbling up out of the hot mud*

bubbly ['bʌbli] **1** *adjective* **(a)** with bubbles; *for a really bubbly bath, pour the soap in under running hot water* **(b)** she has a bubbly personality = she's a lively person **2** *noun* *(informal)* champagne; *come and have a glass of bubbly to celebrate the birth of our son* (NOTE: no plural)

bubonic plague [bjuːˈbɒnɪk ˈpleɪɡ] *noun* often fatal infectious disease transmitted to humans by fleas from rats; *in the Middle Ages, bubonic plague was also called 'the Black Death'*

COMMENT: the symptoms are fever, vomiting, shivering and swelling of the lymph nodes

buck [bʌk] **1** *noun* **(a)** male animal; *a buck rabbit* (NOTE: the females are called **does**) **(b)** *US (informal)* dollar; *it'll cost you ten bucks*; *you couldn't lend me 100 bucks, could you?*; **to make a quick buck** = to get rich quickly; *all he wants is to make a quick buck* **(c)** *(informal)* **to pass the buck** = to pass responsibility to someone else; *the manager is a very weak character, he's always passing the buck*; **the buck stops here** = I am the person who is responsible **(d)** **buck's fizz** see FIZZ **2** *verb* **(a)** **to buck the trend** = to go against the trend; *sales of health books have bucked the trend and risen sharply* **(b)** *(of horse)* to jump in the air; *the horses bucked at the sound of gunfire*

bucket ['bʌkɪt] **1** *noun* **(a)** round container with a handle but no lid, used mainly for liquids; *throw the water on the fire and pass the empty bucket back to me*; *(informal)* **to kick the bucket** = to die; *don't worry - I don't intend to kick the bucket just yet!*; **to come down in buckets** = to pour with rain; *you should have seen the rain - it was coming down in buckets!* **(b)** the contents of a bucket; *he brought a bucket of water from the river*; *they threw buckets of water on the fire* **2** *verb* *(informal)* to pour with rain; *it's bucketing down outside*

bucketful ['bʌkɪtful] *noun* amount contained in a bucket; *the garden is so dry, that we had to pour bucketfuls of water on the fruit trees*; *they picked up bucketfuls of rotten apples*; *(informal)* **by the bucketful** = in large quantities; *they were drinking beer by the bucketful*

buckle ['bʌkl] **1** *noun* metal fastener for a strap; *she wore a black leather belt with a big gold buckle*; *these shoes are fastened with buckles* **2** *verb* **(a)** to attach with a buckle; *he buckled on his seat belt*; *the little girl can buckle her sandals all by herself* **(b)** to bend and collapse; *the whole bridge buckled under the weight of the traffic* **(c)** to become bent; *the front wheel of my bicycle has buckled*

buckle down ['bʌkl 'daun] *verb* to start to work hard; *if we all buckle down (to it) we'll finish the job in time*

buck up ['bʌk 'ʌp] *verb* *(informal)* **(a)** to hurry up; *buck up, or we'll miss the train* **(b)** to improve your performance; *if you don't buck your ideas up, you'll be joining the dole queue!*; **to buck someone up** = to make someone more lively; *a glass of whisky will soon buck you up*

bud [bʌd] *noun* **(a)** place where a new shoot comes on a plant; *it was spring and the buds on the trees were* *beginning to open*; **in bud** = flower which has not yet opened; *the roses are in bud*; **to nip something in the bud** = to sop something before it develops any further; *we must try to nip the staff protests in the bud* **(b)** US *(informal)* friend, buddy; *hey bud! come and have a beer!*

Buddhism ['bʊdɪzm] *noun* religion based on the teaching of Buddha, an Indian religious teacher; *Buddhism began in India in the sixth century BC*

Buddhist ['bʊdɪst] **1** *adjective* referring to the teaching of Buddha; *a Buddhist temple*; *a Buddhist monk* **2** *noun* person who follows the teaching of Buddha; *life in Nepal suits him so much that he's become a Buddhist*

budding ['bʌdɪŋ] *adjective* hoping to be; *he's a budding architect*

buddy ['bʌdi] *noun (informal)* friend, pal; *he's gone fishing with a couple of his old buddies* (NOTE: plural is **buddies**)

budge [bʌdʒ] *verb (informal)* to move; *this box is so heavy that I can't budge it*; *he sits in front of the TV after dinner and doesn't budge until he goes to bed*

budgerigar ['bʌdʒərɪgɑː] *noun* small colourful tropical bird often kept as a pet; *he has two yellow and blue budgerigars in a cage* (NOTE: often called a **budgie**)

budget ['bʌdʒɪt] **1** *noun* **(a)** proposed expenditure; *there isn't enough money in the household budget to pay for a new carpet*; **publicity budget** = money allowed for expected expenditure on publicity; *we've increased the publicity budget by 50%* **(b)** the Budget = the government's plans for spending and tax **2** *adjective* cheap; **budget prices** = low prices; **budget travel** = cheap travel **3** *verb* to plan how you will spend money in the future; *it would be helpful if you learnt to budget*; *they are having to budget carefully before going on holiday in Greece*; **to budget for** = to plan to spend money on something; *we're budgeting for a 10% increase in electricity prices*

budgetary ['bʌdʒətri] *adjective* referring to a budget; **budgetary control** = keeping a check on spending; **budgetary policy** = policy of planned income and expenditure

budgie ['bʌdʒi] *noun (informal)* = BUDGERIGAR

buff [bʌf] **1** *adjective* pale brown colour; *the document you're looking for is in a buff folder* **2** *noun* **(a)** pale brown colour; *this type of folder comes in blue, green and buff only* **(b)** *(informal)* enthusiast; *this is the best dictionary for crossword buffs* **(c)** *(informal)* **in the buff** = naked; *give me time to dress, I'm in the buff just now*; *they all stripped to the buff and plunged into the lake* **3** *verb* to polish and shine; *young recruits have to spend hours buffing their boots*

buffalo ['bʌfələʊ] *noun* **(a)** *(in the Far East)* water buffalo = animal of the cow family, used for ploughing and pulling carts; *the old man was walking behind a plough pulled by a water buffalo* **(b)** *(in North America)* large wild animal with long hair, like a large ox, which used to be common in North America but is reduced in numbers; *buffalo used to roam the plains of the Mid West* (NOTE: also called the **bison**; the plural is **buffaloes** *or* **buffalo**; for a group, you say **a herd of buffalo**)

buffer ['bʌfə] *noun* **(a)** shock-absorbing pad; *the cushion acts as a buffer between the two pieces of*

machinery; *the train failed to stop and crashed into the buffers* **(b)** something placed between two powerful forces, which prevents clashes between them; *the UN tried to establish a buffer zone between the two factions* **(c)** *(old) (informal)* **old buffer** = silly old man

buffer state ['bʌfə 'steɪt] *noun* small country between two large opposing states; *the country found itself acting as a buffer state between the two belligerents*

buffet ['bʊfeɪ] *noun* meal where the food is laid out in dishes on a table, and each person helps himself; *the hotel serves a buffet breakfast*; **hot buffet** = buffet with hot dishes to choose from; **cold buffet** = buffet with cold dishes to choose from

buffet car ['bʊfeɪ 'kɑː] *noun* railway coach where you can buy snacks; *the journey is too short for the train to have a buffet car*

buffoon [bə'fuːn] *noun (old)* someone who acts in a funny or stupid way; *what a buffoon! how can a fool like that run a company?*

bug [bʌg] **1** *noun* **(a)** insect; *what are these bugs on the roses?* **(b)** *(informal)* germ; *she got a stomach bug on holiday* **(c)** hidden microphone; *the secret services left a bug in her bedroom* **(d)** error in a computer program; *you need a special program to remove the bugs in the system*; **millenium bug** = error in a computer in which the year 2000 is not correctly recognized **2** *verb* **(a)** *(informal)* to plant a hidden microphone; *they met in Hyde Park because he was afraid his flat had been bugged* **(b)** *(informal)* to annoy, to bother; *what's bugging him?* (NOTE: **bugging - bugged**)

bugbear ['bʌgbeə] *noun* something that worries people; *government officials are the bugbear of small businesses*

bugging ['bʌgɪŋ] *noun* planting a hidden microphone; *the bugging was carried out when he was away from home*; **bugging device** = a hidden microphone

buggy ['bʌgi] *noun* **(a)** a little electric car for one or two people; *beach buggies have very large tyres so that they can drive on sand*; *some people hire buggies when they play golf* **(b)** light folding carriage for pushing a child in; *she pushed the buggy across the busy road*; **double buggy** = buggy for two children (NOTE: also called a **pushchair**; in American English this is a **baby carriage**; plural is **buggies**)

bugle ['bjuːgl] *noun* brass musical instrument similar to a trumpet, mainly used in the army; *the bugle will be sounded before each meal*

bugler ['bjuːglə] *noun* person who plays a bugle; *the bugler is sick, can anyone else play the bugle?*

build [bɪld] **1** *noun* shape of the body; *she's a girl of slender build*; *he has the same build as his father* **2** *verb* to make something by putting things together; *the house was only built last year*; *they are planning to build a motorway across this field*; *the children built sandcastles on the beach* (NOTE: **building - built** [bɪlt])

builder ['bɪldə] *noun* person who builds houses, blocks of flats, etc.; *he works for a local builder*; *the builders are starting work on the kitchen today*

building ['bɪldɪŋ] *noun* **(a)** something which has been built, such as a house, railway station, factory, etc.; *the flood washed away several buildings*; *his office is on the top floor of the building*; *they will have* *to knock several buildings down to build the new motorway* (b) *(used in names of large office blocks) the Shell Building* (c) action of constructing something; *the building of the pyramids must have taken many years*

building blocks ['bɪldɪŋ 'blɒks] *noun* (a) small pieces of wood, used by children to build castles, etc.; *most children like to play with building blocks* (b) one of the parts which form a whole; *printed books are the essential building blocks of a national library*

building site ['bɪldɪŋ 'saɪt] *noun* site where a large building, such as an office block, is being built; *visitors to the building site must wear helmets*

building society ['bɪldɪŋ sə'saɪəti] *noun* organization which pays interest on deposits and lends money to people buying houses or flats; *he put his savings in the building society; how much do you have in your building society account?*

build up ['bɪld 'ʌp] *verb* to increase; *the pressure is building up on him to resign; gas built up rapidly in the boiler until it exploded*

build-up ['bɪldʌp] *noun* preparations for something; *the children got more and more nervous during the build-up to the exams*

-built ['bɪlt] *suffix* made or constructed; *a solidly-built wall;* **heavily-built** = very large and strong; **well-built** = large and strong; *he's very well-built*

built-in ['bɪltɪn] *adjective* made as part of a room or machine; *the kitchen has built-in cupboards; the computer has a built-in clock*

bulb [bʌlb] *noun* (a) fat underground part of a plant, from which leaves and flowers grow; *she planted daffodil bulbs all round the house* (b) glass ball which gives electric light; *you'll need a ladder to change the bulb; see also* CLEAR, PEARL

bulbous ['bʌlbəs] *adjective* fat and rounded; *he has a bulbous nose*

Bulgaria [bʌ'geəriə] *noun* country in eastern Europe, south of Romania and north of Greece and Turkey (NOTE: capital: **Sofia**; people: **Bulgarians**; language: **Bulgarian**; currency: **lev**)

Bulgarian [bʌ'geəriən] **1** *adjective* referring to Bulgaria **2** *noun* (a) person from Bulgaria (b) language spoken in Bulgaria

bulge [bʌldʒ] **1** *noun* swelling; *there's a little bulge in the carpet - I guess we'll find the missing toy underneath* **2** *verb* **to bulge with** = to be fat with; *her pockets were bulging with bundles of notes; father's briefcase bulged not with important papers but with toys for his children*

bulimia [bʊ'lɪmɪə] *noun* psychological condition where the patient eats too much and is incapable of controlling their eating; *people with bulimia always try to hide their condition*

> COMMENT: although the patient eats a large quantity of food, this is followed by vomiting which is self-induced, so that the patient does not become overweight

bulk [bʌlk] *noun* large amount; **in bulk** = in large quantities; *it is cheaper to buy stationery for the school in bulk;* **bulk purchase** = buying in large quantities; *bulk purchase is much more economical;* **the bulk of**

= most of; *the bulk of our sales are in Europe; she finished the bulk of the work before lunch*

bulkhead ['bʌlkhed] *noun* wall inside a ship or aircraft; *after the accident all ferries were fitted with watertight bulkheads*

bulky ['bʌlki] *adjective* awkwardly large; *the post office does not take very bulky parcels* (NOTE: **bulkier - bulkiest**)

bull [bʊl] *noun* (a) male of the cow family; *be careful when you cross the field - there's a bull in it* (informal) **to take the bull by the horns** = to tackle a difficult problem; *he decided to take the bull by the horns and tell his father that he was leaving the family firm* (b) male of some other species; *a bull walrus; a bull elephant* (c) person who believes that stock market prices will rise; **bull market** = period when prices on the stock market rise as shareholders buy shares because they think share prices will rise still further (NOTE: the opposite is **bear**)

bulldog ['bʊldɒg] *noun* squat strong dog with a flat face; *bulldogs are far from being my favourite breed of dog*

bulldozer ['bʊldəʊzə] *noun* large powerful tractor with a curved plate in front for pushing or moving earth, rubble, etc.; *they hired bulldozers to clear the site*

bullet ['bʊlɪt] *noun* piece of metal fired from a hand gun; *he loaded his gun with bullets; two bullets had been fired*

bulletin ['bʊlɪtɪn] *noun* information on a situation; *the hospital issued a daily news bulletin on the condition of the accident victims*

bulletin board ['bʊlɪtɪn 'bɔːd] *noun* (a) *US* board on which notices can be pinned (NOTE: British English is **noticeboard**) (b) *(on the Internet)* system of sending messages, advertising events, etc.; *she advertised the concert on the bulletin board*

bullion ['bʊljən] *noun* gold or silver bars; *the price of bullion changes daily; the ship sank with a cargo of silver bullion*

bullish ['bʊlɪʃ] *adjective* feeling that the stock market is likely to rise; *buy now before the market turns bullish again* (NOTE: the opposite is **bearish**)

bullock ['bʊlək] *noun* castrated bull; *bullocks are often used as draught animals because they are docile and easy to train*

bull's eye ['bʊlz'aɪ] *noun* (a) centre of the target which you try to hit in archery, darts, rifle shooting, etc.; *this target is not easy, the bull's eye is very small* (b) hitting in the centre of a target; *no one scored a bull's eye* (c) *(informal)* large sweet; *he bought a packet of bull's eyes*

bully ['bʊli] **1** *noun* person who hurts or is unkind to weaker people; *he's a bully and is always trying to frighten smaller children* (NOTE: plural is **bullies**) **2** *verb* to be unkind to someone who is weaker; *she was bullied by the other children in school* (NOTE: **bullying - bullied**)

bum [bʌm] **1** *noun* *(informal)* (a) bottom; *he just sits on his bum all day, doing nothing* (b) *US* person who sits around doing nothing; *can't you bums find something to do?* (c) *US* person who is very keen on something; *a ski bum* **2** *verb* *(informal)* **to bum something off someone** = to ask someone for something; *he always trying to bum cigarettes off his friends; can I bum a cigarette?*

bumblebee ['bʌmblbiː] *noun* large brown furry bee; *bumblebees make quite a lot of noise when they fly*

bumbling ['bʌmblɪŋ] *adjective* awkward and inefficient; *he accused the Foreign Office of bumbling incompetence*

bump [bʌmp] **1** *noun* **(a)** slight knock; *the boat hit the landing stage with a bump* **(b)** raised place; *drive slowly, the road is full of bumps* **(c)** raised place on your body, where something has hit it; *he has a bump on the back of his head* **2** *verb* to hit; *he's crying because he bumped his head on the door*

bumper ['bʌmpə] **1** *adjective* very large; *a bumper crop of corn*; *we're publishing a bumper edition of children's stories*; *1997 was a bumper year for computer sales* **2** *noun* protective bar on the front and rear of a car; *he backed into a lamppost and dented the rear bumper*; *there was a mile-long traffic jam with cars standing bumper-to-bumper*

bump into ['bʌmp 'ɪntʊ] *verb* **(a)** to hit slightly; *be careful not to bump into the wall when you're reversing* **(b)** to bump into someone = to meet someone by chance; *I bumped into him at the station*

bump off ['bʌmp 'ɒf] *verb* (*informal*) to murder someone; *three characters were murdered in the first episode, so we wonder who is going to be bumped off next*

bump start ['bʌmp 'stɑːt] **1** *verb* to start a car engine when the battery is flat by putting it into gear and then pushing it; *we bump started the car and drove to town to get a new battery* **2** *noun* starting a car engine when the battery is flat by putting it into gear and then pushing it; *two passers-by gave me a bump start; compare* JUMP START

bumpy ['bʌmpi] *adjective* uneven (path or flight); *the road is so bumpy that driving at 20 mph seems fast*; *although they announced turbulence, the flight was not bumpy at all* (NOTE: **bumpier - bumpiest**)

bun [bʌn] *noun* **(a)** little round bread or cake; *hamburgers are made of minced beef fried and served in a bun*; *the icing on these buns is too sweet*; **currant bun** = bun with currants in it; *see also* HOT CROSS BUN **(b)** hair wound in a knot; *she wears her hair in a bun*

bunch [bʌntʃ] *noun* **(a)** group of things taken together; *he carries a bunch of keys attached to his belt*; *he brought her a bunch of flowers*; *I work with a nice bunch of people* **(b)** cluster of fruit on the same stem; *a bunch of grapes*; *a bunch of bananas* (NOTE: plural is **bunches**)

bundle ['bʌndl] **1** *noun* parcel of things wrapped up or tied up together; *a bundle of clothes was all she possessed*; *he produced a bundle of papers tied up with green string*; *she left her clothes in a bundle on the floor* **2** *verb* **(a)** to put something somewhere roughly; *he bundled the papers into a drawer*; *she bundled the children off to school*; *the police bundled him into the back of their van* **(b)** to sell a software programme at the same time as you sell hardware, both sold together at a special price; *the word-processing package is bundled with the computer*

bungalow ['bʌŋgələʊ] *noun* house with only a ground floor; *my grandparents have bought a bungalow by the sea*

bungee ['bʌndʒiː] *noun* elastic strap with a hook at each end, used for attaching luggage onto a trolley or onto the back of a bicycle, etc.

bungee-jumping ['bʌndʒiːˈdʒʌmpɪŋ] *noun* sport which consists of jumping from a high point (such as a bridge) when attached by your ankles to a long elastic cable, so that instead of hitting the ground, you bounce up into the air; *I'd like to try bungee-jumping, but my girlfriend won't let me*

bungle ['bʌŋgl] *verb* to do something badly; *they bungled the job so it had to be done all over again*; *they called the officials a group of bungling incompetents*

bunion ['bʌnjən] *noun* inflammation and swelling of the first joint of the big toe; *wearing shoes that were too tight, she ended up with bunions*

bunk [bʌŋk] *noun* **(a)** bed attached to a wall, as in a ship, etc.; *he climbed up into his bunk and fell asleep*; *do you want the top bunk or the bottom one?*; **bunk beds** = two beds one on top of the other, with a ladder to climb to the top one; *we put the children in bunk beds because they take up less space* **(b)** (*informal*) **to do a bunk** = to run away; *as soon as they saw the police van, they did a bunk across some waste land*

bunker ['bʌŋkə] *noun* **(a) coal bunker** = place for storing coal; *he brought in a pail of coal from the bunker* **(b)** fortified room, often underground; *the soldiers defended the bunker for several days*; *as the enemy approached, the ministers hid in a bunker under the presidential palace* **(c)** open pit filled with sand placed on a golf course to trap balls and make difficulties for the players; *that's the second time he's in a bunker on this round*

bunny ['bʌni] *noun* child's name for a rabbit; *what a sweet little bunny!*; *look at all the bunnies in the field* (NOTE: plural is **bunnies**)

Bunsen burner ['bʌnsən 'bɜːnə] *noun* a small gas heater which gives a smokeless flame, used in laboratories; *connect the Bunsen burner to the gas tap and light it*; *you need a beaker and a Bunsen burner for this experiment*

buoy [bɔɪ] **1** *noun* floating marker in the sea, or in a lake or river; *light buoys show the harbour's entrance at night*; *the canoes will race around the buoys at the end of the lake* **2** *verb* **to buoy someone up** = to cheer someone up; *a win in the quarter-finals kept the fans buoyed up*

buoyant ['bɔɪənt] *adjective* **(a)** which can float easily, which helps something float easily; *the raft became waterlogged and was no longer buoyant*; *salt water is more buoyant than fresh water* **(b)** full of confidence; *she left the meeting in a very buoyant mood*

burden ['bɜːdn] **1** *noun* **(a)** heavy load; *he relieved her of her burden*; **beast of burden** = animal which carries heavy loads **(b)** something hard to bear; *I think he finds running the office at his age something of a burden*; **to make someone's life a burden** = to make someone's life difficult **2** *verb* to weigh down with a load; *the whole town was burdened with grief*; *the company is burdened with debt*

burdensome ['bɜːdənsʌm] *adjective* which feels like a heavy load; *family responsibilities can be quite burdensome*

bureau ['bjʊərəu] *noun* **(a)** office; *he filed the report from the New York bureau*; **computer bureau** = office which does computer work for other offices; **(tourist) information bureau** = office which gives information to tourists; *ask for a list of guesthouses at the information bureau* **(b)** *US* chest of drawers; *my socks are in the bureau in the bedroom* (NOTE: plural is **bureaux** ['bjʊərəuz])

bureau de change ['bjʊərəu də 'ʃɒnʒ] *noun* office where you can change foreign currency; *the bureau de change didn't have any Canadian dollars* (NOTE: plural is **bureaux de change**)

bureaucracy [bjʊə'rɒkrəsi] *noun* **(a)** group of officials working for central or local government, or for an international body; *the investigation of complaints is in the hands of the local bureaucracy* **(b)** official system that is run by civil servants; *red tape and bureaucracy slow down charitable work; I'm fed up with all this bureaucracy, just to get an export licence*

bureaucrat ['bjʊərəkræt] *noun* civil servant; *she works as a bureaucrat in Brussels*

bureaucratic [bjʊərə'krætik] *adjective* referring to the civil service; *aid workers are continually fighting against bureaucratic muddle*

burgeon ['bɜːdʒn] *verb* to grow rapidly; *the population of the village has burgeoned so rapidly it will soon be the size of a small town*

burgeoning ['bɜːdʒnɪŋ] *adjective* growing fast; *the burgeoning refugee population is causing problems for the United Nations; her parents are very proud of her burgeoning musical talent*

burger ['bɜːgə] *noun short for* BEEFBURGER, HAMBURGER; *he had a burger and chips for lunch*

burgh ['bʌrə] *noun (Scotland)* = BOROUGH

burglar ['bɜːglə] *noun* person who tries to get into a building to steal; *burglars broke in during the night; she saw the burglar as he was climbing out of the window*; **burglar alarm** = device which rings if someone enters a building illegally

burglary ['bɜːgləri] *noun* robbery by a burglar; *he was charged with burglary; he had committed several burglaries over the previous months; there are many more burglaries during the summer holidays*

burgle ['bɜːgl] *verb* to enter a building and steal things from it; *their flat was burgled while they were on holiday; someone tried to burgle our house*

burgundy ['bɜːgəndi] **1** *noun* **(a)** red and white wine from Burgundy in the central part of France; *would you prefer a white or a red burgundy with your quails?* **(b)** dark red colour; *burgundy is not a colour I would choose for a car* **2** *adjective* dark red; *is this burgundy sports car yours?*

burial ['beriəl] *noun* ceremony of burying a dead person; *he died on Monday but the burial will not take place until next week*; **burial ground** = cemetery; *the burial ground attached to the church contains some very old graves*

burly ['bɜːli] *adjective (person)* strong and solid; *it took three burly policemen to hold him down* (NOTE: **burlier - burliest**)

burn [bɜːn] **1** *noun* burnt area of the skin or a surface; *she had burns on her face and hands; there's a burn on the edge of the table where he left his cigarette* **2** *verb* **(a)** to damage or destroy by fire; *all our clothes were burnt in the hotel fire; she burnt her finger on the hot frying pan; the hotel was burnt to the ground last year; the sun and wind burnt his face*; *look,* **you've burnt the bacon** = you've cooked it too much, so that it is black; *(informal)* **to burn the candle at both ends** = to work much too hard; *he gets up early to go to the office, and comes home late - he's burning the candle at both ends; see also* MONEY **(b)** to be on fire; *the firemen were called to the burning school* **(c)** to use as a fuel; *the cooker burns gas*; **a wood-burning stove** = heater which burns wood (NOTE: **burning - burnt** [bɜːnt] *or* **burned**)

burn down [bɜːn 'daun] *verb* **(a)** to destroy completely by fire; *they were playing with matches and burnt the house down* **(b)** to be destroyed completely by fire; *the building had burnt down before the firemen arrived*

burner ['bɜːnə] *noun* apparatus for making fire; *a gas stove with four burners*; **to put something on the back burner** = to shelve something, so that a decision can be made on it later; *all decisions about the project have been put on the back burner; see also* BUNSEN BURNER

burning ['bɜːnɪŋ] *adjective* **(a)** very hot; *the baby must have a temperature - his face is burning; careful, the pan is burning hot* **(b)** (sensation) which feels like being burnt; *she had a burning pain in her left eye* **(c)** eager; *he had a burning desire to go to Egypt* **(d)** **burning question** = important matter, which is likely to cause controversy; *who will be the new mayor, that is the burning question at the moment*

burn out [bɜːn 'aut] *verb* **(a)** to destroy the inside completely by fire; *the restaurant was completely burnt out* **(b)** **to burn yourself out** = to work so hard that you cannot work any more; *she burnt herself out setting up her own business* **(c)** *(of a fire)* **to burn itself out** = to stop burning because there is nothing left to burn; *after a couple of hours the fire had burnt itself out*

burnout ['bɜːnaut] *noun* state of not being able to work any more because you have worked too hard; *he suffered a burnout and had to go on leave*

burnt [bɜːnt] *adjective* black with fire; *the kitchen smells of burnt toast; all that remained of the house were some burnt walls*

burnt-out case ['bɜːntaut 'keis] *noun* employee who is incapable of doing any more work because he has been overworked; *we had a couple of burnt-out cases in our department during the past year*

burp [bɜːp] **1** *noun* noise when bringing up air from the stomach; *when the baby stops drinking, pat him gently on the back until he makes a burp* **2** *verb* **(a)** to make a burp; *there is nothing like a fizzy drink to make you burp* **(b)** **to burp a baby** = to make a baby burp by gently patting him on the back until he burps; *have you burped the baby yet?*

burrow ['bʌrəu] **1** *noun* rabbit hole; *the rabbits all popped down into their burrow when we came near* **2** *verb* to dig underground; *moles have burrowed under the lawn*

burst [bɜːst] **1** *noun* **(a)** sudden loud sound; *there was a burst of gunfire and then silence; bursts of laughter came from the office* **(b)** sudden effort or activity; *he put on a burst of speed; in one of her periodical bursts of efficiency she sorted out the old stock* **2** *verb* to explode suddenly; *a water main burst in the High*

Street; *when she picked up the balloon it burst*; **to be bursting at the seams** = to be very full, not to have any more space; *the schools are bursting at the seams* (NOTE: bursting - burst)

bursting ['bɜːstɪŋ] *adjective* full of; eager to say something; *he was bursting to tell everyone the news*; *she was bursting with pride at her children's success*

burst into ['bɜːst 'ɪntʊ] *verb* **(a)** to enter unexpectedly, in a rush; *she burst into the meeting waving a bundle of papers* **(b)** to start to do something suddenly; *she opened the letter and burst into tears*; *the building burst into flames*

burst out ['bɜːst 'aʊt] *verb* **(a)** to suddenly start; *she burst out laughing* **(b)** to say something loudly; *he burst out into a string of insults* **(c)** to leave quickly; *she burst out of the shop, and started running down the street*

bury ['beri] *verb* to put into the ground; *he was buried in the local cemetery*; *squirrels often bury nuts in the autumn* (*informal*) **to bury your head in the sand** = to pretend that a danger or problem doesn't exist (NOTE: do not confuse with **berry**)

bus [bʌs] *noun* large motor vehicle which carries passengers; *he goes to work by bus*; *she takes the 8 o'clock bus to school every morning*; *we missed the last bus and had to walk home*; *the number 6 bus goes to Oxford Street*; **airport bus** = bus which takes passengers from a town to the airport and vice versa; **school bus** = bus which takes schoolchildren to school; *the children were waiting for the school bus* (NOTE: plural is **buses**)

busboy ['bʌsbɔɪ] *noun US* boy or young man who helps a waiter in a restaurant by clearing dishes, bringing water, etc.; *I asked the busboy for some more water*

bush [bʊʃ] *noun* **(a)** small tree; *an animal was moving in the bushes*; *a holly bush with red berries* (NOTE: plural is **bushes**) **(b)** (*in Africa, India, etc.*) **the bush** = land covered with bushes or low trees; *they walked through the bush for several days before finding a village*

bushel ['bʊʃl] *noun* measure of dry goods, such as grain (equal to 56 pounds); *wheat is sold by the bushel*

bushy ['bʊʃi] *adjective* (*hair*) growing thickly; *bushy eyebrows*; *a squirrel's bushy tail* (NOTE: **bushier - bushiest**)

busily ['bɪzɪli] *adverb* in a busy way; *she was busily preparing the evening meal when I arrived*

business ['bɪznəs] *noun* **(a)** occupation or trade, the work of buying or selling things; *she works in the electricity business*; *they do a lot of business with European countries*; **business college** *or* **business school** = place where commercial studies are taught; *he's going to a business school in September*; **business letter** = letter about business matters; **business trip** = trip to do with your business; *he's on a business trip to France*; **on business** = on commercial work; *the sales director is in Holland on business* **(b)** commercial company; *she runs a photography business*; *he runs a secondhand car business*; **business address** = details of number, street and town where a company is located; **business card** = card showing a businessman's name and the name and address of the company he works for; **business hours** = time (usually 9 a.m. to 5.30 p.m.) when a business is open (NOTE: plural in this meaning is

businesses) **(c)** affair, concern; **it's none of your business** = it's nothing to do with you

businesslike ['bɪznəslaɪk] *adjective* practical and commercial; *a very businesslike young man answered all my queries*; *they dealt with our order in a businesslike way*

businessman, businesswoman ['bɪznəsmæn *or* 'bɪznəswʊmən] *noun* person who is engaged in business, who runs a business; *the early morning flights to Frankfurt are full of businessmen* (NOTE: plural is **businessmen, businesswomen**)

business park ['bɪznəs 'pɑːk] *noun* group of small offices and warehouses built together; *we have bought a unit in the new business park near the station*

bus pass ['bʌs 'pɑːs] *noun* special ticket allowing you to use a bus at a cheaper rate, or without paying at all; *a student bus pass*; *have you got your OAP bus pass yet?*

bus stop ['bʌs 'stɒp] *noun* place where a bus stops and passengers can get on or off; *there were ten people waiting at the bus stop*

bust [bʌst] **1** *noun* **(a)** sculpture of the head and shoulders; *there's a bust of Shakespeare in Stratford church* **(b)** woman's breasts; **bust size** *or* **bust measurement** = measurement round a woman's breasts **2** *adjective* (*informal*) **(a)** broken; *the washing machine's bust* **(b)** **to go bust** = to fail, to be bankrupt; *thousands of people lost their savings when the bank went bust* **3** *verb* (*informal*) to break; *she's bust my precious vase!*; *he hit the ball hard and it bust a window* (NOTE: **busting - busted** *or* **bust**)

bustle ['bʌsl] **1** *noun* **(a)** rushing around; *it's nice to sit quietly at home after the bustle of the office* **(b)** pad at the back of a Victorian dress **2** *verb* to rush around doing things; *she bustled around the kitchen getting dinner ready*

bustling ['bʌslɪŋ] *adjective* very busy; *the bustling crowds in Oxford Street*; *the marketplace was bustling with activity*

busy ['bɪzi] **1** *adjective* working on something, doing something; *he was busy mending the dishwasher*; *I was too busy to phone my aunt*; *the busiest time for shops is the week before Christmas*; **the line's busy at the moment** = someone is using the phone line (NOTE: **busier - busiest**) **2** *verb* **to busy yourself with something** = to occupy yourself, to keep yourself busy with something; *my sister likes to busy herself with the garden now she's retired*

busybody ['bɪzibɒdi] *noun* person who is busy interfering in what other people do; *some busybody decided to clean up my desk, and now I can't find anything* (NOTE: plural is **busybodies**)

but [bʌt] **1** *conjunction* (*coming before a contrast*) *he is very tall, but his wife is quite short*; *we would like to come to your party, but we're doing something else that evening*; *I'm sorry, but there are no seats left* **2** *preposition* except; *everyone but me is allowed to go to the cinema*; *they had eaten nothing but apples* **3** *adverb* (*formal*) only; *this is but one of his mistakes*; *we can but try*

butane ['bjuːteɪn] *noun* gas derived from distilling petroleum, used for heating and cooking and sold in special pressurized containers; *butane gas is more commonly used in France than in England*; *camping gas cylinders are full of butane*

butch [butʃ] *adjective (slang) (of a woman)* very masculine

butcher ['butʃə] **1** *noun* **(a)** man who prepares and sells meat; *ask the butcher to prepare the pheasants for you*; **the butcher's** = shop where you can buy meat; *can you get me some sausages from the butcher's?* **(b)** *(slang)* look; *go on, let's have a butcher's at it* (NOTE: from **butcher's hook** which means 'look' in rhyming slang; see also RHYMING SLANG) **2** *verb* to kill brutally; *the soldiers set fire to the village and butchered the inhabitants*

butchery ['butʃəri] *noun* brutal killing; *UN troops were sent in to halt the butchery of civilians*

butler ['bʌtlə] *noun* most important male servant in a house, who serves at table, especially dealing with wine; *the same butler worked for the princess for ten years*; **the butler's pantry** = in a large house, the room where a butler works

butt [bʌt] **1** *noun* **(a)** water barrel; *it has rained a lot lately and the rainwater butt is overflowing* **(b)** end of a cigarette which has been smoked; *he picked up old butts from the pavement* **(c)** end of the handle of a gun which presses against the shoulder of the person firing it; *the prisoners were beaten with rifle butts* **(d)** person who is teased; *he will always be the butt of their criticism if he doesn't dress any better* **(e)** push with the head; *the goat came up behind him and gave him a butt with its head* **(f)** *US (informal)* buttocks; *to give someone a kick in the butt* **(g)** *(in carpentry)* **butt joint** = flat joint, which does not overlap **2** *verb* **(a)** to push with the head; *the goat lowered its head and butted him* **(b) to butt in** = to interrupt; *he always butts in while I'm trying to tell a story*

butter ['bʌtə] **1** *noun* yellow fat made from cream, used on bread or for cooking; *could you pass the butter, please?*; *don't spread the butter so thick*; *fry the mushrooms in butter* (NOTE: no plural: **some butter**; a **knob of butter**) **2** *verb* **(a)** to spread butter on something; *she was busy buttering slices of bread for the sandwiches* **(b)** *(informal)* **to butter someone up** = to flatter someone, to praise someone insincerely; *just butter up the boss a bit - tell him how good his golf is*

buttercup ['bʌtəkʌp] *noun* common yellow flower found in fields; *she picked buttercups in the field*

buttered ['bʌtəd] *adjective* covered with butter; *a slice of hot buttered toast*

butter-fingers ['bʌtə'fiŋgəz] *noun (informal)* person who often drops things; *I wouldn't let her carry those glasses, she's a real butter-fingers*

butterfly ['bʌtəflaɪ] *noun* **(a)** insect with large brightly coloured wings which comes out in daylight; *butterflies come out in the sunshine* **(b)** *(informal)* **to have butterflies in the stomach** = to be very nervous; *she had butterflies in the stomach before the interview* (NOTE: plural is **butterflies**; similar insects with rather dull wings, which come out a night, are **moths**)

butterfly stroke ['bʌtəflaɪ 'strəʊk] *noun* swimming stroke where the two arms are lifted forwards at the same time and pushed down into the water while kicking the legs

buttock(s) ['bʌtək(s)] *noun* a person's bottom, the part of the body on which you sit; *he has a boil on his left buttock*

button ['bʌtən] **1** *noun* **(a)** little round disc for fastening clothes; *the wind is cold - do up the buttons*

on your coat; *a button's come off my shirt* **(b)** little round disc which you push to ring a bell, etc.; *press the 'up' button to call the lift*; *push the red button to set off the alarm*; *push the button marked 'black' if you want coffee without milk* **2** *verb* to fasten with buttons; *he buttoned (up) his coat because it was cold*

button-down collar ['bʌtəndaʊn 'kɒlə] *noun* shirt collar held down with a button at each point; *he prefers shirts with button-down collars*

buttonhole ['bʌtənhəʊl] **1** *noun* **(a)** hole through which a button goes to fasten a coat, etc.; *you've put the button in the wrong buttonhole* **(b)** flower worn in a little buttonhole on a lapel; *he wore a buttonhole to the office every day* **2** *verb* *(formal)* to stop someone and start talking to him; *she buttonholed her solicitor outside the court and started asking him for information*

buttress ['bʌtrəs] **1** *noun* wall or strong pillar built against another wall to support it; *there are three buttresses on the side wall of the church* (NOTE: plural is **buttresses**) **2** *verb* to support; *you'll need more evidence than that to buttress your argument*

buxom ['bʌksəm] *adjective* plump and attractive; *we were served by a buxom waitress* (NOTE: only used of women)

buy [baɪ] **1** *verb* to get something by paying money; *I bought a newspaper on my way to the station*; *she's buying a flat*; *she bought herself a pair of ski boots*; *what did you buy your mother for her birthday?* (NOTE: **buying - bought** [bɔːt]) **2** *noun* **a good buy** = something which you have bought which is worth the money spent; *that camera you bought was a very good buy*

buyer ['baɪə] *noun* person who buys; *there were no buyers for his house*; *she works as shoe buyer in a department store*; **head buyer** = most important buyer in a store; **a buyer's market** = market where products are sold cheaply because there are more sellers than buyers; *compare* SELLER'S MARKET

buy off ['baɪ 'ɒf] *verb* **to buy someone off** = to pay someone not to do something; *they were going to print the story in the local newspaper but we managed to buy them off*

buyout ['baɪaʊt] *noun* **management buyout (MBO)** = takeover of a company by a group of employees, usually managers and directors; *see also* LEVERAGE

buy up ['baɪ 'ʌp] *verb* to buy a large quantity of something; *a buyer from a supermarket came to the vineyard and bought up their entire production*

buzz [bʌz] **1** *noun* **(a)** noise like the noise made by a bee; *I can hear a buzz but I can't see the bee*; *the buzz of an electric saw in the garden next door* **(b)** *(informal)* thrill, excitement; *she gets a buzz from skiing fast downhill* **(c)** *(informal)* telephone call; *give me a buzz tomorrow* (NOTE: plural is **buzzes**) **2** *verb* to make a noise like a bee; *wasps were buzzing round the jam*

buzzard ['bʌzəd] *noun* large bird of prey; *birds of prey like owls and buzzards help keep down the numbers of pests*

buzzer ['bʌzə] *noun* device which buzzes; *press the buzzer if you want help*

by [baɪ] **1** *preposition* **(a)** near; *the house is just by the bus stop*; *sit down here by me* **(b)** before, not later than; *they should have arrived by now*; *you must be home by* *eleven o'clock; we must finish this piece of work by Friday* **(c)** *(showing means or way) send the parcel by airmail; get in touch with the office by phone; they came by car; she caught a cold by standing in the rain; you make buck's fizz by adding champagne to orange juice; she paid by cheque, not by credit card* **(d)** *(showing the person or thing that did something) a painting by Van Gogh; 'Hamlet' is a play by Shakespeare; a CD recorded by our local group; the postman was bitten by the dog; she was knocked down by a car* **(e)** **by yourself** = *alone; don't sit at home all by yourself; she made the hat all by herself; can you find your way to the station by yourself?* **(f)** *(showing how much) we sell tomatoes by the kilo; eggs are sold by the dozen; prices have been increased by 5%; they won by 4 goals to 2* **(g)** *(showing dimensions) the table is 60cm long by 25 wide* **2** *adverb past; she drove by without seeing us*

◊ **by and large** [ˈbaɪ n ˈlɑːʒ] in general; *by and large, the trains run on time*

◊ **by the way** [ˈbaɪ ðə ˈweɪ] *(used to mention something not very important) by the way, did you see the TV programme on cars yesterday?; by the way, I shall be home late tonight*

bye *or* **bye-bye** [baɪ(baɪ)] *interjection* goodbye; *bye! see you next week!*

by-election [ˈbaɪɪlekʃən] *noun* election for Parliament when an MP has died or retired; *who do you think will win this by-election?; by-elections are not always good indicators of voting trends*

byelaw *or* **by-law** [ˈbaɪlɔː] *noun* **(a)** rule or law made by a local authority or public body but not by central government; *a local byelaw says that this path*

is a public right of way; byelaws must be made by bodies which have been authorized by Parliament **(b)** one of a set of rules for running a club; *according to the byelaws, the president is elected for three years only*

bygone [ˈbaɪgɒn] **1** *adjective* former; *a painting of a bygone age* **2** *noun* **to let bygones be bygones** = to forget what happened in the past (usually insults or something unpleasant); *after ten years of not speaking to each other they finally decided to let bygones be bygones*

by-line [ˈbaɪlaɪn] *noun* line at the beginning or end of an article in a newspaper, giving the name of the journalist who wrote it; *the article appears under the by-line 'William Heath'*

bypass [ˈbaɪpɑːs] **1** *noun* **(a)** road round a town; *take the bypass if you want to avoid congestion in the town centre* **(b)** **heart bypass** = operation to graft pieces of vein around a diseased part of a coronary artery; *she had a heart bypass ten years ago and is still going strong* **2** *verb* to go round a town, avoiding the centre; *it would be better if you could bypass the town centre on market day; the main road bypasses the town centre*

by-product [ˈbaɪprɒdʌkt] *noun* product made as a result of manufacturing a main product; *butane is a by-product of petroleum distillation*

bystander [ˈbaɪstændə] *noun* person near where something is happening; *mothers and children were among the bystanders injured in the explosion*

byte [baɪt] *noun* group of eight bits (binary digits) which a computer operates on as a single unit (NOTE: usually used in compounds **kilobyte, megabyte, etc.;** do not confuse with **bite**)

Cc

C, c [siː] third letter of the alphabet, between B and D; *remember the rhyme: I before E except after C: so write 'receive' and not 'recieve'*

ca. = CIRCA

cab [kæb] *noun* (a) taxi, a car which takes people from one place to another for money; *he took a cab to the airport; she whistled for a cab; can you phone for a cab, please?; the office is only a short cab ride from the railway station; cab fares are very high in New York*; **black cab** = London taxi **(b)** separate compartment for a driver in a large vehicle, such as a truck; *the truck driver climbed into his cab and started the engine*

cabaret [ˈkæbəreɪ] *noun* entertainment given in a restaurant or club, with dancing and singing; *with all these singers and dancers we should be able to put on an excellent cabaret; I heard that there's a cabaret at the club tonight*

cabbage [ˈkæbɪdʒ] *noun* (a) vegetable with large pale green or red leaves which you eat; *we had red cabbage with our lunch; the school always smells of boiled cabbage; he was planting cabbages in his garden* (NOTE: as food, **cabbage** does not have a plural: **some cabbage; a helping of cabbage**; as plants you can count **one cabbage, two cabbages**, etc.) **(b)** person who has had a brain injury, which makes them unable to think, eat, etc.

cab driver *(informal)* **cabbie** [ˈkæbɪ] *noun* driver of a cab; *cabbies are tested on their knowledge of London's streets*

cabin [ˈkæbɪn] *noun* (a) small room on a ship; *we booked a first-class cabin on the cruise; she felt sick and went to lie down in her cabin*; **cabin cruiser** = comfortable motor boat with cabins where you can sleep; *three cabin cruisers were waiting to go through the lock* **(b)** small hut; *he has a cabin by a lake where he goes fishing* **(c)** interior of an aircraft; *the aircraft is divided into three separate cabins; the first-class cabin is in the front of the plane*; **the cabin crew** *or* **cabin staff** = the hostesses and stewards on a plane

cabinet [ˈkæbɪnət] *noun* (a) piece of furniture with shelves; *a china cabinet*; **filing cabinet** = piece of office furniture with drawers for storing files **(b)** committee formed of the most important members of a government; *the cabinet met at 10 o'clock this morning; there's a cabinet meeting every Thursday morning*; **kitchen cabinet** = private unofficial group of ministers, advisers and friends, who advise a Prime Minister; **shadow cabinet** = senior members of the opposition who cover the areas of responsibility of the actual cabinet, and will form the cabinet if their party is elected to power

cable [ˈkeɪbl] **1** *noun* (a) wire for carrying electricity; *he ran a cable out into the garden so that he could use his lawnmower* **(b)** thick rope or wire; *the ship was attached to the quay by cables; the cable snapped and ten passengers died when the cable car fell to the floor of the valley*; **cable railway** = railway where the carriages are pulled by a cable **(c)** wire for sending messages underground or under the sea; *they've been digging up the pavements to lay cables*; **cable TV** = TV where the programmes are sent along underground wires **(d)** a telegram; *he sent a cable to his office asking for more money* **2** *verb* to send a telegram; *he cabled his office to ask them to send more money*

cable car [ˈkeɪbl ˈkɑː] *noun* (a) vehicle which goes up a mountain, hanging on a wire cable; *ten people were killed when the cable car fell to the floor of the valley* **(b)** *US (in San Francisco)* type of tram which is pulled by a metal cable set in a channel in the road; *we took the cable car down to Fisherman's Wharf*

cache [kæʃ] **1** *noun* (a) hidden store; *the police found a cache of explosives in the shed* **(b) cache memory** = section of high-speed memory which stores data that the computer can access quickly; *file access time is much quicker if the most frequently used data is stored in the cache memory* **2** *verb* to file or store in a cache; *this program can cache any size of font* (NOTE: do not confuse with **cash**)

cacophony [kəˈkɒfəni] *noun* unpleasant mixture of loud sounds; *his latest concerto is a curious cacophony of sounds; the delegates came from all over the world - the dining room was a cacophony of Spanish, Russian and Chinese!*

cactus [ˈkæktəs] *noun* prickly plant which grows in the desert; *cacti don't need much water* (NOTE: plural is **cactuses** *or* **cacti** [ˈkæktaɪ])

cadaver [kəˈdɑːvə] *noun (formal)* corpse, dead body; *it is not easy when you see a cadaver for the first time and have to cut it up in an anatomy lab*

cadaverous [kəˈdævərəs] *adjective (formal)* looking like a corpse; *what has happened to him? - he used to be quite fat, now he's absolutely cadaverous*

caddie [ˈkædi] **1** *noun* person who carries the clubs for a golfer; *some of the best golf professionals started as caddies* **2** *verb* to caddie for someone = to act as a caddie for someone; *my nephew is going to caddie for me this weekend*

cadet [kəˈdet] *noun* young person training for the armed services or the police force; *a group of officer cadets marched past; she joined the police force as a cadet*

cadre [ˈkɑːdə] *noun* active member or group of key members of a party (especially a Marxist party); *the party cadres are no longer as powerful as they were*

caesarean [sɪˈzeəriən] *noun* **caesarean (section)** = surgical operation to deliver a baby by cutting through the abdominal wall into the uterus; *the mother may need a caesarean section, but we'd prefer the baby to be born naturally; she had her baby by caesarean; our baby was born by caesarean section*

café [ˈkæfeɪ] *noun* small restaurant selling snacks or light meals; *we had a snack in the station café*

cafeteria [kæfɪ'tɪərɪə] *noun* self-service restaurant; *there's a cafeteria at the campsite - we can eat there*

cafetiere [kæftj'eə] *noun* coffee pot where you push down a filter to make the coffee; *the waitress brought us a cafetiere of coffee*

caffeine ['kæfi:n] *noun* alkaloid found in coffee, chocolate and tea which acts as a stimulant; *have a herb tea - it doesn't have any caffeine; there's about the same amount of caffeine in tea as in coffee; see also* DECAFFEINATED

cage [keɪdʒ] *noun* box made of wire or with metal bars for keeping birds or animals so they cannot get out; *the rabbit got out of its cage*

cagoule [kæ'gu:l] *noun* lightweight waterproof anorak with a hood, often reaching to the knees; *she carried her cagoule in a bag round her waist in case it rained*

cajole [kə'dʒəʊl] *verb* to cajole someone into doing something = to persuade someone to do something by flattery; *it is unbelievable - she managed to cajole him into paying for her trip to Bermuda*

cake [keɪk] **1** *noun* **(a)** food made by mixing flour, eggs, sugar, etc., and baking it; *a piece of cherry cake; she had six candles on her birthday cake; have another slice of Christmas cake; would you like some chocolate cake?*; **wedding cake** = special cake made with dried fruit, covered with icing, eaten at a wedding reception; **cake mix** = main ingredients for a cake which are bought ready mixed in a packet; *(slang)* **it's a piece of cake** = it's very easy; *the exam was a piece of cake - I finished it in half-an-hour!*; **you can't have your cake and eat it** = you can't benefit from two opposing things (NOTE: as food, cake sometimes has no plural: **some cake, a piece of cake**; when it means a particular item of food it can have a plural: **she made twenty cakes; a plate of cakes; there are no cakes left in the shop**) **(b)** small piece of something; *a cake of soap* **(c)** food made by mixing ingredients together into small round pieces which are then fried; *a meal of fishcakes and chips* **2** *verb* to dry and form a hard crust; **to be caked with** = to be covered with something that has dried hard; *his boots were caked with mud*

calamity [kə'læmɪti] *noun (formal)* disaster; *what calamity has befallen her this time?; the poor people in the desert regions have suffered one calamity after another* (NOTE: plural is **calamities**)

calcium ['kælsɪəm] *noun* **(a)** metallic chemical element which is a major component of bones and teeth and which is essential for blood clotting; *their diet has a calcium deficiency or is deficient in calcium* (NOTE: Chemical element: chemical symbol: **Ca**; atomic number: 20) **(b)** white substance found in water, forming lime, etc.; *calcium deposits form inside pipes and kettles*

> COMMENT: calcium is an important element in a balanced diet. Milk, cheese, eggs and certain vegetables are its main sources

calculate ['kælkju:leɪt] *verb* to find the answer to a problem using numbers; *the bank clerk calculated the rate of exchange for the dollar; I calculate that we have enough money left for a meal; he calculated that it would take us six hours to get to Madrid*

calculated ['kælkjʊleɪtɪd] *adjective* planned; *his speech was calculated to make his opponents very angry*; **a calculated insult** = insult which was made on purpose; **a calculated risk** = risk which you think you can afford to take

calculating ['kælkjʊleɪtɪŋ] *adjective* who plans clever schemes in a careful way; *the MP called the Home Secretary a cool calculating plotter*

calculation [kælkju'leɪʃn] *noun* act of calculating; *according to my calculations, we have enough fuel left for only twenty kilometres*; **rough calculation** = approximate answer to a problem using numbers; *I made some rough calculations on the back of an envelope*

calculator ['kælkju:leɪtə] *noun* machine for doing sums; *he worked out the price on his calculator*; **pocket calculator** = small calculator which you can put in your pocket

calculus ['kælkjʊləs] *noun* **(a)** part of mathematics which is the way of calculating varying rates; *calculus is now taught in sixth forms* **(b)** hard mass like a little piece of stone, which forms inside the body; **renal calculus** = stone in the kidney; *calculi in the kidneys are not uncommon* (NOTE: plural in this meaning is **calculi** ['kælkjʊlaɪ])

caldron ['kɔ:ldrən] *noun US see* CAULDRON

calendar ['kæləndə] *noun* paper showing the days and months of the year, which can be pinned on a wall; *he pinned the calendar to the wall by his desk; turn over to the next page of the calendar - today is November 1st*; **calendar month** = month from the first day to the last; **calendar year** = twelve months from January 1st to December 31st

calf [kɑ:f] *noun* **(a)** young cow or bull; *the cow stood in a corner of the field with her two calves* **(b)** young (of elephant, seal, etc.); *the beach was covered with young seal calves* **(c)** fleshy back part of the leg between the ankle and the knee; *he's strained his calf muscle and won't be able to play on Saturday* (NOTE: plural is **calves** [kɑ:vz]; the meat from a calf is **veal**)

calibre *US* **caliber** ['kælɪbə] *noun* **(a)** interior diameter of a gun; *the two bullets come from same calibre guns* **(b)** intellectual or other ability; *it's work which he thinks is beneath a person of his calibre*

call [kɔ:l] **1** *noun* **(a)** telephone conversation; trying to get in touch with someone by telephone; *were there any calls for me while I was out?*; **local call** = call to a number in the same area; **long-distance call** = call to a number in a different area; **overseas call** *or* **international call** = call to another country; **to make a call** = to dial and speak to someone on the telephone; *she wants to make a (phone) call to Australia*; **to take a call** = to answer the telephone **(b)** telephone call or shout to wake someone; *he asked for an early morning call*; **I want a call at 7 o'clock** = I want someone to wake me at 7 o'clock **2** *verb* **(a)** to say something loudly to someone who is some distance away, to tell someone to come; *call the children when it's time for tea*; **call me at 7 o'clock** = wake me up at 7; **to call a taxi** = to shout to a taxi to come **(b)** to give someone or something a name; *they're going to call the baby Sam; his name is John but everyone calls him Jack; our cat's called Felix; what do you call this computer programme?* **(c)** to telephone; *if he comes back, tell him I'll call him when I'm in the office; Mr Smith is out - shall I ask him to call you back?; call the police - the shop has been burgled!; can you call me a cab, please?* **(d)** to visit; *the doctor called at the house, but* *there was no one there; the whole family called round to see if she was better*

callbox ['kɔːlbɒks] *noun* public telephone box; *I'm phoning from the callbox outside the post office* (NOTE: plural is **callboxes**)

caller ['kɔːlə] *noun* (a) person who comes to visit; *she can't see any callers today* (b) person who telephones; *I picked up the phone and the caller asked for my father*

call for ['kɔːl 'fɔː] *verb* **to call for someone** = to fetch someone before going somewhere; *he called for me to take me to the theatre*

call-girl ['kɔːlgɜːl] *noun* prostitute who can be called by telephone

calligraphy [kə'lɪgrəfi] *noun* the art of fine handwriting; *he practises calligraphy as part of his design course*

calling ['kɔːlɪŋ] *noun* vocation; job; *he followed his calling and became a missionary doctor*

call off ['kɔːl 'ɒf] *verb* to decide not to do something which had been planned; *he called off the visit to the museum; the picnic has been called off because it is raining; when the chairman heard about the deal he called it off*

call on ['kɔːl 'ɒn] *verb* (a) to visit someone; *she called on her mother to see how she was* (b) to ask someone to do something; *the police have called on everyone to watch out for the escaped prisoner*

call up ['kɔːl 'ʌp] *verb* to tell someone to join the army, navy or air force; *thousands of men were called up at the beginning of the war*

call-up ['kɔːlʌp] *noun* order to join the army; *my father remembers the day he got his call-up papers to join the navy*

calm [kɑːm] **1** *adjective* quiet, not rough or excited; *the sea was perfectly calm and no one was seasick; keep calm, everything will be all right* (NOTE: **calmer - calmest**) **2** *noun* period of quiet; *the calm of the Sunday afternoon was broken by the sound of jazz from the house next door* **3** *verb* **to calm (down)** = to make someone quieter; to become quieter and less annoyed; *she stroked his hand to try to calm him down; after shouting for some minutes he finally calmed down*

calmly ['kɑːmli] *adverb* quietly, in an unexcited way; *the doctor explained calmly what would happen during the operation*

calorie ['kæləri] *noun* (a) unit of measurement of energy in food; *she's counting calories to try to lose weight; there are 250 calories in a pint of beer* (b) unit of measurement of heat or energy (the heat needed to raise the temperature of 1g of water by 1°C) (NOTE: the **kilocalorie** (or 1000 calories) is now more usual for calculations on food packets)

COMMENT: one calorie is the amount of heat needed to raise the temperature of one gram of water by one degree Celsius. One kilocalorie is the amount of heat needed to raise the temperature of one kilogram of water by one degree Celsius. The calorie is also used as a measurement of the energy content of food and to show the amount of energy needed by an average person. The average adult in an office job requires about 3,000

calories per day, supplied by carbohydrates and fats to give energy and proteins to replace tissue. More strenuous physical work needs more calories. If a person eats more than the number of calories needed by his energy output or for his growth, the extra calories are stored in the body as fat

calorific value [kælə'rɪfɪk 'væljuː] *noun* heat value of a substance, the number of calories which a certain amount of the substance (such as a certain food) contains; *the tin of beans has a calorific value of 250 calories*

calyx ['kælɪks] *noun* outer green covering of a flower, shaped like a cup, the part which covers a flower bud; *turn the flower over to see the calyx underneath* (NOTE: plural is **calyces** *or* **calyxes**)

cam [kæm] *noun* rotating part on a camshaft, which makes the pistons move up and down; *a camshaft has several cams which move the pistons in turn*

COMMENT: cams are not round, but oval, with a rounded point at one side. This allows a rotating movement to be converted to the up-and-down movement of the pistons

camcorder ['kæmkɔːdə] *noun* small portable camera for taking video pictures with sound; *he took a film of the wedding on his camcorder*

came [keɪm] *see* COME

camel ['kæml] *noun* desert animal with long legs and one or two humps; *when we were on holiday in Kuwait we went to camel races in the desert*

COMMENT: there are two breeds of camel: the Bactrian camel has two humps and lives in Asia; the Arabian camel or dromedary has one hump, and is common in North Africa and the Arab countries

cameo ['kæmiəʊ] *noun* (a) small stone with a design of a head which stands out against a darker background; *for her birthday, she was given a pair of cameo earrings and a matching brooch* (b) small but memorable part in a play or film; *the film is worth seeing if only for the cameo role played by Gielgud*

camera ['kæmrə] *noun* (a) machine for taking photographs; *he took a picture of the garden with his new camera; they went on holiday and forgot to take their camera; did you remember to put a film in your camera?; see also* CINE-CAMERA (b) *(legal)* **in camera** = in private; *the court heard the evidence in camera*

cameraman ['kæmrəmən] *noun* main film camera technician who is in charge of the lighting and photography of a shot; *our cameraman is now in position, and we can go direct to the scene of the accident; a BBC cameraman was injured in the fighting* (NOTE: plural is **cameramen**)

camomile ['kæməmaɪl] *noun* fragrant plant, of which the white and yellow scented flowers are used for making hot drinks; *would you prefer a cup of camomile tea instead of coffee?*

camouflage ['kæməflɑːʒ] **1** *noun* hiding of an animal's shape by colours or patterns; *a leopard's spots are a form of camouflage which makes the animal less easy to see in long grass* **2** *verb* to hide the shape of something by using colours or patterns; *the soldiers camouflaged the gun position with branches of trees*

camp [kæmp] **1** *noun* place where people live in tents or cabins in the open air; *we set up camp half-way up the mountain*; **camp fire** = small bonfire at a camp; **holiday camp** = organized holiday cabins **2** *verb* to spend a holiday or a period of time in a tent; *we go camping in Sweden every summer*; *they had camped by the side of the lake*

campaign [kæm'peɪn] **1** *noun* **(a)** organized military attack; *Napoleon's Russian campaign of 1812* **(b)** organized attempt to achieve something; *a publicity campaign* or *an advertising campaign*; *he's organizing a campaign against the new motorway*; *the government's anti-smoking campaign* **2** *verb* **(a)** to take part in a war; *the ladies stayed at home while the knights were away campaigning against the French* **(b)** to work in an organized way to achieve something; *to campaign for a Scottish Parliament*; *to campaign against nuclear reactors*

campaigner ['kæmpeɪnə] *noun* person who campaigns; *the anti-road campaigners are protesting on the village green*; *she's a well-known campaigner for women's rights*

camp bed ['kæmp 'bed] *noun* light folding bed; *when we have visitors, the children have to sleep on camp beds* (NOTE: American English for this is **cot**)

camped ['kæmpt] *adjective* staying in the open air for a long period waiting for something to happen; *several people had spent the night camped outside the shop's entrance waiting for the start of the sales*; *the protesters were camped outside the gates to the research institute*

camper ['kæmpə] *noun* **(a)** person who goes camping; *dozens of campers had to leave their tents because of flooding* **(b)** **camper (van)** = motor caravan which contains bunks, kitchen equipment, tables, etc., and in which people can drive around and park to stay overnight; *rows of camper vans were parked in the National Park*

camping ['kæmpɪŋ] *noun* going on holiday with a tent or caravan; *camping in North Wales in November is not my idea of fun*; *we go on a camping holiday every Easter*; **camping van** = CAMPER VAN

camping site *or* **campsite** ['kæmpɪŋ saɪt *or* 'kæmpsaɪt] *noun* area specially arranged for camping and caravans, with marked places for tents, central washing and toilet facilities, etc.; *there are several well-equipped campsites near the lake*

campus ['kæmpəs] *noun* land on which a university is built; *the campus covers an area of about 25 square miles*; *the university campus is expanding all the time*; **to live on campus** = to live in a students' residence; *all students live on campus during their first year at university* (NOTE: plural is **campuses**)

camshaft ['kæmʃɑːft] *noun* metal rod with several cams on it, which lift pistons one by one; *a camshaft has several cams which move the pistons in turn*

can [kæn] **1** *noun* **(a)** round metal container for food or drink; *he opened a can of lemonade*; *empty beer cans were all over the pavement*; *can you open a can of beans?* (NOTE: British English also uses **tin** to mean a container of food, but not of drink) **(b)** *(informal)* **to carry the can for something** = to take responsibility or blame for something; *they all ran away and left me to carry the can* **(c)** **watering can** = container similar to a

bucket, with a long spout, used for giving water to plants **2** *verb used with other verbs* **(a)** *(to mean 'be able')* *he can swim well but he can't ride a bike*; *she can't run as fast as I can*; *can you remember what the doctor told us to do?*; *I can't bear to watch any longer* **(b)** *(to mean 'be allowed')* *children under 18 can't drive cars*; *he says we can go in*; *the policeman says we can't park here* **(c)** *(in asking politely)* *can we come in, please?*; *can you shut the door, please?* (NOTE: negative: **cannot**, usually **can't**; past: **could, could not,** usually **couldn't**; **can** and **could** are only used with other verbs, and are not followed by the word **to)** **3** *verb* to put food in cans; *the town has a factory where they can sardines* (NOTE: **canning - canned**)

Canada ['kænədə] *noun* very large country in North America, to the north of the United States; *they live in Canada, though his family comes from France* (NOTE: capital: **Ottawa**; people: **Canadians**; languages: **English, French**; currency: **the Canadian dollar**)

Canadian [kə'neɪdjən] **1** *adjective* referring to Canada; *his mother is Canadian and so is he*; *she kept her Canadian nationality* **2** *noun* person from Canada; *how many Canadians are there living in London?*

canal [kə'næl] *noun* artificial river; *you can take a boat trip round the canals of Amsterdam*

canary [kə'neəri] *noun* small yellow singing bird; *she keeps a canary in a cage*; **canary yellow** = light bright yellow colour; *I'm not sure that I really like his canary yellow waistcoat* (NOTE: plural is **canaries**)

cancel ['kænsl] *verb* **(a)** to stop something which has been planned; *the singer was ill, so the show had to be cancelled*; *there is no refund if you cancel less than three weeks before the date of departure*; *the trip was cancelled because the weather was too bad* **(b)** to mark a postage stamp with a rubber stamp to show that it has been used (NOTE: British English: **cancelling - cancelled** but American spelling is **canceling - canceled**)

cancellation [kænsə'leɪʃn] *noun* **(a)** act of cancelling; *cancellations will be accepted until a week before departure*; *a cancellation fee of £50 will be charged* **(b)** seat, ticket or appointment which is available again because the person who bought it cannot use it; *if we have a cancellation for next week I'll call and let you know*

cancer ['kænsə] *noun* disease in which cells grow abnormally; *she developed skin cancer*; *he died of lung cancer*

Cancer ['kænsə] one of the signs of the Zodiac, shaped like a crab; *my birthday's June 29th, so I'm a* **(a)** *Cancer*; **Tropic of Cancer** = parallel running round the earth at latitude 23°28N

cancerous ['kænsərəs] *adjective* referring to cancer; *the X-ray revealed a cancerous growth in the breast*

candid ['kændɪd] *adjective* frank or open; *I want to have a candid discussion with you*; **to be candid about something** = to be open about something; *he's quite candid about his ambition to be president*; **to be candid** = to speak openly; *to be candid, I don't like his novels at all*

candidacy ['kændɪdəsi] *noun* state of being a candidate; *the Senator has announced his candidacy for the Presidential election*

candidate ['kændɪdət] *noun* **(a)** person who applies for a job; *there are six candidates for the post of* *assistant manager*; *we have asked three candidates to come for an interview* **(b)** person who is standing for election; *she accompanied the candidate round the constituency* **(c)** person who has entered for an examination; *all candidates should answer three questions*; *candidates are given three hours to complete the exam*

candle ['kændl] *noun* stick of wax with a wick in the centre, which you light to make a flame; *he blew out all the candles on his birthday cake*; *we lit a candle in her memory*

candlelight ['kændllaɪt] *noun* light given by candles; *the shimmer of satin in the candlelight*

candlelit ['kændllɪt] *adjective* lit by candles; *he took her out to a candlelit supper*

candour *US* **candor** ['kændə] *noun* frankness, openness; *such candour is unusual in politicians*

candy ['kændi] *noun US* **(a)** sweet food, made with sugar; *eating candy is bad for your teeth* (NOTE: no plural in this meaning) **(b)** one piece of this food; *she bought a box of candies* (NOTE: plural in this meaning is **candies**; British English for this is **sweets**)

candyfloss ['kændiflɒs] *noun* thin threads of melted sugar which are spun in a drum and sold as a mass attached to a stick; *stalls at the fair are selling cold drinks and candyfloss* (NOTE: American English is **cotton candy**)

candy store ['kændi 'stɔː] *noun US* store selling candy (NOTE: the British equivalent is a **sweetshop**)

cane [keɪn] **1** *noun* **(a)** strong stem of a plant, especially of tall thin plants like bamboo; *a field of sugar cane* **(b)** walking stick cut from the stem of a plant; *she was leaning heavily on a cane as she walked up the path* **2** *verb* to beat someone with a stick as a punishment; *he was often caned when he was at school*

canister ['kænɪstə] *noun* round metal container for gas, etc.; *opinions are mixed about the use of spray canisters by the police*; *the cameraman left the film canisters in his hotel room*

cannabis ['kænəbɪs] *noun* **(a)** plant from whose leaves or flowers an addictive drug is produced; *someone told the police that he was growing cannabis plants on his balcony*; *see also* HEMP **(b)** marijuana, an addictive drug made from the dried leaves or flowers of this plant; *in some countries, the sale of cannabis has been legalized*

cannibal ['kænɪbl] *noun* person who eats people; *the survivors of the plane crash were forced to become cannibals in order to survive*

cannon ['kænən] **1** *noun* **(a)** large gun; *the sailors hauled a huge cannon across the ship's deck*; **cannon fodder** = soldiers, considered as objects to be hit during a battle; *thousands of troops were sent into battle - they were just cannon fodder*; (informal) **a loose cannon** = someone who is not easily controlled and may do or say things which are not officially approved; *he described the minister as a loose cannon in the government* **(b)** **water cannon** = machine for spraying water against demonstrators, etc.; *the police turned the water cannon on the group of protesters* **(c)** gun in an aircraft; *the old Spitfire had eight cannon in its wings* (NOTE: usually plural is **cannon**) **2** *verb* to **cannon into someone** *or* **something** = to bump into someone *or* something; *the little boy rushed out of the sweet shop and cannoned straight into a policeman*

cannonball ['kænənbɔːl] *noun* (old) large stone or metal ball fired by a cannon; *cannonballs crashed into the wooden sides of the ship*

cannot ['kænɒt] *see* CAN

canny ['kæni] *adjective* (mainly Scottish) wise or clever; *only a very canny financial adviser could have thought up that idea*; *she's a canny one, she always gets someone else to pay for her* (NOTE: **cannier - canniest**)

canoe [kə'nuː] **1** *noun* boat which is moved forward by one or more people using paddles; *she paddled her canoe across the lake* **2** *verb* to travel in a canoe; *they canoed down the river*; *we're going canoeing on Sunday*

canoeing [kə'nuːɪŋ] *noun* sport of going in a canoe; *canoeing isn't my favourite sport - I don't like falling into cold water*; *canoeing down the rapids sounds a bit too dangerous for me*

canoeist [kə'nuːɪst] *noun* person who paddles a canoe; *we could see the helmets of the two canoeists in the distance*

canon ['kænən] *noun* **(a)** religious rule or instructions; **canon law** = law applied by the church to priests; *is there anything in the canon law about the burial of non-practising Catholics?* **(b)** clergyman attached to a cathedral; *what are the special duties of a canon?*

canonization [kænənaɪ'zeɪʃn] *noun* act of officially declaring that someone is a saint; *the canonization of the Irish saints will take place next Easter*

canonize ['kænənaɪz] *verb* to declare officially that someone is a saint; *will Mother Theresa be canonized?*

can opener ['kæn 'əʊpnə] *noun US* tool for opening cans; *there's a can opener on the wall of the kitchen by the telephone* (NOTE: the British equivalent is **tin opener**)

canopy ['kænəpi] *noun* **(a)** small roof over a platform, balcony, etc.; *the porch is covered with a glass canopy*; *the Queen's bedroom is furnished with a 17th century canopy bed* **(b)** leaves of trees which act as an umbrella over the ground beneath; *the trees join to form a canopy over the terrace of the restaurant* (NOTE: plural is **canopies**)

can't [kɑːnt] *see* CAN

canteen [kæn'tiːn] *noun* **(a)** private self-service restaurant in an office block, factory, etc.; *the food in the office canteen is awful, I prefer to bring my own sandwiches* **(b)** box containing knives, forks and spoons; *as a wedding present they were given a canteen of silver* **(c)** portable bottle for water; *this is the canteen used by my grandfather during World War I*

canter ['kæntə] **1** *noun* gentle gallop; *the horses were going through the park at a canter*; (informal) **to win at a canter** = to win easily **2** *verb* to go at a canter; *my horse doesn't like cantering, it prefers to gallop*

cantilever ['kæntɪliːvə] *noun* support which projects from a building, holding up a balcony, a bridge, etc.; *he designed the cantilever bridge across the harbour*

canton ['kæntɒn] *noun* one of the administrative divisions of Switzerland; *our friends live in the Canton of Vaud, near Geneva*

COMMENT: the cantons are: Appenzell, Aargau, Basel, Berne, Fribourg, Geneva, Glaris, Grisons, Lucerne, Neuchâtel, Saint-Gall, Schaffhausen, Schwyz, Soleure, Tessin, Thurgau, Unterwald, Uri, Valais, Vaud, Zug, Zurich

canvas ['kænvəs] *noun* **(a)** thick cloth for making tents, sails, etc.; *he was wearing a pair of old canvas shoes*; **holiday under canvas** = camping holiday in a tent (NOTE: no plural in this meaning) **(b)** a painting; *three canvases by Picasso* (NOTE: plural is **canvases**; do not confuse with **canvass**)

canvass ['kænvəs] *verb* to visit people to ask them to buy goods or to vote or to say what they think; *party workers are out canvassing voters*; *we have canvassed the staff about raising the prices in the staff restaurant* (NOTE: do not confuse with **canvas**)

canyon ['kænjən] *noun* deep valley with steep sides (usually in North America); *if you go to the West of the USA, try to visit the Grand Canyon*

cap [kæp] **1** *noun* **(a)** flat hat with a flat hard piece in front; *the bus driver was wearing an old black cap*; *an officer's cap with a gold badge*; **England cap** = cap worn by a sportsman who has played for England in an international match **(b)** top which covers something; *screw the cap back on the medicine bottle*; *a red pen with a black cap* **(c)** upper limit for something, such as a maximum rate of interest; *the government has put a cap on local authority spending* **2** *verb* **(a)** to place an upper limit on something; *to cap a local authority's budget* **(b)** to name someone to play for his country in an international match; *he has been capped five times for Wales* (NOTE: **capping - capped**)

capability [keɪpə'bɪlɪti] *noun* being able to do something; *I'm afraid this job is way beyond my capabilities* (NOTE: plural is **capabilities**)

capable ['keɪpəbl] *adjective* competent, able to work well; *she's an extremely capable secretary*; **capable of** = able to do something; *the car is capable of very high speeds*; *she isn't capable of running the department on her own* (NOTE: you are capable **of** something or **of** doing something)

capacitance [kæ'pæsɪtəns] *noun* ability of a component to store an electrical charge

capacitor [kæ'pæsɪtə] *noun* electronic component which stores an electrical charge

capacity [kə'pæsɪti] *noun* **(a)** amount which something can hold; *this barrel has a larger capacity than that one*; *the cinema was filled to capacity*; **a capacity audience** = an audience which fills a cinema, theatre, etc.; **seating capacity** = number of seats in a bus, cinema, etc.; **to work at full capacity** = to do as much work as possible **(b)** **engine capacity** = output of an engine or electric motor **(c)** being able to do something easily; *he has a capacity for making friends with anyone he meets* **(d)** position; **acting in his capacity as manager** = acting as a manager; **speaking in an official capacity** = speaking officially (NOTE: no plural)

cape [keɪp] *noun* **(a)** long cloak; *she wrapped her cape more tightly around her* **(b)** piece of high land jutting into the sea; *we rounded the cape on June 21st at 8 a.m.*; **the Cape (of Good Hope)** = the point at the very south of the African continent; *they almost sank in a storm when they were rounding the Cape*

COMMENT: the cape at the southern tip of South America is Cape Horn, often called simply 'the Horn'

capillary [kə'pɪləri] *noun* **(a)** tiny blood vessel which carries blood and nutrients into the tissues; *blood capillaries have very thin walls* **(b)** any tiny tube carrying liquid, such as lymph, in the body; **capillary attraction** *or* **capillary action** = force by which water rises up a narrow tube (NOTE: plural is **capillaries**)

capital ['kæpɪtəl] **1** *noun* **(a)** main city of a country, usually where the government is based; *the capital is in the eastern part of the country*; *Madrid is the capital of Spain*; *tourists flocked to the Italian capital*; *the capital's traffic has ground to a halt* **(b)** money which is invested; *company with £10,000 capital or with a capital of £10,000*; **capital gains** = profit made when selling shares or other investments **(c)** carved top part of a column; *we visited the cloisters and looked at the carvings on the capitals* **(d)** **block capitals** = capital letters, letters written as A, B, C, D, etc., and not a, b, c, d; *write your name in block capitals at the top of the form* **2** *adjective* **(a)** **capital letters** = letters written as A, B, C, D, etc., and not a, b, c, d; *write your name in capital letters at the top of the form* **(b)** **capital punishment** = killing someone as a punishment for a crime; *capital punishment will never be restored in this country*

capitalism ['kæpɪtəlɪzm] *noun* economic system based on ownership of resources by individuals or companies and not by the state; *capitalism gives us all greater freedom*

capitalist ['kæpɪtəlɪst] **1** *noun* **(a)** person who supports the theory of capitalism; *capitalists are in favour of free enterprise* **(b)** businessman who invests money in a business; *he's a young capitalist who is only twenty-one, but on the way to becoming a millionaire* **2** *adjective* working according to the principles of capitalism; *a capitalist economy*; *the capitalist system*

capitalize on ['kæpɪtəlaɪz 'ɒn] *verb* to take advantage of something; *café owners capitalized on the good weather by putting tables and chairs out on the pavement*

Capitol ['kæpɪtəl] *noun* building in Washington where the US Senate and House of Representatives meet; **Capitol Hill** = hill on which the Capitol stands, used to mean the US Legislature (NOTE: do not confuse with **capital**)

capitulate [kə'pɪtjʊleɪt] *verb* to give in, to surrender; *the terrorists capitulated and accepted the offer made to them*

caplet ['kæplət] *noun* small capsule of a drug; *a packet of caplets of paracetamol*

cappucino [kæpu:'tʃi:nəʊ] *noun* Italian coffee, with hot whipped milk and chocolate on top; *two cappucinos, please!*

capricious [kə'prɪʃəs] *adjective* not stable, likely to change; *capricious April weather*; *she's very capricious - you never know what she's going to do next*

Capricorn ['kæprɪkɔːn] *noun* one of the signs of the Zodiac, shaped like a goat; *if you were born on Christmas Day you must be (a) Capricorn*; **Tropic of**

Capricorn = parallel running round the earth at latitude 23°28S

capsize [kæpˈsaɪz] *verb (of boats)* to turn over; *a big wave caught us sideways and we capsized*; *one of the canoes capsized half way through the race*

capsule [ˈkæpsjuːl] *noun* **(a)** small hollow digestible case, filled with a drug to be swallowed by the patient; *she swallowed three capsules of painkiller* **(b)** space capsule = compartment in a space rocket; *an American naval vessel is waiting to recover the space capsule which is expected to splash down in the sea at about midday*

Capt. [kæptən] *abbreviation for* CAPTAIN (NOTE: used with a surname: **Capt. Smith**)

captain [ˈkæptən] *noun* **(a)** person in charge of a team; *the England captain*; *the two captains shook hands at the beginning of the match* **(b)** person in charge of a ship or of an aircraft; *go and see the captain if you want to use the radio phone*; *Captain Smith is flying the plane* **(c)** rank in the army above a lieutenant and below a major; *a lieutenant has to report to his captain* (NOTE: used as a title with names, and often shortened to **Capt.**)

captaincy [ˈkæpənsi] *noun* **(a)** post of captain of a sports team; *because of the scandal, I don't think he will get the England captaincy* **(b)** rank of captain (in the army or navy); *although he had twenty years of service, he never got his captaincy*

caption [ˈkæpʃn] *noun* phrase printed beneath a picture; *the caption read 'England manager to resign'*

captivate [ˈkæptɪveɪt] *verb* to charm, to seduce; *she gave an excellent speech and captivated her audience*; *I'm reading a captivating book about 16th century France*

captive [ˈkæptɪv] **1** *noun* prisoner; *the two captives were kept in total darkness for hours* **2** *adjective* held captive = held as a prisoner; **to take someone captive** = to take someone prisoner; *they were held captive by the rebels for three months*

captivity [kæpˈtɪvɪti] *noun* imprisonment; *after months of captivity, the hostages will need help from our special medical team*; *is this the first panda to be born in captivity?* (NOTE: no plural)

captor [ˈkæptə] *noun* person who captures someone; *their captors kept a round-the-clock watch over them*

capture [ˈkæptʃə] **1** *noun* being captured; *we must do everything to avoid capture* **2** *verb* **(a)** to take someone or something as a prisoner; *they captured the enemy capital very quickly*; *four soldiers were captured in the attack* **(b)** to take a share of sales from another company; *they have captured 10% of the market*

car [kɑː] *noun* **(a)** small private motor vehicle for carrying people; *she's bought a new car*; *my car was stolen while I was shopping*; *he drove his car into the garage*; *he goes to his office every morning by car*; **company car** = car owned by a company and lent to a member of staff to use for business or other purposes; **car ferry** = boat which carries vehicles and passengers from one place to another (NOTE: American English is also **auto**) **(b)** *US* wagon on a railway; *is there a restaurant car on the train?*; **observation car** = special wagon with a glass roof, so that passengers can see more of the scenery

caramel [ˈkærəmel] *noun* **(a)** sweet made with sugar and butter; *I'm a dentist, and I don't like seeing*

children eating caramel **(b)** burnt sugar; *you can make caramel by heating sugar until it melts and burns*; **caramel custard** = egg custard topped with caramel

carat [ˈkærət] *noun* **(a)** measure of the quality of gold (pure gold being 24 carats); *a 22-carat gold ring* **(b)** measure of the weight of precious stones; *a 5-carat diamond* (NOTE: American spelling is also **karat**)

caravan [ˈkærəvæn] *noun* **(a)** van with beds, table, washing facilities, etc., which can be towed by a car; *we got stuck behind a caravan on a narrow mountain road*; *we rent a caravan in a caravan park* (NOTE: American English is **trailer** *or* **mobile home**) **(b)** group of animals or vehicles travelling together, one behind the other; *a caravan of camels crossing the desert*; *we joined a caravan of lorries going to Romania*

caravanning [kærəˈvænɪŋ] *noun* going on holiday in a caravan; *we had a caravanning holiday in the South of France*

carbohydrate [kɑːbəʊˈhaɪdreɪt] *noun* chemical substance containing carbon, hydrogen and oxygen; *she eats too many carbohydrates*

> COMMENT: carbohydrates are found in particular in sugar and starch; they provide the body with energy. Compare proteins

carbon [ˈkɑːbən] *noun* **(a)** substance found in charcoal, soot or diamonds; *carbon is an essential component of living matter* (NOTE: Chemical element: chemical symbol: **C**; atomic number: **6**) **(b)** **carbon (paper)** = paper with a black coating on one side, used for making copies; *you forgot to put a carbon in the typewriter* **(c)** carbon copy; *make a top copy and two carbons*

carbon copy [ˈkɑːbən ˈkɒpi] *noun* copy made with carbon paper; *give me the original, and file the carbon copy*

carbon dioxide (CO₂) [ˈkɑːbən daɪˈɒksaɪd] *noun* colourless gas produced by an animal's body as the tissues burn carbon, and breathed out by the lungs as waste; *the greenhouse effect is partly caused by carbon dioxide in the upper atmosphere*

carbon monoxide (CO) [ˈkɑːbən mɒˈnɒksaɪd] *noun* poisonous gas produced by car engines; *levels of carbon monoxide were very high in the city yesterday*

carbon paper [ˈkɑːbən ˈpeɪpə] *noun* paper with a black coating on one side, used for making copies; *you forgot to put any carbon paper in the typewriter*; *he put the carbon paper in the typewriter the wrong way round*

car boot sale [ˈkɑː ˈbuːt ˈseɪl] *noun* type of jumble sale, organized in a large car park or sports field, where people sell unwanted items which they bring to the sale in their cars; *there's a car boot sale at the school this Sunday*

carburettor *US* **carburetor** [kɑːbəˈretə] *noun* device in a car which mixes fuel with air before it is injected into the engine; *I think the carburettor has been clogged by dirt in the petrol*

carcass [ˈkɑːkəs] *noun* **(a)** body of a dead animal, especially one ready for the butcher; *rows of sheep carcasses were hanging in the cold store*; *after the flood, we found carcasses of horses in the field* **(b)** bones left after you have eaten a cooked bird; *put the chicken carcass in boiling water with some onions to make chicken soup* **(c)** *(humorous)* body of a living person; *kindly remove your carcass from my chair!* (d) old rotting boat, car, etc.; *carcasses of old fishing boats lay rusting on the beach* (NOTE: plural is **carcasses**)

carcinogen [kɑːˈsɪnʃdʒən] *noun* substance which produces cancer; *some substances which used to be commonly used in cooking are now known to be carcinogens*

carcinogenic [kɑːsɪnəˈdʒenɪk] *adjective* which produces cancer; *tobacco is recognized as carcinogenic*

card [kɑːd] *noun* (a) postcard, a piece of stiff paper with a picture on it which you can send with a message; *they sent us a card from Italy*; *how much does it cost to send a card to Australia?*; *see also* POSTCARD (b) piece of stiff paper, folded so that a message can be written inside; **birthday card** = card which you send someone to wish them a happy birthday; **Christmas card** = card which you send someone at Christmas (c) piece of stiff paper with a picture or pattern on it, used to play games; *a pack of cards*; *they were playing cards in the bar*; *would you like a game of cards?* (d) piece of stiff paper with your name and address printed on it; *he gave me his business card* (e) piece of stiff plastic used for payment; *do you want to pay cash or with a card?*; **cash card** = plastic card used to obtain money from a cash dispenser; **charge card** = plastic card for which you pay a fee, but which does not allow the user to take out a loan (he has to pay off the total sum charged at the end of each month); **cheque (guarantee) card** = plastic card from a bank which guarantees payment of a cheque up to a certain amount, even if the user has no money in his account; **credit card** = plastic card which allows you to buy goods without paying for them immediately; *he paid for the hotel with his credit card*; **smart card** = credit card with a microchip, used for withdrawing money from cash dispensers or for buying at automatic terminals; **store card** = credit card issued by a department store which can only be used for purchases within that store; *see also* PHONECARD (f) **filing card** = card with information written on it, used to classify information in correct order; **index card** = card used to make a card index; *she tipped all the index cards out onto the table*

cardboard [ˈkɑːdbɔːd] *noun* thick card; *have you got a small piece of cardboard which I can use to make this model?*; *we put the glasses into cardboard boxes* (*informal*) **cardboard city** = place where homeless people build themselves shelters out of pieces of cardboard (NOTE: no plural: **some cardboard**; **a piece of cardboard**)

cardiac [ˈkɑːdɪæk] *adjective* referring to the heart; *he was rushed to the cardiac ward of the local hospital*; **cardiac arrest** = stopping of the heart, a condition where the heart muscle stops beating; *the paramedics gave the accident victim heart massage when he suffered a cardiac arrest*

cardigan [ˈkɑːdɪgən] *noun* woollen jacket which buttons at the front; *take a cardigan with you in case it gets cold*; *his mother gave him a hand-knitted cardigan for Christmas*

cardinal [ˈkɑːdɪnl] **1** *adjective* (a) very important (rule, etc.); *her attendance at the meeting is of cardinal importance* (b) **cardinal numbers** = ordinary numbers, one, two, three, etc. (NOTE: numbers which show the position in a series, such as first, second, third, etc., are called **ordinal numbers**) **2** *noun* (a) one of the highest priests in the Catholic church, after the Pope;

the cardinals meet in Rome to elect the Pope; *Cardinal Lamont has written an article in today's paper* (NOTE: used as a title before someone's surname: **Cardinal Wolsey**) (b) bright red bird, native of the southern USA

card index [ˈkɑːd ˈɪndeks] **1** *noun* series of cards with information written on them, kept in a special order so that the information can be found easily; **card-index file** = information kept on filing cards **2** *verb* to put information onto a card index

card-indexing [ˈkɑːd ˈɪndeksɪŋ] *noun* putting information onto a card index; *no one can understand her card-indexing system*

cardiovascular [kɑːdɪəʊˈvæskjʊlə] *adjective* referring to the heart and the blood circulation system; **the cardiovascular system** = the blood circulation system; **cardiovascular disease** = disease which affects the blood circulation; *a cardiovascular disease such as hypertension*

card table [ˈkɑːd ˈteɪbl] *noun* usually square, folding table used to play cards; *she got out the card table and four chairs and they started a game of bridge*

care [keə] **1** *noun* (a) serious attention; *he handled the glass with great care*; **to take care** = to be very careful; *take care when you cross the road*; *he took great care with the box of glasses*; *take care not to be late* (b) (*on a letter*) **care of** = words to show that the person is living at the address, but only as a visitor; **Mr Brown, care of Mrs Green** = to Mr Brown at the address of Mrs Green (NOTE: usually written **c/o** on the envelope) (c) looking after someone; *the care of the elderly*; **child care** = looking after children; **to take care of someone** = to look after someone; *will you take care of mother while I'm away?* **2** *verb* to be worried; *I don't care if my car is dirty*; *she cares a lot about the environment*; **he couldn't care less** = he doesn't worry at all about it

career [kəˈrɪə] **1** *noun* life of professional work; *she is starting her career as a librarian*; *he gave up his career as a civil servant and bought a farm*; *go and see the school careers adviser - she will give you advice on how to become an archaeologist*; **career woman** or **girl** = woman who is working and does not plan to stop working to look after the house or children **2** *verb* to rush forward out of control; *the car careered off the road into a ditch*

care for [ˈkeə ˈfɔː] *verb* (a) to like; *would you care for another cup of coffee?*; *I don't care for this music very much* (b) to look after; *nurses cared for the injured people after the accident*; *people who have to care for their elderly relatives should get a grant from the state*

carefree [ˈkeəfriː] *adjective* without any worries; *not so long ago, I was single and carefree - I'm now married and a father of two*

careful [ˈkeəful] *adjective* taking care; *be careful not to make any noise, the baby is asleep*; *be careful when you're packing those glasses, they're very valuable!*; *she is very careful about what she eats*; *the project needs very careful planning*

carefully [ˈkeəfəli] *adverb* with great care; *carry the box of eggs carefully!*; *drive more carefully in future!*; *it poured with rain and spoilt her carefully arranged hair*

careless [ˈkeələs] *adjective* without taking care; *he is careless about his work*; *he made several careless mistakes when he took his driving test*

carer ['keərə] *noun* someone who looks after an old or sick person or children; *a carer comes to look after my old mother when I'm at work*

caress [kə'res] **1** *noun* gentle touch; *the child touched my cheek in a gentle caress* (NOTE: plural is **caresses**) **2** *verb* to stroke gently; *she gently caressed the baby's head*

caretaker ['keəteɪkə] *noun* person who looks after a building; *go and ask the caretaker to replace the light bulb in the stairway* (NOTE: American English is **janitor**)

cargo ['ka:gəu] *noun* goods carried (especially on a ship); *the ship was taking on cargo*; **cargo boat** *or* **cargo ship** *or* **cargo plane** = ship *or* plane which carries only cargo and not passengers (NOTE: plural is **cargoes**)

Caribbean [kærɪ'bi:ən] **1** *noun* sea to the south of the United States and east of Mexico; *we went on a cruise round the Caribbean*; *holidays in the Caribbean are very popular* **2** *adjective* referring to the area and countries near the Caribbean; *Caribbean holidays are very popular*; *goat is important in Caribbean food*

caribou ['kærɪbu:] *noun* reindeer of North America; *herds of caribou trek south at the beginning of winter* (NOTE: plural is **caribou**)

caricature ['kærɪkətjuə] **1** *noun* funny drawing or description which exaggerates a person's appearance; *he drew a caricature of the Prime Minister*; *her description of the office is nothing less than a caricature of the system*; *with his bowler hat and umbrella he looked the caricature of an Englishman* **2** *verb* to draw a caricature of someone; *the Prime Minister is easy to caricature*

caries ['keəri:z] *noun* decayed place in a tooth or other bone; *this toothpaste is supposed to help prevent caries* (NOTE: plural is **caries**)

caring ['keərɪŋ] *adjective* loving and helping; *she's a very caring person*; *his caring attitude towards his students*

carnage ['ka:nɪdʒ] *noun* bloodshed, massacre, killing; *it is thought that more than 200 people died in the carnage* (NOTE: no plural)

carnation [ka:'neɪʃn] *noun* red, pink or white flower with a strong scent; *he offered me a bouquet of red carnations*

carnival ['ka:nɪvl] *noun* festival, often with music, dancing and eating in the open air; *the carnival procession arrived in the main square*

carol ['kærəl] **1** *noun* **Christmas carol** = special song sung at Christmas; *the children are practising their carols*; *we went to a carol service at our local church* **2** *verb* to sing Christmas carols; *in the week before Christmas we go carolling round the villages* (NOTE: **carolling - carolled** but American spelling is **caroling - caroled**)

carousel [kæru:'sel] *noun* **(a)** circular conveyor belt which distributes luggage; *baggage from flight AC1 is on carousel number three* **(b)** *US* roundabout with wooden horses, etc., in a funfair (NOTE: British English is **merry-go-round**)

carp [ka:p] **1** *noun* type of edible fish; *you can catch carp in this lake* (NOTE: plural is **carp**) **2** *verb* to keep on finding fault with things; *my brother's always carping about the office*; *stop carping and get on with your work!*

carpal bones ['ka:pəl 'bəunz] *noun* the eight little bones which make up the wrist

car park ['ka: 'pa:k] *noun* special public place where you can leave a car when you are not using it; *there's a multi-storey car park next to our office*; *if you're going shopping, you can park your car in one of the car parks in the centre of town* (NOTE: in American English, this is a **parking lot**)

carpenter ['ka:pəntə] *noun* person who works with wood, especially in building; *the carpenter has arrived to fit shelves in the children's bedroom* (NOTE: informally, a carpenter is called a **chippy**)

carpentry ['ka:pəntri] *noun* art of working with wood; *he's studying carpentry and building at college* (NOTE: no plural)

carpet ['ka:pɪt] *noun* thick material for covering the floor, stairs, etc.; *he spilt his coffee on our new white dining-room carpet*

carpeting ['ka:pətɪŋ] *noun* **(a)** covering with a carpet; *we have been quoted £2000 for the carpeting of the office* **(b)** wide piece of carpet; *we bought a length of carpeting to cover the bedroom floor*

carport ['ka:pɔ:t] *noun* shelter for a car, built next to a house; *the car is in the carport, so we won't need to scrape the snow off it in the morning*

carriage ['kærɪdʒ] *noun* **(a)** cost of carrying goods; action of carrying goods; *carriage is 15% of the total cost*; *how much do they charge for carriage?*; **carriage free** = deal where the customer does not pay for the transport of goods; **carriage paid** = deal where the price paid includes transport **(b)** **horse-drawn carriage** = open vehicle pulled by a horse; *the queen rode in an open carriage* **(c)** **railway carriage** = railway wagon for passengers; *he was sitting in a first-class carriage although he only had a second-class ticket*

carriageway ['kærɪdʒweɪ] *noun* surface of the road on which traffic moves; **dual carriageway** = road with two lanes in each direction, with a barrier between the pairs of lanes; *there's a dual carriageway ahead so we'll soon be able to overtake that lorry* (NOTE: the American English for this is **two-lane highway**)

carried, carries ['kærɪd or 'kærɪz] *see* CARRY

carrier ['kærɪə] *noun* **(a)** thing or person that carries; *a procession of water carriers with jars on their heads*; **luggage carrier** = grid on the back of a bicycle on which you can carry a bag or box; **carrier bag** = large paper or plastic bag with handles, for carrying shopping, often given by a shop, with the shop's name on it; *her carrier bag split and all her shopping fell onto the pavement* **(b)** person who carries the germ of a disease without showing any signs of it, and who can infect others with it; *a hepatitis carrier*; *hepatitis A is transmitted by a carrier through food or drink* **(c)** **aircraft carrier** = warship which carries aircraft; *sent an aircraft carrier to the Mediterranean*

carrion ['kærɪən] *noun* rotting meat; *vultures feed on carrion* (NOTE: no plural)

carrion crow ['kærɪən 'krəu] *noun* type of large black crow

carrot ['kærət] *noun* vegetable with a long orange root which can be eaten; *boiled carrots*; *carrot soup*

carry ['kæri] *verb* **(a)** to take something and move it to another place; *they had to carry the chest of drawers up the stairs*; *the plane was carrying 120 passengers*; *that suitcase is too heavy for me to carry* **(b)** to vote to approve; **the motion was carried** = the motion was accepted after a vote; *her proposal was not carried* **(c)** to keep in stock; *a supermarket will carry about 5,000 different lines of goods*

carrycot ['kærikɒt] *noun* open rectangular box with handles for carrying a baby in; *the baby was asleep in his carrycot*

carry on ['kæri 'ɒn] *verb* to go on doing something; *when the policeman came into the restaurant, they all carried on talking as if nothing had happened; they carried on with their work even though the office was on fire*

carry out [kæri 'aut] *verb* to do something which has been planned; *doctors carried out tests on the patients; the police carried out a search for the missing walkers*

carsick ['kɑːsɪk] *adjective* feeling sick because of the movement of a motor vehicle; *she gets carsick if she has to travel long distances*

carsickness ['kɑːsɪknəs] *noun* sickness caused by the movement of a motor vehicle; *all our children suffer from carsickness, which makes long journeys impossible*

cart [kɑːt] **1** *noun* **(a)** vehicle pulled by a horse; *a horse-drawn cart piled high with furniture*; **to put the cart before the horse** = to deal with things the wrong way round **(b)** *US* **baggage cart** = metal holder on wheels, on which baggage can be placed to be moved easily in an airport, train station, etc.; **shopping cart** = metal basket on wheels, used by shoppers to put their purchases in as they go round a supermarket (NOTE: British English for these is **luggage trolley** and **shopping trolley** *or* **supermarket trolley**) **2** *verb* to carry a bulky or heavy thing; *why do we have to cart this folding bed around with us?; they carted all their equipment up three flights of stairs; the police came and carted him off to jail*

carte blanche [kɑːt 'blɒnʃ] *French phrase meaning 'white card'* permission given to someone to do whatever he wants; *we gave the architect carte blanche to design the bridge; he has carte blanche to act on behalf of the government*

cartel [kɑː'tel] *noun* group of companies which try to fix the price of something; *several companies have grouped together to form a cartel; the Colombian drugs cartel*

cartilage ['kɑːtɪlɪdʒ] *noun* gristle, thick connective tissue which lines the joints and acts as a cushion or which forms part of the structure of an organ; *there is a layer of cartilage where a bone forms a joint with another bone; he suffered a torn cartilage during the rugby game*

cartographer [kɑː'tɒɡrəfə] *noun* person who draws maps

cartographic [kɑːtə'ɡræfɪk] *adjective* referring to maps; **cartographic pen** = pen that draws very fine lines which do not vary in thickness; *he used a cartographic pen to draw the contours*

cartography [kɑː'tɒɡrəfi] *noun* art of drawing maps; *he studied cartography and now works on computerized maps*

carton ['kɑːtən] *noun* container made of cardboard; *a carton of yoghurt; a milk carton*

cartoon [kɑː'tuːn] *noun* **(a)** funny, often political, drawing in a newspaper; *he draws a cartoon for the*

'Evening Standard' **(b)** film made of moving drawings; *I like watching Tom and Jerry cartoons*

cartoonist [kɑː'tuːnɪst] *noun* person who draws cartoons; *some cartoonists' early work can fetch very high prices*

cartridge ['kɑːtrɪdʒ] *noun* **(a)** tube packed with gunpowder and a bullet for firing from a gun; *the ground was littered with empty cartridges* **(b)** removable device made of a closed box containing a disk or tape; *the handheld computer has no disk drive but instead uses a ROM cartridge* **(c)** part of a record player which holds the stylus; *a new cartridge for this record player will be quite expensive* **(d) toner cartridge** = box containing toner ink which is attached to a printer to fill it with toner; *look in the manual to see if it tells you how to change the toner cartridge* **(e) cartridge paper** = good quality paper for drawing or printing **(f)** tube of ink which fits into a pen; *most pens are now made to use ink cartridges*

cart-track ['kɑːt 'træk] *noun* track which is not suitable for cars; *a muddy cart-track leads to their cottage*

carve [kɑːv] *verb* **(a)** to cut a joint of meat up at table; *who's going to carve?; Father sat at the end of the table, carving a chicken* **(b)** to cut stone or wood to make a shape; *he carved a bird out of wood; chips of stone flew all over the studio as he was carving the statue*

carver ['kɑːvə] *noun* **(a)** person who carves meat; *with 15 guests sitting round the table, the poor carver only just started to eat when everyone else was ready for a second helping* **(b)** artist who carves stone, wood, etc.; *do we know the names of the stone carvers of these magnificent statues?* **(c)** carving knife; *he used a silver carver to carve the turkey* **(d)** chair with arms, placed at the head of a dinner table; *a set of 6 dining chairs plus a carver*

carving ['kɑːvɪŋ] *noun* **(a)** cutting up cooked meat; **carving knife** = large sharp knife, used for carving; *carving would be much easier with a proper carving knife* **(b)** art of cutting stone or wood into shapes; *stone carving is an option at art school* **(c)** an object which has been made by carving; *he gave me a wood carving for my birthday; the stone carvings in the old church date from the 15th century*

car wash ['kɑː 'wɒʃ] *noun* place where cars are washed automatically; *don't forget to close the windows when you go into the car wash*

cascade [kæs'keɪd] **1** *noun* (artificial) waterfall; *there are plants and trees and even a cascade in the atrium of the hotel* **2** *verb* to fall in large quantities; *pale pink roses cascading down the brick wall*

case [keɪs] *noun* **(a)** suitcase, a box with a handle, for carrying your clothes, etc., in when travelling; *she was still packing her case when the taxi came; my plane went to Chicago, but my case went to New York by mistake; the customs made him open his case* **(b)** special box for something; *put the gun back in its case; I've lost my red spectacle case* **(c)** large wooden box for goods; *he bought a case of wine*; **a packing case =** large wooden box for carrying items which can be easily broken; *the removal men are bringing their packing cases tomorrow* **(d)** situation, occurrence, way in which something happens; *your case is very similar to mine; it was a case of first come, first served* **(e) court case** = legal action or trial; **the case is being**

heard next week = the case is coming to court next week

◊ **in any case** [ɪn 'eni 'keɪs] anyway, whatever may happen; *she missed the bus but in any case it didn't matter because the film started late; they scored a late penalty, but it didn't matter, we were losing 3 - 0 in any case*

◊ **in case** [ɪn 'keɪs] because something might happen; *take your gloves in case it's cold on the mountain; I always carry an umbrella in case it rains;* **in case of fire, break the glass** = if there is a fire, break the glass; **just in case** = because something might happen; *it's still sunny, but I'll take my umbrella just in case*

◊ **in that case** [ɪn 'ðæt 'keɪs] if that happens or if that is the situation; *there is a strike on the underground - in that case, you'll have to take a bus*

case study ['keɪs 'stʌdi] *noun* study of a certain group or institution or person over a long period of time; *a case study reveals that housing estates in large cities produce more cases of juvenile crime*

cash [kæʃ] **1** *noun* money in coins and notes, not in cheques; *we don't keep much cash in the house; I'd prefer to use up my spare cash, rather than pay with a credit card;* **cash box** = metal box for keeping cash; **cash dispenser** *or* **cash machine** = machine which gives out money when a special card is inserted and instructions given; **cash on delivery (COD)** = payment in cash when goods are delivered; **cash register** = machine where you pay, with a drawer for cash; **petty cash** = small amounts of money (NOTE: no plural) **2** *verb* **to cash a cheque** = to change a cheque into cash; *he tried to cash a cheque for seven hundred pounds*

cash and carry ['kæʃə nd 'kæri] *noun* discount warehouse, selling items to the general public; *we went to stock up at the cash and carry*

cash desk ['kæʃ 'desk] *noun* place in a store where you pay for the goods you are buying; *take your purchases to the nearest cash desk*

cashew nut [kə'ʃuː 'nʌt] *noun* small sweetish nut, often eaten salted; *bowls of cashew nuts and olives had been put out for the guests*

cash flow ['kæʃ 'fləʊ] *noun* rate at which money comes into and is paid out of a business; **the company is suffering from cash flow problems** = cash income is not coming in fast enough to pay the cash expenditure going out

cashier [kə'ʃiːə] *noun* person who deals with money (in a bank, supermarket, etc.); *ask the cashier if she can give you change; please pay the cashier*

cash in on [kæʃ 'ɪn 'ɒn] *verb* to profit from; *the company cashed in on the interest in computer games; ice cream sellers are cashing in on the fine weather*

cashmere ['kæʃmɪə] **1** *noun* fine soft goat's wool; *cashmere is soft, light and very warm* **2** *adjective* made of fine soft goat's wool; *the price of cashmere jumpers has soared*

cashpoint *US* **cash station** ['kæʃpɒɪnt *or* 'kæʃ 'steɪʃn] *noun* place where there are cash dispensers where a card holder can get cash by using his cash card; *is there a cashpoint in the High Street?* (NOTE: American English is also **automated teller machine** *or* **ATM**)

casino [kə'siːnəʊ] *noun* building where you can gamble; *she spent every evening playing roulette in the casino* (NOTE: plural is **casinos**)

cask [kɑːsk] *noun* large barrel; *we bought a cask of wine*

casket ['kɑːskɪt] *noun* **(a)** ornamental box for jewels; *the thief stole a casket from beside her bed* **(b)** *mainly US* long wooden box in which a dead person is buried or cremated; *they watched in silence as the casket was lowered into the ground* (NOTE: British English prefers **coffin**)

cassette [kə'set] *noun* **(a)** magnetic tape in a plastic case which can fit directly into a playing or recording machine; *do you want it on cassette or CD?; he bought a cassette of folk songs;* **cassette player** = machine which plays cassettes; **cassette recorder** = machine which records and plays back cassettes **(b)** film in a plastic case which fits directly into a camera; *she quickly put a new cassette into her camera; see also* VIDEOCASSETTE

cast [kɑːst] **1** *noun* all the actors in a play or film; *after the first night the cast went to celebrate in a restaurant* **2** *verb* **(a)** to make a metal or plaster object from a mould; *he cast the statue in bronze* **(b)** to choose actors for a play *or* film; *he was cast as a soldier in 'Henry V'* **(c)** **to cast a vote** = to vote; *the process of counting all the votes cast in the election has just begun* **(d)** *(formal)* to throw; *he has cast aside all his old acquaintances;* **to cast doubts on** = to be unsure about; *he cast doubts on the whole proposal;* **to cast light on something** = to make something easier to understand; *the papers cast some light on how the minister reached his decision* (NOTE: **casting - cast**)

caste [kɑːst] *noun (in Indian society)* hereditary class; *they belong to the lowest caste in society*

caster sugar ['kɑːstə 'ʃʊgə] *noun* very fine white sugar, which is sprinkled on pies, cakes, etc.; *cover the cake with caster sugar*

castigate ['kæstɪgeɪt] *verb (formal)* to punish, to criticize someone sharply; *there is no reason to castigate the checkout staff*

casting ['kɑːstɪŋ] **1** *noun* **(a)** moulding of a shape; *the dentist took a casting of her jaw* **(b)** choosing of actors for a film or play; *they are having problems with the casting of the film* **2** *adjective* **casting vote** = vote used by the chairman in a case where the votes for and against a proposal are equal; *he used his casting vote to block the motion*

cast iron ['kɑːst 'aɪən] *noun* **(a)** iron which is moulded, not bent, and so is quite brittle; *the pipes are made from cast iron, and are very solid; don't let the cast-iron pan soak in water as it will rust; compare* WROUGHT IRON **(b)** **cast-iron alibi** = very solid alibi, that cannot be disproved; **cast-iron excuse** = very good excuse, one that cannot be turned down; *he has a cast-iron excuse and won't get into trouble with the authorities*

castle ['kɑːsl] *noun* **(a)** large building with strong walls; *the Queen is spending the week at Windsor Castle; the soldiers shut the castle gate; see also* SAND CASTLE **(b)** one of two pieces used in chess, shaped like a little castle tower; *she took my last castle* (NOTE: also called a **rook**)

cast off ['kɑːst 'ɒf] *verb* **(a)** to untie the ropes holding a boat; *the boat is ready to cast off* **(b)** *(in knitting)* to remove the stitches from the needles so that your work is finished; *the scarf is long enough, all you have to do is to cast off*

cast-off clothing *or* **cast-offs** ['kɑːstɒf 'kəʊðiŋ or 'kɑːstɒfs] *noun* clothes which are not longer wanted; *being the third daughter in the family, she was always wearing her sisters' cast-offs*; *she buys cast-off clothing from charity shops*

castrate [kæ'streit] *verb* to remove the testicles from a male animal; *a young castrated bull is called a steer*

castration [kæ'streiʃn] *noun* act of castrating

casual ['kæʒjuəl] *adjective* not formal; *he just walked in without knocking in a very casual way; she tried to appear casual at the interview, even though she was very nervous;* **casual labour** = temporary workers; **casual shoes** = light shoes, which are not office shoes; **casual work** = work where workers are hired for a short period

casualty ['kæʒjuəlti] *noun* **(a)** person injured or killed in a battle or in an accident; *casualties were taken to hospital by ambulance and helicopter; the radio reported that there had been heavy casualties;* **casualty department** = department in a hospital for accident victims (NOTE: plural is **casualties**) **(b)** *(informal)* casualty department; *the accident victim was rushed into casualty*

cat [kæt] *noun* animal with soft fur and a long tail, kept as a pet; *she asked her neighbours to feed her cat when she went on holiday; don't forget to get some tins of cat food* (NOTE: cats are often called **Puss** *or* **Pussy**; a baby cat is a **kitten**)

cataclysm ['kætəklizm] *noun (formal)* great disaster

cataclysmic [kætə'klizmik] *adjective* disastrous; *they had a cataclysmic drop in sales*

catalogue *US* **catalog** ['kætəlɒg] **1** *noun* list of things for sale or in a library or museum; *look up the title in the library catalogue; an office equipment catalogue; we got the latest catalogue of home furnishings* **2** *verb* to make a list of things that exist somewhere; *she spent months cataloguing the novelist's correspondence*

catalysis [kə'tæləsis] *noun* activating a chemical process by means of a catalyst

catalyst ['kætəlist] *noun* **(a)** substance which produces or helps a chemical process without itself changing; *an enzyme that acts as a catalyst in the digestive process* **(b)** anything which helps something to take place; *she wasn't responsible for the decision herself, but she reckons she acted as a catalyst*

catalytic [kætə'litik] *adjective* referring to catalysis; *the enzyme produces a catalytic reaction;* **catalytic converter** = device put on the exhaust pipe of a motor vehicle to reduce the emission of carbon monoxide; *all new cars must be fitted with catalytic converters; catalytic converters are far from being 100% efficient in removing pollutants*

catapult ['kætəpʌlt] **1** *noun* strong elastic band on a forked stick, used for throwing stones; *he tried to kill birds with his catapult;* **catapult launching gear** = device which launches an aircraft from the deck of an aircraft carrier **2** *verb* **(a)** to send someone, an aircraft, etc., into the air; *the cyclist was hit by a bus and catapulted to the other side of the road* **(b)** to put someone into a new position quickly; *their team was catapulted to the top of the tennis league*

cataract ['kætərækt] *noun* **(a)** waterfall on a river; *the cataracts on the Nile* **(b)** condition where the lens of the eye gradually becomes hard and opaque; *he has developed a cataract in his right eye; the operation to remove the cataract went smoothly*

catarrh [kə'tɑː] *noun* inflammation of the membranes inside the nose and throat, producing a thick substance; *is there anything I can take to relieve my catarrh?; he always has catarrh in the winter*

catastrophe [kə'tæstrəfi] *noun* disaster, very bad accident; *it's a natural catastrophe to match the scale of the earthquake last year; this is the latest catastrophe to hit the family*

catastrophic [kætə'strɒfik] *adjective* disastrous; *the ice storm caused catastrophic damage to electricity pylons; allowing emissions of greenhouse gases to increase could have catastrophic consequences*

catch [kætʃ] **1** *noun* **(a)** thing which has been grabbed or taken; *the boat brought back a huge catch of fish* **(b)** action of grabbing a ball in the air; *he made a marvellous catch; the wicket-keeper dropped an easy catch* **(c)** hidden disadvantage; *it seems such a good deal, there must be a catch in it somewhere* **(d)** little hook which holds the latch on a door (NOTE: plural is **catches**) **2** *verb* **(a)** to grab hold of something moving in the air; *can you catch a ball with your left hand?; when he knocked a glass off the table he managed to catch it before it hit the floor* **(b)** to grab hold of something; *she caught him by the sleeve as he turned away; as he slipped, he caught the handrail to stop himself falling;* **to catch someone's eye** = to look at someone who is looking at you; *she caught his eye and nodded towards the door* **(c)** to get hold of an animal, especially to kill it; *he sat by the river all day but didn't catch anything; our cat is no good at catching mice; she's too lazy* **(d)** to get on a bus, plane, train, etc., before it leaves; *you will have to run if you want to catch the last bus; he caught the 10 o'clock train to Paris* **(e)** to get an illness; *he caught a cold from standing watching the rugby match; the baby has caught measles* **(f)** to find someone doing something wrong; *she caught the boys stealing in her shop; the police caught the burglar as he was climbing out of the window* **(g)** to arrest someone; *after months of searching, the police finally caught the gang; see also* RED-HANDED **(h)** to hear; *I didn't quite catch what she said* (NOTE: **catching - caught** [kɔːt] **- has caught**)

catcher ['kætʃə] *noun* **(a)** person who catches something; *we are paying a pigeon catcher to get rid of the town's pigeon population* **(b)** *(in sport)* person who catches something, especially the fielder who stands behind the batter in baseball; *the catcher missed the ball and they lost the game*

catch fire ['kætʃ 'faiə] *phrase* to start to burn because of something else which is burning; *the office block caught fire; take those papers away - they might catch fire*

catching ['kætʃiŋ] *adjective* (disease) which can be caught, which is infectious; *don't come near me - your illness may be catching*

catch up [kætʃ 'ʌp] *verb* to move to the same level as someone who is in front of you; *she walked so slowly that he soon caught up with her or caught her up; because she had missed so many weeks of school she found it hard to catch up*

catchy ['kætʃi] *adjective* **catchy tune** = tune which is easy to remember; *the ad has a catchy tune that everyone is humming* (NOTE: **catchier - catchiest**)

categoric(al) [kætɪ'gɒrɪk)] *adjective* straightforward or definite; *his categorical refusal surprised everyone*; *she's quite categorical on this point*; *she gave a categorical 'no' as an answer*

categorically [kætɪ'gɒrɪkli] *adverb* definitely; *he categorically refused to help us*

categorize ['kætɪgəraɪz] *verb* to put into classes or categories; *the government has changed the way people are categorized*

category ['kætɪgəri] *noun* classification of things or people; *we only sell the most expensive categories of watches*; *if there is no room in the hotel mentioned in the brochure, we will put you into a similar category of hotel* (NOTE: plural is **categories**)

caterer ['keɪtərə] *noun* person who supplies food and drink; *we have hired a caterer or caterers for the wedding*

cater for ['keɪtə 'fɔː] *verb* (a) to supply food and drink at a party, etc.; *our firm caters for receptions of up to 250 guests* (b) to provide for; *the store caters mainly for overseas customers*

catering ['keɪtərɪŋ] *noun* supplying of food and drink; *who's doing the catering for your wedding?*; *we got a catering firm to deal with refreshments*; *the catering trade* = the food trade, especially supplying food ready to eat

caterpillar ['kætəpɪlə] *noun* (a) insect larva with many legs, which turns into a moth or butterfly; *caterpillars have eaten most of the leaves on our trees* (b) **caterpillar track** = metal belt running round wheels on a tank, etc.; **caterpillar tractor** = tractor with a metal belt round its wheels

catfish ['kætfɪʃ] *noun* ugly freshwater fish with whiskers (NOTE: plural is **catfish**)

catgut ['kætgʌt] *noun* thread made from the intestines of a sheep, used in certain musical instruments and sports rackets

cathedral [kə'θiːdrəl] *noun* large church which is the seat of a bishop; *we went on a tour of cathedrals in the Midlands*; *you can see the cathedral tower from miles away*; *Canterbury Cathedral is one of the oldest in England*

cathode ['kæθəʊd] *noun* negative electric pole through which electricity leaves a piece of electric equipment; **cathode ray tube** = TV tube in which a cathode produces rays which carry the image to the screen (NOTE: the opposite is an **anode**)

catholic ['kæθlɪk] **1** *adjective* (a) **Catholic** = referring to the Roman Catholic Church; *the local Catholic priest*; *there's a French Catholic church near Leicester Square* (b) wide, general (taste); *his interests have always been quite catholic* **2** *noun* a **Catholic** = a member of the Roman Catholic Church; *she became a very devout Catholic*; *the war between Protestants and Catholics*

Catholicism [kə'θɒlɪsɪzm] *noun* beliefs of the Roman Catholic Church; *she was converted to Catholicism when she was an adult*

catkin ['kætkɪn] *noun* long flower head which hangs down from the branches of certain types of tree, such as hazel and birch

catsup ['kætsəp] *noun US* = KETCHUP

cattle ['kætl] *noun* animals of the cow family (such as bulls, calves, oxen, etc.); *a herd of cattle*; *cattle farmers are complaining about the high cost of foodstuffs*; *the cattle were brought inside for the winter* (NOTE: the word is plural)

catty ['kæti] *adjective* (*informal*) making unpleasant remarks about someone; *don't be so catty about her*; *she made some really catty remarks about the secretary*

catwalk ['kætwɔːk] *noun* (a) raised walkway down which models walk to show off clothes; *the model on the catwalk gave a twirl of her skirt*; *fashion editors stared at the models on the catwalk* (b) open metal gangway running along the outside of a ship or building; *he stepped confidently onto the catwalk*

caucus ['kɔːkəs] *noun* group of people in a political party who are strong enough to influence policy; *caucuses play a very important part in American politics* (NOTE: plural is **caucuses**)

caught [kɔːt] *see* CATCH

cauldron *US* **caldron** ['kɔːldrən] *noun* large deep pan for cooking

cauliflower ['kɒlɪflaʊə] *noun* vegetable with hard white flowers, which are eaten cooked; *would you like some more cauliflower?*; **cauliflower cheese** = dish of cauliflower cooked in the oven with a white sauce and cheese on top (NOTE: no plural when referring to the food: **some cauliflower**; **they served cauliflower with the meat**)

causal ['kɔːzl] *adjective* referring to a cause; *there is a causal link between smoking and cancer*

cause [kɔːz] **1** *noun* (a) thing which makes something happen; *what is the chief cause of traffic accidents?*; *the police tried to find the cause of the fire* (b) organization which people support; *she is fighting for the cause of working mothers* **2** *verb* to make something happen; *the accident caused a traffic jam on the motorway*; *the sudden noise caused her to drop the cup she was carrying*

causeway ['kɔːzweɪ] *noun* road or path built up on a bank above marshy ground or water; *you can drive to and from the island along the causeway at low tide*

caustic ['kɔːstɪk] *adjective* (a) (*substance*) which can burn; *this liquid is caustic and you should wear gloves when using it*; **caustic soda** = sodium hydroxide, a compound of sodium and water used to make soap and to clear blocked drains; *you can use caustic soda as a cleaning agent* (b) sharp (wit); *his caustic remarks didn't go down well with his employees*

caution ['kɔːʃn] **1** *noun* (a) care; *the steps are very slippery - please proceed with great caution* (NOTE: no plural in this meaning) (b) warning not to do something again; *the magistrate let him off with a caution* **2** *verb* to warn; *he was cautioned by the police*; *the doctor cautioned him against working too hard*

cautionary ['kɔːʃənri] *adjective* which warns; *the government has issued a cautionary message about drugs*

cautionary tale ['kɔːʃənri 'teɪl] *noun* (a) story written as a warning; *it's a cautionary tale specially written to warn children not to talk to strangers* (b) something which provides a good example; *the whole sequence of events is a cautionary tale about what not to do when letting your house*

cautious ['kɔːʃəs] *adjective* careful, prudent; *we were warned to be cautious when driving through the safari park*; *she's a very cautious driver*; *he has adopted a cautious approach to his investments*

cautiously ['kɔːʃəsli] *adverb* in a cautious way; *she walked cautiously along the plank*

cavalier [kævə'lɪə] **1** *noun* a **Cavalier** = member of the King's party during the English Civil War (NOTE: the opposite party, the supporters of the Parliament, were called **Roundheads**) **2** *adjective* high-handed, with no respect for other people or customs; *she showed a cavalier attitude to employment law*

cavalry ['kævəlri] *noun* soldiers on horseback; *the cavalry did not attack in time*; *he's joined a cavalry regiment* (NOTE: can be followed by either a singular or plural verb)

cavalryman ['kævəlrimən] *noun* soldier on horseback; *the cavalrymen were killed as they charged the guns* (NOTE: plural is **cavalrymen**)

cave [keɪv] **1** *noun* large underground hole in rock or earth; *when the tide went out we could explore the cave*; **cave paintings** = paintings done by ancient peoples on the walls of caves **2** *verb* **to cave in** = to collapse; *the beam cracked and the roof caved in*

cave-in ['keɪvɪn] *noun* situation where the roof of a tunnel or cave falls in and traps people; *work on the extension to the London Underground was stopped because of a cave-in*

caveman ['keɪvmæn] *noun* primitive man who lived in caves; *remains of cavemen have been found in this region* (NOTE: plural is **cavemen**)

cavern ['kævən] *noun* very large cave, formed by water which has dissolved limestone or other rock; *under the castle, the police discovered a cavern which had been used to hide arms*

cavernous ['kævənəs] *adjective* with a very large interior space, like a cavern; *the meeting took place in a cavernous hall*

caviar(e) ['kævɪɑː] *noun* the eggs of a sturgeon, a very expensive delicacy; *there are several types of caviar, and all are very expensive*; *red caviar is popular and a little less expensive than black*

cavity ['kævɪti] *noun* **(a)** hole, space; *the jewellery was discovered hidden in a cavity in the wall*; **cavity wall** = wall with a gap between the inner and outer rows of bricks **(b)** hole in a tooth; *there is a cavity in one of your back teeth which needs filling* **(c)** abdominal cavity = space in the body below the chest (NOTE: plural is **cavities**)

CBI = CONFEDERATION OF BRITISH INDUSTRY

CCTV = CLOSED-CIRCUIT TELEVISION

CD ['siː 'diː] *abbreviation for* compact disc; *I don't like his new CD - do you?*; *some CDs are expensive so I borrow them from the music library*; *you can get it on CD or cassette*; **CD player** = machine which plays CDs

CD-ROM ['siː diː 'rɒm] *noun* = COMPACT DISC READ ONLY MEMORY small plastic disc used as a high capacity ROM storage device which can store 650Mb of data; **CD-ROM drive** = disc drive which allows a computer to read data stored on a CD-ROM; *most PCs have CD-ROM drives*

cease [siːs] *verb* to stop; *at long last the drilling noise has ceased*; **to cease to exist** = to stop being in existence; *the pub on the corner ceased to exist sometime ago*

ceasefire ['siːsfaɪə] *noun* agreement to stop shooting (in a war); *they agreed a two-week ceasefire to allow negotiations to start*

ceaseless ['siːsləs] *adjective* without stopping; *the ceaseless pattering of the rain kept me awake at night*; *her ceaseless complaints about the office cat*

ceaselessly ['siːsləsli] *adverb* without stopping; *she talked ceaselessly about her son*

cedar ['siːdə] *noun* **(a)** large evergreen tree; *there is a large cedar in front of the house*; **cedar of Lebanon** = very large cedar which comes originally from the Lebanon **(b)** wood from this tree; *a cedar chest*; *cedar wood has a pleasant smell*

cede [siːd] *verb* **to cede something to someone** = to pass possession of a territory to another country; *the Philippines were ceded to the USA by Spain in 1898*; *see also* CESSION (NOTE: do not confuse with **seed**)

ceiling ['siːlɪŋ] *noun* **(a)** inside roof over a room; *he's so tall, he can easily touch the ceiling*; *flies can walk on the ceiling*; *he painted the kitchen ceiling*; *watch out when you go into the bedroom - it has a very low ceiling* **(b)** highest point, such as the highest interest rate, the highest amount of money which a depositor may deposit, etc.; *output has reached its ceiling*; *there is a ceiling of £20,000 on the amount you can hold in premium bonds*; *they set a ceiling of £1000 on the price of their washing machines*

celebrate ['selɪbreɪt] *verb* **(a)** to have a party or do special things because something good has taken place, or because of something that happened in the past; *our team won, so we're all going out to celebrate*; *today we celebrate the five-hundredth anniversary of the founding of our school*; *they celebrated their wedding anniversary quietly at home with their children* **(b)** to perform a religious ceremony; *the priest was celebrating Mass*

celebrated ['selɪbreɪtɪd] *adjective* very famous; *Bath is celebrated for its Roman buildings*; *you must try some of our celebrated raisin cakes - they're a speciality of the town*

celebration [selɪ'breɪʃn] *noun* festivity; *we had my birthday celebration in the local pub*; *after our team won, the celebrations went on late into the night*

celebrity [sə'lebrɪti] *noun* famous person; *the theatre was packed with celebrities from the acting world*; *we hope the new supermarket is going to be opened by a TV celebrity* (NOTE: plural is **celebrities**)

celery ['seləri] *noun* plant with a white or green stem, eaten as a vegetable or raw as a salad; *she bought a bunch of celery in the market*; **a stick of celery** = a piece of the stem of the celery plant (often served raw with cheese) (NOTE: no plural)

celestial [sə'lestjəl] *adjective* (*formal*) referring to the sky; *look at the celestial map to find the position of Venus*; *name two celestial bodies - the sun and the moon*

cell [sel] *noun* **(a)** room in a prison, in a monastery; *he was arrested in the centre of town and spent the night in the police cells*; **condemned cell** = room for prisoners condemned to death **(b)** basic unit of an organism; *you can see the cancer cells under a microscope* (NOTE: do not confuse with **sell**)

cellar ['selə] *noun* underground room or rooms beneath a house; *a flight of stone steps leads down to the cellar*; *we keep our wine in the cellar*

cellist ['tʃelɪst] *noun* person who plays the cello; *she is the cellist in the Elgar Cello Concerto*

cello ['tʃeləʊ] *noun* large stringed musical instrument smaller than a double bass; *a quartet made up of two violins and two cellos* (NOTE: plural is **cellos**)

cellular ['seljʊlə] *adjective* **(a)** made up of many small cells; *cellular tissue is connective tissue with large spaces* **(b)** **cellular phone** = mobile phone that works from a series of radio stations all over the country **(c)** (cloth) with open holes in it; *cellular blankets are light and warm - they look as if they've been knitted with very big needles*

cellulite ['seljʊlaɪt] *noun* deposits of fat under the skin, especially in the thighs and buttocks; *cellulite is not uncommon in women*

Celsius ['selsɪəs] *adjective & noun* scale of temperature where the freezing point of water is 0° and the boiling point is 100°; *do you use Celsius or Fahrenheit in the weather forecasts?*; *what is 75° Fahrenheit in Celsius?* (NOTE: used in many countries, but not in the USA, where the Fahrenheit system is still preferred. Normally written as a **C** after the degree sign: **32°C** (say: 'thirty-two degrees Celsius'). Was formerly called **centigrade**)

COMMENT: to convert Celsius temperatures to Fahrenheit, multiply by 1.8 and add 32. So 20°C is equal to 68°F. To convert Fahrenheit to Celsius, subtract 32 and divide by 1.8

cement [sɪ'ment] **1** *noun* **(a)** powder made from lime and clay, which is mixed with water and dries hard; *he was mixing cement to make a path round the house* **(b)** strong glue; *she stuck the handle back on the cup with cement* **2** *verb* to attach strongly; *he cemented some stones on the top of the wall*; *the two halves should be cemented together*

cemetery ['semətri] *noun* burial ground; *he is buried in the cemetery next to the church*; *there are two cemeteries in the city* (NOTE: plural is **cemeteries**)

censor ['sensə] **1** *noun* person who reads documents or looks at films to see if they are fit to be published or shown; *all imported magazines are examined by the official censor*; *the censor has refused permission for the film to be shown*; *during wartime, military censors read all letters from soldiers to their families* **2** *verb* to read books or plays, to watch films, videos or TV programmes, to see if they are fit to be published or shown, or to ban them or change them; *the film was censored before being shown on TV*; *he was accused of censoring the article*

censorious [sen'sɔːriəs] *adjective* (*formal*) who tends to criticize; *he was very censorious of their actions*

censorship ['sensəʃɪp] *noun* action to ban books or newspapers or remove parts of them; *all imported newspapers are subject to strict censorship*; *the writers' union has set up a committee to monitor censorship*; *after the war, military censorship was lifted*; **press censorship** = censoring of what is written in newspapers; *the government has imposed strict press censorship*

censure ['senʃə] **1** *noun* criticism; *there was widespread public censure of the government*; **vote of censure** = vote on a motion criticizing the government, etc. (NOTE: no plural) **2** *verb* to criticize; *the Opposition put forward a motion to censure the Government*; *the borough architect was censured for failing to consult the engineers*

census ['sensəs] *noun* official count of a country's population; *the next census will be taken in the year 2002* (NOTE: plural is **censuses**)

cent [sent] *noun* **(a)** small coin, one-hundredth part of a dollar; *the stores are only a 25-cent bus ride away*; *they sell oranges at 99 cents each* (NOTE: **cent** is usually written ¢ in prices: **25¢**, but not when a dollar price is mentioned: **$1.25**) **(b)** *see also* PER CENT

centaur ['sentɔː] *noun* animal in Greek mythology, the top half a man, and the bottom part a horse; *the marble sculptures show centaurs fighting*

centenary [sen'tiːnəri] *noun* hundredth anniversary; *the university is celebrating the centenary of its foundation*; *this year is the centenary of the death of the great cellist*

centennial [sen'tenjəl] *adjective* referring to a centenary; *our college is getting ready for the centennial celebrations next month*

centigrade ['sentɪgreɪd] *noun* scale of temperature where the freezing point of water is 0° and the boiling point is 100°; *do you use centigrade or Fahrenheit in the weather forecasts?*; *what is 75° Fahrenheit in centigrade?*; *see note at* CELSIUS

centimetre *US* **centimeter** ['sentɪmiːtə] *noun* measure of length, one hundredth part of a metre; *I need a short piece of string - about 25 centimetres long* (NOTE: written **cm** with numbers: **25cm**: say: 'twenty-five centimetres')

centipede ['sentɪpiːd] *noun* little creeping animal with a large number of legs; *he found a centipede under the flowerpot*

central ['sentrl] *adjective* in the centre; *the hall has one central pillar*; *his offices are very central*; **central government** = the main government of a country, as opposed to local government; **central heating** = heating which heats the whole building from one heater; *the house has gas central heating*; **Central Intelligence Agency (CIA)** = US government agency which organizes spies; **central reservation** = section of road or grass, bushes, etc., between the two carriageways of a major road; *the lorry crashed through the central reservation and hit a car coming in the opposite direction* (NOTE: American English is **median strip**)

centralize ['sentrəlaɪz] *verb* to organize from a central point; *the gathering of all personal records has been centralized in the headquarters of the Department of Health*

centre *US* **center** ['sentə] **1** *noun* **(a)** middle; *they planted a rose bush in the centre of the lawn*; *the town centre is very old*; *chocolates with coffee cream centres*; **centre of gravity** = the point in an object at which it will balance; *a bus has a very low centre of gravity* **(b)** large building containing several different sections; *an army training centre*; **health centre** *or* **medical centre** = building with various doctors and specialists; **sports centre** = place where several different sports can be played; **shopping centre** = several shops in one big building **(c)** important town;

Nottingham is the centre for the shoe industry **(d)** group or political party, such as the Liberals or Democrats, between the left and right; *the centre combined with the right to defeat the proposal*; *the cabinet is formed of right-of-centre supporters of the Prime Minister* **(e)** **job centre** = government office which advertises jobs which are vacant **2** *verb* **(a)** to put something in the middle; *make sure you centre the block of wood on the lathe* **(b)** to concentrate on; *the opposition's attack was centred on the government's reorganization of the social services*; *our report centres on some aspects of the sales team*

centred *US* **centered** [sentəd] *adjective* **(a)** in the middle; *make sure the picture is centred in the frame* **(b)** based in; *the shoe industry is centred on Nottingham*

centre forward ['sentə 'fɔːwəd] *noun* (in football) player in the centre of the forward line; *the leading scorer was the Brazilian centre forward*

centrepiece *US* **centerpiece** ['setəpiːs] *noun* **(a)** main item of a display on a table; *a bowl of fruit will be fine as a centrepiece on the dining table* **(b)** main item of policy; *the project is the centrepiece of the government's policy on pensions*

centre stage *US* **center stage** ['sentə 'steɪdʒ] *adverb* in the middle of the stage, in the middle of some action; *she moved centre stage and started to sing*; *the UN Secretary General has moved centre stage to try to defuse the crisis*

centrist ['sentrɪst] **1** *adjective* in favour of the centre in politics; *the group advocates a return to centrist politics*; *they elected a centrist government* **2** *noun* person who is in favour of the centre in politics; *the centrists formed a coalition to influence government policy on education*; *compare* LEFTIST, RIGHTIST

century ['sentʃəri] *noun* **(a)** one hundred years; **the seventeenth century** = the period from 1600 to 1699; *a 17th-century church*; *the church dates from the 17th century* **(b)** score of 100, especially in cricket; *he's a powerful hitter and rapidly scored a century*; *he scored a century, including four fours and two sixes* (NOTE: plural is **centuries**; note also that the number of a century is always one more than the date number: so the period from **1900 to 1999** is the **20th century,** and the period starting in the year **2000** is the **21st century**)

ceramic [səˈræmɪk] *adjective* made of pottery; *a cooker with a ceramic hob*; *I prefer ceramic tiles to vinyl*

ceramics [səˈræmɪks] *noun* **(a)** the art of making pottery; *she is taking a course in ceramics at the local art college* (NOTE: not plural in this meaning) **(b)** artistic things made in pottery; *our next exhibition will be of ceramics by two local potters*

cereal ['siːriəl] *noun* **(breakfast) cereal** = food made from corn, oats, etc., eaten with milk for breakfast; *would you like some cereal for breakfast?* (NOTE: do not confuse with **serial**)

cerebral ['serɪbrəl] *adjective* **(a)** referring to the cerebrum or to the brain in general; *a cerebral haemorrhage means bleeding inside the brain*; **cerebral hemisphere** = one of the two halves of the cerebrum; **cerebral palsy** = disorder of the brain, mainly due to brain damage occurring before birth, or due to lack of oxygen during birth; *his child was born with cerebral palsy* **(b)** intellectual, rather than

emotional; *I need to take some exercise after all this cerebral work*

cerebrum ['serɪbrʌm] *noun* the main part of the brain, which contains the main mental processes including memory; *the cerebrum is divided into two halves called cerebral hemispheres*; *the cerebral cortex is the outer layer of the cerebrum*

ceremonial [serɪˈməʊniəl] **1** *adjective* referring to a ceremony; *a guard of naval officers carrying their ceremonial swords*; *the ceremonial coach is used in the Lord Mayor's Parade* **2** *noun* way of conducting a ceremony; *the ceremonial for the burial of the dead is laid out in the prayer book*

ceremonious [serɪˈməʊniəs] *adjective* with a lot of ceremony; *it was not a simple meal, but a very ceremonious affair with toasts and speeches*

ceremony ['serɪməni] *noun* important official occasion when something special is done in public; *they held a ceremony to remember the victims of the train crash*; **to stand on ceremony** = to be formal and not relaxed; *don't stand on ceremony* (NOTE: plural is **ceremonies**)

certain ['sɜːtɪn] *adjective* **(a)** which you don't know or are not sure about; *the manager is a certain Mr Arbuthnot*; *certain fungi can make you ill if you eat them* **(b)** **a certain quantity** *or* **a certain amount** = some; *the fire did a certain amount of damage*; *rebuilding the house took a certain amount of time*; *you need to add a certain quantity of water to the paint* **(c)** sure; *are you certain that you locked the door?*; *I'm not certain where she lives*; **to make certain that** = to do something to be sure that something with happen; *he put the money in his safe to make certain that no one could steal it* **(d)** without any doubt; *our team is certain to win the prize*

certainly ['sɜːtənli] *adverb* **(a)** (after a question or order) of course; *can you give me a lift to the station? - certainly*; *tell him to write to me immediately - certainly, sir*; *give me a kiss - certainly not!* **(b)** definitely; *she certainly impressed the judges*; *he certainly knows how to score goals*

certainty ['sɜːtənti] *noun* **(a)** being certain; *I can't tell who won with any certainty - it was a photo-finish*; *there is no certainty that the weather will stay fine for the whole of next week* **(b)** sure or certain thing; *fine weather in November is not an absolute certainty* (NOTE: plural is **certainties**)

certificate [sɜːˈtɪfɪkət] *noun* official document which proves or shows something; *she has been awarded a certificate for swimming*; *he has a certificate of aptitude in English*; **birth certificate** = paper from the registrar's office, showing the date on which someone was born, together with details of the parents; **death certificate** = paper signed by a doctor which shows that someone has died and what was the cause of death; **insurance certificate** = document from an insurance company showing that an insurance policy has been issued; **marriage certificate** = paper from the registrar's office to confirm that two people are married; **savings certificate** = document showing you have invested money in a government savings scheme; **share certificate** = document proving that you own shares

certify ['sɜːtɪfaɪ] *verb* **(a)** to make an official declaration in writing; *the document is certified as a true copy*; *he was certified dead on arrival at hospital*

(b) *(old)* to send a patient to a mental hospital; *his parents had him certified*

certitude ['sɜːtɪtjuːd] *noun (formal)* certainty; *there is no certitude that she will get the job; she went on with her search, helped by the certitude that she would find her daughter one day*

cervical ['sɜːvɪkl] *adjective* **(a)** referring to any neck; *the bones in the neck are the seven cervical vertebrae* **(b)** referring to the cervix of the uterus; *what can be done to prevent cervical cancer?; in your case, you should have a cervical smear test every year*

cervix ['sɜːvɪks] *noun* **(a)** any narrow neck of an organ **(b)** neck of the womb, the narrow lower part of the uterus leading into the vagina; *cancer of the cervix may not show any symptoms for a very long time* (NOTE: plural is **cervixes**)

cessation [se'seɪʃn] *noun* stopping; *cessation of hostilities is the number one objective* (NOTE: no plural)

cession ['seʃən] *noun (formal)* action of ceding something; *the cession of the Philippines to the USA; see also* CEDE (NOTE: no plural; do not confuse with **session**)

cf. ['siː'ef] *abbreviation for 'confer'* used to refer to a footnote or to another part of the text; *cf. illustrations p. 72*

CFC [siːef'siː] *abbreviation for* chlorofluorocarbon, compound of fluorine and chlorine; *CFCs contribute to the destruction of the ozone layer; when CFCs are released into the atmosphere, they rise slowly taking about seven years to reach the stratosphere*

CH = CENTRAL HEATING

chain [tʃeɪn] **1** *noun* **(a)** series of metal rings joined together; *she wore a gold chain round her neck; he stopped when the chain came off his bike;* **chain reaction** = series of reactions which follow on from an event; **chain saw** = saw made of a chain with teeth in it, which turns very fast when driven by a motor **(b)** series of stores, restaurants, pubs, hotels, etc., belonging to the same company; *a chain of hotels or a hotel chain; a do-it-yourself chain; she runs a chain of shoe shops* **(c)** series of people, each buying another's house; *there is a chain of six families involved, so the sale will take some time* **2** *verb* to attach with a chain; *I chained my bike to the lamppost*

chained ['tʃeɪnd] *adjective* **(a)** attached with chains; *even a chained bicycle can be easily stolen if the thief has a chain cutter; the dog is kept chained up in the yard* **(b)** firmly attached; *I don't want to spend my life chained to a desk all day long*

chair [tʃeə] **1** *noun* **(a)** piece of furniture which you can sit on, with a back; *someone has been sitting in my chair, said the bear; he pulled up a chair and started to write; these dining-room chairs are very hard;* **easy chair** = comfortable chair; *see also* ARMCHAIR **(b)** the chairman, the person who presides over a meeting; *please address all your comments to the chair;* **Mr Jones took the chair** = Mr Jones presided over the meeting **(c)** position of professor at a university; *he has been appointed to the chair of English* **2** *verb* to preside over a meeting; *the meeting was chaired by Mrs Smith*

chairman ['tʃeəmən] *noun* **(a)** person who is in charge of a meeting; *Mrs Jones was the chairman at the meeting* **(b)** person who presides over a board of

directors; *the chairman of the bank* (NOTE: plural is **chairmen**)

chairmanship ['tʃeəmənʃɪp] *noun* being a chairman; *the committee met under the chairmanship of Mr Jones*

chalet ['ʃæleɪ] *noun* small (holiday) house, usually made of wood; *a mountain landscape dotted with little chalets; the company offers holidays in chalets in Switzerland*

chalk [tʃɔːk] *noun* **(a)** type of soft white rock made of calcium; *the white cliffs of Dover are formed of chalk (informal)* **they're as different as chalk and cheese** = they are totally different **(b)** stick of white or coloured material for writing on a blackboard; *he wrote the dates on the board in coloured chalk*

chalk up ['tʃɔːk 'ʌp] *verb* to achieve a score *or* a victory; *she chalked up three election victories in a row*

challenge ['tʃæləndʒ] **1** *noun* **(a)** test of skill, strength, etc.; *the action by the union is another challenge to the authority of the government;* **to pose a challenge to someone** = to be a difficult task; *getting the piano up the stairs will pose a challenge to the removal men* **(b)** invitation to a fight or struggle; *our team accepted the challenge to play another game;* **to take up a challenge** = to agree to fight **2** *verb* **(a)** to ask someone to prove that he is right; *when challenged, he admitted that he had seen her get into a car; the committee's conclusions have been challenged by other experts* **(b)** **to challenge someone to a fight** = to ask someone to fight

challenger ['tʃæləndʒə] *noun* person who challenges, especially a boxer; *he's the main challenger for the world title*

challenging ['tʃæləndʒɪŋ] *adjective* difficult, which poses a challenge; *she stared at him in a challenging way; it's a challenging task, making the company profitable again; I found the training course quite challenging*

chamber ['tʃeɪmbə] *noun* **(a)** official room; **council chamber** = room where a council meets **(b)** **chambers** = office of a judge or a lawyer; *we went to see the barrister in his chambers* **(c)** **chamber music** = music for a few instruments which can be played in a small room; **chamber orchestra** = small orchestra which plays chamber music **(d)** empty space inside the heart; *blood collects inside the chambers of the heart and is then pumped out*

chambermaid ['tʃeɪmbəmeɪd] *noun* woman who cleans bedrooms in a hotel; *put a 'Do not disturb' sign outside your door if you don't want the chambermaid to wake you up*

Chamber of Commerce ['tʃeɪmbər əv 'kɒməs] *noun* group of local business people who meet to discuss problems which they have and to encourage business in their town; *the Chamber of Commerce is very concerned about parking problems in the town centre; do you belong to the local Chamber of Commerce?*

chameleon [kə'miːliən] *noun* type of lizard which changes its colour to match its natural surroundings

champ [tʃæmp] **1** *noun (informal)* champion; *he's the champ!* **2** *verb* to chew hard and noisily; **to champ at the bit** = to be impatient to do something; *the* salesmen are champing at the bit because the product is still not ready

champagne [ʃæmˈpeɪn] *noun* sparkling white wine from the north-east of France; *they opened a bottle of champagne to celebrate the baby's birth* (NOTE: informally, also called **champers, bubbly** or **fizz**)

champion [ˈtʃæmpɪən] **1** *noun* best in a particular competition; *a champion cow*; *she was champion two years running*; *he's the world champion in the 100 metres* **2** *verb* to champion a cause = to support a cause strongly; *they are championing the cause of women's rights*

championship [ˈtʃæmpɪənʃɪp] *noun* **(a)** contest to find who is the champion; *the schools' tennis championship was won by a boy from Leeds* **(b)** support for a cause; *her constant championship of the homeless*

chance [tʃɑːns] **1** *noun* **(a)** possibility, likelihood; *has our team any chance of winning? - yes, I think they have a good chance; is there any chance of our getting home tonight?; there is no chance of rain in August; what are her chances of survival in this weather?* **(b)** opportunity; *I've been waiting for a chance to speak to the Prime Minister; I wish I had the chance to visit South Africa* **(c)** luck; *it was pure chance or it was quite by chance that we were travelling on the same bus* (NOTE: the meanings: **chance of +ing** = possibility of doing something; **chance to** = opportunity to do something) **2** *verb* **(a)** to do something by chance; *he chanced to look round as she came up to him; the car in front of us chanced to turn right* **(b)** to chance it = to try to do something which is risky; *the sky looks grey, but I think I'll chance it without an umbrella* **(c)** to chance upon = to find something by accident; *as he was searching in the library he chanced upon an unknown play by Shakespeare*

◊ **by any chance** *phrase* by luck, by accident; *do you by any chance happen to know where the nearest post office is?; have you by any chance seen my glasses?*

chancellor [ˈtʃɑːnsələ] *noun* **(a)** important official; *he became chancellor of the university in 1996* **(b)** (*in Germany or Austria*) head of the government (= Prime Minister)

Chancellor (of the Exchequer) [ˈtʃɑːnsələr əv ðiː ɪksˈtʃekə] *noun* chief finance minister in the British government; *newspapers always carry pictures of the Chancellor on Budget day* (NOTE: in most countries, this is called the **Minister of Finance**; the American equivalent is the **Secretary of the Treasury**)

chancy [ˈtʃɑːnsi] *adjective* (*informal*) risky, not very sure; *he lost all his money in some chancy investments in South America*

chandelier [ʃændəˈlɪə] *noun* light fitting which hangs from the ceiling, with several branches for holding electric bulbs; *during the earthquake the chandeliers started swinging; the ballroom was lit by magnificent chandeliers*

change [tʃeɪnʒ] **1** *noun* **(a)** making something different or becoming different; *there was a last-minute change of plan; we've seen a lot of changes over the years*; **I think it's a change for the better** = I think it has made things better than they were **(b)** something different; *we usually go on holiday in*

summer, but this year we're taking a winter holiday for a change; a cup of tea is a nice change after all those glasses of orange juice; a change of scenery will do you good; **he took a change of clothes with him** = he took a set of clean clothes with him **(c)** money in coins or notes; *I need some change for the parking meter; have you got change for a £5 note?*; **small change** = coins, especially ones with a low value; *I have only two £10 notes - I have no small change at all* **(d)** money which you get back when you have given more than the correct price; *the book is £3.50, so if you give me £5, you should get £1.50 change; the shopkeeper gave me the wrong change*; **keep the change** = keep it as a tip (said to waiters, etc.) (NOTE: no plural for meanings (c) and (d)) **(e)** to ring the changes = to try various things to see which is best; *I don't always buy the same newspaper, I prefer to ring the changes between 'The Times', 'The Independent' and 'The Guardian'* **2** *verb* **(a)** to make something different; to become different; *living in the country has changed his attitude towards towns; London has changed a lot since we used to live there; he's changed so much since I last saw him that I hardly recognized him; the prince was changed into a frog*; **I've changed my mind** = I've decided to do something different **(b)** to put on different clothes; *I'm just going upstairs to change or to get changed; go into the bathroom if you want to change your dress*; **changing room** = room where you can change into or out of sports clothes; **to change a bed** = to put clean sheets, etc., on a bed; *the maid has come in to change the beds* **(c)** to use or have something in place of something else; *you ought to change your car tyres if they are worn; can we change our room for one with a view of the sea?; she's recently changed her job or changed jobs*; **to change trains** *or* **to change buses** = to get off one train or bus and onto another to continue your journey; *to get to Stratford you will have to change (trains) at Birmingham* **(d)** to change gear = to change from one gear to the next when driving a car (NOTE: American English is to **shift gears**) **(e)** to give smaller coins or notes for a larger one; **can you change a £20 note?** = can you give me small change for it? **(f)** to give one type of currency for another; *to change £1,000 into dollars*; *we want to change some traveller's cheques*

changeable [ˈtʃeɪnʒəbl] *adjective* which changes often, which is likely to change often; *the weather will be changeable over the weekend; you never know what she will be like from one moment to the next, her moods are so changeable*

change down [ˈtʃeɪnʒ ˈdaʊn] *verb* to move to a lower gear when driving a car; *change down when you come to the hill*

change up [ˈtʃeɪnʒ ˈʌp] *verb* to move to a higher gear when driving a car; *change up to top gear when you get onto the motorway*

channel [ˈtʃænl] **1** *noun* **(a)** piece of water connecting two seas; *the English Channel; the Channel Tunnel* **(b)** way in which information or goods are passed from one place to another; *the matter was sorted out through the normal diplomatic channels*; **channels of communication** = ways of communicating **(c)** frequency band for radio or TV; station using this band; *we're watching Channel 4; can you switch to Channel 1 for the news?; the new chat show is scheduled to compete with the gardening programme on the other channel* **2** *verb* to send in a certain direction; *they are channelling their funds into research*; *the money from the jumble sale has been channelled into the building project* (NOTE: **channelling - channelled** but American spelling is **channeling - channeled**)

chant [tʃɑːnt] 1 *noun* regular singing of a repeated song or phrase; *he has a recording of chants by Buddhist monks*; *the chants of 'down with the police' could be heard in the streets* 2 *verb* to sing to a regular beat; *the crowds chanted anti-government slogans*

chaos ['keɪɒs] *noun* confusion; *there was total chaos when the electricity failed*; **Chaos Theory** = theory that things happen at random, and one should plan for the unexpected to happen

chaotic [keɪ'ɒtɪk] *adjective* confused, without order; *there were chaotic scenes after the train crash*

chap [tʃæp] 1 *noun* (*informal*) man; *he's a really nice chap*; *I bought it from a chap at work* 2 *verb* (*of the skin*) to crack; *rub an ointment on your chapped lips* (NOTE: **chapping - chapped**)

chapel ['tʃæpl] *noun* (a) part of a large church with a separate altar; *there's a chapel on the west side of the cathedral dedicated to St Teresa* (b) small church attached to a special institution; *they were buried in the prison chapel*

chaplain ['tʃæplɪn] *noun* priest attached to a private individual, to a prison or to one of the armed services; *he had a visit from the prison chaplain*

chapter ['tʃæptə] *noun* (a) division of a book; *the first chapter is rather slow, but after that the story gets exciting*; *don't tell me how it finishes - I'm only up to chapter three*; *see also* VERSE (b) **chapter of accidents** = a series of accidents (c) group of p[riests or monks who run a cathedral or monastery; **chapter house** = special room where a chapter meets

char [tʃɑː] 1 *noun* (a) (*old*) (*informal*) = CHARWOMAN (b) (*old*) (*informal*) tea; *how about a cup o' char?* 2 *verb* (a) to burn black; *the barbecue was too hot and the meat was charred* (b) (*old*) (*informal*) to do housework for someone; *she spent all her life charring for rich people* (NOTE: **charring - charred**)

character ['kærəktə] *noun* (a) the part of a person which makes him or her different from all others; *his character is quite different from yours*; *she is a very strong character* (b) person in a play or novel; *the leading character in the film is an old blind man* (c) letter or symbol used in writing or printing; *the book is printed in Chinese characters*

characteristic [kærəktə'rɪstɪk] 1 *adjective* special, typical; *you can recognise him by his characteristic way of walking*; *that is characteristic of this type of flower* (NOTE: something is **characteristic of** something) 2 *noun* typical feature; *the two cars have very similar characteristics*

characteristically [kærəktə'rɪstɪkli] *adverb* in a typical way, typically; *he was characteristically shy about asking her to go with him*

characterization [kærəktəraɪ'zeɪʃn] *noun* indication of character; *Dickens' characterization of women and girls is his weakest point*

characterize ['kærəktəraɪz] *verb* (a) to be a typical feature of something; *the northern coast is characterized by tall cliffs and tiny beaches* (b) to describe something as; *he didn't like to be*

characterized as weak and inefficient; *how would you characterize her reaction to the film?*

charade [ʃə'rɑːd] *noun* (a) **charades** = game where spectators have to guess a word from a scene acted by others; *we had a game of charades or we played charades* (b) action which has no meaning or which is simply a pretence; *can you make any sense of this charade?*; *why bother with this charade of consultation when we know that a decision has already been taken?*

charcoal ['tʃɑːkəʊl] *noun* (a) black fuel formed from wood which has been burnt slowly, used for barbecues and grills; *we need a bag of charcoal for the barbecue* (b) **charcoal grey** = dark grey; *he wore a charcoal grey suit*; *charcoal (grey) is very fashionable this autumn*

charge [tʃɑːdʒ] 1 *noun* (a) money which you have to pay; *there is no charge for delivery*; *we make a small charge for rental*; *we will send the parcel free of charge* = without asking you to pay for postage; **admission charge** *or* **entry charge** = price to be paid before going into an exhibition, etc.; **service charge** = charge added to a bill in a restaurant to pay for service; *a 10% service charge is added*; *does the bill include a service charge?* (b) claim by the police that someone has done something wrong; *he was kept in prison on a charge of trying to blow up the Houses of Parliament* (c) **in charge** = being in control of; *he is in charge of the sales department*; *who's in charge here?*; **to take charge of something** = to start to be responsible for something; *he took charge of the class while the teacher was out of the room* (d) electric current; *he was killed by an electric charge from the wires* (e) running attack; *the captain led the charge against the enemy camp* 2 *verb* (a) to ask someone to pay; *the restaurant charged me £10 for two glasses of water*; *how much did the garage charge for mending the car?*; *can I charge the restaurant bill to my room number?*; **to charge the packing to the customer** = to ask the customer to pay for the packing (b) (*of the police*) to say that someone has done something wrong; *he was charged with stealing the jewels* (c) to attack while running; *the police charged the rioters*; *if the bull charges, run as fast as you can for the gate!* (d) to run violently; *the children charged into the kitchen* (e) to give someone responsibility; *she was charged with organizing the club's dinner dance* (f) to put electricity into a battery; *you can charge your phone battery by plugging it into the mains overnight*; *my mobile phone doesn't work - the battery probably needs charging*

charge account ['tʃɑːdʒ ə'kaʊnt] *noun* arrangement which a customer has with a store to buy goods and pay for them later; *put this on my charge account, please*

charged [tʃɑːdʒd] *adjective* very emotional or angry; *the atmosphere in the House of Commons was very charged*

charge nurse ['tʃɑːdʒ 'nɜːs] *noun* senior male nurse in charge of a ward; *the charge nurse told me my son was getting better* (NOTE: the female equivalent is a **sister**)

charger ['tʃɑːdʒə] *noun* (a) device which can be plugged into the mains and connected to a storage battery to restore the charge; *how long do you have to connect the battery to the charger before it is recharged?* (b) heavy medieval battle horse; *knights in armour had to be lifted onto their chargers with cranes*

chariot ['tʃæriət] *noun* two-wheeled vehicle pulled by horses; *chariot races were a form of entertainment in Roman times*

charioteer [tʃæriə'tɪə] *noun* person who drives a chariot; *in Ancient Rome, some charioteers earned huge amounts of money*

charisma [kə'rɪzmə] *noun* personal appeal; *he has all the charisma of a dead sheep; the Prime Minister's lack of charisma is rather disappointing*

charismatic [kærɪz'mætɪk] *adjective* who appeals to people; *a charismatic preacher who attracted crowds of people to his church; the party have chosen a charismatic young leader*

charitable ['tʃærɪtəbl] *adjective* (a) referring to a charity; *she was famous for her charitable work* (b) less critical; *commuters ought to be more charitable towards railway staff - they're only doing their best*

charitably ['tʃærɪtəbli] *adverb* in a charitable way; *you should behave more charitably towards the poor waiters*

charity ['tʃærɪti] *noun* (a) organization which collects money to help the poor or support some cause; *charities do not pay tax;* **charity shop =** shop run by a charity, where you can take old clothes, ornaments, etc., which are then sold and the proceeds given to the charity (NOTE: plural is **charities**) (b) help, usually money, given to the poor; *he lost his job and his family have to rely on the charity of neighbours* (NOTE: no plural in this meaning)

charlatan ['ʃɑːlətən] *noun* person who pretends he is an expert, when he is not; *he's just a charlatan - I'm sure that ointment doesn't cure cancer*

charm [tʃɑːm] **1** *noun* (a) attractiveness; *she has great personal charm; the charm of the Devon countryside* (b) supposedly magic object; *she wears a lucky charm round her neck* **2** *verb* (a) to put under a spell; *the old man played a pipe and charmed a snake out of its basket* (b) to attract someone, to make someone pleased; *he always manages to charm the girls at the office; I was charmed by their tiny cottage in the country*

charmed [tʃɑːmd] *adjective* protected as if by magic; *that cat leads a charmed life - it crosses the road several times a day and never gets hit*

charming ['tʃɑːmɪŋ] *adjective* attractive; *she looks charming in a pink shawl; he was such a charming young man; the effect of the little lights in the trees was charming*

charred [tʃɑːd] *adjective* burnt in a fire; *the charred beams of the roof; charred pieces of wood showed that someone had been making a fire on the beach*

chart [tʃɑːt] **1** *noun* (a) map of the sea, a river or a lake; *you will need an accurate chart of the entrance to the river* (b) diagram showing statistics; *a chart showing the increase in cases of lung cancer;* **bar chart =** diagram where quantities are shown as thick columns of different heights; **pie chart =** diagram where information is shown as a circle cut up into sections of different sizes (c) **the charts =** list of the most popular records; *his single is going up in the charts;* **chart show =** TV or radio show where records which are in the charts are played **2** *verb* to make a map of the sea, a river or lake; *he charted the coast of southern Australia in the 18th century*

charter ['tʃɑːtə] **1** *noun* (a) **charter flight =** flight in an aircraft which has been hired for that purpose; *our charter flight for Marbella was ten hours late;* **charter plane =** plane which has been chartered (b) legal document giving rights or privileges to a town or a university; *the university received its charter in 1846* **2** *verb* to hire an aircraft, bus or boat for a particular trip; *we chartered a boat for a day trip to the island*

chartered ['tʃɑːtəd] *adjective* (a) (aircraft, bus, boat) which has been hired for a particular trip; *a fleet of chartered coaches took the group to the beach* (b) (accountant, etc.) who has passed the professional examinations; *he is a chartered surveyor; his wife is a chartered accountant*

charwoman ['tʃɑːwumən] *noun* (*old*) woman who does cleaning work in a private house; *we'd like to find a charwoman who can come and help once a week*

chase [tʃeɪs] **1** *noun* pursuit or hunt; *he was caught after a three-hour chase along the motorway;* **to give chase =** to run after someone; *the robbers escaped and the police gave chase; see also* WILD GOOSE CHASE **2** *verb* (a) to run after someone to try to catch him; *the policeman chased the burglars down the street; the postman was chased by a dog* (b) to try to speed up work by asking how it is getting on; *we are trying to chase the accounts department for your cheque; I will chase up your order with the production department*

chaser ['tʃeɪsə] *noun* (a) **progress chaser =** person whose job is to check that work is being carried out on schedule or that orders are fulfilled on time; *the progress chaser will look into complaints from customers whose orders are late* (b) letter to remind someone of something (especially to remind a customer that an invoice has not been paid); *we send out chasers when invoices are not paid within 30 days* (c) alcoholic drink drunk after another stronger or weaker alcoholic drink; *he had a drink of whisky with a half-pint of bitter as a chaser*

chasm ['kæzəm] *noun* (a) huge difference of opinion; *how can we bridge the chasm between the two sides in the dispute?* (b) (*old*) huge crack in the ground; *the mountaineers were forced to turn back when they reached a chasm in the glacier*

chassis ['ʃæsi] *noun* (a) metal framework of a car; *the car's chassis was damaged in the accident* (b) undercarriage of an aircraft; *the aircraft radioed to say that the chassis had failed* (NOTE: plural is **chassis** ['ʃæsɪz])

chaste [tʃeɪst] *adjective* sexually pure; *she led a chaste life, looking after her family while her husband lived in the South of France*

chasten ['tʃeɪsn] *verb* (*formal*) to make someone behave in a better way; *she was chastened by public criticism of her plan*

chastened ['tʃeɪsnd] *adjective* meek, less proud; *the team returned home, chastened by their defeat*

chastise [tʃæ'staɪz] *verb* (*formal*) to punish; *any boy found stealing will be severely chastised*

chastisement [tʃæ'staɪzmənt] *noun* (*formal*) action of punishing; *in this school, corporal chastisement is practised when necessary*

chastity ['tʃæstɪti] *noun* being chaste; *Catholic priests and nuns take a vow of chastity*

chat [tʃæt] **1** *noun* casual friendly talk; *he likes to drop in for a cup of coffee and a chat*; *I'd like to have a chat with you about your work* **2** *verb* to talk in a casual and friendly way; *they were chatting about their holidays when the bus arrived; (informal)* to chat someone up = to flirt with someone; *he tried to chat up the girl he met in a bar* (NOTE: chatting - chatted)

chateau *or* **château** ['ʃætəʊ] *noun* French word meaning 'castle' **(a)** country house, manor house, castle in France; *a tour of the châteaux of the Loire* **(b)** estate where wine is made, usually referring to the wine-producing estates of the Bordeaux region; *the shop only sells very expensive wine from top-quality chateaux* (NOTE: plural is châteaux ['ʃætəʊz])

chat show ['tʃæt ʃəʊ] *noun* TV show where famous people talk to the host; *she has been invited to appear on the new chat show*

chattels ['tʃætlz] *noun* goods and chattels = moveable objects which you possess (as opposed to buildings or land)

chatter ['tʃætə] **1** *noun* quick talking; *the chatter of children in the corridor* **2** *verb* to talk quickly and not seriously; *she went on chattering on the phone, not realizing that the boss was standing behind her; his teeth were chattering* = his teeth were hitting each other because he was shivering; **the chattering classes** = middle-class people working in the media, who spend their time meeting and gossiping; *the chattering classes have detected a whiff of scandal about the minister*

chatty ['tʃæti] *adjective* **(a)** who likes to chat; *she's a very chatty person, always stopping to gossip with anyone she meets* **(b)** informal; *he has a pleasant chatty style, which goes down well with readers of Saturday papers*

chauffeur ['ʃəʊfə] **1** *noun* person who is paid to drive a car for someone else; *the chauffeur brought the Rolls round to the door* **2** *verb* to drive a car for someone else; *my husband lost his driving licence and I had to chauffeur him everywhere*

chauvinism ['ʃəʊvɪnɪzm] *noun* **(a)** strong feeling of pride in your native country; *chauvinism is a barrier to full integration into the European Union* **(b)** male chauvinism = strong feeling that men are better than women; *the club is a stronghold of male chauvinism*

chauvinist ['ʃəʊvɪnɪst] *noun* **(a)** person who has a strong feeling of pride in his native country; *chauvinists insist that British cooking is better than French* **(b)** *(informal)* male chauvinist pig = person who has a strong feeling that men are better than women; *the boss is just a male chauvinist pig*

chauvinistic [ʃəʊvɪ'nɪstɪk] *adjective* feeling that your country is better than all others; *listen to him criticize the EU - how chauvinistic can you get?*

cheap [tʃiːp] **1** *adjective* which does not cost a lot of money; *if you want a cheap radio you ought to shop around; why do you go by bus? - because it's cheaper than the train; buses are by far the cheapest way to travel; dirt cheap* = extremely cheap; *mangoes are dirt cheap in the street markets* (NOTE: cheaper - cheapest) **2** *adverb* at a low price; *I bought them cheap in the local market*

cheaply ['tʃiːpli] *adverb* without paying much money; *you can live quite cheaply if you don't go out to eat in restaurants*

cheat [tʃiːt] **1** *noun* person who acts unfairly in order to win; *I won't play cards with him again, he's a cheat* **2** *verb* **(a)** to act unfairly in order to be successful; *they don't let him play any more since they found he was cheating; they are sure he cheated in his exam, but can't find out how he did it* **(b)** to cheat someone out of something = to get something by tricking someone; *he was furious, saying that he had been cheated out of the first prize*

check [tʃek] **1** *noun* **(a)** examination or test; *the police are carrying out checks on all cars; a routine check of the fire equipment*; baggage check = examination of passengers' baggage to see if it contains bombs or other dangerous devices **(b)** *US (in restaurant)* bill; *I'll ask for the check* **(c)** *US see* CHEQUE **(d)** *US* mark on paper to show that something is correct; *make a check in the box marked 'R'* (NOTE: British English is tick) **(e)** in check = under control; *we must keep our spending in check* **(f)** check (pattern) = pattern made of small squares; *the restaurant has red check tablecloths* **2** *verb* **(a)** to make sure; to examine; *I'd better check with the office if there are any messages for me; did you lock the door? - I'll go and check; you must have your car checked every 2,000 miles* **(b)** *US* to mark with a sign to show that something is correct; *check the box marked 'R'* (NOTE: British English is tick)

checkbook ['tʃekbʊk] *see* CHEQUEBOOK

checked [tʃekt] *adjective* with a pattern of small squares; *he was wearing a blue checked shirt*

checkers ['tʃekəz] *noun US see* DRAUGHTS

check in ['tʃek 'ɪn] *verb* **(a)** *(at a hotel)* to arrive at a hotel and sign for a room; *he checked in at 12.15* **(b)** *(at an airport)* to give in your ticket to show you are ready to take the flight; *please check in two hours before your departure time* **(c)** to check baggage in = to pass your baggage to the airline to put it on the plane for you; *my bag hasn't been checked in yet*

check-in ['tʃekɪn] *noun* place where passengers give in their tickets and baggage for a flight; *the check-in is on the first floor; holders of valid tickets can go straight through the check-in;* check-in counter *or* desk = counter where passengers check in; check-in time = time at which passengers should check in

checking account ['tʃekɪŋ ə'kaʊnt] *noun US* bank account on which you can write cheques; *here's your new checkbook for your checking account* (NOTE: British English is cheque account)

checklist ['tʃeklɪst] *noun* list of things which have to be done or dealt with before something can be done; *I must just go through my checklist to see if we have covered all the points I wanted to discuss*

checkmate ['tʃekmeɪt] **1** *noun (in chess)* position at the end of a game where the king cannot move; *that's checkmate!* **2** *verb* **(a)** *(in chess)* to put your opponent's king in a position from which he cannot escape; *she managed to checkmate me for the second game running* (NOTE: also shortened simply to mate) **(b)** to put an opponent into an impossible situation; *if the judiciary manages to checkmate the president, he will have to resign*

check out ['tʃek 'aʊt] *verb* **(a)** *(at a hotel)* to leave and pay for a room; *we will check out before breakfast* **(b)** to take luggage out of safe keeping; *the ticket shows that he checked out his bag at 9.15* **(c)** *US* to verify, to see if something is all right; *I thought I heard a noise in a kitchen - I'll just go and check it out*

checkout ['tʃekaʊt] *noun* **(a)** *(in a supermarket)* cash desk where you pay for the goods you have bought; *there were huge queues at the checkouts* **(b)** *(in a hotel)* checkout time is 12.00 = time by which you have to leave your room

checkpoint ['tʃekpɔɪnt] *noun* place on a road where the police or army check cars and people passing; *the guerillas managed to get through three army checkpoints before they were recognized*

checkroom ['tʃekruːm] *noun US* place where you leave your coat in a restaurant, theatre, etc.; *I left my coat and briefcase in the checkroom* (NOTE: British English for this is **cloakroom**)

check up on ['tʃek 'ʌp ɒn] *verb* to make sure that something has been done correctly; *I'll just check up on today's sales figures, since there was a mistake yesterday*

checkup ['tʃekʌp] *noun* **(a)** test to see if someone is fit; general examination by a doctor or dentist; *he had a heart checkup last week; he made an appointment with the dentist for a checkup* **(b)** general examination of a machine; *I'm taking the car to the garage for its six-monthly checkup*

Cheddar ['tʃedə] *noun* smooth hard light yellow cheese, originally from a village of this name in the west of England; *have a piece of Cheddar cheese and brown bread; Cheddar is traditionally made in Somerset*

cheek [tʃiːk] *noun* **(a)** fat part of the face on either side of the nose and below the eye; *a baby with red cheeks; see also* TONGUE **(b)** *(informal)* rudeness; *he had the cheek to ask for more money* (NOTE: no plural in this sense)

cheekbone ['tʃiːkbəʊn] *noun* bone which forms the prominent part of the cheek and the lower part of the eye socket; *she has very high cheekbones*

cheeky ['tʃiːki] *adjective* rude; *don't be cheeky to the teacher; it was a bit cheeky of him to come to the lunch without being asked* (NOTE: **cheekier - cheekiest**)

cheer ['tʃɪə] **1** *noun* shout of praise or encouragement; *when he scored the goal a great cheer went up;* **three cheers** = three shouts of praise for someone; *three cheers for the goalkeeper! hip! hip! hooray!* **2** *verb* to shout encouragement; *the crowd cheered when the first marathon runners appeared*

cheerful ['tʃɪəfʊl] *adjective* happy; *you're looking very cheerful today; 'hi!' he said in a cheerful voice*

cheerio [tʃɪərɪ'əʊ] *interjection (informal)* goodbye; *she shouted 'cheerio!' as the bus pulled out*

cheerleader ['tʃɪəliːdə] *noun* person who directs the cheering of a crowd; *the cheerleaders came onto the pitch before the start of the game; she's one of the college cheerleaders*

cheers! [tʃɪəz] *interjection (informal)* **(a)** thank you!; *can I help you with your bag? - cheers, mate!* **(b)** *(when drinking)* good health!; *they all lifted their glasses and said 'cheers!'*

cheer up ['tʃɪə 'ʌp] *verb* to become happier; **cheer up!** = don't be miserable!; **to cheer someone up** = to make someone happier; *she made him a good meal to try to cheer him up*

cheery ['tʃɪəri] *adjective* happy; *he's in a very cheery mood these days; she waved and shouted a cheery 'hello'* (NOTE: **cheerier - cheeriest**)

cheese [tʃiːz] *noun* solid food made from milk; *she ordered a cheese omelette and chips; at the end of the meal we'll have biscuits and cheese; can I have a pound of Cheshire cheese, please?;* **cream cheese** = soft white cheese; **blue cheese** = cheese with blue mould in it; *(informal)* **'say cheese!'** = asking people to smile when their photo is being taken; *the photographer got us all in a line and then told us to 'say cheese!'* (NOTE: the plural **cheeses** is only used to mean different types of cheese or several large round whole blocks of cheese; usually there is no plural: **some cheese; a piece of cheese**)

cheeseburger ['tʃiːzbɜːgə] *noun* hamburger with melted cheese on top; *the kids all want cheeseburgers with fries*

cheesecake ['tʃiːzkeɪk] *noun* tart with a sweet pastry base and cooked cream cheese on top, often covered with fruit; *two pieces of blackcurrant cheesecake, please*

cheesed off [tʃiːzd 'ɒf] *adjective (informal)* fed up, annoyed with something; *I'm cheesed off at having all this homework to do*

cheetah ['tʃiːtə] *noun* animal like a small leopard, with black spots on pale fur, which can run faster than any other animal; *the cheetah raced through the grass after the gazelle*

chef [ʃef] *noun* cook in a restaurant; *they've got a new chef at the 'King's Head' and the food is much better;* **chef's special** = special dish, sometimes one which the chef is famous for, which is listed separately on the menu

chemical ['kemɪkl] **1** *adjective* referring to chemistry; *if you add acid it sets up a chemical reaction* **2** *noun* substance which is formed by reactions between elements; *rows of glass bottles containing chemicals; chemicals are widely used in agriculture*

chemist ['kemɪst] *noun* **(a)** person who sells medicines and also prepares them; *ask the chemist to give you something for indigestion;* **the chemist's** = shop where you can buy medicine, toothpaste, soap, etc.; *go to the chemist's and get me some cough medicine* (NOTE: in American English this is usually a **drugstore** or **pharmacy**) **(b)** scientist who studies chemical substances; *he works as a chemist in a nuclear laboratory*

chemistry ['kemɪstri] *noun* **(a)** science of chemical substances and their reactions; *she's studying chemistry at university; he passed his chemistry exam* **(b)** **personal chemistry** = reaction of one person to another; *the personal chemistry of the two leaders was very good* (NOTE: no plural)

chemotherapy ['kiːməʊ'θerəpi] *noun* using chemical drugs to fight a disease, especially using toxic chemicals to destroy rapidly developing cancer cells; *chemotherapy is the only treatment for her cancer; one unpleasant side effect of chemotherapy is loss of hair* (NOTE: no plural)

cheque *US* **check** [tʃek] *noun* note to a bank asking for money to be paid from one account to another; *I paid for the jacket by cheque; he made out the cheque to Mr Smith; he's forgotten to sign the cheque;* **pay cheque** or **salary cheque** = monthly cheque by which an employee is paid; **traveller's**

cheque = cheque which you buy at a bank before you travel and which you can then use in a foreign country; *most shops in the USA accept traveller's cheques*; *the hotel will cash traveller's cheques for you*; *the bank guarantees to replace stolen traveller's cheques* (NOTE: the American spelling is **traveler's checks**)

chequebook *US* **checkbook** ['tʃekbʊk] *noun* set of blank cheques attached together in a cover; *I need a new chequebook*

cherish ['tʃerɪʃ] *verb* (a) to love; to treat kindly; *the two persons he cherished most died during the year*; *she cherished the old ring given to her by her grandmother* (b) to cling on to a hope; *she still cherishes the hope of living in a warmer country*

cherry ['tʃeri] *noun* (a) small sweet red fruit, growing usually in pairs on a tree; *she ate half a pound of cherries*; *a pot of cherry jam* (b) the tree which grows this fruit; *we have a beautiful cherry in the middle of the lawn* (NOTE: plural is **cherries**)

cherry stone ['tʃeri 'stəun] *noun* hard little seed inside a cherry

> COMMENT: when children eat cherries, they count the stones using the old rhyme: 'tinker, tailor, soldier, sailor, rich man, poor man, beggarman, thief'. The name you reach when you have counted all the stones is supposed to show what you will grow up to be when you are an adult

Cheshire ['tʃəʃə] *noun* crumbly white cheese, originally from Cheshire in the North-West of England; *a piece of Cheshire cheese and brown bread*

chess [tʃes] *noun* game for two people played on a board with sixteen pieces on each side; *would you like a game of chess?*; *they played chess all evening* (NOTE: no plural)

> COMMENT: the game is played on a board with 64 black and white squares. Each player has sixteen pieces: eight pawns, two castles *or* rooks, two knights, two bishops, one queen and one king. The object is to capture and remove your opponent's pieces, and finally to put your opponent's king in a position where he cannot move without being captured (checkmate)

chessboard ['tʃesbɔːd] *noun* board with black and white squares used to play chess on; *they opened the chessboard and began to set out the pieces*

chessmen ['tʃesmen] *noun* pieces used in chess; *a beautiful set of chessmen carved from ivory* (NOTE: the pieces are: **king, queen, knights, bishops, castles** *or* **rooks, pawns**)

chest [tʃest] *noun* (a) the top front part of the body, where the heart and lungs are; *if you have pains in your chest or if you have chest pains, you ought to see a doctor*; *the doctor listened to the patient's chest*; *she was rushed to hospital with chest wounds*; *he has a 48-inch chest*; **to get something off your chest** = to speak frankly about a problem (b) piece of furniture, like a large box; *he keeps his old clothes in a chest under the bed*; **chest of drawers** = piece of furniture with several drawers for clothes

chestnut ['tʃesnʌt] *noun* (a) (*trees*) large deciduous tree, with large shiny red-brown seeds; **horse chestnut (tree)** = large tree, with large leaves and spikes of white flowers, and seeds which cannot be eaten but which are used for playing games; *horse chestnuts usually flower*

in May; **sweet chestnut (tree)** = large tree with seeds which can be eaten; *a sweet chestnut may grow to over 30 metres* (b) (*fruit*) **horse chestnut** = large shiny nut from a horse chestnut tree which is not edible; *little boys were picking up chestnuts in the road* (NOTE: also called **conkers**) (c) (*fruit*) **sweet chestnut** = chestnut from a sweet chestnut tree which is edible; *in winter, men stand at street corners selling roasted chestnuts*; **chestnut purée** = cooked sweet chestnuts, mashed with added sugar (and sometimes vanilla), served as a dessert; *a dessert of chestnut purée and whipped cream topped with grated bitter chocolate* (d) wood from the chestnut tree; *a chestnut table* (e) red-brown colour; *she has beautiful long chestnut hair* (f) red-brown horse; *do you know the name of the chestnut that came last?* (g) (*informal*) old joke; *his speech was just a series of not very amusing old chestnuts*

> COMMENT: there are two kinds of chestnut tree: the horse chestnut which is very common in Britain, and has large nuts which cannot be eaten, but which are used in children's games (see CONKER), and the sweet chestnut, which has smaller edible nuts but which does not often produce edible fruit in Britain

chevron ['ʃevrən] *noun* (a) a V shape; *a sign with a white chevron indicates a bend in the road* (b) piece of braid, shaped like a V, sewn on the sleeve of an soldier's uniform to show his rank; *now that he has been promoted he has two gold chevrons on his sleeve*

chew [tʃuː] *verb* to make something soft with your teeth; *you must chew your meat well, or you will get pains in your stomach*; *the dog was lying in front of the fire chewing a bone*

chewing gum ['tʃuːɪŋ gʌm] *noun* sweet gum which you chew but do not swallow; *would you like a piece of chewing gum?*; *I've got some chewing gum stuck under my shoe*

chew up ['tʃuː 'ʌp] *verb* to chew something a lot, to make it soft or to ruin it; *the dog has chewed up my slipper*; *a stone got into the gears and they were all chewed up*

chic [ʃiːk] **1** *adjective* elegant and fashionable; *it's very chic these days to have an all white sports car*; *we took our visitors to a very chic restaurant in Mayfair* **2** *noun* elegance; *her special brand of chic is like no one else's*; **radical chic** = fashionable elegance of rich left-wing people

chick [tʃɪk] *noun* baby bird, especially a baby hen; *the chicks came running along in a line behind the mother hen*

chicken ['tʃɪkɪn] *noun* (a) young hen; *chickens were running everywhere in the farmyard* (b) meat from a hen; *we're having roast chicken for lunch*; *would you like another slice of chicken?*; *we bought some chicken sandwiches for lunch* (NOTE: no plural for this meaning: **some chicken; a piece** *or* **a slice of chicken**)

chicken out ['tʃɪkɪn 'aut] *verb* (*informal*) to decide not to do something because you are scared; *he said he would help us get into the chemist's but chickened out at the last minute*; *he was ready to jump but chickened out at the last minute*

chickenpox ['tʃɪkɪnpɒks] *noun* infectious disease of children, with fever and itchy red spots; *she's in bed with chickenpox*; *he got chickenpox and couldn't go* *to school* (NOTE: the scientific name for chickenpox is **varicella**)

> COMMENT: chickenpox is caused by the same virus as causes shingles. In older people, shingles can develop when a person who has already had chickenpox in the past is in contact with a child who has chickenpox

chide [tʃaɪd] *verb (formal)* to criticize; *he chided his sons for being lazy* (NOTE: **chided** or **chid** [tʃɪd] - has **chided** or **chidden**)

chief [tʃiːf] **1** *adjective* most important; *he's the chief planner in the local authority*; *what is the chief cause of air accidents?* **2** *noun* **(a)** person in charge in a group of people or in a business; *he's been made the new chief of our department*; *the fire chief warned that the building was dangerous* **(b)** the leader of a tribe; *all the chiefs came together at a meeting*; *(informal)* **too many chiefs and not enough Indians** = situation where there are too many managers, but not enough people to do the actual work

Chief Constable ['tʃiːf 'kʌnstəbl] *noun* person in charge of a police force; *the Chief Constable made an appeal for witnesses to come forward*

Chief Justice ['tiːf 'dʒʌstɪs] *noun US* main judge in a court, including the main judge in the Supreme Court; *the ruling of the Chief Justice was widely criticized*

chiefly ['tʃiːfli] *adverb* mainly; *our town is famous chiefly for its pork pies*

Chief of Staff ['tʃiːf əv 'stɑːf] *noun* **(a)** high ranking officer who assists an officer who is in command; *he was Chief of Staff to the general during the battle* **(b)** main assistant or adviser to someone who has an important post; *the president's Chief of Staff*

chieftain ['tʃiːftən] *noun* leader of a tribe; *the traders brought presents for the chieftains*

chiffon ['ʃɪfɒn] *noun* type of very thin and light silk material; *she wore a very elegant dark blue chiffon dress*

chilblain ['tʃɪlbleɪn] *noun* condition where the skin on your fingers, toes, nose or ears becomes swollen and itchy, caused by the cold; *she got chilblains on her feet*

child [tʃaɪld] *noun* **(a)** young boy or girl; *there was no TV when my mother was a child*; *here is a photograph of the Prime Minister as a child*; *a group of children were playing on the beach*; **child's play** = something which is very easy; *flying a kite may look like child's play, but it's not as easy as it looks* **(b)** son or daughter; *whose child is that?*; *how many children have they got?*; *they have six children - two boys and four girls* (NOTE: plural is **children** ['tʃɪldrən])

childbearing ['tʃaɪldbeərɪŋ] *noun* giving birth to a child; *45 is considered the upper age limit for childbearing*

child benefit ['tʃaɪld 'benɪfɪt] *noun* money given by the government to the parents of young children; *there is a proposal to increase child benefit for families with low incomes*

childbirth ['tʃaɪldbɜːθ] *noun* act of giving birth to a child; *fortunately, death in childbirth is very uncommon nowadays*; **natural childbirth** = giving birth where the mother is not given any pain-killing drugs or anaesthetic; *pregnant women can attend natural childbirth classes*

childcare ['tʃaɪldkeə] *noun* care of young children; *childcare provision must answer not only the needs of children but also the needs of parents*

childhood ['tʃaɪldhʊd] *noun* time when someone is a child; *he spent his childhood in the country*; *she had a happy childhood living on a farm in Canada*; *she's had all the usual childhood diseases - mumps, measles, chickenpox, etc.*

childish ['tʃaɪldɪʃ] *adjective* like a child; silly or foolish; *it was a bit childish of her to start to cry when the boss told her off*

childless ['tʃaɪldləs] *adjective* with no children; *the couple remained childless*; *childless couples don't always enjoy listening to their friends rabbitting on about their children*

childlike ['tʃaɪldlaɪk] *adjective* innocent like a child; *she has a childlike trust in the bank manager*

childminder ['tʃaɪldmaɪndə] *noun* person who looks after children while the parents are working; *do you know of a good childminder who could look after my little girl from time to time?*

> COMMENT: a childminder usually takes the children into her own home, often in the daytime, while a babysitter stays in the house where the child lives, usually in the evening while the parents are at the cinema, a party, etc.

Chile ['tʃɪli] *noun* country in South America, to the west of Argentina (NOTE: capital: **Santiago**; people: **Chileans**; language: **Spanish**; currency: **Chilean peso**)

Chilean ['tʃɪliən] **1** *adjective* referring to Chile **2** *noun* person from Chile

chill [tʃɪl] **1** *noun* **(a)** illness caused by cold; *you'll catch a chill if you don't wear a coat* **(b)** coldness; *the sun came up and soon cleared away the morning chill* **(c)** atmosphere of gloom; *the death of the bride's father cast a chill over the wedding* **2** *verb* to cool; *he asked for a glass of chilled orange juice*; *(informal)* **chilled to the bone** = very cold; *they were chilled to the bone when they came back from their walk over the moors*

chilli *US* **chili** ['tʃɪli] *noun* dried seed pod of a type of pepper plant, used to make very hot sauces; *you can spice up the dish by adding extra chillies or some chilli powder*; **chilli con carne** = Mexican dish of meat and beans cooked in a hot chilli sauce (NOTE: do not confuse with **chilly**)

chilling ['tʃɪlɪŋ] *adjective* frightening; *a chilling tale of torture and killing*

chilly ['tʃɪli] *adjective* quite cold; *even summer evenings can be chilly in the mountains* (NOTE: **chillier - chilliest**)

chime [tʃaɪm] **1** *noun* ringing of bells; *the chimes of the church bells woke me up* **2** *verb (of bells)* to ring; *the clock has just chimed four*

chimney ['tʃɪmni] *noun* tall brick column for taking smoke away from a fire; *the house has two tall chimneys*; *if you look up the chimney in an old house you can see the sky*; *(informal)* **he smokes like a chimney** = he smokes cigarettes all the time

chimney pot ['tʃɪmni 'pɒt] *noun* round pottery tube on top of a chimney; *from the windows of my flat, I look out over all the chimney pots of north London*

chimpanzee *(informal)* **chimp** [tʃɪmpæn'ziː or tʃɪmp] *noun* type of African ape; *children love watching the chimpanzees at the zoo*

chin [tʃɪn] *noun* front part of the bottom jaw; *she suddenly stood up and hit him on the chin*; **to keep your chin up** = to stay confident; *even if everything seems to be going wrong, try to keep your chin up!*

china ['tʃaɪnə] *noun* cups, plates, etc., made of fine white clay; *she got out her best china tea-set because she had visitors*; *a china cup and saucer*; *all our china was broken when we moved house* (NOTE: no plural)

China ['tʃaɪnə] *noun* very large country in Asia; *we went to China on business last year*; *visitors to China always go to see the Great Wall* (NOTE: capital: **Beijing**; people: **the Chinese**; language: **Chinese**; currency: **renminbi** *or* **yuan**)

Chinese [tʃaɪ'niːz] **1** *adjective* referring to China; *her husband is Chinese*; *we often go to a Chinese restaurant in the evening* **2** *noun* **(a)** person from China; *the Chinese are very good at mathematics* (NOTE: plural is **Chinese**) **(b)** language spoken in China; *she has been taking Chinese lessons for some weeks*; *the book has been translated into Chinese*

chink [tʃɪŋk] **1** *noun* **(a)** very small hole or crack; *even a tiny chink in the curtains will let light into the darkroom* **(b)** little noise of pieces of something hard hitting each other; *the chink of glasses on the waiter's tray* **2** *verb* to make a little noise; *we could hear the ice cubes chinking as she carried the tray of drinks over to us*

chip [tʃɪp] **1** *noun* **(a)** long thin piece of potato fried in oil; *he ordered chicken and chips and a glass of beer*; **fish and chips** = traditional British food, obtained from special shops, where portions of fish fried in batter are sold with chips; *we're having fish and chips for dinner*; **fish-and-chip shop** = shop selling cooked fish and chips, and usually other food, such as pies (NOTE: in the USA, chips are called **French fries**. Note also that a fish-and-chip shop can also be called a **chip shop**, or, informally, a **chippy**) **(b)** *US* thin slice of potato, fried till crisp and eaten cold as a snack; *he ordered a beer and a packet of chips* (NOTE: In British English, this is called a **crisp**) **(c)** small piece of something hard, such as wood or stone; *chips of stone flew all over the studio as he was carving the statue*; **chocolate chip** = small piece of hard chocolate, used in ice cream, biscuits or cakes; *chocolate chip biscuit*; *mint chocolate chip ice cream;* **(d) a computer chip** = a small piece of silicon able to store data, used in a computer; *computer chip manufacturers are doing very well* **(e) a chip on your shoulder** = a feeling of being constantly annoyed with someone; *he's got a chip on his shoulder because his brother has a better job than he has* **(f)** counter, piece of plastic or metal which stands in for money in gambling; *the croupier raked the chips across the board*; *(informal)* **when the chips are down** = when the situation is serious and important decisions have to be made **2** *verb* to break a small piece off something hard; *he banged the cup down on the plate and chipped it* (NOTE: **chipping - chipped**)

chipboard ['tʃɪpbɔːd] *noun* thick board made of small chips of wood glued together, used in carpentry; *these walls are not solid, they're only made of chipboard* (NOTE: no plural; for one piece say **a sheet of chipboard, a piece of chipboard**)

chippings ['tʃɪpɪŋz] *noun* small bits of stone used with tar to make road surfaces; **loose chippings** = little bits of stone which are left on the surface of a newly made road, and which can fly up and hit passing cars

chippy ['tʃɪpi] *(informal)* = CARPENTER, FISH-AND-CHIP SHOP (NOTE: plural is **chippies**)

chisel ['tʃɪzl] **1** *noun* metal tool for cutting small pieces of wood or stone, when hit with a hammer; *the stone carver tapped the chisel very carefully with his hammer* **2** *verb* **(a)** to cut wood or stone with a chisel; *we watched the sculptor chiselling away at the piece of stone* **(b)** *(old) (informal)* to swindle; *he chiselled the old lady out of all her savings* (NOTE: British spelling is **chiselling - chiselled** and American spelling is **chiseling - chiseled**)

chitchat ['tʃɪttʃæt] *noun* gossip, talk about things which aren't important; *having dinner with the boss means listening to all sorts of office chitchat*

chives [tʃaɪvz] *noun* herb of which the leaves are used as a garnish or in soups or salads; *chives have a flavour similar to that of mild onions*; *add some chives to your salad* (NOTE: a plural noun; there is no singular)

chloride ['klɔːraɪd] *noun* compound of chlorine and another substance; *common salt is sodium chloride*

chlorine ['klɔːriːn] *noun* powerful greenish gas, used to sterilize water and to bleach; *the smell of chlorine hits you as you open the door to the swimming pool* (NOTE: Chemical element: chemical symbol: **Cl**; atomic number: **17**)

chlorofluorocarbon [klɔːrəʊfluərəʊ'kɑːbən] *see* CFC

chlorophyll ['klɒrəfɪl] *noun* green pigment in plants; *chlorophyll is found in all green plants*

chock-a-block ['tʃɒkəblɒk] *adjective* completely full; *trains going to the seaside were chock-a-block at the beginning of the holidays*

chocolate ['tʃɒklət] *noun* **(a)** sweet brown food made from the crushed seeds of a tropical tree; *can I buy a bar of chocolate?*; *her mother made a chocolate cake*; **dark chocolate** *or* **plain chocolate** = dark brown chocolate which is quite bitter; **milk chocolate** = light brown sweet chocolate **(b)** a single sweet made from chocolate; *there are only three chocolates left in the box*; *who's eaten the last chocolate?* **(c)** drink made from chocolate powder and milk; *I always have a cup of hot chocolate before I go to bed* **(d)** dark brown colour, like chocolate; *we have a chocolate-coloured carpet in the sitting room* (NOTE: no plural, except for meaning (b))

choice [tʃɔɪs] **1** *noun* **(a)** thing which is chosen; *Paris was our first choice for our honeymoon* **(b)** act of choosing something; *you must give the customer time to make his choice* **(c)** range of items to choose from; *the store has a huge choice of furniture*; **I hadn't any choice** *or* **I had no choice** = there was nothing else I could do **2** *adjective* specially selected food; *choice meat*; *choice peaches*

choir ['kwaɪə] *noun* group of people who sing together; *he sings in the church choir*

choke [tʃəʊk] **1** *noun* **(a)** *(in a car engine)* valve which increases the flow of air to the engine; knob on the dashboard which makes this valve work; *you need to pull out the choke to start the car*; *this model has an automatic choke* **2** *verb* **(a)** to block a pipe, etc.; *the canal was choked with weeds* **(b)** to stop breathing properly because you have swallowed something into your windpipe; *don't talk with your mouth full or you'll choke*; *he choked on a piece of bread or a piece of bread made him choke*

cholera ['kɒlerə] *noun* serious bacterial disease spread through infected food or water; *he caught cholera while on holiday*; *a cholera epidemic broke out after the flood*

cholesterol [kɒ'lesterɒl] *noun* fatty substance found in fats and oils, also produced by the liver and forming an essential part of all cells; *eggs are high in cholesterol*

COMMENT: excess cholesterol can be deposited on the walls of arteries, causing them to become blocked

choose [tʃuːz] *verb* (a) to pick something which you like best; *have you chosen what you want to eat?*; *they chose him as team leader*; *don't take too long choosing a book to read on holiday*; *there were several good candidates to choose from*; *you must give customers plenty of time to choose* (b) to decide to do one thing when there are several things you could do; *in the end, they chose to go to the cinema* (NOTE: choosing - chose [tʃəʊz] - has chosen ['tʃəʊzn])

choosing ['tʃuːzɪŋ] *noun* act of making a choice; *the menu is so large it makes choosing very difficult*

choosy ['tʃuːzi] *adjective* (*informal*) difficult to please; *my mother is very choosy and won't stay in any hotel she has not inspected herself*

chop [tʃɒp] 1 *noun* piece of meat with a rib bone; *we had lamb chops for dinner* 2 *verb* (a) to cut into small pieces with an axe or knife; *chop the vegetables up into little pieces*; *he spent the afternoon chopping wood for the fire* (b) **to chop and change** = to do one thing, then another; *he keeps chopping and changing and can't make his mind up* (NOTE: chopping - chopped)

chop down ['tʃɒp 'daʊn] *verb* to cut down a tree, etc., with an axe; *they chopped down hundreds of trees to make the motorway*

chop off ['tʃɒp 'ɒf] *verb* to cut off with an axe or knife, etc.; *he chopped off the dead branch*; *the table was too high for the children, so we chopped 6cm off the legs*

chopper ['tʃɒpə] *noun* (a) axe, especially one for cutting meat; *a butcher armed with a chopper was cutting up carcases* (b) (*informal*) helicopter; *a chopper landed in the middle of the motorway to pick up the accident victims*

chopsticks ['tʃɒpstɪks] *noun* pair of small sticks used in the Far East to eat food or to stir food when cooking; *he said he didn't know how to use chopsticks and asked for a knife and fork instead*

choral ['kɔːrəl] *adjective* referring to a choir; *he has hundreds of CDs of choral music*; *the choral society is giving a concert next week*

chord [kɔːd] *noun* (a) several notes played together in harmony; *he sat down at the piano and played a few chords* (b) line which joins two points on a curve; *draw a chord across this circle* (NOTE: do not confuse with cord)

chore [tʃɔː] *noun* piece of routine work, especially housework; *it's a real chore, having to save all our computer files every day*; *she detests having to do the usual household chores*

choreographer [kɒrɪ'ɒgrəfə] *noun* person who works out the steps for a ballet; *many young dancers attended the ceremony because their choreographer was receiving a prize*

choreography [kɒrɪ'ɒgrəfi] *noun* art of arranging the steps for a ballet; *the choreography is by a young Russian choreographer*

chorus ['kɔːrəs] 1 *noun* (a) group of people who sing together; *all the members of the chorus were on the stage* (b) part of a song which is repeated later in the song; *I'll sing the verses and everyone can join in the chorus* (NOTE: plural is choruses) 2 *verb* to say something all together; *there was a knock at the door and they both chorused 'come in'*

chose, chosen [tʃəʊz or 'tʃəʊzn] *see* CHOOSE

chowder ['tʃaʊdə] *noun* US type of American soup, made of fish, milk and vegetables; *a bowl of lobster chowder or clam chowder is a meal in itself*

Christ [kraɪst] 1 *noun* Jesus Christ, the person on whose life and teachings the Christian religion is based 2 *interjection* (*informal*) showing annoyance; *Christ! it's eight o'clock already and I haven't started cooking dinner*

christen ['krɪsn] *verb* (a) to give a name to a Christian baby in church; *she was christened Natasha* (b) to give a name to something; *she was christened the 'Iron Lady' by the press* (c) (*informal*) to use something for the first time; *come and help us christen our new set of champagne glasses*

christening ['krɪsnɪŋ] *noun* ceremony in church where a baby is given a name; *the christening will take place in the village church*

Christian ['krɪstʃn] 1 *noun* person who believes in the teaching of Christ and in Christianity; *the early Christians were victims of the Roman emperors* 2 *adjective* referring to the teachings of Jesus Christ; *there are several Christian churches in the town*; *she practises all the Christian virtues*

Christianity [krɪstɪ'ænɪti] *noun* religion based on the doctrine preached by Jesus Christ and followed by Christians ever since; *the course on religious studies covers Christianity, Judaism and Islam*

Christian name ['krɪstʃn 'neɪm] *noun* a person's first name, the special name given to someone as a child after birth or at baptism; *I know his surname's Smith, but what's his Christian name?*

Christmas ['krɪsməs] *noun* Christian festival on December 25th, the birthday of Jesus Christ; *have you opened your Christmas presents yet?*; *we're going to my grandfather's for Christmas Day*; **what did you get for Christmas?** = what presents were you given?; **Christmas cake** = special fruit cake eaten at Christmas time; **Christmas card** = special card sent to friends at Christmas to wish them a happy time; **Christmas pudding** = special pudding eaten at Christmas time; **Christmas stockings** = large coloured stockings, which children hang up by their beds or under the Christmas tree, and which are filled with presents by Father Christmas; **Christmas tree** = fir tree which is brought into the house at Christmas and decorated with coloured lights and ornaments; **Father Christmas** = man in a long red coat, with a big white beard, who is supposed to bring presents to children on Christmas Day; **Happy Christmas!** or **Merry Christmas!** = way of greeting someone on Christmas Day

Christmas Eve ['krɪstməs 'iːv] *noun* **(a)** 24th December, the day before Christmas Day; *the office is closed on Christmas Eve* **(b)** the evening of the 24th December; *a Christmas Eve party*

chrome [krəʊm] *noun* **(a)** alloy of chromium and other metals, used to give a shiny silver surface; *a 1960s chair with chrome legs and a plastic seat* **(b) chrome yellow** = bright yellow

chromium ['krəʊmiəm] *noun* metallic trace element used to make alloys such as steel; *chromium-plated bicycle handlebars* (NOTE: Chemical element: chemical symbol: **Cr**; atomic number: **24**)

chromosome ['krəʊməsəʊm] *noun* rod-shaped structure in the nucleus of a cell, formed of DNA which carries the genes; *each human cell has 46 chromosomes, 23 inherited from each parent*

chronic ['krɒnɪk] *adjective* **(a)** continual, repeating (illness, etc.); *she has chronic bronchitis; chronic asthma sufferers need to use special drugs* **(b)** always very bad; *we have a chronic shortage of skilled staff*

chronicle ['krɒnɪkl] **1** *noun* record of things which take place; *he wrote a chronicle of the war* **2** *verb* to write the history of events in the order in which they took place; *he has started interviewing local old people to chronicle the history of the village*

chronological [krɒnə'lɒdʒɪkl] *adjective* **chronological order** = arrangement of records (files, invoices, etc.) in order of their dates; *put the invoices in chronological order; the battles are listed in chronological order*

chronologically [krɒnə'lɒdʒɪkli] *adverb* in chronological order; *the important dates in the history of the village are listed chronologically at the back of the book*

chronology [krɒ'nɒlədʒi] *noun* the order in which things happened; *these are the events I can remember from my childhood, but I am not sure of their chronology*

chronometer [krə'nɒmɪtə] *noun* very accurate watch, as used for timing scientifically; *a ship's chronometer*

chrysalis ['krɪsəlɪs] *noun* an insect when it is covered with a hard case as it changes from a grub or caterpillar to a butterfly or moth; *the butterfly spends the winter in the chrysalis stage, and emerges when the weather becomes warm* (NOTE: plural is **chrysalises;** also called a **pupa**)

chrysanthemum [krɪ'sænθəməm] *noun* type of autumn flower with many small petals; *a pot of yellow chrysanthemums*

chubby ['tʃʌbi] *adjective* pleasantly fat; *at eight months, the little girl was quite chubby; the baby has chubby red cheeks* (NOTE: **chubbier - chubbiest**)

chuck [tʃʌk] **1** *noun* part of a drill which holds the bit; *he released the chuck and put in a bigger bit* **2** *verb* (*informal*) to throw; *chuck me that newspaper, can you?; she chucked the book out of the window*

chuckle ['tʃʌkl] **1** *noun* quiet laugh; *we all had a good chuckle over the chairman's speech* **2** *verb* to give a quiet laugh; *he chuckled when she said she wanted a good steady job*

chug [tʃʌg] *verb* to make a regular noise like an engine; *once on the train, you chug along through the countryside for an hour or so; the typhoon warning*

was soon followed by the sound of boats chugging towards the shelter of the harbour (NOTE: **chugging - chugged**)

chum [tʃʌm] *noun* (*informal*) friend; *he's an old school chum of mine*

chunk [tʃʌŋk] *noun* large thick piece; *they tore off chunks of bread and crammed them into their mouths*

chunky ['tʃʌŋki] *adjective* made of large or thick pieces; *that chunky jumper makes her look fatter; the salad contained chunky bits of chicken; chunky earrings don't suit her* (NOTE: **chunkier - chunkiest**)

church [tʃɜːtʃ] *noun* building where Christians go to pray; *we usually go to church on Sunday mornings; the oldest building in the village is St Mary's Church; the times of the church services are given on the board outside* (NOTE: plural is **churches**)

churchman ['tʃɜːtʃmən] *noun* a priest, especially in the Anglican church; *several churchmen voiced their criticism of the proposed government legislation* (NOTE: plural is **churchmen**)

Church of England (C of E) ['tʃɜːtʃ əv 'ɪŋlənd] *noun* the Protestant church which is the official religion of England, with the Queen as its head (NOTE: also called the **Anglican Church**)

churchyard ['tʃɜːtʃjɑːd] *noun* cemetery round a church; *the family and friends gathered in the churchyard for the burial*

churn [tʃɜːn] **1** *noun* large metal container for milk; *churns of fresh milk were lined up at the farm entrance waiting to be picked up* **2** *verb* **(a)** to turn cream to make butter; *do you know of any farm where butter is still churned by hand?* **(b)** to buy and sell shares on someone's behalf, not to make money for that person, but to earn commission for yourself; *few small investors realize how much money they lose through churning*

chute [ʃuːt] *noun* **(a)** slide into water in a swimming pool; *the kids screamed as they slid down the chute into the pool* **(b)** slide to send things down to a lower level; *the parcels are wrapped and labelled and then sent down a chute to where the delivery vans are waiting*

chutney ['tʃʌtni] *noun* highly-flavoured sauce usually made with tomatoes, onions, vinegar and spices; *we bought some homemade tomato chutney at the stall in the market*

CIA [siːaɪ'eɪ] *abbreviation for* CENTRAL INTELLIGENCE AGENCY

CID [siːaɪ'diː] *abbreviation for* CRIMINAL INVESTIGATION DEPARTMENT

cider ['saɪdə] *noun* alcoholic drink made from fermented apple juice; *Somerset and Devon are famous for their cider; in France, cider is served with pancakes*

cigar [sɪ'gɑː] *noun* tight roll of dried tobacco leaves which you can light and smoke; *I like the smell of cigar smoke; he smoked a large cigar after his meal*

cigarette [sɪgə'ret] *noun* chopped dried tobacco rolled in very thin paper which you can light and smoke; *a packet or pack of cigarettes; he's trying to cut down on the number of cigarettes he smokes; the room was full of cigarette smoke;* **cigarette machine** = machine which sells packets of cigarettes when you put the right money in; *have you any change for the cigarette machine?*

ciggy ['sɪgɪ] *noun (informal)* = CIGARETTE

cinders ['sɪndəz] *noun* lumps of coarse ash left after coal has been burnt; *they used cinders from the furnace to make a path*; **burnt to a cinder** = burnt black in cooking; *I forgot my pie and it was burnt to a cinder* (NOTE: usually plural, except in the example above)

cinder track ['sɪndə 'træk] *noun* race track made with cinders; *she achieved a record time on the university's new cinder track*

cine-camera ['sɪnɪkæmrə] *noun* camera for making moving films; *I bought a camcorder to replace my old cine-camera*

cinema ['sɪnəmə] *noun* building where you go to watch films; *we went to the cinema on Friday night*; **what's on at the cinema this week?** = which film is being shown? (NOTE: American English for this is **movie theater**)

cinematic [sɪnɪ'mætɪk] *adjective* referring to films and the cinema; *the cinematic output of Hollywood*

cinematography [sɪnənə'tɒgrəfɪ] *noun* making films; *he is following a cinematography course at college*

cinnamon ['sɪnəmən] *noun* spice made from the inner bark of a tropical tree; *add a pinch of ground cinnamon to the apple pie*; *add a cinnamon stick to the hot wine*; *cinnamon toast is a favourite of American children*

cipher ['saɪfə] *noun (a)* code, secret language for sending messages; *they sent the message in cipher*; **cipher clerk** = person whose job is to send or receive messages written in cipher *(b)* monogram, initials of a name linked together artistically; *the cipher H+A (for Henry and Anne) is used as decoration in parts of Hampton Court Palace*

circa ['sɜːkə] *preposition (used of dates)* about; *the event took place circa 1560* (NOTE: usually written **ca.**)

circle ['sɜːkl] **1** *noun (a)* line forming a round shape; *he drew a circle on the blackboard (b)* thing forming a round shape; *the children sat in a circle round the teacher*; *the soldiers formed a circle round the prisoner (c)* group of people or society; *she went to live abroad and lost contact with her old circle of friends*; *he moves in the highest government circles* **2** *verb* to go round in a ring; *vultures were circling above the dead antelope; compare* ENCIRCLE

circuit ['sɜːkɪt] *noun (a)* trip around something; *his first circuit of the track was very slow (b)* path of electricity; *he's designed a circuit for a burglar alarm*; **printed circuit board (PCB)** = card with metal tracks printed or etched on it, which forms a connection when other electronic elements are fitted onto it; **short circuit** = electrical fault where two wires touch or where the electric current passes through another channel; *the fallen pylon caused a short circuit that blacked out half the town; see also* CLOSED-CIRCUIT TV

circuitous [sə'kjuːɪtəs] *adjective* **circuitous route** = way which takes much longer than usual; *the taxi took me on some circuitous route through the East End*

circular ['sɜːkjʊlə] **1** *adjective* round in shape; *a circular table* **2** *noun* publicity leaflet; *the restaurant sent round a circular offering a 10% discount*

circularize ['sɜːkjʊlərauz] *verb* to send circulars to people; *the members of the committee were all circularized about the meeting*

circular saw ['sɜːkjʊlə 'sɔː] *noun* electric saw with a round blade; *he used a circular saw to cut down the tree*

circulate ['sɜːkjʊleɪt] *verb (a)* to send round to various people; *they circulated a new list of prices to all their customers (b)* to move round; *blood circulates round the body*; *waiters circulated round the room carrying trays of drinks (c) (informal)* to go round a party, talking to people; *I'll talk later - I've got to circulate*

circulation [sɜːkjʊ'leɪʃn] *noun (a)* act of circulating; *the circulation of the new price list to all departments will take several days*; **banknotes which are in circulation** = notes which have been issued and are in use *(b)* movement of blood round the body; *rub your hands together to get the circulation going*; *he has poor circulation (c)* number of copies of a magazine, newspaper, etc., which are sold; *the new editor hopes to increase the circulation*

circumcise ['sɜːkəmsaɪz] *verb* to remove the foreskin from a boy's penis; *in this country, baby boys are not usually circumcised*; *the Jewish law requires that all baby boys be circumcised*

circumcision [sɜːkəm'sɪʒn] *noun* act of removing the foreskin; *circumcision, which was usually performed for religious and ethnic reasons, may now be required for medical reasons*

circumference [sə'kʌmfərəns] *noun* distance round the outside edge of a circle; *you can calculate the circumference of a circle by multiplying the radius by 2π; a sphere with a circumference of 5m*

circumflex ['sɜːkʌmfleks] *noun* accent like an upside down 'v' placed over certain vowels; *the word 'fête' has a circumflex over the 'e'*

circumstances ['sɜːkəmstənsɪz] *noun (a)* way in which something happened; *he described the circumstances leading up to the accident*; *she died in very suspicious circumstances*; **in the circumstances** *or* **under the circumstances** = as this is the case; *under the circumstances, it would probably be wiser to cancel the meeting (b)* state of your finances; *she's been in difficult circumstances since the death of her husband* (NOTE: usually used in the plural)

circumvent [sɜːkəm'vent] *verb* to avoid; *he tried to circumvent the law, and ended up in prison*

circus ['sɜːkəs] *noun (a)* travelling show, often given under a large tent, with animals, clowns, etc.; *we went to the circus last night*; *the circus is coming to town for the bank holiday weekend (b)* busy road junction in the centre of a large town; *Oxford Circus is where Oxford Street crosses Regent Street* (NOTE: plural is **circuses**)

cistern ['sɪstən] *noun* large tank for water; *we have a cold water cistern in our loft*

citadel ['sɪtədəl] *noun (a)* fort guarding a town; *there is a magnificent view over the harbour from the ramparts of the citadel (b)* place where something is kept safely; *Rome is renowned as the citadel of Catholicism*

citation [saɪ'teɪʃn] *noun (a)* words used in giving someone an award or honour explaining why the award is being made; *he received a posthumous citation for* *bravery* **(b)** *US* quotation from a text; *the citation comes from a medical journal* **(c)** official request asking someone to appear in court; *he received a citation to appear before the court on May 10th*

cite [saɪt] *verb* **(a)** to quote a reference, a person, etc., as proof; *she cited several passages from his latest book* **(b)** to call someone to appear in court; *he was cited to appear before the magistrates*

citizen ['sɪtɪzən] *noun* **(a)** person who comes from a certain country or has the same right to live there as someone who was born there; *all Australian citizens have a duty to vote*; *he was born in Germany, but is now a British citizen*; **senior citizen** = old retired person **(b)** person who comes from a certain city; *the citizens of London complained about their taxes*

citizenship ['sɪtɪzənʃɪp] *noun* state of being a citizen; *she has been granted British citizenship*

citrus ['sɪtrəs] *noun* **citrus fruit** = edible fruit, such as oranges, lemons, grapefruit and limes; *oranges, lemons, grapefruit and limes are all citrus fruits*; **citrus trees** = evergreen trees, grown throughout the tropics and subtropics, with sharp-tasting juicy fruit; *the citrus orchards of California*

city ['sɪti] *noun* **(a)** large town; *walking around the hot city streets can be very exhausting*; *which is the largest city in Germany?*; *traffic is a problem in big cities*; **the city centre** = the central part of a town; *he has an office in the city centre* (NOTE: plural is **cities**) **(b) the City** = the main financial district in London; *he works in the City*

city hall ['sɪti 'hɔːl] *noun* (especially *US*) town hall, the building where the offices of a town council are; *the city hall is a splendid old building in the centre of the town*

civic ['sɪvɪk] *adjective* referring to a city; *we must try to encourage a sense of civic pride*; **civic centre** = building with social and sports facilities for a town; **civic authorities** = the mayor and town council, and directors of municipal departments

civil ['sɪvl] *adjective* **(a)** belonging to the general public and not to the armed forces; **civil aviation** = flying commercial or passenger planes, not war planes; *he left the air force and went into civil aviation*; **civil engineer** = person who builds roads, bridges, etc. **(b)** referring to ordinary people; *there have been civil disturbances in the provinces again today*; **civil defence** = defence of a country by ordinary civilians; **civil law** = laws relating to people's rights and agreements between individuals (NOTE: the opposite, laws relating to crimes against the law of the land punished by the state, is **criminal law**); **civil rights** = rights of an ordinary citizen; *she's a well-known campaigner for civil rights*; **civil rights movement** = campaign for equal rights for all citizens **(c)** polite; *she wasn't very civil to the policeman*; **please keep a civil tongue in your head** = please be polite

civilian [sɪ'vɪljən] **1** *adjective* not in the armed forces; *both the military and civilian personnel will be involved*; *the civilian population was advised to take shelter in their cellars* **2** *noun* ordinary private citizen who is not in the armed forces; *it is certain that ordinary civilians will be affected by the war*; *many civilians were killed in the air raids*

civility [sɪ'vɪlɪti] *noun* (*formal*) behaving in a polite way; *they showed us every civility when we came to see them* (NOTE: plural is **civilities**)

civilization [sɪvɪlaɪ'zeɪʃn] *noun* civilized society or civilized way of organizing society; *the civilization of Ancient Greece*; *she is studying Chinese art and civilization*

civilize ['sɪvɪlaɪz] *verb* **(a)** to educate a primitive people to a higher level of society; *missionaries went out with the purpose of civilizing the African tribes* **(b)** to make someone less rude or less uncouth; *we hope that once they are married, she will civilize him a bit*

civilized ['sɪvɪlaɪzd] *adjective* **(a)** organized to a high level of social behaviour; *how can a civilized nation still maintain the death penalty?* **(b)** pleasant; *we had a very civilized evening, chatting over a good meal*; *try to greet my parents in a civilized manner if you can*; *it's so good to be in civilized company again after a day at school*

civil liberties ['sɪvɪl 'lɪbətiz] *noun* freedom of ordinary people to act within the law (liberty of the press, liberty of the individual, etc.); *a campaign to extend civil liberties*; *security cameras on buildings can be seen as an infringement of civil liberties*

civil service [sɪvɪl 'sɜːvɪs] *noun* organization and personnel which administer a country; *you have to pass an examination to get a job in the civil service or to get a civil service job; see COMMENT below*

civil servant ['sɪvɪl 'sɜːvənt] *noun* person who works in a government department; *as a government translator I am considered to be a civil servant*

COMMENT: the words 'civil service' and 'civil servant' only refer to government or local government departments. People such as teachers, lawyers, policemen, soldiers, etc., although they are paid by the government, do not consider themselves to be 'civil servants'. This is different from the situation in many other countries

civil war ['sɪvɪl 'wɔː] *noun* war between citizens inside a country

COMMENT: the English Civil War, from around 1642 to 1651, was fought between supporters of the King (Charles I) and the supporters of Parliament, one of whose leaders was Oliver Cromwell. The king was captured, tried and executed in 1649, and Cromwell took the title of Lord Protector. The members of the King's party were called Cavaliers, and the supporters of the Parliament were called Roundheads because they wore their hair cut short. The American Civil war of 1861 to 1865 was fought when eleven Southern states seceded from the Union (i.e. from the United States) and fought against the North under President Lincoln

clad [klæd] *adjective* **(a)** wearing; *the soldiers were clad in winter greatcoats*; *a group of leather-clad dancers* **(b)** covered with; *the snow-clad fields*; *a white stucco-clad house*

claim [kleɪm] **1** *noun* **(a)** asking for money; *his claim for a pay increase was turned down*; **wage claim** = asking for an increase in wages **(b)** statement; *his claim that the car belonged to him was correct* **(c)** demand for money against an insurance policy; *after the floods, insurance companies received hundreds of claims*; **no claims bonus** = lower insurance premium paid because no claims have been made against the insurance policy; *it's not worth making a small claim as you'll lose your* *no-claims bonus*; **to put in** *or* **to submit a claim** = to ask the insurance company officially to pay damages; *to put in a claim for repairs to the car*; *she submitted a claim for £250,000 damages against the driver of the other car* **2** *verb* **(a)** to demand as a right; *steel workers have claimed huge pay rises*; *if it doesn't work you must claim a refund* **(b)** to state, but without any proof; *he claims he never received the letter*; *she claims that the car belongs to her* **(c)** to say you own something which has been left behind or lost; *no one has claimed the umbrella found in my office, so I am going to keep it*

claimant ['kleɪmənt] *noun* **(a)** person who claims; *benefit claimants will be paid late because of the bank holiday* **(b) rightful claimant** = person who has a legal claim to something; *the legacy can be paid only to the rightful claimant*

claim back ['kleɪm 'bæk] *verb* to claim something which you owned before; *his car was towed away and he had to go to the pound to claim it back*

clairvoyant [kleə'vɔɪənt] *noun* person who says he can see in his mind things which are happening elsewhere or can foretell the future; *have you ever consulted a clairvoyant?*; *the clairvoyant told her that many of her friends would die*

clam [klæm] *noun* large shellfish found in sand, which is dug out with a spade; *clam diggers have to work at low tide*; **clam chowder** = American soup, made of clams, milk and vegetables; *a bowl of clam chowder is a meal in itself*

clamber ['klæmbə] *verb* to climb with difficulty; *she clambered onto the roof*; *he clambered up the ladder*; *they had to clamber across a glacier*

clamour *US* **clamor** ['klæmə] **1** *noun* **(a)** shouting; *the clamour of the crowd at the rugby ground could be heard for miles around* **(b)** loud demand; *a clamour for democratic elections* **2** *verb* to shout or to demand loudly; *people are clamouring for tickets*; *the crowd clamoured to see the manager*

clamp [klæmp] **1** *noun* **(a)** pieces which are screwed tightly to hold something together; *he held the two pieces of wood together with a clamp* **(b)** (wheel) **clamp** = metal frame which is screwed to the wheel of an illegally parked car; *she had to pay £100 to have the wheel clamp removed* **2** *verb* **(a)** to hold tight with a clamp; *he spread glue over the two pieces of wood and then clamped them together* **(b)** to prevent an illegally parked car from moving by attaching a clamp to one wheel; *I parked on a double yellow line and was clamped*

clampdown ['klæmpdaʊn] *noun* severe action to stop something; *the local authority has decided on a clampdown on smoking in restaurants*

clamp down on ['klæmp 'daʊn ɒn] *verb* to take measures to stop crime, etc.; *railway staff are clamping down on people travelling without tickets*

clamper ['klæmpə] *noun* person who attaches a clamp to a car that is illegally parked; *move your car, I can see a clamper van in the next street*

clam up ['klæm 'ʌp] *verb* to stop talking; *he clammed up and we couldn't get an answer out of him* (NOTE: **clamming - clammed**)

clan [klæn] *noun* family tribe, especially in Scotland; *a meeting of the MacDonald clan*

clandestine [klæn'destɪn] *adjective* secret, undercover; *a clandestine operation to smuggle pirate CDs into the country*

clannish ['klænɪʃ] *adjective* supporting your own group; *they have a clannish tendency to appoint other members of the committee to positions of authority*

clansman, clanswoman ['klænzmən *or* 'klænzwʊmən] *noun* member of a clan; *clansmen met in secret to plot the rebellion* (NOTE: plural is **clansmen, clanswomen**)

clap [klæp] **1** *verb* **(a)** to beat your hands together to show you are pleased; *at the end of her speech the audience stood up and clapped*; *he clapped his hands together in delight* **(b) to clap into jail** = to put someone in jail; *he was arrested and clapped into jail* (NOTE: **clapping - clapped**) **2** *noun* **(a)** action of beating your hands together; *he did very well - give him a big clap, everyone* **(b) clap of thunder** *or* **thunderclap** = sudden loud noise made by thunder; *a thunderclap woke us up*; *we were woken by a sudden clap of thunder*

clapper ['klæpə] *noun* metal piece which swings inside a bell and strikes it; *(informal)* **like the clappers** = very fast; *we ran like the clappers to get away from the police*; *he drove like the clappers to get me to the airport on time*

claret ['klærət] *noun* red wine from Bordeaux; *we had a good bottle of claret with our meal*

clarification [klærɪfɪ'keɪʃn] *noun* making clear; *we have asked for clarification of the demand for payment*

clarify ['klærɪfaɪ] *verb* to make clear; *we will have to clarify the situation before taking any further decisions*

clarinet [klærɪ'net] *noun* wind instrument in the woodwind group; *how many of you can play the clarinet?*; *here is a piece Mozart wrote for the clarinet*

clarity ['klærɪti] *noun* clearness; *atmospheric conditions can affect the clarity of the signals*; *this device should improve the clarity of the image on your screen* (NOTE: no plural)

clash [klæʃ] **1** *noun* **(a)** loud noise of metal things hitting each other; *she heard a loud clash like two saucepans being banged together* **(b)** battle, argument; *there were clashes outside the football ground between supporters of the two teams*; *we are getting reports of clashes between government forces and rebel groups* **(c)** shock of two colours seen close together; *if you wear red tights with an orange dress there will be a colour clash* (NOTE: plural is **clashes**) **2** *verb* **(a)** to bang together making a loud noise; *she has to clash the cymbals at the end of the piece of music* **(b)** to argue violently; *she clashed with her mother about wearing a ring in her nose*; *the opposition deputies clashed with the government during the debate* **(c)** to fight; *rioting fans clashed with the police* **(d)** to happen at the same time as something else; *the party clashes with a meeting I have to go to*; *unfortunately, the two meetings clash, so I'll have to miss one* **(e)** *(of colours)* to shock when put side by side; *that bright pink tie clashes with your green shirt*

clasp [klɑːsp] **1** *noun* **(a)** device for holding something shut; *my handbag won't close properly, the clasp is broken* **(b)** piece of women's jewellery worn fastened to clothes; *her shawl was attached with a silver clasp* **(c)** act of holding in your hand; *I could feel* *the firm clasp of his hand on my shoulder* **2** *verb* to hold something tight; *she clasped his hand anxiously*

class [klɑːs] *noun* **(a)** group of people (usually children) who go to school or college together; *there are 30 children in my son's class* **(b)** group of people who were at the same school or college at the same time in the past; *she's organizing a reunion for the class of '76* **(c)** lesson; **evening classes** = lessons given in the evening (usually to adults); *I am going to evening classes to learn German; we have two maths classes a week* **(d)** people of the same group in society; *people from different social classes mixed at the reception;* **working class** = people who mainly work with their hands; **middle class** = people who have taken exams for their jobs, such as doctors, teachers, etc., or people in business **(e)** certain level of quality; *always buy the best class of product; these peaches are Class 1;* **first-class** = very good; *he is a first-class tennis player;* **second-class** = not as good as first class **(f)** quality of seats or service on a plane, train, etc.; **first class** = best quality (and most expensive); *if you travel first class on the train to France, you get free drinks;* **business class** = less expensive than first class; **economy class** *or* **tourist class** = cheapest; *they are staying in a first-class hotel; first-class passengers get free drinks with their meal; the tourist-class fare is much less than the first-class; I travel economy class because it is cheaper* (NOTE: plural is **classes**)

classic ['klæsɪk] **1** *noun* **(a)** great book, play, piece of music, etc.; *'the Maltese Falcon' is a Hollywood classic; we have to study several classics of English literature for our course* **(b)** **Classics** = study of the languages, literature, philosophy, etc., of Ancient Greece and Rome; *she studied Classics at Oxford; he has a Classics degree from Edinburgh* **2** *adjective* **(a)** (style) which is elegant and traditional; *the classic little black dress is always in fashion; the style of the shopfront is classic, simple and elegant* **(b)** *(style of architecture)* which is based on that of Greek or Roman architecture; *the British Museum is built in classic Greek style* **(c)** typical; *it was a classic example of his inability to take decisions*

classical ['klæsɪkl] *adjective* **(a)** which is elegant and based on the style of Greek or Roman architecture, literature, etc.; *a classical eighteenth century villa* **(b)** referring to Ancient Greece and Rome; *classical Greek literature* **(c)** referring to traditional, serious music; *a concert of classical music*

classicism ['klæsɪsɪzm] *noun* Greek or Roman style; *the classicism of the British Museum is much admired*

classification [klæsɪfɪ'keɪʃn] *noun* way of arranging things into categories; *the classification of social classes into various categories; Linnaeus organized the classification of organisms into genera and species*

classified ['klæsɪfaɪd] *adjective* **(a)** which has been put into a category; **classified ads** *or* **classified advertisements** = newspaper advertisements which are listed under special headings, such as 'jobs wanted' or 'household items for sale'; *I never read the classified ads in the papers;* **classified directory** = directory of business addresses listed under various headings, such as 'hairdressers', 'bookshops', etc.; *look for his address under 'plumbers' in the classified directory* **(b)** secret; **classified documents** *or* **classified**

information = documents *or* information marked 'secret'; *he left a box of classified documents in the back of his car; this is classified information, and only a few people have access to it*

classify ['klæsɪfaɪ] *verb* to arrange things into groups; *the hotels are classified according to a star system; now that these plants have been classified, please write a label for each one*

classless ['klɑːsləs] *adjective* with no division into social classes; *the former Prime Minister used to talk of his wish for a classless society*

classmate ['klɑːsmeɪt] *noun* person who is or was in the same class as you at school or college; *he and his classmates went to the zoo; she's meeting an old classmate from her college days*

classroom ['klɑːsruːm] *noun* room in a school where children are taught; *when the teacher came into the classroom all the children were shouting and throwing books*

classy ['klɑːsi] *adjective (informal)* chic and expensive-looking; *this isn't a very classy restaurant but the food is good; she lives in one of the classiest areas of London* (NOTE: **classier - classiest**)

clatter ['klætə] **1** *noun* noise of things hitting together; *the clatter from the kitchen can be heard in the restaurant; there's a constant clatter of machines in the workshop* **2** *verb* to make a rapid noise; *the wooden cart clattered across the square*

clause [klɔːz] *noun* **(a)** paragraph in a treaty or legal document; *according to clause six, payments will not be due until next year* **(b)** part of a sentence; *the sentence has two clauses, separated by the conjunction 'and';* **main clause** = main part of a sentence; **subordinate clause** = clause which depends on the main clause

claustrophobia [klɒstrə'fəubiə] *noun* fear of being shut inside a closed space; *there is nothing like driving through a long tunnel to give you claustrophobia; I get claustrophobia every time I go into that room*

claustrophobic [klɒstrə'fəubɪk] *adjective* feeling or causing claustrophobia; *the thought of going down into a cave makes me feel claustrophobic; please, open the windows - it is very claustrophobic in here*

clavicle ['klævɪkl] *noun* collarbone, one of two long thin bones joining the shoulders to the breastbone; *she was lucky, after the fall all she had was a broken clavicle*

claw [klɔː] **1** *noun* **(a)** nail on the foot of an animal or bird; *the dog dug a hole with its claws; our cat scratched the furniture with its claws* **(b)** arm of a crab or lobster, with pincers; *I got a nasty nip from the lobster's claws* **2** *verb* to scratch or pull with claws; *the keeper was clawed by the tiger and had to have stitches in his arm; the cat has clawed the leg of the kitchen table;* **to claw your way up** = to go up with great difficulty; *she clawed her way up the promotion ladder*

clay [kleɪ] *noun* **(a)** stiff soil found in river valleys; *the soil in our garden has a lot of clay in it* **(b)** stiff soil used for making bricks or china; *the potter threw a lump of clay onto his wheel and started to make a pot*

clean [kliːn] **1** *adjective* **(a)** not dirty; *wipe your glasses with a clean handkerchief; the bedrooms must be spotlessly clean; tell the waitress these cups aren't clean; the maid forgot to put clean towels in the bathroom; (informal)* **to come clean** = to confess to a crime, etc.; *he came clean and owned up to stealing the watch* **(b)** with no record of offences; *the fine for speeding is a blemish on his otherwise clean driving licence*; *candidates should hold a clean driving licence* **(c)** fair, according to the rules; *we played a good clean of football* (NOTE: **cleaner - cleanest**) **2** *verb* to make clean, by taking away dirt; *remember to clean your teeth every morning*; *she was cleaning the kitchen when the telephone rang*; *he cleans his car every Saturday morning* **3** *adverb* (*informal*) completely; *I clean forgot to send the letter* **4** *noun* (*informal*) action of cleaning; *the restaurant kitchen needs a good clean*

cleaner ['kliːnə] *noun* **(a)** machine which removes dirt; **vacuum cleaner** = machine which sucks up dirt from floors (NOTE: usually called a **hoover**) **(b)** substance which removes dirt; *this new oven cleaner doesn't get rid of the worst stains*; *can you buy another bottle of toilet cleaner?* **(c)** person who cleans (a house, office, etc.); *the cleaners didn't empty my wastepaper basket*

cleaner's ['kliːnəz] *noun* **(a)** shop where you take clothes to be dry-cleaned; *when I got my suit back from the cleaner's there was a button missing* (NOTE: also called the **dry-cleaner's**) **(b)** (*slang*) **to take someone to the cleaner's** = to take all someone's money; *I played poker last night and got taken to the cleaner's*

cleaning ['kliːnɪŋ] *noun* **(a)** action of cleaning; *the cleaning of the house after the party took hours* **(b)** clothes which are ready to be sent for dry-cleaning *or* which have been returned after dry-cleaning; *she ran through the rain to her car with an armful of cleaning* (NOTE: also called **dry-cleaning**)

cleanliness ['klenlɪnəs] *noun* state or degree of being clean; *the inspectors criticized the cleanliness of the kitchens*; *a person of rather dubious cleanliness applied for a job as a waiter*

clean out ['kliːn 'aʊt] *verb* to make something empty and clean; *you must clean out your cupboard*; *he was cleaning out the garden shed*

cleanse [klenz] *verb* to make something very clean; **cleansing cream** = cream which cleans the skin

cleanser ['klenzə] *noun* substance which removes dirt; *skin cleansers don't need to be expensive to be good*

clean-shaven ['kliːnʃeɪvən] *adjective* with no beard or moustache; *she described her attacker as tall, clean-shaven, with short grey hair*

clean up ['kliːn 'ʌp] *verb* **(a)** to make everything clean and tidy after a party, etc.; *it took us three hours to clean up after her birthday party* **(b)** to remove corruption; *the police are going to have a hard job cleaning up this town* **(c)** (*informal*) to make a lot of money; *he cleaned up at the races*; *it was such a good scheme that in no time he'd cleaned up £50,000*

clean-up ['kliːnʌp] *noun* making clean; *after the floods had gone down the clean-up took weeks*

clear [klɪə] **1** *adjective* **(a)** with nothing in the way; *you can cross the road - it's clear now*; *from the window, she had a clear view of the street* **(b)** with no clouds, mist, etc.; *a clear blue sky*; *on a clear day, you can see the other side of the lake* **(c)** easily understood; *she made it clear that she wanted us to go*; *the instructions on the computer screen are not very clear*; *will you give me a clear answer - yes or no?* **(d)** which is not covered and which you can easily see through; *a*

clear glass window; **clear light bulb** = bulb which you can see through (NOTE: a bulb with a pale white coating is a **pearl bulb**) **(e)** whole period of time; *it will take a clear week to process the information*; **three clear days** = three whole working days; *allow three clear days for the cheque to be paid into the bank* (NOTE: **clearer - clearest**) **2** *verb* **(a)** to remove something which is in the way; *snowploughs cleared the railway line of snow or cleared the snow from the railway line*; *we'll get a plumber to clear the blocked pipe in the bathroom*; **to clear the table** = to take away knives, forks, plates, etc., after a meal **(b)** (*of a bank*) **to clear a cheque** = to pass a cheque through the banking system, so that the money is transferred from one account to another; *the cheque took ten days to clear or the bank took ten days to clear the cheque* **(c)** to sell cheaply in order to get rid of stock; *'demonstration models to clear'*; *if we reduce the price we'll clear the stock in no time* **(d)** (*of a court*) to find that someone is not guilty; *the court cleared him of all the charges* **(e)** to go over the top of something without touching it; *she cleared 1.3m in the high jump* **3** *adverb* not close; *stand clear of the doors, please*; *I would advise you to stay clear of that dog*

clearance ['klɪərəns] *noun* **(a)** act of removing obstacles, such as trees and shrubs, from land; *the clearance of the slums from the town centre will make land available for building*; *the government has introduced a programme of slum clearance* **(b)** **clearance sale** = sale of items at low prices to get rid of the stock; *the new models will be launched when the clearance sale is over* **(c)** space for something to pass through; *the lorry can get through the entrance with about twenty centimetres clearance on either side*; *is there enough clearance for the bus to get under the bridge?* **(d)** permission to do something; *the control tower gave the plane clearance to land* (NOTE: no plural)

clear away ['klɪə ə'weɪ] *verb* to take something away completely; *can you help to clear the rubbish away from the pavement?*; *would you mind clearing away the plates?*

clear-cut [klɪə'kʌt] *adjective* definite or distinct; *your proposal is too vague, we need something more clear-cut*; *the contract is very clear-cut about what you can and can't do*

clearing ['klɪərɪŋ] *noun* **(a)** act of removing obstacles; *we don't want the public to interfere with the clearing of the wreckage from the railway track* **(b)** area in a wood where the trees have been cut down; *they set up camp in a clearing in the middle of the forest* **(c)** **clearing bank** = bank which issues and processes cheques; *two of the major clearing banks have decided to merge*

clearly ['klɪəli] *adverb* **(a)** in a way which is easily understood or heard; *he didn't speak clearly, and I couldn't catch the address he gave* **(b)** obviously; *he clearly didn't like being told he was too fat*

clear off ['klɪə 'ɒf] *verb* (*informal*) to go away; *clear off! I don't want you here*

clear out ['klɪə 'aʊt] *verb* **(a)** to empty completely; *can you clear out your bedroom cupboard?* **(b)** (*informal*) to go away; *clear out! I don't want you here*

clear-sighted ['klɪə 'saɪtɪd] *adjective* able to think clearly and understand a problem; *he wrote a very clear-sighted report on the currency situation*

clear up ['klɪə 'ʌp] *verb* **(a)** to tidy and clean completely; *the cleaners refused to clear up the mess after the office party* **(b)** to solve a problem; *in the end, we cleared up the mystery of the missing computer disk* **(c)** to get better; *I hope the weather clears up because we're going on holiday tomorrow; he has been taking aspirins, but his cold still hasn't cleared up*

clear-up ['klɪəʌp] *noun* action of clearing up; *after the tanker went aground, a massive clear-up of the beaches was organized*

cleavage ['kliːvɪdʒ] *noun* **(a)** space between the breasts, especially if it can be seen with a low-cut dress; *all the ladies were dressed in black and there was not a cleavage in sight* **(b)** *(formal)* split, difference of opinion; *the cleavage between the two groups became more and more apparent*

clef [klef] *noun* sign at the beginning of a written piece of music which shows how high the range of notes is; **bass clef** = sign showing that the notes are in a low range; **treble clef** = sign showing that the notes are in a high range; *in a normal piano piece the right hand plays notes in the treble clef and the left hand plays notes in the bass clef*

cleft [kleft] **1** *noun* crack in a rock; *small plants were growing in clefts in the rocks* **2** *adjective* **cleft palate** = defect in babies, where there is a gap in the palate

clematis ['klemətɪs or klə'meɪtɪs] *noun* climbing plant with pink, white or purple flowers; *we could plant a clematis that would climb up this bare wall*

clemency ['klemənsi] *noun* mercy shown to someone who has done something wrong; *she appealed for clemency for her son; as an act of clemency, the president granted an amnesty to all political prisoners*

clench [klentʃ] *verb* to close tightly; *the baby's fists are still clenched tight; he clenched his fists ready for a fight;* **clenched fist salute** = holding your fist in the air as a threat; *the fans gave a clenched fist salute;* **through clenched teeth** = with your teeth closed tight together; *he muttered 'I'm sorry' through clenched teeth*

clergy ['klɜːdʒi] *noun* priests; *the clergy have not yet commented on the story; a member of the clergy will also attend the meeting* (NOTE: the word is plural)

clergyman ['klɜːdʒɪmən] *noun* priest or minister, especially of the Anglican Church; *in the film, he plays the role of an old clergyman* (NOTE: plural is **clergymen**; they are usually referred to by the title **Reverend**)

cleric ['klerɪk] *noun (formal)* priest, clergyman; *an eminent cleric*

clerical ['klerɪkl] *adjective* **(a)** referring to office work; *a clerical error made the invoice £300.00 when it should have been £3000.00; she's looking for part-time clerical work* **(b)** referring to clergy; *the newspaper story has been talked about in clerical circles;* **clerical dress** = suit worn by a priest

clerk [klɑːk *US* klɜːk] *noun* person who works in an office; *a ticket clerk; a bank clerk*

clever ['klevə] *adjective* intelligent, able to learn quickly; *he's the cleverest person in the family; she's very clever with money; he is very clever at spotting bargains;* **he's clever with his hands** = he's good at making things with his hands (NOTE: **cleverer - cleverest**)

cleverly ['klevəli] *adverb* in a clever way; *the dog had cleverly worked out how to open the door*

cliché ['kliːʃeɪ] *noun* saying or phrase which is too frequently used; *'absence makes the heart grow fonder' may be an old cliché, but it's true just the same*

click [klɪk] **1** *noun* short sharp sound; *she heard a click and saw the doorknob turn* **2** *verb* **(a)** to make a short sharp sound; *the cameras clicked as she came out of the church; he clicked his fingers to attract the waiter's attention* **(b)** *(informal)* to become clear and easily understood; **suddenly everything clicked** = suddenly it all became clear **(c)** to press the button on a mouse quickly to start a computer function; *the pull-down menu is displayed by clicking on the menu bar at the top of the screen; using the mouse, move the cursor to the start button and click twice*

client ['klaɪənt] *noun* person who you give a service to; *a personal trainer who visits his clients in their own homes; how often do your salesmen visit their major clients?*

clientele [kliːɒn'tel] *noun* all the customers of a shop or business; *a new hairdressing salon which is try to build up its clientele; the pub's clientele is mainly people under 25*

cliff [klɪf] *noun* high rock face, usually by the sea; *he went for a walk along the top of the cliffs; their first view of England was the white cliffs of Dover; colossal heads of presidents are cut into the cliff face*

climate ['klaɪmət] *noun* **(a)** general weather conditions in a certain place; *the climate in the south of the country is milder than in the north; the climate in Central Europe is hot in the summer and cold and dry in the winter* **(b)** general atmosphere; *the current economic climate makes an interest rate rise very likely; we want to get away from this town - we could all do with a change of climate*

climatic [klaɪ'mætɪk] *adjective* referring to climate; *climatic changes such as those produced by el Niño*

climax ['klaɪmæks] *noun* most important and exciting point; *the celebrations reached their climax with a parade through the centre of the town; the film was reaching its climax when the electricity failed* (NOTE: plural is **climaxes**)

climb [klaɪm] **1** *noun* going up; *it's a steep climb to the top of the hill* **2** *verb* **(a)** to go up (or down) using arms and legs; *the cat climbed up the apple tree; the burglars climbed over the wall; he escaped by climbing out of the window* **(b)** to go up; *the road climbs up to 1,000m above sea level* **(c)** to go up mountains as a sport; *when you have climbed Everest, there is no higher mountain left to climb; he goes climbing every weekend*

climb down ['klaɪm 'daʊn] *verb* **(a)** to come down a mountain, a ladder, etc.; *he climbed down from the roof; the firemen helped the hotel guests climb down the ladder* **(b)** not to do what you had previously insisted on doing; *in the end, the government had to climb down and admit there had been an error*

climber ['klaɪmə] *noun* person who climbs mountains; *the climbers roped themselves together and set off up the slope*

climbing ['klaɪmɪŋ] *noun* **(a)** sport of climbing mountains; *climbing is not a sport for young children; we had a climbing holiday last Easter; she brought her climbing equipment with her* **(b)** **climbing frame** =

framework of wooden bars and platforms for children to climb on

climes [klaɪmz] *noun (old, poetic)* a country and its climate; *we are going abroad to live in sunnier climes*

clinch [klɪntʃ] **1** *noun* **(a)** position where two people hold each other tightly; *he found his girlfriend in a clinch with another man* **(b)** *(in boxing)* position where both boxers hold on to each other; *the referee tried to separate the two boxers who were in a tight clinch* (NOTE: plural is **clinches**) **2** *verb* **(a)** *(in boxing)* to hold each other tight; *the referee tried to stop the two boxers clinching* **(b)** to settle (a deal); *he offered an extra 5% to clinch the deal*

cling [klɪŋ] *verb* to cling (on)to something = to hold tight; *she survived by clinging onto a piece of wood; he clung tightly to his mother's arm* (NOTE: **clinging - clung** [klʌŋ])

clingfilm ['klɪŋfɪlm] *noun* thin transparent plastic sheet for covering food; *she wrapped the sandwiches in clingfilm*

clinic ['klɪnɪk] *noun* specialized medical centre or hospital; *a family planning clinic; she had treatment in a private clinic in Switzerland*

clinical ['klɪnɪkl] *adjective* **(a)** medical; **clinical medicine** = treatment of patients in a hospital ward or a doctor's surgery (as opposed to an operating theatre); *I'm more interested in clinical medicine than in surgery* **(b)** to look at things in a clinical way = to look at something coolly, without any prejudices

clinician [klɪ'nɪʃən] *noun* doctor, usually not a surgeon, who has considerable experience in treating patients; *a clinician should be able to see right away what is wrong with the patient*

clink [klɪŋk] *verb* to make a little noise, like pieces of metal hitting each other; **to clink glasses** = to touch your glass against someone else's glass, to wish each other good luck

clip [klɪp] **1** *noun* **(a)** **paper clip** = piece of bent wire for attaching papers, etc., together; *he attached the cheque to the letter with a paper clip* **(b)** *especially US* piece of jewellery which clips onto your clothes; *he wore a gold clip on his tie; she has a diamond clip on her dress* **(c)** *(old) (informal)* **at a good clip** = quite fast; *the car came round the corner at a good clip* **(d)** *(informal)* **a clip round the ear** = a smack on the side of the head; *stop that noise or you'll get a clip round the ear* **(e)** *(informal)* short piece of film; *here is a clip of the president getting into the car* **2** *verb* **(a)** to attach things together with a clip; *she clipped the invoice and the cheque together and put them in an envelope; these earrings are made to clip onto your ears* **(b)** to cut with scissors; *the dog has its fur clipped once a month; he carefully clipped the article out of the newspaper* **(c)** to hit slightly; *the wing of the plane clipped the top of the tree before it crashed* (NOTE: **clipping - clipped**)

clipboard ['klɪpbɔːd] *noun* stiff board with a clip at the top so that a piece of paper can be clipped to it to allow you to write on it easily; *all the researchers were given a clipboard, a pen and an ID card*

clipped [klɪpt] *adjective* **(a)** cut neatly short; *he has a neatly clipped beard; I was admiring your freshly clipped hedge* **(b)** **clipped voice** = way of speaking using short sharp sounds; *he spoke the famous speech from 'Henry V' in clipped tones*

clipper ['klɪpə] *noun* **(a)** **clippers** = shears; *the clippers will need sharpening if you are going to trim the hedge; I don't let the hairdresser use his clippers when he cuts my hair* **(b)** *(in the 19th century)* **tea clipper** = fast sailing vessel, used mainly for carrying tea

clipping ['klɪpɪŋ] *noun* **(a)** reference to someone *or* something in a newspaper or magazine which is cut out of the paper and filed for reference; *can you file away all these newspaper clippings, please?* **(b)** small piece cut off a hedge, etc.; *trim the hedge and put the clippings in a black bag; grass clippings can be piled on top of the compost heap*

clique [kliːk] *noun* small select group of people; *a clique of old soldiers runs the club; people are complaining that the clique round the president is preventing others gaining access to him*

cloak [kləʊk] **1** *noun* **(a)** long outer covering which hangs from your shoulders and has no sleeves; *she wore a long cloak of black velvet; (informal)* **cloak and dagger stuff** = activities that suggest a mystery, or that someone is spying **(b)** **under the cloak of darkness** = at night when everything is hidden; *they left the city under the cloak of darkness;* **a cloak of secrecy** = making something secret so as to hide it; *the whole affair was shrouded in a cloak of secrecy* **2** *verb* to hide; *the whole project is cloaked in secrecy*

cloakroom ['kləʊkrʊm] *noun* **(a)** place where you leave your coat in a restaurant, theatre, etc.; *I left my coat and briefcase in the cloakroom* (NOTE: American English for this is **checkroom**) **(b)** *(informal)* public toilet (i.e. room with lavatories, washbasins, etc.); *the ladies cloakroom is on the first floor*

clobber ['klɒbə] **1** *noun (informal)* **(a)** belongings; *all my tennis clobber was stolen* **(b)** rubbish, useless items; *can't you get rid of all this clobber in the cupboard?* (NOTE: no plural) **2** *verb (informal)* to affect badly, especially financially; *the government's new proposals will clobber the middle classes; the railway company is aiming to clobber the commuters once again*

clock [klɒk] **1** *noun* large instrument which shows the time; *the station clock is always right; your clock is 5 minutes slow; the office clock is fast; the clock has stopped - it needs winding up;* **alarm clock** = clock which rings a bell to wake you up; *see also* GRANDFATHER, O'CLOCK (NOTE: a small instrument for showing the time, which you wear, is a **watch**) **2** *verb* **to clock in** *or* **on** = to arrive for work and register by putting a card into a timing machine; **to clock out** *or* **off** = to leave work and register by putting a card into a timing machine

clockwise ['klɒkwaɪz] *adjective & adverb* in the same direction as the hands of a clock; *turn the lid clockwise to tighten it; he was driving clockwise round the ring road when the accident took place* (NOTE: the opposite is **anticlockwise**)

clockwork ['klɒkwɜːk] *noun* mechanism in a toy, machine, clock, etc., which works using a spring which is wound up with a key; *he invented the clockwork radio; we gave him a clockwork train for his birthday;* **like clockwork** = smoothly, with no problems; *the whole evening went off like clockwork* (NOTE: no plural)

clod [klɒd] *noun* large lump of earth; *he dug the soil and then broke up the clods with a fork*

clog [klɒg] **1** *noun* wooden shoe; *clogs are very popular in Scandinavian countries* **2** *verb* to block; *Trafalgar Square was clogged with traffic as the protest march arrived*; *dead leaves are clogging the drains* (NOTE: **clogging - clogged**)

cloister [ˈklɔɪstə] *noun* covered walk round a square courtyard, for example in a monastery or next to a cathedral; *we visited the cloisters and looked at the carvings on the capitals*

cloistered [ˈklɔɪstəd] *adjective* protected from problems, as if in a monastery; *he lives a very cloistered existence*

clone [kləʊn] **1** *noun* **(a)** organism produced by asexual reproduction (as by taking cuttings from a plant); *a cutting produces a clone of a plant*; *this sheep was the first mammal to survive as a clone* **(b)** computer or circuit that behaves in the same way as the original it was copied from; *they copied our laptop and brought out a cheaper clone* **2** *verb* to reproduce an individual organism by asexual means; *biologists have successfully cloned a sheep*

close 1 [kləʊs] *adjective* **(a)** very near, just next to something; *our office is close to the railway station*; *this is the closest I've ever been to a film star!* **(b)** where only a few votes separate the winner from the losers; *the election was very close*; *it was a close contest* **(c)** hot and airless; *it's very close in here, can someone open a window?* **2** [kləʊs] *adverb* very near; *keep close by me if you don't want to get lost*; *go further away - you're getting too close*; *they stood so close (together) that she felt his breath on her cheek*; *the sound came closer and closer* (NOTE: **closer - closest**) **3** [kləʊz] *verb* **(a)** to shut; *would you mind closing the window, there's a draught?*; *he closed his book and turned on the TV* **(b)** to make something come to an end; *she closed her letter by saying she was coming to see us* **(c)** to come to an end; *the meeting closed with a vote of thanks* **(d)** to close an account = to take all the money out of a bank account and stop the account; *he closed his building society account* **(e)** to close on someone = to come closer to someone, to catch someone up; *the horse in second place was closing on the leader* **4** [kləʊz] *noun* end, final part; *the century is drawing to a close*; **at close of play** = when a cricket match stops for the day

closed [kləʊzd] *adjective* shut; *the shop is closed on Sundays*; *the office will be closed for the Christmas holidays*; *there was a 'closed' sign hanging in the window*

closed-circuit TV (CCTV) [ˈkləʊzd ˈsɜːkɪt ˈtiːviː] system where a TV picture is shown nearby, used for security in factories, shops, banks, etc., and for showing pictures of events to people who are not able to attend the event themselves; *the conference was relayed to the lobby on closed-circuit TV*; *the shoplifters were filmed on closed-circuit TV cameras*; *the premises are protected by closed-circuit TV*

close down [ˈkləʊz ˈdaʊn] *verb* to shut a business; *they're going to close down the factory because they haven't enough work*

closely [ˈkləʊsli] *adverb* **(a)** attentively; *she studied the timetable very closely* **(b)** tightly; *the photographers moved in closely around the car*; *the prisoners were closely guarded by armed soldiers*

close season [ˈkləʊs ˈsiːsən] *noun* period when certain types of wild animal cannot be killed; *it is the close season for deer*

closet [ˈklɒzɪt] **1** *noun US* cupboard; *will you get my coat from the closet, honey?*; (*informal*) **to come out of the closet** = to say openly that you are homosexual **2** *adjective* secret, not revealing something in public; *he's a closet racist* **3** *verb* **to closet yourself with someone** = to shut yourself away in a room with someone; *the directors have been closeted with the VAT inspectors for several hours*

close-up [ˈkləʊsʌp] *noun* photograph taken very close to the subject; *orchids are ideal subjects for close-up photography*; *he has a framed close-up of his daughter on his desk*

closing [ˈkləʊzɪŋ] **1** *adjective* final, at the end; *the frantic activity of the closing days of the election campaign*; **closing bid** = last bid at an auction; **closing date** = last date; *the closing date for applications is May 1st* **2** *noun* shutting (of a shop, etc.); **closing time** = time when a pub, shop, etc., closes

closing down sale [ˈkləʊzɪŋ ˈdaʊn ˈseɪl] *noun* sale of goods when a shop is closing for ever

closure [ˈkləʊʒə] *noun* shutting; *the number of factory closures has increased this year*; *put the radio on so that we can hear if there are any road closures*

clot [klɒt] **1** *noun* **(a)** soft mass of coagulated blood in a vein or an artery; *the doctor diagnosed a blood clot in the brain* **(b)** (*informal*) fool; *you stupid clot, you put the milk carton into the fridge upside down!* **2** *verb* to coagulate, to change from semi-liquid to semi-solid; *in people with haemophilia, blood clots very slowly*; **clotted cream** = cream which has been heated and has become more solid; *scones served with clotted cream and strawberry jam* (NOTE: **clotting - clotted**)

cloth [klɒθ] *noun* **(a)** material; *her dress is made of cheap blue cloth*; *this cloth is of a very high quality* **(b)** piece of material for cleaning; *he wiped up the spill with a damp cloth*; *see also* DISHCLOTH, FACECLOTH, etc. **(c)** tablecloth, a piece of material which you put on the table to cover it; *the waiter spread a white cloth over the table*; *she split some red wine on the cloth*

clothed [kləʊðd] *adjective* dressed in or covered in; *she was clothed in gold robes*; *he was fully clothed when he fell into the pool*; *the fields were all clothed in frost*

clothes [kləʊðz] *noun* **(a)** things (such as shirts, trousers, dresses, etc.) which you wear to cover your body and keep you warm; *he walked down the street with no clothes on or without any clothes on*; *the doctor asked him to take his clothes off*; *the children haven't had any new clothes for years* **(b)** **clothes horse** = frame for hanging wet clothes on to dry; **clothes line** = rope for hanging wet clothes on to dry; **clothes peg** *or* (*US & Scotland*) **clothes pin** = wooden peg for attaching wet clothes to a line; **clothes rail** = rail for hanging clothes on in a shop

clothing [ˈkləʊðɪŋ] *noun* clothes; *take plenty of warm clothing on your trip to Iceland*; *an important clothing manufacturer* (NOTE: no plural: **some clothing; a piece of clothing**)

cloud [klaʊd] *noun* **(a)** mass of white or grey vapour floating in the air; *do you think it's going to rain? - yes, look at those grey clouds*; *the plane was flying above the clouds* **(b)** (*informal*) **on cloud nine** = very happy;

they were on cloud nine when the won the lottery; **under a cloud** = suspected of having done something wrong; *he was under a cloud for some time after the thefts were discovered; see also* LINING **(c)** similar mass of smoke; *clouds of smoke poured out of the burning shop*

cloudburst ['klaʊdbɜːst] *noun* sudden downpour of rain; *we went walking in the hills and got drenched in a cloudburst*

cloudless ['klaʊdləs] *adjective* with no clouds; *a beautiful cloudless sky*

cloud over ['klaʊd 'əʊvə] *verb* to become covered with clouds; *it was fine at breakfast time, but now it has clouded over and looks like rain*

cloudy ['klaʊdi] *adjective* **(a)** with clouds; *the weather was cloudy in the morning, but cleared up in the afternoon; when it's very cloudy it isn't easy to take good photographs* **(b)** not clear, not transparent; *this beer is cloudy; the water in the aquarium turned cloudy and the fish died* (NOTE: **cloudier - cloudiest**)

clout [klaʊt] **1** *noun* **(a)** blow with the fist; *he received a clout on the head* **(b)** *(informal)* power or influence; *because she owns so many shares, she wields a great deal of clout in company meetings; newspaper editors have a lot of political clout* **2** *verb* to give someone a blow with the fist; *he has a habit of clouting his children on the head when they make a noise*

clove [kləʊv] *noun* **(a)** dried flower bud of a tree used for flavouring; *a few cloves stuck into an onion can be used to flavour a stew* **(b)** **clove of garlic** = one of the parts that make up a bulb of garlic; *rub round the salad bowl with a cut clove of garlic*

cloven hoof ['kləʊvn 'huːf] *noun* hoof which is split into two parts; *sheep have cloven hooves*

clover ['kləʊvə] *noun* **(a)** common weed, used as fodder for cattle; *with so much clover in the fields, the bees produce excellent honey;* **four-leaved clover** = lucky rare sort of clover with four leaves instead of three; **to be** *or* **live in clover** = to live comfortably; *after his lottery win he lived in clover* **(b)** **cloverleaf intersection** = crossroads which intersect with curving link roads, in a way which looks like the leaf of a clover

clown [klaʊn] **1** *noun* man who makes people laugh in a circus; *the clown had a big red nose and baggy trousers* **2** *verb* **to clown about** *or* **around** = to behave in a silly way which makes people laugh; *stop clowning around with that hat and sit down to have your meal*

club [klʌb] *noun* **(a)** group of people who have the same interest or form a team; *an old people's club; I'm joining a tennis club; our town has one of the top football clubs in the country* **(b)** place where a club meets; *the sports club is near the river; he goes to the golf club every Friday; see also* NIGHT CLUB **(c)** **club class** = specially comfortable class of seating on a plane, though not as luxurious as first class **(d)** **clubs** = one of the black suits in a pack of cards, shaped like a leaf with three parts; *he had the five of clubs in his hand* (NOTE: the other black suit is **spades; hearts** and diamonds are the red suits) **(e)** large heavy stick; *she was knocked to the ground by a blow from a club;* a **golf club** = stick for playing golf (NOTE: **a golf club** can either mean the place where you play golf, or the stick used to hit the ball) **2** *verb* **(a)** to hit with a club; *she was clubbed to the ground* **(b)** *(of several people)* **to club together** = to contribute money jointly; *they clubbed*

together and bought a yacht **(c)** *(informal)* **to go clubbing** = to go out to night clubs; *on Saturday evenings we go out clubbing in the West End* (NOTE: **clubbing - clubbed**)

clubhouse ['klʌbhaʊs] *noun* house where members of a club meet; *the golf clubhouse is too small for the number of members*

clue [kluː] *noun* information which helps you solve a mystery or puzzle; *the detective had missed a vital clue; I don't understand the clues to this crossword;* **I haven't a clue** = I don't know at all; *the police still haven't a clue who did it*

clump [klʌmp] **1** *noun* group of shrubs, trees, etc.; *we'll walk as far as that clump of trees and come back* **2** *verb* to move making a dull noise; *he was clumping around the kitchen in his clogs; the people in the flat upstairs started clumping about in the middle of the night*

clumsy ['klʌmzi] *adjective* who frequently breaks things or knocks things over; *she's a beautiful dancer, but clumsy once she gets on an ice rink; don't let Ben set the table - he's so clumsy, he's bound to break something* (NOTE: **clumsier - clumsiest**)

clung [klʌŋ] *verb see* CLING

cluster ['klʌstə] **1** *noun* group of objects together; *a brooch with a cluster of pearls; he photographed a cluster of stars* **2** *verb* **to cluster together** = to form a group; *they clustered round the noticeboard to read their exam results*

clustered ['klʌstəd] *adjective* grouped together; *the village consists of ten little cottages clustered round the church; a few houses clustered together at the foot of the hill*

clutch [klʌtʃ] **1** *noun* **(a)** tight clasp; *she felt the clutch of his fingers on her sleeve;* **in the clutches of** = under the control of; *if the company were to get into their clutches it would be a disaster* **(b)** mechanism for changing the gears in a car; *the car has just had a new clutch fitted;* **clutch pedal** = pedal which operates the clutch and allows the driver to change gear; **to let in the clutch** = to make the clutch engage; *let the clutch in slowly, or you'll stall the car* (NOTE: plural is **clutches**) **2** *verb* to grab hold of; *she clutched my arm as we stood on the edge of the cliff*

clutter ['klʌtə] **1** *noun* mass of things left lying about; *all this clutter will be cleared away by the weekend* (NOTE: no plural) **2** *verb* to fill a room, etc., with a mass of things; *her desk is cluttered with papers and invoices; don't clutter your mind with useless information*

cm *see* CENTIMETRE; *yesterday we had 3cm of rain; 25cm of snow had fallen during the night*

co. [kəʊ *or* 'kʌmpəni] *abbreviation for* COMPANY; *J. Smith & Co.*

c/o ['siː'əʊ] *(in addresses)* = CARE OF; *Jane Smith, c/o Mr & Mrs Jonas, 4 Willowbank Road*

coach [kəʊtʃ] **1** *noun* **(a)** large bus for travelling long distances; *there's an hourly coach service to Oxford; they went on a coach tour of southern Spain; the coach driver fell asleep while driving;* **coach party** = group of people travelling together in a coach; *there were no seats left in the restaurant as a coach party had arrived just before us;* **coach station** = place where coaches and buses begin and end their journey; *we had to wait at the coach station for an hour; see also*

SLOWCOACH (b) passenger carriage on a train; *the first four coaches are for Waterloo* (c) *US* category of seat on a plane which is cheaper than first class; *we went coach to Washington* (d) person who trains sportsmen, etc.; *the coach told them that they needed to spend more time practising*; *he's a professional football coach* (NOTE: plural is **coaches**) 2 *verb* (a) to train sportsmen *or* sportswomen; *she was coached by a former Olympic gold medallist* (b) to give private lessons to someone; *all the actors had to be coached separately*

coaching ['kəʊtʃɪŋ] *noun* (a) training of sportsmen; *the England team have been having special coaching* (b) giving private lessons to someone; *in spite of all the coaching he'd had, he still failed the exam*

coachload ['kəʊtʃləʊd] *noun* number of people carried in a coach; *we get so few tourists that a coachload of them is a real surprise*; *coachloads of schoolchildren arrived at the amusement park*

coagulate [kəʊ'ægjʊleɪt] *verb* to clot, to change from semi-liquid to semi-solid; *in haemophilia, blood doesn't coagulate easily*

coal [kəʊl] *noun* black substance which you can burn to make heat; *it's getting cold in here - put some more coal on the fire*; *I do love a good coal fire!*; **coal-fired power station** = electric power station which burns coal (NOTE: no plural: **some coal; a bag of coal; a piece of coal** *or* **a lump of coal**)

COMMENT: coal is a black mineral formed from the remains of fossilized trees which existed in prehistoric times. Sometimes is it still possible to see fossil leaves in coal when it is split

coalesce [kəʊə'les] *verb* (*formal*) to join together into one mass or group; *heating the compounds makes them coalesce*

coalfield ['kæəlfiːld] *noun* area of coal underground; *it is no longer economically viable to mine this coalfield*; *ten years ago, there were ten pits in this coalfield*

coalition [kəʊə'lɪʃn] *noun* combination of several political parties to form a government; *they formed a coalition government*; *a coalition of the Labour and Liberal parties*

coalmine ['kəʊlmaɪn] *noun* mine where coal is dug; *the last remaining coalmine will close next week*; *my grandfather worked in a Welsh coalmine*

coarse [kɔːs] *adjective* (a) not fine, not small; *coarse grains of sand*; *a coarse net* (b) rough, not refined; *he gave a coarse laugh*; *he could hear her coarse voice booming down the corridor* (c) rude (joke); *he made a coarse gesture and walked out*; *don't make any coarse remarks in front of my mother* (d) **coarse fishing** = fishing for fish other than trout or salmon in rivers or lakes, not in the sea; *the coarse fishing season opens next week* (NOTE: **coarser - coarsest**; do not confuse with **course**)

coarsen ['kɔːsn] *verb* to become coarse; *his face, which had been delicate when he was a boy, coarsened as he grew older*

coast [kəʊst] *noun* land by the sea; *after ten weeks, Columbus saw the coast of America*; *the south coast is the warmest part of the country*; *let's drive down to the coast this weekend*; **from coast to coast** = from the sea on one side of a country to the sea on the other side; *he crossed the USA from coast to coast*

coastal ['kəʊstəl] *adjective* referring to the coast; *the coastal resorts of southern England*

coaster ['kəʊstə] *noun* (a) flat dish or small mat for standing a bottle or glass on; *he bought a set of 6 coasters in the museum*; *here's a coaster to put your glass on* (b) ship which sails from port to port along the coast; *we sailed round Africa on a small coaster*

coastguard ['kəʊstgɑːd] *noun* person who guards a piece of coast, watching out for wrecks, smugglers, etc.; *coastguards stopped a fishing boat suspected of carrying drugs*

coastline ['kəʊstlaɪn] *noun* outline of a coast; *the rocky Cornish coastline*

coat [kəʊt] 1 *noun* (a) piece of clothing which you wear on top of other clothes when you go outside; *you'll need to put your winter coat on - it's just started to snow*; *she was wearing a black fur coat* (b) **coat of paint** = layer of paint covering something; *that window frame needs a coat of paint*; *we gave the door two coats of paint* = we painted the door twice 2 *verb* to cover with a layer of something; *we coated the metal disc with platinum*

coated ['kəʊtɪd] *adjective* covered with; *the streets were coated with fine dust from the volcano*; *a biscuit coated with chocolate*

-coated ['kəʊtɪd] *suffix* covered with; *chocolate-coated biscuits*; *sugar-coated almonds*; *a platinum-coated disc*

coat-hanger ['kəʊthæŋə] *noun* piece of wood, wire or plastic on which you hang a piece of clothing; *there were no coat-hangers in the hotel wardrobe*

coating ['kəʊtɪŋ] *noun* covering of paint, etc.; *a cake with a coating of chocolate*; *they spread a coating of tar on the roof to waterproof it*

co-author ['kəʊ'ɔːθə] 1 *noun* person who writes a book together with another author; *one of the co-authors died before the book was published* 2 *verb* to write a book with another author; *she co-authored a book on Churchill*

coax [kəʊks] *verb* **to coax someone into doing something** = to persuade someone to do something; *he was finally coaxed into paying for two tickets*

cob [kɒb] *noun* (a) seed head of maize; **corn on the cob** = a head of maize, with seeds on it, served hot with butter; *corn on the cob is very popular in North America* (b) **cob nut** = large hazel nut; *this bag of mixed nuts includes cob nuts and walnuts* (c) male swan; *don't go near the swans' nest - the cob attacks anyone passing by* (d) sturdy short-legged riding horse (e) round loaf of bread; *could you stop at the bakery and buy a wholemeal cob?*

cobalt ['kəʊbɔːlt] *noun* (a) metallic element used to make alloys; *cobalt 60 is used in radiotherapy* (NOTE: Chemical element: chemical symbol: **Co**; atomic number: **27**) (b) blue colour obtained from this metal; *a tube of cobalt blue paint*

cobbled ['kɒbld] *adjective* covered with cobblestones; *the cobbled courtyards of Hampton Court Palace*; *the narrow cobbled streets in old Montreal*

cobbler ['kɒblə] *noun* (a) person who mends shoes; *ask the cobbler how much it will cost to put new heels* *on these shoes* **(b)** *US* dessert made of cooked fruit with a cake topping; *she baked an apple cobbler*

cobblestone ['kɒblstəʊn] *noun* round stone set in cement to make the surface of a street; *the carriage clattered over the cobblestones*; *in the old town, the streets are paved with cobblestones*

cobra ['kəʊbrə or 'kɒbrə] *noun* large tropical snake with a poisonous bite; *he picked up his young son quickly when he spotted a king cobra near the beach*

cobweb ['kɒbweb] *noun* net of fine thread made by a spider; *the bedroom hadn't been cleaned and everything was covered with cobwebs* (NOTE: American English is also **spiderweb**)

Coca-Cola ['kəʊkə 'kəʊlə] *noun* trademark for a popular fizzy soft drink; *two Coca-Colas, please, and a pint of beer* (NOTE: often just called **coke: two cokes, please**)

cocaine [kə'keɪn] *noun* painkilling drug, which is addictive; *a cocaine addict* (NOTE: no plural; often just called **coke**)

coccyx ['kɒksɪks] *noun* lowest bone in the backbone, formed of four bones which have fused together; *the coccyx is like a triangle in shape* (NOTE: plural is **coccyges** [kɒk'saɪdʒiːz])

cock [kɒk] **1** *noun* male bird, especially a male domestic chicken; *we were woken by the cocks crowing* (NOTE: American English is **rooster**) **2** *verb* to **cock your ears for** = to listen carefully for something; *the dogs sat by the edge of the field, their ears cocked*

cockerel ['kɒkrəl] *noun* young cock; *on our farm holiday, a cockerel woke us up every morning at 5 o'clock* (NOTE: American English is **rooster**)

cockle ['kɒkl] *noun* small edible shellfish; *we bought some cockles from a stall by the seafront; (informal)* to **warm the cockles of your heart** = to make you happy and full of warm feelings; *the cheers from the audience would warm the cockles of your heart*

cockney ['kɒkni] **1** *adjective* referring to the East End of London; *he speaks with a real cockney accent*; **cockney slang** = RHYMING SLANG **2** *noun* **(a)** person from the East End of London; *he was born and brought up as a Cockney* **(b)** form of English spoken in the East End of London; *'let's have a butcher's' is cockney for 'let's have a look'; see* RHYMING SLANG

cockpit ['kɒkpɪt] *noun* place where the pilot sits in an aircraft, racing car or boat; *he climbed into the cockpit and looked at the instruments*

cockroach ['kɒkrəʊtʃ] *noun* black or brown beetle, a common household pest; *in hot damp climates, cockroaches are commonly found in houses* (NOTE: plural is **cockroaches**)

cocktail ['kɒkteɪl] *noun* **(a)** mixed alcoholic drink; *a Bloody Mary is a cocktail of vodka and tomato juice*; **cocktail lounge** = smart bar in a hotel; **cocktail party** = party where drinks and snacks are served, but not a full meal; **cocktail snacks** = little snacks eaten with drinks **(b)** mixture of various things; *she died after taking a cocktail of drugs*; **fruit cocktail** = mixture of little pieces of fruit; **Molotov cocktail** = home-made grenade made of petrol in a glass bottle; **prawn cocktail** = prawns in salad, eaten as a starter

cocky ['kɒki] *adjective (informal)* unpleasantly confident and conceited; *he's such a cocky little boy!; I told him not to be so cocky!*

cocoa ['kəʊkəʊ] *noun* **(a)** brown chocolate powder ground from the seeds of a tree, used for making a drink; *there's a tin of cocoa on the shelf next to the cooker*; **add cocoa powder to icing sugar to make chocolate icing** **(b)** drink made with cocoa powder and hot water or milk; *I'll warm up some milk to make some cocoa; he always has a cup of cocoa before going to bed* (NOTE: no plural)

coconut ['kəʊkənʌt] *noun* **(a)** large nut from a type of palm tree; *I won a coconut at the fair*; **coconut shy** = place at a fair where you throw balls at coconuts balanced on posts **(b)** white flesh from a coconut; *a coconut cake; I don't like biscuits with coconut in them* (NOTE: no plural in this meaning)

cod [kɒd] *noun* large white sea fish; *he ordered a plate of fried cod and chips*; **cod liver oil** = oil from the livers of cod, taken as a vitamin supplement (NOTE: plural is **cod**)

code [kəʊd] **1** *noun* **(a)** set of laws, rules of behaviour; *the hotel has a strict dress code, and people wearing jeans are not allowed in*; **the Highway Code** = rules for driving on the road; **code of practice** = general rules for a group of people, such as lawyers **(b)** secret words or system agreed in advance for sending messages; *we're trying to break the enemy's code; he sent the message in code*; **code word** = secret password **(c)** system of numbers or letters which mean something; *the code for Heathrow Airport is LHR; what is the code for phoning Edinburgh?*; **area code** = numbers which indicate an area when telephoning; **bar code** = system of lines printed on a product which can be read by a computer to give a reference number or price; **international dialling code** = numbers which indicate a country when telephoning; *what's the international dialling code for France?*

coded ['kəʊdɪd] *adjective* written in code; *the spy sent a series of coded messages to the London headquarters*; *convert the text to a secure coded form before sending it via the telephone*

codeine ['kəʊdiːn] *noun* drug taken to relieve headaches, flu, etc.; *he took a couple of codeine tablets before he went to bed*

code of conduct ['kəʊd əv 'kɒndʌkt] *noun* informal (sometimes written) rules by which a group of people work

codification [kəʊdɪfɪ'keɪʃn] *noun (formal)* act of codifying; *he was responsible for the codification of the country's laws*

codify ['kəʊdɪfaɪ] *verb (formal)* to write laws, rules of conduct, etc., in a systematic way; *French laws were codified by Napoleon*

coding ['kəʊdɪŋ] *noun* act of putting a code on something; *the coding of invoices*

coed [kəʊ'ed] **1** *adjective* coeducational, where male and female students are taught together; *the college only became coed in 1990* **2** *noun US* girl student at a coeducational school or college

coeducational [kəʊedjʊ'keɪʃənl] *adjective* (school) where male and female students are taught together; *the college only became coeducational in 1990*

coerce [kəʊ'ɜːs] *verb* to **coerce someone into doing something** = to force someone to do something; *they coerced her into signing the contract*

coercion [kəʊˈɜːʃn] *noun* forcing someone by pressure to do something such as commit a crime; *no coercion was needed to get him to agree to our terms*; *she only agreed under coercion* (NOTE: no plural)

coercive [kəʊˈɜːsɪv] *adjective* using force; *the use of coercive measures to move refugees is condemned in the press*

C of E [ˈsiː əv ˈiː] = CHURCH OF ENGLAND

coffee [ˈkɒfi] *noun* (a) bitter drink made from the seeds of a tropical plant; *would you like a cup of coffee?*; *I always take sugar with my coffee*; *the doctor told me to avoid tea and coffee*; **black coffee** = coffee without milk in it; **instant coffee** = drink which you make by pouring hot water onto a special coffee powder; **white coffee** = coffee with milk or cream in it; **coffee machine** = automatic machine which gives a cup of coffee or other drink when you put in a coin and press a button; **coffee spoon** = very small spoon, used with small cups of coffee (b) a cup of coffee; *I'd like a white coffee, please*; *three coffees and two teas, please* (c) pale brown colour, like white coffee; *we have a coffee-coloured carpet in our sitting room* (NOTE: usually no plural; **coffees** means **cups of coffee**)

coffee cup [ˈkɒfi kʌp] *noun* special small cup for coffee; *let's use coffee cups instead of mugs*

coffee pot [ˈkɒfi pɒt] *noun* special pot for making coffee in; *my grandmother gave me her silver coffee pot*

coffee shop [ˈkɒfi ˈʃɒp] *noun* small restaurant (often in a hotel) serving tea, coffee and snacks; *it will be quicker to have lunch in the coffee shop than in the restaurant*

coffee table [ˈkɒfi ˈteɪbl] *noun* low table in a sitting room, for putting cups, glasses, newspapers, etc., on; *the dog knocked my glass off the coffee table with his tail*; **coffee-table book** = heavy expensive book with many illustrations, which can be left on a table for people to look at

coffers [ˈkɒfəz] *noun* chests for holding money, hence financial resources; *the company has millions of pounds in its coffers which it could use on publicity if it wanted to*

coffin [ˈkɒfɪn] *noun* long wooden box in which a dead person is buried or cremated; *they watched in silence as the coffin was lowered into the ground* (NOTE: American English prefers **casket**)

cog [kɒg] *noun* one of a series of little teeth sticking out from a wheel, which connect with teeth on another wheel to make it turn; *by pulling this lever you will disconnect the cogs*; (informal) **a cog in the machine** = person who plays an unimportant part in a big organization; *I'm not a director or anything like that, just a cog in the machine*

cogency [ˈkəʊdʒənsi] *noun* (formal) being cogent; *we cannot dispute the cogency of his arguments*

cogent [ˈkəʊdʒənt] *adjective* (formal) valid and powerful; *the committee put forward some very cogent arguments for a change in the law*

cognac [ˈkɒnjæk] *noun* brandy made in western France; *we were served an excellent cognac after dinner*

cognition [kɒgˈnɪʃən] *noun* (formal) process by which you sense something and recognize and understand it; *the development of cognition in babies*

cognitive [ˈkɒgnɪtɪv] *adjective* (formal) referring to the process of understanding; *he has made a study of the cognitive processes of young children*

cognizance [ˈkɒgnɪzəns] *noun* (formal) knowledge and understanding of a fact; **to take cognizance of something** = to take something into account

cognizant [ˈkɒgnɪzənt] *adjective* (formal) **cognizant of** = knowing, being aware of; *the court is cognizant of this fact*

cogwheel [ˈkɒgwiːl] *noun* wheel with little teeth round the edge; *this small cogwheel connects with the large wheel, which turns the axle*

cohabit [kəʊˈhæbɪt] *verb* to live together as man and wife, especially when not married; *there may be problems for couples who cohabit when it comes to getting a mortgage on a house*

cohabitation [kəʊhæbɪˈteɪʃn] *noun* (a) living together as man and wife, although not married; *they had three years' cohabitation before they got married* (b) situation where different political parties hold executive power at the same time, especially in France, where the President and Parliament are elected for different periods of time and so may represent different parties; *following the election, we are in for a period of cohabitation*

cohere [kəʊˈhɪə] *verb* (formal) to stick together to form a whole; *gradually his ideas began to cohere*

coherence [kəʊˈhɪərəns] *noun* being coherent; *her story lacks coherence*

coherent [kəʊˈhɪərənt] *adjective* clear and logical (ideas, story, etc.); *she was not able to give a very coherent description of what had happened*

cohesion [kəʊˈhiːʒn] *noun* sticking together; *the lack of cohesion within the opposition means that they cannot be effective in opposing the government*

cohesive [kəʊˈhiːsɪv] *adjective* which sticks together; *the department is working well as a cohesive unit*

cohort [ˈkəʊhɔːt] *noun* (a) large group of people; *the Prince was followed by a cohort of journalists* (b) group of children, students, etc. of the same year; *this year's cohort have a better pass rate than last year's* (c) (informal) comrade, classmate; *my son and his dishevelled cohorts in class 2* (d) division of a Roman army, one tenth of a legion; *a cohort contained between three and six hundred men*

coil [kɔɪl] **1** *noun* (a) roll (of rope); one loop in something twisted round and round; *the sailors stacked the rope in coils on the deck*; *they surrounded the camp with coils of barbed wire* (b) **electric coil** = coil of wire which conducts electricity (c) spiral metal wire fitted into a woman's uterus as a contraceptive; *she went to the clinic to have a coil fitted or to be fitted with a coil* **2** *verb* to twist round something or into a coil; *the snake had coiled itself up in the basket*; *the sailors coiled the ropes on the deck*

coin [kɔɪn] **1** *noun* piece of metal money; *I found a 50p coin in the street*; *he hid the gold coins under his bed*; *this machine only takes 10p coins* **2** *verb* to invent a new word or phrase; *they coined the phrase 'surfing the net' to mean searching for information on the Internet*; (informal) **to coin a phrase** = to emphasize that you are saying something which is a normal everyday phrase; *'it never rains but it pours' - to coin a phrase*

coinage ['kɔɪnɪdʒ] *noun* **(a)** system of money used in a country; *the old coinage will still be used alongside the new for a period of two years* **(b)** new word or phrase which has been invented; *'surfing the net' is a recent coinage*

coincide [kəʊɪn'saɪd] *verb* **to coincide with something** = to happen by chance at the same time as something else; *the conference doesn't coincide with my birthday this year*; *do our trips to Frankfurt coincide? - if they do, we can meet while we're both there*

coincidence [kəʊ'ɪnsɪdəns] *noun* two things happening at the same time by chance; *the two of us happening to be at the same party was pure coincidence*; *by coincidence, she was waiting for a prescription too*; *what a coincidence, I went to that school too!*

coincidental [kəʊɪnsɪ'dentl] *adjective* happening by chance; *any resemblance between the characters in this play and members of the government is purely coincidental*

coincidentally [kəʊɪnsɪ'dentəli] *adverb* by coincidence; *coincidentally both inventors tried to patent the same invention at the same time*; *coincidentally we bumped into each other again at the airport*

coke [kəʊk] *noun* **(a)** fuel processed from coal, which produces a very strong heat; *the steel is produced in coke ovens* (NOTE: no plural in this meaning) **(b)** *(informal)* Coca-Cola, trademark for a type of fizzy soft drink; a glass of this drink; *he drinks nothing but coke*; *three cokes, and a beer, please* (NOTE: plural is **cokes**) **(c)** *(informal)* = COCAINE; *he takes or sniffs coke* (NOTE: no plural in this meaning)

Col. ['kɜːnəl] = COLONEL

cola ['kəʊlə] *noun* fizzy sweet drink; *the kids would like two colas please*

cold [kəʊld] **1** *adjective* **(a)** with a low temperature; not hot or not heated; *they say that cold showers are good for you*; *the weather turned colder after Christmas*; *it's too cold to go for a walk*; *if you're hot, have a glass of cold water*; *start eating, or your soup will get cold*; *he had a plate of cold beef and salad*; *put your slippers on if your feet are cold*; *(informal)* **to give someone the cold shoulder** = not to give someone a friendly welcome; **to get cold feet** = to begin to feel afraid that a plan is too risky; *we wanted to buy an old house and start a hotel business, but my husband got cold feet* **(b)** not friendly; *he got a very cold reception from the rest of the staff*; *she gave him a cold nod* (NOTE: **colder - coldest**) **2** *noun* **(a)** illness, when you sneeze and cough; *he caught a cold by standing in the rain at a football match*; *my sister's in bed with a cold*; *don't come near me - I've got a cold* **(b)** cold temperature (outdoors); *he got ill from standing in the cold waiting for a bus*; *house plants can't stand the cold*; **to be left out in the cold** = not to be part of a group any more

cold-blooded ['kəʊld'blʌdɪd] *adjective* **(a)** **cold-blooded animal** = animal whose body temperature is the same as the temperature of its surroundings; *fish, tortoises and lizards are all cold-blooded animals* **(b)** with no pity; *she's a cold-blooded murderess*

cold-shoulder ['kəʊldʃəʊldə] *verb* **to cold-shoulder someone** = not to give someone a friendly welcome

cold sore ['kəʊld 'sɔː] *noun* inflammation round the lips caused by the herpes virus

collaborate [kə'læbəreɪt] *verb* to work together; *he's collaborating with her on a new book*; *they've never collaborated before, so it will be interesting to see how they get on*; *anyone found collaborating with the enemy will be shot* (NOTE: you collaborate **with** someone **on** something)

collaboration [kəlæbə'reɪʃn] *noun* action of working together on something; *their collaboration on the dictionary lasted 25 years*; *I couldn't have done it without her collaboration*

collaborative ['kɒ'læbərətɪv] *adjective* involving people working together; *putting on an opera is a collaborative effort, involving hundreds of people*

collaborator [kə'læbəreɪtə] *noun* **(a)** person who works together with someone else; *we want to thank all the collaborators on this project* **(b)** person who works with the enemy forces occupying a country; *after the war, collaborators were hunted down and shot*

collage [kɒ'lɑːʒ] *noun* picture made from pieces of paper, etc., which are stuck onto a backing; *there were no collages at the students' art show*

collagen ['kɒlədʒən] *noun* bundles of protein fibres, which form connective tissue, bone and cartilage

collapse [kə'læps] **1** *noun* **(a)** sudden fall; *the collapse of the old wall buried two workmen* **(b)** sudden fall in price; *the collapse of the dollar on the foreign exchange markets* **(c)** sudden failure of a company; *investors lost thousands of pounds in the collapse of the bank* **2** *verb* **(a)** to fall down suddenly; *the roof collapsed under the weight of the snow* **(b)** to fail suddenly; *the company collapsed with £25,000 in debts*

collapsible [kə'læpsɪbl] *adjective* which can be folded up; *he took a collapsible picnic table with him*

collar ['kɒlə] **1** *noun* part of a shirt, coat, dress, etc., which goes round your neck; *I can't do up the top button on my shirt - the collar's too tight*; *she turned up her coat collar because the wind was cold*; *he has a winter coat with a fur collar*; **to get hot under the collar** = to get angry or worried about something **2** *verb* to catch hold of someone; *I managed to collar him as he was leaving the hotel*

collarbone ['kɒləbəʊn] *noun* clavicle, one of two long thin bones joining the shoulders to the breastbone; *she was lucky, after the fall all she had was a broken collarbone*

collate [kə'leɪt] *verb* **(a)** to check one text against another to make sure that it is all there **(b)** to check that the various parts of a book are gathered in the correct order before the book is bound

collateral [kə'lætərəl] **1** *adjective* additional to something, but less important; *there will always be collateral damage to civilian property during a war*; *one collateral benefit from living in the centre of town will be cheaper travel costs* **2** *noun* security used to provide a guarantee for a loan; *he offered his house as collateral*

colleague ['kɒliːg] *noun* person who works in the same company, office, school, etc. as you; *his colleagues gave him a present when he got married*; *I* *know Jane Gray - she was a colleague of mine at my last job*

collect [kə'lekt] **1** *verb* **(a)** to fetch something or bring things together; *your coat is ready for you to collect from the cleaner's*; *the mail is collected from the postbox twice a day*; *I must collect the children from school* **(b)** to buy things or bring things together as a hobby; *he collects stamps and old coins* **(c)** to gather money for charity; *they're collecting for Oxfam* **(d)** to come together; *a crowd collected at the scene of the accident* **2** *adverb* US **to call collect** = to ask the person being phoned to pay for the call; *if you don't have any money you can always try calling collect* (NOTE: British English for this is **to reverse the charges**)

collected [kə'ketɪd] *adjective* calm; *he didn't appear worried, but looked completely cool and collected*

collection [kə'lekʃən] *noun* **(a)** group of things brought together as a hobby; *he allowed me to see his stamp collection*; *the museum has a large collection of Italian paintings* **(b)** money which has been gathered; *we're making a collection for Oxfam* **(c)** action of bringing things together; *debt collection* = collecting money which is owed **(d)** fetching of goods; *your order is in the warehouse awaiting collection* **(e)** taking of letters from a postbox or post office for dispatch; *there are six collections a day from the postbox at the corner of the street*; *the last collection is at 6 p.m.*

collective [kə'lektɪv] **1** *adjective* done together; *they had a meeting and soon reached a collective decision*; **collective bargaining** = wage negotiations between management and unions **2** *noun* business run by a group of workers; *the owner of the garage sold out and the staff took it over as a workers' collective*

collector [kə'lektə] *noun* **(a)** person who collects things as a hobby; *it's an important sale for collectors of 18th century porcelain*; **stamp collector** = person who collects stamps **(b)** person who collects things as a job; **debt collector** = person who collects money which is owed; **ticket collector** = person who takes tickets from passengers

college ['kɒlɪdʒ] *noun* **(a)** teaching institution (for adults and adolescents); *she's going on holiday with some friends from college*; *he's studying accountancy at the local college*; *the college library has over 20,000 volumes*; **college of education** = college where teachers are trained; **college of further education** = teaching establishment for students after secondary school **(b)** US teaching institution for adolescents and adults, which grants degrees at BA level (NOTE: in British English this is a **university**)

collegiate [kə'liːdʒiət] *adjective* made up of several colleges; *Oxford and Cambridge are collegiate universities*

collide [kə'laɪd] *verb* **to collide with something** = to bump into something; *he lost control of the car and collided with a bus*

collie ['kɒli] *noun* type of sheepdog with long hair; *he uses two collies on his mountain farm*

collier ['kɒliə] *noun* **(a)** (*old*) coal miner; *thousands of colliers worked in the mines in the 1930s* **(b)** ship which carries coal; *a collier ran aground just outside the harbour*

colliery ['kɒljəri] *noun* coalmine; *the last colliery in the area is to close at the end of the year*; *almost every man in the village worked at the colliery* (NOTE: plural is **collieries**)

collision [kə'lɪʒən] *noun* bumping into something; *two people were injured in the collision*; *a collision between a lorry and a bus closed the main road for some time*

collocate ['kɒləkeɪt] *verb* (*formal*) (*of a word*) to be used with another word; *'commit' collocates with 'crime' but 'make' does not*

collocation [kɒlə'keɪʃn] *noun* (*formal*) typical occurrence of a word with another word; *'blazing row' and 'blazing fire' are both collocations*

colloquial [kə'ləʊkwiəl] *adjective* used in common speech; *he writes in a very colloquial style*; *'quid' is a colloquial word meaning 'pound'*

colloquialism [kə'ləʊkwiəlɪzm] *noun* expression used in common speech; *'kick the bucket' is a colloquialism meaning 'to die'*

collusion [kə'luːʒn] *noun* illegal cooperation or agreement to cheat someone; *he was accused of working in collusion with the rival company*

cologne [kə'ləʊn] *noun* pleasant-smelling type of perfume; *grandmother came into the room smelling of cologne*; *he sprinkled some cologne on his handkerchief* (NOTE: also called **eau-de-cologne**)

> COMMENT: originally cologne came from the town of Cologne in Germany (the town is called Köln in German)

Colombia [kə'lʌmbiə] *noun* country in central South America (NOTE: capital: **Bogota**; people: **Colombians**; language: **Spanish**; currency: **Colombian peso**)

Colombian [kə'lʌmbiən] **1** *adjective* referring to Colombia **2** *noun* person from Colombia

colon ['kəʊlən] *noun* **(a)** the main part of the large intestine, going from the small intestine to the rectum; *the intestines are divided into two parts: the small intestine and the large intestine or colon* **(b)** printing sign (:); *use a colon before starting a list*; *a colon is used after a letter to indicate one of the drives in a computer*

colonel ['kɜːnl] *noun* officer in charge of a regiment, an army rank above lieutenant-colonel; *he married the colonel's daughter*; *is Colonel Davis in?* (NOTE: used as a title before a surname: **Colonel Davis**; often shortened to **Col.: Col. Davis**) (NOTE: do not confuse with **kernel**)

colonial [kə'ləʊniəl] *adjective* referring to a colony; *Britain was once an important colonial power*; *the colonial status of Hong Kong ended in 1997*

colonialism [kə'ləʊniəlɪzm] *noun* practice of establishing colonies in other lands; *the meeting denounced colonialism, and demanded independence*

colonialist [kə'ləʊniəlɪst] **1** *adjective* believing in colonialism; *they fought for their colonialist ideals* **2** *noun* person who believes in colonialism; *it is hard to believe that there are still some staunch colonialists*

colonization [kɒlənaɪ'zeɪʒn] *noun* act of colonizing; *the colonization of Brazil by the Portuguese in the 16th century*

colonize ['kɒlənaɪz] *verb* to take possession of an area or country and rule it as a colony; *the government was accused of trying to colonize the Antarctic Region*

colonnade [kɒlə'neɪd] *noun* row of columns; *a tall colonnade links the two wings of the house*

colonnaded [kɒlə'neɪdɪd] *adjective* with a colonnade; *the temple has a colonnaded entrance hall*

colony ['kɒləni] *noun* (a) territory ruled by another country; *Roman colonies were established in North Africa and along the shores of the Black Sea*; *the former French colonies in Africa* (b) group of animals or humans living together; *a colony of ants*; *an artists' colony* (NOTE: plural is **colonies**)

color ['kʌlə] *noun & verb US see* COLOUR

colossal [kə'lɒsl] *adjective* very large, huge; *do they realize what a colossal undertaking that is?*; *the company made a colossal profit last year*; *colossal heads of presidents are cut into the cliff face*; *the play was a colossal success*

colour *US* **color** ['kʌlə] **1** *noun* (a) shade which an object has in light (red, blue, yellow, etc.); *what colour is your bathroom?*; *I don't like the colour of his shirt*; *his socks are the same colour as his shirt*; **to be off-colour** = to feel unwell; *he's a bit off-colour today, so he won't be coming to the party* (b) not black or white; *the book has pages of colour pictures*; **colour TV** or **colour film** = TV or film in all colours, not just black and white (c) shade of a person's skin; *people must not be discriminated against on grounds of sex, religion or colour*; **colour bar** = using the colour of someone's skin as an obstacle to something (d) **water colour(s)** = paint which is mixed with water; *I used to paint in oils but now I prefer water colours*; *see also* WATERCOLOUR (e) **local colour** = amusing or unusual details which go with a certain place; *carts pulled by donkeys lend some local colour to the scene* **2** *verb* to add colour to something; *the children were given crayons and told to colour the trees green and the earth brown*

colour-blind ['kʌlə blaɪnd] *adjective* not able to tell the difference between certain colours, such as red and green; *he couldn't become a pilot because he's colour-blind*

coloured *US* **colored** ['kʌləd] *adjective* (a) in colour; *a coloured postcard*; *a book with coloured illustrations* (b) with a skin that is not white; *coloured children make up over 90% of this class*

-coloured *US* **-colored** ['kʌləd] *suffix* with a certain colour; *a flame-coloured tie*; *she was wearing a cream-coloured shirt*

colourful *US* **colorful** ['kʌləfʊl] *adjective* (a) brightly coloured; *I'm trying to create a flowerbed which will remain colourful all year round*; *she tied a colourful silk scarf round her hair* (b) full of excitement and adventure; *she lived a colourful existence as a dancer in an Egyptian nightclub*; *a colourful account of life in Vienna before the First World War*

colouring *US* **coloring** ['kʌlərɪŋ] *noun* (a) way in which something or a plant or animal is coloured; *the bright colouring of parrots*; *the brilliant colouring of woods in autumn* (b) complexion, the colour of your skin and hair; *choose a lipstick that goes with your colouring* (c) **colouring matter** or **artificial colouring** = substance which gives colour to something such as food; *the jam contains no artificial colouring*

COMMENT: colouring additives are shown on labels as E numbers. Some are natural juices, like carrot juice or chlorophyll. Others are not natural and some may be carcinogenic. The commonest colouring additive used in food is caramel

colouring book ['kʌlərɪŋ 'bʊk] *noun* book with black and white drawings which a child can colour with crayons or paint; *the airline provides colouring books and crayons for all passengers under 12 years old*

colourless *US* **colorless** ['kʌlələs] *adjective* (a) with no colour; *he offered me a glass of some colourless liquid* (b) uninteresting; *the main character of the film is fairly colourless*

colour scheme ['kʌlə 'skiːm] *noun* different colours chosen by a designer for a room, a shop, etc.; *he chose a purple and grey colour scheme for the wine bar*

colour supplement ['kʌlə 'sʌpləmənt] *noun* separate section of a newspaper which is entirely in colour, like a magazine; *there should be a colour supplement with our newspaper today, but it's missing*

colt [kəʊlt] *noun* (a) young male horse; *the Irish colt won the race by two lengths* (NOTE: a young female horse is a **filly**) (b) **the colts** = a junior sports team; *the Colts won 2 - 0*; *our colts are top of the league*

column ['kɒləm] *noun* (a) tall pillar; *there is a row of huge columns at the entrance to the British Museum*; *Nelson's Column is in Trafalgar Square* (b) thing which is tall and thin; *a thin column of smoke rose from the bonfire*; **spinal column** = backbone; **control column** = handle for steering an aircraft; **steering column** = the pillar which holds a steering wheel in a car, bus, etc. (c) line of people, one after the other; *a column of prisoners came into the camp*; *columns of refugees crossed the border* (d) *(in the army)* line of soldiers, tanks, etc., moving forward; *two columns of infantry advanced towards the enemy positions*; *an armoured column entered the town* (e) thin block of printing going down a page; *his article ran to three columns on the first page of the paper*; *'continued on page 7, column 4'* (f) series of numbers, one under the other; *to add up a column of figures*; *put the total at the bottom of the column* (g) regular article in a newspaper; *she writes a gardening column for the local newspaper*; *regular readers of this column will know about my problems with drains*; **gossip column** = regular article about famous people and their private lives

columnist ['kɒləmɪst] *noun* journalist who writes regularly for a paper; *our regular columnist is on holiday, so the editor had to write the motoring feature this week*; **gossip columnist** = person who writes a gossip column

coma ['kəʊmə] *noun* state of unconsciousness from which a person cannot be awakened by external stimuli; *he went into a coma and never regained consciousness*; *she has been in a coma for four days*

comatose ['kəʊmətəʊs] *adjective* (a) in a coma; *a comatose patient* (b) *(informal)* sleepy, half-asleep; *after the long meeting they all looked comatose*

comb [kəʊm] **1** *noun* instrument with long teeth used to make your hair straight; *her hair is in such a tangle that you can't get a comb through it* **2** *verb* to smooth your hair with a comb; *she was combing her hair in front of the mirror*

combat ['kɒmbæt] **1** *noun* fighting; *these young soldiers have no experience of combat*; *they exercise with periods of unarmed combat* **2** *verb* to fight against; *they have set up a special police squad to combat drugs*

combatant ['kɒmbətənt] **1** *adjective* who is fighting **2** *noun* person who is fighting

combative ['kɒmbətɪv] *adjective* who likes to get into quarrels or arguments; *a group of combative residents is trying to prevent the building development on farmland by the village*; *she's in a combative mood today - better not ask her for anything*

combination [kɒmbɪ'neɪʃn] *noun* **(a)** several things taken together; *a combination of cold weather and problems with the car made our holiday in Germany a disaster* **(b)** series of numbers which open a lock; *the safe has a combination lock*; *I've forgotten the combination to my briefcase*

combine 1 *noun* ['kɒmbaɪn] **(a)** large financial or commercial group; *a German industrial combine* **(b)** **combine (harvester)** = large farm machine which cuts corn, takes out and keeps the seeds and throws away the straw; *a row of combine harvesters moved across the huge field* **2** *verb* [kəm'baɪn]; **to combine with** = to join together with; *the cold weather combined with high winds has made it a dreadful harvest*

combined [kəm'baɪnd] *adjective* taken together; *the combined customs forces of several countries have tried to prevent cigarette smuggling*

combustible [kəm'bʌstɪbl] **1** *adjective* which can easily catch fire; *the warehouse was full of paint and other combustible substances* **2** *noun* substance which can easily catch fire; *oil and other combustibles must be carefully stored*

combustion [kəm'bʌstʃən] *noun* **(a)** burning **(b)** rapid burning of fuel to create heat, power, etc.; **internal combustion engine** = type of engine in which petrol is burned inside the cylinders of the engine, so forcing the pistons to move

come [kʌm] *verb* **(a)** to move to or towards this place; *come and see us when you're in London*; *the doctor came to see him yesterday*; *some of the children come to school on foot*; *don't make any noise - I can hear someone coming*; *come up to my room and we'll talk about the problem* **(b)** to happen; *how did the door come to be open?*; *(informal)* **how come?** = why?, how?; *how come the front door was unlocked?* **(c)** to occur; *what comes after R in the alphabet?*; *P comes before Q*; *what comes after the news on TV?* (NOTE: **coming - came** [keɪm] **- has come**)

come across ['kʌm ə'krɒs] *verb* to find by chance; *we came across this little restaurant when we were out walking*

come along ['kʌm ə'lɒŋ] *verb* **(a)** to go with someone; *if you walk, the children can come along with us in the car* **(b)** to hurry; *come along, or you'll miss the bus*

come apart ['kʌm ə'pɑːt] *verb* to break into pieces; *the toy simply came apart in my hands*

come back ['kʌm 'bæk] *verb* to return; *they left the house in a hurry, and then had to come back to get their passports*; *they started to walk away, but the policeman shouted at them to come back*

comeback ['kʌmbæk] *noun* **(a)** reaction; *despite the mistakes in the book there has been no comeback yet*

from the readers **(b)** return of a singer or sportsman, etc., after retirement; *she is trying to make a comeback*

comedian [kə'miːdiən] *noun* man who tells jokes to make people laugh; *a well-known TV comedian*

come down ['kʌm 'daʊn] *verb* **(a)** to get lower; *the price of oranges has come down* **(b)** to come downstairs; *she was in bed but had to come down to answer the phone* **(c)** *(informal)* to get a disease; *the children have come down with measles*

comedown ['kʌmdaʊn] *noun* situation making you feel unimportant; *what a comedown! - last year he was a star, and now he works in a record shop*

comedy ['kɒmədi] *noun* play or film which makes you laugh; *'A Midsummer Night's Dream' is one of Shakespeare's comedies* (NOTE: plural is **comedies**)

come in ['kʌm 'ɪn] *verb* to enter; *please come in, and make yourself at home*; *why didn't you ask him to come in?*

come into ['kʌm 'ɪntʊ] *verb* **(a)** to enter; *three people came into the restaurant* **(b)** **to come into money** = to inherit money; *she came into a fortune when she was twenty-one*

comely ['kʌmli] *adjective (old)* attractive; *a comely girl* (NOTE: used only of women)

come of ['kʌm 'ɒv] *verb* to happen as a result of; *nothing came of his plan to paint the kitchen*

come off ['kʌm 'ɒf] *verb* **(a)** to stop being attached; *the button has come off my coat*; *I can't use the kettle, the handle has come off* **(b)** to be removed; *the paint won't come off my coat* **(c)** to do well or badly; *our team came off badly in the competition*

come on ['kʌm 'ɒn] *verb* **(a)** to hurry; *come on, or we'll miss the start of the film* **(b)** to arrive; *a storm came on as we were fishing in the bay*; *night is coming on*; *she thinks she has a cold coming on*

come out ['kʌm 'aʊt] *verb* **(a)** to move outside; *come out into the garden, it's beautifully hot* **(b)** *(of photograph, etc.)* to appear; *the church didn't come out very well on the photo*; *something must be wrong with the camera - half my holiday pictures didn't come out* **(c)** **to come out (on strike)** = to strike; *all the train drivers came out on strike* **(d)** to be removed; *the ink marks won't come out of my white shirt*; *red wine stains don't come out easily* **(e)** to appear for sale; *the magazine comes out on Saturdays* **(f)** to state publicly that you are homosexual; *the minister came out before the newspapers started to print stories about him* **(g)** *(informal)* **to come out in a rash** = to develop a rash; **to come out with** = to say something unexpected; *he came out with a really strange proposal*

comer ['kʌmə] *noun* person who comes; **tournament open to all comers** = tournament which is open to anyone who comes; **latecomers** = people who arrive late; *latecomers won't be allowed in until the first interval*; **newcomers** = people who have just arrived; *could all newcomers please sign the register?*

comet ['kɒmɪt] *noun* moving body in space, visible at night because of its bright tail; *Halley's Comet returns every 76 years*

come through ['kʌm 'θruː] *verb* **(a)** to move through something to get to a place; *come through the kitchen into the dining room* **(b)** *(of information)* to arrive by phone, fax, etc.; *the message came through this morning*

come to [ˈkʌm ˈtuː] *verb* **(a)** to add up to; *the bill comes to £10* **(b)** to become conscious again; *when he came to, he was in hospital*

come up [ˈkʌm ˈʌp] *verb* **(a)** to reach a certain height; *she's getting tall - she already comes up to my shoulders; the water came up to my waist* **(b)** to come close to someone; *the policeman came up to him and asked to see his passport* **(c)** to come up against something = to stop because something is in the way; *we came up against a lot of opposition from the management*

comfort [ˈkʌmfət] **1** *noun* **(a)** thing which helps to make you feel happier; *it was a comfort to know that the children were safe* **(b)** state of being comfortable; *they live in great comfort; you expect a certain amount of comfort on a luxury liner; she complained about the lack of comfort in the second-class coaches; see also* CREATURE **2** *verb* to make someone happier, when they are in pain or miserable, etc.; *she tried to comfort the little girl; he felt comforted by the gentle words of the priest*

comfortable [ˈkʌftəbl] *adjective* **(a)** soft and relaxing; *this chair isn't very comfortable - it has a wooden seat; there are more comfortable chairs in the lounge* **(b)** to make yourself comfortable = to relax; *she made herself comfortable in the chair by the fire*

comfortably [ˈkʌmftəbli] *adverb* **(a)** in a soft or relaxing way; *if you're sitting comfortably, I'll explain to you what the work involves; make sure you're comfortably dressed because it is rather cold outside* **(b)** comfortably off = having plenty of money; *her husband left her comfortably off when he died*

comforting [ˈkʌmfətɪŋ] *adjective* which comforts; *he gave her a comforting hug as she lay on the hospital bed; it's comforting to think that the police patrol the centre of town every night*

comic [ˈkɒmɪk] *noun* **(a)** children's paper with cartoon stories; *he spends his pocket money on comics and sweets* **(b)** comedian, a man who tells jokes to make people laugh; *a well-known TV comic*

comical [ˈkɒmɪkl] *adjective* funny; *it wasn't supposed to be comical, but you couldn't help laughing; the clowns were wearing comical hats*

coming [ˈkʌmɪŋ] **1** *adjective* which is approaching; *their coming silver wedding anniversary; the horoscope tells you what will happen in the coming year* **2** *noun* arrival; **comings and goings** = lots of movement; *the photographers watched the comings and goings at the palace*

comma [ˈkɒmə] *noun* **(a)** punctuation mark (,) showing a break in the meaning of a sentence; *use a comma between each item listed in this sentence*; **inverted commas** = printing signs (" "), which are put round words which are being quoted or round titles; *you can put this French word in italics or in inverted commas; the title Pickwick Papers should be in inverted commas* **(b)** small brown butterfly with ragged wings, and a little white mark, like a comma, on the underside of each wing; *it seems that the number of comma butterflies is dwindling*

command [kəˈmɑːnd] **1** *noun* **(a)** order; *the general gave the command to attack*; **in command of** = in charge of; **second-in-command** = person serving under the main commander **(b)** knowledge (of a language); *she has a good command of French* **2** *verb* **(a)** to order; *he commanded the troops to open fire on the rebels* **(b)** to be in charge of; *he commands a group of guerillas*

commandant [kɒmənˈdænt] *noun* officer in charge of a military base, etc.; *any deserters who are captured will be taken before the camp commandant*

commandeer [kɒmənˈdɪə] *verb* to take property over to be used by the armed forces; *at the beginning of the war, their house was commandeered for army officers*

commander [kəˈmɑːndə] *noun* officer in charge of an army corps or ship; *the commander must make sure that all his soldiers know exactly what they must do*

commander-in-chief [kəˈmɑːndə ɪn ˈtʃiːf] *noun* person who is in charge of all the armed services of a country; *the President is also Commander-in-Chief* (NOTE: plural is **commanders-in-chief**)

commanding [kəˈmɑːndɪŋ] *adjective* **(a)** in authority, in command; **commanding officer** = officer in command; *report to your commanding officer when you arrive at the camp* **(b)** full of authority; *he spoke with a commanding voice and everyone listened* **(c)** commanding lead = position in which you are very likely to win; *the Russian team has a commanding lead in the tournament* **(d)** which dominates; *the castle occupies a commanding position on the hill above the town; the commanding presence of Henry VIII dominated the court*

commandment [kəˈmɑːndmənt] *noun* rule; **the Ten Commandments** = the ten rules given by God to Moses

commando [kəˈmɑːndəʊ] *noun* **(a)** group of soldiers who are specially trained to attack under difficult circumstances; *they planned a commando attack on the harbour* **(b)** member of such a group of soldiers; *masked commandos burst in through the door* (NOTE: plural is **commandos**)

commemorate [kəˈmeməreɪt] *verb* to celebrate the memory of someone, a special occasion, etc.; *we are gathered here today to commemorate those who died in the world wars; the statue was put up to commemorate the 400th anniversary of Shakespeare's birth*

commemorative [kəˈmemərətɪv] *adjective* which commemorates; *they have issued commemorative stamps in honour of the Queen's birthday; a commemorative service took place in the church of St Martin-in-the-Fields; there's a commemorative plaque on the wall of the old town hall*

commence [kəˈmens] *verb* (*formal*) to begin; *the ceremony will commence with the National Anthem*

commencement [kəˈmensmənt] *noun* **(a)** (*formal*) beginning; *at the commencement of the service, the priest asked everyone to stand* **(b)** US Commencement = day when degrees are awarded at a university or college; *we met the parents of some of the other students at Commencement* (NOTE: the British equivalent is **degree day, degree ceremony**)

commend [kəˈmend] *verb* (*formal*) to praise; *she was highly commended by the judges for her painting; I can commend him to you as an excellent salesman*

commendable [kəˈmendəbl] *adjective* (*formal*) which should be praised; *the manager showed commendable patience in dealing with the crowd of people with complaints*

commendably [kəˈmendəbli] *adverb* (*formal*) in a way which should be praised; *his speech at the wedding was commendably short*

commendation [kɒmenˈdeɪʃn] *noun* (*formal*) official report praising someone; *he received a commendation from the chief of police*

comment [ˈkɒment] **1** *noun* (**a**) words showing what you feel about something; *his comments were widely reported in the newspapers*; *the man made a rude comment accompanied by some very offensive gestures*; '*no comment*' = I refuse to discuss it in public (**b**) discussion of a question; *the scandal aroused considerable comment in the press*; *it is a sad comment on modern values that we spend more money on arms than on helping the poor* (NOTE: no plural in this meaning) **2** *verb* to comment on something = to make a remark about something; *he commented on the lack of towels in the bathroom*

commentary [ˈkɒməntri] *noun* (**a**) remarks about a book, a problem, etc.; *for intelligent commentary on current events you should read the 'Spectator'* (**b**) spoken report on a football match, horse race, etc.; *the match is being shown on Channel 4 with live commentary also on the radio* (NOTE: plural is **commentaries**)

commentate [ˈkɒmənteɪt] *verb* to describe what is happening at an event on radio or TV; *he was commentating on the Boat Race*; *this is the last time he will commentate on a horse race*

commentator [ˈkɒmənteɪtə] *noun* person who reports events as they happen, on the radio or TV; *radio commentators are much better at describing details than those on TV*

commerce [ˈkɒmɜːs] *noun* business, the buying and selling of goods and services; *a trade mission went to South America to boost British commerce in the region*; *the government has a blacklist of companies engaged in commerce with certain banned countries*; *see also* CHAMBER OF COMMERCE

commercial [kəˈmɜːʃl] **1** *adjective* (**a**) referring to business; *he is a specialist in commercial law*; **commercial college** = college which teaches business studies; **commercial course** = course where business skills are studied (**b**) used for business purposes, not private or military; *commercial aircraft*; *commercial vehicle* (**c**) profitable; *our commercial future looks doubtful*; **not a commercial proposition** = not likely to make a profit **2** *noun* advertisement on television; *our TV commercial attracted a lot of interest*

commercially [kəˈmɜːʃəli] *adverb* from a business point of view; *to succeed commercially, the product must be realistically priced*; **not commercially viable** = not likely to make a profit

commission [kəˈmɪʃn] **1** *noun* (**a**) group of people which investigates problems of national importance; *the government has appointed a commission to look into the problem of drugs in schools* (**b**) order for something to be made or to be used; *he received a commission to paint the portrait of the Prime Minister* (**c**) percentage of sales value given to the salesman; *she gets 15% commission on everything she sells*; *he charges 10% commission* (**d**) order making someone an officer; *he has a commission in the Royal Marines* (**e**) **out of commission** = not working; *the lift's out of commission* **2** *verb* (**a**) to authorize an artist or architect, etc., to do a piece of work; to authorize a piece

of work to be done; *the magazine commissioned him to write a series of articles on Germany*; *the statue was commissioned by the veterans' association* (**b**) to make someone an officer; *he was commissioned into the guards*

commissionaire [kəmɪʃəˈneə] *noun* doorman, man who stands at the door of a restaurant, hotel, club, etc.; *the commissionaire wouldn't let us in because we were wearing jeans*; *an imposing commissionaire in a top hat opened the car door*

commissioner [kəˈmɪʃnə] *noun* (**a**) representative of authority; **commissioner of police** = highest ranking police officer; **High Commissioner** = ambassador of a Commonwealth country; *the Indian High Commissioner made a speech* (**b**) **commissioner for oaths** = person, such as a solicitor, who is authorized to take sworn statements

commit [kəˈmɪt] *verb* (**a**) to carry out a crime; *the gang committed six robberies before they were caught*; *he said he was on holiday in Spain when the murder was committed* (**b**) **to commit suicide** = to kill yourself (**c**) **to commit someone for trial** = to send someone for trial; *she has been committed for trial at the Central Criminal Court* (**d**) **to commit funds to a project** = to agree to spend money on a project; *the party pledged to commit more funds to the health service* (**e**) **to commit yourself** = to promise to do something; to give your opinion; *he refused to commit himself*; *I can't commit myself to anything until I have more details* (NOTE: **committing - committed**)

commitment [kəˈmɪtmənt] *noun* (**a**) promise to pay money; *he has difficulty in meeting his commitments* (**b**) agreement to do something; *she made a firm commitment to be more punctual in future*; *we have the photocopier on one week's trial, with no commitment to buy*

committed [kəˈmɪtɪd] *adjective* firmly believing in; *he is a committed Christian*; *she is a committed peace campaigner*

committee [kəˈmɪtiː] *noun* official group of people who organize or discuss things for a larger body; *the town council has set up a committee to look into sports facilities*; *committee members will be asked to vote on the proposal*; **to be on a committee** = to be a member of a committee; *he's on the finance committee*

commodity [kəˈmɒdɪti] *noun* thing sold in very large quantities, especially raw materials (such as silver and tin) and food (such as corn or coffee); **basic commodities** = foodstuffs and raw materials; *the country's basic commodities are coffee and timber*; *because of the drought, even basic commodities have to be imported* (NOTE: plural is **commodities**)

commodore [ˈkɒmədɔː] *noun* (**a**) rank in the Navy above a captain; *several retired admirals and commodores attended his funeral* (**b**) person who is in charge of a yacht club; *the Commodore of the yacht club started the race*

common [ˈkɒmən] **1** *adjective* (**a**) which happens often, which you find everywhere; *the plane tree is a very common tree in towns*; *it's very common for people to get colds in winter*; **it is common knowledge** = everyone knows it; *it is common knowledge that he is having an affair with his secretary* (**b**) belonging to two or more people; *the two countries have a common frontier*; *blue eyes are not common to all the members of our family*; **common ownership** = ownership of a property by a group of people; **in common** = shared by two or more people; *they have two things in common - they are both Welsh and they are both left-handed* (NOTE: **commoner - commonest**) **2** *noun* land which belongs to a community; *we went walking on the common* (NOTE: now mainly used in names of places: **Clapham Common, Wimbledon Common,** etc.)

commoner ['kɒmənə] *noun* ordinary citizen, not a nobleman; *the princess married a commoner*

common law ['kɒmən 'lɔ:] *noun* law as laid down in decisions of courts, rather than by statute; **common-law wife** = woman who is living with a man as his wife without being married

commonly ['kɒmənli] *adverb* often; *rats are commonly found in sewers*; *this bird is commonly called the hedge sparrow*

Common Market ['kɒmən 'mɑːkɪt] *noun (old) see* EUROPEAN UNION

common-or-garden ['kɒmən ɔː 'gɑːdən] *adjective (informal)* very ordinary; *they live in a common-or-garden bungalow by the main road*

commonplace ['kɒmənpleɪs] *adjective* ordinary, which happens frequently; *public executions were commonplace in the 17th century*

Commons ['kɒmənz] *noun* **the (House of) Commons** = the lower house of the British Parliament, made up of 659 members; *she was first elected to the Commons in 1979*; *MPs sit in the House of Commons*; *a vote in the Commons defeated the bill*

common sense ['kɒmən 'sens] *noun* ordinary good sense; *use some common sense - switch the machine off before you start poking around inside it with a screwdriver*; *at least she had the common sense to call the police*

commonwealth ['kɒmənwelθ] *noun* **(a)** group of states; **the (British) Commonwealth** = an association of independent countries linked to Britain; *the Queen is the head of the Commonwealth* **(b)** republic; *the Commonwealth of Massachusetts*

commotion [kə'məʊʃən] *noun* confusion or trouble; *there was a sudden commotion in the school yard and the head teacher went to see what was the matter*

communal [kə'mjuːnəl] *adjective* held in common, belonging to several people; *the students have separate bedrooms, but use a communal kitchen*; *there are communal washing facilities on the campsite*

communally [kə'mjuːnəli] *adverb* done by several people together; *we work separately in departments but the main decisions are taken communally*

commune 1 *noun* ['kɒmjuːn] group of people who live together sharing everything; *what is it like to live in a commune?* **2** *verb* [kə'mjuːn] *(formal)* **to commune with someone** *or* **something** = to communicate with the spirit of someone or something; *she just wants to sit on the grassy hill, communing with nature*

communicate [kə'mjuːnɪkeɪt] *verb* **(a)** to send or give information to someone; *although she is unable to speak, she can still communicate by using her hands*; *he finds it impossible to communicate with his staff*; *communicating with our office in London has been quicker since we installed the fax*; *he communicated his wishes to me* **(b)** to connect with; **communicating rooms** = rooms with a connecting door between them; **communicating door** = door between two rooms; *the communicating door is kept locked at all times*

communication [kəmjuːnɪ'keɪʃn] *noun* **(a)** passing of information; *email is the most rapid means of communication*; *it is not a happy school - there is no communication between the head teacher and the other members of staff*; **to enter into communication with someone** = to start discussing something with someone, usually in writing; *we have entered into communication with their solicitors* **(b)** official message; *we had a communication from the local tax inspector* **(c) communications** = being able to contact people; *after the flood all communications with the outside world were cut off*

communion [kə'mjuːnjən] *noun* **(a)** fellowship with someone **(b) Holy Communion** = Christian ceremony where bread and wine are taken in memory of Christ's Last Supper; *the communion service will be taken by the vicar*

communiqué [kə'mjuːnɪkeɪ] *noun* official announcement; *in a communiqué from the Presidential Palace, the government announced that the President would be going on a world tour*

communism ['kɒmjunɪzm] *noun* social system in which all property is owned and shared by the society as a whole and not by individual people

communist ['kɒmjunɪst] **1** *adjective* referring to communism; *the Communist Party is holding its annual meeting this weekend* **2** *noun* person who believes in communism; member of the Communist Party; *he was a Communist all his life*; *the Communists have three seats on the city council*

community [kə'mjuːnɪti] *noun* **(a)** group of people living in one area; *the local community is worried about the level of violence in the streets*; **rural community** = people living in a small area of the countryside; *rural communities will suffer most from the reduced bus service*; **urban community** = a town's inhabitants; **community centre** = building providing sports or arts facilities for a community; *flood victims are being housed in the local community centre*; **religious community** = group of monks or nuns **(b) the Community** *or* **the European (Economic) Community** = THE EUROPEAN UNION (NOTE: plural is **communities**)

community service [kə'mjuːnɪti 'sɜːvɪs] *noun* working unpaid on behalf of the local community, usually as a sentence for some minor crime; *how many hours community service did he get?*; **community service order** = punishment where a criminal is sentenced to do unpaid work in the local community; *he is serving a community service order*

commute [kə'mjuːt] *verb* **(a)** to reduce a legal penalty; *the prison sentence was commuted to a fine*; *his death sentence was commuted to life imprisonment* **(b)** to travel to work from home each day; *he commutes from Oxford to his office in the centre of London* **(c)** to exchange one type of payment for another; *his pension has been commuted to a lump sum payment*

commuter [kə'mjuːtə] *noun* person who travels to work in town every day; *commuters face a 10% increase in rail fares*; **commuter belt** = area round a town where commuters live; *house prices in London's commuter belt have increased by 10% over the last year*; **commuter train** = train which commuters take in the morning and evening; *the commuter trains are full every morning*

compact 1 *adjective* [kəm'pækt] small; close together; *the computer system is small and very compact* **2** *noun* ['kɒmpækt] **(a)** *(formal)* agreement; *the two companies signed a compact to share their research findings* **(b) powder compact** = small box with face powder in it; *she always carries a compact in her handbag* **(c)** small family car; *they sold the four wheel drive and bought a compact*

compact disc (CD) ['kɒmpækt 'dɪsk] *noun* metal recording disc, which can hold a larger amount of music than a plastic record, and which is read by a laser in a special player; *the sound quality on CDs is better than on old records*

companion [kəm'pænjən] *noun* person or animal who lives with someone; *his constant companion was his old white sheepdog*; **travelling companion** = person who travels with someone; *he and his travelling companions were arrested as they tried to cross the border*

companionship [kəm'pænjənʃɪp] *noun* friendship; *she goes to the old people's centre mainly for companionship*; *after retirement, people often miss the companionship of their workmates*

company ['kʌmpni] *noun* **(a)** commercial firm; *it is company policy not to allow smoking anywhere in the offices*; *the company has taken on three secretaries*; *she runs an electrical company*; *he set up a computer company* (NOTE: usually written **Co.** in names: **Smith & Co.** Note also the plural **companies** in this meaning) **(b) company car** = car which belongs to a company and is lent to an employee to use for business or other purposes; **company director** = person appointed by the shareholders to help run a company; **company doctor** = doctor who works for a company and looks after sick workers; **Companies House** = office of the Registrar of Companies, who makes sure that companies are properly registered, and that they report their accounts and other information on time; *the company failed to lodge their accounts with Companies House* **(c)** being together with other people; *I enjoy the company of young people*; *she went to Paris in company with or in the company of three other girls from college*; **he is good company** = he's a very entertaining person to be with; **to keep someone company** = to be with someone to prevent them feeling lonely; *would you like to come with me to keep me company?*; **to part company** = to split up; *we parted company when we couldn't agree on how to develop the business* **(d)** group of people who work together; **a ship's company** = the crew of a ship; **a theatre company** = the actors and directors of a theatre **(e)** *(in the army)* part of a battalion, a group of men commanded by a captain

comparable ['kɒmprəbl] *adjective* which are similar or which can be compared; *the two towns are of comparable size*; *which is the nearest farm comparable to this one in size?*

comparative [kəm'pærətɪv] **1** *adjective* to a certain extent, when considered next to something else; *judged by last year's performance it is a comparative improvement* **2** *noun* form of an adjective or adverb showing an increase in level; *'happier', 'better' and 'more often' are the comparatives of 'happy', 'good' and 'often'*

COMMENT: comparatives are usually formed by adding the suffix -er to the adjective: 'quicker' from 'quick', for example; in the case of long adjectives, they are formed by putting 'more' in front of the adjective: 'more comfortable', 'more expensive', and so on

comparatively [kəm'pærətɪvli] *adverb* to a certain extent, more than something else; *the country is comparatively self-sufficient*; *she is comparatively well-off*; *comparatively speaking, he's quite tall*

compare [kəm'peə] *verb* **(a) to compare something with** *or* **to something else** = to look at two things side by side to see how they are different; *if you compare the situation in France with that in Britain* **(b) to compare something with** *or* **to something else** = to say that something is like something else; *he compared his mother's homemade bread to a piece of wood*

compared [kəm'peəd] *adjective* **compared to** *or* **with** = when you compare it to; *compared with my Rolls Royce, your car is tiny*; *compared to last year, this summer was cold*

comparison [kəm'pærɪsən] *noun* act of comparing; *this year, July was cold in comparison with last year*; **there is no comparison between them** = one is much better than the other

compartment [kəm'pɑːtmənt] *noun* **(a)** division inside a box; *the box is divided into several compartments*; **glove compartment** = little cupboard with a door in the dashboard in front of the passenger's seat in a car; *don't leave anything valuable in the glove compartment* **(b)** separate section in a railway carriage, or in a ship; *there are no compartments in these trains*; *the hold is divided into watertight compartments*

compass ['kʌmpəs] *noun* **(a)** device which indicates the north by means of a magnetic needle on a dial; *they were lost in the mountains, and without a compass had to rely on the sun and stars to go in the right direction* **(b) a pair of compasses** = device for drawing a circle; *set your compasses to 10mm and draw a circle with a diameter of 20mm*

compassion [kəm'pæʃn] *noun* pity, feeling of sympathy for someone unfortunate; *as a last act of compassion, the authorities allowed the prisoner to see his mother*; *the soldiers showed no compassion in separating families and driving them away from their homes*; **to have compassion on someone** = to feel sorry for someone; *the president had compassion on the prisoners and had them released*

compassionate [kəm'pæʃənət] *adjective* showing sympathy with someone who is ill, etc.; *his compassionate reaction to the news impressed her*; **compassionate leave** = permission to have time off work because someone has died, is ill, etc.; *the company granted him two weeks' compassionate leave following the death of his wife*

compassionately [kəm'pæʃənətli] *adverb* showing sympathy with someone; *most people reacted compassionately when they heard about her accident*

compatible [kəm'pætəbl] *adjective* **(a) compatible with something** = able to fit with something; *make sure the two computer systems are compatible* **(b)** able to live or work happily with someone; *how their marriage lasted so long no one knows - they were not at all compatible*

compatriot [kəm'pætrɪət] *noun* person from the same country; *I met many of your compatriots at the French embassy dinner*

compel [kəm'pel] *verb* to force; *he compelled her to sign the paper* (NOTE: **compelling - compelled**)

compelling [kəm'pelɪŋ] *adjective* (a) which forces you to do something; *he used a very compelling argument against capital punishment* (b) very exciting story or film; *the book was so compelling I couldn't put it down*

compensate ['kɒmpenseɪt] *verb* to **compensate someone for something** = to pay for damage, for a loss; *they agreed to compensate her for damage to her car*; *the airline refused to compensate him when his baggage was lost*

compensation [kɒmpen'seɪʃn] *noun* (a) payment for damage or loss; *the airline refused to pay any compensation for his lost luggage*; *you must submit a claim for compensation to the insurance company within two weeks*; **compensation for loss of office** = payment made to someone who is asked to leave a company before his or her contract ends (b) something that makes up for something bad; *working in the centre of London has its compensations*; *four weeks' holiday is no compensation for a year's work in that office*

compere *or* **compère** ['kɒmpeə] **1** *noun* host of a TV show, the person who introduces the performers in a show; *he's just signed a contract as compere of a TV quiz show* **2** *verb* to act as host in a TV show, to introduce the different performers; *she comperes a game show*

compete [kəm'piːt] *verb* to **compete with someone** = to try to beat someone in sport, trade, etc.; *he is competing in both the 100 and 200 metres*; *we have to compete with cheap imports from the Far East*

competence ['kɒmpɪtəns] *noun* (a) being able or efficient at a job; *does she have the necessary competence in foreign languages?*; *after this latest disaster, his competence to handle the job seems doubtful* (b) being legally able to do something, such as to judge a case; *the case falls within the competence of the tribunal*; *this is outside the competence of this court*

competent ['kɒmpɪtənt] *adjective* (a) legally able to do something; **the court is not competent to deal with this case** = the court is not legally able to deal with the case (b) efficient; *she is a very competent manager* (c) quite good, but not brilliant; *he's quite competent at maths*; *she's a competent golfer*

competing [kəm'piːtɪŋ] *adjective* who or which are in competition; **competing firms** = firms which compete with each other; **competing products** = products from different companies which are similar

competition [kɒmpə'tɪʃn] *noun* (a) sport or game where several teams or people enter and each tries to win; *France were winners of the competition*; *he won first prize in the piano competition*; *the competition is open to everybody* (NOTE: plural in this meaning is **competitions**) (b) trying to do better than someone in business; *our main competition comes from the big supermarkets*; *we have to keep our prices low because of competition from cheap imports* (c) **the competition** = people or companies who are trying to do better than you; *we have lowered our prices to try to beat the competition*; *the competition is or are planning to reduce their prices* (NOTE: singular in this meaning, but can take a plural verb)

competitive [kəm'petɪtɪv] *adjective* (a) liking to win competitions; *he's very competitive*; **competitive sports** = sports, like athletics, which are based on competition between people or teams (b) **competitive prices** = prices which are lower or no higher than those of rival firms; *we must keep our prices competitive if we want to stay in business*

competitor [kəm'petɪtə] *noun* (a) person who enters a competition; *all the competitors lined up for the start of the marathon* (b) company which competes; *two German firms are our main competitors*

compilation [kɒmpɪ'leɪʃn] *noun* (a) putting things together in a list or book; *the compilation of a dictionary is a never-ending task* (b) work which has been compiled; *his compilation of jokes from 19th century magazines has just been published*

compile [kəm'paɪl] *verb* (a) to draw up a list; *she compiled a list of all her friends whose names started with the letter 'R'*; *they have compiled a mass of data on space flights* (b) to write a dictionary; *Dr Johnson used many helpers to compile his dictionary*

complacency [kəm'pleɪsənsi] *noun* being complacent; *I am astonished by his complacency towards rival companies*

complacent [kəm'pleɪsnt] *adjective* satisfied with yourself; *this is no time to be complacent about our rivals*

complain [kəm'pleɪn] *verb* to say that something is no good or does not work properly; *the shop is so cold the staff have started complaining*; *she complained about the service*; *they are complaining that our prices are too high*; *she complained that no one spoke English in the hotel* (NOTE: you complain **to** someone **about** something or **that** something is no good)

complaint [kəm'pleɪnt] *noun* (a) saying that something is wrong; *she sent her letter of complaint to the managing director*; *you must file your complaint with the relevant department*; **complaints department** = department which deals with complaints from customers (b) illness; *she was admitted to hospital with a kidney complaint*

complement 1 *noun* ['kɒmplɪmənt] (a) thing which adds to or fits in with something else; *mint sauce is the perfect complement to roast lamb* (b) **a ship's complement** = the full crew of a ship **2** *verb* [kɒmplɪ'ment] to fit in with something; *the two colours complement each other perfectly*; *her jewellery complemented the colour of her hair* (NOTE: do not confuse with **compliment**)

complementary [kɒmplɪ'mentəri] *adjective* which fits in with something by offering things which the other thing does not have; *the two comedians are totally complementary - one is fat and jolly, the other thin and miserable*; **complementary medicine** = type of medicine which is used alongside traditional medicine, such as homeopathy and acupuncture; *more and more people, including some doctors, are turning to complementary medicine* (NOTE: do not confuse with **complimentary**)

complete [kəm'pliːt] **1** *adjective* with all its parts; *he has a complete set of the new stamps*; *we have to study the complete works of Shakespeare* **2** *verb* (a) to finish; *the builders completed the whole job in two days* (b) to fill in a form; *when you have completed the application form, send it to us in the envelope provided*

completely [kʌm'pliːtli] *adverb* totally; *the town was completely destroyed in the earthquake*; *I completely forgot about my dentist's appointment*

completion [kəm'pli:ʃn] *noun* act of finishing; *the bridge is nearing completion*; **completion of a contract** = signing of a contract

complex ['kɒmpleks] **1** *adjective* complicated; *the committee is discussing the complex problem of the site for the new hospital*; *the specifications for the machine are very complex* **2** *noun* **(a)** series of buildings; *the council has built a new sports complex*; *an industrial complex is planned on the site of the old steel works* **(b)** *(in psychiatry)* group of ideas which are based on an experience that you had in the past, and which influence the way you behave; *he has a complex about going bald*; *stop talking about her height - you'll give her a complex about it*; **inferiority complex** = feeling that you are inferior to others; **Electra complex** = love of a woman for her father and hatred for her mother; **Oedipus complex** = love of a man for his mother and hatred for his father (NOTE: plural is **complexes**)

complexion [kəm'plekʃn] *noun* colour of the skin on your face; *she has a beautiful pale complexion*

complexity [kəm'pleksɪti] *noun* **(a)** being complex; *the report was delayed because of the complexity of the problems* **(b)** difficult problems; *the complexities of the peace negotiations are horrendous*; *the complexities of organizing two birthday parties at the same time* (NOTE: plural is **complexities**)

compliance [kəm'plaɪəns] *noun* agreement to do what is ordered; *I am not sure they are acting in (full) compliance with the law*; *the government is asking for compliance from all taxpayers*

complicate ['kɒmplɪkeɪt] *verb* to make things complicated; *she tried to help, but all she did was to complicate things still further*

complicated ['kɒmplɪkeɪtɪd] *adjective* with many small details; difficult to understand; *it is a complicated subject*; *it's all getting too complicated - let's try and keep it simple*; *chess has quite complicated rules*; *the route to get to us is rather complicated, so I'll draw it on a piece of paper*

complication [kɒmplɪ'keɪʃn] *noun* **(a)** being complicated; *it all seems quite simple to me - what's the complication?* **(b)** illness occurring because of or during another illness; *she appeared to be getting better, but complications set in* **(c)** more trouble; *all these forms which we have to fill in just create further complications*

complicity [kəm'plɪsɪti] *noun* *(formal)* being involved in a crime as an accomplice; *her complicity in the robbery has been proved*

compliment 1 *noun* ['kɒmplɪmənt] **(a)** remark which praises someone *or* something; *she blushed when she read his compliments on her dancing*; **to be fishing for compliments** = to try to get someone to say nice things about you; **to pay someone a compliment** = to praise someone, to do something which shows you appreciate someone; *they paid her the compliment of asking her to speak to the meeting* **(b)** **compliments** = good wishes; **send him my compliments** = give him my good wishes; **with the compliments of Apple Co. Ltd** = with good wishes from Apple Co. Ltd; *a box of chocolates with the compliments of the manager or with the manager's compliments*; *please accept these flowers with my compliments* **2** *verb* ['kɒmplɪment] to praise; *I want to compliment the staff on an excellent turnover this year*; *I would like to compliment the chef*

on an excellent meal (NOTE: do not confuse with **complement**)

complimentary [kɒmplɪ'mentəri] *adjective* **(a)** that praises; *he was very complimentary about her dress*; *the reviews of his book were very complimentary* **(b)** **complimentary ticket** = free ticket, sent to a friend or business associate; *resale of complimentary tickets is not allowed by the club* (NOTE: do not confuse with **complementary**)

comply (with) [kəm'plaɪ] *verb* **(a)** to observe a rule; *does it comply with all the EU regulations?* **(b)** to obey an order; *failure to comply with the court order will lead to prosecution*

component [kəm'pəʊnənt] **1** *adjective* which forms part of a larger machine, etc.; *they supply component parts for washing machines* **2** *noun* small piece in a larger machine; *a components manufacturer*; *the assembly line stopped because they ran out of components*

compose [kəm'pəʊz] *verb* **(a)** to write something, using your intelligence; *he sat down to compose a letter to his family*; *it took Mozart only three days to compose his fifth piano concerto*; *who composed the music to 'Doctor Zhivago'?* **(b)** *(formal)* **to compose yourself** = to make yourself calm; *she paused for a while to compose herself before going out on stage again*

composed [kəm'pəʊzd] *adjective* **(a)** **composed of** = made up of; *a group composed of three girls and their boyfriends* **(b)** not flustered; *the accused man sat in the dock looking very calm and composed*

composer [kəm'pəʊzə] *noun* person who writes music; *Elgar, Britten and other British composers*; *that was a marvellous concerto, but who was the composer?*

composite ['kɒmpəzɪt] *adjective* made of several different parts; *using photographs from satellites, they have built up a composite picture of the earth's surface*

composition [kɒmpə'zɪʃn] *noun* **(a)** how something is made up; *scientists are trying to establish the composition of the rock sample from the moon* **(b)** something which has been composed, a poem, piece of music, etc.; *we will now play a well-known composition by Dowland* **(c)** essay, piece of writing on a special subject; *we had three hours to write a composition on 'pollution'*

compost ['kɒmpɒst] *noun* rotted leaves, etc., used as a fertilizer; *she spread the compost over the soil and dug it in*; *plant the bulbs in compost*; **compost heap** = rotting leaves, etc., piled up in a garden and left to rot; *grass clippings can be piled on top of the compost heap*

composure [kəm'pəʊʒə] *noun* calmness; *as the charges were read out she regained her composure*; *at his little son's funeral he did not lose his composure*; *he managed to retain his composure in spite of being constantly heckled*

compound 1 *adjective* ['kɒmpaʊnd] **(a)** made up of several parts; **compound interest** = interest calculated on the original total plus any previous interest; *compare* SIMPLE INTEREST **(b)** **compound fracture** = fracture where the broken bone goes through the surface of the skin **2** *noun* ['kɒmpaʊnd] **(a)** chemical made up of two or more elements; *water is a compound of hydrogen and oxygen* **(b)** buildings and land enclosed by a fence; *guard dogs patrol the compound at night*; *soldiers were guarding the embassy compound* **3** *verb* [kəm'paund] **(a)** to make something worse; *the plane's late arrival was compounded by fog at the airport*; *the problems of getting across London will be compounded by today's bus strike* **(b)** to agree with creditors to pay part of the money owed

comprehend [kɒmprɪ'hend] *verb (formal)* to understand; *it is difficult to comprehend how he could have done such a stupid thing*

comprehensible [kɒmprɪ'hensɪv] *adjective* which can be understood easily; *why he behaved like that is not at all comprehensible*; *the instructions on the form are just about comprehensible*; *his English is supposed to be good, but to me it is barely comprehensible*

comprehension [kɒmprɪ'henʃn] *noun* understanding; *good punctuation will help the comprehension of a difficult text*; *a comprehension test in French showed just how little the students knew*; **beyond your comprehension** = quite impossible to understand; *his actions are beyond my comprehension*

comprehensive [kɒmprɪ'hensɪv] *adjective* which includes everything; *she was given a comprehensive medical examination before being allowed back to work*; *the police made a comprehensive search of all the files*; *the list is really comprehensive - I don't think we've left anything out*; **comprehensive (school)** = state school for children of all abilities; **comprehensive education** = education system for all children without any selection according ability; **comprehensive insurance** = insurance policy which covers you against all risks which are likely to happen

compress 1 *noun* ['kɒmpres] wad of cloth, sometimes soaked in hot or cold liquid, placed on the skin to relieve pain or to force pus out of an infected wound; *she applied a cold compress to the bruise*; *the nurse applied a dry compress to his bleeding knee* (NOTE: plural is **compresses**) **2** *verb* [kəm'pres] **(a)** to squeeze into a small space; *the garden centre sells peat compressed into large bags*; *I tried to compress the data onto one page, but couldn't do it* **(b) compressed air** = air under pressure; *the cleaning machine uses a jet of compressed air*

comprise [kəm'praɪz] *verb* to be made up of; *the course comprises three years at a British university and one year's study abroad*; **to be comprised of** = to be made up of; *the exam is comprised of two written papers and an oral*

compromise ['kɒmprəmaɪz] **1** *noun* agreement between two opposing sides, where each side gives way a little; *they reached a compromise after some discussion*; *there is no question of a compromise with the terrorists* **2** *verb* **(a)** to come to an agreement by giving way a little; *he asked £15 for it, I offered £7 and we compromised on £10*; *the government has refused to compromise with the terrorists* **(b)** to embarrass someone, to put someone in a difficult position; *now that he has been compromised, he has had to withdraw as a candidate* **(c)** to do something which reveals a secret; *the security code has been compromised*

compromising ['kɒmprəmaɪzɪŋ] *adjective* embarrassing; *he found himself in a compromising situation, to say the least*; *a compromising tape of telephone conversations has been discovered*

comptroller [kən'trəulə] *noun (formal)* financial controller; *the company's comptroller himself wrote with his apologies for the mix-up in payments*

compulsion [kəm'pʌlʃn] *noun* force or urge; *she said she felt a compulsion to jump out of windows*; *he said he was acting under a compulsion which he could not control*

compulsive [kəm'pʌlsɪv] *adjective* not able to stop yourself doing something; *she's a compulsive smoker*; *he's a compulsive liar*

compulsory [kəm'pʌlsəri] *adjective* which everyone is forced to do; *a compulsory injection against cholera*; *it is compulsory to wear a crash helmet on a motorcycle*

computation [kɒmpju'teɪʃn] *noun (formal)* action of calculating; *he did some complicated computations on his calculator and came up with a price*

compute [kəm'pju:t] *verb (formal)* to calculate; *they computed the distance of the Sun from Mars*

computer [kəm'pju:tə] *noun* electronic machine which calculates and keeps information automatically; *all the company's records are on computer*; **personal computer (PC)** *or* **home computer** = small computer which can be used in the home; *he wrote his book on his home computer*; **computer bureau** = office which does computer work for other offices; **computer error** = mistake made by a computer; **computer file** = section of information on a computer, such as a list of addresses, a letter, etc.; **computer game** = game you can play on a computer, using a special program; *the boys spent the weekend playing computer games*; **computer program** = instructions to a computer, telling it to do a particular piece of work

computerize [kəm'pju:təraɪz] *verb* **(a)** to change from a manual system to one using computers; *our booking system has been completely computerized* **(b)** to calculate or work by a computer; *we get computerized pay cheques* **(c)** to equip a business, school, etc., with a computer; *the school is becoming computerized*

computer-literacy [kəmpju:tə'lɪtərəsi] *noun* being able to use a computer; *the project aims to improve computer-literacy in the country by 2005*

computer-literate [kəmpju:tə'lɪtərət] *adjective* able to use a computer

computing [kəm'pju:tɪŋ] *noun* using a computer; *all children nowadays learn computing*; *computing is a very important skill*

comrade ['kɒmreɪd] *noun* **(a)** friend or companion, especially a soldier; *we remember old comrades buried in foreign cemeteries* **(b)** fellow member of a socialist or communist party; *all comrades must attend the party meeting* **(c)** form of address to a fellow member of a socialist or communist party; *comrades, we must fight to establish the right to union membership*

comrade-in-arms ['kɒmreɪdɪn'ɑ:mz] *noun* person who has fought with someone; *how many of his comrades-in-arms are still alive?* (NOTE: plural is **comrades-in-arms**)

con [kɒn] **1** *noun* **(a)** *(informal)* trick done to try to get money from someone; *trying to get us to pay him for ten hours' work was just a con*; *see also* CONMAN **(b)** **the pros and cons** = the arguments for and against; *you* have to weigh up all the pros and cons before coming to a decision **2** verb (informal) to trick someone to try to get money; *they conned the bank into lending them £25,000; he conned the old lady out of all her savings* (NOTE: **conning - conned**)

concatenation [kɒnkætəˈneɪʃən] noun (formal) a **concatenation of events** = a chain of events

concave [kɒnˈkeɪv] adjective (surface) which is rounded inwards like the inside of a spoon; *a concave lens spreads light; the fact that the surface is slightly concave explains why there's always water on this part of the pavement* (NOTE: the opposite is **convex**)

conceal [kənˈsiːl] verb to hide, to put something where it cannot be seen; *she concealed the loss from her manager; he tried to conceal the camera by putting it under his coat*

concealed [kənˈsiːld] adjective hidden, difficult to see; *the tiny camera was concealed in his watch*; **concealed entrance** = entrance which you cannot see as you come to it; **concealed lighting** = lighting from bulbs which are hidden

concealment [kənˈsiːlmənt] noun (formal) action of hiding; *his place of concealment was an old shed in the garden*

concede [kənˈsiːd] verb **(a)** to admit that you are wrong; *she conceded that this time she had been mistaken* **(b) to concede defeat** = to admit that you have lost; *with half the votes counted, the presidential candidate conceded defeat; after sixteen moves, the chess champion had to concede defeat*

conceit [kənˈsiːt] noun high opinion of yourself; *his conceit in saying that he is the only person who can help us is astonishing*

conceited [kənˈsiːtɪd] adjective thinking too much of yourself; *I was told he was very conceited, but I haven't seen any evidence of that; how can you be so conceited as to think you are the only person who can run the shop?*

conceivable [kənˈsiːvəbl] adjective which can be imagined; *it is quite conceivable that he will resign*

conceive [kənˈsiːv] verb (formal) **(a)** to become pregnant; *after two years of marriage she was beginning to think she would never conceive* **(b)** (of a child) **to be conceived** = to start existence in the womb; *our little girl was conceived during a power cut in New York* **(c)** to think up a plan; *they conceived the idea for a self-cleaning oven* **(d)** to imagine; *I can't conceive of any occasion where I would wear a dress like that; it is difficult to conceive how people can be so cruel*

concentrate [ˈkɒnsəntreɪt] **1** verb to be very attentive; *the exam candidates were all concentrating hard when someone started to giggle*; **to concentrate on something** = to pay special attention to something; *don't talk - he's trying to concentrate on his homework; the salesmen are supposed to concentrate on getting orders* **2** noun substance which is concentrated, after water has been extracted; *lemon concentrate*

concentrated [ˈkɒnsəntreɪtɪd] adjective **(a)** from which water has been extracted, so giving a very strong taste; *a bottle of concentrated orange juice* **(b)** very determined to do something; *with a little concentrated effort we should be able to do it*

concentration [kɒnsənˈtreɪʃn] noun **(a)** thinking carefully about something; *loud noises disturbed my concentration; his concentration slipped and he lost the next two games* **(b)** grouping of a lot of things in one area; *the concentration of computer companies in the south of Scotland; the concentration of wildlife round the water hole makes it easy for lions to catch their prey* **(c)** **concentration camp** = harsh camp, often for political prisoners

concept [ˈkɒnsept] noun philosophical idea; *it is difficult for some countries to grasp the concept of democratic government; the concept of punctuation and grammar is completely foreign to her; our children have absolutely no concept of tidiness*

conception [kənˈsepʃn] noun **(a)** becoming pregnant; *birth takes place about nine months after conception* **(b)** idea; *she has no conception of the time it takes to learn Russian*

conceptual [kənˈseptjuəl] adjective referring to concepts; *the comment refers not to the style but to the conceptual plan of the novel*

concern [kənˈsɜːn] **1** noun **(a)** worry; *she's a cause of great concern to her family* **(b)** interest; *my main concern is to ensure that we all enjoy ourselves; the teachers showed no concern at all for the children's safety*; **it is no concern of yours** = it's nothing to do with you; *I don't care what they do with the money - it's not my concern* **(c)** company, business; *a big German chemical concern* **2** verb **(a)** to have as the subject; *the letter concerns you* = the letter is about you; *that does not concern him* = it has nothing to do with him; **as far as money is concerned** = referring to money; **to concern yourself with** = to deal with; *you needn't concern yourself with cleaning the shop* **(b)** to worry; *it concerns me that he is always late for work*

concerned [kənˈsɜːnd] adjective worried; *she looked concerned; I could tell something was wrong by the concerned look on her face; we are concerned about her behaviour - do you think she is having problems at school?*

concerning [kənˈsɜːnɪŋ] preposition dealing with; *he filled in a questionnaire concerning holidays; I'd like to speak to Mr Robinson concerning his application for insurance; anyone with information concerning this person should get in touch with the police*

concert [ˈkɒnsət] noun programme of music played in public; *I'm sorry, the concert is sold out; I couldn't go to the concert, so I gave my ticket to a friend*; **concert hall** = large building where concerts are given; **promenade concerts** = inexpensive concerts of classical music where part of the audience stands and can walk about during the performance (NOTE: also simply called **prom concerts** or **proms**)

concerted [kənˈsɜːtɪd] adjective (effort, attack) done or planned jointly; *our success is not due only to me, it was the result of a concerted effort on the part of all the team; we must make a concerted attack on the backlog of paperwork*

concerto [kənˈtʃeətəʊ] noun piece of music for a solo instrument and orchestra, or for a small group of instruments; *a piano concerto by Beethoven; the group played one of Mozart's concertos* (NOTE: plural is **concertos**)

concession [kənˈseʃn] noun **(a)** allowing someone do something you do not really want them to do; *we insist that the children are home by 8 p.m. on weekdays, but as a concession, we let them stay out* *until 11 on Saturdays* **(b) to make concessions to someone** = to change your plans so as to please someone; *the Prime Minister has said that no concessions will be made to the terrorists*

concessionary [kən'seʃnərɪ] *noun* given as a concession; **concessionary fare** = reduced fare for certain types of passenger (such as employees of a transport company); *concessionary rates are offered to OAPs and students*

conciliation [kənsɪlɪ'eɪʃn] *noun* bringing together the parties in a dispute with a third party, so that the dispute can be settled through a series of negotiations; *conciliation in an industrial dispute*; **the Conciliation Service** *or* **the Advisory, Conciliation and Arbitration Service (ACAS)** = a British government service which arbitrates in disputes between management and employees

conciliatory [kən'sɪlɪətrɪ] *adjective* which aims to make people agree to settle a dispute; *his conciliatory remarks were meant to soften the blow; contrary to what was expected, the attitude of the management was very conciliatory*

concise [kən'saɪs] *adjective* short, using only a few words; *this is the concise edition, but there is also a bigger complete edition; her answers were concise and to the point*

conclude [kən'kluːd] *verb* **(a)** to end; to come to an end; *he concluded by thanking all those who had helped arrange the exhibition; the concert concluded with a piece by Mozart* **(b)** to come to an opinion; *the police concluded that the thief had got into the building through the kitchen window* **(c) to conclude an agreement with someone** = to arrange an agreement or treaty with someone

concluding [kən'kluːdɪŋ] *adjective* last; *in the concluding episode of the TV serial all the characters are killed in an air crash*

conclusion [kən'kluːʒn] *noun* **(a)** end; *at the conclusion of the trial all the defendants were found guilty* **(b)** opinion which you reach after careful thought; *she came to or reached the conclusion that he had found another girlfriend; what conclusions can you draw from the evidence before you?*

conclusive [kən'kluːsɪv] *adjective* decisive, which offers firm proof; *the first test was not conclusive so we are running another test; the fact that there was no conclusive evidence allowed him to walk out of the courtroom a free man*

concoct [kən'kɒkt] *verb* **(a)** to make up or invent a story; *however unbelievable the story is, it is not something which he has concocted* **(b)** to make a dish of food; *I'm always a bit dubious about the dishes she concocts for us when she invites us to dinner*

concoction [kən'kɒkʃn] *noun* curious mixture of food or drink; *he served us some strange concoction made with pineapples and cider*

concord [kɒnkɔːd] *noun (formal)* state of harmony and peace; *all we desire is to live in concord with our neighbours*

Concorde [kɒnkɔːd] *noun* British and French supersonic passenger plane; *we flew by Concorde to New York or we flew Concorde to New York; Concorde flies at speeds that are faster than the speed of sound*

concourse [kɒŋkɔːs] *noun* large entrance area in a railways station or airport; *the concourse was thronged with passengers*

concrete [kɒnkriːt] **1** *adjective* **(a)** made of cement and sand; *a concrete path* **(b)** real, important; *he had no concrete proposals to offer; the police are sure he is guilty, but they have no concrete evidence against him* **2** *noun* mixture of cement and sand, used in building; *concrete was invented by the Romans; the pavement is made of slabs of concrete*

concrete mixer [kɒnkriːt 'mɪksə] *noun* machine which turns to mix cement, sand and water to make concrete

concubine [kɒŋkjubaɪn] *noun* woman who lives with a man as his second wife, but who is not married to him; *he lived with his wives and concubines in a splendid palace in the middle of the city*

concur [kən'kɜː] *verb (formal)* to agree; *I concur with your point of view; we all concur in demanding an end to the strike* (NOTE: **concurring - concurred**)

concurrence [kən'kʌrəns] *noun (formal)* agreement; *he signified his concurrence with the plan*

concurrent [kən'kʌrənt] *adjective* taking place at the same time; *the two medical treatments must be concurrent; he is serving two concurrent sentences for robbery*

condemn [kən'dem] *verb* **(a)** to say that you do not approve of something; *she condemned the council for the delay* **(b)** to sentence a criminal; *she was condemned to death* **(c)** to declare a house to be unfit to live in; *the whole block of flats has been condemned and will be pulled down*

condemnation [kɒndem'neɪʃn] *noun* saying that you do not approve of something; *the report contains a strong condemnation of the police action; the government's action in deporting him was greeted with universal condemnation in the press*

condemned [kən'demnd] *adjective* sentenced to die; *the condemned man was visited by the prison chaplain;* **condemned cell** = room where a prisoner is kept before being executed; *compare* DEATH ROW

condensation [kɒnden'seɪʃn] *noun* steam which becomes a film of water on a cold surface; *the room is so cold that condensation has formed on the walls*

condense [kən'dens] *verb* **(a)** to reduce the size of something; *the article was sent back to the author with a note asking her to condense it* **(b)** to reduce the volume of something, to concentrate; *he opened a tin of condensed soup;* **condensed milk** = milk which has been concentrated and sweetened **(c)** *(of steam)* to form drops of water; *vapour will condense when it is cooled*

condiment [kɒndɪmənt] *noun (formal)* seasoning such as salt, pepper or mustard, used to give taste to food; *could you pass the condiments, please; compare* CRUET

condition [kən'dɪʃn] *noun* **(a)** state that something is in; *the car is in very good condition considering it is over thirty years old; he was taken to hospital when his condition got worse* **(b)** state of the surroundings in which someone is living or working; *conditions in the refugee camps are very bad; the meterological office forecast poor weather conditions* **(c)** illness; *he is being treated for a heart condition* **(d)** term of a deal; something which has to be agreed before something else is done; *they didn't agree with some of the* conditions of the contract; one of conditions of the deal is that the company pays all travel costs; **on condition that** = only if; I will come on condition that you pay my fare

conditional [kən'dɪʃənəl] adjective (a) provided that certain things take place; **to give a conditional acceptance** = to accept, provided that certain things happen or certain terms apply (b) **conditional on** = subject to (certain conditions); the offer is conditional on the board's acceptance (c) **conditional clause** = clause beginning with 'if' or 'unless', which refers to something that might happen

conditioner [kən'dɪʃənə] noun (a) liquid which puts hair into good condition; the hairdresser asked me if I wanted some conditioner after the shampoo; I always use a combined shampoo and conditioner (b) **fabric conditioner** = substance which makes fabrics softer after washing or cleaning; add some fabric conditioner to the wash

condo ['kɒndəʊ] noun US see CONDOMINIUM; his cousin has just bought an expensive condo in Malibu

condolences [kən'dəʊlənsɪz] noun expressions of regret, especially at the death of someone; he expressed his condolences to the company on the death of their founder; we sent our condolences to his wife, whom we know very well; letters of condolence are still arriving at his house

condom ['kɒndɒm] noun rubber covering put over the penis before sexual intercourse as a protection against infection and also as a contraceptive; there are condom machines in public toilets

condominium [kɒndə'mɪniəm] noun (a) system of rule of a territory by two countries together (b) US building where each owner of an apartment shares in the ownership of the roof, elevators, etc.; they're building a condominium on the site of the old hospital (c) US apartment in a condominium; his cousin has just bought an expensive condominium in Malibu (NOTE: both meanings (b) and (c) are often shortened to condo)

condone [kən'dəʊn] verb to excuse or forgive a fault, crime, etc.; how can you condone his treatment of the junior staff?

condor ['kɒndɔ:] noun large South American vulture

conducive to [kən'dju:sɪv 'tu:] adjective favourable to; a flat in the town centre is not conducive to quiet study

conduct 1 noun ['kɒndʌkt] way of behaving; his conduct in class is becoming a cause of concern; her conduct during the trial was remarkably calm; he was arrested for disorderly conduct in the High Street **2** verb [kən'dʌkt] (a) to guide; the VIPs were conducted to their seats; **conducted tour** = tour led by a guide (b) to direct an orchestra; the orchestra will be conducted by a Russian conductor (c) to allow electricity, heat, etc., to pass through; copper conducts electricity very well (d) to carry out; they are conducting an experiment into the effect of TV advertising; the chairman conducted the negotiations very efficiently

conduction [kən'dʌkʃn] noun passing of heat, electricity, etc., through metal, water, etc.; the conduction of electricity through copper wire

conductor [kən'dʌktə] noun (a) metal, or other substance which conducts heat or electricity; copper is

a good conductor but plastic is not; **conductor rail** = the electric rail for trains (b) person who directs an orchestra; as the orchestra reached the grand finale, the conductor started to sing; the conductor asked the horns to play more softly (c) **bus conductor** = person who sells tickets on a bus (d) US person in charge of a train (NOTE: British English is **railway guard**)

conductress [kən'dʌktrəs] noun (old) woman who sells tickets on a bus (NOTE: plural is **conductresses**)

conduit ['kɒndɪt] noun tube along which water or gas or electricity wires can be passed; the road is being dug up again - this time it is to repair a gas conduit; the television cables are channelled through green plastic underground conduits

cone [kəʊn] noun (a) shape which is round at the base, rising to a point; he rolled the newspaper to form a cone (b) **ice cream cone** = cone of biscuit, used for serving ice cream; children like to suck the ice cream out of the bottom of a cone (NOTE: also called an **ice cream cornet**) (c) brightly coloured plastic cone, used to keep motorists away from an area of road; part of the motorway has been marked off with cones; traffic cones were placed round the hole in the road (d) **fir cone** = the fruit of a fir tree; you can burn fir cones on the fire in winter

cone off ['kəʊn 'ɒf] verb to cut off part of a road with cones; one lane has been coned off by the police

confectioner's [kən'fekʃənəz] noun shop that sells sweets and sometimes cakes; we bought some sweets from the confectioner's next door to the post office

confectionery [kən'fekʃənri] noun sweets and cakes; the bread shop also sells confectionery

confederacy [kən'fedərəsi] noun group formed of various states; in the Middle Ages several small Swiss cantons came together to form a confederacy (NOTE: plural is **confederacies**)

Confederacy [kən'fedərəsi] noun (American History) group of eleven Southern states which split off from the Union and fought the North in the American Civil War (1861 - 1865)

confederate [kən'fedərət] **1** noun person who has joined with others, usually to do a crime; all over Europe the police are looking for him and his confederates **2** adjective (American History) referring to the southern states which split off during the Civil War; the Confederate Army moved towards Richmond; the **Confederate States** = THE CONFEDERACY

confederation [kənfedə'reɪʃn] noun group of states, trade unions, etc.; Switzerland is a confederation of separate small states or cantons; the **Confederation of British Industry (CBI)** = organization which represents British employers in commerce and industry

confer [kən'fɜ:] verb (a) to discuss; the leader of the Council conferred with the Town Clerk (b) to give power or responsibility to someone; the discretionary powers conferred on the tribunal by statute; **to confer an honour on someone** = to give in a ceremony; the Queen conferred the Order of Merit on him (NOTE: conferring - conferred)

conference ['kɒnfərəns] noun (a) discussion; the managers had a quick conference to decide what action to take; **to be in conference** = to be in a meeting; **conference phone** = telephone so arranged that several people can speak into it at the same time from different places; **press conference** = meeting where newspaper, radio and TV reporters are invited to hear news of something or to talk to a famous person; *he gave a press conference on the steps of Number Ten*; **sales conference** = meeting of sales managers, representatives, publicity staff, etc., to discuss future sales plans; *see also* ROUND TABLE CONFERENCE **(b)** meeting of a group or society; *the annual conference of the Electricians' Union*; *the conference agenda or the agenda of the conference was drawn up by the secretary*; *2000 people attended the conference on genetic engineering*

confess [kənˈfes] *verb* **(a)** to admit that you have done something wrong; *he confessed to six burglaries*; *she confessed that she had forgotten to lock the door* **(b)** to admit your sins to a priest; *she went to church to confess to the priest*

confessed [kənˈfest] *adjective* having admitted to having done something; *he's a confessed burglar*; *see also* SELF-CONFESSED

confession [kənˈfeʃn] *noun* **(a)** admission of fault; *the prisoner said his confession had been forced from him by the police* **(b)** to **make your confession** = to admit your sins to a priest

confessional [kənˈfeʃənəl] *noun* small private booth in a church where a priest hears confessions; *there was a priest waiting in the confessional when I entered the church*

confide [kənˈfaɪd] *verb* to **confide in someone** = to tell someone a secret; *he has always confided in his mother*

confidence [ˈkɒnfɪdəns] *noun* **(a)** feeling sure; *the staff do not have much confidence in their manager*; *I have total confidence in the pilot*; *see also* VOTE **(b)** being secret; **in confidence** = as a secret; *he showed me the report in confidence* **(c)** **confidence trick** = a trick to get money by making the victim believe something; **confidence trickster** = person who tricks people to get money by making them believe something; *some confidence trickster managed to get her to sign the papers* (NOTE: also called **conman**)

confident [ˈkɒnfɪdənt] *adjective* sure that you or something will be successful; *I am confident (that) the show will go off well*; *she's confident of doing well in the exam*

confidential [kɒnfɪˈdenʃl] *adjective* secret, private; *please mark the letter 'Private and Confidential'*; **confidential secretary** = secretary entrusted with private matters

confidentially [kɒnfɪˈdenʃəli] *adverb* in a confidential way; *I'm telling you this confidentially, so don't tell anyone else*

confidently [ˈkɒnfɪdəntli] *adverb* in a way which shows that you are confident; *she walked confidently into the interview room*

configuration [kənfɪgəˈreɪʃn] *noun* **(a)** *(formal)* shape, layout; *just looking at the configuration of the wires on a telephone exchange makes the mind boggle* **(b)** way in which the hardware and software of a computer system are planned; *the machine uses RAM to store system configuration information*

confine [kənˈfaɪn] *verb* **(a)** to keep in one small place; *the tigers were confined in a small cage with no room to move around*; **confined to barracks** = forced to stay in barracks; **confined to bed** = forced to stay in bed; *she wanted to get up, but the doctor has confined her to bed* **(b)** to restrict; *make sure you confine your answer to the subject in the question*

confinement [kənˈfaɪnmənt] *noun* **(a)** imprisonment; *he was kept in solitary confinement for seven weeks* **(b)** *(old)* period when a woman gives birth to a baby

confirm [kənˈfɜːm] *verb* **(a)** to say that something is certain; *the dates of the concerts have been confirmed by the pop group's manager*; *the photograph confirmed that the result of the race was a dead heat*; *we have been told that she left the country last month - can you confirm that?* **(b)** to **confirm someone in a job** = to say that someone is now permanently in the job; **to be confirmed in office** = to be reappointed in your job by a new management **(c)** **to be confirmed** = to be made a full Christian by a bishop; *he was confirmed when he was twelve*

confirmation [kɒnfəˈmeɪʃn] *noun* **(a)** making sure; *we are awaiting official confirmation of the figures* **(b)** document which confirms something; *we have had confirmation from the bank that the payment has been made* **(c)** ceremony where a person is made a full Christian by a bishop; *when is your nephew's confirmation?*

confirmed [kənˈfɜːmd] *adjective* permanently in a certain state, and not wanting to change; *he's a confirmed gambler*; *he's a confirmed bachelor* = he will never marry

confiscate [ˈkɒnfɪskeɪt] *verb* to take away someone's possessions as a punishment; *the court ordered the drugs to be confiscated*; *his parents confiscated his portable but he borrowed one from his friend*

conflagration [kɒnfləˈgreɪʃn] *noun* *(formal)* enormous fire; *two whole blocks of flats were destroyed in the conflagration*

conflict 1 *noun* [ˈkɒnflɪkt] fighting; *the army is engaged in armed conflict with rebel forces*; **to come into conflict with someone** = to start to fight someone; *the decision brought the union into conflict with the management* **2** *verb* [kənˈflɪkt]; **to conflict with** = to clash with, to contradict; *the defendant's version of events conflicts with that of the witness*; **conflicting advice** = pieces of advice from different people which are the opposite of each other

conform [kənˈfɔːm] *verb* to act in the same way as other people; *my son is a bit of a rebel - he hates having to conform*; *life is tough in the army - anyone who doesn't conform is punished*; **he refused to conform to the regulations** = he refused to do what the regulations say; *the machine conforms to EU regulations*

conformist [kənˈfɔːmɪst] *noun* person who acts in the same way as other people; *he's a solid conformist, and shouldn't be a problem in your office* (NOTE: the opposite is **nonconformist**)

conformity [kənˈfɔːmɪti] *noun* **(a)** action of conforming; *it is their passive conformity that is so depressing* **(b)** **in conformity with** = agreeing with; *he has acted in conformity with the regulations*

confound [kənˈfaʊnd] *verb* to confuse or to bother; *his recovery confounded all the specialists*

confront [kənˈfrʌnt] *verb* **(a)** to try to tackle someone; *don't confront a burglar on your own - he may be armed* **(b)** to confront someone with the evidence = to show the evidence to someone; *when the police confronted him with the photographs he confessed*

confrontation [kɒnfrʌnˈteɪʃn] *noun* angry meeting between opposing sides; *to avoid confrontation, the fans of the two opposing teams will be kept as far apart as possible*; *there have been some violent confrontations between students and the police*

confrontational [kɒnfrənˈteɪʃənl] *adjective* always attacking someone; *he displayed an unusually confrontational attitude towards the taxman*; **confrontational politics** = style of political activity, where opposing sides always attack each other; *confrontational politics is not understood in countries where there is a one-party government* (NOTE: opposite is **consensus politics**)

confuse [kənˈfjuːz] *verb* to muddle; *she was confused by all the journalists' questions*; *I always confuse him with his brother - the two are very alike*

confused [kənˈfjuːzd] *adjective* muddled; *I'm a bit confused - did we say 8.00 p.m. or 8.30?*; *grandmother used to get rather confused in her old age*

confusing [kənˈfjuːzɪŋ] *adjective* muddling; *she found the instructions on the computer very confusing*

confusion [kənˈfjuːʒn] *noun* muddle, disorder; *there were scenes of confusion at the airport when the snowstorm stopped all flights*

congeal [kənˈdʒiːl] *verb* (*of liquid*) to become solid; *I hate washing plates covered with congealed fat* (NOTE: when referring to blood, the normal word to use is **to clot**)

congenial [kənˈdʒiːniəl] *adjective* pleasant or friendly; *the meeting took place in congenial surroundings*; *we had a pleasant dinner in congenial company*

congenital [kənˈdʒenɪtl] *adjective* (illness or defect) which exists at or before birth; *he has a congenital heart condition and may die young*

conger eel [ˈkɒŋgə ˈiːl] *noun* very large type of sea eel

congested [kənˈdʒestɪd] *adjective* **(a)** blocked or crowded; *following the accident, all the roads round the station soon became congested*; *something has to be done about London's congested road system* **(b)** with blood or fluid inside; *with bronchitis and a congested nose, he has difficulty in breathing at night*

congestion [kənˈdʒeʃtʃn] *noun* **(a)** traffic **congestion** = blocking of streets with traffic; *traffic congestion makes it almost impossible for buses to run on time* **(b)** blocking with mucus; *this spray should clear bronchial and nasal congestion* **(c)** accumulation of blood in an organ; *congestion of the liver may be due to heart failure*

conglomerate [kənˈglɒmərət] *noun* group of subsidiary companies, each making very different types of products; *the company is part of a large international conglomerate*

congratulate [kənˈgrætjuleɪt] *verb* to give good wishes on a special occasion or for having done something; *he congratulated them on their silver wedding anniversary*; *I want to congratulate you on your promotion*

congratulations [kəngrætjuˈleɪʃnz] *noun* good wishes to someone who has done well; *congratulations - you're our millionth customer!*; *congratulations on passing your exam!*; *the office sent him their congratulations on his wedding*

congregate [ˈkɒŋgrɪgeɪt] *verb* to gather together; *all the tourists congregated in front of the castle*

congregation [kɒŋgrɪˈgeɪʃn] *noun* people who meet together in a church; *there aren't enough hymn books for all members of the congregation*; *the vicar invited the congregation to pray for the victims of yesterday's massacre*

congress [ˈkɒŋgres] *noun* meeting of a group; *the annual congress of the society*; *this year's party congress will be held in Blackpool*

Congress [ˈkɒŋgres] *noun* legislative body of the USA, formed of the House of Representatives and the Senate; *the President has to persuade Congress to pass his budget*

congressional [kənˈgreʃənəl] *adjective* referring to the US Congress; *a congressional hearing*

congressman *or* **congresswoman** [ˈkɒŋgresmən *or* ˈkɒŋgrəwumən] *noun* member of the United States House of Representatives (NOTE: plural is **congressmen, congresswomen**; note also that it can be used as a title with a surname: **Congressman Smith, Congresswoman Murphy**)

conical [ˈkɒnɪkl] *adjective* shaped like a cone; *the clown wore a conical hat*

conifer [ˈkɒnɪfə] *noun* evergreen tree with long thin leaves (called needles) which produces fruit in the form of cones; *planting with conifers has had a noticeable effect on the landscape of the Lake District*

conjecture [kənˈdʒektʃə] (*formal*) **1** *noun* guesswork; *it was pure conjecture on my part* **2** *verb* to guess; *they conjectured correctly that he would run out of money at some point*

conjunction [kənˈdʒʌŋkʃn] *noun* word which links different sections of a sentence; *'and' and 'but' are conjunctions*

conjure [ˈkʌndʒə] *verb* **(a)** to do tricks with cards, rabbits, etc.; *here is a picture of a magician conjuring a rabbit out of a hat* **(b)** to summon; **to conjure up an image** = to bring an image into someone's mind; *his writing about the south of France conjures up scents of lavender and olive oil*; **a name to conjure with** = an important name; *he's a name to conjure with in the advertising industry*

conker [ˈkɒŋkə] *noun* the nut of the horse chestnut tree, used in children's games; *the children were playing conkers in the school yard*

COMMENT: to play conkers, you put a piece of string through a chestnut and hold it up in front of you; your opponent tries to hit it with his conker, until he misses, and then you try to hit his; the one whose conker breaks up first is the loser

conman [ˈkɒnmæn] *noun* confidence trickster, a person who tricks people to get money by making them believe something; *the conman managed to get her to sign the papers*; *the police have warned that conmen are visiting houses, posing as collectors for charities* (NOTE: plural is **conmen**)

connect [kə'nekt] *verb* **(a)** to join; *the computer should have been connected to the printer*; *has the telephone been connected yet?*; *connect the two red wires together* **(b)** to link up with; **the flight from New York connects with a flight to Athens** = the plane from New York arrives in time for passengers to catch the plane to Athens; **this train connects with the 12.45** = this train allows passengers to catch the 12.45

connected [kə'nektɪd] *adjective* joined; *is the telephone connected?*; **they are connected to the Williams family** = they are related to the Williams family; **well-connected** = with influential friends; *to succeed in politics it helps to be well-connected*

connecting flight [kə'nektɪŋ 'flaɪt] *noun* plane which you will be able to catch and which will take you to your final destination; *check at the helicopter desk for connecting flights to the city centre*

connection [kə'nekʃn] *noun* **(a)** link; *there is a definite connection between smoking and lung cancer*; *he said that there was no connection between how much he had had to drink and his falling over in the street*; **in connection with your visit** = referring to your visit **(b)** train, plane, etc., which you catch after getting off another train or plane; *my train was late and I missed my connection to Birmingham* **(c)** **connections** = people you know; *he has business connections in Argentina*

connective tissue [kə'nektɪv 'tɪʃu] *noun* tissue in which fibrous material surrounds the tissue cells, and which forms the main part of bones, cartilage, ligaments and tendons; *cartilage is thick connective tissue which lines the joints and acts as a cushion*

connoisseur [kɒnə'sɜ:] *noun* expert, person who knows a lot about something; *he's a connoisseur of French cooking*; *don't ask me about modern art, I'm not a connoisseur*

connotation [kɒnə'teɪʃn] *noun* additional meaning; *the word 'ghetto' has unpleasant connotations attached to it*

conquer ['kɒŋkə] *verb* to defeat by force; *England was conquered by the Normans in 1066*; *the Romans conquered most of Europe as far east as Romania*

conqueror ['kɒŋkərə] *noun* person who leads the invasion of a country; **William the Conqueror** = William I, the Duke of Normandy who led the invasion of England in 1066

conquest ['kɒŋkwest] *noun* **(a)** capturing; *the Norman Conquest in 1066* **(b)** country *or* person that has been captured; *the Mongols treated their conquests with great cruelty*

conscience ['kɒnʃəns] *noun* feeling which you have that you have done right or wrong; *I can say with a clear conscience that I have done nothing wrong*; *why can't you look me in the eye - have you got a guilty conscience?*; *he refused to serve in the army as a matter of conscience*

conscientious [kɒnʃi'enʃəs] *adjective* **(a)** working carefully and well; *she's very conscientious about getting the invoices right* **(b) conscientious objector** = person who refuses to join the army when conscripted because he feels that it is morally wrong; *what happened to conscientious objectors during the war?*

conscious ['kɒnʃəs] *adjective* aware of things happening around you; *she had a local anaesthetic and was conscious during the operation*; *a conscious*

decision = a decision which you have thought about; *refusing the offer was a conscious decision on his part*; *he made a conscious decision to try to avoid her in future*

consciousness ['kɒnʃəsnəs] *noun* being conscious; **to lose consciousness** = to become unconscious; **to regain consciousness** = to become conscious again; *he never regained consciousness after the accident*

conscript **1** *noun* ['kɒnskrɪpt] person who is legally obliged to join the armed services; *the conscripts had hardly any time to train before being sent to the front* **2** *verb* [kən'skrɪpt] to order someone to join the armed services; *all men under 35 were conscripted into the armed forces*

conscription [kən'skrɪpʃn] *noun* legal obligation to join the armed services; *as soon as war was declared the government introduced conscription* (NOTE: American English for this is **the draft**)

consecrate ['kɒnsɪkreɪt] *verb* **(a)** to bless a new church, king, etc.; *the bishop was consecrated in the cathedral* **(b)** **to consecrate your life to** = to devote your life to; *she consecrated her life to helping the homeless*

consecration [kɒnsɪ'kreɪʃn] *noun* **(a)** blessing; *the consecration of the new cathedral* **(b)** devoting of your life; *the consecration of her life to helping the poor*

consecutive [kən'sekjutɪv] *adjective* one after the other; *the bank sent him reminders for two consecutive weeks*

consecutively [kə'sekjutɪvli] *adverb* one after the other, in the right order; *you should read the three books consecutively, otherwise the story doesn't make sense*

consensus [kən'sensəs] *noun* opinion which most people agree on; *the general consensus is that we all need to go away on holiday*; *after much discussion the meeting reached a consensus on how to proceed*; *it's going to be difficult to get all the parties to reach a consensus*; **consensus politics** = form of politics where different parties work together to try to find answers to problems (NOTE: the opposite is **confrontational politics**)

consent [kən'sent] **1** *noun* agreement; *doctors must obtain a patient's consent before operating*; **to withhold your consent** = not to agree; *her parents withheld their consent to the marriage*; **the age of consent** = age at which someone can legally agree to have sex **2** *verb* **to consent to something** = to agree to something; *the judge consented to the prosecution's request*

consequence ['kɒnsɪkwəns] *noun* **(a)** something which follows, a result; *we walked all day in the rain, with the consequence that all of us got colds* **(b)** importance; **it is of no consequence** = it is not important

consequent ['kɒnsɪkwənt] *adjective* which follows as a consequence; *the heavy rain and consequent flooding has caused a lot of damage*; **consequent on** = as a result of; *the declaration of war was consequent on the country's non-compliance with the UN resolutions*

consequently ['kɒnsɪkwəntli] *adverb* because of this; *we walked all day in the rain and consequently all caught colds*

conservation [kɒnsə'veɪʃn] *noun* saving of energy, natural resources, old buildings, etc.; *the company is spending more money on energy conservation*; a **Conservation Area** = area of a town where the buildings are of special interest and cannot be altered or demolished

conservationist [kɒnsə'veɪʃənɪst] *noun* person who promotes the preservation of the countryside and the careful management of natural resources; *local conservationists are campaigning for the preservation of the woodland area*

conservatism [kə'sɜːvətɪzm] *noun* (a) being conservative; *the basic conservatism of British farmers* (b) *(in politics)* the ideas and beliefs of Conservatives; *Conservatism had a great effect on British society during the 1980s*

conservative [kən'sɜːvətɪv] 1 *adjective* (a) not wanting to change; *he has very conservative views* (b) *(politics)* the **Conservative party** = political party which is in favour of only gradual change in society and is against government involvement in industry and welfare (c) cautious, probably too low; *a conservative estimate of sales*; *at least two hundred people came to the flower show, and that is a conservative estimate* 2 *noun* a **Conservative** = a member of the Conservative Party; *the Conservatives lost their majority in Parliament*

conservatoire [kən'sɜːvətwɑːr] *noun* = CONSERVATORY (b)

conservatory [kə'sɜːvətri] *noun* (a) room with large windows, where you keep tropical flowers and plants; *with its glass roof and windows, our conservatory becomes very hot in the summer* (b) **conservatory of music** = academy where only music is taught; *he studied at the Berlin Conservatory of Music* (NOTE: plural is **conservatories**)

conserve [kən'sɜːv] 1 *verb* (a) to keep, not to waste; *a government programme to conserve energy* (b) to look after and keep in the same state; *our committee aims to conserve the wildlife in our area* 2 *noun* fruit jam; *peach conserve*

consider [kən'sɪdə] *verb* (a) to think carefully about something; *please consider seriously the offer which we are making*; *we have to consider the position of the children after the divorce* (b) to think; *do you consider him the right man for the job?*; *she is considered (to be) one of the best lawyers in town* (c) all things considered = on the whole; *all things considered, the flower show went off quite well*

considerable [kən'sɪdrəbl] *adjective* quite large; *he lost a considerable amount of money on the horse races*

considerably [kən'sɪdrəbli] *adverb* quite a lot; *it is considerably hotter than it was last week*

considerate [kən'sɪdərət] *adjective* full of feeling or understanding towards someone; *he is very considerate towards children with learning difficulties*; *it was not very considerate of him to forget to tell us about the party*

consideration [kənsɪdə'reɪʃn] *noun* (a) careful thought; *we are giving serious consideration to the possibility of moving the head office to Scotland*; to **take something into consideration** = to think about something when making a decision; *the age of the children has to be taken into consideration*; **under consideration** = being thought about; *the matter is*

under consideration (b) thing which has an effect on a decision; *the safety of the children outweighs all other considerations* (c) *(formal)* small sum of money; **for a small consideration** = for a small fee or payment

considered [kən'sɪdəd] *adjective* which has been thought through carefully; *in my considered opinion, we should sell the house*

considering [kən'sɪdrɪŋ] *conjunction & preposition* when you think (of); *he plays the violin extremely well, considering he's only five*; *he ought to be more grateful, considering the amount of help you have given him*

consign [kən'saɪn] *verb* to hand over to someone; *he consigned his collection of silver to the bank*; *she consigned her daughter's first attempts at drawing to the bin*; to **consign goods to someone** = to send goods to someone for him to use or to sell or store for you

consignment [kən'saɪnmənt] *noun* (a) sending of goods to someone who will sell them for you; *the consignment of books to our French distributor was easily organized*; **consignment note** = note saying that goods have been sent; **goods on consignment** = goods kept for another company to be sold on their behalf for a commission; *the stock the American distributor orders from us is on consignment*; *how much stock do they take on consignment per month?* (b) quantity of goods sent for sale; *a consignment of goods has arrived*; *we are expecting a consignment of cars from Japan*

consist [kən'sɪst] *verb* (a) to **consist of** = to be formed of; *the package tour consists of air travel, six nights in a luxury hotel, all meals and visits to places of interest* (b) to **consist in** = to be, to mean; *for him, dieting consists in having two chocolates instead of three*

consistency [kən'sɪstənsi] *noun* (a) being the same throughout; *I wish there was more consistency in his reports* (b) thickness of a paste, etc.; *the consistency of the sauce should be that of thick syrup*; *in order to obtain the desired consistency, it may be necessary to add a little water*

consistent [kə'sɪstənt] *adjective* (a) **consistent with something** = which does not contradict something; *the measures taken must be consistent with government policy* (b) always at the same level; *some of his work is good, but he's not consistent*

consistently [kən'sɪstəntli] *adverb* always; *she has been consistently late for work every day this week*

consolation [kɒnsə'leɪʃn] *noun* comfort after a loss; *if it's any consolation, I lost more money than you did*; *being one of several people who failed their driving tests is no consolation*; **consolation prize** = prize for making an effort; *she got a goldfish as a consolation prize*

console 1 *noun* ['kɒnsəʊl] (a) flat table with the keyboard of an organ, machine, etc.; *the sound engineer at the console controls the sound coming from the stage* (b) cabinet for a TV set; *we have a console which contains both the TV and video* 2 *verb* [kən'səʊl] to comfort someone; *the priest wanted to console her for the loss of her father*; *I tried to console her but she cried herself to sleep*; to **console yourself** = to take comfort; *after hearing he had failed some of his exams, he consoled himself with the thought that his brother had done even worse than he had*

consolidate [kən'sɒlɪdeɪt] *verb* (a) to make firm or sure; *having entered the market, the company spent a* *year consolidating its position*; *the team consolidated their lead with a second goal* **(b)** to join together to make one single unit; *the two businesses consolidated to form one group* **(c)** to group several items from different suppliers together to make one shipment; *the shipment to India is being consolidated, and will leave Southampton Docks on Tuesday*

consolidation [kənsɒlɪ'deɪʃn] *noun* **(a)** making firm; *after a period of consolidation, the company is now ready to expand overseas* **(b)** joining several companies together to make one single unit; *the consolidation of the businesses went smoothly* **(c)** grouping together of items from different suppliers into one large shipment

consommé [kən'sɒmeɪ] *noun* thin clear meat soup; *for a change, add some sherry to your beef consommé*

consonant ['kɒnsənənt] *noun* letter representing a sound which is made using the teeth, tongue or lips; *'b' and 't' are consonants, while 'e' and 'i' are vowels*

> COMMENT: the five vowels are 'a', 'e', 'i', 'o' and 'u'. All the other letters of the alphabet are consonants

consort 1 *noun* ['kɒnsɔːt] husband or wife of a ruling monarch; *a Prince Consort has a difficult role since he has no real power*; *the emperor and his consort waved to the crowd* (NOTE: the only person with the title in recent times was **Albert, Prince Consort,** the husband of Queen Victoria) **2** *verb* [kən'sɔːt] to go around with; *to consort with criminals*

consortium [kən'sɔːtɪəm] *noun* group of companies which work together; *a consortium of French and British companies is planning to construct the new aircraft* (NOTE: plural is **consortia**)

conspicuous [kən'spɪkjuəs] *adjective* very obvious; *towering above everyone else, he was very conspicuous*; *the mistake on the book cover is so conspicuous that we can't sell it as it is*; *they thought nobody would see them, but they couldn't have been more conspicuous since they were the only people in suits*; **he was conspicuous by his absence** = it was very obvious that he was not there; *the manager had insisted that everyone had to attend the meeting, while he himself was conspicuous by his absence* (NOTE: the opposite is **inconspicuous)**

conspiracy [kən'spɪrəsi] *noun* plot; *a conspiracy to murder the leader of the party*; *he's sure there's a conspiracy against him in the office*; **a conspiracy of silence** = plot to say nothing about something which has happened (NOTE: plural is **conspiracies)**

conspirator [kən'spɪrətə] *noun* person who is part of a conspiracy; *after the Gunpowder Plot, the conspirators were rapidly arrested*

conspiratorial [kənspɪrə'tɔːrɪəl] *adjective* like someone who has a secret plan; *'come in and shut the door,' she said in a conspiratorial whisper*

conspire [kən'spaɪə] *verb* to plot, to take part in a conspiracy; *they conspired with other political groups to overthrow the government*

constable ['kʌnstəbl] *noun* policeman of lowest rank; *the constable on duty raised the alarm*; *an off-duty police constable happened to be in the bank when the robbers came in* (NOTE: British English only; American English uses **police officer)**

constabulary [kən'stæbjʊləri] *noun* police force of a district; *two members of the regional constabulary were arrested for fraud*

constancy ['kɒnstənsi] *noun* being faithful; *her constancy in spite of her husband's drunkenness*

constant ['kɒnstənt] **1** *adjective* **(a)** not changing or stopping; *the constant noise of music from the bar next door drives me mad* **(b)** with a value which does not change; *the calculations are in constant dollars* **(c)** faithful; *his dog was his constant companion* **2** *noun* number or thing which does not change; *the speed of light is a constant*; *death and taxes are the only constants in life*

constantly ['kɒnstəntli] *adverb* all the time; *he is constantly changing his mind*; *the telephone rang constantly all morning*

constellation [kɒnstə'leɪʃn] *noun* group of stars in the sky, often forming a pattern; *the 'Plough' or 'Great Bear' is the constellation that everyone recognizes*

consternation [kɒnstə'neɪʃn] *noun* shock or surprise; *considerable consternation was expressed at the decision to close the railway station*; *his remarks caused consternation in the audience*

constipated ['kɒnstɪpeɪtɪd] *adjective* unable to pass faeces often enough; *to avoid being constipated, you should eat plenty of fruit and vegetables and drink more water*

constipation [kɒnstɪ'peɪʃn] *noun* difficulty in passing faeces often enough; *a diet that doesn't contain enough roughage, and lack of exercise are two of the possible causes of constipation*

constituency [kən'stɪtjuənsi] *noun* area of the country which elects a Member of Parliament; *he represents a Welsh constituency*; *MPs from the North of England have to live in London and can only visit their constituencies at weekends* (NOTE: plural is **constituencies)**

constituent [kən'stɪtjuənt] **1** *adjective* **constituent part** = part which goes to make up a whole; *the constituent parts of that sentence are subject, verb, and object*; *what are the constituent parts of an omelette?* **2** *noun* **(a)** part which goes to make up a whole; *before starting the experiment, make sure that all the chemical constituents are ready* **(b)** person who may vote in an electoral area; *a good MP tries to represent the views of his constituents*; *she has had a mass of letters from her constituents about airport noise*

constituent assembly [kɒn'stɪtjuənt ə'sembli] *noun* group which can make or change the constitution of a country

constitute ['kɒnstɪtjuːt] *verb* to be or form; *selling the photographs to the newspapers constitutes a serious breach of security*; *women now constitute the majority of the committee*

constitution [kɒnstɪ'tjuːʃn] *noun* **(a)** ability of a person to stay healthy; *she has a very strong constitution*; *(informal)* **to have the constitution of an elephant** = to be tough, to have a very strong constitution; *Aunt Maud has the constitution of an elephant* **(b)** laws and principles under which a country is ruled, which give the people rights and duties, and which give the government powers and duties; *unlike most states, Britain does not have a written constitution*; *freedom of speech is guaranteed by the*

American Constitution **(c)** written rules or regulations of a society, club, etc.; *under the society's constitution, the chairman is elected for two years*

constitutional [kɒnstɪ'tjʃənl] **1** *adjective* **(a)** according to a country's constitution; *unilateral action by the Minister of Defence is not constitutional*; **constitutional monarchy** = monarchy where the king or queen has limited powers and most power is held by an elected parliament and government; *the United Kingdom is a constitutional monarchy* **(b)** according to a society's constitution; *the reelection of the chairman is not constitutional* **2** *noun* short walk which you think is good for your health; *after a big lunch I went for a constitutional; he always takes his early morning constitutional in the park*

constrain [kən'streɪn] *verb* **(a)** to stop someone doing something which they want to do; *his movements were constrained by his tight suit; entrepreneurs feel constrained by the mass of bureaucracy and red tape* **(b)** to force someone to do something; *her lack of cash constrained her to sell her house; he felt constrained to attend every single meeting*

constrained [kən'streɪnd] *adjective* unnatural; *she sat with a constrained smile on her face*

constraint [kən'streɪnt] *noun* something which limits your ability to act; *the financial constraints placed on a country by the IMF; the legal constraints of my position do not allow me to make any comment*

constrict [kən'strɪkt] *verb* to make something tighter, smaller; *if you bend the garden hose you will constrict the flow of water; the constricted space under the sink made it difficult for the plumber to repair the leak; all the new EU rules constrict farmers' freedom to do what they want*

construct [kən'strʌkt] *verb* to build; *we have tendered for the contract to construct the new airport; the wings are constructed of aluminium*

construction [kən'strʌkʃn] *noun* **(a)** the act of building; *the construction of the new stadium took three years;* **construction company** = company which specializes in building; **under construction** = being built; *the airport is under construction* **(b)** thing which has been built; *the new stadium is a magnificent construction*

constructive [kən'strʌktɪv] *adjective* which aims to help or improve; *she made some constructive suggestions for improving the layout of the shop*

constructor [kən'strʌktə] *noun* company or person who builds; *the constructor of the bridge has been given a prize; the council is suing the constructors for finishing the work twelve months late*

construe [kən'struː] *verb* (formal) to interpret the meaning of words or of a document; *the court construed the words to mean that there was a contract between the parties*

consul ['kɒnsəl] *noun* person who represents a country in a foreign city, and helps his country's citizens and business interests there; *the British Consul in Seville*

consular ['kɒnsjulə] *adjective* referring to a consul; *the consular offices are open every weekday;* **consular agent** = person with the duties of a consul in a small foreign town

consulate ['kɒnsjulət] *noun* house or office of a consul; *there will be a party at the consulate on National Day*

consult [kən'sʌlt] *verb* **(a)** to ask someone for advice; *he consulted his accountant about his tax;* **consulting room** = room where a doctor sees his patients **(b)** to look at something to get information; *after consulting the map they decided to go north; he consulted his watch and said that they had enough time to catch the train*

consultancy [kən'sʌltənsi] *noun* **(a)** act of giving specialist advice; *he offers a consultancy service; she runs a consultancy firm, offering advice on planning; since he's been made redundant, he's been doing consultancy work* **(b)** post of consultant in a hospital; *she was appointed to a consultancy with a London hospital*

consultant [kən'sʌltənt] *noun* **(a)** specialist who gives advice; *his tax consultant advised him to sell the shares* **(b)** medical specialist attached to a hospital; *we'll make an appointment for you to see a consultant*

consultation [kɒnsʌl'teɪʃn] *noun* **(a)** act of consulting; *after consultations with the police, the government has decided to ban the protest march; a 30-minute consultation with my lawyer cost me more than I earn in a week!* **(b)** act of visiting a doctor for advice; *she had a consultation with an eye surgeon*

consultative [kən'sʌltətɪv] *adjective* asked to give advice; *the report of a consultative body; he is acting in a consultative capacity;* **consultative document** = paper which is issued by a government department to people who are asked to comment and make suggestions for improvement

consume [kən'sjuːm] *verb* **(a)** to eat or drink; *the guests consumed over 100 hamburgers* **(b)** to use up; *the world's natural resources are being consumed at an alarming rate; the new car consumes about half the amount of petrol of an ordinary car*

consumer [kən'sjuːmə] *noun* person or company that buys goods or services; *gas consumers are protesting at the increase in prices; consumers are buying more from supermarkets and less from small shops;* **consumer goods** = goods bought by members of the public

consuming [kən'sjuːmɪŋ] *adjective* which takes up all your time and energy; *his consuming passion for racing cars*

consummate 1 *adjective* [kən'sʌmɪt] perfect, highly skilled; *she's a consummate professional; he was a consummate Japanese scholar* **2** *verb* ['kɒnsəmeɪt] to complete; **to consummate a marriage** = to have sexual intercourse after marriage; *the church would not grant an annulment because the marriage had been consummated*

consumption [kən'sʌmpʃn] *noun* **(a)** act of consuming; *the meat was condemned as unfit for human consumption; the consumption of alcohol on the premises is not allowed* **(b)** quantity consumed; *unless you reduce your consumption of fatty foods, you risk having a heart attack;* **petrol consumption** = amount of petrol used by a car to go a certain distance; *a car with a low petrol consumption*

contact ['kɒntækt] **1** *noun* **(a)** touch; *avoid any contact between the acid and the skin; anyone who has been in physical contact with the patient must consult their doctor immediately;* **contact lenses** = tiny lenses worn on the eye **(b)** act of communicating with someone; *we don't have much contact with our old friends in Australia*; **to get in contact with someone** = to communicate with someone you have not spoken to or written to; **he put me in contact with a good lawyer** = he told me the name and address of a good lawyer; **I have lost contact with them** = I do not communicate with them any longer; **contact number** = phone number which you can call to speak to someone **(c)** person whom you know; *he has a lot of contacts in the newspaper world*; *who is your contact in the ministry?* **2** *verb* to get into communication with someone; *he tried to contact his office by phone*; *can you contact the ticket office immediately?*

contagion [kən'teɪdʒn] *noun* spreading of a disease by touching an infected person or things which an infected person has touched; *the contagion spread through the whole school*; *avoid direct physical contact with the patients to prevent contagion* (NOTE: compare **infection**)

contagious [kən'teɪdʒəs] *adjective* **(a)** *(disease)* which can be transmitted by touching an infected person or objects which an infected person has touched; *did you have any contagious diseases when you were a child?*; *your child is no longer contagious and can go back to school* (NOTE: compare **infectious**) **(b)** which can be passed on to someone else; *he's a great music teacher and his enthusiasm for music is very contagious*

contain [kən'teɪn] *verb* **(a)** to hold, to have inside; *the bottle contains acid*; *the envelope contained a cheque for £1000*; *a barrel contains 250 litres*; *I have lost a briefcase containing important documents* **(b)** to restrict; *the army tried to contain the advance of the enemy forces*; *the party is attempting to contain the revolt among its members*

container [kən'teɪnə] *noun* **(a)** box or bottle, etc., which holds something else; *we need a container for all this rubbish*; *the gas is shipped in strong metal containers* **(b)** very large case for easy loading onto a ship, lorry, etc.; *the crane was loading the containers onto the ship*; *we had our furniture shipped out to Singapore in a container*; **a container-load of spare parts** = a shipment of spare parts sent in a container; **container port** = port which only deals with containers; **container ship** = ship which only carries containers

containment [kən'teɪnmənt] *noun* keeping under control; *we are aiming for a successful containment of the epidemic*

contaminant [kən'tæmɪnənt] *noun* substance which contaminates; *this is one of the many contaminants of our drinking water*

contaminate [kən'tæmɪneɪt] *verb* to make something dirty by touching it or by adding something to it; *supplies of drinking water were contaminated by refuse from the factories*; *a party of tourists fell ill after eating contaminated food*

contamination [kəntæmɪ'neɪʃn] *noun* act of contaminating; *the contamination of the water supply was caused by waste from the factory*

contemplate ['kɒntempleɪt] *verb* **(a)** to look at something; *he stood for several minutes contemplating the painting* **(b)** **to contemplate doing something** = to plan to do something; *he's contemplating retiring from his job and buying a shop*

contemplation [kɒntem'pleɪʃn] *noun* deep thought; *he was deep in contemplation and did not notice that I had come in*

contemporaneous [kəntempə'reɪnɪəs] *adjective* *(formal)* happening at the same date or period; *were these two events contemporaneous?*; *we know a lot about the invasion of Britain in 1066 from contemporaneous accounts*

contemporary [kən'temprəri] **1** *adjective* **(a) contemporary with someone** *or* **something** = existing at the same time as someone *or* something; *most of the people I was contemporary with at college have already got jobs* **(b)** modern, present-day; *contemporary art* **2** *noun* person who lives at the same time as someone; *he is one of my contemporaries from school*; *Shakespeare and his contemporaries*

contempt [kən'tempt] *noun* feeling of not respecting someone; *you have shown contempt for the feelings of our family*; *the reviewer had nothing but contempt for the author of the novel*; **to hold someone in contempt** = not to respect someone; *she holds him in contempt and won't have anything to do with him*

contemptible [kən'temptəbl] *adjective* which deserves your contempt; *these contemptible people are trying to suggest what I should do*; *her action was totally contemptible*

contempt of court [kən'tempt əv 'kɔːt] *noun* being rude to a court, as by bad behaviour in court, or by refusing to carry out a court order; *he refused to obey the court order and was sent to prison for contempt (of court)*

contemptuous [kən'temptjʊəs] *adjective* showing contempt, showing that you do not believe someone is important; *she shouldn't be working in a hospital if she treats patients in such a contemptuous way*; **contemptuous of something** *or* **someone** = full of scorn about something *or* someone; *he was contemptuous of our attempts to sail the boat*

contend [kən'tend] *verb* **(a)** **to contend with** = to cope with; *we had to contend with rainstorms, floods, and mosquitoes, so the holiday was not a great success*; *drugs are yet another problem that schools have to contend with* **(b)** to state; *the witness contended that the injury to the head was consistent with being hit with a blunt instrument*

contender [kən'tendə] *noun* person who wants to win a competition or contest; *the three contenders for the post of leader of the party*

content 1 *adjective* [kən'tent]; **content to** = happy to; *she was content to sit in the sun and wait*; **content with** = satisfied with; *if you are not content with the way the car runs, bring it back and we will look at it again* **2** *noun* **(a)** [kən'tent] satisfaction; **to your heart's content** = as much as you want; *you can play billiards to your heart's content*; *living by the sea, they can go sailing to their heart's content* **(b)** ['kɒntent] thing or amount which is contained; *dried fruit has a higher sugar content than fresh fruit*; **the mineral content of water** = the percentages of different minerals contained in a sample of water

contented [kən'tentɪd] *adjective* satisfied, happy; *he gave a contented sigh*; *our milk comes from contented cows*

contentedly [kən'tentɪdli] *adverb* in a contented way; *the cat sat on my lap, purring contentedly*

contention [kən'tenʃn] *noun* **(a)** argument; **bone of contention** = source of an argument; *the fence between the houses has always been a bone of contention* **(b)** statement of what you believe; *it is his contention that they are trying to ruin our business*

contentious [kən'tenʃəs] *adjective* which is a source of dispute; *management made a series of contentious proposals*

contentment [kən'tentmənt] *noun* being satisfied, happy; *she showed her contentment by lying on her back with her eyes shut; he sat down, with a look of contentment on his face*

contents ['kɒntents] *noun* things which are inside something, which are in a container; *he dropped the bottle and the contents spilled onto the carpet; the burglars took the entire contents of the safe; the customs officials inspected the contents of the crate; she kept the contents of the letter secret;* **table of contents** = list of chapters in a book, usually printed at the beginning of the text

contest 1 *noun* ['kɒntest] fight, competition; *only two people entered the contest for the party leadership;* **beauty contest** = competition to see which girl is most beautiful **2** *verb* [kən'test] **(a)** to fight an election; *there are four candidates contesting the seat* **(b)** to query a will, or argue that a will is invalid; *when she died and left all her money to a cats' home, her family contested the will*

contestant [kən'testənt] *noun* person who enters a contest; *the two contestants shook hands before the match*

context ['kɒntekst] *noun* phrase in which a word occurs which helps to show what it means; *even if you don't know what a word means, you can sometimes guess its meaning from the context;* **taken out of context** = quoted without surrounding text; *my words have been taken out of context - if you read the whole speech you will see that I meant something quite different*

contextual [kən'tekstjʊəl] *adjective* referring to a context; *her review was based on close contextual analysis of the text*

contiguous [kən'tɪgjʊəs] *adjective* (*formal*) touching, next to something; *the two states are contiguous*

continent ['kɒntɪnənt] **1** *noun* **(a)** one of the major land areas in the world (Africa, North America, South America, Asia, Australia, Antarctica, Europe) **(b)** (*in Britain*) **the Continent** = the rest of Europe, as opposed to Britain itself which is an island; **on the Continent** = in Europe; **to the Continent** = to Europe; *when you drive on the Continent remember to drive on the right; they go to the Continent on holiday each year, sometimes to France, sometimes to Switzerland* **2** *adjective* able to control the passing of urine or excreta; *the old lady is barely continent* (NOTE: the opposite is **incontinent**)

continental [kɒntɪ'nentl] **1** *adjective* **(a)** referring to a continent; **continental climate** = climate of hot dry summers and very cold winters; *Germany has a continental climate which is quite different from ours in Britain;* **continental shelf** = area of shallow sea round the edges of a continent; *oil companies are keen to explore the waters of the continental shelf* **(b)** referring to Europe (excluding the British Isles); *we've decided to take a continental holiday this year;*

continental breakfast = light breakfast of rolls, croissants, and coffee (as opposed to a 'full English breakfast'); **continental quilt** = bag stuffed with feathers, used as the only covering for a bed; *I prefer a continental quilt to blankets, because it is lighter* (NOTE: British English is **duvet**); *US* **continental plan** = hotel tariff including accommodation and a continental breakfast **2** *noun* (*informal*) **a Continental** = a European; *the Continentals seem to play a different type of football from us*

contingency [kən'tɪndʒənsi] *noun* possible state of emergency when decisions will have to be taken quickly; *you should prepare for any contingency; we keep stocks of oil as a contingency measure* (NOTE: plural is **contingencies**)

contingent [kən'tɪndʒənt] **1** *adjective* **contingent expenses** = expenses which will be incurred only if something happens; **contingent (up)on something** = which depends on something; *the launch of the space shuttle is contingent upon the weather* **2** *noun* group of soldiers, protesters, etc.; *the army was formed of contingents of freedom fighters from various countries; a large contingent of farmers marched to the Parliament building*

continual [kən'tɪnjuəl] *adjective* which goes on all the time; *I am getting fed up with her continual complaints; the computer has given us continual problems ever since we bought it*

continually [kən'tɪnjuːli] *adverb* very often, almost all the time; *the photocopier is continually breaking down*

continuance [kən'tɪnjuəns] *noun* = CONTINUATION (a)

continuation [kəntɪnju'eɪʃn] *noun* **(a)** going on without stopping; *how can we ensure the continuation of the peace talks?* **(b)** extension, thing which has been continued; *Broad Street is in fact a continuation of the High Street*

continue [kən'tɪnjuː] *verb* to go on doing something or happening; *he continued working, even though the house was on fire; the engine continued to send out clouds of black smoke; the meeting started at 10 a.m. and continued until 6 p.m.; the show continued with some children's dances*

continuing [kən'tɪnjuːɪŋ] *adjective* which continues; *the continuing British love of holidays in the sun;* **continuing education** = education of adults after further or higher education; *the government is developing a programme of continuing education in specialist skills*

continuous [kən'tɪnjuəs] *adjective* with no break; *she has been in continuous pain for three days; a continuous white line means that you are not allowed to overtake;* **continuous stationery** = long sheet of computer paper; **continuous tense** = form of a verb showing that something is going on and has not stopped; *'is going' is a continuous form of the verb 'to go'; continuous tenses in English are formed using the present participle*

continuously [kən'tɪnjuəsli] *adverb* without a break; *the children behind me ate popcorn continuously during the film; the lead singer was on stage continuously for four hours*

continuum [kən'tɪnjuəm] *noun* thing which continues and develops gradually, with no clear divisions between its parts; *he sees human intelligence* *as a continuum*; *the sound of water flowing over the rocks formed a continuum to life by the river*

contour ['kɒntuə] *noun* **contour (line)** = line on a map to show ground of the same height above sea level; *closely drawn contours indicate a steep slope*

contraception [kɒntrə'sepʃn] *noun* prevention of pregnancy by using devices (such as a condom or an IUD) or drugs (such as the contraceptive pill) or by other means; *which method of contraception are you using?*; *did you use any form of contraception?*

contraceptive [kɒntrə'septɪv] **1** *adjective* which prevents pregnancy; *the contraceptive pill is available from doctors and clinics*; *a contraceptive device such as an IUD* **2** *noun* drug or condom which prevents pregnancy; *the chemist sells various types of contraceptives*; *an oral contraceptive such as the pill*

contract 1 ['kɒntrækt] *noun* legal agreement; *I don't agree with some of the conditions of the contract*; **under contract** = bound by the terms of a contract; *the company is under contract to a French supermarket*; **breach of contract** = breaking the terms of a contract; **the company is in breach of contract** = the company has failed to do what was agreed in the contract **2** [kən'trækt] *verb* **(a)** to agree to do some work under a legally binding contract; *to contract to supply spare parts or to contract for the supply of spare parts* **(b)** to become smaller; *metal contracts when it gets cold, and expands when it is hot*

contraction [kən'trækʃn] *noun* **(a)** shortening, becoming smaller; *light will provoke the contraction of the pupil of the eye*; *cold will cause the contraction of metal rails* **(b)** movement of the muscles of the uterus, at the beginning of childbirth; *the first strong contractions will come about every twenty minutes*; *she had two contractions in the car on the way to the maternity hospital*

contractor [kən'træktə] *noun* person who does work according to a signed agreement; *a building contractor*; *an electricity contractor*; **haulage contractor** = company which transports goods by contract; *see also* SUBCONTRACTOR

contractual [kən'træktjʊəl] *adjective* according to a contract; *our employer said he has no contractual liability to provide a crèche*; *she is under no contractual obligation to buy*

contradict [kɒntrə'dɪkt] *verb* to say that what someone else says is not true; to be different from what has been said before; *why do you always contradict me?*; *the witness contradicted herself several times*; *what you have just said contradicts what you said yesterday*

contradiction [kɒntrə'dɪkʃn] *noun* stating or being the opposite; *there is a basic contradiction between the government's policies and what it actually does*; **a contradiction in terms** = phrase which is formed of two parts which contradict each other, and so have no meaning; *a truthful politician is a contradiction in terms*

contradictory [kɒntrə'dɪktəri] *adjective* which states or is the opposite; *we were given various contradictory messages*; *the jury was puzzled by a lot of contradictory evidence*

contraflow ['kɒntrəfləu] *noun* system where traffic on one lane of a motorway is made to go down one of the opposite lanes in the wrong direction, used when the road is being repaired; *there's a two mile long contraflow because of road repairs*

contralto [kən'træltəu] *noun* **(a)** low-pitched singing voice; *she spoke in a soft contralto* **(b)** woman with a low-pitched voice; *we need more contraltos in our choir* (NOTE: plural is **contraltos**)

contraption [kən'træpʃn] *noun* (*informal*) odd machine or device; *he invented a strange contraption for lifting blocks of stone*; *I prefer an old-fashioned corkscrew to this newfangled contraption*

contrary ['kɒntrəri] **1** *adjective* **(a)** opposite; *most people agreed with the speaker, but one or two expressed contrary views*; **contrary winds** = winds blowing in the opposite direction; *the ship could not leave harbour because of contrary winds* **(b) contrary to** = in opposition to; *contrary to what you would expect, the desert gets quite cold at night* **(c)** [kən'treəri] always doing the opposite of what you want; *she's such a contrary child* **2** *noun* **the contrary** = the opposite; **on the contrary** = just the opposite; *I'm not annoyed with her - on the contrary, I think she has done the right thing*; **to the contrary** = stating the opposite; *we will go on with the plans for the exhibition unless we hear to the contrary*; *smoking used to be considered harmless, but now the evidence is to the contrary*

contrast 1 *noun* ['kɒntrɑːst] sharp difference between two things; *the contrast in weather between the north and the south of the country*; **in contrast to** = as opposed to; *he is quite short, in contrast to his sister who is very tall*; *the north of the country is green and wooded in contrast to the south which is dry and sandy*; *the two cities are in sharp contrast* **2** *verb* [kən'trɑːst] to be quite visibly different from; *his formal letter contrasted with his friendly conversation on the telephone*

contrasting [kən'trɑːstɪŋ] which are very different; *the room is decorated in contrasting colours*

contravene [kɒntrə'viːn] *verb* to break rules, regulations, etc.; *the company was fined when it contravened exchange control regulations*; *the fire department can close a restaurant if it contravenes safety regulations*

contravention [kɒntrə'venʃn] *noun* **in contravention of a law** = breaking a law; *the restaurant is in contravention of the safety regulations*; *the management of the cinema locked the fire exits in contravention of the fire regulations*

contribute [kən'trɪbjuːt] *verb* **(a)** to help towards; *the government's policies have contributed to a feeling of dissatisfaction among teachers* **(b)** to give money to; *we were asked to contribute to a charity*; *everyone was asked to contribute to the secretary's leaving present* **(c) to contribute to a magazine** = to write articles for a magazine

contribution [kɒntrɪ'bjuːʃn] *noun* **(a)** money, etc., given to help something; *she makes monthly contributions to the Red Cross*; **National Insurance contributions (NIC)** = money paid each month to the government by a worker and the company he or she works for, to go towards the costs of looking after the sick, poor and unemployed **(b)** article submitted to a newspaper; *the deadline for contributions is December 1st*

contributor [kən'trɪbjutə] *noun* person or organization that contributes; *she's a regular* *contributor to the local newspaper; the company is an important contributor to charity*

contrive [kən'traɪv] *verb* to manage to do something; *somehow she contrived a way of getting into the party without an invitation*

contrived [kən'traɪvd] *adjective* artificial, not natural; *his rather contrived excuse was not accepted by the management*

control [kən'trəʊl] **1** *noun* **(a)** keeping in order, being able to direct something; *the club is under the control of three shareholders; he lost control of his business and resigned; the teacher has no control over the class*; **control button** = on a TV, radio, etc., the button which switches it on, changes channel, increases volume, etc. **(b)** restricting something; **under control** = restricted; *we try to keep expenses under tight control*; **to bring something under control** = to reduce or restrict something; *the firemen quickly brought the fire under control*; **out of control** = not restricted; *the car ran down the hill out of control; our spending has got out of control; the fire started in the roof and quickly got out of control; football fans got out of control and started breaking windows in the centre of town* **(c)** **control group** = group against which the results of a test on another group can be compared **2** *verb* **(a)** to keep in order, to direct or restrict; *the police couldn't control the crowds; there was nobody there to control the traffic; we must try to control the sales of foreign cars; the government controls the price of meat* **(b)** **to control a business** = to have the power to direct the way a business is run; *the business is controlled by a company based in Luxembourg* (NOTE: **controlling - controlled**)

controllable [kən'trəʊləbl] *adjective* which can be controlled or changed; *the level of noise made by the machine is not controllable; the controllable amount of light is one of the advantages of this lighting system*

controller [kən'trəʊlə] *noun* person who controls; **air traffic controller** = person who directs planes from a control tower; *the strike by air traffic controllers caused widespread disruption to air services*

controls [kən'trəʊlz] *noun* **(a)** switches, levers, etc., by which you can control a machine; *she took the controls of the aircraft; he was at the controls of the spacecraft at the time* **(b)** **exchange controls** = restrictions on exchanging one currency for another; **price controls** = restrictions on increases in prices

control tower [kən'trəʊl 'taʊə] *noun* high building at an airport with the radio station which directs planes

controversial [kɒntrə'vɜːʃl] *adjective* which starts violent discussions; *he made a highly controversial speech; legalization of drugs is a very controversial issue; she has controversial views on abortion*

controversy [kən'trɒvəsi] *noun* sharp discussion; *there is a lot of controversy about the funding of political parties*

conundrum [kə'nʌndrəm] *noun* difficult problem; *we are trying to solve the conundrum of how to get thirty rugby players into one minibus; repainting the living room without removing the furniture poses something of a conundrum*

convalesce [kɒnvə'les] *verb* to get back to good health after an illness or an operation; *he convalesced for a couple of weeks at his mother's house*

convalescence [kɒnvə'lesəns] *noun* period of time when you are convalescing; *after the operation you will need a long period of convalescence; he has to follow a special diet during his convalescence*

convalescent [kɒnvə'lesənt] **1** *adjective* referring to convalescence; *convalescent patients must have proper nourishment; he's much better but still convalescent*; **convalescent home** = small hospital where people can recover after illnesses or operations; *the only convalescent home with a room available is 25 miles away* **2** *noun* person who is convalescing after an illness or operation; *now that you're not a convalescent any more, you can go back to work as normal*

convene [kən'viːn] *verb* to call a meeting; *he convened a meeting of local shopkeepers*

convenience [kən'viːniəns] *noun* **(a)** being convenient; *I like the convenience of working from home; we bought the house because of the convenience of the area for shopping*; **at your earliest convenience** = as soon as you can easily do it; *please return this form at your earliest convenience* **(b)** **public conveniences** = public toilets; **all modern conveniences** *or* **all mod cons** = all modern facilities such as central heating, telephone, electricity, etc.; *flat is advertised with all mod cons* **(c)** **convenience food** = food which is prepared by the shop before it is sold, so that it needs only heating to be made ready to eat; *sales of convenience foods are booming*

convenient [kən'viːniənt] *adjective* which does not cause any practical problems; *6.30 in the morning is not a very convenient time for a meeting; a bank draft is a convenient way of sending money abroad*

convenor [kən'viːnə] *noun* person who organizes a meeting; *the convenor asked everyone to sit down*

convent ['kɒnvənt] *noun* religious establishment where nuns live; the buildings of such a place; *the number of nuns has fallen sharply and the Mother Superior is afraid the convent may have to close* (NOTE: the equivalent establishment for men is a **monastery**)

convention [kən'venʃn] *noun* **(a)** the usual way of doing things; *it is a convention that the bride wears white to her wedding* **(b)** contract or treaty; *an international convention on human rights* **(c)** general meeting of an association or political party; *they are holding their annual convention in Chicago*; **convention centre** = building with a series of meeting rooms, hotel bedrooms, restaurants, etc., built specially for holding large meetings

conventional [kən'venʃənəl] *adjective* ordinary, usual; *we are planning a conventional Christmas at home; he arrived at the office wearing a very conventional grey suit*; **conventional weapons** = ordinary weapons such as guns, not nuclear weapons

converge [kən'vɜːdʒ] *verb* to come together at a certain place or point; *crowds of protesters converged on the main square; they complained that the decision to increase the tariff on beer was contrary to the idea of converging EU excise rates*

convergence [kən'vɜːdʒəns] *noun* coming together, meeting; *exchange rate differences have made the task of achieving further convergence more difficult; a certain convergence of opinions helped them to move rapidly towards a settlement*

conversation [kɒnvə'seɪʃn] *noun* talk; *we had a long conversation with the bank manager*; *why did he suddenly change the subject of the conversation?*; **to carry on a conversation with someone** = to talk to someone; *she tried to carry on a conversation with him while he was working*; *it's difficult to carry on a conversation with Uncle Harry because he's deaf*

conversational [kɒnvə'seɪʃənəl] *adjective* used in conversation; *he tends to deliver his speeches in a relaxed conversational tone*; *I need more practice in conversational German*

converse 1 *noun* ['kɒnvɜːs]; **the converse** = the opposite; *if this is true then the converse must be false* **2** *verb* [kən'vɜːs] to talk; *they were conversing seriously in French*

conversely ['kɒnvɜːsli] *adverb* in the opposite way; *this cheap machine cannot process large amounts of data: conversely, more expensive machines process more data than you will ever need*

conversion [kən'vɜːʃn] *noun* **(a)** changing of one thing into another; *the conversion of an old chapel into a modern house*; *I need a calculator to work out the conversion of £500 into pesetas* **(b)** turning of a person to another set of ideas or religion; *she underwent a sudden conversion to Catholicism* **(c)** *(in Rugby)* act of converting a try; *his attempted conversion failed, and the scores remained level*

convert 1 *noun* ['kɒnvɜːt] person who has changed his ideas or religion; *he has become a convert to vegetarianism* **2** *verb* [kən'vɜːt] **(a)** to turn or to make someone turn from one set of ideas or religion to another; *when she got married she converted to Islam*; *she tried to convert her husband to vegetarianism* **(b)** to change; *we are converting the shed into a studio*; *these panels convert the heat of the sun into electricity* **(c)** *(in Rugby)* **to convert a try** = to earn extra points by kicking the ball over the crossbar between the posts after a try has been scored; *if he converts the try the scores will be level* **(d)** to change money of one country for money of another; *we converted our pounds into Swiss francs*

converter [kən'vɜːtə] *noun* device which converts; *all new cars must be fitted with catalytic converters*; *see also* CATALYTIC

convertible [kən'vɜːtəbl] **1** *adjective (especially of a currency)* which can easily be changed into another currency; *the dollar, the yen and other convertible currencies* **2** *noun* car with a roof which folds back or can be removed; *you can hire a small convertible for $100 a day*

convex ['kɒnveks] *adjective* (surface) which is rounded outwards like the back of a spoon; *a convex lens concentrates light beams on a point*; *the surface should be perfectly flat but I noticed that it is slightly convex* (NOTE: the opposite is **concave**)

convey [kən'veɪ] *verb (formal)* **(a)** to transport, to carry; *the supplies were being conveyed in lorries* **(b)** to give a message or to express something; *please convey my congratulations to the team*

conveyance [kən'veɪəns] *noun* **(a)** *(formal)* act of transporting; *the conveyance of goods is controlled by several Acts of Parliament* **(b)** *(formal)* means of transport; *various rickety conveyances were waiting outside the station* **(c)** document by which property is transferred from one owner to another; *the conveyance is being drawn up by the solicitor*

conveyancing [kən'veɪənsɪŋ] *noun* action of transferring property from one owner to another; *a solicitor specializing in conveyancing*

conveyor belt [kən'veɪə 'belt] *noun* moving surface in a factory, which takes something from one part of the factory to another; *the finished products come off the conveyor belt and are packed in crates*

convict 1 *noun* ['kɒnvɪkt] criminal who has been sent to prison; *the police are searching for two escaped convicts* **2** *verb* [kən'vɪkt] to find someone guilty; *she was convicted of theft*

conviction [kən'vɪkʃn] *noun* **(a)** being found guilty; *his lawyers are appealing against his conviction* **(b)** being certain that something is true; *it was a common conviction in the Middle Ages that the earth was flat*; *her religious convictions do not allow her to eat shellfish* **(c)** being likely, being convincing; *she gave a string of excuses which completely lacked conviction*

convince [kən'vɪns] *verb* **to convince someone of something** = to persuade someone that something is true; *the lawyer has to convince the jury of his client's innocence*; *you have to convince the interviewer that you are the right person for the job*

convinced [kən'vɪnst] *adjective* very certain; *I am convinced that she knows something about the robbery*; *I'm still not convinced she is telling the truth*

convincing [kən'vɪnsɪŋ] *adjective* which convinces; *we didn't find her explanation very convincing*

convincingly [kən'vɪnsɪŋli] *adverb* in a convincing way; *he argued convincingly for more money for the health service*

convoy ['kɒnvɔɪ] *noun* group of ships, lorries, etc., travelling together in a line with armed protection; *the supplies were transported in a convoy of UN lorries*

convulsions [kən'vʌlʃnz] *noun* a fit, the rapid involuntary contracting and relaxing of the muscles in several parts of the body; *the child has had convulsions before, but not as violent as this time*; *in adults, convulsions are often associated with epilepsy*

coo [kuː] *verb* to make a soft noise like a pigeon; *I wake up in the morning to hear pigeons cooing outside my window*; *the midwife cooed at the new baby boy, then put him into the cot* (NOTE: do not confuse with **coup**)

cook [kʊk] **1** *noun* person who gets food ready; *he worked as a cook in a pub during the summer*; *he's a very good cook* = he makes very good food **2** *verb* **(a)** to get food ready for eating, especially by heating it; *if you want to learn how to cook Chinese food, watch the TV programme*; *don't bother your mother when she's cooking the dinner*; *how do you cook cabbage?*; *see also* BAKE, BOIL, FRY, etc. **(b)** *(of food)* to be got ready by heating; *the chicken is cooking in the oven*; *how long do these vegetables take to cook?*

cookbook ['kʊkbʊk] *noun* book of recipes; *I gave her an Indian cookbook for her birthday*; *if you're not sure how long to cook turkey, look it up in the cookbook*

cooked [kʊkt] *adjective* food which has been heated to prepare it for eating; *the children seem to prefer raw carrots to cooked ones*; *the meat isn't cooked enough - it's tough*; **cooked breakfast** = breakfast which includes bacon, eggs, sausages, etc. (as opposed to a continental breakfast)

cooker ['kʊkə] *noun* device run on gas, electricity, coal, etc., for cooking food; *we have a fridge, a dishwasher and a gas cooker in the kitchen*

cookery ['kʊkəri] *noun* art of cooking; *he's decided to go to cookery classes*; **cookery book** = book of recipes; *if you're not sure how long to cook turkey, look it up in the cookery book* (NOTE: no plural)

cookie ['kʊki] *noun* usually US biscuit, small flat hard sweet cake; *she bought a packet of cookies*; **chocolate chip cookie** = sweet biscuit made with little pieces of hard chocolate inside

cooking ['kʊkɪŋ] *noun* **(a)** action of getting food ready to eat, especially by heating it; *he does the cooking, while his wife serves in the restaurant*; **cooking apple** = sour apple which can be cooked but not eaten raw **(b)** particular style of preparing food; *French provincial cooking*

cool [kuːl] **1** *adjective* **(a)** quite cold; *blow on your soup to make it cool*; *it was hot on deck but cool down below*; *wines should be stored in a cool cellar*; *it gets cool in the evenings in September* **(b)** not enthusiastic; *I got a cool reception when I arrived half an hour late*; *the board was quite cool towards the proposal* **(c)** calm; *the nurses remained cool and professional when dealing with all the accident victims* (NOTE: **cooler - coolest**) **2** *verb* to make cool; to become cool; *she boiled the jam for several hours and then put it aside to cool* **3** *noun* **(a)** colder area which is pleasant; *after the heat of the square, it is nice to sit in the cool of the garden* **(b)** *(informal)* state of being calm; *as soon as the reporters started to ask her questions she lost her cool*

cool down [kuːl 'daʊn] *verb* **(a)** to make or become cool; *although it is very hot in the desert during the daytime, it always cools down in the evening*; *this coffee is too hot - I'm waiting for it to cool down a bit* **(b)** to become calmer; *he was furious with his secretary, but after a while he cooled down*; *we tried to cool him down but it just made him more angry*

cooler ['kuːlə] *noun* **(a)** thing or machine which cools; *it's going to be a hot day, so you had better put the food for the picnic in the cooler*; *a wine cooler will keep white wine at the right temperature* **(b)** *(slang)* prison; *we kept all of them overnight in the cooler*

cooling ['kuːlɪŋ] *adjective* refreshing, which makes you cool; *after a long run what I need is a cooling drink*; *a cooling breeze blew in from the sea*

coop [kuːp] **1** *verb* **to coop someone up** = to keep someone in a small place; *I don't like being cooped up in this little office* **2** *noun* **chicken coop** = little building where chickens are kept

co-op ['kəʊɒp] *noun* *(informal)* cooperative store; *we do all our shopping at the local co-op*

cooperate [kəʊ'ɒpəreɪt] *verb* **to cooperate with someone** = to work with someone; *the governments are cooperating in the fight against drug smuggling*

cooperation [kəʊɒpə'reɪʃn] *noun* action of working together with someone else; *the school is run with the cooperation of the local church*; *he wrote the book in cooperation with one of his students*

cooperative [kəʊ'ɒprətɪv] **1** *adjective* **(a)** working with the profits shared between the workers; *a cooperative farm*; *a cooperative store* **(b)** helpful, willing to work with someone; *the bank manager was*

not at all cooperative **2** *noun* business which works on a profit-sharing basis; *a workers' cooperative*

coordinate 1 *noun* [kəʊ'ɔːdɪnət] **(a)** set of figures which fix a point on a map or graph; *what are the coordinates for that hill? I don't think it is marked on the map*; *draw the X - Y coordinates* **(b)** *coordinates* = matching pieces of ladies' clothing **2** *verb* [kəʊ'ɔːdɪneɪt] to make things work together or fit in with each other; *his job is to coordinate with the work of the various relief agencies*; *the election campaign was coordinated by the party headquarters*

coordination [kəʊɔːdɪ'neɪʃn] *noun* **(a)** action of coordinating; *better coordination between departments would have allowed everyone to know what was happening* **(b)** ability to move parts of your body properly; *she has excellent coordination for a little girl of 18 months*

cop [kɒp] *noun (informal)* policeman; *he was stopped by a cop*; *when the cops came to arrest him he had disappeared*

cope [kəʊp] **1** *noun* long coloured cloak worn by a priest in church **2** *verb* **to cope with something** = to manage to deal with something; *she can cope perfectly well on her own*; *we are trying to cope with the backlog of orders*

copier ['kɒpjə] *noun* machine which makes copies; **copier paper** = special paper used in photocopiers; *see also* COPYING MACHINE, PHOTOCOPIER

copilot ['kəʊpaɪlət] *noun* pilot who is second in command to the captain of an aircraft; *when the pilot felt ill, his copilot took over the controls*

copious ['kəʊpiəs] *adjective* plentiful, in good supply; *we served copious amounts of orange juice to the children*; *he took copious notes during the lecture*

copper ['kɒpə] *noun* **(a)** reddish metal which turns green when exposed to air; *copper is a good conductor of electricity*; *the end of the copper wire should be attached to the terminal* (NOTE: Chemical element: chemical symbol: **Cu**; atomic number: 29) **(b)** *(informal)* policeman; *watch out! there's a copper coming* **(c)** small coin made of copper or other brown metal; *it only costs a few coppers*; *the beggar was asking for any spare coppers*

coppice ['kɒpɪs] **1** *noun* area of trees which have been cut down to the ground, so that shoots will grow up again; *a coppice of willow* **2** *verb* to cut trees down to the ground; *I wonder how long ago these trees were coppiced*; *coppiced wood can be dried and used in stoves or even small power stations*; *compare* POLLARD

copse [kɒps] *noun* wood of young trees; *a small copse hides the farm from the motorway*

copy ['kɒpi] **1** *noun* **(a)** something made to look the same as something else; *this is an exact copy of the painting by Picasso*; **carbon copy** = copy made with carbon paper **(b)** one book; one newspaper; *where's my copy of today's 'Times'?*; *I lent my old copy of Shakespeare to my brother and he never gave it back*; *can I borrow your copy of the telephone directory?* **(c)** text written to be used in a newspaper or advertisement; *he sent in his copy three days late*; *we need more copy for this page* (NOTE: plural is **copies** in meanings (a) and (b)) **2** *verb* to make something which looks like something else; *to knit the pullover, just copy this pattern*; *I get very annoyed because he copies* *everything I do*; **copying machine** = copier, a machine which copies

copyright ['kɒpɪraɪt] *noun* an author's right to publish a book, put on a play, etc., and not to have it copied without permission; *who holds the copyright for the play?*; *she is being sued for breach of copyright*; **book which is in copyright** = book which is protected by the copyright laws; **book which is out of copyright** = book by a writer who has been dead for more than seventy years and which anyone can publish

coral ['kɒrəl] *noun* rock-like substance formed of the skeletons of tiny animals in the sea; *coral takes hundreds of years to form*; *coral comes in many different shapes and colours*

cord [kɔːd] *noun* **(a)** strong thin rope; *pull the cord to open the parachute*; *in an emergency, pull the cord to stop the train* **(b) spinal cord** = part of the nervous system running along spine; *following an injury to her spinal cord she was paralyzed from the waist down* **(c)** (*informal*) **cords** = corduroy trousers; *cords are warmer than jeans*

cordial ['kɔːdiəl] **1** *adjective* friendly; *his greeting was not very cordial* **2** *noun* concentrated juice of a fruit to which water is added; *fruit cordials such as lemon, orange or lime are popular summer drinks*

cordon ['kɔːdən] **1** *noun* **(a)** barrier to prevent someone moving; line of police or soldiers surrounding an area to prevent people entering or leaving; *police formed a cordon round the referee to protect him from the fans*; *there was a police cordon round the courthouse* **(b)** fruit tree grown as a single stem, with little side shoots; *we planted a cordon pear against the wall* **2** *verb* **to cordon off a street** = to block a street to prevent anyone entering it; *the police had cordoned off the side streets and forced the protesters to march down the main road*

corduroy ['kɔːdjʊrɔɪ] *noun* **(a)** cloth with furry ribs on the surface; *he was wearing a corduroy jacket* **(b) a pair of corduroys** = a pair of trousers made of corduroy; *he was wearing a pair of dirty old corduroys and green wellingtons*

core [kɔː] **1** *noun* central part; **apple core** = hard part in the middle of an apple, containing the seeds; *he threw the apple core into the lake*; **rotten to the core** = completely rotten; *the local police force is rotten to the core*; **to take a core sample** = to cut a long round sample of soil or rock for testing (NOTE: do not confuse with **corps**) **2** *verb* to scoop out the central part of an apple, etc.; *peel and core the apples before putting them in the oven*

coriander [kɒrɪ'ændə] *noun* small herb, whose seeds and leaves are used for flavouring; *the smell of fish flavoured with fresh coriander reminds me of the Far East*

cork [kɔːk] **1** *noun* **(a)** material made from the very light bark of a type of oak tree; *she placed little cork mats on the table to stop the wine glasses marking it*; **cork oak** = type of oak tree with thick light bark; *cork oaks are common in Spain and Portugal* **(b)** stopper which closes wine bottles; *he pulled the cork out of the bottle*; *the little boat bobbed up and down on the surface of the water like a cork* **2** *verb* to put a cork into a bottle; *when they had drunk half the bottle, she corked it up to use the following day*

corkscrew ['kɔːkskruː] *noun* special screwing device for taking corks out of bottles; *I've forgotten the corkscrew - how can we get the bottle open?*

corm [kɔːm] *noun* bottom part of the stem of a plant which can be planted and from which new shoots will sprout

> COMMENT: crocuses and cyclamens have corms, not bulbs

cormorant ['kɔːmərənt] *noun* black seabird which eats fish, often near fishing grounds but also on lakes and rivers; *a couple of cormorants are often to be seen by the weir*

corn [kɔːn] *noun* **(a)** cereal plants such as wheat, etc.; *a field of corn* **(b)** maize, a widely grown cereal crop; **sweet corn** = sweet variety of maize; **corn cob** = head of maize with seeds; **corn on the cob** = a piece of maize, with seeds on it, boiled and served hot, with butter and salt **(c)** hard painful lump of skin, usually on the foot or hand, where something, such as a tight shoe, has rubbed; *he has a corn on his little toe*

cornea ['kɔːnɪə] *noun* transparent part of the front of the eyeball; *it is quite possible to graft a cornea*; *corneal tissue from donors is used to repair a damaged cornea*

corneal ['kɔːnɪəl] *adjective* referring to a cornea; **corneal graft** = grafting of corneal tissue to replace diseased tissue

corner ['kɔːnə] **1** *noun* **(a)** place where two walls, sides or streets meet; *the bank is on the corner of London Road and New Street*; *put the plant in the corner of the room nearest the window*; *the number is in the top right-hand corner of the page*; *the motorbike went round the corner at top speed*; **to paint yourself into a corner** = to get yourself into a situation that you cannot get out of; **to turn the corner** = (i) to go round the corner; (ii) to get better after being ill or in difficulties; *as she turned the corner she saw the bus coming*; *he has been in bed for weeks, but he seems to have turned the corner*; **corner shop** = small general store in a town on a street corner; *I still use the local corner shop for newspapers and cigarettes* **(b)** (in games, such as football) free kick taken from the corner of the field near the opponent's goal **2** *verb* **to corner the market** = to own most or all of the supply of a certain thing and so control the price; *the syndicate tried to corner the market in silver*

cornerstone ['kɔːnəstəun] *noun* **(a)** stone at the bottom of a corner of a building, often with an inscription carved on it to show when it was laid; *the mayor laid the cornerstone of the new library* **(b)** strong foundation or basis; *taking a lot of exercise is still one of the cornerstones of a long life*

cornet ['kɔːnɪt] **(a)** *see* CONE **(b)** type of small trumpet; *he plays the cornet in the brass band*

cornflakes ['kɔːnfleɪks] *noun* breakfast cereal of crisp pieces of toasted maize; *I'll just have a bowl of cornflakes and a cup of coffee for breakfast*

cornflour ['kɔːnflaʊə] *noun* very fine flour made from maize, used in cooking to make sauces thicker; *thicken your sauce with cornflour* (NOTE: American English is **cornstarch**)

cornflower ['kɔːnflaʊə] *noun* wild flower, with bright blue flowers; *she has cornflower blue eyes*

Cornish ['kɔ:nɪʃ] *adjective* referring to Cornwall; **Cornish pasty** = type of little pie filled with vegetables and meat

COMMENT: Cornwall is the most southerly and westerly county in England, pointing out into the Atlantic Ocean

cornstarch ['kɔ:nstɑ:tʃ] *noun US* very fine flour made from maize, used in cooking to make sauces thicker; *use some cornstarch to thicken your chocolate cream* (NOTE: British English is **cornflour**)

corolla [kə'rəʊlə] *noun* ring of coloured petals forming the main part of a flower; *a daffodil with a yellow corolla*

corollary [kə'rɒləri] *noun* natural result, something which follows naturally; *larger school classes are the obvious corollary of education cuts; the corollary to this state of affairs is that nothing will be ready before the end of next year*

corona [kə'rəʊnə] *noun* halo, a ring round the moon or sun when seen through mist

coronary ['kɒrənri] 1 *noun (non-medical term)* coronary thrombosis; *he had a coronary and was rushed to hospital* (NOTE: plural is **coronaries**) 2 *adjective* referring to any structure shaped like a crown; **coronary arteries** = arteries which supply blood to the heart muscles; *coronary heart disease is any disease affecting the coronary arteries;* **coronary thrombosis** = blood clot which blocks the coronary arteries, leading to a heart attack; *coronary thrombosis deprives part of the heart muscle of blood*

coronation [kɒrə'neɪʃn] *noun* official ceremony at which a king, queen or emperor is crowned; *the coronation of British kings or queens takes place in Westminster Abbey*

coroner ['kɒrənə] *noun* public official, either a doctor or a lawyer, who investigates sudden or violent deaths; *deaths of prisoners are investigated by a coroner*

COMMENT: coroners investigate deaths which are violent or unexpected, which may be murder or manslaughter, any deaths of prisoners and deaths involving the police

corporal ['kɔ:prəl] 1 *adjective* referring to the body; **corporal punishment** = punishment by beating; *corporal punishment is illegal in state schools* 2 *noun* rank in the army below sergeant; *the major ordered the corporal to take down the flag* (NOTE: can be used with the surname: **Corporal Jones**)

corporate ['kɔ:pərət] *adjective* referring to a body such as a company; *corporate responsibility rests with the whole management; corporate profits are down this year;* **corporate plan** = plan for a whole company

corporation [kɔ:pə'reɪʃn] *noun* (a) town council; *the corporation has privatized the refuse collection service; the corporation swimming pool is closed on Mondays* (b) large firm; *working for a big corporation can be rather impersonal;* **corporation tax (CT)** = tax on profits made by companies

corps [kɔ:] *noun* military group or organized group; **the diplomatic corps** = all the diplomats living in a certain country; **the press corps** = all the journalists working in a certain place (NOTE: plural is **corps** [kɔ:z]; do not confuse with **core**)

corpse [kɔ:ps] *noun* dead body; *after he had poisoned her he didn't know how to dispose of the corpse*

corpulent ['kɔ:pjʊlənt] *adjective (formal)* fat; *in the plane, I sat next to a corpulent middle-aged man*

corpus ['kɔ:pəs] *noun* (a) all the works written by an author or about an author; *the library has a huge Dickens corpus which is available to students; she is studying references to food in the Shakespeare corpus* (b) mass of text and words stored in a computer; *none of the dictionaries in the list state where their corpus comes from* (NOTE: plural is **corpora**)

corpuscle ['kɔ:pʌsl] *noun see* BLOOD CELL

corral [kɒ'rɑ:l] *US* 1 *noun* area surrounded by a fence to enclose cattle; *the cattle were brought to the OK Corral* 2 *verb* to enclose cattle or people in a confined space; *the cattle were corralled before being branded and shipped out; the police corralled the students into the area behind the university*

correct [kə'rekt] 1 *adjective* right; without any mistakes; *can you tell me the correct time?; you have to give correct answers to all the questions if you want to win first prize; you are correct in thinking that the weather in Greece is hot; would it be correct to say that the shop has not made a profit for years?* 2 *verb* to take away mistakes in something; *the boss had to correct the letter which his secretary had typed; you must try to correct your driving mistakes, or you will never pass the test; the computer keeps switching itself off - can you correct this fault?*

correction [kə'rekʃn] *noun* showing a mistake in something, making something correct; *he made a few small corrections to the letter*

corrective [kə'rektɪv] 1 *adjective* which corrects; *corrective surgery will be needed to prevent him having one leg shorter than the other;* **corrective maintenance** = actions to trace, find and repair a fault after it has occurred; *the computer shop offers corrective maintenance for machines bought from them* 2 *noun* thing which corrects; *these figures act as a welcome corrective to the government's very optimistic forecast*

correctly [kə'rektli] *adverb* in a correct way; *you must answer all the questions correctly if you want to win the prize*

correlate ['kɒrəleɪt] *verb* (a) to correspond to something else; *the figures in your report do not correlate with those I got from the warehouse; the number of people affected by asthma appears to correlate to the amount of air pollution* (b) to check to see if something corresponds to something else; *we need to correlate the data from the two sources*

correlation [kɒrə'leɪʃn] *noun* correspondence, link; *they found a correlation between cigarette smoking and cancer; a correlation exists between poverty, bad diet and poor health*

correspond [kɒrɪ'spɒnd] *verb* (a) to correspond to = to fit with; *the findings correspond to my own research* (b) to correspond with someone = to write letters to someone; *she corresponded for years with this man living in New York whom she had never met*

correspondence [kɒrɪ'spɒnəns] *noun* (a) letters; *they had been carrying on a correspondence for years; she was told by her father to break off the correspondence;* **correspondence course** = lessons given by post; **business correspondence =** letters concerned with a business; **to be in correspondence with someone =** to write letters to someone and receive letters back; *I have been in correspondence with the company about a refund but with no success* **(b)** matching; *there isn't much correspondence between theory and practice*

correspondent [kɒrɪˈspɒndənt] *noun* **(a)** journalist who writes articles for newspapers or reports for TV or radio on a particular subject; *he is the Paris correspondent of the 'Telegraph'; the report comes from the BBC's correspondent in the area; a report from our football correspondent* **(b)** person who writes letters; *a correspondent in Australia sent us an email*

corresponding [kɒrɪˈspɒndɪŋ] *adjective* which corresponds; *the approach of winter brings a corresponding rise in the number of people wanting to go on holiday to warm countries*

correspondingly [kɒrɪˈspɒndɪŋli] *adverb* in a way which corresponds; *when he started exercising more often and eating a more balanced diet, he saw his health improve correspondingly; these computers are more expensive but are they correspondingly more efficient?*

corridor [ˈkɒrɪdɔː] *noun* long, narrow passage; *the ladies' room is straight ahead at the end of the corridor; there is an underground corridor to the next building*

corroborate [kəˈrɒbəreɪt] *verb* to confirm a statement, especially a statement made in court; *the witness corroborated the alibi of the accused*

corrode [kəˈrəʊd] *verb* to rust, to change by exposure to water, air or chemicals; *the silver dish has already started to corrode; after being so long in the sea, the metal boxes were badly corroded*

corrosion [kəˈrə ʒn] *noun* changing of metals by exposure to water, air or chemicals; *the silver dish is showing signs of corrosion; corrosion was apparent on the piece of metal we examined; the metal rods were weakened by corrosion*

corrugated [ˈkɒrəgeɪtɪd] *adjective* bent into folds like waves; **corrugated iron =** sheets of metal which are folded into waves; *we used an old piece of corrugated iron as a roof for the hut*; **corrugated cardboard** *or* **corrugated paper =** brown paper folded into waves, used as packing; *the box was lined with corrugated cardboard*

corrupt [kəˈrʌpt] **1** *adjective* **(a)** who is not honest, who takes bribes; *the Prime Minister promised to sack any officials who were found to be corrupt* **(b)** (data on a computer disk) which is faulty; *power loss can make the data corrupt* **2** *verb* **(a)** to make dishonest; *he was corrupted by his rich friends from college; 'power corrupts, absolute power corrupts absolutely'* **(b)** to make data faulty; *the data on this disk has been corrupted*

corruption [kəˈrʌpʃn] *noun* **(a)** paying money or giving a favour to someone (usually an official) so that he does what you want; *bribery and corruption are difficult to control; corruption in the civil service will be rooted out* **(b)** making data faulty; *you have to watch out for corruption of data*

corset [ˈkɔːsɪt] *noun* **(a)** *(old)* tight piece of underwear worn by women to support their bodies; *she was glad to get back home and remove her corset* **(b)** stiff piece of underwear, worn around the waist or the chest to support the body after a back injury; *would an orthopaedic corset help him with his bad back?*

cortege *or* **cortège** [kɔːˈteɪʒ] *noun (formal)* funeral procession; *the cortege passed through Hyde Park and carried on to St Paul's Cathedral*

cortex [ˈkɔːteks] *noun* outer layer of an organ; *the cerebral cortex is the outer layer of the cerebrum, while the renal cortex is the outer covering of a kidney* (NOTE: plural is **cortices**)

cos [kɒz] **1** *noun* **cos lettuce =** type of tall lettuce **2** *conjunction short for* BECAUSE; *you've got to do what I say 'cos I'm bigger than you!*

cosmetic [kɒzˈmetɪk] **1** *adjective* which improves someone's *or* something's appearance; *she uses a cosmetic cream to remove wrinkles; the changes to the organization were purely cosmetic;* **cosmetic surgery =** surgery to improve the appearance of someone **2** *noun* **cosmetics =** substances which improve appearance; *my wife keeps all her cosmetics in a little bag*

cosmic [ˈkɒzmɪk] *adjective* **(a)** referring to the universe; *cosmic rays are radiation entering the Earth's atmosphere from outer space* **(b)** very large, affecting the whole world; *a war which might reach cosmic proportions*

cosmonaut [ˈkɒzmənɔːt] *noun* Russian astronaut; *the cosmonauts entered the space station*

cosmopolitan [kɒzməˈpɒlɪtən] *adjective* **(a)** made up of people from different parts of the world; *Berlin is a very cosmopolitan city* **(b)** at ease in different cities or with people of different nationalities; *her cosmopolitan upbringing has made her a very interesting person; born in Canada, brought up in Hong Kong and in England, by the age of 10 he was more cosmopolitan than other children*

cosmos [ˈkɒzmɒs] *noun (formal)* the universe; *the origins of the cosmos are still being debated*

cost [kɒst] **1** *noun* **(a)** price which you have to pay for something; *what is the cost of a return ticket to London?; computer costs are falling each year* **(b)** **costs =** expenses involved in a court case; **to pay costs =** to pay the expenses of a court case; *the plaintiff has been ordered to pay costs; the judge awarded costs to the defendant =* the judge said that the defendant would not have to pay the cost of the case **2** *verb* to have a price; *potatoes cost 20p a kilo; petrol seems to cost more all the time; what does it cost =* how much is it?; **to cost the earth =** to be very expensive; *caviar costs the earth;* **to cost someone an arm and a leg =** to be very expensive; *don't buy your kitchen there - it'll cost you an arm and a leg; the repairs to his car cost him an arm and a leg; see also* FORTUNE, SMALL (NOTE: **costing - cost - has cost**)

co-star [ˈkəʊstaː] **1** *noun* the other actor or actress starring in a film or play; *his co-star in the film was an Italian actress* **2** *verb* to act in a play or film as a co-star; *she co-starred with James Dean* (NOTE: **co-starring - co-starred**)

cost-effective [ˈkɒstɪˈfektɪv] *adjective* which gives value when compared with its cost; *we find advertising in the Sunday newspapers very cost-effective*

costing [ˈkɒstɪŋ] *noun* calculation of a selling price, based on the costs of making a product; *I can't do the costing until I have all the production expenditure*

costly ['kɒstli] *adjective* very expensive; *our new car is not very costly to run*; **costly mistake** = mistake which results in a lot of money being spent; *telling them we would fight the law suit was a costly mistake* (NOTE: **costlier - costliest**)

cost of living ['kɒst əv 'lɪvɪŋ] *noun* money which has to be paid for food, heating, rent, etc.; *higher interest rates increase the cost of living*; **cost-of-living increase** = increase in salary to allow it to keep up with the increased cost of living; **cost-of-living index** = way of measuring the cost of living which is shown as a percentage increase on the figure for the previous year

costume ['kɒstjuːm] *noun* **(a) bathing costume** *or* **swimming costume** = swimsuit, one-piece item of clothing worn by women or children when swimming; *bother! we forgot to bring the swimming costumes* **(b)** set of clothes worn by an actor or actress in a play or film or on TV; *the costumes for 'Henry V' are magnificent* **(c) national costume** = special clothes worn by people of a certain country; *they all came to the wedding in national costume*

cosy ['kəuzi] **1** *adjective* comfortable and warm; *an open log fire always makes a room feel cosy*; *she wrapped herself up in a blanket and made herself cosy on the sofa* (NOTE: **cosier - cosiest**) **2** *noun* cover put over something to keep it hot; *she knitted a tea cosy for her mother*; *they served boiled eggs, each with an egg cosy shaped like a chicken* (NOTE: plural is **cosies**)

cot [kɒt] *noun* **(a)** child's bed with sides; *the baby was fast asleep in her cot*; *Jimmy's getting too big for his cot - we'll have to get him a proper bed soon*; **cot death** = unexplained death of a sleeping baby; *the risk of cot death is less if babies sleep on their backs* (NOTE: American English for this is **crib, crib death**) **(b)** *US* folding bed for camping (NOTE: British English for this is **camp bed**)

coterie ['kəutəri] *noun* small select group of people; *the Prime Minister is surrounded by a coterie of friends and advisers*

cottage ['kɒtɪdʒ] *noun* little house in the country; *we have a weekend cottage in the mountains*; *my mother lives in the little cottage next to the post office*; **cottage cheese** = moist lumpy white cheese; **cottage industry** = making of handicrafts in the workers' homes; **cottage pie** = minced meat cooked in a dish with a layer of mashed potatoes on top (NOTE: also called **shepherd's pie**)

cotton ['kɒtən] *noun* **(a)** thread from the soft seed heads of a tropical plant; *a reel of cotton* **(b)** cloth made of cotton; *he was wearing a pair of cotton trousers*; *I bought some cotton material to make a skirt*

cotton candy ['kɒtən 'kændi] *noun US* thin threads of melted sugar which are spun in a drum and sold as a mass attached to a stick; *stalls at the fair selling cold drinks and cotton candy* (NOTE: British English is **candyfloss**)

cotton on ['kɒtən 'ɒn] *verb (informal)* **to cotton on to something** = to understand something; *it was some time before he cottoned on to what I meant*

cotton wool ['kɒtən 'wul] *noun* purified cotton fibres used as a dressing on wounds, to clean the skin, to apply disinfectant, etc.; *she dabbed the cut with cotton wool soaked in antiseptic*; *the nurse put a pad of cotton wool over the graze* (NOTE: also called **absorbent cotton**)

couch [kautʃ] *noun* low bed; *she lay down on a couch in the lounge (informal)* **couch potato** = person who lounges on a sofa all day, watching TV or videos (NOTE: plural is **couches**)

cougar ['kuːgə] *noun US* large brown wild cat from North and South America (NOTE: also called a **mountain lion** or **puma**)

cough [kɒf] **1** *noun* sending the air out of your lungs suddenly, for example when you are ill; *take some cough medicine if your cough is bad*; *he ought to see the doctor if his cough is no better*; *he gave a little cough to attract the waitress's attention*; **cough sweet** = sweet with medicine against coughs; *she always carries a tube of cough sweets in her bag* **2** *verb* to send air out of your lungs suddenly because your throat hurts; *the smoke from the fire made everyone cough*; *people with flu go around coughing and sneezing*

cough up ['kɒf 'ʌp] *verb* **(a)** to bring up matter from your throat when coughing; *she became worried when the little girl coughed up blood* **(b)** *(informal)* to pay; *when he was late with the rent, we sent some people round to get him to cough up*

could [kud] *verb* used with other verbs **(a)** *(meaning 'was or would be able')* *the old lady fell down and couldn't get up*; *you could still catch the train if you ran* **(b)** *(meaning 'was allowed')* *the policeman said we could go into the house* **(c)** *(in asking)* *could you pass me the salt, please?*; *could you shut the window?* **(d)** *(meaning 'might happen')* *the shopping centre could be finished by Christmas* **(e)** *(making a suggestion)* *you could always try borrowing money from the bank* (NOTE: negative is **could not**, usually **couldn't**; note also that **could** is the past of **can**; **could** is only used in front of other verbs and is not followed by the word **to**)

council ['kaunsəl] *noun* **(a)** elected committee; **town council** = elected committee which runs a town; *the town council has decided to privatize the refuse service*; *you need to ask the council for planning permission*; **council flat** *or* **council house** = flat *or* house belonging to a town council which is let to a tenant; *they live in a council house, but are hoping to save up enough money to buy a flat*; *see also* PARISH COUNCIL, SECURITY COUNCIL **(b)** official group chosen to advise on a problem; **consumer council** = group representing the interests of consumers (NOTE: do not confuse with **counsel**)

councillor ['kaunsələ] *noun* elected member of a town council; *the mayor is elected from among the councillors*; *the local paper has exposed corruption among the councillors* (NOTE: do not confuse with **counsellor**)

council tax ['kaunsəl 'tæks] *noun* tax charged by a local council to help pay for its services; *the council tax is going up substantially next year*

> COMMENT: the tax is raised on each property, is paid by the occupier of the property, and is calculated according to the estimated value of the property

counsel ['kaunsəl] **1** *noun* **(a)** *(formal)* advice; *I should have listened to his wise counsel* **(b)** lawyer, barrister; **counsel for the defence** *or* **defence counsel**; **counsel for the prosecution** *or* **prosecution counsel**; *GB* **Queen's Counsel (QC)** = senior lawyer; *she was represented by a leading QC* (NOTE: no plural; do not confuse with **counsel**) **2** *verb* to advise; *she counselled us against buying the house* (NOTE: British English counselling - counselled but American English counseling - counseled)

counselling *US* **counseling** ['kaʊnsəlɪŋ] *noun* giving advice; *couples whose marriage is in difficulties often need counselling; after the murder of the little girl, the other children at the school were offered counselling;* **debt counselling** = advising people in debt as to the best way of arranging their finances so as to pay off their debts

counsellor *US* **counselor** ['kaʊnsələ] *noun* adviser; *he was advised to see a counsellor about his drink problem;* **marriage counsellor** = person who gives advice to couples whose marriage is in difficulties (NOTE: do not confuse with **councillor**)

count [kaʊnt] **1** *noun* **(a)** action of counting or of adding; **to lose count** = to no longer have any idea of how many there are; *I tried to add up all the sales figures but lost count and had to start again; I've lost count of the number of times he's left his umbrella on the train* **(b)** adding up the votes after an election; *the candidates paced up and down during the count* **(c)** large amount of something, calculated scientifically; *today there is a high pollen count* **(d)** noble title, used in many European countries, but not in England; *Count Bismarck, the German Chancellor* **(e)** accusation, charge read out against someone in court; *she was found guilty on two counts of embezzlement* **2** *verb* **(a)** to say numbers in order (1, 2, 3, 4, etc.); *she's only two and she can count up to ten; count to five and then start running;* **to count backwards** = to say numbers in the opposite order (9, 8, 7, 6, etc.) **(b)** to find out a total; *did you count how many books there are in the library?; he counted up the sales for the twelve months; see also* HATCH **(c)** to include when finding out a total; *there were sixty people in the boat if you count the children; did you count my trip to New York as part of my expenses?;* **not counting** = not including; *there are three of us, not counting the baby; we have three computers, not counting the old ones that don't work any more* **(d)** to be important; *your appearance counts for a lot in an interview; every little bit of energy saved counts*

count down ['kaʊnt 'daʊn] *verb* to count backwards (9, 8, 7, 6, etc.); *he counted down the seconds to the launch*

countdown ['kaʊntdaʊn] *noun* action of counting time backwards, especially before something will take place; *the countdown to the launch of the rocket went smoothly; the countdown to the next election has begun*

countenance ['kaʊntnəns] *(formal)* **1** *noun (formal)* expression on your face; *the journalists were surprised by the furious countenance of the President* **2** *verb (formal)* to approve of an action; *my father would never countenance borrowing money from friends*

counter ['kaʊntə] **1** *noun* **(a)** small round disc used in games; *you've thrown a six - you can move your counter six places* **(b)** long flat surface in a shop for displaying goods, or in a bank for placing money; *she put her bag down on the counter and took out her cheque book; the cheese counter is over there;* **bargain counter** = counter where things are sold cheaply; **ticket counter** =

place where tickets are sold; **sold over the counter** = sold without a prescription; *some drugs are sold over the counter, but for most you need a prescription;* **sold under the counter** = sold illegally; *he bought the videos under the counter* **2** *verb* to reply in an opposing way; *he accused her of theft and she countered with an accusation of sexual harassment*

counter- ['kaʊntə] *prefix meaning* against, in response; **counter-attraction** = something which attracts people from another attraction; **counter-revolutionary** = person who acts against a revolution

counteract [kaʊntə'rækt] *verb* to neutralize, to stop the effects of something; *the lotion should counteract the irritant effect of the spray on your skin; what can we do to counteract the increasing tendency towards truancy?*

counter-attack ['kaʊntəətæk] **1** *noun* attack against someone who has just attacked you; *24 hours after the enemy attack we launched a counter-attack* **2** *verb* to attack in return; *the enemy counter-attacked fiercely*

counterclockwise [kaʊntə'klɒkwaɪz] *adverb US* in the opposite direction to the hands of a clock; *turn the knob counterclockwise to turn off the oven* (NOTE: British English is **anticlockwise**)

counterfeit ['kaʊntəfɪt] **1** *adjective (money, etc.)* false, fake, not real; *the police have warned shopkeepers that counterfeit £20 notes are in circulation; you can see stands in Oxford Street selling counterfeit jewellery* **2** *verb* to make imitation money; *are the new £10 notes more difficult to counterfeit than the old ones?; only very sophisticated printing machines can be used to counterfeit banknotes* **3** *noun* thing which has been forged; *there is something wrong with this passport - in fact it may be a counterfeit*

counterpart ['kaʊntəpɑːt] *noun* person who has a similar job or who is in a similar situation; *the Foreign Secretary had talks with his French counterpart;* **John is my counterpart at Smith's** = John has the same post at Smith's as I have here

counter-productive [kaʊntəprə'dʌktɪv] *adjective* which has the opposite effect to what you expect; *increasing overtime pay was counter-productive, the workers simply worked more slowly*

countess [kaʊn'tes] *noun* **(a)** *(in European aristocracy)* wife of a count **(b)** *(in the British aristocracy)* wife of an earl

counting ['kaʊntɪŋ] *noun* action of adding up a total; *counting the votes will take all day; your counting aloud drives me crazy!*

countless ['kaʊntləs] *adjective* very many; *I've told you countless times not to use my electric toothbrush; we have had countless complaints about this product*

count on ['kaʊnt 'ɒn] *verb* to be sure that someone will do something; *can I count on you to help wash the dishes?; don't count on having fine weather for the cricket match*

country ['kʌntri] *noun* **(a)** land which is separate and governs itself; *the countries of the EU; some African countries voted against the plan* (NOTE: plural in this meaning is **countries**) **(b)** land which is not the town; *he lives in the country; we went walking in the hill country; road travel is difficult in country areas*

(NOTE: no plural in this meaning) **(c)** **country music** *or* **country and western** = style of music popular in the south-eastern United States, especially Tennessee; *she's the queen of the country and western*

country club ['kʌntri 'klʌb] *noun* club in the country, usually offering special sports facilities such as golf, horse riding, etc.; *there's an ad for a Scottish country club which offers holidays hunting deer and salmon fishing*

country house ['kʌntri 'haʊs] *noun* large house in the country, with gardens and a park, and sometimes a farm; *there are some beautiful country houses advertised for sale but their prices are more than we can afford*

countryman ['kʌntrimən] *noun* **(a)** person who lives in the country, not in the town; *countrymen are protesting about the new tax* **(b)** person who comes from the same country as you; *he felt ashamed of his countrymen when he saw them fighting at the football stadium*; *he asked friends and countrymen to come to his help* (NOTE: plural is **countrymen**)

countrypeople ['kʌntripi:pl] *noun* people who live in the country, not in the town; *countrypeople are protesting about the new tax* (NOTE: the opposite is **townspeople, townsfolk**)

countryside ['kʌntrisaɪd] *noun* land away from towns, with fields, woods, etc.; *the beautiful English countryside in spring*; *the countryside is in danger of being covered in new houses* (NOTE: no plural)

county ['kaʊnti] *noun* administrative district; *the southern counties of England*; *they come from County Down, in Northern Ireland*; **county court** = court which hears minor civil cases; **county town** = main town of a county, where the administrative offices are; *Dorchester is the county town of Dorset* (NOTE: plural is **counties**)

county council ['kaʊnti 'kaʊnsəl] *noun* group of people elected to run a county; *the county council has voted to approve the construction of a new town*; *county council workmen came to dig up the road*

coup [ku:] *noun* **(a)** short *for* coup d'état, the overthrow of a government by force; *the army took over after yesterday's bloody coup*; *the officers who planned the failed coup were all executed* **(b)** great success, successful move; *getting the Minister of Education to open the school exhibition was a coup for the organizers*

coup d'état ['ku: deɪ'tæ] *noun* overthrow of a government by force; *the radio has announced that a new president has been installed following a coup d'état* (NOTE: plural is **coups d'état**)

couple ['kʌpl] **1** *noun* **(a)** two things together; **a couple of** = (i) two; (ii) a few; *I have a couple of jobs for you to do*; *can you move the chairs a couple of yards to the left?*; *do you mind waiting a couple of minutes while I make a phone call?*; *the film lasted a couple of hours* **(b)** two people together; *they are a charming couple*; *several couples strolled past hand in hand*; **married couple** = husband and wife **2** *verb* **(a)** to link; *high tides coupled with strong winds caused flooding along the coast* **(b)** to join two machines together; *couple the trailer to the back of the truck*

couplet ['kʌplət] *noun* two lines of poetry; *the poem is in rhyming couplets which are easy to learn*

coupling ['kʌplɪŋ] *noun* **(a)** part of an engine which joins two parts, especially shafts; *a coupling has to be undone to detach the last three wagons and leave them in the siding* **(b)** action of joining together; *the coupling of talent and hard work is the recipe for his success*

coupon ['ku:pɒn] *noun* piece of paper which is used in place of money or in place of a ticket; *cut out the six coupons from the paper and send them to this address to receive your free travel bag*; *collect all seven coupons and cross the Channel for £1!*; **gift coupon** = coupon from a store which is given as a gift and which must be exchanged in that store

courage ['kʌrɪdʒ] *noun* being brave when in a dangerous situation; *she showed great courage in attacking the burglar* (NOTE: no plural)

courageous [kə'reɪdʒəs] *adjective* brave; *it was courageous of you to speak to the boss like that*; *her courageous action in saving the little boy won her a medal for bravery*

courgette [kʊə'ʒet] *noun* fruit of the marrow at a very immature stage in its development; *we had fried courgettes with our veal* (NOTE: American English is **zucchini**)

courier ['kʊriə] *noun* **(a)** person who carries messages; *a motorcycle courier* **(b)** guide for tourists on a package tour; *we were met at the airport by a courier*; *the courier tried hard to deal with all our complaints about the hotel*

course [kɔːs] *noun* **(a)** **in the course of** = during; *he's got much richer in the course of the last few years* **(b)** series of lessons; *I'm taking a maths course*; *she's going on a painting course*; *she has finished her secretarial course*; *the hotel offers weekend courses in watercolour painting* **(c)** series of treatments, medicines, etc; *he's taking a course of antibiotics* **(d)** separate part of a meal; *a five-course meal*; *the first course is soup, and then you can have either fish or roast lamb* **(e)** **golf course** = area of land specially designed for playing golf; *there is a golf course near the hotel*

◊ **in due course** [ɪn 'dju: 'kɔːs] after a certain amount of time; *if you study for several years at college, in due course you will get a degree*; *put a coin in the slot and in due course the machine will produce a ticket*

◊ **of course** [ɒf 'kɔːs] **(a)** (used to say yes or no more strongly) *are you coming with us? - of course I am!*; *do you want to lose all your money? - of course not!* **(b)** naturally; *he is rich, so of course he lives in a big house*

court [kɔːt] **1** *noun* **(a)** tribunal where a judge tries criminals, sometimes with a jury; *the court was packed for the opening of the murder trial*; *please tell the court what you saw when you opened the door*; *the defendant was in court for three hours*; **court case** = legal action or trial; *the court case is expected to last two weeks*; **to take someone to court** = to tell someone to appear in court to settle an argument **(b)** group of people living round a king or queen; *the people at court were very cold towards the young princess*; *it was dangerous to be a pretty young girl at the court of Henry VIII*; **court card** = king, queen or jack in a set of cards **(c)** area where a game of tennis, basketball, squash, etc., is played; *the tennis courts are behind the hotel*; **to be on court** = to be playing tennis; *they were* *on court for over three hours* **2** *verb* **(a)** *(old)* to try to persuade a woman to marry you; *King Henry courted Anne Boleyn for some months* **(b)** to be often together before getting married; *do you remember when we were courting and you took me to see the sun setting over the sea at Brighton?; they've been courting for three years, and there are still show no signs of them getting married* **(c)** to try to get someone to support you; *he has been courting the shareholders to win their approval for the scheme* **(d) to court disaster** = to risk disaster happening; *you are courting disaster if you try to drive a sports car without a licence*

courteous ['kɜːtjəs] *adjective (formal)* polite; *I found the hotel staff particularly courteous*

courtesy ['kɜːtəsi] *noun* **(a)** politeness; *the hotel staff showed us every courtesy; she might have had the courtesy to apologize; children should show some courtesy towards their grandparents* **(b) (by) courtesy of** = as a gift from; with the kind permission of; *a box of chocolates by courtesy of the management; he arrived home two hours late, courtesy of the train service;* **courtesy bus** *or* **car** *or* **coach** = bus *or* car *or* coach which is provided for people free of charge as a service; *a courtesy coach will pick you up at the airport; the garage lent me a courtesy car to use while mine was being repaired*

courthouse ['kɔːtheaus] *noun especially US* building where trials are held; *there was a police cordon round the courthouse*

courtier ['kɔːtjə] *noun* member of a royal court; *the king and queen appeared, surrounded by a crowd of courtiers*

court-martial [kɔːt'mɑːʃl] **1** *noun* **(a)** court which tries someone serving in the armed forces for offences against military discipline; *he was found guilty by court-martial and sentenced to imprisonment* **(b)** trial of someone serving in the armed forces by the armed forces authorities; *the court-martial was held in the army headquarters* (NOTE: plural is **courts-martial**) **2** *verb* to try someone who is serving in the armed forces; *he was court-martialled for leaving his post when the enemy attacked* (NOTE: **court-martialled** but American spelling is **court-martialed**)

court of appeal ['kɔːt əv ə'piːl] *noun* civil or criminal court to which a person may go to ask for an award or a sentence to be changed; *how many days do they have to decide whether to take their case to the court of appeal?* (NOTE: also called **Appeal Court**)

courtroom ['kɔːtrum] *noun* room where a judge presides over a trial; *the jury left the courtroom to deliberate*

courtship ['kɔːtʃɪp] *noun* **(a)** period when a man and a woman are courting; *their courtship lasted no more than six months which was very short in those days* **(b)** special display put on by animals to attract the opposite sex; *some birds perform very elaborate courtship dances*

courtyard ['kɔːtjɑːd] *noun* small square yard surrounded by buildings; *the hotel is built round a courtyard with fountains and palm trees; there is a paved courtyard behind the restaurant*

cousin ['kʌzɪn] *noun* son or daughter of your uncle or aunt; *our cousins from Canada are coming to stay with us for Christmas; we didn't have a Christmas card from Cousin Charles this year*

couture [kuːˈtjuə] *noun* **(haute) couture** = designing of expensive, fashionable clothes for women; *she was wearing a couture dress; is French couture really in danger of losing out to the British designers?*

couturier [kuːˈtjuriei] *noun* person who designs expensive, fashionable clothes for women; *all the Paris couturiers hold shows in the spring*

cove [kəuv] *noun* **(a)** small bay; *do you remember the small cove where we loved to go swimming?* **(b)** *(old) (informal)* man; *he's a strange cove*

covenant ['kʌvənənt] **1** *noun* legal contract; **deed of covenant** = official signed agreement to pay someone a sum of money each year; *we signed a deed of covenant promising to pay a regular sum of money for seven years* **2** *verb* to agree to pay a sum of money each year by contract; *he covenanted £50 per annum for seven years*

Coventry ['kɒvəntri] *noun* **to send someone to Coventry** = to refuse to speak to someone; *after he told the teacher who broke the window, the other children sent him to Coventry*

cover ['kʌvə] **1** *noun* **(a)** thing put over something to keep it clean, etc.; *keep a cover over your computer when you are not using it; put a cover over the meat to keep the flies off* **(b)** front and back of a book, magazine, etc.; *she read the book from cover to cover* **(c)** place where you can hide or shelter; *they ran for cover when it started to rain;* **under cover** = under a roof, not in the open air; *if it rains the buffet will be served under cover;* **under cover of night** *or* **of darkness** = at night, when everything is hidden; *they crept out of the city under cover of darkness; the commandos attacked under cover of night;* **to take cover** = to shelter; *it started to rain and they took cover under a tree; when the robbers started shooting, the policeman took cover behind a wall* **(d)** *(in a restaurant)* **cover charge** = charge per person in addition to the charge for food; *there is a £3.00 cover charge* **(e)** envelope; **to send something under separate cover** = in a separate envelope; **to send a magazine under plain cover** = in an ordinary envelope with no company name printed on it **2** *verb* **(a)** to put something over something to keep it clean, etc.; *you should cover the furniture with sheets before you start painting the ceiling* **(b)** to hide something; *he covered the hole in the ground with leaves; she covered her face with her hands* **(c)** to provide enough money to pay for something; *the damage was covered by the insurance; the prize covers all the costs of the holiday* **(d)** to write a report on an event for a newspaper, radio programme, etc.; *the journalists covering the story were briefed by the police*

coverage ['kʌvrɪdʒ] *noun* **press coverage** *or* **media coverage** = amount of space or time given to an event in newspapers or on TV; *the company had good media coverage for the launch of its new car; coverage of Wimbledon continues on BBC2* (NOTE: no plural)

covered ['kʌvəd] *adjective* with a roof or lid over; *a covered market in the centre of town; a covered tennis court; an old covered bridge still crosses the narrow valley; the meat should be cooked for a long time in a covered pan*

covering ['kʌvrɪŋ] *noun* thing which covers; *there was a light covering of snow*

covering letter ['kʌvrɪŋ 'letə] *noun* letter explaining what is enclosed with it; *further details of the job are given in the covering letter*

cover note ['kʌvə 'nəʊt] *noun* letter giving agreement for insurance sent before the policy is issued; *this cover note is valid until the day you receive your policy* (NOTE: the American English for this is **binder**)

covert ['kəʊvət or 'kʌvət] *adjective (formal)* hidden or secret; *the police have uncovered a series of covert financial deals* (NOTE: the opposite, meaning 'open', is **overt**)

cover up ['kʌvə 'ʌp] *verb* to cover completely; *he covered up the mark on the wall with white paint*; **to cover up for someone** = to try to hide a mistake that someone has made; *the staff tried to cover up for their boss*

cover-up ['kʌvərʌp] *noun* hiding of a scandal; *the question remains: was there a cover-up, and if so, why?*

covet ['kʌvɪt] *verb (formal)* to want something which belongs to someone else; *with five children and no help in the house, she covets her sister's lifestyle*

coveted ['kʌvɪtɪd] *adjective* which everyone wants; *the Irish team won the coveted Admiral's Cup*

covetous ['kʌvɪtəs] *adjective (formal)* wanting something which belongs to someone else; *she cast covetous glances at her neighbour's new car*

cow [kaʊ] *noun* **(a)** large female farm animal, kept to give milk; *a field of cows*; *the farmer was milking a cow*; *(informal)* **the cows come home** = for a very long time; *you can wait until the cows come home before getting paid* **(b)** female of other animals; *a cow elephant*; *a cow whale* (NOTE: the meat from a cow is **beef**)

coward ['kaʊəd] *noun* person who is not brave; *when it comes to going to the dentist, I'm a coward*

cowardice [kaʊə'dɪs] *noun* not being brave; *he was accused of cowardice in action, and shot*

cowardly ['kaʊədli] *adjective* not brave; *their cowardly attack on the children's school luckily failed*

cowboy ['kaʊbɔɪ] *noun* **(a)** man who looks after cows in the west of the USA; **a cowboy film** = film about the west of the USA in the late 19th century; **a cowboy hat** = large wide-brimmed hat worn by cowboys **(b)** *(informal)* workman who does bad work and charges a high price; *a cowboy builder*; *the people we got in to paint the house were a bunch of cowboys*

cowshed ['kaʊʃed] *noun* shed where cows are milked, or where they are kept during the winter

coy [kɔɪ] *adjective* timid or shy; *don't be coy about your success in the exams*; *she managed a coy smile as she took her prize*

coyote [kɔɪ'əʊti] *noun* American wild animal, like a small wolf

crab [kræb] *noun* **(a)** edible sea animal with ten legs and large pincers, which walks sideways; *they caught several little crabs in the rock pool* **(b)** meat of this animal, used as food; *he ordered a crab sandwich* **(c)** **to catch a crab** = to miss a stroke when rowing; *one of the rowers caught a crab and all the others stopped rowing*

crack [kræk] **1** *noun* **(a)** sharp sound; *the crack of a twig behind her made her turn round* **(b)** long thin break in something hard; *a crack appeared in the ceiling*; *her ring fell down a crack in the floorboards*; *the field is so dry it is full of cracks*; **at (the) crack of dawn** = as soon as it starts to be light; *if we want to miss the traffic we must set off at (the) crack of dawn* **(c)** *(informal)* **to have a crack at something** = to try to do something; *I've never tried windsurfing before but I'm willing to have a crack at it* **(d)** *(informal)* joke; *she made a nasty crack about his bald patch* **(e)** *(slang)* highly addictive form of cocaine **2** *verb* **(a)** to make a sharp sound; *a twig cracked as he stepped on it* **(b)** to make a long thin break in something; *the stone cracked the glass* **(c)** **to crack jokes** = to tell jokes; *he spent the entire lunch break cracking jokes* **(d)** *(informal)* **get cracking!** = get going!, start now!; *if you don't get cracking you'll never finish on time* **(e)** to decipher a code; *they spent months trying to crack the enemy codes*

crack down on ['kræk 'daʊn ɒn] *verb (informal)* to work hard to reduce crime, etc.; *police are cracking down on drivers who go too fast*

crackdown ['krækdaʊn] *noun* campaign against something; *the government wants a crackdown on juvenile crime*

cracked [krækt] *adjective* with a crack in it; *she asked the waiter to change her cup because it was cracked*; *all the eggs in the carton were cracked*

cracker ['krækə] *noun* **(a)** dry biscuit made of flour and water; *after the main course they served cheese and crackers* **(b)** little firework which makes a series of bangs; *crackers were going off all round the procession to the temple* **(c)** **(Christmas) cracker** = colourful paper tube which makes a little bang when it is pulled, given at Christmas parties; *we had mince pies and pulled crackers*; *what did you get in your cracker? - a paper hat and a puzzle*

COMMENT: Christmas crackers have little presents inside them; usually folded paper hats, small plastic toys, and mottoes (pieces of paper with bad jokes written on them)

cracking ['krækɪŋ] *adjective (informal)* **(a)** very fast; **cracking pace** = fast pace; *the marathon leader set a cracking pace and no one else could keep up* **(b)** *(old)* **cracking (good)** = very good; *it was a cracking good story*

crackle ['krækl] **1** *noun* small dry sound; *he was woken by the crackle of flames* **2** *verb* to make little dry sounds, like something burning; *the bonfire crackled away in a corner of the garden*

crackpot ['krækpɒt] *(informal)* **1** *adjective* mad; *it's just one of his crackpot ideas for making money* **2** *noun* mad person; *she looks a real crackpot, but when you get to know her she's sweet*

cradle ['kreɪdl] **1** *noun* baby's bed which is on rockers and can be rocked; *she rocked the baby to sleep in its cradle*; **from the cradle to the grave** = for the whole of your life; *the government is abandoning the cradle-to-grave insurance scheme* **2** *verb* to hold something gently in your arms or hands; *the little girl was cradling her doll*

craft [krɑːft] *noun* **(a)** making something skilfully by hand; *he learnt the craft of furniture-making as a boy*; *traditional rural crafts such as thatching are being revived again* **(b)** ship; *the sleek craft slipped out of harbour*; *all sizes of craft took part in the rescue* (NOTE: plural in this meaning is **craft**)

-craft [krɑːft] *suffix* **(a)** *(meaning vehicle)* **aircraft**; **spacecraft** (NOTE: in this meaning, words ending in **-craft** have the plural form **-craft**) **(b)** *(meaning art)* **stagecraft** *is the art of writing plays and putting them on*; **witchcraft** *is the art of casting spells* (NOTE: in this meaning, words ending in **-craft** do not have a plural form)

craftsman [ˈkrɑːftsmən] *noun* artist who is expert at making things by hand; *the chair is beautifully made by a master craftsman* (NOTE: plural is **craftsmen**)

craftsmanship [ˈkrɑːftsmənʃɪp] *noun* skill of a craftsman; *look at the craftsmanship in the stone carving*

crafty [ˈkrɑːfti] *adjective* sly; *I could tell from the crafty look on her face that she was going to play a trick on me*; *I have a crafty plan for making a lot of money* (NOTE: **craftier - craftiest**)

crag [kræg] *noun* steep rocky cliff; *we'll try to climb that crag this afternoon*

craggy [ˈkrægi] *adjective* rough, with lines like a rock; *his craggy features are easily recognisable on film posters*

cram [kræm] *verb* **(a)** to squeeze into a small space; *she crammed all her clothes into a suitcase*; *don't try to cram so many interviews into one day* **(b)** to learn facts hurriedly before an examination; *everybody's at home cramming for their finals* (NOTE: **cramming - crammed**)

crammed [kræmd] *adjective* full of things or people squeezed tightly together; *they found a box crammed with confidential papers at the rubbish dump*; *the bus was crammed with children from the local school*

cramp [kræmp] **1** *noun* painful involuntary spasm in the muscles, where the muscle may stay contracted for some time; *he went swimming and got cramp in the cold water*; *she woke up with cramp in her right leg* **2** *verb* **to cramp someone's style** = to stop someone doing what he wants, or developing or expanding; *having my mother-in-law for Christmas tends to cramp our style a bit*

cramped [kræmt] *adjective* too small; *on some aircraft, the seating in tourist class can be very cramped*

cranberry [ˈkrænbəri] *noun* bitter wild red berry, used to make a sharp sweet sauce or drink; *she drank a glass of cranberry juice*; **cranberry sauce** = sharp sweet red sauce, eaten with meat, in particular turkey (NOTE: plural is **cranberries**)

crane [kreɪn] **1** *noun* **(a)** tall metal construction for lifting heavy weights; *the container slipped as the crane was lifting it onto the ship*; *they had to hire a crane to get the piano into the upstairs room* **(b)** large bird with long legs **2** *verb* **to crane your neck** = to stretch your neck; *he craned his neck to try to see the procession*

crank [kræŋk] **1** *noun* **(a)** metal arm with a right angle, often mounted on a shaft; *you'll need a crank to start the engine* **(b)** very odd person; *she's a bit of a crank when it comes to food, because there are so many things she won't eat* **2** *verb* to turn an engine by turning it with a handle; *thank goodness I don't have to crank the car every time I use it* (informal) **to crank out** = to produce a series of things as if by a machine; *she cranks out 1000 words every week for her newspaper column*

crankshaft [ˈkræŋkʃɑːft] *noun* part of a car engine connected to the pistons by connecting rods which convert the up-and-down motion of the pistons into a circular motion; *the crankshaft provides the drive to the wheels via the clutch and transmission*

cranky [ˈkræŋki] *adjective especially US* in a bad mood; *the baby is very cranky today* (NOTE: **crankier - crankiest**)

crap [kræp] **1** *noun* **(a)** solid waste matter from the body; *I need a crap* = I must go to the toilet; *he went for a crap and missed the phone call* **(b)** *(slang)* rubbish; *you're talking crap*; *that film was a load of crap* **2** *adjective (slang)* no good, useless; *your team is just crap, ours is miles better*

crash [kræʃ] **1** *noun* **(a)** accident where cars, planes, etc., are damaged; *he was killed in a train crash*; *none of the passengers were hurt in the coach crash*; *his car was badly damaged in the crash*; **crash helmet** = hard hat worn by motorcyclists, etc.; *it is illegal to ride a motorbike without a crash helmet* **(b)** loud noise when something falls over; *the ladder fell down with a crash*; *he said he would go and do the washing up, and then there was a crash in the kitchen* **(c)** collapse of a company; *he lost all his savings in the bank crash* (NOTE: plural is **crashes**) **2** *verb* **(a)** *(of vehicles)* to hit something and be damaged; *the bus crashed into a wall*; *the plane crashed six kilometres from the airport* **(b)** to move, making a loud noise; *the wall came crashing down*; *the ladder crashed onto the floor* **(c)** *(of a company)* to collapse; *he lost all his savings when the bank crashed* **(d)** *(of a computer)* to stop working; *the hard disk has crashed but we think the data can be retrieved* **3** *adjective* **crash course** = course of rapid, hard study; *he took a crash course in German*

crash-land [kræʃˈlænd] *verb (of an aircraft)* to land heavily without using the undercarriage, so that the aircraft is damaged; *the plane crash-landed short of the runway, and three people were seriously injured*; *on crash-landing, the plane caught fire*

crash-landing [kræʃˈlændɪŋ] *noun* act of landing a plane heavily, without the undercarriage; *the crash-landing did not damage the plane as much as the pilot expected*

crass [kræs] *adjective* rude, stupid or coarse, not caring about what people think; *he made some crass remark about her hair*; *all they are interested in is a crass commercialism*

crate [kreɪt] **1** *noun* **(a)** large rough wooden box; *the dinner set arrived safely, carefully packed in a wooden crate* **(b)** container for bottles; *the school orders a crate of milk every day*; *they had a crate of beer in the back of their car* **2** *verb* to put into a crate; *every piece of china was wrapped in paper, and the whole lot was then crated to be sent to the shipper*

crater [ˈkreɪtə] *noun* **(a)** hole made by a bomb; *over the winter, the bomb craters filled up with rainwater* **(b)** round hollow at the top of a volcano; *a group of scientists flew over the crater to monitor the activity of the volcano* **(c)** round hollow on the moon or a planet, where a meteorite has hit it; *a map of the craters of the Moon*

cravat [krəˈvæt] *noun* type of scarf worn by men knotted round the neck inside the shirt collar; *cravats are rarely worn nowadays although you can still buy them in some shops* (NOTE: American English is **ascot**)

crave [kreɪv] *verb* (*formal*) to want something very much; *why do I always crave strawberries in winter?*; *she's not vicious, she just craves love and affection*

craving ['kreɪvɪŋ] *noun* strong desire; *she has a craving for chocolate*; *did you have any odd cravings when you were pregnant?*

crawl [krɔːl] **1** *noun* very slow speed; *the traffic on the motorway was reduced to a crawl* (NOTE: no plural) **2** *verb* (**a**) to move around on hands and knees; *the baby has just started to crawl* (**b**) to go along slowly; *the traffic was crawling along* (**c**) to be crawling with = to be covered with insects, etc.; *the place was crawling with ants*; *the streets were crawling with police*

crayfish ['kreɪfɪʃ] *noun* fresh-water animal like a little lobster; *how do you cook crayfish?*; *crayfish have the habit of hiding under flat stones in shallow water* (NOTE: plural is **crayfish**; note also that American English also uses **crawfish**)

crayon ['kreɪɒn] *noun* coloured wax pencil; *he had a box of crayons and was colouring the pictures in his colouring book*

craze [kreɪz] *noun* mania; *I don't like the current craze for purple shoes*; *she always follows the latest craze*

crazed [kreɪzd] *adjective* mad, acting wildly; *he was crazed by drugs*; *there was a crazed look in her eyes*

crazy ['kreɪzi] *adjective* (**a**) mad; *it was a crazy idea to go mountain climbing in sandals*; **to drive someone crazy** = to have an effect on someone so that they become very annoyed; *the noise is driving me crazy*; *all this work is driving her crazy*; **crazy about** = very enthusiastic about; *he's crazy about her*; *she's crazy about ballroom dancing* (**b**) **crazy paving** = odd-shaped paving stones (NOTE: **crazier - craziest**)

creak [kriːk] **1** *noun* squeaky noise; *she heard a creak on the stairs and sat up in bed* **2** *verb* to make a squeaky noise; *the front gate creaks, which means that we hear when anyone comes into the garden*; *the shed door creaked and banged all night in the high wind* (NOTE: do not confuse with **creek**)

cream [kriːm] *noun* (**a**) rich top part of milk, full of fat; *I like strawberries and cream*; **single cream** = liquid cream, with a lower fat content; **double cream** = thick cream with a high fat content; **whipped cream** = cream, beaten until it is stiff, flavoured with sugar and vanilla; **cream cake** = any cake or pastry filled with whipped cream; **cream cheese** = rich soft cheese; **cream tea** = afternoon tea, with scones, thick cream and jam (**b**) soft stuff for cleaning, oiling, etc.; *face cream*; *shaving cream*; *shoe cream* (**c**) the top few; *the cream of the medical students*

creamy ['kriːmi] *adjective* (**a**) full of cream; *because of my diet, rich creamy puddings are a thing of the past* (**b**) smooth and liquid like cream; *the chocolate pudding is too solid, it is nicer when it is a little creamier*; *a tempting piece of creamy cheese oozing onto the plate* (NOTE: **creamier - creamiest**)

crease [kriːs] **1** *noun* (**a**) fold made by ironing; *trousers should have a crease in front* (**b**) fold made accidentally; *she ironed his shirts to remove the creases* **2** *verb* to make folds accidentally in something; *after two hours in the car, my skirt was badly creased and had to be pressed*; *hang up your clothes as soon as you arrive otherwise everything will stay creased*

create [kriˈeɪt] *verb* (**a**) to make, to invent; *do you believe that God created the world?*; *a government scheme which aims at creating new jobs for young people* (**b**) (*old*) (*informal*) to make a fuss; *Tim's creating again: he hates having to get dressed*

creation [kriˈeɪʃn] *noun* (**a**) thing which has been made; *for dessert they served some sort of chocolate and cream creation*; *the model appeared on the catwalk wearing a pink and blue creation* (**b**) act of creating; *the aim is the creation of new jobs for young unemployed people*; **job creation scheme** = government scheme to encourage new jobs for the unemployed

creative [kriˈeɪtɪv] *adjective* full of ideas; *always making something*; *he's a very creative child*

creator [kriˈeɪtə] *noun* person who makes or invents something; *he's the creator of an award-winning puppet film*

creature ['kriːtʃə] *noun* (**a**) animal; *lift any stone and you'll find all sorts of little creatures underneath*; *we try not to harm any living creature*; *some sea creatures live in burrows in the sand* (**b**) **creature comforts** = things which make life comfortable for you; *he likes his little creature comforts - his pipe and his glass of beer*

crèche [kreʃ] *noun* special room or building where babies and small children can be looked after, often on a company's premises; *I have to pick up little Jimmy from the crèche at 3*; *the company provides crèche facilities for its staff*

credence ['kriːdəns] *noun* belief that something is correct or true; *I don't give much credence to the rumour* (NOTE: no plural)

credentials [krɪˈdenʃəlz] *noun* letters or documents which describe a person's qualities and skills; *the new production manager has very impressive credentials*

credibility [kredɪˈbɪlɪti] *noun* being able to be believed; *he lost all credibility as an interpreter when he couldn't understand what she was saying*; **credibility gap** = situation where people do not believe what they are told; *the government suffers from a credibility gap*

credible ['kredɪbl] *adjective* which can be believed; *the jury did not find the witnesses' stories at all credible*; *the plot of the film is not entirely credible*

credit ['kredɪt] **1** *noun* (**a**) praise for something which is well deserved; *the professor took all the credit for the invention*; *to his credit, he owned up immediately*; **it does you credit** = you must be proud of it; *your daughter does you both credit*; *he's a credit to the school* = he's done well and this gives honour to the school where he studied (**b**) time given to pay; *we give purchasers six months' interest-free credit*; **credit check** = check on a customer's credit rating; **credit controller** = member of staff whose job is to try to get payment of overdue invoices; **on credit** = without paying immediately; *we bought the dining room furniture on credit* (**c**) side of an account showing money in hand or which is owed to you; *we paid in £100 to the credit of Mr Smith*; **credit note** = note showing that money is owed; *she took the jumper back to the shop and got a credit note*; *the company sent the wrong items and had to issue a credit note* (**d**) **credits** = list of people who helped to make a film, TV programme, etc.; *she sued the company when her name did not appear in the credits* **2** *verb* (**a**) to credit someone with = to say that someone has done something good; *he has been credited with making the company profitable again* **(b)** to believe; *I find that hard to credit; would you credit it? - she's got married again!* **(c)** to pay money into an account; *to credit an account with £100 or to credit £100 to an account*

creditable ['kreditəbl] *adjective* which does you credit, which should be praised; *he gave a very creditable performance on the piano*

credit card ['kredit 'kɑːd] *noun* plastic card which allows you to borrow money and to buy goods without paying for them immediately; *how do you want to pay - cash, cheque or credit card?; I bought a fridge and put it on my credit card*

creditor ['kreditə] *noun* person who is owed money; *he is trying to pay off his creditors*

credit rating ['kredit 'reitiŋ] *noun* amount which a bank feels a customer should be allowed to borrow; *we need to know something about the company's credit rating before granting them a loan*

credo ['kreidəu] *noun* (*formal*) creed, statement of what you believe; *attacking capitalists is part of the socialist credo*

credulity [krɪ'djuːlɪti] *noun* (*formal*) believing anything easily; *advertisers play on people's credulity*; **to strain your credulity** = to try to make you believe something which is quite impossible; *her story of being robbed by three masked men on the Underground strains our credulity to the limit*

credulous ['kredjuləs] *adjective* who believes anything easily; *credulous investors thought they would double their money in days*

creed [kriːd] *noun* **(a)** statement of what you believe; *retraining for the unemployed is one of the government's creeds* **(b)** the **Apostles' Creed** = statement of the Christian faith; *we will now say the Creed*

creek [kriːk] *noun* **(a)** little inlet of the sea; *we sailed along the coast exploring all the little creeks; that creek looks too shallow for us to go up* **(b)** *US* small river (*informal*) **up the creek** = in a difficult situation; *if we don't receive the money by tomorrow evening we'll all be up the creek* (NOTE: do not confuse with **creak**)

creep [kriːp] *verb* **(a)** to move around quietly; *they crept softly down the stairs*; **to creep up on someone** = to come up close behind someone without making any noise; *the idea is to creep up on the gang as they are loading the stolen goods into the lorry* **(b)** to go along slowly; *the traffic was creeping along the motorway because of the fog* (NOTE: **creeping - crept** [krept])

creeper ['kriːpə] *noun* plant which grows close to the ground or climbs up walls; *the creeper-covered walls of the old castle; you could plant a creeper to cover the concrete wall*

creepy ['kriːpi] *adjective* (*informal*) which makes you shudder; *that house is really creepy* (NOTE: **creepier - creepiest**)

creepy-crawlies ['kriːpi'krɔːliz] *noun* (*informal*) spiders and insects; *we try to teach children not to be afraid of creepy-crawlies*

cremate [krɪ'meit] *verb* to burn a dead body; *he asked to be cremated and had his ashes buried next to those of his wife*

cremation [krɪ'meiʃn] *noun* burning of a dead body; *cremation will take place on Friday afternoon at the Kingston crematorium*

crematorium *US* **crematory** [kremə'tɔːriəm or 'kremətəri] *noun* place where the bodies of dead people are burnt; *a service will be held in the crematorium chapel* (NOTE: plural is **crematoria**)

crème de la crème ['krem də læ 'krem] *noun* very best workers, especially secretaries

Creole ['kriːəul] **1** *noun* **(a)** person of mixed African and European family from the West Indies or from the southern states of the USA; *thousands of Creoles form the civil service of the country* **(b)** person who is a descendant of one of the original French settlers in the West Indies or the southern states of the USA, especially Louisiana; *she comes from an old Creole family* **(c)** language based on English, with additions from other languages, spoken in the West Indies and the southern states of the USA; *chicken gumbo is a creole term for chicken stew* **2** *adjective* **(a)** creole cuisine = mixed West Indian and European cuisine from the Caribbean or mixed French and Spanish cuisine from the south of the USA **(b)** cooked with tomatoes and red peppers, served with rice; *a dish of chicken creole as main course*

crescendo [krɪ'ʃendəu] *noun* **(a)** increase in sound, especially in music; **to rise to** *or* **to reach a crescendo** = to become much louder; *the music suddenly rose to a crescendo* (NOTE: plural is **crescendos**) **(b)** rising to reach a high point; *a crescendo of complaints came into the office; protests from the public reached a crescendo with a march on Downing Street*

crescent ['kresnt] *noun* **(a)** curved shape, like a new moon; *the new moon hung like a silver crescent over the lake*; **Red Crescent** = organization which provides medical help, the equivalent of the Red Cross in Muslim countries; *Red Crescent officials have been allowed into the war zone* **(b)** street which forms a semicircle; *the beautiful 18th century houses in Bath's famous crescents*

cress [kres] *noun* plant whose seedlings are used for salads, especially together with seedlings of mustard; *the sandwiches were served with a garnish of mustard and cress; see also* WATERCRESS

crest [krest] *noun* **(a)** highest point along the length of a mountain ridge, of a wave; *follow the path along the crest of the hill - the view is splendid; the crests of some of the waves reached 30 feet* **(b)** topmost point; *when the president was elected he was at the crest of his popularity* **(c)** plumes or fleshy growth on the head of a bird; *a peacock has a tall coloured crest; a striking black cockerel with a red crest* **(d)** coat of arms; *his family crest is a red lion; his college crest is still hanging on his bedroom wall*

crested ['krestid] *adjective* with a crest; *a crested toad*

crevasse [krɪ'væs] *noun* deep crack in a glacier; *he fell into a deep crevasse and had to be rescued with ropes*

crevice ['krevis] *noun* small crack in a rock or wall; *creeping plants were growing in the crevices in the wall; push a stick into the crevice to see how deep it is*

crew [kruː] *noun* people who work on a boat, aircraft, bus, etc.; *the lifeboat rescued the crew of the sinking ship; the plane was carrying 125 passengers and a crew of 6*; **stage crew** = workers who move scenery around in a theatre; *the stage crew worked all night to get the set ready for the following morning*

crewcut ['kru:kʌt] *noun* very short haircut; *new recruits to the army are given crewcuts*

crewman ['kru:mæn] *noun* man who is a member of a ship's crew; *three crewmen were taken off by helicopter* (NOTE: plural is **crewmen**)

crib [krɪb] *noun US* baby's bed; **crib death** = unexplained death of a sleeping baby (NOTE: British English is **cot, cot death**)

cricket ['krɪkɪt] *noun* game played between two teams of eleven players using bats and a hard ball; *we haven't played much cricket this year - the weather has been too bad*; *we are going to a cricket match this afternoon*; *when did we last beat the Australians at cricket?*

COMMENT: the game is played between two teams of eleven players with a wicket made up of three stumps at either end of a 22-yard pitch. The aim is for each team to score runs by hitting a ball with a wooden bat while the other team tries to get them out. One team bats, using two batsmen at a time (one at either end of the pitch) and a run is scored when they change ends. All 11 members of the opposing team position themselves in the field and try to prevent the batsmen scoring a run. One member of the fielding side bowls the ball at the batsman and a different bowler takes over from the opposite end after six balls (or an 'over') have been bowled. Matches start at 11.30 in the morning and continue until the early evening with breaks for lunch and tea. One-day matches consist of one innings per side while first-class matches between county sides, and international matches, or test matches, consist of two innings per side and last 3 and 5 days respectively

cricketer ['krɪkətə] *noun* person who plays cricket; *the cricketers left the pitch and gathered for tea*

cricketing ['krɪkɪtɪŋ] *adjective* referring to the playing of cricket; *my cricketing days are over - I'm much too old to play now*

cried, cries [kraɪd or kraɪz] *see* CRY

crime [kraɪm] *noun* illegal act or acts; *we must try to reduce the levels of crime in the inner cities*; *the government is trying to deal with the problem of teenage crime or with the teenage crime problem*; *more crimes are committed at night than during the daytime*

criminal ['krɪmɪnəl] **1** *adjective* referring to illegal acts; *he has a criminal record*; *stealing is a criminal offence*; *the criminal justice system*; **Criminal Investigation Department (CID)** = department of the police which investigates serious crimes; **criminal law** = laws which deal with crimes against the law of the land, which are punished by the state (NOTE: the opposite, actions relating to people's rights and freedoms, and to agreements between individuals, is **civil law**) **2** *noun* person who commits a crime; *the police think two well-known criminals did it*

criminologist [krɪmɪ'nɒlədʒɪst] *noun* person who makes a study of crime and criminals

criminology [krɪmɪ'nɒlədʒi] *noun* academic study of crime and criminals; *she's a professor of criminology at an American university*

crimson ['krɪmzn] **1** *adjective* deep red; *the shop had a large crimson heart in the window on Valentine's Day*; *she was so embarrassed, she turned bright crimson* **2** *noun* deep red colour; *according to the Sunday paper, crimson will be the colour to wear next winter*

cringe [krɪndʒ] *verb* (a) to bend to avoid a blow; *the little boy cringed when he heard his father shouting* (b) to be embarrassed; *seeing the boss trying to make jokes just makes me cringe*; *she cringed when her son started to play the violin*

cripple ['krɪpl] **1** *noun* person who is disabled or has difficulty in walking; *cripples sat outside the hotel, begging for money from tourists* **2** *verb* (a) to disable someone; *he was crippled in a mining accident* (b) to prevent something from working; *the explosion crippled the supertanker and she drifted towards the rocks*; *the bus and rail strike has crippled the capital's transport system*

crippling ['krɪplɪŋ] *adjective* which cripples, which prevents someone from doing something; *crippling taxes have made the middle class poor*

crisis ['kraɪsɪs] *noun* serious situation where decisions have to be taken rapidly; *an international crisis*; *a banking crisis*; **to take crisis measures** = to take measures rapidly to stop a crisis developing; *the government had to take crisis measures to stop the collapse of the currency* (NOTE: plural is **crises** ['kraɪsi:z])

crisp [krɪsp] **1** *adjective* (a) hard, which can be broken into pieces or crunched; *these biscuits are not crisp any more, they have gone soft*; *pick an apple off the tree, they're really very crisp* (b) sharp and cold; *it was a beautiful crisp morning, with frost glinting on the grass*; *she could see her breath in the crisp mountain air* (NOTE: **crisper - crispest**) **2** *noun* **(potato) crisps** = slices of potato fried until they are dry and break easily; *we always take packets of crisps with us on picnics* (NOTE: American English for these is **chips**)

criss-cross ['krɪskrɒs] **1** *adjective* with lines crossing; *what is the meaning of the criss-cross pattern of yellow lines at a road junction?* **2** *verb* to go backwards and forwards in different directions; *we dodged through the cars, bicycles, carts and pedestrians criss-crossing the Beijing street*

criterion [kraɪ'tɪərɪən] *noun* standard by which things are judged; *does the candidate satisfy all our criteria?*; *this is not a reliable criterion on which to base our judgement* (NOTE: plural is **criteria**)

critic ['krɪtɪk] *noun* (a) person who examines something and comments on it, especially a person who writes comments on new plays and films for a newspaper; *she's the TV critic of the 'Times'*; *the film was praised by all the critics* (b) person who says that something is bad or wrong; *the chairman tried to answer his critics at the meeting*

critical ['krɪtɪkəl] *adjective* (a) dangerous and difficult; *with the enemy attacking on all sides, our position was becoming critical* (b) extremely important; *he made a critical decision to break off the negotiations*; *critical relief supplies have been held up at customs* (c) very serious; *the pilot of the crashed plane was in a critical condition last night*; *the hospital said that her condition was critical* (d) unfavourable, which criticizes; *the report was highly critical of the minister*

critically ['krɪtɪkəli] *adverb* in a critical way; *he was critically injured in the accident; she is still critically ill*

criticism ['krɪtɪsɪzm] *noun* (a) comment; *if you have any constructive criticisms to make, I shall be glad to hear them*; **literary criticism** = criticism of works of literature (b) unfavourable comment; *there was a lot of criticism of the government's plan*

criticize ['krɪtɪsaɪz] *verb* to say that something *or* someone is bad or wrong; *she criticized the sales assistant for not being polite; the design of the new car has been criticized*

critique [krɪ'tiːk] *noun* piece of careful literary criticism; *he wrote a critique of the play in a literary magazine*

croak [krəʊk] 1 *noun* deep sound, like the call of a frog or crow 2 *verb* to make a deep sound; *the frogs started croaking in the pool*

Croat ['krəʊæt] 1 *adjective* referring to Croatia 2 *noun* person from Croatia

Croatia [krəʊ'eɪʃə] *noun* country in the Balkans, south of Slovenia (NOTE: capital: **Zagreb**; people: **Croats**; language: **Croatian**; currency: **kuna**)

Croatian [krəʊ'eɪʃən] 1 *adjective* referring to Croatia 2 *noun* person from Croatia

crochet ['krəʊʃeɪ] 1 *noun* type of knitting using one needle with a hook at the end; *the baby was wrapped in a blue crochet shawl* 2 *verb* to make something out of wool, using a hooked needle; *who crocheted the beautiful jumper you are wearing?* (NOTE: **crocheted** ['krəʊʃeɪd]- **crocheting** ['krəʊʃeɪɪŋ])

crockery ['krɒkəri] *noun* cups, saucers, plates, etc., made from pottery; *the crafts shop sells nothing but paintings and crockery; these pieces of old crockery date back to Roman times* (NOTE: no plural)

crocodile ['krɒkədaɪl] *noun* (a) large reptile which lives in or near rivers and lakes and eats other animals; *crocodiles lay on the banks of the river waiting for the antelope to come to drink* (b) long line of children walking in pairs; *a crocodile of schoolchildren crossed the road to the swimming pool*

crocus ['krəʊkəs] *noun* little spring flower, in various colours, especially yellow and purple; *crocuses are one of the first flowers to come out in spring* (NOTE: plural is **crocuses**)

crony ['krəʊni] *noun* old friend; *he spent the afternoon fishing with one of his cronies* (NOTE: plural is **cronies**)

cronyism ['krəʊniɪzm] *noun* giving jobs to your old friends; *the government has been accused of cronyism*

crook [krʊk] 1 *noun* (a) dishonest dealer; *I don't trust the government - they're a bunch of crooks; that secondhand car dealer is a bit of a crook* (b) bend; *she held the baby in the crook of her arm* (c) long stick with a bent top, used by shepherds 2 *adjective (in Australia) (informal)* ill

crooked ['krʊkɪd] *adjective* (a) bent, not straight; *that picture is crooked; I don't think the wallpaper is straight - it looks crooked to me* (b) *(informal)* dishonest; *the police commissioner promised to remove any crooked officers in his force*

croon [kruːn] *verb* to sing in a low voice; *he looks very old but it's still the same voice crooning the love songs as on the records I had when I was a kid*

crooner ['kruːnə] *noun* person who croons; *the next act was a famous crooner*

crop [krɒp] 1 *noun* plants, such as vegetables or cereals, grown for food; *the bad weather has set the crops back by three weeks; we had a wonderful crop of potatoes or a wonderful potato crop this year* 2 *verb* (a) to cut short; *the photograph had to be cropped to fit the space on the page* (b) *(of plant)* to have fruit; *the pear trees cropped heavily this year* (NOTE: **cropping - cropped**)

cropped [krɒpt] *adjective* cut short; *a young woman with cropped hair came to ask what I wanted; she wore her hair cropped short like a boy's*

crop up ['krɒp 'ʌp] *verb* to happen suddenly; *get in touch if any problem should crop up*

croquet ['krəʊkeɪ] *noun* lawn game played with hoops, balls and mallets; *let's have a game of croquet while the weather is fine*

COMMENT: croquet is a game for two to four players who try to hit a ball through a series of small metal hoops using a long mallet, and finish by hitting a stake; shots are taken in turn, but bonus shots are earned by hitting the ball through the hoop or by hitting an opponent's ball with your own

cross [krɒs] 1 *adjective* angry, annoyed; *the teacher will be cross with you for missing school; don't be cross - the children were only trying to help* 2 *noun* (a) shape made where one line has another going across it; *write your name where I have put a cross; there is a cross on the top of the church tower*; **the Red Cross** = international organization which provides medical help; *Red Cross officials have been allowed into the war zone; compare* RED CRESCENT (b) breed of plant or animal which comes from two different varieties; *a cross between two types of cattle* (NOTE: plural is **crosses**) 3 *verb* (a) to go across to the other side; *she just crossed the road without looking to see if there was any traffic coming; he crossed the lake in a small boat; the road crosses the railway line about 10km from here; Concorde only takes three hours to cross the Atlantic* (b) to put one thing across another; *he crossed his arms and looked annoyed; she sat down and crossed her legs*; **crossed line** = fault on a telephone line, where you can hear a conversation from another line; *I can't hear you properly - we've got a crossed line* (c) to breed a new animal or plant, etc., from two varieties; *he crossed two strains of rice to produce a variety which is resistant to disease*

crossbar ['krɒsbɑː] *noun* (a) beam which goes across a space, especially a beam which goes between the posts forming a goal; *he kicked the ball over the crossbar and converted the try; he almost scored, but the ball hit the crossbar* (b) rod which crosses the frame of a man's bicycle, from the seat to the steering column; *she sat on his crossbar; girls' bicycles normally don't have crossbars*

crossbreed ['krɒsbriːd] 1 *noun* animal bred by crossing two animals of different breeds; *these sheep are crossbreeds* 2 *verb* to breed an animal by crossing two animals of different breeds; *a flock of crossbred sheep* (NOTE: **crossbreeding - crossbred**)

cross-country [krɒs'kʌntri] *noun* race across fields and along paths, not on a running track; *the cross-country champion is a favourite to win the marathon*

cross-examination [krɒsɪgzæmɪ'neɪʃn] *noun* questioning witnesses called by the other side in a case; *under cross-examination, he revealed that in fact he was the driver of the white car*

cross-examine [krɒsɪg'zæmɪn] *verb* to question witnesses called by the other side in a case, in the hope that you can destroy their evidence; *there is no need to cross-examine the witness any longer*

crossing ['krɒsɪŋ] *noun* (a) action of going across to the other side of an area of water; *how long is the crossing from England to Germany?*; *they had a rough crossing* = the sea was rough when they travelled (b) place where you go across safely; *cars have to take care at the railway crossing*; **level crossing** = place where a road crosses a railway line without a bridge or tunnel; *the level crossing gates opened when the train had passed* (NOTE: American English is **grade crossing**); **pelican crossing** = place where you can cross a road with traffic lights worked by pedestrians; **zebra crossing** = place marked with black and white lines where you can walk across a road; *it's safer to use a zebra crossing when you're crossing a main road* (NOTE: American English is **crosswalk**)

cross off *or* **cross out** ['krɒs 'ɒf *or* 'krɒs 'aʊt] *verb* to draw a line through something which has been written to show that it should not be there; *he's ill, so you can cross him off the list for the party*; *I had difficulty reading her letter - she'd crossed out so many words*; *she crossed out £250 and put in £500*

crossover ['krɒsəʊvə] *noun* (a) bridge which takes a road or railway over another road, railway or river; *how would a crossover help relieve traffic congestion?* (b) change from one type of artistic work to another; *he made the crossover from pianist to conductor without any difficulty*

cross-question [krɒs'kwestʃən] *verb* to cross-examine, to ask a lot of questions; *all members of staff were cross-questioned several times after the theft*

cross-refer ['krɒs rɪ'fɜː] *verb* to tell the reader to look up something in another part of a book; *you are cross-referred to the list of dates in the supplement*

cross-reference [krɒs'refərəns] 1 *noun* note in a reference book telling the reader to look in another part of the book for further information; *please, check all cross-references for accuracy*; *cross-references are not only useful to readers but also save time* 2 *verb* to cross-refer to; *the entry will be hard to find if it is not cross-referenced*

crossroads ['krɒsrəʊdz] *noun* place where one road crosses another; *turn right at the next crossroads*

cross-section ['krɒssekʃən] *noun* (a) diagram made to show the inside of something, as if it had been cut through; *the picture shows a cross-section of the Channel Tunnel*; *diagram 4 is a cross-section of a diesel engine* (b) sample cut across a specimen for examination under a microscope; *he examined a cross-section of lung tissue* (c) typical group of people; *the team consulted a cross-section of the public in the shopping centre*

crosswalk ['krɒswɔːk] *noun US* place where you can walk safely across a street; *it's safer to use the crosswalk when you're crossing a busy intersection*; *children should never cross a road anywhere else than at a crosswalk* (NOTE: British English is **pedestrian crossing, zebra crossing**)

crossword ['krɒswɜːd] *noun* puzzle where small squares have to be filled with letters to spell words; *I can't do today's crossword - it's too hard*; *he finished the crossword in 25 minutes*

crotch [krɒtʃ] *noun* place between the tops of your legs; *measure the trousers from the crotch to the floor, to see if they will be long enough* (NOTE: plural is **crotches**)

crotchet ['krɒtʃɪt] *noun* note in music half as long as a minim and twice as long as a quaver; *you played the note as a crotchet instead of a minim*

crouch [kraʊtʃ] *verb* to bend down low; *we had to crouch down to get into the cave*; *she sat crouched down in the bottom of the boat*

croup [kruːp] *noun* (a) children's disease, an infection of the upper respiratory passages which blocks the larynx, makes breathing difficult and makes a loud noise when the child coughs; *steam will help relieve mild croup in children* (NOTE: no plural in this meaning) (b) rounded rear part of a horse; *he hit the croup of the horse to make him run*

croupier ['kruːpiə] *noun* person who is in charge of a gaming table in a casino, who deals cards, collects money, etc.; *the croupier raked the chips across the board*

crow [krəʊ] 1 *noun* large black bird; *the crows make such a noise in the trees that it wakes us up*; **as the crow flies** = in a straight line; *it's only a couple of miles as the crow flies, but since there's no bridge over the river, it takes over half an hour to drive there* 2 *verb* (a) *(of a cock)* to make a loud call; *the sound of the cock crowing woke them all up* (b) **to crow about** = to boast about; *he's always crowing about his success with women*; *stop crowing - just because you've won one game doesn't mean you're going to win the competition*; **to crow over someone** = to be happy because you have beaten someone, because someone has made a mistake, etc.

crowbar ['krəʊbɑː] *noun* heavy metal bar for opening crates and lifting things; *you will need a crowbar to lift the paving stones*; *they were carrying crowbars and pickaxes when they were arrested*

crowd [kraʊd] 1 *noun* mass of people; *she was cut off from her friends by a crowd of school children*; *after the election, the crowds were dancing in the streets*; *someone in the crowd threw an egg at the speaker on the platform*; *if you travel early, you will avoid the crowds of Christmas shoppers* 2 *verb* to group together; *all the rugby fans crowded into the pub*; *the children were crowding round her*

crowded ['kraʊdɪd] *adjective* with a large number of people; *the town gets very crowded during the holiday season*; *the stands were crowded before the game started*; *see also* OVERCROWDED

crown [kraʊn] 1 *noun* (a) jewelled metal headdress for an emperor, king, queen, etc.; *the archbishop placed the crown on the head of the young king*; *the queen received the ambassadors wearing a heavy gold crown* (b) *(in Britain)* king or queen representing the state; *in England, all swans belong to the crown*; *the Crown Jewels are kept in the Tower of London*; **counsel for the Crown** = lawyer representing the state in a trial; *the Crown's case was that the defendant passed secrets to an enemy* (c) false top attached to a broken tooth; *I'm going to the dentist to have a crown fitted* **2** *verb* **(a)** to make someone king, queen, emperor, etc., by placing a crown on his or her head; *the Queen was crowned in Westminster Abbey* **(b)** to be a splendid end to something; *to crown it all, he won the lottery* **(c)** to attach a false top to a broken tooth; *the dentist said that the tooth was so badly broken that he would have to crown it instead of trying to fill it*

Crown Court ['kraun 'kɔːt]] *noun* court in various places in England and Wales which tries criminal cases; *the case will be heard before the Crown Court*

crucial ['kruːʃl] *adjective* extremely important; *it is crucial that the story be kept out of the papers*

crucially ['kruːʃəli] *adverb* seriously, extremely; *crucially, he forgot to mention that he had written a note to his boss*; *it is crucially important that this should be kept a secret*

crucifix ['kruːsɪfɪks] *noun* cross with a figure of Jesus Christ on it; *she has an old crucifix on the wall over her bed* (NOTE: plural is **crucifixes**)

crucifixion [kruːsɪ'fɪkʃn] *noun* killing a person by nailing him to a cross; *in Roman times, crucifixion was a way of executing criminals*; *on Good Friday we remember Christ's Crucifixion*

crucify ['kruːsɪfaɪ] *verb* **(a)** to kill someone by nailing to a cross; *Christ was crucified between two thieves* **(b)** *(informal)* to criticize sharply; *my brother would crucify me if he knew I had used his car without asking him*; *I can't call her now, she'd crucify me if I woke her up*

crude [kruːd] **1** *adjective* **(a)** unrefined; *beaches were covered in crude oil from the tanker* **(b)** rude, with no manners; *he made some crude gestures at the fans* (NOTE: **cruder - crudest**) **2** *noun* raw unrefined petroleum, taken from the ground; *the price of Arabian crude has fallen*

cruel ['kruəl] *adjective* who causes pain, who makes a person or animal suffer; *you must not be cruel to your new puppy*; *it was cruel of him to mention her weight problem* (NOTE: **crueller - cruellest** but American spelling is **crueler - cruelest**)

cruelty ['kruəlti] *noun* act of being cruel; *the zoo keeper was accused of cruelty to animals*; *cases of cruelty to children are increasing*; **mental cruelty** = being cruel to someone in a way that does not hurt them physically

cruet ['kruːt] *noun* set of containers for salt, pepper, mustard, etc., which is put on the table; *can you pass me the cruet, please?*; *compare* CONDIMENTS

cruise [kruːz] **1** *noun* long voyage in a ship calling at different places; *when he retired they went on a cruise round the Mediterranean* **2** *verb* **(a)** to go in a boat from place to place; *they spent May cruising in the Aegean*; *the ship cruised from island to island* **(b)** to travel at an even speed; *the car cruises very comfortably at 160 kilometres an hour* **(c)** to win without much difficulty; *he cruised to victory in the race*

cruiser ['kruːzə] *noun* **(a)** large warship, smaller than a battleship; *how many cruisers can the Navy send to the war zone?* **(b) cabin cruiser** = comfortable motor boat with cabins where you can sleep; *three cabin cruisers were waiting to go through the lock*

cruise ship ['kruːz 'ʃɪp] *noun* large passenger ship which takes people on cruises; *they went round the Caribbean on an American cruise ship*

crumb [krʌm] *noun* small piece of bread, cake, etc.; *they left crumbs all over the table* (NOTE: to show different types of crumbs, you can say **breadcrumbs**, **cakecrumbs**, etc.)

crumble ['krʌmbl] **1** *noun* hot cooked dessert made of fruit covered with a mixture of flour, fat and sugar; *we are having apple crumble and custard for pudding* **2** *verb* **(a)** to break up into small pieces; *he picked up a lump of dry earth and crumbled it between his fingers*; *as the waves battered the cliff it began to crumble away* **(b)** to collapse; *as the witness said what he had seen, the defendant's case crumbled*; *all her confidence began to crumble*

crumpet ['krʌmpɪt] *noun* type of round flat uncooked bread, with holes on one side, toasted and covered with butter; *we toasted crumpets by the fire*

crumple ['krʌmpl] *verb* **(a)** to crush or to screw up into a ball; *I heard him crumple up the paper and throw it into the wastepaper basket* **(b)** to become full of lines or creases; *her shirt was crumpled because she had been lying on the grass*; *people arriving at the airport early in the morning have a crumpled look*; *the box was full of crumpled bits of paper*

crunch [krʌntʃ] **1** *noun* **(a)** sound of something dry being crushed; *the crunch of dry snow under his boots* **(b)** *(informal)* crisis point; *the crunch will come when the firm has no cash to pay the wages*; **if it comes to the crunch** = if crisis point is reached; *when it came to the crunch, the other side backed down* **2** *verb* **(a)** to crush something dry; *the snow crunched under his boots* **(b)** to chew something hard which makes a noise when you are eating; *she was crunching an apple when the phone rang*

crunchy ['krʌntʃi] *adjective* which makes a noise when you are eating; *a crunchy apple*; *biscuits should be crunchy not soft*

crusade [kruː'seɪd] **1** *noun* **(a)** strong action to stop or change something; *the government has launched a crusade against drugs* **(b)** *(history)* **the Crusades** = medieval wars against Muslims in the Middle East, led by Christian kings; *the tomb of a knight who died on the Crusades* **2** *verb* to take part in a crusade; *he has been crusading for more government action to reduce unemployment*

crusader [kruː'seɪdə] *noun* person who takes part in a crusade; *he was a well-known crusader for women's right to vote*

crush [krʌʃ] **1** *verb* **(a)** to press flat; *she was crushed against the wall by the car*; *crush a piece of garlic and add it to the soup* **(b)** to end completely; *government troops crushed the student rebellion*; *all her hopes of getting a better job were crushed by the report of the interview board* **2** *noun* **(a)** mass of people; *she was hurt in the crush of people trying to get to the exit*; *he lost his briefcase in the crush on the train*; **crush barriers** = metal fences which are put up to control crowds; *the fans simply climbed over the crush barriers to get at the pop group's car* **(b)** *(informal)* **to have a crush on someone** = to have a feeling of love for someone you do not know very well; *she had a crush on her tennis coach*

crushing ['krʌʃɪŋ] *adjective* which crushes, which takes away all hope; *they suffered a crushing defeat at* *the last election; losing the government subsidy was a crushing blow to the company*

crust [krʌst] *noun* hard outside layer of bread, the earth, etc.; *you can cut the crusts off the sandwiches; the crust of the pie had sagged in the middle; the earth's crust is over 30km thick*

crustacean [krʌ'steɪʃn] *noun* animal with a hard shell, usually living in the sea, such as a lobster, crab, etc.; *the crayfish is a freshwater crustacean*

crusty ['krʌsti] *adjective* **(a)** with a hard crust; *we had an excellent salad with a glass of wine and a piece of fresh crusty bread* **(b)** *(informal)* who gets angry easily; *the club is full of crusty old men nodding in leather armchairs* (NOTE: **crustier - crustiest**)

crutch [krʌtʃ] *noun* strong support for a patient with an injured leg, formed of a stick with a holding bar or a a T-bar which fits under the armpit; *after his accident he spent several weeks on crutches* (NOTE: plural is **crutches**)

cry [kraɪ] **1** *noun* **(a)** loud shout; *no one heard her cries for help* **(b)** sharp sound made by a bird or animal; *the cry of the eagles overhead; we could hear the cries of monkeys in the trees* (NOTE: plural is **cries**) **2** *verb* **(a)** to have tears coming out of your eyes; *the baby cried when her mother took away her toys; cutting up onions makes me cry; many people were crying when they left the cinema* (informal) **to cry over spilt milk** = to be upset because of something which you couldn't prevent; *it's no use crying over spilt milk - what's happened has happened* **(b)** *(formal)* to call out; *'hello there', she cried*

crypt [krɪpt] *noun* cellar under a church; *a church crypt is often the oldest part of the building*

cryptic ['krɪptɪk] *adjective* secret and mysterious; *no one could understand his cryptic message;* **cryptic crossword** = crossword with difficult clues; *a dictionary for cryptic crossword enthusiasts*

crystal ['krɪstl] *noun* **(a)** solid chemical substance with a regular shape; *the salt formed crystals at the bottom of the jar* **(b)** very clear bright glass; *a crystal wineglass*

crystal clear ['krɪstəl 'kliːə] *adjective* very clear, simple to understand; *I want to make this crystal clear: anyone who gets into trouble with the police will be sent home immediately*

crystalline ['krɪstəlaɪn] *adjective* **(a)** made of crystals, shaped like a crystal; *crystalline materials do not always form single regular crystals* **(b)** clear and pure like a crystal; *the crystalline water of the mountain stream*

crystallize ['krɪstəlaɪz] *verb* **(a)** to form crystals; *water crystallizes to form snow* **(b)** to preserve fruit in sugar; *we had a box of crystallized fruit for Christmas* **(c)** to take shape; *following the meeting, our ideas began to crystallize*

CT = CORPORATION TAX

cub [kʌb] *noun* **(a)** young animal, especially a bear or fox; *the cubs played in the sun while the vixen stood guard; the bear led her cubs down to the river* **(b) Cub (Scout)** = member of the young section of Boy Scouts; *he will be joining the Cubs next year*

Cuba ['kjuːbə] *noun* independent country, a large island in the Caribbean; *we went on holiday to Cuba last year; Cuba is famous for its cigars* (NOTE: capital:

Havana; people: **Cubans**; language: **Spanish**; currency: **Cuban peso**)

Cuban ['kjuːbn] **1** *adjective* referring to Cuba; *Cuban cigars are very famous* **2** *noun* person from Cuba; *two Cubans came onto the plane*

cube [kjuːb] **1** *noun* **(a)** *(geometry)* shape where all six sides are square and join each other at right angles; *the design for the library is nothing more than a series of cubes* **(b)** piece of something shaped like a cube; *I take two cubes of sugar in my tea; the ice cubes chinked in the glasses* **(c)** *(mathematics)* the result when a number is multiplied by itself twice; *27 is the cube of 3;* **cube root of a number** = number which when multiplied twice by itself will equal the number; *the cube root of 1728 is 12 (12 x 12 x 12 = 1728)* **2** *verb* **(a)** to cut into little cubes; *wash, peel and then cube the potatoes* **(b)** to multiply a number twice by itself; *if you cube 6 the result is 216 (6 x 6 x 6)*

cubed [kjuːbd] *adjective* **(a)** made in little cubes; *a pack of cubed sugar; put the cubed vegetables into the soup* **(b)** *(mathematics)* which is multiplied by itself twice; *27 is 3 cubed*

cubic ['kjuːbɪk] *adjective* measured in volume by multiplying length, depth and width; *the crate holds six cubic metres* (NOTE: cubic is written in figures as ^{3}: $6m^3$ = six cubic metres; $10ft^3$ = ten cubic feet)

cubicle ['kjuːbɪkl] *noun* **(a)** changing room in a shop, at the swimming baths; *look for an empty cubicle and change there* **(b)** small room which is part of a larger room, such as a dormitory; *the scout leader sleeps in a little cubicle off the main dormitory*

cuckoo ['kʊkuː] **1** *noun* common bird which comes to Britain in summer only; *when you hear the first cuckoo you know that winter is over;* **a cuckoo in the nest** = someone who comes into a family, an organization, etc., and gradually takes control **2** *adjective* *(informal)* mad; *they must be cuckoo!*

COMMENT: the cuckoo is unusual in that it lays its eggs in the nests of other birds; the young cuckoo throws other baby birds out of the nest and is brought up by the parent birds as if it were their own

cuckoo clock ['kʊkuː 'klɒk] *noun* clock where a small bird comes out at each hour and makes a noise like a cuckoo; *Switzerland is famous for its cuckoo clocks*

cucumber ['kjuːkʌmbə] *noun* long dark green vegetable used in salads or for pickling; *we had cucumber sandwiches for tea;* (informal) **as cool as a cucumber** = very calm and relaxed; *he walked out of the prison as cool as a cucumber*

cuddle ['kʌdl] **1** *noun* a hug; *she picked up her daughter and gave her a cuddle* **2** *verb* to hug someone; *the little girl was cuddling her teddy bear; there was a last chance to cuddle in the taxi that took them to the airport*

cuddle up ['kʌdl 'ʌp] *verb* **to cuddle up to someone** = to hug someone; *the children cuddled up together in the big armchair*

cuddly ['kʌdli] *adjective* soft, which you can hug; *she was given a lot of cuddly toys for Christmas*

cudgel ['kʌdʒl] **1** *noun* large stick for hitting people; *policemen carrying cudgels broke up the demonstration* (old) (informal) **to take up the cudgels**

on someone's behalf = to start to defend someone; *who's going to take up the cudgels on behalf of these abandoned children?* **2** *verb* **to cudgel your brains** = to think hard; *he cudgelled his brains to remember the author of the book* (NOTE: **cudgelling - cudgelled** but American spelling is **cudgeling - cudgeled**)

cue [kjuː] *noun* **(a)** *(in a play)* words after which you have to speak or act; *he missed his cue and had to be prompted*; *the gunshot is your cue to rush onto the stage screaming*; **to take your cue from someone** = to do as someone does; *watch the managing director during the negotiations and take your cue from him* **(b)** long stick for playing billiards or snooker; *before playing his shot, he put some chalk on the tip of his cue*; **cue ball** = the white ball which a snooker player hits with his cue (NOTE: do not confuse with **queue**)

cuff [kʌf] **1** *noun* **(a)** end of the sleeve round the wrist; *the collar and cuffs of his shirt were dirty and frayed*; **speaking off the cuff** *or* **an off-the-cuff speech** = speech made without notes; *he was only asked to speak at the last minute, and for an off-the-cuff speech, it was excellent* **(b)** *US* folded part at the bottom of each leg of a pair of trousers; *this year, slacks with cuffs are back in fashion* (NOTE: British English is **turnup**) **(c)** smack with an open hand; *she gave him a cuff on the back of the head to shut him up* **2** *verb* to give someone a smack; *the parents said he had cuffed the child on the head*

cuff-links [ˈkʌflɪŋks] *noun* little objects, usually linked with a chain, which hold shirt cuffs together; *he has cuff-links with his crest on them*

cuisine [kwɪˈziːn] *French noun (meaning 'kitchen')* style of cooking; *Chinese cuisine is very different from European*; *French cuisine is more and more popular in England*

cul-de-sac [ˈkʌldəsæk] *noun* small street which is only open at one end; *the road is a small cul-de-sac with only six houses* (NOTE: plural is **cul-de-sacs**)

culinary [ˈkʌlɪnəri] *adjective* referring to cooking; *what culinary delights are you offering us tonight?*; *I'm no culinary expert but I love good food*

cull [kʌl] **1** *noun* killing a certain number of animals in order to keep the population under control; *the deer cull takes place in early October* **2** *verb* to kill a certain number of animals in order to keep the population under control; *about 10% of the deer population is culled each autumn*

culminate [ˈkʌlmɪneɪt] *verb* **to culminate in** = to reach a climax; *the race culminated in a win for the Canadian driver*

culmination [kʌlmɪˈneɪʃn] *noun* final point, grand ending; *his gold medal was the culmination of six years of hard training*

culpable [ˈkʌlpəbl] *adjective* which is likely to attract blame; *the directors can be held culpable of any financial mismanagement*; **culpable homicide** = murder or manslaughter

culprit [ˈkʌlprɪt] *noun* person or thing that is responsible for a crime, for something which has gone wrong; *the police say that they have not yet caught the culprits*; *I wondered why the fax machine was not working - I think I've found the culprit*

cult [kʌlt] *noun* small religious group; *I'm worried about my daughter - she left joined a cult two years ago and we haven't seen her since*; **cult hero** = person who is admired by a group; **personality cult** = excessive publicity which makes a political leader into a sort of god; *various Communist leaders encouraged the development of the personality cult*

cultivate [ˈkʌltɪveɪt] *verb* **(a)** to dig and water the land to grow plants; *fields are cultivated in early spring, ready for sowing corn* **(b)** to grow plants; *this field is used to cultivate new strains of wheat* **(c)** to do everything to get someone's friendship; *we are cultivating the new director to try to make sure we get the contract*

cultivated [ˈkʌltɪveɪtɪd] *adjective* **(a)** who has been well educated in music, art, literature, etc.; *a really cultivated person wouldn't be seen dead in a karaoke bar* **(b)** *(plant)* which is specially grown and is not wild; *wild strawberries have a more intense flavour than cultivated ones* **(c)** *(land)* prepared for growing crops; *from the air, the cultivated fields were like a brown and green quilt*

cultivation [kʌltɪˈveɪʃn] *noun* **(a)** act of cultivating; *the cultivation of soft fruit is very dependent on the weather*; **land under cultivation** = land which is being cultivated; *he has sixty acres under cultivation* **(b)** good education; *his lack of cultivation was apparent as soon as he began to speak*

cultivator [ˈkʌltɪveɪtə] *noun* **(a)** farmer, person who cultivates land; *cultivators know that unexpected frosts can ruin an entire crop* **(b)** rake, with many small prongs, sometimes powered by a motor; *use a small cultivator to remove weeds between rows of plants*

cultural [ˈkʌltʃərəl] *adjective* referring to culture; *the French cultural attaché opened the exhibition*; *his cultural interests are very wide-ranging - from Mexican art to 12th century Greek paintings*

culture [ˈkʌltʃə] *noun* **(a)** a country's civilization, including music, art, literature, etc.; *he is taking a course in Russian culture*; *is a TV in every home really the peak of western culture?*; **culture shock** = shock which you feel when moving from one type of society to another which is very different; *going from California to live with hill tribes in India was something of a culture shock* **(b)** cultivation of plants; *the culture of orchids must be done in warm damp conditions* **(c)** bacteria grown in a laboratory; *the first part of the experiment is to grow a culture in the lab*

cultured [ˈkʌltʃəd] *adjective* **(a)** civilized; well educated; *our guide was a very cultured lady from Vienna*; *such behaviour is not acceptable in cultured society* **(b)** (pearl) which has been grown artificially; *only an expert can tell the difference between a cultured pearl and a real one*

cumbersome [ˈkʌmbəsəm] *adjective* large and heavy; *this big bag is very cumbersome - you should get something smaller and lighter*

cumulative [ˈkjuːmjʊlətɪv] *adjective* **(a)** which accumulates, which is added each year; *the interest on this account is cumulative*; *the cumulative effect of a series of late nights finally caught up with him and he fell asleep during the dinner* **(b)** which grows by adding new parts; *a cumulative index is made up of several different indexes put together*

cunning [ˈkʌnɪŋ] **1** *noun* cleverness and trickery; *he showed cunning in his attempts to get tickets for the concert* **2** *adjective* clever and sly; *they tried a cunning ploy to get into the exhibition free*

cup

cup [kʌp] *noun* **(a)** small bowl with a handle, used for drinking tea, coffee, etc.; *she put out a cup and saucer for everyone*; **a tea cup** = a large cup for drinking tea; **a coffee cup** = a small cup for drinking coffee **(b)** liquid in a cup; *he drank two cups of coffee*; *can I have a cup of tea?*; **to make a cup of tea** = to prepare tea, usually in a pot; *I'll make you all a cup of tea*; (*informal*) **it's not my cup of tea** = it's not something I like very much; *modern art isn't really my cup of tea* **(c)** tall silver bowl given as a prize for winning a competition; *he has won three cups for golf*; **cup final** = last game in a football or rugby competition, where the winning side is given the cup; *the winners of the two semi-finals will meet in the cup final on May 4th*; **cup tie** = football or rugby game where the winning side will go on to the next round of the competition; *our star player will miss the cup tie because of injury*

cupboard [ˈkʌbəd] *noun* piece of furniture with shelves and doors; *put the jam in the kitchen cupboard*; *the best plates are in the dining room cupboard*; *she painted the cupboard doors white*

cupful [ˈkʌpfʊl] *noun* quantity which a cup can hold; *add two cupfuls of sugar to the water*

cuppa [ˈkʌpə] *noun* (*informal*) cup of tea; *we stopped for a cuppa in the café on the high street*; *I could murder a cuppa!*

cur [kɜː] *noun* (*old*) **(a)** vicious dog; *the cur followed the beggars everywhere* **(b)** nasty person; *you cur!*

curable [ˈkjʊərəbl] *adjective* (*disease*) which can be cured; *some cancers are curable if they are treated early enough*

curate [ˈkjʊərət] *noun* priest who helps a parish priest; *the vicar was assisted by his curate*

curator [kjʊˈreɪtə] *noun* person in charge of a museum; *she is one of the curators of the British Museum*; *he became curator soon after I left my job at the museum*

curb [kɜːb] **1** *noun* something which holds something back; *the company needs to put a curb on its spending* **2** *verb* to hold back; *she needs to curb her enthusiasm to spend money*

curdle [ˈkɜːdl] *verb* **(a)** to make or become solid and sour; *if you add lemon juice to milk it will curdle it*; *milk will curdle in hot weather* **(b)** **to make your blood curdle** = to make you very frightened; *a story frightening enough to make their blood curdle*; *one's blood curdles at the mere thought of it*; *see also* BLOODCURDLING

cure [kjʊə] **1** *noun* something which makes a disease better; *doctors are still trying to find a cure for colds* **2** *verb* **(a)** to make a patient or a disease better; *I don't know what's in the medicine, but it cured my cough very fast* **(b)** to preserve meat, by putting it in salt; *a piece of cured ham*; *this bacon has been cured in salt water*

curfew [ˈkɜːfjuː] *noun* period when no one is allowed out into the street; *the military government has imposed a dusk-to-dawn curfew*

curiosity [kjʊərɪˈɒsɪti] *noun* **(a)** wanting to know about something; *I just asked out of sheer curiosity* **(b)** strange object; *the vase is a real curiosity - I've never seen anything like it before* (NOTE: the plural in this meaning is **curiosities**)

curious [ˈkjʊərɪəs] *adjective* **(a)** strange; *she has a curious high-pitched voice* **(b)** wanting to know; *I'm curious to know if anything happened at the party*

curiously [ˈkjʊərɪəsli] *adverb* **(a)** strangely; *the meat has a curiously fishy smell*; *curiously enough, nobody noticed that he had dyed his hair green* **(b)** wanting to know; *she peeped curiously into the box*

curl [kɜːl] **1** *noun* **(a)** lock of hair which twists; *the little girl looked so sweet with her golden curls* **(b)** twist in the hair; *my hair has a natural curl* **2** *verb* **(a)** to make hair twist round; *she curled her hair round her finger*; *she went to the hairdresser's to have her hair curled* **(b)** to twist; *my hair curls naturally*; *some creepers curl round other plants*

curling [ˈkɜːlɪŋ] *noun* a Winter Olympic sport for two teams of four, similar to bowls on ice; **curling stone** = a large round polished heavy granite disk, with a handle rather like a door handle on the top which when given a twist as it is send forwards makes the stone curl or curve as it slides across the ice

COMMENT: the game is played with granite stones which are slid towards a fixed target, with teams scoring points for the number of stones they get nearer the target than their opponents. When all eight players have delivered their stones, the game is then played back in the opposite direction

curly [ˈkɜːli] *adjective* **curly hair** = hair with natural waves in it; *she has naturally curly hair* (NOTE: **curlier - curliest**)

currant [ˈkʌrənt] *noun* **(a)** small black or red soft fruit; *I have planted some currant bushes*; *see also* BLACKCURRANT, REDCURRANT **(b)** small dried grape; *a currant bun*; *fruit cake with currants, sultanas and raisins in it* (NOTE: do not confuse with **current**)

COMMENT: currants are smaller and blacker than raisins or sultanas; they are all forms of dried grapes

currency [ˈkʌrənsi] *noun* **(a)** money used in a certain country; *I want to change my pounds into French currency*; **foreign currency** = the money of other countries; *for our holiday, we are taking foreign currency in travellers' cheques*; **hard currency** = money which is stable and is easily exchanged for foreign currency; *people in some countries will do anything to get hold of hard currency*; *underdeveloped countries sell raw materials for hard currency*; **soft currency** = currency of a country with a weak economy, which is cheap to buy and difficult to exchange for other currencies **(b)** state of being known or accepted; **to gain currency** = to become better known or more accepted; *the idea that the world was round began to gain currency in the later Middle Ages*

current [ˈkʌrənt] **1** *noun* **(a)** flow of water or air; *don't go swimming in the river - the current is very strong*; *a warm westerly current of air is flowing across the country*; *vultures circle in rising currents of warm air* **(b)** flow of electricity; *switch the current off at the mains* (NOTE: do not confuse with **currant**) **2** *adjective* **(a)** referring to the present time; *what is your current position?*; *who is the current Prime Minister of Japan?*; *do you have a current timetable? - mine is out-of-date*; **the current rate of exchange** = today's rate of exchange; *the current rate of exchange is nine* *francs to the pound* **(b)** widely believed; *the idea that the world was flat was current in the Middle Ages*

current account [ˈkʌrənt əˈkaʊnt] *noun* bank account from which you can take money at any time; *he deposited the cheque in his current account*; *her salary is paid directly into her current account* (NOTE: the American equivalent is a **checking account**)

> COMMENT: current accounts often do not pay any interest, but you can write cheques on them

current affairs [ˈkʌrənt əˈfeəz] *noun* the political situation as it is now; *we are studying current affairs as part of our politics course*

currently [ˈkʌrəntli] *adverb* at the present time; *he is currently the manager of our Paris office*; *we are currently in the process of buying a house*

curriculum [kəˈrɪkjʊləm] *noun* subjects studied in a school, etc.; *I am very glad that music and drama have been added to the curriculum*; *the National Curriculum is followed by all British schools*

curriculum vitae (CV) [kəˈrɪkjʊləm ˈviːtaɪ] *noun* summary of the biographical details of a person, especially details of education and previous jobs; *please apply in writing, enclosing a current curriculum vitae*; *please enclose a curriculum vitae with your application form* (NOTE: plural is **curriculums** or **curricula vitae**. Note also that the American English is **résumé**)

curried [ˈkʌrɪd] *adjective* cooked with curry; *a plate of curried lamb and rice*

curry [ˈkʌri] **1** *noun* **(a) curry powder** or **paste** = hot spicy powder or paste, used to make Indian dishes; **curry house** = restaurant serving Indian food **(b)** Indian food prepared with spices; *I would like a mild curry, please*; *we ordered chicken curry and rice* (NOTE: plural is **curries**) **2** *verb* **to curry favour with someone** = to try to please someone; *he's just trying to curry favour with the boss by coming in at seven o'clock in the morning*

curse [kɜːs] **1** *noun* **(a)** swear word; *he threw the letter down with a curse* **(b)** magic word to make something unpleasant happen to someone; *the witch put a curse on the whole family* **(c)** something which causes you problems; *being on call 24 hours a day is the curse of being a doctor*; *pollution is the curse of industrialized societies* **2** *verb* **(a)** to swear; *he cursed under his breath and marched out of the room* **(b)** to cast an evil spell on someone; *we must be cursed - everything we do seems to go wrong*

cursed [ˈkɜːst] *adjective* **cursed with** = having a problem which is embarrassing or difficult to deal with; *he's cursed with bad breath*; *they're cursed with noisy neighbours*

cursor [ˈkɜːsə] *noun* marker like a little arrow or a bright spot on a screen which shows where the next character will appear; *press the keys with arrows to move the cursor in the direction you want*; *to print your text, point your cursor at the printer icon and click twice*

cursory [ˈkɜːsəri] *adjective* rapid, not very careful; *the inspectors only gave the heating system a cursory inspection*; *even the most cursory examination would have shown the mistakes in the accounts*

curt [kɜːt] *adjective* abrupt (way of speaking); *all I managed to get out of him was a curt 'no'*; *he was very*

curt with his wife in front of his staff, who were terribly embarrassed

curtail [kɜːˈteɪl] *verb* to shorten; to reduce; *at the suggestion of the auditors, they curtailed their publicity expenditure*; *the birthday celebrations had to be curtailed when water began to pour through the ceiling*

curtailment [kɜːˈteɪlmənt] *noun* (*formal*) act of curtailing; *we expect some curtailment of deliveries while the warehouse is being reorganized*; *the outbreak of war brought about some curtailment of the postal services*

curtain [ˈkɜːtən] *noun* **(a)** long piece of cloth hanging in front of a window, etc.; *can you close the curtains, please?*; **to draw the curtains** = (i) to open the curtains; (ii) to close the curtains; *draw the curtains - it's getting cold* (NOTE: American English for this is **drapes**) **(b)** long piece of cloth hanging in front of the stage at a theatre; **the curtain will go up at 8.30** = the play begins at 8.30; **safety curtain** = fireproof curtain in front of the stage in a theatre; *the safety curtain is lowered and raised at the beginning of each performance*; **it will be curtains for him** = he will be sacked, ruined, etc.

curtain call [ˈkɜːtən ˈkɔːl] *noun* time when actors or dancers come out in front of the curtain to take a bow after the end of a performance; *the cast took six curtain calls*; *that evening he took the last curtain call of his career as an actor*

curtain off [ˈkɜːtən ˈɒf] *verb* to separate with a curtain; *the end of the dining room is curtained off to form a private meeting room*

curvature [ˈkɜːvətʃə] *noun* being bent into a curve; **curvature of the spine** = abnormal bending of the spine forwards or sideways; *his back pain is due to curvature of the spine*; **curvature of the earth** = the curving of the horizon which is seen especially at sea and which shows that the earth is round

curve [kɜːv] **1** *noun* **(a)** round shape like part of a circle; *the road makes a sharp curve to the left* **(b)** rounded shape on a graph; **learning curve** = gradual process of learning; **a steep learning curve** = having to learn new skills fast; **sales curve** = graph showing how sales increase or decrease **2** *verb* to make a rounded shape; *the road curves round the side of the mountain*

curved [kɜːvd] *adjective* not straight, with a rounded shape; *a chair with curved legs*

cushion [ˈkʊʃən] **1** *noun* **(a)** bag filled with feathers, etc., for sitting or leaning on; *feel how soft this cushion is*; *put a cushion behind your back if you find your chair is too low* **(b)** money which allows you to get through a difficult period; *we have a little money in the bank which is a useful cushion when cash is tight* **2** *verb* to make soft something which could be hard or painful; *luckily when he fell off the ladder there was a hedge underneath to cushion his fall*; *she made no attempt to cushion the blow, but just told them straight out that they were all being sacked*

custard [ˈkʌstəd] *noun* **(a)** **(egg) custard** = sweet sauce, made with eggs and milk, flavoured with vanilla, baked until set and eaten warm or cold **(b)** (*in the UK*) sweet yellow sauce made with milk and a powder containing cornflour; *stewed rhubarb and custard*; *would you like some custard with your crumble?*

custodian [kʌˈstəʊdiən] *noun* **(a)** person who is legally entrusted to look after someone or something

(b) person who guards a museum or public building; *the museum custodian was sound asleep and didn't hear any noise*

custody ['kʌstədi] *noun* **(a)** keeping; *the jewels were in the custody of the manager, and he had placed them in the hotel safe*; **to take someone into custody** = to arrest someone; *the three fans were taken into police custody* **(b)** right of keeping and looking after a child; *when they were divorced, she was granted custody of the children* (NOTE: no plural)

custom ['kʌstəm] *noun* **(a)** habit, thing which is usually done; *it's a local custom in this part of the world* **(b)** *(formal)* use of a shop; *if the assistants are rude to me again I will take my custom elsewhere*; **to lose someone's custom** = to do something which makes a regular customer go to another restaurant, shop, etc.; *the little corner shops will lose a lot of custom when the new supermarket is built* **(c)** **custom-built** *or* **custom-made** = made to order for a customer; *he drives a custom-built sports car*

customary ['kʌstəməri] *adjective* usual; *it is customary to put money in the collecting box when attending a church service*

customer ['kʌstəmə] *noun* **(a)** person who buys something in a shop; *the shops are lowering their prices to attract customers*; *he was locking up the shop when a customer came in*; *his shop is always full of customers*; **a satisfied customer** = someone who is happy with what he has bought **(b)** person who uses a service, such as a train passenger; *we apologize to customers waiting on Platform 5 for the late arrival of their train*

customize ['kʌstəmaɪz] *verb* to have something changed to fit your special needs; *we use customized computer terminals*

customs ['kʌstəmz] *noun* **(a) H.M. Customs and Excise** = the British government department which organizes the collection of taxes on goods coming into a country (and also collects VAT); *he was stopped by customs*; *her car was searched by customs*; *the customs officer asked her to open her bag*; **customs duty** = tax which you have to pay to take goods into a country; *you may have to pay customs duty on goods imported from outside the EU* **(b)** office of this department at a port or airport; **to go through customs** = to pass through the area of a port or airport where customs officials examine goods; *when you come into the country, you have to go through customs*; **to take something through customs** = to carry something through the customs area without always declaring it; *she said that her boyfriend had asked her to take the case through customs for him*

cut [kʌt] **1** *verb* **(a)** to make an opening using a knife, scissors, etc.; to remove something using a knife, scissors, etc.; *the meat is very tough - I can't cut it with my knife*; *he needs to get his hair cut*; *there were six children, so she cut the cake into six pieces* **(b)** to hurt yourself by making a wound in the skin; *she cut her finger on the broken glass*; *he cut himself while shaving* **(c)** to reduce the size of something; *we are trying to cut the number of staff*; *accidents have been cut by 10%* **(d)** **to cut across** *or* **to cut through** = to take a short cut to get somewhere; *it's quicker if you cut across or through the park* **(e)** **to cut a corner** = to try to go round a corner quickly, by driving on the pavement; *he was trying to cut the corner and hit a fence*; **to cut corners** = to do things rapidly and

cheaply; *she tried to cut corners and the result was that the whole job had to be redone* **(f)** to look at someone and pretend not to recognize them; *when I held out my hand she cut me dead* (NOTE: **cutting - cut - has cut**) **2** *noun* **(a)** place which bleeds when your skin has been broken; *she had a bad cut on her leg*; *put some sticking plaster on your cut* **(b) short cut** = shorter way; *he took a short cut through the park* **(c)** sudden lowering of a price, salary, etc.; *price cuts* *or* *cuts in prices*; **job cuts** = reductions in the number of jobs; *the union is forecasting massive job cuts*; **he took a cut in salary** *or* **a salary cut** = he accepted a lower salary **(d)** stopping the supply of water, electricity, etc.; *there were power cuts again during the night* **(e)** piece of meat; *you can use a cheaper cut of meat if you're making stew* **(f) cut and paste** = *(computing)* taking a section of text from one point and inserting it at another

cut back [kʌt 'bæk] *verb* to reduce spending; *we are having to cut back on staff costs*

cutback ['kʌtbæk] *noun* reduction in expenditure; *the government has ordered cutbacks in departmental spending*

cut down ['kʌt 'daʊn] *verb* **(a)** to make a tree fall down with a saw, etc.; *he cut the tree down or he cut down the tree* **(b) to cut down (on)** = to reduce; *we are trying to get him to cut down the number of cigarettes he smokes each day*; *she's trying to cut down on chocolates*

cute [kjuːt] *adjective (informal)* nice; *what a cute little cottage!*; *Doreen may look cute now, but you should see her when she's in a temper*

cuticle ['kjuːtɪkl] *noun* hard skin at the base of a fingernail or toenail; *she is going to have a manicure to remove the cuticles on her fingernails*

cut in ['kʌt 'ɪn] *verb* **(a)** to interrupt; *he would keep on cutting in while I was telling the story* **(b)** *(informal)* to drive suddenly in front of another car; *did you see how the little white car cut in in front of the black Audi?*

cutlass ['kʌtləs] *noun* short curved sword, used in the navy and by cavalry; *the pirates attacked with cutlasses and knives* (NOTE: plural is **cutlasses**)

cutlery ['kʌtləri] *noun* knives, forks, spoons; *can you put the cutlery out on the tables, please*; *airlines say that passengers often steal pieces of cutlery* (NOTE: no plural)

cutlet ['kʌtlət] *noun* **(a)** slice of meat, usually with a bone attached; *we were served veal cutlets with mushroom sauce* **(b)** fried dish made with minced meat, fish, vegetables, etc., made into the shape of a piece of meat; *she makes delicious fish cutlets*

cut off ['kʌt 'ɒf] *verb* **(a)** to take away a small part of something using a knife, etc.; *she cut off a little piece of string*; *he cut off two slices of ham* **(b)** to stop someone from being with someone or reaching a place; *she was cut off from her friends by a crowd of policemen*; *the village was cut off by the snow*; *the tide came in and cut off a party of schoolchildren* **(c)** to stop a phone call before it is finished; *we were cut off in the middle of our conversation* **(d)** to stop electricity or water from reaching someone; *he didn't pay the bill, so the company cut off his electricity*; *the lightning hit the generator and caused the power to be cut off*

cutoff ['kʌtɒf] *noun* **cutoff point** = point which marks the end of something; *the cutoff point for students* going to the next level is 80% marks in the exam; *what is the cutoff date for applications?*

cut out ['kʌt 'aʊt] *verb* **(a)** to remove a small piece by cutting it from a large piece (of paper, etc.); *she cut an advertisement out of the newspaper*; *he used a pair of scissors to cut out the picture* **(b)** to stop doing or eating something; *she's decided to cut out sweet things so as to lose weight* **(c)** to be cut out for = to be ideally suited for; *I don't think he's cut out for a job in the post office*

cut-price ['kʌt 'praɪs] *adjective* sold at a cheaper price than usual; *supermarkets attract customers with cut-price petrol*; **cut-price store** = store selling goods at cheaper prices

cutter ['kʌtə] *noun* **(a)** person who cuts; *the cutter said he could cut my piece of glass to any size I wanted* **(b)** machine which cuts; *you need a tile cutter to cut your tiles to fit the corners* **(c)** small, fast boat; *the pilot arrived in a cutter*

cutters ['kʌtəz] *noun* **a pair of cutters** = pair of sharp scissors used for cutting; *a pair of wire cutters will be useful if we need to get through the fence* (NOTE: no singular)

cutting ['kʌtɪŋ] **1** *noun* **(a)** small piece of paper cut out of a newspaper; **press cuttings** = references to a person or thing cut out of newspapers or magazines; *she has a file of press cuttings on her son* **(b)** little piece of a plant which will take root if stuck in the ground; *the cuttings I took from your lavender plant are all growing well* **2** *adjective* **cutting remark** = sharply critical remark

cutting edge ['kʌtɪŋ 'edʒ] *noun* **(a)** the sharp edge of a knife; *the cutting edge is blunt and needs sharpening* **(b)** at the cutting edge of = right at the front of; *the company is at the cutting edge of new technology*

cut up ['kʌt 'ʌp] **1** *verb* **(a)** to make into small pieces by cutting; *she cut the old towel up into little pieces*; *can you cut up the meat for the children?* **(b)** (*informal*) to drive suddenly in front of another car; *did you see how the little white car cut up the black Audi?* **2** *adjective* (*informal*) upset, annoyed; *she's rather cut up because her cat has disappeared*

CV *or* **cv** [siː'viː] *noun* = CURRICULUM VITAE; *please apply in writing, enclosing a current CV*; *please enclose a CV with your application form*

cwt   ['hʌndrədweɪt]   *abbreviation*   *for* HUNDREDWEIGHT

cyanide ['saɪənaɪd] *noun* strong poison; *we put cyanide bait down to kill the rats*

cyclamen ['sɪkləmən] *noun* small pot plant growing from a corm, with flowers whose petals turn back near the centre

cycle ['saɪkl] **1** *noun* **(a)** bicycle; *if your bike's got a flat tyre, take it to the cycle shop*; **cycle path** = special path for cyclists; *there are thousands of cycle paths in Holland* **(b)** period during which something develops and then returns to its starting point; *global warming is starting to affect the natural cycle of the seasons*; *the washing machine broke down in the middle of the spin cycle*; **business cycle** *or* **economic cycle** *or* **trade cycle** = period during which trade expands, then slows down, then expands again; **life cycle** = life of an animal or plant from birth to death, which is repeated by the next generation **2** *verb* to go on a bicycle; *it's hard cycling against the wind*; *he thinks nothing of cycling ten miles to work every day*

cyclical *or* **cyclic** ['sɪklɪkl] *adjective* which happen in cycles; *the cyclical nature of the seasons*

cycling ['saɪklɪŋ] *noun* sport or activity of riding a bicycle; *to go on a cycling holiday*

cyclist ['saɪklɪst] *noun* person who rides a bicycle; *the police told the crowds to stand back as the cyclists were passing*

cyclone ['saɪkləʊn] *noun* **(a)** area of low pressure, usually associated with bad weather; *compare* ANTICYCLONE **(b)** tropical storm in the Indian Ocean and Pacific, where the air moves very fast in a circle round a central area; *according to the shipping forecasts, a cyclone is approaching Hong Kong* (NOTE: in the Far East this is called a **typhoon;** in the Caribbean a **hurricane**)

cygnet ['sɪgnət] *noun* baby swan; *these cygnets are almost as big as their parents but still have their grey feathers*

cylinder ['sɪlɪndə] *noun* **(a)** object shaped like a round tube closed at both ends; **gas cylinder** = metal tube containing gas; *the divers carried oxygen cylinders on their backs* **(b)** part of an engine, in which a piston moves; *the engine seems to lack power - maybe it's not firing on all six cylinders*

cylindrical [sɪ'lɪndrɪkl] *adjective* shaped like a cylinder; *soup tins are always cylindrical but corned beef tins are usually rectangular*

cymbals ['sɪmbəlz] *noun* pair of round metal plates which are banged together to make a loud noise; *she has to clash the cymbals at the end of the piece of music* (NOTE: do not confuse with **symbols**)

cynic ['sɪnɪk] *noun* person who doubts that anyone has any good points; *he's a cynic and doesn't think any government can do anything right*

cynical ['sɪnɪkl] *adjective* doubting if anyone is good; *don't be so cynical - I believe him when he says he didn't do it; it was a nice thing to do, but I'm a bit cynical about his motives for doing it*

cynicism ['sɪnɪsɪzm] *noun* being cynical; *he is always being accused of cynicism, but in fact he is often right*

cypher ['saɪfə] *see* CIPHER

cypress ['saɪprəs] *noun* type of evergreen tree of the Mediterranean region; *most houses in the south of France have cypresses in their gardens* (NOTE: plural is **cypresses**)

Cypriot ['sɪpriət] **1** *adjective* referring to Cyprus **2** *noun* person from Cyprus

Cyprus ['saɪprəs] *noun* country in the eastern Mediterranean, formed of a large island (NOTE: capital: **Nicosia;** people: **Cypriots;** language: **Greek;** currency: **Cyprus pound**)

cyst [sɪst] *noun* abnormal growth in the body containing liquid; *my cousin had a cyst removed from the back of his neck*

cystic fibrosis ['sɪstɪk faɪ'brəʊsɪs] *noun* disease of the pancreas, a hereditary disease in which the breathing and digestion are difficult; *cystic fibrosis runs in families but is not a common disease and can be controlled by vitamins and enzymes*

cystitis [sɪs'taɪtɪs] *noun* infection of the bladder which gives a burning sensation when you pass water;

you are recommended to drink cranberry juice if you have cystitis

czar [zɑː] *noun* **(a)** *US* title of the emperor of Russia; *a photograph of the Czar and his family* (NOTE: the British spelling in this meaning is **tsar**) **(b)** person in overall charge of some official organization; *he's the new drugs czar, with complete responsibility for fighting drug traffickers and dealing with drug problems*

Czech [tʃek] **1** *adjective* referring to the Czech Republic **2** *noun* **(a)** person from the Czech Republic; *three Czechs came to visit our office* **(b)** language spoken in the Czech Republic; *if you're going to work in Prague, you will need to take a course in Czech; she speaks Czech quite well*

Czech Republic [ˈtʃek rɪˈpʌblɪk] *noun* country in central Europe, east of Germany and north of Austria (NOTE: capital: **Prague;** people: **the Czechs;** language: **Czech;** currency: **koruna)**

Dd

D, d [di:] fourth letter of the alphabet, between C and E; *you don't spell 'riding' with two d's*

DA ['di: 'eɪ] = DISTRICT ATTORNEY

dab [dæb] **1** *verb* to give something a light tap; *she dabbed her eyes with her handkerchief; she dabbed the cut with cotton wool soaked in antiseptic*; **to dab something on** = to apply by pressing lightly; *you can dab the paint on with a little brush* (NOTE: **dabbing - dabbed**) **2** *noun* **(a)** small quantity; *she put a dab of glue on each corner of the poster* **(b)** little tap; *the nurse gave the cut a dab with some cotton wool* **(c)** type of small flat fish

dabble ['dæbl] *verb* **(a) to dabble with** *or* **in** = to be slightly involved in; *as a young man he dabbled in politics* **(b)** to play around with your hands or feet in water; *the children dabbled their toes in the brook*

dab hand ['dæb 'hænd] *noun (informal)* person who is skilful at something; *he's a dab hand at poker; she's a dab hand at making sandwiches*

daddy *or* **dad** ['dædi or dæd] *noun* child's name for father; *Hi Daddy! look at my exam results!; my dad has bought me a new bike*; compare MUM, MUMMY

daffodil ['dæfədɪl] *noun* bright yellow spring flower; *she planted some daffodil bulbs; he brought her a bunch of daffodils*

daft [dɑːft] *adjective (informal)* silly; *don't be daft - you can't put a plastic dish in the oven!; what a daft thing to do!; it must be the daftest idea that the government has come up with yet* (NOTE: **dafter - daftest)**

dagger ['dægə] *noun* short knife; *she was stabbed with a dagger*; **at daggers drawn** = bitterly hostile; *the MD is at daggers drawn with the rest of the directors*; **to look daggers at someone** = to look angrily at someone

dahlia ['deɪliə] *noun* brightly coloured garden flower; *we have a bed of dahlias in our front garden*

daily ['deɪli] **1** *adjective* happening every day; *daily newspapers such as 'The Times' and 'Daily Mail'; the cooker has been in daily use for ten years; there's a daily flight to Washington* **2** *noun* newspaper published every weekday; *the story was carried on the front page of most of the dailies* (NOTE: plural is **dailies)**

dainty ['deɪnti] *adjective* delicate and small; *the baby has dainty little fingers and toes; she served the cream from a dainty porcelain jug* (NOTE: **daintier - daintiest)**

dairy ['deəri] *noun* place where milk, cream and butter are processed or sold; *you can buy butter and cheese from the dairy*; **dairy farm** = farm which produces milk, cheese, etc.; **dairy produce** = milk, butter, cream, etc. (NOTE: plural is **dairies)**

daisy ['deɪzi] *noun* small white and yellow flower; *the lawn was covered with daisies (informal)* **as fresh as a daisy** = very fresh, not tired; *she was at a party all night, but still came into the office this morning fresh as a daisy* (NOTE: plural is **daisies)**

dam [dæm] **1** *noun* wall of earth or concrete which blocks a river to make a lake; *after the rainstorm people were afraid the dam would burst* **2** *verb* to block a river with a wall of earth or concrete; *when they built the power station, the river had to be dammed* (NOTE: **damming - dammed)**

damage ['dæmɪdʒ] **1** *noun* **(a)** harm (done to things not to people); *the storm did a lot of damage; it will take us months to repair the damage to the restaurant; the fire caused damage estimated at £100,000*; **fire damage** = damage caused by a fire; **flood damage** = damage caused by a flood; **storm damage** = damage caused by a storm; **to suffer damage** = to be harmed; *the car suffered serious damage in the collision* (NOTE: no plural in this meaning) **(b) damages** = payment to someone who has been hurt or whose property has been damaged; *the accident victim claimed £200,000 in damages; after the accident, he sued the hospital for damages; the court awarded the girl damages against the driver of the car* **2** *verb* to harm something; *a large number of shops were damaged in the fire; glasses need to be packed carefully as they are easily damaged*

dame [deɪm] *noun* **(a)** *(in a pantomime)* old woman (played by a man); *the dame was played by a famous boxer* **(b)** US *(informal)* woman; *who's that dame I saw you with last night?* **(c)** title given to women; *she was made a dame in the New Year's honours' list* (NOTE: equivalent to 'Sir' for men; when used as a title, it is written before the woman's Christian name, followed by the surname: **Dame Sybil Thorndike)**

dammit ['dæmɪt] *noun (informal)* **as near as dammit** = very near; *he made £10,000, or as near as dammit*

damn [dæm] **1** *noun (informal)* **I don't give a damn** = I don't care about it at all **2** *verb* **(a)** *(informal)* used to show annoyance; *damn it, we're going to be late; damn him, he's left the front door open!* **(b)** to condemn; to curse; *the new film was damned by the Sunday papers; Galileo was damned by the Church for saying that the Earth turned round the Sun*; **I'll be damned if I'll allow her to do that** = I will certainly never let her do that **3** *interjection (informal)* used to show annoyance; *damn! I've left my umbrella on the train*

damned ['dæmd] *adjective (informal)* very annoying; *that damned woman is always on the phone; he's got a damned nerve, just walking into my room without knocking*; **I'll try my damnedest to get to the meeting** = I'll do everything I can to get to the meeting

damning ['dæmɪŋ] *adjective* which clearly proves that someone has done something wrong; *the prosecution produced some really damning evidence*

damp [dæmp] **1** *adjective* rather wet; *she'd just had a shower and her hair was still damp; the cellar has cold damp walls* (NOTE: **damper - dampest)** **2** *noun* moisture in the air, on a surface; *the damp makes my* *rheumatism worse*; **rising damp** = damp which enters the walls of houses and damages them (NOTE: no plural)

dampen ['dæmpən] *verb* to make slightly wet; *dampen the cloth before you wipe the floor*; *she dampened the shirts before ironing them*

dance [dɑːns] **1** *noun* **(a)** way of moving in time to music; *she teaches dance or she's a dance teacher*; *we learnt a new dance today* **(b)** evening entertainment for a group of people where you can dance; *the club is holding a New Year's dance*; *they met at a youth club dance*; **dance floor** = specially polished floor for dancing on **2** *verb* **(a)** to move in time to music; *there he is - he's dancing with that tall girl*; *she often goes to discos but never dances* **(b)** to move or jump around happily; *she danced into the room and announced she's got the job*; *the football fans were dancing in the streets*

dancer ['dɑːnsə] *noun* person who dances; *she trained as a dancer*; *the dancers hold hands and form a circle*; **ballet dancer** = person who dances in ballet

dancing ['dɑːnsɪŋ] *noun* action of moving to music; *she teaches dancing*; *she goes to dancing classes*; *she's taking dancing lessons* (NOTE: no plural)

dandelion ['dændɪlaɪən] *noun* wild plant, with yellow flowers that have a mass of little narrow petals; *there are hundreds of dandelions all over our lawn*; **dandelion clock** = the mass of little seeds like a fluffy white ball on top of a dandelion

COMMENT: children blow the seeds off the dandelion, and count as they blow: either seeing when something will happen in the future, saying 'this year, next year, sometime, never', or seeing whether someone loves you: 'loves me, loves me not'. The words said when the last seeds are blown off indicate what will happen

dandruff ['dændrʌf] *noun* small pieces of dry skin which come off your head; *he brushed the dandruff off his collar*; **anti-dandruff shampoo** = specially medicated shampoo which is supposed to cure dandruff (NOTE: no plural)

dandy ['dændi] *noun* man who is very interested in clothes; *he's a bit of a dandy, with his stiff collars and wide pink ties* (NOTE: plural is **dandies**)

Dane [deɪn] *noun* person from Denmark; *Danes are often tall and blond*; *see also* GREAT DANE

danger ['deɪnʒə] *noun* possibility of damage, failure, getting hurt, etc.; *when it rains, there's a danger of flooding*; *the broken window is a danger to office security*; *there's a danger we won't get there in time*; *we were warned of the dangers of travelling alone in the desert*; **danger money** = payment for a dangerous job; *the workers said the job was very dangerous and asked for danger money*; **out of danger** *or* **off the danger list** = not likely to die; *she was very ill, but she's off the danger list now*

◊ **in danger** ['ɪn 'deɪnʒə] *phrase* likely to be harmed; *get an ambulance - her life is in danger*; *I don't think he's in any danger*; *the whole building was in danger of catching fire*

dangerous ['deɪnʒərəs] *adjective* which can cause injury or damage; *be careful - that old staircase is dangerous!*; *those electric wires are dangerous*; *children are warned that it is dangerous to go out alone at night*

dangle ['dæŋgl] *verb* **(a)** to hang limply; *the fish dangled at the end of his line*; *dirty sheets were dangling over the balcony* **(b)** to make something hang limply; *she dangled the puppet in front of the baby*

Danish ['deɪnɪʃ] **1** *adjective* referring to Denmark; **Danish pastry** = sweet pastry cake with jam or fruit folded in it (NOTE: also called simply **Danish: an apple Danish**) **2** *noun* language spoken in Denmark

dank [dæŋk] *adjective* cold and damp; *the prisoners were kept in a dank dark dungeon*

dare ['deə] **1** *verb* **(a)** to be brave enough to do something; *I bet you wouldn't dare put your hand into the cage and stroke that tiger*; **I dare say** = very probably; *I dare say you're right* **(b)** *(negative)* *I dare not go out into the street or I don't dare go out into the street while that man is standing there* **(c)** to challenge someone to do something by suggesting it is cowardly not to do it; *I dared him to go the meeting in his pink tracksuit* **2** *noun* act of challenging someone to do something; *he only climbed on the roof for a dare*

daredevil ['deədevəl] **1** *adjective* not worrying about danger; *his daredevil act on the tightrope* **2** *noun* brave person who does not worry about danger; *he's a daredevil - he flew his plane under Tower Bridge*

daring ['deərɪŋ] **1** *adjective* brave, but foolish at the same time; *that was a very daring thing to do*; *it was very daring of you to ask the boss for the day off* **2** *noun* bravery; *the helicopter pilot showed great daring in trying to rescue the boy from the cliff* (NOTE: no plural)

dark [dɑːk] **1** *adjective* **(a)** with little or no light; *the sky turned dark and it started to rain*; *can you switch the light on - it's getting too dark to see*; *in Scotland in the summer it gets dark very late* **(b)** not a light colour; *her eyes are dark*; *she was wearing a dark blue coat*; **a dark horse** = someone who may succeed unexpectedly **(c)** with black or brown hair; *he's quite dark, but his sister has red hair* (NOTE: **darker - darkest**) **2** *noun* **(a)** absence of light; *little children are afraid of the dark*; *they say cats can see in the dark*; **in the dark**, *everything looks different*; **after dark** = at nighttime; *you must put on your car lights after dark* **(b)** **in the dark** = not knowing anything about something; *I'm completely in the dark about the whole business*; *we want to keep everyone in the dark about our plans*

darken ['dɑːkən] *verb* to become dark; *the sky was darkening and we all ran indoors before the rain came*

darkened ['dɑːknd] *adjective* which has been made dark; *he was made to sit in a darkened room*

dark-haired ['dɑːk'heəd] *adjective* with dark hair; *although she is fair herself, all her children are dark-haired*

darkness ['dɑːknəs] *noun* not having any light; *the cat's eyes glowed in the darkness*; *the sun had set and the darkness was closing in*; **the building was in complete darkness** *or* **in total darkness** = there were no electric lights on in the building (NOTE: no plural)

darkroom ['dɑːkruːm] *noun* room with a special red light, in which you can develop and print films; *don't open the door - he's working in the darkroom*

darling ['dɑːlɪŋ] **1** *adjective* lovable, which you can love; *what a darling little car!* **2** *noun* **(a)** name used to talk to someone you love; *Darling! I'm back from the shops* **(b)** lovable person; *she's an absolute darling!*; *be a darling and fetch me the newspaper*

darn [dɑːn] **1** *verb* to mend holes in clothes; *she was darning some socks when the police came* **2** *noun* place where clothes have been mended; *you can easily see the darns because you used a different colour wool*

dart [dɑːt] **1** *noun* small heavy arrow with plastic feathers, used for playing the game of darts; *each player takes turn to throw his three darts* **2** *verb* to rush; *the little boy darted across the street*; *we sat by the river and watched the dragonflies darting about in the rushes*

dartboard [ˈdɑːtbɔːd] *noun* round board which you throw darts at; *he missed the dartboard altogether and the dart stuck in the ceiling*

COMMENT: the board is made of cork, and is divided up into 20 segments radiating out from the centre like a bicycle wheel; the segments are numbered but always alternate between an odd and even number, with a higher number usually next to a lower one: so, for example, the segment with 20 at the top of the board is flanked by the segments with 5 and 1. The centre of the board is a small red circle (the 'bull') which is worth 50 points; it is surrounded by a slightly larger circle, worth 25 points; halfway out from the bull is another ring that trebles the score of the segment the dart lands in, and a similar ring at the edge of the board doubles the score

darts [dɑːts] *noun* game for two or more people, played by each player throwing three darts in turn at a round dartboard; *they had a game of darts*; *I'm not very good at darts*; *he plays darts every evening in the pub* (NOTE: not plural, and takes a singular verb)

COMMENT: games often have to start and finish with a player throwing a double (hitting the narrow outer ring round the edge of the board) although players in tournaments start with 501 points and deduct from it the score their three darts make without having to hit a double; the highest possible score with three darts is 180 (treble 20 three times) and the object is to finish on a double having used fewer darts than your opponent

dash [dæʃ] **1** *noun* **(a)** small amount; *a tomato juice with a dash of sauce* **(b)** little written line; *the reference number is one four six dash seven (146-7)* **(c)** sudden rush; *there was a mad dash to buy tickets*; *while the policeman wasn't looking she made a dash for the door* (NOTE: plural is **dashes**) **2** *verb* to rush; *I can't stop now - I must dash to catch the last post*; *I dashed home to watch the football on television*; *she dashed into a shop so that he wouldn't see her*

dashboard [ˈdæʃbɔːd] *noun* instrument panel in a car; *the dashboard is covered with a polished wood veneer*

dashing [ˈdæʃɪŋ] *adjective* very smart and forceful; *he looked very dashing in cream trousers and a blazer*; *she married a dashing young naval officer*

data [ˈdeɪtə] *noun* statistical information; *the data is stored in our main computer*; *we spent months gathering data on hospital waiting times*; *the data shows that, on average, germination takes place after two weeks*; **data bank** = store of computerized information; **data protection** = making sure that computerized information about people does not get into the wrong hands (NOTE: **data** is usually singular: **the data is easily available**)

database [ˈdeɪtəbeɪs] *noun* data stored in a computer, which can be used to provide information of various kinds; *we can extract the lists of potential customers from our database*; *I'll just add your details to our customer database*

data processing [ˈdeɪtə ˈprəʊsesɪŋ] *noun* selecting and examining data in a computer to produce special information; *the data processing manager*

date [deɪt] **1** *noun* **(a)** number of a day in a month or year (when something happened); *put today's date on the cheque*; *what's the date next Wednesday?*; *the dates of the exhibition have been changed*; *the date of the next meeting has been fixed for Wednesday, June 10th*; *do you remember the date of your girlfriend's birthday?*; **date of birth** = date on which someone was born; *please write your date and place of birth on the registration form*; **arrival date** *or* **date of arrival** = day on which you arrive; **departure date** *or* **date of departure** = day on which you leave **(b)** time agreed for a meeting, usually between a boy and a girl; *we made a date to meet at the Italian restaurant*; *he asked her out for a date*; **blind date** = meeting arranged between two people who have never met before **(c)** small sweet brown fruit of the date palm; **date palm** = a tall tropical tree with very large leaves and sweet fruit **2** *verb* **(a)** to write the date on something; *the cheque was dated the 15th of June*; *you forgot to date the cheque* **(b) to date from** = to exist since; *this house dates from or dates back to the seventeenth century* **(c)** *especially US* to agree to meet someone of the opposite sex regularly; *he's dating my sister*

◊ **out of date** [ˈaʊt əv ˈdeɪt] without recent information; *this guidebook is out of date*; *the information is two years out of date*

◊ **up to date** [ˈʌp tə ˈdeɪt] containing very recent information; *the new telephone directory is completely up to date*; *he is bringing the guidebook up to date*; **to keep someone up to date on** *or* **with something** = to tell someone all the latest information about something; *while I'm on holiday, you must keep me up to date on what goes on at the office*

dated [ˈdeɪtɪd] *adjective* **(a)** with a date written on it; *thank you for your letter dated June 15th* **(b)** old-fashioned; *that advertisement looks a bit dated now*

date line [ˈdeɪt ˈlaɪn] *noun* imaginary line (in the Pacific Ocean) which marks the change in date from east to west

daughter [ˈdɔːtə] *noun* girl child of a parent; *they have two sons and one daughter*; *my daughter Mary goes to the local school*

daughter-in-law [ˈdɔːtərɪnlɔː] *noun* wife of a son; *my daughter-in-law teaches at our local school* (NOTE: plural is **daughters-in-law**)

daunt [dɔːnt] *verb* to discourage, to frighten; *aren't you a bit daunted by the amount of work involved?*; **nothing daunted** = not frightened at all; *he saw the crocodile and, nothing daunted, continued to walk along the river bank*

daunting [ˈdɔːntɪŋ] *adjective* which seems very difficult; *it's a daunting task, counting ballot papers*

dawdle [ˈdɔːdl] *verb* to do something slowly; *don't let the children dawdle on their way to the bus stop*; *I didn't have time to dawdle over a cup of coffee - I had a train to catch*

dawn [dɔːn] **1** *noun* beginning of a day, when the sun rises; *we must set off for the Pyramids at dawn, so you'll have to get up very early*; **at the crack of dawn** = as soon as it starts to be light; *the plane leaves at 6.30 a.m. - it means I'll have to get up at the crack of dawn* **2** *verb* **(a)** *(of day)* to begin; *the day of the cricket match dawned wet and windy* **(b)** **it dawned on him that** = he began to realize that; *it gradually dawned on him that someone else was going to get the job he had applied for*

day [deɪ] *noun* **(a)** period of time lasting 24 hours; *there are 365 days in a year and 366 in a leap year*; *New Year's Day is January 1st*; *they went on a ten-day tour of Southern Spain*; *I spoke to him on the phone the day before yesterday*; *we are planning to meet the day after tomorrow*; **what day is it today?** = is it Monday, Tuesday, etc. **(b)** **every other day** = every two days (i.e., on Monday, Wednesday, Friday, etc.); *he phones his mother every other day*; **the other day** = quite recently; *the other day I went for a walk by the river*; **one day** *or* **some day** = at some time in the future; *one day we'll have enough money to go on holiday* **(c)** period from morning until night, when it is light; *he works all day in the office, and then helps his wife with the children in the evening*; *it took the workmen four days to build the wall*; **day tour** *or* **day excursion** *or* **day trip** = tour *or* excursion which leaves in the morning and returns the same evening **(d)** work period from morning to night; **she took two days off** = she did not come to work for two days; **he works three days on, two days off** = he works for three days, then has two days' holiday; **to work an eight-hour day** = to spend eight hours at work each day; **to work a four-day week** = to work four days each week **(e)** **days** = time in the past; *in the days of Henry VIII kings were very powerful*; **those were the days** = they were good times we had in the past; *do you remember spending all night going round the bars in Hamburg? - ah! those were the days!*

◊ **a day** [ə 'deɪ] every day; *an apple a day keeps the doctor away*; *you should drink a litre of water a day*

◊ **all day** ['ɔːl 'deɪ] the whole day; *it's been raining hard all day*

day care ['deɪ 'keə] *noun* looking after small children during the daytime in a special centre; *now she has gone back to work, she takes her little girls to the day care centre every morning*

daydream ['deɪdriːm] **1** *noun* dream which you have during the day when you are not asleep; *he was sitting in a daydream, with the guidebook on his lap* **2** *verb* to think about other things; not to concentrate; *he was sitting at his desk daydreaming about holidays in Greece*

daylight ['deɪlaɪt] *noun* light during the daytime; *three men robbed the bank in broad daylight* (NOTE: no plural)

day release ['deɪ rɪ'liːs] *noun* system where a worker is allowed time from work to attend a course of study; *she's been sent on a day release course for hotel managers*

daytime ['deɪtaɪm] *noun* period of light between morning and night; *I watched a lot of daytime television when I lost my job*; **during** *or* **in the daytime** = when it is light; *he sleeps during the daytime because he works at night* (NOTE: no plural)

day-to-day ['deɪtə'deɪ] *adjective* normal, taking place as part of normal existence; which goes on all the time; *he has been put in charge of the day-to-day running of the school*

daze [deɪz] **1** *noun* **in a daze** = confused, not mentally alert; *he stumbled out of the room in a daze*; *he was wandering around in an alcoholic daze* (NOTE: no plural) **2** *verb* to make someone confused; *he was dazed by the news that he had won the lottery*

dazed ['deɪzd] *adjective* confused in the mind; *she was found walking about in a dazed condition*; *she looked dazed when she heard the news*

dazzle ['dæzl] **1** *noun* bright light; *the dazzle of the headlights on the wet road caused the driver to swerve* (NOTE: no plural) **2** *verb* to blind for a moment; *she was dazzled by the lights of the cars coming towards her*

dazzling ['dæzlɪŋ] *adjective* very bright (light); *she covered her eyes against the dazzling sunlight*

dble = DOUBLE

DC = DIRECT CURRENT

deacon ['diːkən] *noun* priest who is lower in rank than a parish priest; *he has been appointed deacon in a parish in the east of the country*

dead [ded] **1** *adjective* **(a)** not alive any more; *his parents are both dead*; *dead fish were floating in the water*; *he brushed the dead leaves into piles*; *six people were dead as a result of the accident*; *(informal)* **wouldn't be seen dead in** = would not ever want to be seen in; *I wouldn't be seen dead in a hat like that*; *a really cultivated person wouldn't be seen dead in a karaoke bar*; *(informal)* **as dead as a dodo** = completely dead, not longer workable; *the plan is as dead as a dodo now that the banks have refused their support*; **to drop dead** = to die suddenly; *he dropped dead in the middle of the High Street* **(b)** complete; *there was dead silence in the exam room*; *the train came to a dead stop* **(c)** not working; **the line went dead** = the telephone line suddenly stopped working; *I was talking on the phone when suddenly the line went dead* **2** *adverb* **(a)** completely; *he was dead tired after his long walk* **(b)** exactly; *you're dead right*; *the train arrived dead on time* **3** *noun* **(a)** **the dead** = dead people; *a memorial to the dead of the two world wars* **(b)** **the dead of night** = the middle of the night; *he woke up in the dead of night and thought he heard footsteps*

dead beat ['ded 'biːt] *(informal)* **1** *adjective* tired out; *I was dead beat after moving all those boxes of books* **2** *noun* lazy, unsuccessful person, who has no money

deaden ['dedən] *verb* to make something less intense, to make a sound quieter, a pain less painful, etc.; *the doctor gave her an injection to deaden the pain*; *the double-glazing helps to deaden the sound of the traffic*

dead end ['ded 'end] *noun* **(a)** street or way which leads nowhere; *we drove into a little street and found it was a dead end* **(b)** point when you can go no further; *all their research has come to a dead end*; **dead-end job** = job where there is not hope of promotion; *he ended up in a dead-end job in the packing department*

dead heat ['ded 'hiːt] *noun* race where two people arrive first together; *the 400 metres was a dead heat*; *there was a dead heat for first place*

deadline ['dedlaɪn] *noun* date by which something has to be done; *we've been given an October deadline to finish the job*; **to meet a deadline** = to finish something in time; *I don't think we can meet the deadline*; **to miss a deadline** = not to finish something in time; *they worked as fast as they could but missed the deadline by two days*

deadlock ['dedlɒk] **1** *noun* point where two sides in a dispute cannot agree; *the negotiations have reached a deadlock*; **to break a deadlock** = to find a way to start discussions again after being at a point where no agreement was possible **2** *verb* to be unable to agree to continue negotiations; *talks have been deadlocked for ten days*

deadly ['dedli] *adjective* **(a)** which will kill; *don't eat those mushrooms - they're deadly poisonous*; *the female spider is deadlier than the male* **(b)** very serious or bitter; *they are deadly rivals*; *he was deadly serious* (NOTE: **deadlier - deadliest**)

deaf [def] **1** *adjective* (person) who cannot hear, who has difficulty in hearing; *the old lady is going deaf*; *he's deafer than he used to be*; **stone deaf** = completely deaf (NOTE: **deafer - deafest**) **2** *noun* **the deaf** = people who cannot hear; *their son goes to a school for the deaf*

deafen ['defən] *verb* to make someone deaf for a time; *he was deafened by the explosion*

deafening ['defənɪŋ] *adjective* so loud as to make you deaf; *there was a deafening crack of thunder*; *there was a sudden deafening noise in the street*

deafness ['defnəs] *noun* state of being deaf; *his deafness only came on gradually* (NOTE: no plural)

deal [diːl] **1** *noun* **(a) a good deal** *or* **a great deal** = much; *he's feeling a good deal better after two days off work*; *she didn't say a great deal*; **a good deal of** *or* **a great deal of** = a lot of; *he made a good deal of money from his business*; *there's a great deal of work still to be done* **(b)** business affair, agreement, contract; *we've signed a deal with a German firm*; *they did a deal to supply envelopes*; *the sales director set up a deal with a Russian bank*; **bad deal** *or* **rough deal** *or* **raw deal** = bad treatment; *she got a rough deal from the firm*; **package deal** = agreement where several different items are agreed at the same time **2** *verb* **(a) to deal in** = to buy and sell; *she deals in carpets and rugs imported from India* **(b)** to hand out cards to players; *it's my turn to deal*; *he dealt me two aces* (NOTE: **dealing - dealt** [delt])

dealer ['diːlə] *noun* person who buys and sells; *a secondhand car dealer*; *an antiques dealer*; **drug dealer** = person who sells illegal drugs to other people

dealership ['diːləʃɪp] *noun* **(a)** authorization to sell certain products or services; *he was granted a dealership for Ford cars* **(b)** business run by an authorized dealer; *he has a large car dealership*

dealings ['diːlɪŋz] *noun* business, affairs; *I've had dealings with that company*

deal with ['diːl 'wɪð] *verb* to concern yourself with, to handle; *the job involves dealing with the public*; *leave it to the filing clerk - he'll deal with it*; *we will deal with your order as soon as we can*; *the government has to deal with the problem of teenage crime*

dean [diːn] *noun* **(a)** person in charge of priests in a cathedral; *he was appointed the Dean of St Paul's* **(b)** person in charge of teachers at a university; *the Dean of the Arts Faculty*

dear [dɪə] **1** *adjective* **(a)** well liked, loved; *she's a very dear friend of mine*; *we had a letter from dear old Mrs Smith* **(b)** *(used at the beginning of a letter)* **Dear Sir** *or* **Dear Madam** = addressing a man or woman whom you do not know, or addressing a company; **Dear Sirs** = addressing a company; **Dear Mr Smith** *or* **Dear Mrs Smith** *or* **Dear Miss Smith** = addressing a man or woman whom you know; **Dear James** *or* **Dear Julia** = addressing a friend or a person you do business with **(c)** costing a lot of money; *fresh fruit is always dearer in the winter*; *that restaurant is too dear for me* (NOTE: **dearer - dearest**) **2** *interjection (meaning how annoying)* **oh dear! it's started to rain**; *dear me! is that how late it is!* **3** *noun* (way of referring to someone you like) **be a dear, and pass me my glasses**; *did you have a good day at the office, dear?*; **old dears** = old people (NOTE: do not confuse with **deer**)

dearest ['dɪərəst] *noun see* NEAREST AND DEAREST

dearly ['dɪəli] *adverb* **(a)** very much; *I'd dearly like to go to Cuba on holiday*; *she loved her old cat dearly, and was very sad when he died* **(b)** at a high cost, in terms of pain, suffering, etc.; *she became a highly paid executive, but paid dearly for the privilege*

dearth [dɜːθ] *noun* shortage of something; *there is a dearth of good restaurants near here*

death [deθ] *noun* **(a)** act of dying; *she never got over her mother's death*; *road accidents caused over 1,000 deaths last year*; **US death duty** = tax paid on the value of the things left by a dead person (NOTE: the British equivalent is **inheritance tax**); **death rate** = percentage of deaths per thousand of population; *the region has a death rate of 15 per thousand*; *an increase in the death rate due to accidents* **(b)** *(informal)* **to death** = completely; *I'm bored to death sitting watching football on television*; *she's sick to death of always having to do the housework*

deathly ['deθli] **1** *adverb* as if dead; *as she read the letter she turned deathly pale* **2** *adjective* like death; *he gave a cheery 'hello there!' as he walked in, only to be greeted by a deathly silence*

death row ['deθ 'rəʊ] *noun US* section of a prison for convicts who have been sentenced to death; *he spent ten months on death row waiting for his appeal to be decided*; *compare* CONDEMNED CELL

death sentence ['deθ 'sentəns] *noun* punishment of a court by which a person is sentenced to be executed; *the death sentence was carried out immediately*

death squad ['deθ 'skwɒd] *noun* group of soldiers or other armed people, who are sent to kill enemies of the people in power; *death squads roamed the streets at night*

death toll ['deθ 'təʊl] *noun* number of people who have been killed in an accident, an earthquake, etc.; *the death toll in the floods has risen to 25 as more bodies have been found*

débâcle [deɪ'bɑːkl] *noun* sudden defeat or collapse; *the negotiations ended in a complete débâcle*; *the party is trying recover from the débâcle of their election defeat*

debatable [dɪˈbeɪtəbl] *adjective* not absolutely certain; *it is debatable whether eating less fat is really good for you*

debate [dɪˈbeɪt] **1** *noun* formal discussion; *the Prime Minister spoke in the Commons debate on capital punishment; after his talk the professor had a lively debate with the students; there has been some debate among experts about whether global warming is really taking place* **2** *verb* to discuss; *we sat in the rain and debated what to do next; the House will debate proportional representation next week*

debilitate [dɪˈbɪlɪteɪt] *verb* to make weak; *he was debilitated by a long illness*

debilitating [dɪˈbɪlɪteɪtɪŋ] *adjective* which makes you weak; *he suffered from a debilitating illness*

debit [ˈdebɪt] **1** *noun* (money) which is owed; *a debit balance*; **debit card** = plastic card, similar to a credit card, but which automatically debits your account when you buy something; **debit side** = left-hand side of an account showing money owing to other people; **direct debit** *see* DIRECT **2** *verb* **to debit money to an account** *or* **to debit an account with money** = to deduct money from an account; *the whole bill was debited to my account; my account was debited with the whole bill*

debris [ˈdebriː] *noun* pieces of a demolished building, crashed aircraft, etc.; *debris from the crash littered the ground; she was hit by flying debris* (NOTE: no plural)

debt [det] *noun* money owed to someone; *her debts are mounting up*; **to be in debt** = to owe money; *he is in debt to the tune of £2500*; **to get into debt** = to start to owe money; **to be out of debt** = not to owe money any more; *see also* IN THE RED; **debt collector** = person who collects money owed to other people

debtor [ˈdetə] *noun* person who owes money; *debtors will be allowed one month to pay off their debts*

debunk [dɪˈbʌŋk] *verb* (*informal*) to show that something is not true; *the professor's latest theory was debunked by one of his students*

debut [ˈdeɪbjuː] *noun* first appearance of an actor, etc.; *she made her debut on the stage in the role of Ophelia*

decade [ˈdekeɪd] *noun* period of ten years; *during the first decade of the 20th century*

decadent [ˈdekədent] *adjective* which is declining in moral values; *the decadent Berlin society of the 1920s*

decaff [ˈdiːkæf] *noun* (*informal*) = DECAFFEINATED COFFEE; *I asked for a decaff*

decaffeinated [diːkəˈfeɪneɪtɪd] *adjective* with all caffeine removed; *I drink decaffeinated coffee, because real coffee keeps me awake*

decal [ˈdiːkæl] *noun US* sticker, piece of plastic or paper with a pattern or slogan which you can stick to a surface as a decoration; *she stuck decals on the doors of her closet*

decamp [diːˈkæmp] *verb* (*informal*) to go away unexpectedly; *the manager decamped with thousands of pounds from the till*

decapitate [dɪˈkæpɪteɪt] *verb* to cut off someone's head; *he was sentenced to death and decapitated; she nearly decapitated herself with an electric saw*

decapitation [dɪkæpɪˈteɪʃn] *noun* act of cutting off someone's head; *in some countries decapitation is still the punishment for certain types of crime*

decathlete [dekˈæθliːt] *noun* athlete who competes in the decathlon

decathlon [dɪˈkæθlən] *noun* an athletic contest for men, covering ten events, held over two days

COMMENT: the sports covered are: **day one:** 100m race, long jump, shot put, high jump, 400m race; **day two:** 110m hurdles, discus, pole vault, javelin, 1500m race. Points are awarded according to the athlete's performance in each event. The equivalent for women is the heptathlon

decay [dɪˈkeɪ] **1** *noun* rotting, falling into ruin; *inner city decay; tooth decay; you must treat the wood to prevent decay* (NOTE: no plural) **2** *verb* to rot, to fall into ruin; *sugar makes your teeth decay; the jungle path was blocked by decaying branches*

deceased [dɪˈsiːst] *noun* (*formal*) person who has died; *the deceased's will was read out by the solicitor*

deceit [dɪˈsiːt] *noun* trying to trick someone into paying money or trying to make someone believe something which is not true; *he gained a lot of money through deceit* (NOTE: no plural)

deceitful [dɪˈsiːtful] *adjective* often tricking people; *she's really deceitful - you can never believe anything she says; dishonest or deceitful advertising is banned by law*

deceive [dɪˈsiːv] *verb* to trick someone, to make someone believe something which is not true; *he deceived everyone into thinking that he was a policeman*

decelerate [diːˈseləreɪt] *verb* (*of a vehicle*) to go slower; *the car suddenly decelerated; you should always decelerate before turning a corner*

deceleration [diːseləˈreɪʃn] *noun* action of going slower; *the sudden deceleration threw the passengers onto the floor*

December [dɪˈsembə] *noun* twelfth and last month of the year, after November and before January; *she was born in December; his birthday is December 25th - Christmas Day!; they always go on a skiing holiday in December; today is December 6th US December 6* (NOTE: **December 6th** *or* **December 6:** say 'the sixth of December' *or* 'December the sixth'; American English: 'December sixth')

decency [ˈdiːsənsi] *noun* honour; good morals; *he didn't have the decency to say he was sorry* (NOTE: no plural)

decent [ˈdiːsənt] *adjective* **(a)** honest; *the boss is a hard-working decent man* **(b)** quite good; *she earns a decent salary* **(c)** (*informal*) properly dressed, wearing clothes; *you can't come in - I'm not decent*

decentralize [diːˈsentrəlaɪz] *verb* to move power or authority or action from a central point to local areas; *the decision-making processes have been decentralized to organizations in each regional capital*

deception [dɪˈsepʃn] *noun* telling a lie in order to trick someone, especially into giving you money; *she obtained £10,000 by deception; he was accused of practising deception on a group of old people*

deceptive [dɪˈseptɪv] *adjective* not as it seems; *the distance to the church is deceptive - it is much farther away than you think*; **appearances are deceptive** = things are not always what they appear to be on the surface

deceptively [dɪ'septɪvli] *adverb* not as it seems; *walking a tightrope looks deceptively simple*

decibel ['desɪbel] *noun* degree of measurement of noise; *people living near the airport complained that the noise of aircraft overhead was well over the decibel limit*

decide [dɪ'saɪd] *verb* to make up your mind to do something; *have you decided which restaurant to go to?; they decided to stay at home and watch TV; she decided not to spend her money on a new car*

decide against [dɪ'saɪd ə'genst] *verb* to make up your mind not to do something; *we've decided against going to France this year*

decided [dɪ'saɪdɪd] *adjective* **(a) decided tone** *or* **decided manner** = firm tone *or* manner **(b)** certain, obvious; *there's a decided difference between French and Spanish wines*

decidedly [dɪ'saɪdɪdli] *adverb* **(a)** certainly; *he's decidedly fatter than he was before he went on holiday; it's decidedly colder this week* **(b)** in a firm manner; *'I'm not going with you', she said decidedly*

deciduous [dɪ'sɪdjuəs] *adjective* (tree) which loses its leaves in the winter; *the hills of southern England are covered with deciduous trees such as beeches and oaks* (NOTE: trees which keep their leaves all year round are called **evergreens**)

decimal ['desɪml] **1** *adjective* **decimal system** = system of counting based on the number 10 **2** *noun* fraction expressed as tenths, hundredths and thousandths; *three-quarters is 0.75 in decimals;* **to three places of decimals** *or* **to three decimal places** = with three figures shown after the decimal point; *67 divided by 13 gives 5.154 to three places of decimals*

decimal point ['desɪml 'pɔɪnt] *noun* dot used to show the division between whole numbers and parts of numbers in decimals, such as 2.05; *to multiply by ten, simply move the decimal point one place to the right*

COMMENT: the decimal point is used in the USA and Britain. In most European countries a comma is used to show the decimal, so 4,75% in Germany is written 4.75% in Britain

decimate ['desɪmeɪt] *verb* to kill in large numbers, to reduce by a large amount; *German forests have been decimated by acid rain; our sales have been decimated by the rise in the value of the pound*

decipher [dɪ'saɪfə] *verb* to read or make out something which has been badly written, or written in code; *I'm trying to decipher the address on this order; the embassy staff worked all night to decipher the coded message*

decision [dɪ'sɪʒn] *noun* act of making up your mind to do something; **to come to a decision** *or* **to reach a decision** *or* **to take a decision** = to decide to do something; *they talked for hours but didn't come to any decision; he thought about the job offer, but, in the end, took the decision to stay where he was*

decision-making [dɪ'sɪʒnmeɪkɪŋ] *noun* **the decision-making process** = the action of making up your mind to do something; *we involve all the staff in the decision-making process*

decisive [dɪ'saɪsɪv] *adjective* **(a)** firm (tone of voice); *he was nervous but tried to sound decisive* **(b)** which brings about a result; *the second and decisive round of voting takes place next Sunday; her action was decisive in obtaining the release of the hostages*

deck [dek] *noun* **(a)** floor of a ship, bus, etc.; *I'll stay on deck because I'm feeling seasick; the sailors were washing down the deck of the ship; let's go up to the top deck - you can see the sights better from there;* **main deck** = deck with the most important facilities, such as the restaurant, bars, etc.; *see also* DOUBLEDECKER, FLIGHT DECK, SINGLEDECKER **(b)** *US* set of playing cards; *she shuffled the deck* (NOTE: British English is **pack of cards**) **(c)** *US* wooden platform on the outside of a house; *we had drinks outside on the deck*

deckchair ['dektʃeə] *noun* long folding canvas chair for sitting in the sun; *he spent the afternoon sitting in a deckchair trying to do a crossword*

deckhand ['dekhænd] *noun* sailor who does various jobs on the deck; *deckhands were painting the sides of the ship*

declaration [deklə'reɪʃn] *noun* official statement; *the minister's declaration was broadcast at 6 o'clock; we had to fill in a customs declaration form;* **VAT declaration** = statement declaring VAT income to the VAT office

declare [dɪ'kleə] *verb* **(a)** to state officially; *Mr Clinton declared his intention to run for President; she was declared dead on arrival at hospital; it was declared that Mrs Broom was elected chairman by 46 votes* **(b)** *(at customs)* **to declare goods to customs** = to list the goods you are carrying on which you may need to pay customs duty; *the customs officials asked him if he had anything to declare; go through the green channel if you have nothing to declare*

decline [dɪ'klaɪn] **1** *noun* going downwards; *sales figures have gone into a sharp decline; the decline in the value of the franc; a welcome decline in the number of cases of pollution* **2** *verb* **(a)** to refuse or to turn down (an invitation); *she declined their request; he declined to come to lunch* **(b)** to become weaker; *he declined rapidly after he went into hospital* **(c)** to become less in numbers or amount; *our sales declined over the last year; the fish population has declined sharply*

decode [di:'kəud] *verb* to translate a coded message into normal writing; *we use a special machine to decode enemy signals*

decompose [di:kəm'pəuz] *verb (of organic material)* to rot; *dead leaves decompose quite quickly on the floor of the forest; the police found a decomposing body under the floorboards*

decomposition [di:kɒmpə'zɪʃn] *noun* process of rotting; *decomposition of vegetable matter is speeded up in a warm climate* (NOTE: no plural)

deconstruct [di:kən'strʌkt] *verb* to analyse how language works in literary texts; *his aim is to deconstruct 'Macbeth'*

decor *or* **décor** ['deɪkɔ:] *noun* interior decoration of a room; *the restaurant has an Arabic décor; she brought in a fashionable interior designer to design the decor of her new flat*

decorate ['dekəreɪt] *verb* **(a)** to paint (a building); to put new wallpaper in (a room); *she can't come to the phone - she's decorating the kitchen;* **interior decorating** = the decorating (curtains, paintwork, etc.) of the inside of a house **(b)** to cover something with pretty or colourful things to make it look attractive, or to celebrate an occasion; *the streets were decorated with flags* **(c)** to put coloured icing on a cake; *Christmas cakes are decorated with holly leaves and berries* **(d)** to award someone a medal; *he was decorated for bravery*

decoration [dekə'reɪʃn] *noun* **(a)** action of decorating; *she is charge of the decoration of the church for the wedding* **(b)** action of painting a room, etc.; *the decoration of the town hall took over a year* **(c)** things added to make something more attractive; *the only decoration allowed was a pattern of geometric shapes* **(d)** decorations = flags or lights, etc., used to celebrate an occasion; *we put up the Christmas decorations at the beginning of the holidays; we must go to see the Christmas decorations in Regent Street* **(e)** medal; *he went to Buckingham Palace to receive his decoration from the Queen; old soldiers were wearing their decorations for the November 11th parade*

decorative ['dekərətɪv] *adjective* pleasant to look at; serving as a decoration; *she stuck a decorative border round the edge*

decorator ['dekəreɪtə] *noun* person who paints the inside and outside of buildings; *we had the decorators in all last week*; **interior decorator** = person who paints the interior of buildings, puts up wallpaper, etc.

decorous ['dekərəs] *adjective* very well-behaved; *a group of decorous convent girls walked into the church*

decorum [dɪ'kɔːrʌm] *noun* being well-behaved; *we noticed a lack of decorum on the part of the younger guests at the wedding* (NOTE: no plural)

decoy 1 *noun* ['diːkɔɪ] object which is placed to attract and trap something; *when they go duck shooting, they use wooden duck decoys which they float on the water; they used a woman police officer to act as a decoy to try to trap the mugger* **2** *verb* [dɪ'kɔɪ] to attract and trap something *or* someone; *the soldiers were decoyed into the ruined building*

decrease 1 *noun* ['diːkriːs] falling, lessening; *a decrease in traffic; sales show a 10% decrease on last year; there has been a decrease of 20% in applications to join the club*; **to be on the decrease** = to be falling; *road accidents are on the decrease* **2** *verb* [diː'kriːs] to fall, to become less; *the number of road accidents is decreasing; applications to join the course have decreased by 20 %*

decree [dɪ'kriː] **1** *noun* legal order which has not been voted by Parliament; *the president has issued a decree banning short dresses* **2** *verb* to state as a legal order; *the president has decreed that short dresses may not be worn*

decrepit [dɪ'krepɪt] *adjective* old, feeble and falling to pieces; *the house will be sold cheaply because of its decrepit state; she drives a decrepit Austin Seven; his father is now so decrepit that a nurse comes to visit him every day*

decriminalize [diː'krɪmɪnəlaɪz] *verb* to make something or an action no longer a crime; *proposals to decriminalize soft drugs*

decry [dɪ'kraɪ] *verb* (*formal*) to criticize, to say that something is bad; *he made a speech decrying the behaviour of today's teenagers*

dedicate ['dedɪkeɪt] *verb* **(a)** to place a church under the patronage of a saint; *the chapel was dedicated to St Christopher in the 13th century* **(b)** to offer a book to someone as a mark of respect or affection; *he dedicated his collection of poems to his wife* **(c)** to spend all your life doing something; *she dedicated her life to the service of the poor*

dedicated ['dedɪkeɪtɪd] *adjective* **(a)** giving a lot of time and effort to achieve something; *her life was saved by the dedicated surgical team at the hospital* **(b)** reserved for a particular task; *there's one dedicated graphics workstation in the network*

dedication [dedɪ'keɪʃn] *noun* **(a)** (*formal*) spending your life doing something; *we all admire her dedication to duty* **(b)** note printed at the beginning of a book or play, where the author offers his work to someone as a mark of respect or affection

deduce [dɪ'djuːs] *verb* to conclude from examining the evidence; *we can deduce from the evidence so far that the accused is not necessarily guilty*

deduct [dɪ'dʌkt] *verb* to remove from a sum of money; *we took £60 at the jumble sale, but if we deduct our expenses, we only made £25; she deducted some money to cover breakages*; **tax deducted at source** = tax which is removed from wages, interest payments, etc., before the money is paid

deduction [dɪ'dʌkʃn] *noun* **(a)** conclusion reached; *their deduction was correct*; **by a process of deduction** = by looking at the evidence and reaching a conclusion **(b)** sum of money which is taken away; *there is an automatic deduction for insurance; net wages are wages after deduction of tax and social security payments*; **tax deductions** = money removed from your salary to pay tax

deed [diːd] *noun* **(a)** (*formal*) (noble) act; *stories of great deeds performed during the war* **(b)** title deeds *or* the deeds of a house = legal documents showing who owns a house; *we have deposited the deeds of the house in the bank*

deem [diːm] *verb* (*formal*) to consider; *if the minister deems it necessary, it will be done*

deep [diːp] **1** *adjective* **(a)** which goes a long way down; *the water is very deep in the middle of the river; this is the deepest lake in North America; in the shallow end of the pool, the water is only a few centimetres deep* (NOTE: the use with figures: **the pool is six feet deep; a lake 500m deep**) **(b)** dark (colour); *a deep brown carpet* **(c)** felt very strongly; *we want to express our deepest admiration for what you have done; she sat in a corner, deep in thought* (NOTE: **deeper - deepest**) **2** *adverb* a long way down; *the mine goes deep under the sea*

deepen ['diːpən] *verb* **(a)** to become deeper; *the water deepened as he waded into the river* **(b)** to make something become deeper; *they're going to deepen the channel so that bigger boats can use the harbour*

deep end ['diːp 'end] *noun* end of a swimming pool where the water is deep (*informal*) **to throw someone in at the deep end** = to give someone a difficult job to start with, to start someone on a new job without any preparation; *when she started her teaching career she was thrown in at the deep end by having to teach a class of fifteen-year-old boys*; (*informal*) **to go off the deep end** = to get very annoyed; *he went off the deep end when he heard that his car had been stolen again* (NOTE: the other end is the **shallow end**)

deep-freeze [diːpˈfriːz] 1 *noun* freezer, refrigerator for freezing food and keeping it frozen; *I'll put the chicken in the deep-freeze until next week* 2 *verb* to freeze food and keep it frozen; *we deep-freeze a lot of the vegetables from our garden*; *he bought some deep-frozen shrimps*

deep-fry [ˈdiːpfraɪ] *verb* to cook in deep boiling oil; *deep-fried chicken pieces*

deeply [ˈdiːpli] *adverb* very much; *we deeply regret having to make so many people redundant*

deep-seated [diːpˈsiːtɪd] *adjective* that has lasted a long time and will be difficult to change; *my father had a deep-seated fear of the telephone*

deer [dɪə] *noun* wild animal of which the male has long horns, often hunted; *there is a herd of red deer in the park* (NOTE: do not confuse with **dear**; **the plural is deer**; the female is a **doe**, the male is a **stag**, the young are **fawns**; note also that the meat from a deer is called **venison**)

COMMENT: there are three species of deer which live wild in the UK. The largest is the red deer, found in Scotland and the West Country; the fallow deer is similar, but with flat antlers, and the smallest is the roe deer, of which the young have white spots

de facto [diːˈfæktəʊ] *Latin phrase meaning* 'in fact', existing in fact, even though perhaps not legally; *he is the de facto owner of the property*; *since the coup, the de facto government has been recognized by most countries* (NOTE: the opposite, where you own a property by having a legal right to it, is **de jure**)

defamation [defəˈmeɪʃn] *noun* **defamation of character** = act of ruining someone's character by saying or writing rude things about him

defamatory [dɪˈfæmətri] *adjective* which is done to ruin someone's reputation; *he made several defamatory statements to the newspapers about his former boss*

defame [dɪˈfeɪm] *verb* (*formal*) to say or write bad things about someone, so as to ruin his reputation; *the book defames the Prime Minister*

default [dɪˈfɒlt] 1 *noun* (**a**) *he is in default* = he has failed to carry out the terms of the contract (**b**) *by default* = because someone else fails to do something; *his opponent withdrew and he won by default* (**c**) (*computers*) set way of working; **default drive** = drive which is accessed first 2 *verb* to fail to carry out the terms of a contract; **to default on payments** = not to make payments which are due; *he paid regularly for six months and then defaulted*

defaulter [dɪˈfɒltə] *noun* person who defaults; *there are heavy penalties for defaulters*

defeat [dɪˈfiːt] 1 *noun* loss of a fight, a vote, a game; *the government suffered a defeat in Parliament last night*; *it was the team's first defeat for two years* 2 *verb* to beat someone in a fight, game or vote; *the proposal was defeated by 10 votes to 3*; *the ruling party was heavily defeated in the presidential election*; *our team has not been defeated so far this season*

defecate [ˈdefəkeɪt] *verb* (*formal*) to pass waste matter from the bowels through the anus; *the burglars had ransacked the bedroom and defecated on the floor*

defecation [defəˈkeɪʃn] *noun* (*formal*) action of defecating

defect 1 *noun* [ˈdiːfekt] fault; *there must be a defect in the computer programme* 2 *verb* [dɪˈfekt]; **to defect (to the enemy)** = to leave your country and join the enemy; *she defected while on a tour of South-East Asia*

defection [dɪˈfekʃn] *noun* leaving your country or party and going over to the side of the enemy or opposition; *the defection of three MPs to the opposition will weaken the goverment*

defective [dɪˈfektɪv] *adjective* faulty; *the fridge broke down because of a defective cooling system*

defector [dɪˈfektə] *noun* person who defects to the enemy; *the defectors were caught as they reached the border*

defence *US* **defense** [dɪˈfens] *noun* (**a**) protection against attack, infection, etc.; *several people ran to her defence when she was attacked by muggers*; *these tablets offer a limited defence against the disease* (**b**) protection provided by the armed forces; *some countries spend more on defence than on education*; **the Ministry of Defence** = government department dealing with the army, navy and air force (**c**) part of a team whose job is to protect the goal; *the England defence came under attack from the Brazilian forwards* (**d**) **defences** = walls, trenches, etc., which are made to protect something; *the town is strengthening its defences by building thicker walls*; **when your defences are down** = when you are not prepared for an attack; *pickpockets often strike when you're relaxing and your defences are down* (**e**) (*in a law court*) **the defence** = lawyers acting for the accused person; **defence counsel** = lawyer who represents the defendant in a lawsuit (NOTE: the opposing side in a court is the **prosecution**)

defend [dɪˈfend] *verb* (**a**) to protect someone who is being attacked; *he jumped forward to defend his wife against the robbers*; *she couldn't defend herself against the assault* (**b**) (*in a law court*) to speak on behalf of an accused person; *he hired the best lawyers to defend him*; *the barrister who is defending my uncle*; **to defend a lawsuit** = to appear in court to state your case when accused of something

defendant [dɪˈfendənt] *noun* (*in a law court*) person who is accused of doing something illegal; person who is sued in a civil case; *the defendant says he is innocent*

COMMENT: in a civil case, the defendant faces a complaint from the plaintiff. In a criminal case, the defendant (also called the accused) is being prosecuted for a crime by the prosecution

defender [dɪˈfendə] *noun* (**a**) person who defends a castle, town, etc.; *the defenders surrendered after 90 days, when they ran out of food* (**b**) player who defends the goal; *the defenders were continually passing the ball back to the goalkeeper*

defensive [dɪˈfensɪv] 1 *adjective* which protects; *they built a defensive wall around the camp* 2 *noun* **to be on the defensive about something** = to need to justify having done something; *she's always on the defensive when newspapers mention her huge salary*

defer [dɪˈfɜː] *verb* (**a**) to put back to a later date, to postpone; **to defer payment**; *the decision has been deferred until the next meeting* (**b**) **to defer to someone** *or* **to someone's opinion** = to accept someone's advice; *she defers to her husband in everything* (NOTE: **deferring - deferred**)

deference ['defərəns] *noun* respect; *you are required to show due deference to the President's wife*; **in deference to** *or* **out of deference to** = to show respect for; *in deference to his wife, who is Muslim, he refused to allow alcohol in his house*; *she put a shawl over her head out of deference to the monastery rules*

defiance [dɪ'faɪəns] *noun* very proud action against an opponent; *when he was sentenced he shook his fist in defiance*; **act of defiance** = action which shows you are defying someone; *he kept his hat on in church as an act of defiance*; **in defiance of** = acting proudly against; *their protest march took place in defiance of a police ban on all demonstrations*

defiant [dɪ'faɪənt] *adjective* very proud against an opponent; *opposition MPs are becoming more and more defiant*

deficiency [dɪ'fɪʃənsi] *noun* (a) lack of; *their diet has a deficiency in calcium or has a calcium deficiency* (b) money lacking; *there is a £10 deficiency in the petty cash*

deficient [dɪ'fɪʃənt] *adjective* **to be deficient in something** = to lack something; *the soil is deficient in important nutrients*; *their diet is deficient in calcium or they have a calcium-deficient diet*

deficit ['defɪsɪt] *noun* amount by which expenditure is more than receipts in a firm's or a country's accounts; *the company announced a two-million pound deficit*; **to make good a deficit** = to put money into an account to balance it; **balance of payments deficit** *or* **trade deficit** = situation when a country imports more than it exports; *the UK's balance of payments deficit*

defile 1 *noun* ['di:faɪl] narrow path between mountains; *they were ambushed in a mountain defile and killed* **2** *verb* [dɪ'faɪl] *(formal)* to make something corrupt or no longer pure; *soldiers defiled the holy temple*

define [dɪ'faɪn] *verb* (a) to explain clearly, to give the meaning of something; *how would you define an environmentalist?*; *the memo tried to define the way in which the two departments should work together* (b) to indicate the limits of something; *the police operate within limits that have been clearly defined*

defined [dɪ'faɪnd] *adjective* (a) which has been described exactly; *the committee works within carefully defined terms of reference* (b) clear, not blurred; *the trees stood sharply defined against the snow of the hills behind*

definite ['defɪnət] *adjective* (a) very clear, very sure; *I need a definite answer*; *he was quite definite that he had seen the girl at the bus stop* (b) **definite article** = 'the' (as opposed to the indefinite article 'a' or 'an')

definitely ['defɪnɪtli] *adverb* certainly, surely; *I'll definitely be there by 7 o'clock*

definition [defɪ'nɪʃn] *noun* (a) clear explanation (of a word); *a bilingual dictionary doesn't give definitions, only translations*; *look up the definition of 'democracy' in the dictionary* (b) clearness (of a photograph); *the closeups are clear, but your landscape photos lack definition* (NOTE: no plural in this meaning)

definitive [dɪ'fɪnɪtɪv] *adjective* final, which cannot be improved on; *a definitive production of 'Macbeth'*

deflate [dɪ'fleɪt] *verb* (a) to let the air out (of a tyre, balloon, etc.); *their hot air balloon began to deflate* (b) **to deflate (the economy)** = to reduce activity in the

economy by cutting the supply of money; *the government may be forced to deflate the economy because of rising imports*

deflation [dɪ'fleɪʃn] *noun* reduction of economic activity; *deflation will put millions of people out of work*

deflect [dɪ'flekt] *verb* to turn aside an arrow, a bullet, etc., so that it goes in another direction; *the goalkeeper deflected the ball into his own net*; *to deflect criticism from the banks, the chairman has decided to sack the finance director*

deforest [di:'fɒrɪst] *verb* to cut down forest trees for commercial purposes or to make arable land; *about 40,000 square miles are deforested each year*

deform [dɪ'fɔ:m] *verb* to change the shape of something and make it ugly; *her hands were deformed by arthritis*

defraud [dɪ'frɔ:d] *verb* **to defraud someone of his money** = to cheat someone to get his money; *he defrauded the old lady of £10,000*

defray [dɪ'freɪ] *verb* to provide money to pay someone's costs; *the company will defray all your expenses*

defrost [di:'frɒst] *verb* (a) to remove ice which has formed; *I must defrost the freezer* (b) *(frozen food)* to thaw out; *a large turkey will take 24 hours to defrost*

deft [deft] *adjective* very agile or clever with your hands; *with one deft movement he removed the tablecloth, while leaving the glasses and plates on the table* (NOTE: **defter - deftest**)

defunct [dɪ'fʌŋkt] *adjective* which is no longer used or in existence; *the club lost most of its members and became defunct*; *he and I were members of a now defunct committee*

defuse [di:'fju:z] *verb* (a) to take the fuse out of a bomb so that it cannot explode; *an army unit was brought in to defuse the bomb* (b) to make a situation less tense; *the chairman made some jokes to try to defuse the situation*; *the UN Secretary General has moved to try to defuse the crisis*

defy [dɪ'faɪ] *verb* (a) to refuse to obey the law; *he should never have tried to defy the university authorities* (b) **to defy someone to do something** = to challenge someone to do something; *I defy you to jump higher than that*

degenerate 1 *adjective* [dɪ'dʒenərət] which has become morally weak or bad; *he was shocked by the student art exhibition which he termed 'degenerate scribbling'* **2** *verb* [dɪ'dʒenəreɪt] to get worse; *her condition degenerated quickly once she went into hospital*; *the celebrations rapidly degenerated into rioting* **3** *noun* [dɪ'dʒenərət] person who is morally weak or bad; *the people who did this are moral degenerates*

degrade [dɪ'greɪd] *verb* (a) to make someone do something that is humiliating; *he was forced to do all sorts of degrading work in prison*; *she had no money but refused to degrade herself by working in a bar* (b) to change (a chemical compound) into a simpler form, to decompose; *some plastics will degrade if left in the sun*

degree [dɪ'gri:] *noun* (a) division of a scale; *the temperature of the water is above 20 degrees*; *an angle of 80°* (NOTE: with figures, **degree** is usually written °: **25° Celsius**) (b) level; *to what degree do you think the* *driver was to blame for the accident?*; **to a certain degree** = partly; *it's his own fault to a certain degree* **(c)** diploma from a university; *she has a degree in mathematics from Oxford*; **bachelor's degree** = first degree from a university; **master's degree** = second, more advanced, degree from a university

COMMENT: the main degrees that are awarded at universities are: **Bachelor of Arts (BA), Bachelor of Science (BSc), Master of Arts (MA), Master of Science (MSc)** and, at the highest level, **Doctor of Philosophy (PhD)** and **Doctor of Science (DSc))**

dehydrate [di:haɪ'dreɪt] *verb* **(a)** to remove water from something; *if you want to use dehydrated mushrooms, you must soak them in water for some time* **(b)** to lose water from the body; *after two days without food or drink, he became severely dehydrated*

dehydration [dɪhaɪ'dreɪʃn] *noun* becoming dehydrated; *after a long tennis match in blistering heat both players were suffering from dehydration*

deification [deɪɪfɪ'keɪʃn] *noun* making someone into a god; *in Ancient Rome, the deification of the emperor took place after he died*

deify ['deɪɪfaɪ] *verb* to make something or someone into a god; *Roman emperors were deified after their deaths*

deity ['deɪɪti] *noun* god; *they worship primitive deities who live in forests and streams* (NOTE: plural is **deities**)

de jure ['deɪ 'dʒʊəri] *Latin phrase meaning* 'by law': as a matter of law, where the legal title is clear; *he is the de jure owner of the property* (NOTE: the opposite, where you own a property by reason of holding it, even if the legal right is not clear, is **de facto**)

delay [dɪ'leɪ] **1** *noun* length of time that something is late; *there will be a delay of ten minutes before the meeting starts*; *we are sorry for the delay in replying to your letter* **2** *verb* **(a)** to make late; *the train has been delayed by fog*; *he was delayed because his taxi had an accident* **(b)** to put something off until later; *we will delay making a decision until we see the result of the election*; *the company has delayed payment of all invoices*

delayed-action ['dɪ'leɪd 'ækʃən] *adjective* which is activated later; *they placed a delayed-action bomb in the shopping centre, timed to go off at three o'clock*

delegate 1 *noun* ['delɪgət] person who represents others at a meeting; *the minister met delegates from the union* **2** *verb* ['delɪgeɪt] to pass authority or responsibility on to someone else; *she finds it difficult to delegate*; *he delegated the job of locking up the shop to the junior manager*

delegation [delɪ'geɪʃn] *noun* **(a)** group of representatives; *the minister met a union delegation* **(b)** passing authority or responsibility to someone else; *the secret of good management is delegation* (NOTE: no plural in this meaning)

delete [dɪ'li:t] *verb* to cut out part of a document, a computer file, etc.; *they want to delete all references to the Prime Minister from the report*; *he pressed DEL and deleted the whole file*

deletion [dɪ'li:ʃn] *noun* **(a)** action of deleting something; *the court asked for the deletion of several sentences from the magazine article* **(b)** word or

phrase which has been deleted; *she made several deletions to the original text*; *in spite of all the deletions, the article is still too long*

deli ['deli] *noun (informal)* = DELICATESSEN; *we got some bagels from the deli opposite the hotel*

deliberate 1 *adjective* [dɪ'lɪbərət] **(a)** done on purpose; *it was a deliberate attempt to spoil her birthday party* **(b)** slow and thoughtful in speaking or doing something; *she has a very deliberate way of signing her name* **2** *verb* [dɪ'lɪbəreɪt] **(a)** to debate, to discuss; *the council were deliberating all morning*; *the jury left the courtroom to deliberate* **(b)** to think carefully about something; *I'll need some time to deliberate on the possible ways of solving the problem*

deliberately [dɪ'lɪbərətli] *adverb* **(a)** on purpose; *it was an accident - I didn't hit her deliberately*; *he deliberately left the cage door open* **(b)** slowly and thoughtfully; *she walked deliberately up the steps onto the platform*

deliberation [dɪlɪbə'reɪʃn] *noun* **(a)** great care; *he moved his king with great deliberation and leant back with a smile* **(b)** discussion; *after lengthy deliberation the meeting voted on the proposal*; *did their deliberations produce any result?*

delicacy ['delɪkəsi] *noun* **(a)** sensitivity; *it is a question which has to be handled with great delicacy* **(b)** state of being delicate; *the delicacy of the glasses means that they have to be handled very carefully* (NOTE: no plural in meanings (a) and (b)) **(c)** rare thing to eat; *they bought all sorts of delicacies for the Christmas party* (NOTE: plural in this meaning is **delicacies**)

delicate ['delɪkət] *adjective* **(a)** easily damaged; *a delicate china vase* **(b)** liable to get illnesses; *little babies are very delicate* **(c)** very soft and fine; *a delicate silk blouse* **(d)** possibly difficult; *he is in a delicate situation*

delicately ['delɪkətli] *adverb* with great care; *he delicately picked up the tiny baby*

delicatessen [delɪkə'tesən] *noun* shop selling cold meats and imported food products; *we bought some salad and pies at the delicatessen*

delicious [dɪ'lɪʃəs] *adjective* which tastes very good; *can I have another piece of that delicious cake?*

delight [dɪ'laɪt] **1** *noun* pleasure; *their singing was a pure delight*; *the news was greeted with delight by the waiting crowd*; **to take great delight in something** = to take great pleasure in something **2** *verb* **to delight in something** = to take great pleasure in something; *she delights in teasing her little brother*

delighted [dɪ'laɪtɪd] *adjective* very pleased; *she's delighted with her present*; *we are delighted that you were able to come*; *I'm delighted to meet you at last*

delightful [dɪ'laɪtfʊl] *adjective* very pleasant; *we had a delightful picnic by the river*

delineate [dɪ'lɪnɪeɪt] *verb (formal)* to draw, to describe in detail; *students were asked to delineate the personalities of Othello and Desdemona*

delinquency [dɪ'lɪŋkwənsi] *noun* act of committing a minor crime; **juvenile delinquency** = crimes by young offenders

delinquent [dɪ'lɪŋkwənt] **1** *adjective US* **a delinquent account** = an account which is overdue **2** *noun* **a juvenile delinquent** *or US* **a delinquent** =

young criminal who commits crimes, especially against property

delirious [dɪˈlɪriəs] *adjective* **(a)** suffering from delirium; *she collapsed and became delirious* **(b)** very excited and happy; *they were delirious when they won the lottery*

delirium [dɪˈlɪriəm] *noun (formal)* mental state where a person is confused, restless, very excited and has hallucinations; *after a period of delirium, he fell into a deep sleep*

deliver [dɪˈlɪvə] *verb* **(a)** to bring something to someone; *has today's newspaper been delivered?*; *he delivered the letter himself so as to save buying a stamp* **(b) to deliver a baby** = to help a mother when a baby is born; *the twins were delivered by the midwife*

delivery [dɪˈlɪvri] *noun* **(a)** bringing something to someone; *there is no charge for delivery within the London area*; *use the rear entrance for deliveries*; *the next delivery will be on Thursday*; **delivery van** = goods van for delivering goods to retail customers **(b)** birth of a child; *the midwife will supervise the delivery*

delta [ˈdeltə] *noun* **(a)** triangular piece of land at the mouth of a large river, formed of silt carried by the river; *the Nile Delta*; *the Mississippi Delta*; *deltas are created by alluvial deposits* **(b)** fourth letter of the Greek alphabet (δ); *the word Delphi is spelt with a delta*

deluge [ˈdeljuːdʒ] **1** *noun* **(a)** flood of questions, orders, etc.; *we had a deluge of phone calls after our TV commercial* **(b)** heavy rainfall; *it had been dry for weeks and then last Saturday we had a deluge* **2** *verb* to flood, to overwhelm; *we were deluged with phone calls*

delusion [dɪˈluːʒn] *noun* false belief which a person holds which cannot be changed by reason; *he suffered from the delusion that he was wanted by the police*; **to be under a delusion** = to have a wrong idea; *the boss is under the delusion that everyone really likes him*

de luxe [dɪ ˈlʌks] *adjective* very expensive; of very high quality; *the airline offers first-class passengers a bag of de luxe toiletries*; *as a treat, they went on a de luxe tour of India*

delve [delv] *verb (old)* to dig; **to delve into** = to investigate; *he has been delving into the past history of the family*

demand [dɪˈmɑːnd] **1** *noun* **(a)** asking for something; *a demand for payment*; *her latest demands are quite unreasonable*; **final demand** = last reminder from a supplier, after which he will sue for payment or cut off supplies; *we had a final demand from the gas company* **(b)** need for goods or services at a certain price; **to meet a demand** *or* **to fill a demand** = to supply what is needed; *the factory had to increase production to meet the extra demand*; *we cannot keep up with the demand for our services*; **there is not much demand for this item** = not many people want to buy it; **this item is in great demand** = many people want to buy it; **law of supply and demand** = general rule that the amount of a product which is available is linked to the amount which is wanted by customers **2** *verb* to ask firmly for something; *she demanded a refund*; *I demand an explanation*

demanding [dɪˈmɑːdɪŋ] *adjective* which takes up much time and energy; *he has a very demanding job*; *looking after little children is very demanding*

demeanour *US* **demeanor** [dɪˈmiːnə] *noun (formal)* behaviour or manner; *she maintained a calm demeanour throughout her trial*

demented [dɪˈmentɪd] *adjective* mad; *she rushed about the kitchen like a demented hen*

dementia [dɪˈmenʃə] *noun* loss of mental ability and memory, causing confusion and changes to the personality, due to a disease of the brain; **senile dementia** = form of mental confusion affecting old people; *gradually he began to show signs of dementia and had to be moved into a hospital*

demilitarize [dɪˈmɪlɪtəraɪz] *verb* to remove soldiers from an area; **demilitarized zone** = area which is no longer occupied by soldiers

demise [dɪˈmaɪz] *noun (formal)* death; *on his demise, the estate passed to his daughter*

demo [ˈdeməʊ] *noun (informal)* = DEMONSTRATION; *they organized a protest demo against the government*; **demo disc** = sample computer disc used to show what a full programme is like

demobilize [diːˈməʊbɪlaɪz] *verb* to release someone from the armed forces; *after the war ended thousands of soldiers were demobilized and tried to find jobs*

democracy [dɪˈmɒkrəsi] *noun* country governed by freely elected representatives of the people; *we live in a democracy* (NOTE: plural is **democracies**) **(b)** system of government by freely elected representatives of the people; *the people want democracy, not a dictatorship* (NOTE: no plural in this meaning)

democrat [ˈdeməkræt] *noun* **(a)** person who believes in democracy; *all true democrats will unite against the dictator* **(b)** *US* **a Democrat** = a member of the Democratic Party; *the Democrats lost the election to the Republicans*

democratic [deməˈkrætɪk] *adjective* referring to democracy; *they promised to restore democratic government*

Democratic Party [deməˈkrætɪk ˈpɑːti] *noun* one of the two main political parties in the USA, which is in favour of some social change and state help for poor people; *the Democratic Party's candidate for the presidency*; *compare* REPUBLICAN PARTY

democratically [deməˈkrætɪkli] *adverb* in a democratic way; *he is the first democratically elected president following the end of military rule*

demographic [deməˈgræfɪk] *adjective* referring to demography; *demographic trends suggest that the population will increase by 30% in the 21st century*

demography [dɪˈmɒgrəfi] *noun* study of populations, trends in birth rates, etc.; *he is an expert in demography*

demolish [dɪˈmɒlɪʃ] *verb* **(a)** to knock down; *we demolished the old church and built a new one* **(b)** *(informal)* to eat completely; *he demolished the whole chocolate cake* **(c)** to show that something is completely wrong; *he wrote an article demolishing the professor's theories*

demolition [deməˈlɪʃn] *noun* action of knocking down; *the plans for the new town centre will involve the demolition of all the old houses round the church*; *as soon as permission was given demolition crews moved in with bulldozers*

demon [ˈdiːmən] *noun* **(a)** devil; *the picture shows red demons throwing people into a fire* **(b)** a demon for = very energetic person; *he's a demon for hard work*; *she's a real demon on the hockey pitch*

demoniacal *or* **demonic** [diːməˈnaɪəkl] or diːˈmɒnɪk] *adjective* like a devil; *the play ends with demonic laughter as the villain dies*

demonstrably [dɪˈmɒnstrəbli] *adverb* which can be demonstrated; *his calculations are demonstrably false*

demonstrate [ˈdemənstreɪt] *verb* (a) to show; *this demonstrates how little he has changed*; *he demonstrated how the machine worked* (b) to **demonstrate against something** = to protest against something in public; *a group were demonstrating against the new motorway*

demonstration [demənˈstreɪʃn] *noun* (a) showing (how something works); *can you give me a demonstration of how it works?*; **demonstration model** = car, or other piece of equipment, which has been used by a shop to show how it works, and is then sold cheaply (b) crowd of people who are protesting against something; *we went shopping and got mixed up in a demonstration in Trafalgar Square*; *they staged demonstrations against the government in several towns*

demonstrative [dɪˈmɒnstrətɪv] *adjective* (*person*) who openly shows feelings; *she's not very demonstrative, but I think she appreciated her gift all the same*

demonstrator [ˈdemənstreɪtə] *noun* (a) person who shows how to do something or how pieces of equipment work; *the demonstrator showed how to work the mixer* (b) person who marches, or who forms part of a crowd protesting against something; *a crowd of demonstrators blocked the road*; *the police used water cannon to clear demonstrators from in front of the Parliament building*

demoralize [dɪˈmɒrəlaɪz] *verb* to lower the morale or confidence of someone; *having two players sent off for fouls has demoralized the rest of the team*; *I felt so demoralized after the teacher criticized my work*

demote [diːˈməʊt] *verb* to give someone a less important job or to reduce an employee to a lower rank or grade; *he was demoted from manager to salesman*; *she lost a lot of salary when she was demoted*

demotion [dɪˈməʊʃn] *noun* giving someone a less important job; *he was very angry at his demotion*

den [den] *noun* (a) place where an animal hides away; *a lion's den* (b) (*informal*) small room where you can hide away to work; *Father's in his den, so don't disturb him* (c) meeting place for criminals; *the bar is just a den of thieves*

denial [dɪˈnaɪəl] *noun* statement that something is not true; *despite his repeated denials, people still suspect he is planning to resign*; *the company issued a denial that it was planning to close down the factory*

denigrate [ˈdenɪgreɪt] *verb* to say that someone *or* something is not very good; *her efforts at painting were denigrated by professional artists*

denim [ˈdenɪm] *noun* thick cotton cloth; *he wore a pair of denim overalls*; **denims** = jeans, blue trousers made of thick cotton cloth

Denmark [ˈdenmɑːk] *noun* country in northern Europe, south of Sweden and Norway, and north of Germany; *Legoland is one of the tourist attractions of Denmark* (NOTE: capital: **Copenhagen**; people: **the Danes**; language: **Danish**; currency: **Danish krone**)

denomination [dɪnɒmɪˈneɪʃn] *noun* (a) unit of money written on a coin, banknote or stamp; *coins of all denominations are put in the church collection box*; *the bank has run out of small denomination notes* (b) religious grouping; *the Protestant church is divided into several denominations*; *what denomination does he belong to?*

denominational [dɪnɒmɪˈneɪʃənəl] *adjective* referring to a particular religious denomination; *the children go to a denominational school*

denote [dɪˈnəʊt] *verb* to mean, to be a sign of; *a little circle after a figure denotes a degree*; *heavy selling of the shares denotes concern on the part of investors*

denouement *or* **dénouement** [deɪˈnuːmɒŋ] *noun* ending of a book, play, film, etc., where the affair is finally sorted out; *the tragic denouement of the play left the audience shocked*

denounce [dɪˈnaʊns] *verb* (a) to blame or to accuse someone or something openly; *someone denounced him to the police*; *he was denounced as a racist by a fellow professor* (b) to condemn something openly; *she denounced the council's policy as short-sighted*

dense [dens] *adjective* (a) very thick; *dense fog closed the airport* (b) crowded together; *they tried to find their way through dense forest*; *I find it difficult to read through 100 pages of dense text* (c) (*informal*) stupid; *how can anybody be so dense?* (NOTE: **denser - densest**)

density [ˈdensɪti] *noun* (a) (*in physics*) amount of mass per unit of volume; *heavy density oils*; **relative density** = density of something as compared to the amount of water which would fill the same space (b) number of things in a certain area; *London suffers from high population density*; *the high traffic density in the centre of Rome* (NOTE: plural in this meaning is **densities**)

dent [dent] **1** *noun* slight hollow mark made by hitting; *someone has made a dent in my car door* **2** *verb* to make a slight hollow mark in something; *he backed into a tree and dented the wing*

dental [ˈdentəl] *adjective* referring to teeth; *he's a dental student*; **dental floss** = thread for cleaning teeth; **dental surgery** = a dentist's office

dental surgeon [ˈdentəl ˈsɜːdʒən] *noun* dentist, a person who looks after teeth; *he trained as a dental surgeon in Australia*

dentist [ˈdentɪst] *noun* person who looks after your teeth; *she had to wait for an hour at the dentist's*; *he hates going to the dentist*

dentistry [ˈdentɪstri] *noun* profession of a dentist; branch of medicine dealing with teeth and gums; *she's studying dentistry* (NOTE: no plural)

dentures [ˈdentʃəz] *noun* false teeth, artificial plastic teeth which fit inside the mouth and take the place of teeth which have been taken out

denunciation [dɪnʌnsɪˈeɪʃn] *noun* public accusation or blame; *he made a strong denunciation of the secret police*

deny [dɪˈnaɪ] *verb* (a) to state that something is not correct; *you were there, weren't you? - don't deny it!*; *she denied that she had ever seen him*; *he flatly denied stealing the car* (b) to **deny someone something** = to prevent someone having something; *he was denied access to the secret government papers*; **to deny oneself** = not to eat, not to do something, which you would like to do; *she denied herself a holiday in order to earn enough to pay off her mortgage*

deodorant [diˈəʊdərənt] *noun* substance which hides and prevents unpleasant smells; *I always put on some deodorant before going to a party*; **a deodorant spray** = deodorant that is sprayed on with an aerosol; **a stick deodorant** = deodorant that is rubbed onto the skin directly

deoxyribonucleic acid (DNA) [diːˌɒksɪraɪbəʊnjuːˈkleɪɪk ˈæsɪd] *noun* the basic genetic material in a cell

depart [dɪˈpɑːt] *verb* **(a)** to go away, to leave; *the coach departs from Victoria Coach Station at 0900* **(b) to depart from the normal procedure** = to act in a different way from the normal practice

department [dɪˈpɑːtmənt] *noun* **(a)** specialized section of a large company; *he is in charge of the marketing department*; *write to the complaints department about the service*; **accounts department** = section in a company which deals with money paid or received, borrowed or owed; *if you have a query about your bill, ask to speak to the accounts department* **(b)** one of the sections of the government; *the Department for Education and Employment*; *the Department of Transport* **(c)** part of a large shop; *if you want cheese you must go to the food department*; *you will find beds in the furniture department*

departmental [dipɑːtˈmentl] *adjective* referring to a department; *the decision was taken at departmental level*; **departmental manager** = manager of a department

department store [dɪˈpɑːtmənt ˈstɔː] *noun* a large shop with many departments; *Selfridges is one of the largest department stores in Oxford Street*

departure [dɪˈpɑːtʃə] *noun* **(a)** leaving; *the departure time is 3 o'clock*; *the plane's departure was delayed by two hours* **(b) departures** = (i) list of trains, planes, etc., which are leaving; (ii) part of an airport terminal which deals with passengers who are leaving; **departure lounge** = waiting area at an airport for people who are about to leave **(c) departure from** = working in a different way from usual; **this is a departure from our usual practice** = we are doing something in a different way from the usual one

depend [dɪˈpend] *verb* **(a)** to happen because of something or someone; *the success of the book will depend on the publicity campaign*; *I can't be sure that we will come to lunch - it depends on what time we get home from the party the night before*; (*informal*) **it (all) depends** = it is not certain; *we may go to France on holiday, or Spain, it all depends* **(b) to depend on someone** *or* **something** = to rely on someone *or* something, to be sure of someone *or* something; *you can't depend on Jack - he's always too busy to help*; *you can depend on her to do her best*

dependability [dɪpendəˈbɪlɪti] *noun* being able to be relied on; *the dependability of the train service varies from day to day* (NOTE: no plural)

dependable [dɪˈpendəbl] *adjective* that can be relied on; *people living in small villages need a dependable bus service*; *he's very dependable - everything you ask him to do gets done on time*

dependant [dɪˈpendənt] *noun* member of the family financially supported by another; *the rule applies to all employees and their dependants* (NOTE: do not confuse with **dependent**)

dependence [dɪˈpendəns] *noun* being dependent on someone or something; **drug dependence** *or* **dependence on drugs** (NOTE: no plural)

dependency [dɪˈpendənsi] *noun* **(a)** country which is ruled by another; *Britain and its former overseas dependencies* (NOTE: plural in this meaning is **dependencies**) **(b)** being dependent on someone or something; **drug dependency** *or* **dependency on drugs**

dependent [dɪˈpendənt] *adjective* **(a)** financially supported by someone else; *she has five dependent relatives* **(b)** relying on someone else; *the patients become very dependent on the hospital staff* (NOTE: do not confuse with **dependant**)

depending [dɪˈpendɪŋ] *adjective* **depending on** = which varies according to something; *it takes around one hour to drive, depending on the traffic*

depict [dɪˈpɪkt] *verb* (*formal*) to show, to describe; *a painting depicting a horse and rider*; *newspapers like to depict him as a raving madman, when to his friends he is calm and thoughtful*

depiction [dɪˈpɪkʃən] *noun* act of showing; *the depiction of the heroine of the film as a teenage drug addict was criticized*

deplete [dɪˈpliːt] *verb* to reduce available stocks or stores; *stocks of fish in the North Sea have been seriously depleted*

deplorable [dɪˈplɔːrəbl] *adjective* very bad; *what deplorable behaviour!*; *it was deplorable the way the fans behaved after the match*

deplorably [dɪˈplɔːrəbli] *adverb* in a very bad way; *they are deplorably late in paying their bills*

deplore [dɪˈplɔː] *verb* to say you dislike an action or an attitude or that you are sorry that something has happened; *the priest deplored the violence which had taken place*; *I deplore her way of making fun of the people who work in the office with her*

deploy [dɪˈplɔɪ] *verb* to spread out soldiers, etc., ready for action; *men were deployed all along the top of the hill*; *they are planning to deploy armoured cars at major street intersections*

deployment [dɪˈplɔɪmənt] *noun* act of deploying; *the committee is against the deployment of nuclear weapons*

deport [dɪˈpɔːt] *verb* to expel someone from a country; *he was deported when his visa expired*

deportation [diːpɔːˈteɪʃn] *noun* expulsion of a foreigner from a country; *now that his visa has expired, he risks deportation*

deportee [diːpɔːˈtiː] *noun* person who is deported; *the deportees were put on a plane*

deportment [dɪˈpɔːtmənt] *noun* (*formal*) way of walking, sitting or standing; *in the 1920s, young girls used to go to classes to improve their deportment* (NOTE: no plural; do not confuse with **deport** and **deportation**)

depose [dɪˈpəʊz] *verb* to remove a king from the throne or a ruler from office; *he was deposed by the army commander*; *the deposed president went into exile*

deposit [dɪˈpɒzɪt] **1** *noun* **(a)** money placed (in a bank); *her deposits in the bank had grown over the years*; **deposit account** = bank account which pays an interest if you leave money in it for some time; *compare* CURRENT ACCOUNT; **deposit slip** = piece of paper stamped by the cashier to prove that you have paid money into your account; **on deposit** = in a deposit account; *the money is on deposit in his bank account* **(b)** money given in advance so that the thing which you want to buy will not be sold to someone else; *she had to pay a deposit on the watch*; *can you leave £50 as deposit?*; *I paid a 30% deposit and don't have to pay anything more for six months* **2** *verb* to put money into a bank account; *he deposited £100 in his current account*; *the cheque arrived at long last, and I deposited it in the bank immediately*

deposition [depə'zɪʃn] *noun* **(a)** forcing someone to leave his position; *following his deposition he went to live in his villa in the south of France* **(b)** written statement of evidence of a witness; *the court was given the sworn deposition of five witnesses*

depositor [dɪ'pɒzɪtə] *noun* person who deposits money in a bank, building society, etc.; *depositors lost most of their savings when the bank crashed*; *we are offering specially high interest rates to long-term depositors*

depot ['depəʊ] *noun* **(a)** central warehouse for goods; *freight depot*; *goods depot*; *oil storage depot* **(b)** centre for transport; *bus depot*; *tram depot*

depraved [dɪ'preɪvd] *adjective* *(formal)* wicked or immoral; *these obscene paintings must be the work of a depraved artist*

depravity [dɪ'prævɪti] *noun* *(formal)* wickednes or immoral behaviour; *he inherited a fortune from his grandfather and lived a life of total depravity*

deprecate ['deprəkeɪt] *verb* to disapprove of something; *we deprecate the lack of interest in politics on the part of the young people* (NOTE: do not confuse with **depreciate**)

depreciate [dɪ'priːʃɪeɪt] *verb* **(a)** to lose value; *the pound has depreciated by 5% against the dollar* **(b)** to reduce the value of assets in accounts; *we depreciate our company cars over three years* (NOTE: do not confuse with **deprecate**)

depreciation [dɪpriːʃɪ'eɪʃn] *noun* **(a)** loss of value; *the pound has shown a depreciation of 5% against the dollar* **(b)** reduction in value of an asset; *depreciation rate* = the percentage by which an asset loses its value each year

depress [dɪ'pres] *verb* **(a)** to make sad or miserable; *listening to that particular piece of music always depresses me* **(b)** *(formal)* to push down a button; *to activate the alarm, depress both buttons simultaneously*

depressed [dɪ'prest] *adjective* **(a)** sad, miserable; *she's been feeling depressed since the accident* **(b) depressed area** = part of a country where people are poor and unemployed and living conditions are bad

depressing dɪ'presɪŋ *adjective* gloomy; *a depressing November day*; *that film is deeply depressing - it just made me want to cry*

depression [dɪ'preʃn] *noun* **(a)** mental state where you feel miserable and hopeless; *he was in a state of depression after the exams*; *she is subject to fits of depression* **(b)** low pressure area bringing bad weather; *the depression coming from the Atlantic will bring rain to most parts of the country*; *winds move anticlockwise round a depression* **(c)** economic crisis; *an economic depression*; **the (Great) Depression** = the world economic crisis of 1929-1933; *all economies suffered during the Depression* **(d)** place which is lower than the area round it; *a pool of water had formed in a depression in the rocks*

deprivation [deprɪ'veɪʃn] *noun* **(a)** being deprived of something; **sleep deprivation** = not allowing someone to have enough sleep **(b)** not having any of the things necessary for a normal life, such as food, housing, etc.; *they suffered dreadful deprivation(s) during the war*

deprive [dɪ'praɪv] *verb* **to deprive someone of something** = to take something away from someone, not to let someone have something; *as a writer, it was dreadful for him to be deprived of paper and pen in prison*

deprived [dɪ'praɪvd] *adjective* (person) who has not enjoyed any of society's benefits; *he comes from a very deprived background*

dept. = DEPARTMENT

depth [depθ] *noun* **(a)** how deep something is; *the depth of the lake is 20m*; *the submarine dived to a depth of 200m* **(b)** deepest or most extreme point; *in the depth of the Russian winter, temperatures can reach -45°C*; *they have a house in the depths of rural Wales*; **the depths of despair** = complete lack of hope; *when he was in the depths of despair he thought of committing suicide*

◊ **out of your depth** *phrase* **(a)** to be in deep water and not be able to touch the bottom; *she got out of her depth and had to be rescued by the lifeguards* **(b)** to be unable to understand; *he's quite out of his depth in discussions about monetary theory*

depth charge ['depθ 'tʃɑːdʒ] *noun* type of bomb dropped into the sea which is used to damage submarines by exploding deep beneath the surface; *they dropped depth charges to force the submarine to come to the surface*

depute 1 *verb* [dɪ'pjuːt] to give part of your responsibility to someone else; *he was deputed to attend the meeting on my behalf* **2** *noun* ['depjuːt] *(in Scotland)* deputy, person who takes the place of someone else; *the Depute Lord Provost*

deputize ['depjʊtaɪz] *verb* **to deputize for someone** = to take the place of someone; *he's deputizing for the chairman who has a cold*

deputy ['depjʊti] *noun* person who can take the place of another person; *he appointed her as his deputy*; *she's acting as deputy chairman while the chairman is in hospital*

derail [dɪ'reɪl] *verb* to make a train leave the rails; *the train was derailed by a block of concrete that had fallen on the line*

derailment [dɪ'reɪlmənt] *noun* action of a train leaving the rails; *services will be disrupted because of a derailment at Clapham Junction*

deranged [dɪ'reɪndʒd] *adjective* **mentally deranged** = with a mental illness; *he became mentally deranged and had to be taken to hospital*

derby ['dɑːbi *US* 'dɜːrbi] *noun* **(a) the Derby** = important horse race run each year in June at Epsom in Surrey; *he won the Derby three times*; *she's the owner of the Derby winner* **(b)** *US* important horse race; *he won the Kentucky Derby in 1996* **(c)** *US* bowler hat **(d)** sporting contest between local teams; *there are always crowds at the local derby* (NOTE: plural is **derbies**)

COMMENT: in British football, the most famous local derbies are between Arsenal and Tottenham Hotspur (in North London), Manchester United and Manchester City, Liverpool and Everton and Rangers and Celtic (in Glasgow)

deregulate [dɪˈrɛɡjuleɪt] *verb* to remove government restrictions from an industry; *Parliament is considering a Bill to deregulate the airlines*

deregulation [dɪˈrɛɡjuleɪʃn] *noun* reducing government control over an industry; *the deregulation of the airlines should result in lower fares*

derelict [ˈdɛrəlɪkt] **1** *adjective* ruined and abandoned; *they plan to build the housing development on derelict land near the city centre*; *they bought a derelict cottage to do it up* **2** *noun* tramp, homeless person; *the Salvation Army looks after the derelicts living in shop doorways*

dereliction [derɪˈlɪkʃən] *noun* (*formal*) **dereliction of duty** = failure to do what you ought to do by law; *he was accused of gross dereliction of duty*

deride [dɪˈraɪd] *verb* to laugh at someone; *his attempts to dance were derided by the rest of the class*

derisive [dɪˈraɪsɪv] *adjective* which laughs at someone; *derisive laughter greeted his attempts at tap dancing*

derisory [dɪˈraɪsəri] *adjective* ridiculously small; *they made the staff a derisory pay offer*

derivative [dɪˈrɪvətɪv] **1** *adjective* which is based on and copies something else; *his prize-winning designs are really very derivative* **2** *noun* (a) thing which is obtained from some other substance; *petroleum derivatives* (b) (*finance*) **derivatives** = securities such as options to buy or sell, which are derived from ordinary bonds and shares

derive [dɪˈraɪv] *verb* (a) **to derive from** *or* **to be derived from** = to come from originally; *the name of the plant 'fuchsia' is derived from the name of the German botanist, Fuchs* (b) (*formal*) to get; *the local people derive a good deal of pleasure from watching the antics of the tourists*

dermatological [dɜːmətəˈlɒdʒɪkl] *adjective* referring to dermatology; *they are carrying out dermatological tests*; *she was sent to the dermatological department in the hospital*

dermatologist [dɜːməˈtɒlədʒɪst] *noun* doctor who specializes in the study and treatment of the skin; *she consulted a dermatologist about her eczema*

dermatology [dɜːməˈtɒlədʒi] *noun* study and treatment of diseases of the skin

derogatory [dɪˈrɒɡətri] *adjective* showing contempt for someone; *he made some derogatory remarks about her hair*

descend [dɪˈsɛnd] *verb* (a) to go down (a ladder, etc.); *the president seemed to stumble as he descended the steps from the plane* (b) **to descend from someone** = to have someone as an ancestor; *on his mother's side, he is descended from one of William the Conqueror's knights* (c) **to descend upon** = to visit in large numbers; *his family descended upon us for Christmas*; *crowds of children descended on the ice cream van*

descendant [dɪˈsɛndənt] *noun* member of a family that started with a particular ancestor; *he is the descendant of an Indian prince*

descending [dɪˈsɛndɪŋ] *adjective* going down in steps; *we had three years of descending sales*; **in descending order** = listed with the highest first, and the lowest last; *the towns are listed in descending order of their populations*

descent [dɪˈsɛnt] *noun* (a) going down; *the descent into the mine takes just under three minutes* (b) family ancestry; *he can trace his descent back to William I*; **she is of Irish descent** = her family is from Ireland (NOTE: do not confuse with **dissent**)

describe [dɪˈskraɪb] *verb* to say or write what something *or* someone is like; *can you describe the car which hit the old lady?*; *she described how the bus suddenly hit a bridge*; *the police asked him to describe what happened*

description [dɪˈskrɪpʃn] *noun* saying or writing what something *or* someone is like; *she gave the police a clear description of the car*; **job description** = official document from a company which says what a job involves

descriptive [dɪˈskrɪptɪv] *adjective* which says what something is like; *we have a full descriptive catalogue with pictures of all our range*

desecrate [ˈdɛsɪkreɪt] *verb* to use a church, a grave, etc., in a disrespectful way; *they were accused of desecrating the churchyard by spraying slogans on the tombstones*

desecration [desɪˈkreɪʃən] *noun* act of desecrating; *the paper reported several cases of desecration of soldiers' graves*

desert 1 [ˈdɛzət] *noun* very dry area of the world; *from Los Angeles you can drive into the Mojave Desert*; *she plans to cross the Sahara Desert on a motorbike*; *it hardly ever rains in the desert*; *we watched a TV programme on desert animals* (NOTE: do not confuse with **dessert**) **2** *verb* [dɪˈzɜːt] (a) to leave the armed forces without permission; *the general ordered that all soldiers who had deserted should be captured and shot* (b) to leave someone all alone; *he deserted his wife when she was expecting their second child*

deserted [dɪˈzɜːtɪd] *adjective* with no one in or near; *a deserted farmhouse*; *the exhibition was completely deserted*

deserter [dɪˈsɜːtə] *noun* person who leaves the armed forces without permission; *they recaptured the deserters and brought them to the barracks*

desertification [dɪzɜːtɪfɪˈkeɪʃn] *noun* process by which an area of land becomes desert, through change of climate or intensive farming; *long periods of drought have brought about the desertification of whole areas of central Africa*

desertion [dɪˈzɜːʃən] *noun* (a) act of leaving the armed forces without permission; *during the war, soldiers were shot for desertion* (b) act of leaving someone, especially your wife or husband; *he is divorcing his wife because of her desertion* (NOTE: no plural)

desert island [ˈdɛzət ˈaɪlənd] *noun* tropical island with no inhabitants; *Robinson Crusoe was stranded on a desert island*

deserts [dɪˈzɜːts] *noun* (*formal*) what you deserve; **just deserts** = fair reward for what you have done; *the muggers got their just deserts when they were caught and beaten up by the crowd*

deserve [dɪ'zɜːv] *verb* to earn something because of what you have done; *he didn't deserve to win because I think he cheated*; *I've been on my feet all day - I think I deserve a sit-down*; *I'm sure she deserved to be punished*

deservedly [dɪ'zɜːvɪdli] *adverb* in a way which is deserved; *Stratford is deservedly famous for being the birthplace of Shakespeare*; *he was deservedly criticized for not calling the police*

desiccate ['desɪkeɪt] *verb* to make something completely dry; *antelope wander over the desiccated plains looking for food*; *desiccated coconut* = the white flesh of a coconut which has been dried; *she used desiccated coconut to make the cakes*

desiccation [desɪ'keɪʃn] *noun* drying out; *the greenhouse effect has led to the desiccation of parts of Central Africa* (NOTE: no plural)

deserving [dɪ'zɜːvɪŋ] *adjective* which ought to be supported or helped; *we contribute each year to several deserving causes*

design [dɪ'zaɪn] 1 *noun* (a) plan or drawing of something, before it is made or built; *here are the designs for the book cover*; *the architect has produced the designs for the new opera house* (b) to have designs on something = to plan to try to take something; *I think he has designs on my job* 2 *verb* to draw plans for the shape or appearance of something before it is made or built; *he designed the new university library*; *she designs garden furniture*

designate 1 ['dezɪgneɪt] *verb* to appoint someone to a post; *he has been designated as our representative at the meeting* 2 ['dezɪgnət] *suffix showing* a person who has been appointed but has not started work; *the ambassador-designate*

designation [dezɪg'neɪʃən] *noun* (a) act of designating; *his designation as ambassador* (b) name, title or description given to someone *or* something; *he has the official designation of Chief Medical Officer*

designer [dɪ'zaɪnə] *noun* artist who plans the shape or appearance of goods, clothes, rooms, etc.; *we've chosen an interior designer to plan the inside of the house*; *designer clothes* = clothes designed by a famous designer; *she was wearing designer jeans*; *designer label* = label attached to clothes made by a famous designer; *see also* STUBBLE

desirable [dɪ'zaɪrəbl] *adjective* which a lot of people want; *this has become a very desirable part of the town to live in*

desire [dɪ'zaɪə] 1 *noun* something that you want very much; *it's difficult to satisfy the public's desire for information*; *she had a sudden desire to lie down and go to sleep* 2 *verb* (*formal*) to want; *he will get you anything you desire*; *to leave a lot to be desired* = not to be of the right standard, not to be acceptable; *the sanitary conditions in the hotel leave a lot to be desired*

desirous [dɪ'zaɪrəs] *adjective* (*formal*) *desirous of something* = wanting something; *the envoy is desirous of a meeting at the king's earliest convenience*

desist [dɪ'zɪst] *verb* (*formal*) to desist from doing something = to stop doing something; *would you kindly desist from smoking while we are eating?*; *the man next door persisted in practising the bagpipes until we asked him politely to desist*

desk [desk] *noun* (a) table for writing (often with drawers); *he put the papers away in his desk drawer*;

she was sitting at her desk when the telephone rang; **desk pad** = pad of paper kept on a desk for writing notes (b) **cash desk** *or* **pay desk** = place in a shop where you pay for the goods bought; *please pay at the cash desk* (c) section of a newspaper, of a government department; *he works on the City desk*; *she on the Central Europe desk in the Foreign Office*

desolate 1 ['desələt] *adjective* bleak and deserted; *she crossed the desolate mountainside, carrying her baby* 2 ['desəleɪt] *verb* to make very sad; *she was desolated by the news*

despair [dɪ'speə] 1 *noun* hopelessness; *when he lost his job and his girlfriend left him, he was filled with despair*; *the depths of despair* = complete lack of hope (NOTE: no plural) 2 *verb* **to despair of something** = to give up hope of something; *after two months, he despaired of ever being rescued*

despairing [dɪ'speərɪŋ] *adjective* feeling despair; *the ship's last despairing calls for help were heard by a radio operator*

despatch [dɪs'pætʃ] *see* DISPATCH

desperate ['desprət] *adjective* (a) hopeless; *supplies ran out and the situation was becoming desperate* (b) urgent; *there is a desperate need of medical supplies* (c) wild with despair; *when he didn't phone she became desperate with worry*

desperately ['desprətli] *adverb* (a) urgently; *the hospital desperately needs medical supplies* (b) wildly; *she was desperately worried when her daughter had still not come home at 11 p.m.*

desperation [despə'reɪʃn] *noun* hopelessness that leads you to try anything in order to make things better; *substituting the goalkeeper was an act of desperation*; *their attempts to hire any vehicle showed their desperation to get away before the enemy army arrived*; **in desperation** = because you are desperate; *in desperation, she called the fire brigade*

despicable [dɪ'spɪkəbl] *adjective* unpleasant, which you can despise; *his despicable behaviour towards his wife*

despise [dɪ'spaɪz] *verb* to look down on someone, to think someone is not worth much; *I despise people who always agree with the boss*; *she despised his attempts to speak with a smart accent*

despite [dɪ'spaɪt] *preposition* in spite of; *despite the wet weather we still enjoyed our holiday*

despondent [dɪ'spɒndənt] *adjective* discouraged, unhappy; *being let down by your best friend is enough to make anyone despondent*

despot ['despɒt] *noun* dictator, cruel ruler; *he ruled the country as a despot for twenty years*

dessert [dɪ'zɜːt] *noun* sweet course at the end of a meal; *the meal will end with a dessert of strawberries and cream*; *what's for dessert?*; **dessert menu** = special separate menu for desserts in a restaurant; *can I see the dessert menu please?*; **dessert spoon** = spoon which is larger than a teaspoon, but smaller than a soup spoon, used for eating desserts (NOTE: do not confuse with **desert**; the word **dessert** is mainly used in restaurants. At home, this part of the meal is usually called **the sweet** *or* **afters** *or* **pudding**)

destabilize [dɪ'steɪbɪlaɪz] *verb* to make a country or government less stable; *enemy agents were accused of trying to destabilize the régime*

destination [destɪˈneɪʃn] *noun* place to which a person or vehicle is going; *we reached our destination at eight o'clock*; *the destination is shown on the front of the bus*

destined [ˈdestɪnd] *adjective* **(a) destined for** = being sent to; *all mail destined for Canada is delayed because of the postal workers' strike* **(b)** inevitably going to have, do or experience something; *she's destined for a great career on TV*; *they were destined to fail in their search for gold*

destiny [ˈdestɪni] *noun* **(a)** what will happen to you in the future; *the war affected the destinies of many people* **(b)** power that controls what happens to you in the future; *you never know what destiny has in store for you*

destitute [ˈdestɪtjuːt] *adjective* with no money or belongings; *when her husband died he left her destitute with three little children*

destroy [dɪˈstrɔɪ] *verb* to ruin completely; *the bomb destroyed several buildings*; *a lot of private property was destroyed in the war*

destroyer [dɪˈstrɔɪə] *noun* medium-sized naval ship; *an aircraft carrier and two destroyers moved towards the Mediterranean*

destruction [dɪˈstrʌkʃn] *noun* complete ruining; *the volcano caused enormous destruction*; *the destruction of the village by enemy bombs*; *after the bomb attack there was a scene of total destruction* (NOTE: no plural)

destructive [dɪˈstrʌktɪv] *adjective* which destroys; *the destructive power of a typhoon*

detach [dɪˈtætʃ] *verb* to separate; *detach the bottom part of the form, sign it, and return it to us*

detached [dɪˈtætʃt] *adjective* **(a) detached house** = house which stands alone, not attached to another; *they live in a pleasant detached house with a large garden*; *compare* SEMI-DETACHED **(b)** not under someone's influence; *he is a detached observer of the political scene*; *he tries to take a detached view of each patient who comes to see him*

detachment [dɪˈtætʃmənt] *noun* **(a)** indifference; lack of particular interest; *he glanced at the advancing policemen with an air of detachment* **(b)** small group of soldiers, etc.; *detachments of marines have been sent to the island*

detail [ˈdiːteɪl] **1** *noun* **(a)** small item of information; *send in your CV including full details of your past experience*; *can you give me further details of when the accident took place?*; *I can't make out the details in the photo because the light is bad*; *the policeman noted down the details of the accident* **(b) in detail** = with plenty of details; *the catalogue lists all the furniture in detail*; *please describe the circumstances of the accident in as much detail as possible* **2** *verb* **(a)** to list all the small items; *he detailed the work which had to be done* **(b) to detail someone to do something** = to tell someone to do a job; *he was detailed to wash the kitchen floor*

detailed [ˈdiːteɪld] *adjective* in detail, giving a lot of details; *we need a detailed list of the items which have been stolen*; *the police issued detailed descriptions of the two men*

detain [dɪˈteɪn] *verb* **(a)** to keep someone in a police station or prison; *the police have detained a man for questioning* **(b)** to stop someone from leaving; *I'm sorry I'm late - I was detained by a phone call*

detainee [diːteɪˈniː] *noun* person held in prison; *the government has promised to release all political detainees*

detect [dɪˈtekt] *verb* to discover; to notice; *a smoke detector detects the presence of smoke*; *if breast cancer is detected early enough, it can be cured*; *do I detect a note of optimism in your report?*

detectable [dɪˈtektəbl] *adjective* which can be detected; *a scarcely detectable trace of arsenic*

detection [dɪˈtekʃn] *noun* **(a)** act of detecting, of solving a crime; *he hid under the bed and managed to escape detection for three days*; **detection rate** = the number of crimes solved, shown as a percentage of all crimes; *the detection rate for burglaries has fallen* **(b)** action of detecting something; *the detection of traces of poison in the cup*; *the early detection of breast cancer* (NOTE: no plural)

detective [dɪˈtektɪv] *noun* policeman who investigates crimes; *detectives have interviewed four suspects*; **private detective** = detective who is not part of a police force, and works for a fee; *we hired a private detective to track them down*

detector [dɪˈtektə] *noun* instrument which discovers something; *smoke detectors are fitted in all the rooms*

détente [deɪˈtɑːnt] *noun* relaxation of tension between two or more countries; *after years of suspicion, the new government has adopted a policy of détente*

detention [dɪˈtenʃn] *noun* **(a)** imprisonment; *after he was released from detention he committed the same offence again*; *the internees were kept in detention camps*; **detention centre** = centre where young criminals are kept **(b)** keeping children at school as a punishment; *the children were kept in detention after school* (NOTE: no plural)

deter [dɪˈtɜː] *verb* **to deter someone from doing something** = to discourage someone from doing something; *the heavy rain didn't deter the pilgrims from visiting the shrine*; *we have installed cameras to deter shoplifters* (NOTE: deterring - deterred)

detergent [dɪˈtɜːdʒənt] *noun* cleaning substance which removes grease and bacteria from clothes, dishes, etc.; *this detergent will not harm your skin*; *she started the washing machine and realized she had forgotten to put in any detergent*

deteriorate [dɪˈtɪəriəreɪt] *verb* to go bad; to get worse; *her health has deteriorated since the accident*; *deteriorating conditions on the roads make driving difficult*

determination [dɪtɜːmɪˈneɪʃn] *noun* **(a)** strong wish to do something, and not to let anyone stop you doing it; *his determination to win the prize*; *the government needs to show more determination in their fight against drugs* **(b)** *(formal)* deciding something; *determination of deadlines will be crucial to the planning of the project* (NOTE: no plural)

determine [dɪˈtɜːmɪn] *verb* **(a)** to fix (a date, etc.); *the meeting will be at a date still to be determined* **(b) to determine to do something** = to make up your mind to do something; *I determined not to make the same mistake again*

determined [dɪˈtɜːmɪnd] *adjective* decided; *he had a very determined expression on his face as he entered the ring*; *she is determined to win the prize*

deterrence [dɪˈterəns] *noun* action of discouraging attacks; *the main aim of the new aircraft will be the deterrence of possible bombing attacks* (NOTE: no plural)

deterrent [dɪˈterənt] *noun* thing which discourages; *cameras by the side of the road act as a deterrent to speeding motorists*; **nuclear deterrent** = nuclear weapon which it is hoped will prevent attacks from other countries

detest [dɪˈtest] *verb* to dislike intensely; *he detests having to go to his mother-in-law's for Christmas*; *I detest her constant whistling while she works*

detestable [dɪˈtestəbl] *adjective* which you detest, very unpleasant; *he has the detestable habit of scratching his head when serving food*

detestation [dɪtesˈteɪʃn] *noun* strong dislike; *she showed her detestation of their behaviour by refusing to come to the meeting* (NOTE: no plural)

detonate [ˈdetəneɪt] *verb* **(a)** to set off an explosive; *the police detonated the package found under the car* **(b)** to explode; *a shell landed in their garden but failed to detonate*

detour [ˈdiːtʊə] *noun* roundabout road taken to avoid an obstacle or to see something not on the direct route; *we made a detour to go to visit churches by the coast*; *you'll have to make a detour because the road is under repair*

detract [dɪˈtrækt] *verb* to **detract from something** = to make something less useful, attractive or interesting; *her rudeness to the judges somehow detracted from the prize-giving ceremony*

detractor [dɪˈtræktə] *noun* person who criticizes something; *his book is seen as a reply to his detractors*

detriment [ˈdetrɪmənt] *noun* damage; to the **detriment of** = which will damage; *all that hard work has been to the detriment of their marriage*

detrimental [detrɪˈmentl] *adjective* which can harm; *there are notices everywhere stating that smoking is detrimental to health*

detritus [diːˈtraɪtəs] *noun* rubbish, waste matter; *they spent days clearing the detritus from the bottom of the lake* (NOTE: no plural)

Deutschmark [ˈdɔɪtʃmɑːk] *noun* currency used in Germany; *the book costs 25,00 DM or DM25,00* (NOTE: usually written DM when used with a figure: **DM25,00**)

devaluation [diːvæljuˈeɪʃn] *noun* reducing the international value of a currency; *the devaluation of the Belgian franc*

devalue [diːˈvæljuː] *verb* to reduce the value of a currency in relation to that of other countries; *the pound has been devalued by 7%*; *we will have to devalue to make our goods more competitive*

devastate [ˈdevəsteɪt] *verb* to wreck completely; *the explosion devastated the airline's offices*

devastated [ˈdevəsteɪtɪd] *adjective* **(a)** badly damaged; *relief agencies are trying to help the devastated region* **(b)** upset by news, etc.; *she was devastated when she was made redundant*; *when he read the report in the paper he was completely devastated*

devastating [ˈdevəsteɪtɪŋ] *adjective* **(a)** causing a lot of damage; *the country has still not recovered from the devastating effects of the storm* **(b)** shocking, upsetting; *the news from Paris was devastating*

devastation [devəˈsteɪʃn] *noun* widespread damage; *the storm caused widespread devastation along the coast*

develop [dɪˈveləp] *verb* **(a)** to grow and change; *eventually, a caterpillar will develop into a butterfly* **(b)** to make larger; *she does exercises to develop her calf muscles* **(c)** to start a disease, etc.; *she developed a cold from standing in the rain* **(d)** to produce and fix a photograph from film; *we can develop your film in an hour* **(e)** to plan and produce; *to develop a new product* **(f)** to plan and build; *they are planning to develop the site as an industrial estate*; *the company is developing a chain of motorway service stations*

developed [dɪˈveləpt] *adjective* a **developed area** = an area which has buildings on it; the **developed world** = countries which are industrialized

developer [dɪˈveləpə] *noun* **(a)** liquid for developing photographs; *she put the film into a bath of developer* **(b)** person or company that plans and builds roads, airports, houses, factories or office buildings; *the land has been acquired by developers for an industrial park*; **property developer** = person who plans and builds property

developing [dɪˈveləpɪŋ] *adjective* **(a)** growing; *his rapidly developing network of contacts in government*; *her developing knowledge of the English language* **(b)** **developing countries** = countries which are becoming industrialized

development [dɪˈveləpmənt] *noun* **(a)** growth; *the development of the embryo takes place rapidly*; **economic development** = process by which a country's economy changes and becomes more industrialized; **industrial development** = planning and building of new industries in special areas **(b)** **developments** = things which happen; *the police are waiting for further developments in the case* **(c)** planning the production of a new product; *the development of new pesticides will take some time*; *see also* RESEARCH AND DEVELOPMENT **(d)** planning and building on an area of land; *they are planning large-scale development of the former docks*; **development plan** = plan drawn up by a government or local council showing how an area will be developed over a long period; **housing development** = group of houses built at the same time

developmental [dɪveləpˈmentl] *adjective* at a **developmental stage** = being developed; *the product is at an advanced developmental stage*

deviant [ˈdiːvɪənt] **1** *adjective* deviating from normal; **deviant behaviour** = behaviour which is very bad and different from what is normal **2** *noun* person who deviates from normal behaviour; *they discovered that the new headmaster was a sexual deviant*

deviate [ˈdiːvɪeɪt] *verb* to **deviate from** = to turn away from what is normal or usual; *the celebrations deviated from their normal pattern by being held on a Sunday*; *he did not deviate from the written version of his speech*

deviation [diːvɪˈeɪʃn] *noun* changing from what is normal or usual; *there must be no deviation from the rules laid down by the management*

device [dɪˈvaɪs] *noun* **(a)** small useful machine; *he invented a device for screwing tops on bottles*; *the engineers brought in a device for taking rock samples*

(b) he was left to his own devices = he was left to do whatever he wanted

devil ['devl] *noun* **(a)** evil spirit; *he believes in ghosts and devils and all that sort of thing* **(b)** *(informal: showing surprise)* **what the devil?** = what on earth?; *what the devil has been going on here while we've been away?* **(c)** *(informal)* person; *he's won the lottery, lucky devil!; poor devil! I must go and see him in hospital*

devilish ['devɪlɪʃ] *adjective* wicked, referring to the devil; *he devised a devilish plan to blow up the Houses of Parliament*

devious ['diːviəs] *adjective* **(a)** not honest or straightforward; *it's just a very devious plan to avoid paying the staff more money* **(b)** not going straight; *the taxi took us on a very devious route to Piccadilly Circus*

devise [dɪ'vaɪz] *verb* to think up, to invent; *we've devised a new timetable for the summer term*

devoid [dɪ'vɔɪd] *adjective* **devoid of** = empty of, without; **the book is devoid of literary merit** = the book has no literary merit at all

devolution [diːvə'ljuːʃn] *noun* passing of power from a central government to a local or regional authority; *the majority voted for devolution for Scotland*

devolve [dɪ'vɒlv] *verb* to pass to another authority; *power is devolved to regional assemblies*; *if the chairman is absent his authority devolves on the deputy chairman*

devote [dɪ'vəʊt] *verb* **to devote time to something** = to spend precious time on something; *don't you think you've devoted enough time to your model planes?*; **to devote yourself to** = to spend all your time on; *she devoted herself to looking after refugee children*

devoted [dɪ'vəʊtɪd] *adjective* **(a) devoted to someone** = loving someone; *he is devoted to his children* **(b) devoted to something** = spending all your time on something; *she's devoted to her flower garden*

devotee [devə'tiː] *noun* someone who likes something very much, an enthusiastic follower; *he's a devotee of organic gardening*

devotion [dɪ'vəʊʃn] *noun* **(a)** love; *her devotion to her father*; *his devotion to his stamp collection*; *her devotion to duty is remarkable* **(b)** constant work on behalf of; *she received an award for twenty years' devotion to the needs of the handicapped* **(c)** *(formal)* **devotions** = prayers; *she is at her devotions*

devour [dɪ'vaʊə] *verb (formal)* to eat greedily; *the lions devoured the pieces of meat; they were so hungry after their walk that they devoured everything I put on the table*

devout [dɪ'vaʊt] *adjective* deeply concerned with religion; *she is a devout Catholic*

dew [djuː] *noun* water which forms at night on objects in the open air; *the grass was wet with dew* (NOTE: do not confuse with **due**)

dewy-eyed ['djuːi 'aɪd] *adjective* with eyes that are wet from crying; *she watched dewy-eyed as her son collected his prize*

diabetes [daɪə'biːtiːz] *noun* illness where the body cannot control sugar absorption because of the pancreas does not produce enough insulin; *some people with diabetes give themselves insulin injections* (NOTE: no plural)

diabetic [daɪə'betɪk] **1** *adjective* referring to diabetes; *the hospital provides a special diet for diabetic patients*; *he's on a strict diabetic diet*; **diabetic food** = special food with a low sugar content which can be eaten by people with diabetes **2** *noun* person with diabetes; *she is a diabetic and has to have regular injections of insulin*

diabolical [daɪə'bɒlɪkl] *adjective* **(a)** referring to the devil; evil and wicked; *they devised a diabolical plot to assassinate the Prime Minister* **(b)** *(informal)* very bad; *the food in the staff canteen is diabolical*

diagnose [daɪəg'nəʊz] *verb* to identify a patient's illness by examining him or her and noting symptoms; *the doctor diagnosed cancer*

diagnosis [daɪəg'nəʊsɪs] *noun* identification of an illness; *tests confirmed the doctor's diagnosis*; *the doctor's diagnosis was cancer, but the patient asked for a second opinion* (NOTE: plural is **diagnoses**)

diagnostic [daɪəg'nɒstɪk] *adjective* referring to diagnosis; **diagnostic test** = test which helps a doctor diagnose an illness, or a car mechanic decide if anything is wrong with a car engine

diagonal [daɪ'ægənl] **1** *adjective* slantwise, going from one corner to another; *he drew a diagonal line on the floor, running from one corner of the room to the other*; *areas of the map shaded with diagonal lines indicate cultivated land* **2** *noun* diagonal line; *draw a diagonal from one corner of the square to the other*

diagram ['daɪəgræm] *noun* sketch, plan or accurate drawing; *she drew a diagram to show how to get to her house*; *the book gives a diagram of the circulation of blood*

diagrammatically ['daɪəgrə'mætɪkli] *adverb* in the form of a diagram; *the process is shown diagrammatically on the next page*

dial ['daɪəl] **1** *noun* round face of a clock, meter, telephone, etc.; *modern telephones don't have dials - just buttons* **2** *verb* to call a telephone number; *to call the police you must dial 999; dial 9 to get an outside line*; **to dial direct** = to contact a phone number yourself without asking the operator to do it for you; *you can dial New York direct from London* (NOTE: **dialling - dialled**, but American spelling is **dialing - dialed**)

dialect ['daɪəlekt] *noun* variety of a language spoken in a particular area; *they were speaking in some local dialect which I found very hard to understand*

dialling *US* **dialing** ['daɪəlɪŋ] *noun* making a number on the telephone; **dialling code** = special phone number for a town or country; *the international dialling code for the UK is 00-44*; **dialling tone** = sound made by a telephone to show that it is ready for you to dial

dialogue *US* **dialog** ['daɪəlɒg] *noun* **(a)** conversation between two people; *the next exercise on the tape is a dialogue between a shopkeeper and a customer* **(b)** spoken words in a film or TV drama; *turn the volume up so that we can hear the dialogue more clearly* **(c)** political talks or negotiations; *the government is trying to encourage greater dialogue in the Middle East*

diameter [daɪ'æmɪtə] *noun* distance across the centre of a circle; *each rod is one centimetre in diameter*

205

diametrically [daɪə'metrɪklɪ] *adverb* **diametrically opposite to** *or* **opposed** = totally the opposite of; *what they did was diametrically opposite to what we had agreed; their views are diametrically opposed*

diamond ['daɪəmənd] *noun* **(a)** very hard colourless precious stone; *he gave her a diamond ring; diamonds sparkled on her crown*; **diamond wedding** = 60th anniversary of a wedding day **(b)** one of the red suits in a pack of cards; *he held the ten of diamonds* (NOTE: the other red suit is **hearts; clubs** and spades are the black suits)

diaper ['daɪəpə] *noun US* cloth which is wrapped round a baby's bottom; *she changed the baby's diaper* (NOTE: British English for this is **nappy**)

diaphragm ['daɪəfræm] *noun* **(a)** thin sheet which vibrates with noise; *the diaphragm in a hearing aid* **(b)** thin layer of tissue which separates the chest from the abdomen, and pulls air into the lungs when you breathe; *the stomach lies in the left upper part of the abdomen, just under the diaphragm* **(c)** contraceptive device for women

diarist ['daɪərɪst] *noun* person who writes a diary; *Samuel Pepys, the famous 17th century diarist*

diarrhoea *US* **diarrhea** [daɪə'rɪə] *noun* condition where a patient frequently passes liquid faeces; *he had an attack of diarrhoea after going to the restaurant; she complained of mild diarrhoea*

diary ['daɪərɪ] *noun* **(a)** description of what has happened in your life day by day; *he kept a diary for years; she kept a diary of the places she visited on holiday* **(b)** small book in which you write notes or make appointments for each day of the week; *I've noted the appointment in my desk diary; I can't fix the date immediately because I haven't got my diary with me* (NOTE: plural is **diaries**)

dice [daɪs] **1** *noun* small cube with one to six dots on each face, used for playing games; *shake the dice in the cup and then throw them onto the board; he lost hundreds of pounds playing dice* (NOTE: plural is **dice**) **2** *verb* **(a)** to cut food into small cubes; *diced potato* **(b)** *(informal)* **to dice with death** = to do something very risky; *running across the main road is dicing with death*

dicey ['daɪsɪ] *adjective (informal)* dangerous; *crossing the frozen lake is a bit dicey at this time of year*

dick [dɪk] *noun* **(a)** *US (slang)* detective, especially a private detective; *some dick working for the family of the dead man called me* **(b)** *(slang)* penis

dictate [dɪk'teɪt] *verb* **(a)** to say something to someone who writes down your words; *she dictated a letter to her secretary; he dictated his address to me over the phone* **(b)** to tell someone what to do; *the army commander dictated the terms of the surrender; she's always trying to dictate to us how to run the business*

dictates ['dɪkteɪts] *noun (formal)* ideas or feelings that strongly influence people; *she always follows the dictates of fashion; we must follow the dictates of our consciences*

dictation [dɪk'teɪʃn] *noun* act of dictating something to be written down; *I got nine out of ten for French dictation*; **to take dictation** = to write down what someone is saying; *the secretary was taking dictation from the managing director*; **dictation speed** =

number of words per minute which a secretary can write down in shorthand

dictator [dɪk'teɪtə] *noun* person who rules a country alone; *the country was ruled by a fascist dictator; the rebel army finally overthrew the dictator*

dictatorial [dɪktə'tɔːrɪəl] *adjective* behaving like a dictator; *officials dislike the Minister's dictatorial way of working*

dictatorship [dɪk'teɪtəʃɪp] *noun* rule of a country by one person; *the country was ruled for ten years by a military dictatorship*

diction ['dɪkʃn] *noun* way of speaking; *her clear diction makes her popular for poetry readings*

dictionary ['dɪkʃənrɪ] *noun* book which lists words in alphabetical order, giving their meanings or translations into other languages; *look up the word in the dictionary if you don't know what it means*; **a French dictionary** = book which gives English words with their French translations, and French words with their English translations; *if you want to find the French translation of this word, look it up in a French dictionary*; **pocket dictionary** = small dictionary which you can put in your pocket (NOTE: plural is **dictionaries**)

dictum ['dɪktəm] *noun* well-known saying made by a famous person; *we follow the dictum 'if it's not broken, don't try to mend it'* (NOTE: plural is **dicta** ['dɪktə])

did, didn't [dɪd or dɪdnt] *see* DO

didactic [daɪ'dæktɪk] *adjective (formal)* which teaches morality; *she wrote some didactic stories for small children*

die [daɪ] *verb* **(a)** to stop living; *his mother died in 1995; she died in a car crash; if you don't water the plants they'll die* **(b)** **dying for** *or* **to** = wanting something very much; *we're dying for a cold drink; I'm dying to read his book* (NOTE: do not confuse with **dye**)

die away ['daɪ ə'weɪ] *verb* to become less noisy; *the sound of footsteps died away*

die down ['daɪ 'daʊn] *verb* **(a)** to get less strong; *the wind began to die down; the government is waiting for the street protests to die down* **(b)** *(of plants)* to die and lose their stems and leaves; *chrysanthemums will die down during the winter*

die out ['daɪ 'aʊt] *verb* to disappear gradually; *the habit of having a cooked breakfast is dying out; tigers are likely to die out unless measures are taken to protect them*

diesel ['diːzl] *noun* **(a)** **diesel (oil)** = engine fuel which is thicker than petrol; *my new car runs on diesel; London taxis have diesel engines* **(b)** car with a diesel engine; *his latest car is a diesel*

diet ['daɪət] **1** *noun* **(a)** kind of food you eat; *he lives on a diet of bread and beer; during the war, people were much healthier than now because their diet was simpler* **(b)** eating only certain types of food, either to become thinner or to cure an illness; *the doctor told her to follow a strict diet; because she is pregnant she has to follow a diet*; **salt-free diet** = diet which does not contain salt; **to be on a diet** = to eat only certain types of food, especially in order to become thin or to deal with an illness; *he's been on a diet for some weeks, but still hasn't lost enough weight*; **to go on a diet** = to start to eat less; *she went on a diet before going on holiday* **2** *verb* to eat less food or only one sort of food;

she dieted for two weeks before going on holiday; he is dieting to try to lose weight

dietary ['daɪətrɪ] *adjective* referring to a diet; **dietary fibre** = roughage, fibrous matter in food, which cannot be digested

dieter ['daɪətə] *noun* person who is on a diet; *dieters should try the new low-fat yoghurt*

dietician [daɪə'tɪʃən] *noun* a person who specializes in the study of diets and advises people on what they should eat; *the dietician warned me not to eat too much red meat*

differ ['dɪfə] *verb* **(a)** not to be the same as something else; *the two machines differ considerably - one has an electric motor, the other runs on oil*; **to differ from** = to be different from, not to be the same as; *this car differs from the earlier model; their business differs from ours in one important aspect* **(b) I beg to differ** = I do not agree

difference ['dɪfrəns] *noun* **(a)** way in which two things are not the same; *can you tell the difference between an apple and a pear with your eyes shut?; what is the difference in price between these two cars?; it doesn't make any difference* = it's not important; *you can use any colour you like - it doesn't make any difference*; **to split the difference** = to agree on a figure which is half way between two figures suggested; *twenty's too many, ten's not enough, let's split the difference and say fifteen; you are offering £20 and he wants £40, so why don't you split the difference and settle on £30?* **(b) differences** = arguments between people; *they had a meeting to try to settle their differences*

different ['dɪfrənt] *adjective* not the same; *living in the town is very different from living in the country; I went to three different clothes shops but I couldn't find anything in my size; he looks different now that he has a beard; that's quite a different matter or a different kettle of fish* = it's not at all the same thing

differential [dɪfə'renʃl] **1** *adjective* which shows a difference; *the company has a differential system of pay for various levels of responsibility* **2** *noun* **(a) wage differentials** = differences in salary between workers in different grades of jobs **(b)** *(in a motor)* gears between two drive shafts that allow one shaft to turn at a different speed from the other, while still transmitting power

differentiate [dɪfə'renʃɪeɪt] *verb* **(a)** to recognize the difference between two things; *they couldn't differentiate between cheap champagne and really top-quality stuff* **(b)** to treat two things differently; *in this school, we don't differentiate between boys and girls*

differentiation [dɪfərenʃɪ'eɪʃən] *noun* act of making a difference between things; *there is no differentiation in treatment between male and female staff*

difficult ['dɪfɪkʌlt] *adjective* not easy; which is hard to do; *the German examination was very difficult - half the class got low marks; finding a parking space is difficult on Saturday mornings; the company is finding it difficult to sell their cars in the European market; it's difficult for me to judge my own sister objectively*; **to make things** *or* **life difficult for someone** = to create problems for someone; *his main aim at the office seems to be to make life as difficult as possible for the secretaries*

difficulty ['dɪfɪkʌltɪ] *noun* **(a) to have difficulty with something** *or* **in doing something** to find it hard to do something; *she has difficulty in paying the rent* **(b)** problem; *the difficulty is that nobody has a driving licence; he is in financial difficulties; she went swimming in the rough sea and got into difficulties*; **to create** *or* **make difficulties for someone** = to create problems for someone; *she doesn't realize that going on holiday now is going to make difficulties for everyone* (NOTE: plural is **difficulties**)

diffidence ['dɪfɪdəns] *noun* shyness, being diffident; *when she went into the lecture room for the first time she had difficulty in overcoming her natural diffidence*

diffident ['dɪfɪdənt] *adjective* shy; lacking confidence; *the young assistant is very diffident, and doesn't like talking to the press*

diffuse 1 *adjective* [dɪ'fjuːs] vague or unclear; *his writing tends to be very diffuse* **2** *verb* [dɪ'fjuːz] to spread out; to send out; **diffused light(ing)** = soft light which is spread out and not concentrated in one spot; *diffused lighting is good for intimate conversations but it makes reading difficult*

dig [dɪg] **1** *verb* to make a hole in the ground (with a spade); *she's been digging in the garden all morning; the prisoners dug a tunnel to try to escape; digging holes in the ground is hard work* (NOTE: **digging - dug** [dʌg] **- has dug**) **2** *noun* **(a)** archaeological excavation, making holes in the ground to find something; *they are working on a dig to uncover the remains of a Roman fort* **(b)** funny attack in words; *the song is a dig at the Prime Minister*

digest 1 *verb* [daɪ'dʒest] **(a)** to break down food in the stomach and intestine and convert it into elements which can be absorbed by the body; *I find cabbage salad difficult to digest* **(b)** to think about something and understand it fully; *give me time to digest the news* **2** *noun* ['daɪdʒest] summary; *he published a digest of the conference proceedings*

digestible [daɪ'dʒestəbl] *adjective* which can be digested; *I don't find raw garlic very digestible*

digestion [dɪ'dʒestʃən] *noun* process by which food is broken down and elements absorbed into the body; *brown bread helps the digestion*

digestive [daɪ'dʒestɪv] *adjective* which helps you to digest; *he has troubles in the digestive system*; **digestive biscuit** = sweet wholemeal biscuit; **the digestive tract** = passage formed of the mouth, throat, stomach, intestines and rectum, down which food passes and is digested

digger ['dɪgə] *noun* person or machine that digs; *they brought in mechanical diggers to lay the pipes*

digit ['dɪdʒɪt] *noun* single number; *a seven-digit phone number*

digital ['dɪdʒɪtəl] *adjective* **(a)** which involves figures; **digital clock** = clock where the time is shown by figures, such as 11:52:02, and not by hands **(b)** *(of audio and video signals)* converted into a form that can be processed by computers and accurately reproduced; *there will soon be hundreds of digital channels available on TV*

dignified ['dɪgnɪfaɪd] *adjective* solemn and important-looking; *a dignified old gentleman; she was walking at a dignified pace*

dignitary ['dɪgnɪtri] *noun* important person; *various dignitaries attended to opening ceremony and made speeches*; **civic dignitaries** = the mayor and town council (NOTE: plural is **dignitaries**)

dignity ['dɪgnɪti] *noun* solemn or serious way of behaving; *the dignity of the occasion was spoilt when the mayor got drunk*; **to be beneath your dignity** = to be too proud to do something; *it's beneath his dignity to do the washing up* (NOTE: no plural)

digress [daɪ'gres] *verb* (*formal*) to wander away from the subject when speaking; *the speaker digressed into talking about his childhood in Wales*

digression [daɪ'greʃən] *noun* wandering away from the subject when speaking or writing; *he speech was full of amusing digressions about his private life*

digs [dɪgz] *noun* (*informal*) furnished room or rooms let to students, etc.; *he's living in digs while he's trying to find a flat ot buy*; *she found some nice digs near the college*

dig up ['dɪg 'ʌp] *verb* (**a**) to find by digging; *we dug up a Roman coin in the garden* (**b**) to break a solid surface by digging; *the workmen had to dig the road up to mend the water main* (**c**) to find information with difficulty; *he managed to dig up some old government statistics*

dike [daɪk] *see* DYKE

dilapidated [dɪ'læpɪdeɪtɪd] *adjective* falling into ruin; *she drives a dilapidated old Ford*; *their house is so dilapidated that it has been condemned by the council*

dilate [daɪ'leɪt] *verb* to swell; *the veins in the left leg have become dilated*; *the drug is used to dilate the pupil of the eye*

dilemma [dɪ'lemə] *noun* serious problem, where a choice has to be made between several bad alternatives; *how can we ever solve this awful dilemma?*; **in a dilemma** = not sure what action to take

diligence ['dɪlɪdʒəns] *noun* hard, careful work; *her diligence in searching the records finally produced results*

diligent ['dɪlɪdʒənt] *adjective* hard-working; *she's been a diligent student during all her time at college*

diligently ['dɪlɪdʒəntli] *adverb* in a hard-working way; *he diligently went through all the government statistics for 1978*

dill [dɪl] *noun* common herb used in cooking and in medicine; **dill pickles** = pickled cucumbers flavoured with dill

dilute [daɪ'ljuːt] **1** *verb* (**a**) to add a liquid, usually water, to another liquid to make it weaker; *dilute the disinfectant with water* (**b**) to make something weaker and less effective; *the proposals were thought too radical and were diluted before being announced to the press* **2** *adjective* with water added; *a solution of dilute antiseptic*

dilution [daɪ'luːʃən] *noun* action of diluting; *the dilution of acid with water*; *it's a dilution of what the party promised in their election manifesto*

dim [dɪm] **1** *adjective* (**a**) weak (light); *the lights grew dimmer*; **I have a dim recollection of it** = I can remember it vaguely; **to take a dim view of something** = to disapprove of something; *the boss takes a very dim view of people who arrive late for work* (**b**) rather stupid; *he must be the dimmest sales manager we've*

ever had (NOTE: **dimmer - dimmest**) **2** *verb* (**a**) to make a light less bright; *they dimmed the cabin lights before takeoff* (**b**) to become less bright; *the cinema lights dimmed before the programme started* (NOTE: **dimming - dimmed**)

dime [daɪm] *noun US* ten-cent coin; *they only cost a dime each*

dimension [dɪ'menʃn] *noun* (**a**) **dimensions** = measurements of length, height, etc.; *what are the dimensions of the hall?* (**b**) extent of a problem; *the international dimension of the refugee problem*; *the task is taking on huge dimensions*

diminish [dɪ'mɪnɪʃ] *verb* (**a**) to make something smaller or weaker; *nothing diminishes his enthusiasm for flying* (**b**) to become smaller or weaker; *my income has diminished over the last few years*

diminution [dɪmɪ'njuːʃn] *noun* (**a**) reduction, becoming less powerful; *the engine has been reduced in size with no diminution of power* (**b**) amount by which something is reduced; *the government has proposed a small diminution in emission levels*

diminutive [dɪ'mɪnjʊtɪv] **1** *adjective* very small; *they have bought a diminutive apartment in Central London* **2** *noun* (**a**) word showing that something is small; *'booklet' is a diminutive of 'book'* (**b**) short form of a name; *'Betty' is a diminutive of 'Elizabeth'*

din [dɪn] **1** *noun* loud noise; *the children are making such a din I didn't hear the phone ring*; *what a din! can't you be a bit quieter, please?*; *I couldn't make out what the guide was saying above the din of the machines* **2** *verb* **to din something into someone's head** = to force someone to learn something; *the instructors dinned it into us that keeping detailed records is absolutely vital* (NOTE: **dinning - dinned**)

dine [daɪn] *verb* (*formal*) to have dinner; *we normally dine at 8.30*; **to dine out** = to have dinner away from home; *see also* WINE

diner ['daɪnə] *noun* (**a**) person who is eating an evening meal; *when the restaurant caught fire, the diners ran into the street* (**b**) dining car on a train (**c**) *US* small restaurant selling simple hot food (NOTE: originally, these were made from old dining cars from railway trains)

dinghy ['dɪŋgi] *noun* small boat, either with oars or sails; *we spent the day in the dinghy, pottering around the harbour* (NOTE: plural is **dinghies**)

dingo ['dɪŋgəʊ] *noun* Australian wild dog; *she claimed the baby had been attacked by a dingo* (NOTE: plural is **dingoes**)

dining car ['daɪnɪŋ 'kɑː] *noun* railway carriage where meals are served; *lunch is being served in the dining car*

dining room ['daɪnɪŋ 'ruːm] *noun* room in a house or hotel where you usually eat; *we were sitting in the dining room having supper*; *he was doing his homework on the dining room table*

dining table ['daɪnɪŋ 'teɪbl] *noun* table on which meals are served and eaten; *we bought a Victorian dining table at an auction* (NOTE: **dining table** refers to the piece of furniture; however, when you are eating at it, it is called the **dinner table**)

dinner ['dɪnə] *noun* (**a**) main meal of the day (usually eaten in the evening); *we were having dinner when the telephone rang*; *would you like to come to dinner on Saturday?*; *he ate his dinner quickly because there* *was a TV programme he wanted to watch; what are we having for dinner?* or *what's for dinner?*; *the restaurant is open for dinner or serves dinner from 7.30 to 11.30*; **dinner party** = private dinner to which guests are invited; **dinner plate** = wide flat plate for serving the main course on **(b)** formal evening meal; *the club is organizing a dinner and dance on Saturday*; **dinner jacket (DJ)** = a man's formal black jacket (worn with a bow tie) (NOTE: American English for this is a **tuxedo**) **(c)** meal eaten in the middle of the day (especially at school); *school dinners are awful*; **dinner lady** = woman who helps serve dinners at a school (NOTE: if you call the meal in the middle of the day **dinner**, then you call the evening meal **tea** *or* **supper**; if you call the evening meal **dinner** then you call the meal in the middle of the day **lunch**. In schools, the midday meal is always called **dinner**; in offices, it is always called **lunch**)

dinner table ['dɪnə 'teɪbl] *noun* table where people are eating; *he was late and we were all sitting at the dinner table*; *this is not a suitable subject for dinner table conversation; see note above at* DINING TABLE

dinnertime ['dɪnətaɪm] *noun* time when you usually have dinner; *hurry up, it's almost dinnertime*

dinosaur ['daɪnəsɔ:] *noun* **(a)** large prehistoric reptile; *at the time when dinosaurs roamed the land, England was covered with tropical forests* **(b)** someone who seems to belong to a past age; *he's one of the dinosaurs of British politics*

diocesan [daɪ'ɒsɪzn] *adjective* referring to a diocese; *a diocesan council*

diocese ['daɪəsɪs] *noun* area under the charge of a bishop; *the diocese of Oxford is one of the largest in the country*

dip [dɪp] **1** *noun* **(a)** sudden drop of a road, of land; *watch out - there's a dip in the road which makes it difficult to see oncoming cars* **(b)** savoury paste into which biscuits, etc., can be dipped as cocktail snacks; *a bowl of avocado dip* **(c)** short bathe or swim; *we went for a quick dip before breakfast; are you coming for a dip in the pool?* **(d)** sudden small fall; *last year there was a dip in our sales* **2** *verb* **(a)** to dip something into = to put something quickly into a liquid; *she dipped the biscuit into her coffee; she dipped her hand into the stream* **(b)** to fall suddenly; *shares dipped sharply on the stock exchange; the bird flew overhead then dipped behind the trees* **(c)** to dip your headlights = to lower the beam of the headlights of your car; *please drive with dipped headlights in the tunnel* (NOTE: **dipping - dipped**)

diphtheria [dɪf'θɪəriə] *noun* serious infectious disease of children, caused by a bacillus, with fever and a growth in the throat which makes breathing difficult; *she was vaccinated against diphtheria as a baby*

diphthong ['dɪfθɒŋ] *noun* two vowel sounds which are pronounced together; *when you say 'eye', you are using a diphthong formed of the sounds 'ah' and 'ee'*

diploma [dɪ'pləumə] *noun* document which shows that a person has reached a certain level of skill in a subject; *she has a diploma in personnel management; he is studying for a diploma in engineering; at the end of the course she was awarded a diploma*

diplomacy [dɪ'pləuməsi] *noun* art of negotiating between different parties, especially between different countries; *civil servants skilled in diplomacy are dealing with the negotiations*; **shuttle diplomacy** = going backwards and forwards between countries to try to solve an international crisis (NOTE: no plural)

diplomat ['dɪpləmæt] *noun* person (such as an ambassador) who represents his country abroad; *the ambassador had invited diplomats from other embassies to the reception*

diplomatic [dɪplə'mætɪk] *adjective* **(a)** referring to diplomats or diplomacy; *we are looking for a diplomatic solution to the crisis, rather than sending in troops*; **the Diplomatic Corps** = all foreign diplomats in a country; **diplomatic immunity** = being outside the control of the laws of the country you are living in because of being a diplomat; *the cultural attaché refused to pay his parking fines and claimed diplomatic immunity*; **the Diplomatic Service** = the government department concerned with relations with other countries, including embassies, consulates and other representatives; *he has decided on a career in the Diplomatic Service* **(b)** careful not to give offence; *it wouldn't be very diplomatic to arrive late for the wedding*

diplomatically [dɪplə'mætɪkli] *adverb* in a diplomatic way; *can you tell her, as diplomatically as possible, that we can't come to her party?*

dipstick ['dɪpstɪk] *noun* rod in the engine of a car which shows the level of oil in the engine; *the oil level should be between the minimum and maximum marks on the dipstick*

dire ['daɪə] *adjective* very serious; *the teachers kept on giving us dire warnings of what would happen if we didn't study*; **dire necessity** = urgent need; *only phone the boss at home in case of dire necessity*; **in dire straits** = in a very difficult situation; *the company must be in dire straits because the staff haven't been paid for weeks*

direct [daɪ'rekt] **1** *adjective* **(a)** straight, without any bends or stops; *this phone number will give you a direct line to the minister*; **direct flight** = flight without any stops; *there are direct flights every day to London* **(b)** not involving another person or organization; **direct debit** = system where a customer allows a company to charge costs to his bank account automatically and where the amount charged can be increased or decreased with the agreement of the customer; *I pay my electricity bills by direct debit*; **direct mail** = selling something by sending publicity material to possible buyers through the post; **direct taxation** = tax, such as income tax, which is paid straight to the government **(c)** **direct speech** = what someone actually says; *'I will come' is direct speech, 'he said he would come' is indirect speech* **(d)** not trying to hide the meaning or make a meaning weaker; *I want a direct answer to a direct question* **2** *verb* **(a)** to manage or to organize; *he directs our London operations; the policeman was directing the traffic* **(b)** to aim towards a point; *can you direct me to the nearest post office?; he directed his remarks to the head of the complaints department* **(c)** to tell someone to do something; *the insecticide has to be used as directed on the bottle; he did as he had been directed, and took the plane to Birmingham* **3** *adverb* **(a)** straight, without stopping; *you can telephone New York direct from here; the plane flies direct to Anchorage* **(b)** not involving other people; *they sell insurance direct to the public*

direct current (DC) [daɪ'rekt 'kʌrənt] *noun* electric current which flows in one direction, as opposed to 'alternating current' (AC)

direction [dɪˈrekʃn] *noun* **(a)** point towards which you are going; *you are going in the wrong direction if you want to get to the station*; *the post office is in the opposite direction*; **in all directions** = everywhere; *the wind was blowing bits of old newspapers in all directions*; *see also* SENSE OF DIRECTION **(b) directions** = instructions how to do something; *we couldn't find the railway station, so we asked the postman for directions*; *I can't start the computer because there are no directions telling me how to put it together*; **directions for use** = instructions showing how to use something **(c)** organizing or managing; *he took over the direction of the group*

directive [daɪˈrektɪv] *noun* official instruction; *the ministry has issued a new directive on animal feeds*

directly [daɪˈrektli] **1** *adverb* **(a)** straight, without anything or anyone between; *this door opens directly into the kitchen*; *she reports directly to the managing director himself* **(b)** soon; *I'll be with you directly* **2** *conjunction* as soon as; *I will write the letter directly I get home*

director [daɪˈrektə] *noun* **(a)** person who is appointed by the shareholders to help run a firm; *the sales director gave a report on sales to date*; *there are four directors on the board of the company*; **managing director** = director in charge of a company **(b)** person in charge of an organization, a project, an official institute, etc.; *she's just started her job as director of an international charity*; **director-general** = person in overall charge of a large organization; *the Director-General of the BBC* **(c)** person in charge of making a film or a play; *who was the first female director to win an Oscar?*

> COMMENT: the director organizes the actual making of the film, giving instructions to the actors, dealing with the lighting, sound, etc. The producer is in overall charge, especially of the financing of the film or play, but does not deal with the technical details

directorate [daɪˈrektərət] *noun* **(a)** *(formal)* group of directors; *the directorate will meet next week to discuss the issue* **(b)** official government body which directs something; *a government examinations directorate*

directory [daɪˈrektəri] *noun* book giving lists of professional people, organizations or businesses with their addresses and telephone numbers; **classified directory** = book listing companies classified into groups; **street directory** = map of a town with all the streets listed in alphabetical order in an index; **telephone directory** = book which lists names of people and businesses in alphabetical order with their phone numbers and addresses; *look up his number in the telephone directory*; *his number must be in the London directory*; **directory enquiries** = telephone service which finds phone numbers which you do not know or cannot find; *call directory enquiries on 192*

dirt [dɜːt] *noun* **(a)** mud; earth; *children were playing in the dirt*; *his clothes were covered with dirt from handling potatoes* **(b)** *(informal)* **dirt cheap** = very cheap; *I got the shoes dirt cheap in the market*

dirty *adjective* **(a)** not clean; *playing rugby gets your clothes dirty*; *after the party, someone has to wash all the dirty plates*; *don't come into the kitchen with your dirty boots on* **(b)** not honest, not done according to the rules; *he never uses violence himself, he just gets other*

people to do the dirty work for him; *there was some dirty play from the other team*; *he's one of the dirtiest players in Football League* **(c)** pornographic, thinking about sex; *he keeps the dirty magazines on the top shelf*; *he makes his money selling dirty postcards to tourists*; *(informal)* **dirty old man** = old man who shows a lot of interest in sex (NOTE: **dirtier - dirtiest**)

dirty trick [ˈdɜːti ˈtrɪk] *noun* **(a)** nasty action that upsets someone; *that was a dirty trick to play on an old lady* **(b)** dishonest method of spoiling someone's plans or of ruining his reputation; *they mounted a dirty tricks campaign against the rival company*

disability [dɪsəˈbɪlɪti] *noun* physical handicap; *deafness is a disability which affects old people*; *people with severe disabilities can claim grants from the government*; **learning disability** = mental handicap, being unable to learn as fast as others

disable [dɪsˈeɪbl] *verb* to make someone *or* something unable to function normally; *a fire in the engine room disabled the ship*

disabled [dɪsˈeɪbld] **1** *adjective* **(a)** physically handicapped; *a hospital for disabled ex-servicemen*; *the car crash left him permanently disabled* **(b)** not able to work properly; *a tug went to the help of the disabled cruise ship* **2** *noun* **the disabled** = handicapped people; *the library has facilities for the disabled*; **access for the disabled** = entrances with sloping ramps instead of steps, which are easier for people in wheelchairs to use; **disabled toilets** = public toilet with a larger room than usual to make it easier for people in wheelchairs to use (NOTE: more polite or formal terms for the **disabled** are **people with disabilities** *or* **people with special needs**)

disablement [dɪsˈeɪblmənt] *noun* *(formal)* condition where a person has a physical or mental disability; *benefits payments are calculated according to the degree of disablement*

disabling [dɪsˈeɪblɪŋ] *adjective* which disables; *she suffers from a disabling disease*

disadvantage [dɪsədˈvɑːntɪdʒ] *noun* drawback, factor which makes someone *or* something less likely to succeed; *her main disadvantage is her lack of experience*; *it was a disadvantage not to be able to get to the airport quickly*; *there are certain disadvantages to leaving at 5.30 in the morning*; **at a disadvantage** = handicapped by something, suffering from a disadvantage; *we are at a disadvantage compared with our competitors because we have no sales force*

disadvantaged [dɪsədˈvɑːntɪdʒd] *adjective* **(a)** suffering a disadvantage; *she was disadvantaged by her lack of experience* **(b)** living in a poor environment, without any facilities; *state help for schools in disadvantaged areas*

disaffected [dɪsəˈfektɪd] *adjective* discontented or rebellious; *the coup was led by three disaffected army officers*

disagree [dɪsəˈɡriː] *verb* **(a)** not to agree, to say that you do not think the same way as someone; *we all disagreed with the chairman*; *they all disagreed about what to do next* **(b)** **to disagree with someone** = to make someone feel ill; *raw onions disagree with me*

disagreeable [dɪsəˈɡriːəbl] *adjective* unpleasant; *he's a very disagreeable old man*; *we had a disagreeable meeting with the tax inspectors*

disagreement [dɪsə'griːmənt] *noun* argument; *they had a disagreement about who should sit in the front row*; *nothing could be decided because of the disagreement between the chairman and the treasurer*

disallow [dɪsə'laʊ] *verb* to reject, not to accept; *he claimed £2,000 for fire damage, but the claim was disallowed*; **the goal was disallowed** = the goal was not counted in the score

disappear [dɪsə'piːə] *verb* to vanish, not to be seen any more; *he hit the ball hard and it disappeared into the bushes*; *there was a bottle of orange juice in the fridge this morning and now it's disappeared*; *the two boys disappeared on their way home from school*

disappearance [dɪsə'pɪərəns] *noun* vanishing; *we were all puzzled by the sudden disappearance of our guide*

disappoint [dɪsə'pɔɪnt] *verb* to make someone sad, because things did not turn out as expected; *I don't want to disappoint you, but I don't think I can come to your party*

disappointed [dɪsə'pɔɪntɪd] *adjective* sad, because things did not turn out as expected; *she is disappointed with her exam results*; *he was disappointed because his ticket didn't win a prize*; *you should have seen the disappointed expression on his face*

disappointing [dɪsə'pɔɪntɪŋ] *adjective* which makes you sad because it does not turn out as expected; *the results of the tests were disappointing*; *it's disappointing to see so few young people come to our meetings*

disappointment [dɪsə'pɔɪntmənt] *noun* **(a)** sadness because what was expected did not take place; *she tried hard not to show her disappointment*; *to his great disappointment, he didn't win anything on the lottery* (NOTE: no plural in this meaning) **(b)** something that disappoints someone; *it was a disappointment to his parents when he failed his exam*; *after many disappointments she finally won a prize*

disapprobation [dɪsæprəʊ'beɪʃn] *(formal)* = DISAPPROVAL

disapproval [dɪsə'pruːvəl] *noun* act of disapproving; *the Speaker showed her disapproval of the MP's behaviour*

disapprove [dɪsə'pruːv] *verb* **to disapprove of something** = to show that you do not approve of something, that you do not think something is good; *the junta openly disapproves of the judicial system*; *the head teacher disapproves of members of staff wearing jeans to school*

disarm [dɪs'ɑːm] *verb* to remove weapons from someone; *the soldiers had orders to disarm the terrorists*

disarmament [dɪs'ɑːməmənt] *noun* reducing the number of arms held by a country; *they signed a nuclear disarmament treaty*

disarming [dɪs'ɑːmɪŋ] *adjective* charming, in such a way that you cannot be annoyed; *she gave me such a disarming smile, that I couldn't ask her to pay for the broken plate*

disarray [dɪsə'reɪ] *noun* lack of order; *the protest march broke up in total disarray*

disaster [dɪ'zɑːstə] *noun* **(a)** catastrophe, very bad accident; *the disaster was caused by fog or due to fog*; *ten people died in the air disaster*; *insurance*

companies are paying out millions for flood disaster damage; we're insured against natural disasters such as hurricanes and earthquakes **(b)** something that is completely unsuccessful; *the advertising campaign was a disaster - our sales went down*; *if it rains the village fête will be a complete disaster* **(c)** financial collapse; *the company is heading for disaster or* **is on a disaster course** = the company is going to collapse

disastrous [dɪ'zɑːstrəs] *adjective* very bad, catastrophic; *there have been disastrous floods in the region before*; *the country had a disastrous harvest*; *it would be disastrous if the car didn't start*

disastrously [dɪ'zɑːstrəsli] *adverb* very badly; *he played disastrously in the semifinal*

disband [dɪs'bænd] *verb* **(a)** to split up an organized group and end their activities; *after the successful coup, the former army was disbanded*; *we are disbanding our door-to-door sales team and relying on mail order selling in future* **(b)** to stop working together; *the group disbanded and its members started to go solo*

disbelief [dɪsbɪ'liːf] *noun* extreme surprise, not being able to believe something; *she stared at the letter in complete disbelief*

disc [dɪsk] *noun* **(a)** round flat object, such as a music record; *the setting sun was a huge orange disc on the horizon*; **disc jockey (DJ)** = person who plays recorded music at a night club **(b)** flat round bone which links with others to make the backbone; **slipped disc** = painful back, caused by a disc having moved out of line (NOTE: British English prefers **disc**, but American English is usually **disk**)

discard 1 *verb* [dɪs'kɑːd] to put something *or* someone on one side because they are no longer useful, to throw something away; *discard any damaged or burnt items* 2 *noun* ['dɪskɑːd] thing or person that has been discarded; *the discards from the England team are bound to feel disappointed*

discern [dɪ'sɜːn] *verb* *(formal)* **(a)** to see, to make out something with difficulty; *in the fog, we could barely discern the traffic coming in the opposite direction*; *can you discern any improvement in her pulse rate?* **(b)** to understand, to find out about something; *it's hard to discern what her motives might be*; *it was simple to discern their plan of campaign*

discernible [dɪ'sɜːnəbl] *adjective* which can be seen; *a barely discernible movement of the eyelids*

discerning [dɪ'sɜːnɪŋ] *adjective* (person) who has good judgement; *the colour scheme would shock any discerning client*; *our customers are much more discerning than they were ten years ago*

discharge 1 *noun* ['dɪstʃɑːdʒ] **(a)** liquid which comes out of a pipe, etc.; *the discharge from the factory flows into the river* **(b)** pus which comes out of a wound; *the wound healed well with no further discharge* **(c)** payment (of a debt); *discharge of the debt must take place within thirty days* **(d)** release (of a prisoner); *he was arrested again within a month of his discharge from prison* 2 *verb* [dɪs'tʃɑːdʒ] **(a)** to get rid of waste; *the factory is discharging waste water into the river* **(b)** to send someone away; *the judge discharged the jury*; **he was discharged from hospital** = he was sent home from hospital **(c)** to let a prisoner go free; *the prisoners were discharged by the judge*; *he was discharged after having served eleven months in jail* **(d)** *(formal)* to pay (a debt); *how will she discharge* *this debt if she has no income?* **(e)** to unload a cargo; *several trucks were waiting to discharge their loads* **(f)** *(formal)* to dismiss, to sack; *he was discharged for being late*

disciple [dɪˈsaɪpl] *noun* follower of a religious leader; *the leader came in with a group of his disciples*

disciplinarian [dɪsɪplɪˈneərɪən] *noun* person who believes in strict discipline; *the headmaster was a strict disciplinarian and boys were punished for the slightest mistake*

disciplinary [dɪsɪˈplɪnərɪ] *adjective* which keeps someone under control or which punishes someone; *if your behaviour does not improve, the governors will have to take disciplinary action*

discipline [ˈdɪsɪplɪn] **1** *noun* **(a)** keeping people under control; *the tour leaders are trying to keep discipline among the teenagers*; *we need to enforce stricter discipline in the school* (NOTE: no plural in this meaning) **(b)** branch of learning; *biology and other related disciplines* **2** *verb* to control someone, to punish someone; *as a result of the investigation, one employee was dismissed and three were disciplined*; *she was disciplined for swearing at her supervisor*

disciplined [ˈdɪsɪplɪnd] *adjective* trained and well controlled; *the team played a very disciplined game*; *a highly disciplined police force*

disclose [dɪsˈkləuz] *verb* to reveal a secret; *the journalists refused to disclose their sources*; *the bank has no right to disclose details of my account to the tax office*

disclosure [dɪsˈkləuʒə] *noun* **(a)** piece of information that had been kept secret before; *the newspaper carried sensational disclosures about the pop star's private life* **(b)** action of revealing a secret; *he resigned after the disclosure of his contacts with the Mafia*

disco [ˈdɪskəu] *noun (informal)* place where people dance to recorded music; party where people dance to pop music; *there's a good disco next door to the restaurant*; *you can't have a conversation in the disco because the music is too loud* (NOTE: plural is **discos**)

discolour *US* **discolor** [dɪsˈkʌlə] *verb* to change a colour; *the bath has been discoloured by drips from the hot tap*

discoloured *US* **discolored** [dɪsˈkʌləd] *adjective* which has changed colour; *her teeth were discoloured by chewing tobacco*

discomfort [dɪsˈkʌmfət] *noun* lack of comfort; *we suffered acute physical discomfort on the flight*

disconcert [dɪskənˈsɜːt] *verb* to surprise and worry someone; *he seemed disconcerted by the question, and hesitated before answering*; *the news that she had been arrested disconcerted her colleagues*

disconcerting [dɪskənˈsɜːtɪŋ] *adjective* worrying or surprising; *he has a disconcerting habit of falling asleep in the middle of a conversation*; *it is rather disconcerting to see how much the village has changed while we have been away*; *the news of her sudden resignation was quite disconcerting*

disconnect [dɪskəˈnekt] *verb* to remove the connection to (a mechanical or electrical device); *the computer must be disconnected from the mains before you start poking around inside it*; *if you refuse to pay your gas bill you will be disconnected*

discontent [dɪskənˈtent] *noun* state of not being satisfied; *the change of leadership caused widespread discontent in the party*; *they showed their discontent with the management by staging a short strike*

discontented [dɪskənˈtentɪd] *adjective* not satisfied; *groups of discontented dock workers marched on the offices of the port authority*

discontinue [dɪskənˈtɪnjuː] *verb* to stop stocking, selling, making a product; *we discontinued that line some time ago*

discord [ˈdɪskɔːd] *noun* lack of agreement; *discord between the family members caused the business to be sold*

discordant [dɪsˈkɔːdənt] *adjective* **(a)** not in agreement; *anyone wanting to express discordant opinions was prevented from doing so by the chairman*; **to strike a discordant note** = to say something that other people will not like or agree with; *I don't wish to strike a discordant note, but your suggestions don't seem at all helpful to me* **(b)** out of harmony; *the discordant sounds of oriental music sound odd to western ears*

discount 1 *noun* [ˈdɪskaunt] percentage by which a full price is reduced to a buyer by the seller; *the store gives a discount on bulk purchases*; *we give a discount on summer holidays booked before Christmas*; **to sell goods at a discount** *or* **at a discount price** = to sell goods below the normal price; **10% discount for cash** *or* **10% cash discount** = you pay 10% less if you pay in cash; **student discount** = reduction in price to students; **discount store** = shop selling cheap goods **2** *verb* [dɪsˈkaunt] **(a)** to reduce a price; *we are discounting many items in our January sales* **(b)** not to pay any attention to something; *don't discount all his advice - he is very experienced*

discourage [dɪsˈkʌrɪdʒ] *verb* not to encourage; *we try to discourage people from coming in without tickets*; *don't be discouraged by the small number of people in the audience*

discouragement [dɪsˈkʌrɪdʒmənt] *noun* **(a)** being discouraged; *he gave up in discouragement after failing his exam for the fifth time* **(b)** thing which discourages you from doing something; *in spite of various discouragements, she continued studying and got her degree*

discouraging [dɪsˈkʌrɪdʒɪŋ] *adjective* not encouraging; *it is discouraging to see how few people want to read my books*; *there was a discouraging review of his play in the local paper*

discourse [ˈdɪskɔːs] *noun (formal)* talk, speech; *we listened politely to a lengthy discourse on the history of the southern States*; *grammar mistakes are common in spoken discourse*

discover [dɪsˈkʌvə] *verb* to find something new; *in the year 1492 Columbus discovered America*; *who discovered penicillin?*; *we discovered that the estate agent had sold the house twice*; *the auditors discovered some errors in the accounts*

discovery [dɪsˈkʌvərɪ] *noun* **(a)** act of finding something new; *his discovery of penicillin*; *her discovery that someone had been in her house while she was away* **(b)** new thing which has been found; *the first discovery they made was that the lake contained salt water*; *look at his latest discovery - an antique oak table which he found in a barn*

discredit [dɪs'kredɪt] **1** *noun* loss of respect; *she brought discredit on the whole family* (NOTE: no plural) **2** *verb* to make people doubt or lose respect for someone *or* something; *when stories about his private life appeared in the press he was totally discredited as a minister*; *they set out to discredit his research*

discreet [dɪs'kri:t] *adjective* **(a)** not giving information about other people and their behaviour; *the chairman's secretary never gossips - she is very discreet* **(b)** not intending to attract attention; *I had a discreet word with the vicar before the service*

discreetly [dɪs'kri:tli] *adverb* quietly, without anyone noticing; *he discreetly left the meeting*

discrepancy [dɪs'krepənsi] *noun* lack of agreement between figures or stories; *there seems to be a discrepancy between my figures and yours* (NOTE: plural is **discrepancies**)

discretion [dɪs'kreʃn] *noun* **(a)** power to decide or choose what to do; **I leave it to your discretion** = I leave it for you to decide what to do; *gratuities are left to the discretion of the customer* **(b)** wisdom, tact, or good sense; *he showed great discretion in his handling of the family crisis* **(c)** ability to keep a secret, not to give information about someone; *the chairman's secretary is known for her discretion* (NOTE: no plural)

discretionary [dɪs'kreʃənəri] *adjective* which can be done if someone wants it; **the tribunal has wide discretionary powers** = the tribunal can act in various ways when it decides it is necessary

discriminate [dɪs'krɪmɪneɪt] *verb* to distinguish; **to discriminate between** = to treat two things in different ways; *the selectors must not discriminate between men and women applicants*; *we discriminate between part-time and full-time staff*; **to discriminate against** = to be biased against; *she accused the management of discriminating against female members of staff*

discriminating [dɪs'krɪmɪneɪtɪŋ] *adjective* able to tell the difference between two things, able to tell the value of something; *these cheap souvenirs aren't attractive to discriminating tourists*

discrimination [dɪskrɪmɪ'neɪʃn] *noun* **(a)** judgement, good taste; *the shop sells gifts which appeal to people of discrimination* **(b)** treating people in different ways because of class, religion, race, language, colour or sex; *we try to avoid discrimination against older applicants*; **racial discrimination** = bad treatment of someone because of their race; **sexual discrimination** *or* **sex discrimination** *or* **discrimination on grounds of sex** = treating men and women in different ways (NOTE: no plural)

COMMENT: in Britain, sexual and racial discrimination are against the law. The Equal Opportunities Commission deals with cases of sexual discrimination and the Commission for Racial Equality deals with cases of racial discrimination

discriminatory [dɪs'krɪmɪnətri] *adjective* which shows discrimination; *the appointment of only males to the three posts was clearly discriminatory*

discursive [dɪs'kɜːsɪv] *adjective* which does not keep to the point, which changes from one subject to another; *he's a discursive speaker, and his lectures are quite difficult to follow*

discus ['dɪskəs] *noun* flat round disc which is thrown as a sport; *she won the silver medal in the discus* (NOTE: do not confuse with **discuss**; plural is **discuses**)

discuss [dɪs'kʌs] *verb* to talk about a serious matter or problem; *the point of the meeting is to discuss how to save money*; *they spent hours discussing the details of the wedding*

discussion [dɪs'kʌʃn] *noun* talking about a serious matter or problem; *most problems can be solved by discussion*; *the next programme will feature a discussion between environmental experts*; *the discussion led to a violent argument*; *she had a heated discussion with the bus driver*

disdain [dɪs'deɪn] **1** *noun* showing that you feel that someone *or* something is inferior; *she showed her disdain by refusing to shake his hand* (NOTE: no plural) **2** *verb* **(a)** to look down on something; *she disdains all modern appliances like telephones and answering machines* **(b)** **to disdain to do something** = to refuse to do something because it is beneath you; *he disdained to carry his own luggage, but got a porter to do it for him*

disdainful [dɪs'deɪnful] *adjective* superior, showing disdain; *the waiter showed us to our table with a disdainful air*

disease [dɪ'zi:z] *noun* serious illness (of people, animals, plants, etc.); *hundreds of people caught the disease*; *it is a disease that can be treated with antibiotics*

diseased [dɪ'zi:zd] *adjective* (*person, animal, plant or part of the body*) affected by an illness, not whole or normal; *the doctor cut away the diseased tissue*; *you should remove any diseased branches to stop the rest of the tree being affected*

disembark [dɪsɪm'bɑːk] *verb* to get off a ship, plane, etc.; *the passengers disembarked at the ocean terminal*; *please disembark via the rear doors*

disembarkation [dɪsembɑː'keɪʃn] *noun* getting off a ship, plane, etc.; *please fill in your customs forms before disembarkation*

disenchanted [dɪsɪn'tʃɑːntɪd] *adjective* **to be disenchanted with something** = not to be as pleased as you used to be with something, to start to dislike something; *she's very disenchanted with her new job and is thinking of quitting*

disengage [dɪsɪn'geɪdʒ] *verb* **(a)** (*in a car, etc.*) **to disengage the clutch** = to press down on the clutch pedal, so that the engine is no longer connected with the gears **(b)** to break off a military action; **the troops disengaged** = the troops stopped fighting

disengagement [dɪsɪn'geɪdʒmənt] *noun* stopping fighting; *disengagement will come into effect at 10 o'clock*

disfavour *US* **disfavor** [dɪs'feɪvə] *noun* (*formal*) lack of approval; *the plan found general disfavour*; **to fall into disfavour** = to stop being approved of; *the minister fell into disfavour and was exiled*; *the duke incurred the king's disfavour*

disfigure [dɪs'fɪgə] *verb* to change someone's appearance so as to make it less pleasant; *her beauty was disfigured by burns*; *that satellite dish disfigures the house*

disfigurement [dɪs'fɪgəmənt] *noun* being disfigured; *the doctors think his disfigurement will be permanent*

disfiguring [dɪsˈfɪɡərɪŋ] *adjective* which disfigures; *they propose to put up a series of disfiguring electricity pylons across the valley*

disgrace [dɪsˈɡreɪs] **1** *noun* **(a)** loss of someone's respect because of errors, scandal, corruption, etc.; *the minister's disgrace followed the discovery of the papers in his office*; **the minister fell into disgrace** = he became out of favour **(b)** shameful thing; *he's a disgrace to the teaching profession*; *it was a disgrace to see her lying on the pavement like that* (NOTE: no plural) **2** *verb* to bring shame on; *he disgraced all his family by arriving drunk at the tea party*; **to disgrace yourself** = to do something which brings shame on you; *he disgraced himself by throwing sandwiches at the speakers at the conference*

disgraced [dɪzˈɡreɪst] *adjective* no longer in a position of authority because of errors, corruption, scandal, etc.; *the disgraced president lives quietly in a village in the mountains*

disgraceful [dɪsˈɡreɪsful] *adjective* which you should be ashamed of; *people living near the football stadium complained about the disgraceful behaviour of the fans*; *it's disgraceful that you have to pay £1 for a cup of tea in the museum café*

disgruntled [dɪsˈɡrʌntld] *adjective* annoyed or discontented; *she was asked to deal with a very disgruntled customer*

disguise [dɪsˈɡaɪz] **1** *noun* costume, wig, etc., to make a person look like someone else; *I didn't recognize him as he was wearing a disguise*; **in disguise** = dressed to look like someone else; *the tramp turned out to be a policeman in disguise* **2** *verb* to dress so as to look like someone else; *he entered the country disguised as a fisherman*; *she wore a wig to disguise her hair*

disgust [dɪsˈɡʌst] **1** *noun* **(a)** strong dislike, feeling sick; *the sight of the flies on the meat in the market filled her with disgust* **(b)** strong feeling of annoyance; *to my disgust, the driving test examiner passed my girlfriend and failed me*; **in disgust** = because you are upset and annoyed; *she walked out of the interview in disgust* **2** *verb* to give someone a strong feeling of dislike or disapproval; *the smell of cooking disgusted her*; *the greediness of these people disgusts me*

disgusted [dɪsˈɡʌstɪd] *adjective* feeling shocked; *disgusted viewers rang the TV studio to complain about the programme*; *I'm disgusted that no one went to see her in hospital*; *she was disgusted at the waste of money*

disgusting [dɪsˈɡʌstɪŋ] *adjective* that fills you with disgust; *there's a disgusting smell in the passageway*; *a disgusting display of violence on the part of the fans*

dish [dɪʃ] **1** *noun* **(a)** large plate for serving food; *she carefully arranged the slices of meat on a dish* **(b)** **dishes** = plates and cups, etc.; **to wash the dishes** *or* **to do the dishes** = to wash plates, glasses, cutlery, etc., after a meal; *he's offered to do the dishes*; *can you dry the dishes for me?* **(c)** part of a meal; plate of prepared food; *we are trying a new Mexican dish*; **side dish** = small dish served on a side plate; *he had a green salad as a side dish* **(d)** round aerial, shaped like a plate, used to get signals from satellites; *almost every house in the street has a satellite dish on the roof* (NOTE: plural is **dishes**) **2** *verb see* DISH OUT, DISH UP

dishcloth [ˈdɪʃklɒθ] *noun* cloth for washing dishes; *she mopped up the red wine with a dishcloth*

dishonest [dɪsˈɒnɪst] *adjective* not honest; *it was quite dishonest of him to tell his wife that he'd given up smoking*; *I've never come across a dishonest policeman*

dishonestly [dɪsˈɒnɪstli] *adverb* not honestly; *he was accused of dishonestly obtaining bank loans*

dishonesty [dɪsˈɒnɪsti] *noun* lack of honesty; *his dishonesty is notorious* (NOTE: no plural)

dishonour *US* **dishonor** [dɪsˈɒnə] **1** *noun* losing your honour; *his actions brought dishonour to the school* (NOTE: no plural) **2** *verb* not to honour; **dishonoured cheque** = cheque which the bank refuses to pay because there is not enough money in the account to cover it

dishonourable *US* **dishonorable** [dɪsˈɒnərəbl] *adjective* with dishonour; *he was given a dishonourable discharge from the army*

dishonourably *US* **dishonorably** [dɪsˈɒnərəbli] *adverb* in a dishonourable way; *he behaved dishonourably by refusing to see his daughter*

dish out [ˈdɪʃ ˈaʊt] *verb* (*informal*) to hand out roughly and in large quantities; *he dished out a piece of bread and a bowl of soup to anyone who asked for it*; *they were dishing out free tickets for the concert*; *they dished out leaflets to everyone at the meeting*; *at the end of the school year, they dish out prizes to the best students*

dish up [ˈdɪʃ ˈʌp] *verb* (*informal*) to serve food; *she dished up the food with a large spoon*; *he was dishing up the meal*

dishwasher [ˈdɪʃwɒʃə] *noun* machine for washing dishes; *I never put the silver in the dishwasher*; **dishwasher-proof** = (china, etc.) which is not harmed by being washed in a dishwasher

disillusion [dɪsɪˈluːʒn] *verb* to make someone feel let down, or sad that something has not turned out as expected; *I don't want to disillusion the children by telling them that Santa Claus doesn't exist*

disillusioned [dɪsɪˈluːʒnd] *adjective* feeling that something has not turned out as expected; *they became disillusioned at working for a large corporation*

disillusionment [dɪsɪˈluːʒnmənt] *noun* feeling of being let down, feeling that something has not turned out as expected; *her enthusiasm for the new leader was quickly followed by disillusionment*

disinclination [dɪsɪnklɪˈneɪʃn] *noun* (*formal*) feeling of being unwilling to do something; *on nice sunny days like this I feel a great disinclination to go to the office*

disinclined [dɪsɪnˈklaɪnd] *adjective* (*formal*) **to be disinclined to do something** = to feel you do not want to do something; *I'm disinclined to lend them any more money*

disinfect [dɪsɪnˈfekt] *verb* to remove germs or bacteria from a place; *she disinfected the cut with surgical spirit*

disinfectant [dɪsɪnˈfektənt] *noun* substance used to kill germs and bacteria; *they poured disinfectant into the drains*

disingenuous [dɪsɪnˈdʒenjuəs] *adjective* (*formal*) trying to hide something; *her remarks about wanting to have everything in the open seemed disingenuous to me* (NOTE: the opposite is **ingenuous**)

disinherit [dɪsɪn'herɪt] *verb* to stop a member of your family from inheriting your money or property when you die; *he disinherited his son and left all his money to his secretary*

disintegrate [dɪs'ɪntɪgreɪt] *verb* to fall to pieces; *the book had been used so much that its cover was disintegrating; most meteorites disintegrate on entering the Earth's atmosphere*

disinter [dɪsɪn'tɜː] *verb* to dig up something which has been buried; *the police asked for permission to disinter the body to carry out tests; the bodies were disinterred and reburied in another part of the cemetery* (NOTE: **disinterring - disinterred**)

disinterested [dɪs'ɪntrəstɪd] *adjective* **(a)** quite impartial, not in favour of one side or the other; *a totally disinterested observer* **(b)** *(informal)* not interested; *she seemed quite disinterested in what was going on* (NOTE: this use is common, but wrong: the correct word in this meaning is **uninterested**)

disk [dɪsk] *noun* any round flat object, especially a piece of plastic used in computers to record information; *don't forget to format the disks first*; **floppy disk** = removable small disk; **hard disk** = large fixed disk; **disk operating system (DOS)** = part of the computer operating system software that controls the disk drives and files storage; *see also* DISC

disk drive ['dɪsk 'draɪv] *noun* device which spins a disk in a computer and controls the access of information; *the disk drive has failed, so we can't do anything*

diskette [dɪ'sket] *noun* small floppy disk; *the data came on a diskette*

dislike [dɪs'laɪk] **1** *noun* **(a)** not liking something *or* someone; *she had never felt such a dislike for someone before*; **to take a dislike to** = to hate; *their dog took a hearty dislike to the postman* **(b)** thing which you do not like; *we try to take account of the likes and dislikes of individual customers* **2** *verb* not to like; *I dislike him intensely; I dislike it when the people behind me at the cinema start whispering; my father dislikes having to get up early on Monday mornings*; **I don't dislike Mozart** = I quite like Mozart

dislocate ['dɪsləkeɪt] *verb* **(a)** to displace a bone from its normal position at a joint; *he fell and dislocated his elbow; the shoulder joint dislocates easily* **(b)** to disorganize something; *train services have been dislocated because of the derailment*

dislocation [dɪslə'keɪʃn] *noun* **(a)** condition where a bone is displaced from its normal position at a joint; *the dislocation of his elbow means that he can't drive* **(b)** disorganization; *the fog will lead to some dislocation of services*

dislodge [dɪs'lɒdʒ] *verb* to move something which is stuck; *by coughing she managed to dislodge the fishbone stuck in her throat*

disloyal [dɪs'lɔɪəl] *adjective* not loyal; *the president accused the general of being disloyal to his country*

disloyalty [dɪs'lɔɪəlti] *noun* lack of loyalty, not being loyal; *he was criticized to his disloyalty to the company*

dismal ['dɪzməl] *adjective* miserable; *the weather in November is usually dismal; we stayed in some dismal hotel in the suburbs; she sat in the corner looking dismal*

dismantle [dɪs'mæntl] *verb* to take to pieces; *the engine is in the garage being dismantled; exhibitors must not start dismantling their stands before 3 p.m.*

dismay [dɪs'meɪ] **1** *noun* horror, great disappointment; *to her great dismay she couldn't find her passport; to the dismay of the supporters, the team played extremely badly* **2** *verb* to strike someone with horror; *his reaction to her letter dismayed her; she was dismayed to find that her passport had been stolen*

dismayed [dɪs'meɪd] *adjective* shocked and upset; *crowds of dismayed depositors rushed to the bank*

dismember [dɪs'membə] *verb* to cut up something into pieces; *the police found her dismembered body under the patio; the victorious countries proceeded to dismember the old empire*

dismiss [dɪs'mɪs] *verb* **(a) to dismiss an employee** = to remove an employee from a job; *he was dismissed for being late; when they found him taking money from the petty cash he was dismissed instantly* **(b)** to send someone away; *at the end of the interview he dismissed her with a brief 'good afternoon'* **(c)** to refuse to consider an idea; *her plan was dismissed as being quite impractical; all his suggestions were dismissed by the MD* **(d)** to refuse a request; *they dismissed my application for a loan*

dismissal [dɪs'mɪsəl] *noun* removal from a job; *he had only been working there three months when he received notice of dismissal*; **unfair dismissal** = removal of someone from a job by an employer who appears not to be acting in a reasonable way

dismissive [dɪs'mɪsɪv] *adjective* showing that you do not consider something or someone important; *he was dismissive of the complaints from the staff*

disobedience [dɪsə'biːdɪəns] *noun* lack of obedience; *little Charles is always getting into trouble at school for disobedience*; **civil disobedience** = not obeying the police, as a sign of protest (NOTE: no plural)

disobedient [dɪsə'biːdɪənt] *adjective* not obedient; *I've never seen such a disobedient group of little children*

disobey [dɪsə'beɪ] *verb* not to obey; *she would never disobey her parents; he disobeyed orders and walked out to talk to the enemy*

disorder [dɪs'ɔːdə] *noun* **(a)** lack of order; *the whole office is in a state of disorder* **(b)** riot, disturbance in the streets; *violent public disorders broke out in the streets* **(c)** illness; *she suffers from a stomach disorder; a doctor who specializes in disorders of the kidneys or in kidney disorders*

disorderly [dɪs'ɔːdəli] *adjective* wild and out of order; *a disorderly crowd of shoppers rushed to the bargain counter; the disorderly scenes in parliament were shown on the TV news*

disorganized [dɪs'ɔːgənaɪzd] *adjective* not well organized; *the whole tour was completely disorganized*

disorientate US **disorient** [dɪs'ɔːrɪənteɪt or dɪs'ɔːrɪənt] *verb* to confuse someone, to make someone lose their sense of direction; *he was quite disorientated by the change in the street names; she was unconscious for some time, and when she found herself in hospital was completely disorientated*

disparage [dɪs'pærɪdʒ] *verb* to say that something is not very good; *he disparaged her efforts to learn the violin*

disparagement [dɪs'pærɪdʒmənt] *noun* act of disparaging; *the other teachers criticized her disparagement of the students' efforts*

disparaging [dɪs'pærɪdʒɪŋ] *adjective* saying that something is not very good; *she made some disparaging remarks about my new hairstyle*

disparate ['dɪspərət] *adjective* (*formal*) varied or different; *he took a disparate group of students and tried to get them to work together as a team*

disparity [dɪs'pærɪti] *noun* (*formal*) difference; *there was hardly any disparity between the results of the two tests; there is still a considerable disparity in pay between graduate trainees and non-graduates*

dispassionate [dɪs'pæʃənət] *adjective* calm, with no emotion; *the reporters tried to send back dispassionate reports of the scenes in the refugee camps*

dispatch [dɪs'pætʃ] **1** *noun* (**a**) sending; *dispatch of the goods will be delayed until Monday*; **dispatch note** = note to say that goods have been sent (**b**) message sent; *the reporters send regular dispatches from the war zone; we received a dispatch from our Calcutta office*; **dispatch box** = box with government papers (NOTE: plural is **dispatches**) **2** *verb* (**a**) to send; *they dispatched the message to all commanding officers; the goods were dispatched to you first thing this morning* (**b**) to finish doing something quickly; *she set to work on the files and dispatched most of them by lunchtime*

dispel [dɪs'pel] *verb* to clear away; *the sun came out during the morning and dispelled the fog; she acted quickly to dispel any rumours about her lack of experience* (NOTE: **dispelling - dispelled**)

dispensation [dɪspən'seɪʃn] *noun* permission not to follow a rule, etc.; *they asked for a special dispensation to get married in church*

dispense [dɪs'pens] *verb* (**a**) to provide; *local magistrates dispense justice in the villages; he sits in his office dispensing good advice to anyone who asks him for it* (**b**) **dispensing chemist** = chemist who prepares and sells medicine (**c**) **to dispense with something** = not to use something any more; *we've dispensed with the services of an accountant*

dispenser [dɪs'pensə] *noun* machine which automatically provides something, when money is put in or a button is pushed; **cash dispenser** = machine which gives out money when a special card is inserted and instructions given

disperse [dɪs'pɜːs] *verb* (**a**) to clear away; *the sun will soon disperse the mist; the police were called in to disperse the crowds of angry fans* (**b**) to scatter in different directions; *the crowd dispersed rapidly once the parade was over*

dispersed [dɪs'pɜːst] *adjective* scattered, not close together; *the museums are dispersed throughout the town; they live in widely dispersed settlements in the mountains*

displace [dɪs'pleɪs] *verb* to move something from its usual place; *who has been in this room? - someone has displaced the ornaments on the mantelpiece*; **displaced persons** = refugees who have left their homes to go to another country

displacement [dɪs'pleɪsmənt] *noun* (**a**) moving of something to a different place; *the invasion resulted in the displacement of thousands of people from their homes* (**b**) amount of water which is removed by a floating ship, used to show the size of the ship; *a ship with a displacement of 20,000 tons*

display [dɪs'pleɪ] **1** *noun* (**a**) show, exhibition; *they have a fine display of Chinese porcelain; a display of local crafts*; **air display** = show of new aircraft; **display case** *or* **display unit** = showcase for goods for sale; **visual display unit (VDU)** = computer screen (**b**) on **display** = shown in an exhibition or for sale; *the shop has several car models on display* **2** *verb* (**a**) to put something on show; *she is displaying her collection of Persian carpets at the antique fair* (**b**) to show; *he displayed considerable courage in meeting the rebel troops; make sure your parking ticket is clearly displayed on the windscreen*

displease [dɪs'pliːz] *verb* not to please; *his reply seemed to displease the examiners; the lack of goals displeased the fans*

displeasure [dɪs'pleʒə] *noun* annoyance; *he showed his displeasure by slamming down the telephone* (NOTE: no plural)

disposable [dɪs'pəuzəbl] *adjective* which can be used and then thrown away; *disposable cups*

disposal [dɪs'pəuzəl] *noun* (**a**) getting rid of; *the disposal of refuse is a problem for large cities* (**b**) **my car is at your disposal** = you can use my car if you want to; **I am at your disposal** = I am ready to do anything you want

dispose [dɪs'pəuz] *verb* **to dispose of something** = to get rid of something; *how are we going to dispose of all this waste paper?; his objections are easily disposed of*

disposed [dɪs'pəuzd] *adjective* **he is well disposed towards us** = he approves of what we are doing; (*formal*) **to be disposed to do something** = to feel like doing something; *they are disposed to accept our terms*

disposition [dɪspə'zɪʃn] *noun* (**a**) character, tendency; *he has a pleasant, easy-going disposition; she has a disposition to argue with her husband* (**b**) (*formal*) act of passing property (land or goods) to another person, especially in a will; *to make testamentary dispositions*

disproportionate [dɪsprə'pɔːʃənət] *adjective* not of the same size, scale, seriousness, etc., as something else; *the punishment was completely disproportionate to the crime*

disprove [dɪs'pruːv] *verb* to prove something is wrong; *the job of the police is to disprove his sworn statement; this seems to disprove the theory that the world is getting warmer*

dispute [dɪs'pjuːt] **1** *noun* argument; *he tried to mediate in the dispute; there was a little dispute over who would pay the bill*; **industrial dispute** *or* **labour dispute** = argument between management and workers; **in dispute** = not agreed; *the ownership of the land is in dispute* **2** *verb* to argue that something is not correct; *I dispute her version of what happened; there is no disputing the fact that Sarah is the best qualified of the candidates*

disqualify [dɪs'kwɒlɪfaɪ] *verb* to make (someone) not able to do something; *being a judge disqualifies you from being a Member of Parliament; after the accident he was fined £1000 and disqualified from driving for two years*

disquiet [dɪs'kwaɪət] *noun* worry; *there is public disquiet about the planning decision*

disquieting [dɪs'kwaɪətɪŋ] *adjective* worrying; *there have been disquieting rumours that the shop may be sold*

disregard [dɪsrɪ'gɑːd] **1** *noun* disregard for something = not paying any attention to something; *he showed a complete disregard for public safety* **2** *verb* to take no notice of; *he disregarded the warning signs and went on along the road*

disreputable [dɪs'repjuːtəbl] *adjective* with a bad reputation, especially for criminal activity; *he lives in a room over some disreputable bar in Barcelona; she went to see a disreputable backstreet doctor; the building trade has been given a bad name by a few disreputable cowboy firms*

disrepute [dɪsrɪ'pjuːt] *noun* bad reputation; **to bring something into disrepute** = to give something a bad reputation; *he was accused of bringing the club into disrepute by his extraordinary behaviour*

disrespect [dɪsrɪ'spekt] *noun* lack of respect to someone; *we didn't mean any disrespect by asking him to stop snoring during the meeting*

disrupt [dɪs'rʌpt] *verb* to break up or to interrupt a meeting; *we are not used to having board meetings disrupted like this*

disruption [dɪs'rʌpʃn] *noun* **(a)** stopping the normal working of something; *the fog has caused disruption to rail timetables* **(b)** breaking up or interruption of a meeting; *we locked the door so that there would no more disruptions*

disruptive [dɪs'rʌptɪv] *adjective* which disrupts; *the disruptive behaviour of a group of fans spoiled the game for everyone*

dissatisfaction [dɪssætɪs'fækʃn] *noun* lack of satisfaction; *I am writing to express my dissatisfaction with the way in which I have been treated by your staff*

dissatisfied [dɪs'sætɪsfaɪd] *adjective* not satisfied; *many ordinary people are dissatisfied with their MP's performance; the shop seems to have a lot of dissatisfied customers*

dissect [dɪ'sekt] *verb* to cut up a body to examine it; *in our biology lesson we had to dissect a frog*

disseminate [dɪs'semɪneɪt] *verb* (*formal*) to spread around; *our aim is to disseminate the truth about the régime*

dissent [dɪ'sent] **1** *noun* lack of agreement; *the chairman wished to avoid dissent; they received many letters of dissent* (NOTE: do not confuse with **descent**) **2** *verb* to dissent from = not to agree with; *the sales director dissented from the majority view;* **there were two dissenting votes** = two people voted against; *the resolution was passed without a single dissenting voice*

dissertation [dɪsə'teɪʃn] *noun* short thesis for a university course; *he wrote a dissertation on the subject of 'Scottish agricultural practices'*

dissident ['dɪsɪdənt] **1** *adjective* not in agreement with the state; *a dissident writer* **2** *noun* person who is not in agreement with the state; *several dissidents tried to set up an underground newspaper; it was a time when dissidents were being arrested and thrown in jail*

dissimilar [dɪ'sɪmɪlə] *adjective* not the same; *the twins are quite dissimilar; they are not dissimilar* = they are alike

dissimilarity [dɪsɪmɪ'lærɪti] *noun* being not the same; *the dissimilarities between the two machines are quite striking*

dissipate ['dɪsɪpeɪt] *verb* **(a)** to clear away; *the hot sun soon dissipated the morning mist; his statement did a lot to dissipate the feeling of annoyance among the members* **(b)** to waste money, talent, etc.; *after winning the lottery he dissipated the lot on drink and expensive cars*

dissipated ['dɪsɪpeɪtɪd] *adjective* living wildly; *he led a dissipated life as an artist in Paris*

dissipation [dɪsɪ'peɪʃn] *noun* wild living; *after university he inherited a fortune and spent it all in a life of dissipation*

dissolution [dɪsə'luːʃn] *noun* ending of a partnership, marriage, etc.; **dissolution of Parliament** = ending of a Parliament, so forcing a general election; *the government lost the vote of no confidence, so the Prime Minister asked for a dissolution*

dissolve [dɪ'zɒlv] *verb* **(a)** to make a solid substance become part of a liquid; *dissolve the sugar in half a litre of boiling water; the powder should be completely dissolved in warm water* **(b)** to become part of a liquid; *the sugar dissolved quite quickly; stir the mixture until the sugar dissolves* **(c)** to bring to an end; **to dissolve a partnership** *or* **a company; to dissolve Parliament** = to close the Parliament, and call new elections

dissonance ['dɪsənəns] *noun* lack of harmony in music which makes it sound unpleasant; *his latest violin works are difficult to listen to because of their dissonance*

dissuade [dɪ'sweɪd] *verb* **to dissuade someone from something** = to persuade someone not to do something; *we tried to dissuade her from entering the beauty competition*

dissuasion [dɪ'sweɪʒn] *noun* persuading someone not to do something; *it took all my powers of dissuasion to stop her selling her shop*

distance ['dɪstəns] *noun* **(a)** space from one point to another; *what is the distance from London to Paris?; the furthest distance I have travelled by train is 800km; the railway line goes underground for a short distance;* **within walking distance** = near enough to walk to; *the hotel is within walking distance of the town centre* **(b) in the distance** = a long way away; *I caught sight of the mountain in the distance; we could hear guns firing in the distance* **(c) distance learning** = studying in your own time away from the place where the course is organized, using radio or TV; *the government is pouring resources into distance learning projects*

distant ['dɪstənt] *adjective* **(a)** far away; *we could hear the sound of distant gunfire;* **a distant relative** = not a member of the immediate family; *she's a very distant relative - her grandfather was my grandmother's cousin;* **in the not too distant future** = quite soon; *we expect to move house in the not too distant future;* **in the dim and distant past** = a long time ago; *it all happened in the dim and distant past when I was at university* **(b)** not very friendly; *the manager was quite helpful but distant*

distaste [dɪsˈteɪst] *noun* dislike; *his expression showed his distaste for the way she was talking*; *the other travellers viewed the drunken football supporters with distaste*

distasteful [dɪsˈteɪstful] *adjective* unpleasant; *they kept making rude and distasteful comments*; *what I find particularly distasteful is the way in which they all ask for more money while trying to do less work*

distil *US* **distill** [dɪˈstɪl] *verb* to make pure water or alcohol by heating and collecting the vapour; **distilled water** = especially pure water that has been purified by distillation, used, for example, to top up car batteries (NOTE: **distilling - distilled**)

distillation [dɪstɪˈleɪʃn] *noun* the process of distilling; *butane is a by-product of petroleum distillation*

distiller [dɪsˈtɪlə] *noun* person who distils alcohol; *he is an important distiller of Scotch whisky*

distillery [dɪsˈtɪləri] *noun* factory for distilling alcohol; *on our tour of the islands we visited several whisky distilleries* (NOTE: plural is **distilleries**)

distinct [dɪˈstɪŋkt] *adjective* **(a)** separate; *there are two distinct varieties of this plant*; *they keep their printing works quite distinct from their publishing company* **(b)** clear; *I got the distinct impression that he was carrying a gun*; *did you notice the distinct tone of anger in his voice?*

distinction [dɪˈstɪŋkʃn] *noun* **(a)** difference; *there is a distinction between being interested in politics and joining a political party*; **to make a distinction between two things** = to recognize that two things are different; *you must try to make a distinction between the police and the secret service* **(b)** special excellence; *he served in the war with distinction*; *she had the distinction of being the first woman to take a degree at the university* **(c)** highest mark; *she got a distinction in her exam*

distinctive [dɪsˈtɪŋktɪv] *adjective* very noticeable, which makes one thing different from others; *the zebra has distinctive black and white stripes*; *what is so distinctive about this plant is that it flowers in winter*

distinctly [dɪsˈtɪŋktli] *adverb* clearly; *I distinctly heard him say that she was his sister*; *she looked distinctly upset*

distinguish [dɪˈstɪŋgwɪʃ] *verb* **(a)** to see clearly; to make out details; *with the binoculars we could easily distinguish the houses on the other side of the lake* **(b) to distinguish between two things** = to recognize the difference between two things; *children must be taught to distinguish between right and wrong*; *it's difficult to distinguish by sight between salt and caster sugar* **(c) to distinguish yourself** = to do something which makes people notice you; *he distinguished himself on the football field*; *she distinguished herself by falling into the river*

distinguished [dɪsˈtɪŋgwɪʃt] *adjective* important and well-known (writer, painter, etc.); *a concert by a distinguished Czech pianist*

distinguishing [dɪsˈtɪŋgwɪʃɪŋ] *adjective* which makes someone *or* something different; *Charles II's most distinguishing feature was his great height - he was well over six feet tall*

distort [dɪˈstɔːt] *verb* **(a)** to twist; *his face was distorted with pain*; **distorting mirrors** = mirrors made of bent glass, which change your appearance **(b)** to give a false impression of; *he distorted the meaning of my speech*

distortion [dɪˈstɔːʃn] *noun* **(a)** bending and twisting out of shape; *the accident was caused by the distortion of the rails in the hot weather* **(b)** something that gives a false impression; *it is a complete distortion of the truth*

distract [dɪˈstrækt] *verb* to attract someone's attention when they should be doing something else; *walking past the school in a bathing costume is bound to distract the students*; **to distract someone's attention** = to make someone look at something different; *if you distract her attention, I'll try to snatch her handbag*

distracted [dɪsˈtræktɪd] *adjective* wild with worry, grief, etc.; *she stared at me with a distracted look*; *distracted parents were phoning the police for news of their children*

distraction [dɪˈstrækʃn] *noun* **(a)** amusement; *we went to London to look for some distraction* **(b)** thing which stops you from concentrating; *how can I do my work properly with all the distractions of the family?* **(c) he loved her to distraction** = he was wildly in love with her

distraught [dɪsˈtrɔːt] *adjective* wild with worry, grief, etc.; *he was distraught with worry over the bill he had received*

distress [dɪˈstres] **1** *noun* **(a)** great sorrow or pain; *I don't want to cause the family any distress*; *the whole family was in distress at grandmother's death* **(b)** difficulty; *we knew the ship was in distress when we saw the flares*; **distress signal** = signal sent when you are in difficulties; *the ship sent out distress signals before she sank* **2** *verb* to make someone very sad and worried; *the news of her grandmother's death distressed her very much*

distressed [dɪˈstrest] *adjective* very sad and worried; *when she came out of the room she was obviously distressed*

distressing [dɪsˈtresɪŋ] *adjective* very sad and worrying; *what distressing news about your mother!*; *it was distressing to see the little bird being eaten by the cat*

distribute [dɪˈstrɪbjuːt] *verb* **(a)** to share out, to give to several people; *she distributed part of her money to the poor*; *the stewardesses came round, distributing immigration forms to non-EU passengers*; *I'll distribute the list to all the committee members* **(b)** to send out goods from a warehouse to retail shops; **we distribute Japanese cars** = we are the agents for Japanese cars

distribution [dɪstrɪˈbjuːʃn] *noun* **(a)** giving to several people; *the newspaper has a wide distribution*; *the staff will organize the distribution of the timetable to the students* **(b)** sending of goods from a warehouse to shops; *our distribution centre is in Oxfordshire*

distributor [dɪsˈtrɪbjutə] *noun* **(a)** company which sells goods for another company which makes them; *who is the local distributor for this make of lawn-mower?* **(b)** (*in a car engine*) mechanism which passes the electric spark to each sparking plug in turn; *the distributor head needs cleaning*

district [ˈdɪstrɪkt] *noun* **(a)** area or region; *it's a district of the town well-known for its Italian* *restaurants*; **the commercial district** *or* **the business district** = part of a town where offices and shops are located; *the shop is well placed right in the main business district of the town* **(b)** official administrative area of a town or country; *US* **district attorney (DA)** = lawyer representing the government in a certain area; **district council** = local council

distrust [dɪs'trʌst] **1** *noun* lack of trust; *the dog showed his distrust of postmen* **2** *verb* not to trust; *I distrust anyone who wears green shoes*; *the police distrusted her motives in making the phone call*

disturb [dɪs'tɜːb] *verb* **(a)** to worry someone; *it disturbed me to see that the plane's wing was wobbling* **(b)** to interrupt someone; *sorry to disturb you but there's an urgent email message just come in*; *don't disturb your mother - she's resting*; **'do not disturb'** = notice placed on a hotel room door, to ask the hotel staff not to come into the room

disturbance [dɪ'stɜːbəns] *noun* **(a)** action of disturbing someone; *I need to work somewhere where there won't be any disturbance* **(b)** noisy riot; *the fans caused a disturbance in the hotel bar*; *there are always disturbances after the local derby*; *there were several instances of looting during the disturbances* **(c)** **mental disturbance** = being mentally ill

disturbed [dɪs'tɜːbd] *adjective* **(a)** worried; *we are disturbed to hear that the company may be forced to close* **(b)** mentally ill; *in her disturbed state of mind, she may do anything*; *some of the patients are mentally disturbed*; *highly disturbed children are taught in this special school*

disturbing [dɪ'stɜːbɪŋ] *adjective* worrying; *a disturbing number of students failed the exam*; *it is a disturbing fact that many children leave school without being able to read*

disused ['dɪsjuːzd] *adjective* not used; *they planned the robbery in a disused warehouse*

ditch [dɪtʃ] **1** *noun* long trench for taking away water; *after the storm, the ditches were full of rainwater*; *he fell into the ditch beside the road* (NOTE: plural is **ditches**) **2** *verb* (*informal*) **(a)** to leave something behind; *we ditched the car and walked to the next town* **(b)** to dismiss; *the company decided to ditch its sales director* **(c)** to land a plane in the sea; *the pilot ran out of fuel and decided to bale out and ditch the plane*

dither ['dɪðə] **1** *noun* **all of a dither** = agitated and worried; *she was all of a dither after getting the letter from the solicitor* **2** *verb* not to be able to make up your mind; *stop dithering and tell me what you want to do*

diurnal [daɪ'ɜːnəl] *adjective* (*formal*) happening during the daytime, awake during the daytime; *there are few diurnal animals in the desert* (NOTE: the opposite, referring to animals that come out at night, is **nocturnal**)

diuretic [daɪjuˈretɪk] **1** *adjective* which makes the kidneys produce more urine; *some mineral waters have a diuretic effect* **2** *noun* substance which produces urine; *she was given diuretics*

diva ['diːvə] *noun* internationally famous woman opera star; *tickets were sold out months in advance to hear the great Italian diva*

divan [dɪ'væn] *noun* low couch or bed with a solid base and no back; *she received visitors lying on a divan, smoking a pipe*

dive [daɪv] **1** *noun* **(a)** plunge downwards head first into water; *he made a beautiful dive into the pool* **(b)** (*informal*) disreputable bar; *he met her in some dive in Frankfurt* **2** *verb* to plunge into water head first; *he dived in and swam across the pool under water* (NOTE: **diving - dived** *or US* **dove** [dəʊv])

dive-bomb ['daɪv'bɒm] *verb* (*of a plane*) to attack by diving out of the sky and dropping a bomb; *the enemy planes dive-bombed the aircraft carrier*

diver ['daɪvə] *noun* **(a)** person who plunges head first into water; *the Australian Olympic diver* **(b)** person who swims and works underwater; *police divers searched the canal*

diverge [daɪ'vɜːdʒ] *verb* **(a)** to go in different directions; *the road and the river diverge at the end of the valley*; *they had shared a flat for some time, then their careers diverged and they saw much less of each other* **(b)** **to diverge from** = to be different from; *this diverges from the plan I was given originally*

divergence [daɪ'vɜːdʒəns] *noun* difference; *there is a noticeable divergence between the results of his research and mine*

divergent [daɪ'vɜːdʒənt] *adjective* which are different; *the two doctors hold divergent views about how the patient should be treated*

divers ['daɪvəz] *adjective* (*old*) various; *he wrote pamphlets on divers political subjects*

diverse [daɪ'vɜːs] *adjective* varied; *the concert was a diverse mix of classical and popular music*; *his reasons for leaving were diverse*

diversify [daɪ'vɜːsɪfaɪ] *verb* to do other sorts of work; to add new types of business to your existing one; *farmers are encouraged to diversify into other forms of land use*; *the company has diversified over the last few years*

diversion [daɪ'vɜːʃn] *noun* **(a)** temporary road system that sends traffic another way; *all traffic has to take a diversion and rejoin the motorway 10km further on* **(b)** amusement; *fishing is one of the most popular diversions for people at weekends*; *it's a quiet country town with very few diversions for teenagers* **(c)** **to create a diversion** = to distract attention, for example so that some else can commit a crime; *she created a diversion by screaming*

diversity [daɪ'vɜːsɪti] *noun* great variety; *the medical journals show a great diversity of opinion among specialists*

divert [daɪ'vɜːt] *verb* **(a)** to send to another place or in another direction; *because of fog in London, flights have been diverted to Manchester*; *traffic has been diverted to avoid the town centre* **(b)** to amuse; *a game of snakes and ladders diverted the children for a little while* **(c)** **to divert someone's attention** = to make someone look away; *try and divert his attention while I steal his keys*

diverting [daɪ'vɜːtɪŋ] *adjective* which entertains; *this evening there's a very diverting series of programmes on TV*

divide [dɪ'vaɪd] *verb* **(a)** to cut into parts; *the cake was divided among the children*; *how can you divide the cake into thirteen pieces?*; *the two companies agreed to divide the market between them*; *our open-plan office is divided up with low partitions* **(b)** to calculate how many of one number there are in another; *ten divided by two gives five* (NOTE: **divide is**

usually shown by the sign ÷ : 10 ÷ 2 = 5: say 'ten divided by two equals five')

dividend ['dɪvɪdend] *noun* part of a company's profits shared out among shareholders; *the company made a loss and there will be no dividend for the shareholders this year*; **to raise** *or* **to increase the dividend** = to pay out a higher dividend than in the previous year

divine [dɪ'vaɪn] **1** *adjective* referring to God; *he prayed for divine help* **2** *verb* to search for hidden sources of water; *in the middle of the drought, they called in someone to divine for water*

diviner [dɪ'vaɪnə] *noun* **water diviner** = DOWSER

diving ['daɪvɪŋ] *noun* **(a)** sport of diving into water from a diving board, with points from 0 - 10 being awarded by a panel of judges; *he won a gold medal for diving* **(b)** swimming underwater with a snorkel or scuba equipment; *we went diving in the Red Sea*

diving board ['daɪvɪŋ 'bɔːd] *noun* plank from which people dive at a swimming pool; *everyone watched as she climbed the ladder up onto the diving board*

divinity [dɪ'vɪnɪti] *noun* **(a)** god; *statues of Egyptian divinities were found in the tomb* **(b)** state of being a god; *the divinity of Christ*

divisible [dɪ'vɪzəbl] *adjective* that can be divided; *36 is divisible by 12*

division [dɪ'vɪʒn] *noun* **(a)** important part of a large organization; *the marketing division*; *the production division* **(b)** splitting into parts; *after his death, the family argued over the division of their father's money* (NOTE: no plural in this meaning) **(c)** calculation, where one figure is divided by another; *my little sister is just learning how to do division*; **long division** = complicated division sum, worked out on paper; **division sign** = printed or written sign (÷) showing that one figure is divided by another **(d)** difference of opinion between groups of people; *the dispute has widened the divisions between the two wings of the party* **(e)** large section of an army; *they have three divisions stationed along the border*; *the general ordered an infantry division to stand by*

divisional [dɪ'vɪʒənəl] *adjective* referring to a division; *he's just been appointed a divisional director*; *the general in charge of divisional headquarters*

divisive [dɪ'vaɪsɪv] *adjective* which produces quarrels; *the government's policy on the disabled has proved divisive*

divorce [dɪ'vɔːs] **1** *noun* legal separation of husband and wife where each is free to marry again; *her parents are getting a divorce*; *since their divorce, they have both remarried* **2** *verb* **(a)** to break off a marriage legally; *they divorced last year* **(b)** to separate from your husband or wife; *she divorced her husband and married the man next door*; *he got divorced after only three years' of marriage* **(c)** to separate (two ideas, etc.); *it is difficult to divorce their financial problems from the problems they are having with the house*

divorced [dɪ'vɔːst] *adjective* no longer married; *they're both divorced, with children from their previous marriages*

divorcee [dɪvɔː'siː] *noun* woman who is divorced; *he's going to marry a divorcee*

divulge [daɪ'vʌldʒ] *verb* to reveal a secret; *she refused to divulge where the papers were hidden*

Diwali [dɪ'wɑːli] *noun* important Hindu festival of lights, celebrated in the autumn

DIY [diːaɪ'waɪ] *abbreviation for* DO IT YOURSELF; *he buys a DIY magazine each week*; *she's very good at DIY*; **a DIY store** = shop which sells paints, tools, etc.

dizzy ['dɪzi] *adjective* **(a)** feeling when everything seems to turn round; *can we stop the car, please, I feel dizzy*; *after standing in the sun, he became dizzy and had to lie down*; *she has started having dizzy spells* **(b)** *(informal)* wild, exciting; *a dizzy round of parties and TV shows* (NOTE: **dizzier - dizziest**)

DJ ['diːdʒeɪ] *abbreviation for* DINNER JACKET, DISC JOCKEY

DNA [diːen'eɪ] *abbreviation for* DEOXYRIBONUCLEIC ACID

COMMENT: many criminal cases can now be solved by DNA testing, identifying the criminal from samples of hair, skin, etc., left at the scene of crime

do [duː] **1** *verb* **(a)** *(used with other verbs to make questions)* **does this train go to London?**; **did the doctor give you any medicine for your cough?**; **where do they live?**; **what did you find there?** **(b)** *(used with other verbs and 'not' to make the negative)* **they didn't laugh at the film**; **it doesn't matter any more**; **his parents don't live in London (c)** *(used to make a verb stronger)* **can I sit down? - please do!**; **why don't you work harder? - I do work hard!**; **why didn't you tell me? - I did tell you! (d)** *(used instead of another verb with* **so** *and* **neither)***; **we don't smoke - neither do I**; **he likes jam sandwiches and so does she (e)** *(used instead of another verb in short answers to questions using the word 'do')* **do you live in London? - yes I do**; **but your parents don't live there, do they? - no they don't**; **does the green colour show? - yes it does**; **did you go to the concert after all? - yes I did (f)** *(used instead of another verb at the end of a question or statement)* **the Russians live here, don't they?**; **it looks very nice, doesn't it?**; **it doesn't rain a lot in Spain, does it? (g)** *(used instead of another verb)* **can you run as fast as he does?**; **he speaks German better than I do**; **she asked me to close the door but I'd already done so**; **they got to the pub before we did (h)** *(telling someone not to do something)* **don't throw away that letter!**; **don't put your coffee cups on the computer! (i)** *(with nouns ending in* **-ing**) **she's doing the shopping**; **he always does the washing up**; **she was doing the ironing (j)** *(used when greeting someone)* **how do you do?** (NOTE: this does not normally expect an answer) **(k)** *(followed by a noun)* to work at something or to arrange something or to clean something; **she's doing her hair**; **have you done the dishes yet?**; **I can't do today's crossword**; **what have you been doing all day?**; **they're a difficult company to do business with**; **what do you do for a living?** = what is your job? **(l)** to succeed, to continue; **she's doing very well in her new job**; **he did badly in the interview**; **how's your business doing?**; **well done!** = congratulations; **I passed my driving test - well done! (m)** to finish being cooked; **the carrots aren't done yet**; **the chicken is done to a turn** = the chicken is cooked and ready to eat **(n)** to be satisfactory; **will this size do?**; **that will do** = that's enough; **that won't do at all** = that's not at all satisfactory **(o) to make do with** = to accept something which is not as good as you wanted; **the ordinary plates are all dirty, so we will have to make do with paper ones (p)** to travel at a certain speed; *the car was doing 100 miles an hour when it hit the tree* (NOTE: **I do; you do; he/she/it does** [dʌz]; **they do; doing - did** [dɪd] **- has done** [dʌn]; negative: **do not** usually **don't** [dəʊnt]; **does not** usually **doesn't** ['dʌznt]; **did not** usually **didn't** ['dɪdnt]) **2** *noun* (*informal*) (a) party; *we've been invited to a do at the Smiths* (b) **the dos and the don'ts** = things you should do and things you should not do; *she told him all the dos and don'ts about working in the office* (NOTE: plural is **dos** [du:z])

do away with ['du: ə'weɪ wɪθ] *verb* to get rid of something; *the government did away with customs inspections*

Doc [dɒk] (*informal*) = DOCTOR; *old Doc Brown came to see me*

docile ['dəʊsaɪl] *adjective* quiet, not aggressive; *some breeds of dog are docile and easy to train*

dock [dɒk] **1** *noun* (a) **the docks** = a harbour where ships are loaded and unloaded; *cars should arrive at the docks 45 minutes before sailing time*; *we used to go down to the docks to watch the ships come in*; **dry dock** = section of a harbour from which the water can be removed, so that ships can be repaired; **the ship is in dock** = (i) the ship is in the harbour; (ii) the ship is being repaired; (*informal*) **my car is in dock** = my car is being repaired (b) box in a law court, where the prisoner sits; *she was in the dock, facing charges of theft* **2** *verb* (a) (*of ship*) to arrive in harbour; *the ship docked at 17.00*; *the cruise liner will dock in Bermuda* (b) to link (two spacecraft) together; *the spacecraft docked with the space station* (c) to remove (money from wages); *I will have to dock your pay if you are late for work again*; *they've docked £20 from my pay!*

docker ['dɒkə] *noun* man who works in a harbour, loading and unloading ships; *the dockers have threatened to strike for more money* (NOTE: also called **stevedore;** American English is **longshoreman**)

dockland ['dɒklənd] *noun* part of a town around docks; *the London docklands have been developed with new offices and blocks of flats*

dockside ['dɒksaɪd] *noun* the side of a dock, where ships load or unload cargo; *the ship left the dockside and moored in the bay*

dockyard ['dɒkjɑːd] *noun* place where ships are built or repaired; *the crippled tanker was towed into the dockyard for repair*

Doc Martens ['dɒk 'mɑːtənz] *noun* trademark for a style of strong flexible laced-up leather boots available in many colours; *she came to the interview in her designer jeans and Doc Martens*

doctor ['dɒktə] **1** *noun* (a) person who looks after people who are ill; *I have a ten o'clock appointment to see the doctor*; *if you have pains in your chest, you ought to see a doctor*; *he went to the doctor's last Friday*; **doctor's certificate** = document written by a doctor to say that a worker is ill and cannot work; *she has been off sick for ten days and has sent in a doctor's certificate*; **ship's doctor** = doctor who travels on a ship and so is ready to treat passengers who become ill (b) person with the highest degree from a university; *she has a doctor's degree in physics* (NOTE: **doctor** is written **Dr** with names: **Dr Thorne is our local GP**) **2** *verb* to change something, so that it is false; *we suspect that he had been doctoring his expenses*; *she was accused of doctoring the test samples*

doctorate ['dɒktərət] *noun* highest degree from a university; *she has a doctorate in engineering*

doctrinal [dɒk'traɪnl] *adjective* referring to a doctrine; *doctrinal arguments split the church*

doctrine ['dɒktrɪn] *noun* statement of what a group of people believe; *he preached the doctrine of nuclear disarmament*; *love of your neighbours is one of the essentials of Christian doctrine*

document ['dɒkjumənt] **1** *noun* piece of paper with written text; *file all the documents away carefully as we may need them again*; *please read this document carefully and sign at the bottom of page two* **2** *verb* to note something in official writing; *cases of this disease are well documented in Africa*; *she sent in a fully documented claim for insurance*

documentary [dɒkju'mentəri] **1** *noun* factual film about a real subject; *did you see the documentary about hippos last night?* (NOTE: plural is **documentaries**) **2** *adjective* referring to documents; **documentary evidence** = evidence in the form of documents *they are searching in the archives for any documentary evidence that the meeting took place*

documentation [dɒkjumen'teɪʃn] *noun* all papers referring to something; *please send me all the documentation concerning the sale* (NOTE: no plural)

dodge [dɒdʒ] **1** *noun* (*informal*) clever trick; *he told me a dodge to avoid paying tax* **2** *verb* (a) to avoid, to get out of the way; *he ran across the street, dodging the traffic*; *she dodged behind a parked car hoping he wouldn't see her* (b) **to dodge the issue** = to avoid answering questions about a problem or trying to do anything about a problem; *we were very disappointed because the council simply dodged the issue*

dodger ['dɒdʒə] *noun* person who avoids something; **fare dodger** = person who travels on public transport without a ticket; *inspectors travel on the underground to try to catch fare dodgers*; **tax dodger** = person who tries to avoid paying tax

dodgy ['dɒdʒi] *adjective* (*informal*) (a) unsafe, risky; *the back wheel on your bike looks a bit dodgy to me*; *I wouldn't go hitchhiking in Russia - it sounds very dodgy* (b) probably dishonest, or dishonestly obtained; *he's a bit of a dodgy customer*; *she paid with a dodgy ten-pound note*

dodo ['dəʊdəʊ] *noun* large bird which lived on the islands in the Indian Ocean: it was not able to fly and became extinct in the 19th century, when it was killed by sailors for food; *see also* DEAD

doe ['dəʊ] *noun* female animal, such as deer, rabbit; *the does are looking after their fawns* (NOTE: do not confuse with **dough;** male rabbits are called **bucks,** male deer are **stags**)

does, doesn't [dʌz or 'dʌznt] *see* DO

doff [dɒf] *verb* (*old*) (*formal*) to take off your hat; *we're expected to doff our caps when the headmaster comes in*

dog [dɒg] **1** *noun* animal kept as a pet, which barks, and wags its tail when it is pleased; *can you take the dog out for a walk?*; *police with dogs were hunting the gang of escaped prisoners*; **to let sleeping dogs lie** = not to disturb things; *I wouldn't investigate any further if I were you - better let sleeping dogs lie* (*informal*) **to go to the dogs** = to get into a bad condition; *the whole place has gone to the dogs*; **it's a dog's life** = life is difficult, with too much work and no play (NOTE: the females are called: **bitches** and the young are **puppies**) **2** *verb* to follow; *all his life he has been dogged by ill-health*; **to dog someone's footsteps** = to follow behind someone closely; *failure seems to dog his footsteps* (NOTE: **dogging - dogged**)

dogfish ['dɒgfɪʃ] *noun* large sea fish (NOTE: also called **huss**)

dogged ['dɒgɪd] *adjective* not giving in easily, continuing to do something, even though people want you to stop; *dogged investigation by the police resulted in an arrest*; *bands of guerrillas put up a dogged resistance in the mountains*

doggedly ['dɒgɪdli] *adverb* not giving in easily; *the reporters questioned him doggedly about the affair*

doggy ['dɒgi] *noun* (*informal*) (*children's word*) dog; *she's brought her little doggy with her*; **doggy bag** = bag in which you can put food which you didn't eat in a restaurant to take home, supposedly for your dog (NOTE: plural is **doggies**)

doghouse ['dɒghaʊs] *noun* US kennel, small house where a dog is kept; *the dogs are kept in the doghouse at night*; (*informal*) **in the doghouse** = in disgrace; *he's in the doghouse because he forgot to buy his daughter a birthday present*

dogma ['dɒgmə] *noun* official belief; *it is part of the Communist Party dogma*

dogmatic [dɒg'mætɪk] *adjective* insistent that what you say is right; *let's not be dogmatic about this, let's just try to find an acceptable solution*

do in ['duː 'ɪn] *verb* (*informal*) (**a**) to kill; *what happened to the gang boss? - he was done in and dumped in the river* (**b**) to hurt; *I think I did my back in digging the garden*

doings ['duːɪŋz] *noun* (*informal*) (**a**) things which are done; *police have been watching the doings of the gang for some time* (**b**) gadget; *have you seen the doings for opening bottles anywhere?*

do-it-yourself (DIY) [duːɪtjə'self] *noun* repairing, building, painting your house by yourself, without employing a professional; *she's good at do-it-yourself jobs*; **do-it-yourself magazine** *or* **DIY magazine** = magazine with articles on work which you can do to repair or paint the house; *he buys a DIY magazine each week*

doldrums ['dɒldrəmz] *noun* area of low pressure over the ocean near the equator where there is very little wind; **in the doldrums** = stagnating, not doing very well; *the economy has been in the doldrums for the last three months*

dole [dəʊl] **1** *noun* (*informal*) money given by the government to people without work; **on the dole** = unemployed and receiving unemployment benefit; *he's been on the dole for four years* **2** *verb* **to dole out** = to hand out or distribute, without much ceremony; *the guide doled out customs forms*

doll [dɒl] *noun* child's toy which looks like a baby; *Susie is upstairs playing with her dolls and teddy bears*; **doll's house** = very small house made as a toy

dollar ['dɒlə] *noun* (**a**) money used in the USA; *a 5-dollar bill*; *the country spends millions of dollars on defence*; *there are two dollars to the pound* (**b**) similar currency used in many other countries; *what is the price in Australian dollars?* (NOTE: when used with a figure, usually written **$** before the figure: **$250**. The currencies used in different countries can be shown by the initial letter of the country: **Can$** (Canadian dollar) **Aus$** (Australian dollar), etc.)

dolly ['dɒli] *noun* (**a**) (*children's speech, informal*) doll; *let's put your dolly in her pram* (**b**) (*filming*) moveable stand on which a camera is mounted so that it can move to follow the action; *the dolly followed the actors across the set* (NOTE: plural is **dollies**)

dolphin ['dɒlfɪn] *noun* sea mammal like a very small whale; *dolphins followed the boat as it crossed the bay* (NOTE: a group of them is a **school of dolphins**)

dolt [dəʊlt] *noun* (*informal*) silly person; *you dolt - you've put the bottle in the fridge upside down*

domain [də'meɪn] *noun* (**a**) area of responsibility; *I don't do the cooking - that's my husband's domain*; **public domain** = property or information which belongs to and is available to the public; *anyone can use this information, it's in the public domain*; **public domain software** = software programs which are available to anyone free of charge (**b**) area, group of nodes in a network; **domain name** = name of a web site *or* computer *or* service provider on the Internet; *the Peter Collin Publishing domain name is www.pcp.co.uk*; *see note on domain names at* INTERNET

dome [dəʊm] *noun* round roof shaped like half of a ball; *you can climb up onto the dome of St Paul's Cathedral*

domed ['dəʊmd] *adjective* with a dome; *the domed ceiling of the library was painted in blue and gold*

Domesday Book ['duːmzdeɪ bʊk] *noun* record of land and population in England, made for William I (the Conqueror) in 1086; *our village is very old - it is mentioned in the Domesday Book*

COMMENT: the Domesday Book gives details of the name and size of each manor, the feudal owner, the number of people living there, either free or serfs, and such items as mills, fishponds, etc. It shows how the ownership of the land had changed in the twenty years since the Norman invasion of 1066. Many present-day English villages and towns are mentioned in the Domesday Book, though some big modern cities such as Manchester or Birmingham, were only little villages then

domestic [də'mestɪk] **1** *adjective* (**a**) referring to the home; *she hated having to do all the domestic work while her husband was out at his job*; **domestic animals** = farm animals and pets; **domestic science** = cooking and housework as subject studied at school; **domestic service** = working as a servant in a house (**b**) inside a country; *sales in the domestic market have risen*; **domestic flights** = flights between airports inside the same country **2** *noun* (*old*) servant in a house; *when the fire broke out all the domestics ran into the house to rescue the furniture*

domesticate [də'mestɪkeɪt] *verb* (**a**) to become domesticated = to be used to doing housework; *he's become totally domesticated since he got married* (**b**) to breed wild animals so that they become tame and can be kept for food or as pets, or wild plants to grow as food or decoration; *early man rapidly domesticated the wild horse and buffalo*; *domesticated forms of wheat were developed by early farmers*

domesticity [dɒme'stɪsɪti] *noun* life at home; *the old couple live a life of simple domesticity*

domicile ['dɒmɪsaɪl] noun (formal) place where someone lives or where a company is registered; *they changed their domicile from Britain to Bermuda for tax reasons*

domiciled ['dɒmɪsaɪld] adjective (formal) living or resident or registered in a place; *she is domiciled in France*; *the company is domiciled in the Cayman Islands*

dominance ['dɒmɪnəns] noun being dominant; *his dominance over his rivals*; *the general election established the party's dominance in the House of Commons*

dominant ['dɒmɪnənt] adjective (a) most important; *the dominant colour in the room is dark red*; *safety will be the dominant theme of the discussion* (b) very powerful, commanding; *he has a very dominant personality and his wife and children have to do what he says*; *the President's party is the dominant force in the country's political system*

dominate ['dɒmɪneɪt] verb (a) to rule; *he is dominated by his wife*; *the Union party dominates the country's political system* (b) to be very obviously seen; *the volcano dominates the town*

domineer [dɒmɪ'nɪə] verb to force your ideas on someone; *he always tries to domineer the meetings*

domineering [dɒmɪ'nɪərɪŋ] adjective forcing your ideas on someone; *he has a very domineering wife*

dominion [də'mɪnjən] noun (a) power of control; *to exercise dominion over a country* (b) a Dominion = an independent state, part of the British Commonwealth; *the Dominion of Canada*

domino ['dɒmɪnəʊ] noun one of a set of small flat blocks used to play a game, each block being divided into two sections, with up to six dots in each section; *to have a game of dominoes*; *they sat playing dominoes in the bar*; **domino effect** = collapse of something, which triggers the collapse of something else; **domino theory** = the theory that if one things happens, other things will follow (NOTE: plural is **dominoes**)

don [dɒn] **1** noun university teacher, especially at Oxford or Cambridge; *his father was an Oxford don* **2** verb (formal) to put on a piece of clothing; *instructions for donning the life jacket are in the pocket in front of your seat*; *visitors to the factory have to don protective clothing* (NOTE: **donning - donned**)

donate [dəʊ'neɪt] verb to give; *he donated a lot of money to a charity for cats*

donation [dəʊ'neɪʃn] noun gift, especially of money; *all donations will be gratefully received*; *I can't afford to make any donations to charity this Christmas*

done [dʌn] verb see DO

donkey ['dɒŋki] noun grey farm animal with long ears, used for riding or pulling; *the old grey donkey stood by himself in a corner of the field*; **to do the donkey work** = to do heavy unpleasant work; *no one wants to do the donkey work, so guess who has to do it?*; **donkey jacket** = thick woollen coat worn by workmen; (informal) **for donkey's years** = for a very long time; *we haven't seen him for donkey's years*

donor ['dəʊnə] noun person who gives; *the donor of the kidney lives in Arkansas*; *the list of the museum's donors is on a board by the entrance*; **blood donor** = person who gives blood regularly for use in transfusions

don't [dəʊnt] see DO

doom [duːm] **1** noun unhappy fate that cannot be avoided; *they marched on to their doom*; *prepare to meet your doom*; *when the knock on the door came at midnight, he felt a sense of doom come over him* **2** verb to condemn someone or something to end in ruin; *the project was doomed (to failure) from the start*; *he was doomed to lose the game*

door [dɔː] noun (a) piece of wood, metal, etc., which closes an entrance; *he went into his office and locked the door behind him*; *she opened the car door and hit a passing cyclist*; **front door** = main door to a building; *she gave him a key to the front door or a front door key*; **back door** = door at the back of a building; *the back door leads out into the garden* (b) used to show where a building is in a street; *he lives three doors down the street* = he lives three houses further along the street; *they live a few doors away from us*; see also NEXT DOOR

doorbell ['dɔːbel] noun bell by a door which you ring to get someone inside to open the door; *the doorbell rang as I was in the bath*; *the postman rang three times on the doorbell*

doorkey ['dɔːkiː] noun key to a door; *don't forget to give me back the doorkey when you leave*

doorknob ['dɔːnɒb] noun handle for opening and shutting a door; *she hung a 'do not disturb' sign on the doorknob*

doorman ['dɔːmən] noun man who stands at the door of a restaurant, hotel, club, etc.; *the doorman would not let us in because we were wearing jeans* (NOTE: plural is **doormen**)

doormat ['dɔːmæt] noun small rough carpet placed in front of or behind a door, on which you wipe your shoes if they are dirty or wet; *the post has come - there are a couple of letters on the doormat*

doorstep ['dɔːstep] noun block of stone, wood, etc., forming the base of a doorway; *leave the empty milk bottles on the doorstep*; **on your doorstep** = very close to where you live; *there's a big supermarket right on our doorstep*

door-to-door ['dɔːtə'dɔː] adjective going from one house to the next, asking people to buy something, to vote for someone, or asking them questions; *the police carried out door-to-door checks to try to find the gunman*; *he has a job selling vegetables door-to-door*; **door-to-door salesman** = salesman who goes from one house to the next, asking people to buy something; *the insurance company uses door-to-door salesmen to sell its policies*

doorway ['dɔːweɪ] noun space where there is a door; *she stood in the doorway, sheltering from the rain*

dope [dəʊp] noun (informal) (a) drug; *a dope peddler*; **to take a dope test** = to take a test to see if you have been taking drugs (b) information; *come on, let's have the dope on the divorce case!* (c) stupid fool; *he's a dope, he should have asked for twice as much!*

dormant ['dɔːmənt] adjective not active; **to lie dormant** = to remain hidden and not active; *some viruses lie dormant for years*; **dormant account** = unused bank account; **dormant period** = winter, the period when plants stop growing; **dormant volcano** = a volcano which is not erupting at the moment; *the volcano has been dormant for many years, but has suddenly started to send out clouds of smoke*; compare EXTINCT

dormitory ['dɔ:mɪtri] *noun* long room full of beds; *the scout leader sleeps in a little cubicle off the main dormitory* (NOTE: plural is **dormitories**)

DOS [dɒs] = DISK OPERATING SYSTEM

dosage ['dəʊsɪdʒ] *noun* correct amounts of a drug calculated by a doctor to be necessary for a patient; *the doctor decided to increase the dosage of antibiotics*

dose [dəʊs] **1** *noun* **(a)** quantity of medicine; *normal daily dose: three tablets*; *it is dangerous to exceed the prescribed dose*; **a fatal** *or* **lethal dose** = amount of drug which can kill; *she took a lethal dose of sleeping tablets* **(b)** *(informal)* attack of a disease; *I've had a dose of bronchitis* **2** *verb* **to dose someone with something** = to give someone medicine; *he dosed himself with hot lemon juice*

dosh [dɒʃ] *noun (informal)* money; *come on, where's the dosh?*

doss down ['dɒs 'daʊn] *verb (informal)* to sleep on the floor, pavement, etc.; *can I stay the night? I don't mind dossing down on the living room floor*

dosser ['dɒsə] *(informal)* tramp; *the Salvation Army looks after the dossers living under railway arches*

dossier ['dɒsɪə] *noun* file of documents; *she has asked to see the dossier of complaints about service*; *the police have a whole dossier on him*

dot [dɒt] *noun* **(a)** small round spot; *a blue tie with white dots* **(b)** **on the dot of** = exactly at a time; *the train left on the dot of four; see also* YEAR

dote on ['dəʊt 'ɒn] *verb* to be very fond of someone; *he dotes on his little granddaughter*

doting ['dəʊtɪŋ] *adjective* very fond of someone; *he showed his prize to his doting grandparents*

dot matrix printer ['dɒt 'meɪtrɪks 'prɪntə] *noun* computer printer that prints characters as a group of little dots

dotted ['dɒtɪd] *adjective* with things here and there; *a landscape dotted with little chalets*

dotted line ['dɒtɪd 'laɪn] *noun* line made of a series of dots; *please sign on the dotted line*; *do not write anything below the dotted line*

double ['dʌbl] **1** *adjective* **(a)** twice the size; *she took a double portion of ice cream*; **double cream** = thick stiff cream **(b)** **in double figures** = with two figures, the numbers from 10 to 99; *inflation is expected to reach double figures next month* **(c)** with two parts, for two people; **double bed** = bed for two people; *do you want a double bed or two single beds?*; **double room** = room for two people **2** *adverb* twice the amount; *it takes double the time*; *her salary is double mine* **3** *noun* **(a)** *(in the army)* **at the double** = running; *the soldiers crossed the square at the double* **(b)** person who looks exactly like someone else; *it was either him or his double we saw at the cinema* **(c)** **doubles** = tennis game for two people on either side; **men's doubles** *or* **women's doubles** = two men against two other men *or* two women against two other women; **mixed doubles** = man and woman against another man and woman

doublebass [dʌbl'beɪs] *noun* musical instrument like a very large violin; *it is awkward for him to take his doublebass with him on a plane* (NOTE: also called simply **bass**)

double-check ['dʌbltʃek] *verb* to check carefully, twice; *we've checked and double-checked the figures*

and still can't find a mistake; *she double-checked to make sure that she had not left her keys in the car*

double-decker [dʌbl'dekə] *noun* **(a)** bus with two decks (an upper as well as a lower one); *double-decker buses are common in London* **(b)** *(informal)* sandwich made of three slices of bread, with a filling of meat, salad, fish, etc., between them; *this double-decker is so thick I can't bite into it*

double-glazed ['dʌbl'gleɪzd] *adjective* with windows made of double panes of glass; *the house is double-glazed, so we hardly hear the trains at all*

double-glazing ['dʌbl 'gleɪzɪŋ] *noun* windows made of two pieces of glass, used to keep out noise or to keep heat inside; *the double-glazing helps to deaden the sound the the the traffic*

double standards ['dʌbl 'stændədz] *noun* quite different moral standards which are applied to different people or situations; *it's a case of double standards - he criticizes us for wasting electricity but leaves the lights on in his office all night long*

doubletalk ['dʌbltɔ:k] *noun (informal)* way of speaking which can be understood in two different ways, either as serious, or as nonsense; *don't believe what MPs say - it's usually just doubletalk*

double up ['dʌbl 'ʌp] *verb* **(a)** to bend because of pain; *she doubled up in pain when he hit her in the stomach* **(b)** to perform two jobs; *the barman doubles up as the cook, when the chef is on holiday*

doubly [dʌbli] *adverb* twice; *he made things doubly difficult by insisting on bringing all his family with him*; *she made doubly sure that she had not left her iron switched on*

doubt [daʊt] **1** *noun* **(a)** not being sure; *even the staunchest believer sometimes has doubts*; **to have doubts about** = to be unsure; *I have my doubts about the accuracy of the figures*; **to cast doubt on** = to be unsure about; *he cast doubt on the whole proposal*; **to give someone the benefit of the doubt** = to allow someone to continue doing something, because you are not sure that accusations made against him are correct; *the referee gave him the benefit of the doubt* **(b)** **no doubt** = certainly; *no doubt they will be suing for damages*; **there's no doubt about** = it is a certain fact; *there's no doubt about it - France is the best place for a holiday*; *there's no doubt that he is guilty*; **in doubt** = not sure; *the result of the game was in doubt until the last minute* **2** *verb* not to be sure of something; *I doubt whether he will want to go to the funeral*; *I doubt her honesty*; *did you ever doubt that we would win?*

doubtful ['daʊtful] *adjective* not sure; *I am doubtful about whether we should go*; *she had a doubtful expression on her face*; *his future with the company looks increasingly doubtful*; *it is doubtful whether the race will take place because of the snow*

doubtless ['daʊtləs] *adverb* certainly; *they have been out climbing in the mountains all day so doubtless they'll appreciate a warm bath when they get back home*

dough [dəʊ] *noun* **(a)** uncooked mixture of water and flour for making bread, etc.; *the chef was kneading the dough for the pizza* **(b)** *(slang)* money; *hurry up, give me the dough!* (NOTE: do not confuse with **doe**)

doughnut ['dəʊnʌt] *noun* small round or ring-shaped cake cooked by frying in oil; *you dip freshly made doughnuts in sugar*

do up ['du: 'ʌp] *verb* **(a)** to attach; *he's still a baby and he can't do his buttons up properly; can you do up the zip at the back of my dress?* **(b)** to repair and make like new; *they bought an old cottage and did it up; he's looking for an old sports car to do up*

dour ['dʊə] *adjective* gloomy or silent; *his dour expression made her think twice about making a joke; he stared out of the window at the dour grey countryside*

douse [daʊs] *verb* to throw water on something; *they tried to douse the fire with buckets of water; she was doused by the garden spray*

dove [dʌv] **1** *noun* **(a)** white domesticated pigeon; *to celebrate the peace treaty they released hundreds of doves* **(b)** person who prefers diplomacy and tries to achieve peace; *curiously, it's the military commanders who are the doves while the president and his advisers are the hawks* (NOTE: the opposite, a person who prefers military action, is a **hawk**) **2** [dəʊv] *verb US see* DIVE

do with ['du: 'wɪθ] *verb* **(a)** to concern; *it has nothing to do with us; it is something to do with my new book* **(b)** to put somewhere; *what have you done with the newspaper?* **(c)** *(informal)* to need; *after that long walk I could do with a cup of tea; the car could do with a wash*

do without ['du: wɪð'aʊt] *verb* not to have something, to manage without something; *if you live in the country can you do without a car?; plants can't do without water*

Dow Jones Index ['daʊ 'dʒəʊnz 'ɪndeks] *noun* index of share prices on the New York Stock Exchange; *see also* FOOTSIE, NIKKEI

down [daʊn] **1** *preposition* **(a)** towards the bottom of; *he fell down the stairs and broke his leg; the ball ran down the hill* **(b)** away from where the person is speaking; *he went down the road to the Post Office; the police station is just down the street* **2** *adverb* **(a)** towards the bottom, towards a lower position; *put the box down in the corner; he sat down on the carpet; she lay down on the bed; I looked in the cellar, but there's no one down there* **(b)** at a lower level; *inflation is down again* **(c)** (put) on paper; *did you write down the number of the car?; the policeman took down her address* **(d)** towards the south; *I'm going down to Brighton tomorrow (from London) they live down on the south coast* **(e)** *(informal)* **down under** = in Australia and New Zealand **(f)** sick; *she is down with flu* **(g)** *(informal)* gloomy; *he's feeling a bit down* **(h)** *(showing criticism)* down with the government!; down with exams!* (NOTE: **down** is often used with verbs: **to go down; to break down; to fall down,** etc.) **3** *noun* **(a)** soft feathers (of a duck); *a duvet filled with down* (NOTE: no plural in this meaning) **(b)** **downs** = grass-covered hills with low bushes and very few trees; *we went for a walk over the downs* (NOTE: usually used in names of areas: **the North Downs, The South Downs**) **4** *verb* **(a)** to swallow quickly; *he downed three pints of beer* **(b)** to down tools = to stop work

downbeat ['daʊnbi:t] **1** *adjective* feeling gloomy; *he was very downbeat when he heard the results* **2** *noun* beat of a conductor's baton to show that the music should begin (NOTE: the opposite is **upbeat**)

downfall ['daʊnfɔ:l] *noun* collapse or ruin; *the recession brought about the downfall of several companies*

downgrade [daʊn'greɪd] *verb* to reduce the importance of a person or of a job; *his job was downgraded in the company reorganization*

downhill [daʊn'hɪl] *adverb* **(a)** towards the bottom of a hill; *the road goes downhill for a while and then crosses the river* **(b)** *(informal)* **to go downhill** = to get worse; *the economy is going downhill; the business started to go downhill when the old manager left* **(c)** it's downhill all the way = it will be easy from now on; *we've done the hardest bit, it's downhill all the way from here*

Downing Street ['daʊnɪŋ 'stri:t] *noun* street in London with the houses of the British Prime Minister (No. 10) and the Chancellor of the Exchequer (No. 11); *they took the petition to Downing Street; see also* NUMBER TEN

down-market ['daʊnmɑ:kɪt] *adjective* cheaper, appealing to a less wealthy section of the population; *the company has decided to launch a more down-market version of the product; she's the editor of one of the more down-market newspapers*

down payment ['daʊn 'peɪmənt] *noun* part of a total payment made in advance; *he made a down payment of $100*

downplay ['daʊnpleɪ] *verb* to make something seem less important; *he tried to downplay the importance of the offer* (NOTE: can also be **to play down**)

downpour ['daʊnpɔ:] *noun* heavy fall of rain; *there was a sudden downpour and all the spectators ran inside*

downright ['daʊnraɪt] **1** *adjective* complete or distinct; *that's a downright lie; the newspaper story was a downright fabrication* **2** *adverb* completely or distinctly; *the waitress wasn't just unpleasant, she was downright rude*

downside ['daʊnsaɪd] *noun* disadvantages of a situation; *the downside is that my mother-in-law is coming to stay for Christmas*; **downside factor** *or* **downside risk** = possibility of making a loss in an investment

downsizing ['daʊnsaɪzɪŋ] *noun* making a company smaller by dismissing staff or making them redundant; *wholesale downsizing has made many companies profitable, but has put hundreds of people out of work*

Down's syndrome ['daʊnz 'sɪndrəʊm] *noun* defect from birth, caused by the existence of an extra chromosome; *their second child has Down's syndrome*

downstage ['daʊnsteɪdʒ] *adverb* to or at the front of the stage; *the hero moves downstage and addresses the audience* (NOTE: the opposite, towards the back of the stage, is **upstage**)

downstairs [daʊn'steəz] **1** *adverb* on or to the lower part of a building; *he heard a noise in the kitchen and went downstairs to see what it was; I left my cup of coffee downstairs* **2** *adjective* on the ground floor of a building; *the house has a downstairs bedroom; you can use the downstairs loo* **3** *noun* the ground floor of a building; *the downstairs has three rooms; the downstairs of the house is larger than the upstairs*

downstream ['daʊnstri:m] **1** *adjective* towards the mouth of the river; *downstream communities have not yet been affected* **2** *adverb* towards the mouth of the river; *the silt is carried downstream and deposited in the delta*

down-to-earth [ˌdaʊntʊˈɜːθ] *adjective* sensible or matter-of-fact; *she has very down-to-earth approach to teaching*

downtown [ˈdaʊntaʊn] **1** *adverb* to the town centre; *you can take the bus to go downtown* **2** *adjective* in the town centre; *the downtown department stores*; *her office is in downtown New York* **3** *noun* the central district of a town; *downtown will be very crowded at this time of day*

downturn [ˈdaʊntɜːn] *noun* movement towards lower prices, sales, profits; *the last quarter saw a downturn in the economy*

downward [ˈdaʊnwəd] **1** *adjective* towards the bottom; *a downward trend in the unemployment figures* **2** *adverb* US see DOWNWARDS

downwards US **downward** [ˈdaʊnwədz] *adverb* towards the bottom; *the path slopes downwards to the stream*; *he went to sleep face downwards on the floor*

dowse [daʊz] *verb* to look for water using a forked twig which moves when it passes over an underground source of water; *we asked a local man to dowse for water on our land*

dowser [ˈdaʊzə] *noun* person who dowses; *the local dowser came and found water under our lawn*

doz [ˈdʌn] = DOZEN

doze [dəʊz] **1** *noun* short sleep; *she had a little doze after feeding the baby* **2** *verb* to sleep a little, to sleep lightly; *she dozed off for a while after lunch*

dozen [ˈdʌzən] *noun* **(a)** twelve; *we ordered two dozen chairs*; **they're cheaper by the dozen** = they are cheaper if you buy twelve at a time; **half a dozen** = six; *half a dozen apples*; **a baker's dozen** = thirteen **(b)** **dozens of** = a lot of; *dozens of people visited the exhibition*; *I've been to New York dozens of times* (NOTE: **dozen** does not become plural after a number: **dozens of chairs**, but **two dozen chairs**)

dozy [ˈdəʊzi] *adjective* **(a)** sleepy; *the children were dozy after their walk, so we put them to bed early* **(b)** **dozy little town** = little town where nothing much happens

Dr *see* DOCTOR

drab [dræb] *adjective* lacking bright colours; brown, grey; *on a rainy November morning the backstreets of London look cold and drab*; *she was wearing a drab olive-green coat* (NOTE: **drabber - drabbest**)

drachma [ˈdrækmə] *noun* unit of money used in Greece; *a meal with wine costs only a few thousand drachmas* (NOTE: usually written **Dr** before a figure: **Dr22,000**)

draconian [drəˈkəʊniən] *adjective* very severe, harsh (law, etc.); *the government took draconian measures against the student protesters*

draft [drɑːft] **1** *noun* **(a)** rough plan of a document; *he quickly wrote out a draft of the agreement*; *it's not the final version, it's just a draft* **(b)** US formerly, military service which most young men had to do; *he left the USA to avoid the draft* **(c)** order for money to be paid by a bank; *she sent me a draft for one thousand pounds* **(d)** US see DRAUGHT **2** *adjective* rough (plan, document); *they brought the draft treaty with them*; *she drew up the draft agreement on the back of an envelope*; *the lawyers were working on the draft contract* **3** *verb* **(a)** to draw up a rough plan of; *we drafted the details of the agreement on a piece of*

paper **(b)** US to call someone for military service; *at the age of eighteen he was drafted into the Marines* **(c)** to ask someone to do something; *the Boy Scouts were drafted in to dig the garden*; *compare* DRAUGHT

draftsman [ˈdrɑːftsmən] US = DRAUGHTSMAN

drag [dræg] **1** *noun* **(a)** boring thing, which stops you doing things you really want to do; *it's a drag, having to write all the Christmas cards* **(b)** *(of a man)* **in drag** = wearing women's clothes **2** *verb* **(a)** to pull something heavy along; *she dragged her suitcase across the platform*; *the police dragged the protesters away from the gate* to hang back, to stay behind; to go slowly; *Tom was dragging along at the end of the line*; *the dinner party seemed to drag on for hours* **(c)** to pull a net along the bottom of (a lake) to try to find something; *the police dragged the lake to try to find the body of the missing boy* **(d)** **drag and drop** = (computers) to move an icon *or* section of text *or* object from one area of the screen to another; *click once on the file icon then keep the mouse button pressed down and drag and drop it onto the printer icon* (NOTE: **dragging - dragged**)

dragon [ˈdrægən] *noun* mythological animal which breathes fire; *the national emblem of Wales is a red dragon*; **dragon boat** = long narrow Chinese boat, with a dragon's head on the bow, paddled by a crew of twenty-two to the beat of a drummer; **dragon boat races** = racing dragon boats as a sport

dragonfly [ˈdrægənflaɪ] *noun* long insect with bright transparent wings which often flies near water; *we sat by the river and watched the dragonflies darting about in the rushes* (NOTE: plural is **dragonflies**)

dragoon [drəˈguːn] **1** *noun* *(old)* armed soldier on horseback; *the dragoons attacked the French cavalry* **2** *verb* to force; *mother dragooned us all into helping move the furniture*

drain [dreɪn] **1** *noun* **(a)** pipe for carrying waste water; *in the autumn the drains get blocked by leaves*; *we had to phone the council to come and clear the blocked drain*; *(informal)* **it's just like pouring money down the drain** = it's a waste of money; *see also* LAUGH **(b)** gradual loss; *the office in Paris is a continual drain on our resources*; *see also* BRAIN DRAIN **2** *verb* **(a)** to remove a liquid; *boil the potatoes for ten minutes, drain and leave to cool* **(b)** to drink the contents of (a glass); *he drained his glass and called for another round*

drainage [ˈdreɪnɪdʒ] *noun* removing water by laying drains; *underground channels and pipes are the usual methods of drainage used on farms*; *drainage is a problem in low-lying meadows*

drained [dreɪnd] *adjective* **to look drained** = to look pale and tired out; *after the interview she looked completely drained*

draining board [ˈdreɪnɪŋ ˈbɔːd] *noun* slightly sloping surface next to a sink; *washed the pans and put them to dry on the draining board*

drainpipe [ˈdreɪnpaɪp] *noun* pipe which takes away waste water; *the burglar climbed up a drainpipe and got into the house through a bedroom window*

drake [dreɪk] *noun* male duck; *the drake is much more brightly coloured than the female* (NOTE: a female duck is called a **duck;** the young are **ducklings**)

drama [ˈdrɑːmə] *noun* **(a)** serious performance in a theatre; *the 'Globe' has put on an unknown*

Elizabethan drama; *I'm reading a book on 19th century French drama*; *a new TV drama series about life in the Lake District*; *she's a drama student or she's studying drama*; **drama department** = department in a college which teaches serious theatre **(b)** series of serious and exciting events; *he always makes a drama out of everything*; *a day of high drama in the court*; *the drama of the rescue of the children by helicopter*

dramatic [drə'mætɪk] *adjective* **(a)** referring to drama; *a dramatic performance which begins at 7.30*; *his latest dramatic work for radio* **(b)** giving a shock; *the door was flung open and she made a dramatic entrance*; *the dramatic moment in the film, when the dinosaurs start to attack children*

dramatically [drə'mætɪkli] *adverb* very surprisingly; *her appearance has altered dramatically during the last few months*

dramatics [drə'mætɪks] *noun* performing plays, usually as a student or amateur; *the local amateur dramatics group is putting on 'Hamlet' in the village hall*

dramatist ['dræmətɪst] *noun* person who writes plays; *Shakespeare was only one of many Elizabethan dramatists*

dramatization [dræmətaɪ'zeɪʃn] *noun* adaptation of something for the TV or theatre; *the BBC is screening a new dramatization of 'Sense and Sensibility'*

dramatize ['dræmətaɪz] *verb* **(a)** to adapt a novel for the theatre or for TV; *the novel was dramatized by J. Smith* **(b)** to make something seem much more dramatic than it really is; *there's no need to dramatize the situation, it's bad enough as it is*

drank [dræŋk] *see* DRINK

drape [dreɪp] **1** *noun US* **drapes** = light curtains; *open the drapes - it's light outside* **2** *verb* to hang cloth around something; *the statue was draped in a white cloth ready to be unveiled*; *he wore a long scarf draped over his shoulders*

draper ['dreɪpə] *noun (old)* person who sells cloth and clothes; *go to the draper's in the High Street and get some red material to make cushions*

drapery ['dreɪpəri] *noun* **(a)** *(old)* **drapery (shop)** = shop selling cloth or clothes; *he runs the drapery in the High Street* **(b)** thin cloth which is draped around something; *she was clothed in thin draperies* (NOTE: plural is **draperies**)

drastic ['dræstɪk] *adjective* severe, which has a sharp effect; *we must take drastic measures to cut costs*; *there has been a drastic fall in sales this month*; *let's not be too drastic - we need only make one or two staff redundant*

drastically ['dræstɪkli] *adverb* severely, with a sharp effect; *they have drastically cut their costs*; *our sales in the Far East have fallen drastically*

draught *US* **draft** [drɑːft] *noun* **(a)** flow of cool air into a room; *he sat in a draught and got a stiff neck* **(b)** **draught beer** *or* **beer on draught** = beer which is served from a barrel, and not in a bottle or can; *I'll have a pint of draught, please* **(c)** **draughts** = game with black and white pieces; *would you like a game of draughts or to play draughts?*; *draughts is a much simpler game than chess* (NOTE: not plural, and takes a singular verb; American English for the game is **checkers**) **(d)** **draught animals** = animals which are used to pull vehicles or carry heavy loads; *bullocks are often used*

as draught animals because they are easy to train **(e)** depth of water which a ship needs to float and not touch the bottom; **shallow-draught boat** = boat which needs only a little water to float

draughtsman *US* **draftsman** ['drɑːftsmən] *noun* person who draws plans for machines or buildings; *the draughtsman produce a set of plans for the new town centre* (NOTE: plural is **draughtsmen** or **draftsmen**)

draughty *US* **drafty** ['drɑːfti] *adjective* with cool air flowing into it; *sitting in that draughty railway carriage has given me a cold* (NOTE: **draughtier - draughtiest**)

draw [drɔː] **1** *noun* **(a)** selecting the winner in a lottery; *the draw is held on Saturdays*; *we are holding a draw to raise money for the local hospital* **(b)** game where there is no winner; *the game ended in a draw, with the score 2 - 2* **(c)** attraction; *the zoo is a great draw for children*; *the new safari park will be the biggest draw in the area* **2** *verb* **(a)** to make a picture with a pen or pencil; *he drew a picture of the house*; *she's drawing a pot of flowers* **(b)** to pull open or to close; *can you draw the curtains - it's getting dark*; *she drew the curtains and let in the sun* **(c)** to move something closer; *draw your chairs up to the table* **(d)** to pull out; *he drew a notepad out of his pocket*; *she was drawing water from a well*; **to draw lots** = to take pieces of paper from a box to decide something (the person who has the marked piece wins); *we drew lots to decide who would go first*; *they drew lots for the bottle of whisky* **(e)** not to have a winner in a game; *the teams drew 2 - 2*; **the match was drawn** = neither side won **(f)** to receive money; *he doesn't draw a salary, but charges us for his expenses*; *in two years' time I'll be drawing my old age pension* (NOTE: **drawing - drew** [druː] **- has drawn** [drɔːn])

drawback ['drɔːbæk] *noun* thing that is inconvenient or an obstacle; *one of the drawbacks of the scheme is that it will take six years to complete*; *the biggest drawback is the we will have to get a flight at 5.30 in the morning*

drawbridge ['drɔːbrɪdʒ] *noun* bridge which can be raised or lowered to give access across water; *they raised the drawbridge as the enemy army came near*; *the knights rode over the drawbridge and entered the castle*

drawer ['drɔːə] *noun* **(a)** part of a desk or cupboard like an open box which slides in and out and which you pull with a handle; *I keep my cheque book in the top drawer of my desk*; **a chest of drawers** = piece of bedroom furniture with several drawers for clothes **(b)** person who writes a cheque or a bill asking money to be paid to someone; **the bank returned the cheque to drawer** = the bank would not pay the cheque because the person who wrote it did not have enough money in the account to pay it (NOTE: the American English equivalent is **nonsufficient funds**)

draw in ['drɔː 'ɪn] *verb* **the nights** *or* **the days are drawing in** = it is becoming darker earlier because winter is approaching

drawing ['drɔːɪŋ] *noun* picture done with a pen or pencil; *I've bought an old drawing of the church*; **drawing board** = large board used by designers to work on; **it's back to the drawing board** = we'll have to start planning all over again

drawing pin ['drɔːɪŋ 'pɪn] *noun* pin with a large flat head, used for pinning papers; *she used drawing pins to pin the poster to the door*; *he put a drawing pin on the teacher's chair* (NOTE: American English is **thumbtack**)

drawing room ['drɔːɪŋ 'rʊm] *noun (formal)* sitting room, a room for sitting and talking in, but not eating; *we were all having a cup of coffee in the drawing room*

drawl [drɔːl] **1** *noun* slow way of speaking; *he spoke with a southern drawl* **2** *verb* to speak slowly, making the words seem long; *'Come up and see me some time', she drawled*

drawn [drɔːn] *adjective* **(a)** tired and ill; *she looked drawn after spending all night with her sick baby* **(b)** see DRAW

drawn-out ['drɔːn 'aʊt] *adjective* **long drawn-out** = taking a very long time; *there was long drawn-out argument about who was going to pay the bill*

draw up ['drɔː 'ʌp] *verb* **(a)** to come close and stop; *as I was standing at the bus stop, a car drew up and asked if I wanted a lift* **(b)** to write down a plan, etc.; *they have drawn up a plan to save money*; *have you drawn up a list of people you want to invite to the party?*

dread [dred] **1** *noun* great fear; *the sound of his voice filled her with dread*; *she has a dread of being touched*; **in dread of** = being very afraid of; *they lived in constant dread of being arrested by the secret police* **2** *verb* to fear greatly; *I'm dreading taking my driving test*; *she dreads her weekly visit to the doctor*

dreaded ['dredɪd] *adjective (humorous)* awful, frightening; *he's been sneezing all day, I think he's caught the dreaded flu*; *she said a dreaded monster will get out of the dustbin to chase naughty little boys*

dreadful ['dredfʊl] *adjective* very bad or unpleasant; *the weather has been dreadful all week*; *what a dreadful colour for a hat!*

dreadfully ['dredfəli] *adverb* awfully, extremely; *we're dreadfully busy this morning*; *I'm dreadfully sorry, but we seem to have lost your ticket*

dreadlocked ['dredlɒkt] *adjective* wearing dreadlocks; *a group of dreadlocked dancers*

dreadlocks ['dredlɒks] *noun* hairstyle where your hair is plaited into thick strands; *he had his hair in dreadlocks*

dream [driːm] **1** *noun* **(a)** things which you think you see happening when you are asleep; *she had a dream about big pink elephants* **(b)** things which you imagine and hope will happen in the future; *the results surpassed our wildest dreams*; *never in your wildest dreams did you imagine you would end up in such an important job* **(c)** something you would really like to do or to see happen; *his dream is to appear on Broadway*; *they finally realized their dream of owning a cottage in the country* **(d)** *(informal)* something very pleasant or delicious; *that chocolate mousse was a dream* **2** *verb* **(a)** to think you see things happening while you are asleep; *he was dreaming of white sand and a blue tropical sea*; *I dreamt about you last night*; *last night I dreamt I was drowning* **(b)** to think about something; **not to dream of doing something** = not to consider doing something; *she wouldn't dream of wearing a big hat like that* **(c)** to imagine something which does not exist; *I never said that - you must have been dreaming!* (NOTE: **he dreamed** *or* **he dreamt** [dremt])

3 *adjective* best possible, that you really want; *their found their dream house in a small town by the sea*; *the game is to select your dream team for the World Cup*

dreamer ['driːmə] *noun* person who is out of touch with practical things; *he's a dreamer rather than a man of action*

dreamy ['driːmi] *adjective* as if you are dreaming; *mention Hawaii and a dreamy look comes into their eyes* (NOTE: **dreamier - dreamiest**)

dreary ['drɪəri] *adjective* sad or gloomy; not interesting; *what a dreary town!*; *he has some sort of dreary job in a bank* (NOTE: **drearier - dreariest**)

dredge [dredʒ] *verb* **(a)** to remove mud or sand from a river bed or harbour, etc.; *they had to spend weeks dredging the channel so that boats can still get to the harbour* **(b)** to sprinkle a cake with powdered sugar, etc.; *when the pie is cooked, dredge it with icing sugar*

dredger ['dredʒə] *noun* boat with a crane and large scoop, used for dredging; *a dredger is working permanently to keep the harbour open*

drench [drentʃ] *verb* to soak; *they came home drenched after the rainstorm*

dress [dres] **1** *noun* **(a)** piece of a woman's or girl's clothing, covering more or less all the body; *she was wearing a blue dress* (NOTE: plural is **dresses**) **(b)** special clothes; **evening dress** = formal clothes worn to an evening banquet or reception (long dresses for women and dinner jacket and bow tie for men); *he was wearing evening dress* (NOTE: no plural in this meaning) **2** *verb* **(a)** to put clothes on; *he got up, dressed and then had breakfast*; *she dressed her little girl all in tartan* **(b)** to clean and put a bandage on a wound; *the nurse will dress the cut on your knee* **(c)** to prepare food; *she dressed the salad with slices of cucumber and tomatoes*

dressage ['dresɑːʒ] *noun* competition in which trained horses show how obedient they are

dressed [drest] *adjective* **(a)** wearing clothes; *I can't come down to see the visitors - I'm not dressed yet*; *he got up, got dressed and then had breakfast*; *she was dressed all in black* **(b) dressed (up) as** = wearing the costume of; *he went to the party dressed (up) as a policeman*; **dressed up to the nines** = wearing your very best clothes; *I saw her going out all dressed up to the nines* **(c) dressed crab** = crab which has been cooked, with the legs and body removed, and the flesh cut up and then put back into the shell

dresser ['dresə] *noun* **(a)** piece of kitchen furniture with open shelves above and cupboards below; *put the plates back in the kitchen dresser* **(b)** *US* a piece of bedroom furniture with a mirror; *she sat at the dresser, combing her hair* (NOTE: British English is **dressing table**) **(c)** person who dresses in a certain way; *he's a very smart dresser* **(d)** person who helps someone dress, in a theatre the person who helps the actors with their costumes; **window dresser** = person who arranges displays in shop windows

dressing ['dresɪŋ] *noun* **(a)** putting on clothes; *dressing the baby takes ages*; **dressing gown** = long robe worn over pyjamas or nightdress before getting dressed **(b)** sauce (for salad); *a bottle of Italian salad dressing*; **French dressing** = mixture of oil and vinegar **(c)** bandage for a wound; *the patient's dressings need to be changed every two hours*

dressing-down ['dresɪŋdaʊn] *noun* action of scolding someone; *he got a good dressing-down from his father*; *the nurse gave him a real dressing-down for not taking his tablets*

dressing room ['dresɪŋ 'rʊm] *noun* room in which you change your clothes, especially a room in a theatre where actors or actresses get dressed in costume, or a room in a sports club where people change into their sports clothes; *the messenger arrived in her dressing room with a huge bunch of flowers*; *the champion was in his dressing room, reading telegrams of congratulations*

dressing table ['dresɪŋ 'teɪbl] *noun* a piece of bedroom furniture with a mirror or mirrors; *she sat at the dressing table, combing her hair* (NOTE: American English is **dresser**)

dress rehearsal ['dres rɪ'hɜːsəl] *noun* **(a)** last rehearsal for a play, where the actors wear costumes, and the scenery is ready; *the dress rehearsal was excellent, I hope they perform as well as that on the first night* **(b)** final practice for something; *the attack on the police station was only a dress rehearsal for the coup d'état which took place the following week*

dress up ['dres 'ʌp] *verb* to put on costumes; *the children love dressing up as doctors and nurses*

drew [druː] *see* DRAW

dribble ['drɪbl] *verb* **(a)** to let liquid flow slowly out of an opening, especially out of your mouth; *the baby dribbled over her dress*; *ketchup dribbled onto the tablecloth* **(b)** to kick a football along as you are running (*in basketball*) to bounce the ball along with one hand as you are running; *he dribbled the ball right down the pitch and scored a goal*

dried, drier, dries, driest [draɪd or 'draɪə or draɪz or 'draɪəst] *see* DRY

dried fruit ['draɪd 'fruːt] *noun* fruit that has been dried to keep it for use later; *you need lots of dried fruit to make a Christmas cake*

> COMMENT the commonest dried fruit are currants, sultanas and raisins, all of which are dried grapes, and dried apricots, figs and prunes (which are dried plums)

drier *or* **dryer** ['draɪə] *noun* machine which dries; *put the shirts in the drier after you have washed them*; *see also* TUMBLE DRIER

drift [drɪft] **1** *noun* **(a)** general meaning; *did you follow the drift of the conversation?*; *my Italian isn't very good, but I got the drift of what they were saying*; *I think she got the general drift of my argument* **(b)** pile of snow blown by the wind; *snow lay in drifts around the farmhouse* **(c)** North Atlantic Drift = current of warm water across North Atlantic (NOTE: also called the **Gulf Stream**) **2** *verb* **(a)** to move with the flow of water, without steering; *the boat drifted down the river for two miles* **(b)** to move aimlessly; *after the match, the spectators drifted towards the exits* **(c)** (*of snow*) to pile up; *the snow began to drift in the high wind* **(d)** to behave aimlessly, to avoid taking any decisions; *the government lost its sense of purpose and started to drift*

drift apart ['drɪft ə'pɑːt] *verb* to move away from each other gradually; *the ice floe broke up and the pieces of ice slowly drifted apart*; *after a time they began to drift apart, and in the end stopped seeing each other at all*

drill [drɪl] **1** *noun* **(a)** tool for making holes in wood, metal, etc.; *he used an electric drill to make the holes in the wall*; **pneumatic drill** = machine driven by compressed air, used for making holes in cement, road surfaces, etc. **(b)** military practice in marching, etc.; *new recruits spend hours practising their drill*; **boat drill** = practice to escape from a sinking boat by getting into lifeboats; **fire drill** = practice to escape from a burning building **2** *verb* **(a)** to make holes; *he drilled two holes for the screws*; *they are drilling for oil* **(b)** to do military practice; *recruits were drilling on the parade ground*

drink [drɪŋk] **1** *noun* **(a)** liquid which you swallow; *if you're thirsty, have a drink of water*; *she always has a hot drink before she goes to bed*; **soft drinks** = drinks like lemonade, that have no alcohol in them **(b)** alcoholic drink; *would you like a drink?*; *come and have a drink*; *I'll order some drinks from the bar* **2** *verb* **(a)** to swallow liquid; *he drank two glasses of water*; *what would you like to drink?*; *do you want something to drink with your meal?* **(b)** to drink alcoholic drinks; *she doesn't drink or she never drinks*; *he drinks like a fish* = he drinks a lot of alcohol **(c)** to **drink a toast to someone** = to drink and wish someone well; *we all drank a toast to the future success of the company* (NOTE: **drinking - drank** [dræŋk] **- has drunk** [drʌŋk])

drinkable ['drɪŋkəbl] *adjective* good enough to drink; *this beer is quite drinkable*; *he ordered some expensive wine and it was hardly drinkable*

drink-driver ['drɪŋk 'draɪvə] *noun* person who drives a car when drunk; *she was knocked down by a drink-driver and killed*

drink-driving ['drɪŋk 'draɪvɪŋ] *noun* driving a car when drunk; *he was had up on a drink-driving charge*

drinker ['drɪŋkə] *noun* person who drinks (too much) alcohol; *she's only a light drinker*; *he's a heavy drinker*; **social drinker** = someone who drinks a little alcohol at parties, but not at other times

drinking chocolate ['drɪŋkɪŋ 'tʃɒklət] *noun* milk drink, made from powdered chocolate; *I have a cup of drinking chocolate before I go to bed*

drinking water ['drɪŋkɪŋ 'wɔːtə] *noun* water which is safe to drink; *don't use that tap, it's not drinking water*

drink to ['drɪŋk 'tʊ] *verb* to give someone good wishes for success, etc., especially by having a drink; *we all drank to the health of the bride and groom*

drink up ['drɪŋk 'ʌp] *verb* to drink all of a liquid; *drink up your orange juice*

drip [drɪp] **1** *noun* **(a)** small drop of water; *there's a hole in the tent - a drip just fell on my nose* **(b)** giving a patient a liquid directly into the body; the tube used to put a liquid into a patient's body; **intravenous drip** = drip which goes into a vein; *she was given an intravenous drip*; **saline drip** = drip containing a solution of distilled water and salt; *she is on a saline drip* **2** *verb* to fall in drops; to let a liquid fall in drops; *the tap is dripping*; *his nose is dripping because he has a cold*; *water was dripping from the roof* (NOTE: **dripping - dripped**)

drive [draɪv] **1** *noun* **(a)** journey, especially in a car; *let's go for a drive into the country*; *the baby gets sick* *on long drives*; *it's a four-hour drive to the coast* **(b)** the way in which power gets from the engine to a car's wheels; *a car with front-wheel drive*; *a four-wheel-drive car* **(c)** place where the driver sits; *car with left-hand drive* (NOTE: British cars are **right-hand drive**) **(d)** part of a computer which works a disk; *the computer has a CD-ROM drive* **(e)** energetic way of working; *we need someone with plenty of drive to run the sales department*; **economy drive** = vigorous effort to save money or materials; **sales drive** = vigorous effort to increase sales **(f)** little road leading to a house; *visitors can park in the drive* **2** *verb* **(a)** to make a car, lorry, etc., travel in a certain direction; *he can swim, but he can't drive*; *he was driving a lorry when the accident happened*; *she was driving to work when she heard the news on the car radio*; **I'll drive your aunt to the airport** = I'll take her to the airport in my car **(b)** to force; *he drove the nail into the wall* **(c)** *(informal)* **to drive someone crazy** *or* **to drive someone mad** = to have an effect on someone so that they become very annoyed; *the noise is driving me mad*; *all this work is driving her frantic* **(d)** **he drives a hard bargain** = he is a tough negotiator (NOTE: **driving - drove** [drəʊv] **- has driven** ['drɪvn])

drive away ['draɪv ə'weɪ] *verb* **(a)** to ride away in a motor vehicle; *the bank robbers leapt into a car and drove away at top speed* **(b)** to force something *or* someone to go away; *the smell of the drains drives away our customers*

drive back ['draɪv 'bæk] *verb* **(a)** to go back *or* to come back in a motor vehicle; *we were driving back to London after a weekend in the country* **(b)** to force someone *or* something back; *the police drove the demonstrators back into the high street*

drive in ['draɪv 'ɪn] *verb* **(a)** to go in by car; *each car that drives in is issued with a ticket* **(a)** to force in; *the shepherd waited for the dogs to drive the sheep in*

drive-in ['draɪvɪn] *adjective & noun* bank, cinema, restaurant, where cars drive up for service; *we went to see the movie at the local drive-in*

driven ['drɪvn] *verb see* DRIVE

drive off ['draɪv ɒf] *verb* **(a)** to ride away in a motor vehicle; *the bank robbers leapt into a car and drove off at top speed* **(b)** to force someone or something to go away; *they drove off the attackers with shotguns*

driver ['draɪvə] *noun* person who drives a car, bus, etc.; *he's got a job as a bus driver*; *the drivers of both cars were injured in the accident*; *US* **driver's license** = DRIVING LICENCE; *see also* DRINK-DRIVER, SLAVE DRIVER

driveway ['draɪvweɪ] *noun* short private road leading to a house; *three cars were parked in the driveway*

driving ['draɪvɪŋ] **1** *adjective (rain or snow)* blown horizontally by the wind; *they were forced to turn back because of the driving rain* **2** *noun* action of driving a motor vehicle; *driving in the centre of London can be very frustrating*; *she's taking driving lessons*; **careless driving** = driving in such a way that other people or vehicles may be harmed; *he was charged with careless driving*; **drunken driving** = offence of driving a car when drunk; *see also* DRINK-DRIVING; **driving school** = school where you can learn to drive a car, lorry, etc.

driving licence *US* **driver's license** ['draɪvɪŋ 'laɪsəns *or* 'draɪvəz 'laɪsəns] *noun* permit which allows

someone to drive a car, truck, etc.; *applicants should hold a valid driving licence*

driving test ['draɪvɪŋ 'test] *noun* test which you have to pass to get a driving licence; *he's taken his driving test three times and still hasn't passed*

drizzle ['drɪzl] **1** *noun* light rain; *a thin drizzle was falling so we took our umbrellas* **2** *verb* to rain lightly; *it's drizzling outside, so you'd better wear a raincoat*

drizzly ['drɪzli] *adjective* when it is raining lightly; *we get a lot of drizzly weather in September*

dromedary ['drɒmədəri] *noun* camel with only one hump; *the tourists went riding on dromedaries* (NOTE: also called the **Arabian camel**. The camel with two humps is a **Bactrian camel**)

drone [drəʊn] **1** *noun* **(a)** male bee; *the workers are busy getting pollen, while the drones do nothing* (NOTE: in a bee colony, the females are **workers**) **(b)** buzz of an insect, of an engine; *I could hear the drone of a small aircraft in the distance* **(c)** monotonous sound; *the drone of the bagpipes sounded across the lake* **2** *verb* **(a)** to buzz; *we could hear a small aircraft droning overhead* **(b)** to talk slowly and in a monotonous voice; *the lecturer droned on and on about population statistics*

droop [druːp] *verb* to hang down; *the flowers are drooping because there's no water in the vase*; *his spirits drooped* = he felt miserable

droopy ['druːpi] *adjective* which hangs down; *he has a droopy white moustache*

drop [drɒp] **1** *noun* **(a)** small amount of liquid which falls; *the roof leaks and we have placed a bucket to catch the drops*; *drops of rain ran down the windows*; **would you like a drop of whisky?** = a small glass of whisky **(b)** distance which you might fall; *there is a drop of three metres from the bathroom window to the ground* **(c)** decrease; *sales show a drop of 10%* **2** *verb* **(a)** to decrease; *prices are dropping*; *take a warm sweater, because at night the temperature can drop quite sharply*; **the wind has dropped** = the wind has stopped blowing **(b)** to let something fall; *he dropped the glass and it broke* **(c)** *(informal)* **to drop someone a line** = to send someone a note; *drop me a line when you are back from the USA* **(d)** to let someone get off a bus or car at a place; *I'll drop you at your house*; *the bus dropped her at the school* **(e)** to give up; *they have dropped the idea of going to settle in Australia*; *the whole plan has been dropped because of the cost* **(f)** **drag and drop** = (computers) to move an icon *or* section of text *or* object from one area of the screen to another; *click once on the file icon then keep the mouse button pressed down and drag and drop it onto the printer icon* (NOTE: **dropping - dropped**)

drop by *or* **drop in** ['drɒp 'baɪ *or* 'drɒp 'ɪn] *verb* to call on someone, to visit someone; *I'll try and drop by next time I'm in the area*; *he just dropped in to see if she was any better*; *drop in for a cup of tea if you're passing*

droplet ['drɒplət] *noun* very small drop of liquid; *droplets of water formed at the end of the icicles*

drop off ['drɒp 'ɒf] *verb* **(a)** to fall asleep; *she dropped off in front of the TV*; *it took me ages to drop off* **(b)** to drop someone off = to let someone who is a passenger in a car get out somewhere; *can you drop me off at the post office?*

drop out [drɒp 'aʊt] *verb* **(a)** to stop competing; *he got as far as the semi-finals but dropped out because of a shoulder injury* **(b)** to give up studies, work, etc.; *he dropped out and went to live on a beach in India*

dropout ['drɒpaʊt] *noun* person who has stopped studying or stopped living conventionally; *pop festivals attract a lot of dropouts and drug addicts*

droppings ['drɒpɪŋz] *noun* solid waste matter from animals; *the grass was covered with rabbit and sheep droppings*

drought [draʊt] *noun* long period when there is no rain and when the land is dry; *relief workers are bringing food to drought-stricken areas*

drove [drəʊv] *see* DRIVE

droves [drəʊvz] *noun* large numbers; *farmers arrived in droves to protest outside the Ministry of Agriculture*

drown [draʊn] *verb* **(a)** to die by being unable to breathe in water; *he drowned in a shallow pool* **(b)** to cover up a sound; *the shouting drowned his speech*

drowse [draʊz] *verb* to be half asleep; *she was drowsing over her computer when the phone rang; he spent the afternoon drowsing in a deckchair watching a cricket match*

drowsy ['draʊzi] *adjective* sleepy; *the injection will make you feel drowsy; if you feel drowsy, don't try to drive the car* (NOTE: **drowsier - drowsiest**)

drug [drʌg] **1** *noun* **(a)** medicine; *they have found a new drug for people with arthritis* **(b)** substance which affects the nerves, and which can be habit-forming; *see also* HARD DRUGS, SOFT DRUGS; *the customs are looking for such things as drugs or alcohol*; **drug addict** = person who takes drugs as a habit; **drug dealer** = person who sells illegal drugs to other people; **Drug Squad** = section of the police force that investigates crime related to drugs (NOTE: the American equivalent is the **Narcotics Squad**) **2** *verb* to give someone a drug; *they drugged him and took him away in a car* (NOTE: **drugging - drugged**)

drugstore ['drʌgstɔː] *noun* US shop where medicines can be bought, as well as many other goods such as shampoo, stationery; *you can buy some toothpaste at the drugstore on the corner* (NOTE: the British equivalent is a **chemist's**, though many chemists do not sell the same variety of goods as an American **drugstore**)

drum [drʌm] **1** *noun* **(a)** large round musical instrument which is hit with a stick; *he plays the drums in the band* **(b)** large barrel or container shaped like a cylinder; *oil drums were piled up in the corner of the yard* **2** *verb* to hit frequently; *he drummed his fingers on the table*; **to drum something into someone** = to make someone learn something; *my grandfather drummed it into me that I had to be polite to customers* (NOTE: **drumming - drummed**)

drummer ['drʌmə] *noun* person who plays the drums; *the band is looking for a new drummer*

drumming ['drʌmɪŋ] *noun* sound like a drum being hit over and over again; *the only sound I could hear was the drumming of the rain on the roof of the car*

drumstick ['drʌmstɪk] *noun* **(a)** wooden stick for playing a drum; *he threw his drumstick in the air between beating time on the bass drum* **(b)** lower part of the leg of a cooked chicken, turkey, etc.; *who wants the drumstick?; he had a cold turkey drumstick for his lunch*

drunk [drʌŋk] *adjective* excited or ill because of drinking too much alcohol; *when he's drunk, he shouts at his children; see also* DRINK

drunken ['drʌŋkən] *adjective* who has drunk too much alcohol; *nurses had to get help to control the drunken patient see also* DRIVING

dry [draɪ] **1** *adjective* **(a)** not wet; *don't touch the door - the paint isn't dry yet; the soil is dry because it hasn't rained for weeks; this cream will help make your skin less dry* **(b)** with no rain; *they are forecasting dry sunny periods*; **dry season** = period of the year when it does not rain much (as opposed to the rainy season) **(c)** not sweet (wine); *a dry white wine is served with fish* (NOTE: **drier - driest**) **2** *verb* **(a)** to stop being wet; *the clothes are drying in the sun; leave the dishes on the draining board to dry* **(b)** to wipe something until it is dry; *if I wash up, can you dry (the dishes)?*

dry-clean [draɪ'kliːn] *verb* to clean clothes or other fabric items with chemicals; *we have sent the curtains away to be dry-cleaned*

dry-cleaner's ['draɪ 'kliːnəz] *noun* shop where clothes are dry-cleaned; *when I got my suit back from the dry-cleaner's there was a button missing*

dry-cleaning ['draɪ 'kliːnɪŋ] *noun* clothes which are ready to be sent for cleaning or which have been returned after cleaning; *she ran through the rain to her car with an armful of dry-cleaning*

dryer ['draɪə] *noun see* DRIER

dry-goods store [draɪ'gʊdz 'stɔː] *noun* US shop selling cloth and clothes

dry out ['draɪ 'aʊt] *verb* **(a)** to become completely dry; *hang up your coat to dry out in front of the fire* **(b)** (*informal*) to try to stop drinking alcohol; *he's went to a clinic in London to dry out*

drystone wall ['draɪstəʊn 'wɔːl] *noun* wall built of stones without using mortar to hold them together; *in the Lake District the fields are enclosed by drystone walls*

dry up ['draɪ 'ʌp] *verb* **(a)** to stop flowing; *the heat wave has made the rivers dry up; the government grants have dried up and it looks as though we will have to close* **(b)** to stop talking, because you can't remember what you were going to say; *he dried up in the middle of his speech, and sat down hurriedly; as soon as she got on the stage she dried up*

dual ['djuəl] *adjective* double, existing as a pair; *driving school cars have dual controls*; **she has dual nationality** = she is a citizen of two countries; *see also* CARRIAGEWAY (NOTE: do not confuse with **duel**)

dub [dʌb] *verb* **(a)** to give someone a nickname; *at college he was dubbed Tom 'Pigpen' Smith because his room was so dirty* **(b)** to add dialogue to a film in a different language from the original; *the film is dubbed into Swedish* (NOTE: **dubbing - dubbed**)

dubious ['djuːbiəs] *adjective* **(a)** suspicious; *there were some dubious characters hanging around outside the off-licence; have you heard about his dubious past in South America?* **(b)** doubtful, hesitating; *I'm dubious about getting involved; everyone else seems to believe her story, but personally I'm dubious about it*

duchess ['dʌtʃes] *noun* wife of a duke; *the Duchess of Westminster* (NOTE: plural is **duchesses**)

duchy ['dʌtʃi] *noun* territory ruled by a duke or duchess; *the Duchy of Cornwall*; *the Grand Duchy of Luxembourg*

duck [dʌk] **1** *noun* **(a)** common water bird; *let's go and feed the ducks in St James' Park; see also* WATER (NOTE: the male is a **drake,** the female a **duck** and the young are **ducklings) (b)** meat of this bird; *we're having roast duck for dinner* **(c)** *(in cricket)* score of zero; *he scored a duck in his last two matches; see also* LAME DUCK **2** *verb* to lower your head quickly to avoid hitting something; *she didn't duck in time and the ball hit her on the head; he ducked as he went through the low doorway*

ducking ['dʌkɪŋ] *noun* accidental fall into water; *he slipped as he was getting into the boat and got a ducking*

duckling ['dʌklɪŋ] *noun* **(a)** baby duck; *the duck with six little ducklings* **(b)** small duck; *we had roast duckling and orange sauce*

duct [dʌkt] *noun* **(a)** tube which carries liquids in the body; *tear duct* = duct which brings tears into the nose and eyes **(b)** tube which carries air, wires, etc., in a building; *the central heating ducts caught fire*

dud [dʌd] **1** *adjective (informal)* false; *he paid me with a dud £10 note* **2** *noun* **(a)** false banknote; *the £50 note was a dud* **(b)** which does not work properly; *most of the fireworks in the box were duds*

dude [djuːd] *noun US* **(a)** dandy, man who is very interested in clothes; *that dude, with his stiff collar and wide pink tie* **(b)** visitor from a city on the East coast to a ranch in the Mid West; *dude ranch* = ranch where city people can come for vacations

due [djuː] *adjective* **(a)** expected; *when is the baby due?; we are due to leave London Airport at 5 o'clock; the plane is due to arrive at 10.30 or is due at 10.30* **(b)** *due to* = because of; *the trains are late due to fog* **(c)** *in due course* = later; *in due course you will have to pass an exam* **(d)** owed; *to fall due or to become due* = to be ready for payment; *balance due to us* = amount owed to us which should be paid **(e)** *due for* = likely to get; *we're due for a thunderstorm after all this hot weather; she must be due for retirement this year* (NOTE: do not confuse with **dew) 2** *adverb* straight; *the plane flew due west; go due east for ten miles and you will see the church on your left*

duel ['djuːəl] **1** *noun* fight between two people with swords, guns, etc.; *they fought a duel over a girl; he challenged the doctor to a duel* (NOTE: do not confuse with **dual) 2** *verb* to fight a duel; *duelling pistols* = old-fashioned pistols used in duels (NOTE: **duelling - duelled** but American spelling is **dueling - dueled)**

duet [djuːˈet] *noun* piece of music played or sung by two people; *they sang duets all evening*

duff [dʌf] *(informal)* that doesn't work, that is no good; *he tried to sell her a duff computer*

duffel ['dʌfl] *noun* **duffel bag** = thick cloth bag closed by a string; **duffel coat** = thick woollen coat, with a hood (NOTE: sometimes also spelt **duffle)**

duff up ['dʌf 'ʌp] *verb (informal)* to beat up; *they took the young man away and duffed him up behind the hut*

dug [dʌg] *verb see* DIG

dugout ['dʌgaut] *noun* **(a)** hole in the ground which is a shelter for soldiers; *they sat in a dugout for hours, waiting for the order to advance* **(b)** bench by the side of a football pitch where the managers and substitutes sit; *the manager was yelling instructions from the dugout* **(c)** **dugout canoe** = canoe made from a hollowed tree trunk; *natives came down the river in dugout canoes*

duke [djuːk] *noun* nobleman of the highest rank; *the Duke of Westminster* (NOTE: the wife of a duke is a **duchess)**

dull [dʌl] *adjective* **(a)** not exciting, not interesting; *the story is rather dull; what's so interesting about old churches? - I find them dull* **(b)** *(weather)* grey and gloomy; *a dull cloudy day* (NOTE: **duller - dullest)**

duly ['djuːli] *adverb* **(a)** properly, as one should; *he duly returned the form to the tax office; I declare Mrs Bond duly elected president* **(b)** as was expected; *we duly received a letter from the police*

dumb [dʌm] *adjective* **(a)** unable to speak; *she was born deaf and dumb or she is deaf and dumb from birth*; **to be struck dumb** = to be so surprised that you cannot say anything; *he was struck dumb by the news* **(b)** *(informal)* stupid; *that was dumb thing to do; how can anyone be so dumb?*

dumbfound [dʌmˈfaund] *verb* to surprise, to astound; *I am dumbfounded at the news*

dummy ['dʌmi] *noun* **(a)** plastic object shaped like a nipple, given to a baby to suck, to prevent it crying; *the baby sat in its pram sucking a dummy* (NOTE: American English is **pacifier) (b)** imitation product to prevent theft, or to test the reaction of potential customers to its design; *that big bottle of whisky isn't real, it's just a dummy*; **dummy run** = practice, before the real thing takes place; *the air raid was a dummy run for the real attack the following night* **(c)** *tailor's* **dummy** = model of a person used to show clothes in a shop window **(d)** *(informal) US* stupid fool; *you dummy! you put the box the wrong way up!* (NOTE: plural is **dummies)**

dump [dʌmp] **1** *noun* **(a)** place for rubbish; *take your rubbish to the municipal dump* **(b)** *what a dump!* = what an awful place!; *his house is a dump* **2** *verb* **(a)** to put something heavily on the ground; *she just dumped her suitcases in the hall* **(b)** to throw away, to get rid of; *someone has dumped an old pram in the car park; the UK dumps its industrial waste into the North Sea*; **to dump goods on a market** = to sell surplus goods at a very cheap price (usually overseas); *old medicines are being dumped in Africa* **(c)** *(informal)* **to dump someone** = to get rid of someone; *she's been dumped by her boyfriend*

dumpy ['dʌmpi] *adjective* short and rather fat; *she's a dumpy little woman but she rules the office with a rod of iron*

dune [djuːn] *noun* **sand dunes** = areas of sand blown by the wind into small hills and ridges which have very little soil or vegetation; *the village was threatened by encroaching sand dunes*

dung [dʌŋ] *noun* solid waste from animals (especially cattle), often used as fertilizer; *they collected the dried dung in the fields and used it as fuel* (NOTE: no plural)

dungarees [dʌŋgəˈriːz] *noun* working clothes, formed of a pair of trousers and a bib covering the chest, usually of thick blue cloth, and worn over ordinary clothes; *the workmen came into the café in their dungarees*

dungeon ['dʌndʒən] *noun* dark and unpleasant underground prison; *the prisoners were kept for years in the dungeons of the Tower of London*

dunno [də'nəʊ] *verb (informal)* = I DON'T KNOW

duo ['djuːəʊ] *noun* (a) two people, usually two performers; *a TV comedy duo* (b) = DUET

dupe [djuːp] 1 *noun* person who has been tricked; *he was the dupe of a Russian businessman* 2 *verb* **to dupe someone into doing something** = to trick someone into doing something; *they duped him into giving them all the cash he had in his wallet*

duplex ['djuːpleks] *noun US* house for two families; **duplex apartment** = apartment on two floors; *they live in a duplex on E56th Street* (NOTE: plural is **duplexes**; Note also that British English is **maisonette**)

duplicate 1 *adjective* ['djuːplɪkət] which is a copy; *put the duplicate invoices in the file* 2 *noun* ['djuːplɪkət] copy; *she sent the invoice and filed the duplicate* 3 *verb* ['djuːplɪkeɪt] to make a copy of a letter, etc.; *she duplicated the letter and put a copy into the file*; **you are just duplicating his work** = you are just doing the same work as he did earlier

duplicity [djuː'plɪsɪti] *noun (formal)* dishonesty, action of tricking someone; *the one thing he can't be accused of is duplicity - he has always been very open about what his plans are* (NOTE: no plural)

durable ['djʊərəbl] 1 *adjective* which lasts, which does not wear away; *you need a really durable floor covering in a kitchen*; *they've signed a peace agreement but will it be more durable than the last one?*; **durable effects** = effects which will be felt for a long time; *the strike will have durable effects on the economy* 2 *noun* **consumer durables** = goods bought by the public which will be used for a long time (such as washing machines or refrigerators)

duration [djʊ'reɪʃn] *noun (formal)* period of time for which something lasts; *they hid in the cellar for the duration of the bombardment*; *luckily the power cut was of short duration*

during ['djʊərɪŋ] *preposition* while something lasts; *he went to sleep during the concert*

dusk [dʌsk] *noun* the period in the evening just before it gets dark; *the gardens close at dusk*

dust [dʌst] 1 *noun* thin layer of dry dirt; *the room had never been cleaned - there was dust everywhere*; *a tiny speck of dust got in my eye* (NOTE: no plural) 2 *verb* to remove dust from something; *don't forget to dust the china ornaments carefully*

dustbin ['dʌstbɪn] *noun* large container for household rubbish; *she put the rest of the dinner in the dustbin*; *he threw the letter into the dustbin* (NOTE: American English is **trashcan**)

duster ['dʌstə] *noun* cloth for removing dust; *rub the surface down with a duster*

dustman ['dʌstmən] *noun* person employed by a town to remove household rubbish; *the dustmen are supposed to come and empty our dustbins once a week* (NOTE: plural is **dustmen**)

dusty ['dʌsti] *adjective* covered with dust; *a dusty path led to the old house*; *his room is full of dusty old books* (NOTE: **dustier - dustiest**)

Dutch [dʌtʃ] 1 *adjective* (a) referring to the Netherlands; *we are going on a tour to visit the Dutch bulb fields* (b) **to go Dutch** = to share the cost of a meal equally between everyone 2 *noun* (a) the language spoken in the Netherlands; *you will need to practise your Dutch if you're going to live in Amsterdam* (b) **the Dutch** = the people living in the Netherlands; *the Dutch are great travellers*

dutiful ['djuːtɪfʊl] *adjective* who does what should be done; *he's a very dutiful son - he always checks to see if his mother needs anything*

duty ['djuːti] *noun* (a) work which you have to do; *one of his duties is to see that the main doors are locked at night*; **to be duty bound to do something** = to be obliged to do something; *if you have any information pertaining to this case, you are duty bound to reveal it to the police* (b) **on duty** = doing official work which you have to do in a job; *he's on duty from 9.00 to 6.00*; *she's been on duty all day* (NOTE: no plural in this meaning) (c) tax which has to be paid; **customs duty** = tax which you have to pay to take goods into a country; *you may have to pay customs duty on goods imported from outside the EU*; **estate duty**; *US* **death duty** = tax paid on the property left by a dead person

duty-free ['djuːti 'friː] *adjective & adverb* sold with no tax to be paid; *he bought a duty-free watch at the airport* or *he bought the watch duty-free*; **duty-free allowance** = amount of goods which you are allowed to take into a country without paying tax on them; **duty-free shop** = shop at an airport or on a ship where goods can be bought free of tax; *he bought some perfume in the duty-free shop*

duty officer ['djuːti 'ɒfɪsə] *noun* officer who is on duty at a certain time; *the duty officer was asleep and didn't see the iceberg*

duvet ['duːveɪ] *noun* bag stuffed with feathers, used as the only covering for a bed; *I prefer a duvet to blankets, because it is lighter*; **duvet cover** = coloured cloth bag used to cover a duvet

dwarf [dwɔːf] 1 *noun* very small person; *Snow White and the Seven Dwarfs* (NOTE: plural is **dwarfs** or **dwarves**) 2 *adjective (plant)* low-growing; *dwarf beans* (NOTE: also called **French beans**) 3 *verb* to make something look very small; *his house is dwarfed by the office block next door*

dwell [dwel] *verb* (a) **to dwell on a problem** = to keep thinking or talking about a problem; *it's best not to dwell too much on your financial situation* (b) *(old)* to live; *there lived a beautiful princess in a castle by the edge of the forest* (NOTE: **dwelling - dwelled** or **dwelt** [dwelt])

dweller ['dwelə] *noun & suffix* person who lives in a place; *many city-dwellers have cottages in the country where they go for weekends*; *prehistoric man was a cavedweller*

dwelling ['dwelɪŋ] *noun (formal)* place to live; *they have had permission to build a dwelling on the site*

dwindle ['dwɪndl] *verb* to get less; *we have to be careful with our dwindling supply of firewood*; *it seems that the number of butterflies is dwindling*; **to dwindle away** = to become much less; *his savings have dwindled away to nothing*

dye [daɪ] 1 *noun* colour used to stain cloth; *synthetic dyes*; *vegetable dyes*; **fast dye** = colour which will not fade when washed 2 *verb* to stain with a colour; *she dyed her hair green* (NOTE: do not confuse with **die**)

dying ['daɪŋ] *see* DIE

dynamic [daɪ'næmɪk] *adjective* very energetic and forceful (person); *a young and dynamic prime minister*

dyke *or* **dike** [daɪk] *noun* (a) long wall of earth to keep water from flooding land; *they built dykes along the river; with this storm blowing from the east, do you think the dykes will hold?* (b) long ditch for rainwater; *it rained all month, and the dykes were full* (c) *(slang)* lesbian

dynamism ['daɪnəmɪzm] *noun* being dynamic; *his dynamism made the sales staff increase sales dramatically*

dynamite ['daɪnəmaɪt] **1** *noun* (a) powerful explosive; *they used dynamite to blow up the old building* (b) something *or* someone that has a very powerful effect; *this news is dynamite!* **2** *verb* to blow up with dynamite; *guerrillas have dynamited stretches of railway line*

dynamo ['daɪnəməʊ] *noun* (a) small electricity generator; *the electric light works by a dynamo attached to the back wheel* (b) very energetic person; *she's a real dynamo* (NOTE: plural is **dynamos**)

dynastic [dɪ'næstɪk] *adjective* referring to a dynasty; *dynastic problems brought about the change of ruling family*

dynasty ['dɪnəsti] *noun* (a) family of rulers, following one after the other; *the Ming dynasty ruled China from 1368 to 1644; Henry VII founded the Tudor dynasty in 1487* (b) period of rule by members of the same family; *the Great Wall of China was built during the Tsin dynasty* (NOTE: plural is **dynasties**)

dysentery ['dɪsəntri] *noun* infection of the intestines, causing bleeding and diarrhoea; *there is a danger of dysentery in the refugee camps*

dyslexia [dɪs'leksiə] *noun* disorder, where a person is not able to read and write properly; *she has dyslexia and has to have special tuition*

COMMENT: dyslexia may be caused by an inherited disability or by damage to the brain; it does not imply any lack of intelligence

dyslexic [dɪs'leksɪk] **1** *adjective* who has difficulty in reading and writing; *she's dyslexic, and needs to go to special classes* **2** *noun* person who has dyslexia; *there are several dyslexics in the family*

dyspepsia [dɪs'pepsiə] *noun (formal)* pains in the stomach caused by not digesting food properly; *she was sucking a tablet for her dyspepsia* (NOTE: means the same as **indigestion**)

dyspeptic [dɪs'peptɪk] *adjective* not digesting food properly; *he's feeling a little dyspeptic this morning*

dystrophy ['dɪstrəfi] *noun see* MUSCULAR

Ee

E, e [iː] fifth letter of the alphabet, between D and F; *do you mean 'dependent' spelt with an 'e' or with an 'a'?; which is it - 'been' with two e's or 'bean' with 'ea'?*

each [iːtʃ] **1** *adjective* every person or thing; *each five pound note has a number; he was holding a towel in each hand; each one of us has a separate office* **2** *pronoun* **(a)** every person; *they have two houses each or each of them has two houses; she gave them each five pounds or she gave them five pounds each or she gave each of them five pounds* **(b)** every thing; *each of the books has three hundred pages or the books have three hundred pages each*

each other ['iːtʃ 'ʌðə] *pronoun* the other one of two people or of two things; *they were shouting at each other; we always send each other presents on our birthdays; the boxes fit into each other*

eager ['iːgə] *adjective* wanting to do something very much; *they are eager to see the exhibition; I am not very eager for Sam to come to live with us*

eagerly ['iːgəli] *adverb* in a way that shows that you want something very much; *the children eagerly awaited the beginning of the school holidays; he reads the appointments vacant columns eagerly every morning*

eagerness ['iːgənəs] *noun* state of wanting to do something very much; *in his eagerness to catch the bus he ran out of the house without his briefcase*

eagle ['iːgl] *noun* large bird of prey; *the eagle is the emblem of the United States*

eagle-eyed ['iːgl'aid] *adjective* with very good eyesight; *an eagle-eyed inspector noticed that my ticket was out of date*

ear [ɪə] *noun* **(a)** part of your head which you hear with; *rabbits have long ears; have you washed behind your ears?; (informal)* **to be up to your ears in** = to be very busy with; *he's up to his ears in work;* **to keep your ear to the ground** = to follow what is happening and know all about something **(b)** ability to sense sound; *he has a good ear for music;* **to play an instrument by ear** = to play without reading the printed notes of music; *she can play the piano by ear; (informal)* **to play it by ear** = to do what you think is right at the time; *we won't make a plan, we'll just play it by ear and see how it goes*

earache ['ɪəreik] *noun* pain in your ear; *if you have (an) earache you should see a doctor*

eardrum ['ɪədrʌm] *noun* membrane inside the ear which vibrates with sound and passes the vibrations to the ossicles in the inner ear

earl [ɜːl] *noun* peer of middle rank, below a marquess and above a viscount; *Princess Diana's brother became Earl Spencer on the death of their father* (NOTE: the wife of an **earl** is a **countess**)

COMMENT: the title of earl is followed directly by the family name; they are addressed as 'Lord' followed by the family name; their wives are addressed as 'Lady' followed by the family name

early ['ɜːli] **1** *adverb* **(a)** before the usual time; *the plane arrived five minutes early; we must get up early tomorrow morning if we want to catch the first boat to France; can you come an hour earlier tomorrow?* **(b)** at the beginning of a period of time; *we went out early in the evening; the snow came early in the year* **2** *adjective* **(a)** which happens at the beginning of a period of time or which happens before the proper time; *we picked some early vegetables; I caught an early flight to Paris; these flowers open in early summer;* **an early date** = soon; *the meeting must be held at the earliest date possible;* **to take early retirement** = to leave a job with a pension before the usual age for retirement **(b)** *(informal)* **an early bird** = someone who likes to get up early and work before breakfast, and who does not stay up late at night; *he's an early bird - he's up at 6.00 every morning; compare* NIGHT OWL (NOTE: **earlier - earliest**)

early warning ['ɜːli 'wɔːnɪŋ] *noun* something which gives advance warning of danger; *they have set up an alarm system which will give early warning of problems with the computer*

earmark ['ɪəmɑːk] *verb* to reserve for a special purpose; *the grant is earmarked for computer systems development*

earn [ɜːn] *verb* **(a)** to be paid money for working; *he earns £20,000 a year; how much does a bus driver earn?* **(b)** to deserve something *or* to be given something; *you can all take a rest now - you've earned it!; his cheeky remarks earned him a reprimand from the teacher* (NOTE: do not confuse with **urn**)

earner ['ɜːnə] *noun* thing or person who earns; *for many families, having one earner in the family is not enough; (informal)* **nice little earner** = small business or clever scheme which gives an easy income; *the corner shop must be a nice little earner - it's in a prime position;* **wage earner** = someone who earns a wage; *the savings scheme is particularly attractive to low wage earners*

earnest ['ɜːnɪst] **1** *adjective* serious; *they were engaged in some earnest conversation* **2** *noun* **(a)** money paid as a down payment **(b)** **in earnest** = seriously; *the discussions began in earnest*

earnestly ['ɜːnəstli] *adverb* seriously; *he talked earnestly about his future plans*

earnings ['ɜːnɪŋz] *noun* salary, the money which you earn from work; *his earnings are not enough to pay the rent*

earphones ['ɪəfəunz] *noun* devices which you put on your ears to listen to music tapes, telephone calls, etc.; *she took off her earphones when I asked her a question*

earplug ['ɪəplʌg] *noun* piece of soft cotton or wax which which you put in your ears to cut out noise, or to prevent water from getting in; *he wore earplugs when he was drilling*

earring ['ɪərɪŋ] *noun* ring worn attached to the lobe of your ear as an ornament; *he has a gold earring in his left ear*; **a pair of earrings** = two similar rings, one worn in each ear; *she was wearing a pair of old earrings which belonged to her mother*

earshot ['ɪəʃɒt] *noun* **within earshot** = near enough to hear something; *everyone within earshot heard the details of her divorce*; **out of earshot** = not near enough to hear something; *now that she's out of earshot, you can tell me what really happened*

earth [ɜːθ] 1 *noun* (a) the planet on which we live; *the earth goes round the sun once in twenty-four hours*; *the space shuttle came back to earth safely*; *(informal)* **it costs the earth** = it costs a great deal of money; *it wouldn't cost the earth to have the house repainted* (b) soil, soft material made up of minerals and rotting vegetable matter, which plants grow in; *put some earth in the plant pot and then sow your cucumber seeds* 2 *verb* to connect an electrical appliance to the earth; *household appliances should be properly earthed* (NOTE: American English is to **ground**)

◊ **on earth** [ɒn 'ɜːθ] *(used to make questions stronger)* *why on earth did you do that?*; *who on earth is going to pay that much for a bottle of wine?*; *how on earth are we going to afford a holiday in Australia?*; *what on earth are they doing digging up the road?*

earthenware ['ɜːðənweə] *noun* pots, dishes, etc. made of clay; *she made a casserole in an earthenware bowl*

earthly ['ɜːθli] *adjective* *(informal)* **he hasn't an earthly (chance)** = he has no possibility of doing it; *realistically, he hasn't an earthly against the champion, but I'm sure he'll still give it a go*

earthquake ['ɜːθkweɪk] *noun* shaking of the earth caused by volcanic activity or movement of the earth's crust; *there have been many earthquakes in or near San Francisco*; *thousands of buildings were flattened in the San Francisco earthquake of 1906* (NOTE: also called simply a **quake**)

earthworm ['ɜːθwɜːm] *noun* worm, little animal which looks like a very small snake and lives in soil; *the earthworms come to the surface when it rains*

earthy ['ɜːθi] *adjective* coarse or rude (humour); *he has an earthy approach to sex* (NOTE: **earthier - earthiest**)

earwig ['ɪəwɪg] *noun* small insect with curved pincers on its tail; *Ugh! there's an earwig in this bag of apples!*

ease [iːz] 1 *noun* (a) lack of difficulty; *he won the first round with the greatest of ease*; *the bottle has a wide mouth for ease of use* (b) to **put someone at their ease** = to make someone feel relaxed and confident; *the policeman offered the children sweets to put them at their ease*; **ill at ease** = nervous, uncomfortable; *she was definitely ill at ease during the interview with the manager* (c) *(in the army)* **at ease!** = command to stand in a relaxed position, with the feet apart, after standing to attention (NOTE: no plural) 2 *verb* (a) to make less painful; *a couple of aspirins should ease the pain* (b) to make easy; *an introduction from his uncle eased his entry into the firm*

easel ['iːzl] *noun* vertical frame on legs (to support a blackboard, painting, etc.); *she was given a blackboard and easel for Christmas*

easier, easiest ['iːziə or 'iːziəst] *see* EASY

easily ['iːzili] *adverb* (a) without any difficulty; *I passed my driving test easily*; *I can get there easily by 9 o'clock* (b) *(for emphasis before comparatives or superlatives)* a lot (compared to something else); *her work was easily better than yours*; *he is easily the tallest man in the team*; *our shop is easily the biggest in the high street*

east [iːst] 1 *noun* (a) direction of where the sun rises; *the sun rises in the east and sets in the west*; *Germany is to the east of France*; *the wind is blowing from the east* (b) part of a country which is to the east of the rest; *the east of the country is drier than the west* (c) **the Far East** = countries to the east of Pakistan and India; **the Middle East** = countries to the east of Egypt and west of Pakistan; **the Near East** = countries to the east of the Mediterranean 2 *adjective* referring to the east; *the east coast is the coldest part of the country*; **East Anglia** = eastern part of England to the north-east of London; **east wind** = wind which blows from the east 3 *adverb* towards the east; *the kitchen windows face east, so we get the morning sun*; *drive east along the motorway for twenty miles*

eastbound ['iːstbaʊnd] *adjective* travelling towards the east; *there has been an accident on the eastbound section of the motorway*; *all eastbound trains have been cancelled*

East End ['iːst 'end] *noun* part of London to the east of the City, the original home of the cockneys; *the taxi took me on some circuitous route through the East End*; *the East End of London is changing rapidly*; *compare* WEST END

Easter ['iːstə] *noun* important Christian festival (in March or April) celebrating Christ's death and resurrection; *we have two weeks' holiday at Easter*; *what are you doing during the Easter holidays?*; *we plan to go walking in the woods on Easter Monday*; **Easter Day** *or* **Easter Sunday** = Sunday celebrating Christ's rising from the dead; **Easter egg** = chocolate or sugar egg eaten at Easter

easterly ['iːstəli] 1 *adjective* (a) (wind) from the east; *there was a light easterly breeze*; *the prevailing easterly airflow across the country* (b) towards the east; *they are heading in a easterly direction* 2 *noun* wind from the east (NOTE: plural is **easterlies**)

eastern ['iːstən] *adjective* from, of or in the east; *Bulgaria is part of Eastern Europe*; *the best snow is in the eastern part of the mountains*

easy ['iːzi] 1 *adjective* not difficult, not needing a lot of effort; *the driving test isn't very easy - lots of people fail it*; *it's easy to see why the shop closed - a big supermarket has opened next door*; *the office is within easy reach of the airport*; *my boss is very easy to get on with*; **easy terms** = conditions which mean that you do not have to pay a lot of money; *the shop is let on very easy terms* 2 *adverb* **to take things easy** = to rest, not to do any hard work; *the doctor told him to take things easy for a time after his operation*; **easy now!** *or* **easy does it!** = be careful!; **go easy on** *or* **with the jam!** = don't take too much jam!; **it's easier said than done** = it's more difficult than you think (NOTE: **easier - easiest**)

easy chair ['i:zi 'tʃeə] *noun* large comfortable armchair; *she settled in an easy chair with a book and a cup of tea*

easy-going ['i:zɪgəʊɪŋ] *adjective* friendly and not very critical; *he's the most easy-going boss I've ever had - he doesn't even mind if we leave a bit early in the evenings*

eat [i:t] *verb* (a) to chew and swallow food; *I'm hungry - is there anything to eat?*; *we haven't eaten anything since breakfast*; *the children ate all the sandwiches*; *eat as much as you like for £5.95!*; *you'll get thin if you don't eat*; **eating apple** = sweet apple which you can eat raw (as opposed to a sour apple which has to be cooked) (b) to have a meal; *he was still eating his breakfast when I arrived*; *we are eating at home tonight*; *have you eaten yet?* (NOTE: eating - ate [et] - has eaten ['i:tn])

eatable ['i:təbl] *adjective* which is good enough to eat; *this meat is hardly eatable* (NOTE: the opposite is **uneatable**)

eat away ['i:t ə'weɪ] *verb* to destroy by wearing away bit by bit; *the metal has been eaten away by the salt water*

eater ['i:tə] *noun* person who eats; *she's a light eater - she just picks at her food*

eatery ['i:təri] *noun* US (*informal*) restaurant, place where you can eat; *a well-known eatery on 5th Avenue* (NOTE: plural is **eateries**)

eat out ['i:t 'aʊt] *verb* to have a meal in a restaurant, and not at home; *there's nothing in the fridge, so we're eating out tonight*

eats [i:ts] *noun* (*informal*) things to eat at a party, picnic, etc.; *look at all those eats on the table!*; *they brought plenty of drinks but not enough eats for the picnic*

eat up ['i:t 'ʌp] *verb* to eat everything; *eat your vegetables up - they're good for you!*

eau-de-cologne ['əʊdəkə'ləʊn] *noun* liquid perfume; *grandmother came into the room smelling of eau-de-cologne*; *he sprinkled some eau-de-cologne on his handkerchief*

eaves [i:vz] *noun* parts of a roof which stick out over the wall underneath; *there are several swallows' nests under the eaves of the roof*

eavesdrop ['i:vzdrɒp] *verb* **to eavesdrop on a conversation** = to listen to a conversation which you are not supposed to hear; *she stood outside the door to eavesdrop on the interview her son had with the manager* (NOTE: eavesdropping - eavesdropped)

eavesdropper ['i:vzdrɒpə] *noun* person who eavesdrops; *he opened the door and looked up and down the corridor to check there were no eavesdroppers*

ebb [eb] **1** *noun* (*of tide*) going down; *if we leave at 3.00 p.m. the tide will be on the ebb*; **to be at a low ebb** = to be in a bad state; *after his interview, his morale was at a low ebb*; *the manager asked them to try harder, just when their energy was at its lowest ebb* **2** *verb* (a) (*of tide*) to go down; *boats at anchor swing round to point upstream when the tide starts to ebb* (b) **to ebb away** = to become weaker gradually; *he couldn't hold on to the life-raft any longer, his strength was ebbing away*

ebb tide ['eb 'taɪd] *noun* tide that is going down; *the raft will float out to sea on the ebb tide*

ebullient [ɪ'bʌliənt] *adjective* very excited or full of life; *he's in a very ebullient mood this morning - has he had some good news?*

eccentric [ɪk'sentrɪk] **1** *adjective* strange, odd; *an eccentric old lady who wears boots all the year round* **2** *noun* strange or odd person; *in his old age, he became something of an eccentric*

eccentricity [eksen'trɪsɪti] *noun* strange habits, odd behaviour; *the professor's eccentricities were well-known to his students*

ecclesiastic [ɪkli:zi'æstɪk] **1** *noun* (*formal*) priest; *he's an important Catholic ecclesiastic* **2** *adjective* = ECCLESIASTICAL

ecclesiastical [ɪkli:zi'æstɪkl] *adjective* referring to the Christian church; *they discovered an ancient ecclesiastical building which was being used as a farm*

echelon ['eʃəlɒn] *noun* (a) group of people at a certain level in an organization; *the upper echelons of management*; *the lower echelons of village society* (b) arrangement of separate things in steps, each behind the other and to one side, and not in a straight line; *the tanks moved forward in echelon*

echo ['ekəʊ] **1** *noun* sound which is repeated (as when you shout in a cave, etc.); *we could hear the echo of voices in the tunnel*; *if you go to the Whispering Galley in the dome of St Paul's Cathedral you can hear the echo very clearly* (NOTE: plural is **echoes**) **2** *verb* (a) (*of sound*) to make an echo; *their voices echoed down the tunnel* (b) to repeat; *the newspaper article echoed the opinions put forward in the minister's speech*

éclair [eɪ'kleə] *noun* long light pastry cake filled with cream and topped with chocolate; *he ate two éclairs*

eclectic [ɪ'klektɪk] *adjective* (*formal*) taking ideas, etc., from several different sources; *he has an eclectic collection of records, everything from reggae to classical music*; *she has an eclectic taste in clothes*

eclipse [ɪ'klɪps] **1** *noun* time when part of the sun or moon disappears, because either the earth's shadow passes over the moon, or the moon passes between the earth and the sun; *there will be a partial eclipse of the moon tonight* **2** *verb* (a) to hide the sun or moon by passing in front of it; *the sun is eclipsed by the moon* (b) to be more successful than someone; *she was eclipsed by her younger sister*

ecological [i:kə'lɒdʒɪkl] *adjective* referring to ecology; *the oil refinery will affect the area's ecological balance*; **ecological disaster** = disaster which seriously disturbs the balance of the environment; *the oil from the tanker caused an ecological disaster*

ecologist [ɪ'kɒlədʒɪst] *noun* person who studies ecology; *the research centre employs two marine biologists and an ecologist*

ecology [ɪ'kɒlədʒi] *noun* study of the relationship between plants and animals and their environment; *books on ecology are in the environmental studies section*

economic [i:kə'nɒmɪk] *adjective* (a) referring to the economy; *I don't agree with the government's economic policy*; *the government has introduced controls to solve the current economic crisis*; *the country enjoyed a period of economic growth in the*

1980s **(b)** which provides enough money; *the flat is let at an economic rent*; *it is hardly economic for us to run two cars*

economical [iːkəˈnɒmɪkl] *adjective* which saves money or resources; *it's more economical to heat the water by gas*; **economical car** = car which does not use much petrol

economics [iːkəˈnɒmɪks] *noun* **(a)** scientific study of how money functions in trade, society and politics; *she is studying for an economics degree* **(b)** the way money is used in a particular activity; *the economics of town planning*; *have you worked out the economics of starting your own business?* (NOTE: takes a singular verb)

economist [ɪˈkɒnəmɪst] *noun* person who specializes in the study of money and its uses; *the university has several internationally famous economists in its teaching staff*

economize [ɪˈkɒnəmaɪz] *verb* **to economize (on)** = to save, not to waste; *the office has been told to economize on electricity*

economy [ɪˈkɒnəmi] *noun* **(a)** way in which a country makes and uses money, the financial state of a country; *the country's economy is in ruins*; *when will the upturn in the economy come about?*; **black economy** = work which is paid for in cash or goods, but not declared to the tax authorities **(b)** something you do to save and not to waste money or materials; *she tried to make a few economies like buying cheaper brands of washing-up liquid*; **an economy measure** = an action to save money or materials; **economy pack** *or* **economy size** = pack which is cheaper than regular size; **economy class** = air fare which is cheaper than first class or business class; **economies of scale** = making a product more profitable by manufacturing it in larger quantities

ecosystem [ˈiːkəʊsɪstəm] *noun* system which includes all the organisms of an area and the environment in which they live; *it is a classic example of an ecosystem that has been influenced by humans*

ecstasy [ˈekstəsi] *noun* great happiness; *these chocolates are pure ecstasy*; *she was in sheer ecstasy over her engagement*

ecstatic [ɪkˈstætɪk] *adjective* very happy or enthusiastic; *she was ecstatic about the job offer*; *the book received some ecstatic reviews*

ecumenical [iːkjuˈmenɪkl] *adjective* concerned with uniting different Christian groups; **an ecumenical service** = service where priests from various churches celebrate together

eczema [ˈeksɪmə] *noun* inflammation of the skin, with itchy rash and blisters, but which is not contagious; *when she gets worried she often gets patches of eczema on her wrists and behind her knees*

eddy [ˈedi] **1** *noun* circular movement of water, dust, etc.; *dust eddies were being raised by the wind*; *he got into an eddy under the waterfall* (NOTE: plural is **eddies**) **2** *verb* to twist round in a circle; *water eddied round the rocks*

edge [edʒ] **1** *noun* **(a)** side of something flat; *he put his plate down on the edge of the table*; *she lay down on the roof and looked over the edge*; *you can stand a £1 coin on its edge*; *the axe has a very sharp edge* **(b)** line between two quite different things; *he lived in a house at the edge of the forest*; *the factory is built right*

on the edge of the town by the motorway **(c)** advantage; **to have the edge on a rival company** = to have a slightly larger share of the market than a rival **2** *verb* to move in a slow, careful way; *he started edging towards the door*

edged [edʒd] *adjective* with something along the edge; *a coat edged with velvet*

edging [ˈedʒɪŋ] *noun* thing whch goes along the edge of something; *a dress with an edging of lace*; *a path with an edging of bricks*

edgy [ˈedʒi] *adjective* nervous or jumpy; *what's the matter with you, you seem very edgy these days?*

edible [ˈedɪbl] *adjective* which can be safely eaten; *how do you know which wild mushrooms are edible and which are poisonous?*

edict [ˈiːdɪkt] *noun* public announcement of a law; *the president issued an edict that opposition parties would be banned*

edifice [ˈedɪfɪs] *noun* (*formal*) large building; *according to the redevelopment plans the main edifice is to be demolished apart from the facade which will be preserved*

edit [ˈedɪt] *verb* **(a)** to be in charge of a newspaper or magazine; *he edited the 'Sunday Express' for more than twenty years* **(b)** to make notes on a text; to change a text to make it better; *the edited text is now ready*; *it took me two hours to edit the first chapter* **(c)** to get a text ready for publication; *I am editing a volume of 20th-century poetry* **(d)** to cut up a film or tape and stick it together in correct order to make it ready to be shown or played; *once the film has been edited it will run for about 90 minutes*

edition [ɪˈdɪʃn] *noun* **(a)** quantity of a book or newspaper printed at the same time; *the book of poems was published in an edition of one thousand copies* **(b)** form in which a book is published; *she bought the hardback edition for her father*; **a first edition** = a copy of the first printing of a book

editor [ˈedɪtə] *noun* **(a)** person who makes notes on a text; person who gets a text, a radio or TV programme, etc., ready for publication; *a dictionary editor*; *the editor of a TV series on French cooking* **(b)** journalist in charge of a newspaper or part of a newspaper; *he wrote to the editor of 'The Times' asking for a job*; *she is the sports editor of the local paper* **(c)** computer program for editing text; *the software contains a basic text editor*

editorial [edɪˈtɔːriəl] **1** *adjective* referring to editors or to editing; *he has overall editorial control of the series*; **editorial board** = group of editors (on a newspaper, etc.) **2** *noun* main article written by the editor of a newspaper; *did you read today's editorial in the 'Times'?* (NOTE: also called a **leading article** or **leader**)

educate [ˈedjʊkeɪt] *verb* to teach someone; *she was educated privately in Switzerland*; *we need to educate young people about the dangers of alcohol*

educated [ˈedjuːkeɪtɪd] *adjective* having been to school and university, having a good knowledge of things; *a well-educated young man*; *the book will appeal to educated members of society*

education [edjuːˈkeɪʃn] *noun* system of teaching, or of being taught; *our children deserve the best education*; *we spent a lot of money on his education, and he's got a job as a dustman!*; **adult education** =

teaching people over the age of 20; **further education** = teaching people who have left school; **higher education** = teaching at colleges and universities; **primary education** = teaching small children; **private education** = teaching in private schools, where the students pay fees; **secondary education** = teaching children from the age of 11 to 16 or 18; **state education** = teaching in schools which belong to the state or local educational authority, where the education is free; **Department for Education and Employment (DfEE)** = British government department which is concerned with education and employment

educational [edju:'keɪʃnl] *adjective* referring to education, teaching, schools, etc.; *this game for 3 to 5 year-olds is very educational; a campaign to improve educational standards*; **educational publisher** = company which publishes school books

educationalist *or* **educationist** [edju:'keɪʃnəlɪst or edju:'keɪʃnɪst] *noun* person who specializes in the study of teaching methods; *the teaching system has been devised by leading educationalists*

educative ['edju:kətɪv] *adjective (formal)* which teaches; *this is part of the educative process*

educator ['edjukeɪtə] *noun* person who teaches, especially someone who teaches people how to teach; *who should educate the educators?*

Edwardian [ed'wɔ:djən] *adjective* referring to the time of Edward VII (1901 - 1910); *they went to a ball where people dressed up in Edwardian clothes*

EEC [i:i:'si:] *noun (old) short for* European Economic Community, now the European Union

eel [i:l] *noun* long thin fish which looks like a snake; *she ordered some smoked eel; he had a plate of jellied eels*

eerie ['ɪəri] *adjective* strange, ghostly, frightening; *it felt very eerie in the old house in the dark* (NOTE: **eerier - eeriest**)

eerily ['ɪərɪli] *adverb* in an eerie way; *somewhere in the trees an owl hooted eerily; he looks eerily like his dead brother*

effect [ɪ'fekt] **1** *noun* **(a)** result or influence; *the cuts in spending will have a serious effect on the hospital; the cream has had no effect on her rash; the effects of the anaesthetic took some time to wear off*; **the order takes effect** *or* **comes into effect from January 1st** = the order starts to have to be obeyed on January 1st; **with effect from** = starting from; *prices will be increased by 10% with effect from January 1st* **(b)** approximate meaning; *the notice said something to the effect that the shop had closed*; **or words to that effect** = or something with that meaning; *she said she wouldn't pay, or words to that effect* **(c)** **sound effects** = artificial sounds in theatre, TV, films; **special effects** = ghosts, cartoon characters appearing with ordinary actors, etc., which are used in films or on stage **(d)** *(formal)* **personal effects** = personal belongings **2** *verb (formal)* to make, to carry out; *she was able to effect a number of changes during her time in charge*; **to effect a payment** = to make a payment

effective ['ɪ'fektɪv] *adjective* **(a)** which produces the required result; *it's a very effective remedy against colds; his method of keeping the children quiet is very effective; advertising on TV is a very effective way of selling* **(b)** which takes effect; *an order which is effective from January 1st*

effectively [ɪ'fektɪvli] *adverb* in a way which produces a good result; *the floodlighting worked very effectively*

effectiveness [ɪ'fektɪvnəs] *noun* state of being effective, of being able to produce an effective result; *tests are being carried out on the new drug to prove its effectiveness in treating certain forms of the disease*

effectual [ɪ'fektjuəl] *adjective (formal)* effective, which produces the required effect; *you need to take more effectual measures against racism*

effervesce [efə'ves] *verb* to make bubbles; *the water will effervesce when you put the tablet in*

effervescence [efə'vesns] *noun* making bubbles; *the effervescence should continue for some minutes*

effervescent [efə'vesent] *adjective* **(a)** which makes bubbles; *the water will become effervescent if you put this tablet into the glass* **(b)** lively and excited; *her effervescent good humour made the party go with a swing*

efficacy ['efɪkəsi] *noun (formal)* effectiveness; the power to produce the correct result; *tests are being carried out on the new drug to prove its efficacy in treating certain forms of the disease*

efficiency [ɪ'fɪʃənsi] *noun* being able to produce a good result without wasting time, money or effort; *how can we improve the efficiency of our working methods?; she is known for her extreme efficiency*; **business efficiency** = making a business work efficiently

efficient [ɪ'fɪʃənt] *adjective* able to work well and do what is necessary without wasting time, money or effort; *he needs an efficient assistant to look after him; the system of printing invoices is very efficient; a fuel-efficient car*

efficiently [ɪ'fɪʃəntli] *adverb* in an efficient way; *the waitresses served the 250 wedding guests very efficiently; the new system of enrolling students is working very efficiently*

effigy ['efɪdʒi] *noun* rough model of a person *(usually unpopular)*; *the crowd burnt effigies of the President* (NOTE: plural is **effigies**)

effluent ['efluənt] *noun* sewage, especially liquid waste from a factory; *the river has been contaminated by effluent from the chemical factory*

effort ['efət] *noun* use of the mind or body to do something; *he's made great efforts to learn Spanish; thanks to her efforts, we have collected more than £10,000 for the children's home; if we make one more effort, we should get all that rubbish cleared away*

effortless ['efətləs] *adjective* without apparently using any energy; *her swimming style is so smooth she makes it look effortless; he gives the impression of effortless superiority*

effortlessly ['efətləsli] *adverb* without apparently using any energy; *he effortlessly rose through the company to become managing director*

effusive [ɪ'fju:sɪv] *adjective* showing too much emotion when talking about something; *we had a letter from our neighbours, full of effusive comments about their holiday*

effusively [ɪ'fju:sɪvli] *adverb* with too much emotion; *she thanked us effusively for having helped her*

eg or **e.g.** ['iː'dʒiː or fɔː igˈzɑːmpl] *abbreviation meaning 'for example'*; *some animals, eg polar bears, live in cold climates* (NOTE: it is short for the Latin phrase **exempli gratia**)

egalitarian [ɪgælɪˈteəriən] *adjective* believing in equality or treating all people equally; *he holds egalitarian views*; *they shared out the proceeds on an egalitarian basis*

egalitarianism [ɪgælɪˈteəriənɪzm] *noun* political theory that all members of society have equal rights and should have equal treatment

egg [eg] *noun* **(a)** oval object with a hard shell, produced by a female bird or reptile, from which a baby comes; *the owl laid three eggs in the nest*; *turtles lay their eggs in the sand* **(b)** a chicken's egg, used as food; *you need three eggs to make this cake*; **boiled egg** = egg which has been cooked by boiling in water; **hard-boiled egg** = egg which has been boiled until it is hard inside; **fried egg** = egg which is fried in fat or butter in a frying pan; **poached egg** = egg which is taken out of its shell and cooked whole in hot water (usually eaten on toast, at breakfast); **scrambled eggs** = eggs which are mixed up with a fork and then cooked in butter; *I had fried eggs and bacon for breakfast*; *do you want sausages with your scrambled eggs?* **(c)** reproductive cell produced by a female, which is fertilized by sperm from a male; *doctors implanted a fertilized egg in her womb*

egg cosy ['eg ˈkəʊzi] *noun* little cover put over a boiled egg to keep it hot; *they served boiled eggs, each with an egg cosy shaped like a chicken* (NOTE: plural is **egg cosies**)

eggcup ['egkʌp] *noun* little cup for a boiled egg; *she had an eggcup with her name on it*

egghead ['eghed] *noun* (*informal*) very intellectual person

egg on ['eg ˈɒn] *verb* to encourage someone to do something, especially something naughty; *stop egging him on - he's bad enough as it is*

eggplant ['egplɑːnt] *noun* dark purple shiny fruit of a small plant, used as a vegetable; *slices of eggplant fried in batter* (NOTE: used mainly in American English; British English is also **aubergine**)

eggshell ['egʃel] *noun* hard outside part of an egg; *I found a big piece of eggshell in my omelette*

egg timer ['eg ˈtaɪmə] *noun* device which is used to time how long an egg boils

ego ['iːgəʊ] *noun* your high opinion of yourself; *all this flattery does wonders for my ego*; **ego trip** = activity designed to boost your good opinion of yourself; *the editor treats the magazine as his own personal ego-trip*

egotist ['egəʊtɪst] *noun* person who thinks he is better than everyone else, who thinks and talks only about himself

egotistic(al) [egəʊˈtɪstɪk(l)] *adjective* thinking you are better than everyone else, thinking and talking only about yourself; *he was so egotistical that he didn't even bother to ask if anyone else needed help*

egregious [ɪˈgriːdʒiəs] *adjective* (*formal*) very bad; *it was an egregious mistake*

Egypt ['iːdʒɪpt] *noun* country in north Africa, at the eastern end of the Mediterranean; *the river Nile is Egypt's main source of water* (NOTE: capital: **Cairo**; people: **the Egyptians**; language: **Arabic**; currency: **Egyptian pound**)

Egyptian [ɪˈdʒɪpʃn] **1** *adjective* referring to Egypt; *the Egyptian pyramids are one of the wonders of the world* **2** *noun* person from Egypt; *the pyramids were built by the ancient Egyptians*

eh [eɪ] *interjection* used when asking questions; *what a laugh, eh?*; *what about a drink, eh?*; *eh? what did he say?*

EHO = ENVIRONMENTAL HEALTH OFFICER

eiderdown ['aɪdədaʊn] *noun* large bag full of feathers, used as a bed covering; *you don't need an eiderdown in the summer, it's too hot*

COMMENT: an eiderdown is put on top of sheets and blankets on a bed, unlike a duvet, which is not used with blankets

eight [eɪt] **(a)** number 8; *he ate eight chocolates*; *the little girl is eight (years old)*; *I usually have breakfast before eight (o'clock)* **(b)** crew of eight rowers in a boat; *our college eight won the race*; *see also* FOUR, PAIR (NOTE: plural in this meaning is **eights**)

eighteen [eɪˈtiːn] number 18; *there are eighteen people in our dance class*; *he will be eighteen (years old) next week*; *the train leaves at eighteen twenty (18:20)*; **the eighteen hundreds** = the years between 1800 and 1899 (NOTE: compare with **the eighteenth century**)

COMMENT: eighteen is the age at which young people in Britain become officially adult, independent of their parents and able to vote

eighteenth (18th) [eɪˈtiːnθ] *adjective & noun* *the eighteenth of April or April the eighteenth (April 18th)*; *today's the seventeenth, so tomorrow must be the eighteenth*; *that's the eighteenth invoice we've sent out today*; *it's his eighteenth birthday next week*; **the eighteenth century** = the years from 1700 to 1799 (NOTE: compare with **the eighteen hundreds**; note also that with dates **eighteenth** is usually written **18th: April 18th, 1999; September 18th, 1866** (American style is **September 18, 1866**), say 'the eighteenth of September' or 'September the eighteenth' (American style is 'September eighteenth'); with names of kings and queens, **eighteenth** is usually written **XVIII: King Louis XVIII** (say: 'King Louis the Eighteenth'))

eighth (8th) [eɪtθ] *adjective & noun* *the eighth of February or February the eighth (February 8th)*; *King Henry the Eighth (Henry VIII) had six wives*; *his eighth birthday is next Monday* (NOTE: with dates **eighth** is usually written **8th: April 8th, 1999; September 8th, 1866** (American style is **September 8, 1866**), say 'the eighth of September' or 'September the eighth' (American style is 'September eighth'); with names of kings and queens, **eighth** is usually written **VIII: King Henry VIII** (say: 'King Henry the Eighth'))

eightieth (80th) ['eɪtiəθ] *adjective & noun* *four and a half days is about an eightieth of a year*; *granny's eightieth birthday is next week*

eighty ['eɪti] number 80; *it's about eighty miles from London to Dover*; *she's eighty (years old)*; **she's in her eighties** = she is between 80 and 89 years old; **the (nineteen) eighties (1980s)** = the period from 1980 to 1989 (NOTE: **eighty-one** (81), **eighty-two** (82) but **eighty-first** (81st), **eighty-second** (82nd), etc.)

either ['aɪðə or 'iːðə] **1** *adjective & pronoun* **(a)** one or the other; *you can use either computer - it doesn't matter which; I don't like either of them* **(b)** each of two; both; *there are trees on either side of the road; some people don't take sugar in their coffee, some don't take milk, and some don't take either; they sat on either side of him* = one sat on each side of him **2** *conjunction (showing one of two possibilities)* **either ... or**; *either you come here or I'll come to see you; it's either a fox or a wolf; you must do it either today or tomorrow* **3** *adverb (with a negative, or to make a statement stronger) he isn't Irish and he isn't Scottish either; she doesn't want to go, and I don't want to go either; the report wasn't on the TV news, and it wasn't on the radio either*

ejaculate [ɪ'dʒækjʊleɪt] *verb* to send out semen from the penis

ejaculation [ɪdʒækjʊ'leɪʃn] *noun* sending out of semen from the penis; *he suffers from premature ejaculation*

eject [ɪ'dʒekt] *verb* **(a)** to throw out; *the chairman called in the police to eject the troublemakers from the meeting* **(b)** to escape from an aircraft using an ejector seat; *the pilot ejected safely*

ejection [ɪ'dʒekʃn] *noun* action of throwing out; *after the ejection of the demonstrators the meeting continued normally* (NOTE: no plural)

ejector seat [ɪ'dʒetə 'siːt] *noun* pilot's seat in an aircraft which in an emergency throws the pilot out; *he escaped using his ejector seat*

eke out ['iːk 'aʊt] *verb (formal)* to use something a little bit at a time, in order to make it last longer; *we eke out a pound of butter to make it last two weeks;* **to eke out a living** = to earn or live on very little money; *she ekes out a miserable existence as a cleaner*

elaborate 1 *adjective* [ɪ'læbərət] very detailed, very complicated; *an elaborate dessert of cream, fruit and cake* **2** *verb* [ɪ'læbəreɪt] to go into details; *it's a very complicated plan so I won't elaborate; he refused to elaborate any further on her reasons for leaving*

elaborately [ɪ'læbərətli] *adverb* in a very complicated or detailed way; *the church has some elaborately carved wooden panels*

elaboration [ɪlæbə'reɪʃn] *noun* giving a detailed explanation; *it's a very complicated plan which needs further elaboration* (NOTE: no plural)

elapse [ɪ'læps] *verb (of time)* to pass; *two years elapsed before they met again*

elastic [ɪ'læstɪk] **1** *adjective* which can stretch and contract; *she was wearing cycling shorts made of some elastic material;* **elastic band** = rubber band which holds cards, papers, etc., together **2** *noun* type of rubber which can stretch; *she threaded a piece of elastic through her waistband*

elasticity [ɪːlæs'tɪsɪti] *noun* being elastic; *the rubber is old and has lost its elasticity*

Elastoplast [ɪ'læstəʊplɑːst] *noun (trademark)* small strip of cloth with gauze in the middle, which can be stuck to the skin to cover a wound; *let me put some Elastoplast on your finger* (NOTE: American English is **BandAid**)

elated [ɪ'leɪtɪd] *adjective* very excited and pleased; *he was elated by his exam results*

elation [ɪ'leɪʃn] *noun* feeling of excitement and pleasure; *her indescribable feeling of elation at having passed the exam* (NOTE: no plural)

elbow ['elbəʊ] **1** *noun* joint in the middle of your arm; *he sat with his elbows on the table; she nudged him with her elbow; (informal)* **to give someone the elbow** = to tell someone you don't want to see them any more; *they had been going out together for some time, and then she suddenly gave him the elbow* **2** *verb* to push with your elbows; *he elbowed his way to the front of the crowd*

elbow-room ['elbəʊ'ruːm] *noun* space to move about; *the seats in tourist class don't give you much elbow-room*

elder ['eldə] **1** *adjective* older; *I have two elder brothers; she brought her elder sister;* **elder statesman** = older and wiser politician (NOTE: **elder** is a comparative, used mainly of brothers or sisters, but is never followed by **than**) **2** *noun* **(a)** older person; *Mary is the elder of the two; which brother is the elder?; children should have respect for their elders and betters* **(b)** common tree with white flowers and bunches of small purple berries; *there's an elder growing in the hedge by the field*

elderberry ['eldəberi] *noun* **(a)** elder tree; *an elderberry was in flower at the corner of the field* **(b)** little black fruit of an elder tree; *some people make wine from elderberries* (NOTE: plural is **elderberries**)

elderly ['eldəli] *adjective* old; *an elderly man sat down beside her; my mother is now rather elderly and doesn't drive any more* (NOTE: used as a polite way of saying **old**)

eldest ['eldəst] **1** *adjective* oldest of a series of people; *this is John, my eldest son* **2** *noun* oldest person of a series of people; *he is the eldest of the three brothers*

elect [ɪ'lekt] *verb* to choose by voting; *she was elected MP for the town; the president is elected for a term of four years; the chairman is elected by the members of the committee*

-elect [ɪ'lekt] *suffix* person who has been elected but has not yet started the term of office; *she is the president-elect* (NOTE: plural is **presidents-elect**)

election [ɪ'lekʃən] *noun* process of choosing by voting; *after the election, the crowds were dancing in the streets; local elections are being held next week; the next item on the agenda is the election of a new treasurer for the club;* **general election** = election for Parliament, where everyone in the country over a certain age can vote

COMMENT: in the UK, a general election to choose a new government and parliament must be held every five years, although the Prime Minister may call one sooner. In the USA, a presidential election is held every four years, always in November. A President can be re-elected once only. The members of Congress are also elected in November elections, each for a two year term, while Senators are elected for six years, one third of the Senate coming up for election every two years

electioneering [ɪlekʃə'nɪərɪŋ] *noun* working for an election campaign, making speeches, writing pamphlets, meeting voters, etc.

elector [ɪ'lektə] *noun* person who votes or who is eligible to vote in an election; *he appealed to the electors to give the government another chance*; **register of electors** = official list of names and addresses of people living in a certain area who are eligible to vote in local or national elections; *if your name does not appear on the register of electors you will not be allowed to vote*

electoral [ɪ'lektərəl] *adjective* referring to an election; *the party suffered a terrible electoral defeat*; **electoral college** = group who elect someone such as a president; **electoral register** *or* **electoral roll** = REGISTER OF ELECTORS

electorate [ɪ'lektərət] *noun* all the people in an area who are qualified to vote; *the village has an electorate of about one thousand*

electric [ɪ'lektrɪk] *adjective* **(a)** worked by electricity; *is your cooker electric or gas?*; *he plays an electric guitar*; *he cut the wood with an electric saw*; *she gave me an electric toothbrush for Christmas* **(b)** making or carrying electricity; *don't touch those electric wires*; *electric plugs in the USA are different from those in Britain*

electrical [ɪ'lektrɪkl] *adjective* referring to electricity; *the college offers courses in electrical engineering*; *a shop selling electrical appliances*; *they are trying to repair an electrical fault*

electric chair [ɪ'lektrɪk 'tʃeə] *noun* chair attached to a powerful electric current, used in some states of the USA to execute criminals; *he was sent to the electric chair*

electrician [ɪlek'trɪʃn] *noun* person who works on electrical repairs, instals electric machines, etc.; *you had better get an electrician to check the wiring*

electricity [ɪlek'trɪsɪti] *noun* energy used to make light, heat, or power; *we haven't paid the electricity bill this month*; *the electricity was cut off this morning*; *the heating is run by electricity*; *the cottage is in the mountains and doesn't have any electricity* (NOTE: no plural)

electrify [ɪ'lektrɪfaɪ] *verb* **(a)** to convert to an electric source of power; *all the most modern railway lines are electrified* **(b)** to startle and excite; *she gave an electrifying performance*

electrocardiogram [ɪlektrəʊ'kɑːdɪəgræm] *noun* chart which shows the electrical impulses of the heart as it is beating

electrocute [ɪ'lektrəkjuːt] *verb* to receive an electric shock; *he touched the wire and was electrocuted*

electrode [ɪ'lektrəʊd] *noun* one of two points on an electric circuit where the current enters or leaves a battery, or other electric source; *make sure the electrodes are clean before connecting them to the battery*; *electrodes attached to his head measure brain impulses*; *compare* ANODE, CATHODE

electromagnetic [ɪlektrəmæg'netɪk] *adjective* generating a magnetic field or magnetic effect when supplied with electrical power; *electromagnetic field*; *electromagnetic wave*

electron [ɪ'lektrɒn] *noun* basic negative particle in an atom

electronic [ɪlek'trɒnɪk] *adjective* using devices such as silicon chips which affect the electric current which passes through them; *my car has electronic ignition*;

electronic engineer = engineer who specializes in electronic devices; **electronic mail** = e-mail, the system of sending messages from one computer to another, via telephone lines

electronics [ɪlek'trɒnɪks] *noun* science of the movement of electricity in electronic devices; *he is studying electronics at university*; *she works for a major electronics company*; **the electronics industry** = the industry which makes TV sets, radios, calculators, etc. (NOTE: takes a singular verb)

elegance ['elɪgəns] *noun* being elegant, being very fashionable; *the rooms have been decorated with taste and elegance*; *he was impressed by the elegance of the ladies at the opera*

elegant ['elɪgənt] *adjective* very fashionable and stylish; *you look very elegant in that dress*; *who is that elegant woman in black at the back of the church?*; *she led us into her elegant drawing room*

elegantly ['elɪgəntli] *adverb* in an elegant style; *an elegantly dressed couple*

elegy ['elədʒi] *noun* sad poem or piece of music about someone who is dead; *he wrote an elegy on his mother* (NOTE: plural is **elegies**)

element ['elɪmənt] *noun* **(a)** basic chemical substance; *magnesium is a metallic element see also* TRACE ELEMENTS **(b)** basic part of something; *I think we have all the elements of a settlement* **(c)** natural environment; *the vicar is in his element when he's talking about cricket*; **the elements** = the weather, usually bad weather; *you don't want to expose your new coat to the elements*

elemental [elɪ'mentəl] *adjective* wild and uncivilized; *the elemental forces of nature*

elementary [elɪ'mentri] *adjective* basic or simple; *elementary physics*

elementary school [elɪ'mentri 'skuːl] *noun* US first school for children up to around eleven years old; *she's an elementary school teacher* (NOTE: the British equivalent is a **primary school**)

elephant ['elɪfənt] *noun* very large African or Indian animal, with large ears, a trunk and tusks; *if you go to the zoo, you can have a ride on an elephant*; *in some countries elephants are used for work in the jungle*; *see also* WHITE ELEPHANT

COMMENT: there are two types of elephant, the African, which is larger and wilder, and the Indian which is found in India and South-East Asia, and is used as a working animal in forests

elevate ['eliveit] *verb* (*formal*) to lift up; *he was elevated to the post of chairman*

elevation [elɪ'veɪʃn] *noun* (*formal*) height above sea level; *at an elevation of 300m, the villa is much cooler than the town below*

elevator ['eliveitə] *noun* **(a)** US device for lifting people from floor to floor inside a building; *take the elevator to the 26th floor* (NOTE: British English is **lift**) **(b) goods elevator** = device for lifting goods from floor to floor inside a building **(c) grain elevator** = tall building for storing grain

eleven [ɪ'levn] **(a)** number 11; *when you're eleven (years old) you will go to secondary school*; *come and see me at eleven (o'clock)*; **the eleven hundreds** = the years from 1100 to 1199 (NOTE: compare with **the**

eleventh century) (b) eleven people, as in a football team; *the England eleven* (NOTE: in this meaning, usually written **XI: the England XI)**

elevenses [ɪˈlevənzɪz] *noun (informal)* snack served in the middle of the morning (about 11 o'clock)

eleventh (11th) [ɪˈlevənθ] *adjective & noun the eleventh of June or June the eleventh (June 11th); his name was eleventh on the list; it's her eleventh birthday tomorrow;* **at the eleventh hour** = at the last minute; *the contract was finally signed at the eleventh hour; his eleventh-hour decision to stand for election;* **the eleventh century** = the years from 1000 to 1099 (NOTE: compare with **the eleven hundreds**; note also that with dates **eleventh** is usually written **11th: April 11th, 1999; September 11th, 1866** (American style is **September 11, 1866)**, say 'the eleventh of September' or 'September the eleventh' (American style is 'September eleventh'); with names of kings and queens, **eleventh** is usually written **XI: King Louis XI** (say: 'King Louis the Eleventh'))

elf [elf] *noun* little man in fairy stories; *he read the children a story about elves and fairies* (NOTE: plural is **elves** [elvz])

elicit [ɪˈlɪsɪt] *verb (formal)* to obtain; *I was unable to elicit any useful information about him* (NOTE: do not confuse with **illicit**)

eligibility [elɪdʒɪˈbɪlɪti] *noun* state of being eligible; *they questioned her eligibility to stand for re-election*

eligible [ˈelɪdʒɪbl] *adjective* **(a) eligible to do something** = able to do something because you are old enough or have the right qualifications; *you aren't eligible to vote until you are eighteen; she's not eligible to enter the competition because she works for the company running it;* **eligible bachelor** = rich bachelor who is thought to be a good person for a girl to marry **(b) eligible for something** = entitled to do something or qualified for something; *the previous president is eligible for re-election; she is not eligible for a grant*

eliminate [ɪˈlɪmɪneɪt] *verb* **(a)** to remove mistakes, waste, etc.; *using a computer should eliminate all possibility of error; smallpox has been eliminated in most parts of the world* **(b)** to remove someone from a competition; *he came last and so was eliminated from the next round of the contest*

elimination [ɪlɪmɪˈneɪʃn] *noun* act of eliminating; *their aim is the elimination of tuberculosis; Spain's elimination from the World Cup disappointed all Spanish football fans*

élite [eɪˈliːt] *noun* group of the best people; *only the élite can afford private education for their children*

elitist [ɪˈliːtɪst] *adjective* believing that an élite should run a group or society; *the head teacher adopted an elitist attitude towards the cleverest children in the class*

Elizabethan [elɪzəˈbiːθən] *adjective* referring to the time of Elizabeth I (1558 - 1603); *Shakespeare was one of many playwrights during the Elizabethan period; Stratford on Avon has many fine examples of Elizabethan architecture*

elk [elk] *noun* large European deer with flat antlers; *elk can be a danger on Swedish roads* (NOTE: similar to the American **moose**; note that the plural is **elk)**

ellipse [ɪˈlɪps] *noun* oval shape; *the path of the satellite is an ellipse*

elm [elm] *noun* large hardwood tree which grows in temperate areas; **Dutch elm disease** = fungus disease which kills elm trees and is spread by bark beetles; *many of the elms in the park have died from Dutch elm disease*

El Niño [ˈel ˈniːnjəʊ] *see* NIÑO

elocution [eləˈkjuːʃn] *noun* art of speaking in a clear and elegant way; *she is taking elocution lessons*

elongated [ˈiːlɒŋɡeɪtɪd] *adjective* longer than normal; *the figures in the painting are curiously elongated*

elope [ɪˈləʊp] *verb* to run away to get married; *he eloped with an heiress*

eloquence [ˈeləkwəns] *noun* art of making speeches which persuade and convince; *his speeches were renowned for their eloquence and wit; the young MP's eloquence impressed the House of Commons* (NOTE: no plural)

eloquent [ˈeləkwənt] *adjective* convincing and persuasive; *he's an eloquent speaker but his views tend to be rather extreme; the damage caused by the volcano is an eloquent reminder of how vulnerable people are to natural disasters*

eloquently [ˈeləkwəntli] *adverb* in an eloquent way; *he eloquently reminded his audience of the great work done by the hospital*

else [els] *adverb* **(a)** *(used after pronouns)* other; *what else can I say?; everyone else had already left; who else was at the meeting?;* **anyone else** = any other person; *is there anyone else who can't see the screen?;* **anything else** = any other thing; *is there anything else you don't like eating?; did you hear anything else?;* **somebody else** *or* **someone else** = some other person, a different person; *she was ill so someone else had to take her place;* **nobody else** *or* **no one else** = no other person; *nobody else's daughter behaved as badly as ours;* **nothing else** = no other thing; *I need one small gold ring - nothing else will do;* **nowhere else** = no other place; *there's nowhere else to go;* **somewhere else** *US* **someplace else** = in some other place, in a different place; *can we go somewhere else?* **(b) or else** = or if not; *come in or else stay outside; you must have a ticket, or else you will be thrown off the train by the inspector; (as informal threat)* **you'd better pay, or else** = if you don't pay, I'll hit you

elsewhere [elsˈweə] *adverb* somewhere else, in another place; *this shop doesn't stock maps, so you'll have to try elsewhere*

elude [ɪˈluːd] *verb (formal)* to escape, to avoid capture; *he eluded his pursuers by diving down an alleyway and leaping over a wall*

elusive [ɪˈluːsɪv] *adjective* difficult to find; *I tried calling the manager of the complaints department but he seems to be very elusive; they spent the summer looking for the elusive white rhino*

emaciated [ɪˈmeɪsieɪtɪd] *adjective* extremely thin; *emaciated prisoners staggered out of the prison camp*

emaciation [ɪmeɪsiˈeɪʃn] *noun* being emaciated; *the inspectors found the horses in a state of emaciation*

e-mail *or* **email** [ˈiːmeɪl] **1** *noun* **(a)** electronic mail, a system of sending messages from one computer to another, using telephone lines; *you can contact me by phone or e-mail if you want; I'll give you my e-mail address* **(b)** message sent by e-mail; *I had two e-mails* *from him this morning* **2** *verb* to send a message using electronic mail; *I e-mailed him about the meeting*

emanate ['eməneɪt] *verb (formal)* to emanate from = to come from; *the smell of onions emanating from the kitchen*; *some of these ideas emanate from the government's own think tank*

emancipate [ɪ'mænsɪpeɪt] *verb* **(a)** to make someone free; *they passed a law to emancipate all slaves* **(b)** to give someone the right to equal treatment; *in the 19th century, women fought to be emancipated*

emancipation [ɪmænsɪ'peɪʃn] *noun* making free, especially making a slave free or giving someone the right to equal status; *Mrs Pankhurst became famous for fighting for the emancipation of women* (NOTE: no plural)

emasculate [ɪ'mæskjʊleɪt] *verb (formal)* to make more weak; *his more radical proposals have been emasculated by the committee*

embalm [ɪm'bɑːm] *verb* to treat a dead body with chemicals to preserve it; *ancient Egyptians were embalmed before being buried*

embankment [ɪm'bæŋkmənt] *noun* **(a)** wall made along a river bank to prevent the river from overflowing; *entire fields were flooded when the river embankment collapsed*; **a motorway embankment** *or* **a railway embankment** = a raised bank of earth to carry a motorway or railway **(b)** road running along the wall along a river; *the Victoria Embankment in London runs along the side of the Thames*

embargo [ɪm'bɑːgəʊ] **1** *noun* official ban on trade; *the oil embargo is still in place*; **to place** *or* **put an embargo on** = to forbid something officially; *they placed an embargo on trade with our country*; **to lift an embargo** = to allow trade to start again; *the government has lifted the embargo on the export of computers*; **to be under an embargo** = to be forbidden (NOTE: plural is **embargoes**) **2** *verb* **(a)** to forbid something officially; *the government has embargoed the sale of arms to Middle Eastern countries* **(b)** not to allow publication of information for a period of time; *the news has been embargoed until next Wednesday*

embark [ɪm'bɑːk] *verb* **(a)** to go onto a ship; *the passengers embarked at Southampton* **(b)** **to embark on something** = to start a project; *the council has embarked on the redevelopment of the town centre*; *we'd better not embark on something new until we have finished this job*

embarkation [embɑː'keɪʃn] *noun* act of going onto a ship or aircraft; *please show your boarding card before embarkation*

embarrass [ɪm'bærəs] *verb* to make someone feel uncomfortable by being rude, indecent, etc.; *he wanted to embarrass me in front of my friends*; *it embarrasses me to have to talk about it in public*

embarrassed [ɪm'bærəst] *adjective* uncomfortable or ashamed, not knowing what to do; *she gave an embarrassed laugh, and said she had forgotten to bring the present*; *he was so embarrassed that he turned bright red*

embarrassing [ɪm'bærəsɪŋ] *adjective* that makes you feel embarrassed; *it was very embarrassing to find that the bride's mother was wearing exactly the same dress as me*

embarrassment [ɪm'bærəsmənt] *noun* feeling of being worried and ashamed; *much to my embarrassment I arrived an hour late*

embassy ['embəsi] *noun* home or offices of an ambassador; *there was a party at the British Embassy in Paris* (NOTE: plural is **embassies**)

embattled [ɪm'bætld] *adjective* under attack; constantly criticized; *the embattled minister refused to come out of his house to face the press*

embed [ɪm'bed] *verb* to fix something into a mass of concrete, into flesh, etc.; *the bullet was embedded in his spine*; *the hook embedded itself in his thumb* (NOTE: **embedding - embedded**)

embellish [ɪm'belɪʃ] *verb* **(a)** to add details which are not true; *he embellished the story of the rescue with details of how he had climbed down the cliff* **(b)** to decorate or to make beautiful; *the ceiling was embellished with gold leaf*

embers ['embəz] *noun* red hot pieces of wood or coal; *she poured water on the embers of the bonfire*

embezzle [ɪm'bezl] *verb* to use money which is not yours, or which you are looking after for someone; *he was sent to prison for six months for embezzling his clients' money*

embezzlement [ɪm'bezlmənt] *noun* act of embezzling; *he was sent to prison for six months for embezzlement* (NOTE: no plural)

embezzler [ɪm'bezlə] *noun* person who embezzles

embittered [ɪm'bɪtəd] *adjective* made bitter; *the divorce left her embittered and angry*

emblem ['embləm] *noun* design which is adopted as the symbol of a country, team, town, etc.; *the national emblem of Wales is a red dragon*

embodiment [ɪm'bɒdɪmənt] *noun* physical expression of an idea; *he is the living embodiment of hard work*

embody [ɪm'bɒdi] *verb* **(a)** to include; *the latest model embodies several new safety features* **(b)** to show an idea in a physical form; *she embodies all the best qualities of children's doctor*

embrace [ɪm'breɪs] **1** *verb* **(a)** to hold and kiss someone to show affection; *they embraced for several minutes before he got on the train* **(b)** to become a convert to a belief; *he embraced communism when he was at university* **2** *noun (literary)* holding someone tightly and kissing them; *she shrank from his embraces*; *they lay on the grass in a close embrace*

embroider [ɪm'brɔɪdə] *verb* **(a)** to make artistic patterns by sewing with coloured threads on cloth; *she embroidered a tablecloth for her mother* **(b)** to invent extra details and add them to a story; *he embroidered the story of his escape from prison with details of how he overpowered three guards and stole their guns*

embroidery [ɪm'brɔɪdri] *noun* **(a)** art of sewing flower designs, patterns, etc., on cloth; *she went to embroidery classes* **(b)** embroidered cloth; *we admired the delicate embroidery on the tablecloth*; *see also* NEEDLEWORK

embroiled [ɪm'brɔɪld] *adjective* involved in an awkward situation; *he became embroiled in a difficult divorce case*

embryo ['embriəʊ] *noun* **(a)** first state of a living organism; *a human embryo* **(b)** **in embryo** = in its early stages; *the plan was presented to us in embryo* (NOTE: plural is **embryos**)

embryonic [embrɪˈɒnɪk] *adjective* in a very early stage of development; *our proposals are still at an embryonic stage*; *the government gives aid to the country's embryonic film industry*

emerald [ˈemrəld] **1** *adjective* bright green; *she was wearing an emerald silk dress* **2** *noun* green precious stone; *her crown was studded with emeralds*

emerge [ɪˈmɜːdʒ] *verb* **(a) to emerge from inside something** = to come out from inside; *they blinked as they emerged into the sunlight from the tunnel* **(b)** to appear, to come into existence, to take on a role; *it was only after the election that he emerged as party leader* **(c)** to become known; *it soon emerged that the Prime Minister knew nothing about what was happening*

emergence [ɪˈmɜːdʒəns] *noun* act of emerging; *the split led to the emergence of a new political party*; *his emergence as leader of the socialists*

emergency [ɪˈmɜːdʒənsi] *noun* dangerous situation where decisions have to be taken quickly (such as a fire, accident, breakdown of law and order, etc.); *phone for an ambulance - this is an emergency!*; **state of emergency** = time when the police or armed forces are in control of a country; *the government has declared a state of emergency*; **emergency exit** = door in a cinema, etc., used in case of fire; **emergency operation** = operation done immediately on a seriously ill patient; **the emergency services** = the police, fire service and ambulance service; **in case of emergency** *or* **in an emergency** = if a dangerous situation develops; *in an emergency or in case of emergency press the red button* (NOTE: plural is **emergencies**)

emergent [ɪˈmɜːdʒənt] *adjective* in a very early stage of development; **emergent nations** = nations that are becoming economically independent

emigrant [ˈemɪɡrənt] *noun* person who emigrates; *Russian emigrants to Israel*; *compare* IMMIGRANT

emigrate [ˈemɪɡreɪt] *verb* to leave your country to live in another; *my daughter and her family have emigrated to Australia*; *compare* IMMIGRATE

emigration [emɪˈɡreɪʃn] *noun* act of leaving your country to live in another; *19th century governments encouraged emigration to the colonies*; *compare* IMMIGRATION

emigré [ˈemɪɡreɪ] *noun* person who has emigrated for political reasons; *after the Revolution many Russian emigrés settled in Paris*

eminence [ˈemɪnəns] *noun* **(a)** *(formal)* high place; *the castle stands on an eminence overlooking the river* **(b)** high rank; *he owed his position of eminence in the government entirely to his friend the Prime Minister*; *she was met by several persons of great eminence in the university hierarchy* **(c)** *(formal)* *(used as a form of address to a cardinal)* *His Eminence, the Cardinal Archbishop of Westminster* (NOTE: when speaking directly to a cardinal, say **Your Eminence**)

eminent [ˈemɪnənt] *adjective* very highly respected because of position or work; *an eminent judge*; *he is eminent in international law*

eminently [ˈemɪnəntli] *adverb* remarkably, particularly; *she is eminently suitable for the job*

emir [ˈemɪə] *noun* Muslim ruler; *the Emir of Kuwait*

emirate [ˈemərət] *noun* country ruled by an emir; *the United Arab Emirates is a group of emirates on the Persian Gulf*

emissary [ˈemɪsəri] *noun* person sent with a message or to act on someone's behalf; *emissaries of the rebel forces were taken into the government offices during the night* (NOTE: plural is **emissaries**)

emission [ɪˈmɪʃn] *noun* **(a)** process of emitting; *they are trying to reduce the emission of carbon monoxide from vehicles* (NOTE: no plural in this meaning) **(b)** substance which is emitted; *gas emissions can cause acid rain*

emit [ɪˈmɪt] *verb* to send out a sound, signal, smoke, etc.; *the machine started to emit a loud buzzing sound*; *the radioactive waste was found to be emitting gamma rays* (NOTE: **emitting - emitted**)

emotion [ɪˈməʊʃn] *noun* strong feeling; *hatred and love are two of the most powerful emotions*; *he tried to hide his emotions when he made his speech*

emotional [ɪˈməʊʃnl] *adjective* which shows emotion; *we bade an emotional farewell to our son and his family*; *the music made her feel very emotional and she started to cry*

emotionally [ɪˈməʊʃnəli] *adverb* **(a)** in an emotional way; *he spoke emotionally of his time as a hostage* **(b)** in a sexual way; *he became emotionally entangled with his secretary*

emotive [ɪˈməʊtɪv] *adjective* which is likely to cause strong feeling; *abortion is a very emotive issue*

empathy [ˈempəθi] *noun* ability to share the feelings of another person, by imagining yourself as that person; *the empathy between father and son*

emperor [ˈemprə] *noun* ruler of an empire; *Napoleon declared himself emperor*; *the Chinese Emperors lived in the Forbidden City*

emphasis [ˈemfəsɪs] *noun* **(a)** showing the importance of something, usually in speech; *don't put too much emphasis on his age*; *she banged the table for emphasis as she spoke* **(b)** loudness of your voice when you pronounce a word or phrase; *his emphasis on the word 'peace' was noticeable* (NOTE: plural is **emphases**)

emphasize [ˈemfəsaɪz] *verb* to show that you feel something is important, by saying it more loudly, slowly, etc.; *please emphasize that the meeting must start on time*; *he emphasized the importance of everyone working together*; *she kept on emphasizing the same point over and over again*

emphatic [ɪmˈfætɪk] *adjective* using emphasis; *he was emphatic in his denials*

emphatically [ɪmˈfætɪkli] *adverb* in a forceful way; *he emphatically denied having anything to do with it*

emphysema [emfɪˈsiːmə] *noun* condition where the surface of the lungs is reduced, making it difficult to breathe; *emphysema is caused by smoking, or by living in a polluted environment*

empire [ˈempaɪə] *noun* several separate territories ruled by a central government; *we're studying the history of the British Empire*; *the Soviet empire covered a huge area from the Pacific Ocean to the middle of Europe*

empirical [emˈpɪrɪkl] *adjective* based on practical experiment and not on theory; *for a theory to be accepted it must be backed by empirical data*

employ [ɪmˈplɔɪ] *verb* (a) to give someone regular paid work; *he is employed as a gardener by the duke*; *she is employed in the textile industry* (b) *(formal)* to use; *if we were to employ more up-to-date methods, would we make more money?*; *how can we best employ our free time on Sunday?*

employed [ɪmˈplɔɪd] **1** *adjective* in regular paid work; *please state the occupations of the employed members of your household*; **self-employed** = working for yourself; *he worked in a bank for ten years but now is self-employed* **2** *noun* **the employed** = people who are working; *the employers and the employed*; **the self-employed** = people who work for themselves (NOTE: the noun is plural)

employee [emplɔɪˈiː] *noun* person who is employed; *the company has decided to take on twenty new employees*

employer [ɪmˈplɔɪə] *noun* person or organization that gives work to people and pays them; *her employer was a Hong Kong businessman*; *the car factory is the biggest employer in the area*

employment [ɪmˈplɔɪmənt] *noun* regular paid work; **in employment** = working; *are you still in employment?*; *everyone in paid employment has to pay tax*; **full-time employment** = work for all of a working day; *he is looking for full-time employment*; **part-time employment** = work for part of a working day; *she is in part-time employment*; **seasonal employment** = work which is available at certain times of the year only (such as in a ski resort); **temporary employment** = work which does not last for more than a few months; **contract of employment** *or* **employment contract** = contract between management and an employee showing all the conditions of work; **employment bureau** *or* **agency** = office which finds jobs for people; **the Department for Education and Employment**; *see* EDUCATION

empower [ɪmˈpauə] *verb* to give someone the power to do something; *she has been empowered by the company to sign the contract*; *the government is empowered to call in the army to deal with the crisis*

empowerment [ɪmˈpauəmənt] *noun* act of giving power to someone; *we are seeking the empowerment of the junior staff*

empress [ˈemprəs] *noun* (a) woman who rules an empire; *Queen Victoria was Empress of India* (b) wife or widow of an emperor; *when the emperor died, the empress decided to rule the country* (NOTE: plural is **empresses**)

emptiness [ˈemptinəs] *noun* being empty; *the vast emptiness of the Russian steppes*; *with his wife and children dead, a terrible feeling of emptiness overwhelmed him* (NOTE: no plural)

empty [ˈemti] **1** *adjective* with nothing inside; *when we opened it, the box was empty*; *take an empty pot and fill it with soil*; *the fridge is empty - we'll have to go out to eat*; *the ski resorts are empty because there is no snow* (NOTE: **emptier - emptiest**) **2** *noun* something, usually a bottle, which has nothing in it; *you can take the empties back to the shop* (NOTE: plural is **empties**) **3** *verb* to make something empty; *she emptied the clothes out of the suitcase*; *he emptied the bottle into the sink*; *they emptied the contents of the petty cash box into a bag*

empty-handed [emptiˈhændɪd] *adjective* having received nothing; *having been unable to open the safe,* *the burglars left the house empty-handed*; *she asked various government departments for grants, but each time came away empty-handed*

emulate [ˈemjʊleɪt] *verb (formal)* to try to do as well as or better than someone; *he tried hard to emulate his older brother*

emulation [emjʊˈleɪʃn] *noun (formal)* act of emulating; *he joined the navy, in emulation of his two brothers*

emulsify [ɪˈmʌlsɪfaɪ] *verb* to mix two liquids together which cannot unite completely (such as oil and water)

emulsion [ɪˈmʌlʃn] *noun* mixture of two liquids which do not unite completely, such as oil and water; *mixing oil and vinegar forms an emulsion*; **emulsion (paint)** = paint made from colour added to oil and water, used for painting walls and ceilings; *use emulsion (paint) for the walls and ceiling, and gloss for the doors and windows*

enable [ɪˈneɪbl] *verb (formal)* to make it possible for someone to do something; *the dictionary should enable you to understand English better*

enact [ɪˈnækt] *verb* to make a law; *once a Bill has been enacted, it becomes law*

enactment [ɪˈnæktmənt] *noun (formal)* (a) making a law; *the enactment of this Bill is likely to take several months* (NOTE: no plural in this sense) (b) an Act of Parliament; *this particular enactment dates back to 1824 and is really no longer applicable*

enamel [ɪˈnæml] **1** *noun* (a) very hard covering of colour; *the enamel of the painting had begun to crack* (b) hard coloured coating fixed to metal by heating (c) hard coating on the teeth; *if the enamel of a tooth gets damaged the tooth will soon start to discolour* **2** *verb* to cover with very hard colour; *this must have taken a long time to enamel* (NOTE: **enamelling - enamelled** but American spelling is **enameling - enameled**)

encamp [ɪnˈkæmp] *verb* **to be encamped** = to be in a camp; *the enemy were encamped around the castle*; *the police tried to remove the protesters encamped on the site of the new motorway*

encampment [ɪnˈkæmpmənt] *noun* large camp; *they bombarded enemy encampments in the valley*

encapsulate [ɪnˈkæpsjʊleɪt] *verb* to summarize, to put in a shortened form; *the peace campaigners' aims were encapsulated in the slogan: 'ban the bomb!'*

encase [ɪnˈkeɪs] *verb* to surround as if in a case; *the faulty nuclear reactor was encased in concrete*; *the pub was full of motorcyclists encased in black leather*

encephalopathy [ensefəˈlɒpəθi] *noun* any disease of the brain; **bovine spongiform encephalopathy (BSE)** = fatal brain disease of cattle, caused by eating contaminated food (NOTE: also called **mad cow disease**)

enchant [ɪnˈtʃɑːnt] *verb* to charm; *she was enchanted by the music of the village choir*

enchanting [ɪnˈtʃɑːntɪŋ] *adjective* very beautiful or magical; *what an enchanting place for a picnic!*

enchantment [ɪnˈtʃɑːntmənt] *noun* mysterious and magic feeling; *the enchantment of summer evenings at Oxford*

encircle [ɪnˈsɜːkl] *verb* to surround completely; *a small lawn encircled by beds of roses*; *the enemy tanks were completely encircled and had to surrender*

encirclement [ɪnˈsɜːklmənt] *noun* action of encircling; *our aim is the encirclement of the enemy camp*

enclave [ˈenkleɪv] *noun* small group of people or small area completely surrounded by another quite different and larger group or area; *they live in a predominantly Chinese enclave in the north of the city*

enclose [ɪnˈkləʊz] *verb* **(a)** to put something inside an envelope with a letter; *I am enclosing a copy of our current catalogue; please find our cheque enclosed herewith* **(b)** to put a wall or fence round an area of land; *the garden is enclosed with high brick walls*

enclosure [ɪnˈkləʊʒə] *noun* **(a)** document enclosed with a letter; *please find details in the accompanying enclosure* **(b)** removal of land from common use, by putting fences round it; area of land which has been enclosed; *much enclosure of common land took place in the 18th and 19th centuries*

encode [enˈkəʊd] *verb* to write something in a code so that it cannot be read or used by other people; *to defeat the hackers, companies try to find sophisticated ways of encoding their programs*

encompass [ɪnˈkʌmpəs] *verb* (*formal*) **(a)** to include; *my talk tonight will encompass all aspects of Shakespeare's comedies* **(b)** to surround; *a flower garden encompassed by high brick walls* **(c)** to cover; *the city encompasses about ten square kilometres*

encore [ˈɒŋkɔː] *noun* **(a)** call by the audience for a performer to repeat a song, a piece of music; *the crowd's cries of 'Encore' were simply deafening* **(b)** song or piece of music repeated at the request of the audience; *at the end of the concert she played or sang two encores*

encounter [ɪnˈkaʊntə] **1** *noun* **(a)** meeting; *I had an unexpected encounter with my former boss at the London Book Fair; she told him about her encounter with the bull* **(b)** short fight; *the encounter only lasted a few minutes, but it seemed longer to the soldiers taking part* **2** *verb* to meet; *on the journey we encountered several amusing people; I have never encountered such hospitality anywhere else*

encourage [ɪnˈkʌrɪdʒ] *verb* **(a)** to make it easier for something to happen; *leaving your credit cards on your desk encourages people to steal or encourages stealing* **(b)** to help someone to do something by giving them confidence; *he encouraged me to apply for the job; I always felt encouraged by his interest in what I was doing*

encouragement [ɪnˈkʌrɪdʒmənt] *noun* giving someone the confidence to do something; *a few words of encouragement and everyone will work better; all he needs is a little encouragement and he will do really well*

encouraging [ɪnˈkʌrɪdʒɪŋ] *adjective* which encourages; *the maths teacher was very encouraging; it's an encouraging sign that so many students have enrolled for the course*

encroach [ɪnˈkrəʊtʃ] *verb* **to encroach (up)on** = to take over someone else's space; *their new wall had encroached on our land; the new town will encroach on areas of green belt land; she accused the professor of encroaching upon her area of study*

encroaching [ɪnˈkrəʊtʃɪŋ] *adjective* which encroaches; *the village was threatened by encroaching sand dunes*

encumber [ɪnˈkʌmbə] *verb* (*formal*) to prevent someone from moving or doing something; *the walkers were encumbered by their heavy rucksacks*

encumbrance [ɪnˈkʌmbrəns] *noun* (*formal*) thing which prevents you from moving or doing something; *all this baggage is just an encumbrance, I prefer to travel light*

encyclopaedia *or* **encyclopedia** [ɪnsaɪkləˈpiːdiə] *noun* **(a)** reference book (sometimes in many volumes) containing articles on all subjects of human knowledge, usually presented in alphabetical order, with an index; *if you need to know something about planets look up the 'Astronomy' article in the encyclopaedia* **(b)** reference book containing articles on a single subject, arranged usually in alphabetical order; *a gardening encyclopaedia; the encyclopaedia of sport*

end [end] **1** *noun* **(a)** last part of something; *she tied the two ends of the ribbon together; the telephone rang and I missed the end of the TV programme; go down to the end of the road and then turn right*; **in the end** = finally, at last; *in the end the teacher let him go home; in the end the shop had to call in the police*; **on end** = with no breaks; *he worked for hours on end*; (*informal*) **no end of** = very many; *the car's caused us no end of problems*; **to come to an end** = to be finished; *the work should come to an end next month*; **to be at a loose end** = to have nothing to do; *I was at a loose end so I decided to go to the cinema*; **to make ends meet** = to have enough money to live on; *after paying tax, we can only just make ends meet* **(b)** final part of a period of time; *can you wait until the end of the week?*; **year end accounts** = accounts prepared at the end of a financial year **(c)** aim, result intended; **the end justifies the means** = you can do anything to achieve your aim; **to this end** *or* **with this end in mind** = in order to do this; *we have decided to sell the house and to this end have put it in the hands of an estate agent* **2** *verb* to be finished, to come to an end; *the film ends with a wedding; the meeting ended with everyone fighting on the floor; the match should end at about 10 o'clock; the game ended in a draw*

endanger [ɪnˈdeɪndʒə] *verb* to put in danger; *pollution from the factory is endangering the fish in the lake*; **endangered species** = any species at risk of extinction; *the tiger is an endangered species*

endear [ɪnˈdɪə] *verb* **to endear someone to someone** = to make someone loved; *the old teacher endeared herself to generations of children*

endearing [ɪnˈdɪːrɪŋ] *adjective* which makes you like someone; *his endearing habit of bringing plants from his garden as presents*

endeavour *US* **endeavor** [ɪnˈdevə] **1** *noun* (*formal*) attempt; *all our endeavours to get the car to start were in vain; in spite of all his endeavours, he could not avoid bankruptcy; we expect staff to make every endeavour to reach the office on days when the public transport system is on strike* **2** *verb* (*formal*) to try hard; *he endeavoured to contact her by phone and fax*

endemic [enˈdemɪk] *adjective* **(a)** (plant or animal) that exists in a certain area; **endemic population** = group of organisms existing in a certain area; *the island's endemic population was devastated by the chance introduction of a pair of rats* **(b)** (pest or disease) which is very common in certain places; *this disease is endemic to Mediterranean countries*

ending ['endɪŋ] *noun* the way a story, film, etc., finishes; *I like films which have a happy ending*; *he told us so much of the story that we could guess the ending*

endless ['endləs] *adjective* with no apparent end; *the afternoon seemed endless, with one boring speech after another*; *we had an endless string of meetings with our suppliers*

endocrine gland ['endəkriːn 'glænd] *noun* gland which secretes hormones directly into the bloodstream

endorse [ɪn'dɔːs] *verb* (a) to show approval of; *I heartily endorse what has just been said*; *they asked us to endorse Mrs Martin as the local candidate* (b) to officially mark or sign the back of a document; **to endorse a cheque** = to sign a cheque on the back to show that you accept it; *the cashier asked him to endorse the cheque before depositing it*; *his driving licence was endorsed* = his licence was marked to show that he had committed a traffic offence

endorsement [ɪn'dɔːsmənt] *noun* (a) approval; *we received a letter inviting our endorsement of his application* (NOTE: no plural in this meaning) (b) note which endorses a driving licence

endow [ɪn'dau] *verb* (a) to give money which will provide a regular income for a school, hospital, etc.; *in her will, she left money to endow a new ward in the children's hospital* (b) **endowed with** = having certain qualities; *he is richly endowed with musical talent*; *she is not endowed with a sense of humour*

endowment [ɪn'daumənt] *noun* (a) giving of money to a charity, etc., to provide a regular income; *he made an endowment to the local animal sanctuary* (b) **endowment policy** = insurance policy where money is paid to the insured person on a certain date, or to his heirs

end product ['end 'prɒdʌkt] *noun* (a) manufactured product, made at the end of a production process; *after six months' trial production, the end product has still not reached an acceptable standard* (b) the result at the end of a process, discussion, etc.; *he works hard, but the end product isn't always satisfactory*

end result ['end rɪ'zʌlt] *noun* the result at the end of a process, discussion, etc.; *the end result of the meeting was a decision to demolish the school*

end up ['end 'ʌp] *verb* to finish; *we ended up with a bill for £10,000*; *after the movie we all ended up at my girlfriend's flat*; *they went to several clubs, and ended up getting arrested by the police in Trafalgar Square*

endurance [ɪn'djurəns] *noun* ability to suffer hardship; *it's a walk that will test the endurance of all but the very fit*

endurance test [ɪn'djurəns 'test] *noun* (a) test to see if a machine or person works well under difficult conditions; *they put the new car through a 1000-kilometre endurance test and it failed* (b) very long and difficult time; *sitting through the five-hour opera was something of an endurance test for the audience*

endure [ɪn'djuə] *verb* (a) to bear; *the prisoners had to endure great hardship*; *the pain was more than she could endure* (b) (*formal*) to last; *the memory of that day will endure for ever in my mind*

enduring [ɪn'djuəɪŋ] *adjective* which continues for a long time; *our enduring impression was of long white beaches and tall palm trees*; *the singing of the little children made an enduring impact on the journalists*; *the enduring appeal of some children's characters like 'Peter Rabbit'*

enemy ['enəmi] *noun* (a) person who hates you; *did your husband have many enemies?* (b) country or people fighting against you in a war; *they attacked enemy airfields with bombs*; *the enemy has or have advanced to three kilometres from the city* (NOTE: plural is **enemies,** but in meaning (b) **enemy** can take a singular or plural verb)

energetic [enə'dʒetɪk] *adjective* using force, lively; *at 82, my grandmother is still astonishingly energetic*; *she's an energetic campaigner for animal rights*

energize ['enədʒaɪz] *verb* to make someone more energetic; *teachers find it increasingly hard to energize students towards the end of the day*

energy ['enədʒi] *noun* (a) force or strength of a person; *he used up a lot of energy rushing around doing the Christmas shopping* (b) power which makes something work; *the use of atomic energy or nuclear energy to make electricity*; *we try to save energy by switching off the lights when the rooms are empty*; *if you reduce the room temperature to eighteen degrees, you will save energy*; *trolley-buses are an energy-efficient method of public transport*; **energy value** = number of calories which a certain amount of a substance, such as a certain food, contains; *a tin of beans has an energy value of 250 calories*

energy-saving ['enədʒɪ'seɪvɪŋ] *adjective* which saves energy; *the college is introducing energy-saving measures*

enforce [ɪn'fɔːs] *verb* to make sure a rule is obeyed; *the police are there to enforce the law*; *this is a regulation which is very difficult to enforce*

enforceable [ɪn'fɔːsəbl] *adjective* which can be enforced; *there's a rule stopping people from walking on the grass, but it is not easily enforceable*

enforcement [ɪn'fɔːsmənt] *noun* act of enforcing; *I must insist on the enforcement of the terms of the contract*; **law enforcement officers** = members of the police force, the drugs squad, etc.

enfranchise [ɪn'fræntʃaɪz] *verb* to give someone the right to vote in elections; *they are proposing to enfranchise immigrants who may not be nationals of the country*

engage [ɪn'geɪdʒ] *verb* (a) to employ a worker; *we have engaged a lawyer to represent us*; *the company has engaged twenty new salesmen* (b) to make parts of a machine fit into each other; *the gears aren't properly engaged*; **to engage a low gear** = to put your car into a low gear (c) **to be engaged in** = to be busy with; *the whole family was engaged in cleaning the car*; *the general is engaged in high-level talks*

engaged [ɪn'geɪdʒd] *adjective* (a) having officially stated your intention to marry; *she was engaged to Tom and then broke it off*; *John and Sue are engaged: they got engaged last week* (b) busy, occupied; *you can't speak to the manager - his line is engaged*; **engaged tone** = ringing sound on a telephone which shows that the line is busy

engagement [ɪn'geɪdʒmənt] *noun* (a) statement that you intend to get married; *my son has announced* his engagement to Pam; the engagement was announced in the paper; **engagement ring** = ring given by a man to a woman at their engagement **(b)** appointment; I have no engagements for the rest of the day; she noted the appointment in her engagements diary; I can't meet you tonight - I have a prior engagement **(c)** agreement to do something; **to break an engagement to do something** = not to do what you have legally agreed to do

engaging [ɪnˈgeɪdʒɪŋ] adjective charming; I liked him - I found him very engaging; she has an engaging smile

engender [ɪnˈdʒendə] verb (formal) to produce; his rise to power engendered feelings of envy among his brothers

engine [ˈendʒɪn] noun **(a)** machine which powers or drives something; the lift engine has broken down again - we shall just have to walk up to the 4th floor; early industrial equipment was powered by steam engines **(b)** vehicle which pulls a train; the engine broke down and the train was stuck in the tunnel

engine driver [ˈendʒɪn ˈdraɪvə] noun person who drives an engine that pulls a train; he always wanted to be an engine driver when he grew up (NOTE: American English is **engineer**)

engineer [endʒɪˈniːə] **1** noun **(a)** person who looks after technical equipment, especially engines; there are comparatively few women telephone engineers; the photocopier's broken down again - we'll have to call the engineer **(b)** person whose profession is designing mechanical, electrical or industrial equipment; **civil engineer** = person who specializes in the construction of roads, bridges, etc. **(c)** US person who drives an engine that pulls a train (NOTE: British English is **engine driver**) **2** verb to arrange something secretly; she engineered the dismissal of her husband's secretary

engineering [endʒɪˈnɪərɪŋ] noun science or study of the design of technical equipment; the college offers courses in electrical engineering; **civil engineering** = science of building, especially of roads, bridges, etc. (NOTE: no plural)

engine room [ˈendʒɪn ˈruːm] noun **(a)** part of a ship where the engines are; the Chief Engineer emerged from the heat of the engine room **(b)** part of a team or organization that does the most work; the midfield is the engine room of a football team

England [ˈɪŋlənd] noun country in the southern part of the island of Great Britain, the largest country in the United Kingdom; how long does it take to cross from England to France?; a lots of Scottish people live in England (NOTE: the word **England** is often used instead of Britain, and this is a mistake, as England is only one part of Great Britain; note also the capital: **London**; people: **the English**; language: **English**; currency: **pound sterling**)

English [ˈɪŋlɪʃ] **1** adjective **(a)** referring to England; the beautiful English countryside; is the English weather really as bad as it is made out to be?; I think she is English although she speaks with an Australian accent **(b)** **English breakfast** = cooked breakfast with bacon, eggs, sausages, etc.; compare CONTINENTAL BREAKFAST (NOTE: the word **English** is often used instead of British, and this is a mistake, as England is only one part of Great Britain; do not say **the English Prime Minister** but **the British Prime Minister**) **2** noun **(a)** language of the United Kingdom, the USA, Australia,

and many other countries; can she speak English?; what's the English for 'Autobahn'?; English is not my first language; we managed to make ourselves understood, even though no one in the hotel spoke English; several of her books have been translated into English **(b)** English language as a subject taught in school or university; she's good at maths but not so good at English; as well as teaching English, he also teaches drama; Mr Smith is our English teacher; she gives English lessons at home in the evenings; there are twenty students in my English class **(c)** **the English** = the people of England; the English on the whole are not a very emotional people

COMMENT: English is spoken as a first language by 415 million people worldwide, and by a further 800 million people as a second language. It was originally a Germanic language, derived from the language of the Angles and Saxons who invaded England in the 4th century AD. However, over the centuries it borrowed heavily from Latin, French and many other languages, and is nowadays a highly mixed language

Englishman, Englishwoman [ˈɪŋglɪʃmən or ˈɪŋglɪʃwumən] noun person from England; 'an Englishman's home is his castle'; a group of young Englishwomen were helping in the relief effort in Africa (NOTE: plural is **Englishmen, Englishwomen**)

engrave [ɪnˈgreɪv] verb to cut a pattern, a letter, etc., on to a hard surface; the name of the winning side is engraved on the silver cup; **to be engraved on your memory** = to be something that you will never forget; the scene at the accident is engraved on my memory = I will always remember the scene at the accident

engraving [ɪnˈgreɪvɪŋ] noun picture made by printing from a plate that has been engraved; he has a collection of old engravings of 18th Century London

engrossed [ɪnˈgrəust] adjective totally interested in something; she was so engrossed by her newspaper that she did not hear him come in

engrossing [ɪnˈgrəusɪŋ] adjective very interesting; I found the novel completely engrossing

engulf [ɪnˈgʌlf] verb **(a)** to swallow up; two villages were engulfed in mud **(b)** (formal) to overwhelm; she was engulfed by feelings of remorse

enhance [ɪnˈhɑːns] verb **(a)** to increase the beauty or value of something; her makeup enhanced the beauty of her dark brown eyes **(b)** to increase the value or power of something; slot in this new memory board to enhance your computer memory; he took steroids to enhance his performance as an athlete

enhancement [ɪnˈhɑːnsmənt] noun increase or improvement in quality, value, etc.; computerized enhancement of photographs provides us with extraordinary detail

enigma [ɪˈnɪgmə] noun mystery or puzzle; we are all trying to solve the enigma; he is an enigma, even to his friends

enigmatic [enɪgˈmætɪk] adjective difficult to explain, difficult to understand; he gave an enigmatic little smile and walked away

enjoy [ɪnˈdʒɔɪ] verb to take pleasure in something; have you enjoyed the holiday so far?; when he asked them if they had enjoyed the film they all answered 'no'; she didn't enjoy the boat trip because she felt seasick all the time; **to enjoy yourself** = to have a good time; *is everyone enjoying themselves?*; *we enjoyed ourselves so much that we're going to the same place for our holiday next year*

enjoyable [ɪnˈdʒɔɪəbl] *adjective* which pleases; *did you have a good holiday? - yes thank you, it was most enjoyable*; *we spent an enjoyable evening playing cards*

enjoyment [ɪnˈdʒɔɪmənt] *noun* pleasure; *the argument spoilt our enjoyment of the concert*; *the book gave me a lot of enjoyment*

enlarge [ɪnˈlɑːdʒ] *verb* (a) to make bigger; *we could enlarge the vegetable plot and grow more potatoes* (b) to make a bigger photograph; *I like this photo best: I'll get it enlarged* (c) to enlarge on *or* upon = to give details of; *even though we asked him twice, he refused to enlarge upon his meeting with the principal*

enlargement [ɪnˈlɑːdʒmənt] *noun* bigger photograph than the original; *I've ordered two enlargements of the photo of the baby*

enlarger [ɪnˈlɑːdʒə] *noun* equipment for enlarging photographs; *the enlarger won't make the photograph any clearer*

enlighten [ɪnˈlaɪtn] *verb* to enlighten someone on *or* about something = to make someone understand something; *will someone please enlighten me on what is happening?*

enlightened [ɪnˈlaɪtən] *adjective* without any prejudice; holding good ideas about people; *the council has an enlightened policy of employing as many disabled people as possible*

enlightenment [ɪnˈlaɪtənmənt] *noun* (a) knowledge, absence of ignorance; *in his search for enlightenment he visited the Buddhist monks of the Himalayas* (b) the Enlightenment = the 18th century in Europe, the period when people did scientific experiments, studied classical literature, planned democracy, etc.; *in France, the Enlightenment led to the revolution of 1789*

enlist [ɪnˈlɪst] *verb* (a) to join up voluntarily as a member of the armed forces; *he left school at 18 and enlisted as a soldier for five years* (b) to enlist someone's help = to get someone to help; *we enlisted our neighbour's help to cut down the tree*

enliven [ɪnˈlaɪvn] *verb* to make more lively; *the talk was enlivened by a number of slides and the introduction of a tame monkey*

en masse [ɒnˈmæs] *adverb* all together in a crowd; *the spectators moved en masse towards the exits*

enmity [ˈenmɪti] *noun* (formal) hatred towards someone; *there is a feeling of enmity between the two leaders* (NOTE: you experience enmity **towards** someone)

enormity [ɪˈnɔːmɪti] *noun* large size of something which is bad or wrong; *they only realized the enormity of the disaster some days after it happened*

enormous [ɪˈnɔːməs] *adjective* very large; *the ballroom is absolutely enormous*; *he ate an enormous lunch*

enormously [ɪˈnɔːməsli] *adverb* very much; *his refusal upset her enormously*; *we were enormously relieved to see her again*

enough [ɪˈnʌf] **1** *adjective* as much as is needed; *have you got enough money for your fare or to pay your fare?*; *there isn't enough light to take*

photographs **2** *pronoun* as much of something as is needed; *I had £20 in my purse to pay the taxi, but it wasn't enough*; *have you all had enough to eat?* **3** *adverb* as much as is needed; *this box isn't big enough for all these books*; *he doesn't work fast enough and so gets behind the others*

enquire [ɪnˈkwaɪə] **enquiry** [ɪnˈkwaɪri] *see* INQUIRE, INQUIRY; *see also* DIRECTORY ENQUIRIES

enrage [ɪnˈreɪdʒ] *verb* to make someone very angry; *he was enraged by the attitude of the council*; *as the noise got louder, so she got more and more enraged*

enrich [ɪnˈrɪtʃ] *verb* (a) to make richer; *he has no scruples about enriching himself at other people's expense* (b) to benefit, to make more fertile; *learning French has enriched his life*; *some crops, such as beans, enrich the soil*

enriched [ɪnˈrɪtʃt] *adjective* made richer; *bread enriched with vitamins or vitamin-enriched bread*; *enriched uranium is used in nuclear reactors*

enrichment [ɪnˈrɪtʃmənt] *noun* making richer; *he treated his job as head of the customs service solely as a means of personal enrichment*

enrol *US* **enroll** [ɪnˈrəul] *verb* to be admitted as a new member or new student; *she was enrolled as a member of the National Association of Dental Surgeons*; *he enrolled for a photography class* (NOTE: enrolling - enrolled)

enrolment *US* **enrollment** [ɪnˈrəulmənt] *noun* (a) action of admitting new members, new students; *enrolment starts next Saturday* (NOTE: no plural in this meaning) (b) number of students who have enrolled; *student enrolments have increased enormously over the past three years*

en route [ˈɒn ˈruːt] *adverb* see ROUTE

ensemble [ɒnˈsɒmbl] *noun* (a) small group of musicians or singers; *a jazz ensemble*; *an ensemble played music by Mozart* (b) set of women's clothes which match; *she lost the hat that went with her ensemble and couldn't find another one to match* (c) group of things which go together to form a whole; *the whole ensemble of church, cottages and pub looks just like a postcard*

enshrine [ɪnˈʃraɪn] *verb* to make something a legal right that cannot be taken away; *freedom of speech is enshrined in the constitution*

ensign [ˈensaɪn] *noun* (a) national flag used by a ship (b) *US* junior naval officer; *this was the young ensign's first sea-going appointment*

COMMENT: ships of the British Royal Navy fly a flag called the white ensign, which is white overall with large red cross and a small Union Jack in the top left-hand corner. Ships of the British merchant navy fly a flag called the red ensign, which is red overall, with a small Union Jack in the top left-hand corner

ensue [ɪnˈsjuː] *verb* (formal) to follow; *after the end of the match, there ensued a fight between rival groups of fans*; to ensue from = to happen as a result of; *several important developments will ensue from the committee's decision*

ensuing [ɪnˈsjuːɪŋ] *adjective* which follows; *the explosion and the ensuing fire*

en-suite ['ɒn 'swiːt] *adjective & adverb* attached; *bedroom with an en-suite shower room*

ensure [ɪn'ʃʊə] *verb* to make sure of; *when taking a shower, please ensure that the shower curtain is inside the bath* (NOTE: do not confuse with **insure**)

entail [ɪn'teɪl] *verb* to involve, to need; *itemizing the sales figures will entail about ten days' work*; *the job will entail going to work in Paris*

entangle [ɪn'tæŋgl] *verb* **(a)** to be catch or tie up in; *her dress became entangled in the machinery*; *the propeller was entangled in seaweed* **(b)** to be caught in a difficult situation from which it is difficult to escape; *he became emotionally entangled with his secretary*; *the country is in danger of getting entangled in the war*

entanglement [ɪn'tæŋglmənt] *noun* **(a)** difficult situation where you are emotionally entangled; *her entanglement with the headmaster affected her career* **(b)** argument, fight; *the group has had several entanglements with the police* **(c)** barbed wire **entanglements** = defences made of coils of barbed wire attached to posts

enter ['entə] **1** *verb* **(a)** to go in, to come in; *he took off his hat as he entered the church*; *did they stamp your passport when you entered the country?* **(b)** to write something in a record; *to enter a name on a list* **(c)** to enter for something = to decide to take part in a race or competition; *she has entered for the 2000 metres* **(d)** to type information on a keyboard, and put it into a computer system; *we will just enter your name and address on the computer* **(e)** to enter into = to begin; *to enter into negotiations with a company*; *to enter into an agreement or a contract; see also* ENTRANCE, ENTRY **2** *noun* key on a keyboard which you press when you have finished keying something, or when you want to start a new line; *to change directory, type CD\ and press enter*

enterprise ['entəpraɪz] *noun* **(a)** business venture, especially something that involves some risk; *his latest enterprise is importing carpets from Turkey* **(b)** method of organizing business; *the state should not interfere with free enterprise*; **private enterprise** = all businesses which are not state-owned **(c)** commercial firm, business organization; *they have merged with another huge industrial enterprise*; **a small-scale enterprise** = a small business; **a state enterprise** = a state-controlled company

enterprising ['entəpraɪzɪŋ] *adjective* using initiative; *an enterprising gardener who makes his own compost*; *an enterprising scheme to get young people into work*

entertain [entə'teɪn] *verb* **(a)** to amuse; *he entertained us with stories of his life in the army*; *we hired a clown to entertain the children*; *the tourists were entertained by the local dance troupe* **(b)** to offer meals, accommodation, a visit to the theatre, etc., to a visitor; *they're entertaining some Swedish friends this evening* **(c)** *(formal)* to be ready to consider a proposal; *they said they would entertain any suggestions we might like to make*

entertainer [entə'teɪnə] *noun* person who entertains; *my brother hired an entertainer for his daughter's birthday party*

entertaining [entə'teɪnɪŋ] *adjective* amusing; *he gave a very entertaining talk about his life in Lebanon*

entertainment [entə'teɪnmənt] *noun* **(a)** amusement; *she sang for their entertainment*; *there's not much entertainment in the village - the nearest cinema is 25km away* **(b)** hospitality; *the entertainment of the visiting managing director and his wife cost us a fortune*; **entertainment allowance** = allowance given to a businessman for entertaining guests

enthral *US* **enthrall** [ɪn'θrɔːl] *verb* to keep someone's attention; *his stories of life on a desert island enthralled his audience*; *we were enthralled to hear of her adventures on holiday* (NOTE: **enthralling - enthralled**)

enthralling [ɪn'θrɔːlɪŋ] *adjective* extremely interesting; *we went to an enthralling lecture on global warming*

enthuse [ɪn'θjuːz] *verb (informal)* **to enthuse about** *or* **over something** = to show great interest in something; *he spent the evening enthusing over his new car*; *she came away from the meeting enthused by the speaker's vision of the future*

enthusiasm [ɪn'θjuːziæzəm] *noun* great interest and liking; *we succeeded thanks to the enthusiasm and hard work of a small group of members*; *she showed a lot of enthusiasm for our new project*

enthusiast [ɪn'θjuːziæst] *noun* person who shows great interest in something; *he's a great opera enthusiast*

enthusiastic [ɪnθjuːzi'æstɪk] *adjective* showing great interest and approval; *the editor was very enthusiastic about my book*; *there were enthusiastic cheers at the end of the performance*

enthusiastically [ɪnθjuːzi'æstɪkli] *adverb* with enthusiasm; *at the end of the concert everyone clapped enthusiastically*

entice [ɪn'taɪs] *verb* to attract or to tempt; *they tried to entice her into signing the document*; *the children were enticed into the car with sweets*

enticing [ɪn'taɪsɪŋ] *adjective* which attracts or tempts; *she received several very enticing offers of jobs in the City*

entire [ɪn'taɪə] *adjective* whole; *we spent the entire day gardening*; *the entire cast came on the stage and bowed to the audience*

entirely [ɪn'taɪəli] *adverb* completely; *I agree with you entirely*; *this is an entirely separate problem*

entirety [ɪn'taɪərəti] *noun* full amount; *is this the entirety of the work you've done this week?*; **in its entirety** = completely; *he read the book in its entirety*

entitle [ɪn'taɪtl] *verb* **(a)** to give the right to; *I am entitled to five weeks' holiday a year* **(b)** to give a title to; *Tolstoy wrote a book entitled 'War and Peace'*

entitlement [ɪn'taɪtlmənt] *noun* right to have something; *when he left the company he lost his entitlement to a share of the profits*; **holiday entitlement** = number of days' paid holiday which you have the right to take; *she has not used up all her holiday entitlement*; *the job carries five weeks' holiday entitlement*; **pension entitlement** = amount of pension which you have the right to receive when you retire

entity ['entɪti] *noun* thing which exists as a separate unit; *the college operates as a separate entity*

entomology [entə'mɒlədʒi] *noun* the study of insects

entourage [ɒntuːˈrɑːʒ] *noun* group of people, secretaries, assistants, advisers, etc., surrounding an important person; *the President's entourage trailed along behind him*

entrails [ˈentreɪlz] *noun* intestines of animals; *Romans used to foretell the future by examining the entrails of animals killed as sacrifices*; *she didn't like to go to the local meat market because of the entrails hanging up for sale*

entrance 1 [ˈentrəns] *noun* **(a)** door for going in; *she was sitting at the entrance to the museum*; *we will meet at the Oxford Street entrance of Selfridges*; **back entrance** = back doorway; **main entrance** = main doorway; *the taxi will drop you at the main entrance* **(b) entrance (charge)** *or* **entrance fee** = money which you have to pay to go in; *entrance is £1.50 for adults and £1 for children* **2** [ɪnˈtrɑːns] *verb* to make someone very happy; *the audience was entranced by his singing*

entrancing [ɪnˈtrɑːnsɪŋ] *adjective* which makes you very happy; *she played an entrancing little piano piece by Mozart*

entrant [ˈentrənt] *noun* person who enters for a race or a competition; *there are over a thousand entrants for the race*

entreat [ɪnˈtriːt] *verb (formal)* to ask; *he entreated her not to do it*

entrée [ˈɒntreɪ] *noun* **(a)** main dish in a meal; *you have the choice of three starters and four entrées* **(b)** *(formal)* right to go in; *becoming director of the National Theatre gave him the entrée to the highest artistic circles*

entrench [ɪnˈtrenʃ] *verb* **(a)** to **entrench yourself** = to establish yourself very firmly; *she rapidly entrenched herself as the key figure in the sales department* **(b)** *(of soldiers)* to dig trenches as a protection; *the enemy forces are entrenched on the top of the hill*

entrenched [ɪnˈtrenʃt] *adjective* **firmly entrenched** = firmly established; *it takes time to change firmly entrenched attitudes*

entrepreneur [ɒntrəprəˈnɜː] *noun* person who directs a company and takes risks commercially; *the conference attracted several young entrepreneurs*

entrepreneurial [ɒntrəprəˈnɜːriəl] *adjective* taking risks in business; *the company tries to encourage an entrepreneurial spirit among its managers*

entrust [ɪnˈtrʌst] *verb* to **entrust something to someone** *or* to **entrust someone with something** = to give someone the responsibility for looking after something; *she entrusted the care of her children to her brother*; *he was entrusted with the keys to the office safe*; *why did she entrust him with all her money?*

entry [ˈentri] *noun* **(a)** going in; *the sign on the door said 'no entry'*; **entry charge** *or* **entry fee** = price to be paid before going into an exhibition, etc.; *the entry charge is £5* (NOTE: no plural in this sense) **(b)** written information in a reference book, an accounts ledger or computer system; *she looked up the entry on 'roses' in the gardening encyclopaedia*; to **make an entry in something** = to write details in a book; *the police looked at the entries in the hotel's register* (NOTE: plural is **entries**)

entryphone [ˈentrifəun] *noun* telephone or intercom at the entrance of a house, block of flats, etc., through which visitors speak to someone inside before entering; *I didn't recognize her voice over the entryphone*; *he pressed the buzzer and spoke to the flat's owner via the entryphone*

E number [ˈiː ˈnʌmbə] *noun* classification number for food additives, used in the EU; *E numbers must be printed on food labels*

enumerate [ɪˈnjuːməreɪt] *verb (formal)* to make a list of things one after another; *the inspector started to enumerate all the defects in the car*; *can you enumerate the essential requirements for the job?*

enumeration [ɪnjuːməˈreɪʃn] *noun (formal)* listing things one after another; *he ended his speech with an enumeration of the benefits that the new regime would bring to the country*

enunciate [ɪˈnʌnsɪeɪt] *verb* to pronounce words clearly; *when giving your name and address over the phone, remember to enunciate each word as clearly as possible*

enunciation [ɪnʌnsɪˈeɪʃn] *noun* clear pronunciation; *she has a beautifully clear enunciation*

envelop [ɪnˈveləp] *verb* to cover, to surround with a covering; *the castle was enveloped in fog*; *the whole scandal is enveloped in mystery*

envelope [ˈenvələup] *noun* folded paper cover for sending letters; *she wrote the address on the envelope and sealed it*; *the shopkeeper wrote down all the information on the back of an envelope*; **airmail envelope** = very light envelope for airmail letters; **a stamped addressed envelope (s.a.e.)** = an envelope with your own address written on it and a stamp stuck on it to pay for return postage; *please send a stamped addressed envelope for further details and our latest catalogue*

enviable [ˈenviəbl] *adjective* which one can envy; *they have the enviable record of not having lost any of their last fourteen matches*; *expatriates have an enviable lifestyle living tax free in the Far East*

envious [ˈenviəs] *adjective* feeling or showing envy; *we're all envious of his new car*; *he gave the yacht an envious look*

environment [ɪnˈvaɪərənmənt] *noun* **(a)** surroundings in which any organism lives, but especially where people live; *the environment in the office is not good for concentrated work*; **the working environment** = the general surroundings in which a person works **(b)** the earth, its natural features and resources, seen as the place where man exists; *they are trying to protect the environment*; **environment protection** = act of protecting the environment against pollution

environmental [ɪnvaɪərənˈmentl] *adjective* referring to the environment; *measures taken to protect against environmental pollution*; *she's joined an environmental group*; **Environmental Health Officer (EHO)** = official of a local authority who examines the environment and tests for air pollution, etc.

environmentalist [ɪnvaɪərənˈmentlɪst] *noun* person who is concerned with protecting the environment; *a group of environmentalists is trying to prevent the trees being cut down*

environs [ɪnˈvaɪərənz] *noun (formal)* area around a place; *a guidebook to Bath and its environs* (NOTE: the word is plural)

envisage [ɪnˈvɪzɪdʒ] *verb (formal)* to imagine something in your mind which could possibly happen in the future; *do you envisage any changes to the design of the car?*; *she could envisage herself as a top model, earning thousands of pounds*; *I envisage a situation where the whole workforce will use computers*

envision [ɪnˈvɪʒn] *verb US see* ENVISAGE

envoy [ˈenvɔɪ] *noun* person sent officially by a country to another; *the United Nations envoy in the area*

envy [ˈenvi] **1** *noun* feeling that you would like to have something which someone else has; *her beautiful long blond hair filled us all with envy* **2** *verb* to feel you would like to be someone else; *I don't envy him with a job like the one he has*; **to envy someone something** = to want to have something which someone else has; *we all envy him his new car*

enzyme [ˈenzaɪm] *noun* protein produced by living cells which makes other substances change, as when digestion takes place; *enzymes are needed to digest food*; *cystic fibrosis runs in families but is not a common disease and can be controlled by vitamins and enzymes*

epaulette *US* **epaulet** [ˈepəlet] *noun* decorative strip on the shoulder of a soldier's uniform; *he looked very dashing in his red coat and gold epaulettes*

ephemera [ɪˈfiːmərə] *noun* things which do not exist for a long time, which people collect; *he collects old tickets, timetables and other train ephemera* (NOTE: the word is plural)

ephemeral [ɪˈfiːmərəl] *adjective* which does not last long; *it was an ephemeral style, popular for a short time in the 1980s*

epic [ˈepɪk] **1** *noun* long poem or film, especially about war; *there's an old Hollywood epic on TV this afternoon*; *the reading was an extract from Homer's epic, the 'Iliad'* **2** *adjective* long and difficult; *his epic struggle against the local planning authority*

epicentre [ˈepɪsentə] *noun* point on the earth's surface above the centre of an earthquake; *the epicentre was 100km south of San Francisco*

epicure [ˈepɪkjʊə] *noun (formal)* person who is fond of, and knows a lot about, food and drink; *he is something of an epicure, he only drinks the most expensive wines*

epidemic [epɪˈdemɪk] *noun* infectious disease which spreads quickly through a large number of people; *the authorities are taking steps to prevent an epidemic of cholera or a cholera epidemic*; *the disease rapidly reached epidemic proportions*

epiglottis [epɪˈglɒtɪs] *noun* cartilage at the back of the throat which moves to block the windpipe when food is swallowed, so that the food goes down the throat, not the windpipe

epilepsy [ˈepɪlepsi] *noun* disorder of the nervous system in which there are convulsions and loss of consciousness; *an epilepsy patient*; *in adults, convulsions are often associated with epilepsy*

epileptic [epɪˈleptɪk] **1** *adjective* referring to epilepsy; *he had an epileptic fit* **2** *noun* person who has epilepsy; *the clinic specializes in the treatment of epileptics*

epilogue *US* **epilog** [ˈepɪlɒg] *noun* short text at the end of a long book, play, etc.; *the epilogue tells what happens to Mr Pickwick and Sam Weller in later life; compare* PROLOGUE

episode [ˈepɪsəʊd] *noun* **(a)** short section of a longer story, one part of a TV series; *do you remember the episode where the ghost appears?*; *the hero's father returns in the third episode* **(b)** short period of your life; *it's an episode in his marriage which he would rather forget*

episodic [epɪˈsɒdɪk] *adjective* which is described in episodes; *an episodic novel of life in the 18th century*

epistle [ɪˈpɪsl] *noun* **(a)** *(formal)* long letter; *I received an epistle from the bank manager* **(b)** **Epistles** = book of the New Testament in the Bible, formed of letters written by Apostles; *the Epistle of St Paul to the Corinthians*

epitaph [ˈepɪtɑːf] *noun* words written on a gravestone; *his epitaph says that he was a loving husband and generous to the poor*

epithet [ˈepːθet] *noun* phrase used to describe a person, such as Ivan the Terrible

epitome [ɪˈpɪtəmi] *noun* person who shows a particular quality very strongly; *she was the epitome of grace as she glided across the ice*

epitomize [ɪˈpɪtəmaɪz] *verb* to show a quality very strongly; *the conviction of two MPs for taking bribes epitomizes the corruption at the heart of this government*

epoch [ˈiːpɒk] *noun* major period of time; *the 1980s and 90s have been one of the most important epochs in European history*

epoch-making [ˈiːpɒkmeɪkɪŋ] *adjective* very important from a historical point of view; *the epoch-making invention of printing*

eponymous [ɪˈpɒnɪməs] *adjective* who has given his or her name to; *Mr Crumstraker, the eponymous owner of Crumstraker's Stores*; *Jane Eyre, the eponymous heroine of the novel*

epoxy resin [ɪˈpɒksiˈrezɪn] *noun* strong synthetic substance, used especially to make glue

equable [ˈekwəbl] *adjective (formal)* calm, not easily worried; *the teacher was astonishingly equable considering she was surrounded by screaming children*

equal [ˈiːkwəl] **1** *adjective* with exactly the same amount as; *his share is equal to mine*; *male and female workers must have equal pay*; *the two sticks are of equal length or are equal in length*; **all things being equal** = assuming nothing else has changed; *all things being equal, I'd prefer to go on holiday in June* **2** *verb* **(a)** to be exactly the same as; *his time for the 100 metres equals the existing record* **(b)** to give a result; *two plus two equals four*; *ten take away four equals six* (NOTE: **equalling - equalled** but American spelling is **equaling - equaled**) **3** *noun* person who is on the same level as someone else; *I don't consider him your equal*; *we're all equals here*

COMMENT: many business and organizations in the UK and USA operate a policy of **equal opportunities**, that is, they employ people on their merits and treat them with equal respect, regardless of age, race, sex, disability, etc. Compare **equality of opportunity**

equality [ɪˈkwɒlɪti] *noun* situation where you are equal; *policies to ensure equality in the workplace*; **equality of opportunity** = situation where everyone, regardless of sex, race, class, etc., has the same opportunity to get a job; *our education policy is designed to promote equality of opportunity* (NOTE: no plural)

equalize [ˈiːkwəlaɪz] *verb* **(a)** *(in a game)* to make a score equal; *they equalized just before half-time* **(b)** to make equal; *we are trying to equalize the availability of medical supplies throughout the region*

equalizer [ˈiːkwəlaɪzə] *noun* goal, etc., which makes the score equal; *he scored the equalizer with a minute still to play*

equally [ˈiːkwəli] *adverb* in exactly the same way; *they are all equally guilty*; *here men and women are paid equally badly*; *they were both equally responsible for the mistake*

equals sign [ˈiːkwəlz ˈsaɪn] *noun* printed or written sign (=) showing that one thing is equal to another

equal to [ˈiːkwəl ˈtuː] *phrase* capable of doing a job; *we all hope the new president will be equal to the task of reforming the government*

equanimity [ekwəˈnɪmɪti] *noun* being calm, not getting flustered; *she took the whole affair with extraordinary equanimity* (NOTE: no plural)

equate [ɪˈkweɪt] *verb* to equate one thing with another = to see the two things as equal; *in his mind, he equates a high salary with a stressful life*

equation [ɪˈkweɪʒn] *noun* **(a)** mathematical or chemical formula showing that two parts are equal; *let me show you how this equation can be solved*; *he formulated the equation for converting mass to energy* **(b)** balancing of various factors in a situation; *making a profit is difficult enough, but when higher interest rates are brought into the equation it becomes impossible*

equator [ɪˈkweɪtə] *noun* imaginary line running round the circumference of the earth at an equal distance from the North and South Poles; *the area of rainforests lies around the Equator*; *Quito, the capital of Ecuador, lies very close to the Equator*

equatorial [ekwəˈtɔːriəl] *adjective* referring to the equator; *the equatorial rainforests of Africa*

equestrian [ɪˈkwestriən] **1** *adjective* referring to horse-riding; *the Olympic equestrian events have been postponed because of an outbreak of flu amongst the horses* **2** *noun* horse rider; *only experienced equestrians should attempt this highly demanding course*

equilateral [iːkwɪˈlætərəl] *adjective* with all sides the same length; *an equilateral triangle*

equilibrium [iːkwɪˈlɪbriəm] *noun* **(a)** state of being perfectly balanced; *the electromagnetic forces are in a state of equilibrium*; *we do not want to disturb the present state of political equilibrium in the region* **(b)** state of being calm; *during the argument, she struggled to retain her equilibrium*

equine [ˈekwaɪn] *adjective* referring to horses; *equine flu*

equinox [ˈiːkwɪnɒks] *noun* one of the two times in the year when the day and night are of equal length (NOTE: plural is **equinoxes**)

COMMENT: the two equinoxes are the spring or vernal equinox, which occurs about March 21st and the autumn equinox, about September 22nd

equip [ɪˈkwɪp] *verb* to equip someone *or* something with something = to provide someone *or* something with something; *the course will equip you with all the skills you need to practise scuba-diving*; *a holiday flat equipped with washing machine and dishwasher*; **well-equipped** = with all necessary equipment; *a well-equipped hospital*; *the hotel has a fully-equipped gymnasium* (NOTE: equipping - equipped)

equipment [ɪˈkwɪpmənt] *noun* all the tools, arms, machinery, etc., which are needed; *he brought all his camera equipment with him*; *do you really need all this fire-fighting equipment on a ship?* (NOTE: no plural: for one item say **a piece of equipment**)

equitable [ˈekwɪtəbl] *adjective* fair or just; *troops have been deployed to ensure equitable distribution of food supplies*

equitably [ˈekwɪtəbli] *adverb* in an equitable way; *the aid workers ensured the food was distributed equitably*

equity [ˈekwɪti] *noun* **(a)** fair system of justice; *she complained about the lack of equity in the company's pay structure*; **in equity** = being fair (NOTE: no plural in this meaning) **(b)** **equities** = ordinary shares; *the equities market has risen sharply during the last month*

equivalent [ɪˈkwɪvələnt] **1** *noun* thing which has the same value or the same strength as something else; *what is the American equivalent of the Chancellor of the Exchequer?*; *I gave him $2000 and he paid me the equivalent in French francs* **2** *adjective* having the same value or the same strength as something else; *two pints and a litre are roughly equivalent*; *she handed me the equivalent amount in Swiss francs*; **to be equivalent to** = to have the same value as, to be the same as; *a litre is roughly equivalent to two pints*

equivocal [ɪˈkwɪvəkəl] *adjective* ambiguous, which misleads on purpose; *he gave an equivocal reply to the judge's questions*

er [ɜː] *interjection* showing that you are hesitating; *what time are you, er, thinking of leaving?*

era [ˈiːrə] *noun* long period of history; *the Victorian era*

eradicate [ɪˈrædɪkeɪt] *verb* to wipe out or to remove completely; *all the errors have now been eradicated from the report*; *international action will be necessary to eradicate tuberculosis*

eradication [ɪrædɪˈkeɪʃn] *noun* *(formal)* complete removal; *the WHO's top priority is the eradication of tuberculosis* (NOTE: no plural)

erase [ɪˈreɪz] *verb* to rub out writing or to remove recorded material from a tape or data from a disk; *he erased the pencil marks with a rubber*; *I've erased your recording of the concert by mistake*

eraser [ɪˈreɪzə] *noun* US piece of rubber for removing writing in pencil (NOTE: British English is **rubber**); **ink eraser** = rubber which rubs out writing in ink

erect [ɪˈrekt] **1** *adjective* straight upright; *she held herself erect as she walked down the aisle* **2** *verb* to put up something vertical, such as a mast or a building; *they are planning to erect a monument to the princess*; *the* *civilians rushed to hide in hastily-erected bomb shelters*

erection [ɪ'rekʃn] *noun* **(a)** action of putting up; *the erection of the tent took about 5 minutes* (NOTE: no plural in this meaning) **(b)** state where the penis becomes stiff and swollen from sexual excitement

erode [ɪ'rəud] *verb* to wear away gradually; *the cliffs have been eroded by the sea*

erosion [ɪ'rəuʒn] *noun* act of wearing away; *erosion of rocks by the wind and sea*; *planting trees provides some protection against soil erosion* (NOTE: no plural)

erotic [ɪ'rɒtɪk] *adjective* strongly sexual; *she paints erotic pictures of naked men and women*

eroticism [ɪ'rɒtɪsɪzm] *noun* quality of being erotic; *the eroticism which is expressed in the movements of the dancers*

err [ɜː] *verb* to make a mistake, to be at fault; *she erred in her judgement of the situation*; **to err on the side of something** = to use more of something than is necessary, as a precaution; *she erred on the side of caution* = she was more cautious than she need have been

errand ['erənd] *noun* being sent out to buy something; *she sent him out on an errand*; **to run errands for someone** = to go to do shopping, take messages, etc., for someone; *the old lady asked him to run an errand for her*

erratic [ɪ'rætɪk] *adjective* irregular or wild; *his erratic behaviour made his neighbours suspicious*; *her driving was erratic and the police stopped her for a breath test*

erratically [ɪ'rætɪkli] *adverb* in a wild manner; *he was driving very erratically so the police stopped him*

erroneous [ɪ'rəuniəs] *adjective* wrong; *the data put into the computer was erroneous*

erroneously [ɪ'rəuniəsli] *adverb* by mistake; *when I was young I erroneously believed politicians were elected to serve the people*

error ['erə] *noun* mistake; *the waiter made an error in calculating the total*; *she must have made a typing error*; *there isn't a single error in the whole document*; *I must have made an error because the screen went blank*; **computer error** = mistake made by a computer; **in error** = by mistake; *the parcel was sent to our Edinburgh office in error*

erstwhile ['ɜːstwaɪl] *adjective (formal)* former; *he gave the police a list of his erstwhile travelling companions*

erudite ['erjudaɪt] *adjective (formal)* learned; *he wrote an erudite thesis on bees*; *this book is too erudite, we need something more popular*

erudition [erju:'dɪʃn] *noun (formal)* great learning

erupt [ɪ'rʌpt] *verb* **(a)** *(of volcano)* to throw out lava, ash, etc.; *the volcano last erupted in 1968* **(b)** to start to become violent suddenly; *a row erupted over the closure of the station walkway* **(c)** *(of person)* to become angry suddenly; *he listened to the discussion for a while and then erupted angrily*

eruption [ɪ'rʌpʃn] *noun* **(a)** *(of volcano)* throwing out of lava, ash, etc.; *several villages were destroyed in the volcanic eruption of 1978* **(b)** breaking through the skin, as in the appearance of spots on the face; *an eruption of pimples on his neck*

escalate ['eskəleɪt] *verb* **(a)** to get worse or more violent; *our financial problems have escalated*; *the conflict escalated into an all-out war* **(b)** to increase steadily; *prices escalated during the year*

escalation [eskə'leɪʃn] *noun* increase; *we want to avoid any escalation of violence*

escalator ['eskəleɪtə] *noun* moving staircase; *they played a game, trying to run down the up escalator*; *one of the escalators at Holborn station is being repaired*

escapade ['eskəpeɪd] *noun* exciting adventure; *the book tells the story of their escapades on the Mississippi*

escape [ɪ'skeɪp] **1** *noun* **(a)** action of getting away from prison or from an awkward situation; *there were three escapes from this jail last year*; *a weekend by the sea was a wonderful escape from the office*; **we had a narrow escape** = we were almost killed **(b)** ESCAPE **(key)** = key which stops what is happening on a computer and returns to the main program; *press the ESCAPE key to get back to the original screen* **2** *verb* to get away from prison or from an awkward situation; *he escaped from the prison by sawing through the bars*; *the police are looking for the escaped prisoners*; *a panther has escaped from the zoo and is roaming the countryside*

escapee [eskeɪ'piː] *noun* person or animal that has escaped

escapement [ɪ'skeɪpmənt] *noun* cogwheels and gears which regulate the mechanism of a watch or clock

escarpment [ɪ'skɑːpmənt] *noun* steep slope; *the fort is built at the stop of a steep escarpment overlooking the river*

eschew [es'tʃuː] *verb (formal)* to avoid; *he eschews tobacco and any form of alcohol*

escort 1 *noun* ['eskɔːt] person or group of people accompanying someone; *she wore red silk and her escort wore a kilt*; *the president had a police escort to the airport* **2** *verb* [es'kɔːt] to accompany someone; *the police escorted the group into the hotel*; *I was escorted around by our local MP*; *the liner entered harbour escorted by a flotilla of yachts*

escudo [es'kuːdəu] *noun* currency used in Portugal; *the book costs 250 escudos*

Eskimo ['eskɪməu] **1** *adjective* referring to the native people living in the north of Canada and Greenland; *he collects Eskimo carvings of whales and polar bears* **2** *noun* one of a native people living in the north of Canada and Greenland; *Eskimos hunt seals and polar bears* (NOTE: plural is **Eskimo** or **Eskimos**; note also that they are generally called by the name they use themselves: **the Inuit**)

esophagus [ə'sɒfəgəs] *noun* US *see* OESOPHAGUS

esoteric [isəu'terɪk] *adjective* understood by very few people because it is too difficult to understand; *the cult's esoteric belief that the day of judgement is June 23rd 2012*; *the details of Chaos Theory are too esoteric for most people*

especial [e'speʃl] *adjective (formal)* = SPECIAL

especially [ɪ'speʃəli] *adverb* particularly, very; *the case is especially heavy*; *do you want to go out? - not especially*

espionage ['espɪənaːʒ] *noun* spying; *the ambassador was accused of carrying out espionage activities near the naval base*; **industrial espionage** = spying on a rival company; *they claimed the cleaning firm had been engaged in industrial espionage* (NOTE: no plural)

espouse [es'pauz] *verb* (*formal*) to support a cause; *they espoused the cause of a united Germany*

espresso [es'presəu] *noun* strong black Italian coffee, served in very small cups; *two espressos please!*

essay ['eseɪ] *noun* piece of prose writing on a particular subject; *a collection of the philosopher's most famous essays*; *for our homework, we have to write an essay on pollution*

essence ['esəns] *noun* (a) pure extract taken from something; *custard flavoured with vanilla essence* (b) central part of an argument; *the essence of what she had to say was very clear* (NOTE: no plural in this meaning)

essential [ɪ'senʃl] **1** *adjective* which is very important or which you cannot do without; *the refugees are lacking essential winter clothing*; *you can survive without food for some time, but water is essential*; *it is essential that we get the delivery on time* **2** *noun* thing which is very important or which you cannot do without; *sun cream is an essential in the desert*; *we've got all the basic essentials - food, water and fuel*; **the bare essentials** = the absolute necessities of life

essentially [ɪ'senʃəli] *adverb* basically, for the most part; *my new job is essentially not so very different from my old one*; *although he's essentially a kind man, he does lose him temper sometimes*

establish [ɪ'stæblɪʃ] *verb* (a) to create, to set up; *the business was established in Scotland in 1823*; *we need to establish a good working relationship with our colleagues* (b) to show something to be true; *if only the police could establish where the car was parked that evening*; *it's difficult to establish what her reasons are for resigning*

established [ɪ'stæblɪʃt] *adjective* which has been shown to be true; *it is an established fact*

establishment [ɪ'stæblɪʃmənt] *noun* (a) creation, setting up; *she helped them with the establishment of the local drama society* (NOTE: no plural in this meaning) (b) business; organization; *it's an establishment which imports radios from China*; *he runs an important teaching establishment* (c) **the Establishment** = people who occupy influential positions in society or who are in authority; *they appointed several Establishment figures to the board of trustees of the museum*; *see also* GREAT AND THE GOOD (d) number of people working in a company; **to be on the establishment** = to be a full-time employee

estate [ɪ'steɪt] *noun* (a) large area of land belonging to one owner; *he owns a 250-acre estate in Norfolk*; **estate car** = large car with a flat space behind the seats where parcels or suitcases can be put through the rear tailgate (NOTE: American English for this is **station wagon**) (b) **real estate** = property (land or buildings); **estate agent** = person who sells houses, flats, land; **housing estate** *US* **housing project** = development of new flats, houses, etc.; **industrial estate** *or* **trading estate** = area of land near a town specially for factories and warehouses (c) property owned by a person at the time of death; *the solicitor announced the value of grandfather's estate*; **estate duty** = tax on property left by a dead person

esteem [ɪ'stiːm] (*formal*) **1** *noun* respect; *I want to assure you of my continuing esteem for your character and work*; *the staff seem to have very little esteem for the directors*; **to hold someone in (high) esteem** = to respect someone; *she is someone whose work we hold in the highest esteem* **2** *verb* to admire; *the accuracy of his work is something we have always highly esteemed*; *my esteemed colleague will now present our findings*

estimate 1 *noun* ['estɪmət] (a) calculation which shows the approximate amount of something, or its worth or cost; *I wasn't in when the man came to read the gas meter, so this bill is only an estimate*; *your estimate of two dozen visitors proved to be correct*; *can you give me an estimate of how much time was spent on the job?*; **rough estimate** = approximate calculation (b) price quoted by a supplier for work to be done; *three firms put in estimates for the job* (NOTE: often simply called a **quote**) **2** *verb* ['estɪmeɪt] (a) to calculate approximately the cost or worth, etc., of something; *I estimate that it will cost £100,000*; *he estimated costs at £50,000* (b) to calculate a price before supplying an item or doing a job; **to estimate for a job** = to state in writing the probable costs of carrying out a job

estimation [estɪ'meɪʃn] *noun* (*formal*) opinion or judgement; *in my estimation, she's the best saleswoman we have ever employed*; *he spoke out at the meeting, and as a result went up in everyone's estimation*

estranged ɪ'streɪnʒd] *adjective* no longer living with a husband or wife; *his estranged wife wrote to ask for more money*

estrogen ['estrədʒən] *US see* OESTROGEN

estuary ['estjuəri] *noun* part of a river where it meets the sea, composed of fresh and salt water; *the birds of the Thames estuary*; *watch out for the sandbank at the mouth of the estuary* (NOTE: plural is **estuaries**)

COMMENT: people in Britain sometimes nowadays talk about **Estuary English**, that is, English spoken with the accent of the counties round London along the estuary of the Thames. This accent is now spreading to other parts of the country, but it is not considered very attractive because some sounds, such as 't' or 'l' are not clearly pronounced: 'a bottle of milk' is pronounced something like [ə 'bɒu əv mɪwk]

---

et al. ['et'æl] and the others; *we'll have to invite John, Joe, Freddy et al., whether we like it or not*

etc. *or* **etcetera** [et'setərə] *Latin phrase meaning* and so on, and other things like this; *fruit such as oranges, bananas, etc.*

etch [etʃ] *verb* to engrave on metal with acid; *the name and date are etched on the plate*; **the scene at the accident is etched in my mind** = I can remember the scene at the accident very clearly

etching ['etʃɪŋ] *noun* (a) art of engraving on metal with acid; *he started with oil colours and has now taken up etching* (NOTE: no plural in this meaning) (b) picture made by printing from metal engraved with acid; *he has several etchings by Whistler*

eternal [ɪˈtɜːnəl] *adjective* everlasting; *she is searching for eternal happiness*; *his eternal complaints really annoy me*

eternally [ɪˈtɜːnəli] *adverb* **(a)** for ever; *I shall be eternally grateful to you* **(b)** *(informal)* all the time; *she's eternally wanting to go the loo*

eternity [ɪˈtɜːnɪti] *noun* never-ending period of time; *insects preserved in amber for all eternity*; *(informal)* **it will take an eternity** = it will take a very long time; *if you insist on correcting every mistake by hand it will take an eternity*; *it seemed to take an eternity for the ambulance to arrive* (NOTE: no plural)

ether [ˈiːθə] *noun (old)* colourless alcohol used formerly as an anaesthetic

ethereal [ɪˈθiːəriəl] *adjective* very light and unreal; *the faint sound of ethereal music came wafting through the trees*; *her ethereal beauty comes out well in her photographs*

ethical [eθɪkl] *adjective* morally right; *is it ethical for the paper to publish the private phone numbers of government ministers?*

ethics [ˈeθɪks] *noun* moral principles; *the ethics of genetic engineering*; *he doesn't care about the ethics of selling arms, provided he can make some money*

ethnic [ˈeθnɪk] *adjective* relating to race; *the census shows the ethnic makeup of the population*; **ethnic food** = food (such as Chinese, Indian, Caribbean food) from a particular country which is not European; **ethnic minority** = minority of the population which is of different racial origin to the majority

ethnic cleansing [ˈeθnɪk ˈklenzɪŋ] *noun* killing people, or removing people from an area, because they are of a different race or religion; *the UN has strongly condemned the ethnic cleansing being carried out in the country*

ethos [ˈiːθɒs] *noun (formal)* beliefs or characteristics, especially those of a group of people; *today's young people are no longer attracted to their parents' conservative ethos*

etiquette [ˈetɪket] *noun* correct way of behaving in society; *she teaches etiquette to young girls before they go into high society*; **professional etiquette** = the rules of behaviour in a profession; *passing the details of the client's will to his brother was a breach of professional etiquette* (NOTE: no plural)

etymological [etɪməˈlɒdʒɪkl] *adjective* referring to etymology; *he is working on an etymological study of plant names*

etymology [etɪˈmɒlədʒi] *noun* study of the ways in which words and their meanings have developed; *the etymology of the word 'bungalow' is curious: it comes from an Indian word meaning 'from Bengal'* (NOTE: plural is **etymologies**)

EU [ˈiːˈjuː] = EUROPEAN UNION; *EU ministers met today in Brussels*; *the USA is increasing its trade with the EU* (NOTE: formerly called the **European Community (EC)**)

eucalyptus [juːkəˈlɪptəs] *noun* Australian hardwood tree with strong-smelling resin; *eucalyptus oil is used in the treatment of colds*

Eucharist [ˈjuːkərɪst] *noun* Christian ceremony of taking bread and wine, in memory of Christ's last supper

eulogize [ˈjuːlədʒaɪz] *verb (formal)* to praise someone

eulogy [ˈjuːlədʒi] *noun (formal)* speech or writing praising someone, especially a speech given at a funeral; *who is going to give the eulogy at the memorial service?*

euphemism [ˈjuːfəmɪzm] *noun* word or phrase used in place of a more offensive or unpleasant word; *'to go to the bathroom' is a euphemism for 'to use the toilet'*

euphonious [juːˈfəʊniəs] *adjective (formal)* which sounds pleasant; *Welsh is a particularly euphonious language*

euphoria [juːˈfɔːriə] *noun* burst of extreme happiness; *euphoria swept through the crowd when their team scored a goal in the last seconds of the game* (NOTE: no plural)

euphoric [juːˈfɒrɪk] *adjective* very happy; *the crowd were in euphoric mood as they turned out to welcome the World Cup winners home*

euro [ˈjʊərəʊ] *noun* monetary unit of the EU; *many articles are priced in euros*; *what's the exchange rate for the euro?* (NOTE: written € before numbers: € 250: say: 'two hundred and fifty euros')

Euro- [ˈjʊərəʊ] *prefix* referring to Europe or the European Union

Eurocheque [ˈjʊərəʊtʃek] *noun* international European cheque which can be cashed in any European bank or used to pay a bill

Euroland [ˈjʊərəʊlænd] *noun* countries of the European Union which have the euro as their currency

Europe [ˈjʊərəp] *proper noun* **(a)** the continent of Europe, the part of the world to the west of Asia, from Russia to Ireland; *most of the countries of Western Europe are members of the EU*; *Poland is in eastern Europe, and Greece, Spain and Portugal are in southern Europe* **(b)** the same area, but not including the UK; *holidays in Europe are less popular than last year* **(c)** the European Union (including the UK); *Canadian exports to Europe have risen by 25%* **(d)** other EU countries but not including the UK; *UK exports to Europe have increased this year*

European [jʊərəˈpiːən] *adjective* referring to Europe; *they do business with several European countries*; *at home we always eat Asian food, not European*; **the European Parliament** = the parliament with members (MEPs) from each country of the EU

European Union (EU) [jʊərəˈpiːən ˈjuːnɪən] *noun* an organization which links several European countries together based on the four freedoms of movement: movement of goods, of capital, of people and of services (NOTE: was formerly called the **European Community** *or* **EC**)

Eurostar [ˈjʊərəʊstɑː] *noun* train service from England to France and Belgium, through the Channel Tunnel; *we took the 8.25 Eurostar to Paris*; *Eurostar is often used by businessmen who want to go to the centre of Brussels*

euthanasia [juːθəˈneɪziə] *noun* mercy killing, the killing of a sick person to put an end to his or her suffering; *euthanasia poses a difficult moral dilemma* (NOTE: no plural)

evacuate [ɪˈvækjʊeɪt] *verb* to make people, troops, etc., leave a dangerous place; *the office staff were evacuated by the fire service*

evacuation [ɪvækjuˈeɪʃn] *noun* removal of people from a dangerous place; *complete evacuation of the aircraft took 12 minutes; we have to practise evacuation drill every week*

evacuee [ɪvækjuˈiː] *noun* person who has been evacuated; *the evacuees were given temporary shelter in the church hall*

evade [ɪˈveɪd] *verb* to avoid or escape something; *the escaped prisoners tried to evade capture; he was trying to evade the press photographers;* **to evade tax** = to try illegally to avoid paying tax; *it is illegal to evade tax although we all try to avoid paying tax if we can*

evaluate [ɪˈvæljueɪt] *verb* (formal) to calculate the value of; *I'm trying to evaluate how useful our visit was; her performance in the classroom will be carefully evaluated*

evaluation [ɪvæljuˈeɪʃn] *noun* (formal) act of calculating a value; *I agreed with everything he said in his evaluation of the play; the inspectors will carry out a careful evaluation of the teacher's performance* (NOTE: no plural)

evanescent [ɪvəˈnesənt] *adjective* (formal) which disappears quickly; *evanescent rays of sunshine appeared through the clouds*

evangelical [iːvænˈdʒelɪkl] *adjective* referring to certain Protestant churches and their teaching of the Bible; *she is a member of an evangelical church*

evangelist [ɪˈvændʒəlɪst] *noun* (a) one of the four men who wrote the Gospels; *Matthew, Mark, Luke and John are the four evangelists* (b) preacher; *the American evangelist is coming to England as part of his world tour*

evaporate [ɪˈvæpəreɪt] *verb* (a) (of liquid) to be converted into vapour; *water gradually evaporates from the soil* (b) to disappear; *as soon as he saw the light at the end of the tunnel all his fears evaporated*

evaporated [ɪˈvæpəreɪtɪd] *adjective* **evaporated milk** = milk reduced by evaporation; *condensed milk is evaporated milk with added sugar*

evaporation [ɪvæpəˈreɪʃn] *noun* process of liquid turning into vapour; *a large percentage of tropical rainfall is lost through evaporation* (NOTE: no plural)

evasion [ɪˈveɪʒn] *noun* avoiding; *his answer was full of evasions and half-truths; the court regards his actions as an evasion of responsibility;* **tax evasion** = illegally trying not to pay tax; *tax evasion is illegal, as opposed to tax avoidance*

evasive [ɪˈveɪsɪv] *adjective* which tries to avoid; *as the child stepped out in front of him the driver took evasive action;* **to give evasive answers** = to try to avoid answering questions directly; *he never replied to the questions directly but always gave evasive answers*

evasively [ɪˈveɪsɪvli] *adjective* trying to avoid a direct answer; *he reacted evasively when asked a direct question about his involvement with her*

evasiveness [ɪˈveɪsɪvnəs] *noun* trying to avoid a direct answer; *his evasiveness gave the impression that he had something to hide* (NOTE: no plural)

eve [iːv] *noun* (a) the night or day before; *on the eve of the election the ministers prepared to celebrate;* **Christmas Eve** = 24th December; **New Year's Eve** = 31st December (b) a short time before; **on the eve of our departure** = just before we left

even [ˈiːvn] **1** *adjective* (a) flat, level; *the road has a smooth even surface* (b) which does not change; *they kept up an even pace for miles; the temperature is an even 28° all through the day* (c) **even numbers** = numbers which can be divided by 2; *on the right-hand side of the street all the houses have even numbers* (d) equal (in a competition); *at the end of the competition three teams were even with 96 points* (e) **to break even** = to make no profit, but no loss either; *the company is just breaking even* **2** *adverb* (showing surprise or making an expression stronger) *he doesn't like strawberries; even the cleverest businessmen can make mistakes; she's overweight, but her sister is even fatter;* **even now** = at this very moment; *even now, he won't admit he was wrong;* **even worse** = worse than before; *that film was bad, but this one is even worse*

◊ **even if** [ˈiːvn ˈɪf] *conjunction* it doesn't matter if; *we'll try and drive there, even if it's snowing*

◊ **even so** [ˈiːvn ˈsəʊ] *adverb* in spite of what has happened; *it was pouring with rain, but even so they decided to go ahead with the village fête*

◊ **even though** [ˈiːvn ˈðəʊ] *conjunction* although, in spite of the fact that; *he didn't take an umbrella, even though it was raining quite hard*

even-handed [ˈiːvn ˈhændɪd] *noun* without any bias; *we are aiming for an even-handed approach to the problem*

even-handedly [ˈiːvn ˈhændɪdli] *adverb* without any bias; *the court attempts to view each case even-handedly*

evening [ˈiːvnɪŋ] *noun* (a) late part of the day, when it is getting dark; *I saw her yesterday evening; the accident took place at 8.30 in the evening; we arrived in London at breakfast time, having left New York the previous evening; we always go to a restaurant on Sunday evenings; they took an evening flight to Madrid; the evening meal is served from 7.30 to 10.30;* **this evening** = today in the evening; *we'll all meet this evening after work* (b) **evening dress** = clothes worn at formal occasions in the evening*

even out [ˈiːvn ˈaʊt] *verb* to make something even or regular; *he tried to even out the payments over a period of twelve months*

evens [ˈiːvnz] *noun* equal chance that something will happen or will not happen (such as a horse winning a race); *the bookmakers are giving evens on the grey horse; compare* ODDS

event [ɪˈvent] *noun* (a) thing which happens; *the events leading up to the war* (b) **in the event** = as it happened; *in the event, the party went off very well;* **in any event** *or* **at all events** = whatever may happen; *I don't know exactly what happened - in any event it doesn't matter; even if he doesn't like the job, at all events he's very well paid* (c) sporting competition; *the last event was the 100 metres hurdles;* **field events** = jumping and throwing competitions; **track events** = running and hurdling races

even-tempered [ˈiːvn ˈtempəd] *adjective* calm, never becoming angry; *luckily he is very even-tempered, or there would be rows every day in the office*

eventful [ɪˈventfʊl] *adjective* (a) with a lot of events taking place; *we had a very eventful journey across India* (b) important; *an eventful decision*

eventual [ɪˈventjuəl] *adjective* in the end; *the eventual result could not have been predicted in the* *early stages*; *our eventual aim is to become the world leader in our field*

eventuality [ɪventjuˈælɪti] *noun* thing which might happen; *we must prepare for every eventuality* (NOTE: plural is **eventualities**)

eventually [ɪˈventjuəli] *adverb* in the end; *after weeks of hesitation he eventually decided to sell the cottage*

even up [ˈiːvn ˈʌp] *verb* to make something balanced; *we've invited three girls and six boys, so we must invite three more girls to even things up*

ever [ˈevə] *adverb* **(a)** *(used with negatives, questions)* at any time; *nothing ever happens here*; *did you ever meet my mother?*; *have you ever been to Germany?*; **hardly ever** = almost never; *I hardly ever go to the theatre* **(b)** *(for emphasis after comparatives)* *she is singing better than ever*; *he went on playing the trumpet louder than ever* **(c)** always; *ever the optimist, he suggested we try once again*; **ever since** *or* **ever since then** = from that time on; *she was knocked down by a car and ever since has been afraid to go out onto the main road* **(d)** *(informal)* **ever so** = extremely; *she's been ever so ill*; *I'm ever so grateful; see also* HOWEVER, WHATEVER, WHENEVER, WHEREVER, WHOEVER

◊ **for ever** [fə ˈevə] *phrase* **(a)** always; *I will love you for ever and ever*; *the good times have gone for ever* **(b)** *(exclamation to show support for a team)* *Scotland for ever!; see also* FOREVER

evergreen [ˈevəgriːn] **1** *adjective* **(a)** (plant) which keeps its leaves all winter; *we need an evergreen climber to cover that wall* **(b)** still popular and successful; *he sang some of the evergreen hits from his repertoire* **2** *noun* **(a)** tree which keeps its leaves all winter; *holly and other evergreens can be used as decorations in winter* (NOTE: trees that lose their leaves in autumn are called **deciduous**) **(b)** person, song, etc., that is still popular and successful; *'My Way', one of evergreens of Sinatra's repertoire*

everlasting [evəˈlɑːstɪŋ] *adjective* going on for ever; *the monks search for everlasting peace*; *I'm sick and tired of her everlasting complaints about the heating*

evermore [evəˈmɔː] *adverb* *(literary)* **for evermore** = for ever, always; *I will be yours for evermore*; *his name will live on for evermore*

every [ˈevri] *adjective* **(a)** each; *it rained every day during the holidays*; *we have a party every New Year's Day*; *every Wednesday, he goes for a swim in the local swimming pool*; *every house in the street has a garden* **(b)** *(showing regular periods of time)* **every two hours** = with a period of two hours in between; *the medicine is to be taken every four hours*; *have your car checked every 10,000 kilometres*; **every other day** = on one day, not on the next, but on the one after that (e.g. on Monday, Wednesday and Friday, etc.)

everybody *or* **everyone** [ˈevribɒdi *or* ˈevriwʌn] *pronoun* all people, or all people involved in a particular situation; *everyone has to die some day*; *if everybody is here, we can start*; *I sent a Christmas card to everybody at work*; *everyone must show their passport* (NOTE: **everybody** and **everyone** are followed by **they, their, themselves**, etc., but the verb stays singular: **is everybody enjoying themselves? not everybody likes pop music, do they?**)

everyday [ˈevriˈdeɪ] *adjective* ordinary or very common; *jeans are fine for everyday wear*; *it's an*

everyday occurrence at our office; compare EVERY DAY

everyone [ˈevriwʌn] *pronoun see* EVERYBODY

everyplace [ˈevripleɪs] *adverb* US everywhere, in all places; *we looked everyplace for that key*

everything [ˈevriθɪŋ] *pronoun* **(a)** all things; *did you bring everything you need?*; *the burglars stole everything of value*; *everything he says annoys me* **(b)** things in general; *everything was dark in the street*; *everything is under control*

everywhere [ˈevriweə] *adverb* in all places; *there were papers lying about everywhere*; *everywhere was white after the first snow fell*; *we've looked everywhere for the key and can't find it* (NOTE: American English is also **everyplace**)

evict [ɪˈvɪkt] *verb* to force someone, especially a tenant, to leave a property; *all the tenants were evicted by the new landlords*; *she was evicted from her council house*

eviction [ɪˈvɪkʃn] *noun* act of forcing someone, especially a tenant, to leave a property; *they are facing eviction for non-payment of rent*

evidence [ˈevɪdəns] *noun* **(a)** fact which indicate that something really exists or has happened; *the bloodstains on his coat were ample evidence of the crime*; *scientists are looking for evidence of life on Mars*; *there is no evidence that he was ever there*; **documentary evidence** = evidence in the form of documents **(b)** written or spoken report given by a witness at a trial; *the victim gave evidence in court this morning*; **to give evidence for someone** = to be a witness, and suggest that someone is not guilty; **to give evidence against someone** = to be a witness, and suggest that someone is guilty; **to turn State's evidence** *or* **Queen's evidence** = to give information against your fellow-criminals; *he hoped to get a reduced sentence by turning Queen's evidence* **(c)** **in evidence** = very visible; *her love of Italy was nowhere more in evidence than in her kitchen* (NOTE: no plural)

evident [ˈevɪdənt] *adjective* obvious; *his annoyance was evident in his tone of voice*; *her evident delight at Tom's arrival, it was quite evident that he didn't want to sign the agreement*

evidently [ˈevɪdəntli] *adverb* **(a)** obviously; *you evidently care more about the football team than me* **(b)** presumably; *evidently his mobile phone is switched off*

evil [ˈiːvl] **1** *adjective* very wicked; *she's an evil old woman*; *his evil intentions were evident as soon as he locked the door*; **evil spirit** = wicked devil which harms people **2** *noun* **(a)** great wickedness; *the struggle between the government and the rebels was seen as a fight between good and evil* (NOTE: no plural in this meaning) **(b)** bad thing; *we are committed to fighting social evils such as juvenile delinquency; see also* LESSER

evocative [ɪˈvɒkətɪv] *adjective* which calls up a sensation in the mind of the onlooker or reader; *the painting is evocative of cold November days in the country*

evoke [ɪˈvəʊk] *verb* to call up an image; *the smell of roses evoked scenes from my childhood in the country*

evolution [iːvəˈluːʃn] *noun* gradual development; *by a slow process of evolution, modern railway engines developed from Stephenson's 'Rocket'*; *the theory of*

evolution = theory, developed by Charles Darwin, that species evolve by a process of natural selection; *see also* SURVIVAL OF THE FITTEST

evolutionary [i:vəˈluːʃənri] *adjective* referring to evolution; *the problem with evolutionary change is that it takes time - revolution is quicker*

evolve [ɪˈvɒlv] *verb* (a) to work out gradually a scientific theory or a way of working; *the research team has evolved its own methods of testing* (b) to develop gradually; *modern dance evolved from classical ballet*; *birds originally evolved from reptiles*

ewe [juː] *noun* female sheep; *we brought the ewes and their lambs out of the snow into the barn* (NOTE: do not confuse with **yew, you**; the male sheep is a **ram**)

ex- [eks] **1** *prefix meaning* (a) former; who used to be; *my ex-boyfriend*; *an ex-policeman* (b) out of; **ex-factory price** = price for delivery direct from the factory **2** *noun* (*informal*) former boyfriend, girfriend, etc.; *how do you get on with your ex?*

exacerbate [ɪɡˈzæsəbeɪt] *verb* (*formal*) to make worse or more painful; *the cold damp weather will only exacerbate his chest condition*; *their annoyance was exacerbated by his refusal to speak to them*; *being rude to the strikers will only serve to exacerbate the situation*

exacerbation [ɪɡzæsəˈbeɪʃn] *noun* making worse; *the dispute is a further exacerbation of an already tense situation*

exact [ɪɡˈzækt] **1** *adjective* completely accurate, not differing at all from what is expected, what has been written, etc.; *what is the exact time of arrival?*; *could you repeat the exact words of the contract?*; *the salesgirl asked me if I had the exact sum, since the shop had no change* **2** *verb* (*formal*) to force someone to give something; *they stopped all the cars on the road and exacted payment from the drivers*

exacting [ɪɡˈzæktɪŋ] *adjective* which demands a lot of effort; *mountain climbing is a very exacting sport*; *I didn't realize how exacting their standards were until I started working for them*

exactly [ɪɡˈzæktli] *adverb* (a) not more, not less, not differing at all from the given amount; *that comes to exactly ten dollars and fifty cents*; *the time is exactly 16.24* (b) completely; *he looks exactly like his father* (c) (*used as an answer*) quite right, I agree; *it's a pity the buses don't run more frequently - exactly!*

◊ **not exactly** [ˈnɒt ɪɡˈzæktli] *phrase* (a) not really; *was it a disaster? - not exactly a disaster, but it didn't go very well*; *it's not exactly the colour I wanted* (b) not at all; *he's not exactly pleased at having to pay out so much money*

exaggerate [ɪɡˈzædʒəreɪt] *verb* to make things seem worse, better, bigger, etc., than they really are; *the wide black belt exaggerates her small waist*; *she exaggerated the importance of my contribution*

exaggerated [ɪɡˈzædʒəreɪtɪd] *adjective* bigger than normal; *he has a very exaggerated opinion of his value to the company*

exaggeration [ɪɡzædʒəˈreɪʃn] *noun* making things seem larger, worse, better; *it wouldn't be an exaggeration to describe his actions as heroic*; **without exaggeration** = quite truthfully; *it was, without any exaggeration, the most perfect summer's day*

exalt [ɪɡˈzɔːlt] *verb* (*formal*) (a) to praise someone excessively; *the letter exalted his qualities as leader* (b) (*literary*) to put someone in a high position; *Joseph was exalted above all his brothers*

exaltation [ɪɡzɒlˈteɪʃn] *noun* state of being very happy in your mind; *her feeling of exaltation as she came out of the interview*

exalted [ɪɡˈzɔːltɪd] *adjective* (a) in a high position in authority; *in his exalted position he should be able to afford a larger car* (b) very happy in your mind; *she came away from the religious meeting in an exalted frame of mind*

exam [ɪɡˈzæm] *noun see* EXAMINATION; *the exam was very difficult - half the students failed*; *she passed all her exams*

examination [ɪɡzæmɪˈneɪʃn] *noun* (a) inspection of something to if it works properly; *he had to have an X-ray examination*; *the examination of the car showed that its brakes were faulty*; **customs examination** = looking at goods or baggage by customs officials; **on examination** = when it was examined; *on further examination, the newspaper report was shown to be quite untrue* (b) written or spoken test; *the examination was very difficult - half the students failed*; *he did badly in his English examination*; *she came first in the final examination for the course* (NOTE: often shortened to **exam** in this meaning)

examine [ɪɡˈzæmɪn] *verb* (a) to inspect something to see if it is correct or healthy, that it works properly, etc.; *the doctor examined her throat*; *we will have to examine the shop's scales to see if they give correct weight*; *the customs officials wanted to examine the inside of the car*; *the water samples were examined in the laboratory* (b) to test a student; *they examined everyone in mathematics and computer skills*

examiner [ɪɡˈzæmɪnə] *noun* person who conducts a test; *a driving test examiner*; *after the test the examiner told her why she had failed*; *the examiners met to agree a system of marking*

example [ɪɡˈzɑːmpl] *noun* (a) something chosen to show something; *this is a good example of French architecture of the eleventh century*; **to set an example** = to do things yourself, so that other people can copy you; *he sets everyone a good example by getting into the office before 8 every morning*; *she sets everyone a bad example by talking for hours to her boyfriend on the phone*; **to make an example of someone** = to punish someone so that others will learn not to do what he did; *the magistrates made an example of him by sending him to prison for two weeks* (b) **for example** = as a typical case; *she is keen on getting her weight down - for example she's stopped eating bread*; *why don't we sell anything to Eastern Europe, to Poland for example?* (NOTE: **for example** can often be replaced by **e.g.**: *countries in Eastern Europe, e.g. Poland*)

exasperate [ɪɡˈzɑːspəreɪt] *verb* to make someone furious; *the constant noise of the machine exasperates me more than you can imagine*

exasperated [ɪɡˈzɑːspəreɪtɪd] *adjective* **exasperated at** *or* **with someone** *or* **something** = extremely annoyed with someone or something; *she was exasperated at getting the engaged tone all the time*; *they were exasperated with the waiter who kept bringing them the wrong dishes*

exasperating [ɪɡ'zɑːspəreɪtɪŋ] *adjective* very annoying; *it's exasperating that there is no train to Paris after 10 o'clock at night*

excavate ['ekskəveɪt] *verb* (a) to dig a hole in the ground; *in order to reinforce the foundations they had to excavate to a depth of 10m* (b) to carry out an archaeological investigation of (a place); *Howard Carter excavated the tomb of Tutankhamen*

excavation [ekskə'veɪʃn] *noun* hole or investigation made by archaeologists; *we went to see the excavations on the site of the old town hall; she's been working on an excavation somewhere in Sicily* (NOTE: often simply called a **dig**)

excavator ['ekskəveɪtə] *noun* machine for making holes in the ground; *bulldozers cleared the site of old buildings and then the excavators moved in*

exceed [ɪk'siːd] *verb* to go beyond; *the car was exceeding the speed limit; our expenses have exceeded our income for the first time; did the UN troops exceed their mandate?*

exceedingly [ɪk'siːdɪŋli] *adverb* very; *this is an exceedingly good wine*

excel [ɪk'sel] *verb* **to excel in** *or* **at something** = to be very good at something; *at school, she excelled in mathematics* (NOTE: **excelling - excelled**)

excellence ['eksələns] *noun* very good quality; *his restaurant is known for the excellence of its cheeses*

Excellency ['eksələnsi] *noun* (*formal*) (*used as a form of address to an ambassador*) *His Excellency, the French Ambassador* (NOTE: the plural **excellencies** is used to refer to several ambassadors, or to an ambassador and his wife: **Their Excellencies, Count and Countess Bismark**)

excellent ['eksələnt] *adjective* very good; *we had an excellent meal in a Chinese restaurant; her handwriting is excellent - it is much clearer than mine*

except [ɪk'sept] **1** *preposition* other than; *she's allowed to eat anything except milk products; everyone was sick on the boat, except (for) me; in Britain, VAT is levied on all goods except books, newspapers, food and children's clothes* (NOTE: do not confuse with **accept**) **2** *conjunction* other than, apart from; *he doesn't do anything except sit and watch football on the TV; everything went well, except that James was sick; everyone enjoyed the birthday party, except (that) there wasn't enough to eat*

exception [ɪk'sepʃn] *noun* (a) thing not included; *all the students failed, with one exception; are there any exceptions to the rule?* (b) **to take exception to** = to be annoyed by something; *he took exception to what she said*

exceptional [ɪk'sepʃənəl] *adjective* (a) outstanding, very good; *she's an exceptional athlete; his skill in debate is really exceptional* (b) being an exception; *in exceptional cases, the fee may be waived*

exceptionally [ɪk'sepʃənəli] *adverb* extremely; *she's an exceptionally gifted musician; it's been exceptionally fine weather for February; what an exceptionally ugly little baby!*

excerpt ['eksɜːpt] *noun* small part (of a larger piece of music or writing); *they played an except from a Mozart symphony; he read excerpts from his latest novel*

excess [ɪk'ses] **1** *noun* (a) too much of something; *he had an excess of alcohol in his bloodstream*; **in excess of** = more than; *quantities in excess of twenty-five kilos*; **to excess** = too much; *he drinks to excess* (NOTE: no plural in this meaning) (b) **excesses** = bad things that you have done; *on Monday mornings he always feels guilty about the weekend's excesses* **2** ['ekses] *adjective* too much, not needed; *the factory has excess capacity and may sell off some of its machines*; **excess baggage** = baggage which is heavier than the weight you are allowed to take free of charge onto a plane

excessive [ɪk'sesɪv] *adjective* more than is usual; *they queried the excessive cost of the wallpaper; I think 500 grams per person is excessive; excessive ultraviolet radiation can cause skin cancer*

excessively [ɪk'sesɪvli] *adverb* too much; *an excessively ornate pattern; he drinks excessively; she is excessively modest about her achievements*

exchange [ɪks'tʃeɪndʒ] **1** *noun* (a) giving one thing for another; *the exchange of rings during the wedding ceremony*; **part exchange** = giving an old product as part of the payment for a new one; *he took my old car in part exchange* (b) **foreign exchange** = changing money of different countries; **exchange rate** = rate at which one currency is exchanged for another; *the current rate of exchange is 9.60 francs to the pound* (c) **telephone exchange** = central telephone switchboard; **Stock Exchange** = place where stocks and shares are bought and sold; *he works on the London Stock Exchange* **2** *verb* (a) to give something and get something similar back; *during the meeting we exchanged ideas on new developments in international law; they exchanged addresses* = they each gave the other their address (b) **to exchange something for something else** = to give one thing and get another in return; *if the trousers are too small you can take them back and exchange them for a larger pair; goods can be exchanged only on production of the sales slip* (c) to change money of one country for money of another; *to exchange francs for pounds*

Exchequer [ɪks'tʃekə] *noun* GB **the Exchequer** = all money received by the government from taxes; **the Chancellor of the Exchequer** = the chief British finance minister

excise 1 *noun* ['eksaɪz]; **excise duty** = tax on certain goods produced in a country (such as cigarettes or alcohol); *they complained that the decision to increase the tariff on beer was contrary to the idea of converging EU excise rates* **2** *verb* [ɪk'saɪz] to cut out; *the surgeon decided to excise the growth*

excision [ɪk'sɪʒn] *noun* cutting out; *the surgeon carried out the excision of the tumour*

excitable [ɪk'saɪtəbl] *adjective* who gets excited easily; *he's a very excitable child and often has headaches*

excite [ɪk'saɪt] *verb* (a) to make someone lively and happy; *his speech excited the crowd* (b) to make someone have a particular feeling; *the thought of going to work in Kuala Lumpur excited his imagination; the case has excited a lot of interest in the press*

excited [ɪk'saɪtɪd] *adjective* lively and happy because you hope something will happen; *she's excited at or by the thought of going on holiday; the children are excited because it's the Christmas holidays; what's everyone excited about?; don't get too excited - not* *everyone wins the lottery; it was lovely to see the children's happy and excited faces*

excitement [ɪk'saɪtmənt] *noun* being excited; *what's all the excitement about?; the children are always in a state of excitement before the holidays*

exciting [ɪk'saɪtɪŋ] *adjective* which gives you a particular feeling; *I couldn't sleep after watching an exciting film on TV; the news about the house is really exciting*

exclaim [ɪk'skleɪm] *verb* to say something loudly and suddenly; *'here it is!' she exclaimed*

exclamation [eksklə'meɪʃn] *noun* action of shouting out; *she read the letter with an exclamation of delight;* **exclamation mark** = written sign (!) which shows surprise; *she was obviously excited, her letter was full of exclamation marks*

exclude [ɪk'skluːd] *verb* **(a)** not to include; *damage by fire is excluded from the policy; don't exclude his name from your list* **(b)** **to exclude something** *or* **someone from a place** = to shut something *or* someone out; *women are excluded from the monastery* **(c)** to send a child away from school; *ten children had to be excluded last term* (NOTE: also called **expel**)

excluding [ɪks'kluːdɪŋ] *preposition* not including; *there were only fifty people at the meeting, excluding the police guards*

exclusion [ɪk'skluːʒn] *noun* **(a)** act of shutting out; *she was hurt at her exclusion from the guest list;* **social exclusion** = shutting someone out of the rest of society; *the government has drawn up plans to prevent social exclusion* **(b)** act of being sent away from school; *the school only considers exclusion as a last resort; see also* EXCLUDE

exclusive [ɪk'skluːsɪv] *adjective* **(a)** select, not open to everyone; *an exclusive Caribbean holiday resort; the new health club is very exclusive* **(b)** **exclusive right** = right which belongs to one person or organization **(c)** **exclusive of** = not including; *the bill was exclusive of service;* **exclusive of tax** = not including tax

exclusively [ɪk'skluːsɪvli] *adverb* solely, only; *the car park is exclusively for the use of residents*

excrement ['ekskrəmənt] *noun (formal)* solid waste matter produced by the body; *the walls of the bedroom were smeared with excrement*

excreta [ɪk'skriːtə] *noun (formal)* faeces and urine, waste matter produced by the body; *everyone laughed at the monkeys playing with their own excreta* (NOTE: the word is plural)

excrete [ɪk'skriːt] *verb (formal)* to produce waste matter; *waste matter is excreted through an animal's anus*

excruciating [ɪk'skruːʃieɪtɪŋ] *adjective* extremely painful; *he had excruciating pains in his head*

excursion [ɪk'skɜːʃn] *noun* short pleasure trip; *we're planning an excursion to the seaside; the whole school went on an excursion to the zoo*

excuse 1 *noun* [ɪk'skjuːs] reason given for doing something wrong or not as expected; *his excuse for not coming was that he forgot the date* **2** *verb* [ɪk'skjuːz] to forgive someone for making a small mistake; *please excuse my arriving late like this*

excuse me [ɪk'skjuːz 'miː] **(a)** *(to attract someone's attention)* excuse me, is this the right bus for Oxford

Circus? **(b)** please forgive me; *excuse me for arriving so late; excuse me for interrupting, but could you repeat what you have just said?*

ex-directory number ['eksdaɪ'rektri 'nʌmbə] *noun* telephone number which is not listed in the telephone book directory; *she has an ex-directory number; the operator wouldn't give me his number because it's ex-directory*

execute ['eksɪkjuːt] *verb* **(a)** to carry out instructions, wishes; *press ENTER to execute the program; they did their best to execute his wishes* **(b)** to do; *as part of the test, drivers are asked to execute an emergency stop* **(c)** to kill someone who has been condemned to death; *murderers are no longer executed in this country*

execution [eksɪ'kjuːʃn] *noun* **(a)** carrying out of an order; *the execution of the order was more complicated than we imagined;* **to put a plan into execution** = to carry out a plan; *the new government wants its financial strategy to be put into execution as soon as possible* (NOTE: no plural in this meaning) **(b)** legal killing of person sentenced to death; *in the 19th century there were still public executions*

executioner [eksɪ'kjuːʃənə] *noun* public official who executes people; *the executioner stepped onto the scaffold, carrying a large axe*

executive [ɪg'zekjʊtɪv] **1** *adjective* which carries out plans and puts things into practice; *he has an executive position on the board of directors;* **executive committee** = committee which runs an organization **2** *noun* **(a)** businessman who makes decisions; *junior executives; middle-ranking executives; top executives;* **Chief Executive** = main director who runs a company **(b)** **the Executive** = the part of Government which runs the state (as opposed to the Judiciary which applies the law, and the Legislature which creates laws); *people are beginning to question the Executive's ability to govern*

executor [ɪg'zekjʊtə] *noun* person appointed in someone's will to make sure that the terms of the will are carried out; *he was named executor by his brother*

exemplary [ɪg'zempləri] *adjective* which serves as an example; *an exemplary performance*

exemplify [ɪg'zemplɪfaɪ] *verb* to show as an example, to be an example; *his lack of fitness is exemplified by his poor goal scoring record; the new library exemplifies modern British architecture at its best*

exempt [ɪg'zempt] **1** *adjective* not forced to obey tax, laws, etc.; **exempt from tax** *or* **tax-exempt** = not required to pay tax; *children's clothes are exempt from VAT; I pay for a medical prescription but pensioners are exempt* **2** *verb* **to exempt someone from something** *or* **from doing something** = to free someone from something; *pensioners are exempted from paying for medical prescriptions*

exemption [ɪg'zempʃn] *noun* act of exempting; **exemption from tax** *or* **tax exemption** = being free from having to pay tax; *you can claim tax exemption in this case*

exercise ['eksəsaɪz] **1** *noun* practice in using physical or mental powers; *she does her piano exercises every morning;* **exercise book** = book for writing out school work; **to take exercise** = to do physical things, like walking or jogging, to keep fit; *you should take some exercise every day if you want to lose weight; she ought to take more exercise* **2** *verb* **(a)** to use a power or right; *the United Kingdom exercised the* *right of veto* (b) to give an animal or person exercise; *she exercised her pony on the race track*; *do some sit-ups to exercise your stomach muscles*

exert [ɪgˈzɜːt] *verb* to use force, pressure, etc.; *in spite of exerting all his strength, he still could not move the rock*; *our group is trying to exert pressure on the council to make it change its decision*

exertion [ɪgˈzɜːʃn] *noun* effort; *we had to lie down in the shade after the exertion of climbing the hill to the church*; *too much exertion strained his heart*; *see also* OVEREXERTION

exhale [eksˈheɪl] *verb* (formal) to breathe out; *as she exhaled, her breath formed a cloud in the frosty air*

exhaust [ɪgˈzɔːst] **1** *noun* **(a)** exhaust (pipe) = the tube at the back of a motor vehicle from which gases produced by the engine are sent out into the air; *clouds of white smoke were coming out of the exhaust pipe*; *fumes from car exhausts pollute the atmosphere* (NOTE: American English is **tailpipe**) *US* gas which is produced by a car engine and is released into the air through the exhaust pipe; *we live downtown and the children are breathing car exhausts all day* **2** *verb* **(a)** to wear out; *the uphill climb had exhausted him* **(b)** to finish; *we've exhausted our supplies of food*

exhausted [ɪgˈzɔːstɪd] *adjective* **(a)** tired out; *I'm exhausted after that run*; *they staggered back home very late, mother, father and three exhausted children* **(b)** completely used up; *exhausted oxygen cylinders*

exhaustion [ɪgˈzɔːstʃn] *noun* state of being very tired; *he collapsed with exhaustion*; *after the match he suffered from heat exhaustion*

exhaustive [ɪgˈzɔːstɪv] *adjective* very thorough; *exhaustive inquiries produced no result*; *they carried out an exhaustive search of the records*

exhaustively [ɪgˈzɔːstɪvli] *adverb* thoroughly; *the police searched exhaustively through the documents without finding any reference to the illegal payment*

exhibit [ɪgˈzɪbɪt] **1** *noun* object displayed in court, at an exhibition, etc.; *Exhibit A is the murder weapon*; *the museum has loaned several exhibits to foreign galleries*; *the buyers admired the exhibits on our stand* **2** *verb* to display; *they are exhibiting at the Motor Show*; *they have rows of vases exhibited on the shelves of the shop*; *she is exhibiting three paintings in the local art show*

exhibition [eksɪˈbɪʃn] *noun* **(a)** display (of works of art, flowers, etc.); *the exhibition is open from 10 a.m. to 5 p.m.*; *opening time for the exhibition is 10 a.m.*; *we stood in line for half an hour waiting to get into the Picasso exhibition* **(b)** show of goods so that buyers can look at them and decide what to buy; *we have a stand at the Ideal Home Exhibition*; **exhibition room** *or* **hall** = place where goods are shown so that buyers can look at them and decide what to buy; **exhibition stand** separate section of an exhibition where a company exhibits its products or services (NOTE: American English is **fair booth**)

exhibitor [ɪgˈzɪbɪtə] *noun* person who displays something at an exhibition; *there are thousands of exhibitors at the Motor Show*

exhilarated [ɪgˈzɪləreɪtɪd] *adjective* extremely excited and happy; *I always feel exhilarated after diving into the cold waves*; *she was exhilarated by the news of her lottery win*

exhilarating [ɪgˈzɪləreɪtɪŋ] *adjective* which makes you full of energy; *an exhilarating walk along the cliff*

exhilaration [ɪgzɪləˈreɪʃn] *noun* extreme excitement and happiness; *she enjoys the exhilaration of racing at over 200 kilometres per hours*

exhort [ɪgˈzɔːt] *verb* (formal) **to exhort someone to do something =** to urge or to encourage someone to do something; *he exhorted his soldiers to stand firm*

exhumation [eksjuˈmeɪʃn] *noun* (formal) act of digging up a dead body from a grave; *the police have requested the exhumation of the body*

exhume [ɪgˈzjuːm] *verb* (formal) to dig up a dead body from a grave; *the police exhumed the three bodies and they are being tested for poison*

exile [ˈegzaɪl] **1** *noun* **(a)** state of being sent away from your home country; *the ex-president went into exile in Switzerland* (NOTE: no plural in this meaning) **(b)** person who is sent away from his own country; *the former king is now an exile in New York*; *the coup was mounted by exiles living across the border* **2** *verb* to send someone away from his home country as a punishment; *the new government exiled the former dictator to Europe*

exist [ɪgˈzɪst] *verb* **(a)** to be; *when I was a child, colour TV didn't exist*; *I don't believe the document exists - I think it has been burnt* **(b)** to live, to survive; *dinosaurs existed on earth for a very long time*; *they got lost in the jungle and managed to exist on berries and roots*

existence [ɪgˈzɪstəns] *noun* **(a)** life, being; *is there anything which proves the existence of life on Mars?*; *they lived a miserable existence in a little coal mining town* **(b)** in existence = which exists, which is actually here; *the original painting is no longer in existence*; *only one version of this car is still in existence in a museum in Geneva*

existent [ɪgˈzɪstənt] *adjective* which is in existence at this moment; *the existent law prevents this from happening*; *the original painting is no longer existent* (NOTE: the opposite is **nonexistent**)

existing [ɪgˈzɪstɪŋ] *adjective* actual, which is in operation at this moment; *can we modify the existing structure in some way?*; *existing regulations do not allow the sale of food in the street*

exit [ˈegzɪt] **1** *noun* **(a)** way out of a building, an aircraft, etc.; *the customers all rushed towards the exits when the fire alarm rang*; **No Exit! =** sign showing that you must not go out this way; **emergency exit** = door used in emergency; **fire exit** = door used in case of fire **(b)** to make your exit = to go out of a place, a room; *I apologized to my host and made my exit*; **exit visa** = visa allowing someone to leave a country **2** *verb* **(a)** to leave a computer system; *press this key to exit the software* **(b)** (informal) to leave; *he exited the room as fast as he could*

exodus [ˈeksədəs] *noun* departure of a crowd of people; *the Easter exodus to ski resorts*; *every Christmas there's a mass exodus to the countryside* (NOTE: no plural)

exonerate [ɪgˈzɒnəreɪt] *verb* to state that someone who was previously blamed for something was not responsible for it; *the official report completely exonerated the driver of the train*

exorbitant [ɪɡ'zɔːbɪtənt] *adjective* very high; *I don't want to pay the exorbitant prices they charge in that restaurant*

exorcism ['egzɔːsɪzm] *noun* forcing an evil spirit or a ghost to leave a place

exorcist ['egzɔːsɪst] *noun* person who drives away evil spirits or ghosts

exorcize ['eksɔːsaɪz] *verb* to say prayers to force evil spirits to leave someone's body or ghosts to leave a haunted house; *they thought she was possessed by evil spirits and called a priest to exorcize her*

exotic [ɪɡ'zɒtɪk] *adjective* unusual, referring to a strange, foreign, often tropical, place; *the silk robes of the dancers give the show an exotic air*; *spices make the meat taste more exotic*

expand [ɪk'spænd] *verb* **(a)** to make something increase in size; *we have had to expand our sales force* **(b)** to become larger; *water expands when it freezes*; *heat caused the metal rods to expand*; *his waistline is expanding fast*

expanse [ɪk'spæns] *noun* large surface covered by something; *the wide expanse of the cornfields of the Mid West*; *the brilliant blue expanse of the lake*; *he took off his T-shirt, revealing a large expanse of white belly*

expansion [ɪk'spænʃn] *noun* increase in size; *the heat of the fire caused the expansion of the metal rods*; *we are preparing for the company's forthcoming expansion into the North American market* (NOTE: no plural)

expansive [ɪk'spænsɪv] *adjective* **(a)** who wants to talk freely about things; *she was in a very expansive mood when she met the TV reporters*; *you would expect someone who works in public relations to be a bit more expansive than she is* **(b)** stretched out wide; *he waved his arms in an expansive gesture of greeting*

expatriate *noun* [ɪk'spætriət] person who is not living in his home country; *the tax implications for expatriates living in the Far East are rather complex*; *the expatriate community feels threatened by the new laws* (NOTE: often shortened to **expat: expats living in the Far East**)

expect [ɪk'spekt] *verb* **(a)** to think, to hope, to assume something is going to happen; *I expect you are tired after your long train journey*; *he expects me to do all the housework*; *I can't talk for long, we're expecting visitors*; *we expect him to arrive at any moment or he is expected at any moment*; *the weather proved to be even worse than (they) expected* **(b)** to be pregnant with; *my sister's expecting twins*

expectancy [ɪk'spektənsi] *noun* **(a)** life expectancy = number of years a person is likely to live; *since 1900 the life expectancy of women has risen by several years* **(b)** feeling that something exciting is going to happen; *there was an air of expectancy in the crowd as the procession approached* (NOTE: no plural)

expectant [ɪk'spektənt] *adjective* **(a)** expecting, hopeful; *as I moved towards the door my dog gave an expectant wag of his tail* **(b)** expectant mother = pregnant woman; *the waiting room of the antenatal clinic was full of expectant mothers*

expectation [ekspek'teɪʃn] *noun* hope, feeling that something will happen; *she lived up to all our expectations*; *we thought our team would do well, but in the end they exceeded all our expectations*

expected [ɪk'spektɪd] *adjective* which is thought will happen, or hoped will happen; *the expected tax cuts didn't take place*

expectorant [ɪk'spektərənt] *noun* medicine which helps you to cough and clear phlegm from the throat and lungs; *the chemist suggested she should take an expectorant*

expectorate [ɪk'spektəreɪt] *verb (formal)* to cough up phlegm from the throat and lungs; *he expectorated loudly and continued with his speech*

expedient [ɪk'spiːdiənt] **1** *noun* convenient way of doing something; *registering as a student was a simple expedient to avoid military service* **2** *adjective* convenient; *colleges find it expedient to have students from other countries because they pay higher fees than local students*

expedite ['ekspɪdaɪt] *verb (formal)* to make something happen faster; *we hope you will be able to expedite delivery of this order*

expedition [ekspɪ'dɪʃn] *noun* **(a)** journey to explore; *he set off on an expedition to the South Pole* **(b)** short trip; *they went on a shopping expedition in the West End*

expeditionary force [ekspɪ'dɪʃnəri 'fɔːs] *noun* army which travels to another country to fight; *they sent an expeditionary force to the area*

expel [ɪk'spel] *verb* **(a)** to throw someone out; *as soon as the generals came to power they expelled all their former allies* **(b)** to send a child away from school; *he was expelled for taking drugs*; *see also* EXPULSION (NOTE: **expelling - expelled**)

expend [ɪk'spend] *verb (formal)* to spend time, energy, etc.; *we seem to have expended a lot of time and energy for nothing*; *they expended all their savings on legal fees*

expendable [ɪk'spendəbl] *adjective (formal)* which is not worth keeping, which can be thrown away; *the booster rocket is expendable*

expenditure [ɪk'spendɪtʃə] *noun* amount of money spent; *the government's heavy expenditure on arms*; *the group objects to the expenditure of public funds on this project* (NOTE: no plural in British English, but American English often uses **expenditures**)

expense [ɪk'spens] *noun* **(a)** amount of money or cost; *I can't afford the expense of a holiday just now*; *the expense of running a household seems to increase every week*; *he furnished the office regardless of expense* = without thinking how much it cost; **expense account** = money which an employee is allowed to spend on personal expenses and entertaining guests, which will be paid for by his or her firm; **at great expense** = having spent a lot of money; *top-quality designers had been hired at great expense*; *the house has been redecorated at great expense* **(b)** at the expense of something = in preference to something, giving something up; *she brought up her three children at the expense of her career in the bank*

◊ **at someone's expense** *phrase* **(a)** with someone paying the cost; *they were flown to Frankfurt at the company's expense* **(b)** making fun of someone; *we all had a good laugh at his expense*

expenses [ɪk'spensɪz] *noun* money spent in doing something; *we are making every effort to cut down on expenses*; *the salary offered is £20,000 plus expenses* = the company offers a salary of £20,000 and will repay any money spent by the employee in the course of his or her work; **all expenses paid** = with all costs paid by the company; *the company sent him to San Francisco all expenses paid* or *he went on an all-expenses-paid trip to San Francisco*; **business expenses** = money spent on running a business, not on stock or assets; **entertainment expenses** = money spent on giving meals, theatre tickets, etc., to business visitors; **legal expenses** = money spent on fees paid to lawyers; **overhead expenses** or **general expenses** or **running expenses** = money spent on the day-to-day cost of a business; **travelling expenses** = money spent on travelling and hotels for business purposes

expensive [ɪk'spensɪv] *adjective* which costs a lot of money; *don't ask her out - she always orders the most expensive things on the menu*; *fresh vegetables are more expensive in winter*; *send your furniture to Australia by sea - it would be much too expensive by air*

experience [ɪk'spiːərɪəns] **1** *noun* **(a)** knowledge got by working or living in various situations; *I have no experience of travelling in the desert*; *you must write down the full details of your past experience on your CV*; *some experience of selling is required for this job* (NOTE: no plural in this meaning) **(b)** event, incident that happens to someone; *going to the top of the Eiffel Tower was a wonderful experience*; *you must write a book about your experiences in prison* **2** *verb* to live through something; *I'm surprised she's so cheerful after all she experienced in prison*; *I have experienced a great deal of pleasure and frustration in my career*; *he is experiencing sharp pains in his left arm*

experienced [ɪk'spiːərɪənst] *adjective* wise from plenty of practice; *she's a very experienced doctor*; *he's the most experienced member of our staff*; *the police are experienced in crowd control*

experiment [ɪk'sperɪmənt] **1** *noun* scientific test; *to carry out experiments on live animals*; *we're offering our customers free samples as an experiment* **2** *verb* to carry out a scientific test; *they are experimenting with a new treatment for asthma*; *the laboratory experiments on live animals*

experimental [ɪksperɪ'mentl] *adjective* used in experiments; still being tested, still on trial; *this process is still at the experimental stage*

experimentally [ɪksperɪ'mentli] *adverb* **(a)** by carrying out experiments; *the new process has been tested experimentally* **(b)** as an experiment; *the system has been introduced experimentally into a few schools*

experimentation [ɪksperɪmən'teɪʃn] *noun* carrying out of experiments; *experimentation on live animals is banned in some cosmetics firms* (NOTE: no plural)

expert ['ekspɜːt] **1** *adjective* **(a)** knowing a lot about a subject; *she can give you expert advice on DIY*; **expert system** = computer program which has been devised for a particular purpose **(b) expert at doing something** = good at doing something; *I'm not very expert at making pastry* **2** *noun* **(a)** person who knows a great deal about a subject; *a TV gardening expert*; *he's a leading expert in tropical medicine* or *on tropical diseases* **(b)** person who is very good at doing something; *she's an expert at getting the children to go to bed*; *he's an expert plumber*

expertise [ekspə'tiːz] *noun* specialist knowledge; *we asked Mr Smith to advise us because of his legal*

expertise; *her expertise in business administration will be of great use to us* (NOTE: no plural)

expertly ['ekspɜːtli] *adverb* in an expert way; *he expertly defused the bomb*

expire [ɪk'spaɪə] *verb* **(a)** to come to an end; *the lease expires in 1999*; *his passport has expired* = his passport is no longer valid **(b)** *(formal)* to die; *after a brief illness, he expired on 28th September*

expiry [ɪk'spaɪri] *noun* coming to an end; *you need to insure your car before the expiry of the previous policy*; **expiry date** = the last date on which something can be used; *what is the expiry date on your credit card?*

explain [ɪk'spleɪn] *verb* **(a)** to give your reasons for something; *can you explain why the weather is cold in winter and warm in summer?* **(b)** to make something clear; *he tried to explain the new pension scheme to the staff*; *she explained what had happened, but the manager still thought she had tried to steal the watch*; *he explained to the customs officials that the drugs were presents for friends*

explanation [eksplə'neɪʃn] *noun* reason for something; *the policeman asked him for an explanation of why the stolen car was in his garage*; *the government has given no explanation for the change of plan*

explanatory [ɪk'splænətəri] *adjective* which explains, which makes clear; *an explanatory diagram at the back of the book shows how a diesel engine works*; *see also* SELF-EXPLANATORY

expletive [ɪk'spliːtɪv] *noun* swear word; *here is the text of the conversation, with the expletives removed*

explicit [ek'splɪsɪt] *adjective* **(a)** straightforward and clear; *could you please be more explicit?*; *their intention to sell the shop was not explicit in the letter* **(b)** showing sex or violence very clearly; *the film contains explicit sex scenes*

explicitly [ek'splɪsɪtli] *adverb* clearly; *I explicitly told you not to speak to any newspaper reporters*; *they issued an explicitly worded statement*

explode [ɪk'spləʊd] *verb* **(a)** *(of bombs, etc.)* to blow up; *a bomb exploded in a crowded train* **(b)** to make a bomb go off; *the army cleared the area and then exploded the bomb*

exploit 1 *noun* ['eksplɔɪt] great or daring achievement; *he told us of his exploits during the war* **2** *verb* [ɪk'splɔɪt] **(a)** to take commercial advantage of something; *we are hoping to exploit the mineral resources of the North Sea* **(b)** to make unfair use of someone, usually by paying them very low wages; *the company was accused of exploiting children by employing them in its shoe factories*

exploitation [eksplɔɪ'teɪʃn] *noun* **(a)** taking commercial advantage of something; *there are plans for the exploitation of the mineral resources of the region* **(b)** unfair use of cheap labour to get work done cheaply; *the exploitation of migrant farm workers*; *the company was accused of the exploitation of children in its shoe factories*

exploration [eksplə'reɪʃn] *noun* **(a)** travelling and discovering unknown parts of the world; *the exploration of Antarctica in the early 20th century*; *he is famous for his exploration of the Himalayas* **(b)** careful investigation; *we recommend further* *exploration of possible alternative solutions to the problem*

exploratory [ɪkˈsplɒrətəri] *adjective* tentative or preliminary; *the surgeon made an exploratory incision*; *we have just started exploratory talks on the possibility of a peace settlement*

explore [ɪkˈsplɔː] *verb* (a) to investigate carefully; *we are exploring the possibility of moving the office to London*; *the minister has set up a group to explore this and other issues* (b) to travel and discover, especially unknown parts of the world; *it is a part of the jungle which has never been explored before*; *we spent our holidays exploring Holland by canal*

explorer [ɪkˈsplɔːrə] *noun* person who explores unknown parts of the world; *a famous Antarctic explorer*

explosion [ɪkˈspləʊʒn] *noun* (a) blowing up of bombs, petrol tanks, etc.; *several explosions were heard during the night as the army occupied the city* (b) sudden increase; *this summer there has been an explosion in the numbers of greenfly*; **population explosion** = rapid increase in population

explosive [ɪkˈspləʊsɪv] **1** *adjective* (a) liable to blow up; *the containers held an explosive mixture*; *the police found an explosive device in the car* (b) tense, likely to be embarrassing; *the situation in the office was explosive, with the clerical staff demanding to see the manager*; *the paper is running an explosive story about the minister* **2** *noun* material, like gunpowder, which can blow up; *tests revealed traces of explosive on his hands*; *the box contained explosives*; *police explosives experts defused the bomb*

exponent [ɪkˈspəʊnənt] *noun* person who practises a certain belief, a certain art; *she is a leading exponent of vegetarianism*; *he is an exponent of the ancient Japanese art of origami*

export 1 *noun* [ˈekspɔːt]; **export(s)** = goods sent to a foreign country to be sold; *the country's major export is tea*; *exports to Africa have increased by 25%*; **export manager** = person in charge of sales to foreign countries (NOTE: usually used in the plural, but the singular form must be used before a noun) **2** *verb* [ɪkˈspɔːt] to send goods to a foreign country for sale; *half of our production is exported*; *the company exports half of what it produces*

exporter [ɪkˈspɔːtə] *noun* person or company which sells goods to foreign countries; *a leading exporter of agricultural machinery*; *Canada is an important exporter of oil or an important oil exporter*; *a meeting of tea exporters*

expose [ɪkˈspəʊz] *verb* (a) to show something which was hidden; *he pulled off his shirt, exposing a huge scar across his chest*; *the plastic coating had rubbed off to expose the metal beneath* (b) to let light go onto a photographic film; *you didn't expose the film for long enough* (c) to reveal a scandal; *he was exposed as the person who wrote the letters*; *the newspaper has exposed several government scandals* (d) **to expose something or someone to** = to place something or someone under the influence of something; *don't expose these plants to direct sunlight*; *she was exposed to a lethal dose of radiation*; *he had inadvertently exposed his children to serious danger*

exposé [ɪkˈspəʊzeɪ] *noun* report which exposes something wrong; *an exposé of corruption in the Finance Ministry*

exposed [ɪkˈspəʊzd] *adjective* open and not protected; *a stretch of exposed mountainside*; *the cottages on the cliff are very exposed*; **a very exposed position** = a position which is not sheltered from the wind

exposition [ekspəˈzɪʃn] *noun* (a) *US* display of works of art, goods for sale, etc.; *the exposition is open from 10 a.m. to 5 p.m.*; *we stood in line for half an hour waiting to get into the book exposition*; **exposition hall** = place where goods are shown so that buyers can look at them and decide what to buy (b) detailed explanation; *she gave a clear exposition of the artist's use of light and shade*

expository [ekzˈpɒzɪtəri] *adjective US* (*formal*) which explains in detail; *he gave an expository lecture on blood circulation*

exposure [ɪkˈspəʊʒə] *noun* (a) placing someone under the influence of something; *the exposure of young children to violence on television*; *the exposure of some workers to radiation* (b) state of not being sheltered from cold, etc.; *the survivors of the crash were all suffering from exposure after spending a night in the snow* (c) time and amount of light needed for a picture to be taken on film; *you need a short exposure to photograph a racing car*; **exposure meter** = device for calculating the exposure for a photograph (d) revealing of corruption, etc.; *the newspaper's exposure of the minister's involvement in the scandal*; *the council was embarrassed by a string of exposures of financial mismanagement*

expound [ɪkˈspaʊnd] *verb* (*formal*) to explain in detail; *the professor expounded his theory of the beginning of the universe to his students*; *she was expounding on the problem of housing shortages*

express [ɪkˈspres] **1** *adjective* (a) rapid (train or postal service); *we have an express delivery service to all parts of the country* (b) done on purpose; *he did it with the express intention of killing me* **2** *noun* rapid train; *we took the express from London to Glasgow* **3** *verb* to put into words or diagrams; *he expressed his gratitude in a short speech*; *the chart shows visitors to our stand expressed as a percentage of all visitors to the exhibition*; **I expressed myself badly** = I did not make clear what I wanted to say

expression [ɪkˈspreʃn] *noun* (a) word or group of words; *'until the cows come home' is an expression which means 'for a very long time'* (b) look on a person's face which shows feeling; *his sad expression showed how miserable he was*; *everyone noticed the expression of surprise on her face*

expressive [ɪkˈspresɪv] *adjective* showing feeling; *comic actors tend to have very expressive faces*; *he gave an expressive wink to the audience*

expressly [ɪkˈspresli] *adverb* on purpose; *I expressly forbade you to go to that club*

expressway [ɪkˈspresweɪ] *noun US* fast road with few junctions; *take the expressway south to junction 20* (NOTE: British English is **motorway**)

expulsion [ɪkˈspʌlʃn] *noun* act of being thrown out or sent away (from school, etc.); *the minister ordered the expulsion of the illegal immigrants*; *the school only considers expulsion as a last resort*; *see also* EXPEL

exquisite [ɪkˈskwɪzɪt] *adjective* very finely made, very refined; *an exquisite glass vase*; *she does some exquisite needlework*

ex-serviceman [eks'sɜːvɪsmən] *noun* man who was a member of the armed forces in the past; *he's the secretary of the local ex-servicemen's club* (NOTE: plural is **ex-servicemen**)

ext. [ɪk'stenʃn] *abbreviation for* EXTENSION; *my number is 967-4971, ext. 23*

extant [ɪk'stænt] *adjective (formal)* still in existence; *according to extant 16th century records, the house belonged to the local doctor*

extend [ɪk'stend] *verb* **(a)** to stretch out; *she extended both arms in welcome*; *the grounds of the house extend over two hectares* **(b)** to make longer or bigger; *we are planning to extend our garden*; *we have asked our landlord to extend the lease for another two years* **(c)** to give; *I want to extend a warm welcome to our guests from China*

extended [ɪk'stendɪd] *adjective* longer than usual; *they went on an extended holiday to Thailand*

extended family [ɪk'stendɪd 'fæmɪli] *noun* family in which relatives outside the central family group, such as aunts and uncles, are included; *she relied on her extended family for help when her husband lost his job*; *compare* NUCLEAR FAMILY

extension [ɪk'stenʃn] *noun* **(a)** act of extending; *my visa has expired, so I have applied for an extension* **(b)** thing added on; *we added an extension at the back of the house*; *I need an extension cable for the electric mower*; *they are planning a further extension of the underground railway* **(c)** subsidiary telephone in an office; *can you get me extension 21?*; *the manager is on extension 23*

extensive [ɪk'stensɪv] *adjective* very widespread, vast; *the grounds of the house are very extensive*; *the church roof needs extensive repair work*

extensively [ɪk'stensɪvli] *adverb* greatly; *the centre of the town was extensively rebuilt after the war*; *when he was young he travelled extensively in China*

extent [ɪk'stent] *noun* degree, size, area; *the extent of the earthquake damage was only revealed later*; *he opened up the map to its full extent*; **to some extent** *or* **to a certain extent** = partly, in some way; *to some extent, the weather was the cause of the failure of the village fair* (NOTE: no plural)

extenuating [ɪk'stenjʊeɪtɪŋ] *adjective* **extenuating circumstances** = events which can partly excuse a wrong action; *he was guilty, but there were extenuating circumstances and the sentence was reduced*

exterior [ɪk'stɪəriə] **1** *adjective* outside; *the exterior walls are of stone* **2** *noun* the outside parts; *the exterior of the house is painted pink*

exterminate [ɪk'stɜːmɪneɪt] *verb* to kill a large number of living things; *cockroaches are difficult to exterminate*; *they were accused of attempting to exterminate the indigenous inhabitants of the land*

extermination [ɪkstɜːmɪ'neɪʃn] *noun* act of killing large numbers; *we are aiming at the total extermination of the rat population* (NOTE: no plural)

external [ɪk'stɜːnl] *adjective* outside; *the external walls of the house are quite solid*; *her injuries were all external*; **external phone** = office phone directly linked to an outside line; **medicine for external use only** = medicine which is used on the skin and must not be drunk or eaten (NOTE: the opposite, referring to the inside, is **internal**)

externally [ɪk'stɜːnəli] *adverb* outside; *externally, the house is in very good condition, but the inside needs a lot of work*

extinct [ɪk'stɪŋkt] *adjective* **(a)** which has died out; *three species of butterfly have become extinct in the last year*; *several species of birds have become extinct since rats were introduced to the island* **(b)** (volcano) which no longer erupts; *the mountain is an extinct volcano*; *compare* DORMANT

extinction [ɪk'stɪŋkʃn] *noun* dying out of a species; *the last remaining pairs of birds were taken to a zoo for breeding purposes, so as to save the species from extinction*; **to face extinction** *or* **to be threatened with extinction** = to be likely to die out; *the tiger is facing extinction unless measures are taken to protect it* (NOTE: no plural)

extinguish [ɪk'stɪŋgwɪʃ] *verb* to put out a fire; *after the fire had been extinguished only the shell of the building remained*

extinguisher [ɪk'stɪŋgwɪʃə] *noun* **fire extinguisher** = can (usually painted red) containing chemical foam which can be sprayed onto a fire to put it out

extol *US also* **extoll** [ɪk'stəʊl] *verb (formal)* to praise very highly; *the inspectors extolled the cooking at the new French restaurant*; *the finance ministers extolled the virtue of thrift* (NOTE: **extolling - extolled**)

extort [ɪk'stɔːt] *verb* **to extort something from someone** = to get money or promises from someone by threatening; *the secret police extorted very valuable information from him*; *the gang extorted money from small shopkeepers by threatening to burn down their shops*

extortion [ɪk'stɔːʃn] *noun* getting money from someone by threats; *she was accused of obtaining money by extortion* (NOTE: no plural)

extortionate [ɪk'stɔːʃənət] *adjective* very high or excessive; *prices in the hotel shopping arcade are simply extortionate*; *extortionate insurance premiums mean that we can't afford to run a car*

extra ['ekstrə] **1** *adjective* more than normal; additional; *we need an extra four teachers* or *four extra teachers for this course*; *the charge for delivery is extra*; *there is no extra charge for heating*; *staff get extra pay for working on Sundays* **2** *adverb* more than normal; in addition; *we need some extra strong string to tie the parcel*; *they charge extra for bulky items*; *if you pay £50 extra you can travel first class* **3** *noun* **(a)** something more than usual; *the price covers the hotels and transport but not extras like drinks and special trips*; *air-conditioning is an extra on this car* **(b)** actor or actress who appears in a crowd scene in a film or play, but is not a star; *the studio hired thousands of extras to make 'Cleopatra'*

extract 1 *noun* ['ekstrækt] **(a)** thing reduced from something larger; *he will be reading extracts from his latest novel* **(b)** something which is reduced to a concentrated form; *she made a soup from meat extract*; *add a drop of vanilla extract to the custard* **2** *verb* [ɪk'strækt] **(a)** to pull something out; *the dentist extracted two teeth*; *we managed to extract £10 from him*; *the police extracted a confession from the accused* **(b)** to produce something from something else; *it is no longer viable to extract tin from Cornish mines*; *the oil is extracted from lavender flowers*

extraction [ɪk'strækʃn] *noun* **(a)** pulling out of a tooth; *an extraction will cost you £40* **(b)** production of coal, etc.; *the extraction of iron ore from this mine is becoming too costly* (c) she is of German extraction = her family originally came from Germany (NOTE: no plural in meanings (b) and (c))

extractor fan [ɪkˈstræktə ˈfæn] *noun* fan which sucks air out (as in a kitchen); *when you switch on the light in the bathroom, the extractor fan comes on automatically*

extracurricular [ekstrəkəˈrɪkjulə] *adjective* outside the normal course of study; *she is involved in all sorts of extracurricular activities, like the drama society and the astronomy club*

extradite [ˈekstrədaɪt] *verb* to bring back an arrested person back from another country to stand trial for a crime committed in his home country; *now the extradition treaty has been signed, he may be extradited back to stand trial in Britain*

extradition [ekstrəˈdɪʃn] *noun* act of bringing back a person to his home country for trial; *he is in prison facing extradition to the USA*; **extradition treaty** = treaty between two countries by which each returns wanted criminals to the other when requested

extraneous [ɪkˈstreɪniəs] *adjective (formal)* (a) not directly connected; *he introduced some extraneous details into his argument* (b) coming from outside; *extraneous material in the blood sample made the test invalid*

extraordinarily [ɪkˈstrɔːdnrəli] *adverb* (a) extremely, very; *her action was extraordinarily brave* (b) in an extraordinary way; *he behaved quite extraordinarily at the party*

extraordinary [ɪkˈstrɔːdnri] *adjective* (a) marvellous, strange and unusual; *seeing her again gave him an extraordinary thrill; a peacock's feathers are quite extraordinary; it's extraordinary weather for June* (b) quite different from everything else; *these are extraordinary costs which will not be charged again; they called an extraordinary meeting of the club*

extra time [ˈekstrə ˈtaɪm] *noun* more time added at the end of a football match in which the scores are level, so that the sides have time to try to score; *they won the match with a goal scored in extra time*

extravagance [ɪkˈstrævəgəns] *noun* excessive expense and luxury; *he must be very rich to be able to afford the extravagance of two Rolls Royces*

extravagant [ɪkˈstrævəgənt] *adjective* (a) who spends a lot of money; *he is extravagant when it comes to buying presents for his wife* (b) expensive and luxurious; *she was criticized for her extravagant way of life* (c) unusual and wild; *the company has made some extravagant claims for its new soap powder*

extravagantly [ɪkˈstrævəgəntli] *adverb* in an extravagant way; *some people spend extravagantly when they win the lottery, others are more cautious*

extravaganza [ɪkstrævəˈgænzə] *noun* expensive and luxurious party, show, film, etc.; *they are going to celebrate her birthday with a lavish extravaganza in a Hollywood night club; his latest extravaganza involves hundreds of dancers and musicians*

extreme [ɪkˈstriːm] **1** *adjective* very great; *the anorak is made to withstand extreme cold; he showed extreme reluctance to get involved*; **at the extreme end** = right at the end **2** *noun* something very unusual, very extraordinary; *you get extremes of temperature here - very hot summers and very cold winters*; **to go to**

extremes = to do everything in an excessive way; **to go from one extreme to the other** = to change to something completely different; *she can go from one extreme to the other - from being happy and excited one minute to being gloomy and depressed the next*

extremely [ɪkˈstriːmli] *noun* very; *it was extremely hot in August; the film is extremely long, and some people walked out before the end; it is extremely difficult to spend less than $50.00 a day on meals in New York*

extremism [ɪkˈstriːmɪzm] *noun (as criticism)* ideas and practices that favour very strong action, such as the use of violence; *with the rapid rise in unemployment, right-wing extremism is on the increase again*

extremist [ɪkˈstriːmɪst] **1** *noun* person who has extreme views, usually about politics; *the government has imprisoned all left-wing extremists* **2** *adjective* having extreme views, usually about politics; *members of an extremist group have taken over the post office*

extremity [ɪkˈstremɪti] *noun* (a) end point; *we set up our camp at the northern extremity of the island* (b) **the extremities** = parts of the body at the ends of the limbs, the fingers, toes, as well as the nose and ears; *her extremities became numb in the cold* (NOTE: plural is **extremities**)

extricate [ˈekstrɪkeɪt] *verb* (a) to get someone out of a difficult situation; *she asked her father to help extricate her from the awkward situation she found herself in* (b) to remove something with difficulty; *the surgeons extricated the bullet which had lodged itself behind her eye*

extrovert [ˈekstrəvɜːt] *noun* person who is very outgoing and likes to be with others; *he's a real extrovert and loves to appear in public; the best salesmen are extroverts* (NOTE: the opposite is **introvert**)

exuberance [ɪɡˈzjuːbərəns] *noun* wild enthusiasm; *the boy's natural exuberance often gets him into trouble; she sometimes finds it difficult to control her natural exuberance* (NOTE: no plural)

exuberant [ɪɡˈzjuːbərənt] *adjective* wildly enthusiastic; *an exuberant performance of the new musical*

exude [ɪɡˈzjuːd] *verb* to send out or to give off a smell, a feeling, in all directions; *he exudes self-confidence*

eye [aɪ] **1** *noun* (a) organ in the head, with which you see; *he has brown eyes; close your eyes and count to ten while we all hide; I've got a bit of dust in my eye*; **as far as the eye can see** = for a very long distance; *grasslands stretch as far as the eye can see*; **to catch someone's eye** = to look at someone who is looking at you; *she caught his eye and nodded towards the door*; **keep your eyes open for!** = watch out for!; *keep your eyes open for burglars!*; **to keep an eye on something** = to watch something carefully to see that it is safe; *can you keep an eye on the house while we are away?*; **to keep an eye out for something** = to watch to see if something is near; *I must keep an eye out for Seville oranges to make some marmalade; can you keep an eye out for the traffic warden while I go into the bank?*; *(informal)* **I'm up to my eyes in work** = I have a lot of work to do; **they don't see eye to eye** = they do not agree; *he doesn't see eye to eye with the boss*; **to have your eye on someone** = to think someone is very good, very attractive, very suspicious; *she's got her eye* on her best friend's brother; the police have had their eye on him for ages **(b)** (informal) a **private eye** = a detective who is not a member of the police force and is employed by an ordinary person **(c)** small hole in the end of a needle, through which the thread goes **2** verb **(a)** to look at something carefully; she sat in a corner, eyeing the arrivals indicator **(b)** (informal) to **eye someone up** = to look at someone showing that you think them attractive; he was eyeing up one of the girls on the other side of the room

eyeball ['aɪbɔːl] **1** noun **(a)** part of the eye, the round ball of tissue through which light passes and which is controlled by various muscles; the retina is a light-sensitive membrane at the back of the eyeball **(b)** **eyeball to eyeball** = facing each other closely; he had an eyeball-to-eyeball confrontation with the referee **2** verb (informal) to stare at someone closely; the security guard eyeballed us as we came near the gate

eyebath ['aɪbɑːθ] noun small cup for bathing the eye; sterilize the eyebath before use

eyebrow ['aɪbraʊ] noun small line of hair above your eye; she has finely arched eyebrows; use some eyebrow pencil to make your eyebrows clearer; he raised his eyebrows = he looked surprised

eye-catching ['aɪkætʃɪŋ] adjective very striking, which makes you look at it; she was wearing an eye-catching dress

eyeful ['aɪfʊl] noun **(a)** amount of something which gets in your eye; he got an eyeful of sand **(b)** (informal) **to get an eyeful of something** = to see something unusual

eyelash ['aɪlæʃ] noun one of the hairs growing round the edge of the eyelids; one of my eyelashes has got into my eye; she had to wear false eyelashes in the film (NOTE: plural is **eyelashes**)

eye level ['aɪ 'levl] noun the height above the floor of the average person's eyes; the little window should have been placed at eye level, not at one metre from the floor

eyelid ['aɪlɪd] noun piece of skin which covers the eye; her eyelids drooped and soon she was fast asleep

eye-opener ['aɪəʊpnə] noun (informal) something which surprises you; the newspaper report on corruption among government ministers was a real eye-opener

eyepiece ['aɪpiːs] noun lens which you look through in a telescope or microscope

eyesight ['aɪsaɪt] noun ability to see; he has got very good eyesight; she suffered from poor eyesight in her old age; her eyesight is failing = she can't see as well as she used to (NOTE: no plural)

eyesore ['aɪsɔː] noun unpleasant sight; that pile of rubbish is an eyesore and should be removed

eyewitness ['aɪwɪtnəs] noun person who has seen something happen; were there any eyewitnesses to the accident?; the police have an eyewitness account of what happened (NOTE: plural is **eyewitnesses**)

eyrie US **aerie** ['ɪəri] noun **(a)** nest of an eagle; the eagles come back to the same eyrie every year **(b)** high place; the general stood in his eyrie, looking at the advancing army through his binoculars

Ff

F, f [ef] sixth letter of the alphabet, between E and G; *'raffle' is spelt with a double 'f' or with two 'f's*

fab [fæb] *adjective (informal)* = FABULOUS

fable ['feɪbl] *noun* moral story, usually about animals, making them seem like human beings; *in 'Animal Farm', Orwell wrote a modern fable about animals who take over a farm and become more human than the humans*

fabled ['feɪbld] *adjective* well-known in stories; *they met the fabled seven-headed monster*

fabric ['fæbrɪk] *noun* (a) cloth, material; *the curtains are made of some expensive fabric*; *we need a fireproof fabric for the chairs* (b) basic structure (of society); *during the revolution, the basic fabric of society collapsed*

fabricate ['fæbrɪkeɪt] *verb* to invent an untrue story; *he claimed that she had fabricated the whole story*

fabrication [fæbrɪ'keɪʃn] *noun* invention of a story that is untrue; *the newspaper story was a complete fabrication from start to finish*

fabulous ['fæbjʊləs] *adjective* (a) imaginary, as in fairy stories; *unicorns and other fabulous animals* (b) *(informal)* marvellous, wonderful; *it was a fabulous party*

facade or **façade** [fə'sɑːd] *noun* (a) front of a large building; *the façade is covered with black marble*; *according to the redevelopment plans the old building is to be demolished apart from the façade, which will be preserved* (b) outward appearance which is intended to give a false impression; *the business seemed prosperous, but it was just a façade*

face [feɪs] **1** *noun* (a) front part of your head; *don't forget to wash your face before you go to the party*; *face to face* = looking at each other; *he turned a corner and came face to face with a policeman*; *I don't like doing business on the phone - I prefer to make deals face to face*; *to lose face* = to feel humiliated; *she can't bear being told off in front of the class - it makes her lose face*; *to make a face* = to make a strange expression; *he made funny faces and all the children laughed*; *he tried to keep a straight face* = he tried not to laugh; *to show your face* = to come to a place; *after what he said about my mother he doesn't dare show his face here* (b) front part of something; *a clock face*; *she put the photograph face down on the desk*; *he has vanished from the face of the earth* = he has disappeared completely **2** *verb* (a) to have the face or front towards; *can everyone please face the camera?*; *the house faces north* (b) to meet someone in an unpleasant situation; *the thought of facing all those journalists frightens me*; *she didn't want to face the committee yet again* (c) to face something or be faced with something = to be likely to have to deal with an unpleasant situation; *she faces a life of poverty*; *will they be able to cope with the problems facing them?*; *not to be able to face something* = not to want to experience something which you expect will be unpleasant; *he couldn't face another meeting*; *to face the facts* = to look at things in a realistic way; *you really ought to face the facts: you'll never get a job if you don't have any qualifications*; *let's face it* = we have to accept it; *let's face it, she's failed her test five times and will probably never pass*; *see also* MUSIC

facecloth or **face flannel** ['feɪsklɒθ or 'feɪs ˌflænəl] *noun* small square of towelling for washing the face or body; *the hotel provides you with a bath towel, a small towel and a facecloth in your bathroom*

faceless ['feɪsləs] *adjective* without a name or face, anonymous and threatening; *at every turn we seem to be up against some faceless local official*

face pack ['feɪs ˌpæk] *noun* thick moist stuff which you put on your face to improve your skin; *don't come in, I've still got my face pack on*

face-saving ['feɪsˌseɪvɪŋ] *adjective* which avoids humiliating someone; *the agreement is a face-saving device to avoid further embarrassment to the minister*

facet ['fæsɪt] *noun* (a) one of the flat sides on a cut gem; *a diamond with forty-four facets* (b) one of many aspects of a problem, etc.; *the problem presents many different facets*; *the film explores several fascinating facets of his life in Africa*

face up to ['feɪs ˌʌp tuː] *verb* to accept an unpleasant state of affairs and try to deal with it; *he had to face up to the fact that he was never going to be rich*; *the problems won't go away - you must try to face up to them*

face value ['feɪs ˌvæljuː] *noun* value written on a coin or banknote; *to take something at (its) face value* = to assume that the apparent meaning is the correct one; *when we booked our holiday we took what the tour company said about the hotel at face value - but it turned out not to be true*

facial ['feɪʃl] **1** *adjective* referring to a face; *her facial expression reflected her feeling of happiness* **2** *noun* beauty treatment in which your face is cleaned and massaged; *she's having a facial*

facile ['fæsaɪl] *adjective* (a) done very easily; *he writes in a facile way which is easy to read, but isn't great literature* (b) done without thinking carefully; *the solution proposed by the town council is simply too facile*

facilitate [fə'sɪlɪteɪt] *verb (formal)* to make something easy; *we need to do everything to facilitate the movement of relief supplies*

facility [fə'sɪlɪti] *noun* (a) ability to do something easily; *she has a facility for languages*; *we offer facilities for payment* (b) facilities = equipment which can be used; *the centre provides facilities for a wide range of sports*; *we have free use of all the club facilities*; *the museum has facilities for the disabled or for the handicapped* = the museum has special ramps, special lifts, etc., to allow disabled or handicapped people to visit it (c) large commercial building; *we have opened our new warehouse facility* (NOTE: plural for meanings (b) and (c) is **facilities**)

facing ['feɪsɪŋ] **1** *adjective* which faces; *our side of the street is in the shade, but the facing side is in full sunlight; the house facing ours belongs to a doctor* **2** *noun* material covering the surface of a building; *the stone facing of the library has started to come off*

facsimile [fæk'sɪmɪli] *noun* **(a)** perfect reproduction or perfect copy; *this is not the real Magna Carta - it is a facsimile; they have published a facsimile edition of one of the earliest printed books* **(b)** *(formal)* fax, copy of a text or picture sent by telephone; *can you confirm the booking by facsimile?*

fact [fækt] *noun* **(a)** thing that is true; *he faced up to the fact that he wasn't fit enough for the race; did you check all the facts before you wrote the article?; it's a well-known fact that it rains more often in the west of the country* **(b) in fact** = really; *he told the police he had seen a man steal a car but in fact he made the whole story up; it rained a lot last month, in fact it rained all month* **(c) the fact of the matter is** = what is true is that; *the fact of the matter is that she is too slow to join the team;* **as a matter of fact** = actually; *have you seen John recently? - as a matter of fact I met him yesterday*

fact-finding ['fæktfaɪndɪŋ] *adjective* which is searching for information; **a fact-finding mission** = group of people who visit a place to search for information about a problem; *they went on a fact-finding mission to Eastern Europe*

faction ['fækʃn] *noun* group of people linked together in opposition to a leader or to a government; *three warring factions are fighting for control; trying to unite the different factions is an impossible task*

factional ['fækʃənl] *adjective* referring to factions; *factional fighting has weakened the structure of the party*

facto *see* DE FACTO

fact of life ['fækt əv 'laɪf] *noun* **(a)** basic principle of life; *it's a fact of life that some people are successful businessmen and others are not* **(b) the facts of life** = details of sexual intercourse, how babies are conceived, etc.; *she had to explain the facts of life to a class of fifteen-year-olds*

factor ['fæktə] *noun* **(a)** one of the numbers which produce a certain other number when multiplied; *4 and 2 are factors of 8;* **by a factor of** = multiplied by; *reported cases of BSE have fallen by a factor of 3* **(b)** number which indicates the strength of something; **factor 20 suncream** = cream which gives twenty times protection against the sun's rays **(c)** thing which has influence or importance; *the key factor is the price; the crucial factor for the success of the village fête is the weather;* **deciding factor** = most important factor which influences a decision **(d)** person who buys debts at a discount and then tries to reclaim the full amount from the debtor

factory ['fæktri] *noun* building where things are made; *she works in a shoe factory; he owns a furniture factory; the factory makes computer terminals;* **factory hand** *or* **factory worker** = person who works in a factory (NOTE: plural is **factories**)

factual ['fæktjʊəl] *adjective* referring to facts; *he presented a straightforward factual report*

faculty ['fækəlti] *noun* **(a)** ability; **mental faculties** = being able to think clearly; *in spite of being over ninety, she is still in possession of all her faculties* **(b)** main division of a university; *the Faculty of Arts or the Arts Faculty* **(c)** *US* teaching staff (of a school, university, college, etc.); *there is a meeting of the faculty tomorrow* (NOTE: plural is **faculties**)

fad [fæd] *noun* strange temporary craze for something; *his latest fad is racing cars; I can't keep up with all her fads - last week it was yoghurt, and now it's tomato juice*

fade [feɪd] *verb* **(a)** to lose colour; *the more you wash your jeans, the more they'll fade; this T-shirt has faded* **(b)** to become less bright or light; *as the light faded, bats came out in the garden; the light from the torch began to fade as the batteries ran out; the islands faded away into the distance*

faded ['feɪdɪd] *adjective* which has lost its colour; *she was wearing a faded T-shirt; the palace has been empty for years, and is a faded shadow of its former glory*

faecal *US* **fecal** ['fiːkəl] *adjective* referring to faeces; *faecal matter was found in the drinking supplies*

faeces *US* **feces** ['fiːsiːz] *noun* *(formal)* solid waste matter passed from the bowels through the anus; *the patient's faeces are not solid*

fag [fæg] *noun* *(informal)* **(a)** tiring or boring work; *it's such a fag, licking all these envelopes* **(b)** cigarette; *he cadged a fag off me; I bought a packet of fags at the kiosk*

fagged (out) ['fægd 'aʊt] *adjective* *(informal)* tired out; *we were fagged out after working all week building the wall*

Fahrenheit ['færənhaɪt] *noun* scale of temperatures where the freezing and boiling points of water are 32° and 212°; *compare* CELSIUS, CENTIGRADE (NOTE: used in the USA, but less common in the UK. Normally written as an **F** after the degree sign: **32°F**: say: 'thirty-two degrees Fahrenheit')

> COMMENT: to convert Fahrenheit to Celsius, subtract 32 and divide by 1.8. To convert Celsius temperatures to Fahrenheit, multiply by 1.8 and add 32. So 68°F is equal to 20°C.

fail [feɪl] **1** *noun* *(formal)* **without fail** = definitely; *I will be there without fail tomorrow morning* **2** *verb* **(a)** not to do something which you were trying to do; *the examination was very difficult - half the students failed; he passed in maths, but failed his English exam; she failed in her attempt to become an MP* **(b)** not to do something; *the car failed to stop at the red light; she failed to notify the tax office of her change of address* **(c)** not to be able to do something; *I fail to see why she can't come the meeting when everyone else can* **(d)** not to work properly; *the brakes failed and he couldn't stop the car;* **if all else fails** = if you can't do anything else; *if all else fails you can always borrow my car* **(e)** to become weaker; *her eyesight is beginning to fail*

failing ['feɪlɪŋ] **1** *noun* weakness, bad point; *she has only one failing - she goes to sleep in front of the TV every night; in spite of his failings, we still think he is a wonderful father* **2** *preposition;* **failing that** = if that does not work; *try some tape to seal the joint, or failing* *that, call a plumber* **3** *adjective* becoming weak; *the cricket match was stopped because of failing light*

failure ['feɪljə] *noun* **(a)** breakdown or stopping; *the accident was caused by brake failure*; *the failure of the plane's engine caused the crash*; **heart failure** = dangerous condition when the heart has stopped beating; **power failure** = breakdown in electricity supplies **(b)** person or thing which does not work satisfactorily; *his attempts to juggle were a complete failure*; *I'm no good at anything - I'm a failure* **(c)** **failure to do something** = not having done something; *his failure to reach the final disappointed his fans*; *failure to pay the bill will mean we will have to take legal action*

faint [feɪnt] **1** *adjective* difficult to see or hear; *we could just see the faint outline of a man in the fog*; *the rescuers could hear a faint tapping in the ruins* **2** *verb* to become unconscious for a short time; *she fainted when she saw the blood*

fair [feə] **1** *adjective* **(a)** light-coloured (hair, skin); *her hair is quite fair*; *she's dark, but her brother is fair* **(b)** not very good; *her work is only fair* **(c)** right, giving something what they deserve; *it isn't fair to go on holiday when we have so much work to do*; *that's not fair - you must let other people play with the ball too* **(d)** bright and warm (weather); *according to the TV it will be fair tomorrow* (NOTE: do not confuse with **fare**; note also: **fairer - fairest**) **2** *noun* **(a)** group of amusements, sideshows, food stalls, etc., set up in one place for a short time; *the fair is coming to the village for the Easter Bank Holiday*; *we went to the fair and won a goldfish at the shooting gallery* **(b)** exhibition for selling and advertising goods; *we are going to the car fair tomorrow* **3** *adverb* in a fair way; *you play fair with me, and I'll play fair with you*

fairground ['feəɡraʊnd] *noun* place in the open air where a fair is held; *every bank holiday, they set up a fairground in our village*; *the children were last seen at the fairground*

fair-haired ['feə'heəd] *adjective* with fair hair; *crowds of little fair-haired children came out of school*

fairly ['feəli] *adverb* quite; *I'm fairly certain I have seen this film before*; *she had been working there a fairly short time*; *the hotel is fairly close to the centre of town* (NOTE: the order of words: **he's a fairly good worker** but **he's quite a good worker**)

fairness ['feənəs] *noun* **(a)** light colouring; *the fairness of her skin makes it difficult for her to stay in the sun for long periods* **(b)** honesty and correctness; *everyone acknowledged his fairness in dealing with staff complaints*

fair play ['feə 'pleɪ] *noun* obeying the rules of a game, or the normal rules of behaviour; *we expect fair play from both sides*

fairway ['feəweɪ] *noun* part of a golf course where the grass is cut; *the ball landed halfway down the fairway*; *the fairway is bordered by the rough, which can be very difficult to hit out of*

COMMENT: on a golf course, the grass on the rough is not cut at all, the grass on the fairway is cut, and the grass on the greens is cut short

fairy ['feəri] *noun* little creature who can work magic; *I believed in fairies when I was little*; **fairy godmother** = kind person who gives you magic presents; *Cinderella's fairy godmother helped her go to the ball*;

what we need is a fairy godmother to get us out of trouble; **fairy lights** = small electric lights for decorating trees, etc. (NOTE: plural is **fairies**)

fairy story ['feəri 'stɔːri] = FAIRYTALE

fairytale ['feəriteɪl] *noun* children's story about fairies, princesses, giants, etc.; **a fairytale castle** = romantic castle like those in fairytales; **a fairytale wedding** = romantic wedding (like that of a prince and princess)

faith [feɪθ] *noun* **(a)** belief, trust; **to have faith in someone** = to believe that someone is good and strong, or will protect you; *I have no faith in advice columns in newspapers*; *you must have faith in the leader of the party*; *I don't have any faith in this government*; **blind faith** = absolute trust in someone, however wicked they may seem to be to other people **(b)** religious belief; *we must respect people of other faiths* **(c)** **in good faith** = honourably, even though perhaps wrongly; *I sold him the car in good faith - I didn't know it would break down the next day*

faithful ['feɪθful] **1** *adjective* **(a)** *(person)* trusting or loyal; *his faithful old dog*; **to be faithful to father's last wishes (b)** *(of husband, wife)* **to be faithful** = not to have love affairs with someone else **(c)** completely correct; *a faithful copy of a document* **2** *noun* **the faithful** = the people who believe in a certain religion; **the party faithful** = the people who believe blindly in a certain political party

faithfully ['feɪθfəli] *adverb* **(a)** loyally, in a trusting way; *her maid had worked faithfully for her for years*; *he faithfully did what the instructor told him to do* **(b)** **Yours faithfully** = used as an ending for business letters, when addressed to no specific person (NOTE: not used in American English)

faith healer ['feɪθ 'hiːlə] *noun* person who heals by the power of prayer; *when she found she wasn't getting any better she stopped going to the doctor and went to a faith healer instead*

faith healing ['feɪθ 'hiːlɪŋ] *noun* healing by the power of prayer; *faith healing can be effective in treating certain conditions*

fake [feɪk] **1** *noun* imitation, forgery; not the real thing; *that picture isn't by Picasso, it's a fake* **2** *adjective* not real; *she was wearing a fake fur coat* **3** *verb* to make an imitation of something, or to imitate something that isn't real; *he faked illness to avoid appearing in court*; *she faked the results of the test*

falcon ['fɔːlkən] *noun* small bird of prey, sometimes trained to catch other birds as a sport; *the king rode out with his falcons*

fall [fɔːl] **1** *noun* **(a)** amount of something which has come down; *there was a heavy fall of snow during the night* **(b)** going to a lower level; *a welcome fall in the price of oil*; *the fall in the exchange rate* **(c)** losing your balance; *he had a fall and hurt his back*; *she had a bad fall while skiing* **(d)** *US* **the fall** = autumn; *we go to New England in the fall to see the trees*; *fall colours are at their best in the first week of October* **2** *verb* **(a)** to drop down to a lower level; *snow fell all night*; *the pound has fallen against the dollar*; *she fell down the stairs*; *he fell off the ladder*; *did he fall into the river or did someone push him?*; *don't put the jug on the cushion - it may fall over* **(b)** **to fall on** = to happen or to take place; *my birthday falls on a Tuesday this year* (NOTE: **falling - fell** [fel] - **has fallen**)

fallacious [fə'leɪʃəs] *adjective* based on a false argument; *his theory is quite fallacious*

fallacy ['fæləsi] *noun* false argument; mistake; *it's a common fallacy to assume that American companies are more efficient than British ones* (NOTE: plural is **fallacies**)

fall apart ['fɔːl ə'pɑːt] *verb* (a) to come to pieces; *my shoes are falling apart; the porcelain dish just fell apart in my hands* (b) to come to an end (in its present form); *when they showed him the letters, his life simply fell apart; when our German partners withdrew, the deal fell apart*

fall asleep ['fɔːl ə'sliːp] *phrase* to go to sleep; *we all fell asleep after dinner*

fall away [fɔːl ə'weɪ] *verb* to become less; *hotel bookings have fallen away since the tourist season ended*

fall back on ['fɔːl 'bæk ɒn] *verb* to use something which you were keeping as a reserve; *the car broke down, so we had to fall back on public transport*

fall behind [fɔːl bɪ'haɪnd] *verb* to be late in doing something; *he fell behind with his mortgage repayments*

fall down ['fɔːl 'daʊn] *verb* to drop to the ground; *the place has been deserted for so long it's falling down*

fall for ['fɔːl 'fɔː] *verb* (a) to fall in love with someone; *she always falls for men twice her age* (b) to be tricked by something; *don't fall for his sales talk*

fall guy ['fɔːl 'gaɪ] *noun* someone who is made to take the blame for a crime committed by someone else; *he realized that he was being set up for a fall guy*

fall ill ['fɔːl 'ɪl] *phrase* to become ill; *the trek through the Himalayas was going well until the leader of the party fell ill; she fell ill, and had to be taken to hospital*

falling-off ['fɔːlɪŋ'ɒf] *noun* becoming less; *a falling-off in the use of the public library; the report mentions a falling-off in international telephone calls*

fall off ['fɔːl 'ɒf] *verb* to become fewer; *the number of visitors to the library has fallen off this year*

Fallopian tube [fə'ləʊpɪən 'tjuːb] *noun* one of two tubes in a woman, which connect the ovaries to the uterus; *they discovered a growth in one of her Fallopian tubes*

fall out ['fɔːl 'aʊt] *verb* to have an argument; *they fell out over the bill for drinks*

fallout ['fɔːlaʊt] *noun* (a) **nuclear fallout** *or* **radioactive fallout** = radioactive material which falls from the atmosphere after a nuclear explosion (b) unfortunate result; *the fallout from the arrest of the party treasurer*

fallow ['fæləʊ] *adjective* (land) which is not used for growing crops for a time so that nutrients can build up again in the soil; *after cropping for four years, we let the land lie fallow for two seasons*

fallow deer ['fæləʊ 'dɪə] *noun* type of deer, slightly smaller than the red deer and with flat antlers; *there are both fallow and red deer in the park*

falls [fɔːlz] *noun* large waterfall; *he tried to go over the falls in a barrel* (NOTE: often used in names of waterfalls: **Niagara Falls, Victoria Falls,** etc.)

fall through ['fɔːl 'θruː] *verb* not to take place as was planned; *our planned holiday in Spain fell through because we had too much work at the office*

false [fɔːls] *adjective* (a) not true; *the story he told was quite false* (b) not real; **false teeth** = artificial teeth; **false alarm** = signal for an emergency when there isn't one; *the fire brigade has answered two false alarms today; she was rushed to hospital, but it turned out to be a false alarm*

falsehood ['fɔːlshʊd] *noun* (*formal*) lie, something which is not true; *it appears that he had told several falsehoods under oath*

false ribs ['fɔːls 'rɪbz] *noun* ribs which are not directly attached to the breastbone; *he fell and fractured one of his false ribs*

false start ['fɔːls 'stɑːt] *noun* start of a race which is not allowed by the judge; *after two false starts, the race got under way*

falsification [fɔːlsɪfɪ'keɪʃn] *noun* act of falsifying; *he was accused of falsification of entries in the accounts*

falsify ['fɔːlsɪfaɪ] *verb* to change something to make it wrong or not real; *he was accused of falsifying the accounts; they said the police had falsified the evidence*

falter ['fɔːltə] *verb* (a) to almost stop moving; *the engine faltered and then stopped; progress in the talks faltered* (b) to speak hesitantly; *she said 'yes' in a faltering voice*

fame [feɪm] *noun* being famous, well known; *he walked to London to seek fame and fortune; fame hasn't spoilt her at all*

famed [feɪmd] *adjective* well-known; *the town is famed for its cheese festival*

familiar [fə'mɪljə] *adjective* (a) heard or seen before; *the dog wagged its tail as it heard its master's familiar voice at the door; he looked round the room, and saw a couple of familiar faces;* **is he familiar with that type of engine?** = does he know that type of engine well? (b) very informal, (too) friendly; *don't try to get familiar with me!; she is getting too familiar with the customers*

familiarity [fəmɪlɪ'ærɪti] *noun* (a) **familiarity with someone** *or* **something** = good knowledge of someone or something; *his familiarity with London makes him an excellent guide* (b) very informal way of speaking to someone; *the manager told her off for familiarity with the customers*

familiarize [fə'mɪljəraɪz] *verb* to **familiarize yourself with something** = to get to know something well; *before starting to work the machine, you will need to familiarize yourself with the control system*

family ['fæmɪli] *noun* (a) group of people who are related to each other, especially mother, father and children; *the Jones family are going on holiday to Spain; they have a very big family - three sons and two daughters;* **family pack** *or* **family size** = larger than normal packet of goods which is cheaper to buy; **family room** = hotel room for a family, with a main bed for the parents and small beds or bunk beds for the children (b) group of animals or plants, etc., which are closely related; *lions and tigers are members of the cat family* (NOTE: plural is **families** but **family** can be used to mean a group and in this case takes the plural: **the family were out**)

family doctor ['fæmɪli 'dɒktə] *noun* general practitioner, especially one who looks after all the members of a family; *who is your family doctor?*

family name ['fæmɪli 'neɪm] *noun* surname, the name of someone's family, shared by all people in the family; *her Christian name or first name is Anne, but I don't know her family name; see also* NAME

family planning ['fæmɪli 'plænɪŋ] *noun* using contraception to control the number of children in a family; *she goes to a family planning clinic*

family tree ['fæmɪli 'triː] *noun* table showing a family going back over many generations; *he's going through the local parish records to try to establish his family tree; they can trace their family tree back to the Norman conquest of 1066*

famine ['fæmɪn] *noun* very serious shortage of food; *famine is widespread in parts of Africa*

famished ['fæmɪʃt] *adjective (informal)* very hungry; *I'm famished - is there anything in the fridge?*

famous ['feɪməs] *adjective* well-known; *he's a famous footballer; this tea shop is famous for its cakes; he owns a famous department store in the centre of London*

famously ['feɪməsli] *adverb* **(a)** as is well-known; *Nelson is famously supposed to have put the telescope to his blind eye and said 'I see no signal'* **(b)** very well; *they got on together famously*

fan [fæn] **1** *noun* **(a)** device for moving air to make things cooler; *we put electric fans in the office to try to keep cool*; **fan belt** = loop of rubber which turns a fan to cool the engine of a car; **extractor fan** = fan which sucks air out; *when you switch on the light in the bathroom, the extractor fan comes on automatically* **(b)** passionate supporter; *there was a crowd of fans waiting for him outside the theatre*; **a Liverpool fan** = a supporter of Liverpool football team **2** *verb* **to fan yourself** = to make yourself cool by making the air move; *he fanned himself with his programme* (NOTE: **fanning - fanned**)

fanatic [fə'nætɪk] *noun* person who is extremely enthusiastic about something; *he's a keep fit fanatic; the tourists were attacked by religious fanatics*

fanatical [fə'nætɪkl] *adjective* very enthusiastic; *she's fanatical about sport*

fanaticism [fə'nætɪsɪzm] *noun* being a religious fanatic; *the government is trying to cope with the rise of religious fanaticism*

fancier ['fænsɪə] *noun* person who has an interest in a certain type of animal; *he's a well-known dog-fancier*; **pigeon fancier** = person who breeds and races pigeons

fanciful ['fænsɪfʊl] *adjective* imaginative, unlikely; *the idea that there was a conspiracy to poison the Prime Minister is just fanciful*

fan club ['fæn 'klʌb] *noun* organized group of admirers of a pop star, actor, etc.

fancy ['fænsi] **1** *noun* **(a)** imagination; *the offer of a part in the film was just her fancy* **(b)** desire; **it took his fancy** = he suddenly wanted it; *the watch took her fancy, so she walked into the shop and bought it* **2** *adjective* **(a)** pretty, decorated; *he wore a fancy waistcoat to the wedding* **(b)** **fancy prices** = high prices (as charged to tourists); *I don't want to pay the fancy prices they ask in London shops* **3** *verb* **(a)** to imagine, to believe; *she fancied she saw a dark figure in the garden* **(b)** to like, to want to have; *I fancy an ice cream - any one else want one?*; *do you fancy sharing a taxi to the airport?*; *(informal)* **I think she fancies you** = I think she is attracted to you **4** *interjection* showing surprise; *fancy meeting you here!*

fancy dress ['fænsi 'dres] *noun* unusual costume worn to a party; **fancy dress party** = party where the guests have to wear costumes

fanfare ['fænfeə] *noun* short piece of music, played especially on trumpets to signal the entrance of an important person or the start of a show; *they played a fanfare as the bride entered the church*

fang [fæŋ] *noun* animal's long tooth; *the wolf bared its fangs and growled*

fanlight ['fænlaɪt] *noun* small window over a door or a larger window; *open the fanlight if you want some more air*; *Georgian houses often have semi-circular fanlights*

fan mail ['fæn 'meɪl] *noun* admiring letters received by a pop star, etc.; *she got sackfuls of fan mail after her TV show*

fantasize ['fæntəsaɪz] *verb* to imagine; *he often fantasizes about how pleasant life would be on a tropical island*

fantastic [fæn'tæstɪk] *adjective* **(a)** strange, like a dream; *his stories are full of fantastic creatures* **(b)** *(informal)* wonderful, amazing; *a holiday surfing in Australia - that's fantastic!*; *it's fantastic working in TV!*

fantasy ['fæntəsi] *noun* invented story, hope which cannot come true; *her story of meeting a rich man in Paris was just a fantasy; he's living in a fantasy world - one day he'll wake up in the real world and it will be a shock* (NOTE: plural is **fantasies**)

fanzine ['fænziːn] *noun* magazine for a fan club; *she edits the pop group's fanzine*

FAO = FOR THE ATTENTION OF

far [fɑː] **1** *adverb* **(a)** a certain distance away; *the railway station is not far from here; how far is it from Paris to London?; the road was blocked by cars as far as we could see*; **as far as I know** *or* **can tell** = I think, but I'm not absolutely sure; *as far as I know, the train is on time; as far as I can tell, the engine is working normally* **(b)** a long time ago; *as far back as 1965, he was making a lot of money* **(c)** much; *it is far cheaper to go by bus than by train; restaurant food is far nicer than the food at college* **2** *adjective* which is a long way away; *the shop is at the far end of the High Street* (NOTE: **far - farther** *or* **further** ['fɑːðə *or* 'fɜːðə] - **farthest** *or* **furthest** ['fɑːðəst *or* 'fɜːðəst])

◊ **far from** ['fɑː frɒm] *adverb* not at all; *the food here is far from cheap*

◊ **by far** ['baɪ 'fɑː] *adverb* very much; *a bike is by far the cheapest way to travel round London; of all small cars, this one uses by far the least amount of petrol*

◊ **so far** ['səʊ 'fɑː] up till now; *so far the weather has been very cold; so far this winter I have managed not to catch flu; have you enjoyed your stay in England so far?*

◊ **in so far as** [ɪn 'səʊ 'fɑː 'æz] *(formal)* to the extent that; *we found the assembly instructions, in so far as they applied to our model, quite easy to understand* (NOTE: also spelt **insofar as**)

faraway ['fɑːəweɪ] *adjective* distant or remote; *he died on active service and is buried in some faraway military cemetery*

farce [fɑːs] *noun* **(a)** comic play based on slapstick and ridiculous situations; *we went to see a 19th century*

French *farce* **(b)** absurd situation; *the meeting rapidly became a farce*

farcical ['fɑːsɪkl] *adjective* absurd; *we got into the farcical situation where we had parked the car backing onto the quayside and it was stuck in reverse gear*

fare [feə] **1** *noun* **(a)** price which you have to pay for a journey; *rail fares have been increased by 10%*; *the tourist class fare is much less than the first class one*; *if you walk to work, you will save £5 a week on bus fares*; **children over 12 must pay the full fare** = they must pay the same price as adults; **single fare** *US* **one-way fare** = fare for a journey from one place to another; **return fare** *US* **round-trip fare** = fare for a journey from one place to another and back again **(b)** *(especially in publicity)* food; *good country fare* **2** *verb* to do, to perform; *how did he fare in his driving test?* (NOTE: do not confuse with **fair**)

Far East ['fɑː 'iːst] *noun* countries to the east of Pakistan and India; *when he was twenty he sailed to the Far East for the first time to work in a Hong Kong shipping company*; *our trade with the Far East has suffered because of exchange problems*

fare-paying ['feəpeɪɪŋ] *adjective* who pays a fare; *fare-paying passengers are furious with the reduction in services*

farewell [feə'wel] *interjection & noun (formal)* goodbye; *it's time to say farewell*; **to bid someone farewell** = to say goodbye to someone; *he left without bidding us farewell*

far-fetched ['fɑːfetʃt] *adjective* difficult to believe; *his story seems extremely far-fetched*

farm [fɑːm] **1** *noun* land used for growing crops and raising animals; *he runs a pig farm*; *we're going to work on a farm during the holidays*; *you can buy eggs and vegetables at the farm shop* **2** *verb* to grow crops, raise animals, etc., on a farm; *he farms 250 acres in Devon*

farmer ['fɑːmə] *noun* person who manages or owns a farm; *farmers are worried that the fine weather won't last until harvest time*; *he is one of the biggest pig farmers in the county*

farmhouse ['fɑːmhaus] *noun* house where a farmer and his family live; *the pig ran out of the barn, straight into the farmhouse*

farming ['fɑːmɪŋ] *noun* work of managing a farm, of growing crops, of keeping animals for sale; *sheep farming is important in Wales*

farm labourer ['fɑːm 'leɪbrərə] *noun* person who does heavy work on a farm; *we used to employ six farm labourers, but now most of the work is done by machine*

farmland ['fɑːmlænd] *noun* land which is used for growing crops or raising animals for food; *thousands of acres of farmland are being set aside for planting trees*

farm out ['fɑːm 'aut] *verb* to hand over work to another person to do; *we farm out our typing to people working from home*

farm worker ['fɑːm 'wɜːkə] *noun* person who works on a farm; *we don't employ as many farm workers as we used to*

farmyard ['fɑːmjɑːd] *noun* area around farm buildings, where tractors are kept, etc.; *hens were pecking at grain in the farmyard*

far off ['fɑː 'ɒf] *adverb* **(a)** a long way away; *we could see the house from far off* **(b) not far off** = almost correct; *you weren't far off in your estimate*

far-off ['fɑːɒf] *adjective* which is a long way away; *a far-off point of light in the darkness*

far out ['fɑː 'aut] *adverb* **(a)** a long way away; *we could see the ships far out at sea* **(b) not far out** = almost correct; *the figure he suggested wasn't very far out*

far-reaching [fɑː'riːtʃɪŋ] *adjective* which has wide effects or results; *a far-reaching investigation into the finances of the local council*

fart [fɑːt] **1** *noun (vulgar)* **(a)** noise made when passing wind from the intestines through the anus; *old Uncle John embarrassed us all after the meal when he belched and then gave a loud fart* **(b)** *(slang)* stupid fool; *he said that the board was just a group of old farts* **2** *verb (vulgar)* to make a fart; *what's that smell - has someone farted in here?*; **to fart around** = to work badly and waste time; *stop farting around and come and help me move this crate*

farther *or* **farthest** ['fɑːðə *or* 'fɑːðəst] *see* FAR; *you're too close to the camera - move farther back*; *how much farther is it to the seaside?*; *which is farther south - New York or Rome?*; *Land's End is the farthest west you can go in England*

fascinate ['fæsɪneɪt] *verb* to interest or to charm greatly; *he's fascinated by Russian music*; *anything to do with stars and space travel fascinates him*

fascinated ['fæsɪneɪtɪd] *adjective* very interested; *she was fascinated to hear about his travels in Asia*; *the children watched fascinated as the clown blew flames out of his mouth*

fascinating ['fæsɪneɪtɪŋ] *adjective* very interesting; *a microscope gives you a fascinating glimpse of life in a drop of water*; *the book gives a fascinating description of London in the 1930s*; *it was fascinating to hear her talk about her travels in India*

fascination [fæsɪ'neɪʃn] *noun* great interest or attraction; *the court heard of his fascination with guns*; *the desert holds a fascination for her*

fascism ['fæʃɪzm] *noun* extreme right-wing political movement; *the rise of fascism in the early 20th century*

COMMENT: fascism emphasizes the power of the state, and the personality of the leader of the nation; it is violently opposed to Communism

fascist ['fæʃɪst] **1** *adjective* referring to fascism; *fascist gangs tried to break up the demonstration*; *the military took power and set up a fascist dictatorship* **2** *noun* person who supports fascism; *the fascists came to power in 1933*

fashion ['fæʃn] **1** *noun* **(a)** most admired style at a particular moment; *it's the fashion today to wear your hair very short*; *she always follows the dictates of fashion*; **in fashion** = popular, following the current style; *high heels are in fashion this year*; **out of fashion** = unpopular, not the current style; *red cars are out of fashion at the moment*; **fashion guru** = person who gives advice on what clothes are fashionable; **fashion victim** = person who follows the current fashion slavishly **(b)** manner or way; *she was treated in a most kindly fashion* **(c) after a fashion** = not very well; *he can speak French after a fashion* **2** *verb* *(formal)* to make; *he fashioned a raft out of old boxes*

fashionable ['fæʃnəbl] *adjective* in fashion; *she lives in the fashionable West End of London*; *it's a fashionable restaurant for film stars and journalists*

fast [fɑ:st] **1** *adjective* **(a)** quick; *this is the fast train to London*; *she was driving in the fast lane of the motorway* **(b)** *(of clock)* to show a time which is later than the correct time; *your clock is fast*; *my watch is five minutes fast* = is showing a time which is five minutes later than it really is (e.g. 6.15 instead of 6.10) **2** *adverb* **(a)** quickly; *walk faster if you want to catch up with the children in front*; *don't go so fast - you almost hit that man on the zebra crossing* **(b)** fast asleep = sleeping so that it is difficult to wake up; *she must have been tired - she's fast asleep already* (NOTE: **faster - fastest**) **3** *noun* period during which you stop eating for religious or health reasons; *he started a 24-hour fast* **4** *verb* to eat nothing for religious or health reasons; *many people fast during Lent*; *he fasted for a week*

fasten ['fɑ:sən] *verb* to close or attach securely; *please fasten your seatbelts*; *these shoes fasten with a buckle*

fastener ['fɑ:snə] *noun* device which fastens; *I must have put on weight - I can't do the fastener up*; zip fastener = sliding fastener for closing clothes, bags, etc.

fastening ['fɑ:snɪŋ] *noun* device which fastens; *the fastening on his skis seems to have come undone*

fast food ['fɑ:st 'fu:d] *noun* food which is prepared and served quickly; *there are several fast-food restaurants near the office*

fastidious [fæ'stɪdɪəs] *adjective* hard to please, careful about tidiness and cleanliness; *put the book back in the right place - the librarian is very fastidious about that sort of thing*

fast-moving [fɑ:st mu:vɪŋ] *adjective* which is moving fast; *the little girl was hit by a fast-moving car*

fast-track ['fɑ:st 'træk] *adjective* (process) which is faster than normal; *they have started a fast-track application scheme*

fat [fæt] **1** *adjective* **(a)** *(person)* round and overweight; *two fat men got out of the little white car*; *you'll have to eat less - you're getting too fat*; *he's fatter than me* *(informal)* fat cats = businessmen who earn enormous salaries and bonuses **(b)** thick; *he pulled a fat wad of notes out of his pocket* **(c)** *(informal)* a fat lot of = none at all; *he's a fat lot of use on a farm - he can't even drive a tractor!*; *she wrote complaining letters to the post office, but a fat lot of good it did her!* (NOTE: **fatter - fattest**) **2** *noun* **(a)** part of meat which is yellowish-white; *if you don't like fat, cut it off* **(b)** cooking fat = white substance from animals or plants, used for cooking; *fry the onions in hot fat*; vegetable fat = fat obtained from peanuts, etc., used for cooking

fatal ['feɪtəl] *adjective* **(a)** which causes death; *there were three fatal accidents on this stretch of road last year* **(b)** which has bad results; *it is fatal to ask him to help with the cooking*

fatality [fə'tælɪtɪ] *noun* *(formal)* death (in an accident); *the floods caused three fatalities*; *train fatalities are on the increase* (NOTE: plural is **fatalities**)

fate [feɪt] *noun* **(a)** destiny, what is certain to happen to you; *they met by chance in a bar in New Zealand, and got married - it must have been fate!*; to tempt fate = to do something which could have bad results; *it's tempting fate to ask him to look after your girlfriend while you are away* **(b)** what happens to someone, especially in the end; *the people of the country have the right to decide their own fate* (NOTE: do not confuse with **fête**)

fated ['feɪtɪd] *adjective* destined by fate; *we seem fated never to be able to have a meal together*; *his book seems fated never to get finished*

fateful ['feɪtful] *adjective* important because of its serious consequences for the future; *the fateful decision was taken in August 1989*

father ['fɑ:ðə] **1** *noun* **(a)** man who has a son or daughter; *ask your father if he will lend you his car*; *she is coming to tea with her father and mother* **(b)** title given to a priest; *Father Thomas is our parish priest* **2** *verb* to become the father of a child, etc.; *he fathered three children by his mistress*

Father Christmas ['fɑ:ðə 'krɪsməs] *noun* man in a long red coat, with a big white beard, who is supposed to bring presents to children on Christmas Day (NOTE: also called **Santa Claus**)

father-in-law ['fɑ:ðəɪn'lɔ:] *noun* father of your wife or husband; *her father-in-law left her all his money in his will* (NOTE: plural is **fathers-in-law**)

fatherland ['fɑ:ðəlænd] *noun* country of your ancestors, especially referring to Germany; *the old people get very sentimental talking about the fatherland*; *compare* MOTHERLAND

fatherly ['fɑ:ðəli] *adjective* like a father; *he kept a fatherly eye on her*

fathom ['fæðəm] **1** *noun* measure of depth of water (6 feet or 1.8 metres); *the ship sank in fifty fathoms of water* **2** *verb* to fathom something out = to understand something *or* someone mysterious; *I can't fathom him out*; *they can't fathom out how the car came to be in the river*

fatigue [fə'ti:g] **1** *noun* **(a)** tiredness; *after a long day walking in the mountains, the group were showing signs of fatigue*; metal fatigue = wearing out of metal used in a construction **(b)** fatigues = (i) cleaning duty in the army; (ii) overalls worn when doing this; *he was put on fatigues because he had been rude to the officer* **2** *verb* *(formal)* to tire someone out; *if you are ill, any physical work is fatiguing*; *I find going to the January sales very fatiguing*

fatstock ['fætstɒk] *noun* cows, sheep, etc., fattened for food; *fatstock prices have risen this month*

fatten ['fætn] *verb* to give animals more food to make them fat for slaughter; *the turkeys are ready to be fattened for Christmas*

fattening ['fætnɪŋ] *adjective* which makes you fat; *low-fat yoghurt isn't fattening*

fatten up ['fætn 'ʌp] *verb* to give animals more food to make them fat for slaughter; *we're fattening up the turkeys for Christmas*

fatty ['fæti] **1** *adjective* (food or tissue) which has a lot of fat in it; *I don't like fatty bacon* **2** *noun* *(informal)* fat person; *come on fatty - move up and let me sit down* (NOTE: plural is **fatties**)

faucet ['fɔːsət] *noun US* device with a knob which, when you twist it, lets liquid come out; *the faucet in the bathroom is leaking* (NOTE: British English is always **tap**)

fault [fɒlt] **1** *noun* **(a)** making a mistake; being to blame for something going wrong; *it isn't my fault if there's nothing in the fridge; it's all your fault - if you hadn't stayed in bed all morning we would be at the seaside by now;* **at fault** = having made a mistake; *the shop is at fault if they sent you the wrong table* **(b)** to **find fault with something** = to criticize something, to find something wrong; *she's always finding fault with my work* **(c)** the fact that something is not working properly; *the invoice was wrong because of a computer fault; the engineers are trying to mend an electrical fault* **2** *verb* to find something wrong with; *you can't fault her work*

faultless ['fɔːltləs] *adjective* perfect; *he played a faultless game of chess; she gave a faultless performance as Cleopatra*

faulty ['fɔːlti] *adjective* with mistakes or imperfections; *the lights are flickering - there must be a faulty connection somewhere; the electrician says that the wiring is faulty*

fauna ['fɔːnə] *noun* wild animals (of an area); *the flora and fauna of South America; compare* FLORA (NOTE: plural is **fauna**)

favour *US* **favor** ['feɪvə] **1** *noun* **(a)** friendly act, act of kindness; *can I ask a favour? will you look after my bike while I'm in the post office?;* **to do someone a favour** = to do something to help someone; *he won't charge for it - he did it as a favour; will you do me a favour and look after my cat when I'm away?* **(b)** approval or popularity; *she tried to win the favour of the committee;* **out of favour** = disliked **(c)** preference or liking; **to be in favour of** = to prefer; *the meeting voted in favour of the resolution;* **the score is 4-1 in our favour** = we are leading 4-1 **2** *verb* **(a)** to like or to prefer; *the managers favour moving to a bigger office* **(b)** to make things easier for someone; *the conditions favour Australian bowlers*

favourable *US* **favorable** ['feɪvrəbl] *adjective* good; *she made a favourable impression at the interview*

favourably *US* **favorably** ['feɪvrəbli] *adverb* well; *this year's exam results compare favourably with last year's*

favoured *US* **favored** ['feɪvəd] *adjective* which is preferred; *the train is his favoured means of travel*

favourite *US* **favorite** ['feɪvrɪt] **1** *adjective* which you like best; *which is your favourite TV programme?* **2** *noun* **(a)** thing or person which you like best; *which ice cream is your favourite?; this chocolate is a favourite with the children* **(b)** person, horse, etc., which most people think is likely to win; *he's the favourite to win the election; that horse is the favourite in the three o'clock race*

favouritism *US* **favoritism** ['feɪvərɪtɪzm] *noun* showing support for one group or one person at the expense of others; *the head teacher was accused of favouritism*

fawn [fɔːn] **1** *noun* **(a)** young deer; *a female deer with two little fawns* **(b)** brownish cream colour; *they painted the kitchen a pale fawn* **2** *adjective* of a brownish cream colour; *she was wearing a fawn coat and dark gloves* **3** *verb* to **fawn on someone** = to try to

get someone's favour by doing everything he wants; *I can't stand all these young people fawning on him all the time*

fax [fæks] **1** *noun* copy of a text or picture sent by telephone; *post it to me, or send a fax; can you confirm the booking by fax?;* **fax machine** = machine attached to the telephone line which sends faxes; **fax paper** = special paper which is used in fax machines; *we need to order some more fax paper* (NOTE: plural is **faxes**) **2** *verb* to send a letter or picture by telephone; *I will fax the design to you or I will fax you the design as soon as it is ready*

faze [feɪz] *verb US* to surprise or shock; *she wasn't fazed by the reporters' questioning*

FBI [efbiːˈaɪ] *noun US* Federal Bureau of Investigation

fear ['fɪə] **1** *noun* **(a)** feeling of being afraid; *fear of the dark is common in small children; she has no fear of heights* **(b)** *(informal)* **no fear!** = certainly not!; *go on, stroke that tiger - no fear!* **2** *verb* **(a)** to be afraid of something; *what do you fear most?* **(b)** to be afraid that something bad will happen; *I fear we are going to get wet - look at those dark clouds; when the little girl had not come back home three days later, everyone began to fear the worst;* **to fear for** = to worry that something might happen; *most parents fear for their children's safety*

fearful ['fɪəful] *adjective* **(a)** *(formal)* **fearful of** = afraid of; *he doesn't want to act because he is fearful of the consequences* **(b)** *(informal)* terrible; *the broken exhaust pipe makes a fearful racket*

fearless ['fɪələs] *adjective* with no feeling of fear; *a fearless lion tamer*

fearsome ['fɪəsəm] *adjective* frightening; *an attack by a band of fearsome pirates*

feasibility [fiːzəˈbɪlɪti] *noun* ability to be done; *he was asked to report on the feasibility of the project;* **to carry out a feasibility study** = to study costs, etc., to see if a project should be started; *the department has produced a feasibility report on the proposed town centre development scheme*

feasible ['fiːzəbl] *adjective* which can be done; *he says it is not feasible to produce draft plans at this stage*

feast [fiːst] **1** *noun* **(a)** special religious day; *today is the Feast of St Nicholas* **(b)** very large meal; *that wasn't an ordinary meal - it was a feast!*

feat [fiːt] *noun* unusually difficult act; *scoring a hat trick is quite a feat;* **no mean feat** = a great achievement; *getting the job done in record time was no mean feat*

feather ['feðə] *noun* one of many light soft parts which cover a bird's body; *a parrot with green feathers; he stuck a feather in his hat;* **as light as a feather** = very light

feathered ['feðəd] *adjective* with feathers; *she wore a strange feathered headdress (humorous)* **our feathered friends** = birds; *don't forget to put some crumbs out for our feathered friends*

featherweight ['feðəweɪt] *noun* weight in boxing between bantamweight and lightweight; *the featherweight champion; a featherweight title fight*

feathery ['feðəri] *adjective* light and delicate like a feather; *the clouds are painted in fine feathery strokes; a fern with feathery leaves*

feature ['fiːtʃə] **1** *noun* **(a)** part of the face, such as the nose or mouth, etc.; *his distinctive features mean that we should find him quite quickly* **(b)** important part of aspect; *the main feature of the castle is its huge tower*; *fjords are a feature of the coastline of Norway* **(c)** important item in a TV news programme; important article on a special subject in a newspaper; *did you see the feature on St Petersburg?* **(d)** feature film = full-length film **2** *verb* **(a)** to have as the main performer, especially in a film, on TV, or in a play; *the film featured Charlie Chaplin as the tramp*; *the circus features Russian clowns* **(b)** to show as the most important item; *the tour features a visit to the Valley of the Kings*; *the next programme will feature a discussion between environmental experts* **(c)** to appear as the main actor or subject in a film or on TV; *she has featured in many TV series*

February ['februəri] *noun* second month of the year, between January and March; *my birthday is in February*; *he died on February 17th US February 17*; *we are moving to new offices next February* (NOTE: **February 17th:** say 'the seventeenth of February' or 'February the seventeenth'; American English: 'February seventeenth')

fecal, feces ['fiːkl or 'fiːsiːz] *US see* FAECAL, FAECES

fecund ['fekənd] *adjective (formal)* productive; *she has a very fecund imagination*

fed [fed] *see* FEED

federal ['fedərəl] *adjective* **(a)** referring to the central government of the United States; *most federal offices are in Washington*; *federal law is more important than state law*; **Federal Bureau of Investigation (FBI)** = main police agency for fighting crime in the USA **(b)** referring to a system where a group of provinces or states exist under a central government; *the Federal Republic of Germany*

federalism ['fedərəlɪzm] *noun* type of government, in which the state is a federation of provinces or states with a central government; *federalism is becoming more powerful in Europe*

federalist ['fedərəlɪst] *noun* referring to federalism; *the government has definite federalist views*

federate ['fedəreɪt] *verb* to join together to form a federation; *the country is formed of seven federated states*

federation [fedə'reɪʃn] *noun* group of states or organizations which have joined together; *the employers' federation*

fed up ['fed 'ʌp] *adjective (informal)* **fed up (with)** = tired of, unhappy because you have had enough of something; *I'm fed up with watching the TV every evening, why can't we go out for a change?*; *she went back to school last Tuesday and she's already fed up*

fee [fiː] *noun* money paid to doctors, schools and lawyers, etc., for work done; *private school fees are very high*; *the lawyer's fee for two days' work was more than I earn in a month!*; **entrance fee** *or* **admission fee** = fee paid to go in

feeble ['fiːbl] *adjective* weak; *the candle only gave a feeble light*; *he gave a feeble excuse for not coming to the party* (NOTE: **feebler - feeblest**)

feed [fiːd] **1** *noun* **(a)** food given to animals; *a bag of cattle feed* **(b)** meal, especially given to a baby or animal; *the poor little thing - she's crying because she*

needs a feed **(c)** means of putting material into a machine; **sheet feed** = device on a printer for inserting single sheets of paper; *the paper feed has jammed* **2** *verb* **(a)** to give food to someone, to an animal; *let's go to the park and feed the ducks*; *how can you feed your family when you haven't any money?* **(b)** to eat; *the lambs are feeding* **(c)** to feed something into a machine = to put something in again and again; *he fed the paper into the printer*; *the grain is fed into the mill through a hopper* (NOTE: **feeding - fed** [fed] **- has fed**)

feedback ['fiːdbæk] *noun* **(a)** information or comments about something which has been done; *I don't know what the sales are like because we haven't had any feedback from our sales people* **(b)** return of a signal in an electronic circuit causing a high-pitched noise

feeder ['fiːdə] *noun* **(a)** container for animals' food; *put the grain in the feeder for the pigs* **(b)** *(old)* baby's bib **(c)** **feeder school** = junior school which provides children for a senior school

feed on ['fiːd 'ɒn] *verb* **(a)** to eat; *sheep feed on grass* **(b)** to grow because of an influence; *the scandal just feeds on rumour*

feedstuff ['fiːdstʌf] *noun* food for farm animals; *cereals form an important part of animal feedstuff*

feel [fiːl] **1** *noun* how something seems when touched; *velvet has a soft feel*; *the rough feel of the wooden floor* **2** *verb* **(a)** to touch (usually with your fingers); *feel how soft the bed is*; **to feel your way** = (i) to try to find the way forward in the dark by putting out your hands; (ii) to act cautiously until you have more experience; *when the lights went out we had to feel our way out of the cinema*; *he hasn't made any decisions yet - he's still feeling his way* **(b)** to seem soft, cold, etc., when touched; *the bed feels hard*; *the stone floor felt cold* **(c)** to sense something with your body or mind; *did you feel the table move?*; *I felt the lift go down suddenly*; *do you feel warmer now that you've had a cup of tea?*; *they felt happy when they saw that all was well*; *by twelve o'clock she was feeling hungry* **(d)** **not to feel yourself** = not to feel very well; *she's not coming to the office, she's not feeling herself today* **(e)** to think; *he feels it would be wrong to leave the children alone in the house*; *the police felt that the accident was due to fog* (NOTE: **feeling - felt** [felt] **- has felt**)

feeler ['fiːlə] *noun* antenna, a long part on an insect's head with which it touches things; *the butterfly senses movement with its feelers*; **to put out feelers** *or* **a feeler** = to explore something, to see if something can be done; *we'll put out some feelers to see what the staff think about the idea*

feel for ['fiːl 'fɔː] *verb* to be sympathetic towards; *I feel for him, he's lost his job and now his wife has been taken to hospital*

feelgood factor ['fiːlgʊd 'fæktə] *noun* general feeling that everything is going well; *they were hoping that the feelgood factor would win them the election*

feeling ['fiːlɪŋ] *noun* **(a)** something which you feel; *I had a feeling that this strange man knew who I was* **(b)** ability to sense something by touching; *my hands were so cold that I lost all feeling in my fingers*

feel like ['fiːl 'laɪk] *verb* **(a)** to want to do something; *I feel like going for a swim*; *do you feel like a cup of coffee?* **(b)** to seem like, when touched; *it feels like* *plastic, not wood* **(c)** *(of weather)* to seem as if it is going to do something; *it feels like snow*

feel up to ['fiːl 'ʌp tʊ] *verb* to be strong enough to do something; *do you feel up to walking round the park?*

feet [fiːt] *see* FOOT

feign [feɪn] *verb (formal)* to pretend; *she feigned surprise*

feisty ['feɪsti] *adjective US* energetic and aggressive; *she's a feisty fighter for women's rights*

fell [fel] *see* FALL

fella ['felə] *noun (informal)* = FELLOW; *a couple of young fellas came up to me in the pub*

fellow ['feləʊ] *noun* **(a)** man; *a young fellow came up to me and asked me the time; who's that fellow with a beard who's watching us?* **(b)** person who belongs to the same group; *I was OK, but several of my fellow passengers were seasick;* **fellow sufferer** = someone who has the same illness as you; *it's the hayfever season, and I sympathize with all fellow sufferers* **(c)** member of a college (at Oxford and Cambridge universities), or of a research institute or academic society; *he's a fellow of Pembroke College, Oxford*

fellowship ['feləʊʃɪp] *noun* **(a)** friendly feeling; *he developed a feeling of fellowship with the other hostages* (NOTE: no plural in this meaning) **(b)** grant to continue studying; *she has a fellowship to research into the causes of skin cancer* **(c)** position of fellow at Oxford and Cambridge Universities; *he got a first, and was immediately offered a fellowship*

felony ['feləni] *noun (old term)* serious crime; *to commit a felony* (NOTE: plural is **felonies**)

felt [felt] **1** *noun* thick material made of wool fibres pressed together; **felt pen** *or* **felt tipped pen** = pen whose writing end is made of hard felt **2** *verb see* FEEL

female ['fiːmeɪl] **1** *adjective* referring to women, girls; referring to the sex which has young; *a female athlete; a female kitten* **2** *noun* **(a)** *(informal)* woman or girl; *three females went into the bar* **(b)** animal, insect, bird which gives birth to young or lays eggs; flower which produces seeds; *the female of the species is larger than the male*

feminine ['femənɪn] *adjective* **(a)** like a woman, suitable for a woman; *her long white silk dress was very feminine* **(b)** *(in grammar)* referring to words which have a particular form or behave in a different way, to show the female gender; *is the French word 'table' masculine or feminine?; 'actress' is the feminine form of 'actor'* (NOTE: the opposite is **masculine**)

feminism ['femɪnɪzm] *noun* being a feminist

feminist ['femɪnɪst] *noun* woman who actively supports the right of women to equal status with men

femininity [femɪˈnɪnɪti] *noun* female qualities; *she uses her femininity to good effect when dealing with the directors at the office* (NOTE: the opposite is **masculinity**)

femur ['fiːmə] *noun* thigh bone, the long bone which goes from the hip to the knee; *she slipped and broke her femur* (NOTE: plural is **femurs** *or* **femora** ['femərə])

fen [fen] *noun* large area of marsh; *we spent a day in the fens, looking for wild duck*

fence [fens] **1** *noun* barrier of wood or wire, used to keep people or animals in or out of a place; *the fence was blown down; the boys looked through the hole in*

the fence; *the builders put up a fence round the construction site;* **to sit on the fence** = to avoid giving a definite answer to a question or giving support to one particular side; *he never takes sides - he just sits on the fence* **2** *verb* **(a)** to put a fence round something; *the police fenced off the accident site* **(b)** to fight with swords as a sport

fencing ['fensɪŋ] *noun* **(a)** material which makes a fence; *the crowd surged forward and flattened the fencing around the football ground* **(b)** sport of fighting with swords; *fencing is one of the sports in the pentathlon*

fend [fend] *verb* **(a)** **to fend off** = to push away; *he spent the morning fending off newspaper reporters* **(b)** **to fend for yourself** = to look after yourself; *we went to Spain and left the children to fend for themselves*

fender ['fendə] *noun* **(a)** rope mat or rubber tyre, etc., hung against the side of a boat to protect it from bumps; *the fender scraped along the side of the quay* **(b)** low guard around a fireplace to stop coal or wood falling out into the room; *she sat by the fender, poking the fire* **(c)** *US* guard over the wheels of a car or bicycle, to prevent mud splashing; *she ran into a tree and bent a fender* (NOTE: British English for this is **wing** for a car, and **mudguard** for a bicycle)

fenland ['fenlænd] *noun* area of land covered by fens; *we love to visit the lonely fenland churches*

fennel ['fenl] *noun* herb with a smell like aniseed; *you can use fennel to flavour fish*

ferment 1 *noun* ['fɜːmənt] upset or agitation; *the university was in a ferment* **2** *verb* [fəˈment] to change into alcohol by the effect of yeast on sugar; *cider has to ferment for at least ten weeks before it is ready to drink*

fermentation [fɜːmenˈteɪʃn] *noun* chemical change brought about in liquids usually leading to the production of alcohol; *they added sugar to encourage fermentation*

fermented [fəˈmentɪd] *adjective* which has been changed to alcohol; *cider is fermented apple juice*

fern [fɜːn] *noun* green plant with feathery leaves which does not have flowers or seeds but is propagated by spores; *she has a collection of ferns in pots*

ferocious [fəˈrəʊʃəs] *adjective* fierce and angry; *a ferocious tiger leapt out of the grass; the newspaper made a ferocious attack on the minister*

ferocity [fəˈrɒsɪti] *noun* fierceness; *everyone was surprised at the ferocity of her attack; the storm beat down on the coast with renewed ferocity*

ferret ['ferɪt] **1** *noun* small animal similar to a weasel, which is half-tamed and used to drive rabbits or rats from holes; *as boys we used to go rat-catching with ferrets* **2** *verb* to look for something; *the police spent two hours ferreting around the office;* **to ferret out** = to find out by endless searching; *he ferreted out some surprising facts about the murderer's family*

Ferris wheel ['ferɪs 'wiːl] *noun* large vertical wheel in a funfair, with seats hanging from it; *you get a marvellous view of the town from the top of the Ferris wheel*

ferry ['feri] **1** *noun* boat which carries cars or trucks or people to and fro across a stretch of water; *the little boat rocked in the wake of the ferry; we are going to take the night ferry to Belgium; there's a ferry across the*

Rhine here; **car ferry** = ferry which carries cars; **passenger ferry** = ferry which only carries passengers (NOTE: plural is **ferries**) **2** *verb* to take across by boat; *small boats ferried the refugees across the lake*

ferryboat ['feribəut] *noun* ferry, a boat which carries cars or trucks or people to and fro across a stretch of water; *the ferryboat was full of passengers when it capsized*

fertile ['fɜːtaɪl *US* 'fɜːtl] *adjective* **(a)** *(soil)* rich enough to produce crops; *the farm has rich black fertile soil*; *along the river valley the soil is very fertile* **(b)** *(of female, or egg)* able to produce young; *the zoo hopes the female panda is fertile, so that she can have cubs*; *the eagle laid several eggs but only two were fertile* **(c)** which produces ideas; *he has a fertile imagination* = he imagines things very easily (NOTE: the opposite is **sterile** *or* **infertile**)

fertility [fə'tɪləti] *noun* being fertile, being able to produce crops or young; *they spread manure to increase the fertility of the soil* (NOTE: the opposite is **sterility** *or* **infertility**)

fertilization [fɜːtɪlaɪ'zeɪʃn] *noun* act of joining male and female cells together; *fertilization took place in the laboratory*

fertilize ['fɜːtɪlaɪz] *verb* **(a)** to spread fertilizer on land; *the soil is poor and needs to be heavily fertilized* **(b)** to join male and female cells together, so that a new animal or plant will be made; *the sheep was fertilized in the laboratory*

fertilizer ['fɜːtɪlaɪzə] *noun* chemical or organic material spread over the soil to make it richer and more able to produce crops; *farmers are being encouraged to use organic fertilizers*; *she spread fertilizer round her carrots*; **liquid fertilizer** = fertilizer in the form of a liquid which is added to water

COMMENT: fertilizers are either 'organic', such as manure, dead plants, seaweed, fishmeal, or 'inorganic', such as lime. Most fertilizers are made from mixtures of chemicals, in particular nitrogen and potassium

fervent *or* **fervid** ['fɜːvənt *or* 'fɜːvɪd] *adjective* passionately enthusiastic; *she's a fervent Chelsea fan*; *it's our fervent desire that he should become an engineer like his father* (NOTE: **fervid** is less common than **fervent**)

fervour *US* **fervor** ['fɜːvə] *noun* passionate enthusiasm; *religious fervour swept the country*; *he spoke with great fervour about his dream of a united country*

fescue ['feskjuː] *noun* type of grass grown in meadows; *fescues are the best types of grass for cattle feed*

fester ['festə] *verb* **(a)** *(of wound)* to become bad and produce pus; *his legs were covered with festering sores* **(b)** to become worse and bitter; *the resentment of the staff continued to fester*

festival ['festɪvl] *noun* **(a)** religious celebration which comes at the same time each year and usually is a public holiday; *the tour will visit Hong Kong for the Lantern Festival* **(b)** artistic celebration or entertainment which is put on at regular intervals; *we saw some excellent plays at the Edinburgh Festival this year*; **arts festival** = competitions in music, drama, painting and handicrafts, etc.; **beer festival** =

competition, tasting and exhibition of different types of beer; **cheese festival** = competition, tasting and exhibition of cheeses; **film festival** = competition where different films are shown; *the film won a prize at the Cannes Film Festival*

festive ['festɪv] *adjective* referring to a celebration; *the country was in festive mood to welcome back the victorious soldiers*; **the festive season** = Christmas and the New Year

festivity [fe'stɪvɪti] *noun* celebration; *the festivities for the President's marriage lasted several days* (NOTE: plural is **festivities**)

festoon [fe'stuːn] **1** *noun* long chain of hanging decorations; *girls put festoons of flowers round the necks of the visitors* **2** *verb* to hang with decorations; *the streets were festooned with banners*

fetch [fetʃ] *verb* **(a)** to go and bring someone *or* something; *it's your turn to fetch the children from school*; *can you fetch me the atlas from the library?* **(b)** to be sold for a certain price; *that car won't fetch more than £200*; *these CDs fetch very high prices on the black market*

fête [feɪt] *noun* small public event, usually in the open air, with stalls, sideshows and competitions; *I hope it doesn't rain for the village fête* (NOTE: do not confuse with **fate**)

fetlock ['fetlɒk] *noun* wide part of a horse's leg just above the pastern; *he had a cut on his right front fetlock; see also* PASTERN

fetus ['fiːtəs] *noun US see* FOETUS

feud [fjuːd] **1** *noun* bitter quarrel; *I don't want to get involved in their family feud* **2** *verb* to quarrel bitterly all the time; *the sisters are feuding over their father's will*

feudal ['fjuːdl] *adjective* referring to feudalism; *the serf had to pay duty to his feudal lord*

feudal system *or* **feudalism** ['fjuːdəl 'sɪstəm *or* 'fjuːdəlɪzm] *noun* medieval system, where land was granted by a king to his nobles and by the nobles to the peasants, on condition that each paid a service to his superior and fought for him; *the feudal system in England began to break down during the fourteenth century, following the Black Death*

fever ['fiːvə] *noun* **(a)** state when the body's temperature is higher than normal; *you must stay in bed until the fever goes down* **(b)** excited state; *the crowd waited in a fever of anticipation*

fevered ['fiːvəd] *adjective (formal)* **(a)** suffering from fever; *the nurse wiped his fevered brow* **(b)** overactive; *the book is the product of a fevered imagination*

feverish ['fiːvərɪʃ] *adjective* **(a)** suffering from fever; *he felt feverish and took an aspirin* **(b)** anxiously quick or excited; *in a burst of feverish activity he finally finished writing the book on time*

few [fjuː] *adjective & noun* **(a)** not many; *she has very few friends at work*; *we go to fewer concerts than last year*; *I wonder why few of the staff stay with us more than six months*; **few and far between** = not very frequent; *trains are few and far between on Sundays* **(b)** **a few** = some, not very many; *I only took a few photographs because it rained all the time*; *I'll call you in a few minutes*; *a few of the wedding guests were sitting playing cards* (NOTE: **fewer - fewest**)

fiancé *or* **fiancée** [fɪˈɒnseɪ] *noun* man or woman who is engaged to be married; *her fiancé is a French lawyer*; *he brought his fiancée to the party*

fiasco [fɪˈæskəʊ] *noun* total failure; *the exhibition ended in a fiasco or was a complete fiasco* (NOTE: plural is **fiascos**)

fibre *US* **fiber** [ˈfaɪbə] *noun* small thread of material; *from the pieces of fibre left at the scene of the murder, the police could work out what the murderer had been wearing*; **optical fibres** = fine threads of glass used for transmitting light signals; *see also* FIBRE OPTICS

fibreglass *US* **fiberglass** [ˈfaɪbəɡlɑːs] *noun* material made from glass fibres, used to make boats and car bodies; *he's bought a new fibreglass boat*; *the car body is made of fibreglass*

fibre optics *US* **fiber optics** [ˈfaɪbə ˈɒptɪks] *noun* using thin strands of glass or plastic for carrying light signals and data; **fibre optic cable** = thin strands of glass or plastic used to carry light signals and information; *they are installing fibre optic cables to bring cable TV to the village*

fibroid [ˈfaɪbrɔɪd] *noun* benign fibrous tumour in the uterus

fibrosis [faɪˈbrəʊsɪs] *noun see* CYSTIC FIBROSIS

fibrous [ˈfaɪbrəs] *adjective* made of fibres; *a fibrous growth*; *fibrous tissue is the strong white tissue which forms ligaments*

fibula [ˈfɪbjʊlə] *noun* thin bone behind the tibia, between the knee and the ankle; *he fractured his fibula*

fickle [ˈfɪkl] *adjective* changeable, not steady; *the fickle public elected him President and is now calling on him to resign*; *we can't rely on the fickle April weather for our garden party*

fiction [ˈfɪkʃn] *noun* (a) novels; *fiction writers such as Graham Greene* (b) story that is not true; *his account of the accident was pure fiction* (NOTE: no plural)

fictional [ˈfɪkʃənəl] *adjective* (a) (character) who exists in fiction; *Mr Pickwick, Sam Weller and other fictional characters from Dickens may have been based on real people* (b) written as a novel; *the book is a fictional account of a real murder*

fictitious [fɪkˈtɪʃəs] *adjective* untrue, not real; *they found he had included bills from fictitious hotels in his expense account*; *his story was fictitious from beginning to end*

fiddle [ˈfɪdl] **1** *noun (informal)* (a) violin; *he plays the fiddle at country dances*; **fit as a fiddle** = very fit; *he's over eighty and still as fit as a fiddle*; **to play second fiddle to someone** = to be in an inferior position to someone; *he always plays second fiddle to his wife* (b) dishonest or illegal dealings; *the whole thing's a fiddle to get money from the EU*; **he's on the fiddle** = he's trying to make money illegally **2** *verb* (a) *(informal)* to play the fiddle; *he was fiddling away at an Irish dance* (b) **to fiddle with something** = to play idly with something; *she was fiddling with her bracelet during the whole interview*; *he fiddled with the radio and managed to get it to work* (c) *(informal)* to record money transactions in a dishonest way; *the company caught him fiddling his expense account*; *she tried to fiddle her tax return*

fiddler [ˈfɪdlə] *noun (informal)* violin player; *a group of Irish fiddlers played at the wedding*

fide *see* BONA FIDE

fidelity [fɪˈdelɪti] *noun* (a) being faithful; *he was rewarded for his fidelity to the president* (b) accuracy of reproduction; *a high fidelity CD player* (NOTE: no plural)

fidget [ˈfɪdʒɪt] **1** *verb* to move all the time; *after an hour he started to fidget in his seat*; *sit still and stop fidgeting!* **2** *noun (informal)* **the fidgets** = moving all the time, not being able to stay still; *the children got the fidgets after sitting still for a few moments*

field [fiːld] **1** *noun* (a) piece of ground on a farm, with a fence or hedge around it; *the sheep are in the field*; *a field of potatoes* (b) **playing field** = piece of ground for playing a game; *the two teams ran onto the field*; **field events** = jumping and throwing competitions; *athletics is made up of both track and field events* (c) special area of interest or study; *what's your field?*; *his field is English language teaching* **2** *verb* (a) to send out a team to play or to negotiate; *England are fielding their strongest side for some years*; *the union fielded a strong negotiating team* (b) **to field questions** = to deal with questions; *he fielded questions from the journalists about his private life*

fielder [ˈfiːldə] *noun (in cricket)* member of the side which is not batting; *two of the fielders ran for the ball and collided*

field glasses [ˈfiːld ˈɡlɑːsɪz] *noun* binoculars; *with his field glasses he could easily see the owl* (NOTE: the word is plural; to show one only, say **a pair of field glasses**)

field gun [ˈfiːld ˈɡʌn] *noun* light gun which can be moved around a place where a battle is taking place; *they brought up more field guns to the top of the hill*

field hockey [ˈfiːld ˈhɒki] *noun US* hockey, a team game played on grass, where you try to hit a small ball into a goal with a curved stick; *the Indian field hockey team* (NOTE: simply called **hockey** in British English)

field marshal [ˈfiːld ˈmɑːʃəl] *noun* officer of the highest rank in the army; *he became a field marshal and retired* (NOTE: can be used as a title with a name: **Field Marshal Haig**)

fieldmouse [ˈfiːldmaʊs] *noun* small type of country mouse with a long tail; *fieldmice have eaten all the peas we planted* (NOTE: plural is **fieldmice**)

field sports [ˈfiːld ˈspɔːts] *noun* outdoor sports, such as hunting and fishing; *she is very keen on field sports*

fiend [fiːnd] *noun* (a) devil; monster; *that boy's a little fiend* (b) *(informal)* person who is very enthusiastic about something; *he's an old car fiend*; *she's an organic food fiend*

fiendish [ˈfiːndɪʃ] *adjective* devilish; very difficult; *you have to pass a fiendish exam to become an accountant*

fiendishly [ˈfiːndɪʃli] *adverb* terribly, very; *the test is fiendishly difficult*; *Hungarian is a fiendishly difficult language*

fierce [fɪəs] *adjective* (a) very angry and likely to attack; *watch out - that dog looks fierce* (b) violent, intense; *a fierce storm broke out as they were leaving the harbour*; *the mountains were the scene of fierce fighting*; *he got into a fierce argument about working conditions*

fiercely [ˈfɪəsli] *adverb* (a) strongly; *she is fiercely independent* (b) violently; *the shop was blazing* *fiercely when the fire brigade arrived; the storm blew fiercely during the night*

fierceness ['fɪəsnəs] *noun* **(a)** violence; *the fierceness of her response surprised everyone* **(b)** heat; *the fierceness of the fire defeated the fire brigade's attempt to put it out*

fiery ['faɪəri] *adjective* **(a)** burning; *a fiery desert sun* **(b)** fierce, angry; *she has red hair and a fiery temper*

fifteen [fɪf'tiːn] **(a)** number 15; *there are fifteen players in a rugby side; she's fifteen (years old); come and see me in fifteen minutes; the train leaves at nine fifteen (9.15);* **the fifteen hundreds (1500s)** = the years from 1500 to 1599 (NOTE: compare **the fifteenth century**) **(b)** group of fifteen people (as in a Rugby team); *the England XV* (NOTE: usually written **XV** in this meaning: **the England XV**: say 'the England fifteen')

fifteenth (15th) [fɪf'tiːnθ] *adjective & noun the fifteenth of July or July the fifteenth (July 15th); that's the fifteenth phone call I've made this morning; it will be her fifteenth birthday next week;* **the fifteenth century** = the years from 1400 to 1499 (NOTE: compare **the fifteen hundreds;** Note also that with dates **fifteenth** is usually written **15th: July 15th, 1935; October 15th, 1991** (American style is **October 15, 1991**), say 'the fifteenth of October' or 'October the fifteenth' (American style is 'October fifteenth'); with names of kings and queens **fifteenth** is usually written **XV: King Louis XV** (say: 'King Louis the Fifteenth'))

fifth (5th) [fɪfθ] **1** *adjective the fifth of May or May the fifth (May 5th); it's his fifth birthday tomorrow;* **the fifth century** = period from 400 to 499 AD **2** *noun* **(a)** a fifth = 20%; *he spends a fifth of the week travelling* **(b)** *(in music)* difference in pitch between D and A (NOTE: with dates **fifth** is usually written **5th: July 5th, 1935; October 5, 1991** (American style is **October 5, 1991**), say 'the fifth of October' or 'October the fifth' (American style is 'October fifth'); with names of kings and queens **fifth** is usually written **V: King Henry V** (say: 'King Henry the Fifth'))

Fifth Amendment ['fɪfθ ə'mendmənt] *noun* the Amendment to the Constitution of the USA which allows citizens not to give evidence in court which might incriminate themselves; *he took the Fifth Amendment and refused to answer any questions*

fifty ['fɪfti] **(a)** number 50; *my mother made fifty pots of jam; she's fifty (years old);* **she's in her fifties** = she's between 50 and 59 years old; **the (nineteen) fifties (1950s)** = the period from 1950 to 1959 **(b) fifty-fifty** = divided into two equal amounts; **to go fifty-fifty** = with each paying half of the cost; *we'll go fifty-fifty on the bill* (NOTE: **fifty-one** (51), **fifty-two** (52), but **fifty-first** (51st), **fifty-second** (52nd), etc.)

fiftieth (50th) ['fɪftɪəθ] *adjective & noun she came fiftieth and last in the race; it's her fiftieth birthday on Monday;* **a fiftieth** = 2%

fig [fɪg] *noun* **(a) fig (tree)** = fruit tree which grows in warm countries; *there's a huge fig growing outside the National Gallery* **(b)** juicy sweet fruit of the fig tree; *we sat under the tree and ate figs and goat's cheese*

fight [faɪt] **1** *noun* **(a)** struggle against someone *or* something; *he got into a fight with boys who were bigger than him; fights broke out between the demonstrators and the police;* **to pick a fight with someone** = to start a fight with someone **(b)** boxing match; *the fight only lasted three rounds* **2** *verb* **(a)** to struggle against someone or something using force; *the*

two boys were fighting over a comic; rival gangs fought in the street; we are committed to fighting crime; doctors are fighting to control the disease **(b) to fight for something** = to struggle on behalf of something; *they are fighting for the right to vote* (NOTE: **fighting - fought** [fɔːt] **- has fought**)

fighter ['faɪtə] *noun* **(a)** person who fights; *the referee stopped the fight when one of the fighters had a cut eye* **(b)** person who is strong; *she's a real fighter - she'll pull through this illness* **(c)** fast attacking aircraft; *two fighters went up to attack the enemy bombers*

fighting ['faɪtɪŋ] *noun* action of struggling; *the meeting ended when fighting broke out among the members; fighting crime is a major priority for the police force*

fight off ['faɪt 'ɒf] *verb* to get rid of an attacker or illness; *the man threw her to the ground but she managed to fight him off; I'm trying to fight off my flu with aspirin and hot drinks*

figurative ['fɪgərətɪv] *adjective* **(a)** *(art)* which shows something as it really it (as opposed to abstract art); *he's a well-known figurative artist* **(b)** which is not the literal meaning of a word; *calling him a 'lump of jelly' was a figurative use of the word; you didn't mean that literally, did you? - no, I was speaking in a figurative sense*

figure ['fɪgə *US* 'fɪgj] **1** *noun* **(a)** written number (such as 35); *I can't read the figure on the order - is it 250?; he added up the figures on the bill; cheques have to be made out in both words and figures; see also* DOUBLE, SINGLE **(b)** geometric shape such as a triangle or circle; *a six-sided figure is a hexagon* **(c)** drawing or diagram in a book; *see figure 2 on page 23* **(d)** shape of a person; *we could see some figures through the mist; the figures in the foreground of the painting* **(e)** attractive shape of a woman's body; *she still has a great figure* **(f)** important person; *he's one of the important figures in the opposition movement* **(g) figure of speech** = colourful figurative expression; *a 'storm in a teacup' is a figure of speech meaning a lot of fuss about nothing* **(h)** pattern of movement (in skating or dancing); *see also* FIGURE SKATING **2** *verb* **(a) to figure out** = to try to think of an answer or to understand something; *try to figure out the answer yourself instead of asking someone else* **(b)** *US (informal)* to consider, to think; *I figure the costs will be high; we figured you'd be late because of the show; had you figured on being there before two o'clock?;* **that figures** = that makes sense **(c)** to appear (in a novel, painting, etc.); *fair-haired girls figure in many of his paintings*

figurehead ['fɪgəhed] *noun* **(a)** wooden figure carved on the front of an old ship; *the museum has a collection of 19th century figureheads* **(b)** person who seems important but who has no real power; *the President is just a figurehead, the Minister of the Interior has the real power*

figures ['fɪgəz] *noun* arithmetic; *I'm just no good at figures*

figure skating ['fɪgə 'skeɪtɪŋ] *noun* international competitions for men and women, involving solo skating and skating in pairs, concentrating on doing jumps and figures of eight, all done to music; *see also* ICE DANCING

COMMENT: the rink used for international competitions is 60m long and 30m wide with rounded corners and the competitors are expected to use all of it. There are nine judges, each judge awarding two marks to a possible maximum of 6.0 for technical merit and artistic presentation

figurine ['fɪgəriːn] *noun* very small statue in china, wood, etc.; *she has a collection of Japanese ivory figurines*

filament ['fɪləmənt] *noun* thin wire; *when the light is switched on, the filament inside the bulb glows*

file [faɪl] 1 *noun* (a) metal tool used for smoothing rough surfaces; *use a file to round off the edges of the metal; see also* NAIL FILE (b) holder for papers and documents; *when you have finished with the papers, put them back in the file; the police have a file on him* (c) section of data on a computer; *type the name of the file and then press ENTER* (d) line of people; **in single file** = one behind the other; *the children entered the hall in single file* 2 *verb* (a) to smooth a surface with a file; *file down the rough edges* (b) to put papers away in a folder or case; *file that letter under SALES* (c) to walk in a line; *they filed past the place where the boy had been shot* (d) to make an official request; *he filed for divorce; she filed a petition in bankruptcy*

filename ['faɪlneɪm] *noun* name given to a computer file; *in the old system, a filename could be made up of letters or numerals, up to eight characters long, followed by a three character extension, such as .DOC*

filial ['fɪliəl] *adjective (formal)* referring to the attitudes or actions of a son or daughter towards his or her parents; *her filial affection for her father; he didn't show his mother proper filial respect*

filibuster ['fɪlɪbʌstə] *noun* attempt to prevent a law being passed by speaking for a very long time in the debate; *the Democrats organized a filibuster in the Senate*

filing ['faɪlɪŋ] *noun* (a) action of putting documents away in the right place; *filing invoices is a job I detest* (b) documents which have to be put in order; *there is a lot of filing waiting to be done at the end of the week*

filing cabinet ['faɪlɪŋ 'kæbɪnət] *noun* piece of office furniture, a tall box with drawers for putting files in; *someone broke open the filing cabinet and removed some documents*

filings ['faɪlɪŋz] *noun* small pieces of metal removed by using a file; *you can demonstrate magnetic fields with iron filings and a magnet*

Filipino [fɪlɪˈpiːnəʊ] *adjective & noun* (person) from the Philippines; *they have two Filipino housemaids* (NOTE: plural is **Filipinos**)

fill [fɪl] *verb* (a) to make something full; *he filled the bottle with water; she was filling the boxes with presents* (b) **to fill a tooth** = to put metal into a hole in a tooth to stop it going bad; *I hate having my teeth filled but it has to be done* (c) **to fill a gap** = to provide something which is needed, but which no one has been provided before; *the new range of small cars fills a gap in the market* (d) **to fill a post or a vacancy** = to find someone to do a job; *your application arrived too late - the post has already been filled*

filler ['fɪlə] *noun* (a) material used to fill holes and cracks in walls, woodwork, etc.; *they used plastic filler*

to repair the cracks in the ceiling (b) thing used to fill a space; **stocking filler** = little gift which can be put into a Christmas stocking

fillet ['fɪlɪt] 1 *noun* (a) piece of good-quality meat, with no bones; *she bought a fillet of lamb* (b) piece of fish from which the bones have been taken out; *we ordered fried fillet of sole* 2 *verb* to remove the bones from a fish; *ask the fishmonger to fillet the fish for you*

fill in ['fɪl 'ɪn] *verb* (a) to fill up a hole; *he dug a hole in the garden, put the box inside, and then filled it in* (b) to write in the empty spaces on a form; *just fill in your name and address; to win the prize you have to fill in the missing words* (c) **to fill in for someone** = to do something which someone else normally does but cannot do; *I'm filling in for the manager who is on holiday*

filling ['fɪlɪŋ] 1 *adjective* which fills; *a meal of salad and a glass of water is not very filling* 2 *noun* (a) metal put into a hole in your tooth by a dentist; *I had to go to the dentist because one of my fillings came out* (b) food used to put into a sandwich, pie, cake, etc.; *a cake with a jam filling*

filling station ['fɪlɪŋ 'steɪʃn] *noun* petrol station, place where you can buy petrol; *let's stop at the next filling station to see if we can get a map*

fill out ['fɪl 'aʊt] *verb* to write in all the empty spaces on a form; *fill out the form and send it back to this address*

fill up ['fɪl 'ʌp] *verb* (a) to make something completely full; *he filled the bottle up with fresh water*; **fill her up** = please fill the car with petrol (b) to write in all the empty spaces on a form; *fill up the form and send it back to this address*

filly ['fɪli] *noun* young female horse; *it was the first time the race had been won by a filly* (NOTE: a young male horse is a **colt**; note also that the plural is **fillies**)

film [fɪlm] *noun* (a) moving pictures shown at a cinema, taken with a cine-camera; *have you seen this old Laurel and Hardy film?; we've seen the film already on TV*; **film rights** = the legal right to make a film from a book (NOTE: American English is **movie**) (b) roll of material which you put into a camera to take photographs or moving pictures; *I must buy another film before the wedding; do you want a colour film or a black and white one?* (c) thin layer of something; *a film of moisture formed on the cold metal surface; everywhere was covered with a film of dust*

filming ['fɪlmɪŋ] *noun* action of making a film; *filming has already started in Spain*

film-maker ['fɪlmmeɪkə] *noun* person who makes films; *a famous American film-maker*

film star ['fɪlm 'stɑː] *noun* well-known film actor or actress; *there are pictures of famous film stars in the cinema foyer*

filter ['fɪltə] 1 *noun* (a) device or material for straining liquids or air, for stopping any solids from passing through; *the filters in the swimming pool have to be cleaned regularly* (b) glass on a camera which allows only certain colours or intensities of light to pass through; *I use an orange filter to give a warm colour to the picture* (c) material at the end of a cigarette, used to remove nicotine 2 *verb* (a) to remove impurities by passing through a filter; *kidneys filter the blood* (b) to move gradually; *watch out for traffic filtering in from the left*; **filter lane** *or* **filter light** = traffic lane *or* light only for cars which are turning **(c)** to go *or* to come slowly through, down, out, etc.; *sunlight filtered through the leaves*; *rumours began to filter out about a boardroom coup*

filter paper ['fɪltə 'peɪpə] *noun* paper used for filtering liquids; *don't forget to put a filter paper in before you put in the coffee*

filter-tip cigarette ['fɪltətɪp 'sɪgəret] *noun* cigarette with a filter at the end

filth [fɪlθ] *noun* **(a)** dirt; *they were horrified at the filth in the streets* **(b)** obscene words, books, etc.; *I don't want you to read any more of this filth*

filthy ['fɪlθi] *adjective* **(a)** very dirty; *where have you been playing - you're filthy!*; *don't touch that filthy old carpet*; *filthy beggars followed the tourists wherever they went* **(b)** very unpleasant and angry; *watch out - the boss is in a filthy temper* **(c)** obscene; *he tried to sell us some filthy postcards* (NOTE: **filthier - filthiest**)

fin [fɪn] *noun* **(a)** thin part on the body of a fish which helps it to swim; *from the beach they could see a shark's fin in the sea* **(b)** similar piece on an aircraft; *the tail fin broke off when the plane crashed*

finagle [fɪ'neɪgl] *verb US (informal)* to get something by dishonest means; *she managed to finagle a free ticket to the show*

final ['faɪnl] **1** *adjective* last, coming at the end; *this is your final warning - if you don't work better you will be sacked*; *the competition is in its final stages*; **my decision is final** = I cannot change my decision; **final date for payment** = last date by which payment should be made **2** *noun* **(a)** last competition in a series between several teams or competitors; *I thought they would win a couple of rounds, but I never imagined they would get to the final*; **cup final** = last game in a series of football games, where the winner is given a silver cup **(b) finals** = last examinations at the end of a university course, after which you get your degree; *after his finals he's planning to travel round Australia*; *everybody's at home cramming for their finals*

finale [fɪ'nɑːli] *noun* last part of a piece of music, of a show; *after the finale the audience applauded enthusiastically*; **grand finale** = final very impressive show; *the grand finale of the party was a firework display*

finalist ['faɪnəlɪst] *noun* person taking part in the final of a competition; *there are four finalists for the title of 'Brain of Britain'*

finalize ['faɪnəlaɪz] *verb* to finish making plans for something; *we hope to finalize the agreement tomorrow*; *if you agree to the plan, we'll finalize the details later*

finally ['faɪnəli] *adverb* at last, in the end; *the police finally cleared up the mystery*; *the little boy finally turned up in Edinburgh*

finance ['faɪnæns] **1** *noun* money, especially money which belongs to the public or to a company; *how are you going to raise the finance for the expansion plan?*; *my finances are in a poor state at the moment*; **Minister of Finance** = government minister in charge of a country's finances (NOTE: in Britain this minister is called **the Chancellor of the Exchequer** and in the USA **the Secretary to the Treasury**) **2** *verb* to provide money for; *how are you going to finance your course at university if you don't have a grant?*; *the*

redevelopment of the city centre is being financed locally

financial [fɪ'nænʃl] *adjective* referring to money; *what is our financial position?*; *the company has got into financial difficulties*; **financial year** = 12-month period for which accounts are calculated

financier [fɪ'nænsɪə] *noun* person who deals with money on a large scale; *a major city financier*

finch [fɪntʃ] *noun* small seed-eating bird; *in the winter lots of finches come to our bird-table* (NOTE: plural is **finches**)

find [faɪnd] **1** *noun* thing which you discover; *what a lucky find! a cheap hotel in the centre of Paris* **2** *verb* **(a)** to discover (something hidden or lost); *I found a £2 coin behind the sofa*; *did she find the book she was looking for?* **(b)** to discover something which was not known before; *no one has found a cure for the common cold yet* **(c)** to have an opinion about something; *I found the book very dull*; *she finds her work too easy* **(d)** to make a legal decision in court; *the tribunal found that both parties were at fault*; *he was found guilty of murder*; **the judge found for the defendant** = the judge decided that the defendant was right **(e) to be found** = to exist; *toadstools are found in woods in the autumn* (NOTE: **finding - found** [faʊnd])

finder ['faɪndə] *noun* person who finds; *he was the finder of the lost tomb of the Inca king*

findings ['faɪndɪŋz] *noun* facts discovered; recommendations; *the findings of the committee of inquiry will be published next week*; *the two companies signed an agreement to share their research findings*

find out ['faɪnd 'aʊt] *verb* to discover information; *your job is to find out if the competition is planning a new model*; *she needs to find out everything she can about Napoleon*; *the police are trying to find out why she went to Scotland*

find time ['faɪnd 'taɪm] *phrase* to do something even though you are short of time; *in the middle of the meeting he still found time to phone his girlfriend*; *we must find time to visit the new staff sports club*

fine [faɪn] **1** *adjective* **(a)** good (weather); *we'll go for a walk tomorrow if it stays fine*; *let's hope it's fine for the village fête next week* **(b)** well, healthy; *I was in bed with flu yesterday, but today I'm feeling fine* **(c)** good; *how are things at home? - fine!*; *it's fine to wear a bikini when you're young and slim, but not when you're old and fat* **(d)** very thin or very small; *use a sharp pencil if you want to draw fine lines*; *I can't read the notice - the print is too fine*; **the fine print** = the conditions on a contract, usually printed in very small letters; *don't forget to check the fine print before you sign the contract* (NOTE: **finer - finest**) **2** *adverb* in very small pieces; *chop up the orange peel very fine* **3** *noun* money which you have to pay for having done something wrong; *I had to pay a £25 fine for parking in a no parking area*; *he was found guilty of embezzlement and got off with a fine* **4** *verb* to make someone pay money for having done something wrong; *he was fined £25 for parking on double yellow lines*

fine art ['faɪn 'ɑːt] *noun* painting, sculpture, etc.; *the Museum of Fine Art*; *she is taking a course in fine art appreciation*

finesse [fɪ'nes] *noun* skill in dealing with awkward situations; *she showed considerable finesse in handling the negotiations*

finger ['fɪŋgə] **1** *noun* **(a)** one of the parts at the end of your hand, but usually not including the thumb; *he wears a ring on his little finger*; *he pressed the button with his finger*; **to keep your fingers crossed** = to hope that something will happen as you want it to happen; *have you heard the exam results yet? - no, but I'm keeping my fingers crossed*; **to put your finger on something** = to point something out correctly; *you put your finger on it when you said that he's afraid of appearing stupid*; **on the fingers of one hand** = five (or less); *the number of times she's offered to buy me a drink can be counted on the fingers of one hand* (*informal*) **to pull your finger out** = to work harder; *I told him to pull his finger out*; **not to lift** *or* **raise a (little) finger to help** = not to do anything to help; *we were trying to move the piano and he didn't raise a finger to help*; *it's unfair to expect her to do all the housework while her sisters don't lift a finger to help* **(b)** part of a glove into which a finger goes; *gloves without fingers are called 'mittens'* **(c)** piece of food shaped like a finger; *a box of chocolate fingers*; *see also* FISH FINGER **2** *verb* **(a)** to touch with your fingers; *don't finger the apples* **(b)** (*informal*) to point out a criminal to the police; *he was fingered by someone else in the gang*

fingernail ['fɪŋgəneɪl] *noun* hard thin part covering the end of a finger; *she painted her fingernails green*; *don't bite your fingernails!*

fingerprint ['fɪŋgəprɪnt] *noun* mark left by a finger when you touch something; *the police found his fingerprints on the car door*

fingertip ['fɪŋgətɪp] *noun* end of the finger; **he has the information at his fingertips** = he knows all about it

finish ['fɪnɪʃ] **1** *noun* **(a)** final appearance; *the table has an attractive finish* **(b)** final appearance which is not real, which is a veneer; *kitchen cupboards with an oak finish* **(c)** end (of a race); *he ran well and came second at the finish* **2** *verb* to do something completely; to come to an end; *haven't you finished your homework yet?*; *tell me when you've finished reading the paper*; *you can't go out until you've finished doing the washing up*; *the game will finish at about four o'clock*

finished ['fɪnɪʃt] *adjective* which has been made, which has come to an end; *the finished product will be on show at the exhibition*; *after the newspapers published the story his career as a politician was finished*; *hang on, I'll be finished in a second*

finishing line ['fɪnɪʃɪŋ 'laɪn] *noun* line marking the end of a race; *she crossed the finishing line at least three metres ahead of the next runner*; *he waved his hands in the air as he came to the finishing line*

finish off ['fɪnɪʃ 'ɒf] *verb* to do something completely; *finish off your homework and then we can go out*

finish up ['fɪnɪʃ 'ʌp] *verb* **(a)** to be in the end; *we got lost and finished up miles from where we wanted to be* **(b)** to eat something completely; *you must finish up all your vegetables*

finish with ['fɪnɪʃ 'wɪð] *verb* to finish using something; *can I have the newspaper when you've finished with it?*; *have you finished with the dictionary?*

finite ['faɪnaɪt] *adjective* **(a)** with an end, with a limit; *the world's coal resources are finite and are forecast*

to run out soon **(b)** **finite verb** = verb which indicates a tense; *'he sat' shows a finite form of 'to sit'*

Finland ['fɪnlənd] *noun* large country in northern Europe, between Sweden and Russia; *we like to go camping and canoeing in Finland in summer* (NOTE: capital: **Helsinki**; people: **the Finns**; language: **Finnish**; currency: **finnmark** *or* **finnmarkka** *or* **markka, euro**)

Finn [fɪn] *noun* person from Finland

Finnish ['fɪnɪʃ] **1** *adjective* referring to Finland **2** *noun* language spoken in Finland; *I bought a Finnish phrase book before going to Helsinki*

fiord ['fiɔːd] *see* FJORD

fir [fɜː] *noun* **fir (tree)** = evergreen tree with needle-shaped leaves; *fir trees are often used as Christmas trees* (NOTE: do not confuse with **fur**)

fir cone ['fɜː 'kəʊn] *noun* hard fruit of the fir tree; *fir cones fall off the trees and get eaten by squirrels*

fire ['faɪə] **1** *noun* **(a)** something which is burning, something which heats; *we have an electric fire in the living room*; *they burnt the dead leaves on a fire in the garden*; **to catch fire** = to start to burn because of something else which is burning; *the office block caught fire*; *take those papers away - they might catch fire*; **to set fire to** = to make something start burning; *his cigarette set fire to the carpet*; **on fire** = burning; *call the emergency services - the house is on fire!* **(b)** shooting with guns; *the soldiers came under fire from the guerrillas*; *see also* GUNFIRE **2** *verb* **(a)** to shoot a gun; *the gunmen fired at the police car*; *we could hear guns firing in the distance* **(b)** to dismiss someone from a job; *she was fired for being late* **(c)** to make someone excited; *he was fired with the desire to make his fortune*

fire alarm ['faɪə ə'lɑːm] *noun* bell or siren which gives warning that a fire has started; *if you see smoke, break the glass to sound the fire alarm*

firearms ['faɪəɑːmz] *noun* any guns that can be held in the hand; *the police raided the club and confiscated firearms such as revolvers and sawn-off shotguns*

fire away ['faɪə ə'weɪ] *verb* to ask someone questions; *go on - fire away!*

fire brigade ['faɪə brɪ'geɪd] *noun* public service organization for preventing or putting out fires; *call the fire brigade - the shop's on fire!*

fire engine ['faɪə 'endʒɪn] *noun* large red van used by the fire brigade, with pumps, hoses, ladders, etc., to fight fires; *six fire engines were at the fire*

fire escape ['faɪə ɪs'keɪp] *noun* stairs or a ladder which can be used by people to get out of burning buildings; *the crowd watched as the hotel guests climbed down the fire escape*

fire extinguisher ['faɪə ɪk'stɪŋgwɪʃə] *noun* tube filled with chemicals or foam which can put out a small fire; *a fire extinguisher should be placed on each floor of the building*

fire fighter ['faɪə 'faɪtə] *noun* fireman, person who tries to put out fires; *dozens of fire fighters tried to put out the forest fire*

fireman ['faɪəmən] *noun* man who tries to put out fires; *the firemen were fighting the fire in the town centre* (NOTE: plural is **firemen**)

fireplace ['faɪəpleɪs] *noun* hole in the wall of a room where you can light a fire for heating; *the dog likes to lie on the carpet in front of the fireplace*

fireproof ['faɪəpruːf] *adjective* which will not burn; *the hotel has fireproof doors at the end of each corridor*

fireside ['faɪəsaɪd] *noun* area around a fireplace in a room; *in the evening we sit by the fireside and listen to the radio*

fire station ['faɪə 'steɪʃn] *noun* centre where fire engines are based; *the fire engines came out of the fire station with their sirens wailing*

firetrap ['faɪətræp] *noun* place which could easily catch fire, in which people could be trapped; *the hotel has no fire escape - it's a real firetrap*

firewood ['faɪəwʊd] *noun* wood for making fires; *they chopped down the dead tree to use for firewood* (NOTE: no plural)

firework ['faɪəwɜːk] *noun* small tube holding chemicals which will sparkle or explode when lit; *there was a big firework display or display of fireworks for Bonfire Night*

firing squad ['faɪrɪŋ 'skwɒd] *noun* group of soldiers who execute someone by shooting; *he was condemned to death and taken before the firing squad immediately*

firm [fɜːm] **1** *adjective* **(a)** solid or fixed; *make sure that the ladder is firm before you climb up*; *my back hurts - I think I need a firmer mattress* **(b)** not going to change; *there is no firm evidence that he stole the money*; *she is a firm believer in hard work*; **to stand firm** = not to give in; *in spite of the offers from the motorway construction company he stood firm and refused to leave his house* **(c)** which cannot be changed; *to place a firm order for two lorries*; *they are quoting a firm price of £1.22 per unit* (NOTE: **firmer - firmest**) **2** *noun* business or company; *when he retired, the firm presented him with a watch*; *the firm was taken over last year*

first [fɜːst] **1** *adjective & noun* (*as a number can be written* **1st**) referring to the thing that comes before all other things; *my birthday is on the first of July* or *July the first (July 1st)*; *King Charles the First (Charles I)*; *it's our baby's first birthday on Tuesday*; *the bank is the first building on the left past the post office*; **first century** = the period from the year 1 to 99 AD; **first name** = a person's Christian name or given name, as opposed to the surname or family name (NOTE: with dates first is usually written **1st: 1st February 1992; December 1st 1670** (American style is **December 1, 1670**), say 'the first of December' or 'December the first' (American style is 'December one'); with names of kings and queens **first** is usually written **I: King Charles I** (say 'King Charles the First')) **2** *adverb* **(a)** at the beginning; *she came first in the exam*; **first come, first served** = dealing with orders, etc., in the order in which they are received; *applications will be dealt with on a first come, first served basis* **(b)** before doing anything else; *wash your hands first, and then you can eat* **(c)** for the first time; *when did you first meet your girlfriend?*

◊ **at first** [æt 'fɜːst] at the beginning; *at first he didn't like the work but later he got used to it*

first aid ['fɜːst 'eɪd] *noun* help given to a person who is hurt, before a doctor or ambulance arrives; *the police gave first aid to the accident victims*; **first aid kit** = box with bandages and dressings kept to be used in an emergency; *we keep a first-aid kit in the car*

first class ['fɜːst 'klɑːs] **1** *adjective* **(a)** very good quality; *you can get a first-class meal in that hotel* **(b)**

using the most expensive seats on a plane or train; *can I have a first-class return to Paris, please?* **(c)** sent using the most expensive and quickest postal service; *a first-class letter is certain to arrive the following day* (NOTE: as an adjective, usually written **first-class**) **2** *adverb* **(a)** in the most expensive seats in a train or plane; *he always travels first class* **(b)** using the most expensive and quickest way of sending a letter; *send that letter first class - I want it to arrive quickly* **2** *noun* travel in the most expensive seats in a train or plane; *first class is always much more comfortable than tourist or business class*

first day cover ['fɜːst deɪ 'dʌvə] *noun* specially stamped envelope which has been franked on the first day of issue of the stamp on it; *he has collected first day covers for some years, and his collection is worth a lot*

first-ever ['fɜːst 'evə] *adjective* the first which has ever been; *it was the first-ever crossing of the Atlantic in a rowing boat*

first floor ['fɜːst 'flɔː] *noun* **(a)** in a building, the floor above the ground floor (NOTE: in American English this is the **second floor**) **(b)** *US* floor in a building which is level with the ground (NOTE: in British English this is the **ground floor**; note the difference between American and British meanings)

first-footing ['fɜːst'fʊtɪŋ] *see note at* HOGMANAY

first half ['fɜːst 'hɑːf] *noun* **(a)** first of two parts, as of a football match; *they scored three goals in the first half* **(b)** first part of a financial year, usually from January to June; *the figures for the first half are up on those for the second part of last year*

firsthand [fɜːst'hænd] **1** *adjective* which comes direct from someone who has experienced something; *we have some firsthand reports of the coup from our reporter in the capital* **2** *adverb* directly; *I heard the news of the accident firsthand from his widow*

First Lady ['fɜːst 'leɪdi] *noun* wife of a president, especially the wife of the President of the USA; *the President and the First Lady have been invited to lunch at Buckingham Palace*

firstly ['fɜːstli] *adverb* to start with; *why are they getting married? - firstly, they're in love, and secondly, her father has offered them a flat*

first mate ['fɜːst 'meɪt] *noun* the main officer in a commercial ship, under the captain; *the captain was asleep in his cabin and it was the first mate who was on duty*

first night ['fɜːst 'naɪt] *noun* evening when a play is performed for the first time; *we went to the first night of the new play at the National Theatre*; *it is impossible to get tickets for the first night*

first person ['fɜːst 'pɜːsən] *noun* word or words referring to the speaker ('I' or 'we'); *have you noticed how she has started to use the first person plural instead of the singular?*; *the whole story is told in the first person*

first-rate ['fɜːstreɪt] *adjective* excellent; *the food here is absolutely first-rate*; *he's a first-rate tennis player*

First World War ['fɜːst 'wɜːld 'wɔː] *noun* war fought from 1914 to 1918; *he was a fighter pilot during* the First World War; they visited the sites of First World War battles

---

COMMENT: the First Wold War began in Sarajevo, when the heir to the throne of the Austro-Hungarian Empire was assassinated on 28th June, 1914. This in turn, brought about a declaration of war between Austria-Hungary and Russia entering the war on the side of Serbia. Germany then declared war on Russia and France in support of Austria, and invaded Belgium. Britain declared war on Germany. Italy joined the war on the side of Britain, Russia and France in 1915, and the United States joined in April 1917. The war lasted from 1914 to November 11th 1918

---

firth [fɜːθ] noun (in Scotland) long arm of the sea; we sailed up the firth to Dundee (NOTE: often used in names: **the Firth of Forth, the Murray Firth, etc.**)

fiscal ['fiskl] adjective referring to tax or to government revenue; the government's fiscal policy; **fiscal year** = 12-month period for tax purposes (in Britain from 6th April of one year to 5th April of the next year)

fish [fɪʃ] **1** noun (a) animal with no legs, which lives in water and which you can usually eat; I sat by the river all day and only caught two little fish; **fish food** = special food which you give to goldfish, etc.; **fish tank** = big container of water for keeping goldfish, etc. (informal) **there are plenty more fish in the sea** = there are lots of other people you could be friends with; **I've got other fish to fry** = I have other more important business to deal with (NOTE: plural is usually **fish: some fish, three fish**, but also sometimes **fishes**) (b) **fish and chips** = traditional British food, obtained from special shops, where portions of fish fried in batter are sold with chips; we're having fish and chips for supper **2** verb (a) to try to catch a fish; we often go fishing in the lake; they fished all day but didn't catch anything (b) to try to find something; he fished around in his suitcase and after some delay produced his passport

fish-and-chip shop ['fɪʃən'tʃɪp 'ʃɒp] noun shop selling cooked fish and chips, and usually other food, such as pies (NOTE: can also be called a **chip shop**, or, informally, a **chippy**)

fishcake ['fɪʃkeɪk] noun round cake of fish and potato mixed together, then fried; he put ketchup on his fishcakes

fisherman ['fɪʃəmən] noun man who catches fish, either as his job or for sport; fishermen are complaining that pollution is wiping out fish stocks (NOTE: plural is **fishermen**)

fishery ['fɪʃəri] noun part of the sea where fish are usually found; the ship sailed for the North Sea fisheries; every year boats go to the rich fisheries off the east coast of Canada (NOTE: plural is **fisheries**)

fish finger ['fɪʃ 'fɪŋgə] US **fish stick** ['fɪʃ 'stɪk] noun frozen finger-shaped piece of fish covered in breadcrumbs; the children don't like fresh fish, but they do like fish fingers

fishing ['fɪʃɪŋ] noun sport or business where you try to catch fish; the sign said 'no fishing'; **fishing boat** = boat used for fishing; **fishing line** = long string used with a hook to catch fish; **fishing rod** US **fishing pole** = long piece of wood to which is attached a line and hook

fishmeal ['fɪʃmiːl] noun ground up bodies of fish, used as a fertilizer

fishmonger ['fɪʃmʌŋgə] noun person who sells raw fish in a shop; his grandfather set up shop as a fishmonger

fishmonger's ['fɪʃmʌŋgəz] noun shop selling raw fish; go to the fishmonger's and get some Dover sole

fish shop ['fɪʃ 'ʃɒp] noun (a) shop selling raw fish; the fish shop has some wonderful fresh salmon (b) (also **fish-and-chip shop**) shop selling cooked fish and chips, and usually other food, such as pies; don't bother cooking - I'll just pop down to the fish shop and get some plaice and chips

fishy ['fɪʃi] adjective (a) like a fish; these eggs have a fishy taste (b) (informal) suspicious or odd; there's something fishy about the whole business; what was she doing there at 2 o'clock in the morning? - it's very fishy if you ask me

fission ['fɪʃən] noun splitting into parts; the fission of cells is part of the development of all organic matter; a nuclear reactor creates heat and energy by fission; **nuclear fission** = splitting a hydrogen atom to create energy; compare FUSION

fissure ['fɪʃə] noun crack or split, especially in a rock or in the ground; fissures opened up in the street after the earthquake

fist [fɪst] noun tightly closed hand; he punched her with his fist; she banged on the table with her fist; see also CLENCH

fit [fɪt] **1** noun sudden sharp attack of illness, etc.; she had a coughing fit or a fit of coughing; in a fit of anger he threw the plate across the kitchen; **by fits and starts** = at odd moments, with continual stoppages; something has gone wrong with the printer - it only prints out by fits and starts **2** adjective (a) healthy; he isn't fit enough to go back to work; you'll have to get fit if you're going to run the marathon; see also FIDDLE, SURVIVAL OF THE FITTEST (b) **fit to do something** = in good enough condition to do something; is he fit to drive?; that car isn't fit to be driven - its brakes don't work and the tyres are worn (c) suitable; is she a fit person to look after small children? (NOTE: **fitter - fittest**) **3** verb (a) to be the right size or shape; he's grown so tall that his jackets don't fit him any more; these shoes don't fit me - they're a size too small (b) to put in place; I want to fit a new fridge in the kitchen; fitting the furniture into the new house was quite a problem (NOTE: **fitting - fitted**)

fit in ['fɪt 'ɪn] verb (a) to find room or time for someone or something; we can't fit a holiday in this year as we have too much work; how can you fit five people into that little car? (b) to be able to go into a space; how will the bed fit into that room? (c) to be comfortable as part of a group; he joined the firm two years ago but has never really fitted in

fitness ['fɪtnəs] noun (a) being physically fit; she does fitness exercises every morning; physical fitness is important in the marines; **fitness centre** = gym, place where you can do exercises to increase your physical fitness; the hotel is equipped with a state-of-the-art fitness centre (b) being suitable; doubts were expressed about her fitness for the job

fit out or **fit up** ['fɪt 'aʊt or 'fɪt 'ʌp] verb to provide someone or something with all the equipment or clothing necessary; he went to the hire firm and got

*fitted up with a tail coat and top hat for the wedding;
the room in the basement has been fitted out as a
gymnasium*

fitted ['fɪtɪd] *adjective* made to fit into a certain space;
fitted carpet = carpet cut to the exact size of the room
and fixed to the floor; **fitted cupboard** = specially
made cupboard which fits into a bedroom, bathroom,
etc., and is attached to the wall; **fitted kitchen** = set of
kitchen cupboards which are attached to the walls

fitter ['fɪtə] *noun* (a) skilled mechanic who adjusts
machines and their parts; *he has trained as an
electrical fitter* (b) person who makes sure clothes or
carpets fit; *the carpet fitters came to put down the
carpet on the stairs*

fitting ['fɪtɪŋ] **1** *adjective* suitable, right; *it's fitting
that grandmother should sit at the head of the table -
it's her birthday party, after all* **2** *noun* (a) action of
making something fit; action of trying on a new piece of
clothing; *she's having the first fitting of her wedding
dress this afternoon*; **fitting room** = small room in a
shop where you can try on clothes before you buy them
(b) size and shape (of shoe, etc.); *do you take a wide or
narrow fitting?* (c) thing which is fixed in a building
but which could be removed; *an electric light fitting;
the shop is being sold with all its fixtures and fittings*

five [faɪv] number 5 (a) *she drank five cups of tea;
he's five (years old) next week; the meeting has been
arranged for five (o'clock)* (b) **fives** = five pound
notes; *he gave me a ten and two fives in change*

fiver ['faɪvə] *noun* (*informal*) five pound note; *she
only had a fiver to pay for a 30p newspaper*

fix [fɪks] **1** *noun* difficult position; *he's in a bit of a fix
- he's got no cash and can't pay for the taxi; that's a
nice fix you've got us into!* (NOTE: plural is **fixes**) **2**
verb (a) to fasten or to attach; *fix one end of the cord to
the tree and the other to the fence* (b) to arrange; *we'll
try to fix a time for the meeting* (c) to mend; *the
telephone people are coming to fix the telephone; do
you know how to fix the photocopier?* (d) *US* to make
or to prepare a drink, meal, etc.; *let me fix you
something to drink; she fixed them some tuna
sandwiches*

fixated [fɪk'seɪtɪd] *adjective* always thinking about
one thing; *he's fixated with motorbikes; she's fixated
on getting a job in a supermarket*

fixation [fɪk'seɪʃn] *noun* state of only thinking about
one thing; *he has this fixation with the pop group;
she's got a fixation about washing her hair*

fixed [fɪkst] *adjective* (a) attached firmly; *the sign is
fixed to the post with six-inch nails* (b) (*price, etc.*)
arranged or agreed upon, which cannot be changed; *we
have a fixed scale of charges*; **fixed rate** = charge or
interest which cannot be changed; *they chose a
fixed-rate mortgage*

fixedly ['fɪksɪdli] *adverb* with eyes fixed on someone
or something; *the cat was staring fixedly at the
goldfish*

fixture ['fɪkstʃə] *noun* (a) sports match; *their next
fixture is against Liverpool on Saturday; season ticket
holders are sent a list of fixtures at the beginning of
the season* (b) **fixtures** = objects permanently fixed in a
house, like radiators, which are sold with the house; *the
shop is for sale with all fixtures and fittings*

fix up with [fɪks ʌp 'wɪð] *verb* to arrange or provide;
*they fixed me up with a car at the airport; can you fix
me up with a room for tomorrow night?*

fizz [fɪz] **1** *noun* (a) sound like that made by bubbles;
the fizz of the rocket as it went up into the air (b)
(*informal*) champagne; *let's have a drink, there's a
bottle of fizz in the fridge*; **buck's fizz** = cold drink of
champagne and fresh orange juice, typically served at
breakfast **2** *verb* to bubble up; *the cider fizzed in the
glasses*

fizzle out ['fɪzl 'aʊt] *verb* (*informal*) to come to
nothing; *they had this great plan, but it soon fizzled out
when they couldn't raise enough money*

fizzy ['fɪzi] *adjective* full of bubbles; *they all ordered
fizzy drinks; I don't like fizzy orange - do you have any
squash?* (NOTE: the opposite is **still: still orange**. Drinks
which should be fizzy but are not are said to be **flat**)

fjord ['fjɔːd] *noun* long arm of the sea among
mountains in Norway; *this summer we're going on a
cruise along the Norwegian fjords*

flab [flæb] *noun* (*informal*) fat flabby flesh on your
body; *she goes to the gym to try to fight the flab; he
eats and drinks too much and it simply turns into flab*

flabbergast ['flæbəgɑːst] *verb* to amaze; *she
flabbergasted us all when she announced she was
getting married*

flabbergasted ['flæbəgɑːstɪd] *adjective* amazed; *he
started to pour paint over the flabbergasted ticket
collector; we were all flabbergasted when she
announced she was getting married*

flabby ['flæbi] *adjective* soft and fat; *sitting at home
doing nothing has made him flabby* (NOTE: **flabbier -
flabbiest**)

flag [flæg] **1** *noun* (a) piece of brightly material with
the emblem of a country or club, etc., on it; *the French
flag has blue, red and white stripes; the ship was flying
the British flag; the flags were blowing in the wind*;
white flag = symbol showing that someone is
surrendering (b) small paper badge sold in aid of a
charity; *pin the flag to your coat to show that you have
given something* **2** *verb* (a) to grow tired; *we've been
travelling all day - no wonder the children are starting
to flag* (b) **to flag down** = to wave to make a taxi stop;
*he stepped out into the street and flagged down a
passing taxi* (c) to insert a marker in a computer file;
*don't forget to flag the addresses so that we can find
them again easily* (NOTE: **flagging - flagged**)

flag day ['flæg 'deɪ] *noun* day on which small paper
flags are sold in aid of a particular charity; *tomorrow is
a flag day in aid of cancer research*

flagpole ['flægpəʊl] *noun* tall pole on which large
flags are flown; *they hoisted the flag on the flagpole in
front of the house*

flagrant ['fleɪgrənt] *adjective* clear, obvious and
shocking; *a flagrant violation of human rights*

flagrantly ['fleɪgrəntli] *adverb* in a flagrant way; *he
flagrantly disobeyed the law on several occasions*

flagstaff ['flægstɑːf] *noun see* FLAGPOLE

flagstone ['flægstəʊn] *noun* large flat stone used for
making pavements or floors; *we put flagstones down to
make a patio; they have redone their kitchen with a
flagstone floor*

flail [fleɪl] **1** *noun* (*old*) hand implement for threshing
corn; *the peasants put the corn on a platform and hit it*

with flails **2** *verb* to wave your arms about; *he lay on his back flailing with his arms at his opponent*

flair ['fleə] *noun* **flair for something** = natural ability; *she has a distinct flair for dress design; he has a flair for languages* (NOTE: do not confuse with **flare**)

flak [flæk] *noun* **(a)** gunfire against aircraft; *we ran into a lot of flak as we approached the enemy stronghold* **(b)** sharp criticism; *he's taken a lot of flak from the reviewers; the programme came in for a lot of flak from the TV critics* (NOTE: no plural)

flake [fleɪk] **1** *noun* **(a)** tiny, thin piece; *the paint came off in little flakes* **(b)** small piece of snow which falls from the sky; *snow fell in large soft flakes all night* **2** *verb* **(a)** **to flake off** *or* **away** = to fall off in little pieces; *the plaster on the wall of the church had flaked away, revealing the old carvings; the paint is beginning to flake off and needs redoing* **(b)** *(informal)* **to flake out** = to collapse with tiredness; *after a hard day at the office, she flaked out on the sofa*

flaky ['fleɪki] *adjective* made up of thin pieces; *it is difficult painting on old flaky plaster;* **flaky pastry** = type of soft pastry which breaks into flakes when cooked

flamboyant [flæm'bɔɪənt] *adjective* **(a)** brightly coloured; *she wore a flamboyant red cape* **(b)** very dramatic; *in a flamboyant gesture, he ordered all the trees in the park to be covered with little lights*

flame [fleɪm] *noun* bright tongue of fire; *flames could be seen coming out of the upstairs windows;* **in flames** = burning; *the building was already in flames when the fire engine arrived*

flamenco [flə'meŋkəʊ] *noun* rapid Spanish dance, to guitar music; *we went to watch some flamenco dancers in the square*

flaming ['fleɪmɪŋ] *adjective* **(a)** in flames; *they ran away from the flaming wreckage* **(b)** **in a flaming temper** = furious, in a very bad mood; *the boss was in a flaming temper when he got back from the meeting* **(c)** *(slang) (used to make what you say stronger) what did you do with the flaming knife?*

flammable ['flæməbl] *adjective* easily set on fire; *household furniture must not be made of flammable materials* (NOTE: means the same as **inflammable**)

flank [flæŋk] **1** *noun* side, especially of an animal, of an army; *he patted the horse's flank; the right flank of the army moved forward* **2** *verb* to be at the side of someone *or* something; *the accused was flanked by two prison warders*

flannel ['flænl] *noun* **(a)** warm material made of wool; *trousers made of grey flannel* or *grey flannel trousers* **(b)** small square of towelling for washing the face or body; *he put his flannel under the hot tap and wiped his face* **(c)** **flannels** = flannel trousers; *he wore a pair of flannels and a blazer*

flap [flæp] **1** *noun* **(a)** flat part which is attached with a hinge; *the pilot tested the wing flaps before taking off;* **cat flap** = little door in the door of a house, which allows a cat to go in or out **(b)** *(informal)* state of worried excitement; *they got into a flap about the new neighbours' dog* **(c)** movement of a bird's wing; *with a flap of its wings, the eagle flew off* **2** *verb* to move up and down like a bird's wing; *flags were flapping in the breeze; the swans stood by the edge of the water, flapping their wings* (NOTE: **flapping - flapped**)

flare ['fleə] **1** *noun* **(a)** device which gives a sudden blaze of light, especially as a signal; *the lifeboat sent up flares; we knew the ship was in distress when we saw the flares* **(b)** **flares** = trousers which are wider at the bottom (NOTE: do not confuse with **flair**) **2** *verb* **(a)** to burn brightly; *the flames from the burning oil refinery flared in the distance* **(b)** *(of a skirt or trousers)* to widen gradually at the bottom; *she wore a long straight skirt which flared from the knees down; flared trousers are back in fashion*

flare up ['fleə 'ʌp] *verb* **(a)** to blaze suddenly; *the bonfire flared up when he poured petrol on it; the flames died down and then flared up again* **(b)** to get angry suddenly; *she flared up when he suggested it was her fault*

flare-up ['fleəʌp] *noun* sudden increase; *a flare-up of fighting in the Middle East*

flash [flæʃ] **1** *noun* **(a)** short sudden burst of light; *flashes of lightning lit up the sky during the thunderstorm;* **in a flash** = very quickly; *in a flash, she said 'yes'; see also* NEWSFLASH **(b)** device for making a bright light, allowing you to take photographs in the dark; *people sometimes have red eyes in photos taken with a flash* **(c)** bright light from a camera; *the scene at the entrance to the film première was lit up with flashes from photographers' cameras* (NOTE: plural is **flashes**) **2** *verb* **(a)** to light up quickly and suddenly; *lightning flashed all around* **(b)** **to flash by** *or* **to flash past** = to move or to pass by quickly; *the champion flashed past to win in record time*

flashback ['flæʃbæk] *noun* scene in a film, showing what happened at an earlier date; *the film starts with a flashback to the hero's childhood*

flash flood ['flʃ 'flʌd] *noun* sudden flood after heavy rain; *flash floods raced down the valleys, sweeping away cars and caravans*

flashlight ['flæʃlaɪt] *noun* small portable electric lamp; *the flashlight caught the eyes of a rabbit in the garden; take a flashlight if you are going to explore the caves*

flashy ['flæʃi] *adjective* showy and bright but of poor quality; *she has some very flashy jewellery; he drives a flashy green sports car* (NOTE: **flashier - flashiest**)

flask [flɑːsk] *noun* small bottle for liquids; *there is a row of labelled flasks on the shelf in the laboratory;* **thermos flask** *or* **vacuum flask** = insulated bottle for keeping liquids hot or cold; *we've brought a thermos flask of coffee*

flat [flæt] **1** *adjective* **(a)** level, not sloping or curved; *a house with a flat roof;* **flat rate** = fixed charge which never changes; *taxi drivers always charge a flat rate of £20 for driving you to the airport; he is paid a flat rate of £2 per thousand* (informal) **as flat as a pancake** = very flat; *the country round Ely is as flat as a pancake* **(b)** **a flat tyre** = a tyre which has lost all the air in it; *he pulled up at the side of the road to change a flat tyre* (NOTE: American English is simply **a flat**) **(c)** **flat racing** = horse-racing over flat ground, without any fences to jump; **the flat season** = the part of the year when flat races are held **(d)** *(of drink)* no longer fizzy; *my lemonade's gone flat* **(e)** with no electric charge left; *the car wouldn't start because the battery was flat* **(f)** *(in music)* playing at a lower pitch than it should; *that violin sounds flat* (NOTE: **flatter - flattest**) **2** *adverb* **(a)** level, not sloping or curved; *lay your clothes out flat on the bed; he tripped over and fell flat on his face*

(b) completely; in a blunt way; *he turned down the offer flat*; **flat broke** = with no money at all; *I can't pay the rent - I'm flat broke* **(c)** exactly; *he ran the mile in four minutes flat* **3** *noun* **(a)** set of rooms for one family, on one floor, usually in a building with several similar sets of rooms; *we have bought a flat in London after selling our house in the country*; *the block of flats where they live is next door to the underground station*; *their flat is on the ground floor* (NOTE: American English for this is **apartment**) **(b)** *US* tyre which has lost its air; *I asked the garage to fix the flat* (NOTE: British English is **flat tyre** *or* **puncture**) **(c)** *(in music)* pitch which is one semitone lower; *they played a Sonata in E flat*; *he played D sharp instead of D flat*

flatly ['flætli] *adverb* in a firm way; *he flatly denied having anything to do with it*

flat-mate ['flætmeɪt] *noun* person who shares a flat with you; *my flat-mate's girlfriend has come to live with him, so I'm having to move out*

flat out ['flæt 'aʊt] *adverb* **(a)** at full speed; *you'll have to drive flat out to get to the airport in time to catch the plane* **(b)** very hard; *he worked flat out to finish his work on time*

flatten ['flætən] *verb* to make flat; *the bomb flattened several houses*; *the tanks advanced across the fields, flattening the corn*; *thousands of buildings were flattened in the San Francisco earthquake of 1906*

flatter ['flætə] *verb* **(a)** to praise someone insincerely; *just flatter the boss a bit, tell him how good his golf is, and he'll give you a rise* **(b) to flatter yourself** = to persuade yourself that something is true, when it is not; *he's flattering himself if he thinks everyone is going to do what he wants*

flattered ['flætəd] *adjective* feeling honoured; *I'm flattered to be invited here tonight*

flattering ['flætərɪŋ] *adjective* which makes you look good or praises you; *she's wearing a very flattering dress*; *there's a flattering article about the restaurant in the evening paper*

flattery ['flætəri] *noun* praising someone too much; *if threats won't get you anywhere, try flattery*

flaunt [flɔːnt] *verb* to display something in a vulgar way to attract attention; *she flaunted her engagement ring all round the office*

flautist ['flɔːtɪst] *noun* person who plays the flute; *James Galway, the famous flautist* (NOTE: the American spelling is also **flutist**)

flavour *US* **flavor** ['fleɪvə] **1** *noun* particular taste; *the tomato soup had an unusual flavour* *(informal)* **the flavour of the month** = the most popular thing at the moment; *all-girl groups are the flavour of the month* **2** *verb* to add things such as spices and seasoning in cooking something, to give it a special taste; *use rosemary to flavour lamb*; *soup flavoured with herbs*

flavoured *US* **flavored** ['fleɪvəd] *adjective* which tastes of something; *a lemon-flavoured drink*

flavouring *US* **flavoring** ['fleɪvərɪŋ] *noun* substance added to food to give a particular taste; *avoid food with artificial flavourings if you can*

flaw [flɔː] **1** *noun* **(a)** defect; *the expert examined the Chinese vase, looking for flaws*; *there must be a flaw in the computer program* **(b)** mistake in an argument; *there's a flaw in your reasoning*; *there was a fundamental flaw in their calculations* **2** *verb* to spoil;

her performance was flawed by her inability to hold the high notes

flawed [flɔːd] *adjective* with mistakes; *we consider the judgement of the court to be flawed*

flawless ['flɔːləs] *adjective* perfect; *he played a flawless game of tennis*

flax ['flæks] *noun* variety of linseed plant, of which the fibres are used for making into linen

flea [fliː] *noun* tiny insect that jumps and sucks blood; *if your cat has fleas, buy a special collar which will get rid of them* (NOTE: do not confuse with **flee**)

flea market ['fliː 'mɑːkɪt] *noun* open-air market for secondhand goods; *you don't often find valuable items in a flea market, but this jug is a genuine antique*

fleck [flek] **1** *noun* small spot; *she tried to brush the flecks of powder off her dress*; *he had flecks of plaster in his hair* **2** *verb* to mark something with small spots; *his hair is flecked with grey*

fled [fled] *verb see* FLEE

fledgling ['fledʒlɪŋ] *noun* baby bird which is ready to fly from the nest; *the fledglings were standing at the edge of the nest, flapping their wings*

flee [fliː] *verb* **to flee (from something)** = to run away (from something); *as the fighting spread, the village people fled into the jungle*; *she tried to flee but her foot was caught in the rope* (NOTE: do not confuse with **flea**; note also: **fleeing - fled** [fled])

fleece [fliːs] **1** *noun* coat of wool covering a sheep; *after shearing, the fleeces are taken away to market* **2** *verb (slang)* to cheat someone and take their money; *the bars round the harbour are waiting to fleece the tourists*; *he was fleeced by two girls he met in a bar*

fleecy ['fliːsi] *adjective* **(a)** made of fleece; *my overcoat has a fleecy lining* **(b)** looking like fleece; *the blue sky was dotted with fleecy clouds*

fleet [fliːt] *noun* **(a)** group of ships belonging together; *when the fleet is in port, the pubs are full of sailors* **(b)** collection of vehicles; *the company replaces its car fleet or fleet of cars every two years*; *the airline's fleet of Boeing 747s*

fleeting ['fliːtɪŋ] *adjective* short and rapid; *she only caught a fleeting glimpse of the princess*

Fleet Street ['fliːt 'striːt] *noun* street in London, leading from the Strand towards the City, the old centre of British newspapers; *a Fleet Street journalist*; *Fleet Street papers put the story on their front pages*

> COMMENT: in fact, very few newspapers still have offices in Fleet Street, but the words are still used to refer to the British national press as a whole

flesh [fleʃ] *noun* **(a)** soft part of the body covering the bones; **a flesh wound** = wound which goes into the flesh but not very deep; **in the flesh** = in real life (not on TV or in photographs); *it was strange to see the TV newsreader in the flesh* **(b)** soft part of fruit; *a melon with pink flesh* (NOTE: no plural)

fleshy ['fleʃi] *adjective* fat or plump; *a basket of fleshy red plums*; *rugby players have big fleshy thighs*

flew [fluː] *see* FLY (NOTE: do not confuse with **flu**, **flue**)

flex [fleks] **1** *noun* flexible insulated cable for carrying electricity; *he tripped over a flex*; *we bought a roll of* *flex to rewire the office* **2** *verb* to bend; **to flex your muscles** = (i) to practise tightening and relaxing the muscles as exercise; (ii) to threaten someone; *the union is flexing its muscles for a fight with the government*

flexibility [fleksɪ'bɪlɪti] *noun* ability to adapt to new circumstances; *he's too rigid in his outlook - he doesn't have the flexibility to change; when negotiating you need to have a certain amount of flexibility* (NOTE: no plural)

flexible ['fleksɪbl] *adjective* **(a)** easy to bend; *soft rubber soles are very flexible* **(b)** able to adapt easily; *my timetable is very flexible - we can meet whenever you want*

flick [flɪk] **1** *noun* little sharp blow or movement; *he shook off the wasp with a flick of his hand* **2** *verb* to hit or move lightly and sharply; *the horse flicked its tail to get rid of flies*

flicker ['flɪkə] **1** *noun* **(a)** trembling or quivering movement; *they saw the flicker of a light in the forest* **(b)** small amount; *there is still a flicker of hope that someone may still be alive under the ruins* **2** *verb* to tremble; to burn unsteadily; *the candles flickered in the draught; the ceremony took place by the flickering light of thousands of candles; we could see the flickering lights of the old harbour in the distance*

flick knife ['flɪk 'naɪf] *noun* knife with a blade which fits inside the handle and which shoots out when a button is pressed; *it is forbidden to carry flick knives to football matches* (NOTE: plural is **flick knives**)

flick through ['flɪk 'θruː] *verb* to glance at the pages of a newspaper or book very rapidly; *I didn't read 'the Times' properly - I just flicked through it*

flier ['flaɪə] *see* FLYER

flies [flaɪz] *see* FLY

flight [flaɪt] *noun* **(a)** flying, travel through the air; *young birds stay in the nest until they are ready for flight* **(b)** travel in a plane; *go to gate 25 for flight AB198; all flights to Paris have been cancelled; she sat next to me on a flight to Montreal; see also* ATTENDANT, CHECK IN **(c) flight of stairs** = set of stairs going in one direction; *go up two flights of stairs and the bathroom is the first door on the left* **(d)** *(literary)* **to take flight** = to run away; **to put to flight** = to chase away

flight deck ['flaɪt 'dek] *noun* **(a)** section at the front of an aircraft where the pilots sit; *the best part of the flight was when we were allowed to go onto the flight deck to watch the pilots* **(b)** long flat deck on an aircraft carrier on which planes land and take off; *smoke covered the flight deck, making it impossible for planes to land*

flight recorder ['flaɪt rɪ'kɔːdə] *noun* device carried in an aircraft which records what happens during a flight, including conversations between pilots and the control tower; *the first priority after a crash is to find the plane's flight recorders* (NOTE: also called the **black box**)

flimsy ['flɪmzi] *adjective* **(a)** *(of material)* light and thin; *he wore only a flimsy cotton jacket* **(b)** *(of excuse)* poor; *she could only offer the flimsiest of excuses* (NOTE: **flimsier - flimsiest**)

flinch [flɪntʃ] *verb* **(a)** to move back in pain or fear; *the reporters flinched at the sight of the corpses* **(b)** **not to flinch from** = to do something, however difficult or painful it may be; *he didn't flinch from his duty*

fling [flɪŋ] **1** *noun* **(a)** wild dance; **the Highland fling** = wild Scottish dance **(b) to have a fling** = to relax, letting off your high spirits; *the boys were having a last fling before joining the army the following morning* *(informal)* **to have a fling with someone** = to have a short sexual relationship with someone; *she had a brief fling with one of the managers* **2** *verb* to throw wildly; *he flung the empty bottle into the sea; she flung herself into an armchair* (NOTE: **flinging - flung** [flʌŋ])

flint [flɪnt] *noun* **(a)** very hard type of rock which makes sparks when struck and can be chipped to make tools; *flints are found in chalky soil; prehistoric people used flints to make knives* **(b)** small piece of metal which makes a spark to light a cigarette lighter; *I need a new flint for my lighter*

flip [flɪp] *verb* to hit lightly; *she flipped a switch and the lights went off;* **to flip over** = to turn over quickly; *before he could do anything the canoe flipped over* (NOTE: **flipping - flipped**)

flip flops ['flɪp 'flɒps] *noun* rubber sandals held on by a strap between the toes; *best wear your flip flops if you're going onto the beach* (NOTE: also called **thongs**)

flippant ['flɪpənt] *adjective* not taking seriously things which should be taken seriously; *he made a lot of flippant remarks about nuclear accidents*

flipper ['flɪpə] *noun* **(a)** long flat piece of rubber which you can attach to your foot to help you swim faster; *you need flippers and a snorkel to go scuba diving* **(b)** limb of a sea animal used for swimming; *a seal's flippers*

flip through ['flɪp 'θruː] *verb* to glance at the pages of a newspaper or book very rapidly; *I didn't read 'the Times' properly - I just flipped through it*

flirt [flɜːt] **1** *noun* woman who often flirts with men; *his new secretary is a bit of a flirt* **2** *verb* to play at attracting people of the opposite sex; *he flirted a lot at the office party*

flirtatious [flɜː'teɪʃəs] *adjective* who flirts a lot; *a flirtatious girl*

flirt with ['flɜːt 'wɪθ] *verb* **(a)** to play at attracting people of the opposite sex for amusement; *she flirted with all the boys at the party* **(b)** to consider a course of action; *he has been flirting with the idea of selling up and going to live in the States* **(c)** to be close to something risky; *she's flirting with danger in standing so close to the fireworks*

flit [flɪt] **1** *noun* **to do a moonlight flit** = to escape quietly at night without paying your bills **2** *verb* **(a)** to move quickly and quietly; *a thought flitted through my mind; bats were flitting around the church tower* **(b)** to go away quietly without anyone noticing; *they had to flit the country to avoid paying tax* (NOTE: **flitting - flitted**)

float [fləʊt] **1** *noun* **(a)** piece of cork, etc., attached to a fishing line which floats on the surface of the water, allowing the line and hook to hang down below; *if the float bobs up and down in the water it means you have caught a fish* **(b)** decorated lorry in a procession; *the long line of carnival floats went down the high street* **(c) milk float** = low electric truck for delivering milk; *it is annoying to be stuck behind a milk float when you're in a hurry* **(d) cash float** = cash put into the cash box at the beginning of the day to allow business to start; *we start the day with a £20 float in the cash desk* **2** *verb* **(a)** to lie or put on the top of a liquid; *dead fish were floating in the river; he floated a paper boat on* *the lake* (b) to start selling shares in a new company; *the company is to be floated on the stock exchange next week* (c) to let a currency find its own exchange rate internationally and not fix it at a certain amount; *the government decided that the best course would be to let the pound float*

floating ['fləʊtɪŋ] *adjective* resting on the surface of a liquid; *floating rubbish on the river makes swimming dangerous*; **floating voter** = person who is not sure which party to vote for in an election

flock [flɒk] **1** *noun* group of similar animals together, such as sheep, goats, or birds; *a flock of sparrows*; *a flock of sheep were grazing on the hillside* (NOTE: **flock** is usually used with sheep, goats, and birds such as hens or geese; for cattle, the word to use is **herd**) **2** *verb* to move in large numbers; *tourists flocked to see the changing of the guard*; *holidaymakers have been flocking to the resorts on the south coast*

floe [fləʊ] *noun* **ice floe** = thick sheet of ice floating on the sea; *the Arctic wind blew across the ice floes* (NOTE: do not confuse with **flow**)

flog [flɒg] *verb* (a) *(informal)* to sell; *I flogged my car to my brother*; *they've been trying to flog the boat for months* (b) to beat hard, usually with a whip; *when he was a little boy he was often flogged at school* *(informal)* **like flogging a dead horse** = which cannot be successful; *trying to get him to change his mind is like flogging a dead horse* (NOTE: **flogging - flogged**)

flood [flʌd] **1** *noun* (a) large amount of water over land which is usually dry; *the floods were caused by heavy rain* (b) large amount of tears, letters, etc.; *the TV station received floods of complaints after the ad was shown*; *she was in floods of tears when they told her that she had to leave her house* (c) **the Flood** = story in the Bible of the time when the earth was covered with water and only Noah and his family and animals were saved in the Ark **2** *verb* (a) to cover with water; *they are going to build a dam and flood the valley*; *fields were flooded after the river burst its banks*; *he forgot to turn the tap off and flooded the bathroom* (b) to overflow; *the Nile floods each year* (c) to come in large numbers; *the office was flooded with complaints or complaints came flooding into the office*

flooded ['flʌdɪd] *adjective* covered with water; *cars couldn't get through the flooded streets after the rainstorm last night*

flooding ['flʊdɪŋ] *noun* covering with water; *several villages have been cut off by flooding*

floodlight ['flʌdlaɪt] **1** *noun* strong electric light used to light in the open air; *they switched on the floodlights for the evening match* **2** *verb* to light with floodlights; *the castle is floodlit at night* (NOTE: **floodlighting - floodlit**)

floodlit ['flʌdlɪt] *adjective* lit by floodlights; *he want to photograph the floodlit castle*

flood tide ['flʌd 'taɪd] *noun* very high tide coming in; *the children were cut off by the flood tide*

floor [flɔː] **1** *noun* (a) part of a room on which you walk; *he put the books in a pile on the floor*; *if there are no empty chairs left, you'll have to sit on the floor* (b) all the rooms on one level in a building; *the bathroom is on the ground floor*; *his office is on the fifth floor*; *there is a good view of the town from the top floor* **2** *verb* **to be floored** = not to be able to answer; *he was floored by one of the questions in the exam paper*

COMMENT: the floors in American buildings are numbered differently from those in Britain: the 'ground floor' in Britain is the 'first floor' in the USA; the 'first floor' in Britain is the 'second floor' in the USA, and so on

floorboard ['flɔːbɔːd] *noun* long flat piece of wood used for making wooden floors; *the engineers took up the floorboards to check the wiring*; *the house has old pine floorboards which need replacing*

flooring ['flɔːrɪŋ] *noun* material used to make a floor; *we've taken up the carpets and put down wooden flooring*

floor lamp ['flɔː 'læmp] *noun* US room lamp on a tall pole standing on the floor (NOTE: British English is **standard lamp**)

floorshow ['flɔːʃəʊ] *noun* entertainment by singers, etc., in a nightclub; *the floorshow starts at 10.30*

floor space ['flɔː 'speɪs] *noun* area of floor taken up by something; *half the floor space in the office is taken up with filing cabinets*; *they bought a flower shop with 400 square metres of floor space*

flop [flɒp] **1** *noun* (a) *(informal)* failure; *his new play was a complete flop and closed after only ten performances*; *the film was a big hit in New York but was a flop in London* (b) noise made when something falls heavily and limply; **belly flop** = poor dive, when your stomach hits the water first **2** *verb* (a) to fall or sit limply or heavily; *the lions lay flopped out in the shade of the trees*; *she got back from the sales and flopped down on the sofa* (b) *(informal)* to be unsuccessful; *the play was a big hit on Broadway but flopped in London* (NOTE: **flopping - flopped**)

floppy ['flɒpi] **1** *adjective* which hangs limply; *a white rabbit with long floppy ears* **2** *noun* floppy disk; *the data is available on 3.5 inch floppies* (NOTE: plural is **floppies**)

floppy disk ['flɒpi 'dɪsk] *noun* small disk used in a computer; *we sent a floppy disk of the data by post*

flora ['flɔːrə] *noun* wild plants (of an area); *the flora and fauna of the deserts* compare FAUNA (NOTE: plural is **flora**)

floral ['flɔːrəl] *adjective* referring to flowers; *wallpaper with a floral pattern*; **floral tributes** = wreaths sent to a funeral

florid ['flɒrɪd] *adjective* (a) reddish; *his florid complexion suggested he drank a lot* (b) elaborate, with too many ornate details; *I don't like the florid style of Baroque architecture*; *he writes in an unpleasantly florid style*

florist ['flɒrɪst] *noun* person who sells flowers; *florists are very busy in the days before Valentine's Day*; *she bought some flowers at the florist's (shop)*

floss [flɒs] *noun* thin thread of silk; **candy floss** = molten sugar spun to make a fluffy mass; *we don't allow the children to eat candy floss because it is bad for their teeth*; **dental floss** = thin waxed thread for pulling between your teeth to remove pieces of food; *the dentist told me to use dental floss every day as well as a toothbrush*

flotation [fləʊˈteɪʃn] *noun* selling shares in a company on the stock exchange for the first time; *the flotation flopped badly, and the price of the shares fell*

flotilla [fləˈtɪlə] *noun* small group of boats; *the liner entered harbour escorted by a flotilla of yachts*

flounder (about *or* **around)** [ˈflaʊndə əˈbaʊt or əˈraʊnd] *verb* **(a)** to move with difficulty in water; *he saw her floundering about in the water and realised she couldn't swim* **(b)** to be uncertain of an answer to a question; *she started to flounder as soon as they started to ask her more technical questions*

flour [ˈflaʊə] *noun* wheat grain crushed to powder, used for making bread, cakes, etc.; *she made the cake by mixing eggs, sugar and flour*

flourish [ˈflʌrɪʃ] **1** *noun* **(a)** wide movement of the arm in the air; *the conductor ended the concert with a flourish* **(b)** large curve in handwriting; *she signed her name with a flourish* (NOTE: plural is **flourishes**) **2** *verb* **(a)** to grow well; to do well; *palms flourish in hot countries*; *the company is flourishing* **(b)** to wave something in the air; *she came in with a big smile, flourishing a cheque*

flourmill [ˈflaʊəmɪl] *noun* place where grain is ground into flour; *we bought some flour at the old flourmill*

floury [ˈflaʊri] *adjective* **(a)** covered with flour; *the baker wiped his hands on his floury apron* **(b)** floury potatoes = potatoes which become soft and powdery when cooked (NOTE: do not confuse with **flowery**)

flout [flaʊt] *verb* to pay no regard to something; *he thinks he can flout the rules without any punishment*; *by selling cigarettes to children, the shop is deliberately flouting the law*

flow [fləʊ] **1** *noun* movement of liquid, air, etc.; *she tried to stop the flow of blood with a tight bandage*; *there was a steady flow of visitors to the exhibition* (NOTE: do not confuse with **floe**) **2** *verb* to move along smoothly; *the river flows into the sea*; *traffic on the motorway is flowing smoothly*

flower [ˈflaʊə] **1** *noun* colourful part of a plant which attracts bees and then produces fruit or seeds; *a plant with bright yellow flowers*; **flower shop** = shop which sells flowers; **flower show** = exhibition of flowers; **in flower** = (plant) which is covered with flowers; *you must visit Japan when the cherry trees are in flower* **2** *verb* to produce flowers; *the cherry trees flowered very late this year*; *a plant which flowers in early summer*

flowerbed [ˈflaʊəbed] *noun* piece of ground specially for flowers; *we use rotted leaves to mulch the flowerbeds*

flowering [ˈflaʊərɪŋ] *adjective* which has flowers for ornament, rather than fruit; *a flowering cherry*

flowerpot [ˈflaʊəpɒt] *noun* container to grow plants in; *the plant has got so big we will have to put it into a larger flowerpot*

flowery [ˈflaʊəri] *adjective* **(a)** decorated with a pattern of flowers; *a flowery dress*; *she chose some very flowery wallpaper* **(b)** using literary or emotional language; *he wrote the most flowery thank you letter* (NOTE: do not confuse with **floury**)

flown [fləʊn] *see* FLY

flu [fluː] *noun* common illness like a bad cold, often with a high temperature; *half of the team are down with flu*; *scores of people have got flu*; *we all caught*

flu, and so did the teacher (NOTE: do not confuse with **flew, flue**: note also that the full word is **influenza**)

fluctuate [ˈflʌktjʊeɪt] *verb* to rise and fall; *the annual temperature in Singapore hardly fluctuates at all*; *the exchange rate has fluctuated between 2.85 and 2.95DM*

flue [fluː] *noun* pipe leading to a chimney; *smoke poured into the room because the flue was blocked* (NOTE: do not confuse with **flew, flu**)

fluency [ˈfluːənsi] *noun* being fluent; *applicants need to show fluency in Japanese*

fluent [ˈfluːənt] *adjective* able to speak easily; *he is fluent in German*

fluff [flʌf] **1** *noun* soft mass of fibres or hair; *she pulled the sofa away from the wall and saw all the fluff which had collected under it* **2** *verb* (*informal*) to do something badly; *he fluffed his speech, and everyone laughed*

fluffy [ˈflʌfi] *adjective* like fluff; covered with fluff; *fluffy little clouds in the blue summer sky*; *the baby loves the fluffy toy you gave her for her birthday*

fluid [ˈfluːɪd] **1** *noun* liquid; *you need to drink plenty of fluids in hot weather* **2** *adjective* which is not settled; *the situation is still fluid - nothing has been agreed yet*

fluke [fluːk] *noun* **(a)** (*informal*) chance, lucky event; *it was a pure fluke that I happened to be there when the phone rang* **(b)** type of parasite, a flat worm living in the liver; *their sheep were attacked by liver fluke*

flung [flʌŋ] *verb see* FLING

flunk [flʌŋk] *verb* US (*informal*) to fail an examination or a candidate; *she flunked math last semester*; *the French professor flunked half his class*

fluorescent [fluəˈresənt] *adjective* **(a)** giving off light when electric current is applied; *we have fluorescent lighting in the office* **(b)** which seems to glow; *she's bought a fluorescent pink tracksuit*

fluoride [ˈfluəraɪd] *noun* compound of fluorine; *they say that if there is fluoride in drinking water, it helps to prevent tooth decay*; **fluoride toothpaste** = toothpaste with small amount of fluoride added in order to prevent tooth decay

fluorine [ˈfluəriːn] *noun* pale greenish yellow gas; *fluorine is poisonous* (NOTE: Chemical element: chemical symbol: **F**; atomic number: **9**)

flurry [ˈflʌri] *noun* **(a)** hurried excitement; *in his flurry to leave he forgot to take his keys* **(b)** sudden small fall of snow when it is windy; *there will be snow flurries during the morning* (NOTE: plural is **flurries**)

flush [flʌʃ] **1** *noun* **(a)** red colour on the face; *a flush of anger*; **hot flush** = red colour on the face and neck, a typical sign of the menopause in women **(b)** rush of water; **flush lavatory** = lavatory which works by allowing rushing water to clean it **(c)** (*at cards*) hand in which all the cards are of the same suit; *she is holding a flush* (NOTE: plural is **flushes**) **2** *verb* **(a)** to go red in the face; *she flushed with pleasure when she heard the results* **(b)** to flush out = to drive out of hiding; *the army brought in helicopters to flush the guerillas out of their mountain bases* **(c)** to flush a lavatory = to wash it out by moving a handle which makes water rush through; *she told the children not to forget to flush the toilet* **3** *adjective* **(a)** flush with = level with; *the door must be flush with the wall* **(b)** (*informal*) having plenty of money to spend; *I've just been paid, so I'm feeling very flush at the moment*

flushed ['flʌʃt] *adjective* red in the face; *she came out of the interview looking flushed*

fluster ['flʌstə] *verb* to confuse someone; *all this rushing about just flusters her*; *she was flustered by the questions from the reporters*

flustered ['flʌstəd] *adjective* confused; *if you all talk at once it makes me flustered*

flute [fluːt] *noun* wind instrument held sideways, and played by blowing across a small hole near the end; *she plays the flute in the local orchestra*

flutist ['fluːtɪst] *noun US see* FLAUTIST

flutter ['flʌtə] **1** *noun* **(a)** light movement, especially of wings; *with a flutter of wings, the robin landed on the bird-table* **(b)** *(informal)* small gamble; *sometimes I have a flutter at our local racetrack* **(c)** very rapid movement of the heart; *we detected a slight heart flutter* **2** *verb* **(a)** to move wings, etc., quickly and lightly; *the little bird fell out of its nest and fluttered to the ground* **(b)** to move softly and quickly; *dead leaves fluttered from the trees*; *the flags fluttered in the breeze*

flux [flʌks] *noun* **(a)** constant change; *the company seems to be in a state of flux* **(b)** metal compound used in soldering; *he took a strip of flux and soldered the pieces of metal together* (NOTE: no plural)

fly [flaɪ] **1** *noun* small insect which lays its eggs on food; *he tried to kill the fly with a newspaper*; *waiter, there's a fly in my soup!* (NOTE: plural is **flies**) **2** *verb* **(a)** to move through the air (with wings, in a plane, etc.); *when the cat came into the garden, the birds flew away*; *I'm flying to China next week*; *he flies across the Atlantic twice a month* **(b)** to make (a plane) move through the air; *the king was flying his own plane* **(c)** to travel fast; *I must fly if I want to get home by 6 o'clock*; *his daughter is already 2 - how time flies!* **(d)** to have a flag up; *the ship was flying the Russian flag* (NOTE: **flying - flew** [fluː] **- has flown** [fləun])

fly-drive ['flaɪ 'draɪv] *adjective* **fly-drive holiday** *or* **fly-drive package** = holiday where the traveller flies to an airport and has a rented car waiting for him to drive; *we have many fly-drive bargains still available*

flyer ['flaɪə] *noun* **(a)** *(informal)* person who flies an aircraft; *he was one of the first flyers to cross the Atlantic; see also* FREQUENT **(b)** paper advertising something; *they sent us a flyer about their home delivery service*

flyhalf ['flaɪhɑːf] *noun* player in rugby who runs fast and passes the ball; *the England flyhalf was brought down by a tackle*

flying ['flaɪɪŋ] **1** *adjective* **(a)** which is flying in the air; *a plague of flying ants* **(b)** **with flying colours** = with great success; *he passed his test with flying colours* **2** *noun* action of going in a plane; *he has a dread of flying*

flying start ['flaɪɪŋ 'stɑːt] *noun* good beginning to a race, etc.; *he got off to a flying start and is still leading the race*

flying visit ['flaɪɪŋ 'vɪzɪt] *noun* very short visit; *I'm just paying a flying visit - I'll be back again next week when I'll be able to stay longer*; *we made a flying visit to our daughter in Kenya on our way to South Africa*

flyover ['flaɪəuvə] *noun* road which passes over another; *the flyover will be closed for three months while the concrete supports are being repaired*

flyweight ['flaɪweɪt] *noun* lightest weight in boxing, below bantamweight; *the flyweight champion*; *a flyweight title fight*

FM ['ef 'em] = FREQUENCY MODULATION; *Radio 4 is on 93.5 FM*

foal [fəul] **1** *noun* young horse; *the mare gently nudged her foal* **2** *verb* to give birth to a foal; *the mare foaled last night*

foam [fəum] **1** *noun* mass of small bubbles; *this detergent makes a huge amount of foam*; **foam rubber** = rubber in blocks with many little holes in it, used for chair cushions, etc.; *the sofa has foam rubber cushions* **2** *verb* to make a mass of small bubbles; *the waitress was carrying mugs of foaming beer*; *the horse was foaming at the mouth after the race*; *(of a person)* **to be foaming (at the mouth)** = to be wildly angry; *the MD was foaming (at the mouth) when he read the report in the paper*

focal ['fəukl] *adjective* referring to a focus; **focal length** = the distance between the centre of an optical lens and the focus; *adjust the focal length until the picture becomes clear*; **focal point** = point which everything is focused on; *the prize-giving was the focal point of the evening*

focus ['fəukəs] **1** *noun* **(a)** point where rays of light from an object meet; *the focus of the beam is a point 20 metres from the spotlight* **(b)** *(of photograph)* point where the details of the photograph are clear and sharp; *adjust the focus so as to get a clear picture*; **in focus** = clear; **out of focus** = blurred, not clear **(c)** centre of attention; *the director brought the star actress to the front of the stage, so that the focus of the audience's attention would be on her* (NOTE: plural is **foci** ['fəusaɪ]) **2** *verb* **(a)** to adjust so as to be able to see clearly; *he focused his telescope on a ship on the horizon* **(b)** **to focus on something** = to look particularly at something, to concentrate on something; *the paper is focusing on the problems of the TV star's marriage* (NOTE: **focusing - focused**)

fodder ['fɒdə] *noun* plants such as grass, hay, etc., which are grown and given to animals as food; *we use the hay from the fields as fodder for the cows; see also* CANNON FODDER

foe [fəu] *noun (formal)* enemy or opponent; *the letters fell into the hands of his deadly foe*; *the sentry called out 'friend or foe?'*

foetal *US* **fetal** ['fiːtl] *adjective* referring to a foetus; *the consultant examined a sample of foetal blood*; **foetal position** = position of a person who is lying curled up on his side, like an unborn baby in the womb

foetus *US* **fetus** ['fiːtəs] *noun* unborn baby human or animal which is developing from an embryo in the womb; *the scan showed that the foetus was normal* (NOTE: plural is **foetuses**)

fog [fɒg] *noun* thick mist made up of millions of drops of water; *all flights out of Heathrow have been delayed by fog*; *the fog is so thick that you can hardly see ten metres in front of you*

fogbound ['fɒgbaund] *adjective* prevented from travelling because of fog; *six planes were fogbound at Heathrow*; *fogbound travellers were advised to take a bus*

foggy ['fɒgi] *adjective* **(a)** covered in fog; *it's often foggier than this in November; they drove slowly along the foggy streets; it's dangerous to drive fast when it's foggy* **(b)** *(informal)* not to have the foggiest (idea) = to know nothing at all; *she hadn't the foggiest idea how to get to the airport* (NOTE: **foggier - foggiest**)

foghorn ['fɒghɔːn] *noun* loud siren which warns boats in fog; *we could hear the foghorn warning the barges on the Rhine*

foglamp *or* **foglight** ['fɒglæmp *or* fɒglait] *noun* very bright car light used in fog; *it was so foggy we could hardly see the foglights of the car in front*

foil [fɔil] **1** *noun* **(a)** thin metal sheet; **tin foil** *or* **cooking foil** = foil used for wrapping food before cooking; *wrap the fish in foil before putting it on the barbecue* **(b)** person who contrasts sharply with another and so makes the other's qualities stand out; *Laurel and Hardy were perfect foils for each other* **2** *verb* to prevent a plan from being put into effect; *the bank robbery was foiled by the police*

fold [fəuld] **1** *noun* crease in paper, cloth, etc.; *she wanted the surgeon to remove the folds of skin under her chin* **2** *verb* **(a)** to bend something so that one part is on top of another; *fold the piece of paper in half; he folded the newspaper and put it into his briefcase* **(b)** **to fold your arms** = to cross your arms in front of your body; *he sat on the stage with his arms folded, looking furious* **(c)** *(of a business)* to stop trading; *his business folded last December; the company folded with debts of over £1m*

-fold [fəuld] *suffix meaning* times; **four-fold** = four times

folder ['fəuldə] *noun* cardboard envelope for holding papers; *she took a folder from the drawer*

folding ['fəuldiŋ] *adjective* which can be folded; *for the picnic he brought a folding table and six folding chairs*

fold up ['fəuld 'ʌp] *verb* to bend something over to make it take up a smaller area than before; *she folded up the map and put it in her bag*

foliage ['fəuliidʒ] *noun* leaves on a tree or plant; *the plant has attractive red and green foliage*

folk [fəuk] *noun* people; *they took the old folk down to the sea for a picnic* (NOTE: **folk** is plural and takes a plural verb; but the plural form **folks** is also used; see below)

folk dance ['fəuk 'dɑːns] *noun* traditional dance; *everyone wears national costume for the folk dances*

folk dancing ['fəuk 'dɑːnsiŋ] *noun* dancing traditional dances; *she goes to folk-dancing classes on Wednesday evenings*

folklore ['fəuklɔː] *noun* traditional stories and beliefs; *folklore has it that fairies come out to dance at full moon; she is making a study of Icelandic folklore*

folk music ['fəuk 'mjuːzik] *noun* traditional music of a people; *Smetana included themes from folk music in his symphonies*

folks [fəuks] *noun* *(informal)* people; *that's all, folks!*; **my folks** = my family; *my folks come from Dorset; wait till I tell my folks about it!*

folk tale ['fəuk 'teil] *noun* traditional story passed down from one generation to the next; *they sat round the fire telling old folk tales of fairies and witches*

follicle ['fɒlikl] *noun* small hole in the skin out of which a hair grows; *rubbing the scalp will encourage hair to grow in the follicles*

follow ['fɒləu] *verb* **(a)** to come after or behind; *the group followed the guide round the town; what follows B in the alphabet?; the dog followed the man across the field; I had the impression I was being followed* **(b)** to be certain because of something; *because I lent you money last week, it doesn't follow that I will lend you some every time you ask; if the owner of the shop is arrested by the police, it follows that his business is likely to close* **(c)** to do what someone tells you to do; *she followed the instructions on the tin of paint; he made the cake following a recipe in the newspaper*

follower ['fɒləuwə] *noun* supporter; *the President's followers came into the capital*

following ['fɒləuwiŋ] *adjective* which comes next; *they arrived on Friday and the following day she became ill; look at the following picture*

follow suit ['fɒləu 'suːt] *phrase* to do what everyone else does; *she jumped into the pool and everyone else followed suit*

follow up ['fɒləu 'ʌp] *verb* to investigate or to research something further; *the police followed up their enquiries by interviewing the woman's husband; that's an interesting idea - it might be worth following it up*

follow-up ['fɒləuʌp] *adjective* which follows something sent earlier; **follow-up letter** = letter sent after a visit or an earlier letter; *the rep came to see us and sent me a follow-up letter the next week*

folly ['fɒli] *noun* **(a)** silly behaviour; *it was utter folly to go out in a small boat in a storm like that* **(b)** strange building, built specially to give a dramatic effect; *he built a gothic folly on the hill overlooking his house* (NOTE: plural is **follies**)

fond (of) ['fɒnd 'ɒv] *adjective* **to be fond of something** = to like something; *I am fond of music; she's very fond of chocolate*

fondle ['fɒndl] *verb* to stroke in a loving way; *she fondled the cat as it sat on her lap*

fondness ['fɒndnəs] *noun* liking for; *her fondness for chocolates is not good for her waistline*

font [fɒnt] *noun* **(a)** basin holding holy water for baptism in a church; *the church has an 11th century font* **(b)** *(in printing)* set of characters all of the same size and typeface

food [fuːd] *noun* things which you eat; *this hotel is famous for its food; do you like German food?; we arrived at the beach and found that we had forgotten to bring the food;* **food poisoning** = poisoning caused by bacteria in food; *the hotel was closed after an outbreak of food poisoning; half the guests at the wedding were ill with food poisoning* (NOTE: **food** is usually used in the singular)

food chain ['fuːd 'tʃein] *noun* series of organisms which pass energy from one to another as each is eaten by the next (grass is eaten by small animals, which are then eaten by larger animals, etc.); *the poison entered the food chain when the fields were sprayed and small insects were killed*

food processor ['fuːd 'prəusesə] *noun* machine for chopping, cutting, slicing, mixing food, etc.; *mix the ingredients by hand or in a food processor*

food stamp ['fʊd 'stæmp] *noun US* stamp given by the government to poor people, which can be used to buy food; *this store does not take food stamps*

foodstuffs ['fuːdstʌfs] *noun* things which can be used as food; *on some islands, most foodstuffs have to be imported*

fool [fuːl] **1** *noun* (a) stupid person; *you fool! why didn't you put the brakes on?; I was a fool to think that I could make her change her mind* (b) type of creamy fruit dessert; *she made some gooseberry fool* **2** *verb* (a) to fool about *or* fool around = to play around in a silly way; *stop fooling around with that knife - you're going to have an accident* (b) to trick someone; *they fooled the old lady into letting them into her house; you can't fool me - I know you're not really ill; you could have fooled me* = I find it hard to believe; *she says she did her best - well, you could have fooled me!*

foolhardy ['fuːlhɑːdi] *adjective* brave, but taking unnecessary risks; *it was foolhardy of her to go into the water when she knew there were sharks about; it would be foolhardy to try to predict which students are going to pass their exams*

foolish ['fuːlɪʃ] *adjective* silly or stupid; *don't be so foolish - you can't go to Paris all alone; playing with matches in a wood store is a foolish thing to do*

foolishly ['fuːlɪʃli] *adverb* stupidly; *foolishly he forgot to ask her for her phone number*

foolishness ['fuːlɪʃnəs] *noun* silliness or stupidity; *it was sheer foolishness to try to stroke the tiger*

foot [fʊt] **1** *noun* (a) end part of your leg on which you stand; *she has very small feet; watch out, you trod on my foot!;* to put your foot down = to say firmly that something is not allowed; *you must put your foot down and stop this habit of everyone arriving late* (informal) to find your feet = to be confident; *she's been with us three months now and has really found her feet;* to put your foot in it = to say something embarrassing; *he really put his foot in it when he said that the mayor's wife was fat; see also* WRONG (b) bottom part, end; *there is a door at the foot of the stairs; there are traffic lights at the foot of the hill; sign your name at the foot of the page* (c) measurement of how long something is (= 12 inches or approximately 30 cm); *the table is four foot or four feet long; she's almost six foot tall; I'm five foot seven (5'7"); see also* INCH (NOTE: plural is **feet**. Note also that as a measurement **foot** often has no plural: **six foot tall; three foot wide**. With numbers **foot** is also often written ' a 6' ladder; he is 5' 6": say 'he's five foot six') **2** *verb* to foot the bill = to pay the bill; *I found I had to foot the bill for the Christmas party*

◊ **on foot** ['ɒn 'fʊt] *phrase* walking; *we left the car in the car park and went to the church on foot; don't wait for the bus - it's quicker to go on foot*

◊ **under foot** ['ʌndə 'fʊt] *phrase* on the ground; *it's very wet under foot after the rain*

footage ['fʊtɪdʒ] *noun* piece of cine film showing an event; *they showed some footage of the volcano erupting; half the footage of the bank robbery was left out of the final film* (NOTE: no plural)

football ['fʊtbɔːl] *noun* (a) ball used for kicking; ball used in the various games of football; *they were kicking a football around in the street;* a rugby football = oval-shaped ball used in rugby (b) game played between two teams of eleven players with a round ball which can be kicked or headed, but not carried; *he's got a new pair of football boots; they went to a football match; the children were playing football in the street; let's have a game of football; he spends all his time watching football on TV* (NOTE: also called **soccer;** American English uses only **soccer** to avoid confusion with **American football**); *see also* AUSTRALIAN RULES FOOTBALL, AMERICAN FOOTBALL, RUGBY

COMMENT: football is a professional sport involving two teams of 11 players who score goals by kicking or heading a round leather ball into their opponents' goal; only the goalkeeper (who usually wears gloves) is allowed to touch the ball with his hands. A game is divided into two 45-minute halves with a 15-minute interval (after which the teams change ends) but in Cup competitions two 15-minute periods of extra time are added if the scores are level at the end of normal time; if they are still level after the end of extra time a penalty shoot-out may take place. Matches are adjudicated by a referee. Minor infringements are penalized by the award of a free kick but players who commit more serious fouls also get shown a yellow card by the referee which denotes an official caution; players who make a dangerous tackle, punch or retaliate on being fouled, or commit a foul to stop an almost certain goal, are shown a red card; if a player receives one red card or a second yellow card during a match he is immediately sent off and cannot be replaced

footballer ['fʊtbɔːlə] *noun* person who plays football; *Pelé was a famous Brazilian footballer*

football field *or* **football ground** ['fʊtbɔːl fiːld *or* graund] *noun* place where football is played; *as they drove past the football field they could see the two teams about to kick off*

footballing ['fʊtbɔːlɪŋ] *adjective* referring to playing football; *he goes to classes every morning to improve his footballing technique*

footbrake ['fʊtbreɪk] *noun* brake on a machine or car which works when you press a pedal with your foot; *press down hard on the footbrake*

footbridge ['fʊtbrɪdʒ] *noun* small bridge for people to walk across, not for vehicles; *to avoid accidents, children must use the footbridge to cross the road on their way to school*

footer ['fʊtə] *noun* (a) words or page numbers printed at the bottom of a page; *compare* HEADER (b) (informal) = FOOTBALL; *we had a game of footer on the beach*

foothills ['fʊthɪlz] *noun* lower slopes; *the foothills of the Alps*

foothold ['fʊthəʊld] *noun* (a) place where you can put your foot when climbing; *he hung in the air at the end of a rope, trying to get a foothold* (b) small position on which you can build; *they gained a foothold in the Spanish market*

footing ['fʊtɪŋ] *noun* (a) safe place for your feet; *she lost her footing on the cliff path, and fell fifty feet into the sea* (b) to be on an equal footing with someone = to be at the same stage or level as someone; *all applicants are on an equal footing;* to put things on a firm footing = to make things solid; *we want to make sure the business is on a firm footing*

footlights ['futlaɪts] *noun* row of lights along the front of the stage in a theatre; *she came down to the front of the stage and looked out across the footlights at the audience*

footman ['futmən] *noun* male servant; *two footmen rushed to open the car door* (NOTE: plural is **footmen**)

footnote ['futnəut] *noun* explanation at the bottom of a page, referring to something on the page; *the asterisk refers to a footnote at the bottom of the page*; *there are so many footnotes that they take up more room than the text*

footpath ['futpɑːθ] *noun* path for people to walk on, but not to ride on; *the footpath leads through the wood and along the edge of a field*

footprint ['futprɪnt] *noun* **(a)** mark left by the foot on the ground; *they followed the footprints in the snow to the cave* **(b)** area covered by something; *the computer has a relatively small footprint*; *a warehouse with a footprint of over 50,000 square feet*

footrest ['futrest] *noun* low bar on which you can rest your feet; *she put her feet up on the footrest in front of her seat*

Footsie ['futsi] = FINANCIAL TIMES STOCK EXCHANGE 100 INDEX index of prices on the London Stock Exchange, based on 100 leading shares; *the Footsie rose seventy points yesterday; see also* DOW JONES, NIKKEI

footstep ['futstep] *noun* **(a)** sound made by a foot touching the ground; *we heard soft footsteps along the corridor* **(b)** to follow in someone's footsteps = to do what someone did before; *he's following in his father's footsteps and going in for a legal career; see also* DOG

footstool ['futstuːl] *noun* small stool on which you can rest your feet; *put your feet up on the footstool*; *she sat on a footstool and talked to her grandmother*

footwear ['futweə] *noun* articles of clothing worn on your feet, such as boots, shoes, sandals, etc.; *you'll need strong footwear if you're going on a walking holiday* (NOTE: no plural)

footwork ['futwɜːk] *noun* way of using your feet (especially in sports); *he used some fancy footwork during the fight* (NOTE: no plural)

for [fɔː] *preposition* **(a)** *(showing the purpose or use of something)* *this plastic bag is for old papers*; *what's that key for?*; **what did she say that for?** = why did she say that? **(b)** *(showing why something is given)* *what did you get for your birthday?*; *what shall we buy her for Christmas?* **(c)** *(showing person who gets something)* *there was no mail for you this morning*; *I'm making a cup of tea for my mother* **(d)** *(showing how long something happens)* *he has gone to France for two days*; *we've been waiting here for hours* **(e)** *(showing distance)* *you can see for miles from the top of the hill*; *the motorway goes for kilometres without any service stations* **(f)** *(showing destination)* *is this the plane for Edinburgh?*; *when is the next bus for Oxford Circus?* **(g)** in exchange; *she gave me £10 for the jug*; *that old computer is no use - I wouldn't give you anything for it* **(h)** in support of, in order to get; *we're striking for higher pay* **(i)** in the place of someone; *can you write this letter for me?* **(j)** with the purpose of; *to go for a walk*; *he was running for the bus*; *all these items are for sale*

◊ **as for** [æz 'fɔː] referring to; *as for him - he will have to take the bus*; *you play cards if you want to - as for me, I'm going to watch TV*

◊ **for ever** [fə 'evə] *phrase* **(a)** always; *I will love you for ever and ever*; *the good times have gone for ever* **(b)** *(exclamation to show support for a team)* *Scotland for ever!*; *see also* FOREVER

◊ **for example** *or* **for instance** ['fɔː ɪg'zɑːmpl *or* fər 'ɪnstəns] *phrase* to mention one thing among many; *some animals, for example polar bears, are not used to hot weather* (NOTE: **for example** can also be written as **e.g.**)

◊ **for good** [fɔː 'gud] for ever; *she left school for good when she was 16*

forage ['fɒrɪdʒ] **1** *noun* crops grown for food for animals such as horses and cattle; *forage crops such as clover and hay* **2** *verb* to search for food or supplies; *they spent the day foraging for food in the jungle*

foray ['fɒreɪ] *noun* sudden attack; *they made a foray into enemy territory*

forbade [fə'bæd] *verb see* FORBID

forbid [fə'bɪd] *verb* to tell someone not to do something; *Parliament has passed a law forbidding the sale of dangerous weapons*; *she forbade her children to go near the pub*; *smoking has been forbidden on trains*; *swimming in the reservoir is strictly forbidden* (NOTE: **forbidding - forbade** [fə'bæd] **- forbidden** [fə'bɪdn])

forbidden [fə'bɪdn] *adjective* which is not allowed; *the staff are forbidden to use the front entrance*; *father's new rock garden is forbidden territory to the children*

forbidding [fə'bɪdɪŋ] *adjective* which looks sinister or dangerous; *the ruined castle looked grey and forbidding*; *the camp is surrounded by a forbidding barbed wire fence*

force [fɔːs] **1** *noun* **(a)** strength or power; *the force of the wind blew tiles off the roof*; *the police had to use force to push back the demonstrators* **(b)** organized group of people; *he served in the police force for twenty years*; **the armed forces** = the army, navy and air force; **a sales force** = a group of salesmen **2** *verb* to make someone do something; *he was forced to stop smoking*; *you can't force me to go if I don't want to*

◊ **in force** ['ɪn 'fɔːs] *phrase* **(a)** in large numbers; *the police were there in force* **(b)** to be in force = to be operating or working; *the rules have been in force since 1986*; **to come into force** = to start to operate or work; *the new regulations will come into force on January 1st*

forced [fɔːst] *adjective* **(a)** done because someone made you do it; *his lawyer said that his confession was forced*; **forced landing** = quick landing of an aircraft because something is wrong **(b)** artificial, not real; *he gave a rather forced laugh*

forceful ['fɔːsful] *adjective* strong or powerful; *she made a forceful speech in favour of increased funding for the arts*; *it is a forceful argument for disarmament*

forcefully ['fɔːsfuli] *adverb* strongly or powerfully; *he argued forcefully against spending more money*

forceps ['fɔːseps] *noun* instrument like tongs with flat ends, used by doctors in surgery; *he needed forceps to deliver the baby* (NOTE: the word is plural)

forcible ['fɔːsɪbl] *adjective* done by or with force; *the forcible removal of protesters from the street*

ford [fɔːd] **1** *noun* shallow part of a river where you can walk across through the water; *there is a ford lower down where you can cross the river easily* **2** *verb* to cross a river by going through a shallow part; *the army forded the river and advanced on the capital*

fore [fɔː] **1** *noun* **(a) to come to the fore** = to become important; *he first came to the fore during the student riots of 1968* **(b)** front part of a ship or plane **2** *adjective & adverb* in the front part of a ship or plane; *the toilets are located fore and aft* **3** *prefix meaning* in front, before; *forearmed; to foresee* **4** *interjection*; **fore!** = word shouted during a golf match, when you think someone is likely to be hit by the ball

forearm 1 *noun* [ˈfɔːrɑːm] part of the arm between the hand and the elbow; *the dog put his paw on her forearm* **2** *verb* [fɔːˈɑːm]; **to be forearmed** = to be prepared in good time for a fight; *he was forearmed with good advice before he went into the interview room; see* FOREWARNED

forebears [ˈfɔːbeəz] *noun (old)* ancestors; *his forebears came from Russia in the 18th century*

foreboding [fɔːˈbəudɪŋ] *noun* feeling that something bad will happen; *he felt a sense of foreboding as he went on board the 'Titanic'*

forecast [ˈfɔːkɑːst] **1** *noun* description of what you think will happen in the future; *his forecast of sales turned out to be completely accurate*; **economic forecast** = description of how you expect the economy will perform in the future; **population forecast** = calculation of how many people will be living in a country or in a town at some point in the future; **weather forecast** = report on what sort of weather there will be in the next few days **2** *verb* to say what will happen in the future; *they are forecasting storms for the south coast; they forecast a rise in the number of tourists* (NOTE: **forecasting - forecast**)

forecaster [ˈfɔːkɑːstə] *noun* person who says what will happen in the future, especially what sort of weather there will be; *the forecasters said it would be fine, and then it rained*

forecasting [ˈfɔːkɑːstɪŋ] *noun* action of making a forecast; *forecasting the weather is not a very accurate science*

forecourt [ˈfɔːkɔːt] *noun* courtyard in front of a building; *he drove into the petrol station forecourt and asked for someone to wash his windscreen*

forefather [ˈfɔːfɑːðə] *noun* ancestor; *he left Canada and returned to the land of his forefathers*

forefinger [ˈfɔːfɪŋgə] *noun* index finger, the first finger next to the thumb; *she pointed at the picture with her forefinger; hold the paintbrush between your thumb and forefinger*

forefront [ˈfɔːfrʌnt] *noun* most advanced position; **to be in the forefront of a campaign** = to be a leader of a campaign; *they are in the forefront of the campaign to save whales*

foreground [ˈfɔːgraund] *noun* part of a picture which seems nearest the viewer; *there is a boat in the foreground against a background of mountains; compare* BACKGROUND

forehead [ˈfɔːhed] *noun* part of the front of the head between the eyes and the hair; *his hair was falling down over his forehead*

foreign [ˈfɒrɪn] *adjective* **(a)** not from your own country; *there are lots of foreign medical students at our college*; **foreign exchange** = exchanging the money of one country for money of another; *the dollar was firm on the foreign exchange markets*; **foreign language** = language spoken by people in another country; *she speaks several foreign languages, such as German and Chinese*; **foreign rights** = legal rights to sell something in another country, such as the translation of a book **(b) foreign body** = something which should not be there, such as a piece of dust in your eye; *the X-ray showed the presence of a foreign body*

foreigner [ˈfɒrɪnə] *noun* person who does not come from the same country as you; *there are crowds of foreigners in London in the summer; you can tell he's a foreigner when you hear him speak*

Foreign Legion [ˈfɒrɪn ˈliːdʒən] *noun* unit of the regular French army made up of foreigners and volunteers, which only serves overseas; *after a miserable childhood he left home at 16 to join the Foreign Legion*

Foreign Minister [ˈfɒrɪn ˈmɪnɪstə] *noun* government minister in charge of a Foreign Ministry; *the Russian Foreign Minister chaired the meeting* (NOTE: in Britain this is **the Foreign Secretary** and in the USA **the Secretary of State**)

Foreign Ministry [ˈfɒrɪn ˈmɪnəstri] *noun* government department dealing with relations with other countries; *the French Foreign Ministry has issued a statement* (NOTE: in Britain this is called **the Foreign Office** and in the USA **the State Department**)

Foreign Office [ˈfɒrɪn ˈɒfɪs] *noun* British government department dealing with relations with other countries (NOTE: in other countries this is **the Foreign Ministry** and in the USA **the State Department**)

Foreign Secretary [ˈfɒrɪn ˈsekrətri] *noun* British government minister in charge of the Foreign Office (NOTE: in other countries this is **the Foreign Minister** and in the USA **the Secretary of State**)

foreman [ˈfɔːmən] *noun* **(a)** *(in a factory)* skilled worker in charge of several other workers; *the foreman came to make a complaint to the manager* **(b) foreman of a jury** = person elected by the other members of the jury as chairman, who pronounces the verdict in court afterwards; *the foreman of the jury stood up and declared the prisoner 'guilty'* (NOTE: plural is **foremen**)

foremost [ˈfɔːməust] *adjective & adverb* first, most important; **first and foremost** = first of all, the most important thing is; *first and foremost we need to get the costs under control*

forensic [fəˈrensɪk] *adjective* referring to the scientific solving of crimes; *the police had very little forensic evidence to show*; **forensic medicine** = medicine concerned with trying to solve crimes

forerunner [ˈfɔːrʌnə] *noun* person or thing coming before another more important or advanced one; *Stephenson's 'Rocket' was the forerunner of modern locomotives*

foresee [fɔːˈsiː] *verb* to think in advance that something will happen; *she foresaw trouble with the staff; do you foresee any problems with the visa?* (NOTE: **foreseeing - foresaw** [fɔːˈsɔː] **- has foreseen**)

foreseeable [fɔː'siːəbl] *adjective* which can be foreseen; *the accident was entirely foreseeable*; **for the foreseeable future** = as far in advance as you can imagine; *I will certainly stay here for the foreseeable future*

foreshorten [fɔː'ʃɔːtən] *verb* to make objects in a drawing appear the wrong size, by drawing the perspective wrongly; *the two main figures are curiously foreshortened*

foresight ['fɔːsaɪt] *noun* ability to see what will probably happen in the future; ability to plan for emergencies; *she had the foresight to put money aside in case she lost her job*

forest ['fɒrɪst] *noun* large area covered with trees; *the country is covered with thick forests*; *in dry weather there's a danger of forest fires*; *in winter bears come out of the forest to search for food* (NOTE: in Britain now usually used with names: **Sherwood Forest, the New Forest**)

forestall [fɔː'stɔːl] *verb* to anticipate and stop someone doing something; *we tried to forestall any legal action which they might take against us*

forestry ['fɒrɪstri] *noun* work of looking after a forest; *we studied forestry at the agricultural college*; *forestry is becoming an important skill in Third World countries*

foretell [fɔː'tel] *verb* (*formal*) to predict, to say what will happen in the future; *the stars at his birth foretold that he would be a great military leader*; *no one could have foretold her strange fate* (NOTE: **foretelling - foretold** [fɔː'təʊld])

forever [fɔː'evə] always; *I will love you forever*; *he's forever making a noise*; *see also* FOR EVER

forewarned [fɔː'wɔːnd] *adjective* warned in advance; *we were forewarned of possible trouble, and took guns to the meeting*; **forewarned is forearmed** = if you know that trouble is going to happen, then you can make preparations to deal with it

forewarning [fɔː'wɔːnɪŋ] *noun* advance warning; *the residents complained that they had no forewarning of the demolition*

foreword ['fɔːwəd] *noun* short section at the beginning of a book, usually written by a person who is not the author, introducing the book and its author to the reader; *compare* PREFACE

forfeit ['fɔːfɪt] **1** *noun* thing taken away as a punishment; *you have to pay a forfeit if you answer wrongly* **2** *adjective* liable to be taken away; *the goods were declared forfeit* **3** *verb* to lose something, especially as a punishment; *she forfeited her deposit*

forgave [fə'geɪv] *verb see* FORGIVE

forge [fɔːdʒ] **1** *noun* blacksmith's workshop where he makes wrought iron objects, such as horseshoes, gates, etc.; *the blacksmith was hammering away in his forge* **2** *verb* (**a**) to copy something illegally; *he forged the signature on the cheque*; *banknotes are not easy to forge* (**b**) **to forge ahead** = to go forward quickly; *the wind blew harder and the yacht forged ahead*; *we are forging ahead with our new project*

forged [fɔːdʒd] *adjective* which has been copied illegally; *he entered the country with a forged passport*

forger ['fɔːdʒə] *noun* person who copies something illegally; *the police arrested the forger of the banknotes*

forgery ['fɔːdʒəri] *noun* (**a**) action of making an illegal copy; *he was sent to prison for forgery* (NOTE: no plural in this meaning) (**b**) illegal copy; *the signature proved to be a forgery* (NOTE: plural in this meaning is **forgeries**)

forget [fə'get] *verb* (**a**) not to remember; *I've forgotten the name of the restaurant*; *I've forgotten how to play chess*; *she forgot all about her doctor's appointment*; *don't forget we're having lunch together tomorrow*; *great scenes at home - I forgot my wife's birthday!* (**b**) to leave something behind; *when he left the office he forgot his car keys* (NOTE: **forgetting - forgot** [fə'gɒt] **- has forgotten** [fə'gɒtən])

forgetful [fə'getful] *adjective* often unable to remember; *I'm getting more and more forgetful in my old age*

forgetfulness [fə'getfulnəs] *noun* being forgetful; *she has sudden attacks of forgetfulness*

forgive [fə'gɪv] *verb* to stop being angry with someone; *don't worry about it - I forgive you!*; *will she ever forgive me for forgetting her birthday?* (NOTE: **forgiving - forgave** [fə'geɪv] **- has forgiven**)

forgiveness [fə'gɪvnəs] *noun* act of forgiving; *he begged for forgiveness*

forgot *or* **forgotten** [fə'gɒt *or* fə'gɒtən] *see* FORGET

fork [fɔːk] **1** *noun* (**a**) object with a handle at one end and several sharp points at the other, used for picking things up, especially when eating; *don't try to eat Chinese food with a knife and fork*; *it's polite to use a fork to eat cake - don't use your fingers*; **garden fork** = very large fork used for digging (**b**) Y-shaped road junction, or one of the roads leading from it; *take the left fork towards the castle and our house is on the right* **2** *verb* (**a**) to turn off a road; *fork left at the next crossroads* (**b**) to split into two parts; *the railway line forks at Crewe and one branch goes to the coast* (**c**) (*informal*) **to fork out** = to pay for something, usually unwillingly; *she didn't bring any money, so I had to fork out for the whole meal*

fork-lift truck ['fɔːklɪft 'trʌk] *noun* type of small tractor, with two metal arms in front, used in warehouses to lift and move pallets

forlorn [fə'lɔːn] *adjective* (**a**) left alone and feeling sad; *she stood all forlorn on the platform, watching the train leave* (**b**) **forlorn hope** = very slight hope; *we'll searching again, but I think it's a forlorn hope*

form [fɔːm] **1** *noun* (**a**) shape; *a decoration in the form of a ring* (**b**) paper with blank spaces which you have to write in; **application form** = form which has to be filled in to apply for something; *don't forget to fill in the customs form* (**c**) state or condition; *their team wasn't in top form and lost*; **in good form** = in a good mood, very amusing; *she's in good form today*; **off form** *or* **out of form** = not performing very well; *he's off form at the moment - he needs more practice* (**d**) class (in school); *she's in the lowest form*; *little children go into the first form*; **sixth form** = class for children who are over 16; **sixth form college** = special college for students aged 16 and over, preparing them for exams that allow them to go to university **2** *verb* (**a**) to make; *the children formed a circle*; *form a queue here, please* (**b**) **formed of** = made of; *the committee is formed of retired schoolteachers* (**c**) to organize; *they got together and formed a club* (**d**) to start to exist; *ice formed on the car windows*

formal [ˈfɔːml] *adjective* **(a)** done according to certain rules; *the formal opening ceremony was performed by the mayor*; **formal dress** = clothes for special occasions, black coats and bow ties for men, long dresses for women; *the guests were all in formal dress* **(b)** official (agreement); *we made a formal offer for the house yesterday*

formality [fɔːˈmælɪti] *noun* thing which has to be done to obey the law or because it is the custom; *we had to go through customs formalities at the docks*; *the chairman dispensed with the formality of reading the minutes* (NOTE: plural is **formalities**)

formalize [ˈfɔːməlaɪz] *verb* to make a situation official; *we have been working together for several years, but we think it would be best to formalize the partnership*

formally [ˈfɔːməli] *adverb* according to rules, done with ceremony; *the exhibition will be opened formally by the mayor*

format [ˈfɔːmæt] **1** *noun* **(a)** shape or size (in which something is made); *what format do you want your invitations printed in?* **(b)** measurements of a page or book; *printers can handle all sorts of book formats* **(c)** style of a computer disk; *my computer can't read that disk - it's the wrong format* **2** *verb* **(a)** to arrange text on a computer, so that it is ready for final printing; *style sheets are used to format documents* **(b)** to set a computer disk so that it is ready to receive data; *you have to format the disk before you can save data on it* (NOTE: **formatting - formatted**)

formation [fɔːˈmeɪʃn] *noun* **(a)** shape, forming of something; *a beautiful cloud formation*; *the formation of ice occurs at temperatures below zero* **(b) in formation** = in a set pattern; *the geese were flying in a V formation*

formative years [ˈfɔːmətɪv ˈjɜːz] *noun* the early years of life when a person's character is being formed; *his formative years were spent as a refugee*

former [ˈfɔːmə] **1** *adjective* who was at an earlier time; *a former army officer*; *the former champion came last in the race* **2** *noun* **the former** = first person *or* thing mentioned (of two); *Mr Smith and Mr Jones are both directors, but the former has been with the company longer* (NOTE: the second of two is called the **latter**)

formerly [ˈfɔːməli] *adverb* at an earlier time; *her house was formerly a railway station*; *he was formerly head of our department*

formidable [ˈfɔːmɪdəbl] *adjective* **(a)** frighteningly difficult; *the castle is surrounded by formidable walls and gates*; *climbing Everest is a formidable feat* **(b)** very impressive (person); *the college principal is a formidable woman*

formula [ˈfɔːmjʊlə] *noun* **(a)** statement of a scientific fact, often shown by means of symbols; *the chemical formula of carbon dioxide is CO_2*; *the drug is made to a secret formula* **(b) Formula I race** = car race where the cars all have engines of the largest classification **(c)** *US* powdered milky food for babies; *don't forget to make up some formula* (NOTE: plural is **formulae** [ˈfɔːmjʊliː])

formulate [ˈfɔːmjʊleɪt] *verb* **(a)** to express an idea clearly; *he had some difficulty in formulating his ideas* **(b) to formulate a plan** = to devise a plan and set it out clearly

formulation [fɔːmjuˈleɪʃn] *noun* devising or expressing clearly; *the formulation of a new management plan*

forsake [fɔːˈseɪk] *verb* (*formal*) to leave behind, to abandon; *what on earth made him forsake his job and family, and go to look for gold in Alaska?*; *don't forsake your ideals for the bright lights of the city!*; *see also* GOD-FORSAKEN (NOTE: **forsook** [fɔːˈsuk] - **has forsaken**)

fort [fɔːt] *noun* **(a)** strong building which can be defended against enemy attacks; *the soldiers rode out of the fort*; *he was posted to a fort in the desert* **(b) to hold the fort** = to be in charge while someone is away; *everyone is away on holiday so I've been left holding the fort*

forth [fɔːθ] *adverb* (*formal*) **(a)** forwards; **back and forth** = backwards and forwards; *I'm fed up with commuting back and forth across town every day* **(b) to go forth** *or* **to set forth** = to go out and onwards; *the expedition set forth in May*; **to hold forth about something** = to talk without stopping about something; *my father was holding forth about the government* (NOTE: do not confuse with **fourth**)

◊ **and so forth** [nd ˈsəʊ ɒn] *adverb* with other things; *he talked about plants: flowers, vegetables, and so forth*

forthcoming [fɔːθˈkʌmɪŋ] *adjective* **(a)** soon to come; *his forthcoming novel will be about London*; *no government grant is forthcoming* **(b)** (*informal*) talkative, full of information; *she wasn't very forthcoming about her wedding*

forthright [ˈfɔːθraɪt] *adjective* direct and blunt (way of speaking); *his forthright condemnation of the terrorist attack*; *he was perhaps a little too forthright, but at least we now know what he thinks*

forthwith [fɔːθˈwɪθ] *adverb* (*formal*) immediately; *your contract of employment is terminated forthwith*

fortieth (40th) [ˈfɔːtɪəθ] *adjective & noun* *he came fortieth and last in the race*; *it's her fortieth birthday tomorrow*

fortification [fɔːtɪfɪˈkeɪʃn] *noun* **(a)** making strong; *he drew up plans for the fortification of the presidential palace* **(b) fortifications** = walls or towers built to defend a city; *archaeologists have uncovered remains of the Roman fortifications*

fortify [ˈfɔːtɪfaɪ] *verb* **(a)** to make a place strong, so that it can be defended against attack; **a fortified town** = a town with strong walls round it to protect it **(b) to fortify yourself with** = to eat or drink something to make you able to continue; *she drank a glass of whisky to fortify herself against the cold*; *we set out on the walk over the mountain, fortified by a good hot meal*; **fortified wine** = wine with extra alcohol added, such as sherry and port

fortnight [ˈfɔːtnaɪt] *noun* two weeks; *see you in a fortnight!*; *she's taking a fortnight's holiday*; *we visit my mother once a fortnight*; *we will be on holiday during the last fortnight of July* (NOTE: not used in American English)

fortress [ˈfɔːtrəs] *noun* strong castle; *the king retreated into his fortress and prepared for battle* (NOTE: plural is **fortresses**)

fortuitous [fɔːˈtjuːɪtəs] *adjective* accidental, which happens by chance and has a good result; *their meeting* *at the restaurant was entirely fortuitous*; *how fortuitous that we happened to see you then!*

fortunate ['fɔːtʃənət] *adjective* lucky; *you are very fortunate to have such a lovely family*; *we've been fortunate with the weather*

fortunately ['fɔːtʃənətli] *adverb* by good luck; *fortunately, he had remembered to take an umbrella*; *he was late getting to the airport, but fortunately the flight had been delayed*

fortune ['fɔːtjuːn] *noun* (a) large amount of money; *he won a fortune on the lottery*; *she left her fortune to her three children*; **to cost a fortune** = to cost a lot of money; *that shop has shoes that won't cost a fortune*; *see also* SMALL (b) what will happen in the future; **to tell someone's fortune** = to say what will happen to someone in the future; *she tells fortunes from cards* (c) luck, chance; *she had the good fortune to be picked for the England team*

fortune-teller ['fɔːtʃən ˌtelə] *noun* person who says what will happen in the future by looking at cards or lines on your hand; *the fortune-teller told her she would meet a tall dark stranger*

fortune-telling ['fɔːtʃən ˌtelɪŋ] *noun* telling people what will happen in the future by looking at cards, tea leaves or lines on the hand; *she makes her money by fortune-telling over the telephone*

forty ['fɔːti] *number* 40; *she's forty (years old)* he has more than forty pairs of shoes; *he's in his forties* = between 40 and 49 years old; **the (nineteen) forties (1940s)** = the period from 1940 to 1949; *see also* WINK (NOTE: **forty-one** (41), **forty-two** (42), but **forty-first** (41st), **forty-second** (42nd), etc.)

forum ['fɔːrəm] *noun* place where matters of general interest can be discussed; *the TV chat shows provide a forum for debate on topical issues*

forward ['fɔːwəd] **1** *adjective* moving in the direction that someone *or* something is facing; *she made a forward pass across the field to the winger* **2** *adverb* (a) in the direction that someone *or* something is facing; *she bent forward to hear what he had to say*; *he took two steps forward*; *he made a sign with his hand and the cars began to go forward* (b) advanced; *thanks to government red tape we're no further forward with our project* (c) **to look forward to something** = to think happily about something which is going to happen; *I'm looking forward to my holidays*; *he isn't looking forward to his exams*; *I'm looking forward to seeing her again* (d) **from that day forward** = from that time on **3** *verb* to send on a letter to another address; *the bank forwarded the cheque to his house in the country*; **forwarding address** = address to which mail can be sent; *they moved and forgot to leave a forwarding address so we can't forward their mail* **4** *noun* player in a team whose job is to attack the other side; *the England defence came under attack from the Brazilian forwards*

forwards *US* **forward** ['fɔːwədz] *adverb* in a forward direction; *he leant forwards and kissed her*; *the cars were moving slowly forwards*; **backwards and forwards** = from one side to the other several times; *the policeman walked backwards and forwards in front of the shop*

fossil ['fɒsl] *noun* remains of a prehistoric animal or plant left in a rock; *they found some fossil shells in the cliffs*; **fossil fuels** = fuels such as coal, which are in fact remains of plants

fossilized ['fɒslaɪzd] *adjective* which has become a fossil; *coal is the fossilized remains of prehistoric tree trunks*

foster ['fɒstə] *verb* (a) to bring up a child who is not your own; *they have fostered several children* (b) to encourage an idea, etc.; *tourism fosters interest in other countries*; *we are trying to foster the interest of the children in the history of the village*

foster-child ['fɒstətʃaɪld] *noun* child brought up by parents who are not his or her own; *the couple had two foster-children and two children of their own* (NOTE: plural is **foster-children**)

foster home ['fɒstə ˈhəʊm] *noun* family where a foster-child is brought up; *the child was not adopted as a baby and now lives in a foster home*

foster-parents ['fɒstəpeərənts] *noun* parents who foster a child; *her foster-parents brought her up as one of their own*

fought [fɔːt] *see* FIGHT

foul [faʊl] **1** *adjective* (a) bad, unpleasant (taste, language, air, etc.); *what foul weather we're having!*; *the boss has been in a foul temper all day*; *a foul-smelling drain ran down the centre of the street* (b) **foul play** = murder; *the body was hanging upside down and the police suspected foul play* (c) **to fall foul of** = to get into trouble with; *the boys fell foul of the police*; *she fell foul of the income tax inspectors* (NOTE: **fouler - foulest**) **2** *noun* action which is against the rules of a game; *the referee gave a free kick for a foul on the goalkeeper*; *look at the action replay to see if it really was a foul* (NOTE: do not confuse with **fowl**) **3** *verb* (a) to make dirty *(of dog)* to leave excreta; *make sure that your dog does not foul the pavements* (b) to do something to another player which is against the rules of a game; *he was fouled inside the penalty box so the ref gave a penalty* (c) *(informal)* **to foul something up** = to make a mess of something *or* to create problems; *don't ask John to do it - he's sure to foul it up*

found [faʊnd] *verb* (a) to establish, to begin something; *the business was founded in 1900* (b) **to be founded on something** = to be bases on something; *the accusations against her are not founded on any definite facts* (c) *see* FIND

foundation [faʊnˈdeɪʃn] *noun* (a) **foundations** = stone or concrete base below ground on which a building is built; *the foundations of the building need strengthening*; **foundation stone** = stone in a wall which records the start of work on a building; *the mayor laid the foundation stone of the new library* (b) establishing, setting up; *ever since its foundation in 1892, the company has been a great success* (c) charitable organization which provides money for certain projects; *a foundation for educational research* (d) **foundation course** = basic course at a university, which allows you to go on to a more advanced course

founder ['faʊndə] **1** *noun* person who establishes or sets up something; *he was one of the founders of the National Trust*; **founder member** = one of the first to establish a club, etc.; *the USA and the UK are both founder members of the United Nations* **2** *verb* (a) to collapse, to fail; *the project foundered for lack of money* (b) *(formal)* to sink; *the ship foundered in heavy seas*

founding ['faʊndɪŋ] *noun* action of setting up; *the anniversary of the founding of the state*; **founding**

father = person who founded a state, especially one of those who signed the American Constitution of 1787

fountain ['fauntɪn] *noun* ornamental jet of water in a street or garden; *there is a statue and a fountain in the middle of the lake; on New Year's Eve people try to jump into the fountains in Trafalgar Square;* **drinking fountain** = public tap where you can drink water

fountain pen ['fauntɪn 'pen] *noun* pen which can be filled with ink; *he rather ostentatiously used a gold fountain pen to sign the contract*

four [fɔː] **(a)** number 4; *he's four (years old) I have an appointment with the doctor at four (o'clock); a square has four corners;* **on all fours** = on hands and knees; *he was creeping around under the desk on all fours* **(b)** crew of four rowers in a boat; *our college four won the race; see also* EIGHT, PAIR **(c)** *(in cricket)* score of four runs for sending the ball over the boundary; *he scored a century, including seven fours and two sixes*

foursome ['fɔːsʌm] *noun* **(a)** golf match played by four people, i.e. two pairs; *they won the foursomes* **(b)** group of four people; *the foursome stole a car and drove to Las Vegas*

fourteen [fɔː'tiːn] number 14; *there are fourteen houses in our street; he's fourteen (years old) next week;* **the fourteen hundreds (1400s)** = the period from 1400 to 1499 (NOTE: compare **the fourteenth century**)

fourteenth, 14th [fɔː'tiːnθ] *adjective & noun she came fourteenth in the race; the fourteenth of July or July the fourteenth (July 14th); it was her fourteenth birthday yesterday;* **the fourteenth century** = the period from 1300 to 1399 (NOTE: that with dates **fourteenth** is usually written **14th:** January 14th, 1985; October 14th 1799 (American style is **October 14, 1991**), say 'the fourteenth of October' or 'October the fourteenth' (American style is 'October fourteenth')

fourth, 4th [fɔːθ] **1** *adjective this is the fourth time he's had to go to hospital this year; it's her fourth birthday tomorrow; the fourth of October or October the fourth (October 4th)* **the fourth century** = the period from 300 to 399 AD **2** *noun* **one fourth** = 25% (NOTE: do not confuse with **forth**; note that instead of **a fourth** or **a fourth part**, you usually say **a quarter**. Note also that with dates **fourth** is usually written **4th:** January 4th, 1985; October 4th 1799 (American style is **October 4, 1991**), say 'the fourth of October' or 'October the fourth' (American style is 'October fourth'); with names of kings and queens **fourth** is usually written **IV:** King Charles IV (say 'King Charles the Fourth'))

Fourth of July ['fɔːθ əv dʒuː'laɪ] *noun* the national day in the United States; *we're having a Fourth of July party*

four-wheel drive (4-wheel drive) ['fɔː wiːl 'draɪv] *noun* type of car where the engine drives all the wheels and not just two of them; *four-wheel drive vehicles are popular with people who live in the country*

fowl [faul] *noun* domestic bird kept to be killed for food or for its eggs (such as chickens, ducks, turkeys and geese); **wild fowl** = game birds, such as grouse, pheasants, etc., which are shot for sport and food (NOTE: do not confuse with **foul**; note that the plural is **fowl**)

fox [fɒks] **1** *noun* wild animal with reddish fur and a bushy tail; *foxes attack lambs in this part of the world;* **urban fox** = fox that lives in a town; *the urban fox has become a menace in parts of London;* **fox cub** = young fox (NOTE: plural is **foxes**; the female is called a **vixen**) **2** *verb* to puzzle; *today's crossword has got me completely foxed; to fox everyone, we used a French company to make the planning application*

foyer ['fɔɪeɪ] *noun* large entrance hall at the front of a hotel, restaurant, theatre; *let's meet in the foyer during the interval; the foyer was full of tourists waiting to register*

fraction ['frækʃn] *noun* **(a)** very small amount; *sales are up a fraction this month; if you move a fraction to the right, you'll all get in the picture* **(b)** *(in mathematics)* less than a whole number; $1/4$ *and* $1/2$ *are fractions*

fractional ['frækʃənl] *adjective* very small; *there's been a fractional increase in sales this month*

fracture ['fræktʃə] **1** *noun* break (especially in bones); *the X-ray showed up the fracture clearly;* **simple fracture** = clean break of a bone; **compound fracture** = fracture where the broken bone has gone through the skin; *simple fractures heal well; compound ones are more difficult to set* **2** *verb* to break a bone; *he fractured his leg in the accident; they put her fractured leg in plaster*

fragile ['frædʒaɪl] *adjective* **(a)** easily broken, delicate; *be careful when packing the glasses - they're very fragile* **(b)** *(informal)* feeling weak and ill after an illness or operation, or after drinking too much alcohol; *she's still very fragile after her recent operation; I don't think I want any breakfast - I'm feeling a bit fragile this morning*

fragility [frə'dʒɪlɪti] *noun* being easily broken; *the fragility of the peace was shown by the riots which broke out when the ambassador's car was stoned*

fragment **1** *noun* ['frægmənt] small piece; *when digging on the site of the old house they found fragments of glass* **2** *verb* [fræg'ment] to break into small pieces; *as soon as the founder died the whole organization fragmented*

fragmentary ['frægməntəri] *adjective* in pieces, not complete; *we found fragmentary remains of a Roman villa*

fragrance ['freɪgrəns] *noun* pleasant smell; *the fragrance of the roses outside our bedroom windows*

fragrant ['freɪgrənt] *adjective* with a sweet smell; *roses are particularly fragrant when the sun is on them*

frail [freɪl] *adjective* weak and thin; *she's getting very frail, and may soon have to go into a nursing home; they set off to cross the Channel in a frail little rowing boat*

frailty ['freɪlti] *noun* **(a)** being weak; *the frailty of human existence; the frailty of my father's health* **(b)** **frailties** = weaknesses of character; *greed is one of the human frailties*

frame [freɪm] **1** *noun* **(a)** border round glasses, a picture, mirror, window, etc.; *he has glasses with gold frames; I think the frame is worth more than the painting* **(b)** one picture in a film; *the book is illustrated with frames from some of his films* **(c)** **climbing frame** = framework of wooden bars and platforms for children to climb on **2** *verb* **(a)** to put a frame round a picture; *the photograph has been framed in red* **(b)** to make someone seem to be guilty; *he says he was framed by the police*; *it wasn't me - I've been framed!* **(c)** to put words together to make a sentence; *he had some difficulty in framing his reply*; *the note was framed in very formal language*

frame house ['freɪm 'haʊs] *noun US* wooden house built round a strong wooden framework; *they live in an old white frame house in Massachusetts*

frame of mind ['freɪm əv 'maɪnd] *noun* way of thinking or feeling, general mood; *you must wait until he's in the right frame of mind before you ask the boss for a rise*

framework ['freɪmwɜːk] *noun* **(a)** structure supporting a building, etc.; *the framework of the shed is sound - it just needs some paint* **(b)** basis of a plan; *they are negotiating the framework of the agreement*

franc [fræŋk] *noun* unit of money used in France, Belgium and Switzerland; *we paid for the meal in Belgian francs*; *how many French francs does it cost?*; *he has a Swiss franc bank account* (NOTE: in English usually written **Fr** before the figure: **Fr2,500** (say: 'two thousand, five hundred francs'). Currencies of different countries can be shown by the initial letters of the countries: **FFr** (French francs); **SwFr** (Swiss francs); **BFr** (Belgian francs))

France [frɑːns] *noun* country in Europe, south of Britain and west of Belgium and Germany; *in 1814 Britain was at war with France*; *last year we went to France on holiday*; *he's visiting friends in France* (NOTE: capital: **Paris**; people: **the French**; language: **French**; currency: **franc** *or* **French franc, euro**)

franchise ['fræntʃaɪz] **1** *noun* **(a)** right to vote; *in some countries women do not have the franchise*; **universal franchise** = the right of everyone in a country to vote **(b)** permit to sell a company's products in a certain region or to trade using a well-known brand name; *he bought a pizza franchise* **2** *verb* to sell licences for people to trade using a brand name and paying a fee for using it; *his sandwich bar was so successful that he decided to franchise it*

franchisee [fræntʃaɪˈziː] *noun* person who runs a business under a franchise; *franchisees have to go through a period of training before they can start their franchises*

frank [fræŋk] **1** *adjective* saying what you think; *he gave her some frank advice*; *to be really frank with you - I think the plan stinks* (NOTE: do not confuse with **franc**) **2** *verb* to stamp a letter with a special machine (instead of using a postage stamp); *the letters were all franked before they left the office*

frankfurter ['fræŋkfɜːtə] *noun* long spiced sausage which is boiled and sometimes eaten with a roll; *we've brought some frankfurters for the barbecue* (NOTE: also called **wieners** in American English)

> COMMENT: frankfurters originally came from Frankfurt in Germany, but are now made all over the world. When they are cooked in hot water and put inside a long roll, they become 'hot dogs'

frankly ['fræŋkli] *adverb* speaking truthfully; *frankly, I don't care what you do*; *she spoke frankly about her childhood in Germany*

frantic ['fræntɪk] *adjective* wild, worried and doing things fast; *where have you been? we were getting frantic*; *we had frantic phone calls from your mother*; *it was a frantic race against time to save the children before the tide came in*

frantically ['fræntɪkli] *adverb* fast in a worried way; *the engineers worked frantically through the night to get the electricity working again*

fraternal [frəˈtɜːnl] *adjective (formal)* **(a)** brotherly; *he started going out with his brother's girlfriend - there's fraternal feeling for you!*; *the comrades sent fraternal greetings to their counterparts in the Romanian union* **(b)** **fraternal twins** = twins who are not identical because they developed from two different ova at the same time (NOTE: twins who are exactly alike are called **identical twins**)

fraternity [frəˈtɜːnɪti] *noun* **(a)** group of people with similar interests or occupations; *members of the banking fraternity have criticized the Chancellor of the Exchequer* **(b)** *US* **student fraternity** = student association for men (NOTE: the equivalent for women is a **sorority**; plural in this meaning is **fraternities**) **(c)** *(formal)* brotherly feeling; *the slogan of the French state is 'Liberty, Equality, Fraternity'*

fraud [frɔːd] *noun* **(a)** making money by making people believe something which is not true; *he is facing trial for fraud*; **Serious Fraud Office** = British government department in charge of investigating fraud in large companies; **fraud squad** = special police department which investigates frauds **(b)** person pretending to be something he is not; *she's a fraud - she says she's a film star, but she's only been in TV commercials*; *he's an old fraud - he didn't build that car himself*

fraudulent ['frɔːdjʊlənt] *adjective* dishonest; *it is fraudulent to claim insurance on something which has not been destroyed or stolen*

fray [freɪ] **1** *noun* fight; **to join the fray** = to join the battle or argument; *the government and opposition argued over the problem, and then the unions joined the fray*; **ready for the fray** = ready to fight; *are we all ready for the fray?* **2** *verb (of material)* to become worn so that threads are loose; *the carpet is fraying at the edges*; *you could see the frayed cuffs on his shirt*; *she stitched tape along the bottom of the hem to stop it fraying*

freak [friːk] **1** *noun* **(a)** unusual type of person, animal or plant; *a white whale is a freak of nature* **(b)** person who is fanatical about something; *my brother's a computer freak* **2** *adjective* extraordinary (weather); *the walkers were caught out by the freak weather conditions on the mountain*; *the vineyards were hit by a freak snowstorm in June*

freakish ['friːkɪʃ] *adjective* unusual or extraordinary; *the freakish weather conditions lasted all week, with snow in the Mediterranean and warm winds in Iceland*

freckles ['freklz] *noun* small brown marks on the skin, often caused by the sun; *you'll recognize her at once, she's tall with fair hair and freckles*; *she's trying to get rid of the freckles on her arms*

freckled ['frekld] *adjective* covered in freckles; *a little freckled red-haired boy came into the room*

free [friː] **1** *adjective* **(a)** not busy, not occupied; *will you be free next Tuesday?*; *there is a table free in the corner of the restaurant* **(b)** not costing any money; *send in four tokens from cereal boxes and you can get a free toy*; *I got a free ticket for the exhibition*;

children are admitted free; **free gift** = present given by a shop to a customer who buys a certain amount of goods; *there is a free gift worth £25 to any customer buying a washing machine* (c) able to do what you want, not forced to do anything; *he's free to do what he wants*; *it's a free country* (d) to be free from *or* of something = to be without something unpleasant; *the country has been declared free of disease*; **free of charge** = with no payment to be made; *see also* DUTY FREE (e) not in prison, not in a cage; *after six years in prison he's a free man again*; *lions roam free in the safari park*; **to set free** = to allow someone to leave prison, to let an animal out of a cage; *the young birds were raised in the zoo and then set free in the wild* (NOTE: **freer - freest**) **2** *verb* (a) to release someone who is trapped; *it took the fire service some time to free the passengers in the bus* (b) to let someone out of prison, an animal out of a cage; *the crowd stormed the jail and freed the prisoners*

freebie ['fri:bi] *noun (informal)* something supplied free of charge (especially as a gift to a customer or journalist); *everyone wants to be a travel writer and enjoy all the freebies given you by travel companies*

freedom ['fri:dəm] *noun* (a) state of being free, not trapped, not in prison; *she felt a sense of freedom being in the country after working all week in the city*; *his lawyer pleaded for his client's freedom* (b) being free to do what you want; *the four freedoms of movement on which the EU is based are the freedom of movement of goods, of capital, of people and of services*; **freedom of information** = making official information held by government departments available to everyone; **freedom of the press** = being able to write and publish in a newspaper what you want, without fear of prosecution, provided that you do not break the law; **freedom of speech** = being able to say what you like without fear of prosecution, provided that you do not break the law

freedom fighter ['fri:dəm 'faɪtə] *noun* guerilla fighting against an oppressive government; *freedom fighters have attacked a government outpost in the north of the country*

free enterprise ['fri: 'entəpraɪz] *noun* system of business where there is no interference from the government; *business people are all in favour of free enterprise*

freehold property ['fri:həʊld 'prɒpəti] *noun* building which the owner can hold for ever (NOTE: the opposite, where the property is not owned outright, is **leasehold**)

free kick ['fri: 'kɪk] *noun* kick which a footballer is allowed to make without anyone opposing him, to punish the other side for something which they have done; *the referee awarded a free kick*

freelance ['fri:lɑːns] **1** *adjective & noun* independent (worker), not employed by one particular company; *she is a freelance journalist*; *he works as a freelance* **2** *adverb* **to work freelance** = to work independently, to be self-employed **3** *verb* to work independently; *she freelances for several newspapers*

freelancer ['fri:lɑːnsə] *noun* freelance worker

freely ['fri:li] *adverb* in an open manner, without being forced; *he freely admitted he had been in the house where the murder took place*; *he gave himself up to the police and freely confessed to the theft of the car*

Freemason ['fri:meɪsən] *noun* member of a secret society whose members help each other and protect each other; *the Freemasons do a lot of work for charity* (NOTE: also simply called **Masons**)

freephone ['fri:fəʊn] *noun GB* system where you can telephone to reply to an advertisement, to place an order or to ask for information and the seller pays for the call

> COMMENT: freephone numbers have the code 0800

freepost ['fri:pəʊst] *noun GB* system where you can write to an advertiser to place an order or to ask for information to be sent, and the seller pays the postage; *write to us freepost at the following address*; *compare* POST FREE

freestyle ['fri:staɪl] *noun (in swimming)* any stroke, but usually the crawl; *the women's 200m freestyle race*

free trade ['fri: 'treɪd] *noun* system where goods can go from one country to another without any restrictions; *the government adopted a free trade policy*; *what he is advocating is an end to the era of protectionism and a return to free trade*; **free trade area** = group of countries practising free trade between them

freeway ['fri:weɪ] *noun US* fast motorway with few junctions; *we took the interstate freeway to San Diego*

free will ['fri: 'wɪl] *noun* **of your own free will** = willingly, without being forced; *he gave himself up to the police of his own free will*

freeze [fri:z] **1** *verb* (a) to change from liquid to solid because of the cold; *the winter was mild and for the first time ever the river did not freeze over*; *it's so cold that the lake has frozen solid* (b) to become very cold; *the forecast is that it will freeze tonight* (c) to make food very cold so that it keeps; *we picked the raspberries and froze them immediately* (d) to freeze to death = to die of cold; *she went out into the snow and froze to death* (e) to keep money or costs, etc., at their present level and not allow them to rise; *we have frozen salaries at last year's level* (f) to freeze a bank account = to issue a court order stopping anyone from using a bank account, especially preventing them from taking money out (NOTE: **froze** [frəʊz] - **has frozen**) **2** *noun* (a) period when it is very cold; *do you remember the great freeze in the winter of 1980?* (b) wages and prices freeze *or* a freeze on wages and prices = period when wages and prices are not allowed to be increased

freezer ['fri:zə] *noun* refrigerator for freezing food and keeping it frozen; *put the ice cream back into the freezer before it starts to melt*

freezing ['fri:zɪŋ] *adjective* very cold; *guests don't appreciate sleeping in freezing bedrooms*; *close the door - it's freezing in here*; **freezing compartment** = part of a refrigerator where food is put to freeze or to be kept frozen; *we've got some frozen pizzas in the freezing compartment in case of emergencies*

freezing point ['fri:zɪŋ 'pɔɪnt] *noun* very low temperature at which a liquid becomes solid; *the freezing point of water is 0°C*

freight [freɪt] **1** *noun* (a) action of transporting goods by air, sea or land; *we sent the order (by) air freight* (b) goods transported; *the government is encouraging firms to send freight by rail*; **freight train** = train used for transporting goods; *US* **freight car** = goods wagon on a train **2** *verb* to transport goods; *we freight goods to all parts of the world*

freighter ['freɪtə] *noun* aircraft or ship which carries goods

French [frentʃ] **1** *adjective* **(a)** referring to France; *the French railways have a system of high speed trains covering the whole country* **(b) to take French leave** = to go away without permission **2** *noun* **(a)** language spoken in France; *he speaks French very well*; *they are learning French at school* **(b) the French** = the people of France; *the French are famous for their wines and their cooking*

French beans ['frentʃ 'biːnz] *noun* beans grown on low bushes and eaten in their pods when still green

French dressing ['frentʃ 'dresɪŋ] *noun* salad dressing made of oil and vinegar, with salt, mustard and other flavourings; *do you want French dressing or mayonnaise?*

French fries *or* **French fried potatoes** ['frentʃ 'fraɪz *or* 'frentʃ 'fraɪd pə'teɪtəʊz] *noun* thin stick-shaped pieces of potato, fried in deep oil or fat; *she ordered a cheeseburger and French fries* (NOTE: also called **chips** in British English, but not in American English; often simply called **fries: hamburger and fries**)

Frenchman *or* **Frenchwoman** ['frentʃmən *or* 'frentʃwʊmən] *noun* person from France; *the average Frenchman drinks more wine per day than the average Englishman* (NOTE: plural is **Frenchmen** *or* **Frenchwomen**)

French horn ['frentʃ 'hɔːn] *noun* brass musical instrument with a tube which is coiled round; *a piece by Mozart for French horn and orchestra*

French polish ['frentʃ 'pɒlɪʃ] **1** *noun* resin polish used on wood; *she gave the table a coating of French polish* **2** *verb* to polish wood with French polish; *the table needs to be French polished*

French toast ['frentʃ 'təʊst] *noun* slice of bread, dipped in beaten egg, and then fried, usually served with sugar; *let's have French toast for supper!*

French window ['frentʃ 'wɪndəʊ] *noun* door made of glass, usually opening on to a garden; *French windows lead from the sitting room onto the patio*

frenetic [frə'netɪk] *adjective* wildly excited; *a day of frenetic dealing on the stock exchange*; *everyone was getting frenetic as the day of the festival approached and nothing was ready*

frenzied ['frenzɪd] *adjective* wild and uncontrollable; *they started a frenzied dance*; *the group launched a frenzied attack on the driver of the bus*

frenzy ['frenzi] *noun* wild excitement; *he killed himself in a frenzy of despair*; *she had a bit of a spending frenzy before the holidays*; *the office was in a frenzy of activity before the visitor from the bank manager*

frequency ['friːkwənsi] *noun* **(a)** rate at which something happens; *the government is becoming alarmed at the frequency of accidents in the construction industry* **(b)** number of vibrations per second made by a radio wave; *what frequency is Radio 3 on?*; **frequency modulation (FM)** = radio system where the number of waves per second varies; *you can pick up Radio 1 on medium wave or FM* (NOTE: plural is **frequencies**)

frequent 1 *adjective* ['friːkwənt] happening often; often seen; *he was a frequent visitor to the library*; *skin cancer is becoming more frequent*; *how frequent are the planes to Birmingham?* **2** *verb* [frɪ'kwent] *(formal)* to go somewhere very often; *he frequents the bar at the corner of the street*

frequent flyer ['friːkwənt 'flaɪə] *noun* person who travels by a certain airline often; *he has a frequent flyer card*; *when making reservations, quote your frequent flyer number*

frequently ['friːkwəntli] *adverb* often; *the ferries don't run as frequently in the winter*; *she could frequently be seen walking her dog in the park*

fresco ['freskəʊ] *noun* painting done on wet plaster on a wall or ceiling; *some 13th century frescoes were damaged in the earthquake* (NOTE: plural is **frescoes;** do not confuse with **alfresco**)

fresh [freʃ] *adjective* **(a)** not used or not dirty; *I'll get you a fresh plate*; **fresh air** = open air; *after ten hours, they came out of the coal mine into the fresh air* **(b)** made quite recently; *a basket of fresh rolls*; *let's ask for a fresh pot of coffee* **(c) fresh water** = water in rivers and lakes which contains no salt (as opposed to salt water in the sea)*; see also* FRESHWATER **(d)** new; *the police produced some fresh evidence* **(e)** not tinned or frozen; *the fishmonger sells fresh fish*; *fresh fruit salad is better than tinned*; *fresh vegetables are difficult to get in winter* **(f)** bright and attractive; *she has a fresh complexion*; *the kitchen is painted a fresh green colour* (NOTE: **fresher - freshest**)

freshen ['freʃən] *verb* **(a)** to make something fresh; *the hot air in the valley was freshened by a mountain breeze* **(b)** to become cooler or fresher; *the wind freshened as night came on* **(c) to freshen (yourself) up** = to wash your hands and face, and tidy your hair; *I must just go to freshen up before the guests arrive*

freshener ['freʃənə] *noun* **air freshener** = substance which makes the air in a room smell fresh and clean; *I've bought some lavender air freshener for the bathroom*

fresher ['freʃə] *noun* *(informal)* freshman, new student in his or her first year at college

freshly ['freʃli] *adverb* newly, recently; *freshly baked bread*; *freshly made coffee*

freshman ['freʃmən] *noun* new student in his or her first year at college or university; *he's a freshman at the local university;* compare SENIOR, SOPHOMORE (NOTE: in American English, **freshman** is also applied to a student at high school; plural is **freshmen**)

freshness ['freʃnəs] *noun* being fresh; *when you buy fruit and vegetables, remember to check them for freshness*

freshwater ['freʃwɔːtə] *adjective* referring to river or lake water, not salt water; *freshwater fish such as trout*

fret [fret] **2** *verb* to worry or be unhappy; *she's fretting about her exams* (NOTE: **fretting - fretted**) **2** *noun* raised metal strip crossing the neck of a guitar against which you press the strings; *place your fingers so that you can feel the fret*

fretful ['fretfʊl] *adjective* always complaining and unhappy; *she's a fretful baby*

friar ['fraɪə] *noun* member of a Christian religious order; *the first friars came to Britain in the early Middle Ages*

COMMENT: both monks and friars were members of religious orders, but monks stayed in their monasteries to pray, while friars went out to collect money or to preach in the streets or in parish churches

friction ['frɪkʃn] *noun* (a) one thing rubbing against another; *you need more oil to reduce friction in the motor* (b) disagreement between two or more people; *there has been a good deal of friction between the members of the board* (NOTE: no plural)

Friday ['fraɪdeɪ] *noun* the fifth day of the week, the day between Thursday and Saturday; *we all had a meal together last Friday*; *we always go to the cinema on Friday evenings*; *we normally have our meetings on Fridays*; *Friday is a day of rest for Muslims*; *today is Friday, June 20th*; **Good Friday** = the Friday before Easter Day; **Man Friday** *or* **Girl Friday** = general helper in an office

fridge [frɪdʒ] *noun* (informal) refrigerator, kitchen machine for keeping things cold; *the fridge is empty - we must buy some more food*; *shall I put the milk back in the fridge?*

fried [fraɪd] *adjective* which is cooked in a little oil or fat; *would you like a fried egg for breakfast?*; *add the fried onions to the meat*; *we had fried rice with our sweet and sour pork*; *see also* FRY

friend [frend] *noun* person whom you know well and like; *she's my best friend*; *we're going on holiday with some friends from work*; **to make friends with someone** = to get to know and like someone; *we made friends with some French people on holiday*

friendly ['frendli] *adjective* like a friend, wanting to make friends; *don't be frightened of the dog - he's very friendly*; *we're not on friendly terms with the people who live next door* (NOTE: **friendlier - friendliest**)

friendship ['frendʃɪp] *noun* state of being friends; *he formed several lasting friendships at school*

fries [fraɪz] *verb see* FRENCH FRIES, FRY

frigate ['frɪgət] *noun* small fast-moving naval ship; *he commanded a frigate during the wars against Napoleon*

fright [fraɪt] *noun* fear; *when she saw the ghost she started shaking with fright*; **to give someone a fright** = to make someone jump with fear; *the sudden noise gave her a fright*; *don't creep up behind me like that - you gave me a real fright*; (old) **to look a fright** = to look awful and not very attractive; *she looks a fright in that bright pink tracksuit*

frighten ['fraɪtn] *verb* to make someone afraid; *take off that horrible mask - you'll frighten the children*; *the cat has frightened all the birds away*

frightened ['fraɪtənd] *adjective* full of fear, scared; *the frightened children ran out of the building*; **frightened of something** *or* **someone** = afraid of someone *or* something; *don't be frightened of the dog - he won't hurt you*

frightening ['fraɪtnɪŋ] *adjective* which causes fear; *a frightening sound of footsteps in the corridor*; *he had a frightening thought - what if no one heard his cries for help?*

frighteningly ['fraɪtnɪŋli] *adverb* in a frightening way; *his new secretary is frighteningly efficient*

frightful ['fraɪtful] *adjective* (informal) terrible or awful; *there was a frightful row at the customs*

frightfully ['fraɪtfuli] *adverb* (informal) extremely, terribly, very; *I'm frightfully sorry that you have had to wait so long*

frigid ['frɪdʒɪd] *adjective* (a) very cold, icy; *I'm not keen on having a shower in their frigid bathroom* (b) unfriendly, not showing any warm feelings; *his frigid response did not give us much hope* (c) (woman) not responsive in sexual relations; *after his marriage he discovered that she was frigid*

frill [frɪl] *noun* (a) piece of material gathered together and sewn on to a dress, etc.; *she sewed a white frill round the hem of her skirt* (b) **frills** = extra things, such as sauces with food; *we had a proper Christmas dinner with all the frills*; *I prefer simple food with no frills*

frilly ['frɪli] *adjective* decorated with a frill; *she wore a frilly skirt*

fringe [frɪndʒ] *noun* (a) hair lying over the forehead; *she has her hair cut in a fringe* (b) edging of a shawl, carpet, etc., consisting of loose threads hanging down; *a lampshade with a yellow fringe* (c) outer edge of an area; *round the fringe of the crowd people were selling souvenirs*; **fringe benefits** = extra benefits on top of a salary (such as a free car, etc.); **fringe theatre** = usually experimental theatre, often not using a traditional theatre building (NOTE: the American equivalent in New York is **off Broadway**)

fringed [frɪndʒd] *adjective* with things along the edge, like a fringe; **fringed with palm trees** = with palm trees growing along the side

fritter ['frɪtə] **1** *noun* piece of meat, fruit or vegetable dipped in a mixture of flour, egg and milk, and fried; *I love apple fritters* **2** *verb* **to fritter away** = to waste time, money, etc., on unimportant things; *he inherited a fortune from his grandfather but had frittered it all away by the time he was thirty*

frivolous ['frɪvələs] *adjective* silly, not serious; *she made some frivolous remarks at the funeral*; *I hope they'll be happy together - she's so serious and he seems very frivolous*; **frivolous complaint** = complaint which is not made for a serious reason; *I'm fed up of listening to all these frivolous complaints about the bus service*

fro [frəʊ] *adverb* **to and fro** = backwards and forwards; *little ferries go to and fro across the Rhine*

frock [frɒk] *noun* (old) dress, a piece of woman's clothing covering more or less all the body; *she looked wonderful in her party frock*; *I decided I'd better wear my blue frock to the wedding*

frog [frɒg] *noun* (a) small tailless animal which lives on both land and water; *he kept some tadpoles in a jar hoping they would turn into frogs*; *can you hear the frogs croaking round the pond?* (b) (informal) **to have a frog in your throat** = to have something in your throat which stops you speaking clearly; *he said 'excuse me, I've a frog in my throat' and coughed several times*

frolic ['frɒlɪk] **1** *noun* happy game or party; *he said that the game of running across the railway lines was just a harmless frolic which went tragically wrong* **2** *verb* to play happily; *the lambs were frolicking in the fields* (NOTE: **frolicking - frolicked**)

from [frɒm] *preposition* **(a)** away; *take three from four and you get one* **(b)** *(showing the place where something starts or started)* *he comes from Germany; the bees went from flower to flower; we've had a letter from the bank; he read the book from beginning to end or from cover to cover* **(c)** *(showing the time when something starts or started)* *I'll be at home from 8 o'clock onwards; the hours of work are 9.30 to 5.30, from Monday to Friday; from now on I'm going to get up early* **(d)** *(showing distance)* *it is more than 3km from here to the railway station* **(e)** *(showing difference)* *can you tell butter from margarine?; his job is totally different from mine* **(f)** *(showing a cause)* *he died from the injuries he received in the accident; she suffers from coughs every winter*

front [frʌnt] **1** *noun* **(a)** part of something which is furthest forward; *the front of the house is on London Road; there is a picture of the Houses of Parliament on the front of the book; she spilt coffee down the front of her dress;* see also **SHOPFRONT** **(b)** line marking the point where two masses of air meet; **cold front** = edge of a mass of cold air, bringing clouds and rain; **warm front** = moving mass of warm air which displaces a mass of cold air and also brings rain **(c)** road or pedestrian walk along the edge of the sea; *we went for a walk along the front; a hotel on the sea front or a sea front hotel* **2** *adjective* which is in front; *she sat in the front seat, next to the driver*

◊ **in front of** [ɪn ˈfrʌnt ɒv] *phrase* before something; *don't stand in front of the car - it may start suddenly; there are six people in front of me in the queue; you can park your car in front of the shop*

frontal [ˈfrʌntəl] *adjective* **(a)** of or in the front; *a frontal attack on the enemy;* **full frontal nudity** = showing the front of the body of a naked person; *the full frontal nude scenes were cut by the censor* **(b)** referring to a cold or warm front; **frontal system** = series of cold or warm fronts linked together

front bench [ˈfrʌnt ˈbentʃ] *noun* the front row of seats on either side of the House of Commons where government ministers or members of the opposition shadow cabinet sit; *the minister stood up from the front bench to answer the question; the Opposition front bench spokesman on the environment asked why the government had been so slow to act;* compare **BACK BENCH**

front door [ˈfrʌnt ˈdɔː] *noun* main door to a house or building; *he came to the front door and rang the bell*

frontier [ˈfrʌntɪə] *noun* **(a)** boundary line between two countries; *the customs men at the frontier didn't even bother to look at our passports* **(b)** the **frontiers of science** = the furthest point in human knowledge; *scientists are trying to push back the frontiers of science*

front line [ˈfrʌnt ˈlaɪn] *noun* line where two armies meet in war; *the army advanced and the front line moved 5 kilometres to the east*

front page [ˈfrʌnt ˈpeɪdʒ] *noun* first page of a newspaper or magazine; *there's a photograph of the house on the front page of today's newspaper;* **front-page story** = an important story which appears on the front page of a newspaper; *it was a front-page story in 'the Independent' yesterday*

front room [ˈfrʌnt ˈrum] *noun* room at the front of a house, used for sitting in; *we all sat in the front room drinking tea*

front-runner [ˈfrʌntˈrʌnə] *noun* person who is currently first in a race or contest; *she is the front-runner for the job of governor; some of the front-runners dropped out*

frost [frɒst] *noun* **(a)** white covering on the ground, trees, etc., when the temperature is below freezing; *the garden was white with frost* **(b)** cold weather, when the temperature is below freezing; *there was a hard frost last night; there's a touch of frost in the air; a late frost can damage young plants*

frostbite [ˈfrɒstbaɪt] *noun* injury caused by very severe cold which freezes your flesh; *after she had frostbite, gangrene set in and she had to have one of her fingers amputated*

frosty [ˈfrɒsti] *adjective* **(a)** very cold; covered with frost; *a frosty night; they walked across the frosty fields* **(b)** cold or unfriendly; *she gave him a frosty stare; the minister got a very frosty reception at the meeting*

froth [frɒθ] **1** *noun* mass of bubbles on top of a liquid; *wait until the froth has settled before drinking your beer* **2** *verb* to make masses of bubbles; *he was lying on the floor, frothing at the mouth*

frown [fraʊn] **1** *noun* pulling your eyebrows together as a sign that you are angry or worried; *take that frown off your face - everything's going to be all right* **2** *verb* to pull your eyebrows together because you are concentrating or worried; *he frowned as he tried to do the calculation;* **to frown on** or **upon something** = to disapprove of something; *the teachers frown on singing in the corridors; the company frowns on people who bring food into the office; this type of behaviour is frowned upon by the municipal authorities*

froze [frəʊz] *verb see* **FREEZE**

frozen [ˈfrəʊzn] *adjective* **(a)** very cold; *come inside - you must be frozen out there* **(b)** at a temperature below freezing point; *we went skating on the frozen lake;* **frozen food** = food stored at a temperature below freezing point; *use frozen peas if you can't get fresh ones* **(c)** not allowed to be changed or used; **frozen account** = bank account where the money cannot be taken out or used because of a court order; *see also* **FREEZE**

frugal [ˈfruːgl] *adjective* **(a)** small and plain; *he had a frugal meal of bread and cheese* **(b)** careful when you spend money or use resources; *he lived a frugal life and died a millionaire; the frugal use of the heating system will cut down on your electricity bills*

frugality [fruːˈgælɪti] *noun* being frugal; *their frugality has allowed them to amass a fortune* (NOTE: no plural)

fruit [fruːt] **1** *noun* **(a)** part of a plant which has seeds and which is often eaten raw and is usually sweet; *I must remember to buy some fruit at the market before we go on our picnic; he has six fruit trees in his garden;* **fruit salad** = pieces of different fruit, cut up and mixed together; *for pudding we had fruit salad and ice cream; see also* **DRIED FRUIT** (NOTE: no plural: **some fruit, a piece of fruit**) **(b)** *(literary)* the **fruits of your labours** = the results of your hard work; *he retired at sixty to enjoy the fruits of his labours* **2** *verb* to produce fruit; *the raspberries have finished fruiting; some pears fruit quite late in the season*

fruitcake ['fruːtkeɪk] *noun* cake with a lot of dried fruit in it; *Christmas cake is a type of fruitcake (informal)* **as nutty as a fruitcake** = completely mad

fruiterer ['fruːtərə] *noun* person who sells fruit; *call at the fruiterers and see if they have any mangoes*

fruitful ['fruːtfʊl] *adjective* which produces good results; *the discussions were serious and fruitful with both sides agreeing on the next steps to be taken*

fruition [fruːˈɪʃn] *noun* **to come to fruition** = to be finished with good results; *after ten years' work, the project finally came to fruition*; **to bring something to fruition** = to finish something with good results

fruit juice ['fruːt dʒuːs] *noun* juice from fruit; *she started breakfast with a glass of fruit juice*

fruitless ['fruːtləs] *adjective* producing no result; *we spent hours in a fruitless search for a hotel*

fruit machine ['fruːt məˈʃiːn] *noun* gambling machine where pictures of different types of fruit appear when you press a button; *he's always playing the fruit machines in the pub*

fruity ['fruːti] *adjective* (a) tasting of fruit; *a dark fruity red wine* (b) deep and tuneful (voice); *he has a fruity voice which is often heard on TV commercials*

frump [frʌmp] *noun (informal)* woman who is badly dressed; *she looks an old frump in that skirt*

frumpish *or* **frumpy** ['frʌmpɪʃ or frʌmpi] *adjective (of women)* wearing old-fashioned clothes; *the lecturer on politics is a frumpish woman in a knitted hat*

frustrate [frʌˈstreɪt] *verb* to prevent someone doing what he wants to do; *the weather frustrated the efforts of the rescuers*

frustrated [frʌˈstreɪtɪd] *adjective* (a) annoyed because of not being able to do things as you want; *she's frustrated at not being able to speak German* (b) **a frustrated artist** = someone who wanted to be an artist but never had the talent or the opportunity; *when he gets behind the wheel of his car you can see the frustrated Grand Prix driver coming out*

frustrating [frʌˈstreɪtɪŋ] *adjective* annoying, because it stops you doing what you want to do; *it's frustrating to be in a town where you don't speak the language*

frustration [frʌˈstreɪʃn] *noun* feeling of anger and impatience when you can't do what you want to do; *we all felt the frustration of not being able to do anything to help*

fry [fraɪ] *verb* to cook in oil or fat in a shallow pan; *fry the onions on a low heat so that they don't burn*; *fry the eggs in some fat* (NOTE: **fries** [fraɪz] - **frying** - **fried** [fraɪd])

frying pan ['fraɪɪŋ pæn] *noun* shallow, open pan used for frying; *she burnt her hand on the hot frying pan*; *put some butter in the frying pan and fry the mushrooms*

ft = FOOT, FEET

fuchsia ['fjuːʃə] *noun* garden plant with colourful hanging flowers; *we planted hanging baskets with fuchsias and geraniums*

fuddy-duddy ['fʌdiˈdʌdi] *noun (informal)* old-fashioned person; *don't be such a fuddy-duddy, you can wear a pink shirt if you want*

fudge [fʌdʒ] **1** *noun* (a) soft sweet made from butter, sugar and milk; *she bought a packet of home made fudge*; **chocolate fudge** = fudge flavoured with chocolate (b) avoiding making a tough decision; *anyone could see that the report was going to be a fudge* **2** *verb* **to fudge the issue** = to avoid making a tough decision on an issue; *for years, the government has been fudging the issue of legalizing drugs*

fuel ['fjʊəl] **1** *noun* substance (coal, gas, oil, petrol, wood, etc.) which can be burnt to give heat or power; *what fuel do you use to heat the house?*; *what's the fuel consumption of your car?*; *we ran out of fuel on the motorway* **2** *verb* (a) to provide fuel for; *the power station is fuelled by coal* (b) to increase; *our money worries were fuelled by news of an increase in the mortgage rate* (NOTE: **fuelling - fuelled** but American spelling is **fueling - fueled**)

fugitive ['fjuːdʒətɪv] **1** *noun* person who is running away; *the two fugitives were captured by the police*; **a fugitive from justice** = a person who is running away from the law **2** *adjective* who is running away from the law; *three fugitive prisoners were found hiding in a shed*

fulcrum ['fʊlkrəm] *noun* point on which a lever rests or on which something balances; *the fulcrum has to be at the centre of a seesaw*

fulfil *US* **fulfill** [fʊlˈfɪl] *verb* to complete something satisfactorily; *did he fulfil his promise and take you to the theatre?*; *he died before he could fulfil his ambition to climb Everest*; *we are so busy that we cannot fulfil any more orders before Christmas* (NOTE: **fulfilling - fulfilled**)

fulfilment *US* **fulfillment** [fʊlˈfɪlmənt] *noun* carrying something out in a satisfactory way; *it is the fulfilment of all my dreams*; **order fulfilment** = supplying items which have been ordered; *rapid order fulfilment is important in keeping the customers happy*

full [fʊl] *adjective* (a) with as much inside as is possible; *is the box full?*; *the bag is full of potatoes*; *we couldn't get on the first bus because it was full*; *all the hotels were full*; **I'm full up** = I've eaten so much that I can't eat any more (b) complete; *you must give the police full details of the accident*; *write your full name and address at the top of the paper*; *he got full marks* = he got 100 out of 100; **full fare** = price of a ticket for an adult, without any reduction; *children over 12 must pay full fare*; **full moon** = time when the moon appears as a complete circle (NOTE: **fuller - fullest**)

fullback ['fʊlbæk] *noun* player who plays at the back of a team near the goal; *the fullbacks managed to get the ball away from the goal*

full-blown [fʊlˈbləʊn] *adjective* (a) *(of a flower)* completely open; *a full-blown rose* (b) fully qualified; *he is a full-blown doctor now* = he has passed all his examinations and is qualified

full English breakfast ['fʊl ˈɪŋglɪʃ ˈbrekfəst] *noun* cooked breakfast, as opposed to a continental breakfast; *see also* the note at BREAKFAST

full-grown [fʊlˈgrəʊn] *adjective* adult, that is mature; *he found himself face to face with a full-grown male gorilla*

full-length [fʊlˈleŋθ] *adjective* (a) covering or showing the whole of someone; *a full-length evening gown*; *a full-length portrait* (b) long film or novel; *it was his first full-length film, made when he was 21*

full-page ['fʊl'peɪdʒ] *adjective* taking up a whole page; *a full-page advertisement*

full-scale [fʊl'skeɪl] *adjective* (a) the same size as in real life; *a full-scale model of a dinosaur* (b) complete; *it started as a dispute over a few islands and soon developed into a full-scale war*

full-size ['fʊl'saɪz] *adjective* the same size as in real life; *a full-size model of the car was sent for testing*

full stop ['fʊl 'stɒp] *noun* (a) punctuation mark like a small dot, showing the end of a sentence or an abbreviation; *when reading, you can take a breath when you come to a full stop* (b) *(meaning 'there's nothing more to say')* *she doesn't like German food, full stop* (NOTE: American English for meanings (a) and (b) is **period**) (c) complete stop; *the car skidded across the road and came to a full stop when it hit a wall*

full-time [fʊl'taɪm] *adjective & adverb* working all the normal working time (i.e. about seven hours a day, five days a week); *she is in full-time work or she works full-time*; *we have 8 full-time and two part-time teachers at our school*; *compare* PART-TIME

fully ['fʊli] *adverb* completely or entirely; *he was fully aware that he had made a mistake*; *she still hasn't fully recovered from her accident*; *the hotel is fully booked for the Christmas week*; *when fully grown, an elephant can weigh several tons*

fully-fledged [fʊli'fledʒd] *adjective* experienced or qualified; *she's a fully-fledged environmental inspector*

fully-grown ['fʊli 'grəʊn] *adjective* adult, that is mature; *he found himself face to face with a fully-grown male gorilla*

fumble ['fʌmbl] *verb* to touch or feel clumsily; *he was fumbling with the door lock in the dark*; *the goalkeeper fumbled the ball*

fume [fjuːm] 1 *noun* **fumes** = smoke or gas; *the children died from inhaling the fumes from the gas cooker* 2 *verb* to be angry; *after he had read the report he was absolutely fuming*

fun [fʌn] 1 *noun* amusement; *having to stay in bed on my birthday is not much fun*; **to have fun** = to enjoy yourself; *we had a lot of fun on the river*; **to make fun of someone** *or* **to poke fun at someone** = to laugh at someone; *don't make fun of her - she's trying her best*; *he poked fun at the Prime Minister*; **for fun** = as a joke; *she poured water down his neck for fun; just for fun, he drove the car through town dressed as a gorilla*; *why did you do that? - just for the fun of it!* 2 *adjective* amusing; *sitting on the grass in St James's Park is a fun way of passing a Sunday afternoon*

function ['fʌŋkʃn] 1 *noun* (a) job or duty; *the function of a goalkeeper is to stop the ball going into the net*; *what's the function of that red switch?* (b) party, gathering of people; *we have two wedding functions in the main restaurant this weekend*; *the Prime Minister is tied up with official functions all week*; **function room** = room in a restaurant or hotel where private parties are held 2 *verb* (a) to work; *the computer is still functioning well after months of constant use* (b) **to function as** = to serve as; *the sofa functions as a bed if we have visitors*

functional ['fʌŋkʃnəl] *adjective* (a) useful but not decorative; *these old saucepans are not works of art but they're very functional* (b) working properly; *the*

heating system will be functional again in an hour or so

function key ['fʌŋkʃn 'kiː] *noun* key on a computer keyboard which activates a set of instructions; *there is a row of function keys along the top of the keyboard*

fund [fʌnd] 1 *noun* (a) sum of money set aside for a special purpose; *she contributes to a pension fund* (b) collection; *he has a fund of stories about his time at sea* 2 *verb* to provide money for a special purpose; *we have asked the government to fund the building of the new library*; *the company is funding her manager's course*

fundamental [fʌndə'mentl] *adjective* basic, essential; *the fundamental difference between us is that I apologize for my mistakes and you don't*; *good air quality is fundamental for children's health*

fundamentalism [fʌndə'mentəlɪzm] *noun* strict orthodoxy, following religious rules very strictly; *the rise of Muslim fundamentalism*

fundamentalist [fʌndə'mentəlɪst] *noun* orthodox person, person who follows religious rules very strictly; *the fundamentalists tried to take power*

fundamentally [fʌndə'mentəli] *adverb* basically; *he's fundamentally ignorant; fundamentally, the plan stays the same but the schedule has been changed*

fundamentals [fʌndə'mentəlz] *noun* basic principles; *the conference will discuss the fundamentals of educational policy*

funding ['fʌndɪŋ] *noun* money for something; *who is providing the funding for the famine relief mission?*; *where is the funding for the new library coming from?*

fund-raising ['fʌndreɪzɪŋ] *adjective* aimed at getting more money, by asking people or organizations to give some; *a fund-raising dinner*; *the mayor launched a fund-raising scheme for the children's club*

funds [fʌndz] *noun* money which is available for spending; *he started a course at college and then ran out of funds*; *the company has the funds to set up the research programme*; *funds are available to get the project off the ground*

funeral ['fjuːnərəl] *noun* (a) ceremony when a dead person is buried or cremated; *the church was packed for her funeral*; *the funeral will take place on Friday morning* (b) *(informal)* **it's your funeral** = it something you alone are responsible for; *if he insists on riding his motorbike without a helmet, then that's his funeral*

funfair ['fʌnfeə] *noun* group of amusements, sideshows, food stalls, etc., set up in one place for a short time; *the funfair is coming to the town for the August Bank Holiday*; *we went to the funfair and won a goldfish at the shooting gallery*

fungal ['fʌŋgəl] *adjective* referring to fungus; *a fungal skin infection*

fungus ['fʌŋgəs] *noun* plant which has no green leaves or flowers and which lives on rotting matter or on other plants; *some fungi, such as mushrooms, can be eaten, but others are poisonous* (NOTE: plural is **fungi** ['fʌŋgaɪ])

funk [fʌŋk] 1 *noun* (a) style of African dance music with a strong rhythm; *the crowd of teenagers were dancing to funk music* (b) *(old) (informal)* fear; **to be in a blue funk** = to be terrified; *she was in a blue funk* *going to her first interview* **2** *verb (old) (informal)* not to do something because you are afraid to do it; *he funked the interview*

funky ['fʌŋki] *adjective (informal)* fashionable, modern; *look at his shoes - aren't they just funky!* (NOTE: **funkier - funkiest**)

funnel ['fʌnl] **1** *noun* **(a)** tube with a wide mouth and narrow bottom used when pouring liquids from one container into another; *using a funnel, she poured the oil from the pan into a bottle* **(b)** chimney on a ship from which the smoke comes; *the liner sailed away, with smoke billowing out of her funnel* **2** *verb* **(a)** to pass through a funnel or through a narrow space; *we funnelled the petrol into the tank* **(b)** to channel, to send in a certain direction; *the money from the jumble sale has been funnelled into the building project* (NOTE: **funnelling - funnelled** but American spelling is **funneling - funneled**)

funny ['fʌni] *adjective* **(a)** which makes you laugh; *we watched a funny programme on children's TV*; *he made funny faces and all the children laughed*; *the clown was wearing a funny hat*; **funny bone** = part of the elbow which gives a painful tingling sensation when hit by accident **(b)** strange or odd; *she's been behaving in a funny way recently*; *there's a funny smell in the bathroom* **(c)** a little bit ill; *I'm feeling funny* (NOTE: **funnier - funniest**)

fur [fɜ:] **1** *noun* soft coat of an animal; *this type of cat has very short fur*; *she was wearing a fur coat*; *have you any fur-lined boots?* (NOTE: do not confuse with **fir**) **2** *verb* **to fur up** = to become covered with a deposit; *the element in the kettle has become furred up*

furious ['fjʊəriəs] *adjective* very angry; *he's furious because someone has scratched his new car*; *the passengers were furious at having to wait four hours*; *she had a furious row with her brother*

furlong ['fɜ:lɒŋ] *noun* measure of length (= 220 yards); *his horse went into the lead at the last furlong* (NOTE: the word is only used when referring to the length of a track for horse-racing)

furnace ['fɜ:nəs] *noun* **(a)** large brick or metal oven which can be heated to a very high temperature; *the ore is heated in a furnace until lead is produced*; **blast furnace** = furnace where iron ore is heated until it produces iron *(informal)* **like a furnace** = it's extremely hot; *can someone open a window, please, it's like a furnace in here!* **(b)** heater which warms the water for central heating; *it's so cold in the office, the furnace seems to have packed up*

furnish ['fɜ:nɪʃ] *verb* **(a)** to put furniture into a house, office, etc.; *we rented a furnished flat for a year*; *his house is furnished with antiques* **(b)** to provide; *he furnished the police with a complete list of addresses*; *the town council furnished details of the improvement plan*

furnishing ['fɜ:nɪʃɪŋ] *adjective* used to furnish; **furnishing fabrics** = special fabrics used to cover chairs, make curtains, etc.

furnishings ['fɜ:nɪʃɪŋz] *noun* furniture, carpets, curtains and fittings in a house; *all the furnishings were removed before the house was demolished*; **soft furnishings** = curtains, cushions, etc. (NOTE: the difference with **furniture**)

furniture ['fɜ:nɪtʃə] *noun* tables, chairs, beds, cupboards, etc.; *the burglars stole all our office furniture*; *you should cover up all the furniture before*

you start painting the ceiling (NOTE: the difference with **furnishings**; note also that there is no plural: **some furniture; a lot of furniture; a piece of furniture**)

furore *US* **furor** [fjuː'rɔːri or fjuː'rɔː] *noun* outburst of anger or excitement; *the book caused a furore when it came out*

furrow ['fʌrəʊ] *noun* **(a)** long trench cut in the soil by a plough; *seagulls followed the plough, looking for food in the furrows* **(b)** deep line in the surface of something; *as he grew older, the furrows on his face deepened*

furrowed ['fʌrəʊd] *adjective* with deep lines; *he peered at the paper with a furrowed brow*

furry ['fɜ:ri] *adjective* covered with fur; *a little furry bear*

further ['fɜːðə] **1** *adverb* a greater distance; *can you all move further back, I can't get you in the picture*; *the police station is quite close, but the post office is further away*; *Edinburgh is further from London than Paris* **2** *adjective* **(a)** more; *the bank needs further information about your salary*; *please send me further details of holidays in Greece*; **further education** = teaching for people who have left school; *she goes to evening classes at the local College of Further Education* **(b)** **further to** = referring to something; **further to our letter of the 21st** = in addition to what we said in our letter; **further to your letter of the 21st** = here is information which you asked for in your letter

furthermore [fɜːðə'mɔː] *adverb* also, in addition; *the party was good fun, and furthermore didn't end too early*

furthest ['fɜːðəst] *adverb & adjective* the greatest distance; *some of the staff live quite close to the office, but James lives furthest away*; *the furthest distance I have ever flown is to Hong Kong*

furtive ['fɜːtɪv] *adjective* as if trying not to be noticed; *he made several furtive glances over his shoulder*; *I had a furtive look at the bill to see how much we were being charged*

furtively ['fɜːtɪvli] *adverb* in a furtive way; *they crept furtively into the club*

fury ['fjʊəri] *noun* fierce anger; *he turned to us in fury and shouted at us to get out*; *in a fit of fury he threw the plate across the kitchen*; *the crowd vented its fury on the president's palace*

fuse [fjuːz] **1** *noun* **(a)** small piece of wire in an electrical circuit which melts and breaks if the circuit is overloaded, and so prevents further damage; *the plug has a 13-amp fuse*; *if the lights go out, the first thing to do is to check the fuses*; **to blow a fuse** = (i) to overload an electric circuit and make the fuse break; (ii) to get very angry; *the lights have gone out - I think we've blown a fuse*; *he's going to blow a fuse when he sees the mess you've made of his car* **(b)** piece of inflammable material, used to light a firework, a bomb, etc.; *he struck a match and lit the fuse*; *a long fuse gives you ten seconds to get out of the way*; *see also* DEFUSE **2** *verb* **(a)** to break an electrical circuit; *she fused the lights by plugging her hair dryer into the wrong socket* **(b)** **to fuse together** = to join things such as wires together to form one single thing; *the heat had fused the metal seats together*

fusebox ['fjuːzbɒks] *noun* box where the fuses are kept; *take each fuse out of the fusebox to see which one has blown*

fuselage ['fjuːzəlɑːʒ] *noun* body of an aircraft; *although the wings came off in the crash, the fuselage remained miraculously intact*

fuse wire ['fjuːz 'waɪə] *noun* very thin wire for putting into fuses; *she bought a roll of fuse wire*

fusillade [fjuːzɪ'leɪd] *noun* series of rapid gunshots or questions; *the troops ran into a fusillade from both sides of the path*; *she faced a fusillade of questions from reporters at the airport*

fusion ['fjuːʒn] *noun* (**a**) melting together of two pieces of metal; *the heat of the explosion was so great that it resulted in the fusion of metal plates*; **nuclear fusion** = joining together of several nuclei to form a single large nucleus, creating energy, as in a hydrogen bomb; *compare* FISSION (**b**) joining together of two or more groups, such as political parties; *the new party has been formed by the fusion of two existing parties*

fuss [fʌs] **1** *noun* unnecessary excitement or complaints; **to make a fuss** *or* **to kick up a fuss about something** = to complain at length about something unimportant; *what's all the fuss about?*; *don't make such a fuss - it's only a little scratch*; **to make a fuss of someone** = to pay great attention to someone; *the children made a fuss of their mother on her birthday* (NOTE: no plural) **2** *verb* **to fuss over something** = to worry about something, or to pay too much attention to something; *don't fuss - it will be all right*; *stop fussing over your hair, you look fine*

fussy ['fʌsi] *adjective* (**a**) too nervous and unnecessarily careful about little things; *she's fussy about what she eats or she's a fussy eater*; *the boss is so fussy about spelling - he's made me do the letter three times* (**b**) with too many small decorations; *I don't like the fussy pattern on this carpet* (NOTE: fussier - fussiest)

futile ['fjuːtaɪl *US* 'fjuːtl] *adjective* useless; *it's futile to expect her to change her way of working immediately*; *he ran around with little cups of water in a futile attempt to put the fire out*

futility [fjuː'tɪlɪti] *noun* uselessness; *everyone is agreed on the complete futility of continuing the discussions*

future ['fjuːtʃə] *noun* (**a**) time which has not yet happened; *what are his plans for the future?*; *you never know what the future will bring*; *can you imagine what London will be like in the future?* (**b**) **in future** = from now on; *try to get to the office on time in future* (**c**) **future (tense)** = form of a verb which shows that something will happen; *'he will eat' and 'he is going to eat' are future forms of the verb 'to eat'*

futuristic [fjuːtʃə'rɪstɪk] *adjective* very modern, which relates to the future; *she produced some futuristic designs for the new city centre*; *a futuristic design for a glass bridge across the river*

fuzz [fʌz] *noun* mass of short hairs; *he had a fuzz of black hair on his chest*

fuzzy ['fʌzi] *adjective* (**a**) fluffy and curly; *she's got dark fuzzy hair, which is difficult to comb* (**b**) blurred, not clear; *the security camera produced a fuzzy photograph of the bank robbers* (NOTE: fuzzier - fuzziest)

Gg

G, g [dʒiː] seventh letter of the alphabet, between F and H; *'jogging' is spelt with two g's*

g = GRAM

gable ['geɪbl] *noun* top part of the wall where it forms a triangle with the roof; *from his hotel window he could see the gables and roofs of the old houses in the town*

gadget ['gædʒɪt] *noun* useful tool; *a useful gadget for taking the tops off bottles*

gag [gæg] **1** *noun* **(a)** something put into or over a person's mouth to stop them speaking; *the burglars tied him up and put a gag in his mouth* **(b)** joke; *the audience laughed at some of his gags, but others fell flat* **2** *verb* **(a)** to put someone over a person's mouth to try to stop him talking; *he was gagged and put into the boot of the car* **(b)** to try to stop someone talking or writing; *the government tried to gag the press* **(c)** to choke, to try to vomit but be unable to do so; *every time the doctor tries to examine her throat, she gags; he gagged on the hamburger* (NOTE: **gagging - gagged**)

gaily ['geɪli] *adverb* happily; *she gaily went ahead and ordered a new Rolls Royce*

gain [geɪn] **1** *noun* **(a)** profit; *he betrayed his country for financial gain*; **capital gains** = profit made by selling assets; **ill-gotten gains** = money made illegally or dishonestly; *thinking of them sitting there with their ill-gotten gains makes me envious* **(b)** increase in weight, quantity, size; *there was no gain in weight*; **gain in experience** = getting more experience **2** *verb* **(a)** to get; *the army gained control of the country; she gained some useful experience working on a farm* **(b)** to increase in value; *the pound gained six cents on the foreign exchange markets* **(c)** *(of a clock, watch)* to move ahead of the correct time; *my watch gains five minutes a day*

gainful ['geɪnfʊl] *adjective* **gainful employment** = employment which pays money

gainfully ['geɪnfʊli] *adverb* **gainfully employed** = working and earning money

gait [geɪt] *noun* way of walking; *he walked with a somewhat unsteady gait into the police station* (NOTE: do not confuse with **gate**)

gal [gæl] **1** *noun (old) (informal)* = GIRL; *she's a big bouncing gal; come on, old gal, we're almost at the top of the hill; I met up with some of the gals at the tennis club* **2** *abbreviation for* GALLON

gala ['gɑːlə] *noun* festive public occasion or performance; *a swimming gala will be held next Saturday; we went to a gala performance at the opera house*

galactic [gə'læktɪk] *adjective* referring to a galaxy; *galactic light*

galaxy ['gæləksi] *noun* **(a)** huge group of stars; *there are vast numbers of galaxies; the speed of stars near the centre of a galaxy may indicate the presence of*

black holes **(b)** **the Galaxy** = the Milky Way, band of what look like tiny stars, easily seen with the naked eye **(c)** mass of film stars, etc.; *there is a galaxy of singers on our show tonight* (NOTE: plural is **galaxies**)

gale [geɪl] *noun* very strong wind; *several trees were blown down in the gale; autumn gales ripped tiles off the roofs; they are forecasting severe gales in the English Channel*; **wintry gales** = gales with snow; **gale force winds** = winds which are strong enough to be called a gale; **gale warning** = weather forecast, warning that there will be strong winds

gall [gɔːl] **1** *noun* **(a)** bile, thick bitter brownish-yellow fluid produced by the liver, which helps to digest fatty substances; **gall bladder** = sac underneath the liver, in which bile produced by the liver is stored; *a gallstone is a hard pebbly growth in the gall bladder* **(b)** growth on a plant, especially on an oak tree, caused by a parasitic insect **(c)** *(informal)* impudence; *he had the gall to say I had cheated* **2** *verb* to annoy; *what galls me is that he is so successful when I'm not*

gallant ['gælənt] *adjective* *(old-fashioned)* **(a)** brave; *a gallant officer* **(b)** polite to women; *it was very gallant of him to offer to take her home* (NOTE: the word is used only of men)

galleon ['gæliən] *noun* large 16th century sailing ship; *divers found the wreck of a Spanish galleon on the seabed*

gallery ['gæləri] *noun* **(a)** **(art) gallery** = place where pictures and sculptures are shown to the public; *the National Gallery is in Trafalgar Square; the Tate Gallery has a collection of modern paintings* **(b)** **(art) gallery** = shop selling pictures, antiques; *she runs an art gallery selling pictures by local artists* **(c)** balcony inside a church, hall or theatre; *a group of musicians played in the gallery*; **public gallery** = place in a court, council chamber, etc., where the public can sit to listen to what is being said (NOTE: plural is **galleries**)

galley ['gæli] *noun* **(a)** *(old)* large ship rowed by slaves; *Roman galleys had five sets of oars on each side* **(b)** kitchen on plane or ship; *the stewardess will get you some water from the galley*

galling ['gɔːlɪŋ] *adjective* annoying; *it's very galling to see him making money out of one of my ideas*

gallivanting ['gælɪvæntɪŋ] *noun (informal)* going out looking for amusement; *I'm off gallivanting round the West End*

gallon ['gælən] *noun* measure of quantity of liquid; *the car was empty and I had to put in seven gallons of petrol; an economical car does 40 miles to the gallon*; **imperial gallon** = size of gallons as used in the Britain (NOTE: **gallon** is written **gal(l)** with figures: **80 gal(l)**)

COMMENT: in Britain one gallon (the imperial gallon) equals 4.55 litres, but in the USA only 3.78 litres

gallop ['gæləp] **1** *noun* **(a)** running pace of a horse; *the horse went off at a gallop* **(b)** fast ride on a horse; *let's go for a gallop along the beach* **2** *verb* **(a)** to go fast; *the riders galloped through the woods*; *he galloped through his lecture* **(b)** galloping inflation = very rapid inflation which cannot be controlled

gallows ['gæləʊz] *noun* wooden support from which criminals are executed by hanging; *he went to the gallows still proclaiming his innocence*

gallstone ['gɔːlstəʊn] *noun* hard mass, like a little piece of stone, which forms inside the gall bladder; *he had an operation for gallstones*

galore [gə'lɔː] *adverb* plenty of; *this autumn we had pears galore* (NOTE: always follows the noun)

galoshes [gə'lɒʃɪz] *plural noun* light rubber shoes worn over other shoes; *it's raining so I'll put on my galoshes*

galvanize ['gælvənaɪz] *verb* **(a)** to coat iron with zinc; *the shed has a galvanized iron roof* **(b)** to give someone a shock so that he acts; *she tried to galvanize him into action*

gambit ['gæmbɪt] *noun* **(a)** something said or done which should give you an advantage in an argument; **opening gambit** = first move in an argument; *his opening gambit was to say that he had made tape-recordings of the previous conversations* **(b)** series of moves which start a game of chess

gamble ['gæmbl] **1** *noun* risk; *this investment is a bit of a gamble*; *he took a gamble with the weather in planning his picnic for the beginning of March* **2** *verb* to bet money on cards, horses, etc.; *he lost all his money gambling on dog races*; **to gamble on something happening** = to do something, hoping that something will happen; *we're gambling on fine weather for the village fête*

gambler ['gæmblə] *noun* person who gambles; *she loves horseracing, and has become something of a gambler*

gambling ['gæmblɪŋ] *noun* betting on cards, horses, etc.; *gambling on dog races is his favourite occupation*

game [geɪm] **1** *noun* **(a)** sport which can be won with skill, strength or luck; *she's not very good at games* **(b)** single match between two opponents; *everyone wanted to watch the game of football*; *do you want a game of snooker?*; *our team have won all their games this year* **(c)** to give the game away = to reveal a secret plan; *so that's his little game!* = now we know what his plans are **(d)** single round in tennis, bridge, etc.; *game, set and match to Becker*; *she's winning by six games to three* **(e)** Games = large organized sports competition; *the Olympic Games*; *the Commonwealth Games* **(f)** wild animals and birds (deer, rabbits, pheasants, etc.) which are killed for sport or food; *our cookery book has several recipes for game*; **big game** = large wild animals, such as lions, elephants, etc.; **game reserve** *or* **game park** = park where wild animals are preserved (NOTE: no plural in this meaning) **2** *adjective* ready and willing; *I'm game to have a go*; *she's always game for anything*

gamebird ['geɪmbɜːd] *noun* bird, such as a pheasant or partridge, which is killed for sport and food; *they raise gamebirds on their farm*

game show ['geɪm 'ʃəʊ] *noun* TV show, where teams play games; *he's the quizmaster on a sports game show*

gaming ['geɪmɪŋ] *noun* gambling, playing games of chance for money; *the council has decided to allow gaming in the town*; **gaming licence** = official permit which allows someone to organize gambling

gamma ['gæmə] *noun* the third letter of the Greek alphabet (γ) mark showing a third level; *he only got a gamma plus for his essay*; **gamma rays** = rays which are shorter than X-rays and are given off by radioactive substances

gammon ['gæmən] *noun* bacon from the leg of a pig; *I had two gammon rashers and a fried egg for breakfast*; **gammon steak** = thick slice of bacon

gander ['gændə] *noun* male goose; *ganders make excellent guards for factories* (NOTE: the females are **geese**, the young are **goslings**)

gang [gæŋ] **1** *noun* **(a)** band of criminals, youths, etc.; *an important South American drugs gang*; *a gang of pickpockets*; *gangs of football fans wandered round the streets breaking shop windows* **(b)** group of workers; *gangs of men worked to repair the railway track* **2** *verb* **to gang up with someone** = to join up with someone to do something; *the different unions are ganging up to put in a joint pay claim*; **to gang up on someone** = to form a group to attack one person; *she felt as if the rest of office staff were ganging up on her*

gangling ['gæŋglɪŋ] *adjective* with long arms and legs; *her son is a tall gangling youth*

gangplank ['gæŋplæŋk] *noun* plank from a quay to a boat; *the passengers walked across the gangplank carrying suitcases*

gangrene ['gæŋgriːn] *noun* condition where tissues die and rot, because the blood supply has been lost through injury; *after she had frostbite, gangrene set in and she had to have one of her fingers amputated*; *he developed gangrene and they had to amputate his leg*

gangster ['gæŋstə] *noun* member of a gang of violent criminals; *gangsters have taken over all the bars in the town*

gangway ['gæŋweɪ] *noun* **(a)** *(in a theatre, cinema, etc.)* passage between rows of seats; *don't block the gangway* **(b)** little movable bridge for going on board a ship; *we went up the gangway carrying our cases*

gaol, gaoler [dʒeɪl *or* 'dʒeɪlə] *see* JAIL, JAILER (NOTE: the American spelling is always **jail**)

gap [gæp] *noun* **(a)** space between two things; *the sheep all rushed through the gap in the hedge*; *his retirement will leave a gap in the committee*; *we need someone to fill a gap in our sales force*; **gap in the market** = place where you may be able to sell; *we're trying to find a gap in the market* **(b)** difference; *the gap is widening between rich and poor*; **age gap** = difference between people of different age groups; **generation gap** = difference between people of different generations; **trade gap** = difference between the value of a country's exports and the value of its imports

gape [geɪp] *verb* to open your mouth wide in surprise or shock; *he gaped when he saw the bill*

gaping ['geɪpɪŋ] *adjective* wide; *a gaping hole appeared in the street in front of our house*

gap year ['gæp 'jɜː] *noun* year between ending secondary school and going to university, when students do not continue their formal studies; *some students use their gap year to go abroad*; *she spent her gap year studying art in Barcelona*

garage ['gærɪdʒ or 'gærɑːʒ] **1** *noun* **(a)** small building where you can keep a car; *he put the car into the garage overnight*; *she drove the car out of the garage*; *don't forget to lock the garage door*; *the hotel has garage space for thirty cars* **(b)** business where petrol is sold and cars, etc., are repaired or sold; *where's the nearest garage? - I need some petrol*; *I can't drive you to the station - my car is in the garage*; *you can hire cars from the garage near the post office* (NOTE: this type of garage is also called a **service station**) **2** *verb* to keep a vehicle in a garage; *the car was garaged overnight in the hotel underground car park*

garb [gɑːb] *noun* (*formal*) clothes worn by a particular category of person; *he was dressed in soldier's garb* (NOTE: no plural)

garbage ['gɑːbɪdʒ] *noun* **(a)** (*informal*) rubbish; *I don't believe a word of what he said - it's just garbage* **(b)** mainly US household waste; *don't forget to put the garbage out* (NOTE: no plural)

garbage can ['gɑːbɪdʒ 'kæn] *noun* US large plastic or metal container for household waste; *the garbage can is too heavy for her to lift* (NOTE: British English for this is **dustbin**)

garbage collector ['gɑːbɪdʒ kə'lektə] = GARBAGE MAN

garbage disposal unit ['gɑːbɪdʒ dɪs'pəuzl 'juːnɪt] *noun* US machine attached to a kitchen sink which grinds up and washes away kitchen rubbish (NOTE: British English is **waste disposal unit**)

garbage man ['gɑːbɪdʒ 'mæn] *noun* US person employed by a town to remove household refuse (NOTE: British English is **dustman**)

garbed [gɑːbd] *adjective* (*formal*) dressed; *the teaching staff sat on the platform garbed in their academic robes*; *brightly garbed Buddhist monks*

garbled [gɑːbld] *adjective* distorted, confused; *he told the police a garbled story about losing his car keys and getting into the wrong flat*; *something went wrong with the e-mail and all I got was a garbled message from Canada*

garden ['gɑːdən] *noun* **(a)** piece of ground near a house, used for growing vegetables, flowers, etc.; *we grow all the vegetables we need in the back garden*; *your sister's outside, sitting in the garden*; *he hurt his foot with a garden fork*; *we keep the lawnmower in the garden shed* (NOTE: American English for this is **yard**) **(b)** **gardens** = large area of garden, usually in several sections; *the hotel is surrounded by flower gardens*; **botanical gardens** = gardens which are set up for the scientific study and display of plants; *when you're in London you must visit Kew Gardens*; **public gardens** = place in a town where there are flowers, trees and grass, where people can go to walk around and enjoy themselves

garden centre ['gɑːdən 'sentə] *noun* place which sells plants, seeds, etc., and equipment for gardening; *we could buy a new wheelbarrow at the garden centre*

gardener ['gɑːdnə] *noun* person who looks after a garden; *he's a keen gardener*; *we can't afford to pay a full-time gardener, so we have to do most of the work ourselves*

gardening ['gɑːdnɪŋ] *noun* looking after a garden; *he reads his gardening magazine every week*; *she does some gardening every Saturday*

gargantuan [gɑː'gæntjuən] *adjective* huge, very big; *we had a gargantuan meal and then lay down to recover*

gargle ['gɑːgl] **1** *verb* to clean or disinfect your mouth by taking liquid into your mouth and blowing air through it before spitting it out; *before every concert he gargles for five minutes with salt water* **2** *noun* action of gargling; *have a good gargle with this mouthwash*

garish ['geərɪʃ] *adjective* too colourful; *she wore a garish orange coat to the funeral*

garland ['gɑːlənd] **1** *noun* circle of flowers or paper decorations; *she wore a garland of flowers in her hair*; *the room was decorated with paper garlands* **2** *verb* to decorate with garlands; *the visitors were garlanded with flowers*

garlic ['gɑːlɪk] *noun* bulb of a plant with a strong smell, a little like an onion; *his breath smelled of garlic*; **garlic bread** = French bread heated with butter and garlic

garment ['gɑːmənt] *noun* piece of clothing; *she was dressed in a long loose garment with wide sleeves*

garner ['gɑːnə] *verb* (*formal*) to collect; *he spent his life garnering data about tropical insects*

garnish ['gɑːnɪʃ] **1** *noun* something used to decorate food; *ham with a garnish of pickled cucumbers* **2** *verb* to decorate (food); *she garnished the fish with slices of tomato*

garret ['gærət] *noun* small room in an attic; *he was born and brought up in a garret in London*

garrison ['gærɪsn] **1** *noun* soldiers defending a castle or town; *the attackers promised the garrison safe passage if they surrendered*; **garrison town** = town where a regiment of soldiers is based **2** *verb* to put troops somewhere as a garrison; *the town was garrisoned by the Scots Guards*

garrulous ['gærjuləs] *adjective* who always talks a lot; *he tends to be very garrulous on the telephone*

garter ['gɑːtə] *noun* elastic strap that holds up stockings

gas [gæs] **1** *noun* **(a)** chemical substance which has no form and which becomes liquid if it is cooled; *decomposing rubbish gives off methane gas*; *air is formed of several gases, mainly nitrogen and oxygen*; **gas attack** = attack on the enemy using poison gas (NOTE: plural in this meaning is **gases**) **(b)** chemical substance used for cooking or heating; *the gas is on*; *there is a smell of gas or it smells of gas in the kitchen*; *turn down the gas or turn the gas down - it's too hot*; *turn up the gas or turn the gas up - the kettle hasn't boiled yet*; *can I borrow your lighter? - mine has run out of gas*; *the hotel is heated by gas*; **gas cooker** = cooker which is heated by gas; *don't play with the gas cooker - it isn't safe*; **gas fire** = fire which heats with gas; *we sat in front of the gas fire, trying to keep warm*; **natural gas** = gas which is found in the earth and not made in a gasworks **(c)** US see GASOLINE; *we ran out of gas on the freeway*; (*informal*) **to step on the gas** = to drive faster; *step on the gas - we'll miss the train!* (NOTE: no plural in meanings (b) and (c)) **2** *verb* to poison or kill someone using gas; *thousands of people were gassed during the war* (NOTE: gassing - gassed)

gaseous ['gæsjəs] *adjective* referring to gas; *the engine is driven by a gaseous mixture of petrol and air*

gash [gæʃ] **1** *noun* deep cut; *he received a gash on his forehead* (NOTE: plural is **gashes**) **2** *verb* to make a gash; *the knife gashed his arm*; *she gashed her hand on the broken glass*

gasket ['gæskɪt] *noun* seal for a part of an engine, which prevents liquid or gas escaping; **cylinder head gasket** = seal between a cylinder and the engine in a petrol engine

gasman ['gæsmæn] *noun* man who comes to check gas appliances, install gas boilers, etc.; *I have to stay at home because the gasman is coming to fix the boiler*; *the old lady was robbed of all her savings by a bogus gasman* (NOTE: plural is **gasmen**)

gasmask ['gæsmɑːsk] *noun* mask which protects against poison gas; *gasmasks were issued to the troops*

gasoline ['gæsəliːn] *noun* US liquid, made from petroleum, used to drive a car engine (NOTE: usually shortened to **gas**; British English is **petrol**)

gasp [gɑːsp] **1** *noun* **(a)** sudden intake of breath showing surprise or pain; *she gave a gasp when she saw the face at the window* **(b)** last gasp = final action, which marks the end of something; *the executions were the last gasp of the army regime*; *he's at his last gasp* = it is almost the end of his life, reign, etc.; *the poor car is at its last gasp - we really must get a new one* **2** *verb* **(a)** to take a short deep breath; *he gasped when he saw the bill* **(b)** to have difficulty in breathing; *after the race he lay on the ground gasping for breath*

gas station ['gæs 'steɪʃn] *noun* US place where you can buy gasoline; *where's the nearest gas station?* (NOTE: British English is **petrol station**)

gassy ['gæsi] *adjective* full of gas; *gassy drinks give me wind*; *this drink is too gassy for my liking*

gas tap ['gæs 'tæp] *noun* tap on a gas cooker, etc., which turns the gas on or off; *make sure the gas taps are all off before you go away on holiday*

gastric ['gæstrɪk] *adjective* referring to the stomach; *gastric juices*; *gastric ulcer*; **gastric flu** = general term for any mild stomach disorder

gasworks ['gæswɜːks] *noun* place where gas is made for domestic use; *the smell from the gasworks is very strong when the wind is in the wrong direction*

gate [geɪt] *noun* **(a)** low door made of bars of wood or metal, in a wall or fence, not in a building; *shut the gate - if you leave it open the sheep will get out of the field*; *there is a white gate leading into the garden* **(b)** door which leads to an aircraft at an airport; *flight AZ270 is now boarding at Gate 23* **(c)** number of people attending a sports match; *there was a gate of 50,000 at the football final* (NOTE: do not confuse with **gait**)

gâteau ['gætəʊ] *noun* large cream cake *see also* BLACK FOREST (NOTE: plural is **gâteaux** ['gætəʊz])

gatecrash ['geɪtkræʃ] *verb* (*informal*) **to gatecrash a party** = to get into a party without being invited; *a group of students tried to gatecrash her party*

gatecrasher ['geɪtkræʃə] *noun* (*informal*) person who gets into a party without being invited

gatepost ['geɪtpəʊst] *noun* vertical piece of wood to which a gate is attached with hinges; (*informal*) **between you, me and the gatepost** = let me tell you this in secret; *between you, me and the gatepost, I think she's pregnant*

gateway ['geɪtweɪ] *noun* **(a)** gap where a gate is fitted; *they crept through the gateway into the garden* **(b)** place which leads to an area; *Washington, gateway to the south*

gather ['gæðə] *verb* **(a)** to bring together; *he gathered his papers together after the lecture*; *she has been gathering information on the history of the local school* **(b)** to come together; *groups of people gathered outside the Parliament Building* **(c)** **to gather speed** = to go faster; *the bus gathered speed as it ran down the hill* **(d)** to understand; *I gather that his father is in hospital*; *I gather he has left the office* **(e)** to pick plants, flowers, fruit, etc.; *the children were gathering blackberries*; *the grape harvest has been gathered*

gathering ['gæðərɪŋ] **1** *noun* group of people who have come together; *a speaker from another association will address the gathering* **2** *adjective* which is coming together; *the gathering crowds did not realize that the president had already left the country*; **the gathering storm** = the storm which is coming

gauche [gəʊʃ] *adjective* awkward when meeting people; *the poor girl was terribly gauche the first time she went out to a grand dinner*

gaudy ['gɔːdi] *adjective* very brightly coloured; *the gaudy blazers of the young men watching the rowing* (NOTE: **gaudier - gaudiest**)

gauge [geɪdʒ] **1** *noun* instrument to measure depth, pressure, etc.; **petrol gauge** or **fuel gauge** = instrument which shows how much petrol there is in a petrol tank; *I don't know how much petrol I have left, because the gauge has stuck*; **tyre gauge** or **pressure gauge** = instrument for measuring the amount of air in a tyre **2** *verb* to measure or to calculate; *this is an instrument which gauges the speed of the wind*; *the chairman tried to gauge the feeling of the meeting*

gaunt [gɔːnt] *adjective* very thin; *he looked gaunt and pale after his years in prison*

gauntlet ['gɔːntlət] *noun* strong glove; *the motorcyclist took off his gauntlet to phone on his mobile*; **to throw down the gauntlet** = to issue a challenge; **to pick up the gauntlet** = to accept a challenge; **to run the gauntlet** = to go through a dangerous crowd; *she ran the gauntlet of news photographers*

gauze [gɔːz] *noun* thin material; *the dancers wore thin gauze dresses*; *the nurse put a gauze dressing on his wound*

gave [geɪv] *see* GIVE

gavel ['gævl] *noun* wooden hammer used by the chairman of a meeting or by an auctioneer; *he banged the gavel on his table for silence*

gawk or **gawp** [gɔːk or gɔːp] *verb* to stare at something with your mouth open; *the tourists stood there gawping at the soldiers in uniform*

gay [geɪ] **1** *adjective* **(a)** homosexual; *did you know her brother is gay?*; *it's a club where gay men and women meet*; *they met in a gay bar in Soho* **(b)** (*old*) bright, lively colours; *the houses along the street are all painted in gay colours* (NOTE: **gayer - gayest**) **2** *noun* homosexual man (or woman); *a club for gays*

gaze [geɪz] **1** *noun* steady look; *she refused to meet his gaze* **2** *verb* to look steadily; *she gazed into his eyes*; *he stood on the cliff, gazing out to sea*

gazelle [gə'zel] *noun* type of small antelope which runs and leaps in the air; *the cheetah raced through the grass after the gazelle* (NOTE: plural is usually **gazelle: a herd of gazelle**)

gazette [gə'zet] *noun* an official newspaper; *his appointment was listed in the gazette*

gazetteer [gæzə'tɪə] *noun* list of names of places

GB ['dʒiː 'biː] = GREAT BRITAIN

GBH ['dʒiːbiː'eɪtʃ] = GRIEVOUS BODILY HARM

GCSE ['dʒiːsiːes'iː] = GENERAL CERTIFICATE OF SECONDARY EDUCATION British school exam taken at the age of around 16; *she's taking her GCSEs this year; she got six grade 'A's in her GCSEs*

g'day [g'daɪ] *(Australia)* see GOOD DAY

GDP [dʒiːdiː'piː] = GROSS DOMESTIC PRODUCT

gear ['gɪə] **1** *noun* **(a)** equipment; *he took all his climbing gear with him; she was carrying her painting gear in a rucksack; landing gear* = wheels of an aircraft and their supports **(b)** *(informal)* clothing; *she was putting on her tennis gear* **(c)** *(of car, bicycle, etc.)* **gears** = arrangement of toothed wheels of different sizes, which control the rate at which the machine moves; **to change gear** = to move from one gear into another; *there was a loud noise as he tried to change gear;* **bottom gear** *or* **first gear** *or* **low gear** = the lowest gear, used when going slowly, or when climbing hills; **top gear** *or* **high gear** = the highest gear, used for fast speeds; *the car is most economical in top gear; always use a low gear when going down steep hills;* **in gear** = with the gears engaged (as opposed to 'in neutral') **2** *verb* **to gear something to** = to fit something to; *the ferry services are geared to the tourist season; lessons must be geared to the students' ability*

gearbox ['gɪəbɒks] *noun* case for gears in a car; *a car with an automatic gearbox*

gear lever *or* **gear stick** ['gɪəliːvə *or* 'gɪəstɪk] *US* **gear shift** ['gɪəʃɪft] *noun* handle in a car used to change gear; *our car has a gear lever with a leather-covered knob*

gear up [gɪər'ʌp] *verb* to get ready; *we are gearing ourselves up for our holiday with my parents-in-law in Scotland; all the hotels are geared up for the tourist season*

geese [giːs] see GOOSE

gee (whizz) ['dʒiː 'wɪz] *interjection showing surprise; gee! that's some automobile!*

geezer ['giːzə] *noun (slang)* man; *this old geezer came to try to sell me firewood*

gel [dʒel] **1** *noun* thick substance, especially one spread on your hair to keep it tidy; *he smoothed the gel over his hair* **2** *verb* to become more certain or more clear; *the details of the plan began to gel* (NOTE: **gelling - gelled**)

gelatin(e) ['dʒelətiːn] *noun* substance made from boiling bones, etc., used to make foods such as jelly; *she made a jelly with a packet of gelatine*

gelatinous [dʒə'lætɪnəs] *adjective* like a jelly; *jellyfish have gelatinous bodies*

gelding ['geldɪŋ] *noun* castrated male horse; *the race was won by a three-year old gelding*

gem [dʒem] *noun* **(a)** precious stone; *she wore a crown set with pearls and gems* **(b)** amusing or interesting item; *here are some gems from yesterday's paper*

Gemini ['dʒemɪnaɪ] *noun* one of the signs of the Zodiac, shaped like twins; *my birthday is on June 1st - oh, you're (a) Gemini, the same as me*

gender ['dʒendə] *noun* **(a)** being male or female; *everyone has the same rights, regardless of race, religion or gender* **(b)** *(in grammar)* system where nouns and adjectives have different forms to indicate if they are masculine, feminine or neuter; *what's the gender of 'Tisch' in German?*

gene [dʒiːn] *noun* part of a chromosome which carries characteristics from parent to offspring; *all the children have red hair like their mother - it must be in their genes;* **dominant gene** = the more important of a pair of genes, where the characteristic is passed on to the offspring; **recessive gene** = the less important of a pair of genes, where the characteristic is only passed on to the offspring if both parents have the gene

genealogical [dʒiːnɪə'lɒdʒɪkl] *adjective* referring to genealogy; *he's doing genealogical research using the local parish records*

genealogy [dʒiːnɪ'ælədʒi] *noun* **(a)** study of the history of families; *he's an expert in the genealogy of Scottish clans* **(b)** the history of a family, showing how different generations are related to each other; *she's drawn up the genealogy of her father's family*

genera ['dʒenərə] *noun* see GENUS

general ['dʒenərəl] **1** *adjective* **(a)** ordinary, not special; *he had a good general education, but didn't specialize in any particular field;* **in general** = normally; *in general, the weather is warmer in the south* **(b)** referring to everything, everybody; *they issued a general instruction to all the staff;* **the General Assembly of the United Nations** = meeting of the representatives of all countries that are members of the UN; **general election** = election where all voters can vote for a government; *do you remember which political party won the 1997 general election?;* **general store** = small country shop which sells a large range of goods; **general strike** = strike of all workers in a country **(c)** **general anaesthetic** = anaesthetic for the whole body; *you don't need a general anaesthetic to have a tooth removed* (NOTE: an anaesthetic for one part of the body only is a **local anaesthetic**) **2** *noun* army officer of high rank; *he has only recently been promoted to general*

generalization [dʒenrəlaɪ'zeɪʃn] *noun* general statement; *she made some sweeping generalizations about racial differences; saying that all seventeen-year-olds take drugs is a bit of a generalization*

generalize ['dʒenrəlaɪz] *verb* to make a general statement about something; *at this moment I prefer to generalize rather than make specific suggestions*

generalized ['dʒenərəlaɪzd] *adjective* **(a)** concerning general ideas, not specific subjects; *after talking about the recent floods, the discussion became generalized about British weather* **(b)** that exists throughout the body; *the cancer became generalized* (NOTE: the opposite in this meaning is **localized**)

generally ['dʒenərəli] *adverb* normally; *the office is generally closed between Christmas and the New Year*

general practitioner (GP) ['dʒenərəl præk'tɪʃənə] *noun* family doctor who does not work in a hospital, and treats all patients, all illnesses, without specializing in any particular branch of medicine; *see your GP first, and he or she will refer you to a consultant*

general public ['dʒenərəl 'pʌblɪk] *noun* all the public; *the general public are not interested in politics;*

the general public is admitted on the second day of the show (NOTE: can take either a singular or plural verb)

generate ['dʒenəreɪt] *verb* to produce power, etc.; *we use wind to generate electricity*

generation [dʒenə'reɪʃn] *noun* **(a)** production of power, etc.; *the generation of electricity from waves* **(b)** all people born at about the same time; *the 1960s generation had an easier life than we did*; *people of my father's generation could not understand computer technology*; **generation gap** = lack of understanding between generations **(c)** members of a family born about the same time; **the younger generation** = the younger members of a family; **the older generation** = the older members of a family **(d)** series of machines made at about the same time; *they are developing a new type of engine for the next generation of aircraft*

generator ['dʒenəreɪtə] *noun* machine which makes electricity; *the hospital had to use the generator because there was a power cut*

generic [dʒə'nerɪk] *adjective* referring to a genus; *generic name; see also* LINNAEAN SYSTEM

COMMENT: organisms are usually identified by using their generic and specific names, e.g. *Homo sapiens* (man) and *Felis catus* (domestic cat). The generic name is written or printed with a capital letter. Both names are usually given in italics or are underlined if written or typed

generosity [dʒenə'rɒsɪti] *noun* being glad to give money, your time, etc., to help someone; *she showed great generosity to her grandchildren*; *the college thanked him for his generosity in giving them a new swimming pool*

generous ['dʒenərəs] *adjective* **(a)** giving money or presents gladly; *a generous birthday present* **(b)** very willing to give your time, etc., to help someone; *he's been very generous with his time* **(c)** large; *a generous helping of pudding*

gene therapy ['dʒiːn 'θerəpi] *noun* prevention of disease by changing human genes

genetic [dʒə'netɪk] *adjective* referring to genes; **genetic code** = information which makes up a cell, stored in the DNA and passed on as the cell divides

genetic engineering [dʒə'netɪk endʒɪ'nɪərɪŋ] *noun* techniques used to change the genetic composition of a cell so as to change certain characteristics which can be inherited; *2000 people attended the conference on genetic engineering*; *scientists are using genetic engineering to produce disease-resistant plants*

genetics [dʒə'netɪks] *noun* the science and study of genes and heredity; *he wrote an article on the latest advances in genetics*

genial ['dʒiːniəl] *adjective* cheerful and friendly; *he greeted her with a genial smile*

genially ['dʒiːniəli] *adverb* in a cheerful and friendly way; *he greeted us genially enough, but the conversation soon became very serious*

genital ['dʒenɪtl] *adjective* referring to the sex organs; *she went to the doctor with a genital infection*; **genital organs;** *see* GENITALIA

genitalia *or* **genitals** [dʒenɪ'teɪliə *or* 'dʒenɪtəlz] *noun* genital organs, the organs on the outside of the body involved in reproduction (the penis and testicles in a man, the vulva in a woman); *he has an irritation round his genitals*

genius ['dʒiːniəs] *noun* **(a)** very intelligent person; person who has great ability; *she's a chess genius*; *Napoleon was a military genius*; *she came top of the class - she's a real genius* (NOTE: plural in this meaning is **geniuses**) **(b)** **evil genius** = wicked person who influences others; *Rasputin was the Empress' evil genius* **(c)** great ability; *he has a genius for keeping people amused*

genocide ['dʒenəsaɪd] *noun* killing of an entire racial group (usually a minority group); *they were accused of the genocide of the other tribes in the region*

genome ['dʒiːnəʊm] *noun* (i) all the genes in an individual; (ii) set of genes which are inherited from one parent

genre ['ʒɒnrə] *noun* type of art, writing, etc.; *he is one of best writers in this genre*; **genre painting** = painting of scenes of everyday life; *Pieter de Hoogh is a master of Dutch genre painting*

gent [dʒent] *noun* (*informal*) = GENTLEMAN; *he's a real gent of the old sort; this old gent came up to me and asked if I could lend him a fiver; see also* GENTS

genteel [dʒen'tiːl] *adjective* refined and respectable; *the two old ladies lived in genteel poverty*; *the houses round the cathedral have an air of genteel respectability*

gentle ['dʒentl] *adjective* **(a)** soft and kind; *the nurse has gentle hands* **(b)** not very strong; *a little gentle persuasion and she agreed to the plan*; *he gave the door a gentle push* **(c)** not very steep; *there is a gentle slope down to the lake* (NOTE: **gentler - gentlest**)

gentleman *noun* **(a)** man, especially a well-behaved or upper-class man; *he's such a gentleman, he always opens the door for me* **(b)** (*polite way of referring to a man*) *this gentleman is waiting to be served*; *well, gentlemen, if everyone is here, the meeting can start*; **'ladies and gentlemen'** = way of starting to talk to a group of men and women (NOTE: plural is **gentlemen**)

gently ['dʒentli] *adverb* **(a)** softly; *he gently put the blanket over her*; *she rocked the cradle gently*; *gently does it!* = be careful! **(b)** not strongly; *the wind blew gently through the bushes* **(c)** not steeply; *the path rises gently to the top of the hill*

gentrification [dʒentrɪfɪ'keɪʃn] *noun* action of making a former poor part of a town more popular with rich people; *the gentrification of Islington*

gentrify ['dʒentrɪfaɪ] *verb* to make a former poor part of town popular with rich people; *the old streets and squares have been gentrified and you wouldn't recognize them any more*

gentry ['dʒentri] *noun* people of high class, below the aristocracy; *the peasants drank beer but the gentry drank wine*; **landed gentry** = old families who own country estates; *he comes from an old family of the landed gentry* (NOTE: the word is plural)

gents [dʒents] *noun* (*informal*) toilet for men; *the gents is down the corridor on the left* (NOTE: it is singular, and takes a singular verb)

genuine ['dʒenjuɪn] *adjective* real, true; *the painting was not a genuine Picasso*; *a genuine leather purse will cost a lot more than that*

genus ['dʒiːnəs] *noun* group of related species of animals or plants; *a Swedish scientist called Linnaeus organized the classification of organisms into genera and species* (NOTE: plural is **genera** ['dʒenərə])

geographer [dʒiˈɒgrəfə] *noun* person who studies geography

geographic *or* **geographical** [dʒiːəˈgræfɪk *or* dʒiːəˈgræfɪkl] *adjective* referring to geography

geography [dʒiːˈɒgrəfi] *noun* study of the earth's surface; *we're studying the geography of the Thames Valley; I'm worse at English than at geography*

geological [dʒiːəˈlɒdʒɪkl] *adjective* referring to geology; *the company is carrying out a geological survey to see if there is any oil in the region*

geologist [dʒiːˈɒlədʒɪst] *noun* person who studies geology

geology [dʒiːˈɒlədʒi] *noun* science and study of the rocks that form the earth's crust; *she studied geology at university and now works for a water company*

geometric *or* **geometrical** [dʒiːəˈmetrɪk *or* dʒiːəˈmetrɪkl] *adjective* referring to geometry; **a geometric design** = a design of squares, triangles, circles, etc.; *the new wallpaper has a geometric design*

geometry [dʒiːˈɒmətri] *noun* science of lines, surfaces and solids; *geometry was first explored by the ancient Greeks*

Georgian ['dʒɔːdʒiən] *adjective* referring to the architecture of the time of George I, George II and George III (i.e. the eighteenth century); *the Georgian squares of Bath; he lives in a beautiful Georgian house in Dublin*

geranium [dʒəˈreɪniəm] *noun* brightly coloured summer flower, usually red or pink; *they put pots of geraniums on the patio*

gerbil ['dʒɜːbl] *noun* desert rat, a small furry animal often kept as a pet; *my little sister has two pet gerbils*

geriatric [dʒerɪˈætrɪk] *adjective* referring to old people; **geriatric hospital** = hospital which specializes in the treatment of old people

geriatrics [dʒerɪˈætrɪks] *noun* the study of old people and their disorders

germ [dʒɜːm] *noun* (a) something which causes disease; *wash your hands after emptying the dustbin so you don't spread any germs* (b) inside part of a seed; **wheat germ** (c) the beginning of something; *he had the germ of an idea*

German ['dʒɜːmən] **1** *adjective* referring to Germany; *there are three German players in the team; do you like German food?; see also* MEASLES **2** *noun* (a) language spoken in Germany, Austria and parts of Switzerland and Italy; *do you know the German for 'one - two - three'?; you must brush up your German if you are going to work in Germany; he took a crash course in German; he works all day in the office, and then goes to German classes in the evening* (b) person from Germany; *our next-door neighbours are Germans*

germane [dʒɜːˈmeɪn] *adjective* (*formal*) relevant, which is directly connected to a matter; *I don't think your question is germane to our discussion*

German shepherd ['dʒɜːmən 'ʃepəd] *noun* US breed of large dog, often used as guard dogs; *German shepherds are excellent guard dogs which look a bit like wolves* (NOTE: British English for this breed is **Alsatian**)

Germany ['dʒɜːməni] *proper noun* large west European country, to the east of France, and west of Poland; *they used to live in Germany; Germany is an important member of the EU* (NOTE: capital: **Berlin**; people: **Germans**; language: **German**; currency: **Deutschmark** *or* **D-mark, euro**)

germinate ['dʒɜːmɪneɪt] *verb* (*of a plant seed*) to start to grow; *sow the seeds in good soil and keep them in a warm place and they will germinate quickly*

germination [dʒɜːmɪˈneɪʃn] *noun* starting to grow; *sow the seeds in good soil and keep them in a warm place and germination will take place quickly*

gerund ['dʒerʌnd] *noun* (*grammar*) verbal noun, formed from the present participle of a verb (NOTE: English, gerunds are formed from the '-ing ' form of verbs, as in **cycling is good exercise; choral singing is very popular in Wales**)

gestation [dʒeˈsteɪʃn] *noun* period when a baby is carried in its mother's womb, or when a book, etc., is being worked on; *the gestation period is almost over and the book should be published next month*

gesticulate [dʒeˈstɪkjʊleɪt] *verb* to make signs with your hands or arms; *she gesticulated wildly to try to attract the attention of the bus driver; when we asked what had happened, he simply gesticulated towards the ruins of the factory; we don't speak Dutch, but we managed to make ourselves understood by gesticulating*

gesticulation [dʒestɪkjʊˈleɪʃn] *noun* sign made with your arms or hands; *the policeman's gesticulations seemed to suggest that it was dangerous to go on*

gesture ['dʒestʃə] **1** *noun* (a) movement of hands, etc., to show feeling; *she made a slight gesture of impatience with her hand* (b) action which shows feeling; *the gift of fruit was a kind gesture on her part; as a gesture to the staff, the management has had the toilets repainted;* **token gesture** = action done to show that you are dealing with a problem; *the motion criticizing the government was simply a token gesture by the opposition parties* **2** *verb* to make a movement with the hands; *he gestured to the audience to sit down*

get [get] *verb* (a) to receive; *we got a letter from the bank this morning; he will get £10 for washing the car; she gets more money than I do* (b) **to get to** = to arrive, to reach (a place); *we only got to the hotel at midnight; when does your train get to London?; the plane gets to New York at 4 p.m.; when you get to my age you'll see why I'm suggesting you should plan for the future* (c) to become; *I'm getting too old for rugby; she's getting deaf; he's got much fatter over the last year or so; the sun got hotter and hotter; the carpet's getting dirty* (d) to have something done; *I must get my suit cleaned; we got the car mended in time to go on holiday* (e) to persuade someone to do something; *can you get the garage to mend the brakes?; I'll try and get her to bring some CDs* (f) **to have got to** = must *or* to be obliged to; **you've got to come** = you must come; *he's got to be at the station at 8 o'clock; have you really got to work all night?* (g) to catch (an illness); *I think I'm getting a cold; he got measles just before the holiday started* (h) to make something become; *he always gets his clothes dirty; she's busy getting the meal ready* (i) (*informal*) to start; *let's get going!* (j) to understand; *do* *you think he got my meaning?*; **got it!** = I've solved the problem! (NOTE: **getting - got** [gɒt] **- has got** *US* **gotten**)

get across ['get ə'krɒs] *verb* **(a)** to manage to cross; *they got across the river on rafts* **(b)** to make someone understand; *I'm trying to get across to the people in the office that they all have to work harder; we just can't seem to get our message across*

get along ['get ə'lɒŋ] *verb* **(a)** to manage; *she got along quite well when her mother was away on holiday; we seem to get along very happily without the telephone; how are you getting along?* **(b) to get along with someone** = to be friendly with someone, to work well with someone; *I don't think they get along*

get around ['get ə'raʊnd] *verb* to move from place to place; *since he had his accident he gets around on two sticks; the news soon got around that they were married*

get at ['get 'æt] *verb* **(a)** to reach; *you'll need to stand on a chair to get at the jam jar on the top shelf* **(b)** *(informal)* **to get at someone** = to criticize someone all the time; *she thinks she's being got at* **(c)** to mean; *what was he really getting at when he said that some people were not working hard enough?*

get away ['get ə'weɪ] *verb* **(a)** to escape; *the robbers got away in a stolen car* **(b) to get away with something** = not to be punished for having done something; *he was rude to the magistrate, but got away with it somehow* *(formal)* **to get away with murder** = to do something really bad and still not be punished for it; *he's the teacher's favourite and she lets him get away with murder* **(c)** *(informal)* **get away with you!** = don't try to make me believe that!

getaway ['getəweɪ] *noun* escape; *they snatched the watches and made a quick getaway on bicycles; a getaway car was waiting for him when he ran out of the bank*

get back ['get 'bæk] *verb* **(a)** to return; *they got back home very late; when did they get back from the cinema?* **(b)** to get something again which you had before; *I got my money back after I had complained to the manager;* **to get your breath back** = to breathe normally after being breathless; *at my age, I can't walk uphill very far without stopping to get my breath back* **(c)** to phone back or reply by post; *I'll find out what the situation is and get back to you as soon as I can*

get by ['get 'baɪ] *verb (informal)* **(a)** to manage to do something with difficulty; *I can just get by in German; how are you going to get by without a car?* **(b)** to manage to live; *it is difficult for them to get by on in New York only $30 a day; they get by somehow on only £50 a week*

get down ['get 'daʊn] *verb* **(a)** to go back down onto the ground; *the cat climbed up the tree and couldn't get down; he got down off the ladder* **(b)** to bring down; *can you get my suitcase down for me?* **(c)** to make someone sad; *rainy weather always gets me down*

get down to ['get 'daʊn tuː] *verb* **to get down to some hard work** = to start working hard; *he will have to get down to work if he wants to pass the test*

get dressed ['get 'drest] *phrase* to put your clothes on; *if the hotel catches fire, don't wait to get dressed, just get out as fast as you can; he got dressed quickly because he had to catch an early train; they were getting dressed when the phone rang*

get in ['get 'ɪn] *verb* **(a)** to go inside (a car, etc.); *get in! - the train's going to leave; the burglars must have got in through the bathroom window* **(b)** to arrive at home, at the office, etc.; *what time did you get in last night?; because of the train strike, we didn't get in until eleven o'clock* **(c)** to ask someone to come to do a job; *we'll get a builder in to mend the wall*

get into ['get 'ɪntu] *verb* **(a)** to go inside (a car, etc.); *they got into the back of the car; I was just getting into bed when the phone rang; the burglars got into the building through a window on the ground floor* **(b)** **to get into the habit of** = to start to do something regularly; *he got into the habit of calling his father 'Boss';* **to get into trouble** *or* **into difficulties** = to start to have problems; *he got into trouble with the police* **(c)** *(informal)* **to get into something** = to become very interested in something; *once he got into the subject, there was no way of getting him to think about anything else*

get off ['get 'ɒf] *verb* **(a)** to come down from *or* out of (a vehicle, etc.); *she got off her bicycle at the red light; if you want the post office, you should get off at the next stop; you have to get off the Underground at South Kensington* **(b)** not to be punished, or only receive a light punishment; *she was lucky to get off so lightly; he was found guilty of embezzlement and got off with a fine* **(c)** *(informal)* **to get off someone's back** = to stop pestering someone; *how can I get him off my back?*

get on ['get 'ɒn] *verb* **(a)** to go inside or onto (a vehicle, etc.); *they got on the bus at the bank; the policeman got on his bike and rode away* **(b)** to become old; *he's getting on and can't work as hard as he used to* **(c) to get on (well)** = to do well; *she's getting on well at university; my son is getting on well in his new job - he has just been promoted* **(d)** to manage; *how is the new secretary getting on?* **(e)** to be friendly with someone; *they don't get on at all well*

get on with ['get ɒn 'wɪð] **(a)** to be friendly with someone; *he gets on very well with everyone; she doesn't get on with her new boss; they don't get on with one another* **(b)** to continue to do some work; *he got on with his work and finished the job early*

get out ['get 'aʊt] *verb* **(a)** to take out; *I'll get the book out of the library; she was getting the car out of the garage and backed into a man on a bicycle* **(b)** to go out of something; *the bus stopped and the driver got out; the burglars got in through a window, but got out through the front door* **(c) to get out of the habit of doing something** = not to do something any more; *I've got out of the habit of eating chocolates* **(d) to get out of (doing) something** = to avoid doing something; *I want an excuse to get out of going to the office party*

get over ['get 'əʊvə] *verb* **(a)** to climb over; *they got over the wall into the garden* **(b)** to become better; *he's got over his flu* **(c)** to recover from a shock; *she never got over the death of her father*

get ready ['get 'redi] *phrase* **(a)** to prepare yourself for something; *how long will it take you to get ready for the wedding?* **(b)** to get something prepared; *we need to get the dinner ready - the guests will be arriving in 30 minutes*

get round ['get 'raʊnd] *verb* **(a) to get round to (doing) something** = to do something at last; *he only got round to sending his Christmas cards in the week before Christmas* **(b)** to persuade someone to do what you want; *she got round the boss by giving him a bottle of wine*

get through ['get 'θruː] *verb* **(a)** to go through; *the cows got through the hole in the fence* **(b)** to be successful; *he got through his exams, so he is now a qualified engineer*

get through to ['get 'θruː tuː] *verb* **(a)** to make someone understand; *I could not get through to her that I had to be at the airport by 2.15* **(b)** to manage to speak to someone on the phone; *I tried to get through to the complaints department but the line was always engaged*

get-together ['getə'geðə] *noun (informal)* meeting of friends; *we are planning a little get-together of people from the office*

get up ['get 'ʌp] *verb* **(a)** to get out of bed; *he went to bed so late that he didn't get up until 11 o'clock*; *it is 9.30 and John still hasn't got up* **(b)** to make someone get out of bed; *you must get everyone up by 7.30 if we are going to leave on time* **(c)** to stand up; *when he had finished his meal, he got up from the table and walked out of the room*

get-up ['getʌp] *noun* odd clothes; *she wore an extraordinary get-up to the wedding*

get-up-and-go ['getʌpənd'gəu] *adjective (informal)* showing enthusiasm; *his get-up-and-go attitude impressed the management*

get up to ['get 'ʌp tuː] *verb* **(a)** to reach; *stop reading when you get up to page 23* **(b)** to get up to something = to do something naughty; *look at the mess in here - whatever did you get up to last night?*

get well card ['get 'wel 'kɑːd] *noun* card sent to someone who is ill, wishing them a fast recovery; *after his operation he received several get well cards*

geyser ['giːzə] *noun* **(a)** natural spring of hot water; *there are famous geysers in Yellowstone National Park* **(b)** gas appliance for heating water

ghastly ['gɑːstli] *adjective* horrible; *what ghastly wine - it tastes of soap*; *we had an absolutely ghastly trip across London on the Underground* (NOTE: **ghastlier - ghastliest**)

ghetto ['getəu] *noun* poor area in a city in which people of a particular race, religion or nationality live; *the problem of crime in inner-city ghettos*; *there are ghettos in many big cities* (NOTE: plural is **ghettos**)

ghost [gəust] **1** *noun* **(a)** image of a dead person which appears; *they say the house is haunted by the ghost of its former owner*; *her face is white - she looks as if she has seen a ghost*; **ghost story** = frightening story about ghosts; **not to have a ghost of a chance** = to have no chance at all; *she's gone in for the competition, but she doesn't have a ghost of a chance of winning* **(b)** **ghost writer** = writer who writes a book for a famous person whose name then appears on the book as the author **2** *verb* to write a book for someone else whose name will appear on the book as the author; *he's ghosting the boxer's memoirs*

ghostly ['gəustli] *adjective* like a ghost; *a ghostly figure appeared out of the mist*

giant ['dʒaɪənt] **1** *noun* **(a)** *(in fairy tales and myths)* very large man; *a story about a giant who lived in a castle at the top of a mountain* **(b)** any very large person, company, plant or building; *he's a giant of a man*; *shares in the computer giant have soared* **2**

adjective very large; *he's grown a giant cabbage*; *they are planning a giant car factory in South Wales*

gibber ['dʒɪbə] *verb* to talk rapidly without making any sense; *after two hours manning the complaints desk and he was a gibbering wreck*

gibberish ['dʒɪbərɪʃ] *noun* nonsense; *she talked a lot of gibberish; what he wrote was complete gibberish* (NOTE: no plural)

gibbon ['gɪbən] *noun* little ape with long legs and arms, native of Asia; *gibbons swung through the trees, chattering and shrieking*

gibe [dʒaɪb] *noun US* nasty remark; *he paid no attention to the gibes of the press* (NOTE: British spelling is **jibe**)

giblets ['dʒɪbləts] *noun* liver, heart, etc., of a bird which are taken out before it is cooked; *the giblets were still inside the pigeons when we bought them*

giddy ['gɪdi] *adjective* dizzy, feeling that everything is turning round; *she had a giddy spell* (NOTE: **giddier - giddiest**)

gift [gɪft] *noun* **(a)** present, something given to someone; *the wedding gifts were displayed on a table*; *she was wrapping up gifts to put under the Christmas tree*; **gift token** = piece of paper given as a present, which you can exchange for goods to a certain value; *I couldn't think of what to buy her, so I gave her a gift token for her birthday*; **gift shop** = shop which sells things which are often given as presents; *see also* LOOK **(b)** special ability for something; *she has a gift for saying embarrassing things*

gifted ['gɪftɪd] *adjective* with a special talent; *he was a gifted artist*

gig [gɪg] *noun (informal)* performance of pop music; *the group started playing gigs in London a year ago*

gigantic [dʒaɪ'gæntɪk] *adjective* very large, huge; *he was eating a gigantic sandwich*; *the staff made a gigantic effort to increase output*

giggle ['gɪgl] **1** *noun* **(a)** little laugh, often showing you are embarrassed; **fit of the giggles** = attack of laughter which you cannot stop; *when the singer came onto the stage, I had a fit of the giggles* **(b)** *(informal)* **for a giggle** = for fun, as a joke; *we did it for a giggle* **2** *verb* to make a little laugh; *when she saw her mother's hat she started giggling; the class giggled at his accent*

gild [gɪld] *verb* to cover with a layer of gold; *the gilded domes of the mosque* (NOTE: do not confuse with **guild**)

gills [dʒɪlz] *noun* **(a)** openings on the sides of a fish's head, through which it breathes; *the fish was still breathing because you could see its gills moving*; *(informal)* **green about the gills** = looking ill, as if you are going to be sick; *when she came out of the abattoir, she looked distinctly green about the gills* **(b)** thin dark ridges on the underside of a mushroom

gilt [gɪlt] *adjective* **(a)** covered with gold; *a picture in a gilt frame* (NOTE: do not confuse with **guilt**) **(b)** **gilt-edged securities** = GILTS

gilts [gɪlts] *noun* gilt-edged securities, British government securities; *she invested the money in gilts; gilts rose on the Stock Exchange*

gimmick ['gɪmɪk] *noun* thing which is intended to attract attention; *they used big green umbrellas as an advertising gimmick*

gin [dʒɪn] *noun* **(a)** colourless alcoholic drink, flavoured with juniper; *a cocktail made with gin* **(b)** a glass of gin; *a gin and tonic; two gins and a bitter lemon, please*

ginger ['dʒɪndʒə] **1** *noun* **(a)** plant whose root has a sharp burning taste and is used in cooking; *fry the meat with spring onions and slices of ginger; add a pinch of powdered ginger to the cake mixture;* **ginger biscuits** = hard biscuits, flavoured with ginger **(b)** *(informal)* name given to someone with orange hair; *hey, Ginger! come and help with these boxes* **(c)** **dry ginger** = type of ginger ale, often mixed with alcohol; *whisky and dry ginger, please* **2** *adjective (of hair)* bright orange in colour; *she has ginger hair and green eyes; a ginger cat sat on the doorstep in the sun* **3** *verb* **to ginger something up** = to make something more lively; *we need something to ginger up the party conference*

ginger ale *or* **ginger beer** ['dʒɪndʒə 'eɪl *or* 'dʒɪndʒə 'bɪə] *noun* fizzy non-alcoholic drink flavoured with ginger; *I'll have a ginger ale and ice, please*

gingerbread ['dʒɪndʒəbred] *noun* dark cake flavoured with ginger; **gingerbread man** = children's cake, made of gingerbread in the shape of a man

gingerly ['dʒɪndʒəli] *adverb* carefully, in case you might get hurt; *she gingerly touched the box with her finger; he gingerly picked up the kettle with a pair of gloves; she stepped gingerly onto the diving board*

gipsy ['dʒɪpsi] *see* GYPSY

giraffe [dʒɪˈrɑːf] *noun* large African animal with a very long neck; *because of their long necks, giraffes can eat leaves from the tallest trees*

girder ['ɡɜːdə] *noun* strong metal beam to hold up a wall or roof; *the crane lifted the huge girders into place*

girdle ['ɡɜːdl] *noun* **(a)** *(old)* belt round a dress **(b)** *(old)* corset, tight piece of underwear worn by women to support their bodies **(c)** **pelvic girdle** = ring formed by the two hip bones to which the thigh bones are attached **(d)** *(in North of England & Scotland)* = GRIDDLE

girl [ɡɜːl] *noun* **(a)** female child; *they have four children - two boys and two girls; a crowd of girls waiting at the bus stop; my sister goes to the local girls' school* **(b)** young woman; **career girl** = woman who is working in business and does not plan to stop working to look after the house or children (NOTE: it is sometimes better to use the word **career woman** in this meaning)

girlfriend ['ɡɜːlfrend] *noun* girl or woman, usually young, that someone is having a relationship with; *he's broken up with his girlfriend; on Saturdays she always has lunch with a group of girlfriends; see also* BOYFRIEND

Girl Guides ['ɡɜːl 'ɡaɪdz] *noun* organization for girls; *she's joined the Girl Guides; she was wearing her Girl Guide uniform* (NOTE: part of the same organization as the **Boy Scouts**; the American equivalent is **Girl Scout**)

girth [ɡɜːθ] *noun* **(a)** measurement round something, especially round your stomach; *the tailor measured his girth* (NOTE: no plural in this meaning) **(b)** leather band round a horse's stomach; *you need to tighten the girths*

gist [dʒɪst] *noun* main meaning of something said or written; *the gist of her complaint is that she seems to be earning less than the other people in the office; I don't understand Chinese very well, but I think this is the gist of what Mr Liu is saying*

git [ɡɪt] *noun (informal)* annoying person; *you stupid git - you've plugged the computer in to the same socket as the washing machine!*

give [ɡɪv] *verb* **(a)** to send or pass something to someone as a present; *we gave her flowers for her birthday; what are you going to give him when he gets married?; we gave ten pounds to the Red Cross* **(b)** to pass something to someone; *give me another piece of cake; can you give me some information about holidays in Greece* **(c)** to do something (to someone); *she gave a deep sigh; he gave me a broad smile; he gave her a kiss; she gave the ball a kick* **(d)** to organize; *they gave a reception for the visiting Foreign Minister; we gave a party to celebrate her twenty-first birthday* **(e)** to do something in public; *she gave a recital of German songs; he will be giving the opening speech at the conference; she has been asked to give a lecture on Shakespeare* **(f)** to bend; *the plank gave as he stepped on it* (NOTE: **giving - gave** [ɡeɪv] - **has given** ['ɡɪvn])

give away ['ɡɪv ə'weɪ] *verb* **(a)** to give as a present; *we are giving away a pocket calculator with each £10 of purchases* **(b)** to lead the bride to the bridegroom at a wedding; *she was given away by her father* **(c)** to reveal something which you are trying to keep secret; *his accent gave him away; she gave herself away by saying that she had never been to France*

giveaway ['ɡɪvəweɪ] *noun* **(a)** gift which is given to a customer; **giveaway paper** = newspaper which is given away free **(b)** thing which reveals something; *her big diamond ring was an absolute giveaway*

give back ['ɡɪv 'bæk] *verb* to hand something back to someone; *give me back my watch or give me my watch back; the burglars gave back everything they had taken; she borrowed my book and hasn't given it back*

give in ['ɡɪv 'ɪn] *verb* to agree to do something even if you didn't want to earlier; *the children kept on asking him if they could go to the cinema and in the end he gave in*

given ['ɡɪvn] **1** *adjective* **(a)** having the habit of; *he is given to sitting at home drinking all by himself* **(b)** particular; **at a given point in time** = at a particular moment **(c)** **given name** = first name *or* Christian name of a person, as opposed to the surname or family name **2** *conjunction;* **given that** = because; *given that it's his birthday, it's a shame he couldn't get to the party*

give off ['ɡɪv 'ɒf] *verb* to produce a smell, steam, etc.; *the fire gave off clouds of black smoke*

give out ['ɡɪv 'aʊt] *verb* **(a)** to give to everyone; *she gave out presents to all the children* **(b)** to come to an end; *the battery has given out so I can't use my watch*

giver ['ɡɪvə] *noun* person who gives; *we want to thank the givers of the prizes for the raffle*

give up ['ɡɪv 'ʌp] *verb* **(a)** to stop doing something; *she's trying to give up smoking* **(b)** **I give up** = I don't know the answer **(c)** **to give yourself up** = to surrender to an enemy, the police, etc.; *he gave himself up to the police; they shouted to the gang to come out of the store and give themselves up*

give way ['ɡɪv 'weɪ] *phrase* **(a)** to let someone go first; *give way to traffic coming from the right* **(b)** to collapse; *the chair gave way when he sat on it*

gizmo ['gɪzməʊ] *noun (informal)* gadget, useful little device; *what's that little gizmo for?*

glacial ['gleɪʃl] *adjective* **(a)** referring to ice; **glacial period** = Ice Age, a long period of time when the earth's temperature was cool and large areas of the surface were covered with ice **(b)** very cold; *the glacial arctic winds blow all winter* **(c)** emotionless; *his expression was glacial*

glacier ['glæsɪə] *noun* mass of ice like a frozen river which moves slowly down a mountain; *we climbed up onto the glacier*

glad [glæd] *adjective* pleased; *Aunt Jane was glad to get your postcard*; *the bank manager is glad you paid*; *after shopping all day, she was glad to find somewhere to sit down*; *(informal)* **glad rags** = party clothes *(old)*; **glad tidings** = good news (NOTE: not usually used before a noun, except in a few set phrases)

gladden ['glædn] *verb* **to gladden your heart** = to make you happy; *the news will gladden the hearts of all gardeners*

glade [gleɪd] *noun (formal)* open grassy place in a wood; *the knights and ladies met in a woodland glade*

glamorous ['glæmərəs] *adjective* attractive, enchanting; *your grandmother looks very glamorous for her age*; *he came to dinner with a glamorous blonde*; *she wants to lead the glamorous life of a film star*

glamour *US* **glamor** ['glæmə] *noun* attractive, dazzling appearance; *the glamour of the big city*; *she wants to lead a life of glamour* (NOTE: no plural)

glance [glɑːns] **1** *noun* quick look; *she gave him an admiring glance*; *she took a quick glance over her shoulder* **2** *verb* **(a)** to look quickly; *he glanced over his shoulder to see who was following him*; *she glanced suspiciously at the waiter* **(b) to glance off something** = to slide off something instead of striking it fully; *the ball glanced off the edge of her racket*

glancing ['glɑːnsɪŋ] *adjective* sliding off to the side; *the sword struck him a glancing blow*

gland [glænd] *noun* organ in the body which produces a chemical substance; *perspiration comes from the sweat glands*; *hormones such as adrenalin are secreted by glands*

glandular ['glændjʊlə] *adjective* referring to glands; **glandular fever** = infectious disease, where the body has an excessive number of white blood cells

glare ['gleə] **1** *noun* **(a)** very bright light; *the glare of the sun on the wet road blinded me*; *pop stars live their lives in the glare of publicity* **(b)** fierce look; *he gave her a glare and walked on* **2** *verb* **(a)** to shine very brightly; *the sun was glaring down on the square* **(b)** to look angrily; *she glared at me and went on reading her book*

glaring ['gleərɪŋ] *adjective* obvious; *the book is full of glaring mistakes*

glass [glɑːs] *noun* **(a)** material which you can see through, used to make windows, etc.; *a bowl made of glass or a glass bowl*; *the roof of the house is made of glass or the house has a glass roof*; *a car with black glass windows*; *see also* FIBREGLASS (NOTE: no plural: **some glass, a piece of glass**) **(b)** thing to drink out of, usually made of glass; *we took plastic wine glasses on the picnic*; *she put the dirty glasses in the dishwasher* **(c)** liquid contained in a glass; *she asked for a glass of water*; *he was so thirsty he drank three*

glasses of lemonade; *add a glass of red wine to the sauce* (NOTE: plural is **glasses** for meanings (b) and (c))

glasses ['glɑːsɪz] *noun* two plastic or glass lenses in a frame which you wear in front of your eyes to help you see better; *have you seen my glasses anywhere?*; *she has to wear glasses to read*; **dark glasses** = glasses made of dark glass, for wearing in sunshine; *he noticed he was being followed by two men wearing dark glasses* (NOTE: **glasses** are also called **spectacles. Dark glasses** are also called **shades**)

glassful ['glɑːsfʊl] *noun* amount contained in a glass; *add two glassfuls of wine to the soup*

glasshouse ['glɑːshaʊs] *noun* **(a)** large greenhouse; *the farm has rows of glasshouses in which they grow tomatoes and peppers* **(b)** *(slang)* military prison; *after ten weeks in the glasshouse he'll be a different man*

glaucoma [glɔːˈkəʊmə] *noun* condition of the eyes, where there is abnormally high pressure of the fluid inside the eyeball; *people with glaucoma have free eye tests*

glaze [gleɪz] **1** *noun* shiny surface on pottery; *the pot has a green-blue glaze* **2** *verb* **(a)** to put glass in a window; *the framework of the greenhouse has been built and now it needs to be glazed* **(b)** to cover with a shiny coating; *she glazed the cake and put six candles on it*

glazed ['gleɪzd] *adjective* **(a)** with a shiny surface; *a floor of glazed tiles* **(b)** with glass windows; *we have built a glazed porch*; **double-glazed** = with windows made of double panes of glass; *the house is double-glazed, so we hardly hear the trains at all* **(c)** a **glazed look** = not showing any expression; *she stared at him with a glazed look on her face*

glazing ['gleɪzɪŋ] *noun* glass in windows; **double-glazing** = windows made of two pieces of glass, used to keep out noise or to keep heat inside; *the double-glazing helps to deaden the sound of the traffic*

gleam [gliːm] **1** *noun* **(a)** small light; *he saw the gleam of a flashlight in the distance* **(b)** slight sign; *he saw a gleam of recognition in the boy's eyes*; *there was a wild gleam in her eyes* **2** *verb* to shine as if polished; *a line of gleaming black cars*

glean [gliːn] *verb* to collect scraps of information; *I managed to glean some information from the newspaper reports*

glee [gliː] *noun* **(a)** great happiness; *she danced and sang with glee when she heard the news* **(b)** short song; **glee club** = club of amateur singers; *he's joined a glee club*

gleeful ['gliːfʊl] *adjective* very happy; *the gleeful supporters cheered as the captain lifted up the cup*

glen [glen] *noun (in Scotland)* narrow valley; *they walked through the glen to the lake*

glib [glɪb] *adjective* easily said, but insincere; *he made some glib remarks about having to get into the European market*; *the committee's reaction to the news was just too glib*

glide [glaɪd] *verb* to move in a smooth way; *skaters were gliding across the ice*; *a bird went gliding past*

glider ['glaɪdə] *noun* aircraft which flies without a motor

gliding ['glaɪdɪŋ] *noun* sport of flying a glider; *he goes gliding every weekend*; *there's a gliding club on the top of the hill*; *see also* HANG-GLIDING

glimmer ['glɪmə] **1** *noun* **(a)** little light; *there was a glimmer of light in one of the upstairs windows* **(b)** very small amount; *the news brought a glimmer of hope to the families of the trapped miners* **2** *verb* to shine weakly; *a light glimmered some distance away in the trees*

glimpse [glɪmps] **1** *noun* brief sight; *we caught a glimpse of the princess as she drove past*; *there was a brief glimpse of the sun during the afternoon* **2** *verb* to catch sight of; *we only glimpsed the back of her head as she was leaving*

glint [glɪnt] **1** *noun* flash; *the glint of sunlight on the waves* **2** *verb* to flash; *the soldiers' swords glinted in the sunshine*

glisten ['glɪsn] *verb* to shine brightly, as if wet; *the dew glistened on the grass*; *his Rolls Royce glistened in the sun*

glitter ['glɪtə] **1** *noun* bright sparkle of light; *the glitter of the sun on the sea*; *she was attracted by the glitter of the West End theatres* **2** *verb* to sparkle; *the jewels in her crown were glittering in the light of the candles*; *her eyes glittered hopefully as she spoke*; *all that glitters is not gold* = things which look very attractive on the surface often turn out not to be so

glittering ['glɪtrɪŋ] *adjective* **(a)** which shines brightly; *a glittering diamond crown* **(b)** very brilliant, very successful; *they threw a glittering reception at the golf club*; *he had a glittering career in the Foreign Office*

glitzy ['glɪtsi] *adjective* (*informal*) brilliant and expensive, but not in good taste; *a glitzy movie première*

gloat [gləut] *verb* to gloat over something = to be happy about something, especially someone else's bad luck; *she gloated over her brother's misfortune in losing his well-paid job*; *he gloated over the bag of gold he kept under his bed*

global ['gləubl] *adjective* **(a)** referring to the whole world; *we offer a global parcel delivery service*; **global warming** = warming of the earth's atmosphere, caused by pollution **(b)** referring to the whole of something; *we are carrying out a global review of salaries*

globally ['gləubəli] *adverb* involving all parts of an organization; *management wants to improve performance globally*

globe [gləub] *noun* **(a) the globe** = the earth; *he is trying to be the first person to fly round the globe in a balloon* **(b)** map of the world on a ball; *he spun the globe round and pointed to Canada*; *see also* ARTICHOKE **(c) the Globe (Theatre)** = one of the original London theatres where Shakespeare's plays were performed, now rebuilt; *have you seen the production of 'Henry V' at the Globe Theatre?*

globetrotter ['gləubtrɒtə] *noun* (*informal*) person who travels all over the world; *do you know my brother, Ian, the globetrotter?*

globetrotting ['gləubtrɒtɪŋ] *adjective* (*informal*) who travels all over the world; *a globetrotting businessman*

globular ['glɒbjulə] *adjective* shaped like a globe; *she was wearing a strange globular hat*

gloom [glu:m] *noun* **(a)** darkness; *it was difficult to see in the gathering gloom* **(b)** deep despair; *a feeling of deep gloom came down on the family*; *when the exam results came out everyone sank into gloom*

gloomily ['glu:mɪli] *adverb* in a gloomy way; *he just sat gloomily watching TV*

gloomy ['glu:mi] *adjective* **(a)** miserable, unhappy; *she was gloomy about her chances of passing the exam*; *he's very gloomy about his job prospects* **(b)** dark; *a gloomy Sunday afternoon in November* (NOTE: **gloomier - gloomiest**)

glorification [glɔːrɪfɪ'keɪʃn] *noun* making more important or special than it really is; *the glorification of war and battle*

glorified ['glɔːrɪfaɪd] *adjective* (*informal*) seeming more important or special than it really is; *the MD's personal assistant is just a glorified typist*; *their new light tank is just a glorified armoured car*

glorify ['glɔːrɪfaɪ] *verb* to make something seem more important or special than it really is; *he was accused of glorifying crime in his report*; *the poem glorifies war and battle*

glorious ['glɔːriəs] *adjective* splendid; *a glorious June afternoon*

glory ['glɔːri] **1** *noun* **(a)** fame; *I did it for the glory of the school, not for myself*; *the team covered themselves with glory* = the team had a marvellous win **(b)** wonderful sight; *it is one of the glories of ancient Rome* **2** *verb* **to glory in** = to take great pride in; *she glories in beating her brother at chess*

gloss [glɒs] **1** *noun* **(a)** shine on the surface; *the metal is polished to give a brilliant gloss* **(b) gloss paint** = paint which is shiny when dry; *use emulsion paint for the walls and ceiling, and gloss for the doors and windows* **(c)** note which explains or gives a meaning to a word, phrase or whole text; *his glosses on the plays of Shakespeare* (NOTE: plural is **glosses**) **2** *verb* **to gloss over** = to try to cover up a mistake or fault; *she tried to gloss over the fact that they had failed*; *the report glosses over the mistakes made by officials*

glossary ['glɒsəri] *noun* list of words and translations; *there's an English-German glossary at the back of the book* (NOTE: plural is **glossaries**)

glossy ['glɒsi] **1** *adjective* shiny; *the glossy coat of a horse*; **glossy magazines** = expensive colour magazines, printed on shiny paper (NOTE: **glossier - glossiest**) **2** *noun* **glossies** = glossy magazines; *photographs of the wedding were in all the glossies*

glottis ['glɒtɪs] *noun* opening in the larynx between the vocal cords, the entry to the main airway

glove [glʌv] *noun* piece of clothing worn on your hand; *she gave him a pair of gloves for his birthday*; *you might have left one of your gloves on the train*; **oven gloves** = thick gloves which you wear to take hot dishes out of an oven; **glove compartment** = little cupboard with a door in the dashboard in front of the passenger's seat in a car; *see also* HAND

glove puppet ['glʌv 'pʌpɪt] *noun* puppet which you put on your hand, with fingers inside the head and arms to make them move; *the children sat entranced by the glove puppet show*

glow [gləu] **1** *noun* soft bright light; *the warm glow of the fire* **2** *verb* to shine dull red; *the logs glowed in the fireplace*; *her face glowed with pride*

glowing ['gləuɪŋ] *adjective* **(a)** bright, shining with fire; *the glowing charcoal in the barbecue* **(b)** full of praise or enthusiasm; *he had a glowing report from his boss*

glucose ['glu:kəuz] *noun* simple sugar found in some fruit; *if you're feeling tired, take a glucose tablet*

glue [glu:] **1** *noun* substance which sticks; *she spread the glue carefully onto the back of the poster; the glue on the envelope doesn't stick very well*; **glue sniffing** = form of drug abuse where addicts inhale the fumes from a strong glue **2** *verb* **(a)** to stick things together; *he glued the label to the box* **(b) to be glued to** = to sit in front of without moving; *the children sat glued to the TV set*

glum [glʌm] *adjective* miserable; *she came out of the interview looking very glum; he's very glum about his chances of getting a job* (NOTE: **glummer - glummest**)

glut [glʌt] **1** *noun* too much of; *there's a glut of fish on the market* **2** *verb* **to be glutted with** = to have too much of; *the market is glutted with cheap cameras* (NOTE: **glutting - glutted**)

glutton ['glʌtn] *noun* **(a)** person who eats too much; *he's just a glutton - look at him finishing off that trifle!* **(b) glutton for punishment** = person who likes doing difficult things; *he's a glutton for punishment - he takes all those computer reports home every evening*

gluttony ['glʌtəni] *noun (formal)* eating and drinking too much; *he preached against the sin of gluttony*

glycerine *US* **glycerin** ['glɪsəri:n] *noun* colourless sweet liquid in fat, used in medicine and explosives; *she took a spoonful of glycerine and honey for her cough; the police found glycerine and timers in the garage*

gm *abbreviation for* GRAM

GMT [dʒi:em'ti:] *abbreviation for* GREENWICH MEAN TIME

gnat [næt] *noun* small fly which bites; *August is the worst month for gnats*

gnaw [nɔ:] *verb* to chew; *the dog was gnawing a bone*

gnome [nəum] *noun* little man with a beard and pointed hat, in children's fairy stories; **garden gnome** = little coloured statue of a gnome, used as a garden decoration

GNP [dʒi:en'pi:] = GROSS NATIONAL PRODUCT

go [gəu] **1** *verb* **(a)** to move from one place to another; *the plane goes to Frankfurt, then to Rome; she is going to London for the weekend; he has gone to work in Washington; they are going on a tour of the south of Spain; she was going downstairs when she fell; the car was carrying so much luggage that it had difficulty going up hills; they went on board at 8 o'clock; how do you go to school - by bike or by bus?; she has gone shopping* **(b)** to work; *can you phone the garage? - the car won't go; he's trying to get his motorbike to go* **(c)** to leave; *get your coat, it's time to go; the last bus goes at half past two* **(d)** to fit; *it's too big to go into the box; this case won't go into the back of the car* **(e)** to be placed; *the date should go at the top of the letter; that book goes on the top shelf* **(f)** to become; *her face went red from sitting in the sun; he went pale and rushed out of the room; you have to shout, my father's going deaf; she's going grey, but it suits her* **(g)** to happen (successfully or not); *the party went very well; things are not going badly at the office* **(h)** to make a sound; *the balloon landed on a candle and went 'pop'; do you remember the song that goes: 'there's no place like home'?* (NOTE: **going - went** [went] - **has gone** [gɒn]) **2** *noun* **(a) on the go** = always busy; *the shop is so busy before Christmas that we're*

on the go from morning till night; **to make a go of something** = to make something work successfully; *they're struggling to make a go of their business* **(b)** try, attempt; *he won the lottery at the first go; she had three goes at the test and still didn't pass; we'll give it one more go, and if the car doesn't start I'll call the garage*

◊ **to be going to** [bi: 'gəuɪŋ tu:] *phrase* **(a)** *(showing future)* we're going to win; I hope it's going to be fine tomorrow; when are you going to wash your hair?; he's going to be a great tennis player when he's older; is she going to sing at the concert?* **(b) to be going to do something** = to be about to do something; *I'm going to be late for the meeting; watch out - that tree is going to fall down!; I am going to sit in bed and read my newspaper*

goad [gəud] **1** *noun* stick used to make animals go forward; *she drove the buffalo forward, poking it with a long goad* **2** *verb* **to goad someone into doing something** = to push someone into doing something which he or she doesn't want to do; *her laughter goaded him into action*

go about ['gəu ə'baut] *verb* to start to do something; *how do you go about getting a new passport?; we'd like to set up a company but I'm not sure how to go about ti*

go ahead ['gəu ə'hed] *verb* to start; *the project went ahead even though there were not enough staff*

go-ahead ['gəuəhed] **1** *noun* **to give something the go-ahead** = to give permission for something to start; *we got the council's go-ahead to build the new supermarket* **2** *adjective* hard-working and enterprising; *a go-ahead publicity firm; the company needs a go-ahead managing director*

goal [gəul] *noun* **(a)** *(in games)* two posts between which you have to send the ball to score a point; *he was unlucky to miss the goal with that shot* **(b)** *(in games)* point scored by sending the ball between the posts; *he scored a goal before being sent off; our team scored three goals* **(c)** aim; *our goal is to open a new pizza restaurant every month; he achieved his goal of becoming a millionaire before he was thirty*

goalkeeper ['gəulki:pə] *noun* player who stands in front of the goal to stop the ball going in; *the goalkeeper dropped the ball and the other team scored*

goalpost ['gəulpəust] *noun* one of the two posts between which you have to send the ball to score a point; *he was unlucky - his shot hit the goalpost*; **to move the goalposts** = to change the way things are done to gain an advantage; *everyone thought the investment was tax-free, and then the government suddenly moved the goalposts*

goat [gəut] *noun* **(a)** small farm animal with horns and a beard, giving milk and wool; *a herd of goats*; **goat's cheese** = cheese made from goat's milk; **to separate the sheep from the goats** = to divide the good from the bad **(b) to get someone's goat** = to annoy someone; *it really got my goat the way he turned up for work at lunchtime* (NOTE: males are **bucks**, also called **billy goats**, females are **does** also called **nanny goats**, and the young are **kids**)

go away ['gəu ə'weɪ] *verb* to leave; *he went away and we never saw him again*

go back ['gəu 'bæk] *verb* to return; *she went back to the shop and asked if she could change the gloves; she worked for two years and then went back to college*

go back on ['gəʊ 'bæk ɒn] *verb* not to do what has been promised; *he promised faithfully to lend me his car, and then went back on his promise*

gobble ['gɒbl] *verb* **(a)** to eat greedily; *he gobbled up his dinner* **(b)** to make a noise like a turkey; *we could hear the turkeys gobbling away in the farmyard*

gobbledygook ['gɒbəldiguːk] *noun (informal)* complicated language with sounds like nonsense; *the expert sent in his report, but it was just gobbledygook to me*

go-between ['gəʊbɪtwiːn] *noun* person who takes messages between two people; *she acted as a go-between, taking messages and ultimatums from one party to the other*

goblet ['gɒblət] *noun* large metal or glass wine glass; *he drank a goblet of red wine*

goblin ['gɒblɪn] *noun* little ugly man in fairy stories; *children love to hear frightening stories about witches and goblins*

go-cart ['gəʊkɑːt] = GO-KART

God [gɒd] **1** *noun* **(a) God** = the most important supernatural being, the being to whom people pray; *do you believe in God?*; *we pray to God that the children will be found alive* **(b)** superhuman being; *Bacchus was the god of wine* **2** *interjection* **(a)** *(showing surprise, annoyance, etc.) God, what awful weather!*; *my God, have you seen how late it is?*; *Good God, that's John from accounts department over there!* **(b)** *(showing thanks)* **Thank God** *no one was hurt in the crash!*; *Thank God you've come!*

god-daughter ['gɒddɔːtə] *noun* girl who has been baptized, and who has godparents; *I'm taking my god-daughter out to tea on her birthday*

goddess ['gɒdes] *noun* female god; *Diana was the goddess of hunting* (NOTE: plural is **goddesses**)

godfather ['gɒdfɑːðə] *noun* **(a)** man who sponsors a child at baptism; *he was godfather to four children* **(b)** *(informal)* head of a mafia gang; *the godfather's word is law*

god-forsaken ['gɒd fɔːseɪkən] *adjective (formal)* desolate; lost; *how do they ever manage to live in this god-forsaken place?*

godly ['gɒdli] *adjective (old)* very religious, like a saint; *he was a godly man*

godmother ['gɒdmʌðə] *noun* woman who sponsors a child at baptism; *my godmother gave me a ring for my birthday*

go down ['gəʊ daʊn] *verb* **(a)** to go to a lower level; *there are thirty-nine steps which go down to the beach*; *be careful when going down the hill*; *after having a rest in her bedroom, she went down to the hotel bar* **(b)** *(informal)* to catch a disease; *half the crew went down with flu*

godsend ['gɒdsend] *noun* helpful thing which arrives just in time; *the new packing machine is an absolute godsend in the office*

godson ['gɒdsʌn] *noun* boy who has been baptized, and who has godparents; *my little godson will be one year old next week*

gofer ['gəʊfə] *noun US (informal)* person who does all types of work in an office, especially taking messages; *he's the chief executive's gofer* (NOTE: do not confuse with **gopher**)

goggles ['gɒgləz] *noun* close-fitting glasses worn to protect your eyes; *you should wear goggles when you use a drill*; *he wore goggles when going scuba diving*

go in ['gəʊ 'ɪn] *verb* to enter; *she opened the door and went in*; *did you see anyone go in?*

go in for ['gəʊ 'ɪn fɔː] *verb* **(a)** to take (an examination); *she went in for her proficiency exam* **(b)** to take up as a career; *he's going in for medicine*

going ['gəʊɪŋ] **1** *adjective* **(a)** working well; *the business is being sold as a going concern* **(b)** normal, usual; **the going rate** = the usual rate, the current rate of payment; *what is the current going rate for a 1996 model?*; *he was happy to pay the going rate*; *the going rate for secretaries is £15.00 per hour* **2** *noun* **(a)** surface of a race track; *the going is soft after last night's rain*; **do it while the going is good** = do it while it is still possible **(b) goings-on** = strange things that happen; *you would never believe the goings-on in the flat upstairs*

go into ['gəʊ 'ɪntʊ] *verb* **(a)** to enter; *she went into the bedroom* **(b)** *(in maths)* to be able to divide a number to give a figure; *seven into three won't go* **(c)** to examine, to look at something carefully; *the bank wants to go into the details of his account* **(d)** to explain in detail; *she said she had a job offer but wouldn't go into any details*

goitre *US* **goiter** ['gɔɪtə] *noun* swelling of the thyroid gland, seen as a swelling in the neck

COMMENT: goitre is caused by lack of iodine

go-kart ['gəʊkɑːt] *noun* low metal frame with an engine, forming a little racing car; *he spends his Saturdays go-kart racing*

gold [gəʊld] *noun* **(a)** very valuable yellow-coloured metal; *that ring isn't made of gold*; *gold is worth more than silver*; *he wears a gold ring on his little finger*; *see also* GOOD (NOTE: no plural: **some gold, a bar of gold**. Note also that gold is a chemical element: chemical symbol: **Au**; atomic number: **79**) **(b) gold (medal)** = medal given to someone who finishes first in a race or competition; *England won three golds at the Olympics*; *see also* BRONZE, SILVER

gold card ['gəʊld 'kɑːd] *noun* special credit card for people with high salaries; *after I was promoted, the bank offered me a gold card*

golden ['gəʊldən] *adjective* coloured like gold; *she has beautiful golden hair*; **golden boy** = young man who is popular and a great success; *he's the golden boy of English football* *(in World Cup football)* **golden goal** = the first goal to be scored in extra time which decides the winner of a match; **golden opportunity** = marvellous chance which will not happen again; *he had a golden opportunity to make his fortune and he didn't take it*; **golden wedding (anniversary)** = celebration when two people have been married for fifty years

goldfish ['gəʊldfɪʃ] *noun* small orange fish, kept as a pet; *he won a goldfish at the fair and brought it home in a plastic bag*; *we have goldfish in our garden pond*; **goldfish bowl** = round glass container of water for keeping goldfish, etc. (NOTE: plural is **goldfish**)

goldmine ['gəʊldmaɪn] *noun* mine which produces gold; *a South African goldmine*; *that shop is a little goldmine* = that shop is a very profitable business

Gold Rush ['gəʊld 'rʌʃ] *noun* rush to find gold in the western USA and Canada in the later part of the 19th century; *we visited some of the old Gold Rush towns in Alaska*

golf [gɒlf] *noun* a game played on a large open course, by hitting a small ball into 18 separate holes with a variety of clubs, using as few strokes as possible; *he plays golf every Saturday; do you want a game of golf?*

COMMENT: the game is for two people, or two couples; a small hard ball is struck with thin long-handled clubs into a series of little holes (either 9 or 18), the object being to use as few strokes as possible. A round of golf (18 holes) takes on average about 4 hours and involves walking about 5 miles. In most big tournaments each player adds up their score for each of the 18 holes, on 4 consecutive days, with the lowest total winning

golf ball ['gɒlf 'bɔːl] *noun* small hard white ball used when playing golf

golf club ['gɒlf 'klʌb] *noun* **(a)** stick to hit the ball with in golf; *she put her golf clubs into the back of the car* **(b)** organization for people who play golf together; *he's joined his local golf club*

golf course ['gɒlf 'kɔːs] *noun* large area of ground for playing golf; *they've cut down a lot of trees to make a new golf course*

golfer ['gɒlfə] *noun* person who plays golf

golfing ['gɒlfɪŋ] *noun* playing golf; *he's gone on a golfing holiday in Spain*

golly ['gɒli] **1** *noun* cloth doll with a black face and black woolly hair; *she went to bed clutching her golly* **2** *interjection* (*old*) showing surprise; *golly! what a big present!; golly! the ship is supposed to sail in ten minutes and we're still not on board*

gondola ['gɒndələ] *noun* narrow boat, used on the canals in Venice, pushed by a man with a long pole; *when we went to Venice we took a trip in a gondola*

gone [gɒn] *see* GO

gong [gɒŋ] *noun* **(a)** metal disc which is sounds like a bell when it is hit; *they sounded a gong to warn visitors that the museum was closing* **(b)** (*slang*) medal; *he got a gong for long service*

goo [guː] *noun* (*informal*) sticky stuff; *what's all this goo in the saucepan?* (NOTE: no plural)

good [gʊd] **1** *adjective* **(a)** not bad; *we had a good breakfast and then started work; did you have a good time at the party?; it would be a good idea to invest in these shares; her Spanish is better than his* **(b)** clever; *he's good at making things out of wood; she's good with her hands; he is good at football* **(c)** well-behaved; *be a good girl and I'll give you a sweet; have you been good while we've been away?; as good as gold* = very well-behaved; *the children were as good as gold* **(d)** a good deal of *or* a good many = a lot of; *he won a good deal of money on the lottery; a good many people saw the accident* **(e)** good for = making better or healthy; *running a mile before breakfast is good for you; they say that eating carrots is good for your eyesight* (NOTE: **good - better** ['betə] **- best** [best]) **2** *noun* **(a)** advantage, making better; *the medicine didn't do me any good; he decided to give up smoking for the good of his health; what's the good of having a big garden if you don't like gardening?; governments*

should work for the good of the people **(b)** for good = for ever; *he's left the town for good* **(c)** no good = useless, not working; *this computer's no good*

good afternoon ['gʊd ɑːftə'nuːn] *interjection* (*used when meeting or leaving someone in the afternoon*) *I just want to say good afternoon to the headmaster*

goodbye [gʊd'baɪ] *noun & interjection* (*used when leaving someone*) *say goodbye to your teacher; goodbye! we'll see you again on Thursday* (NOTE: often shortened to **bye**)

good day *interjection* **(a)** ['gʊd 'deɪ] (*formal, saying goodbye*) *good day to you, my man!* **(b)** [g'daɪ] (*mainly used in Australia, meaning 'hello'*) *good day, everybody!* (NOTE: often written **g'day**)

good evening ['gʊd 'iːvnɪŋ] *interjection* (*used when meeting or leaving someone in the evening*) *good evening, Mrs Smith!*

Good Friday ['gʊd 'fraɪdeɪ] *noun* the Friday before Easter Day

COMMENT: traditionally, hot cross buns are eaten on Good Friday

goodies ['gʊdiz] *noun* (*informal*) **(a)** sweet food; *the children looked at all the goodies on the table* **(b)** presents; *what goodies did Father Christmas bring you?* **(c)** heroes; *in the end, the goodies won* (NOTE: the opposite in this meaning is **baddies**)

good-looking ['gʊd'lʊkɪŋ] *adjective* (*of a person*) pleasant to look at; *she's a very good-looking girl; he's very good-looking, with lots of girlfriends; he's far better-looking than his brother*

good morning ['gʊd 'mɔːnɪŋ] *interjection* (*used when meeting or leaving someone in the morning*) *good morning, Mr Smith!*

good-natured [gʊd'neɪtʃəd] *adjective* pleasant, not cruel; *he made some good-natured jokes about the English weather*

goodness ['gʊdnəs] *noun* **(a)** being good; *she did it out of pure goodness of heart* **(b)** thank goodness! = phrase showing relief; *thank goodness the ambulance arrived quickly!*; for goodness' sake = expression showing you are annoyed, or that something is important; *what are you screaming for? - it's only a little mouse, for goodness' sake; for goodness' sake try to be quiet, we don't want the guards to hear us!*

goodnight [gʊd'naɪt] *interjection* (*used when leaving someone late in the evening*) *goodnight, everyone, sleep well!*

goods [gʊdz] *noun* **(a)** things that are produced for sale; *the company sells goods from various European countries*; goods train = train for carrying freight, not passengers **(b)** possessions, things which you own; *she carried all her worldly goods in a bag*

goodwill [gʊd'wɪl] *noun* **(a)** kind feeling; *the charity relies on the goodwill of people who give money regularly* **(b)** (*of a business*) value of the customers, reputation, site, etc.; *he paid £10,000 for the goodwill of the restaurant and £40,000 for the fittings*

COMMENT: goodwill can include the reputation of the business, any patents which it holds, the trade names it uses, the value of a 'good site', etc.; all this is very difficult to calculate accurately

gooey ['gu:i] *adjective (informal)* soft and sticky; *look at that plate of gooey cakes!; you can toast marshmallows over a barbecue to make them go all hot and gooey*

goof [gu:f] **1** *noun (informal)* stupid person **2** *verb (informal)* to make a stupid mistake; *she really goofed this time!*

go off ['gəʊ 'ɒf] *verb* **(a)** to go to another place; *he went off to look for a parking space; she went off muttering something about buying cheese* **(b)** to start working suddenly; *the burglar alarm went off in the middle of the night* **(c)** to explode; *the bomb went off when there were still lots of people in the building; fireworks were going off everywhere on Bonfire Night* **(d)** to become rotten; *throw that meat away - it's gone off; fish goes off quickly in hot weather* **(e)** *(informal)* not to like something any more; *I've gone off modern music; she went off her new boyfriend quite quickly*

go on ['gəʊ 'ɒn] *verb* **(a)** to continue; *please go on, I like hearing you sing; they went on working in spite of the fire; she went on speaking for two hours; don't ask questions, just go on with your work* **(b)** to happen; *what's been going on here?* **(c)** to base your opinion and actions on; *the police investigating the murder don't have much to go on; we have to go on the assumption that the festival will start on time*

goose [gu:s] *noun* large bird, living near water, both wild and bred on farms; *a flock of wild geese landed on the runway* (NOTE: plural is **geese** [gi:s]) Note also the males are **ganders**, the young are **goslings**)

gooseberry ['guzbri] *noun* little green fruit, with a sharp taste; *gooseberry jam; gooseberry bush* = small bush on which gooseberries grow; *gooseberry fool* = dessert of gooseberries and whipped cream (NOTE: plural is **gooseberries**)

gooseflesh *or* **goose-pimples** ['gu:sfleʃ *or* 'gu:spɪmpəlz] *noun* little bumps on the skin caused by cold, excitement or fear; *just the thought of his strange staring eyes gives me goose-pimples* (NOTE: American English is **goose bumps**)

go out ['gəʊ 'aʊt] *verb* **(a)** to leave a building; *I don't go out often at night; he forgot to lock the door when he went out* **(b)** not to be alight any more; *the fire went out and the room got cold; all the lights in the building suddenly went out* **(c)** to go out of business = to stop trading; *the firm went out of business last week*

go out with ['gəʊ 'aʊt wɪθ] *verb* **(a)** to go to parties, dates, restaurants, etc., with someone as part of a relationship; *he's going out with a girl from work* **(b)** to go to a party, restaurant, etc., with someone; *he's been out with her a couple of times*

go over ['gəʊ 'əʊvə] *verb* **(a)** to cross to the other side; *go over the bridge and turn left* **(b)** to examine something carefully; *she went over the contract with her solicitor*

gopher ['gəʊfə] *noun* fat American rat which lives in holes in the ground; *there's a family of gophers living under that tree* (NOTE: do not confuse with **gofer**)

gore [gɔ:] **1** *noun (formal)* blood; *the final scene of the play was very violent, with lots of gore* **2** *verb* to wound with a horn; *he was gored by a bull*

gorge [gɔ:dʒ] **1** *noun* rocky valley; *the walkers climbed down into the gorge* **2** *verb* to eat too much; *look at her gorging herself on cakes*

gorgeous ['gɔ:dʒəs] *adjective* magnificent; *the peacock spread out its gorgeous tail*

gorilla [gə'rɪlə] *noun* large black African ape; *we are trying to protect the gorillas' natural habitat* (NOTE: do not confuse with **guerrilla**)

go round ['gəʊ 'raʊnd] *verb* **(a)** to turn; *the roundabout went round and round* **(b)** to turn round something; *we went round the roundabout and took the third road on the left* **(c)** to visit; *you'll need at least two hours to go round the museum* **(d)** to be enough; *there wasn't enough ice cream to go round* **(e)** to go to somewhere near; *let's go round to your sister's; we all went round to the pub for a drink*

gorse [gɔ:s] *noun* wild prickly shrub with bright yellow flowers; *the gorse is all in flower on the hillsides* (NOTE: no plural)

gory ['gɔ:ri] *adjective (humorous)* terrible, awful; *she told me all the gory details of her interview*

gosh [gɒʃ] *interjection* showing surprise; *gosh! the plane is supposed to leave in ten minutes*

gosling ['gɒzlɪŋ] *noun* baby goose; *the goose and her three goslings*

go-slow ['gəʊsləʊ] *noun* slowing down of work as a protest against the management; *a series of go-slows in the factory held up production*

gospel ['gɒspl] *noun* **(a)** part of the Bible which tells the life of Jesus Christ; *it's the gospel truth* = it's absolutely true **(b)** *gospel music* = religious music which first became popular in the USA during the Depression

gossip ['gɒsɪp] **1** *noun* **(a)** stories or news about someone, which may or may not be true; *have you heard the latest gossip about Sue?; to spread gossip about someone* = to tell stories about someone (which may or may not be true); *gossip column* = column in a newspaper which tells stories about famous people; *gossip columnist* = person who writes a gossip column **(b)** person who spreads gossip; *be careful what you say to him - he's a great gossip* **2** *verb* to talk about people; *they spent hours gossiping about the people working in the office*

got [gɒt] *see* GET

gothic ['gɒθɪk] *adjective* in a medieval architectural style, with tall pointed arches; *a gothic cathedral*

go through ['gəʊ 'θru:] *verb* to go through with something = to continue with something; *they decided not to go through with their planned pig farm because of the objections from their neighbours*

gotten ['gɒtn] *verb US see* GET

gouge [gaʊdʒ] **1** *noun* chisel; *the gouge bit into the wood* **2** *verb* to cut out; *he gouged out a hole in the plank; the waves have gouged out a cave in the cliff*

goulash ['gu:læʃ] *noun* Hungarian dish of meat and vegetables, flavoured with paprika

go up ['gəʊ 'ʌp] *verb* **(a)** to go to a higher place; *take the lift and go up to the fourth floor* **(b)** to increase, to rise to a higher level; *the price of bread has gone up*

gourd [gʊəd] *noun* round fruit of a climbing plant, dried and used as a bottle or as a decoration

gourmet ['gʊəmeɪ] *noun* referring to good food; *we had a gourmet dinner in a three-star restaurant; this recipe comes from a gourmet cookbook*

govern ['gʌvən] *verb* **(a)** to rule a country; *the country is governed by three generals* **(b)** to influence, to have an effect on; *inflation is governed by interest rates and exchange rates*

governance ['gʌvənəns] *noun* (*formal*) way in which a country or company is governed; *the report made recommendations about the future governance of the country*; **corporate governance** = the correct way in which companies should be run

governess ['gʌvənəs] *noun* private female teacher; *she did not go to school, but was brought up by a series of German governesses* (NOTE: plural is **governesses**)

governing ['gʌvənɪŋ] *adjective* which rules; *the senate is the governing body of the college*; *Republicans are the governing party in the state*

government ['gʌvəmənt] *noun* **(a)** system of ruling a country; *a country struggling to achieve democratic government* (NOTE: no plural in this meaning) **(b)** **central government** = main organization, dealing with the affairs of the whole country; **local government** = organizations dealing with the affairs of small areas of the country, such as towns and counties; **provincial government** *or* **state government** = government of a province or state **(c)** people or political party which governs; *the president asked the leader of the largest party to form a new government*; *everything was working very well until the government stepped in*; *the government controls the price of bread*; *he has an important job in the government*; **the Thatcher government** = the ministers who formed the cabinet when Mrs Thatcher was Prime Minister; **government department** = section of the government with a particular responsibility

governmental [gʌvən'mentl] *adjective* referring to a government; *he chairs the governmental committee on unemployment*

governor ['gʌvnə] *noun* person who runs a state, colony, institution, etc.; *the Governor of Alabama*; **prison governor** = person in charge of a prison; **the Governor of the Bank of England** = person (nominated by the British government) who is in charge of the Bank of England

Governor-General ['gʌvnə 'dʒenrəl] *noun* official head of some Commonwealth countries; *the Governor-General will be sworn in tomorrow*

go with ['gəu 'wɪθ] *verb* **(a)** to match; *blue shoes won't go with a green dress*; *red wine goes best with meat* **(b)** to be linked to; *that remote control goes with the TV*; *he has a big house that goes with his job*

go without ['gəu wɪ'ðaut] *verb* not to have something which you usually have; *after getting lost in the mountains, they went without food for three days*; *she got up late and had to go without breakfast*; *we have too much work, so we'll have to go without a holiday this year*

gown [gaun] *noun* **(a)** (*formal*) woman's long formal dress; *a ball gown* **(b)** robe worn by a judge, person with degree, etc.; *she wore her new gown to the degree ceremony* **(c)** **dressing-gown** = long robe worn over pyjamas or nightdress before getting dressed; *the guests ran out of the hotel in their pyjamas and dressing gowns*

GP ['dʒi: 'pi:] *noun* = GENERAL PRACTITIONER family doctor who does not specialize in any particular branch of medicine; *our son wants to be a GP; see your GP first, and he will refer you to a consultant*

grab [græb] **1** *noun* **to make a grab for something** = to try to seize something; *he made a grab for her wallet* (*informal*) **up for grabs** = available to anyone who wants to get it; *the company is up for grabs*; *now the champion has retired the world title is up for grabs* **2** *verb* **(a)** to pick something up suddenly; *he grabbed his suitcase and ran to the train* **(b)** to get something quickly; *let's grab some lunch in the canteen before the meeting starts* **(c)** (*informal*) how does it grab you? = what do you think of it?; *a weekend in Paris - how does that grab you?* (NOTE: **grabbing - grabbed**)

grace [greɪs] *noun* **(a)** elegance and attractiveness; *the grace of the deer as they ran off into the woods*; **with good grace** = quite cheerfully; *he accepted the criticisms with good grace* **(b)** prayer before a meal; *father always says grace before dinner* **(c)** extra time to pay; *to give a creditor two weeks' grace to pay*

graceful ['greɪsful] *adjective* **(a)** moving smoothly and beautifully; *the swimmer's graceful strokes across the pool* **(b)** behaving politely and smoothly; *he went into the ladies' toilet by mistake and had to beat a graceful retreat*

gracefully ['greɪsfuli] *adverb* smoothly and beautifully; *she moved gracefully across the stage*

gracious ['greɪʃəs] **1** *adjective* **(a)** elegant; *the Edwardian era was a time of gracious living*; *a gracious London square* **(b)** dignified and polite; *she gave him a very gracious welcome* **2** *interjection* (*showing surprise*) **good gracious! is that the time?**

grade [greɪd] **1** *noun* **(a)** level of quality; *grade I eggs*; *what grade of vegetables do you buy?*; **to make the grade** = to succeed *or* to do well; **high-grade** *or* **top-grade** = best quality; **low-grade** = worst quality **(b)** exam mark; *she got top grades in maths* **(c)** *US* class in school; *students in fifth grade*; *she's a fifth grade student* **2** *verb* to sort according to size or quality; *a machine for grading fruit*; *hotels are graded with two, three, four or five stars*

grade crossing ['greɪd 'krɒsɪŋ] *noun US* place where a road crosses a railroad line; *the bus was held up at a grade crossing while a freight train passed* (NOTE: British English is **level crossing**)

graded ['greɪdɪd] *adjective* **(a)** rising in steps; **graded tax** = tax which rises according to income **(b)** **graded hotel** = good quality hotel which has some stars

gradient ['greɪdɪənt] *noun* slope in a road, railway, etc.; *change to low gear - the gradient is very steep*

gradual ['grædjuəl] *adjective* which changes a little at a time; *we're forecasting a gradual improvement in the weather*

gradually ['grædjuəli] *adverb* little by little; *his condition improved gradually day-by-day*; *she gradually learnt how to deal with customers' complaints*

graduate 1 *noun* ['grædjuət] person with a degree from a university *US* person with a degree from a college; *he's a graduate of London University*; *she's a physics graduate*; **graduate training scheme** = scheme which trains graduates for work in business; **graduate trainee** = graduate who is being trained for work in business **2** *verb* ['grædjueɪt] to get a degree; *she graduated from Edinburgh university last year*

graduated ['grædjueɪtɪd] *adjective* **(a)** rising in steps; *graduated income tax* **(b)** with quantities marked on it; *a graduated measuring jar*

graduation [ˌɡrædjuˈeɪʃən] *noun* **(a)** getting a degree from a university; *graduation will take place on June 10th*; **graduation ceremony** = ceremony when degrees are given; *see also* COMMENCEMENT **(b)** *US* leaving high school or college with a diploma

graffiti [ɡrəˈfiːti] *noun* writing on walls in public places; *they're trying to remove the graffiti from railway carriages* (NOTE: a plural noun, though sometimes used as a singular)

graft [ɡrɑːft] **1** *noun* **(a)** *(in surgery)* **skin graft** = piece of skin which is attached to a damaged part of the body so that it will grow there **(b)** piece of a plant which is attached to another plant; *the pear graft has taken* **(c)** *(informal)* **hard graft** = hard work; *selling insurance door-to-door is sheer hard graft* **(d)** *(informal)* bribery and corruption of officials; *graft is widespread at all levels of the civil service; the minister was accused of graft* (NOTE: no plural in meanings (c) and (d)) **2** *verb* **(a)** *(surgery)* to take a piece of skin and attach it to a damaged part of the body so that it grows; *they grafted skin from his arm onto his leg* **(b)** *(gardening)* to take a piece of a plant and attach it to another plant; *he grafted the apple onto the stock*

grain [ɡreɪn] *noun* **(a)** cereal crop; *a field of grain; the grain harvest* **(b)** a very small piece; *a grain of sand* **(c)** patterns of lines in wood; *this old oak table has a beautiful grain*; **to go against the grain** = to go against your natural instincts; *it goes against the grain to throw away all that good food*

gram *or* **gramme** [ɡræm] *noun* weight equal to one thousandth of a kilogram; *you will need 250g of sugar; this piece of fish weighs 500 grams* (NOTE: when used with numbers, **gram** is usually written **g** *or* **gm: 50g**)

grammar [ˈɡræmə] *noun* **(a)** rules of a language; *Russian grammar is very difficult; he's been learning English for years, and still makes grammar mistakes* **(b)** book of rules of a language; *there's a new German grammar coming out in the autumn*

grammar school [ˈɡræmə ˈskuːl] *noun* secondary school where students have to pass an exam to enter; *he went to the local grammar school, and then to university*

grammatical [ɡrəˈmætɪkl] *adjective* referring to correct grammar; *'he didn't never go there' isn't grammatical*

grammatically [ɡrəˈmætɪkli] *adverb* in a correct grammatical way; *'I didn't never do it' is not grammatically correct*

gramophone [ˈɡræməfəʊn] *noun* *(old)* record-player, a device for playing records; *they rolled back the carpet, put a jazz record on the gramophone and danced*

gran [ɡræn] *noun (informal)* grandmother

granary [ˈɡrænəri] *noun* place where grain is stored; **granary loaf** = bread made from whole grain

grand [ɡrænd] **1** *adjective* **(a)** big and important; *his grand plan for making a lot of money* **(b)** imposing; *we went to a very grand wedding; for the grand finale everyone wore gold dresses* **(c)** final; **grand total** = the total of all the figures **2** *noun (informal)* one thousand pounds *or* dollars; *they offered him fifty grand for the information*

grandad [ˈɡrændæd] *noun (informal)* grandfather; *tell me a story, grandad!*

grandchild [ˈɡræntʃaɪld] *noun* child of a son or daughter; *all her grandchildren came to the old lady's eightieth birthday party* (NOTE: plural is **grandchildren** [ˈɡræntʃɪldrən])

granddaughter [ˈɡrændɔːtə] *noun* daughter of a son or daughter; *my granddaughter is nineteen now, and at university; our little granddaughter is adorable*

grandeur [ˈɡrændʒə] *noun* splendour; *the grandeur of the State Opening of Parliament*; **delusions of grandeur** = false impression of being important; *he suffers from delusions of grandeur*

grandfather [ˈɡrænfɑːðə] *noun* father of your mother or father; *tomorrow is grandfather's hundredth birthday; my grandfather can remember seeing the first planes flying*; **a grandfather clock** = a tall clock (NOTE: often called **grandad** *or* **grandpa** by children)

grandiose [ˈɡrændɪəʊs] *adjective* extremely splendid, but too big and complicated; *a grandiose plan for the centre of the town*

grand jury [ˈɡrænd ˈdʒʊri] *noun US* group of jurors (between twelve and twenty-four) who meet as a preliminary to a trial to decide if an indictment should be issued to start criminal proceedings; *the case goes before the grand jury next week*

grandly [ˈɡrændli] *adverb* in a grand way; *the ladies at the wedding were dressed very grandly in hats and gloves; he grandly tipped the taxi driver with a five-pound note*

grandma [ˈɡrænmɑː] *noun (informal)* grandmother; *how old is your grandma?*

grandmother [ˈɡrænmʌðə] *noun* mother of your mother or father; *it will be grandmother's ninetieth birthday next month; grandmother showed me how to make bread* (NOTE: often called **gran** *or* **granny** *or* **grandma** *or* **nan** by children)

Grand National [ˈɡrænd ˈnæʃənəl] *noun* important horse race over fences, run each year at the Aintree racecourse, near Liverpool; *he rode the winner in the Grand National; she won £100 on the Grand National*

grandpa [ˈɡrænpɑː] *noun (informal)* grandfather; *is grandpa coming to the party?*

grandparents [ˈɡrænpeərənts] *noun* parents of your mother or father; *my grandparents are all dead*

grand piano [ˈɡrænd piˈænəʊ] *noun* large horizontal piano; *they had some difficulty in getting the grand piano into their little flat* (NOTE: a smaller piano, with a vertical body, is called an **upright**)

Grand Prix [ɡrɒn ˈpriː] *noun* race for large and powerful racing cars; *did you see the Belgian Grand Prix on TV last night?; he won the French Grand Prix last year*

grand slam [ˈɡrænd ˈslæm] *noun* winning a series of competitions, such as all the main tennis competitions held in a year; *a grand slam winner; the French rugby team are aiming for the grand slam*

grandson [ˈɡrænsʌn] *noun* son of a son or daughter; *our grandson is nearly eighteen, and will be leaving school soon; our grandson is called Nicholas*

grandstand [ˈɡrænstænd] *noun* stand with seats for spectators at games or races; *we have tickets for the grandstand so we should have a good view of the finishing line*

granite ['grænɪt] *noun* hard grey stone; *the granite churches of Aberdeen*

granny ['græni] *noun (informal)* grandmother; *tell me a story, granny!*; **granny flat** = small separate flat in a large house, intended for a relative, not necessarily a grandmother

granola [græ'nəʊlə] *noun US* breakfast cereal made of oats and dried fruit and nuts

grant [grɑːnt] **1** *noun* sum of money to help; *not many students get a full grant*; *my grant only pays for a few books*; *we have applied for a grant to plant trees by the side of the road* **2** *verb* **(a)** to agree to give something; *the government has granted them a loan or a subsidy*; **to take something for granted** = to assume that you will get something, or will keep something, and so not to appreciate it; *the children seem to take it for granted that I will give them big presents every birthday* **(b)** to admit; *I grant you it's going to be difficult, but I'm sure you'll do it well*

grape [greɪp] *noun* fruit of the vine, sometimes used to make wine; *he bought a bunch of grapes; see also* SOUR

grapefruit ['greɪpfruːt] *noun* large yellow citrus fruit, like an orange but not as sweet; *a glass of grapefruit juice*; *I'll start my breakfast with half a grapefruit, please* (NOTE: plural is **grapefruit**)

grapevine ['greɪpvaɪn] *noun* plant on which grapes grow; **I heard it on the grapevine** = someone told me about it when gossiping (NOTE: as a plant, the word **vine** is more usual)

graph [grɑːf] *noun* chart showing figures in the form of a line; *the sales graph is going up*; *he drew a graph to show the number of fatal accidents per thousand cars over the last ten years*; **graph paper** = paper with little squares, for drawing graphs

graphic ['græfɪk] *adjective* **(a)** drawn; *the results are shown in graphic form* **(b)** vivid; *he gave a graphic description of the accident*

graphics ['græfɪks] *noun* pictures on a computer screen or designed on a computer; *the graphics on this game are brilliant*

graphite ['græfaɪt] *noun* natural carbon; *graphite is used in making pencils*

grapple ['græpl] *verb* **(a)** to fight someone; *the two men were grappling on the floor* **(b)** **to grapple with something** = to struggle to solve a problem; *he's trying to grapple with the problem of the company accounts*

grasp [grɑːsp] **1** *noun* **(a)** tight hold; *she pulled his hair, and forced him to loosen his grasp on her arm* **(b)** understanding; *she has a good grasp of physics* **2** *verb* **(a)** to hold tightly; *she grasped the branch of the tree with both hands* **(b)** to understand; *they didn't seem to grasp my meaning*

grasping ['grɑːspɪŋ] *adjective* person who wants to get money; *the landlord is a nasty grasping individual*

grass [grɑːs] **1** *noun* **(a)** low green plant, which is eaten by sheep and cows in fields, or used in gardens to make lawns; *the grass is getting too long*; *the cows are eating the fresh green grass* **(b)** lawn; *keep off the grass!*; *we'll sit on the grass and have our picnic* **(c)** *(informal)* person who gives information to the police; *the police gave the grass special protection* **(d)** *(slang)* marijuana **2** *verb (informal)* **to grass on someone** = to give information about someone to the police; *he grassed on his pals*

grasshopper ['grɑːshɒpə] *noun* insect which jumps and makes a buzzing noise; *grasshoppers make a noise by rubbing their legs and wings together*

grasslands ['grɑːslændz] *noun* land covered with grass; *antelope live in the grasslands covering the central plateau*; *grasslands stretch as far as the eye can see*

grassroots [grɑːs'ruːts] *noun* ordinary members of a political party or of society in general; *what is the grassroots reaction to the proposal?*; *the party has considerable support at grassroots level*

grassy ['grɑːsi] *adjective* covered in grass; *a grassy path*

grate [greɪt] **1** *noun* metal frame for holding coal in a fireplace; *he put some more coal into the grate* **2** *verb* **(a)** to make into small pieces by rubbing against a grater; *she grated nutmeg over the pudding*; *sprinkle grated cheese over your pasta*; *we made a salad of grated carrots and spring onions* **(b)** to make a rough irritating noise; *that door needs oiling - it grates on its hinges*; *the sound of metal grating on stone makes me shudder* **(c)** to irritate, to make someone annoyed; *the way he sings while he works is beginning to grate on my nerves* (NOTE: do not confuse with **great**)

grateful ['greɪtful] *adjective* recognizing and feeling thankful for something that someone has done for you; *we are most grateful to you for your help*

grater ['greɪtə] *noun* kitchen instrument with a rough surface and little holes for grating; *a cheese grater*; *a nutmeg grater*

gratify ['grætɪfaɪ] *verb* **(a)** to satisfy; *it gratifies her need for luxury* **(b)** to please; *we were gratified to see that our work was prominently displayed*

grating ['greɪtɪŋ] **1** *noun* metal frame which covers a hole; *they lifted up the grating to look into the drain* **2** *adjective* **a grating sound** = a rough unpleasant sound

gratis ['grɑːtɪs] *adverb & adjective* free of charge; *we got into the exhibition gratis*; *he sent me two gratis tickets for the show*

gratitude ['grætɪtjuːd] *noun* thankfulness; *we gave her a cheque as an expression of our gratitude*; *the dog showed its gratitude by wagging its tail and licking my hand*

gratuitous [grə'tjuːɪtəs] *adjective* unnecessary, unjustified; *a gratuitous insult*; *the chairman made some quite gratuitous remarks about the secretary*

gratuity [grə'tjuːɪti] *noun* **(a)** *(formal)* tip, money given to someone who has provided a service; *the staff are instructed not to accept gratuities* **(b)** sum of money given to someone who leaves a job; *she received a tax-free gratuity of £10,000 when she retired* (NOTE: plural is **gratuities**)

grave [greɪv] **1** *noun* hole in the ground where a dead person is buried; *at the funeral, the whole family stood by the grave* *(informal)* **to have one foot in the grave** = to be old *(of dead person)* **would turn in their grave** = would be annoyed; *Father would turn in his grave if he saw what they have done to his house* **2** *adjective* **(a)** important, worrying; *it is a very grave offence*; *he is in court facing grave charges* **(b)** quietly serious; *she looked at him with a grave expression* (NOTE: **graver - gravest**)

grave accent ['grɑːv 'æksənt] *noun* accent which slopes backwards over a vowel (à, è) to show that it is pronounced in a special way; *compare* ACUTE ACCENT

> COMMENT: grave accents are used in French to show a change in pronunciation. They are used in other languages to show that the vowel should be stressed

gravel ['grævl] *noun* small stones; *a gravel path* (NOTE: no plural: **a heap of gravel**; for one piece say **a bit of gravel: I've got a bit of gravel in my shoe**)

graveside ['greɪvsaɪd] *noun* at the side of a grave; *a short graveside service was held on the anniversary of his death*

gravestone ['greɪvstəun] *noun* large stone placed on a grave with the name of the dead person written on it; *they walked round the old cemetery reading the inscriptions on the gravestones* (NOTE: also called **headstone** *or* **tombstone**)

graveyard ['greɪvjɑːd] *noun* cemetery; *there's an old graveyard round the church, with some graves dating back to the seventeenth century*

gravitate ['grævɪteɪt] *verb* **to gravitate towards something** = to be attracted towards something; *in the evening the students gravitate towards the bars*

gravitation [grævɪ'teɪʃn] *noun* force of attraction caused by mass; *the gravitation of the moon causes tides*

gravitational [grævɪ'teɪʃnəl] *adjective* referring to gravity; *the planets are held in orbit by the sun's gravitational field*; *tides are caused by the moon's gravitational pull*

gravity ['grævɪti] *noun* **(a)** force which pulls things towards the ground; *apples fall to the ground because of the earth's gravity*; **centre of gravity** = the point in an object at which it will balance; *a bus has a very low centre of gravity*; **specific gravity** = *see* RELATIVE DENSITY **(b)** great seriousness; *no one seems to realize the gravity of the situation*; *due to the gravity of the crimes he is supposed to have committed, his trial will be held in a different town*

gravy ['greɪvi] *noun* sauce from meat during cooking; cooked brown sauce, served with meat; *she poured the gravy over the meat* (NOTE: no plural)

gravy train ['greɪvi 'treɪn] *noun* (*informal*) way of getting money from a large bureaucracy without doing much work; *everyone wants to get on the European gravy train*

gray [greɪ] *adjective US see* GREY

graze [greɪz] **1** *noun* slight wound; *he had a graze on his knee* **2** *verb* **(a)** to feed on grass; *the sheep were grazing on the hillside* **(b)** to hurt the skin slightly; *he fell off his bicycle and grazed his knee*

grazing ['greɪzɪŋ] *noun* grass grown for animals to eat; *the alps provide good summer grazing*

grease [griːs] **1** *noun* **(a)** thick oil; *put some grease on the hinge* **(b)** (*informal*) **elbow grease** = hard work; *it doesn't need any skill, just a lot of elbow grease* **2** *verb* **(a)** to cover with oil; *don't forget to grease the wheels*; *she greased the pan before cooking the eggs* **(b)** (*informal*) **to grease someone's palm** = to give someone a bribe; *we had to grease a few palms to get the contract signed*

greasy ['griːsi] *adjective* **(a)** covered with oil; *he wiped his greasy hands on a piece of rag*; *I don't like*

the chips they serve here - they're too greasy **(b)** (*informal*) **greasy spoon** = small cheap, and often dirty, café; *there was nowhere else to eat, so we had a cup of coffee in a greasy spoon near the railway station* (NOTE: **greasier - greasiest**)

great [greɪt] *adjective* **(a)** large; *we visited the Great Wall of China*; *she was carrying a great big pile of sandwiches*; **a great deal of** *or* **a great many** = a lot of; *there's a great deal of work to be done*; *she earns a great deal of money*; *a great many people will lose their jobs* **(b)** important or famous; *New York is a great city*; *Picasso was a great artist*; *the greatest tennis player of all time* **(c)** (*informal*) wonderful, very good; *we had a great time at the party*; *what did you think of the film? - it was great!*; *it was great of you to help*; *it was great that they could all get to the picnic* **(d)** (*humorous*) **the great and the good** = people who occupy influential positions in society; *the government looked through the ranks of the great and the good to find someone to be chairman of the museum's trustees* (NOTE: **greater - greatest**)

great- [greɪt] *prefix referring to an older generation*; **great-grandfather** = father of a grandfather; **great-great-grandfather** = grandfather of a grandfather

Great Britain (GB) [greɪt 'brɪtən] *noun* country formed of England, Scotland and Wales (which with Northern Ireland makes up the United Kingdom); *they came to live in Great Britain some time ago*; *in Great Britain cars drive on the left hand side of the road* (NOTE: capital: **London**; people: **British**; language: **English**; currency: **pound sterling (£)**)

Great Dane ['greɪt 'deɪn] *noun* breed of very large dog

greatly ['greɪtli] *adverb* very much; *they greatly enjoyed the birthday party*

Greece [griːs] *noun* country in southern Europe; *we go to Greece on holiday every year*; *Greece exports olive oil and wine* (NOTE: capital: **Athens**; people: **Greeks**; language: **Greek**; currency: **drachma**)

greed [griːd] *noun* too much love of food, money, etc.; *their only motive was greed*; *his greed for popularity makes him do all sorts of stupid things*

greedy ['griːdi] *adjective* wanting food or other things too much; *don't be greedy - you've already had two pieces of cake*; *politicians are just greedy for power* (NOTE: **greedier - greediest**)

Greek [griːk] **1** *adjective* referring to Greece; *she married the son of a Greek shipping tycoon*; *he's opened a Greek restaurant near us*; *the letters of the Greek alphabet are used in science* **2** *noun* **(a)** person from Greece; *the ancient Greeks* **(b)** language spoken in Greece; *he reads Plato in ancient Greek*; *she bought a Greek phrasebook before going on holiday*

green [griːn] **1** *adjective* **(a)** of a colour like the colour of grass; *he was wearing a bright green shirt*; *they painted the door dark green*; *go on - the traffic lights are green* **(b)** **to give the green light** = to give permission; *the government gave the project the green light* **(c)** relating to, interested in, or concerned about the environment; *she's very worried about green issues*; *he's a leading figure in the green movement* (NOTE: **greener - greenest**) **2** *noun* **(a)** colour like grass; *the door was painted a very dark green*; *have you any paint of a darker green than this?* **(b)** grassy piece of public land in the middle of a village; *they were* *playing cricket on the village green* **(c)** piece of smooth short grass for playing golf; *the grass on the greens is cut very short*; *his ball landed about two feet from the hole on the tenth green*; *see also* BOWLING GREEN

greenback ['gri:nbæk] *noun (informal) US* dollar bill; *the greenback is acceptable in every country in the world*

Green Belt ['gri:n 'belt] *noun* area of farming land or woods and parks, which surrounds a town, and on which building is restricted or completely banned; *they can't put houses in Old Oak Wood, it's Green Belt land; the Green Belt is supposed to stop the remorseless advance of houses into the countryside*

greenery ['gri:nəri] *noun* trees, plants, etc.; *the parks and squares bring pleasant greenery to the centre of London* (NOTE: no plural)

green fingers ['gri:n 'fiŋgəz] *noun* skill at gardening; *he's got green fingers* (NOTE: American English is **green thumb**)

greenfly ['gri:nflaɪ] *noun* small green aphids which suck sap from garden plants; *the roses are covered with greenfly*; *use a spray to try to get rid of the greenfly*; *there is or are a lot of greenfly on the roses* (NOTE: usually plural)

greengage ['gri:ngeɪdʒ] *noun* variety of green plum; *my mother makes jam with our greengages*

greengrocer ['gri:ngrəusə] *noun* person who sells fruit and vegetables; *the greengrocer's* = shop where you can buy fruit and vegetables; *can you buy some potatoes at the greengrocer's?*; *I went to the greengrocer's in the High Street to buy some fruit*

greenhouse ['gri:nhaus] *noun* glass building for growing plants; *we grow tomatoes in our greenhouse in winter*; *greenhouse effect* = effect of gases in the earth's atmosphere which prevent heat loss (NOTE: plural is **greenhouses** ['gri:nhauzɪz])

greenhouse gases ['gri:nhaus 'gæsɪz] *noun* gases such as carbon dioxide, methane, etc., which are produced by burning fossil fuels and which rise into the atmosphere, forming a barrier which prevents heat loss; *the EU is planning to introduce a tax to inhibit greenhouse gas emissions*

Green Paper ['gri:n 'peɪpə] *noun* report from the British government on proposals for a possible new law; *the government has published a Green Paper on immigration*; *compare* WHITE PAPER

Green Party ['gri:n 'pɑ:ti] *noun* political party concerned mainly with environmental and health issues (NOTE: often called simply **the Greens**)

greens [gri:nz] *noun (informal)* **(a)** green vegetables; *you must eat plenty of greens* **(b)** *see* GREEN PARTY

green thumb ['gri:n 'θʌm] *noun US* skill at gardening; *she has a green thumb for growing vegetables* (NOTE: British English is **green fingers**)

Greenwich ['grɪnɪtʃ] *noun* town to the east of London, on the river Thames; *the Greenwich meridian* = line passing through Greenwich at longitude 0°, from which longitudes are calculated

Greenwich Mean Time (GMT) ['grenɪtʃ 'mi:n taɪm] *noun* local time on the 0° meridian where it passes through Greenwich, England; *at midnight Greenwich Mean Time it is 7 a.m. in Bangkok*

greet [gri:t] *verb* to meet someone and say hello; *she greeted him with a kiss*

greeting ['gri:tɪŋ] *noun* words said when meeting or welcoming someone; *he muttered a few words of greeting to the guests and disappeared into the kitchen*

greetings ['gri:tɪŋz] *noun* good wishes; *we send you birthday greetings or Christmas greetings from all our family*

gregarious [grɪ'geəriəs] *adjective* fond of the company of other people; *she could never go to live in a country cottage, she's too gregarious*; *snow geese are gregarious birds which arrive here in their thousands in spring*

grenade [grɪ'neɪd] *noun* small bomb, usually thrown by hand; *he threw a tear-gas grenade into the crowd*

grenadier [grenə'dɪə] *noun* soldier in the Grenadier Guards, a famous British regiment

grew [gru:] *see* GROW

grey [greɪ] **1** *noun* colour like a mixture of black and white; *he was dressed all in grey*; *charcoal grey* = very dark grey, almost black **2** *adjective* of a colour like a mixture of black and white; *her hair has turned quite grey*; *a grey-haired old lady*; *she was wearing a light grey suit*; *look at the grey clouds - I think it is going to rain* (NOTE: **greyer - greyest**. Note also the American spelling is **gray**)

greyhound ['greɪhaund] *noun* racing dog; *he goes greyhound racing every Friday*

grid [grɪd] *noun* **(a)** set of parallel bars; *we have fitted a metal grid over the top of the well*; *cattle grid* = bars in a road which prevent cattle crossing **(b)** numbered squares on a map; *what's the grid reference of the church?* **(c)** *the national grid* = the national electricity supply system **(d)** *starting grid* = lines marked on the track at the start of a car race; *the cars are all lined up on the grid, with the Ferrari in pole position*

griddle ['grɪdl] *noun* hot metal plate on top of a stove, used for cooking; *he fried the eggs on a griddle*; *griddle cake* = type of little pancake cooked on a griddle

gridiron ['grɪdaɪən] *noun* **(a)** metal frame for cooking over a fire; *they cooked the meat on a gridiron over a charcoal fire* **(b)** *US* football field, marked with white lines; *the teams came onto the gridiron*

gridlock ['grɪdlɒk] *noun* traffic jam; *the gridlock stretched from Hyde Park Corner to the City*

gridlocked ['grɪdlɒkt] *adjective* blocked by traffic jams; *downtown New York was gridlocked for two hours*

grief [gri:f] *noun* sorrow; *she couldn't hide her grief as she watched the pictures on TV*; *to come to grief* = to meet with a disaster; *the project came to grief when the council refused to renew their grant* (informal) *to cause someone grief* = to make someone want to criticize you

grief-stricken ['gri:fstrɪkən] *adjective* very sad; *she was grief-stricken at the news*; *doctors tried to console the grief-stricken parents*

grievance ['gri:vəns] *noun* reason for complaint; *the management has asked staff representatives in to discuss their grievances*; *to air your grievances* = to complain to everyone openly about something; *to nurse a grievance against someone* = to have a reason to complain about someone, and not be able to do anything about it; *she's been nursing a grievance against the boss for some weeks*; **grievance procedure** = agreed way of presenting complaints from a union or an employee to the management of a company; *the company has improved its grievance procedure at the request of its employees*

grieve [griːv] *verb* **(a)** to be sad, especially because someone has died; *she is grieving for her fiancé who was killed in the war* **(b)** to make sad; *it grieves me to say this, but we are going to arrest your daughter*

grievous ['griːvəs] *adjective (formal)* severe, very bad; *the storm caused grievous damage to the apple orchards*; **grievous bodily harm (GBH)** = crime of causing serious physical injury to someone; *he was arrested and charged with GBH*

grill [gril] **1** *noun* **(a)** part of a cooker where food is cooked under the heat; *cook the chops under the grill*; **charcoal grill** = cooker where food is cooked over hot charcoal **(b)** restaurant serving grilled food; *we'll meet up at the Mexican Grill* **(c)** **mixed grill** = dish of different sorts of food grilled together, usually chops, sausages, bacon and mushrooms **2** *verb* **(a)** to cook under a grill; *we're having grilled sardines for dinner* **(b)** *(informal)* to interrogate; *the police grilled him about the missing money*

grille ['gril] *noun* decorative metal grid on the front of a car, with the radiator behind; *the old Ford has a polished chrome grille*

grim [grim] *adjective* **(a)** stern and not smiling; *his expression was grim*; *he gave a grim laugh and went on working* **(b)** unpleasant, worrying; *there is some grim news from the war* **(c)** grey and unpleasant; *the town centre is really grim*; *(informal)* **like grim death** = in a determined way; *she held on to the handrail like grim death* (NOTE: **grimmer - grimmest**)

grimace ['gri'meis] **1** *noun* twisted expression; *he made a grimace when he tasted the medicine* **2** *verb* to make a grimace; *she grimaced as the dentist started up his drill*

grime [graim] *noun* black dirt; *the walls of the cellar are covered with grime*

grimy ['graimi] *adjective* very dirty; *the little boy held out a grimy hand and asked for money*

grin [grin] **1** *noun* broad smile; *she gave me a big grin* **2** *verb* to smile broadly; *he grinned when we asked him if he liked his job*; **to grin and bear it** = to accept a difficult situation; *no one likes doing all these rehearsals, but we've just got to grin and bear it* (NOTE: **grinning - grinned**)

grind [graind] **1** *noun* **the daily grind** = monotonous work done every day **2** *verb* **(a)** to crush to powder; *to grind corn* or *coffee*; *a cup of freshly ground coffee* **(b)** *US*; **ground beef** = beef ground into small pieces (NOTE: British English for this is **mince**) **(c)** to rub surfaces together; **to grind your teeth** = to rub your teeth together and make a noise (usually because you are annoyed); **to grind to a halt** = to stop working gradually; *the men went on strike, and the production line ground to a halt* (NOTE: **grinding - ground** [graund])

grinder ['graində] *noun* **(a)** machine for grinding; *then insert the knife blade into the grinder*; **coffee grinder** = machine for grinding coffee beans into powder for making coffee **(b)** *US* machine for chopping meat (NOTE: British English for this meaning is **mincer** or **mincing machine**)

grip [grip] **1** *noun* **(a)** firm hold; *he has a strong firm grip*; *radial tyres give a better grip on the road surface*; **to lose your grip** = not to be as much in control as before; *she simply doesn't make any decisions - I think she's losing her grip* **(b)** *(informal)* **to get** or **to come to grips with something** = to start to deal with something; *the president is having to come to grips with the failing economy*; **to get a grip on yourself** = to try to control yourself, to try to be less emotional; *get a grip on yourself - you've got an interview in half an hour* **(c)** big soft bag for carrying clothes; *he rolled up some T-shirts and underwear and squeezed them into his grip* **(c)** piece of bent wire used to keep your hair in place; *use a grip to keep your hair off your face* (NOTE: American English is **bobby-pin**) **2** *verb* to hold tight; *she gripped the rail with both hands* (NOTE: **gripping - gripped**)

gripe [graip] **1** *noun* **(a)** complaint; *his list of gripes about the work* **(b)** *(old)* pains in the stomach; *the baby is suffering from gripe*; **gripe water** = liquid tasting of aniseed, given to babies when they have pains in the stomach **2** *verb* **to gripe about something** = to complain about something; *she's always griping about the weather*

grisly ['grizli] *adjective* horrible; *the police made a grisly discovery in the cellar* (NOTE: do not confuse with **grizzly, gristly.** Note: **grislier - grisliest**)

gristle ['grisl] *noun* hard bit of meat; *the pie was full of gristle - I couldn't eat it* (NOTE: no plural)

gristly ['grisli] *adjective* full of gristle; *they served us some awful gristly meat pie* (NOTE: do not confuse with **grisly, grizzly**)

grit [grit] **1** *noun* **(a)** bits of sand; *grit seems to have got into the engine*; *I have a piece of grit in my eye* **(b)** *(informal)* courage; *he had the grit to go mountain climbing with his artificial leg* (NOTE: no plural in meanings (a) and (b)) **(c)** *US* **hominy grits** = ground maize, boiled and eaten at breakfast **2** *verb* **(a)** to put sand on a road that is covered with ice; *lorries have been out all night, gritting the motorway* **(b)** **to grit your teeth** = to be determined; *he gritted his teeth and went on up the mountain* (NOTE: **gritting - gritted**)

gritty ['griti] *adjective* full of grit; *she showed gritty determination in trying to walk again after her accident*

grizzly ['grizli] *noun* **grizzly (bear)** = North American brown and grey bear; *grizzly bears catch salmon in mountain rivers* (NOTE: do not confuse with **grisly, gristly**; plural is **grizzlies**)

groan [grəun] **1** *noun* deep moan; *he uttered a groan and closed his eyes* **2** *verb* **(a)** to moan deeply; *she groaned when she saw how much work had to be done* **(b)** **to groan under a weight** = to carry a heavy weight; *the floor groaned under the weight of the gold bars*

grocer ['grəusə] *noun* person who sells sugar, butter, tins of food, etc.; *the grocer weighed out 500 grams of coffee*; **the grocer's** = shop where you can buy sugar, butter, tins of food, etc.; *can you buy some sugar at the grocer's?*; *we went to the grocer's in the High Street to get some tea*

groceries ['grəusəriz] *noun* things you buy at a grocer's; *a heavy bag of groceries*

grocery ['grəusəri] *noun* general food shop; *he runs the grocery shop in the High Street*

groggy ['grɒgi] *adjective* unsteady, wobbly; *he still felt groggy after his injection*

groin [grɔɪn] *noun* place where the thighs join the abdomen; *he had a dull pain in his groin*; *she strained a muscle in her groin or a groin muscle*

groom [gru:m] **1** *noun* **(a)** person who looks after horses; *she got down from the horse and handed him over to a groom to deal with* **(b)** bridegroom, man who is getting married; *the groom looked nervously over his shoulder, wondering where the best man was* **2** *verb* **(a)** to make smart; *she was grooming her horse*; *a well-groomed young man* **(b)** to make ready; *he is being groomed to take his father's place in the family business*

grooming ['gru:mɪŋ] *noun* being smart and well-brought up; *his good grooming showed as he coped with the crowds at his sister's wedding*

groove [gru:v] *noun* wide line cut into a surface; *the door slides along a groove in the floor*; *the ridges on the nut have to fit into the grooves on the screw*; **to be stuck in a groove** = to be in a routine job, leading a dull life with no excitement

groovy ['gru:vi] *adjective (old slang)* fashionable; *look at that groovy pair of jeans* (NOTE: **groovier - grooviest**)

grope [grəʊp] *verb* to feel with your hands; *he groped in his pockets for his passport*; *it was pitch dark in the cellar and he had to grope for a light switch*; *he tried to grope the girls at the office party*

gross [grəʊs] **1** *adjective* **(a)** total, with no deductions; **gross domestic product (GDP)** = value of goods and services paid for inside a country; **gross income** *or* **gross salary** = salary which is paid without any deductions for tax, insurance, etc.; **gross national product (GNP)** = value of goods and services paid for in a country, including income earned in other countries; **gross profit** = profit before deducting overheads, tax, etc.; **gross weight** = full weight, including the container and packing material (NOTE: the opposite in this meaning is **net**) **(b)** very great and bad; *a gross miscarriage of justice* (NOTE: **grosser - grossest**; in meanings (a) and (b)) **(c)** ugly and vulgar; *he's such a horrible man - he's gross* **2** *adverb* with no deductions; *his salary is paid gross* **3** *verb* to make a gross turnover; *the film grossed $25m in its first week* **4** *noun* twelve dozen (i.e. 144); *we ordered two gross of the bars of chocolate* (NOTE: plural is **gross**)

grotesque [grə'tesk] *adjective* **(a)** strange and ugly; *we got a really grotesque present from our Spanish landlady* **(b)** unnatural and unpleasant; *it was grotesque to see her at the funeral*; *grotesque abuses of justice were commonplace during the civil war*

grotto ['grɒtəʊ] *noun* picturesque cave, especially one made as a garden decoration; *she decorated her grotto with seashells*

ground [graʊnd] **1** *noun* **(a)** soil or earth; *you should dig the ground in the autumn*; *the house is built on wet ground*; *it has been so dry that the ground is hard* **(b)** surface of the earth; *the factory was burnt to the ground*; *there were no seats, so we had to sit on the ground*; *she lay down on the ground and went to sleep*; **to get a project off the ground** = to get a project started; *he played an important role in getting the project off the ground see also* EAR **(c)** land used for a special purpose; *a football ground*; *a sports ground*; *a cricket ground*; *a show ground*; *see also*

FAIRGROUND (d) space between competitors in a race; **to lose ground to someone** = to fall behind someone; **to gain ground** = to catch up on someone; *see also* GROUNDS **2** *verb* **(a)** to put or keep on the ground; *after the mechanical failure was discovered, the fleet of aircraft was grounded* **(b)** to base; *our teaching system is grounded on years of practice* **(c)** US to connect an electrical appliance to the earth; *household appliances should be properly grounded* (NOTE: British English is to **earth**) **(d)** *see also* GRIND

ground beef ['graʊnd 'bi:f] *noun usually US* beef which has been minced into very small pieces; *hamburgers are made of ground beef fried and served in a bun* (NOTE: British English is **minced beef** *or* **mince**)

ground floor ['graʊnd 'flɔ:] *noun* floor (in a shop, block of flats, etc.) which is level with the street; *the men's department is on the ground floor*; *he has a ground-floor office*; **lower ground floor** = **BASEMENT** (NOTE: in America the **ground floor** is called the **first floor**)

groundhog ['graʊndhɒg] *noun* woodchuck, a fat American rodent which lives in holes in the ground and hibernates in winter; **Groundhog Day** = February 2nd, the day when groundhogs are supposed to come out of hibernation, marking the beginning of spring (if the groundhog sees his shadow, he goes back to hibernate for another six weeks because winter has not come to an end)

grounding ['graʊndɪŋ] *noun* basic instruction; *she has a good grounding in pharmacy*

groundless ['graʊndləs] *adjective* without any reason; *her fears proved to be groundless*

ground level ['graʊnd 'levəl] *noun* floor on the level of the ground; *the perfume department is at ground level*

ground rule ['graʊnd 'ru:l] *noun* basic rule; *all staff should follow the ground rules for dealing with complaints by customers*

grounds ['graʊndz] *noun* **(a)** land around a big house, institution, etc.; *the police searched the grounds of the school for the weapon*; *the village fête is held in the grounds of the castle* **(b)** reasons; *does he have any grounds for complaint*; *what grounds have you got for saying that?*; *do they have sufficient grounds to sue us?* **(c)** **coffee grounds** = crushed coffee beans left at the bottom of a filter or coffee jug after the coffee has been served

groundwork ['graʊndwɜ:k] *noun* preliminary work; *we spent months laying the groundwork for the new partnership* (NOTE: no plural)

group [gru:p] *noun* **(a)** a number of people or things taken together; *a group of houses in the valley*; *groups of people gathered in the street*; *she is leading a group of businessmen on a tour of Italian factories*; *there are reduced prices for groups of 30 and over* **(b)** way of classifying things; *these drugs belong to the same group*; **age group** = people of the same age; *children in the 5 to 10 age group*; **blood group** = people with the same type of blood **(c)** people playing music together; *he plays in a jazz group*; *she's the lead singer in a pop group* **(d)** several different companies linked together; *the Shell group of companies*; *a major travel group*

grouping ['gru:pɪŋ] *noun* putting together in a group; **blood grouping** = classifying patients according to their blood groups

group therapy ['gruːp 'θerəpi] *noun* type of therapy where a group of people with the same sort of problems meet together with a therapist to discuss their condition and try to help each other; *he is in a group of alcoholics, undergoing group therapy*

grouse [graʊs] **1** *noun* **(a)** *(informal)* grumble; *all we heard at dinner were his grouses about the office* **(b)** small dark game bird, found in the north of England and Scotland; *we had grouse for supper; they shot six brace of grouse yesterday; grouse shooting starts on August 12th* (NOTE: plural is **grouse**; two of the birds are called **a brace of grouse**) **2** *verb* *(informal)* to grouse about something = to grumble about something; *he's always grousing about the atmosphere in the office*

grove [grəʊv] *noun* small group of trees; *an olive grove or a grove of olive trees*

grovel ['grɒvəl] *verb* to behave very respectfully towards someone, to behave as if you were someone's slave; *he wrote a grovelling letter of apology*

grow [grəʊ] *verb* **(a)** to live (as a plant); *there was grass growing in the middle of the road; roses grow well in our garden* **(b)** to make plants grow; *he grows all his vegetables in his garden; we are going to grow some cabbages this year* **(c)** to become taller *or* bigger; *he's grown a lot taller since I last saw him; rubbing the scalp will encourage your hair to grow; the profit has grown to £1m; the town's population is growing very fast* **(d)** to become gradually; *she grew weak with hunger; the nights are growing colder now; all the time he grew richer and richer* (NOTE: **growing - grew** [gruː] - **grown** [grəʊn])

grower ['grəʊə] *noun* farmer who grows a certain type of plant; *an apple grower; a tomato grower*

grow into ['grəʊ 'ɪntʊ] *verb* to become; *she was a tubby little baby but soon grew into a beautiful tall slim girl*

growl [graʊl] **1** *noun* angry sound made by a dog, or by a person; *as he opened the door he heard a growl* **2** *verb* to make an angry sound; *the dog growled when he tried to take away its bone; when we asked the doorman if we could go in, he just growled 'yes'*

grown [grəʊn] *adjective* (person) full size; *a grown man like you shouldn't be afraid of a little spider* (NOTE: do not confuse with **groan**)

grown-up ['grəʊn 'ʌp] *noun* adult; *the family consists of three grown-ups and ten children; she has a grown-up daughter; the grown-ups had wine with their meal*

grow out of ['grəʊ 'aʊt ɒv] *verb* **(a)** to become bigger so that something doesn't fit; *he's grown out of his coat* **(b)** to become older, and so stop some bad habit; *he plays the drums all day long, but we hope it's something he'll grow out of*

growth [grəʊθ] *noun* increase in size; *the rapid growth of the population since 1980; they measured the tree's growth over the last fifty years;* **the country's economic growth** = rate at which a country's national income grows

grow up ['grəʊ 'ʌp] *verb* to become an adult; *what does your son want to do when he grows up?*

grub [grʌb] *noun* **(a)** little worm which is a young insect; *birds were searching for grubs under the bushes* **(b)** *(slang)* food; *the grub in the canteen is so awful that I take sandwiches to work;* **pub grub** = the sort of food you can get in a pub

---

COMMENT: pub grub will include cold salads, with slices of cooked meat such as chicken or beef, and hot food such as shepherd's pie, chilli con carne, cauliflower cheese, etc. You will almost certainly find sandwiches, and ploughman's lunches

---

grubby ['grʌbi] *adjective* dirty; *a grubby little boy came and asked for money; he was clutching a sweet in his grubby palm* (NOTE: **grubbier - grubbiest**)

grudge [grʌdʒ] **1** *noun* **to have** *or* **bear a grudge against someone** = to have bad feelings about someone because of something he did to you in the past; *since her bag was snatched in Rome, she has a grudge against Italians; he has been nursing a grudge against his boss for the last six years* **2** *verb* to grudge someone something = to be unwilling to give someone something or be angry that he has something; *I grudge having to pay so much for so-called expert advice; no one grudges him his success in the tennis championship*

grudging ['grʌdʒɪŋ] *adjective* reluctant; *they gave him grudging permission to go on holiday; they got a grudging acceptance from the seller*

gruelling ['grʊəlɪŋ] *adjective* tiring; *a gruelling climb*

gruesome ['gruːsəm] *adjective* horrific; *the police made a gruesome discovery in the cellar*

gruff [grʌf] *adjective* harsh and rude (voice or manner); *he told them to go away in a gruff voice* (NOTE: **gruffer - gruffest**)

gruffly ['grʌfli] *adverb* in a gruff way; *the policeman told them gruffly to go away*

grumble ['grʌmbl] **1** *noun* complaint about something; *do you have any grumbles about the food?;* **she's full of grumbles** = she is always complaining **2** *verb* to grumble about something = to complain about something; *he's always grumbling about the noise from the flat above*

grumpy ['grʌmpi] *adjective* bad-tempered; *our boss is always grumpy on Monday mornings* (NOTE: **grumpier - grumpiest**)

grunge [grʌndʒ] *noun* **the grunge look** = untidy and dirty-looking fashion

grunt [grʌnt] **1** *noun* noise like a pig; *he gave a grunt and went on reading his newspaper* **2** *verb* **(a)** *(of a pig)* to make a noise; *the pigs were grunting and squealing in their pen; see also* BLEAT, LOW, NEIGH **(b)** to make a bad-tempered noise, to speak in an unclear way; *I asked if we could have a glass of water and the waiter just grunted; she grunted something and slammed the door*

GSOH = GOOD SENSE OF HUMOUR

guarantee [gærən'tiː] **1** *noun* **(a)** legal document in which someone states that something is going to happen; *the travel agent could not give a guarantee that we would be accommodated in the hotel mentioned in the brochure* **(b)** legal document which promises that a machine is in good condition and will work without problems for a certain length of time; *the fridge is sold with a twelve-month guarantee;* **under guarantee** = covered by a guarantee; *the car is still under guarantee, so the manufacturers will pay for the repairs* (NOTE: also called a **warranty**) **(c)** firm promise that something will happen; *we can't give you a guarantee that the weather will be fine; there is no* guarantee that he will get a job even if he gets through the training course successfully **2** *verb* **(a)** to give a legal assurance that something will work, that something will be done; *the product is guaranteed for twelve months* **(b)** to make a firm promise that something will happen; *I can guarantee that the car will give you no trouble*; *we can almost guarantee good weather in the Caribbean at this time of year*

guaranteed [gærən'ti:d] *adjective* which has been promised legally; *guaranteed delivery within 24 hours*; **guaranteed minimum wage** = minimum wage which all employers must pay

guarantor [gærən'tɔ:] *noun* person who promises to pay the debts of another person; *he stood guarantor for his brother*

guard [gɑ:d] **1** *noun* **(a)** **to be on guard** *or* **to keep guard** = to be looking out for danger; *you must be on your guard against burglars at all times* **(b)** person who protects, often a soldier; *security guards patrol the factory at night*; *our squad is on guard duty tonight*; **changing of the guard** = military ceremony, where one shift of soldiers is replaced by another on guard duty at a palace, etc.; *at 10.30 we're going to watch the changing of the guard at Buckingham Palace* **(c)** man in charge of a train; *the guard helped my put my bike into his van* (NOTE: American English is **conductor**); **guard's van** = van in a train, where the guard is **2** *verb* to protect; *the prison is guarded at all times*

guard dog ['gɑ:d 'dɒg] *noun* dog used to guard a house or other buildings; *Alsatians are often used as guard dogs*

guardian ['gɑ:diən] *noun* person who protects, especially someone who has been legally appointed to look after a child; *when his parents died, his uncle became his guardian*; **guardian angel** = person who looks after and protects someone; *she's his guardian angel and tries to look after him all the time*

guardsman ['gɑ:dzmən] *noun* soldier in a regiment of guards; *the guardsmen marched past in their red uniforms US*; **National Guardsman** = member of the National Guard (NOTE: plural is **guardsmen**)

guerrilla *or* **guerilla** [gə'rɪlə] *noun* soldier who is not part of a regular national army; *the guerrillas fought their way to the capital*; **guerrilla warfare** = type of warfare fought by guerrillas, who attack in small groups in unexpected places (NOTE: do not confuse with **gorilla**)

guess [ges] **1** *noun* trying to give the right answer or figure; *go on - make a guess!*; *at a guess, I'd say it weighs about 10 kilos*; *it is anyone's guess* = no one really knows what is the right answer (NOTE: plural is **guesses**) **2** *verb* **(a)** to try to give the right answer or figure; *I would guess it's about six o'clock*; *neither of them guessed the right answer*; *he guessed right*; *I've bought you a present - shut your eyes and guess what it is* **(b)** *US* to think; *I guess the plane's going to be late*

guest [gest] *noun* **(a)** person who is asked to your home or to an event; *we had a very lively party with dozens of guests*; *none of the guests left the party early*; **be my guest** = help yourself, I'm paying **(b)** person staying in a hotel or guesthouse; **guests' lounge** = special lounge for guests in a hotel

guesthouse ['gesthaʊs] *noun* private house, which takes several guests (like a small hotel); *we stayed three weeks in a guesthouse on the sea front*

guffaw [gə'fɔ:] **1** *noun* loud coarse laugh; *guffaws came from the audience as soon as she started to speak* **2** *verb* to laugh loudly; *the audience guffawed as she tried to ride the bicycle*

guidance ['gaɪdəns] *noun* advice; *an instructor will be on hand to give you guidance*; *he asked the bank manager for guidance about how to fill in his tax form*; **moral guidance** = advice as to what is right or wrong behaviour; *part of a teacher's job is to give the students moral guidance*

guide [gaɪd] **1** *noun* **(a)** person who shows the way; *they used local farmers as guides through the forest* **(b)** person who shows tourists round a place; *the guide showed us over the castle or showed us round the castle*; *the museum guide spoke so fast that we couldn't understand what she was saying* **(c)** book which gives information; *a guide to Athens*; *a guide to the butterflies of Europe* **(d)** the **Guides** *or* **Girl Guides** = organization for girls; *she's joined the Guides*; **a Guide** = a member of the Girl Guides (NOTE: part of the same organization as the **Boy Scouts**) **2** *verb* to show the way; to show tourists round a place; *she guided us up the steps in the dark*; *he guided us round the castle*

guidebook ['gaɪdbʊk] *noun* book with information about a place; *the guidebook lists three hotels by the beach*

guide dog ['gaɪd 'dɒg] *noun* dog which has been trained to lead a blind person; *the only dogs allowed into the restaurant are guide dogs*

guidelines ['gaɪdlaɪnz] *noun* general advice on what to do; *if you follow the government guidelines, you should not have any trouble*; *the minister has issued a new set of guidelines about city planning*

guild [gɪld] *noun* association of craftsmen; *he's a member of the guild of master bakers* (NOTE: do not confuse with **gild**)

guilder ['gɪldə] *noun* currency used in the Netherlands, also called the 'florin'; *the book costs 35fl or 35 guilders* (NOTE: usually written **fl** before or after figures: **fl25, 25fl**)

guildhall ['gɪldhɔ:l] *noun* main civic hall in a town; *the reception was held in the guildhall*

> COMMENT: guildhalls were centres for merchants in the Middle Ages. The Guildhall in London is used for civic receptions by the Lord Mayor

guile [gaɪl] *noun* cunning, the use of trickery to deceive people; *he had to use all his guile to get the committee to pass his proposals*

guillotine ['gɪləti:n] **1** *noun* **(a)** machine which was used in France for executing criminals by cutting off their heads **(b)** machine for cutting paper; *be careful when using the guillotine, so as not to cut your fingers* **(c)** motion in the House of Commons to end a debate at a certain time **2** *verb* (*formerly, in France*) to cut someone's head off as a punishment; *many aristocrats were guillotined during the French Revolution*

guilt [gɪlt] *noun* **(a)** state of having committed a crime; *the prisoner admitted his guilt* **(b)** being or feeling responsible for; *the whole group bears the guilt for his death* (NOTE: do not confuse with **gilt**)

guilty ['gɪlti] *adjective* **(a)** who has committed a crime; *he was found guilty of murder*; *the jury decided*

she was not guilty (b) feeling unhappy because you have done something wrong; *I feel very guilty about not having written to you* (NOTE: **guiltier - guiltiest**)

guinea ['gɪnɪ] *noun* old coin worth 21 shillings (£1.05 in modern currency); *the horse was sold for 10,000 guineas*

> COMMENT: the guinea is still used in auction prices, and in names of prizes for horse races

guinea pig ['gɪnɪpɪg] *noun* **(a)** little furry animal kept as a pet; *she keeps guinea pigs in a hutch in the garden* **(b)** person used in an experiment; *the hospital is advertising for guinea pigs to test the new drug; we're using her as a guinea pig to see if the instructions for making the cake work*

guise [gaɪz] *noun (formal)* appearance, which is sometimes misleading; *the recipe appears in different guises in various cookery books;* **in the guise of =** pretending to be; *the drug was sent in the guise of packets of sugar*

guitar [gɪ'tɑː] *noun* musical instrument with six strings, played with the fingers; *he plays the guitar in a pop group*

guitarist [gɪ'tɑːrɪst] *noun* person who plays a guitar; *he's the lead guitarist with a pop group*

gulch [gʌltʃ] *noun US* narrow rocky ravine with a stream at the bottom; *they rode down into the gulch to cross the stream* (NOTE: plural is **gulches**)

gulf [gʌlf] *noun* area of sea partly surrounded by land; *the Gulf of Mexico;* **the Gulf =** the Persian Gulf (the sea near Iran, Iraq, Saudi Arabia, etc.); *the tanker was carrying crude oil from the Gulf*

Gulf Stream ['gʌlf 'striːm] *noun* warm current which crosses the Atlantic from west to east

gull [gʌl] *noun* any of several types of common white sea birds; *flocks of gulls followed the fishing boat; they were woken by the cries of gulls in the harbour* (NOTE: also called **seagull**)

gullet ['gʌlɪt] *noun* the tube in your throat down which food and drink passes from the mouth to the stomach; *she had a piece of bread stuck in her gullet* (NOTE: also called **oesophagus**)

gullible ['gʌlɪbl] *adjective* ready to believe anything; *he is so gullible: he bought a bottle of the oil because the salesman told him it would make his hair grow again*

gully ['gʌli] *noun* small ravine; *the horsemen rode down the gully towards their camp* (NOTE: plural is **gullies**)

gulp [gʌlp] **1** *noun* quick swallow; *he swallowed the glass of wine in one gulp* **2** *verb* to swallow fast; *she gulped and went onto the stage; he gulped down his drink and ran for the bus*

gum [gʌm] **1** *noun* **(a)** glue; *she spread gum on the back of the photo and stuck it onto a sheet of paper* **(b)** flesh around the base of your teeth; *brushing your teeth every day is good for your gums* **(c) (chewing) gum =** sweet substance which you chew but do not swallow; *he slowly took a piece of gum out of his mouth and put it in the ashtray; I've got some gum stuck to my shoe* **(d)** small fruit sweet which can be sucked until it melts away; *a packet of fruit gums* **2** *verb* to stick with glue; *she gummed the pictures onto a sheet of paper* (NOTE: **gumming - gummed**)

gumbo ['gʌmbəʊ] *noun US* soup made with chicken or fish and vegetables

gummed [gʌmd] *adjective* with glue on it; **gummed label =** label with dry glue on it, which you have to lick to make it stick (NOTE: labels with sticky glue on them are called **sticky labels**)

gumshoe ['gʌmʃuː] *noun US (slang)* detective, especially a private detective; *some gumshoe working for the family of the dead man called me*

gun [gʌn] **1** *noun* **(a)** weapon which shoots bullets; *the robber pulled out a gun; she grabbed his gun and shot him dead;* **starting gun =** gun fired to start a race *(informal)* **to jump the gun =** to start too quickly; *the law on Sunday opening starts in a month's time, but some shops have already jumped the gun;* **to stick to your guns =** to keep to your point of view even if everyone says you are wrong **(b)** large weapon which shoots shells; *we heard the guns firing all night; the ship trained its guns on the town* **(c)** small device which you hold in your hand to spray paint, glue, etc.; *a spray gun gives an even coating of paint* **2** *verb* **(a)** to **gun someone down =** to shoot and kill someone; *the policeman was gunned down in broad daylight* **(b)** *(informal)* to be **gunning for someone =** to try to find a reason to criticize someone; *the papers are gunning for the minister* (NOTE: **gunning - gunned**)

gunfire ['gʌnfaɪə] *noun* shooting of guns; *we could hear gunfire in the distance;* **under gunfire =** being shot at; *he's always very calm, even under gunfire*

gunman ['gʌnmən] *noun* armed robber; *the gunman pulled out a revolver and started shooting* (NOTE: plural is **gunmen**)

gunner ['gʌnə] *noun* soldier who uses artillery guns; *as soon as the order was given, the gunners raced to their guns*

gunpoint ['gʌnpɔɪnt] *noun* **at gunpoint =** with a gun being pointed at you; *he was held at gunpoint by robbers*

gunpowder ['gʌnpaʊdə] *noun* chemical substance used as an explosive and to make fireworks; **the Gunpowder Plot =** plot in 1605 to blow up the Houses of Parliament when King James I was present; *after the Gunpowder Plot, the conspirators were rapidly arrested see also* GUY FAWKES NIGHT

gunshot ['gʌnʃɒt] *noun* firing of a gun; *we heard three gunshots from the street*

gurgle ['gɜːgl] **1** *noun* bubbling sound; *the gurgle of the stream between the rocks* **2** *verb* to make a bubbling sound; *the water gurgled in the pipes; the baby was gurgling in his pram*

guru ['guːruː] *noun* **(a)** respected teacher, often a religious or spiritual teacher; *he was the great guru of the civil disobedience movement* **(b)** *(informal)* person who gives advice; *she's one of the Prime Minister's media gurus;* **fashion guru =** person who gives advice on what clothes are fashionable

gush [gʌʃ] **1** *noun* **(a)** rush of liquid; *a sudden gush of water came out of the pipe* **(b)** *(informal)* effusive praise; *I can't stand all this gush about babies* **2** *verb* **(a)** to spout out; *oil gushed from the hole in the pipeline* **(b)** *(informal)* to speak effusively; *she tends to gush over babies*

gust [gʌst] **1** *noun* **gust of wind =** sudden rush of wind; *a sudden gust blew my hat off* **2** *verb* to blow in gusts; *the wind was gusting at up to 70 miles an hour*

gusto ['gʌstəʊ] *noun* energy and enthusiasm; *they joined in the singing with gusto* (NOTE: no plural)

gusty ['gʌsti] *adjective* with the wind blowing in gusts; *a gusty wind blew leaves into corners*; *it was a gusty March day when we got married*

gut [gʌt] **1** *noun* **(a)** *(informal)* **gut** *or* **guts** = intestines, the tube which passes from the stomach to the anus in which food is digested as it passes through; *he complained of pain in the gut*; **gut reaction** = instinctive reaction; *my gut reaction is to vote for the woman candidate*; **I hate his guts** = I dislike him a lot **(b)** *(informal)* **guts** = courage; *he had the guts to tell the boss what he should do* **2** *verb* **(a)** to remove the insides of an animal or fish before cooking; *the pigeons have not been gutted*; *women stood in the market gutting sardines* *(informal)* **to feel gutted** = to feel extremely upset; *when he missed the penalty kick we all felt gutted* **(b)** to destroy the inside of a building totally; *the house was gutted by fire* (NOTE: gutting - gutted)

gutter ['gʌtə] *noun* **(a)** channel by the side of a road to take away rainwater; *pieces of paper and leaves blowing about in the gutter*; **he was brought up in the gutter** = he was brought up in very poor circumstances **(b)** open pipe under the edge of a roof to catch rainwater; *it rained so hard the gutters overflowed*

guy [gaɪ] **1** *noun* **(a)** *(informal)* man; *she married a guy from Texas*; *the boss is a very friendly guy*; *hey, you guys, come and look at this!* (NOTE: in American English, **you guys** can be used when speaking to men or women) *(in a story or film)* **bad guy** = villain; **good guy** = hero; *the good guys always win* **(b)** rope which holds a tent; *make sure the guys are tight before the storm comes* **(c)** figure of a man burnt on Bonfire Night, 5th November; *the children are collecting clothes to make a guy*; *see note at* GUY FAWKES NIGHT

Guy Fawkes Night ['gaɪ 'fɔːks 'naɪt] *noun* 5th November, when the attempt by Guy Fawkes to blow up the Houses of Parliament in 1605 is remembered; *Guy Fawkes Night is always a busy time for the fire brigade* (NOTE: also called **Bonfire Night**)

COMMENT: bonfires are burnt with a figure of a man on top and fireworks are set off. Children collect money in advance by standing with the guy, and asking for a 'penny for the guy'. See also the rhyme at REMEMBER

guy rope ['gaɪ 'rəʊp] *noun* rope which holds a tent; *make sure the guy ropes are taut*; *he went out in the dark and tripped over a guy rope*

guzzle ['gʌzl] *verb (informal)* to eat or drink greedily; *she's been guzzling cakes all afternoon*

gym *or* **gymnasium** [dʒɪm *or* dʒɪm'neɪziəm] *noun* hall for indoor sports and athletics; *because it rained, we had to hold the school fête in the gym*; *the room in the basement has been fitted out as a gymnasium*

gymkhana [dʒɪm'kɑːnə] *noun* **(a)** GB horse riding competition; *she's competing in the riding club gymkhana* **(b)** US car driving competition; *he won a prize in the local gymkhana, driving his old Ford*

gymnast ['dʒɪmnæst] *noun* athlete who is expert at gymnastics; *an Olympic gymnast*

gymnastic [dʒɪm'næstɪk] *adjective* referring to gymnastics; *her gymnastic ability earned her a gold medal*

gymnastics [dʒɪm'næstɪks] *noun* physical exercises, as a competitive sport; *the children were doing gymnastics in the school yard*; *she is a member of the Romanian gymnastics team* (NOTE: takes a singular verb)

gynaecological US **gynecological** [gaɪnɪkə'lɒdʒɪkl] *adjective* referring to gynaecology; *he gave her a gynaecological examination*

gynaecologist US **gynecologist** [gaɪnɪ'kɒlədʒɪst] *noun* doctor who specializes in disorders of women; *she made an appointment to see the gynaecologist*

gynaecology US **gynecology** [gaɪnɪ'kɒlədʒɪ] *noun* study of women's disorders; *he's studying gynaecology as part of his university course*

gypsy ['dʒɪpsi] *noun* member of a wandering people, perhaps originating in India; *gypsies have camped at the bottom of our field* (NOTE: plural is **gypsies**; also spelled **gipsy**)

gyrate [dʒaɪ'reɪt] *verb* to turn round and round fast; *watching the gyrating lights makes me feel dizzy*

gyratory [dʒaɪ'reɪtəri] *adjective* which goes round in a circle; **gyratory system** = arrangement of roundabouts and one-way streets to take traffic round an area

Hh

H, h [eɪtʃ] eighth letter of the alphabet, between G and I; *the sign for a hospital is a white H on a blue background*

ha [hɑː] **(a)** *interjection showing surprise*; *ha! there's a mistake on page one of the book!* **(b)** *abbreviation for* HECTARE

haberdasher [ˈhæbədæʃə] *noun* **(a)** *(old)* person who sells things for sewing, such as buttons, needles, ribbons, thread **(b)** *US* person who sells men's clothes

haberdashery [ˈhæbədæʃri] *noun* small articles, like needles, ribbon, etc. (NOTE: American English is **notions**)

habit [ˈhæbɪt] *noun* regular way of acting; *he has the habit of going to bed at 9 o'clock and reading until midnight*; **to develop the habit** *or* **to get into the habit of doing something** = to start to do something regularly; *he's getting into the habit of playing football every week*; **to break the habit** = to stop doing something which you used to do regularly; *I haven't had a cigarette for six months - I think I've broken the habit!*; **bad habit** *or* **nasty habit** = regular way of doing something which is not nice; *she has the bad habit of biting her nails*; **from force of habit** = because this is what you do normally; *he switched off all the lights from force of habit*

habitat [ˈhæbɪtæt] *noun* place where an animal or plant lives; *this is an ideal habitat for butterflies*

habitation [hæbɪˈteɪʃn] *noun* place where someone lives; **unfit for human habitation** = not of good enough standard for people to live in; *the house has been condemned as unfit for human habitation*

habitual [həˈbɪtʃuəl] *adjective* **(a)** usual; *she was sitting in her habitual place at the bar* **(b)** regular, who does something by habit; *a habitual liar*; *a habitual offender*

hack [hæk] **1** *noun (slang)* journalist; *a bunch of hacks followed her everywhere* **2** *verb* **(a)** to chop roughly; *he hacked at the tree with an axe* **(b)** to enter a computer system illegally; *he hacked into the bank's computer*

hacker [ˈhækə] *noun* person who enters a computer system via a modem illegally; *to defeat the hackers, companies try to find sophisticated ways of encoding their programs*; *the hackers managed to hack into the government's research data*

hackneyed [ˈhæknɪd] *adjective* (phrase) which is used too often; *no one laughed at his hackneyed jokes*

hacksaw [ˈhæksɔː] *noun* saw for cutting metal; *he used a hacksaw to cut through the bars of the window*

had, hadn't [hæd or ˈhædənt] *see* HAVE

haddock [ˈhædək] *noun* white sea fish; *bake the haddock and serve it with a white sauce*; **smoked haddock** = common smoked fish, coloured yellow (NOTE: plural is **haddock**)

haem- [hiːm] *prefix referring to blood* (NOTE: words beginning with the prefix **haem-** are written **hem-** in US English)

haemoglobin (Hb) *US* **hemoglobin** [hiːməˈɡləubɪn] *noun* protein in red blood cells which gives blood its red colour; *haemoglobin absorbs oxygen and transports it to the tissues*

haemophilia *US* **hemophilia** [hiːməuˈfɪliə] *noun* disease of the blood where the patient's blood clots very slowly, and lengthy and fatal bleeding can occur from the slightest cut; *in people with haemophilia, blood clots very slowly*

> COMMENT: haemophilia only occurs in men. It is passed on a recessive gene to males but females are the carriers

haemophiliac *US* **hemophiliac** [hiːməuˈfɪliæk] *noun* person who has haemophilia; *haemophiliacs can be treated with clotting agents*

haemorrhage *US* **hemorrhage** [ˈhemərɪdʒ] **1** *noun* **(a)** bleeding where a large quantity of blood is lost, especially bleeding from a burst blood vessel; *she had a haemorrhage and was rushed to hospital*; *he died of a brain haemorrhage* **(b)** loss of funds, members, etc.; *we are trying to stem the haemorrhage of the company's resources* **2** *verb* to lose a lot of blood; *the injured man was haemorrhaging from the mouth*

haemorrhoids *US* **hemorrhoids** [ˈhemərɔɪdz] *noun* swollen veins near the anus (NOTE: also called **piles**)

haft [hɑːft] *noun* handle of a knife or axe; *he grasped the axe by its haft and swung it over his head*

haggis [ˈhæɡɪs] *noun* Scottish dish, made of inner parts of a sheep cooked in a bag made from the sheep's stomach; *in Scotland haggis is served on special occasions*

haggle [ˈhæɡl] *verb* to bargain or argue about prices and terms to try to reduce them; *to buy anything in the local market you will have to learn to haggle*; *after two hours' haggling over the price we bought the carpet* (NOTE: you haggle **with** someone **over** something)

ha ha 1 *interjection* [hʌ ˈhɑː] **(a)** showing that you find something funny; *ha ha!, what a funny hat!* **(b)** showing that you find something surprising; *ha ha!, I've caught you stealing from the cash box again!* **2** *noun* [ˈhɑːhɑː]; **ha-ha** = fence at the bottom of a ditch so as not to spoil the view of a landscape; *the lawn in front of the house ends in a ha-ha*

hail [heɪl] **1** *noun* frozen rain; *I thought the hail was going to break the windscreen* (NOTE: do not confuse with **hale**) **2** *verb* **(a)** to fall as frozen rain; *it hailed for ten minutes and then the sun came out* **(b)** to wave, call, etc., to make a taxi stop; *he whistled to hail a taxi* **(c) to hail from** = to come from; *he hails from Montana*

hailstone ['heɪlstəʊn] *noun* piece of frozen rain; *hailstones bounced off the roof of the car*; *huge hailstones covered the road*

hailstorm ['heɪlstɔːm] *noun* storm during which hail falls; *after the hailstorm, the road was white with hailstones*

hair [heə] *noun* **(a)** one of the long threads growing on the body of a human or animal; *waiter, there's a hair in my soup!*; *the cat has left hairs all over the cushion*; *he's beginning to get some grey hairs*; **to split hairs** = to try to find minute differences between things when arguing; *stop splitting hairs, you know you're in the wrong* (NOTE: the plural in this meaning is **hairs**) **(b)** mass of hairs growing on your head; *she has long brown hair or her hair is long and brown*; *she always brushes her hair before washing it*; *you must get your hair cut*; *he's had his hair cut short*; *use some hair spray to keep your hair in place* (informal) **keep your hair on!** = don't get annoyed; **to let your hair down** = to relax and enjoy yourself; *when the exams are finished we're all going to let our hair down* (NOTE: no plural in this meaning)

hairbrush ['heəbrʌʃ] *noun* stiff brush for brushing your hair (NOTE: plural is **hairbrushes**)

haircut ['heəkʌt] *noun* cutting of the hair on your head; *you need a haircut*; *he went to get a haircut*

hairdo ['heəduː] *noun* (informal) style of hair; *she had a new hairdo for the party* (NOTE: usually used referring to women)

hairdresser ['heədresə] *noun* person who cuts, washes, etc., your hair; *he's the President's wife's hairdresser*; *the hairdresser at the new salon is really good*

hairdresser's ['heədresəz] *noun* shop where you have your hair cut, washed, etc.; *I must go to the hairdresser's*; *she recommended her hairdresser's*

hairdressing ['heədresɪŋ] *noun* action of cutting and washing hair; *she was trained in hairdressing*; **a hairdressing salon** = a ladies' hairdresser's

hair drier *or* **hair dryer** ['heədraɪə] *noun* machine for drying wet hair; *each bathroom in the hotel is equipped with a hair dryer*

hairnet ['heənet] *noun* net worn over your hair to keep it in place

hairpiece ['heəpiːs] *noun* small wig, a piece of false hair worn to cover up a place where you are bald; *don't tell anyone, but I think the boss has a hairpiece* (NOTE: also called a **hairpiece**)

hairpin ['heəpɪn] *noun* piece of bent wire used to keep your hair in place; *I need a few more hairpins to get the shape right*; **hairpin bend** = sharp bend on a mountain road (NOTE: also called **grip**; American English is **bobby-pin**)

hair-raising ['heəreɪzɪŋ] *adjective* frightening; *travelling upside down on the fairground ride was a hair-raising experience*

hairstyle ['heəstaɪl] *noun* way of cutting and styling hair; *I have decided to change my hairstyle*; *what do you think of my new hairstyle?*

hairy ['heəri] *adjective* **(a)** covered with hairs; *a hairy dog*; *he's got hairy arms* **(b)** (informal) frightening and dangerous; *crossing the Alps in a snowstorm was the hairiest ride I've ever had* (NOTE: **hairier - hairiest**)

hake [heɪk] *noun* large white sea fish (NOTE: plural is **hake**)

halcyon ['hælsiən] *adjective* (old) beautiful and happy (time); *the halcyon days of summer*; *the halcyon days of youth*

hale [heɪl] *adjective* **hale and hearty** = fit and well; *my grandmother is still hale and hearty at the grand old age of 92* (NOTE: do not confuse with **hail**)

half [hɑːf] **1** *noun* **(a)** one of two parts which are the same in size; *she cut the orange in half*; *one half of the apple fell on the carpet*; *half of six is three* **(b)** (in sport) one of two parts of a match; *our team scored a goal in the first half*; *we thought we were going to win, and then they scored in the final minutes of the second half* **(c)** part of a financial year; *the sales in the first half were down on last year* **(d)** (informal) half a pint (of beer); *an orange juice and two halves of bitter, please* (NOTE: plural is **halves** [hɑːvz]) **2** *adjective* divided into two equal parts; **half a bottle of wine** = half of a bottle of wine; *we drank half a bottle of wine each*; **a half bottle of wine** = a small bottle of wine, containing half the amount of a normal bottle; *he ordered his meal and a half bottle of Bordeaux*; **half an hour** *or* **a half hour** = 30 minutes; *I'll be back in half an hour*; *the journey takes two and a half hours* **3** *adverb* **(a)** **half as big** = only 50 per cent of the size; *this book is half as big* *or* *half the size of that one*; **half as big again** = 50 per cent bigger **(b)** (informal) **not half** = certainly, of course; *this cheese doesn't half smell!*; *did you have a good time at the pub? - not half!*

half-brother ['hɑːfbrʌðə] *noun* a brother who has only one parent the same as another brother; *my half-brother and I never really got on together*

half-day ['hɑːfdeɪ] *adjective* half the day, morning or afternoon; *a half-day tour of the island*

half-dollar [hɑːf'dɒlə] *noun* US fifty cents

half-dozen *or* **half a dozen** [hɑːf'dʌzn *or* 'hɑːf ə 'dʌzn] *noun* six; *I bought half a dozen eggs*

half-empty [hɑːf'empti] *adjective* partly empty; *the bottle is half-empty*

half-full [hɑːf'fʊl] *adjective* partly full; *the room was only half-full*

half-hearted [hɑːf'hɑːtɪd] *adjective* not very enthusiastic; *come on, shout louder - don't be so half-hearted about it!*; *they made a half-hearted attempt to be friendly*

half-holiday ['hɑːf 'hɒlɪdeɪ] *noun* afternoon given as a special holiday to schoolchildren; *the head teacher gave us all a half-holiday on Wednesday*

half-hour ['hɑːf'aʊə] *noun* period of thirty minutes; *there's a bus to town every half-hour*

half-hourly [hɑːf'aʊəli] *adjective & adverb* every thirty minutes; *we have a half-hourly bus service to town*

half-mast ['hɑːf'mɑːst] *noun* **flying at half-mast** = flag raised only half-way up the flagpole, as a mark of respect; *on the day of the King's death flags flew at half-mast on all public buildings* (NOTE: American English is also **at half-staff**)

half past ['hɑːf 'pɑːst] *phrase* 30 minutes after an hour; *I have an appointment with the doctor at half past five* (= 5.30)

half price ['hɑːf 'praɪs] *noun & adjective* 50 per cent of the price; *tours at half price* *or* *half-price tours*; *to sell goods off at half price*; **half-price sale** = sale of all goods at 50% of the usual price; *the shop is holding a half-price sale*

half-sister ['hɑːfsɪstə] *noun* a sister who has only one parent the same as another sister; *she is actually only my half-sister, not my sister*

half-staff ['hɑːfstɑːf] *see* HALF-MAST

half-term ['hɑːf 'tɜːm] *noun* short holiday in the middle of a school term; *we took a few days' holiday at half-term*; *there are hordes of little children in the museums at half-term*; *compare* MIDTERM

half-time [hɑːf'taɪm] *noun* rest period in the middle of a game; *the half-time score or the score at half-time was three all*

halfway [hɑːf'weɪ] *adverb* in the middle; *come on, we're more than halfway there!*; **to meet someone halfway** *or* **to go halfway to meet someone** = to compromise; *I'll meet you halfway: I write the report and you present it at the meeting*

halfwit ['hɑːfwɪt] *noun (informal)* stupid fool; *you halfwit - that was my best coat you've just thrown away!*

half-year [hɑːf'jɜː] *noun* period of six months; **first half-year** *or* **second half-year** = first six months *or* second six months of a company's accounting year; *we look forward to some improvement in the second half-year*

half-yearly [hɑːf'jɜːli] *adjective & adverb* every six months; *a half-yearly report*; *we pay the account half-yearly*

halibut ['hælɪbət] *noun* large flat white fish; *we had grilled halibut* (NOTE: plural is **halibut**)

hall [hɔːl] *noun* **(a)** passageway at the entrance to a house, where you can leave your coat; *don't wait in the hall, come straight into the dining room*; *she left her umbrella in the hall* **(b)** large room for meetings; *the children have their dinner in the school hall*; **concert hall** = large building where concerts are given; **sports hall** = large building for playing indoor sports (like basketball or badminton); **town hall** = building where the town council meets and from where the town is governed; **village hall** = building in a village where meetings, shows, etc., can take place; *the flower show will be held in the village hall* **(c)** **hall of residence** = building where students live at university or college; *how many students live in halls of residence?*

halliard ['hæljəd] *see* HALYARD

hallmark ['hɔːlmɑːk] **1** *noun* **(a)** mark put on gold or silver items to show that the metal is of the correct quality; *the hallmark on this old silver spoon has almost been worn away* **(b)** it bears the hallmark of = it is characteristic of; *the murder bore all the hallmarks of a serial killing* **2** *verb* to put a hallmark on a piece of gold or silver; *the spoon was hallmarked in London in 1790*

hallo [hə'ləʊ] *see* HELLO

hallowed ['hæləʊd] *adjective* **(a)** made holy; *the cemetery is hallowed ground* **(b)** *(humorous)* highly respected; *she entered the hallowed gates of the school*

Halloween [hæləʊ'iːn] *noun* 31st October, eve of All Saints' Day, when witches and ghosts are said to be seen

COMMENT: traditionally, there are parties with apples hung on strings, and pumpkins hollowed out with faces cut into them and candles put inside them; children go from house to house to ask for sweets or fruit. See also TRICK OR TREAT

hallucination [həluːsɪ'neɪʃn] *noun* seeing an imaginary scene or hearing an imaginary sound as clearly as if it were really there; *he had hallucinations and went into a coma*; *she began to have hallucinations*; *hallucination is a common side-effect of the drug*

hallway ['hɔːlweɪ] *noun* hall, a passage at the entrance to a house or flat; *we were met in the hallway by large black dog*; *the postman leaves the letters for all the flats on a table in the hallway*

halo ['heɪləʊ] *noun* **(a)** glowing ring of light round the head of an angel or saint in a painting; *a painting of an archbishop with two saints, each with a golden halo* **(b)** corona, a ring round the moon or sun when seen through mist; *there's a halo round the moon - that means bad weather is on the way* (NOTE: plural is **haloes**)

halogen lamp *or* **halogen bulb** ['hælədʒən 'læmp *or* 'bʌlb] *noun* electric light or bulb, containing a gas which forms a salt when combined with a metal; *halogen lamps give a very bright light*

halt [hɔːlt] **1** *noun* complete stop; **to come to a halt** = to stop dead; *the lorry came to a halt just before the wall*; **to call a halt to something** = to make something stop; *he tried to call a halt to arguments inside the party*; **to grind to a halt** = to stop working gradually; *the whole plan ground to a halt for lack of funds* **2** *verb* to stop; *the car halted when the traffic lights went red*; *we are trying to halt experiments on animals*

halve [hɑːv] *verb* **(a)** to cut into two equal parts; *she halved the cake* **(b)** to reduce by half; *because the town has no cash, its budget has been halved*

halves [hɑːvz] *see* HALF

halyard ['hæljəd] *noun* rope used on a ship to pull up a sail or a flag; *the sailors hauled on the halyards*

ham [hæm] **1** *noun* **(a)** salted or smoked pork; *she cut three slices of ham*; *we had a ham and tomato salad*; *she had a ham sandwich for lunch*; **ham and eggs** = fried ham with fried eggs; **ham roll** = bread roll with ham in it **(b)** **(radio) ham** = person who sends and receives radio messages unofficially; *a radio ham picked up the signals* **(c)** *(old)* bad actor who uses too many gestures and speaks too loudly **2** *verb (informal)* **to ham it up** = to act a piece badly on purpose

hamburger ['hæmbɜːgə] *noun* minced beef grilled and served in a toasted roll; *the children want hamburgers and French fries for lunch*; **hamburger bar** = restaurant selling hamburgers; *we stopped at a hamburger bar*

hamlet ['hæmlət] *noun* little village; *villagers from the surrounding hamlets came to the town on market day*

hammer ['hæmə] **1** *noun* tool with a heavy head for knocking nails; *she hit the nail hard with the hammer*; **to go under the hammer** = to be sold by auction; *all his furniture went under the hammer last week* **2** *verb* **(a)** to knock something into something with a hammer; *it took him a few minutes to hammer the tent pegs into the ground* **(b)** to hit hard, as with a hammer; *he* hammered the table with his fist; she hammered on the door with her stick **(c) to hammer it into someone** = to try to make someone understand by repeating; they're trying to hammer it into schoolchildren that drugs are dangerous

hammering ['hæmərɪŋ] *noun* heavy defeat; *they took a hammering when they played against last year's champions*

hammer out ['hæmər 'aʊt] *verb* **to hammer out an agreement** = to go through long and difficult negotiations in order to reach agreement on something

hammock ['hæmək] *noun* bed made from a piece of canvas hanging between two hooks; *she spent the afternoon lying in a hammock in the shade, drinking lemonade*

hamper ['hæmpə] **1** *noun* large basket; *we packed the hamper with food for the picnic* **2** *verb* to get in the way; *lack of funds is hampering our development project*

hamster ['hæmstə] *noun* small furry animal, kept as a pet; *they keep the hamster in a cage in the classroom*

hamstring ['hæmstrɪŋ] *noun* group of tendons behind the knee, which link the thigh muscle to the bones in the lower leg; *he can't play because of a pulled hamstring; an old hamstring injury stopped him playing*

hand [hænd] **1** *noun* **(a)** part of the body at the end of each arm, which you use for holding things; *she was carrying a cup of tea in each hand; she held out her hand, asking for money;* **to shake hands** = to hold someone's hand to show you are pleased to meet them or to show that an agreement has been reached; *the visitors shook hands and the meeting started;* **to shake hands on a deal** = to shake hands to show that a deal has been agreed; **to give someone a hand** *or* **lend a hand with something** = to help with something; *can you lend a hand with moving the furniture?; he gave me a hand with the washing up;* **the shop has changed hands** = the shop has a new owner; *they walked along hand in hand* = holding each other by the hand **(b) to be hand in glove with someone** = to be working closely with someone; *we discovered he was hand in glove with our main rivals;* **to have your hands full** = to be very busy, totally occupied; *with three little children to look after she has her hands full;* **hand over fist** = in large quantities; *they were making money hand over fist; see also* **WASH (c)** one of the two pieces on a clock which turn round and show the time; *the minute hand is longer than the hour hand* **(d) at hand** = near; *the fire extinguisher is kept close at hand;* **by hand** = using your hands and tools but not using large machines; *he made the table by hand;* **in hand** = supply kept ready; *we have a supply of extra paper in hand for emergencies;* **on hand** = ready; *there's a doctor on hand if accidents occur;* **on the one hand** = showing the first part of a comparison; **on the other hand** = as the second part of a comparison; but; *on the one hand he's a good salesman, on the other hand he can't work out discounts correctly;* **out of hand** = not controlled; *our expenses have got out of hand* **(e)** worker; *to take on ten more hands;* **factory hand** = worker in a factory; **old China hand** = someone who has had a lot of experience in doing business in China **(f)** clapping, action of beating your hands together; *he did very well - give him a big hand, everyone* **2** *verb* to pass something to someone; *can you hand me that box?; she handed me all her money;*

(informal) **you've got to hand it to him** = he has to be admired for; *you've got to hand it to her, she's a great manageress!*

hand back ['hænd 'bæk] *verb* to give something back; *the customs officer handed me back my passport*

handbag ['hænbæg] *noun* small bag which a woman carries to hold her money, pens, handkerchief, etc.; *a robber snatched her handbag in the street* (NOTE: American English is **purse** *or* **pocketbook**)

hand baggage ['hæn(d) 'bægɪdʒ] *noun* small cases carried by passengers onto a plane; *only one piece of hand baggage is allowed* (NOTE: also called **hand luggage**)

handball ['hændbɔːl] *noun* game played with a large ball, which you have to hit only with your hands

> COMMENT: the game is for teams of 5 or 7 seven players and is similar to soccer

handbill ['hænbɪl] *noun* small piece of printed paper advertising something, handed out by hand; *he went round houses distributing handbills for the new restaurant*

handbook ['hænbʊk] *noun* book which gives instructions on how to use or repair something; *look in the handbook to see if it tells you how to clean the photocopier;* **service handbook** = book which shows how a machine should be serviced

handcart ['hændkɑːt] *noun* cart which is pushed or pulled by hand; *an old man used to sell apples from a handcart on the corner of the street*

handcrafted ['hændkrɑːftɪd] *adjective* made in an artistic way by hand; *her silver necklace was handcrafted in the mountains of Peru*

handcuff ['hænkʌf] *verb* to attach with handcuffs; *the prisoner came into the court handcuffed to a policeman; she handcuffed herself to the railings*

handcuffs ['hænkʌfs] *noun* two metal rings linked by a chain, which are locked round the wrists of someone who is being arrested; *he came out of the court house in handcuffs* (NOTE: plural, for one item, say **a pair of handcuffs**)

hand down ['hænd 'daʊn] *verb* **(a)** to pass from one generation to a younger one; *this is one of those folk tales which have been handed down over the centuries; the house has been handed down from father to son since the sixteenth century* **(b)** to announce publicly; *the judge handed down his verdict*

handful ['hænfʊl] *noun* **(a)** as much as you can hold in your hand; *she paid with a handful of loose change* **(b)** very few; *only a handful of people came to the wedding* **(c)** difficult child; *their son is a bit of a handful*

hand grenade ['hænd grə'neɪd] *noun* small bomb usually thrown by hand; *he threw a hand grenade into the trench*

handgun ['hæŋgʌn] *noun* small gun which is carried in the hand; *the police found six handguns when they searched the car; gangsters carrying handguns are a common sight on the streets of the city*

hand-held ['hændheld] *adjective* which can be held in the hand; *the film was shot with a hand-held camera*

handicap ['hændɪkæp] **1** *noun* **(a)** physical or mental disability; *she was born with a physical handicap* **(b)** something which puts you at a disadvantage; *not being able to drive is a handicap in this job* **2** *verb* to put someone at a disadvantage; *she was handicapped by not being able to speak Russian* (NOTE: handicapping - handicapped)

handicapped ['hændɪkæpt] **1** *adjective* with a mental or physical disability; *a school for handicapped children* **2** *noun* **(a)** the handicapped = people with disabilities; *the cinema has facilities for the handicapped*; *there is a toilet for the handicapped on the ground floor* **(b)** mentally handicapped people *or* the mentally handicapped = people with emotional or behavioural problems due to damage to the brain

handicraft ['hændɪkrɑːft] *noun* artistic work done by hand; *handicrafts such as embroidery or pottery are often studied at evening classes*

> COMMENT: many handicrafts are produced by amateurs, working at home and exhibiting at local exhibitions or fairs, often attached to larger exhibitions

hand in ['hænd 'ɪn] *verb* to give in something by hand; *please have the completed form ready to hand in at the reception desk*; *he handed in his notice or his resignation* = he resigned

handiwork ['hændɪwɜːk] *noun* work done or made by yourself; *I was just admiring your handiwork, the detail is beautiful*

handkerchief ['hæŋkətʃiːf] *noun* piece of cloth or thin paper for wiping your nose; *she carries a pack of paper handkerchiefs in her bag*; *he wiped his eyes on his handkerchief* (NOTE: often called a **hanky**, especially by children)

handle ['hændl] **1** *noun* **(a)** part of something which you hold in your hand to carry or use the object held; *I turned the handle but the door didn't open*; *be careful, the handle of the frying pan may be hot*; *the handle has come off my suitcase*; *he broke the cup handle* **(b)** *(informal)* to fly off the handle = to lose your temper; *stop telling him what to do or he'll fly off the handle* **2** *verb* **(a)** to move by hand; *be careful when you handle the bottles of acid* **(b)** to deal with something; *his company handles most of the traffic through the port*; *leave it to me - I'll handle it*; handling charge = charge made for dealing with something **(c)** to sell or to trade in (a sort of service or product); *we do not handle washing machines*

handlebars ['hændlbɑːz] *noun* bar for steering a bicycle or motorcycle; *the handlebars are too low, can you alter their height?* (NOTE: the word is plural)

handler ['hændlə] *noun* baggage handler = person who works at an airport, taking baggage off or putting it on planes

hand luggage ['hæn(d) 'lʌgɪdʒ] *noun see* HAND BAGGAGE

handmade [hæn'meɪd] *adjective* made by hand without using a machine; *he writes all his letters on handmade paper*; *all these items are handmade*

hand out ['hænd 'aʊt] *verb* to distribute; *protesters were handing out leaflets at the station*

handout ['hændaʊt] *noun* **(a)** *(informal)* clothes, money, etc., given to poor people; *the support group exists on handouts from the government* **(b)** printed information sheet; *you will all get handouts after the lecture*

hand over ['hænd 'əʊvə] *verb* to give something to someone; *she handed over all the documents to the lawyers*

handover ['hændəʊvə] *noun* passing of power to someone else; *when the ownership of a company changes, the handover period is always difficult*

handshake ['hænʃeɪk] *noun* act of shaking hands when meeting someone; *he has a firm handshake*; *she gave me rather limp handshake*; golden handshake = large, usually tax-free, sum of money given to a director who retires from a company before the end of his service contract; *the retiring director received a golden handshake of £25,000; see also* SHAKE

handsome ['hænsəm] *adjective* **(a)** good-looking; *her boyfriend is very handsome - I'm jealous!* (NOTE: used of men, rather than women) **(b)** large; *we made a handsome profit on the deal*

hands-on ['hændz'ɒn] *adjective* practical, done by yourself, not theoretical; *the computer firm gives a two-day hands-on training course*; *the new boss has a hands-on approach to the business, he wants to see for himself how everything works*

handstand ['hændstænd] *noun* to do a handstand = to hold yourself upright on you hands, upside down; *she ended her gymnastic show with a couple of handstands*

handwriting ['hændraɪtɪŋ] *noun* writing done by hand; *I can't read her handwriting*

handwritten [hænd'rɪtn] *adjective* written by hand, not typed or printed; *send a handwritten letter of application to the personnel manager*

handy ['hændi] *adjective* practical and useful; *this small case is handy when travelling*; *it's handy having the post office next door*; to come in handy = to be useful; *the knife will come in handy when we are camping* (NOTE: handier - handiest)

hang [hæŋ] **1** *noun* to get the hang of something = to understand how something works; *I don't think I'll ever get the hang of this software package* **2** *verb* **(a)** to attach something to something so that it does not touch the ground; *hang your coat on the hook behind the door*; *he hung his umbrella over the back of his chair*; *he hung the painting in the hall*; *the boys were hanging upside down from a tree* (NOTE: hanging - hung [hʌŋ]) **(b)** to kill someone by tying a rope round his neck and hanging him off the ground; *he was sentenced to be hanged for murder*; to hang yourself = to commit suicide by hanging; *he hanged himself in his prison cell* (NOTE: in this meaning, hanging - hanged)

hangar ['hæŋə] *noun* shed for keeping aircraft in; *the hangars are next to the main airport building* (NOTE: do not confuse with **hanger**)

hang around ['hæŋ ə'raʊnd] *verb* *(informal)* to wait aimlessly in a certain place; *groups of teenagers were hanging around the bar*

hang back ['hæŋ 'bæk] *verb* to stay behind when others go on; *they all ran forward but she hung back*

hang down ['hæŋ 'daʊn] *verb* to hang in a long piece; *her hair hung down to her waist*; *plants were hanging down from the rocks*

hanger ['hæŋə] *noun* device for hanging things on; coat hanger = piece of wood, wire or plastic on which you can hang a coat, shirts, etc.; *keep your clothes on* coat hangers - they won't need ironing twice (NOTE: do not confuse with **hangar**)

hang-glider ['hæŋglaɪdə] noun (a) large cloth wing stretched over a lightweight frame, like a giant kite, under which the pilot hangs in a harness, holding onto a bar which is used for steering; *his hang-glider got caught in a tree* (b) person who flies a hang-glider

hang-gliding ['hæŋglaɪdɪŋ] noun sport of flying a hang-glider; *he goes hang-gliding every weekend; I'd love to have a go at hang-gliding*

COMMENT: to get a hang-glider into the air, it is necessary either to run down a hill or jump off a cliff into the prevailing wind; by pushing the bar away from you, the nose of the glider dips and the glider picks up speed as it descends; by pulling the bar towards you, the nose lifts up and the glider decreases speed until it reaches stalling point

hanging ['hæŋɪŋ] noun (a) **hangings** = pieces of cloth put on a wall as decoration (b) act of executing someone by hanging; *the hangings took place in front of the prison*

hangman ['hæŋmən] noun executioner, person who hangs criminals; *the hangman took the prisoner to the scaffold* (NOTE: plural is **hangmen**)

hang on ['hæŋ 'ɒn] verb (a) to wait; *if you hand on a few minutes you will be able to see her* (b) (while phoning) to wait; *if you hang on a moment, Mr Smith will be off the other line soon* (c) (when thinking again) *hang on! do you mean you're not coming with us?* (d) **to hang onto something** = to hold something tight; *hang onto the ladder and don't look down* (e) to keep; *I've decided to hang on to my shares until the price goes up*

hang out ['hæŋ 'aʊt] verb (a) to hang things outside on a string; *they hung out flags all around the square; mother's hanging out her washing to dry* (b) (informal) to wait aimlessly in a certain place; *teenagers like to hang out round the square*

hangover ['hæŋəʊvə] noun (a) unpleasant feeling after having drunk too much alcohol; *last night's party was good but I've got a dreadful hangover this morning* (b) thing which is left over from the past; *this is a hangover from the old days when inns always provided stables for horses*

hang up ['hæŋ 'ʌp] verb (a) to put something on a hanger or on a hook; *don't leave your jacket on the back of your chair, hang it up!* (b) to stop a telephone conversation by putting the telephone back on its hook; *when I asked him when he was going to pay, he hung up*

hang-up ['hæŋʌp] noun (informal) worry, problem which you have; *he's got a hang-up about going bald; see also* HUNG UP (NOTE: plural is **hang-ups**)

hankie or **hanky** ['hæŋki] noun (informal) = HANDKERCHIEF; *don't sniff, use your hanky*

haphazard [hæp'hæzəd] adjective done at random, without any plan; *his haphazard approach to saving money*

haphazardly [hæp'hæzədli] adverb at random, without any plan; *the books were put on the shelves quite haphazardly*

hapless ['hæpləs] adjective (formal) unlucky, unfortunate; *the hapless goalkeeper managed to head the ball into his own goal; there were not enough beds for the hapless passengers stranded overnight by the snowstorm*

happen ['hæpən] verb (a) to take place; *the accident happened at the traffic lights; how did the accident happen?; something happened to make all the buses late; he's late - something must have happened to him* (b) *what's happened to his brother?* = what is his brother doing now? (c) to be somewhere by chance; *the fire engine happened to be there when the fire started; the shop happened to be empty at the time; we happened to meet at the library; do you happen to have change for £10?; it so happens that* or **happened that** or **as it happens** or **happened** = quite by chance; *as it happens I have the car today and can give you a lift; it so happened that my wife bumped into her at the supermarket*

happening ['hæpnɪŋ] noun event; *tell me about all the happenings in the village while I've been away*

happily ['hæpɪli] adverb in a happy way; *the children played happily in the sand for hours*

happiness ['hæpinəs] noun feeling of being happy; *a feeling of happiness came over her*

happy ['hæpi] adjective (a) (of people) very pleased; *I'm happy to say we're getting married next month; I'm so happy to hear that you are better; she's very happy in her job; happy hour* = period when drinks are cheaper in a bar; *there's a happy hour every day from 6 to 7* (b) (of event) pleasant; *it was the happiest day of my life; by a happy coincidence, we both like Dutch painters and met at the exhibition* (c) **to be happy to do something** = to do something very willingly; *I'd be happy to lend you my car;* **to be happy with something** = to be satisfied with something; *are you happy with your new car?; no one is happy with the plans for the new town centre* (d) (greetings) **Happy Birthday** or **many Happy Returns of the day** = greeting said to someone on their birthday; **Happy Christmas** = greeting said to someone at Christmas; **Happy Easter** = greeting said to someone at Easter; **Happy New Year** = greeting said to someone at the New Year (NOTE: **happier - happiest**)

happy-go-lucky ['hæpigəʊ'lʌki] adjective without any worries; *he's a happy-go-lucky chap, without a care in the world*

harass ['hærəs US hə'ræs] verb to pester and worry someone; *she was harassed by a man at work; they harassed him by phoning every day until he finally paid the bill*

harassed ['hærəst US hə'ræst] adjective bothered and worried; *she was looking harassed as she tried to serve the customers all by herself*

harassment ['hærəsmənt US hə'ræsmənt] noun pestering and worrying; *he complained of police harassment;* **sexual harassment** = pestering someone by making unwanted sexual approaches; *she complained of sexual harassment by her manager*

harbour US **harbor** ['hɑːbə] noun port, place where boats can come and tie up; *the yacht moved away from the harbour; the ship came into harbour last night;* **fishing harbour** = harbour which is used by fishing boats

hard [hɑːd] **1** adjective (a) not soft; *if you have back trouble, you ought to get a hard bed; the ice cream is rock hard* or **hard as a rock**; *the cake she made is so hard I can't bite it* (b) difficult; *today's crossword is too hard - I can't even begin to do it; the exam was* *very hard, and most students failed*; *she finds it hard to cope without any money*; *(informal)* **it's hard to say** = it's difficult to know; *it's hard to say if it's going to rain or not* **(c)** severe; *there was a hard winter in 1962*; *(informal)* **hard lines!** *or* **hard luck!** = I'm sorry you didn't win **(d) he's rather hard of hearing** = he's quite deaf (NOTE: **harder - hardest**) **2** *adverb* strongly; *he hit the nail hard*; *it's snowing very hard*; *they worked hard to finish the order on time*; *they tried hard, but couldn't score enough goals*

hardback ['hɑːdbæk] *noun* book bound in a stiff card binding (as opposed to a paperback or soft cover edition); *the book was published in hardback at £12.95*; *the hardback edition is now out of print*; *compare* PAPERBACK

hardboard ['hɑːdbɔːd] *noun* artificial board, made of little bits of wood mixed with glue and pressed together; *the cupboard is built of hardboard* (NOTE: no plural)

hard-boiled ['hɑːdbɔɪld] *adjective* **(a)** (egg) which has been boiled until the inside is solid; *do you prefer your egg hard-boiled or soft-boiled?* **(b)** *(informal)* tough, not showing any emotion; *she's pretty hard-boiled, that sort of thing doesn't bother her*

hard core [hɑːd'kɔː] **1** *noun* **(a)** rubble, pieces of brick, stones, etc., used as the foundation for roads and buildings; *they dug a hole and filled it with hardcore* **(b)** central group; *most of the guests left before eleven, but the hard core of drinkers stayed till two* (NOTE: no plural) **2** *adjective* referring to a central group; *the hard-core members of the party were all for opposing the government*

hardcover ['hɑːdkʌvə] *noun* book bound in a stiff card binding (as opposed to a paperback or softcover edition); *the hardcover edition is now out of print*

hard currency [hɑːd 'kʌrənsi] *noun* currency of a country with a strong economy, which can be changed into other currencies easily; *these goods must be paid for in hard currency*; *we signed a hard currency deal* (NOTE: the opposite is **soft currency**)

hard disk ['hɑːd 'dɪsk] *noun* disk which is fixed inside a computer; *he downloaded the program onto the hard disk*

hard drugs ['hɑːd 'drʌgz] *noun* strong drugs such as heroin, which people become addicted to and which affect their behaviour; *he started taking hard drugs when he was still at school* (NOTE: the opposite are **soft drugs**)

harden ['hɑːdn] *verb* **(a)** to become hard; *leave the cement for a couple of days to harden*; *attitudes are hardening as the strike continues* **(b)** to make harder and more experienced; *a hardened criminal*

hard hat ['hɑːd 'hæt] *noun* = SAFETY HELMET

hard-hitting ['hɑːd'hɪtɪŋ] *adjective* very critical; *the committee wrote a hard-hitting report about the state of the prison*

hard labour ['hɑːd 'leɪbə] *noun (old)* punishment of sending someone to prison to do hard manual work there; *he was sentenced to five years' hard labour*

hard line ['hɑːd 'laɪn] *noun* **to take a hard line** = to be severe, to follow the rules strictly; *the courts are taking a hard line with football hooligans*

hardline ['hɑːdlaɪn] *adjective* strict and inflexible over policy; *a hardline party member*

hardliner [hɑːd'laɪnə] *noun* inflexible person, person who takes a hard line; *hardliners on the ruling committee voted against the motion*

hardly ['hɑːdli] *adverb* **(a)** almost not; *do you know her? - hardly at all*; *we hardly slept a wink last night*; *she hardly eats anything at all* **(b) hardly ever** = almost never; *I hardly ever see her these days*; *it hardly ever rains in September* **(c) hardly anyone** = almost no one; *hardly anyone came to the party*

hard-pressed ['hɑːdprest] *adjective* acting under a lot of pressure; *they'll be hard-pressed to find the time to go on holiday*; *Eurostar is ideal for the hard-pressed businessman who wants to go straight to the centre of Brussels*

hard put ['hɑːd 'put] *adjective* in a difficult situation; *he will be hard put to pay back the loan*

hardship ['hɑːdʃɪp] *noun* difficult conditions, suffering; *she faced hardship when her husband died and left her in debt*

hard shoulder ['hɑːd 'ʃəʊldə] *noun* hard surfaced strip along the edge of a motorway, used for stopping in an emergency; *he pulled onto the hard shoulder to phone for help*

hard up ['hɑːd 'ʌp] *adjective* with very little money; *I can't lend you anything because I'm rather hard up at the moment*

hardware ['hɑːdweə] *noun* **(a)** tools and pans used in the home; *I bought the paint in a hardware shop* **(b) military hardware** = guns, shells, tanks, etc.; **computer hardware** = processors, printers, keyboards, etc.; *if I had the money I would buy the latest computer hardware*; *compare* SOFTWARE (NOTE: no plural)

hardwood ['hɑːdwʊd] *noun* **(a)** strong hard wood with a fine grain, from trees such as oak or teak; *the demand for tropical hardwood is leading to the destruction of the rainforest* **(b)** slow-growing tree, such as oak or teak, which produces a hard wood with a fine grain; **hardwoods** = (forests of) hardwood trees; *compare* SOFTWOOD

hardworking [hɑːd'wɜːkɪŋ] *adjective* who works hard; *she's a good hardworking member of staff*

hardy ['hɑːdi] *adjective* able to survive in cold weather; *hardy plants such as heather grow high up on the Scottish mountains*; *Icelanders are a hardy people*; **frost-hardy plant** = plant which can stand frost; *can you suggest some frost-hardy plants which would withstand the Canadian winter?* (NOTE: **hardier - hardiest**)

hare ['heə] *noun* **1** wild mammal like a large rabbit; *in the spring mountain hares lose their white winter coats* **2** *verb* **to hare after someone** = to run fast to try to catch someone; *he went haring down the road after the bus*

harebrained ['heəbreɪnd] *adjective (informal)* not serious, not concentrating on essential things; *he made some harebrained suggestion to sell off the shop and buy a farm*

harm [hɑːm] **1** *noun* damage; *he didn't mean to do any harm or he meant no harm*; *there's no harm in having a little drink before you go to bed*; **to do more harm than good** = not to be helpful at all; *talking to him now about the project will do more harm than good* (NOTE: no plural) **2** *verb* to damage; *luckily, the* *little girl was not harmed; the bad publicity has harmed our reputation*

harmful ['hɑːmful] *adjective* which causes damage; *harmful pesticides are banned; smoking is harmful to the health*

harmless ['hɑːmləs] *adjective* which does not hurt; *are you sure this weedkiller is harmless to animals?; our dog barks a lot, but really he's quite harmless;* **harmless fun** = jokes, etc., which are not supposed to harm anyone; *we were just having a bit of harmless fun*

harmonic [hɑː'mɒnɪk] **1** *adjective* referring to harmony; **harmonic series** = series of notes produced by the vibrating string of a musical instrument **2** *noun* **harmonics** = fractions of tones which make up a musical tone

harmonica [hɑː'mɒnɪkə] *noun* mouth-organ, small musical instrument which you play by blowing and sucking, and moving across your mouth to get different notes; *he made some money playing the harmonica outside the shopping centre*

harmonious [hɑː'məʊnɪəs] *adjective* **(a)** which sound well together; *it cannot be said that the band's playing of the national anthem was particularly harmonious* **(b)** which agree together, which go together; *a harmonious discussion between the heads of state; she chose colours and fabrics to create a harmonious scheme of decoration for the room*

harmoniously [hɑː'məʊnɪəsli] *adverb* in agreement; *the meeting ended harmoniously*

harmonium [hɑː'məʊnɪəm] *noun* small moveable organ, like an upright piano; *she accompanied the church choir on an old harmonium*

harmonization [hɑːmənaɪ'zeɪʃn] *noun* standardization; *harmonization of tax policies is one of the EU priorities*

harmonize ['hɑːmənaɪz] *verb* **(a)** to make things similar, to standardize; *to harmonize European VAT systems* **(b)** to play notes which go with a main tune; *he has taken the basic melody and harmonized it for the backing group*

harmony ['hɑːməni] *noun* **(a)** agreeable musical sounds; *the group sang in harmony* **(b)** agreeable colours, etc.; *we are aiming to create a pleasant harmony in the decoration of the room* **(c)** general peace; *they want to live in harmony with their neighbours*

harness ['hɑːnəs] **1** *noun* **(a)** straps used to hold a horse to a cart; **he is still in harness** = he is still working **(b)** straps used to attach something to a person; *his parachute harness slipped and he fell to the ground; make sure that you buy a pushchair with a reliable baby harness* **2** *verb* **(a)** to attach a horse to a cart with straps **(b)** to use resources to make energy; *to harness tidal power*

harp [hɑːp] **1** *noun* musical instrument shaped like a large triangle, played by the fingers plucking the strings; *she plays the harp in the local orchestra* **2** *verb* **to harp on about** = to keep on talking about; *do you have to keep harping on about the mistake I made?*

harpist ['hɑːpɪst] *noun* person who plays a harp; *the solo harpist sat at the front of the orchestra*

harpsichord ['hɑːpsɪkɔːd] *noun* musical instrument like an early form of the piano in which the strings are

plucked, not hit; *they played a Bach piece for violin and harpsichord*

harrowing ['hærəʊɪŋ] *adjective* which causes mental pain; *she tried to forget her harrowing experiences during the siege*

harry ['hæri] *verb* to keep attacking, asking questions, etc.; *the Russian cavalry constantly harried Napoleon's troops during the retreat from Moscow; she was harried with continual orders from her boss*

harsh [hɑːʃ] *adjective* **(a)** severe, cruel; *the prosecutor asked for a harsh sentence to fit the crime* **(b)** rough; *he shouted in a harsh voice* (NOTE: **harsher - harshest**)

harvest ['hɑːvɪst] **1** *noun* **(a)** picking ripe crops; *the corn harvest is in August* **(b)** ripe crops which have been picked; *a bumper harvest of wheat* **2** *verb* to pick ripe crops; *the corn will be ready to harvest next week; they have started harvesting the grapes in the vineyard*

harvester ['hɑːvəstə] *noun* **combine harvester** = farm machine which harvests various types of crops

has, hasn't [hæz or 'hæzənt] *see* HAVE

hash [hæʃ] *noun* **(a)** dish prepared from chopped meat and vegetables; *US* **corned beef hash** = dish made of corned beef, onions and mashed potatoes, cooked in the oven; *US* **hash brown potatoes** *or* **hash browns** = boiled potatoes, diced or mashed and fried till crisp and brown **(b)** *(informal)* **to make a hash of something** = to make a bad job of something; *he was supposed to be the expert, and then he made a hash of it* **(c)** *(informal)* hashish **(d)** **hash** *or* **hashmark** = printed sign (#) which indicates one of a series of numbers, or as an indicator (NOTE: in American usage, # is used to mean 'number': so **#32** means apartment number 32, etc. In computer usage, the pound sign (£) is sometimes used in the United States instead of the hash, to avoid confusion)

hashish ['hæʃɪʃ] *noun* drug made from the hemp plant (NOTE: also called **cannabis, marijuana**, or simply **hash**)

hassle ['hæsl] **1** *noun (informal)* bother; *it was quite a hassle getting tickets; I got to the station early to avoid all the hassle with the luggage* **2** *verb* to bother someone; *her boss is always hassling her to work faster*

haste [heɪst] *noun (formal)* speed of doing something; *why all the haste to get your Christmas cards off? - there's still plenty of time; in his haste to get out of the house, the burglar left his tools behind;* **to make haste** = to hurry; *the ships made haste to get into harbour before the storm came*

hasten ['heɪsn] *verb* **(a)** *(formal)* to go fast; *the chief of police hastened into the room* **(b)** to do something fast; *the government has hastened to deny the report in the paper;* **to hasten to add** = to add something as an explanation; *'someone must have left the keys on the table, and it wasn't me', she hastened to add* **(c)** to make something go faster; *several weeks' rest after your operation will hasten your recovery*

hasty ['heɪsti] *adjective* carelessly fast; *it was a hasty decision, which he regretted afterwards* (NOTE: **hastier - hastiest**)

hat [hæt] *noun* **(a)** piece of clothing which you wear on your head; *take your hat off when you go into a church; he's bought a Russian fur hat for the winter; (informal)* **keep it under your hat** = keep it secret; **to**

take your hat off to someone = (i) to salute someone, by lifting your hat up a little; (ii) to say that you admire someone; *those polar explorers were very brave - I take my hat off to them*; *she's made a great success of her business - I take my hat off to her*; **to be talking through your hat** = to be talking nonsense; *that's rubbish - you're talking through your hat*; *see also* PASS ROUND (b) **hat trick** = score of three goals, etc., by the same person in football, three wickets taken by the same bowler in cricket, etc.; *out of the five goals, Jones scored a hat trick and the other two were by Leonard and Williams*

hatch [hætʃ] **1** *noun* (a) opening in the deck of a ship; cover for this opening; *he opened the hatch and went down into the cabin* (b) **serving hatch** *or* **service hatch** = small opening in a wall between a kitchen and a dining room (NOTE: plural is **hatches**) **2** *verb* (a) *(of a baby bird)* to break out of the egg; *all the chicks hatched on the same day*; *(informal)* **don't count your chickens before they're hatched** = don't be too sure that everything will be all right; *he's a very cautious man, he never counts his chickens before they're hatched* (b) to plan; *they hatched a plot to kidnap the Prime Minister's daughter*

hatchback ['hætʃbæk] *noun* type of car where the back opens upwards as a door; *Rover have brought out a new hatchback*

hatchet ['hætʃɪt] *noun* small axe *(informal)* **to bury the hatchet** = to make peace; *after years of quarrelling, the two brothers decided to bury the hatchet*; *(informal)* **hatchet man** = recently appointed manager, whose job is to make staff redundant and reduce expenditure; *they brought in a hatchet man to oversee the staff cuts*

hate [heɪt] **1** *verb* to dislike intensely; *I think she hates me, but I don't know why*; *I hate going to the dentist*; **hate mail** = letters showing that the writer hates someone; *he received a lot of hate mail after his speech* **2** *noun* intense dislike; *cucumber sandwiches are one of my pet hates*

hateful ['heɪtfʊl] *adjective* which makes people dislike it; *their hateful practice of killing foxes*; *she saw her teacher as a hateful person*

hatred ['heɪtrəd] *noun* great dislike; *he has a hatred of exams*; **racial hatred** = dislike of people of other races

hatter ['hætə] *noun (old)* person who makes hats; *see also* MAD

haughtiness ['hɔːtinəs] *noun* being haughty

haughty ['hɔːti] *adjective* extremely proud and unpleasant; *she speaks to shopkeepers in a haughty way* (NOTE: **haughtier - haughtiest**)

haul [hɔːl] **1** *noun* (a) large quantity of things which have been stolen; *the burglars made off with their haul* (b) distance travelled with difficulty; *it's a long haul up the hill*; **long-haul flight** = long-distance flight (for example, across the Atlantic) **2** *verb* to pull with difficulty; *they hauled the boat up onto the beach*; *the police hauled the body out of the water*

haulage ['hɔːlɪdʒ] *noun* **road haulage** = moving of goods by road; **haulage contractor** = company which arranges for goods to be moved by road or rail under contract

haulier ['hɔːlɪə] *noun* **road haulier** = HAULAGE CONTRACTOR

haunt [hɔːnt] **1** *noun* place which you visit frequently; *I went back to some of my old haunts*; *the pub is a favourite haunt of actors* **2** *verb (of ghosts)* to visit frequently; *the castle is supposed to be haunted by the ghost of a soldier*

haunted ['hɔːntɪd] *adjective* visited by ghosts; *a haunted house*

haunting ['hɔːntɪŋ] *adjective* sad and wonderful; *a haunting melody from Bach's violin concerto*

have [hæv] *verb* (a) *(also* **to have got**) to own or possess; *she has a lot of money*; *they have a new green car*; *she has long dark hair*; *the house has no telephone*; *do you have a table for three, please?* (b) to take, to eat, to play, etc.; *have you had any tea?*; *she has sugar in her coffee*; *they had a meal of bread and cheese*; *she had her breakfast in bed*; *they had a game of tennis*; *I had a long walk* (c) to pay someone to do something for you; *I must have my hair cut*; *she's having the house painted* (d) *(used to form the past of verbs)* *have they finished their work?*; *she has never been to Paris*; *they had finished supper when we arrived*; *I haven't seen him for two days*; *if she had asked me I would have said no* (e) *(greetings)* *have a nice day!*; *have a good trip!* (f) **had better** = it would be a good thing if; *since you have no money, you had better stay here instead of going to the hotel*; *hadn't you better answer the phone?* (NOTE: **have** *or* **has - having - had - has had**)

have got [hæv 'gɒt] *verb* (a) to have; *she's got dark hair*; *have you got a table for three, please?*; *half the people in the office have got flu* (b) to own or possess; *she's got a lot of money*; *they've got a new green car*; *the house hasn't got a telephone* *they haven't got enough to eat* (c) *(used to mean* must*)*; *she's got to learn to drive*; *why have you got to go so early?*

have (got) to do with [hæv gɒt tə 'duː wɪθ] *verb* to concern; *it's got nothing to do with you*

haven ['heɪvn] *noun* safe port or safe place; *the square is a haven of peace in the heart of the town*; **tax haven** = country where taxes are low, encouraging financial companies to set up offices there; *she put most of her money into an offshore tax haven*

haven't ['hævənt] *see* HAVE

have on ['hæv 'ɒn] *verb* (a) to wear; *what did she have on when she left the party?*; *I can't answer the door - I've got nothing on* (b) to have something on = to be busy with visits, meetings, etc.; *I haven't anything on tonight so I'll be able to finish painting the bathroom* (c) *(informal)* **to have someone on** = to trick someone; *I think he's having you on*

haversack ['hævəsæk] *noun* strong bag carried over your shoulders or on your back when walking; *he packed some sandwiches and his binoculars in a haversack and went off birdwatching*

have to ['hæv 'tuː] *verb used with other verbs to mean 'must'*; *in England everyone has to drive on the left*; *he had to walk to work because he missed the bus*; *do we have to get up early?*; *you have to go through customs*; *the car has to have it's 10,000km service*

havoc ['hævək] *noun* damage; *the storm caused considerable havoc to the crops*; **to play havoc with** = to ruin; *the snow has played havoc with the train timetables*

hawk [hɔːk] **1** *noun* (a) large bird of prey; *the hawk was hovering over the motorway*; *she has eyes like a*

hawk = she notices everything **(b)** person who prefers military action to diplomacy; *curiously, it's the military commanders who are the doves and the president and his advisers are the hawks* (NOTE: the opposite, a person who prefers diplomacy and tries to achieve peace is a **dove**) **2** *verb* to sell goods from door to door or in the street; **to hawk something round** = to take an idea or a project to various companies to see if anyone will accept it; *he hawked his idea for a film round all the studios but no one wanted it*

hawker ['hɔːkə] *noun* person who sells goods from place to place; *there was a sign on the door saying: 'No hawkers'; as soon as the policeman came round the corner, the hawkers quickly gathered their goods together and disappeared into the crowd*

hawser ['hɔːzə] *noun* thick rope used on a ship; *the ship was attached to the quay with hawsers*

hawthorn ['hɔːθɔːn] *noun* hedge bush, with spines and little white flowers; *a flowering hawthorn hedge looks very attractive in spring*

hay [heɪ] *noun* dried grass used to feed cattle; *we store our hay in a barn*; **to make hay while the sun shines** = to enjoy yourself while you can

hayfever ['heɪfiːvə] *noun* inflammation of the nose and eyes caused by an allergy to flowers, pollen, scent or dust; *when I have hayfever I prefer to stay indoors; the hayfever season starts in May*

haystack ['heɪstæk] *noun* bales of hay piled up to make a construction like a house; *they built a haystack in the corner of the field*; **it's like looking for a needle in a haystack** = it's a hopeless task

hazard ['hæzəd] **1** *noun* dangerous situation; *don't leave those cardboard boxes in the passage - they're a fire hazard*; **at hazard** = at risk; **hazard warning lights** = warning lights on a car; *he stopped the car and switched on his hazard warning lights* **2** *verb* to risk; **to hazard a guess** = to risk making a guess; *I wouldn't hazard a guess at how many people will come to the concert*

hazardous ['hæzədəs] *adjective* risky or dangerous; *people in hazardous occupations often get paid danger money*; **hazardous to health** = which can harm health; *environmentalists are convinced that the discharges are hazardous to the health of the local people*; **hazardous waste** = rubbish which can pose a risk to people's health; *the dumping of hazardous waste at sea should be banned*

haze [heɪz] **1** *noun* **(a)** mist, smoke or dust suspended in the atmosphere which reduces visibility; *the sun's rays filtered through the haze*; **heat haze** = reduction in visibility caused by warm air rising from the ground; *it's hard to judge distances when you are driving and there's a heat haze* **(b)** not being able to think or remember clearly; *he was in a haze when he came round after the operation* **2** *verb US* to play jokes, especially on a new student; *hazing has become so extreme that it has had to be banned in some colleges*

hazel ['heɪzl] **1** *noun* a small tree which bears small round nuts; *the flowers of the hazel are called catkins* **2** *adjective & noun* light brown colour, with a touch of green; *the little girl had beautiful hazel eyes*

hazelnut ['heɪzlnʌt] *noun* small brown round nut from the hazel tree; *you can have a plain chocolate bar or chocolate with hazelnuts*

hazy ['heɪzi] *adjective* **(a)** misty; *it was too hazy for us to get a good view from the top of the cliff* **(b)** vague; *I have a hazy recollection of the party; he reported the accident to the police but was very hazy about some of the details* (NOTE: **hazier - haziest**)

Hb = HAEMOGLOBIN

he [hiː] *pronoun referring to a man or boy, and some animals*; *he's my brother; he and I met in Oxford Circus; he's eaten all my pudding; don't be frightened of the dog - he won't hurt you* (*see also* HIM, HIS) (NOTE: when it is the object **he** becomes **him**: **he** hit the **ball** *or* the **ball** hit **him**; when it follows the verb to **be**, **he** usually becomes **him**: **who's that? - it's him, the man who borrowed my knife**)

head [hed] **1** *noun* **(a)** top part of the body, which contains the eyes, nose, mouth, brain, etc.; *he says he can relax by standing on his head; she hit her head on the cupboard door*; **head over heels** = over and over; *she rolled head over heels down the hill*; **to be head over heels in love** = to be madly in love; *he's head over heels in love with my sister*; **to shake your head** = to move your head from side to side to mean 'no'; *she asked him if he wanted any more coffee and he shook his head; (informal)* **head and shoulders above** = much better than; *she's head and shoulders above all the others in the class* **(b)** brain, intelligence; *she has a good head for figures; he tried to do the sum in his head; if we all put our heads together we might come up with a solution*; **to take it into your head to do something** = to decide to do something suddenly; *he took it into his head to join the army* **(c)** first place, top part; *an old lady was standing at the head of the queue; his name comes at the head of the list* **(d)** most important person; *she's the head of the sales department; the head waiter showed us to our table* **(e)** top side of a coin, usually with the head of a person on it; **to play heads or tails** = to spin a coin to see which side comes down on top, and so decide something; **heads I win** = if the coin falls with the top side up, then I will win (NOTE: the opposite side is **tails**) **(f)** one person, when counting; *she counted heads as the party got onto the coach*; **a head** *or* **per head** = for each person; *the trip costs £25.00 a head or per head* **(g)** **to come to a head** = to reach a crisis point; *things came to a head when all the family met to discuss grandfather's will* **2** *verb* **(a)** to be the first, to lead; *he heads the list of prize-winners* **(b)** to go towards; *she headed immediately for the manager's office; the car headed east along the motorway; he's heading towards the Channel ports; she's heading for trouble* **(c)** to be the manager, the most important person; *he heads our research department*

headache ['hedeɪk] *noun* **(a)** pain in your head, caused by changes in pressure in the blood vessels; *I must lie down, I've got a dreadful headache; take an aspirin if you have a headache* **(b)** problem; *the lack of resources in the education system is one of the government's biggest headaches*

headboard ['hedbɔːd] *noun* upright panel at the top end of a bed; *a bed with a pink quilted headboard*

headed paper ['hedɪd 'peɪpə] *noun* notepaper with the name and address of a person or company printed at the top of it; *he wrote to his clients on the company's headed paper*

header ['hedə] *noun* **(a)** hitting a ball with your head; *he scored with a header* **(b)** dive; *he took a header into* *the waves* (**c**) words or page numbers at the top of a page of a book, etc.; *compare* FOOTER

head-first ['hed'fɜːst] *adverb* (**a**) with your head first; *he tripped and fell head-first down the stairs* (**b**) hastily; *don't rush head-first into a deal with someone you hardly know*

headhunt ['hedhʌnt] *verb* **to be headhunted** = to be approached by a headhunter and offered a job with another company; *he was headhunted for the job at the German bank*

headhunter ['hedhʌntə] *noun* person or company that looks for top managers and offers them jobs in other companies; *she was approached by a headhunter about a job in a large German bank*

heading ['hedɪŋ] *noun* words at the top of a piece of text; *items are listed under several headings*; *look under the heading 'Hotels and Guesthouses'*; *see also* SUBHEADING

headlamp ['hedlæmp] *noun* one of the headlights, the main white lights on the front of a vehicle; *a car with very powerful headlamps*

headland ['hedlənd] *noun* promontory, piece of high land sticking into the sea; *the ship came round the headland and sailed straight for the harbour*

headlights ['hedlaɪts] *noun* main white lights on the front of a vehicle; *dip your headlights when coming to the crossroads*; **dipped headlights** = headlights with the beam set low so as not to dazzle other drivers

headline ['hedlaɪn] *noun* (**a**) words in large letters on the front page of a newspaper; *did you see the headlines about the accident?*; *the newspaper headline says TAXES TO GO UP* (**b**) **news headlines** = summary of the news on TV or radio; *we will have an interview with the minister following the headlines*

headlined ['hedlaɪnd] *adjective* with a headline; *the article was headlined 'The End of Inflation?'*

headlong ['hedlɒŋ] **1** *adjective* rushing; *the headlong flight of the people of the villages in front of the advancing army* **2** *adverb* (**a**) rushing; *the soldiers rushed headlong into the crowd* (**b**) with your head first; *he fell headlong down the stairs*

headmaster [hed'mɑːstə] *noun* man who is in charge of a school; *the trip was organized by the headmaster*

headmistress [hed'mɪstrəs] *noun* woman who is in charge of a school; *she has retired as headmistress of a large girls' school* (NOTE: plural is **headmistresses**)

head office ['hed 'ɒfɪs] *noun* main office where the directors work and meet; *the company's head office is in Tokyo*

head of state ['hed əv 'steɪt] *noun* king, queen, or president, who is the leader of a state; *the Queen, as head of state, opens parliament each year*

COMMENT: the head of state is not necessarily the head of the government. In the United Kingdom, the Queen is head of state and the Prime Minister is head of government. In the United States, the President combines both roles. Most monarchies, such as Spain or Denmark, split the function of head of state and head of government; some republics, like Germany, do the same

head-on ['hedɒn] *adjective & adverb* (**a**) with the front first; **a head-on collision** = collision where two vehicles run into each other front to front (**b**) directly; *he decided to meet objections head-on*; *we had a head-on confrontation with the police*

headphones ['hedfəʊnz] *noun* devices which you put on your ears to listen to music tapes, etc.; *please use your headphones if you want to listen to the music programme*

headquarters (HQ) [hed'kwɔːtəz] *noun* main offices; *several people were arrested and taken to the police headquarters*; **the headquarters staff** = the staff working in a headquarters

headrest ['hedrest] *noun* cushion on top of a car seat against which you can lean your head; *you can adjust the headrests to the height you want*

headscarf ['hedskɑːf] *noun* square scarf worn over the head and tied under the chin; *she wore a headscarf to go shopping* (NOTE: plural is **headscarves**)

head start ['hed 'stɑːt] *noun* **to have a head start over someone** = to have an advantage over someone; *they had a head start over some other companies because they had a local office*; *his mother is Spanish, so that gave him a head start over the rest of the Spanish class*

headstone ['hedstəʊn] *noun* piece of stone standing at the end of a grave with the name of the dead person written on it; *they walked round the old cemetery looking at the headstones* (NOTE: also called **gravestone** *or* **tombstone**)

headstrong ['hedstrɒŋ] *adjective* determined to do what you want; *a clever but headstrong little girl*

head teacher ['hed 'tiːtʃə] *noun* teacher who is in charge of a school; *the head teacher plans to retire next year*

headway ['hedweɪ] *noun* difficult forward movement; *the boat had difficulty in making any headway against the wind*; *they are not making much headway with their building project* (NOTE: no plural)

headwind ['hedwɪnd] *noun* wind blowing towards you; *the rowers were struggling against the strong headwind*; *the sprinters are running into a slight headwind*; *strong headwinds over the Atlantic meant that the plane was half an hour late* (NOTE: the opposite is a **tail wind**)

heady ['hedi] *adjective* strong and likely to affect your senses, such as making you drunk or excited; *they served some heady concoction of vodka and fruit juice*; *the heady scent of roses hung in the air* (NOTE: **headier - headiest**)

heal [hiːl] *verb* to mend, to become healthy again; *after six weeks, his wound has still not healed* (NOTE: do not confuse with **heel**)

healer ['hiːlə] *noun* person who heals; *healers often work by touching patients with their hands*; **faith healer** = person who claims he can heal those people who believe he can heal them

healing ['hiːlɪŋ] **1** *noun* (**a**) action of making healthy; *healing the sick is her vocation* (**b**) **healing process** = process of getting better; *a substance which will accelerate the healing process* **2** *adjective* which makes better; *the healing power of salt water*

health [helθ] *noun* (**a**) being well, being free from any mental or physical illness; *he has enjoyed the best* *of health for years*; *smoking is bad for your health*; **health club** = club for people who want to improve their health by taking exercise, dieting, etc.; **health farm** = clinic in the country for people who want to improve their health and appearance by taking exercise, dieting, etc.; **health risk** = something which may be bad for people's health; *sewage flowing directly into the river poses a health risk to the population*; **health service** = service in charge of doctors, hospitals, etc.; **health warning** = warning that something may be bad for your health; *each pack of cigarettes carries a government health warning* **(b) your health!** *or* **good health!** = greeting said to someone when drinking

health foods ['helθ 'fʊdz] *noun* natural vegetarian food, such as grains, beans, seeds, etc., grown without chemical fertilizers and so better for you; **health foods store** = shop specializing in health foods

healthy ['helθi] *adjective* **(a)** not ill; *he's healthier than he has ever been* **(b)** which makes you well; *she's keeping to a healthy diet*; *East Anglia is the healthiest place in England* **(c)** good, strong; *he has a healthy contempt for politicians*; *the company's bank account is looking very healthy* (NOTE: **healthier - healthiest**)

heap [hiːp] **1** *noun* pile; *a heap of coal*; *step over that heap of rubbish*; *(informal)* **heaps of** = lots of; *apple pie with heaps of cream*; *don't rush - we've heaps of time* **2** *verb* to pile up; *a pile of presents were heaped under the Christmas tree*; *boxes were heaped up on the station platform*

heaped ['hiːpt] *adjective* piled full; *a heaped spoonful of sugar*

hear [hɪə] *verb* **(a)** to catch sounds with your ears; *he heard footsteps behind him*; *you could hear the sound of church bells in the distance*; *I heard her drive up in the car*; *can you hear him singing in the bath?* **(b)** to listen to something; *did you hear the talk on the radio?*; *I heard it on the BBC news* **(c)** to get information; *I hear he's got a new job*; *have you heard that the Minister has resigned?*; *we have not heard from them for some time* (NOTE: **hearing - heard** [hɜːd])

hear! hear! [hɪə 'hɪə] *interjection* used to show you agree; *several MPs said 'hear hear!'*

hearing ['hɪərɪŋ] *noun* **(a)** being able to hear; *bats have a very sharp sense of hearing*; *she has hearing difficulties* (NOTE: no plural in this meaning) **(b)** **hearing aid** = electric device put in the ear to improve hearing; *she wears a little hearing aid which you can hardly see* **(c)** session of a tribunal or court; *the hearing is expected to last three days*

hear of ['hɪə 'ɒv] *verb* **(a)** to know about something; *I've heard of a new restaurant in the High Street*; *she's never heard of the Rolling Stones* **(b)** *(formal)* **not to hear of it** = not to accept an offer; *I said I would replace the glass I broke, but she wouldn't hear of it*

hearse [hɜːs] *noun* vehicle for carrying a coffin; *the mourners followed the hearse to the cemetery*

heart [hɑːt] *noun* **(a)** main organ in the body, which pumps blood around the body; *she isn't dead - her heart's still beating*; *the doctor listened to his heart*; *he has had heart trouble for years* **(b)** centre, middle; *the house is in the heart of the village* **(c)** centre of feelings; *my heart sank when I realized that he hadn't read my letter*; **with all my heart** = with all my love; **to know something by heart** = to know and remember something; *I don't know his phone number by heart,*

so I'll just look it up for you; **to learn something by heart** = to learn and remember something; *she learnt the poem by heart*; **to lose heart** = to stop being interested in something; *after all the delays she lost heart in the project*; **don't take it to heart** = don't be too sad about it; **his heart isn't in it** = he has lost interest in it; **to set your heart on something** = to want something very much; *he has set his heart on buying a little sailing boat* **(d)** one of the red suits in a game of cards, shaped like a heart; *my last two cards were the ten and the ace of hearts* (NOTE: the other red suit is **diamonds**; **clubs** and **spades** are the black suits)

heartache ['hɑːteɪk] *noun* great sadness and worry; *he was the cause of much heartache to his parents* (NOTE: no plural)

heart attack ['hɑːt ə'tæk] *noun* condition where the heart suffers from defective blood supply because an artery has become blocked; *she had a heart attack but is recovering well*

heartbeat ['hɑːtbiːt] *noun* regular noise made by the heart as it pumps blood; *the hospital doctors were unable to detect a heartbeat and pronounced him dead on arrival*

heartbreak ['hɑːtbreɪk] *noun* great sadness and worry; *the heartbreak of selling the family home almost killed her* (NOTE: no plural)

heartbreaking ['hɑːtbreɪkɪŋ] *adjective* very sad and worrying; *it was heartbreaking to see the whole house burnt to the ground*

heartbroken ['hɑːtbrəʊkn] *adjective* very sad and upset; *the little girl was heartbroken when her cat disappeared*

heartburn ['hɑːtbɜːn] *noun* indigestion causing a burning feeling in the stomach; *he had to take a tablet to get rid of his heartburn*

heart disease ['hɑːt dɪ'ziːz] *noun* any disease affecting the heart; *she has a long history of heart disease*

hearten ['hɑːtn] *verb* to make optimistic, to encourage; *it is heartening to see so many young people marching for peace*

heart failure ['hɑːt 'feɪljə] *noun* failure of the heart to maintain the output of blood to meet the demands of the body; *she died of heart failure*

heartfelt ['hɑːtfelt] *adjective* sincere; *I wish to offer you my heartfelt congratulations*

hearth [hɑːθ] *noun* hole in the wall of a room where you can light a fire for heating; *we were glad to see a fire burning in the hearth when we came in out of the snow*

hearthrug ['hɑːθrʌg] *noun* rug in front of a fireplace; *the dog loves to curl up on the hearthrug in front of the fire*

heartland ['hɑːtlænd] *noun* region where certain activities are concentrated; *Dortmund is in the industrial heartland of Germany*

heartless ['hɑːtləs] *adjective* cruel, not having any pity; *her refusal to meet his mother was heartless*

hearty ['hɑːti] *adjective* big; *you'd better eat a hearty breakfast, as I don't think we'll have time for any lunch*; *he gave a hearty chuckle* (NOTE: **heartier - heartiest**)

heat [hiːt] **1** *noun* **(a)** being hot; *the heat of the sun made the ice cream melt*; *cook the vegetables over a* low heat; **heat wave** = sudden period of high temperature; *the heat wave has made rivers dry up* (NOTE: no plural) **(b)** one part of a sports competition; *there are two heats before the final race*; **dead heat** = race where two competitors finish equal; *the race finished in a dead heat* **2** *verb* to make hot; *can you heat the meal while I'm getting the table ready?*; *the room was heated by a small electric fire*; *heat the milk to room temperature*

heated ['hiːtɪd] *adjective* **(a)** made warm; *the car has a heated rear window*; **a heated swimming pool** = pool where the water is kept warm; *the school has a heated swimming pool* **(b)** angry; *there was a heated discussion after the meeting*; *MPs became very heated during the debate*

heater ['hiːtə] *noun* device for heating; *there is an electric heater in the bathroom*; *I'm cold - I'm going to put the heater on*; **water heater** = device for heating water in a house; **electric heater** = heating device which runs on electricity; *the island can be cool in the winter, so the flat has several portable electric heaters*; **gas heater** = heating device which runs on gas

heath [hiːθ] *noun* area of dry sandy acid soil with low shrubs such as heather and gorse growing on it; *the heaths of Dorset are home to some of Britain's rarest flora and fauna*

heathen ['hiːðn] **1** *adjective* (*old*) who has no religious beliefs, who is not a Christian; *missionaries went out to convert the heathen islanders* **2** *noun* (*old*) person who has no religious beliefs, who is not a Christian

heather ['heðə] *noun* low plant with mainly purple or pink flowers, found on acid soils, common in upland areas; *the mountains of Scotland are beautiful in autumn when the heather is in flower*

heating ['hiːtɪŋ] *noun* way of warming a house, an office, etc.; *we switch the heating off on May 1st*; *I'm cold - I'm going to switch the heating on*; **central heating** = heating of a whole house from one main boiler and several radiators; *our central heating comes on at 6.30*; *the central heating has broken down again*

heave [hiːv] **1** *noun* strong hard pull; *one more heave, and we should pull down the tree* **2** *verb* **(a)** to pull hard; *they heaved on the anchor to pull it up*; (*said when pulling*) **heave ho!** = pull hard; *'all together now, heave ho!'*; (*informal*) **to get the old heave-ho** = to be sacked from your job **(b)** to throw; *he heaved a brick through the window* **(c)** to breathe heavily; *she heaved a sigh, and picked up the phone*; *we all heaved a collective sigh of relief when he left* (NOTE: **heaving - heaved**) **(d)** (*of ship*) **to heave to** = to stop moving; *the ship hove to and dropped anchor in the bay*; **to heave in sight** = to appear; *the ship hove into sight round the headland* (NOTE: **heaving - hove** [həʊv])

heaven ['hevn] *noun* **(a)** paradise, place where good people go after death; *she believes that when she dies she will go to heaven* **(b)** **the heavens** = the sky above; **the heavens opened** = it poured with rain; (*phrase showing surprise*) **good heavens!** *it's almost ten o'clock!*; **for heaven's sake** = expression showing you are annoyed, or that something is important; *what are you screaming for? - it's only a little mouse, for heaven's sake*; *for heaven's sake try to be quiet, we don't want the guards to hear us!*

heavenly ['hevnli] *adjective* **(a)** belonging to heaven; *heavenly choirs of angels singing*; **the**

heavenly host = a group of angels **(b)** (*old*) **heavenly bodies** = stars, planets, moons and comets **(c)** (*old*) (*informal*) very nice; *we had a heavenly holiday by the sea*; *the food she served was simply heavenly*

heavily ['hevɪli] *adverb* **(a)** as if you are heavy; *he sat down heavily on the little chair* **(b)** to a great extent, very much; *the company was heavily criticized in the press*; *she is heavily in debt*; *it rained heavily during the night* **(c)** **to sleep heavily** = to sleep without waking

heavy ['hevi] *adjective* **(a)** which weighs a lot; *this suitcase is so heavy I can hardly lift it*; *she's heavier than I am* **(b)** **a heavy meal** = a meal which is filling and difficult to digest; *don't go to bed just after you've had a heavy meal* **(c)** in large amounts; *there has been a heavy demand for the book*; *there was a heavy fall of snow during the night*; *the radio says there is heavy traffic in the centre of town*; **to make heavy weather of something** = to make something you are doing unnecessarily difficult and complicated to do; *we asked him to sort out the invoices but he's really making heavy weather of it*; **heavy smoker** *or* **heavy drinker** = person who smokes a lot of cigarettes, who drinks a lot of alcohol; *he was a heavy smoker and died of lung cancer* (NOTE: **heavier - heaviest**)

heavy-duty ['hevɪ'djuːti] *adjective* made for rough work; *use heavy-duty plastic to cover the lorry*

heavy goods vehicle (HGV) ['hevi 'gʊdz 'viːkl] *noun* very large lorry; *you need to have an HGV licence if you want to be a lorry driver*

heavy-handed [hevɪ'hændɪd] *adjective* not delicate; *his heavy-handed way of dealing with the problem did not help*

heavy industry ['hevi 'ɪndʌstri] *noun* industry which makes large products (such as steel bars, ships or railway lines); *our heavy industry has been undermined by the low labour costs in the Far East*

heavy metal ['hevi 'metl] *noun* metal such as lead, mercury and zinc, with a high atomic number; *heavy metals can pollute the atmosphere*

heavyweight ['heviweɪt] *noun* **(a)** largest and heaviest class of boxer; *the heavyweight champion*; *a heavyweight title fight*; **light heavyweight** = weight of boxer above middleweight and below heavyweight **(b)** influential person; *he's the director of the National Theatre - a heavyweight in the theatre world*

heck [hek] *noun* (*informal word used to make a phrase stronger*) *what the heck's been going on here?*; *how the heck did he get back?*

heckle ['hekl] *verb* to call out and interrupt a public speaker; *as soon as a few people started to heckle she walked off the stage*

heckler ['heklə] *noun* person who calls out and interrupts a public speaker; *the speaker was constantly barracked by hecklers*

hectare ['hektɑː] *noun* area of land measuring 100 metres by 100 metres, i.e. 10,000 square metres or 2.47 acres; *the farm buildings and 20 hectares of land are for sale by auction* (NOTE: usually written **ha** after figures: **2,500 ha**)

hectic ['hektɪk] *adjective* very active; *a hectic day on the Stock Exchange*; *I'm tired out - the last two weeks have been very hectic*

hecto- ['hektəʊ] *prefix meaning* one hundred; **hectolitre** = 100 litres

hedge [hedʒ] **1** *noun* **(a)** row of bushes planted and kept trimmed to form a screen around a field or garden; *there is a thick yew hedge round the churchyard* **(b)** financial protection; *a hedge against inflation* **2** *verb* **to hedge your bets** = to invest in several areas so as to be protected against loss in one of them

hedgehog ['hedʒhɒg] *noun* small animal with its back covered in spines; *many hedgehogs get killed by cars*

hedgerow ['hedʒrəʊ] *noun* line of bushes forming a hedge round a field or along a country road; *miles of hedgerows are being pulled up each year*

hedonist ['hedənɪst] *noun* person who only lives for pleasure; *he was a hedonist, and refused to get involved in sordid things like work or money*

heed [hi:d] **1** *noun* (*formal*) **to take heed of** *or* **to pay heed to** = to pay attention to; *the company would be wise to take heed of public opinion on this issue*; *he paid no heed at all to what his doctor said* **2** *verb* (*formal*) to pay attention to; *she didn't heed the doctor's warning*

heel [hi:l] **1** *noun* **(a)** the back part of the foot; *after walking, she got a blister on her heel*; **she rolled head over heels down the hill** = she rolled over and over like a ball; **to take to your heels** = to run away; *when they heard the police siren, they took to their heels and disappeared round the corner*; **on the heels of someone** *or* **something** = following immediately behind someone *or* something; *with the police hot on his heels he fled to Argentina*; **to turn on your heel** = to turn suddenly and go in the opposite direction; *she turned on her heel and walked out of the room* **(b)** back part of a sock, stocking or shoe; *he's got a hole in the heel of his sock*; *she always wear shoes with high heels* *or* **high-heeled shoes 2** *verb* to put a new heel on a shoe; *I want these shoes soled and heeled, please* (NOTE: do not confuse with **heal**)

hefty ['hefti] *adjective* **(a)** strong; *we need a couple of hefty lads to move the table* **(b)** (*informal*) large; *he had a hefty pay increase*; *you'll pay a hefty fine if you get caught* (NOTE: **heftier - heftiest**)

hegemony [hɪ'geməni] *noun* leadership or control by one state over others; *the war was fought to prevent the hegemony of one single power over the whole region*; *the cultural hegemony of English is putting some other languages in danger*

heifer ['hefə] *noun* young cow which has not had a calf; *prices for heifers are lower than they were last year*

height [haɪt] *noun* **(a)** measurement of how high something is; *the height of the bridge is only 3m*; *he is of above average height* = he is taller than most men **(b)** highest point; *looking down on the city from the heights around*; *it is difficult to find hotel rooms at the height of the tourist season*; *I don't like heights* *or* *I haven't got a head for heights* = I get dizzy when I am high up

heighten ['haɪtn] *verb* to increase; *the TV programme has helped to heighten public awareness of the drug problem*

heir, heiress ['eə *or* eə'res] *noun* **(a)** man or woman who will inherit from someone after their death; *he's the heir to the banking fortune*; *you've heard of Barbara, the tobacco heiress?*; *his heirs divided the estate between them* (NOTE: the plural of **heiress** is **heiresses**) **(b)** **the heir to the throne** = the man or

woman who will be king or queen when the present king or queen dies; **heir apparent** = person who will certainly inherit a title; **heir presumptive** = person who may be expected to inherit a title (NOTE: do not confuse with **hair, air**)

heirloom ['eəlu:m] *noun* valuable object which has belonged to a family for a long time; *the burglars stole some family heirlooms*

held [held] *see* HOLD

helicopter ['helɪkɒptə] *noun* aircraft which can rise straight up in the air, with a large horizontal propeller; *you can take a helicopter from the airport to the centre of the town*; *it is only a short helicopter flight from the centre of town to the factory site*

helipad ['helɪpæd] *noun* small area where helicopters can land or take off (such as on the roof of a building)

heliport ['helɪpɔ:t] *noun* airport for helicopters; *there's a heliport in the centre of town*

helium ['hi:liəm] *noun* light inert gas, used in balloons, etc.; *scientists sent up a helium balloon to get data from the atmosphere* (NOTE: Chemical element: chemical symbol: **He**; atomic number: **2**)

he'll [hi:l] = HE WILL

hell [hel] *noun* **(a)** place where devils are thought to live, to which wicked people are sent after they die; *medieval pictures show hell as a burning place with red devils pushing wicked people into the fires with pitchforks* (NOTE: does not take the articles **a** *or* **the**) **(b)** (*informal*) miserable place; *it's hell working in the office these days*; **to give someone hell** = to treat someone very badly **(c)** **a hell of a** *or* **one hell of a** = (i) a dreadful thing; (ii) a marvellous thing; *the car's making a hell of a noise*; *that was one hell of a party last night!* **(d)** (*informal* word used to make a phrase stronger) *what the hell's been going on here?*; *am I going to lend you £50? Am I hell!*

hellish ['helɪʃ] *adjective* (*informal*) very unpleasant, like hell; *the journey to Mexico was absolutely hellish*; *I feel hellish, I think I've got flu*

hello [hə'ləʊ] *interjection* showing a greeting; *hello! Mary, I'm glad to see you*; *say hello to her from me*; *she called hello from the other side of the street* (NOTE: also spelt **hallo, hullo**; in American English, use **hi**)

helm [helm] *noun* **(a)** wheel or bar with which a ship or boat is steered; *he put the helm hard to starboard as soon as he saw the iceberg* **(b)** **at the helm** = in charge; **to take the helm** = to take charge; *now that James has taken the helm there shouldn't be any more public relations disasters*

helmet ['helmət] *noun* solid hat used as a protection; *soldiers wear helmets when they are on patrol*; *you must wear a helmet when riding a motorbike*; **crash helmet** = solid hat worn by motorcyclists, etc.; *many cyclists now wear crash helmets*; **safety helmet** = solid hat worn by construction workers, etc.; *visitors to the building site must wear safety helmets* (NOTE: also called **hard hats**)

helmeted ['helmətɪd] *adjective* wearing a helmet; *rows of helmeted police waited for the demonstrators*

help [help] **1** *noun* **(a)** something which makes it easier for you to do something; *she was washing the floor with the help of a big mop*; *do you need any help with moving the furniture?*; *she finds the word-processor a great help in writing her book*; *her* *assistant is not much help in the office - he can't type or drive* **(b)** providing aid and assistance to someone; *people were calling for help from the ruins of the house; the nurses offered help to people injured in the accident;* **to go to someone's help** = to try to rescue someone; *the rescue teams went to the help of the earthquake victims* **(c)** financial assistance; *the government provides help to deprived areas* **2** *verb* **(a)** to make it easier for someone to do something; *he helped the old lady up the steps; the government wants to help small businesses; your father can help you with your homework; one of my friends helped me move the piano into the bedroom* **(b)** *(with* **cannot***)* not to be able to stop doing something; *he couldn't help laughing; she can't help stealing clothes from shops;* **it can't be helped** = nothing can be done to improve the situation; **he can't help it** = it's not his fault; *she can't help it if she has asthma* **(c) to help yourself** = to serve yourself with food, etc.; *she helped herself to some cake; if you feel thirsty just help yourself; (informal)* **to help yourself to** = to steal; *she helped herself to my wallet* **3** *interjection meaning that you are in difficulties;* **help! help! call the police!;** *help! I can't stop the car!*

helper ['helpə] *noun* person who helps; *she works two mornings a week as a helper in a playgroup*

helpful ['helpfʊl] *adjective* which helps; *she made some helpful suggestions; they were very helpful when we moved house*

helping ['helpɪŋ] *noun* **1** portion of food; *the helpings are very small in this restaurant; children's helpings are not as large as those for adults;* **second helping** = another portion of the same food; *can I have a second helping of pudding, please?* **2** *adjective* which helps; **to give someone a helping hand** = to help someone with work; *he gave me a helping hand with the cleaning*

helpless ['helpləs] *adjective* not able to do anything; *the house was burning and I couldn't do anything - I felt so helpless!; he's helpless when his car breaks down*

helplessly ['helpləsli] *adverb* not able to help; *they stood helplessly on the cliffs watching the ship sink*

helpline ['helplaɪn] *noun* special phone number for people to call when they need help; *if you have problems with your purchase, please call our customer helpline*

hem [hem] **1** *noun* the sewn edge of a skirt, tablecloth, etc.; *she was wearing a long skirt, with the hem touching the floor* **2** *verb* **(a)** to make the hem of a skirt, etc.; *I've almost finished the skirt, it just needs to be hemmed* **(b) to hem in** = to surround closely; *the house is hemmed in by big factories; the soldiers were hemmed in by guerrillas* (NOTE: **hemming - hemmed**)

hemisphere ['hemɪsfɪə] *noun* **(a)** half of a sphere; **Northern Hemisphere** *or* **Southern Hemisphere** = the two halves of the earth, north and south, divided by the equator; *it is winter in the Northern Hemisphere when it is summer in the Southern* **(b)** *(in the brain)* **cerebral hemisphere** = one of the two halves of the cerebrum

hemorrhage ['hemərɪdʒ] *US* = HAEMORRHAGE

hemorrhoids ['hemərɔɪdz] *US* = HAEMORRHOIDS

hemp [hemp] *noun* plant used to make ropes and sacking; *fields of hemp;* **marijuana or hashish is derived from the flowers and leaves of hemp**

hen [hen] *noun* **(a)** adult female chicken; *the hens were scared by the fox; look, one of the hens has laid an egg!* **(b)** any female bird; *a hen sparrow* **(c)** *(informal)* **hen night** *or* **hen party** = party for women only; *there's a hen night at the pub on Thursdays; Denise is getting married on Saturday and we've all been invited to her hen night* (NOTE: the opposite, a party for men only, is a **stag party** *or* **stag night**)

hence [hens] *adverb* **(a)** from now; *five months hence, the situation should be better* **(b)** this is why; *he's got flu, hence his not coming to work*

henceforth *or* **henceforward** [hens'fɔːθ *or* hens'fɔːwəd] *adverb* *(formal)* from now on; *henceforth it will be more difficult to avoid customs checks*

henchman ['hentʃmən] *noun* political assistant or bodyguard; *the leader entered the hall followed by his henchmen* (NOTE: plural is **henchmen**)

hepatitis [hepə'taɪtɪs] *noun* inflammation of the liver; **infectious hepatitis** *or* **hepatitis A** = hepatitis transmitted by a carrier through food or drink; *she caught hepatitis A in Africa;* **hepatitis B** *or* **viral hepatitis** = serious form of hepatitis transmitted by infected blood, surgical instruments which have not been properly sterilized, shared needles, sexual intercourse; *he has recently been diagnosed as having hepatitis B*

heptathlon [hep'tæθlən] *noun* an athletic contest for women, covering seven events, held over two days

COMMENT: the sports covered are: **day one:** 100m hurdles, high jump, shot put, 200m race; **day two:** long jump, javelin, 800m race. Points are awarded according to the athlete's performance in each event. The equivalent for men is the decathlon

her [hɜː] **1** *object pronoun referring to a female; did you see her?; he told her to go away; there's a parcel for her in reception* **2** *adjective (belonging to a female, a ship, a country)* someone has stolen all her luggage; *have you seen her father?; the dog doesn't want to eat her food; France is helping her businesses to sell more abroad*

herald ['herəld] **1** *noun (formal)* person who brings a message; *she is a herald of good tidings; if the leaves fall early, that is a herald of cold weather to come; snowdrops are the herald of spring* **2** *verb* to be a sign of something coming; *dark clouds that herald stormy weather; the statistics seem to herald an end to the recession*

herb [hɜːb *US* ɜːb] *noun* plant used to give flavour to food, or as a medicine; *add some herbs to the sauce; rosemary, thyme and sage are some of the herbs we grow in our garden*

herbaceous [hɜː'beɪʃəs] *adjective* (flowering plant) which comes up every year, but does not have permanent stems above the ground; *herbaceous plants have fleshy stems rather than woody ones;* **herbaceous border** = bed of herbaceous plants growing along the edge of a lawn; *you should plant the taller plants at the back of the herbaceous border*

herbal ['hɜːbəl] *adjective* using herbs; *herbal tea; Chinese herbal medicines*

herbicide ['hɜːbɪsaɪd] *noun* chemical which kills plants, especially weeds; *environmentalists want to restrict the use of herbicides and pesticides*

herd [hɜːd] **1** *noun* a group of animals, especially cows; *herds of cattle were grazing on the hillside* (NOTE: do not confuse with **heard**; the word **herd** is usually used with cattle; for sheep, goats, and birds such as hens or geese, the word to use is **flock**) **2** *verb* to gather together into a group; *the prisoners were herded together into a yard*

herdsman ['hɜːdzmən] *noun* farm worker who looks after a herd of animals; *herdsmen drive their cattle down into the plains* (NOTE: plural is **herdsmen**)

here [hɪə] *adverb* **(a)** in this place; *I'll sit here in the shade and wait for you*; *here are the keys you lost*; *I'll put the book down here next to your computer*; *they have been living here in England for a long time*; *here you are* = take this; *here you are, today's newspaper!* **(b)** to this place; *come here at once!*; *can you bring the chairs here, please?*; *here comes the bus!* (NOTE: when **here** comes at the beginning of a sentence, the following subject comes after the verb if the subject is a noun and not a pronoun: **here comes the bus** but **here it comes**)

hereditary [hə'redɪtəri] *adjective* which is inherited, which is passed from parent to child; *haemophilia is a hereditary condition*; *red hair is hereditary in her family*; **hereditary peer** = member of the House of Lords who has inherited his title and will leave it to his heir when he dies; *many people believe that hereditary peers have no place in a democracy*

heredity [hə'redɪti] *noun* occurrence of physical or mental characteristics in children which are inherited from their parents; *a person's physical appearance is usually dependent on heredity*

heresy ['herəsi] *noun* wrong opinion or belief, especially wrong religious belief; *the Arian heresy split the early Christian church*; *shh! it's heresy to talk like that about the president*

heretic ['herətɪk] *noun* person who holds wrong religious beliefs; *in the Middle Ages heretics were burnt*

heretical [hə'retɪkl] *adjective* referring to heresy; *his book contains heretical statements and has been condemned by the church hierarchy*

heritage ['herɪtɪdʒ] *noun* national treasure passed from one generation to the next; *the castle is part of our national heritage*; **heritage attraction** *or* **heritage museum** *or* **heritage park** = tourist facility which is based on a country's historical or cultural background

hermetic [hɜː'metɪk] *adjective* airtight, which does not allow air to get in or out; *the food is in a box with a hermetic seal*

hermetically [hɜː'metɪkəli] *adverb* airtight, not letting air to get in or out; *the films must be kept in hermetically sealed boxes*

hermit ['hɜːmɪt] *noun* person who chooses to live alone outside the community; *this cave used to be inhabited by a hermit*; **hermit crab** = crab that lives in empty sea shells

hermitage ['hɜːmɪtɪdʒ] *noun* place where a hermit lives; *this is the site of an medieval hermitage*

hernia ['hɜːniə] *noun* medical condition where an organ bulges through a hole or weakness in the wall which surrounds it; *you'll give yourself a hernia,*

lifting that suitcase!; *he had a hernia operation last year*

hero ['hɪərəu] *noun* **(a)** brave man; *the hero of the fire was the fireman who managed to rescue the children from an upstairs room* **(b)** main male character in a book, play, film, etc.; *the hero of the story is a little boy* (NOTE: plural is **heroes**; the opposite, the bad character, is the **villain**)

heroic [hɪ'rəuɪk] *adjective* like a hero; *he made a heroic attempt to rescue the dog*

heroically [hɪ'rəuɪkli] *adverb* like a hero; *very heroically she took her driving test again*; *the fireman heroically went back into the burning building*

heroin ['herəuɪn] *noun* strong addictive illegal drug made from poppies; *her daughter is a heroin addict*; *the government has launched a campaign against heroin and other drugs* (NOTE: do not confuse with **heroine**)

heroine ['herəuɪn] *noun* **(a)** brave woman; *the heroine of the accident was a passing cyclist who pulled the children out of the burning car* **(b)** main female character in a book, play, film, etc.; *the heroine of the film is a school teacher* (NOTE: do not confuse with **heroin**)

heroism ['herəuɪzm] *noun* bravery; *it was an act of great heroism*; *she displayed great heroism during the fire* (NOTE: no plural)

heron ['herən] *noun* tall, usually grey, water bird with a long neck and long legs; *the heron stood at the edge of the stream looking for fish*

herpes ['hɜːpiːz] *noun* inflammation of the skin or mucous membrane, forming small blisters, caused by a virus; *herpes round the lips is often called a 'cold sore'*; *chickenpox is caused by the herpes virus*

herring ['herɪŋ] *noun* **(a)** small silver coloured sea fish; *she had grilled herrings for dinner* (NOTE: plural can be **herring: a shoal of herring**) **(b)** a **red herring** = piece of information which is not important, and is given to someone to distract attention from what is really important; *forget about all the clues in the first chapter, they're just red herrings*

hers [hɜːz] *pronoun* belonging to her; *that watch is hers, not mine*; *she introduced me to a friend of hers* = to one of her friends

herself [hɜː'self] *pronoun* referring to a female subject; *the manageress wrote to me herself*; *did your sister enjoy herself?*; *she's too young to be able to dress herself*; **she lives all by herself** = she lives all alone; **she did it all by herself** = she did it with no one to help her; *now she's eight, we let her go to the shops all by herself*

he's [hiːz] = HE HAS, HE IS

hesitant ['hezɪtənt] *adjective* hesitating, not decided yet; *the baby took a few hesitant steps towards the table*; *he is still hesitant about agreeing to the deal*

hesitate ['hezɪteɪt] *verb* to be slow to act, because you are unable to decide; *she's hesitating about whether to accept the job*; *he hesitated for a moment and then said 'no'*

hesitation [hezɪ'teɪʃn] *noun* waiting and not deciding; *after a moment's hesitation he jumped into the water*; *I have no hesitation in recommending him for the job*

heterosexual [hetərəu'seksjuəl] *adjective & noun* (person) attracted to people of the opposite sex; *compare* BISEXUAL, HOMOSEXUAL

hew [hjuː] *verb (literary)* to chop with an axe; *they hewed down the dead tree; we hewed a way through the forest with machetes* (NOTE: do not confuse with hue; note: **hewing - hewed - has hewn**)

hexagon ['heksəgən] *noun (in geometry)* shape with six sides

hexagonal [hek'zægənəl] *adjective* with six sides; *he has built a little hexagonal summerhouse in the garden*

hey! [heɪ] *interjection showing a greeting or surprise; hey! you!, what are you doing there?; hey! that's my chair!*

heyday ['heɪdeɪ] *noun* time of great glory, success, etc.; *in her heyday, she was paid millions for each film; the heyday of the empire lasted until 1914*

HGV *see* HEAVY GOODS VEHICLE

hi! [haɪ] *interjection showing a greeting; Hi! I'm your tour leader; Hi! Mary, how are you today?; say hi to her from me* (NOTE: **hallo, hullo** are more usual in British English, **hi** in American English)

hiccup *or* **hiccough** ['hɪkʌp] **1** *noun* **(a)** spasm in the diaphragm which causes a sudden intake of breath and a characteristic sound; *she had an attack of hiccups; he got the hiccups from laughing too much* **(b)** little thing which goes wrong; *there has been a slight hiccup in our distribution service* **2** *verb* to make a hiccup; *she patted him on the back when he suddenly started to hiccup; he hiccupped so loudly that everyone in the restaurant stared at him* (NOTE: **hiccupping - hiccupped** but American spelling is also **hiccuping - hiccuped**)

hick [hɪk] *US (informal)* **1** *noun* stupid person from the country; *some hick came up and asked me the way* **2** *adjective* backward; *he comes from some hick town*

hid [hɪd] *see* HIDE

hidden ['hɪdn] *adjective* which cannot be seen; *there's a hidden safe in the wall behind his desk; they say there's some hidden treasure in the castle; see also* HIDE

hide [haɪd] **1** *noun* **(a)** thick skin of a large animal, treated to make leather; *how many hides are needed to make that leather sofa?; a real hide wallet* **(b)** place where birdwatchers can sit to watch birds without being seen by them; *birdwatchers set up hides all round the lake* **2** *verb* **(a)** to put something where no one can see or find it; *she hid the presents in the kitchen; they kept some gold coins hidden under the bed; someone has hidden my car keys* **(b)** to put yourself where no one can see or find you; *they hid in the bushes until the police car had gone past; quick! hide behind the door!* (NOTE: **hiding - hid** [hɪd] - **has hidden** ['hɪdn])

hide-and-seek [haɪdn'siːk] *noun* children's game, where one person hides and the others try to find him or her; *the children all played hide-and-seek in the garden*

hideous ['hɪdiəs] *adjective* very ugly; *where did you get that hideous dress?; the accident left him with a hideous scar on his cheek*

hiding ['haɪdɪŋ] *noun* **(a)** action of putting yourself where no one can find you; *he stayed in hiding for three days until the soldiers left the village; they* decided to go into hiding for a time until the police called off their search; **hiding place** = place where you can hide **(b)** *(informal)* beating; *he'll get a hiding from his father when he's caught*

hierarchical [haɪə'rɑːkɪkl] *adjective* arranged in ranks as in a hierarchy; *hierarchical organizations such as the army and the civil service*

hierarchy ['haɪərɑːki] *noun* **(a)** arrangement in ranks; *there is a strict hierarchy in the army* **(b)** people in the upper ranks of an organization; *the party hierarchy met to elect a new leader; the church hierarchy has condemned the attack*

hi-fi ['haɪ'faɪ] = HIGH FIDELITY *noun* very accurate reproduction of sound by equipment such as a record player and amplifier; *the company is a leading manufacturer of hi-fi audio equipment;* **a hi-fi system** *or* **a hi-fi** = equipment for playing records, compact discs or tapes, or for listening to the radio, including tape recorders, turntables, amplifier and speakers; *he played the CD on his hi-fi*

high [haɪ] **1** *adjective* **(a)** reaching far above other things; *Everest is the highest mountain in the world; the new building is 80 storeys high; the kitchen has a high ceiling; the door is not high enough to let us get the wardrobe into the bedroom; they are planning a 10-storey-high hotel next to the royal palace* (NOTE: use with figures: **the mountain is 1000 metres high; high** also refers to things that are a long way above the ground: **a high mountain, high clouds;** for people and buildings use **tall: a tall man**) **(b)** large in quantity; *he earns a high income; the high level of unemployment in the country; high prices put customers off; the car shakes when going at high speeds; the price of petrol is higher every year* **(c)** important; *she occupies a high post in the ministry; he was quite high up in the police force when he retired* **(d)** *(meat, especially game)* which has been kept until it is beginning to rot and has a strong flavour **(e)** *(informal)* **high on drugs** = influenced by drugs; *some of the teenagers were high on drugs when they were arrested* **2** *adverb;* up in the air; *the sun rose high in the sky; the bird flew higher and higher* (NOTE: **higher - highest**)

highball ['haɪbɔːl] *noun US* any long drink, such as whiskey and soda; *the waiters passed round with trays of highballs*

highbrow ['haɪbrau] *adjective* with a high intellectual content; *it was a very highbrow discussion; compare* LOWBROW

high chair ['haɪ 'tʃeə] *noun* baby's chair at a level with a table, sometimes with a tray in front of the baby; *most restaurants provide high chairs these days*

high-class ['haɪ 'klɑːs] *adjective* of very good quality; *a high-class hotel*

high command ['haɪ kə'mɑːnd] *noun* the Commander-in-Chief and his officers; *the British High Command ordered an attack*

High Commissioner ['haɪ kə'mɪʃənə] *noun* **(a)** ambassador of a Commonwealth country; *the Canadian High Commissioner in London* **(b)** top official of the United Nations; *the High Commissioner for Refugees*

High Court ['haɪ 'kɔːt] *noun* main civil court in England and Wales; *the case has been referred to the High Court*

higher education [ˈhaɪə edjəˈkeɪʃn] *noun* education in universities and colleges; *if you pass your A Levels, you can go on to higher education*

> COMMENT: the British higher education system is formed of universities and colleges, where students can take degrees in various specialized subjects. Students need a certain level of passes at 'A' levels to enter a university, and most universities ask students to come for special entrance exams and interviews. Fees in higher education are in some cases met by grants, but many students are required to pay for their tuition fees and take out loans to do this

high fidelity [ˈhaɪ fɪˈdelɪtɪ] *adjective see* HI-FI

high-flyer [ˈhaɪˈflaɪə] *noun* person who has great potential and ambition; *look out for Abel Smith - he's a real high-flyer*

high-flying [ˈhaɪˈflaɪɪŋ] *adjective* **(a)** which is flying high in the sky; *high-flying aircraft leave trails of vapour* **(b)** who has great potential and ambition; *a high-flying business executive*

high ground [ˈhaɪ ˈɡraʊnd] *noun* area of ground which is higher than the rest; *as the river flooded, farmers escaped to high ground with their cattle*; **the moral high ground** = position where one side in an argument feels that they are right in principle; *by attacking corruption, the prime minister has tried to occupy the moral high ground*

high-handed [ˈhaɪˈhændɪd] *adjective* with no respect for other people or customs; *her high-handed attitude to her staff made them dislike her*

high heels [ˈhaɪ ˈhiːlz] *noun* very high thin heels, on women's shoes; *you are not allowed to walk on the polished floor of the museum in high heels*

high jump [ˈhaɪ ˈdʒʌmp] *noun* **(a)** athletic competition (an Olympic event) in which competitors jump over a high horizontal bar set between two vertical supports; *she won a gold medal in the high jump* **(b)** *(informal)* **to be for the high jump** = to be about to be severely punished; *when the sales figures come out, half the sales team will be for the high jump*

> COMMENT: every competitor is allowed three attempts at each height and is eliminated after three unsuccessful attempts, whether at one height or different heights. After all the competitors have jumped the bar is raised to the next height. The winner is the jumper who clears the bar at its greatest height

highland [ˈhaɪlənd] *adjective* from the highlands; *highland cattle* (NOTE: opposite is **lowland**)

highlander [ˈhaɪləndə] *noun* person who lives in the Scottish Highlands

highlands [ˈhaɪləndz] *noun* mountain region; *the Malaysian Highlands*; *the Scottish Highlands* (NOTE: opposite is **lowlands**)

highlight [ˈhaɪlaɪt] **1** *noun* **(a)** most important or interesting event; *the highlight of our tour of Greece was visit to the Parthenon* **(b) highlights** = characters which stand out from the text on a screen by being in bold; *see also* HI-LIGHTS **2** *verb* **(a)** to draw attention to; *the report highlights the problems of inner city housing* **(b)** to make part of the text stand out from the rest; *the headings are highlighted in bold*

highlighter [ˈhaɪlaɪtə] *noun* marker pen, a coloured felt pen used to highlight text; *use a highlighter to show where corrections need to be made*

highly [ˈhaɪlɪ] *adverb* greatly; *the restaurant has been highly recommended*; *their employees are not very highly paid*; **highly-priced** = with a very high price; **he thinks highly of her** = he admires her very much

highness [ˈhaɪnəs] *noun (formal) (used as a form of address to a member of the royal family)* **His Royal Highness, the Prince of Wales** (NOTE: when speaking directly and formally to a member of the royal family, say **Your Royal Highness**. The plural **highnesses** is used to refer to several members of the royal family)

high-pitched [ˈhaɪˈpɪtʃt] *adjective* making a shrill sound; *he speaks in a very high-pitched voice*

high point [ˈhaɪ ˈpɔɪnt] *noun* the best moment; *going to the opera in St Petersburg was the high point of our trip to Russia*

high-powered [ˈhaɪˈpaʊəd] *adjective* very powerful; *a high-powered engine*; *a high-powered businessman*

high-profile [ˈhaɪˈprəʊfaɪl] *adjective* who is often in the news; *Lord Smith, the high-profile chairman of the bank*

high-quality [ˈhaɪ ˈkwɒlətɪ] *adjective* of very good quality; *high-quality steel*

high-ranking [ˈhaɪˈræŋkɪŋ] *adjective* with a high rank in an organization; *he was met by two high-ranking army officers*; *she is the highest-ranking woman in the Civil Service*

high-rise [ˈhaɪˈraɪz] *adjective* with many storeys; *these high-rise blocks of flats were built in the 1960s and have been condemned as unsafe*

high road [ˈhaɪ ˈrəʊd] *noun* main road; *follow the old high road for a mile or so, then turn off when you come to the river*

high school [ˈhaɪ ˈskuːl] *noun* **(a)** secondary school; *she moves from primary school to the high school in the autumn* **(b)** *US* secondary school, from grade 9 to grade 12; *he's in grade 10 or tenth grade at high school*

high seas [ˈhaɪ ˈsiːz] *noun* the ocean, away from the territorial waters of any country; *the ship was attacked by pirate gunboats on the high seas*

high season [ˈhaɪ ˈsiːzən] *noun* period when there are lots of travellers, and when fares are higher (usually the period from July to September); *room rates in high season are 30% higher than in low season* (NOTE: the opposite is the **low season** *or* **off season**)

high-speed [ˈhaɪspiːd] *adjective* which runs or operates at a very high speed; *we took the high-speed train to Paris*

High Street [ˈhaɪ ˈstriːt] *noun* most important street in a village or town, where shops and banks are; *he is the manager of a high street bookshop*; *there are two grocer's shops in the High Street* (NOTE: often written **High St.**; the American equivalent is **Main Street**)

high tea [ˈhaɪ ˈtiː] *noun (in the North of England and Scotland)* early evening meal; *they arrived just in time for high tea*

> COMMENT: 'high tea' is common in hotels and guesthouses in the North of England and

Scotland. It is eaten around 5 o'clock in the afternoon and may consist of cold meat, hot or cold pies, salad, cakes, scones, and of course, tea

high tech ['haɪ 'tek] *adjective* referring to high technology; *high tech industries*

high technology ['haɪ tek'nɒlədʒi] *noun* advanced technology as used in industry, such as the use of electronics, robots, etc.

high-up ['haɪʌp] *noun (informal)* important person; *we met some high-ups in the Ministry of Defence*

high water ['haɪ wɔːtə] *noun* point when the level of the sea or of a river, etc., is at its highest; *what time is high water?*; **high-water mark** = line showing where the high tide reaches; *that slimy green line shows the high-water mark*

highway ['haɪweɪ] *noun* main public road; *a footbridge was built over the highway*

the Highway Code [ðə 'haɪweɪ 'kəʊd] *noun* British government publication containing the rules for people travelling on roads; *you need to know the Highway Code if you're taking your driving test*

hijack ['haɪdʒæk] **1** *noun* taking control of a vehicle by force; *the plane hijack was organized by a group of opponents to the government* **2** *verb* to take control of a vehicle by force; *the bandits hijacked the lorry and killed the driver*; *they hijacked an aircraft and ordered the pilot to fly to Moscow*

hijacker ['haɪdʒækə] *noun* person who hijacks; *the hijackers threatened to blow up the plane unless their demands were met*

hijacking ['haɪdʒækɪŋ] *noun* taking control of a vehicle by force; *there have been six hijackings so far this year*

hike [haɪk] **1** *noun* **(a)** vigorous walk; *we went for a 10-mile hike in the mountains* **(b)** increase; *a price hike* **2** *verb* **(a)** to go for a vigorous walk; *they were hiking in the Pyrenees when the accident happened* **(b)** to increase prices, etc.; *petrol companies have hiked up their prices*

hiker ['haɪkə] *noun* person who goes for long walks in the country for pleasure; *a party of hikers was lost in the mountains*

hiking ['haɪkɪŋ] *noun* going on long walks for pleasure; *we are going for a hiking holiday in Scotland*; *hiking is a very popular sport*

hilarious [hɪ'leəriəs] *adjective* very funny; *I thought the play was hilarious but nobody else seemed to find it funny at all*

hilarity [hɪ'læriti] *noun* great amusement or laughter; *the Prime Minister's speech was greeted with great hilarity*

hi-lights ['haɪlaɪts] *noun* streaks in your hair which have been dyed a pale colour; *is it expensive to have hi-lights at your hairdresser's?*

hill [hɪl] *noun* piece of high land, but lower than a mountain; *the hills are covered with spring flowers*; *their house is on top of a hill*; *if you climb to the top of the hill you will get a good view of the valley*

hillbilly ['hɪlbɪli] *noun (informal, derogatory) US* person from mountain areas in the south of the country *(old)* **hillbilly music** = country music

hillside ['hɪlsaɪd] *noun* sloping side of a hill; *their house is half-way up the hillside*

hilltop ['hɪltɒp] *noun* top of a hill; *low cloud covered the hilltops*; *a hilltop village surrounded by walls*

hilly ['hɪli] *adjective* with many hills; *Wales is no good for cycling - it's far too hilly* (NOTE: **hillier - hilliest**)

hilt [hɪlt] *noun* **(a)** sword handle; *he stood for the photograph with his hand on the hilt of his sword* **(b) to the hilt** = completely, totally; *we're backing him to the hilt*; *the company is up to the hilt in debt*

him [hɪm] *object pronoun* referring to a male; *have you spoken to him today?*; *tell him there's a letter waiting for him*; *that's him! - the man with the beard*

himself [hɪm'self] *pronoun* referring to a male subject; *I was served by the manager himself*; *the doctor has got flu himself*; *did your brother enjoy himself?*; **he lives all by himself** = he lives all alone; **he did it all by himself** = he did it with no one to help him; *now he's eight, we let him go to the shops all by himself*

hind [haɪnd] **1** *adjective* referring to the back part of a four-legged animal; **hind legs** = the back legs of an animal; *deer stand on their hind legs to reach juicy leaves* **2** *noun* female deer; *hinds are very protective of their fawns* (NOTE: also called a **doe**)

hinder ['hɪndə] *verb* to prevent; *the economic situation is hindering any increase in living standards*; *snow hindered the efforts of the rescuers*

hindquarters ['haɪndkwɔːtəz] *noun* the back part of a four-legged animal; *he whipped the horse on its hindquarters*

hindrance ['hɪndrəns] *noun* something which hinders; *having six children is something of a hindrance when arranging holidays*; **without let or hindrance** = without any obstacle; *the police have orders to let anyone through without let or hindrance*

hindsight ['haɪndsaɪt] *noun* realizing something too late, after it has happened; **with (the benefit of) hindsight** = knowing what we know now; *with the benefit of hindsight, I see now that we made a disastrous decision*

Hindu ['hɪnduː] **1** *adjective* referring to Hinduism; *we visited the new Hindu temple in North London* **2** *noun* person who follows Hinduism, the main religion of India; *the Hindus worship several gods; see also* DIWALI

Hinduism ['hɪnduːɪzm] *noun* the main religion of India, in which people worship several gods; *according to Hinduism, the spirit of a person who dies will live again in another person*

hinge [hɪndʒ] **1** *noun* moveable metal bracket used to hold a door, window, lid, etc., so that it can swing; *that squeaky hinge needs oiling*; *they lifted the door off its hinges* **2** *verb* **to hinge on** = to depend on; *everything hinges on her being free on Friday evening*

hinged [hɪndʒd] *adjective* attached with hinges; *the box has a hinged lid*

hint [hɪnt] **1** *noun* **(a)** hidden suggestion, clue; *he didn't give a hint as to where he was going on holiday*; *I don't know what to give her for her birthday - have you any hints?*; **to drop a hint** = to make a suggestion; *she's been dropping hints about what she wants for her birthday*; **to take a hint** = to accept a suggestion; *he took the hint and offered to pay for the lamp he broke* **(b)** very small quantity; *there's just a hint of garlic in the soup* **(c)** piece of advice; *she gave me some useful* *hints about painting furniture* **2** *verb* to say something in a way that makes people guess what you mean; *she hinted that her sister was pregnant*

hip [hɪp] **1** *noun* **(a)** part of the body at the top of your thighs; *the tailor measured him round the hips* **(b)** joint where the thigh bone pivots at the top of the leg; **hip replacement** = operation to replace the whole hip joint with an artificial one; *old people sometimes need to have hip replacements* **2** *adjective* very up-to-date; *that's a very hip shirt she's wearing*

hip hip hooray! ['hɪp 'hɪp huː'reɪ] *interjection said when you cheer someone, giving three shouts*; *three cheers for the goalkeeper! hip! hip! hooray!*

hippie *or* **hippy** ['hɪpi] *noun (informal)* person who does not conform to a normal bourgeois life-style; *the hippie movement in the 1960s*

hippopotamus *(informal)* **hippo** [hɪpə'pɒtəməs or 'hɪpəʊ] *noun* large heavy African animal which spends most of its time submerged in water, but comes onto dry land to graze (NOTE: plurals are **hippopotamuses** *or* **hippopotami** [hɪpə'pɒtəmaɪ] and **hippos** ['hɪpəʊz])

hire ['haɪə] **1** *noun* **(a)** paying money to rent a car, boat, piece of equipment, etc., for a period of time; **boat hire** *or* **cycle hire** *or* **car hire** = lending of boats, cycles, cars to people for money; **car hire firm** *or* **coach hire firm** = company which owns cars *or* coaches and lends them to people for money; **hire car** = car which has been hired; *he was driving a hire car when the accident happened* **(b)** 'for hire' = sign on a taxi showing it is empty and available for hire **2** *verb* **(a)** *(of owner)* **to hire out** = to allow other people to take something and use it, against payment of a fee; *he hires out boats on the river* **(b)** *(of borrower)* to pay money to use a car, boat, piece of equipment, etc., for a time; *she hired a car for the weekend*; *he was driving a hired car when the accident happened* **(c)** to engage someone to work for you; *we've hired three more sales assistants*; *we hired a small company to paint the offices*

hire purchase (HP) ['haɪə 'pɜːtʃəs] *noun* system of buying something by paying a sum regularly each month; *we've planning to buy our new refrigerator on hire purchase*; *she had to sign a hire-purchase agreement* (NOTE: American English uses **to buy on the installment plan**)

his [hɪz] **1** *adjective* belonging to him; *he's lost all his money*; *have you met his mother?*; *our dog wants his food* **2** *pronoun* belonging to him; *that watch is his, not mine*; *he introduced me to a friend of his* = to one of his friends

Hispanic [hɪs'pænɪk] **1** *adjective* referring to countries where Spanish is spoken, especially South American countries; *Hispanic communities in the southern States* **2** *noun* person whose native language is Spanish, especially one living in the United States; *Hispanics form an important community in Florida*

hiss [hɪs] **1** *noun* **(a)** whistling sound like an 's'; *we could hear the hiss of escaping gas* **(b)** saying 's' to show you disapprove; *he left the stage under the hisses of the audience*; *the wicked pirate's appearance was greeted with boos and hisses* (NOTE: plural is **hisses**) **2** *verb* **(a)** to make a hissing sound; *the snake hissed as we came nearer* **(b)** to show disapproval by making an 's' sound; *the audience began to hiss*; *she was hissed off the stage*

historian [hɪ'stɔːriən] *noun* person who studies or writes history; *a historian who specializes in the Chinese Empire*; *the book was written by a French historian*

historic [hɪ'stɒrɪk] *adjective* famous in history; *a historic agreement has been signed*

historical [hɪ'stɒrɪkl] *adjective* referring to history; *he likes books of historical interest*; **historical novel** = story set in a particular period in the past

history ['hɪstəri] *noun* **(a)** study of the past, of past events; *he is studying Greek history*; *she failed her history exam*; *she teaches history at London University* **(b)** book which tells the story of what happened in the past; *he wrote a history of the French Revolution* **(c)** **natural history** = the study of plants and animals

hit [hɪt] **1** *noun* **(a)** very popular song, film, performer, etc.; *the song rapidly became a hit*; *the play was a West End hit*; *she was a hit with the old people's club*; **the hit parade** = a list of hit songs **(b)** blow or knock; *just one more hit on the nail and that will be enough* **(c)** action of visiting a site on the Internet; *how many hits did we have on our web site last week?* **2** *verb* **(a)** to knock; *the car hit the tree*; *she hit him on the head with a bottle*; *she hit the ball so hard that we can't find it*; *I hit my head on the cupboard door*; *(informal)* **to hit the town** = to go and have a night out; *come on, let's hit the town* **(b)** to damage, to affect badly; *the company has been hit by the recession* **(c)** to realize; *it suddenly hit her that now she was divorced she would have to live alone* **(d)** to reach a figure or target; *our sales hit a record high last month*; *new cases of asthma hit two thousand last week* (NOTE: **hitting - hit**)

hit-and-miss ['hɪtənd'mɪs] *adjective* not carefully prepared, not properly planned; *the party was a hit-and-miss affair*; *the experiments were done in a fairly hit-and-miss way*

hit-and-run driver ['hɪtənd'rʌn 'draɪvə] *noun* driver who knocks someone down and does not stop to give help; *the police are searching for a hit-and-run driver in a white Ford*

hit back ['hɪt 'bæk] *verb* **(a)** to hit someone who has hit you; *the muggers hit him so hard that he collapsed before he could hit them back* **(b)** to do something as a reaction to something; *when the supermarket chain lowered their prices, the other chains hit back by lowering prices too*; *he hit back at the inspectors, saying that their report was biased*

hitch [hɪtʃ] **1** *noun* unexpected temporary problem; *there's a hitch, and the wedding has been postponed*; **without a hitch** = with no trouble or problems; *the party went off without a hitch* **2** *verb* **(a)** **to hitch up** = to pull up; *he hitched up his trousers* **(b)** **to hitch (a lift)** = to ask a driver to take you as a passenger, usually by signalling with the thumb or by holding a sign with your destination written on it; *he hitched a lift to Birmingham*; *her car broke down and she hitched a lift from a passing motorist* **(c)** to attach; *the caravan was hitched to the car*

hitch-hike ['hɪtʃhaɪk] *verb* to stand by the road and signal to passing motorists, showing that you want a free ride to a place; *he hitch-hiked his way all across the United States*; *hitch-hiking is forbidden on motorways*

hitch-hiker ['hɪtʃhaɪkə] *noun* person who hitch-hikes; *he picked up two hitch-hikers who were going to Scotland*

hither ['hɪðə] *adverb (old)* to this place; **hither and thither** *or* **hither and yon** = all over the place, in all directions; *the crowd ran hither and thither to escape from the police*

hitherto [hɪðə'tuː] *adverb (formal)* until now; *she discovered a hitherto unknown poem by Shakespeare*

hit list ['hɪt 'lɪst] *noun* list of people who deserve to be punished; *several members of the family are on the Inland Revenue's hit list; the government has drawn up a hit list of schools to be closed*

hit on ['hɪt 'ɒn] *verb* to discover, to get a good idea; *we hit on the idea of taking him to a concert as a birthday present*

hit squad ['hɪt 'skwɒd] *noun* group of gunmen who are ordered to kill people; *hit squads were sent out to get rid of the opposition leaders*

hitter ['hɪtə] *noun* person who hits a ball hard when playing cricket, etc.; *he's a powerful hitter and rapidly scored a century*

HIV ['eɪtʃaɪ'viː] = HUMAN IMMUNODEFICIENCY VIRUS the virus which causes AIDS; *he was diagnosed as being HIV positive*

hive [haɪv] **1** *noun* **(a)** box for bees to make a nest in which makes it easier for the beekeeper to gather the honey; *take the honeycomb carefully out of the hive; the beekeeper opened one of the hives and took out a honeycomb* **(b)** a **hive of activity** = a place where people come and go, where people are very busy; *the school was a hive of activity on Prize Day* **(c) hives** = skin disorder where white, pink or red patches are formed which itch or sting; *hives are caused by an allergy* **2** *verb* **to hive off** = to split off part of a large company to form a smaller subsidiary; *the new managing director hived off the retail sections of the company*

hoard [hɔːd] **1** *noun* store of food, money, etc., which has been collected; *they discovered a hoard of gold coins in the field* **2** *verb* to buy and store supplies in case of need; *squirrels hoard nuts for the winter; everyone has started hoarding fuel in case supplies run out* (NOTE: do not confuse with **horde**)

hoarfrost ['hɔːfrɒst] *noun* white frost, which covers trees, grass, pieces of wood, etc.; *the fields were white with hoarfrost*

hoarse [hɔːs] *adjective* rough-sounding (voice); *she spoke in a hoarse whisper; he shouted so much at the Rugby match that he was quite hoarse* (NOTE: do not confuse with **horse**)

hoary ['hɔːri] *adjective (informal)* very old; **a hoary chestnut** *or* **a hoary joke** = an old joke that everyone knows (NOTE: **hoarier - hoariest**)

hoax [həʊks] **1** *noun* trick played on someone as a joke or to annoy; *the police and fire brigade arrived but the bomb was just a hoax; the ambulance answered a hoax telephone call* (NOTE: plural is **hoaxes**) **2** *verb* to trick someone as a joke; *he hoaxed the inhabitants of the village into thinking he was a famous scientist*

hob [hɒb] *noun* **(a)** flat top on a cooker; *our new cooker has a ceramic hob; do not use abrasive cleaner on the hob* **(b)** metal stand by a fire; *put the kettle on the hob*

hobble ['hɒbl] *verb* **(a)** to walk with difficulty; *he hobbled into the room on crutches* **(b)** to attach a horse's legs together; *the horses were hobbled so that they couldn't run away* **(c)** to be hobbled by something = to be prevented from doing your job by something; *companies cannot expand and are hobbled by government regulations*

hobby ['hɒbi] *noun* favourite thing which you do in your spare time; *his hobby is making model planes* (NOTE: plural is **hobbies**)

hobo ['həʊbəʊ] *noun US* tramp, person who wanders from place to place doing odd jobs, but with nowhere permanent to live; *some came to the ranch looking for farm work* (NOTE: plural is **hoboes**)

hock [hɒk] **1** *noun* **(a)** lower part of a pig's leg, used as food; **boiled hock** = joint of ham from the leg of a pig **(b)** any white wine from the Rhine valley in Germany; *we opened a bottle of hock* **(c)** *(informal)* **in hock to** = in debt to, owing money to; *the company is in hock to the banks* **2** *verb (informal)* to pawn something; *I was so desperate that I hocked my watch*

hockey ['hɒki] *noun* team game played on grass, where you try to hit a small ball into your opponents' goal using a long stick which is curved at the end; *he played in the hockey team at school* (NOTE: called **field hockey** in American English) **(b) ice hockey** = form of hockey played on ice using a hard rubber disc called a puck; *the ice hockey gold medal will be fought out between Canada and Russia* (NOTE: called simply **hockey** in American English)

> COMMENT: hockey is played between two teams of 11 players, each game having two 35-minute halves; ice hockey is played between two teams of six players, each game being made up of three 20-minute periods; *see also note at* ICE HOCKEY

hodgepodge ['hɒdʒpɒdʒ] *noun US* mixture of all sorts of items; *the book is a hodgepodge of ideas and theories taken from various writers* (NOTE: British English is **hotchpotch**)

hoe [həʊ] **1** *noun* garden implement, with a long handle and small sharp blade, used to break up the surface of soil or cut off weeds; *use a sharp hoe to remove the weeds between your peas* **2** *verb* to cultivate land with a hoe; *you must hoe the vegetable patch regularly to keep the weeds down; the gardener was hoeing around the strawberries*

hoedown ['həʊdaʊn] *noun US* party for square dancing and country music

hog [hɒg] **1** *noun* **(a)** *GB* castrated male pig **(b)** *US* any pig; *hogs are traded on the Chicago exchange* **(c)** *(informal)* **to go the whole hog** = to do something completely; *if we're buying two armchairs we might as well go the whole hog and buy a sofa as well* **2** *verb* to monopolize, to take more than you should; *he was hogging the middle of the road; stop hogging the biscuits - we'd like some too!; she's always hogging the limelight* (NOTE: **hogging - hogged**)

Hogmanay ['hɒgmənei] *noun* festival in Scotland on 31st December, celebrating the New Year

> COMMENT: it is a tradition that the first person who comes through the door on New Year's Day (i.e. after midnight on New Year's Eve) should bring luck. If possible the person should be a dark stranger, and should carry a piece of coal for the

fire, as well as food and drink, usually whisky. This tradition also exists in the north of England and is called 'first-footing'

hoist [hɔɪst] **1** *noun* device for lifting; *the fireman rigged up a hoist to get the dog out of the well* **2** *verb* to lift up; *the box was hoisted up on a rope*; *the defenders hoisted a white flag*

hold [həʊld] **1** *verb* **(a)** to keep tight, especially in your hand; *she was holding the baby in her arms*; *she held her ticket between her teeth as she was carrying suitcases in both hands*; *hold tight - the machine is going to start*; *he held the bag close to his chest* **(b)** to contain, to be large enough for something to fit inside; *the bottle holds two litres*; *the box will hold four pairs of shoes*; *will the car hold eight people?*; *the plane holds 250 passengers* **(c)** to make something happen; *they are holding a party for their wedding anniversary*; *the meeting will be held next Tuesday in the town hall*; *we are holding the village fête next week* **(d)** to stay the same; *will the fine weather hold until Saturday?* **(e)** to possess; *she holds a valid driving licence*; *he holds the record for the 2000 metres* **(f)** *(on telephone)* **hold the line please** = please wait; *the chairman is on the other line - will you hold?* **(g)** to keep inside; *the prisoners were held in police cells overnight*; **to hold water** = to be valid, to be true; *his argument doesn't hold water*; **to hold your breath** = to keep air in your lungs to go under water, as a test or because you are afraid that something will happen; *she held her breath under water for a minute*; *we're all holding our breath to see if he wins a gold medal* **(h)** to capture and control a place; *the rebels are holding the airport*; *government forces still hold about half the country* (NOTE: **holding** - **held** [held]) **2** *noun* **(a)** bottom part of a ship or an aircraft, in which cargo is stored; *you can't take all that luggage with you, it has to go in the hold* **(b)** action of gripping something; *he lost his hold on the ladder*; *keep tight hold of the bag, we don't want it stolen*; **to get hold of someone** = to find someone you need by telephone; *I tried to get hold of the doctor but he was out*; **to get hold of something** = to find something which you want to use; *do you know where I can get hold of a ladder?*; **to take hold of something** = to grip something, to take control of something; *the fire took hold rapidly* **(c)** action of having a strong influence over someone; *she has some sort of hold over her husband*

holdall [ˈhəʊldɔːl] *noun* soft bag for carrying clothes, etc., when travelling; *he left the bus carrying a small holdall*

hold back [ˈhəʊld ˈbæk] *verb* **(a)** not to tell; *she held back important information from the police* **(b)** not to go forward; *most of the crowd held back until they saw it was safe*

hold down [ˈhəʊld ˈdaʊn] *verb* **(a)** to keep at a low level; *we are holding our prices down* **(b)** **to hold down a job** = to manage to do a difficult job

holder [ˈhəʊldə] *noun* **(a)** thing which holds; *put the pen back into its holder* **(b)** person who holds; *she is a British passport holder* or *she is the holder of a British passport*; *he is the world record holder in the javelin*

holding [ˈhəʊldɪŋ] *noun* investments owned; *she has holdings in several British companies*; **holding company** = company which owns shares in other companies

hold on [ˈhəʊld ˈɒn] *verb* **(a)** to hold something tightly; *she held on to the rope with both hands*; *hold on to your purse in the crowd*; *hold on tight, we're turning!* **(b)** to wait; *hold on a moment, I'll get my umbrella*; *do you want to speak to the manager? - hold on, I'll find him for you*

hold out [həʊldˈaʊt] *verb* **(a)** to move something towards someone; *hold out your plate to be served*; *he held out his hand but she refused to shake it* **(b)** to resist against; *the castle held out for ten weeks against a huge enemy army*

hold out for [ˈhəʊld ˈaʊt fɔː] *verb* to wait and ask for more; *you should hold out for a 10% pay rise*

hold up [ˈhəld ˈʌp] *verb* **(a)** to lift; *he held up his hand*; *he held the little boy up so that he could see the procession*; *the roof is held up by those pillars* **(b)** to make late; *the planes were held up by fog*; *government red tape is holding up the deal*; *the strike will hold up deliveries* **(c)** to attack and rob; *six gunmen held up the security van*

hold-up [ˈhəʊldʌp] *noun* **(a)** delay, time when something is later than planned; *long hold-ups are expected because of road works on the motorway*; *there's been a hold-up and the shipment won't arrive till next week* **(b)** armed attack; *the gang carried out three armed hold-ups in the same day*

hole [həʊl] *noun* opening, space in something; *you've got a hole in your shoe*; *we all peeped through the hole in the fence*; *rabbits live in holes in the ground*

holiday [ˈhɒlɪdeɪ] *noun* **(a)** day on which no work is done because of laws or religious rules; *the office is closed for the Christmas holiday*; **bank holiday** = special day when most people do not go to work and the banks are closed; *New Year's Day is a bank holiday*; **public holiday** = day when all workers rest and enjoy themselves instead of working; **statutory holiday** = holiday which is fixed by law **(b)** period when you don't work, but rest, go away and enjoy yourself; *when are you taking your holiday* or *when are you planning to go on holiday?*; *he's going to Spain on holiday*; *we always spend our holidays in the mountains*; *how many days' holiday do you have each year?*; *the manager isn't in the office - he's on holiday*; **the job carries five weeks' holiday** = one of the conditions of the job is that you have five weeks' holiday each year; **the summer holidays** = period during the summer when children do not go to school, and when many families go away; *our summer holidays last from July to September*; *the weather was awful during the summer holidays*; *see also* BANK HOLIDAY, PUBLIC HOLIDAY (NOTE: **holiday** is often used without **the**; Note also that the American English is usually **vacation**)

holidaymaker [ˈhɒlɪdɪmeɪkə] *noun* person who is on holiday; *in August the town is full of holidaymakers*

holiness [ˈhəʊlɪnəs] *noun* **(a)** state of being holy **(b)** *(formal) (used as a form of address to the Pope)* **His Holiness, the Pope**

holistic [hɒˈlɪstɪk] *adjective* **(a)** **holistic medicine** = medical treatment involving the whole person, including mental health and family circumstances, rather than just dealing with the symptoms of the illness; *some doctors specialize in holistic medicine* **(b)** *(policy, programme, etc.)* dealing with a social problem as a whole rather than looking at one aspect of it; *the committee has been calling for a more holistic approach to the problem of single parent families*

Holland ['hɒlənd] *noun* another name for the Netherlands (NOTE: strictly speaking, **Holland** is only one of the provinces of the Netherlands (the province to the north of Amsterdam), but the word is very frequently used in English to mean the whole country)

holler ['hɒlə] *verb (informal)* to shout; *she was hollering at the kids to come in*

hollow ['hɒləʊ] **1** *noun* sunken part on a flat surface; *they made a hollow in the ground for a camp fire* **2** *adjective* with a hole inside; *a hollow log*; *if you tap the box it sounds hollow*

hollow out ['hɒləʊ 'aʊt] *verb* to remove the inside part of something so as to make it hollow; *the natives used hollowed-out treetrunks as canoes*

holly ['hɒli] *noun* small evergreen tree with shiny dark green prickly leaves and bright red berries; *at Christmas, we decorate the house with holly and mistletoe*

Hollywood ['hɒlɪwʊd] *noun* town in California, the centre of the American film industry; *she's a Hollywood star*; *he went to Hollywood and became a star*

holocaust ['hɒləkɔːst] *noun* **(a)** total destruction, especially by fire or nuclear war; *a nuclear holocaust would cause unimaginable suffering* **(b)** the Holocaust = mass killing of the Jews during the Second World War; *the horrors of the Holocaust must never be allowed to happen again*

holster ['həʊlstə] *noun* leather holder for a revolver; *he had a revolver in a holster on his belt*

holy ['həʊli] *adjective* **(a)** sacred; *they went to ask a holy man his advice*; **holy water** = consecrated water used when baptizing babies (NOTE: do not confuse with **wholly**; note: **holier - holiest) (b)** the **Holy Father** = the Pope; **the Holy See** = the office of Pope

Holy Communion ['həʊli kə'mjuːnjən] *noun* Christian ceremony where bread and wine are taken in memory of Christ's Last Supper; *Holy Communion will be at 9.30*

Holy Ghost *or* **Holy Spirit** ['həʊli 'gəʊst or 'həʊli 'spɪrɪt] *noun* third member of the Christian Trinity, God in the form of a spirit

homage ['hɒmɪdʒ] *noun* **(a)** *(formal)* respect to someone; **to pay homage to someone** = to show your respect for someone, especially someone who is dead; *the children paid homage to their teacher who had been killed*; *the nation observed a minute's silence as a mark of homage to the dead of two world wars* **(b)** *(formal)* feudal duty; *peasants had to pay homage to their lords*

home [həʊm] **1** *noun* **(a)** place where you live; *their home is a flat in the centre of London*; *will you be at home tomorrow morning?*; *when do you leave home for work in the morning?*; *send the letter to my home address, not to my office*; **make yourself at home** = do as if you were in your own home; *he lay down on the sofa, opened a bottle of beer, and made himself at home*; **home from home** = comfortable and welcoming place, just like your home; *the hotel is a real home from home*; *(informal)* **nothing to write home about** = nothing very exciting or special; *his new job is nothing to write home about* **(b)** area where you come from; *she*

lives in London but her home is the mountains of Wales; *his home is in the West Country* **(c)** house; *they are building fifty new homes on the outskirts of the village* **(d)** house where people are looked after; *my aunt has moved to an old people's home*; **a children's home** = a home for orphaned children or for children from broken homes **(e)** *(in sports)* **at home** = on the local sports ground; *our team is playing at home next Saturday* (NOTE: the opposite is **away**) **(f)** family, household; *she comes from a broken home* **2** *adverb* towards the place where you usually live; *we've got to go home now*; *he usually gets home by 7 o'clock*; *don't send it - I'll take it home with me*; *if you don't want to walk, you can always take the bus home* (NOTE: used without a preposition: **he went home, she's coming home,** etc.) **3** *adjective* **(a)** referring to where you live or where you were born; *my home town is Birmingham*; **home cooking** = style of food as cooked at home, not in restaurants; *I like good home cooking* **(b)** *(in sports)* local; *the home side won*; *our team beat the home team 3 - 0*; *we have a home game next Saturday* **(c)** in this country, not abroad; *home sales were better than exports last month*; *they find it difficult selling into the home market*

Home Counties ['həʊm 'kaʊntɪz] *noun* the area formed of the counties round London; *he comes from the Home Counties*; *there are still some areas of woodland in the Home Counties* (NOTE: always written with **the**)

homegrown ['həʊmgrəʊn] *adjective* grown in your own garden; *homegrown vegetables*

home in on ['həʊm 'ɪn ɒn] *verb* to aim at and go towards a target; *the missile homed in on the enemy plane*

homeland ['həʊmlənd] *noun* home of a people; *the refugees tried to return to their homeland after the war*

homeless ['həʊmləs] **1** *adjective* with nowhere to live; *the council has a duty to house homeless families* **2** *noun* **the homeless** = people with nowhere to live; *the homeless sleep in parks or doorways*

homely ['həʊmli] *adjective* **(a)** simple but pleasant; *the accommodation was homely and unpretentious*; *the pub serves good homely food* **(b)** *US (person)* plain and not very attractive; *she's a homely girl*

homemade [həʊm'meɪd] *adjective* made at home and not bought; *a pot of homemade marmalade*; *they fired a homemade rocket into the police station*

Home Office ['həʊm 'ɒfɪs] *noun* British Government department dealing with internal affairs, such as the police and prisons (NOTE: the department is run by the **Home Secretary**. In other countries this department is usually called the **Ministry of the Interior**; in the USA it is called the **Department of the Interior**)

homeopath ['həʊmiəʊpæθ] *noun* person who practises homeopathy; *she decided to see her local homeopath*

homeopathic [həʊmiəʊ'pæθɪk] *adjective* referring to homeopathy; *she is having a course of homeopathic treatment*

homeopathy [həʊmi'ɒpəθi] *noun* treatment which involves giving very small amounts of a substance which would give a healthy person the symptoms of the condition being treated; *the clinic practises homeopathy and acupuncture*

homeowner ['həʊməʊnə] *noun* person who owns a flat or house; *a homeowner's insurance policy*

home plate ['həʊm 'pleɪt] *noun (in baseball)* the base where the batter stands to hit the ball

home run ['həʊm 'rʌn] *noun (in baseball)* score made when a batter manages to touch all three bases and return to the home plate without stopping

Home Secretary ['həʊm 'sekrətəri] *noun* British government minister in charge of the Home Office (NOTE: in other countries, this minister is usually called the **Minister of the Interior**; in the USA, he is the **Secretary of the Interior**)

homesick ['həʊmsɪk] *adjective* feeling sad because you are away from home; *as soon as she started her job in Australia she felt homesick for London*

homestead ['həʊmsted] *noun* farmhouse and land; *when their parents died, the children put the old homestead up for sale*

home straight ['həʊm 'streɪt] *noun* **(a)** *(on a racetrack)* last straight part of the track before the finish; *the runners are coming into the home straight* **(b)** last part of a project, when it is almost finished; *cheer up, we're in the home straight now!*

home town ['həʊm 'taʊn] *noun* town where you live; *he lives in Canada, but he likes to come back to his home town from time to time*

home truths ['həʊm 'truːðz] *noun (informal)* unpleasant facts about someone, which someone else tells them; *I had to tell her a few home truths*

homeward ['həʊmwəd] *adjective* towards home; *the homeward trip always seems shorter* **2** *adverb* **homeward bound** = heading towards your home; *after many delays we were homeward bound at last*

homewards *US* **homeward** ['həʊmwədz] *adverb (formal)* towards home; *after walking for hours in the hills, they turned back and headed homewards*

homework ['həʊmwɜːk] *noun* work which you take home from school to do in the evening; *have you finished your maths homework?*; *I haven't any homework today, so I can watch TV* (NOTE: no plural)

homeworker ['həʊmwʌkə] *noun* person who works at home for a company

homicidal [hɒmɪ'saɪdl] *adjective* likely to kill someone; *a homicidal maniac got into the hospital*

homicide ['hɒmɪsaɪd] *noun* murder, killing of someone; *he was found guilty of homicide*; *the homicide rate has risen over the past years*; **the Homicide Squad** = special section of the police force which investigates murders

hominy ['hɒmɪni] *noun US* cooked maize seeds; **hominy grits** = ground maize kernels, boiled and eaten at breakfast

homoeopath, homoeopathic, homoeopathy ['həʊmiəʊpæθ or həʊmiəʊ'pæθɪk or həʊmi'ɒpəθi] *see* HOMEOPATH, HOMEOPATHIC, HOMEOPATHY

homogeneous [hɒməʊ'dʒiːniəs] *adjective* all of the same type; *we were a remarkably homogeneous group - all of us were university professors*

homogenized milk [hə'mɒdʒənaɪzd 'mɪlk] *noun* milk which has been treated so that the cream is evenly mixed through the liquid; *we prefer homogenized milk, although it doesn't have cream on top*

homograph ['hɒməʊgrɑːf] *noun* word which is spelt the same as another, but which has a different meaning or pronunciation; *'close' meaning near and 'close' meaning to shut are homographs*

homonym ['hɒmənɪm] *noun* word spelt and pronounced the same as another but which has a different meaning; *'date' meaning a fruit, and 'date' meaning a day in the week, are homonyms*

homophobia [həʊməʊ'fəʊbɪə] *noun* fear of and hostility towards homosexuals; *the police were accused of homophobia*

homophobic [həʊməʊ'fəʊbɪk] *adjective* showing fear of and hostility towards homosexuals; *this homophobic reaction is not uncommon among senior police officers*

homophone ['hɒməfəʊn] *noun* word which is pronounced the same as another, but which is spelt differently or has a different meaning; *'their' and 'there' are homophones*

homosexual [həʊməʊ'seksjʊəl] *adjective & noun* (person) who is attracted to people of the same sex; *compare* BISEXUAL, HETEROSEXUAL

homosexuality [həʊməʊseksjʊ'ælɪti] *noun* being homosexual; *he admitted his homosexuality in public*

hon ['ɒnrəbl] = HONOURABLE

hone [həʊn] *verb* **(a)** to sharpen and smooth; *each arrowhead had been honed to a fine point* **(b)** to improve something over a long period; *his technique has been honed through years of practice*

honest ['ɒnɪst] *adjective* **(a)** truthful; *he was honest with the police and told them what he had done* **(b)** (person) who can be trusted; *I wouldn't buy a car from that garage - I'm not sure they're completely honest*

honestly ['ɒnɪstli] *adverb* truthfully; *honestly, it was John who took the money, not me*; *I honestly don't think she will ever come back to live here*

honesty ['ɒnəsti] *noun* truthfulness; *I admire him for his honesty in saying the job was too difficult for him*; **in all honesty** = speaking truthfully; *in all honesty I don't think we'll be able to finish the job on time*

honey ['hʌni] *noun* sweet substance produced by bees; *I like honey on toast*; *Greek cakes are often made with honey*

honeycomb ['hʌnɪkəʊm] *noun* wax cells inside a beehive that contain honey; *lift the honeycomb carefully out of the hive*; *the beekeeper opened one of the hives and took out a honeycomb*

honeymoon ['hʌnɪmuːn] **1** *noun* **(a)** holiday taken immediately after a wedding; *they went on honeymoon to Corsica*; **honeymoon couple** = two people on honeymoon **(b)** period after an election when the new government is popular; *the president's honeymoon period has come to an end* **2** *verb* to go on a honeymoon; *they plan to honeymoon in Florida*

honeysuckle ['hʌnɪsʌkl] *noun* climbing plant with scented white, pink, yellow or cream flowers; *the luscious scent of honeysuckle around the door*

honorary ['ɒnərəri] *adjective* **(a)** not paid a salary; *she's the honorary secretary of the society* **(b)** *(title which shows respect)* *he's the honorary president of the company*

honour *US* **honor** ['ɒnə] **1** *noun* **(a)** acting according to what you think is right; *he's a man of honour*; **code of honour** = rules of right and wrong which are applied to what people do **(b)** mark of respect; *it is an honour for me to be invited here today* **(c) honours degree** = university degree, showing a high level of study **(d) Your Honour** = way of addressing a judge **(e)** *(informal)* **to do the honours** = to act as host or hostess at a party; *we all need some drinks, will you do the honours, John?* **2** *verb* **(a)** to respect, to pay respect to; *to honour the dead* **(b)** to give an award as a mark of respect; *he was honoured by the university* **(c)** to do what you promised; *he honoured the agreement and gave the staff a pay rise* **(d)** *(of a bank)* **to honour a cheque** = to pay the sum written on the cheque

honourable *US* **honorable** ['ɒnrəbl] *adjective* **(a)** who or which can be respected; *he lived the rest of his life in honourable retirement*; *he did the honourable thing and resigned* **(b)** title used when one MP addresses another in Parliament; *the honourable Member for Putney would do well to remember the conditions in his constituency* (NOTE: usually shortened to **hon.** in this meaning)

hood [hʊd] *noun* **(a)** loose piece of clothing to cover your head; *a coat with a hood* **(b)** folding roof on a car, pram, etc.; *let's put down the hood, it's very hot* **(c)** *US* metal cover for the front part of a car, covering the engine; *he lifted the hood to see what was wrong with the motor* (NOTE: British English is **bonnet**)

hooded ['hʊdɪd] *adjective* wearing a hood; *a hooded figure emerged from the shadows*

hoodlum ['huːdləm] *noun* *(informal)* violent gangster; *hoodlums took over the casinos*

hoof [hːf] **1** *noun* horny part of the foot of a horse, cow, and many other animals; **cloven hoof** = hoof which is split into two parts; *sheep have cloven hooves* (NOTE: plural is **hooves** [huːvz]) **2** *verb* *(informal)* **to hoof it** = to walk; *I am afraid we'll just have to hoof it back to the camp site*

hook [hʊk] *noun* **(a)** bent piece of metal for hanging things on; *hang your coat on the hook behind the door* **(b)** very small piece of bent metal, attached to a line for catching fish; *the fish ate the worm but didn't swallow the hook*; **to get someone off the hook** = to get someone out of a difficult situation; *she got him off the hook by lying to his boss*

hooked [hʊkt] *adjective* **(a)** shaped like a hook; *he had dark eyes and a hooked nose* **(b)** *(informal)* **hooked on** = very fond of; *he's hooked on science fiction* **(c)** *(informal)* **hooked on** = addicted to; *they're both hooked on heroin*

hooker ['hʊkə] *noun* **(a)** *(in Rugby)* player in the centre of a scrum, who has to try to kick the ball backwards; *the English hooker got the ball and from there they scored a try* **(b)** *(informal)* prostitute, woman who receives money for sexual intercourse; *a busy town centre, with bars, and hookers standing on street corners*

hooky ['hʊki] *noun US* **to play hooky** = not to go to school; *they didn't go to school, but played hooky and went fishing instead* (NOTE: British English is **to play truant**)

hooligan ['huːlɪgən] *noun* wild young man; *the police were ready to clamp down on football hooligans during the World Cup*

hooliganism ['huːlɪgənɪzm] *noun* violent behaviour; *at the first sign of hooliganism, the riot police will be sent in*

hoop [huːp] *noun* large ring; *she has trained tigers to jump through hoops* (NOTE: do not confuse with **whoop**)

hooray! [hʊ'reɪ] *interjection showing enthusiasm*; *hooray, it's the first day of the holidays!*; *see also* HIP

hoot [huːt] **1** *noun* **(a)** call made by an owl; *the ghostly hoot of the owl in the night*; **hoots of laughter** = loud laughter; *his imitation of Elvis provoked hoots of laughter* **(b)** sound of a car horn; *the sudden hoot of a car horn made her jump* **(c)** *(informal)* **not to care a hoot** *or* **not to give a hoot about something** = not to worry about something at all; *I don't care a hoot about the meeting - I'm staying in to watch TV* **2** *verb* **(a)** *(of an owl)* to make a loud cry; *an owl hooted in the distance*; **to hoot with laughter** = to laugh wildly; *he had the audience hooting with laughter* **(b)** to sound a car horn; *he hooted at the sheep to get them to move*

hooter ['huːtə] *noun* siren, a device which makes a loud warning noise; *the midday hooter sounded and all the workers came out of the factory*

Hoover ['huːvə] **1** *noun* trade mark for a type of vacuum cleaner; *we need a bigger Hoover - this one isn't powerful enough* **2** *verb* to clean with a vacuum cleaner; *she was hoovering the dining-room*

hop [hɒp] **1** *noun* **(a)** little jump; *magpies walk in a series of little hops*; *(informal)* **to catch someone on the hop** = to catch someone unexpectedly **(b)** short flight; *it's only a short hop from London to Paris* **(c)** bitter fruit of a climbing plant, used in making beer; *hops are used to give the bitter flavour to British beer* **2** *verb* **(a)** to jump on one leg; *he hurt his toe and had to hop around on one foot*; *see also* MAD **(b)** *(of birds, animals, etc.)* to jump with both feet together; *magpies were hopping across the grass*; *the frog hopped onto the lily pad*; *(informal)* **hop it!** = go away! **(c)** *(informal)* **to hop in** = to get in; *I stopped the car and told him to hop in*; **hop on** *or* **to hop off** = to get on *or* off; *with the old London buses, you can hop on and off anywhere along the street, although it can be dangerous* (NOTE: **hopping - hopped**)

hope [həʊp] **1** *noun* wanting and expecting something to happen; *our only hope is that she will get better soon*; *they have given up all hope of rescuing any more earthquake victims*; **in the hope that** = wanting something to happen; *I rang in the hope that you might have a table free for tonight* **2** *verb* **(a)** to want and expect something to happen; *we all hope our team wins*; *she's hoping she will soon be able to drive a car*; *I hope it doesn't rain*; **I hope so** = I want it to happen; *are you coming to the party? - yes, I hope so*; **I hope not** = I don't want it to happen; *it's going to rain tomorrow, isn't it? - I hope not!*; **to hope for something** = to want something to happen; *we are hoping for a change in the weather, it's rained every day this week so far* **(b)** to expect to do something; *the chairman hopes to be at the meeting tomorrow*; *they said they hoped to be back home by 6 o'clock*; *I had hoped to go to the party but in the end I couldn't*

hoped-for ['həʊpt 'fɔː] *adjective* needed and expected; *the day of his eagerly hoped-for release from prison had finally arrived*

hopeful ['həʊpfʊl] **1** *adjective* confident that something will happen; *we are hopeful that the company will accept our offer* **2** *noun* *(informal)* person who hopes to get a job, a place in a team, etc.; *we* *are looking at six young hopefuls for the England team*

hopefully ['həupfuli] *adverb* **(a)** confidently; *they looked hopefully at the lists of lottery winners* **(b)** let us hope; *hopefully the rain will stop*

hopeless ['həupləs] *adjective* **(a)** with no hope; *the invoices are in a hopeless mess*; **he's a hopeless case =** he will never get any better **(b)** no good; *she's hopeless at tennis*; *he's hopeless when it comes to mending cars*

hopelessly ['həupləsli] *adverb* with no hope, very much; *we got hopelessly lost looking for the British Museum*; *the company is hopelessly in debt*

hopper ['hɒpə] *noun* large funnel for channelling flour, sand, etc.; *the grain is poured through a large hopper into the granary*

horde [hɔːd] *noun* large crowd; *hordes of tourists come to London to do their Christmas shopping*; *at half-term, there are hordes of little children in the museum* (NOTE: do not confuse with **hoard**)

horizon [hə'raizn] *noun* line where the earth and the sky meet; *two ships could be seen on the horizon*

horizontal [hɒri'zɒntl] *adjective* flat, level with the ground; *he drew a horizontal line under the text*

hormonal [hɔː'məunəl] *adjective* referring to hormones; *hormonal deficiency*

hormone ['hɔːməun] *noun* substance produced by glands in the body and carried to other parts of the body by the bloodstream to stimulate certain cells into action; **growth hormone =** hormone which stimulates the growth of the long bones in the body; **hormone replacement therapy (HRT) =** treatment to relieve the symptoms of the menopause by supplying oestrogen and thus reducing the risk of osteoporosis

horn [hɔːn] *noun* **(a)** sharp pointed bone growing out of an animal's head; *that bull's horns look very dangerous* **(b)** warning device on a car; **to sound a horn =** to make a warning noise with a horn; *sound your horn when you come to the corner* **(c)** metal musical instrument which is blown into to make a note; *a concerto for horn and orchestra* **(d) the Horn** *or* **Cape Horn =** the cape at the southern tip of South America

hornet ['hɔːnit] *noun* large reddish-brown wasp; *we have a hornets' nest in the roof*

horny ['hɔːni] *adjective* hard, like horn; *the horny pads on the soles of its feet protect the animal from thorns and sharp stones*

horoscope ['hɒrəskəup] *noun* forecast of what will happen, according to the stars; *my horoscope says it's a lucky day for me today*

horrendous [hɒ'rendəs] *adjective* horrible and unpleasant; *a horrendous motorway accident*; *we had to pay horrendous prices for our theatre seats*

horrible ['hɒrəbl] *adjective* awful, terrible; *the victims of the fire had horrible injuries*; *he's a horrible little boy*; *we had a horrible meal at the restaurant*

horribly ['hɒribli] *adverb* very badly; *everything went horribly wrong*; *she was horribly injured in the accident*

horrid ['hɒrid] *adjective* bad and unpleasant; *what a horrid smell!*; *it was horrid of him to shout at you like that*

horrific [hə'rifik] *adjective* which makes you shocked; *the victims of the crash suffered horrific injuries*; *the police uncovered a horrific murder*

horrified ['hɒrifaid] *adjective* frightened or shocked; *when she saw the pictures she was horrified*; *he was horrified by the bill*

horrify ['hɒrifai] *verb* to frighten, to shock; *the pictures of accident victims are meant to horrify*

horrifying ['hɒrifaiŋ] *adjective* frightening, shocking; *they told horrifying tales of their escape from the war zone*

horror ['hɒrə] *noun* **(a)** feeling of being very frightened; *he couldn't hide his horror at hearing the news*; *she has a horror of spiders*; *everyone watched in horror as the planes collided*; **horror film** *or* **horror movie =** frightening film, with ghosts, dead bodies, etc. **(b)** *(informal)* naughty child; *that little boy is a little horror!*

hors d'oeuvre(s) [ɔː'dɜːv] *noun* little pieces of food served at the beginning of a meal (NOTE: a French word, meaning 'outside the main work'; in English, the plural **hors-d'oeuvres** can be used, but not in French)

> COMMENT: hors-d'oeuvres can simply consist of pâté, prawns, radishes, etc., or can be a more complicated dish, such as a salad with scallops, or hard-boiled eggs with mayonnaise. Several items can be served together as 'mixed hors-d'oeuvres', and in some restaurants are brought to the table on an hors-d'oeuvres trolley

horse [hɔːs] *noun* large animal used for riding or pulling; *she was riding a black horse*; *the coach was pulled by six white horses*; *he's out on his horse every morning*; *see also* LOOK (NOTE: do not confuse with **hoarse**)

horseback ['hɔːsbæk] *adverb* **on horseback =** riding on a horse; *there were ten policemen on horseback outside the football ground*

horse-drawn ['hɔːsdrɔːn] *adjective* pulled by a horse; *a horse-drawn sleigh met them at the hotel*

horseman *or* **horsewoman** ['hɔːsmən *or* 'hɔːswumən] *noun* person who rides a horse; *three horsemen came riding down the path*; *she's a very experienced horsewoman* (NOTE: plural is **horsemen, horsewomen**)

horse-racing ['hɔːsreisiŋ] *noun* sport of racing horses and betting on the result; *he loves to watch horse-racing on TV*

horse-riding ['hɔːsraidiŋ] *noun* riding horses for pleasure; *we often go horse-riding in the summer*; *they went on a horse-riding holiday in Ireland*

horseshoe ['hɔːsʃuː] *noun* iron shoe nailed to the hard part of a horse's hoof (also used as a sign of luck); *I found a horseshoe by the path*; *they hung a horseshoe on the back of his car*

horticultural [hɔːti'kʌltʃərəl] *adjective* referring to horticulture; *he showed his vegetables at the local horticultural show*

horticulture ['hɔːtikʌltʃə] *noun* gardening, the growing of fruit, flowers and vegetables for food or decoration; *she's studying horticulture at the local college*

hose [həuz] **1** *noun* **(a)** long flexible tube, either rubber or plastic; *there is a ban on using garden hoses* during the summer; the firemen played their hoses on the burning building **(b)** stockings; **panty hose =** women's tights (NOTE: no plural in this meaning) **2** verb **to hose (down) =** to wash with water from a hose; the sailors were hosing down the decks

hosepipe ['həʊzpaɪp] noun long hose; firemen unrolled their hosepipes to put out the fire; that hosepipe isn't long enough to reach to the bottom of the garden; **hosepipe ban =** ban on using hosepipes and sprinklers to water your garden; a hosepipe ban was introduced three months ago because of the drought

hosiery ['həʊzjəri] noun (in a shop) stockings, socks and tights; you'll find socks in the hosiery department

hospice ['hɒspɪs] noun hospital which cares for terminally ill patients; my mother has been transferred from hospital to a hospice

hospitable [hɒ'spɪtəbl] adjective welcoming and friendly to guests; the people in the village were very hospitable; as a rule, Americans are very hospitable people

hospital ['hɒspɪtəl] noun place where sick or hurt people are looked after; she was taken ill at work and sent to hospital; when is she due to go into hospital?; he was in hospital for several days after the accident; **general hospital =** hospital which deals with all types of injuries and illnesses

hospitality [hɒspɪ'tælɪti] noun welcome to guests; the town is famous for its old-fashioned American hospitality; **the hospitality industry =** the hotel, restaurant and tourism industry; **hospitality room** or **hospitality suite =** special room or series of rooms for entertaining privileged guests; guests are entertained in the hospitality suite before taking their seats for the show

hospitalization [hɒspɪtəlaɪ'zeɪʃn] noun sending someone to hospital; the doctor recommended immediate hospitalization

hospitalize ['hɒspɪtəlaɪz] verb to put someone in hospital; his condition deteriorated and he had to be hospitalized

host [həʊst] **1** noun **(a)** person who has invited guests; the host asked his guests what they wanted to drink **(b)** landlord of a hotel or inn, also sometimes of a restaurant; the host of the 'King's Head' **(c)** (on a TV, radio show) the person who introduces and talks to the guests; the best hosts on Saturday night TV are those that make jokes **(d)** person or animal on which parasites live **(e) a host of =** large number of; we face a host of problems **2** verb **(a)** to act as host; the company hosted a reception for two hundred guests; she hosted a party for the visiting diplomats **(b)** to be the centre where something takes place; Barcelona hosted the Olympic games in 1992

hostage ['hɒstɪdʒ] noun person who is captured and held by someone or an organization, which threatens to kill him unless certain demands are met; three of the hostages will be freed tomorrow; he was held hostage for more than a year by the rebels

hostel ['hɒstl] noun cheap place where people can live; we looked for a hostel near the railway station; a **student hostel =** lodging for students, etc.; **youth hostel =** place where young travellers can stay; we booked in at the youth hostel

hostelry ['hɒstlri] noun (old) inn; we stayed at an old hostelry down by the river (NOTE: plural is **hostelries**)

hostess ['həʊstəs] noun woman who has invited guests; he sat at his hostess's right; **air hostess** US **airline hostess =** woman who looks after passengers on a plane; press the button to call the air hostess (NOTE: also called **flight attendant**)

hostile ['hɒstaɪl] US ['hɒstl] adjective **(a)** referring to an enemy; hostile forces are moving towards the airport **(b)** showing a dislike of someone; the crowd seemed hostile, so the president decided not to go on his planned walkabout; **hostile questioning =** asking questions which attack the person being asked

hostility [hɒ'stɪlɪti] noun **(a)** opposition; the board's hostility towards the plan (NOTE: no plural in this meaning) **(b) hostilities =** war; at the start of hostilities the two armies were about equal in size

hot [hɒt] adjective **(a)** very warm; with a high temperature; the weather is very hot in June but August is the hottest month; if you're too hot, take your coat off; plates should be kept hot before serving the meal (NOTE: the opposite is **cold**) **(b)** very highly spiced (food); this curry is particularly hot; he chose the hottest dish on the menu (NOTE: the opposite is **mild**) **(c) to make things hot for someone =** to make difficulties for someone; **to be hot and bothered =** to be annoyed and nervous about something (informal) **to sell like hot cakes =** to sell very fast; this new toy is selling like hot cakes; **to get into hot water =** to get into trouble; he got into hot water with the local authority after he built a garage without permission; **in the hot seat =** having to take decisions; I pity the club treasurer - he's really in the hot seat **(d)** vigorous and energetic; **in hot pursuit =** chasing someone actively; the rebels retreated into the mountains with the government forces in hot pursuit; see also HOTLY (NOTE: **hotter - hottest**)

hot air ['hɒt 'eə] noun (informal) useless talk; debates in Parliament generate a lot of hot air; don't worry, his threats are just hot air

hot-air balloon ['hɒteə bə'luːn] noun very large balloon which rises into the air as the air inside it is heated, with people travelling in a basket attached underneath; for my birthday, my father took me for a ride in a hot-air balloon

hot chocolate ['hɒt 'tʃɒklət] noun drink made from chocolate powder and hot milk; I like to have a cup of hot chocolate before I go to bed

hotchpotch ['hɒtʃpɒtʃ] noun mixture of all sorts of items; the book is a hotchpotch of ideas and theories taken from various writers (NOTE: American English is **hodgepodge**)

hot cross bun ['hɒt 'krɒs 'bʌn] noun small spicy cake with a cross on it, eaten at Easter; he ate two hot cross buns for breakfast

hot dog ['hɒt 'dɒg] noun snack made of a hot frankfurter sausage eaten in a roll of bread; you can buy hot dogs at the food stall by the station

hotel [həʊ'tel] noun building where travellers can rent a room for the night, eat in a restaurant, drink in a bar, etc.; they are staying at the Grand Hotel, which is the only five-star hotel in town; I'll meet you in the hotel lobby; all the hotel rooms in the town are booked; see also CHECK IN, CHECK OUT

hotelier [həʊ'teliə] *noun* person who owns or manages a hotel; *seaside hoteliers say that the season has been poor so far*

hothouse ['hɒthaʊs] *noun* heated greenhouse; *they grow tomatoes and roses in hothouses during the winter*

hotline ['hɒtlaɪn] *noun* (a) direct emergency phone line between two heads of government; *the president called the prime minister on the hotline* (b) phone line for giving urgent messages, or placing urgent orders; *we get thousands of orders on our Christmas hotline; call the ticket hotline for reservations*

hotly ['hɒtli] *adverb* (a) angrily; *he hotly denied the reports which had been published in the newspapers* (b) close behind; *the enemy fled, hotly pursued by government troops*

hot spot ['hɒt 'spɒt] *noun* (a) place which is exciting; *this café is one of the hottest spots in town* (b) place where fighting is taking place; *he was sent to report from one of the hot spots in the Middle East*

hound [haʊnd] **1** *noun* dog used for hunting; *he has a pack of hounds for hunting* **2** *verb* to attack someone, to victimize someone; *when he came out of prison he was hounded by the press*; **the minister was hounded out of office** = the minister had to resign because of attacks on him in the press

hour ['aʊə] *noun* (a) period of time which lasts sixty minutes; *the train journey takes two hours; it's a three-hour flight to Greece; the train travels at over 150 miles an hour*; **he is paid by the hour** = he is paid for each hour he works; *the pay is £10 an hour; the hours of work are from 9.30 to 5.30; the lunch hour is from 12.30 to 1.30; she works a thirty-five hour week*; **a quarter of an hour** = 15 minutes; **half an hour** = 30 minutes; *I'll be ready in a quarter of an hour; the next train will be in half an hour's time* (b) *(informal)* **hours** = a very long time; *they took hours to serve us; we waited hours for the bus* (c) **on the hour** = at an exact hour, and not before or after that hour; *trains for London leave every hour on the hour* (d) **banking hours** = time when a bank is open for its customers; *you cannot get money from a bank outside banking hours;* **office hours** = time when an office is open; *staff are not allowed to make private calls during office hours;* **outside hours** *or* **out of hours** = when the office is not open; *there is a special number you can ring outside office hours; see also* SMALL

hourglass ['aʊəglɑːs] *noun* device for timing, with two glass containers joined with a narrow neck, one full of sand, which takes exactly one hour to trickle down to fill the other

hourly ['aʊəli] *adjective* happening every hour; *he's paid on an hourly basis;* **hourly-paid workers** = workers paid at a fixed rate for each hour worked; **hourly rate** = amount of money paid for an hour worked; *the minimum hourly rate is £3.60*

house [haʊs] *noun* (a) building in which someone lives; *he has bought a house in London; he has a small flat in town and a large house in the country; all the houses in our street look the same* (b) *(informal)* **they get on like a house on fire** = they're very friendly (c) business; *she runs a publishing house; an important finance house has financed the deal;* **house magazine** *or* **house journal** = magazine produced for the workers or shareholders in a company to give them news about the company (d) part of a Parliament; *the*

British Parliament is formed of the House of Commons and the House of Lords; the American Congress is formed of the House of Representatives and the Senate (e) bar or pub, etc.; **drinks are on the house** = drinks are free to customers; **house wine** = special cheap wine selected by a restaurant; *we'll have a bottle of your house red, please; see also* PUBLIC HOUSE (f) showing of a film, play, etc.; **full house** *or* **house full** = notice showing that a cinema or theatre is full; *the play has played to full houses all week* (NOTE: plural is **houses** ['haʊzɪz])

house arrest ['haʊs ə'rest] *noun* **to be under house arrest** = to be under police guard in your own home, without being allowed to leave it; *the opposition leader has been under house arrest for six years*

houseboat ['haʊsbəʊt] *noun* boat moored on a river, arranged for living in, not for travelling; *they live in a houseboat on the Thames near London*

housebreaker ['haʊsbreɪkə] *noun* person who gets into houses by breaking windows, etc., in order to steal

housebreaking ['haʊsbreɪkɪŋ] *noun* breaking into a house and stealing things; *he was charged with housebreaking*

house fly ['haʊs 'flaɪ] *noun* common insect which lives in houses and lays its eggs in food; *house flies are everywhere in summer, we must get a spray*

household ['haʊshəʊld] *noun* people living together in a house; *this free newspaper is distributed to every household in the borough;* **household goods** = goods which are used in a house; *the household goods department is on the ground floor;* **a household name** = a well-known brand

householder ['haʊshəʊldə] *noun* *(formal)* person who owns a private house; *the householder is responsible for insuring the property*

housekeeper ['haʊskiːpə] *noun* (a) person who looks after a house; *he employs a housekeeper, a chauffeur and two gardeners* (b) person employed to look after the rooms in a hotel, being responsible for the cleaning staff, and providing linen, etc.; *the housekeeper is responsible for the cleanliness of the rooms*

housekeeping ['haʊskiːpɪŋ] *noun* looking after a house; *we asked the nanny to do some light housekeeping* (NOTE: no plural)

houseman ['haʊsmən] *noun* (a) *GB* young doctor who works in a hospital during his final year of training (NOTE: American English is **intern**) (b) *US* man who does odd jobs in a hotel

House of Commons ['haʊs əv 'kɒmənz] *noun* lower house of the British Parliament; *the Bill will come before the House of Commons* (NOTE: members of the House of Commons are called **Members of Parliament** *or* **MPs**)

House of Lords ['haʊs əv 'lɔːdz] *noun* upper house of the British Parliament; *the House of Lords made several amendments to the Bill*

House of Representatives ['haʊs əv repri'zentətɪvz] *noun* lower house of the US Congress; *he's been elected to the House of Representatives* (NOTE: members of the House of Representatives are called **Congressmen**)

house plant ['haʊs 'plɑːnt] *noun* plant that is grown indoors and not in a garden; *they built a conservatory and filled it with house plants*

Houses of Parliament ['hauzız əv 'pɑːrləmənt] *noun* building in London where Parliament meets; *he took a picture of the Houses of Parliament; you can go on a tour of the Houses of Parliament*

house-to-house ['haustə'haus] *adjective* going from one house to the next, asking people to buy something, to vote for someone, or asking them questions; *the police carried out house-to-house checks to try to find the gunman; he has a job selling cleaning products house-to-house*

housewife ['hauswaıf] *noun* woman who looks after the house, and does not go out to work; *being a housewife and mother is a full-time occupation* (NOTE: plural is **housewives** ['hauswaıvz])

housework ['hauswɜːk] *noun* cleaning work in a house or flat; *his wife does all the housework*

housing ['hauzıŋ] *noun* providing places where people can live; *the local council is responsible for housing homeless people*; **housing benefit** = money paid by the government to unemployed people to help them pay their rent; **housing estate** = group of houses and flats belonging to a local authority, and let to tenants at cheap rents

housing project ['hauzıŋ 'prɒdʒekt] *noun* series of houses or flats built by a local municipality; *planning permission has been given for several new housing projects in south London*

hove [həuv] *see* HEAVE

hovel ['hɒvl] *noun* small dirty house; *he was born in a hovel down by the canal*

hover ['hɒvə] *verb* **(a)** to hang in the air without moving forward; *flies hovering over the surface of a pool* **(b) to hover around someone** = to stay near someone; *he hovered around her for the whole evening*

hovercraft ['hɒvəkrɑːft] *noun* type of boat which moves over the surface of the water on a cushion of air; *we are taking the hovercraft from Dover to Calais*

how [hau] *adverb* **(a)** *(showing or asking the way in which something is done)* *how do you switch off the cooker?; can you tell me how to get to the railway station from here?; I don't know how he does it* **(b)** *(showing or asking to what extent)* *how big is their house?; how many people are there in your family?; she showed us how good she was at skiing; how old is your little boy?; how far is it to the church?* **(c)** *(showing surprise)* *how cold it is outside!; how different it is from what I remember!* **(d)** *(informal)* **how come?** = why; *how come you're late?; how come the front door was left open?; how about?* = would you like?; *how about a swim before breakfast?; how about a cup of coffee?;* **how do you mean?** = what do you mean?; *how do you mean, the payment won't be made until next week?*

how are you *or* **how do you do** [hau 'ɑː juː *or* 'hau djə 'duː] **(a)** *(showing a general greeting)* *how do you do, sir?; hi Robert! how are you?* (NOTE: in this meaning a detailed reply is not expected) **(b)** *(asking the state of someone's health)* *how are you today?; the doctor asked me how I was*

however [hau'evə] **1** *adverb* **(a)** to whatever extent; *however many times she tried, she couldn't pass the driving test; I must have the house painted, however expensive it's going to be; however hard he tried, he still couldn't swim* **(b)** *(emphatic form of 'how')*

however did you manage to get in? **(c)** in this case; *we never go out on Saturdays - however, this week we're going to a wedding* **2** *conjunction* in whatever way; *do it however you like*

howl [haul] *verb* to make a long loud cry; *the wolves howled outside the cabin; the wind howled in the chimney*

HP ['haıə 'pɜːtʃəs] = HIRE PURCHASE; *I'm buying the fridge on HP*

HQ ['eıtʃ 'kjuː] = HEADQUARTERS; *we had a call from HQ asking for more details*

hr, hrs = HOUR, HOURS

HRT = HORMONE REPLACEMENT THERAPY

hub [hʌb] *noun* **(a)** centre of a wheel; *the spokes of a wheel meet at the hub* **(b)** business centre; *Frankfurt is hoping to take the place of the City of London as the financial hub of Europe* **(c)** central airport, where domestic flights connect with international flights; *Chicago is the airline's American hub*

hub cap ['hʌb 'kæp] *noun* metal or plastic plate covering the hub of a car's wheel; *someone keeps stealing my hub caps*

huddle ['hʌdl] **1** *noun* **to go into a huddle** = to get together to discuss something; *the players went into a huddle to discuss tactics* **2** *verb* to crowd together; *the refugees huddled in the shade of some trees; the children were huddled together in one room*

hue [hjuː] *noun* **(a)** *(formal)* colour; *the garden is filled with flowers of every hue* **(b) hue and cry** = excited chase after someone; shouts of protest; *the parents raised a great hue and cry when the education committee proposed to close the school* (NOTE: do not confuse with **hew**)

huff [hʌf] *noun (informal)* **in a huff** = in a bad temper; *she went off in a huff*

huffy ['hʌfi] *adjective (informal)* bad-tempered; *when he said her work wasn't good enough she got all huffy*

hug [hʌg] **1** *noun* throwing your arms round someone; *she ran to the little girl and gave her a hug* **2** *verb* **(a)** to throw your arms around someone; *the players hugged each other when the goal was scored* **(b)** to hold something very tightly; *the little girl was hugging a blue blanket* **(c)** to keep very close to something; *the road hugs the foot of the mountain; she drove along slowly, hugging the pavement* (NOTE: **hugging - hugged**)

huge [hjuːdʒ] *adjective* very large; *huge waves battered the ship; the concert was a huge success; failing the test was a huge disappointment for him*

huh [hə] *interjection* to show surprise, disgust, etc.; *huh, you think you can sneak out without paying, do you?*

hulk [hʌlk] *noun* **(a)** big and awkward person or thing; *watch where you're treading, you lumbering great hulk!* **(b)** rotten old ship; *rusting hulks blocked the approaches to the harbour*

hulking ['hʌlkıŋ] *adjective* big and awkward; *two hulking great bouncers stopped us going into the club*

hull [hʌl] **1** *noun* main body of a ship; *the liner is in dry dock for repairs to her hull* **2** *verb* to take peas out of their pods; *if you hull the peas I'll get the potatoes ready*

hullo [hə'ləu] *see* HALLO, HELLO

hum [hʌm] **1** *noun* low buzz; *a loud hum came out of the beehive* **2** *verb* **(a)** to make a low buzz; *bees were humming around the hive* **(b)** to sing without words; *if you don't know the words of the national anthem, you can always hum the tune* (NOTE: **humming - hummed**)

human ['hju:mən] **1** *adjective* referring to people; **human error** = mistake made by a person, and not by a machine; *they concluded that the accident was due to human error*; **he's only human** = he can make mistakes like anyone else; *I know there's a mistake in the exam question, examiners are only human, after all!* **2** *noun* person, a human being; *the animals in the park don't seem to be afraid of humans*; *humans have only existed on earth for a short time compared to fish*

human being ['hju:mən 'bi:ɪŋ] *noun* a person; *the first human beings lived many thousands of years ago*; *I've been walking all day in the forest and you're the first human being I've met*

humane [hju:'meɪn] *adjective* kind to people or animals; *they were praised for their humane treatment of captured soldiers*; *if animal experiments are absolutely necessary then they must be humane*

humanely [hju:'meɪnli] *adverb* in a humane way; *we insist that the animals must be treated humanely when being transported over long distances*

human immunodeficiency virus (HIV) ['hju:mən ɪmju:nəʊdɪ'fɪʃənsi 'vaɪrəs] the virus which causes AIDS

humanism ['hju:mənɪzm] *noun* concern with humans as opposed to religious ideas; *humanism rejects the need for religion*

humanist ['hju:mənɪst] *noun* person who is concerned with humans as opposed to religious ideas; *humanists reject the need for religion*

humanitarian [hju:mænɪ'teəriən] *adjective* helping other human beings; *they brought humanitarian relief to starving people*

humanity [hju:'mænɪti] *noun* **(a)** all people; *a crime against humanity* **(b)** great kindness; *she showed great humanity to the refugees* **(c)** **the humanities** = the arts subjects at university, such as English, History, Philosophy, as opposed to the sciences; *the Dean of the Faculty of Humanities*

humanly ['hju:mənli] *adverb* **humanly possible** = as much as possible; *we did all that was humanly possible to rescue the survivors*

human nature ['hju:mən 'neɪtʃə] *noun* natural feelings which are found in all people; *it's only human nature to feel excited when a little baby is born*

human race ['hju:mən 'reɪs] *noun* all human beings; *the human race has been in existence for several million years*

human resources ['hju:mən rɪ'sɔ:sɪz] *noun* workers in a company, seen as a group; *the human resources manager*

human rights ['hju:mən 'raɪts] *noun* rights which each member of society should enjoy, such as freedom of speech, freedom of movement, etc.; *demonstrators are protesting against abuses of human rights in various parts of the world*

humble ['hʌmbl] *adjective* **(a)** modest, feeling you are not important; *seeing how much work she does for charity makes me feel very humble*; *see also* PIE **(b)** poor, ordinary; *he comes from a humble family; they live in a humble little house in the mountains* (NOTE: **humbler - humblest**)

humdinger [hʌm'dɪŋə] *noun (informal)* marvellous thing; *the match was a real humdinger!*

humdrum ['hʌmdrʌm] *adjective* dull and boring; *he has a humdrum job in an accountant's office*

humerus ['hju:mərəs] *noun* bone in the arm, running from the shoulder to the elbow; *they found the humerus was broken* (NOTE: do not confuse with **humorous**)

humid ['hju:mɪd] *adjective* damp, which contains moisture vapour; *decomposition of organic matter is rapid in hot and humid conditions*; *I don't like humid weather - I much prefer a hot dry climate*

humidifier [hju:'mɪdɪfaɪə] *noun* device which makes the air in a room or house moist; *we switch the humidifier on at night because the central heating makes the air too dry*

humidify [hju:'mɪdɪfaɪ] *verb* to make the air in a room or house moist; *the flat needs to be humidified in winter because the heating dries the air so much*

humidity [hju:'mɪdɪti] *noun* measurement of how much water vapour is contained in the air; *the temperature is 32° with 90% humidity*

humiliate [hju'mɪlieɪt] *verb* to make someone feel unimportant or stupid; *the team was completely humiliated - they lost 10 - 2!*; *she is supposed to be his best friend but she humiliated him in front of everyone*

humiliating [hju:'mɪlieɪtɪŋ] *adjective* which makes you feel embarrassed, unimportant or stupid; *it was humiliating to fail his driving test for the third time*; *it was a humiliating defeat for the French team*

humiliation [hju:mɪlɪ'eɪʃn] *noun* making someone feel unimportant or stupid; *the humiliation of failing his exams once again*

humility [hju:'mɪlɪti] *noun* being humble; *when I look at the snow-capped mountains, I feel a sense of great humility*; *he's too proud, a little humility wouldn't be a bad thing*

humorous ['hju:mərəs] *adjective (formal)* funny; *our host made some humorous remarks to try to make everyone relax*; *she didn't find the book at all humorous*

humour US **humor** ['hju:mə] **1** *noun* **(a)** seeing what is funny; *he has a good sense of humour*; *she has absolutely no sense of humour*; *want to meet male, aged 30 - 35, with a good sense of humour (GSOH)* **(b)** *(formal)* general feeling; *I am in no humour to talk about holidays just now*; *he was not in a humour to discuss what happened during their holiday in Greece*; *his good humour lasted until the end of the party* **2** *verb* **to humour someone** = to say you agree with what someone wants; *when he starts shouting and cursing, you to have to try to humour him to keep him happy*

hump [hʌmp] **1** *noun* **(a)** raised part on the back of a person or animal; *Arabian camels have only one hump, while Bactrian camels have two* **(b)** small raised part in the ground; *they have built humps in the road to slow down the traffic* **(c)** awkward situation; *now that we are over the hump we can perhaps discuss discounts again* **2** *verb (informal)* to carry on your shoulder; *we spent all morning humping sacks of sand*

hump-backed bridge ['hʌmpbækt 'brɪdʒ] *noun* little bridge which rises very steeply

humus ['hjuːməs] *noun* decomposed organic matter in good soil which makes soil dark and makes it bond together; *the humus under the forest trees is excellent for growing bulbs*

hunch [hʌntʃ] **1** *noun (informal)* feeling that something is going to happen; *I've got a hunch that we will win*; *the detective acted purely on a hunch* (NOTE: plural is **hunches**) **2** *verb* to bend forward; *we hunched down behind the wall to get out of the wind*; *the old lady sat hunched over a small fire*

hunched ['hʌntʃt] *adjective* bent forward; *he stood in the corner with hunched shoulders*

hundred ['hʌndrɪd] **(a)** number 100; *the church is over a hundred years old*; *my grandfather will be 100 next month*; *they came in their hundreds to visit the grave*; *do I have to tell you a hundred times to stop that noise?* **(b)** one **hundred per cent** = 100%; **one hundred per cent happy with** = totally satisfied with; *I'm not one hundred percent happy with his work* **(c)** **hundreds of** = very many; *hundreds of birds were killed by the cold weather*; *hundreds of people caught flu last winter* (NOTE: in numbers **hundred** does not change and is followed by **and** when reading: 491 = four hundred and ninety-one; 102 = a hundred and two. Note also: **a hundred and one** (101), **three hundred and six** (306) but **the hundred and first** (101st), **the three hundred and sixth** (306th), etc.)

hundredth (100th) ['hʌndrədθ] *adjective & noun* the clock is correct to one hundredth of a second *(100th of a second); tomorrow is his hundredth birthday; a penny is one hundredth of a pound*

hundredweight ['hʌndrədweɪt] *noun* weight of dry goods such as seeds, equal to 112 pounds; *we ordered a hundredweight of coal* (NOTE: equals approximately 50 kilos; note also that it is abbreviated to **cwt** with figures: **a 5 cwt sack**)

hung [hʌŋ] *adjective* evenly balanced; **a hung parliament** = parliament where no party has a majority; *the result of the election was hung parliament, with the Liberals holding the balance of power; see also* HANG

Hungary ['hʌŋgəri] *noun* country in central Europe, east of Austria and west of Romania; *the river Danube flows north-south through the centre of Hungary* (NOTE: capital: **Budapest**; people: **the Hungarians**; language: **Hungarian**; currency: **forint**)

Hungarian [hʌŋ'geəriən] **1** *adjective* referring to Hungary; *Franz Liszt was a famous Hungarian composer* **2** *noun* **(a)** person from Hungary; *it has been 3 years since a Hungarian last won a gold medal* **(b)** language spoken in Hungary; *I am being transferred to Budapest and want to take a course in Hungarian*

hunger ['hʌŋgə] *noun* wanting to eat, needing to eat; **to die of hunger** = to die because you do not have enough to eat; *there are children dying of hunger in some countries in Africa*

hunger strike ['hʌŋgə 'straɪk] *noun* refusing to eat, as a form of protest; *the prisoners went on hunger strike*

hungry ['hʌŋgri] *adjective* wanting to eat; *you must be hungry after that game of football; I'm not very hungry - I had a big lunch; hurry up with the food - we're getting hungry;* **to go hungry** = not to have enough to eat; *students had to go hungry when their grants were not paid* (NOTE: **hungrier - hungriest**)

hung up ['hʌŋ 'ʌp] *adjective (informal)* worried or bothered about something; *he's really hung up about his promotion prospects; see also* HANG-UP

hunk [hʌŋk] *noun* **(a)** rough piece; *we each had a hunk of bread and a bowl of soup* **(b)** *(informal)* strong athletic man; *Sophie came to the party with that gorgeous hunk of hers*

hunky ['hʌŋki] *adjective (informal)* attractively strong and athletic; *three hunky lifeguards came to rescue us*

hunt [hʌnt] **1** *verb* **(a)** **to hunt for something** = to search for something; *we're hunting for a cheap flat; they came to London in the week after Christmas, hunting for bargains* **(b)** to chase wild animals for food or sport; *we took the dogs out hunting rats; our cat is not very good at hunting mice; they go to Scotland to hunt deer* (NOTE: you hunt animals, but you hunt **for** things) **2** *noun* **(a)** search; *the hunt for new offices has just started* **(b)** group of people who meet together with dogs to hunt foxes; *the hunt will assemble at 10.00 a.m.*

hunter ['hʌntə] *noun* person who hunts; *a deer hunter;* **bargain hunter** = person who looks for bargains; *bargain hunters were queuing outside the shop on the first day of the sales*

hunting ['hʌntɪŋ] *noun* **(a)** sport of chasing wild animals and killing them; *many people are opposed to fox hunting; tiger hunting is strictly controlled* **(b)** action of looking for something; **hunting for bargains** *or* **bargain hunting** = looking for bargains in a store

hunting ground ['hʌntɪŋ 'graʊnd] *noun* **(a)** place where wild animals are hunted; *the island is a fabulous hunting ground for butterfly collectors* **(b)** place where things are often found; *secondhand shops are a good hunting ground for old designer clothes*

huntsman ['hʌntsmən] *noun* man who hunts animals, especially foxes; *the hounds streamed out of the yard, followed by the huntsmen* (NOTE: plural is **huntsmen**)

hurdle ['hɜːdl] *noun* **(a)** small fence which you have to jump over in a race; *she fell at the first hurdle* **(b)** **hurdles** = race where you jump over fences; *the 100 metres hurdles* **(c)** obstacle in the way of something; *only one more hurdle to clear and the house will be ours*

hurdler ['hɜːdlə] *noun* person who races over hurdles

hurl [hɜːl] *verb* to throw; *the crowd hurled stones at the police*

hurrah *or* **hurray** [hʊ'rɑː *or* hʊ'reɪ] *interjection* showing great excitement; *when we heard the news we all shouted 'hurray!'* (NOTE: also spelt **hooray**)

hurricane ['hʌrɪkən] *noun* tropical storm with strong winds and rain in the Caribbean or Eastern Pacific Ocean; *the hurricane damaged properties all along the coast* (NOTE: in the Far East called a **typhoon**; in the Indian Ocean called a **cyclone**)

hurried ['hʌrɪd] *adjective* done in a rush, too quickly; *we just had time to snatch a hurried lunch before catching the train*

hurriedly ['hʌrɪdli] *adverb* in a rush, too quickly; *he finished his speech, and sat down hurriedly*

hurry ['hʌri] **1** *noun* **in a hurry** = doing things fast; *the waiters are always in a hurry*; *can't you drive any faster? - we're in a hurry to catch our plane!*; *he wants the report in a hurry*; *what's the hurry?* = why are you going so fast?; *what's the hurry? it's only two o'clock and the plane doesn't leave until nine*; **there's no hurry** = you need not do it fast; *there's no hurry for the figures, we do not need them until next week* (NOTE: no plural) **2** *verb* **(a)** to go, do or make something fast; *she hurried across the room*; *you'll have to hurry if you want to catch the last post*; *there's no need to hurry - we've got plenty of time* **(b)** to make someone go faster; *don't hurry me, I like to take my time*

hurry up ['hʌri 'ʌp] *verb* **(a)** to go or do something faster; *hurry up - we'll be late for the film*; *can't you get the cook to hurry up, I'm getting hungry?* **(b)** to make someone do something faster; *can you hurry up that order, the customer wants it tomorrow?*

hurt [hɜːt] **1** *verb* **(a)** to have pain; to give pain; *my tooth hurts*; *no one was badly hurt in the accident*; *where did you hurt yourself?*; *is he badly hurt?*; *two players got hurt in the game* **(b)** to harm, to damage; *the bad publicity did not hurt our sales*; *the news report will surely hurt his reputation*; **it won't hurt to** *or* **it never hurts to** = it would be a good thing to; *it wouldn't hurt to complain to the local council*; *it never hurts to be polite to customers* (NOTE: hurting - hurt) **2** *noun* **(a)** *(informal)* *(children's language)* place where you have a pain; *he has a hurt on his toe* **(b)** feeling of sadness because you have been badly treated; *she feels resentful towards him because of the hurt to her pride*

hurtle ['hɜːtl] *verb* to go dangerously fast; *the cart hurtled down the hill*; *she hurtled into the market square on her bike*

husband ['hʌzbənd] **1** *noun* man to whom a woman is married; *her husband is Scottish*; *he's the doctor's husband*; **to live as husband and wife** = to live together as if you were married without being married; *they lived together as husband and wife for twenty years*; *compare* WIFE **2** *verb* *(formal)* not to waste money, supplies, etc.; *we must learn to husband our resources*

husbandry ['hʌzbəndri] *noun* farming, looking after crops and animals; *a new system of intensive husbandry*

hush [hʌʃ] **1** *noun* time of silence; *a hush fell over the people in the hall as the speaker stood up* **2** *verb* **(a)** *(formal)* to make quiet; *she eventually managed to hush the children to sleep*; **hush!** = be quiet! **(b)** **to hush something up** = to hide something so that no one knows about it; *they tried to hush up the scandal*; **to hush someone up** = to make someone keep quiet about something; *we hushed him up with a bribe*

hushed ['hʌʃt] *adjective* quiet, so as not to make too much noise; *she spoke in a hushed whisper*

hush money [hʌʃ 'mʌni] *noun* *(informal)* money paid as a bribe to prevent someone talking about something

hush-hush ['hʌʃhʌʃ] *adjective* *(informal)* secret; *the project was so hush-hush that no one knew anything about it*

husk [hʌsk] **1** *noun* dry outside coating of cereals or nuts; *take the husks off peanuts before you roast them* **2** *verb* to remove the husk from seeds or nuts; *we all sat in front of the house husking corn*

husky ['hʌski] **1** *adjective* **(a)** hoarse, but in an attractive way; *she spoke in a low husky voice* **(b)** *(young man)* tall and strongly built; *a group of husky students cheered when they saw her* (NOTE: **huskier - huskiest**) **2** *noun* dog used to pull sledges; *each sled was pulled by a team of huskies* (NOTE: plural is **huskies**)

huss [hʌs] *noun* large sea fish (NOTE: also called **dogfish**)

hussy ['hʌsi] *noun* *(old)* immoral and indecent woman; *the hussy didn't dare to come back to the village* (NOTE: plural is **hussies**)

hustle ['hʌsl] **1** *noun* movement of people; *it's not a good idea to take suitcases on the Underground at 5.30 with all the hustle of the commuters trying to get home*; **hustle and bustle** = great activity; *the hustle and bustle of Oxford Street in the week before Christmas* **2** *verb* to hurry someone along roughly; *the police tried to hustle the crowd of protesters away*; *don't hustle me - I'm going as fast as I can!*

hut [hʌt] *noun* small rough wooden house; *they found a shepherd's hut where they spent the night*

hutch [hʌtʃ] *noun* box or cage for rabbits, etc.; *she keeps a white rabbit in a hutch in the back garden*

hyacinth ['haɪəsɪnθ] *noun* bulb which produces spikes of bright pink, white or blue scented flowers; *she had a bowl of hyacinths on her windowsill*

hybrid ['haɪbrɪd] *adjective & noun* cross between two varieties of plant or animal; *she is well known for growing hybrid roses*

hybridization [haɪbrɪdaɪ'zeɪʃn] *noun* production of hybrids

hydraulic [haɪ'drɔːlɪk] *adjective* worked by fluid pressure; *the lorry's hydraulic brakes failed*; *the car body is moulded from a metal sheet in a hydraulic press*

hydrocarbon [haɪdrəʊ'kɑːbn] *noun* compound of hydrogen and carbon; *hydrocarbons form part of the exhaust fumes from cars*

hydroelectric [haɪdrəʊɪ'lektrɪk] *adjective* referring to hydroelectricity; **a hydroelectric power station** = power station producing electricity by water power

hydroelectricity [haɪdrəʊelek'trɪsɪti] *noun* electricity from water power; *hydroelectricity is one of Canada's most important exports*

hydrogen ['haɪdrədʒən] *noun* a common gas which combines with oxygen to form water (NOTE: Chemical element: chemical symbol: **H**; atomic number: 1)

hydrophobia [haɪdrə'fəʊbiə] *noun* *(formal)* rabies, frequently fatal disease given to humans by animals; *see also* RABIES

hyena [haɪ'iːnə] *noun* African animal like a large wild dog; *the cry of the hyena sounds like a laugh*

hygiene ['haɪdʒiːn] *noun* being clean and keeping healthy conditions; **personal hygiene** = keeping yourself clean; *nurses have to maintain strict personal hygiene*; *for reasons of hygiene, dogs are not allowed into the shop*; **dental hygiene** = keeping your teeth clean and healthy (NOTE: no plural)

hygienic [haɪ'dʒiːnɪk] *adjective* which is clean and free of germs; *the restaurant kitchen didn't look very hygienic*

hygienist [haɪ'dʒiːnɪst] *noun* **(dental) hygienist** = dentist's assistant, who cleans patients' teeth, removes plaque and gives treatments with fluoride; *I have an appointment with the hygienist on Thursday*

hymn [hɪm] *noun* religious song sung during a Christian religious service; *the priest asked the congregation to stand for the first hymn*

> COMMENT: the Welsh are traditionally great hymn-singers, and Welsh fans often sing hymns as they wait for football or rugby matches to start

hype [haɪp] **1** *noun (informal)* excessive claim in advertising; *no one really believes all the hype surrounding the pop group; there was a lot of hype about the festival and in the end it turned out to be very small* **2** *verb* to make excessive claims in publicity; *the show was hyped (up) in all the newspapers*

hyper- [haɪpə] *prefix* meaning higher, to a greater degree; **hyperactive** = very active; *some food additives make children hyperactive*

hyperbole [haɪ'pɜ:bəli] *noun* exaggerated statement; *you expect a certain amount of hyperbole in any angler's description of the fish he has caught*

hypermarket ['haɪpəmɑːkɪt] *noun* very large supermarket, usually on the outskirts of a large town; *yet another hypermarket is being built near us*

hypertension [haɪpə'tenʃn] *noun* high blood pressure, a condition where the pressure of the blood in the arteries is too high; *hypertension can be treated with drugs such as beta blockers*

hyphen ['haɪfn] *noun* printing sign (-) used to show that two words are joined or that a word has been split; *'coordinate' doesn't take a hyphen but 'high-level' does*

hyphenate ['haɪfəneɪt] *verb* to put a hyphen between two words; to separate a long word at the end of a line with a hyphen or to show that a word has been split at the end of a line; *the word 'coordinate' is not hyphenated; the word 'high-level' is usually hyphenated*

hyphenation [haɪfə'neɪʃn] *noun* act of putting hyphens between words; **hyphenation program** = computer program which automatically divides words correctly at the end of lines

hypnosis [hɪp'nəusɪs] *noun* state like sleep, but caused artificially, where the patient can remember forgotten events in the past or will do whatever the hypnotist tells him to do; *under hypnosis, she was able to recall the traumatic events of the crash*

hypnotherapy [hɪpnəu'θerəpi] *noun* treatment of a patient by hypnosis

hypnotic [hɪp'nɒtɪk] *adjective* **(a)** referring to hypnotism; *hypnotic treatment can be successful for deeply traumatized patients* **(b) hypnotic drug** = drug which makes you go to sleep; *the prescription of hypnotic drugs must be carefully controlled*

hypnotism ['hɪpnətɪzm] *noun* act of hypnotizing people; *hypnotism can be used to treat certain disorders*

hypnotist ['hɪpnətist] *noun* person who practises hypnosis; *the hypnotist put his patient into a hypnotic trance*

hypnotize ['hɪpnətaɪz] *verb* to make someone go into a state where he appears to be asleep and will do anything the hypnotist suggests; *no one can be hypnotized against his will*

hypocrisy [hɪ'pɒkrəsi] *noun* pretending to be what you are not; *it's sheer hypocrisy on her part to criticize him for being lazy when she spends all day reading magazines; for her to say that we are happier than we were last year is pure hypocrisy*

hypocritical [hɪpə'krɪtɪkl] *adjective* referring to hypocrisy; *it was hypocritical of him to criticize others for things he does himself; I hate hypocritical people who say they are glad to see you when you know they aren't*

hypodermic needle *or* **hypodermic syringe** [haɪpə'dɜ:mɪk 'niːdl *or* sɪ'rɪnʒ] *noun* needle or syringe for injecting liquid under the skin; *she needs a hypodermic syringe to give herself an injection*

hypotenuse [haɪ'pɒtənjuːz] *noun* the long side of a right-angled triangle

> COMMENT: according to Pythagoras' theorem, 'the square on the hypotenuse is equal to the sum of the squares on the other two sides'

hypothesis [haɪ'pɒθəsɪs] *noun* something which is probably true, though it cannot be proved; *it's an interesting hypothesis but until you provide some proof I shall remain sceptical; that smoking causes lung cancer is no longer a hypothesis but a matter of established fact* (NOTE: plural is **hypotheses** [haɪ'pɒθəsiːz])

hypothetical [haɪpə'θetɪkl] *adjective* suggested as possible, but not an actual happening; *to take a hypothetical example: what would happen to Britain's coastline if the sea rose by four metres?*

hysterectomy [hɪstə'rektəmi] *noun* surgical removal of the womb, either to treat cancer or because of the presence of fibroids; *she has had a hysterectomy*

hysteria [hɪ'stɪəriə] *noun* neurotic state, where the patient is in a fit of panic or excitement; **mass hysteria** = nervous excitement which affects crowds of people at the same time; *amid scenes of mass hysteria the pop group came onto the stage*

hysterical [hɪ'sterɪkl] *adjective* referring to hysteria; *he burst into hysterical laughter; hysterical fans tried to climb onto the stage; she was hysterical and I had to slap her face to make her stop shrieking*

hysterically [hɪ'sterɪkli] *adverb* in a hysterical way; *she collapsed onto her bed, weeping hysterically*

hysterics [hɪ'sterɪks] *noun* **(a)** attack of hysteria; *she went into hysterics when she saw her daughter covered in blood* **(b)** laughter which you can't control; *the children were in hysterics as they watched the clown tearing up pieces of paper*

Ii

I, i [aɪ] ninth letter of the alphabet, between H and J; *she said 'I' for 'indigo'*; **to dot one's i's and cross one's t's** = to be very careful to get the final details right

I [aɪ] *pronoun used by a speaker when talking about himself or herself; she said, 'I can do it', and she did it*; *she and I come from the same town*; *he told me that I could go home early*; *I said I was going to be late* (NOTE: when it is the object of a verb, I becomes **me: I gave it to him - he gave it to me; I hit him - he hit me;** when it follows the verb **be,** I usually becomes **me: who is it? - it's me!**)

I the Roman numeral for one or first; *King Charles I*

ibid ['ɪbɪd] *used in references to mean 'from the text previously referred to'*

ice [aɪs] **1** *noun* **(a)** water which is frozen and has become solid; *when water freezes, it turns into ice*; *the ice on the lake is dangerous, it isn't thick enough to walk on*; *would you like ice in your drink?*; **her hands are like ice** = her hands are very cold **(b) to break the ice** = to start to talk when everyone has been silent; *the party started quietly, but the hot wine soon broke the ice*; **to keep something on ice** = to shelve something, not to do anything about something for the moment; **to put something on ice** = to file a plan or document as the best way of forgetting about it; *we can't afford the expense at the moment, so we'll put the project on ice until next year* **(c) ice bucket** = bucket of ice in which a wine bottle is placed to keep cool; **ice rink** = special area for ice skating, or for playing ice hockey, etc. **(d)** ice cream; *we had ices during the interval; two coffee ices, please* (NOTE: no plural for meaning (a): **some ice, a lump of ice;** the plural **ices** means **ice creams**) **2** *verb* **(a)** to add ice to a drink; *she asked for a glass of iced water* **(b)** to put icing on a cake; *a cake iced with chocolate*

Ice Age ['aɪs 'eɪdʒ] *noun* long period of time when the earth's temperature was cool and large areas of the surface were covered with ice; *the woolly mammoth is thought to have become extinct during the last Ice Age*

iceberg ['aɪsbɜːg] *noun* huge block of ice floating on the sea; *the ship navigated through the icebergs*; **it's the tip of the iceberg** = it's only a small noticeable part of something (usually unpleasant) that is mostly hidden; *these errors in the accounts were just the tip of the iceberg - the staff had been stealing money and stock for years*

icebox ['aɪsbɒks] *noun* **(a)** box containing ice to keep food or drink cool; *we took the drinks to the picnic in an icebox* **(b)** US (old) see REFRIGERATOR

ice cream ['aɪs 'kriːm] *noun* frozen sweet made from cream and flavouring such as fruit juice; *a lemon ice cream; what sort of ice cream do you want - vanilla or chocolate?*; *can you help me - I can't carry six ice creams at the same time?*

ice cube ['aɪs 'kjuːb] *noun* little block of ice, used to cool a drink; *we could hear the ice cubes chinking as she carried the tray of drinks over to us*

iced [aɪst] *adjective* cold, with ice in it; *she asked for a glass of iced water*

ice dancing ['aɪs 'dɑːnsɪŋ] *noun* Winter Olympic sport for mixed couples, involving skating to music on ice

ice hockey ['aɪs 'hɒki] *noun* form of hockey played on ice; *the ice hockey gold medal will be fought out between Canada and Russia* (NOTE: in American English called simply **hockey**)

COMMENT: ice hockey is a Winter Olympic sport; it is played on ice between two teams of six players wearing skates and using a long-handled stick with a flat blade to try to send a small, hard, flat rubber disk (called the 'puck') into their opponents' goal. Players wear helmets, gauntlets and a large amount of protective padding. Goalkeepers are even more heavily protected with a face visor and stronger gloves, a wider heavier stick. The game is divided into three 20-minute periods

Iceland ['aɪslənd] *noun* independent country, an island in the north Atlantic, north of Britain and west of Norway; *Iceland has many volcanoes* (NOTE: capital: **Reykjavik;** people: **Icelanders;** language: **Icelandic;** currency: **Icelandic krona**)

Icelander ['aɪsləndə] *noun* person from Iceland; *Icelanders are a hardy people*

Icelandic [aɪs'lændɪk] **1** *adjective* referring to Iceland; *fishing is an important Icelandic industry* **2** *noun* language spoken in Iceland; *Icelandic developed from the language spoken by Norsemen*

ice lolly ['aɪs 'lɒli] *noun* mixture of water and flavouring, frozen until solid with a stick in it (NOTE: plural is **ice lollies;** American English is **popsicle**)

ice skate 1 *verb* to glide over ice on ice skates **2** *noun* boot with a steel blade fitted to the sole for skating on ice

COMMENT: skates for figure skating have quite short blades with a serrated edge at the front for making spins and jumps and for stopping; ice hockey skates have flatter blades that allow the skater to skate faster

ice skating ['aɪs 'skeɪtɪŋ] *noun* skating on ice, as opposed to roller skating; *we go ice skating in the park on winter evenings; see also* FIGURE SKATING, ICE DANCING, SPEED SKATING

ice up ['aɪs 'ʌp] *verb* to become covered with ice; *the wings of the plane had iced up*

icicle ['aɪsɪkl] *noun* long piece of ice hanging from a roof, etc., formed of water dripping in freezing weather; *icicles hung down from the roof and dripped onto the pavement; droplets of water formed at the end of the icicles*

icily ['aɪsɪli] *adverb* in a cold and unfriendly way; *'put that back where you found it,' she said icily*

icing ['aɪsɪŋ] *noun* covering of sugar and flavouring, spread over a cake or biscuits; *she made some chocolate icing for the cake*; **icing sugar** = fine powdered white sugar, mixed with water or egg white and flavouring, used to cover cakes or biscuits; *mix the icing sugar with water and vanilla essence to make the white icing*

icon ['aɪkən] *noun* **(a)** little picture used as a symbol on a computer screen; *click twice on the icon of a key to enter the program*; *to print your text, point your cursor at the printer icon and click twice* **(b)** picture of Christ or a saint in the Eastern Christian church; *there is an exhibition of Russian icons in the British Museum*; *the icon of the Virgin Mary is carried in procession round the church* **(c)** person who is admired as a good example of a certain type; *she has become something of a feminist icon*

iconoclast [aɪ'kɒnəklæst] *noun* person who goes against a tradition that many people believe in; *he was something of an iconoclast in his designs for the new cathedral*

icy ['aɪsi] *adjective* covered with ice; *be careful, the pavement is icy* (NOTE: **icier - iciest**)

I'd [aɪd] *short for* I HAD, I SHOULD, I WOULD

ID (card) ['aɪ 'di: kɑːd] *noun* identity card, a card which shows a photograph of the holder, with the name, date of birth and other details, carried by citizens of a country or members of a group to prove who they are; *show your ID card when entering the Ministry*; *in some European countries you are legally required to carry an ID card around with you*; *have you got any ID on you?*

> COMMENT: British citizens are not required to have ID cards, but many firms have them for their employees, and some football clubs have them for their supporters, all for security purposes

idea [aɪ'dɪə] *noun* **(a)** something which you think of; **to have an idea that** = to think that; *I have an idea that the buses don't run on Sundays*; **to have no idea** *or* **not to have the faintest idea** = not to know; *where's your brother? - I've no idea or I haven't the faintest idea*; *I had no idea it was as late as that* **(b)** plan which you make in your mind; *some of his ideas were really original*; *I've had an idea - let's all go for a picnic!*; *that's a good idea!*; **a bright idea** = a good plan; *he had the bright idea of painting the bathroom red*

ideal [aɪ'dɪəl] **1** *noun* highest point of perfection which people try to reach; *my ideal would be to work hard and get rich*; **man of ideals** = person who has standards of perfection **2** *adjective* perfect, extremely suitable; *this is the ideal site for a factory*; *the cottage is an ideal place for birdwatching*

idealism [aɪ'dɪəlɪzm] *noun* aiming at achieving an ideal; *as children grow up they lose their idealism*

idealist [aɪ'dɪəlɪst] *noun* **(a)** person who aims at achieving an ideal; *she's an idealist, and is upset when anyone suggests a solution which is less than perfect* **(b)** impractical person; *he's too much of an idealist to be a government minister*

idealistic [aɪdɪə'lɪstɪk] *adjective* aiming at an ideal; too perfect; *she's young and idealistic and has no idea of the practical problems involved*

idealization [aɪdɪəlaɪ'zeɪʃn] *noun* making someone seem perfect; *his idealization of tall fair women became an obsession*

idealize [aɪ'dɪəlaɪz] *verb* to make someone *or* something seem perfect; *we have a tendency to idealize people after they die*; *the painting is an idealized version of 19th century London*

ideally [aɪ'dɪəli] *adverb* if everything were perfect; *ideally, I'd take three weeks off, but there's too much work at the office*

identical [aɪ'dentɪkl] *adjective* exactly the same; *the twins wore identical clothes for the party*; *their political opinions are identical*; **identical to** = exactly the same as; *her political opinions are identical to mine*; **identical twins** = twins who look exactly alike, because they developed from the same ovum (NOTE: twins who are not alike are called **fraternal twins**)

identically [aɪ'dentɪkli] *adverb* in exactly the same way; *the twins dressed identically for the party*

identifiable [aɪdentɪ'faɪəbl] *adjective* which can be identified; *the body was so decomposed it was no longer identifiable*

identification [aɪdentɪfɪ'keɪʃn] *noun* **(a)** saying who someone is, giving the name, personal details, etc.; *the formal identification of the body was made by the victim's sister*; **identification parade** = line of people at a police station from whom a witness is asked to identify a suspected criminal; *she was asked to pick out the mugger at an identification parade* **(b)** document which shows who someone is; *the bank manager asked him for identification*

identify [aɪ'dentɪfaɪ] *verb* **(a)** to say who someone is or what something is; *can you identify what sort of rock this is?*; *she was able to identify her attacker* **(b)** to state that something belongs to you; *each person was asked to identify his or her baggage* **(c)** **to identify with** = to feel you have the same feelings as someone or to have a feeling of sympathy for someone *or* something; *I can identify with the heroine who spends her life trapped in a small rural town*

identikit [aɪ'dentɪkɪt] *noun* **(a)** method of making a picture of a criminal from descriptions given by witnesses, using pieces of photographs and drawings of different types of faces; *the police issued an identikit picture of the rapist* (NOTE: now replaced by **Photofit pictures**) **(b)** looking identical, doing exactly the same thing as someone else; *the company has a staff of twenty identikit salesmen*

identity [aɪ'dentɪti] *noun* someone's name, personal details, etc.; *he changed his identity when he went to work for the secret services*; **identity card (ID card)** = a card which shows a photograph of the holder, with the name, date of birth and other details, carried by citizens of a country or members of a group to prove who they are; *show your identity card when entering the Ministry*; *in some European countries you are legally required to carry an identity card with you at all times*; **proof of identity** = proof in the form of a document, such as a driving licence, that a person is who he or she claims to be; *the police asked her for proof of identity*

ideological [aɪdɪə'lɒdʒɪkl] *adjective* referring to ideology; *the two wings of the party have important ideological differences*

ideology [aɪdɪ'ɒlədʒi] *noun* theory of life based not on religious belief, but on political or economic philosophy; *her socialist ideology led her to join the party*; *he wrote a study of Communist ideology*

idiocy ['ɪdiəsi] *noun* total stupidity; *the idiocy of the council's decision is obvious*

idiom ['ɪdiəm] *noun* **(a)** particular expression where the words do not have their literal meaning; *'it's raining cats and dogs' is an idiom* **(b)** characteristic way of speaking, of writing; *'How now, what news?' was a common greeting in the idiom of Shakespeare's England*

idiomatic [ɪdiə'mætɪk] *adjective* referring to a natural colloquial way of speaking a language; *he speaks very idiomatic English, but with a strong French accent*

idiosyncrasy [ɪdiəu'sɪŋkrəsi] *noun* particularly odd way of behaving; *singing on her bicycle is one of her little idiosyncrasies*; *this car has some idiosyncrasies, such as the gear change, but once you've got used to it, it is very easy to drive*

idiosyncratic [ɪdiəusɪŋ'krætɪk] *adjective* odd or peculiar; particular to one person; *the chairman was eventually forced to resign because of his increasingly idiosyncratic behaviour*; *the director of the film is famous for his very idiosyncratic style of directing*

idiot ['ɪdiət] *noun* person who is stupid; *if you accepted that offer, you're an idiot*; *don't be an idiot - tell her you're sorry*

idiotic [ɪdɪ'ɒtɪk] *adjective* stupid; *stop throwing the paint around - it's idiotic*; *take that idiotic smile off your face*

idle ['aɪdl] *adjective* **(a)** lazy (person); *he's the idlest man I know - he never does any work at all*; *he's bone idle* = he never does any work **(b)** not working; *the machines stood idle during the strike*; *2,000 employees were made idle by the recession* (NOTE: do not confuse with **idol**; note: **idler - idlest**)

idol ['aɪdl] *noun* **(a)** statue of a god which is worshipped; *the tribesmen danced in front of their idols* **(b)** star performer who is worshipped by fans; *the England captain is many boys' footballing idol* **(c)** favourite person; *my cousin Jimmy was my great idol when I was small* (NOTE: do not confuse with **idle**)

idolatry [aɪ'dɒlətri] *noun* worshipping idols; *bowing down before statues is pure idolatry*

idolization [aɪdəlaɪ'zeɪʃn] *noun* action of idolizing someone; *his idolization of his dead sister turned into an obsession*

idolize ['aɪdəlaɪz] *verb* to admire someone very much; *he idolized his art teacher*

idyll ['ɪdɪl] *noun* (*literary*) scene of peace and happiness in the country

idyllic [ɪ'dɪlɪk] *adjective* happy and pleasant in a romantic way; *what an idyllic spot for a picnic!*

ie *or* **i.e.** ['aɪ 'iː] *abbreviation meaning 'that is'*; *it's best to study Russian in a country where they speak it - i.e. Russia*; *the import restrictions apply to expensive items, i.e. items costing more than £2,500* (NOTE: it is short for the Latin phrase **id est**)

if [ɪf] **1** *conjunction* **(a)** (*showing what might happen*) *if it freezes tonight, the paths will be slippery tomorrow*; *if I'm in London, I'll come and see you*; *if he had told me you were ill, I'd have come to see you in hospital*; *if I won the lottery, I would take a long holiday*; *if he's going to be late, he'll phone to tell us* **(b)** (*asking*

questions) *do you know if the plane is late?*; *I was wondering if you would like to have some tea* **(c)** although; *he is nice, if rather lazy* **2** *noun* question which is not certain; *he'll catch the plane if he gets up in time, and that's a very big if*

◊ **if only** ['ɪf 'əunli] (*exclamation showing regret*) *if only I had some money!*; *if only she'd told me, I could have advised her what to do*

iffy ['ɪfi] *adjective* (*informal*) doubtful, not at all certain; *the whole project looks a bit iffy to me*

igneous rock ['ɪgniəs 'rɒk] *noun* rock originally formed from lava; *those curious rock formations that look like columns are igneous rocks*

ignite [ɪg'naɪt] *verb* **(a)** to light, to set fire to; *the teacher showed us how to ignite the Bunsen burner* **(b)** to catch fire; *there was a loud explosion as the gas ignited*

ignition [ɪg'nɪʃn] *noun* (*in a car*) process which starts the burning of the compressed air-fuel mixture; *the engine doesn't turn over when I switch on the ignition*; **ignition key** = key used to switch on the ignition; *turn the ignition key to start the engine* (NOTE: no plural)

ignominious [ɪgnə'mɪniəs] *adjective* shameful; *the team returned home in disgrace after their ignominious defeat*

ignominy ['ɪgnəmɪni] *noun* disgrace; *he suffered the ignominy of failing his driving test just after he had bought his new car*

ignorance ['ɪgnərəns] *noun* not knowing; *ignorance of the law is no excuse*; **to keep someone in ignorance of something** = not to tell someone about something; *the soldiers were deliberately kept in ignorance of the dangers facing them* (NOTE: no plural)

ignorant ['ɪgnərənt] *adjective* not knowing anything; stupid; *he kept very quiet during the discussion, trying to hide just how ignorant he was*; *the intellectuals in the party refuse to have anything to do with the farmers, whom they think of as ignorant peasants*

ignore [ɪg'nɔː] *verb* not to notice someone *or* something on purpose; *she ignored the red light and just drove straight through*; *when we met he just ignored me*

II the Roman numeral for two or second; *it happened during the reign of King James II*

III the Roman numeral for three or third; *do you know when King George III died?*

ill [ɪl] *adjective* **(a)** sick, not well; *stress can make you ill*; *if you're feeling ill you ought to see a doctor*; **to fall ill** = to become ill; *she fell seriously ill and we thought she was going to die*; **to be taken ill** = to become ill suddenly; *he was taken ill while on holiday in Greece* **(b)** **ill at ease** = embarrassed, not comfortable; *she seemed ill at ease when we started talking about the missing money*; *he felt ill at ease in his new suit at a reception where he knew nobody* (NOTE: **ill - worse** [wɜːs] **- worst** [wɜːst])

I'll [aɪl] *short for* I WILL, I SHALL

ill-advised [ɪləd'vaɪzd] *adjective* not sensible, which is not a good idea; *her ill-advised meeting with her husband's solicitors*

illegal [ɪ'liːgl] *adjective* against the law; *it is illegal to serve alcohol to people under 16*; *illegal immigrants will be deported*

illegally [ɪˈliːgəli] *adverb* against the law; *he was accused of illegally importing arms into the country*; *if he is caught, he will be deported because he entered the country illegally*; *the vehicle was illegally parked*

illegitimate [ɪlɪˈdʒɪtəmət] *adjective* **(a)** born to parents who are not married to each other; *the MP failed in his attempt to hide his illegitimate child from the press* **(b)** forbidden by certain rules, against the law; *we should all be concerned at the illegitimate use of certain prescription drugs*; *the government is cracking down on the illegitimate ownership of firearms*

ill-fated [ɪlˈfeɪtɪd] *adjective* unlucky and bound to fail; *their ill-fated relationship finally ended last Easter*; *his ill-fated attempt to fly round the world in a balloon*

ill-gotten gains [ˈɪlˈgɒtən ˈgeɪnz] *noun* money made illegally or dishonestly; *thinking of them sitting there with their ill-gotten gains makes me envious*

ill health [ˈɪl ˈhelθ] *noun* not being well; *she had a history of ill health*; *he had to retire early for reasons of ill health*

illicit [ɪˈlɪsɪt] *adjective* against the law, not legal; *the illicit sale of drugs*; *he made his money from illicit trading in alcohol* (NOTE: do not confuse with **elicit**)

illiteracy [ɪˈlɪtərəsi] *noun* being unable to read or write; **adult illiteracy** = situation where an adult cannot read or write; *the government is making every effort to reduce adult illiteracy*; compare NUMERACY

illiterate [ɪˈlɪtərət] **1** *adjective* **(a)** not able to read or write; *with so few schools or teachers it is hardly surprising so many children are illiterate* **(b) computer illiterate** = person who does not know how to use a computer; *I am computer illiterate - my son knows more about computers than I do* **2** *noun* person who cannot read or write; *as education facilities have improved, so the percentage of illiterates has been significantly reduced*

illness [ˈɪlnəs] *noun* not being well; *she developed a serious illness*; *a lot of the staff are absent because of illness* (NOTE: plural is **illnesses**)

illogical [ɪˈlɒdʒɪkl] *adjective* not sensible, not reasonable; *it's illogical to increase prices when sales are falling*

illuminate [ɪˈluːmɪneɪt] *verb* **(a)** to make something bright with lights; *the pitch was illuminated by giant floodlights*; *the town looked magical, illuminated with strings of lights along the edge of the sea* **(b)** *(formal)* to explain something to make it clearer; *his talk illuminated several points which I hadn't understood before* **(c)** to draw coloured pictures in a manuscript; *the manuscript was illuminated with pictures from the Bible*

illuminated [ɪˈluːmɪneɪtɪd] *adjective* **(a)** lit up with bright lights; *a brightly illuminated football pitch* **(b)** with small coloured illustrations; *the library has several illuminated manuscripts of the twelfth century*

illumination [ɪluːmɪˈneɪʃn] *noun* **(a) (formal)** action of giving information about something; *I turned to the encyclopaedia for illumination* **(b)** coloured illustration in a manuscript; *the chapter illuminations are real works of art*

illuminations [ɪluːmɪˈneɪʃnz] *noun* floodlighting or coloured lights which decorate a town; *people come from all over the country to see the Blackpool illuminations*

illusion [ɪˈluːʒn] *noun* impression which is not true; *the publicity about the company creates an illusion of seriousness*; **optical illusion** = thing which appears different from what it really is because your eye doesn't recognise it; *the lines are not different lengths - it's just an optical illusion*; **to have no illusions about something** = to know the real unpleasant facts about something; *she has no illusions about her husband being faithful*

illusory [ɪˈluːzəri] *adjective (formal)* not real, which is an illusion; *her hopes of marrying a rich husband proved illusory*

illustrate [ˈɪləstreɪt] *verb* **(a)** to put pictures into a book; *the book is illustrated with colour photographs of birds* **(b)** to show as an example; *the article illustrates his views on the way the company should develop* **(c)** to be an example of; *this poem illustrates the sort of style I prefer*

illustration [ɪləˈstreɪʃn] *noun* **(a)** picture in a book; *the book has 25 colour illustrations* **(b)** example; *his daughter's birthday party is a good illustration of the way he likes to spend money*

illustrative [ˈɪləstrətɪv] *adjective* which illustrates, which is an example; *the dictionary is full of illustrative examples*

illustrious [ɪˈlʌstriəs] *adjective* very famous; *the town erected a statue to their illustrious former mayor*

I'm [aɪm] *short for* I AM

image [ˈɪmɪdʒ] *noun* **(a)** portrait, likeness; *I want the portrait to be a faithful image of my mother*; *(informal)* **he's the spitting image of his father** = he looks exactly like his father **(b)** idea which other people have of a person or of an organization; *the children are so badly behaved that it gives quite a wrong image of the family*; *in an attempt to change his image he bought a lot of trendy clothes*; *they are spending a lot of advertising money to improve the company's image* **(c)** picture produced by a lens, mirror or computer; *the mirror throws an image onto the paper*; *can this software handle images in that format?*; *can you adjust the projector, the image on the screen is out of focus?*

imagery [ˈɪmɪdʒri] *noun* use of comparisons or symbols in writing as a way of making people imagine things; *he uses some very powerful imagery in his war poems*

imaginable [ɪˈmædʒɪnəbl] *adjective* which you can imagine; *the animals were being kept in the worst imaginable conditions*

imaginary [ɪˈmædʒɪnəri] *adjective* false, not real; *in fact the story is imaginary, although most people feel it could be true*; *all his novels are set in an imaginary town in Central Europe*

imagination [ɪmædʒɪˈneɪʃn] *noun* ability to picture things in your mind; *she let her imagination run riot in her stories for children*; **to use your imagination** = to imagine what is possible; *try and use your imagination - think of the money we could make*; **to let your imagination get the better of you** *or* **run away with you** = to think things are possible when they are not; *he let his imagination get the better of him and saw himself as a future Prime Minister*

imaginative [ɪˈmædʒɪnətɪv] *adjective* having or showing a lot of imagination; *she was the most imaginative poet of her generation*; *children often* write very imaginative stories; the decorations for the wedding are tasteful but not very imaginative

imaginatively [ɪˈmædʒɪnətɪvli] adverb in an imaginative way; she imaginatively created the costumes for the play out of old curtains

imagine [ɪˈmædʒɪn] verb to picture something in your mind; imagine yourself sitting on a beach in the hot sun; she though she had heard footsteps, and then decided she had imagined it

imaging [ˈɪmədʒɪŋ] noun technique for creating pictures using scanners attached to computers; to use your computer as a fax machine you will need some imaging software; thermal imaging is used to detect the heat from the bodies lying buried under snow or rubble

imam [ˈɪmæm] noun Muslim religious leader; the crowd listened in silence as the imam addressed them

imbalance [ɪmˈbæləns] noun lack of balance; there is a noticeable imbalance between the money the charity receives and the money it spends

imbecile [ˈɪmbəsiːl] noun (a) person who is mentally subnormal (NOTE: not used by doctors) (b) (informal) stupid person; you imbecile, you threw the envelope with the cheque in it into the rubbish!

imbed [ɪmˈbed] = EMBED

imbibe [ɪmˈbaɪb] verb (humorous) to drink; he's fond of imbibing in the evening

imbue [ɪmˈbjuː] verb (formal) to fill someone with a feeling; when he saw her crying he was imbued with a feeling of pity

IMF [aɪemˈef] abbreviation for INTERNATIONAL MONETARY FUND; the IMF has agreed to allocate more loans to Russia

imitate [ˈɪmɪteɪt] verb to copy something or someone; to do as someone does; he made us all laugh by imitating the head teacher; the company imitates its competitors by making very similar products

imitation [ɪmɪˈteɪʃn] noun (a) act of imitating; she does a very good imitation of the Queen (b) copy made of something; it's not real leather, just imitation; the bag is made of imitation leather; beware of imitations = be careful not to buy low quality goods which are made to look like other more expensive items

immaculate [ɪˈmækjʊlət] adjective (a) extremely clean or tidy; the car looked absolutely immaculate - there wasn't a spot of dirt on it; the nurses all wore immaculate white uniforms; the last house we visited was in immaculate condition, while all the others needed a lot of repairs (b) perfect, with no errors; she did an immaculate driving test

immaculately [ɪˈmækjʊlətli] adverb (a) extremely tidily; it suddenly started to rain, and the immaculately dressed guests had to run from the garden into the house (b) perfectly; she danced her solo immaculately

immaterial [ɪməˈtɪəriəl] adjective not relevant; that information is quite immaterial to the discussion

immature [ɪməˈtʃʊə] adjective (a) not mature, still developing; two immature swans followed their parents across the lake (b) not sensible, not adult; I wish she would grow up and stop being so immature!

immediacy [ɪˈmiːdiəsi] noun being immediately present; the pictures on TV brought the immediacy of the earthquake home to the television viewers

immediate [ɪˈmiːdjət] adjective (a) very soon; he wrote an immediate letter of complaint; you didn't expect an immediate reply, did you?; your order will receive immediate attention (b) closest, (sitting) next to you; he had to share his programme with his immediate neighbour

immediately [ɪˈmiːdiətli] adverb straight away; he got my letter, and wrote back immediately; as soon as he heard the news he immediately phoned his wife

immense [ɪˈmens] adjective huge; very big; enormous; he has an immense black beard; the bill was immense, and we all complained; the president decided to build an immense palace in the mountains

immensely [ɪˈmensli] adverb very much; we enjoyed ourselves immensely

immensity [ɪˈmensɪti] noun huge size; it is difficult to grasp the immensity of the North American prairies; the authorities did not appreciate the immensity of the problem of cleaning up after the tanker went aground (NOTE: no plural)

immerse [ɪˈmɜːs] verb (a) to plunge something in a liquid; he lowered the box into the water until it was completely immersed; to sterilize the bottle, immerse in water and boil for four minutes (b) to immerse yourself in = to concentrate on, to get fully involved in; he immersed himself in the study of Latin literature

immersed [ɪˈmɜːst] adjective immersed in = fully involved in, deeply busy with; the whole family is immersed in politics; he's immersed in his job

immersion [ɪˈmɜːʃn] noun (a) action of plunging something into a liquid; total immersion in the acid bath will remove all traces of paint (b) immersion (heater) = heater inside a water tank; if you want a bath you'll have to switch the immersion on

immigrant [ˈɪmɪɡrənt] noun person who comes to a country to settle; many immigrants came to Britain during the 1930s; immigrants are rushing to Germany because the economy is booming; illegal immigrant = person who has entered a country illegally and wants to settle there; compare EMIGRANT

immigrate [ˈɪmɪɡreɪt] verb to come to settle in a country (NOTE: the opposite is emigrate)

immigration [ɪmɪˈɡreɪʃn] noun (a) settling in a new country; the government is encouraging immigration because of the shortage of workers in key industries; immigration controls = restrictions placed by a country on the numbers of immigrants who can come into the country; many countries have imposed immigration controls (b) Immigration = section of an airport where new arrivals have to show their passports; he was stopped at Immigration; you will need to show all these documents when you go through Immigration; compare EMIGRATION

COMMENT: there was lot of immigration into Britain during the 1950s, 1960s and 1970s, mainly of people from former colonies in the West Indies and South Asia

imminence [ˈɪmɪnəns] noun being about to happen; the imminence of the election made all the parties worried

imminent [ˈɪmɪnənt] adjective which is about to happen; a rise in interest rates is imminent

immobile [ɪˈməʊbaɪl] adjective not moving, not able to move; the heron stood immobile in the stream, *waiting for a fish to come past; she is now completely immobile, and has to be fed by nurses*

immobility [ˌɪməˈbɪlɪti] *noun* state of not moving; *the tourists were impressed by the immobility of the guards lining the route of the procession*

immobilize [ɪˈməʊbɪlaɪz] *verb* to stop something moving; *he immobilized the car by fitting a clamp to the wheel*

immoral [ɪˈmɒrəl] *adjective* not following the usual principles of good behaviour; *it is quite immoral for trustees to use money in their trust for their own purposes; that is a completely immoral suggestion; the minister was accused of having led an immoral life*

immortal [ɪˈmɔːtl] **1** *adjective* **(a)** who never dies; *Roman gods were believed to be immortal* **(b)** very famous, which will always be remembered; *that immortal line from 'Casablanca': 'play it again, Sam'; and now another song from the immortal frank Sinatra* **2** *noun* famous person who will always be remembered; *W.G. Grace, and other cricket immortals*

immortality [ɪmɔːˈtælɪti] *noun* being immortal, never dying; *most religions believe in the immortality of the soul; he achieved immortality by writing one of the funniest plays of the 20th century*

immortalize [ɪˈmɔːtəlaɪz] *verb* to make someone or something be remembered for ever; *this is the tune immortalized in the 'Third Man'*

immune [ɪˈmjuːn] *adjective* **(a)** *(person)* protected against infection; *I seem to be immune to colds - I just never have any; this injection should make you immune to yellow fever;* **immune system** = complex network of cells which protects the body from disease; *in people with AIDS, the immune system gradually deteriorates* **(b)** legally protected against, not liable to; *she believed she would be immune from prosecution* (NOTE: you are immune **to** a disease, and **from** prosecution)

immunity [ɪˈmjuːnɪti] *noun* **(a) immunity to a disease** = ability to resist attacks of a disease because of antibodies produced in the body; *the injection will give immunity to malaria for six months* **(b) immunity from** *or* **against arrest** = protection against being arrested; *when he offered to give information to the police, he was granted immunity from prosecution;* **diplomatic immunity** = freedom from the control of the laws of the country you are living in because of being a diplomat; *the cultural attaché refused to pay his parking fines and claimed diplomatic immunity;* **parliamentary immunity** = protection of Members of Parliament against being arrested

immunization [ɪmjʊnaɪˈzeɪʃn] *noun* injections, etc., to make a person immune to a disease; *check what immunization you need before you travel*

immunize [ˈɪmjʊnaɪz] *verb* to give someone immunity to a disease; *I was immunized against tetanus three years ago* (NOTE: you immunize someone **against** a disease)

immutable [ɪˈmjuːtəbl] *adjective (formal)* which cannot be changed, which does not change; *the immutable laws of nature; all things in modern society change, nothing is immutable*

imp [ɪmp] *noun* **(a)** naughty child; *the little imp - he's put glue on my chair!* **(b)** small devil; *when you go into the cathedral look out for the little imp carved high up near the choir*

impact [ˈɪmpækt] **1** *noun* **(a)** forceful effect; *the TV documentary had a strong impact on the viewers* **(b)** forceful shock; *the car was totally crushed by the impact of the collision;* **on impact** = as soon as it hit; *the plane burst into flames on impact with the ground* **2** *verb* **to impact on something** = to have a strong effect on something; *the fall in the value of the currency will impact strongly on the stock market*

impair [ɪmˈpeə] *verb* to damage something so that it does not work properly; *working with pneumatic drills has impaired his hearing; her accident has impaired her chances of a successful academic career;* **visually-impaired person** = person whose eyesight is not perfect

impale [ɪmˈpeɪl] *verb* to jab a sharp object through the body; *he fell from the balcony and was impaled on the fence beneath*

impart [ɪmˈpɑːt] *verb (formal)* **(a)** to bring a special feeling to something; *the news of the huge order imparted a sense of excitement to the meeting* **(b)** to pass on information, to communicate something to someone; *a teacher tries to impart his knowledge to his students*

impartial [ɪmˈpɑːʃəl] *adjective* not biased; *judges must be strictly impartial*

impartiality [ɪmpɑːʃiˈælɪti] *noun* being impartial; *the lawyers for the accused questioned the judge's impartiality*

impasse [ˈæmpɑːs] *noun* deadlock, state where two sides cannot agree; *negotiations have reached an impasse*

impassioned [ɪmˈpæʃnd] *adjective* showing very deep feelings; *he made an impassioned plea for calm*

impassive [ɪmˈpæsɪv] *adjective* showing no expression of feelings; *the impassive face of the accused as he sat listening to the evidence*

impatient [ɪmˈpeɪʃnt] *adjective* unable to wait for something, always in a hurry to do something; *we were all impatient for the film to start; he's very impatient with anyone who works slowly*

impatiently [ɪmˈpeɪʃntli] *adverb* in a hurried way, not patiently; *'can't you go any faster,' she said impatiently; we are all waiting impatiently for the new book to come out*

impeach [ɪmˈpiːtʃ] *verb* **(a)** formerly, to charge a person with treason or other serious crime before Parliament; *in 1530 Cardinal Wolsey was impeached by the House of Lords before being charged with high treason* **(b)** to charge a head of state or minister with treason or with crimes against the state; *if the president had not resigned, he would have been impeached*

impeachment [ɪmˈpiːtʃmənt] *noun* charge of treason or other serious crime brought against a head of state or government minister; *the president's critics were calling for his impeachment*

impeccable [ɪmˈpekəbl] *adjective* perfect, perfectly correct; *his behaviour on the tennis court has been impeccable; she wrote us a letter in impeccable English*

impecunious [ɪmpɪˈkjuːnɪəs] *adjective (formal)* poor, not having any money; *when I first met him he was an impecunious doctor in one of the large London hospitals*

impede [ɪmˈpiːd] *verb* to stop someone or something going forwards; *his lack of university education does not seem to have impeded his progress up the ranks of the civil service*

impediment [ɪmˈpedɪmənt] *noun* **(a)** obstacle, situation which stops something happening; *is there any just impediment why these two people should not be joined together in matrimony?*; *he finds that not having a car is no impediment to his job as a salesman* **(b)** speech **impediment** = stammer, etc., which prevents you speaking clearly; *he has a slight speech impediment so please be patient when you talk to him*

impel [ɪmˈpel] *verb (formal)* to force someone to do something; *the slow service in the restaurant impelled him to complain to the management*; *she felt impelled to tell him her important family secret* (NOTE: impelling - impelled)

impending [ɪmˈpendɪŋ] *adjective* which will happen soon; *the newspapers carried stories about the impending general election*; *they were filled with a sense of impending disaster*

impenetrable [ɪmˈpenɪtrəbl] *adjective* which you cannot go through or into, or see through; *the impenetrable darkness inside the cave made exploring difficult*; *impenetrable jungle surrounds the site of the ancient city*

imperative [ɪmˈperətɪv] **1** *adjective* urgent, which has to be done; *it is imperative that a reply be given immediately* **2** *noun* **(a)** thing which has to be done; *profitability is an imperative with most companies* **(b)** *(in grammar)* form of a verb when used as a command; *'come here!' is an example of a verb used in the imperative*

imperceptible [ɪmpəˈseptɪbl] *adjective* which you can hardly notice; *the change was imperceptible at first, but became more noticeable six months later*

imperceptibly [ɪmpəˈseptɪbli] *adverb* hardly noticeably; *his behaviour towards us changed imperceptibly over the period of his divorce*

imperfect [ɪmˈpɜːfɪkt] *adjective* not perfect, not complete; *we only have an imperfect understanding of the origins of the universe*

imperfection [ɪmpəˈfekʃn] *noun* fault, flaw; *she examined the whole batch for imperfections*

imperial [ɪmˈpɪəriəl] *adjective* **(a)** referring to an empire; *imperial Russia ended with the Russian Revolution*; *the power of imperial Rome* **(b)** imperial measures = weights and measures used in the UK and the British Commonwealth

> COMMENT: imperial measurements of length include the inch, foot, yard, mile; of weights the ounce, pound; of liquids the pint, quart, gallon. See the note at METRIC

imperialism [ɪmˈpɪəriəlɪzm] *noun (often as a criticism)* **(a)** idea or practice of having an empire formed of colonies; *the main expansion of European imperialism occurred towards the end of the nineteenth century* **(b)** control of other countries as if they were part of an empire; *multinational businesses are accused of economic imperialism* (NOTE: no plural)

imperialist [ɪmˈpɪəriəlɪst] **1** *adjective* referring to imperialism; *they were criticized for their imperialist attitude towards neighbouring countries* **2** *noun* person who builds or favours empires and imperialism; *the nineteenth century Russian tsars were imperialists*

imperialistic [ɪmpɪəriəˈlɪstɪk] *adjective* referring to imperialism; *imperialistic multinational companies*

imperil [ɪmˈperɪl] *verb (formal)* to put in danger; *he drove in a way which imperilled the lives of the bus passengers* (NOTE: imperilling - imperilled but American spelling imperiling - imperiled)

imperious [ɪmˈpɪəriəs] *adjective (formal)* like a commander, expecting people to obey; *her imperious way of giving instructions made the servants afraid of her*

impersonal [ɪmˈpɜːsnl] *adjective* **(a)** not personal, without any personal character; *just stick to the facts and keep the interview impersonal*; *the waiting-room was cold and impersonal* **(b)** impersonal verb = verb used without a subject referring to a particular person or thing; *'it is snowing' is an example of an impersonal verb*

impersonate [ɪmˈpɜːsəneɪt] *verb* to dress like someone, to pretend to be that person; *he impersonated a reporter in order to get close to the president*

impertinence [ɪmˈpɜːtɪnəns] *noun* rudeness, lack of respect; *he actually had the impertinence to ask me if I could lend him £5*

impertinent [ɪmˈpɜːtɪnənt] *adjective* rude, lacking respect; *it was very impertinent of her to give her father tips on how he should drive*

impervious [ɪmˈpɜːviəs] *adjective* **(a)** not bothered by something; *she seems quite impervious to the noise of children all around her*; *not all authors are as impervious to criticism as she is* **(b)** which does not allow liquids to go through; *these rocks are impervious to water*

impetuous [ɪmˈpetjuəs] *adjective* without thinking, thoughtless; *his impetuous reply was quoted in all the newspapers*; *if she had been less impetuous she probably would not be in the difficulties she is in now*

impetus [ˈɪmpətəs] *noun* energy which encourages rapid progress forward; *the new bonus system has provided an impetus for the salesmen*; *signing the contract has given us all an added impetus to get the work finished on time*

impish [ˈɪmpɪʃ] *adjective* wicked, like a naughty imp; *she gave him an impish smile as she handed over the present*

implacable [ɪmˈplækəbl] *adjective* strong, which cannot be satisfied; *her implacable hatred towards all foreigners*; *his implacable opposition to the government*

implacably [ɪmˈplækəbli] *adverb* in an implacable way; *he is implacably opposed to any change*

implant [ɪmˈplɑːnt] **1** *noun* thing which has been fixed inside a person's body; *she has had silicone breast implants* **2** *verb* **(a)** to fix something inside a person very deeply; *a love of his native country was implanted in him from a very early age* **(b)** to fix something inside a person's body; *surgeons implanted a pacemaker in his chest*

implement 1 *noun* [ˈɪmplɪmənt] tool or instrument; *the plumber brought an implement for bending pipes*; garden implements = implements such as forks and spades which are used in the garden **2** *verb* ['ɪmplɪment] to put into effect; *the changes must be implemented immediately*

implementation [ɪmplɪmən'teɪʃn] *noun* putting into effect; *the implementation of the changes requires new software*

implicate ['ɪmplɪkeɪt] *verb* to implicate someone in something = to suggest that someone is connected with something, especially a crime; *the documents seem to implicate the president in the scandal*

implication [ɪmplɪ'keɪʃn] *noun* (a) suggestion that someone is connected with a crime; *the newspaper revealed his implication in the affair of the stolen diamonds* (b) implications = possible effects of an action; *what will be the implications for public spending of the election results?*

implicit [ɪm'plɪsɪt] *adjective* (a) which is not definitely said, but is suggested; *it was implicit in his tone of voice that he wasn't going to agree; implicit in the inspectors' report was the possibility that the restaurant might have to close permanently* (b) implicit faith = total faith ; *he has implicit faith in his teacher's advice*

implicitly [ɪm'plɪsɪtli] *adverb* without asking questions; *I trust her judgement implicitly*

implied [ɪm'plaɪd] *adjective* which has been suggested; *he considered it an implied insult and was very offended*

implore [ɪm'plɔː] *verb* to beg someone to do something; *she implored him to lend her some money; they implored her forgiveness*

imply [ɪm'plaɪ] *verb* to suggest; *he implied that he knew where the papers had been hidden; the lawyer implied that the witness had not in fact seen the accident take place*

import 1 *noun* ['ɪmpɔːt]; imports = goods which are brought into a country for sale; *the volume of imports from Poland has risen by 20% this year; all imports must be declared to customs;* import controls = rules limiting goods which can be brought into a country; *import controls on foreign makes of cars have been lifted;* import duty = tax paid on goods brought into a country; *the government charges an import duty on some items coming into the country;* import licence *or* import permit = official document which allows goods to be imported; *don't try to import guns if you don't have an import licence;* import quota = fixed quantity of a particular type of goods which the government allows to be imported; *the government has imposed an import quota on cars* (NOTE: usually in the plural, **imports,** but always **import** before another noun) **2** *verb* [ɪm'pɔːt] to bring goods into a country; *the company imports television sets from Japan; this car was imported from France*

importance [ɪm'pɔːtns] *noun* seriousness, serious effect or influence; *do not attach too much importance to what he says; the bank attaches great importance to the deal*

important [ɪm'pɔːtənt] *adjective* (a) which matters a great deal; *it's important to be in time for the meeting; I have to go to London for an important meeting; he left a file containing important papers in the taxi* (b) (person) in a high position; *he has an important government job; she's an important government official; he was promoted to a more important position*

importer [ɪm'pɔːtə] *noun* person or company that imports goods; *the company is a big importer of foreign cars*

impose [ɪm'pəʊz] *verb* (a) to ask someone to pay a fine, a tax; *the judge imposed a fine on the shoplifter; the government imposed a 10% tax increase on electrical items* (b) to put something into action; *they have tried to impose a ban on smoking* (c) to impose on someone = to cause someone trouble or inconvenience; *I hope it's not imposing on you too much, but I need to have the report today*

imposing [ɪm'pəʊzɪŋ] *adjective* grand or solemn; *the cathedral is an imposing brick building in the centre of the city*

impossible [ɪm'pɒsəbl] *adjective* (a) which cannot be done; *it's impossible to do all this work in two hours; getting skilled staff is becoming impossible* (b) *(person or situation)* awkward and difficult; *the new secretary is completely impossible*

impossibly [ɪm'pɒsəbli] *adverb* in an impossible way; *the standard required is impossibly high; he found the exam impossibly difficult*

imposter *or* **impostor** [ɪm'pɒstə] *noun* person who pretends to be someone else; *the priest who married them turned out to have been an imposter, so they had to get married again*

imposture [ɪm'pɒstʃə] *noun (formal)* pretending to be someone else; *detectives uncovered the imposture when they asked her for proof of her identity*

impotence ['ɪmpətəns] *noun* (a) being unable to do anything when faced with a problem; *the impotence of the authorities in the face of widespread looting* (b) *(of man)* inability to have an erection or to ejaculate, and so have sexual intercourse; *if a man catches mumps it can lead to impotence*

impotent ['ɪmpətənt] *adjective* (a) *(formal)* not able to do anything; *we were impotent in the face of the typhoon* (b) *(of man)* unable to have sexual intercourse; *her husband was impotent and they were not able to have any children*

impound [ɪm'paʊnd] *verb* to take something away and keep it until the owner claims it; *if you leave your car here it will be impounded by the police*

impoverish [ɪm'pɒvərɪʃ] *verb* to make poor; *the soil has been impoverished by years of neglect*

impoverished [ɪm'pɒvərɪʃt] *adjective* made poor; *after years of famine and war, the impoverished population was reduced to eating insects and small animals*

impractical [ɪm'præktɪkl] *adjective* (a) which is not easy to put into practice; *it is quite impractical to expect three people to move all the furniture in two hours* (b) *(person)* not good at doing things with your hands; *she's totally impractical - she can't even change a light bulb*

impregnable [ɪm'pregnəbl] *adjective* which cannot be captured; *they thought the castle was impregnable until someone showed the enemy the secret passage; after the general election his position as leader of the party was impregnable*

impregnate ['ɪmpregneɪt] *verb* (a) to soak with something, usually with a liquid; *she wiped the floor with a cloth impregnated with insecticide* (b) *(formal)* to make pregnant; *the bull impregnated three cows*

impresario [ˌɪmprɪˈsɑːrɪəʊ] *noun* person who organizes concerts, shows and operas; *a Russian impresario booked the Albert Hall for four nights* (NOTE: plural is **impresarios**)

impress [ɪmˈpres] *verb* **(a)** to make someone admire or respect someone *or* something; *her rapid response to the request impressed her boss*; *she was impressed by his skill with the paintbrush*; *the military government organized the display to impress the neighbouring states* **(b)** **to impress something on someone** = to make someone understand; *I must impress on you just how urgent this is*

impressed [ɪmˈprest] *adjective* full of admiration; *what a beautiful garden - I'm really impressed!*

impression [ɪmˈpreʃn] *noun* **(a)** effect on someone's mind; *blue walls create an impression of coldness*; *the exhibition made a strong impression on her* **(b)** **to get the impression that** = to sense that, to have a feeling that; *I got the impression that she wanted us to leave*

Impressionism [ɪmˈpreʃənɪzm] *noun* French art movement, where painters tried to create an impression of how something really looked, using light and colour but without painting it in exact detail

Impressionist [ɪmˈpreʃənɪst] **1** *adjective* referring to Impressionism; *Renoir and Monet were Impressionist painters*; *the Impressionist movement flourished in the latter half of the 19th century* **2** *noun* painter in the Impressionist movement; *the Impressionists worked mainly in Paris in the late nineteenth century*

impressive [ɪmˈpresɪv] *adjective* which impresses; *he had a series of impressive wins in the chess tournament*; *an impressive display of military hardware*

imprint 1 *noun* [ˈɪmprɪnt] **(a)** mark made by something pressed down; *he looked at the imprint of a foot in the sand* **(b)** name and address of the publisher or printer, which must appear on most printed matter; *this book bears the PCP imprint* **2** *verb* [ɪmˈprɪnt] to stamp, to mark; *the outline of a child's hand was left imprinted on the door*; *the scene of devastation remained indelibly imprinted on her memory*

imprison [ɪmˈprɪzn] *verb* to put or to keep someone in prison; *he was imprisoned by the secret police for six months*

imprisonment [ɪmˈprɪzənmənt] *noun* putting or keeping someone in prison; *the penalty for the first offence is a fine of £200 or six weeks' imprisonment*; a **term of imprisonment** = time which a prisoner has to spend in prison; *he was sentenced to the maximum term of imprisonment*; *the judge sentenced her to a term of imprisonment*; **life imprisonment** = being put in prison for a long time (the penalty for murder)

COMMENT: life imprisonment is a term of many years, but in the UK does not necessarily mean for the rest of the prisoner's life; in the USA it means what it says

improbable [ɪmˈprɒbəbl] *adjective* not probable, not likely; *after last night's disaster, it's highly improbable that we shall ever be invited to their house again*; *the discovery was the result of an improbable coincidence*

impromptu [ɪmˈprɒmptjuː] **1** *adjective* done without any rehearsal or practice; *he gave an impromptu interview on his doorstep* **2** *adverb* without any rehearsal or practice; *they gave her five minutes' notice to speak impromptu in front of six hundred delegates*

improper [ɪmˈprɒpə] *adjective* **(a)** not according to the normal rules of society or of an organization; *it was a quite improper use of our company name* **(b)** rude, indecent; *the old man made some very improper suggestions to the girl* **(c)** used in a wrong way; *the improper use of a drug can cause serious damage to health*

improve [ɪmˈpruːv] *verb* **(a)** to make something better; *we are trying to improve our image with a series of TV commercials*; **to improve on something** = to try to do better than something; *she tried to improve on her previous best time* **(b)** to get better; *the general manager has promised that the bus service will improve*; *it poured down all morning, but in the afternoon the weather improved a little*

improvement [ɪmˈpruːvmənt] *noun* **(a)** making or becoming better; *there has been no improvement in the train service since we complained*; *the new software is a great improvement over the old version* **(b)** thing which is better; *they carried out some improvements to the house*; *we are planning home improvements such as a new kitchen*

improvise [ˈɪmprəvaɪz] *verb* **(a)** to do or to make something without any proper planning; *without a tent, we improvised a shelter using leaves and branches* **(b)** to speak without having any text to read from; *having forgotten the notes for her speech she had to improvise as best as she could*

impudence [ˈɪmpjʊdəns] *noun* being rude or cheeky; *the policeman took down her details, and then she had the impudence to ask him to lend her £10*

impudent [ˈɪmpjʊdənt] *adjective* rude or cheeky; *impudent children shouted names as he drove past*

impulse [ˈɪmpʌls] *noun* **(a)** sudden feeling or decision; *he had a sudden impulse to take the car and drive to France*; **to do something on impulse** = to do something because you have just thought of it, not because it was planned; **impulse buying** = buying goods which you have just seen, not because you had planned to buy them; *everybody goes in for impulse buying during the sales* **(b)** shock which makes something move or work; *electrodes attached to his head measure brain impulses*; *neurons are cells in the nervous system which transmit nerve impulses*

impulsive [ɪmˈpʌlsɪv] *adjective* acting because of a sudden decision, without thinking; *he is too impulsive - always rushing to do things without thinking about the consequences*

impunity [ɪmˈpjuːnɪti] *noun* **with impunity** = without risk of punishment; *no one can flout the law with impunity*

impure [ɪmˈpjʊə] *adjective* which is not pure, which has another substance mixed with it; *using impure drugs is very dangerous*

impurity [ɪmˈpjʊərɪti] *noun* substance which is impure; *you can fit a filter to remove impurities from drinking water* (NOTE: plural is **impurities**)

in [ɪn] *preposition & adverb* **(a)** (showing place) *he lives in the country*; *in Japan it snows a lot during the winter*; *she's in the kitchen*; *he's still in bed*; *don't* *stand outside in the pouring rain* **(b)** at home, in an office; *is the boss in?*; *he isn't in yet*; *my husband usually gets in from work about now*; *the train from Birmingham is due in at 6.30* **(c)** *(showing time)* in autumn the leaves turn brown; *on holiday there was nothing to do in the evenings*; *she was born in 1996*; *he ate his meal in five minutes*; *we went for a skiing holiday in January* **(d)** *(showing time in the future)* *I'll be back home in about two hours*; *she should arrive in twenty minutes' time* **(e)** fashionable; *this year, short skirts are in* **(f)** *(showing a state or appearance)* *he was dressed in black*; *she ran outside in her dressing gown*; *we're in a hurry*; *the words in a dictionary are set out in alphabetical order* **(g)** *(showing a proportion or ratio)* *one in ten of the children wears glasses*

◊ **all in (a)** including everything; *they quoted us an all-in price of £250.00* **(b)** *(informal)* tired out; *after moving all my stuff to my new flat I was all in*

◊ **in for** ['ɪn 'fɔː] *adverb* **to be in for something** = to be about to get something; *I think we're in for some bad weather*; *she's in for a nasty shock*

◊ **in front** ['ɪn 'frʌnt] **1** *adverb* further forwards; *her mother sat in the back seat and she sat in front* **2** *preposition*; **in front of** = placed further forwards than something; *a tall man came and sat in front of me and I couldn't see the screen*

◊ **in on** ['ɪn 'ɒn] *adverb* **to be in on a secret** = to know a secret; *who else was in on the secret?*; **to let someone in on a secret** = to tell someone a secret; *the gang let the driver in on the secret*

◊ **in so far as** ['ɪn səʊ 'fɑː 'æz] *adverb (formal)* to the extent that; *we found the assembly instructions, in so far as they applied to our model, quite easy to understand*

inability [ɪnə'bɪlɪti] *noun* being unable to do something; *his inability to write English correctly is a handicap*

inaccessible [ɪnək'sesɪbl] *adjective* **(a)** impossible to reach or to get to; *they live in a farm which is inaccessible by car*; *the explorers were lost in an inaccessible mountain region*; *the valley is inaccessible to motorists* **(b)** *(formal)* difficult to read or understand; *he writes in a rather inaccessible style*

inaccurate [ɪn'ækjərət] *adjective* not accurate, not exact; *his calculations were wildly inaccurate*

inaccurately [ɪn'ækjərətli] *adverb* not accurately; *my speech was inaccurately reported in the press*

inactive [ɪn'æktɪv] *adjective* not active or not doing anything; *our adviser seems to have been totally inactive when he should have been preparing a report*

inactivity [ɪnæk'tɪvɪti] *noun* not being active; *after a long period of inactivity they have started to send us orders again*

inadequacy [ɪn'ædɪkwəsi] *noun* **(a)** feeling of being inadequate; *being compared with his brother all the time gave him feelings of inadequacy* (NOTE: no plural in this meaning) **(b)** not working well enough; *the report mentions inadequacies in the system used for counting votes* (NOTE: plural is **inadequacies**)

inadequate [ɪn'ædɪkwət] *adjective* **(a)** not enough; *the island has inadequate supplies of water in the summer months* **(b)** not competent, not good enough for a job; *being compared to his brother the MP, made him feel quite inadequate*

inadvertent [ɪnəd'vɜːtənt] *adjective* said or done by mistake and not on purpose; *his inadvertent remark can caused us extreme embarrassment*

inadvertently [ɪnəd'vɜːtəntli] *adverb* said or done by mistake and not on purpose; *she inadvertently put a plastic plate in the oven and it melted*; *he had inadvertently exposed his children to radiation*

inane [ɪ'neɪn] *adjective* silly, senseless; *he just stood in the middle of the room, making inane remarks about the weather*

inappropriate [ɪnə'prəʊprɪət] *adjective* not suitable, not fitting the circumstances; *wearing jeans to the wedding was considered quite inappropriate*; *next Monday is an inappropriate day for the meeting because so many people will be on holiday*

inaugural [ɪn'ɔːgjʊrəl] *adjective* **inaugural address** = speech given at an inauguration or opening ceremony; *the president's inaugural address*; **inaugural ceremony** = opening ceremony; *security was extremely tight during the inaugural ceremony*

inaugurate [ɪn'ɔːgjʊreɪt] *verb* **(a)** to open officially a new building or a festival, etc.; *the Minister was invited to inaugurate the new computer system* **(b)** **to inaugurate someone as president** = to swear in someone as a new president; *each new US president is inaugurated on January 20th*

inauguration [ɪnɔːgjʊ'reɪʃn] *noun* **(a)** official opening; *invitations to the inauguration of the new computer system will be sent out next week* **(b)** swearing in of a new president; *the inauguration of the president will take place on January 20th*; *security was extremely tight during the inauguration*

inborn ['ɪnbɔːn] *adjective* which you have since birth; *she has an inborn love of music*

Inc [ɪn'kɔːpəreɪtɪd] *US abbreviation for* INCORPORATED; *we're dealing with a company called John Doe, Inc.*

incapable [ɪn'keɪpəbl] *adjective* not able to do something; *he is incapable of telling a lie without blushing*; **drunk and incapable** = offence of having drunk so much alcohol that you are not able to act normally

incarcerate [ɪn'kɑːsəreɪt] *verb (formal)* to put in prison; *Anne Boleyn was incarcerated in the Tower of London*

incarnate [ɪn'kɑːnət] *adjective* in the form of a human being; *that little girl is wickedness incarnate*

incarnation [ɪnkɑː'neɪʃn] *noun* **(a)** appearance in human form; *to many people, he was the incarnation of evil* **(b)** **previous incarnation** = what you were in a previous life; *he thinks he was a ballet dancer in a previous incarnation*

incendiary [ɪn'sendjəri] **1** *adjective* which causes fire; *terrorists left incendiary devices in the shopping centre* **2** *noun* bomb which causes fire; *many thousands of incendiaries were dropped on London during the Blitz* (NOTE: plural is **incendiaries**)

incense 1 *noun* ['ɪnsens] powder which when burnt gives a strong smell; *the priests burnt incense round the shrine* **2** *verb* [ɪn'sens] to make someone angry; *his speech incensed the crowd who went on the rampage in the centre of the town*

incensed [ɪnˈsenst] *adjective* very angry; *the incensed crowd attacked the police*; *they were incensed at their treatment by the police*

incentive [ɪnˈsentɪv] *noun* thing which encourages; *the possibility of a bonus is an incentive to the sales force*; **incentive bonus** = extra money paid when production is increased; **incentive scheme** = plan to encourage better work by paying higher commissions or bonuses; *we are setting up an incentive scheme which we hope will increase sales*

inception [ɪnˈsepʃn] *noun (formal)* beginning, start; *since its inception, the scheme has helped thousands of poor families*

incessant [ɪnˈsesnt] *adjective* continuous, not stopping; *our sleep was spoilt by the incessant noise of traffic from the main road*; *incessant rain stopped the cricket match*

incessantly [ɪnˈsesntli] *adverb* continuously, without stopping; *they quarrelled incessantly about the will*

incest [ˈɪnsest] *noun* offence of having sexual intercourse with a close relative (daughter, son, mother, father); *four members of the same family are being tried on charges of incest*

incestuous [ɪnˈsestjuəs] *adjective* referring to incest; *the brother and sister were accused of having an incestuous relationship*

inch [ɪnʃ] **1** *noun* measure of length (= 2.54cm); *snow lay six inches deep on the ground*; *she is five foot six inches tall (5′ 6″)*; *a three and a half inch floppy disk*; *see also* FOOT (NOTE: plural is **inches**. Note also that with numbers **inch** is usually written ″; a 3½″ disk; he is 5′ 9″ : say: 'a three and a half inch disk, he's five foot nine') **2** *verb* **to inch forward** = to go forward little by little; *the queue inched forward slowly*; *the project is inching forward, but it's hard work getting things moving*

incidence [ˈɪnsɪdəns] *noun* **the incidence of something** = how often something happens; *they reported a high incidence of accidents relating to drunken drivers*

incident [ˈɪnsɪdənt] *noun* **(a)** something which happens; *last year six hundred incidents of oil pollution were reported* **(b)** usually violent action or disturbance; *there were several incidents during the demonstration*; **incident room** = special room in a police station to deal with a particular crime

incidental [ɪnsɪˈdentl] **1** *adjective* **(a)** happening in connection with something else, but not important; *breaking the Olympic record was almost incidental - winning the gold medal was the important thing* **(b)** **incidental music** = background music which accompanies a film; *I found the incidental music rather too dominant*; **incidental expenses** = secondary expenses; *don't worry about any incidental expenses - the company will pick up the bill* **(c)** **incidental to something** = resulting from something by chance; *the discovery of penicillin was incidental to research on moulds* **2** *noun* unimportant expense which happens in connection with something else; *take some cash to cover incidentals*

incidentally [ɪnsɪˈdentəli] *adverb* by the way; *incidentally, you didn't see my watch anywhere in the office, did you?*

incinerate [ɪnˈsɪnəreɪt] *verb* to destroy by burning; *hospital rubbish must be incinerated*

incinerator [ɪnˈsɪnəreɪtə] *noun* furnace for burning rubbish; *the lack of incinerators is slowing the disposal of the carcasses*

incipient [ɪnˈsɪpiənt] *adjective (formal)* which is beginning or starting; *his symptoms indicate incipient flu*

incision [ɪnˈsɪʒn] *noun* cut in a patient's body made by a surgeon; *the first incision is made 2 millimetres below the rib*

incisive [ɪnˈsaɪsɪv] *adjective* very perceptive, sharp or cutting; *he made some incisive remarks about the management*

incite [ɪnˈsaɪt] *verb* to encourage something; *his remarks incited violent action on the part of the crowd*; **to incite someone to something** = to encourage or persuade someone to commit a crime; *he was accused of inciting racial hatred*

incitement [ɪnˈsaɪtmənt] *noun* crime of encouraging, persuading or advising someone to commit a crime; *he is facing charges of incitement to murder*; **incitement to racial hatred** = offence of encouraging people, by words or actions or writing, to attack others because of their race

inclination [ɪnklɪˈneɪʃn] *noun* **(a)** tendency; *after a big lunch he had a strong inclination to go to sleep* **(b)** slope, or angle of a slope; *the hill has an inclination of 1 in 15* **(c)** slight movement forwards; *she acknowledged my presence with a slight inclination of her head*

incline 1 *noun* [ˈɪnklaɪn] slope; *a steep incline leads to the garage* **2** *verb* [ɪnˈklaɪn] **(a)** to slope; *the garden inclines gradually down to the river* **(b)** to encourage someone to do something; *the results of the poll inclined newspaper reporters to try to forecast the result of the general election* **(c)** **to be inclined to do something** = to be likely to do something; *she is inclined to try to excuse everything her son does*; *our washing machine is inclined to overheat* **(d)** to bend or to bow; *he inclined his head and murmured a greeting*

inclined [ɪnˈklaɪnd] *adjective* **(a)** sloping; *an inclined plane gives easy access to the warehouse* **(b)** likely to do something; *she is inclined to get very annoyed when anyone criticizes her golf strokes*

include [ɪnˈkluːd] *verb* to count someone *or* something along with others; *the waiter did not include service in the bill*; *the total is £140, not including insurance and handling charges*; *there were 120 people at the wedding if you include the children*

included [ɪnˈkluːdɪd] *adjective* taken together with something else; *the holiday costs £500, all excursions included*; *the service is not included in the bill*

including [ɪnˈkluːdɪŋ] *preposition* taking something together with something else; *the total comes to £25.00 including VAT*; **not including** = not counting; *there were thirty people at the lunch, not including the children*

inclusion [ɪnˈkluːʒn] *noun* counting someone *or* something in among others; *his inclusion in the England team depends on his passing a fitness test*

inclusive [ɪnˈkluːzɪv] *adjective* which counts something in with other things; *the bill is not inclusive of VAT*; **inclusive charge** = charge which includes all costs; *the charge is not inclusive, you will have to pay extra for car parking*; *the conference runs from the 12th to the 16th inclusive* = it starts on the morning of the 12th and ends on the evening of the 16th; *we shall be away from Monday to Friday inclusive*

incoherent [ɪnkəʊ'hɪərənt] *adjective* not able to speak in a way which makes sense; *when the fever was at its height he became incoherent; why do we have to sit here listening to his incoherent waffle?*

income ['ɪŋkʌm] *noun* money which you receive, especially as pay for your work, or as interest on savings; *their weekly income is not really enough to live on;* **income tax** = tax on money earned as wages or salary; *income tax is deducted from his salary each month; she pays income tax at the lowest rate;* **unearned income** = income from investments or rents

income support ['ɪnkʌm sə'pɔːt] *noun* money paid by the government to families with low incomes; *the government wants to reduce the amount spent on income support by encouraging single mothers to go back to work*

incoming [ɪn'kʌmɪŋ] *adjective* **(a)** **incoming call** = phone call that someone receives from someone outside the building; *this line takes incoming calls only;* **incoming mail** = mail which comes into an office; *all incoming mail must be picked up at the front desk* **(b)** recently elected or appointed; *the chairman welcomed the incoming committee; the incoming government has the job of trying to deal with the worsening economic situation* (NOTE: the opposite is **outgoing**)

incomings [ɪn'kʌmɪŋz] *noun* money which is received; *the tax form must show all incomings and outgoings*

incompatible [ɪnkəm'pætɪbl] *adjective* **incompatible with something** = not able to live, work, or fit together, or with something else; *the two computer systems are incompatible; John and Susan are quite incompatible: I don't know how they can stay married; his behaviour is quite incompatible with his position as a manager*

incompetence [ɪn'kɒmpɪtəns] *noun* lack of competence; *she was dismissed for gross incompetence*

incompetent [ɪn'kɒmpɪtənt] *adjective* **(a)** who cannot work well, who is not able to do something; *she was dismissed for being incompetent* **(b)** not legally able to do something; *he is incompetent to sign the contract because he is not a director of the company*

incomplete [ɪnkəm'pliːt] *adjective* not complete, not finished; *the data in the report is incomplete; this puzzle is incomplete - there's a piece missing*

incomprehensible [ɪnkɒmprɪ'hensɪbl] *adjective* which cannot be understood; *it is incomprehensible that the police allowed him to go back into the building; he said something in an incomprehensible accent*

inconceivable [ɪnkən'siːvəbl] *adjective* very unlikely, which cannot be imagined; *how could anybody do such a thing? - it's just inconceivable; it is inconceivable that she did not know he was already married*

inconclusive [ɪnkən'kluːsɪv] *adjective* without any definite result; *the results were inconclusive so she has to go back to the hospital for more tests; after an inconclusive poll, I am afraid there will have to be another general election soon*

incongruous [ɪn'kɒŋgruəs] *adjective* which does not fit with the rest, which seems out of place; *in his dark suit and hat he looked incongruous amongst the crowd of football fans*

inconsequential [ɪnkɒnsɪ'kwenʃl] *adjective* not important; *what he said at the meeting was pretty inconsequential*

inconsistency [ɪnkən'sɪstənsi] *noun* lack of consistency; *his evidence was full of inconsistencies* (NOTE: plural is **inconsistencies**)

inconsistent [ɪnkən'sɪstənt] *adjective* **(a)** **inconsistent with** = which does not follow from, which contradicts something else; *his evidence in court was inconsistent with his earlier statement to the police; owning a night club is inconsistent with being a priest* **(b)** whose behaviour changes often and is unpredictable; *he's inconsistent - sometimes he works hard, sometimes he doesn't; the team's form has been inconsistent of late*

inconspicuous [ɪnkən'spɪkjuəs] *adjective* not at all obvious; *he tried to make himself inconspicuous in the crowd* (NOTE: the opposite is **conspicuous**)

incontinence [ɪn'kɒntɪnəns] *noun* being unable to control your urine or faeces

incontinent [ɪn'kɒntɪnənt] *adjective* unable to control your urine or faeces (NOTE: the opposite is **continent**)

incontrovertible [ɪnkɒntrə'vɜːtəbl] *adjective* which is true and cannot be disproved; *they are looking for incontrovertible evidence that he is the killer*

inconvenient [ɪnkən'viːniənt] *adjective* awkward, causing difficulties; *the evening is a very inconvenient time for a meeting; I find it inconvenient that our bank should be in another town*

incorporate [ɪn'kɔːpəreɪt] *verb* **(a)** to bring something into something else to make one main whole; *we are trying to incorporate the suggestions from the committees into the main proposal* **(b)** to form an official body or a registered company; *the company was incorporated three years ago*

incorporated [ɪn'kɔːpəreɪtɪd] *adjective* US showing that a company has been officially registered; *J. Doe Incorporated (Inc.)* (NOTE: the British equivalents are **Ltd** and **Plc**)

incorporation [ɪnkɔːpə'reɪʃn] *noun* act of incorporating a company; *the company's incorporation dates back to 1980*

incorrect [ɪnkə'rekt] *adjective* wrong, not correct; *he gave three incorrect answers and dropped out of the competition; the minutes of the meeting were incorrect and had to be changed*

incorrectly [ɪnkə'rektli] *adverb* not correctly; *she answered three questions incorrectly*

incorrigible [ɪn'kɒrɪdʒəbl] *adjective* naughty in a way that cannot be changed; *he is an incorrigible liar; you're late again - you're incorrigible!*

increase 1 *noun* ['ɪŋkriːs] **(a)** growth, process of becoming larger; *an increase in tax* or *a tax increase; an increase in the cost of living* **(b)** rise in salary; *she went to her boss and asked for an increase;* **cost-of-living increase** = increase in salary to allow it to keep up with higher cost of living **(c)** **on the increase** = becoming more frequent; *stealing from shops is on the increase* **2** *verb* [ɪŋ'kriːs] **(a)** to rise, to grow, to expand; *the price of oil has increased twice in the past year*; **to increase in price** = to become more expensive; **to increase in size** *or* **in value** = to become larger *or* more valuable **(b)** to make something become bigger; *the boss increased her salary*; *rail fares have been increased by 10%*

increased [ɪnˈkriːst] *adjective* which has become bigger; *these increased rail fares mean that we cannot afford to travel so much*

increasingly [ɪnˈkriːsɪŋli] *adverb* more and more; *he found it increasingly difficult to keep up with the workload at the office*; *his future with the company looks increasingly doubtful*

incredible [ɪnˈkredɪbl] *adjective* **(a)** which you find difficult to believe; *it is absolutely incredible that anyone as rich as he is can avoid paying tax* **(b)** of remarkable size, quantity, etc.; *over the years he has amassed an incredible fortune*; *you should go to see 'Jaws' - it's an incredible film*

incredibly [ɪnˈkredɪbli] *adverb* **(a)** difficult to believe; *incredibly, he passed his driving test first time* **(b)** very, extremely; *she's incredibly tall*; *it is incredibly difficult to find a parking space near my office in the middle of the day*

incredulous [ɪnˈkredjʊləs] *adjective* who does not believe what someone says or what is happening; *he explained the company's decision to a meeting of incredulous shareholders*

increment [ˈɪnkrəmənt] *noun* regular automatic addition to salary; *her salary rises in annual increments of £2000.00*

incriminate [ɪnˈkrɪmɪneɪt] *verb* to show that a person has committed a criminal act; *he was incriminated by the recorded message he sent to the victim*; **to incriminate yourself** = to say something which makes you seem to be guilty; *he refused to testify in case he incriminated himself*

incubate [ˈɪnkjʊbeɪt] *verb* **(a)** to make eggs hatch, either because a bird sits on them or because they are heated in an incubator; *the male penguin incubates the egg standing up for sixty days* **(b)** to make bacteria grow; *in order for the experiment to be acceptable, the bacteria must be incubated in a sterile environment*

incubation period [ɪŋkjuˈbeɪʃn ˈpɪəriəd] *noun* period during which a virus develops in your body after infection, before the symptoms of the disease appear; *the incubation period for measles is 12-14 days*

incubator [ˈɪnkjʊbeɪtə] *noun* **(a)** apparatus for hatching eggs and raising very small chicks **(b)** specially controlled container in which very small babies can be kept in ideal conditions; *she was born five weeks premature and is in an incubator*

incumbent [ɪnˈkʌmbənt] **1** *noun* **(a)** person who holds an official post; *Mrs Jones is our new librarian - she is taking over from the present incumbent next month*; *there will be no changes in the governor's staff while the present incumbent is still in office* **(b)** the priest in charge of a parish; *the former priest was much older than the new incumbent* **2** *adjective* *(formal)* **it is incumbent on you** = it is your responsibility; *it is incumbent on you to seek advice before you buy a house*; *it is incumbent on everyone to check the facts before making an accusation*

incur [ɪnˈkɜː] *verb* **(a)** to get into a position where you have to pay, are in danger, etc.; *the company has*

incurred considerable losses in the USA; *he incurred many debts during his time at college* **(b)** **to incur the anger** *or* **the wrath of someone** = to make someone very annoyed; *she incurred the anger of the authorities by demonstrating outside the parliament building*; **to incur a risk** = to run a risk; *if you put all your money into doubtful investments, you incur the risk of losing everything* (NOTE: **incurring - incurred**)

incurable [ɪnˈkjʊərəbl] **1** *adjective* **(a)** (patient) who will never be cured; (illness) which cannot be cured; *he has an incurable disease of the blood*; *treatment in a hospice is often better for patients with incurable illnesses* **(b)** who cannot change; *he's an incurable optimist - he always thinks everything will turn out fine* **2** *noun* person who will never be cured; *a hospital for incurables*

incurably [ɪnˈkjʊərəbli] *adverb* in a way which cannot be changed; *she's incurably romantic*

incursion [ɪnˈkɜːʃn] *noun* hostile raid into another country's territory; *after numerous rebel incursions the people are beginning to lose confidence in the government*

indebted [ɪnˈdetɪd] *adjective* owing something to someone; *we are indebted to the committee for their help*; *the property company is heavily indebted to the builders*

indecent [ɪnˈdiːsnt] *adjective* **(a)** rude, not decent, offensive; *he was prosecuted for indecent exposure* **(b)** not polite; *as soon as the speeches ended, there was an indecent rush to find something to eat*

indecision [ɪndɪˈsɪʒn] *noun* hesitating, not being able to decide; *he had a moment of indecision, and then picked up the phone*; *the management's indecision is holding back the development programme*

indecisive [ɪndɪˈsaɪsɪv] *adjective* **(a)** without any positive result; *the result of the election was indecisive as no party had a majority* **(b)** who cannot decide anything; *he was criticised for being indecisive*

indeed [ɪnˈdiːd] **1** *adverb* **(a)** *(for emphasis)* greatly, really; *thank you very much indeed for inviting me to stay*; *they have been very kind indeed to their daughter* **(b)** in fact; *they are very poor - indeed they have no money at all* **2** *interjection* showing indignation; *she called me stupid - indeed! the cheek of it!*; *it wasn't you who scratched my car was it? - indeed not!*

indefatigable [ɪndɪˈfætɪgəbl] *adjective* tireless, who does not become tired; *a team of indefatigable aid workers got the supplies through to the area*; *the committee members were absolutely indefatigable in their work on planning the show*

indefinite [ɪnˈdefɪnɪt] *adjective* **(a)** without a definite end; *he has been suspended for an indefinite period, pending an inquiry* **(b)** **the indefinite article** = 'a' or 'an' (as opposed to the definite article 'the')

indefinitely [ɪnˈdefɪnɪtli] *adverb* for an indefinite period; *the construction work has been postponed indefinitely*

indelible [ɪnˈdelɪbl] *adjective* which cannot be removed; *they marked the papers in indelible ink*; *the scene of devastation made an indelible impression on her memory*

indelibly [ɪnˈdelɪbli] *adverb* in a way which cannot be removed; *the image of the eruption of the volcano remained indelibly imprinted on his mind*

indelicate [ɪnˈdelɪkət] *adjective* rude and embarrassing; *he made some rather indelicate remarks about the bride's mother which offended several of the guests*

indemnity [ɪnˈdemnɪti] *noun* compensation for a loss or a wrong; *he had to pay an indemnity of £100; I received a letter of indemnity for £2000* (NOTE: plural is **indemnities**)

independence [ɪndɪˈpendəns] *noun* **(a)** freedom; *the colony achieved independence in 1994; Scotland is aiming for independence in the next few years;* the **American War of Independence** = war by the American colonies against Britain (1775-1786) by which the colonies became independent and formed the United States; **Declaration of Independence** = document written by Thomas Jefferson (1776) by which the former American colonies declared their independence from Britain **(b)** not needing or not relying on anyone else; *she's eighteen and is looking forward to a life of independence from her family*

Independence Day [ɪndɪˈpendəns ˈdeɪ] *noun* July 4th, the National Day of the USA, which commemorates the country's independence

independent [ɪndɪˈpendənt] **1** *adjective* **(a)** free, not ruled by anyone else; *Slovenia has been independent since 1991* **(b)** not owned by a group, not run by the state; *the big chains are squeezing the independent bookshops out of the market;* **independent school** = private school, not run by the state **(c) of independent means** = with enough income from investments, etc., to be able to live without working; *a man of independent means* **(d)** not needing or not relying on anyone else; *she's eighteen and wants to be independent of her family* **2** *noun* **(a)** candidate who does not belong to a political party; *he stood in the general election as an independent* **(b)** shop which is owned by a person and is not part of a chain; *supermarkets have a bad effect on the small independents*

independently [ɪndɪˈpendəntli] *adverb* separately; *we would prefer to deal with the research unit independently of the rest of the firm*

in-depth [ˈɪnˈdepθ] *adjective* very serious and thorough; *they carried out an in-depth examination of the shop's financial problems*

indescribable [ɪndɪˈskraɪbəbl] *adjective* which cannot be described; *her indescribable feeling of joy at having passed the exam; the living conditions of the peasants are indescribable*

index [ˈɪndeks] **1** *noun* **(a)** list, usually in alphabetical order, showing the references in a book; *look up the references to London in the index* (NOTE: plural in this meaning is **indexes**) **(b)** regular report which shows rises and falls in prices, unemployment, etc.; *the economic indices look very promising at the moment;* **cost-of-living index** = way of measuring the cost of living, shown as a percentage increase on the figure for the previous year; *some pensions are linked to the cost-of-living index* (NOTE: plural in this meaning is **indexes** *or* **indices** [ˈɪndɪsiːz]) **2** *verb* to relate pensions, wages, etc., to the cost-of-living index; *the government is considering indexing pensions*

index finger [ˈɪndeks ˈfɪŋɡə] *noun* first finger, the finger next to the thumb; *she cut her index finger in the kitchen, and finds keyboarding difficult*

index-linked [ˈɪndekslɪŋkt] *adjective* calculated according to the cost-of-living index; *she has an index-linked pension; he asked for his pension to be index-linked*

India [ˈɪndjə] *noun* large country in southern Asia, south of China and east of Pakistan; *India is bounded to the north by the Himalayas; India is the largest democracy in the world* (NOTE: capital: **New Delhi**; people: **Indians**; official languages: **Hindi, English, Gujerati, Tamil, etc.**; currency: **rupee**)

Indian [ˈɪndjən] **1** *adjective* **(a)** referring to India; *Indian cuisine is famous for its curries;* **Indian elephant** = large elephant found in India and South-East Asia, slightly smaller than the African elephant, and used as a working animal in forests; **Indian ink** = very black ink which cannot be removed by washing; *Indian ink is used for drawing, and in Chinese calligraphy* **(b)** referring to one of the original peoples of America; *the traditional Indian skills of hunting and tracking;* **Indian corn** = MAIZE; **in Indian file** = in line, one behind the other; *the children walked into the assembly in Indian file;* **Indian summer** = period of hot weather in autumn; *why not take advantage of the Indian summer and visit Scotland for a weekend break?* **2** *noun* **(a)** person from India; *many Indians and Pakistanis emigrated to Britain in the 1960s* **(b)** person from one of the indigenous tribes of America; *the train of settlers' wagons was attacked by Indians* (NOTE: now usually called **Native Americans**) **(b)** *(informal)* ordinary worker, as opposed to a manager; **the company suffers from having too many chiefs and not enough Indians** = the situation in the company is that there are lots of managers, but not enough people to do the actual work

indicate [ˈɪndɪkeɪt] *verb* to show; *can you indicate the position of the enemy camp on this map?; the latest figures indicate a fall in the number of unemployed men*

indication [ɪndɪˈkeɪʃn] *noun* sign; *he gave absolutely no indication that he was thinking of leaving the company*

indicative [ɪnˈdɪkətɪv] **1** *adjective* characteristic, that indicates; *repeated attacks on tourists are indicative of a general breakdown of law and order in the country* **2** *noun* form of a verb showing that the action actually took place or is taking place; *the indicative is used chiefly to make statements of fact*

indicator [ˈɪndɪkeɪtə] *noun* **(a)** something which indicates; *the inflation rate is a good indicator of the strength of the economy* **(b)** flashing light on a car which shows which way the driver is going to turn; *his left indicator was flashing and then he turned right!* **(c) indicator (panel)** = large board which shows details of plane or train departures and arrivals; *we're much too early, the flight isn't even on the indicator panel yet; look on the indicator to see if the train has been delayed*

indict [ɪnˈdaɪt] *verb* to charge someone with a crime; *he was indicted for murder; if she refuses to testify as a witness she may be indicted*

indictment [ɪnˈdaɪtmənt] *noun* written statement of the details of the crime with which someone is charged; *the clerk to the justices read out the indictment*

indifference [ɪnˈdɪfərəns] *noun* lack of interest in something; *the students seem to show a marked indifference as to whether they pass or fail*

indifferent [ɪn'dɪfrənt] *adjective* **(a)** not caring, not interested; *the world cannot remain indifferent to the problems of the starving refugees in central Africa* **(b)** not particularly good, not special; *in view of the school's indifferent exam results, the governors have set up a review of teaching practices*; *they served us a bottle of very indifferent champagne*

indigenous [ɪn'dɪdʒənəs] *adjective* born in or belonging to a place; *imported grey squirrels have driven out the indigenous red squirrels*; *palm trees are not indigenous to northern Europe*

indigent ['ɪndɪdʒənt] *adjective* (*formal*) very poor; *she has to provide for several indigent relatives*

indigestible [ɪndɪ'dʒestɪbl] *adjective* which causes pain because the stomach cannot digest it; *I found the Christmas pudding quite indigestible*

indigestion [ɪndɪ'dʒestʃn] *noun* pain caused when your stomach has difficulty in digesting food; *boiled cabbage always gives me indigestion*

indignant [ɪn'dɪgnənt] *adjective* feeling offended or angry; *he was very indignant when the inspector asked him for his ticket*; *the manager came out to speak to the indignant shoppers who had been queuing for hours in the rain*

indignation [ɪndɪg'neɪʃn] *noun* being indignant; *much to her indignation, she was asked to come for a medical test*; *the crowd showed their indignation at the referee's decision by throwing bottles*

indignity [ɪn'dɪgnɪti] *noun* shameful action against someone's dignity; *the headmaster suffered the indignity of having his car towed away by the police*; *the prisoners suffered terrible indignities in the labour camps*

indigo ['ɪndɪgəʊ] *noun* blue dye; deep blue colour; *my denim shirt started off indigo but has faded to light blue*

indirect [ɪndə'rekt or ɪndaɪ'rekt] *adjective* **(a)** not direct; *the taxi took us to the airport by a very indirect route* **(b) indirect tax** = tax, such as VAT or a sales tax, that is added to the price of goods and not paid directly to the government **(c) indirect speech** = reporting what someone has said; *'he said he would come' is indirect speech, whereas 'I will come' is direct speech*

indirectly [ɪndə'rektli] *adverb* not directly; *he made the suggestion indirectly, through a phone call from his secretary*

indiscriminate [ɪndɪ'skrɪmənət] *adjective* widespread, not selective; *environmentalists are campaigning against the indiscriminate use of pesticides*

indispensable [ɪndɪ'spensəbl] *adjective* which you cannot do without; *water is indispensable for life*; *she has become an indispensable member of our sales team*

indisposed [ɪndɪs'pəʊzd] *adjective* (*formal*) slightly ill; *my mother is indisposed and cannot see any visitors*

indisposition [ɪndɪspə'zɪʃn] *noun* (*formal*) slight illness; *the meeting cannot take place because of the indisposition of the chairman*

indisputable [ɪndɪ'spjuːtəbl] *adjective* which cannot be argued about; *the facts in this case are indisputable*

indistinguishable [ɪndɪ'stɪŋgwɪʃəbl] *adjective* **indistinguishable from something** = which cannot be told apart from something; *to some people margarine is indistinguishable from butter*

individual [ɪndɪ'vɪdjuəl] **1** *noun* **(a)** one single person; *we cater for private individuals as well as for groups* **(b)** (*informal*) person; *the police would like to talk to the individual who was responsible for this* **2** *adjective* **(a)** single, for a particular person; *we treat each individual case on its merits*; *we provide each member of the tour group with an individual itinerary* **(b)** enough for one person; *I want three individual portions of ice cream, please*

individualism [ɪndɪ'vɪdjuəlɪzm] *noun* liking for doing things in your own way, not as other people do; *she likes to display her individualism on the tennis court by wearing bright clothes which no one else wears*

individuality [ɪndɪvɪdju'ælɪti] *noun* quality which makes each person different from all others; *teachers will always emphasize the individuality of each child*

individually [ɪndɪ'vɪdjuəli] *adverb* separately, singly; *the applicants are interviewed individually*; *a box of individually wrapped sweets*

indoctrinate [ɪn'dɒktrɪneɪt] *verb* to teach political or religious ideas and force someone to accept them; *from an early age he was indoctrinated with pacifist ideals by his father*

indoctrination [ɪndɒktrɪ'neɪʃn] *noun* process of indoctrinating someone; *some parents accused the left-wing teachers of indoctrination*

indolent ['ɪndələnt] *adjective* lazy; *he led an indolent existence in his villa on the Mediterranean*

indomitable [ɪn'dɒmɪtəbl] *adjective* which cannot be beaten; *she was praised for her indomitable courage*; *his indomitable will to succeed made him a millionaire*

Indonesia [ɪndə'niːziə] *noun* large country in south-east Asia, formed of several islands south of Malaysia; *Indonesia is the fourth most populous country in the world* (NOTE: capital: **Jakarta**; people: **Indonesians**; language: **Bahasa Indonesia**; currency: **rupiah**)

Indonesian [ɪndə'niːziən] **1** *adjective* referring to Indonesia; *there are over three thousand Indonesian islands*; *the Indonesian economy is going through a period of crisis* **2** *noun* person from Indonesia; *the Indonesians are mainly Muslim*

indoor ['ɪndɔː] *adjective* inside a building; *if it's raining we can play indoor games*; *our school has an indoor swimming pool*

indoors [ɪn'dɔːz] *adverb* inside a building; *if it's cold and wet, you should stay indoors*; *in view of the weather, we had the party indoors*; *everyone ran indoors when it started to rain*

indubitable [ɪn'djuːbɪtəbl] *adjective* (*formal*) which cannot be doubted; *her literary efforts are of indubitable merit*

indubitably [ɪn'djuːbɪtəbli] *adverb* (*formal*) certainly, without any doubt; *he is indubitably the best student in his year*

induce [ɪn'djuːs] *verb* **(a)** to persuade someone to do something; *do you think an extra 10% will induce them to sign the contract?*; *they induced him to steal* the plans by offering him a large amount of money **(b)** to make something, such as the birth of a child, happen; *the baby was ten days late, so had to be induced*

inducement [ɪn'djuːsmənt] *noun* thing which helps to persuade someone to do something; *they offered him a company car as an inducement to stay*

inductance [ɪn'dʌktəns] *noun* ability of an electrical circuit to produce force

induction [ɪn'dʌkʃn] *noun* **(a)** starting a new person in a new job; *induction for all trainees will take place over two weeks in May*; **induction courses** or **induction training** = courses to train people starting new jobs **(b)** installation of a new priest; *his induction into the church will take place next Sunday* **(c)** creation of electricity in an object by placing it near a magnet or near something which is electrically charged; *an induction coil is made of coils of wire and changes the voltage passing through it*

indulge [ɪn'dʌldʒ] *verb* **(a) to indulge in** = to enjoy yourself doing something; *I like to indulge in a sauna once in a while* **(b)** to give someone little luxuries; *she always indulges her little grandson with sweets and presents*; **to indulge yourself** = to give yourself a little luxury; *I love Greek cakes, but I don't often get the chance to indulge myself*

indulgence [ɪn'dʌldʒəns] *noun* pleasant activitiy, especially eating or drinking; *her only indulgence is a fondness for chocolates*

indulgent [ɪn'dʌldʒənt] *adjective* kind, too generous towards someone; *her indulgent parents bought her a sports car for her eighteenth birthday*; *the boss is indulgent towards his family, but very harsh towards his workers*

industrial [ɪn'dʌstriəl] *adjective* referring to manufacturing work; *the Midlands is the main industrial region in Britain*; **industrial action** = strike or protest by workers; *the union members have voted in favour of industrial action*; **industrial estate** = group of factories built together; *we are moving to a new industrial estate near the motorway*

industrialist [ɪn'dʌstriəlɪst] *noun* owner or director of a factory; *the Prime Minister has invited a group of prominent industrialists to Downing Street*

industrialization [ɪndʌstriələ'zeɪʃn] *noun* changing of an economy from being based on agriculture to being based on industry; *the industrialization of the rural areas is proceeding at a rapid rate*; *the government has set out on a country-wide industrialization plan*

industrialize [ɪn'dʌstriəlaɪz] *verb* to set up industries in a country where there were none before; *the government set out to industrialize the agricultural region in the north of the country*; *South-East Asian countries industrialized very rapidly*

industrial relations [ɪn'dʌstriəl rɪ'leɪʃnz] *noun* relations between management and workers; *he carried out a study of industrial relations over the last 10 years*; *we aim to promote good industrial relations*

industrious [ɪn'dʌstriəs] *adjective* who works steadily and hard; *industrious workers are rewarded with bonuses*

industry ['ɪndʌstri] *noun* manufacturing companies, or other types of commercial activity; *oil is a key industry*; *the car industry has had a good year*; *the*

government is helping industry to sell more products abroad; *the tourist industry brings in a lot of foreign currency* (NOTE: plural is **industries**)

ineffective [ɪnɪ'fektɪv] *adjective* which does not have any effect; *most so-called cold cures are quite ineffective*

ineffectual [ɪnɪ'fektjuəl] *adjective* **(a)** which does not have the right effect; *her ineffectual attempts to open the door* **(b)** weak, incapable of asserting your authority; *he's a nice man but quite ineffectual as a salesman*

inefficiency [ɪnɪ'fɪʃnsi] *noun* lack of efficiency; *all this talk of spies is just a way of covering up police inefficiency*

inefficient [ɪnɪ'fɪʃnt] *adjective* not efficient; *this model is very inefficient - its petrol consumption is much higher than it should be*

ineluctable [ɪnɪ'lʌktəbl] *adjective* (*formal*) which cannot be avoided; *the ineluctable progress of the disease*

inept [ɪn'ept] *adjective* incapable of doing something, lacking any skill; *he's an intellectual and so is quite inept at dealing with his students*; *she wrote some inept report on contemporary lifestyles*

inequality [ɪnɪ'kwɒlɪti] *noun* state of not being equal; *the workforce has complained about the inequalities of the company pension scheme*; **inequality of opportunity** = situation where everyone does not have the same opportunities

inequity [ɪn'ekwɪti] *noun* (*formal*) unfairness; *the report highlights the inequities of the present judicial system*

inert [ɪ'nɜːt] *adjective* **(a)** (*formal*) not able to move; *the fallen jockey lay inert on the ground* **(b)** **inert gases** = gases (helium, neon, argon, krypton, xenon and radon) which do not react chemically with other substances

inertia [ɪ'nɜːʃə] *noun* **(a)** lack of wanting to move, lack of being able to do anything; *a feeling of inertia came over the committee as the meeting continued* **(b)** physical force which makes a stationary body remain still, or a moving body remain moving; *an astronaut who pushes himself away from his spaceship will continue to drift away into space under inertia if he is not attached to a safety line* **(c)** lack of energy, laziness; *he became manager of the shop through sheer inertia on the part of everyone else*; **inertia selling** = method of selling goods through the post where it is assumed that they have been bought if they are not returned

inescapable [ɪnɪ'skeɪpəbl] *adjective* which you cannot avoid; *it's an inescapable fact that as you get older, so you work more slowly*; *the inescapable truth is, we are living beyond our means*

inevitability [ɪnevɪtə'bɪlɪti] *noun* being inevitable; *all attempts at negotiating peace failed and there was a sense of inevitability that war would be declared*

inevitable [ɪn'evɪtəbl] *adjective* which must happen, which cannot be avoided; *it was inevitable that the younger children would want to leave home*

inevitably [ɪn'evɪtəbli] *adverb* naturally, of course; *inevitably after walking all day in the mountains they came back hungry and tired*

inexorable [ɪnˈeksərəbl] *adjective* steady, which cannot be stopped; *the glacier's slow but inexorable movement down the valley*; *nothing could stop the inexorable decline of manufacturing industry*

inexpensive [ɪnɪkˈspensɪv] *adjective* cheap, not expensive; *in summer, peaches are relatively inexpensive*; *rice is inexpensive and easy to cook*

inexperienced [ɪnɪkˈspɪəriənst] *adjective* who does not have much experience; *the team is quite inexperienced at playing international football*; *they appointed an inexperienced young man as workshop manager*

inexplicable [ɪnɪkˈsplɪkəbl] *adjective* which cannot be explained; *the inexplicable disappearance of the documents is puzzling the police*; *most of the crowd found the referee's decision completely inexplicable*

inexplicably [ɪnɪkˈsplɪkəbli] *adverb* in a way which cannot be explained; *the president inexplicably refused to answer questions on the subject*

inextricable [ɪnɪkˈstrɪkəbl] *adjective* which is very complicated, very closely connected; *the tax authorities are trying to sort out his inextricable financial affairs*

inextricably [ɪnɪkˈstrɪkəbli] *adverb* in an inextricable way; *the minister is inextricably linked with organized crime*

infallible [ɪnˈfæləbl] *adjective* (a) always correct, which always works; *no one has yet invented an infallible testing system* (b) who never makes mistakes; *the children soon realised that their teacher wasn't infallible*

infamous [ˈɪnfəməs] *adjective* (a) notoriously bad; *tourists were warned not to go near the infamous backstreet moneychangers* (b) *(formal)* very wicked; *she complained of infamous treatment by her bank*

infancy [ˈɪnfənsi] *noun* young childhood; *two of her children died in infancy*; *in its infancy* = in the very early stages of development; *in 1910, the aircraft industry was still in its infancy*

infant [ˈɪnfənt] *noun (formal)* very young child; *infants need feeding every few hours*; **infant school** = school for little children from 4 years old; *see also* PRODIGY

infantry [ˈɪnfəntri] *noun* soldiers who fight on foot, not in tanks, or horses, etc.; *the infantry was advancing to the front line* (NOTE: no plural)

infantryman [ˈɪnfəntrimən] *noun* soldier in the infantry; *the infantrymen were no match for the enemy's machine guns* (NOTE: plural is **infantrymen**)

infect [ɪnˈfekt] *verb* to contaminate with a disease, to transmit infection; *the disease infected his liver*; *his whole arm soon became infected*; *she claimed she was infected by her boyfriend*

infection [ɪnˈfekʃn] *noun* disease which spreads from one person to another; *her throat infection keeps coming back*; *he was sneezing and spreading infection to other people in the office*; *she seems to catch every little infection there is* (NOTE: compare **contagion**)

infectious [ɪnˈfekʃəs] *adjective* (a) (disease) which can be passed from one person to another; *this strain of flu is highly infectious*; *chickenpox is infectious, so children who have it must be kept away from others* (NOTE: compare **contagious**) (b) which can be passed on to someone else; *he's a great music teacher and his enthusiasm for choral music is very infectious*

infer [ɪnˈfɜː] *verb* to reach an opinion about something; *he inferred from the letter that the accused knew the murder victim*; *counsel inferred that the witness had not been present at the time of the accident*; *the article infers that we should not sign the treaty* (NOTE: **inferring - inferred**)

inference [ˈɪnfərəns] *noun* conclusion or deduction; *the inference is quite clear - we ought not to sign the treaty*; **to draw an inference from** = to infer, to deduce that something is probably true; *what inference can we draw from his reaction?*

inferior [ɪnˈfɪəriə] **1** *adjective* (a) not as large as; *the enemy's inferior numbers were a serious drawback* (b) **inferior to** = not as good as something *or* someone else; *this camera is inferior to that one, although they are both the same price*; *the shop was accused of selling cheap inferior goods at inflated prices* **2** *noun* person of a lower rank; *he always addressed his inferiors in a very abrupt way* (NOTE: the opposite is **superior**)

inferiority [ɪnfɪərɪˈɒriti] *noun* state of being less important, less intelligent, not as good as something *or* someone else; *the inferiority of these imported products is reflected in their lower price*; **inferiority complex** = feeling that you are not as good as others (NOTE: the opposite is **superiority**)

infernal [ɪnˈfɜːnl] *adjective* (a) *(informal)* very annoying; *that infernal bank manager keeps phoning me about the overdraft*; *can't you make them stop that infernal noise?* (b) *(formal)* referring to hell; *they believe that after death sinners are sent to the infernal regions*

inferno [ɪnˈfɜːnəʊ] *noun* blaze of fire; *the firemen had to deal with a raging inferno at the plastics factory* (NOTE: plural is **infernos**)

infertile [ɪnˈfɜːtaɪl US ɪnˈfɜːtl] *adjective* (a) not fertile or not able to reproduce; *over the last few years there has been an alarming increase in the number of infertile couples* (b) *(of soil)* barren, not able to produce good crops; *without water, the desert will remain infertile* (NOTE: the opposite is **fertile**)

infest [ɪnˈfest] *verb (of parasites)* to be present in large numbers; *pine forests have been infested with beetles*; *infested plants should be dug up and burnt*; *the child's hair was infested with lice*

infidel [ˈɪnfɪdəl] *noun (old)* person who does not believe in the true religion; *the crusades against the infidel in the twelfth century*

infield [ˈɪnfiːld] *noun* part of a cricket pitch or baseball pitch near where the players are batting (NOTE: the opposite is **outfield**)

infiltrate [ˈɪnfɪltreɪt] *verb* to become, or to make someone become, a member of an organization secretly, without the officials knowing; *the local party has been infiltrated by right-wing agitators*; *they managed to infiltrate one of their top men onto the Prime Minister's private staff*

infinite [ˈɪnfɪnət] *adjective* with no end; *she has infinite patience with little children*

infinitesimal [ɪnfɪnɪˈtesɪml] *adjective* tiny, very small; *they found an infinitesimal amount of bacteria in the drinking water*

infinitive [ɪnˈfɪnɪtɪv] *noun* basic form of the verb, usually shown by using 'to'; *the verb 'to want' is followed by the infinitive; the verb 'can' is followed by the infinitive without 'to'*; **split infinitive** = supposed mistake in English, where it is considered wrong to put another word between the 'to' and the rest of the verb; *the editors went through his text taking out the split infinitives*

> COMMENT: some people feel that to say 'to seriously consider a proposal' is wrong, and that you should say 'to consider a proposal seriously'; it is not always a good idea to avoid a split infinitive, especially when it makes the phrase clumsy; for instance, 'I used to really enjoy it' sounds better than 'I used really to enjoy it'

infinity [ɪnˈfɪnɪti] *noun* space or quantity that never ends; *the space probe headed out past the planets into infinity; if you divide one by three, you get a sequence of threes which carries on to infinity*

infirm [ɪnˈfɜːm] *adjective (formal)* old and weak; *most of the residents in the home are elderly and infirm*

infirmary [ɪnˈfɜːməri] *noun* **(a)** room in a school or factory where people can go if they are ill; *he cut his knee in the playground and was taken to the school infirmary; she was sent to the infirmary to have her hand bandaged* **(b)** old word for a hospital, now used in names; *the Glasgow Royal Infirmary* (NOTE: plural is **infirmaries**)

inflame [ɪnˈfleɪm] *verb* **(a)** *(formal)* to make more violent; *his speech was calculated to inflame public opinion* **(b)** to make part of the body react by becoming red and sore; *his eyes had become inflamed from the chlorine in the water*

inflamed [ɪnˈfleɪmd] *adjective* red and sore; *she put some ointment on his inflamed knee*

inflammable [ɪnˈflæməbl] *adjective* which can easily catch fire; *inflammable materials should not be stored in the corridors* (NOTE: **flammable** has the same meaning)

inflammation [ɪnfləˈmeɪʃn] *noun* being inflamed, having become sore, red and swollen as a reaction to an infection, an irritation, a blow; *she has an inflammation of the bladder; the body's reaction to infection took the form of an inflammation of the eyelid*

inflammatory [ɪnˈflæmətəri] *adjective* **(a)** which makes people behave violently; *his inflammatory speeches caused riots* **(b)** which makes an organ or a tissue become sore, red and swollen; *an anti-inflammatory drug; the ointment produced an inflammatory reaction*

inflatable [ɪnˈfleɪtəbl] *adjective* which can be inflated or blown up; *an inflatable life jacket*

inflate [ɪnˈfleɪt] *verb* **(a)** to fill with air; *he used a small pump to inflate the dinghy* **(b) to inflate prices** = to make prices rise; *the rise in interest rates has had the effect of inflating prices in the shops*

inflated [ɪnˈfleɪtɪd] *adjective* greatly increased or exaggerated; *he has an inflated idea of his own importance; tourists don't want to pay inflated London prices*

inflation [ɪnˈfleɪʃn] *noun* state of the economy where prices and wages are rising to keep pace with each other; *the government is trying to keep inflation down below 3%; we have 15% inflation or inflation is running at 15%*; **rate of inflation** or **inflation rate** = percentage increase in prices over a twelve-month period; **galloping inflation** or **runaway inflation** = very rapid inflation

inflationary [ɪnˈfleɪʃənri] *adjective* which tends to increase inflation; *the report notes inflationary trends in the economy*

inflexible [ɪnˈfleksəbl] *adjective* **(a)** which cannot be bent or changed; *the rules on this point are quite inflexible; negotiation is pointless if everyone maintains an inflexible position* **(b)** who cannot be persuaded to change his mind; *she had a reputation for being totally inflexible in her talks with her EU counterparts*

inflict [ɪnˈflɪkt] *verb* **to inflict pain or damage on someone** = to cause pain or damage to someone; *drugs can inflict serious harm on young people; the bombs inflicted heavy damage on the capital*

in-flight [ˈɪnflaɪt] *adjective* during a flight; **in-flight catering** = preparing food to be served during a flight; **in-flight entertainment** = film shown during a flight

inflow [ˈɪnfləʊ] *noun* action of flowing in; *an inflow of effluent into a river; an inflow of refugees from the war zone*

influence [ˈɪnfluəns] **1** *noun* being able to change someone *or* something; *he has had a good influence on the other staff in the department; the influence of the moon on the tide; he was charged with driving under the influence of alcohol* **2** *verb* to make someone *or* something change; *she was deeply influenced by her old teacher; the moon influences the tides; the price of oil has influenced the price of industrial goods*

influential [ɪnfluˈenʃl] *adjective* **(a)** which causes change; *her speech was influential in changing the opinion of the other members of the committee* **(b)** powerful; *she has influential friends who got the police to drop the charges*

influenza [ɪnfluˈenzə] *noun* infectious disease like a bad cold, with fever and aching muscles, transmitted by a virus and occurring in epidemics; *she is in bed with influenza; half the staff in the office are off with influenza; the latest influenza epidemic has killed several people* (NOTE: usually shortened to **flu**)

> COMMENT: influenza is spread by little drops of moisture in the air, transmitted by coughs or sneezes. It can be quite mild, but there are virulent strains like Hong Kong flu, which weaken patients so much that they catch pneumonia or other infections

influx [ˈɪnflʌks] *noun* sudden flow into; *the influx of immigrant workers into the south of the USA; a huge influx of foreign currency into the country* (NOTE: plural is **influxes**)

info [ˈɪnfəʊ] *(informal)* = INFORMATION; *did you get the info I sent you on the plans for the new leisure centre?*

inform [ɪnˈfɔːm] *verb* **(a)** to tell someone officially; *have you informed the police that your watch has been stolen?; I regret to inform you that your father has died; we are pleased to inform you that your offer has been accepted* **(b) to inform on someone** = to tell the authorities that someone has done something wrong; *he met the police secretly and informed on his colleagues*

informal [ɪnˈfɔːml] *adjective* relaxed, not formal; *dress casually - the party will be informal; the guide gave us an informal talk on the history of the castle*

informant [ɪnˈfɔːmənt] *noun* person who informs or who gives information to someone; *is your informant reliable?*

information [ɪnfəˈmeɪʃn] *noun* **(a)** facts about something; *can you send me information about holidays in Greece?; she couldn't give the police any information about how the accident happened; she gave me a very useful piece or bit of information; for further information, please write to Department 27;* **information bureau** *or* **information office** = office which gives information to tourists and visitors (NOTE: no plural: **some information**; for one item say **a piece of information**) **(b) information retrieval** = storing and then finding data in a computer

information technology (IT)   [ɪnfəˈmeɪʃn tekˈnɒlədʒi] *noun* computers and forms of technology that depend on computers; *the government is determined to increase the resources for information technology in schools*

> COMMENT: information technology covers everything involved in the acquiring, storing, processing and distributing of information by electronic means, including e-mail, the Internet, radio, television, telephone as well as computers

informative [ɪnˈfɔːmətɪv] *adjective* which tells you a lot, which conveys a lot of information; *the brochure about the company is not very informative; he gave a very informative talk on the butterflies of the Eastern Mediterranean*

informed [ɪnˈfɔːmd] *adjective* having the latest information; *informed opinion thinks that the government will lose the vote; he made an informed guess as to the result*

informer [ɪnˈfɔːmə] *noun* person who gives information to the police about a crime or criminals, sometimes someone who is himself a criminal; *the lead came from a police informer*

infraction [ɪnˈfrækʃən] *noun* (*formal*) breaking of the law; *he was stopped by the police for some infraction of motorway regulations*

infrared [ɪnfrəˈred] *adjective* **infrared rays** = long invisible rays below the visible red end of the colour spectrum; *special cameras using infrared rays make it possible to take pictures of wildlife at night; she was advised to take a course of infrared ray treatment*

> COMMENT: infrared rays produce heat in the body, and are used to treat inflammations; infrared radiation is part of the warming radiation which the earth receives from the sun

infrastructure [ˈɪnfrəstrʌktʃə] *noun* basic structure of roads, railways, etc., in a country; *the floods have damaged property and much of the region's infrastructure*

infrequent [ɪnˈfriːkwənt] *adjective* not frequent, not happening very often; *members of the Royal Family are infrequent visitors to this part of the country; my parents' visits became more and more infrequent*

infringe [ɪnˈfrɪndʒ] *verb* to break a law or a right; *newspaper editors protested that their right to freedom of speech was being infringed by the new censorship law;* **to infringe a copyright** = to copy a copyright text illegally; *we reserve the right to prosecute people who infringe our copyrights*

infringement [ɪnˈfrɪndʒmənt] *noun* breaking a law or a right; *infringement of copyright or copyright infringement; infringement of patent or patent infringement*

infuriate [ɪnˈfjʊərieɪt] *verb* to make furious; *the article in the Sunday paper infuriated her*

infuriated [ɪnˈfjʊərieɪtɪd] *adjective* furious, very annoyed; *infuriated commuters asked for their money back*

infuriating [ɪnˈfjʊərieɪtɪŋ] *adjective* which makes you very annoyed; *it is really infuriating to see other companies make so much money when we never seem to have any*

infuse [ɪnˈfjuːz] *verb* **(a)** (*of tea, dried flowers, etc.*) to soak in hot water to make a drink; *leave the lime flowers to infuse for five minutes* **(b)** to pour hot water on tea, lime flowers, etc., to make a drink; *put a pinch of China tea in the cup and infuse it in hot water for four or five minutes* **(c)** (*formal*) to infuse something **into someone or something** = to fill someone or something with a certain feeling; *his speech infused the meeting with great enthusiasm*

infusion [ɪnˈfjuːʒn] *noun* **(a)** addition of something new which will help; *the football club needs an infusion of capital to buy new players; what we need is an infusion of original ideas* **(b)** drink made by pouring boiling water onto a dry substance such as herb tea or a powdered drink; *my grandmother drinks a herbal infusion every evening before bed to help her get to sleep*

ingenious [ɪnˈdʒiːniəs] *adjective* very clever; *he invented an ingenious device for detecting electrical faults; she has an ingenious scheme for winning money on the national lottery* (NOTE: do not confuse with **ingenuous**)

ingeniously [ɪnˈdʒiːniəsli] *adverb* in a very ingenious way; *he ingeniously planted a listening device in the embassy bathroom*

ingenuity [ɪndʒəˈnjuːti] *noun* cleverness, skill in inventing new things; *the students showed great ingenuity in making a raft from branches and vines; even though his robot lawnmower doesn't work very well, he gets full marks for ingenuity*

ingenuous [ɪnˈdʒenjuəs] *adjective* (*formal*) naive, not trying to hide anything; *it was bit ingenuous of her to think he was offering her money just because he admired her work* (NOTE: the opposite is **disingenuous**; do not confuse with **ingenious**)

ingest [ɪnˈdʒest] *verb* (*formal*) to take into the body as if it were food; *if the liquid is ingested, seek immediate medical attention*

ingot [ˈɪŋgət] *noun* bar of gold or silver; *the gold is in the form of ingots, stored in the vaults of the Bank of England*

ingrained [ˈɪngreɪnd] *adjective* deeply fixed; *he had a deeply ingrained love of his native country; it took them weeks to remove years of ingrained dirt*

ingredient [ɪnˈgriːdiənt] *noun* material which goes to make something; *the ingredients are listed on the packet; all the ingredients for the cake can be bought at the local supermarket*

inhabit [ɪn'hæbɪt] *verb* to live in a place; *nobody inhabits the island*; *the area is mainly inhabited by wild goats*

inhabitable [ɪn'hæbɪtəbl] *adjective* which can be lived in; *we are working hard to make the old house inhabitable again*

inhabitant [ɪn'hæbɪtənt] *noun* person who lives in a place; *the local inhabitants do not like noisy tourists in summer*; *London has over seven million inhabitants*; *the local council warned the local inhabitants that they should boil their drinking water*

inhalation [ɪnhə'leɪʃn] *noun* action of breathing in; **smoke inhalation** = breathing in smoke, as in a fire; *two firemen were taken to hospital suffering from smoke inhalation*

inhale [ɪn'heɪl] *verb* to breathe in, to draw something into your lungs when breathing; *he lit a cigarette and inhaled deeply*; *I used to smoke cigars but never inhaled them*

inhaler [ɪn'heɪlə] *noun* small device for administering medicinal substances which can be inhaled; *being an asthmatic he always carries an inhaler with him*

inherent [ɪn'hɪərənt] *adjective* natural, which belongs to someone or something naturally; *quarrelling with your parents is an inherent part of growing up*; *the problem cannot be solved - it is inherent in the software*

inherently [ɪn'hɪərəntli] *adverb* naturally part of something; *there is something inherently wrong with the software*

inherit [ɪn'herɪt] *verb* **(a)** to receive money, etc., from a person who has died; *she inherited a small fortune from her father*; *when her grandfather died she inherited the shop* **(b)** to have characteristics passed on from a parent; *I think she has inherited her father's grumpy character* **(c)** to take over a client or a problem from a predecessor; *when they bought the shop they inherited a lot of ancient equipment*; *the new manager had inherited a lot of financial problems*

inheritance [ɪn'herɪtəns] *noun* property which is received from a dead person; *my grandparents' old home is part of my inheritance*; *the young prince came into his inheritance on reaching the age of 21*

inheritor [ɪn'herɪtə] *noun* person who receives something from a person who has died; *after his death, his collection of silver was divided among five inheritors*; *the choir is the inheritor of a great tradition of choral music* (NOTE: usually called an **heir**)

inhibit [ɪn'hɪbɪt] *verb* to prevent an action happening; *aspirin inhibits the clotting of blood*; **to have an inhibiting effect on someone** *or* **something** = to stop something happening; *if the teacher keeps looking over my shoulder at what I'm doing it has an inhibiting effect on my work*

inhibited [ɪn'hɪbɪtɪd] *adjective* not being able to express yourself freely or to do what you want to do; *she felt inhibited by the fact that she couldn't speak French*

inhibition [ɪnhɪ'bɪʃn] *noun* action of some mental influence which prevents normal reactions; *alcohol helps people lose their inhibitions*

in-house [ɪn 'haus] *adverb & adjective* working inside a company's building; *the in-house staff are all working full-time*; *we do all our catering in-house*; **in-house training** = training given to staff at their place of work

inhuman [ɪn'hju:mən] *adjective* cruel, not human; *the inhuman treatment of prisoners in the prison camps*

inimical [ɪ'nɪmɪkl] *adjective* (*formal*) unfriendly, which does not encourage; *the climate is inimical to wheat growing*

initial [ɪ'nɪʃl] **1** *adjective* first; *the initial stage of the project went off smoothly*; *my initial reaction was to say 'no'*; *he started the business with an initial investment of £500* **2** *noun* **initials** = the first letters of a person's names; *John Smith has a wallet with his initials JS on it* **3** *verb* to write your initials on a document to show you have read and approved it; *can you initial each page of the contract to show that you have approved it?*; *please initial the agreement at the place marked with an X* (NOTE: **initialling - initialled** but American spelling **initialing - initialed**)

initially [ɪ'nɪʃəli] *adverb* at the beginning; *initially we didn't like the new flat, but we have got used to it now*

initiate [ɪ'nɪʃieɪt] *verb* **(a)** to start something; *he initiated the new project last year* **(b)** to introduce someone into something secret, to show someone the basic information about something; *he initiated her into the secrets of digging for gold*

initiation [ɪnɪʃi'eɪʃn] *noun* **(a)** introduction to a new group of people; *new members of the society have to undergo an initiation*; *freshmen protested at the initiation ceremony they had to go through* **(b)** starting to put something into practice; *the initiation of the new project has been delayed*

initiative [ɪ'nɪʃiətɪv] *noun* decision which you hope will get something moving; *the government has proposed various initiatives to get the negotiations moving again*; **to take the initiative** = to decide to do something which other people are reluctant to do; *the manager decided to take the initiative and ask for a meeting with the boss*; *the president took the initiative in asking the rebel leader to come for talks*

inject [ɪn'dʒekt] *verb* **(a)** to force a liquid into something under pressure; *the nurse injected the drug using a needle and syringe*; *he injected himself with a drug* **(b)** to put something new into something; *come on, let's try to inject some life into these rehearsals!*

injection [ɪn'dʒekʃn] *noun* **(a)** act of injecting a liquid into the body; *the doctor gave him a cholera injection* **(b)** liquid which has been injected; *the clinic has ordered another batch of flu injections*

injunction [ɪn'dʒʌŋkʃn] *noun* **(a)** court order compelling someone to stop doing something or not to do something; *he got an injunction preventing his ex-wife from selling his car*; *the company applied for an injunction to stop their rivals marketing a product which was similar to theirs* **(b)** (*formal*) instruction, order; *the children were given strict injunctions not to open the door*; *most people ignored the government's injunction to spend less and save more*

injure [ɪndʒə] *verb* to hurt; *two people were injured in the bank hold-up*; *nurses were caring for the injured people*; *the driver of the car was badly injured in the accident*

injured [ɪndʒəd] *noun* **the injured** = people who have been wounded; *the badly injured were taken to* *hospital by helicopter* (NOTE: plural; for one person say the **injured man**, the **injured girl**, etc.)

injurious [ɪnˈdʒuːriəs] *adjective (formal)* which can harm; *smoking is injurious to your health*

injury [ˈɪndʒəri] *noun* hurt, wound; *he never really recovered from his football injury; she received severe back injuries in the accident* (NOTE: plural is **injuries**)

injustice [ɪnˈdʒʌstɪs] *noun* lack of justice; *the injustice of the court's decision caused a storm of protest in the newspapers; we all believe that an injustice has been done*

ink [ɪŋk] **1** *noun* liquid for writing with a pen; *he has ink marks on his shirt; the ink won't come off the tablecloth; she wrote comments on his work in red ink* **2** *verb* **to ink in** = to write or draw using ink on top of something which was written or drawn in pencil

ink-jet printer [ˈɪŋkdʒet ˈprɪntə] *noun* computer printer that prints characters by sending out little jets of ink

inkstain [ˈɪŋksteɪn] *noun* mark made by ink; *it is difficult to remove inkstains from the tablecloth*

inland [ˈɪnlænd] **1** *adverb* to the interior of a country; *if you go inland from the port, you soon get into the forest* **2** *adjective* in the interior of a country; *they spent a holiday on the inland waterways of Holland;* the **Inland Revenue** = British government department dealing with tax; *he received a threatening letter from the Inland Revenue* (NOTE: the American equivalent is the **Internal Revenue Service** *or* **IRS**)

-in-law [ˈɪnlɔː] *suffix* showing a relationship by marriage; *see* BROTHER-IN-LAW, SISTER-IN-LAW

in-laws [ˈɪnlɔːz] *noun (informal)* parents of your wife or husband; *he visited his in-laws while his wife was in hospital*

inlet [ˈɪnlet] *noun* **(a)** small branch of water off a large stretch of water; *the smugglers could have used any one of the numerous inlets along this stretch of coastline* **(b) inlet pipe** = pipe through which a liquid enters; *turn the water off at the inlet pipe* (NOTE: the opposite is **outlet pipe**)

in-line skates [ˈɪnlaɪn ˈskeɪts] *noun* type of roller skates, with a series of little wheels in line; *two girls on in-line skates zoomed past us at great speed* (NOTE: also called by the trademark, **rollerblades**)

in-line skating [ˈɪnlaɪn ˈskeɪtɪŋ] *noun* sport of going on in-line skates; *in-line skating up and down the street is what the kids do every evening; in-line skating is forbidden in some of the city parks* (NOTE: also called **rollerblading**)

inmate [ˈɪnmeɪt] *noun* person living in a home or in a prison; *five inmates escaped last week*

in memoriam [ˈɪn meˈmɔːriəm] *Latin phrase* meaning 'in memory of' words written on a gravestone to show who is buried; *'In Memoriam, John Smith'*

inmost [ˈɪnməʊst] *adjective* deepest, most private; *his poems reveal his inmost feelings*

inn [ɪn] *noun* small hotel; *we stayed in a little inn in the mountains*

innards [ˈɪnədz] *noun (informal)* **(a)** stomach and intestines; *he caught a trout, cleaned it and took out its innards* **(b)** inside workings of a machine; *he spent the whole morning fiddling around with the innards of his car*

innate [ɪˈneɪt] *adjective* inherited, which is present in someone from birth; *she seems to have an innate talent to be able to make people laugh*

inner [ˈɪnə] *adjective* inside; *go through that archway and you will come to the inner courtyard; heat is conducted from the inner to the outer layer of the material;* **inner tube** = thin rubber tube containing air inside a tyre

inner circle [ˈɪnə ˈsɜːkl] *noun* small group of people closely associated with a president, prime minister, managing director, etc.; *the President is very aloof, and only consults his inner circle of friends*

inner city [ˈɪnə ˈsɪti] *noun* the central part of a city; **inner-city** problems *or* problems of the inner city; *there is always congestion in the inner city at rush hour; inner-city hotels are most convenient, but can be noisy*

inner ear [ˈɪnə ˈiːə] *noun* space inside the head, beyond the middle ear, which controls balance and hearing; *she has an infection in the inner ear or an inner ear infection*

innermost [ˈɪnəməʊst] *adjective* **(a)** furthest inside; *a long dark corridor led to the innermost part of the bank vault* **(b)** deepest, most private; *his poems reveal his innermost feelings*

innings [ˈɪnɪŋz] *noun* **(a)** *(in cricket)* time when a team or a player is batting (NOTE: plural is **innings**. Note too that in American English (in baseball) the singular **inning** is used) **(b) he's had a good innings** = (i) he's been in his job a long time; (ii) he has lived a long time

innocence [ˈɪnəsəns] *noun* **(a)** not being guilty; *the lawyers tried to prove his innocence* **(b)** not having any experience or particular knowledge; *in my innocence, I believed them when they said they were police officers*

innocent [ˈɪnəsnt] **1** *adjective* **(a)** not guilty; *he was found to be innocent of the crime; in English law, the accused is always presumed to be innocent until he is proved to be guilty* **(b)** not having any experience or knowledge; *she's quite innocent when dealing with TV reporters* **2** *noun* person who has no experience or knowledge; *he's a total innocent when it comes to dealing with car salesmen*

innocently [ˈɪnəsəntli] *adverb* in a way which shows that you do not know something, or have any experience or knowledge; *'what is Aunt Jane doing behind the bushes?' the little girl asked innocently; he walked innocently into the bank and found himself in the middle of a robbery*

innocuous [ɪˈnɒkjuəs] *adjective* inoffensive or harmless; *it's a very innocuous drink, just a mixture of fruit juices; I don't know what's the matter with her - she flew into a rage at what was really a very innocuous remark*

innovation [ɪnəˈveɪʃn] *noun* new invention, new way of doing something; *the computer is an innovation which has changed everyone's lives; it was something of an innovation to have the wedding in the local fire station*

innovative [ˈɪnəveɪtɪv] *adjective* which is a new way of doing something; *he has many innovative ideas, and some of them have been produced commercially*

innovator [ˈɪnəveɪtə] *noun* person who brings in new ideas or new methods; *he has a big reputation as an innovator, and some of his ideas have been produced commercially*

Inns of Court [ˈɪnz əv ˈkɔːt] *noun* four societies in London of which the members are lawyers and are called to the bar as barristers

> COMMENT: the four societies are: Gray's Inn, Lincoln's Inn, Inner Temple and Middle Temple

innuendo [ɪnjuˈendəʊ] *noun* remark that suggests someone has done something wrong, but without giving direct details; *the papers were full of innuendoes about his private life* (NOTE: plural is **innuendoes**)

innumerable [ɪˈnjuːmərəbl] *adjective* very many, which cannot be counted; *we have had innumerable complaints about this product*

inoculate [ɪˈnɒkjʊleɪt] *verb* **to inoculate someone against a disease** = to stop someone catching a disease by injecting him or her with a vaccine; *the baby was inoculated against diphtheria*

inoculation [ɪnɒkjʊˈleɪʃn] *noun* **inoculation against a disease** = injection to stop you catching a disease; *has the baby had a diphtheria inoculation?*; *make sure you have the right inoculations before you go to the Far East*

inopportune [ɪnˈɒpətjuːn] *adjective (formal)* at the wrong time, at an awkward moment; *the invitation came at the most inopportune moment*

inordinate [ɪnˈɔːdɪnət] *adjective* excessive, more than is usual; *the shareholders are beginning to question whether the MD should be paid such an inordinate amount of money; we seem to spend an inordinate amount of time discussing money problems*

inordinately [ɪˈnɔːdɪnətli] *adverb* excessively; *he looked inordinately pleased with himself having made a score of 2*

in-patient [ˈɪnˌpeɪʃənt] *noun* person who goes to a hospital for treatment, and stays there in a ward; *he went to the hospital as an in-patient* (NOTE: the opposite, a patient who goes to hospital for treatment but does not stay the night there, is an **outpatient**)

input [ˈɪnpʊt] **1** *noun* **(a)** electric current which goes into an apparatus; *plug the input cable into the computer* **(b)** data fed into a computer; *the input from the various branches is fed automatically into the head office computer* **(c)** contribution to a discussion; *that you very much for your input during the seminar* **(d)** **inputs** = goods or services bought on which you pay VAT (NOTE: the opposite, i.e. goods and services sold on which VAT is charged, are **outputs**) **2** *verb* to put data into a computer; *have you inputted or input the addresses into the database?* (NOTE: **inputting - inputted** *or* **input**)

inquest [ˈɪŋkwest] *noun* legal inquiry into how someone died; *the inquest will be held next week*

inquire [ɪŋˈkwaɪə] *verb* **(a)** to ask questions about something; *the chef inquired if anything was wrong with the meal; she phoned the travel agent to inquire about air fares to Australia; she inquired about my mother's health;* **'inquire within'** = ask for more details inside the office or shop **(b)** to conduct an official investigation into a problem; to investigate, to try to find out about something; *the police are inquiring into his background; the social services are inquiring about the missing girl*

inquiring [ɪŋˈkwaɪrɪŋ] *adjective* interested in finding out information; *even as a little boy you could see he had an inquiring mind*

inquiry [ɪŋˈkwaɪri] *noun* **(a)** formal investigation into a problem; *a government inquiry into bribery in the police force; a public inquiry will be held about plans to build another airport* **(b)** question about something; *I refer to your inquiry of May 25th; all inquiries should be addressed to this department; he made an inquiry about trains to Edinburgh; see also* DIRECTORY ENQUIRIES (NOTE: plural is **inquiries**; also spelt **enquiry**)

inquisitive [ɪŋˈkwɪzətɪv] *adjective* curious, asking a lot of questions; *she was very inquisitive about his home life; don't be so inquisitive: what I do in the evenings is none of your business!*

inquisitiveness [ɪŋˈkwɪzɪtɪvnəs] *noun* being inquisitive; *the inquisitiveness of little children*

inroads [ˈɪnrəʊdz] *noun* **to make inroads into something** = to use up or deal with a large proportion of something; *defending the court case has made considerable inroads into our funds; I've finished painting the kitchen and I hope to start making inroads into the bathroom tomorrow; she finished writing Chapter 3 last week and is making good inroads into Chapter 4*

insane [ɪnˈseɪn] *adjective* mad, with a mental disorder which makes it impossible for you to know what you are doing; *the murderer was declared insane and sent to a secure institution for an indefinite period*

insanity [ɪnˈsænɪti] *noun* severe mental disorder or illness; *he pleaded not guilty by reason of insanity*

insatiable [ɪnˈseɪʃəbl] *adjective* which cannot be satisfied; *my wife had an insatiable desire for peanut butter when she was pregnant; it is difficult to satisfy his insatiable curiosity*

inscribe [ɪnˈskraɪb] *verb* **(a)** to write, especially to write a note inside a book when giving it to someone; *the book is inscribed 'with best wishes to John, from the author'* **(b)** to write permanently, as on stone; *the names of the dead soldiers are inscribed on the walls of the cemetery*

inscription [ɪnˈskrɪpʃn] *noun* **(a)** words cut on a stone, etc.; *the tomb has an inscription in Latin* **(b)** note written in a book which is given to someone; *the inscription in the front of the book is by the author who gave it to his mother*

insect [ˈɪnsekt] *noun* small animal with six legs and a body in three parts; *a butterfly is a kind of insect; insects have eaten the leaves of the cabbages; she was stung by an insect;* **insect bite** = sting caused by an insect which goes through the skin and irritates

insecticide [ɪnˈsektɪsaɪd] *noun* liquid or powder which kills insects; *they sprayed the fruit trees with insecticide*

insecure [ɪnsɪˈkjʊə] *adjective* **(a)** not safe; *she felt insecure when walking down the High Street alone at night* **(b)** not firmly fixed; *be careful! that scaffolding looks insecure*

insecurity [ɪnsɪˈkjʊrɪti] *noun* feeling of not being safe; *job insecurity is usual after a round of redundancies*

insensitive [ɪnˈsensɪtɪv] *adjective* not worrying how other people feel, not sensitive to other people's feelings; *at the funeral, he made some very insensitive remarks about the dead man; she seems quite insensitive to the feelings of the other members of staff*

inseparable [ɪn'sepробl] *adjective* **(a)** which cannot be separated; *in my experience, discos are inseparable from noise and drugs* **(b)** *(of people)* always together; *the twins are absolutely inseparable, they do everything together*

insert 1 *verb* [ɪn'sɜːt] to put something inside; *she inserted another sentence into the letter*; *he inserted each leaflet into an envelope*; *insert a coin into the slot* **2** *noun* ['ɪnsɜːt] paper which is put inside something; *the wedding invitation card had an insert with a map showing how to get to the church*

insertion [ɪn'sɜːʃn] *noun* **(a)** action of putting something in; *the insertion of the words 'not likely' changes the meaning of the phrase completely* **(b)** words added to a text; *the editors have made so many insertions that the book is a lot longer* **(c)** action of putting an ad into a magazine or newspaper; *the ad is charged at £50 per insertion*

inshore [ɪn'ʃɔː] *adjective & adverb* on the water, but near the coast; *whales have been sighted close inshore*; **inshore fishing** = catching fish from boats, but near the coast; *fish stocks have been so depleted that inshore fishing is no longer viable here*; **inshore waters** = water close to the coast; *the inshore waters round this coast are home to three different species of shark*

inside [ɪn'saɪd] **1** *adverb* indoors; *come on inside - it's cold in the street*; *it rained all afternoon, so we just sat inside and watched TV*; *is there anyone there? - the house seems quite dark inside* **2** *preposition* in; *there was nothing inside the bottle*; *she was sitting inside the car, reading a book*; *I've never been inside his office* **3** *noun* part which is in something; *I know their office from the outside, but what is the inside like?*; *the meat isn't cooked - the inside is still quite red* **4** *adjective* **(a)** which is indoors; *the office has an inside garage* **(b)** **inside information** = information which is only known by people working in a certain organization; *she had to sign a confidentiality agreement before being given any inside information*

◊ **inside out** ['ɪnsaɪd 'aʊt] *phrase* **(a)** turned with the inner part facing outwards; *he put his pyjamas on inside out* **(b)** **to know something inside out** = to know something very well; *she knows Central London inside out*

insider [ɪn'saɪdə] *noun* person who works in an organization and therefore knows secret information; *as an insider who has worked there for 15 years, he knows a lot about the company* **insider dealing** = illegal buying or selling of shares by people who have confidential information about a company

insides [ɪn'saɪdz] *noun* *(informal)* the interior of something, especially your stomach; *my insides are upset after last night's Indian meal*

insidious [ɪn'sɪdiəs] *adjective* working secretly to do harm; *I will do everything in my power to fight these insidious rumours and allegations*

insight ['ɪnsaɪt] *noun* clear ideas or knowledge; *we appreciated the insight he was able to bring us into the workings of the Foreign Office*; *her great insight into the customs of the country is invaluable*

insignificant [ɪnsɪg'nɪfɪkənt] *adjective* very small and unimportant; *we can ignore these results, the numbers involved are really insignificant*; *in so far as there has been any disagreement between the brothers, it has been quite insignificant*; *the head of*

the government's anti-terrorism unit is an insignificant little man with a black moustache

insincere [ɪnsɪn'sɪə] *adjective* not sincere; *his speech praising the president sounded very insincere*

insinuate [ɪn'sɪnjʊeɪt] *verb* **(a)** to suggest by hinting at something in a nasty way; *the finance director seemed to be insinuating that the boss was incompetent* **(b)** **to insinuate yourself** = to work your way gradually into a favourable position; *he managed to insinuate himself into the MD's good books*

insinuation [ɪnsɪnju'eɪʃn] *noun* hint or suggestion, which is usually nasty; *I'm fed up with your insinuations - why don't you just say what you mean?* (NOTE: usually used in the plural)

insipid [ɪn'sɪpɪd] *adjective* **(a)** with no flavour; *they served us some insipid tomato soup* **(b)** with no excitement; *her fiancé is a very insipid young man*; *the film is beautifully shot, but it's a pity the story is so insipid*

insist [ɪn'sɪst] *verb* to state firmly; *he insisted that he had never touched the car*; *she insisted that she should be paid compensation for the delay*; **to insist on something** = to state firmly that something must be done or given; *she insisted on (being given) a refund*; *I insist on an immediate explanation*

insistence [ɪn'sɪstəns] *noun* firm demands for something; *his insistence paid off - he got a full refund*; *he attended the meeting at his employer's insistence*

insistent [ɪn'sɪstənt] *adjective* stating or demanding something firmly; *it you are insistent, your case will be dealt with quickly*; *the minister was insistent that there had been no change in policy*

insistently [ɪn'sɪstəntli] *adverb* in a firm or demanding way; *she asked insistently for an explanation from the manager*

insolence ['ɪnsələns] *noun* rudeness and lack of respect; *the boys' insolence to their teacher was astonishing*

insolent ['ɪnsələnt] *adjective* rude and lacking in respect; *the crowd shouted insolent remarks at the referee*

insolvency [ɪn'sɒlvənsi] *noun* not able to pay debts; *the company was officially declared to be in a state of insolvency and was forced to cease trading*

insolvent [ɪn'sɒlvənt] *adjective* not able to pay debts; *if we don't achieve significant sales soon, we shall be insolvent in three months*; **the company was declared insolvent** = the company was officially stated to be incapable of paying its debts

COMMENT: 'insolvency' and 'insolvent' are usually applied to companies and 'bankruptcy' and 'bankrupt' are applied to people. A company is insolvent when its debts are higher than its assets; if this happens it should stop trading

insomnia [ɪn'sɒmniə] *noun* sleeplessness, not being able to sleep; *she suffers from insomnia*; *what does the doctor give you for your insomnia?* (NOTE: no plural)

inspect [ɪn'spekt] *verb* to look at something closely; *the kitchens are regularly inspected by health inspectors*; *she inspected the room to see if it had been cleaned properly*; *the customs officers were inspecting the luggage of all travellers coming from Amsterdam*

inspection [ɪnˈspekʃn] *noun* examining something closely; *they carried out an inspection of the drains*

inspector [ɪnˈspektə] *noun* senior official who examines something closely; *inspectors come onto the trains to check that everyone has a ticket*; **health inspector** = official who inspects buildings to see if they are clean; **police inspector** = officer in the police force above a sergeant and below a chief inspector; *the police inspector made a statement on TV*; **schools inspector** = official of the department of education who examines the teaching in schools; *a team of inspectors visited the school last week*; **inspector of taxes** *or* **tax inspector** = government official who examines tax returns and decides how much tax someone should pay

inspectorate [ɪnˈspektərət] *noun* all inspectors; *former teachers often become members of the schools inspectorate*; **the factory inspectorate** = all inspectors of factories (NOTE: no plural)

inspiration [ɪnspɪˈreɪʃn] *noun* **(a)** sudden urge to write poems, to compose music, etc.; *her inspiration comes from the countryside of her native Cornwall* **(b)** sudden good idea; *we had run out of sugar and all the shops were closed, but she had an inspiration and tried the railway station snack bar*

inspirational [ɪnspɪˈreɪʃnl] *adjective* which inspires; *the coach's half-time talk was inspirational and had a dramatic effect on the team*

inspire [ɪnˈspaɪə] *verb* to make someone feel a desire to do something; *the TV programme inspired him to take up mountain climbing*; *poets were inspired by the beauty of the Lake District*; *in the second half the forwards played as if inspired*

inspired [ɪnˈspaɪəd] *adjective* filled with a desire to do something; *the team played some inspired football, but lost in the end*

inspiring [ɪnˈspaɪrɪŋ] *adjective* who inspires; *he had an inspiring teacher at music school*

instability [ɪnstəˈbɪlɪti] *noun* not being stable or steady; *the instability of the economy does not encourage foreign investors* (NOTE: the adjective is **unstable**)

install [ɪnˈstɔːl] *verb* to put a person into a job, a machine into a workshop, etc.; *it took the plumber a week to install the new central heating system*

installation [ɪnstəˈleɪʃn] *noun* **(a)** putting a machine in place; *the installation of the central heating took six days* **(b)** group of machines which have been put in place; *the harbour installations are very modern*; *the fire seriously damaged the oil installations*

instalment *US* **installment** [ɪnˈstɔːlmənt] *noun* **(a)** payment of part of a total sum which is made regularly; *they are paying for the kitchen by monthly instalments*; *you pay £25 down and twelve monthly instalments of £20*; *US* **installment plan** = system of buying something by paying a sum regularly each month until the purchase is completed; *they bought the car on the installment plan* (NOTE: the British equivalent is **hire purchase**) **(b)** part of something which is being broadcast or delivered in parts; *the next instalment of the thriller will be shown on Monday evening*

instance [ˈɪnstəns] *noun* case, example; *there have been several instances of bullying in our local school*; *in this instance, we will pay for the damage*; **for instance** = as an example; *why don't you take up a new sport - golf, for instance?*

instant [ˈɪnstənt] **1** *noun* moment or second; *for an instant, he stood still and watched the policemen* **2** *adjective* immediate; *a savings account can give you instant access to your money*; **instant coffee** = coffee powder to which you add hot water to make a fast cup of coffee; *she made a cup of instant coffee*; *do you mind if it's instant coffee, we've run out of fresh?*

instantaneous [ɪnstənˈteɪniəs] *adjective* immediate; *we are going over to our political correspondent for an instantaneous reaction to the government's decision*; *the lightning flash and thunderclap were almost instantaneous, because the storm was directly overhead*

instantaneously [ɪnstənˈteɪniəsli] *adverb* immediately; *the fire station reacted instantaneously to the alarm*

instantly [ˈɪnstəntli] *adverb* immediately, at once; *he got my letter, and instantly wrote to the bank*; *as soon as he heard the news he instantly phoned his wife*

instead (of) [ɪnˈsted] *adverb* in place of; *since he's ill, I'm going instead of him*; *instead of stopping when the policeman shouted, he ran away*; *why don't you help me with the housework, instead of sitting and watching TV all day?*; *we haven't any coffee - would you like some tea instead?*; *if you can't go, can I go instead?*

instep [ˈɪnstep] *noun* arched middle part of your foot; *walking in tight boots hurt his instep* (NOTE: do not confuse with **in step**)

instigate [ˈɪnstɪgeɪt] *verb* to make something happen; *he was accused of instigating the riot*; *they have instigated an inquiry into the accident*

instigation [ɪnstɪˈgeɪʃn] *noun* **(a)** making something happen; *we await the instigation of criminal proceedings against those responsible for the violence* **(b)** **at someone's instigation** = when someone suggests it; *at the instigation of the store manager, the opening times were changed*

instil *US* **instill** [ɪnˈstɪl] *verb* to put an idea, etc., into someone's mind gradually; *the teachers tried to instil calm into the crowd of schoolchildren*; *we want to instil a sense of loyalty in our employees* (NOTE: **instilling - instilled**)

instinct [ˈɪnstɪŋkt] *noun* something which you have from birth and have not learnt; *many animals have a hunting instinct*; **by instinct** = from a feeling which you have inside you; *she seems to know by instinct if we have bought any chocolates*; *he seemed to feel by instinct that the plane was dangerous*

instinctive [ɪnˈstɪŋktɪv] *adjective* natural (reaction); *my instinctive reaction was to call the police*

instinctively [ɪnˈstɪŋktɪvli] *adverb* because of something which you feel inside you; *I knew instinctively that the new secretary was going to cause us problems*; *she instinctively locked all the car doors*

institute [ˈɪnstɪtjuːt] **1** *noun* organization set up for a special purpose; *they are proposing to set up a new institute of education*; *she goes to the research institute's library every week* **2** *verb* to set up or to start; *to institute a lawsuit against someone*

institution [ɪnstɪˈtjuːʃn] *noun* **(a)** organization, society set up for a special purpose; *a prison is an institution which houses criminals*; **financial**

institution = bank or trust whose work involves lending or investing large sums of money **(b)** permanent custom; *the lottery has rapidly become a national institution*; *British institutions such as cream teas and the royal family* **(c)** *(formal)* setting up, starting; *the institution of legal proceedings against the president*

institutional [ɪnstɪ'tjuːʃnl] *adjective* referring to institutions; **institutional investors** = financial institutions who invest money in securities

institutionalize [ɪnstɪ'tjuːʃnəlaɪz] *verb* **(a)** to make something into an institution; *the 1970s rock group have been around for so long that they have become institutionalized* **(b)** to put a person into an institution; *she was declared insane and institutionalized*

instruct [ɪn'strʌkt] *verb* **(a)** to instruct someone to do something = to tell someone officially to do something; *the inspectors instructed the restaurant to replace its kitchen equipment*; *the firemen instructed us to leave the building* **(b)** to show someone how to do something; *the stewardess will instruct you in ways of evacuating the aircraft if a fire breaks out* **(c)** to instruct a solicitor = to give information to a solicitor and to ask him to start legal proceedings on your behalf; *(of a solicitor)* **to instruct a barrister** = to give a barrister all the details of a case which he will plead in court

instructional [ɪn'strʌkʃnəl] *adjective* which teaches; *they bought an instructional video on car maintenance*

instructions [ɪn'strʌkʃənz] *noun* **(a)** orders; *he gave instructions to the driver*; **shipping instructions** = details of how goods are to be shipped and delivered; **to await instructions** = to wait for someone to tell you what to do; **in accordance with** *or* **according to instructions** = as the instructions show; **failing instructions to the contrary** = unless someone tells you to do the opposite; *failing instructions to the contrary, everyone should meet at the bus station at 9.00* **(b)** indication of how something is to be done or used; *I can't read the instructions on the medicine bottle - the letters are too small*; *she gave us detailed instructions how to get to the church*; **instruction manual** = booklet which tells you how something should be used

instructive [ɪn'strʌktɪv] *adjective* which gives a lot of information; *I found the accountancy course very instructive*; *it will be very instructive to see what happens*

instructor [ɪn'strʌktə] *noun* teacher, especially of a sport; **driving instructor** = person who teaches people how to drive; **ski instructor** = person who teaches people how to ski; **swimming instructor** = person who teaches people how to swim

instrument ['ɪnstrəmənt] *noun* piece of equipment; *the technical staff have instruments which measure the output of electricity*; **musical instrument** = device which is blown or tapped, etc., to make a musical note; *he doesn't play the piano, the violin or any other musical instrument*; **wind instruments** = musical instruments which you have to blow to make a note; *she plays several wind instruments*; *see also* STRINGED INSTRUMENTS

instrumental [ɪnstrə'mentl] *adjective* **(a)** instrumental in doing something = responsible, playing an important role in getting something done; *the mayor was instrumental in getting our building proposals passed by the planning committee* **(b)** referring to a musical instrument; *I prefer instrumental music to choral music*

instrumentalist [ɪnstrə'mentəlɪst] *noun* person who plays a musical instrument; *the instrumentalists sat in front of the choir*; *compare* VOCALIST

instrumentation [ɪnstrumen'teɪʃn] *noun* **(a)** arranging a piece of music for several instruments; *Tim wrote the lyrics and Andrew was responsible for the instrumentation* **(b)** technical equipment, set of instruments; *we were impressed by the advanced instrumentation of the new fighter*

insufficient [ɪnsə'fɪʃnt] *adjective* not enough; *we have insufficient funds to continue with the research programme*

insufficiently [ɪnsʌ'fɪʃntli] *adverb* not enough; *she's insufficiently experienced for such a responsible job*

insular ['ɪnsjulə] *adjective* **(a)** narrow-minded, thinking only of your own local interests; *opponents of the UK joining the EC were accused of being insular* **(b)** *(formal)* referring to an island; *the insular flora and fauna of the Galapagos are unique*

insularity [ɪnsju'lærɪti] *noun* lack of interest in anything other than your own local interests; *the insularity of the British is gradually being broken down*

insulate ['ɪnsjuleɪt] *verb* to prevent heat or cold or sound escaping or entering; *well-insulated houses need less heating*

insulation [ɪnsju'leɪʃn] *noun* preventing heat or cold or sound escaping or entering; *good insulation saves energy*; **insulation material** = material used to insulate something, especially a building; *glass fibre is a good insulation material*

insulator ['ɪnsjuleɪtə] *noun* **(a)** material which insulates; *rubber makes a good insulator* **(b)** device which insulates; *the high voltage electric cables must have good insulators*

insulin ['ɪnsjulɪn] *noun* hormone which controls the way in which the body converts sugar into energy and regulates the level of sugar in the blood; *she is a diabetic and has to have regular injections of insulin*

insult 1 *noun* ['ɪnsʌlt] rude word said to or about a person; *that is an insult to the government*; *the crowd shouted insults at the police*; **an insult to someone's intelligence** = something which is so obvious or easy that anyone could understand it; *that TV quiz is an insult to the intelligence of the viewers* **2** *verb* [ɪn'sʌlt] to say rude things about someone; *he was accused of insulting the president's wife*

insulting [ɪn'sʌltɪŋ] *adjective* rude; *he made some insulting remarks about the teachers*; *don't be insulting - it's a very beautiful hat*

insultingly [ɪn'sʌltɪŋli] *adverb* in an insulting way; *he laughed insultingly when her name was read out*

insuperable [ɪn'sjuːprəbl] *adjective* *(formal)* which cannot be overcome; *faced by insuperable obstacles, the climbers abandoned their attempt on the summit*; *the problem of getting a loan from the bank proved insuperable*

insurance [ɪn'ʃuːrəns] *noun* agreement with a company by which you are paid compensation for loss or damage in return for regular payments of money; *do you have insurance for your travel?*; **to take out an insurance against fire** = to pay money, so that if a fire happens, compensation will be paid to you; **insurance company** = company which provides insurance; *we contacted the insurance company as soon as the burglary was discovered*; **insurance policy** = document with the details of an insurance; *the insurance policy will be sent to you by post*; **car insurance** *or* **motor insurance** = insuring a car, the driver and passengers in case of accident; *my car insurance only covers drivers named in the policy*; **general insurance** = insurance covering theft, loss, damage, etc. (but not life insurance); **home insurance** *or* **house insurance** = insuring a house and its contents against damage; *house insurance can be arranged by your bank*; **life insurance** = insurance paying a sum of money when someone dies; *the mortgage company requires you to take out a life insurance policy* (NOTE: for life insurance, British English prefers to use the word **assurance**); **National Insurance** = government-run insurance which provides for state medical care, unemployment payments, etc.; *National Insurance contributions are deducted from your salary by your employer*

insure [ɪnˈʃuə] *verb* to agree with a company that if you pay them a regular sum, they will compensate you for loss or damage to property or persons; *she insured her watch for £10,000*; *they forgot to insure the building against fire*; *have you insured the contents of the house?* (NOTE: do not confuse with **ensure**)

insurer [ɪnˈʃuːrə] *noun* person or company which insures; *we contacted the insurer as soon as the burglary was discovered*

insurgency [ɪnˈsɜːdʒənsi] *noun* situation where many groups fight to try to bring down a government over a long period of time; *the year-long insurgency in the north of the island is threatening to bring down the government*

insurgent [ɪnˈsɜːdʒənt] **1** *adjective* fighting to bring down a government by force; *the insurgent army is within ten kilometres of the capital* **2** *noun* person who fights to bring down a government by force; *the army tried to capture the leader of the insurgents*

insurrection [ɪnsəˈrekʃn] *noun* rebellion against a government; *the army was brought in to put down the insurrection*

intact [ɪnˈtækt] *adjective* in one piece, not broken; *the vase arrived intact, but several plates were broken during the move*

intake [ˈɪnteɪk] *noun* (a) thing or things which are absorbed or taken in; *she is trying to reduce her calorie intake* *or* *her intake of calories* (b) group of new students, soldiers, etc.; *we are increasing our intake of mature students again this year*; *this year's intake has more potential officers than ever before*

intangible [ɪnˈtændʒəbl] *adjective* which cannot be defined; *I can't really describe it, I just sensed there was this intangible presence in the room with me*

integer [ˈɪntɪdʒə] *noun* whole number, not a fraction; *integers such as 25 or 161*

integral [ˈɪntɪgrəl] *adjective* which forms part of something; *a year's exchange visit to a French factory is an integral part of the course*

integrate [ˈɪntɪgreɪt] *verb* to link up to form a whole; *to integrate immigrants into the community*; **integrated circuit** = electronic circuit on a microchip

integration [ɪntɪˈgreɪʃn] *noun* act of integrating; *the integration of the two schools will allow for better use of our resources*

integrity [ɪnˈtegrɪti] *noun* (a) honesty, moral principles; *his integrity is in doubt since the report on the company loan scandal* (b) existence as a single thing or group; *we must try to maintain the integrity of the association by avoiding a split among the members*

intellect [ˈɪntəlekt] *noun* (a) power of the brain, ability to think or reason; *you could see at once that she was person of superior intellect* (b) very intelligent person; *Erasmus was one of the great intellects of the sixteenth century*

intellectual [ɪntəˈlektʃuəl] **1** *adjective* (a) referring to the way you use your brain; *'the Times' crossword requires considerably intellectual effort*; *she has great intellectual capacity* (b) *(person)* who is good at using their brain; *she is more intellectual than her husband* **2** *noun* person who believes that the brain is very important, who uses his or her brain to make a living; *left-wing intellectuals have criticized the Prime Minister*

intelligence [ɪnˈtelɪdʒəns] *noun* (a) ability to think and understand; *his intelligence is well above average*; **intelligence quotient (IQ)** = number believed to show how intelligent a person is compared to others; *she has an IQ of 110* (b) information provided by the secret services; *intelligence gathered by our network of agents is very useful to us in planning future strategy*; **the intelligence services** = the government departments involved in spying

intelligent [ɪnˈtelɪdʒənt] *adjective* (a) clever, able to understand things very well; *she is more intelligent than her brother*; *he's the most intelligent child in his class* (b) able to think and reason; *is there intelligent life on Mars?*; *an intelligent computer terminal*

intelligentsia [ɪntelɪˈdʒensiə] *noun* the intellectual, artistic and educated people in a society; *the Russian intelligentsia were subject to strict censorship*

intelligible [ɪnˈtelɪdʒəbl] *adjective* which can be understood; *the guide tried to say something, but it was hardly intelligible*; *the instructions on the packet were quite intelligible, even if written in rather odd English*

intend [ɪnˈtend] *verb* **to intend to do something** = to plan to do something; *we intended to get up early but we all overslept*; *the company intends to sue for damages*; **I intended no insult** = I did not mean my words to be taken as an insult

intended [ɪnˈtendɪd] *adjective* (a) which is aimed at; *they never reached their intended destination*; *the murderer followed his intended victim* (b) provided for a special purpose; *the big plate is intended to be used for serving meat*

intense [ɪnˈtens] *adjective* (a) very strong or vigorous; *there was a period of intense diplomatic activity to try to get the hostages released*; *she had an intense period of study before the exams* (b) extremely serious (person); *she is a very intense young woman*

intensely [ɪnˈtensli] *adverb* strongly; *she despises her husband intensely*

intensification [ɪntensɪfɪ'keɪʃn] *noun* making or becoming stronger; *the intensification of the paper's attacks on the government*

intensify [ɪn'tensɪfaɪ] *verb* **(a)** to become stronger; *the rain intensified and continued all night* **(b)** to make something stronger; *he intensified his attacks on the government*

intensity [ɪn'tensɪti] *noun* strength or violence; *the pain came back with even greater intensity than before* (NOTE: no plural)

intensive [ɪn'tensɪv] *adjective* **(a)** with a lot of effort; *he took a two-week intensive course in German* **(b) intensive care (unit)** = section of a hospital dealing with seriously ill patients who need a lot of attention; *two of the accident victims are still in intensive care*

intent [ɪn'tent] **1** *adjective* determined; *she's intent on becoming a manager* **2** *noun* aim; **with intent to defraud** = with the aim of deceiving; **to all intents and purposes** = virtually, in almost every way; *he is to all intents and purposes the boss of the business*

intention [ɪn'tenʃn] *noun* aim or plan to do something; *I can assure you that I have no intention of going to the party*

intentional [ɪn'tenʃnəl] *adjective* done on purpose; *was it intentional not to invite her to the reception?*

intentionally [ɪn'tenʃnəli] *adverb* on purpose; *were you being intentionally rude?*

intently [ɪn'tentli] *adverb* fixedly; *he stared intently at the girl*

inter [ɪn'tɜː] *verb (formal)* to bury; *a lone bugler played the last post as the general was interred in the military cemetery* (NOTE: **interring - interred**)

inter- ['ɪntə] *prefix meaning* between; *an intergovernmental meeting*; *intercity trains*

interact [ɪntə'rækt] *verb* **to interact with someone** *or* **something** = each person or thing to have an effect on the other; *the students are interacting well with the teachers*

interaction [ɪntə'rækʃn] *noun* effect of two things on each other; *there is little interaction between the two groups*

interactive [ɪntə'ræktɪv] *adjective* **(a)** each having an effect on the others; *we teach drama through interactive groups* **(b)** *(computers)* **interactive system** = system which allows the user to communicate with the computer, which then responds to his commands; *an interactive CD-ROM*

intercept [ɪntə'sept] *verb* to stop something as it is passing; *the defender's pass back to his goalkeeper was intercepted by the opposition striker who then scored*; *we have intercepted a secret message from one of their agents in London*

interchange ['ɪntətʃeɪndʒ] **1** *noun* **(a)** exchange of ideas; *the conference was organized to promote an interchange of ideas in the field of robotics* **(b)** large road junction where motorways cross; *there was a massive pile-up at the interchange* **2** *verb* to exchange one thing for another; *the four wheels can be interchanged (with each other)* *the players are constantly interchanging positions on the field*

interchangeable [ɪntə'tʃeɪndʒəbl] *adjective* which can be exchanged for each other; *the four wheels are interchangeable*

intercity [ɪntə'sɪti] *adjective* (train or plane) between two cities; *intercity rail services have been disrupted by ice*; *hourly intercity trains give a good service between London and Glasgow*

intercom ['ɪntəkɒm] *noun* radio for speaking to people over a short distance; *he pressed the buzzer and spoke to the flat's owner via the intercom*

intercourse ['ɪntəkɔːs] *noun* **(a)** sex act between a man and a woman; *they had intercourse on the first night they met* **(b)** *(formal)* communication between people; *'How do you do?' is a polite expression used in normal social intercourse*

interdict ['ɪntədɪkt] *noun (formal)* official order telling someone not to do something; *the book came under the interdict of the church*

interest ['ɪntrəst] **1** *noun* **(a)** special attention to something; *she takes a lot of interest in politics*; *he has no interest in what his sister is doing*; *why doesn't he take more interest in local affairs?* **(b)** thing which you pay attention to; *her main interest is canoeing*; *list your special interests on your CV* **(c)** percentage which is paid to someone who lends money; *if you put your money in a building society you should get 8% interest on it*; *deposit accounts pay more interest*; *how much interest do I have to pay if I borrow £1000?*; **simple interest** = interest calculated on the capital only, and not added to it; **compound interest** = interest which is added to the capital and then itself earns interest; **interest rate** *or* **rate of interest** = percentage charged for borrowing money; *the Bank of England has raised interest rates*; *savings accounts offer a good interest rate* *or* *a good rate of interest* **(d)** financial share in something; *he has a controlling interest in the company* = he owns more than 50% of the shares and so can direct how the company is run; **majority interest** *or* **minority interest** = situation where someone owns a majority *or* a minority of shares in a company; *he has a majority interest in a supermarket chain*; **to acquire a substantial interest in the company** = to buy a large number of shares in a company; **conflict of interest(s)** = situation where a person may profit personally from decisions which he takes in his official capacity **2** *verb* to attract someone; *he's particularly interested in old cars*; *nothing seems to interest him very much*; *the book didn't interest me at all*; *he tried to interest several companies in his new invention*

interested ['ɪntrəstɪd] *adjective* with a personal interest in something; *he's interested in old churches*; *she's interested in crime fiction*

interesting ['ɪntrəstɪŋ] *adjective* which attracts your attention; *there's an interesting article in the newspaper on European football*; *she didn't find the TV programme very interesting*; *what's so interesting about old cars? - I find them dull*

interestingly ['ɪntrɪstɪŋli] *adverb* it is interesting that; *interestingly, she went red as soon as his name was mentioned*

interface ['ɪntəfeɪs] **1** *noun* **(a)** point where two computer systems connect; program which allows two computer systems to be connected **(b)** area where two different systems meet and interact; *great progress is being made at the interface between medical science and genetic engineering* **2** *verb (of a computer device)* **to interface with** = to communicate with; *my laptop can interface with any other computer in the building*

interfere [ɪntə'fiə] *verb* to interfere in *or* with something = to get in the way of something, to be involved in something in such a way that it doesn't work well; *her mother is always interfering in her life*; *stop interfering with the TV controls*

interference [ɪntə'fiərəns] *noun* (a) involvement, meddling with someone's affairs; *his aunt's interference in his wedding preparations made him very annoyed* (b) noise which affects radio or TV programmes; *the reception isn't good tonight - there's a lot of interference* (NOTE: no plural)

interim ['ɪntərɪm] **1** *adjective* (report) given halfway through a period, before the final result is known; *please send us an interim report on the first year of your research project*; **interim dividend** = dividend paid at the end of a half-year **2** *noun* **in the interim** = meanwhile; *we are still redecorating the offices: in the interim you will have to share an office with your boss*

interior [ɪn'tɪəriə] **1** *adjective* inside; **interior decorating** = the decorating (curtains, paintwork, etc.) of the inside of a house **2** *noun* (a) inner part (of a building, car, etc.); *she cautiously walked into the interior of the cave*; *the interior of the building is fine, but the exterior needs repainting* (b) minister of the interior *or* interior minister = government minister who deals with affairs inside a country, such as police, law and order, etc.; **ministry of the interior** = ministry dealing with affairs inside a country (NOTE: in the UK these are called the **Home Office** and the **Home Secretary**); *US* **Department of the Interior** = government department dealing with the conservation and development of natural resources

interior design [ɪn'tɪːriə dɪ'zaɪn] *noun* planning of the furniture, furnishings, wallpaper, etc. inside a building; *the architects designed the basic structure of the building but left the interior design to us*

interior designer [ɪn'tɪːriə dɪ'zaɪnə] *noun* person who designs the inside of a building, including wall coverings, paint colours, furniture, fabrics, etc.; *we have asked an interior designer to advise us on the design of the restaurant*

interjection [ɪntə'dʒekʃn] *noun* exclamation, a word used to show surprise; *interjections like 'ooh' are usually followed by an exclamation mark*

interlock [ɪntə'lɒk] *verb* to fit together so as not to come apart easily; *the two lovers sat with fingers interlocked and gazed into each other's eyes*; *the Olympic design consists of five interlocking rings*

interlude ['ɪntəluːd] *noun* (a) item such as a dance or piece of music between parts of a performance; *there will now be a short musical interlude* (b) quiet time between two lively periods; *there was a short interlude, then the noise started again*; *during an interlude in the street battle, ambulancemen went to find wounded demonstrators*

intermediary [ɪntə'miːdjəri] **1** *adjective* between two parties; *she played an intermediary role in the negotiations between the two sides* **2** *noun* person who is the link between parties who do not agree or who are negotiating; *he refused to act as an intermediary between the two directors* (NOTE: plural is **intermediaries**)

intermediate [ɪntə'miːdjət] *adjective* (a) halfway between two points; *we are at an intermediate stage in our research work* (b) halfway between beginners and advanced; *she has passed her intermediate level English*

interminable [ɪn'tɜːmɪnəbl] *adjective* which never ends; *the president came on television to make an interminable speech*

intermission [ɪntə'mɪʃn] *noun* especially *US* interval in a play, film or concert, etc.; *the film runs for four hours without intermission*

intermittent [ɪntə'mɪtənt] *adjective* stopping and starting at intervals; *an intermittent banging noise came from the house next door*; *intermittent showers are expected over the weekend*

intern 1 *noun* ['ɪntɜːn] *US* medical school graduate who is working in a hospital while at the same time finishing his studies; *hospital interns work very long hours* (NOTE: British English is **houseman**) **2** *verb* [ɪn'tɜːn] to put someone in a prison or in a camp without trial, usually for political reasons; *many intellectuals and opponents of the military regime have been interned*

internal [ɪn'tɜːnl] *adjective* inside; **internal combustion engine** = engine in which the fuel is burnt inside a closed space (as in the cylinders in a car engine); **internal flight** = flight inside a country; **internal telephone** = private telephone inside a building (NOTE: the opposite, referring to the outside, is **external**)

internally [ɪn'tɜːnəli] *adverb* inside; *please circulate this memo internally - it must not go outside the office*

international [ɪntə'næʃənəl] *adjective* **1** *adjective* between countries; *an international conference on the environment*; *an important international company*; **international call** = telephone call to another country **2** *noun* (a) sportsman who has played for his country's team against another country; *there are three England internationals in our local team* (b) game between two countries; *the Rugby international will be held next Saturday at Twickenham*

internationalist [ɪntə'næʃnlɪst] *noun* person who believes in the need for countries to work together; *he was one of the first internationalists*

International Monetary Fund (IMF) [ɪntə'næʃənl 'mʌnɪtri 'fʌnd] part of the United Nations, a type of bank which helps member states in financial difficulties, gives financial advice to members and encourages world trade; *will the IMF agree to allocate more loans to Russia?*

internee [ɪntɜː'niː] *noun* person who has been interned, usually a political prisoner who has not been tried; *the new government has released hundreds of political internees*

Internet ['ɪntənet] *noun* international network linking thousands of computers; *we send messages over the Internet to hundreds of users of our products*; *he searched the Internet for information on cheap tickets to Alaska*; *see also* SURF, WORLD WIDE WEB (NOTE: also called simply **the Net**)

> COMMENT: Internet addresses (or 'domain names') of companies and other organizations are made up of two or three parts. The first part is the name of the organization (often abbreviated); the second can be .co (for a company), .com (for companies based in the USA), .edu (for educational establishments), .net (for Internet suppliers), .gov for US government organizations

and .mil (for military). With the exception of the USA, all countries add a further two-character country of origin name, such as .au for Australia, .cn for China, .uk for the United Kingdom, or .de for Germany

internment [ɪn'tɜːnmənt] *noun* action of interning, of putting someone into a prison or camp without trial; *in an attempt to stamp out civil unrest, the government has introduced internment of left-wing sympathizers*

interpersonal [ɪntə'pɜːsənl] *adjective* between people; *the company aims to promote good interpersonal relationships*; **interpersonal skills** = skills used when communicating with other people, especially when negotiating; *the successful applicant will have excellent interpersonal skills*

Interpol ['ɪntəpɒl] *noun* international police system; *Interpol works with national police forces to track down drug traffickers*; *they warned Interpol that the criminals might be disguised as women* (NOTE: used without **the**)

interpret [ɪn'tɜːprɪt] *verb* (a) to translate aloud what is spoken in one language into another; *the courier knows Greek, so he will interpret for us* (b) to explain the meaning of something; *his letter was interpreted as meaning that he refused the offer*; *her fit of giggles was interpreted as 'yes'*

interpretation [ɪntɜːprɪ'teɪʃn] *noun* (a) meaning; *a poem can have many interpretations*; *the book puts quite a different interpretation on the meaning of the rule* (b) translating aloud what is being said in one language into another; *she is taking a course in simultaneous interpretation*

interpretative [ɪn'tɜːprətətɪv] *adjective* referring to interpretation; *her interpretative skills will be needed when we all meet at the international conference*

interpreter [ɪn'tɜːprətə] *noun* person who translates aloud from one language to another; *the hotel porter will act as interpreter*; *we need an Italian interpreter*

interpreting [ɪn'tɜːprətɪŋ] *noun* action of translating aloud from one language to another; *she is taking an interpreting course*

interrelate [ɪntərɪ'leɪt] *verb* to be closely connected with something else; *the course is formed of several interrelating subjects*; *we believe that crime and punishment must be interrelated*

interrogate [ɪn'terəgeɪt] *verb* to question someone harshly; *he was interrogated for several hours but still did not give us any new information*

interrogation [ɪntera'geɪʃn] *noun* harsh questioning; *he confessed to the crime during his interrogation*; *under interrogation, she gave the names of her accomplices*

interrogative [ɪntə'rɒgətɪv] *adjective* which asks a question; **interrogative pronoun** = pronoun which asks a question; *'who' and 'which' are interrogative pronouns*

interrupt [ɪntə'rʌpt] *verb* to start talking when someone else is talking; *excuse me for interrupting*

interruption [ɪntə'rʌpʃn] *noun* something that interrupts or stops you from working; *I will never get my work finished with all these interruptions*

intersect [ɪntə'sekt] *verb* to cut across each other; *where the two roads intersect would be a good site for*

a petrol station; *two lines running from opposite corners of a rectangle will intersect at its centre*

intersection [ɪntə'sekʃn] *noun* (a) crossroads; *the accident occurred at one of the busiest intersections in the city* (b) place where lines cut across each other; *the intersection on the graph shows when the pound became weaker than the dollar*

interspersed [ɪntə'spɜːst] *adjective* **interspersed with** = scattered among, alternating with; *the play consisted of short conversations interspersed with long periods of silence*

interstate *adjective* [ɪntə'steɪt] (a) between two countries; *interstate negotiations are continuing to decide on the expansion of the EU* (b) *US* between two states; *we took the interstate freeway to San Diego* **2** *noun* ['ɪntəsteɪt] *US* road between two states; *they took Interstate 80 to Nevada*

intertwine [ɪntə'twaɪn] *verb* to twist things together; to be twisted together; *the two vines had become so intertwined it was impossible to pull them apart*; *her life was closely intertwined with the development of the women's rights movement*

interval ['ɪntəvl] *noun* (a) period of time between two points, between two acts in a play; *there will be a short interval during which the stage will be cleared*; *latecomers won't be allowed in until the first interval*; *there will be bright intervals during the morning, but it will rain in the afternoon* (b) **at intervals** = from time to time; *at intervals, he almost seems sane*; **at regular intervals** = quite often; *at regular intervals during my interview, the phone would ring and the man interviewing me would take down messages* (c) *(in music)* difference in pitch; *the interval between D and A is a fifth*

intervene [ɪntə'viːn] *verb* to come between; *if the police had not intervened so rapidly more people would have been hurt*; *after they left Singapore, several years intervened before they returned to the Far East*; **to intervene in a dispute** = to try to settle a dispute; *the government refused to intervene in the dispute*

intervening [ɪntə'viːnɪŋ] *adjective* which comes between; *in the intervening period the country tried to repair the damage caused to its economy by the war*

intervention [ɪntə'venʃn] *noun* coming between two things; acting to make a change in a system; *the central bank's intervention in the banking crisis*; *the intervention of the army ended the fighting between the two political parties*

interventionist [ɪntə'venʃənɪst] *adjective* policy of intervening in business affairs; *the government's interventionist policies have been criticized in the financial press*

interview ['ɪntəvjuː] **1** *noun* (a) discussion (on radio, TV, in a newspaper) between an important or interesting person and a journalist; *she gave an interview to the Sunday magazine* (b) questioning by one or more people of a person applying for a job; *we asked six candidates for interview*; *he's had six interviews, but still no job offers*; *when will you attend your first interview?* **2** *verb* (a) to ask a famous or interesting person questions and publish them afterwards; *the journalist interviewed the Prime Minister* (b) to talk to a person applying for a job to see if he or she is suitable; *we interviewed ten candidates, but did not find anyone we liked*

interviewee [ɪntəvjuːˈiː] *noun* person who is being or who is going to be interviewed; *the interviewees arrived at 10 o'clock and were asked to wait in reception*

interviewer [ˈɪntəvjuːə] *noun* person who asks the questions at an interview; *the interviewer had prepared a list of questions to ask the candidates*; *he's one of the toughest TV interviewers there are*

interweave [ɪntəˈwiːv] *verb* to weave together; *the author has cleverly interwoven the various strands of the story to produce a fine historical novel* (NOTE: **interweaving - interwove** [ɪntəˈwəʊv] - **interwoven**)

intestinal [ɪnˈtestɪnəl] *adjective* referring to the intestine; *she has an intestinal infection*; *they hope to avoid intestinal surgery*

intestine [ɪnˈtestɪn] *noun* **the small intestine** = top section of the intestines, leading down from the stomach; **the large intestine** = second section of the intestines, leading down to the rectum; **the intestines** = the bowel or gut, the tract which passes from the stomach to the anus in which food is digested as it passes through; *she is in hospital for tests on her intestines*

intimacy [ˈɪntɪməsi] *noun* sexual relationship with someone; *there was no hint of any intimacy between them*

intimate 1 *adjective* [ˈɪntɪmət] **(a)** very close; *she is an intimate friend from my schooldays* **(b)** very detailed; *we will brief you on the intimate details of the investigation*; *the burglars must have had intimate knowledge of the layout of the house* **(c)** sexual; *they have had an intimate relationship for some months* **2** *verb* [ˈɪntɪmeɪt] to announce or to suggest; *he intimated that he was going to resign and go to work in Australia*

intimately [ˈɪntɪmətli] *adverb* closely; *she works in our office, but I don't know her intimately*; *he is intimately acquainted with the details of the case*

intimation [ɪntɪˈmeɪʃn] *noun* suggestion that you will do something; *she gave no intimation of her decision to go to Canada*

intimidate [ɪnˈtɪmɪdeɪt] *verb* to frighten someone by threatening them or appearing to threaten them; *witnesses had been intimidated by local criminals*; *the professor did not realize he intimidated his students*

intimidating [ɪnˈtɪmɪdeɪtɪŋ] *adjective* frightening; *an interview with the headmaster can be quite intimidating*

intimidation [ɪntɪmɪˈdeɪʃn] *noun* action of frightening someone with threats; *there were reports of violence and intimidation inside the prison*

into [ˈɪntuː] *preposition* **(a)** *(showing movement towards the inside)* *she went into the shop*; *he fell into the lake*; *put the cards back into their box*; *you can't get ten people into a taxi*; *we all stopped talking when he came into the room*; *the bus is going into the town centre* **(b)** against, colliding with; *the bus drove into a lamppost* **(c)** *(showing a change)* *the tadpole changed into a frog*; *water turns into steam when it is heated*; *she changed into an evening dress for the party*; **to burst into tears** = to start crying suddenly; *when she opened the box she burst into tears* **(d)** *(showing that you are dividing)* *try to cut the cake into ten equal pieces*; **six into four won't go** = you can't divide four by six **(e)** *(informal)* liking something very much; *he's into reggae*

intolerable [ɪnˈtɒlərəbl] *adjective* which you cannot bear; *she told the doctor that the pain had become intolerable*; *we find it intolerable that there is no bus service on Sundays*

intolerance [ɪnˈtɒlərəns] *noun* refusal to accept the points of view of other people; *the newspaper was accused of stirring up racial intolerance*

intolerant [ɪnˈtɒlərənt] *adjective* refusing to accept the points of view of other people; *the government is intolerant of other political parties*

intone [ɪnˈtəʊn] *verb* to recite in a slow singing voice; *the priest intoned the Lord's Prayer*

intoxicant [ɪnˈtɒksɪkənt] *noun* substance such as alcohol, which makes you intoxicated

intoxicated [ɪnˈtɒksɪkeɪtɪd] *adjective* **(a)** drunk, under the effects of alcohol; *he was charged with driving while intoxicated* **(b)** wildly excited; *intoxicated with their success, they decided to go out to celebrate*

intoxicating [ɪnˈtɒksɪkeɪtɪŋ] *adjective* **(a)** which makes you drunk; *it is illegal to sell intoxicating liquor to people under the age of 18* **(b)** which makes you excited; *excited by the intoxicating atmosphere of the football crowd she stood on her seat and cheered*

intoxication [ɪntɒksɪˈkeɪʃn] *noun* state of being drunk; *he was found on the steps of the police station in a state of intoxication*

intractable [ɪnˈtræktəbl] *adjective (formal)* very difficult to deal with; which is impossible to solve; *intractable differences of opinion are threatening to ruin the negotiations*; *long-term unemployment is one of the most intractable problems the government has to face*; *she had an operation to try to relieve intractable pain in her knee*

intransigence [ɪnˈtrænzɪdʒəns] *noun* being obstinate in refusing to change your mind; *she had a reputation for intransigence in her dealings with the European Commission*

intransigent [ɪnˈtrænzɪdʒənt] *adjective* obstinate in refusing to change your mind; *the union backed down in the face of an intransigent management*

in transit [ˈɪn ˈtrænzɪt] *adverb* which is being transported; *the police seized the goods when they were in transit between London and Manchester*

intransitive verb [ɪnˈtrænsɪtɪv ˈvɜːb] *noun* verb which has no object; *intransitive verbs have no passive voice*; *the verb 'to hit' is transitive: the verb 'to sleep' is intransitive* (NOTE: a verb which has an object is a **transitive verb**)

intrauterine device (IUD) [ɪntrəˈjuːtəriːn dɪˈvaɪs] *noun* contraceptive device which is placed inside a woman's uterus

intravenous [ɪntrəˈviːnəs] *adjective* made into a vein; *an intravenous injection*; **intravenous drip** = drip which goes into a vein; *she was given an intravenous drip*

in-tray [ˈɪntreɪ] *noun* file or basket for incoming letters; *he came back from holiday to find his in-tray full* (NOTE: the file for outgoing letters is the **out-tray** and that for letters which are waiting for a decision is the **pending tray**)

intrepid [ɪnˈtrepɪd] *adjective* fearless, very brave; *an intrepid polar explorer*

intricacy ['ɪntrɪkəsɪ] *noun* state of being very complicated; *we admired the intricacy of the design on the stained glass*; *I've given up trying to follow the intricacies of her love life*

intricate ['ɪntrɪkət] *adjective* very complicated, made of many different parts; *you cannot but marvel at the intricate designs on medieval manuscripts*; *an intricate design of circles and triangles*; *this new system has some extremely intricate programming*

intrigue [ɪn'triːg] **1** *noun* secret plot; *the story is one of intrigues in the court of Mary Queen of Scots* **2** *verb* (a) to plot; *she intrigued to get the ambassador assassinated* (b) to make someone interested; *the girl's story intrigued him*

intrigued [ɪn'triːgd] *adjective* interested in something because it is unusual; *I was intrigued to hear your plan*; *aren't you intrigued to know what happened next?*

intriguing [ɪn'triːgɪn] *adjective* which makes you interested; *it's an intriguing story*

intrinsic [ɪn'trɪnzɪk] *adjective* forming a basic part of something; *fireworks are an intrinsic part of the celebrations on November 5th*

introduce [ɪntrə'djuːs] *verb* (a) to present someone to another person or to people who did not know him or her previously; *he introduced me to a friend of his called Anne*; *she introduced me to her new teacher* (b) to announce a TV or radio programme, etc.; *he introduced the start of the cricket commentary* (c) to bring something to a new place; *several species of plant now common in Britain were introduced by the Romans*; *starlings were introduced to the USA in 1891*

introduction [ɪntrə'dʌkʃn] *noun* (a) act of presenting something for the first time; *the Fair in Chicago was his introduction to the American business scene* (b) letter making someone known to other people who did not know him previously; *I'm going to Moscow next week - can you give me an introduction to anyone there?*; *I'll give you an introduction to Mike Smith - he is an old friend of mine* (c) piece at the beginning of a book which explains the rest of the book; *read the introduction which gives an explanation of the book's layout* (d) elementary book about a subject; *he's the author of an introduction to mathematics* (e) bringing into use; *the introduction of new technology* = putting new computers into a business or industry (f) bringing something to a new place; *before the introduction of grey squirrels, the red squirrel was widespread*

introductory [ɪntrə'dʌktərɪ] *adjective* which introduce; *she made some introductory remarks before the conference opened*; **introductory offer** = offer of a new range of goods at a specially low price; *she took advantage of the introductory offer and bought several boxes of soap powder*

introspective [ɪntrə'spektɪv] *adjective* thinking deeply about yourself; *he wrote some very introspective poetry at the time of his divorce*

introvert ['ɪntrəvɜːt] *noun* person who is not outgoing and does not like to be with other people; *he's something of an introvert - he never goes out and spends every evening playing computer games* (NOTE: the opposite is **extrovert**)

intrude [ɪn'truːd] *verb* to go in or become involved where you are not wanted; *pardon me for intruding,*

but have you finished with the newspaper?; *we condemn TV reporting which intrudes into someone's private life*

intruder [ɪn'truːdə] *noun* person who has got into a place, usually illegally; *she disturbed an intruder in the girls' dormitory*

intrusion [ɪn'truːʒn] *noun* act of intruding; *the television is an unwelcome intrusion into our family life*

intrusive [ɪn'truːsɪv] *adjective* unwanted, which intrudes; *the government is drawing up guidelines to prevent intrusive reporting into people's private lives*; *I found the loud music in the restaurant very intrusive*

intuition [ɪntjuː'ɪʃn] *noun* thinking of something or knowing something naturally, without it being explained; *she couldn't see anyone behind her, but her woman's intuition told her that she was being followed*; *he had an intuition something was wrong before he opened the door*

intuitive [ɪn'tjuːɪtɪv] *adjective* based on intuition; *she had an intuitive feeling that her baby was in danger*

Inuit ['ɪnjuɪt] *noun* a native people living in the north of Canada and Greenland; *the Inuit hunt seals and polar bears* (NOTE: also called **Eskimo** or **Eskimos**, though this may be offensive)

inundate ['ɪnʌndeɪt] *verb* (a) to overwhelm with a lot of things or people; *we have been inundated with requests for tickets*; *the relief camps were inundated with refugees* (b) (*formal*) to flood; *acres of farmland were inundated when the banks of the river gave way*

invade [ɪn'veɪd] *verb* (a) to attack and enter a country with an army; *William the Conqueror invaded England in 1066* (b) (*of the press, official investigators, etc.*) **to invade someone's privacy** = to disturb someone's private life; *she claimed that the photographers had invaded her privacy by climbing over the wall*

invader [ɪn'veɪdə] *noun* person who enters a country by force with an army; *the invaders were beaten back by the defence forces*

invalid 1 *adjective* (a) ['ɪnvəlɪd] sick or disabled; *her invalid mother lives in a nursing home*; **invalid carriage** = small vehicle for one disabled person (b) [ɪn'vælɪd] not valid, not legal; *she was stopped at the frontier because her passport was invalid*; *your library card is invalid, so you need to renew it* **2** *noun* ['ɪnvəlɪd] sick or disabled person; *she has been an invalid since her operation* **3** *verb* ['ɪnvəliːd]; **to invalid someone out** = to make someone retire because of ill health; *he was invalided out of the navy*

invalidate [ɪn'vælɪdeɪt] *verb* to make something invalid; *because the company has been taken over, the contract is invalidated*

invalidity [ɪnvə'lɪdɪtɪ] *noun* (a) being an invalid; *she receives an invalidity pension* (b) state of being invalid; *the invalidity of the contract was discussed* (NOTE: no plural)

invaluable [ɪn'væljuəbl] *adjective* extremely valuable; *I'm most grateful to you - your help has been invaluable*; *the UN soldiers made an invaluable contribution to the relief work*

invariable [ɪn'veərɪəbl] *adjective* always the same, never changing; *she answered with her invariable courtesy*

invariably [ɪnˈveərɪəbli] *adverb* always; *he is invariably late for meetings*

invasion [ɪnˈveɪʒn] *noun* **(a)** entering a country by force with an army; *the invasion took place in early June* **(b)** invasion of privacy = behaviour of the press, official investigators, etc., which disturbs someone's private life; *the photographers climbing over the wall constituted an invasion of privacy*

invasive [ɪnˈveɪsɪv] *adjective (medical)* **(a)** which tends to spread throughout the body; *a malignant tumour is an invasive growth* **(b)** which involves cutting open and entering the patient's body; *invasive surgery will only be used as a last resort*

invent [ɪnˈvent] *verb* **(a)** to create a new process or a new machine; *she invented a new type of computer terminal; who invented shorthand?* **(b)** to think up an excuse; *when she asked him why he was late he invented some excuse*

invention [ɪnˈvenʃn] *noun* **(a)** act of creating a new process or a new machine; *the invention of computers was made possible by developments in electronics* **(b)** new device; *he tried to sell his latest invention to a US car manufacturer*

inventive [ɪnˈventɪv] *adjective* which creates something in an imaginative way; *his excuses for being late have become more and more inventive; the architect's inventive use of space in his design for the airport building*

inventor [ɪnˈventə] *noun* person who invents new processes or new machines; *he's the inventor of the all-plastic car*

inventory [ˈɪnvəntri] *noun* **(a)** list of contents (of a house, etc.); *the landlord checked the inventory when the tenants left* (NOTE: plural in this meaning is **inventories**) **(b)** mainly US stock in a warehouse; *our whole inventory was destroyed by fire; we are carrying a high inventory*; **inventory control** = system of checking that there is not too much stock in a warehouse, but just enough to meet requirements (NOTE: the word 'inventory' is used in American English where British English uses the word 'stock'. So, the American 'inventory control' is 'stock control' in British English)

invert [ɪnˈvɜːt] *verb* **(a)** to turn something upside down or back to front; *invert the mould and ease the jelly onto the dish* **(b)** inverted commas = printed or written marks (" ") showing that a quotation starts or finishes; *that part of the sentence should be in inverted commas; don't forget to put inverted commas round direct speech* **(c)** inverted snobbery = being critical of people of a higher social class, or people who are more intelligent than you are, because you feel that it is better to be inferior; *preferring bangers and mash to French cuisine is just inverted snobbery; some university-educated footballers are victims of inverted snobbery*

invertebrate [ɪnˈvɜːtɪbreɪt] **1** *noun* animal which has no backbone; *fish are vertebrates but worms are invertebrates* **2** *adjective* with no backbone; *can you name any other invertebrate animals besides worms?* (NOTE: the opposite is **vertebrate**)

invest [ɪnˈvest] *verb* **(a)** to put (money) into savings, property, etc., so that it will increase in value; *she was advised to invest in government bonds; he invested all his money in a fish-and-chip restaurant* **(b)** to spend

money on something which you believe will be useful; *we have invested in a new fridge*

investigate [ɪnˈvestɪgeɪt] *verb* to study or to examine something closely; *the detective is investigating the details of the case; we are investigating the possibility of going to live in Costa Rica*

investigation [ɪnvestɪˈgeɪʃn] *noun* close examination; *a police investigation into the causes of the crash*; **on investigation** = when it was examined; *on further investigation, the newspaper report was shown to be quite untrue*

investigative [ɪnˈvestɪgətɪv] *adjective* who or which investigates; *an investigative reporter on a Sunday newspaper*; **investigative journalism** = type of journalism where reporters try to find out and publish the truth about corruption, government mismanagement, etc.; *there is a fine line between investigative and intrusive journalism*

investigator [ɪnˈvestɪgeɪtə] *noun* person who investigates, such as a detective; *crash investigators wrote a report on the causes of the accident*

investment [ɪnˈvesmənt] *noun* **(a)** money in the form of shares, bonds, deposits that are expected to increase in value; *he has been very successful with his investments*; **long-term investments** *or* **short-term investments** = shares, etc., which are likely to increase in value over a long or short period; *buying a house is considered a good long-term investment* **(b)** money spent by a government or a company to improve its resources; *the economy is suffering from a lack of investment in training; investment always declines during a recession*

investor [ɪnˈvestə] *noun* person who puts money into savings or property; *a wise investor has to be cautious sometimes*

invigilate [ɪnˈvɪdʒɪleɪt] *verb* to supervise an examination; *the teachers take it in turns to invigilate*

invigilator [ɪnˈvɪdʒɪleɪtə] *noun* person who supervises an examination; *at the end of the exam the invigilator gathered up all the scripts*

invigorate [ɪnˈvɪgəreɪt] *verb* to make someone feel healthy and full of energy; *they returned thoroughly invigorated by their walk along the cliffs*

invigorating [ɪnˈvɪgəreɪtɪŋ] *adjective* which makes you feel healthy; *he has an invigorating cold shower every morning*

invincible [ɪnˈvɪnsəbl] *adjective* which cannot be defeated; *the champions are proving invincible on their home ground*

invisible [ɪnˈvɪzəbl] *adjective* **(a)** which cannot be seen; *the message was written in invisible ink and hidden inside the pages of the telephone directory* **(b)** invisible earnings = foreign currency earned by a country by providing services, (such as banking, insurance or tourism) but not selling goods

invitation [ɪnvɪˈteɪʃn] *noun* letter or card, asking someone to do something; *he received an invitation to his sister's wedding; she had an invitation to dinner*; **at someone's invitation** = invited by someone; *she spoke to the meeting at the invitation of the committee*

invite [ɪnˈvaɪt] *verb* to ask someone to do something, especially to come to a party, etc.; *we invited two hundred people to the party; she invited us to come in; she's been invited to talk to the club*

inviting [ɪn'vaɪtɪŋ] *adjective* which attracts; *the empty restaurant didn't look very inviting; after the long, hot, dusty walk the water of the lake looked inviting*

invoice ['ɪnvɔɪs] **1** *noun* note sent to ask for payment for services or goods; *our invoice dated November 10th has still not been paid; they sent in their invoice six weeks late; ask the salesman to make out an invoice for £250;* **VAT invoice** = invoice which shows VAT separately **2** *verb* to send a note asking for payment for services or goods; **we invoiced you on November 10th** = we sent you an invoice on November 10th

invoke [ɪn'vəʊk] *verb* to call on someone *or* something for help or support; *he invoked his right to remain silent; Odysseus invoked the gods to help him*

involuntary [ɪn'vɒləntri] *adjective* **(a)** done unconsciously; *his leg gave an involuntary jerk when the doctor tapped his knee; her cry was the involuntary reaction of a mother protecting her young* **(b)** not done willingly; *does the travel insurance cover the involuntary cancellation of the holiday?*

involve [ɪn'vɒlv] *verb* **(a)** to bring someone *or* something into an activity, situation, dispute or crime, etc.; *we want to involve the local community in the decision about the bypass; a competition involving teams from ten different countries; members of the local council are involved in the company which has won the contract for the new road* **(b)** to make necessary; *going to Oxford Circus from here involves taking a bus and then the Underground*

involved [ɪn'vɒlvd] *adjective* complicated; *the new tax forms are very involved; the whole process of getting a visa was terribly involved*

involvement [ɪn'vɒlvmənt] *noun* contact with someone, participating in something; *did she have any involvement with the music festival?; the police were unable to prove his involvement in the crime*

inward ['ɪnwəd] *adjective* on the inside; *she had a feeling of inward calm in spite of the chaos around her;* **inward investment** = money invested in a country by foreign companies

inwards *US* **inward** ['ɪnwədz] *adverb* towards the inside; *as the ball lost speed it moved inwards to the centre of the dish; she turned her thoughts inwards*

iodine ['aɪədiːn] *noun* chemical element which is essential to the body, and often used as an antiseptic; *the nurse dabbed the cut with iodine* (NOTE: Chemical element: chemical symbol: **I**; atomic number: **53**)

ion ['aɪən] *noun* electrically charged atom; *ions can be either positive or negative*

IOU [aɪəʊ'juː] *noun* paper promising that you will pay back money which you have borrowed; *she gave him an IOU for ten pounds* (NOTE: it spells the words **I owe you**)

IQ ['aɪ 'kjuː] = INTELLIGENCE QUOTIENT; *she has an IQ of 110*

Iran [ɪ'rɑːn] *noun* country in the Middle East, between Iraq and Pakistan; *Iran has important oil reserves* (NOTE: capital: **Tehran**; people: **Iranians**; language: **Persian**; currency: **rial**)

Iranian [ɪ'reɪnjən] **1** *adjective* referring to Iran; *Iranian oil exports are an important part of the economy* **2** *noun* person from Iran; *the vast majority of Iranians are Muslims*

Iraq [ɪ'rɑːk] *noun* country in the Middle East, to the west of Iran and east of Jordan; *the rivers Tigris and Euphrates flow through Iraq* (NOTE: capital: **Baghdad**; people: **Iraqis**; language: **Arabic**; currency: **Iraqi dinar**)

Iraqi [ɪ'rɑːki] **1** *adjective* referring to Iraq; *the Iraqi oil wells* **2** *noun* person from Iraq; *UN negotiators discussed sanctions with the Iraqis* (NOTE: plural is **Iraqis**)

irascible [ɪ'ræsɪbl] *adjective* (*formal*) easily made annoyed; *the colonel is an irascible type and you must make sure you keep on good terms with him*

irate [aɪ'reɪt] *adjective* very angry; *the boys were chased out of the orchard by an irate farmer*

Ireland ['aɪələnd] *noun* large island forming the western part of the British Isles, containing the Republic of Ireland and Northern Ireland; *these birds are found all over Ireland;* **Northern Ireland** = the northern part of the island of Ireland, which is part of the United Kingdom

Ireland (the Republic of Ireland) ['aɪələnd] *noun* country to the west of the United Kingdom, forming the largest part of the island of Ireland, a member of the EU; *Ireland was declared a republic in 1949* (NOTE: capital: **Dublin**; people: **the Irish**; languages: **Irish, English**; currency: **Irish pound** *or* **punt, euro**)

iris ['aɪərɪs] *noun* **(a)** plant with tall flat leaves and usually yellow or purple flowers; *irises grow well in damp soil* **(b)** coloured ring in the eye, with the pupil at its centre; *the iris has muscles that adjust the size of the pupil* (NOTE: plural is **irises**)

Irish ['aɪrɪʃ] **1** *adjective* referring to Ireland; *the Irish Sea lies between Ireland and Britain;* **Irish coffee** = hot coffee, served in a glass, with Irish whiskey added to it and whipped cream poured on top **2** *noun* **(a)** Celtic language still spoken in parts of Ireland; *Eire is the Irish name for the Republic of Ireland* **(b) the Irish** = people who live in Ireland; *the Irish are famous for their folk music*

Irishman *or* **Irishwoman** ['aɪrɪʃmən *or* 'aɪrɪʃwʊmən] *noun* person who lives in Ireland, or who comes from Ireland; *George Bernard Shaw and James Joyce were both famous Irishmen; Mary Peters was the first Irishwoman to win an Olympic gold medal in the pentathlon* (NOTE: plurals are **Irishmen, Irishwomen**)

iron ['aɪən] **1** *noun* **(a)** common grey metal; *the old gates are made of iron;* see also CAST IRON, WROUGHT IRON (NOTE: Chemical element: chemical symbol: **Fe**; atomic number: **26**; note also, no plural in this meaning: **some iron, lumps of iron, pieces of iron**) **(b)** electric appliance that is heated to make clothes smooth after washing; *don't leave the iron plugged in, it will burn the clothes; if your iron is not hot enough it won't take the creases out* **(c)** golf club with a metal head **2** *verb* **(a)** to make cloth smooth, using an iron; *she was ironing shirts when the telephone rang; her skirt doesn't look as though it has been ironed* **(b) to iron out** = to sort out, to solve a problem; *we had a very productive morning - all the remaining problems were ironed out*

ironic *or* **ironical** [aɪ'rɒnɪk *or* aɪ'rɒnɪkl] *adjective* **(a)** mocking, meaning something which is the opposite of what you seem to be saying; *she gave an ironic laugh; when I told him I was going to work for Miss Smith, his ironic comment was 'lucky you!'* **(b)** when something happens at the wrong moment, as if deliberately planned; *it was ironic that the rain finally stopped on the last day of our holiday*

ironically [aɪˈrɒnɪkli] *adverb* **(a)** in a mocking way; *'it's no trouble at all,' he said ironically* **(b)** at the wrong time, as if deliberately planned; *ironically, although they had lost both his suitcases, the airline claimed that he owed them for excess baggage*

ironing [ˈaɪənɪŋ] *noun* clothes which have been washed and are ready to be ironed; *she was doing the ironing; there's a lot of ironing waiting to be done*

ironing board [ˈaɪənɪŋ ˈbɔːd] *noun* special narrow table used when ironing clothes

ironmonger [ˈaɪənmʌŋgə] *noun* person who runs a hardware shop, selling tools, paint, buckets, etc.; **ironmonger's** = hardware shop; *I'm just going to the ironmonger's to get some more paint for the kitchen*

ironmongery [ˈaɪənmʌŋgri] *noun* hardware, such as tools, paint, buckets, etc.; *the shop sells all sorts of ironmongery*

irony [ˈaɪərəni] *noun* **(a)** way of referring to something where you say the opposite of what you mean; *do I detect a note of irony in his letter?* **(b)** situation when something happens at the wrong moment, as if deliberately planned; *the irony of it was that the rain finally stopped on the last day of our holiday*

irradiate [ɪˈreɪdɪeɪt] *verb* (i) to subject something to radiation; (ii) to treat food with radiation to prevent it going bad; *in South Africa male mosquitoes have been irradiated to make them sterile and then released back into the environment; some people wonder whether irradiated food is safe to eat*

irrational [ɪˈræʃnl] *adjective* not rational, not sensible, going against commonsense; *I have an irrational fear of being buried alive; his increasingly irrational behaviour worried her*

irregular [ɪˈregjʊlə] *adjective* **(a)** not regular; *an irregular pattern of lines and circles* **(b)** not level; *an irregular stone path leads across the garden* **(c)** not happening always at the same time; *his payments are very irregular; he makes irregular visits to his mother in hospital* **(d)** not according to the rules; *this procedure is highly irregular*

irregularly [ɪˈregjʊləli] *adverb* not regularly; *the buses run fairly irregularly and you can't rely on the service*

irrelevance [ɪˈreləvəns] *noun* not having any connection with the subject; *the irrelevance of her complaints about her room when the hotel was on fire*

irrelevant [ɪˈreləvənt] *adjective* not relevant, with no connection to the subject; *his comments about the weather were quite irrelevant to the subject being discussed; whether he's rich or not is irrelevant - I love him!*

irreparable [ɪˈreprəbl] *adjective* which cannot be repaired; *the fire caused irreparable damage to the church*

irreparably [ɪˈreprəbli] *adverb* in a way which cannot be repaired; *the old town hall was irreparably damaged in the earthquake; the sex scandal has irreparably tarnished his reputation as a politician*

irreplaceable [ɪrɪˈpleɪsəbl] *adjective* which cannot be replaced; *they stole old photographs of 19th-century London which are quite irreplaceable*

irreproachable [ɪrɪˈprəʊtʃəbl] *adjective* which cannot be criticized; *his conduct towards his sister has been irreproachable*

irresistible [ɪrɪˈzɪstəbl] *adjective* which cannot be resisted, which you cannot help accepting; *the tornado was an irresistible force which destroyed everything in its path; that chocolate cake is quite irresistible; he had an irresistible desire to dive into the sea*

irresolute [ɪˈrezəluːt] *adjective (formal)* who cannot decide what to do; *after having asked everyone for advice, they were still irresolute*

irrespective [ɪrɪˈspektɪv] *preposition;* **irrespective of** = taking no account of; *anyone parking on a double yellow line will be fined, irrespective of who they are; the appointment will be made on merit, irrespective of age or sex*

irresponsible [ɪrɪˈspɒnsəbl] *adjective* reckless, senseless, not responsible; *it was quite irresponsible of her to leave the two children alone at home while she went on holiday; some irresponsible drivers park on pedestrian crossings*

irreverence [ɪˈrevrəns] *noun* lack of proper respect; *the irreverence of the puppet show made everyone laugh*

irreverent [ɪˈrevrənt] *adjective* not showing proper respect, often in a humorous way; *the programme takes an irreverent look at religion*

irreversible [ɪrɪˈvɜːsəbl] *adjective* which cannot be changed back to how it was before; *ageing is an irreversible process; she suffered irreversible brain damage*

irrevocable [ɪˈrevəkəbl] *adjective* which cannot be changed; *burning the rain forest will produce an irrevocable change in the environment*

irrigate [ˈɪrɪgeɪt] *verb* to supply water to land to allow plants to grow, usually through a system of little channels; *the small fields are irrigated with water drawn from a well*

irrigation [ɪrɪˈgeɪʃn] *noun* action of irrigating; *irrigation is an absolute necessity in desert areas*

irritable [ˈɪrɪtəbl] *adjective* easily annoyed; *he was tired and irritable, and snapped at his wife*

irritably [ˈɪrɪtəbli] *adverb* in an annoying way; *she has an irritably high-pitched voice*

irritant [ˈɪrɪtənt] *noun* **(a)** thing which annoys; *the mosquitoes were a minor irritant, the big problem was the alligators* **(b)** substance which can irritate; *irritants like chlorine in swimming pool water can make the eyes inflamed*

irritate [ˈɪrɪteɪt] *verb* **(a)** to annoy; *it irritates me when the trains run late* **(b)** to prickle or to make a burning feeling; *some plants irritate the skin*

irritated [ˈɪrɪteɪtɪd] *adjective* annoyed; *'leave me alone,' she said in an irritated voice*

irritating [ˈɪrɪteɪtɪŋ] *adjective* which annoys; *it's irritating to see how badly the work has been done; he has the irritating habit of scratching the top of his head*

irritation [ɪrɪˈteɪʃn] *noun* **(a)** annoyance, thing which annoys; *the irritation of having bad weather every day of the holiday made him quite unbearable* **(b)** rash which causes a burning feeling; *the irritation on his chest got worse during the day*

is [ɪz] *see* BE

Islam ['ɪzlɑːm] *noun* the religion of the Muslims, founded by the prophet Muhammad

Islamic [ɪz'læmɪk] *adjective* referring to Islam; *Islamic law is derived from the Koran*

island ['aɪlənd] *noun* **(a)** piece of land with water all round it; *they live on a little island in the middle of the river*; *the Greek islands are favourite holiday destinations* **(b) traffic island** = small piece of pavement in the centre of the road where pedestrians can safely stand

islander ['aɪləndə] *noun* person who lives on an island; *all the islanders had gathered on the beach to welcome the new arrivals*

isle [aɪl] *noun (poetic)* island; *Ireland is sometimes referred to as 'the Emerald Isle'*; **the British Isles** = the islands which make up Great Britain and Ireland (NOTE: do not confuse with **aisle**)

isn't ['ɪznt] *see* BE

isolate ['aɪsəleɪt] *verb* **(a)** to put something *or* someone in a place alone; *violent prisoners are usually isolated from the others* **(b)** to separate a chemical substance from a compound, to identify a single virus or bacterium among many; *doctors have isolated a new form of the flu virus*; *scientists have been able to isolate the substance which causes the disease*

isolated ['aɪsəleɪtɪd] *adjective* **(a)** separated from others; *they live in an isolated village in the hills* **(b)** one only; **isolated attack** = single attack, which has not been repeated; *an isolated case of mugging*

isolation [aɪsə'leɪʃn] *noun* **(a)** being cut off from communication with other people; *he lived for six months on the island in complete isolation*; **isolation hospital** *or* **isolation ward** = special hospital or ward in a hospital where patients with dangerous infectious diseases can be kept apart from the others **(b) in isolation** = all alone; *the plans for the new bus station should not be seen in isolation - they are part of a major redevelopment scheme for the town centre*

isosceles triangle [aɪ'sɒsɪliːz 'traɪæŋgl] *noun* triangle with two sides which are the same length

isotope ['aɪsətəup] *noun* form of a chemical element which has the same chemical properties as other forms, but a different atomic mass; **radioactive isotope** = an isotope which sends out radiation, used in radiotherapy

issue ['ɪʃuː] **1** *noun* **(a)** problem; *the main issues will be discussed at the meeting*; **to make an issue of something** = to have a big discussion about something; *she's apologized so don't try to make an issue of it*; **the point at issue** = the question which is being discussed; *the point at issue is whether the government is prepared to compromise*; **to take issue with someone** = to disagree with someone **(b)** publication of a book; putting new stamps on sale; putting new coins or notes into circulation; *there will be a new issue of stamps this month* **(c)** giving out of permits, licences, uniforms, etc.; *the issue of ration cards has been delayed* **(d)** one copy of a newspaper or magazine; *we bought the January issue of the magazine* **(e)** giving out new shares; **rights issue** = giving shareholders the right to buy more shares more cheaply **2** *verb* **(a)** to come out; *smoke began to issue from the hole in the ground* **(b)** to put (new stamps) on sale; to publish (books); to put

(new banknotes) into circulation; *the new set of stamps will be issued next week*; *initially the euro will be issued alongside national currencies* **(c)** to give out or to hand out permits, licences, uniforms, etc.; *we issued a writ against the company*; *the government issued a report on London's traffic*; *the Secretary of State issued guidelines for expenditure*

isthmus ['ɪsməs] *noun* narrow piece of land with water on both sides of it, connecting two larger pieces of land; *they cut a canal through the Isthmus of Suez to join the Mediterranean and the Red Sea* (NOTE: plural is **isthmuses**)

it [ɪt] *pronoun referring to a thing* **(a)** *(used to show something which has just been mentioned) what do you want me to do with the box? - put it down*; *where's the box? - it's here*; *she picked up a potato and then dropped it on the ground*; *I put my book down somewhere and now I can't find it*; *where's the newspaper? - it's on the chair*; *the dog's thirsty, give it something to drink* **(b)** *(referring to no particular thing) look! - it's snowing*; *it's miles from here to the railway station*; *is it the 30th today?*; *it's almost impossible to get a ticket at this time of year*; *what time is it? - it's ten o'clock*; *it's dangerous to use an electric saw when it's wet* (NOTE: **it's = it is** or **it has**; do not confuse with **its**)

IT = INFORMATION TECHNOLOGY

Italian [ɪ'tæljən] **1** *adjective* referring to Italy; *my wife loves Italian food like pasta*; *we bought some Italian wine last week* **2** *noun* **(a)** person from Italy; *the Italians are passionate about football* **(b)** language spoken in Italy; *Italian is one of the languages that are derived from Latin*; *we go to Italy on holiday every year, and the children speak quite good Italian*

italic [ɪ'tælɪk] **1** *adjective* sloping (of letters); *the text under the illustrations is printed in italic type* **2** *noun* **italics** = sloping letters; *this example is printed in italics* (NOTE: the other two main styles of print are **roman** and **bold**)

COMMENT: as the name suggests, italics were invented in Italy, in the fifteenth century. Italics are used to show words which you want to highlight in some way, but are not used for whole paragraphs

italicize [ɪ'tælɪsaɪz] *verb* to put a word into italics; *make sure the headings are italicized*

Italy ['ɪtəli] *noun* country in southern Europe, south of France, Switzerland and Austria; *Italy is the home of great sixteenth century painters like Michaelangelo and Raphael* (NOTE: capital: **Rome**; people: **Italians**; language: **Italian**; currency: **lira, euro**)

itch [ɪtʃ] **1** *noun* any irritated place on the skin, which makes a person want to scratch; *I've got an itch in the middle of my back which I just can't reach - it's driving me mad!* (NOTE: plural is **itches**) **2** *verb* **(a)** to produce an irritating sensation, making a person want to scratch; *the cream made his skin itch more than before* **(b)** *(informal)* **to be itching to do something** = to be very eager to do something; *I am itching to have a go at hanggliding but my wife won't let me*

itchy ['ɪtʃi] *adjective* which makes a person want to scratch; *the main symptom of the disease is an itchy red rash*; *(informal)* **itchy feet** = desire to change jobs or to travel; *I'm starting to get itchy feet again - I've been in the same job for too long*

item ['aɪtəm] *noun* **(a)** thing (in a list); *we are discussing item four on the agenda*; *do you have any items of jewellery in your luggage?*; *please find enclosed an order for the following items from your catalogue* **(b)** piece of information, for example on a news programme; *here is a summary of the main items of news* or *the main news items*

itemize ['aɪtəmaɪz] *verb* to make a detailed list of things; *can you itemize your insurance claim?*; *itemizing the sales figures will take about two days*; **itemized invoice** = invoice which lists each item separately

itinerant [ɪ'tɪnərənt] *adjective (formal)* moving from place to place, without settling; *itinerant farm workers travelled from farm to farm looking for work*; *he joined a touring troupe of itinerant actors*

itinerary [ɪ'tɪnərəri] *noun* list of places to be visited on one journey; *he mapped out his itinerary before he set off*; *the members of the group were given a detailed tour itinerary by the courier* (NOTE: plural is **itineraries**)

its [ɪts] *adjective referring to 'it'*; *I can't use the car - one of its tyres is flat*; *the company pays its staff very badly* (NOTE: do not confuse with **it's**)

it's [ɪts] *short for* IT IS, IT HAS

itself [ɪt'self] *pronoun referring to a thing* **(a)** *(referring to an object)* **the dog seems to have hurt itself**; *the screw had worked itself loose*; **all by itself** = alone, with no one helping; *the church stands all by itself in the middle of the street*; *the bus started to move all by itself* **(b)** *(for emphasis)* *if the plug is all right there must be something wrong with the computer itself*

IUD = INTRAUTERINE DEVICE

IV the Roman numeral for four or fourth; *King William IV*

I've [aɪv] = I HAVE

ivory ['aɪvəri] *noun* **(a)** hard whitish substance from an elephant's tusk; *she bought some finely carved ivory chessmen*; *trade in ivory has been banned* **(b)** **ivory tower** = imaginary place where an intellectual can live, isolated from the ordinary world; *just because I'm a university lecturer doesn't mean I live in an ivory tower*

ivy ['aɪvi] *noun* evergreen plant which climbs up walls and trees (NOTE: plural is **ivies**)

IX the Roman numeral for nine or ninth; *what did you learn about King Charles IX?*

Jj

J, j [dʒeɪ] tenth letter of the alphabet, between I and K; *'J' is the first letter of names like Jack, Julia, and Jonathan*

jab [dʒæb] **1** *noun* **(a)** poke with something pointed; *he felt a jab in the back from someone's umbrella* **(b)** *(informal)* injection; *have you had your cholera jabs yet?* **2** *verb* to poke with something sharp; *he jabbed the piece of meat with his fork; she jabbed me in the back with her umbrella* (NOTE: **jabbing - jabbed**)

jabber ['dʒæbə] *verb* to speak fast and not very clearly; *he jabbered something which I couldn't understand; the monkey was jabbering away in the corned of the cage*

jack [dʒæk] *noun* **(a)** instrument for raising something heavy, especially a car; *I used the jack to lift the car up and take the wheel off* **(b)** *(in playing cards)* the card with the face of a young man, with a value between the queen and the ten; *I won because I had the jack of hearts* **(c)** *(at bowls)* small white or black ball for players to aim at; *you need a lot of skill to hit the jack* **(d)** the Union Jack = flag of the United Kingdom; *the Union Jack flew proudly on the ship's stern* **(e)** electric or telephone plug with a single pin; *when he had plugged the jack in he could use the modem*

jackal ['dʒækl] *noun* African wild animal, similar to a dog, which feeds chiefly on dead flesh; *the jackals fought over the carcass*

jacket ['dʒækɪt] *noun* **(a)** short coat worn with trousers; *he was wearing a blue jacket and brown trousers; this orange jacket shows up in the dark when I ride my bike*; dinner jacket (DJ) = man's formal black jacket, worn with a black bow tie (NOTE: American English for this is **tuxedo**) **(b)** paper cover wrapped round a book; *the design of a book jacket has to be very attractive to make people want to buy the book* **(c)** jacket potatoes *or* potatoes in their jackets = potatoes cooked in an oven with their skins on; *she had a jacket potato and salad for lunch; jacket potatoes are healthier than chips*

jackknife ['dʒæknaɪf] **1** *noun* large folding knife; *he pulled out a jackknife and cut the rope* (NOTE: plural is **jackknives**) **2** *verb (of an articulated vehicle)* to go out of control, when the two parts bend in half so that the they are pointing in different directions; *the section of the motorway is closed where a lorry has jackknifed*

jackpot ['dʒækpɒt] *noun* to win *or* to hit the jackpot = to win the highest prize in a lottery; *he won the jackpot and bought himself a new car; last week's lottery jackpot was the highest ever*

jack up ['dʒæk ˈʌp] *verb* **(a)** to lift something up with a jack; *they jacked up the car to remove the exhaust pipe* **(b)** *(informal)* to raise profits or prices; *the newspaper article alleged that dealers had jacked up prices to make bigger profits*

Jacobean [dʒækəbɪən] *adjective* referring to the time of James I (the early seventeenth century); *Ham House is a good example of Jacobean architecture*

jacuzzi [dʒə'kuːzi] *noun* trademark for a type of bath with jets which circulate the water and keep it bubbling; *the health club has two jacuzzis and a whirlpool*

jade [dʒeɪd] *noun* hard green precious stone; *I bought this jade brooch in Hong Kong*

jaded ['dʒeɪdɪd] *adjective* worn out, tired; *she felt a little jaded after years of working in the bank; he made a little dish which would tempt even the most jaded appetite*

jagged ['dʒægɪd] *adjective* with irregular, rough edges; *be careful of the jagged edges on that rusty old can; jagged rocks run down into the sea*

jaguar ['dʒægjuə] *noun* large spotted wild cat of Central and South America; *the jaguar and her cubs hid in the trees*

jail [dʒeɪl] **1** *noun* prison; *she was sent to jail for three months* **2** *verb* to put someone in prison; *she was jailed for six years* (NOTE: also spelled **gaol**)

jailer ['dʒeɪlə] *noun (old)* person who guards prisoners in a jail; *the jailers went round locking the cell doors* (NOTE: also spelled **gaoler**; the modern term is **prison officer**)

jam [dʒæm] **1** *noun* **(a)** sweet food made by boiling fruit and sugar together; *a port of apricot jam; do you want jam or honey on your bread?; we made jam with the fruit in the garden; have you any more jam - the jar is empty?*; *(informal)* it's money for jam = it's a profit which is easy to make (NOTE: no plural in this meaning: **some jam, a pot of jam**; note also the difference with **marmalade** which is made from citrus fruits) **(b)** blockage which happens when there are too many things in too small a space; *there is a paper jam in the printer*; traffic jam = too much traffic on the roads, so that cars and lorries can't move; *the accident on Waterloo Bridge caused traffic jams all over London; there are rush hour jams every evening between 5.00 and 6.30* **(c)** *(informal)* awkward situation; *he's got himself into a jam* **2** *verb* **(a)** *(of machine)* to stick and not to be able to move; *hold on - the paper has jammed in the printer* **(b)** to force things into a small space; *don't try to jam all those boxes into the car boot; the switchboard was jammed with calls* **(c)** *(informal)* to jam on the brakes = to brake suddenly; *he jammed on the brakes and the car went into a spin* (NOTE: **jamming - jammed**)

Jamaica [dʒə'meɪkə] *noun* country consisting of an island in the Caribbean, one of the islands that make up the West Indies (NOTE: capital: **Kingston**; people: **Jamaicans**; language: **English**; currency: **Jamaican dollar**)

Jamaican [dʒə'meɪkən] **1** *adjective* referring to Jamaica; *a bottle of Jamaican rum* **2** *noun* person from Jamaica; *Jamaicans are passionate about football*

jamboree [dʒæmbə'riː] *noun* **(a)** big outdoor party; *are you going to the jamboree in the public gardens tonight?* **(b)** large gathering of people, especially of scouts and guides; *the next world jamboree will be held in Japan*

jam-packed [dʒæm'pækt] *adjective (informal)* extremely full; *the underground train was jam-packed with commuters*; *Trafalgar Square was jam-packed with people seeing the New Year in*

jangle ['dʒæŋgl] **1** *noun* harsh noise of pieces of metal hitting together; *she heard the jangle of keys on the other side of the door* **2** *verb* **(a)** to make a harsh noise of metal; *he jangled the keys in his pocket* **(b)** to **jangle (on) someone's nerves** = to irritate someone's nerves, to make someone nervous; *the sound of the dentist's drill started to jangle my nerves*

janitor ['dʒænɪtə] *noun* especially US person who looks after a building, making sure it is clean, that the rubbish is cleared away, etc.; *tell the janitor that there's a light bulb missing in the stairway* (NOTE: British English is **caretaker**)

January ['dʒænjuəri] *noun* first month of the year, followed by February; *he was born on January 26th* US *on January 26*; *we never go on holiday in January because it's too cold*; *we all went skiing last January* (NOTE: **January 26th** or **January 26**: say 'the twenty-sixth of January' or 'January the twenty-sixth'; American English: 'January twenty-sixth')

Japan [dʒə'pæn] *noun* large country in the Far East, formed of several islands to the east of China and south of Korea; *Japan hosted the 1998 Winter Olympics* (NOTE: capital: **Tokyo**; people: **the Japanese**; language: **Japanese**; currency: **yen**)

Japanese [dʒæpə'niːz] **1** *adjective* referring to Japan; *a typical Japanese meal can include rice and raw fish* **2** *noun* **(a)** the **Japanese** = people from Japan; *the Japanese are very formal people* **(b)** language spoken in Japan; *he has lived in Japan for some time and speaks quite good Japanese*; *we bought a Japanese phrase book before we went to japan*

jar [dʒɑː] **1** *noun* container for jam, etc., usually made of glass; *there was some honey left in the bottom of the jar*; *open another jar of jam - this one is empty*; **jam jar** = special jar for putting jam in; *he kept the money in an empty jam jar* **2** *verb* **(a)** to hit and hurt slightly; *he tripped over the step, jarring his knee* **(b)** to produce an unpleasant effect; *her high-pitched voice jarred on my ears*; *those orange curtains jar with the purple cushions* (NOTE: **jarring - jarred**)

jargon ['dʒɑːgən] *noun* special sort of language used by a trade or profession or particular group of people; *I can't understand half of what the sales director says - it's all marketing jargon*; *he's computer literate, he knows how computers work and understands computer jargon*

jasmine ['dʒæzmɪn] *noun* shrub with little white or yellow flowers which have a sweet smell; *winter jasmine has yellow flowers*; **jasmine tea** = Chinese tea with jasmine flowers in it; *visitors to China are often greeted with a cup of jasmine tea*

jaundice ['dʒɔːndɪs] *noun* condition where there is too much bile in the blood, and the skin and the whites of the eyes become yellow; *when he was younger he had an attack of jaundice*

jaundiced ['dʒɔːndɪst] *adjective* negative, unfavourable because you feel badly treated yourself; *he takes a jaundiced view of modern society*

jaunt [dʒɔːnt] *noun* short trip; *they've gone on a weekend jaunt to the South Coast*

jaunty ['dʒɔːnti] *adjective* cheerful and confident; *he came in with a jaunty step* (NOTE: **jauntier - jauntiest**)

javelin ['dʒævlɪn] *noun* long spear used in battle or in sport; *ancient Greek armies had hundreds of javelin throwers*; *she threw the javelin an enormous distance, it was a new Olympic record*

jaw [dʒɔː] *noun* bones in the face which hold the teeth and form the mouth; **upper jaw** = part of the skull holding the top set of teeth; **bottom jaw** or **lower jaw** = bone holding the lower teeth, which moves to make the mouth open or shut; *she hit him so hard that she broke his lower jaw*

jay [dʒeɪ] *noun* brightly coloured bird, one of the crow family; *the jay doesn't sing, but makes a chattering sound*

jaywalker ['dʒeɪwɔːkə] *noun* pedestrian who crosses a street with paying any attention to the traffic, or who does not cross a street at a pedestrian crossing; *jaywalkers create even more hazards than cyclists*

jaywalking ['dʒeɪwɔːkɪŋ] *noun* crossing a street without paying attention to the traffic; *in some European cities you can be fined for jaywalking*

jazz [dʒæz] *noun* type of music with a strong rhythm, and solo improvisations, first played in the southern United States; *I'm a real jazz fan*; *Louis Armstrong was one of the kings of jazz*

jazz up ['dʒæz 'ʌp] *verb (informal)* to make bright and attractive; *they jazzed up their bedroom with some new curtains*

jazzy ['dʒæzi] *adjective* bright (colour); *that's a jazzy jumper you're wearing!*

jealous ['dʒeləs] *adjective* feeling annoyed because you want something which belongs to someone else; *John was jealous of Mark because all the girls fancied him*; *she was jealous of his new car*; *her new boyfriend is very handsome - I'm jealous!*

jealously ['dʒeləsli] *adverb* in a jealous way, keeping something so that no one else can get it; *the secret recipe was jealously guarded by the family*

jealousy ['dʒeləsi] *noun* feeling of annoyance because someone has something which you don't have; *his jealousy of his wife's success broke their marriage*

jeans [dʒiːnz] *noun* trousers made of a type of strong cotton, often blue; *I like wearing jeans better than wearing a skirt*; *she came into the restaurant in her jeans*; **designer jeans** = fashionable jeans designed by a famous designer (NOTE: sometimes also called **blue jeans**)

jeep [dʒiːp] *noun* trademark for a strong four-wheel drive vehicle used for travelling over rough ground, especially used by the army; *the convoy of jeeps and tanks crossed slowly over the bridge*

jeer ['dʒɪə] **1** *noun* nasty mocking remark; *she left the stage in tears with the jeers of the audience ringing in her ears* **2** *verb* to **jeer at someone** = to mock or to laugh at someone in a nasty way; *because he was fat he was often jeered at and bullied at school*

jellied eels ['dʒelɪd 'iːlz] *noun* traditional London dish, made of cooked eels served cold in jelly

Jell-O ['dʒeləʊ] *see* JELLY

jelly ['dʒeli] *noun* **(a)** type of sweet food which shakes, made with fruit flavouring; *the children had* *fish fingers and chips followed by jelly and ice-cream* (NOTE: plural is **jellies**; note also, in the USA this is often called by a trademark, **Jell-O**) **(b) to turn to jelly** = to tremble and become floppy; *when he heard the sound of the bell his legs turned to jelly* **(c)** type of jam made of fruit juice boiled with sugar; *she loves peanut butter and blackcurrant jelly sandwiches*

jelly baby ['dʒeli 'beɪbi] *noun* sweet of coloured jelly, shaped like a little baby; *she gave the little girl a bag of jelly babies*

jelly bean ['dʒeli 'biːn] *noun* sweet of coloured jelly, shaped like a bean

jellyfish ['dʒelifɪʃ] *noun* animal with a body like jelly, which lives in the sea; *watch out when you're bathing - jellyfish can sting!* (NOTE: plural is **jellyfish**)

jelly roll ['dʒeli 'rəul] *noun US* cake made by rolling a thin sheet of sponge cake covered with jam (NOTE: British English is **Swiss roll**)

jeopardize ['dʒepədaɪz] *verb* to be likely to harm; *her arrest for drunken driving may jeopardize her work as a doctor specializing in child care*; *the murder of the priest will jeopardize the peace negotiations*

jeopardy ['dʒepədi] *noun* **to be in jeopardy** = to be in danger; *the management's attitude to safety has put us all in jeopardy*; *the sale of the company has put thousands of jobs in jeopardy*; *his driving licence is in jeopardy* = he may lose his driving licence

jerk [dʒɜːk] **1** *noun* **(a)** sudden sharp pull; *he felt a jerk on the fishing line* **(b)** *(slang)* stupid person; *don't ask that jerk anything!* **2** *verb* to pull something sharply; *he jerked the rope*

jerkily ['dʒɜːkɪli] *adverb* in a jerky way; *the puppet's arms moved jerkily up and down*

jerkin ['dʒɜːkɪn] *noun* short coat with no sleeves; *he wore a quilted jerkin*

jerky ['dʒɜːki] *adjective* abrupt, sudden; *the car moved forward in a series of jerky movements*

jerry-built ['dʒeribɪlt] *adjective* which has been badly and cheaply built; *after the war they put up thousands of jerry-built blocks of flats in the suburbs*

jersey ['dʒɜːzi] *noun* **(a)** close-fitting woollen sweater; *she was knitting a pink jersey for the new baby* **(b)** special shirt worn by a member of a football team, etc.; *after every game the players swapped jerseys with the other team*; **yellow jersey** = the yellow shirt worn by the leader of the Tour de France

jest [dʒest] *(formal)* **1** *noun* joke, something done or said to make people laugh; *it started off as a jest but turned into something more serious*; **said in jest** = said as a joke; *the remark was said half in jest, but I think he really meant it* **2** *verb* to make jokes; *one should not jest about that sort of thing - it's very serious*

jet [dʒet] **1** *noun* **(a)** long narrow stream of liquid or gas; *a jet of water put out the flames* **(b)** aircraft with jet engines; *jets flew low overhead*; **jet lag** = tiredness felt by travellers who fly by jet aircraft across time zones; *she suffered dreadful jet lag after the flight from New York* **2** *verb (informal)* to travel by jet plane; *she jetted off to Los Angeles for a short holiday*; *Nice airport was busy with stars jetting in for the Cannes Film Festival* (NOTE: **jetting - jetted**)

jet engine ['dʒet 'endʒɪn] *noun* engine which is propelled by a jet of gas; *the two jet engines are located*

on either side of the plane; *before jet engines were invented, planes had propellers*

jet set ['dʒet 'set] *noun* rich people from all round the world; *what a party! - all the international jet set were there*

jet setter ['dʒet 'setə] *noun* person who belongs to the jet set; *she's one of the group of London jet setters*

jet setting ['dʒet 'setɪŋ] *adjective* referring to the jet set; *the club was packed with jet-setting partygoers*

jettison ['dʒetɪzn] *verb* to throw fuel from a plane, or cargo from a ship into the sea to make it lighter; *we were forced to jettison our precious cargo in order to escape from the pirates*; *the plane jettisoned its remaining fuel before making an emergency landing*

jetty ['dʒeti] *noun* small quay where boats can tie up; *there were two boats tied up to the jetty* (NOTE: plural is **jetties**)

jewel ['dʒuəl] *noun* precious stone, such as a diamond; *I'll just lock up these jewels in the safe*; *she owned up to having stolen the jewels*

jeweller *US* **jeweler** ['dʒuːələ] *noun* person who makes or sells jewellery, and usually watches as well; *I must take my ring to the jeweller's to have it repaired*

jewellery *US* **jewelry** ['dʒuːəlri] *noun* ornaments to be worn, made from precious stones, gold, silver, etc.; *the burglar stole all her jewellery* (NOTE: no plural)

jibe [dʒaɪb] *noun* nasty or teasing remark; *he paid no attention to the jibes of the press* (NOTE: American spelling is **gibe**)

jiffy ['dʒɪfi] *noun (informal)* very short time; *you won't have to wait long, I'll have finished in a jiffy*; *just a jiffy, while I put on my shoes*

jig [dʒɪg] **1** *noun* **(a)** type of fast lively dance; *when he heard the news he did a little jig around the office* **(b)** music for this dance; *the band started to play an Irish jig and everyone got up to dance* **(c)** device which guides a tool and holds the material being worked on; *set up the jig so that the holes will be drilled in exactly the same place in each piece of wood* **2** *verb* to jump up and down; to move about jerkily; *the headteacher told the children to stop jigging about and to stand still* (NOTE: **jigging - jigged**)

jiggery-pokery ['dʒɪgəri'pəukəri] *noun (informal)* dishonest dealings; *there's some sort of jiggery-pokery going on among members of the board*

jiggle ['dʒɪgl] *verb (informal)* **(a)** to move rapidly or nervously; *stop jiggling about!*; *I'll never take Jimmy to a concert again - he was jiggling about all the time* **(b)** to move something a little; *if you jiggle the top a bit, it should come off fairly easily*

jigsaw ['dʒɪgsɔː] *noun* **(a)** **jigsaw (puzzle)** = puzzle of odd-shaped pieces of wood or cardboard which when fitted together form a picture; *as its raining, let's stay indoors and try to do this huge jigsaw of the Houses of Parliament* **(b)** saw with a thin blade for cutting designs out of wood; *his electric drill has a jigsaw attachment*

jihad ['dʒihæd] *noun* holy war by Muslims against people who do not believe in Islam; *some terrorist groups are conducting a jihad against this country*

jingle ['dʒɪŋgl] **1** *noun* **(a)** sound made when little pieces of metal knock together; *the jingle of tiny bells on the horse's harness* **(b)** song with a simple rhyme or rhythm; **advertising jingle** = tune which advertises a product **2** *verb* to make a tinkling sound like pieces of metal knocking together; *the doorbell jingled as he went into the shop*

jingoism ['dʒɪŋgəʊɪzm] *noun* excessive feeling that your country is best and feelings of aggression towards other countries; *the jingoism of the tabloid papers came out during the war*

jingoistic [dʒɪŋgəʊ'ɪstɪk] *adjective* showing jingoism; *his jingoistic articles had an effect on government policy*

jinx [dʒɪŋks] *noun (informal)* something which brings bad luck; *I think there's a jinx on this motorbike - everything seems to go wrong with it* (NOTE: plural is **jinxes**)

jinxed [dʒɪŋkst] *adjective (informal)* struck down by bad luck; *the village fête was jinxed - first the vicar got malaria, then the marquee was struck by lightning, what else can go wrong?*

jitters ['dʒɪtəz] *noun (informal)* **to get** *or* **have the jitters** = to be nervous and flustered; *I always get the jitters before an exam*; **to give someone the jitters** = to make someone nervous; *all this talk of bombs gives me the jitters*; *it was a day of jitters on the stock market as the news from Japan began to come in*

jittery ['dʒɪtəri] *adjective (informal)* nervous and flustered; *if I feel myself getting jittery before an interview I do breathing exercises to calm down*

Jnr *US* **Jr** ['dʒuːnɪə] = JUNIOR

job [dʒɒb] *noun* **(a)** regular work which you get paid for; *she's got a job in the supermarket*; *he's finding it difficult getting a job because he can't drive*; *when the factory closed, hundreds of people lost their jobs*; **to be out of a job** = to lose your employment; *if they introduce that new computer system, the secretary will be out of her job*; *(informal)* **jobs for the boys** = the corrupt practice of giving work to your friends or supporters; *there'll be plenty of jobs for the boys when the new government comes in* **(b)** piece of work; *don't sit down, there are a couple of jobs I want you to do*; *he does all sorts of little electrical jobs around the house*; **to make a good job of something** = to do something well; *they made a very good job of mending the table*; **odd jobs** = small items of work, especially repairs, done in the house; *he does odd jobs for us around the house*; **odd job man** = person who does small items of work; *our odd job man will mend the leaking pipe for you* **(c)** *(informal)* **it's a good job that** = it's lucky that; *it's a good job he can drive*; *what a good job you brought your umbrella!*; *it's a good job you're not hungry, as there's nothing in the fridge*; **to give something up as a bad job** = to stop trying to do something; *he tried to get the car to go, and in the end had to give it up as a bad job*; **just the job** = just the right thing, exactly what we need; *that heavy hammer is just the job for breaking up concrete* **(d)** *(informal)* difficulty; *I had a job trying to find your house*; *what a job it was getting a hotel room at the time of the music festival!*

jobbing ['dʒɒbɪŋ] *adjective (of a workman)* doing small jobs which are paid for separately; *he works as a jobbing gardener for various people in the village*

jobcentre ['dʒɒb'sentə] *noun* official office which displays vacant jobs which are available; *every week he went to the local jobcentre to see if there was anything available*

jobless ['dʒɒbləs] **1** *adjective* with no job **2** *noun* **the jobless** = people who have no jobs (NOTE: takes a plural verb)

jobseeker ['dʒɒbsiːkə] *noun* unemployed person who is looking for a job; **jobseeker's allowance (JSA)** = money paid by the government to people who are out of work and actively looking for jobs

jockey ['dʒɒki] **1** *noun* person who rides horses in races; *he's an experienced jockey and knows how to handle a horse over a muddy racecourse*; *he's the youngest jockey to ride in the Grand National*; **disc jockey (DJ)** = person who plays music discs at a disco or on radio; *who's your favourite DJ on Radio One?* **2** *verb (of several people)* **to jockey for position** = to try to improve their positions especially at the expense of the others; *there's a vacancy for managing director, and the sales director and the production director are jockeying for position*

jockstrap ['dʒɒkstræp] *noun* support for the genitals, worn by male athletes under their shorts

jocular ['dʒɒkjʊlə] *adjective* in a good-humoured way, treating things as a joke; *the bride's father made some jocular remarks about the best man*; *I've never seen him in such a jocular mood before*

jocularity [dʒɒkjʊ'lærɪti] *noun (formal)* good humour; *there were moments of jocularity during the press conference*

jodhpurs ['dʒɒdpəz] *noun* trousers for horse riding which are wide above the knee and narrow below it; *she came into the room wearing jodhpurs, and carrying a whip*

joey ['dʒəʊi] *noun (in Australia) (informal)* young kangaroo

jog [dʒɒg] **1** *noun* **(a)** quite slow running pace; *he ran at a jog round the park* **(b)** rather slow run, especially when taken for exercise; *she goes for a jog every morning* **2** *verb* **(a)** to run at an easy pace, especially for exercise; *he jogged along the river bank for two miles*; *she was listening to her personal stereo as she was jogging* **(b)** to move at a steady, but rather slow pace; *the train jogged through the suburbs, stopping at every station* **(c)** to push lightly; *someone jogged my elbow and I spilt my drink*; **it jogged his memory** = it made him remember; *the police are hoping that the reconstruction of the crime will jog people's memories* (NOTE: **jogging - jogged**)

jogger ['dʒɒgə] *noun* person who jogs for exercise; *joggers run round the park every morning*

jogging ['dʒɒgɪŋ] *noun* running at an easy pace for exercise; *jogging every morning is good for you*; **to go jogging** = to run gently for exercise; *they went jogging in the streets near their home*

john [dʒɒn] *noun US (slang)* toilet; *Tom's in the john*

join [dʒɔɪn] **1** *verb* **(a)** to put things together; *you have to join the two pieces of wood together*; *the rooms were joined together by making a door in the wall* **(b)** to come together; *go on for about two hundred metres, until a road joins this one*; *the two rivers join about four kilometres beyond the town* **(c)** to become a member of a club, group, etc.; *after university, he is going to join the police*; *she joined the army because she wanted to travel* **(d)** **to join a firm** = to start work with a company; **he joined on January 1st** = he started work on the January 1st **(e)** to do something with someone; *we're going to have a cup of coffee - would* *you like to join us?*; *won't you join us for a game of golf?* **2** *noun* place where pieces are joined; *can you see the join where I added an extra piece of cloth?*

joiner ['dʒɔɪnə] *noun* person who builds things out of wood, especially windows and doors for houses; *the joiner has come to repair the windows*

joinery ['dʒɔɪnəri] *noun* occupation of being a joiner; *he goes to joinery classes in the evening*

join in ['dʒɔɪn 'ɪn] *verb* to take part in something done as a group; *he started to sing and everyone else joined in*

joint [dʒɔɪnt] **1** *noun* **(a)** place where several pieces are attached, especially in building or woodwork; *the joints of the drawer have worked loose* **(b)** place where bones come together and can move, such as the knee or elbow; *her elbow joint hurt after her game of tennis* **(c)** large piece of meat, especially for roasting; *the joint of lamb was very tender; we all sat round the table while Father carved the Sunday joint* **(d)** *(informal)* club or restaurant; *let's go to Rick's joint* **(e)** *(slang)* cigarette with marijuana; *he smoked a couple of joints during the evening* **2** *adjective* combined, with two or more things linked together; **joint account** = bank account for two people, such as husband and wife; **joint ownership** = owning of a property by several owners

jointly ['dʒɔɪntli] *adverb* together with one or more other people; *this law applies when two or more people own a property jointly*

join up ['dʒɔɪn 'ʌp] *verb* **(a)** to link things together; *she's getting better at writing, and can do joined-up letters* **(b)** to join the army, navy or air force; *he joined up when he was 18 and soon rose to become an officer*

joist [dʒɔɪst] *noun* horizontal beam which supports a ceiling or floorboards; *one of the joists under the kitchen floor was rotten and had to be replaced*

joke [dʒəuk] **1** *noun* thing said or done to make people laugh; *she poured water down his neck as a joke; they all laughed at his jokes; he told jokes all evening*; **practical joke** = action which makes someone uncomfortable to amuse others **2** *verb* to tell jokes; to say or do something to make people laugh; *he used to joke about always being late for the office*; *he was only joking* = he did not mean it seriously; **you're joking!** *or* **you must be joking!** = you are not being serious, are you?; *he's just bought a new Rolls Royce - you must be joking, he's only the office boy!*

joker ['dʒəukə] *noun* extra card, with the picture of a clown on it, used as a bonus in certain card games

jolly ['dʒɒli] **1** *adjective* merry, happy, pleasant, enjoyable; *it was marvellous to see all the jolly faces of the children; her birthday party was a very jolly affair* (NOTE: **jollier - jolliest**) **2** *adverb (informal)* **(a)** very; *it's jolly hard work carrying all those boxes up to the attic* **(b)** *(used to emphasize)* *if you don't want to pay the proper rate for the job, then you can jolly well do it yourself* **3** *verb (informal)* **to jolly someone along** = to encourage someone by keeping him amused; *we tried to jolly the children along, but they just walked slower and slower*

jolt [dʒəult] **1** *noun* sudden shake or shock, or violent jerk; *the train stopped with a jolt* **2** *verb* **(a)** to move with sudden movements; *the train jolted twice before moving off* **(b)** to push or to shake abruptly; *the people in the back of the truck were jolted about from side to side as we bumped over the rocky track* **(c)** to give a sudden shock to; *the sound of the whistle jolted her*

into action; **to jolt someone out of** = to make someone stop doing something; *getting married it will jolt him out of his lazy bachelor habits*

Jordan ['dʒɔːdən] *noun* country in the Middle East, to the east of Israel; *we went to Jordan to visit the old Roman towns* (NOTE: capital: **Amman**; people: **Jordanians**; language: **Arabic**; currency: **Jordanian dinar**)

Jordanian [dʒɔːˈdeɪnɪən] **1** *adjective* referring to Jordan; *the Jordanian capital is Amman* **2** *noun* person from Jordan; *she is married to a Jordanian*

jostle ['dʒɒsl] *verb* to push or to bump into people, especially in a crowd; *we were jostled by other people trying to get onto the train*; **to jostle for position** = to push others so as to get into a good position; *the cars on the starting line were jostling for position*

jot [dʒɒt] **1** *noun (old)* very small amount; *don't worry, it doesn't make a jot of difference; there wasn't a jot of truth in the article* **2** *verb* **to jot something down** = to make quick notes about something; *he jotted down her phone number* (NOTE: **jotting - jotted**)

jotter ['dʒɒtə] *noun* small pad of paper for making notes; *she wrote down the phone number on the jotter next to the telephone*

jottings ['dʒɒtɪŋz] *noun* notes written down at random; *they read some jottings from the famous author's notebooks*

journal ['dʒɜːnl] *noun* **(a)** diary; *he kept a journal during his visit to China; she wrote a journal of the gradual progress of her illness* **(b)** periodical magazine, especially one on a learned subject; *she edits the journal of the Historical Society* **(c)** book for recording each day's business; *she wrote the day's sales in the sales journal*

journalism ['dʒɜːnəlɪzm] *noun* profession of writing for newspapers or periodicals; *she took a journalism course to help her chances of getting a job on a newspaper*

journalist ['dʒɜːnəlɪst] *noun* person who writes for newspapers or periodicals; *journalists asked the policeman some very awkward questions; film stars were greeted by journalists from around the world at the première of the new film*

journalistic [dʒɜːnəˈlɪstɪk] *adjective* referring to journalism; *his journalistic experience has been confined to working on a student newspaper*

journey ['dʒɜːni] **1** *noun* travelling, usually a long distance; *it's at least two days' journey from here; they went on a train journey across China; she has a difficult journey to work every day - she has to change buses twice* **2** *verb (formal)* to travel; *they journeyed many miles to find the treasure; the book tells the story of a man who journeyed from Italy to China in the 13th century*

joy [dʒɔɪ] *noun* very great happiness; *we all wished them great joy on their wedding day; they were full of joy at seeing their son again*

joyful ['dʒɔɪful] *adjective* very happy; *I could tell by her joyful look that the interview had gone well*

joyfully ['dʒɔɪfuli] *adverb* very happily; *the children ran joyfully down onto the beach; he answered joyfully that it was his last day at the office*

joyous ['dʒɔɪəs] *adjective* very happy; *the funeral turned out to be rather a joyous event*

joyride ['dʒɔɪraɪd] *noun* trip for pleasure, especially in a stolen car; *the boys stole a car and went for a joyride; we all went for a joyride in Mark's father's new car*

joystick ['dʒɔɪstɪk] *noun* (a) rod which controls the movements of an aircraft; *pull on the joystick to make the plane rise* (b) device that allows the user to move the cursor round the screen by moving an upright arm

JP ['dʒeɪ'piː] *abbreviation for* JUSTICE OF THE PEACE; *JPs try cases in the magistrate's court*

Jr ['dʒuːnɪə] *abbreviation for* JUNIOR

JSA = JOBSEEKER'S ALLOWANCE

jubilant ['dʒuːbɪlənt] *adjective* full of happiness and triumph; *his parents were jubilant over their son's success*

jubilation [dʒuːbɪ'leɪʃn] *noun* show of great happiness; *there was jubilation in the crowd when they heard the news*

jubilee ['dʒuːbɪliː] *noun* celebration of the anniversary of an important event; *a committee has been set up to organize the jubilee celebrations;* **silver jubilee** = celebration 25 years after an event took place; **golden jubilee** = celebration 50 years after an event took place; **diamond jubilee** = celebration 60 years after an event took place; *street parties were held all over the Great Britain in honour of Queen Victoria's diamond jubilee in 1897*

judder ['dʒʌdə] **1** *noun (of a machine)* shaking; *for some reason, there's a judder when I put the car into third gear* **2** *verb (of a machine)* to shake; *the ferry juddered as it slowed down and reached the pier; he brought the car to a juddering halt*

judge [dʒʌdʒ] **1** *noun* (a) person appointed to make legal decisions in a court of law; *he was convicted for stealing, but the judge let him off with a small fine* (b) person who decides which is the best entry in a competition; *the three judges of the beauty contest couldn't agree* (c) person with good sense; *he's a good judge of character* **2** *verb* (a) to make decisions in a court of law or competition, etc.; *he was judged guilty; her painting was judged the best and she won first prize* (b) to estimate a value, to evaluate a situation; *to be a good driver you need to be able to judge distances well; the Senator judged it would be impossible for him to win the Presidency so he dropped out of the race*

> COMMENT: in Britain the three most senior judges are the Lord Chancellor, the Lord Chief Justice and the Master of the Rolls. They all sit in the House of Lords

judgement *or* **judgment** ['dʒʌdʒmənt] *noun* (a) legal decision by a judge or court; *the judgement of the tribunal was fair; the defendant will appeal against the judgement* (b) ability to see things clearly and to make good decisions; *he trusted his wife's judgement in everything;* **against your better judgement** = although you feel it is not the right thing to do; *he accepted the money against his better judgement; against her better judgement, she reported her son to the police* (c) **Judgement Day** *or* **the Day of Judgement** = day when dead people are judged by God; *members of the cult believe that the Day of Judgement is June 23rd 2012*

judicial [dʒuː'dɪʃl] *adjective* referring to a legal process or to a court of law; *there have been several attempts to reform the country's judicial system*

judiciary ['dʒuː'dɪʃəri] *noun (formal)* the judges, people who apply the law; *the judiciary is one of the three arms of government, the others being the executive and the legislature*

judicious [dʒuː'dɪʃəs] *adjective* based on good judgement; *he wrote a very judicious letter to the lawyers; dividing the prize money equally was a judicious decision; the judicious use of pesticides can greatly increase crop yields*

judo ['dʒuːdəʊ] *noun* Olympic sport, derived from the traditional Japanese art of unarmed combat between two people; *she has a black belt in judo so don't try to threaten her; he's an Olympic judo champion*

> COMMENT: there are twelve grades of judo masters (called Dan), and these are differentiated by the colours of their belts: first to fifth Dan wear a black belt; sixth to eighth Dan wear a red and white belt; ninth to eleventh Dan wear a red belt and a twelfth Dan wears a white belt (only one person has ever reached the level of twelfth Dan)

jug [dʒʌg] *noun* container with a handle, used for pouring liquids; *the cat knocked the milk jug off the table; could we have another jug of water, please?*

juggernaut ['dʒʌgənɔːt] *noun (informal)* very large lorry; *the village high street is impossible to cross, with juggernauts thundering past all the time*

juggle ['dʒʌgl] *verb* (a) to throw and catch several things (such as balls), so that most of them are in the air at the same time; *try and juggle four balls at once* (b) to keep changing things or arrange them in a complicated way; *I will have to juggle my meetings so that I can fit everyone in; she's trying to juggle her investments to get the best interest rate*

juggler ['dʒʌglə] *noun* person who juggles; *the jugglers in Covent Garden market attract a good audience*

juggling ['dʒʌglɪŋ] *noun* art of throwing things in the air and catching them, so that several are in the air at the same time; *he does juggling in his spare time;* **juggling act** = performance where someone throws and catches several things at the same time; *they toured the music-halls with their juggling act*

jugular ['dʒʌgjʊlə] *noun & adjective* **jugular (vein)** = one of the veins running down the side of the neck

juice [dʒuːs] *noun* (a) liquid from fruit, vegetables, meat, etc.; *they charged me £1 for two glasses of orange juice; she had a glass of grapefruit juice for breakfast* (b) **to stew in your own juice** = to suffer because of your mistakes; *don't bother about them - we'll leave them to stew in their own juice*

juicy ['dʒuːsi] *adjective* full of juice; *juicy peaches taste wonderful; these are the juiciest oranges we've had this year* (NOTE: **juicier - juiciest**)

julep ['dʒuːləp] *noun* US **mint julep** = drink made with bourbon and water, with leaves of mint in it

July [dʒuː'laɪ] *noun* seventh month of the year, between June and August; *she was born in July - her birthday is July 23rd US July 23; we went to Spain last July; July is always one of the busiest months for holidays* (NOTE: **July 23rd** *or* **July 23**: say 'July the twenty-third' or 'the twenty-third of July'; American English: 'July twenty-third')

jumble ['dʒʌmbl] **1** *noun* **(a)** confused mess; *his clothes were lying in a jumble on the floor*; *a jumble of thoughts raced through my mind* **(b) jumble sale** = sale of odd second-hand items organized by a club or organization to raise money; *there will be a jumble sale at the village hall on May 2nd* (NOTE: American English is **rummage sale**) **2** *verb* **to jumble up** = to mix; to confuse; *I wish he spent more time on his reports - the details are always rather jumbled up*; *his thoughts were all jumbled up in his head*

jumbo ['dʒʌmbəʊ] **1** *noun* **(a)** child's name for an elephant; *let's go to the zoo to see the jumbos* **(b) jumbo (jet)** = the Boeing 747, a very large jet aircraft; *they live close to the airport, with jumbos roaring overhead all day long; the airline is buying another ten jumbos to add to its fleet* **2** *adjective* very large; *he ordered a jumbo sausage and chips; she bought a jumbo box of fireworks*

jump [dʒʌmp] **1** *noun* sudden movement into the air; *the jump was higher than she thought and she hurt her leg; (in sports)* **long jump** *or* **high jump** = sport where you see who can jump the furthest or highest; *she won a gold medal in the high jump* **2** *verb* **(a)** to go suddenly into the air off the ground; *quick, jump on that bus - it's going to Oxford Circus!; the horse jumped over the fence; she jumped down from the chair* **(b) to jump the gun** = to start before it is your turn, before it is the right time; **to jump the queue** = to go in front of someone who has been waiting longer than you have **(c)** to move upwards suddenly; *the price of oil has jumped from $15.50 to $30.00* **(d)** to make a sudden movement because you are frightened; *she jumped when I came up behind her quietly and said 'Boo!'; when they fired the gun, it made me jump*

jump at ['dʒʌmp 'æt] *verb* to accept eagerly; *she jumped at the chance to work in Australia*

jumper ['dʒʌmpə] *noun* warm woollen knitted sweater; *I bought a pink jumper in the sales*

jump rope ['dʒʌmp 'rəʊp] *noun US* rope which you jump over as you swing it over your head and under your feet (NOTE: British English is **skipping rope**)

jump start ['dʒʌmp 'stɑːt] *verb* to start a car engine when the battery is flat by connecting the battery to the battery of another car; *compare* BUMP START

jumpsuit ['dʒʌmpsuːt] *noun* piece of clothing made of trousers and top joined together; *she was wearing a bright green jumpsuit*

jumpy ['dʒʌmpi] *adjective* nervous and excited; *everyone gets jumpy while waiting for the exam results*

junction ['dʒʌŋkʃn] *noun* place where railway lines or roads meet; *go as far as the next junction and you will see the library on your right; leave the motorway at Junction 5*; **junction box** = box where several electric wires are joined

juncture ['dʒʌŋktʃə] *noun (formal)* point in time; *at this juncture I can't say whether the deal will be accepted or rejected*

June [dʒuːn] *noun* sixth month of the year, between May and July; *she was born in June: her birthday is June 17th US June 17; last June we had a holiday in Canada* (NOTE: **June 17th** *or* **June 17**: say 'June

seventeenth' or 'the seventeenth of June'; American English: 'June seventeenth')

jungle ['dʒʌŋgl] *noun* thick tropical forest which is difficult to travel through; *they explored the jungle, hoping to find rare birds*

junior ['dʒuːniə] **1** *adjective* **(a)** younger, less important; *he was the junior member of the team* **(b)** for younger children; *she sings in the junior choir*; **junior school** = school for children from 7 to 11 years old **2** *noun* **(a) office junior** = young man or woman who does all types of work in an office **(b)** *US* student in his or her third year at college **(c)** son in a family who has the same name as his father; *John Smith, Junior*

juniper ['dʒuːnɪpə] *noun* small coniferous tree of the Northern Hemisphere, whose cones are like berries and are used as a flavouring; *juniper berries are used to flavour gin*

junk [dʒʌŋk] *noun* **(a)** useless articles, rubbish; *don't keep that - it's junk; you should throw away all that junk under your bed* (NOTE: no plural in this meaning) **(a)** large Chinese sailing boat; *Hong Kong harbour was full of junks*

junk bonds ['dʒʌŋk 'bɒndz] *noun* bonds giving a high interest, based on the security of a company which is the target of a takeover bid

junk food ['dʒʌŋk 'fuːd] *noun* bad commercially prepared food with less nutritional value than homemade food; *they just watch TV and live off junk food*

junkie ['dʒʌŋki] *noun* **(a)** *(slang)* heroin addict; *the park is full of junkies and dossers at night* **(b)** *(informal)* person who is very enthusiastic about something and cannot get enough of it; *I'm something of a crossword junkie; some Internet junkies spend a fortune on telephone bills*

junk shop ['dʒʌŋk 'ʃɒp] *noun* shop selling useless old articles; *I bought this old clock for £10 in a junk shop*

junta ['dʒʌntə] *noun* ruling group of ministers, a government which has taken power by force; *the junta came to power six years ago and is formed of representatives of each of the armed forces* (NOTE: used mainly of military governments, and usually referring to South America. The word is correctly pronounced as ['hʊntə] but this pronunciation is not often used in English)

Jupiter ['dʒuːpɪtə] *noun* largest planet in the solar system, more than eleven times the size of the earth

juridical [dʒʊˈrɪdɪkəl] *adjective (formal)* referring to the law and judges

jurisdiction [dʒʊərɪsˈdɪkʃn] *noun* legal power over someone *or* something; *the tribunal has no jurisdiction over the case*; **within the jurisdiction of the court** = in the legal power of the court; **outside the jurisdiction of the court** = not covered by the legal power of the court; *the matter is outside the jurisdiction of the court*

jurist ['dʒʊərɪst] *noun (formal)* person who specializes in the study of law; *he is an eminent jurist who has written many books on legal problems*

juror ['dʒʊərə] *noun* member of a jury; *when I was a juror, the case lasted two weeks*

COMMENT: jurors are selected from people on the register of electors who are aged between 18 and 65 years old. Various categories of people

> cannot be selected to serve on juries: barristers, solicitors, judges, doctors and Members of Parliament, among others

jury ['dʒʊəri] *noun* **(a)** group of twelve citizens who are sworn to decide whether someone is guilty or innocent on the basis of the evidence given in a court of law; *the jury brought in a verdict of not guilty*; **jury service** = service which all citizens may be asked to perform, to sit on a jury **(b) the jury is still out on this** = no one is sure what the result will be

just [dʒʌst] **1** *adjective* fair, showing no bias; *the decision of the court was just* **2** *adverb* **(a)** exactly; *is that too much sugar? - no, it's just right*; *thank you, that's just what I was looking for*; *just how many of students have got computers?*; *what time is it? - it's just seven o'clock* **(b)** barely, scarcely, almost not enough; *she had just enough money to pay the bill*; *he had just enough time to get dressed before the police arrived*; *he's just fifteen - his birthday was yesterday* **(c)** *(showing a very small quantity in space or time)* *your umbrella is just by the door*; *don't come in just yet - we're not ready*; *can you wait just a minute?* **(d)** *(showing the immediate past or future)* *the train has just arrived from Paris*; *she had just got into her bath when the phone rang*; *I don't want any coffee, thank you, I'm just going out*; *thanks for calling - I was just going to phone you* **(e)** only; *we're just good friends, nothing more*; *I've been to Berlin just once*

◊ **just about** ['dʒʌst ə'baʊt] **(a)** nearly, more or less; *I've just about finished my homework*; *the meal's just about ready* **(b) just about to do something** = going to do something very soon; *we were just about to leave*; *they were just about to go to bed when someone knocked on the door*

◊ **just as** ['dʒʌst 'æz] **(a)** at the same time; *just as I got into the car there was a loud bang* **(b)** in exactly the same way; *the film is just as good as the book*; *it is just as hot inside the house as it is outside*; *she loves her cats just as other people love their children*

◊ **just now** ['dʒʌst 'naʊ] **(a)** at the present time; *we're very busy in the office just now* **(b)** a short time ago; *I saw her just now in the post office*

justice ['dʒʌstɪs] *noun* **(a)** fair treatment in law; *justice must always be seen to be done* **(b) to bring someone to justice** = to start legal proceedings against someone; **rough justice** = judging someone in a rough and unfair way **(c) to do justice to** = to treat something as it deserves; *I wasn't very hungry so I couldn't do justice to your marvellous meal*; *his rather prosaic description doesn't do justice to the garden*

Justice of the Peace (JP) ['dʒʌstɪs əv ðə 'piːs] *noun* local magistrate

justifiable [dʒʌstɪ'faɪəbl] *adjective* which can be justified; *the management regards the dismissal as wholly justifiable in the circumstances*; *is it justifiable to kill someone in self-defence?*

justifiably [dʒʌstɪ'faɪəbli] *adverb* in a justifiable way; *she is justifiably proud of her grandson who has been elected to parliament*

justification [dʒʌstɪfɪ'keɪʃn] *noun* **(a)** reason which shows that something has been done correctly; *what was his justification for doing that?*; *they tried to find some justification for what they had done* **(b)** *(in typing and printing)* spacing out the words in the lines so that the right margin is straight; *an American hyphenation and justification program will not work with British English spellings*

justified ['dʒʌstɪfaɪd] *adjective* shown to be right; *he was fully justified in asking for a refund*

justify ['dʒʌstɪfaɪ] *verb* **(a)** to show that something is fair, to prove that something is right; *how can you justify your behaviour?* **(b) the end justifies the means** = if your final aim is good or honourable, you are right to do anything that is necessary to achieve it **(c)** *(in printing)* to space characters on the page so that the ends of lines are neat and straight; *the text should be fully justified*

justly ['dʒʌstli] *adverb* **(a)** with justice; *she was justly punished for her crime* **(b)** with good reason; *he is justly seen as the best British Chancellor this century*

jut [dʒʌt] *verb* **to jut (out)** = to stick out, usually horizontally; *my hotel room has a balcony jutting out over a busy main road*; *the cliff juts out into the lake* (NOTE: **jutting - jutted**)

jute [dʒuːt] *noun* fibre of tropical plants used for making rope, sacks, etc.

juvenile ['dʒuːvənaɪl] **1** *adjective* **(a)** referring to young people; *young offenders are tried before a juvenile court*; **juvenile delinquent** = young person who commits minor crimes, especially crimes against property **(b)** silly, immature, like a young person; *the new comedy series on TV is really juvenile* **2** *noun* *(formal)* young person (officially, one under seventeen years of age); *the police entered the club and arrested four people, two of them juveniles*

juxtapose [dʒʌkstə'pəʊz] *verb* *(formal)* to place side by side, so as to show a difference; *the bright green makes a very sharp contrast when juxtaposed with the pillar-box red*

juxtaposition [dʒʌkstəpə'zɪʃn] *noun* being side by side or very close together; *the juxtaposition of the two contrasting colours highlights the different sections of the painting*

Kk

K, k [keɪ] eleventh letter of the alphabet, between J and L; *K is the eleventh letter of the alphabet*

K [keɪ] *abbreviation for* one thousand; **£20K** = twenty thousand pounds (NOTE: say 'twenty K': 'the salary is around twenty K')

kaleidoscope [kəˈlaɪdəskəʊp] *noun* **(a)** toy formed of a tube with mirrors which reflect small pieces of coloured material and make patterns when you move it while looking into it through an eyepiece **(b)** something which has a series of patterns and colours; *the kaleidoscope of autumn colours which you only see in parts of North America*

kaleidoscopic [kəlaɪdəˈskɒpɪk] *adjective* like a kaleidoscope, with bright colours which change all the time; *the kaleidoscopic scene in the old market*

kangaroo [kæŋɡəˈruː] *noun* large Australian animal, of which the female carries its young in a pouch; *kangaroos are found in Australia*

karaoke [kærəˈəʊki] *noun* entertainment, coming originally from Japan, where people sing to recorded music; *Friday night is karaoke night in our local pub*

karat [ˈkærət] *noun US* measure of the quality of gold (pure gold being 24 karats); *a 22-karat gold ring* (NOTE: the British spelling is **carat**)

karate [kəˈrɑːti] *noun* Japanese style of fighting, where you hit sharp, quick blows with the side of the hand or kicks with the feet; *policewomen are encouraged to take karate lessons*; **karate chop** = blow with the side of the hand, such as to someone's neck; *she brought her attacker down with a karate chop*

> COMMENT: the object of a three-minute karate match is to score points by penetrating your opponent's defence and scoring a hit, in the opinion of the two judges, on one of the target areas: the upper body (including head, face and neck), or the middle of the body (including chest, abdomen and back). In competition, the blows should not actually make contact with the opponent because of potentially lethal consequences

kayak [ˈkaɪæk] *noun* type of small canoe which is pointed at both ends, and almost completely covered, with only a narrow opening for the canoeist; *a group of kayaks from the canoe club raced up the river*

kebab [kɪˈbæb] *noun* small cubes of meat or vegetables, grilled on a skewer; *the Lebanese restaurant has several types of kebab on the menu*

keel [kiːl] **1** *noun* **(a)** long beam in the bottom of a ship, on which the framework is built; *the dolphins swam under the keel and came up the other side of the yacht* **(b) on an even keel** = stable, steady; *after the huge fluctuations in the exchange rate in recent weeks, the pound is back on an even keel now* **2** *verb* (*informal*) **to keel over** = to fall over; *one minute she*

was sitting and talking happily, the next minute she keeled over onto the floor

keen [kiːn] *adjective* **(a) keen on something** *or* **someone** = liking something *or* someone, enthusiastic about something; *he's keen on keeping fit - he goes running every morning; I am not very keen on classical music; I don't think she's very keen on her new maths teacher;* (*informal*) **keen as mustard** = very keen; *the new group of trainees are good to work with, they're keen as mustard* **(b)** very sensitive; *bats have a keen sense of hearing* **(c) keen competition** = strong competition; *we are facing some keen competition from European manufacturers* (NOTE: **keener - keenest**)

keenly [ˈkiːnli] *adverb* acutely, sharply; *she felt his loss keenly; we are keenly aware of the competition coming from supermarkets*

keenness [ˈkiːnnəs] *noun* being keen; *in his keenness to learn the job he arrived at 7.30 in the morning, which annoyed the other trainees*

keep [kiːp] *verb* **(a)** to have for a long time or for ever; *can I keep the newspaper I borrowed from you?; I don't want that hat any more, you can keep it; the police kept my gun and won't give it back* **(b)** to continue to do something; *the clock kept going even after I dropped it on the floor; he had to keep smiling so that people would think he was pleased; keep quiet or they'll hear you; luckily the weather kept fine for the fair; the food will keep warm in the oven* **(c)** to have or put something in a particular place; *I keep my car keys in my pocket; where do you keep the paper for the laser printer?* **(d)** to make someone stay in a place or state; *it's cruel to keep animals in cages; I was kept late at the office; they kept us waiting for half an hour; we put the plates in the oven to keep them warm* **(e)** to prevent someone from doing something or from going somewhere; *she kept him from going out and playing football; he kept her from seeing her friends;* (*informal*) **what kept you?** = why are you so late? **(f)** to stay; **let's keep in touch** = we mustn't lose contact with each other; **she kept him company** = she stayed with him; **to keep an eye on** = to watch carefully; *he's keeping an eye on the shop while I'm away; see also* EAR **(g) to keep a diary** = to write notes every day about what has happened; *she kept a diary of her holiday in Spain* **(h)** to stay in good condition and not to go rotten; *raspberries don't keep* (NOTE: **keeps - keeping - kept** [kept])

keep back [ˈkiːp ˈbæk] *verb* **(a)** to hold on to something which you should give to someone; *they kept back £20 from the deposit to cover damage to the carpet* **(b) to keep something back from someone** = not to tell someone information which you could give to them; *I have the feeling that she's keeping something back from us*

keep down [ˈkiːp ˈdaʊn] *verb* **(a)** to keep at a low level; *keep your voice down, the police will hear us!*

(b) to stay crouched and hidden; *keep down behind the wall so that they won't see us*

keeper ['ki:pə] *noun* **(a)** person in charge of a certain type of animal in a zoo; *an elephant keeper* **(b)** person in charge of a section of a museum; *the keeper of Roman coins in the British Museum* **(c)** *(sport)* = GOALKEEPER, WICKETKEEPER **(d)** fruit which can be kept in good condition for a long time; *you should eat those pears immediately as they are not good keepers*

keep-fit ['ki:pfɪt] *adjective* using exercises to keep you fit; *she goes to keep-fit classes twice a week*

keeping ['ki:pɪŋ] *noun* **(a)** safe keeping = care of something in a safe place; *we left the documents with the bank for safe keeping* **(b)** in keeping with = fitting in with, matching; *the dinner plates are antiques, in keeping with the furniture in the dining room*

keep off ['ki:p 'ɒf] *verb* **(a)** not to walk on; *keep off the grass!* **(b)** not to use; *if he can keep off drink, his health will improve*

keep on ['ki:p 'ɒn] *verb* to continue to do something; *my computer keeps on breaking down; the cars kept on moving even though the road was covered with snow*

keep on at ['ki:p 'ɒn ət] *verb (informal)* to criticize someone constantly; *she keeps on at me about getting a job* = she tells me all the time that I should get a job

keep out ['ki:p 'aut] *verb* **(a)** to stop someone going in; *there were 'Keep Out!' notices round the building site; we put up notices telling people to keep their dogs out of the field where the lambs are* **(b)** not to get involved; *he kept out of the quarrel; try to keep out of trouble with the police*

keepsake ['ki:pseɪk] *noun* thing which is given to you for you to keep to remind you of the giver; *the old pen was given to me by a friend as a keepsake*

keep to ['ki:p 'tu] *verb* **(a)** to stay in a position; *when you drive in France, remember to keep to the right* **(b)** not to move away from a subject; *let's keep to the subject of widening the motorway* **(c)** to keep something to yourself = to keep something secret, not to talk about something; *he doesn't want to talk about his illness, he'd rather keep it to himself*

keep up ['ki:p 'ʌp] *verb* to make something stay at the same high level; *he finds it very difficult to keep up his German; they won't be able to keep up that speed for very long; keep it up!* = continue doing what you doing!; *you're doing very well - keep it up!*

keep up with ['ki:p 'ʌp wɪð] *verb* **(a)** to go at the same speed; *my foot hurts, that's why I can't keep up with the others; his salary hasn't kept up with the cost of living;* to keep up with the Joneses = to try to do the same things as your neighbours or friends to show that you have as much money as they have **(b)** to keep yourself informed about; *have you kept up with the news from Russia?*

keg [keg] *noun* small barrel; *we bought a keg of beer for the party;* keg beer = beer kept in metal kegs under pressure

kennel ['kenl] *noun* small house for a dog; *our dog has a kennel in the garden;* kennels = place where dogs can be left when their owners go away or where dogs are bred; *the left their dog in kennels while they went on holiday*

Kenya ['kenjə or 'ki:njə] *noun* large country in eastern Africa; *Kenya is home to some of Africa's most magnificent big game animals* (NOTE: capital: **Nairobi**; people: **Kenyans**; languages: **Swahili**, **English**; currency: **Kenyan shilling**)

Kenyan ['kenjən] **1** *adjective* referring to Kenya; *Kenyan national parks are famous for their big game* **2** *noun* person from Kenya; *Kenyans are good long-distance runners*

kept [kept] *see* KEEP

kerb [kɜ:b] *noun* stone edging to a pavement; *try not to hit the kerb when you park; she slipped on the edge of the kerb and twisted her ankle*

kerbstone ['kɜ:bstəʊn] *noun* stone edging to a pavement; *she tripped over a kerbstone and hurt her ankle*

kernel ['kɜ:nl] *noun* **(a)** softer edible part inside the hard shell of a nut; *squirrels bite into nuts to get at the kernel* **(b)** the centre, the essential part; *at the heart of every classical myth is a kernel of truth* (NOTE: do not confuse with **colonel**)

kerosene ['kerəsi:n] *noun especially US* paraffin, thin oil for lamps, heaters, etc.; *at night we lit kerosene lamps round the campsite*

ketchup ['ketʃʌp] *noun* spiced tomato sauce, usually available in cafés, etc., in bottles or sachets; *do you want ketchup with your hamburgers?* (NOTE: American spelling is also **catsup**)

kettle ['ketl] *noun* container with a lid and a spout, used for boiling water; *turn the gas up, the kettle hasn't boiled yet; each bedroom has an electric kettle, tea bags and sachets of instant coffee;* to put the kettle on = to start heating the water in a kettle; *I've just put the kettle on so we can all have a cup of tea;* the kettle's boiling = the water in the kettle is boiling; *see also* DIFFERENT

kettledrum ['ketldrʌm] *noun* large metal drum with a round bottom; *the parade started with trumpeters and kettledrums*

key [ki:] **1** *noun* **(a)** piece of metal used to open a lock; *I can't start the car, I've lost the key; where did you put the front door key?;* key ring = ring on which you can put several keys to keep them together; *the garage gave me a key ring with their telephone number on it* **(b)** part of a computer, piano, etc., which you push down with your fingers; *the 'F' key always sticks; there are sixty-four keys on the keyboard;* control key = key on a computer which works part of a program; shift key = key which makes a typewriter or computer move to capital letters **(c)** explanation of a problem; *the key to the signs is written under the diagram* **(d)** system of musical tones; *the symphony is written in the key of F major* **2** *adjective* most important; *the key person in the company is the sales manager; oil is a key industry* **3** *verb* to type letters or figures on a keyboard; *she keyed in the data*

keyboard ['ki:bɔ:d] **1** *noun* set of keys on a computer, piano, etc.; *she spilled her coffee on the computer keyboard; he practises on the keyboard every day* **2** *verb* to put data into a computer, using a keyboard; *she was keyboarding the figures*

keyboarder ['ki:bɔ:də] *noun* person who keyboards data into a computer; *we need another keyboarder to help clear the backlog of data waiting to be keyboarded*

keyed up ['ki:d 'ʌp] *adjective* nervous and tense; *he was very keyed up before the tennis semi-final*

keyhole ['ki:həʊl] *noun* hole in a lock which you put a key into; *they found him outside her bedroom, looking through the keyhole*; **keyhole surgery** = surgery where tiny surgical instruments are sent into the body through a thin tube

keynote ['ki:nəʊt] *noun* main theme; *the keynote of the meeting was the need for political compromise*; **keynote speech** = main speech at a conference; *the keynote speech was delivered by the Home Secretary*

keypad ['ki:pæd] *noun* set of special keys on a computer keyboard, used for various applications; **numeric keypad** = set of nine numbered keys on a computer keyboard; *you can use the numeric keypad to enter the numbers*

kg = KILOGRAM

khaki ['kɑ:ki] **1** *noun* dull yellow-brown cloth used for soldiers' uniforms; *the troops wore khaki uniforms* **2** *adjective* dull yellow-brown colour; *I don't like those dull khaki cushions in the living room*

kick [kɪk] **1** **(a)** *noun* hitting with your foot; *the goalkeeper gave the ball a kick* **(b)** *(informal)* thrill, feeling of excitement; *he gets a kick out of watching a football match on TV*; **he did it for kicks** = to give himself some excitement **(c)** *(informal)* strong effect; *my! this drink has a kick in it!* **(d)** recoil of a gun; *watch out, this rifle has a powerful kick and can hurt your shoulder* **2** *verb* **(a)** to hit something with your foot; *he kicked the ball into the net*; *she kicked her little brother* **(b)** *(informal)* **to kick the habit** = the get rid of a bad habit; *I wish he's kick the habit of whistling while he works*; *he doesn't smoke any more - he kicked the habit a couple of months ago; see also* BUCKET **(c) to kick yourself** = to be annoyed with yourself because of doing something silly, forgetting something, etc.; *I could have kicked myself as soon as I said it; they must be kicking themselves now for not having bought the house when they had the chance*

kickback ['kɪkbæk] *noun* *(informal)* bribe, illegal commission paid to someone who helps a business deal; *he has been suspended on full pay while the allegations that he accepted kickbacks are being investigated*

kick in ['kɪk 'ɪn] *verb* **(a)** to make something open by kicking; *the police kicked the door in* **(b)** *(informal)* to start to have an effect; *the car really moves when the turbocharger kicks in* **(c)** *US (informal)* to contribute money to something; *if everyone kicks in $10, then we will soon get the amount we need*

kick off ['kɪk 'ɒf] *verb* **(a)** to start a game of football; *they kicked off at 3.00 and by half-time there was still no score* **(b)** to start; *let's kick off with a discussion about modern painters*

kick-off ['kɪkɒf] *noun* start of a football game; *what time is the kick-off?*

kick out ['kɪk 'aʊt] *verb* to get rid of someone; *he was kicked out of the club for not paying his subscription*; *they kicked him out of the team because he had started to take drugs*

kick start ['kɪk 'stɑ:t] **1** *noun* pedal lever for starting a motorbike engine; *you'll need the kick start on cold mornings* **2** *verb* **(a)** to start a motorbike using a pedal; *he kick started the engine* **(b)** *(informal)* to give a sharp*

boost to something; *the government's plans to kick start the economy*

kick up ['kɪk 'ʌp] *verb (informal)* **to kick up a fuss** = to make a fuss, a row; *the kids are only messing about - there's no need to kick up a fuss by calling the police*

kid [kɪd] **1** *noun* **(a)** *(informal)* child; *there were a few school kids on their bicycles*; *I saw your kids going off on the bus this morning*; *they've been married a few years, and have got a couple of kids*; **kid brother** = younger brother; *I have to stay in to babysit my kid brother* **(b)** young goat; *a little white kid* **(c)** very soft leather made from the skin of a goat; *he wore a pair of kid gloves*; *(informal)* **to treat someone with kid gloves** = to treat someone very carefully; *he needs to be treated with kid gloves so as not to upset him* **2** *verb (informal)* to make someone believe something which is not true; **I was only kidding** = I didn't mean it; **no kidding?** = is it really true? (NOTE: **kidding - kidded**)

kidnap ['kɪdnæp] *verb* to steal a child or a person and take them away illegally; *the millionaire was kidnapped and held for two weeks* (NOTE: **kidnapping - kidnapped**)

kidnapper ['kɪdnæpə] *noun* person who kidnaps; *the kidnappers were members of an extreme political group*

kidney ['kɪdni] *noun* **(a)** one of a pair of organs in animals that remove impurities from the blood and pass them into the urine; **kidney machine** = apparatus through which a patient's blood is passed to be cleaned when his kidneys have failed; *he has to be linked to the kidney machine for several hours each week*; **kidney stone** = hard mass like a little piece of stone, which forms inside a kidney; **kidney transplant** = operation to transplant a kidney; *the kidney transplant was a success* (NOTE: the technical adjective relating to the kidneys is **renal**) **(b)** this organ from a lamb, pig, etc., used as food; *steak and kidney pie* **(c)** **kidney bean** = type of bean with reddish seeds which look a little like kidneys; *kidney beans are the beans used in chilli con carne*

kill [kɪl] *verb* **(a)** to make someone *or* something die; *he was sentenced to death for killing his wife*; *the lack of rain has killed all the crops*; *the car hit a cat and killed it*; *six people were killed in the plane crash* **(b)** **to kill time** = to spend time while waiting for something important; *I killed some time waiting for the train by having a coffee*; **to kill two birds with one stone** = to get two successful results from one action; *while I'm in London for the conference I could kill two birds with one stone and visit my parents*; *(informal)* **my feet are killing me** = my feet are hurting; *(informal)* **he was killing himself laughing** = he was laughing a lot

killer ['kɪlə] *noun* **(a)** person who kills; *the police are still hunting for the killer*; **serial killer** = person who has committed several murders, one after the other; *because there are similarities between the murders, the police think they are dealing with a serial killer* **(b)** which kills; *a killer flu virus*; **killer whale** = medium-sized black and white whale which eats fish and seals

killing ['kɪlɪŋ] *noun* **(a)** murder, putting a person or animal to death; *the police are investigating the killing of the tourists*; *there have been reports of killings in the villages*; *the killing of rhinos has been banned* **(b)**

to make a killing = to make a very large profit; *he made a killing on the stock market*

killjoy ['kɪldʒɔɪ] *noun* person who stops other people from enjoying themselves; *Aunt Mary is such a killjoy - she's always telling us not to do this, not to do that*

kiln [kɪln] *noun* oven for making pottery, bricks, etc.; *the potter carefully took the jugs and vases out of the kiln*

kilo ['kiːləʊ] *noun* = KILOGRAM; *he weighs 78 kilos*; *I want to buy two kilos of sugar*; *these oranges cost 75p a kilo* (NOTE: plural is **kilos**)

kilobyte ['kɪləʊbaɪt] *noun* unit of storage for a computer equal to 1,024 bytes

kilocalorie ['kiːləʊkælərɪ] *noun* one thousand calories, the amount of heat needed to raise the temperature of one kilogram of water by one degree Celsius

kilogram ['kɪləɡræm] *noun* measure of weight (= one thousand grams) (NOTE: written **kg** after figures: **20kg**)

kilometre *US* **kilometer** [kɪ'lɒmɪtə] *noun* one thousand metres; *the car was only doing 80 kilometres an hour when the accident occurred*; *the two roads join about three kilometres from here*; *the town is about ten kilometres from the sea*; *the car has just had its 10,000 kilometre service* = it has been checked by the garage after having travelled 10,000 kilometres (NOTE: written **km** after figures: **70km**)

kilowatt (kW) ['kɪləwɒt] *noun* one thousand Watts

kilt [kɪlt] *noun* skirt, usually of tartan cloth, worn by men in Scotland, and also by women; *she wore a red kilt*; *Scottish soldiers wear kilts*

kin [kɪn] *noun* **next-of-kin** = nearest relative(s); *after the fatal accident, the police informed the next-of-kin*; *names of the victims will not be released until their next-of-kin have been informed; see also* KITH

kind [kaɪnd] **1** *noun* **(a)** sort, type; *an ant is a kind of insect*; *we have several kinds of apples in our garden*; *we discussed all kinds of things* **(b)** *(informal)* **kind of** = in a certain way; *I was kind of annoyed when she told me that* **(c)** **of a kind** = similar; *the three sisters are three of a kind* **2** *adjective* friendly, helpful, thinking about other people; *it's very kind of you to offer to help*; *how kind of you to invite him to your party!*; *you should always be kind to little children*; *he's a kind old gentleman* (NOTE: **kinder - kindest**)

kindergarten ['kɪndəɡɑːtn] *noun* school for little children; *we send our youngest son to the local kindergarten*

kindhearted [kaɪnd'hɑːtɪd] *adjective* kind and thoughtful towards other people; *she's such a kindhearted person, always ready to help if anyone is ill*

kindle ['kɪndl] *verb* **(a)** to make something catch fire; *a cigarette end must have kindled the dead leaves* **(b)** to make someone start to feel something; *the aim of the class is to kindle an interest in art*

kindly ['kaɪndlɪ] **1** *adjective* thoughtful and pleasant; *a kindly neighbour brought him soup when he was ill* **2** *adverb* in a thoughtful or pleasant way; *he behaved very kindly towards me*; **not to take kindly to** = not to like; *she doesn't take kindly to being told she's fat* **(b)** *(formal)* please, if you don't mind; *kindly shut*

the door; *customers are kindly requested to pay at the cash desk*

kindness ['kaɪndnəs] *noun* being kind; *she was touched by his kindness*

kindred spirit ['kɪndrɪd 'spɪrɪt] *noun* person who thinks in the same way as you do; *Mary and a bunch of kindred spirits got together to form the protest group*

king [kɪŋ] *noun* **(a)** man who governs a country by right of birth; *the king and queen came to visit the town* (NOTE: **king** is spelt with a capital letter when used with a name or when referring to a particular person: **King Henry VIII**) **(b)** main piece in chess; *she moved her knight to place his king in check* **(c)** *(in cards)* the card with the face of a bearded man, coming after the ace and before the queen in value; *he knew he could win when he drew the king of spades* **(d)** champion, top person; *he's king of the pop music scene*; *the lion is king of the jungle*

COMMENT: there have been thirty-five kings of England since William the Conqueror invaded in 1066. The most common names have been Henry and Edward (eight kings each) followed by George (six kings). The first king of England and Scotland was James I (he was previously James VI of Scotland). The most recent English king was George VI, father of the present queen

kingdom ['kɪŋdʌm] *noun* **(a)** land ruled over by a king or queen; *the United Kingdom*; *fairy stories about a magic kingdom* **(b)** part of the world of nature; *the animal kingdom* **(c)** *(informal)* **till kingdom come** = for ever, for a very long time; *on Saturday mornings you can wait till kingdom come to be served*

kingfisher ['kɪŋfɪʃə] *noun* small bright blue bird that dives for fish; *we caught a glimpse of a kingfisher down by the pond*

kingpin ['kɪŋpɪn] *noun* main person in an organization; *she's been the kingpin of the office for years - however are we going to manage without her?*

king-size *or* **kingsized** ['kɪŋsaɪzd] *adjective* very large, much larger than normal; *they have bought a king-size bed*; *we had to take out a king-sized overdraft to buy the car*

kink [kɪŋk] *noun* **(a)** twist in something that should be straight; *can you straighten the flex, it's got a kink in it* **(b)** *(informal)* peculiar mental state; *he must have a kink about women's underwear*

kinky ['kɪŋkɪ] *adjective* *(slang)* sexually odd or strange

kinsman, kinswoman ['kɪnzmən *or* 'kɪnzwʊmən] *noun* relative, someone form your family; *she's a kinswoman of the former president* (NOTE: plural is **kinsmen** *or* **kinswomen**)

kiosk ['kiːɒsk] *noun* small wooden shelter, for selling goods out of doors; *she runs the newspaper kiosk next to the station*; **telephone kiosk** = shelter with a public telephone in it; *turn right at the telephone kiosk on the corner*

kip [kɪp] **1** *noun* *(informal)* short sleep; *I was so tired I lay down on the sofa and had a kip* **2** *verb* *(informal)* to lie down to go to sleep; *you can kip down on the sofa if you want*; *can we kip here tonight? - we've missed the last bus* (NOTE: **kipped**)

kipper ['kɪpə] *noun* split herring, salted and smoked; *I don't like kippers for breakfast, they're usually too bony*

COMMENT: kippers are traditionally eaten for breakfast, grilled, and then served hot with butter

kirk [kɜːk] *noun (in Scotland)* church; *he's the minister at the old kirk*

kiss [kɪs] **1** *noun* **(a)** touching someone with your lips to show love; *she gave the baby a kiss*; **to blow someone a kiss** = to show your love for someone by touching your lips with your hands and making a gesture to the person at a distance; *as the train left, she blew him a kiss* **(b) kiss of life** = bringing someone back to life by breathing into his mouth; **kiss of death** = something which ruins a business, etc.; *the new supermarket is the kiss of death to small businesses in the town* (NOTE: plural is **kisses**) **2** *verb* to touch someone with your lips to show that you love them; *she kissed her daughter and walked away*; *they kissed each other goodbye*; *the politicians are in town, shaking hands with voters and kissing babies*

kit [kɪt] *noun* **(a)** clothes and personal equipment, usually packed for carrying; *did you bring your tennis kit?* **(b) first aid kit** = box with bandages and dressings kept to be used in an emergency; *the doctor rushed to the scene with his first aid kit*; **repair kit** = box with tools for repairing a machine, especially for repairing a car; *there is a repair kit provided in the boot of each car* **(c)** box containing pieces which can be put together to make a piece of furniture, a model, etc.; *he spent the afternoon building a model aircraft from a kit*; *the new garden furniture arrived as a kit and we had to put it together ourselves*

kitbag ['kɪtbæg] *noun* long round bag which a soldier uses for carrying clothes and equipment; *the soldiers crowded into the train, all carrying cases and kitbags*

kitchen ['kɪtʃən] *noun* room where you cook food; *she put the meat down on the kitchen table*; *if you're hungry, have a look in the kitchen to see if there's anything to eat*; *don't come in with dirty shoes on - I've just washed the kitchen floor*; *see also* FITTED

kitchen cabinet ['kɪtʃən 'kæbɪnət] *noun* private unofficial group of advisers and friends, who advise a Prime Minister; *he was criticized for consulting his kitchen cabinet more often than his ministers*

kitchenette [kɪtʃə'net] *noun* small kitchen (in a corner of a living room); *each studio flat is equipped with a bathroom, kitchenette and balcony*

kitchen garden ['kɪtʃən 'gɑːdən] *noun* part of a garden where fruit and vegetables are grown; *he spent the morning weeding in the kitchen garden*

kite [kaɪt] **(a)** *noun* toy made of light wood and paper or cloth which is flown in a strong wind on the end of a string; *he flew his kite from the top of the hill*; *the wind nearly blew the kite away* **(b)** large bird of prey; *red kites have started nesting in the cliffs*

kitsch [kɪtʃ] *noun* popular works of art or decorative objects that are brightly coloured but lack artistic taste; *the market was full of awful kitsch but was crowded with tourists*; *she has a set of really kitsch flying ducks on the wall* (NOTE: no plural)

kitten ['kɪtn] *noun* **(a)** young cat; *the kittens are very playful*; *the cat carefully picked up her kitten by the scruff of its neck* **(b)** *(informal)* **to have kittens** = to be

very nervous; *she was having kittens, waiting for her interview*

kitty ['kɪti] *noun* **(a)** money which has been collected from each member of a group of people to be used for someone later; *we each put £5 into the kitty for the office party* **(b)** child's name for a cat; *she called out 'kitty, kitty, kitty' but the cat didn't come*

kiwi ['kiːwiː] *noun* **(a)** bird which cannot fly, native to New Zealand **(b)** *(informal)* New Zealander

kiwi fruit ['kiːwi 'fruːt] *noun* small tropical fruit, with a hairy skin and green flesh; *kiwi fruit are full of vitamins* **(b)** (NOTE: no plural)

Kleenex ['kliːneks] *noun* trademark for a paper handkerchief; *there is a box of Kleenex in the bathroom* (NOTE: there is a plural form **Kleenexes** which is used when referring to several handkerchiefs, but the word **Kleenex** can also be used as the plural form: **a box of Kleenex**)

km = KILOMETRE; *it is 2km from here to the Post Office*; *the furthest distance I have travelled by train is 800km*; *the road crosses the railway line about 2km from here*

knack [næk] *noun* special skill or ability; *he has the knack of saying exactly the right thing*; *she has a knack of making people feel at home*; *there's a special knack in making Yorkshire pudding*

knackered ['nækəd] *adjective (informal)* tired out; *I've been cleaning the kitchen all day - I'm knackered*

knapsack ['næpsæk] *noun (old)* rucksack, a bag carried on the back of a walker; *he put extra clothes and a bottle of water in his knapsack*

knave [neɪv] *noun (in cards)* jack, the card with the face of a young man, with a value between the queen and the ten; *he played the knave of diamonds*

knead [niːd] *verb* to press and fold dough before it is cooked to make bread; *pizza dough must be kneaded for five minutes*

knee [niː] *noun* **(a)** joint between the thigh and lower leg, where your leg bends; *she sat the child on her knee*; *he went down on one knee and asked her to marry him*; **knee socks** = long socks which go up to your knees **(b)** part of a pair of trousers that covers the knee; *my jeans have holes in both knees*

kneecap ['niːkæp] **1** *noun* little bone in front of the knee; *he hurt his kneecap when he fell* **2** *verb* to punish someone by shooting him in the kneecap; *the terrorists kneecapped the young man*

knee-deep [niː'diːp] *adjective* **knee-deep in** = up to your knees in; *they had to walk knee-deep in snow for several miles*

knee-high ['niːhaɪ] *adjective* reaching up to your knees; *she wore a pair of knee-high boots; (informal, of a child)* **knee-high to a grasshopper** = very small; *when I saw him last he was just knee-high to a grasshopper*

kneel [niːl] *verb* to go down on your knees; *everyone knelt down and the priest gave his blessing*; *she knelt beside his bed and listened to his breathing* (NOTE: kneeling - kneeled *or* knelt [nelt])

knew [njuː] *see* KNOW

knickers ['nɪkəz] *noun* woman's or girl's underwear; *she bought a pair of blue knickers* (NOTE: plural; for one item say **a pair of knickers**)

knife [naɪf] **1** *noun* instrument used for cutting, with a metal blade fixed in a handle; *put out a knife, fork and spoon for each person*; *you need a sharp knife to cut meat*; **bread knife** = special large knife for cutting bread (NOTE: plural is **knives** [naɪvz]) **2** *verb* to stab someone with a knife; *he was knifed in the back during the fight* (NOTE: **knifes - knifing - knifed**)

knight [naɪt] **1** *noun* **(a)** man honoured by a king for services to his country (and taking the title 'Sir'); *he was made a knight*; *see also* BARONET **(b)** *(in medieval times)* brave soldier often devoted to the service of a lady; *King Arthur and his knights*; *many knights were killed in the Wars of the Roses* **(c)** one of two pieces in a chess set with a horse's head; *with a clever move she took his knight* **2** *verb* to make someone a knight; *he was knighted for services to education*

> COMMENT: knights are addressed as 'Sir', followed by their Christian name and family name; their wives are addressed as 'Lady' followed by the family name (hence Sir John Smith's wife is addressed as 'Lady Smith')

knighthood [ˈnaɪthʊd] *noun* position of being a knight; *the actor was given a knighthood in the New Year's honours list*

knit [nɪt] *verb* **(a)** to make a piece of clothing out of wool by linking threads together with the aid of two long needles; *my mother is knitting me a pullover*; *she was wearing a blue knitted hat* (NOTE: **knitting - knitted**) **(b) to knit your brow** = to wrinkle your forehead as you try to do something difficult; *she knit her brow as she tried to understand the guidebook* (NOTE: **knitting - knit**)

knitter [ˈnɪtə] *noun* person who knits; *mother's a marvellous knitter - look at the jumper she gave me for Christmas*

knitting [ˈnɪtɪŋ] *noun* **(a)** action of making something out of wool with knitting needles; *her great hobby is knitting*; **knitting needle** = thin plastic or metal stick used for knitting; **knitting pattern** = detailed instructions for knitting a garment **(b)** piece of work which is in the process of being made by knitting; *she brought her knitting with her to the conference*

knitwear [ˈnɪtweə] *noun* knitted clothes such as jumpers, pullovers, etc.; *the knitwear department is on the first floor* (NOTE: no plural)

knives [naɪvz] *noun see* KNIFE

knob [nɒb] *noun* **(a)** rounded handle on a door, a chest of drawers, etc.; *to open the door, just the knob* **(b)** round button which you turn on a radio, TV, etc.; *turn the knob to increase the volume* **(c)** round lump; *put a knob of butter in the frying pan*

knock [nɒk] **1** *noun* **(a)** sound made by hitting something; *suddenly, there was a knock at the door*; hitting something; *she had a knock on the head* **2** *verb* **(a)** to hit something; *knock twice before going in*; *you'll need a heavy hammer to knock that nail in* **(b)** to criticize; *she wrote an article knocking the Prime Minister* **(c)** *(of car engine)* to ignite badly in the cylinder and made a knocking sound; *the car has started to knock, so the timing needs adjusting*

knock about [nɒk əˈbaʊt] *verb* **(a)** to wander about doing nothing; *he spent several years knocking about the back streets of New Orleans* **(b) to knock someone about** = to beat someone; *he was badly knocked about*

in the fight; *the cathedral was badly knocked about in the bombardment* **(c)** to be in a place; *can you see my hammer knocking about anywhere?*

knock back [nɒk ˈbæk] *verb* **(a)** to drink a drink quickly; *he knocked back his drink and ran outside* **(b)** to cost someone a sum; *it will knock me back a few hundred pounds*

knock down [nɒk ˈdaʊn] *verb* **(a)** to make something fall down; *they are going to knock down the old house to build a new estate* **(b)** to hit; *she was knocked down by a car* **(c)** to reduce a price; *they knocked the price down to £50* **(d)** to sell something to someone at an auction; *it was knocked down to a German buyer for £250*

knock-down [ˈnɒkdaʊn] *adjective* **knock-down price** = very low price; *they're selling off the old stock at knock-down prices*

knocker [ˈnɒkə] *noun* **(a)** knob or ring attached to a door which can be banged against it to call attention; *the bell on the front door doesn't work, so you have to use the knocker* **(b)** *(informal)* person who is always criticizing something; *the letter in the paper should silence the government's knockers*

knock off [nɒk ˈɒf] *verb* **(a)** to make something fall off by hitting it; *the cat knocked the glass off the shelf* **(b)** *(informal)* to stop work; *the workmen all knocked off at 4.30* **(c)** to reduce the price of something (by an amount); *he knocked £1000 off the price of the car*

knock-on [ˈnɒkɒn] *adjective* **knock-on effect** = effect which follows on from something; *the airport strike had a knock-on effect on the tourist industry*

knock out [nɒk ˈaʊt] *verb* **(a)** to hit someone so hard that he is no longer conscious; *she was knocked out by a blow on the head*; *the boxer was knocked out in the third round* **(b)** to make someone go to sleep; *the doctor gave her something which knocked her out*

knockout [ˈnɒkaʊt] *noun* **(a)** *(in boxing)* action of hitting someone so hard that he loses consciousness; *he won by a knockout (KO) in the third round* **(b)** **knockout (competition)** = contest where several teams or players compete against one another and each one that loses then leaves the competition; *there are only eight teams left in the knockout competition*

knock up [nɒk ˈʌp] *verb* **(a)** to waken; *can you knock me up early tomorrow morning?* **(b)** *(informal)* to put something together rapidly; *she knocked up a dinner for six people at half an hour's notice*; *he knocked up a garden shed out of old pieces of timber* **(c)** *(slang)* to make someone pregnant

knock-up [ˈnɒkˌʌp] *noun* *(in tennis)* practise time before a game when the players hit the ball backwards and forwards over the net

knot [nɒt] **1** *noun* **(a)** loop of the ends of a piece of string, rope, etc., fastened together; *Boy Scouts are supposed to be able to tie knots*; *is the knot of my tie straight?*; **to tie the knot** = to get married **(b)** small group; *knots of people stood and watched the firemen* **(c)** measure of speed used to show the speed of a ship or of the wind; *the ship was doing 22 knots when she hit the rocks*; *there's a wind speed of 60 knots* **(d)** round place on a piece of wood where a branch or twig was originally growing; *the plank is full of knots* **2** *verb* **(a)** to tie a knot in something; *he knotted the end of the rope* **(b)** *(slang) (showing annoyance and contempt)* **get knotted!** = go away, don't bother me; *if they ask for* *money again, tell them to get knotted* (NOTE: **knotting - knotted**)

knotty ['nɒti] *adjective* difficult to solve; *this is one of the knottiest problems we've ever had to deal with* (NOTE: **knottier - knottiest**)

know [nəu] **1** *verb* **(a)** to have learned something, to have information about something; *do you know how to start the computer?; he didn't know she had died; how was I to know she wasn't his wife?; you knew it would be expensive; do you know the Spanish for 'one - two - three'?; his secretary doesn't know where he is; he is known to have right-wing views; is she in trouble? - not that I know of* **(b)** to have met someone; *I know your sister - we were at school together; I used to know a man called Jones who worked in your company;* to **know someone by sight** = to know who someone is, even though you have never met him or her **(c)** to have been to a place often; *I know Paris very well; she doesn't know Germany at all* **(d)** to experience; *she knew years of poverty before she became famous; he knows what it is like to be out of work* **(e)** *you never know* = perhaps; *you never know, she may still turn up;* as far as I know = all I know is that; *as far as I know, he left by car at 6 p.m.; is she in trouble? - not as far as I know* **(f)** to **know better than** = to have the experience to avoid making a mistake; *you should know better than to wake grandfather up when he's having his afternoon nap* (NOTE: **knowing - knew** [njuː] - **has known**) **2** *noun (informal)* **in the know** = knowing something that most people do not know; *those in the know say that's the best restaurant in town; someone in the know gave me the tip*

know-all ['nəuɔːl] *noun (informal)* person who claims he knows everything; *I don't like him at all - he's a little know-all*

know-how ['nəuhau] *noun (informal)* knowledge about how something is made or is done; *this book gives you all the know-how you'll need about plumbing*

knowing ['nəuɪŋ] *adjective* showing that you know about something; *he gave her a knowing wink*

knowingly ['nəuɪŋli] *adverb* **(a)** deliberately, on purpose; *he is accused of knowingly handling stolen goods* **(b)** showing that you know about something; *he glanced knowingly in her direction*

knowledge ['nɒlɪdʒ] *noun* **(a)** general facts or information that people know; *an encyclopaedia is supposed to list all human knowledge* **(b)** what a particular person knows about something; *to my knowledge, he left the house at 10 p.m.; the police have no knowledge of the accident;* to the best of my knowledge = as far as I know; *to the best of my knowledge, no one else has seen this document; it is*

common knowledge that = everyone knows that; *it is common knowledge that his wife wants to emigrate*

knowledgeable ['nɒlɪdʒəbl] *adjective* who knows a lot about something; *he's very knowledgeable about the train services*

known [nəun] *adjective* which is known; **a known quantity** = something, a fact or a situation, which you know about; *when trading with American companies, at least you are dealing with a known quantity* (NOTE: the opposite is an **unknown quantity**)

knuckle ['nʌkl] *noun* finger joint; *she hurt her knuckles when she fell;* to **rap someone over the knuckles** = to criticize someone; *he was rapped over the knuckles for having overspent his budget*

knuckle down ['nʌkl 'daun] *verb* to start working hard; *if you don't knuckle down, you'll soon be out of a job*

knuckle under ['nʌkl 'ʌndə] *verb (informal)* to give in to someone; *she refused to knuckle under, and claimed her rights; we will never knuckle under to threats from neighbouring states*

KO = KNOCKOUT

koala [kəu'ɑːlə] *noun* **koala (bear)** = small Australian animal which carries its young in a pouch and lives in trees; *koalas eat eucalyptus leaves*

kookaburra ['kukəbʌrə] *noun* large Australian kingfisher

Koran [kɒ'rɑːn] *noun* holy book of the Muslims; *the mullahs gave readings from the Koran*

Korea [kə'riə] *noun* two countries in the Far East, west of Japan, formed of North Korea and South Korea; *South Korea and Japan are co-hosts of the football World Cup in 2002* (NOTE: capital of South Korea: **Seoul**; capital of North Korea: **Pyongyang**; people: **South Koreans, North Koreans**; language: **Korean**; currency: **won**)

Korean [kə'riən] **1** *adjective* referring to Korea; *Korean cars are exported all over the world* **2** *noun* **(a)** person from Korea; *the Koreans won two medals in the speed skating at the Olympics* **(b)** language spoken in Korea; *Korean is related to Japanese*

korma ['kɔːmə] *noun* type Indian of meat dish made with curry and cream; *we ordered chicken korma and rice*

kph = KILOMETRES PER HOUR

krypton ['krɪptɒn] *noun* inert gas found in very small quantities in the atmosphere (NOTE: Chemical element: chemical symbol: **Kr**; atomic number: **36**)

kudos ['kjuːdɒs] *noun (informal)* glory, fame; *you will win a lot of kudos if you pull this deal off* (NOTE: no plural)

kW = KILOWATT

Ll

L, l [el] twelfth letter of the alphabet, between K and M; *Louise wrote her initial 'L' on the back of the letter;* see also L-PLATES

l = LITRE

lab [læb] *noun short for* LABORATORY

label ['leɪbl] **1** *noun* **(a)** piece of paper, plastic, etc., attached to something to show price, contents, someone's name and address, etc.; **address label =** label with an address on it; **tie-on label =** label with a piece of string attached so that it can be tied on to an item; *put a luggage label on your rucksack if you don't want it to get lost; she stuck a label on the parcel; the price on the label is £25.00* **(b)** especially, the name of a recording company on a record or CD; *the group have made their first single on the Virgin label* **2** *verb* to put a label on something; *all the goods are labelled with the correct price* (NOTE: **labelling - labelled** but American spelling is **labeling - labeled**)

laboratory [lə'bɒrətri *US* 'læbrətɔːri] *noun* place where scientific experiments, testing and research are carried out; *she's a chemist working in the university laboratories; all products are tested in our own laboratories* (NOTE: plural is **laboratories**)

Labor Day ['leɪbə 'deɪ] *noun* American and Canadian national holiday celebrated on the first Monday in September

laborious [lə'bɔːriəs] *adjective* **(a)** involving a lot of work; *I'm afraid it is a very laborious task, moving that pile of sand to the back of the house* **(b)** showing signs of a lot of effort; *his laborious newspaper articles are difficult to read*

laboriously [lə'bɔːriəsli] *adverb* involving a lot of work or effort; *he laboriously copied the chapter of the novel out by hand*

labor union ['leɪbə 'juːniən] *noun US* = TRADE UNION

labour *US* **labor** ['leɪbə] **1** *noun* **(a)** (hard) work; *after digging the garden, it is good to lie on the grass and rest from your labours;* **to charge for materials and labour =** to charge for both the materials used in a job and also the hours of work involved; **hard labour =** prison sentence where the prisoner has to do hard manual work (NOTE: plural can be **labours** in this meaning) **(b)** all workers, the workforce; *cheap labour is difficult to find;* **sweated labour =** workers who work hard for little money; **labour dispute =** argument between management and workers **(c)** the process of childbirth; *she went into labour at home, and her husband drove her to the hospital; she was in labour for 12 hours* **2** *verb* **(a)** to work very hard; *they laboured night and day to finish the project in time* **(b) to labour under an impression** *or* **a delusion =** to have a wrong impression, to assume something which is quite wrong; *he was labouring under the delusion that air fares were cheaper in Europe than in the USA;* **to labour the point =** to discuss something too long; *I*

don't want to labour the point, but may I raise the question for the third time?

Labour *or* **Labour Party** ['leɪbə 'pɑːti] *noun* political party, one of the main political parties in Britain, which is in favour of state involvement in industry and welfare; *the polls showed a strong swing to Labour or to the Labour Party; Labour Party officials denied the reports*

laboured *US* **labored** ['leɪbəd] *adjective* showing signs of too much effort; *his laboured jokes are not really very funny*

labourer *US* **laborer** ['leɪbərə] *noun* person who does heavy work with his hands; *the construction site employs fifty labourers;* **agricultural labourer =** person who does heavy work on a farm

labour force ['leɪbə 'fɔːs] *noun* total number of workers employed in a country, an industry or an organization; *the management has made an increased offer to the labour force; we are setting up a factory in the Far East because of the cheap labour force available*

labour market ['leɪbə 'mɑːkɪt] *noun* supply of workers ready and available for work; *at the end of the school year, another 25,000 young people will come onto the labour market*

labour-saving *US* **labor-saving** ['leɪbəseɪvɪŋ] *adjective* which saves you doing hard work; *a labour-saving device*

labrador ['læbrədɔː] *noun* type of large dog, usually black or pale brown; *she brought along her new labrador puppy*

labyrinth ['læbɪrɪnθ] *noun* complicated paths, alleys, corridors, etc., where it is difficult to find your way about; *it was easy to get lost in the labyrinth of underground passageways*

lace [leɪs] **1** *noun* **(a)** thin strip of leather, cord, etc., for tying up a shoe, etc.; *his laces kept coming undone; she's too little to be able to do up her laces herself* **(b)** decorative fabric with open patterns of threads like a net; *a lace tablecloth; her wedding dress was trimmed with lace* (NOTE: no plural in this meaning) **2** *verb* **(a)** to fasten with laces; *he laced up his boots* **(b)** to add alcohol to a drink; *someone had laced her orange juice with gin*

lace-ups ['leɪsʌps] *noun* shoes which are fastened with laces; *he took off his lace-ups and put on a pair of slip-ons*

lack [læk] **1** *noun* not having enough of something; *the children are suffering from a lack of food; the project was cancelled because of lack of funds* (NOTE: no plural) **2** *verb* not to have enough of something; *the sales staff lack interest; he doesn't lack style - he puts on his sunglasses the moment the sun comes out*

lackey ['læki] *noun* person who acts like a servant; *union officials were accused of being the lackeys of the management*

lacking ['lækɪŋ] *adjective* **lacking in** = without any; *she's completely lacking in business sense*

lacklustre *US* **lackluster** ['læklʌstə] *adjective* dull, not brilliant; *the musicians gave a lacklustre performance*

laconic [lə'kɒnɪk] *adjective* using only a few words; *he gave a laconic reply; all she received from him was a laconic farewell e-mail*

laconically [lə'kɒnɪkli] *adverb* using only a few words; *'we'll see!' she said, laconically*

lacquer ['lækə] **1** *noun* **(a)** type of hard shiny varnish or paint, often used on metals; *the coating of lacquer on the chest had begun to crack* **(b)** *(old)* spray for keeping hair in place; *cover your eyes if you're using hair lacquer anywhere near your face* **2** *verb* to coat with lacquer; *it took a long time to lacquer the whole wardrobe*

lacrosse [lə'krɒs] *noun* team game played with a ball and a long-handled curved stick with a net at the end which can be used to hold or throw the ball; *she's captain of the school lacrosse team*

COMMENT: men's lacrosse is played between two teams of ten; a match is divided into four 25-minute quarters. Women's lacrosse is played with twelve players on each side, and the match is divided into two 25-minute halves. The net at the end of the stick is used to catch, carry and throw the ball; the ball may be knocked down with the hands only by the goalkeeper but may be kicked when on the ground; gloves and protective helmets are compulsory

lacy ['leɪsi] *adjective* like lace, made of a network of fine threads; *he bought her some lacy underwear; the spiders wove lacy webs between the flowers* (NOTE: **lacier - laciest**)

lad [læd] *noun* boy or young man; *don't expect too much - he's just a young lad*

ladder ['lædə] *noun* **(a)** device made of horizontal bars between two uprights, used for climbing; *the ladder was leaning against the wall; he was climbing up a ladder; she got down off the ladder* **(b)** the **promotion ladder** = series of steps by which people can be promoted; *by being appointed sales manager, he moved several steps up the promotion ladder* **(c)** series of little holes in stockings or tights; *bother, I can't wear these tights because they've got a ladder* (NOTE: American English for this is **run**)

laddie ['lædi] *noun* (in the North of England & Scotland) *(informal)* boy or young man; *what's the matter with that little laddie?; compare* LASSIE

laden ['leɪdn] *adjective* **laden with** = containing a cargo, carrying something heavy; *she was laden with shopping bags; heavily laden with* = carrying a heavy load of; *the ship was heavily laden with coal*

ladies ['leɪdɪz] *noun* **(a)** *see* LADY **(b)** *(informal)* women's toilet; *can you tell me where the ladies is, please?; the ladies is down the corridor on the right* (NOTE: is singular, and takes a singular verb)

ladle ['leɪdl] **1** *noun* large deep spoon for serving soup, etc. **2** *verb* **to ladle out** = to serve with a ladle; *she ladled the soup out into bowls*

lady ['leɪdi] *noun* **(a)** *(polite way of referring to a woman)* *there are two ladies waiting to see you US; the First Lady* = the wife of the President (NOTE: plural is **ladies**) **(b)** name given to a female worker; *she was tried by a lady judge; the lollipop lady will see you across the road* **(c)** title given to a woman, either the wife of a lord or knight, or because she is a peer in her own right (NOTE: as a title **Lady** is followed by the family name: Lord and Lady Forbes; Sir Peter and Lady Ross)

COMMENT: the wives of knights, barons, earls and viscounts are addressed as 'Lady' followed by the family name

ladybird *US* **ladybug** ['leɪdɪbɜːd *or* 'leɪdɪbʌg] *noun* type of small beetle, usually red with black spots; *I found a ladybird with six spots in the garden*

ladykiller ['leɪdɪkɪlə] *noun* *(informal)* man who is attractive to women

ladylike ['leɪdɪlaɪk] *adjective* *(way of behaving)* elegant, refined; *I wish she would behave in a more ladylike fashion*

lag [læg] **1** *noun* **(a)** interval of time between two linked happenings; *there's often a long time lag between setting up in business and seeing any results; see also* JET LAG **(b)** *(old)* *(slang)* **old lag** = person who has been put in prison many times **2** *verb* **(a)** to be behind, to fall behind; *she was lagging 10m behind the leaders* **(b)** to cover water pipes, etc., to prevent them losing heat or freezing; *make sure your pipes are lagged before the winter* (NOTE: **lagging - lagged**)

lager ['lɑːgə] *noun* **(a)** type of light beer; *he came to the bar and ordered six pints of lager; lager lout* = young person who drinks a lot of beer and creates a disturbance; *there was a crowd of lager louts on the train from Paris* **(b)** a glass of this beer; *he came to the bar and ordered six lagers*

COMMENT: lager was originally German beer, but is now widely brewed in the UK. It is served cold, while British 'bitter' is served at cellar temperature

lagoon [lə'guːn] *noun* shallow part of the sea in the tropics, surrounded by reefs; *you can swim safely in the lagoon, the sharks are out in the ocean*

laid [leɪd] *see* LAY

laid-back [leɪd'bæk] *adjective* *(informal)* relaxed, not in a hurry; *he's so laid-back, you don't realize he's the boss*

laid up [leɪd 'ʌp] *adjective* unable to work because of illness; *half the staff are laid up with flu*

lain [leɪn] *see* LIE

lair ['leə] *noun* place where a wild animal sleeps; *the lynx returned to its lair*

laird ['leəd] *noun* (in Scotland) owner of a country estate; *the laird does not allow people to camp on his land*

laissez-faire ['leseɪ'fɛə] *French noun* political theory where a government does nothing to control the economy; *laissez-faire policies resulted in increased economic activity, but contributed to a rise in imports*

laity ['leɪɪti] *noun* members of the church who are not priests; *the church may accept divorce for the laity but not for the clergy* (NOTE: no plural)

lake [leɪk] *noun* area of fresh water surrounded by land; *let's take a boat out on the lake; we can sail across the lake; the hotel stands on the shores of Lake Windermere; the Lake District* = area of north-west England where there are several large lakes

lama ['lɑːmə] *noun* Buddhist priest, especially in Tibet (NOTE: do not confuse the spelling with **llama**)

lamb [læm] *noun* **(a)** young sheep; *in spring, the fields are full of sheep and their tiny lambs* **(b)** meat from a lamb or sheep; *a leg of lamb*; *roast lamb and mint sauce* (NOTE: no plural in this meaning)

> COMMENT: The commonest forms of lamb in British cooking are lamb chops and roast lamb; traditionally, lamb is served with mint sauce

lambast [læm'beɪst] *verb* to be very critical of someone *or* something; *his plan was severely lambasted by the opposition*

lambing ['læmɪŋ] *noun* giving birth to lambs; **lambing season** = period in the spring when most lambs are born; *children were given time off school to help during the lambing season*

lame [leɪm] *adjective* **(a)** not able to walk properly; *he is lame in his left leg* **(b)** weak or unsatisfactory; *he produced a very lame excuse for not coming to the meeting* (NOTE: **lamer - lamest**)

lame duck ['leɪm 'dʌk] *adjective* **(a)** **lame duck company** = company which is in financial difficulties; *the government has promised a rescue package for lame duck companies* **(b)** **lame duck president** = president in the last part of his term of office who cannot stand for re-election and so lacks political support; *no foreign policy decisions will be made because of the lame duck presidency*

lamely ['leɪmli] *adverb* weakly; *'I'm sorry,' he said lamely*

lament [lə'ment] **1** *noun* **(a)** song or music for mourning; *a lone piper played a lament at the funeral* **(b)** expression of sadness; *his lament at the demolition of the old church* **2** *verb* to be very sad about; *we are still lamenting the closure of our local post office*

lamented [lə'mentɪd] *adjective* missed because it has gone; *an estate agent's has taken the place of our much lamented post office*; *they took down pictures of the late lamented president*

laminated ['læmɪncɪtɪd] *adjective* with several layers glued together to form a thick surface; *the windscreen is made of laminated glass*

lamp [læmp] *noun* device which makes light; *the camp site is lit by large electric lamps*; **bedside lamp** = small lamp by the side of a bed; *I can't read in bed because my bedside lamp isn't working*; **street lamp** = large light in a street; **table lamp** = lamp on a table; **standard lamp** = room lamp on a tall pole standing on the floor (NOTE: American English is **floor lamp**)

lamppost ['læmpəʊst] *noun* tall post by the side of a road, holding a lamp; *the bus hit a lamppost*; *be careful not to reverse into that lamppost*

lampshade ['læmpʃeɪd] *noun* decorative cover put over a lamp; *I don't like the bright orange lampshade you bought*

lance [lɑːns] **1** *noun* type of long spear carried by a knight in armour **2** *verb* to make a cut in a boil or abscess to remove the pus; *the doctor decided to lance the abscess*

land [lænd] **1** *noun* **(a)** earth (as opposed to water); *they were glad to be back on (dry) land again after two weeks at sea* **(b)** country; *people from many lands visited the exhibition*; *he wants to see his native land* again before he is too old to travel **(c)** piece of ground; *she owns land in the north of the country*; *we bought a piece of land to build a house* **2** *verb* **(a)** to arrive on the ground or a surface; *the flight from Amsterdam has landed*; *we will be landing at London Airport in five minutes* **(b)** to put goods or passengers on to land after a voyage by sea or by air; *the ship was landing goods at the port*; *he landed several passengers at Heathrow Airport* **(c)** to catch a big fish; *we landed three salmon* **(d)** to manage to get something; *he landed a contract with a Chinese company* **(e)** to be successful in hitting someone; *he landed several punches on his opponent's head*

landfill ['lændfɪl] *noun* way of disposing of rubbish by putting it into holes in the ground and covering it with earth; **landfill site** = area of land where domestic rubbish is put into holes in the ground and covered with earth; *landfill sites have to be chosen carefully so that effluent does not leak into the rivers*; *the council has given permission for the old quarry to be used as a landfill site*

landing ['lændɪŋ] *noun* **(a)** *(especially of aircraft)* arriving on the ground or on a surface; *the plane made a smooth landing*; *strong winds meant that landing on the aircraft carrier was difficult* **(b)** flat place at the top of stairs; *she was waiting for me on the landing*

landing craft ['lændɪŋ 'krɑːft] *noun* boat with a flat bottom which can come close to a beach, used for bringing soldiers to land; *the aircraft carriers stayed out at sea, and a force of marines was landed from landing craft* (NOTE: plural is **landing craft**)

landing gear ['lændɪŋ 'gɪə] *noun* wheels of a plane and the mechanism which holds them; *the landing gear didn't come down properly and the pilot had to make an emergency landing*

landing stage ['lændɪŋ 'steɪdʒ] *noun* platform where passengers can get on or leave a boat; *we took a boat trip from Westminster landing stage to Tower Bridge*

landlady ['lændleɪdi] *noun* **(a)** woman from whom you rent a house, room, etc.; *you must pay the rent to the landlady every month* **(b)** woman who is in charge of a hotel or inn, etc.; *the landlady sat behind the bar* (NOTE: plural is **landladies**)

landlord ['lændlɔːd] *noun* **(a)** man or company from whom you rent a house, room, office, etc.; *tell the landlord if your roof leaks*; *the landlord refused to make any repairs to the roof* **(b)** man who is in charge of a hotel or inn, etc.; *there's a new landlord at the 'Half Moon'*

landlubber ['lændlʌbə] *noun* (informal) person who doesn't like going on ships; *it looks as though it's going to be rough, so the landlubbers had better stay on shore*

landmark ['lændmɑːk] *noun* **(a)** building or large object on land which you can see easily; *the Statue of Liberty is a famous New York landmark* **(b)** outstanding or important event, etc.; *the handover of power to China was a landmark in the history of Hong Kong*

landmass ['lændmæs] *noun* large area of land; *storms are approaching the European landmass*; *the continental landmass of the United States* (NOTE: plural is **landmasses**)

landmine ['lændmaɪn] *noun* small bomb hidden under the surface of the soil, which explodes if trodden on; *their jeep ran over a landmine and was blown up*; *the United Nations has proposed a programme to clear landmines*

landowner ['lændəʊnə] *noun* person who owns land, and may let it to a tenant; *landowners are protesting at the government's plans to improve public access to the countryside*

landscape ['lændskeɪp] **1** *noun* **(a)** scenery, appearance of the countryside; *go to the West Country if you want to see beautiful landscapes*; **landscape gardening** = making a garden more beautiful by making artificial lakes, planting trees, etc. **(b)** painting of a country scene; *he collects 18th century English landscapes* **2** *verb* to improve the appearance of a garden by making artificial lakes, planting trees, etc.; *he spent years landscaping his garden*

landscape gardener ['lænskeɪp 'gɑːdnə] *noun* person who designs the layout of large gardens or pieces of land; *he works as a landscape gardener for the local council*

landslide ['lændslaɪd] *noun* **(a)** sudden fall of large amounts of soil and rocks down the side of a mountain; *landslides have blocked several roads through the mountains* **(b)** overwhelming majority obtained in an election; *the Socialists won in a landslide* or *won a landslide victory*

landslip ['lændslɪp] = LANDSLIDE (a)

land up ['lænd 'ʌp] *verb* to end (in a place); *we were trying to go to London and landed up in Southampton*; *he tried to break into a school and landed up in prison*

lane [leɪn] *noun* **(a)** narrow road, often in the country; *a lane with hedges on both sides* **(b)** way for traffic going in a particular direction at a certain speed; *motorways usually have three lanes on either side*; *one lane of the motorway has been closed for repairs*; **bus lane** = part of a road where only buses may go; **inside lane** or **slow lane** = track nearest the side of the road, used by slow-moving vehicles, or by vehicles planning to turn off the road; **middle lane** = track in the centre of a three-lane carriageway; **outside lane** or **fast lane** = track nearest the centre of a road, used by the fast-moving vehicles **(c)** way for one runner in a race; *she is coming up fast on the inside lane*

language ['læŋgwɪdʒ] *noun* **(a)** way of speaking or writing used in a country or by a group of people; *Chinese is a very difficult language to learn, but it is the language spoken by most people in the world*; *we go to English language classes twice a week*; *I don't like travelling in places where I don't know the language*; *his first language is German, but he speaks several other languages very well*; **sign language** = way of communicating with deaf people, making signs with the fingers **(b)** **bad language** = swearing and rude words; *you should have heard the bad language when he ran into her new car* **(c)** **programming language** = system of signs and words used to program a computer

language laboratory ['læŋgwɪdʒ lə'bɒrətri] *noun* room with tape recorders, monitors, etc., where students listen to lessons in foreign languages in order to practise their language skills; *we are supposed to spend two hours a week in the language laboratory*

languid ['læŋgwɪd] *adjective* moving slowly, without any energy; *we spent a languid day on the beach*; *she made a languid movement of her arm and a servant arrived with the tray of drinks*

languish ['læŋgwɪʃ] *verb* to become weaker or more ill, to be in a bad situation; *support for the party has languished since the general election*; *he languished in hospital for two months while they tried to find out what was the matter with him*

languor ['læŋgə] *noun* pleasant lack of energy; *the languor of a summer afternoon in Madrid*

lank ['læŋk] *adjective (hair)* straight and untidy, and possibly dirty; *her hair became dull and lank*

lanky ['læŋki] *adjective* tall, thin and awkward; *she came with her sons, a couple of lanky teenagers* (NOTE: **lankier - lankiest**)

lantern ['læntən] *noun* oil or gas lamp which can be carried in the hand; *instead of a torch, we take a gas lantern when we go camping*

lap [læp] **1** *noun* **(a)** your body from the waist to the knees, when you are sitting; *she listened to the story, sitting in her father's lap* **(b)** **it's in the lap of the gods** = no one knows what will happen; *I can't predict the result of the election - it's all in the lap of the gods*; **in the lap of luxury** = in great luxury; *they live in the lap of luxury* **(c)** circuit, round of a racecourse; *he's finished lap 23 - only two laps to go!* **(d)** part of a long journey; *the last lap of the tour was from Bangkok to Singapore* **2** *verb* **(a)** *(of animal)* to drink with the tongue; *the dog lapped the water in the pond* **(b)** *(of waves)* to wash against something; *little waves lapped against the side of the quay*; *the water was lapping round his ankles* **(c)** to go so fast that you are a whole lap ahead of another competitor in a race; *the winner had lapped three other runners* (NOTE: **lapping - lapped**)

lapel [lə'pel] *noun* one of the two parts of a coat or jacket which are folded back, just above the top button that fastens it; *he wore a rose in the buttonhole in his lapel*; *pin your visitor's badge to your lapel*

lapse [læps] **1** *noun* **(a)** interval of time, especially when something does not take place; *there is a lapse of two seconds between touching the switch and the screen lighting up*; *they have started work on the motorway again after a considerable lapse of time* **(b)** failure of something to work or be done properly; *I must have had a lapse of memory* **2** *verb* **(a)** to stop; *all rubbish collections lapsed during the strike* **(b)** to stop being valid; *my parking permit has lapsed, I must get it renewed* **(c)** **to lapse into something** = to fall into a worse state than before; *the country lapsed into anarchy when the president was assassinated*; *after the brain operation, she lapsed into a coma from which she never recovered*

lapsed [læpst] *adjective* **a lapsed Catholic** = person who was baptized a Catholic, but no longer practises his religion

laptop ['læptɒp] *noun* small computer which can be held on your knees; *I take my laptop with me as cabin luggage so that I can write reports on the plane*

lap up ['læp 'ʌp] *verb* **(a)** to drink greedily with the tongue; *the cat was lapping up the milk* **(b)** *(informal)* to accept something eagerly; *she told him how good his book was, and he just sat there lapping it up*

larceny ['lɑːsni] *noun (old)* crime of stealing goods; *he was convicted of larceny*

COMMENT: larceny no longer exists in English law, having been replaced by the crime of theft

larch [lɑːtʃ] *noun* tree which has cones, but which loses its leaves in winter; *in spring, the larch forest shows new green leaves* (NOTE: plural is **larches**)

lard [lɑːd] *noun* animal fat used in cooking; *you need lard to make the pastry for pies*

larder ['lɑːdə] *noun* cool room or cupboard for storing food; *old houses often have big larders*

large [lɑːdʒ] *adjective* **(a)** big; *she ordered a large cup of coffee; our house has one large bedroom and two very small ones; how large is your garden?; why has she got an office which is larger than mine?* **(b) by and large** = generally speaking; *by and large, it is cheaper living in Madrid than in London* (NOTE: **larger - largest**)

◊ **at large** ['æt 'lɑːdʒ] *phrase* **(a)** in general; *the advertising campaign is aimed at the public at large* **(b)** not in prison; *two prisoners escaped and one is still at large*

largely ['lɑːdʒli] *adverb* mainly, mostly; *the strange weather is largely due to El Niño; his farm is largely grazing land*

large-scale ['lɑːdʒskeɪl] *adjective* involving large numbers of people or large sums of money; *the police are launching a large-scale crackdown on car thefts; compare* SMALL-SCALE

lark [lɑːk] **1** *noun* **(a)** bird which sings and flies high in the sky; *larks were singing high up above the fields;* **to get up with the lark** = to get up very early in the morning **(b)** amusing and daring behaviour; *we all jumped into the fountains at Trafalgar Square - what a lark!* **2** *verb* (*informal*) **to lark about** = to play around noisily like children; *the students were larking about in the snow*

larva ['lɑːvə] *noun* early stage of development of an insect, different in form from the adult; *caterpillars are the larvae of butterflies* (NOTE: plural is **larvae** ['lɑːviː])

larval ['lɑːvəl] *adjective* referring to larvae; *a caterpillar is the larval stage of a butterfly*

laryngitis [lærɪn'dʒaɪtɪs] *noun* inflammation of the larynx; *she's got laryngitis and can hardly speak*

larynx ['lærɪŋks] *noun* upper part of the windpipe, where sounds are made by the voice (NOTE: also called the **voice box**; plural is **larynxes**)

lasagne [læ'zænjə] *noun* type of flat pasta, served cooked with meat or vegetable sauce; *I'll have a some lasagne and a glass of red wine, please*

laser ['leɪzə] *noun* instrument which produces a highly concentrated beam of light; **laser printer** = office printing machine which prints using a laser beam

lash [læʃ] **1** *noun* **(a)** stroke with a whip; *he was sentenced to six lashes* **(b)** flexible part of a whip; *he hit the horse with the tip of his lash* **(c)** eyelash; *she has lovely long lashes* (NOTE: plural is **lashes**) **2** *verb* **(a)** to beat something with a whip; *she lashed at the horse to make it go faster* **(b)** to beat against something, as if with a whip; *the rain was lashing against the windows* **(c)** to fasten or tie down tightly with rope; *containers carried on the deck of a ship must be securely lashed down*

lashings ['læʃɪŋz] *noun* (*informal*) a lot; *they had strawberries with lashings of cream*

lash out ['læʃ 'aut] *verb* **(a) to lash out at** = to try to hit; *he lashed out at the policeman* **(b)** (*informal*) **to lash out on** = to become very extravagant and spend a

large sum of money; *let's lash out on a big party to celebrate the end of the exams*

lass [læs] *noun* (*in the North of England & Scotland*) (*informal*) girl or young woman; *what's the matter, lass?* (NOTE: plural is **lasses**)

lassie ['læsi] *noun* (*in the North of England & Scotland*) (*informal*) girl or young woman; *she's just a wee lassie; compare* LADDIE

lassitude ['læsɪtjuːd] *noun* (*formal*) feeling of great tiredness, where you do not want to do anything; *they suspected anaemia when she complained of continual lassitude*

lasso [lə'suː] **1** *noun* rope with a loop at the end for catching cattle, horses, etc.; *she caught the horse with a lasso* (NOTE: plural is **lassoes**) **2** *verb* to catch an animal with a lasso; *he lassoed the horse* (NOTE: **lassoes - lassoing - lassoed**)

last [lɑːst] **1** *adjective* **(a)** which comes at the end of a list, line or period of time; *the post office is the last building on the right; the invoice must be paid by the last day of the month; she's the last person I would want to take to a chic restaurant* = I would never go to a chic restaurant with her; **last thing at night** = at the very end of the day; *we always have a drink of hot milk last thing at night;* **last but not least** = the last in a list, but by no means the least important; *last but not least, mother topped the cake with chocolate icing;* **the last straw** = the final problem which makes everything seem hopeless; *there was one problem after another with the harvest, and the last straw was when the barn caught fire* **(b)** most recent; *she's been ill for the last ten days; the last three books I read were rubbish;* **last but one** = the one before the last one; *my last car but one was a Rolls Royce;* **last night** = the evening and night of yesterday; *we had dinner together last night;* **last Tuesday** = the Tuesday before today; *I saw her last Tuesday; have you still got last Tuesday's newspaper?;* **last week** = the week before this one; *the fair was in town last week - you've missed it!;* **last month** = the month before this one; *last month it rained almost every day;* **last year** = the year before this one; *where did you go on holiday last year?* **2** *noun* **(a)** thing or person coming at the end; *she was the last to arrive;* **that's the last of the apples** = we have finished the apples **(b)** final words; *that's not the last they've heard from me* **(c) before last** = the one before the most recent; **the Tuesday before last** = two Tuesdays ago; **the week before last** = two weeks ago; **the year before last** = two years ago; *he changed his car the year before last* **3** *adverb* **(a)** at the end; *she came last in the competition; out of a queue of twenty people, I was served last* **(b)** most recently; *when did you see her last?; she was looking ill when I saw her last* or *when I last saw her* **4** *verb* to stay; to go on; *the fine weather won't last; our holidays never seem to last very long; the storm lasted all night; the meeting lasted for three hours*

◊ **at last** or **at long last** [æt 'lɑːst or æt 'lɒŋ 'lɑːst] in the end, after a long time; *we walked for hours and at last got home at six o'clock; I waited for half an hour, and at long last two buses came together*

last-ditch [lɑːst'dɪtʃ] *adjective* final, last before something unpleasant happens; *in a last-ditch attempt to keep the talks going they made a new offer*

lasting ['lɑːstɪŋ] *adjective* which lasts for a long time; *his visit to China made a lasting impression on him;*

I've had these batteries for months - they're very long lasting

lastly ['lɑːstli] *adverb* at the end; *lastly, I would like to say how much I appreciated the letters my friends sent me when I was in hospital*

last-minute [lɑːst 'mɪnɪt] *adjective* very late; *she made some last-minute changes to the wedding dress; people making last-minute bookings can get tours at half-price*

last post ['lɑːst 'pəʊst] *noun* (a) the last collection of mail from a letterbox; *the last post goes at 5.30* (b) bugle call played at military funerals, and at the Remembrance Day ceremonies; *a lone bugler played the last post as the general was buried* (NOTE: the American equivalent is **taps**)

latch [lætʃ] 1 *noun* fastening for a door, etc., consisting of a small bar which fits into a catch; *the burglars pushed on the door and broke the latch; the door is on the latch* = the door is held shut by a latch but is not locked; *leave the door on the latch - I'll be back in a minute* (NOTE: plural is **latches**) 2 *verb* (a) to close with a latch; *it's not enough just to latch the door, it must be locked at night* (b) *(informal)* **to latch on to something** = to understand something or to take up something; *children latch on to their parents' bad habits very quickly; the reporters quickly latched on to the fact that the Prime Minister did not applaud the Chancellor's speech*

latchkey ['lætʃkiː] *noun* key for a front door; *I gave the cleaner a latchkey as we will be away next week;* **latchkey kid** = child who has a key to the front door, because both parents are out at work; *you see latchkey kids with their front-door keys hanging round their necks*

late [leɪt] 1 *adjective* (a) after the usual time; after the time when it was expected; *the plane is thirty minutes late; it's too late to change your ticket; hurry or you'll be late for the show; we apologize for the late arrival of the plane from Amsterdam;* **at the latest** = no later than; *I'll ring back before 7 o'clock at the latest* (b) at the end of a period of time; *the traffic was bad in the late afternoon; he moved to London in the late 1970s* (c) towards the end of the day; *it's late - I'm going to bed* (d) **latest** = most recent; *have you seen his latest film?; he always drives the latest model car; the latest snow reports are published each day in the papers* (e) dead; *his late father was a director of the company; the late president was working on his memoirs when he died* (NOTE: only used before a noun in this meaning) 2 *adverb* (a) after the usual time; *the plane arrived late; I went to bed later than usual last night; our visitors got up late this morning* (b) **later** = at a time after the present; after a time which has been mentioned; *the family came to live in England and she was born a month later; can we meet later this evening?;* **see you later!** = I hope to see you again later today; **later (on)** = afterwards, at a later time; *I'll do it later on; we were only told later that she was very ill* (NOTE: **later - latest**)

latecomer ['leɪtkʌmə] *noun* person who arrives late; *latecomers to the opera will not be allowed in until the first interval*

lately ['leɪtli] *adverb* during recent days or weeks; *have you seen her father lately?; we've been very busy at the office lately*

late-night ['leɪt 'naɪt] *adjective* happening late at night; *there is a late-night bus which leaves at 23.45;* **late-night shopping** = shopping in the late evening, with shops staying open much later than usual (i.e. up to 10 p.m.)

latent ['leɪtənt] *adjective* present but not yet developed; hidden; *I'm sure she has latent acting talent which needs to be encouraged;* **latent heat** = heat needed to change a boiling liquid into a vapour

lateral ['lætərəl] *adjective* referring to the side; *part of the purpose of a ship's keel is to prevent lateral drifting;* **lateral moraine** = deposit of sand and gravel left at the sides of a glacier as it moves forwards; **lateral shoot** = shoot going off from the side of a plant; **lateral thinking** = way of approaching problems by looking at them from an unusual point of view; *let's apply some lateral thinking to this problem*

latex ['leɪteks] *noun* (a) milky juice from a rubber tree; *the raw latex is collected and then heated to make rubber* (b) soft plastic; *the stair carpet is backed with foam latex*

lathe [leɪð] *noun* machine for holding and turning wood or metal so that it can be shaped; *he put the piece of wood into the lathe and made a chair leg*

lather ['lɑːðə] 1 *noun* (a) mass of soap bubbles; *the barber covered my chin with lather* (b) *(especially on horse)* sweat like froth; **to get in(to) a lather** = to get upset or flustered; *he got into a terrible lather about the letter* 2 *verb* (a) to form a lather; *hard water makes it difficult for soap to lather* (b) to cover with lather; *the barber was just lathering my chin when the police rushed in*

Latin ['lætɪn] 1 *noun* language spoken by the ancient Romans; *we learnt Latin at school; the inscription on the tomb is in Latin* 2 *adjective* (a) referring to the language of ancient Rome; *he was reading a book of Latin poetry* (b) referring to Italy, Spain, Portugal and South America; *they always go to one of the Latin countries on holiday;* **Latin America** = countries in South and Central America where Spanish and Portuguese are spoken

latitude ['lætɪtjuːd] *noun* (a) position on the earth's surface measured in degrees north or south of the equator; *pine trees grow in temperate latitudes; see also note at* LONGITUDE (b) freedom or scope to do what you want to do; *the management allows the heads of department considerable latitude in selecting staff*

latter ['lætə] 1 *adjective (formal)* coming at the end of a list; *I'm busy on Monday and Tuesday, but I'll be free during the latter part of the week* 2 *noun* **the latter** = second person *or* thing mentioned of two things; *which do you prefer, apples or pears? - I prefer the latter* (NOTE: the first of two is called the **former**)

latter-day ['lætədeɪ] *adjective* modern, of the present time; *she goes into negotiations like some latter-day Attila the Hun*

Latvia ['lætvɪə] *noun* small country on the Baltic, one of the three Baltic States; *Latvia is sandwiched between Lithuania and Estonia* (NOTE: capital: **Riga**; people: **Latvians**; language: **Latvian**; currency: **lats**)

Latvian ['lætvɪən] 1 *adjective* referring to Latvia; *many Latvian emigrés have returned home now that their country has regained its independence* 2 *noun* (a) person from Latvia; *Latvians voted to leave the* former Soviet Union in 1990 **(b)** language spoken in Latvia; *Latvian is closely related to Lithuanian*

laud [lɔːd] *verb (formal)* to praise; *the police officer was lauded for his bravery*

laugh [lɑːf] **1** *noun* **(a)** sound you make when you think something is funny; *he's got a lovely deep laugh*; *'that's right,' she said with a laugh*; to do something for a laugh = to do something as a joke or for fun; *don't be angry - they only did it for a laugh* **(b)** to have the last laugh = to be successful in the end, after people have laughed at you earlier on; *everyone told him a clockwork radio wouldn't work, but he had the last laugh when it sold in millions* **2** *verb* **(a)** to make a sound to show you think something is funny; *he was very good last night - he had everyone laughing at his jokes*; *she fell off the ladder and everyone laughed*; to laugh like a drain = to laugh a lot; *he laughed like a drain when he was told the story; see also* SLEEVE **(b)** to laugh at someone = to make fun of someone; *don't laugh at her because she's so fat; you mustn't laugh at his hat*

laughable ['lɑːfəbl] *adjective* ridiculous, which can only be laughed at; *the idea that she could be having an affair with the boss is just laughable*

laughing stock ['lɑːfɪŋ 'stɒk] *noun* person who is laughed at by everyone; *if my friends knew what had really happened, I would be the laughing stock of the school*

laughter ['lɑːftə] *noun* sound or act of laughing; *laughter greeted the clowns' appearance in the ring*; *as soon as he opened his mouth, the audience burst into laughter* (NOTE: no plural)

launch [lɔːntʃ] **1** *noun* **(a)** type of small motor boat; *he took the launch out on the lake* **(b)** act of starting off a boat, a rocket, a new product, etc.; *the launch of the new car went off successfully*; *the rocket launch has been delayed by two weeks*; launch pad = *see* LAUNCHING PAD; launch party = party held to advertise the launching of a new product (NOTE: plural is **launches**) **2** *verb* **(a)** to put a boat into the water, especially for the first time and with a lot of ceremony; *the Queen launched the new ship* **(b)** to put a new product on the market; *they are launching their new car at the motor show* **(c)** to give something *or* someone a start; *the TV ad helped to launch her film career* **(d)** to begin; *the enemy launched an attack on our headquarters*

launching ['lɔːntʃɪŋ] *noun* act of starting off a boat, a rocket, a new product, etc.; *the launching of the new car has cost a vast amount of money*; launching pad = platform from which a rocket is launched; launching party = *see* LAUNCH PARTY

launder ['lɔːndə] *verb* **(a)** *(formal)* to wash clothes, sheets, etc.; *he asked to have two shirts laundered* **(b)** to pass money from crime or drugs, or money which has not been taxed, etc., into the normal banking system in such a way that it is not possible to find out where it came from; *the money was laundered through an offshore account*

launderette *US* **laundromat** ['lɔːndret *or* 'lɔːndrəmæt] *noun* shop with coin-operated washing machines which the public can use; *I take my washing to the launderette once a week*

laundry ['lɔːndri] *noun* **(a)** room or building where clothes are washed; *the hotel's sheets and towels are sent to the laundry every day* (NOTE: plural in this

meaning is **laundries**) **(b)** dirty clothes to be sent for washing; *please put any laundry into the bag provided*; laundry basket = large basket in which you put dirty linen waiting to be washed; *the laundry basket is full, so we had better do some washing*; laundry bag = special bag in a hotel room, into which you can put dirty clothes to be taken to be washed; *the laundry bag is emptied twice a day* (NOTE: no plural in this meaning)

laurel ['lɒrəl] *noun* large bush with smooth shiny evergreen leaves; *the ancient Greeks used to crown the victor of a contest with a wreath of laurel leaves*; to rest on your laurels = to enjoy your past success, without trying to do any more; *they've done very well so far but they can't afford to rest on their laurels because their rivals will catch up with them*

lav [læv] *noun (informal)* lavatory; *I'll be ready in a moment, I just need to go to the lav*

lava ['lɑːvə] *noun* molten rock flowing from a volcano which becomes solid when it cools; *nothing could stop the flow of lava down the mountainside towards the village*; lava flow = lava moving down the sides of a volcano; *all buildings in the path of the lava flow simply disappeared*

lavatory ['lævətri] *noun* **(a)** toilet, a small room for getting rid of waste matter or water from the body; *the gents' lavatory is to the right*; *the lavatories are situated at the rear of the plane*; lavatory paper = toilet paper, soft paper for wiping your behind after getting rid of waste matter **(b)** bowl with a seat and water flushing system, for getting rid of waste matter from the body; *the drink was so awful that I poured it down the lavatory* (NOTE: plural is **lavatories**)

lavender ['lævɪndə] *noun* **(a)** shrub with small lilac-coloured flowers and narrow leaves, cultivated for perfume; *my grandmother puts bags filled with dried lavender flowers in her wardrobe to make her clothes smell nice* **(b)** bluish-purple colour; *the bedroom walls have been painted a soothing shade of lavender*

lavish ['lævɪʃ] **1** *adjective* **(a)** extravagant, very generous; *he bought all the children lavish presents* **(b)** generous helping of food, etc.; *grandmother always gives us lavish portions* **2** *verb* to lavish something on someone = to give lots of something to someone; *he lavished presents on his grandchildren*; *she lavishes a lot of care on her collection of orchids*

law [lɔː] *noun* **(a)** the law = the set of rules by which a country is governed; *everyone is supposed to obey the law*; within the law = obeying the laws of a country; against the law = not according to the laws of a country; *it is against the law to drive at night without lights*; to break the law = to do something which is not allowed by law; *he is breaking the law by selling cigarettes to children* **(b)** to lay down the law = to tell someone to do something in a dogmatic way; *he insists on laying down the law, which makes the office staff unhappy*; to take the law into your own hands = to do things to punish someone which are illegal; *they took the law into their own hands and burnt down the rapist's house*; law and order = situation where the laws of the country are obeyed by most people; *the government reacted quickly to the breakdown in law and order* **(c)** one single part of the rules governing a country, usually in the form of an act of parliament; *Parliament has passed a law against the ownership of guns* **(d)** all the laws of a country taken together; civil law = laws relating to arguments between individuals and the rights of individuals; commercial law = laws regarding business; **company law** = laws which refer to the way companies work; **contract law** *or* **the law of contract** = laws relating to private agreements; **copyright law** = laws concerning the protection of copyright; **criminal law** = laws relating to crime; **international law** = laws referring to the way countries deal with each other; **maritime law** *or* **the law of the sea** = laws referring to ships, ports, etc. (NOTE: no plural in this meaning) **(e)** general scientific rule or controlling force; *the law of gravity*; *Einstein's Law of Relativity*; **law of supply and demand** = general rule that the amount of a product which is available is related to what possible customers need

law-abiding ['lɔːəbaɪdɪŋ] *adjective* who obeys the law; *law-abiding citizens do not throw stones at police stations*

law-breaking ['lɔː'breɪkɪŋ] *noun* act of doing something which is against the law

lawcourt ['lɔːkɔːt] *noun* court where cases are heard by a judge and jury, or by a magistrate; *the lawcourts sit from ten to four*

law enforcement ['lɔː ɪn'fɔːsmənt] *noun* enforcing the law; *the police and other law-enforcement agencies*; *who is in charge of law enforcement in this town?*

lawful ['lɔːful] *adjective* acting within the law; **lawful practice** = action which is permitted by the law; **lawful trade** = trade which is permitted by the law

lawless ['lɔːləs] *adjective* not controlled by the law or by the police; *the magistrates criticized the lawless behaviour of the football crowd*

law-making ['lɔːmeɪkɪŋ] *noun* making of laws; *Parliament is the law-making body in Great Britain*

lawman ['lɔːmæn] *noun* US policeman, sheriff (NOTE: plural is **lawmen**)

lawn [lɔːn] *noun* part of a garden covered with short grass; *he lay on his back on the lawn*; *your lawn needs cutting*; *we need to water the lawn every day during the summer*

lawnmower ['lɔːnməʊə] *noun* machine for cutting grass; *the quiet of the Sunday morning was broken by the sound of electric lawnmowers*

lawsuit ['lɔːsuːt] *noun* case brought to a court; **to bring a lawsuit against someone** = to tell someone to appear in court because you think they have acted wrongly towards you; *the parents of the victims brought a lawsuit against the tour company*

lawyer ['lɔːjə] *noun* person who has studied law and can advise you on legal matters; *if you are arrested you have the right to speak to your lawyer*

lax [læks] *adjective* not strict; *the customs officers were very lax in inspecting passengers' baggage* (NOTE: **laxer - laxest**)

laxative ['læksətɪv] **1** *noun* medicine which causes a bowel movement; *the doctor prescribed a laxative to help his constipation* **2** *adjective* which causes a bowel movement; *the laxative properties of fresh fruit are well known*

lay [leɪ] **1** *verb* **(a)** to put something down flat; *he laid the papers on the table*; *a new carpet has been laid in the dining room* **(b)** to produce an egg; *the hens laid three eggs* **(c) to lay the table** = to put knives, forks, spoons, etc., on the table ready for a meal; *the table is laid for four people* **(d)** *see* LIE (NOTE: **laying - laid**) **2**

adjective not trained for a profession or to be a member of a religious order; **lay people often cannot understand doctors' language**; **lay members of the Church help organize the parish**; *see also* LAYMAN

layabout ['leɪəbaʊt] *noun* (*informal*) person who doesn't work; *look at our staff - they're just a bunch of no-good layabouts*

layby ['leɪbaɪ] *noun* place at the side of a road where vehicles can park

layer ['leɪə] *noun* flat, usually horizontal, thickness of something; *she put a layer of chocolate on the cake, then one of cream*; *see also* BRICKLAYER

layered ['leɪəd] *adjective* made in layers; *my daughter wants a three-layered cake for her birthday*; **layered hair** = hair cut in layers of different lengths

layman ['leɪmən] *noun* person who does not belong to a particular profession, who is not an expert in something; *can you explain the theory in words a layman might understand?* (NOTE: plural **laymen**)

lay off ['leɪ 'ɒf] *verb* **(a)** to dismiss workers for a time, until more work is available; *the factory has had to lay off half its workforce because of a temporary lack of orders* **(b)** (*informal*) to stop doing or using something; *you should lay off bread and potatoes if you want to reduce weight*

lay-off ['leɪɒf] *noun* action of dismissing a worker for a time; *the recession has caused hundreds of lay-offs in the car industry*

lay out ['leɪ 'aʊt] *verb* to put out in an orderly way; *the plans were laid out on the table*; *they laid out the children's presents under the Christmas tree*

layout ['leɪaʊt] *noun* design, especially of a garden, a book, etc.; *they have altered the layout of the offices*

laze [leɪz] *verb* to relax, to do nothing or very little; *it's nice to be able to spend the day lazing by the swimming pool once in a while*

lazily ['leɪzɪli] *adverb* in a lazy way; *he walked lazily along the street with his hands in his pockets*

lazy ['leɪzi] *adjective* not wanting to do any work; *she's just lazy - that's why the work never gets done on time*; *he is so lazy he does not even bother to open his mail* (NOTE: **lazier - laziest**)

lb = POUND(S) *it weighs 26lb*; *take 6lb of sugar* (NOTE: written **lb** but said as 'pounds')

LBO = LEVERAGED BUYOUT

LCD ['elsiːdiː] *abbreviation for* liquid crystal display, liquid crystal that turns black when a voltage is applied, used in many watches, calculators and other small digital displays; *when the LCD starts to fade, the battery needs replacing*

lead 1 [led] *noun* **(a)** very heavy soft metal; *tie a piece of lead to your fishing line to make it sink* (NOTE: Chemical element: chemical symbol: **Pb**; atomic number: 82) **(b)** black part in the middle of a pencil; *if your lead's broken then you need to sharpen the pencil* **2** [liːd] *noun* **(a)** string or thin piece of leather to hold a dog; *all dogs must be kept on a lead in the park* **(b)** electric wire, etc., which joins a machine to the electricity supply; *the lead is too short to go across the room* **(c)** first place (in a race); *he went into the lead or he took the lead*; *who's in the lead at the half-way mark?*; *she has a lead of 20m over her nearest rival* **(d)** main part in a play, opera, ballet, etc.; *the understudy had to take over last night when the male* *lead fell and broke his arm* **3** [liːd] *verb* **(a)** to be in first place, to have the most important place; *our side was leading at half time; they were leading by three metres* **(b)** to go in front to show the way; *she led us to the secret box; the road leads you to the top of the hill* **(c)** to be in charge of; to be the main person in a group; *she is leading a group of businesswomen on a tour of Chinese factories* **(d)** **to lead to** = to make something happen; *the discussions led to an international treaty; it led me to think she was lying* = it made me think she was lying (NOTE: **leading - led** [led]) **4** [liːd] *adjective* who sings or plays the main tunes in a pop group; *he's the lead guitarist with a pop group; she's the lead singer of the group*

leaden ['ledn] *adjective* like lead; **a leaden sky** = a dull grey sky

leader ['liːdə] *noun* **(a)** person who leads; *he is the leader of the Labour Party; the leader of the construction workers' union;* **leader of a council** or **council leader** = head of the majority party on a local council (NOTE: this position was created to replace that of mayor, when mayors became largely ceremonial); **leader of an orchestra** = chief violinist in an orchestra **(b)** leading article, one of the main articles in a newspaper, giving the newspaper's views on a topic of current interest; *the rail disaster was featured in the leader*

Leader of the Opposition ['liːdə əv ðə ɒpə'zɪʃn] *noun* head of the main party which opposes a government in parliament; *the Leader of the Opposition replied to the Prime Minister*

leadership ['liːdəʃɪp] *noun* **(a)** ability to be the person who manages or directs others; *we think he has certain leadership qualities* **(b)** position of a leader; *under his leadership the party went from strength to strength* **(c)** group of leaders of an organization; *the leadership was weaker after the president's resignation;* **collective leadership** = group of leaders who take decisions together (NOTE: no plural)

leading ['liːdɪŋ] *adjective* most important; **leading article** = leader, one of the main articles in a newspaper, giving the newspaper's views on a topic of current interest; **leading lady** = actress taking the main role; **leading light** = person who plays an important part in a group; *she's one of the leading lights of the women's lib movement;* **leading question** = question which is worded in order to get a particular answer; *he prepared a few leading questions to use in the interview*

lead on ['liːd 'ɒn] *verb* **(a)** to go first; *lead on, we will all follow!* **(b)** **to lead someone on** = to mislead someone; *they promised him a new car, but they were just leading him on*

lead story ['liːd 'stɔːri] *noun* most important report in a newspaper or broadcast, the story that comes first; *the lead story in this morning's 'Times' is the government's decision to raise taxes*

lead up to ['liːd 'ʌp tuː] *verb* to prepare the way for something to happen; *the events which led up to the war*

leaf [liːf] **1** *noun* one of many flat green parts of a plant; *the leaves of the trees turn brown or red in autumn; caterpillars have eaten the leaves of the roses* **(b)** sheet of paper, especially a page of a book; **to turn over a new leaf** = to make a new start; *after years of wild living he decided to turn over a new leaf and join the family firm* (NOTE: plural is **leaves** [liːvz]) **2** *verb* to

leaf through = to turn the pages of a book rapidly without reading properly; *he leafed through the book, looking at the illustrations*

leaflet ['liːflət] *noun* sheet of paper, often folded, giving information; *opposition groups handed out leaflets at the beginning of the rally; they did a leaflet mailing to 20,000 addresses*

leafy ['liːfi] *adjective* **(a)** with lots of leaves; *these lettuces are really leafy* **(b)** with lots of trees; *we strolled along the leafy avenue*

league [liːg] **1** *noun* **(a)** group joined together for a particular purpose; **to be in league with someone** = to work with someone against someone else **(b)** association of sports clubs which play against each other; *he plays for one of the clubs in the local football league;* **not in the same league as** = not as good or as successful as; *you can't compare our little corner shop to the supermarket, they're not in the same league* **(c)** **league table** = list of things placed in order of merit, efficiency, etc.; *the newspapers published the government's annual league table of schools* **2** *verb* (formal) to join together; *the opposition parties all leagued together to vote against the government*

leak [liːk] **1** *noun* **(a)** escape of liquid or gas, etc., through a hole; *I can smell gas - there must be a gas leak in the kitchen* **(b)** escape of secret information; *the leak of the report led to the minister's resignation* (NOTE: do not confuse with **leek**) **2** *verb* **(a)** (of liquid or gas, etc.) to flow away, to escape; *water must have been leaking through the ceiling for days* **(b)** to pass on secret information; *governments don't like their plans to be leaked to the press; we found that the sales director was leaking information to a rival company*

leakage ['liːkɪdʒ] *noun* **(a)** escape of liquid or gas; *it smells of gas - there must a leakage somewhere* **(b)** revealing a secret; *after the leakage of the report, everyone was ringing up about it*

leaky ['liːki] *adjective* which leaks; *there's a leaky tap in the bathroom*

lean [liːn] **1** *adjective* **(a)** (of person) thin; *he's a lean bearded man* **(b)** (of meat) with little fat; *a slice of lean bacon* (NOTE: **leaner - leanest**) **2** *verb* to be in or to put into a sloping position; *the ladder was leaning against the shed; she leant her bike against the wall; he leaned over and picked up the cushion; it's dangerous to lean out of car windows* (NOTE: **leaning - leaned** or **leant** [lent])

leaning ['liːnɪŋ] **1** *noun* tendency towards; *she has socialist leanings; he has a leaning towards a career in the church* **2** *adjective* which is leaning; *the Leaning Tower of Pisa is one of the most famous buildings in Italy*

lean on ['liːn 'ɒn] *verb* **(a)** to try to influence someone; *someone must have leant on the committee to get them to agree* **(b)** to depend on someone; *if things get difficult she always has her father to lean on*

lean-to ['liːntuː] *noun* small building, such as a shed, attached to a large building; *there's a small lean-to at the side of the house where we keep our bicycles*

leap [liːp] **1** *noun* **(a)** jump; *she took a leap forwards and fell into the water* **(b)** great improvement or progress; **by leaps and bounds** = making rapid progress; *his German has improved by leaps and bounds* **(c)** **a leap in the dark** = an action where you are not sure of what the consequences will be; *the deal* *is something of a leap in the dark, but we hope it will pay off* **2** *verb* **(a)** to jump; *she leapt with joy when she heard the news* **(b)** to go up suddenly; *sales leapt during March* (NOTE: **leaping - leaped** *or* **leapt** [lept])

leap at ['liːp 'æt] *verb* to accept eagerly something which is suggested; *she leapt at the offer of a part in the play*

leap-frog ['liːpfrɒg] **1** *noun* game where one person bends down, and others jump over his back **2** *verb* to advance more rapidly than someone else; **leap-frogging pay demands** = pay demands where each group of workers asks for higher pay to do better than another group

leap year ['liːp 'jɜː] *noun* every fourth year, in which February has 29 days; *the years 2000 and 2004 are both leap years*

learn [lɜːn] *verb* **(a)** to find out about something, or how to do something; *he's learning to ride a bicycle*; *we learn French and German at school*; **to learn something by heart** = to learn and remember something; *she learnt the poem by heart*; **to learn from your mistakes** = to make mistakes and because of them learn how something should be done; *he doesn't want to ask advice, so I only hope he learns from his mistakes* **(b)** to hear (news); *her boss learned that she was planning to leave the company*; *how did you come to learn about the product?* (NOTE: **learning - learnt** [lɜːnt] *or* **learned**)

learned ['lɜːnɪd] *adjective* **(a)** who has a lot of knowledge; *learned professors have written to the paper contradicting the government's calculations* **(b)** **learned journal** = journal for specialists; *once his theory had been published in a learned journal it began to receive more critical attention*

learner ['lɜːnə] *noun* person who is learning; *she's in the learners' class at the swimming pool*; **a learner driver** = someone who is learning to drive

learning ['lɜːnɪŋ] *noun* gaining knowledge of something or of how to do something; *learning how to run the machine will take up most of his first week at work*; **learning curve** = gradual process of learning; **a steep learning curve** = having to learn new skills fast; *being promoted from being a secretary to sales director overnight involved a steep learning curve*

lease [liːs] **1** *noun* **(a)** written contract, allowing someone to use a building, piece of land, etc., for a specified period; *we're renting our offices on a twenty-year lease*; **the lease expires** *or* **runs out in 2020** = the lease comes to an end in 2020 **(b) to give someone a new lease of life** = to make someone want to make a fresh start or to live life more fully; *Alan's retirement has given him a new lease of life* **2** *verb* **(a) to lease (out)** = to give on a lease; *he leased the shop to an Australian company*; *my landlord leases out six other flats* **(b)** to take or hold on a lease; *we're leasing our offices at a good rent*; *we lease our photocopier as it's cheaper than buying one*

leasehold ['liːshəʊld] **1** *noun* holding of property on a lease; *the leasehold was sold last year* **2** *adjective* **leasehold property** = property held on a lease; *my flat is leasehold*; *compare* FREEHOLD

leash ['liːʃ] *noun* leather strap for holding a dog; *when we get to the park I let the dog off the leash*

least [liːst] **1** *adjective* smallest or most unimportant; *this car uses by far the least amount of petrol* **2** *pronoun* **the least** = the smallest or the most unimportant amount; *she was the one who spent the least during their trip round Holland*; **to say the least** = which was worse that I expected; *I thought he was in the office so when I saw him in the supermarket I was surprised to say the least*; **not in the least** = not at all; *it doesn't bother me in the least to work on Sundays* **3** *adverb* less than everyone or everything else; *I liked that part of the book least*; *he was the least conceited man she had ever met*; **least of all** = absolutely less than everyone else; *no one was interested in what I said, least of all my son*

◊ **at least** ['æt 'liːst] *phrase* **(a)** *(mentioning one good thing in a bad situation)* *it rained all day but at least we have brought our umbrellas*; *the children were very naughty but at least no windows were broken* **(b)** *(to correct a statement)* *she lives in Liverpool - at least, she used to* **(c)** as a minimum; *try to tidy yourself up, at least comb your hair* **(d)** not less than; *at least a ninth of the children are ill*; *she can't be sixty - she looks at least eighty*

leather ['leðə] *noun* skin of certain animals used to make shoes, bags, etc.; *a leather bag*; *my shoes have leather soles*

leatherette [leðə'ret] *noun* plastic material which looks like leather; *a leatherette sofa*

leathery ['leðəri] *adjective* tough like leather; *they served us some leathery meat which I think was beef*

leave [liːv] **1** *noun* permission to be away from work; *he has six weeks' annual leave*; **leave of absence** = being allowed to be away from work; **maternity leave** = permission given to a woman to be away from work to have a baby; **sick leave** = period when a worker is away from work because of illness; **to go on leave** *or* **to be on leave** = to go or be away from work; *she is away on sick leave* *or* *on maternity leave* **2** *verb* **(a)** to go away from somewhere; *when they couldn't find what they wanted, they left the shop*; *Eurostar leaves Waterloo for Brussels every day at 8.25*; *when does the next bus leave for Oxford?* **(b)** to forget to do something; to forget to take something with you; *I packed in a rush and left my toothbrush at home* **(c)** to allow something to stay in a certain condition; *did you leave the light on when you locked up?*; *yesterday she left the iron on, and burnt a hole in the ironing board*; *someone left the door open and the dog got out*; *the coffee left a stain on the tablecloth*; *the chickenpox didn't leave any marks on her skin* **(d)** not to take something; *leave some pizza for your brother* **(e)** to go away from someone; *she's left her husband*; **leave me alone** = don't bother me **(f)** to give something to someone to do; *she went out leaving me all the washing up to do* **(g) leave it to me** = let me do it; *leave it to me, I'll find out the address for you*; **I leave it to you to decide** = you are the one who has to decide, not me (NOTE: **leaving - left** [left])

leave behind ['liːv bɪ'haɪnd] *verb* to forget to take something with you; not to take something with you; *he left his car keys behind in the post office*; *the car was too full, so we had to leave Aunt Maud behind at home*

leave off ['liːv 'ɒf] *verb* **(a)** to stop doing something; **leave off!** = stop doing that **(b)** to forget to include; *she left the post code off the address*; *the waitress left the drinks off the bill*

leave out ['liːv 'aʊt] *verb* to forget something; not to put something in; *she left out the date on the cheque*; *she described the accident, but left out the most* *important detail; he was left out of the football team because he had hurt his leg*

leaves [liːvz] *see* LEAF, LEAVE

Lebanese [lebə'niːz] **1** *adjective* referring to the Lebanon; *the Lebanese flag has a picture of a cedar on it* **2** *noun* person from the Lebanon; *many Lebanese speak French*; **the Lebanese** = people from the Lebanon (NOTE: plural is **Lebanese**)

Lebanon ['lebənən] *noun* country at the eastern end of the Mediterranean, north of Israel and west of Syria; *the Lebanon contains some marvellous Roman ruins*; **cedar of Lebanon** = very large cedar which comes originally from the Lebanon (NOTE: usually referred to as **the Lebanon**; capital: **Beirut**; people: **the Lebanese**; language: **Arabic**; currency: **Lebanese pound**)

lecherous ['letʃərəs] *adjective* only interested in sexual intercourse; *her piano teacher was a lecherous old man*

lectern ['lektən] *noun* high desk with a sloping surface on which you put a book, the text of a speech, etc., which you are going to read aloud in public

lecture ['lektʃə] **1** *noun* talk to students or any other group of people on a particular subject; *she gave a lecture on Chinese art; are you going to the lecture this evening?; the lecture lasted thirty minutes, and then there was time for questions*; **lecture tour** = tour with lectures on the places visited, paintings or other objects seen, etc.; *the museum has a programme of lecture tours on 20th-century art* **2** *verb* **(a)** to give a lecture on something; *he will lecture on Roman history next Thursday* **(b)** to teach a subject, by giving lectures; *she lectures on history at Birmingham University*

lecturer ['lektʃərə] *noun* **(a)** person who gives a talk on a particular subject; *this week's lecturer is from Sweden* **(b)** ordinary teacher in a university or college; *he has been a lecturer for five years*

lectureship ['lektʃəʃɪp] *noun* position as a lecturer; *she has got a lectureship at London University*

led [led] *see* LEAD

ledge [ledʒ] *noun* narrow flat part which sticks out from a cliff or building; *every little ledge on the cliff is occupied by a nesting seabird; he climbed up 50 metres and stopped on a narrow ledge just wide enough to stand on*

ledger ['ledʒə] *noun* large book in which accounts are written; **bought ledger** *or* **purchase ledger** = book in which purchases are recorded; **sales ledger** = book in which sales are recorded

lee [liː] *noun* side of a building, hill, ship, etc., sheltered from the wind; *they rested on the lee of the hill, so as to be out of the wind*

leech [liːtʃ] *noun* type of parasitic worm which lives in water and sucks the blood of animals by attaching itself to the skin; *leeches are a nuisance in the swamps of South America* (NOTE: plural is **leeches**)

> COMMENT: leeches are now raised specifically for use in medicine, especially for removing blood after operations and helping wounds to heal. These are called 'medicinal leeches'

leek [liːk] *noun* vegetable of the onion family, with a white stem and long green leaves; *a bowl of leek soup;*

he grows leeks in his garden (NOTE: do not confuse with **leak**)

leer ['lɪə] **1** *noun* nasty look, often expressing sexual desire; *the leers of the men as she came into the bar made her turn round and walk straight out again* **2** *verb* to look with a leer at someone; *the men were sitting in the pavement café, leering at girls passing in the street*

leery ['lɪəri] *adjective (informal)* suspicious; *I'm a bit leery of those builders*

leeward ['liːwəd] *adjective, adverb & noun* (side) sheltered from the wind; *we anchored to the leeward of the island; the boat tied up on the leeward side of the jetty*

leeway ['liːweɪ] *noun* time or space available; *the bank has given us some leeway to find more funds*; **to make up leeway** = to make up for lost time or for a lost opportunity; *you have a lot of leeway to make up after missing so much of the term through illness*

left [left] **1** *adjective* **(a)** not right, referring to the side of the body which usually has the hand you use less often; *I can't write with my left hand; the post office is on the left side of the street as you go towards the church* **(b)** *(in politics)* referring to the socialists; *his politics are left of centre; compare* RIGHT **(c)** **left** *or* **left over** = still there, not used up; *after paying for the food and drink, I've still got £3 left; if you eat three of the sweets, there will be only two left for everyone else; there was nobody left in the building; see also* LEAVE **2** *noun* **(a)** the side towards the left; *remember to drive on the left when you are in Britain; the school is on the left as you go towards the town centre; she was sitting at the chairman's left* **(b)** *(in politics)* **the left** = the socialists and communists, the group supporting the rights of the workers; *we support the left by campaigning for our local Labour candidate*; **swing to the left** = movement of votes towards the left-wing candidates **3** *adverb* towards the left; *go straight ahead and turn left at the traffic lights* **4** *verb see* LEAVE

left-hand ['left 'hænd] *adjective* on the left side; *the cheque book is in the left-hand drawer of his desk; the post office is on the left-hand side as you go towards the station*; **left-hand drive car** = car where the driver sits on the left side of the car

> COMMENT: most cars are left-hand drive: British and Japanese cars are right-hand drive

left-handed ['left 'hændɪd] *adjective* using the left hand more often than the right for doing things; *she's left-handed, so we got her a left-handed cup for her birthday*

left-hander ['left'hændə] *noun* **(a)** person who is left-handed; *both bowlers are left-handers* **(b)** punch with the left hand; *he was knocked out with a powerful left-hander to the chin*

leftist ['leftɪst] **1** *adjective (usually as a criticism)* socialist, referring to the left in politics; *the Minister of Justice was accused of showing leftist tendencies* **2** *noun* person with left-wing ideas; *it is apparent that there is no place for traditional leftists in the new centre government*

left-luggage ['left 'lʌgɪdʒ] *noun* **left-luggage office** = place where suitcases, etc., can be left and collected later for a fee; *don't forget that the left-luggage office closes at 11.00 p.m.; the station doesn't have any* *left-luggage lockers* (NOTE: American English is **baggage room**)

leftover ['leftəuvə] **1** *adjective* which is not used; *I've finished painting the kitchen - what shall I do with the leftover paint?* **2** *noun* **leftovers** = food which is left after a meal; *the children will eat the leftovers tomorrow morning*

leftward ['leftwəd] *adjective* towards the left; *with a leftward movement of his hand he indicated a small door*

left-wing ['leftwɪŋ] *adjective* politically on the left; *his views are very left-wing; a left-wing government was formed*

left-winger [left'wɪŋə] *noun* person who is on the left of a political party; *left-wingers in the party plotted to vote against the government; as a left-winger he does not approve of the Conservative government's policies*

leg [leg] **1** *noun* **(a)** part of the body with which a person or animal walks; *the bird was standing on one leg, asleep; some animals can't stand on their back legs; she fell down the steps and broke her leg; see also* ARM **(b) to pull someone's leg** = to tease someone, to try to make someone believe something that isn't true; *don't worry, she will get here on time - I was only pulling your leg;* **on its last legs** = almost worn out; *the poor old car is on its last legs;* **not to have a leg to stand on** = to be in an awkward situation because you cannot prove what you say; *the children produced a later will, so the claimants to the estate didn't have a leg to stand on* **(c)** one of the parts of a chair, etc., which touch the floor; *the table has four legs* **(d)** leg of an animal used for food; *roast leg of lamb; would you like a chicken leg?* **(e)** stage (of a journey, tour, bicycle race, etc.); *the last leg of the trip goes from Paris to Amsterdam; the first leg of the tour takes in London, Hampton Court and Windsor* **2** *verb (informal)* **to leg it** = to run away; *they legged it round the corner when they saw the police coming*

legacy ['legəsi] *noun* **(a)** what is left to a person after someone's death; *he received a large legacy from his uncle; the legacy can be paid only to the rightful claimant* **(b)** what is left behind by someone; *the company's overdraft is a legacy of the previous finance director* (NOTE: plural is **legacies**)

legal ['li:gl] *adjective* **(a)** according to the law, allowed by the law; *it's legal to drive at 17 if you have a provisional driving licence;* **legal tender** = money which must legally be accepted if you give it in payment; *foreign currency isn't legal tender, but some shops accept it* **(b)** referring to the law; **to take legal action** = to sue someone, to take someone to court; **to take legal advice** = to ask a lawyer to advise about a legal problem; **legal aid** = free legal work done for people without enough money to pay lawyers' fees; *you can apply for legal aid if you want to take the case further*

legalization [li:gəlaɪ'zeɪʃn] *noun* action of making something legal; *a demonstration in favour of the legalization of cannabis*

legalize ['li:gəlaɪz] *verb* to make something legal; *is the government going to legalize soft drugs?*

legally ['li:gəli] *adverb* in accordance with the law; *you must be over 18 to drink in a pub legally*

legatee [legə'ti:] *noun* person who receives a legacy from someone who has died

legation [lɪ'geɪʃn] *noun* **(a)** group of officials below the rank of ambassador, who represent their government in a foreign country **(b)** building where members of a legation work; *he escaped from prison and hid in the Russian legation*

legend ['ledʒənd] *noun* story from the past which may not be based on fact; *the legend of Jason and the Golden Fleece*

legendary ['ledʒəndri] *adjective* **(a)** famous, often talked about; *his meanness is legendary; her legendary dislike of men with beards* **(b)** referring to legends; *a legendary tale of witches and good fairies*

-legged [legd or 'legɪd] *suffix meaning* with legs; *a three-legged chair; a four-legged animal;* **a three-legged race** = a race where two runners run together with the left leg of one tied to the right leg of the other

leggings ['legɪŋz] *noun* **(a)** tight-fitting trousers made from a stretchy material, worn by women and girls; *when my daughter comes home from school she changes out of her uniform and puts on a pair of leggings; a group of women exercising in tops and leggings* **(b)** thick coverings for the legs; *the hunters wore thick leggings and boots* (NOTE: plural; for one item say **a pair of leggings**)

leggy ['legi] *adjective* with long legs; *she looks very different from the leggy models you see in fashion advertisements*

legible ['ledʒɪbl] *adjective* clear, able to be read easily; *the address on the order was hardly legible; you have been practising - your writing is much more legible*

legibly ['ledʒɪbli] *adverb* in a legible way; *I tried to write as legibly as possible*

legion ['li:dʒən] *noun* **(a)** group, especially of soldiers; **the Royal British Legion** = British association of former servicemen; *see also* FOREIGN LEGION **(b)** division of the Roman army; *the Roman legions under Julius Caesar invaded Britain* **(c)** very large number; *many of the legions of fans who support Manchester United will be unable to buy tickets for the Cup Final*

legionary ['li:dʒənəri] *noun* member of a legion, especially the Foreign Legion; *French legionaries were flown in to help the government put down the coup* (NOTE: plural is **legionaries**)

legionnaire [lidʒə'neə] *noun* member of the French Foreign Legion; **legionnaire's disease** = bacterial disease similar to pneumonia, which appears to be spread by droplets of moisture in air-conditioning systems

legislate ['ledʒɪsleɪt] *verb* to make a law or laws; *Parliament has legislated against the sale of drugs or to prevent the sale of drugs*

legislation [ledʒɪ'sleɪʃn] *noun* laws, written rules which are passed by Parliament and applied in the courts; *the new legislation was passed in the Commons yesterday; Congress has voted on the new legislation;* **labour legislation** = laws concerning the employment of workers (NOTE: no plural)

legislative ['ledʒɪslətɪv] *adjective* referring to laws or to law-making; *the legislative system in England and Wales is different from that in Scotland*

legislator ['ledʒɪsleɪtə] *noun* member of a legislature, a person who makes or passes laws, such as an MP, Congressman, etc.; *legislators are working on a law banning the use of firearms*

legislature ['ledʒɪslətʃə] *noun* **(a)** body which makes laws; *members of the legislature voted against the proposal* **(b)** building where a law-making body meets; *the protesters marched towards the State Legislature*

> COMMENT: the Legislature in the UK is Parliament and in the USA, Congress. The Legislature is one of the three arms of Government, the others being the Executive and the Judiciary

legitimate [lɪ'dʒɪtəmət] *adjective* **(a)** according to the law; *he acted in legitimate defence of his rights* **(b)** born to married parents; *the old duke had no legitimate children, so the title passed to his brother* **(c)** **legitimate concern** = reasonable and justifiable concern; *if you think it's a subject of legitimate concern you should tell your manager*

legitimize [lɪ'dʒɪtəmaɪz] *verb (formal)* to make someone *or* something legitimate; *the Prime Minister's speech has legitimized attacks on the party activists*

legroom ['legrum] *noun* amount of space available for the legs of a person sitting down (between the rows of seats in a cinema or aircraft, or inside a car); *there's not much legroom in tourist class* (NOTE: no plural)

legwarmers ['legwɔːməz] *noun* thick woollen coverings without feet, used to keep your legs warm; *gymnasts and ballet dancers often wear legwarmers over their tights when doing their exercises*

leisure ['leʒə] *noun* **(a)** **leisure (time)** = free time when you can do what you want; **leisure centre** = building where people can play sports, put on plays, dance, act, etc.; *she goes to the aerobics class at the local leisure centre* **(b)** **do it at your leisure** = do it when there is an opportunity, without any hurry; *please send in your report at your leisure* (NOTE: no plural)

leisurely ['leʒəli] *adjective* without any hurry; *they had a leisurely holiday sailing along the canals; we enjoyed a leisurely lunch before going round the museum*

leitmotif *or* **leitmotiv** ['laɪtməutiːf] *noun* theme which reappears in a book, piece of music, etc.

lemming ['lemɪŋ] *noun* small Scandinavian mammal which often travels in mass groups (they are said to fall over cliffs into the sea as they follow each other blindly); *the commuters rushed like lemmings out of the trains and to their respective offices*

lemon ['lemən] *noun* **(a)** pale yellow sour-tasting citrus fruit; *oranges are much sweeter than lemons*; **lemon squash** = drink made of concentrated lemon juice and water; **lemon tea** = black tea, served with a slice of lemon and sugar **(b)** tree which produces these fruit; *lemons grow best in hot dry climates*

lemonade [lemə'neɪd] *noun* usually fizzy lemon-flavoured drink; *can I have a glass of lemonade with ice, please?*

lemur ['liːmə] *noun* small animal with a long tail, rather like a monkey; *lemurs sat in the trees, with their long tails hanging down behind them*

lend [lend] *verb* **(a)** to let someone use something for a certain period of time; *he asked me if I would lend him £5 till Monday; I lent her my dictionary and now*

she won't give it back; compare BORROW **(b)** to make a certain effect; *the Christmas decorations lend a festive air to the shopping centre; her new hairstyle lends her an air of authority* **(c)** **to lend a hand** = to help; *can you lend a hand with the cooking?*; **to lend an ear to someone** = to listen sympathetically to what someone has to say; **to lend itself to** = to be able to be used for something special; *the garden lends itself to landscaping; the room lends itself to playing chamber music* (NOTE: **lending - lent** [lent])

lender ['lendə] *noun* person who lends money; *the interest on the loan is paid to the lender every month*

lending rate ['lendɪŋ 'reɪt] *noun* interest rate charged by a bank when lending money; *the bank has increased its base lending rate by 0.5%*

length [leŋθ] *noun* **(a)** measurement of how long something is from end to end; *the table is at least twelve feet in length*; **focal length** = the distance between a lens and a focus; *adjust the focal length until the picture become clear* **(b)** **length of time** = amount of time something takes or lasts; *can you estimate the length of time you need to do this?; she was a bit vague about the length of her visit* = she was not certain how long she was going to stay **(c)** long piece of something; *she bought a length of curtain material in the sale; we need two 3m lengths of copper piping for the new central heating system* **(d)** distance from one end to the other of a swimming pool; *he swam two lengths of the swimming pool* **(e)** **to go to great lengths to get something** = to do anything (even commit a crime) to get something; *he went to considerable lengths to get a photograph of the queen*

◊ **at length** *phrase* **(a)** for a long time and using many words; *he spoke at length about the results of the election* **(b)** with a lot of details; *she explained at great length how the machine worked* **(c)** in the end; *at length he arrived, having taken a later train than we expected*

lengthen ['leŋθən] *verb* **(a)** to make longer; *you can lengthen the skirt by turning down the hem* **(b)** to become longer; *the shadows began to lengthen across the lawn as the sun sank slowly down in the west* (NOTE: the opposite is **shorten**)

lengthways *or* **lengthwise** ['leŋθweɪz *or* 'leŋθwaɪz] *adverb* along the length of something, along the longest side of something; *fold the material lengthwise; they placed the table lengthwise against the wall*

lengthy ['leŋθi] *adjective* (very) long; *she wrote a lengthy note, detailing all the problems involved* (NOTE: **lengthier - lengthiest**)

leniency ['liːniənsi] *noun* not being strict; *the police showed surprising leniency towards the football fans*

lenient ['liːniənt] *adjective* not strict or severe; *the magistrate was surprisingly lenient towards the youths*

lens [lenz] *noun* **(a)** piece of glass or plastic, etc., curved so as to cause light rays to join or spread out, and used in spectacles, telescopes, cameras, etc.; *my eyesight is not very good, and I have to have glasses with strong lenses; if the sun is strong enough you can set fire to a piece of paper using a lens*; see also CONTACT **(b)** part of the eye behind the iris and pupil which focuses light

lent [lent] *see* LEND

Lent [lent] *noun* period of forty days before Easter; *many people try to give something up for Lent*; *see also* ASH WEDNESDAY, SHROVE TUESDAY

lentil ['lentl] *noun* small round dried seed, used especially in soups and stews; *a bowl of lentil soup*; *soak the lentils overnight before cooking them*

Leo ['li:əʊ] *noun* one of the signs of the Zodiac, shaped like a lion; *Simon was born on the 2nd August and is a Leo*; *she's (a) Leo*

leopard ['lepəd] *noun* large wild spotted cat, living in Africa; *a leopard's spots are a form of camouflage which makes the animal less easy to see in long grass* (NOTE: black leopards live in America and are called **panthers**)

leper ['lepə] *noun* person who is has leprosy; *she works in a leper hospital in Africa*

leprosy ['leprəsi] *noun* serious infectious disease which slowly destroys flesh and nerves

> COMMENT: leprosy attacks the nerves in the skin; the patient loses all feeling in a limb, and fingers and toes can drop off

lesbian ['lezbiən] *adjective & noun* (woman) who is sexually attracted to other women; *they went to the Lesbian and Gay Pride march in London*

lesion ['li:ʒn] *noun* wound or sore, or other damage to the body; *the scan showed brain lesions*; *the accident victim had lesions to the chest and neck*

less [les] **1** *adjective & pronoun* a smaller amount (of); *you will get thinner if you eat less bread*; *the total bill came to less than £10*; *she finished her homework in less than an hour*; *he sold it for less than he had paid for it* **2** *adverb* (a) not as much; *I like that one less than this one*; *the second film was less interesting than the first*; *I want a car which is less difficult to drive*; **less and less** = diminishing all the time; *I enjoy my work less and less*; *he's less and less able to look after his garden*; **more or less** = almost; *I've more or less finished painting the kitchen* (b) **in less than no time** = very quickly; *they repaired the car in less than no time*; **nothing less than** = absolutely no less than; *she'll be satisfied with nothing less than a millionaire* **3** *preposition* minus, with a certain amount taken away; *we pay £10 an hour, less 50p for insurance*

lessen ['lesən] *verb* to become less, to make something become less, to reduce something; *the wind lessened in the night and by morning was just a gentle breeze*; *wearing a seat belt lessens the risk of fatal injury* (NOTE: do not confuse with **lesson**)

lesser ['lesə] *adjective* smaller, not as large or important; *the value of the archaeological remains was of lesser importance than the light they shed on the history of Roman Britain*; **the lesser of two evils** = one of two things which is not quite as bad as the other; *faced with the choice of taking a taxi or waiting in the rain for a bus, we chose the lesser of two evils and decided to take the taxi*

lesson ['lesən] *noun* (a) period of time in school, etc., when you are taught something; *he went to sleep during the French lesson*; *we have six lessons of history a week*; *she's taking or having driving lessons*; *he gives Spanish lessons at home in the evenings* (b) something which you learn from experience and which makes you wiser; *he's learnt his lesson, he knows you shouldn't be rude to policemen*; **to teach someone a**

lesson = to punish someone for doing something wrong; *I locked up her bike - that will teach her a lesson* (NOTE: do not confuse with **lessen**)

lest [lest] *conjunction (formal)* (a) in order to avoid; *they had to speak in whispers, lest they be overheard* (b) for fear that; *she is afraid to say what she thinks, lest she might offend someone*

let [let] **1** *verb* (a) to allow someone to do something; *he let her borrow his car*; *will you let me see the papers?*; *let me see what I can do for you* (b) **to let someone know something** = to tell someone about something, to give someone information about something; *please let me know the result as soon as you can*; *can you let me know when the parcel arrives?* (c) to allow someone to borrow a house or office for a while and pay for it; *we're letting our cottage to some friends for the weekend*; **the flat is to let at £1000 a month** = the flat can be rented for £1000 per month (d) *(making a suggestion that you and someone else should do something together)* *let's go to the cinema*; *don't let's leave yet or let's not leave yet* (NOTE: **letting - has let**) **2** *noun* period of the lease of a property; *they took the house on a short let*

let down ['let 'daʊn] *verb* (a) to lower something or someone; *they let him down into the mine on a rope* (b) to make the air go out of a tyre, etc.; *someone had let down my front tyre* (c) not to help when someone expects it; *I asked three people to speak at the meeting but they all let me down*

let go ['let 'gəʊ] *verb* to stop holding on to something; *don't let go of the driving wheel*; *she was holding on to a branch, but then had to let go*

lethal ['li:θl] *adjective* which causes death; *she took a lethal overdose*

lethargic [lə'θɑːdʒɪk] *adjective* showing lethargy; *the heat of the sun makes many animals slow and lethargic*

lethargy ['leθədʒi] *noun* tired feeling, when your movements are slow and you are almost inactive; *lack of ventilation can cause lethargy and drowsiness*

let in ['let 'ɪn] *verb* to allow to come in; *don't let the dog in if she's wet*; *my boots let in water*

◊ **let yourself in for** ['let jə'self 'ɪn fɔː] *verb* to allow yourself to get involved in something difficult or unpleasant; *you're letting yourself in for all sorts of problems*; *she didn't realize what she was letting herself in for when she said she would look after the children*

let off ['let 'ɒf] *verb* (a) to make a gun, etc., fire; *they let off fireworks in the town centre* (b) not to punish someone severely; *he was charged with stealing, but the judge let him off with a fine* (c) to agree that someone need not do something; *she let the class off their homework*

let on ['let 'ɒn] *verb* to tell a secret; *they didn't let on to the police that I was there*

let out ['let 'aʊt] *verb* (a) to allow to go out; *the boys let the pigs out of the field*; *we let the dogs out into the garden in the evening*; *she let the air out of my front tyre* (b) to make a piece of clothing bigger; *can you let out these trousers, they're getting too tight?* (NOTE: in this meaning the opposite is to **take in**)

let's [lets] *see* LET

letter ['letə] *noun* (a) piece of writing sent from one person or organization to another to pass on information; *there were two letters for you in the post*; *don't forget to write a letter to your mother to tell her how we all are*; *we've had a letter from the bank manager* **(b)** one of the signs which make up the alphabet, a sign used in writing which means a certain sound; *Z is the last letter of the alphabet*; *I'm trying to think of a word with ten letters beginning with A and ending with R*; **to the letter** = exactly as indicated; *they followed his instructions to the letter*; *the referee makes sure that the rules of the game are followed to the letter*; *see also* CAPITAL, RED-LETTER DAY

letterbox ['letəbɒks] *noun* **(a)** box in the road where you post letters; *there's a letterbox at the corner of the street* **(b)** hole in a front door through which the postman pushes letters; *the Sunday paper is too big to go through the letterbox*

letterhead ['letəhed] *noun* name and address of a company printed at the top of a piece of writing paper; *the order came on a sheet of paper with the company letterhead*

lettering ['letrɪŋ] *noun* style of letters in an inscription, etc.; *they put the name of the shop over the door in gold lettering*

letting ['letɪŋ] *noun* action of renting out property; **letting agency** = office which deals in property to let; **furnished lettings** = furnished property to let

lettuce ['letɪs] *noun* plant with large green leaves which are used in salads; *he made a salad with lettuce, tomatoes, and cucumber with an oil dressing* (NOTE: no plural except when referring to several plants: **a row of lettuces**)

let up ['let 'ʌp] *verb* to do less, to become less; *the snow didn't let up all day*; *she's working too hard - she ought to let up a bit*

leukaemia *US* **leukemia** [luː'kiːmiə] *noun* any of several malignant diseases where an abnormal number of white blood cells form in the blood; *their daughter has just been diagnosed as having leukaemia*; *she is having a course of radiotherapy to treat her leukaemia*

levee ['levi] *noun US* embankment built along the bank of a river which is liable to flood; *they are strengthening the levees along the Mississippi*

level ['levəl] **1** *noun* **(a)** position relating to height or amount; *I want to lower the level of our borrowings*; *the floodwater has reached a level of 5m above normal*; **decisions taken at managerial level** = decisions taken by managers **(b)** floor in a building; *go up to the next level*; *the toilets are at street level* **(c)** **on the level** = honest, not trying to deceive; *I don't think the salesman is being on the level with us* **2** *adjective* **(a)** flat, even; *are these shelves level, or do they slope to the left?* **(b)** **level with** = at the same level as; *the floor which is level with the street is the ground floor* **3** *verb* **to level off** *or* **to level out** = to stop going up or down; *price increases are starting to level off*; *the road climbs for about two kilometres and then levels out* (NOTE: **levelling - levelled** but American spelling is **leveling - leveled**)

level crossing ['levl 'krɒsɪŋ] *noun* place where a road crosses a railway line without a bridge or tunnel; *the level crossing gates opened when the train had passed* (NOTE: American English is **grade crossing**)

level-headed ['levl'hedɪd] *adjective* sensible; *don't worry, she's a level-headed girl and won't do anything silly*

lever ['liːvə] **1** *noun* instrument like a bar, which helps to lift a heavy object, or to move part of a machine, etc.; *we used a pole as a lever to lift up the block of stone*; **gear lever** = handle in a car which changes the gears; *push the gear lever down and towards you to get into reverse* **2** *verb* to move with a lever; *they levered open the door with an iron bar*

leverage ['liːvrɪdʒ] *noun* **(a)** lifting power of a lever; *they used a longer bar to get better leverage*; *you'll need a longer pole to increase the leverage* **(b)** influence which you can use to get what you want; *his business contacts were useful leverage in discussing terms for the contract*; *she has a majority of the shares in the company and therefore can exert a lot of leverage over the directors* **(c)** **leveraged buyout (LBO)** = takeover by a group of managers and directors by borrowing against the shares in the company to be bought

levitate ['levɪteɪt] *verb* to rise into the air, as if by magic; *it is claimed that some Indian holy men are able to levitate*

levity ['levɪti] *noun (formal)* lack of respect when considering serious things; *the fact that he wears a wig is no cause for levity*

levy ['levi] **1** *noun* tax or other payment demanded and collected; *I think the import levies on luxury goods are too high*; *we paid the levy on time* (NOTE: plural is **levies**) **2** *verb* to demand or to collect a tax or other payment; *the customs levied a large fine*

lewd [luːd] *adjective* rude and indecent; *he made some lewd remarks to the waitress* (NOTE: **lewder - lewdest**)

lexicographer [leksɪ'kɒgrəfə] *noun* person who writes dictionaries

lexicography [leksɪ'kɒgrəfi] *noun* the writing of dictionaries

liability [laɪə'bɪlɪti] *noun* **(a)** legal responsibility; *make sure you understand your legal liabilities before you sign the contract*; **to accept liability for something** = to agree that you are responsible for something; **to refuse liability for something** = to refuse to agree that you are responsible for something; **they couldn't meet their liabilities** = they couldn't pay their debts; *see also* LIMITED (NOTE: plural in this meaning is **liabilities**) **(b)** tendency to do something; *his unfortunate liability to burst into tears when criticized* **(c)** disadvantage; *bad eyesight is a liability if you want to be a pilot* **(d)** person who causes embarrassment or problems; *he has been arrested several times and is something of a liability to his parents*

liable ['laɪəbl] *adjective* **(a)** **liable for** = legally responsible for something; *you will be liable for the payment of the fine*; *parents can be made liable for their children's debts* **(b)** **liable to** = likely to do something; *the trains are liable to be late*; *she is liable to burst into tears at the slightest criticism*

liaise [lɪ'eɪz] *verb* **to liaise with someone** = to inform someone of what is being done so that actions are coordinated; *can you liaise with each individual manager regarding the move to new offices?*

liaison [lɪ'eɪzən] *noun* **(a)** keeping someone informed of what is happening; *there has been a total lack of liaison between the police and the customs department on this case*; **liaison officer** = person whose job is to keep someone else informed of what is happening; *the personnel manager was appointed as liaison officer* *with the unions over relocation* **(b)** sexual affair; *his liaison with the beautiful Hungarian was soon well-known in the embassy*

liar ['laɪə] *noun* person who tells lies; *John is a born liar*

lib [lɪb] *noun (informal) short for* LIBERATION; *see also* WOMEN'S LIB

Lib Dem ['lɪb 'dem] *abbreviation for* LIBERAL DEMOCRAT; *delegates at the Lib Dem party conference* (NOTE: plural is **the Lib Dems**)

libel ['laɪbl] **1** *noun* untrue written statement(s) which can damage someone's reputation; *I will sue you for libel* **2** *verb* **to libel someone** = to damage someone's reputation in writing; *he accused the newspaper of libelling him; compare* SLANDER (NOTE: **libelling - libelled** but American spelling is **libeling - libeled**)

libellous *US* **libelous** ['laɪbələs] *adjective* which libels someone; *the magazine published a libellous article about her*

liberal ['lɪbrəl] **1** *adjective* **(a)** not strict, tolerant of other people's views; *the liberal view would be to let the teenagers run the club themselves* **(b)** generous; *he left a very liberal tip* **(c)** *(in politics)* **Liberal** = referring to or supporting the Liberal Party **2** *noun (in politics)* **a Liberal** = member or supporter of a Liberal Party

liberal arts ['lɪbərəl 'ɑːts] *noun US* subjects other than science, such as English, history, philosophy, languages, etc.; *she has a bachelor's degree in liberal arts*

Liberal Democratic Party ['lɪbrəl demə'krætɪk 'pɑːti] *noun* British political party formed in 1988 from the Liberal Party and some members of the Social Democratic Party; *the Lib Dems have made sweeping gains in the local government elections* (NOTE: often called **the Lib Dems** for short)

liberalism ['lɪbrəlɪzm] *noun* ideals and beliefs of Liberals; *hard-line right-wingers have no time for wishy-washy liberalism*

liberality [lɪbə'ræliti] *noun (formal)* **(a)** being tolerant about opinions you do not agree with; *he was well known for the liberality of his views on divorce* **(b)** generosity; *the liberality of the sheikh's presents astonished everyone*

liberalize ['lɪbərəlaɪz] *verb* to make (laws, etc.) more liberal; *the government has liberalized the divorce laws*

Liberal Party ['lɪbərəl 'pɑːti] *noun* political party which is in favour of some social change, some involvement of the state in industry and welfare, but less centralization of government, with no fixed connections with either workers or employers; *the Liberal Party won an overwhelming victory in the Canadian general election*

liberate ['lɪbəreɪt] *verb* to set someone *or* something free from something; *the hostages were finally liberated by the security forces; the capital was liberated by government troops*

liberation [lɪbə'reɪʃn] *noun* setting free; *the liberation of the country from years of repression;* **women's liberation** *or* **women's lib** = the equal place in society of women with men and actions taken to promote this

libertarian [lɪbə'teəriən] *noun* person who believes in freedom of thought and action; *the latest reported acts of repression in the country will shock libertarians everywhere*

liberty ['lɪbəti] *noun* **(a)** freedom; *when he was in prison he wrote poems about his lost liberty;* anti-terrorist legislation can be seen as an infringement of the liberty of the individual **(b)** at **liberty** = free; not in prison; *two of the escaped prisoners are still at liberty;* **to be at liberty to do something** = to be free to do something; *you are at liberty to go now* **(c)** **to take liberties** = to do something without permission; **to take liberties with something** *or* **someone** = to treat something *or* someone too familiarly; *she borrowed my Walkman without asking - she's always taking liberties with other people's property; the boss felt she was taking liberties by using the office phone to ask about getting another job;* **civil liberties** = freedom of people to act within the law (liberty of the press, liberty of the individual, etc.); *outside security cameras can be seen as an infringement of civil liberties*

Libra ['liːbrə] *noun* one of the signs of the zodiac, shaped like a pair of scales; *John was born on the 11th October and is a Libra*

librarian [laɪ'breəriən] *noun* person who works in a library; *the librarian helped us find what we wanted in the catalogue*

library ['laɪbri] *noun* **(a)** place where books are kept which can be borrowed; *he forgot to take his books back to the library; you can't sell it, it's a library book;* **reference library** = library with reference books, where readers can search for information but not take the books away from the library **(b)** collection of books, records, etc.; *he has a big record library* (NOTE: plural is **libraries**)

libretto [lɪ'bretəʊ] *noun* words of an opera or musical; *who wrote the libretto of 'The Sound of Music'?* (NOTE: plural is **librettos** *or* **libretti**)

Libya ['lɪbjə] *noun* country in North Africa, west of Egypt; *Libya is a major oil exporter* (NOTE: capital: **Tripoli**; people: **the Libyans**; language: **Arabic**; currency: **Libyan dinar**)

Libyan ['lɪbjən] **1** *adjective* referring to Libya; *the Libyan Desert is the north-east part of the Sahara* **2** *noun* person from Libya; *she is married to a Libyan*

lice [laɪs] *see* LOUSE

licence *US* **license** ['laɪsəns] *noun* **(a)** document which gives official permission to possess something or to do something; *she has applied for an export licence for these paintings;* **driving licence** *US* **driver's license** = permit which allows someone to drive a car, truck, etc.; *applicants should hold a valid driving licence; you must apply for a provisional driving licence before taking your first driving lesson; US* **license plate** = plate (one on the front and one on the back of a car) which shows an identifying number (NOTE: British English is **number plate**) **(b)** freedom, especially when used wrongly; *designers should be given the licence to change the whole design whenever they want* **(c)** **under licence** = with a permit from a copyright holder; *the cars are made in South America under licence*

license ['laɪsəns] **1** *noun US see* LICENCE **2** *verb* to give someone official permission to do something; *the* *restaurant is licensed to serve beer, wines and spirits*; *she is licensed to run an employment agency*

licensed ['laɪsənst] *adjective* which has a licence to do something; *most of the traders in the markets aren't licensed*; **licensed hotel** *or* **licensed restaurant** = hotel *or* restaurant which has a licence to sell alcohol; **licensed premises** = building, such as a club, etc., that has a licence to sell alcohol

lichen ['laɪkən or 'lɪtʃən] *noun* primitive plant which grows on the surface of stones or trunks of trees and can survive in very cold climates; *the yellow of the lichens on the rocks makes a very beautiful photograph*

licit ['lɪsɪt] *adjective (formal)* legal

lick [lɪk] **1** *noun* **(a)** a stroke with the tongue; *the dog gave him a friendly lick*; *can I have a lick of your ice cream?* **(b)** *(informal)* quick coat of paint; *the door could do with a lick of paint* **(c)** *(informal)* **a lick and a promise** = a quick wash **2** *verb* **(a)** to stroke with your tongue; *you shouldn't lick the plate when you've finished your pudding*; *they licked their lips when they saw the cakes*; **to lick someone's boots** = to behave very humbly towards someone **(b)** to beat, to hit; **to lick someone into shape** = to train someone to do something properly; *a few weeks with the army and he'll soon be licked into shape*

licorice ['lɪkərɪs] *noun US see* LIQUORICE

lid [lɪd] *noun* covering for a container, sometimes with a handle; *where's the lid of the black saucepan?*; *he managed to get the lid off the jam jar*

lie [laɪ] **1** *verb* **(a)** to say something which is not true; *she was lying when she said she had been at home all evening*; *he lied about the accident to the headmaster* (NOTE: in this meaning: **lying - lied**) **(b)** to be in a flat position; to be situated; *six soldiers lay dead on the ground*; *the dog spends the evening lying in front of the fire*; *there were bits of paper and cigarette packets lying all over the pavement*; *the city of Quito lies near the equator*; **to lie in wait for someone** = to hide and wait for someone to come so as to attack him (NOTE: in this meaning: **lying - lay** [leɪ] - **has lain** [leɪn]) **2** *noun* something which is not true; *that's a lie! - don't believe what he says*; *someone has been telling lies about her*

lie down ['laɪ 'daʊn] *verb* to put yourself in a flat position, especially on a bed; *I'll just go and lie down for five minutes*; *the burglars told him to lie down on the floor*

lie-down ['laɪdaʊn] *noun (informal)* short rest; *after all these arguments about the arrangements for the wedding, mother said she had to have a little lie-down*; *if you're tired, why don't you go and have a lie-down?*

lie in ['laɪ 'ɪn] *verb* to stay in bed late in the morning; *I think I'll lie in this morning*

lie-in ['laɪɪn] *noun (informal)* **to have a lie-in** = to stay in bed longer than usual; *I can't wait until Saturday comes, then I can have a lie-in*

lie low ['laɪ 'ləʊ] *verb* to keep hidden and quiet; *you'd better lie low until the police go away*; *after the robbery, they lay low for a few months*

lieu [ljuː] *noun* **in lieu of** = instead of; *when she was sacked she was given four weeks' pay in lieu of notice*; *he accepted a car in lieu of payment*

lieutenant [lef'tenənt *US* luː'tenənt] *noun* **(a)** rank in the armed forces below a captain; *the lieutenant has to report to his captain*; **lieutenant-colonel** = rank in the armed forces above major and below colonel;

lieutenant-general = rank in the armed forces above major-general and below general **(b)** main helper; *the mayor came into the room with two of his lieutenants*

life [laɪf] *noun* **(a)** time when you are alive; *he spent his whole life working on the farm*; *miners lead a hard life*; **in early life** = when you are a child; *in early life he lived in the country*; **for life** = for as long as someone is alive; *his pension gives him a comfortable income for life*; *(informal)* **not on your life!** = certainly not!; *don't you want to go camping? - not on your life!*; **it's a matter of life and death** = it's a very serious matter; *call the hospital immediately - it's a matter of life and death* **(b)** being a living person; **to lose your life** = to die; *several lives were lost when the ship sank*; *she saved my life* = she saved me from dying; **to take your (own) life** = to commit suicide; *in a fit of despair she took her life* (NOTE: plural is **lives** in meanings (a) and (b)) **(c)** experience; *life can be hard when you don't have much money*; *miners live a hard life* **(d)** living things; *is there life on Mars?*; **there's no sign of life in the house** = it looks as though there is no one in it; **pond life** = animals and plants which live in ponds **(e)** liveliness, energy; *the young actors injected some life into the old play*; *the film comes to life when she appears on the screen* **(f)** biography, the written story of someone's life; *she has written a life of Henry VIII*

life assurance *or* **life insurance** ['laɪf ə'ʃʊərəns *or* 'laɪf ɪn'ʃʊərəns] *noun* insurance which pays an amount of money to your next of kin if you die; *the mortgage company required him to have a life insurance policy*

lifebelt ['laɪfbelt] *noun* large ring which helps you to keep afloat in water; *they threw lifebelts to the passengers from the sinking ferry* (NOTE: American English is also **life preserver**)

lifeboat ['laɪfbəʊt] *noun* special boat used to rescue people at sea; *the lifeboat looked for the crew of the ship which had sunk*

life cycle ['laɪf 'saɪkl] *noun* all the changes an organism goes through during its life; *biology students have to study the life cycle of a locust*

life expectancy ['laɪf ɪk'spektənsi] *noun* number of years a person or animal, etc., is likely to live or survive; *average life expectancy has increased to over 80 for women*; *the life expectancy of this government is short - it only has a majority of one in Parliament*

lifeguard ['laɪfgɑːd] *noun* person who is on duty on a beach or at a swimming pool, and who rescues people who get into difficulty in the water; *lifeguards have raised red flags to show that the sea is dangerous*; *three hunky lifeguards came to rescue us*

life imprisonment ['laɪf ɪm'prɪzənmənt] *noun* being sent to prison for a long time, but not necessarily for the whole of the rest of your life; *he was sentenced to life imprisonment for the murder of his wife*

life jacket ['laɪf 'dʒækɪt] *noun* air-filled or cork-filled coat to keep you afloat; *children must all wear life-jackets on the river*; *instructions for donning the life jacket are in the pocket in front of your seat* (NOTE: American English is also **life preserver**)

lifeless ['laɪfləs] *adjective* **(a)** not alive; *her lifeless body was washed up on the shore* **(b)** not lively; *the dancers' performance was lifeless and the audience booed them at the end of the ballet*

lifelike ['laɪflaɪk] *adjective* just like a living person; *the portrait is very lifelike*

lifeline ['laɪflaɪn] *noun* **(a)** rope thrown to a drowning person; *they threw him a lifeline from the boat* **(b)** help given to someone in difficulties; *the government grant is a lifeline which helps them put on exhibitions of young painters' work at their gallery*

lifelong ['laɪflɒŋ] *adjective* lasting your whole life; *they formed a lifelong friendship at university; he was a lifelong member of the Communist Party*

life preserver ['laɪf prɪ'zɜːvə] *noun* **(a)** *GB* short stick, used in self-defence **(b)** *US see* LIFEBELT, LIFE JACKET

life raft ['laɪfrɑːft] *noun* small raft carried on a ship to carry crew and passengers if the ship sinks; *the ship sank in rough seas and the crew took to the life rafts*

life saving ['laɪfseɪvɪŋ] **1** *noun* rescuing people from drowning; *he took a course in life saving before becoming a guard at the swimming pool* **2** *adjective* which saves lives; *the surgeon performed a life-saving operation on the little girl*

life sciences ['laɪf 'saɪənsɪz] *noun* sciences which involve the study of animals and plants; *biology, botany and medicine are life sciences*

life sentence ['laɪf 'sentəns] *noun* being sent to prison for a long time, but not necessarily for the whole of the rest of your life; *he can expect a life sentence for murdering his wife*

> COMMENT: a life sentence is the penalty for murder, and normally lasts about ten years

life-span ['laɪfspæn] *noun* length of time something exists; *some artificial elements have a life-span of a few millionths of a second*

lifestyle ['laɪfstaɪl] *noun* way in which someone or a group of people live their daily lives; *I don't want to be a film star, I don't envy their lifestyle at all; as an Olympic athlete, his lifestyle involves early-morning training sessions; expatriates have an enviable lifestyle living tax free in the Far East*

life-threatening ['laɪfθretənɪŋ] *adjective* which may kill; *whooping cough is a nasty disease but is rarely life-threatening; he has been diagnosed with a life-threatening disease*

lifetime ['laɪftaɪm] *noun* time when you are alive; *I hope to see men on Mars in my lifetime; he finally won the lottery after a lifetime of poverty; the chance of a lifetime* = the best chance you are ever likely to get; *take the offer - it's the chance of a lifetime*

lift [lɪft] **1** *noun* **(a)** machine which takes people up or down from one floor to another in a building; *take the lift to the tenth floor; push the button to call the lift; your room is on the fifteenth floor, so you had better use the lift* (NOTE: American English for this is **elevator**) **(b)** chair lift *or* ski lift = chairs which take skiers to the top of a mountain slope; *the chair lift takes about ten minutes to reach the top* **(c)** ride in a car offered to someone; *she gave me a lift to the station; to hitch a lift* = to ask a driver to take you as a passenger, usually by signalling with the thumb or by holding a sign with your destination written on it; *he hitched a lift to Birmingham; her car broke down and she hitched a lift from a passing motorist* **2** *verb* **(a)** to pick something up or move it to a higher position; *my briefcase is so heavy I can hardly lift it off the floor; he lifted the little girl up so that she could see the procession; he hurt his back lifting the box down from*

the shelf **(b)** to remove; *the government has lifted the ban on selling guns* **(c)** to go away; *the fog had lifted by lunchtime* **(d)** *(informal)* to copy; *whole sections of his book were lifted from one I wrote two years ago*

lift-off ['lɪftɒf] *noun* vertical launch of a space rocket; *5-4-3-2-1 we have lift-off!*

ligament ['lɪgəmənt] *noun* thick band of fibrous tissue which connects the bones at a joint; *he has a torn ligament in his ankle*

light [laɪt] **1** *noun* **(a)** brightness, the opposite of darkness; *I can't read the map by the light of the moon; there's not enough light to take a photo; to stand in someone's light* = to stand between someone and a source of light **(b)** electric bulb which gives light; *turn the light on - I can't see to read; it's dangerous to ride a bicycle with no lights; in the fog, I could just see the red lights of the car in front of me; (informal)* **there's light at the end of the tunnel** = there is some hope that everything will be all right **(c)** way of making a cigarette, etc., catch fire; *can you give me a light? or do you have a light?* **(d)** **to cast light** *or* **to throw light on something** = to make something easier to understand; *the papers throw light on how the minister reached his decision;* **to come to light** = to be discovered; *documents have come to light which could help the police in their investigations;* **in the light of something** = when something is considered; *in the light of the reports in the press, can the minister explain his decision?* **2** *verb* **(a)** to start to burn, to make something start to burn; *can you light the oven for me?; he couldn't get the fire to light; light a candle - it's dark in the cellar* **(b)** to give light to something; *the full moon lit the village, so we could see the church clearly; floodlights were brought in to light the accident site* (NOTE: **lighting - lit** [lɪt]) **3** *adjective* **(a)** not heavy; *I can lift this box easily - it's quite light or it's as light as a feather; you need light clothing for tropical countries; she's just been ill, and can only do light work* **(b)** *(colour)* pale; *he was wearing a light green shirt; I prefer a light carpet to a dark one* **(c)** having a lot of light so that you can see well; *the big windows make the kitchen very light; it was six o'clock in the morning and just getting light* **(d)** not very serious; *I like to listen to light music when I am doing the cooking; she took some detective novels as light reading on the train* (NOTE: **lighter - lightest**) **4** *adverb* **to travel light** = to travel with very little luggage; *if you're hitching across Australia, it's best to travel light*

light bulb ['laɪt 'bʌlb] *noun* glass ball which gives electric light; *you'll need a ladder to change the light bulb*

lighten ['laɪtən] *verb* **(a)** to make or become brighter, not so dark; *you can lighten the room by painting it white; the sky lightened as dawn broke* **(b)** to make or become lighter, not so heavy; *I'll have to lighten my backpack - it's much too heavy* **(c)** to make someone happier, less gloomy; *the news has lightened the gloom in the office considerably*

lighter ['laɪtə] **1** *noun* **(a)** small device for lighting cigarettes; *can I borrow your lighter? - mine has run out of gas* **(b)** boat for carrying goods from a large ship to land; *cranes were unloading the cargo into lighters* **2** *adjective see* LIGHT

light-fingered ['laɪtfɪŋgəd] *adjective* who tends to steal things; *some light-fingered guest removed two of our silver spoons*

light-headed ['laɪt'hedɪd] *adjective* dizzy; *he felt quite light-headed after he came off the plane*; *a couple of glasses of champagne and she was quite light-headed*

light-hearted [laɪt'hɑːtɪd] *adjective* happy, not very serious; *he told some light-hearted jokes about life in the office*

light heavyweight ['laɪt 'hevɪweɪt] *noun* weight of a boxer between middleweight and heavyweight; *the light heavyweight champion*; *a light heavyweight title fight*

lighthouse ['laɪthaʊs] *noun* tall building near the sea containing a bright light to guide ships away from rocks; *most of the lighthouses on Scottish islands are automatic* (NOTE: plural is **lighthouses** ['laɪthaʊzɪz])

light industry ['laɪt 'ɪndʌstri] *noun* industry which makes small products, such as clothes, books, calculators; *light industry came through the recession quite well*

lighting ['laɪtɪŋ] *noun* the light in a place; *the lighting is very bad in this restaurant - I can't see what I'm eating*

lighting-up time [laɪtɪŋ 'ʌp 'taɪm] *noun* time in the evening when street lamps and car lights have to be switched on; *in the autumn lighting-up time is earlier each day*

lightly ['laɪtli] *adverb* (a) not heavily; *she touched my arm lightly*; *I always sleep lightly and wake up several times each night* (b) without much rich food; *she always eats lightly at lunchtime*

lightning ['laɪtnɪŋ] *noun* (a) flash of electricity in the sky, followed by thunder; *the storm approached with thunder and lightning* (b) **like lightning** = very fast; *deer can run like lightning*

lightning conductor *US* **lightning rod** ['laɪtnɪŋ kən'dʌktə or 'rɒd] *noun* metal strip running from the top of a construction down to the earth, which takes the electrical force of lightning and prevents the building being damaged

lights [laɪts] *noun* red, green and orange lights for making traffic stop and start; *turn left at the next set of lights*; *he drove straight across the crossroads when the lights were red* (NOTE: short for **traffic lights**)

light-sensitive ['laɪt 'sensɪtɪv] *adjective* which reacts to light; *the retina is a light-sensitive membrane at the back of the eyeball*

lightship ['laɪtʃɪp] *noun* ship which carries a large light, and acts as a floating lighthouse; *we passed the lightship on the Goodwin Sands*

light up ['laɪt 'ʌp] *verb* (a) to make something bright; *the flames from the burning petrol store lit up the night sky*; *the firework display lit up the gardens and the lake* (b) to become bright and cheerful; *her face lit up when she saw the presents under the Christmas tree* (c) to start to smoke; *please do not light up until coffee has been served*

lightweight ['laɪtweɪt] **1** *adjective* (a) made of light cloth; *at last we have some hot weather and a chance to wear lightweight clothes* (b) not very influential or important; *he's quite sensible, but only a lightweight member of the committee* **2** *noun* weight of a boxer between featherweight and welterweight; *the lightweight champion*; *a lightweight title fight*

light year ['laɪt 'jɜː] *noun* (a) distance travelled by light during one year (about 9.3 billion kilometres); *stars are light years from earth* (b) **light years apart** = very different; *the new model is light years in advance of its competitors*

like [laɪk] **1** *adjective* (formal) similar, nearly the same; *sociology, psychology and like subjects* **2** *preposition* (a) similar to, in the same way as; *he's like his mother in many ways, but he has his father's nose*; *like you, I don't get on with the new boss*; *the picture doesn't look like him at all*; *he can swim like a fish*; *it tastes like strawberries*; *what's that record? - it sounds like Elgar*; **it feels like snow** = it feels as if it is going to snow; **do you feel like a cup of coffee?** = do you want a cup of coffee? (b) (asking someone to describe something) *what was the weather like when you were on holiday?*; *what's he like, her new boyfriend?* **3** *adverb* **as like as not** = probably; *as like as not, Dan will arrive late* **4** *conjunction* in the same way as; *she looks just like I did at her age* **5** *verb* (a) to have pleasant feelings about something *or* someone; *do you like the new manager?*; *she doesn't like eating meat*; *how does he like his new job?*; *no one likes driving in rush hour traffic*; *in the evening, I like to sit quietly and read the newspaper* (b) to want; *I'd like you to meet one of our sales executives*; *I'd like to go to Paris next week*; *take as many apples as you like* **6** *noun* (a) thing which you like; *we try to take account of the likes and dislikes of individual customers* (b) **the likes of** = someone like; *the likes of him should not be allowed in*

likeable ['laɪkəbl] *adjective* pleasant; *she's a very likeable colleague*

likelihood ['laɪlihʊd] *noun* being probable; *there's every likelihood that he will be late*; *it's cloudy so the likelihood of rain is high*; *the likelihood is that no party will be the outright winner in the elections*

likely ['laɪkli] **1** *adjective* which you think is going to happen; *it's likely to snow this weekend*; *he's not likely to come to the party*; *is that at all likely?* (NOTE: **likelier - likeliest**) **2** *adverb* probably; *most likely he's gone home*

like-minded [laɪk'maɪndɪd] *adjective* who has the same opinions; *she organized a meeting of other like-minded people*

liken ['laɪkən] *verb* **to liken something to something** = to compare two things, by showing how one is similar to the other; *can I liken her to a ray of sunlight?*; *he likened being tackled by the South African forward to being hit by a rhino*

likeness ['laɪknəs] *noun* (a) a portrait, thing which looks like someone; *the sketch is an astonishing likeness of grandmother* (b) being alike; *there is a strong family likeness in all the children* (NOTE: plural is **likenesses**)

likewise ['laɪkwaɪz] *adverb* in the same way, similarly; *John got an 'A' in the maths exam - likewise his sister Penny*

liking ['laɪkɪŋ] *noun* pleasant feeling towards someone *or* something; *she has a liking for chocolate*; *this drink is too gassy for my liking*; **to take a liking to someone** = to start to like someone; *the manager has taken a liking to her*

lilac ['laɪlək] **1** *noun* (a) tree with clusters of purple or white flowers; *they have a pretty lilac in their front garden* (b) pale purple colour; *they painted the* bathroom a deep lilac **2** adjective pale purple; she wore a lilac dress and gloves

lilt [lɪlt] noun way of speaking or singing with a light well-marked rhythm; the Welsh speak with a lilt in their voice

lilting ['lɪltɪŋ] adjective which has a lilt; he song a lilting ballad

lily ['lɪli] noun type of flower shaped like a trumpet, which grows from a bulb; the church was decorated with arrangements of white lilies (NOTE: plural is **lilies**)

lily-of-the-valley ['lɪli əv ðə 'væli] noun spring plant with small white flowers and a strong scent; we picked some lily-of-the-valley on May 1st (NOTE: plural is **lilies-of-the-valley** or **lily-of-the-valley**)

limb [lɪm] noun **(a)** leg or arm; he was lucky not to break a limb in the accident; **danger to life and limb** = danger that someone may be hurt; when he's on his motorbike he's a danger to life and limb **(b)** branch of a tree; **out on a limb** = in a difficult or exposed situation; he feels out on a limb, with no one to share responsibility for running the company

limbo ['lɪmbəʊ] noun **(a)** place between heaven and hell, where people who are not baptized are said to go when they die; in medieval times, some poor souls were condemned to wander in limbo for ever **(b)** position of being halfway between two stages; after losing his seat in the election he now finds himself in political limbo **(c) limbo dancing** = West Indian dance where the dancer bends his body backwards to pass under a low horizontal bar; we spent the evening limbo dancing to music from a steel band

lime [laɪm] noun **(a)** white substance containing calcium, used in making cement; the builder ordered some bags of lime (NOTE: no plural in this meaning) **(b) lime (tree)** = northern deciduous tree with smooth leaves and yellowish flowers; an avenue of limes **(c)** small yellowish-green tropical fruit like a lemon; tree which bears such fruit; you need the juice of two limes to make this recipe

lime green ['laɪm 'griːn] adjective & noun bright green colour of lime, the fruit; they've painted their front door lime green

limelight ['laɪmlaɪt] noun attention or publicity; he seems to enjoy being in the limelight

limerick ['lɪmərɪk] noun type of amusing poem with five lines

COMMENT: the best-known limericks are by Edward Lear: here are two of them: "There was an old man of Dundee/ Who frequented the top of a tree/ When disturbed by the crows,/ He abruptly arose/ And exclaimed 'I'll return to Dundee'" "There was an Old Man of the Hague/ Whose ideas were excessively vague;/ He built a balloon,/ To examine the moon,/ That deluded Old Man of the Hague"

limestone ['laɪmstəʊn] noun common white sedimentary rock; limestone is used in the making of cement

limit ['lɪmɪt] **1** noun furthest point beyond which you cannot go; **age limit** = youngest or oldest age at which you are allowed to do something; we put an age limit of thirty-five on new employees; **speed limit** = highest speed at which you are allowed to drive; the speed limit in towns is 30 miles per hour; the police hope that the

new speed limits will cut down the number of accidents; **weight limit** = heaviest weight which something can stand; the bridge has a weight limit of 3 tonnes; **over the limit** = with more alcohol in your blood than is allowed by law; the breath test showed he was way over the limit; **within limits** = in a modest way, not excessively; we're prepared to help you within limits **2** verb not to allow something to go beyond a certain point; her parents limited the number of evenings she could go out; the treasurer wants to limit expenditure on flowers

limitation [lɪmɪ'teɪʃn] noun **(a)** act of limiting; **damage limitation** = limiting the amount of damage which will occur; **damage limitation exercise** = using the media in response to some bad publicity, so as to make it less harmful; the spin doctors put our photographs of the minister with his family, as part of a damage limitation exercise **(b)** thing which stops you going further; **to know your limitations** = to know what you are capable of doing; I'd love to go hang-gliding but I know my limitations **(c) statute of limitations** = law which allows only a certain amount of time, usually six years, for someone to start legal proceedings to claim damages

limited ['lɪmɪtɪd] adjective which has been limited; **limited (liability) company** = private company in which the shareholders are only responsible for the company's debts up to the amount of capital they have put in (NOTE: limited companies are abbreviated to **Ltd** in the company name: **Jones & Black Ltd**)

limited edition ['lɪmɪtɪd ɪ'dɪʃn] noun something of which only a few copies are printed or made (usually no more than 1,000); a limited edition of 500 copies, each numbered and signed by the artist; he has a priceless collection of limited editions in his library

limiting ['lɪmɪtɪŋ] adjective which limits; **limiting factor** = something which sets a limit to something; the size of the room is a limiting factor - it will only hold fifty people; the limiting factor is the amount of money we can allocate to the project

limitless ['lɪmɪtləs] adjective without any limit; there are limitless opportunities for a young man to make money

limousine (informal) **limo** [lɪmə'ziːn or 'lɪməʊ] noun large luxurious car; as soon as the stars got out of their limos, the photographers' flash bulbs began to pop; we are the only airline to offer free limousine transport to and from your hotel

limp [lɪmp] **1** noun uneven way of walking, when one leg hurts or is shorter than the other; his limp has improved since his operation **2** verb to walk with an uneven step; after the accident she limped badly **3** adjective soft, not stiff; all we had as a salad was two limp lettuce leaves; he gave me a limp handshake; she went limp and we had to give her a glass of water

limpet ['lɪmpɪt] noun small shellfish shaped like a flat cone, which clings to rocks

linctus ['lɪŋktəs] noun sweet cough medicine; take a spoonful of linctus before going to bed

line [laɪn] **1** noun **(a)** long thin mark; she drew a straight line across the sheet of paper; parking isn't allowed on the yellow lines; the tennis ball went over the line; **to draw the line at** = to refuse to do; I don't mind having a cup of coffee with the boss, but I draw the line at having to invite him for a meal at home **(b)** long string; she hung her washing on the (washing) line; *he sat with his fishing line in the river, waiting for a fish* **(c)** wire along which telephone messages are sent; *the snow brought down the telephone lines*; *can you speak louder - the line is bad*; **crossed line** = when two telephone conversations are mixed together; **to be on the line** = to be talking to someone on the telephone; *don't interrupt - I'm on the line to New York*; *do you want to speak to Charles while he's on the line?* **(d)** row of people, etc.; *we had to stand in line for half an hour to get into the exhibition*; *the line of lorries stretched for miles at the frontier* **(e)** row of written or printed words; *he printed the first two lines and showed them to me*; *can you read the bottom line on the chart?*; *(informal)* **to drop someone a line** = to send someone a short letter; *I'll drop you a line when I get to New York*; **line printer** = computer printer which prints each line separately **(f) lines** = words learnt and then spoken by an actor; *he forgot his lines and had to be prompted* **(g) railway line** = rails on which trains run; *don't cross the line when a train might be coming*; **to be on the right lines** = to be doing things the right way **(h)** way of doing things; **in line with** = according to, following (a decision); *we acted in line with the decision taken at the meeting*; **to take a hard line** = not to be weak; *the headmaster takes a hard line with boys who sell drugs in the playground* **(i)** type of work; *what's his line of business?* **(j)** series of different products, all sold or made by the same company; *we sell several lines of refrigerators*; *I'm afraid we don't stock that line any more* **2** *verb* **(a)** to stand side by side in a line; *soldiers were lining the streets* **(b)** to put a lining inside something, especially a piece of clothing; *his jacket is lined with red silk*; *you'll need fur-lined boots in Canada*

lineage ['lɪnɪɪdʒ] *noun (formal)* line of people from whom someone is descended; *her lineage is very distinguished*

linear ['lɪnɪə] *adjective* **(a)** referring to lines; *a linear diagram* **(b)** referring to length; *a metre is a linear measurement*

lined [laɪnd] *adjective* **(a)** with lines on it; **lined paper** = paper with lines printed on it; *a pad of A4 lined paper* **(b) an avenue lined with trees** *or* **a tree-lined avenue** = an avenue with trees along both sides

lineman ['laɪnmən] *noun US* = *see* LINESMAN **(a)**

linen ['lɪnɪn] *noun* **(a)** cloth made from flax; *he bought a white linen suit* **(b) (household) linen(s)** = sheets, pillowcases, tablecloths, etc.; *put clean linen on the bed for the visitors* **(c)** underwear; *you should change your linen more often in hot weather*; **to wash your dirty linen in public** = to tell dreadful personal secrets about yourself and your family; *politicians try to be careful not to wash their dirty linen in public* (NOTE: no plural in meanings (a) and (c))

liner ['laɪnə] *noun* **(a)** thing used for lining; **bin liner** = plastic bag for putting inside a dustbin **(b) eye liner** = makeup for putting round the eyes **(c)** large passenger ship; *they went on a cruise round the Caribbean on an American liner*

linesman ['laɪnzmən] *noun* **(a)** man who looks after electric, telephone or railway lines; *the linesmen struggled for days to restore power to the areas that had been cut off by the storm* (NOTE: American English is **lineman**) **(b)** official who stays on the sideline in a game to see if the ball goes over the line, and helps the referee to spot any breaking of the rules; *after consulting with his linesman, the referee awarded a*

free kick; *the linesman flagged that the ball had gone out of play* (NOTE: plural is **linesmen**)

line up ['laɪn 'ʌp] *verb* to stand in a line; *line up over there if you want to take the next boat*

line-up ['laɪnʌp] *noun* group or list of people; *we've got a great line-up of stars for the concert*

linger ['lɪŋgə] *verb* to stay longer than necessary, longer than expected; *he was still lingering round the back door after six o'clock*

lingerie ['lænʒəri *US* lænʒə'reɪ] *noun* women's underwear; *baby clothes and lingerie are on the second floor*

lingering ['lɪŋgərɪŋ] *adjective* which remains for some time; *I have a lingering doubt about the project*

linguist ['lɪŋgwɪst] *noun* **(a)** person who knows foreign languages well; *only the very best linguists can hope to become interpreters for the EU* **(b)** person who studies linguistics; *linguists have discovered similarities between Sanskrit and ancient Greek*

linguistic [lɪŋ'gwɪstɪk] *adjective* referring to language(s); *translating this letter into Slovenian is going to test her linguistic skills*

linguistics [lɪŋ'gwɪstɪks] *noun* science of language; *he has a degree in linguistics*

lining ['laɪnɪŋ] *noun* **(a)** material put on the inside of something, especially of a piece of clothing; *a pair of boots with a fur lining*; **every cloud has a silver lining** = however gloomy things may seem, there is always some aspect which is good **(b) brake lining** = curved strip round the inside of the brake round a wheel of a car

link [lɪŋk] **1** *noun* **(a)** one of the rings in a chain; *a chain with solid gold links* **(b)** thing which connects two things or places; *the Channel Tunnel provides a fast rail link between England and France*; **telephone link** = direct line from one telephone to another **2** *verb* to join together; *they linked arms and walked down the street*; *his salary is linked to the cost of living*; *all the rooms are linked to the main switchboard*; *Eurostar links London and Paris or Brussels*

linkage ['lɪŋkɪdʒ] *noun* act of linking tow things; *they insisted on a linkage between allowing UN inspectors into the country and the easing of trade sanctions*

link up ['lɪŋk 'ʌp] *verb* to join two or more things together; *we have been able to link up all our computers to from a network*

link-up ['lɪŋkʌp] *noun* joining two things; **a telephone link-up** = joining two people living a very long way apart, by telephone; *we can hold business meetings with our staff in New York by means of a telephone link-up*

Linnaean system [lɪ'neɪən 'sɪstəm] *noun* scientific system of naming organisms devised by the Swedish scientist, Carolus Linnaeus

COMMENT: the Linnaean system gives each organism a name made of two Latin words. The first is the generic name referring to the genus to which the organism belongs, and the second is the specific name referring to the particular species. Organisms are usually referred to by the two names: *Homo sapiens* (man), *Felis catus* (cat), etc.

linseed ['lɪnsiːd] *noun* plant grown for its seeds, from which oil is produced; **linseed oil** = oil used in oil paints

COMMENT: a variety of linseed is the flax plant, used for making linen

lint [lɪnt] *noun* thick cotton wadding used for putting on wounds; *she carefully placed some lint on the wound before bandaging it*

lintel ['lɪntl] *noun* piece of wood or stone forming the top of a doorway or windowframe; *the whole lintel is rotten and will need to be replaced*

lion ['laɪən] *noun* **(a)** large wild animal of the cat family; *lions can be seen in African safari parks* (NOTE: the female is a **lioness** and the young are **cubs**); **mountain lion** = large brown wild cat of North and South America (NOTE: also called **cougar** *or* **puma**) **(b) the lion's share** = the biggest part; *Pat took £750, the lion's share of the £1000 prize*

lip [lɪp] *noun* **(a)** one of the two fleshy parts forming the outside of the mouth; *put some cream on your lips to stop them getting chapped*; **to lick your lips** = to show that you expect something to be enjoyable; *they licked their lips when they saw the cakes*; **my lips are sealed** = I have promised not to say anything **(b)** edge of something round and deep, such as a cup, jug, crater, etc.; *there's a chip on the lip of that cup*; *they stood on the lip of the crater and looked down into the volcano*

lip-read ['lɪpriːd] *verb (of a deaf person)* to understand what someone says by watching the movements of his or her lips; *he learnt to lip-read quickly* (NOTE: **lip-reading - lip-read** ['lɪpred])

lip service ['lɪp 'sɜːvɪs] *noun* **to pay lip service to something** = to give the impression that you respect or obey something when in fact you do not; *the management pays lip service to sexual equality, but none of the directors is a woman*; *he pays lip service to the party's ideas but in reality does very much what he wants*

lipstick ['lɪpstɪk] *noun* substance for colouring the lips; *she was wearing red lipstick*; *she bought a stick of pink lipstick*

liquefy ['lɪkwɪfaɪ] *verb* to become liquid; *a truck carrying canisters of liquefied gas*

liqueur [lɪ'kjuːə *or* lɪ'kɜː] *noun* strong sweet alcohol, made from fruit or herbs, etc.; *a glass of raspberry liqueur*; **liqueur chocolate** *or* **chocolate liqueur** = small chocolate containing a liqueur; *my favourite liqueur chocolates are the ones with cherries in brandy*

liquid ['lɪkwɪd] **1** *noun* substance like water, which flows easily and which is neither a gas nor a solid; *you will need to drink more liquids in hot weather*; **washing-up liquid** = liquid detergent used for washing dirty dishes **2** *adjective* **(a)** which is neither gas nor solid, and which flows easily; *a bottle of liquid soap*; **liquid crystal display** = *see* LCD; **liquid petroleum gas** = *see* LPG **(b) liquid assets** = cash, or items which can easily be changed into cash

liquidate ['lɪkwɪdeɪt] *verb* **(a)** to liquidate a company = to close a company and sell its assets; *the bank has decided to liquidate the company rather than to try and sell it as a going concern* **(b)** to liquidate a debt = to pay a debt in full; *new finance has been arranged, and all our debts have been liquidated* **(c)** to liquidate stock = to sell goods in stock to raise cash; *the company has been forced to liquidate stock to pay off its debts*

liquidation [lɪkwɪ'deɪʃn] *noun* closing of a company and selling of its assets; **the company went into liquidation** = the company was closed and its assets sold

liquidator ['lɪkwɪdeɪtə] *noun* person named to supervise the closing of a company which is in liquidation; *the company was forced to call in the liquidators when its creditors demanded repayment of their debts*

liquidity [lɪ'kwɪdɪti] *noun* having cash or assets which can be changed into cash; *the company's lack of cash flow has led to a temporary liquidity problem*

liquidizer ['lɪkwɪdaɪzə] *noun* machine which makes food liquid; *put the oranges and carrots in the liquidizer*

liquor ['lɪkə] *noun* alcoholic drink; **liquor licence** = licence which allows someone to sell alcohol; *they have had their liquor licence revoked*; *US* **liquor store** = shop which sells alcohol (NOTE: the British equivalent is an **off-licence**)

liquorice *US* **licorice** ['lɪkərɪs] *noun* black substance from the root of a plant, used to make sweets and also in medicine; *she bought a bag of liquorice (sweets)*

lira ['lɪərə] *noun* unit of currency used in Italy; *the book costs L2,700* (NOTE: plural is **lire**; usually written L when used with a figure: **L2,700**)

lisp [lɪsp] **1** *noun* speech defect in which 's' is pronounced as 'th'; *she speaks with a lisp* **2** *verb* to speak with a lisp; *he lisps, which makes him difficult to understand*

list [lɪst] **1** *noun* **(a)** number of items, names, addresses, etc., written or said one after another; *we've drawn up a list of people to invite to the party*; *he was ill, so we crossed his name off the list*; *the names on the list are in alphabetical order*; **address list** *or* **mailing list** = list of names and addresses of people and companies; **black list** = list of people, companies or countries which are banned or disapproved of; **shopping list** = list of things which you need to buy; **to be on the sick list** = to be reported sick; **to be on the danger list** *or* **on the critical list** = to be dangerously ill; *after the accident, she was on the critical list for some hours* **(b)** catalogue; **list price** = price of something as shown in a catalogue; *he asked for a discount on the list price* **(c)** situation where a boat leans to one side; *the trawler had taken in water and had developed a 5° list* **2** *verb* **(a)** to say or to write a number of items one after the other; *she listed the ingredients on the back of an envelope*; *the catalogue lists twenty-three models of washing machine* **(b)** *(of a ship)* to lean to one side; *the ship was listing badly and the crew had to be taken off by helicopter*

listen ['lɪsən] *verb* to pay attention to someone who is talking or to something which you can hear; *don't make a noise - I'm trying to listen to a music programme*; *why don't you listen to what I tell you?*; **to listen out for** = to wait to see if something makes a noise; *can you listen out for the telephone while I'm in the garden?*

listener ['lɪsnə] *noun* person who listens; *the BBC has millions of listeners all over the world*; *Cathy is a good listener - I often go to talk over my problems with her*

listing ['lɪstɪŋ] *noun* published list of information; *cinema listings are found on the back page of the local paper*; **computer listing** = printout of a list of items taken from the data stored in a computer; **listing paper** = paper made as a long sheet, used in computer printers

listless ['lɪsləs] *adjective* with no energy, weak and tired; *a bout of flu often leaves you listless and lethargic*

listlessly ['lɪsləsli] *adverb* in a way which shows lack of energy; *he listlessly turned over the pages of the magazine*

listlessness ['lɪsləsnəs] *noun* being generally weak and tired; *his listlessness is beginning to worry his parents*

lit [lɪt] *see* LIGHT

-lit [lɪt] *suffix* showing where light comes from; *a candlelit table*; *the moonlit lake*

litany ['lɪtəni] *noun* **(a)** series of prayers with repeated responses, used in church; *the priest and congregation recited the litany* **(b)** a litany of = a long list of; *she started on a litany of complaints about the service* (NOTE: plural is **litanies**)

liter ['liːtə] *noun US* = LITRE

literacy ['lɪtərəsi] *noun* being able to read and write; *the project aims to improve literacy in the country by 2005*; *compare* ILLITERACY, NUMERACY

literal ['lɪtərəl] **1** *adjective* keeping to the exact meaning of the original words; *a literal translation usually sounds odd* **2** *noun* mistake made when typing or keyboarding, especially where one letter is put instead of another; *the reviewer found hundreds of literals in the index - who was the proofreader?* (NOTE: American English is **typo**)

literally ['lɪtəli] *adverb* **(a)** in a literal way; *she translated the text literally* **(b)** (*to emphasize*) *she was literally made speechless by the interviewer's questions*

literary ['lɪtrəri] *adjective* referring to literature; *her style of writing is very literary*; **literary critic** = person who writes reviews of books; **literary prize** = prize given to the writer of a novel, poems, etc.

literate ['lɪtərət] *adjective* **(a)** able to read and write; *most people in Britain are literate*; *when he left school he was barely literate*; *compare* ILLITERATE, NUMERATE **(b) computer-literate** = able to use a computer

literature ['lɪtrɪtʃə] *noun* **(a)** books or writing, especially novels, poetry, drama, biography, etc.; *she's studying English and American literature* **(b)** what has been written on a particular subject; *he knows the literature on Roman Britain very well* **(c)** written publicity material about something; *do you have any literature on holidays in Greece?* (NOTE: no plural)

lithograph ['lɪθəɡrɑːf] *noun* print made by pressing paper onto a smooth surface where the design has been made in grease and ink applied; *he was looking at the first proofs of his latest lithograph*

Lithuania [lɪθjuːˈeɪniə] *noun* small country on the Baltic, one of the three Baltic States; *the population of Lithuania is approximately 3.8m* (NOTE: capital: **Vilnius**; people: **Lithuanians**; language: **Lithuanian**; currency: **litas**)

Lithuanian [lɪθjuːˈeɪniən] **1** *adjective* referring to Lithuania; *the Lithuanian president* **2** *noun* **(a)** person from Lithuania; *the majority of Lithuanians are Catholics* **(b)** language spoken in Lithuania; *Lithuanian is closely related to Latvian*

litigant ['lɪtɪɡənt] *noun* person who brings a lawsuit against someone

litigate ['lɪtɪɡeɪt] *verb* to go to law, to bring a lawsuit against someone to have a dispute settled

litigation [lɪtɪˈɡeɪʃn] *noun* going to law, bringing of a lawsuit against someone to have a dispute settled; *he has got into litigation with the county council* (NOTE: no plural)

litmus paper ['lɪtməs 'peɪpə] *noun* paper containing a blue substance which is turned red by an acid and back to blue by an alkali, used to test for acids and alkalis

litre *US* **liter** ['liːtə] *noun* measurement for liquids (almost 2 pints); *I need a 2 litre tin of blue paint*; *this bottle holds two litres* (NOTE: usually written **l** after figures: **25 l** say 'twenty-five litres')

litter ['lɪtə] **1** *noun* **(a)** rubbish left on streets or in public places; *the council tries to keep the main street clear of litter* (NOTE: no plural in this meaning) **(b)** group of young animals born at one time; *she had a litter of eight puppies* **2** *verb* to drop rubbish about; *the street was littered with bits of paper*

litter bin ['lɪtə 'bɪn] *noun* metal container in the street for putting litter; *the men from the council come to empty the litter bins every morning*

little ['lɪtl] **1** *adjective* **(a)** small, not big; *they have two children - a baby boy and a little girl* (NOTE: no comparative or superlative forms in this sense) **(b)** not much; *we drink very little milk*; *a TV uses very little electricity* (NOTE: **little - less - least** ['liːst]) **2** *pronoun* a **little** = a small quantity; *I'm not hungry - just give me a little of that soup*; *can I have a little more coffee please?* **3** *adverb* not much; not often; *it's little more than two miles from the sea*; *we go to the cinema very little these days*

◊ **little by little** ['lɪtlbaɪ'lɪtl] *adverb* gradually, not all at once; *they planted trees here and there, until little by little the garden became like a jungle*; *she's getting better little by little*

little finger ['lɪtl 'fɪŋɡə] *noun* the smallest of the five fingers; *she was wearing a ring on her little finger*; **she can twist him round her little finger** = she can get him to do whatever she wants

little toe ['lɪtl 'təʊ] *noun* the smallest of the five toes; *he has a corn on his little toe*

liturgical [lɪˈtɜːdʒɪkl] *adjective* referring to liturgy; *the differences between the two churches are mainly liturgical*

liturgy ['lɪtədʒi] *noun* form of public service used in church; *we follow the Roman Catholic liturgy* (NOTE: plural is **liturgies**)

live 1 *adjective* [laɪv] **(a)** living, not dead; *there are strict rules about transporting live animals*; *guess who's living next door? - a real live TV star* **(b)** not recorded; *a live radio show* **(c)** carrying electricity; *don't touch the live wires*; *the boys were killed trying to jump over the live rail* **2** *adverb* not recorded; *the show was broadcast live* **3** *verb* [lɪv] **(a)** to have your home in a place; *they have gone to live in France*; *do you prefer living in the country to the town?*; *he lives next door to a film star*; *where does your daughter live?*; *see also* SUITCASE **(b)** to be alive; *King Henry VIII lived in the 16th century*; *the doctor doesn't think she will live much longer*

live in ['lɪv 'ɪn] *verb* to live in the building where you work; *we want a nurse to live in*

live-in ['lɪv'ɪn] *adjective* who lives in the place of work; *we have a live-in nanny who looks after the children*

livelihood ['laɪvlihʊd] *noun* way of earning your living; *they depend on tourists for their livelihood*

liveliness ['laɪvlinəs] *noun* energy, being lively; *she showed remarkable liveliness in spite of her age*

lively ['laɪvli] *adjective* very active; *the boss is still a lively old man*; *it was a very lively party with a dance band and dozens of young people*; *it's the liveliest nightspot in town* (NOTE: **livelier - liveliest**)

live off ['lɪv 'ɒf] *verb* to earn money from; *the whole population of the village lives off tourism*

live on ['lɪv 'ɒn] *verb* to use food or money to stay alive; *they seem to live on tins of fish*; *a family can't live on £50 a week*; *our son is staying with us until he earns enough to live on*

liver ['lɪvə] *noun* (a) large organ in the abdomen which helps the digestion of nutrients and cleans the blood; *her liver was damaged in the car crash* (b) animal's liver used as food; *I'll start with chicken liver pâté*; *he looked at the menu and ordered liver and bacon*

livery ['lɪvri] *noun* (a) special clothing of a group of servants or of an organization; *every employee has to wear the hotel's distinctive livery* (b) special design used to show that something belongs to an organization; *British Airways have changed the livery of all their planes* (c) looking after horses for payment; **livery stable** = place where horses may be looked after and may also be hired; *the livery stables are conveniently situated close to Hyde Park*

lives [lɪvz] *see* LIVE

lives [laɪvz] *see* LIFE

livestock ['laɪvstɒk] *noun* domesticated farm animals, which are reared to produce meat, milk or other products; *mountain farmers move their livestock from place to place to find new grazing* (NOTE: no plural)

live through ['lɪv 'θruː] *verb* to experience something dangerous; *we lived through two earthquakes*

live together ['lɪv tə'geðə] *verb* to live in the same house and have a sexual relationship; *they lived together for two years before they got married*

live up ['lɪv 'ʌp] *verb* to live up to expectations = to succeed as was expected; *the film didn't live up to the hype that preceded it*; *(informal)* **to live it up** = to lead a life when you spend a lot of money on wild parties, etc.; *she won the lottery and immediately started to live it up*

live wire ['laɪv 'waɪə] *noun (informal)* very lively person; *our new sales assistant is a real live wire*

live with ['lɪv 'wɪθ] *verb* (a) to put up with something; *we can't do anything about the noise of the aircraft - you'll just have to live with it* (b) to live with someone = LIVE TOGETHER

livid ['lɪvɪd] *adjective* (a) dark blue grey like the colour of lead; *the livid bruise on her eye where he had hit her* (b) extremely angry; *her father was livid when he heard she had spent the night with her boyfriend*

living ['lɪvɪŋ] **1** *adjective* alive; *does she have any living relatives?* **2** *noun* (a) money that you need for your daily life; *he earns his living by selling postcards to tourists*; **what do you do for a living?** = what job do you do?; **he doesn't earn a living wage** = he does not earn enough to pay for essentials (food, heating, rent, etc.) (b) cost of living = money which a person has to pay for food, heating, rent, etc.; *higher interest rates increase the cost of living*; *see also* COST OF LIVING

living room ['lɪvɪŋ 'ruːm] *noun* comfortable room in a house or flat for sitting in; *they were sitting in the living room watching TV*; *why is the living room door shut?*; *she does her homework on a sofa in the living room*

living standards ['lɪvɪŋ 'stændədz] *noun* quality of personal home life (such as amount of food or clothes bought, size of family car, etc.); *we can't complain about our standard of living, we're really very comfortably off*; *as long as living standards continue to improve, everyone is happy* (NOTE: also the **standard of living**)

lizard ['lɪzəd] *noun* type of small reptile with four legs and a long tail; *little lizards were running around on the walls*

llama ['lɑːmə] *noun* thick-haired camel-like animal found in South America; *Dan went for a ride on a llama when he was in Peru* (NOTE: do not confuse the spelling with **lama**; note also that it is usually pronounced ['lɑːmə] but that in South America it is ['jɑːmə])

lo [ləʊ] *interjection* meaning 'look'; *and lo, the Angel Gabriel appeared*; **lo and behold!** = all of a sudden (something happened); *we had been waiting for hours for a bus when, lo and behold, three came together*; *I turned round, and lo and behold the keys had disappeared*

load [ləʊd] **1** *noun* (a) heavy objects which are carried in a truck, wagon, etc.; *the lorry delivered a load of bricks*; **lorry-load** *or* **van-load** = amount of goods carried on a lorry or van; *they delivered six lorry-loads of coal*; *when we moved we had three van-loads of books* (b) responsibility, thing which is difficult to live with; **that's a load off my mind** = I feel much less worried; *I've finished my exams - that's a load off my mind* (c) *(informal)* **loads of** = plenty, lots of; *it was a wonderful party - there was loads to eat*; *you don't need to rush - there's loads of time before the train leaves*; *John always has loads of good ideas* (NOTE: in this meaning takes a singular verb) **2** *verb* (a) to put something, especially something heavy, into or on to a lorry, truck, etc.; *they loaded the furniture into the van* (b) to put a film into a camera (c) to put a program into a computer; *load the word-processing program before you start keyboarding*

loaded ['ləʊdɪd] *adjective* (a) *(informal)* having a lot of money; *Chris is loaded - he won the lottery!* (b) **loaded question** = question which is worded in such a way as to trap the person who answers; *she asked if I'd had a good time last night - a loaded question, since I was supposed to be at home finishing my homework*

loaf [ləʊf] **1** *noun* (a) large single piece of bread made separately, which you cut into slices before eating it; *he bought a loaf of bread at the baker's*; *we eat about 10 loaves of bread per week*; **sliced loaf** = loaf of bread which has already been sliced mechanically before it is sold (NOTE: plural is **loaves** [ləʊvz]) (b) *(London slang)* head, brains; *use your loaf - it's obvious what she* *wants* (NOTE: from **loaf** of bread which means 'head' in rhyming slang see also RHYMING SLANG) **2** *verb* **to loaf around** = to hang around, doing nothing; *he hasn't any proper job and just loafs around Leicester Square all day*

loafer ['ləʊfə] *noun* (a) trademark for a type of light casual shoe with no laces; *he wore jeans and a pair of brown loafers* (b) person who does nothing all day; *there was no one in the square except a couple of loafers sitting on benches*

loam [ləʊm] *noun* good dark soil which is very fertile and crumbles easily; *the farm is excellent value, being almost all on good loam*

loamy ['ləʊmi] *adjective* crumbly and fertile; *his farm is on good loamy soil*

loan [ləʊn] **1** *noun* (a) act of lending; *I had the loan of his car for three weeks*; **on loan** = being lent; *the picture is on loan to the National Gallery* (b) thing lent, especially a sum of money; *he bought the house with a £100,000 loan from the bank*; **bridging loan** *US* **bridge loan** = short-term loan to help someone buy a new house when he has not yet sold his old one (NOTE: do not confuse with **lone**) **2** *verb* to lend; *the furniture for the exhibition has been loaned by the museum*

loath [ləʊθ] *adjective* **to be loath to do something** = to be reluctant to do something; *personally, I'm very loath to get involved*

loathe [ləʊð] *verb* to hate very much; *why are you wearing that tie, you know how I loathe it!*; *it was well-known that he was loathed by the other teachers*; *I loathe having to make coffee for the boss*

loathing ['ləʊðɪŋ] *noun* feeling of disgust; *he looked at his plate of snails with loathing*; *she has an intense loathing for snakes*

loathsome ['ləʊðsəm] *adjective* disgusting and horrible; *her new boyfriend is really loathsome*

loaves [ləʊvz] *see* LOAF

lob [lɒb] **1** *noun* ball which is hit high into the air; *his lob fell just over the baseline* (NOTE: the opposite, where the ball goes fast down into the ground, is a **smash**) **2** *verb* to throw or hit a ball slowly high into the air; *he lobbed a ball at his sister* (NOTE: **lobbing - lobbed**)

lobby ['lɒbi] **1** *noun* (a) entrance hall; *I'll meet you in the hotel lobby in half an hour* (b) group of people who try to influence important people, especially members of parliament; *the MPs met members of the anti-abortion lobby* (c) hall in the House of Commons used especially for interviews with members of the public; **lobby correspondent** = journalist who reports on parliamentary matters, after confidential briefings from ministers; **division lobby** = corridor where MPs go to vote (NOTE: plural is **lobbies**) **2** *verb* to try to influence someone (especially in order to get a bill through Parliament); *she lobbied her MP with a detailed letter and other documents* (NOTE: **lobbying - lobbied**)

lobbyist ['lɒbiɪst] *noun* person who is paid to represent a pressure group; *lobbyists for the arms manufacturers are trying to organize opposition to the government's proposed ban on arms exports*

lobe [ləʊb] *noun* (a) soft fleshy part at the bottom of the ear; *he has a ring in his right ear lobe* (b) rounded section of an organ, such as the brain, lung or liver; *the right lung has three lobes, the left only two*; *the*

surgeon could see that the right frontal lobe of the brain was affected

lobster ['lɒbstə] *noun* shellfish with a long body, two large claws, and eight legs, used as food; *the lobsters on the market stall were still alive and had their claws tied together*; *we had a bowl of lobster chowder*; **lobster pot** = type of basket put into the sea to catch lobsters

local ['ləʊkəl] **1** *adjective* (a) referring to a place or district near where you are; *she works as a nurse in the local hospital*; *the local paper comes out on Fridays*; *she was formerly the headmistress of the local school*; **local authority** = section of elected government which runs a town or district; *we complained to the local authority about the bus service*; **local call** = telephone call to a number in the same area as the person making the call; **local time** = time of day in a particular place; *it will be 1 a.m. local time when we arrive in Tokyo* (b) **local anaesthetic** = substance which removes the feeling in a certain part of the body only; *my mother was given a pacemaker under local anaesthetic*; *this operation can be carried out under local rather than general anaesthetic* (NOTE: an anaesthetic for the whole of the body is a **general anaesthetic**) **2** *noun* (a) **locals** = people who live in the area; *the restaurant caters for the tourist trade rather than for the locals* (b) *(informal)* pub near where you live; *you can find him in his local every evening*

locale [ləʊ'kɑːl] *noun* place where something happens in a film or book; *the locale of the film is the Sahara desert*

locality [ləʊ'kælɪti] *noun* area of the country or district of a town; **in the locality** = near by; *there are two theatres and four cinemas in the locality* (NOTE: plural is **localities**)

localized ['ləʊkəlaɪzd] *adjective* which occurs in one part of the body only; *the rash appears to be localized around the lower back* (NOTE: the opposite is **generalized**)

locally ['ləʊkəli] *adverb* in the district near where you are; *when we go camping we usually try to buy everything locally*

locate [ləʊ'keɪt] *verb* (a) to find the position of something; *divers are trying to locate the Spanish galleon* (b) **to be located** = to be in a particular position; *the heart is located in the left side of the body*; *the warehouse is located near to the motorway*

location [ləʊ'keɪʃn] *noun* (a) finding the position of something; **echo location** = finding objects in the sea by using echoes (b) place or position; *the hotel is in a very central location* (c) *(filming)* **on location** = in a real setting, not in a studio; *the film was shot on location in North Africa*

loch [lɒx] *noun* (in Scotland) inland lake or arm of the sea; *we plan to go fishing on the loch*; **the Loch Ness monster** = large animal which is supposed to be living in Loch Ness

lock [lɒk] **1** *noun* (a) device which closes a door, safe, box, etc., so that you can only open it with a key; *she left the key in the lock, so the burglars got in easily*; *we changed the locks on the doors after a set of keys were stolen* (b) amount by which the wheels of a car can turn left or right; *the car has an excellent lock - it turns easily in a narrow road* (c) section of a canal or river with gates which can be opened or closed to control the flow of water, and so allow boats to move up or down to different levels; *they passed through dozens of locks* on their trip down the Thames **2** *verb* to close a door, safe, box, etc., so that it has to be opened with a key; *I forgot to lock the safe*; *we always lock the front door before we go to bed*

lockable ['lɒkəbl] *adjective* which can be locked; *each student is allocated a lockable locker*

locked [lɒkt] *adjective* which has been shut with a key; *the burglars managed to break into a locked safe*; *the cash box wasn't locked*

locker ['lɒkə] *noun* small cupboard for personal belongings which you can close with a key; *luggage lockers can be rented at the railway station*; *you will need a £1 coin for the lockers at the swimming pool*

locker-room ['lɒkə 'ruːm] *noun* room where people can change clothes before going to play a game; *the coach gave us a pep talk in the locker-room just before play started*

lock in ['lɒk 'ɪn] *verb* to make someone stay inside a place by locking the door; *I think we've been locked in*

lockjaw ['lɒkdʒɔː] *noun* serious disease caused by infection of a wound by bacteria in the soil, which affects the spinal cord and causes the jaw muscles to stiffen; *see note at* TETANUS

lock-keeper ['lɒkkiːpə] *noun* person who looks after a lock on a canal or river and opens the gates to let boats through; *lock-keepers are busy on summer afternoons when there is a lot of traffic on the river*

lock out ['lɒk 'aʊt] *verb* to make someone stay outside a place by locking the door; *she took the key and locked her husband out*; *he came back late at night and found he was locked out of the hotel*; *I've left the keys inside the car and locked myself out*

lockout ['lɒkaʊt] *noun* time where an employer locks the door of the factory and refuses to let the workers enter unless they agree to his conditions

locksmith ['lɒksmɪθ] *noun* person who makes or mends locks; *he called the locksmith to change all the locks in the house*

lock up ['lɒk 'ʌp] *verb* **(a)** to close a building by locking the doors; *he always locks up before he goes home*; *she was locking up the shop when a man walked in* **(b)** to keep a person or thing inside a place or container by locking the door or lid; *lock up the jewels in the safe or lock the jewels up in the safe* **(c)** to put someone in prison; *they locked him up for a week*

lockup ['lɒkʌp] *noun* **(a)** *(old)* small prison cell; *the police arrested the three boys and put them in the lockup overnight* **(b)** lockup garage *or* shop = garage *or* shop which can be locked and which is not connected to the owner's house

locomotive [ləʊkə'məʊtɪv] *noun* engine of a train; *they electrified the line and got rid of the old diesel locomotives*

locum ['ləʊkəm] *noun* person who does the work of a doctor who is away on holiday; *my regular doctor is in New Zealand so it was his locum who came to see me*

locus ['ləʊkəs] *noun (formal)* place where something is infected; *we need to find the locus of infection* (NOTE: plural is **loci** ['ləʊsaɪ])

locust ['ləʊkəst] *noun* tropical insect, like a large grasshopper, which destroys crops; *a swarm of locusts ate all the millet*

lode [ləʊd] *noun* vein of metal ore in rocks; *a lode of silver runs through this rock*

lodge [lɒdʒ] **1** *noun* small house at the gates of a large building; *if the lodge is as big as that, just imagine the size of the main house!* **2** *verb* **(a)** to rent a room in a house; *he lodges with Mrs Bishop in London Road* **(b)** *(formal)* to lodge a complaint against someone = to make an official complaint about someone; *they lodged a complaint with the local electricity company*; to lodge something with someone = to deposit something with someone to look after for you; *they lodged all the documents with the solicitor* **(c)** to become stuck; *a piece of bread was lodged in her windpipe*; *the bullet was lodged in his spine*

lodger ['lɒdʒə] *noun* person who rents a room in a house; *she has taken in three lodgers for the summer*

lodging ['lɒdʒɪŋ] *noun* **(a)** accommodation; **board and lodging** = room and food; *board and lodging for three nights comes to £175.00* **(b)** lodgings = rented rooms; *are you still looking for lodgings or have you found somewhere to stay?*

loft [lɒft] *noun* **(a)** top part of a house right under the roof; *they converted their loft into a bedroom* (NOTE: also called an **attic**) **(b)** part of a large building, such as a warehouse, converted to living accommodation; *he's bought a loft apartment in the centre of Soho*

lofty ['lɒfti] *adjective* **(a)** very high; *from the lofty height of the church tower the boys could see for miles*; *the lofty ceiling and wide windows gave the studio a wonderful feeling of space* **(b)** proud; *her lofty attitude towards her colleagues does not make her many friends* (NOTE: **loftier - loftiest**)

log [lɒg] **1** *noun* **(a)** thick piece of a tree; *he brought in a load of logs for the fire*; to sleep like a log = to sleep very soundly; *after his 12-mile walk he slept like a log* **(b)** daily detailed record of speed, position, etc., especially on a ship or plane; *the ship's log gave details of their position when the fire broke out* **2** *verb* **(a)** to write down details of something which has happened in a book as a record; *have you logged your day's activities into the book?* **(b)** *(computing)* to log in *or* log on = to enter a password and start to access a computer system; to log off *or* log out = to exit a computer system by entering an instruction (NOTE: **logging - logged**)

loganberry ['ləʊgənberi] *noun* soft fruit, a cross between a blackberry and a raspberry; *we went into the garden and picked a bowl of loganberries* (NOTE: plural is **loganberries**)

logarithm ['lɒgərɪðm] *noun* number which allows calculations to be done by adding instead of multiplying

logbook ['lɒgbʊk] *noun* **(a)** official document showing details of the owners of a car; *check the details in the logbook before buying the car* **(b)** *(on ship, etc.)* book with the records of a journey; *the captain wrote up the logbook every night*

loggerheads ['lɒgəhedz] *noun* to be at loggerheads (with someone) = to constantly arguing (with someone); *he has been at loggerheads with the town council for some months*

logging ['lɒgɪŋ] *noun* cutting trees for timber; *the government is trying to stamp out illegal logging of timber in the national parks*

logic ['lɒdʒɪk] *noun* **(a)** formal reasoning; *your logic is flawed - just because she's an MA doesn't mean she's a good teacher* **(b)** sense, good reason; *I don't see the logic of owning two cars and not being able to drive*

logical ['lɒdʒɪkl] *adjective* **(a)** clearly reasoned; *a logical argument* **(b)** *(of person)* able to reason clearly; *she's a very logical person and thinks everything through carefully*

logically ['lɒdʒɪkəli] *adverb* in a logical or reasonable way; *logically you should be able to get to Manchester by that route, but I don't think it's practical*

logistic(al) [lə'dʒɪstɪk(l)] *adjective* referring to logistics; *there are considerable logistical problems in organizing a protest march by ten thousand disabled people*

logistics [lɒ'dʒɪstɪks] *noun* organization of the movement of supplies, people, etc.; *the logistics of such an enormous relief effort are extremely complicated*

logo ['lɒɡəʊ] *noun* symbol or design used by a company to identify its products; *the hotel group uses a small pine tree as its logo* (NOTE: plural is **logos**)

loin [lɔɪn] *noun* cut of meat, taken from the back of the animal; *we had roast loin of pork for dinner*

loincloth ['lɔɪnklɒθ] *noun* piece of clothing in the form of a long cloth worn round the waist; *he was wearing a loincloth and sandals*

loiter ['lɔɪtə] *verb* to stand or wander about doing nothing; *various suspicious characters were seen loitering near the bar*

loll [lɒl] *verb* **(a)** to sit or lie in a lazy way; *they spent the afternoon lolling about in armchairs, watching the cricket* **(b)** *(of an animal's tongue)* to hang out; *the dogs were lying in the shade with their tongues lolling out*

lollipop ['lɒlɪpɒp] *noun* **(a)** round sweet on the end of a stick; *she bought the children a lollipop each* **(b)** *(informal)* **lollipop man** *or* **lollipop lady** = person employed to stop traffic to let schoolchildren cross a street (NOTE: called this because he or she holds a large round 'stop' sign, rather like a lollipop)

lolly ['lɒli] *noun* **(a)** *(informal)* lollipop, a round sweet on the end of a stick; **ice lolly** = piece of flavoured ice on the end of a stick (NOTE: plural in this meaning is **lollies**) **(b)** *(slang)* money; *what happened to the lolly, then?* (NOTE: no plural in this meaning)

London ['lʌndən] *proper noun* capital of England and the United Kingdom; *the plane arrives in London at 4 o'clock; she went to the railway station to ask about cheap tickets to London; most London buses are red; London has changed a lot in the past few years; London is on the river Thames; Charles II was king at the time of the Fire of London; there is a picture of the Tower of London on the front of the book*

lone [ləʊn] *adjective* single, one alone; *she was the lone Englishwoman in a crowd of Germans; a lone house on the edge of the marsh; a lone rider on the beach; see also* WOLF (NOTE: do not confuse with **loan**)

loneliness ['ləʊnlinəs] *noun* **(a)** feeling sad because you are alone; *after his wife died it took him a long time to get over his feelings of loneliness* **(b)** being alone; *he was attracted to the loneliness of the hotel, all by itself on the top of the cliff*

lonely ['ləʊnli] *adjective* **(a)** feeling sad because of being alone; *it's odd how lonely you can be in a big city full of people;* **lonely hearts ad** = advertisement in a newspaper to try to find a girlfriend or boyfriend; *she*

answered a lonely hearts ad in her local paper **(b)** (place) with few or no people; *the cliff top is a lonely place at night; we spent the weekend in a lonely cottage in the Welsh hills* (NOTE: **lonelier - loneliest**)

loner ['ləʊnə] *noun* person who prefers to be alone; *he doesn't mix with other children much, he's a bit of a loner*

lonesome ['ləʊnsəm] *adjective* especially US lonely, sad because of being alone; *I'm feeling lonesome tonight*

long [lɒŋ] **1** *adjective* **(a)** not short in length; *a long piece of string; the Nile is the longest river in the world; my hair needs cutting - it's getting too long* **(b)** not short in time; *what a long programme - it lasted almost three hours; they've been waiting for the bus for a long time; we don't approve of long holidays in this job* **(c)** *(indicating measurement in time)* how long is it before your holiday starts? (NOTE: the use with figures: **the road is six miles long; a piece of string a metre long**) **2** *adverb* **(a)** for a long time; *have you been waiting long?; I didn't want to wait any longer; long ago, before the war, this was a wealthy farming area* **(b)** **as long as** *or* **so long as** = provided that; *I like going on picnics as long as it doesn't rain* **(c)** **no longer** = not any more; **I no longer have it** = I had it at some time in the past, but not any more (NOTE: **longer - longest**) **3** *verb* to want something very much; *I'm longing for a cup of tea; everyone was longing to be back home*

long-awaited ['lɒŋ ə'weɪtɪd] *adjective* which people have been waiting for for a long time; *at last the government has produced the long-awaited report on prisons*

long-distance [lɒŋ'dɪstəns] *adjective* **(a)** *(in sport)* (race) between two places which are far apart; *a long-distance runner* **(b)** (telephone call) made over a long distance; *in some countries you have to book long-distance calls in advance*

longed-for ['lɒŋdfɔː] *adjective* which people have been hoping will come; *the day of his longed-for release from prison had finally arrived*

longevity [lɒn'dʒevɪti] *noun* *(formal)* very long life; *some species of tortoise are famous for their longevity*

longhand ['lɒŋhænd] *noun* ordinary writing, not shorthand or typing; *she sent in her job application in longhand; compare* SHORTHAND

long-haul [lɒŋ'hɔːl] *adjective* over a large distance, especially between continents; *my feet always swell up on long-haul flights; compare* SHORT-HAUL

longhorn ['lɒŋhɔːn] *noun* old breed of cow with long horns; *compare* SHORTHORN

longing ['lɒŋɪŋ] *noun* great desire for something; *after three months travelling in South America, he had a longing to be back home in Scotland*

longingly ['lɒŋɪŋli] *adverb* showing that you want something very much; *she looked longingly at the swimming pool*

longitude ['lɒndʒɪtjuːd] *noun* position on the earth's surface measured in degrees east or west of an imaginary line running north-south through Greenwich, a town just to the east of London; *see also* GREENWICH

COMMENT: longitude and latitude are used to indicate the exact position of something on the earth's surface. They are measured in degrees, minutes and seconds. London is latitude 51°30'N, longitude 0°5'W

long jump ['lɒŋ 'dʒʌmp] *noun* athletic competition, an Olympic field event in which contestants try to jump as far as possible; *he's the Olympic gold medallist in the long jump*

COMMENT: the contestant sprints down a track and takes off as close to the edge of the take-off board as possible before landing in a sandpit. The jump is measured from the take-off board to the nearest mark in the sand made by the jumper, and competitors are usually allowed six jumps

long jumper ['lɒŋ 'dʒʌmpə] *noun* athlete who competes in the long jump

long-lasting ['lɒŋ'lɑːstɪŋ] *adjective* which lasts a long time; *long-lasting batteries can run for a much longer time than ordinary batteries*; *the effects of exposure to radiation can be very long-lasting*

longlived [ʃɔːt'lɪvd] *adjective* which lives for a long time; *all their family are very longlived*; *compare* SHORTLIVED

long-range [lɒŋ'reɪndʒ] *adjective* which covers a long distance or a long time; *the long-range weather forecast is not very reliable*; *they stationed long-range missiles along the border*; *see also* SHORT-RANGE

long-running [lɒŋ'rʌnɪŋ] *adjective* **(a)** which has been performed for several years without a break; *a long-running musical*; *which is the longest-running TV sitcom?* **(b)** which has been going on for a long time; *our long-running dispute with our neighbours*

longshoreman ['lɒŋʃɔːmən] *noun US* person who works at a port, loading or unloading ships (NOTE: plural is **longshoremen**; British English is **docker**)

longsighted [lɒŋ'saɪtɪd] *adjective* able to see things clearly things which are far away but not things which are close; *he's longsighted and needs reading glasses*; *see also* SHORTSIGHTED

longsightedness [lɒŋ'saɪtɪdnəs] *noun* being able to see things clearly things which are far away but not things which are close; *see also* SHORTSIGHTEDNESS

long-sleeved [lɒŋsliːvd] *adjective* with long sleeves; *he was wearing a blue long-sleeved shirt*; *see also* SHORT-SLEEVED

longstanding [lɒŋ'stændɪŋ] *adjective* which has been in existence for a long time; *we have a longstanding arrangement to have a picnic together on Easter Monday*; *she's a very longstanding customer of ours*

long-stay ['lɒŋ 'steɪ] *adjective* referring to a stay of weeks or months; *long-stay car park* = car park where you can leave your car for a long time (several days or weeks); *compare* SHORT-STAY

long-suffering [lɒŋ'sʌfrɪŋ] *adjective* patient with problems caused by other people; *our neighbours are very long-suffering - they rarely complain about the noise our children make*

long-term [lɒŋ'tɜːm] *adjective* planned to last for a long time; *he asked the bank for a long-term loan*; *they never make any long-term plans*; *see also* SHORT-TERM

long-time ['lɒŋtaɪm] *adjective* who has existed for a long time; *his long-time partner*

long wave ['lɒŋ 'weɪv] *noun* radio wave longer than 1000 metres; *we listened to the BBC on long wave*; *see also* MEDIUM WAVE, SHORT WAVE

loo [luː] *noun (informal)* lavatory; *where's the ladies' loo?*; *he's in the loo, but will be back in a minute* (NOTE: this is the term which is used most often in the UK)

look [luk] **1** *noun* **(a)** seeing something with your eyes; *have a good look at this photograph and tell me if you recognize anyone in it*; *we only had time for a quick look round the town* **(b)** the way someone *or* something appears; *there is a French look about her clothes*; *good looks* = pleasing and beautiful appearance; *his good looks and charm attracted many women* **(c)** searching for something; *we had a good look for the ring and couldn't find it anywhere* **2** *verb* **(a)** to turn your eyes towards something; *I want you to look carefully at this photograph*; *look in the restaurant and see if there are any tables free*; *if you look out of the office window you can see our house*; *he opened the lid of the box and looked inside* **(b)** to *look someone in the eye* = to look straight at someone in a confident way; *he didn't dare look me in the eye*; *don't look a gift horse in the mouth* = don't criticize something which someone has given you for free **(c)** to appear to be; *I went to see her in hospital and she looks worse*; *is he only forty? - he looks much older than that*; *those pies look good*; *it looks as if it may snow*

look after ['luk 'ɑːftə] *verb* to take care of; *nurses look after patients in hospital*; *who's going to look after your dog when you're away?* (NOTE: American English is also to **look out for someone**)

look ahead ['luk ə'hed] *verb* to make plans for the future; *I'm looking ahead to the summer and hoping to get a casual job*

lookalike ['lukəlaɪk] *noun* person who look like someone else, especially someone famous; *they hired a Marilyn Monroe lookalike to open the new cinema*

look back ['luk 'bæk] *verb* **(a)** to turn your head to see what is behind you; *he looked back and saw a police car was following him* **(b)** he never looked back = he was very successful; *the first year after starting the business was difficult, but after that they never looked back*

look back on ['luk 'bæk ɒn] *verb* to think about something which happened in the past; *he looked back on his time with the company with satisfaction*; *looking back on the events of last week, I think we could have handled things more efficiently*

look down ['luk 'daun] *verb* to *look down on someone* = to think you are better than someone; *he looks down on anyone who hasn't been to university*

look for ['luk 'fɔː] *verb* to search for, to try to find; *we looked for the watch everywhere but couldn't find it*; *the police are looking for three escaped prisoners*

look forward to ['luk 'fɔːwəd 'tuː] *phrase* to think happily about something which is going to happen; *the whole family is looking forward to going on holiday*; *she isn't looking forward to taking her driving test*; *I'm looking forward to seeing my parents again*

looking glass ['lukɪŋ 'glɑːs] *noun (old)* mirror; *she stared at herself in the looking-glass and saw how old she looked*

look in (on) ['lʊk 'ɪn ɒn] *verb* to pay a short visit; *I'll look in on my aunt to see how she is; they didn't stay long - they just looked in*

look into ['lʊk 'ɪntʊ] *verb* to try to find out about a matter or problem; *I've asked the manager to look into the question of staff holidays*

look like ['lʊk 'laɪk] *phrase* **(a)** to be similar to; *he looks just like his father* **(b)** *(asking someone to describe something)* *what's he look like, her new boyfriend?; tell me what she looks like so that I can recognize her when she gets off the train* **(c)** to seem to be going to happen; *take an umbrella, it looks like rain; the sky is dark, it looks like snow*

look on ['lʊk 'ɒn] *verb* **(a)** to watch without doing anything; *the police beat up the demonstrators while the tourists just looked on* **(b)** to consider, to think of something as; *we look on trade fairs as a bit of relaxation after the office; he looks on his secretary as simply someone to make coffee and answer the phone*

look out ['lʊk 'aʊt] *verb* **(a)** to look out on *or* over = to have a view towards; *the windows of the office look out over a park* **(b)** to be careful; *look out! - the car is going backwards!*

lookout ['lʊkaʊt] *noun* **(a)** careful watch; *keep a sharp lookout for pickpockets; from their lookout post they could see across the square;* to be on the lookout for = to watch carefully for; *she's always on the lookout for bargains; the police are on the lookout for car thieves* **(b)** person who is on watch; *the captain posted a lookout in the bows*

look out for ['lʊk 'aʊt fɔ:] *verb* **(a)** to keep looking to try to find; *we're looking out for new offices because ours are too small; I'll look out for his sister at the party* **(b)** to be careful about; *look out for ice on the pavement* **(c)** US to look out for someone = to protect someone; *the falling rock missed us by inches - someone was obviously looking out for us!* (NOTE: British English is to **look after someone**)

look over ['lʊk 'əʊvə] *verb* **(a)** to have a view over something; *the office looks over a disused warehouse* **(b)** to examine briefly; *she looked over the figures and said they seemed to be OK*

look round ['lʊk 'raʊnd] *verb* **(a)** to turn to see what is behind you; *she heard footsteps behind her and quickly looked round* **(b)** to go round looking at something; *did you have time to look round the town?; can I help you? - no, I'm just looking round to see what is available*

look up ['lʊk 'ʌp] *verb* **(a)** to turn your eyes upwards; *she looked up and saw clouds in the sky* **(b)** to try to find some information in a book; *I'll look up his address in the telephone book; look up the word in the dictionary if you don't know what it means* **(c)** to get in contact with; *look me up when you're next in London* **(d)** to get better; *things are looking up*

look up to ['lʊk 'ʌp tu:] *verb* to admire, to regard someone with respect; *she looks up to her professor and copies everything he does*

loom [lu:m] **1** *noun* machine on which cloth is woven; *she weaves cloth on a hand loom at home* **2** *verb* to appear in a rather threatening way; *a storm loomed on the horizon; a bus suddenly loomed out of the fog*

looming ['lu:mɪŋ] *adjective* threatening; *the looming financial crisis threatens our expansion plans*

loony ['lu:ni] *(informal)* **1** *adjective* mad; *he had this loony plan to cycle round Africa; that's the looniest idea I've heard yet!* (NOTE: **loonier - looniest**) **2** *noun* mad person; *whoever invented bungee-jumping was a bit of a loony* (NOTE: plural is **loonies**)

loop [lu:p] **1** *noun* curve formed by a piece of thread or ribbon, etc., which crosses over itself; *to tie your laces, start by making a loop* **2** *verb* to attach with a loop; *she looped the cord over the tent pole*

loophole ['lu:phəʊl] *noun* means of avoiding a law; **to find a tax loophole** = to find a means of legally not paying tax; *he spends his time looking for tax loopholes*

loose [lu:s] **1** *adjective* **(a)** not attached; *watch out! - the sail is loose and swinging towards you!; the front wheel is loose and needs tightening; the boat came loose and started to drift away* **(b)** to be at a loose end = to have nothing special to do; *we're at a loose end this weekend* **(c)** loose change = money in coins only; *can you spare some loose change for the charity?* (NOTE: **looser - loosest**) **2** *verb* to start something happening; *the government's proposals loosed off demonstrations in all parts of the country*

looseleaf book ['lu:sli:f 'bʊk] *noun* book with loose pages which can be taken out and put back on metal rings

loosely ['lu:sli] *adverb* not tightly; *the skirt fits loosely round her waist; he tied his horse loosely to the post*

loosen ['lu:sən] *verb* **(a)** to make something less tight; *he loosened his shoelaces and relaxed* **(b)** to loosen your grip on something = to hold something less tightly than before; *the parliament forced the president to loosen his grip on the civil service*

loot [lu:t] **1** *noun* **(a)** things which have been stolen; *the police discovered the rest of the loot under his bed* **(b)** *(slang)* money; *he's got plenty of loot* (NOTE: no plural) **2** *verb* to steal, especially from shops and houses, during a riot or other emergency; *some houses were looted during the floods*

looter ['lu:tə] *noun* person who steals, especially from houses and shops during a riot or other emergency; *looters will be arrested by the police*

looting ['lu:tɪŋ] *noun* stealing from shops and houses during a riot or other emergency; *there were several incidents of looting during the disturbances* (NOTE: no plural)

lop [lɒp] *verb* to cut branches off trees; *the trees are getting too tall and need lopping* (NOTE: **lopping - lopped**)

lopsided [lɒp'saɪdɪd] *adjective* leaning to one side, with one side lower than the other; *he walks in a lopsided way; she trimmed the hedge badly so it is now quite lopsided*

loquacious [lɒ'kweɪʃəs] *adjective* *(formal)* who talks a lot; *she's very loquacious, and a phone call from her can last hours*

loquaciousness *or* **loquacity** [lɒ'kweɪʃəsnəs or lɒ'kwæsɪti] *noun* *(formal)* talking a lot; *his loquacity on the subject of old trains is well-known*

lord [lɔ:d] **1** *noun* **(a)** nobleman, ruler; *he was born a lord; powerful lords forced King John to sign the Magna Carta* **(b)** title for certain peers; *Lord Smith;* the House of Lords = the upper chamber of the British Parliament **(c)** the Lord = God or Jesus Christ; *praise* *the lord for his mercy* **(d)** *(expression of surprise or shock) good lord! I didn't realize it was so late!* **2** *verb* **to lord it over someone** = to treat someone like a servant; *she lords it over the junior staff in the office*

lore [lɔː] *noun* traditional beliefs and knowledge; *it's part of sea lore that it is unlucky to kill an albatross; see also* FOLKLORE (NOTE: no plural)

lorry [lɒri] *noun* GB large motor vehicle for carrying goods; *they put the bricks onto his lorry; big lorries make the house shake when they go past; he drives a five-ton lorry;* **lorry-load** = amount of goods carried on a lorry; *they delivered six lorry-loads of coal; see also* TRUCK (NOTE: plural is **lorries**)

lorry driver [ˈlɒri ˈdraɪvə] *noun* GB person who drives a lorry; *long-distance lorry drivers usually stop at this café* (NOTE: American English is **truck driver**)

lose [luːz] *verb* **(a)** to put or drop something somewhere and not to know where it is; *I can't find my wallet - I think I lost it on the train; if you lose your ticket you'll have to buy another one* **(b)** not to have something any longer; *we lost money on the lottery;* **to lose weight** = to get thinner; *she doesn't eat potatoes as she's trying to lose weight;* **the clock loses 10 minutes every day** = it falls 10 minutes behind the correct time every day; **to lose sight of** = not to see something any longer; *we lost sight of her in the crowd;* **to lose your temper** = to become angry; *he lost his temper when they told him there was no room in the hotel;* **to lose time** = to waste time, not to do something quickly enough; *don't lose any time in posting the letter;* **to lose your way** = to end up not knowing where you are; *they lost their way in the fog on the mountain; see also* HEART **(c)** not to win; *we lost the match 10 - 0; did you win? - no, we lost* (NOTE: **losing - lost** [lɒst])

loser [ˈluːzə] *noun* person who does not win; *the loser gets a consolation prize;* **a bad loser** = person who behaves badly when he loses a game

loss [lɒs] *noun* **(a)** no longer having something; *he was very despondent at the loss of his house;* **it's no great loss** = it doesn't matter now that we no longer have it; *the map's no great loss - I brought two along, just in case* **(b)** money which you have spent and have not got back; *companies often make losses in their first year of operations;* **they sold it at a loss** = they sold it for less than they paid for it **(c)** *(informal)* **that's a dead loss** = it's no use at all; *the plan was a dead loss* **(d)** **to be at a loss what to do** = not to know what to do; *we are at a loss to know how to proceed since our appeal has been rejected; I'm at a loss for something to do now that the party has been cancelled* (NOTE: plural is **losses**)

loss leader [ˈlɒs ˈliːdə] *noun* article which is sold at a loss to attract customers; *we use these cheap films as a loss leader*

lost [lɒst] *adjective* **to be lost** = to end up not knowing where you are; *did you bring a map? I think we're lost!* ◊ **get lost** [ˈget ˈlɒst] *verb* **(a)** not to know where you are; *he's hopeless, he got lost walking from Oxford Circus to Piccadilly; they should be back by now - do you think they've got lost?* **(b)** *(slang)* **get lost!** = go away!; *when she asked him for money he told her to get lost*

lost property office [ˈlɒst ˈprɒpəti ˈɒfɪs] *noun* place where articles which people have left on trains, buses, etc., are stored, and where they can be claimed by their owners; *go to the lost property office tomorrow*

and ask if anyone has found the hat; *have you asked the lost property office if they've got your bag?; we found an umbrella on the train and handed it in at the lost property office* (NOTE: American English for this is **lost and found office**)

lot [lɒt] *noun* **(a) a lot of** *or* **lots of** = a large number *or* a large quantity; *there's lots of time before the train leaves; what a lot of cars there are in the car park!; I've been to the cinema quite a lot recently; she's feeling a lot better now; lots of people are looking for jobs; (informal)* **a fat lot of** = not much; **a fat lot of help you are!** = you are no help at all **(b) the lot** = everything; *that's the lot - there's nothing left; there were old pots and books and newspapers - we sold the lot for £50; we picked pounds of beans and ate the lot for dinner* **(c)** US piece of land, especially one to be used for redevelopment; **parking lot** = place where you can park cars in a town (NOTE: British English is **car park**) **(d)** item or group of items sold at an auction; *lot 23 is a collection of books and pictures* **(e) to draw lots** = to take pieces of paper from a box to decide something (the person who has the marked piece wins); *we drew lots to decide who would go first; they drew lots for the bottle of whisky*

lotion [ˈləʊʃn] *noun* medicinal liquid used on the skin; *he bathed his eyes in a mild antiseptic lotion; use this lotion on your eczema*

lottery [ˈlɒtri] *noun* **(a)** game of chance in which numbered tickets are sold with prizes given for certain numbers; **the National Lottery** = British lottery which takes place twice a week, where you try to forecast a series of numbers; *she won over £2m on the lottery; there were three jackpot winners on this week's lottery; he buys a lottery ticket every week* **(b)** situation where anyone may win; *getting a government contract is something of a lottery* (NOTE: plural is **lotteries**)

loud [laʊd] **1** *adjective* which is very easily heard; *can't you stop your watch making such a loud noise?; turn down the radio - it's too loud* **2** *adverb* loudly; *I can't sing any louder; she laughed out loud in church* (NOTE: **louder - loudest**)

loudly [ˈlaʊdli] *adverb* in a way which is easily heard; *I wish you wouldn't talk so loudly*

loudspeaker [laʊdˈspiːkə] *noun* part of a radio, etc., which allows sound to be heard; *he set up two loudspeakers in opposite corners of the room; the captain called the passengers over the loudspeaker and asked them to go on deck; see also* TANNOY

lounge [laʊnʒ] **1** *noun* **(a)** comfortable room for sitting in; *let's go and watch TV in the lounge;* **lounge bar** = bar in a pub or hotel which has comfortable chairs **(b)** **departure lounge** = room at an airport where passengers wait to board their planes; *as more flights were delayed, the departure lounge filled up with angry travellers* **2** *verb* **to lounge about** = to sit or lie doing nothing or very little; *he doesn't do anything on Saturdays, he just lounges about waiting for the pubs to open; it rained all the time, so we had to spend the day lounging about in the hotel*

louse [laʊs] *noun* small insect which sucks blood and lives on the skin as a parasite on animals and humans; *some of the children in class have head lice* (NOTE: plural is **lice** [laɪs])

louse up [ˈlaʊz ˈʌp] *verb (informal)* **to louse something up** = to ruin something; *he loused up the* whole deal by trying to increase his commission by 25%

lousy ['lauzi] *adjective (informal)* awful; *what lousy weather!; I feel lousy - I think I've got flu; don't watch that lousy programme* (NOTE: **lousier - lousiest**)

lout [laut] *noun* rude and badly behaved man; *a group of louts started throwing stones at cars; see also* LAGER

louvre US **louver** ['luːvə] *noun* sloping wooden strip in a blind or frame which overlaps with other strips and only lets a small amount of light in; *she opened the louvres on the blind*

louvred or **louvered** ['luːvəd] *adjective* with louvres; *the kitchen cupboard has louvred doors*

lovable ['lʌvəbl] *adjective* pleasant, easy to love; *our grandson is a really lovable little boy; I don't find spiders particularly lovable but some people do*

love [lʌv] **1** *noun* **(a)** great liking for someone *or* something; *give my love to your wife; her great love is opera*; **to be in love** = to love each other; *they seem to be very much in love*; **to fall in love with someone** = to start to like them very much; *they fell in love at first sight* **(b) to make love (to someone)** = to have sexual intercourse with someone; *she swore on oath that he had never made love to her or that they had never made love* **(c) there's no love lost between them** = they hate each other; *the partners got on well to begin with, but now there's no love lost between them* **(d)** *(in games such as tennis)* score of zero points; *she lost the first set six - love (6-0)* **2** *verb* **(a)** to have strong feelings for someone *or* something; *she loves little children; the children love their teacher; his wife thinks he loves someone else* to like something very much; *we love going on holiday by the seaside; I'd love to come with you, but I've got too much work to do*

love affair ['lʌv ə'feə] *noun* sexual relationship between two people who are not married to each other; *he's had several love affairs with students but his wife doesn't seem to know about them*

love life ['lʌv 'laɪf] *noun* someone's sexual relationships; *he has a very active love life; she wanted to tell me all about her love life*

lovely ['lʌvli] *adjective* very pleasant; *it's a lovely warm day; she was wearing a lovely pink hat* (NOTE: **lovelier - loveliest**)

lover ['lʌvə] *noun* **(a)** person, especially a man, who is having a sexual relationship with someone; *her lover was arrested when the woman's body was found on the beach* **(b)** person who loves something; *a lover of French food*

love story ['lʌv 'stɔːri] *noun* story about two people in love; *Romeo and Juliet is a tragic love story*

loving ['lʌvɪŋ] *adjective* affectionate, showing love; *they still have a loving relationship after fifteen years of marriage*

low [ləʊ] **1** *adjective* **(a)** not high; *she hit her head on the low branch; the town is surrounded by low hills; we shop around to find the lowest prices; the engine works best at low speeds; the temperature here is too low for oranges to grow; sales were lower in December than in November* **(b)** depressed; *she was very low when I saw her last* (NOTE: **lower - lowest**) **2** *adverb* towards the bottom; not high up; *the plane was flying too low - it hit the trees*; **supplies are running low** =

supplies are becoming scarce; *see also* LIE LOW **3** *noun* point where something is very small; *sales have reached a new low* **4** *prefix meaning* 'with not much of'; **low-calorie diet** = food or drink containing very few calories; *she's on a low-calorie diet*; **low-fat** = containing very little fat; *do you have any low-fat yoghurt?* **5** *verb (formal) (of a cow)* to make a noise; *the cows were lowing in the field*

lowbrow ['ləʊbraʊ] *adjective* not with a very high intellectual content; *he reads some lowbrow newspaper; compare* HIGHBROW

low-class ['ləʊ 'klɑːs] *adjective (old)* not rich or middle-class; *we stayed in a really low-class area of the town*

lower ['ləʊə] **1** *adjective* which is below something else of the same sort; **lower deck** = bottom deck on a ship or bus; *they booked a cabin on the lower deck*; **lower jaw** = bottom jaw, the bone holding the lower teeth, which moves to make the mouth open or shut; *she hit him so hard that she broke his lower jaw* **2** *verb* **(a)** to make something go down; *they lowered the lifeboat into the water* **(b)** to make smaller; *all the shops have lowered their prices to attract customers*; **to lower your voice** = to speak more quietly

lower case ['ləʊə 'keɪs] *noun* small letters (a, b, c, etc.) as opposed to capitals (A, B, C, etc.); *that text should be in lower case, not capitals*

lower class ['ləʊə 'klɑːs] *noun (old)* group of people in society who are not rich, aristocratic or middle-class; *in the Middle Ages, the lower classes worked on the land*

low-key [ləʊ'kiː] *adjective* quiet, without much excitement; *his twenty-first birthday party was a low-key affair, because his mother was very ill in hospital*

lowland ['ləʊlənd] *adjective* referring to a region which is near sea level; *lowland farms are richer than those on the hills; compare* HIGHLAND

lowlands ['ləʊləndz] *noun* low-lying area of the country; *the Lowlands of Scotland*

lowly ['ləʊli] *adjective* humble, poor; *from lowly beginnings, he has risen to become one of the richest men in the country* (NOTE: **lowlier - lowliest**)

low-lying ['ləʊ'laɪɪŋ] *adjective* which is near to sea level, or to the level of a river; *drainage is a problem in low-lying meadows*

low-paid ['ləʊ 'peɪd] **1** *adjective* with low wages; *she has a low-paid job as a cleaner or her job as a cleaner is very low-paid* **2** *noun* **the low-paid** = people who have low wages; *the government has promised to reduce taxes for the low-paid*

low season ['ləʊ 'siːzn] *noun* time of year, usually during the winter, when few people go on holiday, and when air fares and hotel prices are cheaper; *air fares are cheaper in the low season; in February, British Airways was offering special low-season round-the-world fares* (NOTE: also called **off season**; the opposite is **high season**)

lox [lɒks] *noun* US smoked salmon; *he bought bagels and lox for breakfast*

loyal ['lɔɪəl] *adjective* faithful, who supports someone *or* something; *dogs are usually very loyal to their owners; she's a loyal member of the Conservative Party*

loyalist ['lɔɪəlɪst] *noun* person who is loyal to someone *or* something, such as a king; *pro-government loyalists have organized protest marches to demonstrate against the opposition*

loyally ['lɔɪəli] *adverb* in a loyal way; *he loyally agreed to his wife's crazy plan*

loyalty ['lɔɪəlti] *noun* being loyal; *all the staff should show their loyalty by coming to the reception*

lozenge ['lɒzɪndʒ] *noun* **(a)** diamond shape, especially when used in heraldry; *the shield has a pattern of red lozenges* **(b)** sweet medicine tablet; *she was sucking cough lozenges to get rid of her cough*

LPG ['el 'pi: 'dʒi: *or* 'lɪkwɪd pə'trəuliəm 'gæs] = LIQUID PETROLEUM GAS petroleum gases such as propane or butane, stored in liquid form in pressurized canisters, and used as fuel; *a lorry carrying canisters of highly volatile liquid petroleum gas*

L-plates ['el'pleɪts] *noun* two white plastic squares each with a large red L on it, attached to a car driven by a learner driver; *he took off his L-plates as soon as he passed his test*; **green L plates** = similar plastic plates with a green L to show that the driver has passed the driving test recently

Ltd ['lɪmɪtɪd] *short for* LIMITED COMPANY (NOTE: used for private companies. Public companies, that is companies on the Stock Exchange, are called **Plc**)

lubricant ['lu:brɪkənt] **1** *noun* oily or greasy substance used to reduce friction between moving parts; *if there is not enough lubricant, the engine will seize up* **2** *adjective* which makes something run smoothly; *the lubricant properties of oil are well-known*

lubricate ['lu:brɪkeɪt] *verb* to cover something with oil or grease to make it run smoothly; *the bearings must be lubricated regularly*; *the manufacturer claims that this brand of oil has particular lubricating properties*

lubrication [lu:brɪ'keɪʃn] *noun* action of covering with oil or grease; *lubrication should be carried out regularly*

lucid ['lu:sɪd] *adjective* **(a)** clear, easily understood; *the old lady gave a clear and lucid account of the incident to the police* **(b)** able to think clearly; *for most of the time he was delirious but in his few lucid moments he seemed to recognize me*

lucidity [lu:'sɪdɪti] *noun* being clear and easily understood; *the lucidity of his explanation convinced everyone*

luck [lʌk] *noun* something, usually good, which happens to you; *the bus is empty - that's a bit of luck!*; **good luck with your driving test!** = I hope you do well in your driving test; **I wear this ring for luck** = because I hope it will bring me luck; **bad luck** = something bad which happens to you; *it was just my bad luck to have homework when everyone else went swimming*; **bad luck!** *or* **hard luck!** = I am sorry you didn't do well; *you failed the driving test again? - bad luck!*; **to be down on your luck** = to be going through a period of bad luck; *he was down on his luck and thought of emigrating*

luckily ['lʌkɪli] *adverb* which is a good thing; *it started to rain but luckily I had taken my umbrella*; *luckily I was at home when the telephone engineer called*

lucky ['lʌki] *adjective* **(a)** having good things happening to you; *he's lucky not to have been sent to prison*; *how lucky you are to be going to Spain!*; *(informal)* **you'll be lucky!** = it will never happen; *she's hoping to get an extra day off this week - she'll be lucky!* **(b)** which brings luck; *15 is my lucky number* (NOTE: **luckier - luckiest**)

lucrative ['lu:krətɪv] *adjective* bringing in a lot of money or profit; *she has a lucrative consultancy business*; *playing the guitar in the London Underground can be very lucrative*

ludicrous ['lu:dɪkrəs] *adjective* ridiculous, which makes you laugh; *it's ludicrous that we have to carry our bags from the train up three flights of stairs*

lug [lʌg] **1** *verb* to carry or pull something heavy; *I had to lug my cases up two flights of stairs*; *lugging those boxes up into the attic has worn me out* (NOTE: **lugging - lugged**) **2** *noun* small projecting piece on the side of a jar, etc., for carrying it or for attaching something to it; *one of the lugs on the vase has been knocked off*

luge [lu:ʒ] *noun* **(a)** lightweight racing toboggan on which riders lie on their backs, travelling feet first **(b)** racing competition for luges; *he won a bronze medal in the luge*

> COMMENT: the luge is steered by exerting pressure on the tips of the runners with the calves. The track is 1000m long, with a series of bends, and is made of specially prepared ice. Speeds can reach 75 miles per hour (120 kilometres per hour)

luggage ['lʌgɪdʒ] *noun* suitcases, bags, etc., for carrying your belongings when travelling; *check that you haven't left any luggage behind on the coach*; **luggage rack** = space for bags, etc., above the seats in a plane, train, etc.; *she put her suitcase in the luggage rack*; *please place all hand luggage in the overhead luggage racks*; **luggage trolley** = metal holder on wheels, on which luggage can be moved easily in an airport, station, etc.) (NOTE: **luggage** has no plural: to show one suitcase, etc., say **an item of luggage, a piece of luggage**. Note also that American English prefers to use the word **baggage**; **luggage trolley** is **baggage cart** in American English)

lukewarm ['lu:kwɔ:m] *adjective* **(a)** not very hot; *the soup was only lukewarm*; *we sent back the coffee because it was lukewarm* **(b)** not enthusiastic; *he was only lukewarm about our project* (NOTE: means the same as **tepid**)

lull [lʌl] **1** *noun* quiet period; *after last week's hectic rushing around this week's lull was welcome* **2** *verb* to make someone *or* something calmer, to soothe; *she sang a song to lull the baby to sleep*; *the report was not very critical and that lulled them into a false sense of security*

lumbago [lʌm'beɪgəu] *noun* pain in the lower part of the back; *she has been suffering from lumbago for years*; *he has had an attack of lumbago* (NOTE: no plural)

lumber ['lʌmbə] **1** *noun* **(a)** junk, old articles which you are not using at the moment; *I am going to take some of this useless lumber to the jumble sale*; **lumber room** = room in which you keep empty boxes, things which you are not using; *we must clear out the lumber room before we move house* **(b)** *US* trees which have been cut down; *the lumber is tied together in rafts and floated down river to the sawmill* (NOTE: British English is **timber**) **2** *verb* **(a)** *(informal)* to **lumber someone with** = to give someone things he doesn't want; *you* *always manage to lumber me with the worst jobs*; *why do I always get lumbered with doing the shopping?* **(b)** to move slowly and heavily; *the tractor lumbered across the field pulling a trailer full of hay*; *watch where you're treading, you lumbering great hulk!*

lumberjack ['lʌmbədʒæk] *noun* person who cuts down trees; *lumberjacks were busy all summer in the forests of Maine*

luminary ['luːmɪnəri] *noun* important or famous person; *after the lecture I spotted the Lord Chancellor talking with some other legal luminaries in the lobby* (NOTE: plural is **luminaries**)

luminosity [luːmɪ'nɒsɪti] *noun* (*formal*) being full of light; *the luminosity of his landscape paintings*

luminous ['luːmɪnəs] *adjective* which gives out light in the dark; *the luminous hands of her bedside clock glowed faintly in the darkness*

lump [lʌmp] **1** *noun* **(a)** piece of something, often with no particular shape; *a lump of coal*; *a lump of sugar* **(b) lump sum** = money paid in one amount; *he received a lump sum from an insurance policy* **2** *verb* **to lump together** = to bring several different things together; *we lump all the cash purchases together under 'other items' in the account book*

lumpy ['lʌmpi] *adjective* with solid lumps in it; *I want to get rid of this lumpy old mattress*; *I don't like lumpy porridge* (NOTE: **lumpier - lumpiest**)

lunacy ['luːnəsi] *noun* madness, idiotic behaviour; *it's sheer lunacy to go out in the snow without a coat*

lunar ['luːnə] *adjective* referring to the moon; **a lunar eclipse** = time when part of the moon disappears, because the earth's shadow passes over it; **lunar month** = period from one new moon to the next

lunatic ['luːnətɪk] **1** *adjective* mad; *it was a lunatic idea to try to steal the blue light from in front of the police station* **2** *noun* person who acts in a mad way; *don't be such a lunatic - try to talk to her!*; *he drove like a lunatic to catch the ferry*

lunch [lʌnʃ] **1** *noun* meal eaten in the middle of the day; *come on - lunch will be ready soon*; *we always have lunch at 12.30*; *we are having fish and chips for lunch*; *I'm not hungry so I don't want a big lunch*; *the restaurant serves 150 lunches a day*; **business lunch** *or* **working lunch** = lunch where you discuss business; *see also the note at* DINNER (NOTE: plural is **lunches**) **2** *verb* to have lunch; *I'm lunching with my sister today*; *don't forget we're lunching with the agents tomorrow*

luncheon ['lʌnʃən] *noun* (*formal*) lunch, meal eaten in the middle of the day; *luncheon is served in the small dining room from 12.30 to 2 p.m.*; **luncheon meat** = tinned meat loaf containing mostly minced pork; *the canteen offered luncheon meat and salad, or sausage, chips and beans*; **luncheon voucher** = ticket given by an employer to a worker in addition to his wages, which can be exchanged for food in a restaurant; *free luncheon vouchers are one of the perks of the job*

lunch hour ['lʌnʃ 'auə] *noun* period of a working day when lunch is usually eaten; *I try to fit in a game of tennis during my lunch hour*; *the office is closed during the lunch hour*

lunchtime ['lʌnʃtaɪm] *noun* time when you usually have lunch; *it's half past twelve - almost lunchtime*; *the office is closed at lunchtimes*

lung [lʌŋ] *noun* one of two organs in the chest with which you breathe; *the doctor listened to his chest to see if his lungs were all right*

COMMENT: the two lungs are situated in the chest, with the heart between them. Air goes down into the lungs and the oxygen in it is deposited in the blood in exchange for waste carbon dioxide which is breathed out

lunge [lʌndʒ] **1** *noun* sudden movement forwards; *the policeman suddenly made a lunge for the gun* **2** *verb* to make a sudden movement forwards; *the baby suddenly lunged at the candles on the cake*

lurch [lɜːtʃ] **1** *noun* **(a)** sudden unsteady movement; *the ship gave a sudden lurch* (NOTE: plural is **lurches**) **(b)** (*informal*) **to leave someone in the lurch** = to leave someone in time of trouble or crisis; *you've really left me in the lurch by cancelling at such short notice* **2** *verb* to make a sudden unsteady movement; *when the taxi finally lurched to a stop I was shaking all over*; *he lurched over to the bar and ordered another drink*

lure ['ljuə] **1** *noun* thing which attracts a person or animal; *the white beaches are a lure for tourists* **2** *verb* to attract, especially into something bad; *she was lured to the club by reports of high wages for bar staff*

lurid ['ljuərɪd] *adjective* **(a)** glowing with brilliant colours; *the flames gave a lurid glow to the scene*; *she was wearing a lurid pink tracksuit* **(b)** (*of book or film*) sensational, meant to shock; *there were several lurid descriptions of conditions in the refugee camps*

lurk [lɜːk] *verb* to be hidden; *there are all sorts of dangers lurking in the dark*; *she's afraid there may be burglars lurking in the bushes*

luscious ['lʌʃəs] *adjective* very sweet; *a bowl full of the most luscious fruit*; *the luscious scent of honeysuckle around the door*

lush [lʌʃ] **1** *adjective* thick and rich; *the cattle were put to graze on the lush grass by the river*; *lush tropical vegetation rapidly covered the clearing* **2** *noun* (*slang*) alcoholic, drunkard; *she has the reputation of being a bit of a lush*

lushness ['lʌʃnəs] *noun* being lush; *the amazing lushness and luxuriance of tropical vegetation is hard to describe*

lust [lʌst] **1** *noun* **(a)** strong sexual desire; *he looked at her with eyes full of lust* **(b)** great desire for something; *she is driven by a lust for power* **2** *verb* **to lust after** *or* **for someone** *or* **something** = to have a great desire for someone or something; *she has been lusting after Harry ever since she met him*; *I have never really lusted after power or glory*

lustre US **luster** ['lʌstə] *noun* shine and brilliance; *the lustre of a pearl necklace*

lustrous ['lʌstrəs] *adjective* shiny; *use our shampoo to get really lustrous hair*

Luxembourg ['lʌksəmbɜːg] **1** *noun* small country in Western Europe, between France, Belgium and Germany; *Luxembourg is the smallest member of the EU* **2** *adjective* referring to Luxembourg; *the Luxembourg flag is very similar to that of the Netherlands* (NOTE: people: **Luxembourgers**; currency: **Luxembourg franc, euro**)

Luxembourger *or* **Luxemburger** ['lʌksəmbɜːgə] *noun* person from Luxembourg;

because of their unique position at the centre of Europe, Luxembourgers tend to be very cosmopolitan

luxuriant [lʌgˈʒʊriənt] *adjective* growing thickly; *a luxuriant tropical garden*; *he has a luxuriant black beard*

luxurious [lʌkˈʒuəriəs] *adjective* very comfortable; *the flat is furnished with luxurious carpets and fittings*; *business class is not as luxurious as first class*

luxury [ˈlʌkʃəri] *noun* **(a)** great comfort; *he lived a life of great luxury*; *a hot bath is a real luxury after two weeks camping in the mountains*; **luxury hotel** = a five-star hotel, a very good hotel, with luxurious rooms and higher prices **(b)** thing which is pleasant to have but not necessary; *she often buys little luxuries for dessert on Friday nights* (NOTE: plural in this meaning is **luxuries**)

Lycra [ˈlaɪkræ] *noun* trade name for a type of stretchable fabric; *she was wearing Lycra shorts*

lying [ˈlaɪŋ] *see* LIE

lymph [lɪmf] *noun* colourless liquid containing white blood cells which circulates round the body, taking waste matter from the tissues to the veins; **lymph nodes** = collections of lymph tissue found especially under the armpits and in the groin

lymphatic [lɪmˈfætɪk] *adjective* referring to lymph; **lymphatic nodes** = *see* LYMPH NODES

lynch [lɪnʃ] *verb (of a mob)* to catch an accused person and execute him, especially by hanging, without a trial; *the crowd lynched one man, but the actual murderer escaped*

lynx [lɪŋks] *noun* short-tailed animal of the cat family (NOTE: plural is **lynxes**)

lyric *or* **lyrical** [ˈlɪrɪk(l)] *adjective (poem, etc.)* concerned with feeling; *a lyrical description of the countryside in spring*; *(informal)* **to wax lyrical about something** = to be full of enthusiasm about something; *the reviewer waxed lyrical about the young painter*

lyrics [ˈlɪrɪks] *noun* words of a song; *he wrote the lyrics for the musical*

Mm

M, m [em] thirteenth letter of the alphabet, between L and N; *'accommodation' is spelt with two Ms*

ma [mɑ:] *noun (informal)* mother; *let go of my little brother or I'll tell my ma*

MA ['em 'eɪ] = MASTER OF ARTS; *she's taking an MA course in Italian art* (NOTE: written after the name: **Jane Bushell MA**)

mac [mæk] *noun (informal)* coat which keeps off water, which is worn when it is raining; *I took a plastic mac in case it started to rain* (NOTE: short for **mackintosh**; also called **raincoat**)

macabre [mə'kɑːbr] *adjective* very strange and horrifying, referring to dead bodies; *there are aspects of this case that are distinctly macabre*

machete [mə'ʃəti] *noun* large sharp knife; *we hacked our way through the forest with machetes*

machine [mə'ʃiːn] *noun* **(a)** thing which works with a motor; *we have bought a machine for putting leaflets in envelopes; there is a message on my answering machine; she made her dress on her sewing machine; the washing machine has broken and flooded the kitchen* **(b)** organization; *the party machine moved into action to prepare for the general election*

machine gun [mə'ʃiːn 'gʌn] *noun* gun which automatically fires many bullets rapidly, one after the other; *the rapid fire of a machine gun could be heard in the distance; from their lookout post they were able to rake the whole square with machine-gun fire*

machinery [mə'ʃiːnəri] *noun* **(a)** many machines, taken as a group; *the factory has got rid of a lot of old machinery* **(b)** way of organizing; *a review of local government machinery; the machinery for awarding government contracts* (NOTE: no plural: **some machinery, a piece of machinery**)

machine tools [mə'ʃiːn 'tuːlz] *noun* tools driven by motors, used to work on wood or metal; *a factory that manufactures machine tools*

machining [mə'ʃiːnɪŋ] *noun* action of making something with a machine; *machining the metal bodies will take several weeks*

machinist [mə'ʃiːnɪst] *noun* person who works a machine; *the machinists all wear ear protectors because the machines are so noisy*

macho ['mætʃəʊ] *adjective (informal)* aggressively male; *his macho style of management annoys the women staff*

mackerel ['mækrəl] *noun* sea fish with dark flesh, eaten grilled or smoked; also canned and made into pâté; *they went out fishing for mackerel; we had smoked mackerel as a starter* (NOTE: plural is **mackerel**)

mackintosh ['mækɪntɒʃ] *noun (formal)* protective coat worn in the rain; *take a mackintosh in case it rains* (NOTE: usually shortened to **mac**)

macro ['mækrəʊ] **1** *noun* block of instructions for a computer identified by one or more keystrokes; *I do the page layouts using a macro* (NOTE: plural is **macros**) **2** *prefix;* **macro-** = meaning on a large scale

macroeconomics [mækrəʊiːkə'nɒmɪks] *noun* study of economics on a large scale, as applied to countries or regions; *macroeconomics is relevant to small businesses as well as large ones*

mad [mæd] *adjective* **(a)** insane, having a serious mental disorder; *he's quite mad; she became mad and had to be put in a special hospital* **(b)** silly, crazy; *everyone thought he was mad to try to cross the Atlantic in a rowing boat; (informal)* **mad about** = very keen on; *he's mad about jigsaw puzzles;* **mad as a hatter** = totally crazy; *don't ask him for advice - he's as mad as a hatter* **(c)** wildly frantic; *the noise is driving her mad; (informal)* **like mad** = very fast; very enthusiastically; *he drove like mad and managed to get to the station in time to catch the train* **(d)** very angry; *she's mad at or with him for borrowing her car; he was hopping mad when they told him his car had been stolen* (NOTE: **madder - maddest**)

madam ['mædəm] *noun* **(a)** *(way of referring to a lady, often used by waiters or servants)* **after you, madam; would madam like some more tea?** **(b)** *(writing a letter to a lady whom you do not know)* **Dear Madam**

mad cow disease ['mæd 'kaʊ dɪ'ziːz] *noun* bovine spongiform encephalopathy (BSE), a disease affecting the brains of cattle; *the public has lost confidence in beef as a result of mad cow disease*

madden ['mædən] *verb* to exasperate, to annoy; *it maddens me to think that we just missed winning the lottery; the horses were maddened by flies*

maddening ['mædənɪŋ] *adjective* exasperating, annoying; *it's maddening to see a bus sail past just when you're so close to the bus stop*

made [meɪd] *see* MAKE (NOTE: do not confuse with **maid**)

made-to-measure ['meɪd tə 'meʒə] *adjective* (clothes, etc.) which are made specially according to the measurements of one particular person; *I've bought the suit made-to-measure* (NOTE: the opposite is **ready-to-wear** *or* **off-the-peg**)

made-up ['meɪdʌp] *adjective* **(a)** wearing make-up; *she was heavily made-up to try to hide the bruise on her cheek* **(b)** invented; *it was a made-up story - none of the report was true*

madly ['mædli] *adverb* in a wild way; *they were madly in love; as soon as we came through the gate, the dogs rushed across the yard, barking madly*

madman ['mædmən] *noun* person who is mentally ill; *only a madman would attempt something as dangerous as that;* **he drove like a madman** = he drove very fast (NOTE: plural is **madmen**)

madness ['mædnəs] *noun* **(a)** stupid behaviour which may be dangerous; *it's sheer madness to go out in a little boat in this weather* **(b)** being mad; *they say that talking to yourself is the first sign of madness*

madras [mæ'dræs] *noun* type of hot curry; *we ordered chicken madras and rice*

maestro ['maɪstrəʊ] *noun (informal)* **(a)** a musical genius; *he's a maestro on the harmonica* **(b)** conductor; *play it again, maestro!* (NOTE: plural is **maestros**)

mafia ['mæfiə] *noun* secret Italian organization dealing in crime; *many notorious mafia leaders have been arrested; see also* GODFATHER

mag [mæg] *abbreviation* **(a)** = MAGAZINE illustrated publication which comes out regularly; *he found a pile of old car mags in a corner of the shop* **(b)** = MAGNETIC; **mag tape** = special plastic tape on which sounds and pictures can be recorded, also used for recording computer data

magazine [mægə'ziːn] *noun* **(a)** illustrated paper which comes out regularly; *the gardening magazine comes out on Fridays* **(b)** radio or TV programme made up from various items on the same theme, broadcast regularly; *following the news, this week's science magazine has features on space telescopes and the disappearing ozone layer* **(c)** container for ammunition which can be attached to a gun

magenta [mə'dʒentə] **1** *adjective* bright red-purple; *she wore a magenta scarf* **2** *noun* bright red-purple colour; *magenta is one of my favourite colours*

maggot ['mægət] *noun* white worm of a bluebottle which eats rotting meat; *the meat was covered in maggots*

magic ['mædʒɪk] *noun* spells, conjuring tricks, etc., which do not appear to follow normal scientific rules; *the conjuror made a rabbit appear in his hat, and the children all thought it was magic*; **magic wand** = rod held by a fairy or magician to make things happen; *the fairy touched the pumpkin with her magic wand and it changed into a coach*; **as if by magic** = suddenly, without any possible explanation; *he pushed a button and as if by magic lights came on all over the garden*

magical ['mædʒɪkl] *adjective* as if produced by magic; *the magical effect of the evening sun reflected in the waters of the lake; the injection had an absolutely magical effect*

magically ['mædʒɪkli] *adverb* by magic; *the stage was magically transformed into a pirate ship*

magician [mə'dʒɪʃn] *noun* **(a)** wizard; *Merlin was the great magician in medieval legends* **(b)** conjuror; *they hired a magician to entertain the children at the party*

magistrate ['mædʒɪstreɪt] *noun* judge who tries cases in a minor court; *she appeared before the magistrates; the magistrate sent him for trial to the crown court; he was fined £500 by the magistrates*; **magistrates' court** = (i) building where magistrates try cases; (ii) court presided over by magistrates; *the magistrates' court is just opposite the police station; he appeared before the magistrates' court on a charge of theft* (NOTE: unpaid magistrates are also called **Justices of the Peace** or **JPs**)

Magna Carta ['mægnə 'kɑːtə] *Latin for* the 'Great Charter', granted by King John in 1215, which gave his subjects certain political and personal freedoms

COMMENT: the Magna Carta is supposed to be the first step taken towards democratic rule, since it gave political power to the aristocracy and reduced the power of the King to override the law. It did not give power to the ordinary people, but confirmed the rights of the individual to own property and receive impartial justice

magnanimous [mæg'nænɪməs] *adjective* very kind and generous to someone you have defeated or to someone who is weaker than you; *it was a magnanimous gesture on the part of the victors; she had proved her point and so could afford to be magnanimous*

magnate ['mægneɪt] *noun* important and powerful businessman; *he's an important Greek shipping magnate*

magnesium [mæg'niːziəm] *noun* white metal which is used in making alloys and is also an essential element in biological life; *the lifeboat sent off magnesium flares; magnesium burns with a very bright flame* (NOTE: Chemical element: chemical symbol: **Mg**; atomic number: **12**)

magnet ['mægnət] *noun* **(a)** piece of metal which attracts iron and steel and will point roughly north and south when balanced on a pivot; *there is a magnet inside the compass; you can move iron filings around on a piece of paper by holding a magnet underneath; she has a Mickey Mouse which sticks to the fridge door with a magnet* **(b)** anything which attracts; *moths were attracted to the lamp like a magnet; the big city is a magnet for teenagers running away from home*

magnetic [mæg'netɪk] *adjective* **(a)** which attracts metal; *iron and steel can be made magnetic, but wood and paper cannot*; **magnetic field** = area around a magnet which is under its influence; **magnetic north** = the point near the North Pole to which the needle of a compass points; **magnetic pole** = one of the two poles which are the centres of the earth's magnetic field; *see also* STRIP, TAPE **(b)** having a power of attraction; *she has a magnetic personality - everyone looks at her when she enters a room*

magnetism ['mægnətɪzm] *noun* **(a)** quality of being magnetic; **terrestrial magnetism** = the magnetic properties of the earth **(b)** being charming and attractive; *the princess had enormous personal magnetism*

magnification [mægnɪfɪ'keɪʃn] *noun* **(a)** action of making something appear larger; *magnification enables us to see things that are too small to be visible to the naked eye* **(b)** degree to which things appear larger when magnified; *what magnification do you get with these binoculars?*

magnificent [mæg'nɪfɪsənt] *adjective* very fine, very splendid, very luxurious; *he lives in a magnificent 20-bedroom mansion by the lake; she gave a magnificent performance as Cleopatra*

magnificently [mæg'nɪfɪsəntli] *adverb* in a magnificent way; *the stage was magnificently decorated to look like the inside of a Russian palace; she danced magnificently and everyone cheered*

magnify ['mægnɪfaɪ] *verb* to make something appear larger; *distant objects appear magnified when you look at them through a telescope*; **magnifying glass** = lens which makes small objects appear larger; *she used a magnifying glass to read the small print; if the sun is* *strong enough you can set fire to a piece of paper using a magnifying glass*

magnitude ['mægnɪtjuːd] *noun* **(a)** *(formal)* importance; *they did not underestimate the magnitude of the task*; *we will need more staff if we take on a project of this magnitude* **(b)** measure of the brightness of any object in the sky; *a star of the third magnitude*

magnum ['mægnəm] *noun* **(a)** large bottle of wine, especially champagne, containing about one and a half litres; *they ordered magnums of champagne to celebrate their win* **(b)** **magnum opus** = most important work produced by someone, especially by an artist; *the novel in twelve volumes is his magnum opus*

magpie ['mægpaɪ] *noun* common large black and white bird; *magpies are attracted by bright objects and sometimes steal them*

mahogany [mə'hɒgəni] *noun* dark red tropical hardwood, now becoming rare; *we all sat round the mahogany dining table*

maid [meɪd] *noun* female servant; *the chalet has a daily maid to do the cleaning* (NOTE: do not confuse with **made**)

maiden ['meɪdən] **1** *noun* *(formal)* unmarried girl or woman; *the village maidens danced at the wedding* **2** *adjective* **(a)** *(of woman)* unmarried; **maiden aunt** = unmarried aunt; **maiden name** = surname of a woman before she is married; *she still uses her maiden name although she's married* **(b)** **maiden flight** = first flight of a new aircraft; *the test pilot was at the controls for the maiden flight*; **maiden speech** = first speech of a Member of Parliament; *an MP's maiden speech usually deals with a subject which is not particularly controversial*; **maiden voyage** = first voyage of a new ship; *the Titanic sank on her maiden voyage*

mail [meɪl] *noun* **1** *noun* **(a)** letters which are delivered; *the mail hasn't come yet*; *my secretary opens my mail as soon as it arrives*; *the receipt was in this morning's mail* **(b)** service provided by the post office; *the cheque was lost in the mail*; *we sent the parcel by sea mail*; *it's cheaper to send the order by surface mail*; **mail merge** = computer program which allows the same letter to be written to many different addresses; *see also* AIRMAIL **(c)** **(chain) mail** = medieval armour made of small metal rings joined together; *he wore a coat of mail* **2** *verb* to send something by the postal services; *we mailed the catalogue to addresses all over Europe*; *he mailed the order last Wednesday* (NOTE: **mail** is used in both British and American English; British English also uses **post**, while American English does not)

mailbox ['meɪlbɒks] *noun* **(a)** one of several boxes where incoming mail is put in a large building; *I checked the mailbox to see if I had any letters* **(b)** box for putting letters, etc., which you want to mail; *I posted the letter in the mailbox at the corner of the street* (NOTE: plural is **mailboxes**; the British equivalent is a **letterbox** *or* **postbox**)

mailing list ['meɪlɪŋ 'lɪst] *noun* list of names and addresses of people to whom information can be sent; *his name is on our mailing list*; *we are building up a mailing list of potential customers*

mailman ['meɪlmən] *noun US* man who delivers letters; *the mailman's been, but he left nothing for you* (NOTE: plural is **mailmen**; the British equivalent is a **postman**)

mail order [meɪl 'ɔːdə] *noun* ordering and buying by post; *I bought the sofa by mail order or from a mail-order catalogue*

maim [meɪm] *verb* to injure someone so badly that he or she cannot walk, write, etc., ever again; *the car crash maimed him for life*; *hundreds of people are killed or maimed by landmines every year*

main [meɪn] **1** *adjective* most important; *the main thing is to get to work on time*; *their main factory is in Scotland*; *January is the main month for skiing holidays*; *a car will meet you at the main entrance*; *US* **Main Street** = most important street in a town, where the shops and banks are (NOTE: in British English, this is the **High Street**) **2** *noun* **(a)** large pipe for water, gas, etc.; *a water main burst and flooded the street*; *workmen hit a gas main when they were digging a hole in the road* **(b)** **the mains** = electricity brought into a building; *that computer is plugged into the mains*; *our radio can run either on a battery or on the mains*

main course ['meɪn 'kɔːs] *noun* the most important part of a meal, usually a dish of meat and vegetables or fish and vegetables; *we had a starter and a main course, but didn't have a dessert*; *the main course was roast beef and Yorkshire pudding*

mainland ['meɪnlənd] *noun* large solid mass of land, as opposed to an island; *the ferry from the Isle of Wight takes 15 minutes to reach the mainland*; **mainland Europe** = Europe, not counting the British Isles

mainly ['meɪnli] *adverb* **(a)** most often; *we sell mainly to businesses*; *people mainly go on holiday in the summer* **(b)** chiefly; *she is mainly interested in old churches*

main road ['meɪn 'rəʊd] *noun* the largest and busiest road in a place; *we try to keep off the main roads when we're towing a trailer*; *you take a turning off the main road to get to their farm*

mainspring ['meɪnsprɪŋ] *noun* **(a)** central spring of a watch or clock; *the mainspring has snapped and needs replacing* **(b)** most important reason which makes you do something; *ambition seemed to be the mainspring of her professional life*

mainstay ['meɪnsteɪ] *noun* main support that plays the most important part in keeping something going; *experienced employees are the mainstay of the company*; *soya beans are the mainstay of their diet*

mainstream ['meɪnstriːm] *adjective* (group, trend, etc.) most important; *it took him more than ten years to become a mainstream Hollywood director*; *she wants to get into mainstream politics*

maintain [meɪn'teɪn] *verb* **(a)** to keep something going; *we like to maintain good relations with our customers* **(b)** to keep something in good working order; *the boiler needs to be regularly maintained* **(c)** to state as a fact; *throughout the trial he maintained that the car was not his*

maintenance ['meɪntənəns] *noun* **(a)** keeping in working order; *we offer a full maintenance service* **(b)** keeping things going or working; *the maintenance of contacts with government officials* **(c)** money for upkeep, especially paid by a divorced or separated person to help pay for living expenses for children; *he refused to pay maintenance for their children*

maisonette [meɪzə'net] *noun* flat on two floors in a larger house; *they've bought a maisonette near the High Street* (NOTE: American English is a **duplex**)

maître d'hôtel *US* **maître d'** ['metrədəu'tel or metrə'di:] *noun* head waiter; *the maître d'hôtel showed us to our table*

maize [meɪz] *noun* widely grown cereal crop; *maize is the most important food crop grown in the USA* (NOTE: do not confuse with **maze;** note: called **corn** in American English)

majestic [mə'dʒestɪk] *adjective* grand or stately; *the majestic grandeur of the Rocky Mountains*

majesty ['mædʒəsti] *noun* **(a)** beautiful or impressive sight; *the majesty of the snow-covered mountains took his breath away* **(b)** *(formal)* *(used as a form of address to a king or queen) Her Majesty, Queen Elizabeth II* (NOTE: the plural **majesties** is used to refer to several kings and queens: **Their Majesties, the King and Queen of Norway;** when speaking formally to a king or queen, say **Your Majesty**)

major ['meɪdʒə] **1** *adjective* **(a)** important; *inhaled tar is a major cause of lung cancer*; *computers are a major influence on modern industrial society*; *many small roads are blocked by snow, but the major roads are open*; **the major part of** = most of; *the major part of the film takes place in Scotland* **(b)** *(music)* key where there are semitones between the third and fourth, and seventh and eighth notes, and tones between the others; *she played a concerto in B major*; *compare* MINOR **2** *noun* rank of an officer in the army below colonel; *a major and six soldiers* (NOTE: used as a title with a surname: **Major Smith**) **3** *verb US* to specialize in a subject at university; *she majored in English literature*

major-general [meɪdʒ'dʒenərəl] *noun* senior army officer below a lieutenant-general; *he rose to the rank of major-general*

majority [mə'dʒɒrɪti] *noun* **(a)** larger part of a group; *the majority of the members of the club don't want to change the rules*; **in the majority** = being more than half of the members; *women are in a majority on the committee*; *see also* SILENT **(b)** number of voters which is larger than half; *she was elected with a majority of 10,000*; **the government has a majority of one** = the government has one MP more than the opposition; **two-thirds majority** = more than 66%; *you need a two-thirds majority to get the approval of the shareholders* (NOTE: plural is **majorities**)

make [meɪk] **1** *noun* the country or the company which makes something; *Japanese makes of cars*; *what is the make of your refrigerator?* **2** *verb* **(a)** to put together, to build; *he made a boat out of old pieces of wood*; *these knives are made of steel*; *she is making a Christmas cake* **(b)** to get ready; *do you want me to make some tea?*; **to make a bed** = to make a bed tidy after someone has slept in it; *when we got to the hotel, the beds hadn't been made* **(c)** to add up to a total; *six and four makes ten* **(d)** to earn (money); *he made millions of pounds by buying and selling property* **(e)** to give someone a feeling; *the smell of coffee makes me hungry*; *the rough sea made him feel sick*; *looking at old photographs made her sad* **(f)** to force someone to do something; *his mother made him clean his room*; *the teacher made us all stay in after school*; *I can't make the car go any faster*; *what on earth made you do that?* (NOTE: **making - made** [meɪd])

make-believe ['meɪk bɪ'li:v] *noun* pretending that something is true when it is not; *his stories about his love affairs are just make-believe*

make do with ['meɪk 'du: 'wɪθ] *verb* to use something because there is nothing else available; *she forgot her pyjamas, and had to make do with a T-shirt*; *the shop has no brown bread left so we'll have to make do with white*; *all the glasses are broken, so we'll have to make do with plastic beakers*

make for ['meɪk 'fɔ:] *verb* **(a)** to go towards; *the army was making for the capital*; *as soon as the film started, she made straight for the exit* **(b)** to help something to happen; *non-stick pans make for easier washing up*

make of ['meɪk ɒv] *verb* to have an impression or opinion about something; *what did you make of the news on TV?*; *I don't know what to make of this letter*

make off with ['meɪk 'ɒf wɪð] *verb* to steal something; *the burglar made off with all their silver*

make out ['meɪk 'aut] *verb* **(a)** to be able to see clearly; *can you make out the house in the dark?* **(b)** to be able to understand; *I can't make out why he doesn't want to come* **(c)** to claim something which is probably not true; *the English weather isn't really as bad as it is made out to be*; *she tries to make out that she's very poor* **(d)** to write something, such as a name; *the cheque is made out to Mr Smith* **(e)** *(informal) US* to be successful; *he tried opening a fish restaurant but it didn't make out*; *how is Bobby making out at school?*

make over ['meɪk 'əuvə] *verb* to make over something to someone = to pass ownership of something to someone; *he made over the property to his daughter*

maker ['meɪkə] *noun* person who makes something; *the makers of the Mini must have made a lot of money over the years*; *the company is the world's biggest maker of ice-cream*

makeshift ['meɪkʃɪft] *adjective* used temporarily in place of something else; *they used a makeshift ladder to get down into the well*

make time ['meɪk 'taɪm] *phrase* to arrange to do something even though you are short of time; *we must make time to visit the new staff sports club*

make up ['meɪk 'ʌp] *verb* **(a)** to invent a story; *he said he had seen a man climbing into the house, but in fact he made the whole story up* **(b)** to form; *the staff is made up of typists and drivers* **(c)** to make up your mind = to decide; *they can't make up their minds on where to go for their holiday*; *his mind is made up* = nothing will make him change his mind; *it's no use talking to him - his mind is made up* **(d)** to make up for lost time = to act quickly because you did not act earlier; *it's June already - we'll have to plant our beans now to make up for lost time* **(e)** to make yourself up = to put on powder, lipstick, etc.

makeup ['meɪkʌp] *noun* **(a)** face powder, lipstick, etc., which are put on your face to make it more beautiful; *she wears no makeup apart from a little eye shadow*; *he spent hours over his makeup for the part of the monster* **(b)** way in which something is formed or arranged; *by bringing in ministers from another party, the Prime Minister has altered the whole makeup of the Cabinet*; *the census shows the ethnic makeup of the population*

making ['meikiŋ] *noun* construction, formation; *ten tons of concrete were used in the making of the wall*; it was four years **in the making** = it took four years to make; it **has the makings of** = it may develop into; *the situation has all the makings of a political crisis*

maladroit [mælə'drɔit] *adjective (formal)* clumsy when dealing with people or things; *she is still very maladroit at social occasions*

malaise [mæ'leiz] *noun* **(a)** feeling of being slightly ill; *she had a feeling of malaise but couldn't say what caused it* **(b)** feeling of being slightly worried; *there is a general malaise among the middle-class which might make them vote against the government*

malaria [mə'leəriə] *noun* tropical disease caused by a parasite which enters the body after a bite from a female mosquito; *some people going on holiday to African countries come back with malaria*

Malaysia [mə'leizə] *noun* large country in South-East Asia, south of Thailand; *Malaysia exports a lot of rubber* (NOTE: capital: **Kuala Lumpur**; people: **Malaysians**; language: **bahasa Malaysia**; currency: **ringgit** *or* **Malaysian dollar**)

Malaysian [mə'leiʒn] **1** *adjective* referring to Malaysia; *the Malaysian economy* **2** *noun* person from Malaysia; *many Malaysians come to Britain to study*

male [meil] **1** *adjective* **(a)** referring to the sex which does not produce offspring; *a male deer is called a stag* **(b)** referring to men or boys; *the male population is more likely to get flu than the female*; *see also* CHAUVINIST, MENOPAUSE **2** *noun* **(a)** man or boy; *the wreckage contained the bodies of two males and two females* **(b)** animal or insect of the sex which does not give birth to offspring; *with spiders, the female is usually bigger than the male* (NOTE: do not confuse with **mail**)

malevolence [mə'levələns] *noun (formal)* wanting to harm other people; *she did it out of sheer malevolence*

malevolent [mə'levələnt] *adjective* who wants to harm other people; *he gave her a malevolent glare; I don't think his treatment of the children was really malevolent*

malfunction [mæl'fʌŋkʃn] *(formal)* **1** *noun* not working properly; *the data was lost due to a software malfunction* **2** *verb* not to work properly; *some of the keys on the keyboard have started to malfunction*

malice ['mælis] *noun* unfriendly or spiteful feeling towards someone; *the criticism of his book was harsh but there was no malice in it*; **to do something out of malice** = to do something just to hurt someone; *she threw away his diary out of or from pure malice*

malicious [mə'liʃəs] *adjective* **(a)** done because you want to harm someone; *there has been some malicious gossip about her; it was a malicious attempt to make her lose her job* **(b)** *(legal)* done without a lawful reason; **malicious damage** = deliberate damage to property

malign [mə'lain] **1** *verb* to say nasty things about someone or something; *I've no wish to malign my assistant who has generally been doing an excellent job*; he has been much **maligned** = people have criticized him a lot; *their much-maligned extra rapid service is not as bad as all that* **2** *adjective* causing evil; *he came under the malign influence of the old doctor*

malignant [mə'lignənt] *adjective* **(a)** likely to be cause death; **malignant tumour** = tumour which is a cancer and can spread into other parts of the body; *at first they thought the growth was benign, but in fact it was malignant; the hospital diagnosed a malignant tumour in her breast* (NOTE: a tumour which is not cancerous is **benign**) **(b)** wanting to harm someone; *his malignant attitude towards his neighbours because of their dog*

mall *noun* **(a)** [mɔːl]; **shopping mall** = enclosed covered shopping area with shops, restaurants, banks and other facilities; *the new shopping mall is taking customers away from the stores in the town centre* (NOTE: do not confuse with **maul**) **(b)** [mæl]; **the Mall** = street in London leading from Trafalgar Square to Buckingham Palace; *the soldiers paraded down the Mall to Buckingham Palace*

mallet ['mælit] *noun* large wooden hammer; *we drove the tent pegs in with a mallet*

malnutrition [mælnjuː'triʃn] *noun* not having enough to eat; *many of the children in the camp were suffering from malnutrition; malnutrition had reduced the prisoners almost to skeletons*

malpractice [mæl'præktis] *noun (by a doctor, lawyer, accountant, etc.)* acting in an unprofessional or illegal way; *the client felt she had been the victim of legal malpractice*

malt [mɔːlt] **1** *noun* barley grains which have been through the malting process and are used in breweries to make beer and in distilleries to make whisky; **malt whisky** = whisky distilled from malted barley **2** *verb* **(a)** to treat grain, such as barley, by allowing it to sprout and then drying it **(b)** to flavour with malt; **malted milk** = hot drink made from milk powder flavoured with malt

mama [mə'mɑː] *noun (old)* child's name for mother; *my mama says I mustn't play in the street*

mamba ['mæmbə] *noun* poisonous African snake; *the mamba's bite is often fatal*

mammal ['mæml] *noun* type of animal which gives birth to live young and feeds them with milk; *human beings, cats, dolphins and bats are all mammals*

mammalian [mə'meiliən] *adjective* referring to mammals; *some reptiles have mammalian characteristics*

mammoth ['mæməθ] **1** *noun* very large hairy elephant living in prehistoric times; *there's a full-size model of a mammoth in the museum; the woolly mammoth is thought to have become extinct during the last Ice Age* **2** *adjective* enormous, huge; *updating the bank's computer system is a mammoth task*

man [mæn] **1** *noun* **(a)** male human being; *that tall man is my brother; there's a young man at reception asking for Mr Smith* **(b)** any human being; *Stone Age men existed several thousand years ago* **(c)** **the man in the street** = an ordinary person; *the man in the street isn't interested in a united Europe* (NOTE: plural is **men** [men]) **2** *verb* to provide staff to work something; *the switchboard is manned all day; the exhibition stand was manned by three salesgirls; he sometimes mans the front desk when the receptionist is ill* (NOTE: **mans - manning - manned**)

manage ['mænidʒ] *verb* **(a)** to be in charge of something; *she manages all our offices in Europe; we want to appoint someone to manage the new shop* **(b)** **to manage to do something** = to do something successfully; *did you manage to phone the office?*; *the burglars managed to open the door of the safe* **(c)** to be able to work properly or cope with a situation; *can you manage all by yourself?*; *how are we going to manage without a driver?*

manageable ['mænədʒəbl] *adjective* which can be dealt with easily; *his business is easily manageable*; *the financial problems they face are too large to be manageable*

management ['mænɪdʒmənt] *noun* **(a)** directing and control of work; *he's taking a course in management*; *if anything goes wrong now it's just a case of bad management* **(b)** group of people who direct workers; *the management has decided to move to new offices*; **under new management** = with a new owner or manager; *the shop is under new management*; **senior management** = senior managers or directors; **middle management** = departmental managers who are not as important as directors; *there have been redundancies, even at middle management level*; **management buyout (MBO)** = takeover of a company by a group of employees (usually managers and directors)

manager ['mænɪdʒə] *noun* **(a)** person in charge of a department in a shop or in a business; *the bank manager wants to talk about your account*; *the sales manager organized a publicity campaign*; *she's the manager of the shoe department* **(b)** organizer of a sports team; *the club have just sacked their manager* **(c)** person who is employed to organize the work of a singer, sportsman, actor, etc.; *her manager is organizing her tour of North America*

manageress [mænɪdʒə'res] *noun* woman who manages a shop or department; *the assistant called the manageress to help her sort out the problem* (NOTE: plural is **manageresses**)

managerial [mænə'dʒɪəriəl] *adjective* referring to managers; *it's a job with managerial responsibilities*; **to be appointed to a managerial position** = to be appointed a manager; **decisions taken at managerial level** = decisions taken by managers

managing director (MD) ['mænɪdʒɪŋ daɪ'rektə] *noun* director who runs everything in a firm; *she was made managing director of a textile company*; *the MD is in Australia on business*

mandarin ['mændərɪn] *noun* **(a)** small orange with a soft easily-peeled skin; *there are plenty of mandarins in the shops around Christmas* **(b)** *(informal)* **Whitehall mandarin** = top British civil servant (NOTE: compare the American use of **Brahmin: Boston Brahmins**) **(c) Mandarin** = the principal spoken form of Chinese, the official language of China; *I learnt Mandarin before I went to China*

mandate ['mændeɪt] *noun* power given to a person to act on behalf of someone else; *did the UN troops exceed their mandate?*; *the government has a clear mandate from the people to improve the health service* = when they voted for the government people approved of the plan to improve the health service

mandatory ['mændətəri] *adjective* which has to be done, which has to take place because of a rule or law; *the UN voted to impose mandatory sanctions on the country*; *attendance at meetings is mandatory for all committee members*; **mandatory meeting** = meeting which all members have to attend

mandible ['mændɪbl] *noun* lower jaw of birds, insects, etc.; *the bone we found was the fossilized mandible of a small dinosaur*

mandolin ['mændəlɪn] *noun* stringed instrument like a small guitar with eight strings; *he sat on the balcony, playing the mandolin*

mane [meɪn] *noun* long hair on the neck of a lion or horse; *he clung onto the horse's mane as it raced along the edge of the sea* (NOTE: do not confuse with **main**)

maneuver [mə'nu:və] *US see* MANOEUVRE

manfully ['mænfəli] *adverb* in a strong and determined way; *he manfully resisted all attempts to make him change his mind*; *she manfully ate all her pudding even though she felt a bit sick*

manganese ['mæŋgəni:z] *noun* metallic trace element (NOTE: Chemical element: chemical symbol: **Mn**; atomic number: **25**)

mangetout peas ['mɒnʒtu 'pi:z] *noun* type of pea where the pod and little seeds are eaten together; *mangetout peas are eaten in their pods*

mangle ['mæŋgl] **1** *noun (old)* device with rollers for squeezing the water out of clothes, etc., which have been washed; *put the sheets through the mangle before hanging them up to dry* **2** *verb* **(a)** to squash or chop up; *the mangled remains of a dog run over by a lorry* **(b)** to spoil something by doing it badly; *he mangled his part so much that the audience laughed*; *the poem was completely mangled in translation*

mango ['mæŋgəʊ] *noun* large tropical fruit with yellow flesh and a big stone; *they served mango chutney with the curry* (NOTE: plural is **mangoes**)

manhole ['mænhəʊl] *noun* hole in the road or pavement through which you go down into the sewers, etc.; *we have a manhole cover in our front garden which we hide with creeping plants*; *they went down the manhole to inspect the drains*

manhood ['mænhʊd] *noun* state of being a man; *when he reached manhood he was sent out to hunt in the forest with his father* (NOTE: no plural)

mania ['meɪniə] *noun* **(a)** form of mental illness where the patient is very excited and violent; **persecution mania** = state where you feel that everyone is persecuting you **(b)** passion for something; *he has a mania for collecting old cars*; *she has a mania for white clothes*

maniac ['meɪniæk] *noun* **(a)** person with a mania; *a maniac with a gun was holding the family hostage* **(b)** crazy person; *we were nearly killed by some maniac driving a sports car*

manic ['mænɪk] *adjective* **(a)** wildly energetic; *the scene of manic activity in the office as everyone rushed to finish the work before the deadline* **(b)** referring to mania; **manic depression** *or* **manic-depressive illness** = psychological illness where the patient moves between mania and depression and has delusions

manicure ['mænɪkjʊə] **1** *noun* looking after the hands; **to have a manicure** = to have your hands cleaned and nails trimmed; *she offered to give me a manicure* **2** *verb* to look after the hands and nails; *her beautifully manicured hands*

manicurist ['mænɪkjʊrɪst] *noun* person whose job is to look after people's hands; *the manicurist sold me some special hand cream*

manifest ['mænɪfest] **1** *adjective (formal)* obvious, plain for everyone to see; *his manifest lack of interest in the subject, made teaching him difficult* **2** *noun* list of goods, cargo, or passengers; *according to the manifest, the cargo is supposed to be tractor parts*; **passenger manifest** = list of passengers on a ship or plane **3** *verb (formal)* to show; *the cat manifested no interest in her food whatsoever*; **to manifest itself as** = to show itself as; *the disease first manifests itself as a slight skin rash*

manifesto [mænɪˈfestəʊ] *noun* a **political manifesto** = programme of action outlined by a political party and published as a pamphlet; *the Conservative manifesto was published last week*; *compare* PLATFORM (NOTE: plural is **manifestos**)

manifold ['mænɪfəʊld] **1** *adjective (formal)* of varying kinds; *they gave manifold reasons for not continuing with the project* **2** *noun* **exhaust manifold** = tubes that collect the exhaust gases from the cylinders of a car engine and take them to the exhaust pipe

manipulate [məˈnɪpjʊleɪt] *verb* **(a)** to handle; *she found it difficult to manipulate the instruments when wearing protective clothing* **(b)** to influence people or situations so that you get what you want; *by manipulating the media the government made sure its message got across to the people* **(c)** to falsify accounts to make a company seem more profitable; *he was accused of manipulating the sales figures to protect the share price*

manipulation [mənɪpjʊˈleɪʃn] *noun* **(a)** handling of machinery; *manipulation of the machine is best done by an expert* **(b)** influencing people or situations so that you get what you want; *the government made sure its message got across through its manipulation of the media*

manipulative [məˈnɪpjʊlətɪv] *adjective* controlling and using people, so as to get them to do what you want; *the director is an unpleasant manipulative person*

mankind [mænˈkaɪnd] *noun* the human race, all human beings; *one small step for a man, a giant leap for mankind*; *a discovery which should benefit all mankind* (NOTE: no plural)

manly ['mænli] *adjective* looking or behaving as a man should look or behave; *it's not considered manly to cry in public*; *he held her in his manly arms*

man-made [mænˈmeɪd] *adjective* which has been made by human beings; *a shirt made of man-made fibre*; *a shoe with leather uppers and a man-made sole*; *the book lists all man-made disasters since 1990*

mannequin ['mænɪkɪn] *noun* **(a)** model of a person, dressed in clothes to show them to people who might buy them; *her job is to dress the mannequins in the store window* **(b)** *(old)* = MODEL

manner ['mænə] *noun* **(a)** way of behaving; *she has a very unpleasant manner*; *the staff don't like the new manager's manner* **(b)** **manners** = way of behaving in public; *it's bad manners to speak with your mouth full*; *those boys need to be taught some manners* **(c)** sort; **in a manner of speaking** = in some sort of way; *in a manner of speaking, I'm glad to have got the sack, as I won't have to work in that dreadful office again* (NOTE: do not confuse with **manor**)

mannered ['mænəd] *adjective* full of odd unnatural expressions; *I don't like his style, it's too mannered*

mannerism ['mænərɪzm] *noun* gesture or way of speaking which is particular to one person; *she has exactly the same mannerisms as her mother*

manning ['mænɪŋ] *noun* using people to do a work process; **manning levels** = the number of people needed in each department to do the work efficiently

mannish ['mænɪʃ] *adjective (of a woman)* looking or dressing like a man; *with her short hair and deep voice she seemed distinctly mannish*

manoeuvre *US* **maneuver** [məˈnuːvə] **1** *noun* **(a)** planned action to avoid something, or to deceive someone; *the company has carried out various manoeuvres to avoid bankruptcy* **(b)** **manoeuvres** = military exercises; *the fleet is on manoeuvres in the Mediterranean* **2** *verb* **(a)** to move something heavy or difficult to handle; *we manoeuvred the piano into position on the stage* **(b)** to work to put yourself in a good position; *she managed to manoeuvre herself onto the board of the company*

manor ['mænə] *noun* a country house and the land surrounding it; *the lord of the manor owns most of the land round the village*; **manor house** = country house; *the family live in a lovely old manor house near the forest* (NOTE: do not confuse with **manner**)

manpower ['mænpaʊə] *noun* number of workers in a country or industry or organization; *in a labour-intensive industry, manpower is the most important resource*; **manpower requirements** = number of workers needed; *each department has been asked to forecast its manpower requirements for the next three years* (NOTE: no plural)

manservant ['mænsɜːvənt] *noun* male servant; *he has a manservant to look after his clothes and to help him dress*

mansion ['mænʃən] *noun* **(a)** very large private house; *he's bought a mansion overlooking the golf course*; *they live in a mansion in Hampstead with its own swimming pool and tennis courts*; **the Mansion House** = the house of the Lord Mayor of London, in the centre of the City of London **(b)** **mansions** = large block of flats; *his address is Flat 10, Harewood Mansions, London Road*

manslaughter ['mænslɔːtə] *noun* offence of killing someone without having intended to do so or of killing someone intentionally but with mitigating circumstances; *he was acquitted of murder but found guilty of manslaughter*; *compare* MURDER

mantelpiece *or* **mantelshelf** ['mæntlpiːs *or* 'mæntlʃelf] *noun* shelf above a fireplace; *the clock on the mantelpiece struck twelve*

mantle ['mæntl] *noun* **(a)** *(formal)* cloak, covering; *ladies arrived for the ball wrapped in fur mantles*; *the ground was covered by a mantle of snow* **(b)** *(formal)* **to assume the mantle of office** *or* **of power** = to take up an official position *or* to take power; *after the coup, the general assumed the mantle of power* **(c)** **gas mantle** = gauze cover for a gas lamp

mantra ['mæntrə] *noun* phrase which is chanted many times, as in a prayer; *Buddhist monks chanting mantras*; *the strikers walked past, repeating their usual mantra: 'EVERYBODY OUT!'*

manual ['mænjʊəl] **1** *adjective* **(a)** done by hand; **manual work** = work done with your hands; *he has no* *qualifications, so he does some manual work while studying*; **manual worker** = worker who works with his hands **(b)** (car) where the gears are changed by hand; *I prefer a manual model to an automatic* **2** *noun* book of instructions; *look in the manual to see if it tells you how to change the toner cartridge*

manufacture [mænjʊˈfæktʃə] **1** *noun* making of a commercially produced product; *robots are used in car manufacture*; *most of the cars are of foreign manufacture* **2** *verb* to make products commercially; *we no longer manufacture tractors here*

manufacturer [mænjʊˈfæktʃərə] *noun* person or company producing industrial products; *an aircraft manufacturer*; *a shoe manufacturer*

manufacturing [mænjʊˈfæktʃərɪŋ] **1** *noun* the business of making things in large quantities for sale; *only 25% of the nation's workforce is now engaged in manufacturing* **2** *adjective* that manufactures things; *the decline of manufacturing industry*; **manufacturing industries** = industries which take raw materials and make them into finished products; **a manufacturing town** = a town which has many industries based in it; *this used to be a prosperous manufacturing town before the factories closed*

manure [məˈnjʊə] **1** *noun* animal dung used as fertilizer on land; *the farmers were out in the field, spreading manure* **2** *verb* to spread animal dung on the land as fertilizer; *the soil should be well manured before you begin planting*

manuscript [ˈmænjʊskrɪpt] *noun* **(a)** document, letter, poem, which has been written by hand; *one of the original manuscripts of the Domesday Book is kept in London*; *the sale of several manuscript letters by King Charles II* **(b)** handwritten or typed version of a book which has not been printed or published; *he sent his manuscript to several publishers, but no one wanted to publish it* (NOTE: often written **MS**, plural **MSS**, say 'manuscripts')

many [ˈmeni] **1** *adjective* **(a)** a large number of things or people; *many old people live on the south coast*; *so many people wanted rooms that the hotel was booked up*; *she ate twice as many cakes as her sister did* **(b)** *(asking a question)* *how many times have you been to France?*; *how many passengers were there on the plane?* **(c)** **a great many** *or* **a good many** = quite a lot; *a good many people think we should build a bypass round the town*; **too many** = more than necessary; *there were too many people waiting and not enough room on the bus for all of them*; **one too many** = one more than enough (NOTE: **many - more** [mɔː] - **most** [məʊst] Note also that **many** is used with nouns which you can count: **not many apples** but **not much bread**) **2** *pronoun* a large number of people; *many of the students knew the lecturer when he was a student himself*; *many would say that smoking should be banned in all public places*

Maori [ˈmaʊri] *noun* person of the race of the original inhabitants of New Zealand; *the Maoris decorated the prows of their war canoes*

map [mæp] **1** *noun* drawing which shows a place, such as a town, a country or the world as if it is seen from the air; *here's a map of Europe*; *the village where they live is so small I can't find it on the map*; *show me on the map where the mountains are*; *they lost their way because they'd forgotten to take a map*; **physical map** = diagram showing mountains, rivers, etc.;

political map = diagram showing the borders of countries, administrative districts, etc.; **street map** = diagram showing streets with their names; *if you're going to Paris, you'll need a street map* **2** *verb* **(a)** to make a map of a country, etc.; *the explorers mapped the whole of the south of the country* **(b)** to map out = to plan in advance; *we met yesterday to map out our publicity programme*; *he mapped out a route to get to Birmingham using only minor roads, not motorways* (NOTE: **mapping - mapped**)

maple [ˈmeɪpl] *noun* northern tree, growing mainly in Canada and the USA, with sweet sap; *maples are particularly beautiful in autumn, when their leaves turn red*; **maple leaf** = leaf with five points, used as the symbol of Canada on the Canadian national flag; **maple sugar** *or* **maple syrup** = sugar *or* syrup made from the sap of the maple tree; *we had pancakes with maple syrup*

mar [mɑː] *verb* to spoil; *the picnic was marred by clouds of insects*; *a stain on the tablecloth slightly marred the effect the restaurant was trying to achieve* (NOTE: **marring - marred**)

marathon [ˈmærəθən] *noun* **(a)** long distance race; *a marathon is run over 26 miles*; *she's training for the New York marathon* **(b)** anything which lasts a long time and is very tiring; *the marathon meeting of club members lasted for over five hours*; *after a marathon negotiating session, we finally reached agreement*

marble [ˈmɑːbl] *noun* **(a)** very hard type of stone which can be polished so that it shines brilliantly; *the entrance hall has a marble floor*; *the table top is made from a single slab of green marble* **(b)** **marbles** = set of small glass balls for playing with; *children were playing marbles in the school playground*; *I found a marble under the sofa*

march [mɑːtʃ] **1** *noun* **(a)** walking in step by soldiers, sailors, etc.; *the soldiers were tired after their long march through the mountains*; **march past** = ceremonial military parade; *all sections of the armed forces took part in the march past at which the Queen took the salute*; **route march** = long training march; **quick march** = rapid walking pace **slow march** = slow walking pace **(b)** **protest march** = mass of people walking to protest about something; *the police estimate that around 5000 people took part in the protest march* **(c)** music with a regular beat for marching; *at the end of the burial service the band played a slow march*; **wedding march** = music which is played after a wedding; *as the bride and groom came out of the church the organ played the wedding march* (NOTE: plural is **marches**) **2** *verb* **(a)** to walk in step; *the guards marched after the band*; *we were just in time to see the soldiers march past*; **quick march!** = order to soldiers to march at a rapid pace **(b)** **the police marched him off to prison** = they took him away quickly to prison **(c)** to walk quickly and purposefully; *she marched into the shop and asked to speak to the manager* **(d)** to walk in a protest march; *thousands of workers marched to the parliament building*

March [mɑːtʃ] *noun* third month of the year, between February and April; *her birthday is in March*; *today is March 6th US March 6*; *we moved house last March*; *we often have storms in March* (NOTE: **March 6th** or **March 6**: say 'March the sixth' or 'the sixth of March'; American English: 'March sixth')

mare [meə] *noun* female horse; *the mare and her foal were running in the field*

margarine ['mɑːdʒə'riːn] *noun* mixture of animal or vegetable oil which is used instead of butter; *can you tell the difference between butter and margarine?*; *I prefer butter to margarine*

marge [mɑːdʒ] *noun (informal)* = MARGARINE; *we've run out of marge!*

margin ['mɑːdʒin] *noun* **(a)** white space at the edge of a page of writing; *write your comments in the margin*; *we left a wide margin so that you can write notes in it* **(b)** extra space, time, etc.; *leave a margin for error* = allow extra space or time in case you have made a mistake; **safety margin** = space or time left to allow for safety; **by a wide margin** = by a big distance; *the Labour candidate won by a wide margin* **(c)** money received which is more than money paid; *small businesses operate on very narrow margins*; *we have to cut our margins to remain competitive*; **gross margin** = difference between the price received and the cost of manufacture; **net margin** = difference between the price received and all costs, including overheads

marginal ['mɑːdʒinəl] *adjective* **(a)** slight; *there is only a marginal difference between them* **(b)** *(parliamentary seat)* where the opposing parties are almost equal, with very few votes between them; *the party is targetting the most marginal seats in the country* **(c)** **marginal note** = note written in a margin

marginalize ['mɑːdʒinəlaɪz] *verb* to make someone *or* something less important; *employers tried to marginalize the trade unions by dealing with each worker directly*

marginally ['mɑːdʒinəli] *adverb* slightly; *the outlook for business is marginally better than it was last year*; *the baby's rash is marginally better since we tried the new cream*

marigold ['mærigəuld] *noun* common garden plant with yellow or orange flowers; *she planted marigolds all over her front garden*

marijuana [mærɪ'hwɑːnə] *noun* illegal drug made from hemp; *they were demonstrating to force the government to allow the use of marijuana*; *possession of marijuana is illegal* (NOTE: also called **cannabis, grass, hashish, pot**)

marina [mə'riːnə] *noun* special harbour with floating jetties where a large number of yachts and pleasure boats can be tied up; *his yacht was moored in the marina*

marinade [mærɪ'neɪd] **1** *noun* mixture of wine and herbs, etc., in which meat or fish is soaked before cooking; *the marinade gives a delicious flavour to the meat* **2** *verb* to soak meat or fish in a mixture of wine and herbs, etc.; *marinade the meat for twelve hours before cooking*

marinate ['mærineɪt] *verb* = MARINADE

marine [mə'riːn] **1** *adjective* referring to the sea; *a marine biologist* **2** *noun* **(a)** **the merchant marine** = the merchant navy **(b)** soldier serving in the navy; *he decided not to join the Marines, but to become a pilot instead*; *the Marines attacked the enemy air base*

mariner ['mærinə] *noun (formal)* old sailor; *he is an experienced mariner who has sailed single-handed across the Atlantic*

marionette [mæriə'net] *noun* puppet moved by strings attached to its arms and legs; *the children went to see a marionette show*; *she made the marionette*

dance by pulling on a string (NOTE: also called a **string puppet**)

marital ['mæritl] *adjective* referring to a marriage; *their marital happiness was ruined by the behaviour of their son*; *she has been having marital problems*

maritime ['mæritaim] *adjective* referring to the sea or ships; *you should visit the maritime museum at Greenwich*; *Britain has a great maritime tradition*; **maritime law** = laws referring to ships, ports, etc.; **maritime trade** = carrying commercial goods by sea

mark [mɑːk] **1** *noun* **(a)** small spot of a different colour; *the red wine has made a mark on the tablecloth*; *she has a mark on her forehead where she hit her head* **(b)** points given to a student; *she got top marks in English*; *what sort of mark did you get for your homework?*; *no one got full marks - the top mark was 8 out of 10* **(c)** line showing a certain point; *his income has reached the £100,000 mark*; **high-water mark** = line showing where the high tide reaches **(d)** *(order given to runners at the beginning of a race)* **on your marks, get set, go!** **(e)** money used in Germany; *the price is twenty-five marks*; *the mark rose against the dollar* (NOTE: usually written **DM** after a figure: **25DM.** Also called **Deutschmark**) **2** *verb* **(a)** to make a mark; **the box is marked 'dangerous'** = it has the word 'dangerous' written on it **(b)** to correct and give points to work; *the teacher hasn't finished marking our homework*; *has the English exam been marked yet?* **(c)** *(in games)* **to mark an opponent** = to follow an opposing player closely, so as to prevent him getting the ball **(d)** **to mark time** = to stay on one spot, not to move forward; *sales are simply marking time*

mark down ['mɑːk 'daun] *verb* to reduce the price of something; *we have marked all prices down by 30% for the sale*

marked [mɑːkt] *adjective* **(a)** very obvious, definite; *this month's sales showed a marked improvement*; *his performance was first class - in marked contrast to his game last week* **(b)** **a marked man** = man who has been selected by an enemy as a probable target; *he informed on the mafia boss, and since has become a marked man in fear for his life*

markedly ['mɑːkidli] *adverb* very obviously; *her story was markedly different from that of the police officer*

marker ['mɑːkə] *noun* **(a)** thing which marks; *the golfer put down a marker before moving his ball*; **marker buoy** = buoy used to indicate a dangerous spot in a channel; **marker pen** = coloured felt pen which makes a wide mark **(b)** person who gives a mark to a piece of work, an examination, an entry in a competition, etc.; *our teacher is a very hard marker - nobody gets more than seven out of ten*

market ['mɑːkit] **1** *noun* **(a)** place where fruit and vegetables, etc., are sold from small tables, often in the open air; *we buy all our vegetables and fish at the market*; *market day is Saturday, so parking will be difficult*; **covered market** = building in which a market is held; *see also* FLEA MARKET **(b)** sale; **on the market** = for sale; *their house has been on the market for three months*; **to put on the market** = to offer for sale; *we put our house on the market three months ago and no one has even been to look at it* **(c)** place where a product is required, where a product could be sold; *the market for Russian cars has almost disappeared*; *the potential global market for this product is enormous*;

market research = examining the possible sales of a product and the possible customers before it is put on the market; *if we had done proper market research we would have discovered that there were several cheaper products than ours*; **market share** *or* **share of the market** = percentage of possible sales which a company or product has; *they started a nationwide advertising campaign aimed at increasing their market share*; **domestic market** *or* **home market** = the market in the country where you live; *sales in the domestic market have not increased*; **export markets** *or* **overseas markets** = markets outside the country where you live; **the single market** = the EU considered as one single market, with no tariff barriers between its member states **(d) black market** = illegal selling at high prices; *there is a flourishing black market in spare parts for cars*; *we had to pay black market prices*; *you can buy whisky on the black market* **2** *verb* to sell products using marketing techniques; *this product is being marketed in all European countries*

marketable ['mɑːkətəbl] *adjective* which can be sold easily; *speaking several languages is a very marketable skill*

market forces ['mɑːkɪt 'fɔːsɪz] *noun* commercial influences which have an effect on the success of a product or firm; *market forces decide which firms succeed and which fail*

market garden ['mɑːkɪt 'gɑːdən] *noun* small farm which grows vegetables or fruit which are sold in a nearby town (NOTE: American English is **truck farm**)

marketing ['mɑːkɪtɪŋ] *noun* techniques of publicity, packaging, etc., used to sell a product; *our marketing strategy needs to be revised totally*; *they used aggressive marketing to boost sales*; **marketing department** = department in a company which specializes in ways of selling a product; **marketing director** = director in charge of marketing

marketplace ['mɑːkɪtpleɪs] *noun* **(a)** open space in the middle of a town where a market is held; *the marketplace is usually right in the centre of a town* **(b)** the activity of selling of goods or services; *our salesmen find life difficult in the marketplace*; *what is the reaction to the new car in the marketplace?*

market town ['mɑːkɪt 'taʊn] *noun* town where an open-air market is held regularly; *we sell our vegetables in the market town nearby*; *Banbury is a typical English market town*

marking ['mɑːkɪŋ] *noun* **(a)** action of making marks; **marking ink** = black ink which will not wash off **(b)** **markings** = coloured patterns on the coat of an animal or in the feathers of a bird; *the zebra has very distinctive black and white markings* **(c)** correcting exercises, homework, etc.; *marking is not a job I like* **(d)** exercises or exam papers which are waiting to be marked; *he took a pile of marking home with him*

marksman ['mɑːksmən] *noun* person who shoots well; *police marksmen surrounded the house* (NOTE: plural is **marksmen**)

mark up ['mɑːk 'ʌp] *verb* to increase the price of something; *these prices have been marked up by 10%*; *the retailers find the discount too low so they mark the prices up to make a better margin*

mark-up ['mɑːkʌp] *noun* amount added to the cost price to give the selling price; *he buys jeans for £20 a pair and then sells them for £40, which is a 100% mark-up*

marmalade ['mɑːməleɪd] *noun* jam made from oranges, lemons, limes or grapefruit; *I've made fifty pots of lemon marmalade*; **Seville orange marmalade** = marmalade made with bitter oranges; **marmalade cat** = orange and white coloured cat

COMMENT: marmalade is eaten with toast at breakfast, and not at any other time of day. Compare JAM

marmoset [mɑːmə'zet] *noun* small monkey from Central and South America; *she kept a little marmoset as a pet*

maroon [mə'ruːn] **1** *adjective* deep purple red; *he was wearing a maroon tie* **2** *noun* **(a)** deep purple red colour; *maroon is a favourite colour for school uniforms* **(b)** small firework used as a distress signal by ships; *the coastguard let off a maroon as a signal for the lifeboat to be launched* **3** *verb* to leave someone in a place from which there is no escape; *they were marooned on the desert island for ten days*; *the bus broke down, leaving us all marooned miles from anywhere*

marque [mɑːk] *noun* famous brand name for a car; *Porsche, Bentley, Alfa Romeo and other famous marques*; *the luxury marques were particularly well represented at the Car of the Year Show*

marquee [mɑː'kiː] *noun* very large tent; *the wedding reception was held in a marquee in the garden*

marquess *or* **marquis** ['mɑːkwɪs] *noun* member of the nobility, the rank below a duke; *the Marquess of Bath*

marriage ['mærɪdʒ] *noun* **(a)** being legally joined as husband and wife; *a large number of marriages end in divorce*; *she has two sons by her first marriage* **(b)** wedding, the ceremony of being married; *they had a simple marriage, with just ten guests*; *the marriage took place at the registry office*

married ['mærɪd] *adjective* joined as husband and wife; *are you married or single?*; *married life must suit him - he's put on weight*; **married name** = name taken by a woman when she gets married; *after the divorce she stopped using her married name*

COMMENT: in Britain, the USA and many other countries, it is usual for a woman to drop her family name when she gets married and to replace it by her husband's family name. However, many women, especially professional women, nowadays prefer to keep their original family name

marrow ['mærəʊ] *noun* **(a)** **bone marrow** = soft tissue inside bone; *she had a bone marrow transplant* **(b)** large green vegetable of the pumpkin family, similar to a large cucumber; *his marrow was the biggest exhibit in the vegetable show*

marry ['mæri] *verb* **(a)** to make two people husband and wife; *they were married at the registry office* **(b)** to become the husband or wife of someone; *she married the boy next door*; *how long have you been married?*; *she's married to a policeman*; *they're getting married next Saturday*

Mars [mɑːz] *noun* the fourth planet of the solar system, colder than the Earth, with white polar ice caps; *they sent a rocket to Mars*; *is there life on Mars?*

marsh [mɑːʃ] *noun* wet and swampy land; *ducks and geese come to the marshes during winter*; *the* *developers want to drain the marsh and build on it*; **salt marsh** = wet land covered by the sea at high tide (NOTE: plural is **marshes**)

marshal ['mɑːʃl] **1** *noun* **(a)** military officer of the highest rank; **Marshal of the Royal Air Force** = highest rank in the Royal Air Force; *see also* FIELD MARSHAL **(b)** organizer of a race or a show; *marshals tried to direct the crowds to the grandstands; some marshals rushed to the scene of the crash and others waved flags to try to stop the race* **(c)** *US* officer of a court; *federal marshals raided several houses looking for a prisoner who had escaped from jail* **(d)** *US* chief of police or chief of the fire brigade in an area **2** *verb* to organize people, things, etc., into order; *extra police were brought in to marshal the crowds of fans; he tried to marshal the facts but was too sleepy to think clearly* (NOTE: do not confuse with **martial**; note: **marshalling - marshalled** but American spelling is **marshaling - marshaled**)

marsh gas ['mɑːʃ 'gæs] *noun* a colourless gas, produced naturally from rotting organic waste (NOTE: also called **methane**)

marshland ['mɑːʃlænd] *noun* area where the soil is wet and there are many pools of water; *marshland is the favourite habitat of these birds; an area of marshland near the village was drained and used for building*

marshmallow [mɑːʃ'mæləu] *noun* soft white or pink sweet; *you can toast marshmallows over a barbecue to make them go all hot and sticky*

marsupial [mɑː'suːpiəl] *noun* type of animal found in Australia, which carries its young in a pouch of the front of its body; *kangaroos and koalas are both marsupials*

martial ['mɑːʃl] *adjective* referring to war; **martial arts** = oriental fighting techniques using swords, sticks, etc.; *karate is one of the martial arts*; **martial law** = maintenance of law by the army instead of the police; *the government has imposed martial law*; **martial music** = marches played by military bands; *we think a coup may have taken place because all the country's radio stations have started playing martial music* (NOTE: do not confuse with **marshal**)

Martian ['mɑːʃən] **1** *adjective* referring to the planet Mars; *the probe has taken photographs of the Martian landscape* **2** *noun* imaginary person living on or coming from the planet Mars; *a story about Martians who come to invade the Earth*

martinet [mɑːtɪ'net] *noun* person who is very strict about making other people obey rules; *the headmaster's secretary is a bit of a martinet, but she's quite nice when you get to know her*

martini [mɑː'tiːni] *noun* drink made of gin and vermouth; **dry martini** = martini made with a lot of gin and a little vermouth; *a dry martini is James Bond's favourite drink*

martyr ['mɑːtə] **1** *noun* **(a)** person killed or made to suffer because of his or her beliefs; *Christian martyrs were killed by the Romans; St Stephen, the first martyr; she was a martyr in the cause of national liberation* **(b)** person who pretends to suffer in order to get sympathy; *she sat at the switchboard all day, looking a real martyr* **(c) to be a martyr to** = to suffer a lot from; *he's a martyr to indigestion* **2** *verb* to kill someone for his or her religious beliefs; *Saint Catherine was martyred in the 4th century*

martyrdom ['mɑːtədəm] *noun* suffering death for your beliefs; *many Christians suffered martyrdom under the Romans; the martyrdom of St Andrew*

martyred ['mɑːtəd] *adjective* pretending to suffer in order to get sympathy; *he pushed his trolley round the supermarket with a martyred look on his face*

marvel ['mɑːvl] **1** *noun* thing which you think is wonderful; *the building is one of the marvels of the modern age; it's a marvel that she managed to remember my birthday* **2** *verb* **to marvel at someone** *or* **something** = to show wonder or surprise at someone *or* something; *everyone marvelled at the sheer size of the statue* (NOTE: **marvelling - marvelled** but American spelling is **marveling - marveled**)

marvellous *US* **marvelous** ['mɑːvələs] *adjective* wonderful; *the children had a marvellous time at the circus; I've got some marvellous news - Mary is pregnant!; rocking chairs are marvellous for rocking babies to sleep*

mascara [mæ'skɑːrə] *noun* substance for making eyelashes dark; *she put on her mascara; when she cried her mascara ran down her cheeks*

mascot ['mæskət] *noun* object or animal which you think brings good luck; *he took his lucky mascot with him into the exam; the regiment's mascot is a goat*

masculine ['mæskjulɪn] *adjective* **(a)** male, referring to men; *she had a very masculine hair style* **(b)** manly, with qualities that are typical of men; *he answered in a gruff masculine voice* **(c)** *(in grammar)* referring to words which have a particular form to show the male gender; *is the French word 'table' masculine or feminine?* (NOTE: the opposite is **feminine**)

masculinity [mæskju'lɪnɪti] *noun* male qualities, what is typical of a male; *he felt he had to prove his masculinity by taking part in dangerous sports* (NOTE: the opposite is **femininity**)

mash [mæʃ] **1** *noun* **(a)** food mixture made of different ingredients which are crushed together; *they prepared some mash for the pigs* **(b)** *(informal)* mashed potatoes; *a plate of sausage and mash* or *bangers and mash; see also* BANGER **2** *verb* to crush something into a paste; *mash the ingredients together before adding water; she mashed the potatoes with butter and milk*

mashed potatoes ['mæʃd pə'teɪtəuz] *noun* potatoes which have been boiled, then crushed into a soft mass with milk and butter, served hot; *our children prefer chips to mashed potatoes*

mask [mɑːsk] **1** *noun* something which covers or protects your face; *the burglars wore black masks; he wore a mask to go diving;* **gas mask** = mask which covers the face and allows you to breathe when there is poisonous gas about; *the soldiers were told to put on their gas masks;* **oxygen mask** = mask covering the face, which allows you to breathe from a cylinder of oxygen; *in an emergency, oxygen masks will drop down from the panels above your heads* **2** *verb* to cover up or to hide; *she masked her face with her scarf; too much curry powder will mask the flavour of the other spices*

masked ['mɑːskt] *adjective* wearing a mask; *the bank was held up by three masked men*

masochism ['mæsəkɪzm] *noun* **(a)** *(formal)* condition where a person takes sexual pleasure in being hurt or badly treated **(b)** *(informal)* doing something painful and enjoying it; *taking all those children to France sounds more like masochism than a holiday to me; compare* SADISM

masochist ['mæsəkɪst] *noun* **(a)** *(formal)* person who takes sexual pleasure in being hurt or badly treated **(b)** person who enjoys doing something unpleasant or painful; *he's just a masochist - he actually likes doing housework; compare* SADIST

masochistic [mæsə'kɪstɪk] *adjective* taking pleasure in being hurt or badly treated; *he seems to take a masochistic pleasure in being shouted at by the boss; compare* SADISTIC

mason ['meɪsn] *noun* **(a)** person who builds with stone; *no one knows the names of the masons who built the cathedral*; **monumental mason** = person who makes gravestones **(b) Mason** = Freemason, member of a secret society whose members help each other and protect each other; *my grandfather was a Mason; the Masons do a lot of work for charity*

masquerade [mɑːskə'reɪd] **1** *noun* **(a)** action which hides the truth; *her show of grief was a masquerade to hide her involvement in the murder* **(b)** *(formal)* dance or party where people wear masks; *the main event of the carnival season was a grand masquerade* **2** *verb* to **masquerade as someone** = to pretend to be someone; *the car thief was masquerading as a traffic warden*

mass [mæs] **1** *noun* **(a)** large number or large quantity of things; *masses of people went to the exhibition; a mass of leaves blew onto the pavement; I have a mass of letters or masses of letters to write* **(b)** Catholic communion service; *she's a strict Catholic and goes to mass every week;* **high mass** = mass with full ceremony; **low mass** = mass without much ceremony (NOTE: plural is **masses**) **2** *verb* to gather in large numbers; *the rebel army is massing on the border* **3** *adjective* involving a large number of people; *they found a mass grave on the hillside; the group is organizing a mass protest to parliament;* **mass media** = communications such as TV, radio or newspapers, which reach a large number of people; *politicians use the mass media to try to influence the way people think;* **mass meeting** = meeting attended by a lot of people; *the union has called a mass meeting of all workers;* **mass murderer** = killer of a large number of people at one time

massacre ['mæsəkə] **1** *noun* killing of a large number of people or animals; *witnesses to the massacre led reporters to a mass grave in the hillside* **2** *verb* to kill many people or animals; *the soldiers massacred hundreds of innocent civilians*

massage ['mæsɑːʒ] **1** *noun* rubbing of the body to relieve pain or to get someone to relax; *she gave me a massage* **2** *verb* to rub someone's body to relieve pain or to get them to relax; *he asked the nurse to massage his back*

masse *see* EN MASSE

masseur [mæ'sɜː] *noun* man who massages; *the health club employs a qualified masseur; a session with the masseur leaves you feeling really fit*

masseuse [mæ'sɜːz] *noun* woman who massages; *the masseuse gave him a full massage*

massive ['mæsɪv] *adjective* very large; *he had a massive heart attack; the company has massive losses; a massive rock came hurtling down the mountainside towards them*

mass-produced ['mæsprə'djuːst] *adjective* manufactured in large quantities; *imported mass-produced kitchen goods have flooded the market; this porcelain isn't mass-produced, it's all hand-made*

mass production ['mæs prə'dʌkʃn] *noun* manufacturing of large quantities of products; *the factory has gone over to mass production of car components; we need to do more tests before the machine can go into mass production*

mast [mɑːst] *noun* **(a)** tall pole on a ship which carries the sails; *the gale was so strong that it snapped the ship's mast* **(b)** flagpole, tall pole on which large flags are flown; *see also* HALF-MAST **(c)** tall metal construction to carry an aerial; *a television mast* **(d)** seeds of beech, and other trees; *beech mast is often used to feed pigs* (NOTE: no plural in this meaning)

master ['mɑːstə] **1** *noun* **(a)** man who teaches in a school; *Mr Smith is the maths master* **(b)** person in control of a ship; *the ship's doctor asked the master to radio for a helicopter* **(c)** skilled person; *a master craftsman; he's a master of disguise;* **an old master** = painting by a great painter of the past; *the collection of old masters in the National Gallery is priceless* **2** *adjective* **(a)** controlling; *details of the master plan are known to only a few conspirators;* **master disk** = main disk from which copies are made; *keep the master disk in a safe place;* **master key** = main key; *the caretaker has a master key which opens all the doors in the building;* **master switch** = switch which controls all other switches; *the burglars turned off the master switch and all the lights went out* **(b) master bedroom** = main bedroom in a house; *the master bedroom has an en-suite bathroom* **3** *verb* to become skilled at something; *she has mastered the art of TV newscasting; although he passed his driving test some time ago, he still hasn't mastered the art of motorway driving*

masterful ['mɑːstəful] *adjective* **(a)** good at controlling people and giving orders; *her father is a masterful character and takes all the decisions in the household* **(b)** done in an expert way; *he gave a masterful performance of the concerto*

masterly ['mɑːstəli] *adjective* done in an expert way; *everyone praised the masterly way in which she dealt with the problem*

mastermind ['mɑːstəmaɪnd] **1** *noun* very clever person; *a criminal mastermind* **2** *verb* to be the brains behind a plan; *the escape was masterminded by two convicted murderers*

Master of Arts (MA) ['mɑːstə əv 'ɑːts] *noun* person who holds a degree for further study done after a BA (Bachelor of Arts) degree; *she's taking an MA course in Italian art*

Master of Ceremonies (MC) ['mɑːstə əv 'serəmʌnɪz] *noun* person who introduces the speakers at a dinner, or at a prize-giving

masterpiece ['mɑːstəpiːs] *noun* very fine painting, book, piece of music, etc.; *some people think that 'War and Peace' is a masterpiece, but others think it's much too long; the 'Mona Lisa' is a masterpiece, but what about Warhol's picture of Marilyn Monroe?*

master's degree ['mɑːstəz dɪ'griː] *noun* degree for further study after a BA (Bachelor of Arts) degree; *she has a master's degree from Edinburgh University*

mastery ['mɑːstəri] *noun* **(a)** complete understanding of a subject, or great skill at a game; *the French side showed their complete mastery of the game*; *her mastery of Italian is well-known* **(b)** control over someone *or* something; *the two warlords struggled for mastery over the province*

masticate ['mæstɪkeɪt] *verb* *(formal)* to chew; *you should masticate your food slowly before swallowing*

mastiff ['mæstɪf] *noun* breed of large fierce dogs; *mastiffs make very good guard dogs*

masturbate ['mæstəbeɪt] *verb* to rub your own sex organs to excite them and get pleasure

masturbation [mæstə'beɪʃn] *noun* exciting your own sex organs by rubbing

mat [mæt] *noun* **(a)** small piece of carpet, etc., used as a floor covering; *wipe your shoes on the mat before you come in*; **bath mat** = small carpet to step on to when getting out of a bath; *please hang the bath mat up to dry after use* **(b)** **place mat** = small piece of cloth, wood, etc., put under a plate on a table; *the table was laid with glasses, cutlery and place mats*

match [mætʃ] **1** *noun* **(a)** game between two teams, etc.; *we watched the football match on TV*; *he won the last two table tennis matches he played*; *see also* TEST MATCH **(b)** small piece of wood or cardboard with a tip which catches fire when you rub it against a rough surface; *he bought a packet of cigarettes and a box of matches*; *she struck a match and lit a candle* **(c)** thing or person which is equal; *she's met her match* = she has met someone who is as strong, powerful, etc., as she is **(d)** thing which goes together with another; *they make a good match* = they go well together (NOTE: plural is **matches**) **2** *verb* **(a)** to be equal to; *our sales match those of our rivals in the export market* **(b)** to fit or to go with; *the yellow wallpaper doesn't match the bright green carpet*

matchbox ['mætʃbɒks] *noun* small box with matches inside; *most people prefer to use a lighter rather than fiddling around with a matchbox* (NOTE: plural is **matchboxes**)

matched [mætʃt] *adjective* balanced, equal; *the two teams are very evenly matched*

matching ['mætʃɪŋ] *adjective* which fits or goes with something; *she wore a yellow coat with matching hat and shoes*

matchstick US **matchstalk** ['mætʃstɪk *or* 'mætʃstɔːk] *noun* stick of wood which makes a match; *he spent months making a model of the Houses of Parliament out of matchsticks*; **matchstick men** = sketches of people drawn with single lines for each limb; *the figures in Lowry's paintings were just matchstick men*

mate [meɪt] **1** *noun* **(a)** one of a pair of people or animals, male or female, husband or wife; *some birds sing and others show off their feathers to attract a mate* **(b)** *(informal)* friend, companion; *he's gone down to the pub with his mates*; **running mate** = person who stands for election as number two to the main candidate; *if the candidate for president wins, then his running mate becomes vice-president*; *see also* SOUL MATE **(c)** *(in the merchant navy)* **first mate** = second officer after the captain **(d)** *(in chess)* position where the king cannot move, and the game ends; *mate in three moves!* **(e)** *(informal)* *(way of addressing someone)* hey mate, come and look at this!; *sorry, mate, I can't help you!* **2** *verb* **(a)** *(of animals)* to breed; *a mule is the*

result of a donkey mating with a horse **(b)** *(in chess)* to put your opponent's king in a position where he cannot move (NOTE: also, more formally, to **checkmate**)

material [mə'tɪəriəl] **1** *noun* **(a)** substance which can be used to make something; *you can buy all the materials you need in the DIY shop*; **building materials** = cement, wood, bricks, etc.; *the bill for building materials alone came to over £2000*; **raw materials** = materials like wool or iron which have not been made into anything; *the country exports raw materials such as copper, and imports finished products* **(b)** cloth; *I bought three metres of material to make a curtain*; *what material is your coat made of?* **(c)** facts, information; *she's gathering material for a TV programme on drugs* (NOTE: no plural in meanings (b) and (c)) **2** *adjective* **(a)** referring to physical things or to money; *the explosion caused a lot of material damage*; *his success on TV has improved his material life* **(b)** important or relevant; *if you have any material evidence please contact the police*

materialism [mə'tɪəriəlɪzm] *noun* interest only in physical things, especially money and property, not in spiritual ones; *the Church is trying to combat the materialism of modern society*

materialist [mə'tɪəriəlɪst] *noun* person who believes in materialism; *he's a materialist like his father - spiritual values mean nothing to him*

materialize [mə'tɪəriəlaɪz] *verb* **(a)** to become real; *his planned holiday never materialized*; *she promised the staff an extra week's holiday but it never materialized* **(b)** to appear; *a man on horseback suddenly materialized out of the mist*; *after a couple of phone calls, the money we were owed duly materialized*

materially [mə'tɪəriəli] *adverb* in a material way; *the evidence could be materially important*

maternal [mə'tɜːnl] *adjective* **(a)** referring to a mother; **maternal grandfather** = father of your mother **(b)** like or typical of a mother; *she has a very maternal attitude to her staff*; **maternal instincts** = instinctive feelings in a woman to look after and protect her child (NOTE: the equivalent referring to a father, is **paternal**)

maternity [mə'tɜːnɪti] *noun* becoming a mother; *she's in the maternity ward of the local hospital*; **maternity leave** = permission for a woman to be away from work to have a baby; *I'm standing in for Jean while she's on maternity leave* (NOTE: compare **paternity**)

math ['mæθ] US *see* MATHS

mathematical [mæθə'mætɪkl] *adjective* referring to mathematics; *a mathematical problem*; **mathematical model** = representation of a system using mathematical ideas and formulae

mathematician [mæθəmə'tɪʃn] *noun* expert at mathematics; *this is a problem that has baffled mathematicians for centuries*

mathematics *(informal)* **maths** US **math** [mæθə'mætɪks *or* mæθs *or* mæθ] *noun* science of numbers and measurements; *I'm taking a course in mathematics*; *he passed in maths, but failed in English*

mating ['meɪtɪŋ] *noun* *(of animals)* finding partners and having sex; *the mating display of the peacock*; *do not go near the deer during the mating season*

matriarch ['meɪtriɑːk] *noun* respected old woman; *the village is run by a group of matriarchs*; *compare* PATRIARCH

matriarchal ['meɪtriɑːkəl] *adjective* ruled by a matriarch; ruled by older women; *we live in a matriarchal society*

matriarchy ['meɪtriɑːki] *noun* system of rule by the eldest female of the ruling group; *in a matriarchy men have to be content with playing a secondary role*

matrimonial [mætrɪ'məʊniəl] *adjective* referring to marriage; *they took their matrimonial problems to a counsellor*

matrimony ['mætrɪməni] *noun* state of being married; *the priest joined them in holy matrimony*

matrix ['meɪtrɪks] *noun* **(a)** numbers or data items arranged in rows and columns **(b) dot matrix printer** = computer printer that prints characters as a group of little dots **(c)** the conditions or environment in which something develops; *the cultural matrix in which jazz music was developed* **(d)** mould used to cast metal objects (NOTE: plural is **matrices** ['meɪtrɪsiːz])

matron ['meɪtrən] *noun* **(a)** *(formerly)* senior nurse in charge of a hospital; *she was matron of the maternity hospital* **(b)** *(formal)* woman, usually a nurse, who looks after children in a boarding school; *go and see matron and she'll put a plaster on your knee* **(c) matron of honour** = older woman who helps the bride during the wedding ceremony, like an older bridesmaid

matt [mæt] *adjective* not shiny, with a dull surface; *the kitchen chairs are painted in matt black*

matter ['mætə] **1** *noun* **(a)** problem, difficulty; *what's the matter?*; **there's something the matter with the engine** = there is something which makes the engine not work properly **(b)** concern, business; **it's a matter for the police** = it is something which we should tell the police about **(c) as a matter of fact** = to tell you the truth; *I know Paris quite well, as a matter of fact I go there every month on business*; **as a matter of course** = in the usual way; *the police checked his driving licence as a matter of course* **(d)** material; *we put rotting vegetable matter on the garden as fertilizer* **(e) no matter what** = whatever; *no matter what time it is, call the doctor immediately the symptoms appear*; **no matter how** = however; *no matter how hard he tried he couldn't ride a bike* **2** *verb* to be important; *it doesn't matter if you're late*; *his job matters a lot to him*; *does it matter if we sit by the window?*

matter-of-fact ['mætərʌv'fækt] *adjective* practical, not showing any emotion; *they talked about a highly emotional subject in a very matter-of-fact way*; *she has a completely matter-of-fact attitude towards sex*

mattress ['mætrəs] *noun* thick, pad forming the part of a bed that you lie on, made of a canvas case with various fillings; *those who didn't have beds slept on mattresses on the floor*; *the children jump up and down on our mattress*; **sprung mattress** = mattress with springs inside (NOTE: plural is **mattresses**)

mature [mə'tjʊə] **1** *adjective* **(a)** older, adult; *the park has many mature trees*; *only mature stags have a full set of antlers*; **mature student** = student who is older than the usual age for students; *the college is trying to encourage more mature students to enrol* **(b)** ripe; *mature cheese is normally quite strong* **(c)** which is reasonable, like an adult; *she's very mature for her age*; *that's not a very mature way to behave* **2** *verb* **(a)** to become mature; *whisky is left to mature for years*;

he matured a lot during his year in Germany; *girls are supposed to mature faster than boys* **(b)** to become due for payment; *the policy will mature in 20 years' time*

maturity [mə'tjʊrɪti] *noun* **(a)** state of being an adult, or of doing things like an adult; *he's only twelve, yet his painting already shows signs of considerable maturity* **(b)** time when a bond becomes due to be paid; *the bonds have reached maturity*; **maturity date** = date when an insurance policy matures (NOTE: no plural)

maul [mɔːl] *verb* **(a)** to attack or handle someone roughly; *he tried to drive off the leopard and was badly mauled* **(b)** to criticize severely; *the minister was mauled by the tabloid press* (NOTE: do not confuse with mall)

mausoleum [mɔːzə'liəm] *noun* special building in which an important person is buried; *he built the chapel as a mausoleum to his father*; *the Taj Mahal is a mausoleum to the wife of an Indian prince*

mauve [məʊv] **1** *adjective* light pinkish-purple; *the waiters wear mauve shirts* **2** *noun* light pinkish-purple colour; *she had the dining room walls painted in mauve*

maverick ['mævərɪk] **1** *noun* **(a)** person who is unusual and does not fit into a normal pattern; *she's a political maverick* **(b)** *US* animal which has not been branded and is running loose; *the cowboys rounded up the mavericks and brought them back to the ranch to be branded* **2** *adjective* unusual, not fitting into the normal pattern; *he is well-known for his maverick behaviour*

max = MAXIMUM

maxim ['mæksɪm] *noun* wise saying; *'Waste not, want not' was one of my father's favourite maxims*

maximize ['mæksɪmaɪz] *verb* to make as large as possible; *our aim is to maximize profits and minimize expenses*

maximum ['mæksɪməm] **1** *adjective* greatest possible; *what is the maximum number of guests the hotel can take?* **2** *noun* the greatest possible number or amount; *management is aiming to increase profitability to the maximum*; **fifteen at the maximum** = at most fifteen, not more than fifteen (NOTE: plural is **maxiumums** *or* **maxima**)

May [meɪ] *noun* fifth month of the year, after April and before June; *her birthday's in May*; *today is May 15th US May 15*; *we went on holiday last May* (NOTE: **May 15th** *or* **May 15**: say 'the fifteenth of May' or 'May the fifteenth'; American English: 'May fifteenth')

may [meɪ] *verb used with other verbs* **(a)** *(to mean it is possible)* *if you don't hurry you may miss the train*; *take your umbrella, they say it may rain*; *here we are sitting in the bar, and he may be waiting for us outside* **(b)** *(to mean can, it is allowed)* *guests may park in the hotel car park free of charge*; *you may sit down if you want* **(c)** *(asking questions politely)* *may I ask you a question?*; *may we have breakfast early tomorrow as we need to leave the hotel before 8 o'clock?* (NOTE: present: **I may, you may, he may, we may, they may.** Note also that **may** is always used with other verbs and is not followed by to)

maybe ['meɪbiː] *adverb* possibly, perhaps; *maybe the next bus will be the one we want*; *maybe you should ask a policeman*; *maybe the weather forecast was right after all*; **maybe not** = possibly not; *are you coming? - maybe not*

May Day ['meɪ 'deɪ] *noun* May 1st, celebrated as a festival of spring and in many European countries as a festival in honour of workers; *the traditional May Day parade in Red Square*

mayday ['meɪdeɪ] *noun* international distress signal; *the ship sent out a mayday call* (NOTE: do not confuse with **May Day**)

Mayfair ['meɪfeə] *noun* expensive part of the West End of London; *we took our visitors to a very chic Mayfair restaurant; he has a flat in the centre of Mayfair*

mayhem ['meɪhem] *noun* wild confusion; *the sudden snowstorm created mayhem in the city centre*

mayonnaise [meɪə'neɪz] *noun* sauce for cold dishes, made of oil, eggs and lemon juice or vinegar; *would you like some mayonnaise on your salad?; we bought tuna mayonnaise sandwiches*

mayor ['meə] *noun* person who is chosen as the official head of a town, city or local council; *the new leisure centre was opened by the mayor; after his election, the mayor led the procession to a reception in the town hall*; **Lord Mayor** = Mayor of a very large town (such as London, Liverpool); *the Lord Mayor of London* (NOTE: in Scotland the equivalent is the **Provost**; the equivalent for Lord Mayor is **Lord Provost**)

COMMENT: previously, a mayor was the head of the elected government of a town, and the head of the majority party. His responsibilities have now been taken over by the leader of the council, and the office of mayor is largely ceremonial. It is an honour often given to a long-serving or distinguished councillor. In the USA, mayors are elected by popular vote, and appoint their team to run the various departments in a city. Note also that 'Mayor' is used in English to apply to persons holding similar positions in other countries: **the Mayor of Berlin; the Mayor of Paris; the Mayor of New York**

mayoress ['meəres] *noun* (a) wife of a mayor; *the mayor and mayoress rode to the town hall in a horse-drawn carriage* (b) woman mayor; *the mayoress opened the hospital's new children's ward*

maze [meɪz] *noun* (a) network of puzzling paths in which you can get lost; *we couldn't find our way out of the Hampton Court maze; he led me along a maze of corridors* (b) complicated network of things; *we have to try to find our way through the maze of European regulations* (NOTE: do not confuse with **maize**)

Mb = MEGABYTE

MBO = MANAGEMENT BUYOUT

MC ['emsiː] = MASTER OF CEREMONIES

MD ['em 'diː] = MANAGING DIRECTOR director who is in charge of a whole company; *the MD's office is on the first floor; she was appointed MD of a property company*

me [miː] *object pronoun used by the person who is speaking to talk about himself or herself; give me that book; I'm shouting as loud as I can - can't you hear me?; she's much taller than me; who is it? - it's me!*

mead [miːd] *noun* (old) alcoholic drink made from honey; *Ancients Britons drank mead*

meadow ['medəʊ] *noun* large field of grass; *the cows stared at us as we crossed the meadow; the path through the meadow leads to a little bridge over the river*

meagre *US* **meager** ['miːgə] *adjective* small, not enough; *they offered us a meagre lunch; our meagre resources won't pay for more than two weeks' holiday*

meagreness *US* **meagerness** ['miːgənəs] *noun* (formal) small amount; *the meagreness of my budget doesn't allow me to spend money on expensive meals; her main complaint was the meagreness of the salary she was offered*

meal [miːl] *noun* (a) occasion when people eat food at a special time; *most people have three meals a day - breakfast, lunch and dinner; you sleep better if you only eat a light meal in the evening; when they had finished their evening meal they watched TV; you can have your meals in your room at a small extra charge;* (informal) **to make a meal of something** = to spend a lot of time and effort doing something without really doing it well; *she made a meal of repainting the kitchen* (b) **meals on wheels** = municipal service providing hot meals for old or disabled people in their own homes (c) roughly ground flour; *see also* WHOLEMEAL

mealtime ['miːltaɪm] *noun* time when you usually eat; *he doesn't even switch off the TV at mealtimes; each class in school has a set mealtime*

mean [miːn] **1** *adjective* (a) nasty or unpleasant; *he played a mean trick on his mother; that was a mean thing to say* (b) not liking to spend money or to give something; *don't be mean - let me borrow your car; she's very mean with her money* (c) average; *the mean daytime temperature in summer is 20° (d)* (informal) good; *he cooks a mean pasta; that motorbike's a mean machine!* (NOTE: **meaner - meanest) 2** *noun* middle or average figure; *sales are higher than the mean for the first quarter* **3** *verb* (a) to talk about; *did he mean me when he was talking about fat old men?; what do you mean when you when you say she's old-fashioned?* (b) to show, to represent; *when a red light comes on it means that you have to stop; 'Zimmer' means 'room' in German; what does that sign mean with two people with sticks? - it means that old people may be crossing the road* (c) to be meant to; *see* MEANT (NOTE: **meaning - meant** [ment])

meander [mi'ændə] **1** *noun* bend in the course of a river; *the path follows the meanders of the stream* **2** *verb* (a) to wind about; *from the top of the hill you can see how the river meanders around the town; the road meanders through several little villages* (b) to continue without any aim; *the negotiations meandered on without any decision being reached*

meanderings [mi'ændərɪŋz] *noun* winding; *we tried to follow the meanderings of the river on the map*

meaning ['miːnɪŋ] *noun* what something represents; *if you want to find the meaning of the word, look it up in a dictionary; the meaning of a red light is pretty clear to me*

meaningful ['miːnɪŋfʊl] *adjective* full of meaning, significant; *my brother gave me a meaningful look; he's just not capable of forming a meaningful relationship*

meaningless ['miːnɪŋləs] *adjective* not meaning anything; *the child's scribbles are quite meaningless; it was meaningless to try to explain*

means [miːnz] *noun* (a) way of doing something; *is there any means of sending the message to London* *this afternoon?*; *do we have any means of copying all these documents quickly?*; *the bus is the cheapest means of getting round the town* **(b) by all means** = of course; *by all means use my phone if you want to*; **by no means** = not at all; *she's by no means sure of getting the job* **(c)** money; *they don't have the means to buy another shop*; *it is beyond my means* = I don't have enough money to buy it; **means test** = inquiry to find out how much money someone has, to see whether he or she should qualify for a benefit or grant

meant [ment] *verb* **to be meant to** = should, ought to; *we're meant to be at the station at 11 o'clock*; *this medicine is not meant to be used by children*; *trains are meant to leave every half hour; see also* MEAN

meantime ['mi:ntaɪm] *noun* **in the meantime** = meanwhile, during this time; *we waited for her for hours in the rain, and in the meantime, she was happily sitting at home watching TV*; *the new stadium will be finished by Easter but in the meantime we will still have to use the old one*

meanwhile ['mi:nwaɪl] *adverb* during this time; *she hid under the table - meanwhile, the footsteps were coming nearer*

measles ['mi:zlz] *noun* children's disease which gives a red rash and a high temperature; *one of our children has got measles*; *children can be inoculated against measles, mumps and German measles*; **German measles** = usually mild disease which gives a red rash but which can affect an unborn child if caught by a pregnant woman (NOTE: **German measles** is also called **rubella**)

measurable ['meʒrəbl] *adjective* which can be measured; *a measurable quantity of the drug was found in the test*; *the difference between the two is barely measurable*

measure ['meʒə] **1** *noun* **(a)** certain amount or size; *there was a measure of truth in what she said*; *we have no accurate measure of the pressure inside the volcano*; **made to measure** = made specially to fit; *he only wears made-to-measure suits*; **short measure** = less than the correct amount; *the pub was fined for serving short measures* **(b)** thing which shows the size or quantity of something; **tape measure** = long strip of plastic marked in centimetres or inches, etc., used for measuring; *he took out a tape measure and measured the length of the table* **(c)** action; *the government has taken measures to reform the welfare system*; *what measures are you planning to fight air pollution?*; **as a precautionary measure** = as a precaution; *as a precautionary measure we'd better lock the windows as well as the doors*; *it's just a precautionary measure, but you can't be too careful when there's a possibility of fire* **(d)** type of action, especially a law passed by Parliament; *a new government measure to combat crime* **2** *verb* **(a)** to be of a certain size, length, quantity, etc.; *how much do you measure round your waist?*; *the table measures four foot long by three foot wide*; *a package which measures or a package measuring 10cm by 25cm* **(b)** to find out the length or quantity of something; *she measured the window for curtains*; *he measured the size of the garden*; **measuring tape** = TAPE MEASURE **(c) to measure your length on the floor** = to fall flat on your face

measurement ['meʒəmənt] *noun* **(a)** quantity or size, etc., found out when you measure; *he took the measurements of the room*; *the piano won't go through the door - are you sure you took the right*

measurements?; *the measurements of the box are 25cm x 20cm x 5cm* **(b)** the action of measuring; *the measurement of the ozone hole is carried out by satellites*

meat [mi:t] *noun* food from an animal; *would you like meat or fish for your main course?*; *I like my meat well cooked* (NOTE: no plural: **some meat, a piece** *or* **a slice of meat**)

COMMENT: the names of different types of meat are different from the names of the animal from which they come. Full-grown cows or bulls give 'beef'; calves give 'veal'; pigs give 'pork', or if salted, 'bacon' and 'ham'; sheep give 'mutton'; deer give 'venison'. Only birds (chicken, duck, goose, turkey, etc.) and lambs, give meat with the same name as the animal

mecca ['mekə] *noun* **(a)** place which attracts a large number of people; *it's a mecca for motor-racing enthusiasts* **(b) Mecca** = town in Saudi Arabia, where Muhammad was born; *all Muslims should make the pilgrimage to Mecca at least once*

mechanic [mɪ'kænɪk] *noun* person who works on engines; *the mechanics managed to patch up the engine and we went on with the race*

mechanical [me'kænɪkl] *adjective* referring to a machine; *engineers are trying to fix a mechanical fault*

mechanics [me'kænɪks] *noun* **(a)** *(formal)* the study of the effects of force and movement **(b)** the study of machinery; *he is studying aircraft mechanics* **(c)** the way in which something is done or something is made to happen; *he knows nothing about the mechanics of running a business*

mechanism ['mekənɪzm] *noun* **(a)** working parts of a machine; *if you take the back off the watch you can see the delicate mechanism* **(b)** way in which something works; *the mechanism for awarding government contracts*

mechanization [mekənaɪ'zeɪʃn] *noun* action of mechanizing; *the mechanization of the country's farming industry*

mechanize ['mekənaɪz] *verb* to use machines in place of animals or workers; *the country is trying to mechanize its farming industry*; *the manufacturing process has been completely mechanized*

medal ['medl] *noun* metal disc, usually attached to a ribbon, made to commemorate an important occasion or battle, and given to people who have performed well; *the old soldiers put on all their medals for the parade*; **gold medal** *or* **silver medal** *or* **bronze medal** = medal for first, second, third place in competitions; *she won a silver medal at the 96 Olympics* (NOTE: do not confuse with **meddle**)

medallist *US* **medalist** ['medəlɪst] *noun* person who wins a medal in a sports competition, etc.; *she is an Olympic gold medallist*

meddle ['medl] *verb* **to meddle in** *or* **with something** = to interfere in something; *don't meddle in matters that don't concern you* (NOTE: do not confuse with **medal**)

media ['mi:dɪə] *noun* **(a) the (mass) media** = means of passing information to a large number of people, such as newspapers, TV, radio; *the book attracted a lot* *of interest in the media or a lot of media interest* **(b)** *see also* MEDIUM, MULTIMEDIA

median ['miːdiən] **1** *adjective* in the middle; *the median price for shares* **2** *noun* **(a)** point which is in the middle, line which goes through the middle; *the median between two points* **(b)** US median (strip) = section of marked road surface, grass, bushes, etc., between the two carriageways of a major road (NOTE: British English is **central reservation**)

mediate ['miːdɪeɪt] *verb* to intervene to try to bring agreement between two opponents; *he was asked to mediate between the two sides*; *I don't want to get involved in mediating between the manager and his staff*

mediation [miːdɪ'eɪʃn] *noun* trying to make two opponents agree; *the two parties took their dispute to mediation*; *the employers refused an offer of government mediation*

mediator ['miːdiəeɪtə] *noun* person who tries to make two opponents agree; *there seemed to be no hope of a settlement so a mediator was appointed*; *the mediator adjourned the meeting*

medic ['medɪk] *noun (informal)* doctor; *the medics still don't know what's wrong with her*

medical ['medɪkl] **1** *adjective* referring to medicine; *she's a medical student*; *the Red Cross provided medical help*; **medical certificate** = document signed by a doctor to show that a worker has been ill; **medical insurance** = insurance which pays the cost of treatment by a doctor, surgeon, etc. **2** *noun (informal)* examination of someone by a doctor; *you need to pass a medical to join the army*; *after a routine medical, the new forward will be ready to play on Saturday*

medicated ['medɪkeɪtɪd] *adjective* containing something which cures a condition; *wash your hair with a medicated shampoo if you want to get rid your dandruff*

medication [medɪ'keɪʃn] *noun* **(a)** drugs taken by a patient; *are you taking any medication?* **(b)** treatment by giving drugs; *the doctor prescribed a course of medication*

medicinal [me'dɪsɪnl] *adjective* **(a)** referring to medicine; *he has a drink of whisky before he goes to bed for medicinal purposes* **(b)** which can heal or treat a disease; *she made a drink from medicinal herbs*

medicine ['medsɪn] *noun* **(a)** drug taken to treat a disease; *if you have a cough you should take some cough medicine*; *the chemist told me to take the medicine four times a day*; *some cough medicines make you feel sleepy*; *(informal)* **to have a taste of your own medicine** = to be treated in the same way as you have treated others; *he made us fill in all those forms, let's give him a taste of his own medicine* **(b)** study of diseases and how to cure or prevent them; *he went to university to study medicine* (NOTE: no plural in this meaning)

medicine chest ['medsɪn 'tʃest] *noun* cupboard for keeping medicines in; *she fetched some bandages from the medicine chest*

medicine man ['medsɪn 'mæn] *noun* native American believed to have healing powers; *the medicine man was performing a rain dance*

medieval [medɪ'iːvl] *adjective* referring to the Middle Ages; *the ruins of a medieval castle dominate the town*

mediocre [miːdɪ'əʊkə] *adjective* ordinary, not particularly good; *it was a very mediocre performance by our local team*

mediocrity [miːdɪ'ɒkrɪti] *noun* **(a)** not being particularly good; *the game was saved from mediocrity by a thrilling last ten minutes* (NOTE: no plural in this meaning) **(b)** very ordinary person with no special qualities; *she's the only talented minister in a government of mediocrities*

meditate ['medɪteɪt] *verb* **(a)** to remain in a calm, silent state, without thought; *don't disturb him - he's meditating* **(b)** **to meditate on** *or* **about something** = to think deeply about something; *they spent some time meditating on the meaning of life*

meditation [medɪ'teɪʃn] *noun* **(a)** silent, calm state, as part of religious practice; *she's deep in meditation* **(b)** long deep, often religious, thought; *he sat in the corner of the library, lost in meditation*

Mediterranean [medɪtə'reɪnɪən] **1** *noun* **the Mediterranean (Sea)** = the sea between Europe and Africa; *we went for a cruise round the Mediterranean* **2** *adjective* referring to the Mediterranean Sea; *the Mediterranean climate is good for olives*; *she has bought a villa on one of the Mediterranean Islands*

medium ['miːdiəm] **1** *adjective* middle, average; *he is of medium height* **2** *noun* **(a)** middle point; **happy medium** = compromise; *finding a happy medium between the demands of work and the family is not easy* **(b)** type of paint or other materials used by an artist; *he started to experiment with different mediums, such as poster paints* **(c)** means of doing something, of communicating something; *television is the most popular medium of communication*; *deaf people can communicate through the medium of sign language* (NOTE: plural is **media** *or* **mediums**)

medium-sized ['miːdiəm 'saɪzd] *adjective* which is neither very large nor very small; *a medium-sized pack of detergent*; *it was only a medium-sized shark*

medium-term ['miːdjəm 'tɜːm] *adjective* for a period of one or two years

medium wave ['miːdiəm 'weɪv] *noun* radio frequency range between 200 and 1000 metres; *the BBC's medium wave broadcasts*

medley ['medli] *noun* mixture of different things, such as pieces of music; *the orchestra played a medley of popular tunes*

meek [miːk] *adjective* humble, always willing to do what other people want, feeling you are not important; *he looks the meek type, but he rules the office with an iron hand* (NOTE: **meeker - meekest**)

meet [miːt] *verb* **(a)** to come together with someone; *he met her at the railway station*; *we'll meet for lunch before we go to the cinema*; *if you don't know how to get to our office, I'll meet you at the bus stop* **(b)** to come together; *several streets meet at Piccadilly Circus*; *if you draw a diagonal line from each corner of a square, the two lines will meet in the centre* **(c)** to get to know someone; *I've never met your sister - come and meet her then!*; *have you met our sales manager?* **(d)** to pay for; *the company will meet your expenses*; *he was unable to meet his mortgage repayments* **(e)** to be suitable for; *does the car now meet the standards set by the motor racing authorities?* (NOTE: **meeting - met** [met])

meeting ['miːtɪŋ] *noun* **(a)** action of coming together in a group; *the next meeting of the club will be on Tuesday; there were only four people at the committee meeting;* **to hold a meeting** = to organize a meeting of a group of people; *the meeting will be held in the committee room;* **to open a meeting** = to start a meeting; **to conduct a meeting** = to be chairman of a meeting; *as he was going away on business, he asked his deputy to conduct the meeting;* **to close a meeting** = to end a meeting; **to address a meeting** = to speak to a meeting; *see also* ANNUAL GENERAL MEETING **(b)** sports competition or series of horse races held over several days; *Britain won a gold and three bronzes at the athletics meeting*

meeting place ['miːtɪŋ 'pleɪs] *noun* place where you can meet someone; *the simplest meeting place will be under the clock at Waterloo station*

meet up ['miːt 'ʌp] *verb (of several people)* to come together; *we all met up in the local teashop*

meet with ['miːt 'wɪθ] *verb* **(a)** to find, to come up against (a problem); to have (an accident); *the advancing soldiers met with stiff resistance; she met with an accident on the escalator* **(b)** *usually US* to meet someone; *he met with the sales people in New York*

mega- ['megə] *prefix meaning* **(a)** one million; *one megahertz* **(b)** *(informal)* very big; *only the megarich can afford that kind of house; she's a Hollywood megastar*

megabyte (Mb) ['megəbaɪt] *noun* unit of storage for a computer equal to 1,048,576 bytes; *my computer has a 500 megabyte hard disk*

melancholy ['melənkəli] **1** *noun (formal)* great sadness; *there was an air of melancholy as the contents of the house were auctioned* **2** *adjective (formal)* very sad; *she's still feeling melancholy because her cat died*

mellow ['meləʊ] **1** *adjective* **(a)** which has matured and has a full taste; *Burgundy produces some mellow red wines* **(b)** soft, rich (voice); *Shakespeare's lines sound more beautiful when they are read in his lovely mellow voice* **(c)** *(informal)* calm and relaxed; *after a couple of drinks she became quite mellow* (NOTE: **mellower - mellowest**) **2** *verb* **(a)** to become soft or rich; *time has mellowed the brickwork to a soft deep red;* **he has mellowed with age** = as he has got older, so he has become much less angry and unpleasant than he used to be **(b)** to become ripe, to mature; *you should leave the wine to mellow for some years*

melodic [mɪ'lɒdɪk] *adjective* referring to a melody; **the melodic line of a piece of music** = the main tune of a piece of music

melodious [mə'ləʊdiəs] *adjective* full of pleasant tunes; *the melodious song of the blackbird*

melodrama ['melədrɑːmə] *noun* play full of excitement and violent exaggerated emotion; *they're reviving one of the Victorian melodramas*

melodramatic [melədrə'mætɪk] *adjective* full of violent and exaggerated emotions; *the scene in the cemetery was really melodramatic*

melody ['melədi] *noun* tune; *the song has a catchy melody; according to grandfather the old Victorian melodies are still the best* (NOTE: plural is **melodies**)

melon ['melən] *noun* large round fruit which grows on a creeping plant; *we had melon and ham as a starter;* **watermelon** = very large type of melon with red flesh and black seeds; *she cut the watermelon into slices; they sat in the shade eating slices of watermelon*

melt [melt] *verb* to change from solid to liquid by heating; *if the sun comes out your snowman will melt; the heat of the sun made the road melt; glass will melt at very high temperatures*

melting point ['meltɪŋ 'pɔɪnt] *noun* temperature at which a solid becomes liquid; *heat the chocolate to melting point and pour it over the ice cream*

member ['membə] *noun* **(a)** person who belongs to a group; *the two boys went swimming while the other members of the family sat on the beach; three members of staff are away sick* **(b)** organization which belongs to a society; *the member states of the EU; the members of the United Nations*

Member of Parliament ['membə əv 'pɑːləmənt] *noun* person elected to represent a constituency in Parliament; *the Member of Parliament for Bristol East spoke in the debate; she's the Member of Parliament for Richmond* (NOTE: often abbreviated to **MP**. The plural is **MPs**)

> COMMENT: any British subject over 21 years of age is eligible for election as an MP. However, the following are disqualified: peers, persons holding an office of profit (such as judges and civil servants), people who are bankrupt or insane

Member of the European Parliament (MEP) ['membə əv ðə jʊərə'piːən 'pɑːləmənt] *noun* person elected to represent a constituency in the European Parliament

membership ['membəʃɪp] *noun* **(a)** belonging to a group; *I must remember to renew my membership; membership costs £50 a year;* **membership card** = card which shows you belong to a club or to a political party; *bring your membership card with you* **(b)** all the members of a group; *the membership voted to reject the proposal; the club has a membership of five hundred*

membrane ['membreɪn] *noun* **(a)** thin layer of tissue which lines or covers part of the inside of the body; *a membrane connecting the tongue to the bottom of the mouth* **(b)** thin material; *the metal is covered with a waterproof membrane*

memento [mə'mentəʊ] *noun* souvenir, a thing kept to remind you of something; *we brought back a carpet as a memento of our stay in Turkey* (NOTE: plural is **mementoes**)

memo ['meməʊ] *noun* note or short message between people working in the same organization; *did you see the memo from head office?; he sent a memo to all heads of department;* **memo pad** = pad of paper for writing short notes; *he wrote the number down on a memo pad* (NOTE: plural is **memos**)

memoir ['memwɑː] *noun* **(a)** **memoirs** = autobiographical work, written in a less formal way than a full autobiography; *the general spent his retirement writing his memoirs* **(b)** short official or scientific note; *they reported their findings in a memoir to the Geographical Society*

memorabilia [memərə'bɪliə] *noun* things which used to belong to a famous person or organization and are kept to remind you of them; *she collects London tram memorabilia*; *he has a room full of Laurel and Hardy memorabilia*

memorable ['memrəbl] *adjective* which you cannot forget easily; *we didn't have a very memorable holiday as it rained all the time*; *I can still remember that memorable afternoon in 1977 when his horse won the gold cup*

memorandum [memə'rændəm] *noun* short note; *he drew up a memorandum about policy in the Far East* (NOTE: often shortened to **memo**; plural is **memoranda**)

memorial [mɪ'mɔːriəl] **1** *adjective* which reminds you of something *or* someone; **memorial service** = church service to remember someone who has died **2** *noun* monument to remind you of something *or* someone; *the mayor unveiled the memorial to the dead poet*; **war memorial** = monument to soldiers who died in a war; *on Armistice Day a ceremony is held at the local war memorial*

memorize ['meməraɪz] *verb* to learn something by heart; *for homework, we all had to memorize a poem*; *try to memorize your PIN number*

memory ['memri] *noun* **(a)** *(in people)* ability to remember; *he recited the poem from memory*; **if my memory serves me right** = if I can remember it correctly **(b)** *(in computers)* capacity for storing information; *this computer has a much larger memory than the old one* **(c)** *memories* = things which you remember; *we have many happy memories of our holidays in Greece* (NOTE: the plural, only in this meaning, is **memories**)

men [men] *see* MAN; **men's toilet** *(especially US)*; **men's room** = public toilet for men (NOTE: also called **the gents**)

menace ['menəs] **1** *noun* **(a)** someone *or* something which can harm people; *she's an absolute menace on the motorway*; **that little boy's a menace** = he's very naughty **(b)** tone which threatens; *the menace in his voice made her shiver* **2** *verb* (*formal*) to threaten; *the members of the gang were menaced with imprisonment*; *several regions are menaced by drought*

menacing ['menəsɪŋ] *adjective* which threatens; *'Give me the money,' he said in a menacing voice*; **menacing clouds** = clouds which threaten to bring rain

mend [mend] **1** *verb* to make something work which has a fault; to repair something which is broken or damaged; *I dropped my watch on the pavement, and I don't think it can be mended*; *she's trying to mend the washing machine*; *I tore my coat on the fence - can you mend it for me?* **2** *noun* **on the mend** = getting better; *she has been quite ill, but I'm glad to say now she's on the mend*

mending ['mendɪŋ] *noun* **(a)** action of repairing torn clothes, etc.; *she spent all evening doing the mending* **(b)** things which need repairing; *there's a pile of mending waiting to be done*

menial ['miːniəl] **1** *adjective* **menial work** *or* **menial tasks** = boring and trivial jobs which are done by people who are not considered important; *why do I always have to do the menial jobs?* **2** *noun* person who does the lowest type of work; *the manager sent some menials to clear up the mess*

meningitis [menɪn'dʒaɪtɪs] *noun* inflammation of the membranes which surround the brain and spinal cord, where the patient has violent headaches, fever, and stiff neck muscles, and can become delirious; *he had meningitis when he was ten and nearly died*

menopause ['menəpɔːz] *noun* period (usually between 45 and 55 years of age) when a woman stops menstruating and can no longer have children; *hot flushes are often a symptom of the menopause*; *hormone replacement therapy is used to relieve the symptoms of the menopause*; **male menopause** = non-medical term given to a period in a man's life in middle age, when he wants to change his way of life

menstrual ['menstruəl] *adjective* referring to menstruation; **a woman's menstrual cycle** = the period of about 28 days during which a woman ovulates and then menstruates

menstruate ['menstrueɪt] *verb* to bleed from the uterus during menstruation; *she started menstruating at a younger age than most girls*

menstruation [menstru'eɪʃn] *noun* bleeding from the uterus which takes place in a woman each month; *a woman's childbearing years last from the onset of menstruation to the menopause* (NOTE: also called the **periods**)

menswear ['menzweə] *noun* clothes for men; *the menswear department is on the first floor* (NOTE: no plural)

mental ['mentl] *adjective* referring to the mind; **mental age** = method of showing a person's mental development by giving the age when such a stage of development is normally reached; *she is 19 with a mental age of 8*; **mental arithmetic** = calculations which you do in your head; *I can do simple mental arithmetic, but for complicated sums I need a calculator*; **mental cruelty** = being cruel to someone by what you say, rather than by what you do; **mental illness** = illness which affects the mind

mentality [men'tælɪti] *noun* way of thinking which is typical of someone or of a group; *I don't understand the mentality of people who are cruel to animals*

mention ['menʃən] **1** *noun* act of referring to something; *there was no mention of the explosion in the morning papers*; *just the mention of his name made her furious* **2** *verb* **(a)** to refer to something; *the press has not mentioned the accident*; *can you mention to the secretary that the date of the next meeting has been changed?* **(b)** **not to mention** = as well as, not forgetting; *it cost us £20 just to get into the exhibition, not to mention all the expensive meals we had to pay for*

mentor ['mentɔː] *noun* (*formal*) person who teaches, or helps younger people starting their careers; *he was my mentor when I started out in show business*

menu ['menjuː] *noun* **(a)** list of food available in a restaurant; *what's on the menu today?*; *the lunch menu changes every week*; *some dishes are not on the menu, but are written on a blackboard* **(b)** list of options available on a computer program; **menu bar** = series of icons on a computer screen which are the options you can choose; **pull-down menu** = menu which appears as a list on part of the screen; *the pull-down menu is displayed by clicking on the menu bar at the top of the screen*

meow [mi'au] *US* MIAOW

MEP ['emiːˈpiː] = MEMBER OF THE EUROPEAN PARLIAMENT (NOTE: plural is **MEPs**)

mercantile ['mɜːkəntaɪl] *adjective* commercial; *British mercantile history goes back thousands of years*; **mercantile marine** = MERCHANT NAVY

mercenary ['mɜːsənəri] **1** *adjective* interested in money; *I don't want to sound mercenary, but how much did you pay for your ticket?* **2** *noun* soldier who is paid to fight for a foreign country; *he was one of a group of mercenaries hired to protect the president*; *the national army was mainly formed of foreign mercenaries* (NOTE: plural is **mercenaries**)

merchandise ['mɜːtʃəndaɪs] *noun* goods for sale; *we have a wide range of merchandise for sale*

merchandize ['mɜːtʃəndaɪz] *verb* to sell goods by a wide variety of means; *her children's books make more money through merchandizing than through sales in bookshops*

merchandizing ['mɜːtʃədaɪzɪŋ] *noun* organizing the display and promotion of goods for sale; *the merchandizing of a product*

merchant ['mɜːtʃənt] *noun* **(a)** businessman; person who buys and sells a particular product; *a tobacco merchant*; *a wine merchant* **(b) merchant bank** = bank which lends money to companies, not to people; **merchant navy** = a country's commercial ships; *at sixteen he ran away from school to join the merchant navy*; **merchant seaman** = seaman on a commercial ship; **merchant ship** = commercial ship; *he's serving on a merchant ship running between the Caribbean and Europe*

merciful ['mɜːsɪful] *adjective* **(a)** kind and forgiving; *they decided to confess their crime and hope the king would be merciful* **(b) merciful release** = fortunate end to suffering; *his death was a merciful release*

mercifully ['mɜːsɪfəli] *adverb* (*informal*) luckily; *mercifully his speech was very short*

merciless ['mɜːsɪləs] *adjective* showing no mercy; *the coach is merciless towards any player who makes a mistake*

mercurial [mɜːˈkjuəriəl] *adjective* which changes frequently; *the star's mercurial behaviour is causing the other members of the cast some concern*

mercury ['mɜːkjəri] *noun* silver-coloured liquid metal used in thermometers; *as the sun came up, they watched the mercury rising in the thermometer* (Chemical element; symbol: **Hg**, atomic number: **80**)

Mercury ['mɜːkjəri] *noun* the planet nearest to the Sun in the solar system; *Mercury has great extremes of surface temperature*

mercy ['mɜːsi] *noun* **(a)** kindness towards unfortunate people; *the parents of the little boy pleaded with the kidnappers for mercy*; **to have mercy on** = not to want to punish or harm someone; **mercy killing** = killing of someone who is very ill, in pain, and not likely to get better **(b)** gift of fate **at the mercy of** = dependent on; *the success of the garden party is very much at the mercy of the weather*; **we must be thankful for small mercies** = we must be grateful that everything has turned out relatively well so far; *despite lots of things going wrong, at least it didn't rain - we must be thankful for small mercies*; **left to the tender mercies of someone** = left to someone to deal with as he likes; *the courier went back to the hotel, leaving us to the tender mercies of the local guides*

mere ['mɪə] *adjective* simply, only; *the merest hint of garlic makes her ill*; *she could feel the merest breath of wind on her face*; **he's a mere boy** = he's only a boy; **the mere sight of grass makes me sneeze** = simply seeing grass makes me sneeze (NOTE: superlative is **merest**)

merely ['mɪəli] *adverb* simply, only; *I'm not criticizing you - I merely said I would have done it differently*

merge [mɜːdʒ] *verb* to join together with something; *the two motorways merge here*; *the firm has merged with its main competitor*

merger ['mɜːdʒə] *noun* joining together of two companies; *he has a proposed a merger between his manufacturing company and our retail company*; *as a result of the merger, the company is the largest in the field*

meridian [məˈrɪdiən] *noun* imaginary line running from the North Pole to the South Pole at right angles to the equator; **the Greenwich meridian** = line passing through Greenwich near London at longitude 0° from which all longitudes are calculated

meringue [məˈræŋ] *noun* sweet baked dessert made of egg whites and sugar; **lemon meringue pie** = pie with lemon cream inside and meringue on top

merit ['merɪt] **1** *noun* being good, or excellent; *there is some merit in what he says, but I can't agree with all of it*; *this picture has no artistic merit whatsoever*; **to go into the merits of** = to examine the good and bad points of; *the committee spent hours going into the merits of the various development plans*; **merit bonus** = extra pay given because of good work **2** *verb* to be worthy of or to deserve something; *the plan merits further discussion*; *her essay only merited a 'B+'*

meritorious [merɪˈtɔːriəs] *adjective* (*formal*) which should be rewarded; *she received an award for meritorious conduct*

mermaid ['mɜːmeɪd] *noun* imaginary creature, half woman and half fish; *grandmother read us a fairy story about a mermaid who saved a drowning sailor*

merry ['meri] *adjective* **(a)** happy and cheerful; *to wish somebody a Merry Christmas*; **to make merry** = to have a good time; *at harvest festivals the whole village would join in and make merry together*; **the more the merrier** = the more there are the happier everyone is; *invite anyone you like, the more the merrier!* **(b)** (*informal*) slightly drunk; *we all got a bit merry that evening* (NOTE: **merrier - merriest**)

merry-go-round ['merɪgəuraund] *noun* (*in a fairground*) large mechanical amusement machine, which turns round and plays music, usually with horses to sit on which move up and down; *the children wanted to have a ride on the merry-go-round* (NOTE: also called a **roundabout**; American English is **carousel**)

mesa ['meɪsə] *noun* US flat-topped hill with steep sides, found in the southwestern USA; *they rode up to the top of the mesa*

mesh [meʃ] **1** *noun* **(a)** arrangement of threads with spaces in between like a net; *we put wire mesh round the chicken pen to keep foxes out* **(b)** space between the threads of a net; *the boats are supposed to use a net with a half-inch mesh* (NOTE: plural is **meshes**) **2** *verb* (*of gears*) to link together with cogs on another wheel; *for some reason the gears on my bike don't mesh together properly*

mesmerize ['mezmǝraɪz] *verb* to hold the attention of someone so that they don't move; *she seemed mesmerized by the drama taking place before her very eyes*

mess [mes] *noun* **(a)** dirt or disorder; *the milk boiled over and made a mess on the stove*; *we had to clear up the mess after the party* **(b)** **to make a mess of something** = to do something badly; *they made a mess of the repair job* **2** *verb see* MESS ABOUT, MESS UP

mess about ['mes ǝ'baʊt] *verb* **(a)** *(informal)* to spend your spare time doing something without having planned what to do; *he spends his weekends messing about in the garden* **(b)** *(informal)* **to mess someone about** = to treat someone badly; *if you start messing me about, there'll be trouble*; *the garage has messed me her her coat, and so much I'm going to take my car somewhere else for servicing*

message ['mesɪdʒ] *noun* **(a)** information which is sent; *I will leave a message with his secretary*; *can you give the director a message from his wife?*; *we got his message by e-mail*; **message board** = public noticeboard on which messages can be left (such as at a conference, or in a hotel lobby) **(b)** political or religious idea which a group is trying to pass on to the public; *they preached a message of universal peace*; *his message of hard work and simple living did not always find favour* **(c)** *(informal)* **to get the message** = to understand; *she finally got the message when he stood up and handed her her coat*; **to get the message across to someone** = to make someone understand something; *we managed to get the message across, even though no one spoke English*

mess around ['mes ǝ'raʊnd] = MESS ABOUT

messenger ['mesǝndʒǝ] *noun* person who brings a message; *we sent the package by special messenger or by motorcycle messenger*

Messiah [mɪ'saɪǝ] *noun* **(a)** Jesus Christ; *for Christians, Christmas celebrates the birth of the Messiah* **(b)** person whom the Jews expect will come to free them; *the coming of the Messiah is prophesied in the Book of Isaiah* **(c)** **messiah** = person who is expected to come to make the world a better place; *he was seen as the messiah of the ecological movement*

messianic [mesɪ'ænɪk] *adjective* referring to the Messiah; *he preached with messianic fervour*; *he says he has a messianic mission to save the world*

Messrs ['mesǝz] *noun* plural form of Mr used mainly in the names of firms; *Messrs Black & White, Ltd*

mess up ['mes 'ʌp] *verb (informal)* **(a)** to make dirty; *you've messed up your brand new school uniform!* **(b)** to ruin or to spoil; *I'm sorry we can't come - I hope it doesn't mess up your arrangements*

messy ['mesɪ] *adjective* **(a)** dirty; *making pottery is a messy business*; *little children are always messy eaters* **(b)** unpleasant and disorderly; *it was a long messy divorce case* (NOTE: **messier - messiest**)

met [met] *see* MEET

Met [ðǝ 'met] *see* METEOROLOGICAL OFFICE, METROPOLITAN

metabolic [metǝ'bɒlɪk] *adjective* referring to metabolism; **metabolic rate** = amount of energy needed to keep the body functioning

metabolism [me'tæbǝlɪzm] *noun* chemical processes which are continually taking place in organisms and which are essential to life; *there's something wrong with his metabolism - he can't digest fats*

metacarpals *or* **metacarpus** [metǝ'kɑːpǝlz or metæ'kɑːpǝs] *noun* the five bones in the hand between the fingers and the wrist

metal ['metl] *noun* material, such as iron, copper, etc., which can carry heat and electricity and is used for making things; *a metal frying pan*; *these spoons are plastic but the knives are metal*; *these chairs are very heavy - they must be made of metal*

metallic [mǝ'tælɪk] *adjective* **(a)** like metal, referring to metal; *suddenly we heard a quiet metallic sound, like a chain being moved*; **metallic element** = chemical element which is a metal **(b)** shining like metal; *he has had his car resprayed with metallic paint*; **metallic sheen** = shine such as you get on polished metal

metalwork ['metlwɜːk] *noun* **(a)** art of making things with metal; *his hobby is metalwork*; *she goes to a metalwork class on Tuesday evenings* **(b)** pieces of metal which form part of something; *the old car's metalwork gleamed after it was polished*

metalworker ['metlwɜːkǝ] *noun* person skilled in making objects out of metal; *a team of metalworkers designed and produced the palace's iron gates*

metamorphosis [metǝ'mɔːfǝsɪs] *noun (formal)* change to something quite different, especially an insect's change of form; *the metamorphosis of a caterpillar into a butterfly* (NOTE: plural is **metamorphoses** [metǝ'mɔːfǝsiːz])

metaphor ['metǝfǝ] *noun* way of describing something by giving it the qualities of something else, as in 'our eagle-eyed readers soon spotted the mistake'; *he uses an ant's nest as a metaphor for the centre of town on a busy market day*; *compare* SIMILE

metaphorical [metǝ'fɒrɪkl] *adjective* like a metaphor; *I'm using the word in a metaphorical sense*

metaphysical [metǝ'fɪzɪkl] *adjective* referring to metaphysics; *these metaphysical discussions are too complex for me*

metaphysics [metǝ'fɪzɪks] *noun* branch of philosophical study concerned with knowledge and the meaning of existence

metatarsals *or* **metatarsus** [metǝ'tɑːsǝlz or metǝ'tɑːsǝs] *noun* the five bones in the foot between the toes and the ankle

mete out ['miːt 'aʊt] *verb (formal)* to inflict punishment; *he meted out punishments to all the boys in the class*

meteor ['miːtɪǝ] *noun* solid body which enters the earth's atmosphere from outer space, usually burning up and shining brightly as it does so; *in August, watch the sky at night for meteors* (NOTE: also called **shooting star**)

meteorite ['miːtɪǝraɪt] *noun* piece of solid rock which falls from outer space onto the earth's surface; *we think this giant hole is the crater left by a large meteorite*

meteorological [miːtɪǝrǝ'lɒdʒɪkl] *adjective* referring to meteorology, to the climate and weather; *it's the coldest winter since meteorological records began*; **the Meteorological Office** = central government office which analyses weather reports and forecasts the weather (NOTE: often simply called the **Met Office**); **meteorological station** = small local station which notes weather conditions

meteorologist [miːtiə'rɒlədʒɪst] *noun* scientist who studies climate and weather, and forecasts what the weather is going to be like; *meteorologists are forecasting a general warming of the Earth's climate*

meteorology [miːtiə'rɒlədʒi] *noun* the study of climate and weather; *meteorology uses computerized data from weather stations round the world*

meter ['miːtə] **1** *noun* **(a)** device for counting how much time, water, gas, etc., has been used; *he came to read the gas meter*; **parking meter** = device into which you put money to pay for parking for a certain time **(b)** *US* = METRE **2** *verb* to measure with a meter; *the quantity of water used is metered by the water company*

methane (CH₄) ['miːθeɪn] *noun* a colourless gas, produced naturally from rotting organic waste; *a certain amount of methane is produced by rubbish dumps* (NOTE: also called **marsh gas**)

method ['meθəd] *noun* way of doing something; *we use the most up-to-date manufacturing methods*; *what is the best method of payment?*

methodical [mə'θɒdɪkl] *adjective* **(a)** done carefully, in an orderly way; *the police carried out a methodical search of the house room by room* **(b)** who works in a careful orderly way; *no one is more methodical than she is, and even she can't find the documents*

methodically [mə'θɒdɪkli] *adverb* in an orderly way; *he methodically went through all the invoices until he found the right one*

methodology [meθə'dɒlədʒi] *noun* (*formal*) methods used in a certain process or study; *we had to work out our methodology before beginning the actual research*

meticulous [me'tɪkjuləs] *adjective* being very careful about details; *her meticulous attention to detail won her a prize*; *he is not a very meticulous chef, and you never know how his dishes are going to turn out*; **to be meticulous in doing something** *or* **about something** = to pay great attention to detail when you do something; *he is very meticulous in sending off his tax return on time*; *they were not very meticulous about their payments*

meticulously [me'tɪkjuləsli] *adverb* very carefully; *she meticulously files all her bills in chronological order*

metonymy [me'tɒnɪmi] *noun* way of writing, where you use the name of part of something to refer to the whole thing itself

COMMENT: using, for example, the container to mean what it contains: 'he's fond of the bottle'; the material to mean the thing made from it: 'do you take plastic?' (meaning credit cards); 'he's a devotee of the Turf' (meaning horse-racing)

metre *US* **meter** ['miːtə] *noun* **(a)** standard measurement of length (approximately 39.4 inches); *the room is about three metres square*; *the river is 50 metres across*; *the table is more than two metres long*; *the walls are two metres thick*; **ten square metres** = area of 10 metres x 10 metres (NOTE: **ten square**

metres is usually written **10 m²**) **(b)** race over a certain distance; *he holds the world record for the 1000 metres*

metric ['metrɪk] *adjective* using the metre as a basic measurement; **the metric system** = system of measuring, using metres, litres and grams

COMMENT: the metric system is a decimal system, using various basic units multiplied or divided by hundreds, thousands, etc. The basic measurements are: **length**: metre; **weight**: gram; **area**: are (= 10 square metres); **capacity**: litre. Each of these basic units can be divided into hundredths (prefix centi-) or thousandths (prefix milli-), or can be multiplied by one thousand (prefix kilo-). So the basic measurements of length are: millimetre, centimetre, metre and kilometre, and of weight: milligram, gram, kilogram)

metric ton ['metrɪk 'tʌn] *noun* 1000 kilograms; *boat with a load-bearing capacity of 600 metric tons* (NOTE: also called **tonne**)

metro ['metrəu] *noun (in some towns)* underground railway system; *the Paris metro*

metronome ['metrənəum] *noun* device which beats time regularly like a clock, used when practising music; *using a metronome helps you to keep time*

metropolis [mə'trɒpəlɪs] *noun* large capital city; *the plan will provide an integrated transport system suitable for a modern metropolis* (NOTE: plural is **metropolises**)

metropolitan [metrə'pɒlɪtən] *adjective* **(a)** referring to a large capital city; *she spent her childhood in a little village and found it difficult to get used to the metropolitan bustle of central London* **(b)** the **Metropolitan Police** = the police force of Greater London (NOTE: also informally called **the Met**)

mews [mjuːz] *noun* **(a)** row of former stables or garages converted into houses; *she's bought a mews cottage near Marble Arch*; *we live in the mews behind the big houses in the square* **(b)** stables for horses; the **Royal Mews** = stables where horses are kept for use on important occasions, like the State Opening of Parliament

Mexican ['meksɪkən] **1** *adjective* referring to Mexico; *Mexican cooking is hot and spicy*; *the Mexican football team looks like winning*; *have you seen the photos from our Mexican holiday?*; **Mexican wave** = action at a football game or big meeting, when spectators stand up in turn, wave their arms, and then sit down again, giving the impression that a wave is running through the crowd **2** *noun* person from Mexico; *many Mexicans have emigrated to California*

Mexico ['meksɪkəu] *noun* large country in Latin America, south of the United States; *there is a long border between the USA and Mexico* (NOTE: capital: **Mexico City**; people: **Mexicans**; language: **Spanish**; currency: **Mexican peso**)

miaow *US* **meow** [miː'au] **1** *noun* call made by a cat; *we heard plaintive miaows coming from inside the cupboard* **2** *verb* to make a miaow; *the cat was miaowing to be let in*

mice [maɪs] *see* MOUSE

Mickey Mouse ['mɪki 'maus] **1** *noun* popular cartoon character in Disney films; *we watched old Mickey Mouse cartoons on TV* **2** *adjective* small and inefficient; *some Mickey Mouse firm got the contract*

micro- ['maɪkrəʊ] *prefix meaning* on a small scale

microbe ['maɪkrəʊb] *noun* very small organism which can only be seen with a microscope; *microbes that live in the soil can carry tetanus* (NOTE: also called a **microorganism**)

microchip ['maɪkrəʊtʃɪp] *noun* very small piece of silicon with printed circuits on it; *the circuits are printed on microchips*

microorganism [maɪkrəʊ'ɔːgənɪzm] *noun* microbe, a very small organism which can only be seen with a microscope; *these microorganisms are only visible under the microscope*

microphone ['maɪkrəfəʊn] *noun* (a) device which you speak into to transmit sound through loudspeakers, through the radio, or to record on disk or tape; *he had difficulty in making himself heard without a microphone* (b) device for capturing sound and passing it to a listening device; *there was a hidden microphone in the vase of flowers*

microscope ['maɪkrəskəʊp] *noun* instrument which enlarges things which are very small; *he examined the blood sample under the microscope*

microscopic [maɪkrə'skɒpɪk] *adjective* so small as to be visible only through a microscope; *microscopic forms of life are visible in the oldest rocks*

microwave ['maɪkrəweɪv] **1** *noun* small oven which cooks very rapidly using very short electric waves; *put the dish in the microwave for three minutes* **2** *verb* to cook something in a microwave; *you can microwave those potatoes*

mid- [mɪd] *prefix meaning* 'middle'; *from mid-1998* = from the middle of 1998; *the factory is closed until mid-July*

midday ['mɪddeɪ] *noun* noon, twelve o'clock in the middle of the day; *wear a hat if you're going out in the midday sun; I like to eat a hot meal at midday; we were having our midday meal when the builders arrived* (NOTE: also called **noon**)

middle ['mɪdl] **1** *adjective* in the centre; half-way between two ends; *they live in the middle house, the one with the green door* **2** *noun* (a) centre; *she was standing in the middle of the road, trying to cross; Chad is a country in the middle of Africa* (b) (*referring to time*) halfway through; *we were woken in the middle of the night by a dog barking; we were just in the middle of eating our supper when they called; his portable telephone rang in the middle of the meeting; the house was built in the middle of the eighteenth century* (c) waist; *it's quite deep - the water comes up to my middle; how much does he measure round his middle?*

middle age ['mɪdl 'eɪdʒ] *noun* period of life when you are not very young and not very old, between 40 and 60 years old; *when he reached middle age he stopped travelling as much as before*

middle-aged [mɪdl'eɪdʒd] *adjective* not very young and not very old (between 40 and 60 years old); *her brother is much older than she is, he's quite middle-aged; three middle-aged men got on to the bus*

the Middle Ages [ðə 'mɪdl 'eɪdʒɪz] *noun* historical period before the Renaissance (from about 1000 to 1500 AD); *parts of the castle date back to the Middle Ages* (NOTE: the adjective from **Middle Ages** is **medieval**)

middle class ['mɪdl 'klɑːs] *noun* professional class between the upper class and the lower or working class; *as people become more wealthy, so the middle class expands; they live in a middle-class suburb*

Middle East ['mɪdl 'iːst] *noun* area between Egypt and Pakistan; *tensions are running high in the Middle East; the USA has made peace in the Middle East one of its top priorities*

Middle Eastern [mɪdl 'iːstən] *adjective* referring to the Middle East; *the envoy visited several Middle Eastern capitals*

middleman ['mɪdlmæn] *noun* businessman who buys from the manufacturer and sells to customers; *we sell direct from the factory to the public and cut out the middleman* (NOTE: plural is **middlemen**)

middle-of-the-road ['mɪdlʌvðə'rəʊd] *adjective* (*in politics*) of the centre, moderate; *they decided to play safe and adopt a middle-of-the-road policy*

middle-sized ['mɪdl'saɪzd] *adjective* neither big nor small; *many small and middle-sized companies are finding trading conditions difficult*

middleweight ['mɪdlweɪt] *noun* weight of boxer between welterweight and light heavyweight; *the middleweight champion; a middleweight title fight*

middling ['mɪdlɪŋ] *adjective* neither good nor bad; not very large or very small; *there aren't any very large or tiny potatoes, just middling ones; his performance was only of middling quality*

midfield ['mɪdfiːld] *noun* (a) central section of a football pitch; *the goalkeeper kicked the ball to midfield* (b) players who play in the midfield; *the midfield is the most important section of a football team*

the Midlands [ðə 'mɪdləndz] *noun* area in the centre of England; *she was born in the Midlands; he has a Midlands accent*

midnight ['mɪdnaɪt] *noun* twelve o'clock at night; *I must go to bed - it's after midnight; we only reached the hotel at midnight*

midriff ['mɪdrɪf] *noun* front part of your body above the waist and below the chest; *he punched him in the midriff*

midshipman ['mɪdʃɪpmən] *noun* junior trainee officer in the Royal Navy; *he worked his way up from midshipman to admiral* (NOTE: plural is **midshipmen**)

midst [mɪdst] *noun* middle; *in the midst of moving house, she became ill*; **in our midst** = among us; *we have a spy in our midst*

midsummer [mɪd'sʌmə] *noun* middle of the summer; *it's very hot in here in midsummer*; **Midsummer's Day** = June 24th

midterm ['mɪdtɜːm] *noun* US point half-way through an academic term; *we have our midterm exam next week; compare* HALF-TERM

midway [mɪd'weɪ] *adverb* half-way; *we arranged to meet them midway between London and Oxford; the lights went out midway through the performance*

midweek ['mɪdwiːk] *adjective & adverb* in the middle of the week; *if you travel midweek, the fares are higher than if you travel at the weekend*

Midwest [mɪd'west] *noun* central northern part of the United States; *she comes from a small town in the Midwest*

midwife ['mɪdwaɪf] *noun* professional nurse who helps a woman give birth, often at home; *the midwife arrived only just before the baby was born*; *a trained midwife will supervise the delivery*; *the twins were delivered by the midwife* (NOTE: plural is **midwives** ['mɪdwaɪvz])

midwifery ['mɪdwɪfri] *noun* work of being a midwife; *she took a course in midwifery*

might [maɪt] **1** *noun* force; *she pulled at it with all her might, and still could not move it*; *all the might of the armed forces is displayed during the National Day parade* **2** *verb* used with other verbs **(a)** *(to mean it is possible)* *take an umbrella, it might rain*; *if he isn't here, he might be waiting outside*; *I might call in to see you tomorrow if I have time*; *that was a stupid thing to do - you might have been killed!*; *they might win, but I wouldn't bet on it* **(b)** *(to mean something should have been)* *you might try and stay awake next time*; *he* **might have done something to help** = it would have been better if he had done something to help; *you* **might have told me** = I wish you had told me; *you might have told me you'd invited her as well* **(c)** *(asking a question politely)* *might I have another cup of tea?* (NOTE: negative: **might not is** usually **mightn't** Note also that **might** is always used with other verbs and is not followed by **to**)

mighty ['maɪti] *adjective* **(a)** strong, powerful; *with one mighty heave he lifted the sack onto the lorry*; *all she could remember was getting a mighty blow on the head, and then everything went black* **(b)** great; *that's mighty kind of you*; *(informal)* **he's in a mighty hurry** = he's very impatient (NOTE: **mightier - mightiest**)

migraine ['miːɡreɪn] *noun* sharp headache often associated with vomiting and seeing bright lights; *he had an attack of migraine and could not come to work*; *her migraine attacks seem to be worse in the summer*

migrant ['maɪɡrənt] **1** *noun* **(a)** worker who moves from one job to another or from one country to another to look for work; *the government is trying to prevent migrants coming into the country*; **economic migrant** = person who moves to live in another country where living conditions are better **(b)** bird which moves from one country to another with the seasons; *the marshes are an ideal place to see the winter migrants* **2** *adjective* who moves from one job to another or from one country to another; *migrant workers often do the jobs no one wants to do*; *the exploitation of migrant farm workers*

migrate [maɪˈɡreɪt] *verb* to move from one place to another with the seasons; *herds of animals migrate across the desert in search of water*; *the marshes are an ideal place to see migrating geese*

migration [maɪˈɡreɪʃn] *noun* movement of animals and birds from one country to another; *the swallows are starting to gather in groups, ready for their long migration south for the winter*

mike [maɪk] *noun (informal)* = MICROPHONE; *a member of the audience jumped onto the stage and grabbed the mike*; *she tapped the mike to see if it was working*

mild [maɪld] *adjective* **(a)** not harsh, not too bad; *there was some mild criticism, but generally the plan was welcomed*; *he had a mild heart attack and was soon back to work again* **(b)** not severe (weather); *winters in the south of the country are usually milder than in the north* **(c)** not strong-tasting; *we'll choose the mildest curry on the menu* (NOTE: in this meaning the opposite is **hot**); (NOTE: **milder - mildest**)

mildew ['mɪldjuː] **1** *noun* fungus which grows like a white powder on plants, paper, leather, etc.; *we spray the plants to stop them getting mildew*; *the bathroom walls are covered in mildew* **2** *verb* to become **mildewed** = to become covered with mildew; *remove any mildewed leaves from the plants*

mile [maɪl] *noun* **(a)** measure of length (= 1,760 yards or 1.61 kilometres); *he thinks nothing of cycling ten miles to work every day*; *the car can't go any faster than sixty miles per hour*; *the line of cars stretched for three miles from the road works*; **the car was doing 100 miles an hour** = was travelling at 100 miles an hour **(b)** **miles** = long distance; *there are no shops for miles around*; *we walked for miles and came back to the point where we started from* **(c)** *(informal)* **miles** = a lot of; *she's miles better at swimming now than she was six months ago*; **miles of string** = very long piece of string; **it's miles too big** = it's much too big

mileage ['maɪlɪdʒ] *noun* **(a)** distance travelled in miles; **unlimited mileage** = allowance with a hired car, where the driver is not charged for the number of miles driven **(b)** **to get more mileage out of something** = to take as much advantage as possible of something; *can we get any more mileage out of his appearance on TV?*

milestone ['maɪlstəʊn] *noun* **(a)** important point in history, etc.; *this year marks an important milestone in the firm's history*; *1887 was a milestone in the history of road transport when Daimler patented the first internal combustion engine* **(b)** *(old)* stone by the side of a road, showing the distance in miles; *the milestone showed it was 17 miles to Bristol*

milieu ['miːljɜː] *noun* society which surrounds someone; *his social milieu is quite different from hers*; *the offices of a London newspaper was a very different milieu from the one in which she was brought up*

militancy ['mɪlɪtənsi] *noun* vigour in supporting a political party or a cause; *the party was embarrassed by the militancy of some of its left-wing supporters*

militant ['mɪlɪtənt] **1** *adjective* very active in supporting a cause or political party; *he is on the militant wing of the party* **2** *noun* **(a)** person who is very active in supporting a cause or a political party; *the party must keep its militants under control* **(b)** person who supports a policy of using violence to achieve aims; *a few militants in the march started throwing stones at the police*

military ['mɪlɪtri] **1** *adjective* referring to the armed forces; *the two leaders discussed the possibility of military intervention*; *military spending has fallen over the past three years*; **military service** = period of time served in the armed forces; *in some countries there is still compulsory military service for all young men* **2** *noun* **the military** = the army; *faced with riots all over the country, the government called in the military*

military police ['mɪlɪtri 'pliːs] *noun* police force which is part of the army; *a military police jeep arrived as the fight developed*

militia [mɪˈlɪʃə] *noun* emergency police force organized like an army; *the governor called out the militia to deal with the riots*

militiaman [mɪˈlɪʃəmæn] *noun* man who is a member of a militia; *militiamen are required to do* *three weeks military training every year* (NOTE: plural is **militiamen**)

milk [mɪlk] **1** *noun* white liquid produced by female mammals to feed their young, especially the liquid produced by cows; *do you want milk with your coffee?*; *can we have two glasses of milk, please?*; *don't forget to buy some milk, there's none in the fridge*; **milk chocolate** = pale brown chocolate made with milk; *see also* CRY (NOTE: no plural: **some milk, a bottle of milk, a glass of milk**) **2** *verb* **(a)** to take milk from an animal; *the cows are waiting to be milked* **(b)** *(informal)* to get as much advantage as possible from a situation; *the newspapers milked the story for all it was worth*

milkman ['mɪlkmən] *noun* **GB** man who brings milk to each house in the morning; *tell the milkman to leave six pints of milk today*; *we pay the milkman every week* (NOTE: plural is **milkmen**)

milk shake ['mɪlk 'ʃeɪk] *noun* drink made by beating milk with sweet liquid or fruit; *she drank two coffee milk shakes*; *can I have a banana milk shake, please?*

milky ['mɪlki] *adjective* **(a)** made with milk; containing milk; *this coffee is too milky* **(b)** looking like milk; *if you cut the plant, a milky fluid comes out*; **the Milky Way** = band of light across the sky caused by the high concentration of stars in our galaxy; *on a clear night the Milky Way is easily seen* (NOTE: **milkier - milkiest**)

mill [mɪl] *noun* **(a)** small machine for grinding seeds into powder; *there is a pepper mill on the table* **(b)** large machine for grinding corn into flour; *corn is fed into the mill through a hopper* **(c)** building which contains such a machine; *at lunch the visitors were shown round the mill*; *see also* WATERMILL, WINDMILL **(d)** *(informal)* **to go through the mill** *or* **to be put through the mill** = (i) to be fully trained; (ii) to suffer a great deal; *her divorce has really put her through the mill* **(e)** **run-of-the-mill** = ordinary; *it's very much a run-of-the-mill operation which any doctor can do* **(f)** large factory; **paper mill** = factory producing paper; **steel mill** = factory producing steel

millennial [mɪ'leniəl] *adjective* referring to a millennium; *millennial celebrations*

millennium [mɪ'leniəm] *noun* period of a thousand years; *the celebrations for the millennium*; **millennium bug** = error in a computer system in which the year 2000 is not correctly recognized (NOTE: plural is **millennia**)

miller ['mɪlə] *noun* man who makes flour in a mill; *the farmer took his corn to the miller who ground it into flour*

millet ['mɪlɪt] *noun* common cereal crop grown in many of the hot, dry regions of Africa and Asia, where it is a staple food; *millet is boiled and eaten like rice* (NOTE: no plural)

milli- ['mɪli] *prefix meaning* one thousandth

milligram ['mɪlɪɡræm] *noun* one thousandth of a gram; *the product contains 7 milligrams of fat per gram* (NOTE: usually written **mg** after figures)

millimetre *US* **millimeter** ['mɪlɪmiːtə] *noun* one thousandth of a metre; *one inch equals roughly 25 millimetres* (NOTE: usually written **mm** after figures: **35mm**)

million ['mɪljən] **(a)** number 1,000,000; *the population of Great Britain is just over 58 million* **(b)**

millions of = a very large number of; *millions of trees are chopped down for paper*; *the country spends millions of dollars on imports of oil*; *millions of people spend their holidays in Italy* (NOTE: no plural with figures: **sixty million**. With figures, **million** can be written m: £2m, $2m: say 'two million pounds, two million dollars')

millionaire [mɪljə'neə] *noun* person who has more than a million pounds or a million dollars; *if you win the lottery you will become an instant millionaire*; *only a millionaire could afford a yacht like his* (NOTE: to show the currency in which a person is a millionaire, say **a dollar millionaire, a sterling millionaire, a Deutschmark millionaire**, etc.)

millionth (1,000,000th) ['mɪljənθ] *adjective & noun* referring to a million; *a millionth of a second*; *the tourist office gave a prize to the millionth visitor*

mime [maɪm] **1** *noun* **(a)** gestures and facial expressions used in the theatre to tell a story or convey emotions; *a story told in mime* **(b)** story conveyed by gestures; *he did a mime of a man trying to open an umbrella in a high wind* **(c)** actor who does not speak, but tells a story or conveys emotions through gestures; *Marcel Marceau, the famous French mime* **2** *verb* to tell a story or convey emotions through gestures; *he mimed getting into a car and driving off*

mimic ['mɪmɪk] **1** *noun* person who imitates; *a good mimic imitates a person's body language as well as their voice* **2** *verb* to imitate; *he doesn't like it when people mimic the way he talks* (NOTE: **mimicking - mimicked**)

min = MINIMUM, MINUTE

minaret [mɪnə'ret] *noun* tall tower which is part of a mosque; *Muslims are called to prayer from the minaret*

mince [mɪns] **1** *noun* meat which has been ground into very small pieces; *she bought a pound of mince*; *add the mince to the onions and fry till brown* **2** *verb* **(a)** to grind up meat or vegetables until they are in very small pieces; *a pound of minced beef or of minced lamb*; *beefburgers are made of minced beef*; *mince the meat finely and then roll into little balls* (NOTE: American English for **minced beef** and **mince** is **ground beef**) **(b)** *he didn't mince his words* = he said what he had to say in a straightforward way

mincemeat ['mɪnsmiːt] *noun* mixture of suet, apples, spices, dried fruit, etc., used to make mince pies; **to make mincemeat (out) of someone** = to defeat someone, to destroy someone completely; *he made mincemeat of his opponent* (NOTE: no plural)

mince pie ['mɪns 'paɪ] *noun* small pie filled with mincemeat, eaten at Christmas; *go on, have another mince pie*

mincer *or* **mincing machine** ['mɪnsə *or* 'mɪnsɪŋ mə'ʃiːn] *noun* machine for grinding up meat into very small pieces; *badly cleaned mincers are a source of contamination* (NOTE: American English is a **grinder**)

mind [maɪnd] **1** *noun* part of the body which controls memory, reasoning; *his mind always seems to be on other things*; *I've forgotten her name - it just slipped my mind*; *I think of her night and day - I just can't get her out of my mind*; *my mind went blank as soon as I saw the exam paper*; **what do you have in mind?** = what are you thinking of?; *let's do something unusual this weekend - what do you have in mind?*; **she's got something on her mind** = she's worrying about something; *she's not her usual cheery self today - I* think she's got something on her mind; **let's try to take his mind off his exams** = let's try to stop him worrying about the exams; **state of mind** = general feeling; *she was in a very gloomy state of mind*; **to make up your mind (to do something)** = to decide (to do something); *I can't make up my mind whether to take the afternoon off to do some shopping or stay in the office and work*; *she couldn't make up her mind what clothes to wear to the wedding*; **to change your mind** = to decide to do something different; *he was going to go by car but then changed his mind and went by bus*; *he has decided to go on holiday next week and nothing will make him change his mind*; **to be in two minds about something** = not to be sure about something, to be undecided; *I'm in two minds about his proposal* 2 *verb* (a) to be careful, to watch out; *mind the steps - they're slippery!*; *mind you get back early*; *mind the plate - it's hot!* (b) to worry about; *don't mind me, I'm used to working with children*; **never mind** = don't worry; *never mind - you'll get another chance to enter the competition next year*; **mind your own business!** = don't interfere with other people's problems (c) to be bothered or annoyed by; *nobody will mind if you're late*; *there aren't enough chairs, but I don't mind standing up* (d) *(asking politely)* *do you mind if I open the window?* (e) **wouldn't mind** = would rather like; *I wouldn't mind a cup of coffee*

mind-boggling ['maɪndbɒglɪŋ] *adjective* *(informal)* large, complicated and difficult to understand; *the complexities of international trade are quite mind-boggling*

minder ['maɪndə] *noun* person who protects someone, a bodyguard; *the president arrived surrounded by his minders*; *see also* CHILDMINDER

mindful ['maɪndful] *adjective* **mindful of something** = remembering something, thinking about something; *he is always mindful of his responsibilities as chairman*; *you should be mindful of the risks you are taking*

mindless ['maɪndləs] *adjective* stupid, done without thinking; *an act of mindless vandalism*

mindset ['maɪndset] *noun* way of thinking, general attitude to things; *we have to change her mindset if we want her work to improve*; *his mindset makes him very suspicious of foreign ideas*

mine [maɪn] 1 *pronoun* belonging to me; *that book is mine*; *can I borrow your bike, mine's been stolen*; *she's a great friend of mine* 2 *noun* (a) deep hole in the ground from which coal, etc., is taken out; *the coal mine has stopped working after fifty years*; *he has shares in an African gold mine* (b) sort of bomb which is hidden under the ground or under water; *the tank went over a mine and two soldiers were killed*; *it will take years to clear all the mines left by the rebel army*; *see also* LANDMINE 3 *verb* (a) to dig coal, etc., out of the ground; *they mine gold in the south of the country* (b) to place mines in land or water; *the entrance to the harbour has been mined*

minefield ['maɪnfiːld] *noun* (a) area of land or sea where mines have been laid; *minefields lay along both sides of the road* (b) difficult and dangerous situation; *trying to find your way round EU agriculture regulations is an absolute minefield*; *the company got caught up in the minefield of government tax regulations*

miner ['maɪnə] *noun* person who works in a mine; *twelve miners were trapped when the roof of a coal mine collapsed yesterday* (NOTE: do not confuse with minor)

mineral ['mɪnərəl] *noun* (a) substance, such as rock, which is dug out of the earth, or which is found in food, etc.; *what is the mineral content of spinach?*; *the company hopes to discover valuable minerals in the mountains* (b) **mineral water** = water from a spring; *pure mineral water was bubbling up out of the ground*; *do you want orange juice or mineral water?*

minesweeper ['maɪnswiːpə] *noun* ship which specializes in removing mines placed under water

mingle ['mɪŋgl] *verb* (a) to mix together; *the flavours of chocolate and lemon mingle deliciously* (b) to mix, to join in a party; *the host and hostess started to mingle with their guests* (NOTE: mingling - mingled)

miniature ['mɪnɪtʃə] 1 *noun* (a) very small model, portrait, painting, bottle of alcohol, etc.; *we went to an exhibition of Elizabethan miniatures* (b) **in miniature** = reproduced on a very small scale; *the Parliament in the colony is like Westminster in miniature*; *in the model village, everything is in miniature* 2 *adjective* very small; *he has a miniature camera*

minibus ['mɪnɪbʌs] *noun* small bus holding about twelve passengers; *the school minibus had a crash on the motorway*; *we are trying to solve the problem of how to get thirty rugby players into one minibus*

minim ['mɪnɪm] *noun* note in music lasting for two crotchets or half as long as a semibreve; *you played a crotchet instead of a minim*

minimal ['mɪnɪməl] *adjective* very low or small, the smallest possible; *there is a minimal charge to cover some of our expenses*; *the cars were moving very slowly when they hit each other, so damage was minimal*

minimalist ['mɪnɪməlɪst] *noun* artist who does or makes something using the least possible amount of material; *the Japanese minimalist art of flower arranging*

minimize ['mɪnɪmaɪz] *verb* to reduce to the smallest amount; to make something seem very small; *not much can be done to minimize the effects of a nuclear explosion*; *nurses are doing everything to minimize the risk of infection*; *the finance minister minimized the problems facing the country's economy*

minimum ['mɪnɪməm] 1 *adjective* smallest possible; *the minimum amount you can save is £25 per month*; *the minimum age for drivers is 18* 2 *noun* smallest possible amount; *we try to keep expenditure to a minimum*; *she does the bare minimum of study, just enough to pass her exams*

mining ['maɪnɪŋ] *noun* (a) action of taking coal and other minerals out of the land; *a Welsh mining village*; *the company is engaged in mining for diamonds or in diamond mining* (b) placing mines underground or under water; *the mining of the harbour was carried out by marines*

minion ['mɪnjən] *noun* *(informal)* low-grade assistant; *he sent one of his minions to deliver the message*

minister ['mɪnɪstə] 1 *noun* (a) member of a government in charge of a department; *the inquiry is to be headed by a former government minister*; *he was the Minister of Defence in the previous government*;

cabinet minister = minister who is also a member of the cabinet; *see also* PRIME MINISTER (NOTE: in the UK and USA, Ministers are also called **secretaries: the Foreign Secretary, Secretary for Commerce**) **(b)** Protestant clergyman; *the minister gave a very moving sermon at the funeral* **2** *verb* **to minister to someone's needs** = to take care of someone; *nurses went to the country to minister to the needs of the refugees*

ministerial ['mɪnɪ'stɪərɪəl] *adjective* referring to a government minister; *she takes her ministerial responsibilities very seriously*; *he arrived in the ministerial Rolls Royce*

ministry ['mɪnɪstrɪ] *noun* **(a)** government department; offices of a government department; *he works in the Ministry of Defence* (NOTE: plural is **ministries**; in the UK and the USA, important ministries are also called **departments: the Department of Trade and Industry; the Commerce Department**) **(b)** government; *the Conservative Ministry of 1951* (NOTE: you can also say **administration** in this sense: **the Conservative Administration of 1951**)

mink [mɪŋk] *noun* **(a)** small animal whose fur is very valuable; *mink are now found in the wild in Britain*; **mink farm** = farm where mink are reared (NOTE: plural is **mink**) **(b)** *(informal)* coat of mink fur *she wore her mink to the opera* (NOTE: no plural in this meaning: to show a plural say **mink coats**)

minor ['maɪnə] **1** *adjective* **(a)** not very important; *it was just a minor injury*; *she has a minor role in the film*; *he played a minor part in the revolution* **(b) Asia Minor** = Turkey **(c)** *(music)* **minor key** = key where there are semitones between the second and third, and fifth and sixth, and seventh and eighth notes, and tones between the other notes; *she played a concerto in B minor*; *compare* MAJOR **2** *noun* young person under the age of 18; *we are forbidden to serve alcohol to minors* (NOTE: do not confuse with **miner**)

minority [maɪ'nɒrɪtɪ] *noun* number or quantity which is less than half of a total; *although the proposal was carried, a large minority of members voted against it*; **the men are in the minority** = there are more women than men; **minority government** = government with fewer members of parliament than the opposition; *a minority government can be defeated if all the opposition parties vote together*

minstrel ['mɪnstrəl] *noun* **(a)** *(in the Middle Ages)* travelling singer or musician; *a wandering minstrel arrived at the castle* **(b)** *(old)* one of a group of popular singers; *she performed in a troupe of minstrels in the 1920s*

mint [mɪnt] **1** *noun* **(a)** factory where coins are made; *the mint is preparing to make the new coins*; **in mint condition** = perfect, in exactly the same condition as when it was made; *he is offering a camera for sale in mint condition*; *(informal)* **a mint of money** = a great deal of money; *the inventor of the zip must have made a mint of money* **(b)** common herb used as flavouring; **mint sauce** = sauce made of chopped mint, sugar and vinegar, served with lamb; *see also* MINT JULEP **(c)** small white sweet tasting of peppermint; *he always keeps a packet of mints in his pocket to suck when travelling* **2** *verb* to make coins; *British coins are minted by the Royal Mint*

minus ['maɪnəs] **1** *preposition* less; *ten minus eight equals two (10 - 8 = 2) net salary is gross salary minus tax and National Insurance deductions*; *(informal)*

luckily they came minus children = luckily they came without their children **2** *noun* sign (-) meaning less; *minus 10 degrees (-10°)*

minuscule ['mɪnəskjuːl] *adjective* very small; *she was carrying a minuscule amount of the drug*; *the differences between the two models are minuscule*

minute 1 ['mɪnɪt] *noun* **(a)** one sixtieth part of an hour; *there are sixty minutes in an hour, and sixty seconds in a minute*; *the doctor can see you for ten minutes only*; *if you don't mind waiting, Mr Smith will be free in about twenty minutes' time*; *the house is about ten minutes' walk or is a ten-minute walk from the office*; **six minutes to four** = 3.54; **eight minutes past three** = 3.08; **minute hand** = long hand on a clock or watch which shows the minutes **(b)** very short space of time; *I'll be ready in a minute*; *why don't you wait for a minute and see if the dentist is free?*; **I won't be a minute** = I'll be very quick; *I'm just going to pop into the bank - I won't be a minute*; **at any minute** = very soon; *I expect the train to arrive at any minute* **(c) minutes** = notes taken of what has been said at a meeting; *the secretary will take the minutes of the meeting*; *copies of the minutes of the last meeting will be sent to all members of the committee* **2** ['mɪnɪt] *verb* to write the record of a meeting; *my objection to the proposal has been minuted* **3** [maɪ'njuːt] *adjective* very small; *a minute piece of dust must have got into the watch*; **in minute detail** = with all details carefully drawn or explained; *I explained it all to you in the minutest detail, and you still got it wrong* (NOTE: superlative is **minutest**)

miracle ['mɪrəkl] *noun* **(a)** very lucky happening; *it was a miracle she was not killed in the accident* **(b)** marvellous event which happens apparently by the power of God; *she went to the shrine and was cured - it must have been a miracle*

miraculous [mɪ'rækjʊləs] *adjective* wonderful, which cannot be explained; *she has made a miraculous recovery*

miraculously [mɪ'rækjʊləslɪ] *adverb* wonderfully, in a way which cannot be explained; *miraculously no one was killed when the two trains collided*; *miraculously, he landed on a pile of hay when his parachute failed to open*

mirage ['mɪrɑːʒ] *noun* imaginary sight caused by hot air, such as an oasis seen in a desert; *it looked as if there was water on the road ahead but it was only a mirage*

mirror ['mɪrə] **1** *noun* piece of glass with a metal backing which reflects an image; *they looked at themselves in the mirror*; **bathroom mirror** = mirror in a bathroom; **driving mirror** *or* **rear-view mirror** = mirror inside a car which allows the driver to see what is behind without turning his head **2** *verb* **(a)** to be very similar to; *the report mirrors the information given to the committee by local doctors* **(b)** to be the same as; *her astonishment at the news mirrored mine*

mirror image ['mɪrə 'ɪmɪdʒ] *noun* something that looks the same as something else except that it is the other way round, as in a mirror; *our house is a mirror image of the one opposite*

misbehave [mɪsbɪ'heɪv] *verb* to behave badly; *if anyone misbehaves they will be sent home immediately*

misbehaviour *US* **misbehavior** [mɪsbɪ'heɪvjə] *noun* bad behaviour; *she won't tolerate any misbehaviour during lessons*

miscalculate [mɪs'kælkjuleɪt] *verb* to calculate wrongly; *the salesman miscalculated the discount, so we hardly broke even on the deal*

miscarriage ['mɪskærɪdʒ] *noun* **(a) miscarriage of justice** = wrong decision by a court, which can be changed on appeal; *the papers think there has been a gross miscarriage of justice* **(b)** loss of a baby during pregnancy; *she had two miscarriages before having her first child*

miscellaneous [mɪsə'leɪnɪəs] *adjective* various or mixed, not all of the same sort; *a box of miscellaneous pieces of equipment*; *we'll file this under 'miscellaneous expenditure'*

mischief ['mɪstʃɪf] *noun* naughty or wicked action; *be good, and try to keep out of mischief*; *the children were full of mischief last night - they just wouldn't go to bed*; **to make mischief** = to make trouble for other people; *she's always trying to make mischief between me and the boss*; *he is always getting into mischief* = he's always doing something naughty (NOTE: no plural)

mischievous ['mɪstʃɪvəs] *adjective* wicked or naughty; *he has a mischievous way of looking at you*; *those mischievous little boys - whatever are they doing now?*

misconception [mɪskən'sepʃən] *noun* mistaken idea; *is is a popular misconception that eating carrots helps you to see in the dark*

misconduct [mɪs'kɒndʌkt] *noun* action by an employee which could harm someone, such as disobeying instructions; *that kind of misconduct can lead to instant dismissal*; **gross misconduct** = action such as being drunk or molesting women staff, which leads to instant dismissal; **professional misconduct** = behaviour by a member of a profession, such as a lawyer or accountant or doctor, which the body regulating that profession considers to be wrong; *the Board will decide whether the complaint justifies a charge of professional misconduct*

misconstrue [mɪskən'struː] *verb* to understand something wrongly; *the proposal was not very clearly worded and we misconstrued their intentions*; *she misconstrued his attempts at being pleasant*

misdeed [mɪs'diːd] *noun* (*formal*) wicked action; *he is being punished for his misdeeds*

misdemeanour US **misdemeanor** [mɪsdɪ'miːnə] *noun* minor crime; *the magistrates decided to overlook his previous misdemeanours*; *he was charged with several misdemeanours*

miser ['maɪzə] *noun* person who loves his money and refuses to spend it; *in Dickens' 'Christmas Carol', the main character, Ebenezer Scrooge, is a miser who hates Christmas and everything it stands for*

miserable ['mɪzrəbl] *adjective* **(a)** sad, unhappy; *he's in a very miserable state of mind*; *can't you do something to cheer her up?* - *she's very miserable since her boyfriend left her* **(b)** bad or unpleasant (weather); *what miserable weather! will it ever stop raining?* **(c)** very low (salary); *she earns a miserable wage as a library assistant*

miserly ['maɪzəli] *adjective* **(a)** not wanting to spend money; *he's very miserly with his money* **(b)** very small; *her father gave her a miserly allowance*; *for pudding we were given a miserly amount of ice cream*

misery ['mɪzəri] *noun* great unhappiness; *there were scenes of appalling human misery in the refugee camps*; *his life in the home was sheer misery*; **to put someone out of his misery** = not to keep someone waiting any longer, but tell them the result of the exam, etc.; *let's go and put the candidates out of their misery*

misfit ['mɪsfɪt] *noun* person who does not fit in with a group, who does not fit into society; *at school she was a bit of a misfit*

misfortune [mɪs'fɔːtjuːn] *noun* **(a)** bad luck; *it was his misfortune to be born in the year when his father was declared bankrupt* (NOTE: no plural) **(b)** piece of bad luck; *misfortunes never come singly*

misgiving [mɪs'gɪvɪŋ] *noun* doubt, fear that something will go wrong; *she expressed her misgivings about the plan*; *I have considerable misgivings about his suitability for the job*

misguided [mɪs'gaɪdɪd] *adjective* badly advised; wrongly judged; *in a misguided attempt to try to please everybody, the barman offered free drinks all round*; *if that's what she thinks, then she's sadly misguided*

mishap ['mɪshæp] *noun* little accident; *we had a slight mishap on the way to the office*

misinterpret [mɪsɪn'tɜːprɪt] *verb* not to understand correctly; *I misinterpreted the gestures he was making*

misjudge [mɪs'dʒʌdʒ] *verb* **(a)** to judge wrongly; *he misjudged the distance he had to jump and fell into the ditch* **(b)** to form a wrong opinion about someone *or* something; *I thought he was mean with money, but I obviously misjudged him*

mislay [mɪs'leɪ] *verb* to put something down and not to remember where it is; *I seem to have mislaid my glasses, can you help me find them?* (NOTE: **mislaying - mislaid**)

mislead [mɪs'liːd] *verb* to give someone wrong information; *we were misled into thinking that the plan had been approved by the government*; *the brochure misled us when it said the hotel was near the beach* (NOTE: **misleading - misled** [mɪs'led])

misleading [mɪs'liːdɪŋ] *adjective* quite wrong; likely to cause a mistake; *the map was very misleading*; *he gave misleading information to the press*

mismanagement [mɪs'mænɪdʒmənt] *noun* bad organization and management; *the company failed because of the chairman's mismanagement*

misnomer [mɪs'nəʊmə] *noun* wrong name; *to call him a cricket fan is a bit of a misnomer: he watches cricket on TV about twice a year!*

misplace [mɪs'pleɪs] *verb* to lose something temporarily; *I seem to have misplaced my keys*

misplaced ['mɪspleɪst] *adjective* directed at the wrong person or thing; *your trust in his good intentions was sadly misplaced*; *her misplaced loyalty to her boss*

mispronounce [mɪsprə'naʊns] *verb* to pronounce wrongly; *German speakers of English sometimes mispronounce 'th' as 'z'*

misrepresent [mɪsreprɪ'zent] *verb* to report what someone thinks wrongly; *our aims and intentions have been totally misrepresented by the press*; *he claimed to have been misrepresented as a greedy capitalist*

misrepresentation [mɪsreprɪzen'teɪʃn] *noun* wrong account; *the newspaper report was a compete misrepresentation of what was said at the meeting*

Miss [mɪs] *noun* **(a)** title given to a girl or woman who is not married; *have you met Miss Jones, our new sales* *manager?*; *the letter is addressed to Miss Anne Smith* **(b)** way of addressing a teacher; *Miss! John keeps hitting me* (NOTE: with a name, **Miss** can be followed by the surname, or by the Christian name and surname; without a name, **Miss** is used to call a school teacher)

miss [mɪs] **1** *noun* not having hit something; *he hit the target twice and then had two misses*; **let's give it a miss** = let's not go to see it; **a near miss** = situation where you almost hit something; *that was a near miss - we missed the other car by inches* (NOTE: plural is **misses**) **2** *verb* **(a)** not to hit; *he missed the target*; *she tried to shoot the rabbit but missed* **(b)** not to see, hear, notice, etc.; *we missed the road in the dark*; *she missed the last bus and had to walk home*; *I missed the article about books in yesterday's evening paper*; *I arrived late, so missed most of the discussion*; **you didn't miss much** = there wasn't much to see, the film, etc., wasn't very good; **he just missed being knocked down** = he was almost knocked down **(c)** not to catch; *he tried to catch the ball but he missed it* **(d)** to be sad because you don't do something any more, because someone is not there any more; *do you miss living by the sea?*; *I miss going on those long country walks*; *you'll be missed if you go to work in another office*

missile ['mɪsaɪl *US* 'mɪsl] *noun* **(a)** thing which is thrown to try to hit someone; *the students threw missiles at the police* **(b)** explosive rocket which can be guided to its target; *they think the plane was brought down by an enemy missile*

missing ['mɪsɪŋ] *adjective* lost, which is not there; *I'm looking for my missing car keys*; *they found there was a lot of money missing*; *the police searched everywhere for the missing children*

mission ['mɪʃn] *noun* **(a)** aim or purpose for which someone is sent; *the students were sent on a mission to find the best place to camp*; **her mission in life is to help orphans** = her chosen task is to help orphans; **mission statement** = statement which gives the aims of an organization **(b)** group of people sent somewhere with a particular aim; *several firms took part in a business mission to Japan*; *a United Nations peace mission*; *a rescue mission was sent out into the mountains* **(c)** embassy or consulate; *there were riots outside several diplomatic missions*

missionary ['mɪʃənri] **1** *noun* person who tries to convert people to his or her religion; *European missionaries tried to convert the inhabitants of the Pacific Islands* (NOTE: plural is **missionaries**) **2** *adjective* referring to a missionary; like a missionary; *he followed his calling and became a missionary doctor*; *she showed missionary zeal in trying to get people to join her club*

miss out ['mɪs 'aʊt] *verb* to leave out, to forget to put in; *remember not to miss out the news about the wedding when you're writing to your family*

miss out on ['mɪs 'aʊt ɒn] *verb (informal)* not to enjoy something because you are not there; *I missed out on the skiing trip because I had mumps*

mist [mɪst] **1** *noun* thin fog; *early morning mist covered the fields* **2** *verb* to **mist up** = to become covered with condensation; *the steam in the bathroom had misted up the mirror*; *switch on the heated rear window to stop it misting up*

mistake [mɪs'teɪk] **1** *noun* act or thought which is wrong; *she made a mistake in typing the address*; *there are lots of mistakes in this book*; **by mistake** =

wrongly; *they sent the wrong items by mistake*; *by mistake she put my letter into an envelope for the chairman*; *we took the wrong bus by mistake*; *he put my coat on by mistake in the cloakroom* **2** *verb* to think wrongly; **I mistook him for his brother** = I thought he was his brother; *he is mistaken in thinking I am your brother*; *there's no mistaking him, with his red hair and purple anorak* (NOTE: **mistakes - mistaking - mistook** [mɪs'tʊk] - **has mistaken** [mɪs'teɪkən])

mistaken [mɪs'teɪkən] *adjective* wrong; *I am afraid you are mistaken - I was in Edinburgh on that date*; *it must be a case of mistaken identity - it can't have been me she saw because I wasn't there*; *unless I am very much mistaken, that's an eagle up there on top of the pine*; *if I'm not mistaken, Dr James is your brother*

mistakenly [mɪs'teɪkənli] *adverb* by mistake; *he mistakenly believed that she sat next to him because she liked him*

mister ['mɪstə] *noun (informal)* way of addressing a man; *what's the time, mister?*

mistook [mɪs'tʊk] *verb see* MISTAKE

mistress ['mɪstrəs] *noun* **(a)** woman who has a sexual relationship with a man without being married to him; *she had engaged a detective to follow her husband and photograph him with his mistress* **(b)** woman teacher; *the geography mistress* **(c)** woman in charge; *the dog chased after a rabbit but came back when his mistress whistled*; **she's her own mistress** = she is independent (NOTE: plural is **mistresses**)

mistrust [mɪs'trʌst] **1** *noun* not having any confidence; *the occupying army aroused considerable mistrust in the local population* **2** *verb* not to trust someone, to be doubtful about someone; *he's too charming, that's why I mistrust him*

misty ['mɪsti] *adjective* **(a)** covered in mist; *a misty autumn morning* **(b)** not clear; *a misty image appeared on the screen* (NOTE: **mistier - mistiest**)

misunderstand [mɪsʌndə'stænd] *verb* not to understand correctly; *sorry, I misunderstood the question* (NOTE: **misunderstanding - misunderstood** [mɪsʌndə'stʊd])

misunderstanding [mɪsʌndə'stændɪŋ] *noun* not understanding something correctly; *there was a misunderstanding over my tickets*

misunderstood [mɪsʌndə'stʊd] *adjective* not appreciated because people do not understand you; *he felt misunderstood as an artist*

misuse 1 *noun* [mɪs'juːs] wrong use; *the directors of the charity were accused of misuse of funds* **2** *verb* [mɪs'juːz] **(a)** to use something in a wrong way; *she misused the money which she had been given to look after* **(b)** to treat someone badly; *he felt misused when the company refused to help him*

mite [maɪt] *noun* **(a)** tiny animal of the spider family which lives in soil or is a parasite on animals or plants; *house mites can cause allergies* **(b)** very small child; *the poor little mite looks half-starved*

mitigate ['mɪtɪɡeɪt] *verb* to make less serious; *he was provoked, which to some extent mitigates his offence*

mitigating ['mɪtɪɡeɪtɪŋ] *adjective* **mitigating circumstances** *or* **factors** = things which make a crime less serious, which can excuse a crime; *there are mitigating circumstances which the judge should have taken into account*

mitigation [mɪtɪ'geɪʃn] *noun* reduction of a sentence or of the seriousness of a crime; *in mitigation, counsel submitted evidence of his client's work for charity*; *defence counsel made a speech in mitigation*

mitre ['maɪtə] *noun* tall pointed hat, worn by a bishop during religious ceremonies

mitt *or* **mitten** [mɪt *or* 'mɪtn] *noun* **(a)** glove without separate fingers; *she knitted a pair of woollen mittens for the baby* **(b)** **oven mitt** = glove to hold hot dishes with **(c)** glove which covers the main part of the hand but leaves the fingers bare; *it was so cold that he wore mittens when he went sketching*

mix [mɪks] **1** *noun* mixture of things together; *there was an odd mix of people at the party*; **cake mix** = main ingredients for a cake which are bought ready mixed in a packet **2** *verb* **(a)** to blend or to mingle things together; *she made the cake by mixing eggs and flour*; *oil and water do not mix* **(b)** to get along with other people; *he finds it hard to mix with the other staff in the office*

mixed [mɪkst] *adjective* made up of different things put together; *the reaction to the proposal has been rather mixed - some people approve, but others disapprove*; **I have very mixed feelings about the project** = I like some things about the project but not others; **mixed blessing** = something which can have advantages and disadvantages as well; *automation can be a mixed blessing - machines usually tend to be out of order when you need them most*; **in mixed company** = when both men and women are together; *that's not the sort of joke you can tell in mixed company; (in tennis)* **mixed doubles** = doubles match where a man and woman play against another man and woman; **mixed grill** = dish of different sorts of food grilled together, usually chops, sausages, bacon and mushrooms; **a mixed marriage** = marriage between two people of different races; **mixed school** = school with both boys and girls

mixed-up ['mɪkstʌp] *adjective* confused in your mind; *he's just a crazy mixed-up kid*

mixer ['mɪksə] *noun* machine for mixing; *blend all the ingredients together in a mixer*; **a concrete mixer** = machine with a container which turns, mixing cement, sand and water to make concrete

mixture ['mɪkstʃə] *noun* blend of things mixed together; *if the mixture is too thick, add some more water*; *his latest paintings are a strange mixture of shapes and colours*; **cough mixture** = liquid medicine to cure a cough

mix up ['mɪks 'ʌp] *verb* **(a)** to think someone or something is someone or something else; *I always mix her up with her sister* **(b)** **to be mixed up in** *or* **with** = to be part of, involved in; *he was mixed up in the bank scandal; how did she get mixed up with those awful people* **(c)** his notes got all mixed up = the notes were out of order, upside down, etc.

mix-up ['mɪksʌp] *noun (informal)* confusion; *we nearly didn't catch the plane because there was some mix-up over the tickets*

mm *abbreviation for* MILLIMETRE

mmm! [ʌm] *interjection showing that you smell nice food*; *Mmm! - I can smell fish and chips!*

mnemonic [nɪ'mɒnɪk] *noun* word, sentence or little poem which helps you remember something

COMMENT: to remember the order of the colours of the rainbow, think of 'Richard Of York Gained Battles In Vain' (= Red Orange Yellow Green Blue Indigo Violet)

moan [məʊn] **1** *noun* **(a)** low wailing sound; *rescuers could hear moans from inside the wreckage*; *when she read the news she gave a loud moan* **(b)** complaining generally; *the staff are having a moan about their pay* **2** *verb* **(a)** to make a low wail; *they could hear someone moaning in the cellar* **(b)** to complain about something; *they are moaning about working conditions*; *stop moaning, it will be your turn soon*

moat [məʊt] *noun* wide ditch with water in it, made as a protection round a castle or town; *to get into the castle you had to cross the moat*

mob [mɒb] **1** *noun* **(a)** uncontrolled crowd of people; *mobs of looters ran through the streets*; *an angry mob surged towards the palace gates* **(b)** *(informal)* **the mob** = criminal gangs; *New York police are trying to crack down on the mob's activities* **2** *verb* to surround with a wild crowd; *as the stars arrived they were mobbed by teenage fans* (NOTE: **mobbing - mobbed**)

mobile ['məʊbaɪl *US* 'məʊbl] **1** *adjective* which can move; **she is not very mobile** = she can't walk easily; **mobile library** = library in a van which travels around from place to place; **mobile shop** = van fitted out like a small shop which travels round selling meat, fish, groceries, etc. **2** *noun* **(a)** mobile phone; *I'll call him on his mobile; he gave me the number of his mobile* **(b)** artistic construction using small pieces of metal, card, etc. which when hung up move in the slightest draught; *they bought a mobile of clowns to hang over the baby's cot*

mobile home ['məʊbaɪl 'həʊm] *noun* large caravan in which people can live permanently, which is usually based in a special park (NOTE: American English is also **trailer**)

mobile phone ['məʊbaɪl 'fəʊn] *noun* small telephone which you can carry around; *the sound is bad because I'm calling on my mobile phone*

mobility [məʊ'bɪlɪti] *noun* being able to move easily; *people enjoy the mobility they get from owning a car*; *I've got much more mobility in my knee since I've been seeing the physiotherapist*

mobilization [məʊbɪlaɪ'zeɪʃn] *noun* bringing of people together, especially to join the armed forces in wartime; *the government ordered a general mobilization when they realized that the enemy troops were moving towards the border*

mobilize ['məʊbɪlaɪz] *verb* **(a)** to bring people together, especially bringing civilians to join the armed forces in wartime; *as soon as enemy troops were seen on the border, the President gave orders to mobilize* **(b)** to bring resources, etc., together; *unions are trying to mobilize support for a general strike*

mobster ['mɒbstə] *noun especially US (informal)* member of a criminal gang; *mobsters were meeting in a downtown restaurant when the police arrived*

mock [mɒk] **1** *adjective* imitation, false; *her handbag was made of mock crocodile skin*; *the house is built in mock medieval style*; **mock examinations** = trial examinations carried out before the real ones; *she has her mock A Levels next week* **2** *verb* to laugh at someone *or* something in an unkind way; *don't mock the singer - he's doing the best he can*

mockery ['mɒkəri] *noun* **(a)** thing which is only a bad imitation, which is of no use; *the trial was a mockery of justice*; **to make a mockery of something** = to make something seem useless; *the exam makes a mockery of the government's insistence on educational standards* **(b)** action of laughing at someone *or* something in an unkind way; *he could see the mockery in her eyes*

mocking ['mɒkɪŋ] *adjective* which laughs at someone *or* something in an unkind way; *his mocking laugh made her go red*

mock-up ['mɒkʌp] *noun* scale model of a new product for testing purposes; *they produced a mock-up of the new car*

modal ['məʊdəl] *adjective & noun* **modal auxiliaries** *or* **modal verbs** *or* **modals** = verbs used with other verbs to show permission, possibility, intention, duty, etc.; *see also* AUXILIARY

> COMMENT: the modal verbs in English are **can, could, dare, had better, may, might, must, need, ought to, shall, should, used to, will, would**

mod cons ['mɒd 'kɒnz] *noun (informal)* **all mod cons (all modern conveniences)** = all modern facilities such as central heating, cooker, fridge, dishwasher, telephone, etc.; *the flat is advertised to let with all mod cons*

mode [məʊd] *noun* way of doing something; *she will have to change her mode of life when she goes to university*; **mode of payment** = way in which payment is made (such as cash or cheque)

model ['mɒdl] **1** *noun* **(a)** small version of something larger; *the exhibition has a model of the new town hall; he spends his time making model planes* **(b)** person who wears new clothes to show them to customers; *he used only top models to show his designs during the London Fashion Week* **(c)** particular type of car, etc., produced at a particular time; *this is this year's model; he bought a 1979 model Mini*; **demonstration model** = piece of equipment used in demonstrations and then sold cheaply **2** *verb* **(a)** to make shapes in clay; *he modelled a statue of the little girl* **(b)** to copy; *she modelled her way of working on that of her father* = she imitated her father's way of working **(c)** to wear newly designed clothes to show to customers; *she is modelling the autumn collection by Dior* (NOTE: **modelling - modelled** but American spelling is **modeling - modeled**)

modelling *US* **modeling** ['mɒdəlɪŋ] *noun* **(a)** the job of being a fashion model; *with your looks you could take up modelling as a career* **(b)** making models; **modelling clay** = special clay for sculpture

modem ['məʊdem] *noun* device for sending data by telephone linking a computer to the telephone lines; *you'll need a modem to connect to the Internet*

moderate 1 *adjective* ['mɒdərət] not excessive; *she had moderate success in her exams; the economy has ended a period of steady moderate growth; the union's wage demands are really quite moderate* **2** *noun* ['mɒdərət] person whose political ideas are not very violent; *after years of struggle the moderates have gained control of the party* **3** *verb* ['mɒdəreɪt] to make or become less strong; *they moderated their demands; as the wind moderated, the waves became smaller*; **to**

moderate your language = to be less rude or violent in what you say; *she asked him to moderate his language*

moderately ['mɒdərətli] *adverb* **(a)** quite, fairly; *he's not a millionaire but he's been moderately successful; I'm moderately satisfied with the result* **(b)** quite cheap; *a moderately priced hotel*

moderation [mɒdə'reɪʃn] *noun* not being excessive; *she asked him to show some moderation in his language*; **in moderation** = not too much, not excessively; *red wine is good for you, but only in moderation*

modern ['mɒdən] *adjective* referring to the present time; *it is a fairly modern invention - it was patented only in the 1980s; her parents have a very modern attitude to boyfriends; you expect really modern offices to have automatic windows and air-conditioning systems;* **modern languages** = languages which are spoken today; *she's studying German in the modern languages department*

modern-day ['mɒdən'deɪ] *adjective* **(a)** at the present time; *modern-day living is becoming more and more stressful* **(b)** existing now, but very similar to somebody or something that existed in the past; *the army needs a modern-day Napoleon to lead it; he's a modern-day equivalent of a Victorian factory owner*

modernism ['mɒdənɪzm] *noun* the use of modern ideas and methods in art, especially in the mid-twentieth century; *simple, functional design was the main feature of modernism in architecture*

modernist ['mɒdənɪst] **1** *noun* person who uses modern ideas and methods; *the art world was divided into two groups - the modernists and the traditionalists* **2** *adjective* referring to modernism; *he has a collection of 20th century modernist art*

modernize ['mɒdənaɪz] *verb* to make something up to date; *it took a lot of effort to modernize the party; if we want to modernize the factory, we'll have to throw out all the old equipment*

modest ['mɒdɪst] *adjective* **(a)** not boasting; *he was very modest about his gold medal* **(b)** not excessively expensive; *the union's demands were really quite modest; we had a modest meal in a local restaurant*; **a modest flat** = a flat which does not look expensive

modestly ['mɒdɪstli] *adverb* in a modest way; *he modestly gave all the credit for his success to his family; she modestly acknowledged the applause from the audience*

modesty ['mɒdɪsti] *noun* **(a)** being modest, not being boastful; *without any false modesty, I think that our house is the most beautiful in the village; modesty forbids me to mention all my other achievements* **(b)** not being excessive, being quite small; *we think he stole some money from the petty cash box, but in view of the modesty of the sum involved, we won't report it to the police*

modification [mɒdɪfɪ'keɪʃn] *noun* alteration, change to a different type of work; *the latest modification should make the engine 10% more efficient*

modify ['mɒdɪfaɪ] *verb* to change or to alter something to fit a different use; *the management modified its wage proposals in the light of government guidelines; the car will have to be modified if we want to sell it here*

module ['mɒdjuːl] *noun* part of a larger thing made up of various sections; *the science course is made up of a series of modules*; **lunar module** = part of a spacecraft which lands on the moon; *the lunar module separated from the command module and made its way down to the moon's surface*

mogul ['məʊgəl] *noun* (*informal*) boss of a large business organization, especially a film or a TV company; *Mr Goldwyn, the Hollywood movie mogul*

moist [mɔɪst] *adjective* slightly wet; *mushrooms grow well in moist soil*; *to clean the oven, just wipe with a moist cloth* (NOTE: **moister - moistest**)

moisten ['mɔɪsn] *verb* to make slightly wet; *moisten the flap of the envelope and stick it down*; *moisten the flour mixture by adding milk*

moisture ['mɔɪstʃə] *noun* small drops of water in the air or on a surface; *there's a lot of moisture in the air*; *this soil is too dry - it lacks moisture* (NOTE: no plural)

moisturize ['mɔɪstʃəraɪz] *verb* to rub cream onto your skin to prevent it from being dry; *you should apply a moisturizing cream after being in the sun*

moisturizer ['mɔɪstʃəraɪzə] *noun* cream which makes the skin less dry; *moisturizer is supposed to keep your skin looking young and healthy*

molasses [mə'læsɪz] *noun* thick black syrup removed from sugar as it is being refined; *molasses is used in making real American baked beans* (NOTE: in British English is usually called **black treacle**)

mold, moldy [məʊld] *noun & verb US* = MOULD, MOULDY

mole [məʊl] *noun* (a) small mammal with soft dark grey fur, which lives under the ground; *moles are a menace when they make molehills all over my lawn* (b) small dark spot on the skin; *she has a little mole on her cheek*; *the doctor removed a mole from the back of her hand* (c) (*informal*) member of an organization who is in the pay of the enemy; *they planted a mole in our secret service*; *there's a mole in the department who is leaking information to the press*

molecular [mə'lekjʊlə] *adjective* referring to molecules; *the molecular structure of a substance*; **molecular biology** = study of the molecules which form the structure of living matter

molecule ['mɒlɪkjuːl] *noun* smallest unit in a substance that can exist by itself; *a molecule of carbon dioxide has one carbon atom and two oxygen atoms*

molehill ['məʊlhɪl] *noun* little heap of earth pushed up by a mole when digging; *he woke up one morning to find his lawn covered with molehills*; **to make a mountain out of a molehill** = to make a fuss about something which is not serious; *stop making mountains out of molehills, the situation isn't as bad as all that*

molest [mə'lest] *verb* to attack a child or a woman, especially in a sexual way; *he was accused of molesting children in the park*

molester [mə'lestə] *noun* person who molests someone; *the crowd attacked the police van when the child molester appeared in court*

mollify ['mɒlɪfaɪ] *verb* to make someone less annoyed or less upset; *in an effort to mollify the students, the government has changed its plans to charge them for university tuition*

mollusc *US* **mollusk** ['mɒləsk] *noun* animal with no backbone, but usually with a soft body and a shell, such as a snail, an oyster, etc.; *edible molluscs such as clams are often made into soup*; *an octopus is a mollusc though it has no shell*

molt [məʊlt] *US* = MOULT

molten ['məʊltən] *adjective* which has become liquid with heat; *the defenders poured molten lead from the castle walls onto the heads of the attackers*; *gold bars are made by pouring molten gold into moulds*; **molten lava** = liquid rock and minerals which flow out of an erupting volcano

mom [mɒm] *noun US* child's name for mother; *his mom always waits for him outside school* (NOTE: British English is **mum, mummy**)

moment ['məʊmənt] *noun* (a) very short time; *can you please wait a moment - the doctor is on the phone?*; *I only saw her for a moment*; **a moment ago** = just now; *we only heard of it a moment ago* (b) at any moment = very soon; *I expect it to rain at any moment*; **at the moment** = now; *I'm rather busy at the moment*; **at this moment in time** = at this particular point; *at this moment in time, it is not possible for me to answer reporters' questions*; **for the moment** = for a little while; *we won't take any action for the moment*

momentary ['məʊməntəri] *adjective* which only lasts for a short time; *I only caught a momentary glimpse of it*; *a momentary lapse can have appalling consequences*

momentous [mə'mentəs] *adjective* very important; *our hundredth anniversary is a momentous occasion for the school*; *deciding to sell to an American company was a momentous decision*

momentum [mə'mentəm] *noun* forward movement; *he stopped rowing a few metres from the end of the race but his momentum carried him over the finishing line*; **to gain momentum** *or* **to gather momentum** = to go forward faster; *the anti-war movement is gathering momentum*; **to lose momentum** = to go more slowly; *when a spinning top loses momentum, it wobbles and finally falls over*

momma *or* **mommy** ['mɒmæ or 'mɒmi] *US* (*informal*) *noun* child's name for mother; *I love my mommy*; *is your momma at home today?* (NOTE: British English is **Mummy** *or* **Mum**)

monarch ['mɒnək] *noun* king or queen; *France used to have a monarch but is now a republic*

monarchical [mə'nɑːkɪkl] *adjective* referring to a monarchy; *a monarchical government*

monarchy ['mɒnəki] *noun* system of government with a hereditary ruler such as a king or queen; *there's a big debate about whether we should get rid of the monarchy and become a republic*; **constitutional monarchy** = system of government where a king or queen is the head of state, but the country is ruled by an elected government; *all European countries with kings or queens are constitutional monarchies* (NOTE: plural is **monarchies**)

monastery ['mɒnəstri] *noun* religious establishment where monks live; the buildings of such a place; *the old monastery has been completely modernized and turned into a luxury hotel*; *the monks came out of their monastery and made their way down the mountain*; *women tourists are not allowed to visit some Greek monasteries* (NOTE: plural is **monasteries**;

note also that the equivalent establishment for women is a **convent**)

monastic [mɒ'næstɪk] *adjective* referring to monasteries or monks; *he found he was not suited to monastic life*; **monastic orders** = different groups of monks founded in the Middle Ages with different aims and different ways of living; *the Benedictines are one of the most important of the monastic orders*

Monday ['mʌndeɪ] *noun* first day of the week, the day between Sunday and Tuesday; *some supermarkets are shut on Mondays*; *she had to go to the doctor last Monday*; *next Monday is a bank holiday*; *the 15th is a Sunday, so the 16th must be a Monday*

monetary ['mʌnɪtəri] *adjective* referring to money or currency; *the government's monetary policy is in ruins*; **monetary union** = joining various national currencies together to form one single currency

money ['mʌni] *noun* **(a)** coins or notes which are used for buying things; *how much money have you got in the bank?*; *he doesn't earn very much money*; *we spent more money last week than in the previous month*; *we ran out of money in Spain and had to come home early*; *(informal)* **to have money to burn** = to have more money than you know what to do with; *they spent thousands on their house - they simply have money to burn*; *see also* SENSE **(b)** currency used in a country; *I want to change my British pounds into German money* **(c) to make money** = to make a profit; *(informal)* **it's money for old rope** *or* **it's money for jam** = it's a profit which is easy to make (NOTE: no plural)

money belt ['mʌni 'belt] *noun* belt with a purse attached, which is worn round the waist to prevent your money being stolen; *I always keep my passport and money in my money belt*

moneylender ['mʌnɪlendə] *noun* person who lends money as a business; *moneylenders charge a very high rate of interest*

money market ['mʌni 'mɑːkɪt] *noun* market for buying and selling short-term loans; *the international money markets are nervous*

money order ['mʌni 'ɔːdə] *noun* document which can be bought for passing money from one person to another through the post; *they paid by money order*; *I want a money order for £100, made payable to Mr Smith*

money supply ['mʌni sə'plaɪ] *noun* amount of money which exists in circulation in a country; *control of the money supply is seen as the key to reducing inflation*

mongrel ['mʌŋɡrəl] *adjective & noun* (dog) of mixed breed; *they've bought a mongrel puppy*

monitor ['mɒnɪtə] **1** *noun* screen of a computer or a small television screen used for checking what is happening; *the larger the monitor, the less strain it will be on your eyes*; *my computer has a colour monitor*; *a bank of monitors allows the police to see everything which happens in the shopping centre*; *details of flight arrivals and departures are displayed on monitors around the airport* **2** *verb* to check, to watch over (the progress of something); *doctors are monitoring her heart condition*; *how do you monitor the performance of the sales staff?*

monk [mʌŋk] *noun* man who is a member of a religious group and lives in a monastery; *the monks*

lived on a little island off the north coast; see also FRIAR (NOTE: the equivalent women are **nuns**)

monkey ['mʌŋki] **1** *noun* **(a)** a tropical mammal which lives in trees and normally has a tail; *monkeys ran up the trees looking for fruit*; **monkey nuts** = peanuts **(b) monkey wrench** = large spanner with an adjustable grip; *this spanner's too small - we need a monkey wrench* **(c)** *(informal)* **little monkey** = naughty little child **2** *verb* **to monkey around with something** = to play with something; *stop monkeying around with that axe!*

monkish ['mʌŋkɪʃ] *adjective* like a monk; *he was tired of his monkish life at university and wanted to get out into the real world*

mono ['mɒnəʊ] **1** *prefix meaning* one only, single; *monogamy* **2** *adjective* not stereophonic, which reproduces sound through a single channel; *a mono recording*

monogamous [mə'nɒɡəməs] *adjective* where a person has only one husband or wife; *some native tribes on the island are monogamous, but most are polygamous*

monogamy [mə'nɒɡəmi] *noun* system of marriage to only one person at a time; *monogamy is the only legal form of marriage in Western countries*; *compare* BIGAMY, POLYGAMY

monogram ['mɒnəɡræm] *noun* initials of a name linked together artistically; *he had the monogram PC on his signet ring*

monologue *US* **monolog** ['mɒnəlɒɡ] *noun* long speech by one actor or other person alone; *the little boy stood on a chair and recited a long monologue*

mononucleosis [mɒnənjuːklɪ'əʊsɪs] *noun* condition where there is an abnormal number of white blood cells in the body, giving sore throat, swellings and fever (NOTE: also called **glandular fever**)

monopolize [mə'nɒpəlaɪz] *verb* **(a)** to create a monopoly; *they managed to monopolize the market in oil* **(b)** to use something entirely for yourself; *don't monopolize the computer - let some of the others have a go*; **to monopolize the conversation** = to do all the talking and not let anyone else speak

monopoly [mə'nɒpəli] *noun* system where one person or company supplies all of a product in one area without any competition; *the state has a monopoly of the tobacco trade*; *the company has a monopoly of French wine imports* (NOTE: plural is **monopolies**)

monosyllabic [mɒnəsɪ'læbɪk] *adjective* **(a)** (word) with only one syllable; *monosyllabic words such as 'hat' and 'cat'* **(b)** using short simple words and not saying much; *in answer to the reporters' questions he gave a series of monosyllabic replies*

monosyllable ['mɒnəsɪləbl] *noun* word which only has one syllable; *he replied in a couple of monosyllables*

monotonous [mə'nɒtənəs] *adjective* not varied, boring, which does not change; *doing the same job every day is getting rather monotonous*; *the radio played monotonous speeches by the president*

monotony [mə'nɒtəni] *noun* lack of variety, which leads to boredom; *she was trying to find something to break the monotony of her stay in hospital*; *they couldn't stand the monotony of life in the country, and moved back to London as quickly as they could*

monsoon [mɒnˈsuːn] *noun* **(a)** season of wind and rain in tropical countries; *at last the monsoon brought relief after the hot dry summer* **(b)** wind which blows in opposite directions according to the season, especially the wind blowing north from the Indian Ocean in the summer; *they sailed north with the monsoon*

monster [ˈmɒnstə] **1** *noun* **(a)** horrible, strange and frightening creature; *the Loch Ness Monster is said to be a large dinosaur living in the bottom of Loch Ness in Scotland*; *she drew a picture of a green monster with purple horns and huge teeth* **(b)** cruel or wicked person; *her stepfather was a monster who used to beat her with his belt* **2** *adjective (informal)* very large; *look at the monster cabbage Dad's grown in the garden*; *what a monster sandwich!*

monstrosity [mɒnˈstrɒsɪti] *noun* horrible, large, ugly thing; *the building is a monstrosity and ought to be demolished*

monstrous [ˈmɒnstrəs] *adjective* **(a)** huge, ugly, horrible; *a monstrous sea serpent* **(b)** extremely large; *the students left behind a monstrous pile of dirty washing* **(c)** very shocking or unfair; *that's an absolutely monstrous accusation*

month [mʌnθ] *noun* **(a)** one of the twelve parts that a year is divided into; *December is the last month of the year*; *what day of the month is it today?*; *there was a lot of hot weather last month, in fact it was hot all month (long) she's taken a month's holiday to visit her parents in Australia* **(b)** **months** = a long time; *it's months since we went to the cinema*; **for months** = for a very long time; *we haven't had any homework for months*

monthly [ˈmʌnθli] **1** *adjective & adverb* happening every month; *he is paying for his car by monthly instalments*; *my monthly salary cheque is late*; *she gets paid monthly* **2** *noun* magazine which is published each month; *I buy all the computer monthlies* (NOTE: plural is **monthlies**)

monument [ˈmɒnjumənt] *noun* **(a)** stone, building, statue, etc., erected in memory of someone who is dead; *they put up a monument to the people from the village who died in the war*; **the Monument** = tall column erected in the City of London to commemorate the Great Fire of 1666 **(b)** **ancient monument** = building which is officially listed as being very old and is preserved by the state; *the chapel is an ancient monument and is protected*

monumental [mɒnjuˈmentl] *adjective* **(a)** very large and impressive; *Brahms' monumental Fourth Symphony* **(b)** very serious; *he made a monumental error* **(c)** referring to a monument; **monumental arch** = stone arch built to commemorate something such a victory; **monumental mason** = person who makes gravestones

moo [muː] **1** *noun* noise made by a cow; *I heard a moo from behind the cowshed* **2** *verb* to make a noise like a cow; *the cows were mooing because they wanted to be milked*

moo-cow [ˈmuːkau] *noun (children's word for)* cow; *look at the moo-cows in the field!*

mood [muːd] *noun* **(a)** feeling in general; *wait until she's in a good mood and then ask her*; *he's in a foul mood this morning*; *her mood changed as soon as she opened the letter*; *a mood of gloom fell over the office* **(b)** fit of bad temper; *don't talk to the boss - he's in one of his moods*

moody [ˈmuːdi] *adjective* often in a bad temper; changing quickly from being in a good mood to a bad one; *she's very moody - sometimes happy and helpful, sometimes sulky and bad-tempered* (NOTE: **moodier - moodiest**)

moon [muːn] *noun* body in the sky which goes round the earth and shines at night; *the first man walked on the moon in 1969*; *the moon is shining very brightly tonight*; *there's no moon because it's cloudy*; **full moon** = time when the moon is a full circle; *by the light of the full moon they could clearly make out figures moving on the hillside*; **new moon** = time when the moon is visible as only a thin crescent; *the guerillas waited for the new moon to make their attack*; *(informal)* **once in a blue moon** = very rarely; *we only go to the theatre once in a blue moon*; **to be over the moon about something** = to be very happy and excited; *she's over the moon about her exam results*; *they're absolutely over the moon with their first baby*

moonlight [ˈmuːnlaɪt] **1** *noun* light from the moon; *we could see the path clearly in the moonlight*; *(informal)* **to do a moonlight flit** = to go away (at night) leaving many unpaid bills; *they had booked the hotel room for a week, but on the Friday night they did a moonlight flit* **2** *verb* to do a second job, often in the evening, for cash not declared to the Inland Revenue, and separate from your regular job; *he works full-time in a garage, and moonlights as a barman in a pub in the evenings*; *the tax people are stepping up their investigations into people who moonlight*

moonlighting [ˈmuːnlaɪtɪŋ] *noun (informal)* doing a second job, usually in the evening, separate from your regular job; *he makes thousands of pounds a year from moonlighting*; *moonlighting costs the country millions of pounds a year in lost taxes*

moor [ˈmuə or mɔː] **1** *noun* poor land covered with heather and grass and small shrubs; *the horsemen galloped across the moor*; *the Lake District is wild country, full of moors and forests* **2** *verb* to attach a boat to something; *the boat was moored to the river bank*; *he rowed up to the jetty and moored his boat with a piece of rope*

moorings [ˈmuərɪŋz] *noun* **(a)** place where a boat is moored; *the boat had been moved to new moorings* **(b)** ropes used to attach a boat; *we cast off our moorings and rowed out into the river*

moorland [ˈmuələnd] *noun* area of land which is uncultivated and covered with grass and low shrubs such as heather; *roughly half the area is cultivated and the rest is moorland*

moose [muːs] *noun* large deer from North America; *a herd of moose crossed the river*; *three moose came out of the forest* (NOTE: plural is **moose**; similar to the European **elk**)

moot [muːt] **1** *adjective* **moot point** = question which is open to discussion; *it's a moot point whether their action was justified* **2** *verb (formal)* to raise a question; *the idea was first mooted in 1967*

mop [mɒp] **1** *noun* soft brush for washing dishes; brush with a head made of soft string or foam rubber, used for washing floors; **mop of hair** = long and untidy hair; *in spite of his torn clothes and mop of red hair he still looked a sweet little boy* **2** *verb* **(a)** to wash with a mop; *she was mopping the kitchen floor* **(b)** to mop

your brow = to wipe your forehead when you are hot and sweating; *he stopped digging to mop his brow with his handkerchief* (NOTE: mopping - mopped)

mope [məʊp] *verb* to sit miserably, thinking about how bad things are; *don't sit there moping, come and help with the washing up*; *when his girlfriend left him he moped for weeks*

moped ['məʊped] *noun* two-wheeled cycle with a low-powered engine; *it's easier to get through the traffic on a moped* (NOTE: do not confuse with the verb moped ['məʊpd])

mop up ['mɒp 'ʌp] *verb* (a) to clear up spilt liquid; *use a cloth to mop up the water on the floor*; *we spent days mopping up after the floods* (b) to overcome small groups of enemy fighters; *it took our soldiers several days to mop up the last pockets of enemy resistance in the mountains*

moraine [mə'rem] *noun* gravel and earth carried by a glacier and deposited in a valley as the glacier melts

moral ['mɒrəl] **1** *adjective* (a) referring to right and wrong behaviour; *judges have a moral obligation to be impartial*; *he refused to join the army on moral grounds* (b) referring to good behaviour; *she's a very moral person*; **to give someone moral support** = to encourage someone without active help; *motorists showed their moral support for the striking nurses by hooting their horns as they drove past the hospital* **2** *noun* (a) lesson which you can find in a story; *there must be a moral in this somewhere*; *the moral of the story is that if you always tell lies, no one will believe you when you tell the truth* (b) **morals** = way of behaving of society as a whole or of each individual; *some people blame TV for corrupting public morals*

morale [mə'rɑːl] *noun* confident feeling; *the manager gave us a pep talk to try to raise the morale of the workforce*; *low morale has made everyone gloomy*; *after his interview, his morale was at a low ebb*

morality [mə'ræləti] *noun* sense of moral standards; *where is the morality in spending millions on celebrating the president's wedding and not doing anything to help the poor and disabled?* (NOTE: no plural)

morass [mə'ræs] *noun* (a) area which is very muddy, marshy or swampy; *heavy rain had turned the playing field into a morass*; *the vehicle was sinking deeper and deeper into the morass* (b) problems or difficulties which prevent any progress; *we were caught up in a morass of paperwork*

moratorium [mɒrə'tɔːriəm] *noun* temporary stop, such as to repayments of money owed; *the banks called for a moratorium on interest payments*; *the government has declared a moratorium on nuclear testing* (NOTE: plural is moratoriums *or* moratoria)

morbid ['mɔːbɪd] *adjective* (a) showing an unhealthy interest in death or unpleasant things; *even as a little boy he showed a morbid curiosity in dead butterflies*; *all this talk about death and decomposition seems distinctly morbid to me* (b) diseased, referring to disease; *the X rays showed a morbid condition of the kidneys*

more [mɔː] **1** *adjective* extra, which is added; *do you want any more tea?*; *there are many more trains on weekdays than on Sundays* **2** *pronoun* extra thing; *is there any more of that soup?*; *£300 for that suit - that's more than I can afford!*; *we've only got nine men, we need two more to make a football team* **3** *adverb* (a)

(used with adjectives to make the comparative) **the dog was more frightened than I was**; *she is much more intelligent than her sister*; *the dinner was even more unpleasant than I had thought it would be* (b) **more or less** = not completely; *the rain has more or less stopped*; *I've more or less finished my homework* (c) **not...any more** = no longer; *she doesn't write to me any more*; *we don't go to France on holiday any more* (d) **once more** = one more time; *he played the song once more before the show ended* (NOTE: more is used to make the comparative of adjectives which do not take the ending -er)

moreish ['mɔːrɪʃ] *adjective* (*informal*) which makes you want to eat more; *I can't stop eating these biscuits - they're so moreish*

moreover [mɔː'rəʊvə] *adverb* (*formal*) in addition; *we all felt cold, wet and hungry, and moreover, we were lost*; *if you do that again I will report you to the head teacher and moreover tell your parents*

morgue [mɔːg] *noun* building where dead bodies are kept before being buried; *the family had to go to the morgue to identify the body*

moribund ['mɒrɪbʌnd] *adjective* ineffective and likely to come to an end soon; *the custom of wearing top hats at weddings is becoming moribund*

morning ['mɔːnɪŋ] *noun* (a) first part of the day before 12 o'clock; *every morning he took his briefcase and went to the office*; *tomorrow morning we will be meeting our Japanese agents*; *have you read the morning paper?*; *if we want to be in Paris for lunch you have to get the early morning train*; **morning coffee** = coffee served with biscuits as a snack in the middle of the morning; **morning dress** *or* **morning suit** = clothes for men consisting of a black tail coat, light grey waistcoat and striped black and grey trousers, worn by men at weddings; **early morning tea** = tea brought to a hotel guest's bedroom early in the morning, often with the day's newspaper (b) (*showing times*) **I woke up at four in the morning** = at 04.00 (NOTE: in the morning is often written and said as a.m.: we were woken at four a.m.)

Moroccan [mə'rɒkən] **1** *adjective* referring to Morocco; *here are some photographs of our Moroccan holiday* **2** *noun* person from Morocco; *the Moroccans are very proud of their national football team*

Morocco [mə'rɒkəʊ] *noun* country in North Africa; *we went on a business trip to Morocco* (NOTE: capital: Rabat; people: Moroccans; language: Arabic; currency: dirham)

moron ['mɔːrɒn] *noun* (*informal*) very stupid person; *only a complete moron would light a match to find a gas leak*

moronic [mə'rɒnɪk] *adjective* (*informal*) very stupid; *the manager criticized the moronic attitude of his fans towards the opposing team*

morose [mə'rəʊs] *adjective* miserable and bad-tempered; *faced with a group of morose salesmen you need to find something to motivate them*

morphine ['mɔːfiːn] *noun* drug made from opium, used to relieve pain; *the doctor gave him a morphine injection*

Morse code ['mɔːs 'kəʊd] *noun* system of dots and dashes used for sending messages by radio; *the* *message was sent in Morse code; in Morse code, SOS is dot dot dot, dash dash dash, dot dot dot*

> COMMENT: the Morse code was officially abandoned in 1998

mortal ['mɔːtl] **1** *adjective* **(a)** which causes death; *he suffered a mortal blow in the fight*; **mortal enemy** = enemy who wants to kill you **(b)** referring to death; *we are all mortal* = we are all going to die eventually; **mortal remains** = corpse **2** *noun* **an ordinary mortal** = an ordinary human being; *Olympic athletes can run at speeds which we ordinary mortals have no chance of reaching*

mortality [mɔː'tælɪti] *noun* **(a)** being a human, knowing that all human beings must die; *having a heart attack makes you acutely aware of your own mortality* **(b) mortality rate** = number of deaths as a percentage of the total population; *the mortality rate declined dramatically when antibiotics became available*

mortally ['mɔːtli] *adverb* ending in death; *he was mortally wounded in battle*

mortar ['mɔːtə] *noun* **(a)** cement mixture for holding together the bricks or stones used in building; *the wall needs rebuilding - you can see how the mortar is crumbling away* **(b)** bowl for crushing things with a pestle; *crush the seeds with a mortar and pestle*

mortgage ['mɔːgɪdʒ] **1** *noun* **(a)** agreement by which someone lends money on the security of a property; *he took out a mortgage on the house*; *she bought a house with a £200,000 mortgage* **(b)** money lent on the security of a property; *she is behind with her mortgage repayments*; **second mortgage** = second loan obtained using a property which is already mortgaged as a security **2** *verb* to give a property as security for a loan; *he mortgaged his house to set up his business*; *because his house was already mortgaged, he had to take out a second mortgage to pay for his car*

mortician [mɔː'tɪʃn] *noun US* person who prepares a dead body for burial and organizes funerals; *the mortician asked if we wanted a moment to pay our last respects* (NOTE: British English is **undertaker**)

mortuary ['mɔːtjuəri] *noun* place where dead bodies are kept before burial; *the body was removed to the hospital mortuary* (NOTE: plural is **mortuaries**)

mosaic [mə'zeɪɪk] *noun* picture made of tiny pieces of coloured stone stuck to a wall or floor; *the floor was covered with mosaics showing scenes from Greek mythology*

Moslem ['mɒzləm] *see* MUSLIM

mosque [mɒsk] *noun* building where Muslims meet for prayer; *everyone must take off their shoes before entering a mosque*; *Muslims are called to prayer from the minaret of the mosque*

mosquito [məs'kiːtəu] *noun* small flying insect which sucks blood and gives an irritating sting; *her arms were covered with mosquito bites*; *I was woken up by a mosquito buzzing round my head*; *mosquitoes can be carriers of diseases such as malaria*; **mosquito net** = thin net spread over a bed to prevent mosquitoes biting at night; *your mosquito net won't do much good - it's got a big hole in it*; **mosquito repellent** = liquid which is sprayed or applied to the skin, to keep off mosquitoes (NOTE: plural is **mosquitoes**)

moss [mɒs] *noun* small green plant like fur, growing in compact low clumps in damp places on the ground or on stones; *the rocks near the stream are all covered in moss*; *she sat down on a moss-covered bank* (NOTE: plural is **mosses**)

most [məust] **1** *adjective* the largest number of; *most people go on holiday in the summer*; *he spends most evenings watching TV*; *most apples are sweet* **2** *pronoun* very large number or amount; *most of the work was done by my wife*; *she spent most of the evening on the phone to her sister*; *it rained for most of our holiday*; *most of the children in the group can ride bikes* **3** *adverb* **(a)** *(making the superlative)* *she's the most intelligent child in the class*; *the most important thing if you are a salesman is to be able to drive a car* **(b)** very; *I find it most frustrating that the train service is so slow*; *most probably the plane will be held up by the fog*; *thank you, you are most kind* (NOTE: **most** is used to form the superlative of adjectives which do not take the ending **-est**)

mostly ['məustli] *adverb* usually, most often; *we sometimes go to France for our holidays, but we mostly stay in Britain*; *the staff are mostly women of about twenty*

MOT (test) [eməu'tiː] *noun* mechanical test for cars which are more than three years old; *my car failed its MOT because there was a hole in the exhaust pipe*; *you need to have a valid MOT certificate to get a tax disk for your car*

motel [məu'tel] *noun* hotel for car drivers where there is a parking space for every room; *they checked into the motel last Saturday*; *the hotel is full, but there is a motel just out of town near the motorway junction*

moth [mɒθ] *noun* flying insect with large wings like a butterfly, but which flies mainly at night; *moths were flying round the street light*; *she screamed as a moth flew into her face*

mothballs ['mɒθbɔːlz] *noun* **(a)** balls of a chemical substance put among clothes to keep moths away; *my winter coat smells of mothballs* **(b) in mothballs** = stored for future use; *three ships have been put in mothballs*; *they are planning to bring the aircraft carrier out of mothballs*

mother ['mʌðə] **1** *noun* **(a)** woman who has children; *he's twenty-two but still lives with his mother*; *her mother's a dentist*; *Mother! there's someone asking for you on the telephone!* **(b)** *(informal)* **shall I be mother?** = shall I pour the tea?; *who's going to be mother?*; *John, will you be mother?* (NOTE: **Mother** is sometimes used as a name for a **mother**, but in British English **Mum** or **Mummy**, and in American English **Mom** or **Mommy** are more usual) **2** *verb* to look after someone or something very carefully; *the new recruits will have to be mothered along until they get some experience*

motherhood ['mʌðəhud] *noun* being a mother; *how is your daughter coping with motherhood?*

Mothering Sunday ['mʌðərɪŋ 'sʌndeɪ] *noun* = MOTHER'S DAY

mother-in-law ['mʌðərɪn'lɔː] *noun* mother of your wife or husband; *my mother-in-law is visiting us for Christmas*; **mother-in-law's tongue** = type of house plant with a few tall stiff vertical leaves (NOTE: plural is **mothers-in-law**)

motherland ['mʌðəlænd] *noun* country of your ancestors, especially a country from which colonists have emigrated; *the old people get very sentimental talking about the motherland*; compare FATHERLAND

motherly ['mʌðəli] *adjective* maternal, like a mother; *she kept a motherly eye on all the children; the manager's wife is a very motherly woman and looks after the staff as if they were her children; she didn't show much motherly love towards her son when he was in jail*

mother-of-pearl ['mʌðəəv'pɜːl] *noun* shiny substance found on the inside of oyster shells; *a brooch inlaid with mother-of-pearl; a shirt with mother-of-pearl buttons*

Mother's Day ['mʌðəz 'deɪ] *noun* day in the spring when mothers get presents or cards or flowers from their children; *look at the flowers the children brought me for Mother's Day!* (NOTE: also called **Mothering Sunday**)

motif [məʊ'tiːf] *noun* distinctive pattern which is repeated in a design or in a piece of music; *the carpet has a floral motif which is repeated on the wallpaper; the same motif played by the flutes reappears in the final movement*

motion ['məʊʃn] **1** *noun* **(a)** act of moving; *the motion of the ship made him feel ill;* in motion = moving; *do not try to get on or off while the train is in motion; now that we have planning permission for the new sports hall, we can set things in motion to get the foundations laid* **(b)** movement of part of the body; *a slight motion of his head indicated to the auctioneer that he was making a bid; she made a motion as if to get up, but in the end stayed in her seat* **(c)** to go through the motions = to do something for the sake of appearances without believing in it; *he's lost all interest in his job - he's just going through the motions* **(d)** *(formal)* faeces, the solid waste matter in a bowel movement; *the doctor asked her if her motions were regular* **(e)** proposal which is to be put to the vote at a meeting; *the motion was carried by 220 votes to 196;* to second a motion = to support the person who proposed the motion; to table a motion = to put forward a proposal for discussion by putting details of it on the table at a meeting **2** *verb* to make a movement with your hands which means something; *he motioned us to our chairs; she motioned to me to open the window*

motionless ['məʊʃənləs] *adjective* not moving; *herons can stand motionless for hours at the edge of the stream, waiting for a fish to appear; she lay motionless on the ground and everyone thought she was dead*

motion picture ['məʊʃn 'pɪktʃə] *noun* US cinema film; *the 'Third Man' is a classic motion picture starring Orson Welles and Joseph Cotton; the American motion picture industry is based in Hollywood*

motivate ['məʊtɪveɪt] *verb* to encourage someone to do something; *it's the job of the coach to motivate his team; we need some extra incentives to motivate the sales force;* highly motivated = eager; *the staff are all highly motivated and eager to tackle the new job; she's a hard-working, highly-motivated individual;* racially motivated = done because of racial hatred; *the arson attack on the house was racially motivated*

motivation [məʊtɪ'veɪʃn] *noun* encouragement to do something; *the staff lack motivation - hence the poor sales; his only motivation is money*

motive ['məʊtɪv] **1** *noun* reason for doing something; *the police are trying to find a motive for the murder* **2** *adjective* **motive force** = which makes something move; *wind is the motive force which makes a windmill turn*

motley ['mɒtli] *adjective* of varied types or colours; *he came to the meeting with a motley crowd of supporters*

motor ['məʊtə] **1** *noun* **(a)** the part of a machine which makes it work; *the model plane has a tiny electric motor* **(b)** car; motor insurance = insuring a car, the driver and passengers in case of accident **(c)** motor nerve = nerve which carries impulses from the brain to the muscles and makes part of the body move **2** *verb* *(old)* to travel in a car for pleasure; *we motored down to Brighton*

motorbike ['məʊtəbaɪk] *noun* *(informal)* motorcycle, a two-wheeled cycle driven by a motor; *motorbike accidents are quite common; I'm learning to ride a motorbike*

motorboat ['məʊtəbəʊt] *noun* boat driven by a motor; *they watched a motorboat towing a waterskier across the bay*

motorcar ['məʊtəkɑː] *noun* *(old)* = CAR

motorcycle ['məʊtəsaɪkl] *noun* two-wheeled cycle driven by a motor; *he fell off his motorcycle; he learnt to ride a motorcycle when he was 65*

motorcyclist ['məʊtəsaɪklɪst] *noun* person who rides a motorcycle; *all motorcyclists have to wear crash helmets; the police watched as the motorcyclist raced away up the hill*

motoring ['məʊtərɪŋ] **1** *noun* *(old)* driving of a car; school of motoring = driving school; *the costs of motoring or motoring costs seem to increase year by year* **2** *adjective* referring to driving of cars; *the motoring organizations are asking the government for a reduction in tax; he was convicted of a motoring offence*

motorist ['məʊtərɪst] *noun* person who drives a car; *the government is trying to persuade motorists to use their cars less; motorists are warned of long delays on all roads leading to the coast*

motor scooter ['məʊtə 'skuːtə] *noun* small type of motorbike with a curving shield in front of the seat and a platform for the feet; *she dodged through the traffic on her motor scooter* (NOTE: also called simply a **scooter**)

motorway ['məʊtəweɪ] *noun* fast road with several lanes and very few junctions, on which traffic can travel at high speeds; *we drove south along the new motorway; you will get there faster if you take the motorway; there is a lot of traffic on the motorway on bank holidays* (NOTE: the American equivalent is **expressway, freeway**)

COMMENT: in Britain, motorways are given numbers, following the letter M: **take the M3 if you want to go to Wales; the M25 goes right round London**

motto ['mɒtəʊ] *noun* **(a)** short phrase which is used to sum up an attitude; *'Be Prepared' is the motto of the Scouts* **(b)** piece of paper inside a Christmas cracker, with an amusing phrase or bad joke written on it; *every cracker contains a toy, a paper hat and a motto* (NOTE: plural is **mottoes**)

mould US **mold** [məʊld] **1** *noun* **(a)** soft earth; leaf mould = soft earth formed from dead leaves; *plant the* bulbs in pots of leaf mould **(b)** hollow shape into which a liquid is poured, so that when the liquid becomes hard it takes that shape; *gold bars are made by pouring molten gold into moulds*; **jelly mould** = shape for making jelly; *pour the jelly into the mould and put it in the fridge to set* **(c)** grey fungus which looks like powder; *throw that bread away - it's got mould on it* **2** *verb* to shape something; *she moulded a little dog out of clay*

moulding *US* **molding** ['məʊldɪŋ] *noun* thing which has been moulded, especially plaster decorations on the ceiling of a room; *there are elaborate mouldings around the doorways*

mouldy *US* **moldy** ['məʊldi] *adjective* covered with mould; *the health inspectors found mouldy bread in the kitchen*; *these potatoes have gone mouldy*

moult *US* **molt** [məʊlt] *verb* to lose feathers or hair at a certain period of the year; *most animals moult at the beginning of summer*

mound [maʊnd] *noun* **(a)** small hill; *they built a mound of stones to mark the farthest point they reached*; *the castle is built on top of a mound*; *Stonehenge is surrounded by burial mounds* **(b)** heap of things; *there's a mound of letters waiting to be signed*; *(informal)* **mounds of** = a large quantity of; *there's mounds of washing to be done*

mount [maʊnt] **1** *noun* **(a)** *(usually in names)* mountain; *Mount Kilimanjaro*; *Mount St Helens* **(b)** frame for a picture; *he stuck the photograph into a mount and put it on his desk* **(c)** *(formal)* horse, etc., on which a rider sits; *he tried to make his mount jump the fence* **2** *verb* **(a)** to climb on to something; to climb up something; *they mounted their horses and rode off*; *he mounted the stairs two at a time*; *the car skidded, mounted the pavement, and hit a wall* **(b)** to increase; *tension is mounting as the time for the football final approaches* **(c)** to **mount guard over** = to stand on guard to protect something; *soldiers are mounting guard over the shops to prevent looting*; *there were ten security men mounting guard over the president as he went for a walk in the town* **(d)** to set something in a cardboard frame or in a metal brooch, etc.; *mount the photograph in a black frame*; *the diamonds were mounted in silver* **(e)** to organize something; *the unions are mounting a campaign to get the government to back down*; *our forces mounted a surprise attack on the enemy*; *the British Museum is mounting an exhibition of drawings*; *the coup was mounted by exiles living across the border*

mountain ['maʊntən] *noun* **(a)** very high land, rising much higher than the land which surrounds it; *Everest is the highest mountain in the world*; *every weekend we go climbing in the Scottish mountains*; *how far is it to the top of the mountain?*; **mountain railway** = special railway which climbs steep mountains **(b)** large amount; *there is a mountain of letters on the manager's desk*; **mountains of** = a large quantity of; *I have mountains of work to do*

mountain bike ['maʊntən 'baɪk] *noun* specially strong bike with thick tyres, designed for riding over rough ground but not necessarily used on mountains; *all my friends have got mountain bikes*; *mountain bikes are great for going along country paths*

mountaineer [maʊntə'nɪə] *noun* person who climbs mountains as a sport; *three mountaineers were killed by the avalanche*

mountaineering [maʊntə'nɪːrɪŋ] *noun* sport of climbing mountains; *at the age of 20 he decided to take up mountaineering*

mountainous ['maʊntənəs] *adjective* **(a)** with many high mountains; *it is a mountainous region, and very difficult for tanks and artillery*; *parts of Scotland are very mountainous* **(b)** very high; *mountainous waves crashed over the ship*

mountain rescue ['maʊntən 'reskjuː] *noun* service which provides experienced climbers to help people in difficulties on mountains; *the mountain rescue services radioed for helicopters to bring down the injured skiers*

mounted ['maʊntɪd] *adjective* riding on horseback; **mounted police** = policemen on horses; *mounted police were on hand to keep the crowds under control*

mounting ['maʊntɪŋ] *adjective* increasing; *the crowd waited with mounting excitement*; *the committee was horrified at the mounting cost of the exhibition*

mount up [maʊnt 'ʌp] *verb* to increase; *during his absence the unpaid bills mounted up*

mourn [mɔːn] *verb* to feel very sad about someone *or* something; *they are mourning their father who died last week*; *she's mourning for her lost youth*

mourner ['mɔːnə] *noun* person who mourns someone who has died; **the mourners** = people attending a funeral; *members of the royal family were among the mourners*

mournful ['mɔːnfʊl] *adjective* very sad; *he played a mournful tune on the bagpipes*; *he has a permanently mournful expression*; *why is he looking so mournful this morning?*

mourning ['mɔːnɪŋ] *noun* **(a)** period of time when you grieve over the death of a person; *the official period of mourning for the dead president was one week* **(b)** dark clothes worn as a mark of respect for someone who has died; *she is in mourning for her husband who died last week* (NOTE: do not confuse with morning)

mouse [maʊs] **1** *noun* **(a)** small animal with a long tail, often living in holes in the walls of houses; *I saw a mouse sitting in the middle of the kitchen floor*; *our cat is good at catching mice* (NOTE: plural is **mice** [maɪs]) **(b)** device which is held in the hand and moved across a flat surface, used to control a cursor on a computer monitor; *you can cut, paste and copy using the mouse*; *using the mouse, move the cursor to the start button and click twice*

mouselike ['maʊslaɪk] *adjective* small and insignificant, like a mouse; *she's a quiet mouselike woman*

mousetrap ['maʊstræp] *noun* device for catching and killing mice when they have become a pest; *our cat is so slow that we've decided to get a mousetrap for the kitchen*

mousse [muːs] *noun* light food made of whipped eggs, cream and flavouring; *you can have chocolate mousse for dessert*

moustache *US* **mustache** [mə'staːʃ *US* 'mʌstæʃ] *noun* hair grown on the upper lip; *he looks quite different now he's shaved off his moustache*

mousy *or* **mousey** ['maʊsi] *adjective* **(a)** dull brown colour; *he has mousy hair and a little*

moustache (b) small and insignificant; *her secretary is a mousy little woman*

mouth 1 [mauθ] *noun* (a) opening in your face through which you take in food and drink, and which has your teeth and tongue inside; *it's not polite to talk with your mouth full*; *he snored because he slept with his mouth open*; *the cat was carrying a mouse in its mouth*; **to make your mouth water** = to look so good that your mouth fills with saliva; *those cakes make my mouth water*; *his new car made her mouth water* (b) round entrance to a hole; *the mouth of the cave is hidden by bushes*; *the train came out of the mouth of the tunnel* (NOTE: plural is **mouths** [mauðz]) 2 [mauð] *verb* to speak without making any sound; *I could see her mouthing something on the other side of the window*

mouthful ['mauθful] *noun* (a) amount which you can hold in your mouth; *he took a mouthful of meat and chewed hard*; *she had a mouthful of soup* (b) *(informal)* complicated word or phrase; *I'll spell the name for you - it's a bit of a mouthful*

mouth-organ ['mauθ ɔːgən] *noun* small musical instrument which you play by blowing and moving across your mouth to get different notes; *he sat in the corner of the café, playing his mouth-organ* (NOTE: also called a **harmonica**)

mouthpiece ['mauθpiːs] *noun* (a) part of a musical instrument which goes into the mouth; *there is a reed attached to the mouthpiece of a clarinet* (b) the part of a telephone that you speak into; *he put his hand over the mouthpiece so I couldn't hear what he was saying* (c) person who speaks on behalf of someone, especially a political party; *she acts as the mouthpiece for the party*

mouthwash ['mauθwɒʃ] *noun* antiseptic solution used to treat infection in the mouth; *you could try using a mouthwash if you have bad breath*

mouth-watering ['mauθwɔːtrɪŋ] *adjective* which looks and smells so delicious that it makes your mouth water; *a plate of mouth-watering cream cakes*

movable ['muːvəbl] *adjective* which can be moved; *seats in the first class cabin have movable armrests*

move [muːv] 1 *noun* (a) change from one place to another; *the police were watching every move he made*; *it's time to make a move* = we must leave; **on the move** = moving; *after I've been on the move all day I just want to get home and go to bed*; **get a move on!** = hurry up! (b) changing the place of a piece in chess, etc.; *it's your move - I've just moved my queen* (c) action done to achieve something; *it was a clever move to get here early before the crowds arrive*; **what's the next move?** = what do we have to do next?; **who will make the first move?** = who will act first? (d) change of house or office; *luckily, nothing got broken during our move* 2 *verb* (a) to change the place of something; *move the chairs to the side of the room*; *who's moved my drink? - I left it on the table*; *he moved his hand to show he had heard* (b) to change your position; *some animal was moving about outside the tent*; *the only thing moving was the tip of the cat's tail*; **don't move!** = stand still (c) to leave one house, flat or office to go to another; *he got a new job and they had to move from Scotland to London*; *they didn't like living in the country, so they moved back to London*; *the company is moving office, from London Road to the centre of town* (d) to propose formally that a motion

be accepted by a meeting; *I move that the meeting should adjourn for ten minutes* (e) to make someone feel sad; *the sound of the bagpipes moved her to tears*; *we were all deeply moved by the ceremony*

move about ['muːv ə'baut] *verb* to change the place of something often; to change position often; *I can hear someone moving about downstairs*; *he keeps on moving the chairs about*; *crowds of people were moving about in the square*

move away ['muːv ə'weɪ] *verb* to change the place of something to a place further away; *the ship gradually moved away from the quay*; **we're moving away from Oxford** = we are going to live in another town away from Oxford

move back ['muːv 'bæk] *verb* (a) to go back; *after the meeting, please move the chairs back to where they were before* (b) to change house or office to where you were before; *after three years in Central London they decided to move back to the country*

move in ['muːv 'ɪn] *verb* (a) to put your furniture into a new house and start to live there; *they only moved in last week*; *they got married and moved in with her parents* (b) to come together as a group; *the lions moved in for the kill*; *when everything is ready the police will move in on the gang*

movement ['muːvmənt] *noun* (a) moving, not being still; *there was hardly any movement in the trees*; *all you could see was a slight movement of the tiger's tail* (b) **bowel movement** = action of passing faeces from the bowel through the anus; *the patient had a bowel movement this morning* (c) mechanism; *a clock movement* (d) group of people who are working towards the same aims; *the movement for equal pay for women*; *he's a leading figure in the green movement*; *she led the movement for the reunification of the country* (e) one of the sections of a symphony; *they played the slow movement a little too fast*

move off ['muːv 'ɒf] *verb* to start moving; *the car moved off when the lights changed to green*; *she tried to get on the train as it was moving off*

move on ['muːv 'ɒn] *verb* (a) to go forward; *we stopped for a quick visit to the cathedral and then moved on to the next town* (b) to make people move; *the police moved the crowd on* (c) to deal with the next item; *we will now move on to item 10 on the agenda*

movie ['muːvi] *noun* usually *US* cinema film; *we go to the movies most weekends*; **movie theater** = place where films are shown (NOTE: British English is usually **cinema**)

moving ['muːvɪŋ] *adjective* (a) which is changing position; *make sure all the moving parts are clean*; **moving staircase** = escalator (b) which makes you feel sad; *a moving ceremony*; *the funeral was very moving*

mow [məu] *verb* to cut grass, hay, etc.; *I must mow the lawn while it is dry*; *the smell of newly mown hay* (NOTE: **mowing - mowed - has mown** [məun])

mow down ['məu 'daun] *verb* to kill; *the soldiers were mown down by enemy machine-gun fire*; *the car mowed down a dozen people on the street before the police could stop it*

mower ['məu] *noun* **(lawn)mower** = machine which cuts grass; **hand mower** = lawnmower which you push by hand; **motor mower** = lawnmower powered by a motor

MP ['em 'pi:] *noun* = MEMBER OF PARLIAMENT; *I saw our local MP speak in Parliament last night*; *you should write to your MP to complain about the government's plans* (NOTE: plural is **MPs** ['em 'pi:z])

mph = MILES PER HOUR

Mr ['mɪstə] *noun* title given to a man; *Mr Jones is our new sales manager*; *here are Mr and Mrs Smith* (*at the beginning of a letter*) *Dear Mr Smith* (NOTE: Mr is used with a surname, sometimes with both the Christian name and surname)

Mrs ['mɪsɪz] *noun* title given to a married woman; *Mrs Jones is our manager*; *(at the beginning of a letter) Dear Mrs Jones* (NOTE: Mrs is used with a surname, sometimes with both the Christian name and surname)

Ms [mʌz or mɪz] *noun* way of referring to a woman (married or unmarried); *(at the beginning of a letter) Dear Ms Jones* (NOTE: Ms is used with a surname, sometimes with both the Christian name and surname)

MS = MANUSCRIPT (NOTE: plural is **MSS**)

MSc ['emes'si:] = MASTER OF SCIENCE

much [mʌtʃ] **1** *adjective* **(a)** a lot of; *with much love from Aunt Mary*; *how much sugar do you need?*; *I never take much money with me when I go on holiday*; *she eats too much meat*; *as much as* = the same quantity; *you haven't eaten as much fruit as she has*; *he spends twice as much money as I do* **(b)** *(asking the price) how much does it cost to go to Edinburgh?*; *how much is that book?* (NOTE: much is used with nouns you cannot count: **not much money** but **not many boys**) **2** *adverb* very; a lot; *he's feeling much better today*; *it's much less cold in the south of the country*; *does it matter very much?*; *much as I like her, I don't want to share an office with her*; *as much as* = the same amount as; *you haven't eaten as much as she has* (NOTE: **much - more** [mɔː] - **most** [məʊst]) **3** *pronoun* a lot; *he didn't write much in his exam*; *much of the work has already been done*; *do you see much of him?* = do you see him often?

much-loved ['mʌtʃ'lʌvd] *adjective* which someone or everyone loves very much; *she didn't want to let go of her much-loved doll, even if it was dirty and smelly*

muck [mʌk] *noun* farmyard manure; *he came in with his boots covered with muck*; *spreading muck is one of the less pleasant jobs on a farm*

muck about *or* **around** ['mʌk ə'baʊt or ə'raʊnd] *verb* (*informal*) to behave in a silly way, not carefully; *stop mucking around, or we'll never get the work done*; (*informal*) to **muck about with** = to play with; *he loved mucking about with chemicals until he caused a small explosion in the garden shed*

muck in ['mʌk 'ɪn] *verb* (*informal*) to **muck in together** = to do work together; *if we all muck in the job won't take very long*

muck out ['mʌk 'aʊt] *verb* to **muck out a stable** = to clean manure and old straw from a stable

muck up ['mʌk 'ʌp] *verb* (*informal*) to ruin; *she mucked up the arrangements by putting the wrong date on the invitations*

mucous ['mju:kəs] *adjective* referring to mucus, covered in mucus; **mucous membrane** = wet membrane which lines inside passages of the body such as the nose, the mouth, the throat, etc. (NOTE: do not confuse with **mucus**)

mucus ['mju:kəs] *noun* slippery liquid secreted by mucous membranes inside the body, which protects the membranes; *the baby's nose is blocked with mucus*; *the snail left a trail of mucus across the kitchen floor* (NOTE: do not confuse with **mucous**)

mud [mʌd] *noun* very wet earth; *you need a stiff brush to get the mud off your shoes*; *the pigs were lying in the mud*; *the boat got stuck in the mud as the tide went out*

muddle ['mʌdl] **1** *noun* confused mess; *the papers were lying all over the floor in a muddle*; *she tried to put up the tent on her own but she got into a muddle*; *there was some muddle over the tickets* **2** *verb* to confuse, to mix up; *don't muddle the papers up - I've just put them in order*; *granny is 96 so she often muddles up our names*

muddled ['mʌdld] *adjective* confused, not clear and not well organized; *I get muddled if I try to do too many things at once*; *the proposal is just another example of the management's muddled thinking*

muddle through ['mʌdl 'θru:] *verb* to get through your work, to succeed in a confused way; *although we had never done this sort of work before, we managed to muddle through*

muddy ['mʌdi] *adjective* full of mud; covered with mud; *don't come into the kitchen with your muddy boots on*; *the car stopped in the middle of a muddy field* (NOTE: **muddier - muddiest**)

mudflap ['mʌdflæp] *noun* flap hanging behind the wheel of a car to protect the bodywork from damage by dirt or stones

mudguard ['mʌdgɑːd] *noun* strip of metal over the wheel on a bicycle to stop water or dirt from splashing; *I don't have any mudguards on my mountain bike*; *if you don't have a mudguard, you will get covered with mud* (NOTE: American English is **fender**)

muffin ['mʌfɪn] *noun* small round cake eaten warm with butter; *we toasted some muffins for tea*; *they had blueberry muffins for breakfast*

muffle ['mʌfl] *verb* **(a)** to wrap someone up in cloth for warmth; *she muffled herself in a big woollen shawl* **(b)** to make a loud noise quieter; *she wrapped a cloth around the hammer to muffle the sound of the blows*

muffled ['mʌfəld] *adjective* not as loud or clear as usual because the sound has been made quieter; *there was a muffled bang and the police rushed towards the house*; *muffled cries were coming from inside the cupboard*

muffler ['mʌflə] *noun* **(a)** (*old*) long scarf; *he wore a long red muffler round his neck* **(b)** *US* apparatus to stop the noise of the exhaust of a car; *the car is very noisy and needs a new muffler* (NOTE: British English for this is **silencer**)

mug [mʌg] **1** *noun* large china cup with a handle; *she passed round mugs of coffee* **2** *verb* to attack and rob someone in the street; *she was mugged as she was looking for her car keys*; *she's afraid of going out at night for fear of being mugged*; *the gang specializes in mugging tourists* (NOTE: **mugging - mugged**)

mugger ['mʌgə] *noun* person who attacks and robs someone in the street; *the muggers were caught in the next street*

mugging ['mʌgɪŋ] *noun* robbery with violence in the street; *it isn't safe to go out late a night - mugging is quite common*; *there have been three muggings in this*

street this month (NOTE: plural **muggings** means 'cases of mugging')

Muhammad [mə'hæmɪd] *noun* the founder and chief prophet of Islam, the Muslim religion

mulberry ['mʌlbəri] *noun* **(a)** large tree with small black fruit, rather similar to blackberries; *silkworms feed on the leaves of mulberries* **(b)** fruit of this tree; *the ground under the tree was covered with mulberries*

mulch [mʌltʃ] **1** *noun* material, such as dead leaves or straw, used to spread over the surface of the soil to prevent evaporation or to stop weeds growing; *we spread mulch around the stems of the rose bushes* (NOTE: plural is **mulches**) **2** *verb* to spread material, such as straw or dead leaves, over the surface of the soil to prevent evaporation or to stop weeds growing; *we used rotted leaves to mulch the flowerbeds*

mule [mju:l] *noun* **(a)** cross between a donkey and a horse; *he entered the town riding on a mule*; **as stubborn as a mule** = very obstinate; *I can't get her to agree - she's as stubborn as a mule* **(b)** light shoe with no back part at the heel

mull [mʌl] *verb* to heat wine with spices, sugar, etc.; *we sat by the fire drinking glasses of mulled wine*

mullet ['mʌlɪt] *noun* small sea fish; *you can use mullet to make fish stew* (NOTE: plural is **mullet**)

mull over ['mʌl 'əʊvə] *verb* to think about, to consider; *he spent the next few days mulling over the proposals*

multi- ['mʌlti] *prefix* meaning many

multicoloured *US* **multicolored** ['mʌltɪkʌləd *US* 'mʌltaɪkʌləd] *adjective* with many colours; *do you prefer the plain wrapping paper or the multicoloured one?*

multilateral [mʌltɪ'lætərəl] *adjective* between several people or groups; *the three countries signed a multilateral agreement*

multimedia [mʌltɪ'mi:djə] *noun* means of communication using several different media, such as sound, moving images, computer screens, etc.; *the company gave a multimedia presentation to show off its new product range; the pop concert was a spectacular multimedia event*

multimillionaire [mʌltɪmɪljə'neə] *noun* person who has several million pounds or dollars; *many successful film stars have become multimillionaires*

multinational [mʌltɪ'næʃnl] **1** *adjective* referring to several different countries; *the UN sent a multinational peacekeeping force with troops from several countries* **2** *noun* company which operates in several different countries; *our business has been bought by one of the big multinationals*

multiple ['mʌltɪpl] **1** *adjective* involving many people or things; *she was taken to hospital suffering from multiple injuries*; **a multiple birth** = birth of more than one baby at the same time (i.e., twins, triplets, etc.); **multiple crash** = crash involving several cars or lorries; **multiple ownership** = situation where something is shared by several parties jointly; **multiple sclerosis** = disease of the nervous system which gets progressively worse; **multiple store** = chain of stores belonging to the same company **2** *noun* **(a)** number which contains another number several times exactly; *nine is a multiple of three* **(b)** repeated groups of the same number of something; **sold in multiples of five** =

you can buy five, ten, fifteen, etc.; *Premium Bonds are available in multiples of £100*

multiplication [mʌltɪplɪ'keɪʃn] *noun* action of multiplying; *the children are taught addition, subtraction and multiplication*; **multiplication sign (x)** = sign used to show that one number is to be multiplied by another; **multiplication tables** = lists of figures to learn by heart how each number is multiplied

COMMENT: children sometimes learn their multiplication tables by heart, chanting: 'three threes are nine, four threes are twelve, five threes are fifteen', etc.

multiply ['mʌltɪplaɪ] *verb* to calculate the result when several numbers are added together a certain number of times; *square measurements are calculated by multiplying length by width*; *ten multiplied by five gives fifty* (NOTE: **multiply** is usually shown by the multiplication sign x : **10 x 4 = 40**: say 'ten multiplied by four equals forty' *or* 'ten times four is forty')

multi-storey ['mʌlti'stɔːri] *adjective* with several storeys; *there's a multi-storey car park next to our office; multi-storey buildings are going up all over Beijing*

multitude ['mʌltɪtjuːd] *noun* (*formal*) **(a)** very large number; *there are a multitude of reasons why the plan won't work* **(b)** crowd of people; *he stood up to address the assembled multitude*

multitudinous [mʌltɪ'tjuːdɪnəs] *adjective* (*formal*) in very large numbers; *multitudinous swarms of insects*

mum [mʌm] *see* MUMMY

mumble ['mʌmbl] **1** *noun* way of speaking which is difficult to understand because it is not clear; *speaking in a mumble, he thanked everyone for being at the party* **2** *verb* to speak in a low indistinct voice; *he mumbled an excuse and left the room; she mumbled something about the telephone and went to the back of the shop*

mummify ['mʌmɪfaɪ] *verb* to preserve a dead body in a perfect state by using chemicals, etc.; *the mummified body of an Egyptian king was found in the tomb*

mummy, mum ['mʌmi *or* mʌm] *noun* **(a)** child's name for mother; *tell your mum I want to see her; hello, John, is your mummy at home?; Mummy! can I have a biscuit?* (NOTE: American equivalent is **Mom, Mommy**) **(b)** dead body which has been treated with chemicals to stop it decaying; *we went to see the Egyptian mummies in the British Museum* (NOTE: plural is **mummies**)

mumps [mʌmps] *noun* infectious disease of children, where the patient gets swellings on the sides of the neck; *she caught mumps from the children next door; her little boy has come down with mumps; he can't go to school - he's got mumps*

munch [mʌnʃ] *verb* to chew noisily something that is crisp or dry, with a regular movement of your jaws; *he was munching a biscuit when he answered the phone; she didn't answer, and just munched away at an apple*

mundane [mʌn'deɪn] *adjective* ordinary, not exciting; *he's too intellectual to bother much with mundane matters like cooking and cleaning*

municipal [mju:'nɪsɪpl] *adjective* referring to a town which has its own local government; *we're going to play on the municipal golf course; municipal elections* *will be held on June 14th*; *take your household rubbish to the municipal refuse dump*; **municipal gardens** = park which belongs to a town; **municipal buildings** = offices where a town council works

municipality [mjuːnɪsɪ'pælɪti] *noun* *(formal)* town which governs itself; *a small municipality in the north of England*; *the municipality is responsible for the upkeep of the town gardens* (NOTE: plural is **municipalities**)

munificent [mjuː'nɪfɪsənt] *adjective* *(formal)* extremely generous; *she made a munificent donation to the local art gallery*

munitions [mjuː'nɪʃnz] *noun* weapons and ammunition; *she works in a munitions factory*

mural ['mjʊərəl] **1** *adjective* referring to walls; *mural decoration* **2** *noun* painting on a wall; *the murals were painted by Giotto in the fourteenth century*; *see also* FRESCO

murder ['mɜːdə] **1** *noun* **(a)** act of deliberately killing someone; *the murder was committed during the night*; *she was accused of murder*; *they denied the murder charge*; *compare* MANSLAUGHTER **(b)** *(informal)* difficult situation; *it was sheer murder getting to work this morning* **2** *verb* **(a)** to kill someone illegally and deliberately; *he was accused of murdering a policeman* **(b)** *(informal)* to want something to eat or drink very badly; *I could murder a pint of beer!*

murderer ['mɜːdərə] *noun* person who has committed a murder; *the murderer was sentenced to life imprisonment*; **mass murderer** = killer of a large number of people at one time; **serial murderer** = SERIAL KILLER

murderess ['mɜːdrəs] *noun* woman who has committed a murder; *he was horrified to discover he'd married a murderess*

murderous ['mɜːdərəs] *adjective* likely to kill; *she had a murderous look in her eye*; *he was carrying a murderous-looking axe*

murky ['mɜːki] *adjective* dark and dirty; *the police searched the murky waters of the harbour*; *it's a bit murky in here - can't you put the light on?* (NOTE: **murkier - murkiest**)

murmur ['mɜːmə] **1** *noun* low sound of people talking, of water flowing, etc.; *there was a murmur of voices in the hall* **2** *verb* to speak very quietly; *she murmured something and closed her eyes*

muscle ['mʌsl] **1** *noun* part of the body which contracts to make other parts move; *he has very powerful arm muscles*; **to strain a muscle** *or* **to pull a muscle** = to injure a muscle by using it too much; *she strained a muscle in her back* (NOTE: do not confuse with **mussel**) **2** *verb* *(informal)* **to muscle in on something** = to try to interfere with something; *he's always trying to muscle in on our projects and get all the credit for them*

muscular ['mʌskjʊlə] *adjective* **(a)** referring to muscles; *she suffered from muscular pain after working in the garden*; *he has very muscular arms*; **muscular dystrophy** = condition where the muscle tissue wastes away **(b)** with big muscles; *a couple of muscular bouncers stood at the door of the club*

muse [mjuːz] **1** *noun* *(formal)* woman who inspires poets, musicians, etc. **2** *verb* to think deeply; *she spent hours musing about her youth*; *he was sitting in his garden musing on the beauty of the autumn colours*

museum [mjuː'ziːəm] *noun* building which you can visit to see a collection of valuable or rare objects; *the museum has a rich collection of Italian paintings*; *the Natural History Museum is always very popular with school parties who go to see the dinosaurs*

mushroom ['mʌʃruːm] *noun* round white fungus which can be eaten; *do you want fried mushrooms with your steak?*; *she ordered a mushroom omelette* (NOTE: fungi which are poisonous are called **toadstools**)

music ['mjuːzɪk] *noun* **(a)** sound made when you sing or play an instrument; *do you like Russian music?*; *she's taking music lessons*; *her music teacher says she plays the violin very well* **(b)** written signs which you read to play an instrument; *here's some music, see if you can play it on the piano*; *he can play the piano by ear - he doesn't need any music* **(c)** *(informal)* **to face the music** = to receive punishment; *the manager fled abroad when the bank collapsed, but came back to face the music* (NOTE: no plural: **some music; a piece of music**)

musical ['mjuːzɪkl] **1** *adjective* **(a)** referring to music; *do you play any musical instrument?* **(b)** loving music, being able to play musical instruments; *his whole family is very musical - they all either sing or play in orchestras* **2** *noun* play with songs and popular music; *musicals such as 'Cats' and 'Evita' have been playing for years*

musical chairs ['mjuːzɪkl 'tʃeəz] *noun* **(a)** game where people try to sit on chairs when the music stops, with one chair and one person less each time; *after tea we all played musical chairs* **(b)** *(informal)* continuous changing of jobs; *the game of musical chairs which the Prime Minister has to play to keep the members of the coalition happy*

musical instrument ['mjuːzɪkl 'ɪnstrəmənt] *noun* instrument such as piano, trumpet, or violin, that a musician plays; *you're not much use in the band if you don't play any musical instrument*

music-hall ['mjuːzɪk 'hɔːl] *noun* *(old)* type of theatre specializing in variety shows; *they toured the music-halls with their juggling act*

musician [mjuː'zɪʃn] *noun* person who plays music professionally; *a group of young musicians playing the street*; *the actors applauded the group of musicians who had played during 'Twelfth Night'*

musket ['mʌskɪt] *noun* early portable gun with a long barrel; *Napoleon's soldiers were armed with muskets*

musketeer [mʌskə'tɪə] *noun* soldier who was armed with a musket; **the Three Musketeers** = a story of 17th century France where three soldiers, Athos, Porthos and Aramis, are joined by a fourth, D'Artagnan, in various adventures

Muslim ['mʊzləm] **1** *adjective* following the religion of the prophet Muhammad; *he comes from a strict Muslim family* **2** *noun* person who follows the religion of the prophet Muhammad; *Islam is the religion of Muslims or the Muslim religion*; *he comes from a family of strict Muslims*

muss [mʌs] *verb* US *(informal)* to make your hair, etc., untidy; *don't muss my hair, I've just brushed it*

mussel ['mʌsl] *noun* small shellfish, with a blue shell; *we always eat mussels when we're in Belgium* (NOTE: do not confuse with **muscle**)

must [mʌst] **1** *verb* used with other verbs **(a)** *(meaning it is necessary)* *you must go to bed before* *eleven, or your mother will be angry; we mustn't be late or we'll miss the last bus; you must hurry up if you want to see the TV programme; must you really go so soon?* (NOTE: the negative: **mustn't, needn't** Note also the meanings: **mustn't** = not allowed; **needn't** = not necessary: **we mustn't be late; you needn't hurry) (b)** *(meaning it is very likely) I must have left my briefcase on the train; there is someone knocking at the door - it must be the postman; you must be wet through after walking in the rain* (NOTE: negative is **can't; it can't be the doctor;** past is **had to; I must go to the dentist: yesterday I had to go to the dentist;** negative: is **didn't have to;** perfect: **must have; I must have left it on the train;** negative: **can't have; I can't have left it on the train.** Note also that **must** is only used with other verbs and is not followed by **to) 2** *noun* something important; *when in Florida, a trip to the Everglades is a must*

mustache ['mʌstæʃ] *noun US* = MOUSTACHE

mustang ['mʌstæŋ] *noun* wild American horse; *he rode a mustang which he'd broken in himself*

mustard ['mʌstəd] *noun* **(a)** yellow paste made from mixing mustard powder and water, eaten with meat, especially ham and beef; *would you like some mustard on your beef sandwich?; English mustard is yellow and quite strong;* **mustard powder** = sharp-tasting yellow powder made from crushed mustard seeds; **mustard yellow** = dull yellow colour; *see also* KEEN **(b)** plant whose seeds make mustard powder; **mustard and cress** = seedlings of the mustard plant eaten as a salad, together with seedlings of cress; *the sandwiches were served with a garnish of mustard and cress*

muster ['mʌstə] **1** *noun* **(a)** parade and inspection of soldiers; *the colonel called a muster of the country militia* **(b)** **to pass muster** = to be acceptable; *I'm afraid your work just doesn't pass muster* **2** *verb* to gather together; *he tried to muster all his supporters before the vote; he find it difficult to muster enough energy to go for a walk after lunch;* **muster station** = place where passengers on a ship must gather in an emergency

mutability [mjuːtə'bɪlɪti] *noun (formal)* being likely to change; *the mutability of human nature*

mutant ['mjuːtənt] **1** *adjective* in which mutation has occurred; *the mutant cells will affect the other normal cells;* **mutant gene** = gene in which mutation has occurred **2** *noun* organism carrying a gene in which mutation has occurred; *this plant appears to be a mutant*

mutate [mjuː'teɪt] *verb* to undergo a change in structure which changes a gene or chromosome; *bacteria can mutate suddenly and become resistant to antibiotics*

mutation [mjuː'teɪʃn] *noun* genetic change affecting the structure of a living thing; *radiation causes strange mutations in plants and animals*

mute [mjuːt] **1** *adjective* **(a)** not speaking; *a look of mute horror crossed her face* **(b)** which is not pronounced; *in the word 'crumb' the letter 'b' is mute* **2** *adverb* not speaking; *she stood mute throughout all her trial* **3** *noun* **(a)** person who cannot speak, who is dumb; **deaf mute** = person who cannot hear or speak **(b)** device used to soften the sound of a musical instrument; *she fitted a mute into the mouth of the trumpet; the last part of the piece is played with a mute on the violin* **4** *verb* to soften the sound of a musical

instrument; *the violins are muted before playing the final quiet passage*

muted ['mjuːtɪd] *adjective* **(a)** quiet, not noisy; *the press gave the proposal a muted welcome; criticism of the government's proposals has been muted* **(b)** not bright; *I prefer muted colours for the sitting room*

mutineer [mjuːtɪ'nɪə] *noun* person who mutinies; *the mutineers took over the ship and set the officers adrift in a small boat*

mutinous ['mjuːtɪnəs] *adjective* likely to mutiny, likely not to obey; *the soldiers were getting mutinous because they hadn't been paid; the manager decided to try to speak to his mutinous staff*

mutiny ['mjuːtɪni] **1** *noun* rebellion against someone in a position of authority, such as the officers in the army, the government and its ministers, etc.; *the officers kept a lookout for any signs of mutiny among the crew* **2** *verb* to rebel against authority; *the soldiers mutinied and captured the castle; there is a possibility that some MPs will mutiny against the government*

mutter ['mʌtə] **1** *noun* low indistinct way of speaking; *mutters could be heard coming from the back of the hall* **2** *verb* to mumble, to speak in a low and indistinct voice; *don't mutter, I can't understand you; he muttered something about the telephone and went to the back of the shop*

muttering ['mʌtərɪŋ] *noun* complaints, spoken indistinctly; *low muttering started at the back of the hall; there has been some muttering about the service, but nothing serious*

mutton ['mʌtən] *noun (old)* meat of a sheep (NOTE: not very often used: **lamb** is generally used for all meat from sheep as well as lambs)

mutual ['mjuːtʃuəl] *adjective* referring to what is done by two people, countries, companies, etc., to each other; *they have a lot of mutual respect; if we work together, it could prove to be to our mutual advantage; she doesn't like him and the feeling is entirely mutual;* **our mutual friend** = the friend of both of us; **by mutual agreement** *or* **by mutual consent** = with the agreement of both parties; *by mutual agreement they have decided to sell the flat and split the money between them*

mutual fund ['mjuːtʃuəl 'fʌnd] *noun US* organization which takes money from small investors and invests it in stocks and shares for them, the investment being in the form of shares in the fund; *she put her savings into a mutual fund* (NOTE: British equivalent is a **unit trust)**

muzzle ['mʌzl] **1** *noun* **(a)** front part of an animal's head, especially the mouth, jaws and nose; *she stroked the horse's long, silky muzzle* **(b)** straps placed round the mouth of a dog to prevent it from biting; *our dog always has to wear a muzzle when he's taken for a walk* **(c)** mouth of a gun; *she found herself looking down the muzzle of a gun; the army was equipped with muzzle-loading rifles* **2** *verb* **(a)** to tie up the mouth of a dog to prevent it biting; *I always muzzle my dog when I walk him through the children's playground* **(b)** **to muzzle the press** = to stop newspapers from saying what they want

my [maɪ] *adjective* belonging to me; *is that my pen you're using?; have you seen my glasses anywhere?; we went skiing and I broke my leg*

myriad ['mɪriəd] (*formal*) **1** *noun* very large number; *there are myriads of islands in the mouth of the river; the sky was bright with a myriad of stars* **2** *adjective* very many; *these are only a few of the myriad life forms found on a coral reef*

myself [maɪ'self] *pronoun* referring to me; *I hurt myself climbing down the ladder; it's true - I saw it myself; I enjoyed myself a lot at the party;* **all by myself** = all alone, with no one else; *I built the house all by myself; I don't like being all by myself in the house at night*

mysterious [mɪ'stɪəriəs] *adjective* which cannot be explained; *who is the mysterious stranger at the back of the hall?; she died in mysterious circumstances, but the police are not sure it was murder*

mysteriously [mɪ'stɪəriəsli] *adverb* in a strange way which cannot be explained; *'take care tomorrow', she said mysteriously, 'you could be in for a shock'; the red car was there in the evening but by morning it had mysteriously changed colour to yellow*

mystery ['mɪstri] *noun* thing which cannot be explained; *the police finally cleared up the mystery of the missing body; it's a mystery how the box came to be hidden under her bed* (NOTE: plural is **mysteries**)

mystic ['mɪstɪk] **1** *noun* person who attempts to achieve union with God through prayer, meditation, etc. **2** *adjective* in contact with God; *the mystic union between Christ and the Church*

mystical ['mɪstɪkl] *adjective* in contact with God by some process which cannot be understood; *she had a mystical experience in the old cemetery; he wrote about his mystical vision of the universe*

mysticism ['mɪstɪsɪzm] *noun* religion based on attempts to achieve union with God by prayer and meditation; *a follower of Eastern mysticism*

mystify ['mɪstɪfaɪ] *verb* to puzzle, to bewilder; *I'm mystified by the disappearance of the car*

mystique [mɪ'stiːk] *noun* mysterious atmosphere about a person or thing; *in modern times the monarchy has lost a lot of its mystique*

myth [mɪθ] *noun* **(a)** ancient story about gods; *poems based on the myths of Greece and Rome* **(b)** untrue idea, but one which is commonly held; *it was many years before people could disprove the myth that the earth was flat; the sales figures showed up the myth of their so-called super sales force*

mythical ['mɪθɪkl] *adjective* **(a)** referring to ancient tales of gods; *a unicorn is a mythical animal* **(b)** untrue, which does not exist; *he keeps talking about some mythical order from Japan*

mythology [mɪ'θɒlədʒi] *noun* **(a)** ancient folk stories from a particular source; *the floor was covered with mosaics showing scenes from Greek mythology; according to ancient Scandinavian mythology, he cut off the head of the dragon* **(b)** ideas held by the general public; *according to popular mythology, it is unlucky to walk under ladders*

Nn

N, n [en] fourteenth letter of the alphabet, between M and O; *can you think of a five-letter word beginning with N and ending in R?*

nab [næb] *verb* **(a)** *(informal)* to snatch something quickly; *when we came down to the pool we found that the others had nabbed all the best seats; pass me that bottle before anyone else nabs it* **(b)** *(informal)* to arrest someone; *the police nabbed him as he was coming out of the bank* (NOTE: **nabbing - nabbed**)

nadir ['neɪdɪə] *noun* very lowest point; *public confidence in the government has reached its nadir*

nag [næg] **1** *verb* **to nag someone** *or* **to nag at someone** = to complain about someone *or* something all the time; *she was always nagging (at) him to buy a new car; she's been nagging me for an ice cream all afternoon* (NOTE: **nagging - nagged**) **2** *noun (informal)* old horse; *I can't go riding on that nag*

nagging ['nægɪŋ] *adjective* that worries you over a long period of time; *I have a nagging doubt about their plan; she had a nagging suspicion that something was wrong;* **nagging pain** = dull, continuous throbbing pain; *he had a nagging pain in his jaw*

nail [neɪl] **1** *noun* **(a)** little metal spike; *hit the nail hard with the hammer; you need a hammer to knock that nail in (informal)* **to hit the nail on the head** = to judge something accurately **(b)** **as hard as nails** = very hard, uncompromising; *she's as hard as nails* **(c)** hard part at the end of your fingers and toes; *she painted her nails red; he was cutting his nails;* **nail scissors** = special small scissors for cutting nails; *see also* FINGERNAIL, TOENAIL **2** *verb* to attach with nails; *he nailed the notice to the door*

nail down ['neɪl 'daʊn] *verb* to attach something flat with nails; *they nailed down the floorboards or they nailed the floorboards down*

nail file ['neɪl 'faɪl] *noun* flat stick covered with sandpaper, used to smooth your fingernails; *have you got a nail file? - I've broken a nail*

naive [naɪ'iːv] *adjective* innocent, lacking experience; *he is naive for his age; it was very naive of her to think he was offering her money just because he admired her work*

naivety *or* **naiveté** [naɪ'iːvti *or* naɪ'iːvteɪ] *noun* being naive; *the naivety of some young managers is astonishing*

naked ['neɪkɪd] *adjective* **(a)** with no clothes on; *the little children were playing around in the river stark naked; a naked man stood on the balcony* **(b)** without any covering; *a naked electric bulb hung from the ceiling;* **invisible to the naked eye** = which cannot be seen without a magnifying glass; **naked flame** = flame which is burning without any protection round it

name [neɪm] **1** *noun* **(a)** special way of calling someone or something; *hello! my name's James; what's the name of the shop next to the post office?;* **I know him by name** = I have never met him, but I know

who he is; **in the name of someone** = using someone's name; *the table is booked in the name of 'Green';* **to put your name down for** = to apply for; *she put her name down to join the club;* **under the name of** = using the name of; *he wrote his novels under the name 'Saki'; they checked into the hotel under the name of 'Smith';* **to make a name for yourself** = to do something which makes you famous; *he made a name for himself as a criminal lawyer* **(b)** **Christian name** *or* **first name** = special name given to someone as a child after birth or at baptism; *her Christian name or her first name is Natasha, but I don't know her surname;* **family name** *or* **surname** = name of someone's family, shared by all people in the family; *Smith is the commonest name in the London telephone directory; see also* BRAND NAME, SURNAME **(c)** **to call someone names** = to be rude to someone; *don't call the teacher names;* **to give something a bad name** = to give something a bad reputation; *employing waiters who are rude to customers is going to give the restaurant a bad name* **2** *verb* to call someone or something by a name; *can you name three British Prime Ministers?; the Queen named the ship 'Britannia'; they have a black cat named Jonah;* **to name someone after someone** = to give someone the same name as someone else; *they named their son Peter after his grandfather*

namely ['neɪmli] *adverb* that is to say; *only one student failed the exam, namely poor Bruce*

nameplate ['neɪmpleɪt] *noun* metal plate with the name of a person or firm carved on it; *the cleaner polished the nameplate on the door every week*

nan *or* **nana** [næn *or* 'nænə] *noun* child's name for grandmother; *my nan looks after me when my mum and dad are away*

nanny ['næni] *noun* **1 (a)** girl who looks after small children in a family; *she's training to be a nanny; our new nanny starts tomorrow;* **the nanny state** = a state where the government looks after everyone and tells them what to do; *telling people at what time their children should go to bed is another example of the nanny state; compare* WELFARE STATE (NOTE: plural is **nannies**) **(b)** *(children's word)* **nanny goat** = female goat; *a nanny goat and her two kids* (NOTE: a male goat is a **billy goat**) **2** *verb* to look after someone or something very carefully and tell them what to do; *she loves to nanny the new students along*

nap [næp] **1** *noun* **(a)** short sleep; *after lunch he always takes a little nap* **(b)** smooth surface of cloth such as velvet; *just feel the nap on this cloth* **(c)** tip as to which horse is likely to win a race **2** *verb* to sleep a little; **to catch someone napping** = to take someone by surprise; *his sudden offer caught us all napping*

nape [neɪp] *noun* back of the neck; *you can pick up a kitten by the loose skin on the nape of its neck*

napkin ['næpkɪn] *noun* **(a)** **(table) napkin** = square piece of cloth used to protect clothes and wipe your mouth at meal times; *she wiped her fingers on a napkin*; **paper napkin** = napkin made from paper (NOTE: also called a **serviette**, but some people think this is not correct) **(b)** *(formal)* nappy; *the baby must have his napkin changed*

nappy ['næpi] *noun* cloth which is wrapped round a baby's bottom to absorb urine and faeces; *she changed the baby's nappy*; *a pack of disposable nappies* (NOTE: plural is **nappies**; American English for this is **diaper**)

narcissus [nɑː'sɪsəs] *noun* flower similar to a daffodil, with white and orange flowers shaped like trumpets; *he gave her a bunch of narcissi* (NOTE: plural is **narcissi** [nɑː'sɪsaɪ])

narcotic [nɑː'kɒtɪk] **1** *adjective* which makes you sleep or become unconscious; *the narcotic side-effects of antihistamines* **2** *noun* **(a)** pain-relieving drug which makes a patient sleep; *the doctor put her to sleep with a powerful narcotic* **(b)** **narcotics** = dangerous drugs which are sold by criminals; *narcotics are being smuggled into the country from South America*; *US* **Narcotics Squad** = section of the police force that investigates crime related to drugs (NOTE: the British equivalent is the **Drug Squad**)

narrate [nə'reɪt] *verb* to tell a story; *in the novel, the story is narrated by the hero's wife*

narrative ['nærətɪv] **1** *noun* written story; *he's writing a narrative about their journeys in South America* **2** *adjective* describing an action; *the narrative part of the book is very exciting*; *he wrote a narrative poem about the war against Troy*

narrator [nə'reɪtə] *noun* person who tells a story; *the film opens with the narrator's voice*

narrow ['nærəʊ] *adjective* **(a)** not wide; *why is your bicycle seat so narrow?*; *we went down a narrow alleyway to the shop* **(b)** **narrow escape** = near miss, situation where you almost hit something; *she had a narrow escape when her bike was hit by a lorry*; **narrow majority** = majority of only a few votes; *the government had a narrow majority in the vote on the European Union* (NOTE: **narrower - narrowest**) **2** *verb* **(a)** to make less wide, to become less wide; *the road narrows suddenly, and there is hardly enough room for two cars to pass*; *he narrowed his eyes* **(b)** to **narrow something down to** = to reduce something to; *we have narrowed down our choice of restaurants to two*

narrow boat ['nærəʊ 'bəʊt] *noun* long narrow barge used on English canals

narrowly ['nærəʊli] *adverb* very nearly; *she only narrowly escaped being killed by a lion*

NASA *abbreviation for* NATIONAL AERONAUTICAL AND SPACE ADMINISTRATION

nasal ['neɪzl] **1** *adjective* **(a)** referring to the nose; *she used nasal drops to try to cure her cold* **(b)** speaking as if through the nose; *he speaks with a nasal accent* **2** *noun (phonetics)* sound pronounced through the nose, like 'n' or 'm' in English

nasty ['nɑːsti] *adjective* unpleasant; *what a nasty smell!*; *he's in for a nasty shock*; *it was nasty of her to report you to the teacher*; to **turn nasty** = to become unpleasant suddenly; *when she couldn't pay, the manager turned quite nasty* (NOTE: **nastier - nastiest**)

nation ['neɪʃən] *noun* **(a)** country; *such a great nation as the USA has a duty to protect smaller countries from aggression*; *the member nations of the EU*; *see also* UNITED NATIONS **(b)** people living in a country; *the Prime Minister spoke to the nation about the declaration of war*

national ['næʃənl] **1** *adjective* **(a)** belonging to a country; *this is in our national interest*; *the story even appeared in the national newspapers*; *we're going to see a new play at the National Theatre* **(b)** **National Health Service (NHS)** = system of free doctors, nurses, hospitals and clinics, run by the government; **National Insurance** = government-run insurance which provides for state medical care, unemployment payments, etc.; **National Savings** = scheme for saving money by lending it to the government **2** *noun* person from a certain country; *two German nationals were arrested at the scene of the crime*

national anthem ['næʃnl 'ænθəm] *noun* piece of music which is used to represent the nation officially, and is played at official ceremonies; *everyone stood up when the National Anthem was played*; *the band played the National Anthem and then we all sat down*; *the British National Anthem is 'God Save the Queen'*

nationalism ['næʃnəlɪzm] *noun* **(a)** wanting independence for your country; *during the occupation, all feelings of nationalism had to be suppressed* **(b)** feeling of great pride in your country, feeling that your country is better than others; *Danish nationalism as shown by their football supporters*

nationalist ['næʃnəlɪst] **1** *noun* person who wants his country to be independent; *a Welsh nationalist*; *the nationalists have not been invited to the negotiations* **2** *adjective* wanting your country to be independent; *there is a lot of nationalist feeling in the country*

nationalistic [næʃnə'lɪstɪk] *adjective* strongly supporting your own country; *the newspapers criticized the nationalistic fervour of some of the parties*

nationality [næʃə'næləti] *noun* being a citizen of a state; *he is of United Kingdom nationality*; **he has dual nationality** = he is a citizen of two countries at the same time (NOTE: plural is **nationalities**)

nationalization [næʃnəlaɪ'zeɪʃn] *noun* passing the ownership of a business from private individuals to ownership by the state; *after nationalization the railways were run much more efficiently* (NOTE: do not confuse with **naturalization**)

nationalize ['næʃnəlaɪz] *verb* to put a privately-owned industry under state ownership and control; *the government has plans to nationalize the banking system*; **nationalized industry** = industry which was once privately owned, but now belongs to the state; *workers in nationalized industries are to get a 3% pay rise*

national park ['næʃənl 'pɑːk] *noun* area of land protected by the government for people to enjoy; *the Peak District in Derbyshire is a national park*

nation-state ['neɪʃn 'steɪt] *noun* country which is an independent political unit, formed of people with the same nationality and often the same language and traditions; *the 19th century saw the rise of many European nation-states*

nationwide ['neɪʃnwaɪd] *adjective* all over the country; *the union called for a nationwide strike*; *we offer a nationwide delivery service*

native ['neɪtɪv] **1** *noun* **(a)** person born in a place; *he's a native of Cornwall* **(b)** flower, bird, etc., which lives in a place; *the robin is a native of the British Isles* **(c)** original inhabitant; *Captain Cook was killed by natives as he came ashore* **2** *adjective* belonging to a country; *the tiger is native to India*; **native language** = language which you speak from birth; *her native language is Italian*

nativity [nə'tɪvɪti] *noun (formal)* **the Nativity** = the birth of Jesus Christ; **nativity play** = a play about the birth of Jesus, especially one performed by children; *Jenny's playing the Virgin Mary in her school nativity play*

NATO *abbreviation for* NORTH ATLANTIC TRATY ORGANIZAION

natter ['nætə] **1** *noun (informal)* chat, casual friendly talk; *come round for coffee tomorrow and we can have a natter* **2** *verb (informal)* to chat, to talk in a casual and friendly way; *they were nattering about their holidays and didn't see the bus go past; she spends too much time nattering on the phone to her boyfriend*

natural ['nætʃərəl] *adjective* **(a)** ordinary, not unusual; *her behaviour at the meeting was quite natural; it's only natural if you can't sleep the night before your exams; it's natural to worry about your first baby; it was natural for small shopkeepers to feel annoyed when the hypermarket opened* **(b)** coming from nature, and not man-made; *do you think the colour of her hair is natural?; yes, she's a natural blonde; the inquest decided that he died from natural causes*; **natural gas** = gas which is found in the earth and not made in a gasworks; **natural history** = study of plants, animals, etc.

naturalist ['nætʃərəlist] *noun* person who is interested in and studies natural history; *she's a naturalist who has made a special study of beetles*

naturalization [nætʃərəlaɪ'zeɪʃn] *noun* granting of the position of citizen to a foreigner; *you have to fill in the naturalization papers to apply to become a British subject* (NOTE: do not confuse with **nationalization**)

naturalize ['nætʃərəlaɪ] *verb* to make someone a citizen of a country; *she's a naturalized American*

naturally ['nætʃərəli] *adverb* **(a)** of course; *naturally the top team beat the bottom team; do you want to watch the game? - naturally!* **(b)** because of nature, not man-made; *she has naturally fair hair* **(c)** in a normal way; *he behaved quite naturally at the office, so we were surprised when he was arrested for murder*

natural resources ['nætʃrl rɪ'zɔːsɪz] *noun* minerals, energy sources, etc., which can be used commercially, such as coal or water power; *Canada is a country which is very rich in natural resources*

natural selection ['nætʃərəl sə'lekʃn] *noun* the process of evolution of a species, by which the characteristics that help the organism to survive are passed on to its offspring, and those characteristics which do not help to survive are not passed on

nature ['neɪtʃə] *noun* **(a)** plants and animals; *we must try to protect nature and the environment*; **nature study** = school lessons where you learn about plants and animals **(b)** character of a person, thing, animal; *he has a very aggressive nature*; **human nature** = the general character of people; *it's only human nature to want to get on and do better than others*; **better nature** = feelings of kindness which you have inside you; *they appealed to the president's better nature to release the prisoners*

naught [nɔːt] *noun (formal)* nothing; *all our efforts came to naught*

naughty ['nɔːti] *adjective (usually of a child)* behaving badly, not being obedient; *the children are very quiet - they must be doing something naughty; that boy is very naughty - but his sister is worse; it was very naughty of you to put glue on your daddy's chair* (NOTE: **naughtier - naughtiest**)

nausea ['nɔːziə] *noun* feeling sick, feeling that you want to vomit; *she suffers from nausea in the morning; he felt slight nausea in getting onto the boat*

nauseate ['nɔːzieɪt] *verb* to make someone feel sick or disgusted; *the manager's attitude towards the customers simply nauseates me*

nauseating ['nɔːzieɪtɪŋ] *adjective* which makes you sick; *the scenes of violence in the film were absolutely nauseating; the thought of eating raw fish is nauseating*

nauseous ['nɔːziəs] *adjective* US feeling sick, feeling about to vomit; *as soon as I stepped onto the ship I started to feel nauseous*

nautical ['nɔːtɪkl] *adjective* referring to ships and the sea; *he likes to use nautical terms in his conversation to show he's been to sea*; **nautical mile** = unit of measurement of distance, used at sea and in the air (= 1.852 kilometres)

naval ['neɪvl] *adjective* referring to the navy; *he comes from a naval family; we are very interested in naval history*; **naval base** = base for warships; **naval college** = college where students study before entering the navy (NOTE: do not confuse with **navel**)

nave [neɪv] *noun* main part of a church where the congregation sits; *we took our seats in the nave waiting for the service to begin*

navel ['neɪvl] *noun* depression in the middle of the abdomen, just below the waist, where the umbilical cord was detached after birth; *she wore a silver stud in her navel*; **navel orange** = large seedless orange with a depression at one end like a navel (NOTE: in children's language a navel is called a **belly button** or **tummy button**; do not confuse with **naval**)

navigate ['nævɪgeɪt] *verb* **(a)** to guide a ship or aircraft; *he skilfully navigated the boat into the harbour* **(b)** to give directions to the driver of a car; *can you navigate as far as Marble Arch? - I know my way from there*

navigation [nævɪ'geɪʃn] *noun* **(a)** action of guiding and steering; *in the sixteenth century, navigation was done by the stars; thanks to Jim's bad navigation we lost our way twice* **(b)** movement of ships or aircraft; *the canal is open to navigation again*; **inland navigation** = sailing on canals, rivers and lakes

navigator ['nævɪgeɪtə] *noun* **(a)** person who calculates the distances and direction taken by an aircraft or ship; *the navigator estimates that we should reach the coast in about ten minutes* **(b)** person who deals with the maps, signs and timing for a rally driver; *the navigator warned me that there was a sharp right turn ahead*

navy ['neɪvi] **1** *noun* **(a)** military force which fights battles at sea; *he left school and joined the navy; the navy has many ships*; **the Royal Navy** = British warships and men **(b)** dark blue colour; *she was* *dressed in navy* **2** *adjective* **navy (blue)** = of a dark blue colour; *she was wearing a navy skirt; he's bought a navy blue pullover*

nay [neɪ] *adverb (old)* no; *nay, master, it was not I that took the sheep*

NB *or* **n.b.** ['en'biː] *abbreviation meaning 'take note';* *NB: don't forget you have a dentist's appointment tomorrow* (NOTE: it is short for the Latin phrase **nota bene**)

NCO [ensiː'əʊ] *noun* = NON-COMMISSIONED OFFICER (NOTE: plural is **NCOs**)

near [nɪə] *adverb, preposition & adjective* **(a)** close to, not far away from; *our house is near the post office; bring your chair nearer to the table; he lives quite near or quite near here; which is the nearest chemist's?;* a **near miss** = situation where you almost hit something; *that was a near miss - we missed the other car by inches!; (in a car)* **the near side** = the side closer to the side of the road; *someone has scratched the near-side door* **(b)** soon, not far off in time; *her birthday is on December 21st - it's quite near to Christmas; can you phone again nearer the day and I'll see if I can find a few minutes to see you?* (NOTE: **nearer - nearest**)

nearby [nɪə'baɪ] *adverb & adjective* not far away; *he lives just nearby; they met in a nearby restaurant*

Near East ['nɪə 'iːst] *noun* countries at the eastern end of the Mediterranean; *flights to the Near East have been stopped because of fighting in the area*

nearest and dearest ['nɪːrəst n 'dɪːrəst] *noun* *(informal)* your close family; *you don't expect your nearest and dearest to side with your mother-in-law against you*

nearly ['nɪəli] *adverb* almost; *he's nearly 18 - he'll be going to university next year; the film lasted nearly three hours; the book isn't nearly as good as the last one I read; hurry up, it's nearly time for breakfast*

near-sighted ['nɪə'saɪtɪd] *adjective* able to see close objects clearly, but not objects which are further away; *I'm near-sighted and have to wear glasses* (NOTE: also called **short-sighted**)

neat [niːt] *adjective* **(a)** tidy, without any mess; *leave your bedroom neat and tidy; a blouse with a neat lace collar* **(b)** alcohol without any water added; *I prefer my whisky neat* (NOTE: American English only uses **straight** in this meaning) **(c)** *mainly US* **a neat idea** = a good idea (NOTE: **neater - neatest**)

neatly ['niːtli] *adverb* in a neat and tidy way; *she's always very neatly dressed; he folded his clothes neatly and put them on a chair; the little boy gave the teacher a neatly wrapped parcel*

nebula ['nebjulə] *noun* group of very distant stars; *the nebula in the constellation of Andromeda* (NOTE: plural is **nebulae** ['nebjuliː])

nebular ['nebjulə] *adjective* referring to nebulae

nebulous ['nebjuləs] *adjective* vague, not very clear; *when I got married my idea of what married life would be like was still very nebulous; they made us a nebulous proposal suggesting cooperation*

necessarily [nesə'serəli] *adverb* which cannot be avoided; *going to Newcastle from here necessarily means changing trains twice;* **not necessarily** = possibly sometimes but not always; *taking the train isn't necessarily slower than going by plane*

necessary ['nesesri] *adjective* which has to be done; *it's absolutely necessary for taxes to be paid on time; it is necessary to have a current passport if you are going abroad; are you sure all this equipment is really necessary?; does she have the necessary qualifications for the job?*

necessitate [nə'sesɪteɪt] *verb* to make necessary; *the new model will necessitate a complete change of machinery; living alone necessitates dealing with all household chores yourself*

necessity [nə'sesɪti] *noun* what is needed; essential thing; *a car is a necessity if you live in the country; can they afford the simple necessities of life?* (NOTE: plural is **necessities**)

neck [nek] *noun* **(a)** part which joins your head to your body; *she was sitting in a draught and got a stiff neck; the mayor wears a gold chain round his neck;* **pain in the neck** = annoying person; *he's a real pain in the neck;* **to breathe down someone's neck** = to watch what someone is doing and be ready to criticize; *I wish he would stop breathing down my neck all the time;* **to stick your neck out** = to do something risky; *I'll stick my neck out and say that the government will lose the next election* **(b)** **neck and neck** = equal (in a race, in an election); *the two boats finished neck and neck; the result is still unclear - the two parties are neck and neck* **(c)** part of a piece of clothing which goes round your neck; *he takes size 16 neck in shirts* **(d)** narrow part; *the neck of a bottle;* **a neck of land** = narrow piece of land between two pieces of water; *(informal)* **in this neck of the woods** = in this part of the country; *not many people live in this neck of the woods*

-necked [nekt] *suffix* with a certain type of neck; *a V-necked pullover; a polo-necked jumper*

necklace ['nekləs] *noun* string of beads or stones, etc., worn round your neck; *he gave her a necklace for her birthday*

necktie ['nektaɪ] *noun especially US* piece of coloured cloth worn knotted round the neck; *is it the sort of party for which you have to wear a necktie?* (NOTE: British English only uses **tie**)

nectar ['nektə] *noun* **(a)** liquid produced by flowers to attract bees; *honey is made from the nectar collected by bees* **(b)** very delicious-tasting drink; *after a game of tennis this lemonade is absolute nectar*

need [niːd] **1** *noun* what is necessary or wanted; *there's no need for you to wait - I can find my own way;* **in need** = requiring food and help; *the Red Cross is bringing supplies to families in need;* **to be in need of** = to want something; *they're in urgent need of medical supplies* **2** *verb* **(a)** *(meaning to be necessary)* we shall need Spanish pesetas for our holiday; *painting needs a lot of skill; I need someone to help me with the cooking; you don't need to come if you have a cold* **(b)** *(meaning to want to use)* does anyone need any more coffee?; *we don't need all these chairs; will you be needing this hammer any more or can I use it?; do you need any help?; the police need to know who saw the accident* **(c)** *(used with other verbs)* need you make so much noise in the bath?; *need you go now?; the living room needs painting or needs to be painted*

needle ['niːdl] *noun* **(a)** metal tool for sewing, like a long pin, with a hole at one end for the thread to go through; *this needle hasn't got a very sharp point; you must try to pull the piece of wool through the hole in the needle;* **knitting needle** = thin pointed plastic or metal stick used for knitting; **it's like looking for a needle in a haystack** = it's a hopeless task **(b) hypodermic needle** = needle used for injections; *hepatitis B is a serious disease transmitted by infected blood or shared needles* **(c)** leaf of a pine tree; *she had lots of pine needles stuck in her hair*

needless ['niːdləs] *adjective* not necessary; **to cause someone needless worry** = to make someone worried when there is no cause; *don't send a police car to the house - we don't want to cause them needless worry;* **needless to say** = as you might expect; *needless to say, they can't pay for it themselves*

needlework ['niːdlwɜːk] *noun* embroidery, decorative work done using a needle and thread; *she does some exquisite needlework*

needn't ['niːdnt] *verb used with other verbs (to mean it isn't necessary) she needn't come if she has a cold; you needn't have made a cake - I'm not hungry; she needn't make such a fuss about a little spider* (NOTE: **needn't** is only used with other verbs and is not followed by **to**. Note also the difference in meanings: **mustn't** = not allowed; **needn't** = not necessary: **we mustn't be late; you needn't hurry**)

needs [niːdz] *noun* what is basically needed; *the hospital caters to the needs of the local community; it's a full-time job looking after a baby's everyday needs;* **special needs** = special requirements for people who have disabilities; *people with special needs can claim grants from the government*

needy ['niːdi] **1** *adjective* very poor; *an organization dedicated to helping needy people in Africa* (NOTE: **needier - neediest**) **2** *noun* **the needy** = poor people; *he tried to help the needy as much as he could*

nefarious [nɪ'feəriəs] *adjective (formal)* very wicked; *he was engaged in various nefarious plots to overthrow the government*

negate [nɪ'geɪt] *verb* to cancel something out, to remove the effect of something; *the rise in inflation negates the effect of the pay increase*

negative ['negətɪv] **1** *noun* **(a)** meaning 'no'; *the answer was in the negative* **(b)** developed film with an image where the light parts are dark and dark parts light; *don't touch the negatives with your dirty fingers* **2** *adjective* **(a)** showing the absence of something; *her blood test was negative;* **a negative response** = saying 'no' **(b) negative pole** = the end of a magnet which points to the south **(c) negative film** = film where the light parts are dark and the dark parts are light (as opposed to positive film) **(d) negative terminal** = one of the terminals in a battery, shown by a minus (-) sign; *the brown wire should be attached to the negative terminal* (NOTE: the opposite is **positive**)

neglect [nɪ'glekt] **1** *noun* lack of care; *the building has suffered from years of neglect* **2** *verb* **(a)** to fail to look after someone *or* something properly; *he neglected his three children; the building had been neglected by its owners* **(b)** *(formal)* not to do something; *she neglected to return her income tax form; he neglected to tell the police that he had been involved in an accident*

neglected [nɪ'glektɪd] *adjective* not looked after; *as the recession hit the town, more and more shops stood empty and neglected*

negligence ['neglɪdʒəns] *noun* lack of proper care; not doing what you should do; *it was through his negligence that the safe was left unlocked; she is suing*

the car manufacturer for negligence; **criminal negligence** = acting recklessly with the result that harm is done to other people; **gross negligence** = act showing very serious neglect of your duty towards other people

negligent ['neglɪdʒənt] *adjective* showing negligence, not taking proper care; *the defendant was negligent in carrying out his duties as a trustee*

negligible ['neglɪdʒəbl] *adjective* very small, not worth bothering about; *the effect of the strike on the economy was negligible;* **not negligible** = quite large; *the loss was not a negligible one*

negotiable [nɪ'gəʊsiəbl] *adjective* **(a)** which can be changed or decided by discussions between the people involved; *the salary for the job is negotiable;* **negotiable instrument** = document (such as a bill of exchange) which can be exchanged for cash; **not negotiable** = which cannot be exchanged for cash **(b)** (path) which can be used; *the route through the mountains is only negotiable during the summer*

negotiate [nɪ'gəʊsieɪt] *verb* **(a)** to discuss with someone; *we are negotiating with the travel agent about a refund* **(b)** to make a commercial arrangement; *the two parties negotiated the terms of the contract* **(c)** to go round something which is in the way; *we had to negotiate several boulders in the road*

negotiating table [nɪ'gəʊsieɪtɪŋ 'teɪbl] *noun* meeting between parties to negotiate; *our aim is to bring the two sides to the negotiating table*

negotiation [nɪˌgəʊsi'eɪʃn] *noun* **(a)** discussing; *the only answer to this conflict is peaceful negotiation;* **it is open to negotiation** = the terms can be negotiated (NOTE: no plural in this meaning) **(b) negotiations** = discussions; *we have started negotiations with the management over new contracts of employment*

negotiator [nɪ'gəʊsieɪtə] *noun* person who discusses; *union negotiators discussed terms with the directors*

neigh [neɪ] **1** *noun* sound made by a horse; *the horse gave a loud neigh and galloped off* **2** *verb* to make the sound of a horse; *we could hear the horses neighing in the stables; see also* BLEAT, GRUNT, LOW

neighbour *US* **neighbor** ['neɪbə] *noun* **(a)** person who lives near you, who is sitting next to you, etc.; *help yourself and then pass the plate on to your neighbour; he doesn't get on with his neighbours;* **next-door neighbours** = people who live in the house next to yours; **the Swedes and the Norwegians are neighbours** = their countries are close together **(b)** *(old)* another person; *love of your neighbour is one of the essentials of Christian doctrine*

neighbourhood *US* **neighborhood** ['neɪbəhʊd] *noun* **(a)** small area and the people who live in it; *this is a quiet neighbourhood, we don't like noisy parties; the doctor knows everyone in the neighbourhood* **(b) in the neighbourhood of** = (i) near; (ii) approximately; *there are three hotels in the neighbourhood of the Conference Centre; the sum involved is in the neighbourhood of £100,000*

neighbouring *US* **neighboring** ['neɪbərɪŋ] *adjective* which is close to you; *there are no shops where we live, so we go to the neighbouring village to do our shopping; Sweden and Denmark are neighbouring countries*

neighbourly *US* **neighborly** ['neɪbəli] friendly to the people near you; *it's very neighbourly of you to* *lend us your lawnmower*; *people in this street aren't very neighbourly*

neither ['neɪðə or 'niːðə] **1** *adjective & pronoun* not either of two (people, etc.); *neither car or neither of the cars passed the test*; *neither sister is dark or neither of the sisters is dark* **2** *adverb* not either; *he doesn't eat meat and neither does his wife*; *she isn't fat but neither is she really very thin* **3** *conjunction*; **neither...nor** = not one...and not the other; *the water is neither too hot nor too cold - it's just right*; *she's neither Chinese nor Japanese - she comes from Korea*; *neither his mother nor his father is coming to the wedding*; **neither here nor there** = not important; *whether you go by bus or tube is neither here nor there, provided you get to the meeting on time*

neoclassical ['niːəʊ'klæsɪkl] *adjective* in the ancient Greek and Roman style; *his neoclassical design for the library was rejected in favour of a more modern one*

neologism [ni'ɒlədʒɪzm] *noun* new word, one that has come into use very recently; *the dictionary contains quite a few neologisms*

neon ['niːɒn] *noun* inert gas found in very small quantities in the atmosphere and used in illuminated signs; *they installed neon lighting at the motorway junctions*; *there are massive neon signs all round Piccadilly Circus* (NOTE: Chemical element: chemical symbol: **Ne**; atomic number: **10**)

nephew ['nefjuː] *noun* son of a sister or brother; *my nephew has set up his own business*

Neptune ['neptjuːn] *noun* the eighth planet from the sun, much heavier than the Earth; *the orbit of Neptune*

nerve [nɜːv] **1** *noun* **(a)** thread in the body which takes messages to and from the brain; *nerves are very delicate and easily damaged* **(b) to be in a state of nerves** = to be tense and worried; **to get on someone's nerves** = to annoy someone; *that humming noise is really getting on my nerves* **(c)** *(informal)* over-confidence *or* rudeness; *he's got a nerve to ask for a day off, when he was away all last week* **2** *verb* **nerve yourself** = to get all your strength together; *he nerved himself against the meeting with the police*; *she nerved herself to take her driving test*

nervous ['nɜːvəs] *adjective* **(a)** referring to the nerves; *the nervous system*; **nervous energy** = excited tense energy **(b)** worried and timid; *she gets nervous if she is alone in the house at night*; *he's nervous about driving in London*; *to be of a nervous disposition*

nervous breakdown ['nɜːvəs 'breɪkdaʊn] *noun* non-medical term for a sudden mental illness, where a patient becomes so depressed and worried that he or she is incapable of doing anything; *he had a nervous breakdown after he was made redundant*; *our poor accountant seems to be heading for a nervous breakdown*

nervous system ['nɜːvəs 'sɪstəm] *noun* system of nerves in the body, including the spinal cord and nerve centres; *the poison affects the whole nervous system*

nervy ['nɜːvi] *adjective (informal)* worried, uneasy; *she's so nervy, she jumps every time the phone rings*

nest [nest] **1** *noun* construction built by birds to lay their eggs in; *the bird built their nests among the trees*; *the blackbirds have laid three eggs in their nest* **2** *verb (of birds)* to build a nest and lay eggs; *the swans are nesting by the river bank*; **nesting site** = place where a bird may build a nest

nest egg ['nest 'eg] *noun* money which you have saved; *we've saved up a nice little nest egg for our retirement*

nestle ['nesl] *verb* **(a)** to settle in comfort; *the cat nestled down quietly in the cushions*; *the children nestled round their mother as she read them a story* **(b)** to be in a safe and sheltered place; *their cottage nestles at the bottom of the valley*; *a church nestling in the hills*

nestling ['neslɪŋ] *noun* baby bird still in the nest; *the robin is bringing food for its nestlings*

net [net] **1** *noun* **(a)** woven material with large holes; *a long petticoat made of pink net*; **net curtains** = light curtains made of thin material **(b)** piece of this material used for a special purpose; **a butterfly net** = bag of netting with which you can catch butterflies; **a fishing net** = large piece of material with holes, used by fishermen to catch fish; **a tennis net** = piece of material with holes, stretched across the middle of a tennis court; *he hit the ball into the net* **(c) the Net** = INTERNET; *see also* SURF **2** *verb* to make a profit; *we netted £3,000 on the deal* (NOTE: **netting - netted**) **3** *adjective* after deductions; *that figure is net not gross*; **net earnings** *or* **net income** *or* **net salary** = money earned after tax has been deducted; **net price** = final price which is paid by the purchaser; **net profit** = profit calculated after deducting all expenses; **net weight** = weight after deducting the weight of packaging material (NOTE: also spelt **nett weight** in this meaning; the opposite is **gross**)

netball ['netbɔːl] *noun* team game similar to basketball, played by two teams of seven players, usually women, in which the aim is to score points by getting the ball through a horizontal ring into a high net; *she's captain of the school netball team*

COMMENT: a match is made up of four 15-minute quarters. Each player wears a bib with letters indicating the player's position in the side. The ball must be played through each third of the court; it cannot just be lobbed from one end to the other (as in basketball), nor can a player run with the ball nor hold the ball longer than 3 seconds

Netherlands ['neðələndz] *noun* European country, to the west of Germany and north of Belgium; *Amsterdam is the largest city in the Netherlands*; *see also* DUTCH, HOLLAND (NOTE: capital: **Amsterdam**; people: **the Dutch**; language: **Dutch**; currency: **guilder, euro**)

nett [net] *see* NET

netting ['netɪŋ] *noun* loosely woven material; *we put up wire netting to keep out rabbits*

nettle ['netl] **1** *noun* **(stinging) nettle** = type of common weed which stings when you touch it; *he walked bare-legged through the wood and got stung by nettles*; **to grasp the nettle** = to deal with a problem quickly and firmly to settle it before it causes you any more trouble; *no politician has dared grasp the nettle of sponsorship of sport* **2** *verb* to make someone annoyed; *she was clearly nettled by his remarks*

network ['netwɜːk] **1** *noun* **(a)** system of linked roads, railways, etc.; *there is a network of tunnels under the castle*; *the British rail network*; *a satellite TV network* **(b)** linked computer system; *how does this network operate?*; *you can book at any of our hotels throughout the country using our computer network*

(c) group of people linked together; *his rapidly developing network of contacts in government; see also* OLD BOY NETWORK **2** *verb* to link up two or more computers to allow them to exchange information; *workstations are usually networked and share resources*

networking ['netwɜːkɪŋ] *noun* **(a)** broadcasting a TV programme over several stations at the same time; *TV executives are always hoping to find popular programmes suitable for nationwide networking* **(b)** keeping in contact with people who are in the same profession as you and who may be able to help you; *a conference is a good opportunity to do some networking*

neural ['njʊrəl] *adjective* referring to a nerve or the nervous system; *the accident victim suffered severe neural damage*

neurological [njʊərəˈlɒdʒɪkl] *adjective* referring to neurology; *neurological research*

neurology [njuːˈrɒlədʒi] *noun* study of nerves and disorders associated with them; *he specialized in neurology after he had finished his medical training*

neuron *or* **neurone** ['njʊrɒn] *noun* nerve cell, cell in the nervous system which transmits nerve impulses; *brain tissue consists mainly of neurons*

neurosis [njuˈrəʊsɪs] *noun* illness of the personality, in which a patient becomes obsessed with something and experiences strong emotions about it, such as fear of empty spaces; *it is a form of neurosis that has a terrible effect on the sufferer's social life* (NOTE: plural is **neuroses** [njuˈrəʊsiːz])

neurotic [njuˈrɒtɪk] **1** *adjective* worried or obsessed with something; *she has a neurotic dislike of cats; don't get neurotic about the change in the firm's logo* **2** *noun* person who has neurosis; *he's a neurotic who genuinely believes spiders will kill him*

neuter ['njuːtə] **1** *adjective (in grammar)* neither masculine nor feminine (in some languages, such as German and Latin); *strangely enough, the usual word for 'girl' in German is neuter* **2** *verb* to remove an animal's sex organs; *we took our tomcat to the vet to have him neutered*

neutral ['njuːtrəl] **1** *adjective* **(a)** not in favour of one side or the other in a dispute; *the UN sent in neutral observers; the arbitrator has to stay neutral* **(b)** refusing to take part in a war; *during the war, Switzerland remained neutral* **(c)** with a light colour, such as beige or pale grey; *red walls, green upholstery and a neutral carpet* **2** *noun* **(a)** country which does not take part in a war **(b)** citizen of a neutral country; *only neutrals were admitted to the talks* **(c)** *(cars, trucks, etc.)* not in gear; *the car is in neutral*

neutrality [njuˈtrælɪti] *noun* being neutral in a war; *Switzerland maintained its neutrality through two world wars;* **armed neutrality** = state where a country is neutral during a war, but keeps armed forces to defend itself

neutralization [njuːtrəlaɪˈzeɪʃn] *noun* counteracting the harmful effects of something; *the powder should help the neutralization of stomach acid; our first aim was the neutralization of our rival's publicity campaign*

neutralize ['njuːtrəlaɪz] *verb* **(a)** to make an acid neutral; *acid in drainage water can be neutralized by limestone* **(b)** to counteract the effect of something; *we*

acted immediately to neutralize the threat from their navy **(c)** to make a poison harmless; *you need to act quickly to neutralize the effects of the snake bite*

neutron ['njuːtrɒn] *noun* neutral particle in the nucleus of an atom; *the nucleus of an atom is composed of neutrons and protons*

never ['nevə] *adverb* not at any time; not ever; *we'll never forget that restaurant; I've never bought anything in that shop although I've often been inside it; he never eats meat;* **never mind!** = don't worry, don't bother about it

never-ending ['nevə 'endɪŋ] *adjective* which seems as if it will never stop; *there followed a never-ending series of little disputes; the compilation of a dictionary is a never-ending task*

nevertheless [nevəðəˈles] *adverb* in spite of all that; *I know it is raining, but nevertheless I'd like to go for a walk along the beach; she had a cold, but went to the meeting nevertheless*

new [njuː] *adjective* **(a)** made quite recently, never used before; *put some new paper in the printer; this is the new model - it's just come out; are your shoes new?* **(b)** which arrived recently, fresh; *there are two new secretaries in the office;* **new potatoes** = first young potatoes of a year's harvest **(c)** which has just been bought; *she bought herself a new motorbike; he's trying to get his new computer to work* **(d)** quite different from what was before; *we need someone with new ideas; they put some new wallpaper in the bedroom* (NOTE: **newer - newest**)

newborn ['njuːbɔːn] *adjective* which has been born recently; *the mother and her newborn baby survived the crash*

newcomer ['njuːkʌmə] *noun* person who has just come to a place; *the family are newcomers to the village; could all newcomers to the meeting please sign the register?*

new face ['njuː 'feɪs] *noun* person whom you have not seen before, who has not been part of something before; *you're a new face in here, aren't you?; there are several new faces in the England international squad*

newfangled [njuːˈfæŋgld] *adjective* modern and complicated; *I don't like these newfangled ideas of his; I prefer an old-fashioned corkscrew to this newfangled contraption*

new-found ['njuːfaʊnd] *adjective* that has been found recently; *he delighted in his new-found freedom; Jane decided to keep her new-found friend a secret from the rest of her family*

newly ['njuːli] *adverb* recently; *he was showing off his newly acquired car; the house has been bought by a newly married couple*

newly-weds ['njuːliˈwedz] *noun* couple who have just got married

new moon ['njuː 'muːn] *noun* time when the moon is visible as only a thin crescent; *the guerrillas waited for the new moon to make their attack*

news [njuːz] *noun* spoken or written information about what has happened; *what's the news of your sister?; she told me all the latest news about the office; he was watching the 10 o'clock news on TV; I don't want to hear any bad news;* **have you heard the news?** = have you heard what has happened?; *have you had any news about your pay rise?;* **to break the news to**

someone = to tell someone the bad news; *he broke the news to his daughters*; **no news is good news** = if there is nothing new to mention, things must be going well (NOTE: **news** is singular, not plural)

news agency ['njuːz 'eɪdʒənsi] *noun* office which distributes information to newspapers and TV; *he works for an international news agency*

newsagent ['njuːzeɪdʒənt] *noun* person who sells newspapers; *my father has always been a newsagent*

newsagent's ['njuːzeɪdʒənts] *noun* shop selling newspapers, sweets, cigarettes, etc.; *he went to the newsagent's to buy some cigarettes*; *there's a newsagent's next door to the pub*

newsboy ['njuːzbɔɪ] *noun* boy who sells newspapers in the street; *the newsboys were shouting in the street that the government had collapsed*

newscast ['njuːzkɑːst] *noun* news programme on radio or TV; *the report arrived too late for the early-evening newscast*

newscaster ['njuːzkɑːstə] *noun* person who reads the news on radio or TV; *a highly-respected BBC newscaster*

newscasting ['njuːzkɑːstɪŋ] *noun* reading the news on radio or TV; *she is looking for a career in newscasting*

news conference ['njuːz 'kɒnfərəns] *noun* meeting with journalists to give information about something and answer questions; *the mountaineers held a news conference at the airport on their return*

newsflash ['njuːzflæʃ] *noun* short item of news broadcast at an unexpected time; *there was a newsflash about a bomb in central London*; *we interrupt the programme for a newsflash*

newsletter ['njuːzletə] *noun* printed sheet or small newspaper giving news about a company, a club or other organization; *the details of the church fair are in the June newsletter*

news media ['njuːz 'miːdiə] *noun* the media which give news, i.e. TV, radio and the press; *the news media are accused of never telling people what is happening*; *the news media haven't shown much interest in the story*

newspaper ['njuːzpeɪpə] *noun* publication consisting of loose folded sheets of paper, which usually comes out each day, with news of what has happened; **a daily newspaper** = newspaper which is published every day except Sunday; *we saw your picture in the local newspaper*; *I couldn't finish the crossword in yesterday's newspaper*; *the newspapers are full of news of the election* (NOTE: **a newspaper** is often simply called a **paper**)

newspaperman ['njuːzpeɪpəmən] *noun* journalist, a person who works on a newspaper; *he started his career as a newspaperman before moving to television*

newsprint ['njuːzprɪnt] *noun* cheap paper used for newspapers and magazines; *the price of newsprint has risen sharply*; *a shortage of newsprint meant the paper was only half its normal size* (NOTE: no plural)

newsreader ['njuːzriːdə] *noun* person who reads the news on radio or TV; *you don't often hear newsreaders mispronouncing words* (NOTE: also called a **newscaster**)

newsreel ['njuːzriːl] *noun* short film about current events; *in the old days, they used to show a short film and a newsreel before starting the main film*

newsroom ['njuːzruːm] *noun (in a newspaper office, TV or radio station)* room where news reports are received and prepared for publication or broadcasting; *there was frantic activity in the newsroom as reports of the disaster started coming through*

newssheet ['njuːzʃiːt] *noun* simple type of newspaper usually with very few pages; *a friend lent me his computer and I began to produce a newssheet for other members of the fan club*

newsstall *or* **newsstand** ['njuːzstɔːl *or* 'njuːzstænd] *noun* mainly *US* small shop or kiosk selling books, newspapers and magazines; *she bought a magazine at the newsstand at the corner of the street* (NOTE: British English is also **bookstall**)

news vendor ['njuːz 'vendə] *noun* person who sells newspapers in the street; *two news vendors had set up their stalls at the entrance to the station*

newsworthy ['njuːzwɜːði] *adjective* interesting enough to be in the newspapers or on radio or TV; *it's probably the only newsworthy thing that's happened this week*

newt [njuːt] *noun* little lizard-like animal, living in water; *Simon found some newts in our garden pond*; *my brother-in-law breeds newts as a hobby*

New Testament ['njuː 'testəmənt] *noun* the second part of the Bible, which deals with the life of Jesus Christ, his teachings and the work of his followers; *the epistles of St Paul form one of the books of the New Testament*

the New World [ðə 'njuː 'wɜːld] *noun* North and South America; *a plant which comes originally from the New World*

New Year ['njuː 'jɜː] *noun* first few days of the year; *I started my new job in the New Year*; **Happy New Year!** = good wishes for the New Year; **New Year's resolution** = plan to improve your way of living, decided on at the New Year, and usually abandoned shortly afterwards; *each New Year I make the same resolutions, but never manage to keep them*; **to stay up to see the New Year in** = to stay up until after midnight on 31st December to celebrate the beginning of the New Year

New Year's Day [njuː jɜːz 'deɪ] *noun* 1st January; *it's a shame you have to work on New Year's Day*

New Year's Eve [njuː jɜːz 'iːv] *noun* 31st December; *the only time we drink champagne is on New Year's Eve*

New York ['njuː 'jɔːk] *noun* large town on the Eastern coast of the USA; *we are due to arrive in New York at 5 o'clock*; *she's the manager of our New York office*; *New York seems to get busier and busier each time I visit*; *yesterday New York had three inches of snow*

New Zealand ['njuː 'ziːlənd] *noun* country in the Pacific Ocean, to the east of Australia; *the sheep trade is important to the New Zealand economy* (NOTE: capital: **Wellington**; people: **New Zealanders**; language: **English**; currency: **New Zealand dollar**)

New Zealander ['njuː 'ziːləndə] *noun* person from New Zealand; *my niece recently married a New Zealander*

next [nekst] **1** *adjective & adverb* **(a)** coming after in time; *on Wednesday we go to Paris, and the next day we travel to Italy; first you put the eggs into a bowl and next you add some sugar; don't forget to give me a call when you're next in town; next week is the start of our holiday; the next time you go to the supermarket, can you get some coffee?* **(b)** nearest in place; *the ball went over the fence into the next garden; she took the seat next to mine;* **it costs next to nothing** = it doesn't cost very much **2** *pronoun* the thing or person following; *after two buses went past full, the next was almost empty; I'll be back from holiday the week after next; (asking the next person in the queue to come) next, please!*

next door ['nekst 'dɔː] *adjective & adverb* in the house next to this one; *who lives next door to your mother?; the shop is next door to a bank; our next-door neighbours have gone on holiday, and we are looking after their cat*

next of kin ['nekstəv'kɪn] *noun* nearest relative(s); *after the fatal accident, the police informed the next of kin; names of the victims will not be released until their next of kin have been informed*

NGO ['en 'dʒiː 'əʊ] = NON-GOVERNMENTAL ORGANIZATION (NOTE: plural is **NGOs**)

NHS ['en 'eɪtʃ 'es] = NATIONAL HEALTH SERVICE

niacin ['naɪəsɪn] *noun* vitamin of the vitamin B complex, found in milk, meat, liver, yeast, beans, peas and bread

nib [nɪb] *noun* the point of a pen, from which the ink flows; *I've bent the nib of my fountain pen and it won't write properly*

nibble ['nɪbl] **1** *verb* to take small bites; *she was nibbling a biscuit; the mice have nibbled into the flour sacks* **2** *noun* (*informal*) **nibbles** = little snacks, such as peanuts or crisps, served with drinks

NIC = NATIONAL INSURANCE CONTRIBUTIONS

nice [naɪs] *adjective* **(a)** pleasant, fine; *we had a nice time at the seaside; if the weather's nice let's have a picnic; the nicest thing about the town is that it is on the sea; try and be nice to your grandfather* **(b)** pleasant, polite; *that wasn't a very nice thing to say* (NOTE: **nicer - nicest**)

nicely ['naɪsli] *adverb* **(a)** very well; *that will do nicely, thank you* **(b)** politely; *you can have a biscuit if you ask for it nicely*

niche [niːʃ] *noun* **(a)** rounded hollow place in a wall; *there are statues in niches all round the garden* **(b)** to find your niche *or* to find a niche for yourself *or* to carve out a niche for yourself = to find the right job or activity for yourself; *he found his niche working in an animal hospital;* **market niche** = special place in a market, occupied by one company; *they're a niche company making only garden gnomes*

nick [nɪk] **1** *noun* **(a)** small notch; *he made a nick in the stick* **(b)** (*informal*) **in the nick of time** = just in time **(c)** (*slang*) prison; *he's been in the nick for the last year* **(d)** (*slang*) **in good nick** = in good condition; *the car was in quite good nick so I bought it* **2** *verb* **(a)** to make a small notch or cut; *he nicked his finger with a razor blade* **(b)** (*slang*) to steal; *a group of young lads who went around nicking things from the local shops; who's nicked my umbrella?*

nickel ['nɪkl] *noun* **(a)** metallic element, used in making special metal alloys; *we use an alloy of copper and nickel;* **nickel-plated saucepans have some advantages over aluminium** (NOTE: Chemical element: chemical symbol: **Ni**; atomic number: **28**) **(b)** *US* 5-cent coin; *can you lend me a nickel?*

nickname ['nɪkneɪm] **1** *noun* short or informal name given to someone; *her real name's Henrietta, but everyone calls her by her nickname 'Bobbles'* **2** *verb* to give a nickname to; *he was nicknamed 'Camel' because of his big nose*

nicotine ['nɪkətiːn] *noun* toxic substance in tobacco, also used as an insecticide; *nicotine is addictive;* **nicotine-stained fingers** = yellow fingers from smoking cigarettes

niece [niːs] *noun* daughter of a brother or sister; *his niece had just given birth to her second child*

nigh [naɪ] *adverb* (*old*) (*formal*) near; *it was nigh on fifty years since he had left his family and gone to seek his fortune in the West Indies; repent your sins! the end of the world is nigh!*

night [naɪt] *noun* part of the day when it is dark; *it's dangerous to walk alone in the streets at night; burglars got into the office during the night; he is on night duty three days a week; they're planning to have a night out tomorrow; see also* OWL (NOTE: do not confuse with **knight**)

nightclub ['naɪtklʌb] *noun* club which is only open at night; *our daughter will only come with us on holiday if we go to a resort with lots of nightclubs*

nightdress ['naɪtdres] *noun* loose dress worn by a girl or woman in bed; *a cotton nightdress is best in hot climates* (NOTE: usually called a **nightie**)

nightie ['naɪti] *noun* (*informal*) nightdress; *she packed a small suitcase with her sponge bag and nightie*

nightingale ['naɪtɪŋgeɪl] *noun* small singing bird which sings at night; *the nightingale has the most beautiful song*

night life ['naɪtlaɪf] *noun* entertainment in a town at night; *the place is dead - there's no night life; the beaches are fine, but the night life is very dull*

nightly ['naɪtli] *adverb* every night; *car thefts are a nightly occurrence around here*

nightmare ['naɪtmeə] *noun* **(a)** very frightening dream; *I had a nightmare that I was drowning* **(b)** horrible experience; *the dinner party was a nightmare; a nightmare journey across the desert*

nightstick ['naɪtstɪk] *noun US* long stick carried by a policeman; *the policeman walked up swinging his nightstick* (NOTE: British English is **truncheon**)

night-time ['naɪttaɪm] *noun* period when it is night; *the airport has banned night-time flights; night-time phone calls are cheaper*

Nikkei Average [nɪ'keɪ 'ævrɪdʒ] index of prices on the Tokyo Stock Exchange, based on about 200 leading shares; *the Nikkei Average rose seven points; see also* DOW JONES, FOOTSIE

nil [nɪl] *noun* nothing; *our advertising budget has been cut to nil*

nimble ['nɪmbl] *adjective* able to move quickly; *she's still very nimble even though she's 80; her nimble* *fingers counted the pile of notes* (NOTE: **nimbler - nimblest**)

nine [naɪn] **(a)** number 9; *she's nine (years old) tomoroow*; *the shop opens at 9 o'clock*; **nine times out of ten** = very often; *see also* DRESSED **(b) 999** ['naɪn 'naɪn 'naɪn] telephone number to call the emergency services in Britain; *the firemen came quickly when we called 999*; *the ambulance braved the snowstorm to answer the 999 call*

nineteen [naɪn'tiːn] number 19; *he's nineteen (years old) tomorrow*; **the nineteen fifteen train** = the train leaving at 19.15; **the nineteen hundreds (1900s)** = the years from 1900 to 1999; **in the 1950s** = during the years 1950 to 1959 (NOTE: the **1950s**: say 'the nineteen fifties')

nineteenth (19th) [naɪn'tiːnθ] *adjective & noun* referring to nineteen; *it's his nineteenth birthday tomorrow*; **the nineteenth century** = the period from 1800 to 1899; *the nineteenth of August or August the nineteenth (August 19th)* (NOTE: with dates **nineteenth** is usually written **19th: July 19th, 1935; October 19th, 1991** (American style is **October 19, 1991**), say 'the nineteenth of October' or 'October the nineteenth' (American style is 'October nineteenth')

ninetieth (90th) ['naɪntiəθ] *adjective & noun* referring to ninety; *a ninetieth of a second*; *it will be grandfather's ninetieth birthday next month*

ninety ['naɪnti] number 90; *my old aunt will be ninety (years old) next week and her husband is ninety-two: they are both in their nineties*; **the nineteen nineties (1990s)** = the years from 1990 to 1999 (NOTE: **ninety-one** (91), **ninety-two** (92), etc., but **ninety-first** (91st), **ninety-second** (92nd), etc.)

El Niño [el 'niːnjəʊ] *noun* phenomenon which occurs every few years in the Pacific Ocean, where a mass of warm water moves from west to east, causing very high tides along the Pacific coast of South America; *climatic changes such as those produced by El Niño*

> COMMENT: El Niño does not only bring high tides, but has a dramatic effect on rainfall worldwide, with higher than usual rainfall along the coast of the Pacific, and droughts in Africa, India and Australia. After each El Niño, the phenomenon is reversed, with droughts along the Pacific Coast and heavy rain in Africa, India and Australia: this is commonly known as 'La Niña'

ninth (9th) [naɪnθ] *adjective & noun* referring to nine; *tomorrow is his ninth birthday*; *today is the ninth of June or June the ninth (June 9th) he missed the record by a ninth of a second*; **the ninth century** = the period from 800 to 899 AD (NOTE: with dates **ninth** is usually written **9th: July 9th, 1935; October 9th, 1991** (American style is **October 9, 1991**) say 'the ninth of October' or 'October the ninth' (American style is 'October ninth'); with names of kings and queens **ninth** is usually written **IX: King Charles IX** (say: 'King Charles the Ninth')

nip [nɪp] **1** *noun* **(a)** short sharp bite; *the little dog gave him a nasty nip* **(b)** small amount of alcohol; *we sell whisky at £1 per nip* **(c)** **there's a nip in the air** = the air feels cold **2** *verb* **(a)** to pinch sharply; *we nipped off the end of the stalk to stop the plant growing any taller; the crab nipped his thumb as he picked it up; see also* BUD **(b)** to bite sharply; *the dog nipped the postman in the leg* **(c)** *(informal)* to go very quickly;

I'll just nip round to the newsagent's and get the evening paper; we'll nip down to the pub for a drink (NOTE: **nipping - nipped**)

nipple ['nɪpl] *noun* **(a)** darker part in the centre of a woman's breast, through which the milk passes; *she held the baby to her nipple* **(b)** valve for greasing a machine; *a grease nipple*

nippy ['nɪpi] *adjective (informal)* **(a)** cold; *put on your coat, it's quite nippy outside* **(b)** which goes fast; *it's a nippy little car* (NOTE: **nippier - nippiest**)

nitrate ['naɪtreɪt] *noun* chemical compound containing nitrogen and oxygen, existing in all plants; *nitrates are often used in fertilizer*

nitrogen ['naɪtrədʒən] *noun* important gas which is essential for life, and which forms most of the atmosphere; *nitrogen is absorbed into the body from protein* (NOTE: Chemical element: chemical symbol: **N**; atomic number: **7**)

nitwit ['nɪtwɪt] *noun (informal)* stupid idiot; *you nitwit, you're not supposed to tell them what cards you're holding!*

no [nəʊ] *adjective & adverb* **(a)** *(showing the opposite of 'yes')* *I asked my mother if we could borrow her car but she said 'no'; do you want another cup of coffee? - no, thank you* **(b)** not any; *there's no milk left in the fridge; we live in a little village, and there's no post office for miles around; we had no reply to our fax* **(c)** *(signs)* **no entry** = do not go in this way; **no exit** = do not go out this way; **no parking** = do not park; **no smoking** = do not smoke **(d)** *(informal)* **no way** = certainly not; *will you lend me £2000? - no way!* **(e)** not at all; *my new kitchen knife is no sharper than the old one; she no longer works here; I'm no good at maths*

no. ['nʌmbə] *abbreviation for* NUMBER

Nobel prize [nəʊ'bel 'praɪz] *noun* one of several prizes awarded annually for science, literature, peace, etc.; *he won the Nobel Prize for Literature in 1986*

> COMMENT: the Nobel Prizes were founded by Alfred Nobel, the Swedish inventor of dynamite. They are awarded annually by the Nobel Foundation in Stockholm and are given in the fields of chemistry, physics, medicine, literature, economics and peace. The prizes are very prestigious

nobility [nə'bɪlɪti] *noun* **(a)** all noble families, taken as a group; *the king invited members of the nobility to the meeting; the nobility fought hard to protect their privileges* **(b)** *(formal)* being noble, being impressive and admirable; *the nobility of his actions is not in doubt* (NOTE: no plural)

noble ['nəʊbl] **1** *noun* person of high rank; *the nobles forced the king to sign the treaty* **2** *adjective* **(a)** of high rank in society; *she comes from a noble family - her father is an earl* **(b)** with a fine character; *it was very noble of him to lend her his umbrella; she did it for the noblest of reasons* **(c)** **the noble gases** = INERT GASES (NOTE: **nobler - noblest**)

nobleman ['nəʊblmən] *noun* man of high rank; *she is the daughter of a French nobleman* (NOTE: plural is **noblemen**)

noblewoman ['nəʊblwʊmən] *noun* woman of high rank; *as a noblewoman she expects to be treated with great respect* (NOTE: plural is **noblewomen**)

nobody ['nəubədi] *pronoun* no one *or* no person; *there was nobody in the café; we met nobody on our way here; nobody wants to do her job; you'll have to drive the bus - nobody else has a driving licence*

no claims bonus [nəu 'kleɪmz 'bəunəs] *noun* reduced insurance premium because no claims have been made against the policy; *the insurance premium is £300 but I have a 50% no claims bonus*

no-confidence vote ['nəu'kɒnfɪdəns 'vəut] *noun* vote to show that a person or group cannot be trusted; *when the government lost the no-confidence vote, the Prime Minister had to call a general election; the chairman resigned after the vote of no-confidence in the committee*

nocturnal [nɒk'tɜːnl] *adjective* **(a)** referring to the night; *the nocturnal habits of the badger* **(b)** active at night; **nocturnal animals** = animals which are active at night, and sleep during the daytime (NOTE: the opposite, referring to animals that come out during the daytime, is **diurnal**)

nod [nɒd] **1** *noun* little movement of the head up and down, meaning 'yes'; *he gave me a nod as I came in;* (*informal*) **it went through on the nod** = it was accepted without any discussion **2** *verb* **(a)** to move the head slightly up and down, meaning 'yes'; *when he asked her if she understood the question, she nodded or nodded her head; he nodded to show his agreement* (NOTE: the opposite is to **shake** your head, meaning 'no') **(b)** to move the head slightly up and down, to mean 'hello' or 'goodbye'; *she nodded at me as I went past* **(c) to nod off** = to go to sleep; *she was nodding off in front of the television* (NOTE: **nodding - nodded**)

node [nəud] *noun* **(a) leaf node** = the point on the stem of a plant where a leaf is attached **(b)** small mass of tissue; group of nerve cells; **lymph nodes** = collections of lymph tissue found especially under the armpits and in the groin **(c)** point where two lines cross

no-go area ['nəugəu 'eəriə] *noun* area of a town where ordinary people or the police cannot go; *this government will not allow no-go areas to exist anywhere in the country*

noise [nɔɪz] *noun* **(a)** loud or unpleasant sound; *don't make any noise - the guards might hear you; the workmen are making such a lot of noise that we can't use the telephone* **(b)** sound in general; *the baby made a little gurgling noise; is there anything the matter with the washing machine - it's making a funny noise; there was a noise of running water in the bathroom; he woke up when he heard a noise in the kitchen*

noiseless ['nɔɪzləs] *adjective* making no noise; *the engine is virtually noiseless*

noiselessly ['nɔɪzləsli] *adverb* making no noise; *they crept noiselessly up to the house*

noisy ['nɔɪzi] *adjective* which makes a lot of noise; *a crowd of noisy little boys; unfortunately, the hotel overlooks a noisy crossroads; this lawn mower is noisier than our old one* (NOTE: **noisier - noisiest**)

nomad ['nəumæd] *noun* person who moves from place to place in a large area of land without settling in any one spot; *the nomads move their livestock from place to place to feed on available grazing*

nomadic [nəu'mædɪk] *adjective* **(a)** referring to nomads; *nomadic herdsmen wander across the plains with their cattle* **(b)** moving all the time; *families of*

diplomats lead a nomadic existence, moving from country to country

no-man's-land ['nəumænzlænd] *noun* land between two countries or armies, which does not belong to either; *the football match which took place in the no-man's-land between the trenches*

nomenclature [nə'menklətʃə] *noun* (*formal*) system of giving names; *the Linnaean system of nomenclature*

nominal ['nɒmɪnl] *adjective* **(a)** in name, not in fact; *he's the nominal head of the company, but his secretary does all the work; his appointment as director is entirely nominal - I will continue to be in charge* **(b)** involving a small amount of money; *we pay a nominal fee; the subscription is really nominal; we make a nominal charge for our services*

nominally ['nɒmɪnəli] *adverb* in name, not in fact; *she is nominally the managing director, but her son runs the company*

nominate ['nɒmɪneɪt] *verb* to propose someone for a post; *he's been nominated to the committee; she was nominated as Labour candidate in the next election*

nomination [nɒmɪ'neɪʃn] *noun* **(a)** action of nominating; *her nomination to the board of directors;* **nomination papers** = official forms by which someone is nominated as a candidate in an election **(b)** name which has been proposed; *there are three nominations for the post of secretary*

nominee [nɒmɪ'niː] *noun* person who has been proposed; *there are three nominees for the post of secretary;* **nominee account** = bank account held by a bank on behalf of someone

non- [nɒn] *prefix meaning* not

non-alcoholic [nɒnælkə'hɒlɪk] *adjective* not containing alcohol; *a non-alcoholic drink*

non-aligned [nɒnə'laɪnd] *adjective* **non-aligned state** = country which is not allied to a superpower; *after independence, India joined the group of non-aligned states*

nonchalance ['nɒnʃələns] *noun* being calm, not showing any excitement; *he affected an air of nonchalance, when really he was furious with his family*

nonchalant ['nɒnʃələnt] *adjective* not showing any excitement or worry about anything; *he had an innocent, nonchalant air; she's terribly nonchalant about the whole business*

non-commissioned officer (NCO) [nɒnkə'mɪʃnd 'ɒfɪsə] *noun* rank in the army such as a sergeant or corporal, below a full officer; *non-commissioned officers are mainly responsible for maintaining discipline in the ranks*

nonconformist [nɒnkən'fɔːmɪst] *adjective* **(a)** not following normal social conventions; *his nonconformist attitude to staff relations* (NOTE: the opposite is **conformist**) **(b) the Nonconformist Church** = Protestant Church in England which is not part of the Church of England

none [nʌn] *pronoun* **(a)** not any; *how many dogs have you got? - none; can you buy some milk, we've none left in the fridge?; a little money is better than none at all;* **her health is none too good** = it is not very good **(b)** not one; *none of my friends smokes; none of the group can speak Chinese* **2** *adverb* (used with 'the' *and comparative*) not at all; *she seems none the better for her holiday*; *he was none the worse for his accident* = he was not at all hurt in the accident; **to be none the wiser** = to know no more about it than you did before; *I read his report, and I'm still none the wiser*; *his lengthy explanation left us none the wiser about how the system would work*

nonentity [nɒ'nentɪti] *noun* person who is completely unimportant; *she's a beautiful girl, with lots of money and a first-class degree, and now she's married some nonentity in the Ministry of Transport*

nonetheless [nʌnθə'les] *adverb* in spite of all that; *I know it is raining, but nonetheless I'd like to go for a swim before breakfast*; *he had a cold, but went to the meeting nonetheless*

nonexistent [nɒnɪg'zɪstənt] *adjective* which does not exist, which is not real; *the danger of flooding is nonexistent, as the house is well above sea-level*; *the money was sent to a nonexistent company in the Bahamas*

non-fiction ['nɒnfɪkʃn] *noun* books which are about real things, events or people, and are not stories; *a well-known non-fiction author*; *don't send your novel to that publisher, they only publish non-fiction* (NOTE: no plural)

non-governmental organization (NGO) ['nɒn gʌvən'mentəl ɔːgənaɪ'zeɪʃn] *noun* organization, such as a charity or voluntary agency, which is not funded by a government, but which works on an international as well as a national level

> COMMENT: Oxfam, the Red Cross, Médecins sans Frontières, and other NGOs work in many countries to bring aid to people in need

no-no ['nəunəu] *noun* (*informal*) thing which is not allowed; *kissing the boss's secretary at the office party is an absolute no-no*

no-nonsense ['nəu'nɒnsəns] *adjective* sensible, serious and straightforward; *people liked her no-nonsense way of tackling problems*

non-payment [nɒn'peɪmənt] *noun* failure to pay; *he was sent to prison for non-payment of his fine*; **non-payment of a debt** = not paying money which is owed

non-profit ['nɒn'prɒfɪt] *adjective* not making a profit; *we run the club on a non-profit basis*

non-profit-making *US* **non-profit** ['nɒn'prɒfɪtmeɪkɪŋ] *adjective* which does make a profit, or is not allowed to make a profit; *the housing association is a strictly non-profit-making concern*; *non-profit-making organizations such as charities*

nonsense ['nɒnsəns] *noun* silly ideas; *I'm too fat - nonsense!*; *he talked a lot of nonsense*; *it's nonsense to expect people to pay money for that* (NOTE: no plural)

non-smoker ['nɒnsməukə] *noun* person who does not smoke; *this section of the restaurant is reserved for non-smokers*

non-smoking ['nɒnsməukɪŋ] *adjective* where smoking is not allowed; *the non-smoking section of a restaurant*; *all British Airways flights are non-smoking*

non-stick ['nɒnstɪk] *adjective* with a surface which prevents food sticking to it; *a non-stick frying pan*

non-stop ['nɒnstɒp] **1** *adjective* which does not stop; *a non-stop train to Paris*; *they took a non-stop flight to Australia*; *all our flights to the Toronto are non-stop* **2** *adverb* without stopping; *the planes flies to Hong Kong non-stop*; *they worked non-stop to finish the job on time*

nonsufficient funds [nɒnsə'fɪʃənt 'fʌndz] *noun US* not having enough money in an account to pay a cheque; *the check was returned marked 'nonsufficient funds'* (NOTE: the British equivalent is **returned to drawer**)

non-violent [nɒn'vaɪələnt] *adjective* with no violence; *a non-violent demonstration was broken up by the police*

noodles [nuːdlz] *noun* flat strips of pasta; *I ordered spicy meatballs with noodles*; *we started with chicken noodle soup*; **egg noodles** = noodles made with flour, water and egg

noon [nuːn] *noun* twelve o'clock in the middle of the day; *we'll stop for lunch at noon* (NOTE: also called **midday**)

no one ['nəuwʌn] *pronoun* nobody *or* no person; *you can go to the bathroom - there's no one there*; *we met no one we knew*; *no one here takes sugar in their tea*; *no one else has a driving licence so you'll have to be the driver*

noose [nuːs] *noun* loop in a piece of rope which becomes tight as you pull on it; *he felt the noose tightening around his neck*

nope [nəup] *interjection* (*informal*) no; *any luck? - nope!*

nor [nɔː] *conjunction* and not; *I did not meet him that year nor in subsequent years*; *I never went there again, nor did my wife*; *I don't want to go - nor me!*; *see also* NEITHER

norm [nɔːm] *noun* standard; *the machine is built to European norms*; *the output from this factory is well above the norm for the industry or well above the industry norm*

normal ['nɔːməl] *adjective* usual, what usually happens; *we hope to resume normal service as soon as possible*; *look at the rain - it's just a normal British summer*; *what's the size of a normal swimming pool?*; *at her age, it's only normal for her to want to go to parties*

normality [nɔː'mælɪti] *noun* being normal; *this week saw a welcome return to normality*

normalization [nɔːməlaɪ'zeɪʃn] *noun* making something normal again after it has been disrupted, for example by a war or a crisis; *a normalization of relations between the two countries*

normalize ['nɔːməlaɪz] *verb* to make normal again; *we've done what we can to try to normalize the situation*

normally ['nɔːməli] *adverb* usually; *the bus is normally late*; *she doesn't normally drink wine*

Norman ['nɔːmən] **1** *adjective* (**a**) referring to Normandy, the northern part of France; *a typical Norman town* (**b**) referring to the people from Normandy who conquered England in 1066; *after the Norman conquest, French became widely spoken in England*; *the Norman style of architecture is heavy with round arches and thick pillars*; *an old Norman castle stands above the town* **2** *noun* person from

Normandy; *William the Conqueror and the Normans invaded England in 1066*

> COMMENT: the name Norman comes from the fact that Normandy was invaded by the Vikings, or Norsemen, from Scandinavia; the Norman chiefs, such as William the Conqueror, were descended from earlier Norse invaders

normative ['nɔːmətɪv] *adjective (formal)* which sets a standard for other things; *the judgment can be considered as normative for future cases*; **normative grammar** = grammar which tells you how to write correctly

Norse [nɔːs] *adjective* referring to ancient Norway or Scandinavia; *Norse invaders attacked the east of England in the 8th century*

Norseman ['nɔːsmen] *noun* ancient inhabitants of Norway and other parts of Scandinavia, who travelled widely in the early Middle Ages (8th to 10th centuries), and attacked and colonized parts of England and northern France; *see also* VIKINGS

north [nɔːθ] **1** *noun* direction to your left when you are facing the direction where the sun rises; *there will be snow in the north of the country; it's cold when the wind blows from the north* **2** *adjective* referring to the north; *we went on holiday to the north coast of Scotland; the north side of our house never gets any sun; when the north wind blows, you can expect snow* **3** *adverb* towards the north; *they were travelling north at the time; go north for three miles and then you'll see the road to London; our office windows face north*

North America ['nɔːθ ə'merɪkə] *noun* part of the American continent to the north of Mexico, formed of the USA and Canada; *he has travelled widely in North America from Alaska to Florida*

northbound ['nɔːθbaʊnd] *adjective* travelling towards the north; *there has been an accident on the northbound carriageway of the motorway; all northbound trains are subject to delay*

north-east [nɔːθ'iːst] **1** *adverb* direction between north and east; *they were travelling north-east at the time; go north-east for three miles and then you'll come to our village; our office windows face north-east* **2** *noun* part of country to the north and east; *the North-East of England will have snow showers; it's cold when the wind blows from the north-east*

north-eastern [nɔːθ'iːstən] *adjective* referring to the north-east; *the country's north-eastern border with Russia*

northern ['nɔːðən] *adjective* referring the north; *northern countries have more rain; they live in the northern part of the country*

North Pole ['nɔːθ 'pəʊl] *noun* furthest point at the north of the earth; *an explorer who has been to the North Pole*

North Sea ['nɔːθ 'siː] *noun* sea between England and Denmark, Germany, the Netherlands, etc.; *how many oil rigs are there in the North Sea?; there are many ferries crossing the North Sea every day*

north-west [nɔːθ'west] **1** *adverb* direction between west and north; *they were travelling north-west at the time; go north-west for a few miles and then you'll come to our house* **2** *noun* part of the country to the north and west; *the North-West of England is wetter than the east coast; we can expect rain when the wind*

blows from the north-west; *the old castle stood to the north-west of the cathedral*

north-western [nɔːθ'westən] *adjective* referring to the north-west; *the north-western part of the United States*

Norway ['nɔːweɪ] *noun* country in northern Europe, to the west of Sweden; *northern Norway is inside the Arctic circle* (NOTE: capital: **Oslo**; people: **Norwegians**; language: **Norwegian**; currency: **Norwegian krone**)

Norwegian [nɔː'wiːdʒən] **1** *adjective* referring to Norway; *Ibsen was the most famous Norwegian dramatist* **2** *noun* **(a)** person from Norway; *the Norwegians have a very large fishing fleet* **(b)** language spoken in Norway; *Norwegian is similar in many ways to Swedish*

nose [nəʊz] *noun* part of the head which you breathe through and smell with; *he has a cold, and his nose is red; dogs have wet noses; she's got flu - her nose is running; don't wipe your nose on your sleeve, use a tissue*; **to blow your nose** = to blow air through your nose into a handkerchief to remove liquid from your nose; **to speak through your nose** = to talk as if your nose is blocked, so that you say 'b' instead of 'm' and 'd' instead of 'n'; **to look down your nose at something** = to look at something as if you don't think it is very good; *she's got a degree and looks down her nose at the other secretaries*; **to pay through the nose for something** = to pay far too much for something than you should; *he paid through the nose for his ticket to Hong Kong because it was the only seat left*; **to turn your nose up at something** = to show that you don't feel something is good enough for you; *it's a marvellous deal, I don't see why you should turn your nose up at it*

nosebleed ['nəʊzbliːd] *noun* blood coming from the nose; *he had a nosebleed and had to lie down*

nosey *or* **nosy** ['nəʊzi] *adjective (informal)* too interested in other people's affairs; *don't be so nosey, it's none of your business*; **nosey Parker** = person who is too interested in other people's affairs (NOTE: **nosier - nosiest**)

nostalgia [nɒ'stældʒiə] *noun* sad longing for the past; *she sometimes felt nostalgia for the good old days before the war; going back to the village where he spent his childhood filled him with nostalgia*

nostalgic [nɒ'stældʒɪk] *adjective* referring to nostalgia; *I made a nostalgic visit to my old home town*

nostril ['nɒstrɪl] *noun* one of two holes in the nose, which you breathe through; *nosebleeds can usually be controlled by pinching the nostrils*

not [nɒt] *adverb (often shortened to* **n't**) **(a)** *(used with verbs to show the negative)* she can't come; it isn't there; he didn't want any meat; we couldn't go home because of the fog; don't you like coffee?; a service charge is not included **(b) not...either** = and not...also; *she doesn't eat meat, and she doesn't eat fish either; it wasn't hot, but it wasn't very cold either* **(c) not only...but also** = not just this...but this as well; *she isn't only blind, but she's deaf also; the film wasn't only very long, but it was also very bad* **(d)** *(used to make an emphatic negative)* is it going to rain? - I hope not; I don't like bananas - why on earth not?; he begged her not to leave him alone; there was not one single shop open; everyone was invited, not forgetting the bus driver; **not a few** = many; **not very well** = quite ill

notable ['nəʊtəbl] **1** *adjective* which is worth noticing; *it was a notable achievement; she was notable by her absence; the town is notable for its currant cakes* **2** *noun* important person; *a meeting of local notables*

notably ['nəʊtəbli] *adverb* **(a)** especially; *some Western countries, notably Canada and the United States, have a very high standard of living* **(b)** in a way that is easily noticed; *the food was notably better than the last time we ate there*

notary (public) ['nəʊtəri('pʌblik)] *noun* lawyer who has the authority to witness and draw up legal documents and so make them legal (NOTE: plural is **notaries public**)

notch [nɒtʃ] **1** *noun* small V-shaped cut; *he cut two notches in the stick with his penknife* (NOTE: plural is **notches**) **2** *verb* **(a)** to mark with a notch; *the stick was notched in several places* **(b) to notch up** = to score, to make a number; *she's notched up 25 years with the company; he notched up twenty runs in twenty minutes*

note [nəʊt] **1** *noun* **(a)** a few words in writing to remind yourself of something; *she made a few notes before she gave her speech; she made a note of what she needed to buy before she went to the supermarket;* **to take note of** = to pay attention to; *we have to take note of public opinion* **(b)** short message; *she left a note for the managing director with his secretary; he wrote me a note to say he couldn't come* **(c)** piece of paper money; *I tried to pay with a ten-pound note* (NOTE: American English for this is **bill**) **(d)** musical sound or a written sign meaning a musical sound; *he can't sing high notes* **(e)** key on a piano; *she played a tune, using only the black notes on the piano* **(f)** further explanations about a text; *the notes are at the back of the book* **2** *verb* **(a)** to write down something in a few words; *the policeman noted in his notebook all the details of the accident* **(b)** to take notice of; *please note that our prices were raised on January 1st*

notebook ['nəʊtbʊk] *noun* **(a)** small book for making notes; *the policeman wrote down the details in his notebook* **(b)** very small computer which you can carry around with you

noted ['nəʊtid] *adjective* famous; *the town is noted for its public gardens; Mr Smith, the noted local artist*

notepad ['nəʊtpæd] *noun* **(a)** pad of paper for writing notes; *I took a notepad to jot down any interesting points from the lecture* **(b)** part of the screen used to store information even if the terminal is switched off; *use the notepad to make changes to your file*

notepaper ['nəʊtpeɪpə] *noun* **(a)** paper for writing letters; *it must be an official order, it's written on the company's headed notepaper; you'll find some notepaper in the hotel bedroom* **(b)** *US* paper for writing rough notes on (NOTE: no plural: **some notepaper, a piece of notepaper**)

noteworthy ['nəʊtwɜːði] *adjective* remarkable because it is interesting or special; *this was one of the more noteworthy facts to emerge from the investigation; a lot was said, but nothing that was particularly noteworthy*

nothing ['nʌθɪŋ] *pronoun* **(a)** not anything; *there's nothing interesting on TV; she said nothing about what she had seen; there's nothing more we can do;*

nothing much happened = not very much happened; *he has nothing left in the bank* = no money left; **for nothing** = free, without having to pay; *we're friends of the organizer and she got us into the exhibition for nothing* **(b) to think nothing of doing something** = to do something easily; *he thinks nothing of cycling ten miles to work;* **it's nothing to do with you** = it doesn't concern you

notice ['nəʊtɪs] **1** *noun* **(a)** piece of writing giving information, usually put in a place where everyone can see it; *he pinned up a notice about the staff tennis match* **(b)** official warning that something has to be done, that something is going to happen; *they gave us five minutes' notice to leave the office; if you want to resign, you have to give a month's notice; the train times were changed without notice;* **until further notice** = until different instructions are given; *you must pay £200 on the 30th of each month until further notice;* **at short notice** = with very little warning; *it had to be done at short notice; the bank manager will not see anyone at such short notice* **(c)** attention; *it has been brought to my notice that students have been going into town at lunchtime;* **take no notice of what the policeman says** = pay no attention to what he says, don't worry about what he says **2** *verb* **(a)** to take note of; *I wore one blue and one white sock all day and nobody noticed; I didn't notice you had come in; did you notice if John was sitting next to Sarah?*

noticeable ['nəʊtɪsəbl] *adjective* which is easily noticed; *the stain is hardly noticeable; I can't see any noticeable difference between them*

noticeably ['nəʊtɪsəbli] *adverb* obviously, visibly; *after her holiday, she was noticeably fatter*

noticeboard ['nəʊtɪsbɔːd] *noun* flat piece of wood, etc., on a wall, on which notices can be pinned; *did you see the new list of members on the club noticeboard?* (NOTE: American English is **bulletin board**)

notifiable [nəʊtɪ'faɪəbl] *adjective* which should be reported officially; **notifiable disease** = serious infectious disease which has to be reported to the Department of Health (such as cholera, meningitis, etc.)

notification [nəʊtɪfɪ'keɪʃn] *noun* informing someone; *have they received any notification of the date of the court case?; we have had no notification that the sale has taken place*

notify ['nəʊtɪfaɪ] *verb* **to notify someone of something** = to tell someone something formally; *they were notified of the arrival of the shipment; the local doctor notified the Health Service of the case of cholera*

notion ['nəʊʃn] *noun* **(a)** idea; *she has this strange notion that she ought to be a TV star* **(b)** *US* **notions** = small articles used in sewing, like needles, ribbon, etc. (NOTE: British English for this is **haberdashery**)

notional ['nəʊʃnəl] *adjective* assumed to be correct for the purposes of making a calculation; *let us take £6000 as the notional price*

notoriety [nəʊtə'raɪəti] *noun* bad reputation; *the hotel enjoys a certain notoriety as a meeting place for the mafia*

notorious [nəʊ'tɔːriəs] *adjective* well known for something bad; *he comes from a notorious gangster family; it is a house which is notorious for the crimes committed there*

notwithstanding [nɒtwɪθ'stændɪŋ] *adverb & preposition (formal)* in spite of; *the case proceeded notwithstanding the objections of the defendant or the defendant's objections notwithstanding* (NOTE: the word can be placed before or after a noun)

nought [nɔːt] *noun* (a) zero; *one million can be written as '1m' or as one and six noughts* (NOTE: **nought** is commoner in British English; in American English, **zero** is more usual) (b) *(game)* **noughts and crosses** = game where each player puts either a zero or a cross on a grid, the first to get three in a row is the winner (NOTE: American English for this is **tic-tac-toe**)

noun [naʊn] *noun (in grammar)* word which can be the subject of a verb and is used to refer to a person or thing; *nouns such as 'brick' and 'elephant'*; **proper noun** = word which is the name of a place, a person, a building, etc.; *proper nouns such as 'The Tower of London', 'the Mona Lisa', etc.* (NOTE: proper nouns are almost always written with a capital letter)

nourish ['nʌrɪʃ] *verb* (a) to give food to someone; *all the children look very well nourished* (b) to keep ideas, etc., alive; *the news nourished their hopes that their son might still be alive*

nourishment ['nʌrɪʃmənt] *noun* (a) food which nourishes, such as proteins, fats or vitamins; *as a result of poor nourishment they were all weak and underweight; is there enough nourishment in a diet that consists solely of salads?* (b) food in general; *she just lies in bed and refuses to take any nourishment* (NOTE: no plural)

nova ['nəʊvə] *noun* star that suddenly becomes bright when an explosion takes place inside it; *there is a theory that the star of Bethlehem may have been a nova; see also* SUPERNOVA (NOTE: plural is **novae** ['nəʊviː])

novel ['nɒvl] *noun* long story with imaginary characters and plot; *'Pickwick Papers' was Dickens' first major novel*

novelist ['nɒvəlɪst] *noun* person who writes novels; *Jane Austen is one of the most important English women novelists*

novelty ['nɒvəlti] *noun* (a) new thing you have not experienced before; *flying in a plane is still a novelty for them* (b) being new; *the novelty of the new job soon wore off* (NOTE: no plural in meanings (a) and (b)) (c) unusual little ornament; *small shops selling novelties and souvenirs* (NOTE: plural in this meaning is **novelties**)

November [nə'vembə] *noun* eleventh month of the year, the month after October and before December; *today is November 5th US November 5; she was born in November; we never go on holiday in November* (NOTE: **November 5th** or **November 5**: say 'November the fifth' or 'the fifth of November'; American English: 'November fifth')

COMMENT: November 5th is the date of the Gunpowder Plot; a children's rhyme recalls the event: 'remember, remember, the Fifth of November, gunpowder, treason and plot'. *See also* GUY FAWKES NIGHT

novice ['nɒvɪs] *noun* (a) beginner; *he's still a novice at rowing; we send novice salesmen out with an experienced rep to learn the ropes* (b) person who intends to become a monk or nun; *Sister Agnes is in charge of the novices*

now [naʊ] **1** *adverb* at this point in time; *I can hear a train coming now; please can we go home now?; the flight is only two hours - he ought to be in Berlin by now; now's the best time for going skiing; a week from now we'll be sitting on the beach;* **until now** *or* **up to now** = until this point in time; *until now, I've never had to see a doctor* **2** *conjunction;* **now that** = since, because, *now that I know how to drive I can take more holidays by myself; now you've mentioned it, I do remember having a phone call from him last week* **3** *interjection* (a) *(showing a warning)* **now then**, *don't be rude to the teacher!; come on now, work hard!; now, now! nobody wants to hear you crying* (b) *(attracting someone's attention)* **now, everyone, let's begin the meeting**

nowadays ['naʊədeɪz] *adverb* at the present time; *nowadays lots of people go to Spain on holiday; the traffic is so bad nowadays that it takes us an hour to drive to Piccadilly Circus*

nowhere ['nəʊweə] *adverb* (a) not in *or* to any place; *my wallet was nowhere to be found; where are you going? - nowhere; there is nowhere else for them to live;* **to get nowhere** = to be unsuccessful; *I rang six shops to try and find a new dishwasher, but got nowhere;* **to be getting nowhere** = not to have any success; *I'm getting nowhere with my research* (b) **nowhere near** = not at all; *the work is nowhere near finished; he has nowhere near done all his homework*

nozzle ['nɒzl] *noun* fitting at the end of a pipe which controls the flow of liquid; *one of nozzles feeding fuel to the carburettor was blocked*

n/s *abbreviation for* NON SMOKER

NSPCC = NATIONAL SOCIETY FOR THE PREVENTION OF CRUELTY TO CHILDREN

nuance ['njuːɑːns] *noun* slight shade of meaning; *there are some subtle nuances in his writing which are impossible to translate*

nuclear ['njuːkiə] *adjective* (a) referring to energy from atomic particles; *a nuclear power station;* **nuclear fission** = splitting a hydrogen atom to create energy; **nuclear power** = electricity produced by a nuclear power station (b) **nuclear family** = family consisting simply of parents and children; *see also* EXTENDED FAMILY

nuclear reactor ['njuːkliə ri'æktə] *noun* device which creates heat and energy by starting and controlling atomic fission; *this small nuclear reactor provides enough electric power for a whole city*

nucleus ['njuːkliəs] *noun* (a) central core of an atom, formed of neutrons and protons; *electrons orbit the nucleus of the atom* (b) central body in a cell, containing DNA and RNA, and controlling the function and characteristics of the cell; *first the nucleus divides, then the whole cell splits in two* (c) centre around which something gathers; *the six experienced players form the nucleus of the new team* (NOTE: plural is **nuclei** ['njuːklaɪ])

nude [njuːd] **1** *noun* (a) naked person, usually a woman; *a portrait of a nude* (b) painting of a naked woman; *an exhibition of Manet's nudes* (c) **in the nude** = wearing no clothes; *they went swimming in the nude* **2** *adjective* wearing no clothes; *nude sunbathing is allowed on some beaches; would you be willing to appear nude on stage?*

nudge [nʌdʒ] **1** *noun* little push, usually with the elbow; *she gave me a nudge to wake me up* **2** *verb* to give a little push, usually with the elbow; *he nudged me when it was my turn to speak*; **to give someone a nudge** = to try to get someone to do something; *he's late with his work - better give him a nudge*

nudity ['nju:dɪti] *noun* nakedness; *she thinks there's too much nudity in television programmes nowadays* (NOTE: no plural)

nuisance ['nju:səns] *noun* thing which annoys; *the dog's a nuisance because she always wants attention*; *it's a nuisance the bus doesn't run on Sundays*

null [nʌl] *adjective* not valid; **the contract was declared null and void** = the contract was declared to be no longer valid

nullify ['nʌlɪfaɪ] *verb (formal)* **(a)** to make something invalid, to cancel something; *this new amendment to the contract will nullify the conditions we have just agreed* **(b)** to make useless; *his speech has nullified all our attempts at negotiation*

numb [nʌm] **1** *adjective* which has no feeling; *the tips of his ears went numb*; *his hands were numb with cold* **2** *verb* to remove feeling; *the doctor gave him an injection to numb the pain*

number ['nʌmbə] **1** *noun* **(a)** figure; *13 is not a lucky number*; *they live on the opposite side of road at number 49*; *can you give me your telephone number?*; *a number 6 bus goes to Oxford Street*; *please quote your account number*; **box number** = reference number used when asking for mail to be sent to a post office or to a newspaper's offices; *please reply to Box No. 209* **(b)** quantity of people or things; *the number of tickets sold was disappointing*; *a large number of children* or *large numbers of children will be sitting the exam*; *there were only a small number of people at the meeting*; **a number of times** = often; *I've seen that film a number of times*; **any number of times** = very often; *I've been to France any number of times*; *she could take her driving test any number of times but she still wouldn't pass it* (NOTE: when **a number** refers to a plural noun it is followed by a plural verb: **a number of houses were damaged**) **(c)** issue of a magazine, newspaper, etc.; *we keep back numbers of magazines for six months and then throw them away* **(d)** piece of music, song; *she played a selection of numbers by Noel Coward* **2** *verb* **(a)** to give something a number; *the raffle tickets were numbered 1 to 1000*; *I refer to our invoices numbered 234 and 235*; *all the seats are clearly numbered* **(b)** to count; *visitors to the exhibition numbered several thousand*; *he numbers among the most important writers of the 20th century*

number one ['nʌmbə 'wɒn] **1** *adjective* most important; *pollution is the number one issue at the election* **2** *noun* **(a)** yourself, your own interests; *he always remembers to look after number one* = he always thinks of his own interests first **(b)** most important thing, person, etc.; *his latest single is number one in the charts*; *she's number one in the organization*

number plate ['nʌmbəpleɪt] *noun* one of two plates on a car, etc. (one on the front and one on the back), which shows an identifying number; *the thieves had changed the van's number plates* (NOTE: American English is **license plate**)

Number Ten ['nʌmbə 'ten] *noun* No 10 Downing Street, London, the house of the British Prime Minister; *sources close to Number Ten say the plan has not been agreed*; *the plan was turned down by Number Ten*; *it is*

rumoured that Number Ten was annoyed at the story (NOTE: used to refer to the Prime Minister or to the government in general)

numeracy ['nju:mərəsi] *noun* ability to work with numbers; *staff are working hard with pupils to improve numeracy*; *compare* ILLITERACY, LITERACY

numeral ['nju:mərəl] *noun* written sign representing a number; *a filename can be made up of letters or numerals*; **Arabic numerals** = figures such as 2, 3 and 6; **Roman numerals** = figures such as III, IV and XX

numerate ['nju:mərət] *adjective* being able to work with numbers; *after six years at school, she is still barely numerate*; *compare* ILLITERATE, LITERATE

numeric *or* **numerical** [nju:'merɪk or nju:'merɪkl] *adjective* referring to numbers; *the data is stored in numerical form*; **in numerical order** = in the order of figures (such as 1 before 2, 33 before 34); *file these invoices in numerical order*

numerous ['nju:mərəs] *adjective* very many; *he has been fined for speeding on numerous occasions*

nun [nʌn] *noun* woman member of a religious order; *a Tibetan nun*; *nuns served hot soup to the refugees* (NOTE: do not confuse with **none**; note: the equivalent men are **monks**)

nunnery ['nʌnəri] *noun* convent, religious establishment where nuns live; *the buildings of such a place*; *the number of nuns has fallen sharply and the Mother Superior is afraid the nunnery may have to close*; *she entered a nunnery at the age of twenty-one* (NOTE: plural is **nunneries**; the equivalent establishment for men is a **monastery**)

nurse [nɜːs] **1** *noun (woman or man)* person who looks after sick people; *she has a job as a nurse in the local hospital*; *he's training to be a nurse* **2** *verb* **(a)** to look after people who are ill; *when she fell ill her daughter nursed her until she was better* **(b)** to be ill with something; *he's sitting in bed nursing his cold*; *she came back from her holiday nursing a broken arm* **(c) to nurse a grudge** = to have a secret feeling of hatred, etc.; *he has been nursing a grudge against his boss for the last six years*

nursery ['nɜːsəri] *noun* **(a)** home for babies or young children; *my sister went to a nursery every day from the age of 18 months*; **day nursery** = nursery which is open during daytime; **nursery school** = first school for very small children; **nursery rhyme** = children's traditional song **(b) nursery slopes** = easy slope on a mountain where you learn to ski **(c)** place where young plants are grown and sold; *buy some plants from the nursery* (NOTE: plural is **nurseries**)

nursing ['nɜːsɪŋ] **1** *noun* profession of being a nurse; *she decided to go in for nursing*; *have you considered nursing as a career?* **2** *adjective* referring to the job of looking after sick people; **nursing home** = small private hospital

nurture ['nɜːtʃə] *verb (formal)* to bring up and look after carefully (children, plants, ideas); *these houseplants have been carefully nurtured in our greenhouse*; *he nurtured hopes of becoming prime minister*

nut [nʌt] *noun* **(a)** fruit of a tree, with a hard shell; *almonds and brazils are sorts of nut*; **to crack nuts** = to break the shells of nuts to get at the fruit inside; *he cracked the nuts with his teeth* **(b)** metal ring which screws on a bolt to hold it tight; *screw the nut on tightly; (informal)* **the nuts and bolts of something** = the main details of something; *you'll need to master the nuts and bolts of the stock market before going to work as a stockbroker*

nutmeg ['nʌtmeg] *noun* hard round seed of a tropical tree, grated and used as a spice; *add some grated nutmeg to the cake mixture*; **nutmeg grater** = special little kitchen instrument for grating nutmegs

nutrient ['njuːtriənt] *noun (formal)* substance in food which is encourages the growth of living things; *plants find nutrients in rainwater*

COMMENT: proteins, fats, vitamins are all nutrients needed to make animals grow; carbon, hydrogen, phosphorus, etc., are nutrients needed by plants

nutriment ['njuːtrɪmənt] *noun (formal)* food which nourishes; *plants extract the nutriments from the soil*

nutrition [njuː'trɪʃn] *noun* **(a)** receiving food; *a scheme to improve nutrition in the poorer areas* **(b)** study of food; *we are studying nutrition as part of the food science course*

nutritional [njuː'trɪʃənəl] *adjective* referring to nutrition; *it tastes nice but it has no nutritional value*; **nutritional disorder** = disorder, such as obesity, related to food and nutrients

nutritionist [njuː'trɪʃənɪst] *noun* dietician, a person who specializes in the study of nutrition and advises on diets; *the nutritionist warned me not to eat too much red meat*

nutritious [njuː'trɪʃəs] *adjective* valuable as food; *ice cream is not a very nutritious food*

nuts [nʌts] *adjective (informal)* mad; **nuts about someone** *or* **something** = very keen on someone *or* something; *he's nuts about old cars*; **to drive someone nuts** = to make someone crazy; *I wish they'd turn the music down - it's driving me nuts*

nutshell ['nʌtʃel] *noun* hard outside part of a nut; *the squirrels left bits of nutshells under the trees*; **in a nutshell** = as concisely as possible; *it's a long and complicated story, but, in a nutshell, he left his wife and set fire to the house*

nutty ['nʌti] *adjective* **(a)** full of nuts; *a nutty chocolate bar* **(b)** *(informal)* mad, crazy; *he's a typical nutty professor*; *I think it's a bit of a nutty idea myself*; **nutty about someone** *or* **something** = mad about someone *or* something; *he's completely nutty about steam trains*; **she's as nutty as a fruitcake** = she's completely mad

nylon ['naɪlɒn] *noun* type of synthetic material used to make clothing, sheets, etc.; *I hate the feel of nylon against the skin; why are nylon sheets so cold?*

nymph [nɪmf] *noun* **(a)** young insect at the stage in its development between the larva and the adult; *dragonfly nymphs were skimming across the surface of the lake* **(b)** goddess of woods, streams, etc.; *in ancient time, nymphs were thought to live in lakes, rivers and woods*

Oo

O, o [əʊ] fifteenth letter of the alphabet, between N and P; *'cooperate' can be spelt with a hyphen between the Os*

oaf [əʊf] *noun* stupid and clumsy person; *move, you great oaf, you're standing on my foot!*

oak [əʊk] *noun* **(a)** type of large tree which loses its leaves in winter; *oaks produce thousands of acorns each year; a forest of oak trees* **(b)** wood from this tree; *an oak table*

OAP [əʊeɪ'piː] *noun short for* OLD AGE PENSIONER; *have you got your OAP bus pass yet?*

oar [ɔː] *noun* long wooden rod with a flat part at the end, used for moving a boat along; *his oar got stuck in the weeds on the bed of the river;* (*informal*) **to stick your oar in** = to interfere where you are not wanted (NOTE: do not confuse with **ore**)

oarsman ['ɔːzmən] *noun* person who rows a boat, especially as a sport; *he's an Olympic oarsman; the oarsmen were struggling to make progress against the strong headwind* (NOTE: plural is **oarsmen**)

oasis [əʊ'eɪsɪs] *noun* **(a)** place in the desert where water is found, and where plants grow; *after crossing the desert for days they finally arrived at an oasis* **(b)** quiet place which is pleasantly different from everything else around it; *Golden Square is an oasis of calm in the middle of London's West End* (NOTE: plural is **oases** [əʊ'eɪsiːz])

oatcake ['əʊtkeɪk] *noun* round biscuit made of oatmeal; *oatcakes are delicious with cheese*

oath [əʊθ] *noun* **(a)** solemn legal promise that someone will say or write only what is true; *all the members of the jury have to take an oath; the lords swore an oath of allegiance to the king;* **he was on oath** *or* **under oath** = he had promised in court to say what was true; *he was accused of lying to the court when he was under or on oath* **(b)** swear word; *as the police grabbed him, he let out a long string of oaths* (NOTE: plural is **oaths** [əʊðz])

oatmeal ['əʊtmiːl] *noun* rough flakes made from ground oats; *the recipe needs two spoonfuls of oatmeal; have you got any oatmeal?* (NOTE: no plural: **some oatmeal; two ounces of oatmeal**)

COMMENT: oatmeal is used to make porridge

oats [əʊts] *noun* **(a)** cereal plant grown in temperate climates, of which the grain is used as food; *the farmer has decided to grow oats in this field this year* **(b) to sow your wild oats** = to behave in a wild way when young

obdurate ['ɒbdjʊrət] *adjective* (*formal*) stubborn, refusing to yield; *he was obdurate in his refusal to discuss the workers' grievances*

obedience [ə'biːdɪəns] *noun* being obedient, doing what someone tells you to do; *he demanded total obedience from his followers; in obedience to her*

father's wishes, the little girl was buried in the local churchyard

obedient [ə'biːdɪənt] *adjective* doing what your are told to do; *our old dog is very obedient - he always comes when you call him; all students must be obedient to the rules of the college*

obediently [ə'biːdɪəntli] *adverb* in an obedient way; *the teacher went first, with the children following obediently behind*

obese [ə'biːs] *adjective* much too fat or too heavy; *she's not just overweight, she's obese*

obesity [ə'biːsɪti] *noun* being very fat and overweight; *obesity makes you more likely to have a heart attack*

obey [əʊ'beɪ] *verb* to do what someone tells you to do; *if you can't obey orders you shouldn't be a policeman; everyone must obey the law*

obituary [ə'bɪtjʊəri] *noun* written account of someone's life, published after his or her death; *did you read the obituary of the bishop in 'the Times'?* (NOTE: plural is **obituaries**)

object 1 *noun* ['ɒbdʒekt] **(a)** thing; *they thought they saw a strange object in the sky* **(b)** aim; *their object is to take control of the radio station* **(c)** (*in grammar*) noun or pronoun, etc., which follows directly from a verb or preposition; *in the phrase 'the cat caught the mouse', the word 'mouse' is the object of the verb 'caught'* **(d) money is no object** = money is not a problem; *money is no object to them - they're very wealthy* **2** *verb* [əb'dʒekt] **(a) to object (to)** = to refuse to agree to; *she objected to the council's plans to widen the road; I object most strongly to paying extra for my little suitcase* **(b)** to say why you refuse to agree; *he objected that the pay was too low*

objection [əb'dʒekʃn] *noun* reason for refusing to agree to; *do you have any objection to me smoking?; any objections to the plan?;* **to raise an objection to something** = to object to something; *she raised several objections to the proposal*

objective [əb'dʒektɪv] **1** *adjective* considering things from a general point of view and not from your own; *you must be objective when planning the future of your business* **2** *noun* aim, object which you are aiming at; *our long-term objective is to make the company financially sound; the company has achieved its main objectives*

objectively [əb'dʒektɪvli] *adverb* in an objective way, without being influenced by your own feelings; *look at it objectively: if the firm hadn't made half its staff redundant it would have had to close down completely*

objectivity [ɒbdʒek'tɪvɪti] *noun* being objective; *can we rely on the objectivity of his report?*

obligation [ɒblɪ'geɪʃn] *noun* **(a)** duty; legal debt; **to meet your obligations** = to pay your debts; *he cannot meet his obligations* **(b)** duty to do something; *you* *have an obligation to attend the meeting*; **to be under an obligation to someone** = to feel morally obliged to help someone; *she felt under an obligation to look after her friend's cat*; **two weeks' free trial without obligation** = the customer can try the item at home for two weeks without having to buy it at the end of the trial

obligatory [ə'blɪgətəri] *adjective* which has to be done according to rules or laws; *in some countries, military service is obligatory for all men of eighteen or over*

oblige [ə'blaɪdʒ] *verb* (a) to force someone to do something; *he was obliged to hand the money back* (b) **to feel obliged to do something** = to feel it is your duty to do something; *he felt obliged to study medicine at university because his father was a doctor* (c) to do something useful or helpful; *he wanted to oblige you by weeding your garden for you* (d) *(formal)* **to be obliged to someone** = to be grateful to someone for having done something; *thank you - I'm much obliged to you for your help*; *I'd be obliged if you could shut the window*

obliging [ə'blaɪdʒɪŋ] *adjective* ready to help; *an obliging gentleman showed us the way to the hotel*

obligingly [ə'blaɪdʒɪŋli] *adverb* in an obliging way; *he obligingly stood aside to let me pass*

oblique [ə'bliːk] *adjective* (a) slanting, not meeting something at a right angle; **oblique angle** = angle which is not a right angle (b) not direct, not mentioning or referring to something directly; *the speech contained an oblique reference to the president's family problems*

obliquely [ə'bliːkli] *adverb* in an oblique way; *he did mention the minister, but only obliquely*

obliterate [ə'blɪtəreɪt] *verb* to wipe out, to destroy completely; *half the town was obliterated in the explosion*; *the new block of flats completely obliterates the view between our house and the river*

obliteration [əblɪtə'reɪʃn] *noun* act of obliterating or of being obliterated; *we're trying to save the remains of the Roman theatre from total obliteration by the construction company*

oblivion [ə'blɪviən] *noun* (a) being completely forgotten; *after being famous during the war the town fell into complete oblivion* (b) not being aware of what is going on around you; *he sat there in a state of complete oblivion*

oblivious [ə'blɪviəs] *adjective* not noticing; *he seemed completely oblivious of his surroundings*; *she is oblivious to what is going on in the office*

oblong ['ɒblɒŋ] **1** *adjective* rectangular, with two pairs of equal sides, one pair being longer than the other; *he pulled out an oblong folder full of papers* **2** *noun* shape with two pairs of equal sides, one pair being longer than the other; *the screen is an oblong, approximately 30cm by 40cm*

obnoxious [ɒb'nɒkʃəs] *adjective* very unpleasant or very offensive; *the waitress was really obnoxious to the poor old lady*

oboe ['əʊbəʊ] *noun* woodwind instrument, with a smaller range than the clarinet; *she played one of Mozart's oboe concertos*; *he plays the oboe in the school orchestra*

oboist ['əʊbəʊɪst] *noun* person who plays the oboe

obscene [əb'siːn] *adjective* (a) which is likely to deprave or corrupt someone who sees or reads it; *the obscene language in the film makes it unsuitable for children*; *the novel was banned because it was thought to be obscene* (b) which offends moral standards or normal feelings; *it's obscene to spend so much money on a banquet when poor people are starving*

obscenely [əb'siːnli] *adjective* in an obscene way; *they discussed sex openly, but not obscenely*; *she is obscenely rich*

obscenity [əb'senɪti] *noun* (a) being obscene; *the artist narrowly escaped being prosecuted for obscenity* (b) obscene word; *he shouted obscenities at the judge as he was led away* (NOTE: plural in this meaning is **obscenities**) (c) something which is completely unacceptable; *she regards the mere existence of nuclear weapons as an obscenity*

obscure [əb'skjʊə] **1** *adjective* (a) not clear; *there are several obscure points in his letter* (b) not well-known; *they always stay in some obscure village in the Alps which no one has ever heard of* **2** *verb* to hide, especially by covering; *during a solar eclipse, the moon obscures the sun*

obscurity [əb'skjʊərɪti] *noun* being obscure, not being well-known; *he was a famous footballer when he was young, but died in comparative obscurity*; *he rose from complete obscurity to become Prime Minister*

obsequious [əb'siːkwiəs] *adjective* too eager to help or obey; *we were greeted at the door by an extremely obsequious waiter*

observance [əb'zɜːvəns] *noun* (a) action of obeying a law or rule; *professional players should set a good example by strict observance of the rules of the game* (b) following a custom or tradition; *the observance of Christmas is very widespread*

observant [əb'zɜːvənt] *adjective* who notices many details; *only someone who is very observant would have noticed that*

observation [ɒbzə'veɪʃn] *noun* (a) action of observing; *by careful observation, the police found out where the thieves had hidden the money*; **under observation** = being carefully watched; *the patient will be kept under observation for a few days* (b) remark; *he made several observations about the government*

observatory [əb'zɜːvətəri] *noun* place from which stars and planets can be watched; *the Greenwich Observatory is on the east side of London* (NOTE: plural is **observatories**)

observe [əb'zɜːv] *verb* (a) to follow or to obey (a law, rule, custom, etc.); *his family observes all the Jewish festivals*; *the local laws must be observed* (b) to watch or to look at; *they observed the eclipse from the top of the mountain* (c) to notice; *the police observed the car coming out of the garage* (d) to make a remark; *I merely observed that the bus was late as usual*

observer [əb'zɜːvə] *noun* person who attends an event and watches (especially without taking part); *the UN sent observers to the elections*

obsess [əb'ses] *verb* to occupy someone's mind all the time; *he is obsessed by money*

obsession [əb'seʃn] *noun* (a) fixed idea which occupies your mind all the time; *making money is an obsession with him* (b) idea or problem which worries you all the time, often associated with mental illness; *she has an obsession with cleanliness*

obsessive [əb'sesɪv] *adjective* showing an obsession; *he has an obsessive need to make money*; *the inspectors are obsessive about cleanliness in restaurant kitchens*

obsessively [əb'sesɪvli] *adverb* in an obsessive way; *she talks obsessively about their plans for the future*

obsolescence [ɒbsə'lesəns] *noun* going out of date because of advances in technology or changes in fashion; **built-in obsolescence** *or* **planned obsolescence** = making something in such a way that the current model will soon become obsolete and consumers will have to buy a newer one

obsolescent [ɒbsə'lesənt] *adjective* going out of use or out of fashion; *computers are being developed so fast that a new machine is obsolescent almost as soon as you buy it*

obsolete ['ɒbsəliːt] *adjective* no longer used; *when the office was equipped with PCs the old word-processors became obsolete*

obstacle ['ɒbstəkl] *noun* thing which is in the way, which prevents someone going forward; *the truck had to negotiate boulders and other obstacles to cross the mountain pass*; *their incompatible computer system is an obstacle to any linkup with ours*

obstacle course ['ɒbstəkl 'kɔːs] *noun* place for training soldiers, in which various obstacles have to be passed; *Captain Johnson was the first man round the obstacle course*

obstetrician [ɒbstə'trɪʃn] *noun* doctor who specializes in obstetrics; *the obstetrician delivered the baby by Caesarean section*

obstetrics [ɒb'stetrɪks] *noun* branch of medicine dealing with pregnancy, childbirth and the period immediately after childbirth; *she took a course in obstetrics*

obstinacy ['ɒbstɪnəsi] *noun* refusing to change your opinion or be persuaded by anyone; *their obstinacy is nearly driving me mad*; *it's sheer obstinacy that's stopping him from going to see a doctor*

obstinate ['ɒbstɪnət] *adjective* (a) not willing to change your mind, sticking to an opinion or course of action, etc., against all arguments; *she's such an obstinate person, that you can never make her change her mind*; *stop being so obstinate and do what I say!* (b) difficult to remove; *she tried to get rid of the obstinate red wine stain on the tablecloth*

obstinately ['ɒbstɪnətli] *adverb* in an obstinate way; *she obstinately refused any help her with the housework*

obstruct [əb'strʌkt] *verb* (a) to block, to stop something going through; *the artery was obstructed by a blood clot*; *a large black car was obstructing the roadway* (b) to stop someone doing something; *he was fined for obstructing the referee*; *she was accused of obstructing the police in the course of their duties*

obstruction [əb'strʌkʃn] *noun* (a) act of obstructing; *the fullback was penalized for obstruction* (b) thing which gets in the way; *his car broke down and caused an obstruction on the motorway*

obtain [əb'teɪn] *verb* (a) to get; *she obtained a copy of the will*; *he obtained control of the business* (b) *(formal)* to be in existence; *this rule still obtains in cases involving the Inland Revenue*

obtainable [əb'teɪnəbl] *adjective* which can be obtained; *the book is obtainable from any good bookshop*

obtuse [ɒb'tjuːs] *adjective* (a) dull person, who does not understand things very quickly; *he's too obtuse to take a subtle hint, so you'll just have to tell him to move* (b) **obtuse angle** = angle of between 90° and 180°

obverse ['ɒbvɜːs] *noun* side of a coin with the head on it, the main side of a coin; *British coins always have the king or queen's head on the obverse* (NOTE: also called 'heads'; the opposite is the **reverse** *or* **tails**)

obvious ['ɒbviəs] *adjective* clear; easily seen; *it's obvious that we will have to pay for the damage*; *it was obvious to everyone that the shop was not making any money*

obviously ['ɒbviəsli] *adverb* clearly; *obviously we will need to borrow various pieces of equipment*

occasion [ə'keɪʒən] *noun* (a) **a special occasion** = a special event (such as a wedding, etc.); *the baby's first birthday was a special occasion*; *it's an extra-special occasion - she's one hundred years old today!* (b) happening, time when something happens; *it is an occasion for celebrations*; **on occasion** = from time to time; *on occasion, we spend a weekend in the country*

occasional [ə'keɪʒnəl] *adjective* happening now and then, not very often; *he was an occasional visitor to my parents' house*; *we make the occasional trip to London*; **occasional table** = small table used from time to time

occasionally [ə'keɪʒnəli] *adverb* sometimes, not very often; *occasionally he has to work late*; *we occasionally go to the cinema*

Occident ['ɒksɪdənt] *noun* (*old*) **the Occident** = the West, the Western countries (NOTE: the word referring to the East is the **Orient**)

occidental [ɒksɪ'dentl] *adjective* (*formal*) referring to the west; *occidental philosophy never really became rooted in Japan* (NOTE: the word referring to the east is **oriental**)

occult ['ɒkʌlt] **1** *noun* **the occult** = supernatural magic; *he started going to seances and dabbling in the occult*; *she has always been interested in the occult* **2** *adjective* referring to supernatural magic; *he dabbles in occult practices*

occupancy ['ɒkjupənsi] *noun* (*formal*) act of occupying a property, such as a house, an office, a room in a hotel, etc.; *our occupancy of the premises dates from April 1998*; *the hotel had 90% occupancy during the high season*

occupant ['ɒkjupənt] *noun* person or company occupying a property; *the occupant of the flat downstairs*; *the previous occupants left the offices in a terrible state*

occupation [ɒkju'peɪʃn] *noun* (a) act of occupying, of being occupied; *the occupation of the country by enemy soldiers* (b) job, position, employment; *what is her occupation?*; *his main occupation is running a small engineering works*; *my Sunday afternoon occupation is washing the car*

occupational [ɒkju'peɪʃnl] *adjective* referring to a job; *stress is an occupational hazard, I'm afraid*; **occupational therapy** = treating patients by using activities to help them deal with problems or disabilities, used especially for handicapped or mentally ill patients

occupied ['ɒkjupaɪd] *adjective* **(a)** occupied with = busy with; *she is always occupied with her family*; *he is occupied with sorting out the mail* **(b)** being used; *all the rooms in the hotel are occupied*; *all the toilets are occupied, so you'll have to wait*

occupier ['ɒkjupaɪə] *noun* person who lives in a house, flat, etc.; *are you the occupier of this flat?*; *the occupier was out when the police called*

occupy ['ɒkjuːpaɪ] *verb* **(a)** to live in or work in; *they occupy the flat on the first floor*; *the firm occupies offices in the centre of town* **(b)** to be busy with; *dealing with the office occupies most of my time* **(c)** to take control of a place by being inside it; *protesters occupied the TV station*

occur [ə'kɜː] *verb* **(a)** to happen; *when did the accident occur?* **(b)** *it has just occurred to me* = I have just thought that; *did it never occur to you that she was lying?* **(c)** to exist; *iron ore occurs in several parts of the country* (NOTE: **occurring - occurred**)

occurrence [ə'kʌrəns] *noun* happening; *we saw a strange occurrence on our way here*; **it is a daily occurrence** = it happens every day

ocean ['əʊʃn] *noun* very large area of sea surrounding the continents; *ocean currents can be very treacherous*; *ocean liners used to dock here*

> COMMENT: the oceans are: the Atlantic, the Pacific, the Indian, the Antarctic (or Southern) and the Arctic

oceanic [əʊsɪ'ænɪk] *adjective* referring to an ocean; *the oceanic currents in the Atlantic carry warm water north*

ocean-going ['əʊʃn'gəʊwɪŋ] *adjective* which can sail on the open sea; *he bought an ocean-going yacht*

ochre US **ocher** ['əʊkə] **1** *noun* **(a)** yellowish-red natural material used for colouring; *the cloth is dyed with yellow ochre* **(b)** dull yellowish-red colour; *the ochre of the wall of the houses in the village* **2** *adjective* dull yellowish-red; *the houses in the village have ochre walls*

o'clock [ə'klɒk] *phrase (used with numbers to show the time) get up - it's 7 o'clock*; *we never open the shop before 10 o'clock*; *by 2 o'clock in the morning everyone was asleep* (NOTE: **o'clock** is only used for the exact hour, not for times which include minutes. It can also be omitted: **we got home before eight** *or* **we got home before eight o'clock**)

octave ['ɒktɪv] *noun (in music)* the eight notes between the first and last notes of a scale; *a bassoon has a range of over four octaves*

October [ɒk'təʊbə] *noun* tenth month of the year, between September and November; *do you ever go on holiday in October?*; *today is October 18th or US October 18*; *last October we moved to London* (NOTE: **October 18th** *or* **October 18**: say 'October the eighteenth' or 'the eighteenth of October'; in American English: 'October eighteenth')

octopus ['ɒktəpəs] *noun* sea animal with eight long arms or tentacles; *there's a huge octopus in the aquarium* (NOTE: plural is **octopuses**; similar smaller animals are **squid**)

ocular ['ɒkjulə] *adjective* **(a)** *(formal)* referring to the eyes or to sight; *opticians are trained to detect ocular imbalance* **(b)** which can be seen by the eyes; *he refused to believe it without ocular proof*

odd [ɒd] *adjective* **(a)** abnormal, peculiar; *it's odd that she can never remember how to get to their house*; *he doesn't like chocolate - really, how odd!* **(b)** **odd numbers** = numbers (like 17 or 33) which cannot be divided by two; *the odd-numbered buildings or the buildings with odd numbers are on the opposite side of the street* **(c)** roughly, approximately; *she had twenty odd pairs of shoes in cardboard boxes* **(d)** one forming part of a group; **an odd shoe** = one shoe of a pair; *we have a few odd boxes left* = we have a few boxes left out of all the boxes we had (NOTE: **odder - oddest**)

oddball ['ɒdbɔːl] *noun (informal)* person who behaves in an odd way; *here they think I'm an oddball because I like classical music*

oddity ['ɒdɪti] *noun* **(a)** state of being odd; *I was struck by the oddity of the situation, sitting at the same table as my two former wives* **(b)** odd thing or odd person; *this symphony is a bit of an oddity, it only has two movements*

oddly ['ɒdli] *adverb* in an odd way; for odd reasons; *she looked at me rather oddly*; *the restaurant seemed oddly familiar*; **oddly enough** = strangely, surprisingly; *oddly enough, we were just talking about him when he came in*

odds [ɒdz] *noun* **(a)** difference between the amount which can be won and the amount which has been bet; *odds of 10 to 1* **(b)** the likelihood that something will happen; *the odds are against it*; *the odds are that she'll get the job*; compare EVENS **(c)** **it makes no odds** = it makes no difference; **to be at odds with someone** = to quarrel with someone all the time **(d)** **odds and ends** = group of various things that have no connection with each other; *he used odds and ends found on the beach to make a sculpture*; *we made a meal from various odds and ends we found in the fridge*

odds-on ['ɒdz'ɒn] *adjective* likely to happen; *they're odds-on favourites to win the Cup*; *it's odds-on he'll forget to come*

ode [əʊd] *noun* long poem often addressed to a person or thing; *Schiller's 'Ode to Joy'*; *Keats' 'Ode to a Nightingale'*

odious ['əʊdiəs] *adjective (formal)* very unpleasant and hateful; *he's a really odious man*; *she wrote an absolutely odious review of my play*

odium ['əʊdiəm] *noun (formal)* great unpopularity and hatred; *by building a huge palace for himself, the president incurred the odium of the people*

odour US **odor** ['əʊdə] *noun (formal)* **(a)** smell, scent; *I think I can detect a faint odour of cheese*; *see also* BODY ODOUR **(b)** **to be in good** *or* **bad odour with someone** = to be in favour *or* out of favour with someone; *she's not in very good odour with my parents*

odyssey ['ɒdɪsi] *noun* long voyage of adventure; *their journey by raft across the Atlantic was a modern-day odyssey*

> COMMENT: called after the long poem by the ancient Greek poet, Homer, which describes the adventures of Odysseus after the end of the Trojan War

oesophagus US **esophagus** [ɪ'sɒfəgəs] *noun* the gullet, the tube in your throat down which food and drink goes from the mouth to the stomach; *he's being treated for cancer of the oesophagus*

oestrogen US **estrogen** ['iːstrədʒən or 'estrədʒən] *noun* hormone produced in the ovaries which controls sexual development and the reproductive system; *after the menopause a woman's body produces less oestrogen*

of [ɒv] *preposition* **(a)** *(showing a connection)* *she's the sister of the girl who you met at the party; where's the top of the jam jar?; what are the names of Henry VIII's wives?* **(b)** *(showing a part or a quantity)* *how much of the cloth do you need?; today is the sixth of March; there are four boys and two girls - six of them altogether; half of the apples are on holiday; a litre of orange juice* **(c)** *who or which is; the school takes children of ten and over; the town of Edinburgh is important for its festival* **(d)** *(showing position, material, cause)* *he lives in the north of the town; the jumper is made of cotton; she died of cancer* (NOTE: **of** is often used after verbs or adjectives **to think of, to be fond of, to be tired of, to smell of, to be afraid of,** etc.)

of course [ɒv 'kɔːs] **(a)** *(used to make yes or no stronger)* *are you coming with us? - of course I am!; do you want to lose all your money? - of course not!; do you want to lose all your money? - of course not!; do you want to lose all your money? - of course not!* **(b)** naturally; *he is rich, so of course he lives in a big house*

off [ɒf] **1** *adverb & preposition* **(a)** *(showing movement or position away from a place)* *we're off to the shops; the office is just off the main road; they spent their holiday on an island off the coast of Wales; the children got off the bus; take your boots off before you come into the house* **(b)** away from work; *she took the week off; it's my secretary's day off today; half the staff are off with flu* **(c)** not switched on; *switch the light off before you leave the office; is the TV off?* (NOTE: **off** is often used after verbs **to keep off, to break off, to fall off, to take off,** etc.) **2** *adjective* **(a)** switched off; *make sure the switch is in the OFF position* **(b)** not good to eat; *I think this meat's a bit off* **(c)** *(in a restaurant)* not available; *chicken is off today*

◊ **off and on** [ɒf ənd 'ɒn] *adverb* not continuously, with breaks in between; *it's been raining off and on all afternoon*

offal ['ɒfl] *noun* inside organs, such as the heart, liver, etc., of an animal used as food; *offal is cheaper than meat and just as nutritious*

off-balance ['ɒf'bæləns] *adverb* not standing steadily; *the sudden movement of the bus threw her off-balance;* **to catch someone off-balance** = to say or do something to somebody which takes them by surprise; *her question caught him off-balance and he didn't know how to answer*

off-colour US **off-color** [ɒf'kʌlə] *adjective* not well; *John's feeling a bit off-colour today; she's a bit off-colour today, so she won't be coming to the party*

off-duty ['ɒf'djuːti] *adjective* who is not on duty; *the robbery was witnessed by an off-duty policeman*

offence US **offense** [ə'fens] *noun* **(a)** state of being offended; **to take offence at** = to be offended by; *he took offence at being called a coward; don't take offence - I didn't really mean it* **(b)** crime, act which is against the law; *he was charged with committing an offence; since it was his first offence, he was let off with a fine*

offend [ə'fend] *verb* **(a)** to be or to go against public opinion, someone's feelings; *he offended the whole village by the article he wrote in the paper* **(b)** to commit a crime; *he was released from prison and immediately offended again*

offender [ə'fendə] *noun* person who commits an offence against the law; *the job of the police is to bring offenders to justice;* **first offender** = someone who commits an offence for the first time; *since he was a first offender, he was let off with a warning;* **young offender** = young person who commits a crime

offending [ə'fendɪŋ] *adjective* which causes trouble or makes somebody angry; *council workmen came and took down the offending sign*

offensive [ə'fensɪv] **1** *adjective* **(a)** unpleasant, which offends; *what an offensive smell!; the waiter was quite offensive* **(b)** *(in army)* **offensive weapons** = weapons which are used in an attack; *it is against the law to carry offensive weapons* **2** *noun* (military) attack; *the offensive was successful, and the enemy retreated;* **to take the offensive** *or* **to go on the offensive** = to start to attack someone; *he took the offensive and demanded an explanation*

offer ['ɒfə] *verb* **1** *noun* **(a)** thing which is proposed; *she accepted his offer of a job in Paris;* **on offer** = which has been offered; *there are several good holiday bargains on offer* **(b)** **bargain offer** *or* **special offer** = goods which are put on sale at a reduced price; *this week's bargain offer - 30% off all holidays in Egypt; oranges are on special offer today; this supermarket always has special offers* **2** *verb* to say that you will give something or do something; *she offered to drive him to the station;* **to offer someone a job** = to tell someone that he can have a job in your company; *if they offer you the job, take it; he was offered a job, but he turned it down*

offering ['ɒfrɪŋ] *noun* thing which is offered; a present; *it's only a small offering, I'm afraid; all offerings will be gratefully received!*

offhand [ɒf'hænd] **1** *adverb* straightaway, without thinking carefully; *I can't say offhand whether I'll be able to go* **2** *adjective* quite unfriendly, not being really polite; *she gave a very offhand reply; he was very offhand about it* (NOTE: also **offhanded** in this meaning)

office ['ɒfɪs] *noun* **(a)** room or building where you carry on a business or where you organize something; *I'll be working late at the office this evening; why is Miss Jones's office bigger than mine?; we bought some new office furniture;* US **doctor's office** = room where a doctor sees his patients (NOTE: British English for this is **surgery**) **(b)** position, job; *she holds the office of treasurer;* **term of office** = period of time when someone has a position; *during his term of office as President* **(c)** government department; **the Foreign Office** = British government department dealing with relations with other countries; **the Home Office** = British Government department dealing with internal affairs, such as the police and prisons; **Serious Fraud Office** = government department in charge of investigating fraud in large companies; *see also* METEOROLOGICAL OFFICE, POST OFFICE

officer ['ɒfɪsə] *noun* **(a)** person who holds an official position; *the customs officer asked me to open my suitcase* **(b)** person who is in charge of others in the army, navy, airforce, etc.; *ordinary soldiers must*

always salute officers **(c) police officer** = policeman;
there are two police officers at the door

official [ə'fɪʃl] **1** adjective **(a)** referring to any
organization, especially one which is recognized as part
of a government, etc.; he left official papers in his car;
we had an official order from the local authority; he
represents an official body **(b)** done or approved by
someone in authority; she received an official letter of
explanation; the strike was made official by the union
headquarters **2** noun person holding a recognized
position; they were met by an official from the
embassy; I'll ask an official of the social services
department to help you; **customs official** = person
working for the customs

officialdom [ə'fɪʃəldəm] noun bureaucracy,
government officials taken as a group and their work;
his job is to persuade officialdom to deal with
complaints more sympathetically (NOTE: no plural)

officialese [əfɪʃə'liːz] noun pompous official
language, which is difficult to understand; all this
officialese, why can't they write letters in normal
English?

officially [ə'fɪʃəli] adverb **(a)** in an official way; she
has been officially named as our representative at the
meeting **(b)** according to what is said in public;
officially, you are not supposed to take money out of
the country, but everyone does; officially he knows
nothing about the problem, but unofficially he has
given us a lot of advice about it

officious [ə'fɪʃəs] adjective very ready to give advice
or tell people what to do, especially when the advice is
not wanted; some officious person in the planning
office held up our application because it wasn't
correctly worded; an officious parking attendant told
me not to park there

off-licence ['ɒflaɪsəns] noun shop which has a
licence to sell alcoholic drinks to be taken away; he
went round to the off-licence to buy a bottle of wine
(NOTE: the American equivalent is a **liquor store**)

off-peak ['ɒf'piːk] adjective not at the peak period;
off-peak fares are considerably less expensive

off-putting ['ɒfpʊtɪŋ] adjective (informal) rather
unpleasant or annoying; I find the audience's giggling
very off-putting; nothing is more off-putting than a
person who insists he knows how to do something
when really he doesn't

off season ['ɒf 'siːzən] **1** noun time of year when
there are fewer travellers, and when air fares and hotel
prices are cheaper; in February, British Airways was
offering special off-season round the world fares; tour
operators try to get more people to travel during the off
season (NOTE: also called **low season**; the opposite is
high season) **2** adverb in the off season; we travelled
off-season, to take advantage of the low fares

offset 1 noun ['ɒfset] method of printing from a plate
to a rubber surface and then to paper; the book was
printed by offset **2** verb [ɒf'set] to balance one thing
against another; losses in France more than offset our
profits in the domestic market (NOTE: **offsetting - has
offset**)

offshore [ɒf'ʃɔː] adjective **(a)** at a distance from the
shore; we went to visit an offshore oil rig **(b)** offshore
wind = wind which blows from the coast towards the
sea (NOTE: the opposite is an **onshore wind**) **(c)** on an
island which is a tax haven; offshore investments have
produced a good rate of return

off side ['ɒf 'saɪd] noun (in a car) side nearest the
middle of the road; you usually overtake on the off side
of another vehicle (NOTE: the other side, where the
passenger sits, is the **near side**)

offside [ɒf'saɪd] **1** adverb (in football) between the
ball and the opposing team's goal; the goal was
disallowed because he was offside **2** adjective referring
to the side of a car nearest to the middle of the road;
your offside rear light isn't working

offspring ['ɒfsprɪŋ] noun **(a)** young of an animal; the
mother deer produces her offspring in early spring **(b)**
(formal) child or children; her offspring are all very
musical (NOTE: no plural)

off-the-cuff ['ɒfðə'kʌf] adjective & adverb made
without notes; he was only asked to speak at the last
minute, and for an off-the-cuff speech, it was
excellent

off-the-peg ['ɒf ðə 'peg] adjective & adverb
(clothes, etc.) which are mass-produced, ready to fit any
person of a certain size; I buy everything off-the-peg
(NOTE: also called **ready-to-wear**; the opposite, clothes
which are made to fit a particular person, are called
made-to-measure)

off-the-wall ['ɒfðə'wɔːl] adjective (informal) very
unusual and strange; he is famous for his off-the-wall
humour; some of the things she says are totally
off-the-wall

often ['ɒfən] adverb many times, frequently; I often
have to go to town on business; do you eat beef often?;
how often is there a bus to Richmond?; every so often
= from time to time; we go to the cinema every so often

oftentimes ['ɒfntaɪmz] adverb (old) often; as
children we loved to hear the oftentimes repeated story
of Little Red Riding Hood

ogre ['əʊgə] noun **(a)** (in fairy stories) cruel giant who
eats human beings; Puss in Boots knocked at the door
of the ogre's castle **(b)** cruel, terrifying person; the
staff say he is an ogre and don't like working for him

oh [əʊ] interjection (showing surprise, interest,
excitement) Oh look, there's an elephant!; Oh can't
you stop making that noise?; Oh, Mr Smith, someone
phoned for you while you were out; you must write to
the bank manager - oh no I won't

ohm [əʊm] noun standard measure of electrical
resistance; a resistance of thirty ohms

COMMENT: one ohm is the resistance in a
conductor where one volt produces a current of
one amp

oil [ɔɪl] **1** noun **(a)** liquid of various kinds which flows
smoothly, produced from plants and used in cooking;
cook the vegetables in hot oil; **olive oil** = oil made from
olives **(b)** thick mineral liquid found mainly
underground and used as a fuel or to make something
move smoothly; the door squeaks - it need some oil;
some of the beaches are covered with oil; the company
is drilling for oil in the desert **(c)** **oil (paint)** = paint
made with colours and oil; I used to paint in oils but
now I prefer water colours; **oil painting** = picture
painted in oils, not in water colour **2** verb to put oil on or
in (especially to make a machine run more smoothly);
you should oil your bicycle chain; that squeaky door
needs oiling

oiled [ɔɪld] *adjective* covered in or treated with oil; *put the bread on an oiled metal tray; a well-oiled machine will run easily*

oilfield ['ɔɪlfiːld] *noun* area of rock under which oil lies, which can be exploited; *most of Britain's oil comes from North Sea oilfields*

oils [ɔɪlz] *noun* paints made of colours mixed with oil; *he wanted his portrait done in oils*

oil slick ['ɔɪlslɪk] *noun* layer of oil which has spilled into the sea from a tanker or oil rig and which floats on the water; *an enormous oil slick covered the whole surface of the bay*

oil tanker ['ɔɪltæŋkə] *noun* large ship specially constructed for carrying oil; *an oil tanker ran aground on the rocks outside the harbour*

oil well ['ɔɪl 'wel] *noun* hole in the ground from which oil is pumped; *their oil well produces thousands of barrels of oil per day*

oily ['ɔɪli] *adjective* **(a)** containing oil, covered with oil; *he wiped his hands on an oily rag; the tank was full of oily liquid* **(b)** (*of manner*) too polite and insincere; *I can't stand her oily manner; he smiled an oily smile* (NOTE: **oilier - oiliest**)

ointment ['ɔɪntmənt] *noun* smooth healing cream which you spread on the skin; *rub the ointment onto your knee*

OK *or* **okay** ['əu'keɪ] **1** *interjection* all right, yes; *would you like a coffee? - OK!; it's ten o'clock - OK, let's get going* **2** *adjective* all right; *he was off ill yesterday, but he seems to be OK now; it is OK for me to bring the dogs?* **3** *noun* **to give something the OK** = to approve something; *the committee gave our plan the OK* **4** *verb* to approve something; *the committee OK'd or okayed our plan* (NOTE: **OK'd** ['əu'keɪd])

old [əuld] *adjective* **(a)** not young; *my uncle is an old man - he's eighty-four; she lives in an old people's home* **(b)** having existed for a long time; *he collects old cars; play some old music, I don't like this modern stuff* **(c)** not new; which has been used for a long time; *put on an old shirt if you're going to wash the car; he got rid of his old car and bought a new one* **(d)** with a certain age; *he's six years old today; how old are you?* **(e)** (*used as a pleasant way of talking about someone*) *he's a sweet old man; come on, old thing, it's time to go home* (NOTE: **older - oldest**)

old age ['əuld 'eɪdʒ] *noun* period of your life when you are old; *he started writing poetry again in his old age;* **old age pension** = government pension given to a person who is past retirement age; *in two years' time I'll be drawing my old age pension*

old boy ['əuld 'bɔɪ] *noun* **(a)** (*informal*) old man; *I met his father once, he was a funny old boy; you'll have to shout - the old boy's gone quite deaf* **(b)** former pupil of a school; *did you know that the bank manager is an old boy of this school?;* **the old boy network** = system where men who were at school together help each other get ahead in later life; *thanks to the old boy network he got a good job in the City; he got himself a job in the bank through the old boy network* **(c)** (*old*) (*informal*) way of addressing a friend; *I say, old boy, would you like a game of tennis?*

old-fashioned [əuld'fæʃənd] *adjective* not in fashion; out of date; *she wore old-fashioned clothes; call me old-fashioned, but I don't approve of the way*

young people behave; *I prefer an old-fashioned corkscrew to this newfangled contraption*

old girl ['əuld 'gɜːl] *noun* **(a)** (*informal*) old woman; *the poor old girl has to walk with a stick nowadays; come on, old girl, we've got to run for the bus* **(b)** former pupil of a school; *there's a reunion of the old girls of St Ursula's school*

old guard ['əuld 'gɑːd] *noun* people who have been part of an organization for a long time and are opposed to any changes; *the party old guard will expect to have their say in choosing the new leader*

oldie ['əuldi] *noun* (*informal*) old-fashioned or out-of-date person or thing; *we played some 60s music for the oldies*

old lady ['əuld 'leɪdi] *noun* **(a)** lady who is old; *he helped the old lady cross the street* **(b)** (*informal*) mother or wife of someone; *his old lady's in hospital; I've got to take my old lady shopping this afternoon*

old maid ['əuld 'meɪd] *noun* **(a)** (*offensive*) older woman who has never married; *by the time she was forty and still hadn't got married she had resigned herself to being an old maid for the rest of her life* **(b)** (*informal*) man who is very fussy about little things; *he's a real old maid when it comes to keeping his precious car polished*

old man ['əuld 'mæn] *noun* (*informal*) **(a)** father or husband of someone; *he takes after his old man; she is knitting a pullover for her old man* **(b)** boss; *the old man took charge of the operation personally* **(c)** (*old*) way of talking to a friend; *do you fancy a drink, old man?*

old master ['əuld 'mɑːstə] *noun* **(a)** a very famous old painter; *they think the portrait may be by an Italian old master* **(b)** a painting by a very famous old painter; *there are several old masters in the collection*

old-style ['əuldstaɪl] *adjective* of a kind that was common or typical in the past; *he still uses an old-style typewriter; she's just an old-style crime reporter*

Old Testament ['əuld 'testəmənt] *noun* the first part of the Bible that deals with the origins and history of the Jewish people; *one of the books of the Old Testament; Isaiah and other Old Testament prophets*

old-time [əuld'taɪm] *adjective* done in an old-fashioned way; *there's old-time dancing at the hall this evening*

old timer [əuld'taɪmə] *noun* person who has been in a place or a job for a very long time; *only a few of the old timers can remember back that far*

old wives' tale ['əuld 'waɪvz 'teɪl] *noun* old, and often silly, idea; *eating carrots won't make you see in the dark - that's just an old wives' tale*

Old World ['əuld 'wɜːld] *noun* **the Old World =** Europe, Asia and Africa

old-world ['əuldwɜːld] *adjective* which recalls the good times in the past; *this hotel still provides old-world hospitality*

oleaginous [ɒli'ædʒɪnəs] *adjective* (*formal*) (*of manner*) oily, too polite and insincere; *I prefer the blunt-speaking Mr Brass to his oleaginous assistant*

oligarch ['ɒlɪgɑːk] *noun* one of a group of powerful people who run a country

oligarchy ['ɒlɪgɑːki] *noun* government by a small group of powerful people; *the country is run by an oligarchy of thirty families*

olive ['ɒlɪv] *noun* (a) small black or green fruit from which oil is made for use in cooking; *olives are grown in Mediterranean countries like Spain, Greece and Italy*; **black olives** = ripe olives; **green olives** = unripe olives; *which do you prefer - green or black olives?*; **olive oil** = oil made from olives; *add a little olive oil to the pan* (b) tree which produces this fruit; **olive branch** = sign of peace; *the negotiators held out the olive branch* (c) **olive (green)** = dull green colour of unripe olives; *he wore an olive green coat*

Olympics *or* **Olympic Games** [ə'lɪmpɪks or ə'lɪmpɪk 'geɪmz] *noun* international athletic competition held every four years; *he's an Olympic sportsman*; *she broke the world record or she set up a new world record in the last Olympics*; *the Olympic Games were held in Atlanta in 1996*; *see also* WINTER OLYMPICS

COMMENT: originally an ancient Greek festival held every four years in Olympia in honour of the god Zeus, the modern Games were revived in Athens in 1896 and have been held every four years since (with the exception of 1916, 1940 & 1944 because of the two World Wars) in a variety of cities throughout the world. The sports include: archery, athletics (track and field), badminton, basketball, boxing, canoeing, cycling, diving, equestrianism, fencing, gymnastics, handball, hockey, judo, modern pentathlon, rowing, shooting, soccer, swimming, tennis, volleyball, water polo, weightlifting, wrestling and yachting

ombudsman ['ɒmbədzmən] *noun* official who investigates complaints by the public against government departments or other large organizations; *when the government department ignored her complaint, she took her case to the ombudsman* (NOTE: plural is **ombudsmen**)

COMMENT: there are many ombudsmen: the main one deals with cases against government departments, but there are others who deal with complaints against the health service, against banks, etc.

omelette *US* **omelet** ['ɒmlət] *noun* dish made of beaten eggs, cooked in a frying pan and folded over before serving, with various fillings inside; *I had a cheese omelette and chips for lunch*

omen ['əumən] *noun* thing that indicates what will happen in the future; *the sun was shining as we set out, which seemed like a good omen for the trip*; *was it an omen that the car refused to start when we were off to see the specialist?*

ominous ['ɒmɪnəs] *adjective* threatening bad results; *there was an ominous silence as he asked to see the colonel*; *it's rather ominous that they haven't contacted us yet*

ominously ['ɒmɪnəsli] *adverb* in an ominous way; *the sky looks ominously black*

omission [ə'mɪʃn] *noun* (a) act of omitting; *we were surprised at the omission of his name from the list of candidates* (b) thing which has been omitted; *I can think of at least two obvious omissions from your list of famous playwrights: Shakespeare and Shaw!*

omit [ə'mɪt] *verb* (a) to leave something out; *she omitted the date when typing the contract* (b) to omit to do something = not to do something; *he omitted to tell the police that he had lost the documents* (NOTE: omitting - omitted)

omnibus ['ɒmnɪbəs] *noun* (a) book which includes several books all together; *an omnibus edition of Sherlock Holmes stories* (b) radio or TV programme bringing several programmes together which were previously broadcast separately; *don't forget to listen to the omnibus edition on Saturday!* (c) *(old)* bus, large vehicle which carries passengers; *horse-drawn omnibuses started to run in London in 1829*

on [ɒn] **1** *preposition* (a) on the top or surface of something; *put the box down on the floor*; *flies can walk on the ceiling* (b) hanging from; *hang your coat on the hook* (c) *(showing movement or place)* *a crowd of children got on the train*; *the picture's on page three*; *the post office is on the left-hand side of the street* (d) part of; *she's on the staff of the bank*; *he's been on the committee for six years* (e) doing something; *I have to go to Germany on business*; *we're off on holiday tomorrow* (f) *(showing time, date, day)* *the shop is open on Sundays*; *we went to see my mother on my birthday*; *on his arrival* = when he arrived (g) *(means of travel)* *you can go there on foot - it only takes five minutes*; *she came on her motorbike* (h) about; *the committee produced a report on German industry*; *she wrote a book on wild flowers* (i) *(showing an instrument or machine)* *he played some music on the piano*; *the song is available on CD*; *he was on the telephone for most of the morning*; *the film was on TV last night* **2** *adverb* (a) being worn; *have you all got your wellingtons on?*; *the central heating was off, so he kept his coat on in the house* (b) working; *have you put the kettle on?*; *the heating is on*; *she left all the lights on*; *she turned the engine on*; *he switched the TV on* (c) being shown or played; *what's on at the theatre this week?* (d) continuing, not stopping; *he didn't stop to say hello, but just walked on*; *he went on playing the trumpet even though he asked him to stop*; *go on - I like to hear you play the piano* (e) *(showing time has passed)* *later on that evening, the phone rang*; *he almost drowned, and from that time on refused to go near water* (NOTE: **on** is often used after verbs: **to sit on, to jump on, to put on, to lie on,** etc.)

◊ **on and off** ['ɒn ənd 'ɒf] *adverb* not continuously, with breaks in between; *it's been raining on and off all afternoon*

once [wʌns] **1** *adverb* (a) one time; *take the tablets once a day*; *the magazine comes out once a month*; *how many times did you go to the cinema last year? - only once*; *once in a while* = from time to time, but not often; *it's nice to go to have an Indian meal once in a while* (b) formerly, at a time in the past; *once, when it was snowing, the car skidded into a ditch*; *he's someone I knew once when I worked in London*; *(beginning fairy stories)* **once upon a time** = at a certain time in the past; *once upon a time, there was a wicked witch* **2** *conjunction* as soon as (in the future); *once he starts talking you can't get him to stop*; *once we've moved house I'll give you a phone call*

◊ **at once** ['æt 'wʌns] *adverb* (a) straightaway, immediately; *come here at once!*; *the ambulance came at once* (b) at the same time; *don't all speak at once!* (c) **all at once** = suddenly; *all at once the phone rang*

oncoming ['ɒnkʌmɪŋ] *adjective* coming towards you; *she was dazzled by the headlights of the oncoming traffic*

one [wʌn] **1** number 1; *one plus one makes two*; *our grandson is one year old today*; *his grandmother is a hundred and one* **2** noun **(a)** single item; *have a chocolate - oh dear, there's only one left!*; **last but one** = the one before the last; *this is the last weekend but one before Christmas*; **one by one** = one after another; *he ate all the chocolates one by one*; *they came in one by one and sat in a row at the back of the hall* **(b)** (informal) **a quick one** = a quick drink; *let's have a quick one before the meeting starts*; **one for the road** = a last drink before leaving the bar; *let's have one for the road* **(c)** (informal) *she hit him one with the bottle* = she hit him with the bottle **2** adjective & pronoun **(a)** single (thing); *which hat do you like best - the black one or the red one?*; *one of the staff will help you carry the box to your car*; *I've lost my map - have you got one?*; *small cars use less petrol than big ones*; *all the china plates were dirty so we made do with paper ones* **(b)** (formal) you; *one can't spend all the morning waiting to see the doctor, can one?*; *at his age, one isn't allowed to drive a car* **(c) one another** = each other; *we write to one another every week* (NOTE: **one** (1) but **first** (1st))

one-man ['wʌn 'mæn] adjective run or worked by one person with no helpers; **one-man business** or **firm** or **company** or **operation** or **band** = business run by one person alone with no staff or partners; *he's trying to run his department as a one-man operation*

one-off [wʌn'ɒf] adjective & noun (thing) which is done or made only once; *the free pop concert was a one-off*; *it's a one-off bargain*

one-piece ['wʌn 'piːs] adjective **a one-piece swimming costume** = costume made of one piece of clothing (as opposed to a bikini)

onerous ['ɒnərəs] adjective (formal) needing a lot of effort or money; *the duties of the job are not very onerous*; *the repayment terms are particularly onerous* = the loan is particularly difficult to pay back

oneself [wʌn'self] pronoun referring to the person speaking as an indefinite subject; *it's important to be able to look after oneself*; *it's not easy to do it oneself*

one-sided [wʌn'saɪdɪd] adjective dealing with or favouring one side only; *the judge's decision seemed very one-sided*; *it was a one-sided match - half their team was ill with flu*

one-time ['wʌntaɪm] adjective former; *the Minister of Defence, a one-time general, has powerful support in the armed forces*

one-to-one ['wʌntə'wʌn] adjective where one person has to deal with one other person only; *the two presidents had a one-to-one conversation*; *she is taking a one-to-one Spanish conversation course*

one-track mind [wʌn'træk 'maɪnd] noun he has a **one-track mind** = he thinks about only one thing

one-way street ['wʌn 'weɪ 'striːt] noun street where the traffic only goes in one direction; *don't turn left here - it's a one-way street*

ongoing ['ɒnɡəʊɪŋ] adjective which is continuing; *crime among teenagers is an ongoing problem*

onion ['ʌnjən] noun strong-smelling vegetable with a round white bulb; *fry the onions in butter*; *I don't like onion soup*; **spring onion** = young onion eaten raw in salad

online ['ɒnlaɪn] adjective & adverb directly connected to a computer; *you need to know the password to access the data online*

onlooker ['ɒnlʊkə] noun person who watches an event; *a crowd of onlookers gathered at the scene of the accident*

only ['əʊnli] **1** adjective one single (thing or person), when there are no more; *don't break it - it's the only one I've got*; **only child** = son or daughter who has no other brothers or sisters; *she's an only child* **2** adverb **(a)** with no one or nothing else; *we've only got ten pounds between us*; *only an accountant can deal with this problem*; *this lift is for staff only* **(b)** as recently as; *we saw her only last week*; *only yesterday the bank phoned for information* **3** conjunction but, except; *I like my mother-in-law very much, only I don't want to see her every day of the week*

◊ **if only** [ɪf 'əʊnli] (phrase showing a strong wish) *if only we had known you were in town!*; *she's late - if only she'd phone to let us know where she is!*

◊ **only just** ['əʊnli 'dʒʌst] almost not; *we only just had enough money to pay the bill*; *he had to run and only just caught the last bus*

◊ **only too** ['əʊnli 'tuː] very much; *we would be only too glad to help you if we can*

o.n.o. = OR NEAREST OFFER

onomatopoeia [ɒnəmætə'piːə] noun making or using words which imitate a sound; *the poet uses onomatopoeia to convey the sound of gunfire*

onomatopoeic [ɒnəmætə'piːɪk] adjective using onomatopoeia; *the poem ends with the onomatopoeic phrase 'the rifles' rapid rattle'*

on-screen ['ɒn 'skriːn] adjective & adverb on a computer screen rather than on paper; *most of our design work is done on-screen*

onset ['ɒnset] noun beginning; *the onset of his illness was marked by a sudden high temperature*; *travelling in country districts becomes impossible with the onset of the rainy season*

onshore [ɒn'ʃɔː] adjective towards the shore; **onshore wind** = wind which blows from the sea towards the coast (NOTE: the opposite is an **offshore wind**)

onslaught ['ɒnslɔːt] noun sudden severe attack; *our troops retreated under the enemy onslaught*; *the chairman could not answer her onslaught on company policy*

onstage [ɒn'steɪdʒ] adjective & adverb on the stage of a theatre and in view of an audience; *the onstage action is fast and furious*; *people started to laugh as soon as he walked onstage*

on-the-spot ['ɒnðə'spɒt] adjective done immediately, at the scene where something happens; *now we go over to James Barton for an on-the-spot report*; *the police issue on-the-spot fines to people who are illegally parked*

onto ['ɒntuː] preposition on to; *the speaker went up onto the platform*; *the door opens directly onto the garden*; *turn the box onto its side* (NOTE: also spelt **on to**)

onus ['əʊnəs] noun (formal) responsibility for doing something difficult; *the onus is on the prosecution to prove the accused is guilty*; *the onus is on you to find a solution to the problem*

onward [ˈɒnwəd] **1** *adjective* further forward; *nothing can stop the onward march of computer technology*; **onward connection** = train or plane which takes you on the next stage of your journey; *our onward connection to Dusseldorf is in fifteen minutes* **2** *adverb* further forward; *he urged his men onward towards the enemy positions*

onwards *US* **onward** [ˈɒnwədz] *adverb* further forwards; *from that time onwards he looked on her suspiciously*; *from the 1890s onwards, the death rate began to fall*

ooh [uː] *interjection (showing surprise or shock) ooh you are awful!*; *ooh look at that spider!*

ooze [uːz] **1** *noun* soft mud, especially at the bottom of a lake or the sea; *the wreck lay buried in the ooze at the bottom of the lake* **2** *verb (of liquid)* to flow slowly; *a black sticky liquid oozed from under the door*; *a delicious cake oozing with cream*

oozy [ˈuːzi] *adjective* soft, like mud; *pudding was an oozy chocolate cake, covered in cream*

op [ɒp] *short for* OPERATION; *the op was a success*

opacity [əˈpæsɪti] *noun* state of being opaque; *the opacity of the painted glass*; *his writings are notorious for their opacity*

opal [ˈəʊpl] *noun* semi-precious white stone with changing colours; *a ring set with a large opal*

opaque [əʊˈpeɪk] *adjective* **(a)** which you cannot see through, but which does allow light through; *the surface of the glass is treated to make it opaque*; *opaque black tights are the fashion this winter* **(b)** difficult to understand; *the meaning of the document is completely opaque to me*; *her writings are notorious for being opaque to non-specialists*

OPEC [ˈəʊpek] *noun* = ORGANIZATION OF PETROLEUM EXPORTING COUNTRIES group of countries who produce and export oil; *the OPEC meeting will be held in Geneva*

open [ˈəʊpən] **1** *adjective* **(a)** not shut; *the safe door is open*; *leave the window open - it's very hot in here* **(b)** working, which you can go into; *is the supermarket open on Sundays?*; *the show is open from 9 a.m. to 6 p.m.*; *the competition is open to anyone over the age of fifteen* **(c)** without anything to protect you; *the garden is open on three sides*; *we like walking in the open air*; **open space** = area of land which has no buildings or trees on it; *the parks provide welcome open space in the centre of the city* **(d)** **with an open mind** = with no particular opinions; *I'd like to keep an open mind until the investigation is completed* **2** *noun* **(a)** place outside which is not covered or hidden; *keep the plants in the greenhouse during the winter, but bring them out into the open in the summer*; *the police investigation brought all sorts of offences out into the open* **(b)** competition which anyone can enter provided they are good enough; *he has qualified for the British Open* **3** *verb* **(a)** to make something open; *can you open the door for me, I'm trying to carry these heavy boxes?*; *don't open the envelope until I tell you to* **(b)** to start doing something, a business; *a new restaurant is going to open next door to us*; *most shops open early in the morning* **(c)** to make something begin officially; *the new hotel was opened by the Minister of Tourism*; *the exhibition will be formally opened by the mayor*; *the chairman opened the meeting at 10.30*

open air [ˈəʊpən ˈeə] *noun* place outside which is not covered or hidden; *we keep the plants in the greenhouse during the winter, but bring them out into the open air in the summer*

open-air [ˈəʊpən ˈeə] *adjective* in the open, not in a building; *an open-air performance of 'Twelfth Night'*; *an open-air concert in Central Park*

open day [ˈəʊpən ˈdeɪ] *noun* day when a building is open to the public; *the laboratory is having an open day next week*; *we must go to the open day at Simon's school*

open-door [ˈəʊpən ˈdɔː] *adjective* **open-door policy** = trading policy, where a country allows any person or goods to enter the country freely; *a country that suddenly decides to operate an open-door policy risks being flooded with imports*

open-ended [ˈəʊpən ˈendɪd] *adjective* with no fixed limit, with some items not specified; *we have an open-ended agreement with our American partners*

opener [ˈəʊpnə] *noun* device for opening; *where's the bottle opener?*; *I need a tin opener to open this tin of tomatoes*

opening [ˈəʊpnɪŋ] *noun* **(a)** action of becoming open; *the opening of the exhibition has been postponed*; *the office opening times are 9.30 to 5.30* **(b)** hole; *the cows got out through an opening in the wall* **(c)** opportunity, such as a job vacancy; *we have openings for telephone sales staff*

opening night [ˈəʊpnɪŋ ˈnaɪt] *noun* first evening performance when a new film or play is shown; *a host of stars gathered for the film's opening night*; *it is impossible to get tickets for the opening night* (NOTE: for a play also **first night**)

open letter [ˈəʊpən ˈletə] *noun* letter to someone, published as an article in a newspaper and not actually sent to the person it is addressed to; *six professors wrote an open letter to the Prime Minister in 'the Times'*

openly [ˈəʊpənli] *adverb* in a frank and open way; *they discussed the plan quite openly*; *can I talk openly to you about my sister?*

open market [ˈəʊpən ˈmɑːkɪt] *noun* market where anyone can buy or sell; *how much would it fetch on the open market?*

open-minded [ˈəʊpənˈmaɪndɪd] *adjective* not having prejudices or fixed opinions and willing to listen to other people's ideas; *he adopted a very open-minded attitude to the managers' suggestions*; *she's very open-minded about what her daughter does in the evenings*

open on to [ˈəʊpən ˈɒn tuː] *verb* to lead out on to or to look out on to; *the door opens straight onto the street*; *the windows open onto the garden*

open-plan [ˈəʊpənplæn] *adjective* **open-plan offices** = offices in a large space with no internal walls to divide them

Open University [ˈəʊpən juːnɪˈvɜːsɪti] *noun* a university in the UK where students study at home, sending work to their teachers by post and watching lectures on television; *she took a course at the Open University or an Open University course*

opera [ˈɒprə] *noun* performance on the stage with music, in which the words are sung and not spoken; *'the Marriage of Figaro' is one of Mozart's best-known operas*; *we have tickets for the opera tomorrow*; *we are going to see the new production of an opera by Britten*

opera house ['ɒprə 'haʊs] *noun* theatre in which operas are performed; *the old opera house is in the centre of the city; Covent Garden Opera House is one of the most famous in the world*

operate ['ɒpəreɪt] *verb* **(a)** to make something work; *he knows how to operate the machine; she is learning how to operate the new telephone switchboard* **(b)** to **operate on a patient** = to treat a patient by cutting open the body; *she was operated on by Mr Jones*

operatic [ɒpə'rætɪk] *adjective* referring to opera; *he joined the local amateur operatic society*

operating system ['ɒpəreɪtɪŋ 'sɪstəm] *noun* basic software that controls the running of the hardware on a computer, and the management of data files, without the user having to operate it; *which operating system do you use?; Apple Macs use a different operating system from PCs*

operating theatre ['ɒpəreɪtɪŋ 'θɪːətə] *noun* special room in a hospital where surgeons carry out operations; *they rushed the patient straight into the operating theatre*

operation [ɒpə'reɪʃn] *noun* **(a)** action of operating; *the rescue operation was successful*; **to come into operation** = to begin to be applied; *the new schedules came into operation on June 1st* **(b)** treatment by cutting open the body; *she's had three operations on her leg; the operation lasted almost two hours*

operational [ɒpə'reɪʃnəl] *adjective* **(a)** referring to the working of something; *the operational procedure is described in the manual* **(b)** ready for use; **the system became operational on June 1st** = the system started working on June 1st

operative ['ɒpərətɪv] **1** *adjective* working, in operation; **to become operative** = to start working; *the new system became operative on June 1st* **2** *noun* worker, especially one who operates a machine, etc.; *the factory used to employ two hundred operatives*

operator ['ɒpəreɪtə] *noun* **(a)** person who works instruments, etc.; *he's a computer operator; she's a machine operator* **(b)** person who works a telephone switchboard; *dial 0 for the operator; you can place a call through or via the operator* **(c)** person who organizes things; **tour operator** = travel agent who organizes package holidays or tours; *(informal)* **a smart operator** = a clever businessman

operetta [ɒpə'retə] *noun* opera with an amusing story in which some words are spoken; *'The Merry Widow' is Lehar's most famous operetta*

ophthalmic [ɒf'θælmɪk] *adjective* referring to the medical treatment of the eye; *an ophthalmic surgeon*

ophthalmologist [ɒfθæl'mɒlədʒɪst] *noun* doctor who treats diseases of the eye; *compare* OPTICIAN, OPTOMETRIST

opinion [ə'pɪnjən] *noun* **(a)** what someone thinks about something; *ask the lawyer for his opinion about the letter*; **he has a very high** *or* **very low opinion of his assistant** = he thinks he is very good *or* very bad; *see also* SECOND OPINION **(b)** **in my opinion** = as I think; *in my opinion, we should wait until the weather gets warmer before we go on holiday; tell me what in your opinion we should do*

opinionated [ə'pɪnjəneɪtɪd] *adjective* with strong fixed opinions; *she's so opinionated she never asks what other people think*

opinion poll [ə'pɪnjən 'pəʊl] *noun* asking a sample group of people questions, so as to get the probable opinion of the whole population; *the opinion poll taken before the election did not reflect the final result; opinion polls showed that people preferred butter to margarine*

opium ['əʊpiəm] *noun* drug made from a type of poppy, used in the preparation of codeine and heroin; *he quickly became addicted to opium; some painkillers still contain opium*

opponent [ə'pəʊnənt] *noun* **(a)** person or group which is against something; *opponents of the planned motorway have occupied the site* **(b)** person who fights someone else; *his opponent in the election is a local councillor; he knocked out his last three opponents*

opportune ['ɒpətjuːn] *adjective* happening by chance at the right time; *arrival of the police was very opportune, otherwise I might have been robbed; I'm waiting for an opportune moment to ask him for his autograph*

opportunist [ɒpə'tjuːnɪst] *noun* person who takes advantage of opportunities, especially at the expense of others; *financial opportunists saw the privatization programme as a way to make a lot of money very quickly; he's not really interested in our work, he's an just an opportunist trying to further his career*

opportunistic [ɒpətjuː'nɪstɪk] *adjective* trying to take advantage from an opportunity which is offered; *his decision was quite opportunistic, not based on principle*

opportunity [ɒpə'tjuːnɪti] *noun* **(a)** chance or circumstances which allow you to do something; *when you were in London, did you have an opportunity to visit St Paul's Cathedral?; I'd like to take this opportunity to thank all members of staff for the work they have done over the past year*; **a good opportunity for doing something** = a good time for doing something; *it is an excellent opportunity to buy the business* **(b)** **equality of opportunity** = situation where everyone, regardless of sex, race, class, etc., has the same opportunity to get a job; *the female staff are demanding equality of pay and opportunities with the men*; **inequality of opportunity** = situation where all people do not have the same opportunities

oppose [ə'pəʊz] *verb* **(a)** to put yourself against someone in an election; *she is opposing him in the election* **(b)** to try to prevent something happening; *several groups oppose the new law*

opposed to [ə'pəʊzd 'tuː] *adjective* **(a)** not in favour of; *he is opposed to the government's policy on education* **(b)** in contrast to; *if you paint the kitchen a light colour as opposed to dark purple, you will find it will look bigger*

opposing [ə'pəʊzɪŋ] *adjective* **(a)** playing, fighting or arguing against you; *the players on the opposing side refused to shake hands with us; he fouled a member of the opposing team* **(b)** which is the opposite; *she holds quite opposing views to mine*

opposite ['ɒpəzɪt] **1** *preposition* on the other side of, facing; *I work in the offices opposite the railway station; she sat down opposite me* **2** *adjective* which is on the other side; *the shop's not on this side of the street - it's on the opposite side; her van was hit by a lorry going in the opposite direction* **3** *noun* something which is completely different; *'black' is the opposite of 'white'; she's just the opposite of her brother - he's tall* *and thin, she's short and fat; he likes to say one thing, and then do the opposite*

opposite number ['ɒpəzɪt 'nʌmbə] *noun* person who is in a similar job to yours in another company; *she's my opposite number at Smith's Ltd*

opposite sex ['ɒpəzɪt 'seks] *noun* the other sex, not the one you belong to; *the scent is supposed to make you attractive to members of the opposite sex*

opposition [ɒpə'zɪʃn] *noun* **(a)** action of opposing; *there was a lot of opposition to the company's plans to demolish the church hall and build a supermarket* **(b)** *(in politics)* the party or group which opposes the government; *the leader of the opposition rose to speak; the party lost the election and is now in opposition; see also* LEADER

oppress [ə'pres] *verb* **(a)** to make people suffer, especially by harsh government; *the barons oppressed the peasants* **(b)** to make someone feel shut in and depressed; *the atmosphere in this office really oppresses me; playing in India for the first time, the members of the team felt oppressed by the heat*

oppressed [ə'prest] *adjective* treated in a cruel and unfair way; *members of the oppressed minority fled into the mountains to escape from government troops*

oppression [ə'preʃn] *noun* cruel and unfair rule and control; *they set up an organization to help victims of oppression; for years the people of the country have been suffering oppression*

oppressive [ə'presɪv] *adjective* **(a)** cruel, using oppression; *under the general's oppressive regime, ordinary citizens were afraid to speak out against the government* **(b)** that makes people feel shut in and depressed; *there's a very oppressive atmosphere in the office; I find the hot, humid July weather very oppressive*

oppressor [ə'presə] *noun* person who oppresses others; *the people rose in rebellion against their oppressors*

opt [ɒpt] *verb* to choose; **to opt for something** = to choose something, to decide in favour of something; *in the end, she opted for a little black dress; we couldn't decide where to go on holiday, and in the end opted for Greece; see also* OPT OUT

optic ['ɒptɪk] *adjective* referring to the eye or to sight; **optic nerve** = nerve which transmits the sensation of sight from the eye to the brain; **fibre optic cable** = thin strands of glass or plastic used to carry light signals and data

optical ['ɒptɪkl] *adjective* **(a)** referring to the eyes or to eyesight; **an optical illusion** = thing which seems real when you see it, but is not; *the sword seemed to go right through his body, but it was just an optical illusion;* **an optical telescope** = telescope which uses mirrors and lenses to magnify enormously the image and light coming from stars (as opposed to a radio telescope) **(b)** referring to optics; **optical fibres** = fine threads of glass used for transmitting light signals; *metal telephone cables are being replaced by optical fibres*

optician [ɒp'tɪʃn] *noun* person who tests your eyesight, prescribes and sells glasses or contact lenses, etc.; *the optician prescribed some reading glasses;* **the optician's** = the shop and offices of an optician; *I must go to the optician's to have my eyes tested* (NOTE: also called an **optometrist**; compare also **ophthalmologist**)

optics ['ɒptɪks] *noun* study of sight and light rays; *Newton's first work was a treatise on optics;* **fibre optics** = the use of optical fibres to send signals and images, to examine the inside of the body, etc.; *advances in fibre optics have enormously increased the speed of communications*

optimism ['ɒptɪmɪzm] *noun* belief that everything is as good as it can be or will work out for the best in the future; cheerful attitude; *he showed considerable optimism for the future of the company; I like your brother - he's always full of optimism*

optimist ['ɒptɪmɪst] *noun* person who believes everything will work out for the best in the end; *he's an incurable optimist - he always thinks everything will turn out fine*

optimistic [ɒptɪ'mɪstɪk] *adjective* feeling that everything will work out for the best; *we are optimistic about the plan or that the plan will succeed*

optimum ['ɒptɪməm] **1** *noun (formal)* best thing or amount; *twenty would be just enough, thirty would be the optimum we should aim for* **2** *adjective (formal)* best; *the market offers optimum conditions for sales; what is the optimum speed for fuel consumption?*

option ['ɒpʃn] *noun* **(a)** choice, other possible action; *one option would be to sell the house; the tour offers several options as half-day visits* **(b)** **to hold an option on something** = to have the opportunity to buy or sell something within a certain time or at a certain price

optional ['ɒpʃnəl] *adjective* which may or may not be chosen; *you don't have to go to the extra classes on Saturday mornings - they're optional; the computer comes with an optional CD-ROM drive;* **optional extras** = extra fittings which can be added to a car, but which are not provided in the basic model; *air conditioning is an optional extra on this model*

optometrist [ɒp'tɒmətrɪst] *noun* person who tests your eyesight, prescribes and sells glasses or contact lenses, etc.; *the optometrist gave him an eye test* (NOTE: also called an **optician**; compare also **ophthalmologist**)

opt out ['ɒpt 'aʊt] *verb* **to opt out of something** = to decide not to take part in something; *she decided to opt out of the pension scheme; he opted out from the trip because he couldn't afford the price of a ticket*

opt-out ['ɒptaʊt] *noun* action of opting out of something; *they negotiated an opt-out from some of the provisions of the treaty*

opulence ['ɒpjʊləns] *noun* great luxury or wealth; *the film shows the opulence of the Titanic's first-class accommodation*

opulent ['ɒpjʊlənt] *adjective* rich, luxurious, splendid; *the palace's interior and furnishings are even more opulent than its facade*

opus ['əʊpəs] *noun (formal)* **(a)** important piece of music which is given a number; *Beethoven's Pastoral Symphony, opus 68* **(b)** large work of art; *the gallery isn't big enough to house his latest opus;* **magnum opus** = work of art to which the artist has devoted a lot of time; *the novel in twelve volumes is his magnum opus* (NOTE: plural is **opuses** or **opera**)

or [ɔː] *conjunction* **(a)** *(linking alternatives, showing other things that can be done)* *you can come with us in the car or just take the bus; do you prefer tea or coffee?; was he killed in an accident or was he murdered?; the film starts at 6.30 or 6.45, I can't* remember which **(b)** *(approximately) five or six people came to the shop; it costs five or six dollars*

◊ **or else** ['ɔː 'els] **(a)** if not; *don't miss the bus, or else you'll have a long wait for the next one; put a coat on to go out, or else you'll catch cold; we'd better get up early or else we'll miss the train* **(b)** *(as a threat) do as I tell you, or else!*

oral ['ɔːrl] **1** *adjective* **(a)** spoken, by speaking; *there is an oral test as well as a written one* **(b)** oral medicine = medicine taken by the mouth (NOTE: do not confuse with **aural**) **2** *noun* examination where you answer questions by speaking, not writing; *he passed the written examination but failed the oral*

orange ['ɒrɪnʒ] **1** *noun* **(a)** sweet tropical fruit, coloured between red and yellow; *she had a glass of orange juice and a cup of coffee for breakfast; roast duck and orange sauce;* orange marmalade = marmalade made from oranges (usually bitter oranges); orange squash = drink made of concentrated orange juice and water; *do you want some orange squash?* **(b)** orange (tree) = tree which bears this fruit; *a grove of oranges and lemons; the orange orchards of Spain; we have a little orange tree in a pot* **(c)** the colour of an orange, a colour between yellow and red; *she painted the bathroom a very bright orange; she wore a dark orange dress* **2** *adjective* of the colour of an orange; *that orange tie is awful*

orangeade [ɒrɪndʒ'eɪd] *noun* fizzy orange-flavoured drink; *which do you want - orangeade or lemonade?; I'm looking for low sugar orangeade*

orang-utang [əˈræŋ uːˈtæŋ] *noun* large ape with red hair found in South-East Asia

orbit ['ɔːbɪt] **1** *noun* curved path of something moving through space; *the rocket will put the satellite into orbit round the earth* **2** *verb* to move in an orbit round something; *the satellite orbits the earth once every five hours*

orbital ['ɔːbɪtl] *adjective* **(a)** referring to the orbit of a planet, satellite, etc.; *the Earth has an orbital velocity round the Sun of about 30km per second* **(b)** that goes all the way around something, especially round a big city; *the M25 is the London orbital motorway*

orchard ['ɔːtʃəd] *noun* field of fruit trees; *the apple orchards of Kent; the orange orchards of California*

orchestra ['ɔːkəstrə] *noun* **(a)** large group of musicians who play together; *the London Symphony Orchestra* **(b)** orchestra pit = part of a theatre, usually next to the stage and just below it, where the musicians sit; *you can see into the orchestra pit from where we're sitting;* orchestra stalls = seats in the ground floor of a theatre nearest the orchestra and the stage

orchestral [ɔːˈkestrəl] *adjective* referring to an orchestra; *they played some orchestral pieces*

orchestrate ['ɔːkɪstreɪt] *verb* **(a)** to arrange a piece of music for an orchestra; *Mussorgsky's 'Pictures at an Exhibition' was orchestrated by Ravel* **(b)** to organize a demonstration, etc.; *they orchestrated the protest marches in such a way as to get them on the TV news every evening*

orchid ['ɔːkɪd] *noun* flowering plant with colourful showy flowers; *he was wearing a green orchid in his buttonhole; she lavishes a lot of care on her collection of orchids*

ordain [ɔːˈdeɪn] *verb* **(a)** to make someone a priest or a clergyman in a formal ceremony; *he was ordained in Canterbury Cathedral* **(b)** *(formal)* to order, to command that something be done; *the king ordained that all children over five had to be registered with the tax authorities; fate ordained that the children would never see their father again*

ordeal [ɔːˈdiːl] *noun* painful test, difficult time; *she's been through a dreadful ordeal; the death of his best friend was a terrible ordeal for Tom*

order ['ɔːdə] **1** *noun* **(a)** instruction to someone to do something; *he shouted orders to the workmen; if you can't obey orders you can't be a soldier* **(b)** *(from a customer)* asking for something to be served or to be sent; *we've had a large order for books from Russia; she gave the waitress her order* **(c)** things ordered in a restaurant; *the waiter brought him the wrong order* **(d)** special way of putting things; *put the invoices in order of their dates;* the stock in the storeroom is all in the wrong order *or* all out of order = it is not in the right place; alphabetical order = arrangement by the letters of the alphabet (A, B, C, etc.); *the books are put in alphabetical order;* chronological order = arrangement in the order of the dates; *the reports are filed in chronological order;* numerical order = arrangement in order of numbers; *put these invoices in numerical order* **(e)** functioning correctly; out of order = not working; *you'll have to use the stairs, the lift is out of order;* in order = correct; *are his papers in order?* **(f)** in order that = so that; *bicyclists should wear orange coats in order that drivers can see them in the dark;* in order to = so as to; *she ran as fast as she could in order to catch the bus; he looked under the car in order to see if there was an oil leak* **(g)** whole group of monks or nuns; *the Benedictines are one of the most important of the monastic orders* **2** *verb* **(a)** to tell someone to do something; *they ordered the protesters out of the building; the doctor ordered him to take four weeks' holiday* **(b)** *(of a customer)* to ask for something to be served or to be sent; *they ordered chicken and chips and some wine; I've ordered a new computer for the office; they ordered a Rolls Royce for the managing director*

order about ['ɔːdə əˈbaut] *verb* to tell someone what to do all the time; *I don't like being ordered about*

orderly ['ɔːdəli] **1** *adjective* **(a)** tidy or well-arranged; *she keeps a really orderly office; the papers were stacked in orderly piles* **(b)** well-behaved; *I want you to all to cross the road in an orderly fashion; the police praised the orderly rugby supporters* **2** *noun* **(a)** person who does general work; hospital orderly *or* medical orderly = person who does heavy work in a hospital, such as moving patients on trolleys, moving equipment from one place to another, etc.; *the nurse sent for an orderly to move the bed* **(b)** soldier who does general work for an officer; *an orderly appeared with a cup of coffee for the general* (NOTE: plural is **orderlies**)

ordinal (number) ['ɔːdɪnl 'nʌmbə] *noun* number indicating the position in a series; *first, second and third are ordinal numbers* (NOTE: ordinary numbers, such as one, two, three, are called **cardinal numbers**)

ordinance ['ɔːdɪnəns] *noun (formal)* special decree of a government; *a council ordinance lists the types of trees which can be planted along the streets* (NOTE: do not confuse with **ordnance**)

ordinarily ['ɔːdnrəli] *adverb* **(a)** normally, usually; *ordinarily we don't allow visitors in here; it's not* something we **ordinarily** do **(b)** in a normal way; *she was dressed quite ordinarily*

ordinary ['ɔːdənri] *adjective* not special; *I'll wear my ordinary suit to the wedding; they lead a very ordinary life;* **out of the ordinary** = very unusual, very different; *their flat is quite out of the ordinary;* **nothing out of the ordinary** = normal; *the weather in June was nothing out of the ordinary*

ordination [ɔːdɪ'neɪʃn] *noun* act or ceremony of ordaining someone as a priest; *his ordination took place in Coventry cathedral; the bishop opposed the ordination of women*

ordnance ['ɔːdnəns] *noun* **(a)** heavy guns; *the army besieging the town directed their ordnance against the weakest part of the city walls* **(b)** military supplies; **the Royal Ordnance** = the former British government department dealing with military supplies (NOTE: no plural; do not confuse with **ordinance**)

Ordnance Survey ['ɔːdnəns 'sɜːveɪ] *noun* British government agency which is responsible for producing detailed maps of the country; *we used an Ordnance Survey map to plot our route*

ore [ɔː] *noun* type of stone found in the earth from which metals are obtained; *iron is produced from iron ore* (NOTE: do not confuse with **oar**)

organ ['ɔːgən] *noun* **(a)** part of the body with a special function, such as the heart, liver etc.; *he was in a coma and some of his organs had stopped functioning* **(b)** musical instrument with keyboard(s) and many pipes through which air is pumped to make a sound; *she played the organ at our wedding; the organ played the 'Wedding March' as the bride and groom walked down the aisle; see also* MOUTHORGAN **(c)** *(formal)* official newspaper; *it is the organ of the book trade; the appointments will be published in the official organs*

organic [ɔː'gænɪk] *adjective* **(a)** referring to living things; **organic chemistry** = chemistry of carbon compounds **(b)** cultivated naturally, without using any chemical fertilizers and pesticides; *organic vegetables are more expensive but are better for you;* **organic farming** = farming using only natural fertilizers and pesticides

organically [ɔː'gænɪkli] *adverb* in an organic way; **organically grown** *or* **organically produced** = (food) which is grown or produced naturally, without any chemical fertilizers or pesticides

organism ['ɔːgənɪzm] *noun* living thing; *with a microscope you can see millions of tiny organisms in ordinary tap water*

organist ['ɔːgənɪst] *noun* person who plays the organ; *he was organist in our local church for twenty-five years*

organization [ɔːgənaɪ'zeɪʃn] *noun* **(a)** action of arranging something; *the organization of the meeting is done by the secretary* **(b)** organized group or institution; *he's chairman of an organization which looks after blind people; international relief organizations are sending supplies; see also* NON-GOVERNMENTAL ORGANIZATION

organizational [ɔːgənaɪ'zeɪʃnl] *adjective* referring to the way in which something is organized; *the chart is a diagram of the company's organizational structure*

organize ['ɔːgənaɪz] *verb* **(a)** to arrange; *she is responsible for organizing the meeting; we organized*

ourselves into two groups; *the company is organized in three sections* **(b)** to put into good order; *we have put her in charge of organizing the city archives*

organized crime ['ɔːgənaɪzd 'kraɪm] *noun* crime which is run as a business, with groups of specialist criminals, assistants, security staff, etc., all run by a group of directors or by a boss; *the police chief was rumoured to have links with organized crime*

organizer ['ɔːgənaɪzə] *noun* **(a)** **personal organizer** = little computer in which you enter your appointments, addresses, etc.; *I'll put the dates in my personal organizer; he was lost when someone stole his organizer* **(b)** little diary or looseleaf book, in which you enter your appointments, addresses, etc. **(c)** person who arranges things; **tour organizer** = company or person who arranges a tour

orgasm ['ɔːgæzəm] *noun* climax of the sexual act, when a person experiences a moment of great excitement

orgy ['ɔːdʒi] *noun* **(a)** uncontrolled party with drinking and dancing; *the celebrations rapidly became a drunken orgy; Jenny's birthday party turned into an all-night orgy* **(b)** uncontrolled activity; *when he won the lottery he indulged in an orgy of spending* (NOTE: plural is **orgies**)

orient ['ɔːriənt] **1** *noun* **the Orient** = the East, Eastern countries (NOTE: the word referring to the West is the **Occident**) **2** *verb* **(a)** **to orient yourself** = to get yourself accustomed to a new place or ready for a new situation or job; *they are still orienting themselves to living in London* **(b)** to put facing a certain direction; *the house is oriented towards the west*

oriental [ɔːri'entl] *adjective* referring to the Far East; *we love oriental food, both Chinese and Japanese; she collects oriental carpets* (NOTE: the word referring to the west is **occidental**)

orientate ['ɔːriənteɪt] *verb* **(a)** to get yourself accustomed to a new place or ready for a new situation or job; *she'll need time to orientate herself after her long trip abroad* **(b)** to put in a certain direction; *the house is orientated towards the west*

orientation [ɔːriən'teɪʃn] *noun* **(a)** attitude, views or aims of a person or organization; **political orientation** = a person's political preferences; *do we know anything about his political orientation?; a party with a socialist orientation;* **sexual orientation** = whether a person is heterosexual or homosexual; *the questionnaire has a section on sexual orientation* **(b)** process of helping people to get to know a place, job, or subject; *all new students take an orientation course in their first week at college* **(c)** being placed along a particular line or facing in a particular direction; *the church's orientation is north-south, instead of the more usual east-west*

origami [ɒrɪ'gæmi] *noun* Japanese art of folding paper to make interesting shapes

origin ['ɒrɪdʒɪn] *noun* beginning, where something *or* someone comes from; *his family has French origins;* **country of origin** = country where a product is manufactured; *there should be a label saying which is the country of origin*

original [ə'rɪdʒɪnl] **1** *adjective* **(a)** from the beginning; *the original ideas for his paintings came from his own garden* **(b)** new and different, made for the first time; with ideas not based on those of other people; *they solved the problem by using a very* original method; the planners have produced some very original ideas for the new town centre (c) not a copy; they sent a copy of the original invoice; he kept the original receipt for reference 2 noun thing from which other things are copied, translated, etc.; the original was lost in the post but luckily I kept a copy; she found that the old painting bought in a jumble sale was an original and not a copy

originally [ə'rɪdʒnəli] adverb in the beginning; originally it was mine, but I gave it to my brother; the family originally came from France in the 18th century

originate [ə'rɪdʒɪneɪt] verb (a) to begin, to start from, to have a beginning; this strain of flu originated in Hong Kong; his problems at work originated in his home life (b) to make for the first time; we have originated a new style of computer keyboard

ornament ['ɔːnəmənt] 1 noun small thing used as decoration; there's a row of china ornaments on the mantelpiece 2 verb to add a decoration to something; the cake was ornamented with flowers in pink and green icing

ornamental [ɔːnə'mentl] adjective (a) acting as an ornament; a box with ornamental carvings on its sides (b) pretty rather than useful; the table is purely ornamental: it's far too small to use as a dining table

ornamentation [ɔːnəmən'teɪʃn] noun ornaments added as decoration; the cover of the book is beautiful as it is and doesn't need any ornamentation; strip away the ornamentation and the room is basically a plain square box

ornate [ɔː'neɪt] adjective with too much ornamentation; the carving round the church door is very ornate; an ornate plaster ceiling with flowers and birds

ornery ['ɔːnəri] adjective US (informal) bad-tempered; he's as ornery as a bear with a sore head

orphan ['ɔːfn] 1 noun child who has no parents; she's an orphan - both her parents were killed in a car crash 2 verb to make someone an orphan; hundreds of children were orphaned during the war

orphanage ['ɔːfənɪdʒ] noun home where orphans are looked after; the event was staged to raise money for the local orphanage

orphaned ['ɔːfnd] adjective (children) whose parents have died; the organization helps orphaned children in African; the old couple brought up their orphaned grandchildren

orthodox ['ɔːθədɒks] adjective (a) holding the generally accepted beliefs of a religion, a philosophy, etc.; the Chancellor of the Exchequer is following orthodox financial principles (b) (people) who observe traditional religious practices very strictly; he was brought up in an orthodox Jewish family (c) the Orthodox Church = the Christian Church of Eastern Europe

orthodoxy ['ɔːθədɒksi] noun (a) the generally accepted beliefs of a religion, a philosophy, etc.; the orthodoxy of some of the bishop's beliefs was questioned in the article (b) opinion that is generally accepted at a particular time; he challenged the orthodoxies of the scientific establishment

orthopaedic [ɔːθə'piːdɪk] adjective referring to the correction of deformed bones and joints; she's an orthopaedic surgeon with the local hospital; would an orthopaedic corset help him with his bad back?

OS = OUTSIZE

oscillate ['ɒsɪleɪt] verb to swing from one side to the other; the needle on the dial started to oscillate wildly

oscillation [ɒsɪ'leɪʃn] noun act of oscillating; the regular oscillations of a pendulum

ossicle ['ɒsɪkl] noun one of the three little bones in the middle ear; the ossicles pick up vibrations from the eardrum and transmit them to the inner ear

ostensible [ɒ'stensɪbl] adjective which seems on the surface to be real, when in fact it is not; the ostensible reason for the delay was that the car wouldn't start

ostensibly [ɒ'stensɪbli] adverb seeming to be real, when in fact it is not; it was ostensibly a trade mission, but several of its members were secret service agents

ostentatious [ɒsten'teɪʃəs] adjective looking showy and expensive, so as to impress; the newspapers criticized the ostentatious display of their new offices; she rejected the first design as too ostentatious; being rather ostentatious, he arrived at the hotel in a chauffeur-driver Rolls Royce

ostentatiously [ɒsten'teɪʃəsli] adverb in a showy and expensive way, aiming to impress; he rather ostentatiously used a gold fountain pen to sign the contract

osteoporosis [ɒstiəʊpə'rəʊsɪs] noun condition where the bones become thin, porous and brittle, because of lack of calcium and lack of physical exercise; hormone replacement therapy reduces the risk of osteoporosis; older women are the chief sufferers from osteoporosis

ostracism ['ɒstrəsɪzm] noun being rejected by a group or by society; they felt they risked ostracism by the local community if they reported the matter to the police

ostracize ['ɒstrəsaɪz] verb to refuse to talk to somebody or allow them to be part of a group; people who worked during the strike were later ostracized by their colleagues; see also COVENTRY

ostrich ['ɒstrɪtʃ] noun very large, fast-running bird which cannot fly and is found in Africa; she wore ostrich feathers in her hat (NOTE: plural is **ostriches**)

other ['ʌðə] adjective & pronoun (a) different (person or thing), not the same; we went swimming while the other members of the group sat and watched; I don't like chocolate cakes - can I have one of the other ones or one of the others?; I'm fed up with that campsite - can't we go to some other place next year? (b) second one of two; he has two cars - one is red, and the other (one) is blue; one of their daughters is fat, but the other (one) is quite thin (c) (showing an idea which is not clear) she went to stay in some hotel or other in London; he met some girl or other at the party (d) the other day or the other week = a day or two ago or a week or two ago; I'm surprised to hear he's in hospital - I saw him only the other day and he looked perfectly well; every other = every second one; he wrote home every other day = on Monday, Wednesday, Friday, etc. (e) one after the other = following in line; the dominoes fell down one after the other; all the family got colds one after the other

otherwise ['ʌðəwaɪz] adverb (a) in other ways; your little boy can be noisy sometimes, but otherwise he's an excellent pupil (b) if not, or else; are you sure you can't come on Tuesday? - otherwise I'll have to cancel my visit to the doctor

OTT ['əʊti:ti:] = OVER THE TOP; *throwing the letter on the floor and stamping on it was a bit OTT*

otter ['ɒtə] *noun* small fish-eating mammal with webbed feet living mainly by rivers; *we saw an otter disappear into its hole in the river bank*

ouch [aʊtʃ] *interjection showing that you have been hurt*; *ouch! that was my foot you trod on!*

ought [ɔːt] *verb used with other verbs* **(a)** *(to mean it would be a good thing to)* *you ought to go swimming more often*; *you ought to see the doctor if your cough doesn't get better*; *he oughtn't to eat so much - he'll get fat*; *the travel agent ought to have told you the hotel was full before you went on holiday* **(b)** *(to mean it is probable that)* *she ought to pass her driving test easily*; *he left his office at six, so he ought to be home by now* (NOTE: **ought** is always followed by **to** and a verb in the infinitive)

ounce [aʊns] *noun* measure of weight (= 28 grams); *the baby weighed 6lb 3oz (six pounds three ounces)* *mix four ounces of sugar with two eggs* (NOTE: usually written **oz** after figures: **3oz of butter:** say 'three ounces of butter')

our [aʊə] *adjective* which belongs to us; *our office is near the station*; *our cat is missing again*; *two of our children caught flu* (NOTE: do not confuse with **hour**)

ours [aʊəz] *pronoun* thing or person that belongs to us; *that house over there is ours*; *friends of ours told us that the restaurant was good*; *can we borrow your car, because ours is being serviced?*

ourselves [aʊə'selvz] *pronoun* **(a)** referring to us; *we all organized ourselves into two teams*; *we were enjoying ourselves when the police came* **(b)** all by ourselves = with no one else; *we built the house all by ourselves*; *we don't like being all by ourselves in the dark house*

oust [aʊst] *verb* to force someone to leave a position; *the head of the company was ousted*; *he ousted his little brother from the chair in front of the TV*

out [aʊt] **1** *adverb* **(a)** away from inside; *how did the tiger get out of its cage?*; *she pulled out a box of matches*; *take the computer out of its packing case*; *see also* OUT OF **(b)** not at home; *no one answered the phone - they must all be out* **(c)** away from here; *the tide is out*; *the fishing boats left the harbour and are now out at sea* **(d)** wrong (in calculating); *the cash in the till was £10 out* **(e)** not in fashion; *long hair is out this year* (NOTE: **out** is often used with verbs: **to jump out, to come out, to get out,** etc. Note also that **out** is often followed by **of**)

outboard ['aʊtbɔːd] *adjective* **outboard motor** = engine which is attached to the outside of a boat; *if there's not enough wind to sail the yacht we will have to use the outboard motor*

outbreak ['aʊtbreɪk] *noun* sudden series of cases of an illness or unrest; *there has been an outbreak of measles at the school*; *there was an outbreak of violence at the prison yesterday*

outbuildings ['aʊtbɪldɪŋz] *noun* buildings near to a main building; *there is a range of outbuildings next to the farmhouse which could be converted into holiday cottages*

outburst ['aʊtbɜːst] *noun* sudden display of violent emotion; *there was a spontaneous outburst of emotion*

at the news; *the boss is prone to sudden outbursts of enthusiasm*; *in an angry outburst in Parliament, the MP called on the Prime Minister to resign*

outcast ['aʊtkɑːst] *noun* person who has been rejected by society, or driven away from a group; *in the early years of the century, unmarried women who became pregnant were treated as social outcasts*

outcome ['aʊtkʌm] *noun* result; *the outcome of the match was in doubt until the final few minutes*; *what was the outcome of the appeal?*

outcry ['aʊtkraɪ] *noun* loud protest from a number of people; *in answer to the public outcry the government has decided to act*; *there was an immediate outcry when the true facts were revealed*

outdated [aʊt'deɪtɪd] *adjective* old-fashioned; *they're using outdated equipment, so it is hardly surprising they are not as efficient as their rivals*; *the methods the police are using are completely outdated*

outdo [aʊt'duː] *verb* to do better than; *not to be outdone by his wife, he planned an even bigger party for his own birthday*; *the team outdid everyone's expectations and reached the final* (NOTE: **outdid** [aʊt'dɪd] - **outdone** [aʊt'dʌn])

outdoor [aʊt'dɔː] *adjective* in the open air; *the club has an outdoor swimming pool*; *the hotel offers all sorts of outdoor activities*

outdoors [aʊt'dɔːz] **1** *adverb* in the open air, not inside a building; *the ceremony is usually held outdoors*; *why don't we take our coffee outdoors and sit in the sun?*; *the concert will be held outdoors if the weather is good* (NOTE: you can also say **out of doors**) **2** *noun* the open air, the open countryside; *the pictures of the snowcapped Rocky Mountains are a typical scene of the great American outdoors*

outer ['aʊtə] *adjective* on the outside; *though the outer surface of the pie was hot, the inside was still cold*; *the outer suburbs of London are full of green spaces*; **outer space** = space beyond the earth's atmosphere

outermost ['aʊtəməʊst] *adjective* furthest out, furthest from the centre; *on a clear night you can see stars shining in outermost space*; *the rocket reached the outermost edge of our galaxy*

outfield ['aʊtfiːld] *noun* part of a cricket pitch or baseball pitch furthest away from the players who are batting (NOTE: the opposite is the **infield**)

outfit ['aʊtfɪt] *noun* **(a)** set of clothes needed for a particular purpose; *she bought a new outfit for the wedding*; *for the fancy dress party she wore a nurse's outfit* **(b)** *(informal)* organization; *I want some really professional builders, not an outfit like my brother's*; *she works for some local government outfit*

outflow ['aʊtfləʊ] *noun* quantity which flows out; *scientists have been measuring the outflow from the dam*

outgoing ['aʊtgəʊɪŋ] *adjective* **(a)** **outgoing call** = phone call going out of a building to someone outside; **outgoing mail** = mail which is sent out (NOTE: the opposite in this meaning is **incoming**) **(b)** lively, who likes to be with others; *he has a very outgoing personality*

outgrow [aʊt'grəʊ] *verb* **(a)** to grow too big for clothes; *she's already outgrown the dress I bought her for Christmas* **(b)** to change your behaviour as you grow up; *we hoped they'd soon outgrow that sort of* *behaviour* (NOTE: you can also say to **grow out of**; note also: **outgrew - outgrown**)

outhouse ['aʊthaʊs] *noun* small building standing near to a main building; *the toilet is in an outhouse in the yard*

outing ['aʊtɪŋ] *noun* short trip; *the children went on an outing to the seaside*

outlandish [aʊt'lændɪʃ] *adjective* strange or different from the usual; *many of the clothes at fashion shows are too outlandish for ordinary people to wear*

outlaw ['aʊtlɔː] **1** *noun (old)* person who has been outlawed; *they read about Robin Hood, the famous English outlaw* **2** *verb* **(a)** to say that something is unlawful; *the government has proposed a bill to outlaw drinking in public* **(b)** *(old)* to declare someone to be beyond the protection of the law; *the leader of the bandits was outlawed and fled into the mountains*

outlay ['aʊtleɪ] *noun* money spent, expenditure; *we expect to recoup our initial outlay within six months*; **capital outlay** = money spent on fixed assets such as property, machinery, furniture, etc.; **for a modest outlay** = for a small sum; *now, for a modest outlay, you can buy a calculator which will do all the calculations for you*

outlet ['aʊtlət] *noun* **(a)** place where something can be sold or distributed; *he owns a small number of clothing outlets in south-east London*; **retail outlets** = retail shops **(b)** means by which an idea or feeling can get out; *he did weight-lifting as a outlet for his stress at work* **(c)** **outlet (pipe)** = pipe through which a liquid goes out; *the outlet pipe takes excess water out of the boiler*; *the sewage outlet goes directly into the sea* (NOTE: the opposite is **inlet pipe**)

outline ['aʊtlaɪn] **1** *noun* **(a)** line showing the outer edge of something; *he drew the outline of a car on the paper* **(b)** broad description without giving much detail; *she gave the meeting an outline of her proposals; I don't have much time - just give me the outline of the story* **2** *verb* to make a broad description of a plan, etc.; *he outlined the plan to the bank manager; she outlined her proposals to the meeting* *adjective* as a broad description, without any details; *the outline proposal was rejected; the council gave outline planning permission for a new house*

outlive [aʊt'lɪv] *verb* to **outlive someone** = to live longer than someone; *he outlived all his brothers and sisters; she outlived her husband by twenty years;* to **outlive its usefulness** = to be no longer any use; *our old telephone system has outlived its usefulness*

outlook ['aʊtlʊk] *noun* **(a)** view of the world in general; *his gloomy outlook shows in his novels* **(b)** view of what will happen in the future; *we think the outlook for the company is excellent; the economic outlook is not good; the outlook for tomorrow's weather is mainly sunny with some rain*

outlying ['aʊtlaɪɪŋ] *adjective* away from a town or city; *some outlying areas of the country have bad bus services; people came in from outlying villages for the weekly market*

outmanoeuvre *US* **outmaneuver** [aʊtmə'nuːvə] *verb* to gain an advantage over someone by acting or working more cleverly; *the union outmanoeuvred us in negotiations about pay and conditions*

outnumber [aʊt'nʌmbə] *verb* to be greater in number than; *women outnumber men on the committee by three to one*

out of ['aʊt 'ɒv] *preposition* **(a)** outside of; *get out of my way!; they went out of the room;* **out of your mind** = mad; *are you out of your mind?* **(b)** from among a total; *she got 60 marks out of 100 for her exam; one out of ten policemen is corrupt;* **nine times out of ten** = nearly all the time; *nine times out of ten it's the other driver who is wrong* **(c)** from; *her dress is made out of a piece of old silk; he made a fortune out of buying and selling antiques* **(d)** no longer available; *we're out of carrots today; I'm out of change - can I borrow £5?;* **out of print** = with no printed copies left

out of date ['aʊt əv 'deɪt] *adjective* **(a)** no longer in fashion; *flared trousers are rather out of date* **(b)** no longer valid; *I'm afraid your bus pass is out-of-date; she tried to travel with an out-of-date ticket*

out of doors ['aʊt əv 'dɔːz] *adverb* in the open air, not inside a building; *the ceremony is usually held out of doors; the concert will be held out of doors if the weather is good* (NOTE: you can also say **outdoors**)

out of pocket ['aʊt əv 'pɒkɪt] *adjective* having lost money which you paid personally; *the lunch left him £25 out of pocket; the accounts department advanced me £100 for out-of-pocket expenses*

out of stock ['aʊt əv 'stɒk] *adverb* with no stock left; *the dresses sold so fast that the shop was soon out of stock*

out of the way ['aʊt əv ðə 'weɪ] *adjective* **(a)** not near any main town; *they live in an out-of-the-way village in the West Country* **(b)** it's nothing out of the **way** = it's not unusual, not extraordinary

out of touch ['aʊt əv 'tʌtʃ] *adjective* **(a)** not having the most recent information about something; *he seems out of touch with what's been happening in his department* **(b)** not communicating with somebody by letter, telephone, etc.; *we've been out of touch with our relations in Canada for several years* (NOTE: the opposite is **in touch**)

out-of-town ['aʊtəv'taʊn] *adjective* not near to a town centre; *they have applied to build an out-of-town shopping centre*

out of work ['aʊtəv'wɜːk] **1** *adverb* with no job, unemployed; *the recession has put millions out of work* **2** *adjective* with no job, unemployed; *the company was set up by three out-of-work engineers*

outpace [aʊt'peɪs] *verb* to walk or go faster than someone; *they soon outpaced us and got to the cave first; we expect orders for the new model will soon outpace supply*

outpatient ['aʊtpeɪʃənt] *noun* person who goes to a hospital for treatment, without staying there overnight; *where is the outpatients department, please?; I went to the hospital as an outpatient* (NOTE: the opposite, a patient who stays in hospital for treatment, is an **in-patient**)

outperform [aʊtpə'fɔːm] *verb* to do something better or more quickly than somebody or something else; *in tests the new model easily outperformed all its rivals*

outpost ['aʊtpəʊst] *noun* small town or small fort in a distant part of an occupied territory; *the outpost signalled that it was under attack by rebel tribesmen*

output ['autpʌt] *noun* **(a)** amount which a firm, machine or person produces; *the factory has doubled its output in the last six months* **(b)** outputs = goods or services sold on which VAT is charged (NOTE: the opposite, i.e. goods and services bought on which VAT is paid, are **inputs**)

outrage ['autreɪdʒ] **1** *noun* offence; vigorous attack against moral standards; *the terrorist attack on the market is an outrage; I think the new tax on food is an outrage* **2** *verb* to shock, to be a cause of great indignation; *his behaviour outraged his parents*

outrageous [aut'reɪdʒəs] *adjective* causing indignation and shock; *it is outrageous that they can charge these prices*

outrageously [aut'reɪdʒəsli] *adverb* in an outrageous way; *the meal was outrageously expensive*

outright ['autraɪt] **1** *adjective* complete; *the play was an outright success; she's the outright winner of the competition* **2** *adverb* straight out, openly; *he told me outright that he didn't like me*

outset ['autset] *noun* beginning; *right from the outset, you could see the team was going to lose; at the outset he didn't have much confidence, but he soon grew more sure of himself*

outside [aut'saɪd] **1** *noun* part which is not inside; *he polished the outside of his car; the apple was red and shiny on the outside, but rotten inside* **2** *adjective* which is on the outer surface; *the outside walls of the house are brick;* **outside line** = line from an internal telephone to the main telephone system; *you dial 9 to get an outside line; see also* BROADCAST **3** *adverb & preposition* not inside a building; *it's beautiful and warm outside in the garden; the dog's all wet - it must be raining outside; I left my umbrella outside the front door*

outsider [aut'saɪdə] *noun* **(a)** person who does not belong to a group, society; *she has always been a bit of an outsider* **(b)** horse which is not expected to win a race; *the outsider won the race by a neck*

outsize (OS) ['autsaɪz] *adjective* larger than normal; *he's so tall that he has to buy his clothes in the outsize department*

outskirts ['autskɜːts] *noun* outer edges of a town, etc.; *workers living in blocks of flats round the outskirts of the city*

outspoken [aut'spəukən] *adjective* speaking very frankly; *MPs were outspoken in their criticism of the minister; she made an outspoken attack on the head teacher*

outstanding [aut'stændɪŋ] *adjective* **(a)** excellent; of very high quality, of a very high standard; *her performance was outstanding; an antique Chinese vase of outstanding quality* **(b)** not yet paid; *the invoice from the solicitor is still outstanding; I have some outstanding bills to settle*

outstay [aut'steɪ] *verb* **to outstay your welcome** = to stay longer than your hosts thought you were going to stay

outstretched [aut'stretʃt] *adjective* which is stretched out; *she tripped over his outstretched leg; his mother stood waiting for him with outstretched arms*

outstrip [aut'strɪp] *verb* **(a)** to go faster than someone; *they outstripped everybody else in their new boat; she outstripped all the other competitors to win*

the race **(b)** to do better than someone; *Japanese firms have been outstripping their American rivals* (NOTE: **outstripping - outstripped**)

out-tray ['aut 'treɪ] *noun* file or basket for outgoing letters; *when he had finished dealing with the mail his out-tray was full; I posted everything that was in your out-tray this morning* (NOTE: the file for incoming letters is the **in-tray** and that for letters which are waiting for a decision is the **pending tray**)

outvote [aut'vəut] *verb* to defeat in a vote; *we were outvoted by the Conservatives on the committee*

outward ['autwəd] *adjective & adverb* **(a)** towards the outside; away from the centre or starting point; *the outward journey takes about six hours;* **outward bound** = leaving home, especially for another country **(b)** on the outside; *his outward appearance belies his true character*

outwardly ['autwədli] *adverb* as it seems on the outside; *outwardly, nothing seemed to have changed at home, but we soon realized that there were problems*

outwards *US* **outward** ['autwədz] *adverb* towards the outside; away from the centre or starting point; *the door opens outwards; the ripples spread outwards across the pond*

outweigh [aut'weɪ] *verb* to be more important than something; *the safety of the children outweighs all other considerations*

ova ['əuvə] *see* OVUM

oval ['əuvl] **1** *noun* long rounded shape like an egg; *he drew an oval on the paper* **2** *adjective* with a long rounded shape like an egg; *the pie was cooked in an oval bowl; a rugby ball isn't round but oval*

Oval Office ['əuvəl 'ɒfɪs] *noun* room in the White House which is the personal office of the President of the USA (NOTE: also used to refer to the President himself: **the Oval Office was pleased by the reaction of the Senate**)

ovarian [əu'veəriən] *adjective* referring to the ovaries; **ovarian cyst** = cyst which develops in the ovaries

ovary ['əuvəri] *noun* one of two organs in a woman or female animal which produce ova or egg cells and secrete the female hormone oestrogen; *she had an operation to remove her ovaries* (NOTE: plural is **ovaries**)

ovation [ə'veɪʃn] *noun* great applause; *the pianist got a terrific ovation from the audience;* **standing ovation** = applause at the end of a speech, concert, etc., where all the audience stand up and clap and cheer; *he received a standing ovation at the end of the concert; all the delegates stood up and gave the president a 10-minute standing ovation*

oven ['ʌvn] *noun* metal box with a door which is heated for cooking; *don't put that plate in the oven - it's made of plastic; supper is cooking in the oven; can you look in the oven and see if the meat is cooked?*

ovenproof ['ʌvənpruf] *adjective* which can be put into a hot oven without any danger of it being cracked by the heat; *the potatoes were served in an ovenproof dish*

over ['əuvə] **1** *preposition* **(a)** above or higher than; *he put a blanket over the bed; planes fly over our house every minute; the river rose over its banks* **(b)**

on the other side, to the other side; *our office is just over the road from the bank*; *he threw the ball over the wall*; *the children ran over the road* **(c)** from the top of; *he fell over the cliff*; *she looked over the edge of the balcony* **(d)** during; *over the last few weeks the government has taken several measures*; *let's discuss the problem over lunch* **(e)** more than; *children over 16 years old have to pay full price*; *the car costs over £40,000*; *we had to wait for over two hours* **2** *adverb* **(a)** several times; *he plays the same CD over and over again*; *she did it ten times over* **(b)** down from being upright; *the bottle fell over and all the contents poured out*; *she knocked over the plant pot*; *he leaned over and picked up a pin from the floor* **(c)** more than; *children of 16 and over pay full price*; *there are special prices for groups of 30 and over* **(d)** not used, left behind; *any food left over after the meal can be given to the poor* (NOTE: **over** is used after many verbs: **to run over**, **to fall over**, **to come over**, **to look over**, etc.) **3** *adjective* finished; *is the match over yet?*; *when the civil war was over everyone had more food to eat*

◊ **all over** ['ɔːl 'əʊvə] *phrase* everywhere; *his trousers were dirty all over*

over- ['əʊvə] *prefix* **(a)** *(meaning extremely)* some *overanxious parents took their children to be examined by the specialist* **(b)** *(meaning more than)* **the over-60s** = people who are more than sixty years old; *tour company which caters for the over-60s*

overall 1 [əʊvə'ɔːl] *adjective* covering or taking in everything; *the overall outlook for the country is good*; *the overall impression was favourable*; **overall majority** = majority over all other parties in Parliament taken together **2** [əʊvə'ɔːl] *adverb* taking in everything; *overall, her work has improved considerably* **3** ['əʊvəɔːl] *noun* light coat worn at work; *he was wearing a white overall as he had just come out of the laboratory*; *put an overall over your clothes before you start painting*

overalls ['əʊvəɔːlz] *noun* one-piece suit of working clothes (trousers and top) worn over normal clothes to keep them clean when you are working; *all the workers wear white overalls*

overboard ['əʊvəbɔːd] *adverb* into the water from the edge of a ship, etc.; *he fell overboard and was drowned*; **man overboard!** = someone has fallen into the water!

overcast ['əʊvəkɑːst] *adjective (of sky)* dull and cloudy; *it's been overcast all afternoon, but at least it hasn't rained*

overcharge [əʊvə'tʃɑːdʒ] *verb* to charge too much for something; *they overcharged us for meals*; *we asked for a refund because we had been overcharged*

overcoat ['əʊvəkəʊt] *noun* thick outdoor coat which you wear over other clothes; *you need an overcoat, it's snowing outside*

overcome [əʊvə'kʌm] *verb* to gain victory over an enemy, a problem, etc.; *the army quickly overcame the invaders*; *do you think the drugs problem can ever be overcome?* (NOTE: **overcame** [əʊvə'keɪm] - **has overcome**)

overcrowded [əʊvə'kraʊdɪd] *adjective* with too many people inside; *this part of the town is badly overcrowded*; *the overcrowded ferry sank in the harbour*

overcrowding [əʊvə'kraʊdɪŋ] *noun* having too many people or things in a small area; *new suburbs were built to relieve overcrowding in the inner city*

overdo [əʊvə'duː] *verb* **(a)** to do to much or to use too much of something; *they overdid the red velvet and made the sitting room look like a bar*; *don't overdo the exercises in the first few weeks* **(b) to overdo it** = (i) to work too hard or make too much of an effort; *the doctor says I've been overdoing it recently and need a rest*; *don't overdo it and strained his back*; *be polite and complimentary, but don't overdo it* (NOTE: **overdid - overdone** [əʊvə'dʌn])

overdone [əʊvə'dʌn] *adjective* **(a)** exaggerated; *all right, it's a tragedy, but all that weeping and wailing was terribly overdone* **(b)** cooked too much; *I complained because my steak was overdone* (NOTE: the opposite in this meaning is **underdone**)

overdose ['əʊvədəʊs] **1** *noun* dose of a drug which is more than normal; *she went into a coma after an overdose of heroin or after a heroin overdose* **2** *verb* **to overdose on** = to take too much of a drug; *it's perfectly possible to overdose on aspirin*

overdraft ['əʊvədrɑːft] *noun* amount of money which you can withdraw from your bank account with the bank's permission, which is more than there is in the account, i.e. you are borrowing money from the bank; *he has an overdraft of £500*; *she arranged an overdraft with her bank manager*; *he had to have an overdraft to buy the car*

overdraw [əʊvə'drɔː] *verb* to take out more money from a bank account than there is in it; *I can't take any money out of my account or I shall be overdrawn*; *the bank phoned to say that her account was overdrawn* (NOTE: **overdrew** [əʊvə'druː] - **overdrawn** [əʊvə'drɔːn])

overdue [əʊvə'djuː] *adjective* **(a)** (debt) which has not been paid at the correct time; *this invoice is overdue - please pay immediately*; *his interest payments are three weeks overdue* = he should have been paid his interest payments three weeks ago **(b)** which is late; *her library books were overdue so she had to pay a fine*; *this visit to my mother is long overdue*

overeat [əʊvə'iːt] *verb* to eat too much; *everyone overeats at Christmas* (NOTE: **overate** [əʊvə'et] - **overeaten**)

overeating [əʊvə'iːtɪŋ] *noun* eating too much food; *overeating is bad for your heart*

overestimate [əʊvə'estɪmeɪt] *verb* to think something is larger or worse than it really is; *he overestimated the amount of time needed to fit out the factory*

overexert [əʊvəɪg'zɜːt] *verb* **to overexert yourself** = to work too hard; *don't overexert yourself!*; *he's in no danger of overexerting himself!*

overexertion [əʊvəɪg'zɜːʃn] *noun* too much effort; *he wasn't fit enough to run the marathon and collapsed from overexertion*

overflow 1 [əʊvə'fləʊ] *verb* **(a)** to flow over the top; *the river overflowed its banks*; *the bath was so full it was overflowing* **(b)** to occupy more space; *the crowd was so big that it overflowed into the street outside the meeting room* **2** ['əʊvəfləʊ] *noun* **(a)** liquid which has overflowed; *this ditch takes away the overflow from the pond* **(b) overflow (pipe)** = pipe to take away overflowing liquid; *the overflow was blocked so the* *water started coming through the ceiling* (c) amount or number which will not fit a given space; *the new towns were built to house the overflow population from the capital; the stadium was full and the overflow watched the match on giant TV screens in the park next door*

overgrown [əuvə'grəun] *adjective* covered with plants; *the garden is completely overgrown*

overhang 1 ['əuvəhæŋ] *noun* part which sticks out from something over a space; *getting past the rock overhang is the most difficult part of the climb; we sheltered from the rain under the overhang of the roof* **2** [əuvə'hæŋ] *verb* to stick out above something else; *the upper storey of the house overhangs the street* (NOTE: **overhanging - overhung**)

overhaul 1 [əuvə'hɔːl] *verb* (a) to examine something carefully and make changes so that it works better; *we need to overhaul the company's union agreements* (b) to overtake another ship, car, etc.; *from being last in the race he gradually moved up and in the end overhauled the leaders* **2** ['əuvəhɔːl] *noun* act of examining and repairing; *my car's in the garage for a complete overhaul*

overhead 1 [əuvə'hed] *adverb* above you, above your head; *look at that plane overhead* **2** [əuvə'hed] *adjective* (a) above (your head); *please stow your hand luggage in the overhead lockers*; **an overhead reading light** = a small light directly over your head; **overhead projector** = projector which projects a picture from a flat surface onto a screen (b) **overhead expenses** = general expenses incurred by a business as a whole, such as salaries, heating, rent, etc.; *the accounts department is calculating the overhead expenses for next year's budget* **3** ['əuvəhed] *noun US* overhead expenses; *by cutting back on the overhead we should make a profit* (NOTE: British English in this meaning is **overheads**)

overheads ['əuvəhedz] *noun* overhead expenses; *by cutting back on overheads we should make a profit* (NOTE: American English uses the singular **overhead**)

overhear [əuvə'hiə] *verb* to hear accidentally something which you are not meant to hear; *I couldn't help overhearing what you said just then* (NOTE: **overheard** [əuvə'hɜːd])

overheat [əuvə'hiːt] *verb* to get too hot; *the engine overheated and we had to pull into the side of the road to let it cool down*

overjoyed [əuvə'dʒɔɪd] *adjective* extremely happy; *his parents were overjoyed to hear that he was safe*

overland ['əuvəlænd] *adverb & adjective* by land; *you can travel to India overland; the overland route to South Africa takes you right through the heart of the African continent*

overlap 1 [əuvə'læp] *verb* to cover part of something else; *try not to let the pieces of wallpaper overlap; the two meetings are likely to overlap, so I will ask for one to be put back* (NOTE: **overlapping - overlapped**) **2** ['əuvəlæp] *noun* amount by which something overlaps; *the overlap of the wallpaper was so small that no one noticed it*

overlay ['əuvəleɪ] **1** *noun* covering for the surface of something; *they put an overlay of gold leaf on the statue* **2** *verb* to overlay something with something = to cover the surface of something with something; *a stone floor overlaid with brilliantly coloured mosaics*

overload [əuvə'ləud] *verb* to put too heavy a load on something; *with so many refugees trying to get on board, there was a danger of the boat being overloaded; the washing machine broke down because you overloaded it*

overlook [əuvə'luk] *verb* (a) not to notice; *she overlooked several mistakes when she was correcting the exam papers* (b) to pretend to not notice; *in this instance the bank will overlook the delay in making payment* (c) to look out on to; *my office overlooks the factory; I want a room overlooking the hotel gardens, not the car park*

overly [əuvə'laɪ] *adverb* too much; *I'm not overly worried about what they think*

overnight [əuvə'naɪt] **1** *adverb* for the whole night; *we will stay overnight in France on our way to Italy; will the food stay fresh overnight?* **2** *adjective* lasting all night; *they took an overnight flight back from China; there are three sleeping cars on the overnight express*

overpass ['əuvəpɑːs] *noun* road which crosses over the top of another road; *they built an overpass to ease congestion at the busy junction* (NOTE: the opposite, i.e. a road built under another, is an **underpass**)

overpower [əuvə'pauə] *verb* to control someone by force; *she managed to overpower the man who attacked her; the police chased the robbers and overpowered them in a car park*

overpowering [əuvə'pauərɪŋ] *adverb* very strong; *an overpowering smell of cheese*

overrated [əuvə'reɪtɪd] *adjective* said to be better than it really is; *I think their new 'first-class service' is vastly overrated; it must be the most overrated film of the year*

override [əuvə'raɪd] *verb* (a) to cancel an instruction, etc.; *chairman decided to override the committee's decision* (b) to be more important than other things; *the safety of the children overrides all other considerations* (NOTE: **overrode** [əuvə'rəud] - **overridden** [əuvə'rɪdn])

overriding ['əuvəraɪdɪŋ] *adjective* more important than all others; *our overriding concern is not to spend more than our budget*

overrule [əuvə'ruːl] *verb* (a) *(in a meeting)* not to allow a decision because you are more powerful than the person who took the decision; *Mr Smith tried to object but his objection was overruled by the chairman; the committee overruled the decision made by the secretary* (b) *(of a higher court)* to set a new precedent by deciding a case on a different principle from one laid down by a lower court; *the Supreme Court can overrule any other court in the USA*

overrun [əuvə'rʌn] *verb* (a) to go beyond a certain time limit; *the meeting overran by thirty minutes* (b) to beat someone or occupy their territory very quickly; *the enemy overran our coastal defences and began advancing inland* (c) **to be overrun with something** = to be filled with a crowd of people, animals or things; *the city centre is overrun with tourists every summer* (NOTE: **overran - overrun**)

overseas [əuvə'siːz] **1** *adverb* in a foreign country, across the sea; *he went to work overseas for some years* **2** *adjective* referring to foreign countries, across the sea; *overseas sales are important for our company*

oversee [əʊvəˈsiː] *verb* to superintend or to supervise; *he oversaw the delivery of the cash to the bank*; *can you oversee the children's bath time tonight as I have to go out?* (NOTE: **overseeing - oversaw - has overseen**)

overseer [ˈəʊvəsiːə] *noun* (*formal*) person who supervises other people at work; *the slaves were often beaten by the brutal overseers*

overshadow [əʊvəˈʃædəʊ] *verb* to make someone or something less conspicuous by being more brilliant yourself; *the bride was overshadowed by her sister who was much more glamorous than she was*

oversight [ˈəʊvəsaɪt] *noun* mistake made by not doing something because you forgot it or did not notice it; *through an oversight on the part of the secretary, the minutes of the meeting were not sent out*

oversimplification [ˈəʊvəsɪmplɪfɪkeɪʃn] *noun* making something appear too simple; *his report is a gross oversimplification of the problems involved*

oversize *or* **oversized** [ˈəʊvəsaɪz(d)] *adjective* bigger than usual, or too big for somebody or something; *oversize packages must be sent by special mail*; *she came to the wedding wearing a ridiculously oversized hat*

overspend [əʊvəˈspend] *verb* to spend more than you should; *she overspent on her shopping and ended up £200 overdrawn*; *be careful not to overspend your budget* (NOTE: **overspending - overspent**)

overstate [əʊvəˈsteɪt] *verb* to state too strongly or with too much detail; *the government tends to overstate the case in favour of monetary union*

overt [əʊˈvɜːt] *adjective* open, not hidden; *an overt attempt to bribe government officials*; *without showing overt disapproval, he made his unfavourable opinion pretty clear* (NOTE: the opposite is **covert**)

overtake [əʊvəˈteɪk] *verb* to go past someone travelling in front of you; *she overtook three trucks on the motorway*; *we were going so slowly that we were overtaken by cyclists* (NOTE: **overtaking - overtook - has overtaken**)

over-the-top (OTT) [ˈəʊvəðəˈtɒp] *adjective* excessive and exaggerated; *her behaviour at the fashion show was quite over-the-top*

overthrow 1 [ˈəʊvəθrəʊ] *noun* removal of a government or dictator from power; *the revolution led to the overthrow of the dictator* **2** [əʊvəˈθrəʊ] *verb* to defeat; *do you think the rebels can overthrow the military government?*; *the former régime was overthrown and the President fled* (NOTE: **overthrew** [əʊvəˈθruː] **- overthrown**)

overtime [ˈəʊvətaɪm] **1** *noun* hours worked more than normal working time; *he worked six hours' overtime*; *the overtime rate is one and a half times normal pay*; **overtime pay** = money paid for working beyond normal hours; *overtime pay is calculated at one and a half times the standard rate*; *I'm owed lots of overtime pay* **2** *adverb* more than normal hours of work; *the staff had to work overtime when the hotel was full*; *how much extra do I get for working overtime?*

overtones [ˈəʊvətəʊnz] *noun* suggestion of something which is not directly stated; *his whole speech was full of racial overtones*

overture [ˈəʊvətʃə] *noun* (**a**) short piece of music played at the beginning of an opera, concert, etc.; *the orchestra played the overture to the 'Magic Flute'* (**b**) **to make overtures to someone** = to try to begin negotiations with someone; *the socialists made overtures to the communists with the aim of forming a left-wing alliance*

overturn [əʊvəˈtɜːn] *verb* (**a**) to make something fall over; to turn upside down; *the baby accidentally overturned the goldfish bowl* (**b**) to vote against a previous decision; *the decision to raise subscriptions was overturned by the council*

overvalue [əʊvəˈvæljuː] *verb* to give a higher value than is right; *perhaps the judges overvalued originality and neglected traditional drawing skills*; **these shares are overvalued at £1.25** = the shares are worth less than the £1.25 for which they are selling

overview [ˈəʊvəvjuː] *noun* general view of a subject; *his book is a good overview of the history of the period*; *can you give me an overview of the progress which has been made so far?*

overweight [əʊvəˈweɪt] *adjective* too heavy; *the doctor says I'm overweight and must go on a diet*; **the package is sixty grams overweight** = the package weighs sixty grams too much

overwhelm [əʊvəˈwelm] *verb* (**a**) to conquer completely; *the enemy was overwhelmed by our troops*; *his enthusiasm overwhelms me* (**b**) **overwhelmed with work** = having more work than you can do; *the new receptionist was overwhelmed by her job*

overwhelming [əʊvəˈwelmɪŋ] *adjective* enormous; *there was an overwhelming response to their appeal for money*; *they got an overwhelming 'yes' vote*

overwork [əʊvəˈwɜːk] **1** *noun* too much work; *he is suffering from stress caused by overwork* **2** *verb* (**a**) to work too hard; *you've been overworking, that's why your eyes hurt* (**b**) to make someone work too hard; *he overworks the kitchen staff dreadfully*; *like everyone else in the company, I'm overworked and underpaid*

overwrought [əʊvəˈrɔːt] *adjective* very worried, under a lot of stress; *don't ask her to comment - she's too overwrought to be able to think clearly*

ovulate [ˈɒvjuleɪt] *verb* (*of woman or female animal*) to produce an egg inside the body; *a woman's temperature rises slightly just before she ovulates*

ovulation [ɒvjuˈleɪʃn] *noun* release of an ovum into one of the Fallopian tubes; *there are drugs you can take to assist ovulation*

ovum [ˈəʊvəm] *noun* female egg cell which can develop into an embryo inside the mother's body when fertilized; *the ovum is released into one of the Fallopian tubes* (NOTE: plural is **ova** [ˈəʊvə])

owe [əʊ] *verb* (**a**) **to owe money to someone** = to be due to pay someone money; *he still owes me the £10 he borrowed last month* (**b**) **to owe something to something** = to have something because of something else; *he owes his good health to taking a lot of exercise*

owing to [ˈəʊɪŋ ˈtuː] *preposition* because of; *the plane was late owing to fog*; *I am sorry that owing to staff shortages, we cannot supply your order on time*

owl [aʊl] *noun* bird of prey which is mainly active at night; *an owl hooted somewhere in the wood*; (*informal*) **a night owl** = someone who likes to work, eat, etc., until late at night, and does not get up early in the morning; *she's a night owl and finds it difficult to get up in time for work*; *compare* EARLY BIRD

own [əʊn] **1** *adjective* belonging to you alone; *I don't need to borrow a car - I have my own car*; *he has his own hairdressing shop* **2** *noun* **(a)** of my own *or* of his own, etc. = belonging to me *or* to him alone; *he has an office of his own*; *I have a car of my own*; *they got married and now have a house of their own* **(b)** on my own *or* on his own, etc. = alone; *I'm on my own this evening - my wife's playing bridge*; *he built the house all on his own* **3** *verb* to have, to possess; *there's no sense in owning two cars, since my wife doesn't drive*; *who owns this shop?*

owner ['əʊnə] *noun* person who owns something; *the police are trying to find the owner of the stolen car*; *insurance is necessary for all house owners*

owner-occupier ['əʊnə 'ɒkjʊpaɪə] *noun* person who owns the house that he or she lives in; *the majority of the population are owner-occupiers*; *owner-occupiers have certain advantages over people who live in rented accommodation* (NOTE: plural is owner-occupiers)

ownership ['əʊnəʃɪp] *noun* situation where someone owns something; *the ownership of the land is in dispute*; *the hairdresser's shop has been sold and is under new ownership*; **private ownership** = situation where a company is owned by private shareholders; *the company is being sold into private ownership*; **public ownership** = situation where an industry is owned by the state, or has been nationalized

own goal ['əʊn 'gəʊl] *noun* **(a)** goal scored against your own side by mistake; *he tried to pass back to the goalkeeper and scored an own goal* **(b)** *(informal)* something that is intended to help you do something but has the opposite effect; *their attempts to show that the government was financially incompetent led to a spectacular own goal* (NOTE: plural is own goals)

own up (to) ['əʊn 'ʌp tʊ] *verb* to say that you have done something wrong; *she owned up to having tried to steal the jewels*; *the teacher asked who had thrown ink bombs but no one would own up*

ox [ɒks] *noun* male or female domestic cattle, especially when used as a draught animal; *in the country areas, pairs of oxen are used to pull heavy loads* (NOTE: plural is oxen)

oxide ['ɒksaɪd] *noun* chemical compound formed with oxygen; *copper oxide*

oxidize ['ɒksɪdaɪz] *verb* to form an oxide by the reaction of oxygen with another chemical substance; *in damp conditions iron soon oxidizes and forms rust*

oxtail ['ɒksteɪl] *noun* meat from the tail of a cow, etc., used as food; **oxtail soup** = soup made by boiling the tail of a cow, etc.; *a bowl of oxtail soup*

oxygen ['ɒksɪdʒən] *noun* common gas which is present in the air and is essential for plant and animal life; *hydrogen combines with oxygen to form water*; *the divers ran out of oxygen and had to end their dive early*; **oxygen mask** = mask which appears from a panel above your head if there is a drop in pressure in a plane; *if there is an emergency an oxygen mask will automatically drop down in front of you* (NOTE: Chemical element: chemical symbol: O; atomic number: 8)

oyster ['ɔɪstə] *noun* type of shellfish with two shells, highly valued as food; *don't eat oysters if you're allergic to shellfish*; **oyster bed** = part of the sea floor where oysters are found

oz ['aʊnsɪz] *abbreviation for* OUNCES; *according to the recipe I need 12oz flour and 5oz butter* (NOTE: say 'twelve ounces of flour', 'five ounces of butter')

ozone ['əʊzəʊn] *noun* harmful form of oxygen, which is found in the atmosphere and which is poisonous to humans when concentrated; **ozone hole** = gap which forms in the ozone layer, allowing harmful radiation from the sun to reach the earth; *the ozone hole is getting larger every year*; **ozone layer** = layer of ozone in the upper atmosphere, formed by the action of sunlight on oxygen, which acts as protection against harmful rays from the sun

Pp

P, p [piː] **(a)** sixteenth letter of the alphabet, between O and Q; *you spell 'photo' with a PH and not an F* **(b)** letter used to show a price in pence; *this book costs 60p*; *you should get a 20p ticket from the machine*; *I bought the children 50p ice creams each*; *see also* PENNY

pa [paː] *noun* (*informal*) child's name for father; *my pa won't let me stay out after ten o'clock*

PA [ˈpiː ˈeɪ] = PERSONAL ASSISTANT

pace [peɪs] **1** *noun* **(a)** distance covered by one step; *walk thirty paces to the north of the stone*; *step three paces back* **(b)** speed; **to keep pace with** = to keep up with; *she kept pace with the leaders for the first three laps*; *wages haven't kept pace with inflation*; *(of a runner, driver, horse, etc.)* **to set the pace** = to decide how fast a race should be run; *the German driver set the pace in his Ferrari* **2** *verb* **(a)** to walk; *he paced backwards and forwards in front of the door* **(b)** to measure by walking; *he paced out the distance between the tree and the house* **(c)** to set the pace for a runner, etc.; *to help him train for the race she paced him on her bicycle*

pacemaker [ˈpeɪsmeɪkə] *noun* electronic device which is implanted in a patient's chest and which stimulates and regulates the heartbeat; *surgeons have fitted him with a pacemaker*

pacific [pəˈsɪfɪk] *adjective* preferring peace and calm; **the Pacific Ocean** *or* **the Pacific** = huge ocean between North America and Asia and South America and New Zealand; *they set out to cross the Pacific on a raft*; **the Pacific Rim** = the countries of South-East Asia, Japan, the Western States of the USA, South America, Australia and New Zealand

pacifier [ˈpæsɪfaɪə] *noun US* plastic teat given to a baby to suck, to prevent it crying; *the baby won't be quiet without her pacifier* (NOTE: British English is **dummy**)

pacifist [ˈpæsɪfɪst] **1** *adjective* supporting pacifism; *the pacifist movement had many new members* **2** *noun* person who supports pacifism; *my father was a pacifist and refused to do military service*

pacify [ˈpæsɪfaɪ] *verb* to make someone calm; *the manager was only trying to pacify an angry customer*

pack [pæk] **1** *noun* **(a)** set of things put together in a box; *he bought a pack of chewing gum*; **a pack of cards** = set of playing cards (NOTE: American English is **a deck of cards**) **(b)** group of wild animals together; *a pack of wild dogs* **(c)** bag which you can carry on your back; *see also* BACKPACK **(d)** **face pack** = thick substance which you put on your face to improve your skin; *don't come in, I've still got my face pack on* **(e)** *(in Rugby)* the group of forward players who form the scrum **2** *verb* **(a)** to put things into a suitcase ready for travelling; *the taxi's arrived and she hasn't packed her suitcase yet*; *I've finished packing, so we can start*; *he packed his toothbrush at the bottom of the bag*; *(informal)* **to tell someone to pack their bags** = to tell someone to leave, to sack someone; *when he got home,*

she told him to pack his bags **(b)** to put things in containers ready for sending; *the books are packed in boxes of twenty*; *fish are packed in ice* **(c)** to put a lot of people or things into something; *how can you pack ten adults into one tent?*; *the streets are packed with Christmas shoppers*; *the supermarket shelves are packed with fruit and vegetables*

package [ˈpækɪdʒ] **1** *noun* **(a)** parcel which has been wrapped up for sending; *there was a package for you in the post*; *we mailed the package to you yesterday* **(b)** box or bag in which goods are sold; *instructions for use are printed on the package* **(c)** **package holiday** *or* **package tour** = holiday where everything (hotel, food, travel, etc.) is arranged and paid for before you leave; *they went on a package holiday to Greece* **(d)** **salary package** = salary and other benefits offered with a job **2** *verb* to put into packages; *the chocolates are attractively packaged in silver paper*

packaging [ˈpækɪdʒɪŋ] *noun* **(a)** wrapping of goods; *the packaging is all done by machines* **(b)** paper, cardboard, etc., used to wrap goods; *the boxes are sent in dust-proof packaging*

packed [pækt] *adjective* **(a)** full of people; *the restaurant was packed and there were no free tables* **(b)** put in a pack; **packed lunch** = sandwiches, etc., put ready in a box

packer [ˈpækə] *noun* person who packs goods; *there are packers at the supermarket check-outs to help the customers*; *we are slow in sending out goods because one of the packers in the warehouse is off sick*

packet [ˈpækɪt] *noun* small bag, parcel or box; *a packet of cigarettes*; *a packet of soup*

packing [ˈpækɪŋ] *noun* **(a)** putting things into suitcases, etc.; *my wife's in the hotel room doing our packing* **(b)** **packing case** = special wooden box for sending goods; **packing list** *or* **packing slip** = list of goods which have been packed, sent with the goods to show they have been checked **(c)** material used to protect goods which are being packed; *the goods are sealed in airtight packing* **(d)** to send someone **packing** = to send someone away; *when the boys started to throw stones at her cat she soon sent them packing*

pack off [ˈpæk ˈɒf] *verb* to send someone away; *as soon as they were old enough, she packed her children off to boarding school*; *we've packed the children off to their grandparents for the summer holidays*

pack up [ˈpæk ˈʌp] *verb* **(a)** to put things into a box before going away; *they packed up all their equipment and left* **(b)** to stop working; *I'll pack up now and finish the job tomorrow morning* **(c)** to break down; *an engine packed up when we were taking off*

pact [pækt] *noun* agreement, treaty; *the two countries signed a defence pact*

pad [pæd] **1** *noun* **(a)** soft cushion which protects; *put a pad of cotton on your knee*; **shoulder pads** = thick pads put inside the shoulders of a coat, to make it look bigger **(b)** set of sheets of paper attached together; **desk pad** = pad of paper kept on a desk for writing notes; **memo pad** *or* **note pad** = pad of paper for writing memos or notes; **phone pad** = pad of paper kept by a telephone for noting messages; *I scribbled down his address on the phone pad* **2** *verb* to walk heavily and softly; *the tiger was padding up and down its cage; see also* PAD OUT (NOTE: **padding - padded**)

padded ['pædɪd] *adjective* with soft material in it; *I like chairs with padded seats*; *send the diskette in a padded envelope*

padding ['pædɪŋ] *noun* **(a)** soft material which protects, used in dressmaking, or to make cushions, chairs, etc.; *the tailor put some more padding in the shoulders of the jacket*; *we put cotton wool under the bandage as padding* **(b)** words added to a speech or article to make it longer; *the speech was over an hour long, but most of it was just padding*; *your essay has got too much padding in it* (NOTE: no plural)

paddle ['pædl] **1** *noun* **(a)** short oar used to make a boat move through the water; *help, I've dropped my paddle in the river!* **(b)** walk in shallow water; *the little children went for a paddle in the sea* **2** *verb* **(a)** to make a boat move forward using a paddle; *we stopped paddling and let the canoe drift with the current* **(b)** to walk about in very shallow water; *they all took off their shoes and socks and paddled in the lake*

paddle steamer ['pædl 'stiːmə] *noun* boat driven by large wheels on either side; *we took a trip up the river on an old-fashioned paddle steamer*; *compare* STERNWHEELER

paddle wheel ['pædl 'wiːl] *noun* side wheel on a paddle steamer; *the paddle wheels churned up the water*

paddling pool ['pædlɪŋ 'puːl] *noun* small shallow pool for little children; *the little ones love playing in the paddling pool*

paddock ['pædək] *noun* **(a)** small enclosed field, usually near farm buildings, where horses can run; *she keeps her pony in the paddock* **(b)** enclosed area at a racecourse where racehorses parade before a race; *the jockeys mount up in the paddock*

paddy ['pædi] *noun* **(a)** **paddy (field)** = field filled with water, in which rice is grown; *rice paddies are breeding grounds for mosquitoes* (NOTE: plural is **paddies**) **(b)** *(old) (informal)* fit of bad temper; *he got into a paddy and threw his toys out of the pram*

padlock ['pædlɒk] **1** *noun* small portable lock with a hook for locking things together; *the gate is fastened with a padlock* **2** *verb* to lock with a padlock; *he padlocked his bicycle to the lamppost*

pad out ['pæd 'aʊt] *verb* to add text to a speech or article, just to make it longer; *he padded out his talk to last half an hour*

padre ['pɑːdri] *noun* chaplain in the armed forces; *the padre conducted the burial service*

pagan ['peɪgn] **1** *adjective* believing in a form of religion which is not one of the main religions; *the missionaries tried to ban pagan religious practices*; *the explorers visited a pagan temple* **2** *noun* **(a)** person who believes in a pagan religion; *the kings of Britain were pagans until they were converted by Christian missionaries* **(b)** *(informal)* person who does not believe in any religion, person who does not go to

church; *doesn't anybody want to go to church? - you're just a lot of pagans!*

page [peɪdʒ] **1** *noun* **(a)** a side of a sheet of paper used in a book, newspaper, etc.; *it's a short book, it only has 64 pages*; *the crossword is on the back page*; *start reading at page 34* (NOTE: with numbers the word **the** is left out: **on the next page** but **on page 50**) **(b)** **page (boy)** = little boy who attends the bride at a wedding, in the same way as a bridesmaid does **2** *verb* to call someone by radio, over a loudspeaker, etc.; *Mr Smith isn't in his office at the moment - I'll page him for you*

pageant ['pædʒənt] *noun* grand display of people in historical costumes; *they held a medieval pageant*; *the school held a pageant showing the history of the town*

pager ['peɪdʒə] *noun* small electronic device that makes a noise or displays a message when someone is trying to contact you; *if you can't reach me on my home number, try my pager*

pagoda [pə'gəʊdə] *noun* tall tower made of several storeys, used as a temple, found in China, Korea, Japan, etc.

paid [peɪd] *see* PAY

paid-up ['peɪd'ʌp] *adjective* having paid all the money owing; *she's a fully paid-up member of the teachers' union*; **paid-up shares** = shares which have been completely paid for by the shareholders

pail [peɪl] *noun* bucket, round container with a handle but no lid, used mainly for liquids; *every morning she brings the milk from the dairy in a pail*; *he took a pail of water to the horse* (NOTE: do not confuse with **pale**)

pain [peɪn] **1** *noun* **(a)** feeling of being hurt; *if you have a pain in your chest, you ought to see a doctor*; *she had to take drugs because she could not stand the pain*; *I get pains in my teeth when I eat ice cream* **(b)** **to take pains over something** *or* **to do something** = to take care to do something well; *they took great pains over the organization of the conference*; *she took pains to make everyone feel at home* **(c)** *(informal)* a **pain (in the neck)** = annoying person; *he's a real pain in the neck*; *she's a pain - she's always gets top marks* (NOTE: do not confuse with **pane**) **2** *verb* *(formal)* to hurt; *it pains me to have to do this, but we must report you to the police*

pained [peɪnd] *adjective* annoyed or upset; *judging by her pained expression, we must have done something wrong*; *his teacher was pained to hear that he had been arrested*

painful ['peɪnfʊl] *adjective* which hurts, which causes pain; *she got a painful blow on the back of the head*; *I have very painful memories of my first school*

painfully ['peɪnfʊli] *adverb* **(a)** in a way which hurts; *he twisted his ankle painfully*; *I am painfully aware that most people are blaming me for the accident* **(b)** with great difficulty; *so far, progress on building the dam has been painfully slow*

painkiller ['peɪnkɪlə] *noun* drug which stops someone feeling pain; *I'll get you a painkiller for your migraine*; *she keeps a bottle of painkillers by her bed*

painless ['peɪnləs] *adjective* which does not hurt; *he has a painless method of removing warts*

painlessly ['peɪnləsli] *adverb* in a painless way; *the dentist promised to take the tooth out quickly and painlessly*

painstaking ['peɪnsteɪkɪŋ] *adjective* working very carefully and thoroughly; *she's a very painstaking worker*; **painstaking work** = careful and delicate work; *cleaning a painting by Rembrandt is slow and painstaking work*

painstakingly ['peɪnsteɪkɪŋli] *adverb* very carefully and thoroughly; *the police painstakingly went through all their records*

paint [peɪnt] **1** *noun* coloured liquid which you use to give something a colour or to make a picture; *we gave the ceiling two coats of paint*; *she was given a box of paints for her birthday*; *I need a two-litre tin of green paint*; *the paint's coming off the front door* **2** *verb* **(a)** to cover something with paint; *we got a firm in to paint the house*; *they painted their front door blue*; *she painted her toenails bright red* **(b) to paint yourself into a corner** = to get yourself into a situation that you cannot get out of; *(informal)* **to paint the town red** = to have a wild party in the town; *after the exam results come out we are all going up to London to paint the town red* **(c)** to cover with a liquid; *the nurse painted his knee with antiseptic* **(d)** to make a picture of something using paint; *she painted a picture of the village*; *he's painting his mother*; *the sky is not easy to paint*

paintbrush ['peɪntbrʌʃ] *noun* brush used to put paint on something; *I dropped my paintbrush in the can of paint*; *he used a very fine paintbrush to paint the branches of the trees* (NOTE: plural is **paintbrushes**)

painter ['peɪntə] *noun* **(a)** person who paints (a house, etc.); *the painter is coming next week to paint the kitchen* **(b)** person who paints pictures; *he collects pictures by 19th century French painters*

painting ['peɪntɪŋ] *noun* **(a)** action of putting on paint; *painting the kitchen always takes a long time* **(b)** picture done with paints; *do you like this painting of the old church?*

paints [peɪnts] *noun* set of tubes of paint or cubes of watercolour paint, in a box; *she bought me a box of paints for my birthday*

paintwork ['peɪntwɜːk] *noun* surface which has been painted; *the old paintwork needs to be cleaned*; *the car's paintwork is in very good condition*

pair [peə] **1** *noun* **(a)** two things taken together; *a pair of socks*; *a pair of gloves*; *she's bought a new pair of boots*; *these socks are a pair* = they go together **(b)** two things joined together to make a single one; *he took a pair of binoculars with him when he went out walking*; *I'm looking for a clean pair of trousers*; *where's my pair of green shorts?*; *this pair of scissors is blunt* **(c)** two rowers in a boat; *the British pair won the silver medal; see also* EIGHT, FOUR **(d)** *(in the House of Commons)* MP who has an agreement with an MP from the opposite party not to vote if either is absent from Parliament **2** *verb* **to pair up** = to join with another person to do something; *everyone paired up to start the treasure hunt*

pairing ['peərɪŋ] *noun* agreement between two members of parliament from opposite sides of the House of Commons by which if one is absent and cannot vote the other will not vote either

paisley ['peɪzli] *noun* pattern on fabric, scarves, cushions, etc., made of curved shapes like drops of water; *she wore a paisley scarf round her head*

pajamas [pɪ'dʒɑːməz] *US see* PYJAMAS

Pakistan [pækɪ'stɑːn] *noun* country in the Indian sub-continent, to the west of India; *Karachi is the largest city in Pakistan* (NOTE: capital: **Islamabad**; people: **Pakistanis**; languages: **Urdu, Punjabi, English**; currency: **rupee**)

Pakistani [pækɪ'stɑːni] **1** *adjective* referring to Pakistan; *a Pakistani cricketer* **2** *noun* person from Pakistan; *many of the local shops are owned by Pakistanis*

pal [pæl] *noun (informal)* friend; *a pal of mine told me the story*; *he's gone out to the pub with his pals from work*; *they used to be great pals, but then they quarrelled*

palace ['pæləs] *noun* large building where a king, queen, president, etc., lives; *the presidential palace is in the centre of the city*; *the Queen lives in Buckingham Palace*

palaeontologist [pælɪɒn'tɒlədʒɪst] *noun* person who studies fossils; *the dinosaur bone was found by an amateur palaeontologist*

palaeontology [pælɪɒn'tɒlədʒi] *noun* study of fossils; *the museum has a large palaeontology section*

palatable ['pælətəbl] *adjective* nice to eat, tasting good; *this medicine is actually quite palatable*

palate ['pælət] *noun* **(a)** top part of the inside of the mouth; *I burnt my palate with the hot soup*; **a cleft palate** = defect in babies, where there is a gap in the roof of the mouth **(b)** being able to judge the quality of food or drink; *a trained palate easily distinguishes different types of wine* (NOTE: do not confuse with **palette, pallet**)

palatial [pə'leɪʃl] *adjective* magnificent, like a palace; *his palatial villa overlooks the bay*; *they took up residence in a palatial suite at the Savoy Hotel*

pale [peɪl] **1** *adjective* light-coloured; *what colour is your hat? - it's a pale blue colour*; *when she read the letter she went pale* (NOTE: do not confuse with **pail**; note: **paler - palest**) **2** *verb* to become pale; *the sky paled as dawn broke*

palette ['pælət] *noun* **(a)** flat board on which an artist mixes his colours; *she squeezed a blob of paint onto her palette*; **palette knife** = long flat knife with a rounded end; *he put on the paint with a palette knife* **(b)** range of colours available, especially on a computer graphics program; *you can create your own colours and add them to the palette* (NOTE: do not confuse with **palate, pallet**)

pall [pɔːl] **1** *noun* **(a)** *(formal)* **a pall of smoke** = a thick layer of smoke; *a pall of smoke hung over the burning building* **(b)** cloth put over a coffin; **to cast a pall over something** = to make something seem gloomy; *the illness of the bride's father cast a pall over the wedding* **2** *verb* to become less interesting; *her bright chatter began to pall after a while*

pallbearer ['pɔːlbeərə] *noun* person who walks beside a coffin or carries a coffin in a funeral procession; *the pallbearers were members of the general's old regiment*

pallet ['pælət] *noun* flat wooden frame on which goods can be stacked to be moved by a fork-lift truck (NOTE: American English is **skid**; do not confuse with **palate, palette**)

palliate ['pælɪeɪt] *verb (formal)* to try to reduce a pain

palliative ['pælɪətɪv] *noun* something done to try to help a situation, but which does not make it any better; *the government's remedies for unemployment are simply palliatives*

pallid ['pælɪd] *adjective* sickly pale; *her husband was shocked at her pallid face after the operation; pallid light of the moon lit the garden*

palm [pɑːm] *noun* (a) soft inside surface of your hand; *she held out some crumbs in the palm of her hand and the birds came and ate them* (b) tall tropical tree with long leaves; *an oasis surrounded by date palms; the boy climbed a coconut palm a brought down a nut*

palmist ['pɑːmɪst] *noun* person who says what will happen in the future by looking at the lines on your palm; *the palmist told her she would meet a tall dark stranger*

palmistry ['pɑːmɪstri] *noun* telling people what will happen in the future by looking at the lines on the palms of their hands

palpable ['pælpəbl] *adjective* which can be felt, which can be easily seen; *it was a palpable error to mix up the two customers' names; the tension in the room was almost palpable; her story was palpable nonsense*

palpably ['pælpəbli] *adverb* in a palpable way; *their claims are palpably false*

palsy ['pɔːlzi] *noun* paralysis; **cerebral palsy** = disorder of the brain, mainly due to brain damage occurring before birth, or due to lack of oxygen during birth; *their son was born with cerebral palsy*

paltry ['pɔːltri] *adjective* very small; *it's such a paltry sum that I won't lose any sleep over it; it's an insult to be offered such a paltry fee* (NOTE: **paltrier - paltriest**)

pamper ['pæmpə] *verb* to treat someone too well, by giving them too much food or making their life too comfortable; *your grandparents are allowed to pamper you a little; never once in her pampered existence had she had to boil an egg; pamper yourself with a luxurious bubble bath*

pamphlet ['pæmflət] *noun* small booklet giving information about something; *before the election, political pamphlets were handed out in the street; the tourist board produces a range of pamphlets about local places of interest*

pan [pæn] **1** *noun* metal cooking container with a handle; *boil the potatoes in a pan of water; she burnt her hand on the hot frying pan; see also* FRYING PAN, SAUCEPAN **2** *verb* (a) *(informal)* to criticize; *his latest film has been panned by the critics* (b) to **pan for gold** = to sift mud in a stream hoping to find gold in it (NOTE: **panning - panned**)

panacea [pænə'siːə] *noun* **(universal) panacea** = thing which cures everything or which solves every problem; *a tight monetary policy is not the universal panacea everyone thought it was*

panache [pə'næʃ] *noun* confident and showy way of doing things; *he organized the festival with great panache*

pancake ['pænkeɪk] *noun* (a) thin soft flat cake made of flour, milk, and eggs; *we ate pancakes and maple syrup for breakfast* (b) **as flat as a pancake** = very flat; *the country round Cambridge is as flat as a pancake*

Pancake Day ['pænkeɪk 'deɪ] *noun* Shrove Tuesday, the Tuesday before Lent starts; *you must have pancakes on Pancake Day*

COMMENT: it is the last day before Lent, and so a day when feasts are held. In Britain, pancakes are traditionally eaten on Pancake Day, usually with lemon and sugar, but also with other sweet fillings. In France and French-speaking countries, the festival is called 'Mardi Gras'

pancreas ['pæŋkriəs] *noun* gland which lies across the back of the body between the kidneys; *insulin is produced in the pancreas* (NOTE: plural is **pancreases**)

COMMENT: the pancreas produces juices which help digest proteins and carbohydrates, as well as insulin which regulates the use of sugar by the body

panda ['pændə] *noun* (a) **(giant) panda** = large black and white animal found in China, which looks like a bear (b) **panda car** = police patrol car with black and white check markings (NOTE: do not confuse with **pander**)

pander ['pændə] *verb* to **pander to something** = to try to satisfy something; *the book panders to the low taste of the reading public* (NOTE: do not confuse with **panda**)

pane [peɪn] *noun* sheet of glass in a window, etc.; *we need a new pane of glass for the conservatory; he threw some stones and broke three panes in the window* (NOTE: do not confuse with **pain**)

panel ['pænl] **1** *noun* (a) flat rectangular piece which forms part of something; *unscrew the panel at the back of the washing machine;* **instrument panel** = flat part of a car in front of the driver, with dials which show speed, etc. (b) section of different-coloured material; *a pink skirt with white panels* (c) group of people who answer questions or who judge a competition; *she's on the panel that will interview candidates for the post;* **panel of experts** = group of people who give advice on a problem **2** *verb* to cover with sheets of wood; *he decided to panel the study in oak; the room is panelled in walnut* (NOTE: **panelling - panelled**) but American spelling is **paneling - paneled**)

panel game ['pænl 'geɪm] *noun* game on radio or TV where a group of people guess the answers to questions, give their opinions on subjects, etc.; *a popular radio panel game*

panelled ['pænəld] *adjective* covered with panels; *the panelled walls of the study make the room dark and cosy*

panelling *US* **paneling** ['pænəlɪŋ] *noun* sheets of wood used to cover walls, etc.; *we have oak panelling in the dining room*

pang [pæŋ] *noun* sudden strong feeling; *he suffered pangs of conscience after sending her away; hunger pangs reminded her it was past her lunchtime*

panic ['pænɪk] **1** *noun* terror, great fear; *the weather forecast caused panic in towns near the river;* **panic buying** = rush to buy something at any price because stocks may run out or because the price may rise **2** *verb* to become frightened; *don't panic, the fire engine is its way* (NOTE: **panicking - panicked**)

panicky ['pænɪki] *adjective (informal)* terrified, caused by panic; *we all had a panicky feeling that the* *plane was going to crash*; *she gets panicky if she can't find her glasses*

pannier ['pæniə] *noun* one of a pair of bags carried on the side of an animal or the back wheel of a bicycle; *we managed to pack all the camping gear into our cycle panniers*

panorama [pænə'rɑːmə] *noun* view over a wide expanse of landscape; *he looked out of the upstairs window at the wonderful panorama of mountains*

panoramic [pænə'ræmɪk] *adjective* looking out over a wide area; *there's a panoramic view over the mountains*

pansy ['pænzi] *noun* (a) small garden plant with large brightly coloured petals; *she planted pansies in her window boxes* (b) *(informal)* man who is weak like a woman; *they called him a pansy because he thought rugby was a rough dirty game* (NOTE: plural is **pansies**)

pant [pænt] *verb* to breathe fast; *he was red in the face and panting as he crossed the finishing line*

pantheon ['pænθiən] *noun* (a) all the gods of an ancient pagan religion; *the Greek pantheon* (b) group of people who are considered to be exceptionally talented or heroic; *he has his place in the pantheon of British sporting heroes*

panther ['pænθə] *noun* large black leopard from North America; *panthers live mainly in the mountains*

panties ['pæntiz] *noun* *(informal)* women's brief knickers; *a pair of panties were left on the washing line*; *she carries a spare pair of panties in her handbag*

pantomime ['pæntəmaɪm] *noun* funny Christmas play for children, with songs and dances on a traditional fairy-tale subject; *we took the children to the pantomime as a Christmas treat*

COMMENT: the best-known stories for pantomimes are 'Jack and the Beanstalk', 'Aladdin', 'Puss in Boots', 'Cinderella', etc. Certain things are traditional: the hero is always played by a girl, the 'dame' (a funny old woman) is always played by a man; the villain is always hissed by the audience

pantry ['pæntri] *noun* cool cupboard or small room for keeping food in; *my grandmother didn't own a refrigerator and kept all her food in the pantry*; the **butler's pantry** = in a large house, the room where a butler works (NOTE: plural is **pantries**)

pants [pænts] *noun* (a) *GB (informal)* briefs, shorts worn on the lower part of the body under other clothes; *she was standing by the window in her bra and pants*; *I put on clean pants and socks every morning* (b) *US (informal)* trousers; *the waiter was wearing a black jacket and a pair of striped pants*; *I need a belt to keep my pants up*

panty hose ['pænti 'həʊz] *noun* *US* women's tights; *I must buy a pack of panty hose*

papa [pə'pɑː] *noun* *(old)* child's name for father; *my papa bought me this bracelet*

papacy ['peɪpəsi] *noun* position of pope; *John Paul II was elected to the papacy in 1978*

papal ['peɪpl] *adjective* referring to the pope; *the papal apartments in the Vatican*

paparazzi [pæpə'rætsi] *noun* photographers who follow famous people to take pictures of them for newspapers; *the paparazzi were lying in wait for the*

couple as they left the hotel (NOTE: plural, the singular is **paparazzo**)

papaya [pə'pæjə] *noun* green tropical fruit with yellow flesh; *a slice of papaya makes a lovely refreshing breakfast* (NOTE: also called **pawpaw**)

paper ['peɪpə] *noun* (a) thin piece of material which you write on, and which is used for wrapping or to make books, newspapers, etc.; *he got a letter written on pink paper*; *I need another piece of paper or sheet of paper to finish my letter*; *there was a box of paper handkerchiefs by the bed* (NOTE: no plural for this meaning: **some paper, a piece of paper, a sheet of paper**) (b) newspaper; *I buy the paper to read on the train every morning*; *my photo was on the front page of today's paper*; *our local paper comes out on Fridays*; *the Sunday papers are so big that it takes me all day to read them* (c) **papers** = documents; *she sent me the relevant papers*; *he has lost the customs papers*; *the office is asking for the VAT papers* (d) **on paper** = in theory; *on paper the system is ideal, but no one has ever seen it working* (e) exam; *the English paper was very difficult*; *she wrote a good history paper* (f) scientific essay; *he wrote a paper on economics which was published in one of the learned journals*

paperback ['peɪpəbæk] *noun* cheap book with a paper cover; *I took a couple of paperbacks to read on the plane*; *the novel is only in hardback at the moment, but will come out in paperback in the spring* (NOTE: American English is also **pocketbook**)

paper boy ['peɪpə 'bɔɪ] *noun* boy whose job is to deliver newspapers to houses; *the paper boy left us 'the Times' instead of the 'Telegraph'*

paperclip ['peɪpəklɪp] *noun* piece of bent wire for holding pieces of paper together; *she fastened the documents together with a paperclip*

paper mill ['peɪpə 'mɪl] *noun* factory where paper is made; *most of the people in the village work in the paper mill*

paper round ['peɪpə 'raʊnd] *noun* group of streets or houses where one paper boy or girl delivers newspapers; *she does a paper round to earn some extra pocket money*

paperwork ['peɪpəwɜːk] *noun* office work; *exporting involves a large amount of paperwork* (NOTE: no plural)

paprika ['pæprɪkə] *noun* red spice made from powdered sweet peppers; *paprika is an essential ingredient of Hungarian goulash*

papyrus [pə'paɪrəs] *noun* (a) tall reed growing in the Middle East, used by the ancient Egyptians to make a type of paper; *as you go along the Nile you can see the beds of papyrus beside the river* (NOTE: no plural in this meaning) (b) piece of paper made from this reed, with writing on it; *a collection of Ancient Egyptian papyri* (NOTE: plural is **papyri** [pə'paɪriː])

par [pɑː] *noun* (a) being equal; **to be on a par with** = to be equal to; *it isn't really on a par with their previous performances* (b) to buy shares at par = to buy shares at their face value; **the shares are below par** = they are less than their face value (c) **below par** = not very well; *he's feeling a bit below par after his illness* (d) *(in golf)* number of strokes usually needed by a good golfer to hit the ball into the hole; *he went round in five under par*

COMMENT: each hole on the golf course is given a par rating, i.e. the number of strokes a good golfer should take from the tee to the hole; a par 3 is up to 250 yards long from tee to green, a par 4 is from 251-475 yards, while a par 5 is over 475 yards long

para ['pærə] = PARATROOPER; *the paras went in and attacked the rebel stronghold*

parable ['pærəbl] *noun* short story with a religious or moral point; *the parables of Jesus*; *the story is a parable of an unjust society*

paracetamol [pærə'si:təmɒl] *noun* common drug, used to stop the symptoms of flu, colds, headaches, etc.; *she always keeps a bottle of paracetamol (tablets) in her bag*

parachute ['pærəʃu:t] **1** *noun* large piece of thin material shaped like an umbrella, with cords attached, which allows you to float down slowly and safely from a plane; *his parachute did not open and he was killed* **2** *verb* **(a)** to jump from an aircraft with a parachute; *the pilot parachuted safely from the burning plane* **(b)** to drop something attached to a parachute; *they parachuted supplies to the villages*

parachutist ['pærəʃu:tist] *noun* person who jumps from an aircraft with a parachute; *parachutists landed on the fairground with bright coloured parachutes*

parade [pə'reid] **1** *noun* **(a)** display of soldiers; *a sergeant inspects the men before they go on parade*; **parade ground** = square area on a military camp where parades are held **(b)** series of bands, decorated cars, etc., passing in a street; *the parade was led by a brass band*; *Independence Day is always celebrated with a military parade through the centre of the capital*; **fashion parade** = display of new clothes by models **2** *verb* to march past in rows; *the soldiers paraded down the Mall to Buckingham Palace*; *the winning horse paraded round with its rosette*

paradigm ['pærədaim] *noun* example which others can copy; *our intention was to provide a paradigm of good labour relations*

paradise ['pærədais] *noun* **(a)** wonderful place where good people are supposed to live after death; *for a moment, I thought I must have died and gone to paradise* **(b)** any beautiful place or a place where you feel very happy; *their grandparents' farm was a paradise for the children*

paradox ['pærədɒks] *noun* thing which appears to contradict itself but may really be true; *it's a paradox, but people with very different characters can often work together better than people who are similar*; *scientists have struggled to understand and explain this paradox* (NOTE: plural is **paradoxes**)

paradoxical [pærə'dɒksikl] *adjective* contradictory like a paradox; *it is paradoxical that she should want to go to live in the one town which her parents dislike the most*

paradoxically [pærə'dɒksikli] *adverb* in a paradoxical way; *paradoxically, the system seems to work best in unfavourable conditions*

paraffin ['pærəfin] *noun* thin liquid used as a fuel for lamps, heaters, etc.; *we lit a paraffin lamp in the tent*; *they poured paraffin over the rubbish and set it alight*; **liquid paraffin** = refined oil taken as a laxative;

paraffin wax = solid white substance used for making candles

paragon ['pærəgən] *noun* a perfect human being; *he's a paragon of virtue*; *I don't believe she's quite such a paragon as everyone seems to think*

paragraph ['pærəgrɑ:f] *noun* section of several lines of writing, which can be made up of several sentences; *to answer the first paragraph of your letter* or *paragraph one of your letter*; *please refer to the paragraph headed 'shipping instructions'*

COMMENT: a paragraph always starts with a new line, often with a small blank space (or 'indent') at the beginning. A blank line is usually left between paragraphs

parallel ['pærəlel] **1** *adjective* (lines) which are side by side and remain the same distance apart without ever touching; *draw two parallel lines three millimetres apart*; *the road runs parallel to* or *with the railway*; **parallel bars** = pair of horizontal bars in a gym, on which athletes do exercises **2** *noun* imaginary line running round the earth, linking points at an equal distance from the equator; *the 49th parallel marks most of the border between Canada and the United States*

parallelogram [pærə'leləgræm] *noun* shape with four sides where each side is parallel to the one opposite; *the opposite angles of a parallelogram are equal to 180°*

paralysis [pə'ræləsis] *noun* condition where the muscles of part of the body cannot move because the motor nerves have been damaged; *the condition causes paralysis of the lower limbs*; *he suffered temporary paralysis of the right arm*

paralytic [pærə'litik] **1** *adjective* **(a)** paralyzed in all or part of the body; *a paralytic patient* **(b)** *(slang)* so drunk you cannot stand up or move; *this is the second time this week he's gone out and got absolutely paralytic* **2** *noun* person who is paralyzed; *he dreaded spending the rest of his life as a helpless paralytic*

paralyze or **paralyse** ['pærəlaiz] *verb* to weaken muscles or harm the nerves supplying them, so that they cannot function; *his arm was paralyzed after the stroke*; *she is paralyzed from the waist down*

paramedic [pærə'meik] *noun* person who works in a medical profession linked to that of nurse or doctor, such as ambulancemen, therapists, etc.; *the paramedics did a heart massage when the patient had a cardiac arrest in the ambulance*

parameter [pə'ræmitə] *noun* figure which shows the limits of something; *pay increases have to keep within parameters set by the government*

paramilitary [pærə'militri] **1** *adjective* organized in the same way as the army, but not a part of it; *members of paramilitary organizations were asked to surrender their arms* **2** *noun* member of a paramilitary organization; *paramilitaries supporting the president were blamed for the attack*; *paramilitaries set up road blocks on all the roads leading into the area* (NOTE: plural is **paramilitaries**)

paramount ['pærəmaunt] *adjective* (formal) supreme, most important; *it is of paramount importance that the job be finished on time*

paranoia [pærə'nɔiə] *noun* mental disorder where the patient has fixed delusions, usually that he is being persecuted or attacked; *his paranoia is so acute he doesn't even trust members of his own family*

paranoiac [pærə'nɔɪæk] *noun* person with paranoia; *they decided he was a paranoiac and disregarded his stories that he was constantly being followed*

paranoid ['pærənɔɪd] *adjective* suffering from a fixed delusion; *she's absolutely paranoid about cleanliness in the home*; **paranoid schizophrenia** = form of schizophrenia where the patient believes he is being persecuted

parapet ['pærəpet] *noun* small wall at the edge of a bridge, balcony, etc.; *we sat on the parapet looking down into the river*; *if you put your head over the parapet you were likely to get shot at*

paraphernalia [pærəfə'neɪlɪə] *noun* mass of bits and pieces of equipment; *I make him store all his photographic paraphernalia in the attic* (NOTE: no plural)

parasite ['pærəsaɪt] *noun* **(a)** animal or plant which lives on or inside another organism and draws nourishment from it; *many diseases are carried by parasites* **(b)** person who does no useful work and gets money from others; *we aim to get rid of beggars and other parasites on society*

parasitic [pærə'sɪtɪk] *adjective* referring to parasites; *fleas and other parasitic insects*

paratrooper ['pærətru:pə] *noun* soldier who is a parachutist; *paratroopers were dropped behind enemy lines* (NOTE: often shortened to **para**)

paratroops ['pærətru:ps] *noun* paratroopers; *a small group of paratroops led the attack*

paratyphoid [pærə'taɪfɔɪd] *noun* infectious disease which is similar to typhoid, and caused by bacteria

parcel ['pɑ:səl] **1** *noun* package (to be sent by post, etc.); *the postman has brought a parcel for you*; *the parcel was wrapped up in brown paper*; *if you're going to the post office, can you post this parcel for me?* **2** *verb* to wrap and tie something up to send by post; *I parcelled the books up yesterday but I haven't posted them yet* (NOTE: **parcelling - parcelled** but American spelling is **parceling - parceled**)

parcel out ['pɑ:səl 'aʊt] *verb* to divide up between several people; *the land was parcelled out between the groups of immigrants*

parched [pɑ:tʃt] *adjective* very dry due to lack of water; *at last rain fell on the parched earth*; *can I have a drink, I'm parched?*

parchment ['pɑ:tʃmənt] *noun* **(a)** skins of animals which were treated and used for writing on; *monks wrote books by hand on parchment* **(b)** high quality thick cream-coloured writing paper

pardon ['pɑ:dən] **1** *noun* **(a)** forgiving someone; *I beg your pardon!* = excuse me, forgive me; *I beg your pardon, I didn't hear what you said*; *I do beg your pardon - I didn't know you were busy* **(b)** act of legally forgiving an offence which someone has committed; *the prisoners received a free pardon from the president* **2** *verb* **(a)** to forgive someone for having done something wrong; *pardon me for interrupting, but you're wanted on the phone*; *please pardon my rudeness in not answering your call earlier* **(b)** to forgive an offence which someone has committed, and allow them to leave prison; *some political prisoners were pardoned and set free* **3** *interjection*; **pardon!** = excuse me, forgive me

pare ['peə] *verb* **(a)** to take the skin or peel off a fruit or vegetable, etc., with a knife; *she took a sharp knife to pare the apple*; *he pared a thin slice off the block of cheese* **(b)** to make something smaller by cutting off a small amount; *he managed to pare three seconds off his previous best time*; **to pare something to the bone** = to reduce something as much as possible; *margins have been pared to the bone to keep our prices low*

parent ['peərənt] *noun* father or mother; **single parent** = one parent (mother or father) who is bringing up a child alone; *single parent families are more and more common* (NOTE: **parent** is not often used in the singular)

parentage ['peərəntɪdʒ] *noun* someone's origin; *his parentage is unknown*; *the heroine sets out to discover her true parentage*

parental [pə'rentl] *adjective* referring to parents; *parental guidance seems to have been totally lacking*; *if grants are reduced, the parental contribution to students' maintenance will have to increase*

parenthesis [pə'renθəsɪs] *noun* **(a)** phrase in the middle of a sentence which is placed in brackets or between dashes; *he referred to it only in a brief parenthesis* **(b) parentheses** = round brackets, printing symbol ( ) which encloses words or characters and separates them from the rest of the text; *she put the phrase in parentheses* (NOTE: plural is **parentheses** [pə'renθəsi:z])

parenthetical [pærən'θetɪkl] *adjective* added as a parenthesis; *he made some parenthetical remarks*

parenthood ['peərənthʊd] *noun* state of being a parent; *they are so young, I am not sure they are ready for parenthood*

parenting ['peərəntɪŋ] *noun* activity of looking after children; *people with young children sometimes attend parenting classes*

parents ['peərənts] *noun* mother and father; *his parents live in Manchester*; *did your parents tell you I had met them in London?*

parish ['pærɪʃ] *noun* **(a)** area served by a church; *he's the vicar of a country parish* **(b)** administrative district in a county with a church as its centre; **parish council** = elected committee which runs a parish; **parish councillor** = elected member of a parish council; *he's been a parish councillor for the last four years* (NOTE: plural is **parishes**; the adjective is **parochial**)

parishioner [pə'rɪʃənə] *noun* person who lives in or belongs to a parish; *the new vicar isn't very popular with his parishioners*

parity ['pærɪti] *noun* (*formal*) being equal, especially having the same rates of pay and conditions as others; *we aim to achieve parity with our rivals*; *the female staff want parity with the men*

park [pɑ:k] **1** *noun* **(a)** open space with grass and trees; *Hyde Park and Regents Park are in the middle of London*; *you can ride a bicycle across the park but cars are not allowed in* **(b) national park** = area of land protected by the government for people to enjoy; *the Peak District in Derbyshire is a national park*; *we went camping in the national park* **(c) car park** = area where you can leave a car when you are not using it; *he left his car in the hotel car park*; *the office car park is full* (NOTE: American English is **parking lot**) **2** *verb* **(a)** to leave your car in a place while you are not using it; *you can park your car in the street next to the hotel*;

you mustn't park on a yellow line **(b)** *(informal)* **to park yourself** = to put yourself in a place, especially where you are not wanted; *he came and parked himself next to me*

parka ['pɑːkə] *noun US* warm waterproof jacket with a hood; *you need a parka when climbing mountains in winter*

parked [pɑːkt] *adjective (of vehicle)* left in a car park, standing at the side of the road etc.; *the bus crashed into two parked cars*

Parker ['pɑːkə] *see* NOSEY PARKER

parking ['pɑːkɪŋ] *noun* action of parking a car; *parking is difficult in the centre of the city*; **no parking** = sign showing that you must not park your car; **parking meter** = device into which you put money to pay for parking; *US* **parking lot** = area where you can leave a car when you are not using it (NOTE: British English is **car park**)

parkland ['pɑːklænd] *noun* open land with grass and trees; *the house stands amid twenty acres of parkland*

parliament ['pɑːləmənt] *noun* group of elected representatives who vote the laws of a country; *Parliament has passed a law forbidding the sale of dangerous drugs*; **Act of Parliament** = law which has been passed by parliament; **Houses of Parliament** = building in London where Parliament meets; *he took a picture of the Houses of Parliament*

parliamentarian [pɑːləmənˈteəriən] *noun GB* member of one of the Houses of Parliament; *a delegation of British parliamentarians was invited to visit Canada*

parliamentary [pɑːləˈmentəri] *adjective* referring to parliament; *parliamentary procedure*; *parliamentary elections*

parlour *US* **parlor** ['pɑːlə] *noun* **(a)** *(old)* sitting room, room in a house where visitors are entertained; *my aunt invited us into the parlour for tea* **(b)** **beauty parlour** = shop where women can have their hair done and their faces made up; *I spent all morning at the beauty parlour and my boyfriend didn't notice any difference*; **funeral parlour** = shop where dead bodies are taken to be made ready to be buried

Parmesan [pɑːmɪˈzæn] *noun* type of hard Italian cheese that is often grated and sprinkled on pasta dishes; *would you like Parmesan on your spaghetti?*

parochial [pəˈrəʊkiəl] *adjective* **(a)** referring to a parish; *the parochial church council*; *the vicar takes his parochial duties very seriously* **(b)** restricted and narrow-minded; *her outlook is too parochial*

parody ['pærədi] **1** *noun* poetry, play, song, which imitates someone to make fun; *he wrote a parody of Wodehouse* (NOTE: plural is **parodies**) **2** *verb* to imitate in order to make fun; *his writing style is very easy to parody*

parole [pəˈrəʊl] **1** *noun* (i) allowing a prisoner to leave prison for a short time, on condition that he or she behaves well; (ii) allowing a prisoner who has behaved well to be released from prison early on condition that he or she continues to behave well outside prison; *he was given a week's parole to visit his mother in hospital*; *she will be eligible for parole in three weeks' time*; *he was let out on parole and immediately offended again*; **parole board** = group of people who advise on whether a prisoner should be released on parole **2** *verb* to let a prisoner out of prison on condition

that he or she behaves well; *after six months he was paroled*

parrot ['pærət] *noun* **(a)** colourful tropical bird with a large curved beak; *he keeps a green parrot in a cage in his sitting room* **(b)** *(informal)* **sick as a parrot** = very annoyed and upset; *I put all my money on the favourite and he came in last - I was sick as a parrot*

parry ['pæri] *verb* **(a)** to try to prevent a blow from hitting you; *he tried to parry the blows which rained down on his head* **(b)** to try to avoid giving an answer to a question; *she skilfully parried the questions from the journalists*

parsimonious [pɑːsɪˈməʊniəs] *adjective (formal)* not liking to spend money; *he lives a very parsimonious existence*

parsimony ['pɑːsɪməni] *noun (formal)* being a miser; *her parsimony is notorious*

parsley ['pɑːsli] *noun* green herb used in cooking; *sprinkle some chopped parsley on top of the salad*

parson ['pɑːsn] *noun* clergyman in charge of a parish in the Church of England; *the parson was getting ready to write his sermon*; *go and see the parson and tell him your problems*

part [pɑːt] **1** *noun* **(a)** piece; *parts of the film were very good*; *they live in the downstairs part of a large house*; *they spend part of the year in France*; **spare parts** = pieces used to put in place of broken parts of a car, etc. **(b) in part** = not completely; *to contribute in part to the costs or to pay the costs in part* **(c)** character in a play, film, etc.; *he played the part of Hamlet*; **to play a part** = to be one of several people or things which do something; *the guests played an important part in putting out the hotel fire*; **to take part** = to join in; *they all took part in the game*; *did he take part in the concert?* **2** *verb* **(a)** to divide into sections; *he parts his hair on the right side* **(b) to part company** = to leave, to split up; *we all set off together, but we parted company when we got to Italy*; *see also* PART WITH

part exchange ['pɑːt ɪksˈtʃeɪndʒ] *noun* giving an old product as part of the payment for a new one; *they refused to take my old car in part exchange for the new one*

partial ['pɑːʃl] *adjective* **(a) partial to** = with a liking for; *everyone knows he is partial to a slice of cheesecake* **(b)** not complete; *he got partial compensation for the damage to his house*; *the treatment was only a partial success* **(c)** in a biased way; *the judge was accused of being partial*

partiality [pɑːʃiˈælɪti] *noun* **(a)** being in favour of someone rather than someone else; *apart from a natural partiality to members of his own family, he treated everyone the same* **(b) partiality for something** = great liking for something; *his partiality for good French cooking is well-known*

partially ['pɑːʃəli] *adverb* not completely; *he is partially deaf*; *I partially agree with what they are proposing*

participant [pɑːˈtɪsɪpənt] *noun* person who takes part; *all participants should register with the organizers before the race starts*; *conference participants are asked to meet in the foyer of the conference hall*

participate [pɑːˈtɪsɪpeɪt] *verb* to take part in something; *he refused to participate in the TV discussion*

participation [pɑːtɪsɪ'peɪʃn] *noun* taking part in something; *their participation is vital to the success of the talks; his participation in the show will ensure that we get a good audience*

participle ['pɑːtɪsɪpl] *noun* word formed from a verb, used either to form compound tenses or as an adjective or noun; *in English, present participles are formed by adding -ing to a verb 'gone' is the past participle of 'to go'*

particle ['pɑːtɪkl] *noun* very small piece; *they found tiny particles of glass in the yoghurt*

particular [pə'tɪkjuːlə] **1** *adjective* **(a)** special, referring to one thing or person and to no one else; *the photocopier only works with one particular type of paper* **(b) in particular** = especially; *fragile goods, in particular glasses, need special packing* **(c)** fussy; *she's very particular about her food; give me any room you have available - I'm not particular* **2** *noun* **particulars** = details; *the sheet which gives particulars of the house for sale; the inspector asked for particulars of the missing car*

particularize [pətɪkjulə'raɪz] *verb (formal)* to list things in detail; *please particularize your grievances*

particularly [pə'tɪkjuːləli] *adverb* specially; *I particularly asked them not to walk on the lawn; it's a particularly difficult problem; he isn't particularly worried about the result*

parting ['pɑːtɪŋ] **1** *noun* **(a)** leaving someone; *our final parting took place outside the railway station* **(b)** line which marks where your hair is separated when you comb it; *my parting is on the left side* **2** *adjective* done when leaving a place or person; *it was a parting gift from my brother before he went abroad;* **parting shot** = last, often unpleasant, words spoken when leaving someone; *as a parting shot he told her he was going to divorce her*

partisan [pɑːtɪ'zæn] **1** *adjective* **(a)** strongly supporting a certain point of view; *his partisan views are obvious in the article; she's too partisan to be trusted to make an objective assessment of the situation* **(b)** referring to local armed resistance against an occupying army; *the invaders found themselves up against a partisan army* **2** *noun* **(a)** person who supports a policy forcefully; *she's a partisan of having more women Members of Parliament* **(b)** member of a local armed resistance movement, fighting against an occupying army; *the town was captured by partisans*

partition [pɑː'tɪʃn] **1** *noun* **(a)** division of a country into separate parts; *did you agree with the partition of the country after the war?* **(b)** thin wall between two spaces, especially one splitting a large room into sections; *we put a partition across the centre of the room to make two separate bedrooms for the boys* **2** *verb* **(a)** to divide; *the country was partitioned in 1947 to form the new independent states of India and Pakistan* **(b) to partition something off** = to divide a room, especially by means of a partition; *the open-plan office has been partitioned off into smaller areas*

partly ['pɑːtli] *adverb* not completely; *the house is partly furnished; I'm only partly satisfied with the result; we're selling our house in London, partly because we need the money, but also because we want to move nearer to the sea*

partner ['pɑːtnə] *noun* **(a)** person who works in a business and has a share in it with others; *he became a partner in a firm of solicitors;* **sleeping partner** = partner who has a share in a business but does not work in it **(b)** person you live with, without necessarily being married; *we invited him and his partner for drinks* **(c)** person who plays games or dances with someone; *take your partners for the waltz; Sally is my usual tennis partner*

partnership ['pɑːtnəʃɪp] *noun* business association between two or more people where the risks and profits are shared according to a letter of agreement between the partners; **to go into partnership with someone** = to join with someone to form a partnership; *they went into partnership to market his new invention*

parts of speech ['pɑːts əv 'spiːtʃ] *noun* different types of words, such as nouns, verbs, etc., which are classified according to grammatical use; *nouns, adjectives and verbs are different parts of speech; what part of speech is 'this'?*

part payment ['pɑːt 'peɪmənt] *noun* paying of part of a whole payment; *I gave them £500 in part payment*

partridge ['pɑːtrɪdʒ] *noun* small brown and grey wild bird, shot for sport and food; *he came home with a brace of partridges for supper*

part-time [pɑːt'taɪm] *adjective & adverb* not for the whole working day; *he is trying to find part-time work when the children are in school; we are looking for part-time staff to work our computers; she works part-time in the local supermarket*

part-timer [pɑːt'taɪmə] *noun* person who works for part of a day; *most of our staff are part-timers; part-timers do not have the same security of employment as permanent staff*

part with ['pɑːt 'wɪθ] *verb* to give or sell something to someone; *he refused to part with his old bicycle; I'm reluctant to part with the keys to the house*

party ['pɑːti] *noun* **(a)** special occasion when several people meet, usually in someone's house; *we're having a party on New Year's Eve; our family Christmas party was a disaster as usual; she invited twenty friends to her birthday party;* **to gatecrash a party** = to get into a party without being invited; *a group of students tried to gatecrash her party* **(b)** group of people doing something together; *parties of tourists walking round the gardens* **(c)** **political party** = organization of people with similar political opinions and aims; *which party does he belong to?; she's a member of the Labour Party; see also* THIRD PARTY, WORKING PARTY (NOTE: plural is **parties**)

party line ['pɑːti 'laɪn] *noun* **(a)** telephone line shared by two subscribers **(b)** official policy of a political party, which must be followed by its members; *the party line is that there will be no new taxes until the economy improves;* **to toe the party line** = to say what the party experts expect you to say and not to have a different view from the official party policy; *you won't get anywhere if you don't toe the party line*

party political ['pɑːti pə'lɪtɪkl] *adjective* referring to or involving party politics; *tonight there is a party political broadcast on behalf of the Labour party; we don't want to make this a party political issue*

party politics ['pɑːti 'pɒlɪtɪks] *noun* **party politics** = working to promote the interests of a political party, by taking power in a local or national government; *the man in the street isn't interested in party politics; the head of state should be above party politics*

party wall ['pɑːti 'wɔːl] *noun* wall between two houses or flats, which belongs to both properties; *the party wall is so thin, we can hear everything our neighbours say*

pass [pɑːs] **1** *noun* **(a)** *(in football, etc.)* sending the ball to another player; *he sent a long pass across the field and Smith headed it into goal* **(b)** low area where a road can cross between two mountain peaks; *the Brenner Pass is closed by snow*; *the road winds steeply up to the pass* **(c)** season ticket on a bus or train; *I left my pass at home, so I had to pay for a ticket* **(d)** permit to go in or out regularly; *you need a pass to enter the ministry offices*; *all members of staff must show a pass* (NOTE: plural is **passes**) **2** *verb* **(a)** to go past; *if you walk towards the bank you will pass the office on your right*; *I passed her on the stairs*; *if you're passing the bookshop, can you pick up the book I ordered?* **(b)** to move something towards someone; *can you pass me the salt, please?*; *he passed the ball back to the goalkeeper* **(c)** to be successful in a test or examination; *he passed in English, but failed in French*; *she passed her driving test first time!* **(d)** to vote to approve something; *Parliament has passed a law against the ownership of guns*; *the proposal was passed by 10 votes to 3*

passable ['pɑːsəbl] *adjective* **(a)** which you can travel along; *the roads across the mountains have been cleared of snow and are passable again* **(b)** fairly good; *he did a passable imitation of the prime minister*

passage ['pæsɪdʒ] *noun* **(a)** corridor; *she hurried along the passage*; *there's an underground passage between the two railway stations* **(b)** section of a text; *she quoted passages from the Bible*; *I photocopied a particularly interesting passage from the textbook* **(c)** action of moving from one place to another; *the attackers promised the garrison safe passage if they surrendered* (NOTE: no plural in this meaning)

passageway ['pæsɪdʒweɪ] *noun* corridor; *there's a narrow passageway between the houses*; *his pile of luggage is blocking the passageway*

pass away ['pɑːs ə'weɪ] *verb* to die; *mother passed away during the night* (NOTE: also **pass on**)

passbook ['pɑːsbʊk] *noun* book which records how much money you put in or take out of your savings account at a bank or building society; *when you make a deposit you hand your passbook to the cashier to have it stamped*

passenger ['pæsɪndʒə] *noun* person who is travelling in a car, bus, train, plane, etc. but who is not the driver or one of the crew; *his car's quite big - it can take three passengers on the back seat*; *the plane was carrying 104 passengers and a crew of ten*; **foot passenger** = passenger on a ferry who is not travelling with a car; **passenger side** = the side of the car nearest to the kerb; **passenger train** = train which carries passengers but not freight

passer-by [pɑːsə'baɪ] *noun* person who is walking past; *a passer-by saw what happened and called the police*; *she was looked after by passers-by until the ambulance came* (NOTE: plural is **passers-by**)

passing ['pɑːsɪŋ] *adjective* **(a)** not permanent; *it's just a passing fashion* **(b)** which is going past; *the driver of a passing car saw the accident and called the police on his mobile phone*

passion ['pæʃn] *noun* very strong emotion or enthusiasm; *she has a passion for motor racing*; *he didn't put enough passion into the love scene*

passionate ['pæʃənət] *adjective* strongly emotional; *he's passionate about cleanliness*; *she has a passionate love for Italian art*

passionately ['pæʃnetli] *adverb* strongly; *they are passionately in love*

passive ['pæsɪv] **1** *adjective* allowing things to happen to you and not taking any action yourself; *he wasn't one of the ringleaders, he only played a passive role in the coup*; **passive resistance** = protesting against something by refusing to do it, but not by using violence; *the protesters organized a programme of passive resistance*; **passive smoking** = breathing in smoke from other people's cigarettes, when you do not smoke yourself; *passive smoking is believed to be one of the causes of lung cancer* **2** *noun* form of a verb which shows that the subject is being acted upon (NOTE: also called the **passive voice**; if you say 'the car hit him' the verb is active, but 'he was hit by the car' is passive)

pass off [pɑːs 'ɒf] *verb* **(a)** to take place; *the meeting passed off without any problems* **(b)** to pass something off as something else = to pretend that it is another thing in order to cheat; *he passed the wine off as French*; **to pass yourself off as** = to pretend to be; *he passed himself off as a rich banker from South America*

pass on ['pɑːs 'ɒn] *verb* **(a)** to move something on to someone else; *she passed on the information to her boss* **(b)** to die; *my father passed on two years ago* (NOTE: also **pass away** in the same meaning)

pass out ['pɑːs 'aʊt] *verb* to faint, to become unconscious for a short time; *she passed out when she saw the blood*; *when he told her that her mother was seriously ill in hospital, she passed out*

Passover ['pɑːsəʊvə] *noun* Jewish spring festival which celebrates the release of Jews from captivity in Egypt

passport ['pɑːspɔːt] *noun* official document allowing you to pass from one country to another; *if you are going abroad you need to have a valid passport*; *we had to show our passports at customs*; *his passport is out of date*

pass round ['pɑːs raʊnd] *verb* **(a)** to hand something to various people; *she passed the box of chocolates round the table*; *the steward passed round immigration forms* **(b)** to pass the hat round = to ask for money; *we don't have the funds to put on the school play this year, so we'll have to pass the hat round*

pass up ['pɑːs 'ʌp] *verb (informal)* not to make use of a chance or opportunity which is offered; *he passed up the chance of going to work in our office in Australia*

password ['pɑːswɜːd] *noun* secret word which you need to know to be allowed to go into a military camp or to use a computer system; *the soldiers stopped him at the gate and asked him for the password*; *you need to know the password to access the data online*

past [pɑːst] **1** *preposition* **(a)** later than, after; *it's past the children's bedtime*; *it's ten past ten (10.10) - we've missed the TV news* **(b)** from one side to the other in front of something; *if you go past the bank, you'll see* the shop on your left; she walked past me without saying anything; the car went past at at least 60 miles an hour (NOTE: **past** is used for times between o'clock and the half hour: **3.05** = five past three; **3.15** = a quarter past three; **3.25** = twenty-five past three; **3.30** = half past three. For times after **half past** see **to**. **Past** is also used with many verbs: **to go past, to drive past, to fly past**, etc.) **2** adjective which has passed; he has spent the past year working in France; the time for talking is past - what we need is action **3** noun **(a)** time before now; in the past we always had an office party just before Christmas **(b) past (tense)** = form of a verb which shows that it happened before the present time; 'sang' is the past (tense) of the verb 'to sing'

pasta ['pæstə] noun Italian food made of flour and water, cooked by boiling and eaten with oil or sauce; spaghetti, macaroni, etc., are all types of pasta; I'll just have some pasta and a glass of wine (NOTE: no plural: **some pasta, a bowl of pasta**; note that **pasta** takes a singular verb: **the pasta is very good here**)

paste [peɪst] **1** noun **(a)** thin liquid glue; spread the paste evenly over the back of the wallpaper **(b)** soft food; the cake is covered with almond paste; mix the flour, eggs and milk to a smooth paste; add tomato paste to the soup **(c)** hard shining glass, used to make imitation jewellery; those aren't real diamonds, they're just paste **2** verb to glue paper, etc.; she pasted a sheet of coloured paper over the front of the box; he pasted the newspaper cuttings into his scrapbook; see also CUT

pastel ['pæstl] noun **(a)** coloured crayon like chalk; a portrait done in pastels; **pastel colours** = soft, light shades; the whole house was decorated in light pastel colours **(b)** picture done with coloured crayons like chalk; this pastel was used as a sketch for the finished painting

pastern ['pæstɜːn] noun narrow part of a horse's leg just above the hoof; the horse sank into mud up to its pasterns; see also FETLOCK

pasteurization [pɑːstʃəraɪˈzeɪʃn] noun action of pasteurizing; pasteurization kills off harmful bacteria

pasteurize ['pɑːstʃəraɪz] verb to kill the germs in milk by heating it; only pasteurized milk should be given to babies

pastiche [pæˈstiːʃ] noun poem, piece of music, etc., which is deliberately done in the style of another artist; it's an amusing pastiche of 1930s gangster movies

pastime ['pɑːstaɪm] noun hobby, thing you do to pass your spare time; the national pastime seems to be watching football on TV

pastor ['pɑːstə] noun Protestant clergyman; the pastor of our local church came to see my mother

pastoral ['pɑːstərəl] adjective **(a)** referring to country life; Virgil was famous for his pastoral poetry **(b)** referring to guidance in connection with someone's personal problems; there's an important pastoral side to a teacher's job

pastry ['peɪstri] noun **(a)** pie crust made of flour, fat and water; she was in the kitchen making pastry **(b) pastries** = sweet cakes made of pastry filled with cream or fruit, etc.; **Danish pastries** = sweet pastry cakes with jam or fruit folded inside

pasturage ['pɑːstʃərɪdʒ] noun land used as pasture; there's not enough pasturage for a bigger herd (NOTE: no plural)

pasture ['pɑːstʃə] noun grassy area where animals such as horses, cows and sheep can graze; every summer the cows are driven up to the mountain pastures

pat [pæt] **1** noun **(a)** little tap with the hand; I didn't hit her - I just gave her a little pat; **a pat on the back** = praise; the committee got a pat on the back for having organized the show so well **(b) a pat of butter** = small round piece of butter **2** verb to give someone or something a pat; he patted his pocket to make sure that his wallet was still there; **to pat someone on the back** = to praise someone (NOTE: **patting - patted**)

patch [pætʃ] **1** noun **(a)** small piece of material used for covering up a hole; his mother sewed a patch over the hole in his trousers (informal) **not a patch on** = not nearly as good as; the 1998 model isn't a patch on the old one **(b)** small area; they built a shed on a patch of ground by the railway line; **a cabbage patch** = small piece of ground where you grow cabbages (NOTE: plural is **patches**) **2** verb to repair by attaching a piece of material over a hole; her jeans are all mended and patched; we patched the curtains with some material we had left over

patch up ['pætʃ 'ʌp] verb **(a)** to mend with difficulty; the mechanics managed to patch up the engine; the surgeon patched him up but warned him not to fight with knives again **(b) to patch up a quarrel** = to become more friendly again after quarrelling; they had a bitter argument, but patched up their quarrel in time for the party

patchwork ['pætʃwɜːk] noun **(a)** a piece of needlework made by sewing small pieces of material together in patterns; all the women in the family came together to sew a patchwork quilt **(b)** area which looks like a patchwork quilt; a typical English landscape with a patchwork of small fields

patchy ['pætʃi] adjective **(a)** not all good; this year's exam results have been patchy **(b)** in small areas; if you don't prepare the surface properly, the paint will look patchy; there may be some patchy rain in the southwest (NOTE: **patchier - patchiest**)

pâté ['pæteɪ] noun paste made of cooked meat or fish finely minced; I'll start with chicken liver pâté; he brought some pâté home with him from France

patella [pəˈtelə] noun (formal) kneecap, the small bone in the front of the knee joint

patent ['peɪtənt or 'pætənt] **1** noun (only ['pætənt]) official confirmation that you have the sole right to make or sell a new invention; to take out a patent for a new type of light bulb; they have applied for a patent for their new invention **2** adjective **(a)** covered by an official patent; **patent medicine** = medicine made under a trade name by one company **(b) patent leather** = leather with an extremely shiny surface **3** verb **to patent an invention** = to register an invention with the patent office to prevent other people from copying it

paternal [pəˈtɜːnəl] adjective **(a)** referring to a father; **my paternal grandfather** = my father's father **(b)** like a father; the younger workers disliked his paternal attitude; he kept a paternal eye on the young people working in his department (NOTE: the equivalent referring to a mother, is **maternal**)

paternity [pəˈtɜːnɪti] noun **(a)** being a father; **paternity leave** = permission for a man to be away from work when his wife has a baby; I'm standing in for John while he's on paternity leave **(b)** the identity of a father; *the court had first to establish the child's paternity* (NOTE: compare **maternity**)

path [pɑ:θ] *noun* **(a)** narrow track for walking; *there's a path across the field; follow the path until you get to the sea* (NOTE: also called a **footpath**) **(b)** bicycle path = narrow lane for bicycles by the side of a road **(c)** direction in which something is moving or coming; *people in villages in the path of the hurricane were advised to get away as fast as possible; the school stands right in the path of the new motorway*

pathetic [pə'θetɪk] *adjective* **(a)** which makes you feel pity or contempt; *he made a pathetic attempt at a joke; she looked so pathetic I hadn't the heart to scold her* **(b)** *(informal)* extremely bad; *her performance in the semi-final was absolutely pathetic*

pathological [pæθə'lɒdʒɪkl] *adjective* **(a)** referring to a disease or which is caused by a disease; *a pathological condition* **(b)** extreme or uncontrollable; *she has an almost pathological hatred of German men*; **pathological liar** = person who tells lies all the time

pathologist [pə'θɒlədʒɪst] *noun* **(a)** doctor who specializes in the study of diseases and the changes in the body caused by disease; *a pathologist took samples for examination in the laboratory* **(b)** doctor who examines dead bodies to find out the cause of death; *the pathologist found traces of poison in the corpse*

pathology [pə'θɒlədʒi] *noun* study of diseases and the changes in structure and function which diseases cause in the body; *blood samples were sent to the pathology laboratory for testing*

pathos ['peɪθɒs] *noun* quality in something which makes you feel pity; *there is tremendous pathos in the hero's dying speech* (NOTE: the adjective is **pathetic**)

pathway ['pɑ:θweɪ] *noun* track for walking along; *a concrete pathway connected the two buildings*

patience ['peɪʃns] *noun* **(a)** being patient; *with a little patience, you'll soon learn how to ride a bike; I don't have the patience to wait that long*; **to try someone's patience** = to make someone impatient; *looking after a class of thirty little children would try anyone's patience* **(b)** card game for one person; *she sat by herself in her hotel room, playing patience*

COMMENT: the simplest form of children's patience is when you lay out nine cards, face upwards, and cover with other cards any pairs of cards which add up to eleven (9 and 2, or 10 and ace, for example). You also cover up the king, queen and jack if all three are there. You continue to do this until you only have two cards left, and can calculate from the cards in front of you which cards you are holding in your hand

patient ['peɪʃnt] **1** *adjective* **(a)** being able to wait a long time without getting annoyed; *you must be patient - you will get served in time* **(b)** careful and thorough; *weeks of patient investigation by the police resulted in his arrest* **2** *noun* sick person who is in hospital or who is being treated by a doctor, dentist, psychiatrist, etc.; *there are three other patients in the ward; the nurse is trying to take the patient's temperature*

patiently ['peɪʃəntli] *adverb* without getting annoyed; *they waited patiently for the bus to arrive*

patio ['pætɪəʊ] *noun* paved area outside a house or other building for sitting or eating; *it was such a lovely morning we had breakfast on the patio* (NOTE: plural is **patios**)

patriarch ['peɪtriɑ:k] *noun* **(a)** bishop of an Eastern church; *the Patriarch of Constantinople* **(b)** respected old man who is considered the head of a village or community; *we were taken to see an old man who was obviously the village patriarch*; compare MATRIARCH

patriarchal [peɪtri'ɑ:kl] *adjective* referring to a patriarchy; *a patriarchal system*

patriarchy ['peɪtriɑ:ki] *noun* system of government by the eldest male of the ruling group; *in a patriarchy women have to be content with playing a secondary role*

patrician [pə'trɪʃn] **1** *adjective* referring to aristocrats, like an aristocrat; *the old East Coast patrician families lost influence when Texas and California became economically powerful; the magazine article described his patrician style of living* **2** *noun* *(formal)* member of an old aristocratic family; *the patricians lost influence when the Roman Republic was replaced by the Empire*

patriot ['peɪtriət] *noun* person who is proud of his country and is willing to defend it; *he's a real patriot; all true patriots must vote in the referendum*

patriotic [pætri'ɒtɪk] *adjective* proud of your country and willing to defend it; *they sang patriotic songs before the football match; I'm not ashamed of being patriotic - I think this is a wonderful country*

patriotism ['peɪtriətɪzm] *noun* feeling of great pride in your country; *feelings of patriotism made many young men join the army when their country was invaded*

patrol [pə'trəʊl] **1** *noun* **(a)** keeping guard by walking or driving up and down; *they make regular patrols round the walls of the prison; he was on patrol in the centre of town when he saw some youths running away from a bank* **(b)** group of people keeping guard; *each time a patrol went past we hid behind a wall* **2** *verb* to keep guard by walking or driving up and down; *armed security guards are patrolling the warehouse* (NOTE: **patrolling - patrolled**)

patrol car [pə'trəʊl 'kɑ:] *noun* police car which drives up and down the streets; *they hid in doorways every time they saw a patrol car coming*

patrolman [pə'trəʊlmən] *noun* *(especially US)* policeman on patrol; *the patrolman asked to see my driver's licence* (NOTE: plural is **patrolmen**)

patron ['peɪtrən] *noun* **(a)** person who protects or supports someone *or* something; *she's a great patron of the arts*; **patron saint** = saint who is believed to protect a particular group of people; *St Christopher is the patron saint of travellers* **(b)** person who goes regularly to a shop, hotel, restaurant, theatre, etc.; *the car park is for the use of hotel patrons only*

patronage ['pætrənɪdʒ] *noun* giving support or encouragement to an artist, etc.; *in those days artists depended on the patronage of a few rich noble families*; **political patronage** = right to give government posts or honours to people who have supported you

patronize ['pætrənaɪz] *verb* **(a)** to support or to encourage an artist, etc.; *King Charles I patronized several Flemish painters, especially Van Dyck* **(b)** to act in a way which shows you think you are superior; *he* thinks he can patronize us because we're younger than he is (c) to go regularly to a shop, public house, theatre, etc.; *we believe it's important to patronize small local shops*; *the restaurant is mainly patronized by local businessmen*

patronizing ['pætrənaɪzɪŋ] *adjective* showing that you feel you are superior; *his patronizing attitude really annoys me*; *she asked to see the manager in a patronizing tone of voice*

patter ['pætə] 1 *noun* (a) light tapping noise; *the patter of raindrops on the roof*; *I heard a patter of feet in the corridor* (b) rapid talk by a conjuror, salesman, trickster, etc., to keep your attention; *he kept up a continuous patter as he shuffled the cards* 2 *verb* to make a light tapping noise; *the rain pattered on the windows*

pattern ['pætən] *noun* (a) instructions which you follow to make something; *she copied a pattern from a magazine to knit her son a pullover* (b) design of lines, flowers, etc., repeated again and again on cloth, wallpaper, etc.; *she was wearing a coat with a pattern of black and white spots*; *do you like the pattern on our new carpet?* (c) general way in which something usually happens; *a change in the usual weather pattern*

patterned ['pætənd] *adjective* with a repeated pattern; *we have put patterned wallpaper all over the hallway*; *a patterned carpet won't show stains*

paucity ['pɔːsɪti] *noun (formal)* lack of something; *we suffer from a paucity of information about the research being carried out*; *there are several job vacancies at the moment, but a paucity of good candidates* (NOTE: no plural)

paunch [pɔːnʃ] *noun* man's fat stomach; *he's developing a paunch* (NOTE: plural is **paunches**)

pause [pɔːz] 1 *noun* short stop during a period of work, etc.; *the exercise consists of running on the spot for ten minutes, with a short pause after each 100 steps*; *he read his speech slowly, with plenty of pauses* 2 *verb* to rest for a short time; to stop doing something for a short time; *she ran along the road, only pausing for a second to look at her watch*

pave [peɪv] *verb* (a) to cover a road or path, etc., with a hard surface; *in the old town, the streets are paved with cobblestones*; *there is a paved courtyard behind the restaurant* (b) to pave the way for something = to prepare the way for something to happen; *the election of the new president paves the way for a change of government*

pavement ['peɪvmənt] *noun* (a) hard path for walkers at the side of a road; *walk on the pavement, not in the road*; *look out! - the pavement is covered with ice* (NOTE: in American English this is **sidewalk**) (b) *US* hard road surface (NOTE: British English for this is **roadway**)

pavilion [pə'vɪljən] *noun* (a) small building for sportsmen to rest in between games; *the rest of the team watched from the pavilion as he scored the winning run* (b) separate building at a large exhibition; *have you seen the Canadian pavilion yet?*

paving stone ['peɪvɪŋ 'stəʊn] *noun* large flat stone slab used for making paths, patios, etc.; *she tripped over a loose paving stone*

paw [pɔː] 1 *noun* (a) hairy foot of an animal with claws; *the bear held the fish in its paws* (b) *(informal)*

hand; *keep your paws off my food!* 2 *verb* (a) to pat with a foot; *the horse pawed the ground impatiently* (b) *(informal)* to touch with the hands; *he tried pawing the girls at the office party*

pawn [pɔːn] 1 *noun* (a) smallest piece on the chessboard; *he took two of my pawns*; *she sacrificed a pawn in order to put his king in check* (b) person who is controlled by someone more powerful; *he was just a pawn in the hands of powerful bankers* (c) in pawn = left in exchange for money which has been borrowed; *he left his watch in pawn for twenty pounds* 2 *verb* to leave an object in exchange for borrowing money: you claim back the object when you pay back the money; *I was so desperate that I pawned my mobile phone; he was in a bad state, even his dinner jacket had been pawned*; *she pawned her ring to get money for food*

pawnbroker ['pɔːnbrəʊkə] *noun* person who lends money in exchange for valuables left with him; *families relied on the pawnbroker to help them through hard times*

pawnbroker's *or* **pawnshop** ['pɔːnbrəʊkəz *or* 'pɔːnʃɒp] *noun* shop where goods can be pawned; *I was sent to fetch the silver teapot back from the pawnbroker's*

pay [peɪ] 1 *noun* wages or salary; *they're on strike for more pay*; *I can't afford luxuries on my miserable pay*; **basic pay** = normal salary without extra payments; **take-home pay** = pay left after tax and insurance have been deducted; **holidays with pay** = holiday which a worker can take by contract and for which he is paid; **unemployment pay** = money given by the government to someone who is unemployed; *see also* RISE 2 *verb* (a) to give money for something; *how much did you pay for your car?*; *how much rent do you pay?*; *please pay the waiter for your drinks*; *she paid him £10 for his old bike* (b) to give money to someone for doing something; *we pay secretaries £10 an hour*; *I paid them one pound each for washing the car*; *I'll pay you a pound to wash my car* (NOTE: you **pay someone to wash the car** before he washes it, but you **pay someone for washing the car** after he has washed it) (c) to pay attention to = to note and think about something carefully; *pay attention to the following instructions*; **to pay a visit** = to visit; *we'll pay my mother a visit when we're in town* (NOTE: **paying - paid** [peɪd])

payable ['peɪəbl] *adjective* which must be paid; *the invoice is payable at 30 days*; *no tax is payable on these items*

pay back ['peɪ 'bæk] *verb* (a) to give someone money which you owe; *he borrowed ten pounds last week and hasn't paid me back* (b) to pay someone back for = to take revenge on someone for having done something; *'that will pay them back for ruining our party,' he said as he smashed their car window*

paycheque *US* **paycheck** ['peɪ 'tʃek] *noun* regular salary cheque given to an employee; *it's three weeks until I get my next paycheque*

payday ['peɪdeɪ] *noun* day when workers get paid; *can you lend me £10 till payday?*

payer ['peɪə] *noun* person who pays money to someone; *the company is usually a very prompt payer*

pay in ['peɪ 'ɪn] *verb* to put money into an account; *I've got several cheques and some cash to pay in*

paying-in slip ['peɪɪŋ 'ɪn slɪp] *noun* form which is filled in when money is deposited in a bank account or building society account; *she forgot to put the amount being deposited on the paying-in slip*

payment ['peɪmənt] *noun* **(a)** giving money for something; *I make regular monthly payments into her account; she made a payment of £10,000 to the solicitor* **(b)** money paid; *did you receive any payment for the work?; if you fall behind with your payments, they will take the car back*

pay off ['peɪ 'ɒf] *verb* **(a)** to finish paying money which is owed; *he's aiming to pay off his mortgage in ten years; she said she couldn't pay off the loan* **(b)** to pay all the money owed to someone and terminate his employment; *when the company was taken over the factory was closed and all the workers were paid off* **(c)** *(informal)* to be successful; *their more cautious approach eventually paid off; all that hard work paid off when she came out top of her class*

pay-off ['peɪɒf] *noun* **(a)** money paid to finish paying something which is owed, such as money paid to a worker when his employment is ended; *each of the directors received a pay-off of twenty thousand pounds* **(b)** benefit which is deserved; *one of the pay-offs of a university degree is increased earning power*

payola ['peɪəʊlə] *noun* US *(slang)* bribery; *the disc jockey expects some payola for plugging a record*

pay out ['peɪ 'aʊt] *verb* **(a)** to give money to someone; *the insurance company paid out thousands of pounds to claimants after the storm; we have paid out half our profits in dividends* **(b)** to unroll a rope; *they paid out the rope gradually as I climbed down the cliff*

payroll ['peɪrəʊl] *noun* **(a)** the people employed by a company and paid by it; *the company has 250 people on the payroll* **(b)** the total wages paid by a company

pay up ['peɪ 'ʌp] *verb* to pay all the money which you owe; *the tourist paid up quickly when the taxi driver called the police*

PC ['piː'siː] = PERSONAL COMPUTER, POLICE CONSTABLE, POLITICALLY CORRECT

PCB = PRINTED CIRCUIT BOARD

PE ['piː 'iː] = PHYSICAL EXERCISE; *a PE class*

pea [piː] *noun* climbing plant of which the round green seeds are eaten as vegetables; *what vegetables do you want with your meat? - peas and carrots, please*; **pea soup** = green soup, made with peas; **sweet peas** = plant of the pea family with scented flowers; **like two peas in a pod** = very similar; *no one can tell the twins apart, they're like two peas in a pod*

peace [piːs] *noun* **(a)** state of not being at war; *the UN troops are trying to keep the peace in the area; both sides are hoping to reach a peace settlement*; **peace process** = negotiations, concessions, discussions, etc., which take place over a long time, with the aim of ending a state of war **(b)** calm, quiet state; *noisy motorcycles ruin the peace and quiet of the village*

Peace Corps ['piːs 'kɔː] *noun* an organization that sends young volunteers from the USA to help with technical projects in developing countries; *he first went to Africa with the Peace Corps* (NOTE: the British equivalent is **VSO (Voluntary Service Overseas)**

peaceful ['piːsfʊl] *adjective* **(a)** calm; *we spent a peaceful afternoon by the river* **(b)** liking peace; *the Swiss seem to be a very peaceful nation*; **peaceful coexistence** = living side by side without making war

peacefully ['piːsfʊli] *adverb* **(a)** calmly; *the baby is sleeping peacefully in its cot* **(b)** without fighting, without making war; *we hope the dispute can be settled peacefully*

peacekeeper ['piːskiːpə] *noun* person who tries to maintain peace; *United Nations peacekeepers are stationed in the town*

peacekeeping ['piːskiːpɪŋ] *adjective & noun* trying to maintain peace; *a peacekeeping force; the army is involved in peacekeeping rather than in fighting wars*

peacetime ['piːstaɪm] *noun* period when a country is not fighting in a war; *in peacetime, you can travel anywhere, provided you have a valid passport*

peach [piːtʃ] *noun* **(a)** sweet fruit, with a large stone and velvety skin; *we had peaches and cream for dessert* **(b)** **peach (tree)** = tree which bears peaches; *he's planted two peaches in his back garden; the peach orchards were all in flower* (NOTE: plural is **peaches**)

peacock ['piːkɒk] *noun* large bird, of which the cock has a huge tail with brilliant blue and green feathers; *they keep peacocks in their garden and they make a lot of noise*

peahen ['piːhen] *noun* female peacock

peak [piːk] **1** *noun* **(a)** top of a mountain; *can you see that snow-covered peak in the distance? - it's Mont Blanc* **(b)** highest point; *the team has to reach a peak of fitness before the match; the graph shows the peaks and troughs of pollution over the last month*; **peak period** = period of the day when most electricity is used, when most traffic is on the roads, etc.; *see also* OFF-PEAK **(c)** front part of a cap which juts out; *he wore a white cap with a dark blue peak* **2** *verb* to reach the highest point; *sales peaked in January* (NOTE: do not confuse with **peek**)

peal [piːl] **1** *noun* **(a)** sudden loud noise; *she could hear peals of laughter from the next room; a peal of thunder woke me up* **(b)** sound of bells ringing; *peals rang out from the church tower on Christmas morning* **(c)** set of bells of different sizes, playing different notes; *the church has a lovely peal of bells* **2** *verb* **(a)** to ring loudly; *the church bells pealed out as the couple came out into the sunlight* **(b)** to make a loud noise like bells; *the audience pealed with laughter* (NOTE: do not confuse with **peel**)

peanut ['piːnʌt] *noun* **(a)** nut which grows in the ground in pods like a pea; *I bought a packet of peanuts to eat with my beer*; **peanut butter** = paste made from crushed peanuts; *she made peanut butter sandwiches for the children* **(b)** *(informal)* very small amount of money; *why does he stay in that job, when he only earns peanuts?*

pear [peə] *noun* **(a)** fruit like a long apple, with one end fatter than the other; *when are pears in season?* **(b)** **pear (tree)** = tree which bears pears; *we've planted a pear and an apple in the garden* (NOTE: do not confuse with **pair**)

pearl [pɜːl] *noun* **(a)** precious round white gem formed inside an oyster; *she wore a string of pearls which her grandmother had given her* **(b)** **pearl bulb** = light bulb which is not clear, but covered with a pale white coating (NOTE: a bulb without this coating is a **clear bulb**)

peasant ['pezənt] *noun* farm labourer or farmer living in a backward region; *the peasants still use traditional farming methods*

peasantry ['pesəntri] *noun* peasants seen as a group; *the peasantry still use oxen to plough their land* (NOTE: no plural)

peat [piːt] *noun* wet soil in a bog, made from partly-decayed mosses and other plants; *the garden centre sells compressed peat in large bags*; *they burn peat on the fire*; **a peat bog =** soft wet area of land which is covered with peat

pebble ['pebl] *noun* small round stone; *the boys were throwing pebbles into the water*; *there's no sand on the beach - it's all pebbles*

peck [pek] **1** *noun* **(a)** bite with a bird's beak; *be careful when you feed the parrot - he can give a nasty peck* **(b)** *(informal)* little kiss; *he gave her a peck on the cheek* **2** *verb* **(a)** *(of birds)* to bite with a beak; *hens were pecking around in the yard*; **pecking order =** unwritten order of importance of people in a firm or office, or animals in a farm **(b) to peck at food =** to eat a little, taking little bites; *she's not feeling very well - she's pecking at her food*

peckish ['pekɪʃ] *adjective (informal)* slightly hungry; *hurry up with the sandwiches, I'm feeling peckish after my long walk*

peculiar [pɪ'kjuːliə] *adjective* **(a)** odd, strange; *it's peculiar that she refuses to have a TV in the house*; *there's a peculiar smell coming from the kitchen* **(b) peculiar to =** only found in one particular place or person; *French fries with mayonnaise is a dish which is peculiar to Belgium*

peculiarity [pɪkjuːli'ærɪti] *noun* odd feature or detail which makes something different; *it's a peculiarity of the British system that judges and lawyers wear wigs in court* (NOTE: plural is **peculiarities**)

pedal ['pedəl] **1** *noun* **(a)** lever worked by the foot; *if you want to stop the car put your foot down on the brake pedal*; **pedal bin =** rubbish bin with a lid worked by a pedal **(b)** flat rest which you press down on with your foot to make a bicycle go forwards; *he stood up on the pedals to make the bike go up the hill* **2** *verb* to make a bicycle go by pushing on the pedals; *he had to pedal hard to get up the hill* (NOTE: **pedalling - pedalled** but American spelling is **pedaling - pedaled**)

pedant ['pedənt] *noun* person who insists on having every small detail correct; *don't be such a pedant, I can drink red wine with my fish if I like*

pedantic [pɪ'dæntɪk] *adjective* who worries too much about small details; *she's fussy to the point of being pedantic when it comes to setting a table and seating the guests*

peddle ['pedl] *verb* to sell goods from door to door or in the street; *he makes a living peddling cleaning products door-to-door*; *he was accused of peddling drugs*; *she tried to peddle the information to various newspapers* (NOTE: do not confuse with **pedal**)

pedestal ['pedɪstl] *noun* base for a statue; *after the earthquake, they found that the statue of the emperor had fallen off its pedestal*; **to put somebody on a pedestal =** to treat somebody as if they were very special or important, even if they have faults; *he always put his wife on a pedestal and was horrified to hear the stories about her which came out in court*

pedestrian [pə'destriən] **1** *noun* person who walks by a road; *two pedestrians were also injured in the accident*; **pedestrian crossing =** place where pedestrians can cross a road (NOTE: American English is **crosswalk**); **pedestrian precinct =** street or group of streets closed to traffic, where people can walk about freely **2** *adjective* **(a)** referring to pedestrians; *the street is open to pedestrian traffic only* **(b)** heavy, done without any imagination; *she gave a terribly pedestrian performance as Juliet*

pedigree ['pedɪgriː] *noun* table showing the ancestors of an animal bred by a breeder; *you should study a dog's pedigree before deciding whether to buy it*; **pedigree bull =** bull with a certificate showing it is pure bred

pee [piː] **1** *noun (informal)* **(a)** waste water from the body; *this drink's horrible, it tastes like pee!* **(b)** passing waste water from the body; *I need to go for a pee*; *he had a quick pee and then went back to the meeting* **2** *verb (informal)* to pass waste water from the body; *the cat's peed all over my flowerbed*

peek [piːk] **1** *noun (informal)* quick look; *he opened the fridge door and had a peek at the dessert* (NOTE: do not confuse with **peak**) **2** *verb (informal)* to look at something quickly; *she peeked through the window and saw there was no one in the kitchen*

peel [piːl] **1** *noun* outer skin of a fruit, etc.; *throw the banana peel into the rubbish bin*; *this orange has got very thick peel* (NOTE: no plural; do not confuse with **peal**) **2** *verb* to take the outer skin off a fruit or a vegetable; *he was peeling a banana*; *if the potatoes are very small you can boil them without peeling them*

peelings ['piːlɪŋz] *noun* bits of skin from vegetables or fruit that have been peeled; *throw the potato peelings into the rubbish*

peep [piːp] **1** *noun (informal)* quick look; *he opened the fridge door and had a peep inside* **2** *verb* to look quickly and secretly at something; *she peeped into the box*; *we found him peeping through the keyhole*

peer ['pɪə] **1** *noun* **(a)** member of the nobility; *peers sit in the House of Lords* **(b)** person of the same rank or class as another; *he's always trying to compete with his peers*; **peer group =** group of people of equal (social) status (NOTE: do not confuse with **pier**) **2** *verb* to look at something hard when you cannot see very well; *she peered at the screen to see if she could read the figures*

peerage ['pɪərɪdʒ] *noun* **(a)** all peers taken as a group; *the book lists all the members of the British peerage* **(b)** position of being a peer; *three new peerages were created in the New Year's Honours List*

peeress ['pɪəres] *noun* woman peer; *the peers and peeresses processed into Westminster Abbey* (NOTE: plural is **peeresses**)

peeved [piːvd] *adjective (informal)* annoyed and bothered; *he was pretty peeved that you didn't invite him*

peevish ['piːvɪʃ] *adjective* bad-tempered, always complaining; *she wrote me a peevish letter saying how badly she was paid*

peg [peg] **1** *noun* **(a)** small wooden or metal stake or pin; *the children hang their coats on pegs in the cloakroom*; *they used no nails in building the roof - it is all held together with wooden pegs*; **tent peg =** metal peg driven into the ground, to which ropes are attached to keep a tent firm; *the ground was so hard that we had* *to bang the tent pegs in with a hammer* (b) **clothes peg** = little wooden clip, used to attach wet clothes to a washing line (NOTE: American English is **clothes pin**); *see also* OFF-THE-PEG **2** *verb* (a) to attach with a peg; *she pegged the washing out on the line* (b) to hold prices, etc., stable; *prices will be pegged at the current rate for another year* (NOTE: **pegging - pegged**)

pejorative [pə'dʒɒrətɪv] *adjective (formal)* showing that you feel something is bad; *he used the word 'bird' in a pejorative meaning*; *I didn't mean it in a pejorative sense*

pekinese [pɪkɪ'niːz] *noun* small dog with a short flat nose and wrinkled face; *she carried her pekinese about under her arm* (NOTE: no plural)

pelican ['pelɪkən] *noun* (a) large white water bird, which catches fish and keeps the fish in a bag of skin under its beak; *the zoo keeper brought a bucket of fish to feed the pelicans* (b) **pelican crossing** = pedestrian crossing with traffic lights which come on when a pedestrian presses a button; *compare* ZEBRA CROSSING

pellet ['pelɪt] *noun* (a) small ball of lead, used in shotguns; *there may still be pellets left in the pheasant so be careful when you eat it* (b) small ball; *the boys made bread pellets and threw them across the room*; *the cattle feed comes in the form of pellets*

pelmet ['pelmɪt] *noun* decorative strip of wood, cloth, etc., above a window which hides the curtain fittings; *you have to remove the pelmets before you start painting the ceiling*

pelt [pelt] **1** *noun* (a) skin of an animal with fur on it; *the trappers sold the pelts at the trading post* (b) **at full pelt** = going as fast as possible; *he was running at full pelt down the street* **2** *verb* (a) **to pelt someone with something** = to throw things at someone; *the crowd pelted the speaker with rotten tomatoes* (b) **the rain was pelting down** = it was raining very hard (c) to run very fast; *I pelted after her to try and catch her up*

pelvic ['pelvɪk] *adjective* referring to the pelvis; **pelvic girdle** = ring formed by the two hip bones to which the thigh bones are attached

pelvis ['pelvɪs] *noun* group of bones and cartilage which form a ring and connect the thigh bones to the spine; *Elvis Presley drove the fans wild when he wiggled his pelvis*; *the tip of the femur fits into a socket in the pelvis* (NOTE: plural is **pelvises**)

pen [pen] **1** *noun* (a) object for writing with, using ink; *I've lost my red pen - can I borrow yours?*; *if you haven't got a pen you can always write in pencil*; **felt pen** = pen with a point made of hard cloth; **marker pen** = pen which makes a wide coloured mark; *see also* BALLPOINT (b) fenced enclosure for animals, such as sheep; *they put the sheep in a pen overnight*; *somehow the goats managed to get out of their pen* **2** *verb* (a) to put in a pen; *the sheep were penned while waiting to be taken to the market* (b) **to be penned in** = to be in a small space, closely surrounded by other things; *she felt penned in, living in the same house as her husband's parents* (NOTE: **penning - penned**)

penal ['piːnl] *adjective* referring to punishment; *the first European settlement in Australia was a penal colony*; **penal code** = set of laws governing crime and its punishment; **penal laws** *or* **the penal system** = system of laws relating to different crimes

penalize ['piːnəlaɪz] *verb* to punish; *he was penalized for being rude to the referee*; *the Inland Revenue penalizes people for making late tax returns*

penalty ['penəlti] *noun* (a) punishment; *the maximum penalty for this offence is two years imprisonment*; *the deal failed and he had to pay the penalty*; **death penalty** = punishment by death; *the judge passed the death penalty on the murderer* (b) punishment in sport, especially a kick at goal awarded to the opposite side in football; *he was awarded a penalty kick*; *they scored from a penalty* (c) disadvantage; *being chased by photographers is one of the penalties of being rich and famous* (NOTE: plural is **penalties**)

penalty area ['penəlti 'eərɪə] *noun (in football)* the area in front of the goal where if a player breaks the rules the other team is given a free shot at the goal from a short distance away; *a free kick from just outside the penalty area*

penance ['penəns] *noun* punishment which someone accepts as a way of acknowledging a bad action; *the priest told him to do penance for his sins*; *as a penance, I agreed to clean the bathroom*

pence [pens] *see* PENNY

penchant ['pɑːnʃɑːn] *noun* special liking for something; *for this job, we need someone with a penchant for detail*; *he has a penchant for pretty secretaries*

pencil ['pensəl] **1** *noun* object for writing with, made of wood, with a strip of coloured material in the middle; *I want a knife to sharpen my pencil with*; *examination answers must be written in ink, not in pencil* **2** *verb* to write with a pencil; **to pencil in** = to write something with a pencil, which you rub out later if it isn't correct; *I'll pencil in the meeting for next Wednesday* (NOTE: **pencilling - pencilled** but American spelling is **penciling - penciled**)

pencil sharpener ['pensəl 'ʃɑːpnə] *noun* instrument for sharpening pencils; *can I borrow your pencil sharpener?*

pending ['pendɪŋ] **1** *adjective* which has not happened or been dealt with; which will happen or be dealt with soon; *a judgement is still pending in the fraud case*; *an official announcement is pending*; **pending tray** = tray for papers and letters waiting to be dealt with **2** *preposition*; **pending advice from our lawyers** = while waiting for advice from our lawyers

pendulum ['pendjuləm] *noun* (a) weight on the end of a chain which swings from side to side, making a clock work; *if you look in the clock case, you can see the pendulum swinging back and forth* (b) trend from one extreme to another; *a few years ago every household had two cars, now the pendulum has swung in the opposite direction and more people are using public transport*

penetrate ['penɪtreɪt] *verb* to go into *or* through something; *the knife penetrated his lung*; *a bullet which can penetrate three centimetres of solid wood*

penetrating ['penɪtreɪtɪŋ] *adjective* deep and searching; *he gave her a penetrating look*; *the inspector asked her some very penetrating questions*

penetration [penɪ'treɪʃn] *noun* (a) action of penetrating something; *the tank's armour-plating resists penetration by machine-gun fire*; *the leg is bruised but there is no penetration of the skin*; *our aim* *is complete penetration of the enemy's air defences* **(b)** being able to think deeply; *it is a work of extraordinary penetration for such a young scholar*

penfriend ['penfrend] *noun* somebody, often in another country, whom you write to regularly without ever meeting; *I'm writing to my penfriend in Jamaica* (NOTE: American English is **pen pal**)

penguin ['peŋgwɪn] *noun* black and white bird found in the Antarctic, which swims well but cannot fly; *colonies of penguins nest on the ice*

penicillin [penɪ'sɪlɪn] *noun* common antibiotic, made from a mould; *some bacteria have developed a resistance to penicillin*

peninsula [pə'nɪnsjulə] *noun* large piece of land which goes out into the sea; *the Malay Peninsula*; *Cornwall is a peninsula jutting out into the Atlantic Ocean*

peninsular [pə'nɪnsjulə] *adjective* referring to a peninsula; **Peninsular Spanish** = Spanish as spoken in Spain, as opposed to the Spanish spoken in South America

penis ['piːnɪs] *noun* male organ used for passing urine and for sexual intercourse (NOTE: plural is **penises**)

penitence ['penɪtəns] *noun* regretting something you have done; *do you think her penitence is truly sincere?*; *as an act of penitence, he offered to pay £1000 to charity*

penitent ['penɪtənt] **1** *adjective* being sorry for having done something wrong; *if you are penitent, God will forgive you* **2** *noun* person who is sorry for having done something wrong; *penitents in white robes walked in procession to the cathedral*

penitentiary [penɪ'tenʃəri] *noun US* prison; *he was sentenced to eight years in the state penitentiary* (NOTE: plural is **penitentiaries**)

penknife ['pennaɪf] *noun* small pocket knife which folds up; *he was peeling an apple with a penknife*; *she cut her name on the table with her penknife* (NOTE: plural is **penknives** ['pennaɪvz])

pennant ['penənt] *noun* long thin triangular flag; *a pennant was flying from the top of the mast*

penniless ['penɪləs] *adjective* with no money; *after paying the legal fees we were left virtually penniless*

penny ['peni] *noun* **(a)** smallest British coin, one hundredth of a pound; *it cost £4.99, so I paid with a five-pound note and got a penny change*; *I came out without my purse and I haven't got a penny on me*; *a cup of tea is cheap - it only costs 50 pence* (NOTE: plural is **pennies** or **pence**; **pennies** is used to refer to several coins, but **pence** refers to the price. In prices, **pence** is always written **p** and often said as [piː] **this book only costs 60p**: say 'sixty p' or 'sixty pence') **(b)** *(informal)* **the penny's dropped** = he's understood at last; *it took ages for the penny to drop*; **to spend a penny** = to go to the toilet; *wait a moment, I want to spend a penny*

penology [piː'nɒlədʒi] *noun* study of punishments in relation to crimes; *modern penology condemns the use of corporal punishment*

pen pal ['pen 'pæl] *noun US (informal)* = PENFRIEND; *I'm writing to a pen pal of mine in Jamaica*

pension ['penʃn] **1** *noun* money paid regularly to someone who has retired from work, to a widow, etc.;

he has a good pension from his firm; *she finds a teacher's pension quite enough to live on*; **old age pension** = money paid regularly by the state to people over a certain age **2** *verb* **to pension someone off** = to make someone stop working and live on a pension; *they pensioned him off at the age of 55*

pensionable ['penʃnəbl] *adjective* referring to the right to have a pension; **pensionable age** = age at which a pension begins to be paid; **pensionable job** = job which gives you the right to have a company pension; *I only found out after I joined that the job was not pensionable*

pensioner ['penʃnə] *noun* person who gets a pension; *we offer special discounts for pensioners*; *he's a pensioner, so he has to be careful with his money*; **old age pensioner (OAP)** = person who has retired and lives on a pension

pensive ['pensɪv] *adjective* thoughtful; *he was in a pensive mood and hardly said a word all day*; *she sat looking pensive*

pensively ['pensɪvli] *adverb* thoughtfully; *she was sitting pensively looking out of the window*

pentagon ['pentəgən] *noun* **(a)** geometrical figure with five sides; *he drew a pentagon on the blackboard* **(b) the Pentagon** = the US Ministry of Defence; *the Pentagon is considering sending more troops to the area* (NOTE: so called because it is in a building with five sides)

pentathlete [pen'tæθliːt] *noun* athlete who competes in a pentathlon; *an Olympic pentathlete*

pentathlon [pen'tæθlən] *noun* athletic competition where competitors have to compete in five different sports; *he won the Olympic pentathlon*

COMMENT: the pentathlon was the main competition in the original Greek Olympic Games. The modern pentathlon includes riding over a 800m course with jumps, fencing, shooting, swimming 300m, and a 4000m cross-country race

penthouse ['penthaus] *noun* flat on the top floor of a high building; *they took a penthouse suite in the hotel for three weeks*; *they live in a penthouse overlooking Central Park*

pent-up ['pentʌp] *adjective* held back by a barrier; *the dam broke, releasing the pent-up waters into the valley*; *when she left school, all her pent-up creative force was suddenly released*; **pent-up emotions** = strong emotions which are repressed

penurious [pɪ'njuəriəs] *adjective (formal)* very poor; *she ekes out a penurious existence cleaning toilets*; *after five penurious years as a student, he was glad to be earning again*

penury ['penjuri] *noun (formal)* **(a)** being extremely poor; *he ended his days living in penury*; *the job offered an escape from penury* **(b)** great lack; *the government is suffering from a penury of new ideas* (NOTE: no plural)

penultimate [pe'nʌltɪmət] *adjective* next to last; *the sun finally came out on the penultimate day of our holiday*

people ['piːpl] **1** *noun* **(a)** men, women or children taken as a group; *there were at least twenty people waiting to see the doctor*; *so many people wanted to see the film that there were queues every night*; *a group of people from our office went to Paris by train* **(b)**

inhabitants of a country; *the people of China are very hard-working*; *government by the people, for the people* **2** *verb* **peopled with** = filled with inhabitants; *the island was peopled with tribes from the mainland*

pep [pep] **1** *noun (informal)* energy, liveliness; *the dancers' performance had plenty of pep*; **pep pill** = drug used to give a feeling of being fit and energetic; *some students take pep pills before going into the examinations*; **pep talk** = talk designed to encourage people to work hard, to win a match, etc.; *the trainer gave the school team a pep talk*; *the coach gave us a pep talk just before play started* **2** *verb (informal)* **to pep someone up** = to make someone livelier and more energetic; *you need a bit of brisk exercise to pep you up*; *the whole team needs pepping up* (NOTE: **pepping - pepped**)

pepper ['pepə] *noun* **(a)** sharp spice used in cooking, made from the seeds of a tropical climbing plant; *add salt and pepper to taste* (NOTE: no plural in this meaning) **(b)** green or red fruit used as a vegetable; *we had stuffed green peppers for lunch* (NOTE: these are called **bell peppers** in American English)

COMMENT: there are basically two types of the spice: black pepper from whole seeds, and white pepper from seeds which have had the outer layer removed. You can buy pepper in the form of seeds or already ground. There is no connection between the spice and the plants which give green and red peppers. Small red peppers are dried and crushed to make red pepper or paprika

peppercorn ['pepəkɔːn] *noun* whole seed which is ground to make pepper

peppermint ['pepəmɪnt] *noun* **(a)** herb which is cultivated to produce an oil used in confectionery, drinks and toothpaste; *I always use peppermint-flavoured toothpaste* **(b)** sweet flavoured with peppermint; *a bag of peppermints*

pepperpot ['pepəpɒt] *noun* little pot for holding pepper; **pepperpot tower** = round tower with a conical pointed roof, rather like a pepperpot, found in medieval castles; *the old castle with its pepperpot towers*

COMMENT: in Britain, pepperpots have several holes at the top, and salt cellars only one. In the USA it is the other way round

peppery ['pepri] *adjective* **(a)** food with a lot of pepper in it; *they served us a hot peppery peasant stew* **(b)** very easily made angry; *that was not the right thing to say to a peppery old naval officer like my father*

per [pɜː] *preposition* **(a)** out of each; **twenty per thousand** = twenty out of every thousand; *there are about six mistakes per thousand words* **(b)** for each; *I can't cycle any faster than fifteen miles per hour*; *potatoes cost 10p per kilo*; *we paid our secretaries £7 per hour*

perambulator [pə'ræmbjuleɪtə] *noun (old)* baby carriage (NOTE: now called a **pram**)

perceive [pə'siːv] *verb* to notice through the senses; to become aware of something; *the changes are so slight that they're almost impossible to perceive with the naked eye*; *I perceived a worsening in his condition during the night*; *some drugs are perceived as being a danger to health*

per cent [pə 'sent] **1** *noun* out of each hundred; **twenty-five per cent (25%)** = one quarter, twenty-five parts out of a total of one hundred; **fifty per cent (50%)** = half, fifty parts out of a total of one hundred; *sixty two per cent (62%) of the people voted*; *eighty per cent (80%) of the cars on the road are less than five years old* **2** *adjective* showing a quantity out of a hundred; *they are proposing a 5% increase in fares* **3** *adverb* **one hundred per cent happy with** = totally satisfied with; *I'm not one hundred percent happy with his work* (NOTE: **per cent** is written % when used with figures: **30%** (say 'thirty per cent')

percentage [pə'sentɪdʒ] *noun* figure shown as a proportion of a hundred; *a low percentage of the population voted*; *what percentage of businesses are likely to be affected?*; **percentage point** = 1 per cent; **half a percentage point** = 0.5 per cent

perceptible [pə'septɪbl] *adjective* which can be noticed by the senses, ie. seen, heard, smelled, etc.; *there was a perceptible change in public feeling*; *his pulse was so weak it was barely perceptible*

perception [pə'sepʃn] *noun* ability to notice or realize; *he doesn't have a very clear perception of what he is supposed to do*

perceptive [pə'septɪv] *adjective* showing that you understand something clearly; *she made some very perceptive comments about the plan*; *it was very perceptive of the inspectors to notice that the waiters had dirty fingernails*

perch [pɜːtʃ] **1** *noun* **(a)** branch or ledge on which a bird can sit; *the parrot flew down from his perch and landed on the back of my chair* (NOTE: plural is **perches**) **(b)** type of small freshwater fish (NOTE: plural is **perch**) **2** *verb* **(a)** *(of bird)* to sit; *the parrot was perched on a high branch* **(b)** *(of person, building)* to be placed high up; *she was sitting perched on a bar stool*; *a castle perched high on the mountainside*

percolate ['pɜːkəleɪt] *verb* to filter through; *it was some time before the news percolated through to the warehouse*; *leave the coffee to percolate for a minute or two*

percolator ['pɜːkəleɪtə] *noun* coffee pot where the water boils up and filters down through the ground coffee

percussion [pə'kʌʃn] *noun* **(a)** **percussion cap** = piece of paper with a small amount of explosive powder which explodes when hit **(b)** **percussion instruments** = musical instruments which are hit, such as drums, triangles, etc.; **the percussion section** *or* **the percussion** = section of an orchestra with percussion instruments; *you have just heard a piece with Rich Nix on piano and Art Daley on percussion*; *the work provides a lot of scope for the percussion section*; *see also* BRASS, STRINGS, WIND

perennial [pə'renɪəl] **1** *adjective* which continues from year to year; *a perennial plant*; *it's a perennial question* **2** *noun* plant which flowers every year without needing to be sown again; *most of the plants in this bed are perennials*; *compare* ANNUAL, BIENNIAL

perfect 1 ['pɜːfɪkt] *adjective* **(a)** which is good in every way; *your coat is a perfect fit*; *don't change anything - the room is perfect as it is* **(b)** ideal; *she's the perfect secretary*; *George would be perfect for the job of salesman*; *I was in a perfect position to see what happened* **(c)** **perfect (tense)** = past tense of a verb which shows that the action has been completed; *in*

English the perfect is formed using the verb 'to have'
2 [pə'fekt] *verb* to make something new and perfect;
*she perfected a process for speeding up the bottling
system*

perfection [pə'fekʃn] *noun* state of being perfect;
perfection is not always easy to achieve; **to perfection**
= perfectly; *he timed his kick to perfection*

perfectionist [pə'fekʃənɪst] *noun* person who
insists that everything has to be perfect; *he's too much
of a perfectionist to leave a job before he's got
everything just right*

perfectly ['pɜːfɪktli] *adverb* very well; *she typed the
letter perfectly*; *it fits you perfectly*; *I'm perfectly
capable of finding my own way home*; *she's perfectly
willing to take the test*

perfidious [pə'fɪdiəs] *adjective* (formal)
treacherous, not loyal; *their perfidious guide had led
them into a trap*

perform [pə'fɔːm] *verb* **(a)** to carry out an action; *she
performed a perfect dive*; *it's the sort of task that can
be performed by any computer* **(b)** to act in public; *the
group will perform at the arena next week*; *the play
will be performed in the village hall*

performance [pə'fɔːməns] *noun* **(a)** how well a
machine works, a sportsman runs, etc.; *we're looking
for ways to improve our performance*; *after last
night's miserable performance I don't think the team
is likely to reach the semi-finals* **(b)** public show; *the
next performance will start at 8 o'clock*; *there are
three performances a day during the summer*

performer [pə'fɔːmə] *noun* person who gives a
public show; *in Covent Garden, street performers
entertain the tourists*

perfume ['pɜːfjuːm] *noun* liquid which smells nice,
and which is put on the skin; *do you like my new
perfume?*

perfumed ['pɜːfjuːmd] *adjective* which has a nice
smell; *a heavily perfumed rose*; *the letter was written
on perfumed notepaper*

perfunctory [pə'fʌnktəri] *adjective* superficial and
rapid; *he gave the letter a perfunctory glance and went
on with his dinner*

perhaps [pə'hæps] *adverb* possibly; *perhaps the
train is late*; *they're late - perhaps the snow's very
deep*; *is it going to be fine? - perhaps not, I can see
clouds over there*

peril ['perəl] *noun* (formal) great danger; *the country
is facing the greatest peril it has ever seen*; **at your
peril** = you risk everything if you do this; *you disregard
your doctor's advice at your peril*; **in peril** = facing a
risk; *the ship was on the rocks and the lives of the crew
were in peril*

perilous ['perɪləs] *adjective* (formal) very
dangerous; *without a helicopter there was no way of
rescuing them from their perilous position*

perilously ['perɪləsli] *adverb* dangerously; *the car
was balanced perilously on the very edge of the cliff*;
she came perilously close to getting fired

perimeter [pə'rɪmɪtə] *noun* outside boundary round
an enclosed area; *the protesters tried to break through
the camp perimeter fence*; *guards were posted all
around the airport perimeter*

period ['pɪəriəd] *noun* **(a)** length of time; *she swam
under water for a short period*; *the offer is open for a

limited period only*; *it was an unhappy period in her
life* **(b)** time during which a lesson is given in school;
we have three periods of English on Thursdays **(c)** US
punctuation mark like a small dot, showing the end of a
sentence or an abbreviation; *when reading, you can
take a breath at a period* (NOTE: British English is **full
stop**) **(d)** *meaning* 'and that's all'; *she doesn't like
German food, period* (NOTE: also used in British English
in this sense) **(e)** bleeding from the uterus which occurs
in a woman each month; *some women experience
abdominal pain during their periods* (NOTE: formally
called **menstruation**)

periodic [pɪəri'ɒdɪk] *adjective* repeated after a regular
period of time; *periodic attacks of an illness*; *we carry
out a periodic review of the financial position*;
periodic table = list of chemical elements arranged in
order of their atomic numbers

COMMENT: the periodic table of the elements
was first described by Mendeleyev in 1860. He
suggested that all elements could be grouped into
a table according to the number of protons in the
nucleus of each element. Hydrogen (the lightest
element, with one proton) is number 1, and
uranium (the heaviest natural element with 92
protons) is number 92. Since the table was
established, further elements have been created
by bombarding a uranium atom with neutrons, so
creating several artificial elements, none of which
exists for more than a fraction of a second. These
elements based on uranium have numbers up to
100, and even more artificial elements have been
created by combining the nuclei of elements such
as lead and nickel

periodical [pɪəri'ɒdɪkl] **1** *adjective* = PERIODIC **2**
noun magazine which appears regularly; *he writes for
several London periodicals*

periodically [pɪəri'ɒdɪkli] *adverb* from time to time;
you need to check the oil level periodically; *it happens
periodically, but not often enough to cause alarm*

peripheral [pə'rɪfərəl] **1** *adjective* minor, not very
important; *the shop is peripheral to our main business*;
*do all these peripheral activities take up too much of
his time?* **2** *noun* **peripherals** = items of hardware, such
as printers, which are attached to and controlled by a
computer

periphery [pə'rɪfəri] *noun* edge, not the centre; *they
are proposing a new housing development on the
southern periphery of the town*; *they operate on the
periphery of the mafia*

periscope ['perɪskəup] *noun* long tube which allows
someone in a submarine under water to look above the
surface of the water; *the captain ordered the periscope
to be raised*

perish ['perɪʃ] *verb* **(a)** (formal) to die; *the ship sank
and twenty-five sailors perished* **(b)** to rot; *the rubber
has perished and the lid isn't airtight any more* **(c)**
(informal) **I'm perished** = I'm cold; **it's perishing in
here** = it's very cold in here **(d)** (informal) **perish the
thought** = this is something I don't want to happen or
don't want to do; *go into work on a Sunday morning -
perish the thought!*

periwinkle ['perɪwɪŋkl] *noun* **(a)** small creeping
plant with blue flowers; *periwinkles had spread all
along the bottom of the fence* **(b)** winkle, small edible
snail which lives in the sea; *a stall selling mussels and
periwinkles*

perjury ['pɜːdʒəri] *noun* crime of telling lies when you have sworn an oath to tell the truth in court; *he's accused of having committed perjury*; *she appeared in court on a charge of perjury or on a perjury charge*

perk [pɜːk] *noun* extra item given by a company to workers in addition to their salaries, such as company cars, private health insurance; *use of the company chalet in Switzerland is one of the perks of the job*; *she gets various perks including a company car*

perk up ['pɜːk 'ʌp] *verb* to become more cheerful or more interested; *he immediately perked up when I suggested we should go out for a drink*

perm [pɜːm] **1** *noun (informal)* (a) curls or a wave put into your hair artificially; *she's had a perm and it's changed her appearance* (b) combination of football teams on a football pools coupon; *selecting these games gives you twenty-four perms* **2** *verb (informal)* (a) to put a wave or curl into someone's hair; *she's had her hair permed* (b) to select several football teams in various combinations on a football pools coupon; *he permed numbers 7, 10, 17, 23 and 28*

permanent ['pɜːmənənt] *adjective* (a) lasting for ever; supposed to last for ever; *he has found a permanent job*; *she is in permanent employment*; *they are living with her parents temporarily - it's not a permanent arrangement* (b) Permanent Secretary = title of the chief civil servant in a government department

permanently ['pɜːmənəntli] *adverb* for ever; always; *the shop seems to be permanently closed*; *you can never speak to him on the phone - he's permanently in meetings*

permeate ['pɜːmieit] *verb (formal)* to filter right through something; *the surface is treated to stop damp from permeating into the wood*; *a smell of fried fish permeated the whole house*

permissible [pə'misəbl] *adjective (formal)* which can be allowed; *the food contains additives above the permissible level*

permission [pə'miʃn] *noun* freedom which you are given to do something; *you need permission from the boss to go into the storeroom*; *he asked the manager's permission to take a day off*

permit 1 ['pɜːmit] *noun* paper which allows you to do something; *you have to have a permit to sell ice cream from a van*; **parking permit** = paper which allows you to park a car **2** [pə'mit] *verb* to allow; *this ticket permits three people to go into the exhibition*; *smoking is not permitted in underground stations* (NOTE: **permitting - permitted**)

permutation [pɜːmjuː'teiʃn] *noun (formal)* grouping of several items together in various combinations; *I've tried all the possible permutations and none of them opens the lock*; *we offer 65 different shades of paint, which allows endless permutations of colour*

pernicious [pə'niʃəs] *adjective (formal)* (a) harmful; *the teachers said the TV programmes were having a pernicious effect on the children* (b) very severe (disease), which may result in death; *she was diagnosed as having pernicious anaemia*

perpendicular [pɜːpən'dikjulə] **1** *adjective* (a) standing stright up, at right angles to a base; *the y-axis is perpendicular to the x-axis* (b) style of late medieval English church architecture, with tall pointed arches and large windows; *there are many Perpendicular churches in East Anglia*; *the nave is Norman and the chancel is Perpendicular* **2** *noun* vertical line which stands a right angles to a base line; *the tower is several degrees out of the perpendicular*

perpetrate ['pɜːpitreit] *verb* to commit a crime; *who perpetrated this act of vandalism?*

perpetrator ['pɜːpitreitə] *noun* person who does something harmful or immoral, especially a person who commits a crime; *our task is to ensure that the perpetrators of this terrible crime are brought to justice*

perpetual [pə'petʃuəl] *adjective* continuous, without any end; *I don't drive in Central London because of the perpetual traffic jams*; *I'm fed up with these perpetual arguments*

perpetually [pə'petʃuəli] *adverb* always; *he's perpetually complaining about having nothing to do*

perpetuate [pə'petʃueit] *verb* to make something continue; *this will merely perpetuate the existing unhappy state of affairs*; *the book has perpetuated the story of the bad treatment of prisoners*

perplex [pə'pleks] *verb* to puzzle, to make someone confused; *the constant changes in the rules perplexed her*; *he was perplexed to see so many staff leaving*; *I'm perplexed by this letter from the bank*

perplexed [pə'plekst] *adjective* puzzled and confused; *the police explained to the perplexed driver that she was driving on the wrong side of the road*

perplexing [pə'pleksiŋ] *adjective* which puzzles; *we found the reaction of the bank manager very perplexing*

persecute ['pɜːsikjuːt] *verb* to treat someone badly on political or religious or racial grounds; *early Christians were persecuted by the Romans*; *she said that her family was being persecuted by the media*

persecution [pɜːsi'kjuːʃn] *noun* bad treatment for political, religious or racial reasons; *the persecution of the early Christians by the Romans*; *victims of government persecution tried to escape across the border*

persevere [pɜːsi'viə] *verb* to persevere with *or* in something = to continue doing something in spite of obstacles; *if you persevere with your exercises you should lose weight*

persist [pə'sist] *verb* to continue to exist; *the fog persisted all day*; **to persist in doing something** = to continue doing something, in spite of obstacles; *he will persist in singing while he works although we've told him many times to stop*; *she persists in refusing to see a doctor*

persistence [pə'sistəns] *noun* refusal to stop doing something; *her persistence paid off when she finally got a refund*

persistent [pə'sistənt] *adjective* continuing to do something, even though people want you to stop; *he can be very persistent if he wants something badly enough*; *she broke down under persistent questioning by the police*

persistently [pə'sistəntli] *adverb* in a persistent way; *she persistently refuses to go and see a doctor*; *the reporters questioned him persistently about the affair*

person ['pɜːsən] *noun* (a) man or woman; *the police say a person or persons entered the house by the* *window*; *his father's a very interesting person*; *the manager was there in person* = he was there himself; **missing person** = someone who has disappeared, and no one knows where he is; *her name is on the police Missing Persons list* **(b)** *(in grammar)* one of three forms of verb or pronoun; **first person singular** = I; **first person plural** = we; **second person singular, second person plural** = you; **third person singular** = he *or* she *or* it; **third person plural** = they

persona [pɜːˈsəʊnə] *noun* a person's character as seen by other people; *his public persona is very different from his character in real life*; **persona non grata** = foreign person, especially a diplomat, who is not acceptable to a government; *he was declared persona non grata and asked to leave the country immediately*

personage [ˈpɜːsənɪdʒ] *noun* important person; *we invited various important personages from the world of arts and entertainment*

personal [ˈpɜːsnəl] *adjective* **(a)** belonging or referring to a particular person or people; *they lost all their personal property in the fire*; **personal best** = best time, speed, etc., which a sportsman has achieved, though not necessarily a record; **personal computer (PC)** = small computer used by a person at home; **personal organizer** = little computer or looseleaf book in which you enter your appointments, addresses, etc.; *I'll put the dates in my personal organizer*; **personal stereo** = small stereo set which you can carry around **(b)** referring to someone's private life in an offensive way; *the attacks on the minister became increasingly personal*

personal assistant (PA) [ˈpɜːsənəl əˈsɪstənt] *noun* person who works as a high-level secretary to an important businessman; *I'll ask my personal assistant to draft an agenda*

personality [pɜːsəˈnælɪti] *noun* **(a)** character; *he has a strange personality*; *she's got lots of personality* = she's a lively and interesting person **(b)** famous person, especially a TV or radio star; *the new supermarket is going to be opened by a famous sporting personality*; **personality cult** = publicity given to a political leader, making him into a kind of god

personalize [ˈpɜːsənəlaɪz] *verb* **(a)** to mark something to show that it belongs to a particular person; *can you think of a way of personalizing the gift?*; **personalized briefcase** = briefcase with the initials of the owner on it; **personalized number plate** = car number plate which spells the name or the initials of the person who owns the car **(b)** to make personal; *the article in the paper personalized the whole affair*

personally [ˈpɜːsnəli] *adverb* **(a)** from your own point of view; *personally, I think you're making a mistake* **(b)** in person; *he is sorry that he can't be here to accept the prize personally* **(c)** **don't take it personally** = don't think it was meant to criticize you

personification [pəsɒnɪfɪˈkeɪʃn] *noun* **(a)** good example of a quality in a person; *for many people she was the personification of youthful innocence*; *little children looked on him as the personification of wickedness* **(b)** *(in a work of art)* representing an abstract thing in the form of a person; *the poet's personification of winter as an old man covered in snow and ice*

personify [pəˈsɒnɪfaɪ] *verb* **(a)** to be a good example of; *he seemed to personify all that was best in American life* **(b)** to use a character in art to represent a quality; *the artist personified the wind as a fat red-faced man, blowing hard*

personnel [pɜːsəˈnel] *noun* staff, the people employed by a company; *we've made some changes to the personnel in the last few weeks*; **personnel manager** = manager who deals with pay, sick leave, administration, etc., for all the staff (NOTE: now often called a **human resources manager**)

perspective [pəˈspektɪv] *noun* **(a)** *(in art)* way of drawing objects or scenes, so that they appear to have depth or distance; *he's got the perspective wrong - that's why the picture looks so odd* **(b)** way of looking at something; *a French politician's perspective on the problem will be completely different from mine*; *she was looking at the situation from the perspective of a parent with two young children*; **to put things in perspective** = to show things in an objective way; *you must put the sales figures in perspective - they look bad, but they're much better than last year*

perspiration [pɜːspəˈreɪʃn] *noun* sweat, drops of liquid which come through your skin when you are hot; *I was bathed in perspiration after my exercises*

perspire [pəˈspaɪə] *verb* to sweat, to produce moisture from the sweat glands; *I started perspiring the moment I stepped outside the front door*

persuade [pəˈsweɪd] *verb* to get someone to do what you want by explaining or asking; *she managed to persuade the bank manager to give her a loan*; *after ten hours of discussion, they persuaded him to leave*

persuading [pəˈsweɪdɪŋ] *noun* action of getting someone to do what you want; *it took a lot of persuading to get her to change her mind*

persuasion [pəˈsweɪʒn] *noun* **(a)** act of persuading; *it took a lot of persuasion on his part to get her to change her mind*; *with a bit of gentle persuasion, he agreed to be chairman* **(b)** firm, usually religious, belief; *people of that persuasion refuse to do military service*; *people of varying political persuasions have signed the petition*

persuasive [pəˈsweɪzɪv] *adjective* which persuades; *they employed some very persuasive arguments to get us to agree to the plan*; *she can be very persuasive when she wants to*

pertain [pəˈteɪn] *verb (formal)* **to pertain to** = to refer to, to relate to; *if you have any information pertaining to this case, you are duty bound to reveal it*

pertinent [ˈpɜːtɪnənt] *adjective (formal)* which is relevant; *here is a list of all the facts that are pertinent to the case*; *she made several pertinent comments on the plan*

pertinently [ˈpɜːtɪnəntli] *adverb* in a pertinent way; *as she pertinently remarked, it takes two to make a quarrel*

perturb [pəˈtɜːb] *verb* to make someone anxious; *scenes of violence on TV perturb me*

perturbed [pəˈtɜːbd] *adjective* made anxious; *she was greatly perturbed at the news*

Peru [pəˈruː] *noun* country in South America, along the Pacific coast; *Lima is the capital of Peru* (NOTE: capital: **Lima**; people: **Peruvians**; language: **Spanish**; currency: **inti**)

Peruvian [pə'ruːvɪən] **1** *adjective* referring to Peru; *they visited ancient temples in the Peruvian mountains* **2** *noun* person from Peru; *the Peruvians are sending a delegation to the conference*

pervade [pə'veɪd] *verb* to spread everywhere; *an air of despondency pervaded the whole company*

pervasive [pə'veɪzɪv] *adjective* found or seen everywhere; *there was a pervasive smell of gas in the house*; *I tried my best to dispel the pervasive mood of pessimism in the office*

perverse [pə'vɜːs] *adjective* continuing to do something even if it is wrong; *it was perverse of her to refuse to see him*; *children have a perverse love of dirt*

perversion [pə'vɜːʃn] *noun* **(a)** behaviour that is considered unnatural and unacceptable; *sexual perversion* **(b)** changing something to make it bad or wrong; *her story is a perversion of the truth*

pervert 1 *noun* ['pɜːvɜːt] person who commits unnatural sexual acts; *a sexual pervert* **2** *verb* [pə'vɜːt] **(a)** to change someone or something to make them wicked; *does pornography pervert the minds of people who read or watch it?* **(b)** to attempt to pervert the course of justice = to try to influence the outcome of a trial by tampering with the evidence, bribing the jurors, etc.; *the officers could be charged with perverting the course of justice*

perverted [pə'vɜːtɪd] *adjective* which has been made bad or wrong; *his perverted mind thought that she was trying to kill him*

pervious ['pɜːvɪəs] *adjective* US *(formal)* which allows radiation or heat to pass through; *a pervious membrane* (NOTE: the opposite **impervious** is used in both British and American English)

peseta [pe'seɪtə] *noun* unit of currency used in Spain; *the book costs 4000ptas*; *I changed my pounds into pesetas* (NOTE: usually written **ptas** when used with a figure: **400ptas**)

peso ['peɪzəʊ] *noun* currency used in Argentina, Bolivia, Chile, Colombia, Cuba, Mexico, the Philippines, Uruguay and other countries

pessimism ['pesɪmɪzm] *noun* state of believing that only bad things will happen; *he sits alone in his bedroom all day, full of pessimism at his prospects of finding another job*; *her pessimism is starting to affect the other members of the team*

pessimist ['pesɪmɪst] *noun* person who thinks only bad things will happen; *pessimists thought the policy was bound to fail*

pessimistic [pesɪ'mɪstɪk] *adjective* believing that only bad things will happen; *his pessimistic attitude is affecting the whole family*; *I'm pessimistic about our chances of success*

pest [pest] *noun* **(a)** troublesome plant, animal, or insect; *many farmers look on rabbits as a pest* **(b)** *(informal)* person who annoys; *that little boy is an absolute pest - he won't stop whistling*

pester ['pestə] *verb* to annoy or bother someone; *beggars sit in the entrances to the Underground, pestering travellers for money*; to pester someone into doing something = to bother someone until they do what you want; *she pestered him into getting his hair cut*

pesticide ['pestɪsaɪd] *noun* poison to kill pests; *you need to spray the apple trees with pesticide*

pestilence ['pestɪləns] *noun* *(formal)* plague, disease; *war and pestilence wiped out half the population*

pestilential [pestɪ'lenʃl] *adjective* *(informal)* very unpleasant; *these flies are a pestilential nuisance*

pet [pet] **1** *noun* **(a)** animal kept in the home to give pleasure; *the family has several pets - two cats, a dog and a hamster* **(b) teacher's pet** = school child who is the favourite of the teacher and so is disliked by the other children **2** *adjective* **(a)** favourite; *the weather is his pet topic of conversation*; **pet name** = special name given to someone you are fond of; *ever since he was a baby he's been called by his pet name 'Bootsie'* **(b)** tame (animal); *you can't keep a pet crocodile in the bath!* **3** *verb* to caress sexually; *couples were petting in the back seats of the cinema*

petal ['petl] *noun* colourful part of a flower; *a bowl of rose petals*; *daffodils have bright yellow petals*

peter out ['piːtə 'aʊt] *verb* to come to an end, to fade away; *the path petered out in the middle of a wood*

petite [pə'tiːt] *adjective* *(of a woman)* small and dainty; *she wished she was petite like her younger sister, not built like an Olympic swimmer*

petition [pə'tɪʃn] **1** *noun* **(a)** official request, often signed by many people; *she wanted me to sign a petition against the building of the new road*; *we went to the town hall to hand the petition to the mayor* **(b)** legal request; *a divorce petition* **2** *verb* to ask someone for something officially, to make an official request; *they petitioned the town council for a new library*; *he petitioned the government to provide a special pension*

petitioner [pə'tɪʃənə] *noun* person who presents a petition; *the person applying for a divorce is known as the petitioner*

petrified ['petrɪfaɪd] *adjective* **(a)** changed to stone; *you can find petrified trees at the bottom of the gorge* **(b)** *(informal)* unable to move because you are afraid; *I thought he was going to shoot me, I was absolutely petrified*

petrify ['petrɪfaɪ] *verb* **(a)** to change something to stone; *a petrifying spring* **(b)** to make someone so afraid that he or she cannot move; *the idea of appearing on stage absolutely petrifies me*

petrochemical [petrəʊ'kemɪkl] *noun* chemical derived from petroleum or natural gas; *petrochemicals have many industrial uses* **2** *adjective* referring to production from petroleum or natural gas; *a petrochemical plant*; **the petrochemical industry** = the industry which processes petroleum or natural gas and produces petrochemicals

petrol ['petrəl] *noun* liquid used as a fuel for engines; *this car doesn't use very much petrol*; *the bus ran out of petrol on the motorway*; *petrol prices are lower at supermarkets*; **petrol pump** = machine which supplies petrol at a petrol station (NOTE: no plural: **some petrol, a litre of petrol** Note also that American English is **gas** or **gasoline**)

petrol bomb ['petrəl 'bɒm] **1** *noun* bomb made of a glass jar containing petrol, with a wick which is lit just before the bomb is thrown **2** *verb* to attack or destroy with a petrol bomb; *the police station was petrol bombed last night*

petroleum [pə'trəʊlɪəm] *noun* raw mineral oil (from the earth); *there are large deposits of petroleum under* the North Sea; **petroleum products** = substances like petrol, plastics, etc., which are made from petroleum

petrol station ['petrəl 'steɪʃn] *noun* place where you can buy petrol for your car; *I'll have to stop at the next petrol station - the tank is almost empty* (NOTE: American English is **gas station**)

petrol tank ['petəl 'tæŋk] *noun* tank in a vehicle where the fuel is stored; *I accidentally put diesel into the petrol tank; the reason your car won't start is that the petrol tank is empty*

petticoat ['petɪkəut] *noun* piece of women's underwear, a light skirt worn under another skirt; *do I need to wear a petticoat with this dress?; the edge of your petticoat is showing*

petty ['peti] *adjective* **(a)** unimportant; *I haven't time to deal with petty points of detail;* **petty cash** = small amounts of cash, in an office **(b) petty officer** = non-commissioned officer in the Royal Navy **(c)** with a narrow point of view; *it was very petty of her to ask for her money back*

petulant ['petjulənt] *adjective* irritable, peevish; *his petulant remarks were quoted in all the daily papers*

pew [pju:] *noun* long wooden seat in a church; *we sat down on an empty pew at the back of the church* (informal) **take a pew** = please sit down

pewter ['pju:tə] *noun* mixture of tin and lead, used for making mugs, plates, etc.; *we drank beer from pewter tankards*

pH [pi:'eɪtʃ] *noun* measure of the concentration of hydrogen ions in a solution, which shows how acid or alkaline it is; *there was a sudden increase in pH; polluted water with a low pH value is more acid and corrosive;* **pH factor** *or* **number** *or* **value** = number which indicates how acid or alkaline a solution is

COMMENT: acidity and alkalinity are measured according to the pH scale. pH7 is neutral; numbers above pH7 show alkalinity, while pH6 and below is acid

phallic ['fælɪk] *adjective* like a phallus; *we all laughed, because the carrot did look incredibly phallic;* **phallic symbol** = thing which resembles a penis, and is taken to symbolize male sex; *the sculpture is obviously supposed to be a phallic symbol*

phallus ['fæləs] *noun* (formal) penis; *the cave drawing represents an erect phallus* (NOTE: plural is **phalluses**)

phantom ['fæntəm] **1** *noun* ghost; *phantoms were supposed to have been seen in the churchyard at dead of night* **2** *adjective* **(a)** not real, ghostly; *she felt a phantom presence standing beside her* **(b)** (humorous) who secretly does annoying or amusing things; *the phantom eater of my biscuits has been at it again*

pharmaceutical [fɑːmə'sjuːtɪkl] *adjective* referring to medicines; *the pharmaceutical industry*

pharmacist ['fɑːməsɪst] *noun* person who prepares and sells medicines; *ask the pharmacist for advice on which suntan lotion to use* (NOTE: also called a **chemist**)

pharmacological [fɑːmək·ə'lɒdʒɪkl] *adjective* referring to pharmacology; *pharmacological research*

pharmacologist [fɑːmə'kɒlədʒɪst] *noun* person who studies pharmacology; *the pharmacologists think the drug will have no side effects*

pharmacology [fɑːmə'kɒlədʒi] *noun* study of drugs and medicines; *modern pharmacology has found several new uses for this plant*

pharmacy ['fɑːməsi] *noun* **(a)** study of medicines; *the six pharmacy students are taking their diploma examinations this year; she's studying pharmacy; he has a diploma in pharmacy* **(b)** shop which makes and sells medicines; *he runs the pharmacy in the High Street* (NOTE: plural in this meaning is **pharmacies**; also called a **chemist's**)

pharynx ['færɪŋks] *noun* passage at the back of the nose leading to the oesophagus; *something seems to have lodged in the pharynx* (NOTE: plural is **pharynxes**)

phase [feɪz] **1** *noun* period or stage in the development of something; *the project is now in its final phase; it's a phase she's going through and hopefully she will grow out of it; I'm sure dyeing his hair green is just a phase;* **critical phase** = important point where things may go wrong; *negotiations have reached a critical phase* **2** *verb* **to phase something in** *or* **to phase something out** = to introduce *or* to remove something gradually; *the new telephone system will be phased in over the next two months*

PhD [pi:eɪtʃ'di:] = DOCTOR OF PHILOSOPHY advanced degree from a university in an arts subject; *she has a PhD in Italian* (NOTE: written after the name: **Alec Smart PhD**)

pheasant ['fezənt] *noun* large brightly-coloured bird with a long tail, shot for sport and food; *she bought a brace of pheasants*

phenomenal [fə'nɒmɪnəl] *adjective* remarkable; *the marrow grew to a phenomenal size; the success of the book has been absolutely phenomenal*

phenomenon [fə'nɒmɪnən] *noun* very remarkable thing which happens; *a strange phenomenon which only occurs at high altitudes; scientists have not yet found an explanation for this phenomenon;* **natural phenomenon** *or* **phenomenon of nature** = remarkable thing which happens naturally; *eruptions of volcanoes are natural phenomena* (NOTE: plural is **phenomena**)

pheromone ['ferəməun] *noun* chemical substance produced and released into the environment by an animal which influences the behaviour of another animal of the same species; *pheromones play a vital part in marking an animal's territory*

phew [fju:] *interjection* showing surprise or relief; *phew, it's hot in here!; phew, that was a narrow escape!*

philanthropist [fɪ'lænθrəpɪst] *noun* person who does good deeds to help people; *the factory owner was a philanthropist who often helped poor people find jobs*

-phile [faɪl] *suffix meaning* 'who likes'; **Francophile** = person who likes the French

philharmonic [fɪlɑː'mɒnɪk] *adjective meaning* 'liking music'; *the Berlin Philharmonic Orchestra* (NOTE: used mainly in the names of orchestras, concert halls, etc.)

Philippines ['fɪlɪpiːnz] *noun* large country made up of several large islands in the Pacific Ocean; *a typhoon struck the central part of the Philippines; see also* FILIPINO (NOTE: capital: **Manila**; people: **Filipinos**; language: **Filipino**; currency: **Philippine peso**)

philistine ['fɪlɪstaɪn] **1** *adjective* not sympathetic to the arts; *the concert of medieval church music was* *wasted on a philistine audience* **2** *noun* person who is not sympathetic to the arts; *he thinks people who don't appreciate modern jazz are simply philistines*

philological [fɪlə'lɒdʒɪkl] *adjective* referring to philology; *we're studying the philological developments that transformed Old English into Middle English*

philologist [fɪ'lɒlədʒɪst] *noun* expert in philology; *Finnish is a language of special interest to philologists because it is different from other European languages*

philology [fɪ'lɒlədʒi] *noun* study of language or of the history of languages; *he knows more about German philology than he does about modern German slang*

philosopher [fɪ'lɒsəfə] *noun* person who studies the meaning of human existence; *as a famous philosopher once said: 'I think, therefore I am'*

philosophical [fɪlə'sɒfɪkl] *adjective* **(a)** thoughtful; calm in the face of problems; *to take a philosophical attitude*; *it's best to be philosophical about it and not get too upset* **(b)** referring to philosophy; *she was involved in a philosophical argument*

philosophically [fɪlə'sɒfɪkli] *adverb* thoughtfully; calmly; *he accepted his defeat philosophically*

philosophy [fɪ'lɒsəfi] *noun* **(a)** study of the meaning of human existence; *he's studying philosophy* **(b)** Doctor of Philosophy (PhD) = advanced degree from a university in an arts subject **(c)** general way of thinking; *my philosophy is that you should treat people as you want them to treat you*

phlegm [flem] *noun* **(a)** mucus, slimy substance in the nose and throat, etc., when you have a cold; *she sneezes a lot and coughs up phlegm from the throat*; *the cough mixture should loosen the phlegm on your chest* **(b)** calmness; *he responded to the latest disaster with traditional British phlegm*

phlegmatic [fleg'mætɪk] *adjective* calm, not flustered; *his phlegmatic reply to the rebels' demands calmed the situation*

-phobe [fəub] *suffix* meaning 'who does not like'; **xenophobe** = person who dislikes foreigners

phobia ['fəubiə] *noun* extreme fear; *he has a phobia about spiders*; *fear of snakes is one of the commonest phobias*

phone [fəun] **1** *noun* telephone, a machine which you use to speak to someone who is some distance away; *if someone rings, can you answer the phone for me?*; *she lifted the phone and called the ambulance*; **by phone** = using the telephone; *to place an order by phone* **2** *verb* to call someone using a telephone; *your wife phoned when you were out*; *can you phone me at ten o'clock tomorrow evening?*; *I need to phone our office in New York*; **to phone for something** = to make a phone call to ask for something; *he phoned for a taxi*; **to phone about something** = to make a phone call to speak about something; *he phoned about the message he had received*

◊ **on the phone** [ɒn ðə 'fəun] **(a)** speaking by telephone; *don't make such a noise - the boss is on the phone*; *she has been on the phone all morning* **(b)** with a telephone in the house; *don't look for their address in the phone book - they're not on the phone*

phone back ['fəun 'bæk] *verb* to reply by telephone; *the manager is out - can you phone back in about fifteen minutes?*

phone book ['fəun buk] *noun* book which gives the names of people and businesses in a town in alphabetical order, with their addresses and phone numbers; *the restaurant must be new - it isn't in the phone book*

phone booth or **phone box** ['fəun bu:θ or bɒks] *noun* small glass shelter in a public place, containing a public telephone; *call me from the phone box outside the station, and I'll come and pick you up*; *there was a queue of people waiting to use the phone box*

phone call ['fəun 'kɔ:l] *noun* telephone call, speaking to someone by telephone; *I had a phone call from an old friend today*; *I need to make a quick phone call before we leave*

phonecard ['fəunkɑ:d] *noun* plastic card which you use in a cardphone; *you can buy phonecards at post offices and newsagents*

phone-in ['fəunɪn] *noun* radio show, where members of the public telephone a speaker to ask questions or put their points of view; *the Prime Minister was on a phone-in answering questions about unemployment* (NOTE: plural is **phone-ins**)

phoneme ['fəuni:m] *noun* single speech sound that makes a word different from other words; *the same letter of the English alphabet can represent different phonemes, for example the two letter 'Cs' in 'circus'*

phone number ['fəun nʌmbə] *noun* number of one particular phone; *what's the phone number of the garage?*; *if I give you my phone number promise you won't forget it*; *his phone number's Birmingham 878 1405*

phonetic [fə'netɪk] *adjective* referring to spoken sounds; **phonetic alphabet** = special series of characters which show phonemes; *the pronunciation is shown using a phonetic alphabet*

phonetician [fəunə'tɪʃn] *noun* person who studies phonetics; *phoneticians made recordings of people speaking the dialect so that they could study its sounds*

phonetics [fə'netɪks] *noun* **(a)** study of the sounds of a language; *every linguist has to take a course in basic phonetics* **(b)** written signs which show how words are pronounced; *each word is followed by its phonetics which show you how the word should be pronounced*

phoney ['fəuni] *(informal)* **1** *adjective* not real, not what it seems to be; *he gave a phoney address in Paris*; *she made a lot of phoney claims in her story in the newspaper* **2** person who is not what he or she seems to be; *he's just an old phoney - he doesn't have any experience of TV reporting at all*

phonograph ['fəunəgrɑ:f] *noun* US gramophone or record-player, a device for playing records; *the phonograph was one of Thomas Edison's most successful inventions*

phony ['fəuni] *see* PHONEY

phosphate ['fɒsfeɪt] *noun* salt of phosphoric acid, which is an essential plant nutrient formed naturally by weathering of rocks, and produced artificially to make fertilizers; *when phosphates used in fertilizers are washed into rivers, they encourage the growth of weeds and algae*

phosphorus ['fɒsfərəs] *noun* poisonous yellow element, which is essential to biological life, being present in bones and nerve tissue; it also burns easily; *phosphorus is used in making safety matches* (NOTE:

photo 563 **pianist**

Chemical element: chemical symbol: **P**; atomic number: 15)

photo ['fəʊtəʊ] *noun* photograph, a picture taken with a camera; *here's a photo of the village in the snow*; *I've brought some holiday photos to show you* (NOTE: plural is **photos**)

photocopier ['fəʊtəʊkɒpiə] *noun* machine which makes photocopies; *I'll just take this down to the photocopier and run off six copies*; *the paper has jammed in the photocopier*; *you can make colour photocopies on a colour photocopier*

photocopy ['fəʊtəʊkɒpi] **1** *noun* copy of a document made by photographing it; *she made six photocopies of the contract* **2** *verb* to copy something and make a print of it; *can you photocopy this letter, please?*

photo-finish ['fəʊtəʊ'fɪnɪʃ] *noun* result of a horse race where two horses finish close together, and a photograph is taken to see who was the winner; *I can't tell who won with any certainty - it was a photo-finish*

Photofit ['fəʊtəʊfɪt] *noun* method of making a picture of a criminal from descriptions given by witnesses, using pieces of photographs of different types of faces; *the police issued an Photofit picture of the rapist*

photograph ['fəʊtəgrɑːf] **1** *noun* picture taken with a camera; *I've found an old black and white photograph of my parents' wedding*; *she's trying to take a photograph of the cat*; *he kept her photograph in his wallet*; *you'll need two passport photographs to get your visa* **2** *verb* to take a picture with a camera; *she was photographing the flowers in the public gardens*

photographer [fə'tɒgrəfə] *noun* person who takes photographs; *the photographer asked us to stand closer together*; *she's a photographer for a local newspaper*

photographic ['fəʊtəʊ'græfɪk] *adjective* **(a)** referring to photography; *photographic paper* **(b)** **photographic memory** = ability to remember things in exact detail, as if you were still seeing them

photography [fə'tɒgrəfi] *noun* taking pictures on sensitive film with a camera; *she bought a camera and took up photography*; *an exhibition of 19th-century photography*; *photography is part of the art and design course*

photon ['fəʊtɒn] *noun* unit of electromagnetic energy

photo opportunity ['fəʊtəʊ ɒpə'tjuːnɪti] *noun* arranged situation where a famous person can be filmed or photographed by journalists; *the minister visited the children's hospital because it provided plenty of photo opportunities*

phrasal verb ['freɪzl 'vɜːb] *noun* type of verb which has two or three parts, usually a verb plus an adverb or preposition, which together have a meaning different from that of the main verb; *a dictionary of phrasal verbs can be very useful*; *'dwell on', 'lift off' and 'put up with' are all phrasal verbs*

phrase [freɪz] *noun* short sentence or group of words; *try to translate the whole phrase, not just one word at a time*; *I'm trying to remember a phrase from 'Hamlet'*; **phrase book** = book of translations of common expressions; *we bought a Japanese phrase book before we went to Japan*; **to coin a phrase** = to say something

which everyone says; *it's a case of 'the pot calling the kettle black', to coin a phrase*

physical ['fɪzɪkl] *adjective* **(a)** referring to matter, energy, etc.; *a lump of lead can't float - it's a physical impossibility*; **physical geography** = study of rocks and earth, etc.; **physical chemistry** = study of chemical substances **(b)** referring to the human body; *the illness is mental rather than physical*; *he has a strong physical attraction for her*; **physical exercise** = exercise of the body; *you should do some physical exercise every day*

physically ['fɪzɪkli] *adverb* **(a)** referring to the body; *she is physically handicapped, but manages to look after herself*; *I find him physically very attractive* **(b)** referring to the laws of nature; *it is physically impossible to get a piano into that little car*

physician [fɪ'zɪʃn] *noun* US (formal) doctor; *consult your physician before taking this medicine*

physicist ['fɪzɪsɪst] *noun* person who studies physics; *an atomic physicist*

physics ['fɪzɪks] *noun* study of matter, energy, etc.; *she teaches physics at the local college*; *it's a law of physics that things fall down to the ground and not up into the sky*

physio ['fɪziəʊ] *noun* (informal) = PHYSIOTHERAPIST; *I have to see the physio once a week*

physiological [fɪziə'lɒdʒɪkl] *adjective* referring to physiology; *researchers are studying the physiological change brought about by the drug*; *I think the cause is physiological rather than psychological*

physiologist [fɪzi'ɒlədʒɪst] *noun* person who studies physiology; *you need a physiologist to explain how hormones work*

physiology [fɪzi'ɒlədʒi] *noun* study of the way in which living things work; *the physiology of the digestive system*

physiotherapist [fɪziə'θerəpɪst] *noun* trained specialist who gives physiotherapy; *a physiotherapist travels with the team to all its matches* (NOTE: often shortened to simply **physio**)

physiotherapy [fɪziəʊ'θerəpi] *noun* treatment for problems with joints, muscles and nerves by exercise, massage, heat treatment, infrared lamps, etc.; *after the operation she needed an extensive course of physiotherapy*

physique [fɪ'ziːk] *noun* shape of a person's body, especially the muscles; *he's trying to improve his physique by exercising daily*

pi (π) [paɪ] *noun* Greek letter used in mathematics to indicated the quantity 3.14159; *you can calculate the circumference of a circle by multiplying the radius by 2π*

COMMENT: the Ancient Greeks calculated that the circumference of a circle was $2\pi r$ (where *r* is the radius) and that the area of a circle is $2\pi r^2$ but they were not able calculate an exact value for π. They knew it was slightly less than $3^{1}/$, In fact, π does not have a finite value, being 3.14159... with a series of figures continuing to infinity

pianist ['piːənɪst] *noun* person who plays the piano; *he had a brilliant career as a concert pianist before becoming a conductor*

piano ['pjænəʊ] *noun* large musical instrument with black and white keys which you press to make music; *she's taking piano lessons*; *she played the piano while her brother sang*; **grand piano** = large horizontal piano; **upright piano** = smaller piano which stands vertically

piazza [pɪ'ætsə] *noun* Italian square, often surrounded by arcades; *we sat in the piazza drinking coffee and planning the rest of the tour*

pic [pɪk] *noun* (*informal*) photograph; *do you want to look at the pics at the party?* (NOTE: the plural is sometimes written **pix**)

pick [pɪk] **1** *noun* (**a**) something which you choose; **take your pick** = choose which one you want; *we've got green, red and blue balloons - just take your pick!* (**b**) a large heavy tool with a curved metal head with a sharp end that you lift up and bring down like an axe; *they started breaking up the concrete path with picks and shovels* (NOTE: also called a **pickaxe**) **2** *verb* (**a**) to choose; *the captain picks the football team*; *she was picked to play the part of Hamlet's mother*; *the Association has picked Paris for its next meeting* (**b**) to take fruit or flowers from plants; *they've picked all the strawberries*; *don't pick the flowers in the public gardens* (**c**) to take away small pieces of something; *she picked the bits of grass off her skirt*; *he was picking his teeth*; **to pick at your food** = to eat little bits as if you have no appetite; *she's a light eater - she just picks at her food* (**d**) **to pick someone's brains** = to ask someone for advice or information; **to pick someone's pocket** = to take something from someone's pocket without them noticing; *I lost my wallet - my pocket was picked!*

pickaxe *US* **pickax** ['pɪkæks] *noun* pick, a large heavy tool with a curved metal head with a sharp end that you lift up and bring down like an axe; *they were carrying crowbars and pickaxes when they were arrested*; *I had to break up the old concrete with a pickaxe*

picker ['pɪkə] *noun* person who picks fruit, flowers, etc.; *he worked as an apple-picker in France during summer vacations*

picket ['pɪkɪt] **1** *noun* (**a**) striking worker who stands at the gate of a factory to try to persuade other workers to not go to work; *the pickets at the main gate tried to stop lorries from entering*; **picket line** = line of pickets; *many non-union workers refused to cross the picket line* (**b**) group of pickets; *they organized a picket of the factory* (**c**) protester, person who stands outside a place to protest against what is going on inside; *pickets stood outside the laboratory* (**d**) pointed stake; *they put a picket fence round the field* **2** *verb* **to picket a factory** = to put pickets at the gate of a factory to try to prevent other workers from going to work; *groups of strikers picketed the factory*

picketing ['pɪkətɪŋ] *noun* action of posting strikers at the entrance of a factory to try to prevent workers going to work; *the government has banned mass picketing*; *picketing is legal so long as it is non-violent*

pickle ['pɪkl] **1** *noun* **pickle(s)** = vegetables preserved in a vinegar sauce, etc.; *a cheese and pickle sandwich*; *do you want some pickle with your pork pie?* **2** *verb* to preserve (vegetables, etc.) in vinegar; *she bought some small onions for pickling*; **pickled beetroot** = beetroot which has been cooked and kept in vinegar

pick-me-up ['pɪkmiʌp] *noun* (*informal*) tonic, medicine or alcohol drunk to make you feel less tired; *I occasionally drink a glass of brandy as a pick-me-up*

pick on ['pɪk 'ɒn] *verb* to choose someone to attack or criticize; *why do you always pick on children who are younger than you?*; *the manager is picking on me all the time*

pick out ['pɪk 'aʊt] *verb* to choose; *he picked out all the best fruit*

pickpocket ['pɪkpɒkɪt] *noun* person who steals things from people's pockets; *'Watch out! Pickpockets are operating in this area!'*

pick up ['pɪk 'ʌp] *verb* (**a**) to lift something up which is lying on the surface of something; *she dropped her handkerchief and he picked it up*; *he bent down to pick up a pound coin which he saw on the pavement* (**b**) to learn something easily without being taught; *she never took any piano lessons, she just picked it up*; *he picked up some German when he was working in Germany* (**c**) to give someone a lift in a vehicle; *the car will pick you up from the hotel*; *can you send a taxi to pick us up at seven o'clock?* (**d**) to meet someone by chance and start a relationship with them; *she's a girl he picked up in a bar* (**e**) to arrest; *he was picked up by the police at the airport*, to get better; *she's been in bed for weeks, but is beginning to pick up*; *business is picking up after the Christmas holiday* (**g**) **to pick up speed** = to go faster; *the truck began to pick up speed as it went down the hill* (**h**) (*informal*) **to pick up the bill** = to pay the bill; *don't worry about the hotel expenses - the company will pick up the bill*

pick-up ['pɪkʌp] *noun* (**a**) light van with an open back; *they loaded all their gear into the back of a pick-up* (**b**) act of collecting someone or something; *the customer pick-up point is behind the store*; *I've got several pick-ups to do before I can go home* (**c**) (*informal*) person who has been picked up; *she wasn't his regular girlfriend - probably just a pick-up*

pick-your-own (PYO) ['pɪkjər'əʊn] *adjective* where fruit or vegetables are gathered by people who then pay for them; *we stopped at a pick-you-own farm to pick some strawberries*

picnic ['pɪknɪk] **1** *noun* meal eaten in the open air; *if it's fine, let's go for a picnic*; *they stopped by a wood, and had a picnic lunch* **2** *verb* to eat a picnic; *people were picnicking on the bank of the river* (NOTE: **picnicking - picnicked**)

picnicker ['pɪknɪkə] *noun* person who goes on a picnic; *the river bank is a favourite spot for picnickers*

pictorial [pɪk'tɔːriəl] *adjective* referring to pictures; *the book is a pictorial history of the life of Sir Francis Drake*; *a unique pictorial record of life in the village during the last century*

picture ['pɪktʃə] **1** *noun* (**a**) drawing, painting, photo, etc.; *she drew a picture of the house*; *the book has pages of pictures of wild animals*; *she cut out the picture of the President from the magazine* (**b**) (*informal*) **to put someone in the picture** = to give someone all the information about a problem; *let me put you in the picture*; **to get the picture** = to understand the problem; *I get the picture - you want me to arrange for him to be disposed of* (**c**) **the pictures** = the cinema; *we went to the pictures twice last week* **2** *verb* to imagine; *it takes quite an effort to picture her in a bikini*

picturesque [pɪktʃə'resk] *adjective (of scenery, houses)* attractive, like in a picture; *the bedroom windows look out onto a picturesque landscape of mountains and waterfalls; they live in the centre of a picturesque village on the Rhine*

pie [paɪ] *noun* **(a)** meat or fruit cooked in a pastry case; *for pudding, there's apple pie and ice cream; if we're going on a picnic, I'll buy a big pork pie (informal)* **to eat humble pie** = to apologize, to say you are sorry for having made a mistake; **pie in the sky** = ideal situation which you can never reach **(b) cottage pie** *or* **shepherd's pie** = minced meat cooked in a dish with potatoes on top; **fisherman's pie** = cooked fish in a dish with potatoes on top

piece [piːs] **1** *noun* **(a)** (small) bit of something; *would you like another piece of cake?; I need two pieces of black cloth; she played a piece of music by Chopin* **(b) to be a piece of cake** = to be very easy; *that test was simple - a piece of cake!* **(c) pieces** = broken bits of something; *the watch came to pieces in my hand; the plate was in pieces on the floor; you will have to take the clock to pieces to mend it* (NOTE: **piece** is often used to show one item of something which has no plural: **equipment: a piece of equipment; stone: a piece of stone; cheese: a piece of cheese; news: a piece of news; advice: a piece of advice**) **2** *verb* **to piece together** = to put things together to form a whole; *the police are trying to piece together the events which took place during the evening of the murder*

piecemeal ['piːsmiːl] *adjective & adverb* separately, done bit by bit; *the work was carried out on a piecemeal basis; they had bought all sorts of paintings piecemeal*

piecework ['piːswɜːk] *noun* work for which you are paid by the amount of work done and not by the hour; *if you're a fast worker you can earn more money on piecework*

pie-chart ['paɪtʃɑːt] *noun* diagram shaped like a circle with slices cut out showing how something is divided up; *the company report was illustrated with graphs and pie-charts; figure three is a pie-chart showing the percentages of people in each category*

pier ['pɪə] *noun* construction built from the shore out into the sea, often with amusements on it; *if you go to Brighton, you must go on the pier; we went for a stroll along the pier; he spent his holiday fishing from the end of the pier* (NOTE: do not confuse with **peer**)

pierce ['pɪəs] *verb* to make a hole in something; *she decided to have her ears pierced; he pierced the metal cap on the jar with the point of a kitchen knife*

piercing ['pɪəsɪŋ] *adjective* **(a)** very loud, shrill; *they suddenly heard a piercing cry; he let out a piercing yell* **(b)** very severe; *you need to shelter from the piercing east wind; they sat huddled together for protection against the piercing cold* **(c)** very intensely; *he looked at her with his piercing blue eyes*

pig [pɪg] *noun* pink or black farm animal with short legs which gives meat (NOTE: fresh meat from a **pig** is called **pork; bacon, gammon** and **ham** are types of smoked or cured meat from a pig)

pigeon ['pɪdʒn] *noun* fat greyish bird which is common in towns; *let's go and feed the pigeons in Trafalgar Square*

pigheaded [pɪg'hedɪd] *adjective (informal)* obstinate, refusing to change your mind; *he's too pigheaded to listen to good advice*

piglet ['pɪglət] *noun* little pig; *there are six little piglets in the pen with the mother pig*

pigment ['pɪgmənt] *noun* substance which colours; *in a case of jaundice, excess bile pigments flow into the blood and make the skin turn yellow*

pigmentation [pɪgmən'teɪʃn] *noun* colouring of the skin; *skin naturally increases its pigmentation in response to sunlight*

pigmy ['pɪgmɪ] *noun see* PYGMY

pigsty US **pigpen** ['pɪgstaɪ *or* 'pɪgpen] *noun* **(a)** little building where a pig is kept (NOTE: also called a **sty**; plural is **pigsties**) **(b)** messy place; **like a pigsty** = dirty and in a mess; *he left his room looking like a pigsty*

pigtail ['pɪgteɪl] *noun* hair twisted into a plait, hanging down at the back of the head; *the little girls had pink ribbons in their pigtails*

pike [paɪk] *noun* **(a)** large ferocious freshwater fish (NOTE: plural is **pike**) **(b)** *(old)* long spear

pikestaff ['paɪkstɑːf] *noun (old)* the long handle of a pike *(informal)* **as plain as a pikestaff** = very obvious; *you must be able to see the answer - it's as plain as a pikestaff!*

pile [paɪl] **1** *noun* **(a)** heap; *look at that pile of washing; the pile of plates crashed onto the floor; the wind blew piles of dead leaves into the road; he was carrying a great pile of books* **(b)** *(informal)* **piles of** = a lot of; *they brought piles of food with them; there's no need to hurry, we've got piles of time* **(c)** thick wooden post, driven into the ground; *they drove piles into the river bank to hold up the wharf* **(d)** soft surface of cloth like velvet; *just feel the pile on these cushions; we have put a thick pile carpet in the sitting room* **2** *verb* **to pile (up)** = to heap up; *all the Christmas presents are piled (up) under the tree; complaints are piling up about the service*

piles [paɪlz] *noun* swollen veins in or near the anus; *if you don't eat enough roughage, you risk getting piles* (NOTE: also called **haemorrhoids**)

pile-up ['paɪlʌp] *noun* crash involving a series of vehicles which have smashed into each other; *there was a massive pile-up on the motorway this morning; he was in a seven-car pile-up*

pilfer ['pɪlfə] *verb* to steal small objects or small amounts of money from the office or shop where you work; *they pilfered stationery from office stores for their personal use*

pilfering ['pɪlfərɪŋ] *noun* stealing small objects or amounts of money; *pilfering by staff goes on in most large companies*

pilgrim ['pɪlgrɪm] *noun* person who goes to visit a holy place; *pilgrims came to Rome from all over the world*; **the Pilgrim Fathers** = emigrants who left England to settle in America in the 1620s

pilgrimage ['pɪlgrɪmɪdʒ] *noun* **(a)** journey to an important religious place for religious reasons; *the church is organizing a pilgrimage to Rome in April; all Muslims should make the pilgrimage to Mecca at least once* **(b)** journey to any important place associated with a person; *many tourists make the pilgrimage to Dickens' house in London*

pill [pɪl] *noun* **(a)** small round tablet of medicine; *take two pills before breakfast* **(b)** *(informal)* **on the pill** = taking a course of contraceptive tablets; *it she's not on the pill, you must use a condom*; *she went on the pill when she was seventeen*

pillage ['pɪlɪdʒ] **1** *noun* plundering, stealing goods, especially done by soldiers; *in the Middle Ages, the country was devastated by bands of English soldiers who lived by pillage* **2** *verb* *(of soldiers)* to plunder, to steal goods from a captured town, etc.; *the invaders pillaged the monastery buildings, then set fire to them*

pillar ['pɪlə] *noun* column which supports part of a building; *the roof is supported by a row of wooden pillars*; *one of the pillars supporting the bridge collapsed*

pillar box ['pɪlə 'bɒks] *noun* round red metal container into which you can post letters; *there's a pillar box at the corner of the street*; *the postman was emptying the pillar box when I came with my letter*; **pillar-box red** = bright red; *she has a pillar-box red coat, so she's easy to see in a crowd*

pillion ['pɪljən] *noun* **pillion (seat)** = rear saddle for a passenger behind the driver of a motorcycle; *he came on his motorbike with his girl-friend on the pillion*; **pillion passenger** = person riding on the pillion seat; *the motorcyclist was badly hurt and his pillion passenger was killed*; **to ride pillion** = to ride on the pillion seat; *she's got a spare crash helmet for anyone who rides pillion*

pillow ['pɪləʊ] *noun* rectangular bag full of soft material which you put your head on in bed; *I like to sleep with two pillows*; *she sat up in bed, propped up on pillows*

pillowcase *or* **pillowslip** ['pɪləʊkeɪs *or* 'pɪləʊslɪp] *noun* cloth bag to cover a pillow with; *the maids change the room and put clean sheets and pillowcases on the beds every night*

pilot ['paɪlət] **1** *noun* **(a)** person who flies a plane; *he's training to be an airline pilot*; *he's a helicopter pilot for an oil company* **(b)** person who guides boats into or out of a harbour; *ships are not allowed into the harbour without a pilot* **(c)** made or used as a test; *a pilot for a new TV series*; **pilot scheme** = small scheme used as a test before starting a full-scale scheme; *he is running a pilot scheme for training unemployed young people* **(d)** **pilot light** = little gas flame, which burns all the time, and which lights the main gas jets automatically when a heater or oven is switched on; *there's a smell of gas in the kitchen - the pilot light has gone out* **2** *verb* **(a)** to guide a boat, aircraft, etc.; *he safely piloted the ship into harbour* **(b)** to guide someone; *he piloted her through a maze of passageways to the meeting room*

pimento [pɪˈmentəʊ] *noun* green or red fruit with a mild spicy taste used as a vegetable; *green olives stuffed with pimento* (NOTE: plural is **pimentos**)

pimp [pɪmp] **1** *noun* man who organizes and makes money from prostitutes; *the pimps are supposed to protect the girls if customers turn nasty* **2** *verb* to work as a pimp; *the police think he has been pimping in the West End*

pimple ['pɪmpl] *noun* small bump on the surface of the skin, containing pus; *you've got a pimple on your chin*

pimply ['pɪmpli] *adjective* covered with pimples; *try this cream for your pimply skin*

pin [pɪn] **1** *noun* **(a)** small thin sharp metal stick with a round head, used for attaching clothes, papers, etc., together; *she fastened the ribbons to her dress with a pin*; **drawing pin** = pin with a large flat head, used for pinning papers; *give me some drawing pins so that I can pin the poster to the door* (NOTE: American English is **thumbtack**); **safety pin** = pin whose point fits into a cover when it is fastened, and so can't hurt you **(b)** *US* **clothes pin** = little wooden clip, used to attach wet clothes to a washing line (NOTE: British English is **clothes peg**) **(c)** **pins and needles** = prickling feeling in your hand or foot after it has been numb for a time; *wait a bit - I've got pins and needles in my foot* **2** *verb* **(a)** to attach with a pin; *she pinned up a notice about the meeting*; *he pinned her photograph on the wall*; *he pinned the calendar to the wall by his desk* **(b)** to trap someone so that they cannot move; *several people were pinned under the fallen roof*; *the car pinned her against the wall* (NOTE: **pinning - pinned**)

pinafore ['pɪnəfɔː] *noun* **(a)** large apron with a bib, worn over a dress; *all the waitresses wear starched white pinafores* **(b)** full dress worn to cover ordinary clothes when working

pincers ['pɪnsəz] *noun* **(a)** **(pair of) pincers** = tool for holding something tight, shaped like scissors; *we pulled the nails out of the wood with pincers* **(b)** claws of a crab or lobster; *a crab can give you a nasty nip with its pincers*

pinch [pɪntʃ] **1** *noun* **(a)** squeezing tightly between finger and thumb; *he gave her arm a pinch* **(b)** **at a pinch** = if really necessary; *at a pinch, we can manage with only one sales assistant*; **to feel the pinch** = to find you have less money than you need; *we really started to feel the pinch when my father lost his job* **(c)** small quantity of something held between finger and thumb; *add a pinch of salt to the boiling water* (NOTE: plural is **pinches**) **2** *verb* **(a)** to squeeze tightly, using the finger and thumb; *Ow! you're pinching me!* **(b)** *(informal)* to steal; *someone's pinched my pen!*

pin down ['pɪn 'daʊn] *verb* **to pin someone down** = to get someone to say what he or she really thinks, to get someone to make his or her mind up; *I'm trying to pin the chairman down to make a decision*; *she's very vague about dates - it's difficult to pin her down*

pine [paɪn] **1** *noun* **(a)** **pine (tree)** = type of evergreen tree with needle-shaped leaves; *they planted a row of pines along the edge of the field* **(b)** wood from a pine tree; *we've bought a pine table for the kitchen*; *the pine cupboards in the children's bedroom* **2** *verb* **to pine for something** = to feel sad because you do not have something any more; *she's pining for her cat*

pineapple ['paɪnæpl] *noun* large sweet tropical fruit, shaped like a large pine cone with stiff prickly leaves on top; *she cut up a pineapple to add to the fruit salad*

pine cone ['paɪn 'kəʊn] *noun* hard case containing the fruit of a pine tree; *you can spray pine cones with gold paint to make Christmas decorations*

ping [pɪŋ] **1** *noun* noise made when a small bell, a glass, etc., is hit; *the glass went ping and cracked*; *there was a ping as a stone hit the windscreen* **2** *verb* to make a ping; *a little bell pings when the oven reaches the right temperature*

ping pong ['pɪŋpɒŋ] *noun* *(informal)* table tennis; *let's have a game of ping pong*; *he was playing ping pong with the children*

pink [pɪŋk] **1** *adjective* **(a)** pale red or flesh colour; *she uses pink paper when she writes to her friends*; **shocking pink** = very bright pink, which seems to glow; *he wore a pair of shocking pink socks* **(b)** *(informal)* **tickled pink** = very much amused; *we were tickled pink to get our first letter from our little granddaughter* **2** *noun* **(a)** pale red colour; *the bright pink of the geraniums shows clearly across the garden* **(b)** scented garden flower like a small carnation; *there was bunch of pinks on the table*

pinkie [ˈpɪŋki] *US noun (informal)* little finger

pin money [ˈpɪn ˈmʌni] *noun (informal)* money earned by a woman for part-time work; *she earns some pin money typing at home*

pinnacle [ˈpɪnəkl] *noun* **(a)** topmost point of someone's career; *by becoming Lord Chief Justice he reached the pinnacle of his legal career* **(b)** topmost point of a pointed rock; *a narrow ridge connected the two pinnacles* **(c)** tall, thin stone spire or tower; *looking down on the domes and pinnacles of the old Italian city*

PIN number [ˈpɪn ˈnʌmbə] *noun* = PERSONAL IDENTIFICATION NUMBER special number which is allocated to the holder of a credit card or cash card; *try to memorize your PIN number*

pinpoint [ˈpɪnpɔɪnt] **1** *noun* **a pinpoint of light** = a tiny spot of light **2** *verb* to indicate exactly; *we can pinpoint the ship's exact position by radar*

pinstripe [ˈpɪnstraɪp] *noun* thin light line on a dark cloth; **pinstripe suit** = suit made of dark cloth with a pinstripe in it; *his father is a company director and always wears pinstripe suits*

pint [paɪnt] *noun* liquid measure (= .568 of a litre); *he drinks a pint of milk a day*; *two pints of bitter, please*

pioneer [paɪəˈnɪə] **1** *noun* **(a)** person who is among the first to try to do something; *he was one of the pioneers of radar*; *the pioneers in the field of laser surgery* **(b)** person who is among the first to explore or settle in a new land; *the first pioneers settled in this valley in about 1860* **2** *verb* to be first to do something; *the company pioneered developments in the field of electronics*; *she pioneered a new route across the Andes*

pioneering [paɪəˈnɪːrɪŋ] *adjective* opening up a new area of activity; *he was awarded the Nobel Prize for his pioneering work in genetics*; *his father was a pioneering aviator in the early years of this century*

pious [ˈpaɪəs] *adjective* **(a)** showing great respect for religion; *a pious benefactor gave the money to build a new church* **(b)** **pious hope** = hope for something that is unlikely to happen; *expecting the children to behave well was something of a pious hope*

pip [pɪp] **1** *noun* **(a)** small seed in some fruits; *take out all the pips when you cut up the grapefruit* (NOTE: apples, pears, oranges, lemons, etc., all have pips) **(b)** short high-pitched call used on radio to show a time signal; *I'm waiting for the pips to set my watch right* **(c)** star on the shoulder showing an officer's rank; *the three pips showed he was a captain* **2** *verb* to beat, to defeat; *she pipped me for first place*; **to pip someone at the post** = to beat someone at the last minute; *he put on a final spurt and pipped me at the post*

pipe [paɪp] *noun* **(a)** tube; *he's clearing a blocked pipe in the kitchen*; *the water came out of the hole in the pipe*; *see also* DRAINPIPE **(b)** tube for smoking tobacco, with a bowl at one end in which the tobacco burns; *he only smokes a pipe, never cigarettes* **(c)** **the pipes** = BAGPIPES; **pipe band** = band of bagpipes

pipeline [ˈpaɪplaɪn] *noun* **(a)** very large tube for carrying oil, natural gas, etc., over long distances; *an oil pipeline crosses the desert* **(b)** **in the pipeline** = being worked on, coming; *the company has a series of new products in the pipeline*; *she has two new novels in the pipeline*

piper [ˈpaɪpə] *noun* person who plays the bagpipes; *a solitary piper played a lament as the funeral procession moved off*

pipette [pɪˈpet] *noun* thin glass measuring tube used in laboratories; *she drew off some of the fluid with a pipette*

piping [ˈpaɪpɪŋ] **1** *noun* **(a)** tubes in general; *the old lead piping was removed and replaced with plastic*; **a piece of piping** = a section of plastic or metal tube **(b)** decoration like tubes on a cake or on a dress; *a scarlet uniform with white piping* **2** *adverb* **piping hot** = extremely hot; *porridge should be served piping hot*

piracy [ˈpaɪrəsi] *noun* **(a)** robbery at sea, when ships are attacked; *piracy is on the increase in the South China Sea* **(b)** illegal copying of books, records, computer programs or patented works; *the government is trying to stamp out video piracy*

pirate [ˈpaɪərət] *noun* **(a)** sailor who attacks and robs ships; *pirates attacked the ship*; *pirates buried treasure on the island hundreds of years ago* **(b)** person who copies a patented invention or a copyright work; **pirate radio** = illegal radio station; **video pirates** = people who organize the copying of videos to make a profit **2** *verb* to copy a book, disk, design, etc., which is copyright; *the designs for the new dress collection were pirated in the Far East*; *I found a pirated copy of my book on sale in a street market*

Pisces [ˈpaɪsiːz] *noun* one of the signs of the zodiac, shaped like fish; *he's (a) Pisces, his birthday is on the first of March*

piss [pɪs] **1** *noun (informal & vulgar)* waste water from the body; **to take the piss** = to make fun of someone; *I thought he was taking the piss, but he was deadly serious* **2** *verb (informal & vulgar)* to pass waste water from the body

pissed [pɪst] *adjective (slang)* **(a)** drunk; *he was too pissed to know what he was doing*; **pissed as a newt** = extremely drunk **(b)** **pissed off** = annoyed; *he's a bit pissed off with all the criticism he's had at the office*

pistachio (nut) [pɪˈstæʃɪəʊ ˈnʌt] *noun* small green tropical nut; **pistachio ice cream** = ice cream flavoured with pistachio, coloured green; *she had pistachio ice cream for dessert* (NOTE: plural is **pistachios**)

pistol [ˈpɪstl] *noun* small gun which is held in the hand; *he pointed a pistol at the cashier*; **starting pistol** = small handgun which you fire to start a race

piston [ˈpɪstn] *noun (in an engine)* metal disc which moves up and down in a cylinder; *if you have a cracked piston we'll have to take the whole engine apart*; **piston rod** = rod which is attached to a piston and which drives other parts of the engine

pit [pɪt] *noun* **(a)** deep, dark hole in the ground; *they dug a pit to bury the rubbish* **(b)** coalmine; *my grandfather spent his whole life working down a pit* **(c)** *US* hard stone inside a fruit; *a date pit*; *see also* PITTED

pitch ['pɪtʃ] **1** *noun* **(a)** ground on which a game is played; *I'll time you, if you run round the football pitch*; *the pitch is too wet to play on*; *he dribbled the ball the whole length of the pitch and scored* (NOTE: plural is **pitches**) **(b)** *(music)* being able to sing or play notes correctly; *he's got perfect pitch* **2** *verb* **(a)** to put up a tent; *they pitched their tent in a field by the beach* **(b)** to throw a ball; *I pitched him a high ball to see if he could catch it* **(c)** *(of boat)* to rock with the front and back going up and down; *the little boat was pitching up and down on the waves* (NOTE: the other movement of a boat, from side to side, is to **roll**)

pitch black *or* **pitch dark** ['pɪtʃ 'blæk *or* 'pɪtʃ 'dɑːk] *adjective* very black; very dark; *we couldn't see anything in the pitch black night*; *give me a torch - it's pitch dark down here*

pitched battle ['pɪtʃt 'bætl] *noun* battle where the opposing sides stand and face each other

pitcher ['pɪtʃə] *noun* **(a)** *especially US* large earthenware jug; *my aunt brought out a pitcher of lemonade* **(b)** person who throws the ball in baseball; *the Dodgers are without their regular pitcher this afternoon*

pitfall ['pɪtfɔːl] *noun* hidden trap, danger; *as a manager, you must tread carefully to avoid any hidden pitfalls*; *I warned you about the pitfalls of trying to make money fast*

pitiable ['pɪtiəbl] *adjective* which deserves pity; *the animals were in a pitiable condition*

pitiful ['pɪtɪful] *adjective* deserving pity; *the poor cat was in a pitiful state*

pitifully ['pɪtɪfuli] *adverb* **(a)** in a pitiful way; *he moaned pitifully and kept asking for water* **(b)** extremely, in a way which is pitiful; *the pension she has to live on is pitifully small*; *her little arms and legs were pitifully thin*

pitiless ['pɪtɪləs] *adjective* **(a)** not showing any pity; *his voice was harsh and pitiless* **(b)** very severe; *the pitiless wind blew across the ice floes*

pitted ['pɪtɪd] *adjective* with the stones removed; *a box of pitted dates*

pity ['pɪti] **1** *noun* **(a)** feeling of sympathy for someone unfortunate; *have you no pity for the homeless?*; **to take pity on someone** = to feel sorry for someone; *at last someone took pity on her and showed her how to work the machine* **(b)** **it's a pity that** = it is sad that; *it's a pity you weren't there to see it*; *it's such a pity that the rain spoiled the picnic*; **it would be a pity to** = it would be unfortunate to; *it would be a pity not to eat all this beautiful food* **2** *verb* to feel sympathy for someone; *I pity his children*

pivot ['pɪvət] *noun* point on which something turns; *this little spike is the pivot on which the compass needle turns*

pivotal ['pɪvətəl] *adjective* central, of great importance; *he played a pivotal role in getting the project off the ground*; *this was undoubtedly the pivotal moment of the whole election campaign*

pivot on ['pɪvət 'ɒn] *verb* **(a)** to turn on a point; *the heavy door pivots on a metal point in the floor* **(b)** to depend on something; *the whole process pivots on the accuracy of the measurements*

pix [pɪks] *see* PIC

pixel ['pɪksəl] *noun* single point on a computer display; *a high resolution screen can display 640 x 450 pixels*

pizza ['piːtsə] *noun* Italian savoury dish, consisting of a flat round piece of dough cooked with tomatoes, onions, etc., on top; *we can pick up a pizza for supper tonight*

placard ['plækɑːd] **1** *noun* **(a)** notice on a large piece of cardboard; *the protesters carried placards bearing anti-government slogans* **(b)** poster, large notice, picture or advertisement stuck on a wall; *placards appeared in shop windows announcing that the circus was coming to town* **2** *verb* to stick posters on; *they placarded every tree and lamppost in the street*

placate [plə'keɪt] *verb* to calm someone, to make someone less angry; *he tried to placate her by offering to pay for the damage*

place [pleɪs] **1** *noun* **(a)** where something is, or where something happens; *here's the place where we saw the cows*; *make sure you put the file back in the right place*; **all over the place** = everywhere; *there were dead leaves lying all over the place* **(b)** home; *would you like to come back to my place for a cup of coffee?* **(c)** seat; *I'm keeping this place for my sister*; *I'm sorry, but this place has been taken*; **to change places with someone** = to take each other's seat; *if you can't see the screen, change places with me* **(d)** space for one person at a table; *please set two places for lunch* **(e)** position (in a race); *the British runners are in the first three places* **(f)** page where you have stopped reading a book; *I left a piece of paper in the book to mark my place*; *I've lost my place and can't remember where I got to* **(g) to take place** = to happen; *the fight took place outside the football ground*; *the film takes place in China* **(h)** name given to a smart street in a town; *they live in Regent Place* **2** *verb* to put; *the waitress placed the teapot on the table*; *please place the envelope in the box*

placebo [plə'siːbəʊ] *noun* tablet which appears to be a drug, but has no medicinal substance in it; *in the test, no one knew for certain which patients were given the drug and which the placebo* (NOTE: plural is **placebos**)

placemat ['pleɪsmæt] *noun* mat which a person's plate is put on; *you'll need a placemat - the dish is very hot*

placement ['pleɪsmənt] *noun* action of finding a job for someone; *the placement service tries to find jobs for all students*

placenta [plə'sentə] *noun* tissue that grows inside the uterus during pregnancy, linking the baby to its mother

COMMENT: the placenta allows an exchange of oxygen and nutrients to be passed from the mother to the foetus through the umbilical cord

place setting ['pleɪs 'setɪŋ] *noun* set of knife, fork and spoon, etc., for one person; *we need an extra place setting - Frank's bringing his girlfriend*

placid ['plæsɪd] *adjective* calm; *luckily, our nanny is a very placid person or she would be driven frantic having to cope with our three little boys*; *the normally placid life of the village was suddenly disrupted by a TV crew*

placidly ['plæsɪdli] *adverb* calmly; *he stood placidly smoking a cigar*

placing ['pleɪsɪŋ] *noun* position of something in a list; *the two teams share top placings in the championship*

plagiarism ['pleɪdʒərɪzm] *noun* copying another person's written work and passing it off as your own

plagiarize ['pleɪdʒəraɪz] *verb* to copy the work of another author and pretend it is your own; *he was accused of having plagiarized a book by an American author*

plague [pleɪg] 1 *noun* (a) fatal infectious disease transmitted by fleas from rats; **to avoid someone like the plague** = to try not to meet someone; *I avoid him like the plague* (b) great quantity of pests; *a plague of ants* 2 *verb* to annoy or to bother someone; *we were plagued with wasps last summer; she keeps plaguing me with silly questions*

plaice [pleɪs] *noun* common flat sea fish; *we ordered plaice and chips* (NOTE: plural is **plaice**)

plaid [plæd] *noun* (a) tartan cloth; *he wore plaid trousers* (b) *(in Scotland)* long piece of tartan cloth; *the highlanders traditionally wore the plaid wrapped around their whole body*

plain [pleɪn] 1 *adjective* (a) easy to understand; *the instructions are written in plain English* (b) obvious; *it's perfectly plain what he wants; we made it plain to them that this was our final offer* (c) simple and uncomplicated; *we put plain wallpaper in the dining room; the outside is decorated with leaves and flowers, but the inside is quite plain*; **plain cover** = envelope without any company name on it (d) not pretty; *his two daughters are rather plain* (e) **plain chocolate** = dark bitter chocolate; **plain flour** = white flour with no baking powder in it (NOTE: do not confuse with **plane**; note: **plainer - plainest**) 2 *noun* flat area of country; *a broad plain bordered by mountains*

plainly ['pleɪnli] *adverb* (a) obviously; *he's plainly bored by the whole business; plainly, the plan is not working* (b) clearly; *it is plainly visible from here; the sounds of a violent argument could be heard plainly from behind the door* (c) in a simple way; *she always dresses very plainly*

plaintiff ['pleɪntɪf] *noun* person who starts a legal action against someone in the civil courts; *she's the plaintiff in a libel action; the court decided in favour of the plaintiff* (NOTE: the other party in an action is the **defendant**)

plaintive ['pleɪntɪv] *adjective (of sounds)* sad and complaining; *the plaintive cries of the gulls by the harbour*

plait [plæt] 1 *noun* three strands of hair, woven into a long rope; *she wears her hair in a plait or in plaits* 2 *verb* to weave hair, etc., to form a plait; *my mother used to plait my hair before I went to school in the morning; they make plaited baskets which they sell to tourists in the market*

plan [plæn] 1 *noun* (a) organized way of doing things; *he made a plan to get up earlier in future; she drew up plans for the village fête;* **according to plan** = in the way it was arranged; *the party went off according to plan* (b) drawing of the way something is arranged; *here are the plans for the kitchen; the fire exits are shown on the plan of the office;* **town plan** *or* **street plan** = map of a town; *can you find London Road on the town plan?* 2 *verb* (a) to arrange how you are going to do something; *she's busy planning her holiday in Greece* (c) to intend to do something; *they are*

planning to move to London next month; we weren't planning to go on holiday this year; I plan to take the 5 o'clock flight to New York (c) to arrange how to build something; *she planned the bathroom herself; a new town is being planned next to the airport* (NOTE: **planning - planned**)

plane [pleɪn] 1 *noun* (a) aircraft, vehicle which flies; *when is the next plane for Glasgow?; how are you getting to Paris? - we're going by plane; don't panic, you've got plenty of time to catch your plane; he was stuck in a traffic jam and missed his plane* (b) tool with a sharp blade for making wood smooth; *he smoothed off the rough edges with a plane* (c) **plane (tree)** = large tree with broad leaves, often grown in towns; *the bark of plane trees comes off in large pieces; many London squares are planted with planes* (NOTE: do not confuse with **plain**) 2 *verb* to make wood smooth with a plane; *he planed the top of the table*

planet ['plænɪt] *noun* (a) one of the bodies which revolve round the sun; *is there life on any of the planets?; Earth is the third planet from the sun* (b) the planet Earth; *an environmental disaster which could affect the whole planet*

COMMENT: the planets in the solar system are (in order of their distance from the Sun): Mercury, Venus, Earth, Mars, Jupiter, Saturn, Uranus, Neptune, and Pluto

planetarium [plænɪ'teərɪəm] *noun* building with a dome, where the stars and planets are shown using lights; *we visited the planetarium with a school party*

planetary ['plænɪtri] *adjective* referring to the planets; **a planetary system** = a number of planets revolving around a star, such as the nine planets which orbit the Sun

plank [plæŋk] *noun* long flat rectangular piece of wood used in building; *hold the plank steady while I saw it in half; the floor of the house is made of pine planks; see also* THICK

plankton ['plæŋktn] *noun* tiny animals and plants which live and drift in the sea, and are the food of large animals; *most whales live mainly on plankton* (NOTE: the word is plural)

planner ['plænə] *noun* (a) person who draws up plans; *the planners made the car park too small;* **town planner** = person who designs the layout of a town (b) **wall planner** = chart which is pinned on a wall, showing days and weeks for the whole year, allowing work to be planned

planning ['plænɪŋ] *noun* making plans; *the trip will need very careful planning; the project is still in the planning stage;* **family planning** = decision by parents on how many children to have; *a family planning clinic; the clinic gives advice on family planning;* **town planning** = designing how a town should develop

planning permission ['plænɪŋ pə'mɪʃn] *noun* official document allowing a person or company to build new buildings on empty land or adapt old ones; *you need planning permission to build an extension to your house*

plant [plɑ:nt] 1 *noun* (a) living thing which grows in the ground and has leaves, a stem and roots; *he planted a row of cabbage plants; sunflower plants grow very tall;* **house plants** *or* **pot plants** = plants which you grow in pots in the house; *will you water my house plants for me while I'm on holiday?;* **plant pot** =

special pot for growing plants in (b) machinery; *investment in buildings and plant accounts for 90% of our setting up costs*; **plant-hire firm** = company which lends large machines (such as cranes and tractors) to building companies (NOTE: no plural in this meaning) (c) large factory; *they are planning to build a car plant near the river* 2 *verb* (a) to put a plant in the ground; *we've planted two pear trees and a peach tree in the garden* (b) to put in a place; *they phoned to say that a bomb had been planted in the High Street*

plantation [plɑːnˈteɪʃn] *noun* (a) area of trees specially planted; *a plantation of pines* (b) tropical estate growing a particular crop; *a coffee plantation*; *a rubber plantation*

planter [ˈplɑːntə] *noun* (a) person in charge of a plantation; *as a young man he went out to Ceylon as a tea planter* (b) decorative container to hold plants in pots; *a set of planters for indoor plants*

plaque [plæk] *noun* (a) flat stone, metal or earthenware plate with an inscription on it; *they put up a plaque to commemorate the soldiers who died*; *the Princess unveiled a plaque commemorating her visit and the opening of the new library*; **blue plaque** = blue plate put on the wall of a building to show that someone famous once lived there (b) deposit which forms on the teeth; *use dental floss every morning to control plaque* (NOTE: no plural in this meaning)

plasma [ˈplæzmə] *noun* yellow watery liquid which makes up the main part of blood; *supplies of plasma for blood transfusions were running low*

plaster [ˈplɑːstə] 1 *noun* (a) mixture of fine sand and lime which is mixed with water and is used for covering the walls of houses; *the flat hasn't been decorated yet and there is still bare plaster in most of the rooms* (b) white paste used to make coverings to hold broken arms and legs in place; *he broke his leg and now has his leg in plaster* (c) **sticking plaster** = adhesive tape used for covering small wounds; *she put a piece of sticking plaster on my cut*; *see also* BANDAID, ELASTOPLAST 2 *verb* (a) to cover with plaster; *they had to take off the old plaster and plaster the walls again* (b) to cover thickly as if with plaster; *she plastered her face with makeup*

plastered [ˈplɑːstəd] *adjective* (a) covered with plaster; *we painted the plastered walls pink* (b) covered with; *after the rugby match he was plastered in mud* (c) *(slang)* drunk; *he got completely plastered at his brother's party*

plastic [ˈplæstɪk] 1 *noun* (a) man-made material used to make many things; *we take plastic plates when we go to the beach*; *the supermarket gives you plastic bags to put your shopping in*; *we cover our garden furniture with plastic sheeting when it rains* (NOTE: no plural: **a bowl made of plastic**) (b) *(informal)* **plastic (money)** = credit cards and charge cards; *I don't have any cash with me, do you take plastic?* 2 *adjective* **plastic surgery** = surgery to repair deformed parts of the body

COMMENT: plastic surgery is used especially to treat accident victims or people who have suffered burns. When surgery is used simply to improve your appearance in some way, it is called cosmetic surgery

Plasticine [ˈplæstɪsiːn] *noun* (trademark for a type of) coloured plastic material like clay, which children

use to make model figures; *the children spent the afternoon making animals out of Plasticine*

plate [pleɪt] 1 *noun* (a) flat round dish for putting food on; *put one pie on each plate*; *pass all the plates down to the end of the table*; **dinner plate** = large plate for serving a main course on; **tea plate** = smaller plate for serving cakes and sandwiches, etc. (b) food which is served on a plate; *they passed round plates of sandwiches*; *she ate two plates of cold meat* (c) flat piece of metal, glass, etc.; *the dentist has a brass plate on his door*; **number plate** = plate (one on the front and one on the back of a car) which shows the number (NOTE: American English is **license plate**) (d) picture in a book; *the book is illustrated with twenty colour plates* (e) objects made of copper with a thin layer of gold or silver put on electrically; *the spoons aren't sterling silver - they're just plate* 2 *verb* to cover a metal object with a thin layer of gold or silver electrically; *the metal cross is plated with gold*

plateau [ˈplætəʊ] *noun* (a) area of high flat land; *the high plateau region of southern Argentina*; *the town lies on a plateau about 2000 feet above sea level* (b) highest point that will be reached; *house prices seem to have reached a plateau* (NOTE: plural is **plateaux** [ˈplætəʊz])

-plated [ˈpeɪtɪd] *suffix* covered with a layer of metal; *a copper-plated saucepan*; *those forks are not silver, just silver-plated*

plateful [ˈpleɪtful] *noun* quantity held by a plate; *he's eaten three platefuls of beans and he's still hungry*

plate glass [ˈpleɪt ˈglɑːs] *noun* glass made in vary large flat sheets, used for windows; **a plate glass window** = a very large window, such as in a shop

platelet [ˈpleɪtlət] *noun* blood cell which helps blood to coagulate

platform [ˈplætfɔːm] *noun* (a) high flat structure by the side of the railway lines at a station, to help passengers get on or off the trains easily; *crowds of people were waiting on the platform*; *the train for Liverpool will leave from platform 10*; *the next train at this platform is the Circle Line to Paddington* (b) high wooden floor for speakers to speak from; *the main speakers sat in a row on the platform* (c) **platform shoes** = shoes with very thick soles; *I can't imagine how she can totter along in those platform shoes* (d) *US* programme of action outlined by a political party at an election; *compare* MANIFESTO

platinum [ˈplætɪnəm] *noun* (a) valuable metal which does not corrode, and is used in jewellery; **platinum disc** = prize given to a singer or pop group when one of their records has sold more than two million copies (NOTE: Chemical element: chemical symbol: Pt; atomic number: 78) (b) **platinum blonde** = woman with silvery blonde hair; *his latest girlfriend was a gorgeous platinum blonde*

platitude [ˈplætɪtjuːd] *noun* remark considered to be uninteresting and ordinary; *he said nothing new in his TV broadcast, just the same old boring platitudes*

platoon [pləˈtuːn] *noun* small group of soldiers commanded by a lieutenant, part of a company; *our platoon was ordered out on patrol*

platter [ˈplætə] *noun* (a) large flat serving plate; *a huge joint of meat was carried in on a platter* (b) large plate of prepared food, arranged in a decorative way; *we ordered a seafood platter*

plausible ['plɔːzɪbl] *adjective* **(a)** which sounds as though it could be correct or true; *he couldn't produce any plausible excuse to explain why he was in the warehouse* **(b)** good at telling lies, although sounding as though you could be right; *he sounds very plausible over the phone*

play [pleɪ] **1** *noun* **(a)** written text which is acted in a theatre or on TV; *did you see the play on TV last night?*; *we went to the National Theatre to see the new play*; *two of Shakespeare's plays are on the list for the English exam* **(b)** taking part in a game; *play will start at 3 o'clock*; **out of play** = not on the field; *the ball was kicked out of play* **(c)** way of amusing yourself; *they watched the children at play*; *all right, you children, it's time for play*; **it's child's play** = it is very easy; *it's child's play if you've got the right tools for the job* **2** *verb* **(a)** to take part in a game; *he plays rugby for the university*; *do you play tennis?* **(b)** *(of a game)* to be held; *the tennis match was played on the Centre Court*; *cricket isn't played in the winter* **(c)** to make music on a musical instrument or to put on a disk; *he can't play the violin very well*; *let me play you my new Bach CD* **(d)** to amuse yourself; *the boys were playing in the garden*; *when you've finished your lesson you can go out to play*; *he doesn't like playing with other children* **(e)** to act the part of a person in a film or play; *Orson Welles played Harry Lime in 'The Third Man'*

play back ['pleɪ 'bæk] *verb* to listen to something which you have just recorded on tape; *he played back the messages left on his answerphone*

Play-doh ['pleɪdəʊ] *noun* (trademark for a type of) coloured plastic material like clay, which children use to make model figures; *the children spent the afternoon making animals out of Play-doh*

player ['pleɪə] *noun* **(a)** person who plays a game; *you only need two players for chess*; *rugby players have to be fit*; *four of the players in the opposing team are ill* **(b)** person who plays a musical instrument; *a famous horn player*

playful ['pleɪfʊl] *adjective* lively and enjoying playing; *a playful kitten*; *he was in playful mood, chasing the children round the garden*

playground ['pleɪgraʊnd] *noun* place, at a school or in a public area, where children can play; *the little girls were playing quietly in a corner of the playground*; **adventure playground** = children's playground with climbing frames, slides, wooden houses, etc.

playgroup ['pleɪgruːp] *noun* group of small children who play together under the supervision of a teacher; *she goes to the playgroup while her mother is at work*

playhouse ['pleɪhaʊs] *noun* **(a)** theatre; *there's a brand new play on at the playhouse* **(b)** model house for children to play in (NOTE: also called a **Wendy house**)

playing cards ['pleɪɪŋ 'kɑːdz] *noun* set of 52 pieces of card with pictures or patterns on them, used for playing various games; *a pack of playing cards*; *US a deck of cards*; *he can do tricks with playing cards*; *see also* CARD

playing field ['pleɪɪŋ 'fiːld] *noun* large field where sports can be played; *two rugby matches can be played at the same time on our playing field*; **level playing field** = situation where all competing groups compete on the same terms and conditions; *we are quite happy to compete in European markets provided we do so on a level playing field*

play off ['pleɪ 'ɒf] *verb* **to play someone off against someone** = to try to benefit by making two people compete against each other; *children try to get what they want by playing their parents off against each other*

playoff ['pleɪɒf] *noun* game to decide the final result, played between two players or teams what have the same score

playpen ['pleɪpen] *noun* type of light wooden or plastic cage in which a baby can be left to play safely; *he keeps throwing his toys out of the playpen*

playroom ['pleɪrʊm] *noun* room in which children can play; *we converted the basement into a playroom for the kids*

plaything ['pleɪθɪŋ] *noun* **(a)** something or someone that a person uses simply for his own pleasure; *luxury yachts are the playthings of the rich* **(b)** *(old)* toy for a child to play with; *I keep all the children's playthings in this cupboard*

playtime ['pleɪtaɪm] *noun* time in school when children can play; *as it was wet, the children had to stay in during playtime*

playwright ['pleɪraɪt] *noun* person who writes plays; *he's a playwright who mainly writes for the television*; *the latest works by modern British playwrights*

Plc [piːel'siː] *abbreviation for* PUBLIC LIMITED COMPANY

plea [pliː] *noun* **(a)** answer to a charge in court; *he entered a plea of 'not guilty'*; **plea bargaining** = arrangement where an accused person pleads guilty to some charges so as to be let off others **(b)** *(formal)* request; *her pleas for clemency were rejected*

plead [pliːd] *verb* **(a)** to answer a charge in a law court; *he pleaded guilty to the charge of murder* **(b)** to give an excuse; *she said she couldn't come, pleading pressure of work* **(c) to plead with someone** = to try to change someone's mind by asking again and again; *I pleaded with her not to go*

pleading ['pliːdɪŋ] **1** *adjective* asking in a emotional or very humble way; *the dog sat next to me with a pleading look in his eyes* **2** *noun* **(a)** action of asking for something in a emotional or very humble way; *he finally gave in to her pleading* **(b)** action of speaking in court on someone's behalf; *in English courts, a solicitor prepares the case and a barrister does the actual pleading*

pleasant ['plezənt] *adjective* which pleases; *what a pleasant garden!*; *how pleasant it is to sit here under the trees!*; *he didn't bring the pleasantest of news* (NOTE: **pleasanter - pleasantest**)

pleasantly ['plezəntli] *adverb* in a pleasant way; *he smiled at me pleasantly*; *I was pleasantly surprised that she had remembered my birthday*

please [pliːz] **1** *interjection* used to ask politely; *can you close the window, please?*; *please sit down*; *can I have a ham sandwich, please?*; *do you want some more tea? - yes, please!*; *compare* THANK YOU **2** *verb* to make someone happy or satisfied; *she's not difficult to please*; **please yourself** = do as you like; *shall I take the red one or the green one? - please yourself*

pleased [pliːzd] *adjective* happy; *we're very pleased with our new house*; *I'm pleased to hear you're feeling better*; *he wasn't pleased when he heard his exam results*; *see also* PUNCH

pleasing ['pliːzɪŋ] *adjective* which pleases; *she's made very pleasing progress this year*; *the whole design of the garden is very pleasing*

pleasurable ['pleʒərəbl] *adjective* pleasant, which gives pleasure; *having to do jury service is hardly a pleasurable experience*; *she worked hard to make their stay a pleasurable one*

pleasure ['pleʒə] *noun* pleasant feeling; *his greatest pleasure is sitting by the river*; *it gives me great pleasure to be able to visit you today*; **with pleasure** = gladly; *I'll do the job with pleasure*; **pleasure cruise** = cruise taken for enjoyment

pleat [pliːt] **1** *noun* fold in a skirt, etc.; *his shirt front was decorated with a row of small pleats* **2** *verb* to make vertical folds in something; *pleating the skirt makes it hang better*

pleated ['pliːtɪd] *adjective (of fabric)* made with pleats; *she wore a dark blue pleated skirt*

plebiscite ['plebɪsɪt] *noun* type of vote, where the whole population of a town, region or country is asked to vote to decide a particular issue; *the province decided by plebiscite to lower the voting age to eighteen*

plectrum ['plektrəm] *noun* small piece of wood, bone, etc., for plucking the strings of a guitar; *he accidentally dropped the plectrum into the guitar* (NOTE: plural is **plectrums** *or* **plectra** ['plektrə])

pledge [pledʒ] **1** *noun* **(a)** object given to a lender when borrowing money, and which will be returned to the borrower when the money is paid back; *any unclaimed pledges will be sold* **(b)** promise; *they made a pledge to meet again next year, same time, same place*; *the government never fulfilled its pledge to cut taxes* **(c)** **to take the pledge** = to swear never to drink alcohol again **2** *verb* **(a)** to promise formally; *she pledged £50 to the charity*; *thousands of people have pledged their support for the scheme* **(b)** to give something as a pledge when borrowing money; *she had to pledge her ring to buy food for the children*

plenary ['pliːnəri] *adjective* complete, covering everything; *a special investigative committee with plenary powers*; **plenary session** = session of a conference where all the delegates meet together; *the working parties reported back at the plenary session the next day*

plentiful ['plentɪfʊl] *adjective* abundant; in large quantities; *she took a plentiful supply of tissues with her*; *apples are plentiful and cheap this year*

plenty ['plenti] *noun* large quantity; *you've got plenty of time to catch the train*; *plenty of people complain about the bus service*; *have you enough bread? - yes, we've got plenty* (NOTE: no plural)

plenum ['pleməm] *noun* meeting at which all members must be present; *a plenum was required for constitutional changes to be discussed*

plethora ['pleθərə] *noun (formal)* **a plethora of** = too many; *there has been a plethora of books about the 'Titanic' following the success of the film*

pliable *or* **pliant** ['plaɪəbl *or* 'plaɪənt] *adjective* **(a)** which can be bent easily; *she has a pair of slippers in soft pliable leather*; *soak the material to make it more pliable* **(b)** who can be easily influenced; *she would prefer someone a bit more pliable as her assistant*; *although he seems quite pliant, he defends his point of view very strongly*

pliers ['plaɪəz] *noun* **(pair of) pliers** = tool shaped like scissors for pinching, pulling, or cutting wire; *I need a pair of pliers to pull out these rusty nails*

plight [plaɪt] **1** *noun* bad state; *you must pity the plight of the people made homeless by the war* **2** *verb (formal)* to promise; **to plight your troth** = to promise faithfully to love and support the person you are marrying

plimsolls ['plɪmsɒlz] *noun* canvas shoes with thin rubber soles, worn when doing gymnastics; *I forgot my plimsolls and had to do gym in my bare feet*

plod [plɒd] *verb* **(a)** to walk slowly and heavily; *the camels plodded across the desert*; *he plodded round the department stores but didn't find anything he wanted* **(b)** to work steadily; *the police plodded slowly through a list of people who had to be interviewed* (NOTE: **plodding - plodded**)

plonk [plɒŋk] **1** *noun (slang)* cheap wine; *I bought a bottle of Spanish plonk from the supermarket* **2** *verb (informal)* to put down; *the waiter just plonked the plates down in front of us and went off*; *a big fat man plonked himself down in the seat next to me and went to sleep*

plot [plɒt] **1** *noun* **(a)** small area of land for building, for growing vegetables, etc.; *they own a plot of land next to the river*; *the plot isn't big enough to build a house on* **(b)** basic story of a book, play, film; *the novel has a complicated plot*; *I won't tell you the plot of the film in case I spoil it for you* **(c)** wicked plan; *they hatched a plot to steal money from the security van* **2** *verb* **(a)** to mark on a map; *we plotted a course to take us to the island* **(b)** to draw a graph; *they plotted the rise in house prices on a graph* **(c)** to draw up a wicked plan; *they plotted to assassinate the Prime Minister* (NOTE: **plotting - plotted**)

plotter ['plɒtə] *noun* person who plots; *the plot was uncovered and the plotters were arrested*

plough *US* **plow** [plaʊ] **1** *noun* **(a)** farm machine for turning over soil; *the plough is pulled by a tractor* **(b)** **snow plough** = machine like a tractor with a large blade in front, used for clearing snow from streets, railway lines, etc.; *the snow ploughs were out all night clearing the main roads* **2** *verb* to turn over the soil; *some farmers still use horses to plough the fields*

ploughman *US* **plowman** ['plaʊmən] *noun* **(a)** farm worker who drives a plough (NOTE: plural is **ploughmen**) **(b)** **ploughman's (lunch)** = bread, cheese and pickles; *I'll have a ploughman's and a pint of beer, please*

plough on *US* **plow on** ['plaʊ 'ɒn] *verb* to continue with something difficult; *in spite of the heckling, the minister ploughed on with his speech*; *it's a difficult job, but we'll just have to plough on until it's finished*

plover ['plʌvə] *noun* type of wader found near the sea or in fields and on moors; *a flock of plovers landed in the field*

plow [plaʊ] *noun & verb US see* PLOUGH

ploy [plɔɪ] *noun* clever trick; *it's just a ploy to get you to spend more money*

pluck [plʌk] **1** *noun (old)* courage; *it took a lot of pluck to leave home and go to Australia* **2** *verb* **(a)** to pull out feathers; *to pluck a chicken*; *ask the butcher to pluck the pheasants for you* **(b)** to pick flowers, etc.; *she plucked an apple from the tree* **(c)** to pull and release the strings of a guitar or other musical instrument, to make a sound; *he was idly plucking the strings of his guitar* **(d) to pluck up courage** = to get ready to face a danger; *he finally plucked up courage and asked to see the boss*

plucky ['plʌki] *adjective* brave; *he's a plucky little boy!* (NOTE: **pluckier - pluckiest**)

plug [plʌg] **1** *noun* **(a)** flat rubber disc which covers the hole for waste water in a bath or sink; *can you call reception and tell them there's no bath plug in the bath; she pulled out the plug and let the dirty water drain away;* **ear plugs** = pieces of soft wax which you put in your ears to stop you hearing loud sounds **(b)** device with pins which go into an electric socket, and allows the electric current to pass through; *the vacuum cleaner is supplied with a plug* **(c)** *(in a car)* **(sparking) plug** = device which passes the electric spark through the petrol vapour; *if the plugs are dirty, the engine won't start; the garage put in a new set of sparking plugs* **(d)** *(informal)* piece of publicity; **to give a plug to a new product** = to publicize a new product; *during the radio interview, she got in a plug for her new film* **2** *verb* **(a)** to block up (a hole); *we plugged the leak in the bathroom; he plugged his ears with cotton wool because he couldn't stand the noise* **(b)** *(informal)* to publicize; *they ran six commercials plugging holidays in Spain; they paid the radio station to plug their new album* (NOTE: **plugging - plugged**)

plug away at ['plʌg ə'wei 'æt] *verb* *(informal)* to work hard doing something; *he plugged away at his exercises and learnt a few words of Arabic every day*

plug in ['plʌg 'in] *verb* to push an electric plug into a socket and so attach a device to the electricity supply; *the computer wasn't plugged in - that's why it wouldn't work*

plum [plʌm] *noun* **(a)** gold, red or purple fruit with a smooth skin and a large stone; *she bought a pound of plums to make a pie* **(b)** plum (tree) = tree which bears this fruit **(c)** *(informal)* **plum job** = important well-paid job; *he's landed a plum job in the BBC* (NOTE: do not confuse with **plumb**)

plumage ['plu:mɪdʒ] *noun* feathers on a bird; *a small bird with light brown plumage* (NOTE: no plural)

plumb [plʌm] **1** *verb* **(a)** to measure the depth of water by using a plumb line; *to plumb the ocean's depths;* **to plumb the depths of something** = to reach the lowest point ; *her mood changes all the time, plumbing the depths of despair one minute and wildly optimistic the next* **(b)** to try to understand something fully; *scientists are still trying to plumb the mysteries of the beginning of the universe* **(c) to plumb (in)** = to attach something to the water pipes in a building; *I can't wash any clothes because the washing machine still hasn't been plumbed in* **2** *noun* **plumb line** = string with a lead weight attached to see how deep water is, or if something is straight; *the plumb line showed that they were in two fathoms of water; they used a plumb line to see if the wall was straight* (NOTE: do not confuse with **plum**) **3** *adverb* **(a)** exactly (in the middle); *he hit the target plumb in the middle* **(b)** *US* completely; *that's plumb crazy; I plumb forgot you were coming*

plumber ['plʌmə] *noun* person who installs or mends water pipes, radiators, etc.; *there's water dripping through the kitchen ceiling, we'll have to call a plumber*

plumbing ['plʌmɪŋ] *noun* system of water pipes in a house; *the plumbing's very old and makes strange noises at night*

plume [plu:m] *noun* **(a)** long feather worn in a hat, etc.; *a hat with ostrich plumes* **(b)** long cloud of smoke from a factory chimney or volcano; *a plume of smoke rose from the burning oil depot*

plummet ['plʌmɪt] *verb* to fall sharply; *share prices plummeted on the news of the devaluation*

plump [plʌmp] **1** *adjective* **(a)** fat and tender; *we had a plump chicken for dinner* **(b)** *(person)* round and fat; *he's easy to spot, he's a short fair-haired boy with a plump red face; is she pregnant or is she just plumper than she was?* (NOTE: **plumper - plumpest**) **2** *verb* **(a) to plump up cushions** = to shake squashed cushions until they are fat again **(b)** *(informal)* **to plump for** = to decide on; *after a lot of thought we've plumped for an orange carpet* **(c)** to drop down heavily; *he plumped himself down on the sofa*

plunder ['plʌndə] **1** *noun* booty, goods stolen, especially in wartime; *the pirates returned from the voyage laden with plunder* (NOTE: no plural) **2** *verb* to steal goods by force, especially in wartime; *many of the exhibits in the museum were plundered from foreign palaces and churches; half the ideas in his book were plundered from a book that came out in 1978*

plunge [plʌndʒ] **1** *noun* **to take the plunge** = to decide suddenly to do something; *I've decided to take the plunge and buy a satellite dish* **2** *verb* **(a)** to throw yourself into water; *he plunged into the river to rescue the little boy* **(b)** to fall sharply; *share prices plunged on the news of the devaluation*

plunger ['plʌndʒə] *noun* **(a)** device which goes up and down in a cylinder; *he pressed the plunger to set off the explosion* **(b)** handle with a soft rubber cup at the end, used for clearing blocked pipes by suction; *he tried to unblock the drain with a plunger*

plural ['plʊrəl] *adjective & noun* *(in grammar)* form of a word showing that there are more than one; *does 'government' take a singular or plural verb?; what's the plural of 'mouse'?; the verb should be in the plural after 'programs'*

plurality [plʊə'ræliti] *noun* **(a)** *US* a larger number of votes than that received by any other candidate in an election; *he received a plurality of the votes cast* **(b)** *(formal)* more than one of something; *we are aiming to contact a plurality of social groups*

plus [plʌs] **1** *preposition* **(a)** added to; *his salary plus commission comes to more than £25,000* (NOTE: in calculations **plus** is usually shown by the sign + : **10 + 4 = 14**: say 'ten plus four equals fourteen') **(b)** more than; **houses valued at £100,000 plus** = houses valued at over £100,000 **2** *adjective* favourable, good and profitable; *being able to drive is certainly a plus factor;* **on the plus side** = this is a favourable point; *the weather wasn't very good, but on the plus side, it didn't actually rain* **3** *noun* **(a) plus (sign)** = sign (+) meaning more than; *she put in a plus instead of a minus* **(b)** *(informal)* favourable sign, a good or favourable point; *it's a definite plus that the hotel has room service*

plush [plʌʃ] **1** *noun* soft cloth for furnishings, with a pile like velvet; *curtains made of red plush* **2** *adjective* *(informal)* luxurious; *the car's got a very plush interior; they always stay at the plushest hotel they can find* (NOTE: **plusher - plushest**)

Pluto ['pluːtəʊ] *noun* the ninth and smallest of the planets in the solar system, and the one which is furthest away from the Sun

plutonium [pluːˈtəʊnɪəm] *noun* radioactive element, also used to produce nuclear power; *they've got enough plutonium to build several atom bombs* (chemical symbol is **Pu**; atomic number: **94**)

ply [plaɪ] **1** *noun* **(a)** one thickness of wood in plywood; *the table top is made of four-ply wood* **(b)** strand of wool made up of a certain number of threads; *three-ply wool* **2** *verb* **(a)** to go backwards and forwards; *the little ferry plies between Birkenhead and Liverpool* **(b) to ply someone with** = to keep giving someone something to eat or drink; *they plied the boys with drink and cigarettes, and then started asking them questions*

plywood ['plaɪwʊd] *noun* sheet of wood made of several thin layers of wood stuck together; *we used plywood for the shelves* (NOTE: no plural)

PM ['piː 'em] *noun* = PRIME MINISTER, POST MORTEM

p.m. *US* **P.M.** ['piː 'em] *adverb* in the afternoon, after midday; *the exhibition is open from 10 a.m. to 5.30 p.m.*; *if you phone New York after 6 p.m. the calls are at a cheaper rate*

pneumatic drill [njuːˈmætɪk 'drɪl] *noun* drill driven by compressed air; *you can't hear yourself speak when that pneumatic drill starts up*

pneumonia [njuːˈməʊnɪə] *noun* illness caused by inflammation of a lung, where the lung becomes filled with fluid; *he developed pneumonia and had to be hospitalized*; *she died of pneumonia*

PO ['piːˈəʊ] = POST OFFICE; **PO Box number** = reference number given for delivering mail to a post office, so as not to give the actual address of the person who will receive it

poach [pəʊtʃ] *verb* **(a)** to cook eggs without their shells, or fish, etc., in gently boiling water; *would you like your eggs boiled or poached?*; *they served lightly poached salmon as a first course* **(b)** to catch game, i.e. animals, birds or fish, illegally on someone else's land; *the gamekeeper suspected that someone was poaching his rabbits* **(c)** to entice a worker to leave his jobs and work for another employer; *they poached our best salesman*

poacher ['pəʊtʃə] *noun* person who catches game illegally; *the poacher had two pheasants hidden inside his coat*

pocket ['pɒkɪt] **1** *noun* **(a)** one of several little bags sewn into the inside of a coat, etc., in which you can keep your money, handkerchief, keys, etc.; *she looked in all her pockets but couldn't find her keys*; *he was leaning against a fence with his hands in his pockets*; **breast pocket** = pocket on the inside of a jacket; **hip pocket** *or* **back pocket** = pocket at the back of a pair of trousers; **pocket calculator** = small calculator which you can put in your pocket; **pocket dictionary** = small dictionary which you can put in your pocket **(b) to be £25 in pocket** = to have made a profit of £25; *when we counted the takings we found we were over £100 in pocket*; **to be out of pocket** = having lost money which you paid personally; **to be £25 out of pocket** = to have lost £25; *the lunch left him £25 out of pocket*; *if you are out of pocket you can always get some cash from the accounts department*; *nobody paid my expenses, so I was £100 out of pocket at the end of the day* **2** *verb* to

put in your pocket, to keep; *at the end of the jumble sale, she pocketed all the money*

pocketbook ['pɒkɪtbʊk] *noun* *US* **(a)** small paperbound book (NOTE: British English is **paperback**) **(b)** small bag which a woman carries to hold her money, pens, handkerchief, etc.; *my pocketbook was stolen and I'm left without any money* (NOTE: British English is **handbag**)

pocket money ['pɒkɪt 'mʌni] *noun* money which parents give to their children each week; *she gets more pocket money than I do*

pockmarked ['pɒkmɑːkt] *adjective* covered with round scars; *his pockmarked face shows he has had smallpox*; *the surface of the moon is pockmarked with craters*

pod [pɒd] *noun* long case in which peas or beans, etc., are formed; *mangetout peas are eaten in their pods*

podium ['pəʊdɪəm] *noun* small raised platform for winning sportsmen, orchestral conductors, etc., to stand on; *the three winners stood on the podium*

poem ['pəʊɪm] *noun* piece of writing, with words carefully chosen to sound attractive and convey themes and emotions, set out in lines usually of a regular length which sometimes end in words which rhyme; *he wrote a long poem about an old sailor*; *the poem about the First World War was set to music by Britten*

poet ['pəʊɪt] *noun* person who writes poems; *Lord Byron, the famous English poet*; *the poet gives a wonderful description of a summer morning*

poetic *or* **poetical** [pəʊˈetɪk or pəʊˈetɪkl] *adjective* referring to poetry; imaginative and rhythmic as in poetry; *she uses wonderfully poetic language to describe her journey to the island*; *what he said sounded so poetic*

poetry ['pəʊɪtri] *noun* poems taken as a type of literature; *reading poetry makes me cry*; *this is a good example of German poetry* (NOTE: no plural)

poignancy ['pɔɪnjənsi] *noun* sadness, conveying a feeling of deep emotion; *the poignancy of the scene where the father arrives to find his son dying*

poignant ['pɔɪnjənt] *adjective* moving, making you sad; *the old photographs are a poignant reminder of how peaceful country life used to be*

poignantly ['pɔɪnjəntli] *adverb* sadly, in a way which makes you sad; *the picture evokes poignantly country life before the First World War*; *her sense of loss is poignantly described in her memoirs*

point [pɔɪnt] **1** *noun* **(a)** sharp end of something long; *the point of my pencil has broken*; *the stick has a very sharp point* **(b) decimal point** = dot used to show the division between whole numbers and parts of numbers in decimals; *to multiply by ten, you simply move the decimal point* (NOTE: three and a half is written: **3.5** (say 'three point five'). Note also that in many other languages, this is a comma) **(c)** particular place; *the path led us for miles through the woods and in the end we came back to the point where we started from*; *we had reached a point 2000m above sea level*; **starting point** = place where something starts **(d)** particular moment in time; *from that point on, things began to change*; *at what point did you decide to resign?*; **at that point** = at that moment; *all the lights went off at that point*; **at this point in time** = at this particular moment; *at this point in time, it is not possible for me to answer reporters' questions*; **on the point of doing something** = just about to do something; *I was on the point of phoning you* **(e)** meaning or reason; *there's no point in asking them to pay - they haven't any money*; *the main point of the meeting is to see how we can continue to run the centre without a grant*; *what's the point of doing the same thing all over again?*; I see your point = I see what you mean; *I see your point, but there are other factors to be considered*; *I can't see the point of doing that* **(f)** score in a game; *their team scored three points*; *in rugby, a try counts as five points* **(g)** temperature; *what's the boiling point of water?* **2** *verb* **(a)** to aim a gun or your finger at something; to show with your finger; *the teacher is pointing at you*; *it's rude to point at people*; *don't point that gun at me - it might go off*; *the guide pointed to the map to show where we were* **(b)** to put mortar between bricks in a completed wall, so as to make the surface smooth; *after the wall was built they pointed it with grey mortar*

point-blank ['pɔɪnt'blæŋk] **1** *adjective* **point-blank range** = at very close range; *he was shot at point-blank range* **2** *adverb* sharply, directly and rudely; *I told him point-blank that his work was no good*

pointed ['pɔɪntɪd] *adjective* **(a)** sharpened to a sharp point; *a pointed stick* **(b)** sharp and critical; *he made some very pointed remarks about the waitress*

pointedly ['pɔɪntɪdli] *adverb* in a pointed way; *he pointedly refused to shake her hand*

pointer ['pɔɪntə] *noun* **(a)** something which points; *the pointer moved quickly around the dial*; *he used a pointer to show us our positions on the wall map* **(b)** piece of advice or information; *she asked her teacher for some pointers to help her with her project* **(c)** dog which is trained to point out game with its nose; *the pointer suddenly stopped, staring at a clump of bushes*

pointless ['pɔɪntləs] *adjective* with no sense; *it's pointless to wait any longer, the last bus must have gone*; *the whole business seems utterly pointless to me*

point of view ['pɔɪnt əv 'vjuː] *noun* particular way of thinking about something; *from our point of view, it's been a great success*; *try to see things from their point of view*

point out ['pɔɪnt 'aut] *verb* **(a)** to show; *the tour guide will point out the main things to see in the town*; *the report points out the mistakes made by the agency over the last few years* **(b)** to give a point of view; *she pointed out that the children in her class were better behaved than in previous years*

point up ['pɔɪnt 'ʌp] *verb* to make something seem very obvious; *it just points up the difference between the two brothers*

poise [pɔɪz] **1** *noun* balance, graceful way of holding your head or of standing upright; *she has the grace and poise of a ballet dancer* **2** *verb* **to be poised to do something** = to be ready to do something; *the army is poised to capture the city*; *the tiger was poised to spring on the antelope*

poison ['pɔɪzn] **1** *noun* substance which kills or makes you ill if it is swallowed or if it gets into the blood; *there's enough poison in this bottle to kill the whole town*; *don't drink that - it's poison* **2** *verb* **(a)** to kill with poison; *she was accused of poisoning her husband* **(b)** to put poison in; *he didn't know the wine was poisoned*; *chemicals from the factory are poisoning the river*

poisoner ['pɔɪznə] *noun* person who murders people by poisoning them; *the trial of the notorious poisoner*

poisoning ['pɔɪznɪŋ] *noun* **(a)** taking poison into your system; **blood poisoning** = condition caused by bacteria in the blood; *wash the wound with disinfectant or you might get blood poisoning*; **food poisoning** = poisoning caused by bacteria in food; *the hotel was closed after an outbreak of food poisoning*; *half the guests at the wedding were ill with food poisoning* **(b)** using poison to kill or harm people; *he was accused of the poisoning of several old ladies*

poisonous ['pɔɪsənəs] *adjective* which can kill or harm with poison; *a poisonous snake*; *these plants are deadly poisonous*

poke [pəuk] **1** *noun* jab with something sharp; *he got a poke in the eye in the street from someone's umbrella* **2** *verb* **(a)** to push with your finger or with a stick; *he poked the pig with his stick* **(b)** **to poke fun at someone** *or* **something** = to laugh at someone; *he poked fun at the Prime Minister*; *she poked fun at his odd hat* **(c)** **to poke about for** = to search for; *she poked about in her desk to see if she could find the papers* **(d)** **to poke out of somewhere** = to come out through a hole, etc.; *a red-faced man poked his head out of the window*; *a red handkerchief was poking out of his pocket*

poker ['pəukə] *noun* **(a)** long metal rod for stirring up a fire; *she stirred the dying fire with the poker* **(b)** card game in which the players gamble on the cards in their hands, at the same time trying to hide their position from other players; *they played poker until 3 o'clock in the morning*; *he won £25 at poker*

poker-faced ['pəukə'feɪst] *adjective* not showing any feeling; *he sat with a poker-faced expression*

Poland ['pəulənd] *noun* large country in Eastern Europe, between Germany and Russia; *Poland is an important agricultural country* (NOTE: capital: **Warsaw**; people: **the Poles**; language: **Polish**; currency: **zloty**)

polar ['pəulə] *adjective* referring to the North Pole or South Pole; *an expedition to the polar region or a polar expedition*; **polar bear** = big white bear found in the Arctic

polarize ['pəuləraɪz] *verb* to divide into two opposite groups; *the court case has polarized the country into two opposing camps: those who think he did it, and those who think he is innocent*

pole [pəul] *noun* **(a)** long wooden or metal rod; **telegraph pole** = pole which holds up a telegraph line; *the telegraph poles which were brought down by the storm have not yet been replaced*; **tent pole** = pole which holds up a tent; *one of the tent poles snapped in the gale* **(b)** one of the points at each end of the earth's axis; **magnetic pole** = one of the two poles which are the centres of the earth's magnetic field; **North Pole** = furthest point at the north of the earth; **South Pole** = furthest point at the south of the earth

Pole [pəul] *noun* person from Poland; *Pope John Paul II is a Pole*

polemic [pə'lemɪk] *noun* (*formal*) **(a)** fierce written or spoken attack; *the book seems to be a polemic against marriage*; *her speech was a polemic against government policies on abortion* **(b)** style of making fierce attacks; *his very effective use of polemic in his speeches*

polemical [pə'lemɪkl] *adjective* controversial, likely to start an argument; *a polemical book about the Vatican*

pole position ['pəʊl pə'zɪʃn] *noun* position of the first car in a race; *he was in pole position at the start of the Grand Prix*

pole star ['pəʊl 'stɑː] *noun* star which appears to be over the North Pole; *at night you know where north is by looking at the pole star*

pole vault ['pəʊl 'vɒlt] *noun* sport where you have to jump over a high bar with the help of a long pole; *he won a silver medal in the pole vault*

police [pə'liːs] **1** *noun* organization which controls traffic, tries to stop crime and tries to catch criminals; *the police are looking for the driver of the car*; *the police emergency number is 999*; *call the police - I've just seen someone drive off in my car*; **military police** = police force which is part of the army; *a military police jeep arrived as the fight between the soldiers and airmen developed into a riot*; **secret police** = part of the police force which spies on people; **traffic police** = branch of the police force dealing with traffic on roads (NOTE: usually takes a plural verb) **2** *verb* to make sure that rules or laws are obeyed; *we need more constables to police the area*; *the problem is how to police the UN resolutions*

police constable ['pliːs 'kʌnstəbl] *noun* ordinary member of the police; *the superintendent was accompanied by a sergeant and three police constables* (NOTE: used as a title, followed by a name: **Police Constable John Smith** *or* **PC John Smith**; usually abbreviated to **PC** and women police constables are abbreviated to **WPC**)

police force ['pliːs 'fɔːs] *noun* group of police in a certain area; *he joined the police force after leaving university*; *the local police force is trying to cope with drug dealers coming from London*

policeman, policewoman ['pliːsmən *or* 'pliːswʊmən] *noun* ordinary member of the police; *three armed policemen went into the building*; *if you don't know the way, ask a policeman* (NOTE: plurals are **policemen, policewomen**)

police officer ['pliːs 'ɒfɪsə] *noun* member of the police force; *I'm a police officer, madam, please get out of the car*; *an off-duty police officer chased the robbers as they tried to escape from the bank*

police state ['pliːs 'steɪt] *noun* country whose government controls the freedom of the people through the police; *these new laws will turn the country into a police state*

police station ['pliːs 'steɪʃn] *noun* building with the offices of a particular local police force; *three men were arrested and taken to the police station*

policy ['pɒlɪsi] *noun* **(a)** decisions on the general way of doing something; *government policy on wages or government wages policy*; *it is not our policy to give details of employees over the phone*; *people voted Labour because they liked their policies* **(b)** insurance **policy** = document which shows the conditions of an insurance contract; **an accident policy** = an insurance contract against accidents; **a comprehensive** *or* **all-in policy** = an insurance which covers all risks; **to take out a policy** = to sign the contract for an insurance and start paying the premiums; *she took out a house insurance policy* (NOTE: plural is **policies**)

policy-making ['pɒlɪsimeɪkɪŋ] **1** *noun* deciding what the policies of a party or government should be; *the committee reports to the Cabinet, but plays no part in actual policy-making* **2** *adjective* which makes policy decisions; *a policy-making committee*

polio ['pəʊlɪəʊ] *(informal)* = POLIOMYELITIS; *she caught polio when she was ten years old*

poliomyelitis [pəʊlɪəʊmaɪə'laɪtɪs] *noun* infection of cells in the spinal cord caused by a virus which attacks the motor neurons and can lead to paralysis; *Dr Salk developed an effective vaccine against poliomyelitis*

polish ['pɒlɪʃ] **1** *noun* substance used to make things shiny; *wash the car thoroughly before you put the polish on*; **floor polish** = wax used to make wooden floors shiny; **furniture polish** = wax used to make furniture shiny; **shoe polish** = wax used to make shoes shiny (NOTE: plural is **polishes**) **2** *verb* to rub something to make it shiny; *he polished his shoes until they shone*

Polish ['pəʊlɪʃ] **1** *adjective* referring to Poland; *the Polish Army joined in the manoeuvres* **2** *noun* language spoken in Poland; *I know three words of Polish*; *you will need an English-Polish phrasebook if you're visiting Warsaw*

polished ['pɒlɪʃt] *adjective* **(a)** shiny; *be careful, that polished floor is very slippery* **(b)** made perfect by practice; *he gave a polished performance as Hamlet* **(c)** very polite, with sophisticated manners; *she's a very polished young lady who has obviously been taught how to speak in public*

polish off ['pɒlɪʃ 'ɒf] *verb* **(a)** to finish off a job quickly; *he polished off his essay in half an hour* **(b)** to eat a meal quickly; *they polished off the scrambled eggs and then asked for baked beans*

polish up ['pɒlɪʃ 'ʌp] *verb* to improve a skill; *she spent a term in Spain polishing up her Spanish*

polite [pə'laɪt] *adjective* respectful, not rude; *sales staff should be polite to customers* (NOTE: **politer - politest**)

politely [pə'laɪtli] *adverb* in a respectful way; *she politely answered the tourists' questions*

political [pə'lɪtɪkl] *adjective* referring to government or to party politics; *I don't want to get involved in a political argument*; *she gave up her political career when she had the children*; **political refugee** = person who has left his country because he is afraid of being persecuted for his political beliefs; *these political refugees are afraid that they will be imprisoned if they go back to their country*

political asylum [pə'lɪtɪkl ə'saɪləm] *noun* the right to stay in another country and be protected by its government because it would be dangerous for you to return to your own country for political reasons; *he asked for political asylum in Britain*

political correctness [pə'lɪtɪkl kə'reknəs] *noun* acting in an exaggerated way to avoid giving offence for racial, sexist or other reasons; *she insisted that all official documents should be checked for political correctness*

political economy [pə'lɪtɪkl i'kɒnəmi] *noun* study of politics and economics and their relationship to each other; *he is taking a course in political economy*

politically correct (PC) [pə'lɪtɪkli kə'rekt] *adjective* done in an exaggerated way to avoid giving offence for racial, sexist or other reasons; *it's not politically correct to say that someone is black*; *what's the politically correct term for a backward child?*

political party [pəˈlɪtɪkl ˈpɑːti] *noun* organized group of people who have the same beliefs about how a country should be governed; *he joined a political party*; *the military government has banned all political parties*; *compare* PARTY POLITICAL

political prisoner [pəˈlɪtɪkl ˈprɪznə] *noun* person kept in prison because he is an opponent of the political party in power; *the group is working for the release of political prisoners all over the world*

political science [pəˈlɪtɪkl ˈsaɪəns] *noun* study of governments and their use of political power; *she has a degree in political science from an American university*

political scientist [pəˈlɪtɪkl ˈsaɪəntɪst] *noun* person who studies political science; *political scientists have studied the voting intentions of a group of 1000 people*

politician [pɒlɪˈtɪʃn] *noun* person who works in politics, especially a Member of Parliament; *politicians from all parties have welcomed the report*; **local politician** = member of a local political party, especially one who is a member of the town council

politicize [pəˈlɪtɪsaɪz] *verb* **(a)** to make someone more aware of politics; *the revolutionaries' first aim was to politicize the mass of the population* **(b)** to deal with something from a party political point of view; *the issue is becoming increasingly politicized*

politics [ˈpɒlɪtɪks] *noun* **(a)** ideas and methods used in governing a country; *see also* PARTY POLITICS **(b)** study of how countries are governed; *he studied politics and economics at university*

poll [pəʊl] **1** *noun* **(a)** vote, voting; *we are still waiting for the results of yesterday's poll*; *a poll of factory workers showed that more than 50% supported the union's demands* **(b)** number of votes cast in an election; *the poll was lower than usual - only 35% of the voters bothered to vote* **(c)** **opinion poll** = asking a sample group of people questions, so as to get the probable opinion of the whole population; *the opinion poll taken before the election did not reflect the final result*; *opinion polls showed that most people preferred butter to margarine* **(d)** **the polls** = places where people vote in an election; *the polls close at 9 o'clock*; **to go to the polls** = to vote in an election; *the people of France go to the polls next Sunday to elect a new President* **2** *verb* **(a)** to get a number of votes in an election; *she polled more than ten thousand votes* **(b)** **to poll a sample of the population** = to ask a sample group of people what they feel about something

pollard [ˈpɒlɑːd] *verb* to cut back the branches of a tree every year at a height of about two metres from the ground; *a wood of pollarded oaks*; *compare* COPPICE

pollen [ˈpɒlən] *noun* usually yellow powder on the stamens of a flower which fertilizes a female flower; *bees carry pollen from one flower to the next*; **pollen count** = number showing the amount of pollen in the air, which can cause hayfever; *it's going to rain tomorrow, so the pollen count should be low*

polling [ˈpəʊlɪŋ] *noun* voting in elections; *polling started at 8.00 in the morning*; **polling booth** = small compartment in which each voter goes alone to write his or her vote; **polling day** = day when an election is held; **polling station** = place where you vote in an election

> COMMENT: polling stations are usually in public buildings, such as a library or school

pollster [ˈpəʊlstə] *noun* (*informal*) expert in understanding what polls mean; *the pollsters are predicting a Labour victory*

poll tax [ˈpəʊl ˈtæks] *noun* tax which is levied equally on each person in a population; *a poll tax is unfair because poor people pay as much as the rich*

pollutant [pəˈluːtənt] *noun* substance which pollutes; *pollutants from the factory have drained into the river*; **air pollutant** *or* **atmospheric pollutant** = substance which pollutes the air and the atmosphere, such as gas or smoke

pollute [pəˈluːt] *verb* to make the environment dirty by discharging harmful substances into it; *the company was fined for polluting the lake with chemicals*

polluted [pəˈluːtɪd] *adjective* made dirty; *the river is so polluted that all the fish have died*; *what can we do to clean up our polluted beaches?*; *polluted soil must be removed and buried before houses can be built on the site*

pollution [pəˈluːʃn] *noun* **(a)** action of making the environment dirty; *pollution of the atmosphere has increased over the last 50 years* **(b)** dirty or harmful materials that are put into the environment; *it took six months to clean up the oil pollution on the beaches*; *the pollution in the centre of town is so bad that people have started wearing face masks*; **air pollution** *or* **atmospheric pollution** = dirt and gas in the air; **noise pollution** = spoiling people's enjoyment of the outdoors by making a lot of noise

polo [ˈpəʊləʊ] *noun* **(a)** ball game in which the two teams ride on ponies, trying to hit a small hard ball with clubs like long hammers; *there's a polo match in the park this afternoon*; *he plays polo every Saturday*; **water polo** = ball game played by two teams in the water, who try to throw a ball into a goal **(b)** **polo neck (pullover)** = pullover with a high rolled neck; *it's silly to wear a tie under a polo neck pullover*

polyester [pɒlɪˈestə] *noun* type of synthetic fibre used especially to make clothing; *he bought two polyester shirts in the sale*; *the dress is made of a mixture of cotton and polyester*

polygamous [pəˈlɪɡəməs] *adjective* referring to polygamy; **a polygamous society** = social group where the men are allowed to have more than one wife at a time

polygamy [pəˈlɪɡəmi] *noun* custom of having several wives at the same time; *the Mormons used to practice polygamy*; *compare* BIGAMY, MONOGAMY

polyglot [ˈpɒlɪɡlɒt] **1** *adjective* speaking or writing several languages; written in several languages; *our polyglot guide had to translate everything into three or four languages* **2** *noun* person who speaks several languages; *it's useful to have a polyglot on the staff*

polymer [ˈpɒlɪmə] *noun* natural or artificial chemical compound whose large molecules are made of smaller molecules combined in repeated groups; *a great many modern plastics are based on polymers*

polysyllabic [pɒlɪsɪˈlæbɪk] *adjective* with several syllables; *in polysyllabic words like 'interdepartmental' the stress does not always fall on the first syllable*

polysyllable [ˈpɒlɪsɪləbl] *noun* word with several syllables; *his dissertation on agricultural practices was riddled with polysyllables*

polytechnic [pɒlɪˈteknɪk] *noun* educational establishment for school-leavers, giving degrees, especially in technical subjects; *he's taking an engineering course at the local polytechnic*

COMMENT: most British polytechnics have converted to universities; there are still polytechnics in many other countries

polythene [ˈpɒlɪθiːn] *noun* type of strong transparent plastic used in thin sheets; *pack the sandwiches in a polythene bag*; *cover the carpet with polythene sheeting before you start to paint the ceiling*

polyunsaturated [pɒlɪʌnˈsætjʊreɪtɪd] *adjective* which is capable of absorbing more hydrogen; **polyunsaturated fat** = fat which is less likely to be converted into cholesterol in the body; *vegetable oils and fish oils are polyunsaturated*

Pom *or* **Pommie** [ˈpɒm *or* ˈpɒmi] *noun (Australian slang)* English person; **whingeing Poms** = English people who go to live in Australia and then complain about life there

pomegranate [ˈpɒmɪgrænɪt] *noun* tropical fruit with many black seeds covered in juicy red flesh; *pomegranate juice stains badly*

pomp [pɒmp] *noun* splendid ceremony; *he was greeted with all the pomp due to a visiting head of state* (NOTE: no plural)

pomposity [pɒmˈpɒsɪti] *noun* being pompous; *I can't stand his arrogance and pomposity*

pompous [ˈpɒmpəs] *adjective* using very dignified language to make yourself sound more important; *when he talks to us about morality he always ends up sounding pompous*

pond [pɒnd] *noun* small lake; *there's a duck pond in the middle of the village*; *children sail their boats on the pond in the park*

ponder [ˈpɒndə] *verb* to think deeply; *let me ponder over the problem and I'll try and give you an answer tomorrow*

ponderous [ˈpɒndərəs] *adjective* (a) very heavy and slow-moving; *she walked with ponderous steps across the stage*; *he imitated the ponderous way of walking of a Japanese wrestler* (b) heavy and dull (style); *the piece is supposed to be brisk and light-hearted and this CD makes it sound ponderous and slow*

pong [pɒŋ] *(slang)* 1 *noun* unpleasant smell; *what's that terrible pong in here?* 2 *verb* to make an unpleasant smell; *this cheese doesn't half pong!*

pontoon [pɒnˈtuːn] *noun* (a) boat used to support a floating temporary bridge; *one of the pontoons broke loose and floated downstream*; **pontoon bridge** = bridge built on pontoons; *the engineers built a pontoon bridge across the river* (b) card game, the object being to get a combination of cards totalling twenty-one; *when it was too wet to go out, we played endless games of pontoon*

pony [ˈpəʊni] *noun* small horse; *my best friend lets me ride her pony sometimes* (NOTE: plural is **ponies**)

ponytail [ˈpəʊniteɪl] *noun* hairstyle where your hair is tied at the back and falls loosely; *she usually wears her hair in a ponytail*

poo [puː] *noun (children's slang)* faeces, solid waste matter passed from the body; *there's a pile of dog's poo*

on the pavement; *Mum, the cat's done a poo on the carpet!*; *I want to do a poo*

poodle [ˈpuːdl] *noun* type of curly-haired dog, with its fur usually cut in a curious way; *she's taking her poodle to be clipped*

pool [puːl] 1 *noun* (a) small lake; *he dived in and swam across the pool* (b) (swimming) **pool** = large bath of water for swimming in; *we have a little swimming pool in the garden*; *he swam two lengths of the pool*; **an indoor pool** = swimming pool inside a building; *our school has an indoor swimming pool*; **an outdoor pool** = swimming pool in the open air; **a heated pool** = pool where the water is kept warm (c) group where people share facilities; *we belong to a pool of people who baby-sit for one another*; **car pool** = arrangement where several people share cars; **typing pool** = group of typists working for several departments (d) unused supply; *we can draw on a pool of unemployed talent* (e) **football pools** = system of gambling where you bet on the results of football matches; *she won £1500 on the pools* (f) game rather like snooker, where you hit balls into pockets using a cue; *we were playing pool in the bar* 2 *verb* **to pool resources** = to group resources together; *the only way we can afford it will be to pool our resources*

poolroom [ˈpuːlruːm] *noun* public room where you can play pool; *the poolroom is a favourite meeting place for out-of-work young men*

poor [pɔː] *adjective* (a) with little or no money; *the family is very poor now that the father has no work*; *the poorer students find it difficult to get through university without grants*; *this is one of the poorest countries in Africa* (b) **poor in** = with very little of something; *the soil in my garden is very poor in nutrients* (c) not very good; *vines can grow even in poor soil*; *they were selling off poor quality vegetables at a cheap price*; *she's been in poor health for some months* (d) (showing you are sorry) *poor old you!* - *having to stay at home and finish your homework while we go to the pictures*; *my poor legs - after climbing up the mountain!* (NOTE: **poorer - poorest**)

poorly [ˈpɔːli] 1 *adverb* in quite a bad way; *the offices are poorly laid out*; *the job is very poorly paid*; **poorly-paid staff** = staff with low wages 2 *adjective* ill; *she felt quite poorly and had to go home*

pop [pɒp] 1 *noun* (a) noise like a cork coming out of a bottle; *there was a pop as she lit the gas*; **to go pop** = to make a noise like a cork; *the car engine went pop and we stopped suddenly*; *the balloon landed on the candles and went pop* (b) (informal) **pop (music)** = modern popular music; *she prefers jazz to pop*; *he spends all day listening to pop records*; *we went to a pop concert last night*; **pop chart** = list showing the most popular songs at a certain time; *the record is at number ten in the pop charts*; **pop group** = group of singers and musicians who play pop songs; *he was lead singer in a 1980s pop group* (c) (informal) fizzy drink; *a bottle of pop* (d) *US* (informal) name for a father; *I'll ask my Pop if we can borrow his ladder* 2 *verb* (a) to make a noise like 'pop'; *champagne corks were popping as the result was announced* (b) (informal) to go quickly; *I'll just pop down to the town*; *he popped into the chemist's*; *I'm just popping round to Jane's*; *I'd only popped out for a moment* (c) to put quickly; *pop the pie in the microwave for three minutes* (NOTE: **popping - popped**)

popcorn ['pɒpkɔːn] *noun* corn seed which is heated (sometimes with sugar) until it bursts, eaten as a snack; *we always buy a carton of popcorn when we go to the cinema*

Pope [pəʊp] *noun* the head of the Roman Catholic Church; *the Pope said mass in a stadium before 50,000 people*; *security was very tight for the Pope's visit*

poplar ['pɒplə] *noun* common tall and slender tree; *a road lined on each side with poplars*

poplin ['pɒplɪn] *noun* strong cotton cloth used for making shirts; *a pale blue poplin shirt*

popper ['pɒpə] *noun* (*informal*) little metal fastener for clothes, in two parts which you press to attach together; *this anorak fastens with poppers* (NOTE: American English is **snap**)

poppy ['pɒpi] *noun* common red wild flower which often grows in fields; *she picked a bunch of poppies on her way home through the fields* (NOTE: plural is **poppies**)

Poppy Day ['pɒpi 'deɪ] *noun* (*informal*) November 11th, or the nearest Sunday, celebrating the end of the First World War and remembering the dead of both World Wars; *we all bought poppies for Poppy Day* (NOTE: formally called **Remembrance Day** or **Armistice Day**)

COMMENT: during the ceremonies marking Remembrance Day, wreaths of red poppies are laid at war memorials, and many people wear poppies in their buttonholes. The tradition of associating poppies with the Armistice goes back to the First World War, when soldiers remembered seeing the red poppies flowering in the battlefields. See also the comment at REMEMBRANCE

Popsicle ['pɒpsɪkl] *noun* US (trademark for a) mixture of water and flavouring, frozen until solid with a stick in it; *I keep some Popsicles in the freezer for the kids* (NOTE: British English is **ice lolly**)

populace ['pɒpjʊləs] *noun* (*formal*) **the populace =** the ordinary people; *the rest of the populace envied the privileges of the rich*

popular ['pɒpjʊlə] *adjective* (**a**) liked by a lot of people; *the department store is popular with young mothers*; *the South Coast is the most popular area for holidays* (**b**) referring to the mass of ordinary people; *he was elected by popular vote*; *it is a popular belief that it is unlucky to walk under a ladder*

popularity [pɒpjʊ'lærɪti] *noun* being liked by a lot of people; *the scandal doesn't seem to have affected the President's popularity*; *science-fiction films are enjoying renewed popularity*

popularize ['pɒpjʊləraɪz] *verb* to make something understood or liked by a lot of people; *television has helped to popularize the sport*

popularly ['pɒpjʊləli] *adverb* (**a**) by most people; *she was popularly supposed to possess magic powers* (**b**) by the ordinary people; *the plant popularly known as 'old man's beard' is in fact wild clematis*

populate ['pɒpjʊleɪt] *verb* (**a**) to go and live in an area; *settlers moved away from the coast and began to populate the interior* (**b**) to put people to live in an area; *the king decided to populate the colony with retired soldiers*

populated ['pɒpjʊleɪtɪd] *adjective* with a certain type of population; *the area is populated by peasant farmers*; *Hong Kong is one of the most densely-populated cities in the world*

population [pɒpjʊ'leɪʃn] *noun* number of people who live in a place; *the population of the country is 60 million*; *Paris has a population of over three million*

populist ['pɒpjʊlɪst] **1** *adjective* believing that ordinary people should have more say in government; *the movement was led by a young populist politician*; *it was a rousing populist speech* **2** *noun* person who believes that ordinary people should have more say in government; *the populists in the party supported the lowering of the voting age*

populous ['pɒpjʊləs] *adjective* densely populated; *it's the most populous area of the country*

pop-up ['pɒpʌp] *noun* (**a**) (*book*) with cut-out pictures that stand up when the book is opened; *a children's pop-up book* (**b**) a pop-up toaster = toaster that pushes the toast up when it is ready (**c**) pop-up menu = list of possible actions shown on a computer screen when you press a key

porcelain ['pɔːslɪn] *noun* fine china; *she keeps her collection of precious Chinese porcelain in a glass case*; *they served tea in a porcelain tea service*

porch [pɔːtʃ] *noun* (**a**) GB shelter over a doorway; *you weren't in when I called, so I left the parcel in the porch* (**b**) US balcony at ground level around a house; *they like to sit out on the porch on summer evenings* (NOTE: plural is **porches**)

porcupine ['pɔːkjʊpaɪn] *noun* American rodent with long sharp spikes covering its body; *the porcupine raises its quills when it is attacked*

pore [pɔː] **1** *noun* tiny hole in the skin or in a leaf, through which moisture such as sweat passes; *I was sweating from every pore as I waited for the results of the test*; *water evaporates from the pores of the leaves* **2** *verb* to pore over = to look at a book, etc., very closely; *he spent days in the library poring over old documents* (NOTE: do not confuse with **poor, pour**)

pork [pɔːk] *noun* fresh meat from a pig, eaten cooked; *we're having pork for dinner tonight*; pork pie = pie with pork filling; *let's buy a pork pie to eat on the picnic* (NOTE: no plural; note also that salted or smoked meat from a pig is **ham** or **bacon**)

COMMENT: roast pork is traditionally served with apple sauce and sage and onion stuffing

pornographic [pɔːnə'græfɪk] *adjective* obscene, aiming to arouse sexual excitement; *he was charged with selling pornographic films*

pornography [pɔː'nɒgrəfi] *noun* books, films, etc., with obscene subject matter; *it's very difficult to stop pornography getting onto the Internet*

porous ['pɔːrəs] *adjective* which has many little holes in it, allowing water or air to seep through slowly; *terracotta flowerpots are porous while plastic ones are not*; *after thousands of years, rainwater will make caves in porous rock*

porpoise ['pɔːpəs] *noun* sea mammal which swims in groups; *porpoises followed the ship* (NOTE: a group of them is a **school of porpoises**)

porridge ['pɒrɪdʒ] *noun* oatmeal cooked in water or milk, eaten for breakfast; *he had a bowl of porridge for breakfast* (NOTE: no plural)

port [pɔːt] *noun* **(a)** harbour, or town with a harbour; *the ship is due in port on Tuesday*; *we left port at 12.00*; **to call at a port** = to stop at a port to load or unload cargo; **port of call** = port at which a ship stops; *our next port of call is Hamburg*; **fishing port** = port which is used mainly by fishing boats **(b)** left side (when looking forward on board a ship or aircraft); *passengers sitting on the port side of the plane can see Tower Bridge*; *the ship turned to port to avoid the iceberg* **(c)** opening in a computer for plugging in an attachment; *a mouse port* **(d)** strong sweet wine from Portugal; *at the end of the meal the port was passed round*

portable ['pɔːtəbl] **1** *adjective* which can be carried; *he used his portable computer on the plane*; *portable phones won't work in the Underground* **2** *noun* small computer which can be carried; *I keyboard all my orders on my portable*

portal ['pɔːtl] *noun (formal)* imposing entrance; *many famous people have passed through the portals of this college*

porter ['pɔːtə] *noun* **(a)** person who carries luggage for travellers at railway stations; *find a porter to help us with all this luggage* **(b)** person who does general work in a hospital, including moving the patients around; *the nurse asked a porter to fetch a wheelchair*

portfolio [pɔːt'fəuliəu] *noun* **(a)** large cardboard case for carrying drawings, designs, etc.; *he brought a portfolio of samples of his work* **(b)** a portfolio of shares = all the shares owned by someone **(c)** minister's position in a government; *she's taken over the defence portfolio* = she has become Minister of Defence (NOTE: plural is **portfolios**)

porthole ['pɔːthəul] *noun* round window in the side of a ship; *I opened the porthole to let some air into the cabin*

portico ['pɔːtɪkəu] *noun* roof supported by columns forming a porch in front of the entrance to a building; *a large stone portico led into the inner courtyard*; *we sheltered under the portico until the rain eased off* (NOTE: plural is **porticoes** *or* **porticos**)

portion ['pɔːʃn] **1** *noun* **(a)** part; *this is only a small portion of the material we collected*; *our carriage was in the rear portion of the train* **(b)** serving of food, usually for one person; *the portions in that French restaurant are tiny*; *ask the waitress if they serve children's portions* **2** *verb* **to portion out** = to share out; *we portioned out the money between the four of us*

portrait ['pɔːtreɪt] *noun* painting or photograph of a person; *he has painted a portrait of the Queen*; *old portraits of members of the family lined the walls of the dining room*

portray [pɔː'treɪ] *verb* to paint or to describe a scene or a person; *in the book he is portrayed as gloomy and miserable, while in real life he was nothing like that at all*

portrayal [pɔː'treɪəl] *noun* description of a scene or person; *many people disagreed with his portrayal of Hamlet*; *an unusual portrayal of the Nativity scene*

Portugal ['pɔːtjugəl] *noun* country is Southern Europe, to the west of Spain; *Portugal is Britain's oldest ally* (NOTE: capital: **Lisbon**; people: the Portuguese; language: **Portuguese**; currency: **Portuguese escudo, euro**)

Portuguese [pɔːtju'giːz] **1** *adjective* referring to Portugal; *a Portuguese explorer* **2** *noun* **(a)** person from Portugal; *she married a Portuguese*; **the Portuguese** = people from Portugal **(b)** language spoken in Portugal, Brazil, etc.; *I don't know the word for it in Portuguese*

pose [pəuz] **1** *noun* **(a)** way of standing, sitting, etc.; *she is painted standing in an elegant pose*; *he struck a funny pose as I was taking the photo* **(b)** way of behaving which is just a pretence; *he'd like you to think he's an expert but it's just a pose* **2** *verb* **(a) to pose for someone** = to stand or sit still while someone paints or photographs you; *he posed for her in his uniform* **(b)** to pretend to be; *he got into the prison by posing as a doctor* **(c)** to set a problem; to put a question; *what to do with illegal immigrants poses a problem for the immigration services*

posh [pɒʃ] *adjective* **(a)** very smart; *I decided I'd better wear my poshest frock to the wedding*; *we dined out in a posh restaurant* **(b)** belonging to a high social class; *he puts on a posh voice when he's talking on the phone* (NOTE: **posher - poshest**)

position [pə'zɪʃən] **1** *noun* **(a)** place where someone or something is; *from his position on the roof he can see the whole of the street*; *the ship's last known position was 200 miles east of Bermuda* **(b)** job; *the sales manager has a key position in the firm*; *he's going to apply for a position as manager*; *we have several positions vacant* **(c)** situation or state of affairs; *what is the company's cash position?* **(d) to be in a position to do something** = to be able to do something; *I am not in a position to answer your question at this point in time* **2** *verb* to put, to place in a position; *she positioned herself near the exit*

positive ['pɒzɪtɪv] **1** *adjective* **(a)** meaning 'yes'; *a positive answer* **(b)** certain, sure; *I'm positive I put the key in my pocket*; *are you positive he said six o'clock?* **(c)** plus, more than zero; *a positive quantity* **(d)** *(in a test)* showing that something is there; *the cancer test was positive* **(e) positive film** = film where the light parts are light and the dark are dark (as opposed to negative film) **(f) positive terminal** = one of the terminals in a battery, shown by a plus (+) sign; *the wire should be attached to the positive terminal* **2** *noun* photograph printed from a negative, where the light and dark appear as they are in nature (NOTE: the opposite is **negative**)

positively ['pɒzɪtɪvli] *adverb* absolutely; *that's positively the last time I come out with you*; *it's positively disgraceful to waste money like that*

posse ['pɒsi] *noun* **(a)** *especially US* group of armed men or police; *the sheriff organized a posse to hunt down the outlaws* **(b)** group of people; *a posse of TV reporters followed them to their hotel*

possess [pə'zes] *verb* **(a)** to own; *he possesses several farms in the south of the country*; *he lost all he possessed in the fire* **(b)** to occupy someone's mind and influence their behaviour; *she was possessed by fear when she realized the baby wasn't breathing*; *what possessed him to do it?* = why on earth did he do it? **(c)** *(of an evil spirit)* to control someone in mind and body

possessed [pə'zest] *adjective* controlled by an evil spirit; *they thought she was possessed and called a* *priest to exorcise her*; **like a man possessed** = like a madman; *he was driving like a man possessed*

possession [pə'zeʃn] *noun* **(a)** ownership; **in someone's possession** = being held by someone; *the jewellery came into my possession when my mother died*; *when he couldn't keep up the mortgage payments the bank took possession of the house* **(b) possessions** = things which you own; *they lost all their possessions in the flood*

possessive [pə'zesɪv] *adjective* **(a)** *(person)* who treats someone *or* something as if he owns them; *his girlfriend's very possessive and hates it when he goes out with his mates*; *he gets very possessive about his gold pen and won't let anyone else use it* **(b)** *(in grammar)* **possessive pronoun** = pronoun such as 'his' or 'my', which indicates possession

possibility [pɒsə'bɪlɪti] *noun* being likely to happen; *is there any possibility of getting a ticket to the show?*; *there is always the possibility that the plane will be early*; *there is no possibility of the bank lending us any more money*

possible ['pɒsəbl] *adjective* which can be; *that field is a possible site for the factory*; *it is possible that the plane has been delayed*; *a bicycle is the cheapest possible way of getting round the town*

◊ **as possible** [æz 'pɒsəbl] *(used to make a superlative)* *I want to go as far away as possible for my holiday*; *please do it as quickly as possible*; *they will need as much time as possible to finish the job*

possibly ['pɒsəbli] *adverb* **(a)** perhaps; *the meeting will possibly finish late*; *January had possibly the worst snowstorms we have ever seen* **(b)** *(used with 'can' or 'can't' to make a phrase stronger)* *you can't possibly eat twenty-two pancakes!*; *how can you possibly expect me to do all that in one day?*

post [pəʊst] **1** *noun* **(a)** long piece of wood, metal, etc., put in the ground; *the fence is attached to concrete posts*; *his shot hit the post*; *see also* DOORPOST, GATEPOST, GOALPOST **(b)** job; *he applied for a post in the sales department*; *we have three posts vacant*; *they advertised the post in 'the Times'* **(c)** letters, etc., sent; *the morning post comes around nine o'clock*; *there were no cheques in this morning's post*; *has the post arrived yet?*; **to open the post** = to open the envelopes and parcels which have arrived; *she usually opens the post before the rest of the staff arrive* **(d)** system of sending letters, parcels, etc.; *it is easier to send the parcel by post than to deliver it by hand*; **letter post** *or* **parcel post** = service for sending letters or parcels **2** *verb* **(a)** to send a letter, parcel, etc.; *don't forget to post your Christmas cards*; *the letter should have arrived by now - we posted it ten days ago* **(b)** to send someone to another place, often overseas, to work; *he was posted to an air base in East Anglia*; *she has been posted overseas* (NOTE: referring to the postal services, American English only uses **mail** where British English uses both **mail** and **post**)

post- [pəʊst] *prefix meaning* later than, after; *post-Christmas sales*; *post-holiday gloom*

postage ['pəʊstɪdʒ] *noun* money which you pay to send something by post; *what is the postage for an airmail letter to India?*; **postage stamp** = piece of paper which you buy and stick on a letter, etc., to pay for it to be sent on by the post office

postal ['pəʊstəl] *adjective* referring to the post; *postal charges are going up by 10% in September*; **postal**

ballot = ballot where the votes are sent by post; **postal order** = order to pay money, which can be bought and cashed at a post office; *you can pay by cheque or postal order*; *she enclosed a postal order for £10*

postbag ['pəʊstbæg] *noun* letters sent to a radio programme, TV show, MP, etc.; *here are a few more letters from our postbag*; *we get several thousand letters a week in our postbag*

postbox ['pəʊstbɒks] *noun* box into which you can put letters, which will then be collected and sent on by the post office; *if you're going out, could you put this letter in the postbox for me?*

COMMENT: in Britain, postboxes are red, and can be rectangular or set into a wall. Round boxes are called 'pillar boxes'

postcard ['pəʊstkɑːd] *noun* piece of card (often with a picture on one side) which you send to someone with a short message on it; *send us a postcard when you arrive in China*; *they sent me a postcard of the village where they were staying*

postcode ['pəʊstkəʊd] *noun* system of letters or numbers to indicate a town or street in an address, to help with the sorting of mail; *my postcode is BA2 5NT*; *don't forget the postcode when addressing the envelope* (NOTE: the American equivalent is **zip code**)

poster ['pəʊstə] *noun* large notice, picture or advertisement stuck on a wall; *they put up posters advertising the concert*; *the wall was covered with election posters*; **poster paints** = water paints in bright colours, often used by children

posterity [pɒ'sterɪti] *noun* generations which will follow this one; *we're trying to save these old buildings for posterity*

post free ['pəʊst 'friː] *adverb* without paying for postage; *the set of glasses is obtainable post free from the manufacturer*; *compare* FREEPOST

postgraduate [pəʊst'grædjuət] *noun* person who has a first degree from a university and who is studying for a further degree; *he's taking a postgraduate course in physics*

posthumous ['pɒstjuməs] *adjective* after death; *she received a posthumous award for bravery*; **posthumous son** = son born after his father's death

posting ['pəʊstɪŋ] *noun* new job with the same organization for which you have to move to a different country or district; *he was hoping for a posting to Hawaii*

postman ['pəʊstmən] *noun* person who delivers letters to houses; *the postman comes very early - before eight o'clock*; *can you give this parcel back to the postman - it's not for us* (NOTE: plural is **postmen**; the American equivalent is a **mailman**)

postmark ['pəʊstmɑːk] **1** *noun* mark stamped on a letter to show when and where it was posted; *a letter with a London postmark*; *you can see from the postmark that it was posted two weeks ago* **2** *verb* to stamp a letter with a postmark; *the letter had been postmarked in New York*

post mortem ['pəʊst 'mɔːtəm] **1** *Latin phrase meaning* 'after death'; trying to find out the cause of death; *a post-mortem examination* **2** *noun* **(a)** examination of a corpse to find out the cause of death; *the post mortem revealed that she had been poisoned* **(b)** examination of something which has happened; *the* *government is carrying out a post mortem on the result of the elections*

post office (PO) ['pəʊst 'ɒfis] *noun* **(a)** building where you can buy stamps, send letters and parcels, pay bills, collect your pension, pay your car tax, etc.; *the main post office is in the High Street; there are two parcels to be taken to the post office; post offices are shut on Sundays;* **Post Office box number** *or* **PO box number** = reference number given for delivering mail to a post office, so as not to give the actual address of the person who will receive it **(b)** organization which runs the postal services; *they are planning to privatize the Post Office; he worked for the Post Office for 50 years*

postpaid [pəʊst'peid] *adjective* with postage paid by the sender; *the price is £5.95 postpaid*

postpone [pəs'pəʊn] *verb* to put back to a later date or time; *the meeting has been postponed until next week; he asked if the meeting could be postponed to tomorrow*

postponement [pəs'pəʊnmənt] *noun* putting off until later; *I had to change my appointments because of the postponement of the meeting; we asked for a postponement because we were not ready*

postscript *or* **post scriptum (PS)** ['pəʊstskript or 'pəʊst 'skriptəm] *Latin phrase meaning* 'after what has been written': an additional note at the end of a letter; *he added a postscript to the letter*

postulate ['pɒstjʊleit] *(formal)* **1** *noun* statement upon which a theory is based; *the postulate that the earth was round was in the end accepted as correct; the postulate on which the argument is based is demonstrably false* **2** *verb* to suppose that something is true; *he postulated that the earth was round*

posture ['pɒstʃə] **1** *noun* way of sitting, standing, etc.; *she does exercises to improve her posture* **2** *verb* to take up a particular position for effect; *he was posturing in front of the cameras*

postwar [pəʊst'wɔː] *adjective* referring to the period after a war; *during the postwar period inflation remained very low; the postwar feeling of optimism did not last long*

pot [pɒt] **1** *noun* **(a)** glass or china container, usually without a handle; *the plant is too big - it needs a bigger pot; she made ten pots of strawberry jam; can we have a pot of tea for two, please?;* see also TEAPOT **(b)** *(informal)* **pots of money** = lots of money; *ask him to pay - he's got pots of money* **(c)** *(informal)* **to go to pot** = to become ruined, useless; *my service has gone to pot since I stopped playing tennis regularly* **(d)** *(slang)* marijuana, drug made from hemp; *he started smoking pot when he was at university* **2** *verb* **(a)** to put a plant into a pot; *she potted the geraniums* **(b)** *(in billiards)* to send a ball into one of the pockets; *he potted the black to win the match* (NOTE: **potting - potted**)

potassium [pə'tæsiəm] *noun* soft metal found in rocks, essential to biological life; *potassium occurs naturally only in compounds* (NOTE: Chemical element: chemical symbol: **K**; atomic number: **19**)

potato [pə'teɪtəʊ] *noun* **(a)** common white root vegetable which grows under the ground; *do you want any more potatoes?; we're having roast lamb and potatoes for Sunday lunch;* **to look like a sack of potatoes** = to be badly dressed, with clothes bulging out; *this dress makes me look like a sack of potatoes;* **baked potatoes** = POTATOES IN THEIR JACKETS; **boiled potatoes** = potatoes cooked in boiling water; **mashed potatoes** = potatoes which have been boiled until they are soft and then mashed and mixed with butter and milk; **roast potatoes** = potatoes cooked in the oven with fat; **jacket potatoes** *or* **potatoes in their jackets** = potatoes cooked in the oven with their skins on; **potato crisps** = thin slices of potato fried until they are hard, served as a snack with drinks (NOTE: American English is **chips**); **potato skins** = skins of potatoes, cooked until crisp and filled with cream cheese or other fillings **(b)** **sweet potato** = yam, a tropical vegetable like a long red potato with sweet yellow flesh inside (NOTE: plural is **potatoes**)

potency ['pəʊtənsi] *noun* strength; *people tend to underestimate the potency of this cider*

potent ['pəʊtənt] *adjective* **(a)** which has a strong effect; *don't drink too much of that beer - it's terribly potent; people don't realize how potent these drugs are* **(b)** powerful; *this is a potent argument in favour of the ban on fox hunting*

potential [pə'tenʃl] **1** *adjective* possible; *he's a potential world champion; the potential profits from the deal are enormous;* **potential customers** = people who could be customers; **potential market** = market which could be exploited **2** *noun* **(a)** possibility of developing into something useful or valuable; *the discovery has enormous potential; she doesn't have much experience, but she has a lot of potential; the whole area has great potential for economic growth* **(b)** *(in physics)* difference in voltage between two parts of an electric circuit

pothole ['pɒthəʊl] *noun* **(a)** hole in a road surface; *the council still hasn't filled in the potholes in our street* **(b)** deep hole in rock worn away by water; *they were exploring a pothole in the Mendip Hills*

potholer ['pɒthəʊlə] *noun* person who goes potholing; *several potholers were trapped in the cave by a flash flood*

potholing ['pɒthəʊlɪŋ] *noun* sport of exploring potholes in rock; *we spent the weekend potholing in the limestone hills*

potion ['pəʊʃn] *noun* *(old)* liquid mixture of medicine; *she mixed up a potion that she said would settle my stomach; the wizard concocted a magic potion and gave it to the king*

potter ['pɒtə] **1** *noun* person who makes pots out of clay; *a potter's wheel; the potter makes cups and bowls to sell in craft shops* **2** *verb* **to potter about** = not to do anything in particular, to do little jobs here and there; *he spent Saturday morning pottering about in the garden* (NOTE: American English is **putter around**)

pottery ['pɒtri] *noun* **(a)** workshop or factory where pots are made; *there are several local potteries where you can buy dishes; I bought this vase from the pottery where it was made* (NOTE: plural in this meaning is **potteries**) **(b)** pots made of clay; *a piece of pottery; she brought me some Spanish pottery as a present* **(c)** the making of pots; *she's taking a pottery course at college*

potting shed ['pɒtɪŋ 'ʃed] *noun* shed in a garden where you put plants in pots; *he spends more time in the potting shed than in the house; it's time to plant out the seedlings from the potting shed*

pouch [paʊtʃ] *noun* **(a)** small bag for carrying coins, etc.; *she carried the ring in a small leather pouch round her neck* **(b)** bag in the skin in front of marsupials such as kangaroos, where the young are carried; *the kangaroo carries its young in its pouch* (NOTE: plural is **pouches**)

poultry ['pəultri] *noun* common farm birds such as ducks or hens, reared for eggs or to be eaten; *they raised some poultry in their back garden*; *you should eat more poultry and less red meat* (NOTE: the word is plural)

pounce [pauns] **1** *noun* sudden attack by jumping on something; *in one quick pounce the cat caught the mouse* **2** *verb* **to pounce on something** = to jump on something; *the cat was waiting in the bushes, ready to pounce on any bird that came by*; *he pounced on the mistake I'd made*

pound [paund] **1** *noun* **(a)** measure of weight (about 450 grams); *she bought a pound of onions and five pounds of carrots*; *the baby was tiny - she only weighed three pounds when she was born*; *how much is tea? - it's 50p a pound* (NOTE: with numbers the word **pound** is usually written **lb** after the figure: **it weighs 26lb; take 6lb of sugar:** say 'twenty-six pounds, six pounds') **(b)** money used in Britain and several other countries; *the cheapest lunch will cost you £25 (twenty-five pounds) at that restaurant*; *he earns more than a six pounds an hour*; *the price of the car is over £50,000 (fifty thousand pounds)* *he tried to pay for his bus ticket with a £20 note (twenty pound note)* (NOTE: with numbers **pound** is usually written **£** before figures: **£20, £6,000,** etc. (say 'twenty pounds, six thousand pounds'). Note also that with the word **note, pound** is singular: **twenty pounds** but **a twenty pound note**) **(c)** place where illegally-parked cars are taken; *he had to go to the police pound to get his car back*; *compare* IMPOUND **2** *verb* **(a)** to smash into little pieces; *the ship was pounded to pieces by heavy waves* **(b)** to hit hard; *he pounded the table with his fist* **(c)** to run or walk heavily; *the policeman pounded along after the bank robbers*; *he pounded up the stairs* **(d)** *(of heart)* to beat fast; *her heart was pounding as she opened the door*

pour [pɔː] *verb* **(a)** to make a liquid flow; *the waiter poured water all over the table*; *he poured the wine into the glasses*; *she poured water down his neck as a joke* **(b)** to flow out or down; *clouds of smoke poured out of the house*; *there was a sudden bang and smoke poured out of the engine* **(c) pouring with rain** = raining very hard; *it poured with rain all afternoon* (NOTE: do not confuse with **pore**)

pour down ['pɔː 'daun] *verb* to rain very hard; *don't go out without an umbrella - it's pouring down*

pout [paut] **1** *noun* sulky expression where your bottom lip sticks out; *the smile turned into a pout when she realized she wasn't going to get her way* **2** *verb* to make a sulky expression with your lips; *when she pouts she looks very sexy*

poverty ['pɒvəti] *noun* **(a)** being poor; *he lost all his money and died in poverty*; *poverty can drive people to crime*; **the poverty line** = amount of money which you need to buy the basic necessities; *thousands of families are living below the poverty line* **(b)** *(formal)* **the poverty of** = the very small amount of; *the poverty of our resources means that we are dependent on outside funds*

POW ['piːəu'dʌblju:] = PRISONER OF WAR

powder ['paudə] *noun* **1** very fine dry grains (like flour); *to grind something to powder*; *the drug is available in the form of a white powder*; *face powder* = scented powder for putting on your face; **washing powder** *or* **soap powder** = soap in powder form, used in washing machines or dishwashers; *we've run out of soap powder*; *can you buy some washing powder next time you go to the supermarket?* **2** *verb* to put powder on something; *she was powdering her cheeks*; *(informal) (of a woman)* **to powder your nose** = to go to the toilet; *can you wait a minute, I'm just going to powder my nose*

powdered ['paudəd] *adjective* dried and made into powder; *a tin of powdered milk*

power [pauə] **1** *noun* **(a)** ability to control people or happenings; *he is the official leader, but his wife has all the real power*; *I haven't the power or it isn't in my power to ban the demonstration*; **the full power of the law** = the full force of the law **(b)** driving force; *they use the power of the waves to generate electricity*; *the engine is driven by steam power*; **wind power** = force of the wind (used to drive a windmill) **(c) (electric) power** = electricity used to drive machines or devices; *turn off the power before you try to repair the TV set* **(d)** political control; *the socialists came to power in 1997*; *during the period when he was in power the country's economy was ruined* **(e)** important, powerful country; *China is one of the great powers* **(f)** *(in mathematics)* number of times one number is multiplied by another; *3 to the power 4* (NOTE: written 3^4) **2** *verb* **(a) to be powered by** = to be driven by; *powered by two Olympic oarsmen, the boat raced across the lake* **(b)** to move fast; *with its huge outboard motor the boat powered through the water*

power base ['pauə 'beis] *noun* group or area which supports a politician; *he's trying to build up a power base among the farming community*

powerboat ['pauəbəut] *noun* boat which has a powerful engine, used for racing; *he goes powerboat racing at weekends*; *he sold his yacht and bought a powerboat*

power drill ['pauə 'dril] *noun* powerful electric drill; *they used a power drill to bore a hole in the wall*

-powered ['pauəd] *suffix* meaning driven or worked by a certain type of energy; *gas-powered central heating*; *a solar-powered calculator*

powerful ['pauəful] *adjective* very strong; *this model has a more powerful engine*; *the treasurer is the most powerful person in the organization*; *the raft was swept away by the powerful current*; *this is the most powerful personal computer on the market*

powerhouse ['pauəhaus] *noun* person, place or thing that is full of energy and very productive; *the man is a powerhouse of original ideas*

powerless ['pauələs] *adjective* unable to do anything because of not having any power or authority; *we were powerless to prevent the accident*

power line ['pauəlain] *noun* cable carrying electric current; *the snowstorm brought down power lines all over the country*

power point ['pauəpɔint] *noun* electric socket in a wall; *I put extra power points in my study to run my computer equipment*

power-sharing ['pauəʃeəriŋ] *noun* sharing the powers and responsibilities of government between different parties; *they expect to reach a power-sharing agreement*; *it was hoped that the two communities* *would agree on some form of power-sharing* (NOTE: no plural)

power station *or* **power plant** ['pauə 'steɪʃn *or* 'pauə 'plɑːnt] *noun* factory where electricity is produced; *this power station burns coal*; *a nuclear power station*

power steering ['pauə 'stiːrɪŋ] *noun* steering in a car which is powered by the engine; *the more expensive models have power steering*

PR [piː'ɑː] *noun* = PUBLIC RELATIONS

practical ['præktɪkl] **1** *adjective* **(a)** referring to practice and action rather than ideas; *she needs some practical experience*; *he passed the practical exam but failed the theory*; *I need some practical advice on how to build a wall* **(b) practical joke** = trick played on someone to make other people laugh **(c)** possible or sensible; *it isn't practical to plug the computer into the same socket as the TV*; *has anyone got a more practical suggestion to make?*; *we must be practical and not try anything too ambitious* **2** *noun* examination or test to show how well someone can work in practice; *she passed the written test but failed the practical*

practicality [præktɪ'kælɪti] *noun* **(a)** way in which something works in practice; *we haven't yet got down to discussing the practicalities of selling the shop* **(b)** way in which something is practical or possible; *I have doubts about the practicality of the scheme*

practically ['præktɪkli] *adverb* **(a)** almost; *practically all the students passed the test*; *the summer is practically over*; *his suit is such a dark grey it is practically black* **(b)** in a practical way; *we must try to solve the problem practically*

practice ['præktɪs] **1** *noun* **(a)** actually applying something; **to put something into practice** = to apply something, to use something; *I hope soon to be able to put some of my ideas into practice*; **in practice** = when actually done; *the plan seems very interesting, but what will it cost in practice?* **(b)** repeated exercise; *you need more practice before you're ready to enter the competition*; *he's at football practice this evening*; *the cars make several practice runs before the race*; **out of practice** = not able to do something because of not having done it recently; *I used to be able to play quite well, but I'm a bit out of practice* **(c) medical practice, dental practice, legal practice** = business of a doctor, dentist, lawyer, etc.; *there are three doctors in this practice*; **private practice** = doctor's or dentist's practice where the clients pay, as opposed to one which is part of the National Health Service **(d) practices** = ways of doing things; *he has written a study of burial practices on the Pacific islands*; **code of practice** = rules drawn up which people must follow when doing business **2** *verb US see* PRACTISE

practise *US* **practice** ['præktɪs] *verb* **(a)** to do repeated exercises; *he's practising catching and throwing* **(b)** to carry on a job as a doctor or lawyer; *he's officially retired but still practises part-time*

practitioner [præk'tɪʃənə] *noun* person who does a skilled job; *she's a practitioner of the ancient Japanese art of flower arranging*; *see also* GENERAL PRACTICIONER

pragmatic [præg'mætɪk] *adjective* dealing with facts or practical matters, not concerned with theories; *you need to take a pragmatic approach when trying to solve this problem*; *it's best to be pragmatic and try to reach a compromise acceptable to both sides*

pragmatism ['prægmətɪzm] *noun (formal)* adopting a pragmatic approach to a problem; *she is well-known for her good sense and pragmatism*

prairie ['preəri] *noun* area of grass-covered plain in North America, mainly without trees, where most of the world's grain is produced; *the road crosses the prairie, going straight for hundreds of miles*; *their family had farmed the prairie for decades*; **prairie oyster** = mixture of raw egg, tomato juice and spices, taken to cure a hangover

praise [preɪz] **1** *noun* admiration, showing approval; *the rescue team earned the praise of the survivors*; **to sing the praises of someone** = to praise someone all the time; *she's always singing the praises of the new vicar* **2** *verb* to express strong approval of something; *the mayor praised the firemen for their efforts to put out the fire*

praiseworthy ['preɪzwɜːði] *adjective* which should be praised; *she showed a praiseworthy willingness to admit to having made mistakes*

pram [præm] *noun* light carriage for pushing a baby in; *we put the baby in her pram and went off for a walk*; *she pushed the pram across the busy road* (NOTE: in American English this is a **baby carriage**; in British English, for slightly older children who can sit up, it is also called a **buggy** *or* **pushchair**)

prank [præŋk] *noun* trick; *it was just a childish prank, it wasn't a serious attempt to burn the house down*; **to play a prank on someone** = to play a trick on someone; *the students played a prank on their teacher*

prattle ['prætl] *verb* to chatter a lot about things which aren't important; *she was prattling on about her holidays and her boyfriends*

prawn [prɔːn] *noun* shellfish like a large shrimp; *we went to the rock pools to look for prawns*; *we're having curried prawns and rice this evening*; **prawn cocktail** = starter consisting of shelled prawns in mayonnaise and tomato dressing, served in a glass with shredded lettuce

pray [preɪ] *verb* **(a)** to speak to God, asking God for something; *farmers prayed for rain*; **to pray for someone** = to ask God to protect someone; *we pray for the children from the village, missing in the mountains* **(b)** *(old)* please; **pray be seated** = please sit down

prayer [preə] *noun* speaking to God; *she says her prayers every night before going to bed*; *they said prayers for the sick*

pre- [prɪ] *prefix meaning* before; *we have been invited for pre-lunch drinks*; *the pre-Christmas rush*

preach [priːtʃ] *verb* to give a sermon in church; *she preached to a packed congregation about the need for tolerance*; **to preach to the converted** = to try to convince people of something when they already know about it; *it's a waste of time telling us about the advantages of using computers - you're just preaching to the converted*

preacher ['priːtʃə] *noun* person who gives a sermon in church; *we have a new preacher at church this Sunday*

precarious [prɪ'keəriəs] *adjective* not safe, likely to fall off; *the house is in a precarious position on top of the cliff*; *their financial future is looking very precarious*

precariously [prɪ'keərɪəsli] *adverb* in an unsafe way; *the eagles' nest was perched precariously on a high ledge*

precautionary [prɪ'kɔːʃnəri] *adjective* **precautionary measure** = measure taken to avoid something unpleasant; *we lock the doors at night as a precautionary measure*

precautions [prɪ'kɔːʃnz] *noun* care taken in advance to avoid something unpleasant; *the company has taken precautions to avoid fire in the warehouse*; *the restaurant did not take proper fire precautions*; *what safety precautions must be taken before we can open the swimming pool to the public?*

precede [prɪ'siːd] *verb* to take place before something; *a period of calm often precedes a storm*; *the concert was preceded by a short talk given by the pianist*

precedence ['presɪdəns] *noun* **to take precedence over** = to be more important than, when considered as part of a hierarchy; *presidents take precedence over prime ministers*

precedent ['presɪdənt] *noun* thing which has happened before, and which can be a guide as to what should be done; *the murder case has set a precedent for lawyers*

preceding [prɪ'siːdɪŋ] *adjective* which comes before; *the three weeks preceding the school play were taken up with constant rehearsals*; *they spent the preceding two weeks interviewing candidates*

precinct ['priːsɪŋkt] *noun* **(a) pedestrian precinct** *or* **shopping precinct** = part of a town which is closed to traffic so that people can walk about and shop; *the council plans to turn the main shopping area into a pedestrian precinct* **(b)** *US* administrative district in a town; *the 16th precinct* (NOTE: British English for this is **ward**)

precious ['preʃəs] *adjective* **(a)** worth a lot of money; **precious metal** = metal, such as gold, which is worth a lot of money; **precious stones** = stones, such as diamonds, which are rare and very valuable; *see also* SEMI-PRECIOUS **(b)** of great value to someone; *all her precious photographs were saved from the fire*; *the memories of that holiday are very precious to me* **(c)** *(informal)* which you don't think is valuable; *she can't talk about anything except her precious boyfriend*; *do you think I'm interested in you and your precious car?*

precipice ['presɪpɪs] *noun* high cliff on the side of a mountain, not usually near the sea; *his body was found at the foot of the precipice*; *she was dangling on a rope over the edge of the precipice*

precipitate **1** *verb* [prɪ'sɪpɪteɪt] **(a)** to make something happen suddenly; *the assassination precipitated a political crisis* **(b)** to settle at the bottom of a liquid; *the crystals precipitate at the bottom of the flask* **(c)** *(formal)* to make someone fall or drop suddenly; *the pram tipped over, precipitating the baby into the ditch* **2** *adjective* [prɪ'sɪpɪtət] rushed or hurried; *their decision to marry seems a bit precipitate* **3** *noun* [prɪ'sɪpɪtət] substance which settles at the bottom of a liquid; *the precipitate begins to form as soon as the reagent is added*

precipitous [prɪ'sɪpɪtəs] *adjective* very steep; *the pram slowly started to roll down the precipitous slope with the baby still inside*

précis ['preɪsiː] **1** *noun* summary of the main points of a text; *I made a précis of the report for my boss* (NOTE: plural is **précis** ['preɪsiːz]) **2** *verb* to make a summary of a text; *can you précis this report on global warming for me?*

precise [prɪ'saɪs] *adjective* exact; *we need to know the precise measurements of the box*; *at that precise moment my father walked in*; *can you be more precise about what the men looked like?*

precisely [prɪ'saɪsli] *adverb* exactly; *the train arrived at 12.00 precisely*; *I don't know precisely when it was, but it was about three months ago*; *how, precisely, do you expect me to cope with all this work?*

precision [prɪ'sɪʒn] *noun* accuracy; *her instructions were carried out with the greatest precision*; **precision drawing** = very accurate drawing; **precision instrument** = instrument for very accurate work

preclude [prɪ'kluːd] *verb* to prevent something taking place; *the cancelling of the present agreement does not preclude any further agreement between the parties in the future*

precocious [prɪ'kəʊʃəs] *adjective* (*child*) surprisingly advanced for its age; *she showed a precocious talent for the piano*; *he's a precocious child and should be put into a higher class*

preconception [priːkən'sepʃn] *noun* idea which is formed in advance, without the benefit of information or experience; *I want you to forget any preconceptions you may have about selling techniques when you start working for us*

precondition [priːkən'dɪʃn] *noun* condition which is set in advance; *the negotiators on the government side wanted to set preconditions before the meeting could start*

precursor [prɪ'kɜːsə] *noun* thing which leads to something more important; *Stephenson's 'Rocket' was the precursor of modern high-speed trains*

predator ['predətə] *noun* animal which kills and eats other animals; *small mammals are food for predators like foxes*

predatory ['predətəri] *adjective* **(a)** referring to a predator; *predatory animals such as foxes eat other animals and birds*; *the cat's predatory instincts came out when she caught a mouse* **(b)** (*business*) referring to a business which is trying to ruin another; **predatory pricing** = cutting prices drastically so as to take customers from other businesses

predecease [priːdɪ'siːs] *verb* (*formal*) to die before someone else; *he predeceased her by six years*

predecessor ['priːdɪsesə] *noun* person who has held the same job, etc., before you; *she moved into her predecessor's office*

predestination [priːdestɪ'neɪʃn] *noun* the idea that the fate of everyone is decided in advance by God; *can a belief in predestination be reconciled with a belief in free will?*

predestined [priː'destɪnd] *adjective* (*formal*) whose fate has been decided in advance; *the project seemed predestined to fail*

predetermine [priːdɪ'tɜːmɪn] *verb* (*formal*) to decide in advance; *the committee agreed to meet again but with no predetermined date or time*; *these factors virtually predetermined the outcome of the election*

predicament [prɪˈdɪkəmənt] *noun* trouble or a difficult situation; *he's got himself into a most awkward predicament; she asked me for advice how to get out of her financial predicament*

predicative [prɪˈdɪkətɪv] *adjective* **predicative adjective** = adjective which follows a verb and makes a statement about a noun

COMMENT: in 'the weather is cold' the word 'cold' is predicative (as opposed to 'the cold weather' where it is attributive)

predict [prɪˈdɪkt] *verb* to foretell, to tell in advance what will happen; *the weather forecasters have predicted rain; he predicted correctly that the deal would not last; everything happened exactly as I had predicted*

predictable [prɪˈdɪktəbl] *adjective* which could be predicted; *his reaction was totally predictable*

predictably [prɪˈdɪktəbli] *adverb* in a way which could have been predicted; *predictably, John was late; her reaction was predictably furious*

prediction [prɪˈdɪkʃn] *noun* foretelling; *here are my predictions for the year 2010; most of her predictions turned out to be correct*

predilection [priːdɪˈlekʃn] *noun (formal)* special liking for something; *everyone knows about her predilection for the Far East*

predominate [prɪˈdɒmɪneɪt] *verb* to be more powerful than others; *a cold northerly airstream predominates during the winter months; the grey squirrel predominates in most parts of England*

predominant [prɪˈdɒmɪnənt] *adjective* most striking or obvious; *red is the predominant colour in the design; the predominant mood among the population is one of relief that the war is over*

predominantly [prɪˈdɒmɪnəntli] *adverb* mainly; *the members of the club are predominantly male; a predominantly Welsh-speaking area of the country; blue features predominantly in the colour scheme she has chosen*

preeminence [prɪˈemɪnəns] *noun* being preeminent; *his preeminence in the field of nuclear physics*

preeminent [prɪˈemɪnənt] *adjective* excellent, much better than everything else; *the college is preeminent in the field of modern languages*

pre-empt [prɪˈempt] *verb* to get an advantage by doing something quickly before anyone else; *they staged a management buyout to pre-empt a takeover bid*

preface [ˈprefəs] **1** *noun* text at the beginning of a book, after the title page, in which the author introduces the book and thanks people for helping make it; *she explains in a preface what motivated her to write the book; compare* FOREWORD **2** *verb* to write or say something before the main part of the text; *he prefaced his article with a quotation from Dickens*

prefect [ˈpriːfekt] *noun* **(a)** older school pupil chosen to be in charge of others; *the prefects help to maintain discipline in the school* **(b)** high official; *the Prefect of Police*

prefer [prɪˈfɜː] *verb* **to prefer something to something** = to like (to do) something better than something else; *I prefer butter to margarine; she prefers walking to going on the underground; we went to the pub, but she preferred to stay at home and watch TV; I'd prefer not to go to Germany this summer* (NOTE: **preferring - preferred**)

preferable [ˈprefrəbl] *adjective* which you would prefer; *any exercise is preferable to sitting around doing nothing*

preferably [ˈprefrəbli] *adverb* if possible; *I'd like to book a seat, preferably one next to a window*

preference [ˈprefrəns] *noun* liking for one thing more than another; *the receptionist asked him if he had any preference for a room with a view; the children all showed a marked preference for chocolate ice cream*

preferential [prefəˈrenʃl] *adjective* showing that one person or thing is preferred to another; *why should they get preferential treatment?*

prefix [ˈpriːfɪks] *noun* part of a word put in front of another to form a new word; *the prefix 'anti-' is very common* (NOTE: plural is **prefixes**)

pregnancy [ˈpregnənsi] *noun* state of being pregnant; *smoking during pregnancy can harm your child; her second pregnancy was easier than the first*; **pregnancy test** = test to see if a woman is pregnant

pregnant [ˈpregnənt] *adjective* **(a)** carrying an unborn child; *don't carry heavy weights when you're pregnant; she hasn't told her family yet that she's pregnant; we have a pregnant girl in our class* **(b) pregnant pause** = pause while everyone waits for someone to say something; *Martha's extraordinary announcement was followed by a pregnant pause*

preheat [ˈpriːhiːt] *verb* to make an oven hot before putting something to cook in it; *preheat the oven to 200° Celsius*

prehistoric [priːhɪˈstɒrɪk] *adjective* belonging to the time before there was a written history; *the excavations tell us something about what life was like in prehistoric times; prehistoric people used flints to make knives*

prehistory [priːˈhɪstəri] *noun* time before written history started; *the finds in the cave shed a fascinating light on the prehistory of this region*

prejudice [ˈpredʒudɪs] **1** *noun* (usually unjust) feeling against someone or preference for one person or thing over another; *the committee seems to have a prejudice against women candidates*; **colour prejudice** = prejudice against someone whose skin is not white; **racial prejudice** = prejudice against someone because of race; *he accused his ex-boss of racial prejudice; she was a victim of racial prejudice* **2** *verb* to make someone become unfriendly towards someone *or* something; *the newspaper reports prejudiced the jury against the accused*

prejudiced [ˈpredʒudɪst] *adjective* unfairly biased against someone; *I'm not prejudiced - I treat everyone exactly the same; she's prejudiced against anyone from a working-class background*

prejudicial [predʒuˈdɪʃl] *adjective* which could harm; *he tried to conceal any facts that might be prejudicial to his case*

preliminary [prɪˈlɪmɪnəri] *adjective* which goes before; *the executive committee will hold a preliminary meeting the day before the conference opens; this is only the preliminary report - the main report will be published later*

prelude ['preljuːd] *noun* **(a)** something which takes place before something more important; *putting tanks near the border is a prelude to a full-scale invasion* **(b)** short piece of music on one theme; *a prelude by Bach*

premature ['premətjʊə] *adjective* **(a)** which happens before the right time; *celebrating victory before the votes have been counted is a little premature* **(b)** (baby) born less than nine months after conception; *little John was six weeks premature and only weight three pounds when he was born*

prematurely ['premətʊəli] *adverb* before the right time; *the party celebrated their election win prematurely: when the votes were counted, they found they had lost*

premier ['premiə] **1** *noun* Prime Minister; *the French premier is visiting London* **2** *adjective* first, most important; *the town advertises itself as Britain's premier holiday resort*; **premier league** = group of top football clubs who play against each other; *the team is in the premier league*

première ['premieə] *noun* first performance of a film, play, etc.; *stars attended the film première in Leicester Square*

premiership ['premiəʃip] *noun* **(a)** time when someone is Prime Minister; *the introduction of income tax was the most important event of his premiership* **(b)** premier league, the group of top football clubs who play against each other; *a premiership match*

premise ['premis] *noun* (formal) assumption, thing which you assume to be true; *her argument is based on false premises*; *he argued from the premise that all wars are evil*

premises ['premisiz] *noun* building and the land it stands on; *smoking is not allowed on the premises*; *there is a doctor on the premises at all times*; **business premises** *or* **commercial premises** = building used for commercial use; **office premises** *or* **shop premises** = building which houses an office or shop (NOTE: the word is plural)

premium ['priːmiəm] *noun* **(a)** amount paid for an insurance policy; *the house insurance premium has to be paid this month*; *we pay a monthly premium of £5* **(b)** **at a premium** = scarce, and therefore valuable; *fresh vegetables were at a premium during the winter months*; **to put a premium on something** = to show that something is useful or valuable; *employers put a premium on staff who can speak good English* **(c)** bonus; *they pay a premium for work completed ahead of schedule*; **premium offer** = offer for sale at a specially attractive price

premium bond ['priːmiəm 'bɒnd] *noun* British government bond which pays no interest but gives you the chance of winning a monthly prize; *I won £100 with my Premium Bonds*

premonition [premə'niʃn] *noun* feeling that something is going to happen; *she had a strange premonition that the house would burn down*

preoccupation [priɒkju'peiʃn] *noun* the only thing you think about; *my main preoccupation is working to get my MA*; *her preoccupation with her business meant that she hadn't noticed that her son had stopped going to school*

preoccupied [pri'ɒkjupaid] *adjective* worried, thinking only about one thing; *she can't work properly because she's preoccupied with her tax problems*

prep [prep] *adjective (informal)* **(a)** homework; *the boys aren't allowed out until they've finished their prep* **(b)** **prep school** = preparatory school; *he teaches in a prep school* **(c)** getting a patient ready for an operation; *the prep is finished, so the patient can be taken to the operating theatre*

preparation [prepə'reiʃn] *noun* **(a)** action of getting ready; *the preparations for the wedding went on for months*; *we've completed our preparations and now we're ready to start*; **in preparation for** = to get ready for; *she bought a hat in preparation for the wedding* **(b)** substance which has been mixed; *a chemical preparation*

preparatory [pri'pærətri] *adjective* **(a)** which prepares; *this is a preparatory course in Chinese for beginners*; **preparatory school** = private school for children up to the age of 13 **(b)** *(formal)* **preparatory to** = before, leading up to; *he's undergoing training preparatory to taking up a managerial position*

prepare [pri'peə] *verb* to get something ready; *he is preparing for his exam*; *you'd better prepare yourself for some bad news*; *I have some friends coming to dinner and I haven't prepared the meal*

prepared [pri'peəd] *adjective* **(a)** ready; *be prepared, you may get quite a shock*; *six people are coming to dinner and I've got nothing prepared* **(b)** **prepared to do something** = willing to do something; *they are prepared to sell the house if necessary*; **prepared for something** = ready for something; *she wasn't really prepared for her exam*; *the country is prepared for an invasion*

preparedness [pri'peədnəs] *noun* being prepared for something; *the army is in a state of maximum preparedness*; *everywhere there are signs of the country's preparedness for war*

preposition [prepə'ziʃn] *noun* word with a noun or pronoun as its object to show place or time; *prepositions like 'by' and 'near' are very common, as in 'he was knocked down by a motorbike' or 'she was sitting near me'*

preposterous [pri'pɒstərəs] *adjective (formal)* silly or absurd; *she made several preposterous suggestions which were all refused*; *it's preposterous that he should claim to be an expert after only six weeks' training*

prerequisite [priː'rekwizit] *noun (formal)* thing which you must have before you can do something; *being able to drive is one of the prerequisites of the job of salesman*

prerogative [pri'rɒgətiv] *noun* special right belonging to one person or group; *he exercised his prerogative and asked to see the company's accounts*

prescribe [pri'skraib] *verb* **(a)** *(formal)* to order that something should be done; *three days' notice has been given, as prescribed by law*; *we have to study two prescribed texts for our exam* **(b)** *(of a doctor)* to tell someone to use something; *he prescribed a course of injections*; *she prescribed some antibiotics*

prescription [pri'skripʃn] *noun* order written by a doctor to a pharmacist asking for a drug to be prepared and sold to a patient; *she took the prescription to the chemist*; **available on prescription** = available from a chemist only when prescribed by a doctor; *this medicine is only available on prescription*

presence ['prezns] *noun* **(a)** being present; *the presence of both his wives in court was noted*; *your presence is requested at a meeting of the committee on June 23rd*; **in someone's presence** = when someone is near; *she actually said that in my presence*; *he slapped her face in the presence of witnesses* **(b) presence of mind** = commonsense, calmness; ability to act quickly; *the hotel staff showed great presence of mind in getting the guests out quickly* **(c)** effect you have on other people; *the general has a commanding presence*

present 1 *noun* ['prezənt] **(a)** thing which you give to someone as a gift; *I got a watch as a Christmas present*; *how many birthday presents did you get?*; *the office gave her a present when she got married* **(b)** the time we are in now; *the novel is set in the present*; **at present** = now; *the hotel still has some vacancies at present*; **for the present** = for now; *that will be enough for the present* **(c)** form of a verb showing that the action is happening now; *the present of the verb 'to go' is 'he goes' or 'he is going'* **2** *adjective* ['prezənt] **(a)** being there when something happens; *how many people were present at the meeting?* **(b)** at the time we are in now; *what is his present address?*; **present tense** = form of a verb showing that the action is happening now; *the present tense of 'to stand' is 'he stands' or 'he is standing'* **3** *verb* [prɪ'zent] **(a)** to give formally (as a present); *when he retired after thirty years, the firm presented him with a large clock* **(b)** to introduce a show on TV, etc.; *she's presenting a programme on gardening* **(c) to present yourself** = to go to a place; *he was asked to present himself at the police station the next morning*

presentable [prɪ'zentəbl] *adjective* clean and tidy, suitable to appear in public; *you're still in your dirty overalls: go and make yourself presentable before the guests arrive!*

presentation [prezən'teɪʃn] *noun* **(a)** act of giving; *the chairman will make the presentation to the retiring sales manager* **(b)** demonstration of a proposed plan; *the distribution company made a presentation of the services they could offer*

present-day [prezənt'deɪ] *adjective* modern; *by present-day standards his old car is slow and inefficient*

presenter [prɪ'zentə] *noun* person who presents a TV show; *a quiz show presenter*; *the presenter introduced his guests for the show*

presently ['prezəntli] *adverb* **(a)** soon; *I'll be there presently*; *he'll be making a speech presently* **(b)** US now, at the present time; *he's presently working for a chemical company*; *she's presently in England*; *what is presently being done to correct the problem?*

preservation [prezə'veɪʃn] *noun* action of protecting; *the trust is mainly concerned with the preservation of historic buildings*; *the ship is in an excellent state of preservation after centuries in muddy water*; *salt and sugar are commonly used in the preservation of food*; **preservation order** = court order to prevent a building being demolished; *a preservation order has been placed on the old town hall*

preservative [prɪ'zɜːvətɪv] *noun* substance used to make food keep, to stop food from going bad (in the EU, preservatives are given E numbers); *the label says that the jam contains no artificial preservatives*

preserve [prɪ'zɜːv] **1** *noun* **preserves** = jams, pickles, etc.; *she has a stall in the market where she sells her preserves* **2** *verb* **(a)** *(formal)* to look after and keep in the same state; *our committee aims to preserve the wildlife in our area*; *the doctors' aim is to preserve the life of the unborn child*; *the Inuit would like to preserve their own alphabet rather than use the Roman one* **(b)** to treat food so that it keeps for a long time; *freezing is a common method of preserving meat*

preshrunk ['priːʃrʌŋk] *adjective* which has been shrunk in advance before being sold; *these preshrunk jeans are so tight I can't get them on*

preside [prɪ'zaɪd] *verb* **(a) to preside at** *or* **over a meeting** = to sit at the head of the table and be the chairman of a meeting; *the meeting was held in the town hall, with the mayor presiding*; *the deputy presided in the absence of the chairman who was ill* **(b)** to be in control of; *she presided over one of the world's richest corporations* **(c)** to be in power during a certain period; *he presided over a period of radical change*

presidency ['prezɪdnsi] *noun* **(a)** job of being president; *he has been proposed as a candidate for the presidency* **(b)** time when someone is president; *during Britain's presidency of the European Union*; *the Second World War ended during the Truman presidency*

president ['prezɪdənt] *noun* **(a)** head of a republic; *during his term of office as President* (NOTE: usually used as a title followed by the surname: **President Wilson**) **(b)** chief member of a club; *we're wondering who'll be the next president of the cricket club*; *A. B. Smith was elected president of the sports club*

presidential [prezɪ'denʃl] *adjective* referring to a president; *the presidential palace*; *the presidential car*

preside over [prɪ'zaɪd 'əuvə] *verb* **(a)** to be president or chairman of something; *she presided over the university appointments committee for several years* **(b)** to be in charge when something happens; *he presided over a radical shake-up of the party's organizational structure*

press [pres] **1** *noun* **(a)** newspapers taken as a group; *the election wasn't reported in the British press*; *there has been no mention of the problem in the press*; **freedom of the press** = being able to write and publish in a newspaper what you want, without being afraid of prosecution unless you break the law **(b)** journalists and other people who work for newspapers, or on radio and TV; *everywhere she went she was followed by the press*; *press photographers were standing outside Number 10* (NOTE: no plural in meanings (a) and (b)) **(c)** machine which presses; *the car body is moulded from a metal sheet in a hydraulic press*; **printing press** = machine for printing books, newspapers, etc. (NOTE: plural is **presses**) **2** *verb* **(a)** to push, to squeeze; *press the button for first floor*; *everyone pressed round the film stars* **(b)** to iron; *his jacket needs pressing* **(c)** to **press on** *or* to **press forward** = to continue, to go ahead; *in spite of the weather they pressed on with the preparations for the village fair*

press conference ['pres 'kɒnfərəns] *noun* meeting where newspaper, radio and TV reporters are invited to hear news of a new product, a takeover bid or to talk to a famous person; *he gave a press conference on the steps of Number Ten*

pressed [prest] *adjective* **we're pressed for time** = we are in a hurry; **I'd be hard pressed to do it** = it would be difficult for me to find time to do it

pressgang ['presgæŋ] **1** *noun (old)* group of people who forced men to join the Royal Navy; *without the pressgangs it would have been impossible to find crews for many ships in the 18th century* **2** *verb* to pressgang someone into doing something = to force someone to do something; *I was pressganged into helping her move house*

pressing ['presɪŋ] *adjective* urgent, which needs to be done quickly; *he had to leave because of a pressing engagement in London*

press office ['pres 'ɒfɪs] *noun* office in an organization which is responsible for relations with the media; *to get an interview with the MD you'll have to phone our press office*

press officer ['pres 'ɒfɪsə] *noun* person who works in a press office, in charge of an organization's relations with the media; *the company's press officer declined to comment*

press release ['pres rɪ'liːs] *noun* sheet giving news about something which is sent to newspapers and TV and radio stations; *the company sent out a press release about the launch of the new car*

press-up ['presʌp] *noun* exercise where you lie on the floor and push yourself up with your arms; *he does twenty press-ups before breakfast* (NOTE: American English is **push-up**)

pressure ['preʃə] *noun* **(a)** something which forces you to do something; *pressure from farmers forced the minister to change his mind*; **to put pressure on someone to do something** = to try to force someone to do something; *they put pressure on the government to build a new motorway*; **under pressure** = being forced (to do something); *he did it under pressure*; *we're under pressure to agree to a postponement* **(b)** force of something which is pushing or squeezing; *there is not enough pressure in your tyres*; **blood pressure** = pressure at which the heart pumps blood; *he has to take pills for his high blood pressure* **(c)** stress caused by having a lot of responsibility; *he gave up his job in the bank because he couldn't stand the pressure*

pressure group ['preʃə 'gruːp] *noun* group of people who try to influence the government, the local town council, etc.; *they formed a pressure group to fight for animal welfare*

pressurized ['preʃəraɪzd] *adjective* **pressurized cabin** = aircraft cabin which is kept at a constant atmospheric pressure which is the same pressure as on earth; *the cargo hold of a jet aircraft is not pressurized*

prestige [pre'stiːʒ] *noun* importance because of high quality, high value, etc.; *there's a lot of prestige attached to working for the royal family*; **prestige offices** = expensive offices in a good area of the town; *our offices are old and functional, not prestige offices like theirs*

prestigious [pre'stɪdʒəs] *adjective* which brings prestige; *they are based at a prestigious address in Park Lane*

presumably [prɪ'zjuːməbli] *adverb* probably; as you think is true; *presumably this is what she wanted us to do*; *they've presumably forgotten the date of the meeting*

presume [prɪ'zjuːm] *verb* **(a)** to suppose, to assume; *I presume this little bridge is safe for cars?*; *the jury has to presume he is innocent until he is proved guilty*; *she is presumed to have fled to South America* **(b)** *(formal)* **not to presume to do something** = not to do something because it would be rude to do it; *I wouldn't presume to contradict her - she's the expert*

presumption [prɪ'zʌmpʃn] *noun* **(a)** thing which is assumed to be correct; *we are working on the presumption that what he has said is in fact true*; **presumption of innocence** = assuming that someone is innocent until a court has found him guilty **(b)** disrespectful behaviour, doing something when you have no right to do it; *it's sheer presumption for her to suggest that she could do the job better than me*

pretax ['priːtæks] *adjective* before tax is paid; *pretax profit*

pretence *US* **pretense** [prɪ'tens] *noun* **(a)** making believe something which is untrue, the action of pretending; *he kept up the pretence of being in love with her while he was seeing another girl*; *all this talk about his aristocratic connections is mere pretence or is just a pretence*; *they made a pretence of being interested* **(b) false pretences** = doing or saying something to cheat someone; *he was sent to prison for obtaining money by false pretences*

pretend [prɪ'tend] *verb* to make someone believe you are something else, so as to deceive them; *he got into the house by pretending to be a telephone engineer*; *she pretended she had flu and phoned to say she was having the day off*

pretender [prɪ'tendə] *noun* person who has claims to something, usually a person who claims to be king although this is not accepted by all the people; *the pretender to the throne has invaded the north of the kingdom*

pretensions [prɪ'tenʃnz] *noun* claim; *she's a homely girl with no particular pretensions to beauty*; *I have no pretensions to being an expert on the subject*

pretentious [prɪ'tenʃəs] *adjective* claiming to be more important than you are; *it sounds a bit pretentious to claim that you changed history*

pretext ['priːtekst] *noun* excuse for doing something which is not the real reason for doing it; *he asked to address the meeting on the pretext that he had something important to say*

pretty ['prɪti] **1** *adjective* pleasant to look at; *her daughters are very pretty*; *she is prettier than her mother*; *what a pretty little house!* (NOTE: **prettier - prettiest.** Note also that **pretty** is used of things or girls, but not of boys or men) **2** *adverb (informal)* quite; *the patient's condition is pretty much the same as it was yesterday*; *I'm pretty sure I'm right*; *you did pretty well, considering it's was the first time you had tried rock-climbing*

prevail [prɪ'veɪl] *verb (formal)* **to prevail upon someone to do something** = to persuade someone to do something; *can I prevail on you to make a speech?*

prevailing [prɪ'veɪlɪŋ] *adjective* usual, common; *the prevailing view is that the disease is incurable*; **prevailing wind** = wind which usually blows from a certain direction

prevalence ['prevələns] *noun* being very common or widespread; *we're becoming alarmed at the prevalence of racist attitudes among sections of the police force*

prevalent ['prevələnt] *adjective* common, occurring frequently; *the disease is prevalent in some African* *countries; the prevalent opinion among doctors is that you should not operate in such cases*

prevent [prɪ'vent] *verb* **(a)** to stop something happening; *we must try to prevent any more flooding* **(b) to prevent someone from doing something** = to stop someone doing something; *we can't do much to prevent the river from flooding; the police prevented anyone from leaving the building*

preventive *or* **preventative** [prɪ'ventɪv or prɪ'ventətɪv] *adjective* which is intended to prevent something; *customs officials are taking preventative measures to stop drugs being brought into the country;* **preventive detention** = putting people in prison because they may cause a disturbance; *potential troublemakers were taken into preventive detention;* **preventive medicine** = medical action to prevent a disease from occurring; *the health service is trying to put more emphasis on preventive medicine*

preview ['priːvjuː] *noun* private showing of a film, an exhibition, etc., before it is open to the public; *we've been invited to a preview of her latest film*

previous ['priːviəs] **1** *adjective* former, earlier; *the letter was sent to my previous address; the gang of workers arrived the previous night and started work first thing in the morning; I had spent the previous day getting to know my way round the town; he could not accept the invitation because he had a previous engagement* = because he had earlier accepted another invitation to go somewhere **2** *adverb* **previous to** = before; *what job were you in, previous to this one?*

previously ['priːviəsli] *adverb* before; *this is my first train trip to Paris - previously I've always gone by plane; the arrangements had been made six weeks previously; at that time they were living in New York, and previously had lived in London*

pre-war ['priːwɔː] *adjective* existing or happening before a war; *the restaurant is celebrating its anniversary by offering meals at pre-war prices; the town has been built to its original pre-war state*

prey [preɪ] **1** *noun* animal eaten by another animal; *mice and small birds are the favourite prey of owls;* **birds of prey** = birds which eat other birds or animals **2** *verb* **(a) to prey on** *or* **upon** = to attack animals and eat them; *here the sharks mainly prey on seals* **(b) something is preying on her** *or* **on her mind** = something is worrying her (NOTE: do not confuse with **pray**)

price [praɪs] **1** *noun* money which you have to pay to buy something; *the price of petrol is going up; I don't want to pay such a high price for a hotel room; there has been a sharp increase in house prices during the first six months of the year;* **cut price** = very cheap price; **net price** = price which cannot be reduced by a discount; **retail price** = price at which the shopkeeper sells to a customer; **Retail Price(s) Index (RPI)** = index which shows how prices of consumer goods have increased or decreased over a period of time; **price list** = sheet giving prices of goods for sale; **price war** = sales battle between companies, where each lowers prices to get more customers; **to increase in price** = to become more expensive **2** *verb* to give something a price; *the book is priced at £25; that house won't sell - it is too highly priced;* **the company has priced itself out of the market** = the company has raised its prices so high that its products do not sell

priceless ['praɪsləs] *adjective* **(a)** extremely valuable; *his priceless collection of paintings were destroyed in the fire; this ring is quite priceless* **(b)** *(informal)* very funny; *some of the things she said were absolutely priceless*

price tag ['praɪs 'tæg] *noun* **(a)** ticket with a price written on it; *how much is this shirt? - the price tag has come off it* **(b)** price at which something is for sale; *car with a £50,000 price tag*

pricey ['praɪsi] *adjective* *(informal)* expensive; *this hotel looks a bit too pricey for us* (NOTE: **pricier - priciest**)

prick [prɪk] *verb* **(a)** to jab with something sharp; *she pricked her finger when she was picking roses; I pricked my finger on a pin and had to put a plaster on it* **(b) to prick up your ears** = to listen attentively; *when his name was mentioned I pricked up my ears*

prickle ['prɪkl] *noun* sharp point on a plant or animal; *be careful of the prickles when you're picking blackberries*

prickly ['prɪkli] *adjective* **(a)** covered with prickles; *a prickly holly bush; a prickly hedgehog;* **prickly pear** = type of cactus with fruit shaped like a red pear; **prickly heat** = skin rash caused by hot climate **(b)** *(person)* who takes offence easily; *be careful what you say to her - she's very prickly*

pride [praɪd] **1** *noun* **(a)** pleasure in your own ability or possessions; *he takes great pride in his garden* **(b)** very high opinion of yourself; *his pride would not let him admit that he had made a mistake (saying)* **'pride goes before a fall'** = if you are very proud of yourself, you are likely to find yourself in trouble **2** *verb* **to pride oneself on** = to be extremely proud of; *she prides herself on her cakes*

priest [priːst] *noun* person who has been blessed to serve God, to carry out formal religious duties, etc.; **parish priest** = priest who is in charge of a parish; *they were married by the parish priest*

priestess [priː'stes] *noun* female priest in a non-Christian religion; *the priestess performed an elaborate purification ceremony* (NOTE: plural is **priestesses**)

priesthood ['priːsthʊd] *noun* **(a) the priesthood** = position of a priest; *at thirty he found he had a vocation for the priesthood* **(b)** all priests considered as a group; *the priesthood refused to accept the government's decree*

priestly ['priːstli] *adjective* referring to priests; *he wore his priestly robes*

prima ballerina ['priːmə bælə'riːnə] *noun* main female dancer in a ballet company

prima donna ['priːmə 'dɒnə] *noun* **(a)** main female singer in an opera company **(b)** *(informal)* person who thinks he or she is extremely important and makes a fuss if things are not done in the way they want; *he's a real prima donna when it comes to choosing flowers for his office*

primacy ['praɪməsi] *noun* *(formal)* being in first place, being most important; *nobody had yet been able to challenge the primacy of the Socialist party in the union movement*

primal ['praɪml] *adjective* *(formal)* old, dating from the very earliest period or state; *the behaviour of animals tells us a lot about what primal human* *societies were like*; *soccer fans always seem to give in to their primal urges*

primarily ['praɪmrəli] *adverb* mainly, mostly; *this is primarily a business trip*; *we're examining primarily the financial aspects of the case*

primary ['praɪməri] **1** *adjective* main, basic; *our primary concern is the safety of our passengers*; **primary colours** = basic colours (red, yellow and blue) which can combine to make up all the other colours; *US* **primary election** = first election to choose a candidate to represent a political party in a main election; *a candidate who does not win the primary election in his own state is doomed to fail* **2** *noun US* primary election; *he won the New Hampshire primary* (NOTE: plural is **primaries**)

primary school ['praɪməri 'skuːl] *noun* school for children up to the age of eleven; *John is still at primary school*; *she's a primary school teacher*; *children concentrate on reading, writing and maths in primary school* (NOTE: the American equivalent is the **elementary school**)

primate ['praɪmeɪt] *noun* **(a) primates** = order of mammals containing monkeys, apes and human beings; *all primates are capable of using facial expressions as a means of communication* **(b)** archbishop; *the Archbishop of Canterbury is the Primate of all England*

prime [praɪm] **1** *adjective* **(a)** most important; *the prime suspect in the case is the dead woman's husband*; *she is a prime target for any kidnapper*; *this is a prime example of what is wrong with this country*; **prime position** *or* **prime site** = good position for a commercial property; *the restaurant is in a prime position in the High Street*; **prime time television** = TV programmes shown at the time when most people watch television; *the interview is being shown on prime time TV* **(b)** of best quality; *prime Scottish beef* **(c) prime number** = number (such as 2, 5, 11, etc.) which can only be divided by itself or by 1 **2** *noun* period when you are at your best; *he was at his prime when he won the championship*; **past your prime** = no longer at your best; *at 35, as a tennis player, she's past her prime* **3** *verb* **(a)** to get something prepared; *the bomb had been primed and would have exploded in ten minutes* **(b)** to give wood or metal a first coat of special paint, before giving the top coat; *the paint is coming off because the wood hadn't been primed properly* **(c)** to put water into a water pump or oil into a machine, so as to start it working **(d) to prime someone to do something** = to prepare someone in advance by giving information, advice, etc.; *she came primed with a few questions which would embarrass the speaker*

Prime Minister ['praɪm 'mɪnɪstə] *noun* head of the government in Britain and other countries; *the Australian Prime Minister or the Prime Minister of Australia*; *she cut out the picture of the Prime Minister from the newspaper*; *the Prime Minister will address the nation at 6 o'clock tonight*

primer ['praɪmə] *noun* special paint which is put on bare wood before giving the top coats; *they didn't use a primer and now the paint is coming off the door*

prime rate ['praɪm 'reɪt] *noun US* best rate of interest at which an American bank lends to its customers; *they are charging interest at 3% above prime rate* (NOTE: the British equivalent is the **bank base rate**)

primeval [praɪ'miːvl] *adjective* **(a)** referring to the period at the beginning of the world's existence; *the primeval forest* **(b)** = PRIMAL

primitive ['prɪmɪtɪv] *adjective* **(a)** referring to very early or prehistoric times; *a primitive people who flourished in the Stone Age* **(b)** rough, crude; *they live in a primitive hut in the woods*; *the system is a bit primitive but it works*

primrose ['prɪmrəʊz] *noun* small pale yellow spring flower; *primroses flower in early spring*

prince [prɪns] *noun* son of a king or queen; **Prince of Wales** = title given to the eldest son of a British king or queen, the heir to the throne (NOTE: used as a title with a name: **Prince Edward**)

princess [prɪn'ses] *noun* **(a)** daughter of a king or queen; *once upon a time a beautiful princess lived in a castle by the edge of the forest* **(b)** wife of a prince (NOTE: used as a title with a name: **Princess Sophia**; note also that the plural is **princesses**)

principal ['prɪnsɪpl] **1** *adjective* main, most important; *the country's principal products are paper and wood*; *she played a principal role in setting up the organization* **2** *noun* **(a)** head (of a school, a college); *the principal wants to see you in her office* **(b)** main performer (actor in a play, dancer in a ballet); *the principals were quite good but the chorus was awful* **(c)** money on which interest is paid, capital which has been invested; *up to now you've been paying interest, but now you can start repaying some of the principal* (NOTE: do not confuse with **principle**)

principality [prɪnsɪ'pæliti] *noun* **(a)** country ruled by a prince; *the Principality of Monaco* (NOTE: plural is **principalities**) **(b) the Principality** = Wales

principally ['prɪnsəpli] *adverb* mainly; *the company trades principally in the Far East*; *we are principally interested in buying antique clocks*

principle ['prɪnsɪpl] *noun* **(a)** law; general rule; *the principles of nuclear physics*; *it is a principle in our system of justice that a person is innocent until he is proved guilty*; **in principle** = in agreement with the general rule; *I agree in principle, but we need to discuss some of the details more thoroughly*; *in principle, the results should be the same every time you do the experiment* **(b)** personal sense of what is right; *she's a woman of very strong principles*; *it's against my principles to work on a Sunday*; **on principle** = because of what you believe; *she refuses to eat meat on principle* (NOTE: do not confuse with **principal**)

print [prɪnt] **1** *noun* **(a)** mark made on something; *the print of a dinosaur's foot has been preserved in this rock*; *the police examined the tyre prints left by the vehicle*; *see also* FOOTPRINT, FINGERPRINT **(b)** letters printed on a page; *I can't read this book - the print is too small*; **the small print** *or* **the fine print** = the conditions on a contract, usually printed in very small letters; *don't forget to check the fine print before you sign the contract* **(c)** picture or photograph which has been printed; *the print is very blurred*; *I'm going to have some more prints made of this photo* **2** *verb* **(a)** to mark letters or pictures on paper by a machine, and so produce a book, leaflet, newspaper, etc.; *the book is printed directly from a computer disk*; *we had five hundred copies of the leaflet printed* **(b)** to write capital letters or letters which are not joined together; *print your name in the space below*

printable ['prɪntəbl] *adjective* fit to be printed and published; *most of what he said was not printable*

printed ['prɪntɪd] *adjective* produced on paper using a printing press; **printed matter** = paper with printing on it, such as leaflets, books, newspapers, magazines, etc.; *printed matter can be sent through the post at a lower rate*; **the printed word** = information in a printed form; *people rely more on television and radio for news and less on the printed word*

printed circuit board (PCB) ['prɪntɪd 'sɜːkɪt 'bɔːd] *noun* card with metal tracks printed or etched on it, which forms an electrical connection when other elements are fitted onto it; *printed circuit boards enable many types of electrical goods to be made in very small sizes*

printer ['prɪntə] *noun* **(a)** person or company that prints books, newspapers, etc.; *the book has gone to the printer, and we should have copies next week* **(b)** machine which prints; **dot matrix printer** = printer which forms characters from a series of tiny dots printed close together; **laser printer** = high-quality printer that uses a laser to print dot-matrix characters

printing ['prɪntɪŋ] *noun* **(a)** the art, business and process of printing books, newspapers, etc.; *errors may have crept into the text during printing*; **printing ink** = ink made from carbon and oil, used for printing; **printing press** = machine which prints books, etc.; *Gutenberg invented the printing press in the fifteenth century* **(b)** number of copies of a book printed at the same time; *the book was published with a first printing of 5,000 copies*; *the second printing has sold out and a third has been ordered*

print out ['prɪnt 'aʊt] *verb* to print information from a computer through a printer; *she printed out three copies of the letter*

printout ['prɪntaʊt] *noun* printed information from a computer; *the travel agent gave me a printout of flight details and hotel reservations*

prior ['praɪə] **1** *adjective* **(a)** before; previous; *the house can be visited by prior arrangement with the owner*; *I had to refuse her invitation because I had a prior engagement in London*; **without prior agreement** = without any agreement in advance **(b)** *(formal)* **prior to** = before; *they had left prior to my arrival* **2** *noun* man who is head of a priory; *the prior has been summoned to Rome*

prioress [praɪə'res] *noun* woman who is head of a convent or priory; *the nuns addressed the prioress as Reverend Mother*

priority [praɪ'ɒrɪti] *noun* **(a)** right to be first; **to have priority over** *or* **to take priority over something** = to be more important than something, to need to be done first; *people with serious injuries have priority over those with only cuts and bruises*; **to give something top priority** = to make something the most important item; *we should give top priority to solving our own financial problems*; *the President want us to give the problem top priority* **(b)** thing which has to be done first; *finding somewhere to stay the night was our main priority*

priory ['praɪəri] *noun* building where monks or nuns live; *the ruins of the old priory are said to haunted* (NOTE: plural is **priories**)

prise [praɪz] *verb* **to prise something open** = to lift open with force; *he prised the lid open with a metal bar* (NOTE: American English is **pry**)

prism ['prɪzm] *noun* glass block usually with a cross-section shaped like a triangle, which splits white light up into the colours of the rainbow; *we shone a light through a prism*

prismatic [prɪz'mætɪk] *adjective* using a prism; *prismatic binoculars*

prison ['prɪzn] *noun* building where people are kept when they are being punished for a crime; *the judge sent him to prison for five years*; *his father's in prison for burglary*; *the prisoners managed to escape from prison by digging a tunnel* (NOTE: **prison** is often used without the article **the**)

prisoner ['prɪznə] *noun* person who is in prison; *the prisoners were taken away in a police van*; **prisoner of war (POW)** = soldier, airman, etc., who has been captured by the enemy

prison officer ['prɪzn 'ɒfɪsə] *noun* person who guards prisoners in a jail; *the prison officers went round locking the cell doors* (NOTE: formerly called **jailers**)

pristine ['prɪstiːn] *adjective (formal)* fresh like new; *the old car is in absolutely pristine condition*

privacy ['prɪvəsi] *noun* not being disturbed by other people; *I need some privacy to be able to think what I must do next*; *she read the letter in the privacy of her bedroom*

private ['praɪvət] *adjective* **(a)** which belongs to one person, not to everyone; *he flew there in his private jet*; *(informal)* **private eye** = a detective who is not a member of the police force and is employed by an ordinary person; **private property** = property which belongs to a private person, not to the public; *you can't park here - this is private property*; **the private sector** = companies which are listed on the stock exchange or owned by individuals, and not by the government; *the research is financed by money from the private sector*; **private view** = private showing of an exhibition, etc., before it is open to the public; *we've been invited to a private view of her latest exhibition* **(b)** which refers to one particular person and should kept secret from others; *you have no right to interfere in my private affairs*; *this is a private discussion between me and my son*; **in private** = away from other people; *she asked to see the teacher in private*

private enterprise ['praɪvət 'entəpraɪz] *noun* businesses that are owned and run by individuals or groups, not by the state; *the bus service is now run by private enterprise*; *the economic success of the USA is based on private enterprise*

privately ['praɪvətli] *adverb* **(a)** in private; *I spoke to her privately about it* **(b)** not telling anyone; *privately, he thought she was a fool* **(c)** (owned) by private individuals; *a privately-owned railway*

private school [praɪvət 'skuːl] *noun* a school that is not run by the state and which the students have to pay to attend; *their children are being educated in a private school*; *compare* PUBLIC SCHOOL

private secretary ['praɪvət 'sekrətri] *noun* someone who deals with an important person's correspondence and affairs; *a letter from the Queen's private secretary*

privatization [praɪvətaɪ'zeɪʃn] *noun* act of privatizing; *after privatization the industry was supposed to be run more efficiently*

privatize ['praɪvətaɪz] *verb* to return a nationalized industry to private ownership by selling shares in it on the stock exchange; *the government says it has no plans to privatize the Post Office*

privilege ['prɪvɪlɪdʒ] *noun* favour or right granted to some people but not to everyone; *it is a great privilege being asked to speak to you tonight; I once had the privilege of meeting the Pope*

privileged ['prɪvɪledʒd] *adjective* who has a special advantage; *you must think yourselves privileged to have her as your president; only a privileged few will be able to see the exhibition*

privy ['prɪvi] 1 *adjective (formal)* **to be privy to a secret** = to know the details of a secret; *I'm not privy to their plans for the rest of the day* 2 *noun (informal)* rough toilet outside a house; *it's freezing cold out there in the privy* (NOTE: plural is **privies**)

Privy Council ['prɪvi 'kaʊnsəl] *noun* body of senior advisers who advise the Queen on political matters

Privy Councillor ['prɪvi 'kaʊnsələ] *noun* member of the Privy Council; *Privy Councillors have the title 'the Right Honourable'*

prize [praɪz] 1 *noun* something given to a winner; *he won first prize in the music competition; he answered all the questions correctly and claimed the prize; the prize was awarded jointly to the young British and Russian competitors;* **prize money** = money given to the person who wins a competition; *there is £10,000 in prize money at stake* 2 *adjective* which has won a prize because of being of good quality; *he showed a prize sheep at the agricultural show*

prizewinner ['praɪzwɪnə] *noun* someone who has won a prize; *prizewinners will be notified by post*

prizewinning ['ʊraɪzwɪnɪŋ] *adjective* that has won a prize; *his prizewinning essay was published in the local paper; another work by the prizewinning novelist*

pro [prəʊ] 1 *prefix* meaning in favour of; *the pro-European lobby* 2 *preposition* in favour of; *she's very pro fox-hunting* 3 *noun* (a) **the pros and cons** = the arguments for and against a case; *having considered the pros and cons of the case, we decided to accept their offer* (b) *(informal)* professional sportsman, actor, etc.; *she's a real pro*

proactive [prəʊ'æktɪv] *adjective* working by starting actions yourself, rather than reacting to what other people do; *they decided to adopt a proactive strategy* (NOTE: the opposite in this meaning is **reactive**)

probability [prɒbə'bɪlɪti] *noun* likelihood, being probable; *there is little probability of the work being finished on time; the probability is that there will be no outright winner;* **in all probability** = very probably; *in all probability they will get married at Easter*

probable ['prɒbəbl] *adjective* likely; *it's probable that she left her bag on the train; the police think it is probable that she knew her murderer*

probably ['prɒbəbli] *adverb* likely to happen; *we're probably going to Spain for our holidays; my father is probably going to retire next year; are you going to Spain as usual this year? - very probably*

probation [prə'beɪʃn] *noun* (a) legal system for dealing with criminals (often young offenders) where they are not sent to prison provided that they continue to behave well under the supervision of a probation officer; *she was put on probation for one year or was put on one year's probation;* **probation officer** =

official of the social services who supervises young people on probation; *my probation officer is helping me find a job* (b) period when a new worker is being tested before being confirmed as having a permanent job; **on probation** = being tested; *we are employing him on three months' probation; she can't have a pay rise as she is still on probation*

probe [prəʊb] 1 *noun* (a) thorough investigation; *a police probe into organized crime* (b) **space probe** = spacecraft sent into space for scientific purposes 2 *verb* to examine something deeply; *I don't want the police to start probing into my financial affairs; the surgeon probed the wound to try to find the bullet*

problem ['prɒbləm] *noun* something which is difficult to answer; *half the students couldn't do all the problems in the maths test;* **to pose a problem** = to be a difficult question; *what to do with illegal immigrants poses a problem for the immigration services;* **to solve a problem** = to find an answer to a problem; *the police are trying to solve the problem of how the thieves got into the house; we have called in an expert to solve our computer problem*

problematic(al) [prɒblə'mætɪk(l)] *adjective* difficult to understand, likely to cause a problem; *the relationship between unions and management remains problematic; the situation is a bit problematical and there's no easy solution to it*

proboscis [prəʊ'bɒsɪs] *noun* long tube coming from the head of an animal, such as the trunk of an elephant or the sting of a mosquito (NOTE: plural is **proboscises**)

procedural [prə'siːdʒərəl] *adjective* referring to procedure; *they still have to sort out various procedural difficulties*

procedure [prə'siːdʒə] *noun* (a) way in which something ought to be carried out; *to obtain permission to build a new house you need to follow the correct procedure; this procedure is very irregular* = this is not the correct way to do something (b) medical treatment; *a new procedure for treating cases of drug addiction*

proceed [prə'siːd] *verb* (a) to go further; *he proceeded down the High Street towards the river* (b) to do something after something else; *they then proceeded to shout and throw bottles at passing cars* (c) **to proceed with something** = to go on doing something; *shall we proceed with the committee meeting?*

proceed against [prə'siːd ə'geɪnst] *verb* to start a lawsuit against someone; *the police can't proceed against her without more evidence*

proceedings [prə'siːdɪŋz] *noun* (a) **legal proceedings** = lawsuit or legal action; *if payment is not made within two days, we shall start proceedings against you; the proceedings are expected to last three days* (b) report of what takes place at a meeting; *the proceedings of the Archaeological Society*

proceeds ['prəʊsiːdz] *noun* money which you receive when you sell something; *she sold her house and invested the proceeds in a little shop; all the proceeds of the village fair go to charity*

process ['prəʊses] 1 *noun* (a) method of making something; *a new process for extracting oil from coal; see also* PEACE (NOTE: plural is **processes**) (b) **in the process of doing something** = while doing something; *she interrupted me while I was in the process of writing my report; we were in the process of moving to*

London when I had the offer of a job in Australia **2** *verb* **(a)** to manufacture goods from raw materials; *the uranium has to be processed before it can be used in a nuclear reactor*; **processed cheese** = cheese which has been treated so that it will keep for a long time **(b)** to deal with a claim, bill, etc., in the usual routine way; *to process an insurance claim*; *orders are processed in our warehouse* **(c)** to sort out information, especially using a computer; *the computer processes the data and then prints it out* **(d)** [prə'ses] to walk in a procession; *the peers and peeresses processed into Westminster Abbey*

processing ['prəusesɪŋ] *noun* **data processing** or **information processing** = selecting and examining data in a computer to produce information in a special form; *a data-processing service*; **word processing** or **text processing** = working with words, using a computer to produce, check and change letters, texts, reports, etc.; *she did a course in word processing before taking a job as a secretary*

procession [prə'seʃn] *noun* group of people (with a band, etc.) walking in line; *the procession will march down Whitehall to the Houses of Parliament*; *the funeral procession will arrive at the cathedral at 11.00*; **in procession** = in a line as part of a ceremony; *the people who have received their degrees will walk in procession through the university grounds*

processor ['prəusesə] *noun* **(a)** machine that processes; *mix the ingredients in a food processor* **(b)** computer which processes information; **word processor** = computer which is used for working with words, to produce texts, reports, letters, etc.; *she offered to write the letter for me on her word processor*

proclaim [prə'kleɪm] *verb* to make an official statement in public; *the president proclaimed a state of emergency*

proclamation [proklə'meɪʃn] *noun* official public statement; *the proclamation of a state of emergency*; *the proclamation of independence*

proclivity [prə'klɪvɪti] *noun* (*formal*) natural tendency, usually to do something bad; *he has the unfortunate proclivity to interrupt you and finish your sentences for you*

procrastinate [prəu'kræstɪneɪt] *verb* (*formal*) to delay, to postpone something until later; *don't procrastinate - do it right away*

procure [prə'kjuə] *verb* **(a)** (*formal*) to get, to obtain something; *somehow he had managed to procure the equipment he needed without anyone knowing*; *we need to procure a map of the area* **(b)** to arrange for a woman to provide sexual intercourse for money

procurement [prə'kjuəmənt] *noun* obtaining of equipment, of supplies; *the department in charge of procurement for the navy*

procurer [prə'kjuərə] *noun* (*formal*) person who provides prostitutes for sex; *the hotel porter acted as a procurer for wealthy guests*

prod [prod] **1** *noun* poke; *he gave the pig a prod with his stick*; *he gave me a prod in the ribs*; **to give someone a prod** = to nudge someone, to try to get someone to do something; *he's late with his work - better give him a prod* **2** *verb* **(a)** to poke with a finger or stick, etc.; *he prodded the pig with his stick* **(b)** to **prod someone into doing something** = to do something to persuade someone to take action; *the*

group tried to prod the government into action *or* into taking some sort of action (NOTE: **prodding - prodded**)

prodigal ['prodɪgl] *adjective* wasteful, especially wasteful of money; *if he hadn't been so prodigal with gifts to his friends he could have bought a house by now*

prodigious [prə'dɪdʒəs] *adjective* (*formal*) **(a)** enormous, very powerful; *the children ate a prodigious quantity of cakes*; *he used his prodigious strength to lift up the trunk* **(b)** extraordinary; *he's a prodigious writer of children's stories*

prodigiously [prə'dɪdʒəsli] *adverb* enormously; *she's a prodigiously gifted pianist*

prodigy ['prodɪdʒi] *noun* **(a)** remarkable person, usually a young person; *by the age of ten he was already a mathematical prodigy*; **infant prodigy** or **child prodigy** = child who does remarkable things; *Mozart was an infant prodigy - he gave concerts before he was five years old* **(b)** extraordinary action; *the firemen performed prodigies of bravery* (NOTE: plural is **prodigies**)

produce 1 *noun* ['prodjuːs] things grown on the land; *vegetables and other garden produce* (NOTE: do not confuse with **product**) **2** *verb* [prə'djuːs] **(a)** to show or bring out; *the tax office asked him to produce the relevant documents*; *he produced a bundle of notes from his inside pocket* **(b)** to make; *the factory produces cars and trucks* **(c)** to put on a play, a film, etc.; *she is producing 'Hamlet' for the local drama club* **(d)** to grow crops, to give birth to young, etc.; *the region produces enough rice to supply the needs of the whole country*; *our cat has produced six kittens*

producer [prə'djuːsə] *noun* **(a)** company or country which makes or grows something; *an important producer of steel*; *the company is a major car producer* **(b)** person who puts on a play or a film; *the producers weren't happy with the director's choice of cast*

COMMENT: a producer of a film is the person who has overall control of the making of the film, especially of its financing, but does not deal with the technical details. The director organizes the actual making of the film, giving instructions to the actors, dealing with the lighting, sound, etc.

product ['prodʌkt] *noun* **(a)** thing which is manufactured; *Germany is helping her industry to sell more products abroad* (NOTE: do not confuse with **produce**) **(b)** **gross domestic product (GDP)** = annual value of goods sold and services paid for inside a country; **gross national product (GNP)** = annual value of goods and services in a country, including income from other countries **(c)** (*in mathematics*) number which is the result when numbers are multiplied; *the product of 4 times 10 is 40*

production [prə'dʌkʃn] *noun* **(a)** manufacturing; *we are trying to step up production*; *production will probably be held up by the strike* **(b)** putting on a play or film; *the film is currently in production at Teddington Studios* **(c)** particular way of putting on a play; *have you seen the production of 'Henry V' at the Globe Theatre?* **(d)** showing something; **on production of** = when something is shown; *goods bought can be exchanged only on production of the sales slip*

production line [prə'dʌkʃn 'laɪn] *noun* system of making a product, where each item (such as a car) moves slowly through the factory with new sections being added to it as it goes along; *he works on the production line*

productive [prə'dʌktɪv] *adjective* which produces; *the 1590s were a very productive period for the English theatre*; *how can we make our workforce more productive?*; **a productive meeting** = a useful meeting which should lead to an agreement; *we had a very productive morning - all the remaining problems were ironed out*

productivity [prɒdʌk'tɪvɪti] *noun* rate of output, rate of production in a factory; *bonus payments are linked to productivity*; *productivity has fallen since the company was taken over*; **productivity bonus** = bonus paid for increased rate of production

Prof [prɒf] = PROFESSOR; *Prof Stanley Ridge*

profane [prə'feɪn] **1** *adjective (formal)* **(a)** not religious; *sacred and profane art*; *they considered all music to be profane and banned singing from church services* **(b)** blasphemous, rude towards God or religion; *she was accused of using profane language* **2** *verb (formal)* to treat something sacred with disrespect; *how dare you profane the memory of your great father!*

profanity [prə'fænɪti] *noun (formal)* swearing, blasphemy, bad language; *my aunt was very religious and would never allow any profanity to soil her lips* (NOTE: plural is **profanities**)

profess [prə'fes] *verb (formal)* to declare; *she professed she had no knowledge of the affair*; *everyone professed themselves satisfied with the decision*

profession [prə'feʃn] *noun* **(a)** work which needs special training, skill or knowledge; *the legal profession*; *the medical profession*; *the teaching profession*; *she is an accountant by profession* **(b)** declaration of belief in something; *a profession of faith*

professional [prə'feʃnəl] **1** *adjective* **(a)** referring to a profession; *he keeps his professional life and his private life completely separate*; **professional qualifications** = documents showing that someone has successfully finished a course of study which allows him to work in one of the professions **(b)** expert or skilled; *they did a very professional job in designing the new office* **(c)** *(sportsman)* who is paid to play; *a professional footballer* **2** *noun* **(a)** expert; *don't try to deal with the problem yourself - get a professional in* **(b)** sportsman who is paid to play; *for many years, professionals were not allowed to compete in the Olympics*; *he ran as an amateur for several years, then turned professional* **(c)** sportsman who coaches others; *a golf professional*

professionalism [prə'feʃnəlɪzm] *noun* **(a)** being an expert, having skill; *people admired the professionalism with which he dealt with the problem* **(b)** paying sportsmen to play; *what effect will professionalism have on the game of rugby?*

professionally [prə'feʃnəli] *adverb* **(a)** as a professional; *acting is her hobby, but she'd like to do it professionally* **(b)** by professionals; *we had the house redecorated professionally*

professor [prə'fesə] *noun* **(a)** most senior teacher in a subject at a university; *a professor of English*; *an economics professor* **(b)** title taken by some teachers of music, art, etc.; *she goes to Professor Smith for piano lessons* (NOTE: **professor** is written with a capital letter when used as a title: **Professor Smith**)

professorial [prɒfə'sɔːriəl] *adjective* referring to a professor; *he's been offered a professorial post at Cambridge*

proffer ['prɒfə] *verb (formal)* to offer; *he proffered his hand in friendship*; *they decided not to take the proffered advice*

proficiency [prə'fɪʃənsi] *noun* skill in doing something; *he has a badge of proficiency in swimming*; *she hadn't reached the required level of proficiency in typing*

proficient [prə'fɪʃnt] *adjective* skilful, able to do something well; **to be proficient at** *or* **in something** = to be very capable of doing something well; *I'm not very proficient at mental arithmetic*; *by the summer I had become reasonably proficient in German*

profile ['prəʊfaɪl] *noun* **(a)** view of someone's head, seen from the side; *a photograph showing her in profile* **(b)** **to keep a low profile** = to be quiet, not to be obvious; *it would be better if you kept a low profile until all the fuss has died down*; **to keep** *or* **maintain a high profile** = to keep yourself in the view of the public; *a politician needs to keep a high profile*; *advertising helps to maintain the company's profile* **(c)** short biography of a famous person in a newspaper; *there's a profile of the Chancellor in the Sunday paper*

profit ['prɒfɪt] **1** *noun* money you gain from selling something which is more than the money you paid for it; *the sale produced a good profit or a handsome profit*; **gross profit** = profit calculated as income from sales less the cost of the goods sold (i.e., without deducting any other expenses); **net profit** = profit calculated as income from sales less all expenditure; **profit margin** = percentage of money gained against money paid out; **to make a profit** = to have more money as a result of a deal; *we aim to make a quick profit*; *we made a large profit when we sold our house*; *it you don't make a profit you will soon be out of business*; **to show a profit** = to make a profit and put it in the company accounts; *we are showing a small profit for the first quarter*; **to take your profit** = to sell shares at a higher price than you paid for them, rather than to keep them as an investment **2** *verb* **to profit from** = to gain from; *I profited from her advice*

profitability [prɒfɪtə'bɪlɪti] *noun* being able to produce a profit; *we are worried about the profitability of some of our overseas operations*

profitable ['prɒfɪtəbl] *adjective* likely to produce a profit; *he signed a profitable deal with a Russian company*; *I am sure he will find a profitable use for his talents as a salesman*

profitably ['prɒfɪtəbli] *adverb* **(a)** at a profit; *make sure the money is profitably invested* **(b)** usefully; *I spent the week very profitably doing research in the library*

profit and loss account ['prɒfɪt ənd 'lɒs ə'kaʊnt] *noun* statement of a company's expenditure and income over a period of time, almost always one year, showing whether the company has made a profit or loss; *shareholders examine the profit and loss account to see how the company is doing*

COMMENT: the profit and loss account shows the movements which have taken place since the end of the previous accounting period; the balance sheet shows the state of a company's finances at a certain date

profligate ['prɒflɪgət] *adjective (formal)* very extravagant; *how can this profligate expenditure be justified to the electors?*

profound [prə'faʊnd] *adjective* very serious, very deep; *he showed a profound understanding of the problems of the unemployed; the play is trying to say something profound about modern life*

profusion [prə'fju:ʒn] *noun* very large quantity; *in May, there is a profusion of flowers in the fields;* in **profusion** = in large quantities; *there are wild flowers in profusion in the countryside in early summer* (NOTE: no plural)

progeny ['prɒdʒəni] *noun (formal)* children, offspring; *we saw them shepherding their numerous progeny along the beach* (NOTE: takes a plural verb)

progesterone [prəʊ'dʒestərəʊn] *noun* sex hormone produced in the second part of the menstrual cycle which stimulates the formation of the placenta if an ovum is fertilized; synthetic forms are also used as contraceptives; *compare* TESTOSTERONE

prognosis [prɒg'nəʊsɪs] *noun* opinion of how something, such as a disease, will develop; *the doctor was unable to give a detailed prognosis; the prognosis for the economy is good;* this cancer has a prognosis of about two years = the patient will die within two years unless the cancer is eradicated (NOTE: plural is **prognoses**)

program ['prəʊgræm] **1** *noun* instructions given to a computer; *to load a program; to run a program; a graphics program; a word-processing program* **2** *verb* to give instructions to a computer; *the computer is programmed to print labels;* programming language = system of signs and words used to program a computer (NOTE: **programming - programmed**)

programme US **program** ['prəʊgræm US 'prəʊgrəm] **1** *noun* **(a)** TV or radio show; *we watched a programme on life in the 17th century; there's a football programme after the news; I want to listen to the phone-in programme at 9.15; there are no good television programmes tonight* **(b)** paper in a theatre or at a football match, etc., which gives information about the show; *the programme gives a list of the actors; the match programme costs £5* **2** *verb* to arrange programmes on TV or radio; *the new chat show is programmed to compete with the gardening programme on the other channel*

programmer ['prəʊgræmə] *noun* **(a)** person who programs a computer; *the programmers made a few alterations to our software* **(b)** person who programmes TV or radio shows; *programmers are always trying to win audiences from other channels*

progress 1 *noun* ['prəʊgres] **(a)** movement forwards; *we are making good progress towards finishing the house* (NOTE: no plural) **(b)** in **progress** = which is happening or being done; *the meeting is still in progress; we still have a lot of work in progress* **2** *verb* [prə'gres] to advance; *work on the bypass is progressing slowly*

progression [prə'greʃn] *noun* advance, movement forwards; *the progression from youth to middle age*

has been very hard for her; having studied French, it seemed a natural progression that I should try to find a job in France

progressive [prə'gresɪv] *adjective* **(a)** (movement) in stages; *I have noticed a progressive improvement in your work* **(b)** advanced (ideas); *they elected a leader with progressive views on education*

progressively [prə'gresɪvli] *adverb* by stages; *it's getting progressively more difficult to find qualified staff; over the holiday, the weather got progressively worse; we will introduce the changes progressively*

prohibit [prə'hɪbɪt] *verb* to say that something must not be done; *the rules prohibit singing in the dining room*

prohibition [prəʊhɪ'bɪʃn] *noun* act of forbidding something; *my father issued a stern prohibition on any more trips to the club*

prohibitive [prə'hɪbɪtɪv] *adjective* so expensive that you cannot afford it; *the cost of redoing the kitchen is quite prohibitive*

project 1 ['prɒdʒekt] *noun* **(a)** plan, scheme; *we are working on a building project* **(b)** work planned by students on their own; *her project is to write the history of her village; she asked her teacher for some pointers to help her with her project* **2** [prə'dʒekt] *verb* **(a)** to plan something, to expect to do something; *they are projecting to build a new science park near the university* **(b)** to send a picture onto a screen; *the lecturer projected slides of his visit to the Arctic*

projected [prə'dʒektɪd] *adjective* **(a)** which has been planned; *we had to abandon our projected American trip; this is the site of the projected factory* **(b)** which has been forecast; *here are the projected sales figures for next year*

projectile [prə'dʒektaɪl] *noun (formal)* thing which is thrown or fired from a gun; *most of the projectiles simply bounced off the vehicle's armour-plating*

projection [prə'dʒekʃn] *noun* **(a)** thing which is forecast for the future; *we have made a projection of the additional housing needed in this area by the year 2010* **(b)** thing which sticks out; *she gashed her arm on a sharp projection of rock* **(c)** action of projecting a picture onto a screen; the **projection room** = room in a cinema, with the projector, where the projectionist works

projectionist [prə'dʒekʃənɪst] *noun* person who operates a projector in a cinema; *the projectionist apologized and restarted the film*

projector [prə'dʒektə] *noun* machine which sends pictures on a screen; *the projector broke down so we couldn't see the end of the film*

proletarian [prəʊlɪ'teəriən] *adjective* referring to the working class; *it was the first truly proletarian revolution*

proletariat [prəʊlɪ'teəriət] *noun* the **proletariat** = the working class, especially manual and industrial workers and their families; *in the nineteenth century, in most countries the peasantry still vastly outnumbered the proletariat; the proletariat were considered incapable of organizing themselves as a political force;* urban **proletariat** = working people who live in towns

proliferate [prə'lɪfəreɪt] *verb* to increase quickly in number; *fast-food restaurants have proliferated in recent years*

proliferation [prəlɪfə'reɪʃn] *noun* rapid spread; *the proliferation of charity shops in the city centre*

prolific [prə'lɪfɪk] *adjective* (a) producing many children, fruit or other offspring; *rabbits are notoriously prolific* (b) producing a lot of something; *he's a prolific writer of travel guides*

prologue *US* **prolog** ['prəʊlɒg] *noun* (a) piece spoken as the introduction of a play or poem; *the prologue sets the scene and introduces the main characters; compare* EPILOGUE (b) preliminary event that leads on to something else; *the discussions between Foreign Ministers are a prologue to the signing of a full-scale treaty*

prolong [prə'lɒŋ] *verb* to make something longer; *I don't want to prolong the meeting unnecessarily*

prolongation [prəʊlɒŋ'geɪʃn] *noun* (*formal*) making something longer; *he opposed the prolongation of the agreement*

prolonged [prə'lɒŋd] *adjective* lasting for a long time; *his prolonged absence worried his family; she died after a prolonged illness*

prom [prɒm] *noun* (*informal*) (a) *GB* promenade; *let's go for a stroll along the prom* (b) **prom concerts** *or* **the proms** = promenade concerts (c) *US* school dance; *they met at the High School prom*

promenade [prɒmə'nɑːd] **1** *noun* (a) walkway built along the side of the sea; *we stood on the promenade and looked out to sea; our hotel was right on the promenade* (*on a ship*) **promenade deck** = deck where passengers can walk about (b) **promenade concerts** = inexpensive concerts of classical music where most of the audience stands and can walk about (NOTE: also simply called **prom concerts** *or* **proms**) **2** *verb* to walk about; *we promenaded up and down the Champs Elysées*

prominence ['prɒmɪnəns] *noun* (a) being important or famous; *he first rose to prominence in the 1960s* (b) **to give prominence to** = to emphasise something; *the newspapers gave too much prominence to that part of the speech* (c) (*formal*) piece of land which stands out higher than the rest; *the castle stands on a prominence overlooking a bend in the river*

prominent ['prɒmɪnənt] *adjective* (a) standing out, easily seen; *she has a very prominent nose* (b) famous or important; *a prominent trade unionist; they assassinated a prominent member of the ruling party*

prominently ['prɒmɪnəntli] *adverb* easily seen; *the white walls stand out prominently against the background of the dark blue sea; the story featured prominently in the evening newspapers*

promiscuous [prə'mɪskjʊəs] *adjective* who has sexual relations with many people; *they indulged in promiscuous sex at college; he was very promiscuous as a young man*

promise ['prɒmɪs] **1** *noun* act of saying that you will definitely do something; *but you made a promise not to tell anyone else and now you've told my mother!; I'll pay you back on Friday - that's a promise;* **to go back on a promise** *or* **to break a promise** = not to do what you said you would do; *the management went back on its promise to increase salaries; he broke his promise to take her to Mexico on holiday;* **to keep a promise** = to do what you said you would do; *he says he will pay next week, but he never keeps his promises; she kept her promise to write to him every day; see also* LICK **2**

2 *verb* (a) to give your word that you will definitely do something; *they promised to be back for supper; you must promise to bring the computer back when you have finished with it; he promised he would look into the problem; she promised the staff an extra week's holiday but it never materialized* (b) to look as if something will happen; *the meeting promises to be very interesting*

promising ['prɒmɪsɪŋ] *adjective* (a) who is likely to succeed; *she's the most promising candidate we have interviewed so far* (b) good, and likely to become much better; *the results of the antibiotic have been very promising; the economic situation looks much more promising than it did a year ago*

promontory ['prɒməntəri] *noun* piece of high land jutting out into the sea; *the ship came round the promontory and sailed straight into the harbour; the lighthouse was built at the end of a promontory* (NOTE: plural is **promontories**)

promote [prə'məʊt] *verb* (a) to give someone a better job; *he was promoted from salesman to sales manager* (b) to make sure that people know about a product or service, by advertising it; *there are posters all over the place promoting the new night club* (c) to encourage; *the club's aim is to promote gardening*

promoter [prə'məʊtə] *noun* **boxing promoter** = person who organizes a boxing match, etc.

promotion [prə'məʊʃn] *noun* (a) move to a better job; *he ruined his chances of promotion when he argued with the boss* (b) advertising of a new product; *we're giving away small bottles of shampoo as a promotion*

promotional [prə'məʊʃnəl] *adjective* used in an advertising campaign; *the admen are using balloons as part of their promotional material; they are making a promotional film for the air force*

prompt [prɒmpt] **1** *adjective* done immediately; *thank you for your prompt reply* (NOTE: **prompter - promptest**) **2** *verb* (a) to suggest to someone that he should do something; *it prompted him to write to the local paper* (b) to tell an actor words which he has forgotten; *he had to be prompted in the middle of a long speech* **3** *noun* message to a computer user, telling him to do something; *the prompt came up on the screen telling me to insert the disk in drive A*

prompting ['prɒmptɪŋ] *noun* the action of persuading someone to do something; *she needed no prompting from me to begin; she did it without any prompting from her teacher*

promptly ['prɒmptli] *adverb* immediately; rapidly; *he replied to my letter very promptly*

promulgate ['prɒmʌlgeɪt] *verb* (*formal*) to make a law known to the public; *the law was promulgated in 1792*

prone [prəʊn] *adjective* (a) (lying) flat; *they found her lying prone on the floor* (b) **prone to** = likely to do something, likely to suffer from something; *when you're tired you are prone to make mistakes; he's prone to chest infections;* **accident-prone** = likely to have accidents often; *the new waitress seems to be accident-prone*

prong [prɒŋ] *noun* one of the sharp points of a fork; *he jabbed the prongs of the fork into his sausage*

pronoun ['prəʊnaʊn] *noun* word used instead of a noun, such as 'I', 'you', 'he', 'she' and 'it'; *there are three pronouns in the sentence 'she gave it to me'*

pronounce [prə'naʊns] *verb* **(a)** to speak sounds which form a word; *how do you pronounce 'Paris' in French?* **(b)** to state officially; *he was pronounced dead on arrival at hospital*; *the priest pronounced them man and wife*

pronounced [prə'naʊnst] *adjective* noticeable; *she walks with a pronounced limp*; *there has been a pronounced improvement in his work*

pronouncement [prə'naʊnsmənt] *noun* official or formal statement; *the chairman made a pronouncement that the meeting had not reached any decision on the matter*

pronunciation [prənʌnsi'eɪʃn] *noun* way of speaking words; *what's the correct pronunciation of 'controversy'?*; *I tried to improve my pronunciation by imitating native speakers*; **standard pronunciation** = pronunciation of educated speakers

proof [pruːf] **1** *noun* **(a)** thing which proves or which shows that something is true; *the police have no proof that he committed the murder* **(b)** sheet with text or pictures printed on it, for the publisher, author or designer to look at and make corrections; *she has a pile of proofs to check*; *he was looking at the first proofs of his latest etching* **2** *adjective* **proof against** = safe from, not affected by; *after it has been treated, the wood is proof against insects and rot*; *no one was proof against her charms*

-proof [pruːf] *suffix* meaning which prevents something getting in, getting out or harming; *a dustproof cover*; *a soundproof studio*

proofread ['pruːfriːd] *verb* to read proofs and note corrections to them; *I gave the script to my secretary to proofread* (NOTE: **proofreading - proofread** ['pruːfred])

proofreader ['pruːfriːdə] *noun* person who reads proofs and notes corrections to them; *the reviewer found hundreds of mistakes in the index - who was the proofreader?*

prop [prɒp] **1** *noun* **(a)** support, stick which holds something up; *I used a ruler as a prop to keep the window open* **(b)** **props** = articles used in the production of a play or film; *the only props we need are two chairs and a table* **(c)** (*in Rugby*) forward in the front row of the scrum; *he plays prop in the England pack* **2** *verb* to support; *he propped up the table with a pile of books*; *she propped the door open with a brick* (NOTE: **propping - propped**)

propaganda [prɒpə'gændə] *noun* spreading of (usually false) political ideas; *they conducted a propaganda campaign against the minister*

propagate ['prɒpəgeɪt] *verb* **(a)** to produce new plants; *I tried to propagate the plants by taking cuttings* **(b)** to spread ideas; *it's a view being propagated by certain sections of the press*

propagation [prɒpə'geɪʃn] *noun* action of propagating a plant; *propagation is very rapid in the summer months*

propel [prə'pel] *verb* to push something forward; *a jet-propelled car won the record*; *pressure from the crowd behind was propelling us further and further forward* (NOTE: **propelling - propelled**)

propeller [prə'pelə] *noun* set of blades which turns rapidly to drive a boat or an aircraft; *he fell overboard and was killed by the propeller*; *a propeller-driven aircraft*

propensity [prə'pensɪti] *noun* (*formal*) tendency to do something; *she has a propensity to burst into tears at any moment*; *the minister has a propensity for making promises he can't keep*

proper ['prɒpə] *adjective* right and correct; *she didn't put the sugar back into its proper place in the cupboard*; *this is the proper way to use a knife and fork*; *the parcel wasn't delivered because it didn't have the proper address*

properly ['prɒpəli] *adverb* correctly; *the accident happened because the garage hadn't fitted the wheel properly*; *the parcel wasn't properly addressed*

proper noun ['prɒpə 'naʊn] *noun* noun which is the name of a person, a country, the title of a book, film, etc.; *most proper nouns begin with a capital letter*

property ['prɒpəti] *noun* **(a)** thing that belongs to someone; *the furniture is the property of the landlord*; *the hotel guests lost all their property in the fire*; *the management is not responsible for property left in the restaurant*; *see also* LOST PROPERTY OFFICE **(b)** buildings and land; *the family owns property in West London*; *a lot of industrial property was damaged in the war*; **commercial property** = buildings used as offices or shops **(c)** a building; *we have several properties for sale in the centre of town* (NOTE: no plural for meanings (a) and (b); plural for (c) is **properties**)

prophecy ['prɒfəsi] *noun* **(a)** saying what will happen in the future; *he had the gift of prophecy* **(b)** thing which you say will happen in the future; *none of his gloomy prophecies has come true*; *she made a prophecy that they would be married within a month* (NOTE: plural in this meaning is **prophecies**)

prophesy ['prɒfəsaɪ] *verb* to say what will happen in the future; *he went around prophesying the end of the world*; *she prophesied that the winter would be cold*; *the coming of the Messiah is prophesied in the Book of Isaiah*

prophet ['prɒfɪt] *noun* **(a)** person who says what will happen in the future; *the prophets of doom in the newspapers are forecasting the collapse of the economy* **(b)** great religious leader; *the Hebrew prophets foretold the coming of the Messiah*; *new prophets arose from time to time in various parts of the Roman Empire*; **the Prophet** = Muhammad, the leader of the Muslims (NOTE: do not confuse with **profit**)

prophetic [prə'fetɪk] *adjective* which says what will happen in the future; *we didn't know then how prophetic that speech was to prove*

propitious [prə'pɪʃəs] *adjective* favourable; *this is a propitious time to buy property in London*; *the funeral of his mother was hardly a propitious time to talk to him about his exam results*

proponent [prɒ'pəʊnənt] *noun* (*formal*) person who supports something; *he is one of the proponents of a change in the electoral system*

proportion [prə'pɔːʃn] *noun* **(a)** part of a whole; *only a small proportion of his income comes from his TV appearances* **(b)** relationship between the amount of something and the amount of something else; *mix equal proportions of oil and vinegar*; *what is the proportion of men to women on the committee?* **(c)** in

proportion to = showing how something is related to something else; *our sales in Europe are tiny in proportion to those in the USA*; *the payment is very high in proportion to the time worked*; **out of proportion** = not in a proper relationship; *his salary is totally out of proportion to the work he does* **(d) proportions** = the relative height, length of a building, picture, etc.; *they proposed building a library of gigantic proportions*; *the picture is odd, the artist seems to have got the proportions of the people wrong*

proportional [prəˈpɔːʃnəl] *adjective* **(a)** which is directly related to something; *the amount you get in interest is proportional to the amount invested* **(b) proportional representation** = system of voting where the votes cast for each party are more or less accurately reflected in the number of MPs each party has; *members of the assembly will be elected by proportional representation*

proportionate [prəˈpɔːʃnət] *adjective (formal)* which is in proportion; *he is paid a commission, so his earnings are proportionate to sales*

proportionately [prəˈpɔːʃnətli] *adverb (formal)* in proportion; *sales are down, so our bonus is proportionately smaller than last year*

proposal [prəˈpəuzl] *noun* **(a)** suggestion, plan which has been suggested; *the committee made a proposal to rebuild the club house*; *his proposal was accepted by the committee*; *she put forward a proposal but it was rejected* **(b) proposal (of marriage)** = asking someone to marry you; *she thought he liked her, but she didn't expect a proposal*

propose [prəˈpəuz] *verb* **(a)** to suggest, to make a suggestion; *I propose that we all go for a swim* **(b) to propose to do something** = to say that you intend to do something; *they propose to repay the loan at £20 a month* **(c) to propose to someone** = to ask someone to marry you; *he proposed to me in a restaurant*

proposed [prəˈpəuzd] *adjective* which has been suggested; *the proposed route of the motorway*

proposer [prəˈpəuzə] *noun* person who proposes; *Mr Smith is the proposer of the motion, but who is the seconder?*

proposition [prɒpəˈzɪʃn] *noun* **(a)** thing which has been proposed; *the proposition is not very attractive*; **it will never be a commercial proposition** = it is not likely to make a profit **(b) tough proposition** = problem which is difficult to solve

proprietary [prəˈpraɪətri] *adjective* **(a) proprietary product** = product which is made by a particular company and marketed under a brand name **(b)** acting as though you own something; *she cast proprietary glances over her boyfriend* **(c)** *US* **proprietary company** = company formed to invest in stock of other companies so as to control them **(d)** *(in South Africa and Australia)* **proprietary company** = private limited company

proprietor [prəˈpraɪətə] *noun* owner; *the proprietor of a hotel or a hotel proprietor*; *the proprietors of national newspapers and TV channels control a lot of the information available to the public*

proprietorial [prəpraɪəˈtɔːriəl] *adjective* **proprietorial air** = looking proud, as if you own something; *he looked around him with a proprietorial air*

propriety [prəˈpraɪəti] *noun (formal)* correct behaviour in society; *she behaved with complete propriety during the divorce proceedings*; **the proprieties** = rules of good conduct in society; *they observed the proprieties and welcomed the king with great ceremony*

propulsion [prəˈpʌlʃn] *noun* the force of moving something forward; *the car is powered by rocket propulsion*

prosaic [prəˈzeɪɪk] *adjective* ordinary and rather dull, not poetic or imaginative or romantic; *his rather prosaic description doesn't do justice to the garden*; *ordinary suburban life is apt to seem rather prosaic to anyone who has just come back from an African safari*

prose [prəuz] *noun* writing which is not poetry; *his letters are examples of perfect English prose*

prosecute [ˈprɒsɪkjuːt] *verb* to bring someone to court to answer a criminal charge; *he was prosecuted for a traffic offence*; *shoplifters will be prosecuted*

prosecution [prɒsɪˈkjuːʃn] *noun* **(a)** bringing someone to court to answer a charge; *he faces prosecution for fraud* **(b)** lawyers who represent the party who brings a charge against someone; *the costs of the case will be borne by the prosecution*; *the prosecution argued that the money had been stolen*; **prosecution counsel** *or* **counsel for the prosecution** = lawyer acting for the prosecution (NOTE: the opposing side in a court is the **defence**)

prosecutor [ˈprɒsɪkjuːtə] *noun* lawyer who prosecutes; *it was the prosecutor's turn to question the witness*; **public prosecutor** = government lawyer who brings charges against a criminal in a law court on behalf of the state

proselyte [ˈprɒsəlaɪt] *noun* person recently converted to a religion or to a political party; *proselytes always tend to be more enthusiastic than the older members of the sect*

prospect 1 *noun* [ˈprɒspekt] **(a)** future possibility; *there is no prospect of getting her to change her mind*; *faced with the grim prospect of two weeks at home he decided to go on holiday*; **to have something in prospect** = to expect something to happen **(b) prospects** = future possibilities in a job; *his prospects are very good*; *what are her job prospects?*; *he's very gloomy about his job prospects* **2** *verb* [prəˈspekt] to search for minerals; *the team went into the desert to prospect for oil*

prospective [prəˈspektɪv] *adjective* who may do something in the future; *he's been nominated as prospective candidate for the parliamentary seat*; a **prospective buyer** = someone who may buy in the future; *there is no shortage of prospective buyers for the house - I'm sure we'll sell it easily*

prospector [prəˈspektə] *noun* person who searches for minerals; *a prospector came into the store with a gold nugget*

prospectus [prəˈspektəs] *noun* document which gives information to attract customers; *she got several college prospectuses before deciding which one to apply for*; *I studied the prospectus carefully before investing in the scheme* (NOTE: plural is **prospectuses**)

prosper [ˈprɒspə] *verb* to succeed; to become rich; *he worked hard and prospered*; *her little shop is prospering*

prosperity [prɒsˈperɪti] *noun* being rich; *they owe their present prosperity to the discovery of oil on their land*; **in times of prosperity** = when people are rich (NOTE: no plural)

prosperous [ˈprɒspərəs] *adjective* wealthy, rich; *Salisbury is a very prosperous town*

prostate [ˈprɒsteɪt] *noun* gland in men which produces a secretion in which sperm cells float; *he's got prostate trouble* (NOTE: do not confuse with **prostrate**)

prostitute [ˈprɒstɪtjuːt] *noun* woman who receives money for sexual intercourse; *the red light district is where prostitutes work*

prostitution [prɒstɪˈtjuːʃn] *noun* providing sexual intercourse in return for payment; *some people want to legalize prostitution*

prostrate 1 [ˈprɒstreɪt] *adjective* lying flat on your face; *he was lying prostrate on the floor* (NOTE: do not confuse with **prostate**) **2** *verb* [prəˈstreɪt] **(a) to prostrate oneself before someone** = to fall down in front of someone as a mark of respect, fear, etc.; *anyone who came into the Emperor's presence had to prostrate himself before the throne* **(b)** he was **prostrated by malaria** = he had to stay in bed because he had malaria

protagonist [prəˈtægənɪst] *noun* **(a)** *(formal)* main character in a play or book, etc.; *the protagonist is a Danish prince* **(b)** leader of one side in a conflict; *the two protagonists were finally persuaded to shake hands* **(c)** supporter of a cause; *he was a leading protagonist of the movement for electoral reform*

protect [prəˈtekt] *verb* to keep someone or something safe from dirt, germs, etc.; *the cover protects the machine against dust*; *the injection is supposed to protect you against flu*

protection [prəˈtekʃn] *noun* shelter, being protected; *the trees give some protection from the rain*; *the legislation offers no protection to part-time workers*; *the injection gives some protection against cholera*

protectionism [prəˈtekʃənɪzm] *noun* policy of discouraging imports from abroad in order to protect a country's own industry; *what he is advocating is an end to the era of protectionism and a return to free trade*

protectionist [prəˈtekʃənɪst] *adjective* in favour of protectionism; *half the Senate approves of the government's protectionist policies*

protective [prəˈtektɪv] *adjective* who or which protects; *visitors to the factory must wear protective clothing*; *she's very protective towards her little brother*; *he put a protective arm around her*

protector [prəˈtektə] *noun* **(a)** person or country which protects; *Parliament is supposed to be the protector of the people's rights*; *she needed a protector, that's what attracted her to him*; **the Lord Protector** = title taken by Oliver Cromwell **(b)** thing which protects; *the machinists all wear ear protectors because the machines are so noisy*

protectorate [prəˈtektərət] *noun* country which is protected and usually controlled by another country; *Swaziland was a British protectorate before gaining independence*

protégé [ˈprɒteʒeɪ] *noun* person, usually a young person, who is supported in artistic work with money or advice by someone else; *she arranged a concert at which her young protégés could show off their skills*

protein [ˈprəʊtiːn] *noun* compound which is an essential part of living cells, one of the elements in food which you need to keep the human body working properly; *you need more protein in your diet*

> COMMENT: meat, eggs and fish contain a lot of protein. Compare with carbohydrates, which provide the body with energy

protest 1 *noun* [ˈprəʊtest] **(a)** statement that you object or disapprove of something; *the new bypass went ahead despite the protests of the local inhabitants*; *she resigned as a protest against the change in government policy*; **protest march** = march through streets to show that you protest against something; *we're organizing a protest march to the town hall* **(b) in protest at** = showing that you do not approve of something; *the staff occupied the offices in protest at their low pay*; **to do something under protest** = to do something, but say that you do not approve of it **2** *verb* [prəˈtest] **(a) to protest against something** = to say that you do not approve of something, to raise a violent objection to; *everyone has protested against the increase in bus fares* (NOTE: British English is **to protest against something**, but American English is **to protest something**) **(b)** to insist that something is true, when others think it isn't; *she went to prison still protesting her innocence*

Protestant [ˈprɒtestənt] **1** *adjective* referring to the Christian Church which separated from the Catholic Church at the time of the Reformation; *she belongs to a Protestant parish*; *the Church of England is a Protestant Church* **2** *noun* member of a Christian Church which separated from the Catholic Church at the time of the Reformation

protester [prəˈtestə] *noun* person who protests; *several protesters lay down in the street and were arrested*

protocol [ˈprəʊtəkɒl] *noun* **(a)** correct diplomatic behaviour; *diplomatic protocol dictates which ambassador sits next to the Queen* **(b)** *(formal)* draft agreement; *they drew up a protocol covering the points of agreement*

proton [ˈprəʊtɒn] *noun* particle with a positive charge found in the nucleus of an atom; *see also* ELECTRON, NEUTRON

> COMMENT: it is the number of protons in the nucleus that determines the number of the element in the periodic table. Uranium, the heaviest natural element, has 92 protons, and is number 92 on the periodic table

prototype [ˈprəʊtətaɪp] *noun* first model of a new machine; *we are showing the prototype of the new engine at the exhibition*

protracted [prəˈtræktɪd] *adjective* very lengthy; *a protracted period of negotiations*

protractor [prəˈtræktə] *noun* device in the form of a semicircle of clear plastic, used for measuring angles in geometry; *use your protractor to measure the angle*

protrude [prəˈtruːd] *verb* to stick out; *you can recognize him because his teeth protrude*; *I caught my coat on a nail protruding from the fence*

protrusion [prəˈtruːʒn] *noun* something which protrudes; *a sharp protrusion in the cliff face*

protuberance [prə'tju:bərəns] *noun (formal)* bump or swelling; *the X-ray revealed a protuberance on his spine*

proud [praud] *adjective* **(a)** proud of something = full of pride about something; *you must be very proud of your children*; *he is proud to have served in the navy* **(b)** *(informal)* to do someone proud = to give someone plenty to eat and drink; *the restaurant did us proud*; to do yourself proud = to give yourself an expensive treat; *he did himself proud and bought himself a bottle of champagne*

proudly ['praudli] *adverb* with pride; *she was proudly wearing the dress she had made*

prove [pru:v] *verb* **(a)** to show that something is true; *the police think he stole the car but they can't prove it*; *I was determined to prove him wrong or that he was wrong* **(b)** to prove to be something = to actually be something when it happens; *the weather for the holiday weekend proved to be even hotter than was expected*; *it's proving very difficult to persuade him to sell his house*

proven ['pru:vən] *adjective* tested and shown to be correct; *he has a proven track record as a salesman*; *there is a proven relationship between smoking and lung cancer*

proverb ['prɒvɜ:b] *noun* saying which teaches you something; *'the early bird catches the worm' is a proverb meaning that if you decide quickly, you will succeed*

proverbial [prə'vɜ:biəl] *adjective* **(a)** as mentioned in a proverb; *she's the proverbial early bird that catches the worm* **(b)** well-known; *the committee's proverbial slowness to take any decisions*

provide [prə'vaid] *verb* to supply; *medical help was provided by the Red Cross*; *our hosts provided us with a car and driver*

provided (that) *or* **providing** [prə'vaidid ðæt *or* prə'vaidiŋ] *conjunction* on condition that; as long as, so long as; *it's nice to go on a picnic provided it doesn't rain*; *you can all come to watch the rehearsal providing you don't interrupt*

provide for [prə'vaid 'fɔ:] *verb* **(a)** to provide for someone = to give enough money to feed and clothe someone; *he earns very little and finds it difficult to provide for a family of six children*; *will your family be provided for when you die?* **(b)** to provide for something = to allow for something which may happen in the future; *the contract provides for an annual increase in charges*

providence ['prɒvidəns] *noun* lucky fate, which protects you; *it was providence that brought us together*; to tempt providence = to take a great risk; *it will be tempting providence to buy that car without having had it checked by a garage*

province ['prɒvins] *noun* **(a)** large administrative division of a country; *the provinces of Canada* **(b)** the provinces = parts of a country away from the capital; *there are fewer shops in the provinces than in the capital* **(c)** area of knowledge or of responsibility; *that's not my province - you'll have to ask the finance manager*

provincial [prə'vinʃl] **1** *adjective* **(a)** referring to a province, to the provinces; *a provincial government* **(b)** not very sophisticated; *they're very provincial down in that part of the world*; *he's too provincial to*

appreciate this kind of music **2** *noun* person from the provinces; *you provincials are out of touch with London fashions*

provincialism [prə'vinʃlizm] *noun* narrow-mindedness and lack of sophistication supposed to be found in provincial areas; *she felt stifled by the provincialism of upstate university life and longed to return to New York*

provision [prə'viʒn] *noun* **(a)** providing something; *the provision of medical services is the responsibility of local government*; to make provision for = to see that something is allowed for in the future; *we've made provision for the computer network to be expanded*; *there is no provision for or no provision has been made for car parking in the plans for the office block* **(b)** provisions = food; *people in remote areas need to lay in provisions for the winter* **(c)** condition in a contract; *it's a provision of the contract that the goods should be transported by air*

provisional [prə'viʒnəl] *adjective* **(a)** temporary; *a provisional government was set up by the army* **(b)** not final; *they faxed their provisional acceptance*; *we made a provisional booking over the phone*; provisional licence = temporary driving licence held by someone who is learning to drive

provisionally [prə'viʒnəli] *adverb* temporarily; *the contract has been accepted provisionally*

provocation [prɒvə'keiʃn] *noun* action of provoking someone, of making someone annoyed; *the police only acted under extreme provocation by the crowd*; *witnesses said that there was no provocation for the attack*

provocative [prə'vɒkətiv] *adjective* **(a)** likely to provoke a violent response, to make someone annoyed; *his provocative remarks did not go down well with the management* **(b)** likely to make someone sexually excited; *in some countries it is considered provocative for women to wear short skirts*

provoke [prə'vəuk] *verb* **(a)** to incite someone to do something violent; *she provoked him into throwing a brick through her front window* **(b)** to make a reaction take place; *his reply provoked an angry response from the crowd*

provost ['prɒvəst] *noun* **(a)** person in charge of a university college; *the Provost of Queen's College, Oxford* **(b)** *(in Scotland)* person who is chosen as the official head of a town, city or local council; *the Lord Provost of Glasgow*; *the Provost agreed to perform the ceremony* (NOTE: the equivalent in England is a **mayor**) **(c)** [prə'vəu]; provost marshal = head of a group of military police; *the provost marshal reported that there had been serious lapses in discipline*

prow [prau] *noun (formal)* front end of a boat; *the Maoris decorated the prows of their war canoes*; *we ran the prow up onto the beach*

prowess ['praues] *noun (formal)* skill; *she once again demonstrated her prowess on the running track*

prowl [praul] **1** *noun* on the prowl = creeping about; *a tiger on the prowl in the jungle* **2** *verb* to creep about quietly; *she thinks she saw someone prowling about in the undergrowth*; *the police are on the lookout for looters prowling around the deserted town*

proximity [prɒk'simiti] *noun* being close to something; *being in such close proximity to a tiger made him nervous*; *the main advantage of the hotel is* *its proximity to the beach; they live in close proximity to their parents*

proxy ['prɒksi] *noun* **(a)** document which gives someone the power to act on behalf of someone else; *if you are away from home on voting day, you can cast your vote by proxy*; **proxy vote** = vote made by proxy **(b)** person who acts on behalf of someone else; *to act as a proxy for someone* (NOTE: plural is **proxies**)

prudence ['pruːdns] *noun* (*formal*) great care or caution; *prudence dictates that you should not invest all your money in one company*

prudent ['pruːdnt] *adjective* very careful and very cautious about avoiding risks; *it would be prudent to consult a lawyer before you sign the contract*

prune [pruːn] **1** *noun* dried plum; *he had a bowl of stewed prunes for breakfast* **2** *verb* to cut back a tree or shrub, to keep it in good shape; *that bush is blocking the window - it needs pruning*

pry [praɪ] *verb* **(a)** to look inquisitively into something; *she accused the press of prying into her private life* **(b)** US to pry something open = to lift open with force; *he pried the lid open* (NOTE: British English is **prise**)

PS [piːˈes] *short for* post scriptum, additional note at the end of a letter; *did you read the PS at the end of the letter?*

psalm [sɑːm] *noun* religious poem or song from the Bible; *we shall now sing Psalm 121; she asked for Psalm 25 to be read at her wedding*

psyche ['saɪki] *noun* the subconscious mind; *an impulse lodged deep in the human psyche*

psychedelic [saɪkə'delɪk] *adjective* **(a)** so full of bright moving colours that you become dizzy; *he painted his car in psychedelic colours* **(b)** which makes you have hallucinations; *the drug has a psychedelic effect*

psychiatric [saɪkɪ'ætrɪk] *adjective* referring to psychiatry; *a psychiatric patient; he's receiving psychiatric treatment*

psychiatrist [saɪˈkaɪətrɪst] *noun* person who studies and treats mental disease; *I think she should see a psychiatrist not a doctor*

psychiatry [saɪˈkaɪətri] *noun* study of mental disease; *when he finished his basic medical training he chose to specialize in psychiatry*

psychic ['saɪkɪk] **1** *adjective* referring to supernatural forces; *he spends his time investigating reports of psychic phenomena; she must be psychic if she can tell the result of the lottery in advance* **2** *noun* person who claims to be in contact with supernatural forces or with dead people; *they consulted a psychic to try find what had happened to their daughter*

psychoanalysis [saɪkəʊəˈnæləsɪs] *noun* treatment of mental disorder where a specialist talks to the patient and analyses his condition; *feelings long repressed were revealed under psychoanalysis*

psychoanalyst [saɪkəʊˈænəlɪst] *noun* doctor who is trained in psychoanalysis; *my psychoanalyst says I haven't got an Oedipus complex* (NOTE: also shortened to **analyst**)

psychological [saɪkə'lɒdʒɪkl] *adjective* referring to psychology; *her problems are mainly psychological; this could have a very bad effect on the child's psychological development*

psychologist [saɪˈkɒlədʒɪst] *noun* person who studies the human mind; *psychologists have developed a new theory to explain why some people get depressed*

psychology [saɪˈkɒlədʒi] *noun* study of the human mind; *she's taking a psychology course; the psychology department in the university*

psychosis [saɪˈkəʊsɪs] *noun* general term for any serious mental disorder; *schizophrenia is one of the commoner forms of psychosis* (NOTE: plural is **psychoses** [saɪˈkəʊsiːz])

psychotherapist [saɪkəʊˈθerəpɪst] *noun* person trained to give psychotherapy; *perhaps you ought to see a psychotherapist*

psychotherapy [saɪkəʊˈθerəpi] *noun* treatment of mental disorders by psychological methods, as when a psychotherapist talks to a patient and encourages him to talk about his problems; *my doctor thought that psychotherapy might be of benefit to me*

psychotic [sæɪˈkɒtik] *adjective* referring to psychosis, to mental disorder; *a psychotic killer was on the loose in the neighbourhood; her jealousy towards other women bordered on the psychotic*

pt [paɪnt] = PINT

PTO [piːtiːˈəʊ] *short for* 'please turn over', letters written at the bottom of a page, showing that there is something written on the other side

pub [pʌb] *noun* (*informal*) public house, place where you can buy beer and other alcoholic drinks, as well as snacks, meals, etc.; *I happened to meet him at the pub; we had a sandwich and some beer in the pub; don't tell your mother you've been to the pub*; **pub crawl** = going from pub to pub having a drink in each one; **pub grub** = *see the note at* GRUB

puberty ['pjuːbəti] *noun* time of life when childhood ends and adolescence and sexual maturity begin; *he has reached the age of puberty*

pubic ['pjuːbɪk] *adjective* referring to the area around the sexual organs; **pubic hair** = hair surrounding the sexual organs; *they usually shave off your pubic hair before you give birth* (NOTE: do not confuse with **public**)

public ['pʌblɪk] **1** *adjective* **(a)** referring to the people in general; *the crown jewels are on public display in the Tower of London; it's in the public interest that the facts should be known*; **public gardens** = place in a town where there are flowers and trees and grass, where people can walk around and enjoy themselves; **public holiday** = holiday for everyone, when everyone can rest and enjoy themselves instead of working; *most of the shops are shut today because it's a public holiday*; **public opinion** = general feeling held by most of the public; **public sector** = state-owned companies; **public telephone** = telephone which can be used by anyone; **public transport** = transport (such as buses, trains) which can be used by anyone; *its quicker to go by public transport into central London than by car* **(b)** **to go public** = (i) to tell something to everyone; (ii) to sell shares in a private or nationalized company on the stock exchange; *after the leaks to the press, the government finally went public on the proposal; the plan is for the company to go public next year* **2** *noun* **(a)** people in general; *the public have the right to know what is going on*; **the travelling public** = people who travel frequently; (*humorous*) **the great British public** = the British people; *see also* GENERAL PUBLIC (NOTE: **public** can take either a singular or plural verb) **(b) in public** = in the open; in front of everyone; *this is* *the first time he has appeared in public since his accident; I dare you to repeat those remarks in public*

publican ['pʌblɪkən] *noun* person who manages a pub; *publicans work very long hours*

publication [pʌblɪ'keɪʃn] *noun* **(a)** making public, publishing; *the publication of the official figures has been delayed* **(b)** book or newspaper which has been published; *he asked the library for a list of gardening publications*

public conveniences ['pʌblɪk kən'viːnɪənsɪz] *noun* toilets for the general public; *why are there are no public conveniences in the centre of town?*

public house ['pʌblɪk 'haʊs] *noun (formal)* place where you can buy beer and other alcoholic drinks, as well as snacks, meals, etc.; *the village has the usual church, post office and public house* (NOTE: usually shortened to **pub**)

publicist ['pʌblɪsɪst] *noun* person who attracts people's attention to something through advertising; *she's a skilled publicist for her own work*

publicity [pʌb'lɪsɪti] *noun* advertising, attracting people's attention to a product; *we're trying to get publicity for our school play*; *the failure of the show was blamed on bad publicity*; **publicity campaign** = period when planned publicity takes place

publicize ['pʌblɪsaɪz] *verb* to attract people's attention to something; to make publicity for something; *the advertising campaign is intended to publicize the services of the tourist board*

publicly ['pʌblɪkli] *adverb* in public; *he said publicly that he intended to resign*; *the results were announced publicly last night*

public relations (PR) ['pʌblɪk rɪ'leɪʃnz] *noun* maintaining good connections with the public, especially to put across a point of view or to publicize a product; *the company does not have a public relations department*; *the council needs better public relations to improve its image*; *our public relations department organized the launch of the new model*

public school ['pʌblɪk 'skuːl] *noun* **(a)** *(in Britain)* private fee-paying secondary school which is not part of the state education system; *Eton and Winchester are two famous British public schools* compare PRIVATE SCHOOL, STATE SCHOOL **(b)** *(in the USA)* school which is funded by public taxes; *the state has decided to spend more money on its public school system* (NOTE: British English is **state school**)

public service ['pʌblɪk 'sɜːvɪs] *noun* **(a)** working for the state; **public-service broadcasting** = broadcasting service which is subsidized by the state **(b)** all government agencies and their personnel; *he's hoping for a job in the public service*

public works ['pʌblɪk 'wɜːks] *noun* engineering and building work paid for by the government; *the government has been forced to scrap several large public works projects*; *the local authority is increasing its spending on public works*

publish ['pʌblɪʃ] *verb* to make publicly known; to bring out a book, a newspaper for sale; *the government has not published the figures yet*; *the company publishes six magazines for the business market*; *we publish dictionaries for students*

publishable ['pʌblɪʃəbl] *adjective* suitable to be published; *the manuscript is not yet of publishable quality*

publisher ['pʌblɪʃə] *noun* person who produces books or newspapers for sale; *I'm trying to find a publisher for my novel*; *he's a publisher who specializes in reference works*

publishing ['pʌblɪʃɪŋ] *noun* producing books or newspapers for sale; *she works in publishing or she has a job in publishing*; *if you're interested in books, have you thought of publishing as a career?*; **publishing house** = firm which publishes books

puck [pʌk] *noun* small hard rubber disk used in ice hockey; *he sent the puck skidding across the ice*

pud [pʊd] *(informal)* = PUDDING; *steak and kidney pud; what's for pud?* (NOTE: very informal, used by children, but also sometimes by adults as a joke)

pudding ['pʊdɪŋ] *noun* **(a)** dessert, the sweet course at the end of the meal; *I'll have an ice for my pudding* **(b)** sweet food which has been cooked or boiled; *there's too much sugar in this pudding*; *he helped himself to some more pudding*; **Christmas pudding** = special pudding eaten on Christmas Day; *see also* RICE **(c)** *(not sweet)* **steak and kidney pudding** = dish of steak and kidney cooked in a soft dough, boiled or steamed; **black pudding** = type of dark sausage made with blood

puddle ['pʌdl] *noun* small pool of water, such as a pool on the pavement left after rain; *I stepped into a puddle and got water in my shoe*

puff [pʌf] **1** *noun* **(a)** small breath of air, smoke, etc.; *he took a puff on his cigarette*; *little puffs of smoke came out of the chimney* **(b)** *(informal)* **out of puff** = having difficulty in breathing after running, etc.; *after the race I was completely out of puff* **(c)** **powder puff** = light fluffy pad for powdering the skin; *she dabbed her cheeks with a powder puff* **(d)** **puff pastry** = light sort of pastry; *a pie with a puff pastry crust* **2** *verb* **(a)** to blow; *white smoke was puffing out of the engine*; *he sat in a corner, puffing on his pipe* **(b)** to breathe with difficulty; *he was puffing and panting and he'd only run fifty yards*

puffin ['pʌfɪn] *noun* black and white bird with a large coloured beak, living near the sea; *puffins nest on ledges in the cliff*

puff out ['pʌf 'aʊt] *verb* **(a)** to make something swell by bringing in air; *he puffed out his chest in pride* **(b)** **to be puffed out** = to be tired and out of breath; *slow down a bit, I'm puffed out*

puke [pjuːk] *verb (informal)* **to puke (up)** = to vomit, to bring up partly digested food into your mouth; *the baby puked (up) all over the carpet*; *all these stories about lottery millionaires make me puke*

pull [pʊl] *verb* **(a)** to move something towards you or after you; *pull the door to open it, don't push*; *the truck was pulling a trailer*; *she pulled some envelopes out of her bag*; *these little boys spend their time pulling girls' hair*; **to pull someone's leg** = to make someone believe something as a joke; *don't believe anything he says - he's just pulling your leg* **(b)** **to pull a muscle** = to injure a muscle by using it too much; *she's pulled a muscle in her back*

pull down ['pʊl 'daʊn] *verb* to knock down (a building); *they pulled down the old railway station to build a row of houses*

pull-down menu ['pʊldaʊn 'menjuː] *noun* menu which appears as a list on part of a computer screen; *the* *pull-down menu is displayed by clicking on the menu bar at the top of the screen*

pulley ['pʊli] *noun* apparatus for lifting heavy weights with a rope that runs round several wheels; *we rigged up a pulley to raise the beams to roof level*

pull in(to) ['pʊl 'ɪn] *verb* to drive close to the side of the road and stop; *all the cars pulled into the side of the road when they heard the fire engine coming*

pullman ['pʊlmən] *noun* **(a)** *(old)* luxurious railway carriage; *we reserved our seats in the pullman car* **(b)** *US* sleeping car on a train; *the conductor showed us to our berth in the pullman*

pull off ['pʊl 'ɒf] *verb* to do something successfully; *he pulled off a big financial deal*; *it will be marvellous if we can pull it off*

pull out ['pʊl 'aʊt] *verb* **(a)** to pull something out of something; *they used a rope to pull the car out of the river*; *see also* FINGER **(b)** to drive a car away from the side of the road; *he forgot to signal as he was pulling out*; *don't pull out into the main road until you can see that there is nothing coming* **(c)** to stop being part of a deal or agreement; *our Australian partners pulled out at the last moment*

pull over ['pʊl 'əʊvə] *verb* to drive a car towards the side of the road; *the police car signalled to him to pull over*

pullover ['pʊləʊvə] *noun* piece of clothing made of wool, which covers the top part of your body, and which you pull over your head to put it on; *he's wearing a new red pullover*; *my girlfriend's knitting me another pullover, this time with a V neck*

pull round *or* **pull through** ['pʊl 'raʊnd *or* 'pʊl 'θruː] *verb* to recover from an illness; *she pulled through, thanks to the expert work of the specialists*

pull together ['pʊl tə'geðə] *verb* **to pull yourself together** = to become more calm; *although he was shocked by the news he soon pulled himself together*

pull up ['pʊl 'ʌp] *verb* **(a)** to bring something closer; *pull your chair up to the window* **(b)** to stop a car, etc.; *a car pulled up and the driver asked me if I wanted a lift*; *he didn't manage to pull up in time and ran into the back of the car in front*

pulmonary ['pʌlmənri] *adjective* referring to the lungs; *he has a pulmonary condition*; **pulmonary arteries** = arteries which take blood from the heart to the lungs

pulp [pʌlp] **1** *noun* **(a)** squashy mass; *cook the apples to a pulp*; *if you don't do as I say I'll beat you to a pulp* (NOTE: no plural) **(b) pulp fiction** = cheap novels which are considered to be of poor quality **2** to crush to a pulp; *waste paper can be pulped and recycled*

pulpit ['pʊlpɪt] *noun* little raised platform in a church where the priest preaches; *the archbishop attacked the government from the pulpit*

pulsar ['pʌlsə] *noun* invisible star which sends out radio signals; *pulsars were first discovered by radio telescopes*

pulsate [pʌl'seɪt] *verb* to throb regularly; *they danced all night to the pulsating rhythm of the steel band*

pulsation [pʌl'seɪʃn] *noun* regular throbbing; *each pulsation of the heart forces blood along the arteries*

pulse [pʌls] *noun* **(a)** regular beat of the heart; *the doctor took his pulse*; *her pulse is very weak* **(b)** dried

seed of peas or beans; *pulses are used a lot in Mexican cooking*

puma ['pjuːmə] *noun* large brown wild cat from North and South America; *pumas live mainly in the mountains* (NOTE: also called a **cougar** *or* **mountain lion**)

pumice stone ['pʌmɪs 'stəʊn] *noun* little piece of light grey porous lava used for rubbing your skin; *we keep a piece of pumice stone by the side of the bath*

pump [pʌmp] **1** *noun* machine for forcing liquids or air; **bicycle pump** = small hand pump for blowing up bicycle tyres; **petrol pump** = machine which supplies petrol at a petrol station **2** *verb* **(a)** to force in something, such as liquid or air, with a pump; *your back tyre needs pumping up*; *the banks have been pumping money into the company*; *the heart pumps blood round the body* **(b)** *(informal)* **to pump someone** = to ask someone a lot of questions to try to get information; *we pumped her after the interview to find out the sort of questions she had been asked*

pumpkin ['pʌmpkɪn] *noun* large round orange-coloured vegetable; *pumpkin pie is a favourite American dish*

COMMENT: pumpkins are used as decorations for Halloween (31st October). Each pumpkin is hollowed out, and holes cut to imitate eyes, nose and a mouth with teeth. A lighted candle is put inside so that the whole thing glows orange.; *see also the note at* HALLOWEEN

pun [pʌn] **1** *noun* play with words which have several different meanings; *he made an awful pun about 'ploughing on' with his book on agriculture* **2** *verb* to make puns; *he was punning on the two senses of 'hedge'* (NOTE: **punning - punned**)

punch [pʌnʃ] **1** *noun* **(a)** blow with the fist; *she landed two punches on his head* **(b)** metal tool for making holes; *the holes in the belt are made with a punch* (NOTE: plural is **punches**) **2** *verb* **(a)** to hit someone with your fist; *he punched me on the nose* **(b)** to make holes in something with a punch; *the conductor punched my ticket*

Punch and Judy ['pʌnʃ n 'dʒuːdi] *noun* traditional children's puppet show; *there was a Punch and Judy show on the beach*; **as pleased as punch** = very pleased; *he's as pleased as punch to be chosen to play for the school*

COMMENT: the traditional characters are Punch (a man with a large hooked nose), his wife Judy (whom he beats with a stick), and their dog (who eats a string of sausages)

punchdrunk ['pʌnʃdrʌŋk] *adjective* **(a)** suffering from brain damage from being punched on the head too often; *by the end of his career as a boxer he was obviously punchdrunk* **(b)** tired out and not able to think clearly; *the delegates emerged punchdrunk from the all-night negotiating session*

punchline ['pʌnʃlaɪn] *noun* last part of a joke, which is the part that makes you laugh; *he went through the whole joke and then couldn't remember the punchline*

punctual ['pʌŋktʃuəl] *adjective* on time; *he was punctual for his appointment with the dentist*; *she is never very punctual in bringing her library books back*

punctuality [pʌŋktʃuˈælɪti] *noun* being on time, never being late; *she's well-known for her punctuality*

punctually [ˈpʌŋktʃuəli] *adverb* on time; *the train arrived punctually at three o'clock*

punctuate [ˈpʌŋktʃueɪt] *verb* (a) to interrupt; *their conversation was punctuated with long silences* (b) to add punctuation marks to a text; *the sentence was not punctuated correctly*

punctuation [pʌŋktʃuˈeɪʃn] *noun* dividing up groups of words using special printed symbols; *there's something wrong with the punctuation in this sentence*; **punctuation marks** = symbols used in writing, such as full stop, comma, dash, etc., to show how a sentence is split up; *without any punctuation marks, the sentence would be difficult to understand*

puncture [ˈpʌŋktʃə] **1** *noun* hole in a tyre; *I've got a puncture in my back tyre* (NOTE: American English is a **flat**) **2** *verb* to make a small hole in something; *the tyre had been punctured by a nail*

pundit [ˈpʌndɪt] *noun* expert, especially in political matters; *political pundits tried to forecast the result of the election*; *the pundits got it wrong on this occasion*

pungent [ˈpʌndʒənt] *adjective* (a) with a strong taste or smell; *the pungent odour of curry came from the kitchen*; *a particularly pungent type of goat's cheese* (b) *(of comments)* strong and sharp; *she reserved her most pungent criticism for the way we performed the musical numbers*

punish [ˈpʌnɪʃ] *verb* to make someone suffer because of something he has done; *the children must be punished for stealing apples*; *the simplest way to punish them will be to make them pay for the damage they caused*

punishing [ˈpʌnɪʃɪŋ] *adjective* exhausting, which makes you tired; *he kept up a punishing schedule of visits*

punishment [ˈpʌnɪʃmənt] *noun* treatment given to punish someone; *as a punishment, you'll wash the kitchen floor*

punitive [ˈpjuːnətɪv] *adjective (formal)* which aims to punish; *the army carried out punitive raids on the enemy camps*; *the judge awarded her punitive damages*

punk [pʌŋk] *noun (informal)* person who dresses in unconventional clothes, has brightly coloured hair and pins through the lips, etc.; *she turned up at the party dressed like a punk*; *he has a punk hair style*

punk rock [ˈpʌŋk ˈrɒk] *noun* type of loud music popular in the 1960s

punt [pʌnt] **1** *noun* (a) long flat-bottomed boat, pushed along with a pole; *I took her out in a punt and we picnicked on the river* (b) *(Irish currency)* Irish pound, currency used in the Republic of Ireland; *what is the price in punts?* (c) *(informal)* bet; *that horse is worth a punt* **2** *verb* (a) to push a punt with a pole; *we went punting on the Cam at Cambridge* (b) to kick a ball which is in the air; *he punted the ball into touch*

punter [ˈpʌntə] *noun* (a) person who gambles; *most of the punters had backed the favourite*; *punters lost thousands when the favourite fell at the last fence* (b) *(informal)* customer, person who uses a service; *we have to keep the punters happy* (c) person who pushes a punt along with a pole; *punters tended to stay close to the river bank*

puny [ˈpjuːni] *adjective* (a) weak and feeble; *the puny body of the baby piglet*; *their puny efforts were totally unequal to the task* (b) very small; *this year's pay rise is the puniest we've ever had* (NOTE: **punier - puniest**)

pup [pʌp] **1** *noun* young of certain animals, especially young dog or seal; *our bitch has had pups*; *they went out onto rocky islands looking for seal pups*; **pup tent** = small ridge tent **2** *verb* to have pups; *she's likely to pup in the next couple of days* (NOTE: **pupping - pupped**)

pupa [ˈpjuːpə] *noun* resting period in the life of an insect when it is covered with a hard case as it changes from a larva to a butterfly or moth; *the butterfly spends the winter as a pupa, and emerges when the weather becomes warm*; *the pupae remain attached for long periods to the stems of the plants* (NOTE: plural is **pupae** [ˈpjuːpiː]; also called **chrysalis**)

pupil [ˈpjuːpl] *noun* (a) child at a school; *there are twenty-five pupils in the class*; *the piano teacher thinks she is her best pupil* (b) black hole in the central part of the eye, through which the light passes; *the pupil of the eye grows larger when there is less light*

puppet [ˈpʌpɪt] *noun* doll which moves, used to give a show; *the puppet's movements were extremely lifelike*; **puppet show** = show given using puppets; *we organized a puppet show for the children's party*; **glove puppet** = doll which fits over your hand; **string puppet** = puppet which works by strings attached to its limbs (NOTE: also called a **marionette**); *see also* PUNCH AND JUDY

puppeteer [pʌpɪˈtɪə] *noun* person who gives a performance using puppets; *you couldn't see the puppeteers who were hiding behind a black curtain*

puppy [ˈpʌpi] *noun* (a) baby dog; *our dog has had six puppies* (NOTE: plural is **puppies**) (b) *(informal)* **puppy fat** = fat on the bodies of young children; *she's nine, and is beginning to lose her puppy fat*

purchase [ˈpɜːtʃəs] **1** *noun (formal)* (a) thing bought; *she had difficulty getting all her purchases into the car*; **to make a purchase** = to buy something; *we didn't make many purchases on our trip to Oxford Street*; **purchase ledger** = book in which purchases are recorded; **purchase price** = price paid for something; *we offer a discount of 10% off the normal purchase price*; **purchase tax** = tax paid on things which are bought; **hire purchase (HP)** = system of buying something by paying a sum regularly each month; *he is buying a refrigerator on hire purchase* (b) ability to get a grip on something; *I couldn't get any purchase on the smooth face of the rock*; *it's difficult to get a purchase on a box as large as this one* (NOTE: no plural in this meaning) **2** *verb (formal)* to buy; *they purchased their car in France and brought it back to the UK*; **purchasing power** = quantity that can be bought with a certain amount of money; *the fall in the purchasing power of the pound*

purchaser [ˈpɜːtʃəsə] *noun* person who buys something; *he has found a purchaser for his house*

pure [ˈpjuə] *adjective* (a) very clean; not mixed with other things; *a bottle of pure water*; *a pure silk blouse*; *a pure mountain stream* (b) innocent; with no faults; *she led a pure life* (c) total, complete; *this is pure nonsense*; *it is pure extortion*; *it was by pure good luck that I happened to find it* (NOTE: **purer - purest**)

purée *or* **puree** [ˈpjuəreɪ] **1** *noun* pulp of cooked and sieved vegetables or fruit; *she made some* *strawberry purée to serve with the ice cream* **2** *verb* to make something into a purée; *she decided to purée the potatoes*

purely ['pjʊəli] *adverb* only, solely; *he's doing it purely for the money*; *this is a purely educational visit*

purgatory ['pɜːgətri] *noun* **(a)** place where your soul will suffer temporarily after you die, before entering heaven; *Masses were said for the souls in purgatory* **(b)** *(informal)* experience which makes you suffer; *it was sheer purgatory listening to her singing out of tune*

purge [pɜːdʒ] **1** *noun* removing opponents and unacceptable people from a group; *the party has begun a purge of right-wing elements* **2** *verb* **(a)** to remove something bad or harmful from your mind or body; *I want you to purge your minds of any unhappy memories*; *this special diet is designed to purge the toxins from your body* **(b)** to remove opponents or other unacceptable people from a group; *the activists have purged the party of moderates or have purged the moderates from the party* **(c)** **to purge your contempt** *or* **to purge a contempt of court** = to do something, such as make an apology, to show that you are sorry for the lack of respect you have shown to the court **(d)** *(formal)* to make a patient have a bowel movement; *old-fashioned doctors frequently purged their patients*

purification [pjʊərɪfɪˈkeɪʃn] *noun* making pure; *worshippers went through elaborate ceremonies of purification before entering the temple*; **a purification plant** = installation where impurities are removed from water

purify ['pjʊərɪfaɪ] *verb* to make pure; *these tablets can be used to purify the water before you drink it*; *they aimed to purify the language by removing all foreign words*

purist ['pjʊərɪst] *noun* person who insists that everything has to be done in the correct way; *purists may object to the use of 'they' to refer to a single unspecified person*; *the changes to the text of 'Hamlet' shocked purists*

purity ['pjʊərɪti] *noun* being pure; *a simple test to establish the purity of the metal*; *the purity of tone of the cathedral choir*; *the purity of the drinking water is questionable*

purple ['pɜːpl] **1** *adjective* blue-red (colour); *the sky turned purple as night approached*; *his face was purple with fury* **2** *noun* blue-red colour; *they painted their living room a deep purple*

purport *(formal)* **1** *noun* ['pɜːpɔːt] *(formal)* general meaning; *what was the purport of his remarks?* **2** *verb* [pɜːˈpɔːt] to claim; *he was purported to be a friend of the princess*

purpose ['pɜːpəs] *noun* **(a)** aim or plan; *the purpose of the meeting is to plan the village fair*; **I need the invoice for tax purposes** = I need the invoice so that I can declare it to the tax **(b)** **on purpose** = in a way which was planned; *don't be cross - he didn't do it on purpose*

purpose-built [pɜːpəsˈbɪlt] *adjective* made specially for a purpose; *the school now has a purpose-built theatre and no longer puts on plays in the school hall*

purposeful ['pɜːpəsful] *adjective* with a specific aim in view; *he strode down the corridor with a purposeful look in his eye*

purposeless ['pɜːpəsləs] *adjective* without having any specific aim; *we seem to be leading a completely purposeless existence*

purr [pɜː] **1** *noun* **(a)** noise made by a cat when pleased; *the cat rubbed against my leg with a loud purr* **(b)** low noise made by a powerful engine; *the purr of the boat's engine* **2** *verb* **(a)** *(of cat)* to make a noise to show pleasure; *he purrs when you tickle his stomach* **(b)** to speak in a low voice; *'come up and see me some time', she purred in his ear* **(c)** *(of engine)* to make a low noise as you travel along; *we purred along at seventy miles an hour*

purse [pɜːs] **1** *noun* **(a)** small bag for carrying money; *I know I had my purse in my pocket when I left home*; *she put her ticket in her purse so that she wouldn't forget where it was*; **to control** *or* **hold the purse strings** = to control the money; *as she's the only money-earner, she holds the purse strings in her family* **(b)** *US* small bag which a woman carries to hold her money, pens, handkerchief, etc.; *a robber snatched her purse in the street* (NOTE: British English is **handbag**) **2** *verb* **to purse your lips** = to press your lips together to show you are annoyed

purser ['pɜːsə] *noun* officer on a ship or aircraft who deals with the comfort of the passengers; *see the purser if you have a complaint about your cabin*

pursue [pəˈsjuː] *verb* **(a)** to chase someone *or* something; *the police pursued the stolen car across London*; *the guerrillas fled, hotly pursued by government troops* **(b)** to carry on a career, an activity; *he pursued his career in the Foreign Office*; *we intend to pursue a policy of reducing taxation*

pursuer [pəˈsjuːə] *noun* person who chases someone; *she tried to shake off her pursuers by driving faster and faster*

pursuit [pəˈsjuːt] *noun* **(a)** chase after someone; *the pursuit lasted until the thieves were caught in an alleyway*; **in pursuit of** = looking for; *we set off in pursuit of our friends who had just left the hotel*; *the robbers left in a stolen car with the police in pursuit*; **in hot pursuit** = chasing someone actively; *the rebels retreated into the mountains with the government forces in hot pursuit* **(b)** trying to find something, to do something; *her aim in life is the pursuit of pleasure* **(c)** *(old)* occupation or pastime; *he spends his time in country pursuits like gardening and birdwatching*

pus [pʌs] *noun* yellow liquid formed in the body as a reaction to infection; *there was a lot of pus coming out of the wound*

push [pʊʃ] **1** *noun* **(a)** action of making something move forward; *he gave the pram a little push and sent it out into the road*; *can you give the car a push? - it won't start* **(b)** action of attacking, of moving forward against someone; *our troops made a sudden push into enemy-held territory*; *the company made a big push to get into European markets* **(c)** *(informal)* **at a push** = with some difficulty; *the cottage will sleep ten people at a push* **(d)** *(informal)* **to give someone the push** = to sack someone; *he kept making mistakes with his discounts, so in the end we had to give him the push* **2** *verb* **(a)** to make something move away from you or in front of you; *we'll have to push the car to get it to start*; *the piano is too heavy to lift, so we'll have to push it into the next room*; *did she fall down the stairs or was she pushed?* **(b)** to press with your finger; *push the* *right-hand button to start the computer (in a lift) he pushed fourth floor*

push back ['pʊʃ 'bæk] *verb* to make something *or* someone go back by pushing; *the police struggled to push back the crowd or to push the crowd back; scientists are trying to push back the boundaries of human knowledge*

pushbike ['pʊʃbaɪk] *noun (informal)* bicycle; *he still goes to work every day on his pushbike*

pushcart ['pʊʃkɑːt] *noun* small trolley for pushing things along; *we loaded our luggage into a pushcart to get it to the taxi rank*

pushchair ['pʊʃtʃeə] *noun* light folding carriage for pushing a child in; *we put the baby in her pushchair and went off for a walk; she pushed the pushchair across the busy road* (NOTE: also called a **buggy**)

pusher ['pʊʃə] *noun* person who sells drugs illegally; *it's more important to arrest the pushers than the heroin users*

push off ['pʊʃ 'ɒf] *verb (informal)* to start (on a journey); *we really ought to push off now* = it's time for us to go; **push off!** = go away

push-up ['pʊʃʌp] *noun US* exercise where you lie on the floor and push yourself up with your arms; *he starts his work-out with twenty push-ups* (NOTE: British English is **press-up**)

pushy ['pʊʃi] *adjective (informal)* always trying to push yourself forward, too ambitious; *no one likes him in the office because he's so pushy*

puss *or* **pussy** *or* **pussycat** [pʊs *or* 'pʊsi *or* 'pʊsikæt] *noun* child's names for a cat; *a big black pussy came to meet us; you mustn't pull pussy's tail* (NOTE: plural is **pussies**)

put [pʊt] *verb* (**a**) to place; *did you remember to put the milk in the fridge?; where do you want me to put this book?* (**b**) to say in words; *if you put it like that, the proposal seems attractive; can I put a question to the speaker?* (**c**) **to put the shot** = to throw a heavy ball as a sport; *he has put the shot further than any other athlete in our team* (NOTE: **putting - put - has put**)

put away ['pʊt ə'weɪ] *verb* to clear things away; *put your soccer things away before you go to bed*

put back ['pʊt 'bæk] *verb* to put something where it was before; *go and put that tin of beans back on the shelf; did you put the milk back in the fridge?;* **to put the clocks back** = to change the time on clocks back to one hour earlier at the beginning of summer; *did you remember to put the clocks back last night?*

put by ['pʊt 'baɪ] *verb* to save money; *she has some money put by to live on when she retires*

put down ['pʊt 'daʊn] *verb* (**a**) to place something lower down onto a surface; *he put his suitcase down on the floor beside him* (**b**) to charge, to note; *put that book down on my account; we put it down to her nerves* (**c**) to let passengers get off; *the taxi driver put me down outside the hotel* (**d**) **to put your foot down** = (i) to insist that something is done; (ii) to make a car go faster; *she put her foot down and told them to stop playing music all night; he put his foot down and we soon left the police car behind* (**e**) to make a deposit; *to put down money on a house* (**f**) to kill a sick animal =; *the cat is very old, she'll have to be put down* (**g**) **to put down a rebellion** = to crush a rebellion

put forward ['pʊt 'fɔːwəd] *verb* (**a**) to suggest; *I put forward several suggestions for plays we might go to*

see (**b**) to change an appointment to a earlier time; *can we put forward the meeting from Thursday to Wednesday?* (**c**) to change the time on a clock to a later one; *you have to put the clocks forward by one hour in October*

put in ['pʊt 'ɪn] *verb* (**a**) to place inside; *I forgot to put in my pyjamas when I packed the case* (**b**) to install; *the first thing we have to do with the cottage is to put in central heating* (**c**) to do work; *she put in three hour's overtime work yesterday evening* (**d**) **to put in for** = to apply; *she put in for a job in the accounts department; he has put in for a grant to study in Italy*

put off ['pʊt 'ɒf] *verb* (**a**) to arrange for something to take place later; *we have put the meeting off until next month* (**b**) to distract someone so that he can't do things properly; *stop making that strange noise, it's putting me off my work* (**c**) to say something to make someone decide not to do something; *he told a story about cows that put me off my food; I was going to see the film, but my brother said something which put me off*

put on ['pʊt 'ɒn] *verb* (**a**) to place something on top of something, on a surface; *put the lid on the saucepan; he put his hand on my arm; put the suitcases down on the floor* (**b**) to dress yourself; *I put a clean shirt on before I went to the party; put your gloves on, it's cold outside; put on your wellies if you're going out in the rain* (**c**) to switch on; *can you put the light on, it's getting dark?; put on the kettle* (**d**) to add; *she has put on a lot of weight since I saw her last*

put out ['pʊt 'aʊt] *verb* (**a**) to place outside; *did you remember to put the cat out?* (**b**) to stretch out your hand, etc.; *she put out her hand to stop herself from falling* (**c**) to switch off; *he put the light out and went to bed* (**d**) *(informal)* **to be put out** = to be annoyed; *he was very put out because you didn't ask him to stay for dinner*

putt [pʌt] **1** *noun* short shot on a green in golf; *he sank a fifteen-foot putt to win the game* **2** *verb* to hit a short gentle shot on the green in golf; *he putted much better than his opponent*

putter ['pʌtə] **1** *noun* (**a**) golf club for putting; *he uses a special lightweight putter* (**b**) **shot putter** = athlete who puts the shot; *an Olympic shot putter* **2** *verb US* **to putter around** = not to do anything in particular, to do little jobs here and there; *he likes to putter around in the yard at the weekend* (NOTE: British English is **potter about**)

put through ['pʊt 'θruː] *verb* (**a**) **to put someone through to someone** = to connect them on the phone; *Peter is out so I'll put you through to Simon; I asked to speak to the accounts department and they put me through to sales* (**b**) to make someone undergo something unpleasant; *I don't want to be put through that treatment again*

put up ['pʊt 'ʌp] *verb* (**a**) to attach to a wall, to attach high up; *I've put up the photos of my family over my desk; they are putting up Christmas decorations all along Regent Street* (**b**) to build something so that it is upright; *they put up a wooden shed in their garden* (**c**) to lift up; *the gunman told us to put our hands up* (**d**) to increase, to make higher; *the shop has put up all its prices by 5%* (**e**) to give someone a place to sleep in your house; *they've missed the last train, can you put them up for the night?*

put up with ['pʊt 'ʌp wɪθ] *verb* to tolerate someone *or* something unpleasant; *living near London Airport* *means that you have to put up with a lot of aircraft noise; how can you put up with all those barking dogs?*

puzzle ['pəzl] **1** *noun* **(a)** game where you have to find the answer to a problem; *I can't do today's crossword puzzle* **(b)** something you can't understand; *it's a puzzle to me why they don't go to live in the country* **2** *verb* **(a)** to be difficult to understand; *it puzzles me how the robbers managed to get away* **(b)** to find something difficult to understand; *she puzzled over the crossword for hours*

puzzled ['pʌzld] *adjective* confused, not understanding something; *they were puzzled to hear that the tour had been cancelled; I am puzzled by your decision; he gave the guide a puzzled look*

puzzling ['pʌzlɪŋ] *adjective* which is difficult to understand and does not make sense; *I find the whole thing very puzzling; for the police, the most puzzling aspect of the case is how the robbers managed to get away from the bank*

pygmy ['pɪgmi] **1** *adjective* much smaller than normal; *a pygmy breed of elephant* **2** *noun* member of a race of very small people living in Africa; *there was a tribe of pygmies living in the forest* (NOTE: plural is **pygmies**)

pyjamas *US* **pajamas** [pɪ'dʒɑːməz] *noun* light shirt and trousers which you wear in bed; *I bought two pairs of pyjamas in the sale; when fire broke out in the hotel, the guests ran into the street in their pyjamas* (NOTE: **a pair of pyjamas** means one shirt and one pair of trousers)

pylon ['paɪlən] *noun* tall metal tower for carrying electric cables; *electricity pylons cross the landscape; the plane crashed into a pylon*

PYO = PICK-YOUR-OWN

pyramid ['pɪrəmɪd] *noun* shape with a square base and four sides rising to meet at a point; **the Pyramids** = huge stone buildings, built as tombs or temples by the Ancient Egyptians and Central Americans; *I went to Egypt mainly to see the Pyramids*

pyrotechnics [paɪrəʊ'teknɪks] *noun* **(a)** art of making fireworks; *they called in a pyrotechnics expert to set up the display* **(b)** firework display; *the pyrotechnics lit up the night sky* **(c)** display of amazing skill; *a piece of music notable for the pyrotechnics demanded from the percussion section; she is capable of amazing vocal pyrotechnics when reciting Shakespeare*

python ['paɪθn] *noun* large snake which kills animals by crushing them

Qq

Q, q [kjuː] seventeenth letter of the alphabet, between P and R; *a 'q' is always followed by the letter 'u'*

QC [ˈkjuːsiː] = QUEEN'S COUNSEL *GB* senior British barrister; *she was represented by a leading QC*

quack [kwæk] **1** *noun* **(a)** sound made by a duck; *I heard a quack in the reeds* **(b) quack doctor** = dishonest person who pretends to be a doctor **(c)** *(informal)* doctor; *I went to see the quack and he gave me some pills* **2** *verb* to make a noise like a duck; *we could hear the ducks quacking on the lake*

quadrilateral [kwɒdrɪˈlætərəl] *noun* shape with four sides; *squares, rectangles and parallelograms are all quadrilaterals*

quadruped [ˈkwɒdrʊped] *noun* animal with four legs; *horses, sheep, cows and other quadrupeds*

quadruple [kwɒˈdrʊpl] **1** *adjective* four times as much, in four parts; *she gave him a quadruple dose of the tablets*; **quadruple vaccine** = vaccine which immunizes against four diseases, diphtheria, whooping cough, polio and tetanus **2** *verb* to multiply four times; *our profits have quadrupled since 1996*

quadruplets *(informal)* **quads** [ˈkwɒdrʊplets or kwɒdz] *noun* four babies born to a mother at the same time; *believe it or not, she's had quads!*

quagmire [ˈkwɒɡmaɪə] *noun* **(a)** area of dangerous marshy ground; *be careful when you take the path across the quagmire; after the rain, the football pitch was like a quagmire* **(b)** situation which is very complicated; *the project got bogged down in a quagmire of government restrictions*

quail [kweɪl] **1** *noun* small brown game bird, like a very small partridge; *would you prefer white or red wine with your roast quail?* **2** *verb* to quail at something = to shrink back because you are afraid of something; *she quailed at the thought of having to do all the Christmas shopping*

quaint [kweɪnt] *adjective* picturesque, oddly old-fashioned; *we stopped at a quaint old pub; they live in a quaint little village in Devon*

quake [kweɪk] **1** *noun (informal)* earthquake, shaking of the earth caused by volcanic activity or movement of the earth's crust; *thousands of buildings were flattened in the San Francisco quake of 1906* **2** *verb* **(a)** to shake; *the explosion made the buildings quake* **(b)** to quake with fear, cold, etc. = to shake with fear, cold, etc.; *she was quaking with fear at the thought of going for an interview; he was quaking in his boots at the idea of having to speak to an audience of specialists*

qualification [kwɒlɪfɪˈkeɪʃn] *noun* **(a)** proof that you have completed a specialized course of study; *does she have the right qualifications for the job?*; **professional qualifications** = proof that you have studied for and obtained a diploma for a particular type of skilled work; **what are his qualifications?** = what sort of degree or diploma does he have? **(b)** something which limits the meaning of a statement, or shows that

you do not agree with something entirely; *I want to add one qualification to the agreement: if the goods are not delivered by the 30th of June, then the order will be cancelled* **(c)** being successful in a test or competition which takes you on to the next stage; *she didn't reach the necessary standard for qualification*

qualified [ˈkwɒlɪfaɪd] *adjective* **(a)** with the right qualifications; *she's a qualified doctor*; **highly qualified** = with very good results in examinations; *all our staff are highly qualified* **(b)** not complete, with conditions attached; *the committee gave its qualified approval; the school fair was only a qualified success*

qualifier [ˈkwɒlɪfaɪə] *noun* **(a)** person who qualifies in a sporting comptetition; *how many qualifiers were there from the first round?* **(b)** round of a sporting competition which qualifies a team to go to the next round; *they won their qualifier and went through to the semi-final*

qualify [ˈkwɒlɪfaɪ] *verb* **(a) to qualify as** = to study for and obtain a diploma which allows you to do a certain type of work; *he has qualified as an engineer*; *when I first qualified I worked as a solicitor* **(b) to qualify for** = (i) to be in the right position for, to be entitled to; (ii) to pass a test or one section of a competition and so go on to the next stage; *the project does not qualify for a government grant; she qualified for round two of the competition* **(c)** to attach conditions to; *I must qualify the offer by saying that your proposals still have to be approved by the chairman*; **the auditors have qualified the accounts** = the auditors have found something in the accounts of the company which they do not agree with

quality [ˈkwɒlɪti] **1** *noun* **(a)** how good something is; *we want to measure the air quality in the centre of town; there are several high-quality restaurants in the West End*; **quality control** = checking a product to make sure that it is of the right standard; *a quality controller has to check all goods leaving the factory*; **quality of life** = how good it is to live in a certain town or country, including low pollution and crime levels, good shops, restaurants, schools, recreational activities, etc. **(b) of quality** = of good quality; *they served a meal of real quality; the carpet is expensive because it is of very good quality* **(c)** something characteristic of a person; *she has many good qualities, but unfortunately is extremely lazy; what qualities do you expect in a good salesman?* (NOTE: plural is **qualities**) **2** *adjective* of good quality; *we aim to provide a quality service at low cost*

qualm [kwɑːm] *noun* feeling of doubt or worry; *she accepted the money despite her qualms*; **to have no qualms about something** = not to worry about something; *he has no qualms about asking the bank to lend him money*

quandary [ˈkwɒndri] *noun* **to be in a quandary** = not to be able to decide what to do; *the family doctor was in a quandary when she found that the girl was pregnant and had not told her family; we are still in* *something of a quandary about who to invite to our wedding*

quantify ['kwɒntɪfaɪ] *verb* to measure in quantities; *it is difficult to quantify the value of the work he does for the company*

quantitative ['kwɒntɪtətɪv] *adjective* referring to quantity; *a quantitative analysis of the chemical composition of a cough medicine*

quantity ['kwɒntɪti] *noun* (a) amount; **a quantity of** = (i) a lot of; (ii) a certain amount of; *the police found a quantity of stolen jewels*; *a small quantity of illegal drugs was found in the car*; **quantities of** = a large amount of; *quantities of explosives were found in the garage* (b) **an unknown quantity** = person or thing you know nothing about; *the new boss is something of an unknown quantity* (NOTE: plural is **quantities**)

quantum ['kwɒntəm] *noun (formal)* small amount; **quantum leap** = great movement forwards; *his discovery was a quantum leap forwards in the fight against cancer*; **quantum theory** = theory in physics that energy exists in amounts which cannot be divided

quarantine ['kwɒrəntiːn] **1** *noun* period of time when an animal or a person (usually coming from another country) has to be kept apart from others to avoid the risk of passing on diseases; *the dogs are kept under quarantine for six months*; *the animals were put in quarantine on arrival at the port* **2** *verb* to put someone or an animal in quarantine; *all the passengers and crew were quarantined and not allowed to leave the plane*

quarrel ['kwɒrəl] **1** *noun* argument; *they have had a quarrel and aren't speaking to each other*; *I think the quarrel was over who was in charge of the cash desk*; **to pick a quarrel with someone** = to start an argument with someone; *it was very embarrassing when my father picked a quarrel with the waiter over the bill*; **to patch up a quarrel** = to settle an argument; *after several months of arguing they finally patched up their quarrel*; **to have no quarrel with someone** or **something** = not to have any reason to complain about someone or something; *I have no quarrel with the idea of women priests* **2** *verb* to quarrel **about** or **over something** = to argue about something; *they're always quarrelling over money* (NOTE: **quarrelling - quarrelled** but American spelling is **quarreling - quarreled**)

quarrelsome ['kwɒrəlsəm] *adjective* argumentative, often getting into arguments; *as chairman she has to deal with a lot of quarrelsome committee members*

quarry ['kwɒri] **1** *noun* (a) place where stone, etc., is dug out of the ground; *if you hear an explosion, it is because they're blasting in the quarry* (NOTE: plural is **quarries** in this meaning) (b) animal or person who is being hunted; *as soon as the dogs saw their quarry, they started barking furiously*; *gunmen surrounded the building, but their quarry managed to escape* (NOTE: no plural in this meaning) **2** *verb* to dig stone out of the ground; *the stone used to build the castle was quarried locally*

quart [kwɔːt] *noun* measure of liquid equal to two pints or one quarter of a gallon; *she bought a quart of milk*

quarter ['kwɔːtə] *noun* (a) one of four parts, a fourth, 25%; *she cut the pear into quarters*; *the jar is only a quarter empty*; *he paid only a quarter of the normal*

fare because he works for the airline (b) **three quarters** = three out of four parts, 75%; *three quarters of the offices are empty*; *the bus was three quarters full* (NOTE: **a quarter** and **three quarters** are often written ¼ and ¾) (c) **a quarter of an hour** = 15 minutes; *it's* (a) **quarter to three** = it's 2.45; **at a quarter past eight** = at 8.15 (d) *US* 25 cent coin; *do you have a quarter for the machine?* (e) period of three months; **first quarter** = period of three months from January to the end of March; **second quarter** = period of three months from April to the end of June; **third quarter** = period of three months from July to the end of September; **fourth quarter** or **last quarter** = period of three months from October to the end of the year; **quarter day** = day at the end of a quarter, when rents, fees, etc., should be paid; *the repayments are due at the end of each quarter*; *the first quarter's rent is payable in advance*

COMMENT: in England, the quarter days are 25th March (Lady Day), 24th June (Midsummer Day), 29th September (Michaelmas Day) and 25th December (Christmas Day)

quarterback ['kwɔːtəbæk] *noun US* key player in American football who plays behind the forwards and directs the team's attacks

quarter-final [kwɔːtə'faɪnəl] *noun (in sport)* one of four matches in a competition, the winners of which go into the semi-finals; *Ireland got through to the quarter-finals of the World Cup*

quarterly ['kwɔːtəli] **1** *adjective & adverb* which happens every three months; *a quarterly payment*; *there is a quarterly charge for electricity*; *we pay the rent quarterly* or *on a quarterly basis* **2** *noun* magazine which appears every three months; *he writes for one of the political quarterlies* (NOTE: plural is **quarterlies**)

quarters ['kwɔːtəz] *noun* (a) accommodation for people in the armed forces or for servants; *when they come off duty the staff go back to their quarters*; **married quarters** = accommodation for families in the services (b) **at close quarters** = close to, very near; *I had seen her often on TV, but this was the first time I had seen her at close quarters*

quartet [kwɔː'tet] *noun* (a) four musicians playing together; *she plays the cello in a string quartet* (b) piece of music for four musicians; *a Beethoven string quartet* (c) four people or four things; *a quartet of British archaeologists discovered the tomb*; *have you read his quartet of novels about Egypt?*

quartz [kwɔːts] *noun* hard mineral often found as crystals in rocks and which makes up the major part of sand; *they found a lump of quartz on the beach*; **quartz watch** = watch in which the electric current from a battery is regulated by a quartz crystal

COMMENT: when connected to an electronic circuit, quartz crystals can provide a very regular signal and so are used to make extremely accurate watches and clocks

quasar ['kweɪsɑː] *noun* very distant object in the universe, similar to a star, which gives off intense radiation

quash [kwɒʃ] *verb* (a) *(formal)* to make a judgement or ruling no longer valid; *the appeal court quashed the verdict*; *he applied for judicial review to quash the order* (b) to make something end; *the government* *moved quickly to quash rumours of a split in the Cabinet*

quaver ['kweɪvə] **1** *noun* **(a)** musical note lasting half as long as a crotchet and a quarter as long as a minim **(b)** tremble in the voice; *there was a slight quaver in her voice as she answered the judge's question* **2** *verb* (*of voice*) to tremble; *a quavering voice answered the telephone*

quay [kiː] *noun* stone jetty, place where ships tie up to load or unload; *we went down to the quay to watch the fishing boats unload* (NOTE: do not confuse with **key**)

quayside ['kiːsaɪd] *noun* edge of a quay; *crowds of children lined the quayside to watch the cruise ship dock; we parked the car backing onto the quayside*

queen [kwiːn] *noun* **(a)** wife of a king; *King Charles I's queen was the daughter of the king of France* **(b)** woman ruler of a country; *the Queen sometimes lives in Windsor Castle; Queen Victoria was queen for many years* **(c)** queen ant *or* queen bee = the main ant *or* bee in a colony, which can lay eggs **(d)** second most important piece in chess, after the king; *in three moves he had captured my queen* **(e)** (*in playing cards*) the card with the face of a woman, with a value between the king and jack; *he had the queen of spades* (NOTE: **queen** is spelt with a capital letter when used with a name or when referring to a particular person: **Queen Elizabeth I**)

> COMMENT: there have been six queens of England in their own right since William the Conqueror invaded in 1066. The first was Mary I, daughter of Henry VIII; she was followed by her sister Elizabeth I. Queen Mary II was queen jointly with her husband, William III: this was the only joint monarchy there has been in England. Queen Anne was the last of the Stuart monarchs, and was followed by a series of German kings, from Hanover. The longest reigning English monarch was Queen Victoria, who was queen for sixty-four years. The present queen, Elizabeth II, came to the throne in 1952

Queen Mother ['kwiːn 'mʌðə] *noun* woman who is the mother of a king or queen and is also the widow of a king

Queen's Counsel (QC) ['kwiːnz 'kaʊnsəl] *noun* senior British barrister (NOTE: informally called a **silk**)

> COMMENT: QCs are appointed by the Lord Chancellor

queer ['kwɪə] **1** *adjective* **(a)** (*old*) odd or strange; *there's something very queer about the deal; isn't it queer that she hasn't phoned back?; there's a queer smell in the kitchen* (NOTE: **queerer - queerest**) **(b)** (*pejorative*) (*slang*) homosexual **(c)** slightly ill; *she felt queer and went home to go to bed* **2** *noun* (*pejorative*) (*slang*) homosexual man **3** *verb* to queer the pitch for someone = to upset someone's plans; *his offer has queered the pitch for all the others*

quell [kwel] *verb* **(a)** to calm a riot; *extra police were drafted in to quell the disturbances* **(b)** to hold back feelings; *she tried to quell her fears about the journey; it was difficult to quell a feeling of resentment*

quench [kwenʃ] *verb* to quench your thirst = to have a drink when you are thirsty; *I expect you would like something to quench your thirst*

querulous ['kwerjʊləs] *adjective* complaining in a bad-tempered way; *he always speaks in a querulous tone as if you had just said something to offend him*

query ['kwɪəri] **1** *noun* question; *she had to answer a mass of queries about the tax form* (NOTE: plural is **queries**) **2** *verb* to doubt whether something is true; to ask a question about something; *I would query whether these figures are correct; the committee members queried the payments to the chairman's son*

quest [kwest] *noun* (*formal*) search; *the knight set out on a quest for a fairy princess*; **in quest of** = in search of, looking for; *they set off in quest of shelter*

question ['kwestʃən] **1** *noun* **(a)** sentence which needs an answer; *the teacher couldn't answer the children's questions; some of the questions in the exam were too difficult; the manager refused to answer questions from journalists about the fire* **(b)** problem or matter; *the question is, who do we appoint to run the shop when we're on holiday?; the main question is that of cost; he raised the question of moving to a less expensive part of town*; **it is out of the question** = it cannot possibly be done; *you cannot borrow any more money - it's out of the question; it's out of the question for her to have any more time off* **2** *verb* **(a)** to ask questions; *the police questioned the driver for four hours* **(b)** to query, to suggest that something may be wrong; *we all question how accurate the computer printout is*

questionable ['kestʃnəbl] *adjective* doubtful, which is not certain; *it is questionable whether she will ever really get better; some of his deals in Asia were highly questionable; the purity of the drinking water is questionable*

questioner ['kwestʃnə] *noun* person who asks questions; *the minister refused to give straight answers to his questioners*

question mark ['kwestʃən 'mɑːk] *noun* sign (?) used in writing to show that a question is being asked; *there should be a question mark at the end of that sentence*; **there's a question mark over something** = it is doubtful if something will happen or will be good enough; *there's still a question mark over whether or not he can come; there's a big question mark over the England goalkeeper*

questionnaire [kwestʃə'neə] *noun* printed list of questions given to people to answer, especially used in market research; *we sent out a questionnaire to ask people what they thought of the new carpet cleaner; he refused to answer or to fill in a questionnaire about holidays abroad*

queue [kjuː] **1** *noun* **(a)** line of people, cars, etc., waiting one behind the other for something; *there was a queue of people waiting to get into the exhibition; we joined the queue at the entrance to the stadium*; **to form a queue** = to stand in line; *please form a queue to the left of the door*; *queues formed at ticket offices when the news of cheap fares became known*; **to jump the queue** = to go in front of other people standing in a queue; *are you trying to jump the queue? - go to the back!* **(b)** series of documents (such as orders, application forms) or telephone calls which are dealt with in order; *your call is being held in a queue and will be dealt with as soon as a member of staff is free; his order went to the end of the queue* = his order was dealt with last (NOTE: do not confuse with **cue**) **2** *verb* to queue (up) = to stand in a line waiting for something;

we queued for hours to get the theatre tickets; *queue here for the London sightseeing bus*; **queuing system** = system where telephone calls are held and answered in turn; *your call is in a queuing system* (NOTE: **queuing - queued**)

quibble ['kwɪbl] *verb* **to quibble about something** = to argue about *or* to raise objections to something very unimportant; *they spent hours quibbling about who should pay the bill*

quiche [kiːʃ] *noun* open tart with a filling of eggs, vegetables, etc.; *we had a spinach quiche with some salad*

quick [kwɪk] *adjective* rapid or fast; *I'm trying to work out the quickest way to get to the Tower of London*; *we had a quick lunch and then went off for a walk*; *he is much quicker at calculating than I am*; *I am not sure that going by air to Paris is quicker than taking the train*; **quick as a flash** = very quickly; *I dropped my purse and quick as a flash a little boy picked it up* (NOTE: **quicker - quickest**)

quicken ['kwɪkən] *verb* **(a)** to make something go faster; *he quickened his steps as he neared the house* **(b)** to make more active, to become more active; *the decision is bound to quicken racial tensions*; *the interest of the public began to quicken as it came closer to the time for the festival*

quickly ['kwɪkli] *adverb* rapidly, without taking much time; *he ate his supper very quickly because he wanted to watch the match on TV*; *the firemen came quickly when we called 999*

quicksand(s) ['kwɪksændz] *noun* dangerous area of soft sand where you can sink in easily; *it is dangerous to cross the estuary as there are quicksands or areas of quicksand*

quicksilver ['kwɪksɪlvə] *noun* (*old*) mercury, silver-coloured liquid metal used in thermometers; **like quicksilver** = very fast; *the money seemed to disappear like quicksilver*

quid [kwɪd] *noun* (*slang*) pound (in money); *it only costs ten quid*; *give me a couple of quid and I'll wash your car* (NOTE: no plural form)

quiescent [kwaɪ'esnt] *adjective* (*formal*) calm, not active; *family life has been quiescent since the birth of our second child*; **quiescent volcano** = volcano which is not active, which is dormant; *the volcano erupted yesterday, after being quiescent for almost fifty years*

quiet ['kwaɪət] **1** *adjective* **(a)** without any noise; *can't you make the children keep quiet - I'm trying to work?*; *the brochure said that the rooms were quiet, but ours looked out over a busy main road*; **quiet as a mouse** = very quiet; *she sat in the corner, as quiet as a mouse, watching what was going on* **(b)** with no great excitement; *we had a quiet holiday by the sea*; *it's a quiet little village*; *the hotel is in the quietest part of the town* (NOTE: **quieter - quietest**) **2** *noun* **(a)** calm and peace; *all I want is a bit of peace and quiet*; *the quiet of the Sunday afternoon was spoilt by aircraft noise* **(b)** **on the quiet** = in secret; *they got married last weekend on the quiet* **3** *verb* to make calm; *she tried to quiet the screaming child*

quieten ['kwaɪətən] *verb* make quiet, to calm down; *the noise in the street started to quieten down*; *she tried to quieten the children*

quietly ['kwaɪətli] *adverb* without making any noise; *the burglar climbed quietly up to the window*; *she shut the door quietly behind her*

quietness ['kwaɪətnəs] *noun* calm and peace; *the quietness of the country makes such a difference after living in London*

quiff [kwɪf] *noun* hair which stands up over your forehead; *he looks like a little boy with that quiff of blond hair*

quill [kwɪl] *noun* **(a)** long feather, formerly a feather used as a pen; *in the eighteenth century people wrote with quill pens* **(b)** spine of a porcupine; *the porcupine raises its quills when it is attacked*

quilt [kwɪlt] *noun* padded cover for a bed; *we put a thicker quilt on the bed during the winter*; *from the air, the cultivated fields were like a brown and green quilt*; *see also* PATCHWORK

quilted ['kwɪltɪd] *adjective* made with padding sewn between two layers of cloth; *she wore a quilted jacket*

quinine ['kwɪniːn] *noun* drug made from the bark of a South American tree, formerly used to treat malaria; *quinine is now used to make tonic water*

quins [kwɪnz] (*informal*) = QUINTUPLETS

quintessence [kwɪn'tesns] *noun* essential part, perfect example of something; *pictures of the snowcapped Rocky Mountains are the quintessence of the great American outdoors*

quintessential [kwɪnti'senʃl] *adjective* which is a perfect example of something; *with his bowler hat and umbrella he looked the quintessential Englishman*

quintet [kwɪn'tet] *noun* **(a)** five musicians playing together; *she plays the cello in a string quintet* **(b)** piece of music for five musicians; *a Mozart flute quintet*

quintuple ['kwɪntjupl] **1** *adjective* five times as big; *their profits are quintuple ours* **2** *verb* to multiply five times; *we aim to quintuple the number of staff over the next two years*

quintuplets ['kwɪntjupləts] *noun* five babies born to a mother at the same time; *the doctors told her she was going to have quintuplets* (NOTE: often called **quins**)

quip [kwɪp] **1** *noun* joke, clever remark; *he made some sort of quip about her hair style* **2** *verb* to make a joke or a clever remark; *'hey, big spender!' she quipped as she saw him staggering out of the supermarket laden with plastic bags* (NOTE: **quipping - quipped**)

quirk [kwɜːk] *noun* odd thing; *not being able to open the side windows when the engine is off is one of the little quirks of the car*; **quirk of fate** = strange thing which happens; *by a strange quirk of fate, he found himself in the same hotel room as he had been in with his girlfriend twenty years earlier*

quirky ['kwɜːki] *adjective* strange, odd; *the house is a quirky building full of odd cupboards and doors which don't seem to lead anywhere*

quit [kwɪt] *verb* **(a)** (*informal*) to leave a job, a house, etc.; *when the boss criticized her, she quit*; *I'm fed up with the office, I'm thinking of quitting* **(b)** *US* (*informal*) to stop doing something; *will you quit bothering me!*; *he quit smoking* (NOTE: **quitting - quit** or **quitted**)

quite [kwaɪt] *adverb* **(a)** more or less; *it's quite a long play*; *she's quite a good secretary*; *the book is quite* *amusing but I liked the TV play better* **(b)** completely; *you're quite mad to go walking in a snowstorm; he's quite right; I don't quite understand why you want to go China;* **not quite** = not completely; *the work is not quite finished yet; have you eaten all the bread? - not quite* **(c) quite a few** *or* **quite a lot** = several *or* many; *quite a few people on the boat were sick; quite a lot of staff come to work by car*

quits [kwɪts] *adjective* even; *if you pay the bill and I pay you half, then we'll be quits (informal)* **to call it quits** = (i) to say that you are even; (ii) to decide to stop doing something; *give me £2.50 and we'll call it quits; it's getting late, let's call it quits and start again tomorrow morning*

quiver ['kwɪvə] **1** *noun* **(a)** tremor, slight shake; *the only sign of any emotion was a slight quiver in his hand as he signed the contract; a quiver of excitement ran through the crowd* **(b)** holder for arrows; *Robin Hood carried a quiver of arrows on his back* **2** *verb* to tremble; *the dog watched the snake, quivering with fear; the children rushed to the Christmas tree, quivering with excitement*

quiz [kwɪz] **1** *noun* game where you are asked a series of questions; *she got all the questions right in the quiz; they organized a general knowledge quiz;* **quiz show** = TV or radio programme where people are asked a series of questions (NOTE: plural is **quizzes**) **2** *verb (informal)* to ask someone questions; *the police quizzed him for hours about the missing car*

quizmaster ['kwɪzmɑːstə] *noun* person who asks the questions on a quiz show or game show; *he's the quizmaster on a popular game show*

quorum ['kwɔːrəm] *noun* number of people who have to be present at a meeting to make it valid; **to have a quorum** = to have enough people present for a meeting to go ahead

quota ['kwəʊtə] *noun* fixed amount of goods which can be supplied; *the government has set quotas for milk production;* **import quota** = fixed quantity of a particular type of goods which the government allows to be imported; *the government has set an import quota on cars*

quotation [kwəʊ'teɪʃn] *noun* **(a)** words quoted; *the article ended with a quotation from one of Churchill's speeches* **(b)** estimate of the cost of work to be done; *we asked for quotations for refitting the shop; his quotation was much lower than all the others* **(c) quotation marks** = inverted commas (" "), printed or written marks showing that a quotation starts or finishes; *that part of the sentence should be in quotation marks*

quote [kwəʊt] **1** *noun* **(a)** quotation, words quoted; *I need some good quotes from his speech to put into my report* **(b)** *(informal)* estimate of the cost of work to be done; *we asked for quotes for refitting the kitchen; in the end, we accepted the lowest quote* **(c)** *(informal)* **quotes** = inverted commas (" "); *that part of the sentence should be in quotes* **2** *verb* **(a)** to repeat a number as a reference; *in reply please quote this number; he replied, quoting the number of the invoice* **(b)** to repeat what someone has said or written; *he started his speech by quoting lines from Shakespeare's 'Hamlet'; can I quote you on that?* = can I repeat what you have just said?; *I think the fee will be £15,000, but don't quote me on that* **(c)** to give an estimate for work to be done; *he quoted £10,000 for the job; their prices are always quoted in dollars*

quotient ['kwəʊʃnt] *noun* result when one number is divided by another; **intelligence quotient (IQ)** = number believed to show how intelligent a person is compared to others; *she has an IQ of 110*

Rr

R, r [ɑː] eighteenth letter of the alphabet, between Q and S; **oysters can only be eaten when there is an 'R' in the month** = you are not supposed to eat oysters when the name of the month doesn't have an R in it (May, June, July and August); **the three Rs** = basic skills which should be taught to children in primary school

> COMMENT: the three Rs are Reading, Riting and Rithmetic (note the spellings! - they should of course be Reading, Writing and Arithmetic)

R&D   [ˈɑːənˈdiː]   =   RESEARCH   AND DEVELOPMENT

rabbi [ˈræbaɪ] *noun* Jewish religious leader or teacher; *two rabbis led the prayers* (NOTE: used as a title with a name: **Rabbi Jonathan Blue**)

rabbit [ˈræbɪt] **1** *noun* common wild animal with grey fur, long ears and a short white tail; *the rabbit ran down its hole*; *he tried to shoot the rabbit but missed*; *she keeps a pet rabbit in a cage* **2** *verb* (*informal*) **to rabbit on about something** = to talk for a long time about something; *he was rabbitting on about his collection of toy soldiers*

rabbit warren [ˈræbɪt ˈwɒrən] *noun* **(a)** series of underground tunnels where rabbits live; *there are many rabbit warrens in the park* **(b)** maze of narrow streets, corridors, etc.; *we got lost in the rabbit warren of old streets behind the market*

rabid [ˈræbɪd or ˈreɪbɪd] *adjective* **(a)** referring to rabies, suffering from rabies; *he was bitten by a rabid dog* **(b)** (*informal*) extremely violent; *he's a rabid socialist; the government has been taken over by rabid nationalists*

rabies [ˈreɪbiːz] *noun* frequently fatal viral disease transmitted to humans by infected animals; *dogs have to be put in quarantine in case they are infected with rabies* (NOTE: also called **hydrophobia**)

> COMMENT: rabies affects the mental balance, and the symptoms include difficulty in breathing and a horror of water

RAC [ˈɑː ˈeɪ ˈsiː] = ROYAL AUTOMOBILE CLUB

race [reɪs] **1** *noun* **(a)** contest to see which person, horse, car, etc., is the fastest; *she was second in the 200 metres race*; *the bicycle race goes round the whole country*; **race against time** = struggle to get something finished on time; *they tried to block the hole in the sea wall but with the high tide rising it was a race against time; see also* BOAT RACE **(b)** large group of people with similar skin colour, hair, etc.,; *the government is trying to stamp our discrimination on grounds of race; they are prejudiced against people of mixed race*; **race relations** = relations between different groups of races in the same country; *race relations officers have been appointed in some police forces* **2** *verb* **(a)** to run, ride, etc., to see who is the fastest; *I'll race you to see who*

gets to school first **(b)** to run fast; *they saw the bus coming and raced to the bus stop*; *he snatched some watches from the shop and then raced away down the street*

racecourse [ˈreɪskɔːs] *noun* grass-covered track where horse races are held; *the Grand National is always run at Aintree racecourse*; *the races had to be cancelled because the racecourse was waterlogged*

racehorse [ˈreɪshɔːs] *noun* horse specially bred and trained to run in horse races; *the trainer checked his racehorses before the race*

racer [ˈreɪsə] *noun* **(a)** person who is running in a race; *he's a well-known bicycle racer* **(b)** special bicycle, car, boat, horse, etc., used for racing; *he's bought a new racer*

races [ˈreɪsɪz] *noun* series of horse races held during one single day, or over several days; *we go to the races on Saturday afternoons*; *the races had to be cancelled because the racecourse was waterlogged*

racetrack [ˈreɪstræk] *noun* track where races are run; *we're also going to the races - we'll meet you at the racetrack at 2.00 pm*; *his car ran off the racetrack into the crowd*

racial [ˈreɪʃl] *adjective* referring to different races; *the election was fought on racial issues*; **racial discrimination** = bad treatment of someone because of their race; **racial prejudice** = prejudice against someone because of race; *he accused his ex-boss of racial discrimination or of racial prejudice*; **incitement to racial hatred** = offence of encouraging, through words or actions or writing, people to attack others because of their race

racialism [ˈreɪʃəlɪzm] *noun* = RACISM

racialist [ˈreɪʃəlɪst] *adjective & noun* = RACIST

racing [ˈreɪsɪŋ] *noun* contests to see who is fastest; *we enjoy watching the racing at weekends*; *he was a famous motor racing driver*; *horse-racing is a favourite sport with Londoners*; **flat racing** = horse-racing over flat ground, without any fences to jump; *compare* STEEPLECHASE

racism [ˈreɪsɪzm] *noun* believing that a group of people are not as good as others because they are of a different race, and treating them differently; *there was no question of racism in this instance, it was more just bad temper on the part of the manager*

racist [ˈreɪsɪst] **1** *adjective* believing that some people are not as good as others because of race and treating them differently; *the murder was thought to have been a racist attack* **2** *noun* person who treats someone differently because of race; *he's an old racist and you won't change his views*; *the former regime was full of racists*

rack [ræk] **1** *noun* frame which holds things such as luggage, or letters; *he put the envelope in the letter rack on his desk*; **luggage rack** = space for bags, etc., above the seats in a plane, train, etc.; *the luggage rack* *was full so she kept her bag on her lap; please place all hand luggage in the overhead luggage racks;* **toast rack** = little device for holding slices of toast upright on the breakfast table; *you should put the toast in the rack to prevent it getting soft;* **wine rack** = frame in which bottles of wine can be kept horizontally; *see also* ROOF RACK **2** *verb* **(a) to rack your brains** = to think very hard; *I'm racking my brains, trying to remember the name of the shop* **(b) racked with** = suffering continuously from; *she was racked with pain; he was racked with suspicions about his son*

racket ['rækɪt] *noun* **(a)** light frame with tight strings, used for hitting the ball in games; *she bought a new tennis racket at the start of the summer season; she asked if she could borrow his badminton racket for the tournament* **(b)** (*informal*) loud noise; *stop that racket at once!; the people next door make a terrible racket when they're having a party* **(c)** (*informal*) illegal deal which makes a lot of money; *don't get involved in that racket, you'll pay a hefty fine if you get caught; he runs a cut-price ticket racket*

racketeer [rækɪ'tɪə] *noun* person who runs a racket; *he's a well-known Chicago racketeer*

racketeering [rækə'tɪərɪŋ] *noun* running a racket; *he has been charged with racketeering*

radar ['reɪdɑː] *noun* **(a)** system for finding objects such as ships or aircraft, and judging their position, from radio signals which are reflected back from them as dots on a monitor; *the plane's radar picked up another plane coming too close* **(b) radar trap** = small radar device by the side of a road which senses and notes details of cars which are travelling too fast (NOTE: also called a **speed trap**)

radial ['reɪdɪəl] *adjective* **(a)** which radiates out from a central point; *the streets are arranged in a radial pattern around the roundabout* **(b) radial tyres** = tyres with internal wires which are strong and give a better grip on the road surface

radiance ['reɪdɪəns] *noun* being bright or brilliant; *the radiance of her smile as she left the hospital carrying her baby son*

radiant ['reɪdɪənt] *adjective* **(a)** bright; *she came out of the church with a radiant smile;* **radiant with** = bright with; *he was radiant with joy as he read the results* **(b)** which is sent out in the form of rays; **radiant heat** = heat which is transmitted by infrared rays from something hot; *an electric fire sends out radiant heat from a hot wire coil*

radiate ['reɪdɪeɪt] *verb* **(a)** to send out rays or heat; *light radiates from the sun* **(b)** to spread out from a central point; *the paths radiated from the tree in the centre of the garden; the pain can radiate down both arms and up into the neck and jaw*

radiation [reɪdɪ'eɪʃn] *noun* sending out rays or heat; *local residents were concerned about the effects of radiation from the nearby nuclear base; any person exposed to radiation is more likely to develop certain types of cancer; prolonged exposure to X-rays can cause radiation sickness*

COMMENT: many forms of cancer can be treated by directing radiation at the diseased part of the body; *see also* RADIOTHERAPY

radiator ['reɪdɪeɪtə] *noun* **(a)** metal panel filled with hot water for heating; *turn the radiator down - it's*

boiling in here; when we arrived at the hotel our room was cold, so we switched the radiators on **(b)** metal panel filled with cold water for cooling a car engine; *the radiator overheated causing the car to break down*

radical ['rædɪkl] **1** *adjective* **(a)** thorough, complete; basic (difference); *the government has had a radical rethink about press freedom; he pointed out the radical difference between the two parties' policies on education* **(b)** new and totally different; *his more radical proposals were turned down by the committee;* **radical party** = a party which is in favour of great and rapid change in the way a country is governed; *he's not a radical and doesn't belong to the radical party* **2** *noun* member of a radical party; *two Radicals voted against the government*

radicalism ['rædɪkəlɪzm] *noun* political ideas of a radical party; *the radicalism of some ministers puts off the voters*

radically ['rædɪkli] *adverb* basically, in a radical way; *we are radically opposed to lowering the age of consent*

radio ['reɪdɪəu] **1** *noun* **(a)** method of sending out and receiving messages using air waves; *they got the news by radio; we always listen to BBC radio when we're on holiday;* **radio cab** *or* **radio taxi** = taxi which is in contact with its base by radio, and so can be called quickly to pick up a client; *it will be quicker to phone for a radio cab;* **radio telescope** = telescope which uses radio waves to detect stars and other objects in the universe; *astronomers used a new advanced radio telescope to observe the comet;* **radio waves** = way in which radio signals move through the atmosphere; *the transmission and reception of sound and data by radio waves is called radio communications* **(b)** device which sends out and receives messages using air waves; *turn on the radio - it's time for the weather forecast; I heard the news on the car radio; please, turn the radio down - I'm on the phone* **2** *verb* to send a message using a radio; *they radioed for assistance*

radioactive [reɪdɪəu'æktɪv] *adjective* (substance) which, as its nucleus breaks up, gives off energy in the form of radiation which can pass through other substances; *after the accident, part of the nuclear plant remained radioactive for 20 years; the problems of disposal of radioactive waste*

radioactivity [reɪdɪəuæk'tɪvɪti] *noun* energy in the form of radiation from radioactive substances; *the power station reactor was showing dangerous levels of radioactivity*

radiotherapy [reɪdɪəu'θerəpi] *noun* treating a disease by exposing the affected part to radioactive rays such as X-rays or gamma rays; *she will have to have a course of radiotherapy to reduce the tumour*

radish ['rædɪʃ] *noun* small red root vegetable, eaten raw in salads; *we started with a bowl of radishes and butter* (NOTE: plural is **radishes**)

radium ['reɪdɪəm] *noun* radioactive metal, used to treat certain diseases such as cancer (NOTE: Chemical element: chemical symbol: **Ra**; atomic number: **88**)

radius ['reɪdɪəs] *noun* **(a)** line from the centre of a circle to the outside edge; *we were all asked to measure the radius of the circle* **(b)** distance in any direction from a particular central point; *people within a radius of twenty miles heard the explosion; the school accepts children living within a two-mile radius* **(c)** the shorter and outer of the two bones in the forearm between the* elbow and the wrist; *they found he had fractured his radius* (NOTE: the other longer bone is the **ulna**; note that the plural is **radii** ['reɪdɪaɪ])

radon ['reɪdɒn] *noun* natural inert radioactive gas, formed from the radioactive decay of radium; *radon seeps into the basements of houses built on granite and can cause radiation sickness* (NOTE: Chemical element: chemical symbol: **Rn**; atomic number: **86**)

RAF ['ɑːeɪ'ef] = ROYAL AIR FORCE; *RAF pilots flew their Tornado jets low over the Welsh hillside*

raffle ['ræfl] **1** *noun* lottery where you buy a ticket with a number on it, in the hope of winning a prize; *she won a bottle of perfume in a raffle* **2** *verb* to give a prize in a lottery; *they raffled a car for charity*

raft [rɑːft] *noun* boat made of pieces of wood or logs tied together to form a flat surface; *they took their raft all the way down the Amazon*; *students held a raft race to raise money for charity*

rafter ['rɑːftə] *noun* sloping beam which holds up a roof; *the builders have finished putting up the rafters and will now start on the tiles*

rafting ['rɑːftɪŋ] *noun* **whitewater rafting** = sport of riding strong rubber dinghies down dangerous rivers; *he took her whitewater rafting on the Colorado River*

rag [ræg] **1** *noun* **(a)** piece of torn cloth; *he used an old oily rag to clean his motorbike*; *(informal)* **like a red rag to a bull** = making you very annoyed; *any mention of socialists is like a red rag to a bull to him* **(b) rags** = old torn clothes; *the children were dressed in rags*; *(informal)* **the rag trade** = the dressmaking trade; *the heart of London's rag trade is to be found in the East End* **(c)** *(informal)* newspaper; *I read about it in the local rag* **(d)** *(informal)* **rag day** *or* **rag week** = day or week when students dress up and collect money for charity **2** *verb* to play jokes on someone; *he was ragged a lot at school*; *the other girls ragged her about her rich boyfriend*

ragamuffin ['rægəmʌfɪn] *noun (old)* dirty child in ragged clothes; *a couple of ragamuffins came up to us asking for money*

rage [reɪdʒ] **1** *noun* **(a)** violent anger; *he rushed up to the driver of the other car in a terrible rage*; **to fly into a rage** = to get very angry suddenly; *when he phoned her she flew into a rage*; *see also* ROAD RAGE **(b)** *(informal)* **it's all the rage** *or* **it's the latest rage** = it's very fashionable; *it's all the rage to wear flared trousers again* **2** *verb* to be violent; *the storm raged all night*

ragged ['rægɪd] *adjective* **(a)** torn (clothes); *the old photographs showed poor children standing in ragged clothes* **(b)** uneven (edge of a page); *if you'd used scissors to cut the wrapping paper you wouldn't have made the edge all ragged*

raging ['reɪdʒɪŋ] *adjective* very violent or painful; *she wanted water to quench her raging thirst*; *he has a raging toothache*; *the firemen battled to bring the raging inferno under control*

raid [reɪd] **1** *noun* sudden attack; *robbers carried out six raids on post offices during the night*; *police carried out a series of raids on addresses in London*; **air raid** = sudden attack by planes **2** *verb* to make a sudden attack on a place; *the police raided the club*; *we caught the boys raiding the fridge*

raider ['reɪdə] *noun* person who takes part in a raid; *raiders attacked the farm just before Christmas and drove away with a load of turkeys*

rail [reɪl] **1** *noun* **(a)** straight metal or wooden bar; *the pictures all hang from a picture rail*; *hold on to the rail as you go down the stairs*; *there is a heated towel rail in the bathroom* **(b)** one of two parallel metal bars on which trains run; *don't try to cross the rails - it's dangerous*; *in the autumn, trains can be delayed by leaves on the rails* **(c)** the railway, a system of travel using trains; *six million commuters travel to work by rail each day*; *we ship all our goods by rail*; *rail travellers are complaining about rising fares*; *rail travel is cheaper than air travel* **2** *verb* **(a) to rail off** = to close an area with railings; *police railed off the entrance to the court* **(b) to rail against** = to speak violently against; *he railed against the actions of the authorities*

railings ['reɪlɪŋz] *noun* metal bars used as a fence; *don't put your hand through the railings round the tiger's cage*; *he leant over the railings and looked down at the street below*

railroad ['reɪlrəʊd] *noun US see* RAILWAY

railway *US* **railroad** ['reɪlweɪ *or* 'reɪlrəʊd] *noun* way of travelling which uses trains to carry passengers and goods; *the railway station is in the centre of town*; *the French railway system has high-speed trains to all major cities*; *by the end of the 19th century, the railroad stretched from the east to the west coast of America*

rain [reɪn] **1** *noun* **(a)** drops of water which fall from the clouds; *the ground is very dry - we've had no rain for days*; *yesterday we had 3cm of rain or 3cm of rain fell here yesterday*; *if you have to go out in the rain take an umbrella*; *all this rain will help the plants grow*; **driving rain** = rain which is blown horizontally by the wind; *they were forced to turn back because of the driving rain* (NOTE: no plural in this meaning: **some rain, a drop of rain**) **(b) the rains** = the rainy season; *the rains came late last year* **2** *verb* to fall as drops of water from the clouds; *as soon as we sat down and took out the sandwiches it started to rain*; *it rained all day, so we couldn't visit the gardens*; **to rain hard** *(informal)* **to be raining cats and dogs** = to rain a lot; *it rained hard all morning, but had cleared up by early afternoon* (NOTE: **rain** is only used with the subject **it**; do not confuse with **reign, rein**)

rainbow ['reɪnbəʊ] *noun* semicircle of colour which shines in the sky when it is sunny and raining at the same time; *a rainbow shone across the whole valley when the sun came out*; *can you name the colours of the rainbow?*

COMMENT: the colours of the rainbow are: red, orange, yellow, green, blue, indigo and violet. See MNEMONIC for a useful rhyme to remember them by

rain check ['reɪn 'tʃek] *noun US* agreement to do something later; **I'll take a rain check on that** = I will not accept your offer right now but I may accept it later; *thanks for the invitation, but I'll take a rain check on that as I need to do some studying tonight*

raincoat ['reɪnkəʊt] *noun* coat which keeps off water, which you wear when it is raining; *take a raincoat with you if you think it's going to rain*; *she took off her raincoat in the hall*

raindrop ['reɪndrɒp] *noun* drop of water which falls from a cloud; *raindrops were running down the window panes; if you tilt your umbrella like that the raindrops will fall down your neck*

rainfall ['reɪnfɔːl] *noun* amount of rain which falls in a place over a certain period; *the annual rainfall on the mountains is higher than in the valley*

rain forest ['reɪn 'fɒrɪst] *noun* thick forest which grows in tropical regions where the rainfall is very high; *poor farmers have cleared hectares of rain forest to grow cash crops; tropical rain forests contain over half of all the world's species of animals and plants*

rain off ['reɪn 'ɒf] *verb* to be rained off = to be cancelled, because of rain; *the cricket match was rained off*

rainstorm ['reɪnstɔːm] *noun* storm with a lot of rain; *the rainstorm last night caused some flooding*

rainwater ['reɪnwɔːtə] *noun* water which falls as rain; *it is better to use rainwater to water plants in the garden*; **rainwater butt** = large barrel for collecting rainwater; *it has rained a lot lately and the rainwater butt is overflowing*

rainwear ['reɪnweə] *noun (in a shop)* clothes worn to protect you against rain: mackintoshes, waterproof anoraks, etc.; *we have a special offer on rainwear this week* (NOTE: no plural)

rainy ['reɪni] *adjective* when it rains; *our holiday was spoilt by the rainy weather*; **rainy season** = period of the year when it rains a lot (as opposed to the dry season); *the rainy season lasts from April to August* (NOTE: rainier - rainiest)

COMMENT: the phrase 'rainy season' is only used of areas where there is a very marked difference between the seasons. It is not used of Britain or any other European country

raise [reɪz] **1** *noun* US increase in salary; *she asked the boss for a raise* (NOTE: GB English is **rise**) **2** *verb* **(a)** to make something higher; *he picked up the flag and raised it over his head*; *the newspaper headline says TAXES TO BE RAISED*; *air fares will be raised on June 1st*; *when the shop raised its prices, it lost half of its customers*; **he raised his eyebrows** = he looked surprised **(b)** to mention a subject which could be discussed; *no one raised the subject of politics*; *the chairman tried to prevent the question of redundancies being raised* **(c)** to obtain money; *the hospital is trying to raise £2m to finance its expansion programme*; *where will he raise the money from to start up his business?* **(d)** to grow plants from seed; *the new varieties are raised in special seedbeds* (NOTE: do not confuse with **raze**)

raisin ['reɪzn] *noun* dried grape; *can you buy some seedless raisins for the Christmas pudding?*

COMMENT: raisins are larger than currants or sultanas, and can have seeds in them; they are all forms of dried grapes

rake [reɪk] **1** *noun* **(a)** garden tool with a long handle and metal teeth, used for smoothing earth or for pulling dead leaves together; *he took a rake and hoe to work on his allotment* **(b)** angle of a slope; *the rake of the stage is quite steep* **2** *verb* **(a)** to smooth loose soil; *she raked the flowerbed before sowing her seeds* **(b)** to pull dead leaves together with a rake; *he raked the*

leaves from under the trees **(c)** to move a camera or gun slowly sideways so that it covers a wide area; *from their lookout post they were able to rake the whole square with machine-gun fire*

raked [reɪkt] *adjective* sloping; *the stage is sharply raked towards the back*

rake up ['reɪk 'ʌp] *verb* **(a)** to pull dead leaves together with a rake; *she raked the dead leaves up into a pile* **(b)** *(informal)* to bring together; *we had difficulty in raking up the money to buy the house* **(c)** *(informal)* to bring back something unpleasant from the past; *the newspapers tried to rake up the old scandal*

rally ['ræli] **1** *noun* **(a)** large meeting of members of an association or political party; *we are holding a rally to protest against the job cuts* **(b)** competition where cars have to go through difficult country in a certain time; *he won the Monte Carlo rally by 55 minutes*; *the navigator has to deal with the maps, signs and timing for a rally driver* **(c)** series of shots in tennis; *it was a great final - full of powerful serves and exciting rallies* **(d)** rise in price when the trend has been downwards; *shares staged a rally on the Stock Exchange* (NOTE: plural is **rallies**) **2** *verb* **(a)** to gather together; **to rally round** = to group together to support someone; *when her husband was sent to prison her friends rallied round* **(b)** to recover for a time from an illness, or from a setback; *he was very poorly on Monday, but by the end of the week he had rallied a little* **(c)** to rise in price, when the trend has been downwards; *shares rallied on the news of the latest government figures*

ram [ræm] **1** *noun* male sheep; *we keep the rams separate from the ewes* (NOTE: the female sheep is a **ewe**) **2** *verb* **(a)** to batter something down hard; *he rammed the post into the soil with a heavy hammer*; *he shouted and rammed his fist on the table* **(b)** to hit another ship, car, etc., hard; *the car rammed into the side of the lorry*; *she swerved quickly to avoid ramming the oncoming car* **(c)** to push something hard; *he rammed the envelope into his pocket*; *she rushed into the house, shut the door, and rammed the bolt home* (NOTE: ramming - rammed)

RAM [ræm] *noun* random access memory, computer memory that allows access to any location in any order without having to access the rest of memory; *the file is stored in RAM*; *plug in another RAM cartridge to increase the printer's memory*

Ramadan ['ræmədæn] *noun* Muslim religious festival, the ninth month of the Muslim year, during which believers are not allowed to eat or drink during the daytime

ramble ['ræmbl] **1** *noun* walk for pleasure in the countryside; *we're going for a ramble through the beech woods* **2** *verb* **(a)** to go for a walk for pleasure in the countryside; *we went rambling last weekend* **(b)** **to ramble (on)** = to talk on and on in a confused way; *he has a tendency to ramble, and his phone calls never last less than half an hour*; *she went rambling on about her 'boy', and it wasn't until later that I realized she was talking about her cat*

rambler ['ræmblə] *noun* **(a)** person who goes for walks for pleasure in the countryside; *a group of ramblers came into the pub* **(b)** type of rose which climbs; *we planted a pink rambler round the cottage door*

rambling ['ræmblɪŋ] **1** *adjective* **(a)** long and confused; *he made a rambling speech of thanks* **(b)**

full of little streets, full of rooms and corridors with no proper plan; *we got lost in a maze of rambling alleys down by the harbour*; *we stayed in a rambling old inn in Suffolk* **2** *noun* walking for pleasure in the countryside; *they had a rambling holiday in Yorkshire*; *he lists his hobbies as reading and rambling*

ramifications [ræmɪfɪˈkeɪʃnz] *noun* complicated and unexpected results; *no one has really thought about all the ramifications of European political union*

ramp [ræmp] *noun* **(a)** slightly sloping surface joining two different levels; *you drive up the ramp and tip your rubbish into a hole in the ground*; *they have built a ramp so that wheelchairs can get into the library* **(b)** slight hump in a road surface; *drive carefully - ramps ahead!*

rampage [ræmˈpeɪdʒ] **1** *noun* **to go on the rampage** = to go about breaking things or creating disorder; *after their team's defeat the fans went on the rampage around the town* **2** *verb* **to rampage about** = to create disorder; *she was rampaging about, throwing books and pictures all over the place*

rampant [ˈræmpənt] *adjective* which is widespread and uncontrollable; *the government is trying to bring the rampant corruption in the civil service under control*; *cholera is rampant in the refugee camps*

ramparts [ˈræmpɑːts] *noun* tall walls which protect; *we walked round the castle ramparts*

ramshackle [ˈræmʃækl] *adjective* dilapidated, falling to pieces; *the bridegroom arrived in a ramshackle old Ford*

ran [ræn] *see* RUN

ranch [rɑːntʃ] *noun* **(a)** (*in North or South America*) farm where horses or cattle are reared; *the cowboys returned to the ranch each evening*; *they left the city and bought a ranch in Colorado* **(b)** (*in Australia*) farm where sheep are reared (NOTE: plural is **ranches**)

rancher [ˈrɑːntʃə] *noun* person who owns or runs a ranch; *he's a big cattle rancher in Argentina*

rancid [ˈrænsɪd] *adjective* with a nasty taste because it has gone bad or is stale; *this butter tastes rancid*

rancour *US* **rancor** [ˈræŋkə] *noun* angry feeling against someone or something; *there was considerable rancour on the part of the defeated candidate*; *she spoke about the woman who had taken her baby without any rancour*

random [ˈrændəm] **1** *adjective* done without any planning; **random access memory** *see* RAM; **random check** = check on items taken from a group without choosing them in any particular order; *the customs officer carried out a random check for drugs*; **random sample** = sample for testing taken without any selection; *the random sample of urine obtained from the athlete proved that he had been taking steroids* **2** *noun* done without any planning; **at random** = without choosing; *pick any card at random*

randy [ˈrændi] *adjective* (*informal*) eager to have sexual intercourse; *harbour towns are used to having groups of randy sailors arriving on shore leave* (NOTE: **randier - randiest**)

rang [ræŋ] *see* RING

range [reɪndʒ] **1** *noun* **(a)** series of buildings or mountains in line; *there is a range of outbuildings next to the farmhouse which can be converted into holiday cottages*; *they looked out at the vast mountain range from the airplane window* **(b)** *especially US* wide open pasture; *the cattle were left to feed on the range during the summer* **(c)** **free-range hens** = chickens which are allowed to run about freely; *she always buys free-range chickens, even though they are more expensive* **(d)** choice or series of colours, etc., available; *we offer a wide range of sizes*; *we have a range of holidays at all prices*; *I am looking for something in the £20 - £30 price range* **(e)** distance which you can go; distance over which you can see or hear; *the missile only has a range of 100km*; *the police said the man had been shot at close range*; *the optician told her that her range of vision would be limited* **(f)** large cooking stove, usually with two or more ovens; *the centrepiece of the kitchen was the magnificent new range*; *see also* RIFLE RANGE **2** *verb* **to range from** = to spread; *the sizes range from small to extra large*; *holidays range in price from £150 to £350 per person*; *the quality of this year's examination papers ranged from excellent to very poor*

ranger [ˈreɪndʒə] *noun* person in charge of the management and protection of a forest, park or nature reserve; *there's the ranger's jeep - you can tell him about the lame deer you saw*

rank [ræŋk] **1** *noun* **(a)** row of soldiers; *the soldiers kept rank as they advanced towards the enemy* **(b)** position in society, in the army; *what rank does he hold in the police force?*; *after ten years he had reached the rank of corporal*; **other ranks** = ordinary soldiers; *he rose from the ranks* = from being an ordinary soldier he became an officer; *General Smith rose from the ranks* **(c)** **the rank and file** = ordinary people; *rank-and-file union members voted against the proposal* **(d)** **taxi rank** = place where taxis wait in line; *they queued at the taxi rank for half an hour*; *there's a taxi rank is just outside the station* **2** *verb* to be classified in order of importance; *Shakespeare ranks among the greatest world authors*; *as an artist he doesn't rank as highly as his sister* **3** *adjective* **(a)** complete; *the race was won by a rank outsider* **(b)** growing thickly and wildly; *rank grass surrounded the marsh* **(c)** with a nasty smell; *the rank smell of stale cigar smoke*

ranking [ˈræŋkɪŋ] *noun* place in order of importance; *a high-ranking* or *a top-ranking official*; *she moved several places up the tennis rankings*

ransack [ˈrænsæk] *verb* to cause a lot of damage and mess while searching a place to find something; *while he was out someone had ransacked his room, turning the place upside down*

ransom [ˈrænsəm] **1** *noun* money paid to get back someone who is being held prisoner; *the daughter of the banker was held by kidnappers who asked for a ransom of £1m*; **to hold someone to ransom** = (i) to keep someone secretly until money is paid; (ii) to hold someone in such a way that they have to agree to what you ask; *the striking lorry drivers are holding the country to ransom*; **ransom note** = message sent by kidnappers asking for money to be paid; *the ransom note warned her family not to inform the police* **2** *verb* to pay money so that someone is released; *she was ransomed by her family*

rant [rænt] *verb* to complain or shout loudly; *he was ranting and raving over the planning decision*; *he* *ranted on at his poor secretary, saying it was all her fault*

rap [ræp] **1** *noun* **(a)** sharp tap; *there was a rap on the door* **(b)** *(informal)* **to take the rap** = to accept responsibility, to take the blame; *let me take the rap with the boss for having a long lunch break* **(c)** form of West Indian music where the singer speaks words rapidly over a rhythmic beat, improvising as he or she goes along; *the club played rap all evening*; **a rap artist** = RAPPER **2** *verb* **(a)** to give a sharp tap; *even though he rapped on the door with a stick, no one heard*; **to rap someone over the knuckles** = to criticize someone; *he was rapped over the knuckles by the Prime Minister* **(b)** to sing rap music; *although he couldn't play the guitar or the drums he was great at rapping* (NOTE: **rapping - rapped**)

rape [reɪp] **1** *noun* **(a)** offence of forcing a person to have sexual intercourse without their consent; *there's been a dramatic increase in the number of rapes in this area over the past year*; *he was in court, charged with rape* **(b)** (oilseed) **rape** = vegetable with yellow flowers, whose seeds are used to produce oil; *market prices for rape soared last autumn* **2** *verb* to force someone to have sexual intercourse without their consent; *the girl was raped at the bus stop*; *he was in court, charged with raping the student*

rapid ['ræpɪd] **1** *adjective* fast; *there has been a rapid rise in property prices this year*; *the rapid change in the weather forced the yachts to turn for home* **2** *noun* **rapids** = place where a river runs fast over rocks; *he took her whitewater rafting down the rapids*; **to shoot rapids** = to sail over rapids in a boat; *one of her favourite pastimes is shooting rapids in her kayak*

rapidly ['ræpɪdli] *adverb* quickly; *the new shop rapidly increased sales*; *she read the letter rapidly and threw it away*

rapier ['reɪpɪə] *noun* long, thin sword; *he drew his rapier and stabbed one of the two attackers*; **rapier wit** = vary sharp way of saying clever things; *his rapier wit made him many enemies*

rapist ['reɪpɪst] *noun* person who has raped someone; *the rapist was sentenced to a term of imprisonment*

rapper ['ræpə] *noun* person who speaks words to rap music; *he's the greatest rapper playing today*

rapport [ræ'pɔː] *noun* understanding, close link between two people or groups; *they established a close rapport with the government department*; *she never managed to have any sort of rapport with her manager*

rapprochement [ræ'prɒʃmɒŋ] *noun* French word meaning 'coming closer', used to mean a situation where two states become more friendly after a period of tension; *officials have noted the rapprochement which has taken place between the two countries since the change of government*

rapt [ræpt] *adjective* so attentive that you don't notice anything else; *she sat in the first row staring at the lecturer with a rapt expression on her face*; **with rapt attention** = very attentively; *the audience listened to the lecture with rapt attention*

rare [reə] *adjective* **(a)** unusual, uncommon; *it's very rare to meet a foreigner who speaks perfect Chinese*; *experienced salesmen are rare these days*; *the woodland is the habitat of a rare species of frog* **(b)** (meat) which is very lightly cooked; *how would you like your steak? - rare, please!* (NOTE: **rarer - rarest**)

rarely ['reəli] *adverb* not often, hardly ever; *I rarely buy a Sunday newspaper*; *he is rarely in his office on Friday afternoons*

rarity ['reərɪti] *noun* **(a)** state of being rare; *the rarity of the species means that it must be protected* **(b)** rare thing; *hot sunny days are a rarity in November*; *we get so few tourists that a coachload of them is a real rarity*

rash [ræʃ] **1** *noun* mass of red spots on the skin, which stays for a time and then disappears; *he showed the rash to the doctor*; *she had a rash on her arms*; **to break out in a rash** = to suddenly get a rash; **heat rash** = spots caused by hot weather; *he suffers from heat rash every summer*; **nappy rash** *US* **diaper rash** = rash on a baby's bottom, caused by the baby having a wet nappy; *she puts cream on the baby's bottom to prevent nappy rash* (NOTE: plural is **rashes**) **2** *adjective* not cautious, not careful; done without thinking; *it was a bit rash of him to suggest that he would pay for everyone* (NOTE: **rasher - rashest**)

rasher ['ræʃə] *noun* slice of bacon; *'two rashers of bacon and a sausage, please!'*

rashly ['ræʃli] *adverb* without considering what might happen; *he rashly decided to buy the house without discussing the matter with his wife*

rasp [rɑːsp] **1** *noun* **(a)** rough metal file; *he used a steel rasp to smooth the surface of the table* **(b)** harsh grating noise; *the rasp of the saw on the metal sheet* **2** *verb* to make a grating noise; *the steel bolt rasped as he slid it back*; **rasping cough** *or* **voice** = dry grating cough *or* voice; *the kidnapper spoke with a rasping voice*; *the woman next to me in the waiting room had a rasping cough*

raspberry ['rɑːzbri] *noun* **(a)** common red soft fruit which grows on tall plants; *they picked raspberries and ate them for tea*; *could I have some raspberries and cream, please?*; *we had scones with raspberry jam*; **raspberry canes** *or* **raspberry bush** = plants formed of tall stems which bear this fruit; *there are two rows of raspberries or of raspberry bushes in the garden* **(b)** *(informal)* rude noise made with the mouth to show that you think something is rubbish; *instead of replying, she blew him a raspberry* (NOTE: plural is **raspberries**)

rat [ræt] **1** *noun* common small grey rodent with a long tail, living in cellars, sewers, on ships, etc.; *rats live in the sewers in the city*; *bubonic plague is a disease which is transmitted to people by fleas from rats*; **like rats leaving a sinking ship** = when large numbers of people leave a company or an organization which they think is going to collapse; *ministers are leaving the government like rats leaving a sinking ship* **2** *verb* **to rat on someone** = to betray someone, to harm someone by telling their secrets; *he ratted on his best friend*

rate [reɪt] **1** *noun* **(a)** number shown as a proportion of another; **birth rate** = number of children born per 1000 of the population; *the national birth rate rose dramatically in the second half of the 20th century*; **death rate** = number of deaths per 1000 of population; *the death rate soared during the Great Plague* **(b)** how frequently something is done; *his heart was beating at a rate of only 59 per minute* **(c)** level of payment; *he immediately accepted the rate offered*; *before we discuss the project further, I would like to talk about the rates of payment*; *their rate of pay is lower than ours*; **all-in rate** = price which covers everything; *the hotel offers an all-in rate of £350 a week*; **fixed rate** = charge or interest which cannot be changed; *they chose* *a fixed-rate mortgage*; **flat rate** = fixed charge which never changes; *we charge a flat rate of £10.00 per visit*; *taxi drivers charge a flat rate of £20 for driving you to the airport*; **the going rate** = the usual rate, the current rate of payment; *what is the going rate for a 1996 model Porsche?*; *we are happy to pay you the going rate*; **interest rate** *or* **rate of interest** = percentage charged for borrowing money; *the bank has raised interest rates again*; *savings accounts offer a good interest rate or a good rate of interest* (d) **exchange rate** *or* **rate of exchange** = rate at which one currency is exchanged for another; *the current rate of exchange is 9.60 francs to the pound*; *what is today's rate for the dollar?* (e) speed; *at the rate he's going, he'll be there before us*; *if you type at a steady rate of 70 words per minutes you'll finish copying the text today* (f) **first-rate** = very good; *he's a first-rate tennis player*; *the food here is absolutely first-rate*; **second-rate** = not very good; *I don't want any second-rate actor, I want the best you can find* (g) **at any rate** = whatever happens; *I don't think he really wants to come, at any rate he won't be able to since he's ill*; *the taxi cost more than I expected, but at any rate we got to the airport on time* **2** *verb* to give a value to something; *she's rated in the top 20 players*; *I don't rate his chances of winning very highly*

rather ['rɑːðə] *adverb* (a) quite; *their house is rather on the small side*; *her dress is a rather pretty shade of blue* (b) (*used with* would *to mean* **prefer**); *we'd rather stay in the office than go to the party*; *is your company going to pay for everybody? - we'd rather not*; *I'd rather we stayed with her*; *they'd rather she went with them* (c) (*showing that something is done instead of something else*) *rather than wait for hours for a bus, we decided to walk home*; *he tried to use his credit card rather than pay cash* (d) **or rather** = or to be more precise; *his father is a doctor, or rather a surgeon*

ratification [rætɪfɪˈkeɪʃn] *noun* official approval of something, which then becomes legally binding; *the agreement has to go to the cabinet for ratification*

ratify ['rætɪfaɪ] *verb* to approve something officially; *the decision was ratified at the Annual General Meeting*; *the treaty must be ratified by Congress*

rating ['reɪtɪŋ] *noun* (a) assessment, giving a score; *what rating would you give that film?*; **credit rating** = amount of money which someone feels a customer can afford to borrow; *his credit rating was excellent so he was able to open a charge account with the store* (b) **TV ratings** = estimated number of people who watch TV programmes; *the show is high in the ratings, which means it will attract good publicity* (c) (*Navy*) ordinary seaman; *the new commander joined the navy 20 years ago as a rating*

ratio ['reɪʃiəu] *noun* proportion; *the ratio of successes to failures*; *our athletes beat theirs by a ratio of two to one* (NOTE: plural is **ratios**)

ration ['ræʃn] **1** *noun* amount of food or supplies allowed; *the rations provided for the expedition were more than sufficient*; *the prisoners had to survive on meagre rations* **2** *verb* to allow only a certain amount of food or supplies; *petrol may be rationed this winter*; *during the war we were rationed to one ounce of cheese per person per week*

rational ['ræʃnl] *adjective* sensible, based on reason; *she had made a rational decision*; *you're not being rational when you say you're going to do it all by yourself*

rationale [ræʃəˈnɑːl] *noun* set of reasons for which something is done; *do we know what was the rationale behind his decision?*

rationalization [ræʃnəlaɪˈzeɪʃn] *noun* act of rationalizing, of making something more efficient; *the company is going through a period of rationalization*

rationalize [ræʃnəˈlaɪz] *verb* (a) to find a reason for actions which do not appear to be rational; *he tried to rationalize what he had done* (b) to streamline, or to make more efficient; *the rail company is trying to rationalize its freight services*

rationally ['ræʃnəli] *adverb* in a reasonable way; *sit down and think about it rationally*; *surely, he was not speaking rationally when he said that*

rationing ['ræʃnɪŋ] *noun* system of allowing people only a small amount of food or supplies in war time; *the government has introduced food rationing*; *there may be petrol rationing this winter*

rat race ['ræt 'reɪs] *noun* bitter competition for success in the business world; *he decided to get out of the rat race and buy a small sheep farm*

rattle ['rætl] **1** *noun* toy which makes a loud repeated noise when waved; *the fans stood waving rattles and blowing whistles*; *the baby threw the rattle out of the cot* **2** *verb* (a) to make a repeated clattering noise; *the wind made the windows rattle* (b) (*informal*) to upset; *he didn't seem rattled by the news of the police investigation*

rattle off ['rætl 'ɒf] *verb* (*informal*) to say rapidly; *she rattled off a list of names and numbers*

rattlesnake (*informal*) **rattler** ['rætlsneɪk or 'rætlə] *noun* poisonous American snake which makes a rattling noise with its tail; *look out for rattlesnakes while you are on your walking tour*

raucous ['rɔːkəs] *adjective* rough, hoarse (sound); *the raucous cry of the magpies*; *raucous laughter greeted the appearance of the prime minister*; *a raucous crowd gathered in front of the palace*

raunchy ['rɔːntʃi] *adjective* (*informal*) coarse, openly sexual; *he took us to a bar with a particularly raunchy floorshow* (NOTE: **raunchier - raunchiest**)

ravage ['rævɪdʒ] **1** *noun* **the ravages of** = damage caused by; *the town will have to spend millions to repair the ravages of war*; *you can try to withstand the ravages of time by dyeing your hair* **2** *verb* to devastate or to ruin a town, etc.; *the countryside had been ravaged by years of civil war*

rave [reɪv] **1** *verb* (a) to speak wildly; *he ranted and raved until someone came to see what was the matter* (b) (*informal*) to be very enthusiastic about something; *she raves about this little restaurant in the West End* **2** *adjective* enthusiastic; *the new musical had rave reviews* **3** *noun* huge party for young people, with bright lights, loud music and usually drugs

raven ['reɪvn] *noun* big black bird like a very large crow; *the ravens sat in the trees overlooking the fields below*; *are there still lots of ravens at the Tower of London?*

ravenous ['rævənəs] *adjective* very hungry; *what's for dinner? - I'm simply ravenous*

ravine [rə'viːn] *noun* deep narrow valley; *the car crashed through the fence and ended up at the bottom of a ravine*

raving ['reɪvɪŋ] *adjective & adverb (informal)* **raving (mad)** = wildly mad; *you must be raving, that's far too expensive!*

ravishing ['rævɪʃɪŋ] *adjective* very beautiful; *what a ravishing dress!*

ravishingly ['rævɪʃɪŋli] *adverb* very (beautiful); *he has two ravishingly beautiful daughters*

raw [rɔː] *adjective* **(a)** not cooked; *don't be silly - you can't eat raw potatoes!*; *we had a salad of raw cabbage and tomatoes*; *sushi is a Japanese dish of raw fish*; *they served the meat almost raw* **(b) raw materials** = substances in their natural state which have not yet been made into manufactured goods (such as wool, wood, sand, etc.); *what raw materials are needed for making soap?*; *a Malaysian company provides the raw materials used by the tyre manufacturer* **(c)** cold and damp (weather); *a very raw winter's morning*; *the driving wind was cold and raw* **(d)** *(on the skin)* sensitive because the skin has been rubbed off; *the blister left her skin red and raw*; *(informal)* **to touch a raw nerve** = to mention something which someone is sensitive about; *his mention of the money they owed touched a raw nerve* **(e)** *(informal)* **a raw deal** = unfair treatment; *he got a raw deal from the government when they refused to pay him a pension*

ray [reɪ] *noun* **(a)** beam of light or heat; *a ray of sunshine hit the window pane and lit up the gloomy room*; **a ray of hope** = small hopeful sign **(b) X-rays** = rays which go through the soft tissue, and allow the bones and organs in the body to be photographed; *the dentist took X-rays of his teeth*; *the X-ray examination revealed the presence of a tumour in the colon* **(c)** type of large flat sea fish; *we had ray cooked in butter*

raze [reɪz] *verb* **to raze something to the ground** = to demolish something completely; *the office block will be razed to the ground to make way for the new road*; *whole sections of the town were razed to the ground in the earthquake* (NOTE: do not confuse with **raise**)

razor ['reɪzə] *noun* instrument with a very sharp blade for removing hair; *he was shaving with his electric razor*; *the barber shaved him with an old-fashioned razor*

RC ['ɑː 'siː] = ROMAN CATHOLIC

Rd [rəud] *short for* ROAD; *our address is 1 Cambridge Rd*

reach [riːtʃ] **1** *noun* **(a)** how far you can stretch out your hand; *keep the medicine bottle out of the reach of the children* **(b)** how far you can travel easily; *the office is within easy reach of the railway station* **(c) reaches** = section of a river; *the upper reaches of the Thames* **2** *verb* **(a)** to stretch out your hand to; *she reached across the table and took some meat from my plate*; *he's quite tall enough to reach the tool cupboard*; *can you reach me down the suitcase from the top shelf?* **(b)** to arrive at a place; *we were held up by fog and only reached home at midnight*; *the plane reaches Hong Kong at midday*; *we wrote to tell her we were coming to visit, but the letter never reached her* **(c)** to get to a certain level; *the amount we owe the bank has reached £100,000* **(d)** to do something successfully; **to reach an agreement** = to agree; *the two parties reached an agreement over the terms of*

the sale; **to reach a decision** = to decide; *the board has still not reached a decision about closing the factory*

react [ri'ækt] *verb* to do or to say something in response to words or an action; *how will he react when we tell him the news?*; *when she heard the rumour she didn't react at all*; **to react against something** = to show opposition to something; *the farmers reacted against the new law by blocking the roads with their tractors*; **to react to something** = to have a particular response to something; *how did he react to news of her death?*; *he didn't react at all well to the injection*; **to react with something** = to change chemical composition because of a substance; *acids react with metals*

reaction [ri'ækʃn] *noun* **(a)** act of reacting; *a chemical reaction takes place when sulphuric acid is added* **(b)** thing done or said in response; *his immediate reaction to the news was to burst into laughter*; *there was a very negative reaction to the proposed building development*; **a natural reaction** = a normal way of responding; *bursting into tears is a natural reaction when you pass your exams*; **what was his reaction to the news?** = what did he say? what did he do?; *what was his reaction when you told him you were leaving him?*

reactionary [ri'ækʃənri] **1** *adjective* extremely conservative, opposed to any reforms; *reactionary elements in the government may try to block the president's plan* **2** *noun* person who is extremely conservative, opposed to any reforms; *the proposals have run up against opposition from reactionaries in the armed forces* (NOTE: plural is **reactionaries**)

reactive [ri'æktɪv] *adjective* **(a)** *(chemical)* which reacts easily with other substances **(b)** working by reacting to things which happen, rather than by starting a process yourself; *they decided to adopt a reactive strategy*; *his method of working is purely reactive* (NOTE: the opposite in this meaning is **proactive**)

reactor [ri'æktə] *noun* **nuclear reactor** = device which creates heat and energy by starting and controlling atomic fission; *a nuclear disaster could have happened if the reactor had exploded*

read [riːd] **1** *verb* **(a)** to look at and understand written words; *she was reading a book when I saw her*; *what are you reading at the moment?*; *we're reading about the general election* **(b)** to look at and understand written music; *she can play the piano by ear, but can't read music* **(c)** *(computers)* to take in and understand data from a disk or sent via a modem, etc.; *our PCs cannot read disks which are not compatible with our system*; *the scanner at the cash desk reads the bar code on each product* **(d) to read Braille** = to touch the Braille symbols with your fingers and understand their meaning **(e)** to speak aloud from something which is written; *the chairman read a message from the president during the meeting*; *she read a bedtime story to the children last night*; *can you read the instructions on the medicine bottle - the print is too small for me?* **(f) to read between the lines** = to understand a hidden meaning which is not immediately obvious; *if you read between the lines of his letter you can tell that he is deeply unhappy* **(g)** to study a subject at university; *he read mathematics at Cambridge* (NOTE: **reading - read** [red]) **2** *noun* **(a)** action of looking at and understanding the words in a book, etc.; *I like to have a read in the train on my way to work* **(b)** good book for reading; *his latest novel will be a good* *holiday read*; *you can't beat that book for a fantastic read* (NOTE: do not confuse with **reed**)

readable ['ri:dəbl] *adjective* (a) legible, which can be read easily; *his handwriting is barely readable* (b) which is a pleasure to read; *it's a very readable story*

read aloud *or* **read out** ['ri:d ə'laud *or* 'ri:d 'aut] *verb* to speak the words you are reading; *she read the letter aloud to the family*; *the teacher read out all the students' marks to the whole class*

reader ['ri:də] *noun* (a) person who reads books, newspapers, etc.; *a message from the editor to all our readers*; *she's a great reader of science fiction* (b) senior teacher at a university, position between Professor and senior lecturer; *he was a reader in English at London University* (c) school book to help children to learn to read; *the teacher handed out the new readers to the class*; *I remember one of my first readers - it was about pirates* (d) electronic device which understands data or symbols; *a bar code reader*

readership ['ri:dəʃɪp] *noun* (a) all the people who read a magazine, newspaper, etc.; *the paper is targeting a younger readership* (b) position of reader in a university; *he has been appointed to a readership in Chinese*

readily ['redɪli] *adverb* (a) easily and quickly; *this product is readily available in most shops* (b) willingly, without any hesitation; *is there anyone readily available to help me this weekend?*; *she came readily when I asked her to help me*

reading ['ri:dɪŋ] *noun* (a) act of looking at and understanding written words; *reading and writing should be taught early*; **reading glasses** = glasses that help you to read things which are close; **reading lamp** = small lamp on a desk or beside a bed, for use when reading or writing; *make sure that the reading lamp on your desk is switched off*; *I can't read in bed at night, I haven't got a reading lamp*; **reading room** = room in a library where people can read books or newspapers without taking them away from the library; *there are people who don't like the reading room of the new British Library* (b) material (such as books, etc.) which is read; *this book is too difficult, it's not suitable reading for a child her age* (c) speaking aloud from something which is written; *they gave a poetry reading in the bookshop* (d) way of understanding a text; *a new reading of 'Hamlet'* (e) one of the stages of the discussion of a Bill in Parliament; *the bill had its second reading in Parliament last night*

ready ['redi] *adjective* (a) prepared for something; *hold on - I'll be ready in two minutes*; *are all the children ready to go to school?*; *why isn't the coach here? - the group are all ready and waiting to go*; **ready for anything** = prepared to do anything; *now that I've had some food, I'm ready for anything!* (b) fit to be used or eaten; *don't sit down yet - the meal isn't ready*; *is my dry cleaning ready yet?* (c) *(informal)* **ready cash** *or* **ready money** = cash which is immediately available; *I won't be able to come out tonight as I'm a bit short of ready cash*; *I always keep some ready cash handy in case of emergencies* (NOTE: **readier - readiest**)

ready-made [redi'meɪd] *adjective* which is mass-produced and ready to use; *I don't have time to cook in the evening so I always buy ready-made meals from the supermarket*; *do you want to buy ready-made curtains or are you going to make your own?*

ready-to-wear [redɪtə'weə] *adjective* (clothes, etc.) which are mass-produced, ready to fit any person of a certain size; *the shop sells both ready-to-wear and made-to-measure suits* (NOTE: also called **off-the-peg**)

reaffirm [ri:ə'fɜːm] *verb* *(formal)* to state something formally again; *he reaffirmed his intention of running for president*

reagent [ri'eɪdʒənt] *noun* substance which is used to start a chemical reaction to show if another substance is present; *the precipitate begins to form as soon as the reagent is added*

real ['rɪəl] *adjective* (a) not a copy, not artificial; *is that watch real gold?*; *that plastic apple looks very real or looks just like the real thing*; *he has a real leather case* (b) *(used to emphasize)* that car is a real bargain at £300; *their little girl is going to be a real beauty*; *wasps can be a real problem on picnics* (c) which exists; *have you ever seen a real live tiger?*; *there's a real danger that the shop will be closed* (d) **real estate** = land or buildings which are bought or sold; *he made his money from real estate deals in the 1980s*; US **real estate agent** = person who sells property for customers (NOTE: British English is simply **estate agent**)

realignment [ri:ə'laɪnmənt] *noun* (a) change in relations between political parties or between states in an alliance; *a realignment of the centre parties took place after the election*; *a basic realignment of Caribbean states* (b) changing a system so that different parts are in a different relationship to each other; **a currency realignment** = a change in the international exchange rates

realism ['rɪəlɪzm] *noun* (a) facing facts, accepting things as they are and not trying to change them or fight against them; *my job is to try to bring some realism to their proposals*; *with the arrival of the new managing director an air of realism has finally entered the company* (b) showing things in writing or painting as they really are; *he brought piles of sand and a deckchair into the studio to lend realism to the photos for the holiday brochure*; *realism dominated French painting in the latter part of the nineteenth century*

realist ['rɪəlɪst] *noun* (a) person who accepts life as it really is, and doesn't try to change it or fight it; *he told me that he didn't believe in love at first sight as he was a realist* (b) artist or writer who shows things as they really are; *realist painters were popular in the 19th century*

realistic [rɪə'lɪstɪk] *adjective* (a) which looks as if it is real; *these flowers look so realistic, I can't believe they're made of plastic* (b) accepting life as it really is; *let's be realistic - you'll never earn enough money to buy this house*; *I'm just being realistic when I say that you should reconsider the offer*

realistically [rɪə'lɪstɪkli] *adverb* in a realistic way; *realistically, you will never be able to drive that distance in one day*

reality [rɪ'ælɪti] *noun* what is real and not imaginary; *the grim realities of life in an industrial town*; *he worked fast, and his dream soon became a reality*

realization [rɪəlaɪ'zeɪʃn] *noun* (a) gradual understanding; *the chairman's realization that he was going to be outvoted* (b) making real; **the realization of a project** = putting a project into action; *how long will it take to bring the project to realization?*; *the plan moved a stage nearer realization when the contracts were signed*; *by buying a house by the sea he achieved* *the realization of his greatest ambition* **(c)** **realization of assets** = selling of assets for money; *the realization of the company's assets went to pay some of the creditors*

realize ['riːəlaɪz] *verb* **(a)** to get to a point where you understand clearly; *he didn't realize what he was letting himself in for when he said he would paint the house*; *we soon realized we were on the wrong road*; *when she went into the manager's office she did not realize she was going to be sacked* **(b)** to get money by selling something; *the sale of his stamp collection realized £100,000* **(c)** to make something become real; *after four years of hard work, the motor racing team realized their dream of winning the Grand Prix*; *by buying a house by the sea he realized his greatest ambition*; **to realize a project** *or* **a plan** = to make a project *or* a plan happen; *the plan took five years to realize*

real life ['rɪəl 'laɪf] *noun* everyday existence, as opposed to life in a film or novel, etc.; *he dreams of being a fighter pilot, but in real life he's an insurance salesman*; *in the TV series he plays the part of the effeminate student while in real life he's happily married with three children*; *winning the lottery is the sort of thing you read about in the newspapers, but it never happens to you in real life*

really ['rɪəli] *adverb* **(a)** in fact; *she's not really French, is she?*; *the building really belongs to my father* **(b)** (used to show surprise) *it's really time you had your hair cut*; *she doesn't like apples - really, how strange!*; *did you really mean what you said?*

realm [relm] *noun* **(a)** (formal) kingdom, especially the United Kingdom; *defence of the realm* **(b)** area where something happens; *it is quite within the realms of possibility*

real time ['riːl 'taɪm] *noun* action of a computer which takes place at the same time as the problem it is solving; *a navigation system needs to be able to process the position of a ship in real time*

realtor ['rɪəltə] *noun* US person who sells property for customers (NOTE: British English is **estate agent**)

realty ['rɪəlti] *noun* US real estate, land or buildings which are bought or sold

real world ['rɪəl 'wɜːld] *noun* the world as it actually exists, with all its faults, not an imaginary one; *it's back to the real world now after our holiday*; *she's out of touch with the real world*

ream [riːm] *noun* **(a)** certain number of sheets of paper; *for office paper or printing paper a ream is 500 sheets* **(b)** **reams of** = very large amount of paper; *we had reams of faxes from the tour operator*

reap [riːp] *verb* **(a)** to cut a grain crop; *in September everyone went to the farm to help reap the corn* **(b)** **reap the benefits of something** = to get benefit from something you have done or someone has done for you; *his grandchildren will reap the benefits of all his work in setting up the family company*

reappear [riːə'pɪə] *verb* to appear again; *the waiter disappeared into the kitchen and reappeared a few moments later with our order*; *after university he vanished for a time and then reappeared as a TV producer*

rear ['rɪə] **1** *noun* part at the back; *the rear of the car was damaged in the accident*; *they sat towards the rear of the cinema*; **to bring up the rear** = to walk behind the others; *the military band brought up the rear of the parade* **2** *adjective* at the back; *the children sat in the rear seats in the car*; *he wound down the rear window*; **rear-view mirror** = mirror in the centre of the front of a car, so that the driver can see what is behind him without turning round; *he checked in his rear-view mirror before turning into the side road* **3** *verb* **(a)** to breed animals; *they rear horses on their farm*; *they stopped rearing pigs because of the smell* **(b)** to rise up, to lift up; *a rhino suddenly reared up out of the long grass*; *the walls of the castle reared up before them*; *the spectre of inflation reared its ugly head* **(c)** (of horse, etc.) to rise on its back legs; *the terrified horse reared (up) and threw its rider*

rearrange [riːə'reɪnʒ] *verb* **(a)** to arrange again; *she rearranged the furniture so that the room looked quite different* **(b)** to change the time of a meeting; *can I rearrange my appointment for next week?*

reason ['riːsən] **1** *noun* **(a)** thing which explains why something has happened; *the airline gave no reason for the plane's late arrival*; *the boss asked him for the reason why he was behind with his work*; **for some reason** = in a way which you cannot explain; *for some reason (or other) the builders sent us two invoices* **(b)** the power of thought; *he used reason to solve the mathematical problem* **(c)** ability to make sensible judgements; *she wouldn't listen to reason*; **it stands to reason** = it makes sense; *it stands to reason that he wants to join his father's firm*; **to see reason** = to see the wisdom of someone's argument; *she was going to report her neighbours to the police, but in the end we got her to see reason*; **within reason** = to a sensible degree, in a sensible way; *the children get £5 pocket money each week, and we let them spend it as they like, within reason* **2** *verb* **(a)** to think or to plan carefully and logically; *he reasoned that any work is better than no work, so he took the job*; *if you take the time to reason it out, you'll find a solution to the problem* **(b)** **to reason with someone** = to try to calm someone, to try to make someone change his mind; *the policewoman tried to reason with the man who was holding a knife*

reasonable ['riːzənəbl] *adjective* **(a)** not expensive; *the hotel's charges are quite reasonable*; *the restaurant offers good food at reasonable prices* **(b)** sensible, showing sense; *the manager of the shop was very reasonable when she tried to explain that she had left her credit cards at home*

reasonably ['riːzənəbli] *adverb* in a reasonable way; *the meals are very reasonably priced*; *very reasonably, he asked for a check on the brakes of the car before buying it*

reasoned ['riːzənd] *adjective* carefully thought out; *they produced a series of reasoned arguments for abandoning the project*

reasoning ['riːzənɪŋ] *noun* using your mind; **I don't follow your reasoning** = I can't see how you came to this conclusion

reassert [riːə'sɜːt] *verb* to assert again, to make something obvious again; *he's trying to reassert his authority*

reassess [riːə'ses] *verb* to assess again; *let's meet in two weeks' time to reassess the situation*

reassurance [riːə'ʃʊərəns] *noun* act of reassuring; *he offered her some reassurance after she heard she had lost her job*

reassure [riːəˈʃɔː] *verb* to make someone less afraid or less worried; *he tried to reassure the voters that the bus service would not be cut*; *the manager wanted to reassure her that she would not lose her job*

reassuring [riəˈʃuːrɪŋ] *adjective* which reassures, which makes you less worried; *the reassuring presence of a policeman in the street*; *it is reassuring to hear that beef is safe to eat*; *he put a reassuring arm round her shoulders*

rebate [ˈriːbeɪt] *noun* **(a)** reduction in the amount of money to be paid; *we are offering a 10% rebate on selected goods* **(b)** money returned to someone because he has paid too much; *he got a tax rebate at the end of the year*

rebel 1 *noun* [ˈrebəl] person who fights against a government or against those who are in authority; *the rebels fled to the mountains after the army captured their headquarters*; *he considers himself something of a rebel because he wears his hair in a ponytail* **2** *verb* [rɪˈbel] to fight against someone *or* something; *the peasants are rebelling against the king's men*; *the class rebelled at the idea of doing extra homework* (NOTE: **rebelling - rebelled**)

rebellion [rɪˈbeljən] *noun* revolt, fight against government, against the people in authority; *the rebellion began with a refusal to pay taxes*

rebellious [rɪˈbeliəs] *adjective* fighting against authority; *her high-handed attitude to her staff made them rebellious*; *the government sent troops to quell the rebellious tribes in the north*

rebirth [riːbɜːθ] *noun* being born again, starting again; *the years following the war saw the rebirth of nationalism in many European countries*

reborn [riːˈbɔːn] *adjective* (*formal*) which starts again; *they found reborn hope when they saw the ship in the distance*

rebound 1 *noun* [ˈriːbaʊnd] bouncing back; *the rebound was so fast that he missed the ball altogether*; *there was a rebound in Tokyo share prices yesterday* **2** *verb* [riːˈbaʊnd] **(a)** to bounce back; *the ball rebounded off the goalpost* **(b) to rebound on** = to have a bad effect on; *his attacks on local shopkeepers rebounded on him when they all voted against him in the elections*

◊ **on the rebound** [ˈɒn ðə ˈriːbaʊnd] *phrase* **(a)** as a ball bounces back; *he caught the ball on the rebound and scored a try* **(b)** while still shocked by a disappointment; *she was furious when Oliver left her, and married James on the rebound*

rebuff [rɪˈbʌf] **1** *noun* sharp refusal of an offer; *her offer to baby-sit met with a rebuff* **2** *verb* to refuse sharply; *they rebuffed all offers of help*

rebuild [riːˈbɪld] *verb* to build again; *the original house was knocked down and rebuilt*; *how long will it take to rebuild the wall?* (NOTE: **rebuilding - rebuilt** [riːˈbɪlt])

rebuke [rɪˈbjuːk] (*formal*) **1** *noun* criticizing someone for doing something; *his attempts at forcing a vote earned him a quick rebuke from the chairman* **2** *verb* to criticize sharply; *she rebuked the MD for not doing enough for the shareholders*

rebut [rɪˈbʌt] *verb* (*formal*) to reject an argument, an accusation; *the opposition was quick to rebut the points raised by the Prime Minister* (NOTE: **rebutting - rebutted**)

rebuttal [rɪˈbʌtəl] *noun* act of rebutting; *his accusations met with a quick rebuttal*

recalcitrant [rɪˈkælsɪtrənt] *adjective* (*formal*) stubborn, difficult; *the police were called in to move the recalcitrant tractor drivers*

recall [rɪˈkɔːl] **1** *noun* calling to come back or to be brought back; *the recall of the damaged goods caused the producers some serious problems*; *the recall of the ambassador is expected anytime now*; **recall of Parliament** = bringing MPs back to Parliament when they are on holiday, to discuss an important matter; **to be beyond recall** = gone and will never come back; *those days beyond recall when we were young*. **2** *verb* **(a)** to remember; *I don't recall having met her before*; *she couldn't recall any details of the accident* **(b)** (*of a manufacturer*) to ask for products to be returned because of possible faults; *they recalled 10,000 washing machines because of a faulty electrical connection*; *they have recalled all their 1997 models as there is a fault in the steering* **(c)** to tell an ambassador to come home from a foreign country; *the United States recalled their ambassador after the military coup* **(d)** to ask Parliament to meet during a vacation period; *in the light of the current crisis, the Prime Minister has asked for Parliament to be recalled or has recalled Parliament*

recant [rɪˈkænt] *verb* to admit that your former beliefs were wrong; *Galileo was forced to recant his view that the earth moved round the sun*

recapture [riːˈkæptʃə] **1** *noun* act of recapturing; *the government forces are making the recapture of the capital from the rebels their main priority*; *the recapture of the former Prime Minister's seat was an important win for the opposition party* **2** *verb* **(a)** to capture again a castle, an escaped prisoner, etc.; *our troops recaptured all the ground they had lost the previous day*; *the police succeeded in recapturing all the escaped prisoners* **(b)** to take again a seat in an election; *the opposition recaptured several seats which they had lost in the election four years earlier* **(c)** to have the same feelings again; *if only one could recapture the innocence of youth!*

recede [rɪˈsiːd] *verb* to go away or to move back; *the chance of a compromise has receded*; **receding hairline** = state where a man's hair at the top of his forehead begins to fall out

receipt [rɪˈsiːt] *noun* **(a)** act of receiving; **to acknowledge receipt of a letter** = to write to say that you have received a letter; *we acknowledge receipt of your letter of the 15th*; *we would like you to confirm receipt of the goods*; *invoices are payable within 30 days of receipt*; **on receipt of** = when you receive; *on receipt of the notification, they decided to appeal* **(b)** paper showing that you have paid, that you have received something; *goods cannot be exchanged unless a sales receipt is shown*; *would you like a receipt for that shirt?* **(c) receipts** = money taken in sales; *our receipts are down against the same period last year*

receive [rɪˈsiːv] *verb* **(a)** to get something which has been sent; *we received a parcel from the supplier this morning*; *we only received our tickets the day before we were due to leave*; *the staff have not received any wages for six months*; **'received with thanks'** = words put on an invoice to show that a sum has been paid; (*informal*) **to be on the receiving end of** = to have to suffer; *he was on the receiving end of a lot of criticism*

(b) to greet or to welcome a visitor; *the group was received by the mayor*

receiver [rɪ'siːvə] *noun* **(a)** part of a radio which receives broadcast programmes; *our radio receiver picked up your signal quite clearly* **(b)** official put in charge of a bankrupt company; *the court appointed a receiver for the company*; *the company is in the hands of the receiver* **(c)** part of a telephone which you hold to your ear and listen through; *he shouted 'get stuffed!' and slammed down the receiver* **(d)** person who accepts stolen goods; *the receivers of the stolen jewellery were arrested and jailed*

receivership [rɪ'siːvəʃɪp] *noun* being under the control of a receiver; **the company went into receivership** = a receiver was appointed to look after the affairs of the bankrupt company

receiving [rɪ'siːvɪŋ] *noun* **receiving stolen property** = crime of taking in and disposing of goods which are known to be stolen

recent ['riːsənt] *adjective* new, which took place not very long ago; *we will mail you our most recent catalogue*; *the building is very recent - it was finished only last year*

recently ['riːsəntli] *adverb* only a short time ago; *I've seen him quite a lot recently*; *they recently decided to move to Australia*

reception [rɪ'sepʃn] *noun* **(a)** welcome; *the committee gave the proposal a favourable reception*; *the critics gave the play a warm reception*; *the minister had a rowdy reception at the meeting* **(b)** *(at a hotel)* place where guests register; *let's meet at reception at 9.00 am tomorrow*; **reception clerk** = person who works at the reception desk; **reception desk** = desk where visitors check in; *please leave your key at the reception desk when you go out* **(c)** *(at an office)* place where visitors register and say who they have come to see; **reception clerk** = person who works at the reception desk; **reception desk** = desk where customers or visitors check in; *there's a parcel waiting for you in reception* **(d)** big party held to welcome special guests; *he hosted a reception for the prince*; **wedding reception** = party held after a wedding, including the wedding breakfast, drinks, toasts, cake-cutting, etc.; *only the members of the two families will be at the church, but we've been invited to the reception afterwards*; *will you be attending Anne and John's wedding reception?* **(e)** quality of the sound on a radio or the sound and picture on a TV broadcast; *perhaps you'd get better reception if you moved the aerial*

receptionist [rɪ'sepʃənɪst] *noun* person in a hotel, doctor's office, etc., who meets visitors and answers the telephone; *ask the receptionist for his room number*; *the doctor's receptionist misspelt my name and they couldn't find my blood test result*

receptive [rɪ'septɪv] *adjective* eager to listen; *he spoke to a very receptive audience*; **to be receptive to** = to be eager to take in (new ideas, etc.); *the management was not at all receptive to the employee's suggestions*

receptor [rɪ'septə] *noun* nerve ending which senses a change such as cold or heat, and reacts to it by sending an impulse to the central nervous system; *receptors are sensitive to cold*

recess [rɪ'ses] *noun* **(a)** alcove, part of the wall of a room which is set back; *the large stone urn stands in the recess by the doorway* **(b)** official holiday of the law courts or parliament; *the decision was taken when*

parliament was in recess **(c)** *US* recreation period at school; *they had a game during the recess* **(d)** recesses = hidden inside parts which are difficult to reach; *they found human bones in the furthest recesses of the cave*; *in the deep recesses of his mind, there was still the fear of dogs which he had always had* (NOTE: plural is **recesses**)

recession [rɪ'seʃn] *noun* situation when a country's economy is doing badly; *many businesses failed during the recession*

> COMMENT: the general way of deciding if a recession is taking place is when the country's GNP falls for three quarters running

recharge ['riːtʃɑːdʒ] *verb* to put an electric charge into something again; *the battery needs recharging*; *you recharge the battery simply by plugging it into the mains overnight*

rechargeable [riː'tʃɑːdʒəbl] *adjective* which can be recharged; *my mobile phone has a rechargeable battery*

recipe ['resɪpi] *noun* **(a)** instructions for cooking food; *I copied the recipe for leek soup from the newspaper*; *you can buy postcards with recipes of local dishes*; **recipe book** = book of recipes; *I gave her an Indian recipe book for her birthday*; *if you're not sure how long to cook turkey, look it up in the recipe book* **(b)** effective way to do something; *there is no single recipe for success*; **it's a recipe for disaster** = it's certain to lead to disaster; *the way the management is approaching the problem is a recipe for disaster*

recipient [rɪ'sɪpiənt] *noun* person who receives; *she is the recipient of a company pension*

reciprocal [rɪ'sɪprəkl] **1** *adjective* mutual, which is done by two people, countries, companies, etc., to each other; **reciprocal trade agreement** = agreement on two-way trade between countries **2** *noun* *(in maths)* quantity produced when 1 is divided by a figure; *the reciprocal of 4 is ¼ (which equals 0.25)*

reciprocate [rɪ'sɪprəkeɪt] *verb* to do the same thing to someone in return for something he or she has done to you; *he helped my company with a loan and I reciprocated when he was short of cash*

recital [rɪ'saɪtl] *noun* performance of music by a musician or a small group; *the group will give a recital next Thursday evening*; *we went to a Beethoven recital yesterday*

recitation [resɪ'teɪʃn] *noun* action of reciting something, usually from memory; *everyone clapped his recitation of 'The boy stood on the burning deck'*

recite [rɪ'saɪt] *verb* to speak a poem, etc., aloud in public; *the author will recite two of his poems this evening*

reckless ['rekləs] *adjective* rash, not cautious, done without thinking; *that was a reckless thing to do*; *it was a bit reckless of him to suggest that he would pay for everyone*; **reckless driving** = driving in such a way that you may cause damage to property or people; *he was charged with reckless driving*

recklessly ['rekləsli] *adverb* in a reckless way; *the company recklessly spent millions on a new factory*; *he always drives recklessly - I'm not surprised he's had an accident*

reckon ['rekn] *verb* **(a)** to calculate, to estimate; *we reckon the costs to be about £25,000* **(b)** to think; *we*

reckon *we'll be there before lunch* **(c)** to reckon on = to count on or to depend on; *we can reckon on the support of the Prime Minister*; *don't reckon on me to drive you to the airport* **(d)** to reckon with = to have to deal with; *he didn't foresee that he still had to reckon with the bank manager*; *leave early, don't forget you'll have to reckon with the rush hour traffic*

reckoning ['reknɪŋ] *noun* calculation; *according to my reckoning I owe you £250*; *day of reckoning* = time when you have to pay for your mistakes; *the manager will tell me today whether I've still got a job or not - it's the day of reckoning!*

reclaim [rɪ'kleɪm] *verb* **(a)** to claim something which you owned before; *after he stopped paying the hire purchase instalments, the finance company tried to reclaim his car*; *his car was towed away and he had to go to the pound to reclaim it* (NOTE: also **claim back** in this meaning) **(b)** to take land, such as a marsh or waste sites, and make it suitable for use; *they reclaimed a whole stretch of land along the banks of the river*; *the airport was built on reclaimed land in the bay*

recline [rɪ'klaɪn] *verb* **(a)** to lie back; *she reclined on the sofa and closed her eyes* **(b)** to make something lie further back; *if you feel tired during the plane journey, recline your seat and try to sleep*

recluse [rɪ'kluːs] *noun* person who lives all alone and does not see anyone else; *since he retired he has become something of a recluse*

recognition [rekəg'nɪʃn] *noun* recognizing or acknowledging; *in recognition for his services he was given a watch*; *he's changed beyond all recognition* = he has changed so much that I didn't recognize him

recognizable [rekəg'naɪzəbl] *adjective* who can be recognized; *she was hardly recognizable when she came out of prison*

recognize ['rekəgnaɪz] *verb* **(a)** to know someone or something because you have seen him or it before; *he'd changed so much since I last saw him that I hardly recognized him*; *he didn't recognize his father's voice over the phone*; *do you recognize the handwriting on the letter?* **(b)** to recognize a mistake *or* that you have made a mistake = to admit that you have made a mistake; *she should have recognized her mistake and said she was sorry*; *I recognize that we should have acted earlier* **(c)** to approve of something or someone officially; *the language school has been recognized by the Ministry of Education*; *she is recognized as an expert in the field of genetics*; *to recognize a government* = to say that a new government which has taken power in a country is the legal government of that country; *Germany was one of the first countries to recognize Croatia as a new independent country*

recognized ['rekəgnaɪzd] *adjective* which has been approved officially; *he has a diploma from a recognized language school*; *she's a recognized expert on genetics*

recoil 1 *noun* ['riːkɔɪl] sudden movement backwards of a gun when it is fired; *the recoil bruised my shoulder*; *watch out, this rifle has a powerful recoil* **2** *verb* [rɪ'kɔɪl] **(a)** to move backwards suddenly; *the gun recoils at least two metres after being fired* **(b)** to move away quickly from something unpleasant; *when she saw the dead dog in the road she recoiled in disgust*; *he recoiled from carrying out the captain's orders*

recollect [rekə'lekt] *verb* (*formal*) to remember something from the past; *someone gave me a drink but after that I don't recollect anything*

recollection [rekə'lekʃn] *noun* (*formal*) remembering something from the past; *I only have a vague recollection of what happened at the party*; *she has no recollection of the accident at all*

recommend [rekə'mend] *verb* **(a)** to suggest that someone should do something; *I would recommend you to talk to the bank manager*; *the doctor recommended seeing an eye specialist* **(b)** to praise something *or* someone; *she was highly recommended by her boss*; *I certainly would not recommend Miss Smith for the job*; *can you recommend a good hotel in Amsterdam?*

recommendation [rekəmen'deɪʃn] *noun* **(a)** advice; *my recommendation is that you shouldn't sign the contract*; *he's staying in bed at the doctor's recommendation* **(b)** praise; *we appointed her on the recommendation of her boss*

reconcile ['rekənsaɪl] *verb* **(a)** to reconcile oneself to = to accept; *she seems reconciled to staying at home and looking after her mother* **(b)** to reconcile someone with someone else = to make two people become friendly; *social workers managed to reconcile him with his family* **(c)** to make two accounts agree; *the accounts department is trying to reconcile the bank statements*

reconciliation [rekənsɪlɪ'eɪʃn] *noun* **(a)** bringing together of two people to become friends again; *do you think a reconciliation is at all possible between the two brothers?* **(b)** making two accounts agree; *the reconciliation of the accounts may take a long time*

reconnaissance [rɪ'kɒnɪsns] *noun* survey of enemy territory to get military information; *they carried out a reconnaissance of the enemy positions*; *reconnaissance aircraft flew over the capital*

reconnoitre *US* **reconnoiter** [rekə'nɔɪtə] *verb* to make a survey of enemy land to get information, to make a reconnaissance; *we sent a small party of soldiers ahead to reconnoitre the centre of the town*

reconsider [riːkən'sɪdə] *verb* to think over again; *we asked the chairman of the tribunal to reconsider his decision*; *I know you said 'no' last week, but I'd be very glad if you could reconsider your decision in the light of the new proposal*

reconstitute [riː'kɒnstɪtjʊt] *verb* to form something again as it was before; *the managers got together and reconstituted the old company under another name*; *this is not fresh milk - it has been reconstituted from milk powder*

reconstruct [riːkən'strʌkt] *verb* **(a)** to construct something again; *the centre of the town was reconstructed using old photographs* **(b)** to work out how a crime must have been committed by taking all the known facts and using actors to play the parts of the people involved; *the police are trying to reconstruct the crime, in the hope that it will produce new evidence*

reconstruction [riːkən'strʌkʃn] *noun* **(a)** act of reconstructing, of building again; *they're planning the reconstruction of the old fortress as a tourist attraction*; *the economic reconstruction of the area after the earthquake* **(b)** thing reconstructed; *this is not the original building, it's a modern reconstruction* **(c)** working out how a crime must have been committed by examining all known facts and using an actor to play the part of the victim, etc.; *the police are hoping that the reconstruction of the crime will jog people's memories*

reconvene [riːkɒn'viːn] *verb* to meet again; *the meeting is adjourned and we will all reconvene in two days' time*

record 1 *noun* ['rekɔːd] **(a)** success in sport which is better than any other; *she holds the world record for the 100 metres*; *he broke the world record or he set up a new world record at the last Olympics*; *the college team is trying to set a new record for eating tins of beans*; **at record speed** *or* **in record time** = very fast; *he finished the book in record time* **(b)** success which is better than anything before; **record sales** = sales which are higher than ever before; *we're looking forward to record sales this month*; *1997 was a record year for our shop*; *sales for 1997 equalled our previous record of 1993*; *we broke our record for June* = we sold more than we have ever sold before in June **(c)** written evidence of something which has happened; *we have no record of the sale*; **for the record** *or* **to keep the record straight** = so as to note something which has been done; *for the record, we will not deal with this company again*; *he is on record as saying* = he is accurately reported as saying; **off the record** = in private, not to be made public; *she spoke off the record about her marriage* **(d)** description of what someone has done in the past; *he has a record of dishonest dealings*; **track record** = success or failure of someone or a business in the past; *he has a good track record as a salesman* **(e)** flat, round piece of black plastic on which sound is stored; *she bought me an old Elvis Presley record for Christmas*; *burglars broke into his flat and stole his record collection* **2** *verb* ['rekɔːd] **(a)** to report; to make a note; *first, I have to record the sales, then I'll post the parcels*; **recorded delivery** = postal service where the person receiving the parcel, letter, etc., must sign a receipt to show that it has been delivered; *it is safer to send the parcel by recorded delivery* **(b)** to fix sounds on a film or tape; *the police recorded the whole conversation on a hidden tape-recorder*; *this song has been badly recorded*

record-breaking ['rekɔːdbreɪkɪŋ] *adjective* which breaks records; *she won a record-breaking third gold medal*; *the company has made record-breaking profits*

recorder [rɪ'kɔːdə] *noun* **(a)** instrument which records sound; *my tape recorder doesn't work, so I can't record the concert* **(b)** small wooden musical instrument which you play by blowing; *like most children, I learnt to play the recorder at school* **(c)** part-time judge

recording [rɪ'kɔːdɪŋ] *noun* **(a)** action of fixing sounds on tape or on disc; *be on time - the recording session starts at 3pm* **(b)** music or speech which has been recorded; *did you know there was a new recording of the concerto?*

record-player ['rekɔːdpleɪə] *noun* (*old*) machine for playing back music or speech, etc., from a record; *they rolled back the carpet, put a jazz record on the record-player and danced*

recount 1 *noun* ['riːkaʊnt] counting again, especially counting votes again; *the vote was very close, so the loser asked for a recount*; *after three recounts Edward Jones was declared the winner by eleven votes* **2** *verb* **(a)** [rɪ'kaʊnt] (*formal*) to tell a story; *he recounted his*

story to the police **(b)** [riː'kaʊnt] to count again; *all the votes had to be recounted*

recoup [rɪ'kuːp] *verb* **to recoup your losses** = to get back money which you thought you had lost; *he's still trying to recoup his losses on the Stock Exchange*; *we expect to recoup our initial outlay within six months*

recourse [rɪ'kɔːs] *noun* (*formal*) **to have recourse to something** = to use something in an emergency; *in the end we had to have recourse to the life rafts*; *we hope to settle the dispute without recourse to the courts*

recover [rɪ'kʌvə] *verb* **(a)** to recover from an illness = to get well again after an illness; *she is still recovering from flu* **(b)** to recover from a shock = to get over a shock; *it took him weeks to recover from the shock of seeing his son in court* **(c)** to get back something which has been lost, stolen, invested, etc.; *she's trying to recover damages from the driver of the car*; *you must work much harder if you want to recover the money you invested in your business* **(d)** [riː'kʌvə] to put a new cover on a piece of furniture; *instead of buying a new chair, I had the old one recovered*

recovery [rɪ'kʌvrɪ] *noun* **(a)** getting back something which has been lost, stolen, invested, etc.; *the TV programme led to the recovery of all the stolen goods*; *we are aiming for the complete recovery of the money invested* **(b)** recovery vehicle = truck that goes to find vehicles which have broken down and brings them back to the garage for repair **(c)** getting well again; *she made a quick recovery and is now back at work* **(d)** upwards movement of the economy, of a company's shares; *the British economy staged a rapid recovery*

recreate [riːkri'eɪt] *verb* to create again; *they put in candles to recreate the atmosphere of an eighteenth-century house*

recreation *noun* **(a)** [rekri'eɪʃn] pleasant activity for your spare time; *what is your favourite recreation?*; *doesn't she have any recreations other than going to bars in the evening?*; **recreation ground** = public area with playgorunds for children and sports fields for adults **(b)** [riːkri'eɪʃn] creating again; *we have been given a grant to help pay for the recreation of the 19th century flower garden*

recreational [rekri'eɪʃnəl] *adjective* referring to recreation; *the town has excellent recreational facilities*; *he doesn't sell drugs, he only has them for recreational use*; US **recreational vehicle (RV)** = vehicle (such as a camper van) used for pleasure as opposed to business

recrimination [rɪkrɪmɪ'neɪʃn] *noun* blaming someone else for something; *the announcement of the winner of the raffle resulted in endless recriminations from the losers*; *it was a messy divorce that led to bitter recriminations from both sides*

recruit [rɪ'kruːt] **1** *noun* new soldier, new member of staff, etc.; *recruits are not allowed in the officers' mess*; *the club needs new recruits* **2** *verb* to encourage someone to join the army, a company, etc.; *they have sent teams to universities to recruit new graduates*; **to recruit new staff** = to get new staff to join a company; *we are recruiting staff for our new store*

recruitment [rɪ'kruːtmənt] *noun* action of recruiting; *the army is stepping up the recruitment of 18-year-olds*; **the recruitment of new staff** = looking for new staff to join the company; **graduate recruitment** = recruiting new staff who have university degrees

rectangle ['rektæŋgl] *noun* shape with four sides and right angles at the corners, with two sets of opposing long and short sides; *if all four sides are equal it isn't a rectangle, it's a square; draw a rectangle with sides 6cm x 2cm*

rectangular [rek'tæŋgjʊlə] *adjective* like a rectangle, with two pairs of equal sides, one pair being longer than the other; *he pulled out a rectangular folder full of papers; a rectangular table would look better in this room than a round one*

rectification [rektɪfɪ'keɪʃn] *noun* correction of something which was wrong; *the figures were incorrect, so the office issued a rectification; rectification of the error will take a short time*

rectify ['rektɪfaɪ] *verb* to correct something, to make something right; *he has been asked to rectify the entry in the catalogue*

rectum ['rektəm] *noun* end part of the large intestine leading from the colon to the anus

recuperate [rɪ'kjuːpəreɪt] *verb* to get better after an illness; *she's gone to live in the country to recuperate after her operation*

recuperation [rɪkjuːpə'reɪʃn] *noun* getting better; *recuperation after the operation can take several weeks*

recur [rɪ'kɜː] *verb* to happen again; *the pain recurred two months later; if the problem recurs, ring me up immediately* (NOTE: **recurring - recurred**)

recurrence [rɪ'kʌrəns] *noun* action of happening again; *there has been no recurrence of the symptoms; we do not want a recurrence of the shocking scenes at last night's meeting*

recurrent *or* **recurring** [rɪ'kʌrənt or rɪ'kɜːrɪŋ] *adjective* which happens again; *she has recurrent blackouts* **(b)** *(decimal figure)* **recurring figure** = figure which is repeated to infinity; *divide 10 by 3 and you get 3.33 recurring*

recycle [riː'saɪkl] *verb* to process waste material so that it can be used again; *glass and newspapers are the main items for recycling; the council is encouraging us to recycle more household rubbish;* **recycled paper** = paper made from waste paper; *she always writes to me on recycled paper*

red [red] **1** *adjective* **(a)** coloured like the colour of blood; *she turned bright red when we asked her what had happened to the money; don't start yet - the traffic lights are still red* **(b) red hair** = hair which is a reddish-orange colour; *all their children have red hair and freckles; red-haired girls often wear green clothes* (NOTE: **redder - reddest**) **2** *noun* **(a)** colour, like the colour of blood; *I would like a darker red for the door; don't start yet - the traffic lights are still on red* **(b) in the red** = showing a loss; *my bank account is in the red; the company went into the red* **(c)** a red ball in billiards or snooker; *he's potted a red* **(d)** *(informal)* red wine; *a glass of house red, please*

red carpet ['red 'kɑːpɪt] *noun* carpet put down when an important visitor comes, hence an official welcome; *they rolled out the red carpet for the president's visit; he got the red-carpet treatment*

Red Crescent ['red 'krezənt] *noun* organization which provides medical help, the equivalent of the Red Cross in Muslim countries; *Red Crescent officials have been allowed into the war zone*

Red Cross ['red 'krɒs] *noun* international organization which provides emergency medical help, and also relief to victims of earthquakes, floods, etc.; *Red Cross officials have been sent to the refugee camps; we met a representative of the Red Cross*

redcurrant ['red'kʌrənt] *noun* **(a)** little red berries, a garden fruit; *a jar of redcurrant jelly; the redcurrants need more sugar - they're very sour* **(b)** the small bush this fruit grows on; *I planted six redcurrants in the garden*

red deer ['red 'dɪə] *noun* largest deer found in Britain; *the royal parks round London are famous for their herds of red deer; red deer are common in Scotland*

redden ['redn] *verb* **(a)** to become red, to turn red; *the trees stood out dark against the reddening evening sky; his eyes were reddened from lack of sleep* **(b)** to blush, to go red in the face because you are ashamed or embarrassed; *she reddened slightly as he gave her a kiss*

reddish ['redɪʃ] *adjective* rather red; *his beard isn't black, it's a sort of reddish grey*

redecorate [riː'dekəreɪt] *verb* to decorate again; *we've decided to redecorate the bedroom in green and blue*

redeem [rɪ'diːm] *verb* **(a)** to make something better than it seemed to be at first; *the playing by the orchestra was redeemed by the singing of the soprano and tenor* **(b)** to get back something which you have pledged in order to borrow money; *after we were paid I redeemed the ring from the pawnbroker* **(c)** to get in exchange; *you can redeem this gift coupon for a free lunch* **(d)** to sell something for a cash payment; *bondholders with mature bonds must redeem them within three months* **(e)** *(formal)* **to redeem a promise** = to do what you promised; *we are still hoping that the government will redeem all its election promises* **(e)** to save from sin; *Christians believe that they will be redeemed by Jesus Christ*

redeeming feature [rɪ'diːmɪŋ 'fiːtʃə] *noun* something which makes something appear better than it seemed at first; *his only redeeming feature is that he is a good accountant*

redefine [riːdɪ'faɪn] *verb* to define again; *we need to redefine the terms of reference of the committee*

redemption [rɪ'dempʃn] *noun* **(a)** action of redeeming a debt; *the bond is due for redemption* **(b)** being saved from sin; **to be past redemption** = to be so bad that it cannot be made better; *I'm afraid those two boys are beyond redemption - they will have to be expelled from school; my old jumper is beyond redemption, we'll just have to throw it away*

redesign [riːdɪ'zaɪn] *verb* to design again; *they had another change of government so the coins and notes had to be redesigned*

redevelopment [riːdɪ'veləpmənt] *noun* building new buildings in an area; *they have put forward plans for the redevelopment of the railway station*

red-handed ['red'hændɪd] *adjective* *(informal)* in the act of committing a crime; *the police caught him red-handed*

redhead ['redhed] *noun* person with red hair; *he brought a gorgeous redhead to the party*

red herring ['red 'herɪŋ] *noun* piece of information which is not important, and is given to someone to distract attention from what is really important; *forget about all the clues in the first chapter, they're just red herrings; all this talk of spies is just a red herring to cover up police inefficiency*

red hot [red'hɒt] *adjective* **(a)** *(of metal)* so hot that it is red; *the bar of steel is red hot when it comes out of the furnace* **(b)** *(informal)* very hot; *watch out - that pan is red hot!*

redirect [riːdaɪˈrekt] *verb* **(a)** to send a letter on to another address or a phone call to another number; *we have asked the post office to redirect all our mail when we are away; phone calls can be redirected to our office number; he redirected the e-mail to his boss* **(b)** to use something in another way; *we are trying to get him to redirect his energy towards some more constructive work*

rediscover [riːdɪsˈkʌvə] *verb* to discover again; *we went back to Malaysia to rediscover the places we visited twenty years ago*

redistribute [riːdɪsˈtrɪbjuːt] *verb* to share something out again in a different way; *the government's plans to redistribute wealth from the rich to the poor*

red-letter day ['red 'letə 'deɪ] *noun (informal)* important day, which you will always remember; *today's a red-letter day - she's passed her driving test!*

red-light district ['red laɪt 'dɪstrɪkt] *noun* part of a town where prostitutes work; *it's best to avoid the red-light district after dark*

redo ['riːduː] *verb* to do something again; *this work is no good - it will have to be redone; she redid her application and this time it was accepted; the paint is beginning to flake off and needs redoing* (NOTE: redoing - redone - redid)

red pepper ['red 'pepə] *noun* **(a)** ripe red fruit of the pimento plant; *we made some red pepper and avocado salad* **(b)** hot red spice made from powdered peppers; *don't put too much red pepper into the soup*

redraw [riːˈdrɔː] *verb* to draw something again; *the map had the street in the wrong position so it had to be redrawn* (NOTE: redrawing - redrawn)

redress [rɪˈdres] **1** *noun* compensation done to make up for something wrong; *there is not much hope of getting any redress from his financial advisers* **2** *verb* to correct or to compensate; *they plan to redress the wrongs of society by taxing the rich;* **to redress the balance** = to make something fair again; *last year I gave my daughter some money, so this year I'll give the same amount to my son to redress the balance*

red tape ['red 'teɪp] *noun* official paperwork which takes a long time to complete; *the venture has been held up by government red tape*

reduce [rɪˈdjuːs] *verb* to make smaller or less; *the police are fighting to reduce traffic accidents; prices have been reduced by 15%; I'd like to reduce the size of the photograph so that we can use it as a Christmas card;* **reduced prices** = lower prices; *there are reduced prices for groups of 30 and over;* **to reduce staff** = to sack employees in order to have a smaller number of staff; *unfortunately, the best way to save money is to reduce staff;* **to reduce (weight)** = to get thinner; *she started a new diet in order to reduce weight*

reduction [rɪˈdʌkʃn] *noun* making smaller (price, speed, standards, etc.); *price reductions start on 1st August; the company was forced to make job reductions*

redundancy [rɪˈdʌndənsi] *noun* being no longer employed, because the job is no longer needed; *there were fifty redundancies this month alone;* **redundancy payment** = payment made to a worker to compensate for losing his job; *he received £10,000 redundancy payment when he left his job;* **voluntary redundancy** = situation where the worker asks to be made redundant, usually in return for a large payment; *so many nurses have taken voluntary redundancy that now the hospitals are short of staff*

redundant [rɪˈdʌndənt] *adjective* no longer needed, more than necessary; *two of the offices are redundant - we should sublet them; redundant workers are being offered a retraining package;* **to be made redundant** = to lose your job because you are not needed any more; *five employees were made redundant this week; my son thinks he'll be made redundant, so he's already looking for another job*

redwood [redwʊd] *noun* very tall conifer which grows on the West Coast of the USA; *the forests of redwoods in northern California*

reed [riːd] *noun* **(a)** tall thick grass growing in wet places; *reeds grow by the edge of rivers or lakes* **(b)** thin piece of wood or metal inside a musical instrument, which vibrates when you blow on it; *see also* REED INSTRUMENT (NOTE: do not confuse with **read**)

reed instrument ['riːd 'ɪnstrəmənt] *noun* wind instrument that has a reed in the mouthpiece which vibrates to make a note; *bassoons, clarinets and oboes are all reed instruments*

reef [riːf] **1** *noun* long ridge of rock just above or beneath the surface of the sea; *the yacht hit a reef and sank; the Great Barrier Reef is a coral reef off the north-east coast of Australia* **2** *verb* **to reef a sail** = to tie up a sail or part of a sail, to make the surface caught by the wind smaller

reek [riːk] **1** *noun* strong smell; *there was a reek of alcohol in the kitchen* **2** *verb* to smell strongly of something; *he reeks of garlic*

reel [riːl] **1** *noun* **(a)** round object used for winding thread, wire or film round; *she put a new reel of cotton on the sewing machine* **(b)** wild Scottish dance; *after the wedding breakfast, some of the guests started to dance Highland reels* **2** *verb* to stagger; *two men came out of the pub and went reeling down the street; the punch on the face sent the boxer reeling; the company is still reeling from its losses in the Far East*

reelect [riːɪˈlekt] *verb* to elect again; *she was reelected with a large majority*

reelection [riːɪˈlekʃn] *noun* being reelected; *her reelection was unexpected*

reel in ['riːl 'ɪn] *verb* to pull in a line round a reel; *the trawler reeled in its nets*

reel off ['riːl 'ɒf] *verb* to give a list of names or figures rapidly; *he reeled off a list of hotels and their prices; she reeled off a series of dates and invoice numbers*

reenter [riːˈentə] *verb* to enter again; *the spacecraft is expected to reenter the earth's atmosphere on Sunday; you can leave the exhibition and reenter as often as you wish on showing your ticket*

re-examine [riːɪɡˈzæmɪn] *verb* to examine something again; *the government is re-examining the question of old age pensions; the hospital has decided to re-examine all patients who have been scanned over the last year*

ref [ref] *noun (informal)* **(a)** *(in sports)* = REFEREE; *come on ref - that was foul!* **(b)** = REFERENCE; *your ref:* = way of referring to the number of the letter which you have received, when replying to it; *our ref:* = giving a reference number to a letter you are writing

refectory [rɪˈfektəri] *noun* eating hall in a monastery, school, etc.; *meals are served in the college refectory*; **refectory table** = long narrow dining table (NOTE: plural is **refectories**)

refer to [rɪˈfɜː tu] *verb* **(a)** to mention something; *do you think he was referring to me when he talked about clever managers?*; *the footnote refers you to page 24* **(b)** to look into something for information; *he referred to his diary to see if he had a free afternoon* **(c)** to pass a problem to someone to decide; *we have referred your complaint to our head office*; *he was referred to an ear specialist by his GP*; *see your GP first, and he or she will refer you to a consultant* (NOTE: **referring - referred**)

referee [refəˈriː] **1** *noun* **(a)** *(in sports)* person who supervises a game, making sure that it is played according to the rules; *when fighting broke out between the players, the referee stopped the match*; *the referee sent several players off* **(b)** person who gives a report on your character, ability, etc.; *she gave the name of her former boss as a referee*; *when applying please give the names of three referees* **2** *verb* to act as a referee in a sports match; *there's no one to referee the match this afternoon*

reference [ˈrefrəns] *noun* **(a)** **reference to something** = mention of something; *she made a reference to her brother-in-law*; *the report made no reference to the bank*; **with reference to** = concerning, about; *with reference to your letter of May 25th* **(b)** direction for further information; *there are bibliographic references at the end of the book*; **reference book** = book, such as a dictionary or an encyclopedia, where you can look for information; *we sell far more novels than reference books*; **reference library** = library with reference books, where readers can search for information but not take the books away from the library **(c)** report on someone's character, ability, etc.; *we ask all applicants to supply references*; **to take up references** = to get in touch with referees to see what they think of the person applying for a job; *when she applied for the job we took up her references and found they were not as good as we had hoped* **(d)** person who gives a report on your character; *he gave my name as a reference; please use me as a reference if you wish* **(e)** **terms of reference** = areas which a committee has to examine or discuss; *the terms of reference of the committee do not extend to EU policy*; *under the committee's terms of reference, it cannot investigate complaints from the public*

referendum [refəˈrendəm] *noun* vote where all the people of a country are asked to vote on a single question; *they will hold a referendum on the issue of European Monetary Union* (NOTE: plural is **referenda** or **referendums**)

referral [rɪˈferəl] *noun* passing a problem on to someone else for a decision; *the referral of the case to the planning committee*

refill 1 *noun* [ˈriːfɪl] **(a)** container with a fresh quantity of liquid; *I must get a refill for my cigarette lighter*; *liquid soap is sold in handy refill packs* **(b)** another drink; *your glass is empty - can I get you a refill?* **2** *verb* [riːˈfɪl] to fill again; *the waiter refilled our glasses*;

we stopped twice to refill the car on the way to Scotland

refinance [rifaɪˈnæns] *verb* to extend a loan by replacing it with a new one; *we are proposing to refinance the company's short-term debts*

refine [rɪˈfaɪn] *verb* **(a)** to make more pure; *juice from the sugar cane is refined by boiling* **(b)** to make something better; *the process needs to be further refined before we can introduce it nationally*; *the company needs to refine its sales techniques*; **to refine (up)on** = to make something even better; *we hope to refine upon our existing production methods*

refined [rɪˈfaɪnd] *adjective* **(a)** which has been made pure; *white refined sugar* **(b)** very elegant, polite; *in refined society, you don't drink tea out of your saucer*

refinement [rɪˈfaɪnmənt] *noun* **(a)** elegance; *the drawing room of the old house gives an idea of the refinement of life in the 18th century* **(b)** improvement; *the latest model has various refinements which the earlier models lacked*; *this is a refinement of our previous word-processing program*

refinery [rɪˈfaɪnəri] *noun* plant where a raw material, such as ore, oil or sugar is processed to remove impurities; *there is a sugar refinery just outside the town*; *oil refineries in the Persian Gulf* (NOTE: plural is **refineries**)

refit 1 *noun* [ˈriːfɪt] complete repairs; *the liner has gone into dock for a refit* **2** *verb* [riːˈfɪt] to fit out a shop, a ship, a factory, an office, etc., again; *the shop is closed for refitting*; *the MD has had his office refitted with dark blue furniture* (NOTE: **refitting - refitted**)

reflate [riːˈfleɪt] *verb* **to reflate the economy** = to stimulate the economy by increasing the money supply or by reducing taxes; *the government's attempts to reflate the economy have so far proved singularly unsuccessful*

reflation [riːˈfleɪʃn] *noun* act of stimulating the economy by increasing the money supply or by reducing taxes; *the Chancellor of the Exchequer is aiming for a modest reflation of the economy*

reflect [rɪˈflekt] *verb* **(a)** to send back light, heat, a picture, etc.; *the light reflected on the top of the car*; *white surfaces reflect light better than dark ones*; *a picture of snow-capped mountains reflected in a clear blue lake* **(b)** **to reflect (on something)** = to think carefully about something; *he reflected that this was the sixth time he had been arrested for speeding*; *when you reflect on the events of the past few days, you realize the truth of the saying that 'pride goes before a fall'*; **to reflect badly on someone** = to show someone in a bad way; *the news reflects badly on the way the manager runs his department*

reflection *or* **reflexion** [rɪˈflekʃn] *noun* **(a)** sending back of light or heat; *wear sunglasses because of the reflection of the sun on the snow* **(b)** reflected image in a mirror, in water, etc.; *she saw her reflection in the mirror and smiled* **(c)** thought; *a few moments' reflection convinced her that she had done the right thing*; **on reflection** = on thinking more; *on reflection, I think I'd better leave today rather than tomorrow* **(d)** **to be a reflection on someone** = to show someone in a bad way; *it's no reflection on you if your father is in prison*

reflective [rɪˈflektɪv] *adjective* **(a)** thoughtful; *the poem was written when the poet was in a reflective* *mood* (b) which reflects; *cyclists should wear reflective armbands when cycling in the dark*

reflex ['ri:fleks] **1** *noun* automatic reaction to something; *the doctor tested his reflexes by tapping on his knee with a little hammer; by stopping the car when the little girl ran into the road he showed how good his reflexes were* (NOTE: plural is **reflexes**) **2** *adjective* (a) which is automatic; **reflex action** = automatic reaction to a stimulus, such as a sneeze after sniffing pepper; *pulling out a gun when he heard the police siren was simply a reflex action* (b) which returns as a reflection; **reflex camera** = camera where the picture is reflected from the lens to the viewfinder exactly as it will appear on the photograph; **reflex angle** = angle of more than 180°

reflexology [rifleks'ɒlədʒi] *noun* treatment to relieve tension by massaging the soles of the feet and toes to stimulate the nerves and increase the blood supply; *she has been to a reflexology clinic for treatment for her liver condition*

reform [rɪ'fɔːm] **1** *noun* act of changing something to make it better; *the government is planning a series of reforms to the benefit system* **2** *verb* (a) to change to make better, to improve; *they want to reform the educational system* (b) to stop committing crimes, to change your habits to become good; *he used to drink a lot, but since he got married he has reformed; after his time in prison he became a reformed character*

reformation [refə'meɪʃn] *noun* (a) great change for the better; *the reformation of the prison system* (b) the **Reformation** = religious movement in sixteenth century Europe which led to the setting up of the Protestant church

reformer [rɪ'fɔːmə] *noun* person who tries to make something better; *he's not a great reformer, he's just trying to be fair to everyone; appointing a radical reformer to the post of Home Secretary is a bold move*

reformist [rɪ'fɔːmɪst] **1** *adjective* in favour of making reforms; *the reformist Prime Minister* **2** *noun* person who plans to make reforms; *the reformists have done well in the elections*

refrain [rɪ'freɪn] **1** *noun* lines which are repeated after each section of a song or poem; *at the end of each verse, everyone joined in the refrain* **2** *verb* to refrain from = not to do something; *please refrain from smoking during dinner; we must ask everyone to refrain from applauding until the signal is given*

refresh [rɪ'freʃ] *verb* (a) to make fresh again; *a coat of paint will refresh the room;* **this should refresh your memory** = this will help you remember something which you seem to have forgotten (b) to make less tired; *after a good night's sleep she felt refreshed;* **to refresh yourself** = to do something to make yourself less tired; *I need a drink to refresh myself before the second half*

refresher course [rɪ'freʃə 'kɔːs] *noun* course of study to make you practise your skills again so as to improve them; *he went on a refresher course in computer skills*

refreshing [rɪ'freʃɪŋ] *adjective* (a) which makes you fresh again; *I had a refreshing drink of cold water; a refreshing shower of rain cooled the air* (b) exciting and new; *our new offices are a refreshing change from the old building*

refreshment [rɪ'freʃmənt] *noun* **refreshments** = food and drink; *light refreshments will be served after the meeting; refreshments are being offered in a tent on the lawn*

refrigerate [rɪ'frɪdʒəreɪt] *verb* to keep food cold so that it will not go bad; *meat is sent from New Zealand and Argentina in refrigerated ships; the refrigerated lorry was carrying butter; keep the yoghurt refrigerated after opening*

refrigerator [rɪ'frɪdʒəreɪtə] *noun* electrical kitchen apparatus, a cooling cupboard for keeping food and drink cold; *there's some cold orange juice in the refrigerator; milk will keep for several days in a refrigerator; each hotel bedroom has a small refrigerator with cold drinks* (NOTE: often called a **fridge**)

refuel [riː'fjuːəl] *verb* to put more fuel into a ship, plane or car, etc.; *he stopped on the 19th lap to refuel or for refuelling* (NOTE: **refuelling - refuelled** but American spelling **refueling - refueled**)

refuge ['refjuːdʒ] *noun* place of refuge = place to shelter; **to seek refuge** = to try to find shelter; *during the fighting, they sought refuge in the British embassy;* **to take refuge** = to shelter; *when the tornado approached, they took refuge in the cellar; we took refuge from the rain under a covered bus shelter*

refugee [refjuː'dʒiː] *noun* person who has left his country because of war, religious persecution, etc.; *at the beginning of the war, thousands of refugees fled over the border;* **economic refugee** = person who has left his country because the economic situation is so bad, and it is difficult to find work; **political refugee** = person who has left his country because he is afraid of being persecuted for his political beliefs; *these political refugees are afraid that they will be imprisoned if they go back to their country*

refund 1 *noun* ['riːfʌnd] money paid back; *she got a refund after she complained to the manager;* **full refund** *or* **refund in full** = paying back all the money paid; *he got a full refund when he complained about the service* **2** *verb* [rɪ'fʌnd] to pay money back; *we will refund the cost of postage; the tour company only refunded £100 of the £400 I had paid*

refurbish [rɪ'fɜːbɪʃ] *verb* to renovate, to make something like new; *they spent thousands of pounds refurbishing the minister's office*

refurbishment [rɪ'fɜːbɪʃmənt] *noun* renovation, making like new; *the house is in good condition generally but needs some refurbishment*

refusal [rɪ'fjuːzl] *noun* (a) saying that you do not accept something, saying no; *his refusal to help was unexpected; did you accept? - no! I sent a letter of refusal;* **to meet with a flat refusal** = to be refused completely; *his request met with a flat refusal* (b) to give someone first refusal of something = to let someone have first choice when doing something; *I asked him if I could have first refusal of his flat if ever he decided to sell it*

refuse 1 *noun* ['refjuːs] rubbish, things which are not wanted; *please put all refuse in the bin;* **refuse collection on our road is on Thursdays** (NOTE: no plural) **2** *verb* [rɪ'fjuːz] (a) to say that you will not do something; *his father refused to lend him any more money; he asked for permission to see his family, but it was refused* (b) the car refused to start = the car would not start; *once again this morning the car refused to start* (NOTE: you refuse **to do something** or refuse **something**)

refutation [refjuː'teɪʃn] *noun* proof that something is wrong; *his refutation of the theory put forward by his former teacher*

refute [rɪ'fjuːt] *verb* (a) to prove that something is wrong; *he has tried to refute Einstein's theory* (b) to show that something is untrue; *he refuted her allegations completely*

regain [riː'geɪn] *verb* to get something back which was lost; *she soon regained her strength and was able to walk*; *what can I do to regain any of the money I've lost?*; **to regain consciousness** = to become conscious again; *she went into a coma and never regained consciousness*

regal ['riːgl] *adjective* (a) referring to a king or queen; *the regal splendour of the state opening of parliament* (b) suitable for a king or queen; *they offered us a truly regal banquet*

regard [rɪ'gɑːd] **1** *noun* (a) concern for something; **with regard to** = relating to, concerning; *with regard to your request for extra funds* (b) opinion of someone; *he is held in high regard by his staff* (c) **regards** = best wishes; *she sends her (kind) regards*; *please give my regards to your mother* **2** *verb* (a) **to regard someone** *or* **something as** = to consider someone *or* something to be; *the police are regarding the case as attempted murder* (b) to have an opinion about someone; *she is highly regarded by the manager* (c) **as regards** = relating to, concerning; *as regards the cost of the trip, I'll let you know soon what the final figure is*

regarding [rɪ'gɑːdɪŋ] *preposition* relating to, concerning; *he left instructions regarding his possessions*; *regarding your offer, I think we will have to say no*

regardless [rɪ'gɑːdləs] *adverb* without paying any attention to; **regardless of** = in spite of; *they drove through the war zone regardless of the danger*; *they furnished their house regardless of expense* = without thinking of how much it would cost; **to carry on regardless** = to continue in spite of everything; *although the temperature was well over 40°, they carried on working regardless*

regatta [rɪ'gætə] *noun* sporting event where rowing boats or sailing boats race; *the Henley Regatta is held in June*

regency ['riːdʒənsi] *noun* (a) period of government by a regent; *during the regency the power was in the hands of the regent and his family* (b) *(British history)* **the Regency** = period from 1810 to 1820 when the Prince of Wales was Prince Regent; *he has a collection of Regency furniture*

regenerate [rɪ'dʒenəreɪt] *verb* (a) *(formal)* to revive, to start up again; *the TV programme has regenerated interest in South America* (b) to make something grow strong again; *we hope to regenerate the area by offering grants to new industries*; *after a fire a forest will regenerate itself very quickly*

regent ['riːdʒənt] *noun* person who governs in place of a king or queen (usually when the king or queen is a child or is ill); *the Regent of Hungary was Admiral Horthy*; **the Prince Regent** = the title of the Prince of Wales (later George IV) when he was regent during George III's illness, 1810-1820

reggae ['regeɪ] *noun* type of West Indian music; *the lively sound of reggae music came from the club*

regime *or* **régime** [reɪ'ʒiːm] *noun* (a) usually harsh type of government or administration; *under a military régime, civil liberties may be restricted* (b) government of a country; *the former régime was overthrown and the President fled*

regiment ['redʒɪmənt] *noun* group of soldiers, usually commanded by a colonel or lieutenant-colonel; *an infantry regiment was dispatched to the war zone*

regimented ['redʒɪməntɪd] *adjective* strictly organized, kept under strict discipline; *life in prison is very strictly regimented*

regimental [redʒɪ'mentl] *adjective* belonging to a regiment; *old regimental banners hang in the cathedral*; *the regimental mascot is a white goat*

region ['riːdʒən] *noun* (a) large administrative area; *the South-West region is well known for its apples*; **the London region** = the area around London (b) **in the region of** = about or approximately; *he is earning a salary in the region of £25,000*; *the house was sold for a price in the region of £100,000*

regional ['riːdʒənəl] *adjective* referring to a region; *the recession has not affected the whole country - it is only regional*; *after the national news, here is the regional news for the South West*

register ['redʒɪstə] **1** *noun* (a) list of names; *I can't find your name in the register*; *his name was struck off the register*; **the register of electors** = list of the names of people who can vote in an election (b) book in which you sign your name; *after the wedding, the bride and groom and witnesses all signed the register*; *please sign the hotel register when you check in* (c) **cash register** = machine which shows and adds the prices of items bought in a shop, with a drawer for keeping the money received; *she opened the cash register to put in the money given by the customer* (d) *(in printing)* making sure that two images are printed correctly one on top of the other; **out of register** = when two images are not printed correctly; *the red is out of register* (e) level and style of language used by certain people or in certain situations; *a dictionary will indicate if the register is 'formal' or 'informal' or 'slang'* **2** *verb* (a) to write a name officially in a list; *if you don't register, we won't be able to get in touch with you*; *babies have to be registered with the registrar as soon as they are born*; **to register at a hotel** = to write your name and address when you arrive at the hotel; *they registered at the hotel under the name of Macdonald* (b) to put a letter into the special care of the post office; *she registered the letter*; *he took the letter to the post office to get it registered* (c) to record, to show a feeling, a figure; *temperatures of over 50° were registered in the desert*; *the amount of radioactivity was so small it didn't register on our monitor*; *his face registered anger and pain* (d) *(informal)* to notice, to pay attention; *I told him he was getting a big pay rise, but it didn't seem to register*

registered ['redʒɪstəd] *adjective* (a) which has been noted on an official list; *a registered trademark* (b) **registered post** *or* **registered mail** = system where details of a letter or parcel are noted by the post office before it is sent, so that compensation can be claimed if it is lost; *to send documents by registered mail* *or* *registered post*; **registered letter** = letter which has been officially recorded at the post office; *the registered letter which arrived this morning was not important*

registrar ['redʒɪstrɑː] *noun* (a) person who keeps official records; *the registrar of births, marriages and deaths; they were married by the registrar;* **Registrar of Companies** = government official who is in charge of Companies House, and makes sure that companies are properly registered, and that they report their accounts and other information on time (b) person who keeps the records of a university; *applications for grants have to be sent to the registrar's office by July 1st* (c) qualified doctor or surgeon in a hospital who supervises house doctors; *she's a registrar at our local hospital*

registration [redʒɪ'streɪʃn] *noun* act of registering; *registration of new members will start at 1pm;* **registration plate** = number plate of a car; **registration number** = official number of a car; *we are trying to buy him a car registration number which forms his initials*

registry ['redʒɪstri] *noun* place where official records are kept; *after the wedding, they went to the registry to sign the register;* **registry office** = office where records of births, marriages and deaths are kept and where you can be married in a civil ceremony; *they didn't want a church wedding so they got married in the registry office; to get a copy of your birth certificate you have to apply to the registry office*

regress [rɪ'gres] *verb* to return to an earlier stage or condition; *in spite of the treatment, the patient regressed*

regression [rɪ'greʃn] *noun* going back to an earlier stage

regret [rɪ'gret] **1** *noun* being sorry; *I have absolutely no regrets about what we did; she showed no regret for having made so much mess;* **much to someone's regret** = making someone very sorry; *much to my regret I will not be able to go to Chicago; much to the children's regret or much to the regret of the children, the ice cream van drove away* **2** *verb* to be sorry that something has happened; *I regret to say that you were not successful; I regret the trouble this has caused you; we regret the delay in the arrival of our flight from Amsterdam; we regret to inform you that the tour has been cancelled* (NOTE: **regretting - regretted**)

regretful [rɪ'gretful] *adjective* sorry, sad; *he wrote a regretful letter, apologizing to his victim*

regrettable [rɪ'gretəbl] *adjective* which must be regretted; *the whole incident is regrettable, but we have decided not to take any further action*

regroup [riː'gruːp] *verb* to form groups again; *the enemy retreated in confusion but managed to regroup on the other side of the river*

regular ['regjulə] **1** *adjective* (a) done at the same time each day; *his regular train is the 12.45; the regular flight to Athens leaves at 06.00;* **regular customer** = customer who always buys from the same shop; *he's a regular customer, you don't need to ask for proof of identity;* **regular income** = income which comes in every week or month; *it is difficult to budget if you don't have a regular income* (b) ordinary, standard; *the regular price is $1.25, but we are offering them at 99¢;* **regular size** = ordinary size of goods (smaller than economy size, family size, etc.); *just buy a regular size packet, it will be enough for the two of us* **2** *noun* (*informal*) customer who always goes to the same shop, who drinks in the same pub, etc.; *the regulars were very sorry when the old landlord retired*

regularity [regju'lærɪti] *noun* being regular; *the regularity of the asthma attacks suggests they may be caused by something which recurs regularly*

regularize ['regjulərɑɪz] *verb* to make an existing situation official; *they have been living together for years but have decided to regularize the situation by getting married*

regularly ['regjuːləli] *adverb* in a regular way; *she is regularly the first person to arrive at the office each morning*

regulate ['regjuleɪt] *verb* (a) to adjust a machine so that it works in a certain way; *the heater needs to be regulated to keep the temperature steady; turn this knob to regulate the volume; her heartbeat is regulated by the pacemaker* (b) to maintain something by law; *speed on the motorway is strictly regulated*

regulation [regju'leɪʃn] *noun* (a) act of regulating; *the greenhouse is fitted with an automatic heat regulation system; the regulation of the body's temperature by sweating* (b) **regulations** = laws, rules; *fire regulations; safety regulations; the new government regulations on housing standards*

regulator ['regjuleɪtə] *noun* (a) person whose job it is to see that regulations are followed in an industry; *the industry regulator makes sure that the rules are followed to the letter* (b) instrument which regulates a machine; *this lorry is fitted with a speed regulator*

rehabilitate [riːhə'bɪlɪteɪt] *verb* to train a disabled person, an ex-prisoner, etc., to lead a normal life and fit into society; *prisoners need special training in order to be rehabilitated*

rehabilitation [riːhəbɪlɪ'teɪʃn] *noun* act of rehabilitating; *a period of rehabilitation will be needed before he can start working again*

rehearsal [rɪ'hɜːsəl] *noun* practice of a play or concert, etc., before the first a public performance; *the director insisted on extra rehearsals because some of the cast didn't know their lines; see also* DRESS REHEARSAL

rehearse [rɪ'hɜːs] *verb* to practise a play, a concert, etc., before a public performance; *we're rehearsing the carol concert in the village hall*

reign [reɪn] **1** *noun* (a) period when a king, queen or emperor rules; *during the reign of Elizabeth I* (b) **reign of terror** = period when law and order have broken down and people live in a continual state of fear **2** (a) *verb* to rule; *Queen Victoria reigned between 1837 and 1901; she reigned during a period of great prosperity* (b) to be in existence; *chaos reigned when the town's electricity supply broke down* (NOTE: do not confuse with **rain, rein**)

reigning ['reɪnɪŋ] *adjective* (a) who is on the throne; *the reigning monarch* (b) **reigning champion** = person who is champion (until someone beats him); *I don't think he has any chance of winning, as his opponent is the reigning heavyweight champion*

reimburse [riːɪm'bɜːs] *verb* (*formal*) to reimburse someone his expenses = to pay someone back for money he has spent; *you will be reimbursed for your expenses or your expenses will be reimbursed*

reimbursement [riːɪm'bɜːsmənt] *noun* paying back money; *reimbursement of expenses*

rein [reɪn] **1** *noun* (a) strap which the rider holds to control a horse; *she walked beside the horse holding the reins; the rider pulled hard on the reins to try to* make the horse stop **(b)** to keep something on a tight rein = to control something strictly; *unless you keep your expenses on a tight rein, you'll have problems* **2** *verb* to rein back *or* rein in = to keep under control; *the leader of the opposition tried to rein in his supporters who wanted to attack the President's palace* (NOTE: do not confuse with **rain, reign**)

reincarnate [riːɪnˈkɑːneɪt] *verb (formal)* to be reincarnated = to be born again in another body after you have died; *his followers believed that when he died he was reincarnated as a religious leader*

reincarnation [riːɪnkɑːˈneɪʃn] *noun* **(a)** a person's soul born again in another body or animal after death; *the ancient Egyptians believed that the owl was the reincarnation of the god Horus* **(b)** *(informal)* reappearance of someone in another form; *his latest reincarnation was as an insurance salesman*

reindeer [ˈreɪndɪə] *noun* type of deer which lives in the Arctic; *besides Finland, in which other countries can you find reindeer?* (NOTE: plural is **reindeer**)

COMMENT: traditionally, on Christmas Eve Father Christmas arrives in a sleigh pulled by reindeer

reinforce [riːɪnˈfɔːs] *verb* to make stronger or more solid; *you must reinforce that wall before it collapses; this event has reinforced my decision to leave*; **reinforced concrete** = concrete strengthened with metal rods; *the new bridge was built with reinforced concrete*

reinforcement [riːɪnˈfɔːsmənt] *noun* **(a)** act of reinforcing; *one of the walls needs reinforcement* **(b)** **reinforcements** = new soldiers to support others already fighting; *they brought up reinforcements to the front line*

reinstate [riːɪnˈsteɪt] *verb* to put someone back into a job from which he was dismissed; *the union demanded that the sacked workers should be reinstated*

reinstatement [riːɪnˈsteɪtmənt] *noun* putting someone back into a job from which he was dismissed; *the union demanded the reinstatement of the workers who had been dismissed*

reissue [riːˈɪʃuː] **1** *noun* issuing of something again; *the reissue of the book in paperback is scheduled for next spring* **2** *verb* to issue something again; *the company reissued its catalogue with a new price list; the book was published as a hardback, then reissued as a paperback*

reiterate [riːˈɪtəreɪt] *verb* to say again, to repeat; *he reiterated his threat to resign; she reiterated that she had no intention of selling*

reiteration [riːɪtəˈreɪʃn] *noun* repetition, saying the same thing again; *the constant reiteration of wage demands by the staff made the managers even more annoyed*

reject 1 *noun* [ˈriːdʒekt] thing which has been thrown away as not satisfactory; **rejects** = goods which are not up to standard and are sold at a reduced price; **reject shop** = shop which specializes in the sale of rejects; *I bought these plates in the new reject shop - they were seconds and very cheap* **2** *verb* [rɪˈdʒekt] **(a)** to refuse to accept something; *she flatly rejected his proposal; we rejected the offer for the house because it was too low; she rejected three different wallpaper designs because they were too bright* **(b)** to throw something

away as not satisfactory; *half the batch was rejected and sold off cheaply as seconds* **(c)** *(medical)* not to accept a transplanted organ; *his body rejected the new heart*

rejection [rɪˈdʒekʃn] *noun* refusal to accept; *I applied for five jobs and got five rejections; the rejection of the transplanted kidney*

rejig [riːˈdʒɪg] *verb (informal)* to rearrange, to arrange something in a different way; *the itinerary had to be rejigged to avoid the floods; we'll need to rejig the workshop to get the new machine in*

rejoice [rɪˈdʒɔɪs] *verb* **(a)** to be very happy; *we all rejoiced to hear the news that the baby had been found* **(b)** to rejoice in = to be happy at; *she rejoiced in the warm welcome that her family gave her*; **to rejoice in a name** = to have a curious name; *the café rejoices in the name of 'The Snail and Banana'*

rejuvenate [rɪˈdʒuːvəneɪt] *verb* **(a)** to make someone young again; *she came back from the health farm completely rejuvenated* **(b)** to give something new vigour and strength; *he hopes to rejuvenate the club by attracting younger members*

rekindle [riːˈkɪndl] *verb* to light again; *meeting her again after all these years rekindled our friendship; the TV programme rekindled interest in his book*

relapse [rɪˈlæps] **1** *noun (of patient or disease)* becoming worse after seeming to be getting better; *he had a relapse and had to go back into hospital* **2** *verb* **(a)** to become worse; *he relapsed into a coma* **(b)** to get back into old bad habits; *he promised he would cut down on his drinking but soon relapsed*

relate [rɪˈleɪt] *verb* **(a)** to tell a story; *it took him half an hour to relate what had happened* **(b)** to be concerned with; *the regulations which relate to mooring in the harbour* **(c)** to relate to someone = to understand someone and be able to communicate with them; *do you find it difficult to relate to him?*

related (to) [rɪˈleɪtɪd ˈtuː] *adjective* **(a)** linked; *a disease which is related to the weakness of the heart muscle; he has a drug-related illness; there are several related items on the agenda* **(b)** belonging to the same family; *are you related to the Smith family in London Road?*

relating to [rɪˈleɪtɪŋ ˈtuː] *adverb* referring to, connected with; *documents relating to the sale*

relation [rɪˈleɪʃn] *noun* **(a)** member of a family; *all my relations live in Canada; Laura's no relation of mine, she's just a friend* **(b)** link between two things; *is there any relation between his appointment as MD and the fact that his uncle owns the business?*; in relation to = referring to, connected with; *documents in relation to the sale* **(c)** **relations** = links (with other people); *we try to maintain good relations with our customers; relations between the two countries have become tense; see also* PUBLIC RELATIONS

relationship [rɪˈleɪʃnʃɪp] *noun* **(a)** link or connection; *there is a proven relationship between smoking and lung cancer; we try to have a good working relationship with our staff*; **love-hate relationship** = situation where two people get on well together and then dislike each other in turn **(b)** close friendship; *she decided to end the relationship when she found he had been seeing other women*

relative [ˈrelətɪv] **1** *noun* person who is related to someone; member of a family; *we have several* relatives living in Canada; he has no living relatives **2** adjective **(a)** compared to something else; everything is relative - if you have ten cows you are rich in some African countries; **their relative poverty** = their poverty compared with really wealthy people or with the wealth they used to have; my old uncle lives in relative poverty **(b)** (in grammar) **relative pronoun** = pronoun, such as 'who' or 'which', which connects two clauses

relatively ['relətɪvli] adverb more or less; the children have been relatively free from colds this winter; we are dealing with a relatively new company

relativity [relə'tɪvɪti] noun (in physics) relationship between objects, time, distance and speed; **Einstein's Theory of Relativity** = theory that time, movement and space are relative and not absolute

relax [rɪ'læks] verb **(a)** to rest from work; to be less tense; they spent the first week of their holiday relaxing on the beach; guests can relax in the bar before going to eat in the restaurant; just lie back and relax - the injection won't hurt **(b)** to make less strict; the club has voted to relax the rules about the admission of women members

relaxation [riːlæk'seɪʃn] noun rest from work; do you consider gardening a form of relaxation?; he plays tennis for relaxation or as a relaxation

relaxed [rɪ'lækst] adjective (informal) calm, not upset; even if he failed his test, he's still very relaxed about the whole thing

relaxing [rɪ'læksɪŋ] adjective which makes you less tense; I always enjoy a relaxing hot bath after a game of rugby; if you feel stressed, just close your eyes and listen to relaxing music

relay 1 noun ['riːleɪ] **(a)** group of people working in turn with other groups; a shift is usually composed of groups of workers who work in relays; all the work had been done by the time the next relay arrived **(b) relay race** = running race by teams in which one runner passes a baton to another who then runs on; they won the 400m relay **2** verb [rɪ'leɪ] **(a)** to pass on a message; she relayed the news to the other members of her family; all messages are relayed through this office **(b)** to pass on a TV or radio broadcast through a secondary station; the programmes are received in the capital and then relayed to TV stations round the country

release [rɪ'liːs] **1** noun **(a)** setting free; the release of prisoners from jail; the release of hormones into the bloodstream; **day release** = arrangement where a company allows a worker to go to college to study for one day each week; she is attending a day release course **(b)** setting free from pain; his death was a merciful release **(c) press release** = sheet giving news about something which is sent to newspapers and TV and radio stations so that they can use the information in it; we issued a press release about the opening of the new shop **(d) new releases** = new records or CDs which are put on the market **2** verb **(a)** to set free; six prisoners were released from prison; the customs released the goods after we paid a fine; we nursed the injured fox for a week and then released it in the woods; the endocrine glands release hormones into the bloodstream **(b)** to make public; the government has released figures about the number of people out of work

relegate ['relɪgeɪt] verb **(a)** (in sports) to move a team down from a higher division to a lower one; they were relegated from the premier division **(b)** to put into a worse position; on the arrival of the new manager, I was relegated to the accounts department

relegation [relɪ'geɪʃn] noun **(a)** (in sports) moving down from one division to a lower one; they only scored two points in their last ten games, and now face relegation **(b)** moving into a worse position; with the arrival of a new manager I'm facing relegation to a less important job

relent [rɪ'lent] verb to be less strict; to decide to be less strict than before; at first, he refused to let me go, but he finally relented; however much I begged him to give me the last remaining ticket he wouldn't relent

relentless [rɪ'lentləs] adjective continuing without giving up; the relentless questions from the prosecutor wore her down; the police were relentless in their search for clues

relentlessly [rɪ'lentləsli] adverb continuing without stopping, with no pity; they questioned him relentlessly about his deals in the Far East; the sun shone relentlessly, burning and drying their skin

relevance ['relɪvəns] noun being relevant; do these documents have any relevance to this case?; his answer is of little or no relevance to the question

relevant ['relɪvənt] adjective which has to do with something being mentioned; which is the relevant government department?; can you give me the relevant papers?; is this information at all relevant?

reliability [rɪlaɪə'bɪlɪti] noun being reliable; reliability is not one of his qualities; the product has passed its reliability test

reliable [rɪ'laɪəbl] adjective which can be relied on, which can be trusted; it is a very reliable car; the sales manager is completely reliable

reliably [rɪ'laɪəbli] adverb in a way which can be trusted; I am reliably informed that he was not on the plane that crashed

reliance [rɪ'laɪəns] noun trust, being reliant; her reliance on the dedicated nursing staff

reliant [rɪ'laɪənt] adjective which relies on something; he is totally reliant on his parents for money

relic ['relɪk] noun **(a)** object which has been left over from the past; that cap is a relic of my time as a naval cadet **(b)** parts of the body or possessions of a holy person, such as the bones of a saint; the relics of the saint are kept in a gold casket in the cathedral

relief [rɪ'liːf] noun **(a)** reducing pain or stress; an aspirin should bring relief; he breathed a sigh of relief when the police car went past without stopping; what a relief to have finished my exams! **(b)** help; international aid agencies are trying to bring relief to the starving population; **famine relief fund** = money collected to help victims of a famine; **relief road** = road built to help reduce traffic congestion; if the relief road is not built, the traffic through the village will become unbearable **(c)** person who takes over from another; a relief nurse will take over from you at one o'clock; your relief will be here in half an hour; **relief shift** = shift which comes to take the place of another shift; the relief shift is due in ten minutes **(d)** carving in which the details of design stand out; **in relief** = standing out, prominent; Braille consists of little dots in relief that can be read by touch; **relief map** = map where height is shown by colour, so mountains are brown and plains are green

relieve [rɪ'liːv] *verb* **(a)** to make better, easier; *he took aspirins to relieve the pain*; *symptoms of hayfever can be relieved by taking antihistamines* **(b)** *(formal)* to **relieve oneself** = to urinate or defecate; *he stopped by the roadside to relieve himself*; *people complained about drunken football fans relieving themselves in the street* **(c)** to help; *an agency which tries to relieve famine* **(d)** to take over from someone; *you can go and have something to eat - I'm here to relieve you* **(e)** to remove a difficult job from someone; *let me relieve you of some of these parcels*; *this piece of equipment will relieve you of some of your work*

relieved [rɪ'liːvd] *adjective* glad to be rid of a problem; *everyone is relieved that she has passed her driving test*; *she was relieved to find that she did not owe him any money after all*; *how relieved I am to hear the news!*

religion [rɪ'lɪdʒən] *noun* belief in gods or in one God; *does their religion help them to lead a good life?*; *it is against my religion to eat meat on Fridays*

religious [rɪ'lɪdʒəs] *adjective* **(a)** referring to religion; *there is a period of religious study every morning* **(b)** having strong belief in God; *she's very religious - she goes to church every day*

religiously [rɪ'lɪdʒəsli] *adverb* *(informal)* regularly and carefully, like a religious ritual; *she religiously takes the dog for a walk at eight o'clock every morning*; *he followed all their instructions religiously*

relinquish [rɪ'lɪŋkwɪʃ] *verb* *(formal)* to leave or to let go of something; *he finally relinquished control of the business to his son*; *she relinquished her grip on power when the rioters attacked the presidential palace*

relish ['relɪʃ] **1** *noun* **(a)** spicy pickles, spicy sauce; *eat your sausages with mustard or relish* (NOTE: plural in this meaning is **relishes**) **(b)** enjoyment; *she argued with him with great relish* **2** *verb* to enjoy; *I don't relish having to take my exam again*

relive [riː'lɪv] *verb* to go through something again, especially in your mind; *the witness was forced to relive the terrible accident*

relocate [riːlə'keɪt] *verb* **(a)** to move an office, factory or staff to a different place; *the board decided to relocate the company to Scotland*; *when the company moved its headquarters, 1500 people had to be relocated* **(b)** to move to a different place; *the firm decided to relocate to Scotland*

relocation [riːlə'keɪʃn] *noun* moving to a different place; *the costs of relocation or relocation costs will be very high*

reluctant [rɪ'lʌktənt] *adjective* **reluctant to** = not eager, not willing; *he was reluctant to go into the water because it looked cold*

reluctantly [rɪ'lʌktəntli] *adverb* not willingly; *he reluctantly agreed to do the work*; *after a few months in Spain she found she loved the life there and only came back to England reluctantly*

rely (on) [rɪ'laɪ ɒn] *verb* to depend on; *I'm relying on you to read the map*; *we rely on part-time staff to help out during the Christmas rush*

remain [rɪ'meɪn] *verb* **(a)** to stay; *we expect it will remain fine for the rest of the week*; *she remained behind at the office to finish her work* **(b)** to be left;

half *the food remained uneaten and had to be thrown away*; *after the accident not much remained of the car* **(c)** *it remains to be seen* = we will find out later; *how many people have survived the crash remains to be seen*

remainder [rɪ'meɪndə] **1** *noun* **(a)** what is left after everything else has gone; *what shall we do for the remainder of the holidays?*; *after the bride and groom left, the remainder of the party stayed in the hotel to have supper* **(b)** **remainders** = new books which are sold off cheaply because they are not selling well; *remainders are sold through special bookshops* **2** *verb* to sell off new books cheaply; *a shop full of piles of remaindered books*

remaining [rɪ'meɪnɪŋ] *adjective* which is left; *the only remaining picture was damaged*; *she's not the only remaining member of her family - her sister is still alive*

remains [rɪ'meɪnz] *noun* **(a)** things left over or left behind; *the remains of the evening meal were left on the table until the next morning*; *we're trying to save the Roman remains from total obliteration by the construction company* **(b)** *(formal)* body of a dead person; *the emperor's remains were buried in the cathedral*

remake 1 [riː'meɪk] *verb* to have something remade = to get someone to make something again; *the kitchen units didn't fit, so we had to have them remade* **2** ['riːmeɪk] *noun* new film with the same story as an old film; *they're planning yet another remake of 'David Copperfield'*

remand [rɪ'mɑːnd] **1** *noun* sending a prisoner away for a time when a case is adjourned to be heard at a later date; **prisoner on remand** *or* **remand prisoner** = prisoner who has been told to come back to the court at a later date; *the court ordered the prisoner to be kept on remand*; *a large proportion of the prisoners in this jail are remand prisoners*; **remand centre** = prison where prisoners on remand are held; *the court sent him to a remand centre* **2** *verb* **(a)** to send a prisoner away to reappear later to answer a case which has been adjourned; *he was remanded in custody or remanded on bail for two weeks* = he was sent to prison *or* allowed to go free on payment of bail while waiting to return to court two weeks later **(b)** *US* to send a case back to a lower court

remark [rɪ'mɑːk] **1** *noun* comment; *I heard his remark even if he spoke in a low voice*; **to make** *or* **pass remarks about** = to make sharp or rude comments about; *she made some remarks about the dirty tablecloth* **2** *verb* to notice, to comment on; *she remarked on the dirtiness of the café*

remarkable [rɪ'mɑːkəbl] *adjective* very unusual, which you might notice; *she's a remarkable woman*; *it's remarkable that the bank has not asked us to pay back the money*

remarkably [rɪ'mɑːkəbli] *adverb* unusually; *remarkably, the bank didn't ask for the money to be paid back*; *he did remarkably well in his exams*; *this little girl is remarkably advanced for her age*

remarry [riː'mæri] *verb* to marry again; *they both remarried after their divorce*; *when his wife died he remarried almost immediately*

remedial [rɪ'miːdiəl] *adjective* which cures or which makes something better; *she had remedial therapy for* *her arthritis*; **remedial class** = class where students who are weak in a subject receive special tuition

remedy ['remədi] **1** *noun* thing which may cure; *it's an old remedy for hayfever* (NOTE: plural is **remedies**) **2** *verb* to correct something, to make something better; *tell me what's wrong and I'll try to remedy it right away*

remember [rɪ'membə] *verb* **(a)** to bring back into your mind something which you have seen or heard before; *do you remember when we got lost in the fog?*; *my grandmother can remember seeing the first television programmes*; *she remembered seeing it on the dining room table*; *she can't remember where she put her umbrella*; *I don't remember having been in this hotel before*; *I remember my grandmother very well*; *it's strange that I can never remember my father's birthday*; *did you remember to switch off the kitchen light?* (NOTE: you **remember doing something** which you did in the past; you **remember to do something** in the future) **(b)** to ask someone to pass your good wishes to someone; *please remember me to your father when you see him next*

remembrance [rɪ'membrəns] *noun* memory; *they held a service in remembrance of the people who had died in the earthquake*

Remembrance Day [rɪ'membrəns 'deɪ] *noun* November 11th, or the nearest Sunday, celebrating the end of the First World War and remembering the dead of both World Wars; *the Remembrance Day parade will start at 10.30 outside the Town Hall* (NOTE: also called **Armistice Day** or **Poppy Day**)

COMMENT: Remembrance Day is marked by ceremonies in all towns and many villages, usually with a church service followed by a procession of Scouts, Guides, veterans, etc., to the local war memorial in order to lay wreaths of red poppies. Nationally, the main ceremony is in London, where the Queen, the Prime Minister and other important people lay wreaths at the Cenotaph, the war memorial in Whitehall. Following the laying of the wreaths, at exactly 11.00 a.m., there is two minutes' silence for everyone to remember the dead; the silence is followed by the playing of the Last Post

---

remind [rɪ'maɪnd] *verb* **(a)** to make someone remember something; *now that you've reminded me, I do remember seeing him last week*; *remind me to book the tickets for New York*; *she reminded him that the meeting had to finish at 6.30* **(b)** to remind someone **of** = to make someone think of something; *do you know what this reminds me of?*; *she reminds me of her mother*

reminder [rɪ'maɪndə] *noun* **(a)** thing which reminds you of something; *he tied a knot in his handkerchief as a reminder of what he had to do*; *keep this picture as a reminder of happier days* **(b)** letter to remind a customer to do something; *we had a reminder from the gas board that we hadn't paid the bill*

reminisce [remɪ'nɪs] *verb* to talk about memories of the past; *the two old soldiers sat reminiscing about the war*

reminiscence [remɪ'nɪsəns] *noun* memory of something from the past; *all we heard during dinner were reminiscences of her youth in Canada*

reminiscent [remɪ'nɪsənt] *adjective* which reminds you of the past; *this landscape is reminiscent of paintings by Constable*; *his whole attitude is reminiscent of that of his father*

remission [rɪ'mɪʃn] *noun* **(a)** reduction of a prison sentence; *he was sentenced to five years, but should only serve three with remission*; *he earned remission for good behaviour* **(b)** period when an illness is less severe; *the cancer is in remission* **(c)** *(formal)* the **remission of sins** = forgiving by God of sins which people have committed

remit 1 *verb* [rɪ'mɪt] **(a)** to reduce a prison sentence; *his prison sentence was remitted* **(b)** to send money; *to remit by cheque*; *the money has been remitted to your bank account* (NOTE: **remitting - remitted**) **2** *noun* ['riːmɪt] area of responsibility given to someone; *this department can do nothing with the case as it is not part of our remit* or *is beyond our remit*; *he has been given the remit to deal with his father's affairs*

remittance [rɪ'mɪtəns] *noun* money which is sent; *please send remittances to the treasurer*; *the family lives on a weekly remittance from their father in the USA*

remnant ['remnənt] *noun* quantity or piece left over; *I bought this at a sale of remnants* or *at a remnant sale*; *this remnant of velvet is just the right size to make a cushion*; *there are only a few remnants of meat left on the chicken*

remorse [rɪ'mɔːs] *noun* regret about something wrong which you have done; *the soldier showed no remorse for what he had done*; *she expressed bitter remorse for her actions*

remorseful [rɪ'mɔːsful] *adjective* full of remorse; *his remorseful parents came to collect him from the police station*

remorseless [rɪ'mɔːsləs] *adjective* **(a)** which cannot be stopped; *the Green Belt is supposed to stop the remorseless advance of houses into the countryside*; *there's nothing you can do to hold back the remorseless advance of old age* **(b)** cruel, showing no pity; *a remorseless artillery bombardment pounded the town*

remote [rɪ'məʊt] *adjective* **(a)** far away; *the hotel is situated in a remote mountain village*; **remote control** = device which controls a model plane, TV, etc., by radio signals; *has anyone seen the remote control for the TV* or *the TV remote control?* **(b)** slight, not very strong; *there's a remote chance of finding a cure for his illness*; *the possibility of him arriving on time is remote*; *there is not the remotest likelihood of the plane taking off this morning because of the fog* **(c)** *(person)* who does not communicate very much; *their daughter is difficult to get to know, she seems so remote* (NOTE: **remoter - remotest**)

remotely [rɪ'məʊtli] *adverb* very slightly; *are you remotely interested in meeting the delegation?*; **not remotely** = not at all; *he wasn't remotely interested in what I had to say*

removal [rɪ'muːvəl] *noun* **(a)** taking something away; *the removal of the ban on importing computers*; *refuse collectors are responsible for the removal of household waste*; *the opposition called for the removal of the Foreign Secretary* **(b)** moving to a new home, new office, etc.; **removal men** = workers who move furniture from one house to another; **removal van** = van which takes your furniture from one house to another; *today's the day we move - the removal van is already here*

remove [rɪ'muːv] *verb* to take away; *you can remove his name from the mailing list*; *the waitress removed the dirty plates and brought us some tea*

remover [rɪ'muːvə] *noun* **(a)** person who moves furniture from one house to another; *we're moving house tomorrow - the removers will be here at 7.30 am* **(b)** thing which removes; **nail varnish remover** = liquid which takes off nail varnish; **paint remover** = liquid which removes old paint; *will one tin of paint remover be enough to strip this old chair?*

renaissance [rə'neɪsəns] *noun* **(a)** rebirth, starting again; *British cinema has undergone a renaissance in recent years* **(b) the Renaissance** = period in late medieval Europe when a renewal of interest in the Greek and Roman civilizations led to a new artistic and intellectual movement; *the Renaissance started in the 14th Century in Italy*

renal ['riːnəl] *adjective (formal)* referring to the kidneys; *he had renal failure and had to be put on a kidney machine*; **renal calculus** = stone in the kidney

rename [riˈneɪm] *verb* to give something a new name; *copy the file and rename it*; *they renamed their boat 'Arabella'*

rend [rend] *verb (formal)* to tear to pieces; *the country was rent by civil war* (NOTE: **rending - rent**)

render ['rendə] *verb* **(a) to render an account** = to send in an account or a statement of account; *as per account rendered* **(b)** to translate; *the text was badly rendered in Italian* **(c) to render (down)** = to melt solid meat fat by heating to produce pure fat **(d)** to cover a wall with a coating of plaster or cement **(e)** to make someone *or* something change into a particular state; *she was rendered speechless by their letter*; *the experts rendered the bomb safe*

rendering ['rendrɪŋ] *noun* **(a)** performance of a song, etc.; *she was famous for her rendering of the popular wartime song*; *the choir's rendering of the Beethoven Mass was criticized* **(b)** mixture of cement and fine sand used to cover the outside of a house; *the rendering is beginning to flake off and needs redoing*

rendezvous ['rɒndeɪvuː] **1** *noun* appointment or meeting; *the police arranged a secret rendezvous with the informer* **2** *verb* to arrange to meet; *you go north, and we'll go west and we'll all rendezvous at the camp at 16.00* (NOTE: **rendezvoused** ['rɒndeɪvuːd])

rendition [ren'dɪʃn] *noun (formal)* performance of a song, etc.; *she was famous for her renditions of the popular wartime song*

renegade ['renɪgeɪd] *noun* person who leaves a religion, group or party and joins another; *the renegade priests were caught and tried by the church*; *their leader is a renegade Communist*; *he left the regular army and joined a band of renegade soldiers*

renege [rɪ'neɪg or rɪ'niːg] *verb (formal)* **to renege on** = not to do something which you had promised to do; *he reneged on his promise to pay half the costs*; *I was furious when he reneged on the deal*

renew [rɪ'njuː] *verb* **(a)** to start again; *renew your efforts and don't lose hope* **(b)** to replace something old with something new; *we need to renew the wiring in the kitchen* **(c)** to continue something for a further period of time; *don't forget to renew your insurance policy*; **to renew a subscription** = to pay a subscription

for another year; *I don't think I'll renew my subscription to the magazine*

renewable [rɪ'njuːəbl] *adjective* **(a)** which can be renewed; *the season ticket is renewable for a further year* **(b)** which can be replaced, which can renew itself; *renewable sources of energy such as solar power, and power from wind or water*

renewal [rɪ'njuːəl] *noun* act of renewing; *we noticed a renewal of interest in oak furniture*; **the subscription is up for renewal** = the subscription needs to be renewed

renminbi ['renmɪnbiː] *noun* official name for the currency of China

renounce [rɪ'naʊns] *verb* **(a)** to give up a right or a claim; *she renounced her claim to the property* **(b)** to state publicly that you are going to stop believing in something or are not going to behave in a certain way; *the government has renounced the use of force in dealing with international terrorists*; *they called on the extremists to renounce violence*

renovate ['renəveɪt] *verb* to make a building like new again; *we are planning to renovate our offices this year*; *the house is in good structural condition but the central heating needs renovating*

renovation [renə'veɪʃn] *noun* making a building like new again; *they spent thousands of pounds on the renovation of the minister's office*

renown [rɪ'naʊn] *noun (formal)* being famous; *he won renown on the battlefield of Waterloo*; *her renown as an opera singer soon spread to the United States*

renowned [rɪ'naʊnd] *adjective (formal)* very famous; *the renowned Italian conductor*; *Rome is renowned as the centre of Catholicism* **(b) renowned for** = famous for something; *she's renowned for being late*; *a shop renowned for the quality of its products*

rent [rent] **1** *noun* money paid to live in a flat, house, to use an office, etc.; *rents are high in the centre of the town*; *the landlord asked me to pay three months' rent in advance*; **rent control** = government regulation of rents **2** *verb* **(a)** to pay money to use a house, flat, car, etc.; *he rents an office in the centre of town*; *they were driving a rented car when they were stopped by the police*; *he rented a villa by the beach for three weeks* **(b) to rent (out)** = to let someone use a house, office, flat, etc., for money; *we rented (out) one floor of our building to an American company*

rental ['rentl] *noun* rent, money paid to use a room, flat, office, car, etc.; *the telephone rental has gone up this quarter*; **car rental firm** = company which specializes in offering cars for rent; *there are no reliable car rental firms around here*

reopen [riːˈəʊpən] *verb* **(a)** to open again; *the shop will reopen next week after a refit* **(b)** *(of the police)* to start to investigate a case again; *the case has been reopened because a new witness has come forward*

reorganization [riːɔːgənaɪ'zeɪʃn] *noun* act of reorganizing; *the reorganization of the company will take a long time*

reorganize [riːˈɔːgənaɪz] *verb* to organize in a new way; *do you plan to reorganize the club and accept more members?*; *she reorganized the library and we can't find anything any more*

reorient *or* **reorientate** [riːˈɔːrɪənt or riːˈɔːrɪənteɪt] *verb* to put in another direction; *the company has been* reorientated towards a more upmarket image; *she'll need time to reorientate herself after her long trip abroad*

rep [rep] *(informal)* **(a)** = REPRESENTATIVE salesman who visits clients, trying to sell them something; *they have vacancies for reps in the north of the country*; *we have a reps' meeting every three months* **(b)** = REPERTORY THEATRE theatre with a permanent group of actors who play a series of plays, changing them at regular intervals; *the local rep is doing 'Henry V' this week*

repaid [riːˈpeɪd] *verb see* REPAY

repair [rɪˈpeə] **1** *noun* **(a)** mending something which is broken or has been damaged; *his car is in the garage for repair*; *the hotel is closed while they are carrying out repairs to the air-conditioning system*; **repair kit** = box with tools for repairing a machine, especially for repairing a car; *there is a repair kit provided in the boot of each car* **(b) to be in a good state of repair** *or* **in good repair** = to be in good condition; *this car is still in a very good state of repair, I won't change it yet* **2** *verb* to mend, to make something work which is broken or damaged; *I dropped my watch on the pavement, and I don't think it can be repaired*; *she's trying to repair the washing machine*; *the photocopier is being repaired*

repairer [rɪˈpeərə] *noun* person who mends things; *the TV repairer said the television was too old to be repaired*

reparation [repəˈreɪʃn] *noun (formal)* something which makes up for a wrong; *he agreed to pay £10,000 in reparation for the damage he had caused*; **reparations** = money paid by a defeated enemy after a war to make up for destruction caused and wrongs committed

repast [rɪˈpɑːst] *noun (formal)* meal; *she served us a marvellous repast*

repatriate [riːˈpætrɪeɪt] *verb* to bring or to send someone back to their home country; *when the war broke out, all British subjects were repatriated*

repatriation [rɪpætrɪˈeɪʃn] *noun* action of repatriating; *repatriation of the embassy staff must start as soon as possible*

repay [riːˈpeɪ] *verb* **(a)** to pay back; *I'll try to repay what I owe you next month*; *thank you for your help - I hope to be able to repay you one day*; **he repaid me in full** = he paid me back all the money he owed me **(b)** to be worth; **it will repay close scrutiny** = it would be worth looking at it carefully (NOTE: **repaying - repaid** [riːˈpeɪd])

repayment [rɪˈpeɪmənt] *noun* paying back; *repayment of the loan is by monthly instalments*; **mortgage repayments** = the instalments paid back on a mortgage; *he fell behind with his mortgage repayments*; *my mortgage repayments have increased this month*

repeal [rɪˈpiːl] **1** *noun* officially ending a law, so that it is no longer valid; *MPs are pressing for the repeal of the Immigration Act* **2** *verb* to end a law officially; *the Bill seeks to repeal the existing legislation*

repeat [rɪˈpiːt] **1** *verb* to say something again; *could you repeat what you just said?*; *he repeated the address so that the policeman could write it down*; *she kept on repeating that she wanted to go home*; **to repeat yourself** = to say the same thing over and over

again; *he's getting old - he keeps repeating himself* **2** *adjective & noun* **repeat (performance)** = performance which is done a second time; *the play is being performed on Friday, and there will be a repeat (performance) on Saturday*

repeated [rɪˈpiːtɪd] *adjective* happening again and again; *the repeated warning sound means that you must turn off the machine*

repeatedly [rɪˈpiːtɪdli] *adverb* again and again; *he repeatedly broke the law*

repel [rɪˈpel] *verb* **(a)** to drive back an attack; *the army easily repelled the invaders* **(b)** to drive something away; *the pain has an ingredient that repels water*; *she sprayed the kitchen with a spray to repel flies* **(c)** to disgust, to be so unpleasant that it drives people away; *the taste repelled me so much that I could not finish my meal* (NOTE: **repelling - repelled**)

repellent [rɪˈpelənt] **1** *adjective* which drives people away, which repels; *the colour of the bathroom is really repellent*; *the repellent smell coming from the drains* **2** *noun* **insect repellent** = chemical which keeps insects away; *I still haven't found a really effective mosquito repellent*

repent [rɪˈpent] *verb (formal)* to be very sorry for what you have done, or for what you have not done; *the probation worker said that the boy had repented his actions*

repentance [rɪˈpentəns] *noun (formal)* great regret for something you have done; *as a token of repentance he took all the bottles from his cupboard and threw them away*

repentant [rɪˈpentənt] *adjective (formal)* full of regret for what you have done; *when the head teacher told him off, he didn't look at all repentant*

repercussions [riːpɜːˈkʌʃnz] *noun* result or effect, usually unpleasant; *the government decision on pensions will have widespread repercussions*; *the BBC is trying to deal with the repercussions of the critical programme on India*

repertoire [ˈrepətwɑː] *noun* **(a)** plays, songs, pieces of music, etc., which someone has learned; *she has an extensive repertoire, covering most of the important soprano roles* **(b)** works, such as plays or operas, which a theatre company has ready for performance; *we have added two plays by Noel Coward to our repertoire* **(c)** total number of things which a person can do; *our little daughter has added lying on the floor and screaming to her repertoire of things to annoy her parents*

repertory theatre [ˈrepətri ˈθiːətə] *noun* theatre with a permanent group of actors who play a series of plays, changing them at regular intervals; *the local repertory theatre is doing 'Henry V' this week*

repetition [repɪˈtɪʃn] *noun* **(a)** act of repeating, of saying the same thing again; *the constant repetition of the song made sure we all knew it by heart* **(b)** thing which is repeated; *she simply gave a repetition of the arguments she had used at the previous meeting*; *the police will try to prevent a repetition of the ugly scenes at the football ground*

repetitive [rɪˈpetɪtɪv] *adjective* which is repeated very frequently and is boring; *we find it difficult to keep workers on this type of repetitive work*

repetitive strain injury (RSI) [rɪˈpetɪtɪv ˈstreɪn ˈɪndʒəri] *noun* pain in the arm felt by someone who performs the same movement many times, such as when operating a computer terminal or playing a musical instrument; *she had to stop working as a keyboarder because of RSI*

rephrase [ri'freiz] *verb* to say something again, but in a different way; *he's not easy to deal with - no, let me rephrase that, I think he's the most difficult person I have ever had to deal with*

replace [ri:'pleis] *verb* (a) to put something back where it was before; *please replace the books correctly on the shelves* (b) **to replace something with something else** = to put something in the place of something else; *the washing machine needs replacing; we are replacing all our permanent staff with freelancers; see also* SEARCH

replaceable [ri'pleisəbl] *adjective* which can be replaced; *the photographs stolen are old photographs of the 19th century and are simply not replaceable* (NOTE: **not replaceable** means the same as **irreplaceable**)

replacement [ri'pleismənt] *noun* (a) replacing something with something else; *the mechanics recommended the replacement of the hand pump with an electric model;* **hip replacement** = operation to replace the whole hip joint with an artificial one; *old people sometimes need to have hip replacements; see also* HORMONE (b) thing which is used to replace something; *an electric motor was bought as a replacement for the old one;* **replacement parts** = spare parts of an engine used to replace parts which have worn out (c) person who replaces someone; *my secretary leaves us next week, so we are advertising for a replacement*

replay 1 *noun* ['ri:plei] (a) match which is played again because the first match was a draw; *they drew 2-2 so there will be a replay next week* (b) **action replay** = section of a sporting event which is shown again on TV at a slower speed, so that the action can be examined carefully; *look at the action reply to see if it really was a foul* **2** *verb* [ri:'plei] to play again; *he replayed the message on the answerphone several times, but still couldn't understand it; the match will be replayed next week*

replenish [ri'pleniʃ] *verb (formal)* to fill up again; *the waiter replenished their glasses with wine; we need to replenish our fridge before the family comes for the weekend*

replete [ri'pli:t] *adjective (formal)* completely full; *after dinner we all felt so replete that we decided to go for a walk; it's a fascinating book, replete with reproductions of old photographs*

replica ['replikə] *noun* exact copy; *this isn't the real Domesday Book, it is a replica; they sailed a replica of the 'Mayflower' across the Atlantic*

replicate ['replikeit] *verb (formal)* to copy something exactly; *a cell divides and replicates itself many times; we tried to replicate their experiment but could not do it*

reply [ri'plai] **1** *noun* (a) answer; *I asked him what he was doing but got no reply; we wrote last week, but haven't had a reply yet; send a stamped addressed envelope for a reply; we had six replies to our advertisement* (b) **in reply** = as an answer; *in reply to my letter, I received a fax two days later; she just shook her head in reply and turned away* (NOTE: plural is **replies**) **2** *verb* to answer; *he never replies to my letters; we wrote last week, but he hasn't replied yet;*

he refused to reply to questions until his lawyer arrived

report [ri'pɔ:t] **1** *noun* (a) description of what has happened or what will happen; *we read the reports of the accident in the newspaper; can you confirm the report that the council is planning to sell the old town hall?* (b) **school report** = document from a school, telling how a student has done over a period; *we discussed little Jane's report with her teacher* **2** *verb* (a) to write a description of what happened; *you must report the burglary to the police; she reported that her wallet had been stolen from her bedroom; the British press reported a plane crash in Africa; she reported seeing the missing man in her shop;* **to report back** = to send a report back to the office, etc., on what has happened; *you must report back as soon as you find out what happened; go and visit our suppliers and report back to me on the situation* (b) to present yourself officially; *to report for work; candidates should report to the personnel office at 9.00* (c) **to report to someone** = to be responsible to someone, to be under someone; *she reports directly to the managing director himself*

reportedly [ri'pɔ:tidli] *adverb* according to what has been reported; *he was reportedly killed before he reached the border; you reportedly know who is guilty - is that true?*

reporter [ri'pɔ:tə] *noun* journalist who writes reports of events for a newspaper or for a TV news programme; *the BBC sent reporters to cover the earthquake; all the reporters gathered in a room to interview the president; he works as a reporter for a regional newspaper*

reporting [ri'pɔ:tiŋ] *noun* action of reporting something in the press; *any reporting of the details of the trial has been forbidden; reporting restrictions have been lifted; the BBC is famous for its unbiased reporting*

repository [ri'pɒzitri] *noun* (a) **furniture repository** = warehouse where furniture is stored (b) person or book which is a store of information, etc.; *the old man is an invaluable repository of information and stories about Alaska during the Gold Rush* (NOTE: plural is **repositories**)

repossess [ri:pə'zes] *verb* to take back an item which someone is buying under a hire-purchase agreement, or a house which someone is buying under a mortgage agreement, because the purchaser cannot continue the payments; *when he couldn't make the repayments on his mortgage, the bank repossessed his house; she had a shock when they repossessed her car - she hadn't realized that she had missed a payment*

repossession [ri:pə'seʃn] *noun* action of repossessing; *repossessions are increasing as people find it difficult to meet mortgage payments*

reprehensible [repri'hensəbl] *adjective* which can be criticized; *the newspapers carried articles on the reprehensible behaviour of the fans*

represent [repri'zent] *verb* (a) to indicate, to be a symbol of; *the dark green on the map represents woods* (b) to speak or act on behalf of someone or of a group of people; *he asked his solicitor to represent him at the meeting* (c) to work for a company, showing goods or services to possible buyers; *he represents an American car firm in Europe*

representation [reprɪzen'teɪʃn] *noun* **(a)** way of showing; *the design on the Lebanese flag is a representation of a cedar tree* **(b)** act of selling goods for a company; *we can provide representation throughout Europe* **(c)** having someone to act on your behalf; *the residents' association wants representation on the committee* **(d)** representations = complaints or protests; *we made representations to the manager on behalf of the junior members of staff*

representative [reprɪ'zentətɪv] **1** *adjective* typical; *the sample isn't representative of the whole batch* **2** *noun* **(a)** person who represents, who speaks on behalf of someone else; *he asked his solicitor to act as his representative*; *representatives of the workforce have asked to meet the management* **(b)** travelling salesman; *they have vacancies for representatives in the north of the country* (NOTE: often called simply a **rep**) **(c)** *(in the United States)* **the House of Representatives** = the lower house of Congress (NOTE: the upper house of Congress is the **Senate**)

repress [rɪ'pres] *verb* **(a)** to control a natural impulse; *she had difficulty in repressing a smile* **(b)** to restrict people's freedom, etc.; *the ordinary people have been repressed for so long that they do not know what it is to be free*

repression [rɪ'preʃn] *noun* the use of force to keep people under control; *the repression by the military regime lasted several years*

repressive [rɪ'presɪv] *adjective* severe, strict, using force to keep people under control; *a repressive regime*

reprieve [rɪ'priːv] **1** *noun* **(a)** temporarily stopping a sentence or order by a court; *he was granted a last-minute reprieve* **(b)** saving something which was planned for demolition; *this magnificent building was to be demolished, but the reprieve came just in time to save it* **2** *verb* **(a)** to stop a sentence or court order from being carried out; *the ringleaders of the coup were sentenced to death and then reprieved* **(b)** to save something which was planned for demolition; *the old church has been reprieved and will be converted into an arts centre*

reprimand ['reprɪmɑːnd] **1** *noun* sharp criticism for doing something wrong; *she received a severe reprimand and lost two weeks' pay* **2** *verb* to criticize someone severely for doing something wrong; *the report reprimanded the directors for their negligence*

reprint 1 *noun* ['riːprɪnt] **(a)** printing of copies of a book again after a first printing; *the mistake on the title page will be corrected in the reprint* **(b)** reprinting of an out-of-print book, or of a very old book, now out of copyright; *this is a facsimile reprint of a 17th century copy of Shakespeare's plays* **2** *verb* [riː'prɪnt] to print more copies of a document or book; *the book is being reprinted*

reprisal [rɪ'praɪzl] *noun* punishment of someone in revenge for something; *after the general was assassinated, the army carried out reprisals on the inhabitants of the town*; *all houses were burnt down in reprisal for the attacks on rebel soldiers*

reprise [rə'priːz] *noun* playing a section or a theme from a piece of music again; *there is a reprise of the heroine's song at the end of the first act*

reproach [rɪ'prəʊtʃ] **1** *noun* **(a)** thing which is a disgrace; *the dirty state of the station is a constant reproach to the railway company* **(b)** blame, criticism; *he took her comments as a reproach and was very*

upset; **beyond reproach** = blameless; **a term of reproach** = term which criticizes **2** *verb* **to reproach someone for** *or* **with something** = to criticize someone for something for having done something; *he was reproached for his slowness in answering*; *he reproached her with spending too much time on the telephone*; **to reproach yourself with something** = to criticize yourself for having done something; *you behaved perfectly, you have absolutely nothing to reproach yourself with*

reprocess ['riː'prəʊses] *verb* to process again; *the company has signed a contract to reprocess spent nuclear fuel*

reprocessing ['riː'prəʊsesɪŋ] *noun* action of processing again; *tonnes of spent nuclear fuel are sent for reprocessing*; *radioactive waste is transported to the reprocessing plant at night*

reproduce [riːprə'djuːs] *verb* **(a)** to copy; *his letters have been reproduced in the biography*; *it is very difficult to reproduce the sound of an owl accurately* **(b)** to produce young; *some animals will not reproduce when in captivity*

reproduction [riːprə'dʌkʃən] *noun* **(a)** copy (of a painting, etc.); *this painting is not a real Picasso, it's only a reproduction*; *buy a reproduction, it's much cheaper than the real thing* **(b)** action of reproducing; **the reproduction is bad on this CD** = the quality of the sound is bad **(c)** production of young; *the rate of reproduction of mice is incredible*

reproductive [riːprə'dʌktɪv] *adjective* referring to reproduction; **reproductive organs** = parts of the bodies of humans and animals which are involved in the conception and development of a foetus

reprove [rɪ'pruːv] *verb (formal)* to criticize someone for doing something wrong; *the new recruits were reproved for their unruly behaviour*

reptile ['reptaɪl] *noun* cold-blooded animal with a skin covered with scales, which lays eggs; *tortoises and lizards are reptiles*

reptilian [rep'tɪlɪən] *adjective* like a reptile; *he gave her an unblinking reptilian stare*

republic [rɪ'pʌblɪk] *noun* system of government which is governed by elected representatives headed by an elected or nominated president; *France is a republic while Spain is a monarchy;* compare MONARCHY

republican [rɪ'pʌblɪkən] **1** *adjective* referring to a republic; *the republican movement would like to see the abolition of the monarchy* **2** *noun* person who believes that a republic is the best form of government; *some republicans made speeches against the emperor*

Republican [rɪ'pʌblɪkən] **1** *adjective US* referring to the Republican Party, one of the two main political parties in the USA **2** *noun US* member of the Republican Party, one of the two main political parties in the USA

Republican Party [rɪ'pʌblɪkən 'pɑːti] *noun* one of the two main political parties in the USA, which supports business and is against too much state intervention in industry and welfare; *the Republican Party's candidate for the presidency;* compare DEMOCRATIC PARTY

repudiate [rɪ'pjuːdieɪt] *verb (formal)* to reject, to refuse to accept; *the treaty was repudiated by the new government*; *he repudiated totally the accusation that he had tried to bribe the minister*

repudiation [rɪpjuːdiˈeɪʃn] *noun* action of repudiating; *their repudiation of the peace treaty was greeted with astonishment*

repulse [rɪˈpʌls] *verb* to push back someone who is attacking; *the attack was repulsed by the defending army*; *she repulsed his advances and complained to the management about sexual harassment*

repulsion [rɪˈpʌlʃn] *noun* (a) feeling of dislike; *he looked at the plate of snails with repulsion* (b) *(in physics)* act of pushing something away; *magnetic repulsion can be demonstrated by trying to join the negative ends of two magnets* (NOTE: the opposite in this meaning is **attraction**)

repulsive [rɪˈpʌlsɪv] *adjective* unpleasant, which makes you disgusted; *what a repulsive tie!*; *it's an absolutely repulsive book, and I can't imagine why anyone would want to read it*

reputable [ˈrepjutəbl] *adjective* well thought of, with a good reputation; *we only use reputable suppliers*

reputation [repjuˈteɪʃn] *noun* opinion that people have of someone; *he has a reputation for being difficult to deal with*; *the chef has a reputation for being temperamental*; *his bad reputation won't help him find a suitable job*

repute [rɪˈpjuːt] *noun (formal)* reputation, general opinion; *he is a wine dealer of excellent repute*; *it's an club of ill repute*; *I only know her by repute* = I have never met her, but I have heard or read about her

reputed [rɪˈpjuːtɪd] *adjective* supposed, said to be; *she is the reputed author of several detective novels*; *he is reputed to be very good at managing staff*; *this year's bonus is reputed to be over 20%*

request [rɪˈkwest] **1** *noun* asking for something; *your request will be dealt with as soon as possible*; **on request** = if asked for; *'catalogue available on request'*; **request stop** = bus stop where buses stop only if you signal to them **2** *verb* to ask for something politely; *I am enclosing the leaflets you requested*; *guests are requested to leave their keys at reception*

requiem [ˈrekwiəm] *verb* (a) **Requiem Mass** = mass for all dead people, or for someone who has died recently; *the Requiem Mass will be held next Sunday* (b) music to be sung at a requiem; *they played Verdi's Requiem at the concert*

require [rɪˈkwaɪə] *verb* (a) to demand that someone should do something; *we were required to go to the local police station*; *you are required to fill in the forms in triplicate* (b) to need; *the disease requires careful nursing*; *writing the program requires a computer specialist*

requirement [rɪˈkwaɪəmənt] *noun* (a) what is necessary; *it is a requirement of the job that you should be able to drive* (b) **requirements** = things which are needed; *we try to meet our customers' requirements*; *if you send us a list of your requirements, we shall see if we can supply them*; **manpower requirements** = number of workers needed; *have you established the manpower requirements for this type of industry?*

requisite [ˈrekwɪzɪt] **1** *adjective (formal)* necessary; *does he have the requisite government permits?*; *we need someone with the requisite skills to run the bar* **2** *noun (formal)* thing which is necessary; *patience is a requisite for a happy marriage*

rerun 1 [ˈriːrʌn] *noun* (a) second showing of a programme or film on TV; *during the summer all the TV channels show reruns of old sitcoms* (b) thing which happens again; *we want to avoid a rerun of the trouble we had at the last meeting* **2** [riːˈrʌn] *verb* to show a TV programme again; *they seem to fill in their schedules by rerunning old Westerns*

reschedule [riːˈʃedjuːl] *verb* (a) to arrange an appointment again for a later time; *my plane was delayed by fog, so I had to reschedule all my meetings* (b) **to reschedule debts** = to arrange new repayment terms for debts; *some Third World countries have asked for their debts to be rescheduled*

rescind [rɪˈsɪnd] *verb* **to rescind a contract** *or* **an agreement** = to annul or to cancel a contract or agreement; *the committee rescinded its earlier resolution on the use of council premises*; *both parties agreed that the contract should not be rescinded without the agreement of the tenants*

rescue [ˈreskjuː] **1** *noun* action of saving; *mountain rescue requires well-trained people*; *no one could swim well enough to go to her rescue*; **rescue party** *or* **rescue team** *or* **rescue squad** = group of people who are going to save someone; *rescue parties were sent out immediately after the avalanche* **2** *verb* to save someone from a dangerous situation; *the lifeboat rescued the crew of the sinking ship*; *the company nearly collapsed, but was rescued by the bank*; *when the river flooded, the party of tourists had to be rescued by helicopter*

rescuer [ˈreskjuːə] *noun* person who rescues or tries to rescue someone; *rescuers were delayed by extremely high winds*; *a team of rescuers arrived in time to save the skiers*

research [rɪˈsɜːtʃ] **1** *noun* (a) scientific study, which tries to find out facts; *the company is carrying out research to find a cure for colds*; *the research laboratory has come up with encouraging results*; *our researches proved that the letter was a forgery*; **research worker** = RESEARCHER (b) **market research** = examining the possible sales of a product and the possible customers before it is put on the market; *if we had done proper market research we would have discovered that the market was full of cheaper products than ours*; *before you launch the product, you must do thorough market research* **2** *verb* to study, to try to find out facts; *research your subject thoroughly before you start writing*

research and development (R & D) [rɪˈsɜːtʃ ən dɪˈveləpmənt] *noun* scientific research that leads to making new products or improving existing ones; *the company spends millions of dollars on research and development*

researcher [rɪˈsɜːtʃə] *noun* person who carries out research; *the new drug was developed by two researchers, one British and one American*

resemblance [rɪˈzembləns] *noun* looking like someone; *she bears a strong resemblance to her father*; *the family resemblance between the two brothers is remarkable*

resemble [rɪˈzembl] *verb* to look like; *do you really think she resembles her father?*; *the scene after the office party resembled the aftermath of the Battle of Waterloo*

resent [rɪˈzent] *verb* to feel annoyed because of a real or imaginary hurt; *she resents having to look after her* *father-in-law; we bitterly resent the suggestion that the company has tricked its customers*

resentful [rɪ'zentfʊl] *adjective* feeling anger or bitterness about something someone has done; *try to forget what he said and not be resentful; the resentful attitude of her neighbours shocked her*

resentment [rɪ'zentmənt] *noun* anger or bitterness felt about something someone has done; *they feel resentment towards their neighbours for building a high wall; she showed no resentment and treated him as if nothing had happened; there is lot of resentment at or against the decision to close the school*

reservation [rezə'veɪʃn] *noun* (a) booking of a seat, table, etc.; *I want to make a reservation on the train to Plymouth tomorrow evening;* (room) **reservations** = department in a hotel which deals with bookings for rooms; *can you put me through to reservations?* (b) doubt; *I have no reservations whatsoever that I have made the right decision; if you have any reservations about the contract, please let me know as soon as possible* (c) area kept separate from other areas; **central reservation** = section of road or grass, bushes, etc., between the two carriageways of a major road; *the car had crossed the central reservation and hit a vehicle travelling in the opposite direction* (NOTE: American English is **median strip**)

reserve [rɪ'zɜːv] **1** *noun* (a) amount kept back in case it is needed in the future; *our reserves of coal were used up during the winter;* **in reserve** = waiting to be used; *we're keeping the can of petrol in reserve* (b) *(in sport)* extra player who can play if someone drops out of the team; *one of the players was hurt so a reserve was called up;* **the reserves** = second football team made up of reserve players; *he's playing in the reserves today* (c) **nature reserve** = area of land where animals and plants are protected; *we often go to a nature reserve in Suffolk to do some birdwatching and walk by the sea* (d) self-control, shyness; *he had to break down her reserve before he could have a proper conversation with her* **2** *verb* (a) to keep back for a special use; *put half the cherries into the mixture and reserve the rest for decoration; don't read this book now, reserve it for your holidays* (b) to keep back for use at a later date; *I'm reserving my right to change my mind;* **to reserve judgement** = not to make up your mind about something until later; *I'll reserve judgement until I've heard all the facts* (c) to book a seat or a table; *I want to reserve a table for four people; have you reserved?* - *if not, we have just two tables available; can you reserve two seats for me for the evening performance?*

reserved [rɪ'zɜːvd] *adjective* (a) booked; *there are two reserved tables and one free one; is this seat reserved?* (b) who does not reveal his or her thoughts and feelings; *Clare is very reserved and doesn't talk much; he's a very reserved man and does not mix with other members of staff*

reservist [rɪ'zɜːvɪst] *noun* part-time soldier who is a member of the army reserves; *army reservists have been put on standby*

reservoir ['rezəvwɑː] *noun* (a) large, usually artificial, lake where drinking water is kept for pumping to a city; *there has been very little rain this year and the reservoirs are only half full* (b) large collection of something kept ready; *there is a huge reservoir of skilled labour waiting to be tapped*

reset 1 [riː'set] *verb* to set again; *the local time is 12.15: please reset your watches; his broken leg was set badly, and the doctors had to reset it* **2** ['riːset] *adjective* **reset button** = button you press to set a machine again

resettle [riː'setl] *verb* to settle someone in another place; *the UN is trying to resettle the refugees in special camps*

resettlement [riː'setlmənt] *noun* arrangement to settle someone in a new place; *various agencies are dealing with the problem of the resettlement of the refugees*

reshape [riː'ʃeɪp] *verb* to shape again, to give something a different shape; *by ending the communist regimes in the East, he reshaped the politics of Western Europe*

reshuffle [riː'ʃʌfl] **1** *noun* changing of positions, especially those of cabinet ministers; *in the reshuffle, he was appointed Secretary of State for Education* **2** *verb* (a) to shuffle cards again; *he shuffled and reshuffled and then finally started to deal* (b) to change the positions of cabinet ministers; *the President is expected to reshuffle his Cabinet soon*

reside [rɪ'zaɪd] *verb (formal)* to live somewhere; *they reside in a villa on the shores of Lake Geneva; the police want to contact James Smith, believed to be residing in France*

residence ['rezɪdəns] *noun* (a) especially US *(formal)* place where you live; *this is Mrs Smith's residence; they have a country residence where they spend their weekends* (b) act of living in a place; **hall of residence** = building where students live at university or college; *how many students live in halls of residence?;* **in residence** = living in a place; *when the Queen is in residence, the royal flag flies over Buckingham Palace;* **artist in residence** = artist who lives and works in a place, such as a university, for a time; *she spent six months as artist in residence at Newcastle University*

resident ['rezɪdənt] **1** *adjective* who lives permanently in a place; *there is a resident caretaker* **2** *noun* person who lives in a place, a country, a hotel, etc.; *you need an entry permit if you're not a resident of this country; only residents are allowed to park their cars here*

residential [rezɪ'denʃl] *adjective* **residential area** = part of a town with houses rather than shops or factories; *the flat is not in a residential area, it's above a shoe shop;* **residential street** = street with houses, and no shops or factories; *he lives in a quiet residential street*

residual [re'zɪdjuəl] *adjective* remaining after everything else has gone; *there is a little residual pain in my left leg, but it is hardly noticeable*

residue ['rezɪdjuː] *noun* (a) what is left of an estate after debts and bequests have been made; *after paying various bequests the residue of his estate was split between his children* (b) what is left after a process has taken place; *after the sugar has been refined the residue is used for cattle feed*

resign [rɪ'zaɪn] *verb* (a) to give up a job; *he resigned with effect from July 1st; she has resigned (her position) as finance director* (b) **to resign yourself to something** = to accept something; *I have to resign myself to never being rich; he was still 20 metres* *behind his rival and resigned himself to coming in second*

resignation [rezɪgˈneɪʃn] *noun* **(a)** act of giving up a job; *his resignation was accepted by the Prime Minister*; *have you written your letter of resignation?*; **he tendered** *or* **he handed in his resignation** = he resigned **(b)** accepting an unpleasant or unwanted situation; *he looked at his exam results with resignation*

resigned [rɪˈzaɪnd] *adjective* accepting something unpleasant; *a resigned look appeared on his face*; **resigned to** = accepting that something unpleasant will happen; *I'm resigned to living by myself for the rest of my life*

resignedly [rɪˈzaɪnɪdli] *adverb* accepting something unpleasant without complaining; *she closed her suitcase and resignedly walked out of the house for the last time*

resilient [rɪˈzɪliənt] *adjective* **(a)** which easily returns to its original shape after being squashed; *cork is a surprisingly resilient material* **(b)** *(person)* who is strong or able to recover easily from a shock; *she is a very resilient person, in spite of her age, and has gone back home from hospital to look after herself*

resin [ˈrezɪn] *noun* **(a)** sticky oil which comes from some types of pine tree; *amber is a yellow stone which is fossilized resin* **(b) (synthetic) resin** = solid or liquid organic compound, a polymer used in the making of plastic; *he made some interesting table decorations with gold coins in blocks of transparent resin*

resinous [ˈrezɪnəs] *adjective* referring to resin; *the resinous smell of the pine forest*

resist [rɪˈzɪst] *verb* to fight against something, not to give in to something; *he resisted all attempts to make him sell the house*; *bands of guerrillas resisted doggedly in the mountains*; *they resisted the enemy attacks for two weeks*

resistance [rɪˈzɪstəns] *noun* **(a)** opposition to something, fighting against something; *bands of guerrillas put up a dogged resistance in the mountains*; *the refugees had no resistance to disease*; *skiers crouch down low to minimize wind resistance*; *there was a lot of resistance to the new plan from the local residents*; **resistance movement** = movement of ordinary people against an invader; *the resistance movement was very strong in their area during the war*; **passive resistance** = resisting the police by refusing to do something, but without violence; *the protesters organized a programme of passive resistance to the new presidential decree*; **he took the line of least resistance** = he did the easiest thing **(b)** *(in physics)* measure of the fall in voltage across a component with a current flowing through it; *an electronic component that provides a known resistance is called a resistor*

resistant [rɪˈzɪstənt] *adjective* which resists; *this plate is not heat resistant and shouldn't be used on kitchen hobs*

resistor [rɪˈzɪstə] *noun* electronic component that provides a known resistance; *with a variable resistor you can change the resistance by turning a knob*

resolute [ˈrezəluːt] *adjective* determined, having made up your mind; *he is quite resolute in his determination to sell his business and retire*; *he's famous for his resolute refusal to use any form of modern technology*

resolution [rezəˈluːʃn] *noun* **(a)** decision to be decided at a meeting; **to put a resolution to a meeting** = to ask a meeting to vote on a proposal; *the meeting passed or carried or adopted the resolution*; *the meeting rejected the resolution or the resolution was defeated by ten votes to twenty* **(b)** being determined to do something; *her resolution to succeed is so strong that I am sure she will get through*; **New Year's Resolution** = plan to improve your way of living, decided on at the New Year, and usually abandoned shortly afterwards; *each New Year I make the same resolutions, but never manage to keep them*; *my New Year's resolution was to take more exercise, but it didn't last long* **(c)** clearness of a TV or computer image (calculated as the number of pixels per unit of area); *a high resolution screen can display 640 x 450 pixels*

resolve [rɪˈzɒlv] **1** *noun* determination, what you have firmly decided to do; *the head teacher encouraged him in his resolve to go to university* **2** *verb* to firmly decide to do something; *we all resolved to work harder*

resolved [rɪˈzɒlvd] *adjective* determined, having made up your mind; *they are completely resolved to sell the business*

resonance [ˈrezənəns] *noun* deep loud ringing tone; *the resonance of the great cathedral bell*

resonant [ˈrezənənt] *adjective* **(a)** which sounds, rings or echoes loudly; *he spoke in a deep resonant voice* **(b) resonant with** = full of; *the house is resonant with memories of our childhood*

resonate [ˈrezəneɪt] *verb* *(formal)* to sound or ring out loudly; *the explosion resonated around the valley*

resort [rɪˈzɔːt] **1** *noun* **(a)** place where people go on holiday; *a famous Swiss ski resort*; *crowds have been flocking to the resorts on the south coast* **(b) as a last resort** *or* **in the last resort** = when everything else fails; *having tried everything without success, she accepted her offer as a last resort* **2** *verb* **to resort to** = to use something in a difficult situation, when everything else has failed; *in the end the police had to resort to using tear gas*

resounding [rɪˈzaʊndɪŋ] *adjective* great, complete; *the exhibition was a resounding success*

resource [rɪˈsɔːs] *noun* **(a)** source of supply for what is needed or used; *we have enough resources - financial or otherwise - to build a prototype rocket*; **financial resources** = supply of money for something; **natural resources** = raw materials which come from nature, such as minerals, oil, trees; *the country is rich in natural resources*; **resource centre** = section of a school where reference books and equipment are kept for the use of students; *the school does not have enough funds to buy dictionaries for the resource centre* **(b) left to your own resources** = left to look after yourself; *their parents were away and the children were left to their own resources*

resourceful [rɪˈsɔːsfʊl] *adjective* good at looking after yourself or at dealing with problems; *she's remarkably resourceful, in spite of being only sixteen*

respect [rɪˈspekt] **1** *noun* **(a)** admiration or regard for someone; *he showed very little respect for his teacher*; *no one deserves more respect than her mother*; **to command respect** = to be admired; *her TV documentaries command respect* **(b) with respect to** = concerning; *I have nothing to say with respect to the* *new treatment*; **in some respects** = in some ways; *in some respects, she doesn't act like a mature person* **(c) respects** = polite good wishes; *my father sends you his respects*; **to pay your respects to someone** = to go to visit someone important; **to pay your last respects to someone** = to go to someone's funeral or to visit someone's coffin at the undertaker's before the funeral **2** *verb* **(a)** to admire or to honour someone; *everyone respected her decision to emigrate* **(b)** to show you care about something; *logging companies have been accused of not respecting the environment* **(c)** to do what is required by something; *the landlord has not respected the terms of the contract*

respectability [rɪspektə'bɪlɪti] *noun* being respectable; *the houses round the cathedral have an air of genteel respectability*; *all he wanted was respectability, but he never achieved it*

respectable [rɪ'spektəbl] *adjective* **(a)** considered by people to be good, proper, and worthy of respect; *she's marrying a very respectable young engineer*; *I don't want to bring up my children here, it is not a respectable area* **(b)** fairly large; *he made quite a respectable score*

respected [rɪ'spektɪd] *adjective* admired by many people; *he's a highly-respected professor of physics*; *the book is a very respected work of reference*

respectful [rɪ'spektful] *adjective* full of respect; *children should always be respectful towards their teachers*; *the delegates listened in respectful silence as the chairman spoke*

respective [rɪ'spektɪv] *adjective* referring separately to each of the people just mentioned; *they chatted for a while and then each went back to their respective tables*

respectively [rɪ'spektɪvli] *adverb* in the order just mentioned; *Mr Smith and Mr Jones are respectively owner and manager of the shop*

respiratory [rə'spɪrətəri] *adjective* referring to breathing; **respiratory infection** = infection in the windpipe or lungs

respite ['respaɪt] *noun* **(a)** rest, period when things are slightly better; *the ceasefire provided a brief respite from the fighting*; *there was no respite from the bitter cold* **(b) without respite** = without stopping; *rescue teams worked without respite for three days in their search for survivors*

resplendent [rɪ'splendənt] *adjective* dazzling, very splendid; *the bride looked resplendent in her white satin gown*

respond [rɪ'spɒnd] *verb* **(a)** to give a reply; *she shouted at him, but he didn't respond* **(b)** to show a favourable reaction to; *I hope the public will respond to our new advertisement*; *the government has responded to pressure from industry*; **he is responding to treatment** = he is beginning to get better

respondent [rɪ'spɒndənt] *noun* **(a)** person who answers a questionnaire; *the majority of respondents ticked this box* **(b)** person who answers a case in court, especially someone who is being sued for divorce; *she was the respondent in the divorce case*

response [rɪ'spɒns] *noun* **(a)** answer; *there was no response to our call for help*; **in response to** = as an answer to; *in response to the United Nations' request for aid, the government has sent blankets and tents* **(b)** answers given by the congregation in church; *the litany is a series of prayers with repeated responses*

responsibility [rɪspɒnsɪ'bɪlɪti] *noun* **(a)** being in a position where you look after or deal with something; *the management accepts no responsibility for customers' property*; *there is no responsibility on his part for the poor results*; *who should take responsibility for the students' welfare?*; **he has taken on a lot of responsibility** = he has agreed to be responsible for many things; **position of responsibility** = job where important decisions have to be taken **(b)** thing which you are responsible for; **responsibilities** = duties; *he finds the responsibilities of being treasurer of the club too demanding*

responsible [rɪ'spɒnsɪbl] *adjective* **(a) responsible for** = causing; *the fog was responsible for the accident* **(b)** looking after something, and so open to blame if it gets lost, damaged, etc.; *he is not responsible for the restaurant next door to his hotel*; *we hold customers responsible for all breakages* **(c) responsible to someone** = being under the authority of someone; *she's directly responsible to the head nurse* **(d)** trustworthy (person); *you can rely on him, he's very responsible*; **responsible position** *or* **responsible job** = job where decisions have to be taken; *he is looking for a responsible position in the Post Office*

responsibly [rɪs'pɒnsɪbli] *adverb* in a responsible way; *he acted responsibly when he called the ambulance*; *young people don't always behave responsibly when in a group*

responsive [rɪ'spɒnsɪv] *adjective* **(a)** showing sympathy, reacting favourably to something; *the management was not very responsive to the demands of the staff* **(b)** reacting to; *the cat is very responsive to being stroked*; *his flu seems to be responsive to antibiotics*

respray 1 [riː'spreɪ] *verb* to spray again; *he has had his car resprayed with metallic paint* **2** ['riːspreɪ] *noun* action of respraying; *the car has had a respray*

rest [rest] **1** *noun* **(a)** being quiet and peaceful, being asleep, doing nothing; *all you need is a good night's rest and you'll be fine again tomorrow*; *we took a few minute's rest and started running again*; *I'm having a well-earned rest after working hard all week* **(b)** not moving; *the ball finally came to rest at the bottom of the hill* **(c)** what is left; *here are the twins, but where are the rest of the children?*; *I drank most of the milk and the cat drank the rest*; *throw the rest of the food away - it will go bad* (NOTE: **rest** takes a singular verb when it refers to a singular: **here's the rest of the milk; where's the rest of the string? the rest of the money has been lost**; it takes a plural verb when it refers to a plural: **here are the rest of the children; where are the rest of the chairs? the rest of the books have been lost**) **(d)** thing which supports; *she pulled up a stool as a rest for her foot*; **headrest** = cushion on top of a car seat against which you can lean your head **2** *verb* **(a)** to be quiet and peaceful; *don't disturb your father - he's resting*; *they ran for ten miles, rested for a few minutes, and then ran on again* **(b)** to lean something against something; *she rested her bike against the wall* **(c)** *(formal)* **to let something rest** = to stop discussing something; *after advice from our solicitor, we decided to let the matter rest*

restart [rɪ'stɑːt] *verb* to start again; *the car stalled at the traffic lights and he couldn't restart it or it wouldn't restart*

restate [riː'steɪt] *verb* to state again; *I wish just to restate the facts of the case; he used his speech to restate government policy on immigration*

restaurant ['restərɒnt] *noun* place where you can buy and eat a meal; *I don't want to stay at home tonight - let's go out to the Italian restaurant in the High Street; she's was waiting for me at the restaurant*; **restaurant car** = wagon on a train where you can eat full meals (as opposed to a buffet car)

restaurateur [restəræ'tɜː] *noun* person who runs a restaurant; *he's a French restaurateur with a chain of restaurants in New York and California*

restful ['restfʊl] *adjective* which makes you feel calm and relaxed; *we were glad to get back to the restful calm of the hotel after the crowded streets of the old town*

restive ['restɪv] *adjective* not quiet, disturbed and difficult to control; *after waiting patiently for three hours, people in the queue began to get restive*

restless ['restləs] *adjective* agitated; always moving about; *after five days of rain, the children were restless and really needed to go out to play; she's becoming restless, she's hardly been here two months and she wants to go abroad again*

restlessness ['restləsnəs] *noun* being restless; *he's going through a period of restlessness and can't settle down*

restoration [restə'reɪʃn] *noun* **(a)** repairing something, making something look like new again; *the old castle is in need of extensive restoration* **(b)** giving back; *the restoration of stolen goods to their rightful owners is essential*

the Restoration [restə'reɪʃn] *noun* the period after 1660, when King Charles II was restored to the throne; *they are putting on a Restoration comedy at the National Theatre*

restore [rɪ'stɔː] *verb* **(a)** to repair, to make something like new again; *the old house has been restored and is now open to the public* **(b)** to give back; *after the war the castle was not restored to its rightful owners* **(c)** to make something exist again; *to everyone's delight, the bonus system was restored*

restorer [rɪ'stɔːrə] *noun* person who restores old paintings, etc.; *the damaged tapestry was sent to the restorer for repair*; **hair restorer** = liquid which is supposed to make your hair grow better

restrain [rɪ'streɪn] *verb* to prevent, to try and stop someone doing something; *it took six policemen to restrain him*; **to restrain yourself** = to keep your temper under control; *next time, I won't restrain myself; I'll tell him exactly what I think of him*

restrained [rɪ'streɪnd] *adjective* controlled, calm; *he carried on talking, but in a more restrained voice*

restraint [rɪ'streɪnt] *noun* control; *she showed great restraint when he criticized her work*; **with great restraint** = without losing your temper; *he was furious, but managed to talk with great restraint*; **lack of restraint** = giving people too much freedom; *the lack of restraint in the school doesn't go down well with the parents*; **wage restraint** *or* **pay restraint** = keeping wage increases under control; *the government is planning to impose pay restraints*

restrict [rɪ'strɪkt] *verb* to limit; *you are restricted to two bottles per person; the government is trying to restrict the inflow of foreign workers*

restricted [rɪ'strɪktɪd] *adjective* limited; *there will be a restricted train service next Sunday; these seats are cheaper because you only have a restricted view of the stage*; **restricted area** = (i) area where cars must obey a speed limit; (ii) place where only certain people are allowed

restriction [rɪ'strɪkʃn] *noun* limitation; *the police have placed restrictions on his movements; restrictions have been imposed on certain imports; there is no overall speed restriction on German motorways*

restrictive [rɪ'strɪktɪv] *adjective* which limits; *I find living in the suburbs very restrictive*; **restrictive (trade) practices** = arrangements between companies to fix prices, to share the market, etc., and so cut out other businesses

restroom ['restruːm] *noun mainly US* toilet, lavatory; *could you tell me where the restroom is, please?*

restructure ['riːstrʌktʃə] *verb* to reorganize, especially the financial basis of a company; *the company is planning to restructure its marketing division*

result [rɪ'zʌlt] **1** *noun* **(a)** something which happens because of something else; *what was the result of the police investigation?*; **as a result (of)** = because of; *there was a traffic jam and as a result, she missed her plane* **(b)** final score in a game, final marks in an exam, etc.; *she isn't pleased with her exam results; I had great fun making the rug but I'm only partly happy with the result; he listened to the football results in the radio 2 verb* to **result from** = to happen because of something which has been done; *the increase in debts resulted from the expansion programme*; **to result in** = to produce as an effect; *the doubling of the sales force resulted in increased sales*

resultant [rɪ'zʌltənt] *adjective* which happens as a result; *the traffic lights failed at Piccadilly Circus and the resultant traffic jams went as far as Marble Arch*

resulting [rɪ'zʌltɪŋ] *adjective* which results; *the traffic lights failed, and in the resulting chaos there were several accidents*

resume [rɪ'zjuːm] *verb* to start again after stopping; *the meeting resumed after a short break; normal train services will resume after the track has been repaired; after the fire, the staff resumed work as normal*

résumé ['rezuːmeɪ] *noun* **(a)** short summing up of the main points of a discussion, of a book; *I can't attend the meeting, but I would like a résumé of the discussion; a brief résumé of the book is all I need* **(b)** *US* summary of a person's life story with details of education and work experience; *attach a résumé to your application form* (NOTE: British English is **curriculum vitae** *or* **CV**)

resumption [rɪ'zʌmpʃn] *noun* starting again; **we expect an early resumption of negotiations** = we expect negotiations will start again soon

resurface [riː'sɜːfəs] *verb* **(a)** to put a new surface on a road; *no one can park on our street because they are resurfacing it today* **(b)** to come back to the surface again, to appear again; *the bird dived into the water and resurfaced several minutes later in a different part of the river; he disappeared for a time, then resurfaced as managing director of a TV company*

resurgence [rɪ'sɜːdʒəns] *noun* reappearance, rising again; *the resurgence of terrorist activity in the north of the country; there are signs of the resurgence of nationalism in some parts of Europe*

resurrect [rezə'rekt] *verb* to bring something back to use; to start something up again; *he resurrected his old plan for rebuilding the town centre; she accepted the part of Lady Macbeth in an attempt to resurrect her stage career*

resurrection [rezə'rekʃn] *noun* **(a)** bringing a dead person back to life; *Easter is an important Christian festival celebrating Christ's death and resurrection* **(b)** coming back into existence; *last month saw the resurrection of the civil war in the country*

resuscitate [rɪ'sʌsɪteɪt] *verb* to make someone who appears to be dead start breathing again, and to restart the circulation of blood; *her heart stopped on the operating table but the surgeons managed to resuscitate her*

resuscitation [rɪsʌsɪ'teɪʃn] *noun* action of resuscitating someone; *she was dragged out of the pool but all attempts at resuscitation failed*

retail ['riːteɪl] **1** *noun* selling small quantities of goods direct to the public; *we specialize in the retail of ordinary household goods; the goods in stock have a retail value of £10,000*; **retail outlet** *or* **retail shop** = shop which sells goods direct to the customer; *he buys wholesale and then sells to various retail outlets;* **retail park** = specially built area of shops outside a town; *compare* WHOLESALE **2** *verb* **(a)** to sell goods direct to customers who do not sell them again; **to retail at** *or* **for** = to sell for a certain price; *these glasses retail at £5.95 for two* **(b)** *(formal)* to pass on gossip; *she immediately retailed the story to her friends* **3** *adverb* **he sells retail and buys wholesale** = he buys goods in bulk at a wholesale discount and sells in small quantities to the public

retailer ['riːteɪlə] *noun* shopkeeper who sells goods directly to the public; *as a retailer, I buy either from a wholesaler or direct from the factory; retailers buy goods from wholesalers and then sell them on to the public; compare* WHOLESALER

retailing ['riːteɪlɪŋ] *noun* business of selling goods at full price to the public; *from car retailing the company branched out into car leasing*

retail price ['riːteɪl 'praɪs] *noun* price at which the retailer sells to the final customer; *have you decided on the retail price of the glasses yet?; the retail price is double the wholesale price;* **Retail Price(s) Index (RPI)** = index which shows how prices of consumer goods have increased or decreased over a period of time

retain [rɪ'teɪn] *verb (formal)* **(a)** to keep; *please retain this invoice for tax purposes; one book especially retained my attention - so I bought it; he managed to retain his composure in spite of being constantly heckled;* **retaining wall** = wall which holds back earth or the water in a reservoir **(b) to retain a lawyer to act for you** = to agree with a lawyer that he will act for you, and to pay him a fee in advance

retainer [rɪ'teɪnə] *noun* **(a)** money paid in advance to someone so that he will work for you, and not for someone else; *we pay him a retainer of £1,000* **(b)** old servant; *the old duke and duchess ate in their dining hall, surrounded by elderly retainers*

retake 1 *noun* ['riːteɪk] shooting of a scene of a film again; *after four retakes the director decided that it was good enough to be screened* **2** *verb* [riː'teɪk] **(a)** to capture something again; *the fighting lasted all day, and in the evening we retook the positions we had lost that morning* **(b)** to shoot a scene of a film again; *the director wasn't pleased and we had to retake the whole scene* (NOTE: **retaking - retook - has retaken**)

retaliate [rɪ'tælɪeɪt] *verb* to hit back, to attack someone in revenge; *when the crowd threw stones, the police retaliated with tear gas; do you think the gang will try to retaliate?*

retaliation [rɪtælɪ'eɪʃn] *noun* attacking someone for something they have done to you; *do you expect any sort of retaliation from the German drivers?;* **in retaliation for** = as a punishment in revenge for something; *the pub was bombed in retaliation for attacks by the other side; prices were lowered in retaliation for their competitor's new low prices; he cancelled his subscription in retaliation for the newspaper's racist attitude*

retard [rɪ'tɑːd] *verb (formal)* to make things slow, to keep something back; *the high exchange rate is retarding industrial growth*

retarded [rɪ'tɑːdɪd] *adjective* not having developed mentally as far as others of the same age; *by the age of four, he was showing signs of being mentally retarded*

retch [retʃ] *verb* to try to vomit without bringing up anything from the stomach; *he staggered out of the pub, coughing and retching; the sight of the mass grave made him retch*

retention [rɪ'tenʃn] *noun (formal)* **(a)** keeping something; *the committee voted for the retention of the existing system* **(b)** holding something back; *we are proposing the retention of 10% of salary to cover potential damage to the stock*

rethink [riː'θɪŋk] **1** *noun (informal)* to have a rethink = to think again about a problem; *we had a rethink and have decided to accept their offer* **2** *verb* to think again, to reconsider; *we should rethink the whole plan now that the council has refused planning permission* (NOTE: **rethinking - rethought** [riː'θɔːt])

reticence ['retɪsəns] *noun (formal)* being unwilling to talk; *his reticence about his qualifications is understandable - he doesn't have any*

reticent ['retɪsənt] *adjective* not willing to talk about something; *she is very reticent about her job plans; some children are so reticent that it is difficult to find out what they really think and feel*

retina ['retɪnə] *noun* inside layer of the eye, which is sensitive to light; *the retina expands and contracts according to the amount of light it receives;* **detached retina** = condition where the retina is partly detached from the tissue of the eyeball

retire [rɪ'taɪə] *verb* **(a)** to stop work and take a pension; *he will retire from his job as manager next April; when he retired, the firm presented him with a watch; she's retiring this year* **(b)** to make a worker stop work and take a pension; *they decided to retire all staff over 50* **(c)** to come to the end of an elected term of office; *the treasurer retires from the committee after six years* **(d)** *(literary)* **to retire for the night** = to go to bed; *it was two o'clock in the morning and all the hotel guests had retired to their bedrooms*

retired [rɪ'taɪəd] *adjective* who has stopped work and draws a pension; *the club is run by a retired schoolteacher*

retiree [riːtaɪˈriː] *noun especially US* person who has retired or is about to retire; *all the retirees gathered for a farewell dinner*

retirement [rɪˈtaɪəmənt] *noun* (a) act of retiring from work; *he was given a watch as a retirement present*; *he claims that the pension he'll get on his retirement won't be sufficient*; to take early retirement = to leave work before the usual age; *I enjoy my work and I don't want to take early retirement*; retirement age = age at which people retire (in the UK usually 65 for men and 60 for women); *she reached retirement age last week* (b) period of life when you are retired; *he spent his retirement in his house in France*; *most people look forward to their retirement*

retiring [rɪˈtaɪrɪŋ] *adjective* shy, quiet and reserved; *she's naturally retiring and does not mix with the other students*

retort [rɪˈtɔːt] **1** *noun* (a) sharp reply; *'I can look after myself perfectly well' was her retort* (b) glass bottle with a long, thin neck which is bent, used for heating liquids and collecting condensed vapour **2** *verb* (*literary*) to reply sharply; *she retorted that she had plenty of money and didn't want any gifts from him*

retrace [riːˈtreɪs] *verb* to go back to the origins of something; *he is trying to retrace the route his grandfather used when exploring the Northwest Territory*; to retrace your steps = to go back over the same path again; *she thought she had lost her watch while shopping, so she retraced her steps from shop to shop*

retract [rɪˈtrækt] *verb* (a) to pull back; *the landing gear retracted after take-off* (b) to withdraw something which has been said; *he refuses to retract a single word of his statement*

retrain [riːˈtreɪn] *verb* (a) to train someone for a new job, or to do the same job in a more modern way; *he has been sent to retrain on the new model 747s*; *the staff are sent to be retrained in selling skills* (b) to learn new skills; *he retrained as a house decorator*

retraining [riːˈtreɪnɪŋ] *noun* process of giving new training to someone; *the retraining of existing staff is one of our priorities*

retreat [rɪˈtriːt] **1** *noun* (a) pulling back an army from a battle; *the army's retreat was unexpected and swift*; in retreat = going back from a battle; in full retreat = going back fast; *the army is in full retreat* (*informal*) to beat a retreat = to go backwards; *he went into the ladies' toilet by mistake and had to beat a hasty retreat* (b) quiet place; *they spent the weekend at their retreat in the Scottish hills* (c) time spent in rest and religious thought in a monastery; *he went on a retreat* **2** *verb* (a) to pull back from a battle; *Napoleon retreated from Moscow in 1812* (b) to go to a quiet place; *monks retreat from the outside world*; *our dog retreats to his basket if we shout at him*

retribution [retrɪˈbjuːʃn] *noun* well-deserved punishment; *the informer suffered swift retribution from the other members of the gang*; to exact retribution for = to carry out punishment for; *they are planning to exact retribution for the attacks on their villages*

retrievable [rɪˈtriːvəbl] *adjective* which can be retrieved; *the hard disk has crashed but we think the data is retrievable*

retrieval [rɪˈtriːvəl] *noun* getting something back; *the retrieval of the text is now impossible*; data retrieval = getting back data which is stored in a computer; retrieval system = system which allows information to be retrieved; *to get back this data, you must use a more up-to-date retrieval system*

retrieve [rɪˈtriːv] *verb* (a) to get back something which was lost; *he retrieved his umbrella from the lost property office* (b) to bring back something which has been stored in a computer; *she retrieved the address files which she thought had been deleted*

retriever [rɪˈtriːvə] *noun* type of dog trained to fetch dead birds which have been shot; *he went off with his retriever to shoot pigeons*

retrospect [ˈretrəspekt] *noun* in retrospect = when you look back; *in retrospect, our decision to make him finance director was quite wrong*

retrospective [retrəˈspektɪv] **1** *adjective* (a) which goes back to a time in the past; *she was awarded a retrospective pay increase*; *the management offered an increase, retrospective to last January* (b) retrospective exhibition = exhibition of works of art covering the whole career of an artist **2** *noun* exhibition of works of art covering the whole career of an artist; *this has been the first Henry Moore retrospective for some years*

retroussé [rəˈtruːseɪ] *adjective* retroussé nose = turned up nose; *she was a pretty girl, with a little retroussé nose*

return [rɪˈtɜːn] **1** *noun* (a) going back, coming back to a place; *it snowed on the day of her return from Canada*; *on his return, he'll come and see you*; return ticket *or* a return = ticket which allows you to go to one place and come back; *I want two returns to Edinburgh* (b) action of going back to a former state; *the government wants to encourage a return to old family traditions* (c) sending back; *he asked for the immediate return of the borrowed tools*; *she replied by return of post* = she replied by the next postal service back; to sell something on sale or return = to sell something and give the purchaser the right to return it if he doesn't sell it (d) key on a keyboard which you press when you have finished keying something, or when you want to start a new line; *to change directory, type C: and press return*; carriage return = key on a typewriter which you press to start a new line (e) many happy returns of the day = greetings said to someone on their birthday (f) income from money invested; *this account should bring in a quick return on your investment* (g) official return = official report; to make an income tax return = to send a statement of income to the tax office; *your income tax return should be sent no later than 1st July*; to fill in a VAT return = to complete the form showing VAT receipts and expenditure (h) returns = unsold goods which are sent back to the supplier **2** *verb* (a) to come back or to go back; *when she returned from lunch she found two messages waiting for her*; *when do you plan to return to Paris?* (b) to give back or to send back; *the letter was returned to the sender* (c) to elect an MP for a constituency; *he was returned with an increased majority* **3** *adjective* return address = address to send something back; *there was no return address on the letter so we couldn't send it back*; return fare = fare for a journey from one place to another and back again; *a return fare is cheaper than two one-way fares*;

return match = match played between the same two teams again

reunification [riːjuːnɪfɪˈkeɪʃn] *noun* act of joining again; *she led the movement for the reunification of the country*; *the reunification of Germany in 1990*; compare UNIFICATION

reunion [riːˈjuːnɪən] *noun* meeting of people who have not met for a long time; *we are holding a reunion of our school year next month*; *the family reunion did not go off very well*

reunite [riːjuːˈnaɪt] *verb* to join people or things together again; *the little boy was finally reunited with his family*

rev [rev] **1** *noun* (*informal*) engine revolution; **rev counter** = dial which shows the number of revolutions at which an engine is turning **2** *verb* (*informal*) **to rev (up)** = to make a car engine go quickly while the car is standing still; *I could hear him revving (up) while he was waiting for me in the car* (NOTE: **revving - revved**)

Rev [ˈrevrənd] *short for* REVEREND (NOTE: used as a title with the surname: **the preacher tomorrow will be Rev Wilson**)

revalue [riːˈvæljuː] *verb* to value something again at a higher value than before; *the company's properties have been revalued*; *the dollar has been revalued against all world currencies*

revamp 1 [riːˈvæmp] *verb* (*informal*) to improve the appearance of something which is slightly old-fashioned; *the whole image of the company needs revamping* **2** [ˈriːvæmp] *noun* complete change of the appearance of something; *our headed notepaper has had a complete revamp*

reveal [rɪˈviːl] *verb* to show something which was hidden; *he revealed his ignorance about cars*; *an unexpected fault was revealed during the test*; *the X-ray revealed a brain tumour*

revealing [rɪˈviːlɪŋ] *adjective* which shows something which is usually hidden; *he made a very revealing remark*; **a revealing dress** = dress which shows parts of the body which are normally kept hidden

revel [ˈrevəl] **1** *noun* (*old*) **revels** = happy celebrations; *let the revels commence!* **2** *verb* to have a happy time; **to revel in something** = to take delight in something; *they revelled in the clean air of the Scottish highlands*; *she's revelling in her new-found fame* (NOTE: **revelling - revelled** but American spelling is **reveling - reveled**)

revelation [revəˈleɪʃn] *noun* surprise showing of something which was secret; *her revelation that she had two children took everyone by surprise*

reveller *US* **reveler** [ˈrevələ] *noun* person who is having a good time; *we were kept awake by the revellers celebrating the New Year*

revenge [rɪˈvenʒ] **1** *noun* punishing someone in return for harm he has caused you; *they broke the windows of the judge's house in revenge for the fines he had imposed*; *all the time he spent in prison, his only thought was of revenge*; *he had his revenge in the end, when her car broke down and she had to phone for help*; **to get** *or* **take your revenge on someone** = to punish someone for something he has done to you **2** *verb* **to revenge yourself on someone** = to punish someone for something he has done to you; *she planned to revenge herself on the people who had treated her so badly*; compare AVENGE

revenue [ˈrevənjuː] *noun* (a) money which is received; *his only source of revenue is his shop* (b) money received by a government in tax; **Inland Revenue** *US* **Internal Revenue Service** = government department which deals with tax; *the Inland Revenue wrote again claiming we owe even more tax*

reverberate [rɪˈvɜːbəreɪt] *verb* to echo or to ring out loudly and repeatedly; *the shouting reverberated down the streets*; *the gunfire reverberated round the mountains*

revere [rɪˈvɪə] *verb* (*formal*) to worship or to respect someone very highly; *she was revered by her patients for her kindness to others*

reverence [ˈrevrəns] *noun* great respect; *they showed their reverence for their dead leader by laying flowers on his grave*; *the priest approached the altar in an attitude of reverence*

Reverend [ˈrevrənd] *adjective* title given to a clergyman; *Reverend John Spencer will be preaching tomorrow*; **Reverend Mother** = title given to the head of a convent; *Reverend Mother does not agree with the sale of the land behind the convent* (NOTE: usually shortened to **Rev: the Rev John Spencer**)

reverent [ˈrevrənt] *adjective* showing respect; *the crowd watched in reverent silence as the funeral procession passed by*

reverie [ˈrevəri] *noun* (*formal*) daydream, dream which you have during the day when you are not asleep; *she sat in a reverie, thinking about life on a tropical island*

reversal [rɪˈvɜːsəl] *noun* change to the opposite; *after being very successful, the business suffered a sudden reversal*; **reversal of fortune** = change of luck from good to bad or from bad to good

reverse [rɪˈvɜːs] **1** *adjective* opposite; *the reverse side of the carpet is made of foam rubber*; *the conditions are printed on the reverse side of the invoice*; **in reverse order** = backwards; *they called out the names of the prize-winners in reverse order*; **reverse charge call** = telephone call where the person receiving the call agrees to pay for it; *since I had no money I made a reverse charge call to my mother* (NOTE: American English is **collect call**) **2** *noun* (a) the opposite; *you're mistaken, the reverse is true* (b) opposite side; *didn't you read what was on the reverse of the letter?* (c) side of a coin which does not bear the head of a king, a queen, etc.; *there is a thistle on the reverse of this coin* (NOTE: also called 'tails'; the opposite is the **obverse** *or* **heads**) (d) car gear which makes you go backwards; *put the car into reverse and back very slowly into the garage*; *the car's stuck in reverse!* (e) defeat in battle or in an election; *the army suffered a catastrophic reverse*; *the Conservatives suffered a series of reverses* **3** *verb* (a) to make something do the opposite; *the page order was reversed by mistake*; *don't try to reverse the trend, go along with it* (b) to make a car go backwards; *reverse as far as you can, then go forward*; *be careful not to reverse into that lamppost* (c) (*on the phone*) **to reverse the charges** = to ask the person you are calling to pay for the call; *my father told me to reverse the charges when I call him* (NOTE: American English is to **call collect**) (d) to change a legal decision to another, opposite, one; *the court reversed its decision*

revert [rɪˈvɜːt] *verb* (a) to go back or to come back to; **to revert to type** *or* **to form** = to go back to an original state; *we thought he was becoming a quiet intellectual, then he reverted to form and went out drinking every night* **(b)** *(formal)* **to revert to a subject** = to start talking about the subject again; *I would like to revert to the subject of overdue payments*; *the conversation reverted to the question of planning permission*

review [rɪˈvjuː] **1** *noun* **(a)** written comments on a book, play, film, etc., published in a newspaper or magazine; *did you read the review of her latest film in today's paper?*; *his book got some very good reviews* **(b)** monthly or weekly magazine which contains articles of general interest; *his first short story appeared in a Scottish literary review* **(c)** examination of several things together; *the company's annual review of each department's performance*; **salary review** = examination of salaries in a company to see if the workers should earn more; *let's hope we all get an increase at the next salary review* **(d)** *(formal)* general inspection of the army, navy, etc.; *a naval review will be held on the king's birthday* (NOTE: do not confuse with **revue**) **2** *verb* **(a)** to read a book, see a film, etc., and write comments about it in a newspaper or magazine; *her exhibition was reviewed in today's paper*; *whoever reviewed her latest book, obviously didn't like it*; **review copy** = copy of new book sent to a newspaper or magazine, asking them to review it **(b)** *(formal)* to inspect soldiers, sailors, ships, etc.; *the general rode on horseback to review the troops* **(c)** to examine in a general way; *the bank will review our overdraft position at the end of the month*; *let's review the situation in the light of the new developments* **(d)** *US* to study a lesson again; *you must review your geography before the exam* (NOTE: British English in this meaning is to **revise**)

reviewer [rɪˈvjuːə] *noun* person who writes comments on books, plays, films, etc.; *there's a new film reviewer on the Sunday paper and I don't like him*; *she's the book reviewer for our local newspaper*

revise [rɪˈvaɪz] *verb* **(a)** to study a lesson again; *there isn't enough time to revise before the exam*; *I'm revising for my history test* (NOTE: American English is to **review**) **(b)** to change, to make something correct; *he is revising the speech he is due to give this evening*; *these figures will have to be revised, there seems to be a mistake*

revision [rɪˈvɪʒən] *noun* action of revising; *have you started your revision yet?*; *the revision of his speech allowed him to correct a serious error*; *is it necessary to do a revision of last month's figures?*

revisit [riːˈvɪzɪt] *verb* to visit again; *she has always wanted to revisit Canada*

revitalize [riːˈvaɪtəlaɪz] *verb* to make something more lively; *the government has plans to revitalize the coal industry*

revival [rɪˈvaɪvəl] *noun* bringing something back into existence; *this type of music is going through a revival*; *thatching is an old craft which has experienced an unexpected revival*; **revival of interest** = new interest in something; *we've noticed a revival of interest in sports cars*; **revival of trade** = increase in trade after a recession

revive [rɪˈvaɪv] *verb* **(a)** to recover, to get well again; *after drinking some water he had revived enough to go on with the marathon* **(b)** to bring someone back to life again; *the paramedics managed to revive her on the way to the hospital* **(c)** to make something popular

again; *it won't be easy to revive people's interest in old country crafts*

revoke [rɪˈvəʊk] *verb* to cancel a right, agreement, permission, etc.; *to revoke a clause in an agreement*; *the council revoked its planning permission*

revolt [rɪˈvəʊlt] **1** *noun* mass protest against authority; *the government faces a revolt from its main supporters* **2** *verb* **(a)** to rise up against authority; *the prisoners revolted against the harsh treatment they were receiving* **(b)** to disgust; *it revolted me to see all that food being thrown away* (NOTE: in this meaning the noun is **revulsion**)

revolting [rɪˈvəʊltɪŋ] *adjective* disgusting, which makes you feel ill; *don't ask me to eat that revolting food again*; *look at the state of the kitchen - it's revolting!*

revolution [revəˈluːʃn] *noun* **(a)** armed rising against a government; *the government soldiers shot the leaders of the revolution*; *he led an unsuccessful revolution against the last president*; *during the French Revolution many aristocrats were executed* **(b)** turning around a central point; *the engine turns at 5000 revolutions a minute* **(c)** change in the way things are done; *a revolution in data processing*; **the Industrial Revolution** = the development of industry during the 19th century in western Europe and the United States; **the technological revolution** = the change to computerization and other developments in information technology; *the twentieth century is the century of the technological revolution*

revolutionary [revəˈluːʃənəri] **1** *adjective* **(a)** aiming to change things completely; very new; *there is a new revolutionary treatment for cancer* **(b)** referring to a political revolution; *his revolutionary ideas upset the bourgeoisie* **2** *noun* person who takes part in an uprising against a government; *the captured revolutionaries were shot when the army took control*

revolutionize [revəˈluːʃənaɪz] *verb* to change completely; *computers have revolutionized office work*

revolve [rɪˈvɒlv] *verb* to turn round a fixed point; *the Earth revolves around the Sun*; *the whole conversation revolved around the new baby*

revolver [rɪˈvɒlvə] *noun* small hand gun where the chamber for cartridges turns after each shot is fired, so that another shot can be fired quickly; *British policemen do not usually carry revolvers*

revolving [rɪˈvɒlvɪŋ] *adjective* which turns round; **revolving doors** = doors which turn round a central pillar; *with all her parcels, she got stuck in the revolving doors as she went into the hotel*

revue [rɪˈvjuː] *noun* stage show with satirical sketches, songs, etc.; *they put on a revue when they were still at university* (NOTE: do not confuse with **review**)

revulsion [rɪˈvʌlʃn] *noun* disgust; *her face showed her revulsion at the sight*; *the ambassador expressed his revulsion at the treatment of the captured soldiers*

reward [rɪˈwɔːd] **1** *noun* money given to someone as a prize for finding something, or for information about something; *when she took the purse she had found to the police station she got a £25 reward*; *he is not interested in money - the Olympic gold medal will be reward enough* **2** *verb* to give someone money as a prize for finding something, or for doing something; *he* was rewarded for finding the box of papers; *all her efforts were rewarded when she won first prize*

rewarding [rɪ'wɔːdɪŋ] *adjective* which gives satisfaction; *I've just finished the rewarding, if tiring, job of painting the kitchen*

rewind ['riːwaɪnd] **1** *noun* action of winding back; **(fast) rewind** = mechanism which makes something wind back very fast; *my new camera has an automatic fast rewind* **2** [riː'waɪnd] *verb* to wind back; *after playing the cassette he rewound it*; *the flex will rewind automatically when you press the red button* (NOTE: **rewinding - rewound** [riː'waʊnd])

rewire [riː'waɪə] *verb* to put new electric cables in; *we are having the house rewired*; *we bought a roll of flex to rewire the office*

reword [riː'wɜːd] *verb* to say or write something again using different words; *can you reword the letter to make it sound less rude?*

rework [riː'wɜːk] *verb* to work on something again; *we will have to rework the designs for Act III*

rewrite 1 ['riːraɪt] *noun* act of rewriting; *the film script had been through several rewrites and the director still wasn't happy with it* **2** [riː'raɪt] *verb* to write something again in different words; *she rewrote the essay, adding more references* (NOTE: **rewrote - rewritten**)

rhesus ['riːsəs] *adjective* **rhesus monkey** = small monkey, often used in laboratories for scientific experiments; **rhesus factor** = antigen in red blood cells, which is an element in blood grouping; **rhesus negative** = (person) who does not have the rhesus factor in his blood; **rhesus positive** = (person) who has the rhesus factor in his blood

rhetoric ['retərɪk] *noun* **(a)** art of speaking in a way which is intended to make people change their minds; *she came away from the meeting enthused by the Prime Minister's rhetoric* **(b)** way of speaking that is insincere, without any real meaning; *his speech was full of empty rhetoric*; *all this rhetoric is getting us nowhere*

rhetorical [rɪ'tɒrɪkl] *adjective* referring to rhetoric; **rhetorical question** = question which makes a statement, rather than expecting an answer; *'who knows what the weather will be like next month?' is just a rhetorical question - I didn't expect you to answer it in detail*

rheumatic fever [ruː'mætɪk 'fiːvə] *adjective* disease of young people and children, where the joints hurt, and the patient becomes feverish; *she caught rheumatic fever and was away from college for several weeks*

rheumatics [ruː'mætɪks] *noun* (*informal*) rheumatism; *it's my rheumatics that make me stiff*

rheumatism ['ruːmətɪzm] *noun* pains or stiffness in the joints or muscles; *I get rheumatism in the winter*; *she has rheumatism in her knees*

rheumatoid arthritis ['ruːmətɔɪd ɑː'θraɪtɪs] *noun* general painful disabling disease affecting any joint, but especially the hands, feet and hips, making them swollen and inflamed; *three times more women than men are affected by rheumatoid arthritis*

rhinoceros [raɪ'nɒsərəs] *noun* large Asiatic or African animal with a thick skin and one or two horns on its head (NOTE: plural is **rhinoceroses**; also called a **rhino**, plural **rhinos**)

rhododendron [rəʊdə'dendrən] *noun* large evergreen shrub with clusters of huge pink, red or purple flowers; *you should visit Kew Gardens in May, when the rhododendrons are in flower*

rhombus ['rɒmbəs] *noun* shape with four equal sides but with no right angles; *he drew a rhombus on a sheet of paper* (NOTE: plural is **rhombuses**)

rhubarb ['ruːbɑːb] *noun* plant of which the thick red leaf stalks are cooked and eaten as a dessert; *we're having stewed rhubarb for pudding*

rhyme [raɪm] **1** *noun* **(a)** way in which some words end in the same sound; *can you think of a rhyme for 'taught'?* **(b) without rhyme or reason** = with no explanation; *he changes his mind all the time without rhyme or reason* **(c)** little piece of poetry; *the children tried to learn the rhyme by heart*; **nursery rhyme** = little piece of poetry for children; *because his mother was French, he didn't learn many English nursery rhymes as a child*; *we gave her a book of nursery rhymes for her birthday* **2** *verb* **to rhyme with** = to end with the same sound as another word; *'Mr' rhymes with 'sister'*

rhyming slang ['raɪmɪŋ 'slæŋ] *noun* London slang where words are replaced by words or phrases which rhyme with them

> COMMENT: in London rhyming slang, common words are replaced by other common words which rhyme with them. So 'apples and pears' takes the place of 'stairs': 'he fell down the apples and pears'. To make things more complicated, many of the rhymes are abbreviated, thus losing the part which actually rhymes. So 'butcher's hook' meant 'look', but is now abbreviated to simply 'butcher's': 'let's have a butcher's at it'; 'tit for tat' meant 'hat', but now is reduced simply to 'titfer': 'where's my titfer?'

rhythm ['rɪðəm] *noun* strong regular beat in music, poetry, etc.; *they stamped their feet to the rhythm of the music*

rhythmic *or* **rhythmical** ['rɪðmɪk *or* 'rɪðmɪkl] *adjective* with a regular beat; *the audience started a rhythmic clapping*; *the doublebass played a rhythmical beat while the rest of the band blew on whistles*

rhythmically ['rɪðmɪkli] *adverb* in time to a rhythm; *the children moved rhythmically in time to the music*

rib [rɪb] *noun* **(a)** one of twenty-four curved bones which protect your chest; *he fell down while skiing and broke two ribs* **(b)** these same bones of an animal, cooked and eaten; **spare ribs** = pork ribs cooked in a savoury sauce **(c)** curved thicker stone arch which helps to strengthen a vault

> COMMENT: the upper seven pairs of ribs are the true ribs and are attached to the sternum; the next three pairs of ribs are the false ribs, and these are attached to the ribs above and not directly to the sternum; the last two pairs of ribs are the floating ribs which are not attached to the front of the body

ribbed [rɪbd] *adjective* (*knitting*) with a pattern of raised lines; *she was wearing a ribbed sweater*

ribbon ['rɪbn] *noun* long thin strip of material for tying things or used as decoration; *she had a red ribbon in her hair*; **printer ribbon** *or* **typewriter ribbon** =

thin strip of material or plastic, with ink or carbon on it, used in a printer or typewriter

ribcage *noun* ['rɪbkeɪdʒ] the ribs and the space enclosed by them; *the ribcage is formed of twelve pairs of curved ribs*

riboflavin [raɪbəʊ'fleɪvɪn] *noun* Vitamin B2, found in eggs, liver, green vegetables and yeast

ribonucleic acid (RNA) [raɪbəʊnjuː'kleɪɪk 'æsɪd] *noun see* RNA

rice [raɪs] *noun* **(a)** very common food, the seeds of a tropical plant; *she only had a bowl of rice for her evening meal*; *cook the rice with some saffron to make it yellow*; **rice pudding** = a pudding made of rice, milk and sugar, cooked together (NOTE: no plural: **some rice, a bowl of rice, a spoonful of rice**) **(b)** common food plant, grown mainly in Asian countries; *women were planting rice in the paddy fields*

COMMENT: long-grain rice is grown in tropical countries, such as India; short-grain rice is grown in colder climates such as Japan. There are thousands of varieties of rice, and the world's leading rice exporters are the USA and Thailand. Wild rice is not rice at all, but a form of North American grass

rich [rɪtʃ] **1** *adjective* **(a)** who has a lot of money; *they're so rich that they can afford to go on holiday for six months*; *if only we were rich, then we could buy a bigger house*; *he never spends anything, and so he gets richer and richer* **(b)** thick and dark (colour); *she painted the kitchen a rich chocolate colour* **(c)** with many treasures; *our local museum has an unusually rich collection of watercolours*; **rich in** = containing a lot of; *the area is rich in old churches*; *the south of the country is rich in coal*; *yeast tablets are rich in vitamin B* **(d)** made with a lot of cream, butter, etc.; *this cream cake is too rich for me* (NOTE: **richer - richest**) **2** *noun* **the rich** = rich people; *at that price, this model of car is only for the really rich*

riches ['rɪtʃɪz] *noun* wealth; *in spite of all their riches they are not a happy family*

richly ['rɪtʃli] *adverb* splendidly; *the dress was richly embroidered with gold thread*; **to richly deserve something** = to deserve something very much; *he richly deserved his prison sentence*; *she richly deserved her award as best actress*

Richter scale ['rɪ tə'skeɪl] *noun* scale of measurement of the force of an earthquake; *there were no reports of injuries after the quake which hit 5.2 on the Richter scale*

COMMENT: the scale has values from zero to ten, and measures the force of an earthquake, not the damage which it causes. The strongest recorded earthquake measured 8.9 on the Richter scale

rick [rɪk] **1** *noun* large pile of straw or hay built like a house; *the peasants took the hay to the edge of the field and built ricks* **2** *verb* to twist or sprain; *I can't lift anything - I've ricked my back*

rickets ['rɪkɪts] *noun* disease of children, where the bones are soft and do not develop properly because of lack of vitamin D; *in this part of the world, many children suffer from rickets*

rickety ['rɪkəti] *adjective (informal)* wobbly, likely to fall down; *she sat down gingerly on a rather rickety*

looking chair; *he came to see us riding up on a rickety old bike*

ricochet ['rɪkəʃeɪ] *verb* to bounce off a surface at an angle; *the bullet ricocheted off the metal window frame* (NOTE: **ricocheted** ['rɪkəʃeɪd])

rid [rɪd] *verb* **to get rid of something** = to dispose of something or to throw something away; *do you want to get rid of that old bookcase?*; *we have been told to get rid of twenty staff*; *she doesn't seem able to get rid of her cold* (NOTE: **getting rid - got rid**)

riddance ['rɪdəns] *noun* **good riddance!** = I am glad to get rid of it!; *our neighbours finally moved with all their screaming children - good riddance, I say!*

riddle ['rɪdl] **1** *noun* puzzling question to which you have to find the answer; *here's a riddle for you: 'what's black and white and red all over?'* (NOTE: the answer is 'a book' if you say 'read' instead of 'red') **2** *verb* to make a lot of holes in something; *they riddled the car with bullets*

riddled with ['rɪdld 'wɪθ] *adjective* **(a)** full of; *the chair is riddled with woodworm*; *most of the animals on the farm are riddled with disease* **(b)** full of holes; *the car was riddled with bullets*

ride [raɪd] **1** *noun* **(a)** pleasant trip on a horse, on a bike, in a car, etc.; *does anyone want to come for a bike ride?*; *can I have a ride on your motorbike?*; *he took us all for a ride in his new car*; *the station is only a short bus ride from the office* **(b)** **to take someone for a ride** = to trick someone; *free beer? - there's no free beer, someone's been taking you for a ride!*; *the young recruit was really taken for a ride when the others told him that there was a party at the colonel's house and he believed them* **(c)** action of travelling; *you will enjoy the smoothness of the ride in the new four-wheel drive model* **2** *verb* to go on a horse, on a bike, etc.; *he rode his bike across the road without looking*; *she's never ridden (on) an elephant*; *my little sister is learning to ride, but she's frightened of big horses* (NOTE: **rides - riding - rode** [rəʊd] **- has ridden** ['rɪdən])

rider ['raɪdə] *noun* **(a)** person who rides; *the rider of the black horse fell at the first fence*; *motorcycle riders must wear helmets* **(b)** additional clause; *to add a rider to a contract*

ridge [rɪdʒ] *noun* long narrow raised part; *the mountain ridge stretches for miles*; **ridge tent** = tent with two sloping sides and a horizontal pole

ridicule ['rɪdɪkjuːl] **1** *noun* mocking, laughing at someone; *she was afraid of the ridicule of her colleagues*; **to hold someone up to ridicule** = to laugh at someone; *the press held the minister up to ridicule after he had been found lying on the pavement outside a bar* **2** *verb* to laugh at someone or something; *she ridiculed his attempts at speaking Italian*

ridiculous [rɪ'dɪkjʊləs] *adjective* silly, which everyone should laugh at; *it's ridiculous to tell everyone to wear suits when it's so hot in the office*

ridiculously [rɪ'dɪkjʊləsli] *adverb* in a ridiculous way; *the flat is ridiculously big for two people*

riding ['raɪdɪŋ] *noun* sport of going on horseback; *he loves riding*; *let's go riding in the park*

riding school ['raɪdɪŋ 'skuːl] *noun* school where you can learn to ride horses; *the best way to learn to ride is to join a riding school*

rife [raɪf] *adjective* **(a)** common; *crime is rife in some parts of the town* **(b) rife with** = full of; *the office is rife with rumours about the managing director*

rifle ['raɪfl] **1** *noun* gun with a long barrel; *the gunman was on a roof with a rifle; he was shooting at a target with an air rifle;* **rifle range** = place where you practise shooting with rifles; *she goes to the rifle range every Saturday to practise* **2** *verb* to search for something, usually to steal it; *the burglars rifled through the drawers of her desk*

rift [rɪft] *noun* split or crack; *a rift developed between members of the ruling party; the family tried to heal the rift between the brother and his sisters*

rig [rɪg] **1** *noun* **(a) oil rig** = construction for drilling for oil; *how many oil rigs are there in the North Sea?* **(b)** *(informal)* large articulated truck; *he drives a 16-wheel rig* **2** *verb* to arrange a dishonest result; *they were accused of rigging the election; see also* RIG UP (NOTE: **rigging - rigged**)

rigging ['rɪgɪŋ] *noun* **(a)** ropes on a ship; *the rigging creaked in the storm; sailors ran up the rigging to wave to the crowds on the quayside* **(b)** arranging a vote to give a dishonest result; *vote rigging is very common here*

right [raɪt] **1** *adjective* **(a)** not wrong, correct; *you're right - the number 8 bus doesn't go to Marble Arch; she gave the right answer every time; he says the answer is 285 - quite right!; is the station clock right?; is this the right train for Manchester?; she didn't put the bottles back in the right place; if you don't stand the jar the right way up it will leak; is this the right road to get to the railway station?; see also* ALL RIGHT **(b)** not left, referring to the hand which most people use to write with; *in England cars don't drive on the right side of the road; the keys are in the top right drawer of my desk; he was holding the suitcase in his right hand* **(c)** *(in politics)* referring to the conservatives; *he's on the right wing of the party; his politics are right of centre* **(d)** *(informal)* **Mr Right** = the man who would be the right man to be someone's husband; *she's still waiting for Mr Right to come along* **2** *noun* **(a)** the side opposite to the left; *when driving in France remember to keep to the right; when you get to the next crossroads, turn to the right; who was that girl sitting on the right of your father?; go straight ahead, and take the second road on the right* **(b)** *(in politics)* **the right** = the political group supporting traditional values and rights; *we support the right by campaigning for our local Conservative candidate;* **swing to the right** = movement of votes towards the right-wing candidates **(c)** legal entitlement to do or to have something; *the accused has the right to remain silent; the manager has no right to read my letters; the staff have a right to know why the shop is closing down; see also* RIGHTS (NOTE: do not confuse with **rite**) **3** *adverb* **(a)** straight; *to get to the police station, keep right on to the end of the road, and then turn left; go right along to the end of the corridor, you'll see my office in front of you; instead of stopping at the crossroads, he drove right on across the main road and into a tree* **(b) right (away)** = immediately; *they called the ambulance right after the accident; the ambulance came right away;* **right now** = at this particular point in time; *right now, it is not possible for me to answer reporters' questions* **(c)** exactly; *the pub is right at the end of the road; the phone rang right in the middle of the TV programme; she stood right in front of the TV and no one could see the screen* **(d)** correctly; *she guessed the answer right; everything is going right for her; (informal)* **it serves you right** = you deserve what has happened to you **(e)** towards the right-hand side; *to get to the station, turn right at the traffic lights; children should be taught to look right and left before crossing the road* **4** *verb* **(a) to right a wrong** = to correct something which is wrong; *she campaigned to right the wrongs done to single mothers* **(b) to right itself** = to turn the right way up again; *the boat capsized and then righted itself*

right angle [raɪt 'æŋgl] *noun* angle of 90°; *the two streets meet at a right angle*

right-angled ['raɪtæŋgld] *adjective* with a 90° angle; *go straight on until the road makes a right-angled turn to the left*

righteous ['raɪtʃəs] *adjective* virtuous, seeing things from a moral point of view; *they showed their righteous anger at being cheated by the tour guide*

rightful ['raɪtful] *adjective* legally correct; *anyone with a rightful claim to the property should come forward;* **rightful claimant** = person who has a legal claim to something; *no rightful claimant to the property has come forward; the legacy can be paid only to the rightful claimant;* **rightful owner** = legal owner; *she is the rightful owner of the property*

right-hand ['raɪt 'hænd] *adjective* on the right side; *look in the right-hand drawer of my desk; the pub is on the right-hand side of the street;* **right-hand man** = main assistant; *he's my right-hand man, I couldn't do without him;* **right-hand drive car** = car where the driver sits on the right side of the car

> COMMENT: most cars have left-hand drives: British, New Zealand and Japanese cars have right-hand drives

right-handed [raɪt 'hændɪd] *adjective* using the right hand more often than the left for things like writing and eating; *she's right-handed*

right-hander ['raɪt'hændə] *noun* **(a)** a blow with the right hand; *he was knocked out with a powerful right-hander to the chin* **(b)** person who is right-handed; *both bowlers are right-handers*

Right Honourable ['raɪt 'ɒnərəbl] *noun* title given to Privy Councillors (NOTE: written before the name; often abbreviated to **Rt Hon: the Rt Hon William Gladstone, MP**)

rightly ['raɪtli] *adverb* correctly; *if I remember rightly, he is tall and dark*

right of way ['raɪt əv 'weɪ] *noun* legal right to go across someone else's property; *there is a public right of way through the wood*

rights [raɪts] *noun* **(a)** what you should be allowed to do or to have; *they are working for women's rights or for the rights of women; the rights of ordinary working people are being ignored;* **human rights** = rights which each ordinary member of society should enjoy, such as freedom of speech, freedom of movement, etc.; *demonstrators are protesting against abuses of human rights in various parts of the world* **(b)** legal right to have something; *he has the British rights to the invention; she sold the American rights to an American publisher;* **film rights** = the legal right to make a film from a book; **foreign rights** = legal right to sell something in another country **(c) rights issue** =

issue of new shares in a company which are offered to existing shareholders at a cheap price

right-wing [raɪt'wɪŋ] *adjective* belonging to the conservative political parties; *the defeat was a blow to the right-wing candidate*

right-winger [raɪt'wɪŋə] *noun* person who is on the right politically; *as a right-winger he does not approve of the Labour government*

rigid ['rɪdʒɪd] *adjective* stiff, inflexible, which doesn't bend; *this pole is too rigid, you will need something more flexible; the club's rules are so rigid that a lot of members are leaving*

rigidity [rɪ'dʒɪdɪti] *noun* being rigid; *a lot of recruits are discouraged by the rigidity of the discipline*

rigidly ['rɪdʒɪdli] *adverb* stiffly; *the guard stood rigidly to attention at the entrance of the palace; he's rigidly opposed to the new law*

rigorous ['rɪgərəs] *adjective* very thorough; *the customs inspection is very rigorous, they open every single case; the rules are too rigorous, they should be relaxed a little; these tests are too rigorous for small children*

rigorously ['rɪgərəsli] *adverb* in a rigorous way; *he rigorously followed his diet*

rigour US **rigor** ['rɪgə] *noun* **(a)** being strict or severe; *we will pursue the case with the full rigour of the law* **(b)** rigours = harshness of the climate; *they rapidly succumbed to the rigours of the Siberian winter*

rig up ['rɪg 'ʌp] *verb* to arrange, to construct something quickly; *they rigged up a telescope in the garden*

rim [rɪm] *noun* **(a)** edge of something round, like a wheel or a cup; *the rim of the glass is chipped; see also* PACIFIC **(b)** frame of spectacles; *glasses with steel rims*

-rimmed ['rɪmd] *suffix* with a rim; *gold-rimmed spectacles*

rind [raɪnd] *noun* skin on fruit, bacon or cheese; *add the grated rind of a lemon; can you eat the rind of this cheese?*

ring [rɪŋ] **1** *noun* **(a)** round shape of metal, etc.; *she has a gold ring in her nose; he wears a ring on his little finger* **(b)** circle of people or things; *the teacher asked the children to sit in a ring round her* **(c)** noise of an electric bell; *there was a ring at the door* **(d)** phone call; *give me a ring tomorrow* **(e)** space where a circus show takes place, where a boxing match is held; *the clowns ran into the ring; the ringmaster came into the ring with his top hat and whip;* boxing ring = square area with a stiff canvas floor, surrounded with a rope fence, in which boxing matches take place; *the two boxers climbed into the ring* **2** *verb* **(a)** to make a sound with a bell; *the postman rang the doorbell; at Easter, all the church bells were ringing; if you ring your bicycle bell people will get out of the way; is that your phone ringing?* **(b)** to ring a bell = to remind someone of something; *the name rings a bell; does the name Arbuthnot ring any bells?* **(c)** to telephone; *he rang me to say he would be late; don't ring tomorrow afternoon - the office will be closed; don't ring me, I'll ring you* (NOTE: **ringing - rang** [ræŋ] **- has rung** [rʌŋ]) **3** *verb* **(a)** to draw a ring round something; *I have ringed the mistakes in red* **(b)** to surround; *rebel troops ringed the president's palace* (NOTE: **ringing - ringed**)

ring back ['rɪŋ 'bæk] *verb* to telephone to answer someone; *Mr Smith isn't in - can you ring back in half an hour?; she said she would ring back but she didn't*

ringfence ['rɪŋ 'fens] *verb* to separate something from other things, so that it is not affected by them; *the local authority's education budget has been ringfenced; they tried to ringfence their currency against international exchange rate fluctuations*

ringing ['rɪŋɪŋ] *noun* sound like that of bells; *I can hear a ringing in my ears - should I go to the doctor?*

ringleader ['rɪŋliːdə] *noun* person who organizes a revolt or some crime; *the government troops took control of the capital and arrested the ringleaders of the coup*

ringmaster ['rɪŋmɑːstə] *noun* person in charge of a circus performance; *the ringmaster came into the ring to start the show*

ring off ['rɪŋ 'ɒf] *verb* to put down the phone; *when I answered the phone, the caller rang off*

ring road ['rɪŋ 'rəʊd] *noun* road which goes right round a town; *instead of driving through the town centre, it will be quicker to take the ring road*

ring up ['rɪŋ 'ʌp] *verb* to make a telephone call; *I rang up his office to say I was going to be late; a Mr Smith rang you up while you were out; he rang up the police to say that his car had been stolen*

rink [rɪŋk] *noun* large enclosed area for ice skating, playing ice hockey, roller skating, etc.; *in the evening we all went to the skating rink*

rinse [rɪns] **1** *noun* **(a)** removing the soap from soapy washing or soapy hair by putting it in clean water; *give your shirt a good rinse* **(b)** coloured liquid for rinsing hair; *she used a blue rinse in her hair* **2** *verb* to put soapy or dirty things into clean water to remove the soap or the dirt; *rinse the dishes before putting them on the draining board to dry*

riot ['raɪət] **1** *noun* **(a)** wild disorder by a crowd of people; *the riot was started by some university students;* to run riot = to get out of control; *after the match, the supporters ran riot and the police had to intervene; in her stories for children she lets her imagination run riot;* to read someone the riot act = to warn someone to stop doing something; *I read her the riot act when I found she had been using the office telephone to call her mother in Australia* **(b)** mass of sounds or colours; *the place was decorated in a riot of colours; the colour scheme is a riot of reds and greens* **(c)** very amusing film, play, etc.; *the whole show was a riot, we never laughed so much* **2** *verb* to take part in a riot; to get out of control; *furious farmers rioted when they heard the decision of the Minister of Agriculture*

rioter ['raɪətə] *noun* person who takes part in a riot; *two of the rioters were killed in the clash with police*

rioting ['raɪətɪŋ] *noun* riots, outbreaks of civil disorder; *no rioting will be tolerated after the match*

riotous ['raɪətəs] *adjective* disorderly, as in a riot; *the crowd engaged in riotous behaviour; his birthday party was a riotous evening*

riot police ['raɪət 'pliːs] *noun* police specially trained and equipped to deal with rioters; *the riot police were ready to intervene when the rioters suddenly dispersed*

rip [rɪp] **1** *noun* tear (in cloth); *he lost the race because of a rip in his sail* **2** *verb* **(a)** to tear; *I ripped my sleeve on a nail; she ripped open the parcel to see what he* *had given her; the old bathroom is being ripped out and new units put in* **(b)** to go through something violently; *the tornado ripped through the town* **(c)** *(informal)* **to let rip** = to start to complain, protest, etc., without any restraint; *when he saw the bill for the meal he really let rip;* **to let something rip** = to let something go as fast as possible; *as he came into the last lap he opened up the throttle and let it rip; see also* RIP OFF (NOTE: **ripping - ripped**)

RIP [ɑːɑɪˈpiː] *abbreviation for the Latin phrase Requiescat in Pace meaning* Rest in Peace, often written on tombstones; *Thomas Hood R.I.P.*

ripe [raɪp] *adjective* **(a)** ready to eat or to be harvested; *don't eat that apple - it isn't ripe yet* **(b)** **the time is ripe** = it is the right time to do something; *the time is ripe to take steps to stop imports of the drug* (NOTE: **riper - ripest**)

ripen [ˈraɪpn] *verb* to become ripe; *these apples will ripen in October*

rip off [ˈrɪp ˈɒf] *verb* **(a)** to tear off; *it's the last day of the month so you can rip the page off the calendar;* *someone has ripped off the book's cover* **(b)** *(slang)* **rip someone off** = to cheat someone, to make someone pay too much; *they were ripped off in the market*

rip-off [ˈrɪpɒf] *noun* *(slang)* bad deal, thing which costs too much; *what a rip-off! - it's not worth half the price; that car was a rip-off - it had been involved in an accident and just repainted*

ripple [ˈrɪpl] **1** *noun* little wave; *even a little stone thrown into the water will make ripples; in the desert, the wind creates ripples on the sand; the news caused ripples through the financial world* **2** *verb* to make little waves; *the lake is like a mirror, there is no wind to ripple the water; the news rippled through the financial world*

rise [raɪz] **1** *noun* **(a)** movement or slope upwards; *there is a gentle rise until you get to the top of the hill; salaries are increasing to keep up with the rise in the cost of living; the recent rise in interest rates has made mortgages more expensive* **(b)** **pay rise** = increase in salary; *she asked the manager for a pay rise; he's had two rises this year; if I don't get a rise soon I'll start looking for another job* (NOTE: American English for this is **raise**) **(c)** *(formal)* **to give rise to something** = to make something happen; *the news gave rise to rumours about a coup* **2** *verb* **(a)** to go up; *the sun always rises in the east; the road rises steeply for a few miles; prices have been rising steadily all year; if you open the oven door, the cake won't rise properly* **(b)** *(formal)* to get up, to get out of bed or out of a chair; *he always rises early* **(c)** *(formal)* to stop being in session; *the court rose at one o'clock* (NOTE: **rising - rose** [rəʊz] **- has risen** [ˈrɪzn])

rising [ˈraɪzɪŋ] **1** *adjective* which is moving upwards, which is increasing; *the gliders took advantage of the rising currents of hot air; the magazine is all about the new young rising film stars; rising interest rates will hurt young families;* **the rising generation** = the next generation which will follow the present one; **he's rising fifty** = he's nearly fifty years old; *see also* DAMP **2** *noun* rebellion, revolt; *the government sent troops to put down the rising in the north*

risk [rɪsk] **1** *noun* **(a)** possible harm; *the risk of becoming blind is very remote; there is a financial risk attached to this deal; at the risk of looking foolish, I'm going to ask her to come out with me* **(b)** to run the

risk of = to be in danger of; *they run the risk of being caught by the customs; if you ask for a pay rise now, you run the risk of losing your job;* **to take a risk** = to do something which may make you lose money or suffer harm; *he's so careful, he never takes any risks; drive slowly, we're in no hurry and there's no need to take any risks on the icy road* **(c)** **at owner's risk** = the owner is responsible if something happens to his property; *cars are parked at owners' risk; goods left in the cloakroom are at owners' risk;* **fire risk** = situation or materials which could start a fire; *that room full of waste paper is a fire risk* **2** *verb* to do something which may possibly harm; *the fireman risked his life to save her; he risked all his savings on buying the bookshop*

risky [ˈrɪski] *adjective* which is dangerous; *he lost all his money in some risky ventures in South America; there is ice on the road, driving would be very risky* (NOTE: **riskier - riskiest**)

rissole [ˈrɪsəʊl] *noun* fried ball of minced meat, fish, etc.; *we ordered lamb rissoles and potatoes*

rite [raɪt] *noun* religious ceremony; **last rites** = religious service for someone who is dying; *my mother received the last rites just before she died* (NOTE: do not confuse with **right**)

ritual [ˈrɪtjuəl] **1** *adjective* referring to a religious ceremony; *the tribe performed a ritual rain dance* **2** *noun* **(a)** religious ceremony; *the ritual of the mass* **(b)** something which you do regularly in the same way; *every evening it's the same ritual: he puts the cat out and locks the door; we don't follow any particular ritual on Christmas day, we take the day as it comes*

rival [ˈraɪvl] **1** *adjective* competing, who competes; *two rival companies are trying to win the contract; is this the rival product you were talking about?; Simon and I are friends but we play for rival teams* **2** *noun* person who competes; company which competes; *do you know if he has any rivals?; we keep our prices low to undercut our biggest rival* **3** *verb* to compete with someone; to be of similar quality to someone; *it will not be easy to rival such a good product; 'l'Auberge' rivals any London French restaurant of the same size* (NOTE: **rivalling - rivalled** but American spelling is **rivaling - rivaled**)

rivalry [ˈraɪvəlri] *noun* competition; *there is intense rivalry between the two local teams*

river [ˈrɪvə] *noun* large mass of fresh water which runs across the land and goes into the sea or into a lake; *London is on the River Thames; the river is very deep here, so it's dangerous to swim in it* (NOTE: with names of rivers, you usually say **the River: the River Thames; the River Amazon; the River Nile**)

riverside [ˈrɪvəsaɪd] *adjective* on the banks of a river; *some riverside houses were flooded; we took our friends to a riverside pub on the Thames*

rivet [ˈrɪvɪt] **1** *noun* large metal pin which fastens metal plates together; *the workers were driving rivets into the metal sheets with huge hammers* **2** *verb* **(a)** to fasten metal plates together; *workmen riveted the sheets of metal together* **(b)** to attract someone's attention; *the audience was riveted by his stories; her eyes were riveted on the door, as if she expected someone to come in*

riveting [ˈrɪvɪtɪŋ] *adjective* which holds everyone's attention; *a riveting performance by the American dance company*

RNA [ɑːenˈeɪ] *abbreviation for* ribonucleic acid, one of the acids in the nucleus of all living cells, which takes information from DNA and translates it into enzymes and proteins

roach [rəutʃ] *noun US (informal)* cockroach (NOTE: plural is **roaches**)

road [rəud] *noun* (a) hard pathway used by cars, trucks, etc., to travel along; *the road to York goes directly north from London*; *drivers must be careful because roads are icy*; *children are taught to look both ways before crossing the road*; *what is your office address? - 26 London Road* (NOTE: often used in names: **London Road, York Road**, etc., and usually written **Rd: London Rd**, etc.) (b) **road signs** = signs put at the side of the road giving information to drivers; *if you come to a road sign saying 'Kingston', turn back because you will have gone too far*; *there are no road signs at that junction, but you must turn left* (c) **on the road** = travelling; *as a salesman, he's on the road thirty weeks a year*; *we were on the road for thirteen hours before we finally reached the hotel*

roadblock [ˈrəudblɒk] *noun* barrier put across a road by the police; *the police set up roadblocks round the town*

road hog [ˈrəud ˈhɒg] *noun (informal)* person who drives fast and dangerously; *she was knocked down by some road hog*

road rage [ˈrəud ˈreɪdʒ] *noun* violent attack by a driver on another car or its driver, caused by anger at the way the other driver has been driving; *there have been several incidents of road rage lately*; *in the latest road rage attack, the driver leapt out of his car and knocked a cyclist to the ground*

roadshow [ˈrəudʃəu] *noun* (a) broadcast from a place away from the normal studio; *the BBC holiday roadshow* (b) exhibition or performing group which goes from place to place; *they took their roadshow round the Highlands of Scotland*

roadside [ˈrəudsaɪd] **1** *noun* the side of a road; *we couldn't find a picnic area, so in the end we picnicked on the roadside*; *they had a puncture so they stopped by the roadside to change the wheel* **2** *adjective* the side of a road; *we had some coffee at a roadside café*

road tax [ˈrəud ˈtæks] *noun* tax paid by owners of cars, trucks, etc., to the government for permission to drive their vehicle on the road; *a tax disk shows that you have paid your road tax*

road user [ˈrəud ˈjuːzə] *noun* person who uses a road; *the government is proposing to tax car drivers and other road users*

roadway [ˈrəudweɪ] *noun* main surface of a road; *the lorry skidded and left the roadway*; *the slippery surface of the roadway made driving difficult* (NOTE: American English is **pavement**)

roadworks [ˈrəudwɜːks] *noun* repairs to a road; *it took longer than normal to get to Birmingham because of all the roadworks*

roam [rəum] *verb* to wander about without any particular destination; *drunken fans roamed around the streets smashing windows*; *he roamed the country looking for work*

roar [rɔː] **1** *noun* loud noise of shouting, of an engine, etc.; *the roar of the jet engines made it impossible for me to hear what she said*; *you could hear the roar of the crowd at the football match several miles away* **2** *verb* to make a loud noise; *he roared with laughter at the film*; *the lion roared and then attacked*

roaring [ˈrɔːrɪŋ] **1** *adjective* wild; **roaring fire** = big fire, with flames going up the chimney; *we sat in front of a roaring fire and ate roasted chestnuts*; **it's a roaring success** = it is extremely successful; *thousands of people came to the show, it was a roaring success*; **to do a roaring trade (in)** = to sell something rapidly; *the stand was doing a roaring trade selling home-made cakes and jam* **2** *noun* sound of loud, deep calls; *the roaring of lions near the camp kept us awake*

roast [rəust] **1** *verb* to cook over a fire or in an oven; *if you want the meat thoroughly cooked, roast it for a longer period at a lower temperature*; *you can either roast pigeons or cook them in a casserole*; **roasted chestnuts** = chestnuts cooked over red-hot charcoal **2** *adjective* which has been roasted; *what a lovely smell of roast meat!*; *we had roast chicken for dinner*; **roast potato** = potato baked in fat in an oven; *serve the meat with roast potatoes and green vegetables* (NOTE: although the verb has the forms **roasting - roasted**, when referring to meat, the adjective **roast** is used: **roast meat, roast turkey**, but **roasted peanuts, roasted chestnuts**) **3** *noun* meal with meat cooked in an oven; *we always have a roast on Sundays*

roasting [ˈrəustɪŋ] **1** *adjective* (a) used for roasting meat; *put the chicken in the roasting tin* (b) *(informal)* very hot; *let's go outside - it's roasting in here* **2** *noun (informal)* sharp criticism; *he'll get a roasting when his father hears about it*

rob [rɒb] *verb* to attack and steal from someone; *a gang robbed our local bank last night*; *the old lady was robbed of all her savings by a conman* (NOTE: **robbing - robbed**)

robber [ˈrɒbə] *noun* person who attacks and steals from someone; *the robbers attacked the bank in broad daylight*; *three of the robbers were caught*

robbery [ˈrɒbri] *noun* attacking and stealing; *there was a robbery in our street yesterday*; *did they ever find out who committed the bank robbery?* (NOTE: plural is **robberies**)

robe [rəub] *noun* **1** (a) long, loose dress for men or women; *the professors came onto the platform in their academic robes*; *the Arab sheikh rode up on a camel in his flowing robes* (b) *US* dressing gown, a long dress worn over pyjamas or nightdress **2** *verb (formal)* **to be robed in** = to be dressed in (a robe); *the priests stood robed in white by the altar*

robin [ˈrɒbɪn] *noun* common small brown bird with a red breast; *robins are common birds in Britain*; *every time I work in the garden, a robin comes and sits on the fence*

Robin Hood [ˈrɒbɪn ˈhud] *noun* legendary medieval bandit, who fought against the power of the nobility; *Robin Hood stole from the rich to give to the poor*

COMMENT: according to legend, Robin Hood was a nobleman who became an outlaw during the reign of Richard I, when the king was away at the Crusades and the country was run by his wicked brother John. Robin Hood lived with a band of outlaws in Sherwood Forest, near Nottingham, and fought against injustice by robbing the rich to give to the poor

robot ['rəʊbɒt] *noun* machine which is programmed to perform tasks automatically; *these cars are made by robots*

robust [rə'bʌst] *adjective* **(a)** strong, vigorous; *this young tree is very robust and should survive the winter; my grandmother is not very robust but she still manages to look after herself* **(b)** vigorous and determined; *he gave some robust answers to the journalists' questions*

robustly [rə'bʌstli] *adverb* in a vigorous way; *he answered his critics robustly*

rock [rɒk] **1** *noun* **(a)** large stone, large piece of stone; *the ship was breaking up on the rocks* **(b)** hard pink sweet shaped like a stick, often with the name of a town printed in it, bought mainly by tourists; *a stick of Brighton rock* **(c)** music with a strong rhythm; *rock (music) is the only music he listens to* **2** *verb* **(a)** to sway from side to side; to make something sway from side to side; *the little boat rocked in the wake of the ferry; the explosion rocked the town* (*informal*) **don't rock the boat** = don't do anything to disturb what has been arranged; *everything has been organized, so please don't rock the boat with any new suggestions* **(b)** to move from side to side, holding something; *the baby is crying, I'll try to rock him to sleep*

◊ **on the rocks** *phrase* **(a)** in great difficulties; *the company is on the rocks; their marriage is on the rocks* **(b)** served with ice; *a whisky on the rocks*

rock bottom ['rɒk 'bɒtəm] *noun* the lowest point; *sales have reached rock bottom*; **rock-bottom prices** = the lowest prices possible; *we can't give you a bigger discount - the prices quoted are rock-bottom prices*

rock cake ['rɒk 'keɪk] *noun* small cake with currants in it; *he ordered a cup of coffee and a rock cake*

rocker ['rɒkə] *noun* **(a)** semicircular wooden piece which a rocking chair stands on; *an old cradle with two rockers; she tripped over the rocker and hurt her ankle* **(b)** *US* rocking chair **(c)** (*slang*) **to be off your rocker** = to be mad; *he must be off his rocker to do something like that* **(d)** type of electric switch which rocks; *use the rocker switch to switch off the motor*

rocket ['rɒkɪt] **1** *noun* **(a)** type of firework which flies up into the sky; *we stood in the square and watched the rockets lighting up the sky* **(b)** type of bomb which is shot through space at an enemy; *they fired a homemade rocket into the police station* **(c)** **space rocket** = large device which is fired into space, carrying satellites, etc.; *the Americans are sending an unmanned rocket to Jupiter* **(d)** (*slang*) **to give someone a rocket** = to criticize someone sharply; *the manager gave him a rocket when he was late back from lunch; she'll get a rocket from the boss if he catches her on the phone to her boyfriend again* **(e)** type of green vegetable eaten in salads **2** *verb* to shoot upwards very fast; *prices have rocketed this summer*

rock garden *or* **rockery** ['rɒk 'gɑːdən *or* 'rɒkəri] *noun* small garden made of very large stones with plants growing between them or over them; *we grow alpines in our rock garden*

rocking chair ['rɒkɪŋ 'tʃeə] *noun* chair which rocks backwards and forwards on curved pieces of wood; *rocking chairs are marvellous to rock babies to sleep in*

rocking horse ['rɒkɪŋ 'hɔːs] *noun* child's toy, a large wooden horse on rockers, which you sit on and rock backwards and forwards

rock music ['rɒk 'mjuːzɪk] *noun* loud popular music with a strong rhythm; *he likes to listen to rock music on his Walkman*

rocky ['rɒki] *adjective* **(a)** full of rocks and large stones; *they followed a rocky path up the mountain* **(b)** (*informal*) difficult; *the company has had a rocky year; my brother and sister-in-law are going through a rocky patch at the moment* **(c)** **the Rocky Mountains** *or* **the Rockies** = range of high snow-capped mountains, running south from Canada into the western United States; *the majestic grandeur of the Rocky Mountains*

rod [rɒd] *noun* **(a)** long stick; *you need something rigid like a metal rod to hold the tent upright*; **fishing rod** = long stick with a line attached, used for fishing **(b)** (*informal*) **with an iron rod** *or* **with a rod of iron** = very strictly, without allowing any weakness; *the secretary of state rules his department with an iron rod; she's a tiny little woman but she rules the office with a rod of iron*

rode [rəʊd] *see* RIDE

rodent ['rəʊdənt] *noun* animal which chews and gnaws, such as a mouse, rat, etc.; *mice and rats are probably the best known rodents; did you know that squirrels are also rodents?*

rodeo [rəʊ'deɪəʊ] *noun* display of skill by cowboys; *they took us to a rodeo in Texas* (NOTE: plural is **rodeos**)

roe ['rəʊ] *noun* **(a)** eggs of fish; *they ate salmon roe on toast* **(b)** **roe deer** = type of deer, much smaller than red deer or fallow deer, found in Europe and Asia (NOTE: do not confuse with **row**)

rogue [rəʊg] *noun* **(a)** wicked or dishonest person; *that car dealer is a bit of a rogue - you shouldn't really trust him* **(b)** **rogue elephant** = (i) elephant driven out of the herd by the other elephants; (ii) person who does not act in the same way as others; *he's something of a rogue elephant - wild and unpredictable*

role [rəʊl] *noun* **(a)** part played by someone, in a play or film; *he plays the role of the king*; **title role** = part after which a play is named; *who's playing the title role in 'Hamlet'?* **(b)** part played by someone in real life; *he played an important role in getting the project off the ground* (NOTE: do not confuse with **roll**)

role model ['rəʊl 'mɒdl] *noun* person who should be taken as an example which others can copy; *she was the role model for thousands of young women*

role play ['rəʊl 'pleɪ] *noun* activity in which people each play the part of another person, as part of a training exercise; *part of the test is role playing - each candidate has to play a certain part*

roll [rəʊl] **1** *noun* **(a)** tube of something which has been turned over and over on itself; *a roll of fax paper; a roll of toilet paper or a toilet roll* **(b)** list of names; **to call the roll** = to read out the list of names to see if everyone is there; *see also* ROLLCALL; **roll of honour** = list of people who have done something special, such as students who have won prizes, or soldiers killed in battle **(c)** very small loaf of bread for one person, sometimes cut in half and used to make a sandwich; *will a tuna salad and a bread roll be enough for you?; the airline's continental breakfast was just a roll and a cup of coffee*; **cheese roll** *or* **ham roll** = roll with cheese or ham in it **(d)** **sausage roll** = small pastry with sausage meat inside; **Swiss roll** *US* **jelly roll** = cake made by rolling up a thin sheet of sponge cake covered with jam **(e)** action of rolling; *it takes time to get used to the roll of the ship*; *with a roll of her eyes and a shake of her head, she left the room* (NOTE: do not confuse with **role**) **2** *verb* **(a)** to make something go forward by turning it over and over; *he rolled the ball to the other player* **(b)** to go forward by turning over and over; *the ball rolled down the hill*; *my pound coin has rolled under the piano* **(c)** to make something move on wheels or rollers; *the table is fitted with wheels, just roll it into the room*; *the patient was rolled into the operating theatre ten minutes ago* **(d)** *(of a boat)* to move from side to side; *the ship rolled in the heavy seas*; *she rolled her eyes and pointed at the door* (NOTE: the other movement of a boat, where the front and back go up and down, is to **pitch**) **(e)** *US (informal)* to attack and rob someone

rollcall ['rəʊlkɔːl] *noun* reading of a list of names; *she missed the rollcall and was marked as absent*

rolled-up ['rəʊldʌp] *adjective* which has been rolled tightly; *she hit him with a rolled-up newspaper*

roller ['rəʊlə] *noun* **(a)** round object which rolls, such as one used for making lawns or cricket pitches flat; *the ground is so bumpy, you'll need a roller to flatten it*; *see also* STEAMROLLER **(b)** plastic tube used for rolling hair into curls; *she came to the door in her dressing gown and rollers* **(c)** *(informal)* Rolls Royce car; *hey, come for a ride in my new Roller!* **(d)** long large wave; *the Atlantic rollers in Cornwall are ideal for surfers*

rollerblades ['rəʊləbleɪdz] *noun* trademark for a type of in-line skate; *the young man on rollerblades zoomed past us at great speed*

rollerblader ['rəʊləbleɪdə] *noun* someone who goes on rollerblades

rollerblading ['rəʊləbleɪdɪŋ] *noun* sport of going on rollerblades; *rollerblading up and down the road is their 15-year-old son's favourite pastime* (NOTE: also called **in-line skating**)

roller coaster ['rəʊlə 'kəʊstə] *noun* **(a)** fairground railway which goes up and down steep slopes; *we all went for a ride on the roller coaster* **(b)** dangerous or risky series of events that cannot be controlled; *the government had a roller coaster ride during its first weeks in office*

roller skate ['rəʊlə skeɪt] **1** *noun* shoe with pairs of wheels side by side, on which you can glide along fast; *I have some roller skates but I'd love to have rollerblades* **2** *verb* to glide on roller skates; *I used to roller skate but I prefer rollerblading because it is so much faster*

roller skating ['rəʊlə 'skeɪtɪŋ] *noun* sport of going on roller skates; *is roller skating still popular with young people?*

rolling ['rəʊlɪŋ] *adjective* **(a)** **rolling countryside** = countryside which is a mass of small hills; **rolling pin** = wooden roller with handles, for flattening pastry; *I don't like making pastry so I've never owned a rolling pin*; **rolling stock** = carriages, wagons, engines used on a railway *(informal)* **rolling stone** = person who never lives long in one place **(b)** continuing from one period to another; **rolling plan** = plan which runs for a period of time, and is continuously updated for further periods; *we have a rolling twelve-month management plan* **(c)** *(informal)* **to be rolling in it** = to have a lot of money; *you've just got to see the inside of their house to see that they must be rolling in it*

roll up ['rəʊl 'ʌp] *verb* **(a)** to turn something flat over and over until it is a tube; *he rolled up the carpet* or *he rolled the carpet up*; *a hedgehog will roll up into a ball if you touch it* **(b)** *(informal)* to arrive; *they just rolled up and asked if we could put them up for the night*; *the bridegroom finally rolled up an hour late and said he'd had a puncture*

ROM [rɒm] *noun* = READ ONLY MEMORY computer memory with data programmed into it when it is manufactured, which can only be read, but not changed; *the file is stored in ROM*

Roman ['rəʊmən] **1** *adjective* referring to Rome, the capital of Italy and of the ancient Roman Empire; *a book about Roman emperors*; **Roman alphabet** = the alphabet used in many European languages (A, B, C, D, etc.), as opposed to the Greek or Russian alphabets; *the Inuit would like to preserve their own alphabet rather than use the Roman one*; **Roman candle** = type of firework giving a brilliant fountain of light; **Roman numerals** = numbers written as by the Ancient Romans (I, II, III, IV, etc.) (NOTE: Roman numerals are used for names of kings and queens) **2** *noun* **(a)** person who lives or lived in Rome; *the Romans invaded Britain in AD 43* **(b)** printing type with straight letters; *the book is set in Times Roman* (NOTE: the other two styles of print are **italic** and **bold**)

Roman Catholic ['rəʊmən 'kæθlɪk] **1** *adjective* referring to the Christian church of which the Pope is the head; *the Pope is the head of the Roman Catholic Church* **2** *noun* person who belongs to the Christian church of which the Pope is the head; *when the Pope visited the country thousands of Roman Catholics attended mass*

romance [rə'mæns] **1** *noun* **(a)** love affair; *she told us all about her holiday romance*; *their romance didn't last* **(b)** love story; *you'll enjoy this book if you like romances* **2** *adjective* **romance language** = language which comes from Latin; *French is a romance language, can you name any others?*

Romania [ruː'meɪnɪə] *noun* country in Eastern Europe, on the Black Sea, north of Bulgaria; *Romania is famous for its old monasteries* (NOTE: capital: **Bucharest**; people: **the Romanians**; language: **Romanian**; currency: **leu**)

Romanian [ruː'meɪnɪən] **1** *adjective* referring to Romania; *Romanian wines are exported to many European countries* **2** *noun* **(a)** person from Romania; *Romanians speak a Romance language* **(b)** language spoken in Romania; *she bought an English-Romanian dictionary*

romantic [rə'mæntɪk] **1** *adjective* **(a)** full of mystery and love; *we had a romantic candlelit dinner which I'll never forget*; *the atmosphere on the ship was very romantic*; **romantic novel** = novel which is a love story **(b)** *(literary or artistic style)* which is very imaginative; *which is based on personal emotions*; *his style is too romantic for my liking*; *the romantic period is not my favourite literary period* **2** *noun* **the Romantics** = writers writing at the beginning of the nineteenth century in a romantic style

romanticism [rə'mæntɪsɪzm] *noun* romantic literary style; *the romanticism of Wordsworth's early poetry*

romp [rɒmp] **1** *noun* playing by children energetically and noisily; *it was only a childish romp but it ended tragically* **2** *verb* **(a)** to play about energetically; *she* *was romping with her friends on the sofa when her mother came in* **(b) to romp home** = to win easily; *our local team romped home 6-2; the favourite romped home by several lengths*

roof [ru:f] *noun* **(a)** part of a building, etc., which covers it and protects it; *the cat walked across the roof of the greenhouse; she lives in a little cottage with a thatched roof* **(b)** top of the inside of the mouth; *I burnt the roof of my mouth drinking hot soup* **(c)** top of a car, bus, lorry, etc.; *we had to put the cases on the roof of the car;* **sunroof** = roof which you can open in fine weather; **roof rack** = frame fixed to the roof of a car for carrying luggage; *our car doesn't have a roof rack, so all the luggage had to go in the boot; they took the new table home on the roof rack*

rooftop ['ru:ftɒp] **1** *noun* top of a roof; *the plane flew low over the rooftops of the village* **2** *adjective* on the top of a roof; *the prisoners staged a rooftop protest*

rook [rʊk] *noun* **(a)** large black bird; *what is the difference between a rook and a crow?* - crows usually live in pairs, while rooks live in colonies **(b)** *(in chess)* one of two pieces used in chess, shaped like a little castle tower; *she took my last rook* (NOTE: also called **castle**)

rookery ['rʊkri] *noun* **(a)** group of rooks' nests; *the noise from the rookery next to the church is deafening* **(b)** colony of penguins, seals, etc.; *photographs of penguin rookeries in the Antarctic* (NOTE: plural is **rookeries**)

rookie ['rʊki] *noun (informal)* new recruit in the armed forces or in the police; *he was arrested by a rookie PC*

room [ru:m] *noun* **(a)** part of a building, divided from other parts by walls; *the flat has six rooms, plus kitchen and bathroom; we want an office with at least four rooms;* **dining room** = room where you eat; *see also* BATHROOM, BEDROOM, LIVING ROOM, etc. **(b)** bedroom in a hotel; *your room is 316 - here's your key; his room is just opposite mine;* **double room** = room for two people with a double bed; *do you have a double room for three nights?; do you prefer a double room with a double bed or a twin room with two beds?;* **single room** = room for one person; *I would like to book a single room for tomorrow night;* **twin room** = room for two people with two beds; **room service** = arrangement in a hotel where food or drink can be served in a guest's bedroom; *if we call room service, we can have food sent up to our room* **(c)** space for something; *the table is too big - it takes up a lot of room; there isn't enough room in the car for six people; we can't have a piano in our flat - there just isn't enough room;* **to make room for** = to squeeze up to give space for; *there is no way we can make room for another passenger;* **there's room for improvement** = things could be improved; *the system is better than it was, but there is still room for improvement* (NOTE: no plural in this meaning: **some room, no room, too much room**)

rooming-house ['ru:mɪŋhaʊs] *noun US* house with furnished rooms to let; *she stayed in a rooming-house on Bel Air Street*

room-mate ['ru:mmeɪt] *noun* person who shares a room with you, especially at college; *I'm meeting my old room-mate from college - I haven't seen her for years*

roomy ['ru:mi] *adjective* with plenty of space inside; *the new model is considerably roomier than the last one; they have bought a very roomy apartment overlooking the river* (NOTE: **roomier - roomiest**)

roost [ru:st] **1** *noun* perch where a bird sleeps; **to rule the roost** = be in charge, be the boss; *he's the MD, but it's his secretary who rules the roost in the firm* **2** *verb* **(a)** to perch asleep; *six chickens were roosting in the shed* **(b) to come home to roost** = to come back to have a bad effect on the person who did it; *his mistakes in investing on the stock market have come home to roost*

rooster ['ru:stə] *noun (mainly US)* male domestic chicken; *the rooster crowed in the farmyard and woke us all up* (NOTE: British English is usually **cockerel** or **cock**)

root [ru:t] *noun* part of a plant which goes down into the ground, and which takes nourishment from the soil; *I'm not surprised the plant died, it has hardly any roots (of a cutting)* **to take root** = to make roots; *the cuttings died, none of them took root;* **root crops** or **root vegetables** = vegetables which are grown for their roots which are eaten, such as carrots, turnips, etc.; *it is impossible to grow root vegetables in this kind of soil* (NOTE: do not confuse with **route**)

root about ['ru:t ə'baʊt] *verb* to look for something under a lot of other things; *she rooted about in her bag and finally produced her ticket*

root beer ['ru:t 'bɪə] *noun US* dark fizzy drink, flavoured with roots and herbs; *she bought a root beer and a hamburger*

rooted ['ru:tɪd] *adjective* **(a)** as if with roots; **rooted to the spot** = unable to move; *she stood rooted to the spot as the lorry came towards her* **(b)** strongly felt; *no one knows why she has a deeply rooted or deep-rooted fear of dogs*

root for ['ru:t 'fɔ:] *(informal)* **to root for a team** = to cheer a team on; *we are all rooting for our college team*

root up or **root out** ['ru:t 'ʌp or 'ru:t 'aʊt] *verb* **(a)** to pull up a plant with its roots; *I spent the morning rooting up weeds in the garden* **(b)** to remove something completely; *the police are trying to root out corruption*

rope [rəʊp] **1** *noun* **(a)** very thick cord; *you'll need a rope to pull the car out of the ditch; the burglar climbed down from the balcony on a rope* **(b) to learn the ropes** = to learn how to do something; *we send new salesmen out with an experienced rep to learn the ropes; (informal)* **it's money for old rope** = it's money which is easy to make **2** *verb* **(a)** to tie together with a rope; *the climbers roped themselves together; we roped the sofa onto the roof of the car* **(b) to rope someone in** = to get someone to help or to join in; *rope in as many people as you can, we need all the help we can get; she was roped in to deal with the children's tea* **(c) to rope off** = to cordon off, to stop people going into a place by putting a rope around it; *the VIP area has been roped off - you need a special ticket to get in*

rose [rəʊz] **1** *noun* **(a)** common garden flower with a strong scent; *he gave her a bunch of red roses; these roses have a beautiful scent* **(b)** common shrub with these strongly scented flowers; *wild roses were growing along the path* **2** *verb see* RISE

rosé [rəʊ'seɪ] *noun* pink wine which gets its colour from the black grape skins being left only for a short time in the fermenting mixture; *what sort of wine do you want - red, white or rosé?*

rosemary ['rəʊzməri] *noun* bush herb with spiky green leaves, used in cooking; *we had roast lamb with rosemary*

rosette [rə'set] *noun* ribbon bunched to look like a flower, used as a decoration or as a badge; *the winning horse paraded round the paddock with its rosette*; *the candidates stood on the platform all wearing their party rosettes*

roster ['rɒstə] *noun* list of duties which have to be done and the people who have to do them; *we are drawing up a new roster for the Saturday afternoon shift*; **duty roster** = list of times showing when each person is on duty; *have a look at the duty roster to see when you're next on duty*

rosy ['rəʊzi] *adjective* (a) bright pink and healthy; *the children had rosy cheeks when they came in from their walk* (b) very favourable; *our future is looking rosier than it has done for years* (NOTE: **rosier - rosiest**)

rot [rɒt] **1** *noun* decay; *once rot infects the roots, it will kill the plant quickly*; **dry rot** = decay in the wooden parts of a house caused by a fungus; *get rid of the dry rot before you do any other repairs to the house*; (*informal*) **the rot has set in** = things have begun to go badly wrong; *we thought things were going well, but then the rot set in and the shop had to close* **2** *verb* to decay, to go bad; *the wooden fence is not very old but it has already started to rot*; *see also* ROTTEN (NOTE: **rotting - rotted**)

rota ['rəʊtə] *noun* roster, list of duties which have to be done and the people who have to do them; *we are drawing up a new rota for the Saturday afternoon shift*

rotary ['rəʊtəri] *adjective* which turns round; **rotary lawnmower** = lawnmower which has blades like a propeller underneath; **rotary machine** *or* **rotary press** = printing press whose printing plate is curved and attached to a cylinder

rotate [rəʊ'teɪt] *verb* to turn round an axis like a wheel; *rotate the knob to the right to increase the volume*; *how long does it take the Earth to rotate fully?*

rotation [rəʊ'teɪʃn] *noun* (a) turning; *the rotation of the Earth round the sun* (b) taking turns; **rotation of crops** *or* **crop rotation** = system of cultivation where different crops are planted in consecutive growing seasons; *crop rotation reduces the effect of pests and diseases*

> COMMENT: the advantage of rotating crops are that pests which thrive on one crop are discouraged from spreading, and some crops, such as beans, actually enrich the soil for other crops which follow them

rotor ['rəʊtə] *noun* machinery which rotates, such as the motor that drives the blades of a helicopter; *don't get out until the rotor blades have stopped turning*

rotten ['rɒtən] *adjective* (a) decayed; *the apple looked nice on the outside, but inside it was rotten*; *don't walk on that plank, I think it is rotten* (b) (*informal*) miserable; *I had a rotten time at the party - no one would dance with me*; *we had rotten weather on holiday*; **to feel rotten** = (i) to feel ill; (ii) to feel ashamed; *yesterday I felt slightly unwell, but today I feel really rotten*; *I feel so rotten for having spoiled your party*

rotund [rə'tʌnd] *adjective* round and fat; *the inspector was a rotund little man in a dark coat*

rouble *US* **ruble** ['ru:bl] *noun* currency used in Russia

rouge [ru:ʒ] *noun* pink cream or powder which you put on your face to give yourself more colour; *she put rouge on her cheeks*

rough [rʌf] **1** *adjective* (a) not smooth, uneven; *the sea's rough today - I hope I won't be sick*; *we had a rough crossing from England to France*; *rub down any rough edges with sandpaper* (b) with a sharp, unpleasant taste; *this wine's a bit rough - but what can you expect for £2.99?* (c) approximate, not very accurate; *I made some rough calculations on the back of an envelope* (d) not finished; *he made a rough draft of the new design* (e) not gentle; *don't be rough when you're playing with the puppy* (NOTE: **rougher - roughest**) **2** *noun* (a) design which has not been finished; *she showed me some roughs for the new gardening magazine* (b) (*informal*) **to take the rough with the smooth** = to accept that there are bad times as well as good times (c) part of a golf course where the grass is not cut, the part along the sides of the fairway; *his ball went into the rough* **3** *verb* (a) (*informal*) **to rough it** = to live in uncomfortable conditions; *the four-star hotels are all full, so we'll just have to rough it in a bed and breakfast* (b) **to rough something out** = to make a rough design for something; *he roughed out the plan of the house on the back of an envelope* (c) (*informal*) **to rough someone up** = to attack someone; *when he refused to pay, the landlord sent some people round to rough him up* **4** *adverb* **to sleep rough** = to sleep in the open, on the pavement; *hundreds of young people were sleeping rough in doorways*

roughage ['rʌfɪdʒ] *noun* dietary fibre, fibrous matter in food which cannot be digested and passes out of the body; *bran is an important source of roughage*; *a diet that doesn't contain enough roughage is a possible cause of constipation* (NOTE: no plural)

rough and ready ['rʌf n 'redi] *adjective* approximate; not beautifully finished; *the plan is a bit rough and ready, but it will give you a general idea of what we want*; *I'm not too pleased with the work he did - it is a bit too rough and ready*

roughen ['rʌfn] *verb* to make rough, to become rough; *the sea is roughening - perhaps we should head for the nearest harbour*; *scrape the soles of your new shoes on the pavement to roughen them*

roughly ['rʌfli] *adverb* (a) in a rough way; *don't play so roughly with the children*; *the removal men threw the boxes of china roughly into the back of their van* (b) approximately, more or less; *there are roughly ten francs to the pound*; *the cost of building the new kitchen will be roughly £25,000*

roulette [ru:'let] *noun* game of chance where bets are made on the numbers in boxes on a flat rotating wheel where a small ball will lodge when the wheel stops turning; *he lost all his fortune playing roulette*; **Russian roulette** = game played with a revolver containing a single bullet: the magazine is spun round and the gun is then fired at the player's head; *they got drunk, and someone suggested a game of Russian roulette*

round [raʊnd] **1** *adjective* (a) with a shape like a circle; *in Chinese restaurants, you usually sit at round tables* (b) with a shape like a globe; *soccer is played* with a round ball, while a Rugby ball is oval; *people used to believe that the Earth was flat, not round* (c) in **round figures** = not totally accurate, but correct to the nearest 10 or 100; *expect to pay £5000 in round figures* **2** *adverb & preposition* (a) in a circular way; *the wheels of the lorry went round and round; the Earth goes round the Sun; he was the first person to sail round the world single-handed; we all sat round the table chatting* (b) towards the back; *she turned round when he tapped her on the shoulder; don't look round when you're driving on the motorway; he ran down the street and disappeared round a corner* (c) from one person to another; *they passed round a list of proposals; can you pass the plate of cakes round, please?*; **enough to go round** = enough for everyone; *there aren't enough glasses to go round* (d) in various places, here and there; *they spent the afternoon going round the town* (NOTE: **round** is used with many verbs: **go round, come round, talk round,** etc.) **3** *noun* (a) regular route for delivering; *the milkman starts his round at 5am*; **the postman's round** = the streets where a postman delivers mail every day; **a newspaper round** = the houses which a newspaper boy or girl delivers newspapers to every day; *our son started doing a newspaper round last week* (b) **round (of drinks)** = drinks bought by one person for a group of people; *it's my turn to buy the next round* (c) slice of bread; **a round of toast** = piece or pieces of toast made from one slice of bread; **a round of sandwiches** = two or four sandwiches made from two slices of bread (d) part of a competition; *those who answer all the questions correctly, go on to the next round; he was knocked out in the first round* (e) playing all the holes on a golf course; *I think we have time for one more round before it gets dark* (f) series of meetings; *a round of pay negotiations* (g) one bullet; *the police fired several rounds into the crowd of students* **4** *verb* to go round; *he rounded the corner and saw a crowd in front of him; the boat capsized as it was rounding the buoy*

roundabout ['raʊndəbaʊt] **1** *noun* (a) place where several roads meet, and traffic has to move in a circle; *when you get to the next roundabout, turn right* (NOTE: in American English, this is called a **traffic circle**) (b) *(in a children's playground)* heavy wheel which turns, and which children ride on; *the children all ran to get on the roundabout; a small child fell from the roundabout and hurt his leg badly* (c) *(in a fairground)* large mechanical amusement machine, which turns round and plays music, usually with horses to sit on which move up and down* (NOTE: also called **merry-go-round**; American English is **carousel**) **2** *adjective* not direct; *the taxi took a very roundabout route to get to Trafalgar Square*

round down ['raʊnd daʊn] *verb* to decrease to the nearest full figure; *the figures have been rounded down to the nearest dollar*

rounded ['raʊndɪd] *adjective* with a smooth or round shape; *the road leads up a valley with rounded hills covered with sheep; the table has a smooth rounded edge*

rounders ['raʊndəz] *noun* team game played with a bat and ball, where the batsman has to run round the pitch to score; *the children were playing rounders in the park* (NOTE: the game is similar to the American **baseball**)

Roundhead ['raʊndhed] *noun* nickname for a follower of the parliamentary side in the English Civil War (NOTE: the followers of the king (Charles I) were called **Cavaliers**)

round on ['raʊnd 'ɒn] *verb* to start to criticize someone suddenly; *he suddenly rounded on the poor waitress and reduced her to tears*

rounds [raʊndz] *noun* regular visits; *the doctor made his rounds of the patients*

round table conference ['raʊnd 'teɪbl 'kɒnfərəns] *noun* discussion or conference where all the delegates are on equal terms; *the government is trying to get the leaders of the various factions to come to a round table conference*

> COMMENT: called in this way because when you sit at a round table, everyone is of equal status

round-the-world ['raʊndðə'wɜːld] *adjective* which goes round the world, returning to the original departure point; *a round-the-world ticket allows you to stop in several places; twenty yachts are taking part in the round-the-world yacht race*

round trip ['raʊnd 'trɪp] *noun* journey from one place to another and back again; *by train, the round trip will cost £15; a round-trip ticket is cheaper than two one-way tickets*

round up ['raʊnd 'ʌp] *verb* (a) to gather people or animals together; *the secret police rounded up about fifty suspects and took them off in vans; she rounded up the children and took them into the museum; the farmer is out in the fields rounding up his sheep* (b) to increase to the nearest full figure; *the figures have been rounded up to the nearest dollar; I owed him £4.98 so I rounded it up to £5.00*

roundup ['raʊndʌp] *noun* summary; *here is a roundup of the day's news*

rouse [raʊz] *verb* (a) to wake someone who is sleeping; *the shouts of the firemen roused the sleeping patients* (b) to get someone to act; *the difficulty will be to rouse the chairman into action*; compare **AROUSE**

rousing ['raʊzɪŋ] *adjective* loud and noisy; *the party ended with everyone singing a rousing chorus of 'we won't go home till morning'; the winning team had a rousing reception from their fans*

rout [raʊt] **1** *noun* complete defeat of an army, a team, etc.; *the final match of the series ended in a rout for the home side* **2** *verb* (a) to defeat completely; *the enemy army was routed* (b) to search; **to rout someone** *or* **something out** = to pull someone or something out from where it was hidden; *we are trying to rout out any enemy snipers left hiding in the ruins*

route [ruːt *US also* raʊt] **1** *noun* (a) way to be followed to get to a destination; *we still have to decide which route we will take*; **bus route** = normal way which a bus follows; *the cinema is not on the bus route, we'll have to go there by car* (b) **en route** = on the way; *the tanker sank when she was en route to the Gulf* (c) **route march** = training march by soldiers (NOTE: do not confuse with **root**) **2** *verb* to send someone along a route; *the demonstration was routed along Pall Mall to St James' Park*

routine [ruː'tiːn] **1** *noun* (a) normal, regular way of doing things; *children don't like their routine to be changed; a change of routine might do you good; having a cup of coffee while reading the newspaper is* *part of his morning routine*; **daily routine** = things which you do every day; *buying a newspaper on his way to work and a bar of chocolate on his way home is all part of his daily routine* **(b)** instructions which carry out a task as part of a computer program; *the routine copies the screen display onto a printer*; *the RETURN instruction at the end of the routine sends control back to the main program* **(c)** sequence of dance steps; *the dancers were practising a very complicated routine* **2** *adjective* normal or everyday; *he went to the doctor for a routine checkup*; *we're making a routine check of the central heating boiler*

routinely [ruː'tiːnli] *adverb* in a routine way, done as a routine; *we routinely check the fire fighting equipment*

rove [rəuv] *verb (formal)* to wander about in a place; *the police went out to look for the bands of drunken football supporters roving the suburbs*

roving ['rəuvɪŋ] *adjective* going from place to place; *she is a roving ambassador for the United Nations*; *he's the BBC's roving reporter in South America*

row 1 *noun* **(a)** [rəu] line of things, side by side or one after the other; *he has a row of cabbages in the garden*; *they pulled down an old house to build a row of shops*; *I want two seats in the front row* **(b)** [rau] loud noise; *stop making that dreadful row!* **(c)** [rau] serious argument; *they had a row about who was responsible for the accident* **2** *verb* **(a)** [rəu] to make a boat go forward by using oars; *she rowed across the lake to fetch a doctor* **(b)** [rau] *(informal)* to argue; *they were rowing about who would pay the bill*

rowboat ['rəubəut] *noun US* = ROWING BOAT

rowdy ['raudi] **1** *adjective* making a great deal of noise; *a rowdy party in the flat next door kept us all awake* (NOTE: **rowdier - rowdiest**) **2** *noun (old)* rough person, who makes a lot of noise; *right-wing rowdies broke up the meeting* (NOTE: plural is **rowdies**)

rower ['rəuə] *noun* oarsman, person who rows; *the rowers were struggling to make progress against the strong headwind; see also* SCULLER

rowing ['rəuɪŋ] *noun* making a boat move by the use of oars; *I'm not good at rowing*; *the boys' school has a rowing club*; **rowing boat** = small boat for rowing; *we hired a rowing boat and went down the river* (NOTE: American English is **rowboat**)

royal ['rɔɪəl] **1** *adjective* referring to a king or queen; **the Royal Family** = family of a king or queen; **royal blue** = dark blue; **the royal we** *see* WE **2** *noun (informal)* **the Royals** = the members of the Royal Family; *did you read the latest about the Royals in this morning's paper?*

Royal Automobile Club (RAC) ['rɔɪəl 'ɔːtə'məubaɪl 'klʌb] *noun* British organization which offers services to its members, such as insurance, emergency repairs to vehicles, maps and guide books, etc.

royalist ['rɔɪəlɪst] *noun* person supporting rule by a king or queen; *the royalist army was defeated by Oliver Cromwell*

royalty ['rɔɪəlti] *noun* **(a)** members of a king's or queen's family; *please dress formally, there will be royalty present* (NOTE: no plural in this meaning) **(b)** money paid to the author of a book or an actor in a film, or the owner of land where oil is found, etc., as a percentage of sales; *do you receive royalties on the*

sales of your book?; *all royalty cheques are paid direct to my account in Switzerland* (NOTE: plural is **royalties**)

rpm [ɑːpiː'em] = REVOLUTIONS PER MINUTE

RSI ['ɑː 'es 'aɪ] = REPETITIVE STRAIN INJURY

RSPCA = ROYAL SOCIETY FOR THE PREVENTION OF CRUELTY TO ANIMALS

RSVP ['ɑː es viː 'piː] *abbreviation for the French phrase répondez s'il vous plaît, meaning 'please answer'* letters printed on an invitation asking the person invited to reply

Rt Hon = RIGHT HONOURABLE (NOTE: written before the name; often abbreviated to **Rt Hon**: the **Rt Hon William Gladstone, MP**)

rub [rʌb] **1** *verb* to move something across the surface of something else; *he rubbed his hands together to get them warm*; *these new shoes have rubbed against my heel and given me a blister*; *the cat rubbed herself against my legs* (NOTE: **rubbing - rubbed**) **2** *noun* action of rubbing; *she gave her shoes a quick rub to remove the dust*; *he hit his head on the low ceiling, and gave it a rub*

rubber ['rʌbə] *noun* **(a)** elastic material made from the sap of a tropical tree; *car tyres are made of rubber*; *many years ago, we visited a rubber plantation in Malaysia*; **rubber band** *see* ELASTIC BAND **(b)** piece of rubber used for removing pencil marks; *he used a rubber to try to rub out what he had written* (NOTE: the American equivalent is an **eraser**) **(c)** *especially US (informal)* condom, rubber contraceptive sheath; *did he wear a rubber?*

rubber stamp ['rʌbə 'stæmp] **1** *noun* stamp made of rubber, with words or figures cut on it, which is used for stamping documents; *we use this rubber stamp for marking letters as they are received* **2** *verb* to agree to something automatically without examining it; *the committee simply rubber-stamped the proposal* (NOTE: written with a hyphen when used as a verb)

rubbing ['rʌbɪŋ] *noun* **(a)** action of rubbing; *US* **rubbing alcohol** = pure alcohol used as an antiseptic **(b)** copy made by placing paper on something and rubbing the paper with a coloured pencil or wax crayon; **brass rubbing** = copy of a brass made in this way

rubbish ['rʌbɪʃ] *noun* **(a)** waste, things which are no use and are thrown away; *we had to step over heaps of rubbish to get to the restaurant*; **rubbish bin** = container for putting rubbish; *throw all those old cans into the rubbish bin* **(b)** worthless nonsense; *have you read the new bestseller? - it's rubbish!*; *he's talking rubbish, don't listen to him* (NOTE: no plural; note also American English is **garbage** *or* **trash**)

rubble ['rʌbl] *noun* small stones or broken bricks, etc., from damaged buildings, also used in making paths, etc.; *rescue workers dug through piles of rubble to look for survivors*; *rubble is used as the foundation for roads and walls* (NOTE: no plural)

rubella [ruː'belə] *noun* usually mild disease which gives a red rash but which can affect an unborn child if caught by a pregnant woman (NOTE: also called **German measles**)

rub in ['rʌb 'ɪn] *verb* **(a)** to make an ointment or cream enter the skin by rubbing; *she rubbed sun cream into her skin* **(b)** *(informal)* **don't rub it in** = don't go on talking about my mistake; *yes, I know I made a mistake, but please, don't rub it in*

ruble ['ruːbl] *see* ROUBLE

rub out ['rʌb 'aʊt] *verb* to remove a pencil mark with a rubber; *it's written in pencil so you can rub it out easily*

rub up ['rʌb 'ʌp] *verb (informal)* to rub someone up the wrong way = to make someone irritable; *she's in a bad mood, someone must have rubbed her up the wrong way*

ruby ['ruːbi] **1** *noun* red precious stone; *a necklace of rubies and pearls* (NOTE: plural is **rubies**) **2** *adjective* dark red (colour); *a glass of ruby red wine*

ruck [rʌk] **1** *noun* **(a)** ordinary crowd of people; *he wants to get out of the ruck and become a manager* **(b)** *(in Rugby)* group of players who fight for the ball when it is on the ground; *the big forward broke into the ruck* **(c)** crease in a fabric **2** *verb* to ruck (up) = to move up and make creases; *your shirt is all rucked up*

rucksack ['rʌksæk] *noun* bag carried on the back of a walker; *he put extra clothes and some water in his rucksack*; *a group of walkers with muddy boots and rucksacks came into the pub* (NOTE: larger bags are called **backpacks**)

rudder ['rʌdə] *noun* flat vertical plate at the stern of a boat or on the tail of an aircraft, used for steering; *after the rudder broke off they had to use an oar to steer with*

rudderless ['rʌdələs] *adjective* drifting, without anyone being in control; *the firm has been rudderless since the MD resigned*

ruddy ['rʌdi] *adjective* **(a)** red, fire-coloured; *a ruddy glow hung over the burning city*; *the little boys with their ruddy cheeks* **(b)** *(slang)* awful; *that ruddy dog - he's put dirty paw marks all over the kitchen floor* (NOTE: **ruddier - ruddiest**)

rude [ruːd] *adjective* not polite, likely to offend, trying to offend; *don't point at people - it's rude*; *the teacher asked who had written rude words on the board*; *he was rude to the teacher and has had bad marks ever since* (NOTE: **ruder - rudest**)

rudeness ['ruːdnəs] *noun* being rude; *he was sacked for his rudeness to the customers*

rudimentary [ruːdɪ'mentəri] *adjective* basic; not fully developed; *after a time, tadpoles develop rudimentary legs*; *her knowledge of French is hardly more than rudimentary*

rue [ruː] **1** *noun* bitter herb **2** *verb (formal)* to regret; *I rue the day when I said I would help her*

rueful ['ruːfʊl] *adjective* sorry or regretful; *there was a rueful look on her face when she read the results*

ruefully ['ruːfʊli] *adverb* in a rueful way; *he smiled ruefully and went away without a word*

ruffian ['rʌfiən] *noun (old)* violent man, usually a criminal; *a crowd of ruffians was waiting at the door*

ruffle ['rʌfl] **1** *noun* material or lace gathered into a bunch and used as decoration on clothes or curtains, etc.; *the curtains are edged with ruffles* **2** *verb* to disturb feathers or water or someone's hair; *the breeze ruffled the surface of the lake*; *she ruffled his hair*

ruffled ['rʌfəld] *adjective (informal)* flustered, bothered; *he seemed ruffled by the questions from the reporters*

rug [rʌg] *noun* **(a)** small carpet; *this beautiful rug comes from the Middle East* **(b)** thick blanket, especially one used when travelling; *put a rug over your knees if you're cold*; *we spread rugs on the grass to have our picnic*

rugby ['rʌgbi] *noun* **rugby football** = type of football played with an oval ball which is thrown as well as kicked; *can you tell me when and where the next rugby match is being played?*; **rugby ball** = type of oval ball used in rugby

COMMENT: the game developed from football (soccer) when, in 1823, a pupil at Rugby School picked up the ball and started to run with it. Subsequently, rules of play were developed, and an oval ball introduced. There are two forms of rugby: Rugby Union, which was until 1996 the amateur game, and is also the international game, and Rugby League, which has always been a professional game, played mainly in the north of England. There are fifteen players in a Rugby Union team and thirteen in a Rugby League team. Each match is divided into two 40-minute halves separated by a 10-minute interval. Players can pick up the ball and run with it but are not allowed to pass forward, and players with the ball can be tackled and brought to the ground. Points are scored by touching the ground with the ball behind the opponents' goal line (a try) and by kicking the ball over a crossbar between two posts (a conversion). A try counts as 5 points in Rugby Union and 4 points in Rugby League; a conversion counts as 3 points in Rugby Union and 2 points in Rugby League

rugged ['rʌgɪd] *adjective* **(a)** rough, rocky, uneven; *the rugged landscape of the moon* **(b)** tough and sturdy; *at school, he rapidly developed a rugged independence*

rugger ['rʌgə] *noun (informal)* rugby football; *we beat them at rugger, but they beat us at cricket*; *compare* SOCCER

ruin ['ruːɪn] **1** *noun* **(a)** complete loss of all your money; *he faces complete ruin* **(b)** remains of an old building with no roof, fallen walls, etc.; *the house was a total ruin when I bought it* **2** *verb* **(a)** to wreck or to spoil completely; *our holiday was ruined by the weather* **(b)** to bring to financial collapse; *the bank failure ruined a lot of businesses*

ruined ['ruːɪnd] *adjective* **(a)** in ruins; *smoke rose from the ruined houses* **(b)** bankrupt, not able to pay your debts; *a ruined company director*

ruinous ['ruːnəs] *adjective* extremely expensive; *the cost of living in central London is quite ruinous*

ruinously ['ruːnəsli] *adverb* **ruinously expensive** = so expensive as to make you bankrupt; *hospital treatment in the USA can be ruinously expensive if you don't have health insurance*; *we took my in-laws out for a ruinously expensive meal*

ruins ['ruːɪnz] *noun* remains of old buildings with no roofs, fallen walls, etc.; *the ruins of the house are still smoking*; **in ruins** = wrecked; *the town was in ruins after the war*; *after being arrested at the night club, his career was in ruins*

rule [ruːl] **1** *noun* **(a)** strict order of the way to behave; *there are no rules that forbid parking here at night*; *according to the rules, your ticket must be paid for two weeks in advance*; **against the rules** = not as the rules say; *you can't hold the football in your hands - it's against the rules* **(b)** **as a rule** = usually; *as a rule, we go to bed early during the week* **(c)** **rule of thumb** =

easily remembered way of doing a simple calculation; *as a rule of thumb you can calculate that a pound is half a kilo* **(d)** government; *the country prospered under the rule of the generals* **2** *verb* **(a)** to govern or to control; *the president rules the country according to very old-fashioned principles*; *who rules here, the MD or his wife?* **(b)** to give an official or legal decision; *the judge ruled that the documents had to be brought to the court* **(c)** to draw a straight line using a ruler; **ruled paper** = paper with lines on it

rule of law ['ru:l əv 'lɔ:] *noun* principle that everyone, including the government, has to obey the laws of the land, and that no one shall be punished without a fair trial; *the rule of law has to be enforced*

rule out ['ru:l 'aut] *verb* to leave something out, not to consider something; *you can rule out the possibility of leaving tomorrow*; *you can rule me out - I'm much too tired to go dancing*; *only graduates should apply, so that rules me out*; *I wouldn't rule out the possibility of the voters staying at home on polling day*

ruler ['ru:lə] *noun* **(a)** person who governs; *a ruler should be fair*; *he's the ruler of a small African state* **(b)** strip of wood or plastic with measurements marked on it, used for measuring and drawing straight lines; *you need a ruler to draw straight lines*

ruling ['ru:lɪŋ] **1** *adjective* **(a)** in power, governing; **ruling party** = party which forms the government; *the ruling party is not very popular and will not succeed in winning enough votes* **(b)** in operation at the moment; *we will invoice at ruling prices* **2** *noun* legal decision made by a judge, arbitrator, etc.; *the judge will give a ruling on the case next week*; *according to the ruling of the court, the contract was illegal*

rum [rʌm] **1** *noun* alcoholic drink made from the juice of sugar cane; *she had a glass of rum and pineapple juice* **2** *adjective (old)* odd or strange; *we found ourselves in a very rum situation*

rumble ['rʌmbl] **1** *noun* **(a)** low rolling noise; *we were woken by the rumble of trains passing over the bridge*; *there was a rumble of thunder in the distance* **(b)** *US (informal)* gang fight in the street **2** *verb* **(a)** to make a low rolling noise; *wooden carts full of stone rumbled past*; *thunder rumbled in the distance*; *I'm so hungry my tummy's rumbling* **(b)** *(informal)* to realize that someone is trying to deceive you; *he got away with it for a time but eventually we rumbled him*

rumbling ['rʌmblɪŋ] *noun* **(a)** low rolling noise; *the rumbling of the thunder in the distance* **(b)** **rumblings** = murmuring by people showing that they are not happy; *there were rumblings of discontent among the sales staff*

rummage ['rʌmɪdʒ] **1** *noun* **(a)** searching about for something; *we had a good rummage in the loft but couldn't find the book* **(b)** *US* **rummage sale** = sale of unwanted objects for a charity (NOTE: British English is **jumble sale**) **2** *verb* to search about for something; *she rummaged in her drawer until she found the pair of gloves*

rummy ['rʌmi] *noun* card game where each player tries to collect sets of similar cards or several cards in sequence; *we sat playing rummy all evening*

rumour *US* **rumor** ['ru:mə] **1** *noun* story spread from one person to another but which may not be true; *there's a rumour going around that John's finally getting married* **2** *verb* to spread a story; *it was*

rumoured in the press that they were about to get divorced

rumoured *US* **rumored** ['ru:məd] *adjective* spread by rumour; *the rumoured takeover never took place*

rump [rʌmp] *noun* **(a)** back part of an animal; **rump steak** = thick slice of beef cut from above the leg and considered to have the best flavour **(b)** small number of members of a party left after an election defeat; *the rump of the party met after the election to decide what to do*

run [rʌn] **1** *noun* **(a)** going quickly on foot as a sport; *she entered for the 10-mile run*; *I always go for a run before breakfast*; *you must be tired out after that long run* **(b)** short trip in a car; *let's go for a run down to the coast* **(c)** making a machine work; **test run** = trial made on a machine; *a test run will help you to see if the machine is working properly* **(d)** rush to buy something; *the Post Office reported a run on the new stamps* **(e)** regular route of a plane, bus, etc.; *on this run, the bus does not go as far as the Post Office*; *she's a stewardess on the London - New York run* **(f)** score of 1 in cricket; *he made 45 runs before he was out* **(g)** *US* series of little holes in stockings or tights; *I can't wear these stockings because there's a run in them* (NOTE: British English for this is **ladder**) **2** *verb* **(a)** to go quickly on foot; *when she heard the telephone, she ran upstairs*; *children must be taught not to run across the road*; *she's running in the 200 metre race; see also* CLAPPERS, WIND **(b)** *(of buses, trains, etc.)* to be working; *all underground trains are running late because of the accident*; *this bus doesn't run on Sundays* **(c)** *(of machines)* to work; *he left his car in the street with the engine running*; *my car's not running very well at the moment* **(d)** to go; *the main street of the town runs north and south*; *the film runs for three hours* **(e)** to direct, to organize a business, a club, etc.; *he runs a chain of shoe shops*; *I want someone to run the sales department for me when I'm away on holiday*; *he runs the local youth club*; *the country is run by the army* **(f)** to use a car regularly; *we can't afford to run two cars* **(g)** to drive by car; *let me run you to the station* **(h)** to be in force; *the lease has only six months more to run* **(i)** to amount to; *the costs ran into thousands of pounds* **(j)** **to run a bath** = to fill a bath with water; *don't run a bath now, there is no hot water* **(k)** *(of liquid)* to flow, to move along smoothly; *the river runs past our house*; *this colour won't run* = the colour will not stain other clothes if they are all washed together **(l)** **to run in a family** = to be an inherited trait; *red hair runs in their family* **(m)** to publish a story in several editions of a newspaper; *the paper is running an explosive story about the minister's wife* (NOTE: **running - ran** [ræn] - **has run**)

run across ['rʌn ə'krɒs] *verb* **(a)** to cross quickly on foot; *the little boy ran across the road after his ball* **(b)** to find or to meet by accident; *I ran across it in a secondhand bookshop*

run after ['rʌn 'ɑ:ftə] *verb* to follow someone fast; *he ran after the postman to give back the letter which was wrongly addressed*; *the dog never runs after the dustman, only the postman*

run away ['rʌn ə'wei] *verb* **(a)** to escape, to go away fast; *they were running away from the police*; *she ran away from school when she was 16*; *the youngsters ran away to Paris* **(b)** **to run away with someone** = to go away from your family to live with someone or to marry someone; *she ran away with the postman*; **to let your imagination run away with you** = to think things are possible when they are not; *don't let your imagination run away with you!*

runaway ['rʌnəweɪ] **1** *noun* person who has run away from home; *the police are looking for the runaways* **2** *adjective* which is out of control; *the runaway train stopped at the bottom of the hill*; **runaway success** = great success; *her first exhibition was a runaway success*

run down ['rʌn 'daun] *verb* **(a)** to go down quickly on foot; *she ran down the stairs two at a time*; *can you run down to the village and buy me some bread?* **(b)** *(of clock, machine)* to stop working or go slower because of lack of power; *the clock has stopped - the battery must have run down* **(c)** to criticize someone; *it's not fair to run him down when he's not there to defend himself* **(d)** to reduce the quantity of something; *we're running down our stocks of coal before the summer* **(e)** to knock down with a vehicle; *she was run down by a car which did not stop*

run-down ['rʌndaun] **1** *adjective* **(a)** unwell or tired; *if you feel run-down, ask the chemist for vitamins* **(b)** dilapidated, not looked after; *he drives a run-down old car* **2** *noun* summary; *give me a quick run-down on what happened at the meeting*

runes [ru:nz] *noun* ancient form of writing, used in Germany and then in Northern Europe in the early Middle Ages; **to read the runes** = to try to understand something mysterious; *reading the runes, he decided that the government was planning to hold an early general election*

> COMMENT: runes date back to the 2nd or 3rd century AD, and are based on Greek or Roman letters, adapted to make them suitable for carving on stone or wood

run for ['rʌn 'fɔ:] *verb* **(a)** to go fast to try to catch; *he ran for the bus but it left before he got to the stop* **(b)** to be a candidate for an office; *he's running for president*

rung [rʌŋ] **1** *noun* one of the bars on a ladder; *if you stand on the top rung you can climb onto the roof*; *put your foot on the lower rung to steady the ladder* **2** *verb* see RING

run-in ['rʌnɪn] *noun* (*informal*) argument; *he's had several run-ins with the police*

run into ['rʌn 'ɪntu] *verb* **(a)** to go into a place fast; *she ran into the street, shouting 'Fire!'* **(b)** to go fast and hit something (usually in a vehicle); *he didn't look where he was going and ran into an old lady*; *the bus ran down the hill and into a lamppost* **(c)** to amount to; *costs have run into thousands of pounds*; *her income runs into five figures* **(d)** to find someone by chance; *I ran into him again in a café on the South Bank*

runner ['rʌnə] *noun* **(a)** person or horse running in a race; *my horse came in last of seven runners*; *there are 40,000 runners in the London Marathon* **(b)** shoot of a plant which makes roots where it touches the soil; *strawberry plants are propagated by the runners they produce*; **runner bean** = type of climbing bean **(c)** sharp blade of a skate or of a sledge; *one of the runners of the sledge is damaged, so you can't use it*

runner-up [rʌnə'ʌp] *noun* person who comes after the winner in a race or competition; *Natasha won the competition and her younger brother was runner-up*;

France won the World Cup and Brazil were runners-up (NOTE: plural is **runners-up**)

running ['rʌnɪŋ] **1** *adjective* **(a)** which runs; **running battle** = battle which moves around from place to place; *the police were engaged in running battles with the protesters*; **running commentary** = commentary on an action while the action is taking place; *the BBC reporter gave a running commentary on the riots from his hotel window*; **running total** = total which is carried from one column of figures to the next; *the running total appears at the bottom of the first column and at the top of the next one*; **running water** = water which is available in a house through water mains and taps; *I'm not sure that all the houses in the village have running water*; *there is hot and cold running water in all the rooms* **(b)** used when running a race; **running shorts**; **running shoes** **(c)** **for three days running** = one day after another for three days; *the company have made a profit for the sixth year running* **2** *noun* **(a)** race; **to be in the running for** = to be a candidate for; *three candidates are in the running for the post of chairman*; **out of the running** = with no chance of doing something; *she's out of the running for the job in the bookshop* **(b)** action of managing; *I now leave the running of the firm to my son*

running mate ['rʌnɪŋ 'meɪt] *noun* person who stands for election with another more important candidate (as when two candidates offer themselves for the posts of President and Vice-President); *he chose Senator Brown as his running mate*

runny ['rʌni] *adjective* liquid; *do you prefer honey when it is runny or when it is set?*; **he's got a runny nose** = his nose is dripping because he has a cold

run-of-the-mill ['rʌnəvðəmɪl] *adjective* ordinary; *it's just an ordinary run-of-the-mill Italian restaurant*

run off ['rʌn 'ɒf] *verb* **(a)** to go away fast; *he grabbed the watch and ran off down the street* **(b)** to print using a machine; *she ran off a few photocopies of the leaflet*

run off with ['rʌn 'ɒf 'wɪð] *verb* **(a)** to go away with someone; *he ran off with the girl next door and phoned his parents to say they had gone to Paris* **(b)** to steal something and go away; *the secretary ran off with our petty cash*

run on ['rʌn 'ɒn] *verb* **(a)** to continue; *the text runs on to the next page*; *does the play run on until very late?* **(b)** to use something as a fuel; *the machine runs on electricity*

run out ['rʌn 'aut] *verb* **(a)** to run out of something = to have nothing left of something; *the car ran out of petrol on the motorway*; *I must go to the supermarket - we're running out of butter* **(b)** (*informal*) to run out on someone = to leave someone suddenly; *she ran out on him when he lost his job*

run over ['rʌn 'əuvə] *verb* **(a)** to knock someone down by hitting them with a vehicle; *she was run over by a taxi*; *the car ran over a dog* **(b)** to continue; *the description of the accident runs over two pages*

run through ['rʌn 'θru:] *verb* **(a)** to read a list rapidly; *let's run through the agenda before the meeting starts to see if there are any problem areas*; *she ran through the paragraph again to make sure she understood what it meant*; *we must run through the list of guests to see if we have forgotten anyone* **(b)** to use up; *we have run through our entire stock of wine* *in one weekend* (c) to repeat; *just run through that scene again to see if you all know your lines*

run up ['rʌn 'ʌp] *verb* (a) to go up quickly on foot; *she ran up the stairs carrying a thermometer; the runner have to run up the mountain and back again* (b) **to run up to** = to come closer quickly on foot; *he ran up to the policeman and asked him to call an ambulance* (c) to make debts go up quickly; *the business was running up debts of thousands of pounds each week* (d) to sew something quickly; *I can run up a cushion cover in less than an hour*

run-up ['rʌnʌp] *noun* (a) period leading up to some event; *in the run-up to the election* (b) *(in sport)* run of an athlete before jumping, throwing, etc.; *a long jumper uses his run-up to gather speed before jumping*

run up against ['rʌn 'ʌp ə'genst] *verb* to find your way blocked by something; *whatever we try to do, we seem to run up against local regulations; we ran up against unexpected difficulties*

runway ['rʌnweɪ] *noun* track on which planes land and take off at an airport; *the plane went out onto the runway and then stopped for half an hour*

rupee [ru:'pi:] *noun* currency used in India, Pakistan and some other countries; *the prices in our catalogue are quoted in rupees*

rupture ['rʌptʃə] 1 *noun* (a) hernia, condition where an organ bulges through a hole or weakness in the wall which surrounds it; *you'll give yourself a rupture, lifting that box!* (b) sudden disagreement which ends discussions, etc.; *the rupture of the negotiations has ruined any chance of peace* (c) break or burst; *we are losing pressure, there must be a rupture in the pipeline* 2 *verb* to break or burst; *a water main ruptured and the centre of town was flooded;* **to rupture yourself** = to give yourself a hernia; *he ruptured himself lifting a heavy box*

rural ['ruərəl] *adjective* referring to the countryside; *rural roads are usually fairly narrow; we live quite close to a town but the country round us still looks very rural*

ruse ['ru:z] *noun* clever trick; *it's just a ruse on the part of the police to get him to confess*

rush [rʌʃ] 1 *noun* (a) fast movement; *there was a rush of hot air when they opened the door; there has been a rush to change pounds to francs; when the film ended there was a rush for the loos;* **rush job** = job which has to be done fast; *it is a rush job that needs to be dealt with immediately* (NOTE: no plural in this meaning) (b) type of wild grass growing in water; *rushes grow along the shores of lakes and rivers* (NOTE: plural in this meaning is **rushes**) (c) **rushes** = first prints of a film which are shown before being edited 2 *verb* to hurry, to go forward fast; *the ambulance rushed to the accident; crowds of shoppers rushed to the shops on the first day of the sales;* **don't rush me** = don't keep on making me hurry; *I need time to do this work, please don't rush me*

rushed [rʌʃt] *adjective* done very quickly; *I'm sorry the meal was a bit rushed, but I have to get back to work; he had time for a rushed cup of coffee and then went back to the meeting*

rush hour ['rʌʃ 'auə] *noun* time of day when traffic is bad, when trains are full, etc.; *avoid the rush hour if you don't want to get stuck in the traffic; his taxi was stuck in the rush-hour traffic*

rush into ['rʌʃ 'ɪntu] *verb* (a) to go into a place quickly; *he rushed into the room waving a piece of paper* (b) to get into a position too quickly, without really thinking; *don't rush into marriage if you're doubtful about your partner*

rusk [rʌsk] *noun* hard sweet biscuit given to babies to chew on

Russia ['rʌʃə] *proper noun* large country in Eastern Europe, covering also a large part of Asia up to the Pacific Ocean; *have you ever been to Russia?; he went on a journey across Russia* (NOTE: capital: **Moscow**; people: **Russians**; language: **Russian**; currency: **rouble**)

Russian ['rʌʃn] 1 *adjective* referring to Russia; *she speaks English with a Russian accent; Russian winters can be extremely cold; see also* ROULETTE 2 *noun* (a) person from Russia; *are there any Russians in the group?* (b) language spoken in Russia; *we'll start the Russian lesson by learning the alphabet; he can speak Russian quite well*

rust [rʌst] 1 *noun* orange covering formed on iron or steel which is left in damp air; *there is a bit of rust on the bonnet of the car* 2 *verb* to form rust; *don't leave the hammer and screwdriver in the rain - they'll rust*

rustic ['rʌstɪk] 1 *adjective* (a) of country style; *they live in a little rustic cottage on the edge of a lake* (b) rough, not elegant; *we bought a rustic bench and table for eating in the garden* 2 *noun* peasant; *three rustics sat on a bench outside the village pub*

rustle ['rʌsl] 1 *noun* noise of dry leaves, pieces of paper, etc., rubbing together; *listen to the rustle of the dry leaves in the hedge* 2 *verb* to make a soft crackling noise; *her long skirt rustled as she sat down; don't rustle the newspaper, I can't hear the radio*

rustle up ['rʌsl 'ʌp] *verb (informal)* to get something ready quickly; *can you rustle up some sandwiches?; she rustled up a dinner for six people at half an hour's notice*

rusty ['rʌsti] *adjective* (a) covered with rust; *he tried to cut the string with a pair of rusty old scissors* (b) out of practice; *my German used to be good, but it is very rusty now* (NOTE: **rustier - rustiest**)

rut [rʌt] *noun* (a) deep track made in soft earth by the wheels of vehicles; *the front wheel of the car is stuck in a deep rut* (b) *(informal)* **to get into a rut** = to start to lead a dull life with no excitement; *go out, see friends, travel, but don't allow yourself to get into a rut*

rutabaga ['ru:təbeɪgə] *noun US* swede, a common root vegetable

ruthless ['ru:θləs] *adjective* pitiless, cruel; *the new dictator is just as ruthless as the man he displaced; the manager has the reputation for being ruthless with employees who don't pull their weight*

ruthlessly ['ru:θəsli] *adverb* in a ruthless way; *he behaved ruthlessly towards his family; the accounts department has ruthlessly cut back our expenses*

ruthlessness ['ru:θəsnəs] *noun* cruelty, acting without pity; *his ruthlessness in dealing with waste in the office*

RV = RECREATIONAL VEHICLE

rye [raɪ] *noun* (a) type of dark brown cereal, used to make bread and American whiskey; *they are harvesting the rye today* (b) glass of American whiskey; *a large rye and soda, please* (NOTE: do not confuse with **wry**)

Ss

S, s [es] nineteenth letter of the alphabet, between R and T; *'she sells seashells on the seashore' - how many S's are there in that?*

sabotage ['sæbətɑ:ʒ] **1** *noun* malicious or deliberate destruction; *acts of sabotage were committed against the company's oil installations* (NOTE: no plural) **2** *verb* to destroy, to render useless deliberately; *he sabotaged the whole plan by passing the details to the police*

saboteur [sæbə'tɜ:] *noun* person who commits sabotage; *saboteurs got into the nuclear waste site and set off alarms*

sabre US **saber** ['seibə] *noun* sword with curved blade; *he led the charge on horseback, waving a sabre*

sac [sæk] *noun* part of an animal or plant shaped like a bag

saccharin ['sækərin] *noun* substance used as a substitute for sugar; *I've given up sugar and take saccharin instead*

sachet ['sæʃei] *noun* small plastic or paper bag containing something; *there are sachets of shampoo in the bathroom; each bedroom has an electric kettle, tea bags and sachets of instant coffee*

sack [sæk] **1** *noun* **(a)** large bag made of strong cloth or paper, used for carrying heavy things; *he hurt his back lifting up the sack of potatoes* **(b)** *(informal)* **to get** *or* **to be given the sack** = to be dismissed from a job; *you'll get the sack if you talk to the boss like that* **(c)** complete destruction of a town; *the sack of Rome by the barbarians* **2** *verb* **(a)** *(informal)* to dismiss someone from a job; *he was sacked after being late for work* **(b)** to destroy a town completely; *the town was captured and sacked by the barbarians*

sacking ['sækiŋ] *noun* **(a)** dismissal from a job; *the union protested against the sackings* **(b)** coarse material from which sacks are made hemp is used to make ropes and sacking **(c)** old sacks; *there's a heap of sacking over there in the corner of the warehouse* (NOTE: no plural in meanings (b) and (c))

sacrament ['sækrəmənt] *noun* **(a)** Christian religious ceremony; *the sacrament of marriage* **(b)** the consecrated bread and wine taken at Communion

sacred ['seikrəd] *adjective* **(a)** associated with religion; *the sacred texts were kept locked away;* **sacred art** = paintings of Christian religious scenes; **sacred music** = music to be played at Christian religious ceremonies; *(on a gravestone)* **sacred to the memory of** = remembering someone who has died **(b)** holy; *the hill is considered sacred by the local people; Hindus believe that cattle are sacred* **(c)** respected; *nothing is sacred to a reporter chasing a good story; she believed it was her sacred duty to look after his garden while he was away*

sacred cow ['seikrɪd 'kəʊ] *noun (informal)* belief or idea which is not to be criticized; *the sacred cow of the welfare state was attacked in Parliament for the first time today*

sacrifice ['sækrɪfaɪs] **1** *noun* **(a)** things which you give up to achieve something more important; *he finally won the competition, but at great personal sacrifice; she made many financial sacrifices to get her children through university* **(b)** making an offering to a god by killing an animal or person; *he ordered the sacrifice of two lambs to please the gods* **(c)** animal offered to a god; *cockerels, lambs and goats were all offered as sacrifices to their gods; Romans used to foretell the future by examining the entrails of animals killed as sacrifices* **2** *verb* **(a)** to give up; *I have sacrificed my career to be able to stay at home and bring up my children; she has sacrificed herself for the cause of animal welfare* **(b)** to offer something as a sacrifice; *the priests sacrificed a goat to the goddess*

sacrificial [sækrɪ'fɪʃl] *adjective* as a sacrifice; *they brought a goat to the temple as a sacrificial offering*

sacrilege ['sækrɪlɪdʒ] *noun* **(a)** using something sacred in a way which lacks respect; *the sacrilege committed by the soldiers when they put their horses in the church* **(b)** doing something which is not considered to be correct; *he committed the sacrilege of serving sweet white wine with steak*

sacrilegious [sækrɪ'lɪdʒəs] *adjective* referring to sacrilege; *in India it is considered sacrilegious to harm sacred cows*

sad [sæd] *adjective* **(a)** not happy, miserable; *he's sad because the holidays have come to an end; what a sad film! - everyone was crying; reading his poems makes me sad; it was sad to leave the house for the last time; he felt sad watching the boat sail away; it's sad that he can't come to see her; isn't it sad about her little boy being in hospital?* **(b)** *(slang)* boring, unfashionable; *only sad people collect stamps* (NOTE: **sadder - saddest**)

sadden ['sædn] *verb* to make unhappy; *he was saddened to see the old house in ruins; it saddens me that I will never see England again*

saddle ['sædl] **1** *noun* **(a)** rider's seat on a bicycle or motorbike; *she threw her leg across the saddle and settled herself behind him; my old saddle was very comfortable but this new one is harder* **(b)** rider's seat on a horse; *he leapt into the saddle and rode away;* **in the saddle** = in command; *she's in the saddle now - you have to do what she says* **(c)** cut of meat from the back of an animal; *saddle of lamb* **2** *verb* **(a)** to put a saddle on a horse; *she quickly saddled her pony and rode off* **(b) to saddle someone with** = to give someone a difficult job or heavy responsibility; *he got saddled with the job of sorting out the rubbish in the loft; don't saddle me with all your problems!*

sadism ['seidizm] *noun* getting pleasure from being cruel; *torturing the cat is a form of sadism; compare* MASOCHISM

sadist ['seidist] *noun* person who gets pleasure from being cruel; *the prison guards were simply sadists who* took pleasure in beating the prisoners; compare MASOCHIST

sadistic [sə'dɪstɪk] adjective referring to sadism; he seems to take sadistic pleasure in humiliating his deputy; compare MASOCHISTIC

sadly [sædli] adverb unhappily; after the funeral we walked sadly back to the house; sadly, John couldn't join us for lunch that day

sadness ['sædnəs] noun feeling of being very unhappy; the family experienced a great sadness; her sadness at finding her cat dead

s.a.e. = SELF-ADDRESSED ENVELOPE, STAMPED ADDRESSED ENVELOPE

safari [sə'fɑːri] noun expedition to photograph or kill wild animals in Africa; he went on (a) safari in Kenya; ordinary suburban life is apt to seem rather prosaic to anyone who has just come back from an African safari; **safari park** = park where large wild animals are free to run about, and visitors drive through in their cars to look at them

safe [seɪf] **1** adjective **(a)** not in danger, not likely to be hurt; in this cave, we should be safe from the thunderstorm; all the children are safe, but the school was burnt down; a building society account is a safe place for your money; is it safe to touch this snake?; it isn't safe for women to go into the centre of town alone at night **(b)** in safe hands = in no danger; the guide is very experienced, so we are in safe hands; safe and sound = without being hurt or damaged; we all arrived at our destination, safe and sound; the present reached me safe and sound, thanks to the efficiency of the post office **(c)** to be on the safe side = just in case, to be certain; it should only take an hour to get to the airport, but let's give ourselves an hour and a half, just to be on the safe side (NOTE: **safer - safest**) **2** noun strong box for keeping documents, money, jewels, etc., in; put your valuables in the hotel safe; the burglars managed to open the safe; **wall safe** = safe installed in a wall

safe area ['seɪf 'eəriə] noun place which is specially protected, for example by the armed forces; they established a safe area for refugees away from the fighting

safe deposit box ['seɪf di'pɒzɪt bɒks] noun small box which you can rent to keep jewellery or documents in a bank's strongroom; mother has always kept her jewellery in a safe deposit box at the bank

safeguard ['seɪfgɑːd] **1** noun protection; the metal fence is a safeguard against accidents; there are no safeguards at the moment to prevent the same mistake being made **2** verb to guard or to protect; our aim is to safeguard the interests of the widow and children

safe haven ['seɪf 'heɪvn] noun place which is safe from attack, where someone is protected from danger; they fled from their village looking for a safe haven in the mountains; in times of war, investors look for a safe haven for their money

safely ['seɪfli] adverb **(a)** without being hurt; the rescue services succeeded in getting all the passengers safely off the burning train; we were shown how to handle explosives safely; 'drive safely!' she said as she waved goodbye **(b)** without being damaged; the cargo was unloaded safely from the sinking ship **(c)** without making a mistake or having problems; can we safely say that this is a genuine Picasso?; she got safely through the first part of her exams

safety ['seɪfti] noun **(a)** being safe; the police tried to ensure the safety of the public; I am worried about the safety of air bags in cars; **fire safety** = measures taken to keep a place safe for workers and visitors in case of fire; **road safety** = care taken by drivers on the roads to make sure that accidents don't happen; **safety belt** = belt which you wear in a plane to stop you being hurt if there is an accident; **safety curtain** = fireproof curtain in front of the stage in a theatre; the safety curtain is lowered and raised at the beginning of each performance; **safety helmet** = solid hat worn by construction workers, etc.; visitors to the building site must wear safety helmets (NOTE: also called **hard hats**); **safety pin** = pin whose point fits into a little cover when it is fastened, and so can't hurt anyone; **to take safety precautions** or **safety measures** = to act to make sure something is safe; be sure to take proper safety precautions when handling explosives; **safety regulations** = rules to make a place of work safe for the workers **(b) for safety** = to make something safe, to be safe; put the money in the office safe for safety; keep a note of the numbers of your traveller's cheques for safety (NOTE: no plural)

safety net ['seɪfti 'net] noun **(a)** net stretched under a tightrope walker, etc., to catch him if he falls; he was killed when he walked the tightrope without a safety net **(b)** something which protects you if things go wrong; he has a second job, which is a useful safety net if he is made redundant

safety valve ['seɪfti 'vælv] noun **(a)** valve which allows liquid, gas, steam, etc., to escape if the pressure becomes too high; there was a loud hiss from the safety valve as steam escaped from the boiler **(b)** activity which allows people to get angry or excited without causing any harm; these meetings act as a safety valve for workers to complain about the management

saffron ['sæfrən] **1** noun orange-coloured powder made from crocus flowers, used in cooking to give colour and flavour to food; she made rice with saffron **2** adjective orange-coloured; the saffron robes of the Buddhist monks

saga ['sɑːgə] noun **(a)** old story of heroic achievement or adventure, especially in Norway and Iceland; the sagas of ancient kings of Iceland **(b)** long story; I don't want to hear her tell the saga of the accident all over again

sagacious [sə'geɪʃəs] adjective (formal) very wise; they made a very sagacious decision

sagacity [sə'gæsɪti] noun (formal) great wisdom; he was know throughout the country for his great sagacity

sage [seɪdʒ] **1** noun **(a)** aromatic herb with silvery-green leaves used in cookery; **sage green** = greyish green colour; **sage and onions** or **sage and onion stuffing** = stuffing used especially with roast turkey or pork **(b)** (formal) old wise man; the king invited sages to his castle to give him advice **2** adjective (formal) wise or discreet; she made some very sage remarks

Sagittarius [sædʒɪ'teəriəs] noun one of the signs of the Zodiac, shaped like an archer; my birthday's on 26th November which makes me (a) Sagittarius

said [sed] see SAY

sail [seɪl] **1** noun **(a)** piece of cloth which catches the wind and drives a boat along; the wind dropped so they lowered the sail and started to row; they hoisted the sail and set out across the Channel **(b) to set sail** = to leave by boat; *they set sail for France* **(c)** trip in a boat; *they went for a sail down the Thames* (NOTE: do not confuse with **sale**) **2** *verb* **(a)** to travel on water; *the ship was sailing towards the rocks*; *we were sailing east*; *he was the first person to sail across the Atlantic single-handed*; *she's planning to sail round the world* **(b)** to leave harbour; *the ferry sails at 12.00* **(c)** to travel smoothly; *the car just sailed along the motorway*; *it's maddening to see a bus sail past just when you're getting to the bus stop*; **to sail through** = to pass easily; *he sailed through his driving test*

sailboat ['seɪlbəʊt] *US* = SAILING BOAT

sailing ['seɪlɪŋ] *noun* **(a)** travel in a ship; **sailing boat** *or* **sailing ship** *or US* **sailboat** = boat which uses mainly sails to travel **(b)** sport of going in a sailing boat; *I plan to take up sailing when I retire*; *we have booked to go on a sailing holiday in the Mediterranean* **(c) plain sailing** = easy progress; *once he had passed the first year exams, it was just plain sailing until he got his degree* **(d)** departure (of a ship); *there are no sailings to France because of the strike*; *there are three sailings every day to Dieppe*; **sailing time** = time when a boat leaves the harbour

sailor ['seɪlə] *noun* seaman, person who works on a ship; *the sailors were washing down the deck of the ship*; **good** *or* **bad sailor** = person who is liable or not liable to be seasick; *he doesn't worry about the water being rough - he's a good sailor*

saint [seɪnt] *noun* **(a)** person who led a very holy life, and is recognized by the Christian church; *there are more than 50 statues of saints on the west front of the cathedral*; *St Peter was a fisherman*; *will Mother Teresa be made a saint?*; **patron saint** = saint who is supposed to have a special regard for something; *St Cecilia is the patron saint of music*; *in the car, there's a medal of St Christopher, the patron saint of travellers* **(b)** very good or devoted person; *she has the patience of a saint and never shouts at the children*; *he may be no saint in his personal life but he has the support of the voters* (NOTE: abbreviated with names to **St** [snt])

saintly ['seɪntlɪ] *adjective* very good, like a saint; *Queen Eleanor, the saintly wife of King Edward* (NOTE: **saintlier - saintliest**)

sake 1 [seɪk] *noun* **for the sake of something** *or* **for something's sake** = for certain reasons or purposes, because of something; *for the sake of decency, she wrapped a towel round herself*; *he's not really hungry, he's just eating for eating's sake*; **for the sake of someone** *or* **for someone's sake** = because you want to help someone, because you think someone needs something; *will you come to the party for my sake?*; *the president decided to resign for the sake of the country*; **for old times' sake** = to remember how good the old times were; *let's have a meal together for old times' sake*; **for heaven's sake** *or* **for goodness' sake** = expressions showing you are annoyed, or that something is important; *what are you screaming for? - it's only a little mouse, for heaven's sake*; *for goodness' sake try to be quiet, we don't want the guards to hear us!* **2** ['sɑːkɪ] *noun* Japanese rice wine; *we had a glass of sake with our meal*

salad ['sæləd] *noun* cold food, such as vegetables, often served raw; cold fish or meat served with cold vegetables; *we found some ham, tomatoes and lettuce* in the fridge, and made ourselves a salad; *a chicken salad sandwich*; **salad bar** = self-service bar, where customers help themselves to a wide variety of meat, fish or vegetable salads; **salad cream** = ready-made creamy dressing for salads; **salad dressing** = mixture of oil, vinegar, etc., used on salad; **fruit salad** = pieces of fresh fruit, mixed and served cold

salami [səˈlɑːmɪ] *noun* large dry Italian-style sausage eaten cold in thin slices

salaried ['sælərɪd] *adjective* paid a salary; *the company has 250 salaried staff*

salary ['sælərɪ] *noun* payment for work, made to an employee with a contract of employment, especially in a professional or office job; *she started work at a low salary, but soon went up the salary scale*; *the company froze all salaries for a six-month period*; *I expect a salary increase as from next month*; **basic salary** = normal salary without extra payments; **gross salary** = salary before tax is deducted; **net salary** = salary which is left after deducting tax and national insurance contributions; **starting salary** = amount of payment for an employee when starting work with a company; *he was appointed at a starting salary of £10,000*; **salary cheque** = monthly cheque by which an employee is paid (NOTE: plural is **salaries**)

> COMMENT: in Britain and the USA, salaries are usually paid monthly but are quoted in annual terms. So you say 'her salary is £20,000', 'the job carries a salary of $50,000'. Although bonuses are paid, a regular extra month's salary at Christmas (the 'thirteenth month' in some European countries) is not common in Britain or the USA

sale [seɪl] *noun* **(a)** act of selling, act of giving an item or doing a service in exchange for money, or for the promise that money will be paid; *the sale of the house produced £200,000*; *the shop only opened this morning and we've just made our first sale*; **cash sale** = transaction paid for in cash; **credit card sale** = transaction paid for by credit card **(b)** occasion when things are sold at cheaper prices; *there's a sale this week in the department store along the High Street*; *I bought these plates for £1 in a sale*; *the sale price is 50% of the normal price*; **clearance sale** = sale of items at low prices to get rid of the stock; **half-price sale** = sale of all goods at 50% of the usual price; *see also* CAR BOOT SALE, JUMBLE SALE **(c) for sale** = ready to be sold; **to offer something for sale** *or* **to put something up for sale** = to announce that something is ready to be sold; *they put the factory up for sale*; *these items are not for sale to the general public*; *the office building is for sale at £1m* **(d) on sale** = ready to be sold in a shop; *his latest novel is on sale in all good bookshops*; *these shirts are on sale in the local market* (NOTE: do not confuse with **sail**)

saleroom ['seɪlrʊm] *noun* room where an auction takes place; *there were many foreign collectors in the saleroom that day*

sales [seɪlz] *noun* **(a)** money which a business receives from selling things; *the business has annual sales of over £250,000*; *sales have risen over the first quarter*; **sales appeal** = quality which makes customers want to buy; **sales forecast** = estimate of future sales; **sales ledger** = book in which sales are recorded; **sales manager** = person in charge of a sales department; **sales representative** = person who works for a company, showing goods or services for sale **(b)** time when many shops sell goods at low prices; *the sales start on Saturday; I bought these shirts in the January sales; she bought the cups in the sales or at the sales*

sales assistant ['seɪlz ə'sɪstənt] *noun* person who sells goods to customers in a shop; *the sales assistant will help you*

salesgirl ['seɪlzgɜːl] *noun* girl who sells goods to customers in a shop; *this purse hasn't got a price on it - I'll just go and ask a salesgirl how much it is*

saleslady ['seɪlzleɪdi] *noun* woman who sells goods to customers in a shop; *ask the saleslady if they have that skirt in your size* (NOTE: plural is **salesladies**)

salesman ['seɪlzmən] *noun* (a) man who sells goods to customers in a shop; *the salesman is going to show us the latest model* (b) person who represents a company, selling its products or services to other companies; *we have six salesmen calling on accounts in central London* (NOTE: plural is **salesmen**)

salesperson ['seɪlzpɜːsən] *noun* person who sells goods in a shop; *we need an extra salesperson for Fridays*

sales tax ['seɪlz 'tæks] *noun* tax to be paid on each item sold; *in the USA, sales tax is always added to purchases*

saleswoman ['seɪlzwʊmən] *noun* woman in a shop who sells goods to customers; *our saleswomen are all dressed in pale blue blouses* (NOTE: plural is **saleswomen** ['seɪlzwɪmɪn])

salient ['seɪliənt] **1** *noun* projecting part of a fortification or of a line of battle; *the battle for the salient lasted several days* **2** *adjective* most important; *I asked her to write down the salient points of the talk*

saline ['seɪlaɪn] *adjective* containing salt; **saline drip** = drip containing a solution of distilled water and salt; *she is on a saline drip*

saliva [sə'laɪvə] *noun* fluid in the mouth, secreted by the salivary glands, which starts the process of digesting food; *as he looked in the sweet shop window, saliva came into his mouth*

salivary [sə'laɪvri] *adjective* referring to saliva; **salivary gland** = gland which secretes saliva; *just to see cream cakes sets my salivary glands in motion*

salivate ['sælɪveɪt] *verb* (formal) to produce saliva; *she was salivating over the photos in the fashion magazine*

sallow ['sæləʊ] *adjective* slightly yellow, unhealthy looking; *when he left hospital, his sallow face showed how ill he had been; she has dark hair and a sallow complexion* (NOTE: **sallower - sallowest**)

sally ['sæli] **1** *noun* (a) sudden rush of soldiers out of a position they are defending; *they made a sally and captured some enemy guns* (b) clever remark; *the minister couldn't reply to the opposition sallies about his private life* (NOTE: plural is **sallies**) **2** *verb* to sally forth *or* to sally out = to go out; *I sallied forth in the pouring rain to buy a newspaper*

salmon ['sæmən] **1** *noun* large fish with silver skin and pink flesh; *in Alaska the bears love to catch salmon as they swim up the rivers; we had poached salmon and new potatoes*; **salmon steak** = thick slice of salmon; **smoked salmon** = salmon which has been cured by smoking, and is served in very thin slices, usually with brown bread and lemon (NOTE: plural is

salmon) **2** *adjective* with a pink colour like salmon; *we put a salmon-pink wallpaper in the bathroom*

> COMMENT: salmon live in the sea, but swim up rivers to spawn in the winter. Nowadays, salmon are also farmed in fish farms

salon ['sælɒn] *noun* shop where people can have their hair cut or styled, or have beauty treatments; *the hairdressing salon is on the fifth floor; she went to the beauty salon for a manicure*

saloon [sə'luːn] *noun* (a) **saloon (car)** = car with two or four doors, which can carry four or five people (as opposed to a sports car or convertible); *he bought a Ford saloon* (NOTE: American English for this is a **sedan**) (b) (old) **saloon bar** = comfortable bar in a pub; *we sat in the saloon bar with our friends* (NOTE: now usually called a **lounge bar**) (c) US (old) place which sells alcoholic drinks; *the conversation stopped when the stranger walked into the saloon*

salt [sɒlt] **1** *noun* (a) sodium chloride (NaCl), white crystals used to make food taste better (used especially with meat, fish and vegetables); *there's too much salt in this soup; you don't need to put salt on your fish - it's quite salty enough already*; **to take something with a pinch of salt** = not to believe something entirely; *you have to take everything she says with a pinch of salt* (NOTE: no plural: **some salt, a spoonful** *or* **a pinch of salt**) (b) large crystals used to put on frozen streets to melt ice or snow; *lorries were out all night spreading salt on the streets* (c) **the salt of the earth** = ordinary good honest person; *he's a wonderful man - the salt of the earth!* **2** *adjective* containing salt; *the sea is made up only of salt water* **3** *verb* (a) to add salt to; *you forgot to salt the soup* (b) to spread salt on; *they were salting the streets during the night*

salt cellar US **salt shaker** ['sɒlt 'selə *or* 'sɒlt 'ʃeɪkə] *noun* small pot containing salt usually with a hole in the top so that it can be sprinkled on food; *there's no salt cellar on our table, can you take one from the next table?; see comment at* PEPPERPOT

salt water ['sɒlt 'wɔːtə] *noun* water which contains salt, such as sea water (as opposed to fresh water in rivers and lakes); *she dived into the waves and got a mouthful of salt water; you can float more easily in salt water than in a lake*

saltwater ['sɒltwɔːtə] *adjective* referring to water which contains salt; *the hotel has a saltwater swimming pool*

salty ['sɒlti] *adjective* tasting of salt; *we had a bowl of pea and ham soup which was much too salty; I think you've put too much salt in the carrots - they taste very salty* (NOTE: **saltier - saltiest**)

salubrious [sə'luːbriəs] *adjective* (formal) healthy and pleasant to live in; *Lyme Regis is a particularly salubrious place for anyone who wants to recuperate; we found a hotel in a less salubrious part of the town, down by the railway station*

salutary ['sæljʊtri] *adjective* (formal) which teaches; *the remarks by the judge were a salutary warning to her*

salute [sə'luːt] **1** *noun* (a) movement to express respect, recognition, etc., especially putting your right hand up to touch the peak of your cap; *the officer returned the soldier's salute*; **to take the salute** = to be the person whom soldiers on parade salute; *the general* took the salute at the march past **(b)** firing guns to mark an important occasion; *the birthday of the Queen was marked with a 21-gun salute* **2** *verb* **(a)** to give a salute to someone; *ordinary soldiers must salute their officers* **(b)** to praise someone; *we salute the brave firemen who saved the children*

salvage ['sælvɪdʒ] **1** *noun* **(a)** saving a ship or cargo from being destroyed; **salvage money** = payment made by the owner of a ship or cargo to the person who saved it; *were you paid any salvage for the goods rescued from the boat?*; **salvage vessel** = ship which specializes in saving other ships and their cargoes **(b)** goods saved from a wreck, fire, etc.; *a sale of flood salvage items* **(c)** saving rubbish for use; *a company specializing in the salvage of plastics from household waste* **2** *verb* **(a)** to save from a wreck, fire, etc.; *we are selling off a warehouse full of salvaged goods*; *we managed to salvage the computer discs from the fire* **(b)** to save something from loss; *the company is trying to salvage its reputation after the managing director was sent to prison for* fraud; *the receiver managed to salvage something from the collapse of the company*

salvation [sæl'veɪʃn] *noun* action of saving a person's soul from sin; *he sought his salvation in working for the homeless*

Salvation Army [sæl'veɪʃn 'ɑːmi] *noun* Christian organization run on military lines, which does missionary and welfare work; *my sister has joined the Salvation Army*; *we tracked him down to a Salvation Army hostel in the city centre*

salvo ['sælvəʊ] *noun* simultaneous firing of several guns in a battle at sea or as a salute; *the ships fired a series of salvos at the enemy fortifications* (NOTE: plural is **salvos** *or* **salvoes**)

same [seɪm] *adjective & pronoun* **(a)** being, looking, sounding, etc., exactly alike; *these two beers taste the same*; *you must get very bored doing the same work every day*; *she was wearing the same dress as me*; *this book is not the same size as that one*; **to stay the same** = not to change; *the weather is expect to stay the same for the next few days*; (*informal*) **same again, please!** = please serve us the same drinks or food, etc., as before **(b)** showing that two or more things are in fact one; *they all live in the same street*; *should we all leave at the same time?*; *our children go to the same school as theirs*

◊ **all the same** ['ɔːl ðə 'seɪm] *phrase* **(a)** in spite of this; *I'm not really keen on horror films, but I'll go with you all the same* **(b)** **it's all the same** = it makes no difference; *if it's all the same to you, I won't come to the party*

sameness ['seɪmnəs] *noun* monotony, lack of variety, being always the same; *she gets bored with the sameness of the work in the office*

sample ['sɑːmpl] **1** *noun* specimen, a small part which is used to show what the whole is like; *a sample of the cloth* *or* *a cloth sample*; *try a sample of the local cheese*; *we interviewed a sample of potential customers*; **free sample** = sample given free to advertise a product **2** *verb* **(a)** to test, to try by taking a small amount; *why don't you sample the wine before placing your order?* **(b)** to ask a group of people questions to find out a general reaction; *they sampled 2,000 people at random to test the new soap*

sampler ['sɑːmplə] *noun* piece of embroidered cloth, usually with letters, numbers and simple pictures, made to show your skill at sewing; *they have an old sampler hanging over the fireplace*

sanctify ['sæŋktɪfaɪ] *verb* to make holy; *a chapel sanctified by the relics of a saint*

sanction ['sæŋkʃn] **1** *noun* **(a)** approval, permission; *you will need the sanction of the local authorities before you can knock the house down* **(b)** **economic sanctions** = restrictions on trade with a country in order to try to influence its political development; *to impose sanctions on a country* *or* *to lift sanctions from a country* **2** *verb* to approve; *the committee sanctioned the expenditure of £1.2m on the development project*

sanctuary ['sæŋktjʊəri] *noun* **(a)** place of safety; *the church became a sanctuary for illegal immigrants*; *people escaping from the revolutionary troops sought sanctuary in the church* **(b)** place for the protection of wild animals or birds; *they established several bird sanctuaries near the sea* **(c)** holy place; *the ruins of the sanctuary of the goddess Athene* **(d)** part of a church where the high altar is placed; *the priest turned towards the altar and stepped into the sanctuary* (NOTE: plural is **sanctuaries**)

sand [sænd] *noun* mass of tiny bits of rock, etc., found on beaches, in the desert, etc.; *a beach of fine white sand*; *the black sand beaches of the Northern coast of New Zealand*; *he kicked sand in my face*; **sand castle** = little castle of sand made by children on a beach; *the children built sand castles on the beach with their buckets*; **sand dunes** = area of sand blown by the wind into small hills and ridges which have very little soil or vegetation; *the village was threatened by encroaching sand dunes*

sandal ['sændl] *noun* light shoe with an open top made of straps; *she's bought a pair of white sandals*; *he was wearing sandals and shorts*

sandbag ['sændbæg] *noun* bag filled with sand and used as a protection; *they built a wall of sandbags to try to prevent the river from flooding the village*

sandbank ['sændbæŋk] *noun* area of sand in the sea or a river; *our yacht got stuck on a sandbank as the tide went down*

sandpaper ['sændpeɪpə] **1** *noun* thick paper covered with sand used for smoothing rough surfaces; *use fine sandpaper if you want to get a very smooth finish* **2** *verb* to rub something smooth with sandpaper; *he sandpapered the door before painting it*

sandpit ['sændpɪt] *noun* place in a garden, with sand where children can play; *the twins were sitting playing in their sandpit*

sands ['sændz] *noun* area of sandy beach; *the sands stretch for miles along the coast*

sandstone ['sændstəʊn] *noun* type of reddish-brown rock, formed of tiny pieces of sand; *houses built of sandstone look dark and gloomy*

sandstorm ['sændstɔːm] *noun* high wind in the desert, which carries large amounts of sand with it; *in the morning they saw that the sandstorm had almost buried the jeep*

sandwich ['sændwɪtʃ] **1** *noun* **(a)** snack made with two slices of bread with meat, salad, etc. between them; *she ordered a cheese sandwich and a cup of coffee*; *what sort of sandwiches do you want to take for your lunch?*; *I didn't have a big meal - just a sandwich with some beer in the pub*; **club sandwich** *or* **doubledecker sandwich** = sandwich made of three slices of bread, with a filling of meat, salad, fish, etc., between them (NOTE: plural is **sandwiches**) **(b)** **sandwich boards** = boards carried in front of and behind a person with advertisements on them; **sandwich man** = man who carries sandwich boards **2** *verb* to insert something between two others; *I stood all the way home on the Underground, sandwiched between two fat men*

sandwich course ['sændwɪtʃ 'kɔːs] *noun* course where students spend time working in an office or factory between periods of study at a college; *she's taking a four-year sandwich course in textile design and manufacture*

sandy ['sændi] *adjective* covered with sand; *the resort has miles of safe sandy beaches* (NOTE: **sandier - sandiest**)

sane [seɪn] *adjective* not mad; *he's not mad - he's the sanest person in our group*; *I do embroidery during committee meetings - it's a way of keeping myself sane* (NOTE: **saner - sanest**)

sang [sæŋ] *see* SING

sanguine ['sæŋgwɪn] *adjective* (formal) confident, optimistic; *it would be best not to be too sanguine about our chances of success*

sanitary ['sænɪtəri] *adjective* referring to hygiene or to health; *the sanitary conditions in the hotel leave a lot to be desired*; **sanitary towel** *US* **sanitary napkin** = wad of absorbent cotton used by a woman to absorb blood during her period

sanitation [sænɪ'teɪʃn] *noun* being hygienic, especially referring to public hygiene, removal of household waste, etc.; *poor sanitation in crowded conditions can result in the spread of disease*

sanity ['sænɪti] *noun* state of being sane; *he felt he was losing his sanity among all the arguments in the office*; *in the prisoner-of-war camp they sang songs to preserve their sanity*

sank [sæŋk] *see* SINK

Santa Claus ['sæntə 'klɔːz] *noun* Father Christmas; *the children whooped with delight when Santa Claus came in carrying a big sack full of toys*

sap [sæp] **1** *noun* liquid which flows inside plants and trees; *they cut a notch in the bark of the tree and the sap ran out* **2** *verb* to make weaker; *his strength was sapped by the cold* (NOTE: **sapping - sapped**)

sapling ['sæplɪŋ] *noun* young tree; *we have planted a grove of birch saplings behind the house*

sapper ['sæpə] *noun* soldier whose job is to build roads, bridges, etc., especially one serving in the Royal Engineers; *sappers were brought in to put a bridge across the flooded river*

sapphire ['sæfaɪə] *noun* bright blue precious stone; *he gave her a ring with sapphires and diamonds*

sarcasm ['sɑːkæzəm] *noun* sharp unpleasant remarks which mean the opposite of what they say; *she was hurt by the sarcasm in his review of her book*; *the tone of sarcasm in her voice surprised him*

sarcastic [sɑː'kæstɪk] *adjective* using sarcasm; *don't be so sarcastic*; *'aren't we the clever one?' he said in a sarcastic tone*

sarcastically [sɑː'kæstɪkli] *adverb* in a sarcastic way; *'I'd better remember that,' said James sarcastically*

sardine [sɑː'diːn] *noun* small silvery fish which can be eaten fresh, or commonly bought in tins; *we had*

grilled sardines in a little restaurant overlooking the harbour; *a snack of sardines on toast*; **packed (together) like sardines** = packed very close together; *in the rush hour we were packed like sardines on the Underground*

sardonic [sɑː'dɒnɪk] *adjective* scornful, showing you feel superior to someone; *he gave a sardonic laugh*

sari ['sɑːri] *noun* long piece of cloth, especially silk, which Indian women wear wrapped round their bodies; *a shop which specializes in beautiful saris*

sarong [sə'rɒŋ] *noun* cloth worn wrapped round the waist or under the arms by South East Asian men and women; *a sarong can be very useful to put on over your swimsuit*

sat [sæt] *see* SIT

SAT [sæt] *US* = SCHOLASTIC ASSESSMENT TESTS *(trademark of the College Entrance Examination Board)* pre-college tests

Satan ['seɪtən] *noun* the Devil

satanic [sə'tænɪk] *adjective* referring to Satan; *they indulged in satanic rites by the light of the full moon*

satchel ['sætʃəl] *noun* small leather or canvas bag carried on your shoulders, used mainly by schoolchildren; *a line of schoolchildren each carrying a neat little satchel*

satellite ['sætəlaɪt] *noun* **(a)** device that orbits the earth, receiving and transmitting signals, pictures and data; *the signals are transmitted by satellite all round the world*; **communications satellite** = satellite that relays radio or TV signals from one part of the earth to another; **satellite broadcasting** = sending radio or TV signals from one part of the earth to another using a communications satellite; **satellite dish** = aerial, shaped like a large saucer, used to capture satellite broadcasts; **satellite TV** = television system, where pictures are sent via a space satellite; *we watched the programme on satellite TV* **(b)** body in space which goes round a planet; *the Moon is the only satellite of the Earth*

satin ['sætɪn] **1** *noun* silk material with a glossy surface; *she bought some black satin to make a dress* **2** *adjective* made of satin; *she wore little red satin slippers*

satire ['sætaɪə] *noun* **(a)** way of attacking people in speaking or writing by making them seem ridiculous; *his use of satire in his weekly political column* **(b)** piece of writing which criticizes people by making them seem ridiculous; *'Gulliver's Travels' is a satire on 18th century England*

satirical [sə'tɪrɪkl] *adjective* making use of satire; *he wrote a satirical play about the church*; *the satirical magazines make fun of the Prime Minister*

satirize ['sætɪraɪz] *verb* to attack someone or something in a way which makes them seem ridiculous; *Orwell satirized the Russian Communist state in 'Animal Farm'*

satisfaction [sætɪs'fækʃn] *noun* **(a)** good feeling; sense of comfort or happiness; *after finishing his meal he gave a deep sigh of satisfaction*; *I get no satisfaction from telling you this - you're fired*; **job satisfaction** = feeling which you have that you are happy in your work and pleased with the work you do **(b)** *(formal)* payment of money or goods to someone, who then has no further claim against you; *they demanded satisfaction from the driver of the other car*

satisfactory [ˌsætɪsˈfæktəri] *adjective* quite good, which satisfies; *the result of the election was very satisfactory for big business*; *a satisfactory outcome to the discussions*

satisfied [ˈsætɪsfaɪd] *adjective* contented; *I've finished painting the kitchen, and I hope you're satisfied with the result*; *she gave a satisfied smile*; **satisfied customer** = customer who has got what he wanted

satisfy [ˈsætɪsfaɪ] *verb* (a) to make someone pleased with what he has purchased, with the service he has received; *the council's decision should satisfy most people*; *our aim is to satisfy our customers* (b) to **satisfy a demand** = to fill a demand; *we cannot produce enough to satisfy the demand for the product* (c) to comply with conditions; *the payments received so far do not satisfy the conditions attached to the contract*

satisfying [ˈsætɪsfaɪɪŋ] *adjective* which satisfies; *it was very satisfying to see the two of them getting on so well*; *to grow all our own fruit and vegetables is very satisfying*

SATs [sæts] *GB* = STANDARD ASSESSMENT TESTS

satsuma [sætˈsuːmə] *noun* type of small orange, with peel which is easily removed

saturate [ˈsætʃəreɪt] *verb* to fill something with the maximum amount of a liquid or substance which can be absorbed; *when nitrates leach from forest soils, it shows that the soils are saturated with nitrogen*

saturated [ˈsætʃəreɪtɪd] *adjective* (a) **saturated fat** = butter and other types of animal fat, which contain the largest amount of hydrogen possible (b) as full of a liquid or other substance as can be absorbed; *the ground is saturated and we can't start ploughing yet* (c) containing an overwhelming amount of something; *the media are saturated with scenes of violence*; *it is a marginal seat, and so has been saturated with election posters*; **the market for home computers is saturated** = there are too many home computers available for the number of people who want to buy them

saturation [ˌsætʃəˈreɪʃn] *noun* filling something to the maximum amount possible; **saturation point** = level at which no more of something can be absorbed; *the computer market is nowhere near saturation point*

Saturday [ˈsætədeɪ] *noun* sixth day of the week, day between Friday and Sunday; *he works in a shop, so Saturday is a normal working day for him*; *we go shopping in London most Saturdays*; *Saturday is the Jewish day of rest*; *today is Saturday, November 15th*; *the 15th is a Saturday, so the 16th must be a Sunday*; *we arranged to meet up at the cinema next Saturday evening*

Saturn [ˈsætən] *noun* the sixth planet of the solar system and its largest apart from Jupiter; *Saturn is well-known for its rings*

satyr [ˈsætə] *noun* classical god living in woods, with a human body, but with legs of a goat; *a classical painting of nymphs and satyrs in a forest* (NOTE: do not confuse with **satire**)

sauce [sɔːs] *noun* liquid with a particular taste, poured over food; *ice cream with chocolate sauce*; *we had chicken with a barbecue sauce*; *spaghetti with meat and tomato sauce*; *a bottle of tomato sauce*

saucepan [ˈsɔːspæn] *noun* deep metal cooking pan with a lid and a long handle; *where's the lid of the saucepan?*; *watch the saucepan - I don't want the milk to boil over*; *put the mixture in a saucepan and cook over a low heat*

saucer [ˈsɔːsə] *noun* shallow dish which a cup stands in; *where are the cups and saucers? - they're in the cupboard*; **a saucer of milk** = milk put in a saucer, usually for a cat to drink

Saudi Arabia [ˈsaudi əˈreɪbiə] *noun* large country in the Middle East, to the south of Iraq and Jordan (NOTE: capital: **Riyadh**; people: **Saudis** *or* **Saudi Arabians**; language: **Arabic**; currency: **riyal**)

Saudi (Arabian) [ˈsaudi] **1** *adjective* referring to Saudi Arabia; *Saudi Arabian oil is exported to many countries*; *a Saudi prince* **2** *noun* (a) person from Saudi Arabia; *Saudis speak Arabic*

sauna [ˈsɔːnə] *noun* (a) bath taken by sitting in a room filled with very hot steam; *we all had a sauna and then went for a swim in the lake* (b) room where you can have a very hot steam bath; *there is a sauna in the basement of the hotel*

saunter [ˈsɔːntə] **1** *noun* stroll, slow walk; *we went for a saunter along the sea front* **2** *verb* to walk slowly, to stroll; *she sauntered into the bar and ordered a whisky*

sausage [ˈsɒsɪdʒ] *noun* tube of edible skin full of minced and seasoned meat; *you can't possibly eat all those sausages!*; *I'll have sausages and eggs for breakfast*

sausagemeat [ˈsɒsɪdʒmiːt] *noun* mixture of minced meat and flavourings used for making sausages, and also used in pies and sausage rolls

sausage roll [ˈsɒsɪdʒ ˈrəul] *noun* small roll of pastry with a piece of sausage or some sausagemeat inside; *she made some sausage rolls to hand round at the party*

sauté [ˈsəuteɪ] **1** *adjective* fried quickly in a little fat; *do you want sauté potatoes or new potatoes with your fish?* **2** *verb* to fry in a little fat; *she sautéed some potatoes to go with the meat* (NOTE: **sautéing - sautéed**)

savage [ˈsævɪdʒ] **1** *adjective* fierce, ferocious; *hunger had made the dogs really savage*; *she suffered a savage attack and had to have stitches in her forehead* **2** *noun* wild or uncivilized human being; *how could he turn into such a savage and attack her like that?* **3** *verb* to attack with teeth; *he was savaged by an Alsatian*

savagely [ˈsævɪdʒli] *adverb* in a savage way; *he cut and slashed savagely at the curtains*

savagery [ˈsævɪdʒri] *noun* being savage; *the soldiers attacked the camp with great savagery*

savanna(h) [səˈvænə] *noun* dry grass-covered plain with few trees, usually referring to the grasslands of South America and Africa; *they rode for miles across the savannah, looking for game*

save [seɪv] **1** *noun* (*in football*) stopping the ball from going into the net; *the goalkeeper made a brilliant save, and the result was that the match was drawn* **2** *verb* (a) to stop someone from being hurt or killed; *the firemen saved six people from the burning house*; *how many passengers were saved when the ferry sank?*; **the policeman saved my life** = the policeman helped me and prevented me from being killed (b) to stop something from being damaged; *we managed to save most of the paintings from the fire* (c) to put things such as money to one side so that you can use them later; *I'm saving to buy a car; if you save £10 a week, you'll have £520 at the end of a year; they save old pieces of bread to give to the ducks in the park; he saves bits of string in case he may need them later* (d) not to waste (time, money, etc.); *by walking to work, he saves £25 a week in bus fares; she took the parcel herself so as to save the cost of postage; if you have your car serviced regularly it will save you a lot of expense in the future; going to Scotland by air saves a lot of time* (e) to store data on a computer disk; *don't forget to save your files when you have finished keyboarding them* (f) (*in football*) to stop an opponent from scoring; *the goalkeeper saved two goals* 3 *preposition & conjunction* (*formal*) except for; *everyone was there, save Richard, who was ill*

save on ['seɪv 'ɒn] *verb* not to waste, to use less; *by introducing shift work we find we can save on fuel; by walking to work, you will find that you can save on bus fares*

saver ['seɪvə] *noun* (a) person who saves money; *all savers will receive a bonus this year* (b) special offer or special ticket which allows you to buy something at a lower price; *among this week's savers are baked beans at 50p; saver tickets are not valid on trains before 9.30*

save up ['seɪv 'ʌp] *verb* not to spend the money you get because you are keeping it for a special purpose; *I'm saving up to buy a motorbike; they are saving up for a holiday in the USA*

saving ['seɪvɪŋ] 1 *noun* using less; *we are aiming for a 10% saving in fuel* 2 *suffix* which uses less; *an energy-saving or labour-saving device* = machine which saves energy *or* labour

savings ['seɪvɪŋz] *noun* (a) money which you can save; *he put all his savings into a building society account; she spent all her savings on a round the world trip;* **savings account** = bank account where you can put money in regularly and which pays interest, often at a higher rate than a deposit account; **savings bank** = bank where you can deposit money and receive interest on it (b) money which you do not need to spend; *there are incredible savings on flights to Florida*

saviour *US* **savior** ['seɪvjə] *noun* (a) **our Saviour** = Jesus Christ (b) person who saves; *he was called the Saviour of the West*

savour *US* **savor** ['seɪvə] 1 *noun* (a) characteristic pleasant taste; *some Greek soups have a savour of lemon* (b) feeling of excitement and interest; *office life seems to have lost some of its savour for her* 2 *verb* (a) to appreciate or enjoy something; *he ate slowly, savouring his meal; the general stood at the top of the hill, savouring his victory* (b) **to savour of** = to have a suggestion of something bad; *the whole project savours of tax evasion to me*

savoury *US* **savory** ['seɪvri] 1 *adjective* (a) with a salty taste, or other taste which is not sweet; *I don't particularly like sweets, I prefer savoury things* (b) **not savoury** = unattractive and unpleasant; *the bar doesn't have a very savoury reputation; seeing all those fat men in the sauna was not a very savoury sight* (NOTE: has the same meaning as **unsavoury**) 2 *noun* little salty snack; *they served little savouries with the aperitifs*

saw [sɔː] 1 *noun* tool with a long metal blade with teeth along its edge, used for cutting; *he was cutting logs with a saw; my saw doesn't cut very well - it needs sharpening;* **chain saw** = saw made of a chain with teeth in it, which turns very fast when driven by a motor 2 *verb* (a) to cut with a saw; *she was sawing wood; they sawed the old tree into pieces; you will need to saw that piece of wood in half* (NOTE: **sawing - sawed - has sawn** [sɔːn]) (b) *see also* **SEE**

saw off ['sɔː 'ɒf] *verb* to cut off with a saw; *that branch is too big - it needs to be sawn off;* **sawn-off shotgun** = gun with the barrel cut short; *he was found carrying a sawn-off shotgun*

saxophone ['sæksəfəʊn] *noun* large brass musical instrument with keys; *he plays the saxophone in the school band*

saxophonist [sæk'sɒfənɪst] *noun* saxophone player; *the saxophonist stood up to play a solo*

say [seɪ] 1 *noun* right to speak about something; *the children have no say in the matter; she always wants to have the final say in an argument; they will all expect to have their say in choosing the new leader* 2 *verb* (a) to speak words; *what's she saying? - I don't know, I don't understand Dutch; she says the fee is £3 per person; don't forget to say 'thank you' after the party; the weatherman said it was going to rain and it did; I was just saying that we never hear from my brother, when he phoned* (b) to give information in writing; *the letter says that we owe the bank £200; the notice says that you are not allowed to walk on the grass* (c) to suggest; *choose any number - (let's) say eighteen; let's have another meeting next week - shall we say Thursday?* (NOTE: **says** [sez] - **saying - said** [sed] - **has said**) 3 *interjection US* (to show surprise) *say! haven't we met someplace before?*

saying ['seɪɪŋ] *noun* proverb, phrase which is often used; *it's an old north country saying; my mother was fond of old sayings like 'red sky at night - sailor's delight';* **as the saying goes** = according to the old proverb; *'more haste, less speed' as the saying goes*

say-so ['seɪsəʊ] *noun* (*informal*) permission; *she got the manager's say-so for buying a new photocopier*

scab [skæb] *noun* (a) crust of dry blood which forms over a wound and protects it; *the scab fell off where he had grazed his knee* (b) (*informal*) worker who goes on working when there is a strike; *we don't want scabs here*

scabbard ['skæbəd] *noun* sheath, a cover for a dagger or sword; *he turned round, and pulled his sword out of its scabbard*

scabies ['skeɪbiːz] *noun* very irritating infection of the skin caused by a mite which lives under the skin (NOTE: no plural)

scaffold ['skæfəld] *noun* wooden platform on which an execution takes place; *the executioner stepped onto the scaffold, carrying a large axe*

scaffolding ['skæfəldɪŋ] *noun* construction of poles and planks which makes a series of platforms for workmen to stand on while working; *they put up scaffolding round the building* (NOTE: no plural)

scald [skɔːld] *verb* to burn with hot liquid or steam; *she knocked over a freshly-made pot of tea and scalded her arm*

scalding ['skɔːldɪŋ] *adjective* very hot; *she poured the scalding water over the dirty trays; blow on your soup - it's scalding hot*

scale [skeɪl] **1** *noun* **(a)** proportion used to show a large object in a smaller form; *map with a scale of 1 to 100,000; the architect's design is drawn to scale; a scale model of the new town centre development* **(b)** measuring system which is graded into various levels; *the Richter scale is used to measure earthquakes;* **scale of charges** *or* **scale of prices** = list showing prices for different goods or services; **scale of salaries** *or* **salary scale** = list showing the range and system of salaries in a company; *he was appointed at the top end of the salary scale; see also* SLIDING SCALE **(c)** **large scale** *or* **small scale** = working with large or small amounts of investment or staff, etc.; **to start in business on a small scale** = to start in business with a small staff or few products or little capital **(d)** thin plate protecting the skin of fish and snakes; *don't forget to scrape the scales off the fish before you grill it* **(e)** series of musical notes arranged in a rising or falling order; *she practises her scales every morning* **2** *verb* **(a)** to climb up; *six climbers tried to scale the north face of the mountain* **(b) to scale up** *or* **to scale down** = to increase or to reduce in proportion; *not enough students have passed the exam, so the marks will have to be scaled up; the company is scaling down its operations in Bangkok*

scales [skeɪlz] *noun* weighing machine; *she put two bananas on the scales; the bathroom scales must be wrong - I'm heavier than I was yesterday;* **to tip the scales at** = to weight; *he tipped the scales at 210lb* (NOTE: no singular: for one say **a pair of scales**)

scallions ['skæljənz] *noun US* young onions eaten raw in salad, or used in cooking (NOTE: British English is **spring onions**)

scallop ['skɒləp] *noun* **(a)** type of shellfish with a pair of semicircular flat shells; *we had scallops fried in butter* **(b)** scallops = small semicircles which form an ornamental edge to material

scalp [skælp] **1** *noun* thick skin and muscle with the hair, which covers the skull; *he was taken to hospital with a scalp wound; rubbing the scalp will encourage your hair to grow* **2** *verb* **(a)** to cut off the scalp of an enemy; *they killed the settlers and scalped them* **(b)** *(informal)* to sell tickets at a very high price

scalpel ['skælpl] *noun* sharp pointed knife used in surgery

scalper ['skælpə] *noun (informal)* person who sells tickets at a very high price; *ticket scalpers stood outside the entrances offering tickets at ten times the normal price*

scam [skæm] *noun (informal)* case of fraud; *he was involved in some sort of investment scam*

scamper ['skæmpə] *verb* to run fast with little steps; *when they heard the noise all the children scampered towards the exit; rabbits were scampering across the field*

scampi ['skæmpi] *noun* large prawns; *his favourite meal is scampi fried in batter with chips* (NOTE: can be followed by a singular or plural verb)

scan [skæn] **1** *verb* **(a)** to look very carefully at something all over; *we scanned the horizon but no ships were to be seen; he scanned the map to try to find Cambridge Road* **(b)** to pass a radar beam over (an area); to pass X-rays through part of the body; *first they*

scanned the right side of the brain; the hospital has decided to re-examine all patients who have been scanned over the last year **(c)** to examine a drawing or text and produce computer data from it electronically; *they scanned the text of the book using a hand-held scanner* **(d)** to analyze a line of poetry to identify the rhythm; *some modern poetry is impossible to scan* **(e)** *(of poetry)* to fit a regular rhythm; *the second line of the poem doesn't scan* (NOTE: **scanning - scanned**) **2** *noun* **(a)** examination of part of the body by passing X-rays through the body and analyzing the result in a computer; *she went to have a scan after ten weeks of pregnancy;* **brain scan** = examining the inside of the brain by passing X-rays through the head **(b)** picture of part of the body shown on a screen, derived by computers from X-rays **(c)** examination of an image or an object to obtain data; *a heat scan will quickly show which component is overheating*

scandal ['skændl] *noun* **(a)** talking about wrong things someone is supposed to have done; *have you heard the latest scandal about him?* **(b)** wrong action that produces a general feeling of public anger; *the government was brought down by the scandal of the emperor's diamonds; the government should do something about the scandal of unemployed teenagers; it's a scandal that her father never allowed her to go to university*

scandalize ['skændəlaɪz] *verb* to make people angry by doing something which they think is wrong; *she scandalized her neighbours by wearing very short skirts*

scandalous ['skændləs] *adjective* which is shameful and wrong; *it is scandalous that nothing has been done about the rubbish*

Scandinavia [skændɪ'neɪviə] *noun* area of northern European countries consisting of Norway, Sweden, Denmark, Finland and Iceland

Scandinavian [skændɪ'neɪviən] **1** *adjective* referring to Scandinavia; *we often think of Scandinavian women as being tall with fair hair;* **Scandinavian languages** = languages such as Swedish, Danish, Finnish, etc. **2** *noun* person from Scandinavia

scanner ['skænə] *noun* **(a)** machine which scans part of the body; *the hospital has acquired the most up-to-date scanner;* **brain scanner** = machine which scans only the brain **(b)** electronic device that scans, especially a device that scans images or text and converts them to computer data; *we used a small hand-held scanner to get the photos onto our computer system;* **flatbed scanner** = large scanning device, where images are placed flat on a surface and scanned automatically; **hand-held scanner** = little scanner which is held in your hand and which you pass over an image

scant [skænt] *adjective* not enough; *she paid scant attention to my warning; the government pays scant regard to the needs of the disabled*

scanty ['skænti] *adjective* small, not big enough; *we only had very scanty information about where they lived; she was wearing a scanty nightdress* (NOTE: **scantier - scantiest**)

scapegoat ['skeɪpɡəʊt] *noun* person who carries the blame for someone else; *once the scandal became public, the government started to look for a scapegoat; the company decided to make a scapegoat of the finance director*

scapula ['skæpjʊlə] *noun* shoulderblade, one of the two large flat bones covering the top part of your back

scar [skɑː] **1** *noun* mark left on the skin after a wound has healed; *he still has the scars of his operation* **2** *verb* **(a)** to leave a mark on the skin; *he was scarred for life as a result of the accident* **(b)** to leave a mark on the mind of someone; *the bullying she received at school has scarred her for ever* (NOTE: **scarring - scarred**)

scarce [skeəs] *adjective* **(a)** not enough for the amount needed; *this happened at a period when food was scarce*; *good designers are getting scarce* **(b)** *(informal)* **to make oneself scarce** = to hide, to keep out of someone's way (NOTE: **scarcer - scarcest**)

scarcely ['skeəsli] *adverb* almost not; *he can scarcely walk because of his bad back*; *I can scarcely believe it!*; **scarcely anyone** = almost no one; *scarcely anyone bought tickets for the show*

scarcity ['skeəsəti] *noun* lack of, being scarce; *the country's economic development has been hampered by the scarcity of raw materials*; *the scarcity of jobs in country areas means that more people migrate to the cities*; *there is a scarcity of trained staff*; *there's no scarcity of things to do in London*

scare [skeə] **1** *noun* fright; *what a scare you gave me - jumping out at me in the dark like that!*; **bomb scare** = frightening rumour or announcement that there might be a hidden bomb somewhere **2** *verb* to frighten; *the thought of travelling alone scares me*; *she was scared by the spider in the bathroom*; *(informal)* **to scare the life out of someone** = to frighten someone completely; **to scare away** = to frighten something so that it goes away; *the cat has scared all the birds away from the garden*

scarecrow ['skeəkrəʊ] *noun* figure made to look like a person dressed in old clothes, put up in a field to frighten the birds; *look at the scarecrow with his black coat and funny hat!*; *she looks like a scarecrow in that dress*

scared [skeəd] *adjective* frightened; *don't be scared - the snake is harmless*; *she was too scared to answer the door*; *I'm scared at the idea of driving in London's rush hour traffic*; *she looked round with a scared expression*; **scared stiff** = so frightened that you cannot move; *I was scared stiff when I saw the children playing at the top of the cliff*

scarf [skɑːf] *noun* **(a)** long piece of cloth which is worn round your neck to keep yourself warm; *take your scarf - it's snowing*; *the students were wearing college scarves* **(b)** square piece of cloth which a woman can wear over her head; *put a scarf over your head - it's windy outside* (NOTE: plural is **scarves** [skɑːvz])

scarlet ['skɑːlət] *adjective* brilliant red; *when she accused him of stealing, he turned scarlet*

scary ['skeəri] *adjective (informal)* frightening; *it was a bit scary being left alone in the empty hotel all night*; *the film is too scary for young children* (NOTE: **scarier - scariest**)

scathing ['skeɪðɪŋ] *adjective* very critical; *he made some scathing remarks about the service*

scatter ['skætə] *verb* **(a)** to throw in various places; *the crowd scattered flowers all over the path* **(b)** to run in different directions; *when the police arrived, the children scattered*

scatterbrain ['skætəbreɪn] *noun (informal)* person who often forgets things; *she's a real scatterbrain -*

look, she's left her passport and tickets on the mantelpiece

scatterbrained ['skætəbreɪnd] *adjective (informal)* often forgetting things; *some scatterbrained member of staff forgot to switch on the alarm system*

scattered ['skætəd] *adjective* spread out over a wide area; *there are scattered farms in the hills*; *I found the photos scattered all over the floor*

scattering ['skætərɪŋ] *noun* a small quantity or number of things; *only a scattering of people turned up to the meeting*; *there was a scattering of snow during the night*

scavenge ['skævɪndʒ] *verb* **(a)** to feed on dead and decaying matter; *vultures live by scavenging on the corpses of animals which have died in the desert* **(b)** to get food or other useful items from rubbish; *children were scavenging for food in the heaps of rubbish round the city*

scavenger ['skævɪndʒə] *noun* animal which feeds on dead animals, dead plants or refuse left by other animals; *scavengers like vultures wait in the trees near where the lions are hunting*

scenario [sɪ'nɑːriəʊ] *noun* **(a)** written draft of a film with details of plot, characters, scenes, etc.; *he wrote the scenario for 'Gone with the Wind'* **(b)** general way in which you think something may happen; *the worst scenario would be if my wife's mother came on holiday with us* (NOTE: plural is **scenarios**)

scene [siːn] *noun* **(a)** short part of a play or film; *did you like the scene where he is trying to climb up the skyscraper?*; *it was one of the funniest scenes I have ever seen* **(b)** **behind the scenes** = without being obvious, without many people knowing; *she helped her mother a lot behind the scenes* **(c)** place where something has happened; *the fire brigade were on the scene very quickly*; *it took the ambulance ten minutes to get to the scene of the accident*; *a photographer was at the scene to record the ceremony* **(d)** *(informal)* general area in which something happens; *the British political scene has changed radically over the last twelve months*; *he's king of the pop music scene*; **it's not my scene** = it's not the sort of thing I usually do or like **(e)** view; *he took a photo of the scene from the hotel window* **(f)** display of angry emotion; *she made a terrible scene when she discovered her husband with a girl*; *I can't stand it when people make scenes*

scenery ['siːnri] *noun* **(a)** features of the countryside; *the beautiful scenery of the Lake District* **(b)** painted cloth background used to imitate real buildings, rooms, landscapes, etc., on the stage in a theatre; *they lowered the scenery onto the stage*; *in between the acts all the scenery has to be changed* (NOTE: no plural)

scenic ['siːnɪk] *adjective* referring to beautiful scenery; *welcome to the scenic Scottish Isles*; **scenic route** = (i) road running through beautiful countryside; (ii) long roundabout route

scent [sent] **1** *noun* **(a)** pleasant smell of something which you can recognize; *the scent of roses in the cottage garden* **(b)** perfume; *that new scent of yours makes me sneeze* **(c)** smell; **on the scent of** = following a trail left by; *the dogs followed the scent of the robbers*; **to put someone off the scent** = to give someone wrong information so as to mislead them; *she tried to put the reporters off the scent by saying that her husband had gone into hospital* **2** *verb* **(a)** to give something a pleasant smell; *the lavatory cleaner is*

scented with pine (b) to discover something by smelling; *dogs can scent rabbits in holes in the ground* **(c)** to begin to feel that something exists; *the team raced forward, scenting victory* (NOTE: do not confuse with **cent, sent**)

scented ['sentɪd] *adjective* with a pleasant scent; *strongly scented roses; a slightly scented soap*

sceptic US **skeptic** ['skeptɪk] *noun* **(a)** person who doubts the truth of religion; *in the area of religious belief, he's something of a sceptic* **(b)** person who always doubts the truth of what he is told; *I am a sceptic when it comes to astrology*

sceptical US **skeptical** ['skeptɪkl] *adjective* doubtful, who doubts; *you seem sceptical about his new plan; I'm sceptical of the success of the expedition; he listened to her with a sceptical look on his face*

sceptically US **skeptically** ['skeptɪkli] *adverb* doubtfully; *she listened sceptically to her boyfriend's excuses*

scepticism US **skepticism** ['skeptɪsɪzm] *noun* doubt or uncertainty; *she maintained a healthy scepticism about his plans*

schedule ['ʃedjuːl US 'skedʒuːl] **1** *noun* **(a)** timetable, plan of times drawn up in advance; *he has a busy schedule of appointments; his secretary tried to fit me into his schedule;* **to be ahead of schedule** = to be early; *the building of the hotel was completed ahead of schedule;* **to be on schedule** = to be on time; *the flight is on schedule;* **to be behind schedule** = to be late; *I am sorry to say that we are three months behind schedule* **(b)** list of times of departure and arrival of trains, planes, coaches, etc.; *the summer schedules have been published* **(c)** programme or list of events; *the schedule of events for the music festival* **(d)** list, especially of documents attached to a contract; *please find enclosed our schedule of charges; the schedule of territories to which an insurance policy applies* **2** *verb* **(a)** to put something on an official list; *see the list of scheduled prices; the house has been scheduled as an ancient monument* **(b)** to arrange the times for something; *the building is scheduled for completion in May; the flight is scheduled to arrive at six o'clock; we have scheduled the meeting for Tuesday morning;* **scheduled flight** = flight which is in the airline timetable; *he left for Helsinki on a scheduled flight;* **scheduled service** = regular bus or train service

scheme [skiːm] **1** *noun* plan or arrangement for making something work; *she joined the company pension scheme; he has thought up some scheme for making money very quickly; I think the opposition parties have some scheme to embarrass the government* **2** *verb* to plan something in secret; *she spent most of her time in the office scheming against the finance department; they have been scheming to buy the shop cheaply*

schilling ['ʃɪlɪŋ] *noun* unit of currency used in Austria; *the book costs 16 schillings*

schizophrenia [skɪtsəu'friːniə] *noun* mental disorder where the patient withdraws from other people, has delusions and seems to lose contact with the real world; *he was diagnosed as having schizophrenia;* **paranoid schizophrenia** = form of schizophrenia where the patient believes he or she is being persecuted

schizophrenic [skɪtsəu'frenɪk] *noun & adjective* (person) who has schizophrenia

scholar ['skɒlə] *noun* **(a)** learned person; *he is a well-known scholar of medieval French history* **(b)** student at school or university who has a scholarship; *because I was a scholar my parents didn't have to pay any fees*

scholarly ['skɒləli] *adjective* referring to serious study at a high level; *he wrote an article for a scholarly review*

scholarship ['skɒləʃɪp] *noun* **(a)** deep learning; *the article shows sound scholarship* (NOTE: no plural in this meaning) **(b)** money given to someone to help pay for the cost of his or her study; *the college offers scholarships to attract the best students; she got or won a scholarship to carry out research into causes of cancer*

scholastic [skɒ'læstɪk] *adjective* (*formal*) referring to schools or teaching methods; *his scholastic achievements were small - he left school without passing a single exam*

school [skuːl] **1** *noun* **(a)** place where students, usually children, are taught; *our little boy is four, so he'll be going to school this year; some children start school younger than that; what did the children do at school today?; when he was sixteen, he left school and joined the army; which school did you go to?; we moved here because there are good schools nearby;* **school year** = period which starts in September and finishes in August; **nursery school** = school for very small children, for children under five years old; **primary school** = school for small children; **secondary school** = school for children after the age of eleven or twelve; **grammar school** = school which selects children by an entrance examination; *see also* PUBLIC **(b)** section of a college or university; *the school of medicine is one of the largest in the country; she's studying at law school* **(c)** art school = college where students learn to draw, sculpt, paint, etc.; **music school** = college where students learn to play or write music; *he's been teaching at the London School of Music for two years* **(d)** group of similar artists; *painters who do not belong to the naturalist school* **(e)** group of animals; *a school of porpoises* **2** *verb* (*formal*) to train; *he was schooled in the art of tapping telephones*

school board ['skuːl 'bɔːd] *noun* US committee which runs a local school system

schoolbook ['skuːlbʊk] *noun* book used when learning a subject at school; *schools need more funds to purchase schoolbooks*

schoolboy ['skuːlbɔɪ] *nouns* boy who goes to school; *I haven't worn a cap since I was a schoolboy; we met as schoolboys and have always remained friends*

school bus ['skuːl 'bʌs] *noun* bus which collects children from home in the morning, takes them to school and brings them back home in the afternoon; *the school bus leaves her in front of the house every afternoon; the school bus collects our children every morning*

schoolchildren ['skuːltʃɪldrən] *nouns* children who go to school; *the village schoolchildren are collected by bus every morning*

schoolgirl ['skuːlgɜːl] *nouns* girl who goes to school; *a group of schoolgirls waiting at the bus stop*

schooling ['skuːlɪŋ] *noun* education at school level; *he received his schooling from an old lady in the* village; *his schooling was paid for by the local authority*

school kid ['sku:l 'kɪd] *noun (informal)* child who is at school; *at half past three the shop was full of school kids trying to buy sweets*

school leaver ['sku:l 'li:və] *noun* young person who has just left secondary school; *we have several jobs suitable for school leavers*

schoolmaster ['sku:lmɑ:stə] *noun* male schoolteacher, especially in a private school

schoolmistress ['sku:lmɪstrəs] *noun* female schoolteacher, especially in a private school (NOTE: plural is **schoolmistresses**)

schoolteacher ['sku:lti:tʃə] *noun* person who teaches in a school; *she has taken her degree in history and is now training to be a schoolteacher*

schooner ['sku:nə] *noun* **(a)** sailing ship with two or more masts and sails; *we sailed round the Caribbean in an old schooner* **(b)** tall glass; *they serve sherry in schooners*

science ['saɪəns] *noun* **(a)** study of natural physical things, based on observation and experiment; *she took a science course or she studied science; we have a new science teacher this term; he has a master's degree in marine science; see also* SOCIAL SCIENCE **(b) the sciences** = the science subjects at university, such as physics, chemistry, as opposed to the humanities

science fiction ['saɪəns 'fɪkʃn] *noun* stories of life in the future, based on imaginary scientific developments; *he's mad about science fiction films and anything to do with space travel*

scientific [saɪən'tɪfɪk] *adjective* referring to science; *we employ hundreds of people in scientific research; he's the director of a scientific institute; she loved art and music and was never very scientific*

scientifically [saɪən'tɪfɪkli] *adverb* by using scientific experiments; *we must try to prove our theory scientifically*

scientist ['saɪəntɪst] *noun* person who specializes in a science, often doing research; *scientists have not yet found a cure for the common cold; space scientists are examining the photographs of Mars*

sci-fi ['saɪ 'faɪ] = SCIENCE FICTION; *he's mad about sci-fi and anything to do with space travel*

scissors ['sɪzəz] *noun* tool for cutting paper, cloth, etc., made of two blades attached in the middle, with handles with holes for the thumb and fingers; *these scissors aren't very sharp; have you got a pair of scissors I can borrow?;* **nail scissors** = special small curved scissors for cutting fingernails and toenails; *she cut the story out of the paper with her nail scissors* (NOTE: no singular form: for one, say **a pair of scissors**)

sclerosis [sklə'rəʊsɪs] *noun* hardening of soft tissue; **multiple sclerosis** = disease of the central nervous system which gets progressively worse, causing numbness in the limbs, progressive weakness and paralysis

scoff [skɒf] *verb* **(a) to scoff at something** = to make fun of something in a nasty way; *he scoffed at her attempts at windsurfing; the committee chairman scoffed at my idea for redeveloping the town centre* **(b)** *(informal)* to eat greedily; *the two boys rushed into the dining room and scoffed half the cakes*

Scolastic Assessment Tests (SAT) *US* = (trademark of the College Entrance Examination Board) pre-college tests

scold [skəʊld] *verb* to speak to someone angrily; *the teacher scolded the children for running across the busy road*

scone [skɒn] *noun* type of small round soft bread, sometimes with dried fruit in it, eaten with butter or cream, and jam

scoop [sku:p] **1** *noun* **(a)** deep round spoon with a short handle, for serving ice cream, etc.; *you must wash the scoop each time you use it* **(b)** portion of ice cream, etc.; *I'll have one scoop of strawberry and one scoop of vanilla, please* **(c)** exciting news story which a reporter is the first to find, or which no other newspaper has reported; *he came back from the visit to the footballer's girlfriend with a scoop* **2** *verb* **(a)** to cut out with a scoop; *he scooped out a helping of mashed potato;* **to scoop out the inside of something** = to remove the inside of something with a spoon, etc.; *scoop out the inside of a melon* **(b)** to lift up, as with a scoop; *she scooped up the babies into her arms and ran upstairs; he scooped all the newspapers off the floor* **(c) to scoop a newspaper** = to report a news item before another paper does; *they scooped their rivals with the story of the minister's girlfriend*

scooter ['sku:tə] *noun* **(a)** child's two-wheeled vehicle with a long steering handle, pushed along with one foot while the other foot is on the board **(b)** small type of motorbike with a curving shield in front of the seat and a platform for the feet; *she dodged through the traffic on her scooter*

scope [skəʊp] *noun* **(a)** furthest area covered by observation or action; *these matters are beyond the scope of our investigation* **(b)** opportunity or possibility; *we keep the children busy so there is no scope for them to get bored;* **there is scope for improvement** = it could be improved; *there is considerable scope for expansion into the export market*

scorch [skɔ:tʃ] **1** *noun* **scorch mark** = brown mark where something has been slightly burnt; *the scorch marks showed on the pale blue carpet* **2** *verb* **(a)** to burn slightly, to brown; *he accidentally scorched the tablecloth with the iron* **(b)** to make very hot and dry; *the sun has scorched the grass;* **scorched-earth policy** = tactics in war where you destroy all resources before retreating and giving up land to the enemy

scorching ['skɔ:tʃɪŋ] *adjective* very hot, which scorches; *they walked gingerly across the scorching concrete*

score [skɔ:] **1** *noun* **(a)** number of goals or points made in a match; *the final score in the rugby match was 22 - 10; I didn't see the beginning of the match - what's the score?* **what's the score?** = what is the news?; **I know the score** = I know all the problems involved **(b)** *(formal)* twenty; **three score years and ten** = seventy years **(c) scores of** = many; *scores of people stayed at home during the train strike; I must have seen that film scores of times* **(d)** written music; *he composed the score for the musical* **(e) to settle old scores** = to take revenge for things that happened a long time ago **(f) on that score** = as far as that is concerned; *he likes all sorts of food, so you won't have any trouble on that score* **2** *verb* **(a)** to make a goal or point in a match; *they scored three goals* *in the first twenty minutes; she scored sixty-five!* **(b)** *(music)* to arrange music for certain instruments; *a piece scored for piano and three violins* **(c)** to scratch a flat surface; *score the surface of the wood with a sharp knife so that glue will hold better*

scoreboard ['skɔːbɔːd] *noun* large board on which the score in a game is shown as the game progresses; *the scoreboard showed England needed only 22 runs to win*

scorer ['skɔːrə] *noun* **(a)** person who scores a point, a goal, etc., in a game; *with his hat trick he became the highest scorer in the league this season* **(b)** person who writes down the scores in a game; *we played Scrabble and I was the scorer*

scorn [skɔːn] **1** *noun* feeling of thinking that someone or something is not good enough; *he heaped scorn on the committee's proposal; the suggestion was greeted with scorn* **2** *verb* to refuse to accept an idea, a suggestion; *most young people in the office scorn the idea that smoking can be bad for your health; she scorned his proposal of a lift*

scornful ['skɔːnful] *adjective* considering something not good enough; *the union was scornful of the management's offer*

Scorpio ['skɔːpiəu] *noun* one of the signs of the Zodiac, shaped like a scorpion; *if your birthday is on October 28th you must be (a) Scorpio*

scorpion ['skɔːpiən] *noun* poisonous tropical animal which stings with its long curved tail; *a scorpion was found in a case at the airport*

Scot [skɒt] *noun* person from Scotland; *is she English? - no, she's a Scot; the Scots have voted 'yes' in the referendum*

Scotch [skɒtʃ] **1** *adjective* referring to Scotland (NOTE: 'Scottish' is the usual adjective, but 'Scotch' is always used in the following phrases); **Scotch broth** = thick soup with barley, vegetables and lamb; *a hot bowl of Scotch broth will be very welcome;* **Scotch eggs** = hard boiled eggs covered with sausagemeat and breadcrumbs; **Scotch terrier** = type of black or white terrier; **Scotch whisky** = whisky made in Scotland **2** *noun* **(a)** Scotch whisky; *a bottle of scotch (b)* a glass of this drink; *a large scotch, please* (NOTE: plural is **scotches**) **(c) Scotch tape** = trademark for a type of transparent sticky tape; *can you pass me the reel of Scotch tape, please?; he sealed the parcel with some Scotch tape* **3** *verb* to prove something wrong, to put a stop to something; *by appearing in public, the president scotched rumours of his death*

Scotland ['skɒtlənd] *noun* country to the north of England, forming part of the United Kingdom; *the lochs and moors of Scotland; he was brought up in Scotland; Scotland's most famous export is whisky*

Scotland Yard ['skɒtlənd 'jɑːd] *noun* headquarters of the London Metropolitan Police, or the officers who work there; *the local police were baffled so they called in Scotland Yard; a spokesman for Scotland Yard said that a man was helping police with their enquiries* (NOTE: also called simply **the Yard**)

Scots [skɒts] **1** *adjective* (of the people, laws, etc.) Scottish; *'not proven' is a decision in Scots law* **2** *noun* dialect of English spoken in Scotland; *'Auld Lang Syne' is one of Burns' poems in Scots*

Scotsman ['skɒtsmən] *noun* man from Scotland; *Scotsmen everywhere will be celebrating their team's victory* (NOTE: plural is **Scotsmen**)

Scottish ['skɒtɪʃ] *adjective* referring to Scotland; *is she English? - no, she's Scottish; the beautiful Scottish lochs and moors*

scour ['skauə] *verb* **(a)** to clean by scrubbing with a hard material; *her first job was scouring dirty pans in the restaurant* **(b)** to search everywhere; *we scoured the market and couldn't find any aubergines; the police have been scouring the woods near the village where the little girl lived*

scourer *or* **scouring pad** ['skauərə *or* 'skauərɪŋ 'pæd] *noun* pad of steel wool, plastic thread or other hard material, used to clean pans, etc.

scourge [skɜːdʒ] *noun* thing which causes suffering; *alcohol is the scourge of the business community*

scout [skaut] **1** *noun* boy who belongs to the Boy Scouts' Association; *let Bill light the fire - he was a scout as a boy;* **the Scouts** = the Boy Scouts' Association; *our son has just joined the Scouts* **2** *verb* **to scout (around) for** = to look out for; *he goes to sales in the country, scouting for antiques*

scowl [skaul] **1** *noun* angry look made by wrinkling the forehead; *he gave a scowl and went on eating* **2** *verb* to make a scowl; *when she asked him for a rise the boss scowled; he scowled at the little boy and then told him to run away*

scrabble ['skræbl] **1** *noun* **Scrabble** = trademark for a game where you are given a series of letters and have to make words with them **2** *verb* **to scrabble (about)** = to search wildly with your fingers; *they were scrabbling about in the dustbin, looking for the missing letter; she scrabbled in her shopping bag for the receipt*

scramble ['skræmbl] **1** *noun* **(a)** rush; *there was a last-minute scramble for tickets* **(b)** motorcycle race across rough country; *we went to watch the scramble and got very cold and wet* **2** *verb* **(a)** to hurry, using your hands and knees if necessary; *he scrambled over the wall* **(b)** to rush; *everyone was scrambling to get food* **(c) scrambled eggs** = eggs mixed together and stirred as they are cooked in butter; *we had a starter of scrambled eggs with smoked salmon*

scrap [skræp] **1** *noun* **(a)** little piece; *a scrap of paper; there isn't a scrap of evidence against him; she is collecting scraps of cloth to make a quilt* **(b)** waste materials; *to sell a car for scrap; the scrap value of the car is £200;* **scrap dealer** *or* **scrap merchant** = person who deals in scrap; **scrap heap** = heap of rubbish; *that car's good for the scrap heap;* **scrap metal** *or* **scrap paper** = waste metal *or* waste paper **(c) scraps** = bits of waste food; *they keep the scraps to feed to their pigs* **(d)** *(informal)* fight; *the football fans got into a scrap with local youths* **2** *verb* **(a)** to throw away as useless; *they had to scrap 10,000 faulty spare parts* **(b)** to give up, to stop working on a plan; *we've scrapped our plans to go to Greece* **(c)** to fight; *they were scrapping over who should get the best bit of the chicken* (NOTE: **scrapping - scrapped**)

scrapbook ['skræpbuk] *noun* book with blank pages on which you can stick pictures or stories cut from newspapers, etc.; *she loved looking through her grandmother's old scrapbooks*

scrape [skreɪp] **1** *noun (informal)* awkward situation which is you get into by mistake; *he's always getting* into scrapes **2** *verb* to scratch with a hard object which is pulled across a surface; *she scraped the paint off the door*; *he fell off his bike and scraped his knee on the pavement*

scrape together ['skreɪp tə'geðə] *verb* to gather things together with difficulty; *they scraped together enough money to buy the ticket*

scrape through ['skreɪp 'θruː] *verb* to pass an examination with difficulty; *he thought he was going to fail, but in the end he just scraped through*

scratch [skrætʃ] **1** *noun* **(a)** long wound on the skin; *put some antiseptic on the scratches on your arms*; **without a scratch** = with no injuries; *he came out of the car crash without a scratch* **(b)** long mark made by a sharp point; *I will never be able to cover up the scratches on the car door* **(c) to start from scratch** = to start something new without any preparation; **up to scratch** = of the right quality; *the recording was not up to scratch* (NOTE: plural is **scratches**) **2** *verb* **(a)** to make a long wound on the skin; *his legs were scratched by the bushes along the path* **(b)** to make a mark with a sharp point; *I must touch up the car where it has been scratched* **(c)** to rub a part of the body which itches with your fingernails; *he scratched his head as he wondered what to do next*; *stop scratching - it will make your rash worse!* **(d)** to remove your name from the list of competitors; *one of the players scratched at the last minute* **3** *adjective* collected at the last minute; *our opponents were a scratch side from the nearby village*

scrawl [skrɔːl] **1** *noun* bad, careless handwriting; *I can't read his scrawl* **2** *verb* to write badly or carelessly; *he scrawled a few notes on a bit of paper*

scream [skriːm] **1** *noun* **(a)** loud cry of pain; *he let out a scream of pain*; *the screams of the victims of the fire* **(b) screams of laughter** = loud laughter **(c)** *(informal)* funny person; *she's an absolute scream when she starts talking about the office* **2** *verb* **(a)** to make loud cries; *people on the third floor were screaming for help*; *they screamed with pain*; *she screamed at the class to stop singing* **(b) to scream with laughter** = to laugh very loudly

screech [skriːtʃ] **1** *noun* piercing sound; *I was woken up by the screech of the owl in the tree*; *the car sped away with a screech of tyres* (NOTE: plural is **screeches**) **2** *verb* to make a piercing sound; *the motorbike raced up and screeched to a stop*; *the police car screeched round the corner*

screen [skriːn] **1** *noun* **(a)** flat panel which acts as protection against draughts, fire, noise, etc.; *a screen decorated with flowers and birds*; *the hedge acts as a screen against the noise from the motorway* **(b)** flat glass surface on which a picture is shown; *a computer screen*; *I'll call the information up on the screen*; *a TV screen* **(c)** flat white surface for projecting films or pictures; *we'll put up the screen on the stage*; *a cinema complex with four screens*; **the small screen** = television **2** *verb* **(a)** to protect from draught, fire, noise, etc.; *they planted a row of trees to screen the farm buildings*; *part of the room was screened off*; *put the umbrella up to screen us from the sun* **(b)** to show a film in a cinema *or* on TV; *tonight's film will be screened half an hour later than advertised* **(c)** to consider or investigate people, such as candidates for a job, before making a final choice; *applicants will be screened before being invited to an interview*; **to screen people for a disease** = to examine a lot of

people to see if they have a disease; *all women over 40 should be screened for cervical cancer*

screening ['skriːnɪŋ] *noun* **(a)** showing of a film; *this will be the first screening of the film outside Japan* **(b) the screening of candidates** = examining candidates to see if they are suitable; *Professor Mills will be in charge of the screening of applicants for the job*; **the screening of patients** = examining patients to see if they have an illness; *breast screening is important for women over 40*

screenplay ['skriːnpleɪ] *noun* scenario, a written draft of a film with details of plot, characters, scenes, etc.; *he wrote the screenplay for 'Gone with the Wind'*

screenwriter ['skriːnraɪtə] *noun* person who writes screenplays; *he spent several years as a screenwriter in Hollywood*

screw [skruː] **1** *noun* **(a)** metal pin with a winding groove round it, which you twist to make it go into a hard surface; *I need some longer screws to go through this thick plank*; *the plate was fixed to the door with brass screws*; *(informal)* **to have a screw loose** = to be slightly mad **(b)** propeller of a ship; *a twin-screw trawler* **2** *verb* **(a)** to attach with screws; *the picture was screwed to the wall* **(b)** to attach by twisting; *he filled up the bottle and screwed on the top*; *screw the lid on tightly* *(informal)* **he's got his head screwed on the right way** = he's very sensible

screwdriver ['skruːdraɪvə] *noun* tool with a long handle and special end which is used for turning screws; *she tightened up the screws with a screwdriver*

screwed-up ['skruːdʌp] *adjective* *(informal)* worried and unhappy; *they're just a couple of crazy screwed-up kids*

screw-top jar ['skruːtɒp 'dʒɑː] *noun* jar with a top which screws on and off; *make the salad dressing in a screw-top jar to take with you on the picnic*

scribble ['skrɪbl] **1** *noun* **(a)** meaningless marks written by a child; *the wallpaper was covered with scribbles* **(b)** bad writing; *please excuse my scribble - I'm rushing to get this in the post* **2** *verb* **(a)** to make meaningless marks; *the kids have scribbled all over their bedroom walls* **(b)** to write hurriedly and badly; *she scribbled a few notes in the train*

scribe [skraɪb] *noun* *(old)* person who writes copies of letters, books, etc., by hand; *the letter must have been drafted by a scribe working in the emperor's palace*

script [skrɪpt] *noun* **(a)** written text of a film or play; *the actors settled down with their scripts for the first reading* **(b)** style or system of handwriting; *the Germans used to write in Gothic script* **(c)** written examination answer; *at the end of the exam the invigilator gathered up all the scripts*

scriptural ['skrɪptʃərəl] *adjective* referring to scripture; *the scriptural texts are not always easy to understand*

scripture ['skrɪptʃə] *noun* **(a)** the Bible; *according to Scripture or to the Scriptures, St Peter was a fisherman* **(b)** holy writing; *the story of Vishnu is set down in Hindu scripture*; *a passage translated from Buddhist scriptures*

scriptwriter ['skrɪptraɪtə] *noun* person who writes scripts for films, or TV or radio plays; *the two men are scriptwriters for a popular TV series*

scroll [skrəul] **1** *noun* (a) long piece of paper with writing on it, rolled up; *each graduate was presented with a scroll marking his or her achievement* (b) curved shape, like a roll of paper; *the wallpaper is decorated with little blue scrolls* **2** *verb* to move displayed text up or down the computer screen, one line at a time; *she rapidly scrolled down until she came to the address she wanted*

scrotum ['skrəutəm] *noun* bag of skin hanging from behind the penis, containing the testicles

scrub [skrʌb] **1** *noun* (a) area of land with a few small bushes; *they walked for miles through the scrub until they came to a river* (b) action of scrubbing; *after a game of rugby you will need a good scrub* **2** *verb* (a) to clean by rubbing with soap and a brush; *scrub your fingernails to get rid of the dirt*; *a well-scrubbed kitchen table* (b) *(informal)* to remove something that has been recorded on tape; *can you scrub the last five minutes of the recording?*; **scrub that** = you can forget about that (NOTE: **scrubbing - scrubbed**)

scrubbing brush ['skrʌbɪŋ 'brʌʃ] *noun* stiff brush with no handle, for scrubbing floors, etc.; *you'll need a scrubbing brush to get those marks off*

scruff [skrʌf] *noun* **by the scruff of the neck** = holding someone or an animal by the skin at the back of the neck; *the cat picked up her kittens by the scruff of the neck and took them to her basket*; *the policeman grabbed him by the scruff of the neck and pushed him into the police van*

scruffy ['skrʌfi] *adjective* untidy or dirty; *she was wearing a dark velvet dress and a pair of scruffy sneakers*; *a scruffy-looking boy stole my bike* (NOTE: **scruffier - scruffiest**)

scrum *or* **scrummage** [skrʌm *or* 'skrʌmɪdʒ] *noun* (a) *(in Rugby)* manoeuvre in which two groups of forwards from opposing sides push against each other to get the ball; *there was a scrum just in front of the goal* (b) struggling crowd; *what a scrum! - everyone was trying to get tickets*

scrumptious ['skrʌmʃəs] *adjective (informal)* delicious; *that pudding was scrumptious!*

scruple ['skru:pl] **1** *noun* **to have scruples about doing something** = to have doubts about whether something is right, which prevent you from doing it; *I have considerable scruples about giving money to that particular charity*; *he had no scruples about copying other people's ideas* **2** *verb (formal)* **not to scruple to do something** = not to hesitate to do something, even though it might have a bad effect; *he didn't scruple to threaten his mother with a stick to get her to give him money*

scrupulous ['skru:pjuləs] *adjective* very careful, very honest; *she was well-known for the scrupulous care with which she made dresses for her clients*; *he was scrupulous in all his dealings with the bank*

scrutinize ['skru:tɪnaɪz] *verb* to examine very carefully; *the customs official scrutinized his import permit*

scrutiny ['skru:tɪni] *noun* careful examination; a very close look; *the prisoners are under constant scrutiny*; **it will repay close scrutiny** = it would be worth looking at it carefully; **not to stand close scrutiny** = not to be as good as it seems; *the charity's work will not stand close scrutiny*

scuba diver ['sku:bə 'daɪvə] *noun* person who goes scuba diving; *scuba divers worked round the clock to bring up pieces of the wreckage from the seabed*

scuba diving ['sku:bə 'daɪvɪŋ] *noun* swimming underwater, using breathing apparatus; *we went scuba diving in the Mediterranean*

scuff [skʌf] *verb* to scratch the surface of something; *he was carrying an old scuffed suitcase*; *I scuffed my new shoes on the pedals in the car*

scuffle ['skʌfl] **1** *noun* small fight; *scuffles broke out in the crowd* **2** *verb* to fight; *after the game, fans scuffled with the police*

scull [skʌl] **1** *noun* **sculls** = (i) pair of small oars with which one person rows a boat; (ii) race for boats rowed by people with two oars; **double sculls** = race for boats with two oarsmen, each with two oars **2** *verb* to row in a competition, using two oars (NOTE: do not confuse with **skull**)

sculler ['skʌlə] *noun* oarsman who uses two oars

scullery ['skʌləri] *noun* small room at the back of a kitchen used for cleaning and washing up; *she's in the scullery, polishing the silver* (NOTE: plural is **sculleries**)

sculpt [skʌlpt] *verb* to carve a figure out of wood or stone or make it out of metal; *he spent years sculpting the statue*

sculptor, sculptress ['skʌlptə *or* 'skʌlptrəs] *noun* person who makes figures or shapes out of wood, metal or stone; *we visited the sculptor's studio and watched him working on his next statue*

sculpture ['skʌlptʃə] *noun* figure carved out of stone or wood, etc., or made out of metal; *there is a sculpture of the goddess of love in the centre of the square*

scum [skʌm] *noun* (a) layer of dirty foam on the surface of a liquid; *as the liquid boils, a grey scum forms on the surface and should be removed* (b) person of the worst type; *those muggers are just scum, I hope they get sent to prison* (NOTE: no plural)

scupper ['skʌpə] **1** *noun* hole in the top of the side of a ship to let water run off the deck **2** *verb* (a) *(informal)* to bring to an end, to ruin; *the newspaper article has scuppered his chances of becoming a judge* (b) = SCUTTLE (a)

scurry ['skʌri] **1** *noun* fast movements; *the scurry as the passengers try to get onto the train just before it leaves* (NOTE: no plural) **2** *verb* to run fast, taking short steps; *when the owl appeared overhead, the little animals scurried to their holes*; *she was scurrying to her office with her bag of shopping*

scuttle ['skʌtl] **1** *noun* type of bucket for keeping coal in the house **2** *verb* (a) to sink a ship on purpose by opening holes in the bottom to allow water to come in; *the captain gave orders to scuttle the ship because he did not want her to be captured by the enemy* (b) to run fast, taking short steps; *she scuttled back to her office, afraid that she was late*; **to scuttle off** = to run away fast; *as soon as they saw the policeman in the distance, they all scuttled off down back streets*

scythe [saɪð] **1** *noun* farming implement with a long slightly curved blade attached to a handle with two short projecting hand grips, used for cutting long grass **2** *verb* to cut grass with a scythe; *all the farm workers were in the fields scything the hay*

sea [si:] *noun* **(a)** area of salt water between continents or islands, but not as large as an ocean; *swimming in the sea is more exciting than swimming in a river; the sea's too rough for the ferries to operate; his friends own a house by the sea; the North Sea separates Britain from Denmark and Germany;* **at sea** = travelling by ship; *we were at sea for only five days;* **by sea** = using ships as a means of transport; *when we moved to Australia we sent our furniture by sea;* **sea crossing** = journey across the sea; *the sea crossing between Denmark and Sweden can be quite rough;* **by sea mail** = sent by post abroad, using a ship, not by air; **to run away to sea** = to leave home to work as a sailor; *when he was sixteen he ran away to sea* (NOTE: in names **Sea** is written with a capital letter: **the North Sea,** etc.) **(b)** mass of things; *standing on the beach all I could see was a sea of penguins*

seabird ['si:bɜ:d] *noun* bird which lives near the sea and lives on fish; *gulls and other seabirds*

sea breeze ['si: 'bri:z] *noun* light wind blowing from the sea towards the land; *a sea breeze fluttered the tablecloths on the café tables*

seafood ['si:fu:d] *noun* fish or shellfish which can be eaten; *I never eat seafood - it doesn't agree with me;* a **seafood restaurant** = a restaurant which specializes in seafood (NOTE: no plural)

seafront ['si:frʌnt] *noun* road or wide path which runs beside the sea in a seaside town; *we went for a walk along the seafront; our hotel was right on the seafront; we stayed in a seafront hotel*

seagull ['si:gʌl] *noun* white sea bird; *a flock of seagulls flew around the tractor as it ploughed the field; the ferry was followed by seagulls looking for food; they were woken by the cries of seagulls in the harbour* (NOTE: also called simply **gull**)

seal [si:l] **1** *noun* **(a)** large animal with short fur, which eats fish, living mainly near to or in the sea; *seals lay sunning themselves on the rocks* **(b)** piece of paper, metal, or wax which is used to attach something to close it so that it cannot be opened; *the customs officials attached their seal to the box* **(c)** way in which something is closed; *the screw top gives a tight seal* **2** *verb* **(a)** to close something tightly; *a box carefully sealed with sticky tape;* **sealed envelope** = envelope where the flap has been stuck down to close it; *the information was sent in a sealed envelope* (NOTE: an envelope left open is an **unsealed envelope**) **(b)** to attach a seal; to stamp something with a seal; *the customs sealed the shipment*

sea level ['si: 'levl] *noun* the level of the sea, taken as a point for measuring altitude; *the ski resort is in the mountains, over 1,000m above sea level*

sea lion ['si:laɪən] *noun* large species of seal; *sea lions lay basking on the rocks*

seam [si:m] *noun* **(a)** line where two pieces of cloth, metal, etc., are attached together; *she sewed the seams on the sewing machine; he's got fatter, so can you let out a seam at the back of his coat?* **(b) to be bursting at the seams** = to be extremely full; *the little town was bursting at the seams with thousands of football fans;* **to come apart at the seams** = to fall to pieces; *his plans for a long holiday seem to be coming apart at the seams* **(c)** layer of mineral beneath the earth's surface; *the coal seams are two metres thick; the gold seam was worked out some years ago* (NOTE: do not confuse with **seem**)

seaman ['si:mən] *noun* man who works on a ship; *he works as an ordinary seaman on an oil tanker* (NOTE: plural is **seamen;** do not confuse with **semen**)

seamless ['si:mləs] *adjective* with no visible seams or joins; *a pair of seamless stockings*

seaplane ['si:pleɪn] *noun* plane with floats instead of wheels, which can land on water; *a little seaplane takes supplies to the islands*

search [sɜ:tʃ] **1** *noun* **(a)** action of trying to find something; *our search of the flat revealed nothing; they carried out a search for the missing children; I did a quick search on the Internet for references to Proust;* **search party** = group of people sent to look for someone; *the children haven't come back from the beach - we'll have to send out a search party;* **search warrant** = official document signed by a magistrate which allows police to go into a building and look for criminals, weapons or stolen goods **(b)** examination of records to make sure that a property belongs to the person who is trying to sell it; *the solicitor's search revealed that part of the drive belonged to the neighbouring farm* (NOTE: plural is **searches**) **2** *verb* **(a)** to examine very carefully; *the police searched the house from top to bottom but still couldn't find any weapons; she was stopped and searched by the customs* **(b) to search for** = to try to find; *the police searched for the missing children; I searched the Internet for references to Ireland;* **to search through** = to look for something carefully; *she searched through her papers, trying to find the document* (*computing*) **search and replace** = looking for words or phrases and replacing them automatically with other words or phrases

search engine ['sɜ:tʃ 'endʒɪn] *noun* program which allows you to search for particular words or phrases on the Internet

> COMMENT: some of the most popular search engines on the Internet are Yahoo! (www.yahoo.com), Excite! (www.excite.com), AltaVista (www.altavista.digital.com), HotBot (www.hotbot.com) and Lycos (www.lycos.com)

searcher ['sɜ:tʃə] *noun* person who searches; *the searchers combed the woods but found nothing*

searing ['si:rɪŋ] *adjective* very strong (heat, pain); *she felt a searing pain across her back; they stood in the searing midday heat in the centre of Madrid and looked for somewhere to sit down*

seashell ['si:ʃel] *noun* shell of a shellfish which lives in the sea; *the children walked along the beach collecting seashells*

seashore ['si:ʃɔ:] *noun* sandy area along the edge of the sea; *these types of plants grow on the seashore*

seasick ['si:sɪk] *adjective* ill because of the movement of a ship; *he gets seasick every time he crosses the Channel; she didn't enjoy the cruise because she was seasick all the time; I'll stay on deck because I feel seasick when I go down to my cabin*

seasickness ['si:sɪknəs] *noun* sickness caused by the movement of a ship; *do you suffer from seasickness?;* **seasickness pills** *or* **tablets** = medicine taken to prevent seasickness

seaside ['si:dsaɪd] *noun* area at the edge of the sea; *we always take the children to the seaside in August;*

they'd like a seaside holiday instead of a holiday in the mountains; seaside towns are empty in the winter

season ['siːzən] **1** noun **(a)** one of four parts of a year; the four seasons are spring, summer, autumn, and winter; spring is the season when the garden is full of flowers **(b)** part of the year when something usually happens; the tourist season is very long here - from March to September; the football season lasts from September to May; London is very crowded during the school holiday season; **high season** = period when there are lots of travellers, and when fares and hotels are more expensive; **low season** = time of year (often during the winter) when there are fewer travellers, and so fares and hotels are cheaper; tour operators urge more people to travel in the low season; **dry season** = period of the year when it does not rain much (as opposed to the rainy season); **rainy season** = period of year when it rains a lot (as opposed to the dry season); don't go there in October - that's the beginning of the rainy season; **shooting season** = period of the year when you can shoot pheasants, etc.; the grouse shooting season starts in August **(c)** (of fruit, etc.) **in season** = which is fresh and plentiful and easy to buy; strawberries are cheaper in season; pears are in season just now; **out of season** = more expensive because the growing season is over; oysters are out of season in June **2** verb to add flavouring, spices, etc., to a dish; the meat is seasoned with paprika

seasonal ['siːzənl] adjective **(a)** which only lasts for a season, usually the holiday season; work on the island is only seasonal; **seasonal demand** = demand which exists only during the high season; **seasonal employment** = job which is available at certain times of the year only (such as in a ski resort); **seasonal labour** = workers who work for a season (usually the summer) only **(b)** characteristic of a particular time of year; in December the supermarket shelves are stocked with Christmas decorations and other seasonal goods; we can expect seasonal weather, with temperatures about average for the time of year

seasoned ['siːzənd] adjective **(a)** (food) which has had seasoning put on it; highly seasoned Indian food **(b)** who has had a lot of experience; he's a seasoned traveller, and knows the airlines to avoid **(c)** seasoned wood = wood which has been slowly dried; they did not use seasoned wood for the door frames, and they warped

seasoning ['siːznɪŋ] noun spices which are added to food; the meat seems to lack seasoning

season ticket ['siːzən 'tɪkɪt] noun railway or bus ticket or theatre ticket, which you can use for a whole year or a month at a time; the company will give you an interest-free loan to buy your annual season ticket; season-ticket holders will receive a refund if their train is cancelled

seat [siːt] **1** noun chair, something which you sit on; he was sitting in the driver's seat; can we have two seats in the front row?; please take your seats, the play is about the begin; all the seats on the bus were taken so I had to stand; our kitchen chairs have wooden seats; bicycle seats are narrow and not very comfortable; **to take a seat** = to sit down; please take a seat, the dentist will see you in a few minutes **2** verb to have room for people to sit down; the restaurant seats 75

seat belt ['siːt 'belt] noun belt which you wear in a car or plane to stop you being hurt if there is an

accident; the sole survivor of the crash had been wearing a seat belt; the 'fasten seat belts' sign came on

COMMENT: in Britain, the driver and front-seat passenger in a car are obliged by law to wear seat belts. Rear seat passengers must also wear seat belts if the car has them. All new cars and minibuses are fitted with rear seat belts

seated ['siːtɪd] adjective sitting down; everyone stood up when the chairman came in, except John who remained seated

seating ['siːtɪŋ] noun seats for people; the hall has seating for three hundred people; **seating capacity** = the number of seats (in a bus, cinema, etc.); the hall has a seating capacity of three hundred

sea urchin ['siː 'ɜːtʃɪn] noun small sea animal with a round shell covered with spines

sea water ['siː 'wɔːtə] noun salt water which is found in the sea; some fish, such as salmon, can live both in sea water and fresh water; the hotel has a sea water swimming pool (NOTE: water in rivers and lakes is called **fresh water**)

seaweed ['siːwiːd] noun plant which grows in the sea; the rocks are covered with seaweed (NOTE: no plural: **some seaweed, a piece of seaweed**)

seaworthy ['siːwɜːði] adjective (boat) which is fit to go to sea; the old ferry is scarcely seaworthy

secede [sɪˈsiːd] verb to break away from an organization or a federation; in 1776 the American colonies seceded from Great Britain and formed the United States

secession [sɪˈseʃn] noun act of seceding; the American Civil War began with the secession of several Southern states

secessionist [sɪˈseʃənɪst] **1** noun person who is in favour of secession **2** adjective which has seceded or is proposing to secede; a secessionist state

secluded [sɪˈkluːdɪd] adjective (place) which is quiet, away from crowds; they tried to find a secluded beach; we found a secluded spot by the river for our picnic

seclusion [sɪˈkluːʒn] noun solitude; they left town for the seclusion of the countryside

second ['sekənd] **1** noun **(a)** one of sixty parts which make up a minute; I'll give you ten seconds to get out of my room; they say the bomb will go off in twenty seconds **(b)** very short time; please wait a second; wait here - I'll be back in a second **(c)** something or someone that comes after the first thing or person; today is the second of March or March the second (March 2nd) the Great Fire of London took place when Charles the Second (Charles II) was king (NOTE: in dates **second** is usually written **2nd: August 2nd, 1932, July 2nd, 1666** (American style is **July 2, 1666**), say 'the second of July' or 'July the second' (American style is 'July second'); with names of kings and queens **second** is usually written **II: Queen Elizabeth II** (say 'Queen Elizabeth the Second') **(d)** person who helps a boxer during a fight; **seconds out** = instruction to seconds to leave the ring before a round begins **2** adjective **(a)** coming after the first and before the third; February is the second month of the year; he came second in the race; it's his second birthday next week; B is the second letter in the alphabet; women's clothes are on the second floor; that's the second time the telephone has rung while we're having dinner; the **second century** = the period from 100AD to 199; **second helping** = another helping of the same dish; *after we had finished, the waiter came round with a second helping of fish* (b) second + *superlative* = only one other is more; *this is the second longest bridge in the world; he's the second highest paid member of staff* **3** *verb* (a) ['sekənd]; **to second a motion** = to be the first person to formally support a proposal put forward by someone else in a meeting; *the motion was seconded by Mrs Smith* (b) [sɪ'kɒnd] to lend a member of staff to another company, to a government department, etc., for a fixed period of time; *he was seconded to the Department of Trade for two years; see also* SECONDMENT

secondary ['sekəndri] *adjective* (a) which comes second; **secondary school** = school for children after the age of eleven or twelve (b) **of secondary importance** = not so very important; *the colour of the car is of secondary importance*

second best ['sekʌnd 'best] *noun* something which is not as good as the best; **to come off second best** = to lose in a contest

second-class ['sekənd 'klɑːs] *adjective & adverb* (a) *(of travel, hotels, etc.)* less expensive and less comfortable than first-class; *I find second-class hotels are perfectly adequate; we always travel second-class because it is cheaper* (b) *(of postal service)* less expensive and slower than first-class; *a second-class letter is cheaper than a first-class; send it second-class if it is not urgent* (c) **second-class citizens** = people who have fewer rights, opportunities, etc., than others; *unemployed people are in danger of becoming second-class citizens*

seconder ['sekəndə] *noun* person who seconds a proposal; *there was no seconder for the motion so it was not put to the vote; Mr Smith has proposed the motion, but who is the seconder?*

second half ['seknd 'hɑːf] *noun* (a) second section of two parts, as of a football match; *they scored three goals in the second half* (b) second part of a financial year, from July to December; *the figures for the second half are up on those for the first part of the year*

second hand ['sekənd 'hænd] *noun* long hand on a watch which turns round fast and shows the seconds; *this watch does not have a second hand*

secondhand [sekənd'hænd] **1** *adjective* not new; which someone else has owned before; *we've just bought a secondhand car; we bought this sofa from a secondhand dealer* **2** *adverb* **to buy something secondhand** = to buy something which someone else has owned before; *we bought this car secondhand*

second-in-command ['sekənd ɪn kə'mɑːnd] *noun* chief officer who is under a commanding officer; *after he was wounded he handed over to his second-in-command*

secondly ['sekndli] *adverb* in second place; *I'm not going to his party: firstly it's my mother's birthday, and secondly, I don't really like his family*

secondment [sɪ'kɒndmənt] *noun* being seconded to another job; *he is on three years' secondment to an Australian college*

second nature ['sekənd 'neɪtʃə] *noun* something which has been learned, but which is done so often that it has become an instinctive reaction; *hiding from the*

police has become second nature to him; driving a bus is second nature to her

second opinion ['sekənd ə'pɪnjən] *noun* **to ask for a second opinion** = to ask another doctor or specialist to examine you and give his or her opinion on your medical condition, usually because you are not satisfied with the advice of the first doctor; *I wasn't convinced I needed the operation, so I asked for a second opinion*

second-rate [sekən(d)'reɪt] *adjective* not of very good quality; *never buy anything second-rate; I'm afraid I'm rather a second-rate golfer*

seconds ['sekndz] *noun* (a) *(informal)* another helping of the same dish; *can I have seconds, please?* (b) items which have been turned down as not being of top quality; *the shop has a sale of seconds; we bought our dinner service from a shop selling seconds*

second sight ['seknd 'saɪt] *noun* being able to tell what will happen in the future; *he claims he has the gift of second sight*

second thoughts ['seknd 'θɔːts] *noun* **to have second thoughts about something** = to change your mind about something; *is she having second thoughts about getting married?*; **on second thoughts** = having thought about it again; *I said I didn't want any pudding, but on second thoughts, perhaps I will have some*

Second World War ['sekənd 'wɜːld 'wɑː] *noun* war fought from 1939 to 1945; *he was a fighter pilot during the Second World War; in Northern France, they visited the sites of some of the Second World War battles*

COMMENT: events leading to the Second World War were dominated by Germany's expansionism under Hitler. Other European powers tried to prevent a war by making treaties to protect smaller countries, and it was the treaty between Britain and France with Poland which came into operation when the German troops invaded western Poland in September 1939. Soon, all of Europe was at war, with the exception of Russia, which had signed a treaty with Germany, and only entered the war when Germany invaded Russia in June 1941. The United States remained out of the war for some time, but was drawn in when Japan attacked the American Pacific fleet at Pearl Harbor in December 1941. By that time, Germany had occupied almost all of Western Europe. The war continued until the Allies successfully landed troops in northern France in 1944, gradually pushing the German armies back into Germany at the same time as the Russians were attacking in the east and the Americans were attacking the Japanese in South-East Asia. The war in Europe ended shortly after the suicide of Hitler in May 1945, but continued in the Far East until Japan surrendered following the dropping of atomic bombs on Japanese cities in August 1945

secrecy ['siːkrəsi] *noun* being secret; keeping something secret; *you will see that secrecy is extremely important when we're discussing the new project; why is there so much secrecy about the candidate's age?; the whole project is shrouded in secrecy*

secret ['siːkrət] **1** *adjective* hidden, not known by other people; *there is a secret door into the cellar*; **to keep something secret** = to make sure that no one knows about it; *she kept his birth secret for twenty years* **2** *noun* **(a)** thing which is not known or which is kept hidden; *if I tell you a secret will you promise not to repeat it to anyone?*; **is he in on the secret?** = does he know the secret?; **to keep a secret** = not to tell someone something which you know and no one else does; *can he keep a secret?* **(b) in secret** = without anyone knowing; *they met in secret by the lake in the park*; **he makes no secret of where the money came from** = everyone knows where the money came from; **what's the secret of?** = how do you do something successfully; *what's the secret of making mayonnaise?*

secretarial [sekrə'teəriəl] *adjective* referring to the work of a secretary; *she is taking a secretarial course*; *he is looking for secretarial work*; *we need extra secretarial help to deal with the mailings*; **secretarial college** = college which teaches typing, shorthand and word-processing

secretariat [sekrə'teəriət] *noun* important office and the officials who work in it; *the United Nations secretariat*

secretary ['sekrətri] *noun* **(a)** person who writes letters, answers the phone, files documents, etc., for someone; *both my daughters are training to be secretaries*; *his secretary phoned to say he would be late* **(b)** official who keeps the minutes and official documents of a committee or club; *he was elected secretary of the committee* or *committee secretary* **(c) company secretary** = person who is responsible for a company's legal and financial affairs **(d)** a Secretary of State, a member of the government in charge of a department; **the Secretary for Education** or **the Education Secretary** = the head of the Department for Education (NOTE: plural is **secretaries**)

Secretary General ['sekrtri 'dʒenrəl] *noun* chief administrative officer of an international organization; *the United Nations Secretary General has convened a meeting of the Security Council* (NOTE: plural is **Secretaries General**)

Secretary of State ['sekrətri əv 'steit] *noun* **(a)** *GB* member of the government in charge of a department; *the Secretary of State for Northern Ireland is one of the few women members of the cabinet* **(b)** *US* senior member of the government in charge of foreign affairs; *the US Secretary of State is having talks with the Israeli Prime Minister* (NOTE: the UK equivalent is the **Foreign Secretary**)

secrete [si'kri:t] *verb* **(a)** to produce a liquid substance such as an oil or a hormone; *the gland secretes hormones* **(b)** *(formal)* to hide; *they found packets of drugs secreted under the floor of the car*

secretion [si'kri:ʃn] *noun* **(a)** process by which something is produced by a gland; *this gland stimulates the secretion of hormones* **(b)** substance produced by a gland; *penguins use a secretion from glands near their tails to make their feathers waterproof*

secretive ['si:krətiv] *adjective* liking to keep things secret; *she's very secretive about her holiday plans*

secretly ['si:krətvli] *adverb* without anyone knowing; *they used to meet secretly in the park*; *he secretly photocopied the plans and took them home*

secret police ['si:krət 'pli:s] *noun* part of a police force which spies on members of the public; *two members of the secret police knocked on his door at midnight*

secret service ['si:krət 'sɜ:vis] *noun* government department which spies on other countries; *he was recruited into the secret service when he was at university*

sect [sekt] *noun* religious group; *she has joined a Buddhist sect*

sectarian [sek'teəriən] *adjective* referring to conflicts between religious groups; *there were incidents of sectarian violence over the weekend*

sectarianism [sek'teəriənizm] *noun* existence of religious groups which are violently opposed to each other

section ['sekʃn] *noun* **(a)** part of something which, when joined to other parts, goes to make up a whole; *the brass section of an orchestra*; *the financial section of a newspaper*; *he works in a completely different section of the organization* **(b)** the cutting of tissue in a surgical operation; *see also* CAESAREAN **(c)** diagram showing the inside of something as if cut open; *the drawing shows a section through the main part of the engine*; *see also* CROSS-SECTION **(d)** part of a legal document or Act of Parliament; *we qualify for a grant under Section 23 of the Act*

sectional ['sekʃnəl] *adjective* **(a) sectional diagram** = diagram which shows a section through something; *a sectional diagram of the Channel Tunnel* **(b)** built in sections; *they used sectional building techniques to put up the block of flats quickly* **(c)** referring to the interests of certain groups of people; *a pressure group puts forward a sectional point of view*

sector ['sektə] *noun* **(a)** part of the economy or of the business organization of a country; *all sectors of industry suffered from the rise in the exchange rate*; *computer technology is a booming sector of the economy*; **private sector** = part of industry which is privately owned; *the leisure centre is funded completely by the private sector*; **public sector** = nationalized industries and the civil service; *salaries in the private sector have increased faster than in the public sector* **(b)** part of a circle between two lines drawn from the centre to the outside edge; *the circle had been divided into five sectors*

secular ['sekjʊlə] *adjective* not religious, not connected with religion; *we live in a secular society which pays no attention to moral values*

secure [si'kjuːə] **1** *adjective* **(a)** safe against attack, robbers, etc.; *you need to keep your jewels secure against theft*; *he made all the doors secure by fitting bolts to them* **(b)** firmly fixed; *don't step on that plank, it's not secure*; **secure job** = job which you are sure to keep for a long time **(c) secure institution** = mental hospital in which dangerous prisoners can be kept **2** *verb* **(a)** to make safe, to attach firmly; *secure all the doors before the storm comes*; *she secured herself to the rock with a strong rope* **(b)** to get something safely so that it cannot be taken away; *he secured the backing of a big bank*; *they secured a new lease on very favourable terms*

securely [si'kjuli] *adverb* in a secure way; *don't worry, all the silver is securely locked away*; *she tied the dog securely to a lamppost*

securities [si'kjuərətiz] *noun* investments in stocks and shares; certificates to show that someone owns stocks or shares; **gilt-edged securities** or **government securities** = investments in British government stock;

she invested the remaining money in government securities

security [sɪˈkjuərɪti] *noun* **(a)** safety, protection against criminals; *there were worries about security during the prince's visit; security in this office is nil; security guards patrol the factory at night;* **airport security** = measures to protect aircraft against hijackers or bombs; **hotel security** = measures taken to protect a hotel against theft or fire; **security check** = check to see that no one is carrying a bomb, etc.; **security van** = specially protected van for delivering cash and other valuable items; *six gunmen held up the security van* **(b)** thing given to someone who has lent you money and which is returned when the loan is repaid; *he uses his house as security for a loan; the bank lent him £20,000 without security;* **to stand security for someone** = to guarantee that if the person does not repay a loan, you will repay it for him **(c) job security** *or* **security of employment** = feeling which a worker has that he has a right to keep his job, that he can stay in his job until he retires **(d) social security** = money or help provided by the government to people who need it; *he lives on social security payments* (NOTE: no plural in these meanings)

Security Council [sɪˈkjuərɪti ˈkaunsəl] *noun* ruling body of the United Nations; *France is a permanent member of the Security Council*

> COMMENT: the Security Council has fifteen members, five of which are permanent: these are the United States, Russia, China, France and the United Kingdom. The other ten members are elected for periods of two years. The five permanent members each have a veto over the decisions of the Security Council

sedan [sɪˈdæn] *noun US* two- or four-door car with seating for four or five people (NOTE: British English is a **saloon**)

sedate [sɪˈdeɪt] **1** *adjective* calm, solemn, dignified; *they live in a sedate suburb; the procession moved at a sedate pace through the town* **2** *verb* to calm someone by giving them a drug to make them calm, or which makes them go to sleep; *the patient became violent and had to be sedated*

sedation [sɪˈdeɪʃn] *noun* calming a patient with a drug; **under sedation** = having been given a sedative; *he was still under sedation, and could not be seen by the police*

sedative [ˈsedətɪv] **1** *noun* drug which acts on the nervous system to help a patient sleep or to relieve stress; *she was prescribed sedatives by her doctor* **2** *adjective* which makes you calm or which makes you go to sleep; *this herbal tea has a sedative effect*

sedentary [ˈsedəntri] *adjective* which involves sitting down; **a sedentary occupation** = a job where you have to sit down most of the time; *keyboarding is a very sedentary occupation*

sedge [sedʒ] *noun* type of coarse grass which is common in marshlands

sediment [ˈsedɪmənt] *noun* solid particles which fall to the bottom of a liquid; *you could see a thick sediment at the bottom of the bottle of wine*

sedimentary rock [sedɪˈmentəri ˈrɒk] *noun* rock which has been formed from mud deposited as sediment at the bottom of lakes or the sea, and then subjected to pressure

sedition [səˈdɪʃn] *noun* crime of doing acts, of speaking or publishing words which bring the royal family or the government into contempt and which encourage civil disorder

seditious [sɪˈdɪʃəs] *adjective* which encourages sedition

seduce [sɪˈdjuːs] *verb* **(a)** to persuade someone to have sex; *she was seduced by her French teacher* **(b)** to persuade someone to do something which is perhaps wrong; *he was seduced by the idea of earning a vast salary*

seduction [sɪˈdʌkʃn] *noun* **(a)** act of seducing; *his seduction of the young girl* **(b)** attraction of something; *he was attracted by the seductions of life in the South of France*

seductive [sɪˈdʌktɪv] *adjective* attractive; *they made me a very seductive offer; she gave me a seductive smile*

see [siː] **1** *verb* **(a)** to use your eyes to notice; *can you see that tree in the distance?; they say eating carrots helps you to see in the dark; we ran because we could see the bus coming; I have never seen a badger before* **(b)** to watch a film, etc.; *I don't want to go to the cinema this week, I've seen that film twice already; we saw the football match on TV* **(c)** to go with someone to a place; *the little boy saw the old lady across the road; I'll see her home; my secretary will see you out* **(d)** to understand; *I can't see why they need to borrow so much money; you must see that it's very important for everything to be ready on time; don't you see that they're trying to trick you?; I see - you want me to lend you some money* **(e)** to check to make sure that something happens; *the babysitter will see that the children are in bed by nine o'clock; can you see if a cheque has arrived in the post?* **(f)** to meet; *we see her quite often; she doesn't see much of him; see you next week!; see you again soon!* **(g)** to visit a lawyer, doctor, etc.; *if you have toothache you should see a dentist; he went to see his bank manager to arrange a mortgage* **(h)** *(showing a possibility)* *will you be able to take a holiday this year? - we'll see!* (NOTE: **sees - seeing - saw** [sɔː] **- has seen** [siːn]) **2** *noun* administrative area run by a bishop; *he was appointed to the see of Durham* = he was made bishop of Durham; **the Holy See** = the Vatican, the office of the Pope

seed [siːd] **1** *noun* **(a)** part of a plant which is formed after the flowers die and from which a new plant will grow; *sow the seed(s) in fine earth; a packet of parsley seed; can you eat pumpkin seeds?* **(b)** *(of plant)* **to go to seed** = to become tall and produce flowers and seeds; *the lettuces have gone to seed; he's gone to seed* = he doesn't look after himself properly, he doesn't look as well as he did before (NOTE: **seed** can be plural when it refers to a group: **a packet of lettuce seed; sow the cactus seed in sand**) **(c)** *(in tennis)* player selected as one of the best players in a tournament; *she's the top women's seed; the number one seed was beaten by an unseeded player* **2** *verb* **(a)** **to seed itself** = to produce seed which falls onto the ground and grows; *primroses have seeded themselves all along the side of the motorway* **(b)** to choose the seeds in a tennis competition; *he was seeded No. 5;* compare UNSEEDED (NOTE: do not confuse with **cede**)

seedbed [ˈsiːdbed] *noun* special flowerbed in which you sow seeds; *the new varieties are raised in special seedbeds*

seedless ['siːdləs] *adjective* (fruit) with no seeds in it; *seedless grapes*

seedling ['siːdlɪŋ] *noun* very young plant; *each seedling must then be planted in a separate pot*; *tomato seedlings can be planted outside in May*

seedy ['siːdi] *adjective* **(a)** poor and dirty; *the tour included three nights in a rather seedy hotel* **(b)** *(informal)* quite sick; *she won't be coming to work today as she's feeling rather seedy* (NOTE: **seedier - seediest**)

see in ['siː 'ɪn] *verb* **(a)** to have a midnight party to celebrate; *we stayed up late to see the New Year in* **(b)** **to see something in someone** = to be attracted by someone; *I can't understand what she sees in him*

seeing ['siːɪŋ] **1** *noun* action of sensing with the eyes; *seeing is believing* **2** *conjunction*; **seeing that** = since; *seeing that everyone's here, why don't we open a bottle of champagne?*

seek [siːk] *verb* **(a)** to look for; *the police are seeking a group of teenagers who were in the area when the attack took place*; **to seek refuge** = to try to find shelter; *during the fighting, they sought refuge in the British embassy* **(b)** to ask for; *they are seeking damages from the driver of the car*; *she sought an interview with the minister* (NOTE: **seeking - sought** [sɔːt] **- has sought**)

seeker ['siːkə] *noun* person who looks for something or asks for something; *a band of treasure seekers*; **asylum seekers** = people who are looking for political asylum

seem [siːm] *verb* to look as if; *she seems to like her new job or it seems that she likes her new job*; *everyone seemed to be having a good time at the party*; *the new boss seems very nice*; *it seems to me that the parcel has gone to the wrong house*; *it seemed strange to us that no one answered the phone* (NOTE: do not confuse with **seam**)

seemingly ['siːmɪŋli] *adjective* & *adverb* apparently; *the seemingly unstoppable flow of refugees*; *he had seemingly lost his way*

seen [siːn] *see* SEE

see off ['siː 'ɒf] *verb* to go to the airport or station with someone who is leaving on a journey; *the whole family went to see her off at the airport*

seep [siːp] *verb* *(of a liquid)* to flow slowly through a substance; *water seeped through the rock*; *chemicals seeped out of the container*

seer ['siːə] *noun (old)* person who can see into the future

seesaw ['siːsɔː] **1** *noun* plank with seats at each end, balanced in the middle, so that when one end goes down the other goes up; *the seesaw won't work properly because you're heavier than me* (NOTE: American English is also **teeter-totter**) **2** *verb* to go first one way then the other; *the opinion polls seesawed between the two parties*

seething ['siːðɪŋ] *adjective* **(a)** very angry; *he was seething when he heard the news* **(b)** rapidly moving about like boiling water; *he showed her the seething mass of worms in his bucket*

see through ['siː 'θruː] *verb* to understand everything, not to be tricked by something; *we quickly saw through their plan*

see-through ['siːθruː] *adjective* which you can see through; *a see-through blouse*

see to ['siː 'tuː] *verb* to arrange, to make sure that something is done; *can you see to it that the children are in bed by nine o'clock?*; *my wife will see to the Christmas cards*

segment ['segmənt] *noun* **(a)** part of something which seems to form a natural division; *30- to 40-year-olds are the most affluent segment of the population* **(b)** part of a circle or sphere when a line is drawn across it; **grapefruit segments** = pieces of grapefruit

segregate ['segrɪgeɪt] *verb* to separate into groups; *to avoid crowd trouble, we will have to segregate the fans of the different teams*

segregated ['segrɪgeɪtɪd] *adjective* separated into groups; **segregated schools** = schools which only take children of a certain religion or skin colour

segregation [segrɪ'geɪʃn] *noun* separation into different groups; *the local authority still practises religious segregation in schools*; **racial segregation** = making different races live apart

seismic ['saɪzmɪk] *adjective* referring to earthquakes; **seismic shock** *or* **seismic wave** = shock wave which spreads out from the centre of an earthquake

seismology [saɪz'mɒlədʒi] *noun* scientific study of earthquakes

seize [siːz] *verb* **(a)** to grab something and hold it tight; *she seized the bag of sweets in both hands and would not let go*; **to seize the opportunity** = to take advantage of the situation to do something; *when the President's car slowed down, he seized the opportunity and threw a grenade* **(b)** to take possession of something by force; *the customs seized the shipment of books*

seize on *or* **seize upon** ['siːz ə'pɒn] *verb* to take and use; *she immediately seized upon his suggestion*; *my idea was seized on and developed by a rival inventor*

seize up ['siːz 'ʌp] *verb* to stop working properly; *the car seized up on the hill and we had to call a garage*; *my back seized up after my game of tennis and I couldn't move*

seizure ['siːʒə] *noun* **(a)** taking possession of something; *the court ordered the seizure of the shipment of books* **(b)** sudden contraction of the muscles, especially in a heart attack or epileptic fit; *a member of the audience has had a seizure*; *she has epileptic seizures*

seldom ['seldəm] *adverb* not often; *I seldom get invited to parties*; *seldom do you hear such a beautiful voice* (NOTE the word order when **seldom** is at the beginning of a phrase: **you seldom hear** *or* **seldom do you hear**)

select [sɪ'lekt] **1** *verb* to choose carefully; *she looked carefully at the shelves before selecting a book*; *he was selected for the England squad*; *selected items are reduced by 25%* **2** *adjective* the best, chosen by or for the best people; *she went to a very select school in Switzerland*; *they live in a very select area*; *a select group of players who have scored more than 100 goals in international football*

Select Committee [sɪ'lekt kə'mɪtiː] *noun* special committee of the House of Commons, which examines the work of a single government department; *ministers can be called on to give evidence to select committees*;

the Defence Select Committee or the Select Committee on Defence

selection [sɪ'lekʃn] *noun* **(a)** range; *there is a huge selection of hats to choose from* **(b)** thing which has *or* things which have been chosen; *a selection of our product line*; *a selection of French cheeses*; **selection board** *or* **selection committee** = committee which chooses a candidate for a job; **selection procedure** = general method of choosing a candidate for a job; *see also* NATURAL SELECTION

selective [sɪ'lektɪv] *adjective* **(a)** which chooses (carefully); *I'm very selective about the invitations I accept*; **selective school** = school which chooses pupils by asking them to take an entrance exam **(b)** which only kills certain plants; *use a selective weedkiller on the lawn*

selector [sə'lektə] *noun* person who chooses people to play in a national team; *the England selectors meet today to select the team for the next test match*

self [self] *noun* your own person or character; *she was ill for some time, but now she's her old self again* (NOTE: plural is **selves**)

self- [self] *prefix referring to yourself*; *a self-taught mathematician*

self-addressed envelope (s.a.e.) ['selfə'drest 'envələup] *noun* envelope with your own address on it; *for further information please send a self-addressed envelope*

self-adhesive ['self əd'hiːzɪv] *adjective* covered with a special glue which allows it to be stuck to a surface without being moistened; **self-adhesive envelope** = envelope with a flap which sticks down by pressing

self-assessment ['selfə'sesmənt] *noun* assessing yourself, especially calculating yourself what you owe in tax; *the Inland Revenue has recently introduced self-assessment*

self-catering [self'keɪtrɪŋ] *noun* doing the cooking for yourself; **self-catering holiday** = holiday where you rent accommodation, but cook your own meals; *these cottages are all self-catering*

self-confidence [self'kɒnfɪdəns] *noun* being self-confident; *when she's been in the job a bit longer she will acquire self-confidence*; *the boss's constant criticisms undermined her self-confidence*

self-confident [self'kɒnfɪdənt] *adjective* sure that you are able to do something, sure that what you are doing is well done, etc.; *a very self-confident young salesman*

self-conscious [self'kɒnʃəs] *adjective* embarrassed because you feel you have certain faults; *he's very self-conscious about the size of his nose*

self-contained [selfkən'teɪnd] *adjective* (flat, office) which has its own entrance and kitchen, toilets, etc., and does not share any facilities with others; *the offices we have to let are all self-contained*

self-control [selfkən'trəul] *noun* keeping your feelings under control; *the police showed admirable self-control in face of the screaming fans*; *when he's angry he's liable to lose his self-control*

self-defence ['self dɪ'fens] *noun* defending yourself; *the court decided that he had killed the other man in self-defence*

self-determination [selfdɪtɜːmɪ'neɪʃn] *noun* free choice by the people of a country as to how they should be governed; *countries with powerful neighbours have to fight for the right to self-determination*

self-employed [seklfɪm'plɔɪd] **1** *adjective* working for yourself, not employed by a company; *a self-employed accountant*; *he worked for a bank for ten years but now is self-employed* **2** *noun* the **self-employed** = people who work for themselves; *the self-employed pay a different rate of National Insurance contributions* (NOTE: can be followed by a verb in the plural)

self-esteem [selfɪ'stiːm] *noun* good opinion of yourself and your ability; *after she lost her job her self-esteem vanished*

self-evident [self'evɪdənt] *adjective* obvious; *his guilt was self-evident*

self-governing [self'gʌvənɪŋ] *adjective* which governs itself; *former colonies have become self-governing independent states*

self-government [self'gʌvənmənt] *noun* control of a country by its own government, free from foreign influence; *the colony was granted self-government in 1961*

self-help [self'help] *noun* using your own efforts to help yourself, without relying on other people or the government; *young parents in the area have formed a self-help group*

self-imposed [selfɪm'pəuzd] *adjective* which you have chosen or forced on yourself; *the former president went into self-imposed exile*

self-interest [self'ɪntrəst] *noun* working for your own benefit; *he was acting purely out of self-interest, not to help me*; *it's in your own self-interest to take out insurance*

selfish ['selfɪʃ] *adjective* doing things only for yourself and not for other people; *don't be so selfish - pass the box of chocolates round*

selfless ['selfləs] *adjective* not selfish, not thinking of yourself, only of others; *they praised her selfless devotion to starving children*

self-made man ['selfmeɪd 'mæn] *noun* man who is rich and successful because of his work, not because he inherited money or position; *he's a self-made man who has worked his way up from nothing*

self-pity [self'pɪti] *noun* pity for yourself; *it's no good indulging in self-pity, get out and fight back*

self-portrait ['self'pɔːtreɪt] *noun* painting of the artist done by himself; *a self-portrait of the artist as a young man*

self-respect [selfrɪ'spekt] *noun* pride in yourself; *although he lost his job he managed to keep his self-respect*

self-respecting [selfrɪ'spektɪŋ] *adjective* proud of yourself; *no self-respecting businessman would refuse a deal like that*

self-service ['self 'sɜːvɪs] **1** *noun* system in a shop or restaurant where you help yourself and then pay a cashier; *is there someone to help or is it self-service?* **2** *adjective* (shop, restaurant) where you take things yourself and pay for them when you go out; **self-service restaurant** = restaurant where you take a tray and help yourself to food; **self-service petrol station** = garage where you put the petrol into the car yourself

self-styled [self'staɪld] *adjective* with a title which you have given yourself; *John Jones, the self-styled 'King of South London'*

self-sufficiency [selfsə'fɪʃənsi] *noun* being self-sufficient; *our aim was to achieve self-sufficiency in energy by the year 2000*

self-sufficient [selfsə'fɪʃənt] *adjective* able to provide everything for yourself; *the country is self-sufficient in oil*

sell [sel] **1** *verb* **(a)** to give something to someone for money; *he sold his house to my father; she sold him her bicycle for next to nothing; we managed to sell the car for £500; the shop sells vegetables but not meat* **(b)** to be sold; *those packs sell for £25 a dozen; his latest book is selling very well* (NOTE: **selling - sold** [səʊld]) **2** *noun* the act of selling something; **to give a product the hard sell** = to make great efforts to persuade customers to buy it; **to give a product the soft sell** = to persuade people to buy something, by encouraging and not forcing them to do so (NOTE: do not confuse with **cell**)

sell-by date ['selbaɪ 'deɪt] *noun* date on a packet of food, which is the last date on which the food can be sold and is guaranteed to be good; *don't use that - it's past its sell-by date*

seller ['selə] *noun* **(a)** person who sells something; *there were a few postcard sellers by the cathedral;* **seller's market** = market where a person selling goods or a service can ask high prices because there is a large demand for the product; *prices are high in a seller's market compare* BUYER'S MARKET **(b)** thing which sells; *this book is a steady seller;* **good seller** = thing that sells well; *we've dropped that item from our catalogue - it was never a very good seller; see also* BESTSELLER (NOTE: do not confuse with **cellar**)

selling ['selɪŋ] **1** *noun* action of selling something to someone; *selling secondhand cars is not an easy business these days;* **mail-order selling** = selling by taking orders and supplying a product by post; **selling price** = price at which someone is willing to sell **2** *suffix* **fast-selling items** = items which sell quickly; *see also* BESTSELLING

sell off ['sel 'ɒf] *verb* to sell goods quickly and cheaply to get rid of them; *at the end of the day the market traders sell off their fruit and vegetables very cheaply*

sell-off ['selɒf] *noun* act of selling something to private buyers; *the sell-off of nationalized industries*

Sellotape ['seləʊteɪp] *noun* tradename for a type of sticky tape; *she put the books in a box and sealed it with Sellotape*

sell out [sel'aʊt] *verb* **(a)** to sell your business; *he sold out to his partner and retired to the seaside* **(b)** to sell all the stock of an item; *this item has sold out; have you got it in a size 12? - no, I'm afraid we're sold out* **(c)** *(informal)* to give in to a group of influential people; *the environmental group has accused the government of selling out to the oil companies; see also* SELL OUT OF

sellout ['selaʊt] *noun* **(a)** *(informal)* betrayal of all your principles; *they said his change of policy was a sellout to the forces of the right; it's a sellout - the council should have stood up for our rights* **(b)** performance of a play or film where all the tickets have been sold; *the new musical is a sellout*

sell out of ['sel 'aʊt 'ɒv] *verb* **to sell out of an item** = to sell all the stock of an item; *the shop has sold out of bread; have you got it in a size 12? - no, I'm afraid we're sold out of all the small sizes*

sell up [sel'ʌp] *verb* to sell a business and all the stock; *he sold up and retired to the seaside*

semantics [sɪ'mæntɪks] *noun* **(a)** study of the meanings of words and phrases **(b)** *(informal)* arguing about or raising objections to the meaning of something; *his objections to the wording of the contract are pure semantics*

semblance ['sembləns] *noun* appearance; *she hoovered the sitting room, to try to give it some semblance of tidiness before the guests came; the arrival of the police brought some semblance of order to the chaos*

semen ['siːmən] *noun* thick pale fluid containing spermatozoa, produced by the testes and ejaculated from the penis (NOTE: do not confuse with **seaman**)

semester [sə'mestə] *noun US* term in a school or college year which only has two terms; *they arrived at college for the fall semester; after the spring semester we look for summer jobs*

semi ['semi] *noun (informal)* = SEMI-DETACHED HOUSE

semi- ['semi] *prefix meaning* partly; *he's semi-retired*

semibreve ['semibriːv] *noun* musical note equivalent in length to two minims

semicircle ['semisɜːkl] *noun* half a circle; *the chairs were arranged in a semi-circle round the lecturer's desk; we all sat in a semi-circle round the camp fire*

semicircular [semi'sɜːkjʊlə] *adjective* shaped like half a circle; *the US Congress meets in a semicircular room*

semicolon ['semikəʊlən] *noun* punctuation mark (;) used to separate two parts of a sentence, and also used to show a pause; *you can put a semicolon when you want to show a break in a sentence*

semiconductor ['semikʌn'dʌktə] *noun* material, such as silicon, which has conductive properties between those of a conductor (like metal) and those of an insulator; *semiconductor material is used to make many electronic devices*

semi-detached house [semidɪ'tætʃt 'haʊs] *noun* house which is joined to another similar house on one side, but is not joined to a house on the other; *a street of 1930s semi-detached houses* (NOTE: also called a **semi**)

semi-final [semi'faɪnəl] *noun* one of last two matches in a competition, the winners of which go into the final game; *the two semi-finals will be held on the same day*

seminal ['semɪnl] *adjective* **(a)** which acts as the starting point for something new; *his book was a seminal work for future developments in the field of nuclear physics* **(b)** referring to semen; *seminal fluid*

seminar ['semɪnɑː] *noun* meeting of a small group of university students to discuss a subject with a teacher; *the French seminar is being held in the conference room*

semi-precious stone ['semi'preʃəs] *noun* stone, like an opal, which is not as valuable as other jewels like diamonds; *see also* PRECIOUS

semiquaver ['semikweɪvə] *noun* musical note lasting half as long as a quaver

semitone ['semitəun] *noun* smallest interval between notes in music, the interval between two keys on a piano

senate ['senət] *noun* **(a)** upper house of the legislative body in some countries; *she was first elected to the Senate in 1990* **(b)** body which rules a university; *does Senate concern itself solely with administrative matters?*

senator ['senətə] *noun* member of a senate (in parliament); *she was first elected a senator in 1980* (NOTE: written with a capital letter when used as a title: **Senator Jackson**)

senatorial [senə'tɔːriəl] *adjective* referring to a senate or to senators; *the senatorial elections take place next month*

send [send] *verb* **(a)** to make someone *or* something go from one place to another; *my mother sent me to the baker's to buy some bread; I was sent home from school because I had a headache; he sent the ball into the net; the firm is sending him out to Australia for six months* **(b)** to use the postal services; *the office sends 200 Christmas cards every year; send me a postcard when you get to Russia; send the letter airmail if you want it to arrive next week; send your donations to the following address* **(c)** *(informal)* to make someone act or feel in a certain way; **to send someone crazy** *or* **round the bend** *or* **up the wall** = to make someone extremely annoyed; *the noise of the pneumatic drills outside the office is sending me up the wall* (NOTE: **sending - sent** [sent])

send away for *or* **send off for** ['send ə'weɪ 'fɔː or 'ɒf 'fɔː] *verb* to write and ask someone to send you something, usually something which you have seen in an advertisement; *we sent away for the new brochure; I sent away for a book which was advertised in the Sunday paper*

send back ['send 'bæk] *verb* to return something by post; *if you don't like the shirt, send it back and I'll get you something different*

sender ['sendə] *noun* person who sends; *the sender of the package did not put enough stamps, so we had to pay extra;* **'return to sender'** = words on an envelope or parcel to show that it is to be sent back to the person who sent it

send for ['send 'fɔː] *verb* to ask someone to come; *he collapsed and we sent for the doctor; the restaurant had to send for the police*

send in ['send 'ɪn] *verb* to send a letter to an organization; *he sent in his resignation; she sent in an application for the job*

send off ['send 'ɒf] *verb* to post; *he sent the postcard off without a stamp*

send-off ['sendɒf] *noun* party where you say goodbye to someone who is leaving on a long journey; *we gave the happy couple a rousing send-off*

send off for ['send 'ɒf 'fɔː] *see* SEND AWAY FOR

send up ['send 'ʌp] *verb* **(a)** to make something go up; *they sent up an emergency flare; the cold weather has sent up the price of vegetables* **(b)** *(informal)* to make jokes about; *in one of his TV sketches, he sends up the Foreign Minister*

senile ['siːnaɪl] *adjective (person)* whose mind is getting muddled because of age; *her father is getting a bit senile;* **senile dementia** = form of mental confusion affecting old people (NOTE: the word is now considered derogatory)

senility [sə'nɪlɪti] *noun* being senile; *mental confusion, trembling fingers and other signs of senility*

senior ['siːnjə] **1** *adjective* **(a)** older; *the senior members of the tribe;* **senior citizen** = old retired person; **senior school** = school for older children **(b)** more important in rank, etc.; *a sergeant is senior to a corporal; my senior colleagues do not agree with me;* **senior manager** = manager who has a higher rank than others **2** *noun* **(a)** older person; *he must be at least ten years your senior;* **the seniors** = the older children in a school; *when she's eleven, she'll move up into the seniors* **(b)** *US* student in his or her fourth year or last year at school or college; *compare* FRESHMAN, SOPHOMORE **(c)** the father in a family where the son has the same name; *Harry Markovitz Senior*

seniority [siːnɪ'ɒrɪti] *noun* **(a)** being older or more important; **the professors were listed in order of seniority** = the professor who had been in the department the longest was put at the top of the list **(b)** being a member of a group longer than someone else; *he has several years' seniority over me as a member of the club*

sensation [sen'seɪʃn] *noun* **(a)** general feeling; *I felt a curious sensation as if I had been in the room before* **(b)** physical feeling; *she had a burning sensation in her arm* **(c)** thing *or* person that causes great excitement; *the new ballet was the sensation of the season*

sensational [sen'seɪʃnl] *adjective* **(a)** which causes great excitement; *his sensational discovery shocked the world of archaeology* **(b)** *(informal)* very good; *a sensational new film - don't miss it!; you look sensational in that outfit*

sense [sens] **1** *noun* **(a)** one of the five ways in which you notice something (sight, hearing, smell, taste, touch); *he may be 93, but he still has all his senses; his senses had been dulled by the drugs he was taking; dogs have a good sense of smell* **(b)** general feeling about something; *she had a sense of being cut off from reality; the police seemed to have no sense of urgency* **(c)** meaning; *he was using 'bear' in the sense of 'to carry';* **to make sense** = to have a meaning; *the message doesn't make sense;* **to make sense of something** = to understand something; *I can't make any sense of what she's trying to say* **(d)** being sensible; *at least someone showed some sense and tried to calm the situation; she didn't have the sense to refuse; I thought Patrick would have had more sense than that; (informal)* **to have more money than sense** = to have too much money and not know how to spend it wisely; *did you see what she bought? - she's got more money than sense!* **(e)** in one sense *or* in a sense = up to a point, partly; *in a sense, he was right;* **in no sense** = in no way, not at all; *she's in no sense to blame for what happened* **2** *verb* to be aware of, to feel; *I could sense the feeling of hostility in the room*

senseless ['sensləs] *adjective* **(a)** stupid; *a senseless attack on a little old lady; it's senseless to buy clothes you don't need, just because they are in the sales* **(b)** unconscious; *he lay senseless on the ground*

sense of direction ['sens əv daɪ'rekʃn] *noun* ability to know which way to go in a place which you do not know well; *she has a very good sense of direction: she managed to find her way round London with no difficulty at all*

sense of humour ['sens əv 'hjuːmə] *noun* ability to see the funny side of things; *he has a good sense of humour; she has no sense of humour*

senses ['sensɪz] *noun* rational behaviour; **to take leave of your senses** = to go mad, to do something very strange; *has she taken leave of her senses?*; **to come to your senses** = to become rational again; *in the end he came to his senses and wrote a letter of apology*

sensibility [sensɪ'bɪlɪti] *noun* delicate feeling; *his acute sensibility is felt in his music; the loud music and curious costumes offended my sensibilities*

sensible ['sensɪbl] *adjective* showing good judgement, wisdom; *staying indoors was the sensible thing to do; try and be sensible for once!*; **sensible shoes** = shoes that are strong and comfortable for walking, rather than fashionable

sensibly ['sensɪbli] *adverb* in a sensible way; *very sensibly, they refused to take the boat out in the storm; try and behave a bit more sensibly*

sensitive ['sensɪtɪv] *adjective* **(a)** with keen feelings, easily upset; *she's a very sensitive young woman; some actors are extremely sensitive to criticism;* **price-sensitive** = selling better or worse depending on the price **(b)** controversial, which may provoke an argument; *human rights is a very sensitive issue at the moment* **(c)** which measures very accurately; *we need a more sensitive thermometer; a very sensitive light meter* **(d)** which reacts to light, etc.; *if you have very sensitive skin use plenty of suntan cream; flowers are sensitive to fluctuations in temperature and humidity*

sensitivity [sensɪ'tɪvɪti] *noun* sensitive feelings; *the doctor dealt with the girl with great sensitivity*

sensitize ['sensɪtaɪz] *verb* to make sensitive to light, etc.; *photographs using specially sensitized film*

sensor ['sensə] *noun* electronic device that senses something, such as heat, light, smoke, etc.; *he lit up a cigar and this set off the smoke sensors in the bedroom*

sensory ['sensəri] *adjective* referring to the senses; **sensory nerve** = nerve that transmits impulses regarding the senses (taste, smell, etc.) to the brain

sensual ['sensjul] *adjective* referring to pleasures of the body, not of the mind; *he enjoyed the sensual pleasure of wearing silk next to the skin*

sensuous ['sensjuəs] *adjective* which gives pleasure to the senses; *the band played sensuous Arabic music; her full, sensuous lips*

sent [sent] *see* SEND

sentence ['sentəns] **1** *noun* **(a)** words put together to make a complete statement, usually ending in a full stop; *I don't understand the second sentence in your letter; begin each sentence with a capital letter* **(b)** judgement of a court; *he was given a six-month prison sentence; the judge passed sentence on the accused* **2** *verb* to give someone an official legal punishment; *she was sentenced to three weeks in prison; he was sentenced to death for murder*

sentiment ['sentɪmənt] *noun* **(a)** general feeling; *the government had to take public sentiment into account* **(b)** sentiments = opinions; *I think it's all a waste of time - my sentiments exactly*

sentimental [sentɪ'mentəl] *adjective* showing emotions of love or pity, not reason; *she gets all sentimental on her son's birthday; her father sang a sentimental old love song;* **sentimental value** = being valuable because of the memories attached to it, not because of its actual money value; *the stolen watch was of great sentimental value*

sentinel ['sentɪnl] *noun (formal)* = SENTRY

sentry ['sentri] *noun* soldier on duty at a gate, etc.; *sentries were posted at each gate; he's been on sentry duty all night* (NOTE: plural is **sentries**)

sepal ['sepəl] *noun* part of a plant like a green leaf under the petals of a flower

separate 1 *adjective* ['sepərət] not together, not attached; *they are in separate rooms; the house has one bathroom with a separate toilet; the dogs were kept separate from the other pets; can you give us two separate invoices?*; **to send something under separate cover** = to send something in a different envelope **2** *verb* ['sepəreɪt] **(a)** to divide; *the personnel are separated into part-timers and full-time staff; the teacher separated the class into two groups* **(b)** to keep apart; *the police tried to separate the two gangs; is it possible to separate religion and politics?* **(c)** to break away from a partner and become independent; *they are arguing all the time - it wouldn't surprise me if they were to separate; the Baltic states separated from Russia*

separated ['sepəreɪtɪd] *adjective* not living together any more; *her parents are separated*

separately ['sepərətli] *adverb* in a separate way, individually; *each of us will pay separately*

separation [sepə'reɪʃn] *noun* **(a)** dividing; *he favours the separation of the students into smaller groups; the separation of the house into two flats will require planning permission* **(b)** living apart; *a six-month separation of mother and child may have long-term effects; after my parents' separation I lived with my father*

separatism ['sepərətɪzm] *noun* belief that part of a country should become separate and independent from the rest; *there is not much support for separatism in that part of the country*

separatist ['seprətɪst] **1** *adjective* referring to separatism; *the separatist movement is gaining in popularity* **2** *noun* person who believes that part of the country should become separate and independent; *Basque separatists met the Spanish Prime Minister today*

September [sep'tembə] *noun* ninth month of the year, between August and October; *the weather is usually good in September; her birthday is in September; today is September 3rd US September 3; we always try to take a short holiday in September* (NOTE: **September 3rd** *or* **September 3**: say 'September the third' or 'the third of September'; American English: 'September third')

septic ['septɪk] *adjective* which has been infected with bacteria; *the cut turned septic and had to be disinfected;* **septic tank** = underground tank near a house for collecting sewage

septicaemia [septi'si:miə] *noun* blood poisoning, condition caused by bacteria in the blood; *septicaemia can be dangerous*

sepulchre *US* **sepulcher** ['sepəlkə] *noun* (formal) building containing a tomb or grave; *the body was placed in the sepulchre*

sequel ['si:kwəl] *noun* (a) continuation of a story, play, etc.; *the sequel will be screened tomorrow night* (b) result, thing which follows; *the sequel to the discovery was that the driver of the truck was arrested*

sequence ['si:kwəns] *noun* (a) series of things which happen or follow one after the other; *the sequence of events which led to the accident* (b) in sequence = in order of numbers; *make sure that the invoices are all in sequence according to their numbers* (c) scene in a film; *they showed some sequences from her latest film*

serenade [serə'neɪd] 1 *noun* love song; *he sang a serenade* 2 *verb* to sing a love song to someone; *he serenaded her from the street below her window*

serene [sə'ri:n] *adjective* calm, not worried; *she sat, serene and dignified, watching the ceremony*

serenely [sə'ri:nli] *adjective* calmly, not worried; *he watched serenely from a distance*

serenity [sə'renɪti] *noun* being calm; *we were struck by the serenity of the life of the monks in the abbey*

serf [sɜ:f] *noun* (old) slave working on a farm; *in 18th-century Russia, millions of serfs worked on the land* (NOTE: do not confuse with **surf**)

serge [sɜ:dʒ] *noun* type of thick woollen cloth; *he wore a thick serge jacket*

sergeant ['sɑ:dʒənt] *noun* non-commissioned officer in the army or the police, the rank above a corporal; *Sergeant Jones drilled the new recruits; a police sergeant arrested him* (NOTE: used as a title with a surname: **Sergeant Jones**)

serial ['sɪəriəl] 1 *adjective* in a series; *place the cards in serial order*; **serial murderer** *or* **serial killer** = person who has committed several murders, one after the other; *because there are similarities between the murders, the police think they are dealing with a serial killer*; **serial number** = number in a series; *this batch of shoes has the serial number 25-02* 2 *noun* radio or TV play which is presented in several instalments; *an Australian police serial* (NOTE: do not confuse with **cereal**)

serialize ['sɪəriəlaɪz] *verb* to make into a serial; *the book has been serialized on TV*

series ['sɪəri:z] *noun* (a) group of things which come one after the other in order; *we had a series of phone calls from the bank* (b) TV or radio programmes which are broadcast at the same time each week; *there's a new wildlife series starting this week* (NOTE: plural is **series**)

serious ['sɪəriəs] *adjective* (a) not funny; not joking; *a very serious play; he's such a serious little boy; stop laughing - it's very serious; he's very serious about the proposal; the doctor's expression was very serious* (b) important and possibly dangerous; *there was a serious accident on the motorway; the storm caused serious damage; there's no need to worry - it's nothing serious* (c) carefully planned; *the management is making serious attempts to improve working conditions*

seriously ['sɪəriəsli] *adverb* (a) in a serious way; *she should laugh more - she mustn't always take things so seriously* (b) badly; *the cargo was seriously damaged by water; her mother is seriously ill* (c) with a lot of thought; *they seriously considered emigrating; we are taking the threat from our competitors very seriously*

sermon ['sɜ:mən] *noun* (a) serious talk made by a priest in church; *he gave a sermon about the need to love your neighbours* (b) serious talk giving someone advice; *we all have to listen to the head-teacher's annual sermon about drugs*

serpent ['sɜ:pənt] *noun* (old) snake; *the serpent came down from the tree*

serpentine ['sɜ:pəntaɪn] 1 *adjective* (formal) twisting and winding like a snake; *the path takes a serpentine course through the gardens* 2 *noun* **the Serpentine** = large lake in the middle of Hyde Park, in London; *people go swimming in the Serpentine on Christmas Day*

serrated [sə'reɪtɪd] *adjective* with V-shaped teeth along the edge; *a steak knife with a serrated edge*

serum ['sɪərəm] *noun* **blood serum** = yellowish watery liquid which separates from whole blood when the blood clots

servant ['sɜ:vənt] *noun* (a) person who is paid to work for a family; *they employ two servants in their London home; get it yourself - I'm not your servant!* (b) **civil servant** = person who works in a government department; *as a government translator I was considered a civil servant; the civil servants who advise ministers have a tremendous influence on government policy*

serve [sɜ:v] 1 *verb* (a) to give food or drink to someone; *she served the soup in small bowls; I'll serve the potatoes; it's a buffet lunch - take a plate and serve yourself; has everyone been served?* (b) to bring food or drink to someone at table; *which waitress is serving this table?; I can't serve six tables at once* (c) to go with a dish, etc.; *fish is served with a white sauce; you should serve red wine with meat* (d) to work as an official; *he served in the army for ten years* (e) to help a customer in a shop, etc.; *are you being served?; the manager served me himself; will you serve this lady next, please?; I waited ten minutes before being served* (f) to provide a service; *the local bus serves the villages in the hills; the aim of our organization is to serve the local community; this hospital serves the western side of the city* (g) (in games like tennis) to start the game by hitting the ball; *she served two aces in a row; he served first* (h) **to serve someone with a writ** *or* **to serve a writ on someone** = to give someone a writ officially, so that he has to receive it (i) (informal) **it serves you right** = you deserve what has happened to you; *it serves them right if they missed the train, they shouldn't have taken so long to get ready* 2 *noun* (in tennis) action of hitting the ball first; *she has a very powerful serve; three of his serves were aces*

server ['sɜ:və] *noun* (a) **salad servers** = spoon and fork for serving salad (b) dedicated computer or program which provides a function to a network; **file server** = computer connected to a network, running a network operating system software to manage accounts, files, etc. (c) person who is serving at tennis; *the server stands behind the baseline* (d) person who helps a priest at mass; *the server held the book for the priest*

service ['sɜːvɪs] **1** *noun* **(a)** time when you work for a company, or organization, or in the armed forces; *did he enjoy his service in the army?*; *she did six years' service in the police*; *he was awarded a gold watch for his long service to the company*; *he saw service in Northern Ireland*; **length of service** = number of years someone has worked **(b)** serving or helping someone in a shop or restaurant; *the food is good here, but the service is very slow*; *the bill includes an extra 10% for service*; *is the service included?*; *the bill does not include service*; *to add on 10% for service*; **service charge** = money which you pay for service in a restaurant; *a 10% service charge is added*; **room service** = arrangement in a hotel for food or drink to be served in your bedroom **(c)** regular check of a machine; *the car has had its 20,000-kilometre service*; **after-sales service** = maintenance of a machine carried out by the seller for the buyer; **service centre** = office or workshop which specializes in keeping machines in good working order; **service handbook** *or* **service manual** = book which shows how to keep a machine in good working order **(d)** group of people working together; **civil service** = organization and personnel which administer a country; *you have to pass an examination to get a job in the civil service or to get a civil service job*; **the health service** = doctors, nurses, hospitals, etc., all taken as a group; *we have the best health service in the world*; *I don't want to rely on the National Health Service*; **the (armed) services** = the army, the navy and the air force; *have you thought about a career in the services?*; *service families often have to travel abroad* **(e)** provision of a facility which the public needs; *our train service to London is very bad*; *the postal service is efficient*; *the bus service is very irregular*; *the hotel provides a laundry service*; **the rent includes services** = the rent includes the cost of water, gas and electricity **(f)** favour, something done for someone; *you would do me a great service if you could carry my suitcases for me*; *(formal)* **to be of service to someone** = to help someone; *can I be of service to anyone?* **(g)** religious ceremony; *my mother never misses the nine o'clock service on Sundays* **(h)** *(in tennis)* action of hitting the ball first; *she has a very powerful service* **(i)** set of china for a meal; **dinner service** = big and small plates, serving dishes, etc.; *a complete dinner service costs a lot, so I'll buy it for you bit by bit*; **tea service** = plates, cups, saucers, teapot, etc., **2** *verb* to keep (a machine) in good working order; *the car needs to be serviced every six months*; *the photocopier has gone back to the manufacturer for servicing*

service industry ['sɜːvɪs 'ɪndəstri] *noun* industry which does not make products, but offers a service, such as banking, insurance, transport; *service industries have become much more important in the last decade*

serviceman ['sɜːvɪsmən] *noun* member of one of the services (army, navy, air force) (NOTE: plural is **servicemen**)

services ['sɜːvɪsɪz] *noun* area with a service station, restaurants and sometimes hotel, on a motorway; *no services for 50 miles*; *we'll stop at the next services and have a cup of coffee*

service station ['sɜːvɪsteɪʃn] *noun* garage where you can buy petrol and have small repairs done to a car; *we need petrol - I'll stop at the next service station*

servicewoman ['sɜːvɪswʊmən] *noun* woman member of one of the services (army, navy, air force) (NOTE: plural is **servicewomen**)

servicing ['sɜːvɪsɪŋ] *noun* action of repairing a machine; *I took my car to the garage for servicing*

serviette [sɜːvɪ'et] *noun* square piece of cloth or paper used to protect clothes and wipe your mouth at meals; *he always tucked a large white serviette into his collar before each meal*; *the restaurant is quite down-market - it has paper serviettes* (NOTE: although **serviette** is perfectly correct English, some people prefer to use the word **napkin**)

servile ['sɜːvaɪl] *adjective* acting too much like a slave; *he likes his assistants to be servile - they just have to agree with everything he does*

servility [sɜː'vɪlɪti] *noun* behaviour like that of a slave; *a wife's position should not be one of servility to her husband*

serving ['sɜːvɪŋ] *noun* amount of food served to one person; *500g is enough for two servings*; *she gave him a generous serving of chips*; **serving hatch** = small opening in a wall for passing food and crockery from a kitchen to a dining room; **serving instructions** = instructions on a packet of food, showing how to prepare it

servitude ['sɜːvɪtjuːd] *noun (formal)* having to work hard for other people; *to her, marriage to a farmer seemed like a life of servitude; (formerly, in the 19th century)* **penal servitude** = imprisonment with hard labour; *he was sentenced to penal servitude for life*

sesame ['sesəmiː] *noun* **(a)** tropical plant with seeds that are used in cooking (usually scattered on top of bread or cakes) or to make oil; **sesame seed oil** = oil obtained from crushed sesame seeds, used in oriental cooking **(b)** **open sesame** = magic words, spoken by a magician, which make a magic box or cave open; *the boy said 'Open, sesame' and the rock rolled away to reveal a cave full of gold*

session ['seʃn] *noun* **(a)** time when an activity is taking place; *all these long sessions in front of the computer screen are ruining my eyesight*; **practice session** = time when an athlete, a tennis player, etc., practises; **recording session** = time when music is being recorded **(b)** meeting of a committee, parliament, etc.; *the first session of the all-party talks will be held on Monday*; **opening session** *or* **closing session** = first part *or* last part of a conference; **in session** = in the process of meeting; *the committee has been in session for two hours* (NOTE: do not confuse with **cession**)

set [set] **1** *noun* **(a)** group of things which go together, which are used together, which are sold together; *he carries a set of tools in the back of his car*; *the six chairs are sold as a set*; **a tea set** = cups, saucers, plates, teapot, etc., **(b)** **TV set** = piece of electrical equipment which shows TV pictures; *they have bought a new 15-inch colour set* **(c)** *(in films)* place where a film is shot; *she has to be on set at 7.00 a.m.*; *we went on a tour of the studios and watched a set being built* **(d)** *(in tennis)* one part of a tennis match, consisting of several games; *she won the set 7-5*; *he lost the first two sets* **2** *verb* **(a)** to put in a special place; *she set the plate of biscuits down on the table next to her chair*; **to set the table** = to put the knives, forks, plates, glasses, cups, etc., in their right places on the table **(b)** to fix; *when we go to France we have to set our watches to French time*; *the price of the new computer has been set at*

£500 **(c)** *(surgery)* to fix a broken limb; *the doctor set his broken arm; (of a limb)* to heal; *the broken wrist is setting very well* **(d)** to give work to someone; *the teacher has set us some homework for the weekend; who set this quiz? - it is very difficult;* **this book has been set for the exam** = this book is on the list of those which have to be studied before the exam; **to set someone to work** = to give someone work to do; *the children were set to work washing the dishes* **(e)** to make something happen; *he went to sleep smoking a cigarette and set the house on fire; all the prisoners were set free; I had been worried about her, but the letter set my mind at rest* **(f)** to go down; *the sun rises in the east and sets in the west* **(g)** to write music to go with words; *the poem about cats was set to music* **(h)** *(printing)* to put a text into printed characters; *the idioms in this dictionary have been set in bold* (NOTE: **sets - setting - set - has set**) **3** *adjective* **(a)** fixed, which cannot be changed; *visits are only allowed at set times;* **set book** = book which is on the list of those which have to be studied for an exam; **set menu** = menu which cannot be changed **(b)** ready; *we're all set for a swim; my bags are packed and I'm all set to leave; the government is set to introduce new anti-smoking laws; her latest novel is set to become the best-selling book of the year;* 'on your marks, get set, go!' = orders given to runners at the beginning of a race

set about ['set ə'baʊt] *verb* to start to do something; *they set about making a camp fire; we haven't started yet because we don't know how to set about it*

set aside ['set ə'saɪd] *verb* **(a)** to dismiss, to reject; *the proposal was set aside by the committee* **(b)** to save and keep for future use; *we set money aside every month for the children's holidays*

set-aside ['setəsaɪd] *noun* system of using land previously used for farming for another purpose; *under the set-aside scheme we can plant trees along that side of the field*

set back ['set 'bæk] *verb* **(a)** to delay, to make something late; *the bad weather has set the harvest back by two weeks* **(b)** to place further back; *the house is set back from the road* **(c)** *(informal)* **to set someone back** = to be a cost to someone; *the meal set me back £100*

setback ['setbæk] *noun* problem which makes something late or stops something going ahead; *the company suffered a series of setbacks in 1997; just when we thought he was better, he had a setback and had to go back to hospital*

set down ['set 'daʊn] *verb* **(a)** to let passengers get off; *the bus set down several passengers and two others got on* **(b)** *(formal)* to put something in writing; *the rules are set down in this booklet*

set in ['set 'ɪn] *verb* to start and become permanent; *then the bad weather set in and we couldn't climb any more; winter has set in early this year*

set off ['set 'ɒf] *verb* **(a)** to begin a trip; *we're setting off for Germany tomorrow; they all set off on a long walk after lunch* **(b)** to start something working; *they set off a bomb in the shopping centre; if you touch the wire it will set off the alarm; being in the same room as a cat will set off my asthma*

set out ['set 'aʊt] *verb* **(a)** to begin a journey; *the hunters set out to cross the mountains; we have to set out early tomorrow* **(b)** to explain clearly; *we asked her*

to set out the details in her report **(c)** to aim to do something; *he set out to ruin the party*

set right ['set 'raɪt] *verb* to explain to someone why they are wrong; *he thought I had stolen the money but I soon set him right on that score*

settee [sə'tiː] *noun* sofa, a long seat with a soft back where several people can sit; *my three aunts were sitting on the settee, holding cups of tea*

setter ['setə] *noun* **(a)** hunting dog trained to find game for hunters; *he came into the park with two red setters* **(b)** person who sets a puzzle; *the setter of the crossword in the Sunday paper*

setting ['setɪŋ] *noun* **(a)** background for a story; *the setting for the story is Hong Kong in 1935* **(b)** silver or gold frame in which a precious stone is fixed; *a diamond in a silver setting* **(c) place setting** = set of knives, forks, spoons, etc., for one person; *we only need two place settings on table 6*

settle ['setl] **1** *verb* **(a)** to arrange, to agree; to end (a dispute); *well, I'm glad everything's settled at last; have you settled the title for the new film yet?; it took six months of negotiation for the union and management to settle their differences* **(b) to settle a bill** = to pay the bill; *please settle this invoice without delay; the insurance company refused to settle his claim for damages* **(c)** to go to live in a new country; *they sold everything and settled in Canada* **(d)** to place yourself in a comfortable position; *she switched on the television and settled in her favourite armchair* **(e) to settle money on someone** = to arrange for money to be passed to trustees to hold for someone in the future; *they settled £2,000 a year on their new godson* **(f)** to fall to the ground, to the bottom; *wait for the dust to settle; a layer of mud settled at the bottom of the pond* **2** *noun* long wooden bench with a back; *they sat on a settle by the pub fire, smoking pipes*

settled ['setld] *adjective* fixed or unchanging; *a period of settled weather* (NOTE: the opposite is **unsettled**)

settle down ['setl 'daʊn] *verb* **(a)** to place yourself in a comfortable position; *after dinner, she likes to settle down in a comfortable chair with a good book* **(b)** to change to a calmer way of life; *he has worked all over the world, and doesn't seem ready to settle down; they got married and settled down in Surrey*

settle for ['setl 'fɔː] *verb* to choose or to decide on something which is not quite what you want; *they didn't have any white sofas, so we settled for a beige one*

settle in ['setl 'ɪn] *verb* to become accustomed to a new house, job, etc.; *she's enjoying her job, though she took some time to settle in; the children have all settled into their new school*

settlement ['setlmənt] *noun* **(a)** payment of a bill; *this invoice has not been paid - can you arrange for immediate settlement?* **(b)** agreement in a dispute; *in the end a settlement was reached between management and workers* **(c)** place where a group of people come to live; *a mining settlement in the hills*

settle on ['setl 'ɒn] *verb* **(a)** to decide on, to choose; *after a lot of hesitation we finally settled on the red one* **(b)** *(of insect, etc.)* to sit on; *if only the butterfly would settle on that flower I'd be able to take a picture of it*

settler ['setlə] *noun* person who goes to live in a new country; *the early settlers built log cabins*

settle up ['setl 'ʌp] *verb* to pay a bill, to pay the total of what is owed; *you pay the bill and I'll settle up with you later*

set to ['set 'tuː] *verb* to start to work hard; *if you set to, you should finish the work by this afternoon*

set-to ['set'tuː] *noun (informal)* argument or fight; *I could hear them having a real old set-to on the other side of the fence*

set up ['set 'ʌp] *verb* **(a)** to establish; *to set up a committee or a working party*; *a fund has been set up to receive donations from the public*; *he set himself up as an estate agent*; **to set up a company** = to start a company legally; **to set up home** *or* **to set up house** = to go somewhere to live in your own flat, house, etc.; *they don't intend to set up house yet* **(b)** *(informal)* to deceive someone deliberately; *we were set up by the police*

setup ['setʌp] *noun (informal)* organization; *he works for some PR setup*

seven ['sevən] *number* 7; *there are only seven children in his class*; *she's seven (years old) next week*; *the train is supposed to leave at seven (o'clock)* **the seven hundreds** = the years from 700 to 799 AD (NOTE: compare **the seventh century**)

seventeen [sevən'tiːn] *number* 17; *he will be seventeen (years old) next month*; *the train leaves at seventeen sixteen (17.16)* **the seventeen hundreds (1700s)** = the years from 1700 to 1799 (NOTE: compare **the seventeenth century**)

seventeenth (17th) [sevən'tiːnθ] *adjective & noun today is the seventeenth or the seventeenth of October (October 17th)* Q *is the seventeenth letter of the alphabet*; *it's his seventeenth birthday next week*; *he came seventeenth out of thirty*; **the seventeenth century** = the years from 1600 to 1699 (NOTE: compare **the seventeen hundreds**; Note also that with dates **seventeenth** is usually written **17th: July 17th, 1935; October 17th, 1991** (American style is **October 17, 1991**), say 'the seventeenth of October' or 'October the seventeenth' (American style is 'October seventeenth'); with names of kings and queens **seventeenth** is usually written **XVII: King Louis XVII** (say: 'King Louis the Seventeenth')

seventh (7th) ['sevənθ] *adjective & noun his office is on the seventh floor*; *it's her seventh birthday on Saturday*; *what is the seventh letter of the alphabet?*; *the seventh of July or July the seventh (July 7th)* **Henry the Seventh** (Henry VII) **the seventh century** = the period from 600 to 699 AD (NOTE: in dates **seventh** is usually written **7th: January 7th 1959, April 7th 1797 (American style is April 7, 1797)** say 'the seventh of April' or 'April the seventh' (American style is 'April seventh'); with names of kings and queens **seventh** is usually written **VII: King Henry VII:** say 'King Henry the seventh')

seventieth (70th) ['sevəntiəθ] *adjective & noun don't forget tomorrow is your grandmother's seventieth birthday*

seventy ['sevənti] *number* 70; *she will be seventy (years old) on Tuesday*; *that shirt cost him more than seventy dollars*; **she's in her seventies** = she is between 70 and 79 years old; **the (nineteen) seventies (1970s)** = the years from 1970 to 1979 (NOTE: **seventy-one (71)**,

seventy-two (72) etc., but **seventy-first (71st)**, **seventy-second (72nd)** etc.)

sever ['sevə] *verb* to cut off; *the machine severed his arm at the elbow*; *she has decided to sever all relations with her family*

several ['sevrəl] *adjective & pronoun* more than a few, but not a lot; *several buildings were damaged in the storm*; *we've met several times*; *several of the students are going to Italy*; *most of the guests left early but several stayed on till midnight*

severe [sə'vɪə] *adjective* **(a)** very strict; *he was very severe with any child who did not behave*; *discipline in the school was severe* **(b)** *(illness, weather, etc.)* very bad; *the government imposed severe financial restrictions on importers*; *the severe weather has closed several main roads* (NOTE: **severer - severest**)

severely [sɪ'vɪəli] *adverb* **(a)** strictly; *she was severely punished for being late* **(b)** badly; *train services have been severely affected by snow*; *a severely handicapped child*

severity [sə'verɪti] *noun* being severe; *he attacked the government with increasing severity*; *the severity of the cold has killed many small birds*

Seville oranges ['sevɪl 'ɒrɪndʒɪz] *noun* bitter oranges; **Seville orange marmalade** = marmalade made with bitter oranges

sew [səu] *verb* to attach, make or mend by using a needle and thread; *I've taught both my sons how to sew*; *the button's come off my shirt - can you sew it back on?* (NOTE: **sewing - sewed - sewn** [səun])

sewage ['suːɪdʒ] *noun* waste water and other refuse such as faeces, carried away in sewers; **sewage farm** = place where sewage is treated, especially to make it safe to be used as fertilizer; **sewage treatment plant** *or* **sewage works** = place where sewage is treated to make it safe to be pumped into a river or the sea; **raw sewage** = sewage which has not been treated in a sewage farm; *the municipality was accused of discharging raw sewage into the lake*

sewer ['suə] *noun* large pipe which takes waste water and refuse away from buildings; *the main sewer runs underneath the road*; *the final scene of 'The Third Man' takes place in the sewers of Vienna*

sewerage ['suːərɪdʒ] *noun* system of pipes and treatment plants which collect and dispose of sewage in a town; *part of our local taxes goes to pay for sewerage*

sewing ['səuɪŋ] *noun* clothes, etc., which someone is in the process of sewing; *there was a pile of sewing in the middle of the table*

sewing machine ['səuɪŋ mə'ʃiːn] *noun* machine which sews; *she made her dress with her sewing machine*

sewn ['səun] *see* SEW

sex [seks] *noun* **(a)** one of two groups (male and female) into which animals and plants can be divided; *they've had a baby, but I don't know what sex it is*; *there is no discrimination on the grounds of sex, race and religion*; **the opposite sex** = people of the other sex to yours (ie, men to women, women to men); *he's very attractive to the opposite sex* **(b)** sexual relations; *a film full of sex and violence*; *sex was the last thing on her mind*; **to have sex with someone** = to have sexual intercourse with someone; **safe sex** = having sex in a way that avoids transmission of a sexual disease, for example by using a condom and only having one sexual partner

sex appeal ['seks ə'piːl] *noun* being attractive to the opposite sex; *she had a great deal of sex appeal*

sex education ['seks edjuˈkeɪʃn] *noun* teaching children about adult sexual relations; *sex education starts in primary school*

sexism ['seksɪzm] *noun* unfair treatment because of a person's sex; *the management was accused of sexism because it employed women only in secretarial positions*

sexist ['seksɪst] *adjective* unfair towards one of the sexes, especially women; *his sexist attitude towards his female staff; she complained of sexist remarks passed by the managers*

sextant ['sekstənt] *noun (old)* instrument used to calculate the position of a ship by measuring angles between a star and the horizon; *the captain used his sextant to calculate his position*

sexual ['seksʃʊəl] *adjective* referring to sex; *their relationship was never sexual*; **sexual intercourse** = act of sex between a male and female; **sexual partner** = person you have sex with; *see also* DISCRIMINATION

sexual harrassment ['seksjuːəl ˈhærəsmənt] *noun* pestering someone by making unpleasant sexual approaches; *she complained of sexual harassment by her manager*

sexuality [sekʃuˈælɪti] *noun* awareness of sex; *the normal development of a child's sexuality*

sexually ['sekʃuəli] *adverb* in a sexual way; *do find her sexually attractive?*; **sexually transmitted disease** = disease transmitted by having sexual intercourse

sexy ['seksi] *adjective (informal)* sexually attractive; *she was wearing a very sexy dress; you look very sexy in that suit; he's the sexiest actor in the movies today* (NOTE: **sexier - sexiest**)

sh! [ʃ] *interjection* used to ask for silence; *when they started talking a woman said 'sh'* (NOTE: also spelt **shh!**)

shabby ['ʃæbi] *adjective* **(a)** poor, worn (clothes); *he wore a shabby coat with two buttons missing* **(b)** **shabby trick** = mean trick; *that was a shabby trick to play on a poor old lady* (NOTE: **shabbier - shabbiest**)

shack [ʃæk] **1** *noun* rough wooden hut; *he lived for years in a little shack in the woods* **2** *verb (slang)* to **shack up with someone** = to go to live with someone; *they're shacked up together in a flat in Notting Hill Gate*

shackle ['ʃækl] **1** *noun* **shackles** = chains for attaching a prisoner; *he wore shackles round his ankles; she was desperate to escape from the shackles of her life in the vicarage* **2** *verb* to attach someone with a chain; *the slaves were shackled together*

shade [ʃeɪd] **1** *noun* **(a)** variation of a colour; *her hat is a rather pretty shade of green* **(b)** dark place which is not in the sunlight; *let's try and find some shade - it's too hot in the sun; the sun's so hot that we'll have to sit in the shade* **(c)** to put someone in the shade = to make someone seem less impressive; *his acting puts the rest of the cast in the shade* **(d)** *(informal)* **shades** = sunglasses; *you can take off your shades now we're indoors* **(e)** = LAMPSHADE; *a brass table lamp with a red silk shade* **2** *verb* to protect something from

sunlight; *she shaded her eyes against the sun; the old birch tree shades that corner of the garden*

shaded ['ʃeɪdɪd] *adjective* **(a)** covered in shade; *plants which will do well in a shaded part of the garden* **(b)** made darker with shading; *the shaded part of the plan shows where the new office block will be built*

shading ['ʃeɪdɪŋ] *noun* **(a)** making part of a picture darker; *the shading on the face was particularly fine* **(b)** making a drawing darker by drawing fine lines close together; *on this chart, we use different types of shading to indicate different crops*

shadow ['ʃædəʊ] **1** *noun* **(a)** dark place behind an object where light is cut off by the object; *in the evening, the trees cast long shadows across the lawn; she saw his shadow move down the hall; they rested for a while, in the shadow of a large tree* **(b)** the **shadow cabinet** = senior members of the Opposition in parliament who cover the same areas of responsibility as the ministers in the government and will form the next government if they are elected to power; *the Leader of the Opposition has appointed his shadow cabinet; the shadow Chancellor of the Exchequer* **(c)** *(informal)* **five o'clock shadow** = dark chin, where the beard is starting to grow again after it was shaved in the morning; *the villain is the one with the black hat and the five o'clock shadow* **2** *verb* **(a)** to follow someone closely, but without being seen; *the drugs dealer was shadowed by two undercover policemen* **(b)** to be the Opposition spokesman covering a government department; *she is shadowing the Health Secretary*

shadowy ['ʃædəʊi] *adjective* vague or indistinct; *a shadowy horseman loomed up out of the mist; she is a shadowy figure but apparently wields a lot of influence over the Prime Minister* (NOTE: **shadowier - shadowiest**)

shady ['ʃeɪdi] *adjective* **(a)** in the shade; *at midday in Madrid, it's better to walk on the shady side of the street* **(b)** which provides shade; *they drank beer sitting under a shady tree* **(c)** *(informal)* not honest; *he made several shady deals*; **shady character** = person who may be a criminal

shaft [ʃɑːft] *noun* **(a)** thin stick which is the main part of an arrow or a spear, etc.; *he pulled on the shaft to get the javelin out of the ground* **(b)** long handle of a spade, etc.; *the shaft of the spade was so old it snapped in two* **(c)** thin beam of light; *tiny particles of dust dancing in a shaft of sunlight* **(d)** rod which connects parts of an engine; *the shaft transmits power from the engine to the propeller* **(e)** deep hole; *the ventilation shaft had become blocked*; **lift shaft** = hole inside a building in which a lift moves up and down; **mine shaft** = hole in the ground leading to a coalmine

shaggy ['ʃægi] *adjective* long and untidy; *he had a shaggy grey beard*; **shaggy dog story** = very long story with an unexpectedly silly ending (NOTE: **shaggier - shaggiest**)

shake [ʃeɪk] **1** *verb* **(a)** to move something from side to side or up and down; *shake the bottle before pouring; the house shakes every time a train goes past; his hand shook as he opened the envelope*; **to shake your head** = to move your head from side to side to mean 'no'; *when I asked my dad if I could borrow the car he just shook his head* (NOTE: the opposite, meaning 'yes', is to **nod**) **(b)** to surprise, to shock; *his family was shaken by the news that he had been* *arrested*; *the sight of it really shook me* (NOTE: **shaking - shook** [ʃʊk] **- has shaken**) **2** *noun* (a) action of moving rapidly up and down; *if the tomato sauce won't come out, give the bottle a shake* (b) **milk shake** = drink made by mixing milk and sweet flavouring; *he drank two chocolate milk shakes* (c) moving from side to side; *he indicated 'no' with a shake of his head*

shake hands ['ʃeɪk 'hændz] *verb* to shake hands *or* to shake someone's hand = to greet someone by holding their right hand; *he shook hands with me*; *she refused to shake my hand*; *the negotiators shook hands and sat down at the conference table*; to shake hands on a deal = to shake hands to show that a deal has been agreed; *see also* HANDSHAKE

> COMMENT: in Britain and the USA you shake hands with someone mainly in fairly formal circumstances, for example when you meet them for the first time or when you are saying goodbye to someone and do not expect to see them again soon. You do not normally shake hands with people you see every day

shaken ['ʃeɪkn] *adjective* very upset, disturbed; *after the phone call he looked shaken*

shake off ['ʃeɪk 'ɒf] *verb* to get rid of something, usually something unpleasant; *before you leave the beach, remember to shake the sand off your towel*; *they drove at top speed but couldn't shake off their pursuers*; *I don't seem able to shake off this cold*

shakeout ['ʃeɪkaʊt] *noun* (informal) reorganization of a company, etc., where some employees go and some are left; *he lost his job in the latest management shakeout*; *only three companies are left after the shakeout of the computer market*

shakeup ['ʃeɪkʌp] *noun* (informal) total reorganization; *there's been a shakeup in the finance department*

shaky ['ʃeɪkɪ] *adjective* not very secure, not very reliable; *be careful, that ladder is a bit shaky*; *the champion driver got off to a shaky start*; *your argument sounds a bit shaky to me* (NOTE: **shakier - shakiest**)

shale [ʃeɪl] *noun* sedimentary rock formed from clay, which cracks along horizontal straight lines; *the cliff is of shale and is easily eaten away by the sea*

shall [ʃæl] *verb* used with other verbs (a) *(to make the future)* *we shall be out on Saturday evening*; *I shan't say anything - I shall keep my mouth shut!*; *tomorrow we shan't be home until after 10 o'clock* (b) *(to show a suggestion)* *shall we open the windows?*; *shall I give them a ring?* (NOTE: negative: **shan't** [ʃɑːnt]; past: **should, should not** usually **shouldn't** Note also that **shall** is mainly used with I and we)

shallot [ʃə'lɒt] *noun* small variety of onion; *chop three shallots and cook them in butter*

shallow ['ʃæləʊ] **1** *adjective* (a) not deep, not far from top to bottom; *children were playing in the shallow end of the pool*; *the river is so shallow in summer that you can walk across it* (b) without any serious meaning; *it's a very shallow treatment of a serious subject* (NOTE: **shallower - shallowest**) **2** *noun* **shallows** = parts of a river or the sea where the water is shallow; *the children waded into the shallows looking for little fish*

sham [ʃæm] **1** *adjective* false, not genuine; *a necklace of sham diamonds* **2** *noun* person or thing which is false; *her claim to be a great pianist is just a sham*; *the government's promises were just a sham* **3** *verb* to pretend; *he lay still, shamming death, and the lion went away* (NOTE: **shamming - shammed**)

shamble ['ʃæmbl] *verb* to shamble along = to wander along dragging your feet; *he shambled into the bar and ordered a beer*

shambles ['ʃæmblz] *noun* (a) complete lack of organization; *the whole trip to Paris was a shambles - lost tickets, no hotel booking, everything that could go wrong did go wrong* (b) mess; *she stood at the door looking at the shambles after the office party*; *tidy up your bedroom - it is an absolute shambles*

shame [ʃeɪm] **1** *noun* (a) feeling caused by having done something which you should not have done; *she went bright red with shame*; *to my shame, I did nothing to help*; to die of shame = to feel very ashamed; *I could have died of shame!* (b) what a shame! = how sad; *what a shame you couldn't come to the party!*; *it's a shame your father isn't well - I'm sure he would have enjoyed the play*; *it's a shame to have to go to the office on such a glorious day*; shame on you! = you should be ashamed of yourself **2** *verb* to make someone feel ashamed; *we hope to shame her into contributing to the party*; naming and shaming = publishing the name of someone or an organization that is not working correctly, in the hope that this will make them change their ways; *the government hopes that naming and shaming the councils will lead to a reduction in town hall corruption*; *see also* ASHAMED

shamefaced [ʃeɪm'feɪst] *adjective* embarrassed, showing that you are ashamed; *he gave her a shamefaced grin and handed back the money*

shameful ['ʃeɪmfʊl] *adjective* scandalous or disgraceful, causing shame; *I think it's shameful that those children should have to beg for money in the street*; *they refused to surrender because they considered it shameful to do so*

shameless ['ʃeɪmləs] *adjective* without shame; *when it comes to getting favours from the boss, she's quite shameless*

shampoo [ʃæm'puː] **1** *noun* (a) liquid soap for washing hair, carpets, cars, etc.; *there are sachets of shampoo in the bathroom* (b) action of washing the hair; *she went to the hairdresser's for a shampoo* **2** *verb* to wash your hair, a carpet, a car, etc., with liquid soap; *the hairdresser shampooed her hair, and then cut it*; *they have a machine for shampooing carpets* (NOTE: **shampooing - shampooed**)

shandy ['ʃændi] *noun* drink made by mixing beer and lemonade; *we're all drinking shandies* (NOTE: plural is **shandies**)

shank [ʃæŋk] *noun* (a) straight central stem of a tool (b) meat from the leg of an animal; *I bought a piece of shank to make a stew*

shan't [ʃɑːnt] = SHALL NOT

shanty ['ʃænti] *noun* (a) rough wooden hut; *the immigrants live in shanties round the outskirts of the city*; shanty town = large group of huts belonging to poor people (b) sea shanty = song sung by sailors (NOTE: plural is **shanties**)

shape [ʃeɪp] **1** *noun* **(a)** form of how something looks; *she's got a ring in the shape of a letter S*; *the old table was a funny shape*; *this pullover's beginning to lose its shape* = it is beginning to stretch **(b) in good shape** = in good physical form; *he's in good shape for the race*; *she's in a very bad shape*; **to take shape** = to begin to look as it will do when finished; *after all his hard work, the new garden is beginning to take shape*; **in any shape or form** = of any type; *we do not tolerate criticism in any shape or form* **2** *verb* **(a)** to make into a certain form; *he shaped the cake into the form of a little boat* **(b) to shape up** = to result, to end up; *things are shaping up as we expected*; *it's shaping up to be a fine day*

shaped [ʃeɪpt] *adjective* with a certain shape; *the new art gallery is shaped like a pyramid*; *a square-shaped hole in the floor*

shapeless [ˈʃeɪpləs] *adjective* with no definite shape; *she wore a floppy hat and a shapeless pink dress*

shapely [ˈʃeɪpli] *adjective* with an attractive shape; *a pair of shapely legs*

share [ˈʃeə] **1** *noun* **(a)** part of something that is divided between two or more people; *take your share of the cake and leave me the rest*; *she should have paid her share of the food bill*; *there's a lot of work to do, so everyone must do their share*; **to have a share in** = to take part in, to have a part of; *all the staff should have a share in decisions about the company's future*; *she has her share of the responsibility for the accident*; **market share** *or* **share of the market** = percentage of a total market which the sales of a company cover; *their share of the market has gone up by 10%* **(b)** one of the many equal parts into which a company's capital is divided (the owners of shares are 'shareholders'); *he bought 2000 shares in Marks and Spencer*; *shares fell on the London Stock Exchange* (NOTE: American English often used the word **stock** where British English uses **share**. See the note at STOCK) **2** *verb* **(a) to share (out)** = to divide up something among several people; *let's share the bill*; *in her will, her money was shared (out) among her sons*; *they shared the pencils out amongst them* **(b) to share something with someone** = to allow someone to use something which you also use; *we offered to share our information with them*; *he doesn't like sharing his toys with other children* **(c)** to use something which someone else also uses; *we share an office*; *we shared a taxi to the airport*

shareholder [ˈʃeəhəʊldə] *noun* person who owns shares in a company; *our first duty is to our shareholders*; *he called a shareholders' meeting*; **majority** *or* **minority shareholder** = person who owns more *or* less than half the shares in a company; *the solicitor acting on behalf of the minority shareholders* (NOTE: American English is **stockholder**)

shareholding [ˈʃeəhəʊldɪŋ] *noun* group of shares in a company owned by one owner; *she has sold all her shareholdings*; **a majority shareholding** *or* **a minority shareholding** = group of shares which are more *or* less than half the total; *he acquired a minority shareholding in the company*

share index [ˈʃeə ˈɪndeks] *noun* figure based on the current market price of certain shares on a stock exchange; *all the European share indexes rose following the rise in the Dow Jones Index*

COMMENT: all the stock exchanges publish share indexes. The best known are the Footsie in London, the Dow Jones in New York and the Nikkei in Tokyo

share-out [ˈʃeəaʊt] *noun* dividing something among many people; *a share-out of the profits among the employees*

sharing [ˈʃeərɪŋ] *noun* dividing up among several people; *sharing the workload makes it easier to cope*; **job sharing** = situation where a job is done by more than one person, each working part-time; **profit sharing** = dividing profits among workers; *the company operates a profit-sharing scheme*; **time-sharing** = (i) owning a property together with other people, with the right to use it for a period each year; (ii) sharing a computer system with different users using different terminals; *see also* TIMESHARE

shark [ʃɑːk] *noun* **(a)** large dangerous fish which lives in the sea and can kill people; *the lifeguards shouted when a shark was spotted in the water* **(b) loan shark** = person who lends money at a very high interest rate; *she was so desperate for money that she was forced to borrow from loan sharks*

sharp [ʃɑːp] **1** *adjective* **(a)** with a good edge for cutting or poking; *this needle hasn't got a very sharp point*; *the beach is covered with sharp stones*; *this knife is useless - it isn't sharp enough* **(b)** sudden, great or severe; *there was a sharp drop in interest rates*; *the road makes a sharp right-hand bend*; *he received a sharp blow on the back of his head*; *we had a sharp frost last night*; *it's cold, there's a sharp north wind* **(c)** bitter, unpleasant; *these onions have a very sharp taste* **(d) sharp practice** = way of doing business which is not honest, but not illegal; *we suspect the lawyers of sharp practice but we can't prove anything* **(e)** very keen and acute; *he has a sharp sense of justice*; *she has a sharp eye for a bargain*; *he's pretty sharp at spotting mistakes* **(f)** showing criticism or annoyance; *he got a very sharp reply to his fax*; **a sharp tongue** = a tendency to criticize people openly; *her sharp tongue has landed her in trouble once again* **(g)** *(in music)* playing at a higher pitch than it should be; *that violin sounds sharp* (NOTE: **sharper - sharpest**) **2** *adverb* **(a)** exactly; *the coach will leave the hotel at 7.30 sharp* **(b)** suddenly, at an acute angle; *the road turned sharp right* **(c)** *(in music)* pitch which is one semitone higher; *they played Bach's Sonata in F sharp major*; *he played D sharp instead of D flat*

sharpen [ˈʃɑːpən] *verb* to make something sharp; *the lead's broken - I must sharpen the pencil*; *this saw doesn't cut well - it needs to be sharpened*

sharpener [ˈʃɑːpnə] *noun* **pencil sharpener** = device for making pencils sharp; *a battery-powered pencil sharpener*

sharply [ˈʃɑːpli] *adverb* **(a)** acutely; *he felt his mother's death very sharply* **(b)** completely; *the two groups are sharply divided on this issue* **(c)** in a way that criticizes; *she spoke quite sharply to the poor old lady* **(d)** suddenly; *the temperature fell sharply during the night*; *the road turns sharply to the right*

shatter [ˈʃætə] *verb* **(a)** to break into little pieces; *he knocked the vase with his elbow and it shattered onto the floor*; *the bomb shattered the windows of several houses* **(b)** to destroy, to disturb violently; *his hopes of* *going to university were shattered when he failed the exam*; *a loud sneeze shattered the silence in the library*

shattered ['ʃærəd] *adjective* very upset; *she was shattered when the result of the court case was announced*

shattering ['ʃætərɪŋ] *adjective* which is very worrying, or which makes you very upset; *the letter contained the shattering news that their house had been burnt down*; *the arrest of the managing director had a shattering effect on the staff*

shave [ʃeɪv] **1** *noun* act of cutting off the hair on your face with a razor; *he went to have a shave at the barber's next to the hotel*; **a close shave** = situation where you almost hit something; *it was a close shave - we missed the other car by inches* **2** *verb* **(a)** to cut off the hair on your face with a razor; *he cut himself shaving* **(b)** to cut the hair on your head or legs, etc., very short; *I didn't recognize him with his head shaved* **(c)** to cut a thin piece off something; *you need to shave a bit more off to make the door fit the frame*

shaven ['ʃeɪvn] *adjective (old)* shaved; *shaven-headed monks*; **clean-shaven** = with no beard or moustache; *she described her attacker as tall, clean-shaven, with short grey hair*

shaver ['ʃeɪvə] *noun* electric razor, machine for shaving; *a battery-operated shaver*; **shaver point** *or* **shaver socket** = socket in a bathroom where an electric razor can be plugged in

shaving ['ʃeɪvɪŋ] *noun* **(a)** act of cutting off hair on your face; *shaving only takes me a couple of minutes*; **shaving cream** = cream which you put on your face before shaving **(b) shavings** = small thin slices of wood, cheese, etc., cut off with a knife; *they packed the china in a box of wood shavings*

shawl [ʃɔːl] *noun* large square of warm material for wrapping round your shoulders or your head; *she wrapped herself up in her shawl*

she [ʃiː] *pronoun* referring to a female person, a female animal, and sometimes to cars, ships and countries; *she's my sister*; *she and I are going on holiday to France together*; *I'm angry with her - she's taken my motorbike*; *she's a sweet little cat, but she's no good at catching mice*; *the customs officers boarded the ship when she docked* (NOTE: when it is the object **she** becomes **her: she hit the ball** *or* **the ball hit her;** when it follows the verb to **be, she** usually becomes **her: who's that? - it's her, the girl we met yesterday**)

sheaf [ʃiːf] *noun* **(a)** bundle of papers; *he threw a sheaf of papers onto my desk and told me to sort them out*; *the jury had to examine sheaves of evidence collected by the fraud squad* **(b)** bundle of corn stalks tied together after reaping; *they spent all day picking up sheaves and loading them on carts* (NOTE: plural is **sheaves** [ʃiːvz])

shear ['ʃɪə] **1** *noun* **shears** = very large scissors, used for gardening, cutting wool off sheep, etc.; *he's cutting the hedge with the shears* (NOTE: do not confuse with **sheer**) **2** *verb* **(a)** to cut the wool off sheep; *the sheep have to be brought into the farmyard to be sheared*; *the poor sheep look cold now they've been shorn* **(b)** to cut through something; *the ferry sheared through the nets of the fishing boat* (NOTE: **sheared** *or* **shorn** [ʃɔːn])

sheath [ʃiːθ] *noun* **(a)** cover for a knife, dagger, etc.; *put your knife back in its sheath* **(b)** **(contraceptive) sheath** = condom, rubber covering put over the penis

before sexual intercourse as a protection against infection and also as a contraceptive (NOTE: plural is **sheaths** [ʃiːðz])

sheathe [ʃiːð] *verb* to put something into its sheath; *he sheathed his dagger*; **to be sheathed in** = to be covered in something as a protection; *the cables are sheathed in plastic*

sheath-knife ['ʃiːθnaɪf] *noun* knife which is kept in a sheath; *he carried a sheath-knife on his belt* (NOTE: plural is **sheath-knives**)

sheaves [ʃiːvz] *see* SHEAF

shed [ʃed] **1** *noun* small wooden building; *they kept the mower in a shed at the bottom of the garden*; *she's in the garden shed putting geraniums into pots* **2** *verb* **(a)** to lose something which you are carrying or wearing; *in autumn, the trees shed their leaves as soon as the weather turns cold*; *a lorry has shed its load of wood at the roundabout*; *we shed our clothes and dived into the cool water* **(b)** to lose weight, to become lighter; *he goes on a run every morning to try to shed some weight*; *by stopping eating potatoes, she managed to shed three pounds* **(c)** to let blood, tears, light, etc., flow; *she shed tears of anger as she listened to the speech*; *not one drop of blood was shed* **(d)** to shed light on = to make clearer; *can anyone shed any light on what actually happened?*; *the finds in the cave shed a fascinating light on the prehistory of this region* (NOTE: **shedding - shed**)

she'd [ʃiːd] = SHE WOULD

sheen [ʃiːn] *noun* brilliant shining surface; *the sheen of old polished wood*

sheep [ʃiːp] *noun* common farm animal, which gives wool and meat; *a flock of sheep*; *the sheep are in the field*; *see also* BLACK SHEEP (NOTE: no plural: **one sheep, ten sheep.** A female is a **ewe**, a male is a **ram**, and the young are **lambs**. Note also that the meat from a **sheep** is called **lamb**, or sometimes **mutton**)

sheepdog ['ʃiːpdɒg] *noun* dog trained and used by shepherds to control sheep; *he whistled and his sheepdog ran up the hill and gathered the sheep together*

sheepish ['ʃiːpɪʃ] *adjective* embarrassed, showing that you are ashamed; *he looked sheepish when he realized he had deleted the computer file*

sheepskin ['ʃiːpskɪn] *noun* the skin of a sheep, with the wool still on it, used to make rugs, coats, etc.; *he wore an old sheepskin jacket*

sheer ['ʃɪə] **1** *adjective* **(a)** complete; *it was sheer heaven to get into a hot bath after skiing*; *she was crying out of sheer frustration*; *it's sheer madness to go out without a coat in this weather* **(b)** very steep; *it was a sheer ten-metre drop to the beach below* **2** *adverb* straight up or down; *the cliff drops sheer to the beach below* **3** *verb* **to sheer off** = to move to the side, in a diagonal direction; *the car was speeding towards the tunnel but sheered off into the crowd instead* (NOTE: do not confuse with **shear**)

sheet [ʃiːt] *noun* **(a)** large piece of thin cloth which is put over a bed (you put two of them on a bed, one to lie on, and one to cover you); *she changed the sheets on the bed*; *guests are asked to bring their own towels and sheets* **(b)** large flat piece of paper, cardboard, metal, ice, etc.; *can you give me another sheet of paper?*; **sheet lightning** = lightning where you cannot see the

flash, but the clouds are lit up by it; *see also* BALANCE
SHEET

sheikh [ʃeɪk] *noun* Arab leader; *the sheikh wore
traditional Arab dress*

sheikhdom [ˈʃeɪkdəm] *noun* country ruled by a
sheikh; *Dubai and some of the other sheikhdoms*

shelf [ʃelf] *noun* flat piece of wood attached to a wall
or in a cupboard on which things can be put; *he put up
or built some shelves in the kitchen; the shelves were
packed with books; put that book back on the shelf;
can you reach me down the box from the top shelf?;
the plates are on the top shelf in the kitchen cupboard;*
shelf life = number of days or weeks when a product
can be kept in a shop and still be good to use; *(informal)*
on the shelf = still not married; *she thought she was on
the shelf at thirty-five, and then Mr Right came along*
(NOTE: plural is **shelves** [ʃelvz])

shell [ʃel] **1** *noun* **(a)** hard outside part covering some
animals, such as snails, tortoises, etc.; *snails are
usually served in their shells; the children spent hours
collecting shells on the beach* **(b)** hard outside part of
an egg or a nut; *I found a big piece of shell in my
omelette; see also* EGGSHELL, NUTSHELL **(c)** hard
outside part of a building; *only the shell of the building
remained after the fire* **(d)** metal tube full of explosive,
which is fired from a gun; *a shell landed on the
president's palace* **2** *verb* to attack with shells;
anti-government forces shelled the capital

she'll [ʃiːl] = SHE WILL

shellfish [ˈʃelfɪʃ] *noun* edible animals with shells,
such as crabs, oysters, etc.; *I never eat shellfish - they
don't agree with me* (NOTE: no singular: **a plate of
shellfish, a shellfish restaurant**)

shellsuit [ˈʃelsuːt] *noun* one-piece suit or pair of
matching trousers and top, in bright-coloured shiny
material; *she was wearing a bright purple shellsuit*

shelter [ˈʃeltə] **1** *noun* **(a)** protection; *we stood in the
shelter of a tree waiting for the rain to stop; on the
mountain there was no shelter from the pouring rain;*
to take shelter = to go somewhere for protection; *when
the gunmen started to shoot we all took shelter behind
a wall* **(b)** construction where you can go for protection;
*people ran to the air-raid shelters as soon as they
heard the planes;* **bus shelter** = construction with a
roof where you can wait for a bus **2** *verb* **(a)** to give
someone protection; *the school sheltered several
families of refugees* **(b)** to go somewhere for
protection; *sheep were sheltering from the snow beside
the hedge*

sheltered [ˈʃeltəd] *adjective* protected from wind,
cold, danger, etc.; *our garden is very sheltered; the
cottage is in a sheltered valley; they have lived a very
sheltered life;* **sheltered housing** = small flats provided
for elderly people, often with a resident warden

shelve [ʃelv] *verb* **(a)** to put back to a later date; *the
project was shelved for lack of money; discussion of
the problem has been shelved* **(b)** to slope down; *the
beach shelves gently so it is safe for little children*

shelves [ʃelvz] *noun see* SHELF

shelving [ˈʃelvɪŋ] *noun* **(a)** rows of shelves; *I've
installed metal shelving in the garden shed* **(b)**
postponing; *the shelving of the project has resulted in
chaos*

shepherd [ˈʃepəd] **1** *noun* man who looks after
sheep; *do shepherds still carry a stick with a hooked
end?;* **shepherd's pie** = minced meat cooked in a dish
with a layer of mashed potatoes on top (NOTE: also
called **cottage pie**) **2** *verb* to guide; *the children were
shepherded into the building; the police were
shepherding the crowds away from the scene of the
accident*

sherbet [ˈʃɜːbət] *noun* US type of ice cream made
with more fruit juice than cream; *a raspberry sherbet,
please* (NOTE: British English is **sorbet**)

sheriff [ˈʃerɪf] *noun* **(a)** US official in charge of
justice in a county; *the sheriff of Orange County* **(b)**
(in England) **High Sheriff** = official appointed as the
government's representative in a county **(c)** *(in
Scotland)* chief judge in a district

sherry [ˈʃeri] *noun* **(a)** type of strong wine, made in
Spain; *she brought two bottles of sherry back from
Spain* **(b)** glass of this wine; *I'll have a dry sherry,
please; two sherries and a port please* (NOTE: the plural
sherries can mean types of sherry or glasses of wine)

shh! [ʃ] *interjection* used to ask for silence; *shh! you
mustn't talk like that about the president* (NOTE: also
spelt **sh!**)

shield [ʃiːld] **1** *noun* **(a)** large plate held in one hand,
carried by riot police, knights in armour, etc., as
protection; *the policemen cowered behind their plastic
shields* **(b)** thing which protects from danger; *you need
a shield over your face when welding* **2** *verb* **(a)** to
protect from danger; *he tried to shield her from the
wind* **(b)** to protect someone who has done something
wrong; *she's just shielding her father*

shift [ʃɪft] **1** *noun* **(a)** change of position, of direction,
etc.; *the company is taking advantage of a shift in the
market towards higher priced goods; there has been a
shift of emphasis from confrontation to partnership; I
don't understand this shift in attitude* **(b)** period of
time during which one group of workers works before
being replaced by another group; *which shift are you
working today?; we work an eight-hour shift;* **day
shift** = shift worked during the daytime; **night shift** =
shift worked during the night; *there are 150 men on the
day shift; he works the night shift* **(c)** loose dress; *as it
was so hot she wore only a light cotton shift* **2** *verb* **(a)**
to move; to change position, direction; *we've shifted
the television from the kitchen into the dining room;
the centre of attention shifted to Downing Street* **(b)**
US **to shift gears** = to change from one gear to the next
when driving a car; **to shift up** = to move to a higher
gear when driving a car; *shift up to top gear when you
get onto the expressway;* **to shift down** = to move to a
lower gear when driving a car; *shift down when you
come to the hill* (NOTE: British English is **to change
gear, to change up, to change down**) **(c)** *(informal)* **to
shift for yourself** = to look after yourself; *you'll have
to shift for yourselves while your mother's in hospital*
(d) *(informal)* to sell; *we shifted 20,000 Christmas
trees in one week*

shifting [ˈʃɪftɪŋ] *adjective* moving; *shifting sand
buried the town*

shift key [ˈʃɪftkiː] *noun* key on a typewriter or
computer keyboard which makes capital letters or
switches to another function; *hold down the shift key
while you click the 'help' icon*

shifty [ˈʃɪfti] *adjective (informal)* not looking honest;
*a shifty-looking man tried to sell me tickets to the
World Cup*

shimmer ['ʃɪmə] **1** *noun* soft quivering light; *I could see the shimmer of satin in the candlelight* **2** *verb* to quiver with light; *the lake shimmered in the moonlight*

shin [ʃɪn] **1** *noun* **(a)** front part of your leg below the knee; *he scraped his shin climbing over the wall*; *they kicked him in the shins* **(b) shin of beef** = meat from the bottom part of the front legs of cattle **2** *verb* **to shin up** = to climb up; *the sailors shinned up the mast* (NOTE: **shinning - shinned**)

shine [ʃaɪn] **1** *noun* **(a)** brightness, reflection of light; *the shine of polished tables* **(b)** action of polishing; *give the brass doorknob a shine* **2** *verb* **(a)** to be bright with light; *the sun is shining and they say it'll be hot today*; *she polished the table until it shone*; *the wineglasses shone in the light of the candles*; *why do cats' eyes shine in the dark?*; *the moon shone down on the waiting crowd* **(b)** to make light fall on something; *he shone his torch into the cellar* (NOTE: in these meanings **shining - shone** [ʃɒn]) **(c)** to polish something to make it bright; *she was shining the silver*; *don't forget to shine your shoes* (NOTE: in this meaning **shining - shined**)

shingle [ʃɪŋgl] *noun* **(a)** mass of small pebbles on a beach; *a shingle beach is quite hard to walk on in your bare feet* **(b)** flat piece of wood or asbestos nailed on a wall or roof as a covering; *I must get up on the roof, some of the shingles need replacing* **(c) shingles** = inflammation of a nerve, with pain running along the nerve making a line of blisters form on the skin, usually found mainly on the abdomen or back, or on the face; *she had shingles and could not go to work*

> COMMENT: shingles is caused by the same virus as causes chickenpox. In older people, shingles can develop where a person has already had chickenpox in the past and is in contact with a child who has chickenpox

shining ['ʃaɪnɪŋ] *adjective* brilliant; *the sun glinted on the shining window*; *she turned her shining eyes towards him*; **a shining example of** = a very good example of; *she's a shining example of how to get on in business*

shiny ['ʃaɪni] *adjective* which shines; *the book has a shiny cover*; *he drove up in his new and very shiny car* (NOTE: **shinier - shiniest**)

ship [ʃɪp] **1** *noun* large boat for carrying passengers and cargo on the sea; *she's a fine ship*; *how many ships does the Royal Navy have?*; *the first time we went to the United States, we went by ship*; **cargo ship** = ship which carries only goods and not passengers; **to jump ship** = (i) to leave the ship on which you are working and not come back; (ii) to leave a project or team to go to work for a rival (NOTE: a **ship** is often referred to as **she** *or* **her**) **2** *verb* **(a)** to send goods (or people) but not always on a ship; *we ship goods all over the country*; *the consignment of cars was shipped abroad last week*; *we've shipped the children off to my sister's for two weeks* **(b)** to take on board a ship; *we shipped a lot of water during the storm* (NOTE: **shipping - shipped**)

shipbuilding ['ʃɪpbɪldɪŋ] *noun* building of ships; *shipbuilding is a major industry in Korea*; *the shipbuilding industry was hard hit in the recession*

shipmate ['ʃɪpmeɪt] *noun* sailor on the same ship as you; *this is a photo of me and my shipmates in a bar*

shipment ['ʃɪpmənt] *noun* **(a)** sending of goods; *we make two shipments a week to France* **(b)** goods which

are shipped; *two shipments were lost in the fire*; *a shipment of computers was damaged*

shipper ['ʃɪpə] *noun* person or company that sends goods; *arrange for the shippers to collect the crate tomorrow*

shipping ['ʃɪpɪŋ] *noun* **(a)** sending of goods; *shipping by rail can often work out cheaper*; **shipping company** = company which specializes in the sending of goods; **shipping instructions** = details of how goods are to be shipped and delivered (NOTE: in this meaning, **shipping** does not always mean using a ship) **(b)** cost of transporting goods; *shipping is not included in the invoice* **(c)** ships; *they attacked enemy shipping in the Channel*; **shipping lanes** = routes across the sea which are regularly used by ships; **shipping line** = company which owns ships (NOTE: no plural)

shipshape ['ʃɪpʃeɪp] *adjective (informal)* neat and tidy; *we have to get everything shipshape for the mayor's visit*

shipwreck ['ʃɪprek] *noun* accident which sinks a ship; *ten passengers were drowned in the shipwreck*

shipwrecked ['ʃɪprekt] *adjective* having been on a ship which has been wrecked and sunk; *they were shipwrecked on a little island*; *the shipwrecked crew were rescued by local fishermen*

shipyard ['ʃɪpjɑːd] *noun* factory where ships are built; *let's hope a British shipyard wins the contract for the new liner*

shire ['ʃaɪə] *noun* **(a)** *(old)* county; **the shires** = farming country in the central part of England (NOTE: now used mainly in the names of counties: **Berkshire, Hampshire, etc.**) **(b) shire horse** = large powerful horse, often used for farm work

shirk [ʃɜːk] *verb* to try not to do something, especially work; *he's just shirking, get him to do some work*; **to shirk responsibility** = not to do something which you should do; *she's very conscientious and never shirks her responsibilities*

shirt [ʃɜːt] *noun* light piece of clothing which you wear on the top part of the body under a pullover or jacket; *the teacher wore a blue suit and a blue shirt*; *when he came back from the trip he had a suitcase full of dirty shirts*; *it's so hot that the workers in the fields have taken their shirts off*; *(informal)* **keep your shirt on!** = don't lose your temper

shirtsleeves ['ʃɜːtsliːvz] *noun* **in your shirtsleeves** = not wearing a jacket; *he was sitting at his desk in his shirtsleeves*

shit [ʃɪt] **1** *noun (vulgar)* **(a)** solid waste matter from the body; *I've stepped in some dog shit*; **to scare the shit out of someone** = to frighten someone; *he scares the shit out of me!* **(b)** nonsense; *I've never heard such shit in my life!*; *what a load of shit!* **(c)** unpleasant person; *she's nice, but her brother's a real shit* **2** *verb (vulgar)* to pass solid waste matter from the body; *all babies do is eat, shit and sleep* (NOTE: **shitting - shit**)

shiver ['ʃɪvə] **1** *noun* action of trembling because of cold, fear, etc.; **to send shivers down someone's spine** = to make someone very afraid; *the mere thought of grandfather driving along the motorway at his age sends shivers down my spine* **2** *verb* to tremble with cold, fear, etc.; *she shivered in the cold night air*; *he was coughing and shivering, so the doctor told him to stay in bed*

shoal [ʃəʊl] *noun* (a) **shoal(s)** = bank of sand under the water; *the ship ran aground on a shoal*; *the shoals are clearly marked on the chart of the harbour* (b) group of fish swimming about; *a shoal of herring* (c) large group of people or things, taken together; *shoals of tourists visited the ruins*; *we had shoals of complaints after our TV ad*

shock [ʃɒk] **1** *noun* (a) sudden unpleasant surprise; *it gave me quite a shock when you walked in*; *he's in for a nasty shock* (b) weakness caused by low blood pressure, after an illness or injury or having a sudden surprise; *several of the passengers were treated for shock*; *she was in a state of shock after hearing that her son had drowned* (c) **electric shock** = sudden painful passing of electric current through the body; *I got a shock when I touched the back of the TV set* **2** *verb* to give someone a sudden unpleasant surprise; *the conditions in the hospital shocked the inspectors*

shocked [ʃɒkt] *adjective* unpleasantly surprised; *we were all shocked to hear that he had been arrested*; *she said 'How could you do it?' in a shocked voice*

shocker [ʃɒkə] *noun* (a) story, book or film involving horror and violence; *his latest shocker is available in paperback* (b) *(informal)* shocking event; *finding the bodies in the cellar was a real shocker*

shocking [ʃɒkɪŋ] *adjective* very unpleasant, which gives a sudden surprise; *it is a very shocking film*; *the shocking news of the plane crash*; *it is shocking that no one offered to help*

shockingly [ʃɒkɪŋli] *adverb* in a shocking way; *these patients have been treated shockingly*

shock-proof [ʃɒkpruːf] *adjective* which is not affected by shocks; *my watch is supposed to be shock-proof, so it shouldn't matter if I drop it on the floor*

shock wave [ʃɒk weɪv] *noun* (a) wave of high pressure which comes from an explosion, earthquake, etc.; *three seconds after the explosion, the shock wave smashed the windows on our house* (b) feeling of shock after something has happened; *the shock waves from the collapse of the government will be felt for some time*

shoddily [ʃɒdɪli] *adverb* in a shoddy way; *the gate was shoddily made and doesn't close properly*

shoddy [ʃɒdi] *adjective* (a) badly done; *the shoddy workmanship of these shoes*; *they're selling off shoddy goods at cheap prices* (b) **shoddy trick** = low or nasty trick; *that was a shoddy trick to play on a poor old lady* (NOTE: **shoddier - shoddiest**)

shoe [ʃuː] **1** *noun* (a) piece of clothing which is worn on the foot; *she's bought a new pair of shoes*; *he put his shoes on and went out*; *take your shoes off if your feet hurt*; **tennis shoes** = special shoes worn to play tennis (NOTE: two shoes are called **a pair**) (b) **in his shoes** = in his place, in the situation he is in; *what would you do if you were in his shoes?*; *I wouldn't like to be in her shoes* (c) horseshoe, piece of metal nailed under a horse's hoof; *the horse lost a shoe and couldn't continue the race* **2** *verb* to put a horseshoe on a horse; *the blacksmith was shoeing my horse*; *the horse needs to be shoed*

shoehorn [ʃuːhɔːn] *noun* curved plastic or metal device which you put into the heel of a shoe to make it easier to put on; *it will be easier to put your new shoes on if you use a shoehorn*

shoelace [ʃuːleɪs] *noun* lace for tying up shoes; *your shoelace is undone*; *he bent down and tied his shoelace*

shoeshine [ʃuːʃaɪn] *noun* polishing shoes; **shoeshine boy** = man, or sometimes a boy, who polishes people's shoes

shoestring [ʃuːstrɪŋ] *noun* (a) *US* shoelace (b) *(informal)* **on a shoestring** = done with only a little money; *we're trying to run this business on a shoestring*; *they're living on a shoestring*

shone [ʃɒn] *see* SHINE

shook [ʃʊk] *see* SHAKE

shoot [ʃuːt] **1** *noun* (a) little new part of a plant, growing from a seed; *one or two green shoots are already showing where I sowed my lettuces* (b) new growth on a plant; *the vines have made a lot of new shoots this year*; *after pruning, the roses will send out a lot of strong new shoots* **2** *verb* (a) to fire a gun; *soldiers were shooting into the woods* (b) to hit or kill by firing a gun; *one of the robbers was shot by a policeman when he tried to run away*; *we went out hunting and shot two rabbits* (c) to go very fast; *when the doorbell rang she shot downstairs*; *he started the engine and the car shot out of the garage* (d) to make a film; *they're shooting a gangster film in our street* (NOTE: **shoots - shooting - shot** [ʃɒt])

shoot down [ʃuːt daʊn] *verb* to make an aircraft crash by hitting it with bullets from a gun; *our soldiers shot down the helicopter*

shooting [ʃuːtɪŋ] *noun* action of shooting or killing with a gun; *news is coming in of a shooting in central London*; **shooting gallery** = sideshow at a fair, where you shoot at targets to win prizes; **shooting stick** = stick with a sharp point and a handle which unfolds to make a seat; *see also* SEASON

shooting star [ʃuːtɪŋ stɑː] *noun* meteor, a small object which flashes through space and shines brightly; *in August, watch the night sky for shooting stars*

shoot-out [ʃuːt aʊt] *noun* fight with guns; *the robbers were caught after a shoot-out with the police*

shoot up [ʃuːt ʌp] *verb* to go up fast; *prices shot up during the strike*; *she used to be such a small child but she's really shot up in the last couple of years*

shop [ʃɒp] **1** *noun* (a) place where you can buy things; *quite a few shops are open on Sundays*; *I never go to that shop - it's much too expensive*; *the sweet shop is opposite the fire station*; **corner shop** = small general store in a town, sometimes on a street corner; *we buy all our food from the corner shop*; **shop assistant** = person who serves customers in a shop; *the shop assistant was very helpful when I bought my camera*; **shop window** = large window in a shop where goods are displayed so that customers can see them; *the shop windows are all decorated for Christmas* (NOTE: American English usually uses **store** instead of **shop: a bookstore, a computer store, etc.**) (b) workshop, a place where goods are made or repaired; **body shop** = workshop where car bodies are repaired; **repair shop** = small factory where machines are repaired (c) **closed shop** = system whereby a company agrees to employ only union members in certain jobs; *the union is asking the management to agree to a closed shop* (d) **to talk shop** = to talk about your business; *the dinner party was dull - the men all sat in a corner talking shop* **2** *verb* to look for and buy things in shops; *she's out shopping for his birthday present*; *Mum's gone* *shopping in town; they went shopping in Oxford Street; do you ever shop locally?* (NOTE: **shopping - shopped**)

> COMMENT: in Britain, smaller shops usually open Monday to Saturday from 9 o'clock or 9.30 to 5.30; some close for lunch between 1 o'clock and 2. Some shops close early on Wednesday or Saturday, though this is less frequent that it used to be. Supermarkets and some larger stores are open longer hours, especially on Thursday and Friday evenings, and are also open from 10.00 to 4.00 on Sundays. In big cities there are stores which are open from 7.00 in the morning to midnight. A few supermarkets are open 24 hours a day

shop around ['ʃɒp ə'raʊnd] *verb* to go to various shops to find which one has the cheapest goods before you buy what you want; *if you want a cheap TV set you ought to shop around; you should shop around before getting your car serviced*

shopfront ['ʃɒpfrʌnt] *noun* part of a shop which faces the street, including the entrance and the windows; *we've had our shopfront redone, in dark green paint with gold letters; the style of the shopfront is classic, simple and elegant*

shopkeeper ['ʃɒpkiːpə] *noun* person who owns a shop; *the shopkeeper stood behind the counter adding up the invoices*

shoplifter ['ʃɒplɪftə] *noun* person who steals things from shops; *we saw the shoplifter put a tin of beans in her pocket*

shoplifting ['ʃɒplɪftɪŋ] *noun* stealing from shops; *he was sentenced to three months in prison for shoplifting*

shopper ['ʃɒpə] *noun* person who buys things in a shop; *the store stays open till midnight to cater for late-night shoppers; Oxford Street was crowded with shoppers when the sales started*

shopping ['ʃɒpɪŋ] *noun* **(a)** activity of buying things in a shop; *we do all our shopping at the weekend; he's gone out to do the weekly shopping*; **window shopping** = looking at goods in shop windows, without buying anything; **shopping basket** = basket for carrying shopping; *US* **shopping cart** = metal basket on wheels, used by shoppers to put their purchases in as they go round a supermarket (NOTE: the British English for this is **supermarket trolley**); **shopping spree** = happy time spent buying things in shops **(b)** things which you have bought in a shop; *put all your shopping on the table; she was carrying two baskets of shopping* (NOTE: no plural: **some shopping, a lot of shopping**)

shopping centre *US* **shopping mall** ['ʃɒpɪŋ 'sentə or 'mɔl] *noun* building with several different shops and restaurants, together with a car park; *we must stop them from building any more out-of-town shopping centres*

shopping precinct ['ʃɒpɪŋ 'priːsɪŋkt] *noun* part of town where the streets are closed to traffic so that people can walk about and shop; *the shopping precinct is right next to the car park*

shop-soiled ['ʃɒpsɔɪld] *adjective* dirty because of having been displayed in a shop; *these shop-soiled items have been reduced*

shop steward ['ʃɒp 'stjuːəd] *noun* elected trade union representative; *the shop stewards reported the workers' complaints to the management*

shore [ʃɔː] **1** *noun* land at the edge of the sea or a lake; *she stood on the shore waving as the boat sailed away*; **to go on shore** = to go onto land from a ship; *when we were on shore in Greece our cruise ship sailed without us; see also* ASHORE **2** *verb* **to shore something up** = to hold something up which might fall down; *they had to put in metal beams to shore up the ceiling; the army is trying to shore up the president's regime*

short [ʃɔːt] **1** *adjective* **(a)** *(size, length)* not long; *have you got a short piece of wire?*; **short-sleeved shirt** = shirt with short sleeves **(b)** *(distance)* not far; *she only lives a short distance away; the taxi driver wanted to take me through the high street, but I told him there was a shorter route; the shortest way to the railway station is to go through the park* **(c)** *(period of time)* not long, small; *he phoned a short time ago; we had a short holiday in June; she managed to have a short sleep on the plane* **(d)** *(height)* not tall; *he is only 1m 40 - much shorter than his brother* **(e)** not as much as there should be; *the delivery was three items short; when we counted the cash we were £10 short* = we had £10 less than we should have had **(f) short of** = with not enough; *I can't offer you any tea as we're short of milk; can I pay later as I'm rather short of cash at the moment?*; **to run short of** = to have less and less of; *in the hot weather the pubs ran short of beer* **(g) short for** = written or spoken with fewer letters than usual; *Ltd is short for Limited; his name is Jonathan but everyone calls him Jonty for short* (NOTE: **shorter - shortest**) **2** *adverb* **(a)** suddenly; *I stopped short when I saw her walking towards me* **(b) short of** = without doing something; *short of sacking her, I don't know what we can do* **3** *verb* to short-circuit; *he switched on TV and shorted the whole house*

shortage ['ʃɔːtɪdʒ] *noun* lack of something; *a chronic shortage of skilled staff; what is the government going to do about the housing shortage?; during the war, there were food shortages*

shortbread ['ʃɔːtbred] *noun* thick sweet crumbly biscuit; *a tin of Scottish shortbread; real shortbread must be made of butter* (NOTE: no plural)

shortcake [ʃɔːtkeɪk] *noun US* sponge cake with fruit filling, covered with whipped cream; *he had a strawberry shortcake for his birthday*

short-circuit [ʃɔːt'sɜːkɪt] **1** *noun* bad connection in an electric circuit, making the electric current follow the wrong path; *it was the worn cable which caused the short-circuit* **2** *verb* **(a)** to make a short-circuit; *a faulty contact caused the system to short-circuit* **(b)** to get through something complicated by using a simple short cut; *is there any way of short-circuiting some of the administrative procedures?*

shortcomings ['ʃɔːtkʌmɪŋz] *noun* faults, defects; *any shortcomings in the plan will be noticed by the inspectors*

short cut ['ʃɔːt 'kʌt] *noun* **(a)** way which is shorter than usual; *we can take a short cut through the park* **(b)** quicker way of doing something; *there are no short cuts to learning Russian*

shorten ['ʃɔːtən] *verb* to make shorter; *smoking will shorten your life; I must have these trousers shortened* (NOTE: the opposite is **lengthen**)

shortfall ['ʃɔːtfɔːl] *noun* amount which is missing which would make the total expected sum; *he had to put money into the till to cover the cash shortfall; there was an unexpected shortfall of £50,000 in the accounts*

shorthand ['ʃɔːthænd] *noun* rapid way of writing using a system of signs; *why on earth is he learning shorthand?*; **to take (in) shorthand** = to write using shorthand; *he took the minutes of the meeting in shorthand*; **shorthand typist** = typist who can take dictation in shorthand, then type it; *compare* LONGHAND

short-handed [ʃɔːt'hændɪd] *adjective* without enough staff; *we are rather short-handed at the moment*

short-haul flight ['ʃɔːthɔːl 'flaɪt] *noun* flight over a short distance (up to 1,000 km); *some cabin crew prefer working on short-haul flights; compare* LONG-HAUL

shorthorn ['ʃɔːthɔːn] *noun* breed of cattle with short horns; *he has a herd of pedigree shorthorns; compare* LONGHORN

shortlist ['ʃɔːtlɪst] **1** *noun* list of some of the people who have applied for a job, and who have been chosen to come for an interview; *he's on the shortlist for the job* **2** *verb* to put (someone, someone's name) on a shortlist; *four candidates have been shortlisted; if you are shortlisted you will be asked for an interview*

shortlived [ʃɔːt'lɪvd] *adjective* which does not last for a long time; *their enthusiasm for the project was very shortlived; compare* LONGLIVED

shortly [ʃɔːtli] *adverb* soon; *he left his office shortly before 5 o'clock; don't worry, she'll be here shortly*

short-range [ʃɔːt 'reɪndʒ] *adjective* which covers a short distance or a short time; *a short-range weather forecast; they have put short-range missiles near the border; a short-range weather forecast; see also* LONG-RANGE

shorts [ʃɔːts] *noun* short trousers for men or women, that come down above the knees; *he was wearing a pair of green running shorts; they won't let you into the church in shorts*; **boxer shorts** = men's underwear shaped like sports shorts

shortsighted [ʃɔːt'saɪtɪd] *adjective* **(a)** able to see close objects clearly, but not objects which are further away; *I'm shortsighted and have to wear glasses* (NOTE: also called **nearsighted**) **(b)** not thinking about what may happen in the future; *it is very shortsighted of him to spend all the money on a new car; the government has adopted a very shortsighted policy; see also* LONGSIGHTED

shortsightedness [ʃɔːt'saɪtɪdnəs] *noun* being shortsighted; *the test revealed severe shortsightedness; the Opposition condemned the shortsightedness of current government policy; see also* LONGSIGHTEDNESS

short-sleeved [ʃɔːtsliːvd] *adjective* with short sleeves; *he was wearing a blue short-sleeved shirt; see also* LONG-SLEEVED

short-staffed [ʃɔːt'stɑːft] *adjective* without enough staff; *the service is slow because the restaurant is short-staffed*

short-stay ['ʃɔːt 'steɪ] *adjective* referring to a stay of a short time; **short stay hostel** = hostel where people

can stay for a few weeks or months, rather than years; **short-stay car park** = car park where you can leave your car for a short time, usually not more than one day; *compare* LONG-STAY

short story ['ʃɔːt 'stɔːri] *noun* piece of fiction which is much shorter than a novel; *he has had several short stories published in magazines; Somerset Maugham was a great short-story writer*

short-term [ʃɔːt'tɜːm] *adjective* for a short period only; *staying in a hotel is only a short-term solution; we have taken on more staff on a short-term basis; see also* LONG-TERM

short wave ['ʃɔːt 'weɪv] *noun* radio communications frequency below 60 metres; **short-wave receiver** = radio receiver able to pick up broadcasts on the short wave bands; *see also* MEDIUM WAVE, LONG WAVE

shot [ʃɒt] **1** *noun* **(a)** action of shooting; the sound of shooting; *the police fired two shots at the car; some shots were fired during the bank robbery; a neighbour said she'd heard a shot*; **like a shot** = very rapidly; *he heard a noise and was off like a shot* **(b)** *(informal)* attempt; *he passed the test at the first shot*; **to have a shot at something** = to try to do something; *I'd like to have a shot at water-skiing* **(c)** **mail shot** *or* **mailing shot** = leaflets sent by post to possible customers; *our latest mail shot goes out on Monday* **(d)** *(slang)* injection; *the doctor gave him a tetanus shot* **(e)** *(slang)* small drink of alcohol; *he poured himself a shot of whisky and sat down to wait* **(f)** photograph; *I took several shots of the inside of the house* **(g)** large heavy ball thrown in a sporting competition; *how much does the shot weigh?*; **to put the shot** = to throw a heavy ball in a competition; *see also* SHOT PUTTER **(h)** person who shoots well or badly; *she's a first-class shot; he's a hopeless shot* **2** *past tense and past participle of* SHOOT

shotgun ['ʃɒtɡʌn] *noun* gun which fires small pellets; *the cat was killed by a shotgun pellet*; **sawn-off shotgun** = gun with the barrel cut short; *he was found carrying a sawn-off shotgun*

shot putter ['ʃɒtpʊtə] *noun* person who puts the shot; *an Olympic shot putter*

should [ʃʊd] *verb used with other verbs* **(a)** *(used in giving advice or warnings, used to say what is the best thing to do)* *you should go to the doctor if your cough gets worse; I should have been more careful; she shouldn't eat so much if she's trying to lose weight; should I ask for more coffee?; why should I clean up your mess?* **(b)** *(used to say what you expect to happen)* *if you leave now you should be there by 4 o'clock; their train should have arrived by now; there shouldn't be any more problems now* (NOTE: in meanings (a) and (b) **ought to** can be used instead of **should**) **(c)** *(indicating a possibility)* *if the President should die in office, the Vice-President automatically takes over; I'll be in the next room should you need me* **(d)** *(used instead of* **would***)* *(old)* *we should like to offer you our congratulations; if I had enough money I should like to buy a new car* (NOTE: negative: **should not**, usually **shouldn't**. (Note also that **should** is the past of **shall**: **shall we go to an Indian restaurant? - I suggested we should go to an Indian** restaurant)

shoulder ['ʃəʊldə] **1** *noun* **(a)** part of the body at the top of the arm; *the policeman touched me on the shoulder; he fell and dislocated his shoulder; look* over your shoulder, he's just behind you; **shoulder to shoulder** = side by side; *the three men stood shoulder to shoulder blocking the way; see also* COLD **(b)** piece of clothing which covers the part between top of the arm and the neck; *there's an ink mark on the shoulder of your shirt; a captain has three pips on his shoulders* **(c)** piece of meat from the top part of the front leg of an animal; *we had a shoulder of lamb and new potatoes* **(d) hard shoulder** = extra inside lane on a major road, where you can stop in an emergency; *the engine was making a funny noise, so I pulled over onto the hard shoulder* **2** *verb* to carry responsibility, blame, etc.; *he had to shoulder all the responsibility for the company's collapse; she was left to shoulder the blame for the accident*

shoulder bag ['ʃəuldə 'bæg] *noun* bag with a long strap which can be carried over the shoulder; *you can lengthen the strap and make your bag into a shoulder bag*

shoulderblade ['ʃəuldəbleɪd] *noun* one of two large flat bones covering the top part of your back; *he fell when skiing and broke his shoulderblade* (NOTE: also called the **scapula**)

shout [ʃaut] **1** *noun* yell, loud cry; *she gave a shout and dived into the water; people came running when they heard the shouts of the children* **2** *verb* to make a loud cry, to speak very loudly; *they stamped on the floor and shouted; I had to shout to the waitress to get served; they were shouting greetings to one another across the street*

shove [ʃʌv] **1** *noun* sudden push; *she gave the car a shove and it rolled down the hill* **2** *verb* to push roughly; *he shoved the papers into his pocket; stop shoving - there's no more room on the bus; (informal)* **shove off!** = go away!; *shove off and let me finish my meal*

shovel ['ʃʌvl] **1** *noun* wide spade; *the workmen picked up shovels and started to clear the pile of sand* **2** *verb* **(a)** to lift up with a shovel; *they were shovelling sand into the truck; he collapsed after shovelling snow from the path* **(b)** *(informal)* to put a large amount of food into your mouth; *it wasn't very elegant, the way he was shovelling pasta into his mouth* (NOTE: **shovelling - shovelled** but American spelling **shoveling - shoveled**)

show [ʃəu] **1** *noun* **(a)** exhibition, things which are displayed for people to look at; *the Hampton Court Flower Show opens tomorrow; she has entered her two cats for the local cat show;* **show flat** *or* **show house** = new flat or house which is furnished by the builders so that people can see how other flats or houses will look **(b) on show** = displayed for everyone to see; *is there anything new on show in this year's exhibition?* **(c)** something which is on at a theatre; *'Cats' is a wonderful show; we're going to a show tonight; the show starts at 7.30, so let's have dinner early* **(d) show of hands** = vote where people show how they vote by raising their hands; *the motion was carried on a show of hands* **(e)** *(informal)* planned activity or organization; *she's running the whole show by herself* **2** *verb* **(a)** to let someone see something; *he wanted to show me his holiday photos; she proudly showed me her new car; you don't have to show your passport when you're travelling to Ireland* **(b)** to point something out to someone; *show me where the accident happened; he asked me to show him the way to the railway station; the salesman showed her how to*

work the photocopier; *my watch shows the date as well as the time* **(c)** to prove; *the results show how right we were to invest in the USA* **(d) to show signs of** = to be visible; *the wound doesn't show any signs of infection* **(e)** to be seen, to be obvious; *the repairs were badly done and it shows; her rash has almost disappeared and hardly shows at all* **(f)** *(informal)* **to show someone the door** = to make someone leave, to sack someone; *when we complained we were shown the door* (NOTE: **showing - showed - has shown** [ʃəun])

showbiz ['ʃəubɪz] *noun (informal)* = SHOW BUSINESS; *she's been in showbiz all her life*

show business ['ʃəu 'bɪznəs] *noun* business of providing entertainment for people; *one the great show business events is the annual Oscar ceremony; a famous show business personality*

showcase ['ʃəukeɪs] *noun* **(a)** cupboard with a glass front or top to display items for sale; *the thieves smashed the showcase and went off with a tray of rings* **(b)** event which displays something; *the computer show is a showcase for the latest developments in information technology*

showdown ['ʃəudaun] *noun* final argument which will solve a crisis; *he had a showdown with the boss; they can't go on quarrelling like this - it's bound to come to a showdown*

shower ['ʃauə] **1** *noun* **(a)** slight fall of rain, snow, etc.; *in April there's usually a mixture of sunshine and showers; there were snow showers this morning, but it is sunny again now* **(b)** device in a bathroom for sending out a spray of water to wash your whole body; **power shower** = strong shower driven by an electric pump; **shower cap** = waterproof cap to prevent your hair getting wet when taking a shower; **shower curtain** = piece of waterproof material around a shower; **shower room** = small bathroom with a shower in it **(c)** bath taken in a spray of water from over your head; *she went up to her room and had a shower; he has a cold shower every morning; you can't take a shower now, there's no hot water* **(d)** *US* party where presents are given to a girl about to get married or who has had a baby; *we are holding a shower for Liliane next Saturday* **(e)** *(informal)* group of slow, useless people; *come on, you shower, get a move on!* **2** *verb* **(a)** to wash under a spray of water; *he showered and went down to greet his guests* **(b)** **to shower someone with something** = to give large amounts of something to someone; *he was showered with presents*

showery ['ʃauəri] *adjective* when there are often showers; *in April, we often have showery weather*

show in ['ʃəu 'ɪn] *verb* to bring someone into a room, etc.; *please show the next candidate in; he was shown into a comfortable room with a view over the sea*

showing ['ʃəuɪŋ] *noun* result which shows how well or badly you are doing; *her poor showing in the Olympics was due to lack of preparation; the company's present showing on the stock exchange suggests that it is in difficulties*

show-jumper ['ʃəudʒʌmpə] *noun* horse or rider specially trained for show-jumping; *he trained several Olympic show-jumpers*

show-jumping ['ʃəudʒʌmpɪŋ] *noun* sport in which horses with riders have to jump over different obstacles in a short time; *the British show-jumping team*

shown [ʃəun] *see* SHOW

show off ['ʃəʊ 'ɒf] *verb* **(a)** to show how much better than others you think you are; *don't watch her dancing about like that - she's just showing off* **(b)** to display something you are proud of; *he drove past with the radio on very loud, showing off his new car*

show-off ['ʃəʊɒf] *noun (informal)* person who shows off; *he's just a show-off, don't pay any attention and he'll soon stop*

show out ['ʃəʊ 'aʊt] *verb* to take someone to the door when they are leaving; *let me show you out*

show over *or* **show round** ['ʃəʊ 'əʊvə *or* 'ʃəʊ 'raʊnd] *verb* to lead a visitor round a place; *the old guide showed us over or round the castle; he showed the students round his laboratory; I have to go out now but my mother will show you round*

showpiece ['ʃəʊpiːs] *noun* important item in a collection or an exhibition, used to show how important the rest is; *this beautiful Chinese vase is the showpiece of the museum's collection; this is the government's showpiece research laboratory*

showroom ['ʃəʊruːm] *noun* room or shop where goods are displayed for sale; *a car showroom*

show round *see* SHOW OVER

show up ['ʃəʊ 'ʌp] *verb* **(a)** *(informal)* to come; *we invited all our friends to the picnic but it rained and only five of them showed up* **(b)** to do something which shows other people to be worse than you; *she dances so well that she shows us all up* **(c)** to be seen clearly; *when I ride my bike at night I wear an orange jacket because it shows up clearly in the dark*

showy ['ʃəʊwi] *adjective* which attracts attention because of its bright colours, shiny metal, etc.; *a showy display of orchids; he drove up in a showy pink Cadillac*

shrank [ʃræŋk] *see* SHRINK

shrapnel ['ʃræpnl] *noun* pieces of metal from a shell or bomb which has exploded; *shrapnel was flying in all directions; he had a piece of shrapnel in his arm* (NOTE: no plural)

shred [ʃred] **1** *noun* **(a)** strip torn off something; *she tore his newspaper to shreds; the curtains were on the floor in shreds* **(b)** small amount; *there's not a shred of evidence against him* **(c)** long thin strip of fruit, vegetables, etc.; *marmalade with shreds of orange peel in it* **2** *verb* **(a)** to tear (paper) into thin strips, which can then be thrown away or used as packing material; *they sent a pile of old invoices to be shredded; she told the police that the manager had told her to shred all the documents in the file* **(b)** to cut into very thin strips; *here's an attachment for shredding vegetables; add a cup of shredded carrot* (NOTE: **shredding - shredded**)

shredder ['ʃredə] *noun* machine for shredding paper; *it took her an hour to put all the letters through the shredder*

shrew [ʃruː] *noun* **(a)** little animal like a mouse with a long nose; *shrews form part of the diet of owls* **(b)** *(old)* unpleasant bad-tempered woman who is always criticizing; *Shakespeare's play 'The Taming of the Shrew'*

shrewd [ʃruːd] *adjective* clever or wise; *taking the boss out to lunch was a shrewd move; he's a very shrewd businessman* (NOTE: **shrewder - shrewdest**)

shriek [ʃriːk] **1** *noun* loud high-pitched shout; *we were worried when we heard shrieks from next door; shrieks of laughter came from the girls' changing*

room **2** *verb* to make a shriek; *she ran shrieking into the street; the children were shrieking with laughter*

shrill [ʃrɪl] *adjective* **(a)** high-pitched; *the engine has started to make a shrill whistle when I change gear* **(b)** loud and complaining; *the art gallery is making increasingly shrill complaints about lack of government funding* (NOTE: **shriller - shrillest**)

shrimp [ʃrɪmp] *noun* almost transparent little shellfish with a tail; *the children spent the afternoon fishing for shrimps in the rock pools; we had shrimp salad*

shrimping ['ʃrɪmpɪŋ] *noun* catching shrimps; *they took nets and went shrimping*

shrine [ʃraɪn] *noun* **(a)** holy place connected with a saint; *someone had put flowers at the roadside shrine* **(b)** tomb or chapel where a saint is buried; *pilgrims come to worship at the shrine* **(c)** place greatly admired for something, that attracts a lot of visitors; *Twickenham is a shrine for all Rugby fans*

shrink [ʃrɪŋk] **1** *noun (slang)* psychiatrist; *she's spent thousands on a shrink and she's no better at all* **2** *verb* **(a)** to make smaller; *the water must have been too hot - it's shrunk my shirt* **(b)** to get smaller; *my shirt has shrunk in the wash; the market for typewriters has shrunk almost to nothing* **(c)** not to be willing to do something; *she shrank from speaking to the boss about her suspicions; see also* VIOLET (NOTE: **shrank** [ʃræŋk] - **shrunk** [ʃrʌŋk])

shrinkage ['ʃrɪŋkɪdʒ] *noun* **(a)** action of shrinking; *I have noticed some shrinkage in the pullover after washing* **(b)** amount by which something shrinks; *a noticeable shrinkage in export orders* **(c)** *(informal)* loss of stock from a warehouse or shop through theft, especially by the staff; *shrinkage accounts for 1% of our revenue*

shrink-wrapped ['ʃrɪŋkræpt] *adjective* covered in tight plastic protective cover; *our most expensive books are shrink-wrapped*

shrink-wrapping [ʃrɪŋk'ræpɪŋ] *noun* action of covering a food, books, etc., in a tight plastic cover; *shrink-wrapping is a way of protecting books*

shrivel ['ʃrɪvl] *verb* to make or become dry and wrinkled; *you should water this plant - it's leaves are starting to shrivel; there was nothing for sale in the market, only a few shrivelled apples* (NOTE: **shrivelling - shrivelled** but American spelling **shriveling - shriveled**)

shroud [ʃraʊd] **1** *noun* **(a)** long cloth covering a dead body; *the corpse was wrapped in a white shroud* **(b)** **shrouds** = ropes from a mast to the sides of a ship; *sailors climbed up the shrouds to reef the sails* **2** *verb* to cover; *thick fog shrouded the town; clouds of smoke shrouded the factory*

shrouded ['ʃraʊdɪd] *adjective* **shrouded in** = hidden by; *the whole business of the loan is shrouded in mystery; the valley was shrouded in mist*

Shrove Tuesday ['ʃrəʊv 'tjuːzdeɪ] *noun* the Tuesday before Lent; *tomorrow is Shrove Tuesday, so we'll be having pancakes*

COMMENT: also called 'Pancake Day', it is the last day before Lent, and so a day when feasts are held. In Britain, pancakes are traditionally eaten on Shrove Tuesday, usually with lemon and sugar, but also with other sweet fillings. In France and French-speaking countries, the festival is called 'Mardi Gras'

shrub [ʃrʌb] *noun* small plant with stiff stems; *a flowering shrub would look lovely under that window*

shrubbery ['ʃrʌbri] *noun* part of a garden planted with shrubs; *the children played hide and seek in the shrubbery*

shrug [ʃrʌg] **1** *noun* moving your shoulders up to show you are not sure, not interested, etc.; *he just gave a shrug and walked on* **2** *verb* **to shrug your shoulders** = to move your shoulders up to show you are not sure, not interested, etc.; *when I asked him what he thought about it all, he just shrugged his shoulders and walked off* (NOTE: **shrugging - shrugged**)

shrug off ['ʃrʌg 'ɒf] *verb* to treat something as if it is not something to worry about; *he shrugged off the accusations*

shrunk [ʃrʌŋk] *see* SHRINK

shrunken ['ʃrʌŋkən] *adjective* wrinkled and dried up; *her shrunken cheeks were fixed in a melancholy expression; the bar had no food to offer, just a few shrunken olives*

shudder ['ʃʌdə] **1** *noun* trembling movement; *the car gave a shudder and stopped; she looked at the dead cat and gave a shudder; the thought of going to the dentist sent a shudder down my spine* **2** *verb* to tremble violently with horror; *the thought of eating worms makes me shudder; she shuddered at the thought of spending Christmas with his parents; I shudder to think how much money she spends on clothes each month*

shuffle ['ʃʌfl] *verb* **(a)** to walk dragging your feet along the ground; *he shuffled into the room in his slippers* **(b)** to mix playing cards; *I think he must have done something to the cards when he was shuffling them*

shun [ʃʌn] *verb* to avoid; *he shut himself up in his room and shunned all publicity; after he was caught stealing he was shunned by all his old friends* (NOTE: **shunning - shunned**)

shunt [ʃʌnt] **1** *noun* accident where one car bumps into the back of the car in front of it; *I had a little shunt on the motorway and the front bumper is bent* **2** *verb* **(a)** to put someone or something into a less important place; *the carriages will be shunted into a siding; he was shunted off to our office in Bordeaux* **(b)** to move a vehicle backwards and forwards; *she shunted backwards and forwards until she was parked close to the pavement* **(c)** to move a person from place to place; *they moved several times, and the children were shunted from school to school*

shut [ʃʌt] **1** *adjective* closed, not open; *some shops are shut on Sundays, but most big stores are open; we tried to get into the museum but it was shut; she lay with her eyes shut; come in - the door isn't shut!* **2** *verb* **(a)** to close something which is open; *can you please shut the window - it's getting cold in here; here's your present - shut your eyes and guess what it is* **(b)** to close for business; *in Germany, shops shut on Saturday afternoons; the restaurant shuts at midnight* (NOTE: **shutting - shut**)

shut down ['ʃʌt 'daʊn] *verb* **(a)** to close completely; *the factory shut down for the holiday weekend* **(b)** to

switch off an electrical system; *they had to shut down the nuclear power station because radiation levels were too high*

shutdown ['ʃʌtdaʊn] *noun* action of shutting down; *the shutdown of the works caused huge job losses in the town; computer problems caused a temporary shutdown of the entire rail network*

shut in ['ʃʌt 'ɪn] *verb* to lock inside; *the door closed suddenly and we were shut in; we shut the cat in the kitchen at night*

shut off ['ʃʌt 'ɒf] *verb* **(a)** to switch something off; *can you shut off the water while I mend the tap?* **(b)** to stop access to; *we can shut off the dining room with folding doors; the palace is shut off from the road by a high wall*

shut out ['ʃʌt 'aʊt] *verb* **(a)** to lock outside; *if the dog keeps on barking you'll have to shut him out; I was shut out of the house because I'd left my keys inside* **(b)** to stop light getting inside; to stop people seeing a view; *those thick curtains should shut out the light from the children's room; a high wall shuts out the view of the factory* **(c)** to stop thinking about something; *try to shut out the memory of the accident*

shutter ['ʃʌtə] *noun* **(a)** folding wooden or metal cover for a window; *close the shutters if the sunlight is too bright* **(b)** (*in a camera*) part which opens and closes very rapidly to allow the light to go on to the film; *he released the shutter and took the picture*; **shutter speed** = time when a shutter is open to take a picture; *do I need a high or low shutter speed for a picture in bright sunlight?*

shuttle ['ʃʌtl] **1** *noun* **(a)** thing which moves from one place to another; *there's a shuttle bus from the hotel to the exhibition grounds*; **shuttle service** = bus or plane which goes regularly backwards and forwards between two places; *the ferry operates a shuttle service between the islands*; **shuttle diplomacy** = action of a diplomat going backwards and forwards between two countries to try to make them reach an agreement; *see also* SPACE SHUTTLE **(b)** small device holding thread which goes backwards and forwards under and over the vertical threads when weaving **2** *verb* to go backwards and forwards regularly; *waiters were shuttling backwards and forwards from the kitchen to the dining room*

shuttlecock ['ʃʌtlkɒk] *noun* light little object with feathers stuck in it, which players hit over a net in badminton; *he hit the shuttlecock as hard as he could*

shut up ['ʃʌt 'ʌp] *verb* **(a)** to close something inside; *I hate being shut up indoors on a sunny day* **(b)** (*informal*) to stop making a noise; *tell those children to shut up - I'm trying to work; shut up! - we're tired of listening to your complaints; once he starts talking it's impossible to shut him up*

shy [ʃaɪ] **1** *adjective* **(a)** nervous and afraid to do something; *he's so shy he sat in the back row and didn't speak to anyone;* **once bitten twice shy** = once you have had a bad experience you will not want to do it again; *I'm not getting involved with him again - once bitten twice shy!* **(b)** **to fight shy of doing something** = to avoid getting involved in something **2** *verb* (*of a horse*) to jump nervously; *his horse shied at the noise of the gun* **3** *noun* **coconut shy** = stall in a fair where you throw balls to try and knock coconuts off stands; *you must have a go on the coconut shy*

SI units ['es 'aɪ 'juːnɪts] *noun* international units of physical measurement (NOTE: from the French words **Système International**)

sibling ['sɪblɪŋ] *noun (formal)* brother or sister; *she looks quite different from all her siblings*; **sibling rivalry** = rivalry between brothers or sisters

sic [sɪk] *adverb (used to indicate a mistake)* thus; *she said she's a bit squirmish (sic) about blood and injections* (NOTE: do not confuse with **sick**)

sick [sɪk] **1** *adjective* **(a)** ill, not well; *he's been sick for months*; *we have five staff off sick*; **sick leave** = time when a worker is away from work because of illness **(b) to be sick** = to vomit, to bring up partly digested food from the stomach into the mouth; *the last time I ate oysters I was sick all night*; **to feel sick** = to want to vomit; *when I got up this morning I felt sick and went back to bed*; *the greasy food made her feel sick* **(c) to be sick (and tired) of** = to have had too much of; *I'm sick of listening to all his complaints*; *she's sick and tired of doing housework all day long*; **to make someone sick** = to make someone very annoyed; *all my friends earn more than I do - it makes me sick!* **(d)** referring to something sad, disgusting; *he made some sick jokes about handicapped people* **2** *noun* **the sick** = people who are ill; *nurses were looking after the sick and the dying*

sickbay ['sɪkbeɪ] *noun* room where patients can visit a doctor or nurse for treatment in a school, factory or on a ship; *he sprained his ankle playing deck tennis and was carried down to the sickbay*

sickbed ['sɪkbed] *noun* bed where someone is lying sick; *she sat for hours beside her daughter's sickbed*

sicken ['sɪkn] *verb* **(a)** to make someone disgusted; *it sickens me to think of foxes being killed* **(b)** *(informal)* **to be sickening for something** = to have the first symptoms of an illness; *she's looking pale - she must be sickening for something*

sickening ['sɪknɪŋ] *adjective* which makes you sick; *his head hit the ground with a sickening thud*; *it's sickening to see so much food being wasted*

sickle ['sɪkl] *noun* tool with a curved blade, used for cutting corn or tall weeds; *he used a sickle to cut the weeds along the ditch*

sicklist ['sɪklɪst] *noun* list of the names of people who are sick; *we have five members of staff on the sicklist*

sickly ['sɪkli] *adjective* **(a)** not healthy; *your plants are looking rather sickly, do they need more fertilizer?*; *he turned a sickly yellow colour, and we rushed him to the doctor* **(b)** always slightly ill, never very well; *as a child he was sickly, but is now strong and healthy* (NOTE: **sicklier - sickliest**)

sickness ['sɪknəs] *noun* **(a)** not being well; *there is a lot of sickness about during the winter months* **(b)** feeling of wanting to vomit; **morning sickness** = feeling of wanting to vomit, felt by pregnant women in the morning; **travel sickness** = sickness caused by the movement of a car, aircraft, bus or train, etc.; **travel sickness pills** = pills taken to prevent travel sickness

sick pay ['sɪk 'peɪ] *noun* wages paid to someone who is sick and cannot work; **statutory sick pay** = wages paid by an employer to a person who is sick, and which can then be claimed back from the government

sickroom ['sɪkruːm] *noun* bedroom where someone is ill in bed; *visitors are not allowed into the sickroom*

sick up ['sɪk 'ʌp] *verb (informal)* to vomit, to bring up partly digested food into your mouth; *she sicked up her breakfast*

side [saɪd] **1** *noun* **(a)** one of the four parts which with the top and bottom make a solid object such as a box; *stand the box upright - don't turn it onto its side* **(b)** one of the two parts which with the front and back make a building; *the garage is attached to the side of the house* **(c)** one of the surfaces of a flat object; *please write on both sides of the paper* **(d)** one of two parts or two edges of something; *our office is on the opposite side of the street to the bank*; *London Airport is on the west side of the city*; *the hitchhikers were standing by the side of the road*; *she sat to one side of the fireplace*; **to look on the bright side** = to be optimistic; *you should look on the bright side - you'll have plenty of free time now you've lost your job*; *see also* WRONG **(e)** one of two parts separated by something; *she jumped over the fence to get to the other side*; *in England cars drive on the left-hand side of the road* **(f)** sports team; *the local side was beaten 2 - 0* **(g)** part of the body between the top of the legs and the shoulder; *I can't sleep when I'm lying on my right side*; *the policemen stood by the prisoner's side*; *they all stood side by side* **(h)** one of the sides of an animal, used as a piece of meat; *a side of bacon* **(i)** *(informal)* **on the side** = separate from your normal work, and sometimes hidden from your employer; *her salary is very low, so the family lives on what she can make on the side* **(j)** *(informal)* aspect of something; *the car runs well but it's rather on the small side* **(k) to be on someone's side** = to support someone in a battle or argument, to have the same point of view as someone; *don't attack me - I'm on your side*; *whose side is he on?*; **to take sides** = to say who you agree with; *he refused to take sides in the argument* **(l)** family, ancestors; *on my mother's side everyone has blue eyes* **2** *adjective* which is at the side; *there is a side entrance to the shop*; *can you take that bucket round to the side door?*; **side plate** = small plate placed next to your dinner plate; *they served the vegetables on side plates* **3** *verb* **to side against someone** = to disagree with someone in an argument; *I can't understand why they all are siding against me*; **to side with someone** = to agree with someone in an argument; *why do you always side with the boss?*

◊ **on the right side** [ɒn ðə 'raɪt saɪd] *phrase* **(a)** in the correct relationship with; *you'll be in trouble if you don't keep on the right side of the law* **(b)** *(informal)* not older than; *she's still on the right side of forty*

sideboard ['saɪdbɔːd] *noun* large piece of furniture for holding plates, glasses, etc., like a table with a cupboard underneath; *there was a bowl of fruit on the sideboard*

sideboards *or* **sideburns** ['saɪdwɪskəz] *noun* hair down the side of your face, in front of the ears; *cowboys with long black sideburns*

side drum ['saɪd 'drʌm] *noun* small drum which is used in orchestras and military bands; *the side drums marked the beat for the march*

side effect ['saɪd ɪ'fekt] *noun* effect produced by a drug, treatment, etc., which is not the main effect intended; *one of the side effects of the treatment is that the patient's hair falls out*; *the drug is being withdrawn because of its unpleasant side effects*

sidekick ['saɪdkɪk] *noun (informal)* junior assistant; *he brought along his sidekick to carry the computer*; *Batman and his sidekick, Robin*

sidelight ['saɪdlaɪt] *noun* **(a)** one of the small lights on each side of the front of a car; *switch your sidelights on - it's beginning to get dark* **(b)** piece of information which is given unintentionally; *the letters give some interesting sidelights on life in a Victorian household*

sideline ['saɪdlaɪn] **1** *noun* **(a)** business which you carry out as an extra to your normal job; *he runs a profitable sideline selling postcards to tourists* **(b) sidelines** = white lines along the edge of a tennis court, football pitch, etc.; **to sit on the sidelines** = not to take part in something **2** *verb* **to sideline someone** = to make sure that someone does not take part in something; *he complained that he was being sidelined by the others on the committee*

sidelong ['saɪdlɒŋ] *adjective* from one side; **sidelong glance** = glance loking sideways; *he gave a sidelong glance at the table full of food*

side road ['saɪd 'rəʊd] *noun* small road which leads off a larger road; *he raced towards the town and then suddenly turned off down a side road*; *the motorbike shot out of a side road without stopping*

sideshow ['saɪdʃəʊ] *noun* **(a)** *(old)* small stall with a game of skill at a fair, etc.; *among the sideshows were stalls selling candy floss and a shooting gallery* **(b)** activity that is less important than another activity associated with it; *the European Parliament is just a sideshow - the real decisions are taken by the Council of Ministers*

sidestep ['saɪdstep] *verb* to avoid; *the prime minister is clever at sidestepping all difficult questions* (NOTE: **sidestepping - sidestepped**)

side street ['saɪd 'striːt] *noun* small street which leads off a main street; *he raced towards the market square and then suddenly turned off down a side street*; *the motorbike shot out of a side street without stopping*

sidewalk ['saɪdwɔːk] *noun US* hard path for walkers at the side of a road; *a girl was roller-skating along the sidewalk*; *we sat at a sidewalk café* (NOTE: in British English this is **pavement**)

sideways ['saɪdweɪz] *adverb* to the side or from the side; *crabs walk sideways*; *if you look at it sideways you'll see how bent it is*

sidewhiskers ['saɪdwɪskəz] *noun* long hair down the side of your face; *a photo of great-grandfather with a top hat and white sidewhiskers*

siding ['saɪdɪŋ] *noun* short piece of railway line where trains are kept when they are not being used; *the empty carriages will be shunted into a siding*

sidle ['saɪdl] *verb* to walk in a timid way, not directly forwards; *she sidled up to him and asked him if he knew who she was*

siege [siːdʒ] *noun* surrounding an enemy town or castle with an army to prevent supplies getting in, and so force it to surrender; *the army laid siege to the castle*; *the inhabitants almost starved during the siege of the town*; **siege mentality** = feeling that you are surrounded by enemies; **under siege** = surrounded by an enemy; *the town is under siege*

sieve [sɪv] **1** *noun* kitchen utensil made of a frame with a metal or plastic net, used to strain liquids and to remove lumps; *put the flour through a sieve*; *boil the*

peas for a few minutes and put in a sieve to strain; *(informal)* **he has a memory like a sieve** = he keeps forgetting things **2** *verb* to pass flour, liquids, etc., through a sieve to remove lumps; *she sieved the flour into a bowl*; *boil the peas for a few minutes and sieve them*

sift [sɪft] *verb* **(a)** to sieve; *we sifted the sand to see if there was gold in it* **(b) to sift through** = to examine carefully; *the police sifted through the rubble to see if they could find traces of the bomb*

sigh [saɪ] **1** *noun* long deep breath, showing sadness, tiredness, etc.; *she gave a deep sigh and put the phone down*; *you could hear the sighs of relief from the audience when the heroine was saved* **2** *verb* to breathe deeply showing you are sad, relieved, etc.; *he sighed and wrote out another cheque*

sight [saɪt] **1** *noun* **(a)** one of the five senses, being able to see; *my grandfather's sight isn't very good any more*; **to lose your sight** = to become blind; *he lost his sight in the accident* **(b)** seeing, view; *he can't stand the sight of blood*; *we caught sight of an eagle up in the mountains*; *she kept waving until the car disappeared from sight*; *the fog cleared and the mountains came into sight*; *they waved until the boat was out of sight*; *the house is hidden from sight behind a row of trees*; *the little boy burst into tears at the sight of the dead rabbit*; **at first sight** = when you see something for the first time; *at first sight I thought he was wearing a wig*; *see also* SECOND SIGHT **(c)** something (especially famous) which you ought to see; *they went off on foot to see the sights of the town*; *the guidebook lists the main tourist sights in Beijing*; **to do the sights** = to visit the main tourist attractions; *we did the sights in Barcelona* **(d) to look a sight** = to look awful; *she looks a sight in that old raincoat* **(e) sights** = part of a gun which you look through to aim; *he spent so long adjusting the gun's sights that the stag had disappeared*; **to set your sights on** = to aim for; *she's set her sights on becoming an actress* **2** *verb* to see something a long way away; *we often sight rare birds on the lake*; *they sighted some wreckage from the boat* (NOTE: do not confuse with **cite, site**)

sighted ['saɪtɪd] *adjective & noun* (people) who can see; *the sighted members of the group helped the blind ones*; **partially sighted** = not able to see very well; *see also* LONGSIGHTED, NEARSIGHTED, SHORTSIGHTED

sighting ['saɪtɪŋ] *noun* seeing something; *we had a sighting of the wanted man in Norwich*; *there were two sightings of seals in the Thames this winter*

sightless ['saɪtləs] *adjective (formal)* blind, not able to see; *he raised his sightless eyes towards her face*

sightseeing ['saɪsiːɪŋ] *noun* visiting the sights of a town as a tourist; *I'm too tired to go sightseeing or to do any sightseeing today*; *queue here for the London sightseeing bus*; *we went on a sightseeing tour of the city*

sightseer ['saɪtsiːə] *noun* tourist who visits the sights of a town; *there were fewer sightseers than usual at the Tower of London*

sign [saɪn] **1** *noun* **(a)** movement of the hand which means something; *he made a sign to us to sit down* **(b)** drawing, notice, etc., which advertises something; *the office has a big sign outside it saying 'for sale'*; *a 'no smoking' sign hung on the wall*; **(road) sign** = panel by the side of a road, giving instructions or warnings; *go straight on until you come to a sign pointing left, marked 'to the sea'* (c) something which shows something; *there is no sign of the rain stopping; the economy is showing signs of improvement; the police can find no sign of how the burglars got into the office; he should have arrived by now, but there's no sign of him* (d) printed character; *the pound sign (£) the dollar sign ($) the hash sign (#) see* SIGNS OF THE ZODIAC **2** *verb* to write your name in a special way on a document to show that you have written it or that you have approved it; *the secretary brought him all the letters to sign; sign on the dotted line, please; the letter is signed by the managing director; the cheque is not valid if it has not been signed*

signal ['sɪgnl] **1** *noun* (a) sign or movement which tells someone to do something; *I'll give you a signal to start playing 'Happy Birthday'* (b) device used to tell someone to do something; *the signal was at red so the train had to stop* (c) electronic sound heard on a radio receiver; *we heard a faint signal coming from the mountains* **2** *verb* to make signs to tell someone to do something; *the driver signalled to show that he was turning right; she signalled to me that we were running out of time* (NOTE: British English is **signalling - signalled** but American English is **signaling - signaled**) **3** *adjective (formal)* remarkable; *the conference was a signal success*

signaller *US* **signaler** ['sɪgnlə] *noun* soldier who signals; *he served as a signaller during the desert war*

signalman ['sɪgnlmən] *noun* person who controls railway signals; *the signalman pulled a lever, and the lights turned red* (NOTE: plural is **signalmen**)

signatory ['sɪgnətri] *noun* person who signs a contract; *you have to get the permission of all the signatories to the agreement if you want to change the terms* (NOTE: plural is **signatories**)

signature ['sɪgnətʃə] *noun* (a) name written in a special way by someone to show that a document has been authorized or accepted; *he found a pile of cheques on his desk waiting for his signature; her signature doesn't look like her name at all; the shopkeeper looked very closely at her signature and compared it with the one on the credit card* (b) **signature tune** = tune which is used to identify a radio or TV broadcast; *that programme has had the same signature tune for over 30 years* (c) section of a printed book, usually 16, 32 or 64 pages; *something has gone wrong with this copy of the book, the first signature is missing*

sign for ['saɪn 'fɔː] *verb* (a) to sign a document to show that you have received something; *he signed for the parcel* (b) *(of footballer)* to transfer to a new club; *he signed for Chelsea yesterday*

significance [sɪg'nɪfɪkəns] *noun* meaning; *what is the significance of your logo of a ship?; there was no significance in the fact that her temperature was higher than usual;* **of great significance** = very important; *the contents of the letter were of great significance; his remarks were of little significance*

significant [sɪg'nɪfɪkənt] *adjective* important, full of meaning; *it is highly significant that everyone else was asked to the meeting, but not the finance director; there has been a significant improvement in his condition*

significantly [sɪg'nɪfɪkəntli] *adverb* in a significant way; *my home town has not altered significantly in 20 years; the've re-employed her but on a significantly lower salary*

signify ['sɪgnɪfaɪ] *verb* (a) to mean; *the letter seems to signify that they have accepted our terms* (b) to be important; *it doesn't signify in the least; (informal)* **that signifies** = that makes sense

signing ['saɪnɪŋ] *noun* (a) action of putting your signature on a document; *the signing of the peace treaty took place in the Palace of Versailles* (b) footballer who has just transferred to a new club; *the only goal was by their new signing*

sign on ['saɪn 'ɒn] *verb* (a) to start work; *he signed on and started work immediately* (b) to start drawing unemployment benefit; *she signed on for the dole*

signpost ['saɪnpəʊst] **1** *noun* post with signs showing directions to places; *you should have turned right at that last signpost; the signpost said it was 20 miles to Bristol* **2** *verb* to put signposts along a road to indicate directions; *the way to the harbour is clearly signposted*

Signs of the Zodiac ['saɪnz əv ðə 'zəʊdiæk] *noun* the twelve signs used in astrology, each linked to stars and a period of the year

COMMENT: the twelve signs are (from January onwards): Capricorn, Aquarius, Pisces, Aries, Taurus, Gemini, Cancer, Leo, Virgo, Libra, Scorpio, Sagittarius

Sikh [siːk] *adjective & noun* referring to members of a religious sect from India; *do all Sikh men wear turbans?; over 20% of the students in the college are Sikhs*

silage ['saɪlɪdʒ] *noun* green crops fermented in a silo and used to feed animals; *we cut the hay to make winter silage for the cows*

silence ['saɪləns] **1** *noun* quiet, absence of noise; *I love the silence of the countryside at night; the crowd of tourists waited in silence; the mayor held up his hand and asked for silence; there was a sudden silence as she came in; there will be a minute's silence at 11 o'clock;* **a conspiracy of silence** = plot to say nothing about something which has happened; **wall of silence** = plot by everyone to say nothing about what has happened; *the police investigation met with a wall of silence* **2** *verb* to stop someone saying or writing something; *he tried to silence his critics by taking out an injunction; she refused to be silenced and continued to write her articles about government corruption*

silencer ['saɪlənsə] *noun* (a) device attached to the exhaust of a car to reduce noise; *the car is very noisy and needs a new silencer* (NOTE: American English for this is **muffler**) (b) device attached to a gun to reduce the noise when it is fired; *he was killed with a gun fitted with a silencer*

silent ['saɪlənt] *adjective* not talking, not making any noise; *he kept silent for the whole meeting; she seems rather silent today; a very silent and reserved young man; the house was cold and silent; this new washing machine is almost silent; they showed some old silent films;* **the silent majority** = the majority of people who do not protest, who are not members of political parties, etc., but who vote according to their beliefs

silently ['saɪləntli] *adverb* without any noise, without talking; *they walked silently past the head teacher's office*; *we all silently wondered where Caroline was*

silhouette [sɪluːˈet] **1** *noun* **(a)** black shape of a person or thing against a light background; *we could see two silhouettes in the background, but couldn't make out who they were* **(b)** picture made of the black outline of someone's head in profile; *I bought an 18th century silhouette* **2** *verb* to stand out against a bright background; *she stood silhouetted against the burning house*

silicon ['sɪlɪkən] *noun* chemical element which is used in the electronics industry because of its semiconductor properties; **silicon chip** = a small piece of silicon able to store data, used in a computer; *silicon chips are very important in the manufacture of computers* (NOTE: Chemical element: chemical symbol: **Si**; atomic number: **14**)

silicone ['sɪlɪkəʊn] *noun* chemical compound of silicon used in making various oils or rubber; **silicone implants** = pieces of silicone used in surgery; *hundreds of women are said to be suffering from the after-effects of silicone breast implants*

silk [sɪlk] *noun* **(a)** cloth made from threads produced by silkworms; *she was wearing a beautiful silk scarf*; *I bought some blue silk to make a dress* **(b)** (*informal*) a **silk** = a Queen's Counsel; **to take silk** = to become a Queen's Counsel

silken ['sɪlkən] *adjective* soft and shiny like silk; *she had long black silken hair*

silkworm ['sɪlkwɜːm] *noun* larva of a moth which makes a cocoon of silk; *silkworms are found in China*

silky ['sɪlki] *adjective* soft and smooth like silk; *over the intercom, a silky voice asked him to come in*

sill [sɪl] *noun* flat shelf beneath a window, either inside or outside; *we keep a pot of geraniums on the sill outside the kitchen window*

silly ['sɪli] *adjective* stupid, not thinking; *don't be silly - you can't go to the party dressed like that!*; *she asked a lot of silly questions*; *of all the silly newspaper articles that must be the silliest* (NOTE: **sillier - silliest**)

silo ['saɪləʊ] *noun* **(a)** large container for storing grain, silage, etc.; *they are building huge grain silos near the port*; *the hay is stored in silos until it is needed* **(b)** deep hole in the ground in which missiles are kept; *the missiles were taken out of their silos and destroyed* (NOTE: plural is **silos**)

silt [sɪlt] **1** *noun* soft mud which settles at the bottom of water; *the silt was several inches deep in places* **2** *verb* (*of a harbour or river*) **to silt up** = to become full of silt, so that boats can no longer use it; *the mouth of the river is gradually silting up*

silver ['sɪlvə] **1** *noun* **(a)** precious white metal; *gold is worth more than silver*; *how much is an ounce of silver worth?* (NOTE: Chemical element: chemical symbol: **Ag**; atomic number: **47**) **(b)** coins made of white metal; *he held out a handful of silver* **(c)** knives, forks and spoons made of silver; *she's in the scullery, polishing the silver*; *don't worry, all the silver is securely locked away* **(d)** **silver (medal)** = medal given to someone who finishes in second place in a race or competition; *England won ten silver medals at the Olympics; see also* BRONZE, GOLD **(e)** shiny white colour, like silver; *the car has been resprayed in silver* **(f)** **silver jubilee** = 25th anniversary of an important

event; **silver wedding** = anniversary of 25 years of marriage **2** *adjective* shiny white colour, like silver; *the car has been resprayed with silver paint*; *she wore silver sandals to match her handbag*

silver birch ['sɪlvə 'bɜːtʃ] *noun* common tree with white bark; *the silver birch grows best in a light sandy soil* (NOTE: plural is **silver birches**)

silver-haired ['sɪlvə'heəd] *adjective* with light grey hair; *a distinguished silver-haired man came up to me*

silverside ['sɪlvəsaɪd] *noun* good quality beef, cut from the back part of the animal; *we bought a piece of silverside to roast on Sunday*

silvery ['sɪlvri] *adjective* **(a)** shiny like silver; *her hair was silvery in the moonlight* **(b)** with a light ringing sound; *the silvery sound of the temple bells*

similar ['sɪmɪlə] *adjective* very alike but not quite the same; *here is the old lampshade - do you have anything similar to replace it?*; *the two cars are very similar in appearance*; *our situation is rather similar to yours*

similarity [sɪmɪˈlærɪti] *noun* being similar; *he bears an astonishing similarity to the Prince of Wales*; *there is no similarity whatsoever between the two cases*; *the two children are fair with blue eyes, but the similarity stops there* (NOTE: plural is **similarities**)

similarly ['sɪmɪləli] *adverb* in a similar way; *all these infections must be treated similarly*; *he always writes a nice thank you letter, and similarly so does his sister*

simile ['sɪmɪli] *noun* comparison of one thing to another, using 'like' or 'as'; *'as flat as a pancake' is a simile; compare* METAPHOR

simmer ['sɪmə] *verb* **(a)** to cook by boiling gently; *we left the soup to simmer gently* **(b)** **to simmer down** = to become calmer after being very annoyed; *will you try to simmer down and listen to me, please?*

simple ['sɪmpl] *adjective* **(a)** easy; *the machine is very simple to use*; *she described the accident in a few simple words*; *it turned out to be a simple job to unscrew the door*; *they say the new tax forms are simpler than the old ones* **(b)** ordinary, not very special, not complicated; *they had a simple meal of bread and soup*; *it's a very simple pattern of lines and squares* (NOTE: **simpler - simplest**)

simple interest ['sɪmpl 'ɪntrəst] *noun* interest calculated on the capital only, and not added to it; *the loan will be cheaper because it only attracts simple interest* (NOTE: the opposite is **compound interest**)

simplicity [sɪmˈplɪsɪti] *noun* being simple; *the main attraction of the plan is its simplicity*; *the plan is simplicity itself*

simplification [sɪmplɪfɪˈkeɪʃn] *noun* making something simple; *we're aiming for a simplification of the tariff structures; see also* OVERSIMPLIFICATION

simplify ['sɪmplɪfaɪ] *verb* to make something simple; *we are trying to simplify the procedure*; *in order to simplify matters, why don't we meet at the airport?*

simplistic [sɪmˈplɪstɪk] *adjective* too simple, so simple as to be naive; *the government's simplistic attitude to strikes*

simply ['sɪmpli] *adverb* **(a)** in a simple way; *he described very simply how the accident had happened*; *she always dresses very simply* **(b)** only; *he did it simply to annoy everyone*; *she gave a new look to the* *room simply by painting one wall red* **(c)** *(to emphasize) your garden is simply beautiful; it's simply terrible - what shall we do?*

simulate ['sɪmjʊleɪt] *verb* to copy the way something behaves, or the way something happens; *the actor didn't really kill the cat, it was just simulated although it looked very real on the screen; this software simulates the action of an aeroplane*

simulation [sɪmjʊ'leɪʃn] *noun* operation in which a computer is made to imitate a real life situation or a machine, showing how something works or will work in the future; *simulation techniques have reached a high degree of sophistication; this computer simulation shows how global warming is likely to affect the planet*

simulator ['sɪmjʊleɪtə] *noun* device that simulates something else; **flight simulator** = computer program which allows a user to pilot a plane, showing a realistic control panel and moving scenes, either as a training programme or computer game; *we use flight simulators to train pilots*

simultaneous [sɪməl'teɪnɪəs] *adjective* happening at the same time as something else; *there will be simultaneous radio and TV broadcast of the concert;* **simultaneous translation** = translation of a speech into another language done at the same time as a person is speaking

simultaneously [sɪməl'teɪnɪəsli] *adverb* at the same time; *the concert will be broadcast simultaneously on radio and television*

sin [sɪn] **1** *noun* **(a)** wicked action which goes against the rules of a religion; *greed is one of the seven deadly sins;* **to live in sin** = to live together without being married; *see also* UGLY **(b)** something bad; *it would be a sin to waste all that meat* **2** *verb* to commit a sin, to do something wicked; *the priest told him he had sinned* (NOTE: **sinning - sinned**)

since [sɪns] **1** *preposition* during the period after; *she's been here since Monday; we've been working non-stop since 4 o'clock - can't we have a rest?* **2** *conjunction* **(a)** during the period after; *he has had trouble borrowing money ever since he was rude to the bank manager; since we got to the hotel, it has rained every day* **(b)** because; *since he's ill, you can't ask him to help you; since it's such a fine day, let's go for a walk* **3** *adverb* during the period until now; *she phoned on Sunday and we haven't heard from her since; he left England in 1990 and has lived abroad ever since*

sincere [sɪn'sɪə] *adjective* very honest and genuine; *a politician needs to appear sincere; we send you our sincere best wishes for a speedy recovery*

sincerely [sɪn'sɪəli] *adverb* really, truly; *I sincerely wanted to see her at Christmas; he believed most sincerely that she would come immediately;* **Yours sincerely** *US* **Sincerely yours** = words used as an ending to a letter addressed to a named person

sinew ['sɪnjuː] *noun* ligament or tendon, the tissues which hold together the bones at joints or attach muscles to bones; **to strain every sinew** = to work as hard as possible; *straining every sinew they pulled the boat up onto the shore*

sinewy ['sɪnjuːi] *adjective* full of strength; *his sinewy arms hauled on the rope; she writes strong sinewy prose*

sinful ['sɪnful] *adjective* immoral, wicked; *in the old days, people thought sex before marriage was sinful; building that dome is a sinful waste of money*

sing [sɪŋ] *verb* to make music with your voice; *she was singing as she worked; please sing another song; he always sings in the bath; she sang a funny song about elephants* (NOTE: **singing - sang** [sæŋ] - **has sung** [sʌŋ])

singe [sɪnʒ] *verb* to burn the outside of something; *the iron was too hot and it singed my shirt; she bent over the candles and singed her hair* (NOTE: **singeing**)

singer ['sɪŋə] *noun* person who sings; *she's training to be a professional singer; I'm not a very good singer*

singing ['sɪŋɪŋ] *noun* action of making music with your voice; *everyone joined in the singing; she goes to her singing lessons every Wednesday*

single ['sɪŋgl] **1** *adjective* **(a)** one alone; *he handed her a single sheet of paper; there wasn't a single person I knew at the party;* **the single most important fact about him is that he has no money;** **every single (one)** = each one; *you will need every single penny you have to pay for the house; every single time I asked her out, she refused* **(b)** for one person only; *have you got a single room for two nights, please?; we prefer two single beds to a double bed* **(c)** not married; *she's twenty-nine and still single; are there any single men on the course?;* **single parent** = one parent (mother or father) who is bringing up a child alone **(d)** **single ticket** = ticket for a journey in one direction only; *two single tickets cost more than a return* **(e)** **in single figures** = less than ten; *inflation was over 20% but now it is down to single figures* **2** *noun* **(a)** ticket for one journey; *two singles to Oxford Circus, please* **(b)** **singles** = tennis game played between two people; *the men's singles champion* **(c)** **singles** = people who are not married; *they went to a singles bar* **(d)** record with one piece of music on it; *the group's first single went into the top ten* **(e)** *(in cricket)* one run; *he scored a single and won the match*

singledecker [sɪŋgl'dekə] *noun* bus with only one floor; *the airport bus is a singledecker; see also* DOUBLEDECKER

single-handed [sɪŋgl'hændɪd] *adjective & adverb* all by yourself; *a single-handed yacht race; he sailed single-handed round the world; I can't do all this work single-handed*

single-minded [sɪŋgl'maɪndɪd] *adjective* thinking only of one thing; *they praised his single-minded work to improve the school's reputation; she is so single-minded that she takes no notice of what anyone else says*

single-mindedly [sɪŋgl'maɪndɪdli] *adverb* with only one aim in mind; *he single-mindedly fought the planners and won*

single out ['sɪŋgl 'aʊt] *verb* to notice or choose one person or thing among several; *she singled out a rose bush and bought it; he was singled out as a suitable candidate*

single-sex school ['sɪŋgləseks 'skuːl] *noun* school which takes either girls or boys, not both; *figures seem to show that pupils in single-sex schools do better in some subjects*

singlet ['sɪŋglət] *noun* sleeveless vest worn under a shirt, or when taking part in sports; *the runners had numbers pinned to their singlets*

singly ['sɪŋli] *adverb* one by one; *they each had an interview singly with the board, and then all met up as a group to do tests*

singular ['sɪŋgjʊlə] **1** *adjective* **(a)** odd, strange; *we found ourselves in a really singular position* **(b)** showing that there is only one thing or person; *'she' is a singular pronoun* **2** *noun* form of a word showing that there is only one; *'child' is the singular, and 'children' is the plural; the singular of 'they have' is 'he has'*

sinister ['sɪnɪstə] *adjective* which looks evil, which suggests that something bad will happen; *there's nothing sinister about their getting together; the sinister atmosphere of the castle; his colleague is a sinister character who never smiles*

sink [sɪŋk] **1** *noun* fixed basin for washing dishes, etc., in a kitchen; *the sink was piled high with dirty dishes; he was washing his hands at the kitchen sink;* **sink unit** = arrangement of cupboard, sink, taps, waste pipes, etc., forming a single piece of furniture **2** *verb* **(a)** to go down to the bottom (of water, mud, etc.); *the ferry sank in 30m of water; the paper boat floated for a few minutes, then sank; you should tie a piece of lead to your fishing line to make it sink* **(b)** to drop suddenly; *she was so upset that she just sank into an armchair and closed her eyes; my heart sank when I heard the news; house prices have sunk to an all-time low* **(c)** to invest money in something; *he sank all his savings into a car-hire business* (NOTE: **sinking - sank** [sæŋk] - **sunk** [sʌŋk])

sink in ['sɪŋk 'ɪn] *verb* to become fixed in the mind; *the speaker waited a moment for the meaning of what he had said to sink in*

sinus ['saɪnəs] *noun* empty space inside the body, especially the spaces inside your head behind the cheekbone and nose; *she has sinus trouble; his headaches are due to a sinus infection* (NOTE: plural is **sinuses**)

sip [sɪp] **1** *noun* little drink; *she took a sip of water, and went on with her speech* **2** *verb* to drink taking only a small amount of liquid at a time; *the girl was sipping her drink quietly* (NOTE: **sipping - sipped**)

siphon ['saɪfn] **1** *noun* **(a)** (soda) **siphon** = device for making fizzy water; *the waiter gave him a glass of scotch and put the siphon on the bar next to him* **(b)** bent tube to allow you to take liquid from one container to another placed at a lower level; *using a siphon he removed petrol from the car's tank* **2** *verb* **(a)** to remove liquid by using a siphon; *petrol had been siphoned from the tanks of cars parked in the car park* **(b)** (*informal*) **to siphon money off** = to remove money from a source illegally; *the firm's accountant managed to siphon off the profits into his private bank account*

sir [sɜː] *noun* **(a)** (*usually used by someone serving in a shop or restaurant*) polite way of referring to a man; *would you like a drink with your lunch, sir?; please come this way, sir* **(b)** (*way of addressing a male teacher, in Britain*) *please sir, I forgot to bring my homework* **(c)** (*in letters*) **Dear Sir** = polite way of addressing a man you do not know; **Dear Sirs** = polite way of addressing a company **(d)** title given to a baronet or knight

COMMENT: the title is always used with the man's Christian name, and, in formal address, with the surname as well: you can say 'good morning, Sir George', but 'may I introduce Sir George Smith?'

sire ['saɪə] **1** *noun* **(a)** male horse which is a father; *he was the sire of several Derby winners* **(b)** (*old*) **Sire** = way of addressing a king; *'Sire, spare his life', she cried* **2** *verb* (*of a horse*) to be the father of; *he's a fine horse, and has sired several successful runners*

siren ['saɪrən] *noun* device which makes a loud warning signal; *the siren sounded and everyone ran for shelter; a police car raced past with its siren wailing*

sirloin ['sɜːlɔɪn] *noun* best cut of beef from the back of the animal; *we bought a sirloin of beef for our Sunday roast;* **sirloin steak** = thick piece of beef cut from a sirloin

sister ['sɪstə] **1** *noun* **(a)** girl or woman who has the same father and mother as someone else; *his three sisters all look alike; my younger sister Louise works in a bank; do you have any sisters?* **(b)** senior female nurse in charge of a ward; *the sister told me my son was getting better* (NOTE: the male equivalent is a **charge nurse**) **(c)** title given to a nun (NOTE: can be used with names as a title: **Sister Jones, Sister Josephine**) **2** *adjective* **sister company** = company which forms part of the same group as another company; **sister ship** = ship which is of the same design and belongs to the same company as another ship

sister-in-law ['sɪstəʳɪnlɔː] *noun* wife of your brother; sister of your husband or wife; *my sister-in-law is arriving this afternoon, my brother will come later* (NOTE: plural is **sisters-in-law**)

sit [sɪt] *verb* **(a)** to be resting with your behind on something; to move in into this position; *mother was sitting in bed eating her breakfast; there were no seats left, so they had to sit on the floor* **(b)** to take a test; *she failed her English exam and had to sit it again* **(c)** to **sit for a picture** = to pose, to stand or sit still while someone paints or photographs you; *he sat for his portrait; he sat for her in his uniform* **(d)** (*of bird*) to rest; *the robin always comes and sits on the fence when I'm digging* **(e)** to look after children, to baby-sit; *I'm looking for someone to sit for me tomorrow evening* (NOTE: **sits - sitting - sat** [sæt] - **has sat**)

sit back ['sɪt 'bæk] *verb* **(a)** to rest your back against the back of a chair when sitting; *just sit back and enjoy the film* **(b)** to do nothing; *he just sat back and watched everyone else do the work*

sit by [sɪt 'baɪ] *verb* to do nothing to help; *we can't just sit by and watch these children starve*

sitcom ['sɪtkɒm] *noun* TV comedy series, which always takes place in the same place, with the same characters, each week; *one of the most successful sitcoms takes place in a Boston bar* (NOTE: short for **situation comedy**)

sit down ['sɪt 'daʊn] *verb* to sit on a seat; *if everyone will sit down, the meeting can start; they all sat down and the film began; come and sit down next to me*

sit-down ['sɪtdaʊn] **1** *adjective* **(a)** **sit-down meal** = meal where you sit at a table; *we'd rather have a buffet than a sit-down meal* **(b)** **sit-down protest** or **sit-down strike** = strike where the workers stay in their place of work and refuse to work or to leave; *the factory has been occupied by workers staging a sit-down strike* **2** *noun* (*informal*) little rest; *I've been on my feet all day - I think I deserve a sit-down*

site [saɪt] **1** *noun* **(a)** place where something is or will be; *this is the site for the new factory;* **building site** or **construction site** = place where a building is being built; *all visitors to the site must wear safety helmets*; **camping site** *or* **camp site** = place where you can camp; **green field site** = site for a factory which is in the country, and not surrounded by other buildings **(b)** place where something happened, where something once existed; *this was the site of the Battle of Hastings in 1066*; *they're trying to locate the site of the old Roman fort* **2** *verb* **to be sited** = to be placed on a particular piece of land; *the hotel will be sited between the airport and the new exhibition centre* (NOTE: do not confuse with **cite, sight**)

sit-in ['sɪtɪn] *noun* protest where a place of work is occupied by workers, students, etc., who refuse to leave; *production was halted during the sit-in at the factory* (NOTE: plural is **sit-ins**)

sit on ['sɪt 'ɒn] *verb (informal)* to do nothing about; *they sat on the report for three months*

sitter ['sɪtə] *noun* **(a)** baby-sitter, person who looks after children in a house, while their parents are out; *we won't be able to go to the cinema because I can't find a sitter* **(b)** *(informal)* easy chance to score a goal; *he missed a sitter in the final minutes of the game* **(c)** person who poses, while someone paints or photographs him or her; *the sitter was his mother*

sitting ['sɪtɪŋ] **1** *noun* time when a group of people eat together; *take your seats for the second sitting* **2** *adjective* **sitting MP** = MP who has been elected for a constituency; *six sitting MPs lost their seats in the election*

sitting room ['sɪtɪŋ 'ruːm] *noun* lounge, comfortable room for sitting in; *we spent the evening in the sitting room watching TV*; *please shut the sitting room door*; **bed-sitting room** = room with a bed and also comfortable chairs (NOTE: also called a **bedsit**)

situated ['sɪtjʊeɪtɪd] *adjective* placed, in a certain situation; *the factory is situated next to the railway station*; *the tourist office is conveniently situated in the town centre*

situation [sɪtjuː'eɪʃn] *noun* **(a)** position, way in which something is placed; *what's your opinion of the company's present situation?*; *I wonder how she got herself into this situation* **(b)** job; *I'm looking for a more permanent situation*; **situations vacant** = list of job vacancies in a newspaper **(c)** place where something is; *the hotel is in a very pleasant situation by the sea* **(d) situation comedy** = SITCOM

sit up ['sɪt 'ʌp] *verb* **(a)** to sit with your back straight; *sit up straight!* **(b)** to move from a lying to a sitting position; *he's too weak to sit up*; *he sat up in bed to eat his breakfast* **(c)** to stay up without going to bed; *we sat up playing cards until 2 a.m.*

sit-up ['sɪtʌp] *noun* exercise where you lie on your back on the floor and sit up straight; *he did ten sit-ups and then ran on the spot for five minutes* (NOTE: plural is **sit-ups**)

six [sɪks] **(a)** number 6; *he's six (years old)* *we're having some people round for drinks at six (o'clock)* *there are only six chocolates left in the box - who's eaten the rest?*; **the six hundreds** = the years from 600 to 699 AD (NOTE: compare **the sixth century**) **(b)** *(in cricket)* score of six runs for sending the ball over the boundary without touching the ground; *he scored a century, including four fours and two sixes* **(c) six-pack** = pack containing six bottle or cans; *they brought a six-pack of beer to the party*

sixteen [sɪks'tiːn] number 16; *he'll be sixteen next month*; *the train leaves at seventeen sixteen (17.16)* **the sixteen hundreds (1600s)** = the years from 1600 to 1699 (NOTE: compare **the sixteenth century**)

sixteenth (16th) [sɪks'tiːnθ] *adjective & noun* *she came sixteenth in the race*; *the sixteenth of July* *or* *July the sixteenth (July 16th) her sixteenth birthday is on Tuesday*; **the sixteenth century** = the years from 1500 to 1599 (NOTE: compare **the sixteen hundreds**; Note also that with dates **sixteenth** is usually written **16th**: **July 16th, 1935; October 16th, 1991** (American style is **October 16, 1991**), say 'the sixteenth of October' or 'October the sixteenth' (American style is 'October sixteenth'); with names of kings and queens **sixteenth** is usually written **XVI: King Louis XVI** (say: 'King Louis the Sixteenth'))

sixth (6th) [sɪksθ] *adjective & noun* *his office is on the sixth floor*; *what is the sixth letter of the alphabet?*; *ten minutes is a sixth of an hour*; *the sixth of August* *or* *August the sixth (August 6th) tomorrow is her sixth birthday*; **sixth form** = top class in a school, with students between 16 and 18 years old; **the sixth century** = the period from 500 to 599 AD (NOTE: in dates **sixth** is usually written **6th: October 6th 1923; January 6th, 1984** (American style is **January 6, 1984**), say 'the sixth of January' or 'January the sixth' (American style is 'January sixth'); with names of kings and queens **sixth** is usually written **VI: King Edward VI**; say 'King Edward the Sixth')

sixtieth (60th) ['sɪkstɪəθ] *adjective & noun* *he was sixtieth out of 120 people who entered the race*; *a minute is a sixtieth of an hour and a second is a sixtieth of a minute*; *don't forget - it's dad's sixtieth birthday tomorrow*

sixty ['sɪksti] number 60; *she's sixty (years old) the table cost more than sixty pounds (£60)* **she's in her sixties** = she's between 60 and 69 years old; **the (nineteen) sixties (1960s)** = the years from 1960 to 1969 (NOTE: **sixty-one (61), sixty-two (62)**, etc., but **sixty-first (61st), sixty-second (62nd)**, etc.)

size [saɪz] *noun* measurements of something, how big something is, or how many there are of something; *their garage is about the same size as our house*; *the school has an Olympic size swimming pool*; *he takes size ten in shoes*; *what size collars do you take?*; *the size of the staff has doubled in the last two years*

sizeable ['saɪzəbl] *adjective* quite big; *his salary is quite sizeable now he's been promoted*

sizzle ['sɪzl] *verb* to make a sound like food cooking in oil or fat; *the sausages were sizzling in the pan*; *the wet logs sizzled as he threw them on the fire*

sizzling ['sɪzlɪŋ] *adjective (informal)* very hot; *the streets were sizzling in the afternoon heat*

skate [skeɪt] **1** *noun* **(a) a pair of skates** = a pair of boots with sharp blades attached for sliding on ice *(informal)* **to put your skates on** = to hurry, to get going; *you'll have to put your skates on if you want to catch that train*; *see also* ICE SKATES, ROLLER SKATES **(b)** large flat fish with white flesh; *I love sole but I've never eaten skate* (NOTE: plural in this meaning is **skate**) **2** *verb* **(a)** to move on ice wearing skates; *she skated across the lake*; *we're going skating tomorrow* **(b) to skate around something** = to try to avoid mentioning something; *they skated around the subject of salaries*

skateboard ['skeɪtbɔːd] *noun* board with two pairs of wheels underneath, which you stand on to move about; *put your knee protectors on if you're going out on your skateboard*

skater ['skeɪtə] *noun* person who goes on skates; *there were dozens of skaters on the frozen pond*

skating ['skeɪtɪŋ] *noun* sport of sliding on ice on skates; *skating is very popular in Canada*; **skating rink** = special area for ice skating, or for playing ice hockey, etc.; *there used to be an indoor skating rink in Richmond*

skeletal ['skelətəl] *adjective* very thin, like a skeleton; *the skeletal figures of starving survivors*

skeleton ['skelɪtn] *noun* **(a)** all the bones which make up a body; *they found the skeleton of a rabbit in the garden shed*; *he demonstrated using the skeleton in the biology lab*; **the skeleton in the cupboard** = embarrassing secret that a family is trying to keep hidden **(b) skeleton staff** = a few staff left to carry on with essential work while most of the workforce is away; *only a skeleton staff will be on duty over the Christmas period* **(c) skeleton key** = key which will fit several different doors in a building; *I've locked myself out of my office - could you let me have the skeleton key, please?*

skeptic, skeptical, skepticism   *US* = SCEPTIC, SCEPTICAL, SCEPTICISM

sketch [sketʃ] **1** *noun* **(a)** rough quick drawing; *he made a sketch of the church* **(b)** short comic situation on TV or radio; *the show takes the form of a series of short sketches* (NOTE: plural is **sketches**) **2** *verb* to make a quick rough drawing of something; *she was sketching the old church*; *he sketched out his plan on the back of an envelope*

sketchbook ['sketʃbʊk] *noun* book of drawing paper for sketching; *he was drawing an oak tree in his sketchbook*

sketchmap ['sketʃmæp] *noun* rough map drawn by hand; *they sent us a sketchmap showing how to reach the village*

sketchpad ['sketʃpæd] *noun* pad of sheets of drawing paper for sketching; *he pulled out a little sketchpad and started drawing*

sketchy ['sketʃi] *adjective* not complete, not full; *she could only give a very sketchy description of her attacker*; *the plan is still too sketchy and needs more work before we can consider it* (NOTE: **sketchier - sketchiest**)

skew [skjuː] **1** *noun* **on the skew** = not straight **2** *verb* to make inaccurate or unbalanced; *not using a proper sample has skewed the results of the test*; *tax advantages are always skewed towards the highest earners*

skewed ['skjuːd] *adjective* unbalanced; *the opinion poll is skewed because they didn't interview anyone in rural areas*

skewer ['skjuə] **1** *noun* long thin metal or wooden rod for putting through pieces of meat, fish or vegetables when cooking or grilling; *she put some pieces of chicken and onion on the skewer* **2** *verb* to stick a long metal or wooden rod through something; *he skewered bits of meat and green peppers and grilled them*; *the fish was skewered on a stick*

ski [skiː] **1** *noun* one of two long flat pieces of wood, etc., which are attached to your boots for sliding over snow; *we always hire skis when we get to the ski resort*; *someone stole my new pair of skis*; **ski instructor** = person who teaches people how to ski; **ski boots** = boots to wear when skiing; **ski resort** = town in the mountains where people stay when on a skiing holiday; **water skis** = larger pieces of wood for attaching under your feet for sliding over water **2** *verb* to travel on skis; *the mountain rescue team had to ski to the site of the avalanche*; *we skied down to the bottom of the slope without falling*; *she broke her arm skiing*; **to go skiing** = to slide over snow on skis as a sport; *we go skiing in Switzerland every winter* (NOTE: **skis - skiing- skied**)

skid [skɪd] **1** *noun* **(a)** sideways slide in a vehicle; *the car went into a skid and hit a lamppost*; *there were skid marks on the road* **(b)** *US* flat wooden frame on which goods can be stacked to be moved by a fork-lift truck (NOTE: British English is **pallet**) **2** *verb* to slide sideways in a vehicle suddenly because the wheels do not grip the surface; *he skidded to a halt*; *if you brake to hard on ice you're likely to skid* (NOTE: **skidding - skidded**)

skier ['skiːə] *noun* person who goes skiing; *not a single skier was out on the slopes*

skiff [skɪf] *noun* light rowing boat; *we hired a skiff and rowed up the river*

skiing ['skiːɪŋ] *noun* the sport of sliding on skis; *skiing is a very popular sport*; *have you ever done any skiing?*

ski jump ['skiː 'dʒʌmp] *noun* artificial steep slope covered with snow, with a sudden drop at the bottom to allow a skier to jump high in the air; *they can't jump any more this winter - the rain has melted the snow on the ski jump*

ski jumping ['skiː 'dʒʌmpɪŋ] *noun* a Winter Olympic sporting event using two sizes of jump

> COMMENT: the two sizes of jump are: the 90m (normal hill) and 120m (large hill). Each skier takes two jumps. The sizes refer to the optimum distance that should be jumped from them, not their height

skilful *US* **skillful** ['skɪlful] *adjective* showing a lot of skill; *he's a very skilful carpenter*; *is he skilful enough to use this computer programme?*

skilfully *US* **skillfully** ['skɪlfuli] *adverb* in a skilful way; *it was difficult but he did it very skilfully*

ski lift ['skiː 'lɪft] *noun* device which takes skiers to the top of a slope; *they had a marvellous view from the ski lift*

skill [skɪl] *noun* ability to do something well; *portrait painting needs a lot of skill*; *he acquired management skills through running his own business*; *he's a craftsman of great skill*

skilled [skɪld] *adjective* **(a)** skilful, being able to do something well; *she's a skilled therapist*; *we need skilled programmers*; **skilled workers** *or* **skilled labour** = workers who have special skills or who have had a long period of training; *see also* UNSKILLED **(b)** needing a particular skill; *nursing and other skilled professions*

skim [skɪm] *verb* **(a)** to remove things floating on a liquid; *skim the soup to remove the fat* **(b)** to dash over the surface of something; *flies skimmed across the surface of the lake*; **to skim through a book** = to read a book quickly; *I only had time to skim through the book on the train* (NOTE: **skimming - skimmed**)

skimmed milk ['skɪmd 'mɪlk] *noun* milk from which most of the fat has been removed; *she had cereal with skimmed milk for breakfast*; **semi-skimmed milk** = milk from which half the fat has been removed

skin [skɪn] **1** *noun* **(a)** outer surface of the body; *the baby's skin is very smooth*; **to be just skin and bones** = to be extremely thin **(b)** outer surface of a fruit or vegetable; *this orange has a very thick skin*; *you can cook these new potatoes with their skins on* **(c)** thin layer on top of a liquid; *I don't like the skin on the top of chocolate pudding* **(d)** *(informal)* **to have a thick skin** = to be able to stand a lot of criticism; *luckily he has a thick skin or he would get very annoyed at what the tabloids say about him*; **by the skin of your teeth** = only just; *he escaped from the enemy by the skin of his teeth*; **to jump out of your skin** = to be very frightened or surprised; *the bang made her jump out of her skin* **2** *verb* to remove the skin from an animal, fish, etc.; *ask the fishmonger to skin the sole for you* (NOTE: **skinning - skinned**)

skin-diver ['skɪn 'daɪvə] *noun* person who goes skin-diving; *from the boat we could see skin-divers on the reef*

skin-diving ['skɪn 'daɪvɪŋ] *noun* swimming underwater using breathing apparatus, as a sport; *they went on a skin-diving holiday on the coast of Mexico*

skinhead ['skɪnhed] *noun* usually violent young man, with very short hair or a shaved head; *a crowd of skinheads gathered outside the pub*

skinny ['skɪni] *adjective (informal)* thin; *a tall skinny guy walked in*; *she has very skinny legs* (NOTE: **skinnier - skinniest**)

skint [skɪnt] *adjective (informal)* with no money; *I'm completely skint*

skip [skɪp] **1** *noun* large metal container for rubbish; *the builders filled the skip with old bricks and stones* **2** *verb* **(a)** to run along partly hopping and partly jumping; *the children skipped happily down the lane* **(b)** to jump over a rope which you turn over your head; *the boys played football and the girls were skipping* **(c)** to miss part of something; *she skipped the middle chapters and went on to read the end of the story*; *I'm not hungry, I'll skip the pudding* (NOTE: **skipping - skipped**)

skipper ['skɪpə] **1** *noun* **(a)** captain of a ship; *we reported to the skipper that there was water in the ship's engine room* **(b)** captain of a team; *he's the youngest skipper ever of the national rugby team* **2** *verb* to be the captain of a team; *the youngest man ever to skipper the English rugby team*

skipping rope ['skɪpɪŋ 'rəʊp] *noun* rope which you jump over as you swing it over your head and under your feet; *skipping ropes are used by boxers for training* (NOTE: American English is also **jump rope**)

skirmish ['skɜːmɪʃ] **1** *noun* minor fight between opposite sides; *there were several skirmishes between rival fans, but no serious fighting* (NOTE: plural is **skirmishes**) **2** *verb* to fight small battles with someone; *the opposition was skirmishing with the government*

skirt [skɜːt] **1** *noun* piece of clothing worn by women covering the lower part of the body from the waist down; the lower part of a dress starting at the waist; *she started wearing jeans to work, but the manageress told*

her to wear a skirt **2** *verb* **(a)** to go round; *the main road skirts (round) the town* **(b)** not to touch; *he only skirted round the subject, and didn't deal with it in depth at all*

skirting board ['skɜːtɪŋ 'bɔːd] *noun* decorative board along the bottom edge of a wall in a room; *the wall was painted yellow and the skirting board white* (NOTE: American English is **baseboard**)

skittle ['skɪtəl] *noun* upright target, shaped like a bottle, used in a game where you roll a large ball and try to knock the targets down; *where can we have a game of skittles?* (NOTE: the same game as **ten-pin bowling**)

skull [skʌl] *noun* the bones which are fused together to form the head; *they found a human skull when they were digging*; *the scan showed a fracture of the skull* or *a skull fracture*

sky [skaɪ] *noun* space above the earth which is blue during the day and where the moon and stars appear at night; *what makes the sky blue?*; *it's going to be a beautiful day - there's not a cloud in the sky*; *the wind carried the glider high up into the sky*

sky-blue [skaɪ'bluː] *adjective & noun* bright light blue like the sky; *she wore a sky-blue jacket and a white scarf*

sky-high [skaɪ'haɪ] *adverb* very high; *prices have gone sky-high*; **to blow something sky-high** = to blow something up with explosive

skyline ['skaɪlaɪn] *noun* the shape of buildings seen against the sky; *the Chicago skyline is very distinctive*

skyscraper ['skaɪskreɪpə] *noun* very tall building; *in the old part of the town all the buildings are low and no skyscrapers can be built*; *they're planning a 100-storey skyscraper near the park*

slab [slæb] *noun* flat square or rectangular block of stone, etc.; *a slab of concrete fell from the building*; *his tomb is a slab of black marble*; *we had mugs of tea and thick slabs of cake*

slack [slæk] **1** *adjective* **(a)** not taut or not tight; *the wind had dropped and the sails were slack* **(b)** not busy; *business is slack at the end of the week*; *January is always a slack period for us* **(c)** not working well; *slack workers will be penalized* (NOTE: **slacker - slackest**) **2** *noun* **(a)** loose part of something, such as a rope; **to take up the slack** = to tighten something up; *if you pull on the rope it will take up the slack*; *by reducing the numbers of staff, we will be able to take up some of the slack* **(b)** little pieces of coal; *he threw some slack on the fire* **3** *verb* **to slack (off)** = to be lazy, to do less work; *stop slacking, and get some work done!*; *you can slack off now, as it's past six o'clock*

slacken ['slækn] *verb* **(a)** to loosen; *as the rain started, she slackened the ropes round the tent* **(b)** **to slacken (off)** = to work less, to be less busy, to go slower; *trade slackened off during January*; *he slackened his pace as he turned the corner*

slacks [slæks] *noun (old)* trousers; *he bought a pair of grey slacks and a blue shirt*

slain [sleɪn] *see* SLAY

slalom ['slɑːləm] *noun* type of race where you have to zigzag fast between a series of posts; *she won the slalom in the Winter Olympics*

slam [slæm] **1** *noun* **grand slam** = winning a series of competitions, such as all the main tennis competitions held in a year; *a grand slam winner*; *the French rugby* team are aiming for the grand slam **2** *verb* **(a)** to bang a door shut; to shut with a bang; *when he saw me, he slammed the door in my face*; *the wind slammed the door and I was locked out* **(b)** to slam on the brakes = to apply the brakes fast when driving; *he slammed on the brakes and just stopped in time to avoid an accident* (NOTE: **slamming - slammed**)

slander ['slɑːndə] **1** *noun* untrue spoken statement which damages a person's reputation; *what she said about me is slander*; *to sue somebody for slander*; **action for slander** *or* **slander action** = case in a law court where someone says that another person has slandered them **2** *verb* to damage someone's reputation by saying untrue things about him; *they slandered him at yesterday's meeting*; *compare* LIBEL

slanderous ['slɑːndrəs] *adjective* which could be slander; *he made slanderous statements about the Prime Minister*

slang [slæŋ] *noun* popular words or phrases used by certain groups of people but which are not used in correct style; *'banger' is slang for an old car and also for a sausage*; *don't use slang in your essay*; *slang expressions are sometimes difficult to understand*; *see also* RHYMING

slanging match ['slæŋɪŋ 'mætʃ] *noun* bitter argument where two people call each other rude names; *the TV discussion rapidly developed into a slanging match*

slangy ['slæŋi] *adjective (informal)* using popular language; *he has a very slangy style of writing*

slant [slɑːnt] **1** *noun* **(a)** slope; *the garden is on a slant, which makes cutting the lawn difficult*; **on the slant** = sloping; *the shelves were put up on the slant and had to be taken down* **(b)** point of view; *a TV programme with a decided teenage slant*; *we want to get a new slant on the problem* **2** *verb* **(a)** to slope; *the path slants down the side of the hill*; *the picture seems to be slanting to the right* **(b)** to show news or information in a biased way; *the news was slanted to suit the government*

slanting ['slɑːntɪŋ] *adjective* which slopes; *his slanting handwriting is very easy to recognize*

slap [slæp] **1** *noun* **(a)** blow given with your hand flat; *she gave him a slap in the face*; **a slap on the wrist** = small punishment, slight criticism; *the department had a slap on the wrist from the inspectors, but nothing serious* **(b)** friendly gesture; *he congratulated her with a slap on the back* **2** *verb* **(a)** to hit with your hand flat; *she slapped his face* **(b)** to tap as a friendly gesture; *they all slapped him on the back to congratulate him* **(c)** to put something down flat on a surface; *she slapped the notes down on the table*; *they just slapped some paint on the wall to cover up the marks* (NOTE: **slapping - slapped**) **3** *adverb* **to run slap (bang) into something** = to run right into something; *he rode his bike slap into middle of the procession*

slapstick ['slæpstɪk] *noun* rough comedy which depends on knocking people over, throwing water over someone, etc.; *there is a lot of slapstick in Laurel and Hardy films* (NOTE: no plural)

slash [slæʃ] **1** *noun* **(a)** long cut with a knife; *he had a nasty slash on his forearm*; *she took a knife and made a slash across the painting* **(b)** printing sign (/) used to show an alternative (NOTE: plural is **slashes**) **2** *verb* **(a)** to make a long cut with a knife; *he slashed the painting with a kitchen knife* **(b)** to reduce a price, the number

of something, drastically; *the management has slashed the number of staff*; *prices have been slashed in all departments*

slate [sleɪt] **1** *noun* **(a)** dark blue or grey stone which splits easily into thin sheets; *slate is used for making roofs* **(b)** thin piece of this stone used to cover a roof; *the slates were already piled up on the roof ready for fixing* **(c)** list of candidates for a position; *the Democratic slate in the state elections* **2** *verb* to criticize sharply; *the whole plan was slated by the chairman of the committee*

slaughter ['slɔːtə] **1** *noun* **(a)** killing of animals; *these lambs will be ready for slaughter in a week or so*; *the infected pigs have been slaughtered* **(b)** killing of many people; *the wholesale slaughter of innocent civilians* (NOTE: no plural) **2** *verb* **(a)** to kill animals for meat; *here's the shed where the cattle are slaughtered* **(b)** to kill many people at the same time; *thousands of civilians were slaughtered by the advancing army*

slaughterhouse ['slɔːtəhaus] *noun* place where animals are killed for meat; *all slaughterhouses will be inspected at least once a year*

slave [sleɪv] **1** *noun* person who belongs to someone legally and works for him; *in the old days, slaves worked on the tobacco plantations* (informal) **slave driver** = boss who makes the staff work too hard **2** *verb* **to slave (away)** = to work hard; *here am I slaving away over a hot stove, and you just sit and watch TV*

slavery ['sleɪvri] *noun* **(a)** being a slave; *girls were kidnapped and sold into slavery* **(b)** buying and selling of slaves; *in Britain, slavery was abolished in the 19th century*

slavishly ['sleɪvɪʃli] *adverb* without thinking; *she slavishly follows every change in fashion*

slay [sleɪ] *verb (formal)* to kill; *he slew the giant with his little sword*; *thousands of soldiers were slain in the battle* (NOTE: **slaying - slew** [sluː] - **slain**; do not confuse with **sleigh**)

sleaze [sliːz] *noun* behaviour which is disreputable; *accusations of political sleaze filled the newspapers*

sleazy ['sliːzi] *adjective (informal)* dirty or disreputable; *they went round some of the sleaziest bars in the town* (NOTE: **sleazier - sleaziest**)

sled [sled] *see* SLEDGE

sledge *US* **sled** [sledʒ] **1** *noun* small vehicle with long pieces of wood or metal underneath, for sliding fast over snow; *children dragged their sledges to the top of the snow-covered hill*; *the kids took their sleds to the city park* **2** *verb* to go on a sledge; to play at sliding on the snow on a sledge; *the children were sledging down the hill*; **to go sledging** = to slide fast over snow on sledges as a game; *we went sledging every day till the snow melted*; *the kids sledded down the slope*

sleek [sliːk] **1** *adjective* **(a)** smooth, shiny and well-kept; *an enormous sleek limousine drew up outside the hotel*; *after dinner we walked across the sleek lawns to the river* **(b)** very confident, but not to be trusted; *she gave us some sleek sales talk to try to get us interested in buying a mobile phone*; *sleek salesmen stood round the stand, handing out leaflets* (NOTE: **sleeker - sleekest**) **2** *verb* to make smooth; *he sleeked back his hair*

sleep [sliːp] **1** *noun* rest (usually at night) with your eyes closed, and when you are not conscious of what is happening; *I need eight hours' sleep a night*; *try to get* a good night's sleep - there's a lot of work to be done tomorrow; he always has a short sleep after lunch; to go to sleep or to get to sleep = to start sleeping; don't make all that noise - Daddy's trying to get to sleep; she put the light out and went to sleep (NOTE: you can also say to fall asleep); to send someone to sleep = to make someone go to sleep; her boring speeches would send anyone to sleep; to put someone to sleep = to give someone an anaesthetic; to put an animal to sleep = to kill an animal that is old or ill; my foot has gone to sleep = my foot has lost all feeling; not to lose any sleep over something = not to worry about something; it's such a tiny sum that I won't lose any sleep over it **2** verb (a) to be asleep, to rest with your eyes closed not knowing what is happening around you; she never sleeps for more than six hours each night; he slept through the whole of the TV news; don't make any noise - Daddy's trying to sleep; (informal) to sleep like a log = to sleep very soundly; after his 12-mile walk he slept like a log (b) (informal) to sleep with someone or to sleep together = to have sexual intercourse with someone; they say he's slept with almost all the girls in the office (c) a cottage that sleeps four = a cottage with enough beds for four people (NOTE: sleeps - sleeping - slept [slept])

sleep around ['sliːp əˈraʊnd] (informal) to have sexual intercourse with various people; as a student he slept around but now he has a steady girlfriend

sleeper noun (a) person who sleeps; electrodes are attached to sleepers to record brain waves; he's a heavy sleeper = he always sleeps heavily (b) sleeping car, a carriage on a train where passenger sleep on long journeys; the last two carriages of the train were sleepers (c) overnight train with sleeping cars; the Edinburgh sleeper leaves at 11.30 p.m. (d) heavy piece of wood on which rails are fixed; the track is closed because workmen are laying new sleepers

sleep in ['sliːp 'ɪn] verb to sleep later than usual in the morning; we get up a 6 a.m. every day but on Sundays we sleep in till 9

sleeping ['sliːpɪŋ] **1** adjective (a) who is asleep; the firemen picked up the sleeping children and carried them to safety (b) concerning sleeping in bed; the whole family are coming, and we have to decide on the sleeping arrangements = how the bedrooms are going to be divided between the guests (c) sleeping partner = partner who has a share in a business but does not work in it; sleeping policeman = hump in the road to stop cars going too fast **2** noun state of being asleep or going to sleep; I'm always exhausted so sleeping is never a problem for me; sleeping bag = warm bag for sleeping in a tent, etc.; sleeping pill or sleeping tablet = medicine which makes you go to sleep

sleeping car [sliːpɪŋ 'kɑː] noun carriage on a train with beds where passengers can sleep; there are three sleeping cars on the overnight express

sleepless ['sliːpləs] adjective with no sleep; parents of little babies usually have sleepless nights; she passed a sleepless night thinking about the interview

sleeplessness ['sliːpləsnəs] noun lack of sleep, not being able to sleep (NOTE: also called **insomnia**)

sleep off ['sliːp 'ɒf] verb to get rid of something by sleeping; he went to bed to sleep off his hangover

sleep on ['sliːp 'ɒn] verb to sleep on it = to think about something overnight; let me sleep on it, and I'll give you my answer tomorrow morning

sleepwalking ['sliːpwɔːkɪŋ] noun getting up and walking about even though you are still asleep

sleepy ['sliːpi] adjective (a) feeling ready to go to sleep; sitting in front of the TV made him sleepier and sleepier; the children had a busy day - they were very sleepy by 8 o'clock; the injection will make you feel sleepy; if you feel sleepy, don't try to drive the car (b) quiet; a sleepy little country town (NOTE: sleepier - sleepiest)

sleet [sliːt] **1** noun snow mixed with rain; the temperature fell and the rain turned to sleet **2** verb it is sleeting = it is snowing and raining at the same time; as she went out it began sleeting

sleeve [sliːv] noun (a) part of a piece of clothing which covers your arm; the sleeves on this shirt are too long; he was wearing a blue shirt with short sleeves; see also LONG-SLEEVED, SHORT-SLEEVED (b) (informal) to keep something up your sleeve = to have a plan which you are keeping secret; to laugh up your sleeve = to laugh in secret at something (c) cardboard cover for a record; he designed some of the sleeves for the Rolling Stones

-sleeved [sliːvd] suffix making adjectives having sleeves of a certain style; a short-sleeved shirt; a long-sleeved pullover

sleeveless ['sliːvləs] adjective with no sleeves; a sleeveless pullover; none of my dresses are sleeveless

sleigh [sleɪ] noun large sledge pulled by horses or reindeer; at the ski resort you can go out for sleigh rides (NOTE: do not confuse with **slay**)

slender ['slendə] adjective (a) very thin or slim; a girl with a slender waist; she's wants to be slender, without being too skinny (b) not large; the police held out only a slender hope that the killer would be caught; the government won the vote by only the slenderest of margins (NOTE: slenderer - slenderest)

slept [slept] see SLEEP

slice [slaɪs] **1** noun (a) thin piece cut off something to eat; can you cut some more slices of bread?; have a slice of chocolate cake; would you like another slice of chicken? (b) (in sports) way of hitting a ball, which makes it go in the wrong direction **2** verb (a) to cut into slices; she stood at the table slicing the joint for lunch; sliced bread = loaf of bread which has already been cut into slices before you buy it; (informal) the best thing since sliced bread = the most wonderful new invention in the world (b) to hit a ball so that it spins off to one side; he sliced the ball into the net

slick [slɪk] **1** adjective done in a clever way which tricks people; the politician was a very slick talker; we didn't like his slick manner (NOTE: slicker - slickest) **2** noun oil slick = oil which has escaped into water and floats on the surface; the slick contaminated over 40 miles of coast; an enormous oil slick covered the whole surface of the bay

slid [slɪd] see SLIDE

slide [slaɪd] **1** noun (a) slippery metal or plastic structure for children to slide down; there are swings and a slide in the local playground (b) small piece of film which can be projected on a screen; she put the screen up and showed us the slides of her last trip; there will be a slide show in the village hall; slide

projector = apparatus for showing pictures from slides onto a screen **(c)** steady fall; *the government must act to stop the slide in the pound* **2** *verb* **(a)** to move smoothly over a slippery surface; *the drawer slides in and out easily; the car slid to a stop; the children were sliding on the ice when it broke* **(b)** to move something smoothly; *he slid the money over the table; the door slides open easily; the van has a sliding door which doesn't shut properly* **(c)** to move down steadily; *the pound slid after interest rates were lowered* (NOTE: **sliding - slid** [slɪd])

sliding scale ['slaɪdɪŋ 'skeɪl] *noun* system of marks, points, taxes, etc., which vary according to a scale; *a sliding scale of charges*

slight [slaɪt] **1** *adjective* not very big; *their daughter's a slight young girl; all you could see was a slight movement of the cat's tail; there was a slight improvement in his condition during the night; she wasn't the slightest bit nervous* (NOTE: **slighter - slightest**) **2** *noun* (*formal*) insult; *I treat that remark as a slight on our reputation*

slightly ['slaɪtli] *adverb* not very much; *he was only slightly hurt in the car crash; the American bank is offering a slightly better interest rate; I only know him slightly*

slim [slɪm] **1** *adjective* thin, not fat; *how do you manage to stay so slim?; a slim, fair-haired boy; she looks slimmer in that dress* (NOTE: **slimmer - slimmest**) **2** *verb* to diet in order to become thin; *she started slimming before her summer holidays* (NOTE: **slimming - slimmed**)

slime [slaɪm] *noun* **(a)** slippery substance, which forms on hard damp surfaces; *is there anything which will get this green slime off the paving stones of the patio?* **(b)** trail of slippery matter left by a slug or snail; *the slug left a trail of slime across the kitchen floor*

slimy ['slaɪmi] *adjective* **(a)** unpleasantly slippery; *watch out, the rocks are slimy; what's this slimy mess at the bottom of the fridge?* **(b)** unpleasant, not to be trusted; *I wouldn't trust him an inch, he's a particularly slimy individual* (NOTE: **slimier - slimiest**)

sling [slɪŋ] **1** *noun* **(a)** type of leather loop, used for throwing stones; *David threw a stone with his sling, and killed Goliath* **(b)** triangular bandage attached round the neck, used to support an injured arm and prevent it from moving; *he's going around with his arm in a sling* **(c)** apparatus made of ropes and pulleys for hoisting and carrying goods; *they arranged a sling to lift the piano into the upstairs flat* **2** *verb* **(a)** to throw; *little boys were slinging snowballs at passing cars; he slung his briefcase into the back of the car* **(b)** to hold up or to put something to hang; *he slung his jacket over the back of his chair; they slung the electric cable between the posts; she slung her bag over her shoulder* (NOTE: **slinging - slung** [slʌŋ])

slink [slɪŋk] *verb* to creep about to avoid being noticed; *they saw the photographers waiting at the front of the club, so they slunk out through the back door* (NOTE: **slinking - slunk** [slʌŋk])

slip [slɪp] **1** *noun* **(a)** mistake; *he made a couple of slips in adding up the bill; a slip of the tongue* = a mistake in speaking **(b)** pillow slip = cloth bag to cover a pillow; *the maid had forgotten to change the pillow slips* **(c)** small person; *she was just a slip of a girl* **(d)** woman's underwear like a thin dress or skirt, worn under other clothes; *she bought a black slip* **(e)** men's

underwear which is very short; *he wore a white vest and slip* **(f)** small piece of paper; *as she opened the book a small slip of paper fell out; he handed her the green slip with the reference number on it;* **compliments slip** = piece of paper with the name of the company printed on it, sent with documents, gifts, etc., instead of a letter; **deposit slip** = piece of paper stamped by the cashier to prove that you have paid money into your account; **pay slip** = piece of paper showing the full amount of a worker's pay, and the money deducted as tax, pension and insurance contributions; **paying-in slip** = printed form which is filled in when money is being deposited in a bank; **sales slip** = paper showing that an article was bought at a certain shop on a certain day; *goods can be exchanged only on production of a sales slip* **2** *verb* **(a)** to slide (and fall) by mistake; *he slipped and dropped all his shopping; he was using the electric saw when it hit something hard and slipped* **(b)** to slide out of something which is holding you tight; *the dog slipped its lead and ran away* **(c)** to push something without being seen; *the postman slipped the letters through the letter box; he slipped the keys into his pocket* **(d)** to go down to a lower level; *profits slipped badly last year; the pound slipped on the foreign exchanges* (NOTE: **slipping - slipped**)

slip into ['slɪp 'ɪntu] *verb* to put on clothes quickly; *I'll just slip into a pair of clean trousers and will be with you in a minute*

slip on ['slɪp 'ɒn] *verb* **(a)** to slip because you step on something; *he slipped on the wet leaves and broke his ankle* **(b)** to put clothes on quickly; *she slipped on her dressing gown and ran into the street*

slip-on ['slɪpɒn] *adjective & noun* shoes which can be put on easily, and have no laces; *in the house, he wears a pair of slip-on shoes; he took off his lace-ups and put on a pair of slip-ons*

slipover ['slɪpəʊvə] *noun* light pullover with no sleeves; *he wore a yellow slipover with his blue trousers*

slippers ['slɪpəz] *noun* light comfortable shoes worn indoors; *he ran out into the street in his slippers*

slippery ['slɪpri] *adjective* so smooth that one can easily slip and fall; *watch out! the path's slippery*

slip road ['slɪp 'rəʊd] *noun* small road which leads to or from a motorway; *there was an accident on the slip road so we couldn't get onto the motorway*

slip up ['slɪp 'ʌp] *verb* (*informal*) to make a silly mistake; *we slipped up badly in not checking his facts before publishing his book*

slip-up ['slɪpʌp] *noun* (*informal*) silly mistake; *it was an unfortunate slip-up to leave his name off the list* (NOTE: plural is **slip-ups**)

slipway ['slɪpweɪ] *noun* smooth slope on which ships are built or repaired; *the ship is finished and is on the slipway, waiting to be launched*

slit [slɪt] **1** *noun* long cut or narrow opening; *she peeped through a slit in the curtains* **2** *verb* to make a slit; *he slit open the envelope with a kitchen knife; they robbed him of all his money and then slit his throat* (NOTE: **slitting - slit**)

slither ['slɪðə] *verb* **(a)** to slide about in various directions; *cars were slithering all over the place on the icy streets* **(b)** to slide like a snake; *the snake slithered down the tree trunk*

sliver ['slɪvə] *noun* long thin piece; *slivers of glass were all over the pavement*; *I'm not hungry, I'll just have a sliver of that meat*

slob [slɒb] *noun (informal)* lazy, dirty person; *get a move on, you fat slob!*

slog [slɒg] **1** *noun (informal)* difficult job; *building the wall was quite a slog*; *it's a hard slog from here to the top of the mountain* **2** *verb (informal)* **(a)** to walk with difficulty; *they had to slog through miles of jungle to get to the temple* **(b) to slog away at** = to work hard at something difficult; *he slogged away at his Latin and passed the exam* (NOTE: **slogging - slogged**)

slogan ['sləʊgn] *noun* phrase which is easy to remember and is used in publicity for a product or for a political party, etc.; *we are using the slogan 'Smiths can make it' on all our publicity*; *the walls of the factory were covered with election slogans*

sloop [sluːp] *noun* type of small ship with one mast; *he was the captain of a sloop sailing in the West Indies*

slop [slɒp] *verb* to spill; *the plane ran into turbulence and my coffee slopped into the saucer* (NOTE: **slopping - slopped**)

slope [sləʊp] **1** *noun* **(a)** slanting surface or slanting piece of ground; *the land rises in a gentle slope to the church*; *they stopped halfway down the slope*; **ski slope** = specially prepared and marked slope for skiing down a mountain; **nursery slopes** = gentle snow-covered mountain slopes where people learn to ski **(b)** angle at which something slopes; *the hill has an slope of 1 in 10, put the car in low gear* **2** *verb* to slant upwards or downwards; *the path slopes upwards*

sloping ['sləʊpɪŋ] *adjective (roof, etc.)* which slopes; *the bedrooms all have sloping ceilings*; *she has very recognizable sloping handwriting*

sloppy ['slɒpi] *adjective* **(a)** untidy; *he's such a sloppy eater, he's made a mess all over his pullover* **(b)** loose and untidy; *she was wearing a sloppy jumper* **(c)** badly done; *they said her work was sloppy and had to be done again* **(d)** *(informal)* stupidly sentimental; *she's a sloppy old dog, she's no good at guarding*; *what a sloppy film!* (NOTE: **sloppier - sloppiest**)

slot [slɒt] **1** *noun* **(a)** long thin hole; *a coin has got stuck in the slot of the parking meter*; *put the system disk into the left-hand slot on the front of your computer*; **slot machine** = machine for gambling, or which provides drinks, cigarettes, plays music, etc., when you put a coin into a slot **(b)** set time available for doing something; *the airline has asked for more takeoff and landing slots at the airport* **2** *verb* **to slot into** = to fit into a slot; *the radio slots easily into the dashboard* (NOTE: **slotting - slotted**)

slouch [slaʊtʃ] *verb* to stand or to sit in a bad position, with bent shoulders; *she sat slouched in her chair*; **to slouch along** = to walk along bending forwards

slough 1 *noun* [slaʊ] *(formal)* marshy place; *the guns were bogged down in the slough of the battlefield* **2** *verb* [slʌf] *(of a snake)* to lose its skin; *a snake sloughs its skin each year*

Slovak ['sləʊvæk] **1** *adjective* referring to Slovakia; *the Slovak economy*; *an important Slovak businessman* **2** *noun* person from Slovakia; *three Slovaks came to visit our offices*

Slovakia [sləʊvækiə] *noun* country in Central Europe, to the East of the Czech Republic; *we went on a tour of monasteries in Slovakia* (NOTE: capital: **Bratislava**; people: **the Slovaks**; language: **Slovakian**; currency: **koruna**)

Slovene ['sləʊviːn] **1** *adjective* referring to Slovenia; *the Slovene economy* **2** *noun* **(a)** language spoken in Slovenia; *an English-Slovene Dictionary* (NOTE: in Slovenia, the word **Slovenian** is preferred) **(b)** person from Slovenia; *when we visited Ljubljana, the Slovenes made us very welcome*

Slovenia [sləʊviːniə] *noun* country on the Adriatic Sea, south of Austria and north of Croatia; *they went on a climbing holiday in Slovenia* (NOTE: capital: **Ljubljana**; people: **the Slovenes**; language: **Slovene** or **Slovenian**; currency: **tolar**)

Slovenian [sləʊviːniən] **1** *adjective* referring to Slovenia; *the Slovenian economy is growing fast* **2** *noun* language spoken in Slovenia; *an English-Slovenian Dictionary*

slovenly ['slʌvənli] *adjective* untidy and dirty; *a slovenly waiter came to serve us*; *the manager told her off for her slovenly appearance*

slow [sləʊ] **1** *adjective* **(a)** not fast, needing a long time to do something; *luckily, the car was only going at a slow speed*; *she is the slowest walker of the group*; *the company is very slow at answering my letters*; *sales got off to a slow start but picked up later*; **slow train** = train which stops at each station **(b)** showing a time which is earlier than the right time; *the office clock is four minutes slow* (NOTE: **slower - slowest**) **2** *verb* to go slowly; *the procession slowed as it reached the cathedral*

slowcoach *US* **slowpoke** ['sləʊkəʊtʃ or 'sləʊpəʊk] *noun (informal)* person who is slower than the others; *come on you slowcoaches, get a move on!*

slow down ['sləʊ 'daʊn] *verb* **(a)** to go more slowly; *the van had to slow down as it came to the traffic lights*; *please slow down, I can't keep up with you* **(b)** to make something go more slowly; *the snow slowed the traffic down on the motorway* **(c)** to work less hard; *you should slow down a bit - you're doing too much*

slowdown ['sləʊdaʊn] *noun* slowing down of business activity; *a slowdown in the company's expansion*

slowly ['sləʊli] *adverb* not fast; *luckily, the car was going very slowly when it hit the fence*; *the group walked slowly round the exhibition*; *speak more slowly so that everyone can understand*

slow motion ['sləʊ 'məʊʃn] *noun* showing a film at a slower speed than it was filmed at, so that the action seems to have slowed down; *the film switched to slow motion*; *play the film again in slow motion*

sludge [slʌdʒ] *noun* **(a)** soft muddy material in a liquid; *there's some black sludge at the bottom of the petrol tank* **(b)** solid part of sewage; **raw sludge** = solid sewage before it is treated

slug [slʌg] **1** *noun* **(a)** common garden animal like a snail with no shell; *slugs have eaten all my lettuces*; **slug pellets** = little amounts of poisonous mixture used to kill slugs; *we must put some slug pellets round the lettuces* **(b)** small bullet; *a slug from the rifle hit the wall above my head* **2** *verb (informal)* to hit someone a heavy blow; *he slugged her and she fell to the ground* (NOTE: **slugging - slugged**)

sluggish ['slʌgɪʃ] *adjective* lazy or slow-moving; *we watched the sluggish stream move by*; *the economy is still sluggish, and is taking a long time to get out of recession*

sluice [sluːs] **1** *noun* gate which closes a channel for water, especially through a dam; *they opened the sluices to release the water behind the dam* **2** *verb* to wash something with lots of water; *you'll have to sluice out the pig sty*; *she sluiced the dirty bucket under the tap*

sluice gate ['sluːs 'geɪt] *noun* gate which allows water to enter a channel; *they have to open the sluice gates when the river is in flood*

slum [slʌm] *noun* crowded, dirty district inside a large town; *the children were brought up in the slums of Glasgow*; **slum clearance** = organized demolishing of slum areas to replace them with modern blocks of flats; *the government introduced an urgent programme of slum clearance*

slump [slʌmp] **1** *noun* **(a)** rapid fall; *there has been slump in sales* **(b)** period of economic collapse with high unemployment and loss of trade; *economist argued about the reasons for the slump*; **the Slump** = the world economic crisis of 1929 - 1933 **2** *verb* **(a)** to fall fast; *the pound slumped on the foreign exchange markets* **(b)** to sit or to lie down clumsily or heavily; *he sat slumped on a chair doing his homework*; *at the end of the day, she just slumped down onto the sofa*

slur [slɜː] **1** *noun* **(a)** insult; *she has cast a slur on my reputation* **(b)** *(in music)* action of running several notes together; mark on a musical score to show that notes should run into each other; *there is a slur marked here which I find it difficult to get right* **2** *verb* **(a)** to speak words indistinctly; *you could tell he had been taking drugs by the way he slurred his words* **(b)** *(in music)* to play several notes without a break between them; *the series of notes should be slurred here* (NOTE: **slurring - slurred**)

slurp ['slɜːp] *verb* to drink and make a noise; *don't slurp your soup*

slush [slʌʃ] *noun* **(a)** melting snow; *the snow has started to melt and the roads are covered with slush* **(b)** *(informal)* sentimental writing; *her latest novel is just slush* (NOTE: no plural)

slush fund ['slʌʃ 'fʌnd] *noun (informal)* money kept secretly paid to give to people as bribes, to persuade them to do what you want; *we paid thousands of dollars into a slush fund*

slushy ['slʌʃi] *adjective* **(a)** covered with melting snow; *the path is slushy and slippery* **(b)** very sentimental; *she sits on the sofa all day reading slushy novels*

sly [slaɪ] *adjective* cunning and slightly dishonest; *the sly old thing - he never told me about it*; **on the sly** = without anyone knowing; *she transferred all the money to her Swiss account on the sly* (NOTE: **slyer - slyest**)

slyly ['slaɪli] *adverb* in a sly way; *he looked slyly at her and asked if she had ever been to Brighton*

smack [smæk] **1** *noun* hitting someone with your hand flat; *if you pull the cat's tail you'll get a smack* **2** *verb* **(a)** to hit someone with your hand flat; *she smacked the little girl for being rude* **(b)** to put something down noisily; *she smacked the report down on the table and walked out of the room* **(c)** to smack

your lips = to make a loud noise with your lips to show you are hungry or looking forward to have something; *she smacked her lips as he mentioned diamonds* **(d)** to show signs of; *the whole affair smacks of fraud* **3** *adverb* straight, directly; *the bus ran smack into a tree*

small [smɔːl] **1** *adjective* **(a)** little, not big; *small cars are more economical than large ones*; *the house is too big for us, so we're selling it and buying a smaller one*; *she only paid a small amount for that clock*; *the guidebook isn't small enough to carry in your pocket*; *these trousers are already too small for him*; **small business** = little company with a low turnover and few employees; **small businessman** = man who runs a small business; **small change** = loose coins; *do you have any small change, I only have notes?* **(b)** young; *fireworks can frighten small children* **(c)** a **small fortune** = a lot of money; *those shoes cost me a small fortune*; *she earns a small fortune selling postcards*; **the small hours** = early in the morning; *we went on talking until the small hours (of the morning); see also* WEE (NOTE: **smaller - smallest**) **2** *noun* **the small of the back** = the middle part of the back below and between the shoulder blades; *something is tickling me in the small of my back*

smallholder ['smɔːlhəʊldə] *noun* person who owns a smallholding; *several smallholders round here keep goats*

smallholding ['smɔːlhəʊldɪŋ] *noun* small farm, under 20 hectares in area, usually run as a family concern; *he has a smallholding keeping goats and selling cheese*

small intestine ['smɔːl ɪn'testɪn] *noun* the top section of the intestines, leading down from the stomach; *the doctor diagnosed cancer in the small intestine*

smallpox ['smɔːlpɒks] *noun* formerly a very serious, usually fatal contagious disease, with a severe rash which leaves masses of small scars on the skin; *vaccination has proved effective in eradicating smallpox*

small print ['smɔːl 'prɪnt] *noun* words printed in very small size, such as the conditions on the back of a contract; *he read the small print very carefully before signing the contract*

small-scale ['smɔːlskeɪl] *adjective* working in a small way, with few staff and not much money; *it is a small-scale operation with only 3 full-time staff*; a **small-scale enterprise** = a small business; *compare* LARGE-SCALE

small-time ['smɔːltaɪm] *adjective (informal)* not very important and not very successful; *he's a small-time crook*; *they run a small-time protection racket*

smarmy ['smɑːmi] *adjective (informal)* polite but not sincere; *some smarmy individual came to try to sell me insurance*

smart [smɑːt] **1** *adjective* **(a)** well-dressed or elegant; *a smart young man asked me if he could use my mobile phone*; *he looked very smart in his uniform*; *(informal)* **look smart!** = hurry up! **(b)** clever; *it was smart of her to note the car's number plate*; *he's the smartest of the three brothers*; **smart card** = plastic credit card with a microchip in it **(c)** sharp (blow); *she gave a smart knock on the door* **(d)** rapid; *the horse set off at the smart pace* (NOTE: **smarter - smartest**) **2** *noun* sharp pain from a blow; *he remembered the smart* *of the slap on his cheek* **3** *verb* to hurt with a burning feeling; *the burn on my hand is still smarting*

smarten up ['smɑːtn 'ʌp] *verb* **to smarten yourself up** = to make yourself look smarter; *you'd better smarten yourself up for the interview*

smartly ['smɑːtli] *adverb* **(a)** in a smart way; *he dresses very smartly*; *a smartly dressed young man* **(b)** with a sharp blow; *she knocked smartly on the door and went in*

smash [smæʃ] **1** *verb* **(a)** to break into pieces; *he dropped the plate and it smashed to pieces* **(b)** to break something to pieces; *demonstrators smashed the windows of police cars* **(c)** to break a record, to do better than a record; *she smashed the world record; six records were smashed at the Olympics* **(d)** to go violently; *the train smashed into the car; the crowd smashed through the railings* **(e)** *(in tennis)* to play a fast stroke, sending the ball down to the ground (NOTE: **smashing - smashed**) **2** *noun* **(a)** sound of something breaking into pieces; *we could hear the smash of crockery from the restaurant* **(b)** bad accident; *six people are feared killed in the train smash* **(c)** *(in tennis)* fast stroke, sending the ball down to the ground (NOTE: the opposite, where the ball goes up into the air, is a **lob**)

smash hit ['smæʃ 'hɪt] *noun* *(informal)* play, film, etc., which is very popular; *a new smash hit musical*

smashing ['smæʃɪŋ] *adjective* *(informal)* very good, fantastic; *we had a smashing time at the zoo; I thought the meal was smashing*

smash up ['smæʃ 'ʌp] *verb* to break everything in a place; *the fans smashed up the pub*

smear ['smɪə] **1** *noun* **(a)** dirty mark; *waiter, there's a lipstick smear on this cup!* **(b)** something which is smeared, especially a small amount of something put on glass for examining under a microscope; **smear test** = test for cancer of the cervix; *older women should have a (cervical) smear test every year* **(c)** words about someone which are not true but which are meant to harm his or her reputation; *the report about my wife was just a dirty smear*; **smear campaign** = campaign to discredit someone by spreading gossip about his or her private life **2** *verb* **(a)** to spread something; *she smeared glue all over the piece of wood or she smeared the piece of wood with glue; how did your shirt get smeared with paint?* **(b)** to make dirty marks; *he smeared the kitchen table with his dirty fingers* **(c)** to hurt someone's reputation by saying things which are not true; *the report was just an attempt to smear my wife*

smell [smel] **1** *noun* **(a)** one of the five senses, which you can feel through your nose; *animals have a better sense of smell than humans; these dogs have a very keen sense of smell and can sniff out even a minute quantity of drugs* **(b)** something which you can sense with your nose; *I love the smell of coffee coming from the restaurant; he can't stand the smell of fried onions; there's a smell of burning or there's a burning smell coming from the kitchen; she noticed a smell of gas downstairs* **(c)** unpleasant thing which you can sense with your nose; *there's a smell or a funny smell or a nasty smell in the shed* **2** *verb* **(a)** to notice the smell of something; *can you smell gas?; wild animals can smell humans; my nose is blocked - I can't smell anything; just smell these roses!; Mmm! - I can smell fish and chips!; (informal)* **to smell a rat** = to suspect

that something wrong is happening; *why is he so generous all of a sudden? - I smell a rat!* **(b)** to make a smell; *I don't like cheese which smells too strong; what's for dinner? - it smells very good!; there's something which smells funny in the bathroom; it smelt of gas in the kitchen* **(c)** to bring your nose close to something to smell it; *she bent down to smell the snowdrops* (NOTE: **smelling - smelled** *or* **smelt** [smelt])

smelly ['smeli] *adjective* which has a nasty smell; *I don't want them to build a smelly pig farm next to my house; he goes everywhere with a smelly old dog* (NOTE: **smellier - smelliest**)

smile [smaɪl] **1** *noun* way of showing that you are pleased, by turning your mouth up at the corners; *the dentist gave me a friendly smile; she had a big smile as she told them the good news* **2** *verb* to show that you are pleased by turning your mouth up at the corners; *that girl has just smiled at me; everyone smile please - I'm taking a photo!*

smiley (face) ['smaɪli (feɪs)] *noun* round face with a smile ☺ produced as a computer character or icon; *each item on the list had a smiley in front of it*

> COMMENT: the smiley face is a character in a specialist typeface, but it can also be made by using various sequences of characters; :-) means happy and :-(means sad. Turn your head sideways to see them!

smirk [smɜːk] **1** *noun* unpleasant smile, showing that you think you are better than someone else; *he brought his winning lottery ticket to the office and showed it to her with a smirk* **2** *verb* to give a smirk; *she smirked as the other girls all heard they'd lost their jobs*

smith [smɪθ] *noun* blacksmith, a person who works with red-hot iron, hammering it into different shapes; *she asked the smith to make her a new garden gate*

smithy ['smɪði] *noun* workshop where a blacksmith works; *go to the smithy as ask the blacksmith if he can repair our gate* (NOTE: plural is **smithies**)

smock [smɒk] *noun* long loose overall worn over clothes to protect them; *she put on her smock and started to clean the kitchen; the painter wiped his brushes on his smock*

smog [smɒg] *noun* pollution of the atmosphere in towns, caused by warm damp air combined with exhaust fumes from cars; *do you remember the last smog in London?; as we came into Los Angeles Airport we could see the smog below us*

smoke [sməʊk] **1** *noun* **(a)** white, grey or black product formed of small particles, given off by something that is burning; *the restaurant was full of cigarette smoke; clouds of smoke were pouring out of the upstairs windows; two people died from inhaling toxic smoke; smoke detectors are fitted in all the rooms* **(b)** *(informal)* time when you are smoking a cigarette; *cigarettes aren't allowed in the office, so everyone goes outside for a quick smoke; I'm dying for a smoke!* **(c)** **to go up in smoke** = (i) to be burnt; (ii) to fail, not to work; *his entire art collection went up in smoke in the fire; all her plans for buying a bigger house have gone up in smoke* **2** *verb* **(a)** to give off smoke; *two days after the fire, the ruins of the factory were still smoking* **(b)** to breathe in smoke (from a cigarette, cigar, pipe, etc.); *everyone was smoking even though the signs said 'no smoking'; she doesn't smoke much - only one or two cigarettes a day; you shouldn't* *smoke if you want to play football*; *I've never seen her smoking a cigar before*; **he smokes like a chimney** = he smokes a lot of cigarettes **(c) the chimney smokes** = the fire sends smoke into the room instead of taking it up the chimney **(d)** to preserve food (such as meat, fish, bacon, cheese) by hanging it in the smoke from a fire; *a factory where they smoke fish*; **smoked salmon** = salmon which has been cured by smoking, and is served in very thin slices; *a plate of smoked salmon sandwiches*

smoke-free ['sməuk'fri:] *see* SMOKELESS

smokeless ['sməukləs] *adjective* **(a)** where there is no smoke or where smoke is not allowed; **smokeless** *or* **smoke-free area** = part of a public place, such as a restaurant, aircraft, etc., where smoking is not allowed; **smokeless zone** = area of a town where you are not allowed to produce smoke from chimneys or fires **(b) smokeless fuel** = fuel which does not produce smoke when it is burned

smoker ['sməukə] *noun* person who smokes; *we only have two members of staff who are smokers*; *he's a pipe smoker*

smoking ['sməukɪŋ] *noun* action of smoking cigarettes, etc.; *smoking is bad for your health*; *smoking is not allowed on the London Underground*; **'no smoking'** = do not smoke here; *I always sit in the 'no smoking' part of the restaurant*; **passive smoking** = breathing in smoke from other people's cigarettes, when you do not smoke yourself

smoky ['sməuki] *adjective* **(a)** full of smoke; *a smoky bar* **(b)** with the colour of smoke; *the car windows are slightly smoky grey*

smooth [smu:ð] **1** *adjective* **(a)** with no bumps, with no uneven surface; *the smooth surface of a polished table*; *the baby's skin is very smooth*; *velvet has a smooth side and a rough side*; **to take the rough with the smooth** = to accept that there are bad times as well as good times **(b)** with no jolts or sudden movements; *dirt in the fuel tank can disrupt the smooth running of the engine*; *we had a very smooth ride* **(c)** *(person)* too polite, with manners which are too good; *that car salesman's a bit too smooth for my liking* (NOTE: **smoother - smoothest**) **2** *verb* **(a)** to make something smooth with a tool or with your hand; *she smoothed the sheets and adjusted the pillows*; *the edge of the table needs smoothing, it's still quite rough*; **to smooth the way for someone** *or* **something** = to make things easy for someone *or* something; *the retiring president cut taxes to smooth the way for his successor*; **to smooth things over** = to settle an argument; *after the quarrel, I called round at her house to try and smooth things over* **(b)** to spread something gently over a surface; *smooth the lotion over your face and let it dry*

smoothly ['smu:ðli] *adverb* in a smooth way; *the engine is running smoothly*; *the panther ran smoothly through the grass*

smoothness ['smu:ðnəs] *noun* being smooth; *the fabric has all the smoothness of a baby's skin*; *the smoothness of the ride makes up for the high fare*

smother ['smʌðə] *verb* **(a)** to stifle and kill someone; *they took the kittens and smothered them*; *never put a pillow over someone's face - you may smother them!* **(b)** to cover; *the firemen put out the fire by smothering it with foam*; *a chocolate cake simply smothered in cream*; **to smother someone with affection** *or* **love** = to show too much affection towards someone, especially

your children; *as a child he was brought up by his aunts, who smothered him with affection* **(c)** **to smother a yawn** = to hide the fact that you are yawning, so that people will not think you are bored

smoulder *US* **smolder** ['sməuldə] *verb* **(a)** to burn slowly; *the incense sticks smouldered in the entrance to the temple*; *it took the fire brigade some time to put out the smouldering timbers* **(b)** *(of emotion)* to be violent, but hidden; *his speeches aroused the smouldering ranger of the workforce*; **to be smouldering with rage** = to be extremely angry but try not to show it

smudge [smʌdʒ] **1** *noun* dirty mark; *there is a smudge on the top corner of the photograph*; *he had a smudge of lipstick on his cheek* **2** *verb* to make a dirty mark, such as by rubbing ink which is not dry; *don't touch the artwork until it's dry, otherwise you'll smudge it*

smug [smʌg] *adjective* satisfied with yourself; *he accepted his prize with a smug look on his face* (NOTE: **smugger - smuggest**)

smuggle ['smʌgl] *verb* **(a)** to take goods into a country without declaring them to the customs; *they tried to smuggle cigarettes into the country*; *we had to smuggle the spare parts over the border* **(b)** to take something into or out of a place illegally; *the knives were smuggled into the prison by a someone visiting a prisoner*; *we'll never know how they smuggled the letter out*

smuggler ['smʌglə] *noun* person who smuggles; *customs officers deal with hundreds of smugglers every years*; *he's a known drug smuggler*

smuggling ['smʌglɪŋ] *noun* taking goods illegally into a country; *he made his money in arms smuggling*; *she was accused of smuggling drugs*

smugly ['smʌgli] *adverb* in a smug way; *she said smugly that she had already been given one prize so she didn't want another*

smut [smʌt] *noun* **(a)** small piece of black dirt; *she hung the sheets out to dry and they got covered with smuts*; *I got a smut in my eye from standing close to the bonfire* **(b)** *(informal)* rude stories about sex; *the newspaper seems to be full of smut these days* **(c)** disease of plants, which covers the plants with black spots; *you need to spray the wheat against smut* (NOTE: no plural for (b) and (c))

smutty ['smʌti] *adjective* referring to sex all the time; *he sat in the bar telling us a string of smutty stories* (NOTE: **smuttier - smuttiest**)

snack [snæk] **1** *noun* a light meal, a small amount of food; *we didn't have time to stop for a proper lunch, so we just had a snack on the motorway* **2** *verb* to eat a snack; *she never eats proper meals, she just snacks all the time*

snack bar ['snæk 'bɑː] *noun* small simple restaurant where you can have a light meal; *he met the girl by chance in a snack bar at Waterloo Station*

snag [snæg] **1** *noun* **(a)** obstacle, thing which prevents you from doing something; *we've run into a snag: there are no flights to the island on Sundays*; *the only snag is that he's not a very good driver* **(b)** place where a piece of clothing has been caught on a sharp point; *there's a snag in your jumper* **(c)** sharp point sticking out of something; *she tore her coat on a snag in the fence* **2** *verb* to catch and tear your clothes on a sharp point; *she snagged her coat getting through the hedge* (NOTE: **snagging - snagged**)

snail [sneɪl] *noun* common little mollusc, which has a spiral-shaped shell on its back and moves very slowly; *slugs and snails have ruined all the lettuces in the garden*; **at a snail's pace** = extremely slowly; *negotiations over the sale of the flat have been progressing at a snail's pace*

snake [sneɪk] **1** *noun* long reptile which has no legs and moves along the ground by wriggling; *is this snake safe to handle?*; **snakes and ladders** = children's board game, played with dice, in which landing on a ladder moves you forward and landing on a snake moves you back **2** *verb* to bend and twist; *the Great Wall of China snakes over the mountains*

> COMMENT: only three species of snake are native to Britain: the grass snake and smooth snake which are harmless, and the adder or viper, which is poisonous, though its bite is rarely fatal. There are no snakes in Ireland. There are several species of venomous snakes in the United States

snap [snæp] **1** *noun* (a) **cold snap** = short period of sudden cold weather; *a cold snap can have disastrous effects on my tomatoes* (b) photograph taken quickly; *she showed me an old black-and-white snap of the house*; *he took a lot of snaps of his children* (c) card game where you shout 'snap' if two similar cards are played at the same time; *do you want a game of snap?*; *they played snap all afternoon* (d) **brandy snap** = thin sweet biscuit flavoured with ginger and rolled up; **ginger snap** = round hard biscuit flavoured with ginger (e) *US* (*informal*) little metal fastener for clothes, in two parts which you press to attach together (NOTE: British English is **popper**) **2** *adjective* sudden; **a snap decision** = a decision taken hurriedly; *they carried out a snap check or a snap inspection of the passengers' luggage*; *the government called a snap election* **3** *verb* (a) to say something in a sharp angry tone; *he was tired and irritable, and snapped at the children*; *the manager snapped at the shop assistant, but it wasn't her fault* (b) to break sharply with a dry noise; *the branches snapped as he walked through the wood* (c) **to snap your fingers** = to make a clicking noise with your middle finger and thumb; *they sat snapping their fingers in time to the music*; **to snap into place** = to make a click when fitting together; *push gently on the surface until it snaps into place* (NOTE: **snapping - snapped**)

snappy ['snæpi] *adjective* (a) (*informal*) sharp and fashionable; *she's wearing a very snappy outfit* (b) (*informal*) **make it snappy!** or **look snappy!** = do it quickly!; *make it snappy, there's a policeman coming!* (c) irritable, short-tempered; *the boss tends to be snappy after lunch* (NOTE: **snappier - snappiest**)

snapshot ['snæpʃɒt] *noun* photograph taken quickly; *she took snapshots of the crowd at the wedding*

snap up ['snæp 'ʌp] *verb* to buy quickly; *the toys came into the shops just before Christmas and were snapped up by parents*

snare ['sneə] **1** *noun* (a) trap for catching animals made with a loop of wire which is pulled tight; *he caught a rabbit in the snare* (b) (*formal*) trap; *his offer of a well-paid job in Luxembourg was just a snare* **2** *verb* to catch with a snare; *we snared three rabbits*

snarl [snɑːl] **1** *noun* (a) angry growl; *as she opened the door of the cage she heard a snarl* (b) (*informal*) tangle or knot; *her hair is so full of snarls that it is difficult to comb* **2** *verb* (a) to growl angrily; *the leopard snarled as he approached its cage*; *'take your money, and get out' he snarled* (b) **to snarl something up** = to block something, to make something tangled; *he managed to snarl up all the computer cables*; *the traffic was snarled up from Hyde Park Corner to Marble Arch*

snarl-up ['snɑːl'ʌp] *noun* (*informal*) complicated traffic jam; *there was huge snarl-up on roads leading to the Horse Show*

snatch [snætʃ] **1** *noun* little piece of something heard; *in the evening, I heard snatches of song from across the lake* (NOTE: plural is **snatches**) **2** *verb* to grab something rapidly; *he came beside her on his bike and snatched her handbag*; *I didn't have time for a proper meal, but I snatched a sandwich*; *she snatched a few hours' sleep in the transit lounge*

snazzy ['snæzi] *adjective* (*informal*) bright, modern and colourful; *have you seen her snazzy new car?*; *the book has a really snazzy cover*

sneak [sniːk] **1** *noun* (*informal*) person who tells an adult what another child has done; *you promised not to say anything, you little sneak!* **2** *verb* (a) to go quietly without being seen; *she sneaked into the room*; *the burglar sneaked up to the house, hidden by the trees*; **to sneak up on someone** = to creep up behind someone without being noticed (b) (*informal*) **to sneak on someone** = to tell an adult that another child has done something wrong; *he promised not to sneak on me to my mum* (NOTE: the past tense in British English is **sneaked** and in American English **snuck**)

sneakers ['sniːkəz] *noun US* soft sports shoes with rubber soles; *she came to work in sneakers*

sneaking ['sniːkɪŋ] *adjective* secret; *I have a sneaking suspicion that he made a lot of money out of the deal*

sneaky ['sniːki] *adjective* (*informal*) deceitful and secret; *it was sneaky of him not to tell us he was listening to the conversation*

sneer ['snɪə] **1** *noun* sarcastic, unpleasant smile; *he held the whip in his hand and looked at her with a sneer* **2** *verb* to give someone a sarcastic smile or to speak in a contemptuous way; *he sneered at her attempts to speak French*; *you shouldn't sneer at her clothes - they're by the best designers and are very expensive*

sneeze [sniːz] **1** *noun* reflex action to blow air suddenly out through your mouth and nose because of an irritation inside your nose; *coughs and sneezes spread diseases* **2** *verb* to make a sneeze; *the smell of roses makes me sneeze*; *he has hayfever and can't stop sneezing*; (*informal*) **it's not to be sneezed at** = you should not refuse it; *it's a good offer and not to be sneezed at*

snicker ['snɪkə] **1** *noun* quiet unpleasant laugh; *I heard a little snicker behind my back* **2** *verb* to laugh quietly in an unpleasant way; *they snickered as the teacher came into the room*

sniff [snɪf] **1** *noun* (a) breathing in air through your nose; *the dog gave a sniff at the plate before licking it*; *he gave a little sniff and walked out of the shop* **2** *verb* (a) to breathe in air through your nose; *he sniffed and said 'I can smell fish and chips'*; *the customs* inspection is very strict, a dog is taken round to sniff (at) each bag and suitcase; (informal) it's not to be sniffed at = you should not refuse it; a free ticket with Air Canada is not to be sniffed at; to sniff something out = to discover something by smelling; the dogs sniffed out drugs hidden in her bag (b) to breathe in air through your nose because you have a cold; he's coughing and sniffing and should be in bed (c) to breathe in vapour from solvent or glue; the police caught them sniffing glue; see also GLUE

sniffer ['snɪfə] noun (a) sniffer dog = dog which has been trained to smell things such as drugs; the police brought sniffer dogs to the warehouse (b) person who sniffs solvent or glue; the social workers told her that her son was a glue sniffer

sniffle ['snɪfl] 1 noun noise made when you keep on sniffing, especially when you have a cold or have been crying; you could hear the sniffles from the girls at the back of the room; to have the sniffles = to have a slight cold 2 verb to keep on sniffing because of a cold, or because you want to cry; stop sniffling and get on with your work; he was sniffling and sneezing, and in the end I told him to go home early; stop sniffling! Blow your nose!

snigger ['snɪgə] 1 noun quiet unpleasant laugh; I heard a little snigger behind my back 2 verb to laugh quietly in an unpleasant way; they sniggered as the teacher came into the room; to snigger at something = to laugh unpleasantly at something; what are you sniggering at?

snip [snɪp] 1 noun (informal) bargain, something much cheaper than usual; these typewriters are a snip at £50 2 verb to cut quickly with scissors; she snipped two inches off the hem of the dress (NOTE: snipping - snipped)

snipe [snaɪp] 1 noun large marsh bird with a long beak; we saw several snipe on the marshes (NOTE: no plural) 2 verb to snipe at someone = (i) to shoot at someone from a hiding place; (ii) to criticize someone continuously; gunmen sniped at the soldiers from the rooftops; the MPs kept sniping at the minister

sniper ['snaɪpə] noun hidden soldier who shoots at the enemy; snipers hid on the rooftops; we are trying to root out any enemy snipers left hiding in the ruins; sniper fire = gunfire from snipers; the street was dangerous because of sniper fire

snippet ['snɪpət] noun little bit of gossip, etc.; I heard a snippet of information which you might like to hear

snob [snɒb] noun (a) person who likes people who are of a higher social class than himself or herself; don't ask him to your party, he's such a snob (b) art snob or intellectual snob = person who thinks he or she knows much more about art or is better-educated than other people

snobbery ['snɒbrɪ] noun being a snob; I can't stand the snobbery of the old universities; inverted snobbery = being critical of people of a higher social class, or people who are more intelligent than you are; preferring bangers and mash to French cuisine may just be inverted snobbery

snobbish ['snɒbɪʃ] adjective referring to a snob; we don't associate with them because they're so snobbish; he's snobbish about wine, so we must get him something good

snog [snɒg] verb (informal) to kiss someone lovingly; they were snogging in the back row of the cinema

snooker ['snuːkə] noun game for two players, similar to billiards, played on a table with twenty-two balls of various colours; would you like a game of snooker?; they played snooker all evening; he's the world snooker champion; snooker table = table on which snooker is played

COMMENT: there are 15 red balls (worth 1 point each), a yellow ball (worth 2 points), a green (3 points), a brown (4 points), a blue (5 points), a pink (6 points), a black (7 points) and one white cue ball which the players use to hit the other balls. Each player in turn uses his cue to hit the one white cue ball against one of the 15 red balls in an attempt to pot it (ie, to send it into one of the pockets round the table); having done this he may choose any other non-red ball to pot and score points according to its value; every time a non-red ball is potted it is replaced in (or as near as possible to) its special position on the table whilst the red balls which are potted are never put back on the table. When all the reds have been potted, the rest of the balls must be potted in strict sequence according to their value (finishing with the black); the object is to score more points than your opponent. To make it hard for your opponent to score you can try to leave him without any direct shot at a target ball, forcing him to bounce the cue ball off one or more cushions; this is called 'snookering'

snore [snɔː] 1 noun loud noise produced in the nose and throat when asleep; his snores kept her awake 2 verb to make a snore; I can't get to sleep because my husband snores

snoring ['snɔːrɪŋ] noun action of snoring; his snoring woke me up

snorkel ['snɔːkl] 1 noun tube which allows an underwater swimmer to breathe in air; she could still see Brian's snorkel on the surface of the water 2 verb to swim with a snorkel; the water isn't clear so we can't snorkel here; to go snorkelling = to go swimming with a snorkel for pleasure (NOTE: British English is snorkelling - snorkelled but American English is snorkeling - snorkeled)

snorkelling US **snorkeling** ['snɔːklɪŋ] noun swimming with a snorkel; snorkelling has become my favourite holiday sport

snort [snɔːt] 1 noun (a) noise made when you blow air through your nose; the horse gave a snort and reared up on its hind legs; judging by the snorts coming from the behind the newspaper, I think grandfather has found something he doesn't agree with (b) (informal) amount of drug powder which you breathe through the nose; they had a snort or two during the evening 2 verb (a) to make a loud noise blowing air out through the nose; 'that's just plain stupid', she snorted; the horses snorted and pawed the ground (b) to take powdered drugs by breathing them through the nose; she has been snorting cocaine for some years

snot [snɒt] noun (informal) mucus in the nose; his nose was running and he wiped the snot onto his sleeve

snotty ['snɒti] *adjective (informal)* **(a)** covered with mucus; *a snotty-nosed kid* **(b)** looking down on others who you think are inferior; *don't be so snotty!*

snout [snaʊt] *noun* nose and mouth of some animals, such as pigs; *the pig had its snout in the trough*; *(informal)* **to have your snout in the trough** = to get rich on government money; *all these European officials have their snouts in the trough*

snow [snəʊ] **1** *noun* water which falls as light white flakes of ice crystals in cold weather; *two metres of snow fell during the night*; *the highest mountains are always covered with snow*; *children were out playing in the snow*; *we went for a skiing holiday and there was hardly any snow*; **snow tyres** = special tyres with thick treads, for use when driving on snow (NOTE: no plural: **some snow, a lot of snow**) **2** *verb* to fall as snow; *look! - it's started to snow!*; *it snowed all day, and the streets were blocked*; *they say it's going to snow tomorrow*; *it hardly ever snows here in March* (NOTE: that **to snow** is always used with the subject **it**)

snowball ['snəʊbɔːl] **1** *noun* ball made with snow; *they were throwing snowballs at passing cars*; *I tried to make a snowball but the snow was too dry* **2** *verb* to get steadily bigger; *the protests started slowly and then snowballed into mass demonstrations*

snowboarding ['snəʊbɔːdɪŋ] *noun* sliding down a snow-covered slope while standing on a 6ft x 10in board

> COMMENT: introduced into the Winter Olympics for the first time in Japan in 1998 with giant slalom races for men; in the giant slalom riders wear reinforced gloves to help in the turns and hard boots and bindings

snowbound ['snəʊbaʊnd] *adjective* unable to go out or to travel because of snow; *we were snowbound for four days, not even able to get out to the shops*

snowcapped ['snəʊkæpt] *adjective* with the top covered with snow; *they took pictures of the snowcapped Rocky Mountains*

snowdrift ['snəʊdrɪft] *noun* snow which has been blown into a heap by the wind; *the lane was blocked by a huge snowdrift*

snowdrop ['snəʊdrɒp] *noun* bulb with little white flowers in the early spring; *we went for a walk to look at the snowdrops*

snowed in ['snəʊd 'ɪn] *adjective* blocked by snow and unable to travel; *we were snowed in, and sat indoors playing cards*

snowed under ['snəʊd 'ʌndə] *adjective (informal)* overwhelmed; *we're snowed under with orders*; *he's snowed under with work*

snowed up ['snəʊd 'ʌp] *adjective* blocked by snow, so that you cannot travel; *we were snowed up in our chalet for six days*

snowfall ['snəʊfɔːl] *noun* amount of snow which has fallen; *there was a heavy snowfall during the night*

snowflake ['snəʊfleɪk] *noun* small piece of snow formed of a number of ice crystals; *large snowflakes soon covered the path*

snowman ['snəʊmæn] *noun* model of a man made of snow; *the children made a snowman in the school playground*; *when the sun came out the snowman melted* (NOTE: plural is **snowmen**)

snow plough *US* **snow plow** ['snəʊ 'plaʊ] *noun* heavy truck with a plough on the front used to clear snow off roads, railway tracks, etc.; *the road will remain closed until snowploughs can get through*

snowstorm ['snəʊstɔːm] *noun* storm when the wind blows and snow falls; *all flights are delayed because of the snowstorm*

snow-white ['snəʊ 'waɪt] *adjective* pure white; *she wore a snow-white dress*

snowy ['snəʊi] *adjective* **(a)** with a lot of snow, covered with snow; *I remember walking through the snowy streets to school* **(b)** when there is snow; *this is the snowiest winter I can remember* **(c)** **snowy white** = pure white, as white as snow; *our soap powder will wash your shirts snowy white* (NOTE: **snowier - snowiest**)

snub [snʌb] **1** *noun* behaviour which shows you want to insult someone; *not shaking his hand was a deliberate snub* **2** *verb* to insult someone by refusing to speak to them or by not paying any attention to them; *he snubbed all her attempts to be friendly* (NOTE: **snubbing - snubbed**) **3** *adjective* **snub nose** = small nose which is turned up at the end

snuck [snʌk] *verb US see* SNEAK

snuff [snʌf] **1** *noun* powdered tobacco which is sniffed into the nose; *he took a pinch of snuff* **2** *verb* **(a)** to put out a candle; *before going to bed, remember to snuff the candles* **(b)** *(slang)* **to snuff it** = to die; *just when he thought his father was going to make a fortune, the old man snuffed it*

snug [snʌg] *adjective* warm, comfortable, out of the cold; *here we are sitting by the fire, warm and snug, while it's snowing outside*; *there's a snug little bar I know just near here* (NOTE: **snugger - snuggest**)

snuggle ['snʌgl] *verb* **(a)** to curl yourself up to be warm; *they snuggled under their blankets* **(b)** **to snuggle up to someone** = to curl up close to someone else to be warm; *she snuggled up next to her mother*

so [səʊ] **1** *adverb* **(a)** *(showing how much)* *it's so cold that the lake is covered with ice*; *we liked Greece so much that we're going there again on holiday next year*; *the soup was so salty that I couldn't eat it* **(b)** very much; *she was so kind to us when we were children*; *the film was not so boring, as you said* **(c)** also; *she was late and so was I*; *the children all caught flu, and so did their teacher*; *I like apples - so do I*; *he's a good cook so is his wife*; *the teacher will be late and so will everyone else* **(d)** *(showing that the answer is 'yes')* *does this train go to London? - I think so*; *was your car completely smashed? - I'm afraid so*; *will you be coming to the party? - I hope so!*; *are they going to be at the meeting? - I suppose so* **2** *conjunction* **(a)** and this is the reason why; *it was snowing hard so we couldn't go for a walk*; *she's got flu so she can't come to the office* **(b)** **so that** = in order that; *people riding bikes wear orange coats so that drivers can see them easily*; **so as to** = in order to; *they had to run to the station so as not to miss the train* **3** *adjective* **(a)** *(informal)* **just so** = exactly as it should be; *she always wants everything to be just so* **(b)** *(emphatic, replacing adjective)* *he's very bossy, and his wife is even more so*; *see also* SO-SO

◊ **and so on** [nd 'səʊ ɒn] *adverb* with other things; *he talked about plants - flowers, vegetables, and so on*

◊ **so far** ['səʊ 'fɑː] *adverb* until now; *he said he would lend me his book but so far he hasn't done so; how do you like your new job so far?*

◊ **so there!** [sə 'θeə] *phrase* that's my opinion, and it's none of your business; *I'm not coming, so there!*

◊ **so what** [səʊ 'wɒt] *phrase* what does it matter; *he may be annoyed - so what?; so what if I fail my exam, I can always take it again*

soak [səʊk] **1** *noun* action of lying in a bath for a long time; *after a game of rugby it is good to have a soak in a hot bath* **2** *verb* **(a)** to put something in a liquid for a time; *the beans should be soaked in cold water overnight* **(b)** to get or to make very wet; *I forgot my umbrella and got soaked; the rain soaked the soil*

soaked [səʊkt] *adjective* very wet; *she was soaked to the skin or was soaked through*

soaking ['səʊkɪŋ] *adjective & adverb* wet through; *don't let the dog into the kitchen - he's soaking or he's soaking wet*

soak up ['səʊk 'ʌp] *verb* to take in liquid; *use a dry cloth to soak up the water*

so-and-so ['səʊəndsəʊ] *noun (informal)* **(a)** unpleasant person; *our teacher's a real so-and-so, she won't let us do anything; the so-and-so, he's pinched my ticket!* **(b)** person whose name is not mentioned; *it's the usual story - Mrs So-and-so buys a green hat, and the next thing you know, everyone in the village wants green hats*

soap [səʊp] **1** *noun* **(a)** substance which you wash with, made from oils and usually with a pleasant smell; *there's no soap left in the bathroom; I've put a new bar of soap in the kitchen; there is a liquid soap dispenser in the gents' toilets* (NOTE: no plural in this meaning: **some soap, a bar** *or* **a cake** *or* **a piece of soap**) **(b) soap (opera)** = serial story on television about the daily lives of a set of characters; *he sat in bed watching Australian soaps* **2** *verb* to cover with soap; *there's no need to soap yourself all over, just your legs and feet*

soapbox ['səʊpbɒks] *noun* box used by a politician to stand on when making an informal speech outdoors to passers-by

soap powder ['səʊp 'paʊdə] *noun* soap in the form of powder, used in washing machines or dishwashers; *we've run out of soap powder; can you buy some soap powder next time you go to the supermarket?*

soapy ['səʊpi] *adjective* full of soap; *wash the jeans in hot soapy water*

soar [sɔː] *verb* **(a)** to fly high up into the sky; *the rocket went soaring into the night sky* **(b)** *(of bird)* to glide high in the sky without beating its wings; *we watched the gulls soaring on air currents beside the cliffs* **(c)** to go up very quickly; *food prices soared during the cold weather* (NOTE: do not confuse with **sore**)

soaring ['sɔːrɪŋ] *adjective* rising rapidly; *the soaring cost of living*

sob [sɒb] **1** *noun* short breath like a hiccup, made by someone who is crying; *you could hear the sobs as she lay on her bed; he gave a sob, and put the phone down* **2** *verb* to cry, taking short breaths like hiccups; *she lay sobbing on the bed; the little girl sobbed herself to sleep* (NOTE: **sobbing - sobbed**)

sober ['səʊbə] *adjective* **(a)** not drunk; *I wasn't drunk after the party - I was stone cold sober* **(b)** serious, not frivolous; *the sober truth is that we can't afford it; it was a very sober gathering, nobody laughed or made a joke* **(c)** dark with no bright colours; *she was wearing a sober dark grey suit*

sobering ['səʊbərɪŋ] *adjective* which makes you think seriously; *it's a sobering thought that more people die from lung cancer than from heart disease; the news had a sobering effect on the staff*

sober up ['səʊbə 'ʌp] *verb* **(a)** to recover from being drunk; *I'll talk to you again when you've sobered up a little* **(b)** to make someone sober again who has been drunk; *we gave him several cups of black coffee to sober him up*

sobriety [sə'braɪɪti] *noun (formal)* **(a)** being sober; *sobriety is unusual among English soccer fans* **(b)** serious behaviour; *sobriety is to be praised especially in people in positions of power*

so-called ['səʊkɔːld] *adjective* called by a wrong name; *one of her so-called friends stole her watch*

soccer ['sɒkə] *noun* football, a game played between two teams of eleven players with a round ball which can be kicked or headed, but not carried; *he played soccer at school and then joined his local team; they went to a soccer match last Saturday; let's have a game of soccer; he spends all his time watching soccer on TV; rival soccer fans fought in the street; compare* RUGGER (NOTE: the game is called **football** in most countries, but is generally called **soccer** in the USA to distinguish it from American football)

sociable ['səʊʃəbl] *adjective* friendly, liking the company of other people; *our neighbours are not very sociable - they haven't talked to us once in the last six months; I don't think I'll go to her party - I'm not feeling very sociable at the moment*

social ['səʊʃl] **1** *adjective* **(a)** referring to human society; *inequality leads to social conflict; an area with very serious social problems;* **social science** = study of people and the society they live in, including sociology, history, economics, etc.; **social security** = money or help provided by the government to people who need it; *he lives on social security payments;* **social services** = state services to help people with family problems; *the children are being looked after by social services;* **the social system** = the way in which a society is organized; *see also* EXCLUSION **(b)** referring to friendly contact with other people; *we are organizing some social events for the visiting students; not being able to make conversation is a terrible social handicap; we don't have much social life nowadays* **2** *noun (old)* party for the members of an organization; *the old people's club is holding a social next Saturday*

social democracy ['səʊʃl də'mɒkrəsi] *noun* belief that changes should be made to the structure of society to make it more egalitarian, with some state involvement in industry and welfare, without removing private capitalism

social democrat ['səʊʃl 'deməkræt] *noun* **(a)** person who believes in some social change and some state involvement in industry and welfare **(b) Social Democrat** = person who supports or belongs to a Social Democratic Party; *the Social Democrats are in the majority in some areas of the country*

Social Democratic Party ['səʊʃl demə'krætɪk 'pɑːti] *noun* party that believes in some social change and some state involvement in industry and welfare, but without going as far as a socialist party

socialism ['səuʃəlɪzm] *noun* (a) ideas and beliefs of socialists, that the means of production and distribution should belong to the people, that people should be cared for by the state and that all wealth should be shared equally; *his book explains the principles of socialism* (b) political system where the state is run on socialist principles; *under socialism, this factory was owned by the state*

socialist ['səuʃəlɪst] 1 *adjective* believing in socialism, being in favour of social change, wider sharing of wealth and of state-run industry and welfare; **socialist party** = political party which follow the principles of socialism; *the socialist party won the last elections* 2 *noun* person who believes in socialism; *he's been a socialist all his life*

socialize ['səuʃəlaɪz] *verb* to meet people for friendly talk and activities; *the outing is an opportunity for people to socialize and get to know each other better; we don't socialize much with the people in our street*

social life ['səuʃl 'laɪf] *noun* life involving other people, going to parties, films, etc.; *with two babies under two years old, they have no social life whatsoever*

socially ['səuʃəli] *adverb* (a) in a friendly way, outside business; *I know her from work but I've never met her socially; they get on very well socially* (b) with respect to other people or society; *these policies are socially divisive; the socially unacceptable behaviour of football hooligans*

social order ['səuʃl 'ɔːdə] *noun* arrangement of society, and the classes within it; *the republicans have promised a new social order; with the revolution, the old social order came to an end*

social sciences ['səuʃl 'saɪənsɪz] *noun* academic studies referring to society and people, such as anthropology, sociology, politics, etc.; *the course is given by the Department of Social Sciences*

social work ['səuʃl 'wɜːk] *noun* work done to help people with family or financial problems; *the social work department of the local authority; she does social work among the immigrant population*

social worker ['səuʃl 'wɜːkə] *noun* person who works to help people with family or financial problems; *the old people get a weekly visit by a social worker*

society [sə'saɪəti] *noun* (a) a large group of people, usually all the people living in a country, considered as an organized community; *society needs to be protected against criminals; a free and democratic society; a member of society;* the **affluent society** = type of society where most people are rich; **a consumer society** = type of society where consumers are encouraged to buy goods (b) club or association of people who have the same interests; *he belongs to the local drama society; see also* BUILDING SOCIETY (NOTE: plural is **societies**)

socio-economic ['səusiəuiːkə'nɒmɪk] *adjective* referring to social and economic conditions; *the socio-economic system in capitalist countries;* **socio-economic groups** = groups in society divided according to income and position; *they don't belong to any of the socio-economic groups as defined in this textbook*

sociological [səusiə'lɒdʒɪkl] *adjective* referring to people and society, and the way in which society changes; *he is studying the sociological effects of TV*

sociologist [səusɪ'ɒlədʒɪst] *noun* person who studies people and society and the way society changes; *sociologists studying the urban poor have come to some surprising conclusions*

sociology [səusɪ'ɒlədʒi] *noun* the study of social systems and how people live in society; *he's our new sociology professor; this course is given in the sociology department*

sock [sɒk] 1 *noun* (a) piece of clothing worn on your foot inside a shoe; *he's almost ready - he only has to put on his socks and shoes; I've just bought a pair of socks;* **football socks** = special socks for playing football; **knee socks** = long socks which go up as far as the knees *(informal)* **to pull your socks up** = to try to do better; *he'll have to pull his socks up or he'll lose his job* (b) *(informal)* punch; *she gave him a sock in the jaw* 2 *verb (informal)* to hit someone hard; *she socked the mugger on the jaw*

socket ['sɒkɪt] *noun* (a) **(electric) socket** = holes into which a plug can be fitted; *there is a socket on the wall that you can plug the vacuum cleaner into; this plug doesn't fit that socket;* **light socket** = part of a lamp where the bulb is fitted (b) hollow part in a bone, into which another bone fits; *the tip of the femur fits into a socket in the pelvis*

sod [sɒd] *noun* (a) *(slang)* unpleasant or nasty man; *get away from me, you dirty sod!* (b) *(slang)* person who needs sympathy; *the poor old sod has nowhere to live* (c) *(formal)* piece of soil with grass growing on it; *the mayor cut the first sod for the new town hall*

soda ['səudə] *noun* (a) **soda (water)** = water made fizzy by carbon dioxide into it; *he had a whisky and soda;* **ice cream soda** = sweet fizzy drink mixed with ice cream (b) **baking soda** = sodium bicarbonate, used in baking to make cakes, etc., rise; *add a teaspoonful of baking soda to the cake mixture*

sodden ['sɒdn] *adjective* wet through; *the first priority was to get the children out of their sodden clothing and into a warm bath*

sodium ['səudiəm] *noun* soft white metal, which can catch fire, and is only found combined with other substances; **sodium bicarbonate** = baking soda; **sodium chloride** = salt (NOTE: Chemical element: chemical symbol: Na; atomic number: 11)

sofa ['səufə] *noun* long comfortable seat with a soft back; *he was asleep on the sofa* (NOTE: also called a **settee**)

sofabed ['səufəbed] *noun* type of sofa which can be folded out to form a bed; *you can sleep on the sofabed in the lounge*

soft [sɒft] *adjective* (a) not hard, which moves easily when pressed; *there are big soft armchairs in the lobby of the hotel; I don't like soft seats in a car; do you like soft ice cream?* (b) not loud; *when she spoke, her voice was so soft that we could hardly hear her; soft music was playing in the background* (c) not bright; *soft lighting makes a room look warm* (d) **soft on** = lenient towards; *judges were accused of being soft on crime;* **to have a soft spot for** = to like very much; *she has a soft spot for the PE instructor* (NOTE: **softer - softest**)

soft-boiled ['sɒft'bɔɪld] *adjective* (egg) which has been cooked in boiling water for a short time so that the yolk is hot but still liquid; *I prefer my eggs soft-boiled; here are the two soft-boiled eggs that you ordered*

softcover 729 solely

softcover ['sɒftkʌvə] *noun* **softcover edition** = book bound in paper, as opposed to a hardcover edition; *the hardcover edition is now out of print, and only the softcover is available* (NOTE: also called **paperback**)

soft currency ['sɒft 'kʌrənsi] *noun* currency of a country with a weak economy, which is cheap to buy and difficult to exchange for other currencies; *these goods cannot be paid for in soft currency* (NOTE: the opposite is **hard currency**)

soft drink ['sɒft 'drɪŋk] *noun* drink which is not alcoholic; *I'll just have a soft drink because I'm driving; we've got soft drinks for the children*

soft drugs ['sɒft 'drʌgz] *noun* drugs like marijuana, which are less addictive, but still illegal (NOTE: the opposite, i.e. drugs which are dangerous and addictive, are **hard drugs**)

soften ['sɒfn] *verb* to make something soft, to become soft; *heat the chocolate gently to soften it; her voice softened when she spoke to the children;* **to soften someone up** = to make someone weaker before asking for something, or before launching an attack; *can you try and soften him up a bit before I ask to borrow the car?; bombing raids were made to soften up the enemy defences*

soft fruit ['sɒft 'fruːt] *noun* small fruit, like currants, raspberries, strawberries, etc., which do not have hard skins; *soft fruit should be eaten soon after they've been picked*

soft furnishings ['sɒft 'fɜːnɪʃɪŋz] *noun* curtains, cushions, etc., as opposed to tables and other pieces of furniture; *the soft furnishings department is on the third floor*

softie *or* **softy** ['sɒfti] *noun (informal)* person who is too kind and generous, and who can easily be persuaded to do what you want; *he's just a big softie - his little niece can get him to do anything she wants; our Alsatian is a big softie - he wouldn't hurt anyone*

softly ['sɒfli] *adverb* **(a)** in a gentle way; *I touched her arm softly* **(b)** quietly, not loudly; *she spoke so softly that we couldn't hear what she said; the burglars crept softly up the stairs* **(c)** not brightly; *the lights were shining softly across the lawn*

soft landing ['sɒft 'lændɪŋ] *noun* **(a)** gentle landing (of a parachute, spacecraft, etc.); *the space capsule made a soft landing in the sea* **(b)** way of fighting inflation, which does not cause unemployment or a fall in the standard of living; *the government is still hoping for a soft landing in a year's time*

soft palate ['sɒft 'pælət] *noun* back part of the palate which leads to the uvula (NOTE: the front part is the **hard palate**)

software ['sɒftweə] *noun* computer programs which are put into a computer to make it work, as opposed to the machine itself; *what word-processing software do you use?; compare* HARDWARE (NOTE: no plural)

softwood ['sɒftwʊd] *noun* **(a)** wood from pine trees and other conifers which can be cut easily; *we used softwood panels for the walls of the study* **(b)** fast-growing trees, such as pines or other conifers, which produce such wood; *the softwood forests of Finland; compare* HARDWOOD

softy ['sɒfti] *see* SOFTIE

soggy ['sɒgi] *adjective* wet and soft; *these carrots are overcooked - they're quite soggy; if you put tomato*

sandwiches into plastic bags they will go soggy (NOTE: **soggier - soggiest**)

soil [sɔɪl] **1** *noun* earth in which plants grow; *put some soil in the plant pot and then sow your flower seeds; this soil's too poor for growing fruit trees* **2** *verb* to make dirty; *his overalls were soiled by black oil and rust; use more washing powder if the clothes are heavily soiled; see also* SHOP-SOILED

solace ['sɒləs] *noun (formal)* comfort; *after his wife died he found solace in the study of ancient churches;* **to be a solace to someone** = to comfort someone; *his daughter has been a considerable solace to him*

solar ['səʊlə] *adjective* referring to the sun; **a solar eclipse** = situation when part or all of the sun disappears, because the moon passes between the earth and the sun; **solar energy** *or* **solar power** = electricity produced from the radiation of the sun; *my calculator runs on solar power;* **solar power is a renewable source of energy; solar panel** = a group of special electric cells used to turn the sun's energy into electricity; **solar system** = the sun and the planets which orbit round it; *there are nine planets in the solar system* (NOTE: the similar word referring to the moon is **lunar**, and to the stars is **stellar**)

sold [səʊld] *see* SELL

solder ['səʊldə] **1** *noun* soft metal which melts easily, and is used to attach pieces of metal together; *put a strip of solder along the crack and heat it with a soldering-iron* **2** *verb* to repair or attach using hot metal; *he soldered the broken handle back onto the watering can*

soldering-iron ['səʊldərɪŋ 'aɪən] *noun* device, with a very hot heated tip, which melts solder to attach pieces of metal together

soldier ['səʊldʒə] **1** *noun* person serving in the army; *here's a photograph of my father as a soldier; we were just in time to see the soldiers march past; enemy soldiers blew up the bridge; the children are playing with their toy soldiers* **2** *verb* **to soldier on** = to continue doing something, in spite of difficulties; *even though sales are down, we must soldier on; she's soldiering on with her preparations for the exam*

sold out ['səʊld 'aʊt] *adjective* no longer in stock, because all the stock has been sold; *the book was sold out within a week*

sole [səʊl] **1** *noun* **(a)** underneath side of your foot; *he tickled the soles of her feet* **(b)** main underneath part of a shoe, but not the heel; *these shoes need mending - I've got holes in both soles* **(c)** relatively small flat white sea fish; *he ordered grilled sole* (NOTE: the two varieties of the fish found in Britain are **Dover sole** and **lemon sole**; plural in this meaning is **sole**) **2** *verb* to put a new sole on a shoe; *I want these shoes soled and heeled, please* **3** *adjective* only; belonging to one person; *their sole aim is to make money; she was the sole survivor from the crash; I have sole responsibility for what goes on in this office; he has the sole right to it* = he is the only person allowed to use it; **sole agency** = agreement to be the only person to represent a company or to sell a product in a certain area; *he has the sole agency for Ford cars;* **sole trader** = person who runs a business by himself but has not registered it as a company (NOTE: do not confuse with **soul**)

solely ['səʊli] *adverb* **(a)** only; *the machine was designed solely for that purpose* **(b)** without other people being involved; *he was solely to blame for what happened*

solemn ['sɒləm] *adjective* **(a)** serious and formal, when it would be wrong to laugh; *the doctor looked very solemn and shook his head*; *at the most solemn moment of the ceremony someone's mobile phone rang* **(b)** that should be treated as very serious and not to be broken; *he made a solemn promise never to smoke again*; **solemn and binding agreement** = agreement that is not legally binding, but which all parties are supposed to obey

solemnity [sə'lemnɪti] *noun* being serious; *the children were not at all intimidated by the solemnity of the occasion*

solemnize ['sɒlemnaɪz] *verb (formal)* to perform a marriage or other religious ceremony; *the marriage will be solemnized in the cathedral*

solicit [sə'lɪsɪt] *verb* **(a)** to solicit orders = to ask for orders, to try to get people to order goods **(b)** to offer sex to people; *prostitutes were openly soliciting outside the station*

solicitor [sə'lɪsɪtə] *noun* **(a)** qualified lawyer who gives advice to members of the public and acts for them in legal matters; *I went to see my solicitor about making a will*; *she works as a clerk in a solicitor's office* **(b)** *US* person who comes to the door collecting for charity

solid ['sɒlɪd] **1** *adjective* **(a)** hard, not liquid; *the water in the tank had frozen solid*; *she is allowed some solid food* **(b)** firm, strong; *his wealth is built on a solid base of property and shares*; *is the table solid enough to stand on?* **(c)** made only of one material; *the box is made of solid silver* **(d)** for six hours solid = for six hours without stopping; *negotiations went on for nine hours solid* (NOTE: **solider - solidest**) **2** *noun* **(a)** hard substance which is not liquid; *many solids melt when heated, and become liquids* **(b)** food, as opposed to drink; *the baby is beginning to eat solids*

solidarity [sɒlɪ'dærɪti] *noun* general common interest with other people; *we want to show our solidarity with the strikers*

solidification [səlɪdɪfɪ'keɪʃn] *noun* becoming solid; *cooling causes the solidification of lava*

solidify [sə'lɪdɪfaɪ] *verb* to become solid; *fat solidifies at low temperatures*

solidity [sə'lɪdɪti] *noun* being solid; *the surveyor checked the solidity of the walls*; *the solidity of the Socialist-Green Party alliance is in doubt*

solidly ['sɒlɪdli] *adverb* in a firm way; *their house is very solidly built*; *the staff are solidly behind their manager*

solidus ['sɒlɪdəs] *noun* slash, printing sign (/) used to show an alternative

solitary ['sɒlɪtri] *adjective* **(a)** single, one only; *it was late November, and a solitary tourist was sitting in the waterfront café*; *I don't remember a solitary occasion when he helped with the washing up* **(b)** lonely, living alone; *my sister lives a solitary life in the country*; **solitary confinement** = being kept alone in a cell, without being able to see or speak to other prisoners; *she was kept in solitary confinement for six months*

solitude ['sɒlɪtjuːd] *noun* state of being alone; *she lived in complete solitude on an island in the lake*; *he finds solitude unbearable*

solo ['səʊləʊ] **1** *noun* piece of music played or sung by one person alone; *she played a violin solo* (NOTE: plural is **solos**) **2** *adjective* carried out by one person alone; *she gave a solo performance in the Albert Hall*; *a piece for solo trumpet*; *he crashed on his first solo flight* **3** *adverb* done by one person alone; *he flew solo across the Atlantic* **4** *verb US* to do something solo; *she soloed before a large audience*; *you need hours of flying practice before you can solo*

soloist ['səʊləʊɪst] *noun* musician who plays a solo; *she was the soloist in Elgar's Cello Concerto*

solstice ['sɒlstɪs] *noun* one of the two times of the year when the sun is at its furthest point north or south of the equator; **summer solstice** = 21st June, the longest day in the Northern Hemisphere, when the sun is at its furthest point south of the equator; **winter solstice** = 21st December, the shortest day in the Northern Hemisphere, when the sun is at its furthest point north of the equator

soluble ['sɒljʊbl] *adjective* **(a)** which can be dissolved; *a tablet of soluble aspirin*; **the pill is soluble in water** *or* **is water-soluble** **(b)** which can be solved; *the problem is simply not soluble*; *the difficulties are soluble, given a little money*

solution [sə'luːʃn] *noun* **(a)** action of solving a problem; *the solution of the problem is taking longer than expected* **(b)** answer to a problem; *the programmer came up with a solution to the computer problem*; *we think we have found a solution to the problem of where to stay on holiday*; *the solutions to the quiz are at the back of the book* **(c)** mixture of a solid substance dissolved in a liquid; *bathe your eye in a weak salt solution*

solve [sɒlv] *verb* to find an answer to; *the loan will solve some of his financial problems*; *he tried to solve the riddle*

solvency ['sɒlvənsi] *noun* being able to pay all your debts; *we have doubts about the solvency of the company*

solvent ['sɒlvənt] **1** *adjective* having enough money to pay debts; *when he bought the company it was barely solvent* **2** *noun* **(a)** liquid in which a solid substance can be dissolved **(b)** strong glue used for sticking plastics; **solvent abuse** = form of drug abuse where addicts inhale the fumes from solvent; *deaths among teenagers from solvent abuse* (NOTE: also called **glue sniffing**)

sombre *US* **somber** ['sɒmbə] *adjective* dark and gloomy; *the report painted a sombre picture of the country's economic future*; *the painting of the prison yard is one of Van Gogh's most sombre pictures*

some [sʌm] **1** *adjective & pronoun* **(a)** a certain number of; *some young drivers drive much too fast*; *some books were damaged in the fire*; *some days it was so hot that we just stayed by the swimming pool all day*; *can you cut some more slices of bread?*; *she bought some oranges and bananas*; *we've just picked a basket of apples - would you like some?*; **some of** = a few; *some of the students are ill*; *some of these apples are too green* **(b)** a certain amount; *can you buy some bread when you go to town?*; *can I have some more coffee?*; *to some extent it's an interesting problem*; *her illness is of some concern to her family* **(c)** *(followed by a singular noun)* referring to a person or thing you cannot identify; *some man just knocked on the door and tried to sell me a magazine*; *I read it in some book*

I borrowed from the library; we saw it in some shop or other in Regent Street **(d)** *(referring to a period of time or a distance)* *don't wait for me, I may be some time; their house is some way away from the railway station* (NOTE: **some** is used with plural nouns and with nouns which have no plural: **some people, some apples, some bread,** etc.) **2** *adverb* approximately, more or less; *some fifty people came to the meeting; the house is some sixty years old*

somebody *or* **someone** ['sʌmbədi or 'sʌmwɒn] *pronoun* a certain person; *somebody is sitting on my chair; I can't talk any longer - there's someone waiting outside the phone box; somebody phoned about an order; I know someone who can fix your car*

some day ['sʌm 'deɪ] *adverb* at some time in the future; *some day I'll get round to cleaning out the garage*

somehow ['sʌmhaʊ] *adverb* by some means, although you don't know how; *somehow we must get back home by 6 o'clock; the work has to be done somehow*

someone ['sʌmwɒn] *see* SOMEBODY

someplace ['sʌmpleɪs] *adverb US* somewhere; *haven't I seen you before someplace?; is there someplace else we can talk?*

something ['sʌmθɪŋ] *pronoun* **(a)** a certain thing; *something's gone wrong with the TV; can I have something to drink, please?; there's something about her that I don't like* **(b)** important thing; *come in and sit down, I've got something to tell you* **(c)** approximate amount; *it cost us something around fifty pounds; something like 20% of the students can't spell* **(d)** approximate name; *he's called Nick or Dick, or something like that; it's a fish or mollusc or something, anyway it lives in salt water*

sometime ['sʌmtaɪm] *adverb* at a certain time which is not specified; *the accident happened sometime after midnight*

sometimes ['sʌmtaɪmz] *adverb* occasionally, at various times; *sometimes it gets quite cold in June; sometimes the car starts easily, and sometimes it won't start at all; she sometimes comes to see us when she's in town on business*

somewhat ['sʌmwɒt] *adverb* more than a little, rather; *it's a somewhat difficult question to answer; their system is somewhat old-fashioned; we were somewhat surprised to see him there*

somewhere ['sʌmweə] *adverb* **(a)** in or at a certain place which is not specified; *I left my umbrella somewhere when I was in London; let's go somewhere else, this pub is full; his parents live somewhere in Germany* (NOTE: American English also uses **someplace: we can go someplace else**) **(b)** **somewhere around** *or* **somewhere between** *or* **somewhere in the region of** = approximately; *somewhere between 50 and 60 people turned up for the meeting; he has collected somewhere in the region of 25,000 books*

somnolent ['sɒmnələnt] *adjective* (formal) **(a)** almost asleep; *the museum was guarded by two somnolent caretakers* **(b)** which makes you feel sleepy; *his speech had a somnolent effect on the audience*

son [sʌn] *noun* male child of a father or mother; *they have a large family - two sons and four daughters; her*

son has got married at last; their youngest son is in hospital

sonar ['səʊnɑː] *noun* device that uses sound waves to measure the depth of water or to find objects under water; *with the latest sonar equipment, fishing boats can detect shoals of fish from miles away*

sonata [sə'nɑːtə] *noun* piece of music in three or four movements for one or more instruments, accompanied by an orchestra, piano, harpsichord, etc.; *he was the soloist in Beethoven's Violin Sonata*

song [sɒŋ] *noun* **(a)** words which are sung; *she was singing a song in the bath; the group's latest song has just come out on CD; the soldiers marched along, singing a song* **(b)** (informal) **for a song** = for very little money; *she bought it for a song in a flea market; he made a great song and dance about it* = he made a great fuss about it; *they made a terrible song and dance about having to wait for a taxi* **(c)** special sound made by a bird; *I'm sure that's the song of a robin - look, he's over there!*

songwriter ['sɒŋraɪtə] *noun* person who writes popular songs; *George Gershwin was a famous American songwriter*

sonic ['sɒnɪk] *adjective* referring to sound that can be heard by the human ear; **sonic boom** = loud noise made by an aircraft travelling through the air at or faster than the speed of sound

son-in-law ['sʌnɪnlɔː] *noun* husband of a daughter; *my son-in-law's a mechanic* (NOTE: plural is **sons-in-law**)

sonnet ['sɒnɪt] *noun* poem with fourteen lines; *he composed a series of sonnets to his love; she gave a reading from Shakespeare's sonnets*

COMMENT: sonnets have fixed rhyming patterns. The most usual is to have three stanzas of four lines, rhyming alternately, and then two final lines which rhyme together. This is the form of the sonnet which Shakespeare used

sonny ['sʌni] *noun* (informal) way of addressing a boy; *put that brick down, sonny!*

soon [suːn] *adverb* **(a)** in a short time from now; *don't worry, we'll soon be in Oxford; it will soon be time to go to bed; can't we meet any sooner than that?; the fire started soon after 11 o'clock* **(b)** **as soon as** = immediately; *please phone the office as soon as you get to the hotel; as soon as I put the phone down it rang again; the boss wants to see you as soon as possible* **(c)** **just as soon** = would rather, would prefer; *I'd just as soon stay at the office than go to the party; see also* RATHER, SOONER (NOTE: **sooner - soonest**)

sooner ['suːnə] *adverb* **(a)** **sooner or later** = at some time in the future; *sooner or later, they will realize that they need to save as much money as possible; she drives so fast that sooner or later she'll have an accident; sooner rather than later* = quickly rather than taking a long time; *it would be wise to reduce the staff sooner rather than later* **(b)** **the sooner the better** = it would be better to do it as soon as possible; *she should consult a lawyer, and the sooner the better* **(c)** **would sooner do something** = would prefer to do something; *do you want to come with us? - no, I'd sooner stay at home; we'd sooner live in Chicago than Detroit; would sooner + pronoun* = would prefer that;

I'd sooner she stayed at home than went out with her friends; see also RATHER, SOON

soot [sut] *noun* black deposit of carbon which rises in the smoke produced by burning coal, wood, oil, etc., and which collects on the inside surfaces of chimneys; *I poked a stick up the chimney and brought down a lot of soot*

soothe [suːð] *verb* to relieve pain, to make something less painful, to calm; *the chemist gave me a cream to soothe the rash; she managed to soothe their hurt feelings*

soothing ['suːðɪŋ] *adjective* which relieves pain, which calms; *the nurse put some soothing cream on my rash; I find this piece by Mozart very soothing*

sophisticated [səˈfɪstɪkeɪtɪd] *adjective* **(a)** knowing a lot about the way people behave, and what is stylish or fashionable; *they think smoking makes them look sophisticated* **(b)** cleverly designed, complicated (machine); *his office is full of the latest and most sophisticated computer equipment*

sophistication [səfɪstɪˈkeɪʃn] *noun* **(a)** cultured way of life; *the sophistication of life in the later Roman Empire disappeared under the attacks of the barbarians* **(b)** advanced ideas behind the construction of a machine; *the sophistication of some of these early surgical instruments seems astonishing nowadays*

sophomore [sɒfəˈmɔː] *noun US* **(a)** student in his or her second year at college **(b)** a tenth-grade high school student; *compare* FRESHMAN, SENIOR

soprano [səˈprɑːnəʊ] *noun* **(a)** high-pitched woman's singing voice; *she sings soprano in the local choir* **(b)** woman with such a voice; *the sopranos are too feeble - I can hardly hear them* (NOTE: plural is **sopranos**)

sorbet ['sɔːbeɪ] *noun* soft refreshing dessert made by freezing fruit juice to which the white of an egg is added; *a raspberry sorbet* (NOTE: American English is **sherbet**)

sorcerer, sorceress ['sɔːsərə or 'sɔːsres] *noun (in fairy tales)* person who uses sorcery; *the sorceress seemed to cast a spell over the group*

sorcery ['sɔːsəri] *noun (in fairy tales)* witchcraft, wicked magic; *it wasn't done honestly, it was done by sorcery*

sordid ['sɔːdɪd] *adjective* unpleasant or dirty; *they are trying to clear the sordid squatter huts; the minister is definitely implicated in this sordid scandal*

sore [sɔː] **1** *adjective* **(a)** rough and inflamed; painful; *he can't play tennis because he has a sore elbow* (informal) **to stick out like a sore thumb** = to be easily seen **(b)** *US* angry; *he's sore at her for telling the boss about him* (NOTE: **sorer - sorest**) **2** *noun* small wound on the skin, often producing pus; *he had sores on his back from lying in bed for a long time;* **cold sore** = inflammation round the lips caused by the herpes virus (NOTE: do not confuse with **soar**)

sorely ['sɔːli] *adverb (formal)* very much; *she will be sorely missed; they were sorely afraid that the enemy would attack*

sorghum ['sɔːgəm] *noun* cereal plant grown in arid tropical regions

sorority [səˈrɒrɪti] *noun US* student association for women; *she was asked to join the sorority* (NOTE: the equivalent for men is a **fraternity**; plural is **sororities**)

sorrow ['sɒrəʊ] **1** *noun* sadness; *he expressed his deep sorrow at her death; to his great sorrow, his collection of books was lost in the fire* **2** *verb (formal)* **to sorrow at** *or* **over something** = to be very sad because of something; *we sorrow at the suffering of the refugees*

sorrowful ['sɒrəʊfʊl] *adjective* very sad; *we are gathered together on this sorrowful occasion; the sorrowful look on her face showed how much she missed him*

sorry ['sɒri] **1** *adjective* **to be sorry** = to be sad about; *I'm sorry I can't stay for dinner; he trod on my foot and didn't say he was sorry; everyone was sorry to hear you had been ill;* **not to be sorry** = to be quite happy; *we weren't sorry to see him go* = we were glad when he left; **to feel sorry for someone** = to be sympathetic about someone's problems; to pity someone; *we all feel sorry for her - her family is always criticizing her;* **to feel sorry for yourself** = to be miserable; *he's feeling very sorry for himself - he's just been made redundant* **2** *interjection* used to excuse yourself; *sorry! I didn't see that table had been reserved; can I have another mint, please? - sorry, I haven't any left*

sort [sɔːt] **1** *noun* **(a)** type, kind; *there were all sorts of people at the meeting; I had an unpleasant sort of day at the office; what sorts of ice cream have you got?; do you like this sort of TV show?* **(b)** *(informal)* **sort of** = rather, more or less; *she was sort of expecting your phone call; we're all feeling sort of upset* **(c)** *(informal)* **of sorts** = not very good; *he made a speech of sorts at the prize-giving ceremony* **2** *verb* **(a)** to arrange in order or groups; *the apples are sorted according to size before being packed; the votes are sorted then counted;* **sorting office** = department in a post office where letters are put in order according to their addresses **(b)** to put things in order; *she is sorting index cards into alphabetical order*

sortie ['sɔːtiː] *noun* **(a)** sudden attack or bombing raid by aircraft; *they made several sorties into enemy territory* **(b)** sudden excursion; *we decided to make a sortie into the old part of the town*

sort out ['sɔːt 'aʊt] *verb* **(a)** to settle a problem; *did you sort out the hotel bill?* **(b)** to put things in order or in groups; *I must sort out the papers in this drawer; until they're sorted out, we shan't know which are our files and which are theirs* **(c)** to collect or select things of a particular kind from a mixed group of things; *sort out all the blue folders and bring them to me, please*

SOS [esəʊˈes] *noun* **(a)** the international code for showing that you are in distress (the letters 's', 'o', and 's' are repeated in Morse code); *they sent out SOS messages* **(b)** message broadcast to say that someone is ill and asking a relative to get in contact; *this is an SOS for Mr Smith, at present holidaying in Scotland, to say that his mother is dangerously ill*

so-so ['səʊsəʊ] *adjective & adverb (informal)* not very good, not very well; *how are you today? - only so-so; the results of the test were only so-so*

soufflé ['suːfleɪ] *noun* **(a)** light cooked dish, made from eggs beaten up with a savoury flavouring, eaten hot; *a cheese soufflé* **(b)** cold dessert made from beaten eggs, whipped cream and gelatine; *a lemon soufflé*

sought [sɔːt] *see* SEEK

sought-after ['sɔːt 'ɑːftə] *adjective* wanted by many people; *the skills you have are very sought-after by* *employers nowadays; this has become the most sought-after area of town*

soul [səʊl] *noun* **(a)** the spirit in a person, the part which is believed by some people to go on existing after a person dies; *do you believe your soul lives on when your body dies?; from the depths of his soul he longed to be free;* **to be the life and soul of a party** = to make a party go well **(b)** person; *poor soul! she sits at home all day, and doesn't have anyone to go to see her; she's a cheerful old soul* (NOTE: do not confuse with **sole**)

soulful ['səʊlfʊl] *adjective* with a lot of sad feeling; *try to make your singing more soulful; the soulful chants of the boatmen on the river*

soul mate ['səʊl 'meɪt] *noun* person with whom you have a similar feelings

soul music ['səʊl 'mjuːzɪk] *noun* popular music which conveys deep feelings and which developed from blues and gospel; *a radio station that plays only soul music*

sound [saʊnd] **1** *noun* noise, something which you can hear; *sounds of music came from the street; I thought I heard the sound of guns; please can you turn down the sound on the TV when I'm on the phone?; she crept out of her bedroom and we didn't hear a sound;* **the speed of sound** = the rate at which sound travels; *Concorde flies faster than the speed of sound;* **I don't like the sound of that** = I do not think that is a very good thing **2** *verb* **(a)** to make a noise; *sound your horn when you come to a corner; they sounded the alarm after two prisoners escaped* **(b)** to seem; *it sounds as if he's made an unfortunate choice; the book sounds interesting according to what I've heard;* **that sounds strange** = it seems strange to me; **that sounds like a car** = I think I can hear a car; **that sounds like my father** = (i) that is like the way my father talks; (ii) I think I can hear my father coming; (iii) that's typical of the way my father usually behaves **3** *adjective* **(a)** in good condition, not rotten; *most of the walls of the house are sound;* **sound in wind and limb** = fit and healthy; **he is of sound mind** = he is not mad **(b)** sensible, trustworthy; *he gave us some very sound advice* **(c)** deep (sleep); *I was awoken from a sound sleep by the ringing of the doorbell* (NOTE: **sounder - soundest**) **4** *adverb* deeply; *the children were sound asleep when the police came*

soundbite ['saʊndbaɪt] *noun* short phrase, usually spoken by a politician, especially made so as to be broadcast on radio or TV; *he's a master of the soundbite*

sound effects ['saʊnd ɪ'fekts] *noun* artificial sounds used to give the impression of the real thing; *all the sound effects for the film were produced electronically*

soundly ['saʊndli] *adverb* deeply; thoroughly; *the baby slept soundly during the thunderstorm; they were soundly beaten in the semi-final*

sound out ['saʊnd 'aʊt] *verb* **to sound someone out about something** = to ask someone's opinion about something; *I'll sound out the other members of the committee to see what they think*

soundproof ['saʊndpruːf] **1** *adjective* which does not allow sound to pass through; *the radio commentators sit in a soundproof cabin* **2** *verb* to make a building soundproof; *all the bedrooms in the hotel are soundproofed*

soundtrack ['saʊndtræk] *noun* track of a film on which the sound is recorded; *the music from the soundtrack of the film; the soundtrack wasn't properly synchronized with the pictures*

soup [suːp] *noun* liquid food which you eat hot from a bowl at the beginning of a meal, usually made from meat, fish or vegetables; *we have onion soup or mushroom soup today; does anyone want soup?; a bowl of hot soup is always welcome on a cold day; if you're hungry, open a tin of soup;* **soup bowl** or **soup plate** or **soup spoon** = special bowl or plate or spoon for eating soup (NOTE: no plural: **some soup, a bowl of soup**)

souped-up ['suːpt 'ʌp] *adjective* (car) with an engine which has been adapted to make it go faster; *he was driving a souped-up Mini*

sour [saʊə] **1** *adjective* **(a)** with a sharp bitter taste; *if the lemonade is too sour, add some sugar; nobody likes sour milk;* (*informal*) **sour grapes** = feeling bitter about something which you want but can't have; *he said that the latest model was no better than the older ones, but that was just sour grapes* **(b)** **to go sour** = (i) to take on a sharp taste; (ii) to become unpleasant; *the cream has gone sour; after a few weeks, the whole deal began to go sour* (NOTE: **sourer - sourest**) **2** *verb* to make unpleasant; *relations between the two countries have been soured by the incident*

source [sɔːs] *noun* **(a)** place where something comes from; *I think the source of the infection is in one of your teeth; the source of the river is in the mountains; you must declare income from all sources to the tax office;* **income which is taxed at source** = income where the tax is removed before the income is paid **(b)** person or thing which is the cause of something; *the children are a constant source of worry; polluted water is a possible source of cholera*

sourcing ['sɔːsɪŋ] *noun* getting supplies from a certain place or supplier; *the sourcing of spare parts from Japan*

south [saʊθ] **1** *noun* **(a)** direction facing towards the sun at midday, direction to your left when you are facing the direction where the sun sets; *look south from the mountain, and you will see the city in the distance; the city is to the south of the mountain range; the wind is blowing from the south* **(b)** part of a country to the south of the rest; *the south of the country is warmer than the north; she went to live in the south of England* **2** *adjective* referring to the south; *the south coast is popular for holidaymakers; cross to the south side of the river;* **south wind** = wind which blows from the south **3** *adverb* towards the south; *many birds fly south for the winter; go due south for two kilometres, and you will see the village on your left; the river flows south into the Mediterranean*

South Africa [saʊθ 'æfrɪkə] *noun* large country in the most southerly part of Africa; *South Africa is a major economic power in Africa* (NOTE: capital: **Pretoria**; people: **South Africans**; languages: **Xhosa, Swazi, Zulu, English, Afrikaans**; currency: **rand**)

South African [saʊθ 'æfrɪkən] **1** *adjective* referring to South Africa; *South African wine is exported everywhere; the South African rugby team are called the Springboks* **2** *noun* person from South Africa; *the South Africans beat us again at cricket*

South America ['saʊθ ə'merɪkə] *noun* southern part of the American continent containing Brazil,

Argentina, Chile and several other countries; *Brazil is the largest country in South America*; *he is hiding from the police somewhere in South America*

southbound ['saʊθbaʊnd] *adjective* travelling towards the south; *there has been an accident on the southbound carriageway of the motorway*; *all southbound trains have been cancelled*

south-east [saʊθ'iːst] *adjective, adverb & noun* direction between south and east; *South-East Asia is an important trading area*; *house prices are higher in the south-east than anywhere else in England*; *the river runs south-east from here*

south-easterly [saʊθ'iːstəli] *adjective* (wind) which blows from the south-east; (direction) towards the south-east; *the plane was following a south-easterly route*

south-eastern ['saʊθ'iːstən] *adjective* referring to the south-east; situated in the south-east; *Kent is a south-eastern county where apples grow well*

southerly ['sʌðəli] **1** *adjective* **(a)** (wind) from the south; *the southerly wind melted the snow* **(b)** in a southerly direction = towards the south; *I drove in a southerly direction with the sun shining full in my face* **2** *noun* wind blowing from the south; *the southerlies blew the yacht off course*

southern ['sʌðən] *adjective* of the south; *the southern part of the country is warmer than the north*

southerner ['sʌðənə] *noun* person who comes from or lives in the south; *he was a southerner who had never been to New York before*

South Pole ['saʊθ 'pəʊl] *noun* furthest point at the south of the earth; *they were trying to reach the South Pole*

south-west [saʊθ'west] *adjective, adverb & noun* direction between south and west; *we need to head south-west for two miles*; *Arizona is in the south-west of the United States*

south-westerly [saʊθ'westəli] *adjective* (wind) which blows from the south-west; (direction) towards the south-west; *a south-westerly wind*; *we were following a south-westerly direction*

south-western [saʊθ'westən] *adjective* referring to the south-west; situated in the south-west; *the south-western corner of England includes Cornwall and Devon*

souvenir [suːvə'niːə] *noun* thing bought which reminds you of the place where you bought it; *I bought a tartan scarf as a souvenir of Scotland*; *keep it as a souvenir of your visit*; *they were selling souvenir programmes of the Test Match*; **souvenir shop** = shop which sells souvenirs; *there are too many souvenir shops on the seafront*

sovereign ['sɒvrɪn] **1** *noun* **(a)** ruler, a king or queen; *the sovereign is not supposed to become involved in party politics* **(b)** former British gold coin worth one pound; *I found a bag of gold sovereigns hidden in the attic* **2** *adjective* **sovereign state** = self-governing country

sovereignty ['sɒvrɪnti] *noun* total power of government; *the country has claimed sovereignty over the islands*

sow 1 [saʊ] *noun* mature female pig; *our sow has had eight piglets* **2** [səʊ] *verb* to put seeds into soil so that they germinate and become plants; *peas and beans*

should be sown in April; *sow the seed thinly in fine soil* (NOTE: **sowing - sowed - has sown** [səʊn])

soya *or* **soy** ['sɔɪə *or* sɔɪ] *noun* plant which produces edible beans which have a high protein and fat content and very little starch; *meat substitutes are often made from soya*; **soya sauce** *or* **soy sauce** = salty dark sauce made from soya beans; *Chinese dishes are often seasoned with soy sauce*

spa [spɑː] *noun* **(a)** place where mineral water comes out of the ground naturally and where people go to drink or bathe in it because of its medicinal properties; *he spends two weeks every summer at a French spa*; **spa town** = town which has a spa; *Bath is the oldest spa town in England* **(b)** exercise and health centre in a hotel

space [speɪs] **1** *noun* **(a)** empty place between other things; *there's a space to park your car over there*; *write your name and reference number in the space at the top of the paper* **(b)** area which is available for something; *his desk takes up too much space*; **floor space** = area of the floor in a building; **office space** = area available for offices or used by offices; *we are looking for extra office space for our new staff* **(c)** **(outer) space** = area beyond the earth's atmosphere; *the first man in space was the Russian Yuri Gagarin*; *this is a photograph of the Earth taken from space*; *could someone be sending messages from outer space?* **(d)** **open spaces** = open country, with no buildings; *Canada's wide open spaces* **(e)** in a short **space of time** = in a little time; *you can't do that in a short space of time, you'll need several weeks at least*; *in a very short space of time the burglars had filled their van with furniture* **2** *verb* **to space things out** = to place things at intervals, with gaps between them; *repayments can be spaced out over a period of ten years*; *make sure the text is evenly spaced out on the page*

space bar ['speɪsbɑː] *noun* long bar at the bottom of a typewriter or computer keyboard which inserts a single space into text; *I use my thumb on the space bar when I type*

spacecraft *or* **spaceship** ['speɪskrɑːft *or* 'speɪsʃɪp] *noun* vehicle in which people can travel into space; *they're building a spacecraft for an expedition to Mars*; *in science fiction, spaceships travel at the speed of light*; *the spacecraft is expected to reenter the earth's atmosphere on Sunday*

space shuttle ['speɪs 'ʃʌtl] *noun* type of plane which is launched by a rocket, then flies in space and returns eventually to earth so that it can be used for another trip; *the space shuttle will be launched next week*

space station ['speɪs 'steɪʃn] *noun* satellite which orbits the earth in which people can live and carry out scientific experiments; *a new team of astronauts has moved into the space station*

spacesuit ['speɪssuːt] *noun* specially made clothes for people who travel in space; *the astronauts in their spacesuits waved before entering the spacecraft*

space walk ['speɪs 'wɔːk] *noun* action of getting out of a spacecraft and moving around outside it, usually in order to repair it

spacing ['speɪsɪŋ] *noun* spaces between characters or between lines in printing; *the spacing isn't even in this line*; **double spacing** = typing where a white line is left between lines of text; **single spacing** = typing where there is no white line between lines of text

spacious ['speɪʃəs] *adjective* very large, with plenty of space; *they live in a spacious flat in Hampstead*

spade [speɪd] *noun* **(a)** common gardening tool with a wide square blade at the end of a long handle, used for digging; *he handed me the spade and told me to start digging*; **to do the spade work** = to do the uninteresting work in advance before the main work is done; *I get my assistant to do most of the spade work*; **to call a spade a spade** = to say exactly what you think without trying to hide your opinions by being polite; *if she's not satisfied, she's not afraid to call a spade a spade* **(b)** small spade, used by children; *the children took their buckets and spades to the beach* **(c) spades** = one of the black suits in a pack of cards; *my last two cards were the ten and the ace of spades*; *she played the king of spades* (NOTE: the other black suit is **clubs**; **hearts** and **diamonds** are the red suits)

spaghetti [spə'geti] *noun* long thin strips of pasta, cooked and eaten with a sauce; *I ordered spaghetti with a special cream sauce*; **spaghetti bolognese** = spaghetti with meat and tomato sauce; *she ordered spaghetti bolognese*

Spain [speɪn] *proper noun* country in southern Europe, to the south of France and the east of Portugal; *lots of people go to Spain for their holidays*; *we are going to Spain next July* (NOTE: capital: **Madrid**; people: **the Spanish** or **the Spaniards**; language: **Spanish**; currency: **peseta, euro**)

span [spæn] **1** *noun* **(a)** width of wings, of an arch, etc.; *each section of the bridge has a span of fifty feet* **(b)** length of time; *over a span of five years* or *over a five-year span* **2** *verb* to stretch across space or time; *her career spanned thirty years*; *the bridge will span the river* (NOTE: **spanning - spanned**)

Spaniard ['spænjəd] *noun* person from Spain; *we have several Spaniards working in our office*

spaniel ['spænjəl] *noun* type of dog with large ears that droop down

Spanish ['spænɪʃ] **1** *adjective* referring to Spain; *I want to change my pounds into Spanish money* **2** *noun* language spoken in Spain and many countries of Latin America; *he's studying French and Spanish in the modern languages department*

spank [spæŋk] *verb* to hit a child's bottom as a punishment; *if you do that again I'll spank you!*

spanking ['spæŋkɪŋ] **1** *adjective* (old) **spanking bright** or **spanking new** = very bright or very new; *he gave his grandson a spanking new sports car* **2** *noun* action of being spanked; *if I catch you again you'll get a spanking*

spanner ['spænə] *noun* metal tool with an opening which fits round a nut and which can be twisted to undo the nut or tighten it; *I need a smaller spanner to tighten this nut*; **to throw a spanner in the works** = to stop things happening or to make things difficult by causing problems; *his illness threw a spanner in the works*

spar [spɑː] **1** *noun* **(a)** main beam running along the wing of an aircraft **(b)** ship's mast or a wooden beam for holding the sails; *two spars were broken in the gale* **2** *verb* to practise boxing with someone; *he sparred every morning before the fight* (NOTE: **sparring - sparred**)

spare [speə] **1** *adjective* extra, not being used; *I always take a spare pair of shoes when I travel*; **spare parts** = pieces used to put in place of broken parts of a car, etc.; *I can't get spare parts for that type of washing machine*; **spare time** = time when you are not at work; *he built himself a car in his spare time*; **spare wheel** = fifth wheel carried in a car to replace one that has a puncture; *when he took it out, he found the spare wheel had a puncture as well* **2** *noun* **spares** = spare parts, pieces used to mend broken parts of a car, etc.; *we can't get spares for that make of washing machine*; *it's difficult to get spares for the car because they don't make this model any more* **3** *verb* **(a)** (asking someone if they can to do without something) **can you spare your assistant to help me for a day?**; *can you spare about five minutes to talk about the problem?*; *you have a moment to spare, can you clean the car?*; *can you spare 50p for a cup of tea?* **(b)** not to show or give; *the driving test was awful, but I'll spare you the details* **(c)** **to spare someone** or **someone's life** = not to kill someone; *he pleaded with the soldiers to spare his life*; *no one was spared, all the inhabitants of the village were killed*

spare ribs ['speə 'rɪbz] *noun* pork ribs cooked in a savoury sauce; *we are making spare ribs for the barbecue*

spare room ['speə 'ruːm] *noun* **(a)** unused space; *the car is full, we have absolutely no spare room* **(b)** bedroom which a family does not use; *we can put you up in the spare room*

spare tyre ['speə 'taɪə] *noun* **(a)** extra wheel and tyre carried in a car in case you have a puncture **(b)** (informal) roll of fat round the waist; *he needs to cut down on his lunches, he's developed quite a spare tyre*

sparing ['speərɪŋ] *adjective* **to be sparing with something** = to use very much of something; *be sparing with the wine, we've only got three bottles*

spark [spɑːk] **1** *noun* little flash of fire or of light; *sparks flew as the train went over the junction* **2** *verb* **to spark (off)** = to make something; *the shooting of the teenager sparked off a riot*; *the proposed closure of the station sparked anger amongst travellers*

sparking plug *US* **spark plug** ['spɑːkɪŋ plʌg or 'spɑːk plʌg] *noun* (in an engine) device which is screwed into the top of a cylinder and produces a spark to ignite the fuel; *if the sparking plugs are dirty the engine won't run very well*

sparkle ['spɑːkl] *verb* **(a)** to shine brightly; *her jewels sparkled in the light of the candles*; *his eyes sparkled when he heard the salary offered* **(b)** (of person) to be lively; *she was sparkling with enthusiasm*

sparkler ['spɑːklə] *noun* type of little firework which you can hold in your hand and which sends out bright sparks; *children love holding sparklers*

sparkling ['spɑːklɪŋ] *adjective* **(a)** shining with little lights; *a necklace of sparkling diamonds* **(b)** which has bubbles in it, which is fizzy; *a bottle of sparkling water*; **sparkling wine** = wine which has little bubbles in it; *Champagne is a sparkling wine from France*

sparky ['spɑːki] *adjective* (informal) bright and energetic; *she seems very sparky this morning*

sparring partner ['spɑːrɪŋ 'pɑːtnə] *noun* **(a)** person who a professional boxer practises with; *he has a session with his sparring partner every morning* **(b)** (informal) person with whom you often have discussions or arguments; *they were old sparring partners from the time when they were MPs together*

sparrow ['spærəu] *noun* very common small brown and grey bird; *a flock of sparrows came down onto our lawn*

sparse [spɑːs] *adjective* not thick, not in large quantities; *the plain is covered with sparse vegetation*; *a thin man with sparse grey hair*; *information about the coup has been sparse so far* (NOTE: **sparser - sparsest**)

spartan ['spɑːtən] *adjective* **(a)** harsh or hard; *the report criticized the spartan regime in the labour camps* **(b)** uncomfortable; *we were put up in a spartan hotel by the railway station*

spasm ['spæzəm] *noun* sudden, usually painful, involuntary contraction of a muscle, such as when you have cramp; *the muscles in his leg went into spasm*; *she had painful stomach spasms*

spate [speit] *noun* **(a)** sudden rush of orders, etc.; *we had a spate of inquiries after our ad in 'the Times'* **(b)** *river in spate* = river in flood

spatial ['speiʃəl] *adjective* referring to space; *the architect achieved remarkable spatial effects*

spawn [spɔːn] **1** *noun* **(a)** mass of eggs of a fish, frog, etc.; *the children could see the frog spawn floating on the surface of the pond* **(b) mushroom spawn** = spores of edible mushrooms which are sold to be used to grow mushrooms (NOTE: no plural) **2** *verb* **(a)** *(of a fish or reptile)* to produce a mass of eggs; *salmon swim up the river to spawn* **(b)** to produce a mass of things; *the meetings of the committee spawned a huge amount of documents*

speak [spiːk] *verb* **(a)** to say words, to talk; *she spoke to me when the meeting was over*; *he walked past me without speaking*; *he was speaking to the postman when I saw him*; *the manager wants to speak to you about sales in Africa*; **to speak your mind** = to say exactly what you think; **speak for yourself** = that's what you think, I don't agree; *we both think the decision is crazy - speak for yourself!* **(b)** to be able to say things in (a foreign language); *we need someone who can speak Russian*; *he speaks English with an American accent*; *you will have to brush up your Japanese as my mother speaks hardly any English* **(c)** to make a speech; *do you know who is speaking at the conference*? **(d) so to speak** = as you might say; *he's a very close friend, we're like brothers, so to speak* (NOTE: **speaking - spoke** [spəuk] **- has spoken** ['spəukn])

speaker ['spiːkə] *noun* **(a)** person who speaks; *we need an Arabic speaker to help with the tour*; **he is a popular speaker** = many people come to hear him give speeches at meetings **(b)** loudspeaker; *one of the speakers doesn't work*; *see also* LOUDSPEAKER **(c)** *(in Parliament)* person who presides over a meeting of Parliament; *the Speaker called on the Prime Minister to speak*

COMMENT: the Speaker of the House of Commons is an ordinary MP who is elected by other MPs; similarly in the US House of Representatives, the Speaker is elected by other Congressmen

speaking ['spiːkɪŋ] *noun* action of talking; *politicians have to learn the art of public speaking*;

she and I are not on speaking terms = we have quarrelled and don't speak to each other any more

speak out ['spiːk 'aut] *verb* to make your opinions or feelings known strongly; *she spoke out against the new motorway*; *it's time for those who are in favour of change to speak out*

speak up ['spiːk 'ʌp] *verb* **(a)** to speak louder; to say what you have to say in a louder voice; *can you speak up please - we can't hear you at the back!* **(b)** to make your opinions known strongly; *he's not afraid to speak up when he thinks someone's been unfairly treated*; **to speak up for** = to show your support for; *he was the only person who spoke up for me at the inquiry*

spear ['spiə] **1** *noun* long pointed throwing stick, which formerly was used as a weapon; *they kill fish with spears* **2** *verb* to push something sharp into something to catch it; *spearing fish is not easy*; *she managed to spear a sausage on the barbecue with her fork*; *they served little pieces of cheese speared on toothpicks*

spearhead ['spiəhed] **1** *noun* front part of a force of attackers; *the spearhead of the attack was directed at the castle* **2** *verb* to be in the front of an attacking force; *the minister has spearheaded the attack on the newspapers*

spec [spek] *noun (informal)* **to buy on spec** = without being sure of the value or condition; *I just bought the old painting on spec - no one knew it was by Constable*

special ['speʃəl] **1** *adjective* **(a)** referring to something or someone who is not ordinary but has a particular importance or use; *this is a very special day for us - it's our twenty-fifth wedding anniversary*; *a report from our special correspondent in Hong Kong*; *he has a special pair of scissors for cutting metal* **(b) nothing special** = very ordinary; *there is nothing special about his new car*; *did anything happen at the meeting? - no, nothing special* **2** *noun* particular dish on a menu; **today's special** *or* **special of the day** = special dish prepared for the day and not listed in the printed menu; *I'll have the special, please*; **chef's special** = special dish, sometimes one which the chef is famous for

Special Branch ['speʃl 'brɑːnʃ] *noun* section of the British police dealing with terrorism, spies, crimes against the government; *Special Branch detectives came to investigate*

special effects ['speʃl ɪ'fekts] *noun* the impression of a fire, a snowstorm, an earthquake, etc., made artificially in a film or play; *the special effects in the film were created by computers*

specialist ['speʃəlɪst] *noun* **(a)** person who knows a lot about something; *you should go to a tax specialist for advice* **(b)** doctor who specializes in a certain branch of medicine; *he was referred to a heart specialist* **2** *adjective* specialized; *does he have any specialist knowledge of international currency transactions?*

speciality *US* **specialty** [speʃɪ'ælɪti *or* 'speʃəlti] *noun* **(a)** thing you are very good at doing; *the speciality of the restaurant is its fish soup*; *finding the right partners for people is my speciality* **(b)** particular interest, knowledge or study; *the company's speciality is computer programmes for schools*; *his speciality is the history of Wales in the 15th century*

specialization [speʃəlaɪ'zeɪʃn] *noun* study of a particular subject; subject which you specialize in; *I'm* *not in favour of too much specialization; that's outside my specialization, so you'd better ask someone else*

specialize ['speʃəlaɪz] *verb* to specialize in something = to study one particular subject; to produce one thing in particular; *at university, she specialized in marine biology; the company specializes in electronic components*

specialized ['speʃəlaɪzd] *adjective* which deals with one subject in particular; *the book is too specialized for the ordinary computer user*; **specialized field** = area of study which is very restricted; **a specialized dictionary** = a dictionary referring to one subject only

specially ['speʃəli] *adverb* in particular, more than usual; *the weather has been specially wet this weekend; he is specially good at designing furniture; aren't you tired? - not specially; see also* ESPECIALLY

special needs ['speʃl 'niːdz] *noun* needs of a person with mental or physical disabilities, which are different from the needs of most people; *children with special needs, such as blind or autistic children, require special schooling*

special offer ['speʃl 'ɒfə] *noun* goods put on sale at a specially low price; *we have a range of men's shirts on special offer*

specialty ['speʃəlti] *noun US* = SPECIALITY; **specialty store** = shop selling a limited range of good quality items

species ['spiːʃiːz] *noun* group of living things, such as animals or plants, which can breed with each other; *several species of butterfly are likely to become extinct*; **endangered species** = any species at risk of extinction; *several British species are listed as endangered* (NOTE: plural is **species**)

specific [spə'sɪfɪk] *adjective* referring precisely to something; *can you be more specific about what you're trying to achieve?; I gave specific instructions that I was not to be disturbed; is the money intended for a specific purpose?*; **specific gravity;** *see* RELATIVE DENSITY

specifically [spə'sɪfɪkli] *adverb* particularly; *I specifically said I didn't want a blue door; the advertisement is specifically aimed at people over 50*

specification [spesɪfɪ'keɪʃən] *noun* detailed information about what is needed; *she gave full specifications about how she wanted the kitchen to be laid out*; **job specification** = very detailed description of what is involved in a job; *there was nothing about word-processing in the job specification*; **the work is not up to specification** *or* **does not meet our specifications** = the product is not made in the way which was detailed

specifics [spe'sɪfɪks] *noun* particular details of something; *the minister outlined the plan but refused to go into specifics*

specify ['spesəfaɪ] *verb* to give clear details of what is needed; *please specify full details of the address to which the goods must be sent; do not include VAT on the invoice unless specified*

specimen ['spesɪmən] *noun* (a) sample of something taken as standard; *the bank asked for a specimen signature for their records* (b) example of a particular kind of creature or thing; *he has some very rare specimens in his butterfly collection; this is a fine specimen of this kind of fossil*

speck [spek] *noun* tiny spot; *a speck of dust went into my eye*

speckle ['spekl] *noun* small brown or black spot; *a fish which has dark speckles on its back*

speckled ['spekld] *adjective* covered with speckles; **a speckled hen** = a hen with black and white feathers

specs [speks] *noun (informal)* = SPECTACLES; *I can't see anything without my specs!*

spectacle ['spektəkl] *noun* (a) something very impressive to look at; show; *the firework display is a spectacle not to be missed; for sheer spectacle you can't beat a military parade* (b) **spectacles** = glass lenses worn in front of your eyes to correct defects in vision; *I can't remember where I put my spectacles; he's worn spectacles since he was a child*

spectacular [spek'tækjulə] **1** *adjective* very impressive to see or watch; *the firework display was even more spectacular than last year; she was very ill, but has made a spectacular recovery* **2** *noun* impressive show; *a firework spectacular on November 5th; a musical spectacular featuring over a hundred singers and dancers*

spectacularly [spek'tækjuləli] *adverb* in a spectacular way; *the waterfall plunges spectacularly down a sheer cliff; the rocket launch went spectacularly wrong*

spectator ['spekteɪtə] *noun* person who watches a football match, a horse show, etc.; *thousands of spectators watched the tennis match*

spectator sport [spek'teɪtə 'spɔːt] *noun* sport, like football, where there are thousands of spectators but only a few players, as opposed to fishing, where there are thousands of anglers, but very few people who watch them

spectre *US* **specter** ['spektə] *noun (formal)* (a) ghost; *the spectre of his dead father came to haunt him* (b) image of something which may cause problems in the future; *the spectre of mass unemployment loomed over the country*

spectrum ['spektrəm] *noun* (a) range of colours from red to violet (as seen in a rainbow); *white light passing through a prism breaks up into the colours of the spectrum* (b) range of ideas, etc.; *the bank tries to offer a wide spectrum of services*

> COMMENT: the colours of the spectrum are red, orange, yellow, green, blue, indigo and violet

speculate ['spekjuleɪt] *verb* (a) to speculate about = to make guesses about; *we are all speculating about what's going to happen* (b) to take a risk in business which you hope will bring profit; *he made a lot of money by speculating on the Stock Exchange*

speculation [spekju'leɪʃən] *noun* (a) risky deal which may produce a short-term profit; *she lost all her money in Stock Exchange speculations* (b) trying to guess what will happen; *there's been a lot of speculation in the press about who might get the job* (NOTE: no plural in this meaning)

speculative ['spekjulətɪv] *adjective* (a) made by guessing; *his plans for the future of the business are purely speculative* (b) bought because you think they will make a profit; **speculative share** = share which may go sharply up (or down) in value

speculator ['spekjuleɪtə] *noun* person who buys shares, goods, etc., in the hope that they will rise in price; *most of the land was bought by property speculators*; **currency speculator** = person who buys or sells currency in advance, hoping that the exchange rate will change in his favour; *currency speculators were blamed for making the financial crisis worse*

sped [sped] *see* SPEED

speech [spiːtʃ] *noun* (a) formal talk given to an audience; *he made some notes before giving his speech*; *he wound up his speech with a story about his father*; *who will be making the speech at the prize giving?*; **speech day** = day when children are given prizes at school for good work, etc. (NOTE: plural in this meaning is **speeches**) (b) speaking, making intelligible sounds with the voice; *teaching of speech to deaf children can be a very slow process* (c) spoken language; *this word is more often used in speech than in writing*; **freedom of speech** = being able to say what you want; *the protesters demanded freedom of speech*; **the parts of speech** = different types of words, such as nouns, verbs, etc., which are classified according to grammatical use; *nouns, adjectives and verbs are different parts of speech*

speechless ['spiːtʃləs] *adjective* unable to say anything; *the shock of being sacked left him speechless*; *she was speechless with anger at what he had said*

speed [spiːd] **1** *noun* rate at which something moves or is done; *the coach was travelling at a high speed when it crashed*; *your car will use less petrol if you go at an even speed of 56 miles per hour*; *the speed with which they repaired the gas leak was incredible*; *the train travels at speeds of over 200 km per hour* **2** *verb* **(a)** to move quickly; *the ball sped across the ice* **(b)** to go too fast; *he was arrested for speeding in the centre of town* (NOTE: **speeding - sped** [sped] *or* **speeded - has sped**)

speedboat ['spiːdbəʊt] *noun* small fast motorboat; *the windsurfers were almost killed by the speedboat*

speed limit ['spiːd 'lɪmɪt] *noun* fastest speed at which cars are allowed to go legally; *the speed limit in towns is 30 miles per hour*; *what is the speed limit on German motorways?*

speedometer [spiːˈdɒmɪtə] *noun* instrument which shows how fast a vehicle is travelling; *you're going too fast - look at the speedometer*

speed skating ['spiːd 'skeɪtɪŋ] *noun* Winter Olympic event in which pairs of competing skaters race against the clock round a 400m ice circuit

> COMMENT: speed skaters wear lycra body suits and skate bent forwards with their hands behind their backs to reduce wind resistance

speed skiing ['spiːd 'skiːɪŋ] *noun* skiing fast downhill in a straight line

> COMMENT: racers are timed over a kilometre, and can reach speeds of up to 230kph (145mph)

speed trap ['spiːd 'træp] *noun* small radar device by the side of a road which senses and notes details of cars which are travelling too fast (NOTE: also called a **radar trap**)

speed up ['spiːd 'ʌp] *verb* **(a)** to go faster; *she speeded up as she came to the traffic lights* **(b)** to make

something happen faster; *can't we speed up production?*; *we are aiming to speed up our delivery times*

speedy ['spiːdi] *adjective* very fast; *we all wished her a speedy recovery* (NOTE: **speedier - speediest**)

spell [spel] **1** *noun* **(a)** words which the person speaking hopes will have a magic effect; *the wicked witch cast a spell on the princess* **(b)** short period; *there was a spell of cold weather at the spring bank holiday*; *the warm spell will last until Thursday* **2** *verb* to write or say correctly the letters that make a word; *how do you spell your surname?*; *we spelt his name wrong on the envelope*; *W-O-R-R-Y spells 'worry'*; **to spell out** = to explain very clearly; *let me spell out the consequences of this course of action* (NOTE: **spelling - spelled** *or* **spelt** [spelt] - **has spelled** *or* **has spelt**)

spellchecker ['speltʃekə] *noun* computer program which checks the spelling of text and suggests corrections

speller ['spelə] *noun* person who spells; *he's a very quick writer, but a hopeless speller - you have to check everything he writes*

spelling ['spelɪŋ] *noun* correct way in which words are spelt; *she is a good journalist, but her spelling is awful*

spend [spend] *verb* **(a)** to pay money; *I went shopping and spent a fortune*; *why do we spend so much money on food?* **(b)** to use time doing something; *he wants to spend more time with his family*; *she spent months arguing with the income tax people*; *don't spend too long on your homework*; *why don't you come and spend the weekend with us?* (NOTE: **spending - spent** [spent])

spender ['spendə] *noun* person who spends; *she's a big spender and never has any money left at the end of the month*

spending ['spendɪŋ] *noun* paying money; *government spending on health has increased by 10%*; **consumer spending** = spending by consumers; *interest rates were increased to control consumer spending*; **spending money** = money for ordinary personal expenses; *how much spending money are you taking on holiday?*

spent [spent] *adjective* used; *the ground was littered with spent cartridges*; **spent fuel** = fuel which has been used in a nuclear reactor, which can be reprocessed; *spent nuclear fuel is sent for reprocessing*

sperm [spɜːm] *noun* **(a)** male sex cell which fertilizes the female eggs; *out of millions of sperm only one will fertilize an egg* (NOTE: plural is **sperm**) **(b)** **sperm whale** = species of large whale which is hunted for its oil

spew [spjuː] *verb* (*informal*) **(a)** to **spew (out)** = to pour out; *gallons of toxic waste spewed out into the river*; *he spewed out a stream of racial abuse* **(b)** to **spew up** = to vomit; *he spewed up his dinner*

sphere [sfɪə] *noun* **(a)** object which is perfectly round like a ball; *the earth is not quite a perfect sphere* **(b)** general area; *it's not a sphere of activity that we know very well*; **sphere of influence** = area of the world where a strong country can influence smaller or weaker countries; *some Latin American countries fall within the USA's sphere of influence*

spherical ['sferɪkl] *adjective* shaped like a sphere, perfectly round; *a ball must be spherical to bounce properly*

spice [spaɪs] **1** *noun* **(a)** substance made from the roots, flowers, seeds or leaves of plants, etc., used to flavour food; *cloves, cinnamon and nutmeg are the main spices I use*; *you need lots of spices for Indian cookery* **(b)** thing which excites interest; *I included a murder scene to add a bit of spice to the story* **2** *verb* to **spice something up** = (i) to add spices to something; (ii) to make something more exciting or interesting; *a pinch of mustard will spice up the sauce*; *we need something to spice up the scene where the hero and heroine meet in the rain*

spiced [spaɪst] *adjective* which has had spices added to it; *a dish of spiced chicken wings*

spick-and-span ['spɪkən'spæn] *adjective* very neat and clean; *after all the work they did on it, the car looked spick-and-span*

spicy ['spaɪsi] *adjective* **(a)** with a lot of spices; *he loves spicy Indian food* **(b)** including something which excites sexual interest; *the paper published a spicy story about the MP and two girls* (NOTE: **spicier - spiciest**)

spider ['spaɪdə] *noun* small animal with eight legs, which makes a web and eats insects; *it is fascinating to watch a spider making its web*

spiderweb ['spaɪdəweb] *noun* US web made by a spider (NOTE: British English is **cobweb**)

spike [spaɪk] **1** *noun* **(a)** sharply pointed piece of metal; *the wall was topped with a row of metal spikes* **(b)** **spikes** = sharp points in the soles of running shoes; *spikes give a runner a much better grip on the track* **2** *verb* (*informal*) to add drugs or alcohol to someone's drink; *they spiked his drink but won't admit it*

spiked [spaɪkt] *adjective* with sharp points; *she has a pair of spiked shoes for running*

spiky ['spaɪki] *adjective* standing up in sharp points; *his spiky hairstyle makes him easily recognizable*; *holly has very spiky leaves* (NOTE: **spikier - spikiest**)

spill [spɪl] **1** *noun* pouring of a liquid by accident; *the authorities are trying to cope with the oil spill from the tanker* **2** *verb* **(a)** to pour liquid, powder, etc., out of a container by mistake; *that glass is too full - you'll spill it*; *he spilt soup down the front of his shirt*; *she dropped the bag and some of the flour spilled out onto the floor* **(b)** (*informal*) to **spill the beans** = to reveal a secret (NOTE: **spilling - spilled** *or* **spilt** [spɪlt])

spilt [spɪlt] *see* CRY, SPILL

spin [spɪn] **1** *noun* **(a)** turning movement of a ball as it moves; *he put so much spin on the ball that it bounced sideways* **(b)** (*informal*) to **put a spin on something** = to give something a special meaning; *the PR people have tried to put a positive spin on the sales figures*; *see also* SPIN DOCTOR **(c)** (*informal*) short ride in a car; *let's go for a spin in my new car* **2** *verb* **(a)** to move round and round very fast; *the earth is spinning in space*; *the plane was spinning out of control* **(b)** to make something turn round and round; *the washing machine spins the clothes to get the water out of them*; *he spun the wheel to make sure it turned freely*; to **spin a coin** = to make a coin turn round and round, so as to decide (by guessing which side of the coin will end up on top) which team plays first in a competition, etc. **(c)** to twist raw wool, cotton, etc., to form a thread; *a*

spinning wheel **(d)** (*of a spider*) to make a web; *the spider has spun a web between the two posts* (NOTE: **spinning - spun** [spʌn])

spinach ['spɪnɪtʃ] *noun* annual plant grown for its green leaves eaten raw as salad or cooked as a vegetable; *we had chicken, potatoes and spinach* (NOTE: no plural: **some spinach; a spoonful of spinach**)

spinal ['spaɪnəl] *noun* referring to the spine; *he suffered spinal injuries in the crash*; **spinal column** = backbone; **spinal cord** = part of the central nervous system which runs down the centre of the spine; **spinal nerves** = nerves leading from the spinal cord; *there are 31 pairs of spinal nerves*

spindle ['spɪndl] *noun* **(a)** central pin round which something turns; *the spindle in the wheel broke* **(b)** pin used for twisting thread in a spinning machine; *she was spinning wool, and winding it round a spindle* **(c)** device which holds a disk in its central hole and spins it

spin doctor ['spɪn 'dɒktə] *noun* (*informal*) person who explains news in a way that makes it flattering to the person or organization employing him; *government spin doctors have been having some difficulty in dealing with the news items about the minister's family*

spin-drier [spɪn'draɪə] *noun* machine for removing water from clothes by turning them round very fast in a metal cylinder with holes in it; *if your shirt is still wet, put it back in the spin-drier*

spine [spaɪn] *noun* **(a)** a series of bones linked together to form a flexible support from the base of the skull to the pelvis; *he injured his spine playing rugby* (NOTE: also called the **spinal column** *or* **backbone**; the bones in the spine are the **vertebrae**) **(b)** sharp part like a pin, on a plant, animal, fish, etc.; *the porcupine has dangerous spines*; *did you know that lemon trees had spines?* **(c)** back edge of a bound book, usually with the title printed on it; *the title and the author's name are printed on the front of the book and also on the spine*

spine-chiller ['spaɪntʃɪlə] *noun* film or story which makes you excited and very afraid; *he sat up watching a spine-chiller on TV*

spine-chilling ['spaɪntʃɪlɪŋ] *adjective* which makes you excited and very afraid; *it's a spine-chilling story of murders in a Scottish graveyard*

spineless ['spaɪnləs] *adjective* **(a)** who is weak and cowardly; *he's so spineless - he should say what he thinks to the manager himself* **(b)** with no spine; *insects and molluscs are spineless*

spinner ['spɪnə] *noun* **(a)** person who spins thread **(b)** (*in cricket*) bowler who spins the ball; *the captain has taken off the fast bowlers and put on the spinners*

spinoff ['spɪnɒf] *noun* useful thing which comes from a process, but is not the main aim of the process; *the development of the electric car is a spinoff of the research programme*

spin out ['spɪn 'aʊt] *verb* to make something last as long as possible; *I managed to spin the lecture out to last a full hour*

spin round ['spɪn 'raʊnd] *verb* **(a)** to turn round and round very fast; *the earth spins round in space* **(b)** to turn round fast to face in the opposite direction; *I tapped him on the shoulder and he spun round to face me*

spinster ['spɪnstə] *noun (old)* unmarried woman, usually middle-aged; *she remained a spinster until she was over 60, then suddenly married a retired professor* (NOTE: it is more usual to say **a single girl, a single woman** nowadays)

spiral ['spaɪərəl] **1** *noun* (a) shape which is twisted round and round like a spring; *he drew a spiral on the sheet of paper* (b) thing which turns, getting higher or lower all the time; *smoke was rising in spirals from the top of the chimney*; **inflationary spiral** or **wage-price spiral** = situation where price rises encourage higher wage demands which in turn make prices rise **2** *adjective* which twists round and round; *a spiral staircase leads to the top of the tower* **3** *verb* (a) to move up or down in a spiral; *the firework spiralled up into the air*; *the leaves dropped off the tree and spiralled down to the ground* (b) to move rapidly upwards; *prices of imported goods are spiralling*; **spiralling inflation** = inflation where price rises make workers ask for higher wages which then increase prices again (NOTE: **spiralling - spiralled** but the American spelling is **spiraling - spiraled**)

spire ['spaɪə] *noun* pointed top of a church tower; *you can see the spire of Salisbury Cathedral from miles away*

spirit ['spɪrɪt] **1** *noun* (a) energy and determination; *I like her because she has got such spirit; she fought her case with great spirit* (b) feelings which are typical of a particular occasion; *a good salesman needs to have the spirit of competition; I don't think she approached the task in the right spirit*; **to enter into the spirit of** = to take part in something with enthusiasm; *the managing director entered into the spirit of the party*; **Christmas spirit** = excitement, generosity and friendliness which is supposed to exist at Christmas; *making us all redundant on December 24th didn't show much Christmas spirit*; **public spirit** = feeling that you belong to a certain part of society and have to do things to help others in the group (c) ghost of someone dead; *the spirits of the dead*; **evil spirit** = wicked devil which harms people; **Holy Spirit** = the third person of the Christian Trinity (d) real intention of something; *that's not really in keeping with the spirit of the agreement* (e) alcohol; **surgical spirit** = pure alcohol with an additive which gives it an unpleasant taste, used as a disinfectant or antiseptic; *see also* SPIRITS **2** *verb* to **spirit away** = to remove as if by magic; *they spirited her away before the photographers could get to her*

spirited ['spɪrɪtɪd] *adjective* very lively; *she started doing a spirited Russian dance*

spirit level ['spɪrɪt 'levl] *noun* device for testing if something is level using a glass tube filled with liquid containing an air bubble; *use a spirit level to check if the shelves are straight*

spirits ['spɪrɪts] *noun* (a) strong alcoholic drink (whisky, gin, etc.); *the club is licensed to sell beers, wines and spirits* (b) mood; *the news had an excellent effect on our spirits; their spirits sank when they realized they had no chance of winning*; **in high spirits** = in a very excited mood; *she's been in high spirits since she passed her test*

spiritual ['spɪrɪtjuəl] **1** *adjective* referring to the spirit or the soul; *the church's main task is to give spiritual advice and comfort to its members; to minister to someone's spiritual needs* **2** *noun* **Negro spiritual** = religious song sung by black people in the south of the USA; *the choir sang hymns and spirituals*

spirituality [spɪrɪtjuˈælɪti] *noun* being concerned with thought and beliefs, rather than with the body and the physical world

spirochaete ['spaɪərəukiːt] *noun* bacterium with a spiral shape

spit [spɪt] **1** *noun* (a) metal rod pushed through meat over a fire, which is turned so that the meat is evenly cooked; *they roasted pieces of lamb on spits; a spit-roasted lamb* (b) thin piece of land which goes out into the sea; *the lighthouse was built at the end of a spit of land* (c) liquid which forms in your mouth; *spit is another word for saliva (informal)* **spit and polish** = strenuous cleaning; *he is the dead spit of his father* = he looks like an exact copy of his father **2** *verb* (a) to push liquid or food out of your mouth; *he took a mouthful and immediately spat it out* (b) to spit on = to send liquid out of the mouth to show contempt; *he spat on the car as it drove away* (c) *(informal)* **he is the spitting image of his father** = he looks like an exact copy of his father (d) to rain a little; *it isn't really raining - it's just spitting* (NOTE: **spitting - spat** [spæt])

spite [spaɪt] **1** *noun* (a) bad feeling; *they sprayed his car with white paint out of spite* (b) **in spite of** = although something happened or was done; *in spite of all his meetings, he still found time to ring his wife; we all enjoyed ourselves, in spite of the awful weather* **2** *verb* to annoy someone on purpose; *he did it purely to spite his sister*

spiteful ['spaɪtful] *adjective* full of a nasty feeling to hurt someone; *he made several spiteful remarks about his teacher*

spittle ['spɪtl] *noun (old)* saliva, liquid which forms in your mouth; *he shouted at us, with drops of spittle flying out of his mouth*

splash [splæʃ] **1** *noun* (a) sound when something falls into a liquid or when a liquid hits something hard; *she fell into the pool with a loud splash*; *listen to the splash of the waves against the rocks* (b) sudden show; *the red flowers make a bright splash of colour in the front garden* (c) *(informal)* **to make a splash** = to do something which attracts a lot of publicity; *his new show made a splash on Broadway* **2** *verb* (a) *(of liquid)* to make a noise when something is dropped into it or when it hits something; *I missed the ball and it splashed into the pool; the rain splashed against the windows; the little children were splashing about in the paddling pool* (b) to make someone wet by sending liquid on to him; *the car drove past through a puddle and splashed my trousers* (c) to move through water, making a noise; *he splashed his way through the shallow water to the rocks*

splash out ['splæʃ 'aut] *verb (informal)* to spend a lot of money at one time; *we splashed out on a holiday in Tenerife*

splatter ['splætə] *verb* to splash drops of liquid; *the children's art class splattered paint everywhere on the floor and walls; they had to clean up the pavement splattered with blood*

spleen [spliːn] *noun* (a) organ in the top part of the abdominal cavity behind the stomach; *the spleen cleans the blood and helps fight infection* (b) *(formal)* **to vent your spleen on someone** = to get very angry with someone; *he vented his spleen on his poor assistant*

splendid ['splendɪd] *adjective* magnificent, which impresses; *after a splendid lunch we all had a nap; it was absolutely splendid to see your father again*

splendidly ['splendɪdli] *adverb* in a splendid way; *a splendidly colourful display of flowers*; *we're getting on splendidly*

splendour US **splendor** ['splendə] *noun* magnificence; *they stared at the spendour of the state apartments*; *we dined in splendour on the terrace of the hotel looking out over the sea*

splinter ['splɪntə] 1 *noun* (a) tiny thin piece of wood or metal which can get under the skin and be irritating and cause infection; *I got a splinter in my finger from cutting wood*; *can you try and get this splinter out of my thumb for me?* (b) **splinter group** = group of people who have separated from a main group; *the protesters are from a splinter group which broke away from the Socialist Party some years ago* 2 *verb* to split into thin pointed pieces; *the wooden door splintered as the firemen hit it with hammers and axes*

split [splɪt] 1 *verb* (a) to divide something into parts; *he split the log with an axe*; **to split the difference** = to agree on a figure which is half way between two figures suggested; *you are offering £20 and he wants £40, so why don't you split the difference and settle on £30?*; *see also* HAIR (b) to divide or to come apart; *my trousers were too tight - they split when I bent down*; *after they lost the election, the party split into various factions* (NOTE: **splitting - split**) 2 *noun* (a) division; *they are trying to hide the split between the two factions of the party* (b) **banana split** = dessert made of a banana cut lengthwise, whipped cream, ice cream, chocolate sauce and nuts (c) *(in dancing)* **to do the splits** = to put yourself on the floor, with your legs spread in opposite directions 3 *adjective* which has been broken in half; **split ends** = hair problem, when the end of each hair splits into different strands; *my hair needs to be cut because of my split ends*; **split peas** = dried peas split in half; **in a split second** = very rapidly; *everything happened in a split second*; **to have a split personality** = mental condition where you react from time to time in two totally different and opposing ways

split-level [splɪt'levl] *adjective* with some rooms on different floors to others; *we have a split-level apartment on the top two floors of the block*

splitting ['splɪtɪŋ] *adjective (informal)* very painful; **I have a splitting headache** *or* **my head is splitting** = I have a very bad headache

split up ['splɪt 'ʌp] *verb* (a) to divide; *we must try to split up the class into groups of three or four* (b) to start to live apart; *they had a row and split up*

splutter ['splʌtə] *verb* (a) to speak rapidly, using very short phrases, especially when angry; *'what, what, what ... do you mean by that?' he spluttered in fury* (b) to make a hissing sound; *the wet logs were spluttering on the fire*

spoil [spɔɪl] 1 *verb* (a) to ruin something which was good; *we had such bad weather that our camping holiday was spoilt*; *half the contents of the warehouse was spoiled by floodwater*; **to spoil your appetite** = to make you not want to eat; *don't eat so many crisps - they'll spoil your appetite for lunch* (b) to be too kind to someone, especially a child, so that he or she sometimes becomes badly behaved; *you'll spoil that child if you always give in to him*; *grandparents are allowed to spoil their grandchildren a little* (c) **to be spoiling for a fight** = to be eager to get into a fight; *the socialists were spoiling for a fight with the liberals* (d) to go bad; *if we don't eat this meat today it will spoil*

(NOTE: **spoiling - spoilt** [spɔɪlt] *or* **spoiled**) 2 *noun (formal)* **(a) spoils** = booty, goods taken by soldiers from a defeated enemy; *their spoils filled several train wagons* **(b)** *(humorous)* things bought; *she came back from the jumble sale, laden with spoils* **(c)** spoil heap = heap of rubbish from a mine; *the countryside is littered with spoil heaps from old tin mines*

spoilt ['spɔɪlt] *adjective (child)* who has been treated in a way which is too kind, and so is badly-behaved; *he was acting like a spoilt child*

spoke [spəʊk] 1 *noun* rod which connects the axle of a wheel to the rim; *the wheel wobbles because one of the spokes is bent* 2 *verb see also* SPEAK

spoken ['spəʊkən] *see* SPEAK

spokesman *or* **spokeswoman** *or* **spokesperson** ['spəʊksmən *or* 'spəʊkswuːmən *or* 'spəʊkspɜːsən] *noun* person who speaks on behalf of a party, group, politician, etc.; *a spokesman for the government or a government spokesman* (NOTE: plural is **spokesmen** *or* **spokeswomen**)

sponge [spʌndʒ] 1 *noun* (a) sea animal with a skeleton which is full of holes; *diving down into the Red Sea you could see sponges on the sea floor* (b) the dried soft skeleton of this sea animal, or a block of soft material full of small holes, which soaks up water and is used for washing; *real sponges are very expensive*; *I use a large sponge to wash the car;* *(informal)* **to throw in the sponge** = to admit you have been beaten; *don't throw in the sponge too soon, you've got several other chances* (c) soft material full of small holes used to make cushions, etc.; *the sofa has sponge cushions* (d) **sponge cake** = light soft cake; **sponge pudding** = light soft pudding 2 *verb* (a) to wipe clean with a sponge; *he sponged the kitchen table* (b) *(informal)* **to sponge on** *or* **off someone** = to live by begging for money from someone; *he has no proper job and lives by sponging off his wife's parents*

sponger ['spʌndʒə] *noun* person who doesn't work but begs money from friends

spongiform ['spʌndʒifɔːm] *see* BSE

sponsor ['spɒnsə] 1 *noun* (a) person or company that pays to financially help a sport, an exhibition, a music festival, etc., in return for the right to advertise at sporting events, on sports clothes, programmes, etc.; *the company is the sponsor for the premier division football* (b) company which pays part of the cost of making a TV or radio programme by advertising on the programme (c) person who pays money to a charity when someone else walks, swims, runs, a certain distance, etc.; *he's taking part in the school cross-country and wants sponsors* (d) person who takes responsibility for someone; *she acted as his sponsor when he applied for membership of the club* 2 *verb* (a) to be a sponsor; *the company has sponsored the football match*; *will you sponsor me if I apply to join the club?*; *I sponsored her to take part in a marathon for charity* (b) **to sponsor a child at baptism** = to be the god-parent of a child and promise to help the child to lead a Christian life

sponsored ['spɒnsəd] *adjective* which has been sponsored by people or an organization; *they went on a sponsored walk to raise money for the local hospital*

sponsorship ['spɒnsəʃɪp] *noun* action of sponsoring; *the government is increasing its sponsorship of overseas sales missions*

spontaneity [spɒntə'neɪəti] *noun* behaving in a natural way; *his acting is very stilted - it lacks spontaneity*

spontaneous [spɒn'teɪnɪəs] *adjective* which happens of its own accord, which is not forced or prepared in advance; *in a spontaneous gesture of affection, she flung her arms round him and kissed him*; *what he said sounded more like a prepared statement than a spontaneous comment*

spontaneously [spɒn'teɪnɪəsli] *adverb* in a spontaneous way; *people began clapping completely spontaneously*

spook [spuːk] *noun* **(a)** ghost; *a TV cartoon about spooks who haunted an office block* **(b)** *US* (*informal*) spy; *the spooks planted bugs in the ambassador's car*

spooky ['spuːki] *adjective* (*informal*) frightening, which makes you think there may be ghosts around; *don't go into that old house - it looks so spooky* (NOTE: **spookier - spookiest**)

spool [spuːl] *noun* cylinder round which you wind something; *wind the film back round its spool*

spoon [spuːn] **1** *noun* **(a)** utensil with a handle at one end and a small bowl at the other, used for eating liquids and soft food, or for stirring food which is being cooked; *use a spoon to eat your pudding*; *we need a big spoon to serve the soup*; **coffee spoon** = little spoon used for stirring coffee; **soup spoon** = special larger spoon for eating soup; *see also* DESSERT SPOON, TEASPOON, WOODEN SPOON **(b)** amount held in a spoon; *add two spoons of sugar* **2** *verb* to move something with a spoon; **to spoon something into something** = to put something in with a spoon; *she spooned sugar onto her plate*; *they were spooning soup out into each bowl*

spoonful ['spuːnfʊl] *noun* amount which a spoon can hold; *she always takes her coffee with two spoonfuls of sugar*

sporadic [spə'rædɪk] *adjective* which happens at irregular intervals; *the town was quiet during the night, with only sporadic bursts of gunfire from the army camps*

spore [spɔː] *noun* reproductive body of certain plants and bacteria, which can survive in extremely hot or cold conditions for a long time; *fern spores are often carried long distances by the wind*

sport [spɔːt] **1** *noun* **(a)** any game; all games taken together; *do you like watching sport on TV? or do you like the sports programmes on TV?*; *the world of sport is mourning the death of the racing driver*; **sports facilities** = equipment and buildings for playing sports, such as tennis courts, swimming pools, etc.; *the club has extensive sports facilities* **(b)** game which you play; *the only sport I play is tennis*; *she doesn't play any sport at all* **(c)** **good sport** = person who doesn't mind being teased; *he's a good sport* **2** *verb* to wear something proudly; *he was sporting a red and orange tie*

sporting ['spɔːtɪŋ] *adjective* **(a)** referring to sport; *a big sporting weekend on TV, with tennis matches, the World Cup and a golf tournament* **(b)** pleasant and willing to help, especially when playing a sport; *he's a very sporting chap*; **a sporting chance** = quite a good chance that something will happen; *they have a sporting chance of winning*

sportingly ['spɔːtɪŋli] *adverb* in a pleasant and helpful way; *he sportingly offered us a lift*

sportive ['spɔːtɪv] *adjective* (*formal*) playful, liking to play; *the boat was followed by a school of sportive dolphins*

sports car ['spɔːts 'kɑː] *noun* fast open car; *he bought a flashy green sports car to impress his girl friend*

sports day ['spɔːts 'deɪ] *noun* day at a school where children play various sports for prizes; *sports day is usually just before the end of the summer term*

sportsfield *or* **sportsground** ['spɔːtsfiːld *or* 'spɔːtsgraʊnd] big field where sports are played; *we play football in the local sportsfield*

sportsman, sportswoman ['spɔːtsmən *or* spɔːtswʊmən] *noun* person who plays a sport; *she's an Olympic sportswoman* (NOTE: plurals are **sportsmen, sportswomen**)

sporty ['spɔːti] *adjective* interested in sport and enjoying sport; *she's a sporty type - she's into hockey, canoeing, etc.*

spot [spɒt] **1** *noun* **(a)** particular place; *this is the exact spot where Anne Boleyn was executed*; **black spot** = section of road where accidents often happen; *this road junction is a notorious black spot*; **on the spot** = at a particular place where something happens; *I happened to be on the spot when the incident took place*; *we had twenty policemen on the spot to make sure there was no trouble* **(b)** coloured mark, usually round; *her dress has a pattern of white and red spots*; *he wore a blue tie with white spots*; *see also* SOFT **(c)** small round mark or pimple on the skin; *she suddenly came out in spots after eating fish* **(d)** (*informal*) small amount; *would you like a spot of lunch?*; *we had a spot of luck*; *he's had a spot of bother with the tax authorities* **(e)** buying something for immediate delivery; **spot price** = price for something which is delivered immediately **(f)** **TV spot** = short period on TV which is used for commercials; *we are running a series of TV spots over the next three weeks* **(g)** (*informal*) = SPOTLIGHT **2** *verb* to notice; *the teacher didn't spot the mistake*; *we spotted him in the crowd* (NOTE: **spotting - spotted**)

spot check ['spɒt 'tʃek] *noun* check made suddenly and at random; *customs officers carry out or make spot checks on cars entering the country*

spotless ['spɒtləs] *adjective* very clean; *her kitchen is absolutely spotless*

spotlight ['spɒtlaɪt] **1** *noun* **(a)** bright light which shines on one small area; *she stood in the spotlights on the stage* **(b)** **to turn the spotlight on something** = to draw attention to something; *the TV programme turns the spotlight on the plight of refugees* **2** *verb* to draw attention to something clearly; *we want to spotlight the dangers of riding bicycles without lights*

spot-on [spɒt'ɒn] *adjective* (*informal*) absolutely correct; *his analysis of the situation was spot-on*

spotted ['spɒtɪd] *adjective* covered with spots; *the deer with their little white-spotted fawns*; *the leaves of the roses are spotted with mildew*

spotter ['spɒtə] *noun* person who notes things; **plane-spotter** = person who collects the numbers and makes of planes; **train-spotter** = person who collects the numbers and makes of locomotives

spouse ['spauz] *noun (formal)* husband or wife; *members may be accompanied by their spouses*

spout [spaut] **1** *noun* **(a)** tube which projects out of a container, shaped specially for pouring liquid; *you fill the kettle through the spout; cut here and pull out to form a spout* **(b)** tube for sending rainwater away from the wall of a building; *water was gushing out of the spout* **(c)** *(informal)* **up the spout** = lost or ruined **2** *verb* **(a)** to come out like a jet of water; *blood spouted out of his neck* **(b)** *(informal)* **to spout on about** = to go on speaking about something; *she was spouting on about women's rights*

sprain [spreɪn] **1** *noun* condition where the ligaments in a joint are torn because of a sudden movement; *he is walking with a stick because of an ankle sprain* **2** *verb* to tear the ligaments in a joint, such as your ankle; *he sprained his ankle jumping over the fence*

sprang [spræŋ] *see* SPRING

sprawl [sprɔːl] **1** *noun* **urban sprawl** = area covered by an irregular spread of houses built over what formerly was countryside; *the countryside round the city is slowly disappearing under acres of urban sprawl* **2** *verb* **(a)** to lie with your arms and legs spread out; *he sprawled in his armchair and called the waiter; the boy on the bike hit her and sent her sprawling* **(b)** to spread out in an irregular way; *the housing estates sprawl across the farmland to the east of the town*

sprawled ['sprɔːld] *adjective* lying with arms and legs stretched out; *he lay sprawled on his bed with a glass of water in his hand*

spray [spreɪ] **1** *noun* **(a)** mass of tiny drops of liquid; *the waves crashed against the sea wall sending spray over the road; an aerosol sends out a liquid in a fine spray; she uses a nasal spray to clear her catarrh* **(b)** **spray (can)** = container that sends out liquid in a spray; *this liquid polish is also sold in a spray* **(c)** little branch of a plant with flowers on it; *the room was decorated with sprays of lilac* **2** *verb* to send out liquid in fine drops; *he sprayed water all over the patio with the hose; they sprayed the room with disinfectant*

spray gun ['spreɪ 'gʌn] *noun* device shaped like a gun with a container attached, used for spraying paint, insecticide, etc.; *he borrowed my spray gun to repaint his car*

spread [spred] **1** *noun* **(a)** soft paste of meat, fish or cheese; *as snacks, they offered us water biscuits with cheese spread* **(b)** range; *there is a wide spread of abilities in the class; she has a wide spread of interests* **(c)** *(informal)* attractive mass of food; *you should have seen the spread at her wedding reception!* **(d)** action of moving over a wide area; *doctors are trying to check the spread of the disease* **2** *verb* **(a)** to arrange over a wide area; *spread the paper flat on the table* **(b)** to move over a wide area; *the cholera epidemic has spread to the main towns* **(c)** to cover with a layer of something; *she spread a white cloth over the table; he was spreading butter on a piece of bread* **(d) to spread payments over several months** = to make payments over several months, not all at once (NOTE: **spreading - spread**)

spread out ['spred 'aut] *verb* **(a)** to arrange things over a wide area; *she spread out the clothes on her bed; he spread out the plans on the MD's desk* **(b)** to move away from others over a wide area; *the rioters spread out across the square; the policemen spread out to search the woods*

spreadsheet ['spredʃiːt] *noun* **(a)** computer program which allows calculations to be done in columns of figures; *you can use a spreadsheet to do your household accounts* **(b)** printout of columns of figures on wide computer stationery

spree [spriː] *noun* happy time; **to go on a spending spree** = to have a happy time spending money

sprig [sprɪg] *noun* little branch; *he wore a sprig of heather in his hat; put a few sprigs of thyme on the meat before placing it in the oven*

spring [sprɪŋ] **1** *noun* **(a)** season of the year between winter and summer; *in spring all the trees start to grow new leaves; we always go to Greece in the spring; they started work last spring or in the spring of last year and they still haven't finished; you should come to England in April and see the beautiful spring flowers!* **(b)** wire which is twisted round and round and which goes back to its original shape after you have pulled it or pushed it; *the mattress is so old the springs have burst through the cover; there's a spring to keep the door shut* **(c)** strong coils or discs of special metal which absorb energy and allow a vehicle to travel smoothly over uneven surfaces; *the springs in the car are starting to squeak* **(d)** place where a stream of water rushes out of the ground; *the town of Bath was built in Roman times around hot springs* **(e)** quick jump into the air; *a little spring and he had reached the window sill* **2** *verb* **(a)** to move suddenly; *everyone sprang to life when the officer shouted; the door sprang open without anyone touching it* **(b) to spring from** = to come suddenly from; *where on earth did you spring from?* **(c)** *(informal)* **to spring something on someone** = to surprise someone; *she sprang the question on him and he didn't know how to answer it* (NOTE: **springing - sprang** [spræŋ] **- has sprung** [sprʌŋ])

springboard ['sprɪŋbɔːd] *noun* **(a)** long flexible board used to dive or jump off **(b)** thing used to help you start something; *he bought a small company and used it as a springboard to enter the US market*

springbok ['sprɪŋbʊk] *noun* **(a)** type of small deer found in Africa **(b)** *(informal)* **the Springboks** = the South African international rugby team; *compare* ALL BLACKS, WALLABIES

spring-clean ['sprɪŋ'kliːn] **1** *verb* to clean a house thoroughly; *it took me a week to spring-clean the house* **2** *noun* action of cleaning a house thoroughly; *the house needs a complete spring-clean*

springlike ['sprɪŋlaɪk] *adjective* which is mild like in spring; *the weather in January was unusually mild and springlike*

spring onion ['sprɪŋ 'ʌnjən] *noun* very small onion with long green leaves, used in salads and in cooking; *I chopped some spring onions into the salad* (NOTE: American English is **scallions**)

springtime ['sprɪŋtaɪm] *noun* the time of year when it is spring; *it's springtime, and the fields are full of flowers*

springy ['sprɪŋi] *adjective* **(a) springy step** = quick, light and flexible step; *she walked with a springy step into the room* **(b)** which is very soft to walk on; *we walked across the springy lawn* (NOTE: **springier - springiest**)

sprinkle ['sprɪŋkl] *verb* to scatter around; *sprinkle a little water on the shirt before you iron it; sprinkle the top of the pie with sugar*

sprinkler ['sprɪŋklə] *noun* device for sprinkling water; *we use a sprinkler to keep the lawn green*; **sprinkler system** = system of automatic fire control which sprinkles water on a fire and is set off by heat

sprint [sprɪnt] **1** *noun* fast run, especially at the end of a race; *he must save some energy for the final sprint* **2** *verb* to run very fast over a short distance; *I had to sprint to catch the bus*; *she sprinted down the track*

sprinter ['sprɪntə] *noun* runner who runs in sprint races; *she's a sprinter rather than a long distance runner*; *the sprinters are running into a slight headwind*

sprout [spraʊt] **1** *noun* new shoot of a plant; *the vine is covered with new sprouts*; **bean sprouts** = little shoots of beans, eaten especially in Chinese cooking; **Brussels sprouts** = shoots which look like tiny cabbages **2** *verb* to produce new shoots; *throw those old potatoes away, they're starting to sprout*; *the bush had begun to sprout fresh green leaves*

spruce [spruːs] **1** *noun* softwood tree growing in cold forests; *a forest of spruce* (NOTE: usually no plural) **2** *adjective* smart and clean; *she looks spruce and elegant in her new uniform* **3** *verb* **to spruce yourself up** = to make yourself neat and tidy; *the soldiers spruced themselves up before the general arrived*

sprung [sprʌŋ] *see* SPRING

spud [spʌd] *noun (informal)* potato; *you can peel the spuds while I prepare the meat*

spun [spʌn] *see* SPIN

spur [spɜː] **1** *noun* **(a)** sharp metal point attached to the heel of a rider's boot which jabs the horse to make it go faster; *the cowboy put on his spurs and went to saddle up his horse* **(b) to win your spurs** = to show your qualities for the first time; *it's a chance for this young player to win his spurs at international level* **(c)** thing which stimulates; *the letter from the university was the spur that encouraged him to work harder* **(d) on the spur of the moment** = without being planned in advance; *we decided on the spur of the moment to go to France* **(e)** hill which leads from a higher mountain; *the hill we climbed was a spur of the Rockies* **(f)** minor road or railway line leading off a main one; *a spur road runs off to the power station* **2** *verb* to urge someone on; *the runners were spurred on by the shouts of the crowd* (NOTE: **spurring - spurred**)

spurious ['spjʊəriəs] *adjective* false, not based on facts; *the newspaper made spurious allegations about his private life*

spurn [spɜːn] *verb (formal)* to reject an offer scornfully; *she spurned all our offers of assistance*

spurt [spɜːt] **1** *noun* **(a)** strong jet of liquid; *they tried to block the spurts of water coming out of the pipe* **(b)** sudden rush, sudden effort; *he put on a spurt and won the race* **2** *verb* **(a) to spurt out** = to come out in a strong jet; *oil spurted out of the burst pipe* **(b)** to run fast suddenly; *he spurted past two runners and came in first*

spy [spaɪ] **1** *noun* person who is paid to try to find out secret information about the enemy, a gang, a rival firm; *he was executed as a Russian spy* (NOTE: plural is **spies**) **2** *verb* **to spy on someone** = to watch someone in secret, to find out what they are planning to do; *we discovered that our neighbours had been spying on us*; **to spy for someone** = to find out secret information and

pass it back to someone; *he was accused of spying for the Americans*

spying ['spaɪɪŋ] *noun* trying to find out information about the enemy; *spying is the only way to get information that is vital to national security*

squabble ['skwɒbl] **1** *noun* quarrel or argument; *he got involved in a squabble between the taxi drivers over whose taxi he would take* **2** *verb* to argue; *they spent the whole evening squabbling over money*

squad [skwɒd] *noun* **(a)** small group of soldiers who perform duties together; *Corporal, take your squad and guard the prisoners*; **firing squad** = group of soldiers whose duty is to shoot someone who has been sentenced to death **(b)** department in the police service; *he's the head of the drug squad*; *she's investigating on behalf of the Fraud squad*; **squad car** = police car on patrol duty **(c)** group of players from whom a sports team will be chosen; *the England squad for the World Cup has been selected*

squadron ['skwɒdrən] *noun* group of aircraft or of naval ships; *he commanded a bomber squadron during the war*; **squadron leader** = rank in the air force above flight lieutenant

squalid ['skwɒlɪd] *adjective* unpleasant or dirty; *the refugees are housed in squalid camps on the hills near the border*

squalor ['skwɒlə] *noun* being in a dirty condition; *they live in squalor in a hut on the banks of the river*

squander ['skwɒndə] *verb* to waste money, energy or opportunity; *he inherited a fortune and squandered it in casinos*

square [skweə] **1** *noun* **(a)** shape with four equal sides and four right-angled corners; *a chessboard is made up of black and white squares*; *graph paper is drawn with a series of small squares* *(informal)* **back to square one** = to start again from the point you originally started from; *the test plane crashed, so it's back to square one again* **(b)** open space in a town, with big buildings all round; *the hotel is in the main square of the town, opposite the town hall*; *tourists like feeding the pigeons in Trafalgar Square*; *Red Square is in the middle of Moscow* **(c)** *(mathematics)* result when a number is multiplied by itself; *9 is the square of 3* **2** *adjective* **(a)** shaped like a square, with four equal sides and four right-angled corners; *you can't fit six people round a small square table*; *an A4 piece of paper isn't square*; **a square peg (in a round hole)** = someone whose character means that he does not fit easily into a job, etc. **(b)** making a 90° angle; *there's not one corner in the room that is square* **(c)** honest and fair; *are you being square with me?*; **square deal** = honest treatment in business; *they didn't get a square deal from the tax office*; **a square meal** = a good substantial meal; *(informal)* **now we're all square** = we do not owe each other anything **(d)** multiplied by itself; **square metre** = area of one metre multiplied by one metre; **ten square metres** = space of 10 metres x 10 metres; *the room is 5m by 9m, so its area is 45 square metres ($45m^2$)* (NOTE: **ten square metres** is usually written **10 m^2**) **3** *verb* **(a)** to make something square; **squared paper** = paper with squares drawn on it, for making graphs, etc. **(b)** to pay someone what is owed; to pay someone a bribe; *they had to square a couple of local officials before the deal went through* **(c)** *(informal)* **to square it with someone** = to see that someone gives approval; *let me deal with it - I'll square* *it with the inspector* **(d) to square your shoulders** = to straighten your shoulders; **to square up to someone** = to prepare to fight; *instead of running away, he squared up to the mugger looking very fierce* **(e)** *(mathematics)* to multiply a number by itself; *9 is 3 squared*

square dance ['skweə 'dɑːns] *noun* form of American country dance, where sets of four couples dance forming a square

square dancing ['skweə 'dɑːnsɪŋ] *noun* doing a square dance; *we go square dancing on Friday nights*

squarely ['skweəli] *adverb* **(a)** in a direct, straightforward way; *he looked her squarely in the face* **(b) fairly and squarely** = directly, without any mistakes; *they put the blame fairly and squarely on the bank*

square root ['skweə 'ruːt] *noun* number which, if you multiply it by itself, will produce the number you have; *four is the square root of sixteen*

squash [skwɒʃ] **1** *verb* to crush, to squeeze; *hundreds of commuters were squashed into the train*; *he sat on my hat and squashed it flat* **2** *noun* **(a)** a situation where a lot of people are crowded in a small space; *it's rather a squash with twenty people in the room* **(b)** drink made of concentrated fruit juice to which water is added; *a glass of orange squash* **(c)** large vegetable similar to a marrow or pumpkin

squash (rackets) ['skwɒʃ ('rækɪts)] *noun* fast game for two players played in an enclosed court, with a small, squashy rubber ball and light, long-handled rackets; *he plays squash to unwind after a day at the office*; *let's play a game of squash*

> COMMENT: the ball may be hit against any of the walls but may not bounce on the floor more than once. A game is won by the first player to reach 9 points and a match is usually the best of 5 games

squashy ['skwɒʃi] *adjective* soft, which is likely to turn to pulp; *he threw a squashy tomato at the speaker*

squat [skwɒt] **1** *noun* *(informal)* empty house which people occupy illegally; *the police raided the student squat* **2** *verb* **(a)** to crouch down, sitting on your heels; *she squatted on the floor, trying to get the stains out of the carpet* **(b)** to occupy an empty unused house belonging to another person, without permission and without paying rent; *she squatted for a time with other students from the college* (NOTE: **squatting - squatted**) **3** *adjective* short and thick; *a squat lady in her sixties sat next to me on the bus*; *the table looks too squat and doesn't fit in here* (NOTE: **squatter - squattest**)

squatter ['skwɒtə] *noun* person who squats in someone else's property or illegally on waste ground; *the police had to move in to eject the squatters*; **squatter towns** = towns of wooden or cardboard huts where squatters live; *cholera is rampant in the squatter towns*

squeak [skwiːk] **1** *noun* little high-pitched noise like that of a mouse or a rusty hinge; *you can tell when someone comes into the garden by the squeak of the gate*; *(informal)* **a narrow squeak** = a near miss, a narrow escape; *we had a narrow squeak when a lorry just missed crashing into our car* **2** *verb* to make a squeak; *that door squeaks - the hinges need oiling*

squeaky ['skwiːki] *adjective* **(a)** which squeaks; *he spoke in a little squeaky voice*; *these squeaky hinges*

need oiling **(b) squeaky clean** = (i) extremely clean, as if washed in a dishwasher; (ii) morally pure; *all the work surfaces have to be squeaky clean*; *the minister's squeaky clean image has been tarnished by the scandal*

squeal [skwiːl] **1** *noun* loud high-pitched noise; *angry squeals came from the pigsty*; *the children let out squeals of delight when they saw the cakes*; *the car turned the corner with a squeal of tyres* **2** *verb* **(a)** to make a loud high-pitched noise; *she squealed in delight as she saw the table with cakes and ices*; *as the car turned the corner its tyres squealed* **(b)** *(informal)* **to squeal on someone** = to give the police information about someone

squeamish ['skwiːmɪʃ] *adjective* likely to be upset by nasty things; *I didn't know you were so squeamish - I'll take the dead mouse out of the kitchen!*

squeeze [skwiːz] **1** *noun* **(a)** act of pressing or crushing; *I gave her hand a squeeze*; **a tight squeeze** = a situation where there is very little space to get into or through; *you can get through the hole, but it's a tight squeeze* **(b)** amount pushed out; *he put a squeeze of toothpaste on his brush*; **a squeeze of lemon** = a few drops of lemon juice **(c) credit squeeze** = period when lending by the banks is restricted by the government **2** *verb* **(a)** to press on something; to press or crush a fruit, a tube, etc., to get something out of it; *she squeezed my arm gently*; *he squeezed an orange to get the juice*; *she squeezed some toothpaste out onto her brush* **(b)** to crush, to force into a small space; *you can't squeeze six people into that little car*; *more people tried to squeeze onto the train*; *the cat managed to squeeze through the window*

squeezer ['skwiːzə] *noun* device for pressing lemons, oranges, etc., to let the juice run out; *if I had a squeezer, I'd make some fresh orange juice*

squid [skwɪd] *noun* small sea animal with eight long arms or tentacles; *she ordered fried squid as a starter* (NOTE: plural is **squid**; similar larger animals are **octopuses**)

squint [skwɪnt] **1** *noun* **(a)** state where your two eyes look in different directions; *he has a noticeable squint* **(b)** *(informal)* look or glance; *let's have a squint at that letter* **2** *verb* **(a)** to have eyes which look in different directions; *he squints badly, which makes it difficult to know who he is looking at* **(b)** to half-close your eyes to look at a something; *he squinted through the keyhole but couldn't see anything*

squire ['skwaɪə] *noun* **(a)** country landowner; *he was a gamekeeper, but he married the squire's daughter* **(b)** *(informal)* way of addressing a man; *hello, squire, what can I do for you?* **(c)** formerly, a young man who was the attendant of a knight

squirm [skwɜːm] *verb* to wriggle about; *the little girl squirmed about as her mother tried to put her shoes on*; **it makes me squirm** = it makes me very embarrassed

squirrel ['skwɪrəl] **1** *noun* common small wild mammal with a large bushy tail, living in trees and eating nuts; *the squirrel sat up on a branch nibbling a nut*; *squirrels hoard nuts for the winter* **2** *verb* US **to squirrel something away** = to hide something safely so that you can use it later

COMMENT: the indigenous British squirrel is the red squirrel, but these have largely been ousted except in Scotland and other forest areas by the grey squirrel, which was introduced into the country in the 19th century and is now considered a serious pest in towns. In North America, black squirrels are common

squirt [skwɜːt] **1** *noun* **(a)** thin jet of liquid; *just put a squirt of washing up liquid in the bowl* **(b)** *(informal)* little squirt = small unpleasant person; *that little squirt - you can beat him any day!* **2** *verb* to send out a thin jet of liquid; *don't squirt so much washing-up liquid into the bowl*; *she squeezed the bottle and masses of hand cream squirted out*

ssh! [ʃ] *interjection used to ask for silence*; *ssh! people are trying to work in here*

St *see* SAINT, STREET

St Valentine's Day [sənt ˈvæləntaɪnz ˈdeɪ] *noun* 14th February, the day when you send messages, cards, flowers, etc., to someone you love; *see also* VALENTINE

stab [stæb] **1** *noun* **(a)** deep wound made by the point of a knife; *he died of stab wounds* **(b)** stab in the back = attack by someone who is thought to be loyal; *his speech was a stab in the back for the party leader* **(c)** *(informal)* to have a stab at something = to try to do something; *I'm keen to have a stab at driving the tractor* **2** *verb* **(a)** to wound by jabbing with a sharp knife; *he was stabbed in the chest* **(b)** to stab someone in the back = to do something nasty to someone who thinks you are his friend; *she was stabbed in the back by people who owed their success to her* (NOTE: stabbing - stabbed)

stabbing [ˈstæbɪŋ] **1** *adjective* stabbing pain = pain which comes in a series of short sharp stabs; *he had stabbing pains in his chest* **2** *noun* attack where someone is stabbed; *the stabbing of the young nurse shocked everyone*

stability [stəˈbɪlɪti] *noun* being stable or steady; *the collapse of the stock market threatened the stability of the currency*

stabilize [ˈsteɪbɪlaɪz] *verb* **(a)** to make firm; *we need more weight on this side of the boat to stabilize it*; *the United Nations is sending in troops to try to stabilize the situation* **(b)** to become steady; *prices have stabilized*

stabilizer [ˈsteɪbɪlaɪzə] *noun* **(a)** small wheels attached to a child's bike to stop it falling over; *she says she can ride without stabilizers now* **(b)** piece put on the hull of a ship to prevent it from rolling; *the crossing is much smoother in a ship fitted with stabilizers* **(c)** artificial substance added to processed food to stop a mixture from changing, as in sauces

stable [ˈsteɪbl] **1** *noun* building for keeping a horse; *my horse is not in his stable, who's riding him?*; **stables** = place where horses are kept for breeding, racing, etc.; *she enjoys working in the stables because she loves horses* **2** *adjective* **(a)** steady, which does not shake; *the ladder is not very stable, will you hold it for me*; *put a book under one leg of the desk to keep it stable* **(b)** which does not change; *the hospital said his condition was stable*

stack [stæk] **1** *noun* pile or heap of things one on top of the other; *there was a stack of replies to our advertisement*; *(informal)* **stacks of** = lots of; *you can charge the tourists what you like - they've got stacks of money* **2** *verb* to pile things on top of each other; *the skis are stacked outside the chalet*; *she stacked up the dirty plates*; *the warehouse is stacked with boxes*

stadium [ˈsteɪdɪəm] *noun* large building for sport, with seating arranged around a sports field; *our sports stadium was packed with spectators*; *they are building an Olympic stadium for the next Games;* (NOTE: plural is **stadiums** *or* **stadia**)

staff [stɑːf] **1** *noun* **(a)** all the people who work in a company, school, college, or other organization; *she's on the school staff*; *only staff can use this lift*; *a quarter of our staff are ill*; *their firm pays its staff very badly*; *he joined the staff last Monday*; *three members of staff are away sick*; **clerical staff** *or* **office staff** = people who work in offices; **kitchen staff** = people who work in a kitchen; **staff room** = room for teachers in a school (NOTE: **staff** refers to a group of people and so is often followed by a verb in the plural) **(b)** the general staff = group of senior army officers who work in headquarters **(c)** *(formal)* long stick; *they attacked the beggars and beat them with staffs* **(d)** *(music)* set of five lines on which music is written (NOTE: also spelt **stave**) **2** *verb* to provide workers for an organization; *they are planning to staff the bar with part-timers*; *the shop is staffed by idiots*

staffer [ˈstɑːfə] *noun US* member of the permanent staff; *a White House staffer*

staffing [ˈstɑːfɪŋ] *noun* providing workers for an organization; **staffing levels** = numbers of members of staff required in a department for it to work efficiently

stag [stæg] **1** *noun* **(a)** adult male deer; *don't approach the stags in the autumn - they can be very dangerous* (NOTE: female deer are **does**) **(b)** person who buys a new issue of shares and sells them immediately to make a profit **2** *verb* to stag an issue = to buy a new issue of shares not as an investment, but to sell immediately at a profit

stage [steɪdʒ] **1** *noun* **(a)** raised floor in a theatre where the actors perform; *the pop group came onto the stage and started to sing* **(b)** the stage = the profession of actor; *she is planning to go on the stage*; *he has chosen the stage as a career* **(c)** one of several points of development; *the first stage in the process is to grind the ore to powder*; *the different stages of a production process*; **the contract is still in the drafting stage** = the contract is still being drafted; **in stages** = in different steps; *the company has agreed to repay the loan in stages* **(d)** section of a long journey; *stage one of the tour takes us from Paris to Bordeaux*; **in easy stages** = not doing anything very difficult; *we did the walk in easy stages*; *the tour will cross India by easy stages* **(e)** landing stage = wooden platform for boats to tie up to unload goods or people; *the ferry boat tied up at the landing stage* **2** *verb* **(a)** to put on, to arrange a play, a show, a musical, etc.; *the exhibition is being staged in the conference centre* **(b)** to show; **to stage a recovery** = to recover; *she has staged a remarkable recovery after her accident*

stagecoach [ˈsteɪdʒkəʊtʃ] *noun* (in the 18th and 19th centuries) horse-drawn passenger coach which used to run regularly along certain routes; *how long did it take to get from London to York by stagecoach?*

stage fright [ˈsteɪdʒ ˈfraɪt] *noun* nervousness which actors feel before going onto the stage; *most actors suffer from stage fright at some time in their career*

stagger ['stægə] **1** *noun* unsteady movement when someone walks; *he walked with a noticeable stagger* **2** *verb* **(a)** to walk unsteadily, almost falling down; *she managed to stagger across the road and into the police station*; *three men staggered out of the pub* **(b)** to surprise enormously; *I was staggered at the amount they charge for service* **(c)** to arrange holidays, working hours, so that they do not all begin and end at the same time; *staggered holidays help the tourist industry*; *we have to stagger the lunch hour so that there is always someone on the switchboard*

staggering ['stægrɪŋ] *adjective* very surprising; *there's a staggering amount of corruption going on*

stagnant ['stægnənt] *adjective* **(a)** *(water)* which does not flow, which is not pure enough to drink; *the marsh was full of stagnant pools of brown water*; *mosquitoes breed in stagnant water* **(b)** *(business)* not active, not increasing; *turnover was stagnant for the first half of the year*; *there is a danger of the economy becoming stagnant*

stagnate [stæg'neɪt] *verb* not to increase, not to make progress; *the economy is stagnating*; *after six hours the talks were stagnating*

stag night *or* **stag party** ['stæg 'naɪt *or* 'stæg 'pɑːtɪ] *noun* party for men only, especially a party for a bridegroom, given by his men friends on the night before his wedding (NOTE: the opposite, a party for women only, is a **hen party** *or* **hen night**)

stain [steɪn] **1** *noun* **(a)** mark which is difficult to remove, such as ink or blood; *it is difficult to remove coffee stains from the tablecloth*; *there was a round stain on the table where he had put his wine glass; see also* BLOODSTAIN, INKSTAIN **(b)** liquid paint used to give a different colour to wood; *we bought some dark green stain for the furniture in the conservatory* **2** *verb* **(a)** to make a mark of a different colour on something; *if you eat those blueberries they will stain your teeth*; *the tablecloth was stained with strawberry jam*; *his shirt was stained with blood* **(b)** to colour something with a stain; to put a stain on a surface; *the door will be stained light brown*

stained [steɪnd] **1** *adjective* coloured with a liquid; *he went to change his stained shirt*; **stained glass** = glass which has been coloured, used for making church windows; *Canterbury Cathedral is famous for its stained glass* **2** *suffix meaning* which has been coloured with something; *his ink-stained fingers*; *her blood-stained clothes*

stainless steel ['steɪnləs 'stiːl] *noun* type of steel with a high percentage of chromium in it, which makes it resistant to rust; *a set of stainless steel saucepans*

stair [steə] *see* STAIRS

staircarpet ['steəkɑːpɪt] *noun* long narrow piece of carpet which covers stairs; *the staircarpet's getting badly worn and needs replacing*

staircase ['steəkeɪs] *noun* set of stairs which go from one floor in a building to another; *the staircase is at the back of the building*; *you have to go up a spiral staircase to the top of the tower*

stairs [steəz] *noun* steps which go up or down inside a building; *you have to go up three flights of stairs to get to my office*; *he slipped and fell down the stairs*; *see also* DOWNSTAIRS, UPSTAIRS (NOTE: **stair** is sometimes used in the singular for one step: **he was sitting on the bottom stair**)

stairway ['steəweɪ] *noun* staircase, a set of stairs which go from one floor inside or outside a building to another; *go and ask the caretaker to replace the light bulb in the stairway*; *a stairway leads to the upper terrace*

stake [steɪk] **1** *noun* **(a)** strong pointed piece of wood or metal, pushed into the ground to mark something, or to hold something up; *they hammered stakes into the ground to put up a wire fence*; *the apple trees are attached to stakes* **(b)** money which has been bet or invested; *with a £5 stake he won £100*; **the stakes are high** = a lot of money could be won or lost; **he has a stake in the company** = he has invested money in the company **(c) at stake** = which may be lost if what you do fails; *you must reply to the allegations in the paper, the reputation of the family is at stake!* (NOTE: do not confuse with **steak**) **2** *verb* **(a)** to put sticks in the ground to mark an area; *we staked out the area where the riding events were to take place* **(b) to stake your claim to something** = to say in public that you have the right to own something; *as soon as we arrived at the hotel she staked her claim to the only room with a view of the sea* **(c)** to risk; *he risked his reputation on the libel action*; *I'd stake my life on it, he's not guilty*; *they had staked everything on the success of this product*; **to stake money on something** = to risk *or* bet money on something; *she staked £10,000 on a throw of the dice*

stakeholder ['steɪkhəʊldə] *noun* person who has a stake in a business, such as a shareholder, an employee, a supplier, etc.

stalactite ['stæləktaɪt] *noun* long pointed growth of mineral from the ceiling of a cave, formed by the constant dripping of water which is rich in minerals

stalagmite ['stæləgmaɪt] *noun* long pointed growth of mineral growing from the floor of a cave, formed by the constant dripping of water from the tip of a stalactite

stale [steɪl] *adjective* old and unusable, no longer fresh; *she threw the bread away because it was stale*; *if you don't eat the cakes soon they'll go stale*; *nobody likes the smell of stale tobacco smoke* (NOTE: **staler - stalest**)

stalemate ['steɪlmeɪt] *noun* **(a)** *(in chess)* position where neither player cannot make any move permitted by the rules, and so no one wins **(b)** situation where neither side will compromise; *the discussions have reached a stalemate*; *negotiations are continuing to try to break the stalemate or to find a way out of the stalemate*

stalk [stɔːk] **1** *noun* **(a)** stem of a plant which holds a leaf, a flower, a fruit, etc.; *roses with very long stalks are more expensive*; *cherries often come attached to stalks in pairs* **2** *verb* **(a)** to walk stiffly, proudly or angrily; *she stalked into the committee room* **(b)** to follow someone *or* something secretly in order to catch them; *the hunters stalked the deer*; *the photographers stalked the film star*

stalker ['stɔːkə] *noun* person who follows people or animals; *a stalker followed her as she walked home from the bus stop*

stall [stɔːl] **1** *noun* **(a)** small moveable stand in a market, where a trader displays and sells his goods; *he has a flower stall at Waterloo Station*; *we wandered round the market looking at the stalls* **(b)** compartment for one animal in a building such as a stable; *each horse had its own stall with its name on it* **(c) stalls** = seats on the ground floor in a theatre or cinema; *seats in the* *stalls are expensive, let's get tickets for the balcony* **(d)** **(choir) stalls** = rows of seats for the choir in a church **2** *verb* **(a)** *(informal)* to put off answering a question, making a decision, etc.; *have they got genuine doubts about the plan or are they simply stalling?* **(b)** *(of a car engine)* to stop unintentionally, often when trying to drive off without accelerating; *if he takes his foot off the accelerator, the engine stalls*; *the car stalled at the traffic lights and he couldn't restart it* **(c)** *(of an aircraft)* to go so slowly that the engine cuts out and it falls

stallion ['stæljən] *noun* adult male horse, especially one kept for breeding

stalwart ['stɒlwət] **1** *adjective* strong, vigorous or brave; *a stalwart defence of basic human rights* **2** *noun* person who works hard and is loyal; *there was no one at the meeting except the stalwarts of the parish council*

stamen ['steɪmən] *noun* male part of a flower consisting of a stalk bearing pollen; *each stamen is like a fine stalk bearing an anther*

stamina ['stæmɪnə] *noun* strength to do something over a long period; *does he have the stamina for the job? - it involves travelling around South America for six weeks at a time*

stammer ['stæmə] **1** *noun* hesitating and repeating sounds when speaking; *because of his stammer he was shy and reserved at school* **2** *verb* to hesitate and repeat sounds when speaking; *he stammers badly when making speeches*; *she rushed into the police station and stammered out 'he's - he's - he's after me, he's got - got - a knife'*

stamp [stæmp] **1** *noun* **(a)** little piece of paper with a price printed on it which you stick on a letter, postcard, etc., to show that you have paid for it to be sent by the post; *you need a 26p stamp for that letter*; *she forgot to put a stamp on the letter before she posted it*; *he wants to show me his stamp collection* **(b)** machine for making a mark on something; *we have a stamp for marking letters when they come into the office*; **date stamp** = device with rubber figures which can be moved, used for marking the date on documents or for marking the sell-by date on goods **(c)** mark made on something; *the invoice has the stamp 'received with thanks' on it*; *the customs officer looked at the stamps in his passport* **2** *verb* **(a)** to stick a stamp on a letter or parcel; *all the envelopes need to be sealed and stamped* **(b)** to mark something with a stamp; *they stamped my passport when I entered the country* **(c)** to walk heavily, banging your feet on the ground; *they stamped on the ants to kill them*; *he was so angry that he stamped out of the room* **(d)** to make a noise by banging your feet on the ground; *the audience stamped on the floor in time to the music*

stamp duty ['stæmp 'djuːti] *noun* tax on legal documents, such as the tax paid when buying a property

stamped addressed envelope (s.a.e.) ['stæmpt ə'drest 'envələup] *noun* envelope with your own address written on it and a stamp stuck on it to pay for the return postage; *send a stamped addressed envelope for further details and a catalogue*

stampede [stæm'piːd] **1** *noun* mad rush of animals or people; *after the film finished there was a stampede for the doors* **2** *verb* **(a)** to rush madly; *the herd of buffalo stampeded down the valley* **(b) to stampede**

someone into doing something = to try to force someone into doing something; *they tried to stampede us into voting for their proposal*

stamp out ['stæmp 'aut] *verb* to stop or to remove; *the police are trying to stamp out corruption*

stance [stɑːns] *noun* **(a)** position of someone when standing; *his stance is so awkward I'm surprised he can even hit the ball* **(b)** point of view, opinion; *her stance on environmental issues is surprising*; *the party has adopted a new progressive stance on education*

stand [stænd] **1** *noun* **(a)** something which holds something up; *the pot of flowers fell off its stand* **(b)** seats where you sit to watch a football match, etc.; *the stands were full for the international*; *we have tickets for the North Stand* **(c) display stand** = special set of shelves for displaying goods for sale; **exhibition stand** = separate section of an exhibition where a company exhibits its products or services; *we must book a bigger stand next year - this one is too small* (NOTE: the US English for this is **booth**); **news stand** = small wooden shelter on a pavement, used for selling newspapers **(d)** position; *his stand against the party leader earned him a term in prison*; *she was criticized for her stand against government policy*; **to take a stand against** = to protest against; *they are taking a strong stand against corruption in the party* **(e)** US **witness stand** = place in a courtroom where the witnesses give evidence (NOTE: British English is usually **witness box**) **2** *verb* **(a)** to be upright on your feet, the opposite of sitting or lying down; *she stood on a chair to reach the top shelf*; *they were so tired they could hardly keep standing*; *if there are no seats left, we'll have to stand*; *don't just stand there doing nothing - come and help us* **(b)** to be upright; *only a few houses were still standing after the earthquake*; *the jar was standing in the middle of the table* **(c)** to get up from a seat; *she stood and rushed to the door* **(d)** to put upright; *stand the bookcase over in the corner*; *he stood the pot on the table* **(e)** to tolerate, to put up with; *the office is filthy - I don't know how you can stand working here*; *she can't stand all this noise*; *he stopped going to French lessons because he couldn't stand the teacher* **(f) to stand for election** = to offer yourself as a candidate in an election; *he has stood for parliament several times but has never been elected*; **to stand against someone** = to put yourself against someone in an election; *she is standing against the leader in the election* (NOTE: American English uses to **run for election**) **(g)** to pay for; *he stood us all a round of drinks* (NOTE: **standing - stood** [stud])

standard ['stændəd] **1** *noun* **(a)** the level of quality achieved by something; *the standard of service in this restaurant is very high*; *this piece of work is not up to your usual standard* **(b)** excellent quality which is set as a target; *this product does not meet our standards*; *she has set a standard which it will be difficult to match*; **standard of living** *or* **living standards** = quality of personal home life (such as amount of food or clothes bought, size of the family car, etc.); *we can't complain about our standard of living, we're really very comfortably off* **(c)** tree or bush grown with a tall trunk; *do you prefer an ordinary rosebush or a standard?* **(d)** large official flag; *the royal standard flies over Buckingham Palace* **2** *adjective* **(a)** usual, normal; *she joined on a standard contract*; *you will need to follow the standard procedure to join the association*; **standard authors** = the main classical authors, the authors that everyone usually has to study;

standard pronunciation = pronunciation of educated speakers; **standard rate** = normal charge for something, such as a phone call or income tax; *the standard rate of income tax is 20p in the pound*; **standard work** = book which is the recognized authority on a subject; *he's the author of the standard work on woodland fungi* **(b)** on a tall pole; **standard lamp** = room lamp on a tall pole standing on the floor (NOTE: American English is **floor lamp**); **standard rose** = rose grown with a tall trunk **(c) standard time** = time which applies within a certain area of the world

Standard Assessment Tests (SATs)
['stændəd ə'sesmənt 'tests (sæts)] *noun GB* national tests taken at various ages during secondary school

standardization [stændədaɪ'zeɪʃn] *noun* making sure that everything fits a standard or is produced in the same way; *we are aiming for complete standardization of diskette formats, so that any diskette can be used in* any machine; **standardization of products** = reducing a large number of different products to a few which have the same measurements, design, packaging, etc.

standardize ['stændədaɪz] *verb* to make everything follow the same standard; *components have become standardized throughout the computer industry*

stand around ['stænd ə'raʊnd] *verb* to stand, and not do anything; *they just stood around and watched*

stand aside ['stænd ə'saɪd] *verb* to step sideways; *we stood aside to let the ambulanceman pass*

stand back ['stænd 'bæk] *verb* to take a step or two backwards; *stand well back, the marathon runners are coming*

stand by ['stænd 'baɪ] *verb* **(a)** to confirm, to refuse to change; *I stand by what I said in my statement to the police* **(b)** to stand and watch, without getting involved; *several people just stood by and made no attempt to help* **(c)** to be ready; *we have several fire engines standing by* **(d)** to support, to give help; *she stood by him while he was in prison*

standby ['stændbaɪ] *noun* **(a)** thing which is ready to be used if necessary; *I always have shrimps in the freezer as a standby*; **good standby** = thing which is good to have at hand in case you need it; *an oil lamp is a good standby in case there's a power failure* **(b)** on **standby** = waiting and ready to act if needed; *we have a doctor on standby; army reservists have been put on standby; (at an airport)* **standby ticket** = cheap ticket which you buy just before a plane takes off, allowing you to have a seat if there are any empty seats left at the last minute; *there are no standby tickets for Montreal*

stand down ['stænd 'daʊn] *verb* to agree not to stay in a position or not to stand for election; *the mayor decided to stand down after several years in office*

stand for ['stænd 'fɔː] *verb* **(a)** to have a meaning; *what do the letters DOS stand for?* **(b)** to be a candidate in an election; *she's standing for parliament* **(c)** to accept; *they will never stand for that; I won't stand for any nonsense from the children*

stand-in ['stændɪn] *noun* person who takes the place of someone else; *the preacher is ill so his place has been taken by a stand-in*

stand in for ['stænd 'ɪn fɔː] *verb* to take the place of someone; *she's standing in for the chairman who is ill*

standing ['stændɪŋ] **1** *noun* **(a)** being upright on your feet; *standing all day at the exhibition is very tiring* **(b)** good reputation; *his standing in the* community has never been higher; *a hotel of good standing* **(c) long-standing customer** *or* **customer of long standing** = person who has been a customer for many years **2** *adjective* **(a)** upright, not lying or sitting; *after the earthquake, the few buildings left standing needed to be repaired* **(b)** permanent; *we have a standing agreement with our supplier to send back items we don't want*; **standing order** = order written by a customer asking a bank to pay money regularly to an account, or to a company to send something regularly; *I pay my subscription by standing order; we have a standing order for two dozen eggs every Friday*; **it is a standing joke with us** = it is something we always make jokes about; *his style of dancing is a bit of a standing joke with us*

standing ovation ['stændɪŋ əʊ'veɪʃn] *noun* applause at the end of a speech, concert, etc., where all the audience stand up and clap and cheer; *he received a standing ovation at the end of the concert; all the delegates gave the president a 10-minute standing ovation at the end of his speech*

standing room ['stændɪŋ 'rʊm] *noun* space for people to stand, not to sit; *there is standing room only at the concert*

stand-off ['stændɒf] *noun* situation where two sides cannot agree and neither can win; *the government troops surrounded the university, but the students continued to occupy the building* and the stand-off continued for some hours

stand out ['stænd 'aʊt] *verb* **(a)** to be easily seen; *their house stands out because it is painted pink; her red hair makes her stand out in a crowd* **(b)** to be very clear against a background; *that picture would stand out better against a white wall* **(c)** to be much better than others; *two of the young musicians stood out for their interpretations of Bach*

standpoint ['stændpɔɪnt] *noun* point of view or position from which you look at a problem; *we have to look at this from the standpoint of the children involved*

standstill ['stæn(d)stɪl] *noun* situation where nothing moves; *traffic in Central London was at a standstill; the strike brought the factory to a standstill*

stand up ['stænd 'ʌp] *verb* **(a)** to get up from sitting; *when the teacher comes into the room all the children should stand up; he stood up to offer his seat to the old lady* **(b)** to stand upright, to hold yourself upright; *stand up straight and face forward* **(c)** to put something in an upright position; *stand the books up on the shelf; she stood her umbrella up by the door* **(d)** *(informal)* **to stand someone up** = not to meet someone even though you had arranged to; *we were going to have dinner together and he stood me up*

stand-up ['stændʌp] *adjective* **stand-up buffet** = buffet where you serve yourself and eat standing up; **stand-up fight** = violent argument where people hit each other

stand up for ['stænd 'ʌp fɔː] *verb* to try to defend someone *or* something in an argument; *he stood up for the rights of the small shopkeepers; no one stood up for her when she was sacked*

stanza ['stænzə] *noun* section of a poem made up of a series of lines; *the second stanza begins 'Heard melodies are sweet, but those unheard are sweeter...'*

staple ['steɪpl] **1** *noun* **(a)** piece of wire which is pushed through papers and bent over to hold them together; *he used some scissors to take the staples out of the papers* **(b)** main food in a diet; *rice is the staple of the Chinese diet* **2** *adjective* main; **staple product** = main product of a country, town, etc.; *wheat is the staple crop of several American states*; **staple diet** = main part of what you eat; *rice with fish is the staple diet of many people in the Far East* **3** *verb* to fasten papers together with a staple or with staples; *don't staple the cheque to the order form*; **to staple papers together** = to attach various papers with a staple or with staples; *all these papers need to be stapled together and filed*

stapler ['steɪplə] *noun* little device used to attach papers together with staples; *the stapler needs reloading as it's run out of staples*

star [stɑ:] **1** *noun* **(a)** bright object which can be seen in the sky at night like a very distant bright light; *on a clear night you can see thousands of stars*; *the pole star shows the direction of the North Pole* **(b) star sign** = the sign of the zodiac which marks your birth; *(informal)* **thank your lucky stars** = consider yourself very lucky; *thank your lucky stars that you were not on that plane* **(c)** shape that has several points like a star; *draw a big star and colour it red* **(d)** asterisk, a printing symbol shaped like a star; *a star next to a word refers you to the footnotes* **(e)** classification sign for hotels, restaurants, etc.; **three-star hotel** = hotel which has been classified with three stars, under a classification system; *we stayed in a two-star hotel and found it perfectly comfortable* **(f)** famous person who is very well known to the public; *who is your favourite film star?*; *the film has an all-star cast*; *the Chelsea football star* **2** *verb* to appear as a main character in a film or play; *she starred in 'Gone with the Wind'*; *he has a starring role in the new production of 'Guys and Dolls'* (NOTE: **starring - starred**)

starboard ['stɑ:bəd] *noun* the right-hand side of a ship when facing the bow; also used of the right-hand side of an aircraft; *we turned to starboard to avoid the ferry*; *people on the starboard side of the plane can see the Statue of Liberty* (NOTE: the opposite, ie the left-hand side, is **port**)

starch [stɑ:tʃ] **1** *noun* **(a)** usual form in which carbohydrates exist in food, especially in bread, rice and potatoes; *to get a balanced diet you need to eat both protein and starch* **(b)** white powder mixed with water to make cloth stiff **(c)** *US* **corn starch** = CORNFLOUR (NOTE: no plural) **2** *verb* to make cloth stiff with starch; *she starched his shirt collars*

starchy ['stɑ:tʃi] *adjective* **(a)** (food) which contains a lot of starch; *children eat too much starchy food* **(b)** very formal; *his starchy manner put everyone off*

stardom ['stɑ:dəm] *noun* being a film star, a football star, etc.; *he was very young and couldn't cope with his sudden rise to stardom*

stare [steə] **1** *noun* long fixed look; *he gave her a stare and walked on* **2** *verb* **(a)** to look at someone *or* something for a long time; *she stared unhappily out of the window* **(b)** *(informal)* **to stare someone in the face** = to be very obvious; *he couldn't find the answer even if it was staring him in the face*

starfish ['stɑ:fɪʃ] *noun* flat sea animal, with five arms branching like a star from a central body; *the children found a starfish on the beach and brought it back to the tent in a bucket* (NOTE: plural is **starfish**)

staring ['steərɪŋ] *adjective* which looks steadily for a long time; *we could see rows of staring eyes looking at us from the windows of the prison*; *see also* STARK

stark [stɑ:k] **1** *adjective* **(a)** complete; *he stared at the figures in stark disbelief* **(b)** bare and simple; *the stark outline of the rocks*; *a stark lunar landscape* (NOTE: **starker - starkest**) **2** *adverb* completely; *I don't usually walk round the house stark naked*; **stark staring mad** *or* **stark raving mad** = completely mad; *you must be stark staring mad even to think of swimming in the North Sea on Christmas Day*

starlet ['stɑ:lət] *noun* young film actress who hopes to become famous one day; *pictures of starlets posing by the beach at the Cannes Film Festival*

starling ['stɑ:lɪŋ] *noun* common dark European bird with a green gloss to its feathers; *a flock of starlings were pecking about on the grass*

Stars and Stripes ['stɑ:z n 'straɪps] *noun* the flag of the USA; *the Stars and Stripes is flying over the door of the American Embassy* (NOTE: can take a singular or plural verb)

start [stɑ:t] **1** *noun* **(a)** beginning of something; *building the house took only six months from start to finish*; *things went wrong from the start*; *let's forget all you've done up to now, and make a fresh start*; **for a start** = as the first point; *for a start, tell me the exact time when you made the phone call* **(b)** leaving for a journey; *we're planning on a 6 o'clock start*; *let's make an early start tomorrow* **(c)** place where a race begins; *the cars were lined up at the start* **(d)** being in advance of other competitors; *we'll never catch them, they have three hours' start on us*; *I'll give you four yards' start* **(e)** sudden jump of surprise; *she gave a start when he put his hand on her shoulder* **2** *verb* **(a)** to begin to do something; *the babies all started to cry or all started crying at the same time*; *he started to eat or he started eating his dinner before the rest of the family*; *take an umbrella - it's starting to rain*; *when you learn Russian, you have to start by learning the alphabet*; *we must start packing now or we'll miss the plane*; *at what time does the match start?*; **to start with** = first of all; *we have lots to do but to start with we'll do the washing up* **(b)** to leave on a journey; *we plan to start at 6 o'clock* **(c)** *(of a machine)* to begin to work; *the car won't start - the battery must be flat*; *the engine started beautifully* **(d)** to make something begin to work; *I can't start the car*; *it is difficult to start a car in cold weather* **(e)** to make something begin; *he fired a gun to start the race*; *the police think that the fire was started deliberately* **(f)** to jump with surprise; *she started when she heard the bang*

starter ['stɑ:tə] *noun* **(a)** person who starts doing something; *there were sixty starters in the race, but only twenty finished* **(b)** person who organizes the start of something; *the starter fired his pistol and the race started*; *(of racers)* **under starter's orders** = ready to run just before the start of a race **(c)** *(informal)* first part of a meal; *what do you all want as starters?*; *I don't want a starter - just the main course* **(d)** **starter (motor)** = electric motor in a car which sets the main engine going; *your battery's OK, so maybe the starter is faulty*

starting ['stɑ:tɪŋ] *adjective* at the beginning; **starting date** = date on which something begins; **starting gun** = gun fired to start a race; **starting line** = line at the beginning of a race; *sixty runners were waiting at the starting line*

starting point ['stɑːtɪŋ 'pɔɪnt] *noun* place where something begins; *the starting point of the marathon is in Greenwich; let us take the invasion of England by the Normans in 1066 as our starting point*

startle ['stɑːtl] *verb* to make someone suddenly surprised; *I'm sorry, I didn't mean to startle you; she looked up startled when she heard the knock at the door; we were all startled to hear about his getting married*

startling ['stɑːtlɪŋ] *adjective* suddenly surprising; *everyone was talking about the startling election results*

start off ['stɑːt 'ɒf] *verb* **(a)** to begin; *we'll start off with soup and then have a meat dish* **(b)** to leave on a journey; *you can start off now, and I'll follow when I'm ready*

start out ['stɑːt 'aʊt] *verb* **(a)** to leave on a journey; *she started out for home two hours ago, so I am surprised she hasn't arrived* **(b)** to begin; *I'd like to start out by saying how pleased I am to be here*

start up ['stɑːt 'ʌp] *verb* **(a)** to make a business begin to work; *she started up a restaurant, but it failed* **(b)** to make an engine start to work; *he started up the tractor*

starvation [stɑː'veɪʃn] *noun* illness through lack of food; *people are dying of starvation in parts of Africa*

starve [stɑːv] *verb* **(a)** not to have enough food; *many people starved to death in the desert* **(b)** **to starve someone of something** = not to give enough supplies to someone; *the service is being starved of funds*

starving ['stɑːvɪŋ] *adjective* **(a)** who do not have enough to eat; *relief workers tried to bring supplies to the starving people* **(b)** (*informal*) **I'm starving** = I am very hungry; *isn't dinner ready yet, I'm absolutely starving!*

stash [stæʃ] (*informal*) **1** *verb* **(a) to stash away** = to store in a safe place; *he has thousands of dollars stashed away in overseas bank accounts* **(b)** to put; *make sure you stash all items of hand luggage in the rack above your seat* **2** *noun* hidden store of things; *we found a stash of old love letters in a secret drawer*

state [steɪt] **1** *noun* **(a)** condition (often a bad condition), the way something or someone is; *the children are in a state of excitement; they left the house in a terrible state; look at the state of your trousers; she's not in a fit state to receive visitors* **(b)** condition where you are depressed, worried, etc.; *she's in such a state that I don't want to leave her alone; he was in a terrible state after the phone call* **(c) state of health** = being well or sick; *his state of health has improved with treatment*; **state of mind** = a person's feelings at a particular time; *he's in a very miserable state of mind; in her present state of mind she's unlikely to be able to decide what to do* **(d)** government of a country; *we all pay taxes to the state; the state should pay for the upkeep of museums*; **state-owned** = owned by the country or government and not by private individuals **(e)** independent country; *the member states of the European Union*; **head of state** = official leader of a country, though not necessarily the head of the government **(f)** one of the parts of a federal country; *the State of Arizona; New South Wales has the largest population of all the Australian states; see also* UNITED STATES OF AMERICA **2** *adjective* referring to the state; **state enterprise** = company run by the state **3** *verb* to give information clearly; *please state your name and address; it states in the instructions that you must not open the can near a flame; the document states that all revenue has to be declared to the tax office*

stated ['steɪtɪd] *adjective* made clear; *our stated aim is to expand the retail side of the business*

State Department ['steɪt dɪ'pɑːtmənt] *noun* section of the US government dealing with foreign affairs; *the Russian delegation is meeting State Department officials* (NOTE: in the UK, the equivalent is the **Foreign Office**; in most other countries it is the **Foreign Ministry**)

statehood ['steɪthʊd] *noun* situation of being an independent state; *they fought for their independence and finally achieved statehood last year*

stateless ['steɪtləs] *adjective* who is not a citizen of any country; *he was stateless, with no passport, no documentation at all*

stately ['steɪtli] *adjective* noble or dignified; *the procession walked at a stately pace down the Mall*; **stately home** = palace or large house belonging to a lord, etc.; *we visited several stately homes during our stay in England*

statement ['steɪtmənt] *noun* **(a)** clearly written or spoken description of what happened; *she made a statement to the police* **(b)** list of invoices and credits and debits sent by a supplier to a customer at the end of each month; *I want to query something in last month's statement*; **bank statement** = written document from a bank showing the balance of an account; **monthly** *or* **quarterly statement** = statement which is sent every month *or* every quarter

state of affairs ['steɪt əv ə'feəz] *noun* general situation; *this state of affairs cannot be allowed to continue*

state-of-the-art ['steɪt əv θi 'ɑːt] *adjective* technically as advanced as possible; *the hotel is equipped with a state-of-the-art fitness centre*

States ['steɪts] *noun* (*informal*) the United States of America; *we've lost touch with him now that he's gone to live in the States; they hitched their way across the States*

state school ['steɪt 'skuːl] *noun* school which is funded by the state (as opposed to a private school); *he went to a state school; the state school system needs more funds* (NOTE: in American English this is a **public school**); *compare* PRIVATE SCHOOL, PUBLIC SCHOOL

statesman ['steɪtsmən] *noun* important political leader or representative of a country; *a meeting of world statesmen to agree to a nuclear test ban treaty* (NOTE: plural is **statesmen**)

statesmanlike ['steɪtsmənlaɪk] *adjective* wise and skillful, like a good statesman; *he conducted the negotiations in a thoroughly statesmanlike way*

statesmanship ['steɪtsmənʃɪp] *noun* skill in the government of a country; the ability to be a good statesman; *being able to bring the two leaders together was an act of great statesmanship*

statewide [steɪt'waɪd] *adjective US* referring to the United States as whole; *a statewide hunt for the killer of the little children*

static ['stætɪk] **1** *adjective* not changing, not moving, not growing; *sales have remained static for the last two* *months*; **static electricity** = electric charge that doesn't flow as opposed to electricity which is flowing in a current **2** *noun* **(a)** electrical interference in the air which disturbs a radio signal **(b)** = STATIC ELECTRICITY; *when I touched the car door the static gave me a shock*

station ['steɪʃn] *noun* **(a)** (*railway*) **station** = place where trains stop, where passengers get on or off, etc.; *the train leaves the Central Station at 14.15; this is a fast train - it doesn't stop at every station; we'll try to get a sandwich at the station buffet* **(b)** **bus station** *or* **coach station** = place where coaches or buses begin or end their journeys; *coaches leave Victoria Coach Station for all parts of the country;* **underground station** *or* **tube station** = place where underground trains stop, where passengers get on or off; *there's an underground station just a few minutes' walk away* **(c)** large main building for a service; *the fire station is just down the road from us; he was arrested and taken to the local police station;* **power station** = factory which produces electricity; *the power station chimneys are a local landmark;* **service station** = garage which sells petrol and repairs cars; *luckily I broke down right outside a service station;* **TV station** *or* **radio station** = building where TV or radio programmes are broadcast; *the station broadcasts hourly reports on snow conditions* **(d)** (*in Australia*) **sheep station** = very large farm, specializing in raising sheep **2** *verb* to place someone officially in a place; *soldiers were stationed in the frontier towns; police were stationed all along the route of the procession*

stationary ['steɪʃnəri] *adjective* not moving, standing still; *he collided with a stationary vehicle; traffic is stationary for three kilometres on the M25* (NOTE: do not confuse with **stationery**)

stationer ['steɪʃənə] *noun* person who has a shop which sells stationery; **the stationer's** = show which sells stationery; *go to the stationer's and get me some envelopes*

stationery ['steɪʃnəri] *noun* materials used when writing, such as paper, envelopes, pens, ink, etc.; *the letter was typed on his office stationery* (NOTE: no plural; do not confuse with **stationary**)

station manager *or* **stationmaster** ['steɪʃən 'mænədʒə *or* 'steɪʃnmɑːstə] *noun* person in charge of a railway station

station wagon ['steɪʃən 'wægən] *noun* US large car with a flat space behind the seats where parcels or suitcases can be put through the rear door (NOTE: British English for this is an **estate car**)

statistic [stə'tɪstɪk] *noun* fact given in the form of a figure; *this statistic on its own does not prove your case*

statistical [stə'tɪstɪkl] *adjective* referring to statistics; *she's gathering statistical evidence to prove her case*

statistician [stætɪs'tɪʃn] *noun* person who studies or analyses statistics; *she works as a statistician in a government department*

statistics [stə'tɪstɪks] *noun* study of facts in the form of figures; *we examined the sales statistics for the previous six months; government statistics show an increase in heart disease*

statue ['stætʃuː] *noun* figure of a person or animal carved from stone, made from metal, etc.; *the statue of King John is in the centre of the square*

statuette [stætʃu'et] *noun* very small statue; *she got a statuette as a prize and took it home with her to put on her mantelpiece*

status ['steɪtəs] *noun* **(a)** **legal status** = legal position; **marital status** = position of being married, divorced, or not married **(b)** social importance when compared to other people; *he has a low-status job on the Underground; his status in the company has been rising steadily;* **status symbol** = thing which you use which shows that you are more important than someone else; **the chairman's car is a just status symbol** = the size of his car shows how important he or his company is; **loss of status** = becoming less important in a group **(c)** general position; **status inquiry** = check on a customer's credit rating (NOTE: no plural)

status quo ['steɪtəs 'kwəʊ] *noun* state of things as they are now; *his death does not alter the status quo; the government's aim is to preserve the status quo*

statute ['stætʃuːt] *noun* written law, established in an Act of Parliament; *unlicensed trading is prohibited by a statute of 1979;* **statute book** = list of all the laws passed by Parliament which are still in force; *the law is not yet on the statute book;* **statute of limitations** = law which allows only a certain amount of time, usually six years, for someone to start legal proceedings to claim damages

statutory ['stætʃutri] *adjective* imposed by law; *there is a statutory probationary period of thirteen weeks;* **statutory holiday** = holiday which is fixed by law; **statutory sick pay** = payment made each week by an employer to an employee who is away from work because of sickness

staunch [stɔːnʃ] **1** *adjective* firm; *she's my staunchest friend; they are staunch supporters of the Conservative party* (NOTE: **stauncher - staunchest**) **2** *verb* to stop a flow of blood; *they tied a bandage tightly round his arm in an attempt to staunch the flow of blood*

stave [steɪv] **1** *noun* **(a)** one of several curved pieces of wood which form the sides of a barrel **(b)** (*music*) set of five lines on which music is written (NOTE: also spelt **staff**) **2** *verb* **(a) to stave in** = to batter a hole in a boat or a barrel; *the little boat hit the rocks and one of its sides was staved in* (NOTE: in this meaning the past is **staved** *or* **stove** [stəʊv]) **(b) to stave off** = to hold off or to prevent; *we asked the bank for a further loan to stave off bankruptcy*

stay [steɪ] **1** *noun* **(a)** time during which you live in a place; *my sister's here for a short stay; did you enjoy your stay in London?* **(b) stay of execution** = delay in putting a legal order into effect; *the judge granted a stay of execution* **2** *verb* **(a)** to remain, not to change; *the temperature stayed below zero all day; in spite of the fire, he stayed calm; I won't be able to stay awake until midnight* **(b)** to stop in a place; *they came for lunch and stayed until after midnight; I'm rather tired so I'll stay at home tomorrow; he's ill and has to stay in bed* **(c)** to stop in a place as a visitor; *they stayed two nights in Edinburgh on their tour of Scotland; where will you be staying when you're in New York?; my parents are staying at the Hotel London*

stay away ['steɪ ə'weɪ] *verb* not to come or go to something; *she doesn't like parties, and stayed away*

stay in ['steɪ 'ɪn] *verb* to stop at home instead of going out; *we prefer to stay in rather than go and queue for hours to get into the cinema*

staying power ['steɪɪŋ 'pauə] *noun* energy to keep on doing something until the job is finished; *she has remarkable staying power*

stay out ['steɪ 'aut] *verb* to remain away from home; *the girls stayed out until two o'clock in the morning*

stay put [s'teɪ 'put] *phrase* to stay where you are, not to move; *I'm not going to resign - I'm staying put!*; *stay put! - I'll go and get a doctor*

stay up ['steɪ 'ʌp] *verb* not to go to bed; *we stayed up late to see the New Year in*; *little children are not supposed to stay up until midnight watching TV*

stead [sted] *noun* (a) it stood him in good stead = it was very useful to him; *being able to speak Japanese stood him in good stead* (b) *(formal)* in your stead = in place of you; *when he was ill, she took the chair in his stead*; *see also* INSTEAD

steadfast ['stedfɑːst] *adjective* *(formal)* firm, constant; *the President has always been a steadfast believer in the constitution*

steadily ['stedɪli] *adverb* not changing; regularly or continuously; *things have been steadily going from bad to worse*; *sales have increased steadily over the last two years*

steady ['stedi] **1** *adjective* (a) firm, not moving or wobbling; *you need a steady hand to draw a straight line without a ruler*; *he put a piece of paper under the table leg to keep it steady* (b) continuing in a regular way; *there is a steady demand for computers*; *the car was doing a steady seventy miles an hour*; *she hasn't got a steady boyfriend* (NOTE: **steadier - steadiest**) **2** *interjection*; steady on! = be careful; *steady on! - you almost hit that car*; *(starting a race)* to start the race, *Natasha shouted 'ready! steady! go!'* **3** *verb* (a) to calm; *she took a pill to steady her nerves* (b) to keep firm; *he put out his hand to steady the ladder*

steak [steɪk] *noun* (a) thick slice of beef; *he ordered steak and chips*; *I'm going to grill these steaks* (b) thick slice cut across the body of a fish; *a grilled salmon steak for me, please!* (NOTE: do not confuse with **stake**)

steak and kidney pie ['steɪk ən 'kɪdni 'paɪ] *noun* British dish of cubes of beef and kidney cooked together with onions in a thick sauce covered with pastry; *she ordered steak and kidney pie*

steakhouse ['steɪkhaus] *noun* restaurant serving steak and other grilled food

steak knife ['steɪk 'naɪf] *noun* very sharp knife, knife with a serrated edge, used when eating meat (NOTE: plural is **steak knives**)

steal [stiːl] *verb* (a) to take something which belongs to another person; *someone tried to steal my handbag*; *she owned up to having stolen the jewels*; *did the burglar steal all your CDs? - I'm afraid so*; *he was arrested for stealing, but the judge let him off with a fine* (b) to steal the show = to do better than a star actor; *it was the little dog that stole the show*; *see also* THUNDER (c) to move quietly; *he stole into the cellar and tried to find the safe*; to steal away = to go away very quietly; *he stole away under cover of darkness* (NOTE: **stealing - stole** [stəul] - **stolen** ['stəulən]; do not confuse with **steel**)

stealth [stelθ] *noun* by stealth = in a secret way, without anyone knowing; *they tried to get into the government laboratory by stealth*

stealthily ['stelθɪli] *adverb* without anyone knowing or seeing; *the burglar crept forward stealthily*

stealthy ['stelθi] *adjective* without anyone knowing or seeing; *he crept towards the safe with stealthy footsteps* (NOTE: **stealthier - stealthiest**)

steam [stiːm] **1** *noun* (a) vapour which comes off hot or boiling water; *clouds of steam were coming out of the kitchen*; steam engine = engine which runs on pressure from steam (b) *(informal)* to let off steam = to get rid of energy or annoyance by doing something strenuous; *we sent the children out to play football in the garden to let off steam* **2** *verb* (a) to send off steam; *the kettle is steaming - the water must be boiling* (b) to cook over a pan of boiling water by allowing the steam to pass through holes in a container with food in it; *how are you going to cook the fish? - I'll steam it* (c) to move by steam power; *the ship steamed out of the harbour* (d) to go fast in a certain direction; *we were steaming along at 70 miles an hour when we had a flat tyre*

steamboat ['stiːmbəut] *noun* small boat powered by steam; *steamboats criss-crossed the lake*

steamer ['stiːmə] *noun* (a) large ship powered by steam; *we took the steamer from Cape Town to Mombasa* (b) pan with holes in the bottom which is placed over boiling water to cook food by steaming; *the best way to cook vegetables is in a steamer*

steamroller ['stiːmrəulə] **1** *noun* very heavy vehicle with a large cylinder as a front wheel, used to flatten new road surfaces **2** *verb* *(informal)* to force everyone to do what you want; *they steamrollered the new law through Congress*

steamship ['stiːmʃɪp] *noun* large ship powered by steam; *with the coming of steamships in the 19th century, the journey time to New York was greatly reduced*

steam up ['stiːm 'ʌp] *verb* (a) to become covered with steam; *my glasses got all steamed up when I went into the Palm House at Kew Gardens* (b) *(informal)* to get all steamed up about something = to get angry about something; *don't get all steamed up - it's not a major crisis*

steamy ['stiːmi] *adjective* (a) hot and humid, as if full of steam; *she chose a steamy summer day to visit London* (b) *(informal)* full of descriptions of sex; *this is her steamiest novel yet* (NOTE: **steamier - steamiest**)

steel [stiːl] **1** *noun* strong metal made from iron and carbon; *steel knives are best for the kitchen*; *the door is made of solid steel*; steel band = band which plays West Indian music on steel drums of different sizes which make different notes; *we spent the evening dancing to music from a steel band*; steel grey = the colour of steel; *steel grey will be fashionable next winter*; *see also* STAINLESS **2** *verb* to steel yourself to do something = to get ready to do something which is going to be unpleasant; *he steeled himself for a very awkward interview with the police* (NOTE: do not confuse with **steal**)

steel wool ['stiːl 'wul] *noun* balls of very fine steel wire used to clean metal surfaces; *steel wool is the only thing that will get this saucepan clean*

steely ['stiːli] *adjective* sharp or hard like steel; *she looked at me with her steely blue eyes*; *he gave her a steely look, and asked what she was doing there*

steep [sti:p] **1** *adjective* **(a)** which rises or falls sharply; *the car climbed the steep hill with some difficulty; the steps up the church tower are steeper than our stairs at home* **(b)** very sharp increase or fall; *a steep increase in interest charges; a steep fall in share prices* **(c)** *(informal)* excessive; *their prices are a bit steep; that's a bit steep! - I was trying to help you* (NOTE: **steeper - steepest**) **2** *verb* **(a)** to soak in a liquid; *leave the clothes to steep in soapy water to get the stains out* **(b)** to soak in a liquid to absorb its flavour; *the venison must steep in the marinade for 24 hours; we had pears steeped in red wine* **(c) steeped in history** = full of history, where many historical events have taken place; *Windsor Castle is steeped in history*

steeple ['sti:pl] *noun* church tower with a spire on top; *we climbed up the steeple to look at the view of the surrounding countryside*

steeplechase ['sti:pltʃeɪs] *noun* **(a)** race run across open country, over fences, hedges, etc.; *eighty runners have entered for the steeplechase* **(b)** horse race on a grass track over fences and ditches; *his horse won the Easter Steeplechase; compare* FLAT RACING

steeply ['sti:pli] *adverb* sharply; *the road goes down steeply to the river; prices rose steeply after the budget*

steer ['stɪə] **1** *noun* castrated bull over one year old **2** *verb* **(a)** to make a car, a ship, etc., go in a certain direction; *she steered the car into a ditch; the pilot steered the ship into harbour* **(b) to steer clear of** = to avoid; *I steer clear of greasy food*

steering ['stɪərɪŋ] *noun* parts of a car which control the direction in which it travels; *the car keeps veering to the left, there's something wrong with the steering; our new car is easy to park because it has power steering;* **steering column** = metal column holding the steering wheel; **steering committee** = small committee which manages the early stages of a project and checks on its progress, or which does the preparatory work for another body

steering wheel ['stɪərɪŋ 'wi:l] *noun* wheel which is turned by the driver to control the direction in which a vehicle travels; *in British cars the steering wheel is on the right-hand side*

stellar ['stelə] *adjective (formal)* referring to stars; *stellar light*

stem [stem] **1** *noun* **(a)** stalk, the tall thin part of a plant which holds a leaf, a flower, a fruit, etc.; *trim the stems before you put the flowers in the vase* **(b)** main stalk of a plant or tree; *a shrub with ivy growing up the stem* **(c)** part of a wine glass like a column; *wine glasses with coloured stems* **(d) from stem to stern** = from the front of a boat to the back; *the boat was packed from stem to stern with tourists* **2** *verb* **(a) to stem from** = to be caused by; *his health problems stem from an untreated viral infection* **(b)** to try to prevent something flowing or spreading; *first, try to stem the flow of blood; the police are trying to stem the rising tide of crime* (NOTE: **stemming - stemmed**)

stench [stentʃ] *noun* unpleasant strong smell; *after the flood, the stench of rotting bodies hung over the village*

stencil ['stensl] **1** *noun* **(a)** sheet of cardboard or metal with a pattern cut out of it, so that if it is placed on a surface and colour is passed over it, the pattern will appear on the surface; *he used a stencil with electrical components on it to illustrate his project* **(b)** pattern, letters, numbers, etc., which are painted in this way; *the bathroom is decorated with stencils of fish and shellfish* **2** *verb* to mark with a stencil; *his name was stencilled on each piece of luggage* (NOTE: **stencilling - stencilled** but American spelling is **stenciling - stenciled**)

stenographer [stə'nɒgrəfə] *noun especially US* person who can write spoken words fast in shorthand; *she works as an official stenographer in the Supreme Court*

step [step] **1** *noun* **(a)** movement of your foot when walking; *I wonder when the baby will take his first steps; take a step sideways and you will be able to see the castle;* **to retrace your steps** = to go back the same way as you have just come; *to find the Post Office, he had to retrace his steps to the traffic lights and then turn right* **(b) to take one step forward and two steps back** = not to advance very quickly; **step by step** = gradually, a little at a time; *it's better to introduce the changes step by step; the book takes you step by step through French grammar* **(c)** regular movement of feet at the same time as other people; **in step** = moving your feet at the same rate as everybody else; **out of step** = moving your feet at a different rate from everybody else; *I tried to keep in step with him as we walked along; the recruits can't even march in step; one of the squad always gets out of step;* **in step with something** = at the same rate or speed as something; *house prices have risen in step with salaries;* **out of step with something** = moving at a different rate or speed from something; *wages have got out of step with the rise in the cost of living* **(d)** footstep, the sound made by a foot touching the ground; *we heard soft steps outside our bedroom door; I can always recognize your father's step* **(e)** one stair, which goes up or down; *there are two steps down into the kitchen; I counted 75 steps to the top of the tower; be careful, there's a step up into the bathroom;* **a pair of steps** = STEPLADDER **(f)** one thing which is done or has to be done out of several; *the first and most important step is to find out how much money we can spend;* **to take steps to prevent something happening** = to act to stop something happening; *the museum must take steps to make sure that nothing is stolen* **2** *verb* to move forwards, backwards, sideways, etc., on foot; *he stepped out in front of a bicycle and was knocked down; she stepped off the bus into a puddle; don't step back, there's a child behind you;* **to step on the brakes** = to push the brake pedal hard; *(informal) US* **to step on the gas** = to drive faster; *step on the gas - we'll miss the train!; (informal)* **step on it!** = hurry up! (NOTE: **stepping - has stepped**)

stepdaughter ['stepdɔ:tə] *noun* daughter of your wife or husband by another marriage; *I'm very busy getting ready for my stepdaughter's wedding*

stepfather ['stepfɑ:ðə] *noun* husband of your mother, who is not your father; *he's not her real father, he's her stepfather*

step in ['step 'ɪn] *verb* **(a)** to enter; *please step in and see what we have to offer* **(b)** to do something in an area where you were not involved before; *everything was working fine until the manager stepped in; fortunately a teacher stepped in to break up the fight*

stepladder ['steplædə] *noun* small ladder in two parts, hinged together, which is steady when opened up and does not need to lean on anything; *I need a stepladder to paint the ceiling*

stepmother ['stepmʌðə] *noun* wife of your father, who is not your mother; *she left the house because she didn't get on with her stepmother*

steppe [step] *noun* huge plains covering central Asia and Russia; *the vast emptiness of the Russian steppes*

stepping-stone ['stepɪŋstəʊn] *noun* (a) one of a series of stones which allow you to cross a stream; *I lost my balance going over the stepping-stones* (b) useful stage in your career; *working in head office is a useful stepping-stone to becoming a manager*

stepson ['stepsʌn] *noun* son of your wife or husband by another marriage; *it's a present from my stepson*

step up ['step 'ʌp] *verb* (a) to walk up; *he stepped up onto the platform* (b) to increase the quantity of something; *the company wants to step up production to 2,000 units a day*

stereo ['steriəʊ] 1 *adjective* = STEREOPHONIC; *a stereo disk* 2 *noun* machine which reproduces sound through two different loudspeakers; *I bought a new pair of speakers for my stereo*; **in stereo** = using two speakers to give an impression of depth of sound; **car stereo** = system in a car which reproduces sound in stereo

stereophonic [steriə'fɒnɪk] *adjective* referring to sound which comes through from two different channels and loudspeakers; **stereophonic recorder** = machine that records two audio signals onto magnetic tape

stereotype ['steriətaɪp] *noun* pattern for a certain type of person; *he fits the stereotype of the mad professor*

stereotyped ['steriətaɪpt] *adjective* which fits certain patterns; *the character is just a stereotyped portrait of a feminist*

stereotyping ['steriətaɪpɪŋ] *noun* the idea that people fit certain patterns; *we are trying to get away from the stereotyping of girls and boys in our children's series*

sterile ['sterail] *adjective* (a) free from bacteria, microbes or infectious organisms; *she put a sterile dressing on the wound* (b) infertile, not able to produce offspring; *the flowers on some plants are sterile* (c) not producing any useful results; *they engaged in a sterile debate about human rights* (NOTE: the opposite is **fertile**)

sterility [ste'rɪlɪti] *noun* (a) being free from bacteria, germs, etc.; *it is essential to ensure the sterility of all equipment in the operating theatre* (b) infertility, being unable to produce offspring; *increased sterility has been found in men living near the nuclear site* (NOTE: the opposite is **fertility**)

sterilization [sterɪlaɪ'zeɪʃn] *noun* (a) action of making something free from bacteria or germs; *sterilization of all surgical equipment is essential* (b) action of making a person unable to produce children; *sterilization is used to help reduce the expanding population*

sterilize ['sterɪlaɪz] *verb* (a) to make something sterile by killing microbes or bacteria; *surgical instruments must be sterilized before used*; *the soil needs to be sterilized before being used for greenhouse cultivation* (b) to make a person unable to have children; *a vasectomy is a surgical operation to sterilize men*

sterling ['stɜːlɪŋ] 1 *adjective* (a) of a certain standard, especially of good quality; *she has many sterling qualities*; *this old coat has done sterling service over the years* (b) **sterling silver** = silver of a certain high purity; *we gave her six sterling silver spoons* 2 *noun* British currency; *the prices are quoted in sterling*; **the pound sterling** = official term for the British currency

stern [stɜːn] 1 *adjective* serious and strict; *the judge addressed some stern words to the boys* (NOTE: **sterner - sternest**) 2 *noun* back part of a ship; *the stern of the ship was damaged*; *see also* STEM (NOTE: the front part is the **bow**)

sternum ['stɜːnəm] *noun* bone in the centre of the front of the chest to which most of the ribs are attached; *the false ribs are not directly attached to the sternum, but to the ribs above* (NOTE: also called the **breastbone**)

sternwheeler ['stɜːnwiːlə] *noun* large steamboat with one large wheel at the back (as used on the Mississippi); *we took a trip up the Mississippi on an old-fashioned sternwheeler*; *compare* PADDLE STEAMER

steroid ['stɪərɔɪd] *noun* (a) one of a several natural chemical compounds which affect the body and its functions (b) synthetic chemical compound used to treat some disorders and also used by some athletes to improve their strength; *the random sample of urine obtained from the athlete proved that he had been taking steroids*; *she was banned from competing after tests showed that she had taken steroids*

stethoscope ['steθəskəʊp] *noun* instrument with two earpieces connected to a tube and a metal disc, used by doctors to listen to sounds made inside the body, such as the sound of the heart or lungs; *the doctor listened carefully to the boy's chest with his stethoscope*

stevedore ['stiːvədɔː] *noun* man who works in a harbour, loading and unloading ships; *the stevedores have threatened to strike for more money* (NOTE: also called **docker**; American English is **longshoreman**)

stew [stjuː] 1 *noun* (a) dish of meat and vegetables cooked together for a long time; *this lamb stew is a French recipe* (b) (*informal*) **in a stew** = feeling anxious because of being in an awkward situation; *having lost my wallet, I'm in a bit of a stew* 2 *verb* (a) to cook for a long time in liquid; *stew the apples until they are completely soft* (b) (*informal*) **to stew in your own juice** = to worry about something bad you have done; *don't lend him any more money, leave him to stew in his own juice for a while*

steward ['stjuəd] *noun* (a) man who looks after passengers, and serves meals or drinks on a ship, aircraft, train, or in a club; *the steward served us tea on deck* (b) person who organizes public events such as races, etc.; *the stewards will inspect the course to see if the race can go ahead* (c) **shop steward** = elected trade union representative who reports workers' complaints to the management; *most of the shop stewards favour strike action*

stewardess [stjuːə'des] *noun* woman who looks after passengers and serves food and drinks on a ship or aircraft; *the stewardess demonstrated how to put on the life jacket* (NOTE: plural is **stewardesses**)

stick [stɪk] 1 *noun* (a) thin piece of wood, thin branch of a tree; *he jabbed a pointed stick into the hole*; *I need a strong stick to tie this plant to*; *see also* WRONG (b) **(walking) stick** = strong piece of wood with a handle used as a support when walking; *since she had the accident she gets around on two sticks*; *at last mother has agreed to use a walking stick* (c) a hockey stick = curved piece of wood for playing hockey (d) anything long and thin; *a stick of celery*; *a stick of chewing gum* **2** verb (a) to glue, to attach with glue; *can you stick the pieces of the cup together again?*; *she stuck the stamp on the letter*; *they stuck a poster on the door* (b) to be fixed or not to be able to move; *the car was stuck in the mud*; *the door sticks - you need to push it hard to open it*; *the cake will stick if you don't grease the tin*; *he was stuck in Italy without any money* (c) to poke, to push something into something; *he stuck his hand into the hole*; *she stuck her finger in the jam to taste it*; *she stuck the ticket into her bag*; *she stuck a needle into her finger* (d) to stay in a place; *stick close to your mother and you won't get lost*; **to stick together** = to stay together; *if we stick together they should let us into the club*; **to stick to your guns** = to keep to your point of view even if everyone says you are wrong (e) *(informal)* to bear, to put up with; *I don't know how she can stick working in that office*; *I'm going, I can't stick it here any longer* (NOTE: **sticking - stuck** [stʌk])

sticker ['stɪkə] *noun* small piece of paper or plastic which you can stick on something to show a price, as a decoration or to advertise something; *the salesman charged me more than the price on the sticker*; *she stuck stickers all over the doors of her wardrobe*; **airmail sticker** = blue sticker with the words 'air mail', which can be stuck on an envelope or parcel to show that it is to be sent by air

sticking plaster ['stɪkɪŋ 'plɑːstə] *noun* small strip of cloth with gauze in the middle, which can be stuck to the skin to cover a wound; *I want a piece of sticking plaster to put on my heel* (NOTE: American English calls this by a tradename: **Band-Aid**)

sticking point ['stɪkɪŋ 'pɔɪnt] *noun* point where something stops and which prevents the discussion going forward; *the sticking point is the question of payments*

stick-in-the-mud ['stɪkɪnðə'mʌd] *noun (informal)* old-fashioned person who refuses to change his habits; *an old stick-in-the-mud like you should get out more and see new shows*

stick-on label ['stɪkɒn 'leɪbl] *noun* label which has glue on the back and which you can stick to a surface; *we put stick-on labels on all our luggage*

stick out ['stɪk 'aʊt] *verb* (a) to push something out; **to stick your tongue out at someone** = to make a rude gesture by putting your tongue out of your mouth as far as it will go; *that little girl stuck out her tongue at me!* (b) to be further forward or extended away from something; *your wallet is sticking out of your pocket*; *the balcony sticks out over the road* (c) *(informal)* **to stick out a mile** or **to stick out like a sore thumb** = to be easily seen; *their house sticks out a mile because it is painted pink*

sticks [stɪks] *noun* **in the sticks** = in the depths of the country; *living in the sticks, they know nothing about what is happening in London*

stick up ['stɪk 'ʌp] *verb* (a) to be further up above a surface or to extend beyond a surface; *the aerial sticks up above the roof of the car* (b) to put up a notice, etc.; *she stuck up a notice about the village fête* (c) *(informal)* **stick 'em up!** = put your hands up! (d) **to stick up for someone** or **something** = to defend someone or something against criticism; *he stuck up*

for his rights and in the end won the case; *will you stick up for me if I get into trouble at school?*

sticky ['stɪki] *adjective* (a) covered with something which sticks like glue; *my fingers are all sticky*; *this stuff is terribly sticky - I can't get it off my fingers* (b) with glue on one side so that it sticks easily; **sticky label** = label with sticky glue on one side which you can stick without licking (NOTE: labels with dry glue on them and which you have to lick, are called **gummed labels**); **sticky tape** = plastic strip with glue on one side, used to stick things together, etc.; *she did the parcel up carefully with sticky tape* (c) *(informal)* difficult or embarrassing; *I'm in a rather sticky situation here*; *he came to a sticky end* = he was put in prison, was ruined, killed, etc.; **on a sticky wicket** = in a difficult situation; *the poor man's on a very sticky wicket* (NOTE: **stickier - stickiest**)

stiff [stɪf] **1** *adjective* (a) which does not move easily; *the lock is very stiff - I can't turn the key*; *I've got a stiff neck*; *she was feeling stiff all over after running in the race* (b) with hard bristles; *you need a stiff brush to get the mud off your shoes* (c) **bored stiff** = very bored; *he talked on and on until we were all bored stiff*; *I'm bored stiff with sitting indoors, watching the rain come down* (d) difficult; *he had to take a stiff test before he qualified* (e) formal, not friendly; *his attitude was very stiff towards her* (f) strong, not feeble; *they face stiff competition*; *a stiff breeze was blowing across the bay*; *he got a stiff reprimand from the boss*; **stiff drink** = alcoholic drink with very little water added (NOTE: **stiffer - stiffest**) **2** *noun* US *(informal)* dead body; *we opened the closet door and a stiff fell out*

stiffen ['stɪfn] *verb* (a) to become or make stiff; *as you get older, your joints stiffen* (b) to become cautious or unfriendly; *she stiffened when she heard his voice* (c) *(of wind)* to become stronger; *the boats raced across the bay in the stiffening breeze* (d) to make stronger; *the TV broadcasts helped to stiffen resistance to the government's new measures*

stiffly ['stɪfli] *adverb* in a stiff way; *she walked stiffly up the stairs*; *he bowed stiffly and didn't say a word*

stiffness ['stɪfnəs] *noun* (a) being unable to move easily or having pains in the joints after doing exercises; *arthritis accompanied by a certain amount of stiffness in the joints* (b) being stiff; *the stiffness of the material makes it unsuitable for a dress*

stifle ['staɪfl] *verb* (a) to make someone not able to breathe, not to be able to breathe because of heat, smoke, etc.; *the firemen were almost stifled by the toxic gas* (b) to prevent something taking place; *the plan of the authorities is to stifle any protests before they start*; **to stifle a yawn** = to try to prevent yourself from yawning; *he had difficulty in stifling a yawn*

stifling ['staɪflɪŋ] *adjective* (a) which makes it difficult to breathe; *stifling black smoke made them cough* (b) extremely hot; *he stepped off the plane into the stifling heat of the Louisiana sunshine*

stigma ['stɪgmə] *noun* (a) disgrace, feeling of shame; *the stigma attached to alcoholism makes people try to hide their drinking habits* (b) part of the female organ of a flower that forms seeds after receiving pollen

stigmatize ['stɪgmətaɪz] *verb* to give someone or something a bad name; *he was stigmatized as being difficult*

stile [staɪl] *noun* steps which allow people, but not animals, to get over a wall or fence; *the path led across the field to a stile*

still [stɪl] **1** *adjective* **(a)** not moving; *stand still while I take the photo*; *if you want to see the badgers keep still and don't make any noise*; *there was no wind, and the surface of the lake was completely still* **(b)** *(of drinks)* not fizzy; *can I have a glass of still mineral water, please?* **2** *adverb* **(a)** continuing until now; which continued until then; *I thought he had left, but I see he's still there*; *they came for lunch and were still sitting at the table at eight o'clock in the evening*; *weeks afterwards, they're still talking about the accident* **(b)** *(with comparative)* *we've had a cold autumn, but they expect the winter will be colder still*; **still more** = even more; *there were at least ten thousand people in the football stadium and still more queueing to get in* **(c)** in spite of everything; *it wasn't sunny for the picnic - still, it didn't rain*; *she still insisted on going on holiday even though he had broken his leg*

still life ['stɪl 'laɪf] *noun* painting of objects, such as fruit, bottles, flowers, food, etc.; *Dutch still lifes are well-known* (NOTE: plural is **still lifes**)

stilted ['stɪltɪd] *adjective* forced and unnatural; *the conversation was stilted and difficult*

stilton ['stɪltən] *noun* soft rich white and blue cheese, with a strong flavour, originally from the village of Stilton in Cambridgeshire

stilts [stɪlts] *noun* **(a)** tall poles with rests for your feet, so that you walk high above the ground; *in the circus parade there were elephants, and clowns on stilts* **(b)** tall wooden supports for houses; *their houses are built on stilts on the lake*

stimulant ['stɪmjʊlənt] *noun* **(a)** substance which makes the body function faster; *caffeine is a stimulant* **(b)** something which encourages more activity; *tax cuts should act as a stimulant to the economy*

stimulate ['stɪmjʊleɪt] *verb* to encourage someone or an organ to be more active; *we want to stimulate trade with the Middle East*; *I'm trying to stimulate the students*; *this drug stimulates the heart*

stimulation [stɪmjʊ'leɪʃn] *noun* action of being stimulated; *his job is deadly dull - he needs intellectual stimulation*

stimulus ['stɪmjʊləs] *noun* thing that encourages someone *or* something to greater activity; *what sort of stimulus is needed to revive the tourist trade?*; *a nerve which responds to stimuli* (NOTE: plural is **stimuli** ['stɪmjʊlaɪ])

sting [stɪŋ] **1** *noun* **(a)** wound made by an insect or plant; *bee stings can be very painful*; *have you anything for wasp stings?* **(b)** tiny needle, part of an insect or plant which injects poison into your skin; *he pulled out the sting which had lodged in her arm* **2** *verb* **(a)** to wound with an insect's *or* plant's sting; *I've been stung by a wasp*; *she walked bare-legged through the wood and got stung by nettles*; *see also* NETTLE **(b)** to give a burning feeling; *the antiseptic may sting a little at first* **(c)** *(informal)* **to sting someone (for)** = to charge someone a lot of money; *he was stung for parking on a yellow line*; *they stung me for £100* (NOTE: **stinging - stung** [stʌŋ])

stingy ['stɪndʒi] *adjective* *(informal)* not very generous, not large; *we got a stingy helping of pudding*; *the company is very stingy with its free offers*

stink [stɪŋk] **1** *noun* **(a)** very nasty smell; *there's a terrible stink in the kitchen* **(b)** *(informal)* **to create** *or* **make** *or* **kick up** *or* **raise a stink about something** = to complain vigorously about something; *the neighbours will kick up a stink if you damage their fence* **2** *verb* **(a)** to make a nasty smell; *the office stinks of gas* **(b)** *(informal)* to seem to be dishonest; *the whole affair stinks* (NOTE: **stank** [stæŋk] - **stunk** [stʌŋk])

stinking ['stɪŋkɪŋ] *adjective & adverb* *(informal)* very *(bad)*; *I'm staying at home today because I've got a stinking cold*; *they're stinking rich, they can afford to stay in five-star hotels*

stint [stɪnt] **1** *noun* **(a)** amount of work which you should do; *it's your turn to help now, I've done my stint*; *she had a long stint as a sister in a London hospital* **(b)** *(formal)* **without stint** = in large quantities, with no restriction; *they gave their time to the project without stint* **2** *verb* *(usually negative)* not to stint = to give a large amount; *they didn't stint their help*; *he didn't stint on expense when he had his office redecorated*; **not to stint yourself** = to allow yourself a large amount; *don't stint yourself - there's plenty of food for everyone*

stipend ['staɪpend] *noun* salary of a priest or a magistrate; *how they brought up a family of five children on his tiny stipend I do not know*

stipulate ['stɪpjʊleɪt] *verb* to insist, to make it a condition that; *to stipulate that the contract should run for five years*; *the company failed to pay on the date stipulated in the contract*

stir [stɜː] **1** *noun* **(a)** action of mixing the ingredients of something, or something which is cooking; *add the sugar and give the mixture a stir*; *you should give the porridge an occasional stir* **(b)** excitement; *the exhibition caused a stir in the art world* **2** *verb* **(a)** to move a liquid or powder or something which is cooking, to mix it up; *he was stirring the sugar into his coffee*; *keep stirring the porridge, or it will stick to the bottom of the pan* **(b)** to move about; *the baby slept peacefully without stirring*; *I didn't stir from my desk all day* **(c)** **to stir someone to do something** = to make someone feel that they ought to do something; *we must try to stir the committee into action* (NOTE: **stirring - stirred**)

stir-fry [stɜː'fraɪ] **1** *verb* to cook vegetables or meat quickly in hot oil, while rapidly stirring; *stir-fry the vegetables separately, not all together* **2** *noun* vegetables or meat cooked quickly in a little hot oil; *we had a beef stir-fry*; *she made a stir-fry of vegetables and bamboo shoots*

stirring ['stɜːrɪŋ] *adjective* exciting, encouraging; *he is remembered for his stirring wartime broadcasts to the troops*

stirrup ['stɪrəp] *noun* metal loop hanging from the saddle into which the rider puts his foot; *he lost his stirrups and slipped off*; **stirrup cup** = drink taken on horseback before setting off on a ride, especially before going hunting

stir up ['stɜː 'ʌp] *verb* **to stir up trouble** = to cause trouble; *the fans came with the deliberate intention of stirring up trouble*

stitch [stɪtʃ] **1** *noun* **(a)** little loop of thread made with a needle in sewing or with knitting needles when knitting; *she used very small stitches in her embroidery*; *very fine wool will give you more stitches than in the pattern* **(b)** *(informal)* clothes; *how can I go* *to the party - I haven't a stitch to wear*; **with not a stitch on** = completely naked; *I can't come now, I haven't a stitch on* **(c)** small loop of thread used by a surgeon to attach the sides of a wound together to help it to heal; *she had three stitches in her arm*; *come back in ten days' time to have the stitches removed* **(d)** sharp pain caused by cramp in the side of the body after you have been running; *I can't go any further - I've got a stitch* **(e) in stitches** = laughing out loud; *his story about the school play had us all in stitches* (NOTE: plural is **stitches**) **2** *verb* **(a)** to attach with a needle and thread; *she stitched the badge to his jacket* **(b)** to sew the sides of a wound together; *after the operation, the surgeons stitched the wound*; *his finger was cut off in an accident and the surgeons tried to stitch it back on*

stoat [stəʊt] *noun* small brown animal whose fur turns white in winter, except for the end of the tail which stays black; *stoats eat small animals like mice*

stock [stɒk] **1** *noun* **(a)** supply of something kept to use when needed; *I keep a stock of typing paper at home*; *our stocks of food are running low*; *the factory has large stocks of coal* **(b)** quantities of goods for sale; **stock control** = making sure that enough stock is kept and that quantities and movements of stock are noted (NOTE: the word 'inventory' is used in the USA where British English uses the word 'stock'. So, the British 'stock control' is 'inventory control' in American English) **(b) in stock** = available in the shop or warehouse; *we hold 2,000 items in stock*; **out of stock** = not available in the shop or warehouse; *we are out of stock of this item* or *this item is out of stock*; **to take stock** = to count the items in a warehouse; *they take stock every evening after the store closes*; **to take stock of a situation** = to assess how bad a situation is; *we need to take stock of the situation and decide what to do next* **(c)** investments in a company, represented by shares; **stocks and shares** = shares in ordinary companies; **government stocks** = government securities, bonds issued by a government (NOTE: in the UK, the term **stocks** is generally applied to government stocks and **shares** to shares of commercial companies. In the USA, shares in commercial corporations are usually called **stocks** while government stocks are called **bonds**. In practice, **shares** and **stocks** are interchangeable terms, and this can lead to some confusion) **(d)** family and ancestors; *he comes of old farming stock* **(e)** pedigree farm animals; *stock prices fell at the market last week; see also* LIVESTOCK **(f)** the plant on which a graft is made; *he grafted the apple onto the stock* **(g) on the stocks** = being worked on; *she's finished writing one book and now has another on the stocks* **2** *verb* to keep goods for sale in a warehouse or shop; *they don't stock this book*; *we try to stock the most popular colours* **3** *adjective* normal, usually kept in a store; **stock size** = normal size; *we only carry shoes in stock sizes*; **stock argument** = argument which is frequently used; *she trotted out the stock argument about higher salaries leading to fewer jobs*

stockbreeder ['stɒkbriːdə] *noun* farmer who specializes in breeding livestock

stockbroker ['stɒkbrəʊkə] *noun* person who buys or sells shares for clients; *I know a good stockbroker who can sell your shares*

Stock Exchange ['stɒk ɪks'tʃeɪn(d)ʒ] *noun* place where stocks and shares are bought and sold; *he works on the Stock Exchange*; *shares in the company are traded on the London Stock Exchange*

stockholder ['stɒkhəʊldə] *noun* person who holds shares in a company; *the stockholders voted against the merger*

stocking ['stɒkɪŋ] *noun* long light piece of women's clothing which covers all your leg and your foot; *she was wearing black shoes and stockings*; *the robbers wore stockings over their faces*; **Christmas stockings** = large coloured stockings, which children hang up by their beds or under the Christmas tree, and which are filled with presents on Christmas Eve; **stocking filler** = little gift which can be put into a Christmas stocking

stockist ['stɒkɪst] *noun* person or shop which stocks a certain item; *for spare parts, get in touch with your local stockist*

stockman ['stɒkmən] *noun* farm worker who looks after animals, especially cattle (NOTE: plural is **stockmen**)

stock market ['stɒk 'mɑːkɪt] *noun* place where shares are bought and sold (i.e., a stock exchange); *the stock market crash of 1929*; **stock market valuation** = value of a company based on the current market price of its shares

stockpile ['stɒkpaɪl] **1** *noun* large supplies of something kept by a country or company for future use; *the country's stockpile of weapons* **2** *verb* to collect large supplies of something together in case you need them in the future; *we started to stockpile raw materials in case there was a rail strike*

stock up with ['stɒk 'ʌp wɪð] *verb* to buy supplies for use in the future; *we'll stock up with food to last us over the holiday weekend*

stocky ['stɒki] *adjective (person)* with large shoulders and strong body, but usually not very tall *(animal)* with short, strong legs; *he's a stocky fellow, and very strong*; *a stocky breed of cattle* (NOTE: **stockier - stockiest**)

stockyard ['stɒkjɑːd] *noun* place where animals are kept before they are slaughtered or taken to market

stoke [stəʊk] *verb* to put wood or coal into a fire; *he stoked the stove to warm the log cabin*

stoker ['stəʊkə] *noun* formerly, person who stoked a fire, especially a seaman who looked after a ship's engines

stole, stolen [stəʊl or stəʊlən] *see* STEAL

stolid ['stɒlɪd] *adjective* serious, not easily excited; *he's a stolid type, not exciting but very dependable*; *the cows looked at us with a stolid expression*

stomach ['stʌmək] **1** *noun* **(a)** part of the body shaped like a bag, into which food passes after being swallowed and where it continues to be digested; *I don't want anything to eat - my stomach's upset* or *I have a stomach upset*; *he has had stomach trouble for some time*; **his eyes were bigger than his stomach** = he took too much food and couldn't finish it **(b)** the area round the abdomen; *he had been kicked in the stomach* **2** *verb* to put up with, to tolerate; *they left the meeting because they couldn't stomach any more arguments*

stomach ache ['stʌmək 'eɪk] *noun* pain in the abdomen (caused by eating too much, or by an infection); *I've got a terrible stomach ache*

stomp [stɒmp] *verb* to walk with heavy steps; *he stomped out of the shop, swearing he would never come again*

stone [stəun] **1** *noun* **(a)** very hard material, found in the earth, used for building; *all the houses in the town are built in the local grey stone*; *the stone carvings in the old church date from the 15th century*; *stone floors can be very cold* (NOTE: no plural in these meanings: **some stone, a piece of stone, a block of stone**) **(b)** small piece of stone; *the children playing at throwing stones into the pond*; *the beach isn't good for bathing as it's covered with very sharp stones* **(c)** precious **stones** = stones, such as diamonds, which are rare and very valuable; **semi-precious stones** = stones, like opals, which are not as valuable as other jewels like diamonds; *the ring has two small diamonds and a semi-precious stone, probably an opal* **(d)** British measure of weight (= 14 pounds or 6.35 kilograms); *she's trying tried to lose weight and so far has lost a stone and a half*; *he weighs twelve stone ten* (i.e. 12 stone 10 pounds) (NOTE: no plural in this meaning: **he weighs ten stone;** note also that in the USA, human body weight is always given only in pounds) **(e)** single hard seed inside a fruit; *count the cherry stones on the side of your plate* **2** *adverb* completely; **stone cold** = very cold; *no wonder you're freezing, the radiators are stone cold*; **stone deaf** = completely deaf; *it's no use shouting - she's stone deaf*; *US* **stone broke** = with no money at all **3** *verb* (as a punishment) **to stone someone to death** = to throw stones at someone and kill him or her

stoned [stəund] *adjective* **(a)** (fruit) with the stone removed; *we only buy stoned olives* **(b)** (informal) high on drugs; *he was completely stoned when I met him*

Stonehenge ['stəunhenʒ] *noun* ancient monument in southern England, made of circles of huge standing stones with other stones balanced on top of them

COMMENT: experts are not sure when or how Stonehenge came to be built. The stones come from mountains in Wales, many miles away, and would have had to be dragged long distances to reach the site. Setting them upright would also have been difficult with primitive equipment. The circles are thought to have had some astronomical or astrological purpose, as the sun rises on Midsummer's Day directly over a smaller stone as seen from the centre of the circle

stony ['stəuni] *adjective* **(a)** made of lots of stones; *a stony beach* **(b)** showing no emotion; *they sat with stony faces, listening to the accusation* **(c)** (informal) **stony broke** = with no money at all; *he's stony broke, so I had to pay for the meal* (NOTE: **stonier - stoniest**)

stood [stud] *see* STAND

stool [stu:l] *noun* **(a)** small seat with no back; *when the little girl sat on the piano stool her feet didn't touch the floor*; **bar stool** = high seat used for sitting at a bar or counter; **to fall between two stools** = to have two possible ways of doing something and not to do either successfully; *he tried to please both his wife and his friends and fell between two stools*; *see also* FOOTSTOOL **(b)** (medical) **stools** = faeces, solid waste matter passed from the bowels through the anus; *his stools were an abnormal colour*

stoop [stu:p] **1** *noun* position where you are bent forwards; *she has a stoop*; *he walks with a stoop* **2** *verb* **(a)** to bend forward; *she stooped and picked something up off the carpet*; *I found him standing at the table, stooped over a spreadsheet* **(b)** he **stoops** = he has a

permanently bent back; *he's in his sixties and he stoops* **(c)** **to stoop to do something** = to allow yourself to do something which you feel is not the right thing for you to do; *he would never stoop to begging*

stop [stɒp] **1** *noun* **(a)** end of something, especially of movement; *the police want to put a stop to car crimes*; **to come to a stop** *or* **to a full stop** = to stop moving; *the car rolled on without the driver, and finally came to a stop at the bottom of the hill*; *all the building work came to a stop when the money ran out* **(b)** place where you break a journey; *we'll make a stop at the next service station* **(c)** place where a bus or tram lets passengers get on or off; *we have been waiting at the bus stop for twenty minutes*; *there are six stops between here and Marble Arch* **(d)** **full stop** = punctuation mark like a small dot, showing the end of a sentence or an abbreviation; *when reading, you should take a breath when you come to a full stop* (NOTE: American English is **period**); *see also* FULL STOP **(e)** knob which is pulled on an organ to use different pipes, so making different types of sound (informal) **to pull out all the stops** = to make every effort; *they pulled out all the stops to make sure the work was finished on time* **2** *verb* **(a)** not to move any more; *the motorcycle didn't stop at the red lights*; *this train stops at all stations to London Waterloo*; *the people in the queue were very annoyed when the bus went past without stopping* **(b)** to make something not move any more; *the policeman stopped the traffic to let the lorry back out of the garage*; *stop that boy! - he's stolen my purse* **(c)** not to do something any more; *the office clock has stopped at 4.15*; *at last it stopped raining and we could go out*; *she spoke for two hours without stopping*; *we all stopped work and went home*; *the restaurant stops serving meals at midnight* **(d)** **to stop someone** *or* **something (from) doing something** = to make someone *or* something not do something any more; *the rain stopped us from having a picnic*; *how can the police stop people stealing cars?*; *can't you stop the children from making such a noise?*; *the plumber couldn't stop the tap dripping* **(e)** to stay at a place for a short time; *can you stop at the newsagent's on your way home and buy the evening paper?* **(f)** **to stop at nothing** = to do everything, whether good or bad, to succeed; *he'll stop at nothing to get that job*; **to stop short of doing something** = to stop just in time to avoid doing something; *he stopped short of admitting he was guilty* **(g)** to stay as a visitor in a place; *they stopped for a few days in Paris*; *I expect to stop in Rome for the weekend* **(h)** **to stop an account** = to stop supplying a customer until he has paid what he owes; **to stop a cheque** *US* **to stop payment on a check** = to ask a bank not to pay a cheque that you have written; **to stop someone's wages** = to take money out of someone's wages as a punishment; *we stopped £25 from his pay because he was late* (NOTE: **stopping - stopped**)

stop by ['stɒp 'baɪ] *verb* (informal) to visit someone for a short time; *he said he might stop by on his way home*

stopcock ['stɒpkɒk] *noun* tap which turns off the main supply of water; *turn off the stopcock before you replace the shower fitting*

stopgap ['stɒpgæp] *noun* something used for a short time, while waiting for something better to be found; *as a stopgap, we've sent John to run the shop*; *it's only a stopgap measure until a final decision has been made*

stop off ['stɒp 'ɒf] *verb* to stop for a time in a place before going on with your journey; *we stopped off for a couple of nights in Dallas on our way to Mexico*

stop over ['stɒp 'əʊvə] *verb* to spend a night in a place on a long journey; *we'll stop over in Rome on the flight to Hong Kong*

stopover ['stɒpəʊvə] *noun* short overnight stop on a long journey by air; *the ticket allows you two stopovers between London and Tokyo*

stoppage ['stɒpɪdʒ] *noun* (a) action of stopping something from moving; *deliveries will be late because of stoppages on the production line* (b) money taken from a worker's wages to pay for insurance, tax, etc.

stopper ['stɒpə] *noun* piece of glass, etc., put into the mouth of a bottle or jar to close it; *put the stopper back in the jar*

stop up ['stɒp 'ʌp] *verb* (a) not to go to bed; *we stopped up late to see the New Year in*; *I'm go to stop up to watch the golf on TV* (b) to block; *he tried to stop up the hole in the pipe with some kind of cement*

storage ['stɔːrɪdʒ] *noun* (a) keeping in a store or warehouse; *we put our furniture into storage*; *we don't have enough storage space in this house*; **storage capacity** = space available for storage; **storage facilities** = equipment and buildings suitable for storage; **cold storage** = keeping food, etc., in a cold store to prevent it going bad; **to put a plan into cold storage** = to postpone work on a plan, usually for a very long time (b) cost of keeping things in store; *storage costs us 10% of the value of the items stored* (c) facility for storing data in a computer; *a hard disk with a storage capacity of 200Mb*

store [stɔː] 1 *noun* (a) shop, usually a big shop; *you can buy shoes in any of the big stores in town*; *does the store have a hairdressing salon?*; **department store** = large store, with different sections for different types of goods; **general store** = small (country) shop which sells a wide range of goods (NOTE: British English usually uses **shop** for small businesses; American English uses **store** for any kind of shop) (b) supplies kept to use later; *we keep a big store of coal for the winter*; *they bought stores for their journey* (c) place where goods are kept; *the goods will be kept in store until they are needed*; **cold store** = warehouse or room where supplies can be kept cold; **to be in store for someone** *or* **to have something in store for someone** = to be going to happen to someone; *she's got a big surprise in store*; *we didn't know what would be in store for us when we surrendered to the enemy* 2 *verb* (a) to keep food, etc., to use later; *we store (away) all our vegetables in the garden shed* (b) to put something in a warehouse for safe keeping; *we stored our furniture while we were looking for a house to buy* (c) to keep something in a computer file; *we store all our personnel records on computer*

storefront ['stɔːfrʌnt] *noun* US part of a store which faces the street, including the entrance and the windows; *the style of the storefront is classic, simple and elegant* (NOTE: British English is **shopfront**)

storehouse ['stɔːhaʊs] *noun* (a) (old) place where things are stored; *the Roman grain storehouses were burnt in the fire* (b) place where information, etc., is kept; *the museum is a storehouse of expertise on ancient art*

storeroom ['stɔːrʊm] *noun* room where goods can be stored; *we're running out of paper - can you bring another box from the storeroom?*

storey US **story** ['stɔːri] *noun* whole floor in a building; *a twenty-storey office block*; *the upper storeys of the block caught fire*

stork [stɔːk] *noun* large white bird with long legs and a long thin red beak; *storks build their nests high up*

storm [stɔːm] 1 *noun* (a) high wind and very bad weather; *several ships got into difficulties in the storm*; *how many trees were blown down in last night's storm?*; *March and October are the worst months for storms*; **rainstorm** = storm with a lot of rain; **sandstorm** = high wind in the desert, which carries large amounts of sand with it; **snowstorm** = storm when the wind blows and snow falls; **thunderstorm** = storm with rain, thunder and lightning; *(informal)* **storm in a teacup** = lot of fuss about something which is not important (b) **by storm** = (i) in a sudden rush or attack; (ii) in a whirl of excitement; *the soldiers took the enemy castle by storm*; *the pop group has taken the town by storm* 2 *verb* (a) to rush about angrily; *he stormed into the shop and demanded to see the manager*; **to storm off** *or* **out** = to go away *or* out in anger; *she stormed out of the meeting and called her lawyer* (b) to attack suddenly and capture; *our troops stormed the enemy camp*

stormy ['stɔːmi] *adjective* (a) when there are storms; *they are forecasting stormy weather for the weekend* (b) **stormy meeting** = meeting where there is a lot of argument (NOTE: **stormier - stormiest**)

story ['stɔːri] *noun* (a) description that tells what really happened; *she told her story to the journalist*; **it's a long story** = it is difficult to describe what happened (b) description that tells things that did not really happen but are invented by someone; *the book is the story of two children during the war*; *she writes children's stories about animals* (c) lie, something which is not true; *nobody will believe such stories* (d) US = STOREY (NOTE: plural is **stories**)

storybook ['stɔːrɪbʊk] 1 *noun* book of children's stories; *the library's choice of storybooks for the under fives is excellent* 2 *adjective* as good and perfect as in a children's story; *to her he seemed like a storybook prince*

storyline ['stɔːrɪlaɪn] *noun* plot of a novel, film, etc.; *the film has a very complicated storyline*

storyteller ['stɔːrɪtelə] *noun* person who tells a story; *the children sat in a ring round the storyteller, listening to his tales of old legendary heroes*

stout [staʊt] 1 *adjective* (a) quite fat; *he has become much stouter and has difficulty going up stairs* (b) *(of material)* strong or thick; *take a few sheets of stout paper* (c) *(formal)* brave; *a few stout men held off the enemy attack* (NOTE: **stouter - stoutest**) 2 *noun* strong dark-coloured beer; *he was sitting quietly in the bar, drinking a glass of stout*

stove [stəʊv] *noun* apparatus for heating or cooking; *the hut is heated by an oil stove*; *the milk boiled over and made a mess on the kitchen stove* (NOTE: British English is also **cooker** for the cooking apparatus)

stow [stəʊ] *verb* to put away; *make sure you stow all items of hand luggage in the racks above your seat*

stow away ['stəʊ ə'weɪ] *verb* (a) to put away; *he had stowed all the luggage away in the boot of the car*;

it's June - time you stowed away your skis **(b)** to travel secretly on a ship or aircraft without paying the fare; *they found two students stowing away in a lifeboat*

stowaway ['stəʊəweɪ] *noun* person who stows away; *the stowaways were discovered by the crew and handed over to the police*

straddle ['strædl] *verb* **(a)** to stand with legs apart, on either side of something; *he straddled the ditch* **(b)** be on both sides of something; *the town straddles the main highway to the north*

straggle ['strægl] *verb* **(a)** to move in various directions, not in an orderly fashion; *after the flood went down a few people straggled back to their villages each day* **(b)** to grow or lie in various directions; *her hair was straggling over her face*

straggler ['stræglə] *noun* person or animal who comes after everyone else; *almost all the sheep have been rounded up, there are just a few stragglers left on the mountainside*

straggly ['strægli] *adjective* untidy, not in order; *he has a straggly white beard*

straight [streɪt] **1** *adjective* **(a)** not curved; *Edgware Road is a long straight street*; *the line under the picture isn't straight*; *she has straight black hair*; *stand up straight!* **(b)** not sloping; *is the picture straight?*; *the windowsill should be perfectly straight but it slopes slightly to the left*; *your tie isn't straight* **(c)** clear and simple; *I want you to give me a straight answer*; *a straight fight* = an election contest between two candidates only **(d)** tidy; *can you get the room straight before the visitors arrive?* **(e) to get something straight** = to understand clearly the meaning of something; *before you start, let's get this straight - you are not going to be paid for the work* **(f)** *(slang)* heterosexual, not homosexual; *he met up with two straight guys in Sydney* (NOTE: **straighter - straightest**) **2** *adverb* **(a)** going in a straight line, not curving; *the road goes straight across the plain for two hundred kilometres*; **to go straight on** *or* **to keep straight on** = to continue along this road without turning off it; *go straight on past the crossroads and then turn left*; *keep straight on and you'll find the hospital just after the supermarket*; *the church is straight in front of you* **(b)** immediately, at once; *wait for me here - I'll come straight back*; *if there is a problem, you should go straight to the manager* **(c)** without stopping or changing; *she drank the milk straight out of the bottle*; *the cat ran straight across the road in front of the car*; *he looked me straight in the face*; *the plane flies straight to Washington* **(d)** (alcohol) with no water or any other liquid added; *he drinks his whisky straight* (NOTE: British English also uses **neat** in this sense) **(e)** *(informal)* **to go straight** = to stop committing crimes; *after he left prison he went straight for six or seven months* **3** *noun* (on a racetrack) part of the track which is straight; *the runners are coming into the final straight*; *see also* HOME (NOTE: do not confuse with **straits**)

straightaway ['streɪt ə'weɪ] *adverb* at once, immediately; *I need a lot of money straightaway*; *I had to leave straightaway after the end of the play*

straighten ['streɪtn] *verb* to make straight; *she had surgery to straighten her nose*; *he straightened his tie and went into the interview room*

straighten up ['streɪtn ʌp] *verb* **(a)** to stand straight after bending; *he straightened up and looked at me* **(b)**

to make something tidy; *I must straighten up my bedroom before I leave*

straightforward [streɪt'fɔ:wəd] *adjective* **(a)** honest and frank; *she gave a straightforward answer* **(b)** easy, not complicated; *if you follow the instructions carefully, it's quite a straightforward job*

straight off ['streɪt 'ɒf] *adverb* immediately, at once; *I'll start straight off with the most important question*

straight out ['streɪt 'aʊt] *adverb* directly, without hesitating; *she told him straight out that she didn't want to see him again*

strain [streɪn] **1** *noun* **(a)** force of pulling something tight; *can that small rope take the strain of the boat?* **(b) to put a strain on** = to make something more difficult; *the strong pound will put a strain on our exports*; *his drinking put a strain on their marriage* **(c)** condition where a muscle has been stretched or torn by a sudden movement; *she dropped out of the race with muscle strain* **(d)** nervous tension and stress; *can she stand the strain of working in that office?* **(e)** music, part of a tune; *they all sang to the strains of the accordion* **(f)** variety, breed; *they are trying to find a cure for a new strain of the flu virus*; *he crossed two strains of rice to produce a variety which is resistant to disease* **2** *verb* **(a)** to injure part of your body by pulling too hard; *he strained a muscle in his back or he strained his back*; *the effort strained his heart* **(b)** to make great efforts to do something; *they strained to lift the piano onto the van* **(c)** to put pressure on something, to make something more difficult; *the mortgage repayments will strain our budget*; *the argument strained our relations* **(d)** to pour liquid through a sieve to separate solids from it; *boil the peas for ten minutes and then strain*

strained ['streɪnd] *adjective* **(a)** which has been pulled or worked too hard; *she had to leave the game with a strained calf muscle* **(b)** tense or unfriendly; *relations between them became strained* **(c)** forced, not natural; *he gave a strained laugh, and said he felt fine*

strainer ['streɪnə] *noun* kitchen utensil with metal or nylon mesh, used to separate solids from a liquid; *pass the stewed apples through a strainer*; **a tea strainer** = small utensil placed over a cup to separate tea leaves from the liquid (used when making tea with loose tea leaves)

straitened ['streɪtnd] *adjective* **straitened circumstances** = difficult situation because of not having enough money; *they were living in straitened circumstances*

straits [streɪts] *noun* **(a)** passage of water between two larger areas of sea; *the Straits of Gibraltar can be very rough* **(b)** money difficulties; *after my father died the family was in dire straits* (NOTE: almost always used in the plural)

strand [strænd] **1** *noun* one piece of hair, thread, etc.; *strands of hair kept blowing across her forehead* **2** *verb* to leave or something alone and helpless; *her handbag was stolen and she was stranded without any money*; *the captain stranded the ship on a sandbank*

stranded ['strændɪd] *adjective* alone and unable to move; *the tube strike left thousands of people stranded in central London*; *the airlines are trying to bring back thousands of stranded holidaymakers*

strange [streɪnʒ] *adjective* **(a)** not usual; *something is the matter with the engine - it's making a strange noise; she told some very strange stories about the firm she used to work for; it felt strange to be sitting in the office on a Saturday afternoon; it's strange that no one spotted the mistake; a strange-looking young man was with her* **(b)** which you have never seen before or where you have never been before; *I find it difficult getting to sleep in a strange room; we went to Korea and had lots of strange food to eat* (NOTE: **stranger - strangest**)

strangely [streɪnʒli] *adverb* in a strange way; *your face seems strangely familiar, have we met before?; strangely enough, my birthday's on the same day as his*

stranger [streɪnʒə] *noun* **(a)** person whom you have never met; *I've never met him - he's a complete stranger to me; children are told not to accept lifts from strangers* **(b)** person in a place where he has never been before; *I can't tell you how to get to the post office - I'm a stranger here myself*

strangle [stræŋgl] *verb* **(a)** to kill by squeezing the throat so that someone cannot breathe or swallow; *the marks on his neck showed that he had been strangled* **(b)** to slow the development of something; *the company's expansion is being strangled by lack of funds*

stranglehold [stræŋglhəʊld] *noun* control which prevents you doing what you want to do; *the banks have a stranglehold over small businesses*

strangler [stræŋglə] *noun* person who strangles; *the strangler is still at large and must be caught before he strikes again*

strangulation [stræŋgjʊleɪʃn] *noun* *(formal)* squeezing someone's throat so that he or she cannot breathe or swallow; *the doctor said that death was by strangulation*

strap [stræp] **1** *noun* long flat piece of material used to attach something; *can you do up the strap of my rucksack for me?; I put a strap round my suitcase to make it more secure* **2** *verb* **(a)** to fasten something with a strap; *he strapped on his rucksack; the patient was strapped to a stretcher; make sure the baby is strapped into her seat* **(b)** to wrap a bandage tightly round a limb; *she strapped up his ankle and told him to lie down* (NOTE: **strapping - strapped**)

strapped [stræpt] *adjective* *(informal)* **strapped for cash** = not having any money; *can you lend me a few pounds as I'm a bit strapped for cash at the moment?*

strapping [stræpɪŋ] *adjective* big and strong; *her son is a strapping lad*

stratagem [strætədʒəm] *noun* *(formal)* clever plan, often to trick someone; *you will have to devise a new stratagem to get money quickly*

strategic *or* **strategical** [strəti:dʒɪk(l)] *adjective* referring to strategy; **strategic advantage** = position which gives an advantage over the enemy; *breaking the enemy's secret code gave us an enormous strategic advantage*; **strategic planning** = planning the future work of an organization

strategist [strætədʒɪst] *noun* officer who plans military attacks; *military strategists expected an attack over the mountain pass*

strategy [strætədʒi] *noun* planning of actions in advance; *their strategy is to note which of their rival's models sells best and then copy it; the government has no long-term strategy for dealing with crime*; **business strategy** = planning of how to develop your business

stratosphere [strætəsfɪə] *noun* higher layer of the earth's atmosphere; *when CFCs are released into the atmosphere, they rise slowly taking about seven years to reach the* stratosphere

stratum [strɑ:təm] *noun* **(a)** layer, especially of rock; *as they dug down, they exposed several strata of rock* **(b) social strata** = different levels of society (NOTE: plural is **strata** [strɑ:tə])

straw [strɔ:] *noun* **(a)** dry stalks and leaves of crops left after the grain has been harvested; *you've been lying on the ground - you've got bits of straw in your hair; the tractor picked up bundles of straw and loaded them onto a truck*; **straw poll** = rapid poll taken near voting day, to see how people intend to vote; *a straw poll of members of staff showed that most of them were going to vote for the council's plan* **(b)** thin plastic tube for sucking up liquids; *she was drinking orange juice through a straw* **(c)** *(informal)* **the last straw** = the final and worst problem in a series; *the children had been ill one after another, but the last straw was when the eldest girl caught measles*; **that's the last straw** = I can't stand any more of this

strawberry [strɔ:bri] *noun* common soft red summer fruit growing on low plants; *I picked some strawberries for dessert; a pot of strawberry jam* (NOTE: plural is **strawberries**)

stray [streɪ] **1** *noun* animal which is lost and wandering far away from home; *we have two female cats at home and they attract all the strays in the district* **2** *adjective* **(a)** not where it should be; *he was killed by a stray bullet from a sniper* **(b)** which is wandering away from home; *we found a stray cat and brought it home* **3** *verb* to wander away; *the sheep strayed onto the golf course; the children had strayed too far and couldn't get back*

streak [stri:k] **1** *noun* **(a)** line of colour; *she's had blonde streaks put in her hair* **(b) streak of lightning** = a flash of lightning **(c)** particularly characteristic type of behaviour; *she has a ruthless streak in her; it's his mean streak which makes him not buy any Christmas cards* **(d)** period when a series of things happens; *I was on a winning streak, I won three times in a row; I hope our unlucky streak is coming to an end*; **a streak of luck** = a period when you are lucky; *his streak of luck continued as he won the lottery yet again* **2** *verb* **(a)** to go very fast; *the rocket streaked across the sky* **(b)** *(informal)* to run about naked in public

streaker [stri:kə] *noun* person who runs naked in public; *the rugby match had to be stopped when a streaker ran across the pitch*

streaky bacon [sti:ki beɪkən] *noun* bacon cut in thin strips, with streaks of fat between the meat

stream [stri:m] **1** *noun* **(a)** little river; *can you jump across that stream?* **(b)** things which pass continuously; *crossing the road is difficult because of the stream of traffic; we had a stream of customers on the first day of the sale; streams of refugees tried to cross the border* **(c) to come on stream** = to start production; *output will be doubled when the new factory comes on stream* **2** *verb* to flow continuously; *blood was streaming down his face; cars streamed out* *of the park*; *children streamed across the square*; *he has a streaming cold* = he has a cold where his nose is running all the time

streamline ['striːmlaɪn] *verb* **(a)** to design a car or plane or boat, etc., so that it can move easily through water or air; *the body of the car was streamlined to make it faster* **(b)** to make something more efficient or more simple; *we are trying to streamline the accounting system*

streamlined ['striːmlaɪnd] *adjective* **(a)** designed so as to be able to move faster; *the car has been redesigned with a more streamlined body* **(b)** efficient or rapid; *they have a very streamlined production system*; *the company introduced a more streamlined system of distribution*

street [striːt] *noun* **(a)** road in a town, usually with house on each side; *it is difficult to park in our street on Saturday mornings*; *her flat is on a noisy street*; *the school is in the next street*; **street map** *or* **street plan** = diagram showing the streets of a town, with their names; *you will need a street map to get round New York* **(b)** *(used with names)* *what's your office address? - 16 Cambridge Street*; *Oxford Street, Bond Street and Regent Street are the main shopping areas in London* (NOTE: when used in names, **Oxford Street, Regent Street**, etc., is usually written **St: Oxford St**) **(c)** **High Street** = the main shopping street in a town; *his shop is on the High Street* (NOTE: the American English equivalent is **Main Street**) **(d)** **the man in the street** = the ordinary person, who represents what most people think; *the government's message is not getting through to the man in the street*; *the man in the street isn't interested in Europe* **(e)** **at street level** = at the same height as the street; *the main entrance is at street level*; *(informal)* **streets ahead** = much more advanced or successful; *Japanese firms are streets ahead of us in computer technology*; *(informal)* **it's right up my street** = it's something I know a lot about and can do well; *you're the gardening expert - this job should be right up your street*

streetcar ['striːtkɑː] *noun US* form of public transport, with carriages running on rails laid in the street; *you can take a streetcar from the station to the city centre* (NOTE: British English is **tram**)

streetlamp *or* **streetlight** ['striːtlæmp or 'striːtlaɪt] *noun* electric light on a tall pole, to light a street; *they have been installing new orange street lights in the High Street*

strength [strenθ] *noun* **(a)** being physically strong; *she hasn't got the strength to lift it*; *you should test the strength of the rope before you start climbing* **(b)** being strong, being at a high level; *the strength of the demand for the new car is surprising*; *the strength of the pound increases the possibility of higher inflation* **(c)** **in strength** = in large numbers; *the police were there in strength*; **at full strength** = with everyone present; *the department had several posts vacant, but is back to full strength again*; **in a show of strength** = to show how strong an army is; *in a show of strength, the government sent an aircraft carrier to the area*; **to go from strength to strength** = to get stronger and stronger; *under his leadership the party went from strength to strength*; **on the strength of** = because of; *they employed him on the strength of the references from his previous employer* (NOTE: the opposite is **weakness**)

strengthen ['strenθn] *verb* **(a)** to make something stronger; *the sea wall is being strengthened to prevent another flood*; *this will only strengthen their determination to oppose the government*; *we are planning to strengthen airport security* **(b)** to become stronger; *the wind is strengthening from the south-west* (NOTE: the opposite is **weaken**)

strenuous ['strenjuəs] *adjective* energetic, requiring effort; *the doctor has forbidden him all strenuous exercise*

stress [stres] **1** *noun* **(a)** force or pressure on something; *stresses inside the earth create earthquakes*; **stress fracture** = fracture of a bone caused by excessive force, as in some types of sport **(b)** nervous strain caused by an outside influence; *she has difficulty coping with the stress of the office*; *people in positions of responsibility often have stress-related illnesses* **(c)** loudness of your voice when you pronounce a word or syllable; *in the word 'emphasis' the stress is on the first syllable* (NOTE: plural is **stresses**) **2** *verb* to put emphasis on something; *I must stress the importance of keeping the plan secret*

stressed [strest] *adjective* worried and tense; *when you're feeling stressed it's better to try to get to bed early* *(informal)* **stressed out** = very worried and tense; *he's stressed out with his new job*

stressful ['stresful] *adjective* (situation) which causes stress; *repetitive work can be just as stressful as more varied work*

stretch [stretʃ] **1** *noun* **(a)** long piece of land, road, etc.; *for long stretches of the Transsiberian Railway, all you see are trees*; *stretches of the river have been so polluted that bathing is dangerous*; **the final stretch** *or* **the home stretch** = the last stage of a race or journey; *he was far ahead of the other runners when they came to the final stretch* **(b)** long period of time; *for long stretches we had nothing to do*; **at a stretch** = without a break; *he played the piano for two hours at a stretch* **(c)** *(informal)* time in prison; *he did a stretch in Wormwood Scrubs* **(d)** action of putting out your arms and legs as far as they will go; *I love to lie in bed and have a good stretch before I get up* **(e)** action of pulling something out; *give the sweater a stretch before you hang it up to dry* **(f)** **by no stretch of the imagination** = no one can possibly believe that; *by no stretch of the imagination can you expect him to win* (NOTE: plural is **stretches**) **2** *verb* **(a)** to spread out for a great distance; *the line of cars stretched for three miles from the accident*; *the queue stretched from the door of the cinema right round the corner*; *white sandy beaches stretch as far as the eye can see* **(b)** to push out your arms or legs as far as they can; *the cat woke up and stretched*; *the monkey stretched out through the bars and grabbed the little boy's cap*; *(informal)* **to stretch your legs** = to go for a short walk after sitting for a long time; *in the coffee break I went out into the garden to stretch my legs* **(c)** to pull out so that it becomes loose; *don't hang your jumper up like that - you will just stretch it*; *these trousers are not supposed to stretch*; **he is not fully stretched** = his work is too easy and does not make him work as hard as he could

stretch back ['stretʃ 'bæk] *verb* to go back over a long period; *his interest in music stretches back to when he was at primary school*

stretcher ['stretʃə] *noun* folding bed with handles, on which an injured person can be carried by two people; *some of the injured could walk, but there were* *several stretcher cases*; *the rescue team brought him down the mountain, strapped to a stretcher*; **stretcher bearer** = person who helps to carry a stretcher

stretch to ['stretʃ 'tʊ] *verb* to be enough for; *will your money stretch to paying for a cab ride to the temple?*; **dinner won't stretch to seven** = there won't be enough food for seven people; **to stretch something to the limit** = to be almost too much for; *the new car is going to stretch my finances to the limit*

stretchy ['stretʃi] *adjective* which stretches; *tights are usually made of some stretchy material*

strew [struː] *verb* to scatter over a wide area; *children strewed flowers along the path of the bride and groom*; *burning cars and bodies were strewn all over the motorway* (NOTE: **strewing - strewed** or **strewn** [struːn])

stricken ['strɪkn] *adjective & suffix* struck by disease, emotion, etc.; *half the class was stricken with flu*; *they rushed rescuers to the stricken villages*; *panic-stricken children ran out of the school*; *relief workers are bringing food to drought-stricken areas*

strict [strɪkt] *adjective* **(a)** exact (meaning); *the files are in strict alphabetical order* **(b)** which must be obeyed; *I gave strict instructions that no one was to be allowed in*; *the rules are very strict and any bad behaviour will be severely punished* **(c)** insisting that rules are obeyed; *our parents are very strict with us about staying up late* (NOTE: **stricter - strictest**)

strictly ['strɪktli] *adverb* **(a)** in a strict way; *all staff must follow strictly the procedures in the training manual* **(b)** **strictly confidential** = completely secret; *what I am going to tell you is strictly confidential* **(c)** **strictly speaking** = really, in reality; *strictly speaking, she's not my aunt, just an old friend of the family*

stride [straɪd] **1** *noun* long step; *in three strides he was across the room and out of the door*; **to make great strides** = to advance quickly; *researchers have made great strides in the treatment of asthma*; **to take something in your stride** = to deal with something easily; *other people always seem to have problems, but she just takes everything in her stride* **2** *verb* to walk with long steps; *he strode into the room*; *we could see him striding across the field to take shelter from the rain* (NOTE: **striding - strode** [strəʊd])

strident ['straɪdənt] *adjective* unpleasantly loud and harsh; *the new proposals met with strident protests from the opposition newspapers*; *the strident horns of the fire engines racing through the night*

strike [straɪk] **1** *noun* **(a)** stopping of work by workers because of lack of agreement with management or because of orders from a trade union; *they all voted in favour of a strike*; *the danger of a strike was averted at the last minute*; **general strike** = strike of all the workers in a country; **sit-down strike** = strike where the workers stay in their place of work and refuse to leave; **to take strike action** = to go on strike; *the workers voted to take strike action*; **strike ballot** or **strike vote** = vote by workers to decide if a strike should be held **(b)** **to come out on strike** or **to go on strike** = to stop work; *the workers went on strike for more money*; *the baggage handlers are on strike for higher pay*; **to call the workforce out on strike** = to tell the workers to stop work; *the union called its members out on strike* **(c)** military attack; *they launched an air strike against the enemy positions* **2** *verb* **(a)** to stop working because of disagreement with

management; *the workers are striking in protest against bad working conditions* **(b)** to hit something hard; *he struck her with a bottle*; *she struck her head on the low door*; *he struck a match and lit the fire* **(c)** (*of a clock*) to ring to mark an hour; *the clock had just struck one when she heard a noise in the corridor* **(d)** to come to someone's mind; *a thought just struck me*; *it suddenly struck me that I had seen him somewhere before*; **it strikes me that** = I think that; *it strikes me that we may be charging too much* **(e)** to surprise someone; *he was struck by the poverty he saw everywhere* **(f)** to attack; *the police are afraid the killer may strike again*; *the illness struck without warning* **(g)** to come to an agreement; *we expect to strike a deal next week*; *they struck a bargain and decided to share the costs* (NOTE: **striking - struck** [strʌk])

strikebound ['straɪkbaʊnd] *adjective* not able to move because of a strike; *six ships are strikebound in the docks*

strikebreaker ['straɪkbreɪkə] *noun* worker who goes on working when everyone else is on strike

strike pay ['straɪk 'peɪ] *noun* wages paid to striking workers by their union; *our strike pay is only ten pounds per week*

striker ['straɪkə] *noun* **(a)** worker who is on strike; *strikers picketed the factory* **(b)** football player whose main task is to score goals; *his pass back to the goalkeeper was intercepted by the opposition striker who promptly scored*

striking ['straɪkɪŋ] **1** *adjective* noticeable, unusual; *she bears a striking resemblance to the Queen*; *it is a very striking portrait of Winston Churchill* **2** *noun* hitting; **within striking distance** = quite close, near enough to hit; *the capital is within striking distance of the enemy guns*

strikingly ['straɪkɪŋli] *adverb* very noticeably; *a strikingly handsome man*

string [strɪŋ] *noun* **(a)** strong thin cord used for tying up parcels, etc.; *this string isn't strong enough to tie up that big parcel*; *she bought a ball of string*; *we've run out of string* (NOTE: no plural in this meaning: **some string**; **a piece of string**) **(b)** thread on a musical instrument which makes a note when you hit it; *he was playing the violin when one of the strings broke*; *a guitar has six strings* **(c)** one of the cords in a tennis racket; *one of the strings has snapped* **(d)** long series of things, events; *she's been plagued with a string of illnesses*; *I had a string of phone calls this morning*

string bag ['strɪŋ 'bæg] *noun* shopping bag like a net with handles

stringed instrument ['strɪŋd 'ɪnstrəmənt] *noun* musical instrument where the notes are played on strings; *stringed instruments such as violins and cellos*

stringent ['strɪndʒənt] *adjective* (*formal*) strict or severe; *stringent new customs checks have been introduced at the airport*

stringer ['strɪŋə] *noun* freelance journalist who sends stories regularly to a newspaper, covering events in a particular town or country; *a report from our stringer in the Czech Republic*

strings [strɪŋz] *noun* **(a)** (*informal*) hidden conditions; **are there any strings attached?** = are there any hidden conditions?; *the bank loaned us the money with no strings attached*; (*informal*) **to pull strings** = to use your influence to make something happen; *her* *father pulled strings to get her the job* **(b)** the strings = section of an orchestra with string instruments; *the work provides a lot of scope for the strings; see also* BRASS, PERCUSSION, WIND **(c)** members of an orchestra who play the violin, cello, etc.; *the strings sit at the front of the orchestra, near the conductor*

string vest ['strɪŋ 'vest] *noun* vest made of material woven like a net

stringy ['strɪŋi] *adjective* full of tough fibres; *these beans are too stringy, I can't eat them*

strip [strɪp] **1** *noun* **(a)** long narrow piece of cloth, paper, etc.; *he tore the paper into strips; houses are to be built along the strip of land near the church;* **magnetic strip** = layer of magnetic material on a plastic card, used for recording data **(b) strip cartoon** *or* **comic strip** = cartoon story made of a series of small drawings inside little boxes side by side **(c)** particular clothes worn by football players and fans; *he was wearing the Arsenal strip* **(d) landing strip** *or* **airstrip** = rough place for planes to land; *the soldiers cut a landing strip in the jungle* **2** *verb* **(a)** to take off your clothes; *strip to the waist for your chest X-ray*; *he stripped down to his underpants* **(b)** to remove completely; *the wind stripped the leaves off the trees; first we have to strip the old paint off the cupboards; he was stripped of his title following the scandal* (NOTE: **stripping - stripped**)

stripe [straɪp] *noun* **(a)** long line of colour; *he has an umbrella with red, white and blue stripes* **(b)** piece of coloured cloth sewn to a soldier's jacket to show his rank; *he has just got his sergeant's stripes*

striped [straɪpt] *adjective* with lines of colour; *a red and white striped tie; the clown wore striped trousers*

strip lighting ['strɪp 'laɪtɪŋ] *noun* lighting using long round tubes; *the strip lighting in the office makes my eyes hurt*

striptease ['strɪpti:z] *noun* entertainment where someone takes their clothes off piece by piece; *most striptease clubs are in the West End of London*

stripy ['straɪpi] *adjective (informal)* striped, with lines of colour; *she wore a blue and white stripy shirt; a row of stripy deckchairs*

strive [straɪv] *verb* to try very hard to; *he strove to do as well as his brother; everyone is striving for a solution to the dispute* (NOTE: **striving - strove** [strəʊv] **- has striven** ['strɪvn])

stroke [strəʊk] **1** *noun* **(a)** gentle touch with your hand; *she gave the dog a stroke* **(b)** sudden loss of consciousness caused by a blood clot in the brain; *he was paralyzed after his stroke; she had a stroke and died* **(c)** movement of a pen, brush, etc., which makes a line; *she can draw a cartoon with just a few strokes of the pen*; **oblique stroke** = printing sign (/) used to show an alternative; *all members/visitors must sign the register* (NOTE: say 'all members stroke visitors') **(d)** act of hitting something, such as a ball; *it took him three strokes to get the ball onto the green*; **to put someone off his stroke** = to distract someone's attention so that he does something wrong; *people kept on shouting while the minister was speaking and that put him off his stroke* **(e)** sound made when hitting something (such as a bell); *on the stroke of midnight* = when the clocks are striking twelve **(f) stroke of luck** = piece of luck; *I had a stroke of luck yesterday - I found my wallet which I thought I had lost; it was a stroke of luck that you happened to come along at that moment*; **stroke of work** = action of working; *he hasn't done a*

stroke of work all day **(e)** style of swimming; *she won the 200m breast stroke* **2** *verb* to run your hands gently over; *she was stroking the cat as it sat in her lap*

stroll [strəʊl] **1** *noun* short relaxing walk; *we went for a stroll by the river after dinner* **2** *verb* to walk slowly for relaxation; *people were strolling in the park; on Sunday evenings, everyone strolls along the boulevard*

stroller ['strəʊlə] *noun* **(a)** *US* light chair with wheels for pushing babies in (NOTE: British English is **pushchair**) **(b)** person who strolls along; *crowds of strollers were in the streets, looking at the shop windows*

strong [strɒŋ] **1** *adjective* **(a)** (person) with a lot of strength; *I'm not strong enough to carry that box* **(b)** which has a lot of force or strength; *the string broke - we need something stronger; the wind was so strong that it blew some tiles off the roof*; **strong currency** = currency which is high against other currencies (NOTE: the opposite is a **weak currency**) **(c)** with a powerful smell, taste, etc.; *I don't like strong cheese; you need a cup of strong black coffee to wake you up; there was a strong smell of gas in the kitchen* **(d) strong drink** = alcohol; *have an orange juice, or would you prefer something stronger?* (NOTE: **stronger - strongest**) **2** *suffix* (used to show a number of people) *a 50-strong party of marines landed on the beach; a 20-strong group of shift workers* **3** *adverb* **going strong** = still very active, still working; *she had a heart bypass ten years ago and is still going strong*

strong box ['strɒŋ 'bɒks] *noun* small heavy safe for keeping valuable documents, jewels, etc.; *thieves broke open the strongbox and stole the jewels*

stronghold ['strɒŋhəʊld] *noun* **(a)** fortress, place which is difficult to capture; *the enemy stronghold finally surrendered* **(b)** place which is noted for something; *Rome is renowned as the stronghold of Catholicism; the club is a stronghold of male chauvinism*

strongly ['strɒŋli] *adverb* in a strong way; *the castle is strongly defended; they objected very strongly to the plan*

strong-minded ['strɒŋ'maɪndɪd] *adjective* with clear ideas which are not easily changed; *is he strong-minded enough to resist their offer?*

strong point ['strɒŋ 'pɔɪnt] *noun* particular good characteristic that someone has; *maths is not my strong point; try to emphasise your strong points when writing your CV*

strongroom ['strɒŋrʊm] *noun* special room in a bank where valuable documents, money, gold, etc., can be kept; *the title deeds of the house are in a strongroom in the bank*

strontium ['strɒntiəm] *noun* metallic element, occurring as part of the fallout from nuclear explosions (NOTE: Chemical element: chemical symbol: **Sr**; atomic number: **38**)

strove [strəʊv] *see* STRIVE

struck [strʌk] *see* STRIKE

structural ['strʌktʃrəl] *adjective* referring to a structure; *the surveyor reported several structural defects;* **structural unemployment** = unemployment caused by the changing structure of an industry or of society

structurally ['strʌktʃrəli] *adverb* referring to the basic structure of something; *the house is structurally sound*

structure ['strʌktʃə] **1** *noun* **(a)** way in which things are organized; *a career structure within a corporation*; *the company is reorganizing its discount structure* **(b)** building; *they want to demolish a couple of old structures to make a swimming pool* **2** *verb* to arrange according to a certain system; *we've tried to structure the meeting so that there is plenty of time for discussion*

struggle ['strʌgl] **1** *noun* **(a)** fight; *after a short struggle the burglar was arrested* **(b)** hard effort to do something, because of difficulties; *setting up a new company during a recession was always going to be a struggle*; *her constant struggle to bring up her children*; *their struggle against ill-health* **2** *verb* **(a)** to fight with an attacker; *two men were struggling on the floor* **(b)** to try hard to do something difficult; *she's struggling with her maths homework*; *she struggled to carry all the shopping to the car*; **to struggle to your feet** = to stand up with great difficulty; *after the blast from the bomb she struggled to her feet and started running*

strum [strʌm] *verb* to play a stringed instrument by running your fingers across the strings in an informal way; *he was quietly strumming his guitar when I arrived* (NOTE: **strumming - strummed**)

strut [strʌt] **1** *noun* bar of wood, metal, etc., which supports something; *they pulled away the struts and the wall collapsed* **2** *verb* to walk in a proud and important way; *he strutted across the stage to collect her prize*; *he refused to accept their offer and strutted out of the room* (NOTE: **strutting - strutted**)

stub [stʌb] **1** *noun* **(a)** small piece left after something has been used; *he walked along the gutter looking for cigarette stubs* **(b)** piece of paper left after a cheque or a ticket has been torn out of a book; *look at your cheque stubs to see when you wrote the cheque* **2** *verb* **(a)** to **stub your toe on something** = to hurt your toe by hitting it against something; *I stubbed my toe on a rock on the beach* **(b)** to **stub out a cigarette** = to put out a cigarette by pressing the burning end against something; *here's an ashtray if you want to stub out your cigarette* (NOTE: **stubbing - stubbed**)

stubble ['stʌbl] *noun* **(a)** short stems left in the ground after harvesting a crop of cereals; *burning stubble removes weed seeds and creates natural fertilizer*; **stubble field** = field where the stubble has been left in the ground after the crop has been harvested; *flocks of birds came to feed on the stubble fields* **(b)** short hairs which grow on a man's chin if he does not shave for several days; *she told him to shave, as she didn't like his stubble*; **designer stubble** = unshaved beard which gives you a fashionable look

stubborn ['stʌbən] *adjective* **(a)** obstinate, not willing to change your mind; *he's so stubborn - he only does what he wants to do* **(b)** difficult to remove; *to get rid of really stubborn stains you will need to use bleach*

stubbornly ['stʌbənli] *adverb* in an obstinate way; *he stubbornly refuses to see a doctor*

stucco ['stʌkəu] *noun* hard plaster covering the outside of a building; *many houses in London are built of brick, covered with stucco* (NOTE: no plural)

stuck [stʌk] *see* STICK

stuck-up ['stʌk'ʌp] *adjective (informal)* proud and superior; *she's so stuck-up, she won't speak to any of us*

stud [stʌd] *noun* **(a)** nail with a head that stands out above a surface; *he had a pattern of studs on his belt* **(b)** spikes or nails on the soles of boots; *his boots have specially large studs* **(c)** type of button with two heads for passing through two holes to fasten a shirt; *I can't wear my dinner shirt - I've lost my dress studs* **(d)** small gold ornament or earring for pierced ears, like a little nail; *she wears a stud in her nose* **(e)** horses which are kept for breeding; **to put a horse out to stud** = to use a male horse for breeding; **stud book** = register of pedigree horses, etc.; **stud (farm)** = farm where horses are kept for breeding

studded ['stʌdɪd] *adjective* **(a)** decorated with many small things, nails, etc.; *old church doors are often studded with huge nails* **(b)** full of, covered with; *the film has a star-studded cast*; *the valley was studded with little cottages*

student ['stjuːdənt] *noun* **(a)** person who is studying at a college or university; *all the science students came to my lecture*; *she's a brilliant student*; *two students had to sit the exam again*; **student card** = identification card, showing that you are a student, which allows you special discounts on certain items; **students' union** = (i) building where university students meet to drink, eat, see films, etc.; (ii) group representing the students at a university **(b)** *US* boy or girl studying at high school

studio ['stjuːdɪəu] *noun* **(a)** room where an artist paints; *she uses this room as a studio because of the good light*; **design studio** = independent firm which specializes in creating designs for companies **(b)** place where photographers take photographs; *a studio photograph of the bride and groom* **(c)** place where films, broadcasts, recordings, etc., are made; *the TV series was made at Teddington Studios*; *and now, back to the studio for the latest news and weather report*; *they spent the whole day recording the piece in the studio* **(d)** very small flat for one person, usually one room with a small kitchen and bathroom; *you can rent a studio overlooking the sea for £300 a week in high season* (NOTE: plural is **studios**)

studious ['stjuːdɪəs] *adjective* enjoying study, spending a lot of time studying; *she's a very studious girl, and hardly ever goes out in the evening*

study ['stʌdi] **1** *noun* **(a)** work of examining something carefully to learn more about it; *the company asked the consultant to prepare a study into new production techniques*; *the review has published studies on the new drug*; **to carry out a feasibility study on a project** = to examine the costs and possible profits to see if the project should be started; **nature study** = learning about plants and animals at school **(b)** room in which someone reads, writes, works, etc.; *when he says he is going to his study to read, it usually means he's going to have nap* **(c)** **studies** = attending college or university; *she interrupted her studies and went to work in Kenya for two years*; *he has successfully finished his studies* **2** *verb* **(a)** to learn about a subject at college or university; *he is studying medicine because he wants to be a doctor*; *she's studying French and Spanish in the modern languages department* **(b)** to examine something carefully to learn more about it; *we are studying the possibility of setting up an office in New York*; *the* government studied the committee's proposals for two months; *doctors are studying the results of the screening programme*

stuff [stʌf] **1** *noun* **(a)** substance, especially something unpleasant; *you've got some black stuff stuck to your shoe* **(b)** *(informal)* things, equipment; *dump all your stuff in the living room*; *take all that stuff and put it in the dustbin*; *all your photographic stuff is still in the back of my car* **(c)** ideas; *she talked about the dangers of smoking and all that stuff about lung cancer* **(d)** *(informal)* **to do your stuff** = to do what you are supposed to do or what you're good at; *come on, England, do your stuff!*; *everyone must do their stuff quickly if we want the work to be finished tonight*; **to know your stuff** = to know your subject well, to be good at what you are doing; *it was fascinating to listen to him, he really knows his stuff* **2** *verb* **(a)** to push something into something to fill it; *he stuffed his pockets full of peppermints*; *the banknotes were stuffed into a small plastic wallet* **(b)** to put breadcrumbs, chopped meat, etc., inside meat or vegetables before cooking them; *they served stuffed vine leaves as a starter*; *we had roast veal stuffed with mushrooms* **(c)** *(informal)* **to stuff yourself** = to eat a lot; *they were stuffing themselves on chocolate pudding* **(d)** to fill the skin of a dead animal so that it looks alive; *there was a stuffed tiger at the top of the staircase in the old castle* **(e)** *(informal, rude)* **(go and) get stuffed** = go away, stop interfering; *you can tell the manager to go and get stuffed*

stuffing ['stʌfɪŋ] *noun* **(a)** mixture of bread, fat, onions, herbs, etc., put inside a chicken, fish or vegetables before cooking them; *I prepared the stuffing for the fish according to my mother's recipe* **(b)** soft material used to fill cushions, chair seats, etc.; *the stuffing's coming out of this cushion* **(c)** *(informal)* **to knock the stuffing out of someone** = to make someone lose their confidence; *when his wife ran away with his best friend it seemed to knock all the stuffing out of him*

stuffy ['stʌfɪ] *adjective* **(a)** without any fresh air; *can't you open a window, it's so stuffy in here?*; *I dislike commuting into town every day on stuffy underground trains* **(b)** dull and old-fashioned; *we want to change the stuffy image of the firm* **(c)** (nose) which is blocked with mucus; *his stuffy nose is caused by an allergy* (NOTE: **stuffier - stuffiest**)

stumble ['stʌmbl] *verb* **(a)** to trip, to almost fall by hitting your foot against something; *he stumbled as he tried to get down the stairs in the dark* **(b)** to walk in an unsteady way; *he was stumbling around in the cellar, looking for the light switch* **(c)** **to stumble across something** = to find something by accident; *I stumbled across this letter which someone had hidden* **(d)** to make mistakes when reading; *he managed to stumble through the reading test*; *she read the TV news without stumbling over any of the foreign words*

stumbling block ['stʌmblɪŋ 'blɒk] *noun* thing which prevents you doing what you want to do; *their attitude is the main stumbling block to the peace negotiations*

stump [stʌmp] **1** *noun* **(a)** short piece of something left sticking up, such as the trunk of a tree that has been cut down; *after cutting down the trees, we need to get rid of the stumps* **(b)** one of the three sticks placed in the ground as a target in cricket; *the ball hit the stumps and the last man was out*; **stumps were drawn** = the

game of cricket came to an end (temporarily) **2** *verb* **(a)** **to stump along** = to walk along with heavy steps; *he stumped angrily out of the shop* **(b)** *(informal)* to ask someone a difficult question which he can't answer; *the MD was stumped when the committee asked him how many hours the average packer worked*; *today's crossword has stumped me completely or has got me stumped*

stump up ['stʌmp 'ʌp] *verb (informal)* to pay money; *you promised him five pounds so you'd better stump up*; *she stumped up the money we needed to get the car repaired*

stumpy ['stʌmpɪ] *adjective* short and fat; *some dogs have stumpy little legs*

stun [stʌn] *verb* **(a)** to knock someone out, to make someone lose consciousness with a blow to the head; *the blow on the head stunned him* **(b)** to shock someone completely; *she was stunned when he told her that he was already married* (NOTE: **stunning - stunned**)

stung [stʌŋ] *see* STING

stunning ['stʌnɪŋ] *adjective* extraordinary, marvellously beautiful; *this is a stunning photograph of your mother*; *they have a stunning house in the country*

stunt [stʌnt] **1** *noun* trick or dangerous act done to attract attention; *climbing up the outside of the building was just a publicity stunt*; *he's so fit that he insists on doing all the stunts in his films himself* **2** *verb* to prevent something from growing; *the trees on the top of the cliff are stunted by strong winds*; *the children's development was stunted by malnutrition and disease*

stunt man ['stʌnt 'mæn] *noun* man who carries out dangerous acts in films in place of a film star; *he was the stunt man for the scene where the motorcycle jumps across the river*

stupendous [stjuːˈpendəs] *adjective* extraordinary, very large or magnificent; *he has been offered a stupendous salary*; *his acting was simply stupendous*

stupid ['stjuːpɪd] *adjective* **(a)** not very intelligent; *what a stupid man!* **(b)** not showing any sense; *it was stupid of her not to wear a helmet*; *he made several stupid mistakes*

stupidity [stjuːˈpɪdɪtɪ] *noun* being stupid; *the driver's stupidity was the cause of the accident*

stupidly ['stjuːpɪdlɪ] *adverb* in a stupid way; *I stupidly left my umbrella at home*

stupor ['stjuːpə] *noun* state of being almost unconscious

sturdy ['stɜːdɪ] *adjective* strong and vigorous; *she has two sturdy little boys*; *don't climb on that chair, it's not very sturdy* (NOTE: **sturdier - sturdiest**)

stutter ['stʌtə] **1** *noun* speech defect where someone repeats the sound at the beginning of a word several times; *he is taking therapy to try to cure his stutter* **2** *verb* to repeat the same sounds when speaking; *he stuttered badly when making his speech*

sty [staɪ] *noun* pigsty, little building where a pig is kept; *he leant on the gate of the sty, looking at the pig and her piglets*; *see also* PIGSTY

stye *or* **sty** [staɪ] *noun* inflammation of the gland at the base of an eyelash

style [staɪl] **1** *noun* **(a)** way of doing something, especially way of designing, drawing, writing, etc.; *the room is decorated in Chinese style; the painting is in his usual style; that style was fashionable in the 1940s* **(b)** elegant or fashionable way of doing things; *she always dresses with style; they live in grand style; see also* HAIRSTYLE **(c)** way someone behaves, thinks or lives; *it's not her style to forget an appointment; their style of life wouldn't suit me* **2** *verb* to design something; **to have your hair styled** = to go to the hairdresser's to have your hair cut and set in a particular way

styling ['staɪlɪŋ] *noun* way in which something is designed; *the styling of the car's interior was much admired*

stylish ['staɪlɪʃ] *adjective* attractive and fashionable; *he drives a stylish sports car; we ate in a very stylish new restaurant*

stylist ['staɪlɪst] *noun* person who gives a style to something; **hair stylist** = hairdresser

stylistic [staɪ'lɪstɪk] *adjective* referring to style in art; *she raised some interesting stylistic points about the poem*

stylized ['staɪlaɪzd] *adjective* drawn or designed in a fixed unnatural way; *Egyptian columns were simply stylized trees; the design is a series of stylized maple leaves*

sub [sʌb] *noun (informal)* = SUBMARINE, SUBSCRIPTION, SUBSTITUTE

sub- [sʌb] *prefix meaning* below, under

subcommittee ['sʌbkəmɪti] *noun* small committee which is set up by a main committee and deals with a specific topic; *the next item on the agenda is the report of the finance subcommittee*

subconscious [sʌb'kɒnʃəs] **1** *adjective* referring to mental processes, such as memory, which people are not aware of all the time, but which can affect their actions; *aggression serves a subconscious desire to do better than others* **2** *noun* part of your mind which has ideas or feelings of which you are not aware; *somewhere, deep in his subconscious, was a feeling of hatred for his family*

subcontract **1** [sʌb'kɒntrækt] *noun* contract between the main contractor for a whole project and another firm who will do part of the work; *they have been awarded the subcontract for all the electrical work in the new building; we will put the plumbing work out to subcontract* **2** [sʌbkən'trækt] *verb* to agree with a company that they will do part of the work for a project; *the electrical work has been subcontracted to Smith Ltd*

subcontractor [sʌbkən'træktə] *noun* company which has a contract to do work for a main contractor; *the contractor blamed the delays on the subcontractor*

subdue [sʌb'djuː] *verb* to overcome, to bring under control; *their attempts to subdue the terrorists failed; he learnt to subdue his desire for revenge*

subdued [sʌb'djuːd] *adjective* **(a)** very quiet, not excited; *the audience was very subdued* **(b)** not bright, not loud; *the room has been painted in subdued colours; a subdued discussion was going on in a far corner of the restaurant*

subheading ['sʌbheɪŋ] *noun* heading used to divide a chapter or main entry into smaller sections; *look under the subheading 'Travel expenses'*

subject ['sʌbdʒɪkt] *noun* **(a)** thing which you are talking about or writing about; *he suddenly changed the subject of the conversation; the newspaper has devoted a special issue to the subject of pollution* **(b)** thing shown in a painting, etc.; *the same subject is treated quite differently in the three paintings* **(c)** area of knowledge which you are studying; *maths is his weakest subject; you can take up to five subjects at 'A' Level* **(d) to be the subject of** = to be the person or thing talked about or studied; *the painter Chagall will be the subject of our lecture today; advertising costs are the subject of close examination by the auditors* **(e)** *(grammar)* noun or pronoun which comes before a verb and shows the person or thing that does the action expressed by the verb; *in the sentence 'the cat sat on the mat' the word 'cat' is the subject of the verb 'sat'* **(d)** person who is born in a country, or who has the right to live in a country; *she is a British subject but a Canadian citizen*

subject to **1** *adjective* ['sʌbdʒɪkt 'tu] **(a)** depending on something; *we want you to go on a study tour to France, subject to getting your parents' permission; the contract is subject to government approval* = the contract will be valid only if it is approved by the government; *sale subject to contract* = sale which is not legal until a proper contract has been signed; **offer subject to availability** = the offer is valid only if the goods are available **(b)** affected by; *the timetable is subject to change without notice; these articles are subject to import tax; after returning from the tropics he was subject to bouts of malaria* **2** *verb* [sʌb'dʒekt 'tu]; **to subject to** = to make something *or* someone suffer something unpleasant; *the guards subjected the prisoners to physical violence; we were subjected to a barrage of questions by reporters*

subjection [sʌb'dʒekʃn] *noun* being subjected to; *the subjection of the civilian population to constant air attacks*

subjective [sʌb'dʒektɪv] *adjective* seen from your own point of view, and therefore possibly biased; *this is a purely subjective impression of what happened* (NOTE: the opposite is **objective**)

subjectivity ['sʌbdʒek'tɪvɪti] *noun* being subjective, biased because you see things from your own point of view; *there will always be a certain amount of subjectivity in his reports*

subject-matter ['sʌbdʒektmætə] *noun* subject dealt with in a book, TV programme, etc.; *the subject-matter of the book is very delicate and handled in a sympathetic way*

subjunctive [sʌb'dʒʌŋktɪv] *noun (grammar)* form of a verb used to show doubt, wish, etc.; *in the phrases 'wish you were here', and 'if she were to die tomorrow' the verb 'were' is in the* subjunctive

sublet [sʌb'let] *verb* to let a property you are renting to another tenant; *we have sublet part of our office to a financial consultant* (NOTE: **subletting - sublet**)

sublime [sə'blaɪm] **1** *adjective* **(a)** grand, wonderful; *the sublime music of Beethoven's Ninth Symphony; the sublime sight of snow-capped mountains towering above the lake* **(b)** complete; *he showed sublime indifference to the demands of the staff* **2** *noun* **from the sublime to the ridiculous** = from a very good thing to a very silly thing in comparison; *to leave your Rolls Royce in the garage and go everywhere on a pushbike is really going from the* sublime to the ridiculous

submarine [sʌbməˈriːn] **1** *adjective* which is under the water; *a submarine pipeline* **2** *noun* special type of ship which can travel under water; *the submarine dived before she was spotted by enemy aircraft*

submerge [sʌbˈmɜːdʒ] *verb* **(a)** to cover with something, especially with water; *at high tide the rocks are completely submerged*; *the office is completely submerged with orders* **(b)** to go under water; *the submarine submerged and disappeared from view* **(c) to submerge yourself in something** = to become completely involved in a type of work to forget about other problems; *after the death of her mother she submerged herself in her medical work*

submission [sʌbˈmɪʃn] *noun* **(a)** state of giving in or having to obey someone; *their plan was to starve the enemy into submission* (NOTE: no plural in this meaning) **(b)** evidence, document, argument used in court; *in his submission, he stated that the council had always acted within the law*

submit [sʌbˈmɪt] *verb* **(a) to submit to** = to yield to; *he definitely won't submit to blackmail* **(b)** to put something forward for someone to examine; *you are requested to submit your proposal to the planning committee*; *he submitted a claim to the insurers*; *reps are asked to submit their expenses claims once a month* **(c)** to plead in court; *the defence submitted that there was no case to answer* (NOTE: **submitting - submitted**)

subordinate 1 *adjective* [səˈbɔːdnət] **(a)** under the control of someone else; less important; **subordinate to** = which is under the control of; *the new arrangement will make our department subordinate to yours* **(b) subordinate clause** = clause in a sentence which depends on the main clause **2** *noun* [səˈbɔːdnət] person who is under the direction of someone else; *his subordinates find him difficult to work with* **3** *verb* [səˈbɔːdneɪt]; **to subordinate something to** = to put something in a less important position than something else; *we were taught to subordinate our personal feelings to the needs of the state*

subordination [sʌbɔːdɪˈneɪʃn] *noun* act of subordinating; *the subordination of safety requirements to the need to make quick profits*

subpoena [sʌbˈpiːnə] **1** *noun* court order telling someone to appear in court; *she has been served a subpoena to appear in court next month* **2** *verb* to order someone to appear in court; *the finance director was subpoenaed by the prosecution* (NOTE: **subpoenaed**)

subscribe [səbˈskraɪb] *verb* **(a) to subscribe to a magazine** = to pay in advance for a series of issues of a magazine **(b)** to give money to; *he subscribes to several charities* **(c)** *(formal)* **to subscribe to a view** = to agree with a view; *I subscribe to the view that government expenditure should be reduced* **(d) to subscribe for shares** = to apply for shares in a new company; *if you wish to subscribe for shares, fill in the application form and return it with your cheque*

subscriber [səbˈskraɪbə] *noun* **(a) subscriber to a magazine** *or* **magazine subscriber** = person who has paid in advance for a series of issues of a magazine; *the extra issue is sent free to subscribers* **(b)** person who pays regularly to use a service; *telephone subscribers who don't pay their bills have their phones cut off* **(c) subscriber to a share issue** = person who has applied

for shares in a new company; *there were very few subscribers to the recent share issue*

subscription [səbˈskrɪpʃn] *noun* **(a)** money paid in advance to a magazine for a series of issues; *did you remember to pay the subscription to the computer magazine?*; **to take out a subscription to a magazine** = to start paying for a series of issues of a magazine; **to cancel a subscription to a magazine** = to stop paying for a magazine **(b)** money paid to a club for a year's membership; *he forgot to renew his club subscription* **(c) subscription to a new share issue** = offering new shares in a company for sale

subsequent [ˈsʌbsɪkwənt] *adjective (formal)* which comes later; *the rainstorm and the subsequent flooding disrupted the cricket match*; *all subsequent reports must be sent to me immediately they arrive*

subsequently [ˈsʌbsɪkwəntli] *adverb (formal)* afterwards; *I subsequently discovered that there had been a mistake*; *what happened subsequently proved that our forecast had been correct*

subservient [səbˈsɜːviənt] *adjective* **(a)** always giving in to others; *stand up for your rights - you shouldn't be so subservient* **(b)** not as important as; *each state is subservient to the federation*

subside [sʌbˈsaɪd] *verb* **(a)** to go down, to become less loud or strong; *after the rainstorms passed, the flood waters gradually subsided*; *his anger subsided and he began to try to find out what had happened*; *he waited for the noise to subside before going on with his speech* **(b)** *(of a piece of ground, a building)* to sink, to fall to a lower level; *the office block is subsiding because it is built on clay*

subsidence [ˈsʌbsɪdəns] *noun (of a piece of ground or a building)* sinking, falling to a lower level; *the main road was closed because of subsidence*; *check the house for subsidence before you buy it*

subsidiarity [sʌbsɪdɪˈærɪti] *noun (in the European Union)* principle that decisions should be taken at the level of each individual government and not at the level of the European Commission

subsidiary [sʌbˈsɪdjəri] **1** *adjective* which is less important; *they queried one or two subsidiary items in the estimate*; **subsidiary company** = company which is more than 50% owned by another company, which controls it **2** *noun* company which is owned by a parent company; *most of the profit comes form subsidiaries in the Far East*

subsidize [ˈsʌbsɪdaɪz] *verb* to help by giving money; *the government has agreed to subsidize the coal industry*

subsidy [ˈsʌbsɪdi] *noun* money given to help pay for something which is unprofitable; *the government has increased its subsidy to the coal industry* (NOTE: plural is **subsidies**)

subsist [sʌbˈsɪst] *verb* **(a)** to stay alive, to manage; *some people can subsist on very little food* **(b)** *(formal)* to continue to exist; *doubts subsist in my mind as to his true identity*; *some traces of the old dialect still subsist in the islands*

subsistence [sʌbˈsɪstəns] *noun* minimum amount of food, money, housing, etc., which a person needs; *the company pays its salesmen £50 a day as subsistence money when they are travelling*; **subsistence agriculture** *or* **subsistence farming** = growing just enough crops to feed the farmer and his family, with nothing left to sell; **to live at subsistence level** = to have only just enough money to live on; *people living below subsistence level are eligible for government grants*

substance ['sʌbstəns] *noun* **(a)** solid or liquid material, especially one used in chemistry; *a secret substance is added to the product to give it its yellow colour; toxic substances got into the drinking water* **(b)** truth behind an argument; *there is no substance to the rumour that he was controlled by the mafia; she brought documents to add substance to her claim* **(c)** *(formal)* **a man of substance** = a rich man **(d)** drug; *he was found to have certain illegal substances in his suitcase*

substandard [sʌb'stændəd] *adjective* not up to the usual standard; *quality control is supposed to remove substandard products from the production line*

substantial [sʌb'stænʃl] *adjective* **(a)** large, important; *she was awarded substantial damages; he received a substantial sum when he left the company; a substantial amount of work remains to be done* **(b)** large, which satisfies; *we had a substantial meal at the local pub* **(c)** solid, strong; *this wall is too flimsy, we need something much more substantial*

substantially [sʌb'stænʃəli] *adverb* **(a)** mainly, mostly; *their forecast was substantially correct* **(b)** by a large amount; *the cost of raw materials has risen substantially over the last year*

substantiate [sʌb'stænʃɪeɪt] *verb* to prove that something which has been stated is true; *she made a claim which has never been substantiated*

substantive 1 *adjective (formal)* **(a)** ['sʌbstəntɪv] real, which is serious; *the two countries held substantive discussions at ministerial level* **(b)** [sʌb'stæntɪv] permanent military rank; *he holds the substantive rank of colonel* 2 *noun* ['sʌbstəntɪv] *(formal) (grammar)* a noun; *some substantives such as 'child' and 'man' have irregular plural forms*

substitute ['sʌbstɪtjuːt] 1 *noun* person or thing that takes the place of someone *or* something else; *this type of plastic can be used as a substitute for leather; the substitute teacher was better than the teacher himself; when the goalkeeper was injured they sent on a substitute* 2 *verb* **to substitute something** *or* **someone for something** *or* **someone else** = to put something *or* someone in the place of something *or* someone else; *he secretly substituted the fake diamond for the real one;* **to substitute for someone** = to replace someone; *who will be substituting for the sales manager when she's away on holiday?*

substitution [sʌbstɪ'tjuːʃn] *noun* act of substituting a person for someone else; *the substitution of the understudy for the main actor provoked a riot in the audience (in sport) there were three substitutions in the second half*

subterfuge ['sʌbtəfjuːdʒ] *noun (formal)* trick, clever way of doing something; *I think it is just a subterfuge to get us to pay more*

subterranean [sʌbtə'reɪnɪən] *adjective* under the ground; *a subterranean explosion shook the town*

subtitle ['sʌbtaɪtl] *noun* translation of the spoken text printed over a film; *they were showing 'Gone with the Wind' with subtitles in Japanese*

subtitled ['sʌbtaɪtld] *adjective* with subtitles; *they are showing the subtitled version* (NOTE: compare **dubbed**)

subtle ['sʌtl] *adjective* **(a)** not obvious or easily seen; *there's a subtle difference between the two political parties* **(b)** difficult to analyze because of being complicated or delicate; *a sauce with a subtle taste of lemon; a subtler shade would be better than that bright colour* (NOTE: **subtler - subtlest**)

subtlety ['sʌtlti] *noun* careful thought processes which are difficult to explain; *his way of dealing with protesters may lack subtlety but is very effective; I'm not sure that I have grasped all the subtleties of his argument* (NOTE: plural is **subtleties**)

subtotal ['sʌbtəʊtl] *noun* total of one section of a set of figures; *adding together all the subtotals you get a grand total of just over £10,000*

subtract [sʌb'trækt] *verb* to take one number away from another; *subtract 10 from 33 and you get 23*

subtraction [sʌb'trækʃn] *noun* act of subtracting one figure from another; *he tried to do the subtraction in his head*

suburb ['sʌbɜːb] *noun* residential area on the edge of a town; *he lives in a quiet suburb of Boston;* **the suburbs** = area all round a town where a lot of people live; *people who live in the suburbs find the air quality is better than in the centre of town*

suburban [sə'bɜːbən] *adjective* referring to the suburbs; *this is a very a suburban area - almost all the men commute to London every day;* **suburban line** = railway line between the suburbs to the centre of a town; *services on suburban lines have been disrupted by the strike*

suburbia [sə'bɜːbɪə] *noun* middle-class suburban districts around a city; *life in suburbia is very different from life in a high-rise flat in the town centre*

subversion [sʌb'vɜːʃn] *noun* secret acts against a government; *the government stated that the power of the state was being undermined by enemy subversion*

subversive [sʌb'vɜːsɪv] 1 *adjective* acting secretly against the government or people in authority; *the police are investigating subversive elements in the student organizations* 2 *noun* person who acts secretly against the government; *the police have arrested several known subversives*

subvert [sʌb'vɜːt] *verb* to bring about the downfall of something, or the ruin of the existing political system

subway ['sʌbweɪ] *noun* **(a)** passage under ground along which pedestrians can pass (as under a busy road); *there's a subway from the bus station to the shopping centre* **(b)** *US* underground railway system; *the New York subway; it will be quicker to take the subway to Grand Central Station* (NOTE: the London equivalent is the **Tube** or **Underground**)

succeed [sʌk'siːd] *verb* **(a)** to do well or to be profitable; *his business has succeeded more than he had expected* **(b)** **to succeed in doing something** = to do what you have been trying to do; *she succeeded in passing her driving test; I succeeded in getting them to agree to my plan* **(c)** *(informal, humorous)* to manage to do something which is rather stupid; *they succeeded in getting lost in the centre of London* **(d)** to follow on after someone who has retired, left the job, etc.; *Mr Smith was succeeded as chairman by Mr Jones;* **to**

succeed to the throne = to become king or queen; *he succeeded to the throne when his grandfather died*

success [sʌk'ses] *noun* **(a)** achieving what you have been trying to do; *she's been looking for a job in a library, but without any success so far* **(b)** doing something well; *her photo was in the newspapers after her Olympic success*; *the new car has not had much success in the Japanese market* **(c)** somebody *or* something that succeeds; *the launch of the new model was a great success*; *he wasn't much of a success as a manager*; *the cataract operation was a complete success* (NOTE: plural is **successes**)

successful [sʌk'sesful] *adjective* who *or* which does well; *he's a successful business man*; *she's very successful at hiding her real age*; *their selling trip to German proved successful*

successfully [sʌk'sesfəli] *adverb* achieving what was intended; *the new model was successfully launched last week*; *she successfully found her way to the British Museum*

succession [sək'seʃn] *noun* **(a)** series of the same sort of thing; *I had a succession of phone calls from my relatives*; **in succession** = one after the other; *three people in succession have asked me the same question*; *he won the title five times in succession* **(b)** acquiring property or a title from someone who has died; *the question of the succession to the throne is often mentioned in the newspapers*

successive [sək'sesɪv] *adjective* which come one after the other; *successive delays have meant that we are now ten months behind schedule*; *in three successive matches the goalkeeper was injured*

successively [sək'sesɪvli] *adverb* one coming after the other; *she was successively assistant manager, deputy manager and then head of department*

successor [sək'sesə] *noun* person who takes over from someone; *Mr Smith's successor as chairman will be Mr Jones*; *he handed the keys of the safe over to his successor*

success story [sʌk'ses 'stɔːri] *noun* person, invention, etc., which has been a great success in spite of problems; *the jet engine has been one of the great success stories of the century*

succinct [sək'sɪŋkt] *adjective* concise, not using many words; *a succinct description is given under each item in the catalogue*

succulent ['sʌkjulənt] **1** *adjective* delicious; full of juice; *the succulent dinner was much appreciated*; *they served each of us a succulent slice of roast chicken* **2** *noun* type of plant with thick fleshy leaves and stems, like a cactus; *she has a collection of succulents in her conservatory*

succumb (to) [sə'kʌm] *verb* **(a)** to give in, to yield; *whenever I pass a sweet shop I succumb to temptation and buy some chocolates*; *the stronghold finally succumbed after it was bombed*; *he succumbed to pressure from his family and took a holiday* **(b)** to die from; *cholera struck the refugee camps and thousands succumbed*; *they rapidly succumbed to the rigours of the Siberian winter*

such [sʌtʃ] **1** *adjective* **(a)** of this sort; *the police are looking for such things as drugs or stolen goods* **(b)** **no such** = not existing; *there is no such day as April 31st*; *someone was asking for a Mr Simpson but there is no such person working here* **(c)** **such as** = like; *some shops such as food stores are open on Sundays* **(d)** very; so much; *there was such a crowd at the party that there weren't enough chairs to go round*; *it's such a shame that she's ill and has to miss her sister's wedding*; *she's such a slow worker that she produces about half as much as everyone else*; *these days, people can't afford to buy such expensive meals* **2** *pronoun* this type of person or thing; *she's very competent, and is thought of as such by the management*; *the noise was such that it stopped me sleeping*

suchlike ['sʌtʃlaɪk] *pronoun & adjective* similar (people or things); *he collects small items connected with cars - old number plates, keys, horns and suchlike*; *we buy eggs, cream and suchlike items at the farm shop*

suck [sʌk] **1** *noun* action of sucking; *he's had a lick of my ice cream and now he wants a suck of my ice lolly* **2** *verb* **(a)** to hold something with your mouth and pull at it (with your tongue); *the baby didn't stop sucking his thumb until he was six* **(b)** to have something in your mouth which makes your mouth produce water; *he bought a bag of sweets to suck in the car* **(c)** to pull liquid into your mouth by using the muscles in your mouth; *she sucked the orange juice through a straw*; *she carries a bottle of apple juice everywhere and the baby sucks some when she's thirsty*

sucker ['sʌkə] *noun* **(a)** part of an animal which sticks to a surface by sucking; *an octopus has rows of suckers on its arms* **(b)** little plastic cup which sticks to a surface by suction; *some hooks can be glued to the wall, others stick with suckers* **(c)** *(informal)* person who is easily fooled into doing something; *he's a sucker for any pretty girl who asks him for a loan* **(d)** *(informal)* person who can't resist something; *he's a sucker for chocolate desserts* **(e)** *(of plant)* shoot which comes from the bottom of the stem or from a root; *you need to cut all those suckers off the roses*

suckle ['sʌkl] *verb* to give a child milk from the breast; to give a baby animal milk from the udder; *a mother suckling her newborn baby*; *the sow was lying down, suckling her piglets*

suck up ['sʌk 'ʌp] *verb* **(a)** to swallow; *the new vacuum cleaner sucks up dust very efficiently* **(b)** *(informal)* **to suck up to someone** = to flatter someone so as to get good treatment; *you should see the way he sucks up to the boss*

suction ['sʌkʃən] *noun* action of sucking out air, so that two surfaces stick together; *the plastic hooks stick to the tiles by suction*; *put your hand to the end of the tube to see if you can feel any suction*; **suction cup** = sucker, a plastic cup which sticks to a surface by sucking

sudden ['sʌdən] *adjective* **(a)** which happens very quickly or unexpectedly; *the sudden change in the weather caught us unprepared*; *the bus came to a sudden stop*; *his decision to go to Canada was very sudden* **(b)** **all of a sudden** = suddenly, quickly and giving you a shock; *all of a sudden the room went dark*

sudden death playoff ['sʌdən 'deθ 'pleɪɒf] *noun* ending of a game in which the scores are level, when each player or side tries to score and the one who scores first wins

suddenly ['sʌdənli] *adverb* quickly and giving you a shock; *the car in front stopped suddenly and I ran into* *the back of it; suddenly the room went dark; she suddenly realized it was already five o'clock*

sue [suː] *verb* to take someone to court, to start legal proceedings against someone to get compensation for a wrong; *she is suing the driver of the other car for damages; he sued the company for $50,000 compensation; we are still debating whether to sue or not*

suede [sweɪd] *noun* leather with a soft surface that looks like velvet; *he was wearing blue suede shoes; a pair of black suede gloves*

suet ['suːɪt] *noun* hard fat from around an animal's kidneys, used in cooking; *suet is used to make mincemeat*

suffer ['sʌfə] *verb* (a) to be in a bad situation, to do badly; *the harvest has suffered during the rainy weather; exports have suffered during the last six months* (b) to receive an injury; *he suffered multiple injuries in the accident* (c) to feel pain; *he didn't suffer at all, and was conscious until he died* (d) to suffer from = to have a disease or a fault; *she suffers from arthritis; the company's products suffer from bad design; our car suffers from a tendency to overheat* (d) not to suffer fools gladly = to be impatient with stupid people; *her main problem when answering customer complaints is that she doesn't suffer fools gladly*

sufferer ['sʌfrə] *noun* person who has a certain disease; *a drug to help asthma sufferers or sufferers from asthma;* **fellow-sufferer** = person who suffers from the same thing as you; *she often gets migraine and likes to talk with fellow-sufferers*

suffering ['sʌfrɪŋ] *noun* feeling pain over a long period of time; *the doctor gave him an injection to relieve his suffering;* **to put an animal out of its suffering** = to kill an animal which is very ill; *see also* LONG-SUFFERING

suffice [sə'faɪs] *verb* (*formal*) to be enough; *his earnings more than suffice to cover their household expenses;* **suffice it to say** = it is enough to say; *suffice it to say that we are not at all happy with the results*

sufficiency [sə'fɪʃənsi] *noun* (*formal*) enough of something; *I think we have a sufficiency of food; see also* SELF-SUFFICIENCY

sufficient [sə'fɪʃənt] *adjective* (*formal*) as much as is needed; *does she have sufficient funds to pay for her trip?; there isn't sufficient room to put the big sofa in here; allow yourself sufficient time to get to the airport; see also* SELF-SUFFICIENT

sufficiently [sə'fɪʃəntli] *adverb* (*formal*) enough; *if he isn't sufficiently careful he might injure himself with that chain saw; it is not sufficiently warm to grow orange trees here*

suffix ['sʌfɪks] *noun* letters added to the end of a word to make another word; *the suffix '-ish' can be added to a noun to form an adjective such as 'childish' or 'boyish'* (NOTE: plural is **suffixes**; the opposite, letters which are added in front of a word, is a **prefix**)

suffocate ['sʌfəkeɪt] *verb* (a) to make someone stop breathing by cutting off the supply of air; *the children must have suffocated in the smoke-filled room; she was accused of suffocating the old lady* (b) to be uncomfortable because of heat and lack of air; *we're suffocating in this little room*

suffocating ['sʌfəkeɪtɪŋ] *adjective* (a) which makes breathing difficult; *he stepped out of the plane into Delhi's suffocating heat* (b) unbearable because of being too confined; *she found it difficult to work in the suffocating atmosphere of the head office*

suffocation [sʌfə'keɪʃn] *noun* making someone become unconscious by cutting off his supply of air; *to avoid the danger of suffocation, keep plastic bags away from small children* (NOTE: also called **asphyxia**)

sugar ['ʃugə] *noun* (a) substance that you use to make food sweet; *how much sugar do you take in your tea?; a spoonful of sugar will be enough; can you pass me the sugar, please?;* **brown sugar** = unrefined or partly refined sugar; **Demerara sugar** = light brown sugar with large crystals; **muscovado sugar** = soft brown sugar with fine crystals; **white sugar** = refined sugar; **caster sugar** = white sugar with finer crystals than granulated sugar, used in cooking; **granulated sugar** = normal white sugar; **icing sugar** = fine powdered white sugar, used to cover cakes; *cover the fruit with icing sugar and caramelize under a grill; if you're in a hurry, just dust the cake with icing sugar;* **sugar lump** *or* **lump of sugar** = cube of white sugar (NOTE: no plural: **some sugar; a bag of sugar; a lump of sugar; a spoonful of sugar**) (b) (*informal*) spoonful of sugar; *how do you take your coffee? - milk and one sugar, please*

sugar beet ['ʃugə 'biːt] *noun* type of beet grown for its high sugar content; *lorries full of sugar beet on their way to the refinery* (NOTE: no plural)

sugar bowl ['ʃugə 'bəʊl] *noun* small bowl for sugar; *the sugar bowl we gave her as a wedding present was cracked*

sugarcane ['ʃugəkeɪn] *noun* tall perennial grass, whose thick stems contain a sweet sap from which sugar is made; *sugarcane is grown in many tropical regions*

sugary ['ʃugri] *adjective* (a) very sweet, containing a lot of sugar; *don't serve sugary drinks to children* (b) very sentimental; *the film is a sugary story of adolescent love*

suggest [sə'dʒest] *verb* to mention an idea to see what other people think of it; *the chairman suggested that the next meeting should be held in October; might I suggest a visit to the museum this afternoon?; what does he suggest we do in this case?*

suggestion [sə'dʒestʃn] *noun* idea that you mention for people to think about; *we have asked for suggestions from passengers; the company acted upon your suggestion; whose suggestion was it that we should go out in a boat?; I bought those shares at the stockbroker's suggestion*

suggestive [sə'dʒestɪv] *adjective* (a) **suggestive of** = which suggests; *the music is suggestive of a calm evening in the country* (b) which suggests sex; *he sang some very suggestive songs*

suicidal [suːɪ'saɪdl] *adjective* (a) wanting to kill yourself; *he has suicidal tendencies; after her son's death she became suicidal* (b) very dangerous; *his suicidal habit of driving at high speed along little country roads*

suicide ['suːɪsaɪd] *noun* (a) act of killing yourself; *whether her death was murder or suicide is not yet known;* **to commit suicide** = to kill yourself; *he killed his two children and then committed suicide;* **suicide note** = letter left by someone who has committed suicide; *her suicide note was left on the kitchen table*; **attempted suicide** *or* **suicide attempt** = trying to kill yourself, but not succeeding; *she is still in hospital after her suicide attempt* **(b) political suicide** = action which ends your political career; *by voting against the government he effectively committed political suicide* **(c)** person who has killed himself

suit [suːt] **1** *noun* **(a)** set of pieces of clothing made of the same cloth and worn together, such as a jacket and trousers or skirt; *a dark grey suit will be just right for the interview; the pale blue suit she was wearing was very chic;* **shell suit** = jacket and trousers for jogging; **ski suit** = one-piece suit, or jacket and trousers, for skiing; **three-piece suit** = suit of jacket, trousers and waistcoat **(b)** one of the four sets of cards with the same symbol in a pack of cards; *clubs and spades are the two black suits and hearts and diamonds are the two red suits* **(c) to follow suit** = to do what everyone else does; *she jumped into the pool and everyone else followed suit* **(d)** lawsuit, legal action or claim **2** *verb* **(a)** to look good when worn by someone; *green usually suits people with red hair; that hat doesn't suit her* **(b)** to be convenient; *he'll only do it when it suits him to do it; Thursday at 11 o'clock will suit me fine*

suitability [suːtəˈbɪlɪti] *noun* the extent to which someone *or* something is suitable; *I still have doubts about his suitability for the job*

suitable [ˈsuːtəbl] *adjective* which fits or which is convenient; *the most suitable place to meet will be under the big clock at Waterloo Station; we advertised the job again because there were no suitable candidates; a blue dress would be more suitable for an interview; I'm looking for a suitable present for her 30th birthday; is this a suitable moment to discuss the office move?*

suitably [ˈsuːtəbli] *adverb* in a convenient or fitting way; *I must find a way of suitably rewarding her for finding my purse; I hope you were all suitably impressed by his new car*

suitcase [ˈsuːtkeɪs] *noun* box with a handle which you carry your clothes in when you are travelling; *I never pack my suitcase until the last minute; the customs officer made him open his three suitcases* (*informal*) **to live out of a suitcase** = to travel so frequently, that you don't spend much time at home

suite [swiːt] *noun* **(a)** set of rooms, especially expensive rooms; *their offices are in a suite of rooms on the eleventh floor; they booked a suite at the Savoy Hotel;* **honeymoon suite** = specially attractive hotel rooms for honeymoon couples; **VIP suite** = specially luxurious suite at an airport or in a hotel **(b)** set of pieces of furniture; **bathroom suite** = bath, washbasin and toilet; *a new bathroom suite could cost over £3000;* **bedroom suite** = bed, chest of drawers and wardrobe; **living room suite** = sofa and armchairs **(c)** several short pieces of music played together as one item; *the 'Planets Suite' by Gustav Holst* (NOTE: do not confuse with **sweet**)

◊ **en-suite** [ˈɒn ˈswiːt] *adjective* attached; *bedroom with an en-suite shower room; is the bathroom en-suite?*

suited [ˈsuːtɪd] *adjective* suitable; *he is well suited for the job; she isn't really suited to being a personal assistant*

suitor [ˈsuːtə] *noun (old)* person who wants to marry a girl; *three suitors came to woo the princess, each bringing costly gifts*

sulfate, sulfur [ˈsʌlfeɪt or ˈsʌlfə] *noun US see* SULPHATE, SULPHUR

sulk [sʌlk] **1** *noun (informal)* **a sulk** *or* **the sulks** = period when you are grumpy or annoyed in silence; *she had a fit of the sulks and refused to talk to anyone; I don't mind if she goes into a sulk, but she has to learn to do as she's told* **2** *verb* to show you are annoyed by not saying anything; *they're sulking because we didn't invite them*

sulky [ˈsʌlki] *adjective* showing that you are annoyed; *she is in one of her sulky moods* (NOTE: **sulkier - sulkiest**)

sullen [ˈsʌln] *adjective* silent and bad-tempered; *a sullen waitress took our order*

sulphate *US* **sulfate** [ˈsʌlfeɪt] *noun* salt of sulphuric acid and an element; *sulphate of potash is a fertilizer used by potato growers and market gardeners*

sulphur *US* **sulfur** [ˈsʌlfə] *noun* non-metallic element, which is usually found in the form of yellow powder, and smells of rotten eggs (NOTE: Chemical element: chemical symbol: **S**; atomic number: **16**)

sulphuric acid *US* **sulfuric acid** [sʌlˈfjʊərɪk ˈæsɪd] *noun* very powerful acid which attacks all metals except gold and platinum

sulphurous *US* **sulfurous** [ˈsʌlfərəs] *adjective* full of or containing sulphur; *clouds of sulphurous smoke rose from the volacano*

sultana [sʌlˈtɑːnə] *noun* type of pale seedless raisin; *we will need sultanas for the Christmas cake; compare* CURRANT, RAISIN

sultry [ˈsʌltri] *adjective* **(a)** hot and damp; *a massive thunderstorm brought the sultry weather to an end* **(b)** attractive in a dark and passionate way; *her sultry good looks attracted the eye of her boss* (NOTE: **sultrier - sultriest**)

sum [sʌm] *noun* **(a)** quantity of money; *he only paid a small sum for the car; a large sum of money was stolen from his office; we are owed the sum of £500;* **lump sum** = money paid in one payment, not in several small payments; *you can take part of your pension as a lump sum* **(b)** simple problem in arithmetic; *she tried to do the sum in her head* **(c)** total of two or more figures added together; *the sum of all four sides will give you the perimeter of the field* **(d) sum total** = total amount of something which may not be as much as you want; *that was the sum total of what we saw*

summarize [ˈsʌməraɪz] *verb* to make a brief account of what has happened or what has been said; *could you just summarize what the driver of the lorry said?*

summary [ˈsʌməri] **1** *noun* short description of what has been said or written, or of what happened, without giving all the details; *she gave a summary of what happened at the meeting; here's a summary of the book in case you don't have time to read it; it is 7.30 and here is a summary of the news* (NOTE: plural is **summaries**) **2** *adjective* which happens immediately; *he was given a summary trial* (NOTE: do not confuse with **summery**)

summer [ˈsʌmə] *noun* hottest time of the year, the season between spring and autumn; *next summer we are going to Greece; the summer in Australia* coincides with our winter here in England; I haven't any summer clothes - it's never hot enough here; **Indian summer** = warm period in early autumn; we had an Indian summer this year in late September; the summer holidays = period during the summer when children do not go to school; holidays taken by workers during the period from June to September; I'm starting my summer holidays on July 20th; the weather was awful during our summer holidays; **summer school** = classes held at a school, college or university during the summer holiday; she is organizing a summer school in Florence on 'The Italian Renaissance'

summerhouse ['sʌməhaʊs] noun small building in a garden, where people can sit when it is warm; you'll find him reading the paper in the summerhouse

summer time ['sʌmə 'taɪm] noun system where the clocks are set forward one hour in March to take advantage of the longer period of daylight; summer time begins at the end of March and ends in October

summertime ['sʌmətaɪm] noun the time of year when it is summer; it's summertime, and the farmers are making hay

summery ['sʌmri] adjective like the summer, which is suitable for the summer; we've had some beautiful summery weather lately; she came in a summery dress with a big straw hat (NOTE: do not confuse with **summary**)

summing-up ['sʌmɪŋ'ʌp] noun speech by the judge at the end of a trial, where he reviews all the evidence and arguments, and points out important points of law to the jury; in his summing-up, the judge warned the jury that some of the witnesses must have been lying

summit ['sʌmɪt] noun (a) top of a mountain; it took us three hour's hard climbing to reach the summit (b) **summit (meeting or conference)** = meeting of heads of state or government leaders to discuss international problems; the question was discussed at the last European summit

summon ['sʌmən] verb (a) (formal) to tell people to come to a meeting; the president summoned a meeting of the supreme council; she was summoned to appear before the committee (b) **to summon up courage** = to force yourself to have enough courage to do something; he summoned up enough courage to do his first solo flight; **to summon up strength** = to manage to have enough strength to do something; he summoned up all his strength and climbed the last few metres to the top

summons ['sʌmənz] **1** noun (a) official order to go to see someone; he received a summons to see the president (b) official command telling someone to appear in court to be tried for a criminal offence or to defend a civil action; he threw away the summons and went on holiday to Spain; **to serve a summons on someone** = to give someone a summons officially (NOTE: plural is **summonses**) **2** verb to order someone to appear in court; he was summonsed as a witness at the magistrates' court

sumo ['suːməʊ] noun Japanese style of wrestling, where two very large wrestlers try to throw each other out of a ring; he imitated the heavy gait of a sumo wrestler

sump [sʌmp] noun bowl attached to the bottom of a car engine, into which oil drains; we went over a large stone and cracked the sump

sumptuous ['sʌmptʃʊəs] adjective very luxurious or splendid; he lives in a sumptuous flat in Park Lane; a sumptuous meal was served after the wedding

sums [sʌmz] noun arithmetic, making simple calculations with figures; she is much quicker at sums than her sister

sum up ['sʌm 'ʌp] verb (a) to make a summary of what has been said; I'd just like to sum up what has been said so far; can you sum up the most important points in the speech for me? (b) (of a judge) to speak at the end of a trial and review all the evidence and arguments for the benefit of the jury; I was surprised the judge did not mention that when he summed up (NOTE: **summing - summed**)

sun [sʌn] **1** noun (a) very bright star round which the earth travels and which gives light and heat; the sun was just rising when I got up; I'll try taking a photograph now that the sun's come out; don't stare at the eclipse of the sun, even with sunglasses (b) light from the sun; I'd prefer a table out of the sun; we're sitting in the shade because the sun's too hot; she spent her whole holiday just sitting in the sun; **everything under the sun** = absolutely everything; we talked about everything under the sun **2** verb **to sun yourself** = to sit in the sun and get warm; the cat was sunning herself on the window sill (NOTE: **sunning - sunned**)

sunbathe ['sʌnbeɪð] verb to lie in the sun to get your skin brown; don't forget to put suncream on if you're going to sunbathe

sunbather ['sʌnbeɪðə] noun person who lies in the sun; the pool was surrounded by sunbathers

sunbathing ['sʌnbeɪðɪŋ] noun lying in the sun to get your skin brown; sunbathing on the beach at midday is not recommended

sunburn ['sʌnbɜːn] noun damage to the skin caused by being in the sun for too long; don't touch me - my sunburn is very sore

sunburnt ['sʌnbɜːnt] adjective damaged or made red by the sun; I stayed on the beach too long and got sunburnt

suncream ['sʌnkriːm] noun cream which you put on your skin to prevent it being sunburnt; if you're going to the beach don't forget to take the suncream

Sunday ['sʌndi] noun the seventh day of the week, the day between Saturday and Monday; last Sunday we went on a picnic; most shops are now open on Sundays; can we fix a lunch for next Sunday?; the 15th is a Saturday, so the 16th must be a Sunday; today is Sunday, November 19th; **in your Sunday best** = wearing your smartest clothes; all the children came in their Sunday best

Sunday school ['sʌndi 'skuːl] noun classes held on a Sunday, where children are taught about the Christian religion; her Sunday school teacher gave her a book of hymns

sundial ['sʌndaɪəl] noun type of outdoor clock with a central column whose shadow points to the time when the sun shines on it; there is an old stone sundial on the wall of the church

sundown ['sʌndaʊn] noun sunset, the time when the sun goes down in the evening; the bats come out at sundown

sun-dried ['sʌndraɪd] *adjective* which has been dried in the sun to preserve it; *a jar of sun-dried tomatoes*

sundry ['sʌndri] **1** *adjective* various; *the tourists made sundry purchases in the market*; **sundry items** = SUNDRIES **2** *noun* **(a)** **all and sundry** = everyone; *he told all and sundry about his operation* **(b)** **sundries** = small articles or small items not listed in detail; *don't list all the small items individually, just put them under 'sundries'*

sunflower ['sʌnflauə] *noun* very large yellow flower on a very tall stem; *in France you often see whole fields of yellow sunflowers*; *the children are having a competition to see who can grow the tallest sunflower*; **sunflower oil** = oil made from the seeds of sunflowers; *can you remember to buy some sunflower oil?*; **sunflower seeds** = seed produced by sunflowers; *add a few sunflower seeds to the salad*

sung [sʌŋ] *see* SING

sunglasses ['sʌnɡlɑːsɪz] *noun* dark glasses worn to protect your eyes from the sun; *I always wear sunglasses when I'm driving*

sunhat ['sʌnhæt] *noun* hat worn to protect your head from the sun; *the baby keeps taking his sunhat off*

sunk [sʌŋk] *see* SINK

sunken ['sʌŋkən] *adjective* **(a)** which is beneath the surface; *the boat must have hit a sunken log*; *the channel is blocked by sunken wrecks* **(b)** lower than the area around; *a sunken garden*

sunlamp ['sʌnlæmp] *noun* lamp which gives off ultraviolet rays like those of the sun, used to make your skin brown; *don't stay too long under the sunlamp, set the timer*

sunlight ['sʌnlaɪt] *noun* light which comes from the sun; *sunlight was pouring into the room*; *there's not really enough sunlight to take a picture*; *sunlight is essential to give the body Vitamin D* (NOTE: no plural)

sunlit ['sʌnlɪt] *adjective* bright with the light of the sun; *a sunlit balcony*

sunny ['sʌni] *adjective* **(a)** with the sun shining; *another sunny day!*; *they forecast that it will be sunny this afternoon* **(b)** where the sun often shines; *we live on the sunny side of the street*; *their sitting room is bright and sunny, but the dining room is dark* **(c)** US (*informal*) **sunny side up** = (egg) fried on one side without being turned over, so you can see the yolk (NOTE: **sunnier - sunniest**)

sunrise ['sʌnraɪz] *noun* time when the sun comes up in the morning; *we get up at sunrise to milk the cows*

sunroof ['sʌnruːf] *noun* part of the roof of a car which opens to let in light and air; *we drove along with the sunroof open*

sunscreen ['sʌnskriːn] *noun* cream which you put on your skin to prevent sunburn; *the children will need sunscreen if they're going to the beach*

sunset ['sʌnset] *noun* time when the sun goes down in the evening; *at sunset, bats come out and fly around*

sunshade ['sʌnʃeɪd] *noun* parasol, a light umbrella to protect you from the rays of the sun; *Virginia was sitting in a deckchair under a sunshade, reading a book*

sunshine ['sʌnʃaɪn] *noun* pleasant light from the sun; *we have had very little sunshine this July*; *the*

west coast of France has more than 250 days of sunshine per annum (NOTE: no plural)

sunspot ['sʌnspɒt] *noun* dark patch on the surface of the sun, which is cooler than the rest of the sun; *sunspot activity is at its peak every 22 years*

sunstroke ['sʌnstrəʊk] *noun* serious medical condition caused by too much exposure to sunlight; *in cases of sunstroke patients should lie down in a dark room*

suntan ['sʌntæn] *noun* brown colour of the skin caused by sunlight; *I have to get a suntan before I go back to the office otherwise no one will think I have been on* holiday; **suntan oil** = oil to put on the body to help give a suntan, and avoid burning; *can you put some suntan oil on my back?*

suntanned ['sʌntænd] *adjective* brown from having been in the sun; *he was with two very suntanned Spanish girls*

super ['suːpə] *adjective* (*informal*) very good; *we had a super time in Greece*; *thank you for being such super hosts*; *let's go away for the weekend - what a super idea!*

superb [suːˈpɜːb] *adjective* marvellous, wonderfully good; *he scored with a superb volley from just outside the penalty area*; *I'll have another helping of that superb chocolate cake of yours*

superbly [suːˈpɜːbli] *adverb* in a superb way; *the musicians played superbly*

superficial [suːpəˈfɪʃl] *adjective* **(a)** which affects only the top surface; *the damage was only superficial*; *she suffered a few superficial grazes but nothing serious* **(b)** dealing only with the most obvious and simple matters *I can't answer your question because I only have a very superficial knowledge of the subject* **(c)** not serious; *he's very superficial, you can't have a serious conversation with him*

superficially [suːpəˈfɪʃəli] *adverb* in a superficial way; *the offer is superficially attractive, but there could be a catch in it somewhere*; *he dealt with several topics, but only very superficially*

superfluous [suːˈpɜːfluəs] *adjective* which is more than is needed; not necessary, not needed; *we decided that several members of staff were superfluous to our requirements*; *surely his presence at the meeting was superfluous*; **superfluous hair** = hair which is growing in places where it is not thought to be beautiful; *you can get a cream for removing superfluous hair*

superhighway [suːpəˈhaɪweɪ] *noun* US express highway with many lanes; **information superhighway** = world-wide transfer of information via the Internet

superimpose [suːpərɪmˈpəʊz] *verb* **(a)** to place on top of something else; *they tried to superimpose a new level of management on top of the old one* **(b)** to lay one picture over another so that they are both visible; to print one thing on top of another; *if you superimpose one picture on the other you get the impression of a ghost in the room*

superintend [suːpərɪnˈtend] *verb* (*formal*) to be in charge of work, to watch carefully, to see that work is well done; *Miss Jones is superintending the move to the new offices*

superintendent [suːpərɪnˈtendənt] *noun* **(a)** person who is responsible for work, or for a place; *go and see the building superintendent if a pipe is leaking* **(b)**

police superintendent = senior police officer, above a chief inspector

superior [suːˈpɪəriə] **1** *adjective* **(a)** of very high quality; *he gave her a very superior box of chocolates*; **superior to** = better than; *our products are vastly superior to theirs*; *their distribution service is much superior to ours* **(b)** in a higher rank; *soldiers should always salute superior officers*; **superior to someone** = of a higher rank than someone; *she is superior to him in the office hierarchy* **(c)** thinking you are better than other people; *he gives himself such superior airs* **2** *noun* person in a higher rank; *each manager is responsible to his superior* (NOTE: the opposite is **inferior**)

superiority [suːpɪərɪˈɒrɪti] *noun* **(a)** numerical superiority *or* superiority in numbers = being more than others; *despite their vast superiority in numbers they lost the battle* **(b)** being more important, more intelligent, better than someone else; *the superiority of the Brazilians in the World Cup was obvious*; *he gives the impression of effortless superiority*; **superiority complex** = feeling that you are much better than everyone else (NOTE: the opposite is **inferiority**)

superlative [suːˈpɜːlətɪv] **1** *adjective* extremely good; *he's a superlative goalkeeper* **2** *noun* form of an adjective or adverb showing the highest level when compared with another; *'biggest' is the superlative of 'big'*; *put a few superlatives in the ad to emphasize the superiority of the product*

> COMMENT: superlatives are usually formed by adding the suffix -est to the adjective: 'quickest' from 'quick', for example; in the case of long adjectives, they are formed by putting 'most' in front of the adjective: 'most comfortable', 'most expensive', and so on. Some superlatives are irregular, such as 'worst' and 'best'. You can also form superlatives by adding phrases like 'as possible' (as big as possible)

supermarket [ˈsuːpəmɑːkɪt] *noun* large store selling mainly food and household goods, where customers serve themselves and pay at a checkout; *we've got no tea left, can you buy some from the supermarket?*; *we do all our shopping in the local supermarket*; **supermarket trolley** = metal basket on wheels, used by shoppers to put their purchases in as they go round a supermarket (NOTE: American English for this is **shopping cart**)

supermodel [ˈsuːpəmɒdəl] *noun* (*informal*) top fashion model who earns high fees; *she left school at 16 and became a supermodel*

supernatural [suːpəˈnætʃərəl] **1** *adjective* which cannot be explained by the laws of nature; *he believes in supernatural occurrences like ghosts* **2** *noun* **the supernatural** = things which happen which cannot be explained by the laws of nature; *you can't dismiss the supernatural completely*

supernova [suːpəˈnəʊvə] *noun* explosion of large star; *a galaxy such as ours has a supernova every few decades*; *some supernovae are very bright indeed*; *see also* NOVA (NOTE: plural is **supernovae** [suːpəˈnəʊviː])

superpower [ˈsuːpəpaʊə] *noun* extremely powerful country with great economic strength and large armed forces; *at present there is only one superpower, the USA*

supersede [suːpəˈsiːd] *verb* to take the place of something which has become outdated; *the new price list supersedes the old one*; *the old program has been superseded by the latest version which is much faster*

supersonic [suːpəˈsɒnɪk] *adjective* going faster than the speed of sound; *Concorde flies at supersonic speeds*

superstar [ˈsuːpəstɑː] *noun* extremely famous filmstar or other performer

superstition [suːpəˈstɪʃn] *noun* belief in magic and that some things are lucky and others unlucky; *he always refuses to walk under ladders out of superstition*; *according to an old superstition when the tree in front of the house dies the last member of the family will also die*

superstitious [suːpəˈstɪʃəs] *adjective* believing in magic and the supernatural; *she's so superstitious that she will never walk under a ladder*; *I see you crossed your fingers - are you superstitious?*

superstore [ˈsuːpəstɔː] *noun* very large self-service store selling a wide range of goods or specializing in one line; *they have asked for planning permission to build a new superstore*; *a computer superstore*

supervise [ˈsuːpəvaɪz] *verb* to watch carefully, to see that work is well done; *she supervises six trainee receptionists*; *our move to the new bungalow was supervised by my wife*

supervision [suːpəˈvɪʒn] *noun* act of supervising; *prisoners are allowed out under strict supervision to work on the prison farm*; *new staff work under supervision for the first three months*; *she is very experienced and can be left to work without any supervision*

supervisor [ˈsuːpəvaɪzə] *noun* person who supervises work, a student's thesis, etc.; *if you have any questions, ask your supervisor*; *my supervisor says I am getting on very well*

supervisory [suːpəˈvaɪzəri] *adjective* in a supervisory capacity = as a supervisor

supper [ˈsʌpə] *noun* meal which you eat in the evening; *what do you want for your supper?*; **to have supper** = to eat an evening meal; *we'll have supper on the terrace*; *we usually have supper at about 7 o'clock*; *come and have some supper with us tomorrow evening*; *see note at* DINNER

supplant [səˈplɑːnt] *verb* (*formal*) to take the place of someone or something; *he is plotting to supplant his boss and take over the department*; *the biro and felt tip have supplanted the fountain pen*

supple [ˈsʌpl] *adjective* flexible, which bends easily; *ballet dancers should exercise regularly to keep supple*; *slippers are made of supple leather*

supplement 1 *noun* [ˈsʌplɪmənt] **(a)** thing which is in addition, an additional amount; *the company gives him £200 per month as a supplement to his pension*; *you need to take a vitamin supplement every morning* **(b)** additional section at the back of a book; *there is a list of Prime Ministers in the supplement at the back of the book* **(c)** magazine which is part of a newspaper; *I read his article in the Sunday supplement* **2** *verb* [ˈsʌplɪment] to add to; *we will supplement the ordinary staff with six part-timers during the Christmas rush*

supplementary [sʌplɪˈmentri] *adjective* in addition to what is already there; *there are no supplementary charges - the price covers everything*

supplier [səˈplaɪə] *noun* person, company, or country which supplies; *they are major suppliers of spare parts to the car industry*; *a supplier of disk drives or a disk drive supplier*

supply [səˈplaɪ] **1** *noun* **(a)** stock of something which is needed; *we have two weeks' supply of coal*; **in short supply** = not available in large enough quantities to meet the demand; *fresh vegetables are in short supply during the winter*; **the law of supply and demand** = general rule that the amount of something which is available is linked to the amount wanted by potential customers **(b) supplies** = stock of food, etc., which is needed; *after two months at sea, their supplies were running out*; *the government sent medical supplies to the disaster area*; *we buy all our office supplies from one firm* **(c)** something which is needed, such as goods, products or services; *the electricity supply has failed again*; *they signed a contract for the supply of computer equipment*; *rebel forces have cut off the town's water supply* **2** *verb* to provide something which is needed; *details of addresses and phone numbers can be supplied by the store staff*; *he was asked to supply a blood sample*; *she was asked to supply the names of two referees*; *they have signed a contract to supply online information*; **to supply someone with something** = to provide something to someone; *he supplies the hotel with cheese or he supplies cheese to the hotel*

support [səˈpɔːt] **1** *noun* **(a)** thing which stops something from falling; *they had to build wooden supports to hold up the wall* **(b)** something which helps keep something else in place; *the bandage provides some support for the knee* **(c)** encouragement; *the chairman has the support of the committee*; *she spoke in support of our plan* **(d)** financial help, money; *we have had no financial support from the bank*; **income support** = payments from the government to people with very low incomes **2** *verb* **(a)** to hold something up to stop it falling down; *the roof is supported on ten huge pillars* **(b)** to provide money to help; *we hope the banks will support us during the expansion period* **(c)** to encourage; *which football team do you support?*; *she hopes the other members of the committee will support her* **(d)** to accept; *the public will not support another price increase* **(e)** to give help, to help to run; *the main computer system supports six workstations*

supporter [səˈpɔːtə] *noun* person who encourages; *it sounds a good idea to me - I'm surprised it hasn't attracted more supporters*; **football supporter** = person who encourages a football team; *he's a Liverpool supporter*

supportive [səˈpɔːtɪv] *adjective* who supports or gives encouragement; *he is very supportive of his children*

suppose [sʌˈpəʊz] *verb* **(a)** to think something is probable; *where is the secretary? - I suppose she's going to be late as usual*; *I suppose you've heard the news?*; *what do you suppose they're talking about?*; *will you be coming to the meeting this evening? - I suppose I'll have to; I don't suppose many people will come* **(b)** *(showing doubt)* what happens if?; *suppose it rains tomorrow, do you still want to go for a walk?*; *he's very late - suppose he's had an accident?*;

suppose I win the lottery!; *(giving a doubtful yes)* *please can I go on the roundabout? - oh, I suppose so*; *(giving a doubtful no)* *it doesn't look as though anyone is coming to the meeting - I suppose not*

◊ **supposed to be** [səˈpəʊzd ˈtə ˈbiː] *phrase* **(a)** should, ought to; *the children were supposed to be in bed*; *how I am supposed to know where he is?* **(b)** believed to be; *he's supposed to be a good dentist*; *the film is supposed to be awful*

supposedly [səˈpəʊzɪdli] *adverb* as we suppose; *she's supposedly going to phone us later*

supposing [səˈpəʊzɪŋ] *conjunction* what happens if?; *supposing it rains tomorrow, do you still want to go for a walk?*; *he's very late - supposing he's had an accident?*

supposition [sʌpəˈzɪʃn] *noun* something which is assumed, but cannot be proved; *we can only make a supposition regarding the fate of the ship and her crew*

suppress [səˈpres] *verb* **(a)** to limit something, such as a person's freedom; *the rebellion was ruthlessly suppressed and its leaders executed* **(b)** to stop something being made public; *all opposition newspapers have been suppressed*; *they tried to suppress the evidence but it had already got into the newspapers* **(c)** to stop yourself showing what you really feel; *she suppressed her feeling of annoyance and tried to look happy*; *he couldn't suppress a smile*

suppression [səˈpreʃn] *noun* act of suppressing; *the government's ruthless suppression of all forms of opposition*

supremacy [suˈpreməsi] *noun* position of being the highest power; *they built a range of new warships to achieve naval supremacy*; *American air supremacy won the war*

supreme [suˈpriːm] *adjective* **(a)** greatest, in the highest position; *her dog was supreme champion*; *it meant one last supreme effort, but they did it* **(b) Supreme Court** = highest court in a country; *the Supreme Court was asked to rule on his case*

supremely [suˈpriːmli] *adverb* to the greatest extent; *he was supremely confident of winning*; *she is supremely ignorant of the law*

supremo [suˈpriːməʊ] *noun* *(informal)* person in charge of a very large organization; *he has been named as World Fair supremo*

surcharge [ˈsɜːtʃɑːdʒ] **1** *noun* extra charge; *there is a 10% surcharge on goods entering the country*; **import surcharge** = extra duty charged on imported goods, to try to stop them from being imported and to encourage the manufacture of goods locally **2** *verb* to charge an extra amount; *we have been surcharged because of a fall in the exchange rate*

sure [ʃʊə] **1** *adjective* **(a)** certain; *is he sure he can borrow his mother's car?*; *I'm sure I left my wallet in my coat pocket*; *it's sure to be cold in Russia in December*; **make sure** *or* **be sure** that your computer is switched off before you leave*; *when taking a shower, please make sure that the shower curtain is inside the bath* **(b)** which can be relied on; *it's a sure remedy for hayfever* **(c) sure of yourself** = confident that what you do is right; *he's only just starting in business, so he's still not very sure of himself* (NOTE: **surer - surest**) **2** *adverb* **(a)** mainly US *(meaning yes)* *can I borrow your car? - sure, go ahead!*; *I need someone to help* with this computer program - sure, I can do it **(b)** US (as emphasis) he sure was mad when he saw what they'd done to his car **(c)** for sure = certainly; if you sell the house you'll regret it, and that's for sure! **(d)** sure enough = as was expected; no one thought he would pass his exams and sure enough he failed

surely ['ʃʊəli] adverb (used mostly in questions where a certain answer is expected) of course, I'm certain; surely they can't expect us to work on Sundays?; but surely their office is in London, not Oxford?; they'll surely complain about the amount of work they have to do

surf [sɜːf] **1** noun (i) white foam from waves breaking along a shore; (ii) waves breaking along a shore; the surf is too rough for children to bathe (NOTE: do not confuse with **serf**) **2** verb **(a)** to ride on breaking waves on a surfboard; I'd like to be able to surf, it's too dangerous to go surfing today **(b)** to surf the Internet or to surf the Net = to explore a website looking at the pages in no particular order

surface ['sɜːfɪs] **1** noun top part of something; when it rains, water collects on the surface of the road; the surface of the water was completely still; he stayed a long time under water before coming back to the surface; he seemed calm but under the surface he was furious; dinosaurs disappeared from the surface of the earth millions of years ago **2** verb **(a)** to come up to the surface; the captain gave orders for the submarine to surface; his fear of failure has surfaced again **(b)** to cover a road, etc., with hard surface material; we've had the drive surfaced with asphalt; the kitchen floor is supposed to be surfaced with non-slip material **(c)** (informal) to wake up; if you haven't surfaced by 8.30, I'll come and wake you up

surface mail ['sɜːfɪs 'meɪl] noun post which is sent by van, train, ship, etc., and not by air; we sent the package by surface mail

surfboard ['sɜːfbɔːd] noun long specially designed board on which you stand to ride on top of breaking waves; when they went on holiday they took their surfboards on the roof of the car

surfer ['sɜːfə] noun person who surfs; the beach is known as the surfers' paradise

surfing or **surf-riding** ['sɜːfɪŋ or 'sɜːfraɪdɪŋ] noun **(a)** riding on top of breaking waves as a sport; surfing is the most popular sport in Hawaii **(b)** surfing the Internet or surfing the Net = exploring a website

surge [sɜːdʒ] **1** noun **(a)** sudden increase in the quantity of something; the fine weather has brought a surge of interest in camping; the TV commercials generated a surge of orders **(b)** sudden rising up of water; the surge of the sea between the rocks **(c)** sudden increase in electrical power; power surges can burn out systems **(d)** sudden rush of emotion; he felt a sudden surge of anger at the thought of having been cheated **2** verb **(a)** to rise suddenly; the waves surged up onto the rocks **(b)** to move in a mass; the crowd surged (forward) onto the football pitch; the fans surged around the pop star's car

surgeon ['sɜːdʒən] noun doctor who specializes in surgery; she has been sent to see an eye surgeon; house surgeon = young surgeon working in a hospital in his last year of training; dental surgeon = DENTIST

surgery ['sɜːdʒəri] noun **(a)** treatment of disease which requires an operation to cut into or remove part of the body; she had surgery to straighten her nose;

the patient will need surgery to remove the scars left by the accident (NOTE: no plural in this meaning) **(b)** room where a doctor or dentist sees and examines patients; I phoned the doctor's surgery to make an appointment (NOTE: American English is **doctor's office**) **(c)** time when an MP receives visitors who ask him to solve their problems; instead of writing to your MP why don't you go to one of her surgeries? (NOTE: plural is **surgeries**)

surgical ['sɜːdʒɪkl] adjective referring to surgery; surgical gloves = thin rubber gloves worn by a surgeon; see also SPIRIT

surmount [sɜːˈmaʊnt] verb **(a)** to overcome an obstacle; it took us some time to surmount the obstacles in our path **(b)** to be on top of; the summit is surmounted by an observatory

surname ['sɜːneɪm] noun name of someone's family, shared by all people in the family; her Christian name or first name is Anne, but I don't know her surname; Smith is the commonest surname in the London telephone directory

surpass [səˈpɑːs] verb to do better than; the results surpassed our wildest expectations; her record is unlikely to be surpassed

surplus ['sɜːpləs] **1** adjective extra, left over; surplus butter is on sale in the shops; we are holding a sale of surplus stock; surplus to requirements = more than is needed; these copper pipes are surplus to our requirements **2** noun extra stock; material left over; the problem of agricultural surpluses in the EU (NOTE: plural is **surpluses**)

surprise [səˈpraɪz] **1** noun **(a)** feeling when something happens which you did not expect to happen; he expressed surprise when I told him I'd lost my job; to his great surprise, a lot of people bought his book; what a surprise to find that we were at school together! **(b)** unexpected event; they baked a cake for her birthday as a surprise; what a surprise to see you again after so long! **(c)** to take someone by surprise = to shock someone by saying or doing something which they did not expect; her question took him by surprise and he didn't know how to answer **2** adjective which is unexpected; a surprise fall in the value of the dollar; they gave a surprise party for the retiring college principal **3** verb **(a)** to make someone surprised; it wouldn't surprise me if it rained; what surprises me is that she left without saying goodbye **(b)** to find someone unexpectedly; she surprised the two boys smoking in the yard

surprised [səˈpraɪzd] adjective astonished; she was surprised to see her former boyfriend at the party; we were surprised to hear that he's got a good job

surprising [səˈpraɪzɪŋ] adjective astonishing, which you do not expect; there was a surprising end to the story; wasn't it surprising to see the two sisters together again?; it's hardly surprising she doesn't want to see you again after what you said

surprisingly [səˈpraɪzɪŋli] adverb in a way which surprises; considering she's just had an operation she looks surprisingly fit; not surprisingly, goods of this quality are very expensive; the magistrate was surprisingly lenient towards the youths

surreal [səˈriːəl] adjective totally unreal, as if in a dream; it was really surreal to see all the office staff dressed in white suits

surrealism [sə'rıəlızm] *noun* artistic movement in the 1920s where artists tried to portray real things in a surreal way, as if existing in dreams

surrealist [sə'rıəlıst] **1** *adjective* following the principles of surrealism; *the surrealist movement was important in the 1920s* **2** *noun* artist following the principles of surrealism; *Dali and other surrealists*

surrender [sə'rendə] **1** *noun* **(a)** giving in to an enemy because you have lost; *the surrender of the enemy generals* **(b)** giving up of an insurance policy before the final date when it should mature; **surrender value** = money which an insurer will pay if an insurance policy is given up **2** *verb* **(a)** to give in to an enemy because you have lost; *our troops were surrounded by the enemy and were forced to surrender* **(b)** *(formal)* to give up a ticket, insurance policy, etc.; *he was asked to surrender his passport to the police*

surreptitious [sʌrəp'tıʃəs] *adjective* done in secret; *she had a surreptitious peep to see the amount written on the cheque*

surreptitiously [sʌrəp'tıʃəsli] *adverb* done in secret; *she surreptitiously looked at her watch; he left surreptitiously and no one noticed that he had gone*

surrogate ['sʌrəgıt] *noun* person who acts in place of someone, thing that takes the place of something else; *the children's uncle and aunt became surrogate parents to them after their mother and father were killed; school became a surrogate home to him because his parents spent all their time travelling;* **surrogate mother** = woman who has a child by artificial insemination for a couple where the wife cannot bear children, with the intention of handing the child over to them when it is born

surround [sə'raund] *verb* to be all round someone *or* something; *the Prime Minister has surrounded himself with a group of yes-men; floodwater has surrounded the village*

surrounded [sə'raundıd] *adjective* with something all around; *the villa is outside the town, surrounded by vineyards; the surgeon, surrounded by his team of experts, started the operation at 9.30; the government collapsed, surrounded by scandals*

surrounding [sə'raundıŋ] *adjective* which is all round a place; *from the balcony we had a marvellous view over the surrounding countryside*

surroundings [sə'raundıŋz] *noun* area around a person or place; *the surroundings of the hotel are very peaceful; she found herself in very unpleasant surroundings*

surveillance [sɜ:'veıləns] *noun* careful watch over someone *or* something; *the car was under police surveillance; the week-long surveillance operation produced no results;* **surveillance camera** = camera which takes photographs of people, cars, etc., for the police

survey 1 *noun* ['sɜ:veı] **(a)** general report on a subject; general investigation by asking people questions; *we carried out a survey among our customers; the government has produced a survey of education needs* **(b)** careful examination of a building to see if it is in good enough condition; *they asked for a survey of the house before buying it; the insurance company is carrying out a survey of the damage caused by the storm;* **a damage survey** = a report on damage done **(c)** taking accurate measurements of land, so as to produce a plan or map **(d) quantity survey** =

calculating the cost of materials and labour needed for a construction project **2** *verb* [sə'veı] **(a)** to ask people questions to get information about a subject; *roughly half the people we surveyed were in favour of the scheme* **(b)** to make a survey of a building; *a buildings surveyor was called in to survey the damage caused by the fire* **(c)** to measure land in order to produce a plan or map; *they're surveying the area where the new runway will be built* **(d)** to look at something so that you see all of it; *he stood on the balcony surveying the crowd in the square*

surveying [sə'veıŋ] *noun* taking accurate measurements, especially of land heights, distances, roads, buildings, etc., to produce accurate plans or maps

surveyor [sə'veıə] *noun* person who examines buildings to see if they are in good condition; person who surveys land; *the surveyor's report was favourable*

survival [sə'vaıvəl] *noun* continuing to exist; *the survival of the crew depended on the supplies carried in the lifeboat; the survival rate of newborn babies has started to fall;* **the survival of the fittest** = the process of evolution of a species, by which the characteristics that help the organism to survive are passed on to its offspring, and those characteristics which do not help survival are not passed on

survive [sə'vaıv] *verb* **(a)** to continue to be alive after an accident, etc.; *it was such a terrible crash, it was miracle that anyone survived; the President has survived two assassination attempts this year; he survived a massive heart attack; not all the litter of piglets survived more than a few days* **(b)** to continue to exist; *it is one of the three surviving examples of his work* **(c)** to live longer than someone else; *he survived his wife by ten years; she had no surviving relatives; he is survived by his only son*

survivor [sə'vaıvə] *noun* person who is still alive after an accident, etc.; *lifeboats were sent out to look for survivors*

susceptibility [səseptə'bılıti] *noun* **(a)** lack of resistance to a disease, etc.; *her susceptibility to infection means that she cannot go to any place where there are crowds* **(b) susceptibilities** = feelings which may be hurt; *we must be careful not to offend the susceptibilities of the female members of staff*

susceptible [sə'septıbl] *adjective* **(a) susceptible to** = likely to catch a disease; *she is susceptible to colds and throat infections* **(b)** easily influenced; *he's very susceptible to pretty women* **(c)** *(formal)* **susceptible of proof** = which can be proved

suspect 1 *adjective* ['sʌspekt] which might be dangerous; *don't eat any of that crab - it looks a bit suspect to me;* **suspect package** = package which might contain a bomb **2** *noun* ['sʌspekt] person who is thought to have committed a crime; *the police arrested several suspects for questioning* **3** *verb* [sə'spekt] **(a) to suspect someone of doing something** = to think that someone may have done something wrong; *I suspect him of being involved in the robbery; they were wrongly suspected of taking bribes* **(b)** to guess, to think that something is likely; *I suspect it's going to be more difficult that we thought at first; we suspected all along that something was wrong*

suspected [sʌs'pektıd] *adjective* which is thought to be; *several cases of suspected meningitis have been* reported; *the police rounded up a group of suspected terrorists*

suspend [sə'spend] *verb* (a) to hang something; *the ham is suspended over a smoky fire for some time, which gives it a particular taste* (b) to stop something for a time; *work on the construction project has been suspended; sailings have been suspended until the weather gets better* (c) to stop someone from doing something, such as working; *he has been suspended on full pay while investigations are continuing*

suspender [sʌ'spendə] *noun* (a) *GB* **suspender belt** = belt with elastic straps to hold up a woman's stockings (b) *GB* elastic strap going round your leg for holding up your sock (NOTE: American English is **garter**) (c) *US* **suspenders** = straps which go over your shoulders to hold up your trousers; *he wore bright red suspenders with his jeans* (NOTE: British English for this is **braces**)

suspense [sə'spens] *noun* impatient wait for something to happen or for someone to do something; *friends and relatives of the passengers waited in suspense at the airport for news of the plane; the film uses eerie music to build up suspense*

suspension [sə'spenʃn] *noun* (a) system of springs, etc., which supports a car and insulates it and the passengers from shocks; *hydraulic suspension gives you a very smooth ride* (b) action of hanging from something; **suspension bridge** = bridge which hangs from tall towers by ropes, chains, etc.; **suspension file** = cardboard file which can be hooked inside the drawer of a filing cabinet so that it hangs loose (c) stopping something for a time; *suspension of payments by the bank; there has been a temporary suspension of deliveries*

suspicion [sə'spɪʃn] *noun* (a) feeling that something is wrong, that someone has committed a crime; *his actions immediately aroused suspicion on the part of the police; the bank regards his business deals with considerable suspicion; they were arrested on suspicion of exporting stolen goods* (b) general feeling that something is going to happen; *I have a suspicion that he's coming to see me because he wants to borrow some money; her suspicions proved to be correct when she saw the wedding announced in the paper*

suspicious [sə'spɪʃəs] *adjective* (a) which seems to be wrong, dangerous or connected with a crime; *the police found a suspicious package on the station platform; that the secretary seemed to know all about the deal before everyone else was very suspicious; we became suspicious when we realized we hadn't seen him for three days* (b) **suspicious of** = not trusting; *I'm suspicious of people who tell me they know a way of getting rich quickly*

suspiciously [sə'spɪʃəsli] *adverb* (a) in a suspicious way; *he was behaving very suspiciously and the bank staff called the police* (b) as if you suspect something is wrong; *she glanced suspiciously at the waiter*

suss out ['sʌs 'aʊt] *verb* (informal) to discover; *I want you to suss out everything you can about him*

sustain [sə'steɪn] *verb* (a) to make something continue; *how long can this level of activity be sustained?* (b) to receive an injury; *he sustained severe head injuries* (c) to give you strength; *you need a good breakfast to sustain you through the day* (d) (formal)

to support; *will the roof sustain the weight of the snow?*

sustainable [sʌs'teɪnəbl] *adjective* which does not damage natural resources and which leaves the environment in good condition; *they make conservatories from sustainable timber; the table is made of hardwood from a sustainable source*

sustained [sə'steɪnd] *adjective* which continues for a long time; *a sustained effort*

sustaining [sə'steɪnɪŋ] *adjective* (a) which will support; *a sustaining wall* (b) which will nourish; *a bowl of sustaining soup*

sustenance ['sʌstənəns] *noun* (formal) food; *they were eager for lack of sustenance; the football team came into the pavilion looking for sustenance*; **means of sustenance** = way of keeping someone alive or of keeping strong; *by the time they were found, their only means of sustenance was berries they found on bushes*

suture ['su:tʃə] **1** *noun* stitch used to attach the sides of a wound so that it can heal; *the sutures will be removed the following day* **2** *verb* to attach the sides of a cut together with thread so that it can heal; *the wound was cleaned, then sutured*

swagger ['swægə] **1** *noun* proud way of walking, where you swing your shoulders as you walk; *the crowd of youths walked past with a particular swagger* **2** *verb* to walk in a proud way, swinging your shoulders; *he swaggered into the office, showing off his new suntan*

swallow ['swɒləʊ] **1** *noun* common bird with pointed wings and tail, which flies fast; *there are several swallows' nests under the eaves of the roof* **2** *verb* (a) to make food or liquid pass down your throat from your mouth to the stomach; *he swallowed his beer and ran back to the office; she swallowed hard and knocked on the door to the interview room* (b) to accept something; *he finds being made redundant hard to swallow*

swallow up ['swɒləʊ 'ʌp] *verb* to make something disappear into something; *he stepped out of the door and was swallowed up in the crowds; more than half my salary is swallowed up in mortgage repayments*

swam [swæm] *see* SWIM

swamp [swɒmp] **1** *noun* area of permanently wet land and the plants that grow in it; *you can't build on that land - it's a swamp* **2** *verb* (a) to cover something with water; *the waves nearly swamped our little boat* (b) **swamped with** = having so much, that it is impossible to deal with it all; *the office is swamped with work; the switchboard has been swamped with calls*

swan [swɒn] **1** *noun* large white water bird with a long curved neck; *there are swans on the Thames near Windsor* **2** *verb* (informal) to go swanning off or around = to go off or travel about lazily, not doing any work; *instead of going to university he spent a year swanning around the States*

swansong ['swɒnsɒŋ] *noun* last performance, last appearance of someone; *the concert is the group's swansong before they retire*

swap or **swop** [swɒp] **1** *noun* (a) exchange of one thing for another; *I'll do a swap with you - one of my CDs for your T-shirt* (b) **swaps** = things, such as stamps, coins, etc., which you have ready to exchange for others; *I have a few swaps left but nobody wants them* **2** *verb* to exchange something for something else;

can I swap my tickets for next Friday's show?; *let's swap places, so that I can talk to Susan*; *after every game the players swapped jerseys with the other team*; **they swapped jobs** = each of them took the other's job (NOTE: **swapping** or **swopping** - **swapped** or **swopped**)

swarm [swɔːm] **1** *noun* large group of insects, etc., flying around together; *a swarm of flies buzzed around the meat* **2** *verb* **(a)** to move about in various directions; *police were swarming all over the presidential palace*; *Oxford Street was swarming with shoppers* **(b)** *(of bees)* to move as a large group, looking for a place to nest; *it's the time of year when bees swarm*

swarthy [ˈswɔːði] *adjective* with a dark skin; *with his dark hair and swarthy complexion he looks terrific in a white T-shirt* (NOTE: **swarthier** - **swarthiest**)

swathe [sweɪð] **1** *noun* **(a)** long broad band of land, grass, etc.; *great swathes of forest were destroyed in the fire* **(b)** **to cut a swathe through something** = to destroy a lot of something; *by working hard, they managed to cut a swathe through the outstanding work*; *cholera has cut a swathe through the refugee population* **2** *verb* to wrap someone up; *the baby was swathed in blankets*; *she went to the rugby match swathed in jumpers and scarves*

sway [sweɪ] **1** *noun* **to hold sway over someone** = to hold power over someone; *he held sway in Russia for several years* **2** *verb* **(a)** to move gracefully from side to side; *the crowd swayed in time to the music*; *the palm trees swayed in the breeze* **(b)** to have an influence on; *the committee was swayed by a letter from the president*

swear [sweə] *verb* **(a)** to make a solemn public promise; *he swore he wouldn't touch alcohol again*; *the witnesses swore to tell the truth*; **to swear someone to secrecy** = to make someone swear not to tell a secret; *he was sworn to secrecy* **(b)** to take an oath; **to swear someone in** = to make an official take an oath; *he was sworn in as governor*; **I could have sworn** = I was totally sure; *I could have sworn I put my keys in my coat pocket* **(c)** to shout curses; *they were shouting and swearing at the police*; *don't let me catch you swearing again!*; **he swears like a trooper** = he swears all the time, using extremely bad language **(d)** *(informal)* **to swear by** = to believe completely in something; *he swears by an old Chinese herbal medicine* (NOTE: **swearing** - **swore** [swɔː] - **sworn** [swɔːn])

swearing [ˈsweəɪŋ] *noun* action of shouting curses; *swearing is not allowed in the school*

swear word [ˈsweə ˈwɜːd] *noun* word used as a curse, which most people think should not be spoken; *where on earth did the children learn those swear words?*

sweat [swet] **1** *noun* drops of salt liquid which come through your skin when you are hot or when you are afraid; *after working in the vineyard he was drenched with sweat*; *he broke out into a cold sweat when they called his name*; **sweat gland** = gland in the body that produces sweat **2** *verb* to produce sweat; *he ran up the hill, sweating and red in the face*

sweatband [ˈswetbænd] *noun* narrow strip of towelling worn round your head or wrist to stop sweat trickling down, such as when you are playing tennis; *he usually wears white sweatbands when playing in a tournament*

sweated labour [ˈswetɪd ˈleɪbə] *noun* **(a)** people who work hard for little money; *of course the firm makes a profit - it employs sweated labour* **(b)** hard work which is very badly paid; *working here is more like sweated labour than a proper office job*

sweater [ˈswetə] *noun* knitted pullover with long sleeves; *you'll need a sweater in the evenings, even in the desert*

sweatshirt [ˈswetʃɜːt] *noun* thick cotton shirt with long sleeves; *a sweatshirt is comfortable if the evening is cool*

sweaty [ˈsweti] *adjective* damp with sweat; *the little boy clutched the coin in his sweaty hand*; *she came back from the marathon all hot and sweaty*

Swede [swiːd] *noun* **(a)** person from Sweden; *the Swedes have a very high standard of living* **(b)** **swede** = common vegetable with a round root and yellow flesh, used mainly in soups and stews (NOTE: American English is **rutabaga**)

Sweden [ˈswiːdən] *noun* country in northern Europe, between Norway and Finland; *we went for a camping holiday in Sweden*; *summer evenings in Sweden can be quite cool* (NOTE: capital: **Stockholm**; people: **the Swedes**; language: **Swedish**; currency: **the Swedish krona**)

Swedish [ˈswiːdɪʃ] **1** *adjective* coming from Sweden; referring to Sweden; *have you bought the new Swedish stamps?*; *Swedish roads do not have as much traffic as ours* **2** *noun* language spoken in Sweden; *can you translate this letter into Swedish, please?*; *their children spoke Swedish with their grandmother*

sweep [swiːp] **1** *noun* **(a)** act of sweeping with a brush; *I'll just give the hall floor a sweep* **(b)** **to make a clean sweep of something** = (i) to clear something away completely; (ii) to win everything; *he made a clean sweep of all the old files*; *they made a clean sweep at the local government elections* **(c)** person who cleans chimneys; *sweeps are always busy in the autumn, cleaning chimneys ready for the winter* **(d)** wide expanse; *the green sweep of the lawn running down to the lake* **(e)** wide movement of your arm; *with a sweep of his arm he knocked all the glasses off the table* **2** *verb* **(a)** to clear up dust, dirt, etc., from the floor with a brush; *have you swept the kitchen floor yet?* **(b)** **to sweep the board** = to win completely; *the British team swept the board in the Grand Prix* **(c)** to clean a chimney with a brush; *we must get the chimney swept before we start having fires again* **(d)** to move rapidly; *she swept into the room, with a glass of champagne in her hand*; *the party swept to power in the general election*; *a feeling of anger swept through the crowd*; **to sweep past** = to go past quickly; *the motorcade swept past*; *she swept past without saying a word* **(e)** to follow a curve; *the motorway sweeps round the mountain*; *the road sweeps down to the harbour* **(f)** **to sweep something away** = to carry something rapidly away; *the river flooded and swept away part of the village* (NOTE: **sweeping** - **swept** [swept])

sweeper [ˈswiːpə] *noun* person or machine that sweeps; *the street sweeper cleans our street once a week*

sweeping [ˈswiːpɪŋ] *adjective* which affects many things or people; *the government is proposing sweeping changes to the education system*; *she made some sweeping generalizations about young people*; **sweeping statement** = statement which may be partly true but has no facts to support it; *it's a rather sweeping statement to say that all politicians tell lies*

sweet [swiːt] **1** *adjective* **(a)** tasting like sugar, and neither sour nor bitter; *these apples are sweeter than those green ones*; **to have a sweet tooth** = to like sweet food; *he's very fond of puddings - he's got a real sweet tooth!* **(b)** charming, pleasant; *he sent me such a sweet birthday card*; *it was sweet of her to send me flowers*; *what a sweet little girl!*; *how sweet of you to help me with my luggage!* (NOTE: **sweeter - sweetest**) **2** *noun* **(a)** small piece of sweet food, made with sugar; *she bought some sweets to eat in the cinema*; *he likes to suck sweets when he is driving*; **cough sweets** = sweet-tasting tablets to soothe a cough (NOTE: American English for this is **candy**) **(b)** last course in a meal, sweet food eaten at the end of a meal; *what's on the menu for sweet?*; *we haven't had our sweet yet*; *I won't have any sweet, thank you, just some coffee*; **sweet trolley** = trolley with different sweet dishes, brought to your table in a restaurant for you to choose from; *the waiter brought a tempting sweet trolley to our table* **(c)** (*old term used to someone you love*) *yes, my sweet, I'll be with you in a minute* (NOTE: do not confuse with **suite**)

sweet and sour ['swiːt ənd 'sauə] *adjective* made with a sauce of sugar and vinegar; *we had fried rice with our sweet and sour pork*

sweet corn ['swiːt 'kɔːn] *noun* the large yellow seeds of maize, eaten cooked; *sweet corn covered with melted butter*

sweeten ['swiːtn] *verb* **(a)** to make sweet; *use honey to sweeten your cereal instead of sugar* **(b)** (*informal*) to give someone money or a present to make sure they help you; *we told her to sweeten up the inspector by taking him out for a meal*

sweetener ['swiːtnə] *noun* **(a)** artificial substance, such as saccharin, added to food to make it sweet **(b)** (*informal*) bribe; *she was accused of taking sweeteners from building contractors*

sweetheart ['swiːthɑːt] *noun* **(a)** way of addressing someone you love; *look, sweetheart, I can't lend you any more money* **(b)** (*old*) boyfriend or girlfriend; *they were sweethearts when they were at school* or *they were childhood sweethearts*

sweetie ['swiːti] *noun* (*informal*) **(a)** sweet; *the children were all given bags of sweeties* **(b)** lovely little thing or person; *I must send the cleaning lady a birthday card, she's such a sweetie*

sweet pea ['swiːt 'piː] *noun* climbing plant of the pea family, with scented pink, white or red flowers; *she put a vase of sweet peas on the table*

sweet potato ['swiːt pə'teɪtəu] *noun* vegetable like a long red potato with sweet yellow flesh inside; *baked sweet potatoes are delicious with butter* (NOTE: in American English also called a **yam**)

sweetshop ['swiːtʃɒp] *noun* shop which sells sweets and chocolates; *I'll stop at the sweetshop to buy a box of chocolates* (NOTE: the American equivalent is a **candy store**)

sweet-smelling ['swiːt 'smelɪŋ] *adjective* with a pleasant smell; *a bouquet of sweet-smelling roses*

swell [swel] **1** *adjective US* (*informal*) very good; *we had a swell time in New York City*; *that sounds like a swell idea* **2** *verb* to get bigger, to make bigger; *more and more people arrived to swell the crowd outside the palace gates*; **to swell (up)** = to become larger or to increase in size; *she was bitten by an insect and her hand swelled (up)* (NOTE: **swelling - swollen** ['swələn] **- swelled**) **3** *noun* movement of large waves in the open sea; *the boat rose and fell with the swell*; *there's a heavy swell running*

swelling ['swelɪŋ] *noun* condition where fluid forms in part of the body, making that part swell up; *the swelling will go down in a day or so*

swelter ['sweltə] *verb* to be very hot; *there was no air-conditioning in the courtroom, so we just sat and sweltered*

sweltering ['sweltrɪŋ] *adjective* very hot; *he stepped out of the air-conditioning into the sweltering heat*

swept [swept] *see* SWEEP

swerve [swɜːv] **1** *noun* sudden movement to one side; *he made a swerve to the right to get past the defender* **2** *verb* to move suddenly to one side; *they think the car swerved to the left and hit a wall*; *she had to swerve to avoid the bicycle*

swift [swɪft] **1** *adjective* rapid; *their phone call brought a swift response from the police* (NOTE: **swifter - swiftest**) **2** *noun* little bird like a swallow but with shorter wings and tail, which flies very fast

swiftly ['swɪftli] *adverb* rapidly; *the puzzle was swiftly solved*

swig [swɪg] (*informal*) **1** *noun* mouthful of liquid; *he took a swig from the bottle of water* **2** *verb* to drink in large mouthfuls; *they stopped and swigged water from a bottle* (NOTE: **swigging - swigged**)

swim [swɪm] **1** *noun* moving in the water, using your arms and legs to push you along; *what about a swim before breakfast?*; *it's too cold for a swim* **2** *verb* **(a)** to move in the water using your arms and legs to push you along; *she can't swim, but she's taking swimming lessons*; *she swam across the English Channel*; *salmon swim upstream to get to their spawning grounds* **(b)** **my head is swimming** = I feel dizzy; *my head was swimming after working at the computer all day* **(c)** **to swim against the tide** = to do things differently from everyone else; *carry on as you are, even if you think you're swimming against the tide* **(d)** **swimming in** or **with** = in a lot of liquid; *a plate of lamb swimming in sauce*; *sausages swimming in hot fat* (NOTE: **swimming - swam** [swæm] **- has swum** [swʌm])

swimmer ['swɪmə] *noun* person who is swimming; *one of the swimmers got into difficulties and was saved by the lifeguard*

swimming ['swɪmɪŋ] *noun* action of swimming; **swimming costume** = clothing worn by women when swimming; *we forgot to bring our swimming costumes*; **swimming trunks** = short trousers worn by men and boys when swimming

swimming baths ['swɪmɪŋ 'bɑːðz] *noun* large building with a public swimming pool; *the teacher took the whole class to the swimming baths for a swimming lesson*

swimming pool ['swɪmɪŋ 'puːl] *noun* large pool for swimming; *the school has an indoor swimming pool*; *she swam two lengths of the swimming pool*

swimsuit ['swɪmsuːt] *noun* one-piece swimming costume for women and girls; *she was wearing her blue swimsuit*

swindle ['swɪndl] **1** *noun* illegal deal in which someone is cheated out of money; *she was caught up in some swindle involving imported cars* **2** *verb* to get money from someone by a trick; *she said she had been swindled by the bank*; *he swindled the old lady out of £10,000*

swindler ['swɪndlə] *noun* person who swindles someone; *the car that swindler sold me broke down after I'd only done two miles*

swine [swaɪn] *noun* **(a)** *(old)* collective term for pigs (NOTE: no plural) **(b)** *(informal)* unpleasant man; *he's a swine - he keeps us working all day long and pays us peanuts; you rotten swine!*

swing [swɪŋ] **1** *noun* **(a)** movement of your arm forwards and backwards; **to take a swing at someone** = to try to hit someone; *someone took a swing at him with a stick* **(b)** change in opinion which can be measured; *there was a swing of 10% to the socialists in the elections* **(c)** **to go with a swing** = to go very well, to be very enjoyable; *the party went with a swing*; **to get into the swing of things** = to enjoy being involved; *he'd never been to a night club before but soon got into the swing of things*; **in full swing** = going very well; *when we arrived the party was in full swing* **(d)** seat held by two ropes or chains, to sit on and swing backwards and forwards, usually outdoors; *she sat on the swing and ate an apple* **2** *verb* **(a)** to move from side to side or forwards and backwards, while hanging from a central point; *she picked up the baby and swung him round and round*; *he swung up and down on the garden swing*; *a window swung open and a man looked out* **(b)** to change direction or opinion; *the car swung off the road into the hotel car park*; *the voters swung to the right in Sunday's elections*; *he swung round to face the crowd* **(c)** to move with a swing; *they were swinging the bags one after the other into the rubbish van*; *he swung his suitcase up onto the rack* (NOTE: **swinging - swung** [swʌŋ])

swing door ['swɪŋ 'dɔː] *noun* door which opens in either direction when you push it; *there's a swing door between the kitchen and the dining room*

swinging ['swɪŋɪŋ] *adjective* *(informal)* exciting, fashionably modern; *the swinging London scene of the 1960s*

swipe [swaɪp] **1** *noun* punch; *he took a swipe at the man who tried to steal his wallet* **2** *verb* **(a)** to hit or try to hit; *he took a newspaper and tried to swipe the wasp* **(b)** *(informal)* to steal; *someone's swiped my umbrella* **(c)** to pass a credit card or charge card through a reader; *the cashier swiped my card through the machine*

swirl [swɜːl] **1** *noun* whirling or twisting movement; *swirls of smoke came out of the chimney* **2** *verb* to move with a whirling or twisting motion; *clouds of smoke were swirling round the factory*

swish [swɪʃ] **1** *adjective* *(informal)* smart and expensive; *he took me to dinner in a very swish restaurant* **2** *noun* soft rustling sound of a dress, of dead leaves; *with a swish of his brush, he swept the broken glass into a heap* **3** *verb* to make a whistling noise with a whip or stick; *we sat by the motorway, listening to the cars swishing past*

Swiss [swɪs] **1** *adjective* **(a)** referring to Switzerland; *we eat a lot of Swiss cheese; the Swiss banking system protects the identity of its customers* **(b) Swiss roll** = cake made by rolling up a thin sheet of sponge cake covered with jam or cream (NOTE: American English is **jelly roll**) **2** *noun* person from Switzerland; **the Swiss** = people from Switzerland; *the Swiss celebrate their national day on August 1st*

switch [swɪtʃ] **1** *noun* **(a)** small device that you push up or down to stop or start an electrical device; *the switch to turn off the electricity is in the cupboard*; *there is a light switch by the bed* **(b)** sudden change in opinion; *a switch in government policy* (NOTE: plural is **switches**) **2** *verb* **(a)** to do something quite different suddenly; *we decided to switch from gas to electricity* **(b)** to exchange; *let's switch places*; *he switched flights in Montreal and went on to Calgary*; *the job was switched from our British factory to the States*

switchboard ['swɪtʃbɔːd] *noun* central point in a telephone system, where all internal and external lines meet; *you should phone the switchboard if you can't get the number you want*; **switchboard operator** = person who works the central telephone switchboard by connecting incoming and outgoing calls to various lines

switch off ['swɪtʃ 'ɒf] *verb* **(a)** to make an electrical device stop; *don't forget to switch off the TV before you go to bed*; *she forgot to switch her car lights off* *or* *switch off her car lights*; *the kettle switches itself off automatically when it boils* **(b)** *(informal)* to stop listening to what someone is saying; *if you talk too slowly, everyone starts to switch off; I just switched off once the discussion started getting too technical*

switch on ['swɪtʃ 'ɒn] *verb* **(a)** to make an electrical device start; *can you switch the radio on - it's time for the evening news?*; *when you put the light on in the bathroom, the fan switches itself on automatically* **(b)** *(informal)* **switched on** = with it, knowing all that is happening; *she's very switched on to what is happening on the fashion scene*

switch over to ['swɪtʃ 'əʊvə tuː] *verb* to change to something quite different; *we have switched over to gas for our heating*

Switzerland ['swɪtsələnd] *noun* European country, south of Germany, east of France and north of Italy; *many people go on skiing holidays in Switzerland*; *we went to Switzerland last summer* (NOTE: capital: **Berne**; people: **the Swiss**; languages: **French, German, Italian**; currency: **the Swiss franc**)

swivel ['swɪvl] **1** *noun* joint between two parts which allows each to turn separately; *the monitor is mounted on a swivel, so that you can turn it in any direction* **2** *verb* to turn around a point; *swivel your chair to face the monitor*; *he swivelled round in his chair and looked out of the window* (NOTE: **swivelling - swivelled** but American spelling **swiveling - swiveled**)

swollen ['swəʊlən] *adjective* much bigger than usual; *she can't walk with her swollen ankle*; *the swollen river burst its banks; see also* SWELL

swollen-headed ['swəʊlən'hedɪd] *adjective* *(informal)* thinking you are much better than all the others; *he's got so swollen-headed now he's been promoted; I don't like being told what to do by some swollen-headed accountant*

swoop [swuːp] **1** *noun* coming rapidly down to attack; *several gang leaders were arrested in police swoops on bars in the city centre*; **at** *or* **in one fell swoop** = in a sudden move, all at once; *by pressing these keys I could make your data disappear in one fell swoop* **2** *verb* to come down rapidly to make a sudden attack; *the planes swooped (down) low over the enemy camp*

swop [swɒp] *noun & verb see* SWAP

sword [sɔːd] *noun* weapon with a handle and a long sharp blade; *he rushed onto the stage waving a sword*

swore [swɔː] *see* SWEAR

sworn [swɔːn] *adjective* under oath; *in his sworn statement he said something quite different*; **sworn enemies** = people who will always be enemies; *see also* SWEAR

swum [swʌm] *see* SWIM

swung [swʌŋ] *see* SWING

sycamore ['sɪkəmɔː] *noun* large tree of the maple family; *sycamore seeds are lying all over the garden*

-syllabic [sɪ'læbɪk] *suffix* referring to syllables; **monosyllabic** = having just one syllable

syllable ['sɪləbl] *noun* a whole word or part of a word which has one single sound; *there a three syllables in the word 'syllabus' and the stress is on the first syllable; see also* MONOSYLLABLE

syllabus ['sɪləbəs] *noun* list of subjects to be studied; *astronomy is not on the school syllabus* (NOTE: plural is **syllabuses**)

symbol ['sɪmbl] *noun* sign, letter, picture or shape which means something or shows something; *they use a bear as their advertising symbol; the crown was the symbol of the empire; the olive branch is a symbol of peace; Pb is the chemical symbol for lead* (NOTE: do not confuse with **cymbal**)

symbolic *or* **symbolical**   [sɪm'bɒlɪk or sɪm'bɒlɪkl] *adjective* used as a symbol; *an olive branch is symbolic of peace*

symbolism ['sɪmbəlɪzm] *noun* **(a)** using symbols to express feelings, etc.; *the symbolism of chopping down the orchard as the old man watched was obvious* **(b)** movement in literature and art in the 19th century in which feelings, etc., were not expressed in a straightforward way

symbolist ['sɪmbəlɪst] *noun* writer or painter belonging to the school of symbolism; *symbolist painters conveyed emotions by colours and light*

symbolize ['sɪmbəlaɪz] *verb* to be a symbol of something; *a lion symbolizes strength and courage*

symmetrical [sɪ'metrɪkl] *adjective* with two sides exactly the same; *the wallpaper has a repeated symmetrical pattern*

symmetry ['sɪmətri] *noun* state where two sides of something are exactly the same; *the symmetry of a leaf*

sympathetic [sɪmpə'θetɪk] *adjective* showing that you understand someone's problems; *I'm very sympathetic to her problems; he wasn't very sympathetic when I told him I felt ill*

sympathetically [sɪmpə'θetɪkli] *adverb* in a sympathetic way; *the boss listened to the workers' complaints sympathetically*

sympathize ['sɪmpəθaɪz] *verb* **to sympathize with someone** = to show that you understand someone's problems; *I sympathize with you, my husband snores too*

sympathizer ['sɪmpəθaɪzə] *noun* person who agrees in general with the policies of a group, without being a member of it; *the government is made up of communists and communist sympathizers*

sympathy ['sɪmpəθi] *noun* **(a)** feeling of understanding for someone else's problems, or after someone's death; *we received many messages of sympathy when my wife died; I find it difficult to express my sympathy when someone whom I hardly know dies; he had no sympathy for his secretary who complained of being overworked* **(b)** agreement with or support for someone *or* something; *I have a good deal of sympathy with the idea*; **to come out on strike in sympathy** = to stop work to show that you agree with another group of workers who are on strike; *the postal workers went on strike and the telephone engineers came out in sympathy* (NOTE: plural is **sympathies**)

symphonic [sɪm'fɒnɪk] *adjective* referring to music for a large orchestra; **symphonic poem** = piece of music for a large orchestra, but without the various movements which you find in a symphony

symphony ['sɪmfəni] *noun* long piece of music in several parts, called 'movements', played by a full orchestra; *Beethoven's Fifth Symphony; Smetana included themes from folk music in his symphonies* (NOTE: plural is **symphonies**)

symphony orchestra ['sɪmfəni 'ɔːkestrə] *noun* large orchestra which has enough musicians to be able to play symphonies (NOTE: usually used in titles: **the London Symphony Orchestra**, etc.)

symposium [sɪm'pəʊziəm] *noun* meeting organized to discuss a specialized subject; *the symposium on nuclear energy will be held in London* (NOTE: plural is **symposia**)

symptom ['sɪmptəm] *noun* **(a)** change in the way the body works, or change in the way the body looks, showing that a disease is present and has been noticed by the patient or doctor; *he has all the symptoms of measles* **(b)** visible sign which shows that something is happening; *rubbish everywhere on the pavements is a symptom of the economic crisis facing the borough*

symptomatic [sɪmptə'mætɪk] *adjective* **symptomatic of** = which is a symptom of; *the rash is symptomatic of measles; her rudeness is symptomatic of a general unease among the staff*

synagogue ['sɪnəgɒg] *noun* building where people of the Jewish faith pray and study their religion; *this is the oldest synagogue in London*

synchronize ['sɪŋkrənaɪz] *verb* **(a)** to adjust watches to the same time; *synchronize your watches to the town hall clock* **(b)** to arrange things so that they happen at the same time; **synchronized swimming** = sport where swimmers move about in the water in time to music

syndicate 1 *noun* ['sɪndɪkət] group of people or companies working together to make money; *a German finance syndicate* **2** *verb* ['sɪndɪkeɪt] to produce an article, a cartoon, etc., which is then published in several newspapers or magazines; *his cartoon strip is syndicated across the US; she writes a syndicated column on personal finance*

syndrome ['sɪndrəʊm] *noun* **(a)** group of symptoms which taken together show that a particular disease is present; *their daughter has Down's syndrome* **(b)** general feeling or way of approaching a problem, etc.; *it's an example of the 'let's go home early on Friday afternoon' syndrome*

synod ['sɪnəd] *noun* meeting of religious leaders; *the synod voted to allow women to become priests*

synonym ['sɪnənɪm] *noun* word which means nearly the same thing as another word; *find more than one synonym for the word 'different'*; *'to take industrial action' is often a synonym for 'to go on strike'* (NOTE: a word which means the opposite of another is an **antonym**)

synonymous [sɪ'nɒnɪməs] *adjective* meaning the same; *the words 'error' and 'mistake' are synonymous*

synopsis [sɪ'nɒpsɪs] *noun* short text, giving the basic details of something; *he sent in a detailed synopsis of his new novel*; *she wrote several film synopses* (NOTE: plural is **synopses**)

syntactically [sɪn'tæktɪkli] *adverb* in relation to syntax; *the two constructions are syntactically very different*

syntax ['sɪntæks] *noun* grammatical rules for putting words together into phrases; *English syntax is relatively simple compared to that of Russian* (NOTE: no plural)

synthesis ['sɪnθəsɪs] *noun* producing something by combining a number of smaller elements; *the plan is a synthesis of several earlier proposals* (NOTE: plural is **syntheses**)

synthesize ['sɪnθəsaɪz] *verb* (a) to produce something by combining a number of smaller elements; *synthesized voice* = artificial speech created by an electronic synthesizer that uses phonemes, the separate sounds that make up speech; *a synthesized voice answers their telephone* (b) to make a chemical compound artificially from its separate components; *essential amino acids cannot be synthesized*; *the body cannot synthesize essential fatty acids and has to absorb them from food*

synthesizer ['sɪnθəsaɪzə] *noun* (a) electronic device which can make musical sounds similar to different musical instruments; *the group use a guitar, drums and a synthesizer* (b) **voice synthesizer** *or* **speech synthesizer** = electronic device which generates sounds that are similar to the human voice

synthetic [sɪn'θetɪk] *adjective* artificial, made by man; *the coat she was wearing was made of synthetic fur*

synthetically [sɪn'θetɪkli] *adverb* made artificially; *synthetically produced hormones are used in hormone replacement therapy*

syphilis ['sɪfəlɪs] *noun* serious sexually transmitted disease; *he caught syphilis when he was a young man*;

congenital syphilis = syphilis which is passed on from a mother to her unborn child

syphilitic [sɪfə'lɪtɪk] *adjective & noun* (person) with syphilis

syringe [sɪ'rɪndʒ] **1** *noun* surgical instrument made of a tube with a plunger which slides down inside it, forcing the contents out through a needle to give an injection, or slides up the tube, sucking a liquid up into it; *I close my eyes when I see the dentist's syringe ready* **2** *verb* to wash out using a syringe; *she had her ears syringed*

syrup ['sɪrəp] *noun* (a) sweet liquid; *to make the syrup, dissolve the sugar in a cup of water; see also* COUGH (b) **(golden) syrup** = thick golden juice from sugar (used to make treacle tart, etc.); *compare* MOLASSES, TREACLE

syrupy ['sɪrəpi] *adjective* (a) very sweet, containing a lot of sugar; *syrupy drinks are bad for your teeth* (b) very sentimental; *the film is a syrupy story of adolescent love*

system ['sɪstəm] *noun* (a) group of things which work together; *the system of motorways or the motorway system*; *the London underground railway system*; **computer system** = set of programs, commands, etc., which run a computer; **the central nervous system** = the brain and the spinal cord which link together all the nerves (b) the body as a whole; *amputation of a limb gives a serious shock to the system* (c) way in which things are organized; *I've got my own system for dealing with invoices*; **decimal system** = system of mathematics based on the number 10; **filing system** = way of putting documents in order for easy reference

systematic [sɪstə'mætɪk] *adjective* well-organized; *a more systematic approach is needed*; *he organized a systematic attempt to bring down the government*; *she ordered a systematic report on the distribution service*

systematically [sɪstə'mætɪkli] *adverb* in a systematic way; *go through the report again systematically, checking all the statistics*; *he systematically got rid of anyone who disagreed with him*

systematize ['sɪstəmətaɪz] *verb* to arrange into a systematic order; *you should systematize your files*

systemic [sɪs'temɪk] *adjective* which affects a whole body or system; *blood poisoning is a systemic infection*; **systemic weedkiller** = weedkiller which is absorbed into a plant through its leaves, and kills it

Tt

T, t [tiː] twentieth letter of the alphabet, between S and U; *don't forget - you spell 'attach' with two Ts*; **to dot the i's and cross the t's** = to settle the final details of an agreement; **T-junction** = junction where one road joins another at right angles; *go down the road and turn right at the T-junction*

ta [tɑː] *interjection (informal)* thank you; *say 'ta' to the nice lady* (NOTE: mainly used in the North of England)

tab [tæb] *noun* **(a)** small piece of paper or cloth which sticks out from a surface, used, for example, for pulling open a box; *pull the tab up to lift the cover off the box* **(b)** piece of metal which you pull to open a drinks can; *the tab of the beer can came off when I tried to open it* **(c)** little coloured marker attached to index cards so that they can be found easily; *write the first three letters of the addressee on the tab* **(d)** *(informal)* **to pick up the tab** = to pay the bill; *I'll take you all out to lunch - the company will pick up the tab*; **to keep tabs on someone** = to keep watch on someone; *I'm not too happy about the performance of our new man in the Far East - you had better keep tabs on him for a while* **(e)** tabulator, a key on a computer or typewriter which you press to jump forward to a set place on the line; *press TAB to move the cursor to the next tab stop*

tabby (cat) ['tæbi(kæt)] *noun* striped black, brown, and grey cat; *our cat is always fighting with the tabby from next door*

table ['teɪbl] **1** *noun* **(a)** piece of furniture with a flat top and legs, used to eat at, work at, etc. ; *we had breakfast sitting round the kitchen table*; *he asked for a table by the window*; *she says she booked a table for six people for 12.30*; **to lay the table** *or* **to set the table** = to put knives, forks, spoons, plates, etc., on a table ready for a meal; *can someone set the table please, the food's almost ready*; *the table was laid for six*; **to clear the table** = to take away the dirty knives, forks, spoons, plates, etc., after a meal; *the waitress cleared a table for us and we sat down* **(b)** list of figures, facts, information set out in columns; **table of contents** = list of contents in a book **(c)** **(multiplication) tables** = lists of figures to learn by heart how each number is multiplied; *he's learnt his nine times table* **2** *verb* to put items of information on the table before a meeting; *the report of the finance committee was tabled*; **to table a motion** = to put forward a proposal for discussion by putting details of it on the table at a meeting

tableau ['tæbləʊ] *noun* scene where actors represent a historic occasion, etc., without moving; *a group of actors presented a series of tableaux on the history of the town* (NOTE: plural is **tableaux** ['tæbləʊ or 'tæbləʊz])

tablecloth ['teɪblklɒθ] *noun* cloth which covers a table during a meal; *put a clean tablecloth on the table*

table-mat ['teɪblmæt] *noun* mat put on the surface of a table, so that hot plates will not damage it; *put hot dishes on a table-mat, not directly on the table itself*

tablespoon ['teɪblspuːn] *noun* **(a)** large spoon for serving food at table **(b)** amount held in a tablespoon; *add two tablespoons of sugar*

tablespoonful ['teɪblspuːnfʊl] *noun* amount held in a tablespoon; *add two tablespoonfuls of sugar*

tablet ['tæblət] *noun* small round pill taken as medicine; *take two tablets before meals*

table tennis ['teɪbl 'tenɪs] *noun* game similar to tennis, but played on a large table with a net across the centre, with small round bats and a very light white ball; *do you want a game of table tennis?* (NOTE: also called **ping-pong**)

tabloid ['tæblɔɪd] *noun* newspaper with a small page size, usually aimed at a popular readership; *the picture of the England soccer hero is on the front pages of all the tabloids*; *the tabloids all put the story on their front pages* (NOTE: large format newspapers are called **broadsheets**)

taboo [tə'buː] **1** *adjective* not talked about because it is rude or embarrassing; *talking about baldness is taboo in this office*; *money used to be a taboo subject at home* **2** *noun* custom which forbids something; *there is a taboo against cartoons of the royal family*

tabulator ['tæbjʊleɪtə] *noun* key on a computer or typewriter which you press to jump forward to a set place on the line; *when you press the tabulator, the cursor moves to the next tab stop*

tacit ['tæsɪt] *adjective* (agreement, etc.) which is understood but not actually said; *the committee gave their tacit agreement to the proposal* or *gave the proposal their tacit approval*

taciturn ['tæsɪtɜːn] *adjective* not saying much and seeming to be unfriendly; *he's a reserved, taciturn sort of chap - not at all talkative*

tack [tæk] **1** *noun* **(a)** small nail with a wide head; **carpet tack** = nail for attaching a carpet to the floor; *(informal)* **to get down to brass tacks** = to start discussing the real problem **(b)** *(in sewing)* loose stitch used to hold cloth in place when making clothes, which can be removed later; *she put in a row of tacks to show where the pockets were to go* **(c)** movement of a sailing boat in a certain direction as it sails against the wind; **to change tack** = to start doing something different; *originally he offered to pay the all costs of the party and then changed tack and asked everyone to pay for themselves* **2** *verb* **(a)** to nail something down using tacks; *he tacked down the edge of the carpet* **(b)** to make a loose stitch which will be taken out later; *she tacked up the hem of her skirt* **(c)** *(in a sailing ship)* to change direction so that wind blows the sails from the other side; *the yacht had to keep tacking because the wind was blowing away from the harbour*; **they were tacking up the river** = they sailed up the river changing direction all the time because the wind was against them

tackle ['tækl] **1** *noun* **(a)** equipment; *he brought his fishing tackle with him* **(b)** *(in football, etc.)* trying to take the ball from an opposing player; *(in Rugby)* grabbing an opposing player so that he falls down and drops the ball **2** *verb* **(a)** to grab someone to stop him doing something; *he tried to tackle the burglar himself* **(b)** to try to deal with a problem or job; *you can't tackle a job like changing the central heating system on your own*; *you start cleaning the dining room and I'll tackle the washing up* **(c)** *(in football, etc.)* to try to get the ball from an opposing player; *(in Rugby)* to grab hold of an opposing player so that he falls down and drops the ball; *he was tackled before he could score*

tack on ['tæk 'ɒn] *verb (informal)* to add something at the end; *he tacked on a couple of paragraphs at the end of the letter*

tacky ['tæki] *adjective* **(a)** sticky; *don't touch the paint, it's still tacky* **(b)** looking cheap and of bad quality; *the decorations look expensive, but they're really very tacky*; *this Christmas we got some pretty tacky presents* (NOTE: **tackier - tackiest**)

tact [tækt] *noun* being careful not to offend people, being careful to say the right thing; *being a manager requires a lot of tact*

tactful ['tæktful] *adjective* showing tact; *it would be tactful not to mention cars - he's just had an accident with his father's Rolls Royce*

tactfully ['tæktfuli] *adverb* in a tactful way; *he suggested tactfully that it was time to leave*

tactic ['tæktɪk] *noun (often plural)* **(a)** way of doing something so as to get an advantage; *his tactic is to wait until near closing time, when the supermarket reduces the price of bread* **(b)** way of fighting a war; *guerrilla tactics were successful against the advancing army*

tactical ['tæktɪkl] *adjective* **(a)** referring to tactics; *cutting all our prices was a clever tactical move*; *the decision was taken for tactical reasons*; **tactical error** = mistake which will affect your future plans; **tactical withdrawal** = moving back to be able to attack better later on **(b) tactical weapon** = weapon which is used at a relatively short range; *tactical weapons can be used against enemy troops on the ground*

tactical voting ['tæktɪkl 'vəutɪŋ] *noun* way of voting, which aims not at voting for the candidate you want to win, but at voting to prevent the candidate who you do not want to win from being elected; *during the last General Election there was a lot of tactical voting by the two main opposition parties*

> COMMENT: in a case where the three candidates A, B and C, have 47%, 33% and 20% of the vote according to an opinion poll, C's supporters might all vote for B, to prevent A winning

tactician [tæk'tɪʃn] *noun* person who is an expert at tactics; *he has been added to the party team as an experienced tactician in local elections*

tactile ['tæktaɪl] *adjective (formal)* which can be sensed by touch; *the tactile pleasure you get from touching velvet*

tactless ['tæktləs] *adjective* being offensive, not always intentionally; *it was tactless of him to invite John at the same time as his old girlfriend*

tactlessly ['tæktləsli] *adverb* in a tactless way; *they tactlessly kept on calling her Susan, which was the name of her boyfriend's previous girlfriend*

tadpole ['tædpəul] *noun* frog in its first stage after hatching, when it has a body and tail; *the children caught tadpoles in the pond and took them to school in a jar; after a time, tadpoles develop rudimentary legs*

taffy ['tæfi] *noun* **(a)** *US* sweet made from sugar, like toffee; *he gave the children some pieces of taffy* **(b)** *(offensive) (slang)* Welshman; *the English team beat the Taffies by a record score*

tag [tæg] **1** *noun* **(a)** label, a piece of paper, plastic, etc., attached to something to show a price, contents, someone's name and address, etc.; **gift tag** = little label put on a parcel to show who it is for and who it is from; **name tag** = label with a name printed on it; *visitors to the factory are given name tags*; **price tag** = label with the price printed on it; *the car has a £50,000 price tag* **(b)** children's game where the first child has to try to touch another one who then chases the others in turn; *they were playing tag in the school playground* **2** *verb* **(a)** to attach a label to something; *these coats need to be tagged before you put them on the racks; we tag birds so that we can study their migration routes* **(b)** *(informal)* **to tag along behind someone** = to follow close behind someone; *whenever we go out for a walk my sister insists on tagging along* **(c) to tag something on to something** = to attach something at the end of something else; *he tagged on an extra section at the end of the letter* (NOTE: **tagging - tagged**)

tail [teɪl] **1** *noun* **(a)** long thin part at the end of an animal's body, which can move; *all you could see was a slight movement of the cat's tail*; *the dog rushed up to him, wagging its tail*; **to turn tail** = to turn round and run away; *as soon as they heard the dog barking, the burglars turned tail and ran off* (NOTE: do not confuse with **tale**) **(b)** end or back part of something; *the tail of the queue stretched round the corner and into the next street* **(c) tails** = the side of a coin without the head of a king, etc., on it; **heads or tails** = throwing a coin in the air to see which side comes down on top; *let's toss heads or tails for the bill!* **(d)** long back part of a coat or shirt; *he tucked the tail of his shirt back into his trousers* **(e) tails** = man's evening dress, a black coat with a long tail, black trousers, white bow tie, etc.; *all the men wore tails to the ball* **2** *verb* to follow close behind someone; *the police tailed the lorry from the harbour to the warehouse*

tail away ['teɪl ə'weɪ] = TAIL OFF

tailback ['teɪlbæk] *noun* long line of cars held up on a road; *because of the crash, there's a six-mile tailback on the motorway from junction 4*

tail end ['teɪl 'end] *noun* last part, back part (of a film, queue, etc.); *we came in late and just caught the tail end of the programme; the people at the tail end of the queue have no hope of getting in*

tail fin ['teɪl 'fin] *noun* vertical fin on the tail of a plane which helps the steering of the plane; *the tail fin of the crashed plane could be seen sticking up out of the water*

tailgate ['teɪlgeɪt] *noun* door at the back of a car, that opens to give access to the storage space; *he had difficulty shutting the tailgate over the box*

tailgating ['teɪlgeɪtɪŋ] *noun* following closely behind another car; *tailgating at high speeds is potentially very dangerous*

tail off ['teɪl 'ɒf] *verb* to become fainter or less; *the number of overseas visitors starts to tail off in September; he started speaking, but his voice tailed off into a whisper*

tailor ['teɪlə] **1** *noun* person who makes clothes for men, such as suits, coats, etc.; *he gets all his clothes made by a tailor in Oxford Street* **2** *verb* **(a)** to make clothes which fit closely; *she wore a tailored jacket* **(b)** to adapt something to fit a particular requirement; *the payments can be tailored to suit your requirements*; *this course is tailored to the needs of women going back to work*

tailor-made ['teɪləmeɪd] *adjective* made to fit certain needs; *the computer programme is tailor-made for our purposes*

tailpipe ['teɪlpaɪp] *noun US* the tube at the back of a motor vehicle from which gases produced by the engine are sent out into the air; *clouds of white smoke were coming out of the tailpipe* (NOTE: British English is **exhaust pipe**)

tailplane ['teɪlpleɪn] *noun* horizontal wing forming part of the tail of an aircraft

tail wind ['teɪl 'wɪnd] *noun* wind blowing from behind which makes an aircraft, vehicle or runner go faster; *the flight will be slightly early because of a tail wind across the Atlantic* (NOTE: the opposite is a **headwind**)

taint [teɪnt] **1** *noun* trace of evil or of corruption; *we need a new finance director who is totally free of the taint of corruption* **2** *verb* **(a)** to damage; *his political reputation has been permanently tainted by the scandal* **(b)** to make rotten; **tainted food** = food which has become rotten by touching other rotten food

take [teɪk] **1** *verb* **(a)** to lift and move something; *she took the pot of jam down from the shelf*; *the waiter took the tablecloth off the table* **(b)** to carry something to another place; *can you take this cheque to the bank for me, please?* **(c)** to go with someone or something to another place; *he's taking the children to school*; *they took the car to the garage*; *we took a taxi to the hotel* **(d)** to steal; *someone's taken my watch* **(e)** to go away with something which someone else was using; *someone has taken the newspaper I was reading*; *who's taken my cup of coffee?* **(f)** to use or occupy; *sorry, all these seats are taken*; **to take your seats** = to sit down; *please take your seats, the play is about to start* **(g)** to do a test; *you must go to bed early because you'll be taking your exams tomorrow morning*; *she had to take her driving test three times before she finally passed* **(h)** to eat or to drink (often); *do you take sugar in your tea?*; *take the medicine three times a day after meals* **(i)** to accept; *if they offer you the job, take it immediately* **(j)** to do certain actions; *we took our holiday in September this year*; *she's taking a shower after going to the beach*; *she took a photograph or took a picture of the Tower of London*; *she needs to take a rest*; **to take action** = to do something; *you must take immediate action if you want to stop shoplifting*; **to take a call** = to answer the telephone; *I was out of the office so my secretary took the call*; **to take the chair** = to be chairman of a meeting; *in the absence of the chairman his deputy took the chair*; **to take dictation** = to write down what someone is saying; *the secretary was taking dictation from the managing director*; **to take place** = to happen; *the reception will take place on Saturday*; **to take stock** = to count the items in a warehouse; **to take stock of a situation** = to examine the state of things before deciding what to do; *when we had taken stock of the situation, we decided the best thing to do was to sell the house* **(k)** to need; *it took three strong men to move the piano*; *they took two days*

or it took them two days to get to London; *when he wants to watch a TV programme it never seems to take him long to finish his homework* **(l)** to accept or to hold; *the ticket machine takes 10p and 20p coins*; *the lift can take up to six passengers* (NOTE: **taking - took** [tʊk] **- has taken** ['teɪkn]) **2** *noun* **(a)** money received in a shop; *today's take was less than yesterday's* **(b)** scene which has been filmed; *the actors took a break between takes*

take after ['teɪk 'ɑːftə] *verb* to look like a parent or relative; *she takes after her mother*

take away ['teɪk ə'weɪ] *verb* **(a)** to remove something *or* someone; *take those scissors away from little Nicky - he could cut himself*; *the ambulance came and took her away*; *the police took away piles of documents from the office* **(b)** to subtract one number from another (NOTE: **take away** is usually shown by the sign - : **10 - 4 = 6**: say 'ten take away four equals six')

takeaway ['teɪkəweɪ] *noun & adjective (informal)* **(a)** shop where you can buy cooked food to eat somewhere else; *there's an Indian takeaway round the corner* **(b)** hot meal which you buy to eat back home; *we had a Chinese takeaway* (NOTE: American English is **takeout**)

take back ['teɪk 'bæk] *verb* **(a)** to go back with something; *if the trousers are too short you can take them back to the shop*; *if you don't like the colour, you can take it back and change it* **(b)** to accept something which someone has brought back; *I took my trousers to the shop where I had bought them, but they wouldn't take them back because I didn't have a receipt* **(c)** to withdraw something which has been said, and apologize for it; *I take it all back - they're a marvellous team*

take down ['teɪk 'daʊn] *verb* **(a)** to reach up and bring something down; *I took the jar down from the shelf* **(b)** to bring something down which had been put up; *on January 6th we take down the Christmas decorations*; *they have finished the roof and are taking down the scaffolding* **(c)** to write down; *the policeman took down his name and address*

take-home pay ['teɪkhəʊm 'peɪ] *noun* amount of money you actually receive in wages after tax, etc., has been deducted; *his take-home pay is about £750 per week*

take in ['teɪk 'ɪn] *verb* **(a)** to bring inside something which was outside; *the boat was taking in water*; *in October they took in the lemon trees from the gardens* **(b)** to understand; *I don't think she took in anything of what you said* **(c)** to deceive; *thousands of people were taken in by the advertisement* **(d)** to make a piece of clothing smaller; *can you take these trousers in? - they're much too loose round the waist* (NOTE: the opposite in this meaning is to **let out**)

take into ['teɪk 'ɪntu] *verb* to take inside; *to take items into stock or into the warehouse*

taken with ['teɪkn 'wɪθ] *adjective (informal)* attracted by; *her parents were quite taken with her new boyfriend*; *she's suddenly taken with the idea of starting a hairdresser's salon*

take off ['teɪk 'ɒf] *verb* **(a)** to remove, especially your clothes; *he took off all his clothes or he took all his clothes off*; *take your dirty boots off before you come into the kitchen*; see also **HAT** **(b)** to remove *or* to deduct; *he took £25 off the price* **(c)** *(of plane)* to leave the ground; *the plane took off at 4.30* **(d)** to remove someone in a plane or helicopter; *the ship was listing badly and the crew had to be taken off by helicopter* **(e)** to start to rise fast; *sales took off after the TV commercials* **(f) she took the day off =** she decided not to work for the day **(g)** to imitate someone in a funny way; *he likes to make everyone laugh by taking off the headmaster*

takeoff ['teɪkɒf] *noun* **(a)** *(of an aircraft)* leaving the ground; *the takeoff was without any problems*; *I always ask for a seat by the window, so that I can watch the takeoff* **(b)** *(informal)* amusing imitation of someone; *he did a wonderful takeoff of the headmaster*

take on ['teɪk 'ɒn] *verb* **(a)** to agree to do a job; *she's taken on a part-time job in addition to the one she's already got* **(b)** to agree to have someone as a worker; *the shop has taken on four trainees*; *we need to take on more staff to cope with work* **(c)** to fight someone; *it seems he is taking on the whole government*

take out ['teɪk 'aʊt] *verb* **(a)** to pull something out; *he took out a gun and waved it around*; *the dentist had to take his tooth out* **(b)** to invite someone to go out; *I'm taking all the office staff out for a drink* **(c)** **to take out a patent for an invention =** to apply for and receive a patent; **to take out insurance against theft =** to pay a premium to an insurance company, so that if a theft takes place the company will pay compensation; **to take out £50 =** to remove £50 in cash from a bank account **(d) the hot weather takes it out of you =** the hot weather makes you very tired; **to take it out on someone =** to make someone suffer because you are upset or worried; *he keeps on taking it out on his secretary*

takeout ['teɪkaʊt] *noun US* hot meal which you buy to eat back home; *we had a takeout Chinese meal* (NOTE: British English is **takeaway**)

take over ['teɪk 'əʊvə] *verb* **(a)** to start to do something in place of someone else; *Miss Black took over from Mr Jones on May 1st*; *thanks for looking after the switchboard for me - I'll take over from you now*; *when our history teacher was ill, the English teacher had to take over his classes*; *the Socialists took over from the Conservatives* **(b)** to buy a business by offering to buy most of its shares; *the company was taken over by a big group last month*

takeover ['teɪkəʊvə] *noun* **(a)** buying of a controlling interest in a business by buying more than 50% of the shares; *the takeover may mean that a lot of people will lose their jobs*; **takeover bid =** offer to buy all or most of the shares of a business so as to control it; **to make a takeover bid for a company =** to offer to buy most of the shares in a company; **hostile takeover** = takeover where the board of the company being bought do not recommend the sale and try to fight it **(b)** occupying a country and removing the government; *many people were killed during the military takeover*

taker ['teɪkə] *noun* **(a)** person who wants to buy or take something; *at that price, I'm not surprised there were no takers for the painting*; *any takers for this last piece of chocolate cake?* **(b)** person who takes someone *or* something; *the hostage takers asked for a huge ransom*; *drug takers are being targeted by the government publicity campaign*

take to ['teɪk 'tuː] *verb* **(a)** to start to do something as a habit; *he's taken to looking under his bed every night to make sure no one is hiding there*; *she's recently*

taken to wearing trousers to work; **he took to drink =** he started to drink alcohol regularly **(b)** to start to like someone; *she took to her boss right away*

take up ['teɪk 'ʌp] *verb* **(a)** to occupy or to fill a space; *this settee takes up too much room*; *being in charge of the staff sports club takes up too much of my time* **(b)** to remove something which was down; *you will need to take up the rugs if you want to polish the floor* **(c)** to start to do a certain activity, sport, etc.; *she was over fifty when she took up long-distance running* **(d) to take someone up on something =** to accept an offer made by someone; *he asked me if I wanted two tickets to Wimbledon and I took him up on his offer*

takings ['teɪkɪŋz] *noun* cash received in a shop or business; *the day's takings were stolen from the cash desk*; *this week's takings were less than last week's*

talcum powder ['tælkʌm 'paʊdə] *noun* soft scented powder, used to soften the skin or reduce rubbing; *she put some talcum powder between her toes*

tale [teɪl] *noun* *(literary)* story; *a tale of princesses and wicked fairies*; **old wives' tale =** old, and often silly, idea; *eating carrots won't make you see in the dark - that's just an old wives' tale* (NOTE: do not confuse with **tail**)

talent ['tælənt] *noun* **(a)** natural ability or skill; *she has a talent for getting customers to spend money* **(b)** people with natural ability; *the club is always on the lookout for fresh talent*; **talent contest =** contest to find new performers, singers, etc.

talented ['tæləntɪd] *adjective* with a lot of talent; *she's a very talented pianist*

talk [tɔːk] **1** *noun* **(a)** conversation, discussion; *we had a little talk, and she agreed with what the committee had decided*; *I had a long talk with my father about what I should study at university* **(b) talks =** negotiations; *we have entered into talks with the union leaders* **(c)** lecture about a subject; *he gave a short talk about the history of the town* **(d)** general rumour; *there has been talk of a change of government* **2** *verb* to say things, to speak; *the guide was talking French to the group of tourists*; *I didn't understand what he was talking about*; *we must talk to the neighbours about their noisy dog - he kept me awake again last night*; *they're talking of selling their house and going to live by the sea*

talkative ['tɔːkətɪv] *adjective* who likes to talk a lot or to gossip; *the new secretary is not very talkative*

talker ['tɔːkə] *noun* person who talks a lot; *he's a great talker*

talking ['tɔːkɪŋ] *noun* action of speaking; **let me do all the talking =** don't say anything, just let me say what needs to be said

talking shop ['tɔːkɪŋ 'ʃɒp] *noun* place where things are talked about but where no action is ever taken; *people will soon lose respect for Parliament if they think it is just a talking shop*

talking-to ['tɔːkɪŋtuː] *noun* *(informal)* criticizing someone; *the teacher gave her a good talking-to*

talk into ['tɔːk 'ɪntuː] *verb* **to talk someone into doing something =** to persuade someone to do something; *the salesman talked us into buying a new car*

talk over ['tɔːk 'əʊvə] *verb* to discuss; *we've talked it over and decided not to leave*; *if you want to borrow*

money, go and talk it over with the bank manager;
why don't you come and talk it over with your mother?

talk round ['tɔːk 'raʊnd] *verb* to persuade someone
to change his mind; *he wanted to resign immediately,*
but I managed to talk him round

talk show ['tɔːk 'ʃəʊ] *noun* chat show, TV show
where famous people talk to the host; *he is the host of a*
popular talk show

tall [tɔːl] *adjective* **(a)** high, usually higher than
normal; *the bank building is the tallest building in*
London; can you see those tall trees over there?; he's
the tallest boy in his class; how tall are you? - I'm six
foot two (6' 2'') **(b)** *(informal)* **tall order** = difficult
task; *asking all the staff to move to Edinburgh is a*
really tall order (NOTE: **taller - tallest**. Note also the use
with figures: **the tree is two metres tall; he's six foot tall;**
tall is used with people and thin things like trees or
skyscrapers; for things which are a long way above the
ground use **high: high clouds, a high mountain**)

tally ['tæli] **1** *noun* note, account or score; *what's the*
tally in the race so far? - we've had 2 crashes and 4
retirements through mechanical failure; the scorer
keeps a tally of the runs scored; I hope you kept a tally
of all your travelling expenses? (NOTE: plural is **tallies**)
2 *verb* to agree with; *the totals in the two columns*
don't tally; the figures in my notebook tally with the
computer figures

talon ['tælən] *noun* big claw of a bird of prey; *the*
eagle held the mouse in its talons

tambourine [tæmbə'riːn] *noun* small drum with
metal disks attached to the rim, so that they jangle when
it is hit; *he played the tambourine while she danced*

tame [teɪm] **1** *adjective* **(a)** which is not wild; *don't be*
afraid of that fox - he's perfectly tame **(b)** *(informal)*
available, who is always called in to help; *she's our*
tame accountant **2** *verb* to make a wild animal tame;
they tame wild elephants so that they can use them for
work in the forests

tamper ['tæmpə] *verb* **to tamper with** = to meddle
with something; *someone has been tampering with the*
weighing machine; I hope no one tampered with the
test sample

tampon ['tæmpɒn] *noun* **(a)** tube of absorbent
material placed inside the vagina used to soak up blood
from the menstrual flow; *I need to buy a packet of*
tampons from the chemist **(b)** pad of absorbent
material used in operations to soak up blood; *the*
surgeon put a tampon into the wound to absorb some
of the blood

tan [tæn] **1** *adjective* brownish-yellow; *he was*
wearing tan shoes **2** *noun* **(a)** brownish-yellow colour;
have you got the same shoes, but in tan? **(b)**
brownish-yellow colour of the skin after being in the
sun; *she got a tan from spending each day on the*
beach; see also SUNTAN **3** *verb* to get brown from
being in the sun; *she tans easily - just half an hour in*
the sun and she's quite brown (NOTE: **tanning -**
tanned)

tandem ['tændəm] *noun* **(a)** bicycle for two people;
I'm sure that's the second time today we've passed
that couple on their tandem **(b) in tandem** = together,
in pairs; *they worked in tandem for many years*

tang [tæŋ] *noun* sharp taste or smell; *I love to smell*
the tang of the sea

tangent ['tændʒənt] *noun* **(a)** line which touches a
curve without cutting through it; *the line AB forms a*
tangent to the circle at the point P **(b)** to fly *or* to go off
at a tangent *US* to go off on a tangent = to start
talking about something quite different; *he suddenly*
flew off at a tangent and started talking about his car;
she went off at a tangent almost from the beginning of
the discussion

tangerine ['tændʒə'riːn] *noun* small orange with soft
skin which peels easily; *there was a bowl of tangerines*
on the table

tangible ['tændʒəbl] *adjective* which is real or
noticeable; *have the anti-pollution measures had any*
tangible results?; there is no tangible evidence that he
was responsible; **tangible assets** = assets which are
visible, such as property, jewels, machines, etc.; *he*
does not seem to possess any tangible assets

tangle ['tæŋgl] **1** *noun* mass of threads, string, hair,
etc., all mixed together; *the tangle of shrubs in the*
back garden needs clearing; **in a tangle** = all mixed
up; *all my wool is in a tangle* **2** *verb* **(a)** to get things
mixed together in knots; *her hair is so tangled that it's*
impossible to comb **(b) to tangle with someone** = to
get into an argument with someone; *tourists are*
advised not to tangle with the police

tango ['tæŋgəʊ] *noun* South American dance for two
people, where you glide sideways; *couples were doing*
the tango; the band played a tango (NOTE: plural is
tangos)

tangy ['tæŋi] *adjective* with a sharp taste or smell; *the*
tangy smell of the sea; the cake had a tangy lemon
taste

tank [tæŋk] *noun* **(a)** large container for liquids; *how*
much oil is left in the tank?; **petrol tank** = container
built into a car, for holding petrol; **water tank** = tank
for holding water **(b)** armoured vehicle with caterpillar
tracks and powerful guns; *tanks rolled along the main*
streets of the town

tankard ['tæŋkəd] *noun* large metal mug for drinking
beer; *in this club, they serve beer in silver tankards*

tanker ['tæŋkə] *noun* ship or lorry for carrying
liquids, especially oil; *an oil tanker ran onto the rocks*
in the storm; a petrol tanker broke down on the
motorway

tanned [tænd] *adjective* with skin which has been
burnt brown by the sun; *my white legs looked out of*
place among all the tanned bodies on the beach

tanner ['tænə] *noun* person who makes animal skins
into leather; *the tanner hung the animal skins up to*
dry

tannery ['tænri] *noun* factory where skins are made
into leather; *from the roof you could see the vats of the*
tannery (NOTE: plural is **tanneries**)

tannoy ['tænɔɪ] *noun* trademark for a public
loudspeaker system; *the tannoy gave details of special*
offers in the fruit department; they warned over the
tannoy that train services would be delayed

tantalize ['tæntəlaɪz] *verb* to tease someone by
offering them something which they can't have; *the*
little boys were tantalized by the apples hanging just
out of reach

tantalizing ['tæntəlaɪzɪŋ] *adjective* which makes
you want it; *a tantalizing bunch of grapes hung down*
over the wall; the tantalizing smell of fresh bread
coming out of the baker's shop

tantamount ['tæntəmaʊnt] *adjective* **to be tantamount to** = to be the equivalent to in a negative way; *it was tantamount to a declaration of war*

tantrum ['tæntrəm] *noun* sudden attack of uncontrollable bad temper; *she had* or *she threw a tantrum and lay screaming on the carpet*

tap [tæp] **1** *noun* (a) device with a knob which, when you twist it, lets liquid or gas come out; *he washed his hands under the tap in the kitchen*; *she forgot to turn the gas tap off*; **tap water** = water which comes through pipes into a building and not from a well; *we haven't got any bottled water, will tap water be all right?*; **cold tap** = tap which produces cold water; **hot tap** = tap which produces hot water; **on tap** = available when you need it; *we should have all this information on tap*; **to turn a tap on** = to allow water to run; **to turn a tap off** = to stop water running (NOTE: American English is also **faucet**) (b) little knock; *as a signal, he gave three taps on the door* **2** *verb* (a) to hit something gently; *she tapped him on the knee with her finger*; *a policeman tapped him on the shoulder and arrested him* (b) to attach a secret listening device to a telephone line; *the police tapped his phone because they thought he was a spy* (c) to take liquid out of something; *they tap the rubber trees in the plantations*; *he's going down to the cellar to tap a new barrel of beer* (d) to take energy or resources and use them; *the resources of Northern Siberia have not yet been tapped*; *compare* UNTAPPED (NOTE: **tapping - tapped**)

tap-dancer ['tæp 'dɑːnsə] *noun* person who goes in for tap-dancing; *the last act was a group of South American tap-dancers*

tap-dancing ['tæp 'dɑːnsɪŋ] *noun* dancing with special shoes with metal heels and toes, so that the dancer dances vigorously and beats time to the music with his or her feet; *my daughter has tap-dancing classes every Monday*

tape [teɪp] **1** *noun* (a) long narrow strip of cloth, plastic, etc.; *she stitched tape along the bottom of the hem to stop it fraying*; **tape measure** or **measuring tape** = long strip of plastic marked in centimetres or inches, etc., used for measuring; *he took out a tape measure and measured the length of the table*; **sticky tape** = strip of plastic with glue on one side, used to stick things together, etc. (b) **magnetic tape** = special plastic tape on which sounds and pictures can be recorded, also used for recording computer data; **audio tape** = special magnetic tape on which sounds can be recorded; *she lent me her Beatles tape*; *I play a lot of tapes when I'm driving by myself*; **on tape** = recorded on magnetic tape; *we have the whole conversation on tape*; *see also* VIDEOTAPE **2** *verb* (a) to record something on tape or on video; *the whole conversation was taped by the police*; *I didn't see the programme because I was at work, but I've taped it* (b) to attach with sticky tape; *she taped up the box before taking it to the post office*

tape measure ['teɪp 'meʒə] *noun* measuring tape, a long strip marked in centimetres or inches, etc., used for measuring; *the tailor took out his tape measure to measure my waist*

taper ['teɪpə] **1** *noun* long thin candle, made of a wick covered with a thin layer of wax; *if you have a lot of candles to light, use a taper rather than wasting matches* **2** *verb* (a) to make something thinner at the end; *you will need to taper the piece of wood to make it fit into the hole* (b) to become thinner at the end; *her shoes taper to a point*; **to taper off** = to become less strong; *the fuss about the minister's wife seems to have tapered off*

tape-record ['teɪprɪkɔːd] *verb* to record something on audio tape; *I tape-recorded the concert*

tape-recorder ['teɪprɪ'kɔːdə] *noun* machine which is used to record sounds on magnetic tape and which can play back what has been recorded; *he recorded the conversation on his pocket tape-recorder*

tape-recording ['teɪprɪkɔːdɪŋ] *noun* recording done on tape; *they played back a tape-recording of the conversation*

tapestry ['tæpɪstri] *noun* (a) thick woven cloth with a picture or design, usually hung on walls or used to cover chairs; *the walls were hung with tapestries* (b) *(humorous)* **the rich tapestry of life** = life in all its varied forms; *being made manager one week and being switched back to your old job the next is all part of the rich tapestry of life in this office* (NOTE: plural is **tapestries**)

taps [tæps] *noun US* bugle call to put out lights, also played at military funerals (NOTE: the British equivalent is the **last post**)

tar [tɑː] **1** *noun* (a) thick hard black substance which comes from coal and is melted to use with sand to make road surfaces; *they were spreading tar and sand on the road*; *they spread a coating of tar on the roof to waterproof it* (b) similar black oily substance which comes from burning tobacco; *cigarettes with low tar* **2** *verb* to cover with melted tar; *a special machine for tarring roads* (NOTE: **tarring - tarred**)

target ['tɑːgɪt] **1** *noun* (a) object which you aim at with a gun, etc.; *his last shot missed the target altogether*; *she hit the target three times in all*; **target practice** = practising at shooting at a target; *he put an old tin can on top of the post and used it for target practice* (b) goal which you try to reach; **to set targets** = to fix amounts or quantities which workers have to produce; **to meet a target** = to produce the quantity of goods or sales which are expected; *we need to set targets for our salesmen to meet*; **to miss a target** = not to produce the amount of goods or sales which are expected; *the factory missed its production targets again this year*; **target language** = language which a student is learning, the language into which something is translated; **target market** = market to which a company is planning to sell its service **2** *verb* to aim at customers, possible markets, etc.; *the advertising campaign is targeting the student market*

tariff ['tærɪf] *noun* (a) tax to be paid for importing or exporting goods; **to impose a tariff on something** = to make a tax payable when you buy something; **to lift tariff barriers** = to reduce import taxes (b) list of prices for electricity, gas, water, etc.; *the new winter tariff will be introduced next week*

tarmac ['tɑːmæk] *noun* (a) hard road surface made of tar mixed with small stones; *the sun was so hot, the tarmac was starting to melt* (b) runway of an airport; *the snow ploughs were working flat out to clear the snow from the tarmac*

tarnish ['tɑːnɪʃ] *verb* (a) *(of metal)* to become discoloured; *silver tarnishes easily in contact with the air* (b) to ruin a reputation; *the sex scandal has irreparably tarnished his reputation as a politician*

tarot ['tærəʊ] *noun* special set of cards with pictures on them, used in telling fortunes; *the fortune-teller placed the tarot cards on the table*

> COMMENT: originally from the Middle East or Far East, tarot cards have been used by fortune-tellers for many centuries. A modern set of cards consists of a series of picture cards with figures on them (the Emperor, the Pope, the Hanged Man, the Fool, etc.) and a set of cards similar to modern playing cards in four suits. The fortune-teller deals cards and interprets them according to the way they appear on the table. Tarot cards were the originals of the modern playing cards

tarpaulin [tɑːˈpɔːlɪn] *noun* piece of thick waterproof canvas, used to cover things left in the open; *they put a tarpaulin over the trailer*

tarragon ['tærəgən] *noun* herb used often with chicken and to make sauces

tarsal bones ['tɑːsəl 'bəʊnz] *noun* group of seven little bones in the ankle; *the seven tarsal bones are part of the total of twenty-six bones in the human foot* (NOTE: also called by their Latin name **tarsus**)

tart [tɑːt] **1** *noun* **(a)** small pie with a sweet filling; *an apple tart* **(b)** *(informal)* prostitute **2** *adjective* **(a)** bitter, sour; *these apples are very tart* **(b)** sharp and sarcastic; *he gave her a very tart reply* (NOTE: **tarter - tartest**) **3** *verb* **to tart something up** = to make something look smarter, but in a tasteless way; *the new management has tarted up the restaurant and increased all the prices*

tartan ['tɑːtən] *noun* **(a)** cloth woven into a special pattern for one of the Scottish clans; *she wore a tartan kilt; (informal)* **the tartan army** = Scottish football supporters **(b)** distinctive pattern in such a cloth, worn by members of a Scottish clan; *my Scottish grandmother gave me a rug with the Mackay tartan on it or a Mackay tartan rug*

tartar sauce ['tɑːtə 'sɔːs] *noun* sauce made of mayonnaise with chopped olives and herbs, served with fish

task [tɑːsk] *noun* **(a)** job of work which has to be done; *there are many tasks which need to be done in the garden; he had the unpleasant task of telling his mother about it* **(b)** **to take someone to task for** = to criticize someone for; *she took him to task for not cleaning the bathroom*

task force ['tɑːsk 'fɔːs] *noun* special group of people chosen to carry out a difficult task; *they sent in a task force to sort out the problem school*

taste [teɪst] **1** *noun* **(a)** one of the five senses, by which you can tell differences of flavour between things you eat, using your tongue; *I've got a cold, so I've lost all sense of taste* **(b)** flavour of something that you eat or drink; *the pudding has a funny or strange taste; do you like the taste of garlic?; this milk shake has no taste at all* **(c)** being able to appreciate things that are beautiful; *my taste in music is quite different from hers; I don't share his taste for bright green shirts; she showed great taste in furnishing her dining room;* **to someone's taste** = in a way that someone likes; *modern jazz is not to everyone's taste* **2** *verb* **(a)** to notice the taste of something with your tongue; *can you taste the onions in this soup?; she's got a cold so she can't taste anything* **(b)** to have a certain taste; *this*

cake tastes of soap; what is this green stuff? - it tastes like cabbage; the pudding tastes very good **(c)** to try something to see if you like it; *would you like to taste the wine; she asked if she could taste the cheese before buying it*

tasteful ['teɪstfʊl] *adjective* showing good taste; *the decorations for the wedding are tasteful but not very imaginative*

tasteless ['teɪstləs] *adjective* **(a)** with no special flavour; *frozen chicken can be quite tasteless unless you add herbs to it* **(b)** showing bad taste; *she made some tasteless remark about her mother's dress*

taster ['teɪstə] *noun* person whose job is to taste food to test its quality; *he likes his job as a food taster with a big supermarket*

tasty ['teɪsti] *adjective* with a specially pleasant taste; *I liked that pie - it was very tasty* (NOTE: **tastier - tastiest**)

ta-ta [tə'tɑː] *interjection (informal)* goodbye (NOTE: used mainly in the north of England)

tattered ['tætəd] *adjective* torn and old; *it's about time you threw away that tattered old raincoat and bought a new one; the tattered remains of a flag flew from the flagpole*

tattoo [tə'tuː] **1** *noun* **(a)** decoration on skin made by pricking with a needle and putting colour into the wound; *she has a little tattoo of a rose on her left shoulder* **(b)** military parade; *crowds went to see the tattoo last night* **2** *verb* to make decorations on someone's skin by pricking it and putting colour into the wound; *she has had a little rose tattooed on her left shoulder*

taught [tɔːt] *see* TEACH

taunt [tɔːnt] **1** *noun* sarcastic jeering; *she disregarded the taunts of the other secretaries* **2** *verb* to jeer at someone sarcastically; *he taunted the minister with or about his financial problems*

Taurus ['tɔːrəs] *noun* one of the signs of the Zodiac, shaped like a bull; *if your birthday is May 1st, then you're (a) Taurus*

taut [tɔːt] *adjective* stretched tight; *turn the handle until the rope becomes quite taut; his face was taut with concentration*

tauten ['tɔːtn] *verb* **(a)** to stretch tight; *you must tauten the canvas on the frame before you start to paint* **(b)** to become tight; *the ropes tautened as they became wet*

tavern ['tævən] *noun* inn, public house; *Shakespeare's Falstaff was often to be found drinking in a tavern*

tawdry ['tɔːdri] *adjective* cheap and in bad taste; *the market was full of stands selling tawdry jewellery* (NOTE: **tawdrier - tawdriest**)

tax [tæks] **1** *noun* **(a)** money taken by the government from incomes, sales, etc., to pay for government services; *the government is planning to introduce a tax on food; you must pay your tax on the correct date; the newspaper headline says 'TAXES TO GO UP';* **airport tax** = tax added to the price of an air ticket to cover the cost of running an airport; **income tax** = tax which is paid according to how much you earn; *income tax is deducted from your salary every month;* **value added tax (VAT)** = tax on goods and services, added as a percentage to the invoiced sales price; *see also*

ROAD TAX **(b) exclusive of tax** = not including tax; **inclusive of tax** = including tax; *all prices are shown inclusive of value added tax* (NOTE: plural is **taxes**) **2** *verb* **(a)** to put a tax on something *or* someone; *income is taxed at 25%* **(b)** to pay tax on something; *the car is for sale, taxed till next April* **(c)** to demand a great deal; *moving all this furniture taxed her strength* **(d)** *(formal)* **to tax someone with something** = to accuse someone of doing something; *she taxed him with neglecting her*

taxable ['tæksəbl] *adjective* which can be taxed; *all taxable income must be declared to the Inland Revenue*; *all income above a certain level is taxable*

taxation [tæk'seɪʃn] *noun* action of imposing taxes; *money raised by taxation pays for all government services*; **direct taxation** = taxes (such as income tax) which are paid direct to the government; **indirect taxation** = taxes (such as VAT) which are added to the price of goods and not paid directly to the government

tax avoidance ['tæks ə'vɔɪdəns] *noun* trying legally to minimize the amount of tax you have to pay; *tax avoidance, as opposed to tax evasion, is not illegal*

tax break ['tæks 'breɪk] *noun* special legal way of avoiding tax; *the government gives tax breaks to investors*

tax disk ['tæks 'dɪsk] *noun* round piece of paper which is attached to a car windscreen to show that you have paid tax on the car for the current year; *you need to have a valid MOT certificate to get a tax disk for your car if it is more than three years old*

tax evasion ['tæks ɪ'veɪʒn] *noun* illegally trying not to pay tax; *he was accused of tax evasion*

tax-free ['tæksfriː] *adjective* with no tax payable; *he has been offered a tax-free post in the European Union*

tax haven ['tæks 'heɪvən] *noun* place where taxes are low, encouraging companies to set up their main offices and people to go and live there

taxi ['tæksi] *noun* car which you can hire with a driver; *can you call a taxi to take me to the airport?*; *why aren't there any taxis at the station today?*; *there are no buses on Sunday afternoons, so we had to take a taxi to the party* (NOTE: also often called a **cab** and sometimes **taxicab**) **2** *verb (of an aircraft)* to go slowly along the ground before taking off or after landing; *the aircraft taxied out onto the runway*

taxicab ['tæksikæb] *see* TAXI

taxi driver ['tæksi 'draɪvə] *noun* person who drives a taxi; *the taxi driver helped me with my luggage*

taxi rank ['tæksi 'ræŋk] *noun* place in the street where taxis can wait; *there's a taxi rank just outside the hotel*

taxpayer ['tækspeɪə] *noun* person who pays tax, especially income tax; *I don't think the government's plan will be very popular with taxpayers*

tax point ['tæks 'pɔɪnt] *noun* date on which goods are supplied and VAT becomes chargeable

tax relief ['tæks rɪ'liːf] *noun* allowing someone to pay less tax because of other payments he or she is making, such as interest on a mortgage; *you get tax relief on payments into a pension fund*; *there's full tax relief on mortgage interest payments*

tax return ['tæks rɪ'tɜːn] *noun* form to be filled in to report your earnings and allowances to the tax office; *tomorrow is the final date for sending in your tax return*

tax year ['tæks 'jeə] *noun* twelve-month period on which taxes are calculated (in the UK, 6th April to 5th April of the following year); *what was your income from freelance work during the 1997/98 tax year?*

TB ['tiː biː] = TUBERCULOSIS; *outbreaks of TB have started to reappear in Europe*

tea [tiː] *noun* **(a)** drink made from hot water which has been poured onto the dried leaves of a tropical plant; *can I have another cup of tea or some more tea?*; *I don't like tea - can I have coffee instead?* **(b)** a cup of tea; *can we have two teas and two cakes, please* **(c)** the dried leaves of a tropical plant used to make a warm drink; *we've run out of tea, can you put it on your shopping list?*; *put a spoonful of tea into the pot and add boiling water* **(d)** dried leaves or flowers of other plants, used to make a drink; *mint tea* **(e) (afternoon) tea** = afternoon meal at which you drink tea and eat bread, cake, etc.; *why don't you come for tea tomorrow?*; *the children have had their tea*; *we've been asked out to tea by my sister or my sister has asked us to tea*; *tea is served at 4 o'clock in the hotel lounge*; **cream tea** = afternoon tea, with scones, thick cream and jam **(f)** *(in the North of England and Scotland)* **(high) tea** = early evening meal; *they arrived just in time for tea*; *I'm having a baked potato for my tea*; *see also the note at* HIGH TEA (NOTE: generally no plural: **teas** means **cups of tea**, or **meals**)

tea bag ['tiː 'bæg] *noun* small paper bag with tea in it which you put into the pot with hot water

teacake ['tiːkeɪk] *noun* type of little bun with raisins in it, usually toasted and eaten hot with butter; *we ordered toasted teacakes*

teach [tiːtʃ] *verb* **(a)** to give lessons, to show someone how to do something; *she taught me how to dance*; *he teaches maths in the local school*; *she taught herself to type*; *who taught her to swim?* **(b)** *(informal)* **to teach someone a lesson** = to punish someone for doing something wrong; *I locked up her bike - it will teach her a lesson not to go out when she should be doing her homework*; *that'll teach you* = that will be a punishment for you; *that'll teach you for forgetting to do the washing up* (NOTE: **teaching - taught** [tɔːt])

teacher ['tiːtʃə] *noun* person who teaches, especially in a school; *Mr Jones is our maths teacher*; *the French teacher is ill today*; *he trained as a primary school teacher*; *see also* PET

teaching ['tiːtʃɪŋ] *noun* **(a)** work of being a teacher, of giving lessons; *the report praised the high standard of teaching at the college*; *he was working in a bank, but has decided to go into teaching instead*; **the teaching profession** = all teachers, taken as a group; *the teaching profession is often blamed by parents if their children do badly at school* **(b) teachings** = political or moral ideas which are taught; *Christianity is based on the life and teachings of Jesus Christ*; *the teachings of Gandhi*

teacloth ['tiːklɒθ] *noun* cloth which you use for drying plates, dishes, etc.

tea cosy ['eg 'kəʊzi] *noun* cover put over a teapot to keep it hot; *she knitted a tea cosy for her mother* (NOTE: plural is **tea cosies**)

teacup ['tiːkʌp] *noun* cup for drinking tea out of; *she put the teacups and saucers out on a tray* *(informal)*

storm in a teacup = lot of fuss about something which is not important

teak [tiːk] *noun* **(a)** hard wood of a tropical tree, which is resistant to water, and is used for making outdoor furniture, etc.; *we bought some teak furniture for the patio*; *the table is solid teak* **(b)** large tropical tree which produces this wood; *the teak forests of Indonesia*

tealeaf ['tiːliːf] *noun* little piece of a leaf of the tea plant, used to make tea; *there's a tealeaf floating in my cup*; *the fortune-teller looked at the tealeaves in his cup* (NOTE: plural is **tealeaves** ['tiːliːvz])

team [tiːm] **1** *noun* **(a)** group of people who play a game together; *there are eleven people in a football team and fifteen in a rugby team*; *he's a fan of the local football team*; *our college team played badly last Saturday* **(b)** group of people who work together; *they make a very effective team*; *in this job you have to be able to work as a member of a team*; **management team** = all the managers who work together in a company; **sales team** = all representatives, salesmen and sales managers working together in a company; *he has a sales team of twenty salesmen* (NOTE: the word **team** is singular, but can be followed by a singular or plural verb: **the team has** *or* **have come out of the pavilion**) **2** *verb* **to team up with someone** = to join someone to work together; *I teamed up with George to tackle the German project*

team-mate ['tiːmmeɪt] *noun* someone in the same team as you; *he gets on well with his team-mates*

team spirit ['tiːm 'spɪrɪt] *noun* feeling of loyalty to the team on the part of those who play or work together; *the players have trained together and their team spirit is excellent*

teamster ['tiːmstə] *noun US* truck driver; *the Teamsters' Union*

teamwork ['tiːmwɜːk] *noun* working together as a group; *the secret of their success is good teamwork*

teapot ['tiːpɒt] *noun* pot which is used for making tea in; *put two spoonfuls of tea into the teapot and add boiling water*

tear 1 *noun* **(a)** [tɪə] drop of salt water which forms in your eye when you cry; *tears were running down her cheeks*; **in tears** = crying; *all the family were in tears*; **she burst into tears** = she suddenly started crying **(b)** [teə] place where something has a hole in it from being torn; *can you mend the tear in my jeans?*; *see also* WEAR AND TEAR **2** [teə] *verb* **(a)** to make a hole in something by pulling; *he tore his trousers climbing over the fence*; *my anorak is torn - can it be mended?* **(b)** to pull something into bits; *he tore the letter in half*; *she tore up old newspapers to pack the cups and saucers* **(c)** to go very fast; *he tore across the platform, but just missed his train*; *she grabbed the dress and tore out of the shop* (NOTE: **tearing - tore** [tɔː] - **torn** [tɔːn])

tear down [teə 'daʊn] *verb* **(a)** to knock something down; *they tore down the old town hall and replaced it with a supermarket* **(b)** to remove a piece of paper or cloth which is hanging up; *the crowd tore down the posters of the president*; *the police tore down the opposition party's election posters*

tear duct ['tɪə 'dʌkt] *noun* tube which carries tears from the tear gland to the eye and the nose

tearful ['tɪəfʊl] *adjective* sad, crying; *they said a very tearful farewell to their grandparents*; *she was very tearful during the funeral service*

tear gas ['tɪə 'gæs] *noun* gas which makes your eyes burn, used by police to control crowds; *the police used tear gas to force the crowd to disperse*; *he threw a tear-gas grenade into the crowd*

tear gland ['tɪə 'glænd] *noun* gland which produces tears

tearoom ['tiːruːm] *noun* small restaurant which serves mainly tea, coffee, sandwiches, scones and cakes; *there's a tearoom attached to the baker's shop*

tease [tiːz] **1** *verb* to say or do something to annoy someone on purpose; *he teased her about her thick glasses*; *stop teasing that poor cat* **2** *noun (old)* person who teases; *he's such a tease*

teashop ['tiːʃɒp] *noun* small restaurant which serves mainly tea, coffee, sandwiches, scones and cakes; *our village teashop has the best chocolate cake I've ever tasted*

teaspoon ['tiːspuːn] *noun* **(a)** small spoon for stirring tea or other liquid; *can you bring me a teaspoon, please?* **(b)** the amount contained in a teaspoon; *I take one teaspoon of sugar in my coffee*

teaspoonful ['tiːspuːnfʊl] *noun* amount contained in a teaspoon; *just one teaspoonful of sugar, please*

teat [tiːt] *noun* **(a)** rubber cap on a baby's feeding bottle through which the baby sucks milk; *the baby's bottle and teat should be sterilized before each feed* (NOTE: also called **nipple** in American English) **(b)** nipple on a cow's udder through which the calf drinks milk; *a cow is milked by squeezing and pulling on the teats*

teatime ['tiːtaɪm] *noun* time when tea is served; *hurry up, it'll soon be teatime!*; *the children's TV programmes are on at teatime*

tea towel ['tiː 'taʊəl] *noun* cloth which you use for drying plates, dishes, etc.; *she wiped her hands on a tea towel and went to answer the phone*

tech [tek] *noun (informal)* technical college, further education college for older students and adults; *he's doing an engineering course at the local tech*

technical ['teknɪkl] *adjective* referring to industrial processes or practical work; *don't bother with the technical details of how the machine works, just tell me what it does*; *the instructions are too technical for the ordinary person to understand*; **technical college** = further education college for older students and adults, teaching technical skills and other subjects such as languages; **technical subjects** = practical skills taught in schools or colleges, such as car maintenance, woodwork, engineering, etc.; **technical term** = specialized term used in a particular science or industry

technicality [tekni'kælɪti] *noun* little unimportant detail which makes something happen; *their application to build a garage was rejected because of a technicality*

technically ['teknɪkli] *adverb* **(a)** in a technical way; *it's technically possible to make a light bulb that would never wear out* **(b) technically (speaking)** = according to the exact meaning; *technically he isn't a member of the club because he hasn't paid this year's subscription*

technician [tek'nɪʃn] *noun* person who is a specialist in a particular area of industry or science; *she's a computer technician*; *we have a team of technicians working on the project*; **laboratory technician** = person who deals with practical work in a laboratory

technique [tek'niːk] *noun* way of doing something; *he developed a new technique for processing steel*; *she has a specially effective technique for dealing with complaints from customers*

technocrat ['teknəkræt] *noun* person with particular technical skills, brought in to run a country or an organization; *the prime minister has appointed a group of technocrats to run the government*

technological [teknə'lɒdʒɪkl] *adjective* referring to technology; *the company has reported making an important technological breakthrough*

technologist [tek'nɒlədʒɪst] *noun* technical expert; *the government has asked a team of technologists to advise on the new telephone system*

technology [tek'nɒlədʒi] *noun* use or study of industrial or scientific skills; *we already have the technology to produce such a machine*; *the government has promised increased investment in science and technology*; **the introduction of new technology** = putting new electronic equipment into a business or industry; *see also* HIGH TECHNOLOGY, INFORMATION TECHNOLOGY

teddy (bear) ['tedɪ('beə)] *noun* child's toy bear; *she won't go to bed without her teddy bear*; *the little boy was clutching his old teddy*

tedious ['tiːdɪəs] *adjective* boring; *the lectures on medieval manuscripts are so tedious I have skipped most of them*; *filing invoices is a tedious job but it has to be done*

tediously ['tiːdɪəsli] *adverb* in a tedious way; *the meeting was tediously boring and a complete waste of time*

tedium ['tiːdɪəm] *noun* boredom, being boring; *there's nothing worse than being stuck in a huge traffic jam without even the car radio to relieve the tedium*

tee [tiː] **1** *noun* **(a)** raised grass area on a golf course where the ball is placed when you begin to play each hole; *he is walking towards the sixteenth tee* **(b)** little peg which is pushed into ground, on which the golf ball is placed to start playing a hole; *the ground is so hard I can hardly stick my tee in* **2** *verb* **to tee off** = to hit the ball from a tee; *at what time do we tee off?*

teem [tiːm] *verb* **(a)** to be full of something; *in spring the rivers are teeming with salmon*; *Oxford Street was teeming with shoppers* **(b)** *(informal)* **it's teeming (down)** = it's pouring with rain

teenage ['tiːneɪdʒ] *adjective* **(a)** *(also* **teenaged)** aged between 13 and 19; *he has two teenage(d) daughters* **(b)** referring to young people aged between 13 and 19; *the government is trying to deal with the problem of teenage crime*; *the teenage market for their records is enormous*

teenager ['tiːneɪdʒə] *noun* young person aged between 13 and 19; *most of the people who come to the club are teenagers*

teens [tiːnz] *noun* age between 13 and 19; *she joined the bank when she was still in her teens*

teeny ['tiːni] *adjective* *(informal)* very small; *there was just a teeny amount left in the bottom of the bottle*

teeny-bopper ['tiːni'bɒpə] *noun* *(informal)* teenaged girl pop fan

teeny-weeny ['tiːni'wiːni] *adjective* *(informal)* very, very small; *can I have a teeny-weeny bit more pudding, please?*; *the waist of this skirt needs to be a teeny-weeny bit bigger*

teeshirt *or* **T-shirt** ['tiːʃɜːt] *noun* light shirt with no buttons or collar, usually with short sleeves; *no wonder you're cold if you went out in just a teeshirt*; *she was wearing jeans and a teeshirt*

teeter ['tiːtə] *verb* to wobble, to be very unstable; *the little boys teetered dangerously on the top of the wall*; *the economy is teetering on the edge of a recession*; *she teetered along on her extremely high heels*

teeter(-totter) ['tiːtə(tɒtə)] *noun* US see SEESAW

teeth [tiːθ] *see* TOOTH

teethe [tiːð] *verb* **(a)** *(of a baby)* to have the first teeth starting to grow; *the baby wakes up at night because he is teething* **(b) teething problems** *or* **teething troubles** = problems which happen when a new process or system is being introduced; *we are experiencing some teething problems with the new software system*

teetotal [tiː'təʊtl] *adjective* who never drinks alcohol; *the family is strictly teetotal*

teetotaller *US* **teetotaler** [tiː'təʊtlə] *noun* person who never drinks alcohol; *she's a teetotaller*

tel = TELEPHONE

tele- ['teliː] *prefix meaning* over a distance

telecommunications [telɪkəmjuːnɪ'keɪʃnz] *noun* communication system using telephone, radio, TV, satellites, etc.; *thanks to modern telecommunications, the information can be sent to our office in Japan in seconds* (NOTE: also shortened to **telecoms**)

telegram ['telɪgræm] *noun* message sent by telegraph; *we sent a telegram to my grandmother on her birthday*; *she received a telegram from the office*

telegraph ['telɪgrɑːf] **1** *noun* **(a)** system of sending messages along wires; *the order telling him to return home was sent by telegraph*; **telegraph line** *or* **telegraph wire** = wire along which telegraph messages are sent; *telegraph lines had been brought down by the storm*; **telegraph pole** = pole which holds up a telephone line; *telegraph poles were snapped off in the storm* **(b)** *(informal)* **the bush telegraph** = information which is passed by chatting, usually on the phone; *I heard the news on the bush telegraph* **2** *verb* to send a message by telegraph; *they telegraphed him to tell him to return immediately*; *can you telegraph the money to our office in Australia?*

telegrapher [tə'legrəfə] *noun* = TELEGRAPHIST

telegraphic [telɪ'græfɪk] *adjective* referring to a telegraph system; **telegraphic address** = short address to which telegrams are sent; **telegraphic transfer** = system of sending money from one bank account to another by telegraph; *the bank charges a flat fee of £10 per telegraphic transfer*

telegraphist [tə'legrəfɪst] *noun* person who sends messages by telegraph; *my sister trained as an army telegraphist*

telegraphy [tə'legrəfi] *noun* *(old, formal)* sending messages by telegraph; *he was trained in telegraphy*

telepathic [telɪ'pæθɪk] *adjective* (a) referring to telepathy; *she said she could receive telepathic messages from members of the audience* (b) appearing to know what other people are thinking; *how did you know I like yellow roses - you must be telepathic!*

telepathy [tə'lepəθi] *noun* sending thoughts or mental images from one person to another without using the senses; *she uses telepathy to communicate with the audience*

telephone ['telɪfəʊn] 1 *noun* machine which you use to speak to someone who is some distance away; *can't someone answer the telephone - it's been ringing and ringing; I was in the garden when you called, but by the time I got to the house the telephone had stopped ringing; she lifted the telephone and called the ambulance;* by telephone = using the telephone; *he booked his plane ticket by telephone; she reserved a table by telephone* 2 *verb* to call someone using a telephone; *your wife telephoned when you were out; can you telephone me at ten o'clock tomorrow evening?; I need to telephone our office in New York* (NOTE: telephone is often shortened to phone: phone call, phone book, etc., but not in the expressions telephone switchboard, telephone operator, telephone exchange)

◊ **on the telephone** ['ɒn ðə 'telɪfəʊn] (a) speaking by telephone; *don't make such a noise - Daddy's on the telephone; William! - there's someone on the telephone who wants to speak to you; the receptionist is on the telephone all the time* (b) with a telephone in the house; *don't look for their address in the phone book - their cottage isn't on the telephone*

telephone book *or* telephone directory
['telɪfəʊn 'bʊk or daɪ'rektəri] *noun* book which gives the names of people in a town in alphabetical order with their addresses and telephone numbers; *the restaurant must be new - it isn't in the telephone book; look up his number in the telephone directory* (NOTE: is often shortened to phone book)

telephone box ['telɪfəʊn 'bɒks] *noun* shelter with windows round it containing a public telephone; *call me from the telephone box outside the station, and I'll come and pick you up; there was a queue of people waiting to use the telephone box* (NOTE: often shortened to phone box)

telephone number ['telɪfəʊn 'nʌmbə] *noun* number of one particular telephone; *what's the telephone number of the garage?; his telephone number's Birmingham 987 1234* (NOTE: is often shortened to phone number)

> COMMENT: British telephone numbers are formed of a town or area code followed by the number of the actual telephone. Area codes always start with 0, and may have three further digits for large towns (Central London is 0171, Liverpool is 0151) or several digits for smaller towns (Oxford is 01865). Numbers for the actual telephones are usually seven digits. These are spoken as area code + three + four: so 0181 943 1673 is spoken as 'oh one eight one, nine four three, one six seven three'

telephonist [tə'lefənɪst] *noun* person who works a telephone switchboard; *she works as a telephonist at a local insurance company; there's nobody on the switchboard, the telephonist has been taken ill*

telephoto lens [telɪ'fəʊtəʊ 'lenz] *noun* large lens for a camera, which gives a picture of something which is some distance away; *the picture was taken from three hundred feet away using a telephoto lens*

telescope ['telɪskəʊp] *noun* tube with a series of lenses for looking at objects which are very far away; *with a telescope you can see the ships very clearly; he discovered a comet using the telescope in his back garden;* optical telescope = telescope which uses mirrors and lenses to magnify enormously the image and light coming from stars; radio telescope = telescope which uses radio waves to detect stars and other objects in the universe

telescopic [telɪ'skɒpɪk] *adjective* (a) referring to a telescope; *a sniper's rifle has telescopic sights* (b) with parts which slide together like a telescope; *the radio has a telescopic aerial; a telescopic umbrella should be small enough to fit into your bag*

televise ['telɪvaɪz] *verb* to broadcast something by television; *some of the debates in parliament are now televised;* the show is being televised live = the show is being broadcast as it takes place, and not recorded and broadcast later

television (TV) [telɪ'vɪʒən] *noun* (a) sound and pictures which are sent through the air or along cables and appear on a special machine; *we don't watch television every night - some nights we go to the pub; is there any football on television tonight?; Saturday evening television programmes are never very interesting; he stayed in his room all evening, watching television;* cable television = television system, where pictures are sent by cable (b) piece of electrical equipment which shows television pictures; *we can't watch anything - our television has broken down; switch off the television - that programme's stupid; when my husband comes home in the evening he just pours himself a beer, turns on the television and goes to sleep* (NOTE: television is often written or spoken as TV ['ti: 'vi:])

television set [telɪ'vɪʒn 'set] *noun* piece of electrical equipment which shows television pictures; *my father has bought a new television set*

telex ['teleks] 1 *noun* (a) message sent using telephone lines and a special printer; *have you seen the telex that has just come in?* (NOTE: plural in this meaning is telexes) (b) system of sending messages this way; *the order came by telex* 2 *verb* to send a message to someone, using telephone lines and a special printer; *can you telex the Canadian office before they open?*

tell [tel] *verb* (a) to communicate something to someone, for example a story or a joke; *she told me a long story about how she got lost in London; I don't think they are telling the truth* (b) to give information to someone; *the policeman told them how to get to the post office; he told the police that he had seen the accident take place; don't tell my mother you saw me at the pub; nobody told us about the picnic* (c) to tell someone what to do = to give someone instructions; *the teacher told the children to stand in a line; give a shout to tell us when to start* (d) to notice; *he can't tell the difference between butter and margarine; you can tell he is embarrassed when his face goes red* (NOTE: telling - told [təʊld])

teller ['telə] *noun* (a) clerk in a bank who takes in money or pays it out to customers; *the teller told me* *that I couldn't cash the cheque* (b) MP who counts votes in the House of Commons

telling ['telɪŋ] *adjective* which has a certain effect; *when he asked the question there was a telling silence before anyone answered*

tellingly ['telɪŋli] *adverb* in a telling way; *tellingly, he refused to answer some questions at the tribunal*

tell off ['tel 'ɒf] *verb (informal)* to speak to someone angrily about something wrong he has done; *the students were told off for being late*; *the teacher will tell you off if you don't do your homework*

telltale ['telteɪl] *adjective* which shows something; *those marks on his arm are telltale signs of drug addiction*

telly ['teli] *noun (informal)* television; *is there anything on the telly tonight?*; *the telly's broken down again - when are you going to buy a new one?*

temp [temp] **1** *noun (informal) short for* temporary secretary; *we have two temps working in the office this week* **2** *verb (informal)* to work as a temp; *she has done some temping jobs*; *I'm temping for the moment until I can find something permanent*

temper ['tempə] **1** *noun* (a) state of becoming angry; *you have to learn to control your temper*; *he has a violent temper*; *she got into a temper* (b) general calm state of mind; *he lost his temper* = he became very angry; *she tried to keep her temper* = she tried to stay calm and not get angry **2** *verb* (a) *(formal)* to temper something with = to make something have a less harsh effect; *we try to temper the strict prison regime with sports and other recreational activities* (b) to make a metal hard by heating and cooling; *a tempered steel blade*

temperament ['tempramant] *noun* nature of a person; *she has an artistic temperament*

temperamental [tempra'mentəl] *adjective* (a) like to have bad moods, likely to be in a bad temper for no particular reason; *the chef has a reputation for being temperamental* (b) *(humorous)* likely to break down; *our washing machine's a bit temperamental*

temperate ['temprət] *adjective* (a) which is neither very hot nor very cold; *the temperate forests of northern Europe have been badly affected by acid rain*; *temperate climate* = climate where the summers are not very hot and the winters are not very cold; *these plants do well in temperate climates* (b) *(formal)* sober, not given to drinking much alcohol; *he's a man of temperate habits and would be ideally suited to the post of church caretaker*

temperature ['temprətʃə] *noun* (a) heat measured in degrees; *the temperature of water in the swimming pool is 25°*; *temperatures in the Arctic can be very low*; *I can't start the car when the temperature is below zero*; *put the thermometer in the patient's mouth - I want to take her temperature* (b) illness where your body is hotter than normal; *she's off work with a temperature*; *the doctor says he's got a temperature and has to stay in bed*

-tempered ['tempəd] *suffix meaning* having a certain temper; *he's a good-tempered little boy*; *the boss is in one of his bad-tempered moods today*

temple ['templ] *noun* (a) building for worship, usually Hindu or Buddhist, or ancient Greek or Roman, but not Christian or Muslim; *we visited the Greek temples on the islands* (b) flat part of the side of the head between the top of the ear and the eye; *he had a bruise on his right temple*

tempo ['tempəʊ] *noun* (a) rhythm, beat of music, etc.; *the tempo of the band speeded up as midnight approached* (b) speed at which something happens; *he found it difficult to keep up with the tempo of life in the City* (NOTE: plural is **tempos**, and **tempi** ['tempi:] for music)

temporal ['temprəl] *adjective (formal)* (a) referring to the temple, to the flat part of the side of the head near the forehead; *there are two temporal bones, one on each side of the skull*; *temporal lobe* = the rounded part of the brain above each ear (b) referring to this world, not the spiritual world; *the state is concerned with only temporal matters, not with spiritual ones* (c) *(formal)* referring to time; *human beings have a limited temporal existence*

temporarily ['temprərəli] *adverb* for a short time only; *he's temporarily out of work*; *train services have been temporarily interrupted while the track is being repaired*

temporary ['temprəri] *adjective* which is not permanent, only lasting a short time; *she has a temporary job with a construction company*; *this arrangement is only temporary*; **temporary employment** = work which does not last for more than a few months; **temporary staff** = staff who are appointed for a short time; *we usually hire about twenty temporary staff during the Christmas period*

tempt [temt] *verb* (a) to try to persuade someone to do something, especially something pleasant or wrong; *can I tempt you to have another cream cake?*; *they tried to tempt him to leave his job and work for them* (b) **to be tempted to** = to feel like doing something; *he was tempted to send the food back to the kitchen*; *I am tempted to accept their offer* (c) **to tempt providence** *or* **to tempt fate** = to take a great risk; *it would be tempting providence to buy that car without having had it checked by a garage*

temptation [tem'teɪʃn] *noun* being tempted; thing which attracts; *putting chocolates near the cash desk is just a temptation for little children*; *the temptation is just to do nothing and hope the problem will simply go away*

tempting ['temptɪŋ] *adjective* which attracts; *a tempting offer of work in California*; *those cream cakes look very tempting*; *it is tempting just to say nothing and hope no one will notice*

ten [ten] (a) number 10; *in the market they're selling ten oranges for two dollars*; *she's ten (years old) next week*; *the next plane for Paris leaves at 10 (o'clock) in the evening*; **the ten hundreds (1000s)** = the years from 1000 to 1099 (NOTE: compare **the tenth century**) (b) *(informal)* **ten to one** = very likely; *ten to one he finds out about the payment* (c) *(informal)* **tens** = £10 notes; *he gave me two twenties and four tens*

tenacious [tɪ'neɪʃəs] *adjective* (a) holding on tightly to something, determined to have your own way; *we have to deal with several very tenacious tenants* (b) holding on to an idea tightly; *her tenacious belief in socialist principles*

tenaciously [tɪ'neɪʃəsli] *adverb* in a tenacious way; *he clung tenaciously to his old belief in Communist principles*

tenacity [tɪ'næsɪti] *noun* being determined to do something; *he showed great tenacity in continuing with his work*

tenancy ['tenənsi] *noun* period during which a tenant has an agreement to rent a property; *we have signed a two-year tenancy agreement*

tenant ['tenənt] *noun* person *or* company that rents a room, flat, house, office, land, etc., in which to live or work; *the previous tenants left the flat in a terrible state*; **sitting tenant** = person who is living in a property and paying rent for it when the property is sold; *he bought the flat with a sitting tenant in it*

tend [tend] *verb* **(a)** to look after something; *his job is to tend the flower beds in front of the town hall* **(b)** to **tend to do something** = to be likely to do something; *she tends to lose her temper very easily* **(c)** to **tend towards something** = to lean in a certain direction; *he's certainly not a Conservative - if anything, he tends towards the Liberals*

tendency ['tendənsi] *noun* way in which someone *or* something is likely to act; *the photocopier has a tendency to break down if you try to do too many copies at the same time*; *he has an unfortunate tendency to sit in a corner and go to sleep at parties*

tender ['tendə] **1** *adjective* **(a)** (food) which is easy to cut or chew; *a plate of tender young beans*; **tender meat** = which can be chewed or cut easily; *the meat was so tender, you hardly needed a knife to cut it* (NOTE: the opposite is **tough**) **(b)** delicate, easily damaged; *the baby has very tender skin* **(c)** showing love; *the plants need a lot of tender loving care* **(d)** which cannot stand frost; *keep the tender seedlings in the greenhouse until June* **2** *noun* **(a)** **legal tender** = coins or notes which can be legally used; *old pound notes are no longer legal tender in England* (NOTE: no plural in this meaning) **(b)** offer to do something at a certain price; **to put in a tender** *or* **to submit a tender for a job** = to offer to do work at a certain price **(c)** (old) coal wagon attached to a steam engine **3** *verb* **(a)** **to tender for a job** = to offer to do work at a certain price; *the company is tendering for a construction job in Saudi Arabia* **(b)** (formal) to offer; *he tendered his resignation* **(c)** (formal) to offer money; *please tender the correct fare*

tenderhearted [tendə'hɑːtɪd] *adjective* kind to others; *he is too tenderhearted to be a personnel manager*

tendon ['tendən] *noun* piece of strong tissue which attaches a muscle to a bone; *he strained a tendon and had to drop out of the race*

tenement ['tenəmənt] *noun* large old building which is divided into flats; *they are proposing to demolish some tenement buildings and replace them with a housing estate*

tenner ['tenə] *noun* (informal) ten pound note; *I offered him a tenner for it and he refused*

tennis ['tenɪs] *noun* **(a)** game for two or four players who use rackets to hit a ball backwards and forwards over a net; *he's joined the local tennis club*; *would you like a game of tennis?*; *I won the last two tennis matches I played*; *tennis players have to be fit*; **tennis ball** = ball for playing tennis; *that onion's the size of a tennis ball*; **tennis court** = specially marked area for playing tennis; **tennis racket** = racket used to play tennis; **tennis shoes** = special light shoes worn when playing tennis (NOTE: also formally called **lawn tennis** to

distinguish it from **real tennis**) **(b)** **real tennis** = original medieval form of tennis, played by two players inside a court with high walls

COMMENT: A game starts with the server standing behind the baseline and hitting the ball over the net; this is the only time during a rally when the ball must bounce before being hit. The odd way of counting the score originated with the ancient game of real tennis: the first point won by a player is 15, the second 30 and the third 40; a fourth point wins the game unless the score reaches 40 - 40 ('deuce'); after the next point, the umpire calls 'advantage' to the server or receiver (depending on who has won the point), and if they also win the next point, they win the game; if not, the score reverts to deuce. The first player to win 6 games wins the 'set' unless the score reaches 5 - 5 in which case a player must win the next two games to win the set; if the score reaches 6 - 6, a 'tie-break' comes into operation. A men's match is played over the best of 3 or 5 sets; women's and mixed doubles competitions are always played over the best of 3 sets

tenor ['tenə] **1** *noun* **(a)** man who sings with the highest male voice; *the tenors start the song, followed by the sopranos* **(b)** (formal) general meaning; *we were upset by the threatening tenor of his speech* **(c)** (formal) general way of doing something; *the dangerous tenor of life in the refugee camps* **2** *adjective* with a high pitch, similar to that of a tenor; *he plays the tenor saxophone*; *he has a pleasant tenor voice*

ten-pin bowling ['ten 'pɪn 'bəʊlɪŋ] *noun* game where you roll a large ball and try to knock down ten targets, shaped like bottles; *we went ten-pin bowling after work* (NOTE: the same game as **skittles**)

tense [tens] **1** *adjective* nervous and worried; *I always get tense before going to a job interview*; *the atmosphere in the hall was tense as everyone waited for the result of the vote* (NOTE: **tenser - tensest**) **2** *noun* (grammar) form of a verb which shows the time when the action takes place; **future tense** = form of a verb which shows a time in the future; **past tense** = form of a verb which shows a time in the past; **present tense** = form of a verb which shows the time we are in now; *the present tense of 'to sit' is 'he sits' or 'he is sitting'; the future tense is 'he will sit' or 'he will be sitting'; the past tense is 'he sat' or 'he was sitting'* **3** *verb* to become nervous and worried; *he tensed suddenly, as he heard a footstep outside*

tension ['tenʃn] *noun* **(a)** being tight; *you need to adjust the tension in your tennis racket* **(b)** state of nervous anxiety; *tension built up as we waited for the result* **(c)** state of hostility between countries or races; *there is tension in the area caused by fighting between tribes*

tent [tent] *noun* shelter made of cloth, held up by poles and attached to the ground with ropes; *we went camping in the Alps and took our tent in the back of the car*; *their tent was blown away by the wind*; *the flower show was held in a tent in the grounds of the castle*; **to pitch a tent** = to put up a tent; *we pitched our tent in a field by a little mountain stream*

tentacle ['tentəkl] *noun* long arm with suckers, such as that of an octopus; *in the story, an octopus catches the little boat in its tentacles*

tentative ['tentətɪv] *adjective* which has been suggested but not accepted, done in an uncertain way because you are not sure what will happen; *this is only a tentative suggestion*; *we suggested Wednesday May 10th as a tentative date for the wedding*; **tentative proposal** = proposal made to find out what the response is; *we put forward a tentative proposal for the committee to consider*

tentatively ['tentətɪvli] *adverb* in a tentative way; *they tentatively suggested Wednesday as the date for our next lunch*

tenth (10th) [tenθ] *adjective & noun* the tenth of April *or* April the tenth (April 10th) *that's the tenth phone call I've had this morning*; *we spend a tenth of our income on food*; **the tenth century** = the period from 900 to 999 (NOTE: compare **the ten hundreds**; Note also that with dates **tenth** is usually written **10th: July 10th, 1935; April 10th, 1991** (American style is **April 10, 1991**), say 'the tenth of April' or 'April the tenth' (American style is 'April tenth'); with names of kings and queens **tenth** is usually written **X: King Charles X** (say: 'King Charles the Tenth'))

tenuous ['tenjuəs] *adjective* not strong, very slight; *the evidence linking him to the crime is still very tenuous*

tenure ['tenjə] *noun* **(a)** right to hold property or a position; *freehold farmers have tenure of their land*; **security of tenure** = right to keep a job or rented accommodation, provided certain conditions are met; *the contract guarantees security of tenure* **(b)** period when you hold an office; *during his tenure as honorary secretary* **(c)** *(in a college or university)* right to hold a job permanently; *he's on a contract but hopes to get tenure next year*

tepid ['tepɪd] *adjective* **(a)** slightly warm; *there was no hot water left so my bath was only tepid*; *she had a long phone call during dinner and when she came back the food on her plate was tepid*; *there's only a bit of coffee left in your mug and it's probably tepid* **(b)** not very enthusiastic; *his tepid reaction to my great plan disappointed me* (NOTE: means the same as **lukewarm**)

term [tɜːm] **1** *noun* **(a)** official length of time; *his term as President was marked by a lot of disagreement*; *she was sent to prison for a term of three years*; **in the long term** = for a long period from now; **in the short term** = for a short period from now; *in the long term, this investment should be very profitable*; **term of office** = period of time when someone has a position; *during his term of office as President; see also* LONG-TERM, SHORT-TERM **(b)** one of the parts of a school or university year; *a school year has three terms: autumn, spring and summer*; *cricket is played during the summer term only, and football in both the autumn and spring terms*; *the autumn term ends on December 15th*; *next term I'll be starting to learn the piano*; **half-term** = short holiday in the middle of a school term; *we took a few days' holiday at half-term* **(c)** word or phrase which has a particular meaning; *he used several technical terms which I didn't understand*; *some people use 'ducks' as a term of affection* *see also* TERMS **2** *verb (formal)* to call something by a certain word; *you say it is acceptable behaviour - I would term it a disgrace*

terminal ['tɜːmɪnl] **1** *adjective* **(a)** in the last period of a fatal illness; *he has terminal cancer*; **terminal illness** = illness from which the patient will soon die **(b)** at the

end; **terminal shoot** = shoot at the end of a branch **2** *noun* **(a)** building at an airport where planes arrive or depart; *the flight leaves from Terminal 4* **(b)** building where you end a journey; **air terminal** = building in the centre of a town where passengers arrive from an airport; **bus terminal** *or* **coach terminal** = place where coaches or buses begin or end their journeys; *coaches leave the terminal every fifteen minutes* **(c)** electric **terminal** = connecting point in an electric circuit; *the positive terminal of a battery, or anode, is indicated by a plus sign* **(d)** computer **terminal** = keyboard and monitor, attached to a main computer system

terminally ['tɜːmɪnəli] *adverb* in a final way; **terminally ill** = in the last stages of an illness before death

terminate ['tɜːmɪneɪt] *verb (formal)* to finish, to end something; *the offer terminates on July 31st*; *the flight from Paris terminates in New York*

termination [tɜːmɪˈneɪʃn] *noun* bringing something to an end; *the termination of a contract*

terminological [tɜːmɪnəˈlɒdʒɪkl] *adjective* referring to specialist terms used; *examiners must be certain of the terminological accuracy of their questions*

terminology [tɜːmɪˈnɒlədʒi] *noun* special words or phrases used in a particular field; *if you're studying law you have to know some legal terminology*

terminus ['tɜːmɪnəs] *noun* **(a)** station at the end of a railway line; *Waterloo Station is the terminus for the Eurostar trains from Paris and Brussels* **(b)** place at the end of a journey by bus or coach; *we got off two stops before the terminus* (NOTE: plural is **termini** ['tɜːmɪnaɪ])

termite ['tɜːmaɪt] *noun* tropical white insect, like a large ant, that eats wood; *the foundations of the house have been eaten away by termites*

terms [tɜːmz] *noun* **(a)** conditions which are agreed before something else is done; *we bought the shop on very favourable terms*; *what are the terms of the agreement?* **(b)** **to come to terms** = to reach an agreement; *when it became obvious that neither side would win, they came to terms*; **to come to terms with something** = to accept that something has happened and cannot be changed; *it took him some time to come to terms with the fact that he would never walk again* **(c)** **terms of payment** = condition for paying something; *the terms of payment are 50% discount, payable in 60 days*; **our terms are cash with order** = we will supply the goods you want if you pay cash at the same time as you place the order **(d)** **terms of reference** = areas which a committee has to examine or discuss; *the terms of reference of the committee do not extend to EU policy* **(e)** way of getting on with someone; *they're on bad terms with the people next door*; *the company is on good terms with all its suppliers*; **they're not on speaking terms** = they refuse to talk to each other **(f)** **in terms of** = (i) expressed as; (ii) as regards; *how much is 5% per month in terms of an annual percentage rate?*; **we are talking in terms of a salary plus bonuses** = the job is offered with a salary plus bonuses

terrace ['terəs] *noun* **(a)** flat paved area which is raised above another area; *the guests had drinks on the terrace before going into dinner*; **roof terrace** = flat paved area on the roof of a building; *there is a bar on the roof terrace of the hotel* **(b)** row of similar houses connected together; *they live in an early nineteenth century terrace in Islington* **(c)** **terraces** = rows of wide steps in a sport stadium on which the spectators stand; *the terraces were packed with Liverpool fans* **(d)** flat field cut out of the side of a hill; *farmers make terraces for their rice paddies*

terraced ['terəst] *adjective* **(a)** made into a flat raised area; *the sides of the valley are terraced to form small rice fields* **(b)** **terraced houses** = houses built all in a similar style and joined in a row

terracing ['terəsɪŋ] *noun* building earth terraces on the side of a mountain, to create small flat fields; *terracing is widely used in tropical countries to allow more land to be used*

terracotta [terə'kɒtə] *noun* **(a)** red clay used to make little statues, pots and tiles; *terracotta flower pots can crack in very cold weather* **(b)** dull red brown colour; *she brightened up her fence by painting it blue and terracotta* **(c)** statue made of red clay; *a display of Greek terracottas*

terrain [tə'reɪn] *noun* particular type of land surface; *four-wheel drive vehicles are good in rough terrain*; *buffalo are useful for cultivating land on difficult terrains*

terrestrial [tə'restriəl] *adjective* **(a)** referring to the planet Earth; **terrestrial magnetism** = the magnetic properties of the earth; *satellites must be programmed to take account of terrestrial magnetism*; **terrestrial TV (channels)** = TV channels which use cable or radio links, but not satellites; *compare* LUNAR, SOLAR, STELLAR **(b)** *(animal or plant)* which lives on land, not in water; *mice and rats are terrestrial animals* (NOTE: animals and plants that live in water are **aquatic**)

terrible ['terɪbl] *adjective* **(a)** very bad; *we shouldn't have come to this party - the music's terrible*; *there was a terrible storm last night* **(b)** frightening; *it must have been terrible to be in the car which plunged into the river*

terribly ['terɪbli] *adverb (informal)* **(a)** very; *I'm terribly sorry to have kept you waiting*; *the situation is terribly serious* **(b)** in a very bad way; *the peasant farmers suffered terribly from drought*

terrier ['teriə] *noun* small dog, originally one used in hunting; *a little terrier was barking and snapping at the postman's heels*; *the Scotch terrier is one of several types of terriers*

terrific [tə'rɪfɪk] *adjective (informal)* **(a)** wonderful; *we had a terrific time at the party* **(b)** very big or loud; *there was a terrific bang and the whole building collapsed*

terrifically [tə'rɪfɪkli] *adverb (informal)* extremely; *it was a terrifically exciting game*; *it's been a terrifically long time since I was in York*

terrified ['terɪfaɪd] *adjective* very frightened; *terrified women ran out of the burning building*; *the inhabitants of the island are terrified that the volcano might erupt again*; *she's terrified that the baby will fall into the pond*

terrify ['terɪfaɪ] *verb* to make someone very frightened; *the sound of thunder terrifies me*

terrifying ['terɪfaɪɪŋ] *adjective* very frightening; *a terrifying ride at the funfair*

territorial [terɪ'tɔːriəl] *adjective* referring to territory; *they made territorial gains at the end of the war*; **territorial waters** = sea waters near the coast of a

country, which are part of that country and which are governed by the laws of that country

territory ['terɪtri] *noun* **(a)** large stretch of land; land which belongs to a country; *they occupied all the territory on the east bank of the river*; *a group of soldiers had wandered into enemy territory* **(b)** area which an animal or bird thinks belongs only to it; *animals often fight to defend their territory* **(c)** area visited by a salesman; *his territory covers all the north of the country* (NOTE: plural is **territories**)

terror ['terə] *noun* **(a)** great fear; *they live in constant terror of racist attacks*; **reign of terror** = period when law and order have broken down and people live in a continual state of fear **(b)** *(informal)* naughty child; *their daughter's a little terror* **(c)** *(informal)* a terror for = very insistent on; *the new manager is a terror for hygiene in the shop*

terrorism ['terərɪzm] *noun* policy of using violence in a political cause; *acts of terrorism continued during the whole summer*; *the government has said that it will not give in to terrorism*

terrorist ['terərɪst] **1** *noun* person who practises terrorism; *terrorists hijacked a plane and told the pilot to fly to Rome* **2** *adjective* referring to terrorism; *terrorist attacks have increased over the last few weeks*

terrorize ['terəraɪz] *verb* to frighten someone very much by threatening to use violence; *a group of youths has been terrorizing the neighbourhood*

terse [tɜːs] *adjective* concise, short, using few words; *the government has issued a terse statement denying all knowledge of the letter*

tertiary ['tɜːʃəri] *adjective* **(a)** referring to a third stage, especially to the level of education after the secondary; *she's studying at the local tertiary college* **(b)** **tertiary sector** *or* **tertiary industry** = section of the economy which provides services such as banking or insurance

test [test] **1** *noun* **(a)** examination to see if you know something, etc.; *we had an English test yesterday*; *she passed her driving test* **(b)** examination to see if something is working well; *the doctor will have to do a blood test*; *it is a good test of the car's ability to brake fast* **(c)** = TEST MATCH; *England lost the third test against Pakistan* **2** *verb* **(a)** to try to see if you can do something, etc.; *the teacher tested his spoken German* **(b)** to try to see if everything is working well; *we need to test your reactions to noise and bright lights*; *he has to have his eyes tested*; *she tested her new car in the snow*

testament ['testəmənt] *noun* **(a)** **last will and testament** = document written by someone which says what they want to happen to their property after they die; *this is the last will and testament of the late James Smith* **(b)** **the Old Testament** = the first part of the Bible, which deals with the origins and history of the Jewish people; *Isaiah and other Old Testament prophets*; **the New Testament** = the second part of the Bible, which deals with the life of Jesus Christ and his teachings; *the Gospels are the main part of the New Testament*; *the letters of St Paul form part of the New Testament*

test case ['test 'keɪs] *noun* court case where the decision will establish a principle which other cases can follow; *a test case to see if the new law is really effective*

test-drive ['testdraɪv] *verb* to drive a car before buying it to see if it works well; *I went along to the car showroom to test-drive the new Rover*

tester ['testə] *noun* person who tests; *he's a tester for a drug company*

testes ['testiːz] *see* TESTIS

testicle ['testɪkl] *noun* one of the two male sex glands which produce sperm; *it is important for men to consult their GP right away if they notice swelling of the testicles* (NOTE: also called by the Latin name **testis**)

testicular [tes'tɪkjʊlə] *adjective* referring to the testicles; *testicular cancer*

testify ['testɪfaɪ] *verb* to give evidence in court; *she testified against her former boss*; *he refused to testify because he was afraid*

testimonial [testɪ'məʊniəl] *noun* **(a)** written report about someone's character or ability; *she asked her boss if he would give her a testimonial* **(b)** written document praising someone's good qualities, often one which is presented at a ceremony; *at a function in the Town Hall, the mayor presented testimonials to six members of the staff*; **testimonial dinner** = dinner organized to give a present to someone; *the mayor was guest of honour at the testimonial dinner for six retiring council workers*

testimony ['testɪməni] *noun* statement given in court about what happened; *lawyers tried to persuade the jury that her testimony was false*

testing ['testɪŋ] **1** *adjective* which is difficult to deal with; *this has been a testing time for the whole family*; *in the second interview they will ask you more testing questions* **2** *noun* examining something to see if it works well; *during the testing of the engine several defects were corrected*

testis ['testɪs] *noun* (*formal*) testicle; *sperm is produced by the testes* (NOTE: plural is **testes** ['testiːz])

test match ['test 'mætʃ] *noun* international cricket or rugby match; *England beat Australia in the last test match*

testosterone [tes'tɒstərəʊn] *noun* male sex hormone; *testosterone is secreted by the testes; compare* PROGESTERONE

COMMENT: testosterone causes physical changes such as a deep voice and body hair, which occur when a male becomes sexually mature

test pilot ['test 'paɪlət] *noun* pilot who flies new aircraft to see if they work properly

test tube ['test 'tjuːb] *noun* **(a)** small glass tube, open at the top with a rounded bottom, used in laboratories to hold liquids during experiments; *position the base of the test tube over the flame* **(b) test tube baby** = baby which develops after the mother's ova have been removed, fertilized with the father's sperm in a laboratory, and replaced in the mother's womb to continue developing normally; *the first test tube babies are now adults*

tetanus ['tetənəs] *noun* serious disease caused by infection of a wound by bacteria in the soil, which affects the spinal cord and causes the jaw muscles to stiffen; *I was immunized against tetanus three years ago*; *when was the last time you had a tetanus jab?* (NOTE: also called **lockjaw**)

COMMENT: people who work on the land or with soil, such as farm workers and construction workers, should be immunized against tetanus

tether ['teðə] **1** *noun* **(a)** rope which attaches an animal to a post; *the horse had slipped its tether and was galloping away down the street* **(b) he's at the end of his tether** = he can't stand any more, he has lost all patience; *she was at the end of her tether and resigned after just one month in the job* **2** *verb* to attach an animal to a post with a rope; *he tethered his horse to a post*

text [tekst] *noun* **(a)** main written section of a book, not the notes, index, pictures, etc.; *it's a book for little children, with lots of pictures and very little text*; **text processing** = using a computer to produce, check and change documents, reports, letters, etc. **(b)** original words of a speech; *the text of the Gettysburg Address*

textbook ['tekstbʊk] *noun* book used by students to get information about the subject they are studying; *we've been recommended to buy this English textbook*; *which is the best maths textbook?*

textile ['tekstaɪl] *noun* cloth; *they export textiles all over the world*; *the textile industry is influenced by world commodity prices*

textual ['tekstʃuəl] *adjective* referring to a text; *a textual study of Milton's poems*; *the editor made several textual changes to the proofs*

texture ['tekstʃə] *noun* **(a)** the way in which a surface can be felt; *the soft texture of velvet* **(b)** the way a substance is formed; *this bread has a light texture*; *the heavy texture of clay soil*

textured ['tekstʃəd] *adjective* with a certain texture; *a smooth-textured stone*; *this year's fashion favours rough-textured materials*

Thai [taɪ] **1** *adjective* referring to Thailand; *if you're fond of Thai food let's go to a Thai restaurant* **2** *noun* **(a)** inhabitant of Thailand; *Thais are famous for their hot, spicy cooking*; *the two economics students are Thais* **(b)** language spoken in Thailand; *if you're posted to Bangkok, you'll have to learn Thai*

Thailand ['taɪlænd] *noun* country of south-east Asia, north of Malaysia; *Thailand is a favourite holiday destination* (NOTE: capital: **Bangkok**; people: **the Thais**; language: **Thai**; currency: **baht**)

than [ðæn *or* ðən] **1** *conjunction* (*used to indicate an action or state which is being compared with something else*) *it's hotter this week than it was last week* **2** *preposition* (*used to link two parts of a comparison*) *his car is bigger than mine*; *she was born in London, so she knows it better than any other town*; *you can't get more than four people into this lift*; *it's less than five kilometres to the nearest station*

thank [θæŋk] *verb* **(a)** to say or do something that shows you are grateful to someone for doing something for you; *she thanked the policeman for helping her to cross the street*; *don't forget to thank Aunt Ann for her present*; *'Thank you for your letter of June 25th'* **(b) thank goodness!** *or* **thank God!** *or* **thank heavens!** = expressions used to show relief; *thank goodness it didn't rain for the school sports day!*; *thank God the ambulance turned up quickly!*

thankful ['θæŋkful] *adjective* glad because a worry has gone away; *we'll all be thankful to get back into* harbour safely; *I'm thankful that the firemen arrived so quickly*

thankfully ['θæŋkfʊli] *adverb* showing that you are glad that a worry has gone away; *thankfully the X-rays showed that no bones had been broken*

thankless ['θæŋkləs] *adjective* for which no one will thank you; *he has the thankless job of writing to all these candidates to tell them they did not get the job*

thanks [θæŋks] 1 *noun* word showing that you are grateful; *we sent our thanks for the gift; we did our best to help but got no thanks for it; the committee passed a vote of thanks to the secretary for having organized the meeting; many thanks for your letter of the 15th* 2 *interjection* showing you are grateful; *do you want some more tea? - no thanks, I've had two cups already; anyone want a lift to the station? - thanks, it's a long walk from here*

Thanksgiving [θæŋks'gɪvɪŋ] *noun* American festival, celebrating the first harvest of settlers in the United States (celebrated on the fourth Thursday in November); *all the family will be here for Thanksgiving*

> COMMENT: the traditional menu for Thanksgiving dinner is roast turkey, with cranberry sauce, followed by pumpkin pie

thanks to ['θæŋks 'tu:] *preposition* because of, as a result of; *thanks to the map which he faxed to us, we found his house without any difficulty; thanks to the fog, all planes were diverted to Manchester*

thank you ['θæŋk ju:] 1 *interjection* showing that you are grateful; *thank you very much for your letter of the 15th; did you remember to say thank you to your grandmother for the present?; would you like another piece of cake? - no thank you, I've had enough*; **thank-you letter** = letter written to thank someone for something 2 *noun* words or applause, etc., to show you are grateful; *let's say a big thank you to the people who organized the show*

that [ðæt] 1 *adjective* (used to show something which is further away) *can you see that white house on the corner over there?; do you remember the name of that awful hotel in Brighton?* (NOTE: the opposite is **this**; the plural is **those**) 2 *pronoun that's the book I was talking about; do you know who that is sitting at the next table?* 3 *relative pronoun where is the parcel that she sent you yesterday?; can you see the man that sold you the ticket?; there's the suitcase that you left on the train!* (NOTE: when it is the object of a verb **that** can be left out: **where's the letter he sent you? here's the box you left in the bedroom.** When it is the subject, **that** can be replaced by **which** *or* **who: a house that has red windows** *or* **a house which has red windows; the man that stole the car** *or* **the man who stole the car**) 3 *conjunction* (a) *(after verbs like* hope, know, tell, say *and adjectives like* glad, sorry, happy); *they told me that the manager was out; she said several times that she wanted to sit down; I don't think they knew that we were coming; I'm glad that the weather turned out fine; I am sorry that you have been kept waiting* (b) *(after* so *or* such *+ adjective or noun) the restaurant was so expensive that we could only afford one dish; it rained so hard that the street was like a river; we had such a lot of work that we didn't have any lunch; there was such a long queue that we didn't bother waiting* (NOTE: **that** is often left out: **he didn't know we were**

coming; **it's so hot in here we all want a drink of water**) 4 *adverb* (usually with negative) so, to such an extent; *you must remember him, it's not all that long ago that we had a drink with him; his new car is not really that big*

thatch [θætʃ] 1 *noun* straw and reeds used to make a roof; *thatch needs to be redone every ten years or so* (NOTE: no plural) 2 *verb* to cover a roof with reeds or straw; *the house will need to be thatched again this year*

thatched [θætʃt] *adjective* covered with a straw roof; *he lives in a little thatched cottage, just like the ones you see in postcards of English villages*

thaw [θɔ:] 1 *noun* warm weather which makes snow and ice melt; *the thaw came early this year* 2 *verb* (a) to melt; *the ice is thawing on the village pond* (b) to unfreeze something which is frozen; *can you thaw those raspberries?* (c) to become less formal; *after a period of tension, relations between the two countries have begun to thaw*

the [ðə *or before a vowel* ðɪ] *article* (a) (meaning something in particular) *where's the book you brought back from the library?; that's the cat from next door; the town centre has been made into a pedestrian zone* (b) (used with something of which only one exists) *the sun came up over the hills; they want to land a spacecraft on the moon* (c) (meaning something in general) *there's nothing interesting on the television tonight; she refuses to use the telephone; the streets are crowded at lunchtime; many people were out of work during the 1990s* (d) [ðɪː] (meaning something very special) *it's the shop for men's clothes; she's the doctor for children's diseases; that's not the Charlie Chaplin, is it?* (e) (used to compare) *the more he eats the thinner he seems to get; the sooner you do it the better; this is by far the shortest way to London; she's the tallest person in the office*

theatre *US* **theater** ['θɪətə] *noun* (a) building in which plays are shown; *I'm trying to get tickets for the theatre tonight; what is the play at the local theatre this week?; we'll have dinner early and then go to the theatre* (b) *US* **movie theater** = building where films are shown (NOTE: British English for this is only **cinema**) (c) **the theatre** = (i) art of presenting plays on the stage; (ii) business of presenting plays on the stage; *I like the theatre better than the cinema; she wants to work in the theatre as a designer* (d) **operating theatre** = special room in a hospital where surgeons carry out operations; *they rushed him straight into the operating theatre* (NOTE: American English is **operating room**)

theatregoer *US* **theatergoer** ['θɪətəgəʊə] *noun* person who goes to the theatre; *Shaftesbury Avenue was full of theatregoers trying to find taxis*

theatrical [θɪ'ætrɪkl] *adjective* (a) referring to the theatre; *she had a distinguished theatrical career before going into films* (b) exaggerated, dramatic and not natural; *throwing the letter on the floor and stamping on it was a bit theatrical*

theft [θeft] *noun* (a) stealing (in general); *we brought in security guards to protect the hotel against theft; they are trying to stop theft by members of the public* (b) act of stealing; *thefts in supermarkets have increased enormously*

their [ðeə] *adjective* (a) belonging to them; *after the film, we went to their house for supper* (b) referring to them; *the family were eating their dinner when the fire broke out* (NOTE: do not confuse with **there, they're**)

theirs [ðeəz] *pronoun* the one that belongs to them; *which car is theirs - the Ford?*; *she's a friend of theirs*; *the girls wanted to borrow my car - theirs wouldn't start*

them [ðem] *object pronoun* (a) *(referring to a people or things which have been mentioned before)* *do you like cream cakes? - no, I don't like them very much*; *there's a group of people waiting outside - tell them to come in* (b) *(referring to a singular, used instead of* **him** *or* **her***)*; *if someone phones, ask them to call back later*

thematic [θɪˈmætɪk] *adjective* referring to themes; *the exhibits are arranged in thematic groups rather than chronologically*

theme [θiːm] *noun* (a) the main subject of a book or article; *the theme of the book is how to deal with illness in the family* (b) main idea; *the theme of the exhibition is 'Europe in the twenty-first century'* (c) main tune in a piece of music; *the theme comes again at the end of the symphony*; **theme tune** *or* **theme song** = tune or song played several times in a film or TV serial by which you can recognize it

theme park [ˈθiːm ˈpɑːk] *noun* amusement park based on a single theme (such as a medieval castle, etc.); *a visit to the theme park is included in the package tour*

themselves [ðəmˈselvz] *pronoun* (a) *(referring to the same people or things that are the subject of the verb)* *cats always spend a lot time cleaning themselves*; *it's no use going to the surgery - the doctors are all ill themselves* (b) **by themselves** = all alone; *the girls were all by themselves in the tent*; *they did it all by themselves*

then [ðen] **1** *adverb* (a) at that time in the past or future; *he had been very busy up till then*; *ever since then I've refused to eat oysters*; *we're having a party next week - what a pity! I'll be in Scotland then* (b) after that, next; *we all sat down, and then after a few minutes the waiter brought us the menu*; *it was a busy trip - he went to Greece, then to Italy and finally to Spain* (c) and so, therefore; *if there isn't any fish on the menu, then we'll have to have omelettes*; *then he was already at home when you phoned?* **2** *adjective* who or which existed at a certain time in the past; *the then headmaster was a man called Jones*

theologian [θɪəˈləʊdʒiən] *noun* person who specializes in the study of religion or religious beliefs; *several leading theologians will take part in the discussion on the Bible*

theological [θɪəˈlɒdʒɪkl] *adjective* referring to theology; *she started a theological discussion with her parish priest*; **theological college** = college where people study to become priests; *she spent four years in theological college before being sent to a parish in south London*

theology [θɪˈɒlədʒi] *noun* study of religion and the belief in God; *he studied Muslim theology at university*

theorem [ˈθɪərəm] *noun* statement which can be proved in mathematics; **Pythagoras's theorem** = statement that in a right-angled triangle, the square on the hypotenuse is equal to the sum of the squares on the other two sides

theoretical [θɪəˈretɪkl] *adjective* (a) referring to theories; *a theoretical study of the universe* (b) not proved in practice; *she has the theoretical power to dismiss any of the staff*

theoretically [θɪəˈretɪkli] *adverb* in theory, but not in practice; *it is theoretically possible for them to win, but very unlikely*; *you should, theoretically, be able to touch the wire without getting an electric shock*

theoretician *or* **theorist** [θɪːərəˈtɪʃn *or* ˈθɪːərɪst] *noun* person who forms theories, especially political theories; *the government is setting up a committee of eminent theoreticians to advise on political reform*

theorize [ˈθɪːəraɪz] *verb* to make up a theory about something; *he spent his life theorizing about how to become rich and in the end died very poor*

theory [ˈθɪəri] *noun* (a) explanation of something which has not been proved but which you believe is true; *I have a theory which explains why the police never found the murder weapon* (b) careful scientific explanation of why something happens; *Galileo put forward the theory that the earth turns round the sun*; **the theory of evolution** = theory, developed by Charles Darwin, that species evolve by a process of natural selection (c) statement of general principles which may not apply in practice; *in theory the treatment should work, but no one has ever tried it* (NOTE: plural is **theories**)

therapeutic [θerəˈpjuːtɪk] *adjective* which is given in order to cure a disease or disorder; *massage of the back may be therapeutic in some cases*

therapist [ˈθerəpɪst] *noun* person who is specially trained to give therapy; *the therapist said I should rest my leg as much as possible*; **occupational therapist** = person who treats patients by making them do certain activities and exercises

therapy [ˈθerəpi] *noun* treatment of a patient to help cure a disease or condition; *they use heat therapy to treat muscular problems*; **group therapy** = type of treatment where a group of people with the same disorder meet together with a therapist to discuss their condition and try to help each other; **occupational therapy** = treating patients by using activities to help them deal with problems or disabilities, used especially for handicapped or mentally ill patients; **speech therapy** = treatment to cure a speech disorder, such as stammering; *see also* HORMONE

there [ðeə] **1** *adverb* (a) in that place; *is that black van still there parked outside the house?*; *where have you put the tea? - there, on the kitchen counter* (b) to that place; *we haven't been to the British Museum yet - let's go there tomorrow*; *have you ever been to China? - yes, I went there last month* (c) *(used when giving something to someone)* *there you are: two fish and chips and a pot of tea* (NOTE: do not confuse with **their, they're**) **2** *interjection* (a) *(showing pity)* *there, there, don't get upset*; *there, sit down for a little while and you'll soon feel better* (b) *(showing you were right)* *there, what did I say? the plane's late* (c) *(making a decision)* *if you don't want to come with me, I'll go all by myself, so there!* **3** *pronoun* *(used usually with the verb* **to be**, *when the real subject follows the verb)* *there's a little door leading onto the patio*; *there's someone at the door asking for you*; *there are some pages missing in my newspaper*; *were there a lot of people at the cinema?*; *there seems to have been a lot* *of rain during the night; there isn't any jam left in the cupboard*

thereabouts [ðeərə'bauts] *adverb* **(a)** near that place; *they live in Glasgow or thereabouts* **(b)** about that number; *they owe us £250 or thereabouts*

thereafter [ðeər'ɑːftə] *adverb (formal)* after that; *some time thereafter he went back to the house and set it on fire; there were several accidents during the first week, but thereafter things went much better*

thereby [ðeə'baɪ] *adverb (formal)* by doing that; *a truck crashed into the bridge, thereby blocking the road; the company lowered its prices, thereby winning market share from its competitors*

therefore ['ðeəfɔː] *adverb* for this reason; *I therefore have decided not to grant his request; they have reduced their prices, therefore we should reduce ours if we want to stay competitive*

therein [ðeə'rɪn] *adverb (formal)* in that; *therein lies the cause of all our problems*

thermal ['θɜːməl] **1** *adjective* referring to heat; **thermal baths** = baths of natural hot water; **thermal current** = current of warm air or water; **thermal underwear** = thick underwear which keeps you warm **2** *noun* rising current of warm air; *hang-gliders rose into the air on thermals*

thermometer [θə'mɒmɪtə] *noun* instrument for measuring temperature; *put the thermometer in your mouth - I want to take your temperature; the thermometer outside shows 20°*

Thermos (flask) ['θɜːmɒs 'flɑːsk] *noun* trademark for a vacuum flask, a type of bottle which keeps liquids hot or cold; *we took thermoses of hot coffee to drink when we went walking*

thermostat ['θɜːmə'stæt] *noun* instrument which controls heating according to a set temperature; *we set the thermostat at 20°, so that the house stays the same temperature all the time*

thesaurus [θə'sɔːrəs] *noun* book with words collected into groups under different subjects and not in alphabetical order; *a thesaurus is useful for finding words with similar meanings; don't keep using the word 'like' - try to find another verb in your thesaurus* (NOTE: plural is **thesauruses** or sometimes **thesauri** [θə'sɔːraɪ])

these [ðiːz] *see* THIS

thesis ['θiːsɪs] *noun* **(a)** long piece of written research prepared by a candidate for a higher university degree; *she is writing her thesis on the place of women in Spanish literature* **(b)** particular point of view; *his thesis is that, the lower the income tax rate, the more people will spend* (NOTE: plural is **theses** ['θiːsiːz])

they [ðeɪ] *pronoun* **(a)** *(referring to people or things)* where *do you keep the spoons? - they're in the right-hand drawer; who are those people in uniform? - they're traffic wardens; the children played in the sun and they all got sunburnt* **(b)** *(referring to people in general) they say it's going to be fine this weekend* **(c)** *(referring to a singular, used after someone, etc.) if someone else joins the queue, they'll just have to wait* (NOTE: when it is the object, **them** is used instead of **they: we gave it to them; the police beat them with sticks**; also when it follows the verb **to be: who's that? - it's them!**)

they're [ðeə] = THEY ARE (NOTE: do not confuse with **their, there**)

thick [θɪk] **1** *adjective* **(a)** bigger than usual when measured from side to side, not thin; *he cut a slice of bread which was so thick it wouldn't go into the toaster; the walls of the castle are three metres thick; some oranges have very thick skins; he took a piece of thick rope* **(b)** close together; *they tried to make their way through thick jungle; the field was covered with thick grass; (informal) (of two people)* **they're as thick as thieves** = they are great friends, they share each other's secrets **(c)** *(of liquids)* which cannot flow easily; *if the paint is too thick add some water; a bowl of thick soup is just what we need on a cold day like this* **(d)** which you cannot see through easily; *thick fog had closed the airport* **(e)** *(informal)* stupid, not very intelligent; *he's a bit thick or he's as thick as two (short) planks* (NOTE: **thicker - thickest**) **2** *adverb* thickly *(informal)* **to lay it on thick** = to praise someone excessively; *it was laying it on a bit thick to say that she plays the violin like Menuhin*; **thick and fast** = rapidly and often; *the faxes came in thick and fast*

thicken ['θɪkn] *verb* **(a)** to make thick; *thicken the sauce with cornflour* **(b)** to become thick; *as you heat the custard it will thicken*

thicket ['θɪkɪt] *noun* small wood of trees and bushes growing close together; *the songs of blackbirds and a robin could be heard coming from the thicket; the deer moved cautiously along the hedgerow and disappeared into a thicket*

thickly ['θɪkli] *adverb* in a thick layer; *he's putting the paint on too thickly; the surface was thickly covered with dust;* **thickly wooded** = with a lot of trees close together; *thickly wooded valleys*

thickset [θɪk'set] *adjective* **(a)** short and stocky; *her father is a solid thickset man* **(b)** **thickset hedge** = hedge planted with bushes close together; *the garden is surrounded by a thickset hedge of holly and yew*

thick-skinned ['θɪk'skɪnd] *adjective* **(a)** with a thick skin; *a rhinoceros is very thick-skinned* **(b)** able to stand a lot of criticism; *luckily he's a thick-skinned individual or he would be very upset at what the tabloids say about him*

thief [θiːf] *noun* person who steals; *the police are certain they will catch the thief; see also* THICK (NOTE: plural is **thieves** [θiːvz])

thieving ['θiːvɪŋ] **1** *noun* act of stealing things; *thieving from shops has become widespread* **2** *adjective* who steals; *we have to watch those thieving students if they come into the shop again*

thigh [θaɪ] *noun* part at the top of the leg between your knee and your hip; *she was wearing a very short skirt and everyone could see her thighs*

thighbone ['θaɪbəun] *noun* long bone in the top part of the leg, between the hip and the knee; *she slipped and broke her thigh bone* (NOTE: also called by its Latin name **femur**)

thimble ['θɪmbl] *noun* small cup worn to protect the end of your finger when sewing

thimbleful ['θɪmblful] *noun* very small amount of liquid; *I'll just have a thimbleful of whisky*

thin [θɪn] **1** *adjective* **(a)** not fat; *the table has very thin legs; he's too thin - he should eat more;* **as thin as a rake** = very thin; *she's a supermodel and is as thin as a rake* **(b)** not thick; *a plate of thin sandwiches; the book is printed on very thin paper; the parcel was sent* *in a thin cardboard box* **(c)** not placed or growing close together; *the hill was covered with thin grass; the audience is a bit thin tonight* **(d)** *(of liquid)* which flows easily, which has too much water; *all we had for lunch was a bowl of thin soup; add water to make the paint thinner* **(e)** which you can see through; *they hung thin curtains in the windows; a thin mist covered the valley* (NOTE: **thinner - thinnest**) **2** *adverb* thinly; *don't spread the butter too thin* **3** *verb* **(a)** to make more liquid; *if you want to thin the soup just add some water* **(b)** to become fewer; *the crowds began to thin by evening* **(c) to thin out** = to make plants grow less close together; *these lettuces need to be thinned out*

thing [θɪŋ] *noun* **(a)** something which is not living, which is not a plant or animal; *can you see that black thing in the pan of soup?; what do you use that big blue thing for?* **(b)** usually kind way of talking to or about a person or animal; *the lady in the sweet shop is a dear old thing; you silly thing! - why on earth did you do that?* **(c)** something in general; *they all just sat there and didn't say a thing; the first thing to do is to call an ambulance; that was a stupid thing to do!*; **a good thing** = something lucky; *it's a good thing there was no policeman on duty at the door* **(d)** problem, worry; *it never stops, it's just one thing after another* **(e)** *(informal)* **to have a thing about something** = to have strong feelings about something; *he has a thing about spiders; she's got a thing about men with beards* **(f)** *(informal)* **to do your own thing** = to be independent, to do what you want to do; *he pays lip service to what the manager says but quietly does his own thing*

things [θɪŋz] *noun* **(a)** clothes, equipment; *did you bring your tennis things?; she left her painting things in the car* **(b)** general situation; *things aren't going well at the office; he always takes things too seriously*

think [θɪŋk] **1** *verb* **(a)** to use your mind; *we never think about what people might say, we always do what we think is right*; **to think twice** = to consider very carefully; *think twice before you sign that contract* **(b)** to have an opinion; *I think London is a nicer town to live in than Frankfurt; everyone thinks we're mad to go on holiday in December; the weather forecasters think it's going to rain; he didn't think much of the film; the gang is thought to be based in Spain* **(c)** to make a plan to do something; *we're thinking of opening an office in New York* (NOTE: **thinking - thought** [θɔːt]) **2** *noun* period when you think, the act of thinking; *let me have a little think and I'll tell you what we should do; have a think about what I've just said; we really need to have another think about the plan*

think about [ˈθɪŋk əˈbaʊt] *verb* **(a)** to have someone or something in your mind; *I was just thinking about you when you phoned; all she thinks about is food* **(b)** to consider a plan in your mind; *have you ever thought about writing children's books?*; **to think twice about** = to consider very carefully; *I'd think twice about spending all the money you've saved* **(c)** to have an opinion about something; *what do you think about the government's plans to increase taxes?*

think back [ˈθɪŋk ˈbæk] *verb* to remember something in the past; *think back to last Wednesday - do you remember seeing me sign the letter?*

thinker [ˈθɪŋkə] *noun* person who thinks, a philosopher; *great thinkers of ancient Greece such as Socrates, Plato and Aristotle*

thinking [ˈθɪŋkɪŋ] *noun* process of reasoning about something; *I don't understand the thinking behind the decision*; **to my way of thinking** = my opinion is; *to my way of thinking, it shouldn't be allowed*

think of [ˈθɪŋk ˈɒv] *verb* **(a)** to consider a plan in your mind; *we are thinking of going to Greece on holiday* **(b)** to remember something; *now I think of it, he was at the party last week* **(c)** to have an opinion about something; *what do you think of the government's plans to increase taxes?; I didn't think much of the play; she asked him what he thought of her idea*; **to tell someone what you think of something** = to criticize; *he went up to her and told her exactly what he thought of her stupid idea*; **to think highly of someone** = to have a high opinion of someone; **to think nothing of doing something** = to consider something normal, easy; *she thinks nothing of working ten hours a day; (as a response to an apology)* **think nothing of it!** = please don't bother to thank me for it; *he thought better of it* = he changed his mind; *he was going to pay the whole cost himself, and then thought better of it*

think out [ˈθɪŋk ˈaʊt] *verb* to consider something carefully in all its details; *have you thought out all the implications of the plan?; they submitted a well thought-out design*

think over [ˈθɪŋk ˈəʊvə] *verb* to consider a plan or proposal very carefully; *that's the proposal: think it over, and tell me what you decide tomorrow*

think tank [ˈθɪŋktæŋk] *noun* group of advisers who are appointed to discuss important problems and suggest how they should be solved; *the government has set up an education think tank to plan new policies for schools; some of these ideas were put forward by the government think tank*

think through [ˈθɪŋk ˈθruː] *verb* to consider something carefully in all its details; *they didn't think through all the implications of their plan*

think up [ˈθɪŋk ˈʌp] *verb* to invent a plan or new idea; *he thought up a mad plan for making lots of money*

thinly [ˈθɪnli] *adverb* not thickly; *he spread the butter thinly on the bread; smoked salmon should be thinly sliced; sow the seed thinly in fine soil*

thinner [ˈθɪnə] *noun* liquid added to oil paint to make it less thick; *add thinner until you get the right consistency*

thinning [ˈθɪnɪŋ] *adjective* which is getting thinner; *he rubbed some lotion into his thinning hair*

third (3rd) [θɜːd] **1** *adjective* referring to three; *she came third in the race; the cake shop is the third shop on the right; it will be her third birthday next Friday; her birthday is on the third of March or March the third (March 3rd)* **the third century** = the period from 200 to 299 A.D. (NOTE: with dates **third** is usually written **3rd**: May 3rd, 1921: June 3rd, 1896 (American style is **June 3, 1896**), say 'the third of June' or 'June the third' (American style is 'June third'); with names of kings and queens **third** is usually written **III**: King Henry III: say 'King Henry the Third')) **2** *noun* one part out of three equal parts; *a third of the airline's planes are jumbos; two-thirds of the staff are part-timers*

thirdly [ˈθɜːdli] *adverb* as the third item on a list; *I can't come to the party for three reasons: firstly my car isn't working, secondly I'm meeting my girlfriend that evening, and thirdly I haven't anything to wear*

third party ['θɜːd 'pɑːti] *noun* any person other than the two main parties involved in a contract or a civil case; *if possible we want to prevent third parties becoming involved in the dispute*; **third party insurance** = insurance which pays compensation if someone who is not the insured person incurs loss or injury

Third World ['θɜːd 'wɜːld] *noun* countries of Africa, Asia and South America which do not have highly developed industries and where people are generally poor; *we sell tractors into the Third World or to Third World countries*; *some Third World countries have asked for their debts to be rescheduled*

thirst [θɜːst] **1** *noun* (a) feeling of wanting to drink; *digging the garden has given me such a thirst!*; *they ran to the mountain stream to quench their thirst* (b) feeling of wanting something; *he studied at night to satisfy his thirst for knowledge* **2** *verb* (*formal*) to **thirst after** *or* **for something** = to want something strongly; *he thirsts after excitement*

thirsty ['θɜːsti] *adjective* feeling that you want to drink; *it's so hot here that it makes me thirsty*; **are you thirsty?** = would you like a drink?; **thirsty work** = hard work which makes you thirsty; *moving all this furniture is thirsty work* (NOTE: **thirstier - thirstiest**)

thirteen [θɜːˈtiːn] *number* 13; *he's only thirteen (years old), but he can drive a car*; *she'll be thirteen next Monday*; **the thirteen hundreds (1300s)** = the period form 1300 to 1399 (NOTE: compare **the thirteenth century**)

thirteenth (13th) [θɜːˈtiːnθ] *adjective & noun* **the thirteenth of September** *or* **September the thirteenth (September 13th)**; *it's her thirteenth birthday on Monday*; **Friday the thirteenth (Friday 13th)** = day which many people think is unlucky; **the thirteenth century** = the period from 1200 to 1399 (NOTE: compare **the thirteen hundreds**; Note also that with dates **thirteenth** is usually written **13th**: July 13th, 1935; October 13th, 1991 (American style is **October 13, 1991**), say 'the thirteenth of October' or 'October the thirteenth' (American style is 'October thirteenth'); with names of kings and queens **thirteenth** is usually written **XIII**: King Louis XIII (say: 'King Louis the Thirteenth'))

thirtieth (30th) ['θɜːtɪəθ] *adjective & noun* he came **thirtieth out of thirty-five in the race**; **the thirtieth of March** *or* **March the thirtieth (March 30th)**; *it was my thirtieth birthday last week* (NOTE: with dates **thirtieth** is usually written **30th**: May 30th, 1921: June 30th, 1896 (American style is **June 30, 1896**), say 'the thirtieth of June' or 'June the thirtieth' (American style is 'June thirtieth'))

thirty ['θɜːti] *number* 30; *he's thirty (years old)* *she must have more than thirty pairs of shoes*; *she and her partner are both in their thirties* = they are both aged between 30 and 39 years old; **the (nineteen) thirties (1930s)** = the period from 1930 to 1939 (NOTE: **thirty-one** (31), **thirty-two** (32), etc., but **thirty-first** (31st), **thirty-second** (32nd), etc.)

this [ðɪs] *adjective & pronoun* (a) (*used to show something which is nearer - in contrast to* **that**); *this is the shop that was mentioned in the paper*; *this little girl is a friend of my daughter*; *I think we have been to this pub before*; *this is Angela Smith, our new sales manager* (b) (*used to refer to a part of today, the recent past or a period of time which will soon arrive*) *I saw him on the train this morning*; *my mother is coming*

for tea this afternoon; *I expect to hear from him this week*; *he's retiring this August*; *this year, our sales are better than last year*; *they're going to Spain this summer* (NOTE: plural is **these**)

thistle ['θɪsl] *noun* large wild plant with prickly leaves and purple flowers; *he sat down on a patch of thistles and jumped up again*

thong [θɒŋ] *noun* rubber sandal held on by a strap between the toes; *best wear thongs if you're going onto the beach* (NOTE: also called **flip flops**)

thorn [θɔːn] *noun* (a) sharp spine on a prickly plant; *most roses have thorns* (b) **a thorn in someone's flesh** = a constant annoyance to someone; *she's been a thorn in the management's flesh ever since she joined the company*

thorny ['θɔːni] *adjective* (a) covered with thorns; *we planted thorny bushes round the garden to deter burglars* (b) **thorny problem** = problem which is difficult to solve; *trying to solve the thorny racial problems in some East European countries is very difficult* (NOTE: **thornier - thorniest**)

thorough ['θʌrə] *adjective* (a) very careful and detailed; *the police have carried out a thorough search of the woods* (b) total; *they made a thorough mess of it*; *it was a thorough waste of time*

thoroughbred ['θʌrəbred] *adjective & noun* pure-bred (horse); *the race is only open to thoroughbreds or to thoroughbred horses*

thoroughfare ['θʌrəfeə] *noun* main road through a town, usually where there is a lot of traffic; *the high street is the main thoroughfare through the town*; **no thoroughfare** = sign showing that the public cannot use a certain road; *I hadn't seen the 'no thoroughfare' sign and found myself in the garden of the town hall*

thoroughgoing [θʌrəˈgəʊɪŋ] *adjective* complete and careful; *the auditors made a thoroughgoing check on the company's books*; *the restaurant kitchen needs a thoroughgoing clean*

thoroughly ['θʌrəli] *adverb* (a) in a complete and careful way; *we searched the garden thoroughly but couldn't find his red ball* (b) totally; *I'm thoroughly fed up with the whole business*

those [ðəʊz] *see* THAT

though [ðəʊ] *adverb & conjunction* (a) in spite of the fact that; *though tired, she still kept on running*; *we don't employ a computer programmer, though many companies do* (b) **as though** = as if; *his voice sounded strange over the telephone, as though he was standing in a cave*; *that shirt doesn't look as though it has been ironed*; *it looks as though there is no one in* (c) **even though** = in spite of the fact that; *he didn't wear a coat, even though it was snowing*; *he wouldn't come with us, even though we asked him twice*; *we managed to make ourselves understood, even though no one spoke English*

thought [θɔːt] **1** *noun* (a) idea which you have when thinking; *he had an awful thought - suppose they had left the bathroom taps running?* (b) process of thinking; *he sat deep in thought by the window* (c) opinion; *he expressed his thoughts on the subject in a letter to the newspaper* (d) **to have second thoughts about something** = to change your mind about something; *I think she's beginning to have second thoughts about accepting the job*; **on second thoughts** = having thought about it again; *I asked for coffee, but* *on second thoughts I think I'll have tea* **2** *verb see* THINK

thoughtful ['θɔːtful] *adjective* **(a)** thinking deeply; *he looked thoughtful, and I wondered if there was something wrong* **(b)** being sensitive to what other people want; *it was very thoughtful of you to come to see me in hospital*

thoughtfully ['θɔːtfuli] *adverb* in a considerate way; *she had thoughtfully put some batteries with the present; they thoughtfully provided us with an English translation*

thoughtless ['θɔːtləs] *adjective* without thinking about other people; *it was very thoughtless of them to have a party on the same day as Uncle Charles' funeral*

thousand ['θauzənd] *number* 1000; *we paid two hundred thousand pounds for the house (£200,000) thousands of people had their holidays spoilt by the storm* (NOTE: after numbers **thousand** does not take the plural ending **-s: two thousand, ten thousand**)

thousandth (1000th) ['θauzənθ] **1** *adjective* referring to a thousand; *the tourist office gave a prize to their thousandth visitor* **2** *noun* one part out of a thousand; *a thousandth of a second*

thrash [θræʃ] *verb* **(a)** to beat with a stick; *his father caught him stealing and thrashed him* **(b)** to beat another team decisively; *our team thrashed the visitors 7 - 0*

thrash out ['θræʃ 'aut] *verb* **(a)** to try to hit wildly in all directions; *he thrashed out at the youths with his stick* **(b)** to discuss something until a solution is found; *we sat down with the management and thrashed out a compromise; they spent all day thrashing out a solution to the problem*

thread [θred] **1** *noun* **(a)** long strand of cotton, silk, etc.; *a spider spins a thread to make its web; wait a moment, there's a white thread showing on your coat* **(b) to lose the thread of a conversation** = to miss what the conversation is about **(c)** ridge going round and round a screw or the inside of a nut; *it's difficult to tighten the nut because the thread is very worn* **2** *verb* **(a)** to put a piece of cotton through the eye of a needle; *my eyesight is getting so bad, I can't even thread a needle* **(b)** to make something go through a hole; *put the reel on the projector and then thread the end of the film through this aperture* **(c) to thread your way** = to go carefully between things; *she threaded her way through the piles of boxes; we threaded our way through the crowds of Christmas shoppers*

threat [θret] *noun* **(a)** warning that you are going to do something unpleasant, especially if you do not do what you want; *her former husband had been making threats against her and the children; the police took the threat to the Prime Minister very seriously; do you think they will carry out their threat to bomb the capital if we don't surrender?;* **death threat** = warning to someone that he or she will be killed **(b)** person or thing which may harm; *defective cars are a threat to other road users*

threaten ['θretn] *verb* **(a)** to warn that you are going to do something unpleasant, especially if someone doesn't do what you want; *she threatened to go to the police; the teacher threatened her with punishment* **(b)** to be likely to have a bad effect on something; *the collapse of the stock market threatened the stability of the currency*

threatening ['θretnɪŋ] *adverb* suggesting that something unpleasant will happen; *the weather looks threatening; the crowd made threatening gestures at the referee*

three [θriː] *number* 3; *she's only three (years old), so she can't read yet; come and see me at three (o'clock) three men walked into the bank and pulled out guns* (NOTE: **three** (3) but **third** (3rd))

three-dimensional *or* **three-D** *or* **3-D** [θriːdaɪ'menʃnəl *or* 'θriː'diː] *adjective (picture)* which has depth as well as length and breadth; *to see all the 3-D effects in the film the audience have to wear special glasses*

three-quarter [θriː'kwɔːtə] **1** *noun* **three-quarters** = three fourths of one whole; *I'm three-quarters of the way through the book; about three-quarters of the members are in favour;* **three-quarters of an hour** = forty-five minutes; *we had to wait an hour and three-quarters* **2** *adverb* **three-quarters** = 75%, three fourths; *the bottle was three-quarters full* **3** *adjective* covering three quarters of a whole; **three-quarter length dress** = dress which comes down to below the knee

thresh [θreʃ] *verb* to separate grains from stalks of corn and other plants; *in many tropical countries, rice is still threshed by hand;* **threshing machine** = formerly, a machine which was used to thresh corn, now replaced by a combine harvester; *it is amusing to see the old photographs of the threshing machines they used on grandfather's farm*

threshold ['θreʃəuld] *noun* **(a)** bar across the floor of a doorway; *she stopped at the threshold and looked back into the room* **(b)** point where something begins; *she's on the threshold of a great career in teaching;* **tax threshold** = point at which a higher level of tax is charged; *the government has raised the minimum tax threshold from £6,000 to £6,500* **(c)** point at which you start to react; *he's got a very low boredom threshold* = he gets bored easily; **pain threshold** = point at which a person cannot bear pain without crying

threw [θruː] *see* THROW (NOTE: do not confuse with **through**)

thrice [θraɪs] *adverb (old)* three times; *when the clock strikes thrice the prince will become a frog again*

thrift [θrɪft] *noun* **(a)** saving money and spending it carefully; *through hard work and thrift the family became rich* **(b)** small plant with little pink flowers, growing by the sea; *small clumps of thrift were flowering in the dunes* (NOTE: no plural in meanings (a) and (b)) **(c)** *US* private local bank which accepts and pays interest on deposits from small investors

thrifty ['θrɪfti] *adjective* careful with money; *thrifty hard-working people are ideal for mortgages* (NOTE: **thriftier - thriftiest**)

thrill [θrɪl] **1** *noun* feeling of great excitement; *it gave me a thrill to see you all again after so many years; the thrill of sailing near to a waterfall* **2** *verb* to make someone very excited; *we were thrilled to get your letter*

thriller ['θrɪlə] *noun* exciting novel, film, etc.; *I'm looking for a good thriller to read on the plane*

thrilling ['θrɪlɪŋ] *adjective* which makes you very excited; *it was thrilling to land in New York for the first time*

thrive [θraɪv] *verb* to grow well and be strong; *she thrives on her work as a doctor*; *a thriving black market in car radios*

throat [θrəʊt] *noun* **(a)** tube which goes from the back of your mouth down the inside of your neck; *I've got a sore throat today*; *she got a fish bone stuck in her throat*; **to clear your throat** = to give a little cough; *he cleared his throat and started to speak*; **a lump in your throat** = feeling unable to speak because you are so upset or so happy; *she had a lump in her throat as she saw her little girl dance across the stage* **(b)** your neck, especially the front part; *he put his hands round her throat and pressed hard*

throb [θrɒb] **1** *noun* beating of the heart, drum, machine, etc.; *the steady throb of the engine could be heard somewhere deep down in the ship* **2** *verb* **(a)** to beat regularly, like the heart; *she stopped running, and stood still with her heart throbbing*; *the engine started to throb more regularly and the great ship started to move* **(b)** to have a pain which comes regularly like a heartbeat; *when I woke up I had a sore throat and my head was throbbing* (NOTE: **throbbing - throbbed**)

throbbing [ˈθrɒbɪŋ] **1** *adjective* which comes again and again like a heartbeat; *the next morning he had a throbbing headache*; *she has a throbbing pain behind her left eye* **2** *noun* pain which comes again and again like a heartbeat; *there is a continual throbbing in my right ear*

throes [θrəʊz] *noun* **(a)** **in the throes of** = in the middle of; *he can't do anything - he's in the throes of getting a divorce*; *the country is in the throes of a general election* **(b)** **death throes** = great suffering just before death; *we stood on deck watching the death throes of the whale*

thrombosis [θrɒmˈbəʊsɪs] *noun* blood clotting which blocks an artery or vein; **cerebral thrombosis** = condition where a blood clot enters and blocks a brain artery (NOTE: also called a **stroke**); **coronary thrombosis** = blood clot which blocks the coronary arteries, leading to a heart attack; *coronary thrombosis deprives part of the heart muscle of blood*

throne [θrəʊn] *noun* chair on which a king or queen sits during ceremonies; **to succeed to the throne** = to become king or queen; *he succeeded to the throne when his grandfather died*; **to give up the throne** = to resign from being king or queen; *he gave up the throne and retired to live in the country* (NOTE: do not confuse with **thrown**)

throng [θrɒŋ] **1** *noun* great crowd of people; *the stars had difficulty making their way through the throng of fans outside the cinema* **2** *verb* to crowd together; *the children thronged round the TV star*; *the shopping precinct was thronged with shoppers in the days before Christmas*

throttle [ˈθrɒtl] **1** *noun* valve on a pipe in an engine, which allows variable quantities of petrol, etc., to pass into an engine; *he had to retire from the race when his throttle jammed*; **to open up the throttle** = to make the engine go faster; *open the throttle right up and let's see how fast the boat can go*; **at full throttle** = as fast as possible; *he had the engine going at full throttle* **2** *verb* to strangle someone by squeezing the neck, and preventing them breathing; *I could throttle him sometimes when he gives me that sort of answer*

through [θruː] **1** *preposition* **(a)** across the inside of something; going in at one side and coming out of the other; *she looked through the open door*; *cold air is coming in through the hole in the wall*; *the street goes straight through the centre of the town*; *she pushed the needle through the ball of wool* **(b)** during a period of time; *they insisted on talking all through the film* **(c)** by; *we sent the parcel through the ordinary mail*; *we heard of his wedding through the newspaper* **(d)** caused by; *we marked him as absent through illness*; *we missed the deadline through her forgetting to mark it in her diary* **(e)** *US* up to and including; **Monday through Friday** = from Monday to Friday inclusively **2** *adverb* **(a)** going in at one side and coming out of the other side; *someone left the gate open and all the sheep got through* **(b)** speaking by telephone; *I can't get through to New York*; *can you put me through to the person who deals with customer complaints?* **(c)** **to see something through** = to make sure that something is finished (NOTE: do not confuse with **threw**; **through** is often used after verbs: **to go through, to fall through, to see through**, etc.) **3** *adjective* **(a)** not stopping; **through traffic** = traffic which is going through a town and doesn't stop; *through traffic is being diverted to the bypass* **(b)** **through with something** = finished using something, not wanting something any more; *are you through with the newspaper?*; *she's through with her boyfriend*

throughout [θruːˈaʊt] *preposition & adverb* everywhere, all through; *throughout the country floods are causing problems on the roads*; *heavy snow fell throughout the night*

throughput [ˈθruːpʊt] *noun* amount of work done or goods produced during a certain period; *we hope to increase our throughput by putting in two new machines*

throughway [ˈθruːweɪ] *noun US see* THRUWAY

throw [θrəʊ] **1** *verb* **(a)** to send something through the air; *how far can he throw a cricket ball?*; *they were throwing stones through car windows*; *she threw the letter into the wastepaper basket*; *he was thrown into the air by the blast from the bomb* **(b)** **to throw a party** = to organize a party; *they threw a reception for the prize winners* **(c)** *(informal)* to shock; *at first, what the boss said threw me* (NOTE: **throwing - threw** [θruː] - **has thrown** [θrəʊn]) **2** *noun* **(a)** act of throwing; *her javelin throw beat the world record*; *he hurt his back after a throw from his horse* **(b)** **only a stone's throw from** = very near; *the hotel is only a stone's throw from the beach* **(c)** piece of material which you put over a chair, use as a carpet, etc.; *she gave me a piece of old Chinese silk as a throw to cover the sofa*

throw away [ˈθrəʊ əˈweɪ] *verb* to get rid of something which you don't need any more; *don't throw away those old newspapers - they may come in useful*; *she threw away all her winter clothes*

throw in [ˈθrəʊ ˈɪn] *verb* to add something extra as a bargain; *when we bought our new oven, they threw in a set of saucepans as a free gift*

throw-in [ˈθrəʊɪn] *noun (in football)* throwing the ball back into play from the touch-line; *he made a long throw-in*

thrown [θrəʊn] *see* THROW (NOTE: do not confuse with **throne**)

throw off [ˈθrəʊ ˈɒf] *verb* **(a)** to remove something quickly; *she threw off the bedclothes and ran out of the room* **(b)** to recover from an illness; *she's had a cough for several days, and can't throw it off*

throw out ['θrəʊ 'aʊt] *verb* **(a)** to push someone outside; *when they started to fight, they were thrown out of the restaurant* **(b)** to get rid of something which you don't need; *I'm throwing out this old office desk* **(c)** to refuse to accept; *the proposal was thrown out by the planning committee*

throw up ['θrəʊ 'ʌp] *verb* **(a)** *(informal)* to vomit; *the cat threw up all over the sofa* **(b)** to give up something; *she's thrown up her job and gone to live in Australia*

thru [θruː] *preposition, adverb & adjective US (informal)* = THROUGH

thrush [θrʌʃ] *noun* common brown bird with brown spots on its light-coloured breast (NOTE: plural is **thrushes**)

thrust [θrʌst] **1** *noun* **(a)** force which pushes; *the thrust of the engines pushed him back in his seat* **(b)** act of pushing; *he was killed with a thrust of his opponent's sword* **2** *verb* **(a)** to push suddenly and hard; *he thrust the newspaper into his pocket*; *she thrust the documents into her briefcase* **(b)** *(formal)* to **thrust yourself on someone** = to force someone to accept you as a guest, companion, etc.

thruway ['θruːweɪ] *noun US* fast main road; *it is much faster if you take the thruway south* (NOTE: also spelled **throughway**)

thud [θʌd] **1** *noun* dull, heavy noise; *his head hit the ground with a sickening thud*; *they could hear the thud of gunfire in the distance* **2** *verb* to make a dull noise; *a stone thudded into the wall behind him* (NOTE: **thudding - thudded**)

thug [θʌg] *noun* violent person; *gangs of thugs roamed the streets, breaking shop windows and attacking passers-by*

thumb [θʌm] **1** *noun* **(a)** short thick digit which is slightly apart from the other four fingers on each hand; *the baby was sucking its thumb*; *how she cried when she hit her thumb with the hammer!* **(b)** his fingers are all thumbs = he is awkward when trying to do something with his hands; *can you help me untie this knot, my fingers are all thumbs!*; **rule of thumb** = easily remembered way of doing a simple calculation; *divide by eight and multiply by five is a useful rule of thumb when converting kilometres into miles* **(c)** *(informal)* **thumbs up (sign)** = gesture to show that you approve, that things are all right; *he gave us the thumbs up to show that we were through to the next stage of the competition* *(informal)* **thumbs down (sign)** = gesture to show you disapprove; *the project got the thumbs down from the minister* **(d)** **under someone's thumb** = dominated by someone; *she's got him under her thumb* = he has to do what she tells him to do **2** *verb* **(a)** **to thumb a lift** = to ask a car driver or truck driver to take you as a passenger, usually by signalling with the thumb while holding a sign with your destination written on it; *her car broke down and she thumbed a lift from a passing motorist* **(b)** **to thumb through** = to turn over pages; *I was just thumbing through this old accounts book*

thumbnail sketch ['θʌmneɪl 'sketʃ] *noun* little drawing or description of something, giving just a few details; *his book contains thumbnail sketches of various members of the government*

thumbtack ['θʌmtæk] *noun US* pin with a large flat head, used for pinning papers to a wall or a surface; *she used thumbtacks to pin the poster to the door*; *he put a thumbtack on the teacher's chair* (NOTE: British English is **drawing pin**)

thump [θʌmp] **1** *noun* **(a)** dull noise; *there was a thump from upstairs as if someone had fallen out of bed* **(b)** punch, a heavy blow with the fist; *she was so annoyed she gave him a good thump on the arm* **2** *verb* **(a)** *(informal)* to hit someone hard with your fist; *he rushed up to the policeman and started thumping him on the chest*; *she thumped him on the back when he choked* **(b)** to make a dull noise; *how can we possibly get to sleep with the music thumping away next door?*; *I was very frightened and I could feel my heart thumping furiously*

thumping ['θʌmpɪŋ] *adjective (informal)* very large; *the government had a thumping majority at the last general election*

thunder ['θʌndə] **1** *noun* **(a)** loud noise in the air following a flash of lightning; *a tropical storm accompanied by thunder and lightning*; *he was woken by the sound of thunder* **(b)** loud noise; *the thunder of horses' hooves on the paving stones*; *he took his bow to a thunder of applause* *(informal)* **to steal someone's thunder** = to spoil what someone is planning to do by doing it first, and so getting applauded for it **2** *verb* **(a)** to make a loud noise in the air following lightning; *it thundered during the night* **(b)** to make a loud rumbling noise; *lorries thundered past on the motorway all night* **(c)** to speak in a very loud voice; *'shut up' he thundered to the little boy in the back row*

thunderclap ['θʌndəklæp] *noun* sudden loud noise made by thunder; *a thunderclap woke us up*

thundercloud ['θʌndəklaʊd] *noun* large black cloud which brings rain and a thunderstorm; *thunderclouds were gathering over the mountains*

thunderous ['θʌndrəs] *adjective* very loud noise, often of applause, etc.; *the actors came back on stage to thunderous applause*

thunderstorm ['θʌndəstɔːm] *noun* storm with rain, thunder and lightning; *there was a terrible thunderstorm last night and our house was struck by lightning*; *don't shelter under a tree during a thunderstorm*

thunderstruck ['θʌndəstrʌk] *adjective* very surprised; *he was thunderstruck when he found out that she was already married*

thundery ['θʌndri] *adjective* (weather) when thunder is likely; *people say that milk turns sour quickly in thundery weather*; *they are forecasting thundery showers for the afternoon*

Thursday ['θɜːzdeɪ] *noun* day between Wednesday and Friday, the fourth day of the week; *last Thursday was Christmas Day*; *shall we arrange to meet next Thursday?*; *today is Thursday, April 14th*; *the club meets on Thursdays* or *every Thursday*; *the 15th is a Wednesday, so the 16th must be a Thursday*

thus [ðʌs] *adverb (formal)* **(a)** in this way; *the two pieces fit together thus* **(b)** as a result; *she is only fifteen, and thus is not eligible for the over-sixteens competition*

thwart [θwɔːt] **1** *noun* seat across a rowing boat, for a rower to sit on; *they sat side-by-side on the thwart and each took an oar* **2** *verb (formal)* to prevent someone doing something; *he was thwarted by the police in his attempt to get into the building*; *his career move was thwarted by the new manager*

thyme [taɪm] *noun* common herb used as flavouring; *put a few sprigs of thyme on the meat before placing it in the oven*

thyroid (gland) [ˈθaɪrɔɪd (ˈglænd)] *noun* gland in the neck which influences the body's metabolism

> COMMENT: the thyroid gland requires iodine to function properly, and lack of it can lead to goitre

tick [tɪk] **1** *noun* **(a)** sound made every second by a clock; *the only sound we could hear in the room was the tick of the grandfather clock* **(b)** *(informal)* a short moment; *wait a tick, my shoelace has come undone*; *wait there, I'll be with you in a tick* **(c)** mark written to show that something is correct; *put a tick in the box marked 'R'* (NOTE: American English for this meaning is **check**) **(d)** *(informal)* credit; *all the furniture in the house is bought on tick* **(e)** small insect which lives on the skin and sucks blood; *sheep can be affected by ticks* **2** *verb* **(a)** to mark with a tick to show that you approve; *tick the box marked 'R' if you require a receipt* (NOTE: American English for this meaning is **check**) **(b)** to make a regular little noise; *all you could hear was the clock ticking in the corner of the library*; *watch out! that parcel's ticking!*

ticket [ˈtɪkɪt] *noun* **(a)** piece of paper or card which allows you to travel; *they won't let you get on to Eurostar without a ticket*; *we've lost our plane tickets - how can we get to Chicago?*; **season ticket** = ticket which can be used for any number of journeys over a period (usually one, three, six or twelve months); **single ticket** *US* **one-way ticket** = ticket for one journey from one place to another; **return ticket** *US* **round-trip ticket** = ticket for a journey from one place to another and back again **(b)** piece of paper which allows you to go into a cinema, an exhibition, etc.; *can I have three tickets for the 8.30 show please?*; *we tried several theatres but there were no tickets left anywhere* **(c)** **parking ticket** = paper which you get when you leave a car parked wrongly, telling you that you will have to pay a fine; *if you leave your car on the yellow line you'll get a ticket!* **(d)** label, piece of paper which shows something; *keep the ticket in case you want to change the trousers later*; **price ticket** = piece of paper showing a price **(e)** *US* a party's list of candidates for election to political office; *he ran for governor on the Republican ticket*

ticket office [ˈtɪkɪt ˈɒfɪs] *noun* office where tickets can be bought (either for travel or for theatres or cinemas.); *there was a long queue at the ticket office*; *if the ticket office is shut you can buy a ticket on the train*

tickle [ˈtɪkl] **1** *noun* irritation which makes you cough; *I've got a nasty tickle in my throat* **2** *verb* to touch someone in a sensitive part of the body in order to make them laugh; *she tickled his toes and made him laugh*

ticklish [ˈtɪklɪʃ] *adjective* **(a)** easily tickled; *she's very ticklish, you've just got to wave your finger at her and she starts to giggle* **(b)** *(informal)* tricky, not easy to deal with; *we're in rather a ticklish situation*

tick off [ˈtɪk ˈɒf] *verb* *(informal)* **to tick someone off** = to say that you are annoyed with someone; *the policeman ticked them off for running across the road in front of a bus*

tick over [ˈtɪk ˈəʊvə] *verb* **to be ticking over** = to go on working in the usual way; *make sure the office keeps ticking over while the boss is on holiday*

tick-tack-toe *or* **tic-tac-toe** [tɪktækˈtəʊ] *noun US (game)* game where each player puts either a zero or a cross on a grid, the first to get three in a row being the winner (NOTE: British English for this is **noughts and crosses**)

tick-tock [ˈtɪktɒk] *noun* the sound made by a clock; *all you could hear was the tick-tock of the clock in the hall*

tidal [ˈtaɪdəl] *adjective* **(a)** referring to the tide; *the river below the lock is tidal*; **tidal energy** *or* **tidal power** = electricity produced by turbines driven by the movement of the tide; *the group is calling for more resources to be put into the development of wave power and tidal energy*; **tidal stretch of a river** = part of a river near its mouth where the movement of the tides is noticeable; *the tidal stretch of the Thames reaches over 40 miles from the sea to Teddington Lock* **(b)** **tidal wave** = huge wave in the sea, caused by an underwater earthquake and not by the tide; *a tidal wave has caused widespread flooding along the coast of Bangladesh* (NOTE: also called **tsunami**)

tidbit [ˈtɪdbɪt] *noun US see* TITBIT

tide [taɪd] **1** *noun* **(a)** regular rising and falling movement of the sea; *the tide came in and cut off the children on the rocks*; *the tide is out, we can walk across the sand*; **high tide** *or* **low tide** = points when the level of the sea is at its highest *or* at its lowest; *high tide is at 6.05 p.m. today*; **the tide has turned** = the tide has started to go up or down **(b)** **the tide of public opinion** = the general trend of feeling among the public **2** *verb* **to tide someone over** = to help someone get through a difficult period; *can you lend me £50 to tide me over until pay day?*

tidemark [ˈtaɪdmɑːk] *noun* **(a)** mark showing the top limit of the tide on a beach **(b)** *(informal)* dirty line round a bath showing where the water reached to, or on someone's neck, showing which part of the body has been washed and which has not; *you can tell from the black tidemark in the bath how dirty the children must have been*; *he needs a bath, look at the tidemark round his neck*

tidings [ˈtaɪdɪŋz] *noun (formal)* information, news; *she is the bearer of good tidings*; *I bring you bad tidings from the field of battle*

tidy [ˈtaɪdi] **1** *adjective* neat, in order; *I want your room to be completely tidy before you go out*; *she put her clothes in a tidy pile* (NOTE: **tidier - tidiest**) **2** *verb* **to tidy up** = to make everything completely tidy; *mother asked us to help her tidy up after the party*

tie [taɪ] **1** *noun* **(a)** long piece of coloured cloth which men wear round their necks under the collar of their shirts; *he's wearing a blue tie with red stripes*; *they won't let you into the restaurant if you haven't got a tie on*; **old school tie** = tie with a special design which shows which school you went to (NOTE: American English prefers **necktie**) **(b)** result in a competition or election where both sides have the same score; *the result was a tie and the vote had to be taken again*; **there was a tie for second place** = two people were equal second (NOTE: also **draw**) **(c)** **cup tie** = sports match between two teams as a result of which one is eliminated from a competition; *we're expecting a big crowd for the cup tie next week* **(d)** thing which prevents you from doing what you want to do; *the big house has become something of a tie to my parents* **2** *verb* **(a)** to attach with string, rope, etc.; *the parcel was* *tied with a little piece of string; he tied his horse to the post; the burglars tied his hands behind his back* (b) to have the same score as another team in a competition; *they tied for second place*

tie-break ['taɪbreɪk] *noun (in tennis)* game played when the score reaches 6-6

tie-on label ['taɪ ɒn 'leɪbl] *noun* label with a piece of string attached so that it can be tied to an item of luggage or something for sale

tier ['tɪə] *noun* (a) one of a series of steps, usually a row of seats in a theatre; *they sat on the topmost tier of seats* (b) **wedding cake with two tiers** = cake made of two separate cakes balanced one on top of the other; *they ordered a four-tiered wedding cake*

tie up ['taɪ 'ʌp] *verb* (a) to put string or rope round something; *the parcel was tied up with thick string; you should tie that dog up or it will bite someone* (b) to **be tied up** = to be busy; *he's rather tied up at the moment - can we try to meet next week some time?*

tiger ['taɪgə] *noun* large striped wild animal of the cat family living mainly in India and China

tight [taɪt] **1** *adjective* (a) fitting too closely; *these shoes hurt - they're too tight* (b) packed close together; **a tight fit** = situation where there is not enough space to fit; *we can get one more person into the taxi but it will be a tight fit;* **a tight schedule** = a schedule where many meetings are very close together; *the doctor has a very tight schedule today and cannot fit in any more appointments* (c) *(informal)* **money is tight** = there is not very much money available (d) holding firmly; *keep a tight hold of the bag, we don't want it stolen* (e) *(informal)* drunk; *he got rather tight at the Christmas party* (NOTE: **tighter - tightest**) **2** *adverb* (a) closely, firmly (shut); *make sure the windows are shut tight* (b) **to hold tight** = to hold something firmly; *hold tight - we're about to take off*

tighten ['taɪtn] *verb* to make tight; to become tight; *I tightened the straps on my rucksack;* **to tighten your belt** = to be ready to spend less, eat less, etc.; *the government warned that we must tighten our belts*

tighten up on ['taɪtn 'ʌp ɒn] *verb* to control something more carefully; *the government is tightening up on tax evasion*

tight-fisted ['taɪt 'fɪstɪd] *adjective* miserly, not wanting to spend money; *he's very tight-fisted when it comes to birthday presents*

tightfitting [taɪt'fɪtɪŋ] *adjective* which fits the body tightly; *she wore a tightfitting dress*

tightly ['taɪtli] *adverb* in a tight way; *she kept her eyes tightly shut; tie the string as tightly as you can*

tightrope ['taɪtrəʊp] *noun* rope stretched between two poles on which someone can walk or perform tricks; *if she falls off the tightrope the safety net will catch her;* **to walk a tightrope** = (i) to walk on a tightrope; (ii) to go carefully in a difficult situation; *it takes a lot of practice to be a tightrope walker; the government has to walk a tightrope between pleasing the unions and pleasing the employers*

tights [taɪts] *noun* piece of clothing made of thin material, covering your hips, and your legs and feet separately, worn by girls, women, dancers, etc.; *look - you've got a hole in your tights!* (NOTE: American English is **panty hose**)

tigress ['taɪgrəs] *noun* female tiger; *the tigress stalked through the jungle with her cubs* (NOTE: plural is **tigresses**)

tikka ['tɪkə] *noun* type of Indian cooking done in a hot clay oven with red curry sauce; *we ordered chicken tikka and rice*

tilde ['tɪldə] *noun* printed accent (~) used over certain letters; *España is written with a tilde over the 'ñ'*

> COMMENT: the tilde is used over the ñ in Spanish, or over ã and õ in Portuguese

tile [taɪl] **1** *noun* (a) flat piece of baked clay used as a covering for floors, walls or roofs; *the floor is covered with red tiles;* *we are putting white tiles on the bathroom walls* (b) similar piece of another kind of material used to cover a floor, etc.; *they put cork tiles on the walls;* **carpet tiles** = square pieces of carpet which can be put down on the floor like tiles **2** *verb* to cover the surface of a roof, a floor or a wall with tiles; *they have tiled the kitchen with red floor tiles; a white-tiled bathroom*

till [tɪl] **1** *noun* drawer for keeping cash in a shop; *there was not much money in the till at the end of the day* **2** *preposition & conjunction* until, up to the time when; *I don't expect him to be home till after nine o'clock; they worked from morning till night to finish the job; we worked till the sun went down* **3** *verb (formal)* to plough and cultivate soil, to make it ready for growing crops; *in some parts of the world farmers are still using oxen to till the land*

tiller ['tɪlə] *noun* handle which is attached to a rudder and so steers a boat; *he pushed the tiller to one side and the boat moved to starboard; the sailing boat lost her tiller in the storm*

tilt [tɪlt] **1** *noun* (a) sloping or slanting position; *the table has a noticeable tilt* (b) **(at) full tilt** = at full speed; *he was going full tilt when he tripped over; the car ran full tilt into a lamppost* **2** *verb* (a) to slope; *the shelf is tilting to the right; you'll have to change places - the boat is tilting* (b) to put in a sloping position; *he tilted the barrel over to get the last drops of beer out*

timber ['tɪmbə] *noun* (a) *(general)* wood cut ready for building; *these trees are being grown to provide timber for houses* (NOTE: no plural: for one item say **a piece of timber;** American English is **lumber**) (b) one large piece of wood used in building; *the roof was built with timbers from old ships; some of the timbers are rotten and need to be replaced*

timbre ['tæmbə] *noun* quality of the sound, of a voice, musical instrument, etc.; *the timbre of the brass in the orchestra*

time [taɪm] **1** *noun* (a) amount of hours, days, weeks, etc.; *there's no need to hurry - we've got plenty of time; do you have time for a cup of coffee?; he spent all that time watching the TV; if the fire alarm rings, don't waste time putting clothes on - run out of the hotel fast; see also* FIND TIME, MAKE TIME (b) certain period; *we haven't been to France for a long time; we had a letter from my mother a short time ago;* **in ... time** = during a period from now; *we're going on holiday in four weeks' time;* **to take time** = to need a certain amount of time; *it didn't take you much time to get dressed; don't hurry me, I like to take my time;* **your time's up** = the amount of time allocated to you is over; *bring back your boat, your time's up; (informal)* **to do time** = to serve a prison sentence; *he's doing time* for theft **(c)** particular point in the day shown in hours and minutes; *what time is it?* or *what's the time?*; *can you tell me the time please?*; *the time is exactly four thirty*; *departure times are delayed by up to fifteen minutes because of the volume of traffic*; **to tell the time** = to read the time on a clock or watch; *she's only three so she can't tell the time yet* **(d)** system of hours on the clock; **Summer Time** or **Daylight Saving Time** = system of putting the clocks forward one hour in summer to provide extra daylight in the evening; **time difference** = difference in time between one time zone and another; *there is two hours time difference between Moscow and London*; *see also* GREENWICH MEAN TIME **(e)** particular moment when something happens; *they didn't hear anything as they were asleep at the time*; *by the time the ambulance arrived the man had died*; *you can't do two things at the same time*; **for the time being** = temporarily; *for the time being I'm staying at my mother's while I'm waiting for my flat to be redecorated*; **at times** = on some occasions; *at times I think he's quite mad*; *see also* SOMETIMES **(f)** hour at which something usually happens; *the closing time for the office is 5.30*; *it's must be nearly time for dinner - I'm hungry*; *is it time for the children to go to bed?*; *see also* BEDTIME, DINNERTIME, LUNCHTIME, TEATIME **(g)** period when things are pleasant or bad; *everyone had a good time at the party*; *we had an awful time on holiday - the hotel was dreadful, and it rained solidly for ten days* **(h)** one of several moments or periods when something happens; *I've seen that James Bond film on TV four times already*; *that's the last time I'll ask them to play cards*; *next time you come, bring your swimming things*; **time after time** = repeatedly, again and again; *I've told her time after time not to do it* **(i)** **times** = multiplied by; *six times twenty is one hundred and twenty*; *this book is three times as expensive as that one*; *she's a hundred times more efficient than the old secretary* **(j) in time** = not late; *they drove fast and got to the station just in time to catch the train*; *you'll have to hurry if you want to be in time for the meeting*; *we got to Buckingham Palace just in time to see the Changing of the Guard*; **in good time** = early, before the time needed; *we drove fast and got to the airport in good time* **(k) on time** = happening at the expected time; *the plane arrived on time*; *she's never on time for meetings*; *you will have to hurry if you want to get to the wedding on time or if you want to be on time for the wedding* **(l) times** = a period in the past; *in Elizabethan times, most men carried swords*; **behind the times** = not up-to-date, old-fashioned; *he's way behind the times* = he's very old-fashioned **2** *verb* to count in hours and minutes; *I timed him as he ran round the track*; *don't forget to time the eggs - they have to cook for only three minutes*; *the police cameras timed the car - it was going at more than 100 miles an hour*

time bomb ['taɪm 'bɒm] *noun* **(a)** bomb with a clock attached, which can be set to explode at a certain time; *they said that they had left a time bomb in the railway station* **(b)** difficult situation which will happen in the future; *the rapid increase in the world's population is a time bomb for future governments*

time frame ['taɪm 'freɪm] *noun* period of time during which something should take place; *the project may not be completed with the time frame allowed*

timeless ['taɪmləs] *adjective (formal)* which is not affected by time; *the timeless quality of Botticelli's painting*; *the timeless beauty of the Lake District*

time limit ['taɪm 'lɪmɪt] *noun* point in time by which something should be done; *we will set a time limit of two days for the project to be completed*

timely ['taɪmli] *adjective* which happens at the right moment; *a very timely reminder from the bank*

time out ['taɪm 'aʊt] *noun* **to take time out for something** = to take a rest from some activity; *she took time out from her work to come and say hallo to the visitors*

timepiece ['taɪmpiːs] *noun (old)* watch or clock; *the old admiral always used to consult the ancient timepiece in the hall before going outside*

timer ['taɪmə] *noun* **(a)** device which times; *the timer buzzed to show that the five minutes were up*; **egg timer** = device which is used to time how long an egg boils **(b)** time-switch; *I set the timer so that the oven came on at 6 o'clock*; *don't forget to change the central heating timer when the clocks are put back*; *the police found explosives and timers in the garage*

timeshare ['taɪmʃeə] *noun* property which you own together with other people, each having the right to use it for a period each year; *he has a timeshare in Spain*

time-switch ['taɪmswɪtʃ] *noun* switch which can be set to switch electricity on or off, to start a machine, switch off a light, etc., at a particular time; *the time-switch puts on the floodlights at 8 o'clock in the evening*

timetable ['taɪmteɪbl] **1** *noun* printed list which shows the times of classes in school, of trains leaving, etc.; *we have two English lessons on the timetable today*; *the airline has issued its summer timetable, and all the times have changed*; *according to the timetable, there should be a train to London at 10.22* **2** *verb* to schedule, to arrange the times for something; *you are timetabled to speak at 4.30*

time trial ['taɪm 'traɪəl] *noun* testing competitors by timing each one over a track, especially in car and bicycle races; *the Tour de France is formed of a series of long-distance stages, interspersed with time trials*

time zone ['taɪm 'zəʊn] *noun* one of 24 bands in the world in which the same standard time is used; *when you fly across the USA you cross several time zones*

timid ['tɪmɪd] *adjective* afraid to do something; *he wanted to take her out for a meal, but was too timid to ask*; *she gave him a timid smile and asked him what his name was*

timidly ['tɪmɪdli] *adverb* in a timid way; *she timidly bet two pounds on the race*

timing ['taɪmɪŋ] *noun* controlling the time at which something happens; *the timing of the conference is very convenient, as it comes just before my summer holiday*; *that was good timing - to arrive just as I was opening a bottle of wine!*

timpani ['tɪmpəni] *noun* set of kettledrums in an orchestra; *the timpani came in at the end of the piece*

tin [tɪn] *noun* **(a)** silver-coloured soft metal; *bronze is a mixture of copper and tin*; *there have been tin mines in Cornwall since Roman times* (NOTE: Chemical element: chemical symbol: **Sn**; atomic number: 50) **(b)** metal container in which food is sold and can be kept for a long time; *I'm lazy - I'll just open a tin of soup*;

she bought three tins of cat food; we'll need three tins of white paint for the ceiling (NOTE: in British English also called **can**, especially for drinks; American English is only **can**) **(c)** any metal box; keep the biscuits in a tin or they'll go soft; she puts her spare coins into a tin by the telephone

tin can ['tɪn 'kæn] noun round metal box in which food or drink is sold and can be kept for a long time; the alley was full of old newspapers and rusty tin cans; as they drove off from the wedding they realised that someone had tied a tin can to the back of the car

tine [taɪn] noun **(a)** sharp prong of a tool such as a fork or rake; this fork has four tines **(b)** sharp pointed part of a deer's antler

tinfoil ['tɪnfɔɪl] noun thin sheet of aluminium, used to cover food; wrap the salmon in tinfoil and place in the oven

tinge [tɪnʒ] **1** noun slight colour or feeling, etc., of something; she's has blond hair with tinges of red; the fabric is red with a blue tinge; the family didn't show the slightest tinge of excitement about her wedding; there was a slight tinge of sadness in the air as they left the house for the last time **2** verb to give a slight colour or taste to something; the setting sun tinged everything orange; her mother's ill health tinged her last trip home with sadness

tinged [tɪnʒd] adjective **tinged with** = with a little of; she said goodbye in a voice tinged with sadness; a yellow peach tinged with pink

tingle ['tɪŋgl] **1** noun sharp prickling feeling; it didn't hurt, I just felt a tingle in my leg; we felt a tingle of excitement as we queued for the roller coaster **2** verb **(a)** to have a sharp prickling feeling; 'are your fingers tingling?' asked the doctor; it will tingle when I put some iodine on your knee **(b)** **to tingle with excitement** = to be very excited; the children are tingling with excitement as Christmas approaches

tinker ['tɪŋkə] **1** noun (old) mender of saucepans who travels from place to place; see also the comment at CHERRY STONE **2** verb **to tinker with something** = to try to make something work better, but not very successfully; he spent Saturday morning tinkering with his car; the government are just tinkering with the economy when they should be taking strong action

tinkle ['tɪŋkl] **1** noun **(a)** noise like the ringing of a little bell; the gentle tinkle of cow bells on alpine pastures **(b)** (informal) telephone call; I'll give you a tinkle when we've sorted out the details **2** verb to make a little ringing noise; the little bell tinkled as she went into the shop

tinned [tɪnd] adjective preserved and sold in a tin; I like tinned pineapple better than fresh

tin opener ['tɪn 'əupnə] noun device for opening tins of food; we took several tins of soup with us when we went camping, but forgot the tin opener! (NOTE: American English is **can opener**)

tinsel ['tɪnsl] noun thin strips of glittering metal used as Christmas decorations; the children were putting tinsel on the Christmas tree (NOTE: no plural)

tint [tɪnt] **1** noun **(a)** slight shade of colour; a rosy tint in the eastern sky was the first sign of dawn; do you prefer this blue with a tint of grey in it? **(b)** dye used to colour hair; her hair is such a dull colour - she should put a tint in it **2** verb to give something a slight shade of colour; windows of aircraft are tinted to reduce the

glare from the sun; how much would it cost to have my hair tinted?; **tinted glass** = glass which has a slight shade of brown, blue, etc.; he was wearing tinted spectacles; our new car has tinted windows

tiny ['taɪni] adjective very small; can I have just a tiny bit more pudding?; the spot is so tiny you can hardly see it; she lives in a tiny village in the Welsh mountains (NOTE: **tinier - tiniest**)

tip [tɪp] **1** noun **(a)** end of something long; she reads Braille by touching the page with the tips of her fingers; he poked the pig with the tip of his walking stick; (informal) **it's on the tip of my tongue** = I'll remember it in a moment, I'm trying hard to remember it; **it's the tip of iceberg** = it's only a small part of something (usually unpleasant) while the rest is hidden; those errors in the accounts were just the tip of the iceberg - the staff had been stealing money and stock for years **(b)** money given to someone who has provided a service; the taxi driver was annoyed because I only gave him a 20p tip; the service hasn't been very good - should we leave a tip for the waiter?; the staff are not allowed to accept tips **(c)** advice on something which could be profitable; he gave me a tip about a horse which was likely to win; she gave me a tip about a cheap restaurant just round the corner from the hotel **(d)** place where household rubbish is taken to be thrown away; I must take these bags of rubbish to the tip **(e)** (informal) dirty place; look at your bedroom - it's a tip! **2** verb **(a)** to pour something out; he picked up the box and tipped the contents out onto the floor; she tipped all the food out of the bag **(b)** to give money to someone who has helped you; I tipped the waiter £1; should we tip the driver? **(c)** to predict that something may happen, especially who will win; he's tipped to win the election; which horse are you tipping in the next race? (NOTE: **tipping - tipped**)

tip off ['tɪp 'ɒf] verb (informal) **to tip someone off** = to warn someone; we think he tipped the burglars off that the police were outside

tip-off ['tɪpɒf] noun (informal) piece of useful information, given secretly; acting on a tip-off from a member of the public, customs officials stopped the truck; the police received a tip-off about a bomb in the building

tip over ['tɪp 'əuvə] verb **(a)** to lean and fall over; the lorry tipped over in the wind; my cup tipped over and all the coffee spilled on to the tablecloth **(b)** to make something lean so that it falls over; the wind was so strong that it tipped over the caravan

tiptoe ['tɪptəu] **1** noun **on tiptoe** = on your toes, with your heels in the air; by standing on tiptoe he could just see into the window; he crept past the sleeping dog on tiptoe **2** verb to walk quietly on tiptoe; she tiptoed into the room and looked at the baby

tip up ['tɪp 'ʌp] verb **(a)** to lean and fall over; the cup tipped up and all the tea went into the saucer **(b)** to turn something over so that the contents fall out; he tipped up the bottle to see if there was any tomato sauce left inside

tirade [taɪ'reɪd] noun long speech attacking something; he was expecting his mother to launch into a tirade about the mess in his room, but she didn't say anything

tire [taɪə] **1** noun US see TYRE **2** verb to become tired; to make someone become tired; he is getting old *and tires easily; we went for a long cycle ride to tire the children out*

tired ['taɪəd] *adjective* **(a)** feeling sleepy; *I'm tired - I think I'll go to bed; if you feel tired, lie down on my bed* **(b)** feeling that you need rest; *we're all tired after a long day at the office* **(c)** to be (sick and) tired of something = to be bored with something, to have had enough of something; **to get tired of something** = to become bored with something; *I'm sick and tired of waiting for the doctor; they're tired of always having to do all the washing up; can't we do something else - I'm getting tired of visiting museums*

tiredness ['taɪədnəs] *noun* feeling tired; *a continual feeling of tiredness could be the symptom of something*

tired out ['taɪəd 'aʊt] *adjective* feeling very sleepy, feeling that you must have rest; *they were tired out after their long walk; come and sit down - you must be tired out*

tireless ['taɪələs] *adjective* full of energy, never needing to rest; *she has been a tireless campaigner for human rights all her life*

tiresome ['taɪəsəli] *adjective* annoying or bothering; *he has the tiresome habit of singing while he works; it's really tiresome having to wait for him to finish his tea before we can go out*

tiring ['taɪrɪŋ] *adjective* which makes you tired; *after a tiring day in the office all I want to do is sit down and watch TV*

tissue ['tɪʃuː] *noun* **(a)** soft paper handkerchief; *there is a box of tissues beside the bed* **(b)** tissue paper = thin soft paper used for wrapping glass and other delicate objects; *wrap the glasses in tissue paper before you put them away in the box* **(c)** groups of cells which form an animal or plant; *animal tissue grown in a laboratory; they took a sample of tissue from the growth*

tit [tɪt] *noun* **(a)** type of common small bird, usually with blue and yellow or black plumage; *several varieties of tit come to our bird table to feed; we haven't had blue tits in the garden for a long time* **(b)** *(slang)* woman's breast **(c)** tit for tat = paying back a blow with another blow; *one gang kills someone of the rival gang, then the rivals kill one of theirs, it's just tit for tat; the gang violence shows no sign of coming to an end, with this latest in the series of tit-for-tat killings*

titan ['taɪtn] *noun* very large, important person; *he is one of the titans of the opera world*

titanic [taɪ'tænɪk] *adjective* very large, important; *they made titanic efforts to get the building finished on time*

titanium [tɪ'teɪniəm] *noun* light grey metal which does not rust, used in making aircraft and satellites; *the surgical use of titanium is not new* (NOTE: Chemical element: chemical symbol: **Ti**; atomic number: **22**)

titbit *US* **tidbit** ['tɪtbɪt] *noun* special little piece of food, of gossip; *here is a special little titbit of information which you will enjoy; the children gave the baby hedgehog titbits of bread soaked in milk*

titchy ['tɪtʃi] *adjective (informal)* very small; *she's got a titchy little car*

titillate ['tɪtɪleɪt] *verb* to excite; *the pictures of naked women in newspapers are there purely to titillate the male readership*

title ['taɪtl] *noun* **(a)** name of a book, play, painting, film, etc.; *he's almost finished the play but hasn't found a title for it yet;* **title page** = page at the beginning of a book, which gives the title (usually in large letters), the name of the author and the name of the publisher; **title role** = part in a play or film which gives the name to the play or film; *she played the title role in 'Mrs Warren's Profession'* **(b)** word (such as Dr, Mr, Professor, Lord, Sir, Lady, etc.) put in front of a name to show an honour or a qualification **(c)** *(in sport)* official position of champion; *what are his chances of retaining the Formula One title for a second year running?* **(d)** right to own a property; *he holds the title to the property;* **title deeds** = document showing who is the owner of a property

titled ['taɪtld] *adjective* with a title, such as Lord, Sir, etc., put in front of a name; *a titled lady has come to live in the village*

to [tuː] **1** *preposition* **(a)** *(showing direction or place)* *they went to the police station; do you know the way to the beach?; the river is to the north of the town; everyone take one step to the right, please* **(b)** *(showing a period of time)* *the office is open from 9.30 to 5.30, Monday to Friday; she slept from 11.30 to 8.30 the following morning* **(c)** *(showing time in minutes before an hour)* *get up - it's five to seven; the train leaves at a quarter to eight* (NOTE: **to** is used for times between the half hour and o'clock: **3.35** = twenty-five to four; **3.45** = a quarter to four; **3.55** = five minutes to four. For times after the hour see **past**) **(d)** *(showing person or animal that receives something)* *take the book to the librarian; pass the salt to your grandfather; you must be kind to cats* **(e)** *(showing connection)* *they lost by twelve to nine; the exchange rate is ten francs to the pound; there are four keys to the office; in this class there are 28 children to one teacher* **(f)** *(showing that you are comparing)* *do you prefer butter to margarine?; you can't compare tinned pineapple to fresh fruit* **2** *(used before a verb)* **(a)** *(following verbs)* *did you remember to switch off the light?; the burglar tried to run away; she agreed to go to work in Australia; they all decided to go home early* **(b)** *(showing purpose)* *the nurses came to help at the scene of the accident; the doctor left half an hour ago to go to the hospital* **(c)** *(used after adjectives)* *I'd be glad to help; is the water OK to drink?; I'm sorry to be so late for the meeting* **(d)** *(used after a comparison)* *she was too tired to do anything except sit down* **(e)** *(used after nouns)* *this is the best way to do it; his absolute determination to succeed*

toad [təʊd] *noun* **(a)** animal like a large frog, which lives mainly on land; *toads have to cross the road to get to their pond* **(b)** toad in the hole = sausages cooked in batter

toadstool ['təʊdstuːl] *noun* small fungus shaped like an umbrella, but usually not edible, and sometimes poisonous; *that's not a mushroom, it's a toadstool, so don't eat it* (NOTE: white edible fungi are called **mushrooms**)

to and fro [tuː ən 'frəʊ] *adverb* backwards and forwards; *he walked to and fro in the corridor*

toast [təʊst] *noun* **(a)** slices of bread which have been cooked at a high temperature until they are brown; *can you make some more toast?; she asked for scrambled eggs on toast;* **brown toast** or **white toast** = toast made from brown bread or white bread; *I always have a piece of brown toast and marmalade for breakfast; see also*

WARM (NOTE: no plural in this meaning: **some toast, a piece of toast** *or* **a slice of toast**) **(b) to drink a toast to someone** = to take a drink and wish someone success; *let's drink a toast to the bride and groom!*; *we all drank a toast to the future success of the company* **2** *verb* **(a)** to cook bread, etc., in a toaster or under a grill, until it is brown; *we had toasted teacakes* **(b)** to wish someone success and drink at the same time; *they all toasted the happy couple in champagne*

toaster ['təʊstə] *noun* electric device for toasting bread; *that slice of bread is too thick to fit in the toaster*

toast rack ['təʊstræk] *noun* little object for holding slices of toast upright on the table at breakfast; *the waiter brought a toast rack with six pieces of toast*; *you should put the toast in the rack to prevent it getting soggy*

tobacco [tə'bækəʊ] *noun* dried leaves of a plant used to make cigarettes and cigars, and for smoking in pipes; *he bought some pipe tobacco*; *tobacco causes lung cancer* (NOTE: no plural)

tobacconist [tə'bækənɪst] *noun* person who sells tobacco, cigars, cigarettes, etc.; *tobacconists are not allowed to sell cigarettes to people under sixteen*

tobacconist's [tə'bækənɪsts] *noun* shop selling tobacco, cigarettes, etc.; *you can buy newspapers at the tobacconist's on the corner of the High Street*

toboggan [tə'bɒgən] **1** *noun* sledge made of a long flat piece of wood curved upwards at the front, designed for sliding downhill on snow or ice; *the children pulled their toboggans to the hill* **2** *verb* to slide on a toboggan; *they tobogganed down the hill*

tobogganing [tə'bɒgənɪŋ] *noun* sport of sliding on toboggans; *we went tobogganing on the hill behind the farmhouse*

today [tə'deɪ] **1** *noun* this day; *today's her sixth birthday*; *what's the date today?*; *there's a story in today's newspaper about a burglary in our road* **2** *adverb* on this day; *he said he wanted to see me today, but he hasn't come yet*; **today week** *or* **a week today** = in exactly seven days' time; *a week today, and we'll be sitting on the beach* (NOTE: no plural. Note also that when you refer to the morning or afternoon, etc., of **today**, you say **this morning, this afternoon**, etc.; the day before today is **yesterday** and the day after today is **tomorrow**)

toddle ['tɒdl] *verb* **(a)** *(of little child)* to walk unsteadily; *the little girl toddled across the pavement and into the road* **(b)** *(informal)* to walk; *I'll just toddle down to the post office*

toddler ['tɒdlə] *noun* child who has just learnt to walk; *now he's eighteen months old we're sending him to a toddlers' playgroup*; *he's been fascinated by cars ever since he was a toddler*

to-do [tə'duː] *noun* *(informal)* excitement, confusion, bother; *she made such a to-do about a little scratch on her car*; *you should have seen the to-do in the market when someone knocked over a pile of melons*

toe [təʊ] **1** *noun* one of the five parts like fingers at the end of the foot; *she trod on my toe and didn't say she was sorry*; **big toe** = the largest of the five toes; **little toe** = the smallest of the five toes; **to keep someone on their toes** = to keep someone ready or alert; *my job is to make sure the staff are always on their toes* **2** *verb* **to toe the line** = to do what you are told to do; *he was*

sacked because he refused to toe the line (NOTE: do not confuse with **tow**)

toehold ['təʊhəʊld] *noun* place where you can put the toe of your boot when climbing; *he hung in the air at the end of a rope, trying to get a toehold* **(b)** small position on which you can build; *they gained a toehold in the Spanish market*

toenail ['təʊneɪl] *noun* hard nail covering the end of a toe; *one of my toenails hurts*; *she painted her toenails red*

toff [tɒf] *noun* *(old)* *(informal)* rich, aristocratic person; *let's have some beer - wine is for the toffs*

toffee ['tɒfi] *noun* sticky sweet made by cooking sugar and butter; *he went to the sweet shop and bought a bag of toffees*; **toffee apple** = apple covered with toffee, sold on a stick

tofu ['təʊfuː] *noun* bean curd, a soft white paste made from soya beans

together [tə'geðə] *adverb* **(a)** doing something with someone else or in a group; *tell the children to stay together or they'll get lost*; *if you're going to the cinema, and we're planning to go too, why don't we all go together?* **(b)** joined with something else, or with each other; *tie the sticks together with string*; *do you think you can stick the pieces of the cup together again?*; *if you add all the figures together, you'll get the total sales*; *we've had three sandwiches and three beers - how much does that come to all together?*; *compare* ALTOGETHER

toggle ['tɒgl] **1** *noun* **(a)** short piece of wood attached to a coat with string, used in place of a button; *a duffel coat has toggles not buttons* **(b)** **toggle switch** = electrical switch which is moved by a lever and has only two positions, on and off; *the circuit is opened and closed by means of a toggle switch* **2** *verb* (in computers) to change between two states; *the symbol can be toggled on and off the display*

toil [tɔɪl] **1** *noun* *(formal)* hard work; *a life of endless toil* **2** *verb* to work hard; *they toiled for months to try to improve the conditions of the workers*; *she was toiling away at a hot stove*

toilet ['tɔɪlət] *noun* **(a)** bowl with a seat on which you sit to get rid of waste matter from your body; *there is a shower and toilet in the bathroom*; **to go to the toilet** = (i) to use a toilet to remove waste matter from the body; (ii) to remove waste matter from the body; *the children all want to go to the toilet at the same time*; *Mum! the cat's been to the toilet on the sitting room carpet*; **toilet paper** = soft paper for wiping your bottom after going to the toilet; **toilet roll** = roll of toilet paper; **to flush a toilet** = to press a handle to make water flow through the toilet bowl to clear it; *don't forget to flush the toilet* **(b)** room with this toilet bowl in it; *the ladies' toilet is at the end of the corridor*; *the gents toilets are downstairs and to the right*; *there's a public toilet at the railway station*

token ['təʊkən] *noun* **(a)** thing which is a sign or symbol of something; *please accept this small gift as a token of our gratitude*; **by the same token** = in the same way; *you have every right to complain about him, but, by the same token, you mustn't get upset if he complains about you*; **token charge** = small charge which does not cover the real costs; **token gesture** = small and insignificant action done to show that you are intending to deal with a problem; *the motion criticizing the government was simply a token gesture by the* *opposition parties*; **token payment** = small payment to show that a payment is being made; **token strike** = short strike to show that the workers have a grievance; **token woman** *or* **token black** = woman *or* black person appointed to a position on a committee, etc., in an attempt to show that there is no sexual or racial discrimination **(b)** piece of paper, card, etc., which is used in the place of money; *you can use these tokens to pay for meals*; **book token** *or* **flower token** = card which is bought in a shop and given as a present: it can only be exchanged for books or flowers; **gift token** = card bought in a shop which is given as a present and which must be exchanged in that shop for goods **(c)** plastic or metal disk, used instead of money; *she put a token into the slot machine*

told [təʊld] *see* TELL

tolerable ['tɒlərəbl] *adjective* **(a)** bearable; *the noise in the ironworks was barely tolerable* **(b)** fairly good; *we had a tolerable meal in the hotel restaurant*

tolerance ['tɒlərəns] *noun* **(a)** tolerating unpleasant behaviour, etc.; *the police showed great tolerance faced with a crowd of youths throwing bottles and stones* **(b)** allowing something to exist which you do not agree with; *tolerance of other people's views* **(c)** ability of the body to stand the effect of a drug or a poison; *he has been taking the drug for so long that he has developed a tolerance to it* **(d)** amount by which something can vary from a particular size; *the specifications allow for a tolerance of 0.005mm*

tolerant ['tɒlərənt] *adjective* who shows tolerance; *she is very tolerant of her husband's little mistakes*; *the parents have a very tolerant attitude towards their children and the noise they make*

tolerate ['tɒləreɪt] *verb* **(a)** to allow something which you do not like to happen without complaining about it; *she does not tolerate singing in the classroom* **(b)** to allow something which you do not agree with to exist; *opposition parties are not tolerated in that country*; *he is not known for tolerating people with opposing views to his* **(c)** to accept the effect of a drug or a poison; *the body can tolerate small amounts of poison*

toleration [tɒlə'reɪʃn] *noun* allowing something which you do not agree with to exist; *religious toleration increased during the 18th century*

toll [təʊl] **1** *noun* **(a)** payment for using a service, usually a road, bridge or ferry; *you have to pay a toll to cross the bridge*; *there's an office at the bridge where the man collects the tolls*; **toll bridge** = bridge where you have to pay a toll to cross **(b)** number of people hurt, of buildings damaged, etc.; **to take a toll of** = to destroy or damage; *the storm took a heavy toll of ships in the harbour*; *the wind took a toll of trees in the park*; **death toll** = number of people who have died; *the death toll in the disaster has risen to three hundred* **(c)** solemn ringing of a bell; *the toll of the great bell could be heard across the marshes* **2** *verb* to ring a bell slowly, as for a funeral; *the bell was tolling as the coffin arrived at the church*

toll call ['təʊl 'kɔːl] *noun US* long-distance telephone call; *I made a toll call to Seattle*

toll free ['təʊl 'friː] *adjective & adverb US* without having to pay the charge for a long-distance telephone call; *a toll-free number*; *to call someone toll-free*

tom ['tɒm] *noun* male cat; *our poor little cat was chased by a huge ginger tom*

tomato [tə'mɑːtəʊ *US* tə'meɪtəʊ] *noun* **(a)** small, round red fruit used in salads and cooking; *tomatoes cost 30p per kilo*; *we had a salad of raw cabbage and tomatoes*; *someone in the crowd threw a tomato at the speaker on the platform*; **tomato sauce** = sauce made with tomatoes and herbs; *do you want tomato sauce with your fish and chips?* **(b)** tomato plant, a plant which produces tomatoes; *he planted six tomatoes in his back garden* (NOTE: plural is **tomatoes**)

tomb [tuːm] *noun* grave, sometimes one with an underground vault; *archaeologists were excited when they discovered the tomb of Tutankhamen*

tomboy ['tɒmbɔɪ] *noun* girl who enjoys playing boys' games; *he's quiet and studious but his sister's a bit of a tomboy*

tombstone ['tuːmstəʊn] *noun* large stone placed on a grave with the name of the dead person written on it; *he loves wandering round churchyards and noting the dates on the tombstones* (NOTE: also called **gravestone** *or* **headstone**)

tomcat ['tɒmkæt] *noun* male cat; *we were woken by two tomcats screeching outside our window*

tome [təʊm] *noun* *(formal)* large book; *he wrote a tome about the history of the village*

tomorrow [tə'mɒrəʊ] **1** *adverb* referring to the day after today; *are you free for lunch tomorrow?*; *I mustn't forget I have a dentist's appointment tomorrow morning*; *we are going to an Italian restaurant tomorrow evening* **2** *noun* the day after today; *today's Monday, so tomorrow must be Tuesday*; *tomorrow is our tenth wedding anniversary*; **the day after tomorrow** = two days after today; *we're going to Paris the day after tomorrow*

ton [tʌn] *noun* **(a)** measure of weight equal to 2240 pounds; *a ship carrying 1000 tons of coal*; **metric ton** = 1000 kilograms **(b)** *(informal)* **it weighs a ton** = it is very heavy; *your suitcase weighs a ton, what have you got in it?*; *(informal)* **tons of** = lots of; *I've tons of work to do*; *she had tons of cards on her twenty-first birthday* **(c)** *(slang)* **to do a ton** = to drive at 100 miles per hour; *he was doing a ton on the motorway when the police stopped him*

tone [təʊn] **1** *noun* **(a)** way of saying something, or of writing something, which shows a particular feeling; *his tone of voice showed he was angry*; *she said hello in a friendly tone of voice*; *you could tell from the tone of his letter that he was annoyed* **(b)** *(in music)* the difference in pitch between five pairs of notes, which together with the semitones go to make an octave **(c)** special noise which indicates something; *please speak after the tone* (on the phone); **dialling tone** = noise made by a telephone to show that it is ready for you to dial a number; **engaged tone** = sound made by a telephone when the line dialled is busy; *every time I call her number I get the engaged tone* **(d)** slight difference in colour; *she prefers soft tones like pink or pale mauve* **(e)** **muscle tone** = normal slightly tense state of a healthy muscle; *exercising every day will improve muscle tone* **(f)** general spirit of an area, a meeting, etc.; *having all those rusty old fridges and cookers in their front garden lowers the tone of the neighbourhood* **2** *verb* **to tone in with** = to fit in well or to harmonize with; *the colour of the carpet tones in well with the curtains*

tone down ['təʊn 'daʊn] *verb* to make something less offensive; *she asked him to tone down his* *language*; *the magazine won't print the article unless you tone it down a bit*

toner ['təʊnə] *noun* (a) black powder, like dry ink, used in photocopiers and laser printers; *the printer has run out of toner*; **toner cartridge** = sealed box containing toner; *she made a real mess when she dropped the toner cartridge on the floor* (b) substance used on your skin to clean it or to remove grease (NOTE: no plural)

tone up ['təʊn 'ʌp] *verb* to make firmer or fitter; *he does exercises to tone up his leg muscles*

tongs [tɒŋz] *noun* (pair of) **tongs** = device for picking things up, with small claws on the end of two arms which you can move together; *she picked up the burning log with the tongs and put it back on the fire*; **sugar tongs** = tongs for picking up lumps of sugar; *my grandmother insists we use sugar tongs to serve sugar lumps at teatime*

tongue [tʌŋ] *noun* (a) long muscular organ in your mouth, which can move and is used for tasting, swallowing and speaking; *the soup was so hot it burnt my tongue*; **to say something with your tongue in your cheek** *or* **to say something tongue in cheek** = to say something which you do not mean seriously; **it's on the tip of my tongue** = I'll remember it in a moment, I'm trying hard to remember it (b) similar part in an animal, used for food; *we had tongue and salad* (c) way of speaking; *she can have a sharp tongue when she wants to* (d) language; **mother tongue** *or* **native tongue** = language which you spoke when you were a little child; *she speaks English very well, but German is her mother tongue*

tongue-in-cheek ['tʌŋɪn'tʃiːk] *adjective* not meant seriously; *it was just a tongue-in-cheek remark*

tongue-twister ['tʌŋtwɪstə] *noun* phrase (like 'red lorry, yellow lorry') which is difficult to say quickly; *have I got his name right? - it's a bit of a tongue-twister*

tonic ['tɒnɪk] *noun* (a) something which makes you stronger; *he's taking a course of iron tonic tablets*; *going on holiday will be a tonic for you* (b) **tonic (water)** = fizzy water made with quinine, used as a cooling drink; *she asked for a gin and tonic*

tonight [tə'naɪt] *adverb & noun* the night or the evening of today; *I can't stop - we're getting ready for tonight's party*; *I'll be at home from eight o'clock tonight*; *I don't suppose there's anything interesting on TV tonight*

tonne [tʌn] *noun* metric ton, weight of one thousand kilograms; *they harvested over one hundred tonnes of apples*

tonsil ['tɒnsl] *noun* one of two soft lumps of tissue at the back of the throat; *the doctor found there were white spots on her tonsils*

COMMENT: the tonsils protect the body from germs which enter through the mouth

tonsillitis [tɒnsɪ'laɪtɪs] *noun* inflammation of the tonsils; *our daughter will have to see the doctor since she keeps getting tonsillitis*

too [tuː] *adverb* (a) more than necessary; *there are too many people to fit into the lift*; *I think we bought too much bread*; *it's too hot for us to sit in the sun* (b) (*often at the end of a clause*) also; *she had some coffee and I had some too*; *she, too, comes from Scotland or she comes from Scotland too*

took [tʊk] *see* TAKE

tool [tuːl] *noun* instrument which you hold in the hand to do certain work, such as a hammer, spade, etc.; *a set of tools for mending the car*

toot [tuːt] **1** *noun* short sound made by a horn; *as he went past us he gave a toot on his horn* **2** *verb* to blow a horn sharply; *she tooted as she turned the corner*

tooth [tuːθ] *noun* (a) one of a set of hard white objects in the mouth which you use to bite or chew food; *children must learn to clean their teeth twice a day*; *I'll have to see the dentist - one of my back teeth hurts*; *the dentist took one of her teeth out*; **false teeth** = dentures, artificial plastic teeth which fit inside the mouth and take the place of teeth which have been taken out; **milk teeth** = a child's first twenty teeth, which are gradually replaced by permanent teeth; *see also* WISDOM TOOTH (b) **to have a sweet tooth** = to like sweet food; *he's very fond of puddings - he's got a real sweet tooth!*; *don't put the chocolates next to her - she's got a very sweet tooth* (c) **in the teeth of something** = in spite of some problem or obstacle; *the housing development was approved in the teeth of violent opposition from the preservation society*; **long in the tooth** = old; *she's getting a bit long in the tooth for scuba diving*; **armed to the teeth** = carrying lots of weapons; *the robbers were armed to the teeth* (d) one of the row of pointed pieces on a saw, comb, zip, etc.; *throw that comb away, half its teeth are broken* (NOTE: plural is **teeth** [tiːθ])

toothache ['tuːθeɪk] *noun* pain in a tooth; *he went to the dentist because he had toothache* (NOTE: no plural)

toothbrush ['tuːθbrʌʃ] *noun* small brush which you use to clean your teeth; *use your toothbrush twice a day*; *I forgot to pack a toothbrush*; *she gave him an electric toothbrush for his birthday* (NOTE: plural is **toothbrushes**)

toothpaste ['tuːθpeɪst] *noun* soft substance which you spread on a toothbrush and then use to clean your teeth; *I must buy a little tube of toothpaste to take when I'm travelling*; *there's no toothpaste left - use soap!* (NOTE: no plural: **some toothpaste, a tube of toothpaste**)

toothpick ['tuːθpɪk] *noun* little pointed piece of wood, used for cleaning between the teeth; *they served little pieces of cheese speared on toothpicks*

top [tɒp] **1** *noun* (a) highest place, highest point of something; *he climbed to the top of the stairs and sat down*; *the blackbird is sitting on the top of the apple tree*; *there is a roof garden on top of the hotel*; *look at the photograph at the top of page four*; *Manchester United are still at the top of the premier league* (b) flat upper surface of something; *do not put coffee cups on top of the computer*; *the desk has a black top*; *a birthday cake with sugar and fruit on top* (c) cover for a jar, bottle, etc.; *take the top off the jar, and see what's inside*; *she forgot to screw the top back on the bottle* (d) best position in a contest, a profession, etc.; *she came top in the competition* (e) child's toy which turns very rapidly on a point; *when a spinning top loses momentum, it wobbles and finally falls over* (f) (*informal*) **big top** = very large circus tent **2** *adjective* (a) in the highest place; *the restaurant is on the top floor of the building*; *jams and marmalades are on the top shelf* (b) best; *she's one of the world's top tennis* players **3** verb **(a)** to put something on top; *cheesecake topped with whipped cream* **(b)** to do better than; *I don't think anyone else will top his score;* (informal) **to top it all** = on top of everything else; *to top it all, a pipe burst in the bathroom and the whole house was flooded* (NOTE: **topping - topped**)

◊ **on top of** phrase **(a)** on; *he put the book down on top of the others he had bought* **(b)** in addition to; *on top of all my office work, I have the clean the house and look after the baby*

topaz ['təʊpæz] noun usually yellow precious stone; *she was wearing a beautiful topaz ring*

top-class ['tɒpklɑːs] adjective of the highest class; *she's a top-class marathon runner*

top-heavy ['tɒphevi] adjective with the top part heavier than the bottom, and so likely to fall over; *the load was top-heavy, and the lorry turned over as it went round the corner*

topic ['tɒpɪk] noun subject of a discussion or conversation; *can we move on to another topic?*; **to bring up a topic** = to start to discuss something; *she brought up the topic of where to go on holiday*

topical ['tɒpɪkl] adjective interesting at the present time; *the question of global warming is very topical*

topless ['tɒpləs] adjective not wearing any clothes on the top part your body; *topless sunbathing is allowed at the local swimming pool*

top-level ['tɒplevl] adjective involving the most important people; *a top-level delegation*

topography [tə'pɒɡrəfi] noun study or description of the physical features of a place, its rivers, mountains, valleys, etc.; *the topography of the desert was quite unlike anything we had ever seen before*

topping ['tɒpɪŋ] noun cream, melted cheese, etc., put on the top of food such as cakes, pizzas, ice cream, etc.; *a sponge cake with a cream topping*; *what sort of topping would you like on your ice cream?*; *the cheese topping on the cauliflower isn't hot enough*

topple ['tɒpl] verb **(a)** to fall down; *he lost his balance and toppled forwards* **(b)** to make a government or dictator lose power; *the government was toppled after three days of street fighting*

topple over ['tɒpl 'əʊvə] verb to fall down; *the vase toppled over and smashed onto the floor*

top secret ['tɒp 'siːkrət] adjective absolutely secret; *he left a file of top secret documents in the taxi*

topsy-turvy ['tɒpsi'tɜːvi] adjective in disorder, all upside down; *the house is really topsy-turvy since we had the decorators in*

top up ['tɒp 'ʌp] verb to add liquid to fill completely something which is half empty; *let me top up your glass*; *I topped the bottle up with tap water*

top-up ['tɒpʌp] noun liquid which you add to a half-empty cup or glass to make it full again; *can I give you a top-up?*

torch [tɔːtʃ] **1** noun **(a)** small portable electric lamp; *take a torch if you're going into the cave*; *I always carry a small torch in the car* (NOTE: American English only uses **flashlight**) **(b)** flaming light, carried in the hand; *the demonstrators marched through the streets carrying torches* (NOTE: plural is **torches**) **2** verb to set fire to something on purpose; *the rioters torched the police station*

torchlight ['tɔːtʃlaɪt] noun light from a torch; *they were trying to dig a hole in the garden by torchlight*; **torchlight procession** = procession of people carrying burning torches

tore, torn [tɔː or tɔːn] see TEAR

torment 1 noun ['tɔːmənt] extreme pain; *the torment of parents who are separated from their children*; **in torment** = in great pain; *after days in torment with his back pain, he finally went to see the doctor* **2** verb [tɔː'ment] to make someone suffer; *the old couple were tormented by their neighbours' children and in the end moved to a different street*; *he was constantly tormented by doubt*

torn [tɔːn] see TEAR

tornado [tɔː'neɪdəʊ] noun violent storm with a whirlwind; *a tornado struck the southern coast* (NOTE: plural is **tornadoes**)

torpedo [tɔː'piːdəʊ] **1** noun missile like a shell which travels under the water; *the submarine fired a torpedo*; *the ship was hit by three torpedoes and sank immediately* (NOTE: plural is **torpedoes**) **2** verb **(a)** to sink a ship using a torpedo; *the ship was torpedoed by an enemy submarine* **(b)** to ruin someone's plans; *his grandiose scheme for a leisure complex was torpedoed by the council planning department*

torpor ['tɔːpə] noun being half-asleep and slow to react; *after lunch they sat outside to watch cricket and torpor soon set in*

torrent ['tɒrənt] noun **(a)** fast rushing stream; *to get to the farm we had to cross a mountain torrent* **(b)** fast flow; *the rain came down in torrents* **(c)** **torrent of abuse** = large number of insults which are spoken rapidly; *she let out a torrent of abuse*

torrential [tə'renʃəl] adjective like a torrent; *the storm was accompanied by a torrential downpour*

torrid ['tɒrɪd] adjective **(a)** (formal) very hot; *the torrid tropical afternoon* **(b)** (love affair) intensely sexual; *a tale of torrid romance and intrigue*

torso ['tɔːsəʊ] noun main part of the body, not including the head, arms and legs; *his torso was covered with tattoos*; *the police found a human torso in the river* (NOTE: plural is **torsos**)

tortoise ['tɔːtəs] noun reptile covered with a hard shell, which moves very slowly on land and can live to be very old; *the giant tortoises of the Galapagos Islands* (NOTE: British English uses the word **turtle** for similar animals which live in water; American English uses **turtle** for both)

tortoiseshell ['tɔːtəʃel] adjective & noun speckled brown material from the shell of a turtle used for making combs, frames for glasses, etc.; *she keeps her pins in a little tortoiseshell box*; **tortoiseshell cat** = brown, yellow, white and black cat

tortuous ['tɔːtʃuəs] adjective which twists and turns; *because of the roadworks we have to take a long and tortuous route back home*; *I won't start explaining the tortuous procedure we had to go through to recover our money*

torture ['tɔːtʃə] **1** noun making someone suffer pain as a punishment or to make them reveal a secret; *they accused the police of using torture to get information about the plot* **2** verb to inflict mental or physical pain on someone; *the soldiers tortured their prisoners*; *the policeman tortured the girl by refusing to tell her where her mother was*

Tory ['tɔːri] **1** *adjective* referring to the Conservative party; *a Tory government; the last Tory Prime Minister* **2** *noun* member of the Conservative party; *the Tories have recently elected a new leader* (NOTE: plural is **Tories**)

toss [tɒs] **1** *noun* **(a)** act of throwing something into the air; *(in sport)* **to win the toss** = to guess correctly which side of the coin comes down on top and so have first choice or play first **(b)** sharp movement up and down of the head; *with a toss of its head, the horse galloped off* **2** *verb* **(a)** to throw something up into the air; *he tried to toss the pancake and it fell on the kitchen floor; she tossed me her car keys;* **to toss a coin** = to throw a coin to decide something according to which side is on top when it comes down; *we tossed a coin and I had to do the washing up;* **let's toss for it** = let's throw a coin in the air and the person who guesses right starts to play first or has first choice **(b)** to move something about; *the waves tossed the little boat up and down;* **the horse tossed its head** = made a sharp movement of the head

toss up ['tɒs 'ʌp] *verb* to throw a coin to see which side is on top when it comes down; *we tossed up, and I had to do the washing up; let's toss up to see who pays for the taxi*

toss-up ['tɒsʌp] *noun (informal)* **(a)** situation where either of two things is possible; *it's a toss-up who's going to win* = either of them can win; *Chelsea and Arsenal are both on top form, so it's a toss-up which side will win* **(b)** throwing a coin in the air to guess which side comes down on top and so deciding which team starts first, etc.; *the two captains stood with the referee in the centre circle for the toss-up*

tot [tɒt] **1** *noun* **(a)** little child; *she took the tot by the hand and led him back into the house; there are special classes where they teach tiny tots to swim* **(b)** small glass of alcohol; *a tot of whisky before dinner won't do you any harm* **2** *verb* **to tot up** = to add up; *I'll be with you in a minute - I've just got to tot up these invoices* (NOTE: **totting - totted**)

total ['təʊtəl] **1** *adjective* complete, whole; *the expedition was a total failure; their total losses come to over £400,000* **2** *noun* whole amount; *the total comes to more than £1,000;* **grand total** = final total made by adding several items **3** *verb* to add up to; *the bill totalled £600; he was declared bankrupt, with debts totalling more than £1m* (NOTE: British English **totalling - totalled** but American English spelling is **totaling - totaled**)

totalitarian [təʊtælɪ'teəriən] *adjective* having total power and not allowing any opposition or personal freedom; *the junta abolished the constitution and set up a totalitarian régime*

totalitarianism [təʊtælɪ'teəriənɪzm] *noun* political system where the state has total power over the citizens; *although the government was elected by popular vote, it rapidly moved towards totalitarianism*

totalizator *or* **totalizer** [təʊtəlaɪ'zeɪtə or 'təʊtəlaɪzə] *noun (formal)* official system of betting on horseraces where the amount of money bet on a race is divided between the winners (NOTE: usually referred to as the **tote**)

totally ['təʊtəli] *adverb* completely; *the house was totally destroyed in the fire; I had totally forgotten that I had promised to be there; he disagrees totally with what the first speaker said*

tote [təʊt] **1** *noun (informal)* **the tote** = TOTALIZATOR; *she bet £25 on the tote* **2** *verb US* to carry something; *she had to tote her suitcase around town looking for somewhere to stay*

tote bag ['təʊt 'bæg] *noun US* large canvas bag for carrying clothes, etc.

totem pole ['təʊtəmpəʊl] *noun* tall wooden post with carved symbolic figures often painted, found mainly on the Northwest Pacific coast, the work of native North Americans; *it was a very bad omen for the village's totem pole to have been struck by lightning*

totter ['tɒtə] *noun* **(a)** to walk unsteadily, to wobble; *I cannot bear to look at her tottering along in those platform shoes; the old lady manages to totter over to the bakery to get some fresh bread every day* **(b)** to be in a weak condition, likely to collapse; *the company is tottering and we wonder how long it will survive; the IMF has proposed ways of improving the country's tottering economy*

toucan ['tuːkæn] *noun* tropical bird from South America, with a huge coloured beak

touch [tʌtʃ] **1** *noun* **(a)** one of the five senses, the sense of feeling with the fingers; *the sense of touch is very acute in blind people* **(b)** contact, the passing of news and information; **to get in touch with someone** = to contact someone; *I'll try to get in touch with you next week;* **to lose touch with someone** = to lose contact with someone; *they used to live next door, but we've lost touch with them now that they've moved to London;* **to put someone in touch with someone** = to arrange for someone to have contact with someone; *the bank put us in touch with a local lawyer;* **to stay in touch with someone** = to keep contact with someone; *we met in Hong Kong thirty years ago but we have still kept in touch; see also* OUT OF TOUCH (NOTE: no plural in meanings (a) and (b)) **(c)** gentle physical contact; *I felt a light touch on my hand* **(d)** very small amount; *he added a few touches of paint to the picture; there's a touch of frost in the air this morning;* **finishing touches** = final work to make something perfect; *we're just putting the finishing touches to the exhibition before we open tomorrow morning* **2** *verb* **(a)** to feel with your fingers; *the policeman touched him on the shoulder; don't touch that cake - it's for your mother* **(b)** to be so close to something that you press against it; *his feet don't touch the floor when he sits on a big chair; there is a mark on the wall where the sofa touches it* **(c)** to eat or drink; *I never touch coffee; we never touch food which has not been washed* **(d)** to make someone feel sad; *his sad song touched all the people in the church* **(e)** *(informal)* **to touch someone for** = to try and get someone to give you money; *how much did he touch you for?*

touch-and-go ['tʌtʃənd'gəʊ] *adjective* possible that anything can happen; *my sister is slightly better, but it's still touch-and-go; it was touch-and-go who would get the first prize*

touch down ['tʌtʃ 'daʊn] *verb* **(a)** to land; *the plane touched down at 13.20* **(b)** to score a try in Rugby, by touching the ground behind the opponents' line with the ball; *he touched down behind the posts*

touchdown ['tʌtʃdaʊn] *noun* **(a)** landing of a plane or spacecraft; *the plane veered across the runway as one of its tyres burst on touchdown* **(b)** *(in Rugby)* scoring a try by touching the ground behind the opponents' line with the ball; *he burst through for a*

touchdown between the posts **(c)** US scoring a goal in (American) football by taking the ball over the opponents' line; *he completed a pass for the winning touchdown*

touched [tʌtʃt] *adjective* grateful, pleased with; *she was touched to get your phone call on her birthday*

touching ['tʌtʃɪŋ] *adjective* which affects the emotions; *a touching letter from my sister*

touchline ['tʌtʃlaɪn] *noun* white line along the side of a football field; *the linesmen run along the touchline; he kicked the ball over the touchline*

touch up ['tʌtʃ 'ʌp] *verb* to add a small amount of paint; *you will need to touch up the car where it has been scratched*

touchy ['tʌtʃi] *adjective* (informal) **(a)** easily offended; *don't mention his red hair - he's very touchy about it* **(b)** which is likely to cause offence; *don't mention his driving test - it's a very touchy subject at the moment*

tough [tʌf] *adjective* **(a)** difficult to chew or to cut; *my steak's a bit tough - how's yours?; (informal) this meat is as tough as old boots* = it is extremely tough (NOTE: the opposite is **tender**) **(b)** difficult; *the exam is extremely tough* (NOTE: the opposite is **easy**) **(c)** strict; *the police are getting tough on drunk drivers* **(d)** (informal) unfortunate; *it's tough that you can't come to the party; having three little children to look after is tough on the parents; tough luck!* = hard luck! (NOTE: **tougher - toughest**)

toughen ['tʌfn] *verb* **(a)** to make tough or harder; *cooking the meat too much will simply toughen it;* **toughened glass** = specially strengthened glass; *toughened glass is used for shop windows* **(b)** to make more strict or severe; *the aim is to toughen university entrance requirements* **(c) to toughen up** = to make someone tougher, stronger or harder; *the hard work and fresh air on the farm will toughen him up*

toupée or **toupee** ['tu:peɪ] *noun* small wig, covering part of the head; *I'm sure he wears a toupee; he couldn't understand why his audience was giggling, until he realised his toupee had slipped* (NOTE: similar to a **hairpiece**)

tour [tuːə] **1** *noun* **(a)** holiday journey to various places coming back eventually to the place you started from; *there are so many tours to choose from - I can't decide which one to go on; she gave us a tour round the old castle;* **conducted tour** or **guided tour** = tour with a guide who shows places to tourists; **package tour** = tour where everything (hotel, food, travel, etc.) is arranged and paid for before you leave **(b)** journey on business to various places coming back eventually to the place you started from; *he is leading a group of businessmen on a tour of Italian factories* **(c)** journey round various places where you perform, speak, etc.; *the pop group is on an American tour; the Prime Minister went on a tour of the North east* **2** *verb* **(a)** to go on holiday, visiting various places; *they toured the south of France* **(b)** to visit various places to perform or speak; *the opera company toured Eastern Europe last year*

tourism ['tuːrɪzm] *noun* business of providing travel, accommodation, food and entertainment for tourists; *tourism is the country's main source of income*

tourist ['tuːrɪst] *noun* person who goes on holiday to visit places away from his home; *the tourists were*

talking German; *there were parties of tourists visiting all the churches; Trafalgar Square is always full of tourists;* **tourist bureau** or **tourist information office** or **tourist information centre** = office which gives information to tourists about the place where it is situated; *you can get a map of the town from the tourist bureau;* **tourist class** = type of seating in an aircraft which is cheaper than first class; *he always travels first class, because he says tourist class is too uncomfortable; the tourist class fare is much less than the first class;* **tourist trap** = place which charges tourists too much; *it used to be a quiet little town, but now it's just a tourist trap*

tournament ['tuːnəmənt] *noun* sporting competition with many games where competitors who lose drop out until only one is left; *the Wimbledon tennis tournament; the badminton tournament starts on Saturday*

tour operator ['tuːə 'ɒpəreɪtə] *noun* travel agency which organizes and sells package holidays or tours; *hundreds of people were stranded in Spain when the tour operator went bust*

tout [taut] **1** *noun* **ticket tout** = person who sells tickets at high prices to people in the street; *tickets are in great demand but you should still be able to get one from the touts; the authorities are cracking down on ticket touts outside the football ground* **2** *verb* **(a)** to praise something in the hope that people will believe you; *the book was touted as a masterpiece* **(b)** to tout for business or custom = to try to find new customers; *as soon as we left the airport building we were surrounded by taxi drivers touting for business* **(c)** to tout something around = to take something to various people to try to get them to buy it; *he touted his idea for a plastic car round several car companies but no one was interested in it*

tow [təu] **1** *noun* action of pulling something; *we got a tractor to give us a tow to the nearest garage* (NOTE: do not confuse with **toe**) **2** *verb* to pull a car or a ship which cannot move by itself; *the motorways were crowded with cars towing caravans; they towed the ship into port*

towards US also **toward** [təˈwɔːdz] *preposition* **(a)** in the direction of; *the crowd ran towards the police station; the bus was travelling south, towards London; the ship sailed straight towards the rocks* **(b)** near (in time); *do you have any free time towards the end of the month?; the exhibition will be held towards the middle of October* **(c)** as part of the money to pay for something; *he gave me £100 towards the cost of the hotel* **(d)** in relation to; *she always behaved very kindly towards her father*

towel ['tauəl] *noun* large piece of soft cloth for drying; *there's only one towel in the bathroom; after washing her hair, she wound the towel round her head; I'll get some fresh towels;* **to throw in the towel** = to give up, not to continue a contest; **bath towel** = very large towel for drying yourself after having a bath; **beach towel** = coloured towel used to dry yourself after swimming in the sea, and also for sitting on; **tea towel** = cloth which you use for drying plates, dishes, etc.; **towel rail** = bar of metal or wood in a bathroom on which you can hang a towel

towelling US **toweling** ['tauəlɪŋ] *noun* absorbent type of soft cloth used mainly for making towels; *he was wearing a yellow towelling bathrobe*

tower ['taʊə] **1** *noun* **(a)** tall construction; *the castle has thick walls and four square towers*; **tower block =** very tall block of flats; *they live in a tower block south of the Thames*; **control tower =** tall building at an airport where the radio station is **(b)** the **Tower of London =** castle in London, built by William the Conqueror; *there is a picture of the Tower of London on the front of the book* **2** *verb* **to tower over =** to rise very high above; *he towers over his wife who is very small*

towering ['taʊərɪŋ] *adjective* **(a)** very tall; *towering cliffs* **(b)** **towering rage =** very great rage; *when he read the letter he went into a towering rage*

town [taʊn] *noun* place, larger than a village, where people live and work, with houses, shops, offices, factories, etc.; *there's no shop in our village, so we do our shopping in the nearest town*; *the town is known for its chocolate*; *they moved their office to the centre of town*; **town centre =** central part of a town, where main shops, banks and places of interest are situated; *the traffic in the town centre has got so bad that I walk everywhere* (NOTE: this is called **downtown** in American English); **town plan** *or* **town map =** diagram showing the streets of a town with their names; **market town =** town which has a regular market; **seaside town =** town by the sea; *(informal)* **to go to town on something =** to spend a lot of money or time on something; *she really went to town on buying furniture for the new house*; *(informal)* **to paint the town red =** to have a wild party in town

town council ['taʊn 'kaʊnsəl] *noun* representatives elected to run a town; *she's been elected to the town council*; *the next meeting of the town council will be on Thursday*

town hall ['taʊn 'hɔːl] *noun* main building in a town, where the town council meets, and where many of the council departments are; *I got a letter from the town hall about street cleaning*

town house ['taʊn 'haʊs] *noun* **(a)** house in a town belonging to someone who also has a house in the country; *he has a castle in Northumberland, and a town house in London* **(b)** expensive modern terraced house; *they're building a row of town houses behind the police station*

townsfolk ['taʊnzfəʊk] = TOWNSPEOPLE

township ['taʊnʃɪp] *noun* **(a)** *(in the USA and Canada)* local administrative area formed of a small town and the area round it **(b)** *(formerly, in South Africa)* urban area where black people live

townspeople ['taʊnzpiːpl] *noun* people who live in a town; *the townspeople flocked to see the circus*

toxaemia *US* **toxemia** [tɒk'siːmiə] blood poisoning, condition caused by bacteria in the blood

toxic ['tɒksɪk] *adjective* poisonous, harmful; *caution: this product is toxic*; **toxic waste =** waste which is poisonous or harmful to the environment; *environmentalists want to ban the dumping of toxic waste in the sea*

toxin ['tɒksɪn] *noun* poisonous substance produced inside the body by germs; *this special diet is designed to purge the toxins from your body*

toy [tɔɪ] **1** *noun* thing for children to play with; *we gave him a box of toy soldiers for Christmas*; *the children's toys are all over the sitting room floor*; *she won't let me play with any of her toys* **2** *verb* **to toy**

with something = to play with something (not seriously); *she had no appetite and only toyed with her meat*

toy boy ['tɔɪ 'bɔɪ] *noun (informal)* younger man who is the companion of an older woman; *she came to the party with her latest toy boy*

toyshop ['tɔɪʃɒp] *noun* shop which sells toys; *we saw the doll in the toyshop window*

trace [treɪs] **1** *noun* **(a)** something which shows that something existed; **without trace =** leaving nothing behind; *the car seems to have vanished without trace* **(b)** very small amount; *there was a trace of powder on his coat*; *she showed no trace of anger* **2** *verb* **(a)** to follow an animal's tracks; *we traced the badger back to its hole* **(b)** to find where someone or something is; *they couldn't trace the letter*; *the police traced him to Dover* **(c)** to copy a drawing, etc., by placing a sheet of transparent paper over it and drawing on it; *she traced the map and put it into her project on the history of the village*

trace element ['treɪs 'eləmənt] *noun* chemical element which a plant or animal needs to grow properly, but only in very small amounts

COMMENT: plants require traces of copper, iron, manganese and zinc; human beings need chromium, cobalt, copper, magnesium, manganese, molybdenum, selenium and zinc, but all in tiny quantities

trachea [trə'kiːə] *noun* main air passage which runs from the larynx to the lungs, where it divides into the two main bronchi; *the bronchi are the air passages leading from the trachea into the lungs*; *the trachea is about 10 centimetres long* (NOTE: also called the **windpipe**)

tracing ['treɪsɪŋ] *noun* drawing which has been traced; *he made a tracing of the plan*

tracing paper ['treɪsɪŋ 'peɪpə] *noun* transparent paper for copying drawings, etc.; *this is a copy I made on tracing paper*

track [træk] **1** *noun* **(a)** **tracks =** series of footprints left by an animal, marks left by wheels, etc.; *we followed the tracks to the forest*; *those are the tracks of a tiger*; **to make tracks for =** to go towards; *they made tracks for the nearest hotel* **(b)** **to be on someone's track =** to follow someone; *the police are on his track* **(c)** **to keep track of =** to keep an account, to keep yourself informed about; *I like to keep track of new developments in computer technology*; **to lose track of someone** *or* **something =** not to know where someone or something is; *we lost track of him after he went to work in Turkey*; **we lost track of the time =** we didn't know what time it was **(d)** rough path; *we followed a track through the forest*; **off the beaten track =** in a place which is not normally visited by many people; **you're on the right track =** you're working the right way in order to succeed, you're doing the right thing; *we haven't solved the problem yet, but we're certainly on the right track*; **you're on the wrong track =** you're working in the wrong way **(e)** path for races; **track events =** running competitions in athletics; **track suit =** warm two-piece suit of soft cloth, worn when practising sports; *see also* RACETRACK **(f)** line of parallel rails for trains; *the train will be late because of repairs to the track*; **single-track railway =** railway where trains go up and down the same rails but with places where two trains can pass; *(informal)* **to have a one-track mind** = to think about only one thing or to have only one thing which interests you **(g)** one of the sections on a disk; *one of the tracks from their disk has been released as a single* **2** *verb* to follow someone *or* an animal; *the hunters tracked the bear through the forest*; *the police tracked the gang to a flat in south London*

track down ['træk 'daʊn] *verb* **to track someone down** = to follow and catch (a criminal); **to track something down** = to manage to find something; *I finally tracked down that file which you were looking for*

tracker ['trækə] *noun* animal or person who follows tracks; *native trackers helped them find the missing hikers*; **tracker dog** = dog which is trained to follow the scent of a person's tracks; *the police hunted the gunmen with tracker dogs*

trackless ['trækləs] *adjective* with no paths; *the trackless wastes of Antarctica*

track record ['træk 'rekəd] *noun* success or failure of someone or a business in the past; *he has a good track record as a salesman*

tracksuit ['træksuːt] *noun* pair of matching trousers and top, in warm material, worn when practising sports; *the athletes were warming up in their tracksuits*

tract [trækt] *noun* **(a)** large area of land; *whole tracts of forest have been contaminated by acid rain* **(b)** short pamphlet, usually on a religious subject; *someone pushed a tract on the dangers of alcohol through our letterbox* **(c)** system of organs and tubes in the body which are linked together; *the respiratory tract takes air into the lungs*; **the digestive tract** = passage from the mouth to the rectum down which food passes and is digested; *the digestive tract is formed of the mouth, throat, stomach and intestines, etc.*

tractable ['træktəbl] *adjective* which can be controlled easily, made to do what you want; *I wish the children were more tractable*

traction ['trækʃn] *noun* **(a)** pulling a broken leg, etc., with weights and pulleys so as to straighten it; *after we have set the bone, the leg will require traction*; **in traction** = having a broken limb attached and pulled so that it becomes straight; *she was in traction for several weeks* **(b)** *(of tyre)* gripping power between a tyre and the road surface; *these tyres are so old they have no traction at all on ice* **(c)** force of pulling; **traction engine** = large steam-driven engine which used to be used for pulling heavy loads; *the star of the village fair was a huge old traction engine belching smoke and steam*

tractor ['træktə] *noun* heavy vehicle with large back wheels, used for work on farms; *he was driving a tractor down the village street*

trade [treɪd] **1** *noun* **(a)** business of buying and selling; *Britain's trade with the rest of Europe is up by 10%*; **export trade** = the business of selling to other countries; **import trade** = the business of buying from other countries; **free trade** = system where goods can go from one country to another without any restrictions; **to do a good trade in a range of products** = to sell a large number of a range of products; **to do a roaring trade** = to sell a lot very fast; *the ice cream sellers have been doing a roaring trade during the hot weather* **(b)** people or companies that deal in the same type of product or service; *he is in the secondhand car trade*;

trade price = special wholesale price paid by a retailer to a wholesaler or manufacturer **2** *verb* **(a)** to buy and sell, to carry on a business; *the company has stopped trading*; *they trade in furs* **(b)** to exchange something for something; *I'll trade the car for your motorbike*

trade in ['treɪd 'ɪn] *verb* to give in an old item, such as a car or washing-machine, as part of the payment for a new one; *he traded in his old Rolls Royce for a new model*

trade-in ['treɪdɪn] *noun* old item, such as a car or washing-machine, given as part of the payment for a new one; *he gave his old car as a trade-in*; **trade-in price** = amount allowed by the seller for an old item being traded in for a new one

trademark *or* **trade name** ['treɪdmɑːk or 'treɪd neɪm] *noun* particular name, design, etc., which has been registered by the manufacturer and which cannot be used by other manufacturers; *Acme is a registered trademark*; *their trademark is stamped on every item they produce*

trade off ['treɪd 'ɒf] *verb* to balance one thing against another to get a final result; *we needed to trade off the disadvantages of staying where we are against the cost of moving to new premises*

trade-off ['treɪdɒf] *noun* exchanging one thing for another as part of a deal; *the two sides agreed a trade-off: one convicted terrorist for two captured airmen*

trade on ['treɪd 'ɒn] *verb* to exploit or to use something to your advantage; *he trades on the fact that he is so good-looking*; *the company trades on its reputation for reliable products*

trader ['treɪdə] *noun* person who does business; *he was a fur trader in northern Canada*

tradesman ['treɪdzmən] *noun* person who runs a shop; *local tradesmen are furious with the council because they have restricted parking in the centre of the village* (NOTE: plural is **tradesmen**)

Trades Union Congress (TUC) ['treɪdz 'juːnɪən 'kɒŋgres] *noun* organization linking all British trade unions; *the Trades Union Congress holds its annual meeting in September*

trade union *or* **trades union** ['treɪd 'juːnɪən or 'treɪdz 'juːnɪən] *noun* organization which represents workers who are its members in discussions with employers about wages and conditions of employment; *the staff are all members of a trades union or they are trade union members* (NOTE: American English is **labor union**; although **Trades Union Congress** is the official name for the organization representing unions, **trade union** is commoner than **trades union** in British English)

trade unionist ['treɪd 'juːnɪənɪst] *noun* member of a trade union

trading ['treɪdɪŋ] *noun* business of buying and selling; *trading was brisk on the stock exchange this morning*

trading estate ['treɪdɪŋ e'steɪt] *noun* group of warehouses and factories built together; *we have a warehouse on the new trading estate near the station*

tradition [trə'dɪʃn] *noun* beliefs, customs and stories which are passed from one generation to the next; *it's a family tradition for the eldest son to take over the business*; *according to local tradition, two murderers were hanged at the crossroads*

traditional [trəˈdɪʃnəl] *adjective* according to tradition; *on Easter Day it is traditional to give chocolate eggs to the children; villagers still wear their traditional costumes on Sundays*

traditionalist [trəˈdɪʃnəlɪst] *noun* person who does things in a traditional way; *traditionalists criticized the modern dress production of 'Hamlet'; the art world was divided into two groups - the modernists and the traditionalists*

traditionally [trəˈdɪʃnəli] *adverb* according to tradition; *chocolate eggs are traditionally given as presents on Easter Day*

traffic [ˈtræfɪk] **1** *noun* **(a)** cars, lorries, buses, etc., which are travelling on a street or road; *I leave the office early on Fridays because there is so much traffic leaving London; the lights turned green and the traffic moved forward; rush-hour traffic is worse on Fridays*; **traffic-calming measures** = ways used to make traffic less or slower, such as imposing speed limits, building humps in roads, etc.; **traffic offences** = offences committed by drivers of vehicles; **traffic police** = branch of the police force dealing with traffic on roads **(b) air traffic** = aircraft flying around; *air traffic round London will increase when they build the new airport* **(c)** illegal trade; *the South American drugs traffic* (NOTE: no plural: **some traffic; a lot of traffic**) **2** *verb* to deal in drugs, weapons, etc., illegally; *he made a fortune trafficking in cocaine* (NOTE: **trafficking - trafficked**)

traffic circle [ˈtræfɪk ˈsɜːkl] *noun US* place where several roads meet, and traffic has to move in a circle round a central area (NOTE: British English is **roundabout**)

traffic jam [ˈtræfɪk ˈdʒæm] *noun* situation where cars, lorries, etc., cannot move forward on a road because there is too much traffic, because there has been an accident, because of roadworks, etc.; *a lorry overturned, causing a big traffic jam; there are traffic jams on the roads out of London every Friday evening*

trafficker [ˈtræfɪkə] *noun* **drugs trafficker** = person who deals illegally in drugs; *the customs stopped him because they suspected he was a drugs trafficker*

traffic lights [ˈtræfɪk ˈlaɪts] *noun* red, green and amber lights for making the traffic stop and start; *to get to the police station, you have to turn left at the next traffic lights; he drove across the junction when the traffic lights were red* (NOTE: often shortened to just **lights**)

traffic warden [ˈtræfɪk ˈwɔːdən] *noun* person whose job it is to see that cars are legally parked, and to give parking tickets to those which are parked illegally; *I'm just going to the post office - shout if you see a traffic warden coming*

tragedian [trəˈdʒiːdiən] *noun* (formal) actor who acts in tragedies; *Olivier, the great Shakespearean tragedian*

tragedy [ˈtrædʒədi] *noun* **(a)** serious play, film, novel which ends sadly; *Shakespeare's tragedy 'King Lear' is playing at the National Theatre* **(b)** very unhappy event; *tragedy struck the family when the mother was killed in a car crash* (NOTE: plural is **tragedies**)

tragic [ˈtrædʒɪk] *adjective* **(a)** very sad; *a tragic accident on the motorway* **(b)** referring to a tragedy; *one of the greatest tragic actors*

tragically [ˈtrædʒɪkli] *adverb* very sadly; *she was married last week, and tragically died in an accident two days later; running across the railway lines was just a harmless game which went tragically wrong*

trail [treɪl] **1** *noun* **(a)** tracks left by an animal, by a criminal, etc.; *we followed the trail of the bear through the forest; the burglars left in a red sports car, and a police car was soon on their trail* **(b)** path or track; *keep to the trail otherwise you will get lost;* **mountain trail** = path through mountains; **nature trail** = path through the countryside with signs to showing interesting features, such as plants, trees, birds or animals **(c)** something that follows behind; *the car left a trail of blue smoke; the dogs followed the trail of drops of blood to a warehouse; the storm left a trail of destruction across the south of the country* **2** *verb* **(a)** to follow the tracks left by an animal or a person; *the police trailed the group across Europe* **(b)** to trail behind = to follow slowly after someone; *she came third, trailing a long way behind the first two runners; the little children trailed behing the older ones* **(c) trailing plant** = plant whose stems hang down or creep along the ground **(d)** to let something drag behind; *she stormed out, trailing her coat on the floor behind her*

trailer [ˈtreɪlə] *noun* **(a)** small goods vehicle pulled behind a car; *we carried all our camping gear in the trailer* **(b)** *US* van with beds, table, washing facilities, etc., which can be towed by a car; *a trailer park* (NOTE: also called a **mobile home;** British English is **caravan**) **(c)** parts of a full-length film shown as an advertisement for it; *we saw the trailer last week, and it put me off the film*

train [treɪn] **1** *noun* **(a)** engine pulling a group of coaches on the railway; *the train to Paris leaves from platform 1; hundreds of people go to work every day by train; the next train to London will be in two minutes; to get to Glasgow, you have to change trains at Crewe;* **intercity train** = train which goes fast between two cities; **stopping train** = train which goes slowly, stopping at each station; **suburban train** = train which goes from the centre of a town to the suburbs; **train set** = child's toy train with engines, coaches and rails; **train timetable** = list showing times of arrivals and departures of trains **(b)** series of things, one after the other; *the police are trying to piece together the train of events which led to the accident;* **train of thought** = series of thoughts, one after the other; *my wife asked me to help with the baby, thus breaking my train of thought* **2** *verb* **(a)** to teach someone or an animal how to do something; *she's being trained to be a bus driver; guide dogs are trained to lead blind people* **(b)** to make a plant grow in a certain way; *we've trained the clematis up the wall* **(c)** to become fit by practising for a sport; *he's training for the 100 metres; she's training for the Olympics*

trained [treɪnd] *adjective* who has been through a course of training; *the factory employs a doctor and a trained physiotherapist*

trainee [treɪˈniː] *noun* person who is being taught; *graduate trainees come to work in the laboratory when they have finished their courses at university; we employ trainee salesgirls to help in the shop at peak periods*

trainer [ˈtreɪnə] *noun* **(a)** person who trains an athlete; *his trainer says he's in peak condition for the fight* **(b) trainers** = light sports shoes; *she needs a new pair of* *trainers for school*; *he comes to work every morning in trainers* **(c)** small aircraft in which pilots learn to fly

training ['treɪnɪŋ] *noun* **(a)** being taught a skill; *the shop is closed on Tuesday mornings for staff training*; *there is a ten-week training period for new staff* **(b)** practising for a sport; **to be in training** = to practise for a sport; *she's in training for the Olympics*

training camp ['treɪnɪŋ 'kæmp] *noun* camp where people go to train, either for a sport or for the army; *the England squad are spending four days together at a training camp before their next international match*

training college ['treɪnɪŋ 'kɒlɪdʒ] *noun* college where teachers are trained; *after university she took an education course at a training college*

trait [treɪ(t)] *noun* particular characteristic of someone; *his rudeness is one of the more unpleasant traits of his character*

traitor ['treɪtə] *noun* person who betrays his or her country, especially by giving secret information to the enemy; *he was accused of being a traitor to the cause*; **Traitors' Gate** = entrance to the Tower of London by which political prisoners were brought into the castle; *Traitor's Gate is reached from the river*

traitorous ['treɪtrəs] *adjective (formal)* like a traitor; *Guy Fawkes was executed for his traitorous attempt to blow up Parliament*

trajectory [trə'dʒektri] *noun* curving movement of something which has been thrown or shot through the air; *the firework's trajectory described a perfect arc*; *the golf ball followed an unexpected trajectory*

tram [træm] *noun* public transport vehicle, which runs on rails laid in the street; *you can take the tram from the station to the city centre* (NOTE: American English is **streetcar**)

tramcar ['træmkɑː] *noun* single carriage in a tram; *in Germany, most trams consist of two tramcars linked together*

tramlines ['træmlaɪnz] *noun* **(a)** rails in a street along which a tram runs; *don't stand on the tramlines - a tram may come round the corner* **(b)** the two side lines on a tennis court; *he sent a passing shot down the tramlines*

tramp [træmp] **1** *noun* **(a)** noise of heavy feet hitting the ground; *the streets were filled with the tramp of marching soldiers* **(b)** long walk; *we went for a tramp along the cliffs last Sunday* **(c)** person who has nowhere to live and walks from place to place looking for work or begging for food or money; *the farmer was surprised to find a tramp asleep in one of his barns* (NOTE: American English is **hobo**) **(d)** *(old)* **tramp steamer** = cargo ship that goes from port to port as the company instructs, not following a regular route; *we spent a holiday as passengers on an old tramp steamer sailing round the Mediterranean* **2** *verb* **(a)** to walk with heavy feet; *they tramped through the snow to get to the camp*; *you could hear soldiers tramping through the streets at night*; *all day long, we had the workmen tramping through the house with their dirty boots* **(b)** to walk for a long distance; *they tramped for miles before they came to a little inn*

trample ['træmpl] *verb* **to trample on something** = (i) to crush something by walking on it; (ii) to crush something violently; *they trampled on the enemy flag and then burnt it*; *several children were trampled to death in the riot*; *the government has trampled on the rights of the ordinary citizen*

trampoline ['træmpəliːn] *noun* large sheet of elastic material stretched across a frame, which you can bounce or jump on; *the children were bouncing around on the trampoline*

tramway ['træmweɪ] *noun* rails on which a tram runs

trance [trɑːns] *noun* state when you are in a dream but not asleep, and do not notice what is going on around you; *he walked round the room in a trance*; *the hypnotist waved his hand and she went into a trance*

tranquil ['træŋkwɪl] *adjective* calm or peaceful; *her face was tranquil in death*; *the tranquil scene was shattered by fighter jets suddenly roaring past overhead*

tranquillity *US* **tranquility** [træŋ'kwɪlɪti] *noun* being calm or peaceful; *it is the peace and tranquillity of the mountains I like most*

tranquillizer ['træŋkwɪlaɪzə] *noun* drug which makes a person calm down; *she's taking tranquillizers to calm her nerves*; *he's been on transquillizers ever since he started his new job*; **tranquillizer dart** = little arrow with a tranquillizer inside, used to put large dangerous animals to sleep; *vets with tranquillizer darts went up to the tiger's cage*

transact [træn'zækt] *verb* **to transact business** = to carry out a piece of business; *he has been banned from transacting business on the Stock Exchange*; *the council will meet next week to transact the following business*

transaction [træn'zækʃn] *noun* piece of business; *the whole transaction was conducted in French*; **cash transaction** = business which is paid for in cash

transatlantic [trænzət'læntɪk] *adjective* **(a)** across the Atlantic; *transatlantic flights take about six hours depending on the wind*; *prices for transatlantic phone calls have been reduced* **(b)** on the other side of the Atlantic; *our transatlantic trading partners*

transcend [træn'send] *verb (formal)* to go better or further than something, to be much more important than something; *the seriousness of the crisis transcends all party politics*

transcendent [trən'sendənt] *adjective (formal)* very great; *she was a woman of transcendent beauty*

transcribe [træn'skraɪb] *verb* **(a)** to write out the text of something which is heard; *his speech was transcribed from the radio tape*; *the sound of each word has been transcribed into phonetic characters* **(b)** to rewrite a piece of music for a different instrument than the one for which it was originally written; *the piece was originally written for the violin and then transcribed for piano*

transcript ['trænskrɪpt] *noun* written record of something which has been noted in shorthand, text of what was said on a radio programme, at a meeting, etc.; *he asked to see a transcript of the interview*

transcription [træn'skrɪpʃn] *noun* words which have been transcribed; *a phonetic transcription is given for each word*

transfer 1 *noun* ['trænsfə] **(a)** action of moving something *or* someone to a new place; *I've applied for a transfer to our London branch*; **on the transfer list** = on the list of footballers who can transfer to other teams **(b)** changing to another form of transport; **transfer**

passenger = traveller who is changing from one aircraft or train or bus to another, or to another form of transport **(c)** decoration which is taken off a piece of paper and is stuck on to a surface; *she has little transfers of flowers and animals on her arms* **2** *verb* [træns'fɜː] **(a)** to move something *or* someone to another place; *the money will be transferred directly to your bank account*; *she transferred her passport from her handbag to her jacket pocket*; *he's been transferred to our Manchester office* **(b)** to change from one type of travel to another; *when you get to London airport, you have to transfer onto an internal flight* (NOTE: **transferring - transferred**)

transferable [træns'fɜːrəbl] *adjective* which can be transferred; **transferable skills** = skills which you can use in several different types of job; **this ticket is not transferable** = this ticket cannot be given or lent to anyone else to use

transform [træns'fɔːm] *verb* to change the appearance of someone *or* something completely; *after her marriage she was transformed*; *the frog was transformed into a handsome prince*

transformation [trænzfə'meɪʃn] *noun* complete change of appearance; *after her marriage she underwent a complete transformation*

transformer [trænz'fɔːmə] *noun* device for changing the voltage of an alternating current; *you will need a transformer to use a halogen lamp*

transfusion [trænz'fjuːʒn] *noun* **blood transfusion** = transferring blood which has been donated by another person into a patient's body; *she had to have two blood transfusions*

transient ['trænziənt] **1** *adjective* (*formal*) which will not last; *fame for most pop groups is very transient* **2** *noun* US **transients** = people who stay in a hotel or guest house for a short time

transistor [træn'zɪstə] *noun* **(a)** device made of semi-conductors which can control the flow of electric current in a circuit **(b)** (*old*) **transistor (radio)** = small pocket radio which uses transistors; *the schoolboy had a transistor radio hidden under his pillow* (NOTE: old usage, since all radios use transistors nowadays)

transit ['trænzɪt] *noun* movement of passengers or goods on the way to a destination; *some of the party's luggage was lost in transit*; **goods in transit** = goods being transported from one place to another; **transit lounge** = waiting room in an airport where passengers wait for connecting flights; **transit passengers** = travellers who are changing from one aircraft to another

transition [træn'zɪʃn] *noun* process of moving from one state to another; *she easily made the transition from being a poor student to a rich executive*

transitional [træn'zɪʃnəl] *adjective* referring to transition; *she will be in charge during the transitional period between the retirement of the old manager and the appointment of a new one*; **transitional government** = temporary government between two different regimes; *the commander-in-chief of the army has been appointed head of the transitional government*

transitive verb ['trænzɪtɪv 'vɜːb] *noun* verb which has an object; *the verb 'to hit' is transitive: the verb 'to sleep' is intransitive*

transitory ['trænzɪtri] *adjective* which does not last for long; *the drug gives you a transitory feeling of happiness*

translate [trænz'leɪt] *verb* to put words into another language; *can you translate what he said?*; *he asked his secretary to translate the letter from the German agent*; *she translates mainly from Spanish into English, not from English into Spanish*

translation [trænz'leɪʃn] *noun* text which has been translated; *I read Tolstoy's 'War and Peace' in translation*; *she passed the translation of the letter to the accounts department*; **translation bureau** = office which translates documents for companies

translator ['trænsleɪtə] *noun* person who translates; *she works as a translator for the European Parliament*

translucent [trænz'luːsnt] *adjective* which light can pass through, but which you cannot see through; *fine bone china has a translucent quality*

transmission [trænz'mɪʃn] *noun* **(a)** (*formal*) passing of disease from one person to another; *patients must be isolated to prevent transmission of the disease to the general public* **(b)** radio or TV broadcast; *we interrupt this transmission to bring you a news flash* **(c)** (*in a car*) series of moving parts which pass the power from the engine through the gearbox and clutch to the axles; *there's a strange noise coming from the transmission*

transmit [trænz'mɪt] *verb* **(a)** to pass a disease from one person to another; *the disease was transmitted to all the people he came into contact with*; *the disease is transmitted by fleas* **(b)** to send out a programme or a message by radio or TV; *the message was transmitted to the ship by radio* (NOTE: **transmitting - transmitted**)

transmitter [trænz'mɪtə] *noun* apparatus for sending out radio or TV signals; *TV reception is bad here because the transmitter is on the other side of the mountain*

transparency [træns'pærənsi] *noun* **(a)** quality of being transparent; *the transparency of the water allows you to see the coral reefs* **(b)** being clear when making decisions, and being open to the public about official actions; *the government insists on the importance of transparency in all its actions* **(c)** photograph which is printed on transparent film so that it can be projected on to a screen; *transparency is another name for 'slide'*; *do you want to have prints or transparencies?* (NOTE: plural in this meaning is **transparencies**)

transparent [trænz'peərənt] *adjective* **(a)** which you can see through; *the meat is wrapped in transparent plastic film* **(b)** which is completely obvious; *his explanation was a transparent lie* **(c)** clear and open about official actions; *the government insists on the importance all its actions being transparent*

transpire [træn'spaɪə] *verb* **(a)** to become obvious; *it transpired that she had never seen the letter* **(b)** (*of a plant*) to lose water through the surface of a leaf; *in tropical rainforests, up to 75% of rainfall will transpire into the atmosphere*

transplant 1 *noun* ['trɑːnsplɑːnt] **(a)** act of taking an organ such as the heart, or tissue such as a piece of skin, and grafting it onto a patient to replace an organ or tissue which is diseased or damaged; *he had a heart transplant* **(b)** organ or piece of tissue which is transplanted; *the kidney transplant was rejected* **2** *verb* [træns'plɑːnt] **(a)** to move a plant from one place to another; *you should not transplant trees in the summer* **(b)** to graft an organ or piece of tissue onto a patient to replace an organ or tissue which diseased or damaged; *they transplanted a kidney from his brother*

transport 1 *noun* ['trænspɔːt] movement of goods or people in vehicles; *air transport is the quickest way to travel from one country to another*; *rail transport costs are getting lower*; *what means of transport will you use to get to the hotel?*; **public transport system** = system of buses, trams, trains, etc., used by the general public; *the government's policy is to persuade people to use public transport instead of their cars*; *how can we get to Kew Gardens by public transport?* **2** *verb* [træn'spɔːt] to move goods or people from one place to another in a vehicle; *the company transports millions of tons of goods by rail each year*; *the visitors will be transported to the factory by helicopter*

transportation [trænspɔːˈteɪʃn] *noun* action or means of moving goods or people; *the company will provide transportation to the airport*; **ground transportation** = buses, taxis, etc., available to take passengers from an airport to the town

transvestite [trænzˈvestaɪt] *noun* person who wears the clothes of the opposite sex; *see also* DRAG

trap [træp] **1** *noun* **(a)** device to catch an animal; *we have a mouse in the kitchen so we will put down a trap* **(b)** device to catch a person by surprise; **police radar trap** = small radar device by the side of a road which senses and notes details of cars which are travelling too fast **(c) trap door** = door in a floor or in a ceiling; *there's a trap door leading to the loft* **(d)** *(informal)* mouth; **keep your trap shut!** = don't say anything **2** *verb* to catch or hold; *several people were trapped in the wreckage of the plane*; *he was trapped on video as he tried to burgle the bank* (NOTE: **trapping - trapped**)

trapeze [træˈpiːz] *noun* bar which hangs like a swing from ropes high up in a circus tent, used by acrobats; *she performs daring acts on the trapeze without a safety net*

trapezium [træˈpiːziəm] *noun* **(a)** *GB* flat four-sided geometric shape, where two of the sides are parallel and the other two sides are not (NOTE: this is a **trapezoid** in American English) **(b)** *US* flat four-sided geometric shape, where none of the sides are parallel (NOTE: this is a **trapezoid** in British English) **(c)** one of the eight little bones (the carpal bones) in the wrist, one at the base of the thumb

trapezoid ['træpɪzɔɪd] **(a)** *see* TRAPEZIUM **(b)** one of the eight little bones (the carpal bones) in the wrist, one at the base of the index finger

trapped [træpt] *adjective* in an awkward situation and unable to move; *I want to get out of this house - I feel trapped here*

trappings ['træpɪŋz] *noun* ornaments, clothes and ceremonies which are associated with a particular position; *at the end of his time as mayor, he had to give up the chain, the chauffeur-driven car and all the other trappings of office*; *enjoy all the trappings of power while you can - they won't last for ever*

trash [træʃ] **1** *noun* **(a)** useless things; *throw out all that trash from her bedroom* (NOTE: British English prefers **rubbish**) **(b)** *US (informal, derogatory)* poor useless people; **white trash** = poor white people (NOTE: no plural) **2** *verb US* **(a)** to smash up; *someone trashed the telephones* **(b)** to ruin someone's reputation; *she wrote an article trashing the pop singer*

trashcan ['træʃkæn] *noun US* large plastic or metal container for household rubbish; *they come to empty the trashcans once a week*; *she put the rest of the dinner in the trashcan* (NOTE: also called **garbage can**; British English for this is **dustbin**)

trauma ['trɔːmə] *noun* mental shock caused by a sudden unpleasant experience, which was not expected to take place; *she was in trauma after the crash*; *in court, he had to relive the trauma of the accident*

traumatic [trɔːˈmætɪk] *adjective* which gives a sharp and unpleasant shock; *witnessing an accident can be as traumatic as being involved in it*; *I will never forget the traumatic events of 1989*

traumatize ['trɔːmətaɪz] *verb* to shock someone; *hearing that her husband had been sent to prison was a traumatizing experience for her*; *hypnotic treatment can be successful for deeply traumatized patients*

travel ['trævəl] **1** *noun* **(a)** action of moving from one country or place to another; *air travel is the only really fast method of going from one country to another*; **travel insurance** = insurance taken out by a traveller against accident, loss of luggage, illness, etc.; **travel sickness** = sickness caused by the movement of a car, aircraft, bus or train, etc. (NOTE: no plural in this meaning) **(b) travels** = long journey abroad; *she is someone he met on his travels in India* **2** *verb* to move from one country or place to another; *he travels fifty miles by car to go to work every day*; *he has travelled across the United States several times on his motorbike*; *the bullet must have travelled several metres before it hit the wall* (NOTE: **travelling - travelled** but American spelling is **traveling - traveled**)

travel agency ['trævl 'eɪdʒənsi] *noun* office which arranges tickets and accommodation for travellers; *can you get foreign currency from the travel agency?*; *I have to collect my tickets from the travel agency*

travel agent ['trævl 'eɪdʒənt] *noun* person or company that arranges tickets and accommodation for its customers; *I asked the travel agent for details of tours to Greece*; *the tour was arranged by our local travel agent*; *the travel agent called to say that the tickets were ready*

traveller *US* **traveler** ['trævlə] *noun* **(a)** person who travels; *travellers on the 9 o'clock train to London*; *travellers to France are experiencing delays because of the dock strike* **(b)** person who has no fixed home and who travels around the country; *the fields were full of hippies and travellers*

traveller's cheque *US* **traveler's check** ['trævləz 'tʃek] *noun* cheque which you buy at a bank before you travel and which you can then use in a foreign country; *most shops in the USA accept traveller's cheques*; *the hotel will cash traveller's cheques for you*

travelling *US* **traveling** ['trævlɪŋ] *adjective* who travels; *the travelling public is fed up with delays on the trains service*

traverse [trəˈvɜːs] *verb (formal)* to go across; *she was the first woman to traverse the polar continent on foot*

trawl [trɔːl] **1** *noun* long net shaped like a bag, pulled behind a trawler to catch fish; *a trawl is used for fishing in deep waters* **2** *verb* **(a) to trawl through something for something** = to search for something; *he spent hours trawling through boxes of files until he* came to the letter he was looking for **(b)** to fish with a trawl; *they went trawling for herring*

trawler ['trɔːlə] *noun* fishing boat which pulls a net behind it; *the harbour was filling up with trawlers returning home with their catches*

tray [treɪ] *noun* **(a)** flat board for carrying food, glasses, cups and saucers, etc.; *he had his lunch on a tray in his bedroom; she bumped into a waitress carrying a tray of glasses* **(b)** flat open container on a desk for documents which have to be dealt with; *there was a pile of letters in my tray when I returned to work*; **in tray** = basket on a desk for letters or memos which have been received and are waiting to be dealt with; **out tray** = basket on a desk for letters or memos which have been dealt with and are ready to be sent out; **pending tray** = basket on a desk for documents which cannot be dealt with immediately

treacherous ['tretʃrəs] *adverb* **(a)** dangerous; *there are treacherous reefs just offshore; black ice is making the roads very treacherous* **(b)** likely to betray; *his treacherous behaviour led to the downfall of the minister*

treachery ['tretʃəri] *noun* act of betraying, of being a traitor to your country, friends, etc.; *his treachery led to the deaths of many of our agents* (NOTE: no plural: for the plural say **acts of treachery**)

treacle ['triːkl] *noun* **(a)** thick dark-brown liquid produced when sugar is being refined; *you can use treacle in Christmas cakes and Christmas puddings* (NOTE: American English is **molasses**) **(b) treacle pudding** *or* **treacle tart** = pudding or tart made with golden syrup (not with treacle)

treacly ['triːkli] *adjective* dark, thick and sticky like treacle; *we had to make our way through treacly mud*

tread [tred] **1** *noun* **(a)** top part of a stair or step which you stand on; *the carpet on the bottom tread is loose*; *metal treads are noisy* **(b)** pattern of lines on the surface of a tyre; *you need to change your tyres - the tread's worn* **(c)** way of walking; *he walked up to the door with a firm tread* **2** *verb* to step, to walk; *she trod on my toe and didn't say she was sorry; watch where you're treading - there's broken glass on the floor* (NOTE: **treading - trod** [trɒd] **- has trodden** ['trɒdən])

treadmill ['tredmɪl] *noun* **(a)** device turned by animals as they walk around a circular path or inside a large wheel; *our pet hamster often uses the treadmill in his cage* **(b)** dull work which has to be done every day; *his wife complains that her life is a boring treadmill of cooking, cleaning and washing* **(c)** an exercise machine with a moving belt on which you walk or jog without actually moving forward; *after ten minutes on the treadmill I'm ready for the jacuzzi*

treason ['triːzn] *noun* the crime of betraying your country, by giving your country's secrets to the enemy or by helping the enemy during wartime; *he was arrested and accused of treason; it is treason to pass secrets to the enemy; the treason trial lasted several weeks*

treasure ['treʒə] **1** *noun* jewels, gold, or other valuable things; *the treasures in the British Museum*; **buried treasure** = gold, silver, etc., which someone has hidden; *they are diving in the Caribbean looking for pirates' treasure*; **treasure hunt** = game where clues lead you from place to place until you come to a hidden prize; *we organized a treasure hunt for the children's party* **2** *verb* to value something; *I treasure the calm*

life of the fishing village where I live; she treasures her three cats and wouldn't part with them for anything

treasurer ['treʒərə] *noun* **(a)** person who looks after the money of a club, society, etc.; *please send your subscriptions to the treasurer by May 1st*; **honorary treasurer** = treasurer who does not receive any fee; *for a statement of the charity's finances I shall hand over to our honorary treasurer* **(b)** *(in Australia)* minister of finance

treasury ['treʒri] *noun* **(a)** **the Treasury** = government department which deals with the country's finance; *all government departments have to have their spending plans approved by the Treasury* (NOTE: the term is used in both the UK and the USA; in most other countries this department is called the **Ministry of Finance**) **(b)** place where treasure is kept; *robbers broke into the royal treasury and stole boxes of gold*

treat [triːt] **1** *noun* special thing which gives pleasure; *it's always a treat to sit down quietly at home after a hard day in the shop*; **a treat in store** = special future enjoyment; *if you've never seen this film before you've got a treat in store*; **this is our treat** = we are paying the bill **2** *verb* **(a)** to deal with someone; *she bas badly treated by her uncle; it you treat the staff well they will work well* **(b)** **to treat someone to something** = to give someone a special meal or outing as a gift; *come along - I'll treat you all to ice creams!* **(c)** to look after a sick or injured person; *after the accident some of the passengers had to be treated in hospital for cuts and bruises; she is being treated for rheumatism* **(d)** to process in some way to make safe or to protect; *sewage is treated in the council sewage works; the wood has been treated to make it resistant to rot*

treatise ['triːtɪz] *noun* long piece of formal writing on a specialized subject; *his treatise on heat is the foundation of our knowledge of the subject*

treatment ['triːtmənt] *noun* **(a)** way of behaving towards something or someone; *the report criticized the treatment of prisoners in the jail; what sort of treatment did you get at school?; we got VIP treatment when we visited China* **(b)** way of looking after a sick or injured person; *he is having a course of heat treatment; the treatment for skin cancer is very painful*

treaty ['triːti] *noun* **(a)** written legal agreement between two or more countries; *the treaty was signed in 1845; countries are negotiating a treaty to ban nuclear weapons* **(b)** legal agreement between individual persons; **to sell a house by private treaty** = to sell by an agreement between the seller and the purchaser, and not by auction (NOTE: plural is **treaties**)

treble ['trebl] **1** *noun* **(a)** boy's high-pitched soprano voice; *the treble solo rose above the sound of the basses* **(b)** boy who sings with a soprano voice; *the tenors start the hymn, followed by the trebles* **(c)** high-pitched musical instrument; *the school has six recorders: two bass, two tenors and two trebles* **(d)** thing which gives three times as many points; *he hit the inner ring on the dart board and scored a treble* **2** *adjective* **(a)** referring to a high-pitched voice or music; *the treble part of the piece is to be sung by boy sopranos; see also* CLEF **(b)** three times as large; *their garden is treble the size of ours* **3** *adverb* three times as much; *a dart in the inner ring counts treble* **4** *verb* to increase by three times; *the council is planning to* *treble the amount it spends on education; the value of our house has trebled in the last fifteen years*

tree [triː] *noun* **(a)** very large plant, with a thick trunk, branches and leaves; *the cat climbed up an apple tree and couldn't get down; in autumn, the trees in our park turn brown and red; he was sheltering under a tree and was struck by lightning* **(b)** family tree = table showing a family going back over many generations; *he's going through the local parish records to try to establish his family tree; they can trace their family tree back to the Norman conquest of 1066*

tree house [triː 'haʊs] *noun* little building built in the branches of a tree for children to play in

treetops ['triːtɒps] *noun* tops of trees; *monkey were playing round in the treetops*

treetrunk ['triːtrʌŋk] *noun* main stem of a tree; *the natives used hollowed-out treetrunks as canoes*

trek [trek] **1** *noun* long hard journey; *it's quite a trek to the centre of town from here* **2** *verb* to make a long hard journey; *they trekked across the desert in search of water* (NOTE: **trekking - trekked**)

trellis ['trelɪs] *noun* frame of criss-crossed pieces of light wood, used for plants to climb up; *we put a trellis for the roses to climb over*

tremble ['trembl] **1** *noun* shaking movement; *there was a tremble in her voice* **2** *verb* to shake because you are cold or afraid; *she was trembling with cold; I tremble at the thought of how much the meal will cost*

tremendous [trɪ'mendəs] *adjective* **(a)** enormous, very big; *there was a tremendous explosion and all the lights went out; there's tremendous excitement here in Trafalgar Square as we wait for the election result* **(b)** wonderful; *it would be absolutely tremendous if you won; her birthday party was tremendous fun*

tremendously [trɪ'mendəsli] *adverb* greatly, extremely; *I enjoyed the play tremendously; all the brothers and sisters get on tremendously well together, he has a tremendously difficult job*

tremor ['tremə] *noun* **(a)** slight shaking, making slight movements of your hands, feet, etc.; *you can see a tremor in her hands* **(b)** earth tremor = slight earthquake; *the instruments detected an earth tremor somewhere under the Pacific Ocean*

trench [trentʃ] *noun* **(a)** long narrow ditch; *they dug trenches for drainage round the camp; he fought in the trenches during the First World War* **(b)** deep valley at the bottom of an ocean; *at more than 10,000m deep, the Mariana Trench in the Pacific is the deepest place on the surface of the Earth* (NOTE: plural is **trenches**)

trend [trend] *noun* general tendency; *there is a trend away from old-established food stores; the government studies economic trends to decide whether to raise taxes or not*

trendy ['trendi] **1** *adjective* (*informal*) very fashionable; *she's always wearing the trendiest clothes; it's trendy nowadays to care about the environment* (NOTE: **trendier - trendiest**) **2** *noun* (*informal*) person who follows the latest fashion; *it's the restaurant all the trendies go to* (NOTE: plural is **trendies**)

trepidation [trepɪ'deɪʃn] *noun* (*formal*) nervous worry; *she was full of trepidation at the thought of the*

interview; they embarked on their new venture with fear and trepidation

trespass ['trespəs] **1** *noun* going onto someone's land or property without permission; *the farmer accused him of trespass* **2** *verb* to trespass on property = to go onto property without the owner's permission; *the farmer accused him of trespassing on his land*

> COMMENT: note that trespass is not a crime in British law, but a civil action can be brought by a property owner against a trespasser

trespasser ['trespəsə] *noun* person who trespasses on someone else's land; *the notices said 'Trespassers will be prosecuted', but they went through the gate just the same*

trial ['traɪəl] *noun* **(a)** court case held before a judge; *the trial will be heard next week*; to stand trial *or* to be on trial = to appear in court; *she stood trial, accused of murder; he's on trial for theft* **(b)** act of testing something; *the new model is undergoing its final trials*; on trial = being tested to see if it is acceptable; *the system is still on trial*; trial period = time when a customer can test a product before buying it; *at the end of the trial period we weren't satisfied and sent the machine back*; trial and error = testing and rejecting various things until you find the one which works; *we found out the best way of working was simply by trial and error* **(c)** game played to select the best players for a team; *trials to select the England Rugby team will be held this weekend*

triangle ['traɪæŋgl] *noun* **(a)** shape with three sides and three angles; *the end of the roof is shaped like a triangle* **(b)** musical instrument made of a metal rod bent into the shape of a triangle which you play by hitting it with a little metal bar; *playing the triangle is not as easy as it looks*

triangular [traɪ'æŋgjʊlə] *adjective* shaped like a triangle; *the Turkish restaurant served little triangular cakes*

triathlon [traɪ'æθlən] *noun* Olympic endurance sport in which competitors must complete a 1500-metre swim, then cycle 40 kilometres and finally run 10,000 metres; *compare* BIATHLON

tribal ['traɪbl] *adjective* referring to tribes; *tribal customs; tribal lands*

tribe [traɪb] *noun* **(a)** group of people with the same race, language and customs; *she went into the jungle to study the jungle tribes* **(b)** (*informal*) large family group; *they came with all their tribe of children*

tribesman ['traɪbzmən] *noun* man who is a member of a tribe; *tribesmen from all over the desert came to see the explorers* (NOTE: plural is **tribesmen**)

tribunal [traɪ'bjuːnl] *noun* specialist court outside the main judicial system which examines special problems and makes judgements; *a special tribunal has been set up to investigate these complaints*; industrial tribunal = court which decides in disputes between employers and workers; *the case of unfair dismissal went to the industrial tribunal*; rent tribunal = court which adjudicates in disputes about rents and can decide a fair rent

tributary ['trɪbjʊtəri] **1** *adjective* (*formal*) who pays tribute to a ruler; *envoys from tributary states came to the emperor with their gifts* **2** *noun* stream or river which flows into a larger river; *the Mole is one of the tributaries of the Thames* (b) *(formal)* person who pays tribute to a ruler; *tributaries came to the emperor with their gifts* (NOTE: plural is **tributaries**)

tribute ['trɪbjuːt] *noun* (a) words or gifts, etc., to show respect to someone, especially someone who has died; *tributes to the dead president have been received from all over the world*; **floral tributes** = flowers sent to a funeral (b) **to pay tribute to** = to praise; *speaker after speaker paid tribute to her work for charity*

trick [trɪk] 1 *noun* (a) clever act to deceive or confuse someone; *the recorded sound of barking is just a trick to make burglars think there is a dog in the house*; **to play a trick on someone** = to deceive or confuse someone; *he played a mean trick on his sister*; *my memory seems to be playing tricks on me*; *(informal)* **card tricks** *or* **conjuring tricks** = clever games with cards, with hats, handkerchiefs, rabbits, etc., to amuse an audience who try to work out how it is done; *(informal)* **that should do the trick** = that should do what we want to be done; *'there, that should do the trick' he said as he tightened the last nut*; **Trick or Treat** = children's game at Halloween, where children visit houses asking for fruit, sweets, etc., otherwise they will do something naughty (b) round of a card game; *she trumped his ace and won the trick*; *see also* HAT TRICK 2 *adjective* which deceives; *trick photography makes a tiny insect look like a giant monster*; **trick question** = question which is intended to deceive people 3 *verb* to deceive, to confuse someone; *we've been tricked, there's nothing in the box*; **to trick someone into doing something** = to make someone do something which he did not mean to do by means of a trick; *he tricked the old lady into giving him all her money*; **to trick someone out of something** = to get someone to lose something by a trick; *she tricked the bank out of £100,000*

trickery ['trɪkri] *noun* deceiving by using tricks; *the soldiers used trickery to get into the castle*

trickle ['trɪkl] 1 *noun* (a) small flow of water; *in the summer the stream dries up to a trickle* (b) small amount of letters, orders, information, etc.; *a trickle of applications came in after our advertisement* 2 *verb* (a) to flow gently; *water trickled out of the cave* (b) to come in small numbers; *orders still came trickling in two months after the ad appeared on TV*

trickle charger ['trɪkl 'tʃɑːdʒə] *noun* small device which charges a car battery, operated from the mains; *leave the battery on the trickle charger overnight*

trickster ['trɪkstə] *noun* **confidence trickster** = person who tricks or deceives people to get money from them; *some confidence trickster managed to get her to sign the papers*

tricky ['trɪki] *adjective* (a) difficult to do; *getting the wire through the little hole is quite tricky* (b) *(informal)* who cannot be trusted; *he's a tricky individual* (NOTE: **trickier - trickiest**)

tricycle ['traɪsɪkl] *noun* vehicle like a bicycle with three wheels, two at the back and one at the front; *a tricycle is best for little children because you can't fall off* (NOTE: often called a **trike**)

tried, tries [traɪd or traɪz] *see* TRY

trifle ['traɪfl] 1 *noun* (a) pudding made of cake or biscuits with jelly, jam, fruit, sherry and cream; *do you want chocolate pudding or trifle for dessert?* (b) *(old)* small thing which is not important; *the president does*

not bother himself with trifles (c) *(formal)* **a trifle** = a little; *she was a trifle bothered by the letter* 2 *verb* **trifle with someone** = not to treat someone seriously; *I wouldn't trifle with that gang if I were you*; *he's a dangerous opponent and certainly not someone to be trifled with*

trifling ['traɪflɪŋ] *adjective* unimportant; *he always has some trifling illness or other which prevents him from coming to the office*

trigger ['trɪgə] 1 *noun* little lever which you pull to fire a gun; *he pointed the gun at her and pulled the trigger* 2 *verb* **to trigger something (off)** = to start something happening; *the police are afraid the demonstration may trigger off a full-scale riot*; *the explosion was triggered by a spark*

trigonometrical [trɪgənə'metrɪkl] *adjective* referring to trigonometry; **trigonometrical point** *or* **trig point** = point used by surveyors to measure distances when making maps

trigonometry [trɪgə'nɒmɪtri] *noun* branch of mathematics which deals with the relationships between the sides and angles of triangles; *trigonometry is used in surveying, navigation and engineering*

trike [traɪk] *noun (informal)* = TRICYCLE

trillion ['trɪljən] *noun* one million millions (NOTE: British English now has the same meaning as American English; formerly in British English it meant one million million millions, and it is still sometimes used with this meaning)

trilogy ['trɪlədʒi] *noun* novel or play in three separate parts which are linked together; *the third and final volume of the trilogy will be published in May* (NOTE: plural is **trilogies**)

trim [trɪm] 1 *noun* (a) being fit; *he's in very good trim after a week at the health farm* (b) cutting of your hair, a plant, etc.; *he went to the barber's for a trim*; *can you give my beard a trim, please?* (c) decoration on a car, a piece of clothing, etc.; *the car is white with a dark blue trim* 2 *adjective* (a) tidy, cut short; *she always keeps her hedges trim* (b) slim and fit; *he keeps himself trim by going for a long walk every day* (NOTE: **trimmer - trimmest**) 3 *verb* (a) to cut something to make it tidy; *ask the hairdresser to trim your beard* (b) to cut back; to reduce; *to trim expenditure* (c) to decorate; *she wore a white blazer trimmed with blue* (NOTE: **trimming - trimmed**)

trimmer ['trɪmə] *noun* device which trims; *we have so many hedges in our garden that I've bought an electric hedge trimmer*

trimmings ['trɪmɪŋz] *noun* (a) ornament such as braid or lace, added to decorate something; *she wore a white blazer with blue trimmings* (b) the usual sauces and vegetables which go with a dish; *roast turkey with all the trimmings*

Trinidad & Tobago ['trɪnɪdæd n tə'beɪgəu] *noun* country in the Caribbean, formed of two islands in the West Indies (NOTE: capital: **Port of Spain**; people: **Trinidadians**; language: **English**; currency: **Trinidad & Tobago dollar**)

Trinidadian [trɪnɪ'dædiən] 1 *adjective* referring to Trinidad; *I met the Trinidadian High Commissioner* 2 *noun* person from Trinidad; *Trinidadians are passionate about cricket*

trinity ['trɪnɪti] *noun* **the Trinity** = the three entities who form the Christian God: the Father, the Son and the Holy Ghost

trio ['triːəʊ] *noun* **(a)** group of three people, especially a group of three musicians **(b)** piece of music for three instruments; *Mozart's trio for piano, clarinet and viola* (NOTE: plural is **trios**)

trip [trɪp] **1** *noun* **(a)** short journey; *our trip to Paris was cancelled*; *we're going on a trip to the seaside*; **business trip** = journey to visit business contacts; **coach trip** = excursion by coach; **day trip** = journey lasting one day **(b)** *(slang)* sensation experienced after taking drugs; *she had a bad trip* **2** *verb* to catch your foot in something so that you stagger and fall down; *she tripped as she was coming out of the kitchen with a tray of food* (NOTE: **tripping - tripped**)

tripe [traɪp] *noun* **(a)** part of an animal's stomach used as food; *the local dish is tripe and onions* **(b)** *(informal)* rubbish, nonsense; *his article was a load of tripe* (NOTE: no plural)

triple ['trɪpl] **1** *adjective* with three parts; *the three brothers are marrying three sisters in a triple wedding* **2** *verb* to become three times as large; to make something three times as large; *output has tripled over the last year*; *we've tripled the number of visitors to the museum since we reduced the entrance fee*

triplet ['trɪplət] *noun* one of three children born to a mother at the same time; *my sister gave birth to triplets last night*; *she produced triplets after having fertility treatment*

triplicate ['trɪplɪkət] *noun* **in triplicate** = with an original and two copies; *all these forms have to be filled in in triplicate*

tripod ['traɪpɒd] *noun* stand with three legs; *put the camera on a tripod if you want to take a photograph of yourself*

trip over ['trɪp 'əʊvə] *verb* **(a)** to catch your foot in something so that you stagger and fall; *she was running away from him when she tripped over and fell down* **(b) to trip over something** = to catch your foot in something so that you stagger and fall; *she tripped over the wire and fell down the stairs*

trip up ['trɪp 'ʌp] *verb* **(a) to trip someone up** = to make someone fall down; *she put her foot out and deliberately tripped the waiter up* **(b)** *(informal)* to make a silly mistake; *we tripped up badly in not inviting her to the party*; **to trip someone up** = to force someone to make a mistake; *he tried to trip me up by asking a question on a completely different subject*

trite [traɪt] *adjective* very ordinary and unexciting, which is used too often; *he made some trite remarks about students needing to work hard to get good jobs*

triumph ['traɪəmf] **1** *noun* great victory, great achievement; *they scored a triumph in their game against the French*; *the bridge is a triumph of modern engineering*; **in triumph** = celebrating a great victory; *after the battle the army entered the city in triumph* **2** *verb* **(a)** to win a victory, to achieve something; *she triumphed in the 800 metres* **(b) to triumph over something** = to be successful in spite of difficulties which could have stopped you; *he triumphed over his disabilities to become world champion*; **to triumph over someone** = to win a victory over someone; *our local team triumphed over their old rivals*

triumphal [traɪ'ʌmfl] *adjective* referring to triumph; *the team made a triumphal return to their home town*; **triumphal arch** = archway set up to commemorate a victory

triumphant [traɪ'ʌmfənt] *adjective* victorious, happy because you have won; *she came out of the courtroom triumphant at having won the case*; *he gave a triumphant wave as he crossed the finishing line*

triumphantly [traɪ'ʌmfəntli] *adverb* in a triumphant way; *she waved triumphantly to the crowd*

trivia ['trɪvɪə] *noun* details which are not important; *newspapers should report serious issues, not just trivia*; *why do you waste your time on such trivia* (NOTE: the word is plural)

trivial ['trɪvɪəl] *adjective* not important; *most of the complaints are so trivial I don't bother answering them*; *don't waste my precious time with trivial matters*

triviality [trɪvɪ'ælɪti] *noun* **(a)** being unimportant; *the triviality of her complaint meant that it was passed to a junior clerk to deal with* **(b)** unimportant detail; *I don't have time to deal with trivialities*

trod, trodden [trɒd or 'trɒdn] *see* TREAD

trolley ['trɒli] *noun* small cart on wheels; *they put the piano onto a trolley to move it out of the house*; **drinks trolley** = trolley on an aircraft, with various drinks which are served by stewards or stewardesses; **luggage trolley** = small cart with wheels, for carrying luggage at an airport or railway station (NOTE: American English for this is **baggage cart**); **supermarket trolley** = small cart with wheels for pushing round a supermarket (NOTE: American English for this is **shopping cart**); **dessert trolley** *or* **sweet trolley** = table on wheels on which desserts are taken to each table in a restaurant

trolley bus ['trɒlibʌs] *noun* bus which takes electricity from overhead wires; *trolley-buses are an energy-efficient method of public transport*

trombone [trɒm'bəʊn] *noun* brass musical instrument like a large trumpet, where different notes are made by sliding a tube in or out; *he plays the trombone in the city orchestra*

troop [truːp] **1** *noun* **(a) troops** = soldiers; *enemy troops occupied the town* **(b)** large group of people; *she took a troop of schoolchildren to visit the museum* (NOTE: do not confuse with **troupe**) **2** *verb* to go all together in a group; *after the play the whole cast trooped off to the local restaurant*; *all the students trooped into the hall* **3** *adjective* referring to soldiers; **troop ship** *or* **troop train** = ship *or* train which transports soldiers

trooper ['truːpə] *noun* **(a)** cavalry soldier; *Cromwell's troopers defeated the king's infantry*; **to swear like a trooper** = to swear loudly, using extremely bad language; *she swears like a trooper* **(b)** *US* **state trooper** = policeman from a state police force; *the governor called out the state troopers to stop the strikers blocking the entrance to the hospital* (NOTE: do not confuse with **trouper**)

Trooping the Colour ['truːpɪŋ ðə 'kʌlə] *noun* military parade where the flag of a guards regiment is paraded before the Queen; *can you get me tickets to the Trooping the Colour?*

trophy ['trəufi] *noun* prize given for winning a competition; *his mantelpiece is full of trophies which he won at golf* (NOTE: plural is **trophies**)

tropic ['trɒpɪk] *noun* **(a) Tropic of Cancer** = parallel running round the earth at latitude 23°28N; **Tropic of Capricorn** = parallel running round the earth at latitude 23°28S **(b) the tropics** = the hot areas of the world lying between these two imaginary lines; *he lived in the tropics for ten years*; *people work more slowly in the tropics*

tropical ['trɒpɪkl] *adjective* **(a)** referring to hot countries; *in tropical countries it is always hot*; **tropical storm** = violent storm occurring in the tropics **(b) tropical fish** = brightly coloured little fish coming from hot countries; *I'm going to the library to find out how to look after tropical fish*

trot ['trɒt] **1** *noun* **(a)** action of running with short regular steps; *let's start today's exercises with a short trot round the football field*; **at a trot** = running steadily; *every morning he runs round the block of flats at a gentle trot*; **to break into a trot** = to start to run; *as the children turned the corner and saw the ice-cream van, they broke into a trot* **(b)** *(informal)* **on the trot** = one after the other; *if we have to play six matches on the trot, we're bound to lose the last one because we'll be too tired*; *it is a scandal how junior hospital doctors are sometimes kept working for over sixteen hours on the trot*; *(informal)* **to be on the trot** = to work without stopping; *it's 5pm and she's been on the trot since 6 o'clock this morning - she must be dead* **(c)** *(informal)* **the trots** = diarrhoea; *he didn't want to come, he said he had the trots* **2** *verb* **(a)** to run with short regular steps; *we've got no butter left, so I'll trot off to the shop to buy some*; *she trotted down the path to meet us* **(b)** *(informal)* **to trot out** = to say the same thing again; *I'm tired of hearing the government trot out the same old excuse time and time again*; *she trotted out the stock argument about higher salaries leading to fewer jobs* (NOTE: **trotting - trotted**)

troth ['trəuθ] *noun (old)* **to plight your troth** = to promise faithfully to love and support the person you are marrying

trotters ['trɒtəz] *noun* pig's feet cooked for food; *pig's trotters are on the menu tonight*

trouble ['trʌbl] **1** *noun* **(a)** problems, worries; *the trouble with old cars is that sometimes they don't start*; *looking after your cat is no trouble - I like animals*; *the children were no trouble at all*; *we are having some computer trouble or some trouble with the computer*; *he's got his old back trouble again*; **it's asking for trouble** = it is likely to cause problems; *if you don't take out insurance, it's just asking for trouble* **(b) to get into trouble** = to start to have problems with someone in authority; *he and his friends got into trouble with the police*; *she got her best friend into trouble* **(c) to take the trouble to** = to make an extra effort and do something; *he didn't even take the trouble to write to thank us*; *if you had taken the trouble to look at the train timetable, you would have seen that there aren't any trains on Sundays* **2** *verb* **(a)** to make someone worried; *I can see that there's something troubling him but I don't know what it is* **(b)** to cause inconvenience; *can I trouble you for a light?*; *I'm sorry to have to trouble you with this, but I don't know how to switch my computer off*; **not to trouble to do something** = to make no effort to do

something; *he didn't even trouble to tell us he was going to cut down the tree*

troubled ['trʌbld] *adjective* **(a)** where there are problems; *he comes from a troubled family background*; *we live in troubled times* **(b)** worried; *he has a troubled look on his face*; *they seem troubled but I don't know why*

troublemaker ['trʌblmeɪkə] *noun* person who causes problems for other people; *the chairman called in the police to eject the troublemakers from the meeting*

troubleshooter ['trʌblʃuːtə] *noun* person who you ask to sort out problems for you; *they called in James Smith as troubleshooter when they got into difficulties with the local council*

troublesome ['trʌblsəm] *adjective* which causes trouble; *he still can't get rid of that troublesome cough*; *one or two troublesome kids can disturb the whole class*; *having your son arrested is just one of those troublesome situations some parents have to face*

trough [trɒf] *noun* **(a)** large narrow open container for animal food or drink; *the pigs were so greedy for their food, some of them even got into the trough*; **horse trough** *or* **water trough** = large container with water for horses to drink; *(informal)* **to have your snout in the trough** = to get rich on government money; *all these European officials have their snouts in the trough* **(b)** low point between two high points on a graph; *the graph shows the peaks and troughs of pollution over the last month* **(c)** low point in an economic cycle; *the government is trying to get the economy out of its current trough* **(d)** area of low pressure with cold air in it; *a trough of low pressure is approaching from the west* **(e)** low part of the sea between two waves; *the waves were so high that the boat seemed to disappear in the troughs*

troupe [truːp] *noun* group of actors, circus clowns, etc., who perform together; *he joined a touring troupe of itinerant actors* (NOTE: do not confuse with **troop**)

trouper ['truːpə] *noun* **old trouper** = old experienced actor or performer; *she's an old trouper - a little thing like an electricity blackout wouldn't put her off* (NOTE: do not confuse with **trooper**)

trousers ['trauzəz] *noun* clothes which cover your body from the waist down; *he tore his trousers climbing over the fence*; *she was wearing a red jumper and grey trousers*; *he bought two pairs of trousers in the sale*; *(informal)* **who wears the trousers in that family?** = who makes the decisions in the family? (NOTE: plural; to show one piece of clothing say **a pair of trousers**)

trout [traut] *noun* type of edible freshwater fish; *we had grilled trout with almonds* (NOTE: plural is **trout**)

trowel ['trauəl] *noun* hand tool, like a large spoon, used in gardening; *she made holes with a trowel before planting her bulbs*

troy weight ['trɔɪ 'weɪt] *noun* system of measurement formerly used for gold, silver and other precious metals, but no longer in legal use

truancy ['truːənsi] *noun* action of not going to school; *truancy rates are high in our borough*

truant ['truːənt] *noun* **to play truant** = not to go to school; *they didn't go to school, but played truant and* *went fishing instead* (NOTE: American English is **to play hookey**)

truce [truːs] *noun* agreement between two armies or enemies, etc., to stop fighting for a time; *when it got dark, they decided to call a truce*

truck [trʌk] **1** *noun* goods vehicle for carrying heavy loads; *trucks thundered past the house all night; they loaded the truck with bricks* (NOTE: British English also uses **lorry**) **2** *verb* to transport in a truck; *they trucked supplies to the refugees in the mountains*

truck driver *or* **trucker** ['trʌk 'draɪvə *or* 'trʌkə] *noun* person who drives a truck; *a truck driver gave us a lift into town* (NOTE: British English also uses **lorry driver**)

truck farm ['trʌk 'fɑːm] *noun US* small farm which grows vegetables or fruit which are sold in a nearby town (NOTE: British English is **market garden**)

trucking ['trʌkɪŋ] *noun US* carrying of goods by truck; *trucking goods across the United States is cheaper than sending them by rail; he works for a trucking company*

truckload ['trʌkləʊd] *noun* amount carried in a truck; *a truckload of bricks* (NOTE: British English also uses **lorryload**)

trudge [trʌdʒ] **1** *noun* long and tiring walk; *it was a long trudge back to camp through the mud* **2** *verb* to walk slowly with heavy footsteps; *the defeated army trudged back through the snow; he missed the bus and had to trudge to the village to get some milk*

true [truː] *adjective* correct, right; *what he says is simply not true; it's quite true that she comes from Scotland; is it true that he's been married twice?* (NOTE: **truer - truest**)

truffle ['trʌfl] *noun* **(a)** type of round black edible fungus found under the earth near trees; *specially trained pigs are trained to sniff out the best truffles* **(b)** soft sweet made of chocolate, often flavoured with rum; *we bought our hosts a bottle of wine and a box of (chocolate) truffles*

truly ['truːli] *adverb* **(a)** really; *he truly believes that was what happened; I'm truly grateful for all your help; do you love me, really and truly?* **(b) Yours truly** *US* **Truly yours** = words written at the end of a slightly formal letter; *(informal)* **yours truly** = me myself; *who had to pay for all the damage, why yours truly, of course!*

trump [trʌmp] **1** *noun* **(a)** *(in card games)* suit which is chosen to have a higher value than the other suits; *hearts are trumps; she should play a trump* **(b)** *(informal)* **to turn up trumps** = to be very generous or helpful; *when my car wouldn't start, my neighbour turned up trumps and gave me a lift to the station* **2** *verb* **(a)** **to trump a card** = to play a card of the suit which is trumps, and so win; *she trumped his ace and won the trick* **(b)** **to trump up** = to invent something false to harm someone; *he maintains the charges were trumped up by the police*

trump card ['trʌmp 'kɑːd] *noun* advantage which is kept ready for use in an emergency; *the terrorists' trump card is that they can cut off the country's supply of oil*

trumped-up charge ['trʌmpt'ʌp 'tʃɑːdʒ] *noun* charge which is based on false information, or on information which has been invented; *the opposition*

leaders were arrested on some trumped-up charge the week before the elections were due to take place

trumpet ['trʌmpɪt] *noun* **(a)** brass musical instrument with three pistons which are worked by pressing down on keys; *he plays the trumpet in the school orchestra; she practises the trumpet in the evenings* **(b)** *(informal)* **to blow your own trumpet** = to boast about what you have done; *he's an awful man, always blowing his own trumpet*

trumpeter ['trʌmpɪtə] *noun* person who plays the trumpet; *Louis Armstrong was a famous American jazz trumpeter*

truncheon ['trʌntʃən] *noun* short, thick stick used by policemen as a weapon; *most British police officers are just armed with truncheons, and not guns;* **to draw your truncheon** = to pull your truncheon out of its holder, ready for use; *the police drew their truncheons as they came close to the barricade* (NOTE: American English is also **nightstick**)

trundle ['trʌndl] *verb* to push or roll along something heavy; to move in a heavy way; *the gardener trundled the wheelbarrow along the path; the horse-drawn caravan trundled along the country lane*

trunk [trʌŋk] *noun* **(a)** thick stem of a tree; *ivy was climbing up the trunk of the oak tree* **(b)** an elephant's long nose **(c)** large box for storing or sending clothes, etc.; *she sent a trunk of clothes in advance to the new house* **(d)** *US* space at the back of a car, where you put luggage; *they stowed the boxes in the trunk* (NOTE: British English is **boot**)

trunk call ['trʌŋk 'kɔːl] *noun (old)* long-distance telephone call; *he made several trunk calls to Scotland*

trunk road ['trʌŋk 'rəʊd] *noun* main road; *all trunk roads leading out of the city have been blocked by protesting farmers*

trunks [trʌŋks] *noun* **(swimming) trunks** = shorts worn by a man when swimming

trust [trʌst] **1** *noun* **(a)** belief that something or someone is strong, will work well, etc.; *don't put too much trust in his skills as a plumber;* **to take something on trust** = to take something without looking to see if it is all right; *we took his statement on trust* **(b)** legal arrangement to pass valuables or money to someone to look after; *he left his property in trust for his grandchildren* **(c)** company which manages money for its clients; **unit trust** = organization which takes money from small investors and invests it in stocks and shares under a trust deed, the investment being in the form of units or shares in the trust **2** *verb* **(a)** to be sure of someone, to be confident that someone is reliable; *you can trust his instructions - he knows a lot about computers; I wouldn't trust him farther than I could kick him* **(b)** *(informal)* **trust you to** = it is typical of you to; *trust him to be late!; trust them to forget to bring the food!* **(c)** *(formal)* to hope or to believe; *I trust she will not get lost* **(d)** **to trust someone with something** = to give something to someone to look after; *can she be trusted with all that cash?*

trustee [trʌs'tiː] *noun* person who administers a trust or who directs a charity or other public institution; *the lease has to be agreed with the trustees of grandfather's estate; the director is appointed by the trustees of the museum*

trustful *or* **trusting** ['trʌstful *or* 'trʌstɪŋ] *adjective* showing that you trust someone and are not suspicious;

she's a simple trusting soul, and he easily conned her out of all her savings

trustworthiness ['trʌstwɜːðinəs] *noun* being trustworthy; *can you rely on the trustworthiness of the courier?*

trustworthy ['trʌstwɜːði] *adjective* who can be depended upon; *our cashiers are completely trustworthy*

truth [truːθ] *noun* thing which is true, a true story; *do you think he is telling the truth?; the police are trying to work out the truth about what happened; I don't think there is any truth in his story; see also* HOME TRUTHS

truthful ['truːθful] *adjective* (a) who always tells the truth; *she's a very truthful child* (b) giving true facts; *to be truthful, I'm not quite sure where we are; the young man gave a truthful account of what happened*

try [traɪ] 1 *noun* (a) making an effort to do something; *she's going to have a try at water skiing; he had two tries before he passed his driving test; let's give it a try* = let's see if it works (b) goal scored in rugby; *they scored two tries* (NOTE: plural is **tries**) 2 *verb* (a) to make an effort to do something; *the burglar tried to climb up the tree; don't try to ride a motorbike if you've never ridden one before; why don't you try to get a ticket yourself?* (b) to test, to see if something is good; *you must try one of my mother's cakes; I tried the new toothpaste and I didn't like the taste; have you ever tried eating cheese with fruit?* (c) to hear a civil or criminal case in court; *the case will be tried by a judge and jury*

trying ['traɪɪŋ] *adjective* annoying and difficult to deal with; *we had a very trying weekend looking after my sister's three children*

try on [traɪ 'ɒn] *verb* (a) to put on a piece of clothing to see if it fits; *you must try the trousers on before you buy them; did you try on the shoes at the shop?* (b) *(informal)* **to try it on** = to try to trick someone; *don't believe him - he's just trying it on*

try out ['traɪ 'aʊt] *verb* to test something, to see if it is good; *it's best to try a car out before you buy it*

tsar *or* **tzar** [zɑː] *noun* formerly, the title of the emperor of Russia; *the last tsar and his family were killed after the Russian Revolution* (NOTE: the American spelling is **czar**)

tsarina *or* **tzarina** [zɑːˈriːnə] *noun* formerly, the title of the empress of Russia; *the last tsarina, the wife of Nicholas II, was killed with him in 1918*

T-shirt *or* **teeshirt** ['tiːʃɜːt] *noun* light shirt with no buttons or collar, usually with short sleeves; *she was wearing jeans and a T-shirt; no wonder you're cold if you went out in just a T-shirt*

T-square ['tiː ˌskweə] *noun* piece of wood or plastic, shaped like a T, used to draw parallel lines; *a T-square is a often used by draughtsmen*

tsunami ['tsuːˈnɑːmi] *noun* huge wave in the sea, caused by an underwater earthquake; *a tsunami caused widespread flooding along the coast*

tub [tʌb] *noun* (a) round wooden container; *there's a tub of daffodils by their front door* (b) small, round cardboard box for ice cream; *girls went round the audience during the interval, selling small tubs of ice cream; our kids prefer ice cream cones to tubs* (c) *generally US* bath; *the children splashed so much in the tub that the bathroom floor was awash* (d)

(informal) old ship; *the tramp steamer was a rusty old tub which was ready to be scrapped*

tubby ['tʌbi] *adjective (informal)* short and fat; *the landlord is a tubby little man* (NOTE: **tubbier - tubbiest**)

tube [tjuːb] *noun* (a) long pipe for carrying liquids or gas; *he was lying in a hospital bed with tubes coming out of his nose and mouth; air flows down this tube to the face mask*; **inner tube** = rubber tube which is inflated inside a tyre (b) soft container with a screw top which contains paste, etc.; *I forgot to pack a tube of toothpaste; she bought a tube of mustard* (c) *(in London)* the underground railway system; *it's quicker to take the tube to Oxford Circus than to go by bus; you'll have to go by bus because there's a tube strike* (NOTE: the American English equivalent is **subway**) (d) *(in Australia)* can of beer

tuber ['tjuːbə] *noun* fat part of an underground root or stem which has buds from which new shoots grow; *when planting the dahlias be careful not to damage the tubers*

> COMMENT: tubers such as potatoes can be planted in the spring and will produce a crop later in the year

tubercular [tjuːˈbɜːkjʊlə] *adjective* with tuberculosis; *the number of tubercular patients has increased*

tuberculosis (TB) [tjuːbɜːkjʊˈləʊsɪs] *noun* infectious disease of the lungs, caused by a bacillus which creates infected lumps; *in Europe, cases of tuberculosis are starting to reappear; tuberculosis can be cured by long-term treatment with antibiotics*

> COMMENT: tuberculosis can be caught by breathing in germs, but is often caught from infected food, such as unpasteurized milk

tubing ['tjuːbɪŋ] *noun* tubes in general; *he bought some copper tubing; they are digging up the pavement to lay plastic tubing for cable TV* (NOTE: no plural)

tubular ['tjuːbjʊlə] *adjective* (a) shaped like a tube; *she wore a tubular pink skirt* (b) made of tubes; *the house is furnished with tubular steel chairs from the 1930s*; **tubular bells** = 18 metal tubes of varying lengths which are hung in a frame and hit with a hammer, giving different notes; *tubular bells are part of the percussion section of an orchestra*

TUC ['tiː 'juː 'siː] = TRADES UNION CONGRESS; *the TUC holds its annual meeting in September*

tuck [tʌk] 1 *noun* little fold in a piece of cloth; *I put a tuck in the shirt to make it fit better round the waist* 2 *verb* to put into a narrow or small place; *the shop is tucked away down a little lane; I offered him a £10 note, which he tucked away into his shirt pocket*

tucker ['tʌkə] *noun (in Australia) (informal)* food; *have you got your tucker bag?*

tuck in ['tʌk 'ɪn] *verb* (a) to fold something around and push the ends in; *she tucked the blanket in around the baby or she tucked the baby in; he tucked his trousers into his boots* (b) *(informal)* to start eating enthusiastically; *come on, the food's ready, everyone can tuck in; after our long walk we all tucked in to a huge lunch*

tuck shop ['tʌk ˈʃɒp] *noun (old)* shop attached to a school, selling sweets, drinks, etc., to the students; *the* *tuck shop opens every Friday afternoon after school*; *his mother gave him some money to spend in the tuck shop*

tuck up ['tʌk 'ʌp] *verb* **to tuck someone up in bed** = to push the edge of the bedclothes around someone to keep them warm; *by eight o'clock the children were all tucked up in bed*

Tudor ['tjuːdə] *adjective* referring to the time of Henry VII, Henry VIII, Edward VI, Mary I and Elizabeth I (i.e., the later fifteenth century and the sixteenth centuries); *the magnificent Tudor palace at Hampton Court* (NOTE: although, strictly speaking, Elizabeth I was a Tudor monarch, the adjective used to refer to her period is usually **Elizabethan**)

Tuesday ['tjuːzdeɪ] *noun* day between Monday and Wednesday, the second day of the week; *I saw him in the office last Tuesday*; *the club always meets on Tuesdays*; *shall we meet next Tuesday evening?*; *today is Tuesday, April 30th*; *the 15th is a Monday, so the 16th must be a Tuesday*

tug [tʌg] **1** *noun* **(a)** sudden pull; *he felt a tug on the line - he had caught a fish!* **(b)** powerful boat which pulls other boats; *two tugs helped the liner get into the harbour* **2** *verb* to pull hard; *he tugged on the rope and a bell rang* (NOTE: **tugging - tugged**)

tugboat ['tʌgbəʊt] *noun* powerful boat which pulls other boats; *two tugboats helped the ferry get into the harbour*

tug-of-war [tʌgəv'wɔː] *noun* **(a)** competition in which two teams pull against each other on a rope; *there will be a tug-of-war between teams from the two village pubs* **(b)** bitter struggle between two sides; *after the divorce the children were caught in a tug-of-war between their parents*

tuition [tjʊ'ɪʃn] *noun* teaching of students; *many students now have to pay their tuition fees themselves*; *as part of his scholarship, he has free tuition*; **individual tuition** = being taught alone by a teacher; *these students are lucky - they have individual tuition*

tulip ['tjuːlɪp] *noun* common spring bulb with flowers in brilliant colours, shaped like cups; *go to Holland to see the tulip fields in bloom*

tumble ['tʌmbl] **1** *noun* fall; *she took a tumble on the ski slopes* **2** *verb* to fall; *he tumbled down the stairs head first*; *she arrived home late after the party and just tumbled into bed*

tumble drier ['tʌmbl 'draɪə] *noun* machine which dries clothes after they have been washed, by turning them over and over inside a heated metal cylinder

tumbler ['tʌmblə] *noun* glass with a flat base and straight sides, used for serving drinks, etc.; *he handed her a tumbler of whisky*

tummy ['tʌmi] *noun* (*informal*) (*children's language*) stomach; *my tummy hurts*; *she had a tummy upset after eating too much ice cream*; **tummy ache** = stomach ache, pain in the stomach; *the little girl is crying because she has a tummy ache*; **tummy button** = navel, the depression in the middle of the abdomen, just below the waist, where the umbilical cord was detached after birth (NOTE: plural is **tummies**)

tumour *US* **tumor** ['tjuːmə] *noun* abnormal swelling or growth of new cells in the body; *the doctors discovered a tumour in the brain* *or* *a brain tumour*; **malignant tumour** = tumour which is cancerous and can grow again or spread into other parts of the body,

even if removed by surgery; *the hospital diagnosed a malignant tumour in the colon*

tumultuous [tjʊ'mʌltjʊəs] *adjective* noisy and excited; *the dancers left the stage to tumultuous applause*; *the local team was given a tumultuous welcome when the came back with the cup*

tuna ['tjuːnə] *noun* very large sea fish used for food; *a tuna salad* (NOTE: plural is **tuna**)

tune [tjuːn] **1** *noun* **(a)** series of musical notes which have a recognizable pattern; *he wrote some of the tunes for the musical*; *she walked away whistling a little tune* **(b) to change your tune** = to change your way of thinking; *he used to say that managers had an easy life, but when he was promoted he soon changed his tune*; (*informal*) **to the tune of £100** = at least £100; *we are paying rent to the tune of over £500 a week* **(c) in tune** = with the correct musical tone; *the various sections of the orchestra weren't playing in tune*; **in tune with** = harmonizing with, similar to; *his speech was in tune with the changing policies of the party*; **out of tune** = not harmonizing with; *the wind instruments seem to be playing out of tune* **2** *verb* **(a)** to adjust a musical instrument so that it plays at the correct pitch; *the man has come to tune the piano* **(b)** to adjust a radio to a particular station; *he keeps the radio tuned to Radio 4* **(c)** to adjust a car engine so that it works as efficiently as possible; *you'd use less petrol if you had the engine properly tuned*

tune in ['tjuːn 'ɪn] *verb* to adjust a radio so that it takes broadcasts from a particular station; *I've just tuned in to Radio 3*

tungsten ['tʌŋstən] *noun* hard metal used in making steel (NOTE: Chemical element: chemical symbol: **W**; atomic number: **74**)

tunic ['tjuːnɪk] *noun* **(a)** loose top shirt, without sleeves; *she was wearing a matching tunic and skirt* **(b)** short uniform jacket worn by soldiers, policemen, etc.; *the guardsmen spent hours polishing the buttons on their tunics*

tuning fork ['tjuːnɪŋ 'fɔːk] *noun* metal fork with two prongs which gives a pure note when it is hit; *a piano tuner uses a tuning fork to help him tune the piano*

Tunisia [tjuː'nɪzɪə] *noun* country in North Africa, between Algeria and Libya; *we fancy a bit of sunshine this winter so we're going to Tunisia for two weeks* (NOTE: capital: **Tunis**; people: **Tunisians**; language: **Arabic**; currency: **Tunisian dinar**)

Tunisian [tjuː'nɪzɪən] **1** *adjective* referring to Tunisia; *over 99% of the Tunisian population is Muslim* **2** *noun* person from Tunisia; *many Tunisians speak French as well as Arabic*

tunnel ['tʌnl] **1** *noun* long passage under the ground; *the Channel Tunnel links Britain to France*; *the road round Lake Lucerne goes through six tunnels*; *they are digging a new tunnel for the underground railway*; *taking the tunnel through the Alps is quicker than driving up the roads over the mountains*; **tunnel vision** = (i) seeing only the area immediately in front of the eye; (ii) having the tendency to concentrate on only one aspect of a problem **2** *verb* to dig a long passage underground; *they decided to tunnel under the hill rather than build the road round it* (NOTE: **tunnelling - tunnelled** but American spelling is **tunneling - tunneled**)

turban ['tɜːbən] *noun* long piece of cloth worn wrapped round your head; *Sikhs wear turbans*

turbaned ['tɜːbənd] *adjective* wearing a turban; *a group of turbaned soldiers followed the Indian president's car*

turbine ['tɜːbaɪn] *noun* machine which produces power from the action of water, gas or steam turning a wheel with blades which runs a generator; *water turbines create electricity from the force of water power*; **gas turbine** = unit in a car engine where the exhaust gases from the engine are used to drive a turbine and so increase engine power

turbocharger *(informal)* **turbo** ['tɜːbəʊ(tʃɑːdʒə)] *noun* gas turbine which turns at a very high speed and is powered by the gases from a car's exhaust, increasing the power of the engine; *power increases dramatically as soon as the turbocharger starts functioning*

turbojet ['tɜːbəʊdʒet] *noun* **(a)** powerful jet engine driven by a turbine; *they are developing a new type of turbojet engine for the next generation of aircraft* **(b)** aircraft powered by this type of engine; *a new generation of turbojets is being developed*

turbulence ['tɜːbjʊləns] *noun* disturbance in air or water currents; *turbulence can make an aircraft rock suddenly*; *fasten your seat-belts as we are expecting some turbulence*

turbulent ['tɜːbjʊlənt] *adjective* **(a)** which is moving violently; *watch out for turbulent water near the rocks* **(b)** likely to have riots or civil war; *a turbulent period in the country's history*

turd [tɜːd] *noun (informal)* lump of excreta; *there's a dog's turd on the pavement outside the office door*

tureen [tjuˈriːn] *noun* large bowl for serving soup; *the waitress arrived with a tureen of vegetable soup and put it on the table*

turf [tɜːf] **1** *noun* **(a)** area of grass which is mown and looked after; *after the rain, the dry springy turf suddenly turned wet and sticky underfoot* **(b)** piece of grass and soil which can be planted to form a lawn; *make sure the ground is flat before laying the strips of turf*; *it is quicker to lay turfs than to sow grass seed* **(c)** *(in Ireland)* block of peat for burning (NOTE: plural for (b) and (c) is **turfs** *or* **turves** [tɜːvz]) **(d) the turf** = the world of horse-racing; *enthusiasts of the turf are flocking to Epsom for the Derby*; *(formal)* **turf accountant** = bookmaker, person who takes bets on the result of races; *if the favourite always won, turf accountants would soon go out of business* **2** *verb* **(a)** to make a lawn by putting turfs on flat soil; *spring is the best time of year to turf a lawn* **(b)** *(informal)* **to turf someone out** = to throw someone out; *he was turfed out of the restaurant for refusing to wear a tie*; *we turfed out our old office furniture*

Turk [tɜːk] *noun* **(a)** person from Turkey; *many Turks travel to Germany in search of work* **(b) young turks** = ambitious young managers or army officers; *the new leader has surrounded himself with young turks who support his radical policies*

Turkey ['tɜːki] *noun* country in the eastern Mediterranean, south of the Black Sea; *Turkey lies partly in Europe and partly in Asia*; *Turkey has applied to join the EU*; *we're going sailing off the coast of Turkey this summer* (NOTE: capital: **Ankara**; people: **the Turks**; language: **Turkish**; currency: **Turkish lira**)

turkey ['tɜːki] *noun* **(a)** large farm bird, similar to a chicken but much bigger, often eaten at Christmas; *we had roast turkey and potatoes*; *who's going to carve the turkey?* **(b)** *US (informal)* failure; *his latest film was a complete turkey*

COMMENT: roast turkey is traditionally served with roast potatoes, bread sauce, chestnut stuffing, Brussels sprouts and cranberry sauce

---

Turkish ['tɜːkɪʃ] **1** *adjective* referring to Turkey; *the Turkish flag is red with a white crescent and star*; **Turkish delight** = sweet substance made of jelly, flavoured with scented water and containing chopped nuts; *there are lots of stalls in the bazaar selling Turkish delight* **2** *noun* language spoken in Turkey; *I couldn't understand what they were saying since they were speaking Turkish*

turmoil ['tɜːmɔɪl] *noun* state of disorder and confusion; *the devaluation caused turmoil on the foreign exchange markets*; *Parliament was in turmoil after the bomb attack*

turn [tɜːn] **1** *noun* **(a)** movement in a circle; *he gave the bottle top a couple of turns*; *don't forget to give the key an extra turn to double-lock the door* **(b)** change of direction, especially of a vehicle; *the bus made a sudden turn to the left*; *see also* U-TURN **(c)** road which leaves another road; *take the next turn on the right* **(d)** doing something in order, one after the other; *you have to wait for your turn to see the doctor*; *it's my turn on the piano now*; *let me go now - no, it's my turn next*; **in turn** = one after the other in order; *each of the children will sing a song in turn*; **out of turn** = not in the correct order; *people don't like it if you go out of turn* **(e) to take turns** *or* **to take it in turns** = to do something one after the other, to help each other; *they took it in turns to push the car* or *they took turns to push the car* **(f) the meat is done to a turn** = properly cooked all through **(g)** performance in a show; *their juggling act is one of the most popular turns of the evening* **(h) to do a good turn** = to do something to help; **one good turn deserves another** = if you do something to help someone they should do something to help you **2** *verb* **(a)** to go round in a circle; *the wheels of the train started to turn slowly*; *be careful - the blades of the lawnmower go on turning for a few seconds after the engine has been switched off* **(b)** to make something go round; *turn the handle to the right to open the safe* **(c)** to change direction, to go in another direction; *turn left at the next traffic lights*; *the car turned the corner too fast and hit a lamppost*; *the path turns to the right after the pub*; *the tide has turned* = the tide has started to go up or down **(d)** to move your head or body so that you face in another direction; *can everyone turn to look at the camera, please* **(e)** to change into something different; *leaves turn red or brown in the autumn*; *when he was fifty, his hair turned grey* **(f)** to go past a certain time; *it's turned nine o'clock, and they still haven't come home*; *she's turned sixty* = she is more than 60 years old **(g)** to find a page in a book; *please turn to page 65*

turn aside ['tɜːn əˈsaɪd] *verb* to move to one side; *they turned aside from the main path to follow a little path through the woods*; *she turned aside to let other cars go past*

turn away ['tɜːn əˈweɪ] *verb* **(a)** to send people away; *the restaurant is full, so we have had to turn people away* **(b)** to turn so as not to face someone; *he turned away because he didn't want to be photographed*

turn back ['tɜːn ˈbæk] *verb* **(a)** to go back in the opposite direction; *the path was so muddy that we had* *to turn back and go home* **(b)** to tell someone to go back; *the police tried to turn back the people who had no tickets*

turn down ['tɜːn 'daʊn] *verb* **(a)** to refuse something which is offered; *he was offered a job in Australia, but turned it down; she has turned down a job or turned a job down in the town hall* **(b)** to make less noisy, less strong; *can you turn down the radio - I'm trying to work; turn down the gas or turn the gas down - the soup will burn*

turn in ['tɜːn 'ɪn] *verb* **(a)** to take someone *or* something to someone in authority; *everyone was asked to turn in their guns; he caught the thief and turned him in to the police* **(b)** *(informal)* to go to bed; *it's after eleven o'clock - time to turn in!*

turning ['tɜːnɪŋ] *noun* road which goes away from another road; *take the next turning to the right; after taking several wrong turnings we were hopelessly lost*

turning point ['tɜːnɪŋ 'pɔɪnt] *noun* time when an important or decisive change takes place; *it was a turning point in the history of Europe*

turn into ['tɜːn 'ɪntʊ] *verb* **(a)** to change to become something different; *the witch turned the prince into a frog; we are planning to turn this room into a museum* **(b)** to change direction and go into something; *we went down the main road for a short way and then turned into a little lane on the left*

turnip ['tɜːnɪp] *noun* common vegetable, with a round white root; *slice a turnip and add it to the stew*

turn off ['tɜːn 'ɒf] *verb* **(a)** to switch off; *don't forget to turn the TV off when you go to bed; turn off the lights or turn the lights off - father's going to show his holiday films* **(b)** to leave a road you are travelling on; *you can turn off the High Street into one of the car parks; when you get to the next crossroads turn off the main road and go down a little path towards the river*

turn on ['tɜːn 'ɒn] *verb* **(a)** to switch on; *can you turn the light on or turn on the light - it's too dark to read; turn on the TV or turn the TV on - it's time for the news* **(b)** to attack someone suddenly; *the dog suddenly turned on the girl; the newspapers suddenly turned on the prime minister*

turn out ['tɜːn 'aʊt] *verb* **(a)** to force someone to go out; *they were turned out of their house when they couldn't pay the rent* **(b)** to produce or make; *the factory turns out more than 10,000 cars a week* **(c)** to switch off; *turn out the lights or turn the lights out - father's going to show a film of our holidays* **(d)** to happen in the end; *we got talking, and it turned out that she was at school with my brother; the party didn't start very well, but everything turned out all right in the end* **(e)** to come out; *the whole town turned out to watch the cycle race* **(f)** well *turned-out* = well dressed; *they haven't much money but their children are always well turned-out*

turnout ['tɜːnaʊt] *noun* crowd of people who come to a show, a meeting; *the football match attracted only a small turnout; there was a record turnout for the flower show*

turn over ['tɜːn 'əʊvə] *verb* **(a)** to roll over; *the lorry went round the corner too fast and turned over; their boat turned over in the storm* **(b)** to turn the page of a book; *turn over the page or turn the page over; she turned over two pages together* **(c)** to have a certain amount of sales; *we turn over about three million pounds per annum*

turnover ['tɜːnəʊvə] *noun* **(a)** amount of sales of goods or services by a business; *our turnover is rising each year* **(b)** type of small sweet pie made with pastry containing a fruit filling; *an apple turnover* **(c)** staff **turnover** = changes in staff, with some leaving and new people coming; *high staff turnover is a sign that a company is in trouble*

turn round ['tɜːn 'raʊnd] *verb* to move your head or body so that you face in another direction; *he turned round when the policeman touched his shoulder; she turned round to see who was following her*

turnround *US* **turnaround** ['tɜːnraʊnd *or* 'tɜːnəraʊnd] *noun* processing orders and sending out goods; **turnround time** = time taken from receiving an order and supplying the goods; *if we can reduce our turnround time it should improve profits*

turnstile ['tɜːnstaɪl] *noun* little revolving gate which has a counter to record the number of people going through it; *over 10,000 people went through the turnstiles to see the exhibition*

turntable ['tɜːnteɪbl] *noun* **(a)** flat part of a record player which turns with the record on it; *I don't think the turntable is aligned correctly - the records seem to turn at the wrong speed* **(b)** flat turning platform with rails on it, which allows a railway engine to be turned round to face a different direction; *there is a turntable at the end of the line so that the engines can turn round*

turn up ['tɜːn 'ʌp] *verb* **(a)** to arrive; *the food was spoiled because half the guests didn't turn up until nine o'clock; he turned up unexpectedly just as I was leaving the office* **(b)** to be found; *the police searched everywhere, and the little girl finally turned up in Edinburgh; the keys turned up in my trouser pocket* **(c)** to make louder, stronger; *can you turn up the radio or turn the radio up - I can't hear it; turn up the gas or turn the gas up, the potatoes aren't cooked yet*

turnup ['tɜːnʌp] *noun* folded part at the bottom of each leg of a pair of trousers; *trousers with turnups went out of fashion in the 1960s and are now back in fashion again* (NOTE: the American English is **cuffs**)

turpentine ['tɜːpəntaɪn] *noun* oil from fir trees, used for thinning oil paint; *clean your paintbrush with turpentine*

turps [tɜːps] *noun (informal)* = TURPENTINE

turquoise ['tɜːkwɔɪz] **1** *noun* blue-green precious stone; *her earrings are made of turquoise; she was wearing a turquoise ring* **2** *adjective* blue-green; *I bought a pale turquoise silk dress to go to the wedding; from the top of the cliff the sea looked turquoise in the sunshine*

turret ['tʌrɪt] *noun* **(a)** small tower; *from here, you can see the castle's pointed turrets* **(b)** small armoured structure with a gun inside, on a ship, tank, etc.; *the turret of the tank swung round until the barrel of the gun was pointing directly at the president's palace*

turtle ['tɜːtl] *noun* **(a)** sea animal with a hard shell, similar to a tortoise; *turtles come up onto the beach to lay their eggs;* **to turn turtle** = to turn over, to capsize; *the raft turned turtle and threw us all into the water; a big wave caught us sideways and we turned turtle* **(b)** *US* = TORTOISE

tusk [tʌsk] *noun* long tooth of some animals such as elephants, walruses, etc.; *poachers still kill elephants for their tusks*

tussle ['tʌsl] **1** *noun* fight or argument; *he got into a tussle with his friend over the motorbike*; *after a short tussle with the manager she got a refund* **2** *verb* to fight or to struggle; *they tussled with the administration over payment of expenses*

tutor ['tjuːtə] **1** *noun* teacher, especially a person who teaches only one student or a small group of students; *his first job was as private tutor to some German children* **2** *verb* to teach a small group of students; *she earns extra money by tutoring students after school*

tutorial [tjuˈtɔːriəl] *noun* teaching session between a tutor and one or more students; *we had a tutorial on Russian history*

tuxedo [tʌkˈsiːdəʊ] *noun US* a man's formal black or white jacket, worn with a bow tie; *all the men were wearing tuxedos and the women were in long evening gowns* (NOTE: British English for this is a **dinner jacket**)

TV ['tiː 'viː] *noun* **(a)** television; *they watch TV every night*; *the TV news is usually at nine o'clock*; *some children's TV programmes are very dull*; *the daughter of a friend of mine was on TV last night*; **cable TV** = television system where the programmes are sent along underground cables; **satellite TV** = television system, where pictures are sent via space satellites; **TV lounge** = room in a hotel, college, hospital, etc., where residents can watch TV **(b)** television set; *he's bought a portable TV*; *our TV is broken so we had to listen to the radio instead*; *we have a TV in our bedroom*

twang [twæŋ] **1** *noun* **(a)** sound made as when the string of a musical instrument or a taut wire is pulled and released; *you could hear the twang of his guitar*; *there was a loud twang as the cable snapped* **(b)** nasal **twang** = accent made when you speak through your nose; *he speaks with a South African twang* **2** *verb* to make a twang; *he was twanging away at his guitar*

tweak [twiːk] *verb* **(a)** to pinch and pull with your finger and thumb; *she tweaked his nose* **(b)** *(informal)* to adjust something carefully; *with a little tweaking we got the graphics right*

tweed [twiːd] *noun* rough woollen cloth made with strands of different coloured wool; *he was wearing a tweed jacket*

tweezers ['twiːzəz] *noun* little metal pincers for pulling our a hair or splinter; *she pulled the hair out with her tweezers*

twelfth (12th) [twelfθ] *adjective & noun* he came *twelfth out of two hundred in the competition*; *today is the twelfth of August or August the twelfth (August 12th)* *it's her twelfth birthday next week*; **the twelfth century** = the period from 1100 to 1199 (NOTE: compare **the twelve hundreds;** Note also that with dates **twelfth** is usually written **12th: July 12th, 1935; October 12th, 1991** (American style is **October 12, 1991**), say 'the twelfth of October' or 'October the twelfth' (American style is 'October twelfth'); with names of kings and queens **twelfth** is usually written **XII: King Louis XII** (say: 'King Louis the Twelfth'))

twelve [twelv] *number* 12; *she's twelve (years old) tomorrow*; *come round for a cup of coffee at twelve o'clock*; *there are twelve months in a year*; **the twelve hundreds** = the period from 1200 to 1299 (NOTE: **twelve o'clock** is also called **midday; twelve o'clock at night** is **midnight**)

twentieth (20th) ['twentiəθ] *adjective & noun* she *was twentieth out of twenty in the race*; *today is the twentieth of June or June the twentieth (June 20th)* *it's her twentieth birthday on Wednesday*; **the twentieth century** = the period from 1900 to 1999 (NOTE: with dates **twentieth** is usually written **20th: July 20th, 1935; October 20th, 1991** (American style is **October 20, 1991**), say 'the twentieth of October' or 'October the twentieth' (American style is 'October twentieth'))

twenty ['twenti] *number* 20; *she's twenty (years old) next week*; *he's in his twenties* = he is between 20 and 29 years old; **the (nineteen) twenties (1920s)** = the years from 1920 to 1929; **the twenty-first century** = the period from the year 2000 to 2099 *(informal)* **twenties** = £20 notes; *he gave me two twenties and four tens* (NOTE: **twenty-one (21), twenty-two (22),** etc., but **twenty-first (21st), twenty-second (22nd),** etc.)

twice [twais] *adverb* two times; *turn it off - I've seen that programme twice already*; *twice two is four, twice four is eight*; *I'm fifteen, she's thirty, so she's twice as old as I am*

twiddle ['twidl] *verb* **(a)** to twist something aimlessly; *she twiddled the knobs, hoping to find a German radio station* **(b)** to **twiddle your thumbs** = holding your hands together, to turn your thumbs round and round as a sign of not having anything to do; *why should we pay them wages when they just sit there twiddling their thumbs?*

twig [twig] **1** *noun* little branch of a tree; *there is a bud at the end of each twig*; *the blackbird made its nest of twigs and leaves* **2** *verb (informal)* to understand at last; *it took ages for him to twig what had happened*; *at last she twigged*

twilight ['twailait] *noun* time when the light is weak, between sunset and night; *the twilight hours are dangerous for drivers*

twin [twin] **1** *adjective & noun* **(a)** one of two babies born at the same time to the same mother; *he and his twin brother*; *she's expecting twins*; **identical twins** = twins who look exactly alike, because they developed from the same ovum; *I'm not surprised you were confused, they're identical twins*; **fraternal twins** = twins who are not identical because they developed from two different ova at the same time **(b) twin beds** = two single beds placed in a bedroom **2** *verb* to **twin one town with another town** = to arrange a special relationship between a town in one country and a similar town in another country, to encourage international understanding; *Richmond is twinned with Fontainebleau* (NOTE: **twinning - twinned**)

twine [twain] **1** *noun* strong rough string; *he tied the roses to the wall with thick twine* **2** *verb* to wind around; *she twined her arms round him*

twinge [twindʒ] *noun* short sharp pain; *he sometimes has a twinge in his right shoulder*; **twinge of anxiety** = short feeling of worry; *she felt a twinge of anxiety as she stood at the top of the ski slope*

twinkle ['twiŋkl] **1** *noun* little glitter; *there was a twinkle in his eyes as he gave her the present* **2** *verb (of stars, eyes)* to glitter; *his eyes twinkled as he showed the children the sweets he had bought*; *we could see the lights of the harbour twinkling in the distance*

twirl [twɜːl] **1** *noun* **(a)** movement of making something spin; *the model on the catwalk gave a twirl of her skirt*; *start it moving by giving the wheel a twirl* **(b)** curly shape; *the pattern was full of twists and twirls* **2** *verb* **(a)** to spin round; *models twirled round on the* *catwalk* (b) to twist something round in your hand; *I wish I could twirl a baton like the cheerleader*

twist [twɪst] **1** *noun* (a) thing which has been twisted; *put a twist of lemon (peel) in the drink*; *the twists and turns of the road through the mountains*; *it is difficult to follow the twists and turns of government policy* (b) different way of telling a story; *he put a new twist on the story about the princess* **2** *verb* (a) to turn in different directions; *the path twisted between the fields* (b) to wind something round something; *she twisted the string round a piece of stick* (c) to bend a joint in the wrong way; *she twisted her ankle running to catch the bus*; (*informal*) to **twist someone's arm** = to put pressure on someone to persuade them to do what you want; *I had to twist his arm to get him to lend me his car*

twister ['twɪstə] (b) *US* tornado, whirlwind; *houses in the path of the twister had their roofs ripped off*

twitch [twɪtʃ] **1** *noun* sudden little movement; *he has a nervous twitch than makes him look as if he's winking* **2** *verb* to make a sudden little movement; *one side of his face kept on twitching*

twitcher ['twɪtʃə] *noun* (*informal*) fanatical birdwatcher; *twitchers came from all over the country when there were reports of a cardinal in the Welsh hills*

two [tuː] number 2; *there are only two peppermints left in the box*; *his son's only two (years old), so he can't read yet*; *she didn't come home until after two (o'clock)* **one or two** = some, a few; *only one or two people came to the exhibition* (NOTE: **two (2)** but **second (2nd)**)

two-bit ['tuːbɪt] *adjective US* (*informal*) second-rate; *she's just some two-bit singer*

two-lane highway ['tuː leɪn 'haɪweɪ] *noun US* road in two parts, with a barrier between them; *the traffic on the two-lane highway was bumper-to-bumper* (NOTE: the British English for this is **dual carriageway**)

two-piece ['tuːpiːs] *adjective* made of two pieces; **two-piece suit** = suit made of a jacket and skirt or trousers; *I need a new lightweight two-piece suit for the office this summer*

two-time ['tuːtaɪm] *verb* (*informal*) to **two-time someone** = to be unfaithful to your spouse or lover; *you dirty two-timing rat!*

two-way ['tuːweɪ] *adjective* going in two directions; *this is a two-way street*; **two-way radio** = radio where both users can talk to each other; *all the taxis in the fleet are fitted with two-way radios*

tycoon [taɪˈkuːn] *noun* very rich businessman; *a wealthy tycoon has offered to buy the football club for £100m*; *these new flats all belong to a property tycoon*; *he's a very well known shipping tycoon*

tying ['taɪɪŋ] *see* TIE

type [taɪp] **1** *noun* (a) sort or kind; *this type of bank account pays 10% interest*; *what type of accommodation are you looking for?*; **blood type** = classification of blood into a certain group (b) characters used in printing; *the chapter headings are in bold type* (NOTE: no plural in this meaning) **2** *verb* to write with a typewriter; *please type your letters - your writing's so bad I can't read it*; *she only typed two lines and made six mistakes*

typecast ['taɪpkɑːst] *verb* to give an actor the same sort of part to play all the time; *since she played the stupid schoolgirl in the TV series, she's been typecast in that sort of part* (NOTE: **typecasting - has typecast**)

typed [taɪpd] *adjective* written on a typewriter; *we prefer to get typed applications rather than handwritten ones*

typeface ['taɪpfeɪs] *noun* set of printed characters which have been designed with a certain style and have a certain name; *most of this dictionary uses the Times Roman typeface*

typescript ['taɪpskrɪpt] *noun* manuscript of a book, typed on a typewriter; *the author sent in his typescript six months late*

typesetter ['taɪpsetə] *noun* person who sets text in type ready for printing; *the text is ready to be sent to the typesetter*

typewriter ['taɪpraɪtə] *noun* machine which prints letters or figures on a piece of paper when keys are pressed; *keep a cover over your typewriter when you are not using it*

typewritten ['taɪprɪtn] *adjective* which has been written with a typewriter; *it's better to send in a typewritten job application letter*; *all entries must be typewritten with double spacing*

typhoid fever ['taɪfɔɪd 'fiːvə] *noun* serious and possibly fatal disease caused by infected food or water; *contaminated water was probably the cause of the recent outbreak of typhoid fever*

typhoon [taɪˈfuːn] *noun* the name for a violent tropical storm in the Far East; *the typhoon caused immense damage in the regions along the coast* (NOTE: in the Caribbean it is called a **hurricane**)

typhus ['taɪfəs] *noun* serious fever, where the virus is carried by fleas and lice; *aid workers fear that a typhus epidemic may erupt if conditions in the refugee camps deteriorate any further*

typical ['tɪpɪkl] *adjective* having the usual qualities of a particular group or occasion; *describe a typical day at school*; *he's definitely not a typical bank manager*; **that's typical of him** = that's what he always does; *it's typical of them to be late*

typically ['tɪpɪkli] *adverb* in a typical way; *I want to buy something which is typically Welsh*; *typically, he arrived for dinner a hour late*

typify ['tɪpɪfaɪ] *verb* to be a good example of something; *this report typifies her conscientious attitude towards all her school work*; *that sexist remark typifies his attitude towards women*

typing ['taɪpɪŋ] *noun* action of writing letters with a typewriter; *she taught herself typing*; **typing pool** = group of typists who work for several departments in a company; **typing paper** = special paper for typewriters

typist ['taɪpɪst] *noun* person whose job is to type letters on a typewriter; *she's quite a good typist*

typo ['taɪpəu] *noun US* (*informal*) mistake made when typing or keyboarding, especially where one letter is put instead of another; *the reviewer founds hundred of typos in the index - who was the proofreader?* (NOTE: British English is also **literal**)

typographer [taɪˈpɒgrəfə] *noun* person who designs the printed pages of a book, or who designs a typeface; *the typographer and the publisher disagree about which typeface to use*

typographic or **typographical** [taɪpəˈgræfɪk or taɪpəˈgræfɪkl] *adjective* referring to typography; *a typographical error made when typesetting is often called a 'typo'*

typography [taɪˈpɒgrəfi] *noun* **(a)** arranging the text on a printed page in a pleasing way or in a way which best conveys the meaning; *I like the typography of this magazine - it makes it very easy to read* **(b)** study of the design of typefaces; *as part of his printing course he has to learn about typography*

tyrannical [tɪˈrænɪkl] *adjective* cruel and unjust; *the people rose up against the tyrannical dictator*

tyranny [ˈtɪrəni] *noun* **(a)** the use of force and fear to rule a country; *to arrest so many protesting students was an act of tyranny* **(b)** unfair strict control over someone; *the tyranny of the hospital manager over the nursing staff*

tyrant [ˈtaɪrənt] *noun* ruler who rules by force and fear; *the tyrant was overthrown and a democratic republic was set up*

tyre *US* **tire** [taɪə] *noun* ring made of rubber and a hard case, which is put round a wheel and which is filled with air; *check the pressure in the tyres before starting a journey; they used an old tyre to make a seat for the garden swing*; **flat tyre** = a tyre which has lost all the air in it; *he pulled up at the side of the road to change a flat tyre; my bike got a flat tyre and I had to walk home* (NOTE: American English is simply a **flat**); **snow tyres** = special tyres with thick treads, for use when driving on snow; *when hiring a car in the winter, check if it has snow tyres*; **spare tyre** = (i) extra tyre carried in a car in case you have a flat tyre; (ii) *(informal)* roll of fat round the waist

Uu

U, u [juː] twenty-first letter of the alphabet, between T and V; *the letter 'q' is always followed by a 'u'*; **U-bend** = bend in a pipe shaped like a U; *see also* U-TURN

ubiquitous [juˈbɪkwɪtəs] *adjective* which is or which seems to be everywhere; *business executives and their ubiquitous mobile phones*

udder [ˈʌdə] *noun* gland which produces milk, a bag which hangs under the body of a cow or female goat; *the newborn calf was looking for the cow's udder*

UFO [juː ef ˈəʊ] = UNIDENTIFIED FLYING OBJECT

ugh [ɜː] *interjection showing a feeling that something is unpleasant*; *Ugh, I don't think I could ever eat snails!*

ugliness [ˈʌglinəs] *noun* the state of being ugly; *we were struck by the ugliness of the town with its grey snow and puddles of dirty water*

ugly [ˈʌgli] *adjective* **(a)** not beautiful, not pleasant to look at; *what an ugly pattern!*; *the part of the town round the railway station is even uglier than the rest*; **ugly as sin** = very ugly **(b) ugly mood** = dangerous mood; *the mood of the crowd turned ugly* (NOTE: **uglier - ugliest**)

uh huh [əˈhə] *interjection showing that you agree or that you are listening*; *'Want to come?' - 'Uh huh!'*

UK [juːˈkeɪ] *abbreviation for* United Kingdom; *exports from the UK or UK exports rose last year*

Ukraine (the) [ðə juːˈkreɪn] *noun* large country in Eastern Europe, south of Russia, on the north coast of the Black Sea; *he's going to the Ukraine to see business contacts in Kiev* (NOTE: capital: **Kiev**; people: **Ukrainians**; language: **Ukrainian**; currency: **Ukrainian rouble**)

Ukrainian [juːˈkreɪniən] **1** *adjective* referring to the Ukraine; *Ukrainian exports to Germany* **2** *noun* **(a)** person from the Ukraine; *a party of Ukrainians visited our stand at the exhibition* **(b)** language spoken in the Ukraine; *if you're going to the Ukraine, you will need an English-Ukrainian phrase book*

ulcer [ˈʌlsə] *noun* open sore on or inside the body; *he's on a special diet because of his stomach ulcers*

ulcerous [ˈʌlsrəs] *adjective* referring to ulcers; *an ulcerous sore*

ulna [ˈʌlnə] *noun* the inside bone of the two bones of the forearm between the elbow and the wrist; *she broke both the radius and the ulna* (NOTE: the other bone is the **radius**)

ulterior motive [ʌlˈtɪəriə ˈməʊtɪv] *noun* hidden reason for doing something which will give you an advantage; *she had an ulterior motive for writing to the newspaper to compliment it on the quality of its articles - she was hoping to get a job as a reporter*

ultimate [ˈʌltɪmət] **1** *adjective* last, final; *this is the ultimate game in the series* **2** *noun* the most valuable or desirable thing; *our first-class cabins are the ultimate in travelling luxury*

ultimately [ˈʌltɪmətli] *adverb* in the end; *ultimately, the manager had to agree to refund her money*

ultimatum [ʌltɪˈmeɪtəm] *noun* final demand, proposal sent to someone stating that unless he does something within a period of time, action will be taken; *unless they respond to our ultimatum we will consider ourselves to be at war*; *the union delivered an ultimatum to the management*

ultrasound [ˈʌltrəsaʊnd] *noun* very high frequency sound wave, used to detect objects in the body or under water; *ultrasound scanning can provide pictures of a woman's ovaries*; *ultrasound treatment is used to treat inflammation of soft tissue*

ultraviolet rays (UV rays) [ʌltrəˈvaɪələt ˈreɪz] *noun* invisible short light rays which are beyond the violet end of the spectrum and form the burning and tanning part of sunlight; *when in the sun, you should protect your skin against ultraviolet rays*; **ultraviolet lamp** = lamp which gives off ultraviolet rays which tan the skin and help the skin produce Vitamin D; *don't stay under the ultraviolet lamp longer than the recommended time*

um [ʌm] **1** *interjection showing that you are not sure what to say*; *um, perhaps it's - no I don't know the answer* **2** *verb* (informal) **to um and ah** = to hesitate about what to do; *I can't stand all this umming and ahing - why can't they make their minds up?*

umbilical [ʌmˈbɪlɪkl] *adjective* referring to the navel; **umbilical cord** = cord which links the foetus to the placenta inside the womb

umbrella [ʌmˈbrelə] *noun* **(a)** round frame covered with cloth which you hold over your head to keep off the rain; *can I borrow your umbrella?*; *the company gives away umbrellas with red, green and white spots*; *as it was starting to rain, he opened his umbrella*; *the wind blew my umbrella inside out*; **beach umbrella** = parasol, a large umbrella to protect you from the sun **(b) umbrella organization** = large organization which includes several other smaller ones

umpire [ˈʌmpaɪə] **1** *noun* person who acts as a judge in a game to see that the game is played according to the rules; *the umpire ruled that the ball was out*; *he was disqualified for shouting at the umpire* **2** *verb* to act as umpire; *he umpired the match very fairly*

umpteen [ʌmpˈtiːn] *adjective* (informal) a large number; *I've been to France umpteen times*; *there are umpteen forms to fill in*

umpteenth [ʌmpˈtiːnθ] *adjective* (informal) latest in a long series; *that's the umpteenth wrong number we've had this morning*; *for the umpteenth time, can't you turn that radio down!*

UN [ˈjuːen] *abbreviation for* United Nations; *UN peacekeeping forces are in the area*; *the British Ambassador to the UN spoke in the debate*

unable [ʌnˈeɪbl] *adjective (formal)* not able to (do something); *I regret than I am unable to accept your suggestion*; *she was unable to come to the meeting* (NOTE: **be unable to** is rather formal; otherwise use **can't**)

unacceptable [ʌnəkˈseptəbl] *adjective* which you cannot allow because it is too bad; *there were an unacceptable number of errors in the test*; *the terms of the contract are quite unacceptable*

unaffected [ʌnəˈfektɪd] *adjective* **(a)** unaffected by = not affected by; *he seemed totally unaffected by the publicity about his marriage*; *some of the plants were killed by the frost, but these were quite unaffected* **(b)** sincere or natural; *she's totally unaffected, and genuinely interested in our work*

unalike [ʌnəˈlaɪk] *adjective* not at all similar; *the two brothers are completely unalike*

unambiguous [ʌnæmˈbɪgjuəs] *adjective* clear, not ambiguous; *the message was unambiguous and no one could have mistaken what was meant*

unanimity [juːnəˈnɪmɪti] *noun* being unanimous; *we could not find any unanimity within the committee*

unanimous [juˈnænɪməs] *adjective* with everyone agreeing; *there was a unanimous vote against the proposal*; *the jury reached a unanimous verdict of not guilty*

unanimously [juˈnænɪməsli] *adverb* with everyone agreeing; *the proposals were adopted unanimously*

unannounced [ʌnəˈnaʊnst] *adjective* which has not been announced; *they arrived totally unannounced*

unanswered [ʌnˈɑːnsəd] *adjective* which has not had an answer; *piles of unanswered letters lay on his desk*; *this important question still remains unanswered*

unarmed [ʌnˈɑːmd] *adjective* with no weapons; *should policemen who patrol the streets be armed or unarmed?*

unashamed [ʌnəˈʃeɪmd] *adjective* not ashamed; *he is quite unashamed of his wealth*; *in spite of being criticized, she remains unashamed of what she did*

unattached [ʌnəˈtætʃt] *adjective* not married, or not in a sexual relationship with anyone; *he's very attractive, and apparently unattached*

unattractive [ʌnəˈtræktɪv] *adjective* not attractive; *a rather unattractive young man dealt with our query*; *the house is unattractive from the outside, but the inside is quite extraordinary*; *I find the idea of spending the weekend with my wife's family a very unattractive proposition*

unauthorized [ʌnˈɔːθəraɪzd] *adjective* which has not been permitted; *this expenditure was unauthorized*; *she wrote an unauthorized biography of the pop star which has been criticized by his family*

unavailable [ʌnəˈveɪləbl] *adjective* not available; *the following items on your order are temporarily unavailable*; *we tried to phone the manager, but he was unavailable*

unavoidable [ʌnəˈvɔɪdəbl] *adjective* which cannot be avoided; *once the teacher fell ill it was unavoidable that the whole class should get flu*

unaware [ʌnəˈweə] *adjective* **unaware of** = not knowing, not aware of; *he said he was unaware of any rule forbidding animals in the restaurant*

unawares [ʌnəˈweəz] *adverb* without being expected; **to catch someone unawares** = to catch someone by surprise; *the TV cameras caught her unawares as she slept through the reception*; *the security cameras caught him unawares as he was putting a packet in the rubbish bin*

unbalanced [ʌnˈbælənst] *adjective* **(mentally) unbalanced** = erratic or slightly mad; *I think her husband is a bit unbalanced*

unbearable [ʌnˈbeərəbl] *adjective* which cannot be borne; *old people find this heat unbearable*; *the noise was unbearable and no one could work*

unbearably [ʌnˈbeərəbli] *adverb* impossible to bear; *it was unbearably hot and noisy in the restaurant*

unbeatable [ʌnˈbiːtəbl] *adjective* which cannot be beaten; *their team is too good - they're simply unbeatable*

unbeaten [ʌnˈbiːtn] *adjective* which has not been defeated; *our local team has been unbeaten so far this season*; *his unbeaten record for the high jump was set in 1996*

unbelievable [ʌnbɪˈliːvəbl] *adjective* incredible, which is difficult to believe; *it's unbelievable that she didn't know that the drugs were hidden in her suitcase*; *he has an unbelievable number of pop records*

unbelievably [ʌnbɪˈliːvəbli] *adverb* incredibly, extremely; *the scent is unbelievably powerful*

unbeliever [ʌnbɪˈliːvə] *noun* person who does not believe in God; *as an unbeliever, I don't mind if the baby is christened or not*

unbiased [ʌnˈbaɪəst] *adjective* without any bias; *the BBC is famous for its unbiased reporting*

unblinking [ʌnˈblɪŋkɪŋ] *adjective* without blinking; *she gave him an unblinking stare*

unborn [ʌnˈbɔːn] *adjective* not yet born; *a pregnant woman and her unborn child*

unbroken [ʌnˈbrəʊkn] *adjective* which has not been broken; *after weeks of unbroken sunshine the rains came as a relief*; *his record is still unbroken after ten years*

uncanny [ʌnˈkæni] *adjective* mysterious, which seems unnatural; *there is an uncanny resemblance between her and her aunt*; *it's uncanny how he seems to be able to remember things which happened more than half a century ago*

unceasing [ʌnˈsiːsɪŋ] *adjective* which never stops; *the unceasing sound of the sea on the rocks outside our window*; *the unceasing support of my brother helped me through my divorce*

uncertain [ʌnˈsɜːtən] *adjective* **(a)** doubtful, not sure; *she is uncertain as to whether her father will come to stay*; *their plans are still uncertain* **(b) in no uncertain terms** = rudely; *he told him in no uncertain terms what he could do with his offer* **(c)** which will probably change for the worse; *she faces an uncertain future*

uncertainty [ʌnˈsɜːtənti] *noun* being uncertain or doubtful; *there is some uncertainty about the date of the meeting*

unchallenged [ʌnˈtʃælənʒd] *adjective* without a challenge; *he's the only candidate, and it looks as though he'll remain unchallenged*; *she entered the hospital premises unchallenged but was stopped by* *the surveillance system when she reached the baby unit*; **to let something go** or **pass unchallenged** = to let something be said or written without questioning it; *if we let this ruling pass unchallenged we will regret it later*

unchanged [ʌn'tʃeɪndʒd] *adjective* not changed, without any changes; *the time of the meeting is now 10.30, but all the other details remain unchanged*

uncharacteristic [ʌnkærəktə'rɪstɪk] *adjective* odd, not in character; *it's uncharacteristic of her not to send me a birthday card*; *following the treatment an uncharacteristic reaction was noticed*

unchecked [ʌn'tʃekt] *adjective* which has not been checked; *he seems to have got in through the entrance quite unchecked*; *some items of unchecked baggage remained in the check-in area*

uncle ['ʌŋkl] *noun* brother of your father or mother; husband of an aunt; *he was brought up by his uncle in Scotland*; *we had a surprise visitor last night - old Uncle Charles*

unclear [ʌn'klɪə] *adjective* not clear; *the result of the election is still unclear - the two parties are neck and neck*

uncomfortable [ʌn'kʌmftəbl] *adjective* **(a)** not comfortable, not soft and relaxing; *what a very uncomfortable bed!*; *plastic seats are very uncomfortable in hot weather* **(b)** **to feel uncomfortable about** = to feel worried about; *I still feel uncomfortable about asking her to carry all that cash to the bank*

uncommon [ʌn'kɒmən] *adjective* strange or odd; rare; *it's a very uncommon bird in the north of Scotland*; *it's not uncommon for us to have hundreds of phones calls during the morning* (NOTE: **uncommoner - uncommonest**)

uncomplicated [ʌn'kɒmplɪkeɪtɪd] *adjective* not complicated; *children live simple uncomplicated lives*

uncompromising [ʌn'kɒmprəmaɪzɪŋ] *adjective* unwilling to give in or to change your ideas; *he was quite uncompromising in his attitude towards his grandchildren*

unconditional [ʌnkən'dɪʃnl] *adjective* with no conditions attached; *they demanded the unconditional surrender of the enemy general*; *her unconditional trust in her children*

unconditionally [ʌnkən'dɪʃnəli] *adverb* without any conditions; *the union accepted the offer unconditionally*; *the army surrendered unconditionally*

unconfirmed [ʌnkən'fɜːmd] *adjective* which has not been confirmed; *according to unconfirmed reports, a bomb has exploded at the airport*; *the disappearance of the plane is still unconfirmed*

unconscious [ʌn'kɒnʃəs] **1** *adjective* not conscious, not aware of what is happening; *he was found unconscious in the street*; *she was unconscious for two days after the accident*; **unconscious of something** = not realizing something; *he was quite unconscious of how funny he looked* **2** *noun* **the unconscious** = the part of the mind which stores thoughts, memories or feelings which you are not conscious of, but which influence what you do

unconsciously [ʌn'kɒnʃəsli] *adverb* without realizing; *he unconsciously offended her by calling her 'Sally' which was the name of his last girlfriend*

unconstitutional [ʌnkɒnstɪ'tjuːʃənl] *adjective* action which is against a country's constitution, which is not allowed by the rules of a club or society; *the chairman ruled that the meeting was unconstitutional*; *the court decided that the action of the government was unconstitutional*

uncontrollable [ʌnkən'trəʊləbl] *adjective* which cannot be controlled; *the uncontrollable spread of a disease through the population*; *uncontrollable children pose a particular problem to teachers*

uncontrolled [ʌnkən'trəʊld] *adjective* which has not been controlled; *the council is planning to cut down on uncontrolled parking round the main square*

unconventional [ʌnkən'venʃnl] *adjective* not usual; *the treatment may be unconventional but it seems to work*; *she's always been unconventional, so don't be surprised at the way she's dressed*

unconvinced [ʌnkən'vɪnst] *adjective* not convinced; *I remain quite unconvinced of her innocence*

unconvincing [ʌnkən'vɪnsɪŋ] *adjective* which does not convince; *his argument for cutting benefits is totally unconvincing*

uncooked [ʌn'kʊkt] *adjective* raw, not cooked; *some Japanese dishes consist of uncooked fish*; *shrimps are grey when uncooked and become pink when cooked*

uncouth [ʌn'kuːθ] *adjective* rude, with bad manners; *he is so uncouth that no one invites him to parties*; *her parents were shocked when she appeared with this uncouth young man*

uncover [ʌn'kʌvə] *verb* **(a)** to take a cover off something; *leaving the pots of jam uncovered will simply attract wasps* **(b)** to find something which was hidden; *they uncovered a secret store of gold coins*; *the police have uncovered a series of secret financial deals*

undecided [ʌndɪ'saɪdɪd] *adjective* who has not made up his mind; *he's undecided as to whether he should accept the post or not*; *have you fixed your departure date or are you still undecided about it?*

undemocratic [ʌndemə'krætɪk] *adjective* not democratic; *the action of the president was completely undemocratic*

undeniable [ʌndɪ'naɪəbl] *adjective* which cannot be denied, which is quite clearly true; *there are undeniable tax advantages in working abroad*; *it's undeniable that the government is not taking strict enough measures*

under ['ʌndə] **1** *preposition* **(a)** in or to a place where something else is on top or above; *we all hid under the table*; *my pen rolled under the sofa*; *she can swim under water* **(b)** less than a number; *no one wanted the old table - it was sold for under £10*; *it took under two weeks to sell the house*; *the train goes to Paris in under three hours*; *under half of the members turned up for the meeting* **(c)** younger than; *she's a managing director and she's still under thirty* **(d)** according to; *under the terms of the agreement, the goods should be delivered in October* **(e)** controlled by a ruler; *the country enjoyed a period of peace under the rule of the British governors* (NOTE: **under** is often used with verbs: **to look under**, **to go under**, etc.) **2** *adverb* **(a)** in a lower place; **to go under** = to fail, to go bankrupt; *the company went under during the recession* **(b)**

(informal) **down under** = in Australia and New Zealand; *we get a lot of tourists from down under*

undercarriage [ˈʌndəkærɪdʒ] *noun* landing gear of an aircraft, the aircraft's wheels and their supports; *the undercarriage was damaged and the plane had to make an emergency landing*

underclass [ˈʌndəklɑːs] *noun* the lowest class in society; *the benefits system has created an underclass of homeless poor*

underclothes *or* **underclothing** [ˈʌndəkləʊðz or ʌndəˈkləʊðɪŋ] *noun* clothes which you wear next to the skin, under other clothes; *he ran out of the house in his underclothes; the doctor asked him to strip down to his underclothes*

undercover [ˈʌndəkʌvə] **1** *adjective* acting in disguise; *two undercover policemen were sent to the night club to monitor the sale of drugs* **2** *adverb* in secret; *he was working undercover for the British government at the time*

undercurrent [ˈʌndəkʌrənt] *noun* **(a)** current of water under the surface; *there are strong undercurrents in this part of the river* **(b)** hidden feelings; *there is an undercurrent of antagonism to management in the factory*

undercut [ˈʌndəkʌt] *verb* to sell more cheaply than someone; *some cheap travel agents undercut air fares; our prices are the lowest and we won't allow anyone to undercut us* (NOTE: **undercutting** - **undercut**)

underdeveloped [ʌndədɪˈveləpt] *adjective* not developed; not industrially advanced; *underdeveloped countries sell raw materials for hard currency*

underdog [ˈʌndədɒg] *noun* person or team that is weaker, that is going to lose; *this newspaper will always champion the underdog*

underestimate **1** *noun* [ʌndərˈestɪmət] estimate which is less than the actual figure; *the figure of £50,000 was a considerable underestimate* **2** *verb* [ʌndərˈestɪmeɪt] to think that something is smaller or not as bad as it really is; *he underestimated the amount of time needed to finish the work; don't underestimate the intelligence of the average voter*

undergarment [ˈʌndəgɑːmənt] *noun (old)* piece of clothing worn next to the skin, under other clothes; *she couldn't really come to the door in her undergarments*

undergo [ʌndəˈgəʊ] *verb* to suffer, to have something happen to you; *she will probably have to undergo another operation soon* (NOTE: **underwent** [ʌndəˈwent] - **undergone** [ʌndəˈgɒn])

undergraduate [ʌndəˈgrædjʊət] *noun* student at university who is studying for his or her first degree; *lots of undergraduates are trying to get summer jobs*

underground [ˈʌndəgraʊnd] **1** *adverb* **(a)** under the ground; *the ordinary railway line goes underground for a short distance; worms live all their life underground; if power cables were placed underground they would be less of an eyesore* **(b)** to **go underground** = to go into hiding; *they had to go underground for a time until the police called off their search* **2** *adjective* under the ground; *there's an underground passage to the tower* **3** *noun* railway in a town, which runs under the ground; *thousands of people use the underground to go to work; take the underground to go to Oxford Circus; it's usually quicker to get to Waterloo by underground* (NOTE: the

London underground is often called the **Tube**. In the USA, an underground railway is called a **subway**)

undergrowth [ˈʌndəgrəʊθ] *noun* shrubs and other plants which grow thickly under large trees; *they had to cut a path through the forest undergrowth; if we clear the undergrowth away the newly planted trees will grow better*

underlie [ʌndəˈlaɪ] *verb* to be beneath, to be the basic cause of something; *hard work underlies their business success* (NOTE: **underlying** - **underlay** [ʌndəˈleɪ] - **has underlain**)

underline [ˈʌndəlaɪn] *verb* **(a)** to write a line under a word, a figure; *he wrote the title and then underlined it in red* to emphasize; *this just underlines the urgent need for more medical supplies; I want to underline the fact that we need an experienced sales force*

underlying [ʌndəˈlaɪɪŋ] *adjective* which is the reason for everything; *it is difficult to solve the underlying problem of bad housing*

undermine [ʌndəˈmaɪn] *verb* to make weaker; *the documents undermined his case; our heavy industry has been undermined by the low labour costs in the Far East*

underneath [ʌndəˈniːθ] **1** *preposition* under; *she wore a long green jumper underneath her mac; can you lie down and see if my pen is underneath the sofa?* **2** *adverb* under; *he put the box of books down on the kitchen table and my sandwiches were underneath!* **3** *noun* base, the part of something which is under; *the underneath of the car is showing signs of rust*

underpants [ˈʌndəpænts] *noun* men's short underwear for the part of the body from the waist to the top of the legs; *the doctor told him to strip down to his underpants; his wife gave him a pair of bright red white and blue underpants for his birthday*

underpass [ˈʌndəpɑːs] *noun* road which is built under another; *turn left at the lights when you come out of the underpass* (NOTE: the opposite, i.e. a road built over another, is an **overpass**)

underpin [ʌndəˈpɪn] *verb* to support; *their success was underpinned by a lot of hard work* (NOTE: **underpinning** - **underpinned**)

underpinning [ʌndəˈpɪnɪŋ] *noun* supporting from underneath; *it's a major job if the house needs underpinning*

underrate [ʌndəˈreɪt] *verb* to value something less than you ought; *her achievements have been underrated; don't underrate the ability of the British voter to spring a surprise on the party in government*

underscore [ʌndəˈskɔː] *verb* to emphasize, to underline; *the report underscores the importance of office security*

Undersecretary [ʌndəˈsekrətri] *noun* GB **Parliamentary Undersecretary (of State)** = junior member of the government, working in a government department under the Secretary of State

undershirt [ˈʌndəʃɜːt] *noun* US light piece of underclothing for the top half of the body; *he wears a thick undershirt in winter; if you don't have a clean undershirt, wear a T-shirt instead* (NOTE: British English is **vest**)

underside [ˈʌndəsaɪd] *noun* side that is underneath; *the underside is painted a dark colour; the plane skidded across the runway on its underside*

understand [ʌndəˈstænd] *verb* **(a)** to know what something means; *don't try to talk English to Mr Yoshida - he doesn't understand it; I hardly speak any Japanese, but I managed to make myself understood* **(b)** to have information, to think something is true because someone has told you so; *we understand that they're getting married next month; it was understood that the group would meet at the pub* **(c)** to have sympathy for someone; *she's a good teacher - she really understands children* **(d)** to know why something happens or how something works; *I can easily understand why his wife left him; I still don't understand how to operate the new laser printer* (NOTE: **understanding - understood** [ʌndəˈstʊd])

understandable [ʌndəˈstændəbl] *adjective* normal, which is easy to understand; *her response was quite understandable in the circumstances*

understandably [ʌndəˈstændəbli] *adverb* in a way which you can understand; *she was understandably upset when her cat was run over by a car*

understanding [ʌndəˈstændɪŋ] **1** *noun* **(a)** ability to understand something; *my understanding of how the Internet works is severely limited* **(b)** sympathy for someone else and their problems; *the boss showed no understanding when she told him about her financial difficulties; the aim is to promote understanding between the two countries* **(c)** private agreement; *we reached an understanding with the lawyers; the understanding was that we would all go to the office after lunch* **(d)** on the understanding that = on condition that, provided that; *we accept the terms of the treaty, on the understanding that it has to be passed by Parliament* **2** *adjective* sympathetic; *his understanding attitude was much appreciated*

understate [ʌndəˈsteɪt] *verb* to make something seem less important than it really is; *the report understates the danger of using this product*

understated [ʌndəˈsteɪtɪd] *adjective* which makes something seem less strong than it really is; *the room is decorated in very understated colours*

understatement [ʌndəˈsteɪtmənt] *noun* statement which does not tell the facts forcefully enough; *saying that the government has had a few difficulties is the understatement of the year*

understood [ʌndəˈstʊd] *see* UNDERSTAND

understudy [ˈʌndəstʌdi] **1** *noun* actor who learns a part in the play so as to be able to act it if the usual actor cannot perform; *the understudy had to take over last night when the male lead fell and broke his arm* **2** *verb* to be the understudy for an actor; *who is understudying Judi Dench?; he is understudying Hamlet*

undertake [ʌndəˈteɪk] *verb* **(a)** to agree to do something; *he has undertaken to pay her £100 a week for twelve weeks* **(b)** to do something; *they undertook a survey of the market on our behalf* (NOTE: **undertook** [ʌndəˈtʊk] - has **undertaken**)

undertaker [ˈʌndəteɪkə] *noun* person who organizes funerals; *there is a firm of undertakers next door to our office* (NOTE: American English is also **mortician**)

undertaking [ˈʌndəteɪkɪŋ] *noun* **(a)** business; *the Post Office must be considered as a commercial undertaking, not as a public service* **(b)** promise; *she gave him an undertaking that she would continue to work for a further six months; they have given us a written undertaking that they will not play loud music*

after ten o'clock at night **(c)** large-scale job; *it was quite an undertaking* = it was a very difficult job

undervalued [ʌndəˈvæljuːd] *adjective* not valued highly enough; *the dollar is undervalued on the foreign exchanges; at that price, the property is considerably undervalued; he felt his work was undervalued at the office*

underwater [ʌndəˈwɔːtə] *adjective* below the surface of the water; *how long can you stay underwater?; he dived and swam underwater for several seconds; she goes on holiday to the Red Sea to do underwater photography*

under way [ˈʌndə ˈweɪ] *adverb* in progress; *the show finally got under way after a lot of delays*

underwear [ˈʌndəweə] *noun* clothes worn next to your skin under other clothes; *it's December, so I'd better get out my winter underwear; the nurse asked her to strip to her underwear and put on a hospital gown; each child will need to bring a change of underwear* (NOTE: no plural)

underweight [ʌndəˈweɪt] *adjective* not heavy enough, which weighs less than usual; *the pack is 20 grams underweight; he is several pounds underweight for his age; an underweight baby is more likely to catch infections than a normal baby*

underworld [ˈʌndəwɜːld] *noun* **(a)** *(in mythology)* place inhabited by the dead; *Orpheus went down into the Underworld to search for his wife* **(b)** world of criminals; *the police superintendent is an expert on London's underworld gangs; underworld killing* = murder of a criminal by other criminals

underwrite [ʌndəˈraɪt] *verb* **(a)** to insure something, such as a risk; *they underwrote the insurance policy* **(b)** to accept responsibility for something; *the share issue was underwritten by one of the merchant banks* **(c)** to agree to pay for the costs; *the government is underwriting the costs of the exhibition* (NOTE: **underwrote** [ʌndəˈrəut] - has **underwritten** [ʌndəˈrɪtən])

underwriter [ˈʌndəraɪtə] *noun* person who underwrites an insurance; *it was a difficult year for insurance underwriters as there were so many storms and floods; a marine underwriter* = person who insures ships and cargoes

undesirable [ʌndɪˈzaɪərəbl] **1** *adjective* **(a)** not wanted; *it's highly undesirable that they should build a factory in the national park; undesirable alien* = person who is not a citizen of the country, and who the government considers should not be allowed to stay in the country; *he was deported as an undesirable alien* **(b)** not pleasant; *taking the medicine produces no undesirable effects* **2** *noun* person who is not wanted, who is considered a bad influence; *we are tightening the immigration law to keep undesirables out of the country*

undid [ʌnˈdɪd] *see* UNDO

undies [ˈʌndɪz] *noun (informal)* underwear, especially women's underwear; *I've just washed my undies, I hope they'll be dry by the morning*

undisclosed [ʌndɪsˈkləuzd] *adjective* which has not been told to anyone; *the house was sold for an undisclosed sum; the family has moved to an undisclosed address*

undisputed [ʌndɪsˈpjuːtɪd] *adjective* which no one disputes; *he is the undisputed master of the country; she is the undisputed world champion*

undisturbed [ʌndɪsˈtɜːbd] *adjective* without being disturbed; *we will leave him to go on sleeping undisturbed; the thieves ransacked the office undisturbed - the security guards were watching the World Cup; your mother seems quite undisturbed by the news*

undo [ʌnˈduː] *verb* (a) to unfasten something which is tied or buttoned; *the first thing he did on getting home was to undo his tie; undo your top button if your collar is too tight* (b) to upset the good effect of something; *his off-the-cuff remarks undid all the good work done to increase racial cooperation* (NOTE: **undid** [ʌnˈdɪd] - has **undone** [ʌnˈdʌn])

undoubted [ʌnˈdaʊtɪd] *adjective* certain, true; *his undoubted enthusiasm for the project helped get it off the ground*

undoubtedly [ʌnˈdaʊtɪdli] *adverb* quite certainly; *this is undoubtedly the best investment deal on the market*

undress [ʌnˈdres] *verb* to take your clothes off; *the doctor asked the patient to undress or to get undressed; he undressed and got into the bath; they carried him upstairs, undressed him and put him to bed*

undue [ˈʌndjuː] *adjective* (*formal*) excessive, too much; *some parents feel the school is putting undue pressure on the children to do well; he got through his test without any undue problems;* **undue influence =** pressure put on someone which prevents him from acting independently; *the government was accused of exerting undue influence on the committee*

undulate [ˈʌndjuleɪt] *verb* to rise and fall like waves; *the fields of golden wheat undulating in the breeze*

unduly [ʌnˈdjuːli] *adverb* (*formal*) excessively, too much; *the court's sentence seems unduly severe; ring us up as often as you can so that we don't worry unduly about you*

undying [ʌnˈdaɪɪŋ] *adjective* which lasts for ever; *he earned the undying hatred of his boss; her undying love for her fiancé who was killed in battle*

unearth [ʌnˈɜːθ] *verb* to dig up; to discover; *the team of archaeologists unearthed a fine Roman pot; where did you unearth this document from? - everyone said it was lost*

unearthly [ʌnˈɜːθli] *adjective* (a) wild and strange; *unearthly shrieks came from the empty church* (b) (*informal*) much too early; *I had to get up at some unearthly hour to catch the plane to Milan*

unease [ʌnˈiːz] *noun* feeling uncomfortable and worried; *he couldn't hide his unease at having to talk in front of the all the other delegates; after the theft of the money a certain unease is affecting the staff*

uneasy [ʌnˈiːzi] *adjective* nervous and worried; *I'm rather uneasy about lending her so much money* (NOTE: **uneasier - uneasiest**)

uneatable [ʌnˈiːtəbl] *adjective* not good to eat; *the food at the conference was absolutely uneatable*

unemployed [ʌnɪmˈplɔɪd] **1** *adjective* without a job; *the government is encouraging unemployed teenagers to apply for training grants* **2** *noun* the **unemployed =** people with no jobs; *the government is offering special grants to help the unemployed*

unemployment [ʌnɪmˈplɔɪmənt] *noun* lack of work; *the unemployment figures or the figures for unemployment are rising;* **mass unemployment =** situation where large numbers of people are out of work; **unemployment benefit =** money paid by the government to someone who is unemployed

unending [ʌnˈendɪŋ] *adjective* which is going on for ever, with no end; *their unending struggle to earn enough money to live on; children always need something new - school uniforms, bikes, pop CDs, the list is unending*

unequal [ʌnˈiːkwəl] *adjective* (a) not equal; *the management was accused of applying unequal conditions to male and female employees* (b) **unequal to =** not good enough, not strong enough for; *their feeble efforts were totally unequal to the task*

unequalled [ʌnˈiːkwəld] *adjective* which has no equal; *she is unequalled at tennis; her score remains unequalled; you can rely on the unequalled expertise of our staff*

unequivocal [ʌnɪˈkwɪvəkl] *adjective* (*formal*) clear, which cannot be misunderstood; *the unequivocal 'no' from the negotiators took everyone by surprise; there can be no mistake - the meaning of his letter is quite unequivocal*

uneven [ʌnˈiːvn] *adjective* not smooth, not flat; *don't try to pitch the tent where the ground is uneven*

unevenly [ʌnˈiːvnli] *adverb* not evenly; *the paint had been put on very unevenly*

unexpected [ʌnɪkˈspektɪd] *adjective* which is surprising and not what was expected; *we had an unexpected visit from the police; his failure was quite unexpected*

unexpectedly [ʌnɪkˈspektɪdli] *adverb* in an unexpected way; *just as the party was starting his mother walked in unexpectedly*

unexplained [ʌnɪksˈpleɪnd] *adjective* which has not been explained; *how the suitcase got past the customs is still unexplained; the unexplained late arrival of the plane from Paris*

unfair [ʌnˈfeə] *adjective* not right, not fair; *it's unfair to expect her to do all the housework while her sisters don't life a finger to help;* **unfair dismissal =** removing of a person from his job for reasons which are not fair; *he made an appeal against the company on the grounds of unfair dismissal*

unfaithful [ʌnˈfeɪθfəl] *adjective* having sex with someone who is not your husband or wife; *he was unfaithful to his wife on many occasions; he divorced his unfaithful wife*

unfamiliar [ʌnfəˈmɪliə] *adjective* not knowing at all well; *I am quite unfamiliar with the US tax regulations; we found ourselves in a totally unfamiliar part of the town*

unfashionable [ʌnˈfæʃnəbl] *adjective* not fashionable; *it was the trendiest restaurant last year, but now is quite unfashionable; according to the fashion magazines, it is now unfashionable to wear baggy trousers*

unfasten [ʌnˈfɑːsn] *verb* to undo a belt, tie, button, etc., which is fastened; *he unfastened his belt and tucked his shirt into his trousers; watch the screen to see how your seatbelt should be fastened and unfastened*

unfavourable US **unfavorable** [ʌnˈfeɪvrəbl] *adjective* not favourable; *the judgement was unfavourable to her; unfavourable winds pushed the boat several miles off course; some MPs were unfavourable to the proposed amendment*

unfinished [ʌnˈfɪnɪʃt] *adjective* which has not been finished; *the builders were so slow that the annexe was still unfinished six months after they started work; there is some unfinished business which I have to clear up*

unfit [ʌnˈfɪt] *adjective* **(a)** not fit, not in good physical condition; *I used to play a lot of tennis but I've got unfit during the winter; he's so unfit, he goes red in the face if he simply bends down to pick something up off the floor* **(b)** unfit for = not suitable for; *he was classed as unfit for service in the police force*; unfit for human consumption = not good enough to be eaten by people; *the meat was found to be unfit for human consumption*; unfit for human habitation = not of good enough standard for people to live in; *the house has been condemned as unfit for human habitation; the old houses were declared unfit for human habitation and pulled down*

unfold [ʌnˈfəʊld] *verb* **(a)** to spread out something which is folded, such as a newspaper; *she unfolded the tablecloth and put it on the table* **(b)** *(of story)* to become clear; *as the full extent of the disaster unfolded, so it became clear that the emergency services could not cope*

unforeseeable [ʌnfɔːˈsiːəbl] *adjective* which could not be foreseen; *we will arrive at 6.30, barring any unforeseeable delays on the motorway; unforeseeable circumstances prevented him from attending the show*

unforeseen [ʌnfɔːˈsiːn] *adjective* not foreseen, not anticipated; *barring any unforeseen hitches the new shop should be open to the public next Monday*

unforgettable [ʌnfəˈgetəbl] *adjective* which cannot be forgotten; *going to an open-air performance was an unforgettable experience*

unfortunate [ʌnˈfɔːtʃənət] *adjective* **(a)** which is not lucky; *he made some rather unfortunate purchases on the stock exchange* **(b)** which makes you sad; *it was very unfortunate that she couldn't come to see us* **(c)** embarrassing; *he made some very unfortunate friendships when he was in the army; she made some unfortunate remarks about the bride's feet*

unfortunately [ʌnˈfɔːtʃənətli] *adverb* sadly, which you wish was not true; *unfortunately the train arrived so late that she missed the meeting*

unfounded [ʌnˈfaʊndɪd] *adjective* without any basis in truth; *a quite unfounded rumour spread through the town; he thought he had cancer, but was told his fears were unfounded*

unfriendly [ʌnˈfrendli] *adjective* not like a friend; *the old teachers were very unfriendly towards the new recruits; he acted in such an unfriendly manner that I wondered what I had done to make him annoyed* (NOTE: **unfriendlier - unfriendliest**)

unfulfilled [ʌnfʊlˈfɪld] *adjective* which has not been carried out; *there are stacks of unfulfilled orders waiting in the warehouse; the opposition has made a list of the government's unfulfilled promises*

unfurl [ʌnˈfɜːl] *verb* **(a)** to unroll like a flag; *the petals of the flower slowly unfurled; the crew were getting ready to unfurl the sail* **(b)** to develop gradually; *we watched fascinated by the events which unfurled on our TV screens*

unfurnished [ʌnˈfɜːnɪʃt] *adjective* with no furniture; *we are looking for an unfurnished house to rent; he let his house unfurnished*

unhappily [ʌnˈhæpɪli] *adverb* in a sad way; *she sat there, staring unhappily out of the window*

unhappy [ʌnˈhæpi] *adjective* sad, not happy; *he's unhappy in his job because his boss is always criticizing him; she looked very unhappy when she came out of the hospital; the children had an unhappy childhood* (NOTE: **unhappier - unhappiest**)

unharmed [ʌnˈhɑːmd] *adjective* not harmed, not hurt; *the children were found two days later, quite unharmed*

unhealthy [ʌnˈhelθi] *adjective* **(a)** not healthy; which does not make you healthy; *the office is very unhealthy, and most of the staff seem to be ill all the time; sitting around smoking and not doing any sport is very unhealthy; their children have a very unhealthy diet* **(b)** unnatural; *she has an unhealthy interest in dead bodies* (NOTE: **unhealthier - unhealthiest**)

unheard of [ʌnˈhɜːdɒv] *adjective* strange or odd; *to be accepted at a university at the age of fifteen was quite unheard of; in their family, it is quite unheard of to vote Conservative*

unhelpful [ʌnˈhelpfəl] *adjective* not helpful; *her unhelpful comments made me depressed; the person I talked to about my plane ticket was rather unhelpful*

unhurt [ʌnˈhɜːt] *adjective* not hurt; *the little girl crawled out of the wrecked car quite unhurt; all four people in the two cars escaped unhurt*

unicorn [ˈjuːnɪkɔːn] *noun* imaginary animal, a white horse with one long, straight horn growing from the centre of its head; *a lion and a unicorn stand on either side of the British coat of arms*

unidentified [ʌnaɪˈdentɪfaɪd] *adjective* which you do not recognize, which you cannot identify; *the photograph stayed in a drawer unidentified for years*; unidentified flying object (UFO) = mysterious object in the sky which cannot be identified; *there are fewer sightings of UFOs than there were some years ago*

unification [juːnɪfɪˈkeɪʃn] *noun* act of joining two countries together to form one; *the unification of the two countries took place in 1989*; compare REUNIFICATION

uniform [ˈjuːnɪfɔːm] **1** *noun* special clothes worn by all members of an organization or group; *he went to the fancy dress party dressed in a policeman's uniform; who are those people in French army uniform?; what colour is her school uniform?; the holiday camp staff all wear yellow uniforms*; in uniform = wearing a uniform; *the policeman was not in uniform at the time* **2** *adjective* all the same, never changing; *the supermarket wants vegetables of uniform size and colour*

uniformed [ˈjuːnɪfɔːmd] *adjective* wearing a uniform; uniformed staff = staff who wear uniforms (such as hotels porters, railway staff, etc.)

uniformity [juːnɪˈfɔːmɪti] *noun* being uniform; *the newspapers reflect the uniformity of views held by the public; the uniformity of style of modern terraced houses*

unify ['juːnɪfaɪ] *verb* to join separate countries together to form one; *the country was finally unified after years of civil war*

unilateral ['juːnɪlætərəl] *adjective* done by one side only; *a unilateral cancellation of the contract; the decision was unilateral not taken jointly*

unilaterally [juːni'lætərəli] *adverb* in a unilateral way; *they decided unilaterally to leave the association*

unimaginable [ʌnɪ'mædʒɪnəbl] *adjective* which cannot be imagined; *they live in unimaginable luxury; the amount of money he lost gambling is unimaginable; a nuclear holocaust would cause unimaginable suffering*

unimportant [ʌnɪm'pɔːtənt] *adjective* not important; *don't apologize for being late - it's quite unimportant; I have an unimportant meeting at the office which I can easily cancel*

unimpressed [ʌnɪm'prest] *adjective* not impressed; *I was quite unimpressed by or with his work; her singing was not up to her usual standard, and the judges were left unimpressed*

uninformed [ʌnɪn'fɔːmd] *adjective* without enough knowledge; *I can't stand uninformed criticism; he was kept uninformed of the decision*

uninhibited [ʌnɪn'hɪbɪtɪd] *adjective* able to express yourself freely, able to do what you want to do; *her dance performance was totally uninhibited*

uninitiated [ʌnɪ'nɪʃieɪtɪd] *adjective* the uninitiated = people who do not have specialist knowledge of something; *to the uninitiated, computer jargon seems difficult to understand*

unintelligible [ʌnɪn'telɪdʒəbl] *adjective* which cannot be understood; *I read the book and found her theories unintelligible; the committee drew up such complicated and unintelligible rules that no one follows them*

unintentional [ʌnɪn'tenʃənl] *adjective* which is not intended; *the pun was quite unintentional*

uninterested [ʌn'ɪntrestɪd] *adjective* not having any interest in something; *she seemed quite uninterested in what was going on*

uninterrupted [ʌnɪntə'rʌptɪd] *adjective* continuous, with no breaks; *he spoke for four hours uninterrupted; from the top floor, you have an uninterrupted view of the park*

union ['juːniən] *noun* (a) state of being joined together; *we support the union of these various groups under one umbrella organization* (b) group of countries or independent states which are linked into a federation; *the union between England and Scotland is over 300 years old;* Union Flag *see* UNION JACK; *see also* EUROPEAN UNION (c) *(specifically)* the United States of America; *the President will give his State of the Union message in January* (d) *(formal)* marriage; *their union will be celebrated on 1st November* (e) (trade) union = organization which represents workers who are its members in discussions with employers about wages and conditions of employment; *the staff are all members of a union or they are (trade) union members; the union called a meeting to discuss the company's takeover by a German company* (NOTE: American English for trade union is labor union)

unionism ['juːniənɪzm] *noun* believing in the principle of trade unions; *he is a great believer in unionism*

unionist ['juːniənɪst] *noun* (a) member of a trade union; *all her family were trade unionists* (b) Unionist = member of a party which wants to preserve the union between Britain and Northern Ireland

Union Jack ['juːniən 'dʒæk] *noun* national flag of the United Kingdom; *the Union Jack was flying over the embassy* (NOTE: also called the **Union Flag**)

unique [ju'niːk] *adjective* different to everything else, the only one that exists; *the stamp is unique, and so worth a great deal; he's studying the unique vegetation of the island*

uniqueness [ju'niːknəs] *noun (formal)* state of being unique; *the uniqueness of his paintings*

unison ['juːnɪsn] *noun* in unison = (i) doing something all together; (ii) in total agreement; *the children all shouted 'yes, please' in unison; unions and employers must learn to work in unison*

unit ['juːnɪt] *noun* (a) one part of something larger; *if you pass three units of the course you can move to the next level* (b) one piece of furniture, such as a cupboard, or set of shelves, etc., which can be matched with others; *the kitchen is designed as a basic set of units with more units which can be added later;* wall unit = cupboard which matches other units and is attached to the wall; corner unit = unit which matches other units and fits into a corner (c) monetary unit = main item of currency of a country (such as the dollar, peseta, pound, etc.); *the pound is the monetary unit in Britain* (d) specialized section of a hospital; *she is in the intensive care unit; the burns unit was full after the plane accident*

unitary ['juːnɪtəi] *adjective* referring to a single unit; *they are planning a unitary authority for the whole London area*

unite [ju'naɪt] *verb* to join together into a single body; *the office staff united in asking for better working conditions; workers of the world, unite!*

united [ju'naɪtɪd] *adjective* joined together as a whole; *relief workers from various countries worked as a united team; they were united in their desire to improve their working conditions*

United Kingdom (UK) [ju'naɪtɪd 'kɪŋdəm] *noun* independent European country, formed of England, Wales, Scotland and Northern Ireland; *he came to the United Kingdom to study; does she have a UK passport?; French citizens do not need work permits to work in the United Kingdom; see also* BRITISH, ENGLISH (NOTE: capital: **London**; people: **British**; language: **English**; currency: **pound sterling (£)**

United Nations (UN) [ju'naɪtɪd 'neɪʃnz] *noun* international organization including almost all sovereign states in the world, where member states are represented at meetings; *the countries of the United Nations; see also* GENERAL ASSEMBLY, SECURITY COUNCIL

United States of America (USA) [ju'naɪtɪd steɪts ʌv ə'merɪkə] *noun* independent country, a federation of states (originally thirteen, now fifty) in North America, south of Canada and north of Mexico; *she now lives in the United States with her husband and two sons; as a student, I worked in the USA during my summer holidays; which is the largest city* *in the United States?*; *we went across to the United States by ship*; *he never had the chance to visit the United States*; *see also* AMERICAN (NOTE: capital: **Washington DC**; people: **Americans**; language: **English**; currency: **US dollar**)

unit trust ['juːnɪt 'trʌst] *noun* organization which takes money from small investors and invests it in stocks and shares under a trust deed, the investment being in the form of units or shares in the trust; *unit trusts must be authorized by the government* (NOTE: the American equivalent is a **mutual fund**)

unity ['juːnɪti] *noun* being one whole; *the aim of the government is to preserve national unity*

universal [juːnɪ'vɜːsəl] *adjective* which is understood or experienced by everyone; *there is a universal desire for peace in the region*; **universal suffrage** = situation where all adults have the right to vote; **universal product code (UPC)** = bar code, printed lines which can be read by a computer

universally [juːnɪ'vɜːsəli] *adverb* everywhere; by everyone; *the universally accepted view that too much sun can cause skin cancer*

universe ['juːnɪvɜːs] *noun* all space and everything that exists in it, including the earth, the planets and the stars; *scientists believe the universe started as an explosion of matter*

university [juːnɪ'vɜːsɪti] *noun* highest level of educational institution, which gives degrees to successful students, and where a wide range of specialized subjects are taught; *you need to do well at school to be able to go to university* (NOTE: plural is **universities**)

unjust [ʌn'dʒʌst] *adjective* not fair; *they complained that the tribunal's decision was unjust*; *it is unjust to treat her as they do - she doesn't deserve it*

unjustified [ʌn'dʒʌstɪfaɪd] *adjective* **(a)** which is not justified; *her criticism of the minister was completely unjustified* **(b)** *(in printing)* not justified, without an even edge to the text; *we left the right-hand edge unjustified*

unkempt [ʌn'kempt] *adjective* not looked after, especially referring to hair; *he's easy to recognize with his straggly unkempt hair*; *the unkempt lawn in front of the church spoils its appearance*

unkind [ʌn'kaɪnd] *adjective* nasty, cruel; *it was unkind of him to keep talking about her weight* (NOTE: **unkinder - unkindest**)

unknown ['ʌnnəʊn] *adjective* **(a)** not known; *she was killed by an unknown attacker*; *the college received money from an unknown benefactor* **(b)** **unknown quantity** = person whose ability and track record you know nothing about; *the new sales director is an unknown quantity* (NOTE: the opposite is a **known quantity**)

unlawful [ʌn'lɔːfəl] *adjective* which is against the law; *the unlawful selling of fireworks to small children*; *it is unlawful to drive a car without being insured*

unleaded petrol [ʌn'ledɪd 'petəl] *noun* petrol without lead additives; *more and more car engines are built to use unleaded petrol*

unleash [ʌn'liːʃ] *verb* **(a)** to allow a violent force to become free; *the government's decision unleashed a wave of protests throughout the country* **(b)** to let a

dog go free after it was attached by a leash; *as soon as the security guards heard the siren they unleashed the dogs*

unless [ʌn'les] *conjunction* if not; except if; *unless we hear from you within ten days, we will start legal action*; *I think they don't want to see us, unless of course they're ill*

unlike [ʌn'laɪk] *adjective & preposition* **(a)** totally different from; *he's quite unlike his brother* **(b)** not normal, not typical; *it is unlike him to be rude* = he is not usually rude

unlikely [ʌn'laɪkli] *adjective* **(a)** not likely; *it's unlikely that many people will come to the show* **(b)** *(story)* which is probably not true; *he trotted out some unlikely story about how his train ticket had been eaten by the dog*

unlimited [ʌn'lɪmɪtɪd] *adjective* with no limits; *your membership card gives you unlimited access to the gym and swimming pool*; *this Internet account provides you with unlimited e-mail addresses*; **unlimited mileage** = allowance with a rented car, where the driver is not charged for the number of miles he drives; *it is more economical to hire a car with unlimited mileage*

unload [ʌn'ləʊd] *verb* to remove a load from a ship, truck, etc.; *the ship is unloading at Hamburg*; *we need a trolley to unload the lorry*

unlock [ʌn'lɒk] *verb* to open something which was locked; *I can't unlock the car door, I think I've got the wrong key*; *scientists have unlocked the secrets of DNA*

unlucky [ʌn'lʌki] *adjective* not lucky, which brings bad luck; *they say it's unlucky to walk under a ladder* (NOTE: **unluckier - unluckiest**)

unmanned [ʌn'mænd] *adjective* not manned, with no crew; *the Americans are sending an unmanned rocket to Jupiter*

unmarked [ʌn'mɑːkt] *adjective* with no mark on it which could identify it; *she was buried in an unmarked grave*; *he was stopped by police officers in an unmarked police car*

unmarried [ʌn'mærɪd] *adjective* not married; *because of tax incentives, they decided to remain unmarried*; **unmarried mother** = woman who has a child but is not married

unmistakable [ʌnmɪs'teɪkəbl] *adjective* which is easily recognized, which cannot be mistaken; *his unmistakable Scottish accent gave him away*; *his old red car is unmistakable*

unmoved [ʌn'muːvd] *adjective* not touched or not affected; *he was unmoved by his daughter's plea for more money*

unnamed [ʌn'neɪmd] *adjective* who has not been named; *the girl, who remains unnamed for legal reasons, was accused of killing the baby*

unnatural [ʌn'nætʃərəl] *adjective* **(a)** which is not as it is in nature; *his face was an unnatural blue colour* **(b)** which does not follow the usual pattern; *it seems unnatural that he should take his father to court*; *their behaviour seemed unnatural to me*

unnecessary [ʌn'nesəsəri] *adjective* which is not needed, which does not have to be done; *it is unnecessary for you to wear a suit to the party*; *she makes so many unnecessary phone calls*

unnerve [ʌn'nɜːv] *verb* to make someone lose his nerve or his courage; *he was unnerved at the thought of flying on his own for the first time*; *the examiner's questions unnerved her completely*

unnerving [ʌn'nɜːvɪŋ] *adjective* which frightens you; *it is rather unnerving to fly a plane by yourself for the first time*; *all you could hear were these unnerving high-pitched screams*

unnoticed [ʌn'nəʊtɪst] *adjective* **(a)** not noticed; *the bomb lay unnoticed by the door of the supermarket* **(b)** without anyone noticing; *the whole affair passed unnoticed by the press*

unobtainable [ʌnəb'teɪnəbl] *adjective* which cannot be obtained; *the book is quite unobtainable*; *I tried to ring the phone number you gave me but it was unobtainable*

unobtrusive [ʌnəb'truːsɪv] *adjective* not obvious; not easily noticed; *the pattern on the carpet is quite unobtrusive*; *she dresses with unobtrusive elegance*; *the unobtrusive police presence along the route of the protest march*

unofficial [ʌnə'fɪʃl] *adjective* not approved by an administration or by people in power; *we have had some unofficial meetings with people from the ministry*; **unofficial strike** = strike by local workers which has not been approved by the union

unofficially ['ʌnə'fɪʃəli] *adverb* in an unofficial way; *he was told by the Foreign Office unofficially that it would be better if he left the country*

unorthodox [ʌn'ɔːθədɒks] *adjective* not usual; *her approach to the problem is very unorthodox*; *his unorthodox views have caused quite a stir amongst the congregation*

unpack [ʌn'pæk] *verb* to take things out of containers in which they were transported; *his two suitcases were already unpacked*; *I've just come back from Canada and I'm still unpacking*; *the items in the box are fragile, and should be unpacked with care*

unpaid [ʌn'peɪd] *adjective* **(a)** (person) who is not paid a salary; *he works as unpaid secretary for the sports club* **(b)** (bill) which has not been settled; *piles of unpaid bills littered his desk*

unparalleled [ʌn'pærəleld] *adjective* with no parallel or no equal; *such a speech by a member of the government is quite unparalleled in modern parliamentary history*; *the tour offers an unparalleled opportunity to study Indian culture*

unpleasant [ʌn'plezənt] *adjective* not nice, not pleasant; *there's a very unpleasant smell in the kitchen*; *the boss is a very unpleasant man and shouts at his secretary all the time*; *try not to be unpleasant to the waitress*

unpopular [ʌn'pɒpjʊlə] *adjective* not liked by other people; *the new working hours were very unpopular with the staff*

unpopularity [ʌnpɒpjuˈlærɪti] *noun* not being liked; *politicians have to expect periods of unpopularity* (NOTE: no plural)

unprecedented [ʌn'presɪdentɪd] *adjective* which has never happened before, or with such force; *the rain and floods which followed were quite unprecedented for August*; *there followed a period of unprecedented prosperity*

unpredictable [ʌnprɪ'dɪktəbl] *adjective* which cannot be predicted or forecast; *the weather can be quite unpredictable in March*; *his moods are unpredictable*

unprepared [ʌnprɪ'peəd] *adjective* not ready; *they were totally unprepared for the arrival of the police*; **unprepared to do something** = not willing to do something; *the students are unprepared to pay the increased tuition fees*

unpretentious [ʌnprɪ'tenʃəs] *adjective* modest, not showing off; *his office is in an elegant but unpretentious old building*

unproductive [ʌnprə'dʌktɪv] *adjective* **(a)** (discussion) which does not produce any result; *the debate was quite unproductive* **(b)** (land) which does not produce any crops; *their land had become unproductive and they'd stopped farming it*

unprofitable [ʌn'prɒfɪtəbl] *adjective* **(a)** which does not make a profit; *the international show was unprofitable, and had to be subsidized by the government* **(b)** (formal) which does not bring any advantage; *she made an unprofitable visit to her lawyer*

unprotected [ʌnprə'tektɪd] *adjective* which is not protected; *the security guards went off to lunch leaving the bank completely unprotected*; *the borders to the south are dangerously unprotected against invaders*; **unprotected sex** = sexual intercourse without using a condom

unpublished [ʌn'pʌblɪʃt] *adjective* which has not been published; *he's trying to find a publisher for his unpublished novel*; *the book has been advertised but is as yet unpublished*

unqualified [ʌn'kwɒlɪfaɪd] *adjective* **(a)** (person) who has not passed the examinations to qualify for a profession; *the hospital is said to be employing unqualified nursing staff* **(b)** total or complete; *the school sports day was an unqualified success*

unquestionable [ʌn'kwestʃənəbl] *adjective* which is certain, not doubtful; *the young musician has an unquestionable talent*; *it is unquestionable that she is the best candidate for the job*

unravel [ʌn'rævl] *verb* **(a)** to disentangle something knotted; *we spent hours trying to unravel the ball of string* **(b)** (knitting or woven material) to become undone; *don't cut that bit of wool or the jumper will unravel* **(c)** to come to pieces; *his elaborate plan began to unravel* **(d)** to solve a mystery; *no one has ever been able to unravel the mystery of her disappearance* (NOTE: British spelling is **unravelling - unravelled**, American spelling is **unraveling - unraveled**)

unreal [ʌn'rɪəl] *adjective* not like the real world; *looking round the garden at night, with the lights in the trees and the candles on the tables, I felt the whole scene was somehow unreal*

unrealistic [ʌnrɪə'lɪstɪk] *adjective* impractical, not facing facts; *expecting everyone to work more for less pay is quite unrealistic*; *it's unrealistic of the government to hope that people will be glad to pay more tax*

unreasonable [ʌn'riːznəbl] *adjective* not reasonable, unfair; *the union made unreasonable demands to the management*; *it was unreasonable of the minister to refuse to meet the delegation*

unrelated [ʌnrɪ'leɪtɪd] *adjective* **(a)** not related, with no connection; *two unrelated incidents occurred during the night*; *the sudden increase in temperature is quite unrelated to her heart condition* **(b)** not belonging to the same family; *they have the same surname, but as far as I know are unrelated*

unrelenting [ʌnrɪ'lentɪŋ] *adjective* which never stops or weakens; *she only survived because of her parents' unrelenting care*; *the unrelenting pain kept him awake all night*

unreliable [ʌnrɪ'laɪəbl] *adjective* which cannot be relied on; *don't count on her, she's too unreliable*; *read the instructions in Spanish - the English translation is unreliable*; *the bus service is so unreliable that I think I'll go by car*

unrepentant [ʌnrɪ'pentənt] *adjective (formal)* with no regrets for what you have done; *when the head teacher told him off, he looked quite unrepentant*

unresolved [ʌnrɪ'zɒlvd] *adjective* which has not been solved; *there is still the unresolved problem of who owns the land*

unrest [ʌn'rest] *noun* situation where people protest to try to get political or industrial change; *the announcement of the election followed a period of unrest*; *the government has sent in troops to deal with the unrest in the south of the country* (NOTE: no plural)

unrestricted [ʌnrɪs'trɪktɪd] *adjective* without any restrictions; *they demanded unrestricted access to the company's books*; *you can take an unrestricted amount of money out of the country*

unruly [ʌn'ruːli] *adjective* wild, with no discipline; *a couple of unruly kids disrupted the wedding service*; *he can do nothing with his unruly hair except shave it off!* (NOTE: unrulier - unruliest)

unsafe [ʌn'seɪf] *adjective* dangerous; *don't go into the building - the floor's unsafe*; *the police say it is unsafe to go out at night*; *it's unsafe to swim in the river because of the strong current*; **to feel unsafe** = to feel you are in danger; *she doesn't like to be alone at night, she says she feels unsafe* (NOTE: unsafer - unsafest)

unsatisfactory [ʌnsætɪs'fæktri] *adjective* not satisfactory; *the reply from the complaints department was quite unsatisfactory*; *she found that the service in the restaurant was unsatisfactory*

unsavoury *US* **unsavory** [ʌn'seɪvəri] *adjective* not pleasant; *he has an unsavoury reputation*; *the football ground is situated in a rather unsavoury part of town*

unscathed [ʌn'skeɪðd] *adjective* not harmed; *their house remained quite unscathed after the battle*; *she walked through the minefield unscathed*

unscrew [ʌn'skruː] *verb* **(a)** to open by twisting a top which screws on; *the top of this bottle opens by unscrewing so you don't need a bottle opener* **(b)** to unfasten by taking out screws; *my screwdriver is much too big to unscrew the back of the TV*

unscrupulous [ʌn'skruːpjʊləs] *adjective* not worrying too much about honesty; *he made the mistake of buying a car from an unscrupulous dealer*; *it was unscrupulous of her to suggest that she had documents which could ruin him*

unsealed ['ʌnsiːld] *adjective* which is not closed with a seal; **unsealed envelope** = envelope where the flap has not been stuck down but is simply tucked

inside; *the information was sent in a unsealed envelope* (NOTE: an envelope where the flap is stuck down is a **sealed envelope**)

unseat [ʌn'siːt] *verb* **(a)** to make a sitting MP lose his seat in an election; *she only needs a small swing to have a good chance of unseating him* **(b)** to make someone fall off a horse; *he was unseated as he tried to jump the fence*

unsecured creditor [ʌnsɪ'kjuːəd 'kredɪtə] *noun* creditor who is owed money but has no security from the debtor for it; *being an unsecured creditor, I lost all the money owed to me when the company crashed*

unseeded player [ʌn'siːdɪd 'pleɪjə] *noun (in tennis)* player who has not been seeded; *the last unseeded player was knocked out in the semi-finals*; *the number one seed was beaten by an unseeded player*; *compare* SEEDED

unseen [ʌn'siːn] *adjective* not seen, invisible; *he managed to get into the office unseen by the caretaker*; *a large number of paintings are stored unseen in the basement of the museum*

unselfish [ʌn'selfɪʃ] *adjective* thinking only of other people; *his unselfish work for poor families*; *her unselfish refusal to take any credit for the project*

unsettle [ʌn'setl] *verb* to upset, to make worried; *seeing their mother taken off in an ambulance unsettled the children*; *they hope the news from the Far East will not unsettle the stock market*

unsettled ['ʌnsetəld] *adjective* **(a)** (weather) which changes often; *unsettled weather is forecast for the next few days* **(b)** not calm; *the present unsettled market shows no sign of becoming more stable*

unsettling [ʌn'setlɪŋ] *adjective* which makes you nervous and worried; *it's an unsettling period, when we've sold our house and not found another one*; *the divorce was unsettling for the children*; *the longer the problem remains unsolved, the more unsettling it is*

unsightly [ʌn'saɪtli] *adjective* ugly, unpleasant to see; *she has an unsightly rash across her forehead*; *the council is planning to move the unsightly refuse dump*

unskilled ['ʌnskɪld] *adjective* without any particular skill; *some of these unskilled jobs pay very bad wages*; **unskilled staff** = employees who have no particular skills, and do general work such as cleaning, taking the post to the post offices, etc.; *the hospital employs a number of unskilled staff*

unsociable [ʌn'səʊʃəbl] *adjective* not friendly, wanting to meet other people; *I'm feeling unsociable, so I'm staying at home to read*; *he's a painter and like many artists he's rather unsociable*

unsold [ʌn'səʊld] *adjective* not sold; *several of the items in the auction remained unsold*; *any unsold food items will be sold off cheaply at the end of the day*

unsolved ['ʌnsɒlvd] *adjective* (problem) which has not been solved; *the film is about an unsolved murder*; *the mystery has remained unsolved to this day*

unspeakable [ʌn'spiːkəbl] *adjective* extremely unpleasant; *did you hear what she did to the baby? - it's unspeakable!*; *the whole thing was an unspeakable disaster*

unspecified [ʌn'spesɪfaɪd] *adjective* which has not been specified; *they said our query would be dealt with at some unspecified date in the future*

unspoken [ʌn'spəʊkən] *adjective* which is not said; *there was an unspoken agreement between them that if any one of them was in difficulties, the others would come to their help*

unstable [ʌn'steɪbl] *adjective* **(a)** not stable; *they put scaffolding round the chimney because it had become unstable*; *the weather can be very unstable in August*; *we have to take account of the very unstable exchange rate* **(b)** likely to change suddenly; *the economic situation has become very unstable*; *neighbouring states were worried that the unstable military regime could be overthrown* **(c)** with a mental state that is likely to change quickly; *the patient is mentally unstable*

unstoppable [ʌn'stɒpəbl] *adjective* *(informal)* which cannot be stopped; *when he starts talking about his stamp collection, he's unstoppable*; *the seemingly unstoppable flow of refugees escaping from the war zone*

unsuccessful [ʌnsək'sesfəl] *adjective* which does not succeed; *he was unsuccessful in his attempt to get elected to Parliament*; *your application for the job was unsuccessful*

unsuitable [ʌn'suːtəbl] *adjective* not suitable; *the path is unsuitable for motor vehicles*; *several people complained that the TV film was unsuitable for children*

unsure [ʌn'ʃʊə] *adjective* **(a)** not sure; *she was unsure whether to go to work or to stay at home*; *I'm unsure as to which route is the quickest* **(b)** unsure of yourself = lacking self-confidence; *he's still very unsure of himself, but he'll get more confident as time goes by*

unsurprising [ʌnsɜː'praɪzɪŋ] *adjective* which is not at all surprising; *they came to the rather unsurprising conclusion that some French restaurants are better than others*; *why do you find the verdict unsurprising?*

unsuspecting ['ʌnsəs'pektɪŋ] *adjective* (person) who does not realize something, who does not realize that a danger is imminent; *many unsuspecting people sent money to the advertiser and never received the goods*

untapped ['ʌntæpt] *adjective* not yet exploited; *the untapped resources of the Antarctic*

untenable [ʌn'tenəbl] *adjective* (position or theory) which cannot be defended; *his position is untenable and he must resign as soon as possible*

unthinkable [ʌn'θɪŋkəbl] *adjective* **(a)** which cannot be considered or thought of; *it would be unthinkable not to celebrate Christmas with the children*; *going to live in a foreign country was unthinkable only a few years ago* **(b)** to think the unthinkable = to consider plans which go totally against what is normal practice

untidy [ʌn'taɪdi] *adjective* not tidy; *his bedroom is untidier than ever*; *he'll never be promoted, he always looks so untidy* (NOTE: **untidier - untidiest**)

untie [ʌn'taɪ] *verb* to unfasten something which is tied with a knot; *since her shoelaces are always untied, she'd be better off wearing sandals*; *someone untied the canoe and it drifted away down the river*; *can you help her untie the parcel?*

until [ʌn'tɪl] **1** *conjunction* up to the time when; *she was perfectly well until she ate the strawberries*; *he blew his whistle until the police came* **2** *preposition & conjunction* up to the time when; *I don't expect to be back until after ten o'clock*; *until yesterday, I felt very well* (NOTE: the word **till** means the same)

untold [ʌn'təʊld] *adjective* **(a)** which has not been told; *his story was to remain untold for years, until we discovered the old diary* **(b)** very large; so large that it cannot be counted; *the lottery offers people the possibility of untold wealth*; *the new treatment should help untold numbers of asthma sufferers*

untouchable [ʌn'tʌtʃəbl] **1** *adjective* which cannot be touched or affected; *the President's son is quite untouchable by the police* **2** *noun* person from the lowest caste in the old Indian social system

untouched [ʌn'tʌtʃt] *adjective* **(a)** not touched; *one small area of the forest was untouched by the fire*; *she left the meat untouched on her plate* **(b)** not influenced by; *we discovered a beautiful part of the countryside still untouched by the 20th century*

untoward [ʌntə'wɔːd] *adjective* disturbing and unexpected; *I hope nothing untoward will disrupt our plans*

untreated [ʌn'triːtɪd] *adjective* **(a)** not treated medically; *if left untreated, the disease can be fatal* **(b)** which has not been processed; *the council dumps untreated sewage into the sea*; *they used untreated wood for the fence and it rotted very quickly*

untrue [ʌn'truː] *adjective* false, wrong; *his statement was untrue - the real story was in yesterday's paper*

untutored [ʌn'tjuːtəd] *adjective* *(formal)* not having been taught; *to my untutored eye, his paintings look like absolute rubbish*

unused *adjective* **(a)** [ʌn'juːzd] new or clean; which has not been used before; *we found a packet of unused stamps in his desk drawer* **(b)** [ʌn'juːst]; unused to = not accustomed to; *she's quite unused to committee work*; *getting up early is something he's unused to*

unusual [ʌn'juːʒʊəl] *adjective* strange, not normal; *it is unusual to have rain at this time of year*; *she chose a very unusual colour scheme for her sitting room*

unusually [ʌn'juːʒʊəli] *adverb* strangely, abnormally; *the weather is unusually warm for January*; *unusually, she was very talkative*

unveil [ʌn'veɪl] *verb* **(a)** to take a cover off something, to open it formally; *the statue was unveiled by the mayor* **(b)** to reveal details of a new plan, etc.; *the committee will unveil its proposals next week*

unwanted [ʌn'wɒntɪd] *adjective* which is not wanted; *take any unwanted Christmas presents to the charity shop*; *nobody spoke to him all evening, and made him feel unwanted*

unwarranted [ʌn'wɒrəntɪd] *adjective* which is not justified; *his rude comments were totally unwarranted*

unwelcome [ʌn'welkʌm] *adjective* which is not welcome; *her boss gave her all sorts of unwelcome presents*; *we felt unwelcome and left within a few minutes*; *some people have the knack of making you feel unwelcome*

unwell [ʌn'wel] *adjective* sick, ill, not well; *she felt unwell and had to go home* (NOTE: not used before a noun: **the baby was unwell** but **a sick baby**)

unwieldy [ʌnˈwiːldi] *adjective* large and awkward; *schoolchildren with unwieldy sports bags filled the bus*; *they are trying to streamline their unwieldy administrative system*

unwilling [ʌnˈwɪlɪŋ] *adjective* not wanting to do something; *he was unwilling to pay any more*

unwind [ʌnˈwaɪnd] *verb* (a) to undo something which has been wound; *pull to unwind the flex - it will rewind automatically when you press the red button* (b) (*informal*) to relax; *gardening at the weekend helps him to unwind* (NOTE: **unwinding - unwound** [ʌnˈwaʊnd])

unwise [ʌnˈwaɪz] *adjective* rash or imprudent; not wise; *it would be unwise to put all your savings into one account*; *it was unwise of her to go out on her own late at night*

unwitting [ʌnˈwɪtɪŋ] *adjective* (*formal*) not knowing or intending; *ten per cent of the population are believed to be unwitting carriers of the disease*

unwittingly [ʌnˈwɪtɪŋli] *adverb* without knowing or intending; *she unwittingly deleted all the sales files*

unworkable [ʌnˈwɜːkəbl] *adjective* which will not work; *the plan seemed very clever on paper but proved to be unworkable in practice*

unworthy [ʌnˈwɜːði] *adjective* which does not deserve; *the plan is unworthy of further consideration*; *she said she was unworthy of the honour given her*

unwrap [ʌnˈræp] *verb* to take the wrapping off something; *here is a photo of the little girl unwrapping her Christmas presents* (NOTE: **unwrapping - unwrapped**)

unwritten [ʌnˈrɪtən] *adjective* **unwritten law** = custom which has grown up over a period of time but which is not written down

up [ʌp] 1 *adverb* (a) in or to a high place; *put your hands up above your head*; *what's the cat doing up there on the cupboard?* (b) to a higher position; *his temperature went up suddenly*; *the price of petrol seems to go up every week* (c) not in bed; *the children were still up when they should have been in bed*; *they stayed up all night watching films on TV*; *he got up at six because he had an early train to catch*; *it's past eight o'clock - you should be up by now*; *she's getting better - the doctor says she will be up and about quite soon* (d) towards the north; *I'll be going up to Scotland next week* (e) in London; *give me a call next time you're up in town*; *I'm up in London next week for a meeting* (f) **your time's up** = you have had all the time allowed (g) (*informal*) happening in an unpleasant or dangerous way; *something's up - the engine has stopped!*; **what's up?** = what's the matter?; **what's up with him?** = what is the matter with him?; *what's up with the cat? - it won't eat anything* 2 *preposition* (a) in or to a high place; *they ran up the stairs*; *she doesn't like going up ladders* (b) along; *go up the street to the traffic lights and then turn right*; *the house is about two hundred metres up the road* (NOTE: that **up** is often used after verbs: **to keep up, to turn up**, etc.) 3 *verb* (a) to raise prices, etc.; *they upped their offer to £1000* (b) (*informal*) to stand up, to get up; *she upped and left him when she heard he had been seen with his best friend* (NOTE: **upping - upped**)

◊ **up-and-coming** [ʌpənˈkʌmɪŋ] *adjective* (*informal*) becoming fashionable and likely to succeed; *they live in a very up-and-coming part of town*; *he's one of the most up-and-coming young MPs*

◊ **up and down** [ˈʌp ənd ˈdaʊn] 1 *preposition* in one direction, then in the opposite direction; *the policeman was walking up and down in front of the bank*; *she looked up and down the street but couldn't see her little boy* 2 *noun* **ups and downs** = the times of good luck and bad luck; *his book describes the ups and downs of life in a circus*

◊ **up and running** [ˈʌp ənd ˈrʌnɪŋ] *adjective* (*informal*) working; *he played an important role in getting the project up and running*; *the project is up and running at long last*

◊ **up for** [ˈʌp ˈfɔː] *preposition* (a) ready for; *my house insurance is up for renewal* (b) **up for sale** = on sale, going to be sold; *he's put his flat up for sale*

◊ **up front** [ʌp ˈfrʌnt] *adverb* in advance; **money up front** = payment in advance; *they are asking for £100,000 up front before they will consider the deal*; *we had to put money up front before we could get them to sign the deal*

◊ **up to** [ˈʌp ˈtuː] *preposition* (a) as many as; *the lift will take up to six people* (b) **what are you up to these days?** = what are you doing? (c) **it's up to you** = it is your responsibility (d) capable of doing something; *it's a very demanding job and I wonder if she's up to it*

upbeat [ˈʌpbiːt] 1 *adjective* feeling optimistic and happy; *the conference ended on a very upbeat note*; *we're all very upbeat about the potential sales of the new model* 2 *noun* beat of a conductor's baton at the end of a bar (NOTE: the opposite is **downbeat**)

upbringing [ˈʌpbrɪŋɪŋ] *noun* education, the way a child is brought up; *he had a rather unorthodox upbringing on his grandfather's farm in Brazil*

UPC = UNIVERSAL PRODUCT CODE

update [ʌpˈdeɪt] 1 *noun* latest information; *the manager gave us an update on the latest sales figures* 2 *verb* to add the latest information to something so that it is quite up-to-date; *she was asked to update the telephone list*; *the figures are updated annually*; *they have updated their guidebook to Greece to include current prices*

upgrade [ʌpˈgreɪd] *verb* (a) to improve the quality of something; *she has upgraded her computer* (b) to put someone into a more important job; *his job has been upgraded to senior manager*

upheaval [ʌpˈhiːvəl] *noun* disturbance, great change; *it was a time of great upheavals in the family, with the children leaving to work abroad and the parents getting divorced*; *young parents find that the arrival of a second baby is a bigger upheaval than the first one*

uphill [ʌpˈhɪl] 1 *adjective* going upwards; difficult; *from here the road is uphill all the way to the house*; *he faces an uphill struggle to get elected* 2 *adverb* upwards; *at my age, I can't walk uphill very far without stopping to get my breath back*

uphold [ʌpˈhəʊld] *verb* (a) **to uphold the law** = to make sure that a law is obeyed (b) to reject an appeal and support an earlier judgement; *the appeal court upheld the decision of the lower court* (NOTE: **upholding - upheld** [ʌpˈheld])

upholster [ʌpˈhəʊlstə] *verb* to cover furniture in padding and cloth, etc.; *we have asked him to upholster the settee in white cotton*; *the chairs are upholstered in red velour*

upholsterer [ʌpˈhəʊlstərə] *noun* person who covers furniture with cloth, etc.; *the upholsterer has said he will come and pick up the chairs to be repaired*

upholstery [ʌpˈhəʊlstri] *noun* (a) work of covering chairs, etc., with padded seats and covers; *he has an upholstery shop, repairing old chairs and sofas* (b) covers for chairs; padded seats and cushions; *the upholstery matches the colour scheme in the sitting-room*

upkeep [ʌpˈkiːp] *noun* (cost of) keeping a house, a car, etc., in good order; *we're forced to sell the house because its upkeep is so expensive; the upkeep of the car costs me more than £50 a week; how much are you getting from your ex-husband for the upkeep of the children?*

upland [ʌpˈlənd] *noun* mountainous area of a country; *heather is common in upland areas*

uplift [ˈʌplɪft] *noun* sudden optimistic feeling; *there was an uplift in the morale of the team after they scored the first goal*

uplifting [ʌpˈlɪftɪŋ] *adjective* which makes you feel in a better mood; *he gave a very uplifting talk to the children who were leaving school*

up-market [ʌpˈmɑːkɪt] *adjective* more expensive, appealing to the wealthy section of the market; *the company has decided to launch a more up-market version of the product; the new shop is very up-market and everything is extremely expensive* (NOTE: the opposite is **down-market**)

upon [əˈpɒn] (a) *(formal)* on; *the church is built upon a grassy hill* (b) imminent, likely to happen soon; *the summer holidays will soon be upon us again*

upper [ˈʌpə] 1 *adjective* (a) higher or further up; *the upper slopes of the mountain are covered in snow;* **upper arm** = part of the arm from the shoulder to the elbow; *he had a rash on his right upper arm* (b) more important; **the upper classes** = the nobles *(in a school)* **the upper forms** = classes with older pupils; **upper house** *or* **upper chamber** = more senior of the two houses in a parliament (in Britain, the House of Lords, in the USA, the Senate); *the bill has been passed in the lower house and now goes to the upper house for further discussion* (NOTE: opposite is **lower**) 2 *noun* top part of a shoe; *a pair of shoes with leather uppers and man-made soles*

upper-class [ˈʌpəklɑːs] *adjective* referring to the highest class in society; *he speaks with an upper-class accent; she comes from a very upper-class family*

uppercut [ˈʌpəkʌt] *noun* punch given by the fist coming upwards on someone's chin; *he was knocked out by an uppercut in the third round*

uppermost [ˈʌpəməʊst] 1 *adjective* (a) highest; *the birds are nesting in the uppermost branches of the apple tree* (b) most important; *which plan has the uppermost significance for you?;* **what is uppermost in your mind** = the subject you think about most; *when I see these youngsters taking their exams, I wonder what is uppermost in their minds* 2 *adverb* in the top position; *carry the box with this side uppermost; which side of the painting should be uppermost?*

upright [ˈʌpraɪt] 1 *adjective* standing straight up, vertical; *he got dizzy as soon as he stood upright; put your seats into the upright position for landing; she picked up the vase and placed it upright on the table* 2 *noun* (a) vertical post; *the goalkeeper was leaning*

against one of the uprights (b) piano with a vertical body (NOTE: the other type of piano, with a large horizontal body is called a **grand piano**)

uprising [ˈʌpraɪzɪŋ] *noun* rebellion or revolt; *an uprising against the government; the uprising was crushed by the army*

uproar [ˈʌprɔː] *noun* loud noise, disturbance; *there was (an) uproar in Parliament when the report was published; the whole school was in uproar over the decision*

uproarious [ʌpˈrɔːriəs] *adjective* noisy with laughter; *the sound of uproarious singing was coming from the bar; the whole audience broke into uproarious laughter*

uproariously [ʌpˈrɔːriəsli] *adverb* noisily; *the audience laughed uproariously at my jokes*

uproot [ʌpˈruːt] *verb* (a) to pull a plant out of the ground with its roots; *everywhere you could see trees uprooted by the storm* (b) to make a family move to a totally new area; *families were uprooted from their homes and taken to camps many miles away*

upset [ʌpˈset] 1 *adjective* (a) very worried, unhappy, anxious; *she gets upset if he comes home late* (b) slightly ill; *she is in bed with an upset stomach* 2 *noun* (a) slight illness; **stomach upset** = slight infection of the stomach; *she is in bed with a stomach upset* (b) unexpected defeat; *there was a major upset in the tennis tournament when the number three seed was beaten in the first round* 3 *verb* (a) to knock over; *he upset all the coffee cups* (b) to make someone worried or unhappy; *don't upset your mother by telling her you're planning to go to live in Russia*

upside down [ˈʌpsaɪd ˈdaʊn] *adverb* (a) with the top underneath; *don't turn the box upside down - all the papers will fall out; the car shot off the road and ended up upside down in a ditch; bats were hanging upside down from the branches* (b) in disorder; *while he was out someone had ransacked his room, turning the place upside down*

upstage [ʌpˈsteɪdʒ] 1 *adverb* to or at the back of the stage; *the hero moves upstage and hides behind a tree* (NOTE: the opposite, towards the front of the stage, is **downstage**) 2 *verb* to take attention away from someone who should be more important; *in last night's performance, the prima ballerina was completely upstaged by the youngest dancer*

upstairs [ʌpˈsteəz] 1 *adverb* on or to the upper part of a building, bus, etc.; *she ran upstairs with the letter; I left my glasses upstairs; let's go upstairs onto the top deck - you can see London much better* 2 *adjective* on the upper floors of a building; *we have an upstairs kitchen; we let the one of the upstairs offices to an accountant* 3 *noun* the upper floors of a building; *the upstairs of the house needs decorating*

upstart [ʌpˈstɑːt] *noun* inexperienced person who has just started a job and feels he knows everything about it; *these young upstarts think they can run the company; why should I do what that little upstart says?*

upstate [ˈʌpsteɪt] *adjective* US in the northern part of a state; *he lives in a small town in upstate New York*

upstream [ʌpˈstriːm] *adverb & adjective* (moving) towards the source or a river, against the flow of the current; *the ship was sailing upstream from the Atlantic towards the Great Lakes; the river has been polluted somewhere upstream*

upsurge ['ʌpsɜːdʒ] *noun* sudden increase; *an upsurge in demand has kept the factory very busy this month*; *major cities report an upsurge in violence*

uptight ['ʌptaɪt] *adjective (informal)* nervous and angry; *as soon as I mentioned money he got all uptight*

up to date *or* **up-to-date** ['ʌp tə' deɪt] **1** *adverb* with the latest information; *I keep myself up to date on the political situation by reading the newspaper every day* **2** *adjective* with very recent information; *I don't have an up-to-date timetable*

up-to-the-minute ['ʌptəðə'mɪnɪt] *adjective* very recent; *we got an up-to-the-minute traffic report*

uptown ['ʌptaʊn] *adverb US* in or to the outer residential parts of a town; *he lives in uptown New York*

upturn ['ʌptɜːn] *noun* movement towards higher sales or profits; *there has been a sharp upturn in the economy since March*

upward ['ʌpwəd] **1** *adjective* moving towards a higher level; *the spacecraft's engines generate enormous upward thrust* **2** *adverb US* = UPWARDS

upwards *US* **upward** ['ʌpwədz] *adverb* **(a)** towards the top; *the path went upwards for a mile then levelled off* **(b) upwards of** = more than; *upwards of a thousand people answered the advertisement*

uranium [jʊ'reɪnɪəm] *noun* radioactive metal used in producing atomic energy (NOTE: Chemical element: chemical symbol: U; atomic number: 92)

Uranus ['jʊərənəs] *noun* seventh planet in the solar system, a very large planet, fifteen times the size of the Earth

urban ['ɜːbən] *adjective* **(a)** referring to towns; *they enjoy an urban lifestyle* **(b)** living in towns; *the urban fox has become a menace in parts of London*

urbanization [ɜːbənaɪ'zeɪʃn] *noun* act of urbanizing; *the urbanization of the land along the coast*

urbanize ['ɜːbənaɪz] *verb* to build houses in open country, to make open country into towns; *the whole area round London was rapidly urbanized in the nineteenth century*

urchin ['ɜːtʃɪn] *noun (old)* dirty little boy; **sea urchin** = small sea animal with a round shell covered with spines

urge [ɜːdʒ] **1** *noun* strong wish to do something; *she felt an urge to punch him on the nose* **2** *verb* **(a)** to advise someone strongly to do something; *he urged her to do what her father said*; *I would urge you to vote for the proposal*; *our lawyer urged us to be careful and avoid breaking the law* **(b) to urge someone on** = to encourage someone to do better, to do more; *the runners were urged on by their supporters*

urgency ['ɜːdʒənsi] *noun* being very important, needing to be done quickly; *there was a note of urgency in his voice*; **there's no great urgency** = there's no need to rush

urgent ['ɜːdʒənt] *adjective* which is important and needs to be done quickly; *he had an urgent message to go to the police station*; *she had an urgent operation*; *the leader of the council called an urgent meeting*; *this parcel is urgent and needs to get there tomorrow*

urgently ['ɜːdʒəntli] *adverb* needed immediately; *the relief team urgently requires more medical supplies*

urinal [jʊ'raɪnəl] *noun* **(a)** place where men can go to pass waste liquid from the body; *there's a public urinal at the corner of the street* **(b)** bowl to catch waste liquid passed from the body by men; *the men's room is very modern, with stainless steel urinals*

urinary ['jʊərɪnəri] *adjective* referring to urine; *cystitis is a urinary infection more common in women than in men*; **urinary system** = system of organs which remove waste liquids from the blood and excrete them as urine; *the kidneys and bladder form part of the urinary system*; **urinary tract** = tubes down which the urine passes from the kidneys to the bladder and from the bladder out of the body

urinate ['jʊərɪneɪt] *verb* to pass waste liquid from the body; *the patient has difficulty in urinating*

urination [jʊərɪ'neɪʃn] *noun* passing of urine out of the body; *she said that urination was painful*

urine ['jʊərɪn] *noun* yellowish liquid which is passed out of the body, containing water and waste matter; *he was asked to produce an urine sample for testing*

urn [ɜːn] *noun* very large vase; **tea urn** *or* **coffee urn** = large metal container with a tap, in which large quantities of tea or coffee can be made in advance and then kept hot (NOTE: do not confuse with **earn**)

Uruguay ['jʊərəgwaɪ] *noun* country in Latin America, north of Argentina; *he's going to Uruguay on business* (NOTE: capital: **Montevideo**; people: **Uruguayans**; language: **Spanish**; currency: **Uruguayan peso**)

Uruguayan [jʊərə'gwaɪən] **1** *adjective* referring to Uruguay; *Uruguayan exports to the USA* **2** *noun* person from Uruguay

us [ʌs] *object pronoun (meaning me and other people)* *mother gave us each 50p to buy ice cream*; *who's there? - it's us!*; *the company did well last year - the management have given us a bonus*

US *or* **USA** ['juː'es *or* 'juː'es'eɪ] *see* UNITED STATES; *they're thinking of going to the US on holiday next year*; *we spent three weeks travelling in the USA*

usable ['juːzəbl] *adjective* which can be used; *the handle's broken, but the kettle's still perfectly usable*

usage ['juːsɪdʒ] *noun* **(a)** custom; way of doing things; *it still is the usage in France to shake hands when you meet someone* **(b)** way of using a word; *it is a technical term that is now in common usage*; *the book clearly explains common legal terms and their usage* **(c)** the way something is used; *the shampoo is for normal usage*; *with constant usage, you can expect the machine to need replacing every two years*

use 1 *noun* [juːs] **(a)** purpose, usefulness; *can you find any use for this piece of cloth?* **(b)** being used; *the coffee machine has been in daily use for years* **(c)** possibility of using something; *room 51 has no bathroom, but you have the use of the bathroom next door*; *the lounge is for the use of the hotel guests*; *don't worry, he'll soon recover the use of his arm* **(d)** being useful; *he kept the old chair, thinking it might be of use some day*; *what's the use of telling the children to shut up - they never do what I say*; *it's no use just waiting and hoping that someone will give you a job* **(e) to make use of something** = to use something; *he didn't make use of his phrase book once*; *you should make more use of your bicycle* **2** *verb* [juːz] **(a)** to take a tool, etc., and do something with it; *did you use a* sewing machine to make your curtains?; the car's worth quite a lot of money - it's hardly been used; do you know how to use a computer?; can I use this knife for cutting the meat? **(b)** to take a service; guests used the fire escape to get out of the building; she used the money she had saved to pay for a trip to Greece; I don't use the underground much because I can walk to the office; we use second-class mail for all our correspondence **(c)** to take a substance and do something with it; don't use the tap water for drinking; does this car use much petrol?; turn down the heating - we're using too much gas **(d)** to take advantage of someone; he works every evening until late - I think they're just using him

used [juːzd] adjective which is not new; a shop selling used clothes; a used car salesman

used to ['juːzd 'tuː] **(a)** to be used to something or to doing something = not to worry about doing something, because you do it often; farmers are used to getting up early; we're used to hard work in this office; I'm not used to eating such a large meal at lunchtime **(b)** to get used to something or to doing something = to do something often or for a period of time, so that it is not a worry any more; she'll soon get used to her new job; we lived in Canada for six years, so we got used to very cold temperatures; even though he had to catch the 6.15 train for years, he never got used to getting up early **(c)** (showing that something happened often or regularly in the past) there used to be lots of small shops in the village until the supermarket was built; when we were children, we used to go to France every year for our holidays; the police think he used to live in London; he used not to smoke a pipe; didn't she use to work in London? (NOTE: the forms used in the negative and questions: he used to work in London; he didn't use to work in London or he used not to work in London; didn't he use to work in London?)

useful ['juːsful] adjective who or which can help you do something; I find these scissors very useful for opening letters; she's a very useful person to have in the office; to make yourself useful = to do something to help

usefulness ['juːsfulnəs] noun how useful something is; I don't see the usefulness of doing that

useless ['juːsləs] adjective which is not useful; these scissors are useless - they won't cut anything; I found it useless to try to persuade her to do something different; she's useless at numbers = she is no good at mathematics

user ['juːzə] noun person who uses a tool or a service; we have mailed the users of our equipment about the possible design fault; road user = motorist, cyclist, etc., who uses the road; user's guide or handbook = book showing someone how to use something; I find the computer user's guide very useful

user-friendly [juːzə'frendli] adjective (computers) (program or machine) which a user finds easy to use; these programs are really user-friendly

use up ['juːz 'ʌp] verb to use all of something; she's used up all the glue; paying for the house has used up all her savings

usher ['ʌʃə] **1** noun man who shows people to their seats in a cinema or at a wedding; at her wedding, the two ushers were her brothers **2** verb to usher in = (i) to bring someone in; (ii) to be the beginning of; they were

ushered into the chairman's office; the end of the war ushered in a period of great prosperity

usherette [ʌʃə'ret] noun (old) woman who shows people to their seats in a cinema; the usherette used her torch to show us to our seats; the usherettes will be selling small tubs of ice cream during the interval

usual ['juːʒuəl] **1** adjective **(a)** which is done or used often; she took her usual bus to the office; we'll meet at the usual time, usual place; his usual practice is to get up at 6.30 and run round the park; the usual hours of work are from 9.30 to 5.30 **(b)** as usual = as is normal, in the usual way; the post was late today as usual; as usual, it rained for the school sports day; business as usual = everything still working in the usual way in spite of difficulties; although their warehouse burnt down within twenty-four hours it was business as usual **2** noun (informal) drink or food which someone has most often in a restaurant, pub, etc.; a pint of the usual, please; will you have your usual, sir?

usually ['juːʒəli] adverb very often or mostly; there's usually someone in the office at 9 o'clock; we usually have sandwiches for lunch; the restaurant is usually full on Friday evenings

usurp [juː'zɜːp] verb (formal) to take and use a right which is not yours, especially to take the throne from a rightful king; King Henry IV usurped the throne from Richard II; the council said that the new government committee would usurp their powers

usurpation [juːzɜː'peɪʃn] noun taking and using a right which is not yours

usurper [juː'zɜːpə] noun person who usurps power; the army attacked the palace and killed the usurper

utensils [juː'tenslz] noun kitchen utensils = tools, pans, knives, etc., used for work in the kitchen; she has a number of cooking utensils in her kitchen which she uses all the time

uterine ['juːtəraɪn] adjective referring to the uterus; uterine wall = wall of the uterus; a fertilized egg becomes implanted in the uterine wall

uterus ['juːtərəs] noun hollow organ in a woman's body where a fertilized egg is lodged and an unborn baby is carried; at the time of birth, strong contractions of the wall of the uterus will help push the baby out (NOTE: also called the **womb**)

utilitarian [juːtɪlɪ'teəriən] adjective used for a practical purpose not decoration; there's no decoration in the office - it is all very utilitarian; his utilitarian designs for bathroom furniture are well-known

utility [juː'tɪlɪti] noun **(a)** how useful something is; does your gadget have any practical utility?; utility van = small van for carrying goods; utility room = room in a house where you put the washing machine, freezer, etc. **(b)** utilities = essential public services (such as electricity, gas, water, etc.)

utilization [juːtɪlaɪ'zeɪʃn] noun (formal) making use of something; the utilization of electricity for cooking is very common

utilize ['juːtɪlaɪz] verb (formal) to make use of something; he's keen to utilize his programming skills

utmost ['ʌtməust] **1** adjective greatest that can be; it is of utmost importance that the police be kept informed; the situation is of the utmost urgency **2** noun greatest action possible; they did their utmost to save the children from the fire

utopia [juˈtəupiə] *noun* imaginary perfect world; *the new government came to power thinking it would create a utopia*

utopian [juˈtəupiən] *adjective* very perfect, but not at all practical; *his vision of the future is quite utopian*

utter [ˈʌtə] **1** *adjective* complete, total; *the exhibition was an utter waste of time*; *he's an utter fool* **2** *verb* to speak; to make a sound; *she only uttered a few words during the whole evening*

utterance [ˈʌtrəns] *noun (formal)* something which is said; *do not believe any of his public utterances*

utterly [ˈʌtəli] *adverb* completely; *he was utterly worn out after the test*

U-turn [ˈjuːtɜːn] *noun* **(a)** turning round to go back in the opposite direction; *the police car did or made a U-turn and went back to the hotel*; *U-turns are not allowed on motorways* **(b)** to do a U-turn = to change policy completely; *the papers were surprised at the government's U-turn on defence expenditure*; *the government has done a complete U-turn on pensioners' rights*; *the council did a U-turn and passed the development plan for the town centre*

UV rays [ˈjuː ˈviː] *see* ULTRAVIOLET

uvula [ˈjuːvjulə] *noun* piece of soft tissue which hangs down at the back of the mouth

Vv

V, v [vi:] twenty-second letter of the alphabet, between U and W; *I know his name's Stephen but I don't know if it is spelt with a 'ph' or a 'v' (Stephen or Steven); see also* V-NECK

v ['vɜːsəs or vi:] = VERSUS

V (a) the Roman numeral for five or fifth; *King George V* **(b)** = VOLT

vacancy ['veɪkənsi] *noun* **(a)** job which is not filled; *we have vacancies in several departments*; *we advertised a vacancy for a secretary in the local paper*; **job vacancies** = jobs which are empty and need people to do them **(b)** empty place, empty room; *all the hotels had signs saying 'No vacancies'* **(c)** not showing any interest or emotion; *the vacancy of her expression showed how shocked she was*

vacant ['veɪkənt] *adjective* **(a)** empty, available for you to use; *we have six rooms vacant in the annexe*; *is the toilet vacant yet?*; **with vacant possession** = empty, with no one living in it; *the house is for sale with vacant possession* **(b) situations vacant** *or* **appointments vacant** = list in a newspaper of jobs which are available **(c)** *(expression)* not showing any interest or liveliness; *he sat with a vacant expression on his face*

vacate [və'keɪt] *verb* to leave something empty; *guests are requested to vacate their rooms before 12.00*; **to vacate the premises** = to leave a building so that it is empty; *the staff had to vacate the premises as soon as the fire alarm went off*

vacation [və'keɪʃn] **1** *noun* **(a)** *especially US* holiday; *the family went on vacation in Canada* **(b)** *GB* period when the universities and law courts are closed; *I'm spending my vacation working on a vineyard in Italy*; **long vacation** = summer holiday in a British university; **vacation job** = job taken by a student during the vacation to earn money to help pay for the costs of a university or college course **2** *verb US* to take a holiday; *they are vacationing in Mexico*

vaccinate ['væksɪneɪt] *verb* to vaccinate someone **against a disease** = to use a vaccine to give a person immunization against a specific disease; *she was vaccinated against smallpox as a child*; *make sure you are vaccinated before you travel to Africa* (NOTE: you vaccinate someone **against** a disease)

vaccination [væksɪ'neɪʃn] *noun* action of vaccinating; *he had a vaccination against smallpox or a smallpox vaccination*

vaccine ['væksiːn] *noun* substance which contains the germs of a disease and which is used to inoculate or vaccinate; *the hospital is waiting for a new batch of vaccine to come from the laboratory*; *new vaccines are being developed all the time*

vacuum ['vækjuəm] **1** *noun* **(a)** space which is completely empty of all matter, including air; *the experiment has to be carried out in a vacuum*; **vacuum-packed food** = food packed in a plastic envelope from which all air has been removed;

vacuum-packed cheese will keep for months **(b)** **to create a vacuum** = to empty a space completely; **power vacuum** = situation where there is no one left in control; *the death of the Foreign Minister creates a power vacuum in the government* **(c)** **working in a vacuum** = working in a situation where you have no connection with anyone else **(d)** *US* = VACUUM CLEANER **2** *verb (informal)* to clean using a vacuum cleaner; *she vacuums the hall every day*; *I must vacuum the living room before my mother arrives*

vacuum cleaner ['vækjuəm 'kliːnə] *noun* machine which cleans by sucking up dust; *our cat hides under the bed when she hears the vacuum cleaner*

vacuum flask ['vækjuəm 'flɑːsk] *noun (formal)* type of bottle which keeps liquids hot or cold; *we took vacuum flasks of hot coffee to drink when we went walking* (NOTE: also commonly called by a trade name, **thermos**)

vagabond ['vægəbɒnd] *noun* person who travels from place to place and has no home; *after a few years of a vagabond existence, he longed to settle somewhere*

vagaries ['veɪgəriz] *noun* strange unpredictable behaviour; *investors are nervous about the vagaries of the stock market*; *the vagaries of the English summer*

vagina [və'dʒaɪnə] *noun* passage in a female body connecting the uterus to the vulva and through which a baby is born; *the lower end of the uterus opens into the vagina*

vaginal [və'dʒaɪnəl] *adjective* referring to the vagina; *she experienced vaginal bleeding*

vagrancy ['veɪgrənsi] *noun* crime of being a vagrant; *he was charged with vagrancy*

vagrant ['veɪgrənt] *noun (formal)* tramp, a person who travels from place to place with no home or work; *the council has set up a home for vagrants*

vague [veɪg] *adjective* not clear, with no precise details; *he's very vague about what he wants to do after university*; *we've made some vague plans to go to Greece in August*; *she hadn't the vaguest idea what to do* = she had no idea at all (NOTE: **vaguer - vaguest**)

vaguely ['veɪgli] *adverb* **(a)** more or less; *there's something vaguely dishonest about the affair* **(b)** in a vague way; *they were talking vaguely about going to Tunisia on holiday*

vain [veɪn] *adjective* **(a)** which does not succeed; *she went to the pub in the vain hope of finding him there* **(b) in vain** = without any success; *we waited in vain for a bus and had to walk home*; *he did not die in vain* = his death had an immense moral effect on people **(c)** very proud of your appearance, clothes, achievements, etc.; *he's very vain, and is always combing his hair* (NOTE: do not confuse with **vein**; note: **vainer - vainest**)

vainly ['veɪnli] *adverb* without any success; *she vainly attempted to get him to change his mind*

valentine ['væləntaɪn] *noun* **(a) valentine (card)** = card sent to someone you love on Valentine's Day **(b)** *(old)* person you say you love particularly; *he asked her to be his valentine*

Valentine's Day ['væləntaɪnz 'deɪ] *noun* 14th February, day when people send cards and flowers to loved ones; *the price of flowers doubles in the days before Valentine's Day*; *he bought her a Valentine's card*

valet ['væleɪ *US* væl'eɪ] *noun* **(a)** *(old)* servant who looks after a man's clothes; *his valet unpacked his suits* **(b)** person who parks your car at a restaurant or hotel; **valet parking** = service at a hotel or restaurant where a member of the staff parks guests' cars for them; *valet parking is available for our clients* **(c) valet service** = service in a hotel for cleaning and pressing clothes; *ring our valet service to have your suit pressed for tomorrow morning*

valeting ['vælɪtɪŋ] *noun* cleaning the inside of a car; *the garage offers a full valeting service*; *prices for valeting your car vary according to what you want to be done*

valiant ['væliənt] *adjective* brave; *in spite of all their valiant efforts, the rescuers were not able to save the crew of the yacht*

valid ['vælɪd] *adjective* **(a)** which is acceptable because it is true; *that is not a valid argument or valid excuse*; *she made several valid points in her speech* **(b)** which can be lawfully used for a time; *travellers must have a valid ticket before boarding the train*; *I have a season ticket which is valid for one year*; *he was carrying a valid passport*

validate ['vælɪdeɪt] *verb* **(a)** to check to see if something is correct; *the document has to be validated by the bank* **(b)** to make something valid; *the ticket has to be stamped to validate it* **(c)** to certify officially that something is acceptable; *the new course has not yet been validated by the academic board*

validation [vælɪ'deɪʃn] *noun* act of certifying that something is acceptable; *we're still waiting for course validation before we can start enrolling students*

validity [və'lɪdɪti] *noun* **(a)** truth; *the police questioned the validity of her confession* **(b)** being valid; **period of validity** = length of time for which a ticket or document can be used lawfully; *my visa for China has a thirty-day period of validity*

valley ['væli] *noun* long piece of low land through which a river runs; *fog forms in the valleys at night*; *a lot of computer companies are based in the Thames Valley*

valour *US* **valor** ['vælə] *noun* *(formal)* courage, especially in war time; *his valour on the battlefield was recognized with a medal*

valuable ['væljubl] **1** *adjective* worth a lot of money; *be careful, that glass is valuable!*; *the burglars stole everything that was valuable* **2** *noun* **valuables** = items which are worth a lot of money; *you can deposit valuables in the hotel safe*

valuation [vælju'eɪʃn] *noun* **(a)** estimate of the worth of something; *a £350 valuation for this ring is much too low* **(b)** act of estimating the worth of something; *at the end of a financial year, we have to do a stock valuation*; *we asked for a valuation of the property or for a property valuation*

value ['vælju:] **1** *noun* **(a)** amount of money which something is worth; *he imported goods to the value of £500*; *the fall in the value of the yen*; *items of value can be deposited in the hotel safe overnight*; **to rise in value** = to become worth more; **to fall in value** = to become worth less; *houses have fallen in value in some parts of the country*; **good value (for money)** = a bargain, something which is worth the price paid for it; *that restaurant gives value for money*; *holidays in Italy are good value because of the exchange rate* **(b)** quantity shown as a number; **calorific value** *or* **energy value** = number of calories which a certain food contains; *the tin of beans has a calorific value of 250 calories*; **pH value** = number which indicates how acid *or* alkaline a solution is **(c) practical value** = usefulness; *the gadget is of no practical value at all* **2** *verb* **(a)** to estimate the value of something; *the jewels have been valued at £5000* **(b)** to consider something as being valuable; *she values her friendship with him*

value added tax (VAT) ['vælju: 'ædɪd tæks] *noun* tax imposed on the value of goods or services; *see* **VAT**

valueless ['væljuləs] *adjective* which has no value; *her jewels were all imitations, they were quite valueless*

valve [vælv] *noun* **(a)** device in a tube (in a machine) which allows air or liquid to pass through in one direction only; *the problem was caused by a faulty valve*; **safety valve** = valve which allows liquid, gas, steam, etc., to escape if the pressure becomes too high **(b)** flap in the heart, in a blood vessel, or other organ which opens and closes to allow liquid to pass in one direction only; *surgery was needed to repair a valve in the heart*

vampire ['væmpaɪə] *noun* evil person who supposedly sucks blood from his victims; *do you really enjoy watching vampire films?*; **vampire bat** = large bat which bites other animals and sucks their blood

van [væn] *noun* covered goods vehicle; *a delivery van ran into the back of my car*; *our van will call this afternoon to pick up the goods*; **van-load** = amount of goods carried on a van; *when we moved we had three van-loads of books*; **security van** = specially protected van for delivering cash and other valuable items; *six gunmen held up the security van*

vandal ['vændl] *noun* person who destroys property, especially public property, for the pleasure of destruction; *vandals pulled the telephones out of the call boxes by the station*

vandalism ['vændəlɪzm] *noun* meaningless destruction of property; *the railway company is employing guards to prevent vandalism to trains*; *we condemn all acts of vandalism however small*

vandalize ['vændəlaɪz] *verb* to destroy property for no reason at all; *none of the emergency telephones work because they have been vandalized*

vanguard ['vængɑːd] *noun* **(a)** front part of an army; *the vanguard should reach the capital within a few days* **(b)** **in the vanguard** = in the front of a movement; *we are in the vanguard of the operations to control drug smuggling*

vanilla [və'nɪlə] *noun* flavouring made from the seed pods of a tropical plant; *add a few drops of vanilla (essence) to the batter*; *this recipe uses* *vanilla-flavoured sugar*; *I want vanilla ice cream with chocolate sauce*

vanish ['vænɪʃ] *verb* to disappear suddenly; *the magician made the rabbit vanish*; **to vanish into thin air** = to disappear completely; *all the money the depositors had put into the bank simply vanished into thin air*

vanishing point ['vænɪʃɪŋ 'pɔɪnt] *noun* (a) point in a picture where lines appear to meet at the horizon (b) point where something disappears completely; *profits have fallen to vanishing point*

vanity ['vænɪti] *noun* (a) being excessively proud of your appearance, feeling that you are very handsome; **to tickle your vanity** = to make you amused and proud; *her constant phone calls rather tickled his vanity* (b) *(formal)* uselessness; *the vanity of all human possessions*

vanquish ['væŋkwɪʃ] *verb (literary)* to defeat; *the enemy army was vanquished*

vantage point ['vɑːntɪdʒpɔɪnt] *noun* place from which you can see well; *from your vantage point on the roof, you can easily see what is happening in the Boat Race*

vaporization [veɪpəraɪˈzeɪʃn] *noun* changing into vapour; *the vaporization of water*

vaporize ['veɪpəraɪz] *verb* to change a solid or liquid into vapour; *water vaporizes when heated*

vapour *US* **vapor** ['veɪpə] *noun* substance in the form of a gas, usually caused by heating; *you can see water vapour rising from the swimming pool in cold weather*; **vapour trail** = line of white vapour left in the sky by an aircraft; *the planes' vapour trails criss-crossed the sky*

variable ['veəriəbl] **1** *adjective* which may change frequently; *the weather forecast is for variable winds*; *the weather can be very variable on the coast* **2** *noun* thing which varies; *we have to take a great many variables into account*

variance ['veəriəns] *noun (formal)* amount of difference between two things; *the variance in temperature during the summer months is shown on the chart*; **to be at variance with** = not to agree, to be slightly different; *the actual sales are at variance with the sales reported by the reps*

variant ['veəriənt] *noun* spelling of a word or name, etc., which is slightly different; *the surname has two or three variants but all the families are related*

variation [veəriˈeɪʃn] *noun* (a) change from one state or level to another; *the variation in colour or the colour variation is because the cloth has been dyed by hand*; *there is a noticeable variation in temperature in the desert regions*; *the chart shows the variations in price over a period of six months* (b) **variations** = short pieces of music which take the same theme but repeat it in different styles

varicella [værɪˈselə] *noun see* CHICKENPOX

varicose veins ['værɪkəʊs 'veɪnz] *noun* veins, especially in the leg, which have become twisted and swollen; *she wears stockings specially made for people with varicose veins*

varied ['veərɪd] *adjective* made up of different sorts and kinds; *the menu isn't very varied - there are only three starters and two main courses*; *a varied programme of music*

variegated ['veərɪgeɪtɪd] *adjective* striped, marked in contrasting colours; *we have planted variegated shrubs to brighten up this corner of the garden*; *this variegated holly has yellow and green leaves*

variegation [veərɪˈgeɪʃn] *noun* state of being variegated; *why is it that some of the leaves have no variegation?*

variety [vəˈraɪəti] *noun* (a) differences; *her new job, unlike the old one, doesn't lack variety*; **a variety of** = a lot of different sorts of things or people; *she's had a variety of boyfriends*; *we had a variety of visitors at the office today*; *we couldn't go on holiday this year for a variety of reasons*; **variety is the spice of life** = if you meet lots of different people, visit lots of different places, etc., then this makes your life exciting (b) different type of plant or animal in the same species; *do you have this new variety of rose?*; *is this a new variety of potato?* (c) type of entertainment which includes several different short performances by different types of entertainer (such as singers, conjurors, ventriloquists, etc.); *at Christmas, the TV has nothing but a series of variety shows* (NOTE: American English is **vaudeville**)

various ['veəriəs] *adjective* different; *the shop sells goods from various countries*; *I'll be out of the office today - I have to see various suppliers*

variously ['veəriəsli] *adverb* in different ways; *the children were variously affected by the virus*; *the box contains variously coloured folders for easy identification*

varnish ['vɑːnɪʃ] **1** *noun* (a) liquid which when painted on something gives it a shiny surface; *he applied two coats of varnish to the door*; **nail varnish** = coloured liquid which is put on fingernails or toenails; *she was putting red nail varnish on* (b) shiny surface made by painting with varnish; *be careful with that knife - you'll scratch the varnish* **2** *verb* to paint with a liquid varnish; to give a shiny surface to something; *can you varnish our front door?*

vary ['veəri] *verb* (a) to change what you do often; *it will help your digestion if you vary your diet* (b) to be different; *prices of flats vary from a few thousand pounds to millions*

vase [vɑːz] *noun* container used for cut flowers, or simply for decoration; *she put the flowers into a vase*; *we were given a beautiful Japanese vase as a wedding present*

vasectomy [væˈsektəmi] *noun* surgical operation to sterilize a man; *he had a vasectomy*

vast [vɑːst] *adjective* enormous, very large; *the moor was so vast - it stretched as far as the eye could see*; *a vast tanker suddenly appeared out of the fog*

vastly ['vɑːstli] *adverb* very much; *the meal ended up costing vastly more than I expected*; *I think their new 'first-class service' is vastly overrated*

vat [væt] *noun* large container for liquids; *the vats of whisky are stored in a cellar*

VAT [væt or viːeɪˈtiː] *abbreviation for* Value Added Tax, a tax imposed as a percentage of the invoice value of goods or services; *VAT is an indirect tax*; *the invoice includes VAT at 17.5%*; *hotels and restaurants have to charge VAT like any other business*; *in Britain there is no VAT on books*; **VAT inspector** = government official who examines VAT returns and checks that VAT is being paid; **VAT invoice** = invoice which shows VAT separately

Vatican ['vætɪkən] *noun* **(a)** state in Italy, ruled by the Pope (NOTE: also called the **Holy See**) **(b)** palace in Rome, where the Pope lives; *when we went to Rome we visited the Vatican museum*

vaudeville ['vɔːdəvɪl] *noun US see* VARIETY SHOW; *at Christmas, TV shows nothing but a series of vaudeville acts*

vault [vɔːlt] **1** *noun* **(a)** arched stone ceiling; *the 11th century vault of the chapel in the Tower of London* **(b)** **vault** *or* **vaults** = underground room for keeping valuables safe; *the documents are kept in the bank vaults* **(c)** underground room for burying people; *she is buried in the family vault* **(d)** high jump; **pole vault** = leap over a high bar, using a pole to swing you up; *he won the pole vault for the first time* **2** *verb* to jump over something by putting one hand on it to steady yourself; *he vaulted over the fence and ran across the garden*

veal [viːl] *noun* meat from a calf; *some people refuse to eat veal; we had roast veal for lunch;* **veal cutlet** = flat cake of minced veal, fried; **veal escalope** = thin slice of veal, covered in breadcrumbs and fried; *we went to an Italian restaurant and had veal escalope; see also* WIENER SCHNITZEL

COMMENT: veal is not as popular in Britain as in some other European countries

veer ['vɪə] *verb* **(a)** to turn in a direction suddenly; *the car suddenly veered to the right and crashed through a wall; she veered away off the main road into a little lane* **(b)** to change plans, ideas, etc.; *the government seems to be veering towards the left* **(c)** *(of wind)* to change direction; *the wind suddenly veered to the south*

veg [vedʒ] *(informal)* = VEGETABLES; **meat and two veg** = traditional lunch with roast meat served with two sorts of vegetables

vegan ['viːgən] *noun* person who does not eat meat, dairy produce, eggs or fish, but only eats vegetables and fruit and other non-animal products; *his wife is a vegan, so we'll make a special meal for her* (NOTE: also called a **strict vegetarian**)

vegetable ['vedʒɪtəbl] *noun* **(a)** plant grown to be eaten, but not usually sweet; *we grow potatoes, carrots and other sorts of vegetables in the garden; what vegetables do you want with your meat? - beans and parsnips, please; the soup of the day is vegetable soup;* **green vegetables** = vegetables which are green, especially cabbage, spinach, Brussels sprouts, etc.; *green vegetables are a good source of dietary fibre;* **root vegetables** = vegetables, such as carrots, of which you eat the roots **(b)** **vegetable oil** = oil which is extracted from plants

vegetarian [vedʒɪ'teəriən] **1** *noun* person who eats only fruit, vegetables, bread, eggs, etc., but does not eat meat, and sometimes not fish; *our children are all vegetarians;* **strict vegetarian** = person who does not eat any animal products, including eggs and milk (NOTE: **strict vegetarians** are also called **vegans**) **2** *adjective* not eating meat; *he is on a vegetarian diet; she asked for the vegetarian menu;* **vegetarian dish** = dish which does not contain meat

vegetation [vedʒɪ'teɪʃn] *noun* plants; *there is very little vegetation in the Arctic regions; all the vegetation has been eaten by wild goats* (NOTE: no plural)

vehement ['viːəmənt] *adjective* forceful; *we didn't expect such a vehement attack on our plans; he made a vehement denial of all involvement in the plot*

vehemently ['viːəməntli] *adverb* very strongly, forcefully; *she vehemently denied the accusations*

vehicle ['viːɪkl] *noun (formal)* car, truck, bus, etc., a machine which carries passengers or goods; *a three-wheeled vehicle;* **goods vehicles can park at the back of the building;** **commercial vehicle** = vehicle which carries passengers or goods; **heavy goods vehicle (HGV)** = very large truck

vehicular [vɪ'hɪkjulə] *adjective (formal)* referring to vehicles; *no vehicular traffic is allowed on the island;* **vehicular access** = access for cars, lorries, etc.; *vehicular access is limited to residents with special permits; there is no vehicular access to the rear of the building*

veil [veɪl] **1** *noun* **(a)** light cloth which can cover a woman's head or face; *at the funeral she wore a hat with a black veil; the bride lifted her veil as she came out of the church;* **to take the veil** = to become a nun; *she took the veil when she was twenty-three* **(b)** **to draw a veil over something** = not to mention something which is wrong or unpleasant; *I think we had better draw a veil over her attempts to pass her driving test* **(c)** something which stops you seeing or understanding; *a veil of mist lay over the valley; a veil of secrecy has prevented us finding out what really happened* **2** *verb* to cover something, as if with a veil; *the moon was veiled by clouds; the whole affair is veiled in mystery*

veiled [veɪld] *adjective* partly hidden; *you could just see the temple in the distance, veiled in mist; the report is a thinly-veiled criticism of the tourist industry*

vein [veɪn] *noun* **(a)** small tube in the body which takes blood from the tissues back to the heart; *the veins in her legs are swollen* **(b)** mood shown in speaking or writing; *he went on in the same vein for twenty minutes;* **in poetic vein** = feeling poetic **(c)** thin tube forming part of the structure of a leaf **(d)** thin layer of mineral in rock; *they struck a vein of gold* (NOTE: do not confuse with **vain**)

Velcro ['velkrəu] *noun* tradename for a material with stiff fibres which cling tight when pressed together; *her sandals have Velcro straps; the rucksack fastens with Velcro*

velocity [və'lɒsɪti] *noun (formal)* speed; *the rocket reached its maximum velocity in three seconds; high velocity rifles are now forbidden by law*

velour [və'luːə] *noun* fabric similar to velvet, but usually made of cotton; *the chairs are upholstered in red velour*

velvet ['velvət] *noun* cloth made from silk, with a soft furry surface on one side; *he wore a velvet jacket for dinner*

vendetta [ven'detə] *noun* private quarrel between families or persons; *she is conducting a personal vendetta against her boss*

vending ['vendɪŋ] *noun* action of selling; **automatic vending machine** = machine which provides cigarettes, bars of chocolate, etc., when a coin is put into a slot; *she bought some sandwiches from a vending machine at the station*

vendor ['vendə] *noun* **(a)** person who sells a property; *the vendor's solicitor is trying to get the* purchaser to hurry up **(b)** **street vendor** = person who sells food or small items in the street; *outside the hotel, street vendors were selling toys and fruit*

veneer [vəˈnɪə] **1** *noun* **(a)** thin layer of expensive wood glued to the surface of ordinary wood; *the table has a mahogany veneer* **(b)** **a veneer of** = thin layer of something which hides your real feelings; *his veneer of politeness soon disappeared as the old lady asked more and more questions* **2** *verb* to cover wood with a veneer; *the table is veneered in oak*

venerable [ˈvenrəbl] *adjective (formal)* very old and likely to be respected; *the monarchy is a venerable institution*; *he died at a venerable age*

venerate [ˈvenəreɪt] *verb* to respect greatly; *his memory is venerated throughout the area*; *the festival when the Chinese venerate their ancestors*

veneration [venəˈreɪʃn] *noun (formal)* great respect; *they speak of their ancestors with veneration*; **to hold someone** *or* **something in veneration** = to respect someone *or* something greatly; *the people hold their president in veneration*

Venezuela [venɪˈzweɪlə] *noun* country in the north of South America, on the Caribbean; *he's going to Venezuela on business* (NOTE: capital: **Caracas**; people: **Venezuelans**; language: **Spanish**; currency: **bolivar**)

Venezuelan [venɪˈzweɪlən] **1** *adjective* referring to Venezuela; *Venezuelan exports to Spain are increasing* **2** *noun* person from Venezuela

vengeance [ˈvendʒəns] *noun* **(a)** harm caused to someone in return for harm they have caused you; *he has vowed to exact vengeance for the wrong done to his family*; *she is seeking vengeance for the killing of her child* **(b)** *(informal)* **with a vengeance** = very strongly; *the rain came down again with a vengeance*

vengeful [ˈvendʒful] *adjective (formal)* eager to have revenge on someone; *his vengeful brother set fire to the house*; *she was in a vengeful mood*

venison [ˈvenɪzn] *noun* meat from a deer; *roast venison and mushrooms*; *try the venison pâté as a starter* (NOTE: no plural)

venom [ˈvenəm] *noun* **(a)** poison from the bite of a snake, etc.; *the venom of certain snakes may cause paralysis* **(b)** bitter hatred; *the venom in her reply was obvious*

venomous [ˈvenəməs] *adjective* **(a)** with poison in its bite; *this snake is particularly venomous*; *she was bitten by a venomous spider* **(b)** showing bitter hatred; *she gave him a venomous look*; *his venomous letter was printed in the newspaper*

venous [ˈviːnəs] *adjective* referring to veins in the body; *the venous system brings blood back to the heart and lungs*; **venous blood** = dark blood from which most of the oxygen has been removed and which is taken by the veins back to the heart

COMMENT: blood pumped from the heart to the tissues via the arteries is called arterial blood

vent [vent] **1** *noun* **(a)** hole through which air or gas can escape; *the gas heater is connected to a vent in the wall*; **air vent** = vent which allows air to come in; *there should be an air vent in the machine room* **(b)** **to give vent to** = to let an emotion come out; *when the crowd heard the news they gave vent to their feelings* **(c)** slit

in the back of a coat, etc., allowing you to sit down more easily; *he always wears jackets with double vents* **2** *verb* **to vent your anger on someone** = to make someone the target of your anger; *he vented his anger on the poor ticket collector*

ventilate [ˈventɪleɪt] *verb* **(a)** to allow fresh air to come into; *the freshly painted kitchen needs to be ventilated for several hours*; *children tend to fall asleep in poorly ventilated classrooms* **(b)** *(formal)* to discuss a question openly; *they thoroughly ventilated their worries regarding money*

ventilation [ventɪˈleɪʃn] *noun* bringing fresh air into a place; *the ventilation of the lecture room could be improved*; *the ventilation system seems to be functioning badly*; **ventilation shaft** = tube which allows fresh air to go into a building

ventilator [ˈventɪleɪtə] *noun* **(a)** machine which pumps in fresh air; *you need to install ventilators in this kitchen* **(b)** opening which allows fresh air to come into a building; *there is a little ventilator in the wall of the bathroom* **(c)** machine which pumps air into the lungs of a person who has difficulty in breathing; *the newborn baby was put on a ventilator*

ventriloquist [venˈtrɪləkwɪst] *noun* person who can make his voice appear to come from another place; *a ventriloquist and his puppet*

venture [ˈventʃə] **1** *noun* business or commercial deal which involves risk; *the venture failed and all the partners lost money*; *she has started a new venture - a computer shop* **2** *verb (formal)* **(a)** to risk doing something dangerous; *she ventured into the cave*; *they ventured out into the blizzard* **(b)** to say something, even though other people may criticize you for saying it; *at last she ventured to say that the whole thing was a failure*

venue [ˈvenjuː] *noun* agreed place where a meeting will be held; *what is the venue going to be for the exhibition?*; *the meeting will be held on Wednesday, 10th May, but the venue has not been fixed yet*

Venus [ˈviːnəs] *noun* second planet of the solar system, slightly smaller than the Earth

verandah [vəˈrændə] *noun* covered terrace along the side of a house; *it is nice to have breakfast on the verandah in the summer*; *they loved to sit on the verandah facing the river after dinner*

verb [vɜːb] *noun (grammar)* word which shows an action, being or feeling, etc.; *in the sentence 'she hit him with her fist' the word 'hit' is a verb*

verbal [ˈvɜːbəl] *adjective* **(a)** spoken; not written down; *the head teacher gave the boys a verbal warning*; **verbal agreement** = agreement which is spoken (such as one made over the phone) **(b)** *(grammar)* referring to a verb; *when you say 'to X-ray' the noun has taken a verbal form*; **verbal noun** = gerund, a noun formed from the present participle of a verb (NOTE: in English, verbal nouns are formed from the '-ing' form of verbs, as in **cycling is good exercise**; **choral singing is very popular in Wales**)

verdict [ˈvɜːdɪkt] *noun* **(a)** decision of a magistrate or jury; *the jury returned a guilty verdict after one hour*; **to come to a verdict** *or* **to reach a verdict** = to decide whether the accused is guilty or not **(b)** *(informal)* opinion, what you think about something; *she gave her verdict on the soup*

verdigris ['vɜːdɪɡrɪs] *noun* green mould on copper, etc., caused by damp; *an old bronze statue covered with verdigris*

verge [vɜːdʒ] **1** *noun* **(a)** border of grass along the side of a road; *you can park on the verge outside the house*; *wild flowers were growing all along the motorway verges* **(b)** edge; *on the verge of* = near to; *the company is on the verge of bankruptcy*; *she was on the verge of a nervous breakdown* **2** *verb* **to verge on** = to be close to; *his sharp comments about her clothes verged on rudeness*

verification [verɪfɪ'keɪʃn] *noun* action of verifying; *we had to wait for verification of the documents*

verify ['verɪfaɪ] *verb* to check to see if documents or a statement are correct; *the police are trying to verify all the witnesses' statements*; *is it possible to verify that what he said was true?*

veritable ['verɪtəbl] *adjective* true or real; *the garden needs weeding - it's a veritable jungle out there*

vermillion *US* **vermilion** [və'mɪlɪən] *adjective & noun* bright orange-red (colour); *she wanted a striking colour so she chose vermillion*; *the vermillion cushions give a touch of warmth to the room*

vermin ['vɜːmɪn] *noun* **(a)** insects which live on other animals; *his head was covered with vermin* **(b)** animals or insects (mice, cockroaches, etc.) which eat crops, bring disease into houses, etc.; *grey squirrels are considered as vermin and so are foxes* (NOTE: no plural)

vermouth ['vɜːməθ] *noun* type of strong red or white wine flavoured with herbs; *I'd love a glass of red vermouth with ice, please*

vernal ['vɜːnl] *adjective* (*formal*) referring to the spring; **the vernal equinox** = moment around March 21st, when the sun crosses the celestial equator and night and day are each twelve hours long (NOTE: also called the **spring equinox**. The other equinox is the **autumn equinox**)

versatile ['vɜːsətaɪl] *adjective* **(a)** (*person*) good at doing various things equally well; *he's very versatile - he can play the piano, the guitar and he's the lead singer as well* **(b)** (*machine, material, etc.*) which is suitable for various uses; *the car is extremely versatile: it can be used on rough mountain tracks, but is equally suitable for town use*

verse [vɜːs] *noun* **(a)** group of lines which form a part of a song or poem; *we sang all the verses of the National Anthem*; *she read the first verse to the class* **(b)** poetry, writing which has a certain rhythm and sometimes rhymes; *he published a small book of verse* compare PROSE (NOTE: no plural in this meaning) **(c)** one short sentence from the Bible, each of which has a number; *the reading in church was some verses from St John's Gospel*; **to give** *or* **to quote chapter and verse for something** = to say exactly where to find a piece of information

versed ['vɜːst] *adjective* **to be well versed in something** = to know a lot about something, to be skilled at doing something; *she's well versed in British law*

version ['vɜːʃn] *noun* **(a)** description of what happened as seen by one person; *the victim told her version of events to the jury* **(b)** type of a work of art, model of car, etc.; *this is the film version of the novel*;

he bought the cheapest version available **(c)** translation; *here is the Chinese version of the book*

versus ['vɜːsəs] *preposition* (*in a sports match, a civil court case*) against (NOTE: usually written **v:** **Manchester United v Arsenal; Smith v the Inland Revenue**, sometimes **vs**)

vertebra ['vɜːtɪbrə] *noun* one of the twenty-four bones which link together to form the vertebral column or backbone; *the backbone or spine is formed of twenty-four vertebrae* (NOTE: plural is **vertebrae** ['vɜːtɪbreɪ])

vertebral column ['vɜːtɪbrəl 'kɒləm] *noun* the series of bones and disks linked together to form a flexible column running from the skull to the pelvis (NOTE: also called the **backbone** *or* **spine**)

vertebrate ['vɜːtɪbrət] **1** *noun* animal which has a backbone; *fish are vertebrates but worms are invertebrates* **2** *adjective* with a backbone; *can you name any other vertebrate animals besides birds and fish?* (NOTE: the opposite is **invertebrate**)

vertical ['vɜːtɪkl] **1** *adjective* standing straight up; *he drew a few vertical lines to represent trees* **2** *noun* the **vertical** = position of something pointing straight up and down; *the ship was listing several degrees from the vertical*

vertigo ['vɜːtɪɡəʊ] *noun* **(a)** dizziness or loss of balance where everything seems to rush round you; *some ear conditions may cause vertigo* **(b)** feeling of dizziness felt when high up, especially inside a tall building; *he refuses to sit near the window - he suffers from vertigo*

verve [vɜːv] *noun* enthusiasm, feeling of liveliness; *he spoke with great verve*

very ['veri] **1** *adverb* (*used to make an adjective or adverb stronger*) *it's very hot in the car - why don't you open a window?*; *can you see that very tall pine tree over there?*; *the time seemed to go very quickly when we were on holiday* **2** *adjective* exactly the right one, exactly the same; *she's the very person you want to talk to*; *the scene takes place at the very beginning of the book*; *he did his very best to get tickets*

◊ **very many** ['veri 'meni] *adjective* **not very many** = not a lot of; *there weren't very many visitors at the exhibition* (NOTE: **not very many** is used with things you can count: **not very many cars**)

◊ **very much** ['veri 'mʌtʃ] **1** *adverb* greatly; *I don't like chocolate very much*; *thank you very much for your cheque*; *it's very much hotter today than it was yesterday* **2** *adjective* **not very much** = not a lot of; *she doesn't have very much work to do at the office*; *they haven't got very much money* (NOTE: **not very much** is used with things you cannot count: **not very much money**)

vessel ['vesl] *noun* **(a)** (*formal*) container for liquid; *archaeologists think it was a form of ancient drinking vessel*; **blood vessel** = any tube which carries blood round the body; *arteries and veins are both blood vessels* **(b)** ship; *vessels from all countries crowded into the harbour*; **merchant vessel** = commercial ship which carries a cargo

vest [vest] *noun* **(a)** light piece of underclothing for the top half of the body; *he wears a thick vest in winter*; *if you don't have a clean vest, wear a T-shirt instead* (NOTE: American English is **undershirt**) **(b)** *US* short coat with buttons and without any sleeves, which is worn over a shirt and under a jacket; *he wore a pale* *grey vest with a black jacket* (NOTE: British English is **waistcoat**)

vested interest ['vestɪd 'ɪntrəst] *noun* special interest in keeping an existing state of affairs; *she has a vested interest in keeping the business going; the unions have a vested interest in seeing a socialist government in power*

vestibule ['vestɪbjuːl] *noun* **(a)** entrance hall to a large building; *we met in the vestibule of the bank* **(b)** *US* inside hall of a house; *there's a large vestibule, specially useful for leaving boots and coats in the winter* (NOTE: also called **lobby**)

vestige ['vestɪdʒ] *noun* trace, remains; *no vestiges remain of the old palace of Henry VIII; is there any vestige of truth in the report?*

vet [vet] **1** *noun (informal)* veterinary surgeon; *we have to take the cat to the vet; the vet has a surgery in the High Street* **2** *verb* to examine carefully; *all candidates have to be vetted by the managing director* (NOTE: **vetting - vetted**)

veteran ['vetrən] **1** *noun* **(a)** soldier, sailor, etc., who has fought in a war; *the veterans visited war graves on the 50th anniversary of the battle* **(b)** person who has a lot of experience; *he is a veteran of many takeover bids* **2** *adjective* who has a lot of experience; *she's a veteran war correspondent; the veteran American film director died this week;* **veteran car** = car made before 1905 (or, according to some people, before 1916)

veterinarian [vetərɪ'neərɪən] *noun* *US* = VETERINARY SURGEON

veterinary ['vetrɪnrɪ] *adjective* referring to the treatment of sick animals; *he always wanted to study veterinary medicine*

veterinary surgeon ['vetrɪnrɪ 'sɜːdʒən] *noun* doctor who specializes in treating sick animals; *the sign over the door says 'Veterinary Surgeon'* (NOTE: always shortened to **vet** when speaking)

veto ['viːtəʊ] **1** *noun* ban, order not to allow something to become law; *the president exercised his veto; the UK used its veto in the Security Council;* **power of veto** = power to forbid something; *the President has (the) power of veto over bills passed by Congress* (NOTE: plural is **vetoes**) **2** *verb* to forbid; *the proposal was vetoed by the president; the council has vetoed all plans to hold protest marches in the centre of town*

vex [veks] *verb (old)* to make someone annoyed; *she was very vexed at not having been invited to the wedding; I found it very vexing that there was no one to help me with my luggage*

vexation [vek'seɪʃn] *noun (formal)* being annoyed; *she slammed the door out of pure vexation*

vexatious [vek'seɪʃəs] *adjective (formal)* done to annoy someone; *what I find most vexatious are the constant phone calls when I'm trying to work*

vexed question ['vekst 'kwestʃən] *noun* question which is often discussed but which is difficult to solve; *now we come to the vexed question of what present to get Aunt Mary for her 90th birthday*

VI the Roman numeral for six or sixth; *King George VI*

via ['vaɪə] *preposition* through; *we drove to London via Windsor; we are sending the payment via our office in London; the shipment is going via the Suez Canal*

viable ['vaɪəbl] *adjective* **(a)** able to work in practice; *the project is certainly viable;* **not commercially viable** = not likely to make a profit; *if we follow his proposals, the project will certainly not be commercially viable* **(b)** *(of foetus)* which can survive if born; *a foetus is viable after about 28 weeks of pregnancy*

viaduct ['vaɪədʌkt] *noun* long bridge carrying a road or railway across a valley; *the railway viaduct is still under repair and the trains have to slow down when crossing it*

vibrant ['vaɪbrənt] *adjective* **(a)** *(person)* full of energy; *a teacher with a vibrant personality* **(b)** bright; *my husband likes vibrant blues and greens while I prefer much more subdued colours*

vibrate [vaɪ'breɪt] *verb* to move slightly, but rapidly and continuously; *the windows vibrate whenever a plane flies over the house; you can feel the machine vibrating if you put your hand on it*

vibration [vaɪ'breɪʃn] *noun* rapid and continuous movement; *speech is formed by the vibrations of the vocal cords; the vibrations of a pneumatic drill can cause circulation problems*

vicar ['vɪkə] *noun (in the Church of England)* priest in charge of a parish; *we have to see the vicar to arrange a date for the wedding*

vicarage ['vɪkrɪdʒ] *noun* house of a vicar; *the village fête was held in the vicarage gardens*

vice [vaɪs] *noun* **(a)** wickedness, especially involving sex; **vice squad** = police department dealing with prostitution, etc. **(b)** particular type of wickedness; *gluttony is a vice* **(c)** bad habit; *I have all the usual vices - I smoke, I drink, I drive too fast* **(d)** tool that screws tight to hold something, so that a workman can work on it; *he put the piece of wood in a vice before cutting it* (NOTE: spelled **vise** in American English in this meaning)

vice- [vaɪs] *prefix meaning* person who is second in rank to someone

vice-president ['vaɪs'prezɪdənt] *noun* **(a)** deputy to a president; *when President Kennedy was assassinated, Vice-President Johnson became president* **(b)** *US* one of the executive directors of a company

COMMENT: in the USA, the Vice-President is the president (i.e. the chairman) of the Senate. He also succeeds a President if the President dies in office (as Vice-President Johnson succeeded President Kennedy)

vice versa ['vaɪsɪ 'vɜːsə] *adverb* the other way from what has just been mentioned; *would you like the report before the final figures or vice versa?*

vicinity [vɪ'sɪnɪtɪ] *noun* **(a)** area around something; *the police are searching the vicinity of the lake* **(b)** **in the vicinity** = nearby; *were there any suspicious characters in the vicinity?;* **in the vicinity of** = near; *the body was found in the vicinity of the church; the price paid was somewhere in the vicinity of £200,000*

vicious ['vɪʃəs] *adjective* **(a)** cruel and wicked; *a vicious attack on an elderly lady* **(b)** **vicious circle** = situation where one problem leads to another which is worse than the first; *he found it hard to break out of the vicious circle of drugs, followed by crime and imprisonment*

victim ['vɪktɪm] *noun* person who is attacked, who is in an accident; *the victims of the train crash were taken to the local hospital*; *she was the victim of a brutal attack outside her front door*; *earthquake victims were housed in tents*

victimization [vɪktɪmaɪ'zeɪʃn] *noun* action of victimizing someone; *the victimization of one child by the others*

victimize ['vɪktɪmaɪz] *verb* to treat someone more unfairly than others; *the prison governor was accused of victimizing young prisoners*; *she was victimized at school because she was fat*

victor ['vɪktə] *noun (formal)* person who wins a fight, game, battle; *the victor ran round the track waving a flag*

Victorian [vɪk'tɔːrɪən] **1** *adjective* referring to the reign of Queen Victoria (1837 - 1901); *they live in a Victorian house*; **Victorian values** = qualities valued by the Victorians, such as hard work, thrift, temperance, etc. **2** *noun* person living at the time of Queen Victoria; *he wrote the biography of several eminent Victorians*

victorious [vɪk'tɔːrɪəs] *adjective* (person, general) who has won a game or a battle; *the victorious army marched into the town*

victory ['vɪktri] *noun* winning of a battle, a fight, a game, etc.; *they won a clear victory in the general election*; *the guerrillas won a victory over the government troops*; *the American victory in the Olympics*

video ['vɪdɪəu] **1** *noun* **(a)** electronic system which records, stores and reproduces pictures and sound; *using video, it is possible to show students the mistakes they have made and get them to correct them* **(b)** text, film or graphics which can be viewed on a television or monitor; *he was watching a video of the film*; *she borrowed the video from the public library* **2** *verb* to record pictures, a TV programme or film, etc., on magnetic tape; *I didn't see the programme because I was at work, but I've videoed it*

videocamera [vɪdɪəu'kæmərə] *noun* special camera for filming onto videotape; *he took his new videocamera to the wedding*

videocassette [vɪdɪəukə'set] *noun* small cassette containing a videotape; *he borrowed a videocassette of the wedding*; **videocassette recorder** = VIDEORECORDER

videorecorder [vɪdɪəurɪ'kɔːdə] *noun* machine which records television pictures on videotape, which can be played back later on your TV; *did you remember to set the videorecorder before we went out?*

videotape ['vɪdɪəuteɪp] **1** *noun* magnetic tape on which pictures and sound can be recorded for playing back on a television set; *he made a videotape of the film* **2** *verb* = VIDEO

vie [vaɪ] *verb* **to vie with someone** = to rival someone, to try to beat someone; *they vied with the German team for the gold medal*; *the best students are vying for the scholarship* (NOTE: **vying - vied**)

Vietnam [vjet'næm *US* [vjet'nɑːm]] *noun* country in south-east Asia, south of China (NOTE: capital: **Hanoi**; people: **the Vietnamese**; language: **Vietnamese**; currency: **dong**)

Vietnamese [vjetnə'miːz] **1** *adjective* referring to Vietnam **2** *noun* **(a)** person from Vietnam; **the Vietnamese** = people from Vietnam **(b)** language spoken in Vietnam; *if you are going to Vietnam you will need an English-Vietnamese phrase book*

view [vjuː] **1** *noun* **(a)** what you can see from a certain place; *you can get a good view of the sea from the church tower*; *we asked for a room with a sea view and were given one looking out over the bus depot* **(b)** photograph or picture; *here is a view of our house taken last year* **(c)** way of thinking about something; *in his view, the government ought to act now*; **point of view** = way of thinking; *try to see it from a teacher's point of view*; **to take a dim view of something** = not to think very highly of something; *he takes a dim view of members of staff turning up late for work* **(d)** **in view of** = because of; *in view of the stormy weather, we decided not to go sailing*; *(formal)* **with a view to** = with the aim of; *they bought the shop with a view to converting it into a restaurant* **2** *verb* **(a)** to watch; *the Queen viewed the procession from a special stand* **(b)** to consider; *he views the change of government as a disaster for the country*

viewer ['vjuːə] *noun* **(a)** person who watches TV; *the programme attracted ten million viewers* **(b)** small device through which you can look at colour slides; *she bought a little viewer to look at her slides*

viewfinder ['vjuːfaɪndə] *noun* small window in a camera through which you look when taking a picture, and which shows the exact picture you are about to take; *if you look through the viewfinder, you'll see a dot that will help you focus on the subject you want to photograph*

viewpoint ['vjuːpɔɪnt] *noun* particular way of thinking about things; *his viewpoint is not the same as mine*; *she looks at the project from the viewpoint of a mother with young children*

vigil ['vɪdʒɪl] *noun* **(a)** keeping awake, on guard all night; *nurses kept vigil by her bedside* **(b)** quiet remembrance of someone or something, held at night; *they are holding a candlelit vigil for children missing in the war*

vigilance ['vɪdʒɪləns] *noun* being on your guard to look out for crimes; *her vigilance paid off, and the police were able to catch the shoplifters*

vigilant ['vɪdʒɪlənt] *adjective* watchful, on guard; *the public was asked to be specially vigilant and tell the police about any suspect packages*; *parents must be vigilant and look out for the first signs of meningitis*

vigilante [vɪdʒɪ'lænti] *noun* person who is a member of group which tries to enforce law and order in their area, especially when the police seem to find it impossible to do so; *vigilantes travel on the underground late at night*

vigorous ['vɪgrəs] *adjective* very energetic, very strong; *he went for a vigorous run round the park*; *the plant has put out some vigorous shoots*

vigorously ['vɪgrəsli] *adverb* in a vigorous way; *she shook the blanket vigorously*; *if you exercise too vigorously, you may damage your heart*

vigour *US* **vigor** ['vɪgə] *noun* energy; *at the age of eighty-five he is still astonishingly full of vigour*; *they attacked the job of removing the rubbish with great vigour*

VII the Roman numeral for seven or seventh; *King Edward VII*

VIII the Roman numeral for eight or eighth; *King Henry VIII*

Vikings ['vaɪkɪŋz] *noun* ancient inhabitants of Scandinavia, who travelled widely in the early Middle Ages (8th to 10th centuries), and attacked and colonized parts of England and northern France

COMMENT: the Vikings (or Norsemen) invaded the north of England, Scotland and Ireland in the 8th and 9th centuries. They also were the invaders of Normandy, and the Norman chiefs, such as William the Conqueror, were descended from them

vile [vaɪl] *adjective* extremely unpleasant or bad; *it was a vile evening, drizzly, cold and with a dense fog*; *he came back from the office in a vile temper*

villa ['vɪlə] *noun* large country or seaside house, usually in a warm country; *he is staying in a villa on the Mediterranean*; *they are renting a villa in Greece for August*

village ['vɪlɪdʒ] *noun* small group of houses in the country, like a little town, with a church, and usually some shops; *they live in a little village in the Swiss Alps*; *the village shop sells just about everything we need*; *they are closing the village school because there aren't enough children*

villager ['vɪlɪdʒə] *noun* person who lives in a village; *the villagers were very surprised to see tourists in the middle of the winter*

villain ['vɪlən] *noun* (a) wicked character in a film, novel, etc.; *he plays the villain in the pantomime* (NOTE: the opposite, the good character, is the **hero**) (b) (*informal*) criminal; *the villains must be caught*

villainous ['vɪlənəs] *adjective* (*literary*) wicked; *the villainous landlord came to throw the family out of the house*

villainy ['vɪləni] *noun* (*formal*) wicked behaviour; *an old woman was attacked in her house - who could be capable of such villainy?*

vindicate ['vɪndɪkeɪt] *verb* to justify; to show that someone was right; *the report completely vindicated the action taken by the train driver*

vindication [vɪndɪ'keɪʃn] *noun* justification, proof that someone was right; *the result was a complete vindication of the captain's strategy*

vindictive [vɪn'dɪktɪv] *adjective* wanting to take revenge; spiteful; *she's particularly vindictive towards her former husband*

vine [vaɪn] *noun* climbing plant which produces grapes; *the hillsides along the Moselle are covered with vines*; *see also* GRAPEVINE

vinegar ['vɪnɪgə] *noun* liquid with a sharp taste, made from sour wine or cider, used in cooking and for pickling; *you can pickle onions in vinegar*

vinegary ['vɪnɪgri] *adjective* tasting like vinegar; *this wine is a bit vinegary*

vineyard ['vɪnjəd] *noun* area planted with vines for making wine; *there are some vineyards in southern England*; *we visited vineyards along the Moselle and bought some wine*

vintage ['vɪntɪdʒ] *noun* (a) fine wine made in a particular year; *1995 was a very good vintage*; *what vintage is it? - it's a 1968*; **vintage wine** = fine, expensive old wine made in a good year (b) year when something was made; **vintage car** = one made between

1917 and 1930 (c) of typical high quality of a certain person; *the film is vintage Laurel and Hardy*

vinyl ['vaɪnl] *noun* type of strong plastic sheet which can be made to look like other materials such as leather, tiles, etc.; *vinyl is not biodegradable*; *they covered the floor with vinyl tiles to look like marble*

viola [vaɪ'əʊlə] *noun* (a) small pansy-like garden flower (b) stringed instrument slightly larger than a violin; *she plays the viola in the city orchestra*

violate ['vaɪəleɪt] *verb* to break a rule, to go against the law; *the council has violated the planning regulations*; *the rebels violated the conditions of the peace treaty*; *the country has violated the international treaty banning the testing of nuclear weapons*

violation [vaɪə'leɪʃn] *noun* action of violating; *the attacked the fishing boats, in violation of the peace treaty*

violence ['vaɪələns] *noun* (a) action which is intended to hurt someone; *acts of violence must be punished* (b) great force; *the violence of her reaction surprised everyone*

violent ['vaɪələnt] *adjective* (a) very strong; *the discussion led to a violent argument*; *a violent snowstorm blew all night* (b) very severe; *he had a violent headache* (c) who commits acts of violence; *he husband was a very violent man* (d) **violent death** = death caused by an act of violence; *she died a violent death*

violently ['vaɪələntli] *adverb* (a) roughly, with force; *this horse threw him violently onto the ground*; *she hurled the bottle violently across the table* (b) strongly, with great feeling; *she violently rejected the accusations made against her*; *he reacted violently to the injection*; *the oysters made her violently sick*

violet ['vaɪələt] *noun* (a) small wild plant with bluish purple flowers which have a strong scent; *we picked a bunch of violets in the woods* (b) (*informal*) **no shrinking violet** = not a shy or timid person; *she's certainly no shrinking violet!* (c) bluish purple colour; *her lips turned violet as she gasped for breath*

violin [vaɪə'lɪn] *noun* stringed instrument played with a bow, smaller than the viola; *everyone listened to him playing the violin*

violinist [vaɪə'lɪnɪst] *noun* person who plays the violin; *she's a world renowned violinist*; *the school's looking for a violinist to teach small children*

VIP [viːaɪ'piː] = VERY IMPORTANT PERSON; *seats have been arranged for the VIPs at the front of the hall*; *we laid on VIP treatment for our visitors*; **VIP lounge** = special room at an airport for important travellers

viper ['vaɪpə] *noun* small European poisonous snake; *the viper is the only poisonous snake in England* (NOTE: also called an **adder**)

viral ['vaɪrəl] *adjective* caused by a virus, referring to a virus; *he caught viral pneumonia when travelling*; *it is often said that antibiotics have no effect against viral infections*

virgin ['vɜːdʒɪn] **1** *noun* (a) person who has never had sex; *she was a virgin until she was married* (b) (*Christian religion*) **the Virgin** = the mother of Jesus Christ; *an icon of the Virgin hung beside the altar* **2** *adjective* untouched by humans; in its natural state; *virgin rainforest is being cleared at the rate of 1,000* hectares per month; *we walked over fields of virgin snow*; **virgin land** = land which has never been cultivated

virginal ['vɜːdʒɪnəl] *adjective* pure, like a virgin; *her virginal innocence had disappeared long ago*

Virgin Mary ['vɜːdʒɪn 'meəri] *noun (Christian religion)* the mother of Jesus Christ; *an icon of the Virgin Mary hung beside the altar*; *the cult of the Virgin Mary has a prominent place in the Roman Catholic Church*

Virgo ['vɜːgəʊ] *noun* one of the signs of the Zodiac, shaped like a girl; *her birthday is at the beginning of September so that means she's (a) Virgo*

virile ['vɪraɪl] *adjective* with strong male characteristics; *his virile good looks attract young girls and some who are not so young*

virtual ['vɜːtʃuəl] *adjective* almost, nearly; *the company has a virtual monopoly of French wine imports*; *his grandfather has become a virtual recluse*

virtually ['vɜːtʃuəli] *adverb* almost; *these shirts have been reduced so much that we're virtually giving them away*; *it's virtually impossible to get tickets for the concert*

virtual reality ['vɜːtʃuəl rɪ'æliti] *noun* simulation of a real-life scene or real events on a computer; *this new virtual reality software can create a three-dimensional room*

virtue ['vɜːtjuː] *noun* **(a)** particular goodness of character; good quality; *honesty is his principal virtue* **(b)** special thing which gives you an advantage; *the virtue of the train link to France is that you arrive right in the centre of Paris* **(c)** *(formal)* **by virtue of** = as a result of; *he's eligible for British citizenship by virtue of his father who was born in Newcastle*

virtuoso [vɜːtʃu'əʊsəʊ] *noun* person who is skilled in an art, especially who can play a musical instrument extremely well; *the virtuoso cellist will give a series of concerts*; *he was given a standing ovation for his virtuoso performance* (NOTE: plural is **virtuosos** or **virtuosi** [vɜːtʃu'əʊsi])

virtuous ['vɜːtʃuəs] *adjective* **(a)** very good, very honest; *she was a virtuous old lady who never said a bad word against her neighbours* **(b)** feeling satisfied because you think that you have done something good; *there is nothing virtuous about going to the office on Saturday morning - we do it as a matter of course*; *she said she felt virtuous doing her exercises first thing in the morning*; *I won't have any pudding - I'll be virtuous*

virulent ['vɪrjʊlənt] *adjective* **(a)** violent (form of a disease, organism); *the new flu virus is said to be particularly virulent*; *he contracted a virulent form of the disease* **(b)** very harsh; *the newspaper carried a virulent attack on the Foreign Minister*

virus ['vaɪrəs] *noun* **(a)** tiny germ cell which can only develop in other cells and often destroys them; *scientists have isolated a new flu virus*; *shingles is caused by the same virus as chickenpox* **(b)** hidden routine placed in a computer program, which corrupts or destroys files; *you must check the program for viruses* (NOTE: plural is **viruses**)

COMMENT: many common diseases such as measles or the common cold are caused by viruses; these diseases cannot be treated with antibiotics

visa ['viːzə] *noun* special stamp on a passport allowing you to enter a country; *she filled in her visa application form*; *he applied for a tourist visa*; *you will need a visa to go to China*; **entry visa** = visa allowing someone to enter a country; **multiple entry visa** = visa allowing someone to enter a country many times; **tourist visa** = visa which allows a person to visit a country for a short time on holiday; **transit visa** = visa which allows someone to spend a short time in one country while travelling to another country

viscera ['vɪsərə] *noun* internal organs, such as the heart, lungs, stomach and intestines

visceral ['vɪsərəl] *adjective (formal)* **(a)** referring to the internal organs inside the body; *visceral muscles are muscles in the wall of the intestine which makes it contract* **(b)** strong and emotional, felt very deeply; *I have a visceral dislike of his paintings*

viscosity [vɪs'kɒsɪti] *noun* state of a liquid which moves slowly; *water and milk have low viscosity*

viscount ['vaɪkaʊnt] *noun* peer of lower rank, below an earl

COMMENT: viscounts are addressed as 'Lord' followed by the family name; their wives are addressed as 'Lady' followed by the family name

viscous ['vɪskəs] *adjective* thick, slow-moving; *honey is a viscous liquid*

vise [vaɪs] *noun US see* VICE (d)

visibility [vɪzɪ'bɪlɪti] *noun* ability to see clearly; *drivers are recommended to drive slowly because of poor visibility*; **good visibility** = ability for things to be seen at long distances because the air is clear; *the visibility is so good you can see the tower of the castle at least twenty kilometres away*

visible ['vɪzɪbl] *adjective* which can be seen; *the marks of the bullets were clearly visible on the car*; *everywhere in the forest there are visible signs of the effects of acid rain*; **visible imports** or **exports** = real products which are imported or exported; *compare* INVISIBLE

visibly ['vɪzɪbli] *adverb* in a way which everyone can see; *she was visibly annoyed by the television cameras*

vision ['vɪʒn] *noun* **(a)** eyesight, your ability to see; *after the age of 50, the vision of many people begins to fail*; **field of vision** = area which you can see over clearly; **tunnel vision** = (i) seeing only the area immediately in front of the eye; (ii) having the tendency to concentrate on only one aspect of a problem; **twenty/twenty vision (20/20 vision)** = perfectly normal eyesight **(b)** what you can see from where you are; *from the driver's seat you have excellent all round vision* **(c)** ability to look and plan ahead; *her vision of a free and prosperous society*; *we need a man of vision as college principal* **(d)** thing which you imagine; *he had visions of himself stuck in London with no passport and no money*; *she had visions of him being arrested for drug smuggling* **(e)** ghost; strange sight; *she saw a shadow-like vision walking along the castle walls*

visionary ['vɪʒnəri] **1** *adjective* idealistic, with original ideas; *his visionary designs influenced a whole generation* **2** *noun* person whose plans are idealistic and original; *as a biologist he was a pioneer and a visionary* (NOTE: plural is **visionaries**)

visit ['vɪzɪt] **1** *noun* short stay with someone, short stay in a town or a country; *they had a visit from the police*; *we will be making a short visit to London next week*; *the manager is on a business visit to China*; **to pay a visit to** = to go and see; *while we're in town, let's pay a visit to the local museum*; *we will pay my sister a visit on her birthday*; see also FLYING VISIT **2** *verb* to stay a short time with someone, to stay a short time in a town or country; *I am on my way to visit my sister in hospital*; *they are away visiting friends in the north of the country*; *the group of tourists are going to visit the glass factory*; *he spent a week in Scotland, visiting museums in Edinburgh and Glasgow*; **visiting hours** *or* **visiting times** = times of day when friends are allowed into a hospital to visit patients; **visiting team** = opposing team that have come to play against the home team

visitor ['vɪzɪtə] *noun* **(a)** person who comes to visit; *how many visitors come to museum each year?*; *we had a surprise visitor yesterday - the bank manager!*; **visitors' book** = book in which visitors to a museum or guests to a hotel write comments about the place; **visitors' bureau** *or* **visitor information centre** = office which deals with visitors' questions; **health visitor** = nurse who visits people in their homes to check their health; **prison visitor** = member of a group of people who visit, inspect and report on conditions in a prison; **summer visitor** = someone or a bird that only comes to this country in the summer; *the cuckoo is a summer visitor to Britain* **(b)** the visitors = VISITING TEAM

visor ['vaɪzə] *noun* **(a)** part of a helmet, which is hinged and can drop down to cover and protect the eyes; *he lifted his visor to talk to the policeman* **(b)** sun visor = little screen which folds down in front of a car driver, to keep the sun out of his eyes; *the visor's no use - the sun is coming from the side of the car*

vista ['vɪstə] *noun* wide view; *from the top of the tower a vista of snow-covered mountains opened up*; *the job offer opens up vistas of travel to all parts of the Pacific Rim*

visual ['vɪʒuəl] *adjective* referring to seeing; **visual aids** = maps, slides, films, etc., used to illustrate a lecture; *using slides or other visual aids would make the lecture more interesting*; **visual arts** = arts such as painting, sculpture, etc., which can be seen, as opposed to music which is listened to; *photography is one of the visual arts*

visualize ['vɪʒuəlaɪz] *verb* to have a picture of something in your mind; *I can just visualize myself driving a sports car down the motorway*; *can you visualize her as manager of the shop?*

vital ['vaɪtl] *adjective* **(a)** very important; *it is vital that the murderer should be caught*; *oxygen is vital to human life* **(b)** vigorous, energetic; *his vital energy comes out in his paintings* **(c)** vital organs = the most important organs in the body (such as the heart, lungs, brain) without which a human being cannot live

vitality [vaɪ'tælɪti] *noun* great energy; *her incomparable vitality is the key to her success*; *he started working at the new project with renewed vitality*

vital statistics ['vaɪtl stə'tɪstɪks] *noun* **(a)** official statistics concerning births, marriages and deaths in a certain area; *a government publication with vital statistics about the changing population* **(b)** (*informal, as a joke*) measurements of a woman's bust, waist and hips; *her vital statistics are in all the tabloid newspapers*

vitamin ['vɪtəmɪn] *noun* essential substance which is not synthesized by the body but is found in food and is needed for growth and health; *make sure your diet contains enough vitamins*; **vitamin deficiency** = lack of necessary vitamins; *he is suffering from Vitamin A deficiency*

vivid ['vɪvɪd] *adjective* **(a)** very bright; *vivid yellow sunflowers*; *the vivid colours of the Mediterranean beach* **(b)** very lively, very lifelike; *she has a vivid imagination*; *the play is a vivid portrayal of country life*; *I had a really vivid dream last night*; *she gave a vivid account of her experiences at the hands of the kidnappers*

vividly ['vɪvɪdli] *adjective* in a vivid way; *she described vividly how the family had been attacked*; *I vividly remember that trip to China*

vixen ['vɪksn] *noun* female fox; *a vixen and her cubs*

V-neck ['viːnek] *noun* dress, pullover, etc., with a neck shaped like a V; *he's wearing a dark blue V-neck pullover*

vocabulary [və'kæbjuləri] *noun* **(a)** words used by a person or group of persons; *reading stories to little children helps them expand their vocabulary*; *she reads a lot of French newspapers to improve her vocabulary*; *the dictionary will give you some of the specialist legal vocabulary you will need in your job* **(b)** printed list of words; *there is a German-English vocabulary at the back of the book* (NOTE: plural is **vocabularies**)

vocal ['vəukl] **1** *adjective* **(a)** referring to the voice; *singers need to do vocal exercises daily*; **vocal cords** = folds in the larynx which are brought together to make sounds when air passes between them **(b)** very loud (in protest); *the protesters were very vocal at the demonstration* **2** *noun* **vocals** = the part of a piece of pop music that is sung; *on this track the group is joined by Graham doing the vocals*

vocalist ['vəukəlɪst] *noun* singer, especially in a pop group; *she is the vocalist with a Scottish pop group*; *compare* INSTRUMENTALIST

vocation [və'keɪʃn] *noun* work which you feel you have been called to do or for which you have a special talent; *for her, being a nurse is a vocation*; **she missed her vocation** = she should be in another job for which she is better suited; *I think she missed her vocation - she would have been an excellent doctor*

vocational [və'keɪʃnl] *adjective* referring to a vocation; *the college offers vocational studies for mature students*; **vocational training** = training for a particular job, such as doctor, nurse, dentist, etc.; *consider vocational training if you want to become a dental nurse*

vociferous [və'sɪfərəs] *adjective* shouting loudly; *the vociferous protests from the crowd*; *some vociferous fans in the stand shouted abuse at the opposing side*

vodka ['vɒdkə] *noun* **(a)** strong, colourless alcohol made from grain or potatoes, originally in Russia and Poland; *we talked over a glass of vodka* **(b)** glass of this alcohol; *a couple of vodkas, please*

vogue [vəug] *noun* fashion; *are these shoes the latest vogue?; the vogue for wearing bright red braces seems to have disappeared;* in vogue = fashionable; *this year, black is back in vogue again*

voice [vɔɪs] **1** *noun* **(a)** sound made when you speak or sing; *I didn't recognize his voice over the telephone; the chairman spoke for a few minutes in a low voice* **(b)** to lose your voice = not to be able to speak; *she's got a sore throat and has lost her voice;* to raise your voice = to start to shout; at the top of your voice = very loudly; *he suddenly said 'look at that funny hat' at the top of his voice* **(c)** *(grammar)* passive voice *see* PASSIVE **2** *verb* to tell what you think; *she voiced her objections to the plan*

voice box ['vɔɪs 'bɒks] *noun* the larynx, the upper part of the windpipe, where sounds are made by the voice

void [vɔɪd] *(formal)* **1** *adjective* **(a)** invalid, which cannot be used lawfully; *after the revelations of cheating, the competition was declared void;* null and void = no longer valid; *the contract was declared null and void* **(b)** to be void of = to lack completely; *the sentence is void of any meaning* **2** *noun* emptiness; *he tried to fill the void in his life caused by the death of his wife; she stood on the bridge for a few minutes, looking down into the void* **3** *verb* **(a)** to mark a document to show that it cannot be used lawfully; *the airline voided the ticket and issued a new one* **(b)** to void a contract = to make a contract invalid; *their action had the effect of voiding the contract*

volatile ['vɒlətaɪl] *adjective* **(a)** *(substance)* which can easily change into gas at normal temperatures; *canisters of highly volatile liquid petroleum gas* **(b)** changing your mind or mood frequently; *the voters are very volatile* **(c)** not stable, likely to move up or down sharply; *a volatile stock market*

volcanic [vɒl'kænɪk] *adjective* referring to volcanoes; *scientists are expecting another volcanic eruption*

volcano [vɒl'keɪnəu] *noun* mountain with a hole on the top through which lava, ash and gas can come out; *the volcano erupted last year* (NOTE: plural is **volcanoes**)

COMMENT: volcanoes occur along faults in the earth's surface and exist in well-known chains. Some are extinct, but others erupt relatively frequently. Some are always active, in that they send out gas and smoke, without actually erupting. Volcanoes are popular tourist attractions: the best-known in Europe are Vesuvius, Stromboli and Etna in Italy and Helgafell in Iceland; the best-known in North America is Mount St Helen's in Washington State. There are no volcanoes in the British Isles

vole [vəul] *noun* small animal, like a mouse, but with a shorter tail; *voles form part of the diet of owls*

volley ['vɒli] **1** *noun* **(a)** series of shots fired at the same time; *the police fired a volley into the crowd; volleys of gunfire could be heard in the distance* **(b)** *(in sport)* hitting the ball before it touches the ground; *he managed to return a very difficult volley* **2** *verb* *(in sport)* to hit the ball before it touches the ground; *he volleyed to win the match*

volleyball ['vɒlibɔːl] *noun* Olympic sport played on a rectangular court between two teams of six, in which a large inflated ball is hit over a high net with the hands, and the object is to prevent the ball touching the floor of the court; *we all played volleyball on the beach*

COMMENT: volleyball can be played by men and women, both indoors and outdoors, although competitive matches take place indoors.

volt [vəult] *noun* standard unit of for measuring electric force; *in most of Europe, electric appliances work on 240 volts (240V)*

voltage ['vəultɪdʒ] *noun* electric force expressed in volts; *fluctuations in voltage can affect your computer; the plane touched a high-voltage cable; the voltage is different in Canada, so make sure your hair dryer can be switched from 240V to 110V*

COMMENT: the voltage in many countries (USA, Canada, Japan, etc.) is 110V. In Europe, South-East Asia and Africa, voltage is usually 220V or 240V. You sometimes need a transformer to get electrical appliances to work in different countries

voluble ['vɒljubl] *adjective* who talks a lot, who talks very quickly; *her voluble friend was on the phone for hours; he suddenly switched into voluble Arabic*

volubly ['vɒljubli] *adverb* talking very quickly; *she spoke volubly about her research*

volume ['vɒljuːm] *noun* **(a)** one book, especially one in a series; *have you read the third volume of his history of medieval Europe?* **(b)** capacity, amount which is contained inside something; *what is the volume of this barrel?* **(c)** amount of something; *the volume of traffic on the motorway was far more than usual* **(d)** amount of sound; *she turned down the volume on the radio; he drives with the car radio on at full volume*

voluminous [və'ljuːmɪnəs] *adjective* large; which takes up a lot of space; *she put the packets into the pockets of her voluminous coat; the voluminous report was handed out to the journalists*

voluntarily ['vɒləntrəli] *adverb* willingly; *he surrendered voluntarily to the police*

voluntary ['vɒləntri] *adjective* **(a)** done because you want to do it, and without being paid; *many retired people do voluntary work;* voluntary organization = organization which does not receive funding from the government but relies on contributions from the public or from business; *see also* VSO **(b)** done willingly, without being forced; *he made a voluntary contribution to the fund;* voluntary redundancy = situation where a worker asks to be made redundant usually in return for a large payment

volunteer [vɒlən'tɪə] **1** *noun* **(a)** person who offers to do something without being paid or being forced to do it; *the school relies on volunteers to help with the sports day; the information desk is manned by volunteers* **(b)** soldier who has joined the army willingly, without being forced; *the volunteers had two weeks' intensive training and then were sent to the front line* **2** *verb* **(a)** to offer to do something without being paid or being forced to do it; *he volunteered to collect the entrance tickets; will anyone volunteer for the job of washing up?* **(b)** to join the armed services because you want to, without being forced; *he volunteered for the Royal Navy* **(c)** to give information without being forced to do so; *she volunteered a statement to the police*

voluptuous [vəˈlʌptʃuəs] *adjective* evoking sensual pleasure; *he watched the voluptuous dancing girls*; *voluptuous music mingled with exotic perfumes*

vomit [ˈvɒmɪt] **1** *noun* partly digested food which has been brought up into the mouth from the stomach; *there was vomit all over the bathroom floor*; *he choked on his own vomit* **2** *verb* to bring up partly digested food into your mouth; *he vomited last night and now has a high temperature*; *she vomited her breakfast*

vortex [ˈvɔːteks] *noun* (*formal*) flow of a liquid or a gas which is turning round and round very fast in a whirlpool or whirlwind (NOTE: plural is **vortices** [ˈvɔːtɪsiːz])

vote [vəʊt] **1** *noun* (**a**) marking a paper, holding up your hand, etc., to show your opinion or who you want to be elected; *how many votes did you get?*; *there were only ten votes against the plan*; **to take a vote on a proposal** *or* **to put a proposal to the vote** = to ask people present at a meeting to say if they agree or do not agree with the proposal; **to cast a vote** = to vote; *the number of votes cast in the election was 125,458* (**b**) act of voting; **vote of no confidence** = vote to show disapproval of the government, etc.; *they passed a vote of no confidence in the chairman*; **postal vote** = election where the voters send in their voting papers by post; *the result of the postal vote will be known next week* (**c**) the right to vote in elections; *only in 1928 were women given the vote* (**d**) number of votes made by a group of voters; *no one knows where the youth vote will go* **2** *verb* to mark a paper, to hold up your hand, etc., to show your opinion or who you want to be elected; *fifty per cent of the people voted in the election*; *we all voted to go on strike*; **to vote for a proposal** *or* **to vote against a proposal** = to say that you agree *or* do not agree with a proposal; *twenty people actually voted for the proposal to demolish the old church*

vote of thanks [ˈvəʊt əv ˈθæŋks] *noun* situation where someone has done something and is thanked officially by the whole committee; *she proposed a vote of thanks to the outgoing treasurer*

voter [ˈvəʊtə] *noun* person who votes or who has the right to vote; *voters stayed at home because of the bad weather*; *the voters were queuing outside the polling stations from early morning*; **floating voter** = person who is not sure which party to vote for in an election

vote-rigging [ˈvəʊtˈrɪgɪŋ] *noun* arranging a vote to give a dishonest result

voucher [ˈvaʊtʃə] *noun* paper which is given instead of money; *enclosed is a voucher to be presented at the reception desk of the hotel when you arrive*; *with every £20 of purchases, the customer gets a cash voucher to the value of £2*; **gift voucher** = card bought in a store, which you give as a present and which must be exchanged in that store for goods; *it will be simpler to give her a gift voucher since we can't decide on a present*; **luncheon voucher** = ticket given by an employer to a worker which can be exchanged for food in a restaurant; *the sandwich bar will accept luncheon vouchers*

vouch for [ˈvaʊtʃ ˈfɔː] *verb* to guarantee that something is true, that someone will behave well; *we can't vouch for the statement put out by the publicity department*; *I can vouch for Miss Smith - she's one of the best cashiers we ever had*

vow [vaʊ] **1** *noun* solemn promise; *he made a vow to go on a pilgrimage to Jerusalem*; *she vowed to have her revenge but she died before she could keep her vow* **2** *verb* (*formal*) to make a solemn promise to do something; *he vowed to pay the money back*

vowel [ˈvaʊəl] *noun* one of the five letters (a, e, i. o, u) which represent sounds made without using the teeth, tongue or lips; *'b' and 't' are consonants, while 'e' and 'i' are vowels* (NOTE: the letters representing sounds which are not vowels are **consonants**; note also that in some languages 'y' is a vowel)

voyage [ˈvɔɪdʒ] *noun* long journey, especially by ship; *the voyages of Sir Francis Drake*

voyager [ˈvɔɪdʒə] *noun* person who goes on a long journey by ship; *the book is about a Jewish voyager who travelled from Italy to China in the thirteenth century*

vs [ˈvɜːsəs] *see* VERSUS

VSO [viːˈesəʊ] = VOLUNTARY SERVICE OVERSEAS British organization which sends people to developing countries overseas to help to improve the living standards of the people; *she went to work for the VSO in Kenya*; *he's a VSO teacher in a college in Ethiopia* (NOTE: the American equivalent is the **Peace Corps**)

vulgar [ˈvʌlgə] *adjective* (**a**) rude or indecent; *don't use that sort of vulgar language in front of the children*; *he made a vulgar gesture at the policeman* (**b**) not in good taste; *his pink Rolls Royce is particularly vulgar* (**c**) **vulgar fraction** = fraction written as one number above and another below a line

vulgarity [vʌlˈgærɪti] *noun* being vulgar; not being in good taste; *the vulgarity of TV Christmas shows is so depressing*

vulnerable [ˈvʌlnərəbl] *adjective* which can be easily hurt; *she is vulnerable to criticism*; *children of that age are particularly vulnerable*; *premature babies are vulnerable to infection*

vulture [ˈvʌltʃə] *noun* (**a**) large bird that mainly eats dead animals; *vultures live by scavenging on the corpses of animals which have died*; *scavengers like vultures wait in the trees near where the lions are hunting* (**b**) greedy person; *when she died, all the relatives descended on her flat like vultures*

vulva [ˈvʌlvə] *noun* the external sexual organs of a woman; *this is a common infection of the vulva*

Ww

W, w ['dʌbl juː] twenty-third letter of the alphabet, between V and X; *'one' is pronounced as if it starts with a W*

W = WATT

wacky ['wæki] *adjective* (*informal*) crazy or silly; *he's wacky, but he's very clever and very interesting; who do you think wrote this wacky article for April Fool's Day?* (NOTE: **wackier - wackiest**)

wad [wɒd] **1** *noun* (**a**) thick piece of soft material; *the nurse put a sterile wad on the sore* (**b**) thick pile of banknotes or papers; *he had a wad of banknotes in his hand; the hole was blocked with a wad of old papers* (**c**) (*informal*) thick sandwich **2** *verb* US to press something into a thick ball; *wad up some newspapers to help light the fire* (NOTE: **wadding - wadded**)

wadding ['wɒdɪŋ] *noun* material used to cover a wound or to wrap delicate objects; *there wasn't enough wadding in the box* (NOTE: no plural)

wade [weɪd] *verb* (**a**) to walk through water; *the explorers had to wade across a river* (**b**) to wade into someone = to attack someone fiercely; *in his article he waded into the government*; **to wade through a technical journal** = to read through a boring technical journal

wader ['weɪdə] *noun* (**a**) bird which spends most of its time in or near shallow water; *we saw several types of waders near the estuary* (**b**) **waders** = long waterproof boots worn by fishermen; *he pulled on an old pair of waders*

wafer ['weɪfə] *noun* (**a**) thin sweet biscuit eaten with ice cream; *a cup of vanilla and chocolate ice cream, with a wafer in it* (**b**) **communion wafer** = thin round piece of bread eaten at mass or communion

wafer-thin ['weɪfə'θɪn] *adjective* very thin, as thin as a wafer; *the government has only a wafer-thin majority in Parliament*

waffle ['wɒfl] **1** *noun* (**a**) type of crisp pancake cooked in an iron mould and eaten with syrup; *we bought waffles at the stall in the fairground; waffles are very popular in Belgium* (**b**) unnecessary or muddled speaking or writing; *you don't need to read the article, it is just waffle; don't tell me you listened to all his waffle!* (NOTE: no plural in this meaning) **2** *verb* to talk too much without saying anything clearly; *what are you waffling on about?; if someone mentions the word 'ecology', our lecturer will waffle on for 20 minutes*

waft [wɒft] **1** *noun* gentle smell; *when I opened the box, a waft of spices reminded me of the Far East* **2** *verb* to carry something gently through the air; *the delicious smell of strawberry jam wafted through the window to where I was sitting*

wag [wæg] **1** *verb* (**a**) to move from side to side or up and down; *the dog ran up to him, wagging its tail; the grandmother wagged her finger at the little boy who was picking the flowers* (**b**) (*informal*) **tongues are wagging** = people are talking about something they do not approve of; *you can imagine that her being seen with him set tongues wagging in the village* (NOTE: **wagging - wagged**) **2** *noun* (**a**) movement from side to side or up and down (**b**) (*old*) (*informal*) person who likes making jokes or facetious remarks; *he's a bit of a wag and likes to make silly jokes during lectures*

wage *or* **wages** [weɪdʒ *or* 'weɪdʒɪz] **1** *noun* money paid, usually in cash each week, to a worker for work done; *all work came to a stop when the firm couldn't pay the workers' wages; her wages can't keep up with the cost of living; the company pays quite good wages; she is earning a good wage or good wages in the pizza restaurant*; **wage freeze** = period when wages are not allowed to increase; **basic wage** = normal pay without any extra payments; *the basic wage is £110 a week, but you can expect to earn more than that with overtime*; **hourly wage** *or* **wage per hour** = amount of money paid for an hour's work workers; *they are paid by the hour and the hourly wage is very low*; **a living wage** = enough money to live on; *he doesn't earn a living wage*; **minimum wage** = lowest hourly wage which a company can legally pay its; *a statutory minimum wage has existed in some countries for years* (NOTE: used both in the singular and the plural: **he doesn't earn a living wage; her wages are £500 a week**) **2** *verb* **to wage war on** = to fight against; *the government is waging war on homelessness; the police are waging war on drug dealers*

wage-earner ['weɪdʒ 'ɜːnə] *noun* person who is paid a wage; *the average wage-earner can't afford a car*

wage packet ['weɪdʒ 'pækɪt] *noun* envelope containing a worker's weekly wages; amount of money a worker earns each week; *he used to give his entire wage packet to his wife*

wager ['weɪdʒə] **1** *noun* bet, money which you promise to pay if something you expect to happen does not take place; *she made a wager that the government would lose the election* **2** *verb* to bet; *I'll wager that they will arrive late*

waggle ['wægl] *verb* to move from side to side quickly; *she waggled her hips as she walked across the stage; he waggled the letter in front of my face and asked me what I was going to do about it*

wagon ['wægn] *noun* (**a**) railway truck used for carrying heavy loads; *the container wagons are leaving the freight terminal* (**b**) (*informal*) **on the wagon** = not drinking alcohol; *he's been on the wagon for the last three months* (**c**) (*old*) heavy cart pulled by horses or oxen (NOTE: also spelt **waggon** in British English)

wail [weɪl] **1** *noun* high-pitched sad cry; *the wails of the mourners at the funeral* (NOTE: do not confuse with **whale**) **2** *verb* to make a high-pitched mournful cry; *at the news, she just sat down and wailed*

waist [weɪst] *noun* (**a**) narrower part of the body between the bottom of the chest and the hips; *she*

measures 32 inches round the waist *or* she has a
32-inch waist **(b)** part of a piece of clothing such as a
skirt, trousers or dress, that goes round the middle of the
body; *the waist of these trousers is too small for me*
(NOTE: do not confuse with **waste**)

waistcoat ['weɪskəʊt] *noun* short coat with buttons
and without any sleeves, which is worn over a shirt and
under a jacket; *a three-piece suit has a jacket, trousers
and waistcoat* (NOTE: American English is **vest**)

waistline ['weɪstlaɪn] *noun* measurement around
your waist, showing how fat you are; **he has to watch
his waistline** = he's trying not to get fat

wait [weɪt] **1** *verb* **(a)** to stay where you are or not do
anything until something happens or someone comes;
wait here while I call an ambulance; *they had been
waiting for half an hour in the rain before the bus
finally arrived*; *wait a minute, my shoelace is undone*;
don't wait for me, I'll be late; *we gave our order half
an hour ago, but are still waiting for the first course*;
*the man didn't come on Friday, so we had to wait until
Monday to have the fridge repaired* **(b)** to keep
someone waiting = to make someone wait because you
are late; *the boss doesn't like being kept waiting*; *sorry
to have kept you waiting!* **(c)** to wait on someone = to
serve food and drink to someone, especially in a
restaurant; **to wait on someone hand and foot** = to do
everything for someone; *he just sits around watching
TV, and his mother waits on him hand and foot* **(d)** to
wait a meal for someone = not to serve a meal at the
usual time because you are waiting for someone to
arrive; *don't wait dinner for me, I'm going to be late* **2**
noun time spent waiting until something happens or
arrives; *you've just missed the bus - you will have a
very long wait for the next one*; **to lie in wait for
someone** = to hide and wait for someone to come so as
to attack him; *the lions were lying in wait near the
waterhole* (NOTE: do not confuse with **weight**)

waiter ['weɪtə] *noun* man who brings food and drink
to customers in a restaurant; *the waiter still hasn't
brought us the first course*; *shall we give the waiter a
tip?*; **head waiter** = person in charge of other waiters;
see also WAITRESS

waiting ['weɪtɪŋ] **1** *noun* **(a)** action of serving people
in a restaurant, etc.; *I find waiting very boring* **(b)**
action of parking by the side of a street; *he stopped his
car in front of a 'no waiting' sign* **2** *adjective* who is
waiting; *she came out of the meeting to speak to the
waiting journalists*

waiting list ['weɪtɪŋ 'lɪst] *noun* list of people waiting
for a service or medical treatment; *we have been put on
the waiting list for a council flat*; *there is a waiting list
of people hoping to get on the flight*; *hospital waiting
lists are going to be reduced*

waiting room ['weɪtɪŋ 'ruːm] *noun* room where you
wait at a doctor's, dentist's or at a railway station; *take
a seat in the waiting room - the dentist will be free in a
few minutes*

waitress ['weɪtrəs] *noun* woman who brings food
and drink to customers in a restaurant; *the waitress
brought us the menu*; *shall we give the waitress as a
tip?*; *see also* WAITER (NOTE: plural is **waitresses**)

wait up ['weɪt 'ʌp] *verb* not to go to bed because you
are waiting for someone; *don't wait up for us - we'll be
very late*

waive [weɪv] *verb* to give up a right or a claim; *the
police waived the fine because it was an emergency*

delivery; *in exceptional cases, the fee may be waived*
(NOTE: do not confuse with **wave**)

waiver ['weɪvə] *noun* document showing that
someone is willingly to give up a right or claim; *if you
want to work without a permit, you will have to apply
for a waiver*; *they signed a waiver giving up their right
to the land* (NOTE: do not confuse with **waver**)

wake [weɪk] **1** *verb* **(a)** to stop someone's sleep; *the
telephone woke her or she was woken by the
telephone*; *I banged on her door, but I can't wake her*;
he asked to be woken at 7.00 **(b)** to stop sleeping; *he
woke suddenly, feeling drops of water falling on his
head* (NOTE: **waking - woke** [wəʊk] **- has woken**) **2**
noun **(a)** white waves following a boat as it goes
through the water; *the ferry's wake rocked the little
boat* **(b) in the wake of** = following something,
immediately after something; *the management has to
decide what to do in the wake of the sales director's
resignation*

wakeful ['weɪkfʊl] *adjective* not at all sleepy, not
wanting to sleep; *we spent several wakeful nights by
his bed in hospital*; *the children were excited and still
wakeful at 10 o'clock*

waken ['weɪkn] *verb (formal)* to make someone wake
up; *she wakened the sleeping children and led them to
safety*; *I wonder what wakens me every night at 3
o'clock*; *he always sleeps soundly, even an earthquake
wouldn't waken him*

waken up ['weɪkn 'ʌp] *verb (formal)* to stop
sleeping; *splash cold water on your face to try to
waken up*

wake up ['weɪk 'ʌp] *verb* **(a)** to stop someone's
sleep; *he was woken up by the sound of the dog
barking* **(b)** to stop sleeping; *she woke up in the middle
of the night*; *come on, wake up! it's past ten o'clock*;
*he woke up to find water coming through the roof of
the tent*; **wake-up call** = phone call from the hotel
switchboard to wake a guest up **(c)** to wake up to = to
realize; *when is he going to wake up to the fact that he
is never going to be promoted?*

waking ['weɪkɪŋ] *adjective* awake, not asleep; *all his
waking hours were spent looking for his lost daughter*

Wales [weɪlz] *noun* country to the west of England,
forming part of the United Kingdom; *there are some
high mountains in North Wales*

walk [wɔːk] **1** *verb* **(a)** to go on foot; *the baby is ten
months old, and is just starting to walk*; *she was
walking along the high street on her way to the bank*;
the marchers walked across Westminster Bridge; *the
visitors walked round the factory*; **to walk someone
home** = to go with someone who is walking home; *it
was getting late, so I walked her home* **(b)** to take an
animal for a walk; *he's gone to walk the dog in the
fields* **2** *noun* **(a)** usually pleasant journey on foot; *let's
all go for a walk in the park* **(b)** going on foot; *it's only
a short walk to the beach*; *it's only a five minutes'
walk from the office to the bank or the bank is only a
five minutes' walk from the office* **(c)** path where you
can walk; *we hiked along one of the long-distance
walks in the hills* **(d)** organized route for walking; *we
went on a walk round Dickens' London*; *are you
coming on the sponsored walk for refugees?* **(e)** way
of walking; *he has the walk of an old man, even if he's
not 50 yet*

walk about ['wɔːk ə'baʊt] *verb* to walk in various
directions; *we walked about looking for a restaurant*

walkabout ['wɔːkəbaut] *noun* informal walk among a crowd, by an important person; *the Queen looked relaxed during her walkabout*; *the crowd seemed hostile, so the president decided not to go on his planned walkabout*

walker ['wɔːkə] *noun* person who goes walking for pleasure and exercise; *he's a keen walker, and goes walking in Scotland every summer*

walkie-talkie [wɔːki'tɔːki] *noun (informal)* portable two-way radio; *he called another security guard on his walkie-talkie*

walk-in ['wɔːkɪn] *adjective* big enough for you to walk into; *there's a walk-in cupboard leading off the kitchen*

walking ['wɔːkɪŋ] *noun* going on foot as a relaxation, along paths, up mountains, etc.; *they like to go walking at the weekends*; *we went on a walking holiday in the Lake District*; **walking shoes** = heavy shoes, suitable for walking long distances; *buy a pair of proper walking shoes if you plan to go walking in the Alps*

walking stick ['wɔːkɪŋ 'stɪk] *noun* strong wooden or metal stick with a handle used as a support when walking; *at the age of 93, she finally agreed to use a walking stick*

walk into ['wɔːk 'ɪn] *verb* to enter on foot; *she walked into the waiting room and sat down*

Walkman ['wɔːkmən] *noun* trademark for a small portable cassette player which you can carry around with you and which has headphones for you to listen to music with; *the chap next to me in the Underground had his Walkman on full blast*; *he likes to listen to rock music on his Walkman*

walk off ['wɔːk 'ɒf] *verb* **(a)** to go away on foot; *she walked off and left him holding the shopping*; *the builders walked off the site because they said it was too dangerous* **(b) to walk off your dinner** = to go for a walk to help you digest your dinner

walk off with ['wɔːk 'ɒf wɪð] *verb* **(a)** to win; *she walked off with first prize* **(b)** to steal; *the burglar walked off with all my silver cups*

walk of life ['wɔːk əv 'laɪf] *noun* occupation or social position; *people from all walks of life came to his funeral*

walk-on part ['wɔːkɒn 'pɑːt] *noun* part in a play where the actor doesn't have to speak; *he pleaded with his teacher and was given a walk-on part in the school play*

walk out ['wɔːk 'aut] *verb* **(a)** to go out on foot; *she walked out of the house and down the street* **(b)** to go out angrily; *he walked out of the restaurant, saying that the service was too slow* **(c)** *(of workers)* to go on strike, to stop working and leave your office or factory; *the office staff walked out in protest* **(d) to walk out on someone** = to leave someone suddenly; *she walked out on her husband and went to live with her mother*; *our head salesman walked out on us just as we were starting our autumn sales campaign*

walkout ['wɔːkaut] *noun* strike of workers; *the staff staged a walkout in protest*

walk up ['wɔːk 'ʌp] *verb* **(a)** to climb on foot; *I never take the lift - I always walk up the three flights of stairs to my office* **(b) to walk up to someone** = to go up to someone on foot; *she walked up to me and asked if I needed any help*

walkway ['wɔːkweɪ] *noun* outdoor path where you can walk between buildings, usually raised above ground level; *there's a covered walkway between the car park and the hotel*; *a row erupted over the closure of the walkway linking the station to London Road*

wall [wɔːl] *noun* **(a)** bricks, stones, etc., built up to make one of the sides of a building, of a room or to surround a space; *the walls of the restaurant are decorated with pictures of film stars*; *there's a clock on the wall behind my desk*; *he got into the house by climbing over the garden wall*; *the garden is surrounded by an old stone wall* **(b)** *(informal)* **to drive** *or* **send someone up the wall** = to make someone very annoyed; *the noise of the pneumatic drills outside the office is sending me up the wall* **(c) wall of silence** = plot by everyone to say nothing about what has happened; *the police investigation met with a wall of silence* **(d) walls** = thick stone construction round an old town; *you can walk all round York on the old town walls*

wallaby ['wɒləbi] *noun* **(a)** Australian animal like a small kangaroo **(b)** *(informal)* the Australian international rugby team; *compare* ALL BLACKS, SPRINGBOKS

walled [wɔːld] *adjective* surrounded with walls; *they visited several old walled towns in South-West France*

wallet ['wɒlɪt] *noun* small flat leather case for credit cards and banknotes, carried in your pocket; *my wallet was pinched in the crowd*; *his wallet was stolen from his back pocket*; *do not leave your wallet on the car seat* (NOTE: American English is **billfold**)

wallow ['wɒləu] *verb* **(a)** *(of animals)* to roll delightedly around in mud; *when I hear of animals wallowing in mud, I immediately think of hippos* **(b)** *(of person)* to take too much pleasure in; *he positively wallows in gossip about media people*; *it's time she stopped wallowing in self-pity*

wallpaper ['wɔːlpeɪpə] **1** *noun* paper with different patterns on it, covering the walls of a room; *the wallpaper was light green to match the carpet* **2** *verb* to stick wallpaper on walls; *she spent the weekend wallpapering the dining room*

Wall Street ['wɔːl 'striːt] *noun* **(a)** street in New York where the Stock Exchange is situated; *he walked along Wall Street, looking for the company's offices* **(b)** American finance centre in New York; *Wall Street reacted cautiously to the interest rise* (NOTE: here the name of the street is used to mean the American financial markets in general)

wall-to-wall ['wɔːltu'wɔːl] *adjective* covering the entire floor of a room; *the floor is covered with a thick pale wall-to-wall carpet*

wall up ['wɔːl 'ʌp] *verb* to block a door, an entrance, etc., with a wall; *the entrance to the tomb was walled up and forgotten for centuries*

walnut ['wɔːlnʌt] *noun* **(a)** hard round nut with a wrinkled shell; *he cracked the walnuts with the nutcrackers*; *a scoop of maple and walnut ice cream* **(b)** tree on which walnuts grow; *the walnuts or walnut trees have produced a huge crop this year* **(c)** wood from a walnut tree; *the beautifully dark walnut panelling in my office*

walrus ['wɒlrəs] *noun* animal which looks like a large seal, with two long tusks pointing downwards; *(informal)* **walrus moustache** = long drooping moustache (NOTE: plural is **walruses**)

waltz [wɒls] 1 *noun* (a) slow dance in which a man and woman turn around together as they move forward; *the next dance is a waltz, so I'll ask her to dance* (b) music suitable for such a dance; *listen, the orchestra is playing a waltz; the 'Blue Danube' is one of Strauss' most famous waltzes* (NOTE: plural is **waltzes**) 2 *verb* (a) to dance together; *couples were waltzing elegantly around the ballroom* (b) (*informal*) to do something smoothly or happily; *she waltzed into the bank and said she wanted to withdraw $200,000 in cash; he waltzed off with first prize*

wan [wɒn] *adjective* (*formal*) pale, looking ill; *it was sad to see her wan little face at the window*

wand [wɒnd] *noun* thin stick used to make magic; *the fairy waved her magic wand and the pumpkin turned into a coach*

wander ['wɒndə] *verb* (a) to walk around without any particular aim; *they wandered round the town in the rain*; to wander away *or* wander off = to walk away from where you are supposed to be; *two of the party wandered off into the market* (b) to stop thinking about the current problem and think about something else; *sorry - my mind was wandering, thinking about the garden; he is old and his mind is wandering* = he no longer thinks clearly

wanderer ['wɒndrə] *noun* person who wanders from place to place, with no permanent home; *he's a wanderer and can't settle down*

wanderings ['wɒndrɪŋz] *noun* (*formal*) long journeys, visiting various places; *he wrote a book about his family's wanderings in Europe during the Second World War*

wane [weɪn] 1 *noun* the moon is on the wane = appears to be getting smaller; his influence is on the wane = his influence is diminishing 2 *verb* to appear smaller; to decrease; *his influence over his family is waning; he takes vitamin tablets to boost his waning energy*

want [wɒnt] 1 *verb* (a) to hope that you will do something, that something will happen, that you will get something; *she wants a new car for her birthday; where do you want to go for your holidays?; he wants to be a teacher; do you want any more tea?* (b) to ask someone to do something; *the manager wants me to go and see him; I want those windows painted* (c) to need; *with five children, what they want is a bigger house; the kitchen ceiling wants painting* (d) to look for someone; *the bank manager has disappeared and is wanted by the police* 2 *noun* (a) lack of something; *a want of funds has hindered the development programme*; in want of something = needing something; *the kitchen is in want of a good clean; he looks as though he's in want of a good meal*; for want of something better = as something better is not available; *for want of something better to do we went to the cinema* (b) desire for something; *their greatest want is for new clothes*; wants = things needed; *their wants are too numerous to count*; to draw up a wants list = to make a list of things which you need

wanton ['wɒntn] *adjective* wild or undisciplined; *the wanton destruction of the old palaces; reports of wanton killings reach us every day*

war [wɔː] *noun* (a) fighting between countries; *millions of soldiers and civilians were killed during the war; in 1914 Britain was at war with Germany or Britain and Germany were at war*; to declare war on = to state formally that a war has begun; civil war = situation inside a country where groups of armed people fight against each other or against the government; prisoner of war (POW) = member of the armed forces captured by the enemy in time of war (b) strong action against something; *the police have declared war on the drug dealers* (c) argument between companies; price war *or* price-cutting war = competition between companies to get a larger market share by cutting prices; *at the moment there's a price war between the two airlines*

ward [wɔːd] 1 *noun* (a) room or set of rooms in a hospital, with beds for patients; *the children's ward is at the end of the corridor; she was taken into the accident and emergency ward* (b) division of a town for administrative purposes; an electoral ward = area of a town represented by a councillor on a local council; *Councillor Smith represents Central Ward on the council; the ballot boxes from each ward were brought to the council offices* (NOTE: the American equivalent is precinct) (c) young person protected by a guardian or a court; ward of court = young child who is under the protection of the High Court; *the High Court declared the girl a ward of court* 2 *verb* to ward something off = to keep something away; *they keep a flock of geese in the warehouse to ward off thieves*

warden ['wɔːdən] *noun* (a) person in charge of an institution, an old people's home, a students' hostel, etc.; *ask the warden if we can visit on Sundays* (b) person who looks after or guards something; park warden *or* forest warden = person who looks after a park or forest; *the park warden told us to keep our dog on the leash* (c) traffic warden = person who controls the parking of cars, etc., in a town; *move your car - there's a traffic warden coming*

warder, wardress ['wɔːdə or 'wɔːdrəs] *noun* prison officer, a person who guards prisoners; *he works as a prison warder in one of the most dangerous prisons*

wardrobe ['wɔːdrəub] *noun* (a) fixed or moveable tall cupboard in which you hang your clothes; *he moved the wardrobe from the landing into the bedroom* (b) clothes; *she bought a whole new wardrobe for her holiday*

ware ['weə] *noun* 1 suffix meaning goods made of a certain material or for a special purpose; *you'll find the kitchenware department on the third floor; this is a new product for cleaning silverware* 2 *noun* wares = things that have been made and are for sale; *women from the surrounding villages come to the market on Saturdays to sell their wares*

warehouse ['weəhaus] 1 *noun* large building where goods are stored; *our goods are dispatched from the central warehouse to shops all over the country* 2 *verb* to store goods in a warehouse; *they have offered to warehouse for us on a temporary basis*

warehousing ['weəhauzɪŋ] *noun* action of storing goods; *warehousing costs are rising rapidly*

warfare ['wɔːfeə] *noun* fighting a war, especially the method of fighting; *the arguments between the clans soon developed into open warfare; the enemy resorted to guerrilla warfare; governments are trying to ban chemical warfare*

warhead ['wɔːhed] *noun* explosive top end of a missile; *a missile with a nuclear warhead*

warlike ['wɔːlaɪk] *adjective* which likes war; *the country adopted a warlike attitude towards their neighbours*

warlord ['wɔːlɔːd] *noun* military leader who rules part of a country; *two warlords struggled for control of the province*

warm [wɔːm] **1** *adjective* **(a)** quite hot; *the temperature is below freezing outside but it's nice and warm in the office; the children tried to keep warm by playing football; are you warm enough, or do you want another blanket?; the winter sun can be quite warm in February (informal)* **warm as toast** = nice and warm; *it may be snowy outside, but we're as warm as toast in our little cottage* **(b)** pleasant and friendly; *we had a warm welcome from our friends; she has a really warm personality* (NOTE: **warmer - warmest**) **2** *verb* **(a)** to make hotter; *come and warm your hands by the fire; I'll warm some soup; the greenhouse effect has the result of warming the general temperature of the earth's atmosphere; see also* COCKLES **(b)** to become interested in something, to start to like someone; *she never really warmed to the subject of her thesis; I think everyone is warming to the new boss* **3** *noun* place where it is warm; *I'm not going out for a walk - I'm staying here in the warm*

warm-hearted [wɔːm'hɑːtɪd] *adjective* friendly and kind; *she's really warm-hearted and looked after me when I had flu*

warming ['wɔːmɪŋ] *noun* making warmer; **global warming** = gradual rise in temperature over the whole of the earth's surface, caused by the greenhouse effect

warmth [wɔːmθ] *noun* **(a)** being or feeling warm; *it was cold and rainy outside, and he looked forward to the warmth of his home* **(b)** enthusiasm for something; *the management's lack of warmth for the project*

warm up ['wɔːm 'ʌp] *verb* **(a)** to make hotter; *a cup of coffee will soon warm you up; I'll just warm up some soup for supper* **(b)** to practise or exercise; *the orchestra is just warming up before the concert*

warn [wɔːn] *verb* **(a)** to inform someone of a possible danger; *we were warned to boil all drinking water; children are warned not to play on the frozen lake; the group was warned to look out for pickpockets; the guide warned us that there might be snakes in the ruins* **(b)** to inform someone in advance; *the railway has warned that there will be a strike tomorrow; the weather forecast warned of storms in the English Channel* (NOTE: you warn someone **of** something, or **that** something may happen)

warning ['wɔːnɪŋ] **1** *noun* **(a)** information about a possible danger; *he shouted a warning to the children; the government issued a warning about travelling in some countries in the area; each packet of cigarettes has a government health warning printed on it* **(b)** written or spoken notice to an employee telling them that they will be dismissed or punished if they don't stop behaving in a certain way; *when he was late for the third time this week, he got a written warning* **(c)** **without warning** = unexpectedly; *the car in front braked without warning and I couldn't stop in time* **2** *adjective* which informs about a danger; *red warning flags are raised if the sea is dangerous; warning notices were put up round the building site*

warn off ['wɔːn 'ɒf] *verb* **to warn someone off something** = to advise someone not to do something; *two men came to see him and warned him off going to*

the police; they hope that this tragedy will warn other adolescents off drugs

warp [wɔːp] **1** *noun* **(a)** twisting out of shape of a piece of wood or metal; *put the two planks together, and the warp in one of them is obvious* **(b)** threads running lengthwise in a piece of woven material; *the warp of the fabric consists of a red thread* (NOTE: the threads running across the material are the **weft**) **2** *verb* **(a)** to twist out of shape; *cycling across potholes can warp your front wheel; if you leave the planks out in the rain they will warp* **(b)** to have a bad effect on someone's mind or character; *the beatings he had from his father seem to have warped his mind*

warpath ['wɔːpɑːθ] *noun* (*informal*) **to be on the warpath** = to be annoyed and want to fight someone; *keep out of the way - the headteacher's on the warpath!*

warped ['wɔːpt] *adjective* strange and twisted; *his drawings are the product of a warped imagination; he must have a warped sense of humour to make that sort of joke*

warplane ['wɔːpleɪn] *noun* armed plane used for fighting or dropping bombs; *enemy warplanes flew over our ships at night*

warrant ['wɒrənt] **1** *noun* **(a)** official document from a court permitting someone to do something; *the magistrate issued a warrant for her arrest* **(b)** **warrant officer** = rank in the armed forces below commissioned officers and above non-commissioned officers **2** *verb* **(a)** to guarantee that something is of good quality, will work properly, etc.; *all the spare parts are warranted for six months* **(b)** to be a good reason for; *our sales in France do not warrant six trips a year to Paris by the director*

warranty ['wɒrənti] *noun* guarantee, a legal document which promises that goods purchased will work properly or that an item is of good quality; *the car is sold with a twelve-month warranty; the warranty covers spare parts but not labour costs* (NOTE: plural is **warranties**)

warren ['wɒrən] *noun see* RABBIT WARREN

warring ['wɔːrɪŋ] *adjective* at war; *the United Nations is trying to mediate between the various warring parties in the dispute*

warrior ['wɒrɪə] *noun* (*formal*) person who fights in battle; *thousands of warriors charged at the enemy waving spears*

warship ['wɔːʃɪp] *noun* armed ship which is used for fighting, not for carrying passengers or goods; *the government is sending two warships to the area*

wart [wɔːt] *noun* small hard benign lump on the skin; *the doctor burnt away the small wart he had on his hand* (*informal*) **warts and all** = with all faults shown; *his book is a warts-and-all description of life with the former Prime Minister*

> COMMENT: the expression is supposed to come from Oliver Cromwell, who told a painter to paint him 'warts and all', instead of an idealized image

wartime ['wɔːtaɪm] *noun* time of war; *in wartime, food was rationed; he is remembered for his stirring wartime broadcasts to the troops*

wary ['weəri] *adjective* careful because of possible problems; *I am very wary of any of his ideas for* *making money; you should be wary of going on the ice in the spring* (NOTE: warier - wariest)

was [wɒz] *see* BE

wash [wɒʃ] **1** *noun* **(a)** action of cleaning, using water; *the car needs a wash; he's in the bathroom, having a quick wash* **(b)** to do a wash = to wash some clothes in a washing machine; *I'll do a wash this morning;* **in the wash** = (i) being washed; (ii) in a pile of things waiting to be washed; *all my T-shirts are in the wash;* **to come out in the wash** = to lose colour; *all the colour of my pyjamas came out in the wash; (informal)* **it will all come out in the wash** = everything will work out correctly, in spite of various mistakes having been made; *don't worry too much about the mistakes in your report - it'll all come out in the wash* **(c)** the wake of a ship, the waves made by a ship moving through water **(d)** mixture of paint and water; *they started to put a pale yellow wash on the front of the house; see also* MOUTHWASH **2** *verb* **(a)** to clean using water; *cooks should always wash their hands before touching food!; I must wash the car before we go to the wedding; the moment I had washed the windows it started to rain; his football shirt needs washing; see also* LINEN **(b)** to wash your hands of someone *or* something = to refuse to be responsible for something; *she's washed her hands of her son since he was put in prison for drugs dealing; he's washed his hands of the whole affair* **(c)** *(formal)* to flow or splash against something; *the waves washed against the steps leading to the quay* **(d)** to be washed overboard = to be pulled off a boat by waves; *he was washed overboard during the night*

washable ['wɒʃəbl] *adjective* which can be washed in water (as opposed to being dry- cleaned); *is this a washable fabric?*

wash away ['wɒʃ ə'weɪ] *verb* to remove with water; *use a hosepipe to wash away the mud from under the car; several houses were washed away by the floods*

washbasin ['wɒʃbeɪsn] *noun* container, with taps, for holding water for washing the hands and face, usually attached to the wall of a bathroom; *each room has a washbasin*

washcloth ['wɒʃklɒθ] *noun* US small square of cloth for washing the face or body; *he took a clean washcloth and a towel in the cupboard and had a shower* (NOTE: British English is **facecloth** *or* **flannel**)

wash down ['wɒʃ 'daʊn] *verb* **(a)** to wash with a large amount of water; *they washed down the van with buckets of water; the sailors were washing down the deck* **(b)** to have a drink with food; *he had a pizza washed down by a glass of beer*

washed out ['wɒʃt 'aʊt] *adjective (informal)* **to look washed out** = to look pale and tired out; *after the interview she looked completely washed out*

washer ['wɒʃə] *noun* **(a)** rubber ring inside a tap which prevents water escaping when the tap is turned off; *the tap is leaking, and I think the washer needs replacing* **(b)** metal ring under a nut or bolt; *put a washer on the bolt to make it screw tight* **(c)** **windscreen washer** = system on a car that operates the wipers and squirts water on to the windscreen at the same time; *see also* DISHWASHER

washing ['wɒʃɪŋ] *noun* **(a)** clothes which have been washed, or which are ready to be washed; *put the washing in the washing machine; she hung out the washing to dry; washing left out in the morning will be*

delivered to the room within 12 hours; to do the washing = to wash dirty clothes; *I'm not doing the washing today* **(b)** action of washing; **washing powder** = soap in powder form, used in washing machines or dishwashers; *can you buy some washing powder next time you go to the supermarket?* (NOTE: no plural)

washing machine ['wɒʃɪŋ mə'ʃiːn] *noun* machine for washing clothes; *he took the clothes out of the washing machine and hung them up to dry* (NOTE: a machine for washing plates and cutlery is a **dishwasher**)

washing up ['wɒʃɪŋ 'ʌp] *noun* **(a)** cleaning of dirty dishes, glasses, cutlery, etc., with water; *can someone help with the washing up?; it took us hours to do the washing up after the party; use this little brush for the washing up;* **washing-up liquid** = liquid detergent used for washing dirty dishes; *don't squirt so much washing-up liquid into the bowl* **(b)** dirty dishes, glasses, cutlery, etc., waiting to be cleaned; *there is a pile of washing up waiting to be put into the dishwasher*

wash off ['wɒʃ 'ɒf] *verb* to take off by washing; *wash the mud off your shoes before you come into the house; the stain won't wash off*

washout ['wɒʃaʊt] *noun* **(a)** failure due to rain; *the village fête was a complete washout* **(b)** failure; *no one turned up for the memorial service - it was a washout*

washroom ['wɒʃruːm] *noun* US toilet; *where's the washroom, please?*

washstand ['wɒʃstænd] *noun (old)* table on which a bowl and jug of water used to stand in a bedroom; *we bought an old-fashioned washstand with a bowl and a jug in the antique shop*

wash up ['wɒʃ 'ʌp] *verb* **(a)** to clean dirty cups, plates, knives, forks, etc., with water; *it took us hours to wash up after the party; my brother's washing up, while I'm sitting watching the TV* **(b)** *(of the sea)* to bring something up onto the beach; *it's interesting to walk along the shore to see what has been washed up onto the beach during the night* **(c)** US to wash your face and hands; *he went into the bathroom to wash up*

wasn't [wɒznt] *see* BE

wasp [wɒsp] *noun* insect with black and yellow stripes, which can sting; *wasps buzzed around the kitchen as she was making jam*

wastage ['weɪstɪdʒ] *noun* **(a)** act of wasting; *there is an enormous wastage of natural resources;* **natural wastage** = losing workers because they resign or retire, not because they are made redundant or are sacked; *the reductions in staff will be achieved through natural wastage* **(b)** amount lost by being wasted; *allow 10% extra material for wastage*

waste [weɪst] **1** *noun* **(a)** unnecessary use of time or money; *it is a waste of time asking the boss for a rise; that computer is a waste of money - there are plenty of cheaper models* **(b)** rubbish, things which are no use and are thrown away; *put all your waste in the rubbish bin; the dustmen collect household waste once a week;* **industrial waste** = rubbish from industrial processes; *the company was fined for putting industrial waste into the river;* **kitchen waste** = rubbish from the kitchen, such as bits of vegetables, tins, etc.; **nuclear waste** = radioactive waste from a nuclear reactor; *the disposal of nuclear waste is causing problems worldwide;* **waste pipe** = pipe which takes used or dirty water to the drains; *the waste pipe from the kitchen sink is blocked* (NOTE: no plural; do not confuse with

waist) 2 *verb* to use more of something than you need; *they wasted so much food at the reception and had to throw it away*; *don't waste time putting your shoes on - jump out of the window now*; *we turned off all the heating so as not to waste energy*; *(old saying)* **waste not, want not** = if you don't waste anything, you will never lack things when you really need them **3** *adjective* **(a)** useless, ready to be thrown away; *we have heaps of waste paper to take to the dump*; *waste products should not be dumped in the sea* **(b)** *(of land)* not used for cultivation or building; **waste ground** = area of land which is not used for any purpose; *the plan is to build houses on the waste ground*; **to lay waste** = to destroy the crops and buildings in an area in wartime, so that it cannot be used again

waste away ['weɪst ə'weɪ] *verb* to become much thinner, to lose weight; *after he caught the disease he simply wasted away*

wasteful ['weɪstfʊl] *adjective* extravagant, which wastes a lot; *this new washing machine is less wasteful of hot water*; *you could have cooked those apples, it was very wasteful to throw them away*

wastepaper basket *US* **wastebasket** ['weɪst'peɪpə 'bɑːskɪt] *noun* small box or basket where useless papers can be put; *throw those papers into the wastepaper basket*

wasteland ['weɪstlænd] *noun* land which is not used for anything; *people got into the habit of taking old fridges, car tyres, etc., and dumping them on the wasteland behind the factory*; *the council is planning to redevelop the industrial wastelands as business parks*

watch [wɒtʃ] **1** *noun* **(a)** device like a little clock which you wear on your wrist; *she looked at her watch impatiently*; *what time is it? - my watch has stopped* (NOTE: plural in this meaning is **watches**) **(b)** looking at something carefully; *visitors should be on the watch for pickpockets*; *keep a watch on the potatoes to make sure they don't burn* (NOTE: no plural for this meaning) **(c)** period when a soldier or sailor is on duty; *the men on the night watch didn't see anything unusual* **2** *verb* **(a)** to look at and notice something; *did you watch the TV news last night?*; *we went to the sports ground to watch the football match*; *everyone was watching the children dancing* **(b)** to look at something carefully to make sure that nothing happens; *watch the saucepan - I don't want the potatoes to burn*; *can you watch the baby while I'm at the hairdresser's?*

watchdog ['wɒtʃdɒg] *noun* **(a)** dog used to guard a house or other buildings; *Alsatians are often used as watchdogs* **(b)** person or committee that examines public spending, public morals, etc.; *the report of the watchdog committee on water pricing*

watchful ['wɒtʃfʊl] *adjective* very careful; *the children were playing under the watchful eye of the au pair*; *I feel I must be watchful all the time when the baby is awake*

watchman ['wɒtʃmən] *noun* person who guards a building, usually when it is empty; *they tied up the watchman and then proceeded to load the boxes onto a van* (NOTE: also called **nightwatchman**, plural is **watchmen**)

watch out [wɒtʃ 'aʊt] *verb* **(a)** to be careful; *watch out! there's a car coming!* **(b)** **to watch out for** = to be careful to avoid; *you have to watch out for children playing in the road*; *watch out for pickpockets!*

water ['wɔːtə] **1** **(a)** common liquid (H_2O) which forms rain, rivers, lakes, the sea, etc., and which makes up a large part of the bodies of organisms and which you drink and use in cooking, in industry, etc.; *can we have three glasses of water please?*; *cook the vegetables in boiling water*; *is the tap water safe to drink?*; *you are advised to drink only bottled water*; *the water temperature is 60°*; **drinking water** = water which you can drink safely; **running water** = water which is available in a house through water mains and taps; *I'm not sure that all the houses in the village have running water*; *there is hot and cold running water in all the rooms*; **under water** = (i) swimming under the surface of water; (ii) covered by floods; *she can swim well, even under water*; *parts of the town are under water after the river flooded*; **to keep your head above water** = (i) to swim with your head out of the water; (ii) to be able to keep out of trouble; **to spend money like water** = to spend large amounts of money; *when they were furnishing the house they just spent money like water* *(informal)* **it's all water under the bridge** = a long time has passed and the situation has changed completely; **like water off a duck's back** = having no effect at all; *he was told off several times for being late, but it was like water off a duck's back* (NOTE: no plural: **some water**; **a drop of water**) **(b)** mass of water forming a lake, river, sea, etc.; *they live right on the water's edge*; *when you fly across Finland, you realize how much water there is*; *living surrounded by water, they became good sailors* **(c)** **waters** = areas of sea; **in international waters** *or* **outside territorial waters** = in that part of the sea which is outside any country's jurisdiction; **territorial waters** = sea near the coast of a country, which is part of that country and governed by the laws of that country; *the attack happened in British territorial waters* **2** *verb* **(a)** to pour water on the soil round a plant to make it grow; *because it is hot we need to water the garden every day*; *she was watering her pots of flowers* **(b)** *(of your eyes)* to fill with tears; *(of your mouth)* to fill with saliva; *peeling onions makes my eyes water*; **to make your mouth water** = to look so good that your mouth fills with saliva; *those cakes make my mouth water*; *his new car made her mouth water*

water biscuit ['wɔːtə 'bɪskɪt] *noun* thin hard biscuit made of flour and water, eaten with cheese; *the guests were offered cheese and water biscuits after supper*

water buffalo ['wɔːtə 'bʌfələʊ] *noun* large Asian animal of the cow family, with a hump, used for farm work in some countries; *we saw water buffaloes ploughing on small farms in the Far East*

water cannon ['wɔːtə 'kænən] *noun* machine for sending out jets of water under pressure; *the police used water cannon to clear demonstrators* (NOTE: usually no plural form, but sometimes **water cannons**)

water closet ['wɔːtə 'klɒsɪt] *see* WC

watercolour *US* **watercolor** ['wɔːtəkʌlə] *noun* **(a)** paint which is mixed with water and used by artists; *he prefers using watercolours to oils* **(b)** picture painted using watercolours; *there is an exhibition of Turner's watercolours in the Tate Gallery*; *she bought a watercolour of the village church*

watercress ['wɔːtəkres] *noun* creeping plant grown in water streams and eaten in salads and soup; *watercress has round green leaves with a slightly sharp taste*; *she made us a delicious watercress soup*; *see also* CRESS (NOTE: no plural)

watered-down ['wɔːtəd'daʊn] *adjective* weaker and less powerful than the original; *this is a watered-down version of what was actually said at the summit meeting*; *he was accused of serving watered-down wine*

waterfall ['wɔːtəfɔːl] *noun* place where a stream falls down a steep vertical drop; *let's climb up to the waterfall and picnic there*; *is Niagara the largest waterfall in the world?*

waterfowl ['wɔːtəfaʊl] *noun* birds (such as ducks, geese, etc.) that live around ponds and lakes; *the big reservoirs are excellent places to see waterfowl* (NOTE: the word is plural)

waterfront ['wɔːtəfrʌnt] *noun* bank of a river or shore of the sea and the buildings along it; *gangs of dock workers stood around on the waterfront, waiting for the ship to tie up*; *lets have lunch on the terrace of one of the waterfront restaurants*

waterhole ['wɔːtəhəʊl] *noun* small pool in the jungle, where animals come to drink; *the lions were lying in wait near the waterhole*

watering can ['wɔːtrɪŋ 'kæn] *noun* container similar to a bucket, with a long spout, used for watering plants, etc.; *he filled the watering can and watered the pots on the balcony*

waterline ['wɔːtəlaɪn] *noun* line marking where the water reaches on the hull of a ship; *the barge was empty and the waterline was well above the level of the water*

waterlogged ['wɔːtəlɒgd] *adjective* **(a)** full of water, and so unable to float; *the boat became waterlogged and we all had to get off* **(b)** flooded, full of water; *after so much rain, the waterlogged golf course had to be closed*; *most plants cannot grow in waterlogged soil*

water main ['wɔːtə 'meɪn] *noun* main pipe that carries water underground along a road, and into buildings; *we have no water - they turned it off while they were repairing the water main*

watermark ['wɔːtəmɑːk] *noun* **(a)** hidden mark in paper, which identifies the paper; *if you hold a banknote up to the light you will see the watermark* **(b)** line showing the level water has reached; *on the wall by the river you can see various watermarks showing the level of floods in different years*

watermelon ['wɔːtəmelən] *noun* very large type of melon with red flesh and large black seeds; *she cut the watermelon into slices*

watermill ['wɔːtəmɪl] *noun* mill driven by a flow of water over a large wheel; *there is an old watermill just outside the village*

water polo ['wɔːtə 'pəʊləʊ] *noun* ball game played in water by two teams, each trying to throw a ball into a goal

waterproof ['wɔːtəpruːf] **1** *adjective* which does not let water go through; *these boots aren't waterproof - my socks are wet through*; *divers wear waterproof watches*; *you will need plenty of waterproof clothing if you are going sea fishing* **2** *verb* to cover something with a substance to prevent water getting in; *they spread a coating of tar on the roof to waterproof it* **3** *noun* piece of clothing made of material that does not let water through; *the fishermen were all dressed in their yellow waterproofs*

watershed ['wɔːtəʃed] *noun* **(a)** high ground separating different rivers and the streams that run into

them; *the ridge of hills marks the watershed between the Rhine and Rhone* **(b)** point where an important permanent change takes place; *failing the exams for the Civil Service was a watershed in his career*; *the nine o'clock watershed* = the time (9.00 p.m.) when adult programmes can start on TV

waterskier ['wɔːtəskiːə] *noun* person who goes waterskiing; *waterskiers swept past the beach*

waterskiing ['wɔːtəskiːɪŋ] *noun* sport of gliding along the surface of a lake or river on large skis, pulled by a fast boat; *she goes waterskiing every Saturday*

watertight ['wɔːtətaɪt] *adjective* **(a)** made so that water cannot get in or out; *the food has to be kept in watertight containers*; *is the seal round the radiator watertight?* **(b)** which cannot be shown to be false; *she has a watertight alibi for the time when the crime was committed*

waterway ['wɔːtəweɪ] *noun* canal or deep river along which boats can easily travel; *an inland waterway which goes from London direct to Birmingham*

waterworks ['wɔːtəwɜːks] *noun* **(a)** buildings with pumps for pumping water to houses and factories; *this red brick building is the waterworks for the whole area* **(b)** *(informal)* the urinary system, the system for passing urine; *the doctor says there's nothing wrong with his waterworks* **(c)** *(informal)* to turn on the waterworks = to start to cry because you want sympathy; *she just has to turn on the waterworks and her mother always gives in*

watery ['wɔːtri] *adjective* like water, which has a lot of water in it; *all I had was a cup of unpleasant watery coffee*; *the watery winter sun shone through the mist*; *to go to a watery grave* = to be drowned at sea; *the ship sank in the storm, and all the crew went to a watery grave*

Watt [wɒt] *noun* standard unit of electrical power; *use a 60 Watt (60W) bulb in the desk lamp*

wattage ['wɒtɪdʒ] *noun* power of an electric appliance measured in Watts; *what is the wattage of this appliance?*

wave [weɪv] **1** *noun* **(a)** ridge of water on the surface of the sea, a lake or a river; *waves were breaking on the rocks*; *watch out for big waves on the beach*; *the sea was calm, with hardly any waves*; *see also* MEXICAN **(b)** up and down movement of your hand; *she gave me a wave* = she waved her hand to me **(c)** regular curve on the surface of hair; *his hair has a natural wave* **(d)** sudden increase in something; *a wave of anger surged through the crowd*; *crime wave* = increase in the number of crimes; *heat wave* = sudden spell of hot weather; *the temperature went up to 40° during the heat wave in Athens* **(e)** groups of people, machines, etc., rushing forwards; *wave after wave of soldiers attacked the fort*; *they sent in waves of bombers to destroy the harbour* **(f)** air waves = way in which radio signals move through the air; *long wave* = radio wave longer than 1000 metres; *we listened to the BBC on long wave*; *medium wave* = radio frequency range between 200 and 1000 metres; *the BBC's medium wave broadcasts*; *short wave* = radio frequency below 60 metres **2** *verb* **(a)** to move up and down in the wind; *the banners were waving outside the town hall* **(b)** to make an up and down movement of the hand (usually when saying goodbye); *they waved until the car was out of sight*; *they waved goodbye as the boat left the harbour*; *to wave to someone* = to signal to someone by moving your hand up and down; *when I saw him I waved to him to cross the road*; **to wave someone on** = to tell someone to go on by a movement of the hand; *the policeman waved the traffic on* **(c)** *(of hair)* to have a wave; *I wish my hair would wave naturally* (NOTE: do not confuse with **waive**)

waveband ['weɪvbænd] *noun* group of radio waves which are close together; *this receiver can pick up signals on FM wavebands*

wavelength ['weɪvleŋθ] *noun* **(a)** distance between corresponding points on radio waves; *they used a short wavelength for transmitting messages* **(b)** *(informal)* **they're not on the same wavelength** = they do not understand each other at all; *she operates on quite a different wavelength from her husband*

waver ['weɪvə] *verb* **(a)** to tremble or to move from side to side; *the needle on the dial wavered around the 200km mark* **(b)** to hesitate; *he is still wavering about which hotel to go to in Paris*; *she wavered between the two possible colour schemes and finally decided to paint the kitchen white* (NOTE: do not confuse with **waiver**)

wavy ['weɪvɪ] *adjective* which goes up and down; *her hair is not at all wavy*; *he drew a wavy line across the bottom of the page* (NOTE: **wavier - waviest**)

wax [wæks] **1** *noun* **(a)** solid substance made from fat or oil, used for making candles, polish, etc.; *she brought a tin of wax polish and started to polish the furniture* **(b)** soft yellow substance made by bees to build their honeycomb; *he separated the honey from the wax and put it into jars* **(c)** soft yellow substance that forms in your ears **2** *verb* **(a)** to put wax polish on furniture, etc.; *she was waxing the dining room table* **(b)** *(informal)* **to wax lyrical about something** = to be full of enthusiasm about something; *the reviewer waxed lyrical about the young painter*

waxworks ['wækswɜːks] *noun* exhibition of wax models of famous people; *if you're in London you must go and see the famous waxworks at Madame Tussauds*

way [weɪ] **1** *noun* **(a)** path or road which goes somewhere; *our neighbours across the way*; *I'll walk the first part of the way home with you* **(b)** correct path or road to go somewhere; *do you know the way to the post office?*; *she showed us the way to the railway station*; *they lost their way and had to ask for directions*; *I'll lead the way - just follow me* **(c)** on the way = during a journey; *I'll stop at the post office on my way to the restaurant*; *she's on her way to the office*; **well on the way to** = nearly; *the repairs to the house are well on the way to being finished*; **to go out of your way to help someone** = to make a special effort to help someone **(d)** **to make your way** = to go to (a place) with some difficulty; *can you make your way to the passport control?*; *he made his way to the tourist information office* **(e)** particular direction from here; *a one-way street*; *can you tell which way the wind is blowing?*; *this way please, everybody!* **(f)** means of doing something; *my mother showed me the way to make marmalade*; *isn't there any other way of making it?*; *he thought of a way of making money quickly*; *the way she said it implied I was at fault*; *(informal)* **to get your own way** = to do what you want to do, even if other people don't want you to do it; *she always seems to get her own way* **(g)** **to have it both ways** = to take advantage from two courses of action; *he wants to have it both ways, but he'll soon realize he can't*; *you can't*

have it both ways - going out to the club every evening and saving money; **in many ways** = almost completely; *in many ways, I think she is right*; **in some ways** = not completely; *in some ways she may be wrong* **(h)** manner of behaving; *he spoke in a pleasant way*; *you will have to get used to the manager's funny little ways* **(i)** distance; *the bank is quite a long way away*; *he's got a long way to go before he qualifies as a doctor* **(j)** space where someone wants to be or which someone wants to use; *get out of my way - I'm in a hurry*; *it's best to keep out of the way of the police for a moment*; *I wanted to take a short cut, but there was a lorry in the way* **(k)** progress, forward movement; **under way** = moving forwards; *the project is under way at last* **(l)** **in a bad way** = very ill; *she's in hospital and in a really bad way* **2** *adverb* *(informal)* far, a long distance away; *the bank is way beyond the Post Office*; *the financial problems started way back in 1992*; *the price was way too high for me*; **way over your head** = difficult to understand; *the book was way over my head*

◊ **by the way** ['baɪ ðə 'weɪ] *(used to introduce something which is not very important or to change the subject which is being talked about) by the way, have you seen my keys anywhere?*

◊ **no way** ['nəʊ weɪ] not at all; *can I have a table for lunch? - no way!*; *there's no way that the government is going to get involved*

◊ **out of the way** ['aʊt əv ðə 'weɪ] **(a)** not near any large town; *the village is a bit out of the way* **(b)** strange, unusual; *what she proposed was nothing out of the way*

way in ['weɪ 'ɪn] *noun* entrance; *this is the way in to the theatre*; *the way in is through the gates by the park*

waylay ['weɪleɪ] *verb* **(a)** to stop and attack someone; *the gang waylaid the cashier as she was walking back to the office* **(b)** to stop to talk to someone; *I was waylaid by an old friend on my way to the Post Office*

way out ['weɪ 'aʊt] *noun* **(a)** exit; *this the way out of the car park*; *he couldn't find the way out in the dark* **(b)** **a way out of a difficulty** = a solution to a problem; *the leave the country and live abroad was probably the easiest way out*

way-out [weɪ'aʊt] *adjective (slang)* strange, exciting; *they played some really way-out music*

way up ['weɪ 'ʌp] *noun* way in which something stands; *keep the jar the right way up or the contents will spill*; *he was pretending to read the book, but was holding it the wrong way up*

wayward ['weɪwəd] *adjective* wild, who does what he wants; *he was a particularly wayward child*

WC ['dʌbljuː'siː] *noun* short for 'water closet', meaning toilet (NOTE: mainly used on signs)

we [wiː] *pronoun* **(a)** *(used by a speaker referring to himself and others) he said we could go into the exhibition*; *we were not allowed into the restaurant in jeans*; *we had a wonderful holiday - we all enjoyed ourselves enormously* (NOTE: when it is the object **we** becomes **us**: **we gave it to him**; **he gave it to us**; when it follows the verb to **be**, we usually becomes **us: who is it? - it's us!**) **(b)** *(used instead of I)* **the royal we** = using 'we' instead of 'I'; *Queen Victoria said 'we are not amused'*

weak [wiːk] *adjective* **(a)** not strong; *after his illness he is still very weak*; *I don't like weak tea - put another teabag in the pot* **(b)** not good at, not having knowledge or skill; *she's weaker at science than at maths*; *French* is his weakest subject; she gave the weakest of excuses for not finishing the work on time (NOTE: do not confuse with **week**; note: **weaker - weakest**)

weaken ['wiːkn] verb to make or to become weak; she was very weakened by the disease; if you remove that wall you'll weaken the whole structure; living outside the borough weakens his chances of getting a place in that school (NOTE: the opposite is **strengthen**)

weakly ['wiːli] adverb in a weak way; instead of resisting their demands, they weakly gave in (NOTE: do not confuse with **weekly**)

weakness ['wiːknəs] noun (a) state of being weak; the doctor noticed the weakness of her pulse (NOTE: the opposite is **strength**) (b) (informal) weakness for = liking for; she has a weakness for tall men with dark hair; I have a weakness for Danish pastries

wealth [welθ] noun riches, a large amount of money; his wealth was inherited from his grandfather (NOTE: no plural)

wealthy ['welθi] adjective very rich (person); is she really wealthy, or just rich?; 50% of the land is in the hand of the ten wealthiest families (NOTE: **wealthier - wealthiest**)

wean [wiːn] verb (a) to make a baby start to eat solid food after only drinking milk and other liquids; at what age should you start to wean a baby? (b) (informal) to wean someone off or away from something = to get someone to drop a bad habit; we must try to wean him off the TV for a period

weapon ['wepən] noun object such as a gun or sword, which you fight with; the crowd used iron bars as weapons

weaponry ['wepənri] noun weapons; the army is equipped with the latest weaponry (NOTE: no plural)

wear [weə] 1 verb (a) to have (especially a piece of clothing) on your body; what dress are you wearing to the party?; when last seen, he was wearing a blue raincoat; she's wearing her mother's earrings; she wears her hair very short (b) to become damaged or thin through being used; the tread on the car tyres is worn; I've worn a hole in the heel of my sock (c) (informal) not to wear something = not to allow or put up with something; you can't put that picture up in the office - the female staff will never wear it (NOTE: **wearing - wore** [wɔː] - **has worn** [wɔːn]) 2 noun (a) (formal) clothes; the menswear department is on the ground floor (b) action of wearing clothes; this anorak is suitable for summer wear; a little black dress is perfect for evening wear (c) amount of use which something may have; the carpet on the stairs will have a lot more wear than the one in the bedroom (d) action of damaging something through use; fair wear and tear = damage through normal use which is accepted by an insurance company; the policy covers most forms of damage but not wear and tear to the machine

wear away [weə ə'wei] verb to disappear gradually, to make something disappear by rubbing; the carvings have worn away over the centuries

wearer ['weərə] noun person who wears clothes, shoes, etc.; wearers of sandals must watch out for nettles

wear off [weə 'ɒf] verb to disappear gradually; the effects of the drug wore off after a few hours

wear on [weə 'ɒn] verb to continue, with difficulty; as the evening wore on, we realized that there was not going to be very much to eat

wear out [weə 'aut] verb (a) to use something so much that it is broken and useless; walking across the USA, he wore out three pairs of boots (b) to wear yourself out = to become very tired through doing something; she wore herself out looking after the old lady; see also WORN OUT

weary ['wɪəri] adjective (formal) very tired; we were all weary after a day spent walking round London; to grow weary of (doing) something = to get tired of doing something; we grew weary of always eating in the same restaurant (NOTE: **wearier - weariest**)

weasel ['wiːzl] noun (a) small thin furry wild animal which kills and eats birds and small mammals; the weasel chased the rabbit into its burrow (b) weasel words = dishonest way of speaking where you avoid saying what you really think

weather ['weðə] 1 noun (a) conditions outside, i.e., if it is raining, hot, cold, windy, sunny, etc.; what's the weather going to be like today?; the weather in Iceland is usually colder than here; rain every day! - just normal English summer weather!; if the weather gets any better, then we can go out in the boat (b) to make heavy weather of something = to make something you are doing unnecessarily difficult and complicated; we asked him to sort out the invoices but he's really making heavy weather of it; under the weather = miserable or unwell; she's feeling a bit under the weather (NOTE: no plural; do not confuse with **whether**) 2 verb (a) (of sea, frost, wind, etc.) to wear down rocks, to change the colour of wood, etc.; the rocks have been weathered into curious shapes; the wooden fence was dark brown but now it has weathered to a light grey colour (b) to survive a storm, crisis; I don't know if we can weather this crisis without any extra cash

weatherbeaten ['weðəbiːtn] adjective (of face) made brown by the wind and sun; the weatherbeaten faces of the old mountain farmers (b) worn and marked by rain, sun and wind; there are a few weatherbeaten fishermen's cottages down by the harbour

weather bureau or **weather centre** ['weðə 'bjuːrəʊ or 'weðə 'sentə] noun bureau which notes weather conditions and forecasts the weather; the weather centre is forecasting a period of dry sunny weather

weather forecast or **weather report** ['weðə 'fɔːkɑːst or 'weðə rɪ'pɔːt] noun description of the sort of weather which is going to come in the next few hours or days; the weather forecast is good; switch on the radio - I want to hear the weather forecast

weather girl, weatherman ['weðə 'gɜːl or 'weðəmæn] noun (informal) a meteorologist, person who describes the coming weather usually on TV or radio; the map of the British Isles behind the weatherman was covered with little black clouds (NOTE: plural for **weatherman** is **weathermen**)

weave [wiːv] 1 verb (a) to make cloth by winding threads in and out; the cloth is woven from the wool of local sheep; the new weaving machines were installed last week (b) (informal) get weaving! = get going!, start now!; if you don't get weaving you'll never finish on time; come on, don't just sit around, let's get *weaving* **(c)** to make something by a similar method, but using straw, etc.; *she learnt how to weave baskets* (NOTE: **wove** [wəuv] - **has woven** [wəuvn]) **2** *noun* pattern made on cloth as it is being woven; *the coat has a very fine weave*

weaver ['wiːvə] *noun* person who weaves cloth; *we visited a small textile factory and watched the weavers at work*

web [web] *noun* **(a)** net spun by spiders; *the garden is full of spiders' webs in autumn* **(b)** pieces of skin between the toes of ducks, frogs, etc. **(c) the Web** = the World Wide Web, the thousands of web sites and web pages that display text and images within the Internet, which users can visit; **web browser** = special software that allows a person to view the contents of a web page and move between pages; **web page** = single file of text and graphics, forming part of a web site; **web site** = collection of related web pages, which is created by a company, organization or individual, and which anyone can visit; *how many hits did we have on our web site last week?*; *see also* DOMAIN, INTERNET

webbed feet ['webd 'fiːt] *noun* feet with skin between the toes; *having webbed feet helps ducks and swans to swim*

wed [wed] *verb* *(formal, used mainly in newspapers)* to marry; *'PRINCESS TO WED POP STAR'*; *he wed his childhood girlfriend* (NOTE: **wedding - wed** *or* **wedded**)

wedded ['wedɪd] *adjective* **(a) to be wedded to something** = to believe firmly that something is right; *the party is firmly wedded to the idea of European integration* **(b)** *(formal)* **his lawful wedded wife** = his wife whom he had married legally

wedding ['wedɪŋ] *noun* marriage ceremony, when two people are officially made man and wife; *they rang the church bells at the wedding*; *don't count on having fine weather for your wedding*; *the film ends with a wedding*; *this Saturday I'm going to John and Mary's wedding*; **a church wedding** = a wedding held in a church, and performed by a clergyman; **a registry wedding** *or* **a civil wedding** = wedding held in a registry office or other place, but not a church, which is performed by a registrar; **silver wedding** = day when you have been married for twenty-five years; **golden wedding** = day when you have been married for fifty years; *it's my parents' golden wedding next Tuesday*; **white wedding** = wedding where the bride wears a white dress; **wedding anniversary** = date which is the date of a wedding in the past; *don't tell me that for once you remembered our wedding anniversary!*; **wedding breakfast** = special meal for the bride, the groom, their families and guests, eaten after the wedding ceremony; **wedding cake** = special cake made with dried fruit, covered with icing, eaten at a wedding reception; *did you get a piece of wedding cake?*; **the 'Wedding March'** = piece of music by Mendelssohn played at weddings; *the organist played the 'Wedding March' as the bride and groom walked down the aisle*; **wedding reception** = party held after a wedding; *the wedding reception was held in the gardens of the hotel*; **wedding ring** = ring which is put on the finger during the wedding ceremony

COMMENT: at a wedding, the bride is usually assisted by bridesmaids (young girls), pages (little boys) and possibly a matron of honour, who is an older married woman. The bridegroom is always helped by his best man, who is usually an old school friend. The bride is 'given away' by her father, that is, she goes down the aisle of the church on his arm, and leaves the church on the arm of her new husband. Weddings are often on Saturdays; weddings are always followed by the wedding breakfast, and then the bride and groom go away on honeymoon. The costs of the wedding are usually borne by the parents of the bride, and the parents of the bridegroom have very little to do with the organization of the wedding, apart from being there

wedge [wedʒ] **1** *noun* **(a)** solid piece of wood, metal, rubber, etc., that has a V-shape; *put a wedge under the door to hold it open* **(b)** piece of anything with a V-shape; *a wedge of cheese* **(c) the thin end of the wedge** = something which seems small and unimportant but which will make things change dramatically later; *allowing the children to stay out till 10.30 is just the thin end of the wedge - in a couple of years' time they'll not come home until after midnight!* **2** *verb* **(a)** to put a wedge under something fix it firmly open or shut; *she wedged the door open with a piece of wood* **(b)** to force something into a small space; **to become wedged** *or* **to get wedged** = to become tightly stuck; *he got his head wedged between the railings*

Wednesday ['wenzdi] *noun* day between Tuesday and Thursday, the third day of the week; *she came for tea last Wednesday*; *Wednesdays are always busy days for us*; *can we meet next Wednesday afternoon?*; *Wednesday the 24th would be a good date for a meeting*; *the 15th is a Tuesday, so the 16th must be a Wednesday*; *see also* ASH WEDNESDAY

wee [wiː] **1** *adjective* (in Scotland) very small; *he's only a wee bairn*; *I've had a big meal so I'll just have a wee piece of cake*; **a wee bit** = a little; *he was just a wee bit annoyed by my letter*; **in the wee small hours** = very early in the morning **2** *noun* (child's word) urine; *the cat did a wee on the lawn* **3** *verb* (child's word) to urinate; *do you want to wee, Tommy?* (NOTE: also **wee-wee** in meanings 2 and 3)

weed [wiːd] **1** *noun* wild plant that you do not want in a garden; *weeds grew all over the flowerbeds while he was on holiday* **2** *verb* **(a)** to pull out plants which you do not want from a garden; *she spent all afternoon weeding the vegetable garden* **(b) to weed out** = to remove something which is not wanted; *weed out any old newspapers you don't want*

weedkiller ['wiːdkɪlə] *noun* chemical which kills weeds; *use weedkiller to get rid of the grass along the paths*; *are you sure this weedkiller is harmless to animals?*; *see also* SELECTIVE

weedy ['wiːdi] *adjective* **(a)** thin and weak; *his opponent was a weedy little man who looked as though he had never had a fight before* **(b)** covered with weeds; *we've been away and the garden is so weedy*

week [wiːk] *noun* **(a)** period of seven days, usually from Monday to Sunday; *there are 52 weeks in the year*; *the firm gives us two weeks' holiday at Easter*; *it's my aunt's 80th birthday next week*; *I go to the cinema at least once a week*; **a week from now** *or* **a week today** = this day next week; *a week from now or in a week's time, I'll be on holiday*; **a week tomorrow**

= in eight days' time; *a week tomorrow I'll be in Greece*; **yesterday week** = a week ago yesterday; *they came back from holiday yesterday week*; **what day of the week is it today?** = is it Monday, Tuesday, etc.? **(b)** part of a seven day period, when people work; *he works a 35-hour week* or *he works 35 hours every week* (NOTE: do not confuse with **weak**)

weekday ['wiːkdeɪ] *noun* any of the days from Monday to Friday, when most offices are open (but not Saturday or Sunday); *the banks are only open on weekdays*

weekend ['wiːkend] *noun* Saturday and Sunday, or the period from Friday evening to Sunday evening; *we're going to Brighton for the weekend*; *why don't you come to spend next weekend with us in the country?*; *at weekends, we try to spend time in the garden*; **long weekend** = weekend, including Friday night and Sunday night; *we took a long weekend in Paris*

weekly ['wiːkli] **1** *adjective & adverb* which happens or is published once a week; *we have a weekly paper which tells us all the local news*; *the weekly rate for the job is £250*; *do you pay the milkman weekly?* (NOTE: do not confuse with **weakly**) **2** *noun* magazine published once a week; *he gets a gardening weekly every Friday* (NOTE: plural is **weeklies**)

weep [wiːp] *verb (formal)* to cry, to have tears coming out of your eyes; *seeing them cut down the trees to make a new motorway is enough to make you weep*; *my mother wept with joy when I came back home safe and sound after the ordeal*; *crowds of weeping mourners followed the coffin* (NOTE: **weeping - wept** [wept])

wee-wee ['wiː 'wiː] *noun (child's word)* urine; *the cat's done a wee-wee on the carpet*; *I want to go wee-wee*; *she did a quick wee-wee and then went back to the playground*

weft [weft] *noun* threads that go across a length of woven material; *a blue thread was used for the weft* (NOTE: the threads running up and down the material are the **warp**)

weigh [weɪ] *verb* **(a)** to use scales or a weighing machine to measure how heavy something is; *can you weigh this parcel for me?*; *they weighed his suitcase at the check-in desk*; *I weighed myself this morning* **(b)** to have a certain weight; *this piece of meat weighs 100 grams*; *the packet weighs twenty-five grams*; *how much do you weigh?*; *he weighs 120 pounds*; *she only weighs 40 kilos*

weigh down ['weɪ 'daʊn] *verb* to be weighed down with = to be bent because you are carrying something heavy; *the car was weighed down with all our luggage*; *the branches of the pear trees were weighed down with fruit*

weigh in ['weɪ 'ɪn] *verb (of boxers, jockeys)* to have your weight measured before a fight or horse race; *the boxer weighed in at 200lbs*

weigh-in ['weɪɪn] *noun* time when boxers or jockeys are weighed before a fight or race; *the weigh-in will take place on the morning of the race*

weighing machine ['weɪɪŋ məˈʃiːn] *noun* device for weighing someone or something; *she placed the bag of sweets on the weighing machine*

weigh out ['weɪ 'aʊt] *verb* to measure something by weight; *she weighed out the dried fruit according to the recipe*

weight [weɪt] **1** *noun* **(a)** how heavy something is; *what's the maximum weight of parcel the post office will accept?*; **to sell fruit by weight** = to sell for a certain price per pound or kilo; **gross weight** = weight of both the container and its contents; **net weight** = weight of goods without the packing material and container **(b)** how heavy a person is; *his weight is less than it was a year ago*; **to lose weight** = to get thinner; *he's trying to lose weight*; **to put on weight** = to get fatter; *she's put on a lot of weight since her holiday* **(c)** **to pull your weight** = to work as hard as everyone else; *the manager has the reputation for being ruthless with employees who don't pull their weight*; *(informal)* **to throw your weight about** = to use your authority to tell people what to do in an arrogant way; *she loves to throw her weight about at management meetings*; **she's worth her weight in gold** = she's a very useful person and we couldn't do without her **(d)** something which is heavy; *if you lift heavy weights like paving stones, you may hurt your back*; *have you got a weight to put on the papers to stop them blowing away?*; **that's a weight off my mind!** = that is something I need not worry about any longer **2** *verb* **(a)** to attach something heavy to something; *they weighted down the sack with bricks and threw it into the river* **(b)** to add an amount to a total to produce a certain result; *the figures are weighted to take account of seasonal variations* (NOTE: do not confuse with **wait**)

weighting ['weɪtɪŋ] *noun* additional salary paid to compensate for living in an expensive part of the country; *salary plus a London weighting*

weightlifter ['weɪtlɪftə] *noun* person who lifts heavy weights as exercise or sport

weightlifting ['weɪtlɪftɪŋ] *noun* sport or exercise of lifting heavy weights

weighty ['weɪti] *adjective* **(a)** important, serious; *we now face the weighty problem of trying to expand into new markets* **(b)** heavy; *she's tired after lugging her weighty bag round London* (NOTE: **weightier - weightiest**)

weigh up ['weɪ 'ʌp] *verb (informal)* to form an opinion of someone or something; *she weighed up the character of the bride's mother within ten minutes of meeting her*; **to weigh up the pros and cons** = to look at all the arguments for and against something; *he weighed up the pros and cons of what was being suggested very carefully*

weir ['wɪə] *noun* **(a)** small dam built across a river to control the flow of water; *from here, you can see the weir and the lock* **(b)** fence put across a lake or river to trap fish

weird ['wɪəd] *adjective* strange, different from normal; *I don't like her new boyfriend - he's really weird*; *wasn't it weird that he phoned just when we were talking about him?*; *this meat has a weird taste* (NOTE: **weirder - weirdest**)

weirdo ['wɪədəʊ] *noun (informal)* strange person; *some weirdo asked me to dance, but I said I was just leaving* (NOTE: plural is **weirdos**)

welcome ['welkʌm] **1** *adjective* **(a)** met or accepted with pleasure; *the rain was welcome after months of drought*; *a bowl of warm soup would be welcome* **(b)** **welcome to** = willingly allowed to *you're welcome to* *use the library whenever you want* **(c)** *(informal) (as a reply to 'thank you') thanks for carrying the bags for me - you're welcome!* **2** *verb* **(a)** to greet someone in a friendly way; *the staff welcomed the new secretary to the office; when we arrived at the hotel we were welcomed by a couple of barking guard dogs* **(b)** to be glad to hear news; *I warmly welcome the result of the election; I would welcome any suggestions as to how to stop the water seeping into the basement* **3** *noun* action of greeting someone; *there was not much of a welcome from the staff when we arrived at the hotel*; a warm welcome = a friendly welcome; *they gave me a warm welcome*; to outstay your welcome = to stay longer than your hosts thought you were going to stay

welcoming ['welkʌmɪŋ] *adjective* making you feel happy to have arrived; *she greeted them with a welcoming cup of tea; a welcoming group of ministry officials*

weld [weld] **1** *verb* to join two pieces of metal together by heating them together; *the chassis can be repaired by welding the two pieces together* **2** *noun* joint made by welding two pieces of metal together; *the weld was badly done and came apart*

welder ['weldə] *noun* person whose job is to weld metal; *gangs of welders worked on the new ship*

welfare ['welfeə] *noun* **(a)** providing comfort and freedom from want; *the club looks after the welfare of the old people in the town; we take the children to a child welfare clinic; the government has taken measures to reform the welfare system* **(b)** money paid by the government to people who need it; *he exists on welfare payments; the family is on welfare*

welfare state ['welfeə 'steɪt] *noun* state which spends a large amount of money to make sure that its citizens all have adequate housing, education, public transport and health services; *Britain is a welfare state; compare* NANNY

well [wel] **1** *adverb* **(a)** in a way that is satisfactory; *he doesn't speak Russian very well; our business is small, but it's doing well; is the new computer working well?* **(b)** a lot (more); *he got back from the office late - well after eight o'clock; you should go to the Tower of London - it's well worth a visit; there were well over sixty people at the meeting; she's well over eighty* **(c)** as well = also; *when my aunt comes to stay she brings her two cats and the dog as well; you can't eat fish and chips and a meat pie as well!*; as well as = not only, but also; *some newsagents sell groceries as well as newspapers; she ate a slice of cheesecake as well as two scoops of ice cream* **(d)** *(to emphasize)* he may well be right; *she's well aware of how serious the situation is* **2** *adjective* healthy; *she's looking well after her holiday!; the secretary's not very well today - she's had to stay off work; it took him some weeks to get well after his flu; see also* GET WELL CARD **3** *interjection* (which starts a sentence, and often has no meaning) well, I'll show you round the house first; *well now, we've done the washing so we can sit and watch TV (showing surprise)* well, well! what is Mr Smith doing here! **4** *noun* very deep hole dug in the ground with water or oil at the bottom; *we pump water from the well in our garden; Middle Eastern oil wells*

well- [wel] *prefix meaning* in a satisfactory way; *well-attended; well-chosen* (NOTE: **well-** is used in front of many adjectives, see the following words. Note also the comparative in these compounds: **well-advised - better advised; well-off - better off**)

well-advised [weləd'vaɪzd] *adjective* to be well-advised to do something = to be sensible to do something; *you would be well advised to buy now before prices go up in the autumn*

well-balanced [wel'bælənsd] *adjective* **(a)** well-balanced diet = diet containing all the things you need to be healthy; *it is important that children should have a well-balanced diet* **(b)** steady or sensible; *she's a well-balanced girl, and won't make any rash decisions*

well-behaved [welbɪ'heɪvd] *adjective* good, having good manners; *they have two very well-behaved children; a well-behaved crowd of fans swarmed round the bus; the computer screen used to keep changing colour but is now better behaved*

well-being [wel'biːɪŋ] *noun* feeling of being healthy and happy; *the well-being of all the children in a school is the responsibility of the teachers*

well-bred [wel'bred] *adjective* polite and well brought up; *what's a well-bred girl like her doing with these people?*

well-built ['wel'bɪlt] *adjective* strong and sturdy; *he always has a couple of well-built men with him as minders; Victorian furniture was heavy but well-built*

well-defined ['weldɪ'faɪnd] *adjective* which is clearly laid out; *we need a well-defined objective to aim for; you can see the well-defined outline of the mountains in the distance*

well done ['wel 'dʌn] **1** *interjection* showing congratulations; *well done, the England team!; well done to all of you who passed the exam!* **2** *adjective* (meat) which has been cooked a long time; *can I have my steak well-done, please?*

well-dressed ['weldrest] *adjective* dressed in good clothes, in the latest fashion; *what is the well-dressed businessman wearing these days?; she's no longer the well-dressed career girl she used to be*

well-earned [wel'ɜːnd] *adjective* which has been deserved; *after doing all that gardening I think I can take a well-earned rest; she received a well-earned medal for coming second*

well-established [welɪs'tæblɪʃt] *adjective* which has been established for some time; *'Smith & Co.', the well-established women's dress shop in the High Street; the series of jazz concerts in July is a well-established feature of our summer festival*

well-informed [welɪn'fɔːmd] *adjective* knowing a lot about a subject; *she seems very well-informed about our financial problems; it is always good to have a well-informed audience*

wellingtons *(informal)* **wellies** ['welɪŋtənz or 'welɪz] *noun* long rubber boots going almost up to your knees, often green; *put your wellies on - it's pouring down*

well-known [wel'nəʊn] *adjective* famous, known by a lot of people; *she lives next door to a well-known TV star*

well-meaning [wel'miːnɪŋ] *adjective* done with good intentions; *in a well-meaning attempt to be helpful, she pulled up all my little lettuce plants as well as the weeds*

well-off [wel'ɒf] *adjective (informal)* rich; *I thought his wife came from a well-off family; our neighbours have always been better off than us*

well-paid ['wel'peɪd] *adjective* earning a good salary; *well-paid secretaries can earn really high salaries; what I want is not just a well-paid job but one that is interesting*

well-to-do [weltə'duː] *adjective (informal)* rich, wealthy; *she comes from a very a well-to-do family*

Welsh [welʃ] **1** *adjective* referring to Wales; *we will be going climbing in the Welsh mountains at Easter*; **Welsh rarebit** = bread with toasted cheese on top **2** *noun* **(a) the Welsh** = the people of Wales; *the Welsh are proud of their heritage; the Welsh are magnificent singers* **(b)** language spoken in Wales; *Welsh is used in schools in many parts of Wales*

Welshman, Welshwoman ['welʃmən or 'welʃwumən] *noun* person from Wales (NOTE: plurals are **Welshmen, Welshwomen**)

welterweight ['weltəweɪt] *noun* weight of boxer between lightweight and middleweight; *the welterweight champion; a welterweight title fight*

Wendy house ['wendi 'haus] *noun* model house for children to play in; *the girls want a Wendy house, but they're very expensive* (NOTE: also called a **playhouse**)

went [went] *see* GO

wept [wept] *see* WEEP

were, weren't [wɜː or wɜːnt] *see* BE

west [west] **1** *noun* direction of where the sun sets; *the sun sets in the west and rises in the east; we live in a village to the west of the town; their house has a west-facing garden* **2** *adjective* in or to the west; *she lives on the west coast of the United States; the west part of the town is near the river*; **west wind** = wind which blows from the west; *a wet west wind blowing from the Atlantic* **3** *adverb* towards the west; *go west for about ten kilometres, and then you'll come to the national park; the river flows west into the ocean*

westbound ['westbaund] *adjective* travelling towards the west; *there has been an accident on the westbound section of the motorway; all westbound trains have been cancelled*

West End ['west 'end] *noun* **(a)** the fashionable part of London, where the main shops can be found; *I bought all my Christmas presents in West End shops; crowds go shopping in the West End on Sunday afternoons; compare* EAST END **(b)** central London theatres, which put on major plays; *his first play was a hit in the West End; he wrote three West End musicals compare* FRINGE (NOTE: the American equivalent for main theatres is **Broadway**)

westerly ['westəli] **1** *adjective* **(a)** (wind) from the west; *there was a light westerly breeze* **(b)** towards the west; *they are heading in a westerly direction* **2** *noun* wind blowing from the west; *the westerlies blow many ships onto the rocks* (NOTE: plural is **westerlies**)

western ['westən] **1** *adjective* from or in the west; *Great Britain is part of Western Europe; the Western part of Canada has wonderful scenery* **2** *noun* film about cowboys; *she likes watching old westerns on TV*

westerner ['westənə] *noun* person who comes from the west, ie, from Europe or from America; *Westerners find it more difficult to get jobs in Hong Kong, now that it has become part of China*

Westminster ['wesmɪnstə] *noun* **(a)** borough in London where Westminster Abbey and the Houses of Parliament are; *tourists always go to Westminster as part of their visit to London* **(b)** the British Parliament itself; *the news was greeted with surprise at Westminster; MPs returned to Westminster after the summer recess*

wet [wet] **1** *adjective* **(a)** covered in water or other liquid; *she forgot her umbrella and got wet walking back from the shops; the chair's all wet where he knocked over his beer; the baby is wet - can you change her nappy?*; **wet through** *or* **soaking wet** = very wet; *change your shirt - it's wet through; I was soaking wet after falling into the river* **(b)** when it is raining; *the summer months are the wettest part of the year; there's nothing I like better than a wet Sunday in London* **(c)** not yet dry; *watch out! - the paint's still wet* **(d)** *(informal)* feeble, and incapable of taking decisions; *don't be so wet - phone the manager and tell him what you think!* (NOTE: **wetter - wettest**) **2** *verb* **(a)** to make something wet; *the rain didn't really wet the soil* **(b)** to sprinkle with water; *wet the shirt before you iron it* **(c)** *(of child)* **to wet the bed** = to urinate in bed and make it wet; *she's started to wet her bed* **3** *noun (informal)* feeble person, especially a politician who prefers compromise; *she got rid of all the wets in her cabinet*

wetland ['wetlənd] *noun* marshy areas which are often covered by water; *every effort has been made to halt the draining of the wetlands; there are two important wetland sites in the area*

wetsuit ['wetsuːt] *noun* rubber suit worn by swimmers and divers to keep themselves warm in the water; *police divers in wetsuits were ready to search the river*

we've [wiːv] = WE HAVE

whack [wæk] **1** *verb* **(a)** to hit hard, making a loud noise; *she whacked her head on the low doorway; he whacked the ball hard with his bat* **(b)** to defeat in a match; *we whacked them 7 - 0 last time we played them* **2** *noun* **(a)** hard, noisy blow; *he gave the ball a whack and it went over the wall* **(b)** *(informal)* **have a whack (at it)!** = try to do it **(c)** *(informal)* amount of money; *we each paid the full whack*

whale [weɪl] *noun* **(a)** huge mammal that lives in the sea; *you can take a boat into the mouth of the river to see the whales* (NOTE: do not confuse with **wail**) **(b)** *(informal)* **to have a whale of a time** = to enjoy yourself very much; *the children had a whale of a time at the zoo*

whaling ['weɪlɪŋ] *noun* hunting of whales; *commercial whaling is severely restricted; the major whaling countries include Japan and Norway*

wharf [wɔːf] *noun* place by the sea where a ship can tie up to load or unload; *the fishing boats were tied up at the wharf* (NOTE: plural is **wharfs** *or* **wharves** [wɔːvz])

what [wɒt] **1** *adjective (asking a question)* **what time is it?**; *what type of food does he like best?* **2** *pronoun* **(a)** the thing which; *did you see what was in the box?; what we like to do most on holiday is just to visit old churches* **(b)** *(asking a question)* **what's the correct time?**; *what did he give you for your birthday?; what's the name of the French restaurant in the High*

Street?; *what's the Spanish for 'table'?*; *what happened to his car?* **(c)** *(informal)* **to know what's what** = to know everything about the situation; *the builder knows what's what, so he'll tell you the details* **3** *adverb* **(a)** *(showing surprise)* *what a huge meal!*; *what beautiful weather!* **(b)** *(giving a reason)* *what with the children being ill one after another, and my husband being away, I've got my hands full at the moment* **4** *interjection (showing surprise)* *what! the restaurant's full?*; *what! did you hear what he said?*; *I won the lottery! - What!* (NOTE: after **what** used to ask a question, the verb is put before the subject: **what's the time** but **they don't know what the time is**)

what about [wɒt ə'baʊt] *phrase (showing a suggestion) what about having some lunch?*; *they invited everybody - are you sure, what about Fiona?*

whatever [wɒt'evə] *pronoun (form of 'what' which emphasizes)* **(a)** it doesn't matter what; *you can have whatever you like for Christmas*; *she always does whatever she feels like doing*; *I want that car whatever the price* **(b)** *(in questions)* what, why; *whatever made him do that?*; *whatever does that red light mean?*; *I've sold the car - whatever for?*

what for ['wɒt 'fɔː] **(a)** why; *what are they all shouting for?*; *he's sold his car - what for?*; *what did he phone the police for?* **(b)** for what use; *what's this red button for?*

whatsoever [wɒtsəʊ'evə] *adjective & pronoun (form of 'whatever' which emphasizes) there is no truth whatsoever in the report*; *the police found no suspicious documents whatsoever*; **none whatsoever** = none at all; *do you have any idea why the computer suddenly stopped working? - none whatsoever* (NOTE: always used after a noun and after a negative)

wheat [wiːt] *noun* cereal plant of which the grain is used to make flour; *after the storms much of the wheat lay flat on the ground*; *use wheat flour to make the muffins* (NOTE: no plural)

wheedle ['wiːdl] *verb* to try to persuade someone to do something, using a flattering tone of voice; *she managed to wheedle a promise out of him*

wheel [wiːl] **1** *noun* **(a)** round piece which turns round an axle and on which a bicycle, a car, etc., runs; *the front wheel and the back wheel of the motorbike were both damaged in the accident*; *we got a flat tyre so I had to get out to change the wheel*; **on wheels** = with wheels attached; *hospital beds are on wheels so they are easy to move*; *see also* MEALS **(b)** any similar round piece for turning; **steering wheel** = wheel which is turned by the driver to control the direction of a vehicle; *the steering wheel is on the right-hand side of the car in British cars*; **to be at the wheel** = to be driving; *she was at the wheel when the car went off the road*; **to take the wheel** = to start to drive a car; *she took the wheel because her husband was falling asleep* **2** *verb* **(a)** to push something along that has wheels; *he wheeled his motorbike into the garage*; *she was wheeling her bike along the pavement*; *the waiter wheeled in a sweet trolley* **(b)** **to wheel round** = to turn round suddenly; *she wheeled round and went straight up to the counter* **(c)** to fly in circles; *gulls were wheeling above the fishing boats* **(d)** **to wheel and deal** = to negotiate to make business deals

wheelbarrow ['wiːlbærəʊ] *noun* small cart with one wheel in front, and two handles, used by builders and gardeners to carry heavy loads; *he filled the wheelbarrow with soil and wheeled it to the end of the garden*

wheelchair ['wiːltʃeə] *noun* chair on wheels which people who cannot walk use to move around; *he manages to get around in a wheelchair*; *she has been confined to a wheelchair since her accident*; **wheelchair entrance** = special entrance with a ramp instead of steps, which can be used by people in wheelchairs

wheeled [wiːld] *adjective* with wheels; *a motorbike is a two-wheeled vehicle*

wheelhouse ['wiːlhaʊs] *noun* construction on a small ship where the captain stands at the wheel, steering; *he was in the wheelhouse when the big wave hit the boat*

wheely bin ['wiːli 'bɪn] *noun (informal)* large dustbin on wheels

wheeze [wiːz] **1** *noun* **(a)** whistling noise made when breathing; *I'm full of coughs and wheezes* **(b)** *(informal)* clever trick; *he thought he had discovered a clever wheeze how to avoid paying tax until he got caught* **2** *verb* to make a whistling sound when breathing; *the little boy had an attack of asthma and started to wheeze*

whelk [welk] *noun* type of edible sea snail; *we bought some whelks at a stall on the pier*

when [wen] **1** *adverb (asking a question)* at what time; *when is the last train for Paris?*; *when did you last go to the dentist?*; *when are we going to get paid?*; *since when has he been wearing glasses?*; *I asked her when her friend was leaving* (NOTE: after **when** used to ask a question, the verb is put before the subject: **when does the film start?** but **he doesn't know when the film starts**; **when is he coming?** but **they can't tell me when he is coming**) **2** *conjunction* **(a)** at the time that; *when he was young, the family was living in London*; *when you go on holiday, leave your key with the neighbours so they can feed the cat*; *do you remember the day when we all went for a picnic in Hyde Park?*; *let me know when you're ready to go* **(b)** after; *when the speaker had finished, he sat down*; *wash up the plates when you've finished your breakfast* **(c)** even if; *the salesman said the car was worth £5000 when he really knew it was worth only half that* **(d)** although; *I said I knew nothing about it when in fact I'd known about it for some time*

whence [wens] *adverb (formal)* from where; *she returned to Canada whence she had come in 1958*

whenever [wen'evə] *adverb* **(a)** at any time that; *come for tea whenever you like*; *we try to see my mother-in-law whenever we can or whenever possible* **(b)** *(form of 'when' which emphasizes) whenever did she learn to drive?*

where [weə] *adverb* **(a)** *(asking a question)* in what place, to what place; *where did I put my glasses?*; *do you know where the restaurant is?*; *where are the knives and forks?*; *where are you going for your holiday?* **(b)** *(showing place)* in a place in which; *stay where you are and don't move*; *they still live in the same house where they were living twenty years ago*; *here's where the wire has been cut* **(c)** whenever; *use fresh tomatoes where possible* (NOTE: after **where** used to ask a question, the verb is put before the subject: **where is the bottle?** but **he doesn't know where the bottle is**)

where- ['weə] *prefix* which thing (NOTE: some of the following words formed from **where-** are used in their formal meanings in legal documents)

whereabouts 1 *noun* ['weərəbauts] the place where someone *or* something is; *she knew nothing of her son's whereabouts* **2** *adverb* [weərə'bauts] (*asking a question*) in what place?; *they live in London - oh! whereabouts in London?*

whereas [weər'æz] *conjunction* (a) if you compare this with the fact that; *he likes tea whereas she prefers coffee* (b) (*formal*) taking the following fact into consideration; *whereas the contract between the two parties stipulates that either party may withdraw at six months' notice*

whereby [weə'bai] *adverb* (*formal*) by which; according to which; *a deed whereby ownership of the property is transferred; a teaching method whereby students can measure their own progress*

wherein [weər'ın] *adverb* (*formal*) in which; *we visited the house wherein Shakespeare once lived*

whereupon [weərə'pɒn] *conjunction* at that point, after that; *the orchestra started playing, whereupon he immediately fell asleep*

wherever [weə'evə] *adverb* (a) to or in any place; *you can sit wherever you want; wherever we go on holiday, we never make hotel reservations; the police want to ask her questions, wherever she may be* (b) (*form of 'where' which emphasizes*) *wherever did you get that hat?*

whet [wet] *verb* to whet your appetite = to make you more interested in something by giving you a little sample of it; *the brochures whet your appetite for holidays by the sea* (NOTE: **whetting - whetted**)

whether ['weðə] *conjunction* (a) (*showing doubt, or not having reached a decision*) if; *do you know whether they're coming?; I can't make up my mind whether to go on holiday now or later* (b) (*applying to either of two things*) both; *all employees, whether managers or ordinary staff, must take a medical test* (NOTE: do not confuse with **weather**)

which [wıtʃ] *adjective & pronoun* (a) (*asking a question*) what person or thing; *which dress are you wearing to the wedding?; which boy threw that stone?* (b) **which is which** = what is the difference between the two; *there are two switches, one for the light and one for the fan, but I don't know which is which* (c) (*only used with things, not people*) that; *the French restaurant which is next door to the office; they've eaten all the bread which you bought yesterday* (d) **in which case** = if that is the case; *he's ill, in which case he'd better stay at home* (NOTE: with an object, **which** can be left out: *here's the bread we bought yesterday*)

whichever [wıtʃ'evə] **1** *pronoun* (a) anything that; *you can take several routes, but whichever you choose, the journey will still take three hours* (b) (*emphatic form of 'which'*) no matter which; *take whichever one you want* **2** *adjective* no matter which; *whichever newspaper you read, you'll get the same story*

whiff [wıf] *noun* slight smell; *there was a whiff of lavender as the old lady came in; I thought I could detect a whiff of melons; the tabloids have detected a whiff of scandal about the minister*

Whig [wıg] *noun* (*old*) name of a member of the political party which eventually became the Liberal Party in Britain; *the Whigs came to power for the first time in 1721*

while [wail] **1** *noun* (a) some time; *it's a while since I've seen him*; **in a while** = in a short time, soon; *I'll be ready in a while*; **a little while** = short period of time; *do you mind waiting a little while until a table is free?*; **quite a while** = a longer period of time; *he changed jobs quite a while ago*; **once in a while** = from time to time, but not often; *it's nice to go to have an Indian meal once in a while* (b) **to be worth someone's while** = to be worth doing; *it's worth your while keeping copies of your work, in case your computer goes wrong*; see also WORTHWHILE **2** *conjunction* (a) when, at the time that; *he tried to cut my hair while he was watching TV; while we were on holiday someone broke into our house; shall I clean the kitchen while you're having a bath?* (b) (*showing difference*) *he likes meat, while his sister is a vegetarian; she only earns £120 a week while everyone else in the office earns twice that; everyone is watching TV, while I'm in the kitchen making the dinner* (c) (*formal*) although; *while there may still be delays, the service is much better than it used to be*

while away ['wail ə'wei] *verb* **to while away the time** = to do something to make the time pass more quickly; *I had two hours to wait between planes and had several cups of coffee to while away the time*

whilst [wailst] *conjunction* (*formal*) while; *she went to London whilst he remained in their cottage in the country*

whim [wım] *noun* sudden wish or desire; *she had this sudden whim to go to Bangkok*; **your every whim** = all your desires; *after she got married, she expected her husband to indulge her every whim*; **a passing whim** = desire which will change quickly to something else; *don't do what he says - it's only a passing whim*

whimper ['wımpə] **1** *verb* (*of person or small animal*) to make low weak cries; *she whimpered that she would be OK; the dog was whimpering because it was tied up* **2** *noun* sad, weak cry; *I could still hear her whimpers through the bedroom door*

whimsical ['wımzıkl] *adjective* odd or fanciful, not very serious; *we expected a serious report but the result was whimsical; we were wondering what to do in the evening, and he made some whimsical suggestions*

whine [wain] **1** *verb* (a) to make a loud high-pitched noise; *you can hear the engines of the racing cars whining in the background* (b) to complain in a loud high voice; *she's always whining about how little money she has* **2** *noun* loud high-pitched noise; *we could hear the whine of the engines long before we got to the racetrack* (NOTE: do not confuse with **wine**)

whinge [wındʒ] *verb* (*informal*) to complain in a whining voice; *what are they whingeing about?; if you don't stop whingeing, I'll go off without you* (*Australian: informal*) **whingeing Poms** = English people who go to live in Australia and then complain about life there

whinny ['wını] **1** *noun* quiet neigh made by a horse; *did you hear the horse's whinnies in the middle of the night?* **2** *verb* (*of a horse*) to make a quiet neigh; *I heard the horses whinnying in their stables*

whip [wıp] **1** *noun* (a) long, thin piece of leather with a handle, used to hit animals to make them do what you want; *jockeys use the whip to make their horses run* *faster* (b) **to crack the whip** = to make everyone do what you want; *the boss had to crack the whip to get the job finished on time* (c) MP who controls the attendance of other MPs of his party at the House of Commons and who makes sure that all MPs vote; **Chief Whip** = main whip, who organizes the other whips; *the Government Chief Whip made sure the MPs were all present for the vote* (d) sweet pudding made with whipped cream or eggs and fruit or chocolate; *she made a chocolate whip* 2 *verb* (a) to hit someone or an animal with a whip; *he whipped the horse to make it go faster* (b) to beat cream, eggs, etc., until firm; *whip the eggs and milk together; it is easier to whip cream if it is cold* (c) to go quickly; *he whipped round to the newsagent's to buy some cigarettes* (d) to do something quickly; *he whipped off his hat when he saw her coming towards him; she whipped out her chequebook* (e) *(slang)* to steal; *someone's whipped my newspaper!* (NOTE: whipping - whipped)

whiplash ['wɪplæʃ] *noun* injury to the bones in your neck, caused when your head moves suddenly backwards, as in a car which has been hit from behind; *one of the passengers suffered whiplash injuries*

whipped cream ['wɪpt 'kriːm] *noun* cream which has been beaten to make it thicker; *whip the cream at the last minute, and put the whipped cream on the cake and decorate it with strawberries*

whipping cream ['wɪpɪŋ 'kriːm] *noun* cream which has enough fat in it to be whipped; *I forgot to buy some whipping cream*

whip up ['wɪp 'ʌp] *verb* (a) to encourage, to make something increase; *loudspeaker messages whipped up the crowd's enthusiasm before the match* (b) *(informal)* to get food ready; *I'll just whip up a salad* (c) to beat things together; *whip up the eggs and milk in a bowl; the wind whipped up the waves on the lake*

whirl [wɜːl] 1 *noun* rapid turning movement; *a whirl of activity* *(informal)* **let's give it a whirl** = let's try it out 2 *verb* to turn round quickly, to spin; *she put on her new skirt and whirled around for every one to see; the children's paper windmills whirled in the wind*

whirlpool ['wɜːlpuːl] *noun* stream of water that turns round and round very fast; *be careful, there are whirlpools in the river*

whirlwind ['wɜːlwɪnd] *noun* (a) column of air that turns round and round very fast in the centre of an area of very low pressure; *whirlwinds come in the summer months and cause a huge amount of damage* (NOTE: in American English also called a **twister**) (b) *(informal)* something which happens more quickly than usual; *they had a whirlwind romance, and got married on holiday*

whirr *US* **whir** [wɜː] 1 *noun* low sound like something turning; *I was woken up by the whirr of a small plane* 2 *verb* to make a low sound like something turning; *the journalists' cameras were whirring and clicking as she stepped out of the church*

whisk [wɪsk] 1 *noun* kitchen tool used for whipping cream, eggs, etc.; *she was looking for the whisk to beat some eggs* 2 *verb* (a) to move something very fast; *she whisked the plate of cakes away before I could take one; they came in, said hello to us, and whisked our daughter off to the restaurant* (b) to beat cream, eggs, etc., very quickly; *next, whisk the mixture until it is creamy; I always whisk egg whites by hand*

whiskers ['wɪskəz] *noun* moustache and beard on the side of an animal's or a man's face; *it's not only cats that have whiskers, rabbits have them too; that's a family portrait - my great-grandfather's the one with a top hat and whiskers*

whiskey ['wɪski] *noun* Irish or American whisky

whisky ['wɪski] *noun* (a) alcoholic drink, made in Scotland, distilled from barley or other grains; *the distillery produces thousands of bottles of whisky every year; I don't like whisky - I prefer gin* (b) a glass of this drink; *two whiskies, please* (NOTE: plural is whiskies)

whisper ['wɪspə] 1 *noun* quiet voice, words spoken very quietly; *she spoke in a whisper* 2 *verb* to speak very quietly, to make a very quiet sound; *he whispered instructions to the other members of the gang; she whispered to the nurse that she wanted something to drink*

whist [wɪst] *noun* card game for four people, playing in pairs; *I don't know how to play whist, I've never played it*

whistle ['wɪsl] 1 *noun* (a) high-pitched sound made by blowing through your lips when they are almost closed; *she gave a whistle of surprise; we heard a whistle and saw a dog running across the field* (b) simple instrument which makes a high-pitched sound, played by blowing; *he blew on his whistle to stop the match;* **penny whistle** *or* **tin whistle** = simple metal flute; *he stood at the corner of the street, playing a tune on a penny whistle* 2 *verb* (a) to blow through your lips to make a high-pitched sound; *they marched along, whistling an Irish song; the doorman whistled for a taxi* (b) to make a high-pitched sound using a small metal instrument; *the referee whistled to stop the match*

whistlestop tour ['wɪslstɒp 'tʊə] *noun* tour where you stop for a short time in many different places; *we went on a whistlestop tour of the French vineyards*

white [waɪt] 1 *adjective* of a colour like snow or milk; *a white shirt is part of the uniform; a white car will always look dirty; her hair is now completely white;* **white wine** = wine which is clear or slightly yellow; *I'll have a glass of white wine with the fish;* **white meat** = (i) breast of chicken or turkey; (ii) pale coloured meat like veal, as opposed to red meat like beef; **white Christmas** = Christmas when there is snow on the ground; **white coffee** = coffee with milk added; *do you take your coffee black or white?;* **white goods** = large household electrical equipment like fridges and washing machines; *(informal)* **white as a sheet** = completely white, very pale; *are you all right? - you look as white as a sheet* (NOTE: **whiter - whitest**) 2 *noun* (a) colour of snow or milk; *the white of the snow-capped mountains stood out against the deep blue of the sky* (b) person whose skin is pale; *whites are in the minority in African countries* (c) light-coloured meat (on a chicken); *do you want a leg or some white?* (d) white part of something; *the white of an egg; the whites of his eyes were slightly red; (informal)* **wait until you see the whites of their eyes** = wait until they are very close to you (e) *(informal)* white wine; *a glass of house white, please*

whitebait ['waɪtbeɪt] *noun* type of very small sea fish; *we had fried whitebait as a starter* (NOTE: plural is whitebait)

whitecollar worker [waɪt'kɒlə 'wɜːkə] *noun* worker in an office, not in a factory; *our staff are all whitecollar workers* (NOTE: factory workers are called **blue collar workers**)

white elephant ['waɪt 'elɪfənt] *noun* something which cost a lot of money and is no use; *the new airport is a complete white elephant*

Whitehall ['waɪthɔːl] *noun* **(a)** street in London, leading from Trafalgar Square to the Houses of Parliament, where several ministries are situated; *as you walk down Whitehall you pass Downing Street on your right* **(b)** *(informal)* the British government and civil service; *Whitehall sources suggest that the plan will be adopted; there is a great deal of resistance to the idea in Whitehall;* **Whitehall mandarins** = top British civil servants

white-hot ['waɪt 'hɒt] *adjective* extremely hot; *the molten iron was white-hot*

White House ['waɪt 'haʊs] *noun* **(a)** building in Washington D.C., where the President of the USA lives and works; *the President invited the Prime Minister to lunch at the White House; the new First Lady is planning to redecorate only a few rooms in the White House; see also* OVAL OFFICE **(b)** *(informal)* the US government, the president himself; *a White House spokesman gave a statement to the press; White House officials refused to confirm the report*

whiten ['waɪtn] *verb* to make whiter or to become whiter; *the soap ads say that their products will whiten your washing; he whitened when he saw the police car outside his house*

whiteness ['waɪnəs] *noun* being white; *the whiteness of the snow all round us*

White Paper ['waɪt 'peɪpə] *noun* report issued by the government as a statement of government policy on a particular problem; *the government has published a White Paper on immigration; compare* GREEN PAPER

white pepper ['waɪt 'pepə] *noun* pepper from seeds which have had the outer layer removed; *she put salt and white pepper on her omelette* (NOTE: pepper from whole dried pepper seeds is **black pepper**)

white stick ['waɪt 'stɪk] *noun* stick carried by a person who is blind or partially sighted

whitewash ['waɪtwɒʃ] **1** *noun* **(a)** mixture of water and lime used for painting the walls of houses; *one coat of whitewash should be enough for this wall* **(b)** attempt to cover up mistakes or corruption; *everyone said the report was a whitewash and nobody was ever arrested* **2** *verb* **(a)** to paint with a mixture of water and lime; *a landscape of fields and little whitewashed cottages* **(b)** to try to cover up mistakes or corruption; *the report was just an attempt to whitewash the officials at the children's home*

whitewater ['waɪtwɔːtə] *noun* rapids, part of a river which flows very fast over rocks; *we went whitewater rafting in Canada*

whither ['wɪðə] *adverb* *(formal)* to which place; *he left not saying whither he was going;* **whither the EU?** = what is the future of the EU?

whiting ['waɪtɪŋ] *noun* type of small sea fish (NOTE: plural is **whiting**)

whittle ['wɪtl] *verb* **(a)** to shape a piece of wood by cutting off small pieces with a knife; *he was whittling a stick with his penknife* **(b)** to whittle something away

or **down** = to make something gradually smaller; *he found his authority as chairman being gradually whittled away by the secretary; their aim is to whittle the staff down to half the actual number*

whiz [wɪz] *verb* to move very fast; *someone whizzed past me but I didn't see who it was; she's been whizzing around all afternoon trying to sort out her trip to the Caribbean* (NOTE: **whizzing - whizzed**)

who [huː] *pronoun* **(a)** *(asking a question)* which person or persons; *(who was it) who phoned?; who are you talking to?; who was she going home with?; who spoke at the meeting?* **(b)** the person or the people that; *the men who came yesterday morning work for the electricity company; anyone who didn't get tickets early won't be able to get in; there's the taxi driver who took us home last night; do you remember the girl who used to work here as a waitress?* (NOTE: with an object, **who** can be left out: **there's the man I saw at the pub**. Note also that when **who** is used as an object, it is sometimes written **whom** [huːm] **whom are you talking about? the man whom I saw in the office**. After **who** used to ask a question, the verb is put before the subject: **who is that man over there?** but **I don't know who that man is over there**)

WHO ['dʌblju: 'eɪtʃ 'əʊ] = WORLD HEALTH ORGANIZATION; *the WHO's top priority is the eradication of tuberculosis*

whoever [huː'evə] *pronoun (emphatic form of 'who')* no matter who, anyone who; *whoever finds the umbrella can keep it; go home with whoever you like*

whole [həʊl] **1** *adjective* all of something; *she must have been hungry - she ate a whole apple pie; we spent the whole winter in the south; a whole lot of people went down with flu* **2** *noun* all, everything; *she stayed in bed the whole of Sunday morning and read the newspapers; the whole of the north of the country was covered with snow; did you watch the whole of the programme?* (NOTE: do not confuse with **hole**) **3** *adverb* in one piece; *the heron swallowed the fish whole*

wholehearted [həʊl'hɑːtɪd] *adjective* complete or total; *I found it difficult to give her my wholehearted attention*

wholeheartedly [həʊl'hɑːtɪdli] *adverb* completely; *I agree wholeheartedly with what he has said*

wholemeal ['həʊlmiːl] *noun* **wholemeal flour** = flour which contains a large proportion of the original wheat grain; **wholemeal bread** = bread made from wholemeal flour; *I have two slices of wholemeal toast for breakfast*

whole number ['həʊl 'nʌmbə] *noun* number which is not a fraction (1, 3, etc.); *if your answer is a fraction, round it up to the next whole number; the answer must be a whole number: 5.97 should be given as 6*

wholesale ['həʊlseɪl] **1** *adverb* buying goods from manufacturers and selling them in large quantities to traders who then sell them in smaller quantities to the general public; *he buys wholesale* (NOTE: the opposite is **retail**) **2** *adjective* **(a)** in large quantities; **wholesale discount** **(b)** on a large scale; *the wholesale killing of wild birds*

wholesaler ['həʊlseɪlə] *noun* person who buys goods in large quantities from manufacturers and sells them to retailers; *wholesalers ask for very big discounts; the shop doesn't buy direct from the manufacturer but from a wholesaler*

wholesome ['həʊlsəm] *adjective* **(a)** healthy, good for your health; *you should stick to a more wholesome diet and stop eating all that junk food*; **wholesome food** = food that is good for your health; *you should eat fresh fruit and vegetables and other wholesome food* **(b)** good for your morals; *those videos are not what I would call good wholesome entertainment for youngsters*

wholewheat ['həʊlwiːt] *noun* mainly *US* = WHOLEMEAL

wholly ['həʊli] *adverb (formal)* completely, totally; *I don't think she has wholly recovered from her illness*; *we were talking about two wholly different subjects* (NOTE: do not confuse with **holy**)

whom [huːm] *see* WHO

whoop [wuːp or huːp] **1** *noun* loud cry; *the boys let out whoops as they ran down the hill* (NOTE: do not confuse with **hoop**) **2** *verb* to make loud cries; *the gang ran along the main street, shouting and whooping at passers-by*

whooping cough ['huːpɪŋ 'kɒf] *noun* infectious disease which affects the bronchial tubes, common in children, and sometimes very serious; *she caught whooping cough from her brother*

> COMMENT: the patient coughs very badly, and makes a characteristic 'whoop' when breathing in after a fit of coughing

whoops [wuːps] *interjection* used to show that an accident has almost happened *(informal)* **whoops!** *you nearly hit that tree!*; *she went charging across the kitchen on her trike and whoops! just missed Mum carrying a pile of plates*

whose [huːz] *pronoun* **(a)** *(asking a question)* which belongs to which person; *whose is that car?*; *whose chequebook is this?*; *whose money was stolen?* **(b)** of whom; *the family whose house was burgled*; *the girl whose foot you trod on* (NOTE: do not confuse with **who's**)

why [waɪ] **1** *adverb* **(a)** *(asking a question)* for what reason; *why did he to phone me in the middle of the TV film?*; *I asked the ticket collector why the train was late* **(b)** *(giving reason)* she told me why she couldn't go to the party **(c)** *(showing something else is preferred)* why go by plane to Paris when you can take the train?; *why don't we go for a picnic as it's fine?* (NOTE: after **why** used to ask a question, the verb is put before the subject: **why is the sky blue?** but **they don't know why the sky is blue**) **2** *interjection showing surprise*; *why, if it isn't old Mr Smith!*

wick [wɪk] *noun* piece of string in the middle of a candle or in an oil lamp, which you light and which burns slowly; *the wick is too short and I can't light it*

wicked ['wɪkɪd] *adjective* **(a)** very bad; *what a wicked thing to say!*; *it was wicked of them to steal the birds' eggs* **(b)** mischievous; *she gave a wicked little laugh* **(c)** dangerous; *he came in carrying a wicked axe* **(d)** *(informal)* very good; *they do a wicked line in French pastries*

wicker ['wɪkə] *adjective* (made of) thin pieces of wood or twigs woven together; *we've bought a wicker basket*; *wicker furniture is fashionable again*

wickerwork ['wɪkəwɜːk] *noun* things made of thin pieces of wood or twigs woven together; *a wickerwork chair*; *there's a shop in the village that sells baskets and other types of wickerwork* (NOTE: no plural)

wicket ['wɪkɪt] *noun* **(a)** *(in cricket)* set of three sticks put in the ground with two small sticks on top, used as the target; *the first ball hit his wicket* **(b)** *(in cricket)* main playing area between two sets of these sticks; **fast wicket** = wicket where the ball moves fast off the ground; **slow wicket** = wicket where the ball moves slowly off the ground; *(informal)* **to be on a sticky wicket** = to be in an awkward situation **(c)** *US* position or opening with a window at a post office, bank, etc.

wicket-keeper ['wɪkɪtkiːpə] *noun* *(in cricket)* player who stands behind the wicket to stop the balls that the batsman does not hit; *the wicket-keeper dropped an easy catch*

wide [waɪd] **1** *adjective* **(a)** which measures from side to side; *the table is three foot or three feet wide*; *the river is not very wide at this point* **(b)** extensive, enormous; *the shop carries a wide range of imported goods*; *she has a wide knowledge of French painting* (NOTE: **wider - widest**) **2** *adverb* **(a)** as far as possible, as much as possible; *she opened her eyes wide*; *the door was wide open so we just walked in*; **wide apart** = separated by a large space; *he stood with his legs wide apart*; **wide awake** = very much awake, not at all sleepy; *at eleven o'clock the baby was still wide awake* **(b)** not on the target; *the shells fell wide of their target*; **to be wide of the mark** = to be very wrong; *he's wide of the mark when he says that that old car is worth £2000* **3** *noun* *(in cricket)* ball which goes too far to the side of the batsman

widely ['waɪdli] *adverb* **(a)** by a wide range of people; *it is widely expected that he will resign* **(b)** over a wide area; *contamination spread widely over the area round the factory*; *she has travelled widely in Greece*; **he is very widely-travelled** = he has travelled in many places

widely read ['waɪdli 'red] *adjective* **(a)** (book) which many people have read; *it must be the most widely read travel book of the year* **(b)** (person) who has read many books; *the students are not as widely read as we would like*

widen ['waɪdn] *verb* **(a)** to make wider; *we need to widen the road to take larger lorries* **(b)** to become wider; *further along, the road widens into two lanes in each direction*

wide-ranging [waɪd'reɪndʒɪŋ] *adjective* which covers a wide range of topics; *we had a wide-ranging discussion on various topics*

widespread ['waɪdspred] *adjective* over a large area; *there was widespread flooding in the south of the country*; *there is a widespread idea that exercise is good for you*

widget ['wɪdʒɪt] *noun (informal)* little device; *do you know what this widget's for?*; *let's suppose you're running a company that makes widgets in the West Midlands*

widow ['wɪdəʊ] *noun* woman whose husband has died and who has not married again; *she was left a widow at a very early age*; **grass widow** = woman whose husband is often away from home

widowed ['wɪdəʊd] *adjective* (woman) who has become a widow; (man) who has become a widower; *she has been widowed twice and married for the third time at the age of 60*

widower ['wɪdəuə] *noun* man whose wife has died and who has not married again; *she married again, this time a widower aged 62*

width [wɪdθ] *noun* **(a)** measurement of something from one side to another; *I need to know the width of the sofa; the width of the garden is at least forty feet or the garden is at least forty feet in width* **(b)** distance from one side to another of a swimming pool; *she swam three widths easily*

wield ['wiːld] *verb* **(a)** to hold something, usually by its handle, and use it; *her attacker was wielding a knife* **(b)** to use or have power to control people; *the state wields enormous power over the ordinary citizen*

wiener ['wiːnə] *noun US* frankfurter, a long spiced sausage which is cooked and sometimes eaten with a roll; *we cooked wieners on the barbecue*

Wiener Schnitzel ['viːnə 'ʃnɪtzəl] *noun* slice of veal, covered in breadcrumbs and fried; *I've been in Germany for four days and all I've eaten are Wiener Schnitzels*

wife [waɪf] *noun* woman who is married to a man; *I know Mr Jones quite well but I've never met his wife; they both came with their wives*; *see also* OLD WIVES' TALE (NOTE: plural is **wives** ['waɪvz])

wig [wɪg] *noun* false hair worn on the head; *she wore a green wig for the carnival*

wiggle ['wɪgl] *verb (informal)* to move slightly up and down or from side to side; *try to wiggle your toes to see if the shoes are big enough; she wears high heels and wiggles her hips as she walks*

wiggly ['wɪgli] *adjective (informal)* which is not straight; *this wiggly line isn't what we wanted - it should be straight; the road is very wiggly here, so drive slowly*

wild [waɪld] **1** *adjective* **(a)** living naturally, not tame; *wild dogs roam over parts of Australia*; **wild animals** = animals which are living in natural surroundings, as opposed to pets or farm animals; *we watched a TV programme on wild animals in Africa*; **wild flower** = flower which grows naturally, not a garden plant; *the book has several pictures of wild flowers* **(b)** **wild mountain scenery** = mountains with high cliffs, waterfalls, etc. **(c)** *(informal)* very angry; very excited; *he will be wild when he sees what I have done to the car; the fans went wild at the end of the match*; *(informal)* **to be wild about something** = to be very interested in something; *she's wild about motorbikes*; **beyond your wildest dreams** = even better than you could expect; *the results surpassed our wildest dreams* **(d)** not thinking carefully; *she made a few wild guesses, but didn't find the right answer; they had the wild idea of walking across the Sahara* **2** *noun* **(a)** **in the wild** = living in nature; *in the wild, elephants can live to a great age* **(b)** **the wilds of** = the remote parts of; *they have a cottage in the wilds of the Scottish Highlands* **3** *adverb* **(a)** freely; *in the safari park we let the animals run wild* **(b)** without any control; *the crowds were running wild through the centre of the town*

wild cat ['waɪld 'kæt] *noun* small wild animal of the cat family, living in forests; *wild cats come down from the pine woods and eat our chickens*

wildcat strike ['waɪldkæt 'straɪk] *noun* strike organized suddenly by workers without the permission of the main union office; *the wildcat strike caused chaos with the bus service*

wilderness ['wɪldənəs] *noun* uncultivated and uninhabited country or desert; *he spent years exploring the Arctic wilderness*

wildfire ['waɪldfaɪə] *noun* **like wildfire** = very fast; *the news spread like wildfire through the crowd*

wildfowl ['waɪldfaul] *noun* wild birds, such as ducks and geese, that are shot for sport; *we shoot pheasants and other wildfowl in these fields; thousands of wildfowl come to nest in these marshes* (NOTE: the word is plural)

wild goose chase [waɪld 'guːs tʃeɪs] *noun* hopeless search; *they set off on a wild goose chase for new kitchen furniture*

wildlife ['waɪldlaɪf] *noun* birds, plants and animals living free and untouched by humans; *they spent the summer studying the wildlife in the national park*; **wildlife park** = large park surrounded by high fences, where wild animals are kept and are allowed to run wild inside (NOTE: no plural)

wildly ['waɪldli] *adverb* **(a)** in a wild way; *the crowd cheered wildly as the pop group started to sing* **(b)** **wildly inaccurate** = completely wrong; *his prediction of a fine summer was wildly inaccurate*

wilful *US* **willful** ['wɪlful] *adjective* **(a)** determined to do what you want; *she's a wilful child and very difficult to control* **(b)** done because someone wants to do it; *they caused wilful damage to several telephone kiosks*; **wilful murder** = murder which was planned in advance; *this was a wilful murder and had been well planned*

wilfully *US* **willfully** ['wɪlfuli] *adverb* done because someone wants to do it; *he wilfully set fire to the building*

will [wɪl] **1** *verb, used with other verbs* **(a)** *(to form the future)* the party will start soon; *will they be staying a long time?; we won't be able to come to tea; if you ask her to play the piano, she'll say 'no'* **(b)** *(emphasizing)* the dog will keep eating the cat's food **(c)** *(polite way of asking someone to do something)* **will everyone please sit down?; will someone close the curtains?;** *(formal)* **won't you sit down? (d)** *(showing that you are keen to do something)* don't call a taxi - I'll take you home; the car will never start when we want it to; don't worry - I will do it* (NOTE: the negative: **will not** is usually written **won't** [wəunt] The past is: **would**, negative: **would not**, usually written **wouldn't**. Note also that **will** is often shortened to **'ll: he'll** = he will) **2** *noun* **(a)** power of the mind and character; **to work with a will** = to work very earnestly and willingly; **with the best will in the world** = however much you want to do something; *even with the best will in the world, I don't see how we can finish it in time* **(b)** wish; **against your will** = without your agreement; *he was forced to sign the document against his will*; **of your own free will** = willingly, without being forced; *he signed the document of his own free will*; **at will** = whenever you want to; *visitors can wander around the gardens at will* **(c)** legal document by which a person gives instructions to his or her executors as to what should happen to the property after he or she dies; *he wrote his will in 1984; according to her will, all her property is left to her children; has she made a will yet?*

COMMENT: to make a valid will, a person must be sane, and the will must be signed and witnessed by two witnesses who will not benefit from the will. In English law, you have complete freedom to leave your property as you wish. You may, for example, not leave anything to your children, but leave your fortune to a home for stray cats, although in this case, your children would probably contest the will in the courts

willing ['wɪlɪŋ] **1** *adjective* keen to help; *is there anyone who is willing to drive the jeep?*; *I need two willing helpers to wash the car* **2** *noun* eagerness to help; **to show willing** = to show you are eager to help

willingly ['wɪlɪŋli] *adverb* readily, in a eager way; *I would willingly do the shopping but my foot hurts too much*

willingness ['wɪlɪŋnəs] *noun* being ready to do something; *he may be a bit slow, but at least he shows willingness*

willow ['wɪləu] *noun* tree with long thin branches often found near rivers and streams; *she sat in the shade of an old willow, watching the river flow past*; **weeping willow** = type of large willow tree with long drooping branches

willowy ['wɪləuwi] *adjective* tall and slender; *a tall willowy girl on a grey horse*

willpower ['wɪlpauə] *noun* strength of will; *does she have the willpower to do it?*; *you need very strong willpower not to drink when everyone else is drinking*

wilt [wɪlt] **1** *noun* disease of plants which makes them droop; *the lettuces are all suffering from wilt* **2** *verb* to become weak and droop; *we've had no rain for days and the plants in the garden have started to wilt*; *we all started off at a fast pace, but after the first mile or so some of us began to wilt*

wily ['waɪli] *adjective* crafty, full of tricks; *a wily politician* (NOTE: **wilier - wiliest**)

Wimbledon ['wɪmbəldʌn] *noun* town in the south of London, where a tennis tournament is held each summer; *coverage of Wimbledon on TV*; *the Wimbledon women's champion*

wimp [wɪmp] *noun* weak individual; *he never does anything exciting, he's such a wimp*

win [wɪn] **1** *noun* beating someone in a game; *the local team has only had two wins so far this year*; *we're disappointed, we expected a win* **2** *verb* **(a)** to beat someone in a game; to be first in a race; *I expect our team will win tomorrow*; *the local team won their match yesterday*; *she won the race easily* **(b)** to get (a prize, etc.); *she won first prize in the art competition*; *he won two million pounds on the lottery*; *she's hoping to win a new car in a competition in the paper* (NOTE: **winning - won** [wʌn])

wince [wɪns] **1** *noun* reaction on your face which shows you feel pain; *he gave a wince as the nurse cleaned his wound* **2** *verb* to show signs of pain, especially on the face; *he winced as the nurse gave him an injection*; *she still winces as the memory of the awful mistake she made*

winch [wɪnʃ] **1** *noun* device which pulls things up by winding a rope around a drum; *the recovery vehicle has a winch at the back* **2** *verb* to pull up or to lift by using a winch; *the sailors were winched from the yacht by helicopter*

wind 1 [wɪnd] *noun* **(a)** air moving outdoors; *the wind blew two trees down in the park*; *there's no point trying to use an umbrella in this wind*; *there's not a breath of wind - the sailing boats aren't moving at all*; **to run like the wind** = to run very fast; *he ran like the wind and won the race* **(b)** ability to breathe; **to get your wind back** = to breathe properly again after running fast; *just give me a moment to get my wind back and I'll give you the message*; **wind instruments** = musical instruments, like the flute, which you have to blow to make a note; *he doesn't play any wind instrument, just the piano* **(c)** **the wind section** = section of an orchestra with wind instruments; *the work provides a lot of scope for the wind section*; see also BRASS, PERCUSSION, STRINGS **(d)** gas which forms in the digestive system; *the baby is suffering from wind*; **to break wind** = to let gas escape from the intestines **(e)** **to get wind of something** = to hear a rumour about something; *somehow, our rivals got wind of our plan to expand our chain of stores* **2** [waɪnd] *verb* **(a)** to turn a key, etc., to make a machine work; *do you need to wind (up) the clock twice a week?* **(b)** to twist round and round; *he wound the towel round his waist*; *she wound the string into a ball* (NOTE: **winding - wound** [waund])

windbag ['wɪndbæg] *noun* (*informal*) someone who talks a lot

windcheater *US* **windbreaker** ['wɪndtʃiːtə or 'wɪndbreɪkə] *noun* waterproof jacket, usually with a hood; *you'll need to wear a windcheater if you're going walking today*

windchill factor ['wɪndtʃɪl 'fæktə] *noun* way of calculating the risk of exposure in cold weather by adding the speed of the wind to the number of degrees of temperature below zero; *it is supposed to be around $0°$, but with the windchill factor it will feel even colder than that*

wind down ['waɪnd 'daun] *verb* to turn a handle to make something go down; *you can wind down the window if it is too hot*

windfall ['wɪnfɔːl] *noun* **(a)** fruit which has fallen to the ground from a fruit tree; *there are a lot of windfalls this year* **(b)** money which you receive unexpectedly; *his premium bond suddenly produced a windfall*

winding ['waɪndɪŋ] *adjective* which turns and twists; *they took a winding road up the mountain*

windless ['wɪnləs] *adjective* with no wind; *it was a beautiful windless day - no good for sailing*

windmill ['wɪnmɪl] *noun* mill driven by sails which turn when the wind blows; *they live in an old windmill in East Anglia*; *windmills were used to grind corn into flour*

window ['wɪndəu] *noun* **(a)** opening in a wall, door, etc., which is filled with glass; *when I fly, I always ask for a seat by the window, so that I can watch the landing and takeoff*; *I looked out of the kitchen window and saw a fox*; *it's dangerous to lean out of car windows*; *the burglar must have got in through the bathroom window*; **shop window** = large window in a shop where goods are displayed so that customers can see them; *she bought the dress she had seen in the shop window* **(b)** **window of opportunity** = short moment when the conditions for something are especially favourable **(c)** section of a computer screen used to display special information; *open the command window to see the range of possible commands*

window box ['wɪndəʊ 'bɒks] *noun* long narrow box for plants which is put on a windowledge outside a window; *she has a beautiful display of flowers in her window boxes*

windowframe ['wɪndəʊfreɪm] *noun* wooden or metal frame around a window; *all the windowframes need repainting*

windowledge *or* **windowsill** ['wɪndəledʒ *or* 'wɪndəsɪl] *noun* flat shelf beneath a window, either inside or outside; *he stood nervously on the windowledge, wondering if he could jump; she had a bowl of hyacinths on her windowsill*

window shopping ['wɪndəʊ 'ʃɒpɪŋ] *noun* looking at shop windows without buying anything; *we'll go window shopping in Regent Street*

windpipe ['wɪndpaɪp] *noun* main air passage from the nose and mouth to the lungs; *he had a piece of bread stuck in his windpipe* (NOTE: also called the **trachea**)

windscreen ['wɪndskriːn] *noun* glass window in the front of a car, bus, lorry, etc.; *the windscreen broke when a stone hit it; see also* WIPER (NOTE: the American English is **windshield**)

windshield ['wɪndʃiːld] *noun* (a) screen on the front of a motorcycle; *the windshield protects the rider from the rain* (b) *US* glass window in the front of a car, bus, lorry, etc.; *see also* WIPER (NOTE: British English is **windscreen**)

windsurfer ['wɪndsɜːfə] *noun* person who rides on water on a surfboard with a sail; *windsurfers were waiting for some wind to make really big waves*

windsurfing ['wɪndsɜːfɪŋ] *noun* sport of riding on the sea on a surfboard with a sail attached; *this is a very popular beach for windsurfing*

windswept ['wɪndswept] *adjective* blown by the wind; *they live in a tiny cottage on the windswept Yorkshire moors; they staggered into the hotel, looking windswept after their day's sailing*

wind up ['waɪnd 'ʌp] *verb* (a) to twist round and round; *she was winding the string up into a ball* (b) to turn a key to make a machine work; *when did you wind up the clock or wind the clock up?* (c) to turn a key to make something go up; *wind up your window if it starts to rain* (d) to end up; *they wound up owing the bank thousands of pounds* (e) to finish; *the meeting wound up at five o'clock* (f) **to wind up a company** = to put a company into liquidation; *the court ordered the company to be wound up* (g) (*informal*) to make someone annoyed; *he only did it to wind you up*

wind-up ['waɪndʌp] **1** *adjective* which works by clockwork; *a wind-up toy; it is not a wind-up clock - it works on a battery* **2** *noun* (*informal*) something done to annoy you; *I didn't believe him at first, I thought it was just a wind-up*

windward ['wɪnwəd] *noun, adjective & adverb* on or to the side of a ship from which the wind is blowing; *the windward side of the boat was constantly hit by waves; compare* LEEWARD

windy ['wɪndi] *adjective* when a strong wind is blowing; *we have a lot of windy weather in March; dress warmly, it's a cold windy day outside* (NOTE: windier - windiest)

wine [waɪn] **1** *noun* alcoholic drink made from grapes; *we had a bottle of French red wine; two glasses of white wine, please; should we have some white wine with the fish?*; **house wine** = special wine selected by a restaurant, cheaper than other wines on the wine list; **wine list** = list of wines and other drinks available in a restaurant (NOTE: usually singular: **some wine, a glass of wine**. Note that the plural **wines** means different sorts of wine) **2** *verb* **to wine and dine someone** = to invite someone for an expensive meal; *he seems to spend most of his time wining and dining potential customers*

wine bar ['waɪn 'bɑː] *noun* bar serving mainly wine, and food; *I don't like the food in the hotel restaurant, let's go to the wine bar round the corner*

wine glass ['waɪn 'glɑːs] *noun* glass for serving wine; *these wine glasses are very expensive*

wing [wɪŋ] *noun* (a) one of the two parts of the body which a bird or butterfly, etc., uses to fly; *the little birds were flapping their wings, trying to fly; which part of the chicken do you prefer, a leg or a wing?* (b) (*informal*) **to take someone under your wing** = to help someone by showing them what to do, especially someone who is new to the work or in training (c) one of the two flat parts sticking from the side of an aircraft, which hold an aircraft in the air; *he had a seat by the wing, so could not see much out of the window* (d) part of a large building which leads off to the side of the main building, often built as an extension; *they are building a new wing for the hospital* (e) body panel over the wheel of a car, which protects against splashing water and mud; *the front wing was dented in the crash* (NOTE: American English for this is **fender**) (f) side of a football or hockey pitch; *he ran along the left wing* (g) winger, player who plays on the wing; *he passed the ball out to the wing* (h) part of a political party which has a certain tendency; *she is on the right wing of the Conservative party*

winged [wɪŋd] *adjective* with wings; *winged insects were flying round the lamp*

winger ['wɪŋə] *noun* (a) (*in football, hockey, etc.*) person who plays on the side of the field; *one of the wingers kicked the ball into the net* (b) *suffix* showing a person on the right or left wing politically; *a right-winger*

wingspan ['wɪŋspæn] *noun* measurement from the tip of one wing to the tip of another; *the largest albatrosses can have a wingspan of up to three metres*

wink [wɪŋk] **1** *verb* (a) to shut and open one eye quickly, as a signal; *she winked at him to try to tell him that everything was going well* (b) (*of lights, stars*) to flash on and off; *the lights of the harbour were winking in the distance* **2** *noun* (a) opening and shutting one eye quickly; *she gave him a wink to show that she had seen him take the piece of cake* (b) (*informal*) **forty winks** = a very short sleep; *he closed his eyes and had forty winks*; **to sleep hardly a wink** = almost not to sleep at all; *we hardly slept a wink last night because the children kept waking us up*

winkle ['wɪŋkl] **1** *noun* small edible snail which lives in the sea; *we bought winkles and jellied eels from the stall on the pier* **2** **to winkle something out** = to get something out with a lot of difficulty; *it took them some time to winkle out the information*

winner ['wɪnə] *noun* (a) person who wins; *the winner of the race gets a silver cup* (b) something which is successful; *his latest book is a winner*

winning ['wɪnɪŋ] *adjective* (a) which has won; *the winning team go on to the next stage of the tournament; she had the winning lottery ticket;*

winning post = post which indicates the end of a horse race; *the first past the winning post was 'White Lady'* (b) pleasant, attractive; *she has a very winning smile*

winnings ['wɪnɪŋz] *noun* money which has been won at betting; *he collected all his winnings and went to book a holiday in Spain*

win over ['wɪn 'əʊvə] *verb* to persuade someone who was previously reluctant; *we argued with them, but finally won them over*

winter ['wɪntə] **1** *noun* the coldest season of the year, the season between autumn and spring; *in some countries winter usually means snow*; *it's too cold to do any gardening in the winter*; *we're taking a winter holiday in Mexico*; **winter sports** = sports which are done in the winter, such as skiing, skating, etc. **2** *verb* to spend the winter in a place; *these birds normally winter in Southern Portugal*

Winter Olympics ['wɪntə ə'lɪmpɪks] *noun* part of the Olympic Games, played in the winter, at a different venue from the true Olympic Games.

> COMMENT: first held in France in 1924. The following events are among those included: cross-country skiing, snowboarding, ski jumping, bobsleigh, luge, figure skating, speed skating, curling, ice hockey, etc.

wintry ['wɪntrɪ] *adjective* (a) cold like winter; *they are forecasting more wintry weather tonight* (b) unfriendly and cold; *he gave them a wintry smile which made conversation difficult*

wipe [waɪp] **1** *verb* to clean or dry with a cloth; *wipe your shoes with a cloth before you polish them*; *here's a hanky to wipe your nose*; *use the blue towel to wipe your hands*; *I'll do the washing up, but someone else must wipe* **2** *noun* action of cleaning or drying with a cloth; *she gave the table a quick wipe*

wipe out ['waɪp 'aʊt] *verb* (a) to kill, to destroy; *the tidal wave wiped out half the villages along the coast* (b) to remove completely; *the costs of moving to the new office have completely wiped out our profits*

wiper ['waɪpə] *noun* **windscreen wiper** *US* **windshield wiper** = device on a car which removes rainwater away from the windscreen; *it rained so much the wipers couldn't cope*

wipe up ['waɪp 'ʌp] *verb* to clean liquid which has been spilt, with a cloth; *wipe up that milk which you spilt on the floor*

wire ['waɪə] **1** *noun* (a) thin piece of metal or metal thread; *he used bits of wire to attach the apple tree to the wall*; *the chip basket is made of woven wire* (b) **(electric) wire** = thin metal thread along which electricity flows, usually covered with coloured plastic; *the wires seem to be all right, so there must be a problem with the dishwasher itself*; **live wire** = wire with electricity running through it; *be careful - that's a live wire*; *see also* LIVE WIRE (c) (*informal*) **to get your wires crossed** = to get two messages confused; *we seem to have got our wires crossed - I thought we were meeting today, and he thought it was tomorrow* (d) (*informal*) telegram; *he sent me a wire to say that he couldn't come* **2** *verb* (a) to put in wires to carry electricity round a building; *the office has been wired for computers* (b) to send a telegram; *he wired his office to say that the deal had been signed*

wireless ['waɪələs] **1** *noun* (*old*) radio receiver; *during the war, families huddled around their wirelesses to listen to the news*

wiring ['waɪrɪŋ] *noun* all the wires which make up a system to carry electricity round a building; *the wiring is old and needs to be replaced*

wisdom ['wɪzdəm] *noun* general common sense; *I doubt the wisdom of allowing her to go out alone at night*; **words of wisdom** = sound advice; *just a few words of wisdom: don't get involved!*

wisdom tooth ['wɪzdəm 'tuːθ] *noun* one of the four back teeth which only grow after the age of 20, or sometimes not at all

wise [waɪz] *adjective* (a) having intelligence and being sensible; *I don't think it's wise to ask her to invest all that money in his business*; *it was a wise decision to cancel the trip* (b) **to be none the wiser** = to know no more about it than you did before; *I read his report, and I'm still none the wiser*; *his lengthy explanation left us none the wiser about how the system would work* (NOTE: **wiser - wisest**)

wise guy ['waɪz 'gaɪ] *noun* someone who seems to know the answer to everything, but in reality doesn't; *he's just some wise guy who hangs around the bar giving advice*

wish [wɪʃ] **1** *noun* (a) desire; *I have no wish to get involved* (b) what you want to happen; *close your eyes and make a wish*; **to make a wish** = to think of something you would like to have or to see happen; *close your eyes and make a wish*; *make a wish when you blow out the candles on your birthday cake*; **her wish came true** = what she wanted to happen did happen (c) greetings; *best wishes for the New Year!*; *please give my good wishes to your family* (NOTE: plural is **wishes**) **2** *verb* (a) to desire something (which is almost impossible to have); *I wish I were blonde*; *I wish we didn't have to go to work on Christmas Day*; *I wish my birthday wasn't in June when I'm taking exams* (b) to want something to happen; *she sometimes wished she could live in the country*; *I wish some of you would help me with housework*; **I wouldn't wish it on anyone** = it is so awful, I wouldn't want anyone, even someone I don't like, to have it; *this flu is awful, it's not something I would wish on anyone* (c) to hope something good will happen; *she wished him good luck in his interview*; *he wished me a Happy New Year*; *wish me luck - it's my exam tomorrow* (d) (*formal*) to want; *the headmaster wishes to see you in his study*

wishbone ['wɪʃbəʊn] *noun* bone in the shape of a V at the end of a chicken breast

> COMMENT: when the bone is dry, two people can pull it until it breaks, each making a wish, and the wish of the one who has the larger piece is supposed to come true

wishful thinking ['wɪʃfʊl 'θɪŋkɪŋ] *noun* thinking that something will actually happen because you want it to; *expecting to win first prize was just wishful thinking on her part*

wishy-washy [wɪʃɪ 'wɒʃɪ] *adjective* without any bright colours, or firm ideas; *there's was nothing I liked at the exhibition, just a lot of wishy-washy paintings*; *hard-line right-wingers have no time for the wishy-washy wets on the left of the party*

wisp [wɪsp] *noun* small strand; little piece; *a wisp of hair kept falling into his eyes*; *we knew someone was* there when we saw a wisp of smoke coming out of the chimney

wistful ['wɪstful] *adjective* longing for something, but sad because there is no hope of getting it; *she had a wistful look on her face when the children talked of their grandfather*

wit [wɪt] *noun* (a) ability to say clever and funny things; *his wit comes out all through his book* (b) wits = intelligence; at your wits' end = not knowing what to do next; *they were at their wits' end when the builders reported even more structural problems in the house*; to keep your wits about you = to keep calm in a difficult situation and think hard what to do next; *don't panic, keep your wits about you, and everything will be all right*

witch [wɪtʃ] *noun* woman believed to have magic powers; *witches are supposed to fly over the city on Halloween* (NOTE: plural is **witches**; the male equivalent is a **wizard**)

witchcraft ['wɪtʃkrɑːft] *noun* art of magic; *she was accused by her neighbours of practising witchcraft*

witchdoctor ['wɪtʃ'dɒktə] *noun* man in a primitive tribe who seems to cure illnesses by magic

with [wɪθ or wɪð] *preposition* (a) (showing things or people that are together) *she came here with her mother*; *my sister is staying with us for a few days* (b) (showing something which you have) *he went into the church with his hat on*; *you know the girl with blue eyes who works in the accounts department*; *they live in the house with the pink door* (c) (showing something which is used) *he was chopping up wood with an axe*; *since his accident he walks with a stick*; *the crowd attacked the police with stones and bottles* (d) because of; *her little hands were blue with cold*; *half the people in the office are ill with flu* (e) and; *he always has ice cream with apple pie*; *I want a sheet of paper with an envelope* (NOTE: **with** is used with many adjectives and verbs: **to agree with, to be pleased with,** etc.)

withdraw [wɪθ'drɔː] *verb* (a) to move back; *the crowd slowly withdrew as the soldiers advanced*; *he talked to the guests for a few moments, then withdrew into his library* (b) to take back; *the old coins have been withdrawn from circulation* (c) to take money out of a bank account; *you can withdraw up to £100 from any cash machine* (d) to take back something which has been said; *she withdrew her offer to provide the food for the party* (NOTE: **withdrew** [wɪθ'druː] - **withdrawn**)

withdrawal [wɪθ'drɔːəl] *noun* (a) removing of money from a bank account; *she made three withdrawals last week* (b) going back; *his withdrawal from the election surprised his friends* (c) withdrawal symptoms = unpleasant physical condition which occurs when someone stops taking an addictive drug; *she is trying to give up smoking, and is having difficulty in coping with the withdrawal symptoms*

withdrawn [wɪθ'drɔːn] *adjective* shy, not liking to meet other people; *she became withdrawn after the death of her son*

wither ['wɪðə] *verb* (of plants) to grow weaker and dry up, to shrivel; *in autumn, the leaves start to wither and fall*; *the flowers withered because nobody watered them*

withering ['wɪðərɪŋ] *adjective* disapproving, which makes someone feel embarrassed; *a withering look*

from her father made her stop; *she made some withering remarks about his painting skills*

withhold [wɪθ'həuld] *verb* to refuse to let someone have something; *they suspect him of withholding important information from the police* (NOTE: **withholding - withheld** [wɪθ'held])

within [wɪ'ðɪn] *preposition* (a) (in space or time) in; *the house is within easy reach of the station*; *we are within walking distance of the shop*; *I must go back for a check-up within three months*; *they promised to deliver the sofa within a week*; within sight = able to be seen; *we are almost there, the house is within sight*; *the ship sank within sight of land* (b) within the law = legal; *is parking on the pavement within the law?*

with it ['wɪð ɪt] *phrase* (informal) knowing all about something; *she's very with it when it comes to what is happening on the fashion scene*; *I'm just not very with it today - I seem to be forgetting everything*

without [wɪ'ðaut] *preposition* (a) not with; *they came on a walking holiday without any boots*; *she managed to live for a few days without any food*; *he was stuck in Germany without any money*; *they were fined for travelling without a ticket* (b) not doing something; *she sang for an hour without stopping*; *they lived in the hut in the forest without seeing anybody for weeks* (c) without doubt = certainly; *it is, without any doubt, his best film ever*

withstand [wɪθ'stænd] *verb* to resist, to stand up to; *hardy plants can withstand the coldest winter*; *can the government withstand all this pressure from the business community?*; to withstand the test of time = to survive; *Shakespeare's comedies have withstood the test of time remarkably well* (NOTE: **withstanding - withstood**)

witness ['wɪtnəs] **1** *noun* (a) person who sees something happen or who is present when something happens; *the witness happened to be outside the house when it was burgled* (b) person who appears before a court or committee to give evidence; *the secretary appeared as a witness in the libel case* (c) person who is present when someone signs a document; *the contract has to be signed in front of two witnesses*; *his sister signed as a witness* (d) to bear witness to = to be evidence of; *his reaction bore witness to his interest in the matter* (NOTE: plural is **witnesses**) **2** *verb* (a) to be present when something happens, and see it happening; *did anyone witness the accident?* (b) to sign a document to show that you guarantee that the other signatures on it are genuine; *one of his colleagues witnessed his signature*

witness box *US* **witness stand** ['wɪtnəs 'bɒks or 'wɪtnəs 'stænd] *noun* place in a courtroom where the witnesses give evidence; *he was called to the witness box to answer questions from the prosecuting counsel*

witty ['wɪti] *adjective* clever and funny; *he made a witty speech at the wedding*; *she made some witty remarks which helped defuse the situation* (NOTE: **wittier - wittiest**)

wives [waɪvz] *see* WIFE

wizard ['wɪzəd] *noun* (a) man who is believed to have magic powers; *the wizard made the frog change into a prince* (NOTE: the female equivalent is a **witch**) (b) clever person, expert; *he's a wizard at chess*

wizardry ['wɪzədri] *noun* being clever; *by some financial wizardry he managed to convert a huge loss into a profit*

wobble ['wɒbl] **1** *verb* to move unsteadily from side to side; *the children made the jelly wobble in their bowls*; *don't wobble the table when I'm pouring coffee* **2** *noun* unsteady shaking movement; *the front wheel has a wobble*

wobbly ['wɒbli] *adjective* **(a)** unsteady, shaking from side to side; *his bike has a wobbly back wheel*; *she sat on a wobbly armchair* **(b)** *(of person)* shaky, not very steady; *she's a lot better, but still a bit wobbly* **(c)** *(voice)* as if wanting to cry; *her voice sounded wobbly over the phone*

woe [wəʊ] *noun* **(a)** sadness or trouble; *money cannot cure all the woes of the world*; *she stopped me and told me her tale of woe* **(b)** *(formal, humorous)* **woe betide** = trouble will come to; *woe betide anyone who tries to contradict my mother!*

woeful ['wəʊful] *adjective* **(a)** bad, annoying; *his woeful lack of interest in environmental problems is infuriating* **(b)** *(formal)* full of sadness; *they sang woeful songs about their lost land*

wok [wɒk] *noun* Chinese round-bottomed frying pan used in stir-fry cooking; *you'll need a wok to make some fried rice*

woke *or* **woken** [wəʊk or wəʊkn] *see* WAKE

wolf [wʊlf] **1** *noun* **(a)** wild animal like a large dog, usually living in groups in the forest; *at night the wolves came and howled outside the hut*; **a pack of wolves** = group of wolves living together; **wolf cub** = young wolf **(b)** *(person)* **lone wolf** = person who prefers to be alone, who has no friends; *he's a bit of a lone wolf who enjoys travelling on his own* **(c)** **wolf in sheep's clothing** = person who seems inoffensive but really is wicked; **to cry wolf** = to call for help when you do not need it, so that when you really need help no one believes you; **to keep the wolf from the door** = to have enough food to live on; *with prices rising all the time they have difficulty in keeping the wolf from the door* (NOTE: plural is **wolves**) **2** *verb* *(informal)* to eat fast without chewing your food properly; *he wolfed his food down and ran out to catch the bus*

wolf whistle ['wʊlf 'wɪsəl] *noun* whistle made by a man when he sees an attractive girl; *you should hear the wolf whistles when I walk past the building site*

woman ['wʊmən] *noun* **(a)** adult female person; *the manageress is an extremely witty woman*; *there were two middle-aged women in the seats next to ours*; *there are very few women in government*; *there are more and more women bus drivers* **(b)** wife, female companion; *he still has no woman in his life* (NOTE: plural is **women** ['wɪmɪn])

womanhood ['wʊmənhʊd] *noun* state of being a woman; *when she reaches womanhood she will leave her family*

womb [wuːm] *noun* hollow organ in a woman's body where a fertilized egg is lodged and an unborn baby is carried; *pregnancy is the period when a woman carries a baby in her womb*; *the surgical removal of the womb is called a hysterectomy* (NOTE: also called the **uterus**)

women's lib ['wɪmɪnz 'lɪb] *noun* the equal place in society of women with men, and actions taken to promote this

women's movement ['wɪmɪnz 'muːvmənt] *noun* grouping of women who are involved in the movement to promote women's rights and their equality with men

won [wʌn] *see* WIN

wonder ['wʌndə] **1** *verb* **(a)** to want to know something; *I wonder why the room has gone quiet*; *she was wondering how many French francs you get for a pound*; *if you don't ring home, your parents will start wondering what has happened* **(b)** to think about something; *I wonder how I can earn more money*; *he's wondering what to do next*; **to wonder about** = (i) to think about; (ii) to worry about; *we've been wondering about moving house*; *I'm wondering about the children, they don't look well* **(c)** *(asking a question politely)* *we were wondering if you would like to come for dinner on Saturday* **2** *noun* **(a)** amazing thing; **to do wonders for** = to help make something better; *an evening out would do wonders to cheer him up*; *the cream did wonders for her skin problem*; **no wonder** = it isn't surprising; *it's no wonder you had difficulty in getting tickets for the show with so many tourists in London* **(b)** feeling of surprise and admiration; *the little girl stared at the elephant in wonder*

wonderful ['wʌndəful] *adjective* very good, splendid; *they had a wonderful holiday by a lake in Sweden*; *the weather was wonderful for the whole holiday*; *you passed your driving test first time? - wonderful!*

wonderfully ['wʌndəfuli] *adverb* in a wonderful way; *the experiment worked wonderfully well*

wonderland ['wʌndəlænd] *noun* marvellous imaginary place; *they drove into the mountain wonderland*

wondrous ['wʌndrəs] *adjective (old)* wonderful; *the wondrous beauty of the countryside in spring never fails to give me pleasure*

won't [wənt] *see* WILL NOT

woo [wuː] *verb* **(a)** to try to get someone to support you, to vote for you, etc.; *the government is wooing the younger voter*; *the supermarket is trying to woo customers with special offers* **(b)** *(old)* to try to attract a girl to marry you; *Henry VIII wooed Anne Boleyn during the summer of 1533*; *three suitors came to woo the princess, each bringing costly gifts*

wood [wʊd] *noun* **(a)** hard material which comes from a tree; *the kitchen table is made of wood*; *she picked up a piece of wood and put it on the fire*; *a wood floor would be just right for this room* (NOTE: no plural for this meaning: **some wood, a piece of wood**) **(b)** many trees growing together; *the path goes straight through the wood*; *their house is on the edge of a wood*; *(informal)* **not to see the wood for the trees** = not to see what is important because you are concentrating only on details; **we're not out of the wood(s) yet** = we still have problems; *there's still so much to do to the house, we're not out of wood yet* **(c)** large wooden ball, used in bowls **(d)** large-headed wooden club, used in golf to drive off from the tee and hit the ball as far as possible; *he's trying a new wood* (NOTE: do not confuse with **would**)

woodchuck ['wʊdtʃʌk] *noun* US fat rodent which lives in holes in the ground and hibernates in winter (NOTE: also called a **groundhog**)

wooded ['wʊdɪd] *adjective* covered in trees; *there's a family of foxes living in the wooded land next to our farm*

wooden ['wʊdən] *adjective* **(a)** made out of wood; *in the market we bought little wooden dolls for the children* **(b)** *(of an actor, etc.)* showing no emotion when acting; *he was very wooden on stage, not at all natural*

wooden spoon ['wʊdən 'spuːn] *noun* **(a)** spoon made of wood, used when cooking; *she used a wooden spoon to stir the porridge* **(b)** silly prize given to someone who is last in a competition; *the wooden spoon goes to the team from the Police Force*

woodland(s) ['wʊdlənd(z)] *noun* area of land covered in woods; *they walked through the woodlands to the lake*; *woodland birds are affected by climate change*

woodpecker ['wʊdpekə] *noun* bird with a long sharp beak which makes holes in trees to find insects under the bark; *she heard the woodpecker hammering and then saw it in the tree*

woodwind ['wʊdwɪnd] *noun* smaller instruments in an orchestra which are played by blowing; *the woodwind section of the orchestra*

> COMMENT: the main woodwind instruments are the flute, clarinet, oboe and bassoon

woodwork ['wʊdwɜːk] *noun* **(a)** carpentry, the art of working with wood; *woodwork classes were the ones I liked best at school* **(b)** parts of a building which are made of wood; *all the woodwork will be painted white* (NOTE: no plural)

woodworm ['wʊdwɜːm] *noun* little insect that eats wood; *the chair is riddled with woodworm*

woof [wʊf] **1** *noun* **(a)** = WEFT **(b)** the sound made by a dog when it barks; *your father must be back, I've just heard a woof from the garden*; *(children's speech) a dog goes 'woof, woof', a cat goes 'miaow'* **2** *verb* (*of dog*) to bark; *this great black dog rushed out and woofed at me*

wool [wʊl] *noun* **(a)** long threads of twisted animal hair, used to make clothes or carpets, etc.; *the carpet is made of wool*; *I need an extra ball of wool to finish this pullover* **(b)** to pull the wool over someone's eyes = to deceive someone by not telling them the true facts; *the estate agent tried to pull the wool over our eyes about the house, but luckily the surveyor pointed out some structural defects; see also* COTTON WOOL, STEEL WOOL

woollen *US* **woolen** ['wʊlən] *adjective* made of wool; *she was wearing a red woollen jumper*

woollens ['wʊlnz] *noun* clothes made of knitted wool; *woollens need to be washed carefully, or they will lose their shape*

woolly ['wʊli] **1** *adjective* **(a)** made out of wool; *she wore a woolly hat* **(b)** not clear; *his explanation was really very woolly* (NOTE: **woollier - woolliest**) **2** *noun* (*informal*) knitted piece of clothing made of wool; *don't forget to take a woolly - it's quite cold today; October - it's time to get your winter woollies out* (NOTE: plural is **woollies**)

word [wɜːd] *noun* **(a)** separate piece of language, either written or spoken; *this sentence has five words*; *he always spells some words wrongly, such as 'though'*; *a word-for-word translation often doesn't make any sense* **(b)** something spoken; *she passed me in the street but didn't say a word*; *I'd like to say a few words about Mr Smith who is retiring today*; **to have a word with** = to speak to; *I must have a word with the manager about the service*; *the salesgirl had made so*

many mistakes, *I had to have a word with her*; **without a word** = without saying anything; *she went out of the room without a word* **(c)** something written; *we received a word from my sister - she's now in Canada*; *we've not heard a word from the lawyers* **(d)** promise which you have made; **to give your word** = to promise; *he gave his word that the matter would remain confidential*; **to keep your word** = to do what you promised to do; *he kept his word, and the cheque arrived the next day*; **to take someone's word for it** = to accept what someone says as being true; *OK, I'll take your word for it* **(e)** **to breathe a word** = to mention something; *we want to keep our plans secret for the moment, so don't breathe a word to anyone*; **to have words with someone** = to argue with someone; *they were good friends until one day they had words about the fence*; **in other words** = to that is to say; *it's seven o'clock - in other words, time for dinner*; *I'm going on holiday next month, in other words I'll be away from the office for about four weeks*; **you took the words out of my mouth** = you've said exactly what I was going to say; **not to mince your words** = to say exactly what you think; *I didn't mince my words - I told them exactly what I thought of their wretched plan*

wording ['wɜːdɪŋ] *noun* words and phrases used in a piece of writing; *did you read the wording on the contract?*; *the wording for the ad must be changed*

word processing ['wɜːd 'prəʊsesɪŋ] *noun* using a computer to produce, check and change texts, reports, letters, etc.; *load the word-processing program before you start keyboarding*; **word-processing bureau** = office which specializes in word-processing for other companies

word processor ['wɜːd 'prəʊsesə] *noun* **(a)** small computer which is used to produce texts, reports, letters, etc.; *she offered to write the letter for me on her word processor*; *you can use my word processor to type your letter if you like* **(b)** word-processing programme which allows you to create texts, edit them and print them

wore ['wɔː] *see* WEAR

work [wɜːk] **1** *noun* **(a)** something done using your strength or your brain; *there's a great deal of work still to be done*; *there's too much work for one person*; *she tries to avoid doing too much work in the house*; *if you've finished that piece of work, there's plenty more to be done*; *cooking for two hundred people every day is hard work*; **to have your work cut out to do something** = to find it difficult to do something; *they'll have their work cut out to get the job finished on time* **(b)** job done regularly to earn money; *he goes to work every day on his bicycle*; *work starts at 9 a.m. and finishes at 5 p.m.*; *her work involves a lot of travelling*; *he is still looking for work*; **at work** = working; *the builders are still hard at work*; *she's at work today, but will have the day off tomorrow*; **out of work** = without a job; *hundreds of people were out of work when the factory closed*; *she has been out of work for six months* (NOTE: no plural for meanings (a) and (b)): **some work, a piece of work** **(c)** something which has been made, painted, written, etc., by someone; *an exhibition of the work of local artists*; *the complete works of Shakespeare*; **standard work** = book which is the recognized authority on a subject; *he's the author of the standard work on woodland fungi* **2** *verb* **(a)** to use your strength or brain to do something; *I can't work in the garden if it's raining*; *he's working well at school,* *we're very pleased with his progress; work hard and you'll soon get a better job;* **to set to work** = to start working; *if we all set to work early, we should finish the job this evening* **(b)** to have a job; *she works in an office in London; he used to work in his father's shop; she had to stop working when her mother was ill* **(c)** *(of machine)* to run; *the computers aren't working; the machine works by electricity* **(d)** to make a machine run; *she works the biggest printing machine in the factory; do you know how to work the microwave?* **(e)** to succeed; *will the plan work?; if the cough medicine doesn't work, you'll have to see a doctor* **(f)** to move a little; **to work loose** = to become loose by constant movement; *the nut holding the wheel must have worked loose*

workable ['wɜːkəbl] *adjective* which can work; *do you think that his plan is really workable?; we'll have to rewrite the timetable to make it more workable*

work against ['wɜːk ə'genst] *verb* to have the opposite effect; *being highly qualified seems to work against her when she's looking for a job*

workaholic [wɜːkə'hɒlɪk] *noun (informal)* person who cannot stop working; *he's a workaholic, and hardly sees anything of his family*

work at ['wɜːk 'æt] *verb* **to work at something** = to work hard; *if you want to become a concert pianist you will have to work at it*

work bench ['wɜːk 'bentʃ] *noun* table in a workshop at which someone works; *the carpenter was standing at his workbench*

workbook ['wɜːkbʊk] *noun* book of exercises to help teach a subject; *the workbook should be used together with the textbook*

worked up ['wɜːkd 'ʌp] *adjective (informal)* **all worked up about something** = excited or annoyed about something; *the people in the village got all worked up about the plan for the new airport*

worker ['wɜːkə] *noun* **(a)** person who works in a certain way; *she's a good worker; he's a fast worker* **(b)** person who works, especially in a certain job; *the factory closed when the workers went on strike; office workers usually work from 9.30 to 5.30* **(c)** female bee which goes to find pollen to provide the queen with honey; *workers go out of the hive to search for pollen* (NOTE: in a bee colony, the males are called **drones**)

workforce ['wɜːkfɔːs] *noun* all the workers in an office or factory; *the management has made an increased offer to the workforce; the company cannot continue production with half its workforce off sick* (NOTE: no plural)

working ['wɜːkɪŋ] **1** *adjective* referring to a job or to work; *the working population of a country; the unions have complained about working conditions in the factory; he came to the party in his working clothes;* **working breakfast** = breakfast where you discuss business; **working class** = group in society consisting of people who work with their hands, usually earning wages not salaries; **working life** = the years a person has worked; *I was a commuter all my working life;* **working week** = the part of the work when people usually go to their jobs; *the government is planning to reduce the working week to 35 hours* **2** *noun* **(a)** way or ways in which something works; *the workings of a car engine are a complete mystery to him; I wish I could understand the workings of local government!*

(b) workings = place where mineral has been dug; *that hole is the entrance to some old iron workings*

working party ['wɜːkɪŋ 'pɑːti] *noun* group of experts who study a problem and report on how to deal with it; *a working party was set up to study the question of building a new airport*

workload ['wɜːkləʊd] *noun* amount of work which a person has to do; *don't give him any more work - he has difficulty in coping with his workload as it is; everyone will have an extra workload until we find replacements for those who are ill*

workman ['wɜːkmən] *noun* man who works with his hands; *workmen came to mend the gas heater* (NOTE: plural is **workmen**)

workmanship ['wɜːkmənʃɪp] *noun* skill of a good workman; *look at the workmanship in this table - they don't make them like that any more!*

workmate ['wɜːkmeɪt] *noun* person who works with you; *after retirement, people often miss the companionship of their workmates*

work on ['wɜːk 'ɒn] *verb* to work hard to make something better; *you'll have to work on your French if you want to get through the exam*

work out ['wɜːk 'aʊt] *verb* **(a)** to calculate; *I'm trying to work out if we've sold more this year than last; the waiter couldn't work out the total bill* **(b)** to succeed; *everything worked out quite well in the end* **(c)** to do exercises; *he works out every morning in the gym* **(d)** *(of mine)* to exhaust a seam of coal, etc., and not be able to continue working there; *the gold seam was worked out some years ago*

workout ['wɜːkaʊt] *noun* exercise or sports practice; *he goes to the gym for a workout twice a week*

workplace ['wɜːkpleɪs] *noun* place where work is done; *more work is done if the workplace is in pleasant surroundings*

workroom ['wɜːkruːm] *noun* room where you work; *come into my workroom, that's where all the computers are; she's in her workroom designing fabrics*

works [wɜːks] *noun* **(a)** factory; *the steel works will be closed next week for the Christmas holidays* **(b)** parts of a machine; *I looked inside the clock and there seems to be dust in the works* **(c) public works** = constructions done by a government or local council; **road works** = repairs to a road **(d)** *(informal)* **the works** = everything; *they built a conservatory with a fountain, automatic lighting, a barbecue - the works!*

works council ['wɜːks 'kaʊnsəl] *noun* committee of managers and workers which discusses the organization of work in a factory

workshop ['wɜːkʃɒp] *noun* very small factory where things are made or repaired; *he runs a workshop for repairing bicycles; the chairs are upholstered in the workshop behind the shop*

workstation ['wɜːksteɪʃn] *noun* desk with terminal, monitor, keyboard, etc., where a computer operator works; *the system has five workstations linked in a network*

work surface *or* **worktop** ['wɜːk 'sɜːfɪs *or* 'wɜːktɒp] *noun* top of a kitchen cupboard, etc., for working on; *there is a marble worktop where you can prepare meals; the work surface is too small*

work-to-rule ['wɜːk tə 'ruːl] *noun* form of protest, where employees work strictly according to the rules agreed by the union and management, in such a way that the work is done very slowly; *because of the work-to-rule all deliveries are late*

work up ['wɜːk 'ʌp] *verb* **(a)** to develop; *I find it difficult to work up any enthusiasm for my job* **(b)** to do some hard work to make something happen; *I'm doing some digging to work up an appetite* **(c)** to work yourself up into a state = to make yourself annoyed and worried by something; *he's worked himself up into such a state about his exams; see also* WORKED UP

world [wɜːld] *noun* **(a)** the earth on which we live; *here is a map of the world; she flew round the world twice last year; he has to travel all over the world on business; a round-the-world ticket allows several stopovers;* **the Old World** = Europe, Asia and Africa; **the New World** = North and South America; **the Third World** = countries of Africa, Asia and South America which do not have highly developed industries; **World War** = war in which many countries all over the world take part; *see* FIRST WORLD WAR, SECOND WORLD WAR **(b) to come into the world** = to be born; **to bring a child into the world** = to give birth to a baby; **who in the world is John Sparrow?** = do you have any idea who John Sparrow is?; **to be all alone in the world** = to have no family; *he isn't married, an only child, both his parents are dead, so he's all alone in the world; (informal)* **to be on top of the world** = to feel very happy; *she's got a new boyfriend and is on top of the world;* **out of this world** = magnificent; *the cooking in the restaurant was out of this world;* **to think the world of someone** = to respect or love someone; *they think the world of their daughter;* **to do someone a world of good** = to make someone feel much better; *his holiday has done him a world of good* **(c)** people with a particular interest or who work in a particular business; *he's very interested in the world of music; she wants to get into the world of big business* **(d)** particular group of animals, etc.; *the insect world; the world of mammals*

world-class ['wɜːld 'klɑːs] *adjective* so good as to be amoung the best in the world; *he's a world-class violinist*

World Cup ['wɜːld 'kʌp] *noun* football tournament, held every four years, where teams from all over the world can compete against each other; *the police are ready to clamp down on football hooligans during the World Cup*

world-famous [wɜːld'feɪməs] *adjective* known everywhere; *you've never heard of her? - she's world-famous!*

World Health Organization (WHO) ['wɜːld 'helθ 'ɔːɡənaɪ'zeɪʃn] *noun* organization, a part of the United Nations, which aims to improve health in the world by teaching and publishing information about diseases; *her father used to work in the World Health Organization; at the present time, the WHO's top priority is the eradication of tuberculosis*

worldly ['wɜːldli] *adjective* **(a)** referring to the material world; *all her worldly possessions fitted into two small suitcases* **(b)** not idealistic, with a lot of experience; *she's worldly enough to know exactly what she's doing*

worldwide [wɜːld'waɪd] *adjective & adverb* over the whole world; *the company has a worldwide network of*

distributors; *a worldwide energy crisis; the TV news programme is available worldwide*

World Wide Fund for Nature (WWF) ['wɜːld 'waɪd fʌnd fə 'neɪtʃə] *noun* international organization, set up in 1961, to protect endangered species of animals and plants and their habitats, and now also involved with projects to control pollution

World Wide Web (WWW) ['wɜːld 'waɪd 'web] *noun* web sites and web pages within the Internet, which users can visit (NOTE: usually shortened to **the Web**)

worm [wɜːm] **1** *noun* **(a)** small boneless animal which has no limbs and lives in the soil; *birds were pecking at the soil for worms;* **the early bird catches the worm** = if you are the first to do something you will beat your rivals (NOTE: also called **earthworm**) **(b)** similar tiny animal living inside an animal's body, usually in the intestines; *we had to give the dog a tablet to get rid of its worms* **2** *verb* **(a)** to get worms out of an animal; *the cat needs to be wormed* **(b)** to get through by twisting and turning; *they managed to worm their way into the exhibition* **(c) to worm something out of someone** = to get information out of someone by continually asking questions; *they managed to worm the combination of the safe out of her*

worn [wɔːn] *see* WEAR

worn out ['wɔːn 'aut] *adjective* **(a)** very tired; *he was worn out after the game of rugby; she comes home every evening, worn out after a busy day at the office* **(b)** old and which has been used a lot; *the tyres on the back wheels are worn out; she was wearing a pair of worn out trainers; see also* WEAR OUT

worried ['wʌrid] *adjective* anxious; *he had a worried look on his face; she's looking worried; I'm worried that we may run out of petrol;* **worried to death** = extremely worried; *they were worried to death about her*

worry ['wʌri] **1** *noun* **(a)** some thing which makes you anxious; *go on holiday and try to forget your worries* **(b)** being anxious; *she is a great source of worry for her family* **2** *verb* to be anxious because of something; *he's worrying about his driving test; I worry when the children stay out late; don't worry, I'll be back on time; she's always pale and that worries me*

worrying ['wʌriɪŋ] *adjective* which makes you worried; *there has been a worrying increase in the number of thefts*

worse [wɜːs] **1** *adjective* **(a)** less good (as compared to something else); *it rained for the first week of our holidays, and the second week was even worse; I think this film is worse than the one I saw last week; both children are naughty - but the little girl is worse than her brother; both children are ill, and to make matters worse, their mother has broken her arm* **(b)** more ill; *he's much worse since he started taking his medicine* **2** *adverb* not as well; *he drives badly enough but his sister drives even worse* (NOTE: **worse** is the comparative of **bad, badly** and **ill**) **3** *noun* something which is worse; *they thought their problems were over, but worse was to follow;* **to take a turn for the worse** = to suddenly become more ill; *everyone thought she was getting better and then she took a turn for the worse*

worsen ['wɜːsn] *verb* to become worse, to make worse; *I think the pain has worsened today; we are watching the worsening situation carefully*

worse off ['wɜːs 'ɒf] *adjective* with less money than before; *the family is much worse off since he was made redundant*

worship ['wɜːʃɪp] **1** *noun* (a) praise and respect to God; *prayer is the most important part of worship*; *an act of worship* = a religious ceremony (b) praise and love for someone or something; *her worship of her boss isn't healthy* **2** *verb* (a) to praise and respect God; *the ancient peoples worshipped stone statues of their gods* (b) to take part in a church service; *they worship regularly in the parish church* (c) to praise and love someone; *she absolutely worships her boyfriend* (NOTE: **worshipping - worshipped**)

worshipper ['wɜːʃɪpə] *noun* person who worships; *our church is closed and worshippers now have to attend services in the next village*; *sun worshipper* = person who loves sunbathing

worst [wɜːst] **1** *adjective* worse than anything else; *this summer is the worst for fifty years*; *I think this is the worst film he's ever made* **2** *adverb* less well than anything or anyone else or than at any other time; *it's difficult to say which team played worst*; *she works worst when she's tired* **3** *noun* very bad thing; *the worst of the bad weather is past now*; *to prepare for the worst* = to get ready to have bad news; *your father was very badly injured - you must prepare for the worst* (NOTE: **worst** is the superlative of **bad** and **badly**)

worsted ['wustɪd] *noun* fine woollen cloth; *he's still wearing the same old worsted jacket he had at university*; *after looking at several samples of cloth, I chose a blue and grey worsted for my suit*

worth [wɜːθ] **1** *adjective* (a) **to be worth** = to have a certain value or price; *this ring's worth a lot of money*; *gold is worth more than silver*; *the house is worth more than £250,000*; *the car is worth £6,000 on the secondhand market* (b) **for all you are worth** = with as much effort as possible; *they dug for all they were worth to try to find people trapped by the explosion* (c) **it is worth while** = it is good to do, it may be profitable; *it's worth while keeping copies of your work, in case your computer goes wrong*; *it's well worth while trying to get a ticket for the show*; **it is worth your while** = it is worth the effort; **I'll make it worth your while** = I'll pay you a lot to do it; *it's an awful job, but if you agree to do it I'll make it worth your while* (d) **to be worth doing something** = to find something good or helpful to do; *it's worth taking a map with you, as you may get lost in the little streets*; *his latest film is well worth seeing*; *the old castle is well worth visiting or is well worth a visit* **2** *noun* value; *its worth will increase each year*; *she lost jewellery of great worth in the fire*; *can you give me twenty pounds' worth of petrol?*

worthless ['wɜːθləs] *adjective* having no worth, no use; *I got this free ticket, but at the door I was told it was worthless*; *their paper money is absolutely worthless*

worthwhile [wɜːθ'waɪl] *adjective* which is worth the effort spent on it; *taking handicapped children to the seaside is a very worthwhile project*; *was your trip to London worthwhile?*

worthy ['wɜːði] *adjective* deserving; *it's a worthy cause, and I'm ready to help*; *the plan is worthy of careful consideration* (NOTE: **worthier - worthiest**)

would [wud] *verb* used with other verbs (a) (polite way of asking someone to do something) *would you please stop talking?*; *would someone please tell me*

where the library is?; *would you like some more tea?* (b) (*past of 'will'*) *he said he would be here for lunch*; *she hoped she would be well enough to come*; *he wouldn't go even if I paid him* (c) (*past of 'will'*, showing something which often happens) *he would bring his dog with him, even though we asked him not to*; *naturally the car wouldn't start when we were in a hurry*; *my husband forgot my birthday again this year - he would!* (d) (showing something which often happened in the past) *every morning she would go and feed the chickens*; *he would always be there waiting outside the station*; *they would often bring us flowers* (e) (following a condition) *I'm sure that if they could come, they would*; *I would've done it if you had asked me to*; *if she were alive, she'd be a hundred years old today*; *if it snowed we would or we'd go skiing* (NOTE: the negative **would not** is usually written **wouldn't**. Note also that **would** is often shortened to **'d: she'd be a hundred, he'd stay at home.** Note also that **would** is only used with other verbs and is not followed by **to**)

would-be ['wudbiː] *adjective* who hopes to become; *she's a would-be publisher*

would rather ['wud 'rɑːðə] *verb* to prefer; *I would rather live in London than anywhere else*; *are you all going to pay? - we'd rather not*; *they'd rather we stayed at home than go with them*

wound 1 [waund] *see* WIND **2** [wuːnd] *noun* (a) cut made on someone's body, usually in fighting; *the soldier had a bullet wound in his leg*; *he was admitted to hospital with a knife wound in his chest* (b) hurt to someone's feelings; *the wounds caused by the divorce will take years to heal* **3** [wuːnd] *verb* (a) to hurt someone badly in a fight, a war; *two of the gang were wounded in the bank robbery*; *as a young soldier he was badly wounded in the battle of the Somme* (b) to hurt someone's feelings; *she was deeply wounded by what he said*

wound up ['waund 'ʌp] *adjective* tense and anxious; *she was so wound up before her exam that she did badly*

wove, woven [wəuv or 'wəuvn] *see* WEAVE

wow [wau] **1** *interjection* showing surprise and pleasure; *Wow! have you seen his new girlfriend!* **2** *noun* (a) (*informal*) great success; *her latest film is a real wow* (b) fluctuation of sound frequency when playing back tapes; *wow is usually caused by uneven tape movement* **3** *verb* (*informal*) (of a singer, etc.) to excite (an audience); *the new singing group wowed their fans*

WPC = WOMAN POLICE CONSTABLE (NOTE: used as a title, followed by a name: **WPC Smith**)

wrangle ['ræŋgl] **1** *noun* argument or dispute; *a bitter wrangle developed between the partners* **2** *verb* to argue; *they're always wrangling over money*; *they wrangled for months before the treaty was finally signed*

wrap [ræp] **1** *noun* (a) type of shawl that is put round the shoulders or the top part of the body; *she pulled her wrap closer around her* (b) piece of material used to cover something; *remove the wrap before putting the dish in the microwave* (c) (*informal*) **to keep something under wraps** = to keep something secret; *the whole project is still under wraps* **2** *verb* (usually **wrap up**) (a) to cover something all over; *we're wrapping up the Christmas presents for the children*;

the parcel is wrapped (up) in brown paper; if you're cold, wrap yourself (up) in your blanket (b) to wear warm clothes; wrap up warmly if you're going for a walk in the snow (c) (informal) to finish off; that just about wraps up the points we have to make (d) to wrap round = to put right round something; she wrapped her arms around the little boy; it's cold - wrap your scarf round your neck (NOTE: **wrapping - wrapped** [ræpt])

wraparound ['ræpəraʊnd] adjective which goes right round something; I dislike wraparound skirts - they're awkward when you want to sit down; young people with their wraparound sunglasses

wrapped up ['wræpt 'ʌp] adjective so busy doing something, that you don't notice anything else; she is so wrapped up in her work she sometimes forgets to eat

wrapper ['ræpə] noun piece of paper used to wrap round something; he took the wrapper off the sweet; the pavement was littered with sweet wrappers

wrapping ['ræpɪŋ] noun paper, cardboard, plastic, etc., used to wrap something up; the children tore the wrapping off the box; **wrapping paper** = brightly coloured paper used to wrap presents; I bought two rolls of Christmas wrapping paper

wrath [rɒθ] noun (formal) great anger; the wrath of the authorities descended on him; she incurred the government's wrath by demonstrating outside the parliament building

wreak [riːk] verb to do something violent; the winds wreaked or wrought havoc on the power lines; he left prison, vowing to wreak revenge on the judge who had sentenced him (NOTE: **wreaking - wreaked** or **wrought** [rɔːt])

wreath [riːθ] noun (a) circle of flowers or leaves especially given at a funeral in memory of the dead person; the wreaths came from all his friends; the Queen laid a wreath at the tomb of the Unknown Soldier (b) circle of holly decorated with coloured balls, hung on a door as a Christmas decoration; a lot of people hang holly wreaths on their front doors at Christmas (c) circle of leaves put round someone's head; the emperor rode past in triumph, with a wreath of laurel round his head (d) winding clouds of smoke or mist; wreaths of smoke rose from the smouldering village (NOTE: plural is **wreaths** [wriːðz])

wreathe [riːð] verb to surround with; because of the forest fires, these hills are wreathed in smoke; **wreathed in smiles** = smiling broadly; the faces of the children were wreathed in smiles

wreck [rek] 1 noun (a) ship which has been sunk or badly damaged; divers have discovered the wreck on the seabed; the wreck of the 'Mary Rose' was found in the sea near Southampton (b) anything which has been damaged and cannot be used; the police towed away the wreck of the car; their new car is now a total wreck (c) (informal) nervous, tired and worried person; after the interview with the boss he was a nervous wreck; two hours manning the complaints desk and you're a gibbering wreck 2 verb (a) to damage something very badly; the ship was wrecked on the rocks in the storm; the bank was wrecked by the explosion (b) to ruin something; the children catching chickenpox has wrecked our plans to go to Greece

wreckage ['rekɪdʒ] noun what is left of a building, ship, plane, etc., after it has been wrecked; wreckage of the cars and lorries covered the motorway; rescuers searched the wreckage of the hotel looking for survivors (NOTE: no plural)

wrecker ['rekə] noun (a) person who wrecks something; there he goes, the wrecker of my marriage! (b) US truck which goes to move cars which have broken down on the road; the police called a wrecker to remove the damaged cars after the accident on the highway (NOTE: British English is a **recovery vehicle**)

wren [ren] noun very small brown bird; a pair of wrens have built a nest near our back door

wrench [renʃ] 1 noun (a) large spanner which can be adjusted to undo various sizes of nut; see also MONKEY WRENCH (b) sadness at leaving; it will be a wrench to leave the old office 2 verb to twist and pull something violently; she wrenched the box from his hands and ran off

wrest [rest] verb (formal) to twist, to wrench away; he finally managed to wrest power from the former dictator

wrestle ['resl] verb (a) to fight with someone to try to throw him to the ground; the guards wrestled with protesters (b) to fight or struggle with a problem; he's wrestling with his tax forms

wrestler ['reslə] noun person who wrestles as a sport; the two wrestlers entered the ring

wrestling ['reslɪŋ] noun sport of fighting, but without punching; **wrestling match** = sporting contest between wrestlers watched by crowds of people

wretched ['retʃɪd] adjective (a) miserable and ill; I won't go to the office today, I feel wretched (b) terrible or annoying; it's this wretched contract - we still can't get the terms agreed; those wretched squirrels have eaten all our tulip bulbs

wretchedly ['retʃɪdli] adverb miserably; she sat wretchedly looking out of the window

wriggle ['rɪgl] verb (a) to twist from side to side; the baby wriggled in her father's arms; the worm wriggled back into the soil (b) to wriggle free = to twist from side to side and get free; the burglars had tied his hands and legs, but he managed to wriggle free; to wriggle out of something = to get out of a difficult situation by making clever excuses; somehow he managed to wriggle out of having to do the washing up

wring [rɪŋ] verb (a) to twist something, especially to get water out of it; wring the face cloth (dry) after you have used it; he wrung out his shirt before putting it to dry (b) to wring information from someone = to manage to get information with difficulty; the police managed to wring a confession out of him (c) to wring your hands = to twist and turn your hands, showing sadness and emotion, but not being able to do anything; she sat there wringing her hands as her house went up in flames (NOTE: do not confuse with ring; note: **wringing - wrung** [rʌŋ])

wrinkle ['rɪŋkl] 1 noun (a) fold in the skin; she had a facelift to remove wrinkles round her eyes (b) line or crease in cloth, etc.; she tried to iron out the wrinkles in his trousers 2 verb (a) to make lines or creases in the skin; her face has started to wrinkle; she wrinkled her nose at the smell (b) to make lines or creases in; sitting in the hot bus all day has wrinkled her shirt

wrinkled ['rɪŋkld] adjective full of lines or creases; at 93 her wrinkled face was still beautiful; he was *wearing a wrinkled old shirt; whatever happened to this letter, it's all wrinkled?*

wrinkly ['rɪŋkli] **1** *adjective* covered with wrinkles; *his wrinkly face broke into a smile* **2** *noun (informal)* **the wrinklies** = old people

wrist [rɪst] *noun* joint between the arm and the hand; *he sprained his wrist and can't play tennis tomorrow*

wristwatch ['rɪstwɒtʃ] *noun* small watch worn on a strap around the wrist; *he's one of the rare people not to wear a wristwatch* (NOTE: plural is **wristwatches**)

writ [rɪt] *noun* legal document which starts an action in the High Court; *the company issued a writ to prevent the union from going on strike; she issued writs for libel against two Sunday newspapers;* **to serve someone with a writ** = to give someone a writ officially; *they served a writ on the owner of the shop*

write [raɪt] *verb* **(a)** to put words or numbers on paper, etc., with a pen, word processor, etc.; *she wrote the address on the back of an envelope; someone wrote 'down with the management' on the wall of the staff canteen; write the reference number at the top of the letter; did you know she used to write for the 'Sunday Times'?; he wrote a book on keeping tropical fish;* **(b)** to write a letter and send it to someone; *have you written to your MP yet?; she writes to me twice a week; don't forget to write as soon as you get to your hotel; he wrote a letter to the management to complain about the service; don't forget to write a postcard when you get to New York; (informal)* **it's nothing to write home about** = it's not very special; *the food in the hotel is nothing to write home about* (NOTE: **writing - wrote** [rəʊt] **- has written** ['rɪtn])

write back ['raɪt 'bæk] *verb* to answer by letter; *she got my postcard, and wrote back immediately*

write down ['raɪt 'daʊn] *verb* to write on paper, etc.; *she wrote down the registration number of the car; please write down all the necessary details on a piece of paper*

write in ['raɪt 'ɪn] *verb* **(a)** to write a letter to an organization; *hundreds of people wrote in to complain about the programme* **(b)** *US* to vote for a candidate whose name does not appear on the ballot paper, by writing his or her name there

write off ['raɪt 'ɒf] *verb* **(a)** to cancel a debt; *the bank couldn't trace him so they had to write the debt off* **(b)** to remove an asset from a company's accounts because it no longer has any value; **the car was written off** = the insurance company considered it a total loss

write-off ['raɪtɒf] *noun (informal)* total loss, removing an asset from a company's accounts; *after the accident the car was a total write-off*

write out ['raɪt 'aʊt] *verb* to write something in full; *can you write out a list of all the things you want?;* **to write out a cheque** = to write the words and figures on a cheque and then sign it

writer [raɪtə] *noun* person who writes; *who is the writer of this letter?; she's the writer of books on gardening*

write up ['raɪt 'ʌp] *verb* to write a text fully from notes which you have taken; *I took masses of notes, and now I have to write them up for the local newspaper*

write-up ['raɪtʌp] *noun (informal)* article about someone *or* something in a newspaper; *have you read the write-up about our local restaurants; the film has got a good write-up in today's paper*

writhe [raɪð] *verb* to twist and turn when pain is very severe; *she was writhing in pain when the doctor arrived*

writing ['raɪtɪŋ] *noun* **(a)** something which is written; *please don't phone, reply in writing; put everything in writing, then you have a record of what has been done* **(b)** *(informal)* **the writing is on the wall** = there are signs that a disaster is about to happen; *the writing is on the wall for old-fashioned grocer's shops* **(c)** writing done by hand; *his writing's so bad I can't read it; see also* HANDWRITING **(d)** being a writer; *he earns his living from writing*

writing paper ['raɪtɪŋ 'peɪpə] *noun* good quality paper used for writing letters; *he bought some writing paper and envelopes*

written ['rɪtn] *adjective* which has been put in writing; *he had a written reply from the Prime Minster's office*

wrong [rɒŋ] **1** *adjective* **(a)** not correct; *he gave three wrong answers and failed the test; that's not the right time, is it? - no, the clock is wrong; there is something wrong with the television;* **wrong number** = telephone number which is not the one you wanted to dial; *we tried dialling several times, but each time got a wrong number; I want to speak to Mr Cousin please - sorry, you've got the wrong number* **(b)** **to start on the wrong foot** = to start to do things the wrong way; **to get out of bed on the wrong side** = to start the day badly; **to get the wrong end of the stick** = to misunderstand what someone is saying **(c)** not suitable; *you came just at the wrong time, when we were bathing the children; she was wearing the wrong sort of dress for a wedding* **(d)** bad; *it's wrong to talk like that about her; cheating in exams is wrong* **(e)** making someone worried; **what's wrong?** = what is the matter?; *what's wrong with my handwriting? - nothing, it's just that I find it difficult to read; I hope nothing's wrong or there's nothing wrong, is there?* = I hope there is no problem **2** *adverb* badly; *everything went wrong yesterday; she spelt my name wrong;* **don't get me wrong** = don't put the wrong meaning on what I'm trying to say; *don't get me wrong, I love him dearly but at times he can be infuriating* **3** *noun* incorrect thing; **to be in the wrong** = to have made a mistake; *I apologize - I was clearly in the wrong*

◊ **on the wrong side of** [ɒn ðə 'rɒŋ saɪd əv] *phrase* **(a)** going against; *he got on the wrong side of the law* **(b)** *(informal)* older than; *she's on the wrong side of fifty*

wrongdoer ['rɒŋduːə] *noun (formal)* person who has committed a crime; *the measures are meant to punish wrongdoers but in fact they punish everyone*

wrongdoing ['rɒŋduːɪŋ] *noun (formal)* crime or unlawful act; *they arrested him for some wrongdoing but I'm not sure what it was*

wrongful ['rɒŋful] *adjective* unjust; unlawful; **wrongful dismissal** = removing someone from a job for a reason which does not justify dismissal; *the tribunal was agreed that it was a case of wrongful dismissal*

wrongfully ['rɒŋfuli] *adverb* unfairly and illegally; *can you imagine how he feels at being wrongfully accused of abusing his children?; the paper had* *wrongfully reported that the firm had collapsed; he complained that he had been wrongfully arrested*

wrongly ['rɒŋli] *adverb* not correctly; *she added up the bill wrongly; the manager spelt my name wrongly; the parcel was wrongly addressed*

wrote [rəut] *see* WRITE

wrought iron ['rɔːt 'aɪən] *noun* iron which is bent to make gates, fences, etc.; *he made the wrought iron gates for the palace; compare* CAST IRON

wry [raɪ] *adjective* showing amusement and mockery by twisting your mouth; *he listened to her story with a wry smile* (NOTE: do not confuse with **rye**)

WWF *see* WORLD WIDE FUND FOR NATURE

www *or* **WWW** *see* WORLD WIDE WEB

Xx

X, x [eks] **(a)** twenty-fourth letter of the alphabet, between W and Y **(b)** multiplication sign; *3 x 3 = 9* (NOTE: say 'three times three equals nine') **(c)** showing size; *the table top is 24 x 36cm* (NOTE: say 'twenty-four by thirty-six centimetres') **(d)** used to indicate an unknown person; *let's take the example of Mrs X, who is a widowed lady 40 years old* **(e)** mark of a cross; *'X' is written on the map to show where the treasure is hidden*

X the Roman numeral for ten or tenth; *Pope Pius X*

xenon ['ziːnɒn] *noun* heavy rare inert gas (NOTE: Chemical element: chemical symbol: **Xe**; atomic number: 54)

xenophobe ['zenəfəub] *noun* person who dislikes foreigners

xenophobia [zenə'fəubiə] *noun* dislike of foreigners

xerox ['zɪərɒks] **1** *noun* **(a)** trademark for a type of photocopier; *a new xerox machine will be installed tomorrow* **(b)** photocopy made with this machine; *we have sent xeroxes to each of the agents*; *please, give the other party a xerox of the contract* **2** *verb* to make a photocopy with a Xerox machine; *she xeroxed all the files*; *I was asked to xerox the document* (NOTE: **xeroxing - xeroxed**)

XI the Roman numeral for eleven or eleventh; *Pope Pius XI*

XII the Roman numeral for twelve or twelfth; *Pope Pius XII*

Xmas ['krɪsməs *or* 'eksməs] *noun (informal)* = CHRISTMAS

X-ray ['eksreɪ] **1** *noun* **(a)** radiation with a very short wavelength, which is invisible, but can go through soft tissue and register as a photograph on a film; *the X-ray examination showed the key inside the baby's stomach*; *the X-ray department is closed for lunch* **(b)** photograph taken with X-rays; *the X-ray showed that the bone was broken in two places*; *they will take an X-ray of his leg*; *she was sent to hospital for an X-ray* **2** *verb* to take an X-ray photograph of someone; *there are six patients waiting to be X-rayed*; *they X-rayed my leg to see if it was broken*

xylophone ['zaɪləfəun] *noun* musical instrument consisting of wooden or metal bars of different lengths which make different notes when you tap them with a little hammer; *she plays the xylophone in the school orchestra*

Yy

Y, y [waɪ] twenty-fifth letter of the alphabet, between X and Z; *not many words begin with a Y*

yacht [jɒt] *noun* **(a)** sailing boat, used for pleasure and sport; **yacht club** = private club for people who sail yachts **(b)** large luxurious boat with a motor; *she spent her holiday on a yacht in the Mediterranean*

yachting [ˈjɒtɪŋ] *noun* activity of sailing on a yacht; *yachting holidays in the Greek Islands are very popular*

yachtsman [ˈjɒtsmən] *noun* person who sails a yacht; *one of the boats capsized but the three yachtsmen are safe* (NOTE: plural is **yachtsmen**)

yak [jæk] **1** *noun* large hairy type of cattle, found in mountain regions in India and China **2** *verb US* to chat; *they were yakking away on the street corner*

yam [jæm] *noun US* sweet potato, a vegetable like a long red potato with yellow flesh inside

yank [jæŋk] **1** *noun (informal)* short sharp pull; *he gave the rope a yank and it came away in his hands* **2** *verb (informal)* to pull hard and sharply; *yank that string and it should ring a bell in the bar*; *she tried to yank the pram out of the mud*

Yank *or* **Yankee** [ˈjæŋk *or* ˈjæŋki] *noun (informal)* American, especially one from the northern states; *half the delegates were Yanks and we got along very well*; *posters with 'Yankees go home' appeared on the walls*

yap [jæp] **1** *verb (of small dog)* to bark; *her wretched little dog was yapping all the time* **2** *noun* little bark; *when the door bell rang the dog gave a yap*

yard [jɑːd] *noun* **(a)** measurement of length, 36 inches (= 0.914 metres); *the police station is only yards away from where the fight took place*; *can you move your car a couple of yards as it is blocking the entrance to our garage?*; **square yard** = measurement of area measuring one yard on each side **(b)** area of concrete at the back or side of a house; *we keep our bikes in the yard* **(c)** *US* garden round a house; *let's have a barbecue in our back yard* **(d)** large area where stores are kept outside, where lorries can load and unload; *he went to the builder's yard to buy some bricks* **(e)** **Scotland Yard** *(informal)* **the Yard** = headquarters of the London Metropolitan Police; *they called in the Yard to investigate*; *Scotland Yard officers were called in*

yardstick [ˈjɑːdstɪk] *noun* standard for measurement; *if we apply the normal yardstick, then the business cannot be said to be a success*

yarn [jɑːn] *noun* **(a)** long piece of wool used in knitting or weaving; *she sells yarn from the wool of her sheep* **(b)** *(informal)* long story; *he told me or he spun me some yarn about his time in the navy*

yawn [jɔːn] **1** *verb* to open your mouth wide and breathe in and out deeply when you are tired or bored; *he went on speaking for so long that half the people at the meeting started yawning or started to yawn* **2** *noun* **(a)** opening the mouth when you are bored or going to sleep; *his yawns made everyone feel sleepy*; **to stifle a yawn** = to try to prevent yourself from yawning **(b)** *(informal)* something which is very boring; *the concert was just one big yawn*

yeah [jeə] *(informal) interjection meaning* YES

year [jɜː] *noun* **(a)** period of time, lasting twelve months, from January 1st to December 31st; *Columbus discovered America in the year 1492*; *the great celebrations planned for the year 2000*; *last year we did not have any holiday*; *next year she's going on holiday in Australia*; *the weather was very bad for most of the year*; **year in, year out** *or* **year after year** = every year, over a long period of time; *year in, year out he sends me a plant for my birthday*; **all year round** = working or open for the whole year; *the museum is open all year round* **(b)** *(informal)* **since the year dot** = for a very long time; *we've been going on holiday to Wales since the year dot*; *see also* NEW YEAR, NEW YEAR'S DAY **(c)** a period of twelve months from a particular time; *we spent five years in Hong Kong*; *he died two hundred years ago today*; *she'll be eleven years old tomorrow*; *how many years have you been working for the company?* **(d)** **years** = a long time; *I haven't seen him for years or for donkey's years* = I haven't seen him for a very long time **(e)** *(in Britain)* **school year** *or* **academic year** = period which starts in September and finishes in July; *the school year starts in September*; *it's her last year at college*; **tax year** = the twelve-month period which starts on April 6th, used to calculate personal tax; *see also* CALENDAR, FINANCIAL, LEAP YEAR

yearbook [ˈjɜːbʊk] *noun* reference book which is published each year with updated or new information

year-long [ˈjɜːlɒŋ] *adjective* which lasts a year; *they got married after a year-long engagement*; *his year-long trial for embezzlement*

yearly [ˈjɜːli] *adjective & adverb* which happens every year or once a year; *they make a yearly trip to London to do their Christmas shopping*; *my yearly subscription to the museum is only £25.00*

year-round [ˈjɜːraʊnd] *adjective* happening all the year; *the museum offers year-round entertainment to schoolchildren*

yeast [jiːst] *noun* living fungus used to make bread and to ferment alcohol; *yeast is a good source of Vitamin B*

yell [jel] **1** *verb* to shout very loudly; *the policeman yelled to her to get out of the way* **2** *noun* loud shout; *he gave a yell and everyone came running to see what he had found*

yellow [ˈjeləʊ] **1** *adjective* of a colour like that of the sun or of gold; *his new car is bright yellow*; *she's wearing yellow sandals*; *at this time of year the fields are full of yellow flowers* (NOTE: **yellower - yellowest**) **2** *noun* the colour of the sun or gold; *do you have any hats of a lighter yellow than this one?*; *the yellow of the lichens on the rocks makes a very beautiful* photograph **3** *verb* to become yellow; *the pages of the diary have yellowed with time but it is still legible*

yellow fever ['jeləu 'fiːvə] *noun* infectious disease, found especially in Africa and South America; *yellow fever is an infectious disease transmitted by mosquitoes*

yellow line ['jeləu 'laɪn] *noun* line painted along the side of a street, showing that you are not allowed to park; *he got a ticket for parking on a double yellow line*

yellow pages ['jeləu 'peɪdʒɪz] *noun* section of a telephone directory printed on yellow paper, which lists businesses under various headings, such as computer shops, newsagent's, etc.; *he looked up 'airlines' in the yellow pages*

yelp [jelp] **1** *verb (usually of animals)* to give a short cry of pain or excitement; *the dogs were yelping in the back of the car* **2** *noun* short cry of pain; *the dog gave a yelp when the little boy pulled its tail*

yen [jen] *noun* **(a)** currency used in Japan; *it cost two thousand yen* (NOTE: no plural; usually written ¥ after figures: **2000¥**) **(b)** *(informal)* strong desire; *he has a yen to go walking along the Great Wall of China*

yes [jes] *adverb (word showing that you agree, accept, etc., the opposite of 'no')* *they asked her if she wanted to come and she said 'yes'; anyone want more coffee? - yes, please; you don't like living in London? - yes I do!; didn't you work in Scotland at one time? - yes, I did; I need a clear answer - is it 'yes' or 'no'?*

yes-man ['jesmæn] *noun* person who always agrees with someone in authority; *the Prime Minister has surrounded himself with a group of yes-men*

yesterday ['jestədeɪ] *adverb & noun* the day before today; *yesterday was March 1st so today must be the 2nd; she came to see us yesterday evening; the day before yesterday* = two days before today; *it rained the day before yesterday; the shop only opened the day before yesterday*

yet [jet] **1** *adverb* **(a)** already, until now; *has the manager arrived yet?; I haven't seen her yet this morning; don't throw the newspaper away - I haven't read it yet* **(b)** as yet = up till now; *they have not managed to repair the fault as yet; as yet, he hasn't given me any explanation* **(c)** still, even; *the police charged and yet more fans were arrested; she ate yet another cake* **(d)** *(formal)* in the future; *all hope is not lost, we may yet win the championship* **2** *conjunction* but, still; *he's very small and yet he can kick a ball a long way; it was starting to snow, and yet he went out without a coat*

yew [juː] *noun* large evergreen tree with flat green needles and poisonous red berries; *you often find yews growing near churches* (NOTE: do not confuse with **ewe, you**)

yield [jiːld] **1** *noun* **(a)** interest produced by an investment; *the yield on these bonds is higher than average* **(b)** quantity of a crop or a product produced from a plant or from an area of land; *what is the normal yield per hectare?* **2** *verb* **(a)** to produce money; *the investment has yielded a good interest up till now* **(b)** to produce a crop or a product; *this variety of rice can yield up to 2 tonnes per hectare; the North Sea oil deposits yield 100,000 barrels a month* **(c)** to produce a result; *their researches finally yielded the information they were looking for* **(d)** to yield to someone = to give up, to give way to; *(of traffic)* to yield to another car = to

allow another car to go first; **to yield to pressure** = to give in to pressure; *the government yielded to pressure from the unions and did not proceed with the planned legislation* **(e)** *(of material)* to bend; *we need a stiff material, something that will not yield*

yielding ['jiːldɪŋ] *adjective* soft and flexible; *this material is too stiff, you need something more yielding; the manager needs to learn to be more yielding when dealing with customers' complaints*

yob *or* **yobbo** [jɒb *or* 'jɒbəu] *noun (informal)* badly behaved young man; *a group of yobbos came into the pub*

yoga ['jəugə] *noun* system of exercises and meditation practised by Hindu thinkers, now popular in western countries as a way of keeping fit and relaxing; *he does yoga every morning before going to work*

yoghurt *or* **yogurt** ['jɒgət] *noun* milk which has become slightly sour after bacteria are added, often flavoured with fruit; *a pot of raspberry yoghurt*; **plain yoghurt** = yoghurt without any flavouring

yoke [jəuk] **1** *noun* **(a)** piece of wood placed over the necks of two animals when they walk side by side, pulling a cart, etc.; **a yoke of oxen** = two oxen attached together **(b)** piece of wood placed over a person's shoulders, with baskets or buckets at each end **(c)** part of a dress or shirt around the shoulders from which the rest of the dress falls; *the yoke of her little girl's dress is embroidered with flowers* (NOTE: do not confuse with **yolk**) **2** *verb* to join together; *the water buffaloes were yoked together in pairs and taken to plough the fields; now that they are married she feels she's yoked to him for the rest of her life*

yolk [jəuk] *noun* yellow part inside an egg; *in my boiled egg, the yolk was soft and the white was hard; beat the yolks of three eggs and add sugar* (NOTE: do not confuse with **yoke**)

yon *or* **yonder** [jɒn *or* 'jɒndə] *adjective & adverb (old)* over there; *yon lad is our blacksmith's son; can you see that house yonder, past the bridge?; see also* HITHER

Yorkshire pudding ['jɔːkʃə 'pudɪŋ] *noun* mixture of eggs, flour and milk, cooked in the oven, the traditional accompaniment to roast beef; *we had a satisfying lunch of roast beef and Yorkshire pudding*

> **COMMENT:** Yorkshire pudding may be cooked in the oven in one large dish or in several small ones. It used to be cooked in the oven in a pan under the roasting beef, so that the juices of the meat dripped onto the pudding. The pudding is served with the meat as part of the main course

you [juː] *pronoun* **(a)** *(referring to someone being spoken to)* *are you ready?; you look tired, you should rest a bit; if I give you my address will you give me yours?; hello, how are you?; are you both keeping well?* **(b)** *(referring to anybody)* *you never know when you might need a penknife; you have to be very tall to be a policeman* **(c)** *(addressing someone directly)* *you with the red scarf over there, I need to see your ticket!; hey you! leave my bicycle alone* (NOTE: **you** is both singular and plural)

you'd = YOU HAD, YOU WOULD

you'll = YOU WILL

young [jʌŋ] **1** *adjective* not old; *she's very young, she's only six; he became Prime Minister when he was* *still a young man*; *my little brother's much younger than me or than I am*; *in the afternoon there are TV programmes for very young children*; *this is where your Daddy used to live when he was a young boy*; *your new haircut makes you look younger* (NOTE: **younger** - **youngest**) **2** *noun* **(a)** young animals or birds; *animals fight to protect their young* **(b)** *the young* = young people; *today, the young have great need of spiritual guidance* (NOTE: no plural)

youngster ['jʌŋstə] *noun* young person; *the youngsters went to the park to play football*

your [jɔː] *adjective* belonging to you; *I hope you didn't forget to bring your toothbrush*; *this letter is for your brother*

yours [jɔːz] *pronoun* **(a)** belonging to you; *this is my car - where's yours?*; *my car's in the garage, can I borrow yours?*; **a friend of yours** = one of your friends; *you said she was a friend of yours, but she says she's never met you* **(b)** *(greetings used at the end of a letter)* **Yours faithfully** = used as an ending for business letters, when addressed to no specific person; **Yours sincerely** *US* **Sincerely yours** = used as an ending to a letter addressed to a named person; **Yours truly** *US* **Truly yours** = words written at the end of a slightly formal letter; *(informal)* **yours truly** = me myself; *who had to pay for all the damage, why yours truly, of course!*

yourself [jɔː'self] *pronoun* **(a)** *(referring to 'you' as a subject)* *why do you wash the car yourself, when you could easily take it to the car wash?*; *watch out for the broken glass - you might hurt yourself*; *I hope you are all going to enjoy yourselves* **(b)** **by yourself** = alone, with no one to help you; *will you be all by yourself at Christmas?*; *did you find your way back to the hotel all by yourself?*; *(for emphasis)* *did you yourself see what*

happened? (NOTE: the plural **yourselves** refers to **you** as a plural subject)

youth [juːθ] *noun* **(a)** young man; *gangs of youths were causing trouble in the village*; *a youth, aged 16, was arrested for possessing drugs*; **youth club** = club where young people meet; *she runs the youth club attached to the church*; *see also* YOUTH HOSTEL **(b)** period when you are young, especially the time between being a child and being an adult; *in his youth he was a great traveller*; *I haven't done that since the days of my youth!*

youthful ['juːθful] *adjective* young; *your mother still looks so youthful!*; *with his youthful impatience he said he would buy the car, without thinking to ask the price*

youth hostel ['juːθ 'hɒstəl] *noun* building where young travellers, walkers, etc., can stay the night cheaply; *if you can find places at youth hostels, that's the cheapest way of travelling*

you've = YOU HAVE

yo-yo ['jəʊjəʊ] **1** *noun* toy made of two round pieces and a string which you make the toy run up and down; *yo-yos were very popular when I was at school* **2** *verb* to go up and down; *share prices have been yo-yoing all week*

yuan ['juən] *noun* currency of China (NOTE: officially called the **renminbi**)

Yule log ['juːl 'lɒg] *noun* large log burnt on the fire at Christmas

Yuletide ['juːltaɪd] *noun* *(literary)* Christmas time

yummy ['jʌmi] *adjective* *(informal)* delicious; *just look at all those yummy cakes!*

yuppy ['jʌpi] *noun* *(informal)* young professional person who earns a large salary; *the restaurants are full of yuppies and their mobile phones*

Zz

Z, z [zed or *US* ziː] last and twenty-sixth letter of the alphabet; *he can say his alphabet from A to Z*

zap [zæp] *verb (informal)* **(a)** *(on a computer)* to hit, to kill; *he zapped all the monsters and got to the end of the game*; *press Control Z and you'll zap all the text* **(b)** to shut down the television using the remote control (NOTE: **zapping - zapped**)

zeal [ziːl] *noun* keenness or eagerness; *he showed great zeal in searching for political opponents of the government*

zealot ['zelət] *noun* fanatic, person who shows excessive zeal, especially for religion; *he's a very religious man, but I wouldn't call him a zealot*

zealous ['zeləs] *adjective* eager, too efficient; *parking for 3 minutes on a yellow line cost me £10 thanks to some zealous traffic warden*

zebra ['zebrə or ziːbrə] *noun* **(a)** African animal like a horse, with black and white stripes; *zebras' stripes help them hide in the long grass of the African bush* (NOTE: usually no plural: **a herd of zebra**) **(b)** zebra crossing = place marked with black and white lines where you can walk across a road; *it's safer to use a zebra crossing when you're crossing a main road*

zenith ['zenɪθ] *noun* **(a)** highest point, point of greatest achievement; *the soprano retired at the zenith of her career; the British Empire reached its zenith at the beginning of the 20th century* **(b)** highest point in the sky reached by the sun or moon; *the sun is now at its zenith*

zero ['zɪərəʊ] *noun* **(a)** number 0; *to make an international call you dial zero zero, followed by the number of the country* **(b)** freezing point of water on a Celsius thermometer; *the temperature stayed below zero for days* **(c)** nothing at all; *they lost ten - zero* (NOTE: plural is **zeros**)

zero hour ['zɪərəʊ 'aʊə] *noun* time fixed to start something important, such as a battle; *the soldiers were warned that zero hour would be early the next morning*

zero in on ['zɪərəʊ 'ɪn ɒn] *verb* to go straight to something; *she zeroed in on the main weakness of the plan*

zest [zest] *noun* **(a)** enthusiasm or enjoyment; *her zest for playing football made her apply to join the local club* **(b)** added pleasure or spice; *it all adds zest to the occasion* **(c)** thin piece of orange or lemon peel; *grate the zest of one lemon and add it to the cake mix*

zestful ['zestfʊl] *adjective* enthusiastic; *it was a fabulous evening, thanks to our zestful orchestra*

zigzag ['zɪgzæg] **1** *adjective & noun* (line) which turns one way, then the opposite way; *there are zigzag lines painted at pedestrian crossings to show that cars must not stop there* **2** *verb* to move from left to right, then from right to left; *the car zigzagged up the motorway until the police managed to stop it* (NOTE: **zigzagging - zigzagged**)

zilch [zɪltʃ] *noun (informal)* nothing; *I've heard absolutely zilch from him since he has left; how much were you paid for this work? - zilch!*

zinc [zɪŋk] *noun* hard bright light-coloured metal; *galvanized iron is coated with zinc* (NOTE: Chemical element: chemical symbol: **Zn**; atomic number: **30**)

zip [zɪp] **1** *noun* device for closing openings on trousers, dresses, bags, etc., consisting of two rows of teeth which lock together; *the zip of my anorak is broken; can you do up the zip at the back of my dress?* (NOTE: also called a **zip fastener**; in American English it is a **zipper**) **2** *verb* **(a)** to go fast; *cars were zipping past us on the motorway* **(b)** to zip up = to close something using a zip; *she zipped up her anorak; he zipped up his bag* (NOTE: **zipping - zipped**)

zip code ['zɪp 'kəʊd] *noun US* numbers used to indicate a postal delivery area in an address on an envelope; *don't forget the zip code - it's a very important part of the address* (NOTE: the British English for this is **postcode**)

zipper ['zɪpə] *see* ZIP

zodiac ['zəʊdɪæk] *noun* imaginary division of the sky into twelve sections, through which the sun and planets are said to travel during the year; **signs of the Zodiac** = signs for the twelve sections of the sky, named after groups of stars; *see also* AQUARIUS, ARIES, CANCER, CAPRICORN, GEMINI, LEO, LIBRA, PISCES, SAGITTARIUS, SCORPIO, TAURUS, VIRGO

zombie ['zɒmbi] *noun (informal)* someone who is unable to think; *after thirteen hours in the plane I felt like a zombie*

zone [zəʊn] **1** *noun* area or part which is different from others, or which has something special; *police cars are patrolling the inner city zones*; **pedestrian zone** = part of a town where cars are not allowed; *the town centre has been made into a pedestrian zone*; **time zone** = one of 24 bands in the world in which the same standard time is used; *when you fly across the USA you cross several time zones* **2** *verb* to divide a town into parts for planning purposes; *the land is zoned for industrial use*

zonked ['zɒŋkt] *adjective (informal)* (i) very tired; (ii) under the influence of alcohol or drugs; *he looks completely zonked*

zoo [zuː] *noun* place where wild animals are kept, and where people can go to see them; *let's go to the zoo this afternoon; we went to the zoo to see the pandas and penguins*

zoological [zuːə'lɒdʒɪkl or zəʊə'lɒdʒɪkl] *adjective* referring to the study of animals; *he brought back zoological specimens from his trip to the Galapagos*; **zoological gardens**; *see* ZOO

zoologist [zuː'ɒlədʒɪst or zəʊ'ɒlədʒɪst] *noun* person who studies animals; *zoologists are concerned about the effects of forest fires on the monkey population*

zoology [zuːˈɒlədʒi or zəʊˈɒlədʒi] *noun* study of animals; *he studied zoology at Edinburgh University; currently we have fifty zoology students*

zoom [zuːm] **1** *noun* = ZOOM LENS **2** *verb* **(a)** to go very fast; *cars were zooming past me on the motorway* **(b)** *(of prices, etc.)* to rise suddenly and steeply; *the exchange rate zoomed up last month* **(c)** to zoom in on something = to focus a camera lens so that it makes a distant object appear to come closer; *he zoomed in on the yacht*

zoom lens [ˈzuːm ˈlenz] *noun* camera lens which allows you to change quickly from distant to close-up shots while still keeping in focus; *using a zoom lens can give you close-ups of lions from quite a long way away*

zucchini [zʊˈkiːni] *noun US* fruit of the marrow at a very immature stage in its development (NOTE: British English is **courgette**)

zwieback [ˈzwiːbæk] *noun US* type of biscuit made of bread baked hard

SUPPLEMENT

International Telephone Codes

Albania	355	Guyana	592
Algeria	213	Haiti	509
Andorra	33 628	Honduras	504
Angola	244	Hungary	36
Argentina	54	Iceland	354
Australia	61	India	91
Austria	43	Indonesia	62
Bahamas	1 809	Iran	98
Bahrain	973	Iraq	964
Bangladesh	880	Ireland	353
Barbados	1 809	Italy	39
Belgium	32	Ivory Coast	225
Benin	229	Jamaica	1 809
Bolivia	591	Japan	81
Brazil	55	Jordan	962
Bulgaria	359	Kenya	254
Burma	95	Korea	82
Burundi	257	Kuwait	965
Cameroon	237	Lebanon	961
Canada	1	Liberia	231
Central African		Libya	218
Republic	236	Liechtenstein	41 75
Chad	235	Luxembourg	352
Chile	56	Madagascar	261
China	86	Malawi	265
Colombia	57	Malaysia	60
Congo	242	Mali	223
Costa Rica	506	Malta	356
Croatia	38	Mauritius	230
Cuba	53	Mexico	52
Cyprus	357	Monaco	33 93
Czech		Morocco	212
Republic	42	Mozambique	258
Denmark	45	Namibia	264
Dominican		Nepal	977
Republic	1 809	Netherlands	31
Ecuador	593	New Zealand	64
Egypt	20	Nicaragua	505
El Salvador	503	Niger	227
Ethiopia	251	Nigeria	234
Falkland Is	500	Norway	47
Finland	358	Oman	968
France	33	Pakistan	92
French Guiana	594	Panama	507
Gabon	241	Paraguay	595
Gambia	220	Peru	51
Germany	49	Philippines	63
Ghana	233	Poland	48
Gibraltar	350	Portugal	351
Great Britain	44	Puerto Rico	1 809
Greece	30	Romania	40
Guatemala	502	Russia	7
Guinea	224	Rwanda	250

International Telephone Codes

Rwanda	250	Togo	228
Saudi Arabia	966	Trinidad & Tobago	1 809
Senegal	221	Tunisia	216
Sierra Leone	232	Turkey	90
Singapore	65	Uganda	256
Slovakia	42	Ukraine	7
Slovenia	38	United Arab	
Somalia	252	Emirates	971
South Africa	27	United Kingdom	44
Spain	34	U.S.A.	1
Sri Lanka	94	Uruguay	598
Sweden	46	Venezuela	58
Switzerland	41	Vietnam	84
Syria	963	Zaire	243
Tanzania	255	Zambia	260
Thailand	66	Zimbabwe	263

Local times around the world

London time	*1200*	*London*	*1200*
Adelaide	2100	Luxembourg	1300
Algiers	1300	Madeira	1200
Amsterdam	1300	Madrid	1300
Ankara	1500	Malta	1300
Athens	1400	Mexico	0600
Beijing	2000	Montreal	0700
Beirut	1400	Moscow	1500
Berlin	1300	Nairobi	1500
Bern(e)	1300	New York	0700
Bombay	1730	Oslo	1300
Brasilia	0900	Ottawa	0700
Brussels	1300	Panama	0700
Bucharest	1400	Paris	1300
Budapest	1300	Perth	2000
Buenos Aires	0900	Prague	1300
Cairo	1400	Quebec	0700
Calcutta	1730	Rangoon	1830
Cape Town	1400	Rio de Janeiro	0900
Chicago	0600	Riyadh	1500
Copenhagen	1300	San Francisco	0400
Delhi	1730	Santiago	0800
Dublin	1200	Singapore	2000
Gibraltar	1300	Stockholm	1300
Helsinki	1400	Sydney	2200
Hong Kong	2000	Tehran	1530
Istanbul	1500	Tokyo	2100
Jerusalem	1400	Toronto	0700
Kuwait	1500	Tunis	1300
Lagos	1300	Vienna	1300
Lima	0700	Warsaw	1300

You say

Numbers

one, two, three, four	1, 2, 3, 4
five, six, seven, eight	5, 6, 7, 8
nine, ten, eleven, twelve	9, 10, 11, 12
thirteen, fourteen	13, 14
fifteen, sixteen	15, 16
seventeen, eighteen	17, 18
nineteen, twenty	19, 20
twenty-one, twenty-two, twenty-three	21, 22, 23
thirty, thirty-one, thirty-two	30, 31, 32
forty, fifty, sixty	40, 50, 60
seventy, eighty, ninety	70, 80, 90
one hundred, a hundred and one	100, 101
two hundred, three hundred	200, 300
four hundred, five hundred	400, 500
six hundred, seven hundred	600, 700
eight hundred, nine hundred	800, 900
one thousand	1,000
ten thousand	10,000
one million	1,000,000
one billion	1,000,000,000
one trillion	1,000,000,000,000

Decimals

0.5	zero point five
0.23	zero point two three
2.5	two point five

Money

£1	one pound
30p	thirty pence *or* thirty pee
£1.25	one pound twenty-five *or* one twenty-five
£27.36	twenty-seven pounds thirty-six (pee)
$1	one dollar
10¢	ten cents *or* a dime
25¢	twenty-five cents *or* a quarter
30¢	thirty cents
$1.25	one dollar twenty-five *or* one twenty-five

Telephone numbers

0171-921 3567	oh-one-seven-one, nine-two-one, three-five-six-seven

Year

1998	nineteen ninety-eight
2000	the year two thousand
1905	nineteen five *or* nineteen hundred and five *or* nineteen oh five

Date

2.1.98 or 2/1/98	the second of January nineteen ninety eight *or* (US) February first nineteen ninety eight

NOTE:
American dates are written as: month/day/year
European & British dates as: day/month/year

Weights and Measures - Metric Measures

Length
1 millimetre (mm)		= 0.0394 in
1 centimetre (cm)	= 10 mm	= 0.3937 in
1 metre (m)	= 100 cm	= 1.0936 yds
1 kilometre (km)	= 1000 m	= 0.6214 mile

Weight
1 milligramme (mg)		= 0.0154 grain
1 gramme (g)	= 1000 mg	= 0.0353 oz
1 kilogramme (kg)	= 1000 g	= 2.2046 lb
1 tonne (t)	= 1000 kg	= 0.9842 ton

Area
1cm^2	= 100 mm^2	= 0.1550 sq.in.
1m^2	= 10,000 cm^2	= 1.1960 sq.yds
1 are (a)	= 100 m^2	= 119.60 sq.yds
1 hectare (ha)	= 100 ares	= 2.4711 acres
1km^2	= 100 hectares	= 0.3861 sq. mile

Capacity
1 cm^3	= 0.0610 cu. in	
1 dm^3	= 1000 cm^3	= 0.0351 cu. ft
1 m^3	= 1000 dm^3	= 1.3080 cu. yds
1 litre	= 1 dm^3	= 0.2200 gallon
1 hectolitre	= 100 litres	= 2.7497 bushels

Imperial Measures

Length
1 inch		= 2.54 cm
1 foot	= 12 inches	= 0.3048 m
1 yard	= 3 feet	= 0.9144 m
1 rod	= 5.5 yards	= 4.0292 m
1 chain	= 22 yards	= 20.117 m
1 furlong	= 220 yards	= 201.17 m
1 mile	= 1760 yards	= 1.6093 km

Weight
1 ounce	= 437.6 grains	= 28.350 g
1 pound	= 16 ounces	= 0.4536 kg
1 stone	= 14 pounds	= 6.3503 kg
1 hundredweight	= 112 pounds	= 50.802 kg
1 ton	= 20 cwt	= 1.0161 tonnes

Area
1 sq.inch		= 6.4516 cm^2
1 sq.foot	= 144 sq.ins	= 0.0929 m^2
1 sq. yard	= 9 sq.ft	= 0.8361 m^2
1 acre	= 4840 sq.yds	= 4046.9 m^2
1 sq.mile	= 640 acres	= 259.0 hectares

Capacity
1 cu.inch		= 16.387 cm^3
1 cu.foot	= 1728 cu.ins	= 0.0283 m^3
1 cu.yard	= 27 cu.ft	= 0.7646 m^3
1 pint	= 4 gills	= 0.5683 litre
1 quart	= 2 pints	= 1.1365 litres
1 gallon	= 8 pints	= 4.5461 litres
1 bushel	= 8 gallons	= 36.369 litres
1 fluid ounce	= 8 fl.drachms	= 28.413 cm^3
1 pint	= 20 fl.oz	= 568.26 cm^3

Irregular Verbs

verb	past tense	past participle
arise	arose	arisen
awake	awoke	awoken
be	was, were	been
bear	bore	borne
beat	beat	beaten
become	became	become
befall	befell	befallen
begin	began	begun
behold	beheld	beheld
bend	bent	bent
beseech	besought, beseeched	besought, beseeched
beset	beset	beset
bet	bet	bet
bid	bid	bid
bind	bound	bound
bite	bit	bitten
bleed	bled	bled
blow	blew	blown
break	broke	broken
breed	bred	bred
bring	brought	brought
broadcast	broadcast	broadcast
build	built	built
burn	burned, burnt	burned, burnt
burst	burst	burst
buy	bought	bought
can	*see main dictionary text*	
cast	cast	cast
catch	caught	caught
chide	chided, chid	chidden
choose	chose	chosen
cling	clung	clung
come	came	come
cost	cost	cost
could	*see main dictionary text*	
creep	crept	crept
cut	cut	cut
deal	dealt	dealt
dig	dug	dug
dive	dived, *US* dove	dived
do	did	done
draw	drew	drawn
dream	dreamed, dreamt	dreamed, dreamt
drink	drank	drunk
drive	drove	driven
dwell	dwelt, dwelled	dwelt, dwelled
eat	ate	eaten
fall	fell	fallen
feed	fed	fed
feel	felt	felt
fight	fought	fought
find	found	found
fit	fit, fitted	fit, fitted
flee	fled	fled
fling	flung	flung
fly	flew	flown
forbid	forbade	forbidden
forecast	forecast	forecast
forget	forgot	forgotten
forgive	forgave	forgiven
forsake	forsook	forsaken
freeze	froze	frozen
get	got	got, *US* gotten
give	gave	given
go	went	gone
grind	ground	ground

Irregular Verbs - *continued*

verb	past tense	past participle
grow	grew	grown
hang	hung	hung
have	had	had
hear	heard	heard
heave	heaved, hove	heaved, hove
hide	hid	hidden
hit	hit	hit
hold	held	held
hurt	hurt	hurt
input	inputted, input	inputted, input
interweave	interwove	interwoven
keep	kept	kept
kneel	knelt, kneeled	knelt, kneeled
knit	knit, knitted	knit, knitted
know	knew	known
lay	laid	laid
lead	led	led
lean	leaned, leant	leaned, leant
leap	leaped, leapt	leaped, leapt
learn	learned, learnt	learned, learnt
leave	left	left
lend	lent	lent
let	let	let
lie	lay	lain
light	lit	lit
lose	lost	lost
make	made	made
may	*see main dictionary text*	
mean	meant	meant
meet	met	met
might	*see main dictionary text*	
mislead	misled	misled
mistake	mistook	mistaken
misunderstand	misunderstood	misunderstood
mow	mowed	mowed, mown
outdo	outdid	outdone
outgrow	outgrew	outgrown
overcome	overcame	overcome
overdo	overdid	overdone
overdraw	overdrew	overdrawn
overeat	overate	overeaten
overhang	overhung	overhung
overhear	overheard	overheard
overlay	overlaid	overlaid
oversee	oversaw	overseen
overtake	overtook	overtaken
overthrow	overthrew	overthrown
pay	paid	paid
put	put	put
quit	quit, quitted	quit, quitted
read	read	read
redo	redid	redone
remake	remade	remade
rend	rent	rent
repay	repaid	repaid
rerun	reran	rerun
reset	reset	reset
rethink	rethought	rethought
rewind	rewound	rewound
rewrite	rewrote	rewritten
rid	rid	rid
ride	rode	ridden
ring	rang	rung
rise	rose	risen
run	ran	run
saw	sawed	sawed, sawn

Irregular Verbs - *continued*

verb	past tense	past participle
say	said	said
see	saw	seen
seek	sought	sought
sell	sold	sold
send	sent	sent
set	set	set
sew	sewed	sewed, sewn
shake	shook	shaken
shall	*see main dictionary text*	
shear	sheared	sheared, shorn
shed	shed	shed
shine	shone	shone
shoot	shot	shot
should	*see main dictionary text*	
show	showed	shown
shrink	shrank	shrunk
shut	shut	shut
sing	sang	sung
sink	sank	sunk
sit	sat	sat
sleep	slept	slept
slide	slid	slid
sling	slung	slung
slink	slunk	slunk
slit	slit	slit
sow	sowed	sown
speak	spoke	spoken
speed	sped	sped
spell	spelt, spelled	spelt, spelled
spend	spent	spent
spill	spilled, spilt	spilled, spilt
spin	spun	spun
split	split	split
spread	spread	spread
spring	sprang	sprung
stand	stood	stood
steal	stole	stolen
stick	stuck	stuck
sting	stung	stung
stink	stank	stunk
stride	strode	strode
strike	struck	struck
strive	strove	striven
swear	swore	sworn
sweep	swept	swept
swell	swelled	swelled, swollen
swim	swam	swum
swing	swung	swung
take	took	taken
teach	taught	taught
tear	tore	torn
tell	told	told
think	thought	thought
throw	threw	thrown
thrust	thrust	thrust
tread	trod	trodden
understand	understood	understood
undertake	undertook	undertaken
underwrite	underwrote	underwritten
undo	undid	undone
unwind	unwound	unwound
uphold	upheld	upheld
upset	upset	upset
wake	woke	woken
wear	wore	worn
weave	wove	woven

Irregular Verbs - *continued*

verb	*past tense*	*past participle*
wed	wedded, wed	wedded, wed
weep	wept	wept
will	*see main dictionary text*	
win	won	won
wind	wound	wound
withdraw	withdrew	withdrawn
withhold	withheld	withheld
withstand	withstood	withstood
wreak	wreaked, wrought	wreaked, wrought
wring	wrung	wrung
write	wrote	written

This *English Dictionary for Students* has a companion workbook to help improve vocabulary using a range of exercises, puzzles and word-games. This dictionary also has a companion thesaurus to help improve and extend vocabulary.

Check Your Vocabulary for English ISBN 1-901659-11-9
English Thesaurus for Students ISBN 1-901659-31-3

Our range of specialist English dictionaries provide comprehensive coverage of specialist subject areas, and clearly define complex terms and expressions. Many titles are available on CD-ROM - visit our website (www.pcp.co.uk) for further details.

❑ Accounting 0-948549-27-0
❑ Aeronautical 1-901659-10-0
❑ Agriculture, 2nd ed 0-948549-78-5
❑ American Business 0-948549-11-4
❑ Automobile Engineering 0-948549-66-1
❑ Banking &Finance 0-948549-12-2
❑ Business, 2nd ed 0-948549-51-3
❑ Computing, 3rd ed 1-901659-04-6
❑ Ecology &Environment, 3rd ed 0-948549-74-2
❑ Government &Politics, 2nd ed 0-948549-89-0
❑ Hotel, Tourism, Catering Managemnt 0-948549-40-8
❑ Human Resource &Personnel, 2ed 0-948549-79-3
❑ Information Technology, 2nd ed 0-948549-88-2
❑ Law, 3rd ed 1-901659-43-7
❑ Library &Information Management 0-948549-68-8
❑ Marketing, 2nd ed 0-948549-73-4
❑ Medicine, 3rd ed 1-901659-45-3
❑ Printing &Publishing, 2nd ed 0-948549-99-8

Our range of workbooks help improve and understand specialist English vocabulary.

❑ Banking &Finance 0-948549-96-3
❑ Business 1-901659-27-5
❑ Computing 0-948549-58-0
❑ Colloquial English 0-948549-97-1
❑ English 1-901659-11-9
❑ Hotels, Tourism, Catering 0-948549-75-0
❑ Law, 2nd ed 1-901659-21-6
❑ Marketing 1-901659-48-8
❑ Medicine, 2nd ed 1-901659-47-X

Professional Series and General Interest dictionaries.

❑ Astronomy 0-948549-43-2
❑ Economics 0-948549-91-2
❑ Multimedia, 2nd ed 1-901659-01-1
❑ PC&the Internet, 2nd ed 1-901659-12-7
❑ Bradford Crossword Solver, 3rd ed 1-901659-03-8
❑ International Food &Cooking 0-948549-87-4

Our range of bilingual specialist dictionaries provides accurate translations to specialist vocabulary.

❑ Chinese-English bilingual
❑ French-English bilingual
❑ German-English bilingual
❑ Greek-English bilingual
❑ Hungarian-English bilingual
❑ Italian-English bilingual
❑ Polish-English bilingual
❑ Portuguese-English bilingual
❑ Slovene-English bilingual
❑ Spanish-English bilingual
❑ Swedish-English bilingual

For further details about our range of specialist English or bilingual dictionaries, please complete the form above and return to:

Peter Collin Publishing Ltd
1 Cambridge Road, Teddington, TW11 8DT, UK
tel: (+44) 020 8943 3386 fax: (+44) 020 8943 1673 email: info@pcp.co.uk
Details on all our titles are available on our web site: **www.pcp.co.uk**